WHO'S WHO IN SCOTLAND
1999 (NINTH EDITION)

Who's Who in Scotland 1999

Carrick Media

Published by Carrick Media
2/1 Galt House, 31 Bank Street, Irvine KA12 0LL
01294 311322

Printed in Great Britain by Bookcraft, Midsomer Norton, Avon

British Library Cataloguing-in-Publication Data
A catalogue record for this book is available from the British Library

ISBN 0 946724 42 3

Preface

Publication of this, the ninth of the series, has fallen rather awkwardly some weeks in advance of elections to the Scottish Parliament. We considered the possibility of delaying publication in order to carry biographies of the chosen ones, but decided against: why hold up a national reference work in order to accommodate a few more politicians? We shall endeavour to include details of the chosen ones in the tenth of the series.

Meanwhile, the population of the wee Scottish burgh known as Who's Who in Scotland grows encouragingly. This edition is 50 pages longer than last year's, making it the heftiest volume since the book was established in 1986.

On two occasions in the quite recent past we have been asked to co-operate in the compilation of "Power Lists" – attempts by the popular press to identify the Scottish establishment. We looked at preliminary versions of the lists and decided on both occasions not to co-operate. One, a list of about 400 names, included six representatives of the Christian churches, yet found room for several night-club proprietors. I am not sure that a single night-club proprietor has ever been admitted to Who's Who in Scotland. We may be in the position of the bishop who, upon arrival at Kennedy Airport, was asked whether he intended to visit any night clubs while in New York. "*Are* there any night clubs in New York?" he asked with mock innocence.

Perhaps the best "Power List" is the superior address book and telephone directory known as Who's Who in Scotland.

The Editor
Irvine, Ayrshire
19 March 1999

THE DIRECTORY

AGRICULTURE, HORTICULTURE AND BOTANY

MYLNEFIELD RESEARCH SERVICES LTD
INVERGOWRIE, DUNDEE DD2 5DA.
TEL.: 01382 568568. FAX: 01382 568501. e-mail: n.kerby@scri.sari.ac.uk
Contact: Dr. Nigel W. Kerby, Managing Director; Dr. Jonathan B. Snape, Commercial Manager; Professsor John R. Hillman, Deputy Chairman.
Mylnefield Research Services Ltd acts as the gateway to unique skills and services available in biology, agriculture and horticulture at the Scottish Crop Research Institute (SCRI). Considerable emphasis is placed on developing successful partnerships between SCRI's research community and industry. Expertise in plant breeding, plant health, diagnostics, environmental impact analysis, molecular analysis, advisory packages, licensing and technology transfer is available. Core crops include cereals, potatoes, soft-fruit, brassicas, trees and certain tropical crops.

SCOTTISH AGRICULTURAL SCIENCE AGENCY
82 CRAIGS ROAD, EAST CRAIGS, EDINBURGH EH12 8NJ.
TEL.: 0131-244 8890. FAX: 0131-244 8940. e-mail: library@sasa.gov.uk
Contact: Dr. R.K.M. Hay, Director, 0131-244 8843; Mrs L. Clark, Librarian, 0131-244 8826, e-mail: clark@sasa.gov.uk; S. Cooper, Deputy Director, 0131-244 8932, e-mail: cooper@sasa.gov.uk
The purpose of SASA is: to provide government with scientific information and advice on agricultural and horticultural crops, and aspects of the environment; to perform statutory and regulatory work in relation to national, European Community (EC) and other international legislation and agreements on plant health, bee health, plant variety registration, crop improvement, genetic resources, the protection of crops, food and the environment; to conduct research and development in support of statutory work undertaken above.

SCOTTISH CROP RESEARCH INSTITUTE
INVERGOWRIE, DUNDEE DD2 5DA.
TEL.: 01382 562731. FAX: 01382 562426. e-mail: wmacfa@scri.sari.ac.uk
Contact: Professor J.R. Hillman, Director; Dr. R.J. Killick, Secretary; Dr. W.H. Macfarlane Smith, Scientific Liaison Officer.
The Institute is financed principally by the Scottish Office Agriculture, Environment and Fisheries Department and external contracts (c. £13m. per annum). It undertakes research to advance knowledge in the biological sciences, to improve the quality of crops, and to control losses due to pests and diseases with due regard to the environment. It is the lead centre in the UK for research on potatoes and soft fruit, and has major inputs into barley, beans and brassicas, and other temperate, tropical and subtropical crops.

ANIMALS AND WILDLIFE

CANINE CONCERN SCOTLAND TRUST
UNIT 10, HAZELBURN BUSINESS PARK, MILLKNOWE, CAMPBELTOWN, ARGYLL PA28 6PM.
TEL.: 01586 553399. FAX: 01586 553399.
Contact: Mrs Patricia McCulloch, Administrator; Mrs M.J. Henley Price, Chairman of Trustees; Mr James Macdonald, 18 Mannering Road, Shawlands, Glasgow G41 3SW, 0141-632 4893.
Exists to improve the image of the dog by promotion of responsible and caring ownership,

mainly by education with posters, leaflets, specially made video, etc., and visits to schools and any interested groups in society. Our Therapet Scheme is carried out by volunteer members with suitably selected dogs visiting homes for the elderly, mentally handicapped, long-term geriatric wards and psychiatric wards in hospitals, patients in hospices, etc, sometimes with almost miraculous results.

ROYAL ZOOLOGICAL SOCIETY OF SCOTLAND
EDINBURGH ZOO, MURRAYFIELD, EDINBURGH EH12 6TS.
TEL.: 0131-334 9171. FAX: 0131-316 4050.

Contact: Dr David Waugh, Director; Dr Mauvis Gore, Curator.

Exists to promote, through the presentation of our living collections, the conservation of animal species and wild places by captive breeding, environmental education and scientific research. The Royal Zoological Society of Scotland is a charitable, non-profit making organisation devoted to the study and conservation of wildlife. Founded in 1909 to promote a greater knowledge of animal life among the Scottish people, today it is one of the nation's foremost conservation organisations, owning both Edinburgh Zoo and the Highland Wildlife Park.

RSPB SCOTLAND
DUNEDIN HOUSE, 25 RAVELSTON TERRACE, EDINBURGH EH4 3TP.
TEL.: 0131-311 6500. FAX: 0131-311 6569.

Contact: Stuart Housden, Director; Steve Sankey, Head of Policy and Advisory; David Sexton, Head of Reserves Management.

The RSPB is involved with the conservation of wild birds and the environment in a number of ways including: (a) management of nature reserves; (b) education, both formal and informal; (c) promotion of sustainable land use and development; (d) assisting police with wildlife law enforcement; (e) offering advice to land users and government; (f) co-operating with other bodies, both nationally and internationally through the Birdlife International partnership; (g) carrying out and commissioning research, both biological and socio-economic. Web: www.rspb.org.uk

SCOTTISH WILDLIFE TRUST (SWT)
CRAMOND HOUSE, KIRK CRAMOND, CRAMOND GLEBE ROAD, EDINBURGH EH4 6NS.
TEL.: 0131-312 7765. FAX: 0131-312 8705. e-mail: scottishwt@cix.co.uk

Contact: Stan Blackley, Press and Information Officer, Ext. 259, e-mail: sblackley@scottishwt.cix.co.uk

Established in 1964, the Scottish Wildlife Trust is the leading voluntary body protecting all forms of Scottish wildlife and Scotland's natural environment. The SWT owns and manages over 120 wildlife reserves, protects over 2,000 wildlife sites, trains 800 individuals in practical conservation work each year and runs high-profile campaigns on a wide variety of environmental issues. As a registered charity, the SWT relies on public support for its funding. The SWT has a network of offices, staff, conservation teams, branches and groups throughout Scotland.

ARTISTIC AND CULTURAL

BBC SCOTTISH SYMPHONY ORCHESTRA
Chief Conductor: Osmo Vänskä
BBC BROADCASTING HOUSE, QUEEN MARGARET DRIVE, GLASGOW G12 8DG.
TEL.: 0141-338 2606. FAX: 0141-307 4312. e-mail: bbcsso@bbc.co.uk
Contact: Hugh Macdonald, Director; Alan Davis, Manager.
Founded in December 1935, the BBC Scottish Orchestra as it was then called, was Scotland's first full-time professional orchestra. Since then it has developed an international reputation with concert tours throughout Europe and to Canada and Hong Kong, and regular appearances at the Edinburgh International Festival and BBC Proms in London. The orchestra is particularly noted for its performances of contemporary music and it has an ambitious commissioning policy, giving special prominence to Scottish composers. In recent years it has recorded extensively, winning *Gramophone* Awards in 1992 and 1993.

BORDERLINE THEATRE COMPANY
NORTH HARBOUR STREET, AYR KA8 8AA.
TEL.: 01292 281010. FAX: 01292 263825.
Contact: Eddie Jackson, Chief Executive; Leslie Finlay, Artistic Director.
Borderline is one of Scotland's most dynamic and innovative touring theatre companies. Based in Ayr, the company tours throughout the country, playing to in excess of 35,000 people per year. Borderline presents high quality, exuberant theatre that is accessible and seeks to stimulate, enlighten and, above all, entertain. In addition to the touring work the company is unique in having a year-round programme of workshops and projects in schools and communities.

THE BRITISH COUNCIL
3 BRUNTSFIELD CRESCENT, EDINBURGH EH10 4HD.
TEL.: 0131-447 4716. FAX: 0131-452 8487.
The British Council Scotland works in partnership with Scottish institutions and the British Council's network of 228 offices in 109 countries to establish long-term, world-wide partnerships. We aim to increase global understanding of the unique aspects of Scottish culture, in particular the arts, education, governance and law, taking a lead role in developing and encouraging Scottish participation in international initiatives in these areas. Please see our website for further information: http://www.britcoun.org

CHARLES RENNIE MACKINTOSH SOCIETY
QUEEN'S CROSS CHURCH, 870 GARSCUBE ROAD, GLASGOW G20 7EL.
TEL.: 0141-946 6600. FAX: 0141-945 2321.
Contact: David Mullane, Director.
To encourage a greater interest in the work of this important Scottish architect, artist and designer. In 1977 the Society undertook the care of Queen's Cross, the only church designed by CRM which was built. It is now the Society's headquarters with reference library, shop and information centre.

COMUNN NA GAIDHLIG
5 MITCHELL'S LANE, INVERNESS IV2 3HQ.
TEL.: 01463 234138. FAX: 01463 237470. e-mail: ailean@cnag.org.uk
Contact: Allan Campbell, Chief Executive; Donald Martin, Director of Community Development; Margaret MacIver, Education Director.
Comunn na Gàidhlig, established in 1984 with Scottish Office support, is a co-ordinating Gaelic development agency with specific emphasis on education, arts and social/economic development. Operating at local, regional and national levels, Comunn na Gàidhlig is a company with charitable status and a management board which includes representatives from Highlands and Islands Enterprise, local authorities, An Comunn Gaidhealach, all major Gaelic development bodies and co-opted individuals.

featuring works by members and non-members. The RSA also gives financial and material encouragement to young artists, through the unique Students' Art Exhibition and the valued Kinross and Salvesen Scholarships. All exhibitions are held in the RSA Galleries at The Mound, Princes Street, Edinburgh.

ROYAL SCOTTISH ACADEMY OF MUSIC AND DRAMA
100 RENFREW STREET, GLASGOW G2 3DB.
TEL.: 0141-332 4101. FAX: 0141-332 8901. e-mail: registry@rsamd.ac.uk
Contact: Dr Philip Ledger, CBE, Principal; Mrs Isobel Fowler, Director of Finance and Administration.
The RSAMD is Scotland's only conservatoire and is one of the four Royal Schools of Music and one of the two Royal Academies of Drama in the United Kingdom. Its mission is to produce musicians, actors and other professionals in music and drama well equipped to pursue a diversity of careers at national and international level. Its facilitics include concert halls, theatres and television, broadcasting and recording studios and, within the Alexander Gibson Opera School, a state-of-the-art opera studio and extensive rehearsal facilities.

SCOTS LANGUAGE RESOURCE CENTRE
A.K. BELL LIBRARY, 2-8 YORK PLACE, PERTH PH2 8EP.
TEL.: 01738 440199. FAX: 01738 477010. e-mail: slrc@sol.co.uk
Contact: Stuart McHardy, Director; Gordon Beange, Development Officer; Professor Graham Caie, Convenor, (Glasgow University, Department of English).
To support and promote all activities in and about the Scots language.

SCOTTISH BOOK TRUST
137 DUNDEE STREET, EDINBURGH EH11 1BG.
TEL.: 0131-229 3663. FAX: 0131-228 4293.
e-mail: scottish.book.trust@dial.pipex.com
Contact: Lindsey Fraser, Executive Director; Kathryn Ross, Deputy Executive Director; Chris Young, Administrator/Librarian.
SBT promotes books, reading and writers throughout Scotland and beyond. It has a particularly strong reputation for its work in the field of children's books, but offers a comprehensive Book Information Service, publishes a wide range of resources and administers the prize for the Scottish Writer of the Year. In 1998/99 SBT is co-ordinating the National Year of Reading in Scotland.

SCOTTISH CHAMBER ORCHESTRA
4 ROYAL TERRACE, EDINBURGH EH7 5AB.
TEL.: 0131-557 6800. FAX: 0131-557 6933. e-mail: info@sco.org.uk
Contact: Donald MacDonald, Chairman; Roy McEwan, Managing Director; Fiona McLeod, Business Relations Director.
Recognised as one of the world's finest chamber orchestras, the SCO celebrates its 25th anniversary in 1999 with concerts throughout Scotland, further recordings, its fourth US tour and innovative community and education projects.

SCOTTISH MUSEUMS COUNCIL
20-22 TORPHICHEN STREET, EDINBURGH EH3 8JB.
TEL.: 0131-229 7465. FAX: 0131-229 2728. e-mail: inform@scottishmuseums.org.uk
Contact: Jane Ryder, Director, e-mail: jryder@scottishmuseums.org.uk; Patricia Andrew, Assistant Director, e-mail: patriciaa@scottishmuseums.org.uk
The Scottish Museums Council is the national agency for central government support to Scotland's local museums. The 200-strong membership cares for some 330 museums and galleries. The Council aims to improve the quality of museum and gallery provision in Scotland by providing advice, services and grant-aid to its members and by promoting recognition of the role museums play in the country's cultural, social and economic life.

THE SCOTTISH NATIONAL DICTIONARY ASSOCIATION LIMITED
27 GEORGE SQUARE, EDINBURGH EH8 9LD.
TEL.: 0131-650 4149. FAX: 0131-650 4149. e-mail: mail@snda.org.uk
web: http://snda.org.uk
Contact: Iseabail MacLeod, Editorial Director.
The SNDA was founded in 1929 and the 10-volume Scottish National Dictionary, covering Scots from 1700 to the present, was completed in 1976. Since then the SNDA has produced works of reference for the general public, including The Concise Scots Dictionary (1985) and, most recently, the Scots School Dictionary. The results of a new research programme on Scots are stored in an electronic database, and there are plans to create electronic versions of all SNDA dictionaries. The first of these, the Electronic Scots School Dictionary was published in 1998.

SCOTTISH POETRY LIBRARY
5 CRICHTON'S CLOSE, CANONGATE, EDINBURGH EH8 8DT.
TEL.: 0131-557 2876. e-mail: spl_queries@presence.co.uk
Contact: Tessa Ransford, Director; Penny Duce, Librarian.
A free reference and lending library for Scotland's poetry in its three languages throughout the centuries and up-to-date, and for British and international poetry. Stock includes books, audio and video tapes, CDs, magazines and newscuttings. Specialist lists, indexes and bibliographies may be produced by the computer catalogue, INSPIRE. Lending is free to the public; also by post, and from travelling van and branches. The Library has charitable status: membership £15 (organisations £20) for reading room, newsletter and to support the work.

THE SCOTTISH TARTANS SOCIETY
SEVEN OAKS, SCHOOL LANE, MOFFAT DG10 9AX.
TEL.: 01683 220584. FAX: 01683 220584. e-mail: mfelliott@aol.com
President: Duncan W. Paisley of Westerlea, FRSA, FSA Scot. Contact: Mrs Marilyn F. Elliott, Membership Secretary, as above; Research Officer, Hall of Records, Port-na-Craig Road, Pitlochry PH16 5ND, Tel.: 01796 474079, Fax: 01796 474090, e-mail: research.enquiries@perth.almac.co.uk
An Incorporation Noble in the Noblesse of Scotland Inaugurated on 13th May 1963 by Sir Thomas Innes of Learney, GCVO, Lord Lyon King of Arms 1945–1969. The Scottish Tartans Society is a long established worldwide authority on Scottish tartans and dress. The Society maintains two museums, one in Edinburgh (Scotch House) and one in Franklyn, North Carolina, USA, comprising unique collections of tartan and tartan-related artefacts. Holding the Register of *all publicly known tartans*, the Society conducts research, records, registers and accredits new tartans, as well as providing advice and information on all tartan related subjects including clans and families. The Society publishes the journal *Tartans* bi-annually. Membership is welcome.

SOCIETY OF ANTIQUARIES OF SCOTLAND
ROYAL MUSEUM OF SCOTLAND, CHAMBERS STREET, EDINBURGH EH1 1JF.
TEL.: 0131-247 4115/4133. FAX: 0131-247 4163.
Contact: Fionna Ashmore, Director.
The Society, founded in 1780, is the second oldest antiquarian society in Britain; an active body, it organises lectures, conferences, seminars and excursions, publishes an annual *Proceedings*, a twice-yearly Newsletter and a Monograph series. It plays an important role in the cultural life and heritage of Scotland, sponsoring all aspects of archaeological and historical research. Drawing on its wide range of available expertise, it provides an impartial and independent voice on heritage matters and is represented on many committees and councils.

TOSG THEATRE COMPANY
SABHAL MOR OSTAIG, SLEAT, ISLE OF SKYE IV44 8RQ.
TEL.: 01471 844443. FAX: 01471 844447.

Contact: Simon Mackenzie, Director; Annette Kerr, Administrator.
Scotland's only professional Gaelic theatre company. Mainly touring productions, with an emphasis on new writing. The company has a support and advice system for new Gaelic writers.

BUSINESS

BARR HOLDINGS LIMITED
HEATHFIELD, AYR KA8 9SL.
TEL.: 01292 281311. FAX: 01292 618678.

Contact: W.J. Barr, OBE, CEng, FICE, FCIOB, FIMgt, Chairman and Chief Executive; Sir W. Francis, CBE, DSc, LLD, FEng, Director; S.H. Ingall, MA, FCA, Director.
Construction, development, steelwork, quarries, homes, precast concrete, ready mix concrete, ports, joinery, cranes, waste management, facilities management, plant and transport.

CLYDEPORT PLC
16 ROBERTSON STREET, GLASGOW G2 8DS.
TEL.: 0141-221 8733. FAX: 0141-248 3167.

Contact: Tom Allison, Chief Executive; Euan Davidson, Commercial Director; David Green, Finance Director.
Clydeport is Scotland's premier west coast port operator. With comprehensive facilities designed to cater for the needs of both importers and exporters, Clydeport offers unrivalled facilities, speedy turnaround times and above all, excellent service. Our facilities at Glasgow, Greenock, Ardrossan and Hunterston, are each dedicated to specific cargoes such as coal, dry bulks, forest products, containers and cruise liners. The company is also involved in road transport, property acquisition and development. At Clydeport, you can always be assured of the best possible service.

EDINBURGH CONVENTION BUREAU
4 ROTHESAY TERRACE, EDINBURGH EH3 7RY.
TEL.: 0131-473 3666. FAX: 0131-473 3636. e-mail: convention@edinburgh.org

Contact: Stewart Walker, Director; Sue Stuart, Head of Sales; Ellen Colingsworth, Sales Manager Associations.
Edinburgh Convention Bureau represents the conference and meetings industry in the Edinburgh and Lothians area, Scotland's top conference destination. We provide free and impartial advice and assistance with all aspects of event and meeting planning and can help with venue finding, familiarisation visits and site inspections; provision of delegate literature, accommodation booking and suggestions for social programmes and tours.

E | I
C | C

EDINBURGH INTERNATIONAL CONFERENCE CENTRE
THE EXCHANGE, EDINBURGH EH3 8EE. TEL.: 0131-300 3000. FAX: 0131-300 3030.
e-mail: sales@eicc.co.uk

Contact: Hans Rissmann, Chief Executive; Trevor McCartney, Sales and Marketing Director; Geoff Fenlon, Total Quality Management Facilitator.

Since opening in 1995, the purpose-built Edinburgh International Conference Centre has firmly established itself in the international meetings market. The Centre was set up with the aim of generating economic benefit by attracting additional national and international conferences to the city of Edinburgh. EICC has hosted many prestigious events, gaining a worldwide reputation for quality and service. The Centre's flexible facilities can accommodate events for up to 1,200 people from conferences, sales meetings and AGMs to banquets, product launches and private dinners.

GLASGOW OPPORTUNITIES
7 WEST GEORGE STREET, GLASGOW G2 1BQ.
TEL.: 0141-221 0955. FAX: 0141-221 3244.

Contact: Bob Rowan, Chairman; Agnes Samuel, Executive Director.
Glasgow Opportunities offers advice and support to those wishing to start their own business or to developing and growing existing businesses. We can offer advice on finance, business planning, marketing, human resource development, training, support for innovation and design, support for the retail sector, and other specialist support services. Glasgow Opportunities is supported by Glasgow City Council, Glasgow Development Agency and European funding.

INVERESK PLC
KILBAGIE MILLS, ALLOA, CLACKMANNAN FK10 4AF.
TEL.: 01259 455000. FAX: 01259 455070.

Contact: S.G. Kay, Managing Director, e-mail: sgkay@hq.inveresk.co.uk; G.W. Cassels, Finance Director, e-mail: gwcassels@hq.inveresk.co.uk; G.J. Lawson, Company Secretary, e-mail: gjlawson@hq.inveresk.co.uk
Manufacture of speciality coated and uncoated papers and boards.

MURRAY JOHNSTONE LIMITED
7 WEST NILE STREET, GLASGOW G1 2PX.
TEL.: 0141-226 3131. FAX: 0141-248 5420.

Contact: Giles Weaver, Managing Director; David MacLellan, Deputy Managing Director; Bill Johnstone, Marketing Director.
MJ is a leading Scottish investment management group managing over £4bn. for a broad range of UK and international clients. These include investment trusts, venture capital trusts, unit trusts, OEICs, institutional and charity funds and private clients. With no other business activities to distract us from our investment role, our sole intention is to maximise returns for our clients. We have five offices in the UK as well as offices in Chicago, Singapore and Bahrain. Our headquarters are in Glasgow where most of the investment management is undertaken.

POST OFFICE COUNTERS LTD
THE ATHENAEUM, 8 NELSON MANDELA PLACE, GLASGOW G2 1BT.
TEL.: 0345 223344. FAX: 0141-353 7244.

Contact: Mrs Wendy Goldstraw, Regional General Manager, Scotland and Northern Ireland, 0345 223344.
Post Office Counters Ltd runs the country's largest retail chain – the nationwide network of Post Offices. We offer a wide range of retail services and products, are committed to

providing excellent personal service to our customers and are proud of our unmatched presence in local communities.

SCOTTISH EQUITABLE PLC
EDINBURGH PARK, EDINBURGH EH12 9SE.
TEL.: 0131-339 9191. FAX: 0131-339 9567.

Contact: Graham Dumble, Managing Director; Shona Johnstone, Head of Group Communications; Scott White, Group PR Manager.

Scottish Equitable is an investment and financial services group which specialises in pensions and investment products and services. By combining investment management expertise with innovative product design, Scottish Equitable has acquired a particularly strong reputation, underpinned by the group's continued focus on effective communication with all its customers. Scottish Equitable distributes its range of products and services via a dedicated, well trained sales force and focuses its attention on the IFA distribution channel.

SCOTTISH SALMON BOARD
DRUMMOND HOUSE, SCOTT STREET, PERTH PH1 5EJ.
TEL.: 01738 635973. FAX: 01738 621454.

Contact: Mr Mike Lloyd, Marketing Manager.

The Scottish Salmon Board is the marketing arm of the Scottish salmon industry. It represents 13 fresh salmon farm organisations and seven smoked salmon companies, embracing 70 per cent of the industry. It markets behind the Tartan Quality Mark in the UK, with the addition of Label Rouge in France.

THE WISE GROUP
72 CHARLOTTE STREET, GLASGOW G1 5DW.
TEL.: 0141-303 3131. FAX: 0141-303 0070. e-mail: itwise@aol.com

Contact: Peter McKinlay, Chairman; Alan Sinclair, Chief Executive; Allan Watt, Group Funding Manager.

Limited Company with charitable status, set up in 1983. Holding Company with subsidiaries providing training work experiences and job search as an integrated package contributing to urban and social development. Wise Group pioneered the Intermediate Labour Market concept. There are 215 employees and 600 trainees at any time in the Wise Group. Wise Group aims to get long term unemployed people back to work using the Intermediate Labour Market and other programmes. In 1997 over 1,000 people passed through the Wise Group with 63 per cent of those on the ILM moving into work.

CHARITABLE AND VOLUNTARY

AGE CONCERN SCOTLAND
113 ROSE STREET, EDINBURGH EH2 3DT.
TEL.: 0131-220 3345; FAX: 0131-220 2779. e-mail: acs@ccis.org.uk

Contact: Maureen O'Neill, Director; Lucie McKenzie, Information Manager.

Age Concern is committed to working throughout Scotland to ensure that all older people have their rights upheld, their needs addressed, their voices heard, and have choice and control over all aspects of their lives. We support a network of local groups providing practical services and friendship to older people. ACS is a campaigning organisation, seeking to influence policy and practice in all areas that affect older people.

APEX SCOTLAND
9 GREAT STUART STREET, EDINBURGH EH3 7TP.
TEL.: 0131-220 0130. FAX: 0131-220 6796.

Contact: Jeane Freeman, Director; Philip Dunion, Assistant Director; Martin Currie, Assistant Director.

APEX Scotland aims to create equality of access to employment and to employment opportunities for individuals with a criminal record. In achieving this aim, APEX Scotland will work co-operatively with employers, individuals and all relevant agencies, and will make a critical contribution to the long-term reduction of crime. In all of its services and its approach, APEX Scotland will demonstrate the strongest commitment to cost efficiency, innovation, quality and customer service.

ASH SCOTLAND
8 FREDERICK STREET, EDINBURGH EH2 2HB.
TEL.: 0131-225 4725. FAX: 0131-220 6604. e-mail: ashscotland@dial.pipex.com

Contact: Maureen Moore, Chief Executive; Wendy Ugolini, Press and Campaigns Manager; Sheila Duffy, Information and Resources Manager.

ASH Scotland is the leading voluntary organisation campaigning for effective tobacco control policies. Our main activities centre on an expert information service, action-based research projects and campaigning.

CHILDREN IN SCOTLAND
PRINCES HOUSE, 5 SHANDWICK PLACE, EDINBURGH EH2 4RG.
TEL.: 0131-228 8484. FAX: 0131-228 8585.
e-mail: info@childreninscotland.org.uk

Contact: Dr Bronwen Cohen, Director; Heather Walker, Information and Publications Manager.

Children in Scotland is an independent agency representing over 300 voluntary, statutory and professional organisations and individuals. It works with its members to identify and promote the interests of children and their families. Its activities include information, training, policy and practice development and research. Specific development areas include early years (including rural childcare), disability/special needs, HIV/AIDS and parenting. web:http://www.childreninscotland.org.uk/children

EX-SERVICES MENTAL WELFARE SOCIETY
HOLLYBUSH HOUSE, HOLLYBUSH, BY AYR KA6 7EA.
TEL.: 01292 560214. FAX: 01292 560871.

Contact: Wing Commander D. Devine, Assistant Director (Welfare) Scotland and Ireland.

The Ex-Services Mental Welfare Society is the only organisation specialising in the mental problems of ex-Service men and women of HM Forces and the Merchant Navy. In undertaking this work it fills a void. Men and women breaking down through service to their country, have either to go into a mental hospital, or to have treatment in their own homes. The Society visits ex-Service men and women at home or in mental hospital, runs its own nursing homes, provides a veterans' home and a pensions appeal department. Support is vital and the Society asks everybody to "remember those who can't forget". Some of its patients are only 19, some are 90, and all need the Society's help because there's no one else.

HANSEL ALLIANCE
SYMINGTON, AYRSHIRE KA1 5PU.
TEL.: 01563 830340. FAX: 01563 830019.

Contact: Nancy Findlay, Development Manager, Residential Services; Richard Wilkinson, Development Manager, Day Services; Nan Smith, Development Manager.

Hansel Alliance is a leading Scottish voluntary organisation providing residential, vocational and community services in support of people with learning (and other) disabilities. Through our facilities at Hansel Village and our highly successful Community Support Services, we work alongside service users supporting them to fulfil their hopes and expectations for the future courses of their lives. Capital funding for new projects is generated by Hansel Foundation (see separate entry). Hansel Alliance – built on 37 years of experience and commitment. Registered Charity No.: SCO 27681.

HANSEL FOUNDATION
SYMINGTON, AYRSHIRE KA1 5PU.
TEL.: 01563 830340. FAX: 01563 830019.

Contact: Judith Young, Fundraising Organiser.

Founded in 1962 as "Hansel Village", Hansel Foundation is recognised as one of Scotland's leading voluntary sector organisations in the field of learning disabilities. It is the driving force for Hansel Alliance (see separate entry) "pump priming" new initiatives such as £385,000 of community housing projects and a £900,000 courtyard development, both scheduled for early completion. "A Strong Foundation for Alliance", Hansel Foundation relies entirely on capital funds generated from trusts, legacies and other donations.

OXFAM IN SCOTLAND
FLOOR 5, FLEMING HOUSE, 134 RENFREW STREET, GLASGOW G3 6ST.
TEL.: 0141-331 2724. FAX: 0141-331 2264. e-mail: glascamp@oxfam.org.uk

Contact: Marie Hearle, Head of Campaigns; Donald Easson, Scottish Retail Manager, glastrad@oxfam.org.uk; Iain Gray, Deputy Head of Campaigns, e-mail: edincamp@oxfam.org.uk

Oxfam is a development and relief agency working to put an end to poverty worldwide. Oxfam believes that poverty is not inevitable; it can be tackled. In partnership with local groups, Oxfam works with poor people to help them help themselves.

QUARRIERS
HEAD OFFICE, QUARRIERS VILLAGE, BRIDGE OF WEIR, RENFREWSHIRE PA11 3SX.
TEL.: 01505 612224. FAX: 01505 613906. e-mail: enquiries@quarriers.org.uk

Contact: Mr Gerald E. Lee, Chief Executive; Dr. Tony Williams, Director of Fundraising and Publicity; Ms Zara Ross, Director of Human Resources.

Quarriers works to overcome personal and social disadvantage, inspire optimism, create opportunity and offer choice to needy and disabled people. Established in 1871, Quarriers is now one of Scotland's largest care charities providing a wide range of services to children, families and young people and people with a disability. The charity also works in Russia and other parts of Eastern Europe and has strong historical connections with Canada.

ROYAL NATIONAL INSTITUTE FOR DEAF PEOPLE (SCOTLAND) (RNID SCOTLAND)
9 CLAIRMONT GARDENS, GLASGOW G3 7LW.
TEL.: 0141-332 0343 (VOICE), 0141-332 5023 (TEXT). FAX: 0141-331 2640.

Contact: Lilian Lawson, Service Director, Scotland; Dorothy Davidson, Regional Information Officer; Linda Richards, Communication Services Manager.

The Royal National Institute for Deaf People (RNID) is the largest charity representing the 8.7 million deaf and hard of hearing people in the UK. We aim to achieve a radically better quality of life for deaf and hard of hearing people. We do this by campaigning and lobbying vigorously, by raising awareness of deafness and hearing loss, by providing services and through social, medical and technical research.

ROYAL NATIONAL LIFEBOAT INSTITUTION (SCOTLAND)
BELLEVUE HOUSE, HOPETOUN STREET, EDINBURGH EH7 4ND.
TEL.: 0131-557 9171. FAX: 0131-557 6943.

Contact: Mrs Maren L. Fitzgerald, LLB, MICFM, National Organiser, Scotland; Mr Dick Richardson, Fundraising and Publicity Co-ordinator, Scotland.

The RNLI is a voluntary organisation that relies entirely on public donations. It exists solely to save lives at sea. The RNLI has given a commitment to the British and Irish governments to provide cover to 50 miles offshore; this is achieved with a modern fleet of 299 fast lifeboats. The crews are all highly trained local volunteers, who will turn out 24 hours a day, 365 days a year – no matter what the weather! Some 50 lifeboats are based in Scotland. In 1997 they launched 975 times, and saved 161 lives.

Contact: Miss M.A. Stewart, Honorary Librarian; Miss J.P.S. Ferguson, Honorary Secretary; Sales Secretary.
The aims are to promote research into Scottish family history and to collect, exchange and publish material relating to genealogy, but the Society does not engage in professional research. *The Scottish Genealogist* is published quarterly and lectures are held monthly from September until April. The library holds books, periodicals, microfilm and microfiche. Publications include transcriptions of gravestones which are a valuable adjunct to pre-1855 records.

SCOTTISH HUMAN RIGHTS CENTRE
146 HOLLAND STREET, GLASGOW G2 4NG.
TEL.: 0141-332 5960. FAX: 0141-332 5309. e-mail: shrc@dial.pipex.com
Contact: Professor Alan Miller, Director; John Scott, Chair.
Independent voluntary organisation which promotes human rights in Scotland. A membership organisation constantly and actively seeking new people to join and organisations to affiliate. Maintains a library which is freely available to the public.

SCOTTISH MARRIAGE CARE
50 GREENOCK ROAD, PAISLEY PA3 2LE.
TEL.: 0141-849 6183. FAX: 0141-849 6183.
Contact: Mrs Mary Toner, Chief Executive.
Scottish Marriage Care offers a confidential counselling service to couples and individuals experiencing relationship difficulties. Short courses for marriage preparation are also provided. We aim to help people to prepare for marriage, accomplish and sustain fulfilling marriages, and support couples or individuals if their marriages or relationships are under pressure or break down. There are 96 volunteer counsellors in Scotland working out of nine centres. Service is free but we welcome donations.

SCOTTISH NATIONAL WAR MEMORIAL
THE CASTLE, EDINBURGH EH1 2YT.
TEL.: 0131-226 7393. FAX: 0131-225 8920.
Contact: Lieutenant Colonel H.D.R. Mackay, Secretary to the Trustees; Mrs Janey Whitson, Administrative Assistant.
Maintains and amends the Rolls of Honour of Scots who fell in the two World Wars and Campaigns after 1945. Administers the memorial building in Edinburgh Castle.

THE SCOTTISH SOCIETY FOR AUTISM
(FORMERLY SCOTTISH SOCIETY FOR AUTISTIC CHILDREN)
HILTON HOUSE, ALLOA BUSINESS PARK, WHINS ROAD, ALLOA FK10 3SA.
TEL.: 01259 720044. FAX: 01259 720051.
Contact: Donald Liddell, Chief Executive; Helen Petrie, Appeals and Marketing Manager.
Autism is a complicated lifelong communication disorder which isolates the child or adult from the world as we know it. People with autism have great difficulty acquiring any form of communication, forming relationships or understanding emotions. Many are unable to speak and around 75 per cent have other learning difficulties. Having to cope with autism can have a devastating effect on families' lives. The Scottish Society for Autism are the leading provider of services for autism in Scotland. Family support services, home visits, carers' workshops, information and respite care are heavily dependent upon your generosity. Once you have provided for your family, please see if there is some extra room for us. Communicate your concern by considering a donation, covenant or legacy.

SEAD (SCOTTISH EDUCATION AND ACTION FOR DEVELOPMENT)
23 CASTLE STREET, EDINBURGH EH2 3DN.
TEL.: 0131-225 6550. FAX: 0131-226 6384. e-mail: sead@gn.apc.org
Contact: Fiona Sinclair, Director; Liz Ferguson, Information and Membership Development Officer; Amanda Hunter, Programme Leader.
Sead promotes the potential of community voice within Scotland, set within a global

perspective. By working alongside diverse groups of Scottish society, Sead works to challenge poverty and inequality by promoting social inclusion. Its aim is to inspire a Scottish culture of everyday political awareness and so foster a climate in which ideas can be exchanged and a wider debate strengthened. Its programme of activities, "Striking a Chord" is a community celebration of democracy and solidarity through the arts.

SENSE SCOTLAND
5TH FLOOR, 45 FINNIESTON STREET, CLYDEWAY CENTRE, GLASGOW G3 8JU.
TEL.: 0141-564 2444. FAX: 0141-564 2443. e-mail: kay51@dial.pipex.com
Contact: Gillian Morbey, OBE, Director; Joyce Wilson, Depute Director; John Calder, Information Officer.
Sense Scotland works with deafblind and multiply impaired children and adults who have: impairments to both sight and hearing whether or not they have other disabilities; impairment to sight with other disabilities; impairment to hearing with other disabilities. Sense Scotland has experience developing and providing: support and advice to families and professionals; community living for adults; day services; respite; holidays; community support; training; information; representation, consultation and policy development.

VOLUNTEER DEVELOPMENT SCOTLAND
72 MURRAY PLACE, STIRLING FK8 2BX.
TEL.: 01786 479593. FAX: 01786 449285. e-mail: vds@vds.org.uk
Contact: Liz Burns, OBE, Director; Lesley Greenaway, Senior Development Officer, Training; Isabel Bryce, Parliamentary and Media Officer.
Volunteer Development Scotland is Scotland's national centre for volunteering. We are committed to extending the range and effectiveness of voluntary work by giving volunteering a voice, promoting good practice and developing new initiatives. We work across all sectors and through national and local networks. Our services include the provision of specialist training, information, advice on policy development, consultancy, publications and development projects with specific groups such as volunteering in the health service, youth and employee volunteering.

CHILD CARE

THE CENTRE FOR RESIDENTIAL CHILD CARE
UNIVERSITY OF STRATHCLYDE, 74 SOUTHBRAE DRIVE, GLASGOW G13 1SU.
TEL.: 0141-950 3683. FAX: 0141-950 3681. e-mail: margaret.lindsay@strath.ac.uk
Contact: Meg Lindsay, Director, 0141-950 3683, e-mail: margaret.lindsay@strath.ac.uk; Alan Macquarrie, Information Officer, 0141-950 3683, e-mail: a.macquarrie@strath.ac.uk; Tracy Leckenby, Administrator, 0141-950 3683, e-mail: t.a.leckenby@strath.ac.uk
The Centre for Residential Child Care, founded in 1994 as a result of a recommendation from the Scottish Office Report *Another Kind of Home – a review of residential child care* (Skinner, 1992) provides consultancy, advice, information, research and training to the field of residential child care. The Centre acts as a catalyst for the development of good and innovative practice and creates networks to promote this via seminars, conferences, a library service, current awareness bulletin and publications.

CONSERVATION

EDINBURGH NEW TOWN CONSERVATION COMMITTEE
13A DUNDAS STREET, EDINBURGH EH3 6QG.
TEL.: 0131-557 5222. FAX: 0131-556 6355.

Contact: Richard Griffith, MA(Cantab), Dip Arch(Cantab), RIBA, RIAS, Director; Caroline Sibbald, Grant Case Officer.

Established 1970 to halt decay of residential buildings in Georgian New Town. Funded by Scottish Office (Historic Scotland) and City of Edinburgh Council. Remit: to award grants for appropriate external repairs, promote building maintenance, and advise central and local government on major policy issues. Committee representation: City of Edinburgh Council; Historic Buildings Council for Scotland; Scottish Civic Trust; Cockburn Association; Architectural Heritage Society of Scotland; New Town Residents.

EDINBURGH OLD TOWN RENEWAL TRUST
343 HIGH STREET, EDINBURGH EH1 1PW.
TEL.: 0131-225 8818. FAX: 0131-225 8636. e-mail: eotrt@edinburgholdtown.org.uk

Contact: Kirsteen Thomson, Executive Director.

The Trust's work is to promote and co-ordinate a conservation led economic regeneration strategy for the Old Town of Edinburgh. The aim is to ensure that the Old Town is a place in which people live, work and spend leisure time. The Trust works closely with other agencies to focus resources to achieve development, conservation and town centre management initiatives. In addition, the Trust manages a £500,000 conservation grants programme.

HISTORIC SCOTLAND
LONGMORE HOUSE, SALISBURY PLACE, EDINBURGH EH9 1SH.
TEL.: 0131-668 8600.

Historic Scotland is a government agency within The Scottish Office. It is responsible for safeguarding and promoting Scotland's built heritage including listing of historic buildings and scheduling of ancient monuments, designed landscapes, grants to owners of listed buildings and ancient monuments. Historic Scotland manages a programme of rescue archaeology and is a leading authority in technical conservation and research. Historic Scotland is the country's largest operator of visitor attractions including Edinburgh Castle, Stirling Castle, Fort George and the Border Abbeys at Melrose, Dryburgh and Jedburgh.

NATIONAL PLAYING FIELDS ASSOCIATION
20 QUEEN STREET, EDINBURGH EH2 1JX.
TEL.: 0131-225 4307. FAX: 0131-225 5763.

Contact: Stephen Barr, Secretary/Treasurer.

Our Royal Charter tasks us with the protection and preservation of playing fields and recreational space and in Scotland we are the guardian trustees of 85 King George V Memorial Playing Fields. The Association's objectives are to provide, maintain, promote and assist in the provision and maintenance of playing fields, recreational grounds, playgrounds, open spaces and other facilities for play and recreation, for the benefit of the community at large and particularly in areas of greatest social need. The Association awards grants and loans to organisations whose aims and objectives are basically in line with our own.

THE NATIONAL TRUST FOR SCOTLAND
5 CHARLOTTE SQUARE, EDINBURGH EH2 4DU.
TEL.: 0131-226 5922. FAX: 0131-243 9501.
e-mail: information@thenationaltrustforscotland.org.uk

Contact: Trevor A. Croft, Director; Ian Gardner, Head of Public Affairs, 0131-243 9386; Peter Reekie, Press Officer.

Established in 1931, The National Trust for Scotland preserves places of historic interest and natural beauty throughout the country. Over 100 varied properties come under the Trust's care and the organisation is supported by 228,000 members, making it Scotland's leading conservation charity.

NORTH ATLANTIC SALMON CONSERVATION ORGANIZATION (NASCO)
11 RUTLAND SQUARE, EDINBURGH EH1 2AS.
TEL.: 0131-228 2551. FAX: 0131-228 4384. e-mail: hq@nasco.org.uk

Contact: Dr. Malcolm L. Windsor.

NASCO is an international, inter-governmental, treaty organization. It is the only inter-governmental organization with its headquarters in Scotland. NASCO is dedicated to the conservation, restoration, enhancement and rational management of wild Atlantic salmon stocks. NASCO has as its member parties: Canada, Denmark (in respect of the Faroe Islands and Greenland), the European Union, Iceland, Norway, the Russian Federation, and the United States of America. All international negotiations on any aspect of conservation of wild Atlantic salmon are now organised through Scotland.

ROYAL COMMISSION ON THE ANCIENT AND HISTORICAL MONUMENTS OF SCOTLAND
JOHN SINCLAIR HOUSE, 16 BERNARD TERRACE, EDINBURGH EH8 9NX.
TEL.: 0131-662 1456. FAX: 0131-662 1477/1499.

Chairman: Sir William Fraser, GCB, MA, LLD, FRSE; Contact: Mr R.J. Mercer, MA, FSA, FRSE.

The aims of the Royal Commission on the Ancient and Historical Monuments of Scotland are: to survey and record the man-made environment of Scotland; to compile and maintain in the National Monuments Record of Scotland a record of the archaeological and historical environment; and to promote an understanding of this information by all appropriate means.

THE SCOTTISH CIVIC TRUST
THE TOBACCO MERCHANTS HOUSE, 42 MILLER STREET, GLASGOW G1 1DT.
TEL.: 0141-221 1466. FAX: 0141-248 6952. e-mail: sct@scotnet.co.uk

Contact: John N.P. Ford, Director of Administration and Finance; John Gerrard, Technical Director; Mary Miers, Buildings at Risk Officer.

The Scottish Civic Trust is a national charity concerned with improving the quality of Scotland's built environment. It encourages high quality in planning, the conservation and, where necessary, adaptation for re-use of older buildings of distinction or historic interest. It publishes, on behalf of Historic Scotland, *The Buildings at Risk Bulletin*, illustrating a wide variety of all kinds of buildings in need of rescue and re-use. It co-ordinates Doors Open Day in September, when interesting buildings not normally open, give free access to the public. The Trust is the umbrella organisation for local civic and amenity groups.

SCOTTISH CONSERVATION PROJECTS
BALALLAN HOUSE, 24 ALLAN PARK, STIRLING FK8 2QG.
TEL.: 01786 479697. FAX: 01786 465359. e-mail: scp@btcv.org.uk

Contact: Nick Cooke, Director, e-mail: n.cooke@dial.pipex.com; Peter Blackburn, Co-ordinator, Conservation Volunteers, e-mail: p.blackburn@dial.pipex.com; Russell Hampton, Technical Services Manager, e-mail: r.hampton@dial.pipex.com

SCP is the Scottish division of BTCV, the UK's leading practical conservation charity, supporting the activities of over 95,000 volunteers in positive action to improve the environment. SCP's activities including week-day and weekend projects, Action Breaks – conservation residential projects, environmental training, and providing advice and support for community groups and schools.

ECONOMIC DEVELOPMENT AND PLANNING

CORROM TRUST
DAVIDSON HOUSE, DRUMMOND STREET, COMRIE, PERTHSHIRE PH6 2DW.
TEL.: 01764 670333. FAX: 01764 670333. e-mail: corrom@btinternet.com
Contact: Alan Caldwell, Executive Director.
The Corrom Trust was established in 1994 to promote sustainable community based regeneration. The Trust has five areas of work: community strategic planning – preparing and implementing plans for the future; policy development and advocacy – creating frameworks for sustainable communities; community consultation – facilitating the process; training and research – supporting communities and agencies; support to local organisations – ensuring continued success. The Trust works in Scotland and throughout the UK with communities and their partners in the public, private and charitable sectors.

GLASGOW DEVELOPMENT AGENCY
ATRIUM COURT, 50 WATERLOO STREET, GLASGOW G2 6HQ.
TEL.: 0141-204 1111. FAX: 0141-248 1600.
Contact: Michael Lunn, Chairman; Stuart Gulliver, Chief Executive; Gordon Kennedy, Director, Corporate Development.
Glasgow is the largest city in Scotland in terms of population, jobs, companies and investment. Its sphere of influence affects almost half of the Scottish population. Within the Scottish Enterprise network, Glasgow Development Agency's task of delivering economic development in Glasgow is unique, since it is the only Local Enterprise Company to serve an exclusively inner city area. Glasgow's urban context and scale presents a special set of challenges and problems, as well as genuine advantages and opportunities.

LANARKSHIRE DEVELOPMENT AGENCY
NEW LANARKSHIRE HOUSE, STRATHCLYDE BUSINESS PARK, BELLSHILL ML4 3AD.
TEL.: 01698 745454. FAX: 01698 842211.
e-mail: lda@scotent.co.uk web: www.lda.co.uk
Contact: Iain Carmichael, Chief Executive.
Lanarkshire Development Agency is part of the Scottish Enterprise Network and is the principal economic development body in Lanarkshire. Working with a range of partners, LDA is active in areas such as local company development, new business creation, exporting, product development, inward investment and property development. LDA and its partners recently unveiled "Changing Gear", a new 10-year economic strategy which provides a framework for building a dynamic, healthier and more prosperous Lanarkshire.

LEEL (LOTHIAN AND EDINBURGH ENTERPRISE LTD)
APEX HOUSE, 99 HAYMARKET TERRACE, EDINBURGH EH12 5HD.
TEL.: 0131-313 4000. FAX: 0131-313 4231.
Contact: David Crichton, Chief Executive; Mike Walker, Chairman.
LEEL is the local enterprise company serving Edinburgh and Lothian. Across a range of activities, LEEL contributes to the economic well-being of the whole community and focuses on growing existing and new businesses, attracting new investment, improving skills and developing a modern infrastructure and environment.

THE PLANNING EXCHANGE
TONTINE HOUSE, 8 GORDON STREET, GLASGOW G1 3PL.
TEL.: 0141-248 8541. FAX: 0141-248 8277. e-mail: info@planex.co.uk
Contact: Tony Burton, OBE, Managing Director.
Since 1973 the Planning Exchange has gathered and managed information, especially on good and innovative practice, with the aim of improving access to and encouraging the use of information and good practice in urban and rural development, among both policy makers and practitioners for the benefit of the communities they serve. The Exchange covers urban and rural development and regeneration issues including: local economic development; planning and environment; housing; social services; education, skills and training; transportation and infrastructure; estates and property; recreation and leisure; youth and

community. The Planning Exchange is an independent not-for-profit company. Our information dissemination services are used by local government, public agencies, academic and research institutions, enterprise initiatives, consultants, development corporations and private sector firms.

THE SCOTTISH CHAMBERS OF COMMERCE
CONFERENCE HOUSE, THE EXCHANGE, 152 MORRISON STREET, EDINBURGH EH3 8EB.
TEL.: 0131-477 8025. FAX: 0131-477 7002. e-mail: mail@scottishchambers.org.uk
Contact: Mr Lex Gold, Director.
The Scottish Chambers of Commerce (SCC) is the most extensive business support organisation in Scotland with 21 member Chambers and 8,000 member companies who, in turn, employ more than 50 per cent of the Scottish workforce. SCC co-ordinates member Chamber activities at national and international level. It encourages development of Chamber services such as Export Support and Training and Education. It is the authentic national voice of the business community and plays a major role in influencing Government policy and decisions at all levels.

SCOTTISH ENTERPRISE
120 BOTHWELL STREET, GLASGOW G2 7JP.
TEL.: 0141-248 2700. FAX: 0141-221 3217.
e-mail: scotentcsd@scotent.co.uk web: http://www.scotent.co.uk
Scottish Enterprise, Scotland's premier economic development agency, reports to The Scottish Office. Its aim is to help the people of Scotland create and sustain jobs, prosperity and a high quality of life. The Scottish Enterprise Network consists of Scottish Enterprise and 13 Local Enterprise Companies. Working in partnership with the private and public sectors Scottish Enterprise aims to build more and better businesses, to develop the skills and knowledge of Scottish people and to make Scottish business internationally competitive. Through Locate in Scotland, it helps attract jobs to Scotland and through Scottish Trade International assists Scottish companies compete in world export markets. The Local Enterprise Companies deliver a wide range of economic development services to meet local needs, including company development, business start-up and skills development programmes.

EDUCATION
(see also Schools)

ASSOCIATION OF SCOTTISH COLLEGES
ARGYLL COURT, THE CASTLE BUSINESS PARK, STIRLING FK9 4TY.
TEL.: 01786 892100. FAX: 01786 892109. e-mail: enquiries@ascol.org.uk
Contact: Tom Kelly, Chief Officer; Sarah Chisnall, Policy Co-ordinator.
The Association of Scottish Colleges (ASC) represents Further Education colleges throughout Scotland. ASC is the policy and lobbying voice for the work of Scottish FE and fulfils this role by: informing and advising Government and senior politicians about the work of FE and responding to government consultations; making sure that the FE sector is involved in policy and decision making in Scotland; consulting with members on key policy issues and developing a sense of collective purpose.

CARDONALD COLLEGE
690 MOSSPARK DRIVE, GLASGOW G52 3AY.
TEL.: 0141-272 3333. FAX: 0141-272 3444. e-mail: executive@cardonald.ac.uk
Contact: Ros Micklem, Principal, Ext. 201; Eleanor Harris, Depute Principal, Ext. 240; David Baillie, Secretary to Board of Management, Ext. 208.
The College's mission is "to meet the aspirations of each student or client by providing a valuable and enjoyable learning experience". It provides a wide variety of courses at both

non-advanced and advanced levels in a range of disciplines, from aromatherapy to water operations. There is increasing emphasis on community outreach and open learning. Most subjects are available on a full-time or part-time basis and a business development unit keeps the College close to market realities.

CENTRE FOR EDUCATION FOR RACIAL EQUALITY IN SCOTLAND
ROOM 2.5, CHARTERIS BUILDING, FACULTY OF EDUCATION, MORAY HOUSE, EDINBURGH UNIVERSITY, HOLYROOD ROAD, EDINBURGH EH8 8AQ.
TEL.: 0131-651 6371. FAX: 0131-651 6511. e-mail: ceres@ed.ac.uk

Contact: Rowena Arshad, Director, 0131-651 6371, e-mail: rowena.arshad@ed.ac.uk; Edna Sommerville, Senior Adminstrator, 0131-651 6371, e-mail: edna.sommerville@ed.ac.uk

CERES is a Scottish Office Education and Industry funded initiative. Its main aim is the promotion of multicultural and anti-racist education in Scottish schools and the wider education community. It provides consultancy, training, and houses one of the most extensive libraries on academic multi-cultural education publications for public lending. CERES contributes to curriculum development work with parents and conducts research into race equality issues within Scottish education. Web: http://www.mhie.ac.uk/-ceres/index.html

COMMITTEE OF SCOTTISH HIGHER EDUCATION PRINCIPALS (COSHEP)
ST. ANDREW HOUSE, 141 WEST NILE STREET, GLASGOW G1 2RN.
TEL.: 0141-353 1880. FAX: 0141-353 1881.
e-mail: coshep@gcal.ac.uk

Contact: Dr Ronald L. Crawford, Secretary; Ms Jane Denholm, Deputy Secretary.

"The most effective regional organisation of its kind in the UK" (Commission on Scottish Education). COSHEP is the official "voice" of the Scottish universities and higher education colleges. The present Convener (1998-2000) is Dr Ian Graham-Bryce, Principal and Vice-Chancellor of the University of Dundee. web: http://www.coshep.gcal.ac.uk

DUMFRIES AND GALLOWAY COLLEGE
HEATHHALL, DUMFRIES DG1 3QZ.
TEL.: 01387 261261. FAX: 01387 250006.

Contact: Mr J.W.M. Neil, OBE, Principal, 01387 243808; Mrs A.C. Sinyard, Depute Principal, 01387 243801; Mrs V.P. Quinn, Assistant Principal, 01387 243906.

We pride ourselves on our friendly atmosphere and excellent facilities. We are able to offer courses and training in a wide variety of occupational areas, so whatever your chosen career path or your personal development needs, there is something on offer for everyone at Dumfries and Galloway College. We care for your educational and personal development through the provision of student support services, a mobile learning resource, childcare facilities and a wide range of opportunities for adults.

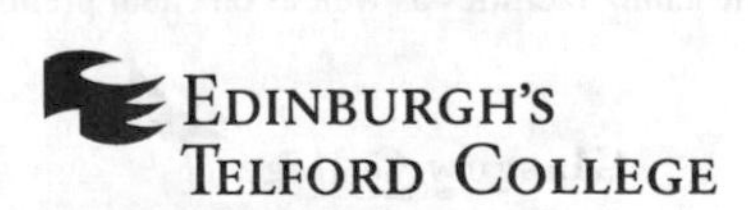

EDINBURGH'S TELFORD COLLEGE
CREWE TOLL, EDINBURGH EH4 2NZ.
TEL.: 0131-332 2491. FAX: 0131-343 1218. e-mail: @ed.coll.ac.uk

Contact: Mrs Fiona M. Baikie, Principal and Chief Executive, Ext. 7201, e-mail: fionab@ed-coll.ac.uk; Mr Joe Mooney, Depute Principal, Ext. 7302, e-mail: joem@ed-coll.ac.uk; Mr Jim Haluch, Facilities and Marketing, Ext. 7478, e-mail: jimh@ed-coll.ac.uk

The College mission is "to be accessible, responsive and flexible, and to achieve excellence". It aims to meet the educational and training needs of individuals, industry and the wider community. In pursuit of these goals, it works in partnership with a wide range of local, national and international organisations. The number of students enrolled with the College in 1997-98 exceeded 18,000, many of them studying part-time and by distance learning.

THE UNIVERSITY OF EDINBURGH
OLD COLLEGE, SOUTH BRIDGE, EDINBURGH EH8 9YL.
TEL.: 0131-650 1000. FAX: 0131-650 2147.

Contact: Professor Sir Stewart Sutherland, Principal, 0131-650 2150; Dr Martin Lowe, Secretary, 0131-650 2144, e-mail: Dr. M.J.B.Lowe@ed.ac.uk; Mr Ray Footman, Director of Communications and Public Affairs, 0131-650 2249, e-mail: R.Footman@ed.ac.uk

The University of Edinburgh, with some 17,500 students and over 2,000 academic and research staff, is one of Europe's leading centres of higher education, devoted to excellence in teaching and research across a broad range of disciplines and professions. It especially values its intellectual and economic relationship with the Scottish community that forms its base and provides a wide range of research, educational, commercial and cultural services for its client groups.

FALKIRK COLLEGE OF FURTHER AND HIGHER EDUCATION
GRANGEMOUTH ROAD, FALKIRK FK2 9AD.
TEL.: 01324 403000. FAX: 01324 403222.
e-mail: marketing@falkirkcollege.demon.co.uk

Contact: Ms Linda MacKay, Principal; Dr. Maxwell Sharp, Depute Principal.

A large comprehensive provider of further and higher education and vocational training in central Scotland. 15,000 students/trainees per year of which half undertake HNC, HND, AD or SVQ level III/IV. Validated by OUVS for BA and BSc vocational degree programmes. A member of Scotland's Polytechnic Colleges Group. SQA Approved Centre, accredited under SQMS, an Investor in People and Chartermark Award winners.

FIFE COLLEGE OF FURTHER AND HIGHER EDUCATION
ST. BRYCEDALE AVENUE, KIRKCALDY, FIFE KY1 1EX.
TEL.: 01592 268591. FAX: 01592 640225. FREEPHONE: 0800 413280.
e-mail: enquiries@fife.ac.uk

Contact: Mrs Joyce Johnston, Principal; Mr Douglas Law, Depute Principal; Mrs Joy Boyle, Access Information Officer, Ext. 2401.

The mission of Fife College is to provide each student with the highest possible quality of opportunity, helping them to achieve success in their personal education and training objectives. Fife College of Further and Higher Education is one of Scotland's foremost education and training organisations. From our four campuses in Kirkcaldy, we serve local, regional, national and international clients. Services are provided out of our own offices, consultancy rooms and teaching facilities as well as on client premises.

GLASGOW COLLEGE OF NAUTICAL STUDIES
21 THISTLE STREET, GLASGOW G5 9XB.
TEL.: 0141-565 2500. FAX: 0141-565 2599. e-mail: enquiries@glasgow-nautical.ac.uk

Contact: Chris Hunter, Principal; Alan Hinch, Director Quality and Marketing; James Burns, Quality and Marketing Manager.

Glasgow College of Nautical Studies is a further education community college which has an extensive portfolio of courses including: engineering; social sciences; computing; business and management; telecommunications; sports coaching; information technology; care studies; manufacturing; instrumentation and electrical engineering. The College is also the sole provider of the full range of maritime education courses both for deck officers and engineering officers. Glasgow College of Nautical Studies enjoys a worldwide reputation for the quality of its education and training.

GLASGOW SCHOOL OF ART
167 RENFREW STREET, GLASGOW G3 6RQ.
TEL.: 0141-353 4500. FAX: 0141-353 4746.

Contact: Jane McAllister, Academic Services, Ext. 4515, e-mail: j.mcallister@gsa.ac.uk; Sally Stewart, Admissions Officer, Mackintosh School of Architecture, Ext. 4665, e-mail: s.stewart@gsa.ac.uk; Gail McAulay, Development/Alumni Office, Ext. 4689/4710, e-mail: m.mcaulay@gsa.ac.uk

Glasgow School of Art is one of the very few remaining independent art schools in the UK and offers undergraduate and postgraduate degrees in a broad range of art, design and architecture related disciplines. The School has enjoyed a long, distinguished history of producing innovative, creative and successful artists, designers and architects. Today, the School seeks to provide courses that are professionally relevant and intellectually challenging, and introduce our students to a broad spectrum of critical and theoretical perspectives.

HEADTEACHERS' ASSOCIATION OF SCOTLAND
UNIVERSITY OF STRATHCLYDE, JORDANHILL CAMPUS, SOUTHBRAE DRIVE, GLASGOW G13 1PP.
TEL.: 0141-950 3298. FAX: 0141-950 3434. e-mail: head.teachers@strath.ac.uk

Contact: George Ross, General Secretary; Lyn Honnan, Admin and Finance Officer.

Professional support to head teachers, depute head teachers and assistant head teachers in Scottish secondary schools and the enrichment of education in Scotland.

HERIOT-WATT
UNIVERSITY
Edinburgh

HERIOT-WATT UNIVERSITY, EDINBURGH
RICCARTON CAMPUS, EDINBURGH EH14 4AS.
TEL.: 0131-451 3530. FAX: 0131-451 3441.

Contact: Gordon Gillies, Head of Public Affairs, e-mail: g.r.gillies@hw.ac.uk; Dr. Kevin Cullen, Acting Director, Institute of Technology Management, e-mail: k.cullen@hw.ac.uk; Vickie Allan, Manager, Edinburgh Conference Centre, e-mail: v.allan@hw.ac.uk

The university's main task is to research new knowledge in contemporary issues of engineering, science, management and languages with the funding and suppport of industry and the research councils. The university is respected, modern and valued in the marketplace. It seeks to become the Scottish institution which is recognised for outstanding success in academic-industrial collaboration. Conferene venue: with superb year-round facilities, the Edinburgh Conference Centre is a leading venue within Scotland's meeting industry.

JAMES WATT COLLEGE OF FURTHER AND HIGHER EDUCATION
FINNART STREET, GREENOCK PA16 8HF.
TEL.: 01475 724433. FAX: 01475 888079.

Contact: T. Davies, Principal.

A member of Scotland's Polytechnic Colleges Group. Sixty per cent of the work of the College is at advanced HNC/D level. A large community college offering an all through provision for its community.

MOTHERWELL COLLEGE
DALZELL DRIVE, MOTHERWELL ML1 2DD.
TEL.: 01698 232323. FAX: 01698 275430.

Contact: Richard Millham, Principal and Chief Executive.

Motherwell College will develop its role as a key provider of local, national and international learning opportunities, making a full contribution to the economic, social and cultural life of the local community and meeting the needs of individual learners.

NAPIER UNIVERSITY
219 COLINTON ROAD, EDINBURGH EH14 1DJ.
TEL.: 0131-444 2266. FAX: 0131-455 4666. e-mail: info@napier.ac.uk
Contact: Professor John Mavor, FRSE, FEng, Principal, 0131-455 4600, e-mail: j.mavor@napier.ac.uk; Professor Michael Thorne, BSc, PhD, FIMA, FBCS, Vice-Principal, 0131-455 4607, e-mail: m.thorne@napier.ac.uk; Ian Miller, MA, LLB, Secretary and Registrar, 0131-455 4603, e-mail: i.miller@napier.ac.uk
Napier University is the sixth largest HEI in Scotland with 11,500 students following professional, technical and vocational courses. Its five faculties – Arts & Social Science, Engineering, Health Studies, Science, and the Business School – offer degree, honours degree, and postgraduate programmes, diploma and certificate courses, and short courses for industry and commerce. Napier is a vocational university with a strong reputation for applied research and consultancy in biomedicine, building technology, electronics, international law, management, new materials, statistics, tourism and transportation.

QUEEN MARGARET UNIVERSITY COLLEGE
CORSTORPHINE CAMPUS, CLERWOOD TERRACE, EDINBURGH EH12 8TS.
TEL.: 0131-317 3000. FAX: 0131-317 3256. e-mail: admissions@mail.qmced.ac.uk
Contact: Dr Joan Stringer, Principal and Vice Patron; Rosalyn Marshall, Vice Principal (Strategic Planning and Development) Dr. Gordon Duncan, Director, External Relations.
Queen Margaret University College is a university with around 3,000 full-time students as well as over 2,000 part-time and short-course students. In 1992, the University College was granted Degree Awarding Powers by the Privy Council. The University College's courses fall into the categories of Business, Management and Information; Theatre Arts and Health Care which together reflect the vocational and professional emphasis of the University College's mission. QM is located on three sites, with the majority of teaching taking place at the Corstorphine and Leith campuses. Drama occupies premises in the Gateway Theatre on Leith Walk.

SCET (SCOTTISH COUNCIL FOR EDUCATIONAL TECHNOLOGY)
74 VICTORIA CRESCENT ROAD, GLASGOW G12 9JN.
TEL.: 0141-337 5000. FAX: 0141-337 5050. e-mail: scet@scet.com
Contact: Bronagh Bell, Marketing Manager.
SCET aims to enhance the quality of education and training in Scotland, helping people learn effectively through technology. We are actively involved in software and internet development, multi-media production, consultancy, training and providing information and support on all aspects of learning through technology.

SCOTTISH CONSULTATIVE COUNCIL ON THE CURRICULUM
GARDYNE ROAD, BROUGHTY FERRY, DUNDEE DD5 1NY.
TEL.: 01382 455053. FAX: 01382 455046. e-mail: Reception@sccc.ac.uk
Contact: Michael Baughan, Chief Executive; Tegwen Wallace, Senior Information Officer; Anne Gerono, Public Relations and Promotions Officer.
The Scottish Consultative Council on the Curriculum is the principal advisory body to the Secretary of State on all curriculum matters relating to 3-18 year olds in Scottish schools. It has three main functions: to keep the curriculum under review and inform the government on those areas requiring attention; to consult with local authorities, teachers, parents and other representatives of the community; to provide guidance on curriculum development and practice. The Council publishes support materials for government programmes as well as guidance and discussion documents for teachers on aspects of the curriculum.

SCOTTISH COUNCIL FOR RESEARCH IN EDUCATION
15 ST. JOHN STREET, EDINBURGH EH8 8JR.
TEL.: 0131-557 2944. FAX: 0131-556 9454. e-mail: scre@scre.ac.uk
Contact: Professor Wynne Harlen, OBE, Director, e-mail: wynne.harlen@scre.ac.uk; Mr David Gilhooly, Head of Admin Services, e-mail: david.gilhooly@scre.ac.uk; Ms Rosemary Wake, Head of Information Services, e-mail: r.wake@scre.ac.uk.
SCRE's mission is to conduct research for the benefit of education in Scotland and elsewhere. It supports research through disseminating its own and others' research by

conventional and electronic publications and conferences. It supplies information and consultancy to help others conduct and disseminate research and provides training in research methods through workshops and seminars. web: http://www.scre.ac.uk

SFEU
SCOTTISH FURTHER
EDUCATION UNIT

SCOTTISH FURTHER EDUCATION UNIT
ARGYLL COURT, THE CASTLE BUSINESS PARK, STIRLING FK9 4TY.
TEL.: 01786 892000. FAX: 01786 892001. e-mail: sfeu@sfeu.demon.co.uk

Contact: Alison Reid, Chief Executive, 01786 892030; John Laird, Director, 01786 892004; John Young, Director, 01786 892051; Brian Wright, Director, 01786 892003.

The Scottish Further Education Unit is the primary national agency supporting the continued development of further education in Scotland. The Unit works in partnership with all 43 FE colleges in Scotland as well as other national agencies involved in vocational education and training and life-long learning. It undertakes its development role through the provision of consultancy, training and development and its focus of activity is on teaching, learning and assessment, quality, organisation and professional development, research and design development. SFEU: Working for Scotland's colleges.

SCOTTISH PRE-SCHOOL PLAY ASSOCIATION
14 ELLIOT PLACE, GLASGOW G3 8EP.
TEL.: 0141-221 4148. FAX: 0141-221 6043.

Contact: Martha Simpson, Chief Executive; Mary Wales, Development Manager; Robert Walters, Network Manager.

Scottish Pre-School Play Association is a charity committed to the development of quality care and education in pre-school groups which respect the rights, responsibilities and needs of all children and their parents. In SPPA groups children learn and develop through the provision of quality play experience. This voluntary organisation works in partnership with other agencies and plays a major part in the mixed provision of services for pre-school children.

SCOTTISH QUALIFICATIONS AUTHORITY
HANOVER HOUSE, 24 DOUGLAS STREET, GLASGOW G2 7NQ.
TEL.: 0141-242 2214. FAX: 0141-242 2244. e-mail: mail@sqa.org.uk

Contact: Ron Tuck, Chief Executive; David Miller, Chairman; Amanda Cornish, Head of Marketing and PR.

The Scottish Qualifications Authority offers a framework for education and training for the whole population of Scotland from school age onwards. It develops and awards most of Scotland's qualifications including Standard and Higher Grades, normally taken at school; Higher National Certificates (HNCs) and Higher National Diplomas (HNDs), usually taken at college; and Scottish Vocational Qualifications (SVQs), the workplace based qualification. The qualifications on offer cover a huge range of skills – both academic and vocational – at all levels.

SCOTTISH SECONDARY TEACHERS' ASSOCIATION
15 DUNDAS STREET, EDINBURGH EH3 6QG.
TEL.: 0131-556 5919. FAX: 0131-556 1419. e-mail: sstateach@aol.com

Contact: David H. Eaglesham, BEd, General Secretary.

The Association was founded to advance education in Scotland and to safeguard and promote the interests of Scottish secondary teachers especially regarding salaries and conditions of service. We represent members within schools, at local authority levels, and nationally through bodies such as the SJNC and GTC. This representation is carried out for individuals as well as the whole membership, and involves shaping the future of education in Scotland as well as offering a comprehensive range of services to members.

SSERC LIMITED (TRADING AS SSERC AND STS SUPPORT SERVICES)
ST. MARY'S BUILDING, 23 HOLYROOD ROAD, EDINBURGH EH8 8AE.
TEL.: 0131-558 8180. FAX: 0131-558 8191. e-mail: sserc@mhie.ac.uk
Contact: John Richardson, Executive Director.
Technical resource support for education. Advisory, information, consultancy, testing and training services on anything connected with the purchase, use (including health and safety), maintenance and repair of equipment and materials for education, health and safety, management training and consultancy.

ENERGY

BRITISH ENERGY PLC
10 LOCHSIDE PLACE, EDINBURGH EH12 9DF.
TEL.: 0131-527 2000. FAX: 0131-527 2277.
Contact: John Robb, Chairman; Peter Hollins, Chief Executive; Robert Armour, Company Secretary.
British Energy is the UK's largest electricity generator with around one fifth of the market. British Energy owns and operates the UK's eight modern nuclear power stations – with two in Scotland at Hunterston B in Ayrshire and Torness in East Lothian – and is seeking to establish partnerships with other UK and international energy companies.

ENERGY ACTION SCOTLAND
SUITE 4A, INGRAM HOUSE, 227 INGRAM STREET, GLASGOW G1 1DA.
TEL.: 0141-226 3064. FAX: 0141-221 2788.
Contact: Ann Loughrey, Director; Norman Kerr, Development Officer; Allana Parker, PR/Information Officer.
The national organisation in Scotland promoting affordable warmth and investment in practical energy-efficiency solutions in the domestic sector. EAS assists local authorities and housing associations in developing integrated strategies to make dwellings more energy-efficient. The charity offers training in energy advice, energy auditing and consultancy services. It campaigns for warm, dry homes and provides information on fuel poverty. Publications include: *Energy Review* (quarterly journal); *Developing an Energy-Efficiency Strategy* (for local authorities); and *Fuel Poverty in Scotland.*

≡Scottish and Southern Energy plc

SCOTTISH AND SOUTHERN ENERGY PLC
10 DUNKELD ROAD, PERTH PH1 5WA.
TEL.: 01738 455040. FAX: 01738 455045. web: www.hydro.co.uk
Contact: Jim Forbes, Chief Executive; Carolyn McAdam, Director of Corporate Communications.
Scottish and Southern Energy plc was formed by the merger of Scottish Hydro-Electric and Southern Electric. The company has 3.3 million customers from Shetland to the Isle of Wight. It operates the largest network of lines in the UK and has an expanding fleet of power stations throughout the UK. It is the largest generator of renewable energy and its power stations are the youngest and most efficient of the major generators. Our aim is to deliver exceptional products, services and value for money to all our customers and therefore provide attractive returns for our shareholders.

FINANCIAL

ACCOUNTS COMMISSION FOR SCOTLAND
18 GEORGE STREET, EDINBURGH EH2 2QU.
TEL.: 0131-477 1234. FAX: 0131-477 4567.

Contact: Ian Percy, Chairman; Robert W. Black, Controller of Audit; William F. Magee, Secretary.

The Accounts Commission is a statutory, independent body which, through the audit process, assists local authorities and NHS bodies to achieve the highest standards of financial stewardship and the economic, efficient and effective use of their resources.

ADAM & COMPANY GROUP PLC
22 CHARLOTTE SQUARE, EDINBURGH EH2 4DF.
TEL.: 0131-225 8484. FAX: 0131-225 5136.

Contact: Ray Entwistle, Group Managing Director; Mark Hedderwick, Managing Director, Adam & Company Investment Management Limited; Douglas Corner, Director (Glasgow).

Adam & Company is a private bank that effectively combines banking with investment management – providing a full asset and liability management service. As well as all the normal facilities expected from a bank, Adam holds in great store the old-fashioned courtesies that were a hallmark of banking in bygone days and endeavours to provide guidance in most aspects of the financial life of their clients.

ASSOCIATION OF BRITISH INSURERS
51 GRESHAM STREET, LONDON EC2V 7HQ.
TEL.: 0171-600 3333. FAX: 0171-696 8996.

Contact: Vic Rance, Manager, Media, 0171-216 7440 (After-hours: 0181-647 5188); Suzanne Moore, Assistant Manager, Media, 0171-216 7411 (After-hours: 0370 441277); Malcolm Tarling, Assistant Manager, Media, 0171-216 7410 (After-hours: 0181-297 9510).

The Association of British Insurers represents around 440 insurance companies, which between them account for over 95 per cent of the business of UK insurance companies. The Association represents insurance companies to the Government and to regulatory and other agencies, and it provides a wide range of services to its members.

THE CHARTERED INSTITUTE OF BANKERS IN SCOTLAND
DRUMSHEUGH HOUSE, 38B DRUMSHEUGH GARDENS, EDINBURGH EH3 7SW.
TEL.: 0131-473 7777. FAX: 0131-473 7788. e-mail: info@ciobs.org.uk

Contact: Dr. Charles W. Munn, Chief Executive; Colin A. Morrison, Director of Education; Derek J. Langley, Business Development Manager.

The Chartered Institute of Bankers in Scotland is the professional and educational body for the Scottish Financial Services Industry. The main aims of the Institute are to: encourage the highest standards of professionalism and conduct amongst its members; improve and extend the knowledge and expertise of those engaged in the financial services industry; conduct examinations and promote the continued study of financial services; establish links, co-operate with other professional or educational bodies and represent the financial services industry both nationally and internationally. web: http://www.ciobs.org.uk

CIPFA (THE CHARTERED INSTITUTE OF PUBLIC FINANCE & ACCOUNTANCY)
8 NORTH WEST CIRCUS PLACE, EDINBURGH EH3 6ST.
TEL.: 0131-220 4316. FAX: 0131-220 4305. e-mail: cipfa.scotland@cipfa.org

Contact: Ian P. Doig, CPFA, Director (Scotland); Valerie Davidson, CPFA, Depute Director (Scotland).

GEOLOGY

HEALTH

0131-662 8109.
The British Medical Association, founded in 1832, represents doctors from all branches of medicine in the UK. It is a voluntary professional association, independent trade union, scientific and educational body and a publishing house. The BMA and the BMJ Publishing Group, which is one of the most influential medical publishers in the world, produce a wide range of journals, reports and medical books. With a UK membership of 111,000, and nearly 12,000 in Scotland, the BMA is regarded as the voice of the medical profession.

CHEST, HEART AND STROKE SCOTLAND
65 NORTH CASTLE STREET, EDINBURGH EH2 3LT.
TEL.: 0131-225 6963. FAX: 0131-220 6313. e-mail:chss@dial.pipex.com
Contact: Mr David H. Clark, Chief Executive; Professor Charles Forbes, FRCP, FRSEd; Chairman; Mrs Janet Buncle, Director of Public Relations.
Chest, Heart and Stroke Scotland is an independent Scottish medical charity which aims to improve the quality of life for people affected by chest, heart and stroke illness, and their carers. We seek to achieve this through programmes of medical research, health promotion, advice and information, and the provision of services in the community.

ERSKINE HOSPITAL
BISHOPTON, RENFREWSHIRE PA7 5PU.
TEL.: 0141-812 1100. FAX: 0141-812 3733.
Contact: Colonel M.F. Gibson, OBE, Chief Executive; Dr T. McFadyen, Director, Medical Services; Mr I.W. Grimmond, Director of Finance.
Founded in 1916, now operates as an integrated nursing home with physiotherapy, occupational therapy and speech therapy and a wide range of activities for disabled ex-Service men and women requiring medical, nursing and residential care, including respite. Also has a holiday home in Dunoon, three ground floor self-catering flats for the disabled at moderate cost, two supported workshops providing paid employment for disabled people and 55 cottages within the estate for War Pensioners and their families. Erskine 2000 project to provide modern care facilities at Erskine and Scotland-wide underway. Appeal to raise additional £5m. launched October 1997.

HEALTH EDUCATION BOARD FOR SCOTLAND
WOODBURN HOUSE, CANAAN LANE, EDINBURGH EH10 4SG.
TEL.: 0131-536 5500. FAX: 0131-536 5501.
Contact: Martin Raymond, Deputy Director of Programmes and Communications/Head of Public Affairs; Graham Robertson, Deputy Chief Executive/Director of Programmes and Communications; Professor Andrew Tannahill, Chief Executive.
The Health Education Board for Scotland gives leadership to the health education effort in Scotland. Its aim is to promote good health through the empowerment of individuals, groups and communities. HEBS is committed to the development, implementation and support of effective, efficient and ethical health education, responsive to the needs and priorities of the population and its sub-groups. As well as providing programmes of health education at the national level, the Board facilitates the development and co-ordination of complementary initiatives sub-nationally across Scotland. It contributes to the education and training of relevant professionals and others, reviews, undertakes and commissions relevant research, and gives advice on policies which affect health. The Board's tasks involve communication and collaboration with a wide range of partners, in Scotland and beyond.

HIGH BLOOD PRESSURE FOUNDATION
DEPT. OF MEDICINE, WESTERN GENERAL HOSPITAL, EDINBURGH EH9 1JN.
TEL.: 0131-332 9211. FAX: 0131-537 1012. e-mail: hbpf@hbpf.org.uk
Contact: Rosalind Newton, Director; Dr. Paul Padfield, Chairman.

The High Blood Pressure Foundation is dedicated to improving the basic understanding, assessment, treatment and public awareness of high blood pressure, and, in so doing, help promote the welfare of people with high blood pressure.

LEUKAEMIA RESEARCH FUND
43 WESTBOURNE GARDENS, GLASGOW G12 9XQ.
TEL.: 0141-339 0690. FAX: 0141-339 0690.

Contact: Mrs Mae Naddell, Scottish Secretary, 0141-339 1101; Mrs Shirley Carnegie, Chairman, Glasgow, 0141-637 8384; Mrs Claire Mulholland, Secretary, Glasgow, 0141-339 0690.

Founded in 1960, we want to improve treatments, find cures and prevent all forms of leukaemia and related cancers including Hodgkin's disease and other lymphomas, myeloma, the myelodysplasias, myeloproliferative disorders and aplastic anaemia. We are committed to nationally organised research of the highest calibre, guided by strict impartial expert advice, and to international collaboration. We aim to co-ordinate fundraising throughout the UK towards these ends. Our administration costs are five per cent.

NATIONAL BOARD FOR NURSING, MIDWIFERY AND HEALTH VISITING FOR SCOTLAND
22 QUEEN STREET, EDINBURGH EH2 1NT.
TEL.: 0131-226 7371. FAX: 0131-225 9970.

Contact: Mrs Isobel Mackinlay, Chairman, Ext. 214; Mr David Benton, Chief Executive, Ext. 211; Mr David Ferguson, Board Secretary, Ext. 202.

The National Board is the statutory body responsible in Scotland for ensuring professional standards of education and training for nurses, midwives and health visitors.

ROYAL COLLEGE OF PHYSICIANS AND SURGEONS
232-242 ST. VINCENT STREET, GLASGOW G2 5RJ.
TEL.: 0141-221 6072. FAX: 0141-221 1804.

Contact: Mr Colin MacKay, President; Dr Colin Semple, Honorary Secretary; Mr Robert Littlejohn, Registrar, e-mail: registrar@rcpsglasg.ac.uk.

The College is responsible for postgraduate medical and dental training in the West of Scotland. Through its examinations in medicine, surgery and dentistry, and regular inspections of hospital posts which are accredited for training purposes, the College ensures that the highest standards are maintained. The College has a full programme of training courses, symposia and guest lectures on both general and specialist topics, which are attended by medical students, junior doctors, consultants, dentists and general practitioners. In addition the College offers lectures of wider interest (eg to schools) and there is an annual open day.

THE ROYAL COLLEGE OF SURGEONS OF EDINBURGH
NICOLSON STREET, EDINBURGH EH8 9DW.
TEL.: 0131-527 1600. FAX: 0131-557 6406. e-mail: library@rcsed.ac.uk

The Royal College of Surgeons of Edinburgh is a body incorporated by Royal Charter and is concerned with education and training for medical and surgical practice and with the maintenance of high standards of professional competence and conduct.

SCOTTISH ASSOCIATION OF HEALTH COUNCILS
24A PALMERSTON PLACE, EDINBURGH EH12 5AL.
TEL.: 0131-220 4101. FAX: 0131-220 4108. e-mail: sahc@sol.co.uk

Contact: Patricia Dawson, Director; Andrew Gardiner, Convener; John Taylor, Vice Convener.

The SAHC seeks to be the national voice of the public in health matters.

Scottish Heart and Arterial Risk Prevention (SHARP)
University Department of Medicine, Ninewells Hospital and Medical School, Dundee DD1 9SY. Tel.: 01382 660111, Ext. 33124. Fax: 01382 660675.
e-mail: s.r.mcewan@dundee.ac.uk

Contact: Dr Shirley R. McEwan, MBE, Chairman and Medical Administrator; Dr Fergus Daly, Senior Research Fellow, e-mail: f.daly@dundee.ac.uk; Ms Elaine Anderson, Secretary.

SHARP is a Scottish medical charity founded and run by clinicians, whose aim is to reduce the incidence of premature diseases of the heart and arteries, which lead to heart attacks, strokes and gangrene. The aims of the organisation are pursued through research, the identification through screening of high risk individuals, the education of health professionals at scientific meetings, and the raising of awareness in the public of the need for a healthy lifestyle, through the production of educational materials.

Tak Tent Cancer Support Scotland
Block C, 20 Western Court, 100 University Place, Glasgow G12 6SQ.
Tel.: 0141-211 1930. Fax: 0141-211 1879.

Contact: Mrs Carol Horne, Manager, 0141-211 1931; Mrs Una Gibson, Counselling Co-ordinator, 0141-211 2734.

Tak Tent seeks to provide emotional support to cancer patients, their relatives and friends, through a network of local support groups giving self-help; through information and counselling in the resource centre; and through the youth project which supports patients, carers and friends who are 16 to 25 years old.

Housing

Scottish Council for Single Homeless
Wellgate House, 200 Cowgate, Edinburgh EH1 1NQ.
Tel.: 0131-226 4382. Fax: 0131-225 4382. e-mail: robert@scsh.demon.co.uk

Contact: Laurie Naumann, Director; Robert Aldridge, Information Officer; Alison Brown, Research and Development Officer.

Campaigns throughout Scotland, firstly, to highlight the wide-ranging needs of single homeless people for access to secure accommodation according to individual requirements and, secondly, for the prevention of homelessness. SCSH also presses for improvements in the law and in the practices of service providers, publishes a monthly newsletter, undertakes training and research, publishes reports and offers advice and information to individuals and agencies. SCSH works closely with others in the voluntary, statutory and independent sectors and has a particular interest in community care issues.

Scottish Federation of Housing Associations
38 York Place, Edinburgh EH1 3HU.
Tel.: 0131-556 5777. Fax: 0131-557 6028.
e-mail: sfha@sfha.co.uk

Contact: David Orr, Director; Dave Alexander, Depute Director; Jimmy Black, Communications Officer.

The SFHA aims to contribute to the provision of high quality, affordable housing and housing related services, and to the creation of sustainable communities, by promoting, representing and providing services to housing associations and co-operatives in Scotland, and by campaigning on their behalf.

SCOTTISH HOUSING ASSOCIATIONS CHARITABLE TRUST
38 YORK PLACE, EDINBURGH EH1 3HU.
TEL.: 0131-556 5777. FAX: 0131-557 6028.

Contact: Alison Rigg Campbell, Director; Jayne Gross, Development Officer.
Aims to provide good quality housing and support throughout Scotland by giving grants and loans to voluntary organisations. Funds are raised from housing associations, individuals and the corporate sector. Funds are also distributed on behalf of other trusts. SHACT depends on donations to support its work.

LOCAL GOVERNMENT

ANGUS COUNCIL
THE CROSS, FORFAR DD8 1BX.
TEL.: 01307 461460. FAX: 01307 461874.

Contact: Mr A.B. Watson, Chief Executive, 01307 473023.
Scottish local authority providing full range of services, with the following key themes: to promote the identity of and represent the interests of Angus locally, nationally and internationally; to aim to provide excellent public services, maximising the use of available resources to meet local needs; to improve economic prosperity in Angus; to improve the environment and the quality of life in Angus, with an emphasis on sustainability; to promote equal opportunities/reduce inequalities in Angus; to value staff as the Council's most important asset, and seek to ensure long-term employment prospects for a locally based and directly employed workforce; to develop partnerships.

COMMISSIONER FOR LOCAL ADMINISTRATION IN SCOTLAND
(LOCAL GOVERNMENT OMBUDSMAN)
23 WALKER STREET, EDINBURGH EH3 7HX.
TEL.: 0131-225 5300. FAX: 0131-225 9495.

Contact: Janice Renton, Deputy Commissioner.
The Commissioner (Local Government Ombudsman) investigates complaints of injustice against local authorities arising from maladministration and also Scottish Homes in connection with housing matters. The Ombudsman will not normally accept a complaint unless it has first been raised formally with the authority. The service is independent and impartial and there is no charge. Information, leaflets and complaint forms are available on application.

Dumfries
& Galloway
COUNCIL
Serving South West Scotland

DUMFRIES & GALLOWAY COUNCIL
COUNCIL OFFICES, ENGLISH STREET, DUMFRIES DG1 2DD.
TEL.: 01387 260000. FAX: 01387 260034.

Contact: Philip N. Jones, Chief Executive, 01387 26006; Liz Manson, Research Assistant, 01387 260074, e-mail: lizma@ dumgal.gov.uk
Dumfries & Galloway Council is the single local authority serving south west Scotland. The Council's stated aim is to develop the diverse areas of Dumfries & Galloway to their full and sustainable potential to provide a high level of services and quality of life for all its people. The Council will achieve this through our corporate commitments to service improvement, quality and performance, communications and a shared policy agenda (health, governance, regeneration and community safety).

EAST AYRSHIRE COUNCIL
COUNCIL HEADQUARTERS, LONDON ROAD, KILMARNOCK KA3 7BU.
TEL.: 01563 576000. FAX: 01563 576500.

Contact: Douglas Campbell, Head of PR and Marketing, 01563 576165, e-mail: douglas.campbell@east-ayrshire.gov.uk; David Montgomery, Chief Executive; Councillor David Sneller, Leader of the Council.

Built on the four core values of quality, equality, access and partnership, the Council delivers local government services within East Ayrshire including the communities of: Kilmarnock, Stewarton, Crosshouse, Fenwick, Galston, Darvel, Newmilns, Mauchline, Auchinleck, Cumnock, Muirkirk, New Cumnock, Dalmellington, Patna, Ochiltree, Catrine, Stair, Rankinston.

GLASGOW CITY COUNCIL
CITY CHAMBERS, GEORGE SQUARE, GLASGOW G2 1DU.
TEL.: 0141-287 2000. FAX: 0141-287 5666.

Contact: James Andrews, Acting Chief Executive; John Brown, Head of Public Relations and Marketing.

Scotland's largest "unitary" council serving City of Glasgow. Population 617,000. Budget 1998/99 £1.7bn. (gross). Main services – education, social work, housing, environmental health, local roads, parks and recreation, planning, licensing, economic development, museums and art galleries and libraries.

MIDLOTHIAN COUNCIL
MIDLOTHIAN HOUSE, BUCCLEUCH STREET, DALKEITH, MIDLOTHIAN EH22 1DJ.
TEL.: 0131-270 7500. FAX: 0131-271 3251.

Contact: Trevor Muir, Chief Executive, 0131-270 7500.

Midlothian is situated to the south of Scotland's capital city of Edinburgh. Midlothian Council serves a population of 80,000, covering a geographical area of over 35,515 hectares, incorporating the main towns of Penicuik, Bonnyrigg, Dalkeith, Mayfield and Easthouses, Loanhead and Gorebridge. The Council employs over 4,000 people.

MARINE AND COASTAL

DUNSTAFFNAGE MARINE LABORATORY –
CENTRE FOR COASTAL AND MARINE SCIENCES
P.O. BOX 3, OBAN, ARGYLL PA34 4AD
TEL.: 01631 562244. FAX: 01631 565518. e-mail: mail@ccms.ac.uk

Contact: Mrs Helen Anderson, Activities Manager.

Dunstaffnage Marine Laboratory (DML) is a host laboratory of the Natural Environment Research Council. It hosts the Scottish Association for Marine Science (SAMS) and is one of the Centre for Coastal and Marine Sciences' Institutes. Scientists from the Laboratory play a major role in many national and international marine scientific programmes. The Laboratory operates two research vessels with state-of-the-art navigation, remote sensing and marine sampling equipment. Dr. Graham Shimmield is the Director of both DML and SAMS.

NORTHERN LIGHTHOUSE BOARD
84 GEORGE STREET, EDINBURGH EH2 3DA.
TEL.: 0131-473 3100. FAX: 0131-220 2093.
e-mail: nlb@dial.pipex.com

Contact: Captain James Taylor, Chief Executive; Douglas Gorman, Director of Finance; Lorna Grieve, Public Relations and Information Officer.

The Board provides marine aids to navigation – lighthouses, buoys, beacons and a precision satellite navigation system in Scotland and the Isle of Man. It receives no public monies and is funded entirely by light dues paid by merchant shipping and fishing vessels.

Scottish Association for Marine Science
P.O. Box 3, Oban, Argyll PA34 4AD.
Tel.: 01631 562244. Fax: 01631 565518. e-mail: mail@ccms.ac.uk
Contact: Mrs Helen Anderson, Activities Manager.
The Scottish Association for Marine Science (SAMS) is based at Dunstaffnage Marine Laboratory (DML). SAMS promotes education and research in marine science and scientists from SAMS and DML play a major role in many national and international scientific programmes. The Laboratory operates two research vessels with state-of-the-art navigation, remote sensing and marine sampling equipment. SAMS is an academic partner in the University of the Highlands and Islands Project. Dr. Graham Shimmield is the Director of both SAMS and DML.

Media and Publishing

Grampian Television
Queen's Cross, Aberdeen AB15 4XJ.
Tel.: 01224 846846. Fax: 01224 846800. e-mail: gtv@grampiantv.co.uk
Contact: Derek Thomson, Controller; Hilary Buchan, Head of Public Relations.
Grampian Television serves North Scotland as a producer licensee, with 99 per cent of its wide range of regional programmes made in the area. It produces additional Gaelic programmes funded by the Gaelic Broadcasting Committee, schools programmes for Channel Four, and ITV Network shows which include the highly popular *National TV Awards*. For 36 years, Grampian Television has ensured that its area, larger than Belgium or Denmark, enjoys a service that meets its distinctive regional requirements. The Station has a licence to continue this service until 2002 but it can apply for a 10 year extension before that date.

Independent Television Commission
123 Blythswood Street, Glasgow G2 4AN.
Tel.: 0141-226 4436. Fax: 0141-226 4682.
Contact: Brian Marjoribanks, Head of ITC, Scotland; Alan Stewart, Deputy Head of ITC, Scotland; Veronica McDowall, Assistant Head of ITC, Scotland.
The Independent Television Commission (ITC) is the public body responsible for licensing and regulating all non-BBC television services operating in or for the UK. These include ITV, Channel 4, Channel 5, digital services, a range of cable, satellite, text and data services. The National Office in Scotland has a particular responsibility to liaise with the licensees in Scotland and to promote awareness and understanding of the ITC's functions.

Northsound Radio
45 Kingsgate, Aberdeen AB15 4EL.
Tel.: 01224 632234. Fax: 01224 400003. e-mail: webster@srh.co.uk
Contact: Rod Webster, Managing Director; Fiona Stalker, Head of News; Lewis Carnie, Sales Director.
Commercial radio station serving NE Scotland, broadcasting local and national news and weather, local information. Split into two services, Northsound One on FM, and Northsound Two on AM, the station provides entertainment and information as the top-rated broadcaster in national research.

Scottish Publishers Association
Scottish Book Centre, 137 Dundee Street, Edinburgh EH11 1BG.
Tel.: 0131-228 6866. Fax: 0131-228 3220. e-mail: enquiries@scottishbooks.org
Contact: Lorraine Fannin, Director; Alison Rae, Marketing Services; Allan Shanks, Scottish Book Marketing Group and Training.
The SPA aims to help publishing concerns in Scotland to conduct their book publishing businesses in a professional manner, to market their output to a wide readership within Scotland, the UK and overseas, and to encourage the development of a literary culture in

Scotland. A programme of activities is planned annually, including marketing, publicity, advertising, provision of training, and attendance at book fairs. These are provided to all member publishers whatever their size, scope, speciality or geographical location.

POLITICAL

SCOTTISH LABOUR PARTY
KEIR HARDIE CAMPAIGN OFFICE, 4TH FLOOR, DELTA HOUSE, 50 WEST NILE STREET, GLASGOW G1 2NA.
TEL.: 0141-572 6900. FAX: 0141-572 2566. e-mail: general@scottish-labour.org
Contact: Alex Rowley, General Secretary; Lorraine Davidson, Director of Communications; Lesley Quinn, Assistant General Secretary.
The official organisation of the Labour Party in Scotland – organising campaigns, events and publicity for a Labour victory at elections. Youth Section, election candidates and party staff can all be contacted via the head office.

SCOTTISH LIBERAL DEMOCRATS
4 CLIFTON TERRACE, EDINBURGH EH12 5DR.
TEL.: 0131-337 2314. FAX: 0131-337 3566. e-mail: scotlibdem@cix.co.uk
Contact: Willie Rennie, Chief Executive; Rae Grant, Party Administrator; Dawn Williamson, Administrative Officer.
Scotland's second strongest Party with 10 MPs and over 130 councillors. Led by Jim Wallace MP, the Party is trying to raise the standard of Scottish politics by dealing with the issues that matter, such as health and education, and not the constitutional arguments of the past. The Liberal Democrats play important roles in the running of Aberdeenshire, Dumfries and Galloway, and Borders Councils. The Party is likely to hold the balance of power in the new Parliament.

SCOTTISH NATIONAL PARTY
6 NORTH CHARLOTTE STREET, EDINBURGH EH2 4JH.
TEL.: 0131-226 3661. FAX: 0131-226 7373. e-mail: snp.hq@snp.org.uk
Contact: Michael W. Russell, Chief Executive, e-mail: michael.russell@snp.org.uk
Scotland's only political party with the aim of independence within the European Union. Six MPs, two MEPs and hundreds of councillors; branches all over Scotland. web: www.snp.org.uk

PROFESSIONAL SERVICES

1. CHARTERED ACCOUNTANTS

THE McCABE PARTNERSHIP
56 PALMERSTON PLACE, EDINBURGH EH10 5AY.
TEL.: 0131-225 6366. FAX: 0131-220 1041.
e-mail: enquiries@mccabe-partnership.org.uk
Contact: Barry Laurie, Tax Partner, 0131-225 6366; Jeffrey A.C. Meek, Managing Partner, 0131-225 6366.
One of Scotland's foremost firms of chartered accountants with clients throughout the UK. Focussed on consultancy services that help businesses to set and attain their goals. Key growth services, strategic planning, business finance and tax consultancy and accountancy. Key markets: hospitality and leisure, technology and media, charities.

2. Chartered Surveyors

DM|HALL

DM Hall & Son
36 Melville Street, Edinburgh EH3 7HA.
Tel.: 0131-477 6000. Fax: 0131-477 6016.

Contact: I.D. Sutherland, Managing Partner; M.J. Mendelssohn, Commercial Partner; M.S. Ramsay, Residential Partner.

Chartered Surveyors with 27 offices in Scotland. Over 100 years experience of general practice surveying work. The majority of the current workload lies in the residential sector although there are separate divisions dealing with commercial work, building surveying, quantity surveying and rural practice. There are 41 partners and 40 professional staff.

3. Legal Firms

BIGGART BAILLIE
SOLICITORS

Biggart Baillie
Dalmore House, 310 St. Vincent Street, Glasgow G2 5QR.
Tel.: 0141-228 8000. Fax: 0141-228 8310. e-mail: info@biggartbaillie.co.uk

Contact: Campbell Smith, Managing Partner; Gordon Wyllie, Head of Private Client Department; David Ross, Head of Corporate Department.

Biggart Baillie provide practical legal advice on business and personal matters including contracts, company law, MBOs/MBIs, property sale, purchase or lease, employment, construction, intellectual property, matrimonial and family law from our offices in Glasgow and Edinburgh.

Burnside Kemp Fraser
4 Queens Terrace, Aberdeen AB10 1XL.
Tel.: 01224 624602. Fax: 01224 624011. e-mail: sandy@bkfak.demon.co.uk

Contact: David M. Burnside, Partner; Alexander Kemp, Partner; Charlie Fraser, Partner.

A three partner specialist legal firm providing a range of legal services including employment law and personal injury claims together with divorce and family law and a full house purchase and sale service. David Burnside and Sandy Kemp are certified by the Law Society of Scotland as specialists in employment law and are members of the Personal Injury Panel. The firm has been involved in a number of high profile cases.

Golds Solicitors
8 Newton Terrace, Glasgow G3 7PJ.
Tel.: 0141-300 4300. Fax: 0141-300 4350. e-mail: golds@golds.co.uk

Contact: Stephen H. Gold, Senior Partner; Jonathan Edwards, Managing Partner; Louise Irvine, Client Services Manager.

Golds Solicitors, Glasgow, is a leading Scottish law firm recommended by all the independent guides. Our core areas are company and commercial work; banking; building society; and commercial finance; housing association; commercial property; and litigation. We are market leaders in providing innovative, IT-based work, in particular for the lending industry. The firm is active throughout Scotland.

PROFESSIONAL AND TRADE ORGANISATIONS

THE LAW SOCIETY OF SCOTLAND
26 DRUMSHEUGH GARDENS, EDINBURGH EH3 7YR.
TEL.: 0131-226 7411. FAX: 0131-225 2934. e-mail: lawscot@lawscot.org.uk

Contact: Philip J.S. Dry, President; Michael Scanlan, Vice President; Douglas R. Mill, Secretary.

The Law Society of Scotland is the governing body of the Scottish legal profession. The Society promotes the interests of solicitors and the public in relation to the Scottish solicitors profession. It regulates its members and administers the master insurance policy for all practising solicitors. It provides services including: continuing legal education; advice on professional practice, European law, mediation, a solicitor referral service; and Dial-A-Law, a telephone information and referral service. The Society promotes law reforms and undertakes legal research. Web: http://www.lawscot.org.uk

THE ROYAL INSTITUTION OF CHARTERED SURVEYORS IN SCOTLAND
9 MANOR PLACE, EDINBURGH EH3 7DN.
TEL.: 0131-225 7078. FAX: 0131-226 3599. e-mail: scot@rics.org.uk

Contact: Eileen Masterman, Director; Graeme Hartley, Deputy Director; Elizabeth Bruce, Assistant Director (Communications).

The principal objectives of the RICS in Scotland are to: promote the knowledge and skills of chartered surveyors and the services they offer; maintain high standards of qualification for membership of the Institution; maintain high standards of professional conduct; and ensure the continuing development of the knowledge and skill base of chartered surveyors.

SCOTTISH DAIRY ASSOCIATION
46 UNDERWOOD ROAD, PAISLEY PA3 1TL.
TEL.: 0141-848 0009. FAX: 0141-848 5559.
e-mail: scotdairy@dial.pipex.com

Contact: K.J. Hunter.

Representing the interests of dairy companies active in the Scottish market.

THE SCOTTISH PHARMACEUTICAL FEDERATION
135 WELLINGTON STREET, GLASGOW G2 2XD.
TEL.: 0141-221 1235. FAX: 0141-248 5892; 0141-226 5047.
e-mail: secretary@spf.netkonect.co.uk

Contact: F.E.J. McCrossin, Secretary/Treasurer; G.E. Allan, Chairman; I.J. Johnston, Vice Chairman.

The SPF represents owners of community pharmacies in Scotland, looking after the interests of some 550 members who own approximately 1,050 pharmacies. It runs a monthly Clearing House service for members and in conjunction with the National Pharmaceutical Association, to which it is affiliated, provides professional indemnity cover, business and financial services, commercial insurance, information and guidance on pharmaceutical and business matters. The SPF is run by an Executive Council of 16 members from all parts of Scotland.

SOCIETY FOR COMPUTERS & LAW
10 HURLE CRESCENT, CLIFTON, BRISTOL BS8 2TA.
TEL.: 0117-923 7393. FAX: 0117 923 9305. e-mail: ruth.baker@scl.org

Contact: John Sibbald, Scottish Group Chairman; Miss Rosemary Colquhoun, WS, Scottish Group Secretary; S.P. Riddell, Scottish Group Meetings Convener.

The Society exists to develop information technology for lawyers and information technology law. It is run by an elected council supported by secretariat in Bristol. Membership is available to anyone interested in the Society's aims and objectives. Established in 1988, the Scottish Group represents members' interests within the Scottish jurisdiction and holds regular events throughout the year. For further information contact the General Manager, Mrs Ruth Baker at the above address or visit website: http://www.scl.org

RELIGIOUS

THE CHURCH OF SCOTLAND
121 GEORGE STREET, EDINBURGH EH2 4YN
TEL.: 0131-225 5722. FAX: 0131-220 3113.

Contact: Rev. Dr. Finlay A.J. Macdonald, Principal Clerk of the General Assembly.

The Church of Scotland, part of the one Holy, Catholic and Apostolic Church, is the national church in Scotland, recognised by the State but independent in spiritual matters. Trinitarian in doctrine, Reformed in tradition and Presbyterian in polity, it exists to glorify God, to work for the advancement of Christ's kingdom throughout the world and to provide religious services for the people in Scotland, through parish ministry. It co-operates with other churches in various ecumenical bodies in Scotland and beyond.

FREE PRESBYTERIAN CHURCH OF SCOTLAND
133 WOODLANDS ROAD, GLASGOW G3 6LE.
TEL.: 0141-332 9283. FAX: 0141-332 4271.
e-mail:gentreas@compuserve.com

Contact: Rev. J. MacLeod, MA, Clerk of Synod, 16 Matheson Road, Stornoway, Isle of Lewis HS1 2LA, Tel.: 01851 702755. Fax: 01851 702919, e-mail: j.macl@aol.com; Mr R.A. Campbell, General Treasurer, as above; Rev. D.A. Ross, Moderator of Synod, 1998/99, Free Presbyterian Manse, Laide, Achnasheen IV22 2NB.

The Free Presbyterian Church of Scotland exists to promote the biblical doctrines of the Christian faith in the UK and abroad by preaching the Gospel, administering the Sacraments and exercising ecclesiastical discipline, and by publishing and selling Christian literature and providing educational and medical facilities, along with care for the elderly and for orphans.

NATIONAL BIBLE SOCIETY OF SCOTLAND
7 HAMPTON TERRACE, EDINBURGH EH12 5XU.
TEL.: 0131-337 9701. FAX: 0131-337 0641. e-mail: nbss@nat-bible-society.org

Contact: Rev. Dr. Graham Houston, Executive Director; Mr David Cochrane, Bibleworld Co-ordinator; Mrs Sheila Fraser, Bibleworld Co-ordinator.

The Bible Society exists to translate, produce and distribute the Bible in a language people can understand and at a price they can afford to pay. The Society is also involved in programmes and products which enable people to use and interact with God's Word.

RURAL, CROFTING, LAND

CROFTERS COMMISSION
4-6 CASTLE WYND, INVERNESS IV2 3EQ.
TEL.: 01463 663450. FAX: 01463 711820. e-mail: crofters_commission @cali.co.uk

Contact: Brian MacDonald, Information Officer, 01463 663447.

The Commission is a non-departmental public body set up in 1955 by the Crofters (Scotland) Act. We aim to promote a thriving crofting community by regulating crofting effectively, increasing contact with people in crofting communities, working closely with partner organisations, encouraging the best use of croft land, developing crofting and advising the Secretary of State for Scotland on matters relating to crofting.

RURAL FORUM SCOTLAND
HIGHLAND HOUSE, 46 ST. CATHERINE'S ROAD, PERTH PH1 5RY.
TEL.: 01738 634565. FAX: 01738 638699. e-mail: rural@ruralforum.org.uk

Contact: Sally Moschard, Secretary; Deirdre Hutton, Chairman; Barbara Kelly CBE, President.

Rural Forum is an alliance of non-governmental organisations that includes agricultural, environmental, business, trade union, consumer and community interests. A membership organisation, it brings together local authorities, community councils, government agencies and departments as well as individuals active in rural areas. It aims to address rural matters in an integrated way involving people living and working in the countryside. Three main areas of work: policy and innovation (includes undertaking and commissioning research, organising conferences, seminars, exchanges, etc); Rural Action Network (aims to support action at the local level by providing grants, advice and information); and Rural Housing Service (incorporates both a research and a community involvement element in respect of rural housing issues). Has a number of publications including a quarterly magazine, conference reports, case studies in rural development and reports on research and demonstration projects.

SCOTTISH LANDOWNERS' FEDERATION
STUART HOUSE, ESKMILLS BUSINESS PARK, MUSSELBURGH EH21 7PH.
TEL.: 0131-653 5400. Fax: 0131-653 5401. e-mail: slfinfo@slf.org.uk

Contact: Andrew Dingwall-Fordyce, Convener; Maurice S. Hankey, BSc, PhD, Director.
Represents the whole spectrum of landowners in Scotland. There are approximately 4,000 members. The aims of the Federation are: to promote high standards of management and use of land; to ensure proper communication on matters relating to the ownership of land between its members, other organisations and the wider public; and to ensure that legislation and policies affecting landownership and use are prepared with proper consideration for the responsibilities and rights of landowners, in addition to the well-being of rural communities, the environment, and the wider public interests.

SCHOOLS
(see also Education)

ALBYN SCHOOL FOR GIRLS
17-23 QUEENS ROAD, ABERDEEN AB15 4PB.
TEL.: 01224 322408. FAX: 01224 209173.

Contact: Mrs Jenny Thomson, Assistant to Head; Mrs Sheena B. Taylor, Head; Mrs Louie Parker, Head of Lower School.
Albyn School provides a caring, supportive and happy atmosphere where girls are enabled to achieve excellence in academic subjects and participate in a wide range of extra-curricular activities. There is a high staff-pupil ratio from totally committed teachers meeting the needs of individual pupils. Girls leaving Albyn have confidence, poise and high regard of their personal worth to equip them for the modern world. Albyn School for Girls exists to provide education on a non-profit making basis.

BELMONT HOUSE SCHOOL
SANDRINGHAM AVENUE, NEWTON MEARNS, GLASGOW G77 5DU.
TEL.: 0141-639 2922. FAX: 0141-639 9860.

Contact: Stuart McCulloch, Headmaster.
Our principal aim is to serve as well as we can the boys who are pupils with us. We believe that each boy is able to make a contribution to the school community. We aim to encourage this talent in every possible way and to open up new opportunities wherever they might exist. The life of the school is based upon a personalised approach and a caring attitude in the classroom where we seek to give the maximum amount of individual attention.

FETTES COLLEGE
CARRINGTON ROAD, EDINBURGH EH4 1QX.
TEL.: 0131-332 2281. FAX: 0131-332 3081.

Contact: Mr Michael Spens, Headmaster.
The purpose of the school is to provide an education based on Christian principles which will enable each pupil to develop his or her own individual talents to the full. Particular emphasis is placed on academic excellence, good personal relationships and strong pastoral

care. Thriving artistic, dramatic and musical traditions coupled with a wide range of sporting activities exist. The school is coeducational with 490 pupils aged between 8 and 18.

GEORGE HERIOT'S SCHOOL
LAURISTON PLACE, EDINBURGH EH3 9EQ.
TEL.: 0131-229 7263. FAX: 0131-229 6363.

Contact: Mr A.G. Hector, Headmaster.

Heriot's Hospital was founded in 1628 to maintain and educate fatherless sons of Edinburgh burgesses. Today it is an independent, coeducational day school, deeply rooted in the Scottish tradition. The School which has a unique setting close to the Royal Mile, Edinburgh University and the Castle, has long enjoyed a reputation for educational excellence, pastoral care and sporting achievement. Our aim is to introduce all our pupils to the broadest possible spectrum of academic, cultural and sporting interests and experiences.

HIGH SCHOOL OF DUNDEE
EUCLID CRESCENT, DUNDEE DD1 1HU.
TEL.: 01382 202921. FAX: 01382 229822.
e-mail: admin@thehighschool. dundeecity.sch.uk

Contact: Mr A. Michael Duncan, MA, BPhil, DipEd, Rector.

A fully co-educational independent school of 1,100 pupils (junior school 400 pupils) offering all through education for pupils from five to 18. Emphasis is placed upon the needs and welfare of the individual. Pupils are prepared for SQA examinations with over 90 per cent of final leavers entering university. There is an extensive range of sporting, cultural and social activities with games, music, drama and debating particularly strong.

KELVINSIDE ACADEMY
33 KIRKLEE ROAD, GLASGOW G12 0SW.
TEL.: 0141-357 3376. FAX: 0141-357 5401.

Contact: J.L. Broadfoot, Rector; Mrs T. Littlefield, Head of Lower School; Miss J. Martin, Head of Nursery.

A leading independent day school for boys and girls aged three to 18. The aim is to encourage each pupil to achieve his or her fullest potential in all academic, sporting and cultural fields, in what is a friendly but disciplined environment. Small classes and individual attention are main features. A rich and rounded education produces confident and articulate young people ready and skilled for Higher Education and the world of work.

LAUREL PARK SCHOOL
4 LILYBANK TERRACE, GLASGOW G12 8RX.
TEL.: 0141-339 9127. FAX: 0141-357 5530. e-mail: lpark@rmplc.co.uk

Contact: Mrs E. Surber, Headmistress; Mrs L. Coupar, Admissions Secretary; Mrs E. Doig, Bursar.

This is a school dedicated to the education of girls. It has long enjoyed a reputation for producing well-rounded, articulate and confident young women. There is a warm atmosphere, lots of hard work and plenty of fun. Each girl is known as an individual and encouraged to develop her interests and talents to the full. The school is housed in elegant, listed buildings next to the University in the West End of Glasgow. A superb new Sports Club was opened in 1998.

LOMOND SCHOOL
10 STAFFORD STREET, HELENSBURGH, ARGYLL & BUTE G84 9JX.
TEL.: 01436 672476. FAX: 01436 678320. e-mail: admin@lomond-school.demon.co.uk

Contact: Mr A. Macdonald; Mr W. MacKenzie; Mr I. McKellar.

An independent co-educational day and boarding school with a strong academic reputation and commitment to developing the whole person. Brand new facilities. An excellent school in an ideal setting.

MERCHISTON CASTLE SCHOOL
COLINTON, EDINBURGH EH13 0PU.
TEL.: 0131-312 2200. FAX: 0131-441 6060. e-mail: headmaster@mcsch.org.uk
Contact: A.R. Hunter, Headmaster, 0131-312 2202; K.J. Houston, Deputy Head, 0131-312 2208; Mrs S.J. McGuckin, Admissions Secretary, 0131-312 2201.
Merchiston Castle School is a leading Scottish independent boys' boarding school (with some day pupils), situated in 100 acres of grounds, four miles west of the centre of Edinburgh. The school offers academic and sporting excellence, complemented by modern teaching and recreational facilities with first-class accommodation and pastoral care.

ST. COLUMBA'S SCHOOL, KILMACOLM
DUCHAL ROAD, KILMACOLM, RENFREWSHIRE PA13 4AU.
TEL.: 01505 872238. FAX: 01505 873995.
Contact: Mr A.H. Livingstone, Rector.
Founded in 1897, St. Columba's is one of Scotland's foremost schools with a roll of 600 students. The school is non-denominational and has equal numbers of boys and girls at all stages. It has an excellent academic reputation and, in addition, is strong musically, on the sporting front and in its participation in the Duke of Edinburgh Awards' Scheme.

ST. MARGARET'S SCHOOL FOR GIRLS
17 ALBYN PLACE, ABERDEEN AB10 1RU.
TEL.: 01224 584466. FAX: 01224 585600.
Contact: Miss Anne C. Ritchie, Headmistress.
St. Margaret's School for Girls in Aberdeen (age range three to 18 years) is one of the leading girls' schools in Scotland. We aim to make the education of pupils a happy and rewarding experience, where talents are encouraged and goals are set. We pride ourselves on working in partnership with parents and the community. Our academic results are excellent. A thoroughly modern curriculum is delivered, using up-to-date methodology and resources. We educate for life with a wide extra-curricular and personal development programme.

ST. MARY'S MUSIC SCHOOL
COATES HALL, 25 GROSVENOR CRESCENT, EDINBURGH EH12 5EL.
TEL.: 0131-538 7766. FAX: 0131-467 7289.
Contact: Mrs Jennifer Rimer, Headteacher; Mr John Grundy, Director of Music.
Independent specialist music school, day and boarding, offering integrated music and academic education to instrumental pupils and the choristers of St. Mary's Cathedral. Sixty-six pupils, age nine to 19, supported by the Aided Places scheme or by scholarships. Entry by audition at any stage, including 6th or 7th year. Prospectus available. Also runs Saturday morning community classes.

SPORT

SCOTTISH LAWN TENNIS ASSOCIATION
177 COLINTON ROAD, EDINBURGH EH9 2DE.
TEL.: 0131-444 1984. FAX: 0131-444 1973.
Contact: Gloria Grosset, Secretary and Treasurer; Judy Murray, National Coach; Ian Woodcraft, Development Manager.
Aims: to foster and encourage the game of tennis in Scotland including tournaments and events; training of players and coaches; developmental, educational and schools-related activity.

Tourism

Greater Glasgow and Clyde Valley Tourist Board
11 George Square, Glasgow G2 1DY.
Tel.: 0141-204 4480. Fax: 0141-204 4772. e-mail: TourismGlasgow@ggcvtb.org.uk

Contact: Professor Eddie Friel, Chief Executive, e-mail: friel@ggcvtb.org.uk; Scott Taylor, Director, Convention Bureau, e-mail: taylors@ggcvtb.org.uk; Ms Nancy McLardie, Director, Communications, e-mail: mclardien@ggcvtb.org.uk

The official destination marketing organisation of the Greater Glasgow and Clyde Valley area. The primary function is to increase the number of leisure tourists and convention delegates to the area and provide quality visitor servicing through a network of Tourist Information Centres that are linked to the national network operated by the 14 Area Tourist Boards. Our Ambassador programme is designed to provide support to local people in membership of national and international associations in attracting conferences to the destination.

Trades Unions

Banking, Insurance & Finance Union
146 Argyle Street, Glasgow G2 8BL.
Tel.: 0141-221 6475. Fax: 0141-204 3315.

Contact: Sandy Boyle, Joint Deputy General Secretary; Andy Colognori.

The Banking, Insurance & Finance Union (BIFU) is Europe's largest financial services union. Membership exceeds 118,000. Sole recognition in Bank of Scotland, Clydesdale Bank, The Royal Bank of Scotland, Royal Bank of Scotland International and TSB.

ISTC
20 Quarry Street, Hamilton, Lanarkshire ML3 7AR.
Tel.: 01698 422924. Fax: 01698 286322.

Contact: Jim Brandon, Divisional Officer; Steve McCool, Organiser; M.J. Leahy, General Secretary, 0171-837 6691.

ISTC – the "family" union with 80 years' experience. Exists to: represent its members, to bring about stability and orderly industrial relations to those in need where employees feel the management systems have failed them; and to secure an independent voice on our members' behalf.

UNISON, Scotland
14 West Campbell Street, Glasgow G2 6RX.
Tel.: 0141-332 0006. Fax: 0141-331 1203.

Contact: Matt Smith.

UNISON is the largest trade union in the country, representing a range of members across the public services – local government, the National Health Service, higher and further education, the electricity, gas, water and transport industries and a range of public and voluntary organisations. UNISON provides a range of membership services in addition to its professional negotiation and representation role. It has offices in Glasgow, Edinburgh, Aberdeen and Inverness. UNISON is committed to campaigning actively in support of public services in Scotland.

Transport

FirstGroup plc
395 King Street, Aberdeen AB24 5RP.
Tel.: 01224 650100. Fax: 01224 650140.

Contact: Moir Lockhead, OBE, Chief Executive, 01224 650102; Robbie Duncan, Director – UK Bus, 01224 650114.

FirstGroup is a leading UK-based international passenger transport group, employing over 30,000 people with an annualised turnover of £1.5bn. With a fleet of over 8,000 buses and 22% market share, it is the UK's largest bus operator. In 1998 the Group was awarded a franchise to provide bus services in Hong Kong. Through Great Eastern Railway, Great Western Trains and North Western Trains, it is one of the UK's largest train operators. Since 1997, it has extended into airport management, owning a majority stake in Bristol International Airport.

Rail Users' Consultative Committee for Scotland
Caledonian MacBrayne Users' Consultative Committee
5th Floor, Corunna House, 29 Cadogan Street, Glasgow G2 7AB.
Tel.: 0141-221 7760. Fax: 0141-221 3393.

Contact: Helen Millar, Chairman; Bill Ure, Secretary; Sharon Hume, Assistant Secretary.

Exists to represent rail and ferry users' interests, to monitor quality of service provided by train operating companies and Caledonian MacBrayne; to undertake investigations into rail quality of service matters as directed by the Rail Regulator and Franchise Director; to act as "Court of Appeal" for passengers who are dissatisfied with how their complaints are handled by train operators. Holds four public meetings each year to question senior railway managers on quality of service matters. Reports annually to the Secretary of State for Scotland on rail matters.

Railtrack plc
Buchanan House, 58 Port Dundas Street, Glasgow G4 0LQ.
Tel.: 0141-335 2424. Fax: 0141-335 2070.

Contact: Janette Anderson, Director (Scotland); Fiona Callison, Head of Corporate Affairs (Scotland); Nigel Wunsch, Business Development Manager.

As the owner/operator of Britain's rail infrastructure of track, stations, signals, structures and overhead equipment, it is Railtrack's mission to work with our industry partners to create a safe, reliable and efficient rail network of world standard, and which forms the heart of Britain's 21st century transport system.

Water

North of Scotland Water Authority

North of Scotland Water Authority
Cairngorm House, Beechwood Park North, Inverness IV2 3ED.
Tel.: 0345 437437. Fax: 01463 245405.

Contact: Joe Moore, Customer Services Manager, 01463 245404.

The Authority supplies water and wastewater services in the areas covered by the unitary authorities of the City of Aberdeen, Aberdeenshire, Moray, Highland, Orkney, Shetland, Angus, Western Isles, City of Dundee, and Perth and Kinross (excepting Kinross). We are committed to serving our customers with the highest quality and best value water for life in Scotland.

West of Scotland Water
419 Balmore Road, Glasgow G22 6NU.
Tel.: 0141-355 5333. Fax: 0141-355 5146.
e-mail: customer.services@westscotlandwater.org.uk

Contact: Ernest Chambers, Chief Executive, 0141-355 5177; Jarvis McFadzean, Customer and Environmental Services Director, 0141-355 5238; Charlie Cornish, Corporate Services Director, 0141-355 5305.

As a public Water Authority, West of Scotland Water aims "to provide water and sewerage services to the people of the West of Scotland to the standard which they seek at the least possible cost". The water supply service collects, treats and delivers in excess of 1,000 megalitres of water each day to 2.5 million domestic customers and over 80,000 industrial and commercial customers. The sewerage service collects, treats and discharges some 1,000 megalitres of waste water each day from in excess of 1,000,000 domestic and non-domestic properties, the associated surface water and road drainage.

Youth

The Boys' Brigade
Scottish Headquarters, Carronvale House, Carronvale Road, Larbert, Stirlingshire FK5 3LH.
Tel.: 01324 562008. Fax: 01324 552323. e-mail: carronvale@boys-brigade.org.uk

Contact: Mr Ian McLaughlan, Secretary for Scotland; Mr Sydney Jones, OBE, Brigade Secretary; B.B. UK Headquarters, 01442 231681, e-mail: felden@boys-brigade.org.uk

By the year 2000, The Boys' Brigade will be known for its leading Christian Youth Work which cares and challenges young people for life. The Boys' Brigade uses and will continue to use methods of working which are attractive to boys, both those boys from within the family of the church and those from without. It seeks to provide an atmosphere in which boys can find enjoyment and fulfilment and in which they will respond to challenges – physical, intellectual and spiritual. The Boys' Brigade will maintain its position in seeking to inculcate Christian moral and spiritual values in its membership in an increasingly secular world.

A

Abbott, Mollie Pearson, CBE (1984), DPE, MEd; b. 4.2.28, Peebles. Educ. Edinburgh Ladies' College; Dunfermline College of Physical Education. Assistant Teacher of Physical Education in Edinburgh schools; Temporary Lecturer, Moray House College of Education, Edinburgh, 1952-56; Senior Lecturer, Ripon Training College, 1956-62; Principal Lecturer, Aberdeen College of Education, 1962-63; HM Inspector of Schools, 1964-70; Principal, Dunfermline College of Physical Education, 1970-83. Past Chairman: Association of Higher Academic Staff in Colleges of Education in Scotland, Scottish Central Committee on Physical Education, Scottish Joint Consultative Committee on Physical Education; former Member: General Teaching Council for Scotland, Court of Heriot Watt University, National Committee for the In-Service Training of Teachers, Scottish Arts Council, Scottish Council of Physical Education, Scottish Sports Council. Recreations: gardening; handbell-ringing; swimming. Address: (h.) Janefield House, Kirkcudbright DG6 4UR; T.-01557 330119.

Abercrombie, Ian R., QC, LLB (Hons); b. 7.7.55, Bulawayo. Educ. Milton High School; Edinburgh University. Recreations: travelling; walking. Address: (h.) 7 Lauder Road, Edinburgh EH9 2EW; T.-0131-668 2489.

Aberdeen and Temair, June Marchioness of, CBE, DL, GCStJ, FRCM, FRSE. Musical Director and Conductor, Haddo House Choral and Operatic Society, since 1945. Educ. Southlands School, Harrow; Royal College of Music. Chairman: Scottish Children's League, 1969-84, NE Scotland Music School, since 1975, Advisory Council, Scottish Opera, 1979-90. Address: Haddo House, Aberdeen AB41 0ER; T.-01651 851216.

Abernethy, Hon. Lord (John Alastair Cameron). Senator, College of Justice, since 1992; b. 1.2.38, Newcastle-upon-Tyne; m., Elspeth Mary Dunlop Miller; 3 s. Educ. St. Mary's School, Melrose; Glenalmond College, Perth; Pembroke College, Oxford. National Service, 2nd Lt., RASC, Aldershot and Malta, 1956-58. Called to the Bar, Inner Temple, 1963; admitted Member, Faculty of Advocates, 1966; Advocate-Depute, 1972-75; Standing Junior Counsel to Department of Energy, 1976-79, Scottish Development Department, 1978-79; QC (Scotland), 1979; Vice-Dean, Faculty of Advocates, 1983-92; President, Pensions Appeal Tribunals for Scotland, 1985-92 (Legal Chairman, 1979-85); Chairman, Faculty Services Ltd., 1983-89 (Director, 1979-89); Hon. Fellow, Pembroke College, Oxford, 1993; Chairman, Judges' Forum, International Bar Association, 1994-98; Member, Executive Committee, Society for the Welfare and Teaching of the Blind (Edinburgh and South East Scotland), 1979-92; Trustee, Arthur Smith Memorial Trust, since 1975, Chairman, since 1990; President, Scottish Medico-Legal Society, since 1996. Publications: Medical Negligence: an introduction, 1983; Reproductive Medicine and the Law (Contributor). Recreations: travel; sport; nature conservation; Africana. Address: (b.) Court of Session, Parliament House, Edinburgh EH1 1RQ; T.-0131-225 2595.

Abram, Henry Charles, LLB, WS. Solicitor, Tods Murray WS, since 1973; b. 11.8.51, Glasgow; m., Leslie Anne Hamilton; 2 s.; 1 d. Educ. Merchiston Castle School; Aberdeen University. Articled Tods Murray WS; qualified, 1976; Partner, 1978; Chairman, Management Board, 1994-97; Chairman, 1998. Member, Council, Law Society of Scotland, 1983-86; Vice-Chairman of Governors, Merchiston Castle School; Member, High Constables and Guard of Honour of Holyrood House. Recreations: shooting; stalking; golf; skiing; running. Address: (b.) 66 Queen Street, Edinburgh EH2 4NE; T.-0131-226 4771.

Adam, Edmund Ian, MBChB, DRCOG. Medical Officer, Company of Merchants of City of Edinburgh, since 1973; b. 26.5.31, Edinburgh; m., Norma Barbara; 2 s. Educ. Daniel Stewart's College, Edinburgh; University of Edinburgh. House Officer (Surgery), General Hospital, Kirkcaldy, 1956-57; House Officer (Medicine), Bangour General Hospital, 1957; Medical Officer (Captain, RAMC), Intelligence Corps Depot, Sussex, 1957-59; House Officer (Obstetrics), Craigtoun Maternity Hospital, St. Andrews, 1959-60; Trainee Assistant, general practice, Dunkeld, 1960-61; Partner, general practice, Edinburgh, 1961-85; School Medical Officer, Daniel Stewart's and Melville College, Edinburgh, 1972-85; Medical Adviser, Lothian Regional Council, 1985-95; Clinical Assistant, Department of Medicine, Western General Hospital, Edinburgh, 1969-97. Moderator, Society of High Constables of Edinburgh, 1987-89; Honorary Physician: Scottish Schools Rugby Union, 1977-94, Scottish Badminton Union, 1977-90. Recreation: golf. Address: (h.) Norian, 60 Hillview Terrace, Edinburgh EH12 8RG; T.-0131-334 3498.

Adam, Ian Simpson Thomson, OBE, QFSM, HonFIFireE. Firemaster, Central Scotland Fire Brigade, since 1984; b. 4.5.40, Dunfermline; m., Norma; 1 s. Educ. Beath Secondary, Cowdenbeath. Retained Firefighter, Fife, 1960; wholetime Firefighter, Fife, 1964; Leading Firefighter, Fife, 1968; Sub Officer, Fife, 1969; Station Officer, Fife, 1972; Assistant Divisional Officer, Fife, 1974, Divisional Officer, Fife, 1978; Third Officer, SDO, Fife, 1979; Depute Firemaster, Central, 1982. Recreations: gardening; photography. Address: (b.) Main Street, Maddiston, Falkirk FK2 0LG.

Adam, James Seymour, FIOD. Author, broadcaster and poet; b. 4.12.07, Dundee; m., Flora MacDonell; 1 s.; 1 d. Educ. Dens Road School, Dundee; Hyndland Academy, Glasgow; School of Accountancy, Glasgow. Advertisement department, Scottish Daily Express; advertising agency Account Executive; Staff Captain, War Office; Features Editor, Glasgow Evening News then Daily Record; Assistant Editor, Evening Times; Editor, Weekly Scotsman; General Manager, Scotsman Publications; Managing Director, Chester Chronicle Newspapers; Managing Director, Middlesbrough Evening Gazette. Produced Claymore with Sir Alastair Dunnett in 1933, an adventure magazine for boys which led him to make first solo crossing of the Minch by kayak; organiser of first ever International Gathering of the Clans, 1977. Publications: Declaration of Arbroath; New Verses for an Auld Sang; Laughter in the Kirk; More Laughter in the Kirk; Gaelic Scots Wordbook; Business Diaries of Sir Alexander Grant; A Fell Fine Baker; Over the Minch; poetry in Scots and Gaelic. Address: 4 Southlawn Court, Easter Park Drive, Edinburgh EH4 6SJ; T.-0131-312 8445.

Adams, Professor Carol Alison, BA, MSc, CA. Professor of Accounting, University of Glasgow, since 1998; b. 11.9.59, Driffield; m., Adrian; 1 s.; 1 d. Educ. Queen Elizabeth Grammar School, Hexham, Northumberland; University of Stirling; London School of Economics. KPMG, 1981-85 (qualified CA, 1984); Financial Controller, Company Secretary, John Graham Shoes Ltd., 1985-86; Supervising Senior, KPMG, 1986-87; Senior Lecturer, Polytechnic of West London, 1987-91; University of Glasgow: Lecturer, 1992-95, Senior Lecturer, 1995-98. Recreations: running; swimming. Address: (b.) Stair Building, 5–9 The Square, Glasgow G12 8QQ; T.-0141-330 6855.

Adams, Professor (Charles) David, MA, MCD, PhD, MRTPI, FRSA. Professor and Head of Department of Land Economy, University of Aberdeen, since 1997; b. 10.9.54, Menston, England; m., Judith Banks; 1 s.; 1 d. Educ.

Rossall School; University of Cambridge; University of Liverpool. Planning Assistant, Leeds City Council, 1978-83; Research Assistant, University of Reading, 1983-84; Lecturer, University of Manchester, 1984-93; University of Aberdeen: Senior Lecturer, 1993-95, Reader, 1995-97. Publications: Urban Planning and the Development Process, 1994; Land for Industrial Development (Co-author). Recreations: walking; listening to classical music. Address: (b.) University of Aberdeen, St. Mary's, King's College, Old Aberdeen AB24 3UF; T.-01224 273692.

Adams, David Anstey, MA. Principal, Northern College of Education, formerly Aberdeen College of Education, since 1983; b. 2.3.42, Wakefield, Yorkshire; m., Margaret Ishbel; 1 s.; 1 d. Educ. Harris Academy, Dundee; St. Andrews University. Teacher of English and History, High School of Dundee; Principal Teacher of English, Arbroath Academy; Assistant Director of Education: Angus County Council, Tayside Regional Council. Member, Committee of Scottish Higher Education Principals, General Teaching Council for Scotland, Open University Validation Board. Recreations: fishing; shooting. Address: (b.) Northern College of Education, (Aberdeen Campus), Hilton Place, Aberdeen AB9 1FA; T.-01224 283500.

Adams, Douglas William, MA, MBA. Business Planning Director Europe, Templeton Global Investors Ltd, since 1988; b. 17.5.53, Perth; m., Jacqueline Mary Ferguson; 1 s.; 1 d. Educ. Perth Academy; Glasgow University; Strathclyde University. Economic Assistant, Scottish Office, Edinburgh, 1975-78; Economist, European Commission, Brussels, 1978-82; Head of Industrial Programmes, Scottish Development Agency, Glasgow, 1982-86; Economist, Scottish Provident, Edinburgh, 1986-88. Recreation: golf. Address: (b.) Saltire Court, 20 Castle Terrace, Edinburgh EH14 1ER; T.-0131-469 4000.

Adams, Irene, JP. MP (Labour), Paisley North, since 1990; b. 1947; m., Allen Adams (deceased); 1 s.; 2 d. Former local councillor. Address: House of Commons, London SW1A 0AA.

Adams, James Gordon Leitch, MA, PhD. Director of Planning and Development, Scottish Tourist Board, since 1988 (formerly Director of Development); b. 17.10.40, Glasgow; m., Rowan Hopwood; 1 s.; 1 d. Educ. Dundee High School; St Andrews University; Queen's University, Canada; McGill University. Economist: Canadian Federal Government, 1966-70, Highlands and Islands Development Board, 1970-75; Lecturer, Glasgow University, 1975-82; Visiting Lecturer in Poland, 1978, and India, 1981. Recreations: mountaineering; golf. Address: (h.) 5 Corrennie Drive, Edinburgh; T.-0131-447 8073.

Adams, Ralph Gange, LLB, CA. Partner in Charge, Scottish and Northern Ireland Offices, Deloitte & Touche, Chartered Accountants, since 1993; b. 30.10.55, Calcutta; m., Kirstine Mary Park; 2 s.; 1 d. Educ. Trinity College, Glenalmond; University of Dundee. Deloitte & Touche: indentured student, 1976-79; qualified as CA, 1979; seconded to Melbourne Office, 1980; seconded to Bank of Scotland, Glasgow and Edinburgh, 1984, Partner, 1986; Partner in Charge, Edinburgh Office, 1990-93, Scottish Offices, since 1993; Member, Board of Partners. Recreations: tennis; golf; music; theatre. Address: (b.) Deloitte & Touche, 39 George Street, Edinburgh EH2 2HZ; T.-0131-225 6834.

Adams, Robert William, OBE, FCMA, FCCA, JDipMA. Director, John Cairney & Co. Ltd., since 1983; Chairman, Hanover Housing Association, 1995-98; b. 27.9.22, Glasgow; m., Mary Ann Ritchie; 2 s.; 1 d. Educ. Shawlands Academy, Glasgow. H.C. Stewart & Co., CA, Glasgow; Lieutenant, Parachute Regiment; South of Scotland Electricity Board; James Colledge (Cocoa) Ltd., West Africa; Highland Home Industries Ltd.; Managing Director, A.H. McIntosh & Co. Ltd., until 1982. Member, Glenrothes Development Corporation, 1976-84; former Member: Scottish Sports Council; Council, Institute of Cost and Management Accountants; Scottish Sports Council; former Convenor, Scottish Athletic Coaching Committee; former Scottish Chairman, Writers' Guild. Recreations: tennis; golf. Address: (h.) Achray, Shore Road, Aberdour, Fife; T.-01383 860269.

Adams, Sheenagh, MA (Hons), MCIH. Secretary, Historic Buildings Council for Scotland, since 1995; Head, Grants and Heritage Policy, Historic Scotland, since 1995; b. 31.8.57, Dundee; m., Peter Craig; 2 d. Educ. Harris Academy, Dundee; St. Andrews University. Welfare Rights Officer, Strathclyde Regional Council, 1979-82; Tenant Participation Officer, Clydebank Council and TPAS, 1982-85; Principal Management Officer, Falkirk District Council, 1985-90; Principal, Scottish Office, since 1990. Address: (b.) Longmore House, Salisbury Place, Edinburgh EH9 1SH; T.-0131-668 8799.

Adamson, James G., CBE, FRSA. Chairman, AMF Insight Ltd., Edinburgh; b. 25.5.41, Rosyth; m., Ann May; 2 s.; 2 d. Educ. Heriot-Watt University. MoD (Navy), Rosyth; Honeywell Computer Systems; ITT; Marconi Space & Defence; NCR, AT&T (now NCR). President, Fife Society for the Blind; Non-Executive Director, East Board, Bank of Scotland; Member: Scottish Economic Council, Advisory Board, SCDI. Recreations: sailing; singing. Address: (b.) 20 Stafford Street, Edinburgh EH3 7BD.

Adamson, Rev. Sidney, MA, BD. Minister, Church of Scotland; b. 3.8.11, Arbroath; m., Margaret T. Sharpe, JP; 1 s. Educ. Dumbarton Academy; Glasgow University and Trinity College; Royal Scottish Academy of Music and Drama. Ministries: St Ninian's, Sanquhar, 1937-47 (including war service), Trinity Church, Renfrew, 1947-54, High Kirk of Rothesay, 1954-59, St Michael's Inveresk, Musselburgh, 1959-85. Moderator of Presbytery: Dumfries, 1939, Dunoon, 1958, Dalkeith, 1964 and 1965; former Moderator, Synod of Lothian and Tweeddale; Army Chaplain, India, 1944-47; Territorial Army Chaplain, 1952-66; Chaplain, Royal British Legion (Scotland), Paisley, Renfrew, Rothesay, Musselburgh, and Honorary Vice President, Edinburgh & Lothian Area Council, 1973; Industrial Chaplain, Babcock & Wilcox Ltd., Renfrew, 1948-54; Chaplain, British Sailors' Society, 1955-85; Editor, Homeward Bound (Forces magazine, India), 1946-47. Publications: Two Centuries of Service (history of Sanquhar congregation), 1939; St Michael's Kirk at Inveresk (four editions between 1963 and 1984). Recreations: (at suitable periods) ballroom dancing; shooting; swimming; (always) reading; theatre; freelance journalism; ex-service welfare. Address: 48 Hailes Gardens, Colinton, Edinburgh EH13 0JH; T.-0131-441 2471.

Addison, Alexander, MBE, MB, ChB, FRCGP, DObstRCOG. Senior Partner, Addison, Scott, Kane & Ferguson, 1978-95; Chairman, Lanarkshire LMC, 1989-95; Member, Scottish Committee, BMA, since 1984, and Fellow, BMA, since 1993; b. 23.8.30, Kerala; m., Joan Wood; 3 s. Educ. Keith Grammar School; Aberdeen Grammar School; Aberdeen University. House Surgeon and Physician, Woodend General Hospital, Aberdeen, 1954-55; Captain, RAMC; Junior Medical Specialist, Cowglen MH, 1955-58; SHO, Bellshill MH, 1958-59; GP in Douglas and Physician to Lady Home Hospital, 1959-95; Member, West of Scotland Faculty of GP College, 1967-79 and of Scottish Council, 1976-78; Member, Lanarkshire LMC, since 1972, and of AMAC, since 1975; Chairman, Lanarkshire AMAC, 1982-86; Chairman, Scottish Association of General Practitioner Hospitals, 1985-87; Member, Scottish Committee of Medical Commission on Accident Prevention, since 1976; Member, National Medical Consultative Committee, 1977-83; Honorary Surgeon, St. Andrews Ambulance Association, 1959-89. Recreations:

curling; golf; reading. Address: (h.) 7 Addison Drive, Douglas, Lanarkshire ML11 0PZ; T.-01555 851302.

Addison, Gordon, LLB, DipLP, NP. Solicitor, since 1989; Partner, Nelsons, Falkirk, since 1996; Secretary, Falkirk District Faculty of Solicitors, since 1995; b. 4.3.67, Lanark; m., Pauline Heather Proudfoot. Educ. Lanark Grammar; Aberdeen University. Traineeship, Drummond & Co. W.S., 1988-90; Associate, More & Co., 1991-92; Partner, Caesar & Howie, 1994-96. President, Corstorphine Curling Club, since 1998; Director, Edinburgh Curling Club Ltd., 1994-96; Founder Member, Scottish Court Lawyers' Association, 1997. Recreations: curling; golf; the countryside. Address: (b.) Nelsons, 326 Main Street, Camelon, Falkirk; T.-01324 613316.

Ager, Professor Alastair Kenneth St. Clair, BA, PhD, MSc, CPsychol. Director, Centre for International Health Studies, Queen Margaret College Edinburgh, since 1997; Professor of Applied Psychology, Queen Margaret College Edinburgh, since 1992; Honorary Consultant Psychologist, Edinburgh Healthcare NHS Trust, since 1994; Research Associate, Queen Elizabeth House, University of Oxford, since, 1996; b. 24.6.56, Birmingham; m., Wendy; 1 s.; 1 d. Educ. Coleshill Grammar School; University of Keele; University of Wales, Cardiff; University of Birmingham. Posts in clinical and applied psychology; Lecturer in Clinical Psychology, University of Leicester, 1985; Senior Lecturer and Head of Psychology, University of Malawi, 1988; Head, Department of Management and Social Sciences, Queen Margaret College, 1992. British Psychological Society: Member, Professional Affairs Board, 1994-96, Member, Division of Clinical Psychology – Scottish Branch, 1994-97, Standing Conference Committee, since 1995. Publications: The Life Experiences Checklist, 1990; Microcomputers and Clinical Psychology, 1991; Refugees: Perspectives on the Experience of Forced Migration, 1999. Recreations: music; golf; skiing; church affairs. Address: Queen Margaret College Edinburgh, Clerwood Terrace, Edinburgh EH12 8TS; T.-0131-317 3491.

Agnew of Lochnaw, Sir Crispin Hamlyn. 11th Baronet (created 1629); Chief of the Agnews; Advocate 1982; Queen's Counsel (1995); Unicorn Pursuivant of Arms, 1981-86, Rothesay Herald of Arms, since 1986; Trustee, John Muir Trust; Chairman, Crofting Law Group; b. 13.5.44, Edinburgh; m., Susan Rachel Strang Steel; 1 s.; 3 d. Educ. Uppingham School; Royal Military Academy, Sandhurst. Commissioned Royal Highland Fusiliers, 1964, as 2nd Lieutenant; Major, 1977; Retired, 1981. Member: Royal Navy Expedition to East Greenland, 1966; Joint Services Expedition to Elephant Island, Antarctica, 1970-71; Army Nuptse Himal Expedition, 1975; Army Everest Expedition, 1976; Leader: Army East Greenland Expedition, 1968; Joint Services Expedition to Chilean Patagonia, 1972-73; Army Api Himal Expedition, 1980. Publications: Licensing (Scotland) Act 1976 (4th edition) (Co-author); Agricultural Law in Scotland, 1996; Connell on the Agricultural Holdings (Scotland) Acts (Co-author) 1996; Land Obligations, 1999; articles in various newspapers and journals. Recreations: mountaineering; offshore sailing. Address: 6 Palmerston Road, Edinburgh EH9 1TN; T.-0131-668 3792.

Agnew, Ian, MA (Hons) (Cantab). Rector, Perth High School, 1975-92; b. 10.5.32, Newcastle-upon-Tyne; m., Gladys Agnes Heatherill; 1 d. Educ. King's College School, London; Pembroke College, Cambridge. Assistant Teacher of Modern Languages, Melville College, Edinburgh, 1958-63; Assistant Teacher of Modern Languages, then Principal Teacher of Russian, George Heriot's School, Edinburgh, 1964-70; Housemaster, Craigmount Secondary School, Edinburgh, 1970-73; Deputy, Liberton High School, Edinburgh, 1973-75. Non-Executive Director, Perth and Kinross Healthcare NHS Trust; Minute Secretary, Headteachers Association of Scotland, 1979-81; Committee Member, SCCORE; President: Perthshire Musical Festival, 1978-88, Perth Chamber Music Society, 1982-89; Past President, Rotary Club of Perth St. John's; Past Chairman: Barnton and Cramond Conservative Association and West Edinburgh Conservative and Unionist Association; Serving Officer (OStJ), Priory of Scotland of the Most Venerable Order of St. John; Member, Society of High Constables, City of Perth; Governor: Balnacraig School, Perth, since 1981, Kilgraston School, Convent of the Sacred Heart, Bridge of Earn, since 1990; Chairman: Friends of Pskov, Friends of St. John's Kirk, Perth; Secretary, Friends of Perth Festival of the Arts; Member, Advisory Group, Perth College Development Trust. Recreations: music (opera); reading; tennis; gardening. Address: (h.) Northwood, Heughfield Road, Bridge of Earn, Perthshire PH2 9BH; T.-01738 81 2273.

Ailsa, 8th Marquess of (Archibald Angus Charles Kennedy); b. 13.9.56; 2 d. Address: Cassillis House, Maybole KA19 7JN.

Ainslie, Allan, MA (Hons), FRICS. Chief Valuer Scotland, since 1998; b. 16.2.51, Edinburgh; m., Jennifer Anne Park; 1 s.; 1 d. Educ. Broxburn Academy; Napier College; Edinburgh University. Valuer, Valuation Office, Inland Revenue, 1976-79; Senior Valuer, 1980-85; Principal Valuer, 1986-90; First Class Valuer, 1991-92; Director Valuer (Fife and Central), 1992-95; District Valuer Scotland South East, 1996-97. Recreations: tennis; badminton; gardening. Address: (b.) 50 Frederick Street, Edinburgh EH2 1NG; T.-0131-225 9602.

Airlie, 13th Earl of (David George Coke Patrick Ogilvy), KT, GCVO, PC, KStJ, JP. Former Lord Chamberlain of Her Majesty's Household; Ensign, Queen's Body-Guard for Scotland (Royal Company of Archers), since 1975; Chancellor, University of Abertay, Dundee, since 1994; Director, Baring Stratton Investment Trust plc, since 1986; Lord Lieutenant, Angus; Chancellor of the Royal Victorian Order; President, National Trust for Scotland, since 1997; Hon. President, Scottish Council, The Scout Association; b. 17.5.26, London; m., Virginia Fortune Ryan; 3 s.; 3 d. Educ. Eton College. Lieutenant, Scots Guards, 1944; serving 2nd Bn., Germany, 1945; Captain, ADC to High Commissioner and C-in-C Austria, 1947-48; Malaya, 1948-49; resigned commission, 1950; Chairman, Ashdown Investment Trust Ltd., 1968-82; Director, J. Henry Schroder Wagg & Co. Ltd., 1961-84 (Chairman, 1973-77); Chairman, Schroders plc, 1977-84; Scottish and Newcastle Breweries plc, until 1983; Director, Royal Bank of Scotland Group, 1983-93; Director, Royal Bank of Scotland plc, 1991-93; Chairman, General Accident Fire & Life Assurance Corporation plc, 1987-97; Trustee, Royal Collection Trust, 1993; Captain, Queen's Body Guard for Scotland (Royal Company of Archers), 1996. Address: (h.) Cortachy Castle, Kirriemuir, Angus.

Airlie, Countess of (Virginia Fortune Ryan), DCVO. Lady in Waiting to HM The Queen, since 1973; Chairman, National Galleries of Scotland, since 1997 (Trustee since 1995); President, Angus Red Cross, since 1988; b. 9.2.33, London; 3 s.; 3 d. Educ. Brearley School, New York City. Commissioner, Royal Fine Arts Commission; Trustee, Tate Gallery, 1983-95; Trustee, National Gallery, London, 1989-95; Member, Industrial Design Panel, British Rail, 1974-91; Trustee, American Museum in Britain, since 1985; Founder/Governor, Cobham School. Address: (b.) Cortachy Castle, Kirriemuir, Angus; T.-01575 540231.

Aitchison, James Douglas, MA (Hons), MEd (Hons). Head Teacher, Boclair Academy, Bearsden, since 1991 (Head Teacher, Gleniffer High School, Paisley, 1984-91); b. 2.7.47, Glasgow. Educ. High School of Glasgow; Glasgow University; University of Marburg. Teacher, Lycee Faidherbe, Lille; Principal Teacher, Bearsden

Academy; Assistant Head Teacher, Gryffe High School, Houston. Recreations: curling; walking; travel. Address: (h.) 44 Keystone Road, Milngavie, Glasgow G62 6QG; T.-0141-956 6693.

Aitchison, Thomas Nisbet, MA, MSc. Chief Executive, City of Edinburgh Council, since 1995; b. 24.2.51, Edinburgh; m., Kathleen Sadler; 1 s.; 2 d. Educ. Glasgow University; Heriot-Watt University. Lothian Regional Council: Policy Planning, 1975-78, PA to Chief Executive, 1978-81, seconded to Chief Executive's Co-ordination Team, 1981-82, Department of Manpower Services, 1982-85, Department of Management and Information Services, 1985-87, Corporate Planning Manager and Depute Director, 1987-91, Depute Chief Executive, 1991-94, Chief Executive, 1994-95. Honorary Secretary, Council, Edinburgh International Festival; Member, Court, Napier University. Recreations: hill-walking; football; music. Address: (b.) Council Headquarters, Wellington Court, 10 Waterloo Place, Edinburgh EH1 3EG.

Aitken, Rev. Ewan, BA (Hons), BD (Hons). Parish Minister, St. Margaret's Church of Scotland, Edinburgh, since 1995; b., 27.4.62, Paisley; m., Hilary Brown; 1 s. Educ. Woodmill High School, Dunfermline; University of Sussex; University of Edinburgh. Youth Worker, Ruchill Parish Church, 1980-81; Vice President (sabbatical), University of Sussex Union, 1982-83; Regional Secretary, Student Christian Movement, 1985-87; Pastor, West Avenue Presbyterian Church, Buffalo, NY, 1990-91; Assistant Minister, South Leith Parish Church, Edinburgh, 1991-93; Staff Member, St. Andrews Church of Scotland, Tiberias, Israel, 1993-94; Locum Minister, St. Andrews, Gisborne, New Zealand, 1994-95. Branch Secretary, Links/Restalrig Labour Party; Convener, Iona Community Finance and Staffing Committee. Recreations: following Dunfermline Athletic F.C.; vegetarian cookery; laughter; collecting earrings. Address: (b.) 176 Restalrig Road South, Edinburgh EH7 6TD; T.-0131-554 7400.

Aitken, Joan Nicol, JP, MA (Hons), SSC. Solicitor, since 1978; Mediator; former Editor, Journal of the Law Society of Scotland; b. 26.2.53, Glasgow; m., Alistair Bruce Dodds; 1 d. Educ. James Gillespie's High School for Girls; Dundee University. Former Member: Scottish Consumer Council and Council, Law Society of Scotland; part-time Chairman, Industrial Tribunals (Scotland), Disability Appeal Tribunal, and Child Support Appeal Tribunal; family law mediator and Convener, CALM; Member, General Dental Council; was first woman member, Society of Solicitors in the Supreme Courts of Scotland. Address: (h.) Shepherd's Lodge, Kiltarlity, Beauly IV4 7HR; T.-01463 741369.

Aitken, Keith, MA. Freelance Journalist and Broadcaster, since 1995; b. 31.10.57, Edinburgh; m., Christine Willett; 1 d. Educ. George Watson's College, Edinburgh; University of Edinburgh. The Scotsman: Graduate Trainee, 1979-82, Parliamentary Correspondent, 1982-85, Labour Correspondent, 1985-88, Columnist, 1985-97, Industrial Editor, 1988-92, Economics Editor and Chief Leader Writer, 1992-95; Columnist, The Herald, 1997-99; Presenter, Head Lines, Radio Scotland, since 1995, and documentary series and programmes for BBC Radio Scotland, World Service and Radio 4; Editor, Enterprise Scotland magazine, since 1995. Member, Court, Napier University. Awards include Business and Industry Writer of the Year, Scottish Press Awards, 1986 and 1987. Publications: The Bairns o' Adam, 1997; How Scotland's Parliament Will Work, 1999. Recreations: walking; cycling; reading; deplorable Blues Guitar. Address: 25 Bridge Road, Colinton Village, Edinburgh EH13 0LH; T.-0131-441 7982.

Aitken, Professor Robert Cairns Brown, CBE, MB, ChB, DPM, MD, DSc (Hon), FRCPEdin, FRCPsych. Chairman, Royal Infirmary of Edinburgh NHS Trust, 1994-97; Professor of Rehabilitation Studies, Edinburgh University, 1974-94 (Dean, Faculty of Medicine, 1990-91, Vice-Principal, 1991-94); Honorary Consultant in Rehabilitation Medicine, Lothian Health Board, 1974-94; b. 20.12.33, Dunoon; m., Audrey May Lunn; 1 s.; 1 d. Educ. Dunoon Grammar School; Cargilfield School, Edinburgh; Sedbergh School, Yorkshire; Glasgow University. Institute of Aviation Medicine, RAF, 1959-62; Orpington and Maudsley Hospitals, 1962-66; Senior Lecturer/Consultant Psychiatrist, Royal Infirmary and Royal Edinburgh Hospital, 1967-74. President, International College of Psychosomatic Medicine, 1985-87; Chairman, Napier Polytechnic of Edinburgh Governors, 1983-90; Member, Council for Professions Supplementary to Medicine, 1983-90; Member, General Medical Council, 1991-96; Director, Lothian Health Board, 1991-93; Editor, Journal of Psychosomatic Research, 1979-85; occasional WHO consultant; Foundation Secretary, then President, Society for Research in Rehabilitation, 1981-83; Member, Human Genetics Advisory Commission, since 1996. Publications: papers on measurement of mood; flying phobia; management of disability. Recreations: people, places and pleasures of Edinburgh, Scotland and beyond. Address: (h.) 11 Succoth Place, Edinburgh EH12 6BJ; T.-0131-337 1550.

Aitken, William Duff, MM (FG). Director, William Aitken Highland Exports Ltd., since 1973; Member, Board of Directors, Eden Court Theatre, 1984-88; Member, Inverness District Council, 1984-88; b. 12.3.27, Newton Mearns; m., Eva Alexandra Kjellsson; 2 d. Educ. Terra Nova, Birkdale; Merchant Taylors'; Liverpool Nautical College. Seafaring, 1943-53; tanning industry, 1953-72. Member, SSAT. Recreations: philately; swimming; RNXS; TNAUK. Address: (h) The Thistles, 24 MacLeod Road, Balloch, by Inverness IV1 2JW; T.-01463 791234.

Aitken, William Mackie, JP, DL, ACII. Councillor, City of Glasgow, since 1976; Magistrate, since 1985; Deputy Lord Lieutenant; b. 15.4.47, Glasgow. Educ. Allan Glen's School, Glasgow. Chairman, Scottish Young Conservatives, 1975-77; Convenor, City Licensing Committee and Vice-Convenor, Personnel Committee, 1977-79; Leader of the Opposition, City Council, 1980-84 and 1992-96; Bailie of the City, 1980-84, 1988-92, since 1996. Recreations: football; reading; foreign travel. Address: (h.) 35 Overnewton Square, Glasgow G3 8RW; T.-0141-357 1284.

Aitkin, John, TD, CA. Partner, John J. Welch & Co., Chartered Accountants, 1961-97, now a Consultant with the firm; National Chairman, Royal British Legion Scotland, 1995-98; b. 10.9.33, Denholm; m., Elizabeth Charlotte Fraser; 1 s.; 1 d. Educ. Hawick High School. Qualified as a CA, 1956; National Service (commissioned 2nd Lt.), 1956-58; joined John J. Welch & Co., CA, Hawick, 1958; served in TA, 1958-73; Committee of Management, Royal British Legion Housing Association Ltd., 1978-91 (Chairman, 1986-91); Hon. Treasurer, Royal British Legion Scotland, 1985-90; Member, Executive Committee, Earl Haig Fund Scotland, since 1992; Regimental Trustee, King's Own Scottish Borderers, since 1980; Member, Management Committee, Ex-Services Mental Welfare Society, since 1998; Member, Central Advisory Committee on War Pensions, 1995-98; Committee Member, British Commonwealth Ex-Services League, since 1998. Recreations: gardening; reading; walking. Address: (h) Appletreehall House, Hawick TD9 8PW; T.-01450 372424.

Alexander, Professor Alan, MA. Professor of Local and Public Management, Strathclyde University (Head, Department of Human Resource Management, 1993-96, Professor of Local Government, 1987-93); b. 13.12.43, Glasgow; m., Morag MacInnes (Morag Alexander, qv); 1 s.; 1 d. Educ. Possil Secondary School, Glasgow; Albert Secondary School, Glasgow; Glasgow University. Lecturer/Assistant Professor, Political Science, Lakehead University, Ontario, 1966-71; Lecturer in Politics, Reading University, 1971-87. Member of Board, Housing

Corporation, 1977-80; Member, Standing Research Committee on Local and Central Government Relations, Joseph Rowntree Memorial Trust, 1988-92; conducted inquiry into relations between Western Isles Islands Council and BCCI, 1991; Director, Scottish Local Authorities Management Centre, 1987-93; Member, Commission on Local Government and the Scottish Parliament, since 1998; Chair, Glasgow Regeneration Fund, since 1998; Trustee, Quarriers, since 1995. Publications: Local Government in Britain since Reorganisation, 1982; The Politics of Local Government in the UK, 1982; L'amministrazione locale in Gran Bretagna, 1984; Borough Government and Politics: Reading, 1835-1985, 1985; Managing the Fragmented Authority, 1994; The Future of DLOs/DSOs in Scotland, 1998. Recreations: theatre; cinema; hill-walking; avoiding gardening. Address: (b.) Scottish Local Authorities Management Centre, The Graham Hills Building, 50 Richmond Street, Glasgow G1 1XT; T.-0141-553 4167.

Alexander, Professor David Alan, MA (Hons), CPsychol, FBPS, PhD. Professor of Mental Health, University of Aberdeen, since 1994; Hon. Consultant, Police and Fire Services, since 1989; b. 28.8.43, Ellon. Educ. George Watson's College, Edinburgh; Morgan Academy, Dundee; University of St. Andrews; University of Dundee. MRC Research Scholar; Lecturer then Senior Lecturer in Mental Health; Visiting Lecturer, FBI Academy, Virginia, USA; Visiting Professor to universities in USA, Russia, Croatia, Spain and West Indies. Publications: co-author of three books; numerous professional articles. Recreations: badminton; squash; hill-walking. Address: (b.) Medical School, Foresterhill, Aberdeen AB25 2ZD; T.-01224 681818.

Alexander, Major-General David Crichton, CB. Commandant, Scottish Police College, 1979-87; b. 28.11.26, Aberdour; m., 1, Diana Joyce (Jane) Fisher (deceased); 2, Elizabeth Patricia Fleming; 1 s.; 1 step-s.; 2 d. Educ. Edinburgh Academy; Staff College, Camberley; Royal College of Defence Studies. Royal Marines, 1944-77 (2nd Lieutenant to Major-General, including Equerry and Acting Treasurer to Duke of Edinburgh); Director-General, English Speaking Union, 1977-79. President, Corps of Commissionaires, 1994-97; Member, Civil Service Final Selection Board, 1978-88; Chairman, Edinburgh Academy, 1985-90; Freeman, City of London; Liveryman, Painter Stainers' Company; Member, Transport Users Consultative Committee for Scotland, 1989-93; President, SSAFA Fife, 1990-94. Recreations: fishing; golf; gardening. Address: (h.) Baldinnie, Park Place, Elie KY9 1DH; T.-01333 330882.

Alexander, Douglas Gavin. MP (Labour), Paisley South, since 1997; b. 26.10.67. Educ. University of Edinburgh; University of Pennsylvania. Admitted, Solicitor, 1995. Address: House of Commons, London SW1A 0AA.

Alexander, Rev. Douglas Niven, MA, BD. Minister, Erskine Parish Church, Bishopton, 1970-99, retired; b. 8.4.35, Eaglesham; m., Dr. Joyce O. Garven; 1 s.; 2 d. Educ. Hutchesons' Boys' Grammar School, Glasgow; Glasgow University (President, SRC, 1958); Union Theological Seminary, New York. Assistant Minister, St. Ninian's Church, Greenock, 1961-62; Warden, Iona Community House, Glasgow, 1963-70. Secretary, Scottish Union of Students, 1958; Assessor to Lord Rector, Glasgow University, 1969-71; Chaplain to Erskine Hospital, since 1970; Moderator, Paisley Presbytery, 1984; Mair Memorial Lecturer, Glasgow University, 1987; Chairman, British Churches Committee for Channel 4 TV, 1986-88; Convener, Church of Scotland Board of Communication, 1987-91; Member: Scottish Committee, IBA, 1988-90; National Religious Advisory Committee, IBA, 1988-90; Central Religious Advisory Committee, 1988-92; National Religious Advisory Committee, ITC, 1991-92; Scottish Viewers Consultative Committee, ITC, 1991-92; Member, Church of Scotland Board of Social Responsibility, since 1997. Recreation: researching ways of salmon poachers! Address: West Morningside, Main Road, Langbank PA14 6XP; T.-01475 540249.

Alexander, Ian W., BA, BD, STM. Europe, Middle East, North Africa Secretary, Board of World Mission, Church of Scotland, since 1995; b. 28.11.64, Dumfries. Educ. Douglas Ewart High School; Glasgow College; University of Edinburgh; Union Theological Seminary, New York City. Assistant Minister, Palmerston Place Church of Scotland, Edinburgh, 1989-91; Communication and Education Officer Presbyterian United Nations Office, New York City, 1992-95. Member, Shared Interest Council; Member, United Nations Association (Edinburgh Committee). Recreations: travel; reading; dancing. Address: (h.) 5 Comiston Gardens, Edinburgh EH10 5HQ; T.-0131-447 4519.

Alexander, Professor James, BSc, PhD. Professor, Department of Immunology, Strathclyde University, since 1994; b. 14.11.49, Glasgow; m., Margaret Jean Wendon; 1 s. Educ. St. Mungo's Academy, Glasgow University. Scientific Staff, Division of Leprosy and Mycobacterial Research, National Institute for Medical Research, London, 1975-79; Research Fellow, Department of Biology, Imperial College of Science and Technology, London, 1979-85; Strathclyde University: Wellcome Trust Lecturer, Immunology, 1985, Senior Lecturer, 1989, Reader, 1990; Visiting Professor, School of Veterinary Medicine, University of Pennsylvania, 1998-99. Recreations: gardening; reading. Address: (b.) Todd Centre, Taylor Street, Strathclyde University, Glasgow G4 0NR; T.-0141-552 4400.

Alexander, John Huston, BLitt, MA, DPhil Oxon. Reader in English, Aberdeen University, since 1996; b. 5.4.41, Coleraine, Northern Ireland; m., Flora Ross; 2 s.; 2 d. Educ. Campbell College, Belfast; St. Edmund Hall, Oxford. Sessional Lecturer in English, University of Saskatchewan, Canada, 1966-67; Lecturer then Senior Lecturer in English, Aberdeen University, 1968-96. Editor, The Scott Newsletter, since 1982; Session Clerk, St. Machar's Cathedral, Aberdeen, since 1975. Publications: Two Studies in Romantic Reviewing, 1976; The Lay of the Last Minstrel: Three Essays, 1978; The Reception of Scott's Poetry By His Correspondents: 1796-1817, 1979; Marmion: Studies in Interpretation and Composition, 1981; Scott and his Influence (Editor, with David Hewitt), 1983; Reading Wordsworth, 1987; The Tavern Sages (Editor), 1992; Walter Scott, Kenilworth: A Romance (Editor), 1993; Scott in Carnival (Editor, with David Hewitt), 1993; Walter Scott, The Bride of Lammermoor (Editor), 1995; Walter Scott, A Legend of the Wars of Montrose (Editor), 1995; Walter Scott, The History of France (Second Series) (Co-Editor), 1996; General Editor, Edinburgh Edition of the Waverley Novels. Recreations: music; walking. Address: (h.) 45A Queen's Road, Aberdeen AB15 4ZN; T.-01224 317424.

Alexander, Keith, BSc (Hons), BArch, RIBA, ARIAS, FCIOB, CFM, IFMA Fellow. Director, Centre for Facilities Management, Strathclyde University, since 1990; b. 20.9.49, Nottingham; m., Marie-Yvonne; 2 s.; 1 d. Educ. Wellingborough Grammar School; Welsh School of Architecture; University of Wales Institute of Science and Technology. Architect, new town development authorities, 1971-75; Principal, private practice, Northern Ireland and Scotland, 1975-78; Senior Lecturer, Ulster College, Northern Ireland Polytechnic, 1975-78; Consultant, Building Performance Design and Appraisal, 1978-90; Strathclyde University: Lecturer, Department of Architecture and Building Science, 1978-90, Director, Building Performance and Research Unit, 1984-90; Visiting Lecturer, School of Architecture, National University of Singapore, 1982-84; Architect, private practice, Singapore, 1982-84. Chairman, EUROFM, since 1995; Editor, International Journal of Facilities Management.

Recreations: rugby; golf. Address: (b.) Centre for Facilities Management, Strathclyde Graduate Business School, 199 Cathedral Street, Glasgow G4 0QU. T.-0141-553 4165.

Alexander, Sir Kenneth John Wilson, BSc (Econ), LLD, DUniv, FRSE, CBIM, Hon. Fellow, RIAS; b. 14.3.22, Edinburgh; m., Angela-May; 1 s.; 4 d. Educ. George Heriot's School, Edinburgh; School of Economics, Dundee. Taught at Universities of Leeds, Sheffield and Aberdeen; Professor of Economics, Strathclyde University, 1963-80; Principal and Vice-Chancellor, Stirling University, 1981-86; Chancellor, Aberdeen University, 1986-87. Member, Advisory Committee on University of the Air, 1965; Chairman: Committee on Adult Education in Scotland, 1970-73, Social Science Research Council, 1975-76; President, Section F, British Association, 1974; Chairman, Govan Shipbuilders, 1974-76; Chairman, Highlands and Islands Development Board, 1976-80; Economic Consultant to the Secretary of State for Scotland, 1968-89; Member, Scottish Development Agency, 1975-85; Chairman, Council for Applied Science in Scotland, 1980-85; Governor, Technical Change Centre, 1981-87; Director, Scottish Television Ltd., 1981-92; Member, Council for Tertiary Education in Scotland, 1981-82; Deputy Chairman, Scottish Council (Development and Industry), 1982-91; Honorary President: The Highland Fund, since 1983; Scottish National Dictionary Association Ltd., since 1983; President, Town and Country Planning (Scottish Section), since 1982; Director, Stakis plc, 1987-93; Chairman, Edinburgh Book Festival, 1987-91; Chairman, Scottish Industrial Trade Exhibitions, since 1990; Trustee, Aegean Archipelago, since 1994. Publications: The Economist in Business, 1967; Fairfields, a study of industrial change (with C.L. Jenkins), 1971; The Political Economy of Change (Editor), 1976. Recreation: Scottish antiquarianism. Address: (h.) 9 West Shore, Pittenweem, Fife KY10 2NV; T.-01333 310593.

Alexander, Professor Michael Joseph, BA, MA (Oxon). Berry Professor of English Literature, St. Andrews University, since 1985; b. 21.5.41, Wigan; m., 1, Eileen Mary McCall (deceased); 2, Mary Cecilia Sheahan; 1 s.; 2 d. Educ. Downside School; Trinity College, Oxford; Perugia University; Princeton University. Editor, William Collins, London, 1963-65; Lecturer, University of California, 1966-67; Editor, Andre Deutsch, London, 1967-68; Lecturer: East Anglia University, 1968-69, Stirling University, 1969; Senior Lecturer, 1977; Reader, 1985. Publications: Earliest English Poems (Translator), 1966; Beowulf (Translator), 1973; Twelve Poems, 1978; The Poetic Achievement of Ezra Pound, 1979; History of Old English Literature, 1983; Macmillan Anthology of English Literature, 1989; Beowulf (Editor), 1995; Sons of Ezra (Editor), 1995; Beowulf and Grendel (Translator), 1995; The Canterbury Tales – The First Fragment (Editor), 1996; The Canterbury Tales : Illustrated Prologue (Editor), 1996. Address: (b.) School of English, St. Andrews University, St. Andrews KY16 9AL; T.-01334 462666.

Alexander, Morag, BA (Hons). Director, Equal Opportunities Commission, Scotland, since 1992; b. 10.10.43, Kilwinning; m., Professor Alan Alexander (qv); 1 s.; 1 d. Educ. Lourdes Secondary School, Glasgow; Glasgow University; Lakehead University, Ontario. Research Assistant, ASTMS, 1971-73; Editor and Researcher, RIPA, 1973-82; freelance journalist and consultant, 1982-90; Founding Editor, Women in Europe, 1985-89, and UK Correspondent, Women of Europe, 1987-92; Founding Director, Training 2000 (Scotland) Ltd., Scottish Alliance for Women's Training, 1990-92; Member, Board, Children in Scotland, Chair, Early Years Advisory Group, since 1995; Member, Scottish Committee, Turning Point, since 1996; Member, Board, Partnership for a Parliament, 1997. Recreations: music; opera; visiting art galleries and museums; hill-walking. Address: (b.) E.O.C., Stock Exchange House, 7 Nelson Mandela Place, Glasgow G2 1QW; T.-0141-248 5833.

Alexander, Samuel, BL. Honorary Sheriff, Dumbarton, since 1983; b. Glasgow; m., Isabella Kerr Ligertwood; 2 s. Educ. Govan High School; Glasgow University. Formerly Consultant and Senior Partner, Keyden Strang & Co., Solicitors, Glasgow. Recreations: golf; reading. Address: (h.) 1 Hillneuk Avenue, Bearsden, Glasgow G61; T.-0141-942 4674.

Alexander, Walter Ronald, CBE. Chairman, Walter Alexander plc, 1979-90 (Managing Director, 1973-79); Company Director; b. 6.4.31; m., 1, Rosemary Anne Sleigh (m. diss.); 2 s.; 2 d.; 2, Mrs Lorna Elwes. Educ. Loretto School; Cambridge University (MA Hons). Chairman and Managing Director, Tayforth Ltd., 1961-71; Chairman, Scottish Automobile Company Ltd., 1971-73; Director: Scotcros plc, 1965-82 (Chairman, 1972-82); Investors Capital Trust plc, since 1967; Clydesdale Bank plc, 1970-96; RIT and Northern plc, 1973-84; Dawson International plc, 1979-96; Chairman, Scottish Appeals Committee, Police Dependants' Trust, 1974-81; President, Public Schools Golfing Society, 1973-79; Chairman: PGA, 1982-85; Royal and Ancient Golf Club of St. Andrews Trust, since 1987; Governor, Loretto School, 1961-89; Comr., Queen Victoria School, 1987-92; Scottish Free Enterprise Award, 1977. Recreation: golf. Address: Moonzie Mill, Balmullo, St. Andrews KY16 0AH; T.-01334 870990.

Alexander, Wendy, MA (Hons), MA (Econ), MBA. Special Adviser to Secretary of State for Scotland, since 1997; b. 27.6.63, Glasgow. Educ. Park Mains School, Erskine; Glasgow University; Warwick University; INSEAD, France. Research Officer, Scottish Labour Party, 1988-92; Senior Associate, Booz Allen & Hamilton Int., 1994-97. Address: (b.) Scottish Office, St. Andrew's House, Regent Road, Edinburgh EH1 3DG; T.-0131-244 2029.

Ali, Nasir, MB, BS, DPM, FRCPsych. Consultant Psychiatrist, since 1973; Honorary Senior Lecturer, Aberdeen University, since 1982; b. 21.8.39, Lucknow, India; m., D. Rosemary; 1 s.; 1 d. Address: (h.) Balmachree House, Dalcross, Inverness IV1 2JQ; T.-Inverness 790602.

Allan, Bob. Chief Executive, Clackmannanshire Council. Address: (b.): Greenfield, Alloa FK10 2AD.

Allan, Charles Maitland, MA. Journalist, Economist and Farmer; b. 19.8.39, Stirling; m., Fiona Vine; 2 s.; 2 d. Educ. Dartington Hall; Aberdeen University. Lecturer in Economic History, Glasgow University, 1962-63; Lecturer in Economics, St. Andrews University, 1963-65; Lecturer and Senior Lecturer, Strathclyde University, 1965-74; Producer/Presenter, BBC, 1982-86; Editorial Adviser, Leopard Magazine; Managing Editor, Ardo Publishing Co. Publications: Theory of Taxation; Death of a Papermill; Farmer's Diary I, II, III, IV, V; Neeps and Strae. Recreation: cycling; World Caber Tossing Champion, 1972. Address: (h.) Whinhill of Ardo, Methlick, Ellon, Aberdeenshire; T.-01651 806 218.

Allan, D. Stuart, LLB, NP. Solicitor and Notary Public; Head, Law and Administration, Fife Council; b. 11.11.49, Dundee. Educ. Morgan Academy; Dundee University. Chairman, Society of Directors of Administration in Scotland, 1991-92. Address: (b.) Fife House, Glenrothes KY7 5LT; T.-01592 414141.

Allan, Eric, MA (Hons). Head Teacher, St. Michael's Academy, Kilwinning, since 1994; b. 6.9.55, Inverness; m., Elaine; 2 d. Educ. Dingwall Academy; Glasgow University; Jordanhill College. Teacher: St. Andrew's Academy, Saltcoats, St. Brendan's High School, Linwood (Principal Teacher, Geography); Assistant Head Teacher, St. Brendan's, 1987-92; Depute Head Teacher, Trinity High

School, Renfrew, 1992-94. Recreations: golf; supporting Kilmarnock FC; reading; music. Address: (h.) 3 Holmes Crescent, Kilmarnock; T.-01563 524199.

Allan, George Alexander, MA (Hons). Headmaster, Robert Gordon's College, Aberdeen, 1978-96; b. 3.2.36, Edinburgh; m., Anne Violet Veevers; 2 s. Educ. Daniel Stewart's College, Edinburgh; Edinburgh University. Teacher of Classics, Glasgow Academy, 1958-60; Daniel Stewart's College: Teacher of Classics, 1960-63, Head of Classics, 1963-73 (appointed Housemaster, 1967); Schoolmaster Fellow Commoner, Corpus Christi College, Cambridge, 1972; Deputy Headmaster, Robert Gordon's College, 1973-77. Former Chairman and former Secretary, Headmasters' Conference (Scottish Division) (Member, National Committee, 1982 and 1983); Governor, Welbeck College, 1980-89; Council Member, Scottish Council of Independent Schools, 1988-96 and since 1997; Director, Edinburgh Academy, since 1997. Recreations: gardening; golf; music. Address: 5 Abbey View, Kelso, Roxburghshire TD5 8HX.

Allan, James Morrison, FRICS, ACIArb, MIPS. Chartered Surveyor; b. 1.10.43, Edinburgh; m., Elizabeth Howie Sneddon Jack; 2 s. Educ. George Watson's College; Heriot Watt College. Joined Phillips Knox & Arthur as Apprentice Quantity Surveyor, 1960; qualified ARICS, 1965; FRICS, 1975; RICS: Chairman, National Junior Organisation, 1975-76; Chairman, Quantity Surveyors Committee in Scotland, 1988-89; Chairman, RICS in Scotland, 1991-92; Member, RICS General Council; Member, RICS Management Board, 1992-95; Chairman, RICS Business Services Ltd. Recreations: family; caravanning and motoring; golf. Address: (h.) 4 Stevenson Way, Longniddry, East Lothian EH32 0PF; T.-01875 852377.

Allan, Sheriff John Douglas, BL, DMS, FBIM. Sheriff of Lanark, since 1988; b. 2.10.41, Edinburgh; m., Helen E.J. Aiton; 1 s.; 1 d. Educ. George Watson's College, Edinburgh; Edinburgh University. Solicitor in private practice, Edinburgh, 1963-67; Procurator Fiscal Depute, Edinburgh, 1967-71; Solicitor, Crown Office, Edinburgh, 1971-76; Assistant Procurator Fiscal, then Senior Assistant Procurator Fiscal, Glasgow, 1976-79; Solicitor, Crown Office, Edinburgh, 1979-83; Procurator Fiscal for Edinburgh and Regional Procurator Fiscal for Lothians and Borders, 1983-88. Part-time Lecturer in Law, Napier College, Edinburgh, 1963-66; Holder, Scout "Medal of Merit". Recreations: Scouts; youth leadership; walking; Church. Address: (b.) Sheriff Court House, Lanark ML11 7NE; T.-01555 661531.

Allan, Richard James Paul, BSc, PhD, FSA (Scot). Chairman, Executive Committee, Royal Zoological Society of Scotland, since 1995; Hon. Vice President: Shetland Sheep Breeders Group, since 1992, Eriskay Pony Society, since 1997; b. 26.5.30, Glasgow; m., Norma Adam Dick; 3 s. Educ. High School of Glasgow; University of Glasgow; Royal Technical College, Glasgow. Technical service with ICI Fibres Division in man-made fibres and development of commercial computing; left industry to develop countryside and wildlife interests and farming; fronted development of rare breeds in Scotland, assisted by Royal Zoological Society of Scotland. Founder Chairman, Border Country Life Association; Member, Scottish Borders Council Heritage Steering Group (preparing series of booklets on Borders history and archaeology). Publications: The Scottish Borderland (Co-Editor, Contributor), 1988; Wool Quality (Co-Author), 1992; many articles on rare breeds. Recreations: photography; gardening; walking; reading; classical music. Address: (h.) Buskinburn House, Coldingham, Eyemouth, Berwickshire TD14 5UA; T.-018907 71215.

Allan, Robert, MBE. Chief Executive, Scottish Fishermen's Federation, 1982-98; b. 14.11.33, Peterhead; m., Moira W. Morrison; 2 d. Educ. Aberdeen Grammar School. Audit Assistant, R.C. Kelman & Shirreffs, CA, Aberdeen, 1949-62; Assistant Secretary, latterly Secretary, Aberdeen Fishing Vessel Owners' Association Ltd. and Scottish Trawlers' Federation, 1962-71; Chief Executive, Aberdeen Fishing Vessel Owners' Association Ltd. and Aberdeen Fish Producers' Organisation Ltd., 1971-82. Address: (h.) 40 Parkhill Circle, Dyce, Aberdeen AB21 7FN; T.-01224 724366.

Allan, W. Douglas, MA (Oxon). Chairman, Crossroads (Scotland), Caring for Carers, since 1997; Director, J. & P. Coats Ltd., 1984-93; b. 1.11.39, Tongshan, China; m., Joan Blakeborough; 3 s. Educ. Trinity College, Glenalmond; St. John's College, University of Oxford; London Business School. Graduate Trainee, Coats Patons Ltd., 1962; Managing Director, Coats Chile, then Venezuela and Brazil; Chief Executive, Coats South America. Chairman, Cargilfield School, Edinburgh, 1986-88. Recreations: hill-walking; travel; Hispanic affairs; sport. Address: (h.) Fidra, Gryffe Road, Kilmacolm PA13 4BA; T.-01505-872 772.

Allen, Professor John Walter, MA, FSAS, FRSE. Professor of Solid State Physics, St. Andrews University, since 1980; b. 7.3.28, Birmingham. Educ. King Edward's High School, Birmingham; Sidney Sussex College, Cambridge. RAF, 1949-51; Staff Scientist, Ericsson Telephones Ltd., 1951-56; Services Electronics Research Laboratory, 1956-68; Visiting Associate Professor, Stanford University, 1964-66; joined Department of Physics, St. Andrews University, 1968. Recreations: archaeology; country dancing. Address: (b.) Department of Physics and Astronomy, St. Andrews University, North Haugh, St. Andrews, Fife KY16 9SS; T.-01334 463331.

Allison, Professor Arthur Compton, BSc, DipNumMath, PhD, FBCS. Vice Principal, Information Services and Professor of Computing Science, Glasgow University, since 1986; b. 24.3.41, Belfast; m., Dr. Joyce Allison; 3 d. Educ. Queen's University, Belfast; Glasgow University. Glasgow University, 1962-67; Smithsonian Institution, Boston, 1967-73; Glasgow University, 1973-83; Northeastern University, Boston, 1983-84; Glasgow University, since 1984. Elder, Church of Scotland. Recreations: running; curling. Address: (b.) Glasgow University, Glasgow G12 8QQ; T.-0141-330 4453.

Allison, Charles William, MBChB, FFARCS. Consultant Anaesthetist, Stracathro Hospital, Brechin, since 1982; Consultant, Dundee teaching hospitals; Honorary Senior Lecturer, Dundee University; b. 1.7.52, Newport on Tay; m., Elspeth Stratton; 2 d. Educ. Madras College, St. Andrews; Dundee University. Training grades in anaesthesia, Dundee, 1976-81; Clinical Research Fellow, Hospital for Sick Children, Toronto, 1982. Publications: papers and book chapter. Recreations: golf; photography. Address: Summerbank House, Brechin, Angus DD9 6HL; T.-01356 623624.

Allison, Glenn Fraser Whyte, CA. Financial Director, Stewart Milne Group Limited, since 1989; b. 27.1.56, Montrose; m., Sheila Katherine; 1 s.; 1 d. Educ. Dundee High School; Dundee College of Technology. Trained Thomson McLintock, Dundee; Scottish Agricultural Industries plc: Management Accountant, 1979-81, Financial Accountant, 1981-84; Financial Director: CALA Homes (Aberdeen) Limited, 1984-86, CALA Homes (Lothian) Limited, 1986-89. Member, Council, Institute of Chartered Accountants of Scotland, since 1997; Member, North-East Committee, Scottish Council Development and Industry; Member, Grampian Area Committee, ICAS; Member, IoD. Recreations: golf; hillwalking; football. Address: 442 North Deeside Road, Cults, Aberdeen AB15 9ET; T.-01224 861096.

Allison, John Andrew, MA, LLB. Honorary Sheriff, Cupar, since 1986; Solicitor (retired 1993); b. 10.5.36, Glasgow; m., Elizabeth; 2 s.; 1 d. Educ. Paisley Grammar School; Glasgow University. Legal apprenticeship, McGrigor, Donald and Co., Glasgow; Legal Assistant, Glenrothes Development Corporation; Partner, Pagan Osborne and Grace, WS, Fife; Member, Council, Law Society of Scotland; Dean, Society of Solicitors for Eastern District of Fife. Past President, Glenrothes Rotary Club. Recreations: oil painting; hillwalking; Rotary. Address: (h.) Craigrothie House, by Cupar, Fife; T.-01334 828606.

Allsop, Rev. Thomas Douglas, MA, BD. Minister, Beechgrove Church, Aberdeen, since 1977; b. 2.3.34, Kilmaurs; m., Marion Morrison Urie; 2 s.; 1 d. Educ. Kilmarnock Academy; Glasgow University and Trinity College. Assistant Minister, St. Marnock's, Kilmarnock; Minister: Kirriemuir South (after a union called Kirriemuir St. Andrew's), 1959-65; Minister, Knightswood St. Margaret's, Glasgow, 1965-77. Founder Chairman, Kirriemuir Round Table; Moderator, Dumbarton Presbytery, 1975, Aberdeen Presbytery, 1994-95; Burgess, City of Aberdeen. Recreations: photography; golf; musical appreciation. Address: 156 Hamilton Place, Aberdeen AB15 5BB; T.-01224 642615.

Almaini, Professor A.E.A., BSc(Eng), MSc, PhD, CEng, FIEE. Professor, School of Engineering, Napier University, since 1991, Professor, since 1991; b. 1.7.45, Baghdad; m., Shirley May; 2 s.; 1 d. Educ. London University; Salford University; Loughborough University. Research Scientist, Scientific Research Foundation, 1970-78; Lecturer, then Senior Lecturer, Napier University, 1980-91. Publication: Electronic Logic Systems (book); many papers published. Recreation: gardening. Address: (b.) School of Engineering, Craiglockhart Campus, Edinburgh EH14 1DJ; T.-0131-455 4364.

Alstead, Brigadier (Francis) Allan (Littlejohns), CBE, DL, MPhil, FCIT, FIMgt, FIPD, FInstAM, FRSA, FInstD. Chief Executive, Scottish Sports Council, since 1990; b. 19.6.35, Glasgow; m., Joy Veronica Edwards; 2 s. Educ. Glasgow Academy; Royal Military Academy, Sandhurst; Royal Naval Staff College; Joint Services Staff College; Edinburgh University; University of Wales, Aberystwyth. Commissioned into King's Own Scottish Borderers, 1955; commanded 1st Bn., KOSB, 1974-76 (Mention in Despatches); Military Assistant to Quarter-Master-General,, 1976-79; Instructor, Army Staff College, Camberley, 1979-81; Assistant Chief of Staff, BAOR, 1981-84 (Colonel); Commander, 51st Highland Brigade, 1984-87 (Brigadier); NATO Research Fellow, Edinburgh University, 1987-88; NATO Reinforcement Co-ordinator, 1988-90. Member, Royal Company of Archers (Queen's Bodyguard in Scotland); Deputy Lieutenant, City of Edinburgh; Regimental Trustee, KOSB; Trustee, Youth Sport Trust; Deputy Hon. Colonel, City of Edinburgh Universities OTC; Governor: Moray House College, 1991-97, Glasgow Academy; Member, Executive, Scottish Council, Development and Industry; Member, Lowland TAVRA; President, SSAFA, Edinburgh and Midlothian, 1990-98. Recreations: running; swimming; tennis. Address: (b.) South Gyle, Edinburgh EH12 9DQ; T.-0131-317 7200.

Amyes, Dorothy Mary Gregory, BSc, MSc, MRTPI. Director, Scottish Farm and Countryside Educational Trust, since 1991; b. 17.3.52, Warrington; m., Sebastian Giles Becket Amyes; 1 s.; 1 d. Educ. Warrington High School; Sir John Cass College; University of Strathclyde; University of Edinburgh. Planning Assistant, Lanarkshire, Surrey and Strathclyde, 1973-78; Project Supervisor, Scottish Wildlife Trust, 1985-87; Scottish Executive/Director, Association of Agriculture/Scottish Association of Agriculture, 1988-91. Address: (b.) Royal Highland Centre, Ingliston, Edinburgh EH28 8NF; T.-0131-335 6226.

Amyes, Professor Sebastian Giles Becket, BSc, MSc, PhD, DSc, FRCPath, FIBiol. Professor of Microbial Chemotherapy and Head of Medical Microbiology Department, Edinburgh University; b. 6.5.49, Stockton Heath; m., Dorothy Mary Gregory; 1 s.; 1 d. Educ. Cranleigh School; University College, London. Edinburgh University, since 1977; Reader, 1988; Professor, 1992. Royal Pharmaceutical Society annual conference award, 1984; C.L. Oakley lectureship, Pathological Society, 1987. Recreations: fishing; opera; golf; exploring parts of the world that the tour companies have not yet found. Address: (b.) Department of Medical Microbiology, Medical School, Teviot Place, Edinburgh EH8 9AG; T.-0131-650 3163.

Ancram, Earl of (Michael Andrew Foster Jude Kerr), DL. Advocate; MP (Conservative), Devizes, since 1992; Minister of State, Northern Ireland Office, 1994-97; b. 7.7.45; m.; 2 d. Educ. Ampleforth; Christ Church, Oxford; Edinburgh University. MP: Berwickshire and East Lothian, 1974, Edinburgh South, 1979-87; Parliamentary Under Secretary of State, Scottish Office, 1993-94; Minister of State, Northern Ireland Office, 1994-97; Chairman, Conservative Party in Scotland, 1980-83. DL, Roxburgh District.

Anderson, Alastair, CA. Director of Finance, Napier University, since 1989; b. 10.8.49, Glasgow; m., Maureen Wilson; 1 s.; 1 d. Educ. Hutchesons' Boys Grammar School. CA apprentice and audit assistant, 1967-74; Assistant Accountant, 1975; Retail Trade Accountant, 1975-89. Recreations: sailing; squash. Address: (b.) 219 Colinton Road, Edinburgh EH14 1DJ; T.-0131-455 4656.

Anderson, Alex, DipTP, MRTPI. Director of Planning and Transport, Angus Council, since 1995; b. 21.3.47, Dundee; m., Maureen; 2 s. Educ. Grove Academy, Dundee; Duncan of Jordanstone College. Address: (b.) Department of Planning, Transport and Economic Development, St. James House, St. James Road, Forfar DD8 2ZP; T.-01307 473405.

Anderson, Professor Anne Harper, MA, PhD. Professor of Psychology, University of Glasgow, since 1997; Director, ESRC Cognitive Engineering Programme, since 1995; b. 19.2.54, Glasgow; m., Ian K. Anderson; 1 s.; 1 d. Educ. Hutchesons' Girls' Grammar School; University of Glasgow. Research Associate/Fellow, University of Edinburgh; Lecturer/Senior Lecturer, University of Glasgow; Principal Investigator, Human Communication Research Centre. Recreations: reading; relaxing. Address: (b.) Department of Psychology, University of Glasgow, 52 Hillhead Street, Glasgow G12 8BQ; T.-0141-330 4938.

Anderson, Professor Annie S., BSc, PhD, SRD. Research Professor of Food Choice, University of Dundee, since 1996; b. 24.12.57, Torphins; m., Professor Mike Lean; 1 s.; 2 d. Educ. Cults Academy, Aberdeen; RGIT; University of Aberdeen. Dietitian, Cambridge Area Health Authority, 1979-81; Research Assistant, Medical School, University of Cambridge, 1982-84; Research Dietitian, Grampian Health Board, 1985-86; Postgraduate Research Student, Department of Obstetrics, University of Aberdeen, 1987-91; Research Fellow (Human Nutrition), University of Glasgow, 1991-96. Recreation: genealogy. Address: (b.) Centre for Applied Nutrition Research, University of Dundee, Dundee; T.-01382 345383.

Anderson, Arthur Andrew, MBE, FRAgS, FGAJ. Producer, Landward, BBC Scotland, since 1979; b. 21.11.44, Dumfries; m., Andrea Jane MacKenzie; 2 s.; 2 d. Educ. Barnard Castle School. Copy Boy, The Scotsman, 1961-64; Reporter, Scottish Farmer, 1964-65; Sub-Editor, Glasgow Herald, 1965-66; Agricultural Reporter, The Scotsman, 1967-69; Scottish Correspondent, Farmers Weekly, 1970-73; News/Farming Producer and Reporter, BBC Radio Carlisle, 1973-75; General Programme Producer, BBC Radio Scotland, 1975-77; joined BBC TV,

Aberdeen, 1977; former Head of Production, BBC Aberdeen. Winner RICS TV Award, John Deere Journalism Award, Norsk Hydro TV Award, One World Broadcasting Trust Prize, Netherthorpe Award; Member, Aberdeen Children's Panel, 1982-89; Chairman, Guild of Agricultural Journalists, 1997-99; UK Delegate, International Federation of Agricultural Journalists. Recreation; hill-walking. Address; (h.) Denmill Cottage, Burnett Street, Auchenblae AB30 1WP; T.-01561 320248.

Anderson, David Alexander, BA (Hons), MEd, FIPD, FRSA. Chief Executive, Dunbartonshire Enterprise, since 1998; b. 2.12.54, Perth; m., Tricia; 3 s.; 1 d. Educ. Arbroath High School; University of Stirling; University of Newcastle; University of Sheffield. Graduate Management Trainee, Department of Employment; Local Office Manager, Newcastle, Department of Employment, 1980-84; Manpower Services Commission: Programme Development Manager, Newcastle, 1984-86, Policy Manager, Head Office, Sheffield, 1986-90; Operations Manager, Training Agency, Ayrshire, 1990-91; Director of Skills Development, Enterprise Ayrshire, 1991-97. Director, Keynote Trust; Member, Institute of Economic Development. Recreations: golf; music. Address: (b.) Spectrum House, Clydebank Business Park, Clydebank G84 2DR; T.-0141-951 2121.

Anderson, David Rae, MA (Hons), LLB, LLM, WS, NP. Solicitor, since 1961 (Senior Partner, Allan Grant Solicitors); part-time Legal Chairman, Industrial Tribunals, since 1971; Honorary Sheriff, since 1981; accredited solicitor-mediator; b. 27.1.36, Stonehaven; m., Jean Strachan. Educ. Mackie Academy, Stonehaven; Aberdeen University; Edinburgh University; Australian National University, Canberra. Barrister and Solicitor of Supreme Court of Victoria, Australia, 1962; Legal Officer, Attorney-General's Department, Canberra, 1962-65; part-time research student, Law Faculty, Australian National University, Canberra, and part-time Lecturer in Legal History, 1962-65; returned to Scotland, 1965, in private legal practice, Edinburgh, 1965-67, Alloa and Central Scotland, since 1967; Interim Town Clerk, Burgh of Alva, 1973; former part-time Reporter to Secretary of State for Scotland for public enquiries; twice Dean, Society of Solicitors of Clackmannanshire; Member, Council, Law Society of Scotland: former Convener, International Relations Committee, 1992 Committee, Committee on the Constitution, and Convener, Specialist Accreditation Committee; Law Society of Scotland Representative, Council, Commonwealth Lawyers Association; former Member, UK Delegation, Council of the Bars and Law Societies of the European Community; Member, Stirling University Conference; Elder, Church of Scotland; Parliamentary candidate, 1970 and 1971; formerly served, RNVR; Past President, Alloa Rotary Club. Recreations: climbing and hill-walking; reading, especially historical biography and English literature; music, especially opera; interested in current affairs, architecture, stately homes and travel. Address: (h.) 3 Smithfield Loan, Alloa FK10 1NJ; T.-01259 213096; (b.) 8 Shillinghill, Alloa FK10 1JT; T.-01259 723201.

Anderson, Dorothy Elizabeth, BSc (Hons), MB, ChB, MRCP(UK), DMRD, FRCR, FRCP(Glas). Consultant Radiologist, Glasgow Royal Infirmary, since 1981; Honorary Clinical Lecturer, then Senior Lecturer, Glasgow University, since 1982; b. 26.9.50, Glasgow; m., David Anderson; 1 s.; 1 d. Educ. Glasgow High School for Girls; Glasgow University. Pre-registration posts, Stobhill Hospital and Glasgow Royal Infirmary; post-registration year, Respiratory Unit, Knightswood Hospital; trained in radiology, Western Infirmary, Glasgow (Registrar, then Senior Registrar). Recreation: choral singing; walking; aerobics. Address: (h.) 18 Milverton Avenue, Bearsden, Glasgow G61 4BE; T.-0141-942 7510.

Anderson, Douglas Kinloch, OBE, MA. Chairman, Kinloch Anderson (Holdings) Ltd., Edinburgh, since 1975; Board Member, Scottish Tourist Board, 1986-92; Deputy Chairman, Edinburgh Marketing Ltd., 1990-92; Director: Lothian and Edinburgh Enterprise Ltd., 1990-95, Scottish Eastern Investment Trust PLC, Fidelity Special Values PLC; b. 19.2.39, Edinburgh; m., Deirdre Anne; 2 s.; 1 d. Educ. George Watson's Boys College; St. Andrews University. Joined Kinloch Anderson Ltd., 1962 (fifth generation in family business); Assistant on Master's Court, Edinburgh Merchant Company, 1976-79; elected Honorary Member, St. Andrew's Society of Washington DC, 1985; Member, Edinburgh Festival Council, 1988-90; President, Edinburgh Royal Warrant Holders Association, 1987-88; former Member, Scottish Committee, Institute of Directors; President, Edinburgh Chamber of Commerce, 1988-90; Master, Edinburgh Merchant Company, 1990-92; President, Royal Warrant Holders Association, 1994; elected Leith High Constable, 1993; Freeman, City of London. Recreations: golf; fishing; watching rugby; travel (non-business). Address: (b.) Commercial Street/Dock Street, Leith, Edinburgh EH6 6EY; T.-0131-555 1355.

Anderson, Gavin Alan, DipArch, MPhil. Head, Community Care Division, Social Work Services Group, Scottish Office, since 1994; b. 5.7.39, Bridge of Allan; m., Margaret Clarke; 1 s.; 1 d. Educ. St. Modan's High School, Stirling; Edinburgh College of Art; Edinburgh University. Architect, Edinburgh University Architecture Research Unit, 1966-73; Architect, then Principal Architect, Scottish Development Department, 1973-85; Assistant Secretary, Scottish Home and Health Department, 1985-90; Deputy Chief Executive, NHS in Scotland, 1990-93. Recreations: reading; listening to music; art; walking. Address: (b.) James Craig Walk, Edinburgh EH1 3BA; T.-0131-244 5452.

Anderson, Gordon Alexander, CA, FCMA. Chartered Accountant; b. 9.8.31, Glasgow; m., Eirene Cochrane Howie Douglas; 2 s.; 1 d. Educ. High School of Glasgow. Apprentice CA, Moores Carson & Watson, Glasgow, 1949-54; qualified CA, 1955; National Service, Royal Navy, 1955-57 (Sub Lieutenant); Partner, Moores Carson & Watson, 1958 (firm name changed to McClelland Moores, 1958, Arthur Young McClelland Moores, 1968, Arthur Young, 1985, Ernst & Young, 1989); Chairman, Arthur Young, 1987-89; Deputy Senior Partner, Ernst & Young, 1989-90; Director: Lloyds TSB Group plc, since 1993, TSB Bank Scotland plc, since 1991 (Chairman, since 1994), High School of Glasgow Ltd., 1975-81 and since 1990 (Chairman of Governors, since 1992), Merchants House of Glasgow, since 1996; Member, Council on Tribunals and of its Scottish Committee, 1990-96; Chairman, Bitmac Ltd., 1990-96; Director: Douglas Firebrick Co. Ltd., 1960-70; Member, Scottish Milk Marketing Board, 1979-85; Institute of Chartered Accountants of Scotland: Member, Council, 1980-84, Vice President, 1984-86, President, 1986-87. Recreations: golf; gardening; rugby football (as spectator). Address: (h.) Ardwell, 41 Manse Road, Bearsden, Glasgow G61 3PN; T.-0141-942 2803.

Anderson, Rev. Professor Hugh, MA, BD, PhD, DD, FRSE. Professor of New Testament Language, Literature and Theology, Edinburgh University, 1966-85; b. 18.5.20, Galston, Ayrshire; m., Jean Goldie Torbit; 1 s.; 1 s. (deceased); 1 d. Educ. Kilmarnock Academy; Glasgow University. Chaplaincy work, Egypt and Palestine, 1945-46; Lecturer in Old Testament, Glasgow University, 1946-51; Minister, Trinity Church, Pollokshields, Glasgow, 1951-57; Professor of Biblical Criticism, Duke University, North Carolina, 1957-66; special appointments including A.B. Bruce Lecturer in New Testament, Glasgow University, 1954-57; Katharine McBride Visiting Professor, Bryn Mawr College, Pennsylvania, 1972-73; Kenan Distinguished Visiting Professor, Meredith College, North Carolina, 1982-83; Pendergrass Visiting Professor, Florida

Southern College, 1985-86, 1987-88. Awarded Schweitzer Medal from North Carolina History and Science Foundation. Publications: Psalms 1-45; Historians of Israel; The New Testament in Historical and Contemporary Perspective (Editor with W. Barclay); Jesus and Christian Origins; Jesus; The Gospel of Mark: Commentary; 3 and 4 Maccabees (Commentary). Recreations: golf; gardening; music. Address: (h.) Morningside Way, 23/13 Maxwell Street, Edinburgh EH10 5HT.

Anderson, Iain Buchanan, MA, DipEd, LGSM. Music Presenter/Sports Commentator, BBC, since 1985; m., Marion Elizabeth; 3 s.; 1 d. Educ. Bellahouston Academy, Glasgow; Glasgow University; Guildhall School. Lecturer in Speech and Drama, Jordanhill College, 1967; Arts Editor/Presenter, Radio Clyde, 1974. Former Rugby Correspondent, Scotland on Sunday. Address: (h.) Elmhurst, Station Road, Langbank PA14 6YA; T.-0147 554 0733.

Anderson, Ian Wilson Russell, MBChB, FRCS (Glasgow), FRCS (England), FFAEM. Consultant, Accident and Emergency, Victoria Infirmary, Glasgow; Honorary Clinical Senior Lecturer, University of Glasgow; b. 4.5.51, Prestwick. Educ. Ayr Academy; University of Glasgow. House Officer posts, Glasgow; completed general professional training in surgery, 1980; completed specialist training in accident and emergency medicine and surgery, 1984; main interest in initial assessment and resuscitation of trauma. Member, Council, Medical and Dental Defence Union of Scotland; President Elect, Faculty of Accident and Emergency Medicine; Member, Council, Royal College of Physicians and Surgeons of Glasgow. Recreations: travel; golf; motoring. Address: Accident and Emergency Department, Victoria Infirmary, Glasgow G42 9TY; T.-0141-201 5305.

Anderson, James A., MA, MEd, DipEd. Director of Education, Angus Council, since 1995; b. 21.8.49, Aberdeen; m., Linda; 1 s.; 1 d. Educ. Aberdeen Grammar School; Aberdeen University; Edinburgh University; Stirling University. Teacher, Assistant Principal Teacher, Principal Teacher of Mathematics, 1973-84; Tayside Regional Council: Assistant Director of Education, 1984-87, Area Education Officer, 1987-91, Senior Assistant Director of Education, 1991-95, Director of Education, 1995-96. Recreations: golf; bridge. Address: (b.) Angus Council, County Buildings, Market Street, Forfar DD8 3WE; T.-01307 473235.

Anderson, James Frazer Gillan, CBE, JP, DL. Member, Scottish Development Agency, 1986-89; Convener, Central Regional Council, 1974-86; b. 25.3.29, Maddiston, by Falkirk; m., May Harley; 1 s.; 1 d. Educ. Maddiston School; Graeme High School, Falkirk. Convener, Stirling County Council, 1971-75; Member: Health and Safety Commission, 1974-80; Montgomery Committee, 1982-84; Scottish Economic Council, 1983-87; awarded Hononary Degree, Doctor of University (Stirling). Recreations: gardening; walking; reading. Address: California Road, Maddiston, Falkirk.

Anderson, James Killoch, OBE, MB, ChB, FFCM, FCR, JP. Former Unit Medical Officer, Glasgow Royal Infirmary and Royal Maternity Hospital, Glasgow (retired, 1988); b. 3.2.23, Johnstone; m., Irene Webster Wilson; 1 s.; 2 d. Educ. High School of Glasgow; Glasgow University. Deputy Medical Superintendent, Glasgow Royal Infirmary and Associated Hospitals, 1954; appointed Medical Superintendent, 1957; District Medical Officer, Eastern District, Greater Glasgow Health Board, 1974; Unit Medical Officer, Unit East 1, Greater Glasgow Health Board, 1984. Corps Commandant and Council Member, St. Andrew's Ambulance Association, 1957-82; Member of Committee, Scottish Ambulance Service, 1957-74; Director, North Parish, Washing Green Society, Glasgow, since 1957; Member, Scottish Technical Education Council, since 1974; Member, Science Development Team, 16-18s Action Plan, Scottish Education Department. Recreations: gardening; golf. Address: (h.) 15 Kenilworth Avenue, Helensburgh G84 7JR; T.-01436 3739.

Anderson, Janette, BAcc, CA. Director Scotland, Railtrack; b. 16.4.64, Glasgow; m., Brian Anderson; 1 d. Arthur Andersen and Co., 1984-88; Digital Equipment Scotland, 1988-90; Price Waterhouse, 1990-92; Chief Accountant, ScotRail, 1992-93; Railtrack: Financial Controller, 1993-97, Business Development Manager, 1997. Recreations: jazz; travel; eating out; toddler activities. Address: (b.) Buchanan House, 58 Port Dundas Road, Glasgow G4 0LQ; T.-0141-335 3555.

Anderson, Professor Kathleen Janette, OBE, FRSE, BSc, PhD, DSc(H), FScotvec, FSQA, CBiol, FIBiol, CChem, FRSC. Depute Principal, Napier Polytechnic of Edinburgh, 1983-92; b. 22.5.27, Glasgow; m., Mark Elliot Muir Anderson; 1 s.; 1 d. Educ. Queens Park School, Glasgow; Glasgow University. Lecturer, West of Scotland Agricultural College, Glasgow, 1948-54; Johnson and Florence Stoney Research Fellow, University of Sydney, Australia, 1952-53; Commonwealth Travelling Research Fellow, Australia and New Zealand, 1953; Sir James Knott Research Fellow, Durham University, 1955-57; King's College, Durham University: Lecturer in Biochemistry, 1958-59, Lecturer in Microbiology, 1962-63, Lecturer (part-time) in Landscape Horticulture, 1963-65, Lecturer (part-time), Extra-Mural Department, 1959-65; Lecturer (part-time), Department of Extra-Mural Studies, Edinburgh University, 1965-68; Napier College, Edinburgh: Senior Lecturer, Department of Biological Sciences, 1968-69, Head of Department, Biological Sciences, 1969-83. Crown Trustee, National Library for Scotland, since 1981; Deacon, Church of Scotland, 1974-78, Elder, since 1978; CNAA Environmental Sciences Board, 1978-84; Chairman, Joint Committee for Biology, SCOTEC, 1979-85; Institute of Biology: Chairman, Scottish Branch, 1977-79, Member of Council, 1977-80, Fellowship Committee, 1980-83, Environment Division, 1982-86; Founder Chairman, Heads of Biology in Tertiary Education, 1975-77; Heads of Biology in Polytechnics, 1974-83; Nurse Education Committee, Royal Edinburgh Hospital, 1974-77; SCOTVEC: Council Member and Chairman, Education Policy Committee, 1984-92, Vice Chairman, 1989-92; Chairman, Edinburgh Branch, Glasgow Graduates Association, 1985-86; Trustee, Royal Observatory (Edinburgh) Trust, since 1987; Member: Scottish National Committee, English Speaking Union, 1987-92, Radioactive Waste Management Advisory Committee, 1988-92, Agriculture Industries Training Board, 1989-92, Scottish Committee, University Funding Council, 1989-92, Canon Foundation, since 1991, British Council, Scottish Committee, 1991-96, Governing Body, Independent Girls Schools, since 1996, Eastern Board, Scottish Environment Protection Agency, since 1996; Governor, St George's School, since 1989; Governor, George Watson's School, since 1990; founder Chairman, Women of Lothian Lunch, since 1987; Governor, Edinburgh's Telford College, 1992-97. Publications: Discover Lothian Beaches; Holyrood Park Teachers Handbook; Safety in Biological Laboratories. Recreations: grand-children; charity work; gardening; foreign travel. Address: (h.) 40 Barony Terrace, Edinburgh EH12 8RD.

Anderson, Kenneth, MBChB, MD, FRCP (Glasgow). Consultant Physician with special interest in respiratory medicine; b. Glasgow. Educ. Allan Glen's School; Glasgow University. Visiting Physician, University of Colorado Hospitals, Denver. Honorary Clinical Subdean, Medicine, University of Glasgow; Honorary Lecturer, Environmental Health, University of Strathclyde; Member, Scottish Council, British Lung Foundation; Member, Scottish, British and American Thoracic Societies. Recreations: Marr

Rugby Club; Kilmarnock (Barassie) Golf Club; Troon Tennis Club. Address: (b.) Law Hospital, Carluke ML8 5ER; T.-01698 361100; (h.) Fairhaven, 14 Sarazen Drive, Troon KA10 6JP.

Anderson, Professor Michael, MA, PhD, FBA, FRSE. Professor of Economic History, University of Edinburgh, since 1979; b. 21.2.42, Woking; m., Rosemary Elizabeth Kitching; 1 s.; 1 d. Educ. Kingston Grammar School; Queen's College, Cambridge. University of Edinburgh: Assistant Lecturer, 1967-69, Lecturer, 1969-75, Reader, 1975-79, Dean of Faculty of Social Sciences, 1985-89, Vice-Principal, 1989-93, and since 1997, Acting Principal, 1994. Member: Scottish Records Advisory Council, 1984-93, Economic and Social Research Council, 1990-94, Follett Committee on Libraries and Follett Implementation Group, 1993-97, British Library Board, since 1994, Council of British Academy, 1995-98; Curator, Royal Society of Edinburgh, since 1997. Publications: Family Structure in Nineteenth Century Lancashire, 1971; Approaches to the History of the Western Family, 1981; Population Change in North-Western Europe 1750-1850; many papers on family sociology and history and historical demography. Recreations: natural history; gardening; study of ancient civilisations. Address: (b.) Department of Economic and Social History, University of Edinburgh, William Robertson Building, George Square, Edinburgh EH8 9JY; T.-0131-650 3844.

Anderson, Moira, OBE. Singer; b. Kirkintilloch; m., Dr. Stuart Macdonald. Educ. Ayr Academy; Royal Scottish Academy of Music, Glasgow. Began with Kirkintilloch Junior Choir, aged six; made first radio broadcast for BBC in Scotland, aged eight; was Teacher of Music in Ayr before becoming professional singer; made first professional broadcast, White Heather Club, 1960; has toured overseas, had her own radio and TV series; has introduced Stars on Sunday, ITV; appeared in summer shows, cabaret, pantomime and numerous other stage shows; several Royal Variety performances.

Anderson, Peter David, MA, PhD, FSA Scot, FRHistS. Deputy Keeper, National Archives of Scotland (formerly Scottish Record Office), since 1993; b. 10.3.47, Greenock; m., Jean Johnstone Smith; 1 s.; 1 d. Educ. Hutchesons' Grammar School, Glasgow; St. Andrews University; Edinburgh University. Teacher of History, Cranhill Secondary School, Glasgow, 1972-73; Research Assistant, Scottish Record Office, 1974-80; Registrar, National Register of Archives (Scotland), 1980-83; Secretary, NRA(S), 1984-85; Conservation Officer, 1985-89; Head, Records Liaison Branch, 1989-93. Member, International Council on Archives Committee on Electronic Records; Convener, Society of Archivists Legislation Panel, since 1996; Chair, International Council on Archives Committee on Archive Buildings and Equipment, since 1996; Secretary, Scottish Oral History Group, 1984-88, Deputy Convener, since 1988; Chair, Linlithgow Players, 1994-97. Publications: Robert Stewart, Earl of Orkney, Lord of Shetland, 1533-93, 1982; Black Patie, 1993. Recreations: drawing and painting; drama. Address: (b.) National Archives of Scotland, HM General Register House, Edinburgh EH1 3YY; T.-0131-535 1406.

Anderson, Robert Alexander, LLB, DipLP, NP. Solicitor, since 1983; Partner, Lindsay & Kirk, Aberdeen, since 1988; President, Aberdeen Bar Association,1996-98; b. 31.5.60, Nairn; m., Nicola Mary; 1 s.; 1 d. Educ. Nairn Academy; University of Glasgow. Trained at J.A. McGoogan & Co., Coatbridge, 1981-83, Legal Assistant, 1983-85; Legal Assistant, Lindsay & Kirk, Aberdeen, 1985-88. Involved on voluntary basis with Aberdeen Women's Aid; Tutor in Criminal Court Practice, Aberdeen University. Recreation: orienteering. Address: (b.) 39 Huntly Street, Aberdeen AB10 1TJ; T.-01224 641402.

Anderson, Professor Robert David, MA, DPhil. Professor of Modern History, Edinburgh University, since 1994; b. 11.7.42, Cardiff. Educ. Taunton School, Somerset; Queen's and St. Antony's Colleges, Oxford. Assistant Lecturer, Glasgow University, 1967-69; Lecturer, then Senior Lecturer and Reader, Edinburgh University, 1969-94. Publications: Education in France 1848-1870, 1975; France 1870-1914: Politics and Society, 1977; Education and Opportunity in Victorian Scotland, 1983 (winner, Scottish Arts Council Literary Award, 1984); The Student Community at Aberdeen, 1860-1939 (1988); Universities and Elites in Britain since 1800, 1992; Education and the Scottish People 1750-1918, 1995. Address: (b.) Department of History, Edinburgh University, Edinburgh; T.-0131-650 3786.

Anderson, Rev. Robert Scott, MA, BD (Hons). Director, Scottish Churches World Exchange, since 1986; b. 11.11.57, Glasgow; m., Jennifer Jane Paterson; 1 s.; 2 d. Educ. Hutchesons' Boys' Grammar School; Glasgow University. Assistant Manager, Glen Dairy Co. Ltd.; Assistant Minister, St. John's Renfield Church. Member, Glasgow Eastern Merchants and Tradesmen's Society; Member, Incorporation of Tailors of Rutherglen. Recreations: skiing; walking; orchid growing; reading poetry; literature. Address: St. Colm's International House, 23 Inverleith Terrace, Edinburgh.

Anderson, EurIng Professor Thomas Alfred, CEng, FICE, FCIWEM, FIHT, FIOSH, FIMgt. Member and West Area Chairman, Scottish Water and Sewerage Customers' Council; Independent Adviser to Secretary of State on appointments to executive Non-Departmental Public Bodies; National Council Member and Director, Chartered Institution of Water and Environmental Management; Director: Scottish Greenbelt Foundation, Land Trust Co. Ltd.; Public Sector Management Consultant, Joint Board for Engineering Management; Visiting Professor, Department of Civil, Structural and Environmental Engineering and Department of Biology, Paisley University, since 1992; b. 9.11.34, Glasgow; m., Margaret; 3 d. Educ. Strathbungo Senior Secondary School; Royal Technical College, Glasgow; Paisley College of Technology. City Engineer's Department, Corporation of the City of Glasgow: Senior Civil Engineer, 1964-68, Assistant Chief Civil Engineer, 1968-75; Strathclyde Regional Council: Assistant Director of Sewerage, 1975-81, Depute Director of Sewerage, 1981-91, Director of Sewerage, 1991-94. Institution of Municipal Engineers National Medal and Prize Winner, 1980; Examiner/Reviewer, Institution of Civil Engineers, since 1977; Freeman, City of London – Company of Water Conservators; Member, Industrial Advisory Committee/ Specialist Visiting Lecturer, Glasgow Caledonian University; Elder, Church of Scotland. Publications: technical papers. Recreations: gardening; golf; cricket. Address: (h.) Craigela, Ryefield Avenue, Drumpellier, Coatbridge ML5 1LG; T.-01236 424146.

Anderson, William, CBE. Managing Editor, The Sunday Post (Editor, 1967-90); b. 10.2.34, Motherwell; m., Margaret Cross McClelland (deceased); 3 s. Educ. Dalziel High School; Glasgow University. Journalist since first producing school newspapers, with interruptions as cook steward, male nurse, medical student and Army officer. Address: (b.) 2 Albert Square, Dundee DD1 9QG; T.-01382 223131.

Anderson, Professor Sir (William) Ferguson, Kt (1974), OBE, KStJ, MD, FRCP(Lond), (Glas), (Edin), (C), (I), FACP. Professor Emeritus, Geriatric Medicine, Glasgow University; Vice-President, Scottish Retirement Council; Honorary President, Crossroads (Scotland) Care Attendant Scheme; Honorary Vice-President, Age Concern (Scotland); Vice-President, Marie Curie Cancer Care; b. 8.4.14, Glasgow; m., Margaret Gebbie; 1 s.; 2 d. Educ. Glasgow Academy; Glasgow University. Assistant

Lecturer, Materia Medica, Glasgow University, 1939-41; Major, RAMC, 1941-46; Senior Lecturer, Materia Medica, Glasgow University, 1946-48; Senior Lecturer, Medicine, Welsh National School of Medicine, 1948-52; Honorary Consultant Physician, Cardiff Royal Infirmary, 1948-52; Consultant Physician in Geriatric Medicine and Advisor in diseases of old age and chronic sickness, Western Regional Board, 1952-65; Professor of Geriatric Medicine, Glasgow University, 1965-79. St. Mungo Prize, City of Glasgow; Ed Henderson Award, American Geriatrics Society; Brookdale Award, Gerontological Society of America. Recreation: golf. Address: (h.) 11 Craigfern Drive, Blanefield, Glasgow G63 9DP; T.-Blanefield 770862.

Anderson, Very Rev. Canon William Rutherfoord Turnbull, MA, FTCL. Administrator, St. Mary's R.C. Cathedral, Aberdeen; b. 7.1.31, Glasgow. Educ. George Watson's College, Edinburgh; University of Edinburgh; Sidney Sussex College, Cambridge. Curate, St. David's, Dalkeith, 1960-61; staff, St. Mary's College, Blairs, Aberdeen, 1961-69; Producer, BBC Scotland Religious Department, 1969-77; Spiritual Director, Pontifical Scots College, Rome, 1977-85; staff, St. Mary's College, Blairs, Aberdeen, 1985-86; R.C. Chaplain, University of Aberdeen, 1986-93. Canon, R.C. Diocese of Aberdeen; former Major Scholar, Sidney Sussex College, Cambridge; Poetry Society Gold Medal for verse-speaking, 1980; Preacher of the Year, The Times and College of Preachers, 1996; Warrack Lecturer, Aberdeen University, 1998. Recreations: walking; music and poetry; cats! Address: (b.) 20 Huntly Street, Aberdeen AB10 1SH; T.-01224 640678.

Anderson, Willie. Managing Director, John Smith & Son, since 1994; b. 7.4.48, Glasgow; m., Pat; 2 d. Educ. Sedbergh School. Bookseller for 24 years; President, Booksellers Association of Great Britain and Ireland, 1995-97; Joint Chair, World Book Day Steering Committee, 1997-98; Member, Booker Prize Management Committee, since 1993. Recreations: books; wine; art; keeping my weight down. Address: (h.) Crossburn, Milngavie; T.-0141-221 7472.

Andonovic, Professor Ivan, BSc, PhD, CEng, FIEE, SMIEEE, MOSA. Chair in Broadband Networks, Department of Electronic and Electrical Engineering, University of Strathclyde, since 1985; b. 16.9.57, Belgrade, Yugoslavia; m., Lynda Elizabeth; 1 s.; 1 d. Educ. Bishopbriggs High School; University of Strathclyde; University of Glasgow. Research Scientist, Barr and Stroud, 1982-85. Publications: two books; over 150 technical papers. Recreations: football; golf; skiing; reading. Address: (h.) 48 Schaw Drive, Bearsden, Glasgow G61 3AT; (b.) 204 George Street, Glasgow G1 1XW; T.-0141-942 9211.

Andrew, Hugh, BA (Oxon), FSA Scot. Joint Managing Director, Canongate Books, since 1994; b. 8.4.62. Educ. Glasgow Academy; Magdalen College, Oxford. Set up own sales business, 1990; set up own publishing company, Birlinn Ltd., 1992; bought Canongate Books with colleague, 1994. Recreations: reading; music; archaeology; islands. Address: (b.) Unit 8, Canongate Venture, 5 New Street, Edinburgh EH8 8BH; T.-0131-558 1500.

Andrew, John Anthony, MA, FRICS. Chief Estates Officer, Scottish Office, since 1996; b. 10.10.52, Ormskirk; m., Mary MacLeod Mackay; 3 s. Educ. Ormskirk Grammar School; Heanor Grammar School; Downing College, University of Cambridge. Valuation Office, Inland Revenue, Cleveland North, 1976-78; Lecturer in Land Economy, University of Aberdeen, 1978-81; Valuation Office, Inland Revenue, Aberdeen and Dumfries, 1981-89; Principal Estates Surveyor, Scottish Office, 1989-92 and 1994-96; Principal, Scottish Office Agriculture and Fisheries Department, Land Use and Conservation Division, 1992-94. Member: RICS Chairman's Committee, since 1996, Castle Rock Housing Association Ltd. Management Committee, since 1997. Recreations: reading; fishing. Address: (b.) Scottish Office Land and Property Division, 1-H42, Victoria Quay, Edinburgh EH6 6QQ; T.-0131-244 7943.

Andrews, June, RMN, RGN, MA(Hons). Secretary to Scottish Board, Royal College of Nursing, since 1993; nurse, since 1980; b. Kilwinning. Educ. Ardrossan Academy; Glasgow University; Nottingham University. NHS nursing and management posts, Nottingham and London; adviser on ethics and Aids, RCN; Assistant Director Policy and Research, Royal College of Nursing. Member, Nuffield Council on Bioethics; regular contributor to nursing press. Address: (b.) RCN, 42 South Oswald Road, Edinburgh EH9 2BB; T.-0131-662 1010.

Angus, Rev. James Alexander Keith, LVO, TD, MA. Extra Chaplain to HM The Queen, since 1996; b. 16.4.29, Aberdeen; m., Alison Jane Daly; 1 s.; 1 d. Educ. High School of Dundee; St. Andrews University. Assistant Minister, Glasgow Cathedral, 1955-56; Minister: Hoddam Parish Church, 1956-67, Gourock Old Parish Church, 1967-79; Minister, Braemar and Crathie Parish Churches, 1979-95. TA: Captain, Royal Artillery, 1950-56, Chaplain, 1957-77; Convener, Committee of Chaplains to HM Forces, General Assembly, 1981-85; LVO, 1990; Domestic Chaplain to HM The Queen in Scotland, 1979-96. Recreations: hill-walking; fishing; golf. Address: (h.) Darroch Den, Hawthorn Place, Ballater, Aberdeenshire AB35 5QH; T.-013397 56260.

Angus, Rae, MA (Hons), MLitt, MITD. Principal, Aberdeen College, since 1993; b. 1947, Ellon; m., Alison Hay; 2 d. Educ. Peterhead Academy; Aberdeen University. Further Education Lecturer, 1975; Research Fellow, Aberdeen University, 1978-80; Aberdeen College of Commerce, 1981-90, latterly as Depute Principal; Depute Principal, Aberdeen College of Further Education, 1991-93. Recreations: reading; walking; computing. Address: (b.) Gallowgate, Aberdeen AB25 1BN; T.-01224 612000.

Angus, Col. William Turnbull Calderhead, CEng, MRAeS, FIMgt, FIQA. Honorary Sheriff, North Strathclyde, since 1986; b. 20.7.23, Glasgow; m., Nola Leonie Campbell-Gillies; 2 s.; 2 d. Educ. Govan High School; Glasgow University; Royal Military College of Science. Commissioned Royal Regiment of Artillery, 1944; King's African Rifles and GSO2, DAAG (Major), HQ East Africa Command, 1945-47; Technical Staff Course, Royal Military College of Science, 1949-51; TSO2 (Major), Inspectorate of Armaments, 1951-54; BAOR and Cyprus, 1954-57; GSO2 (Major), G(Tech) HQ BAOR, 1957-60; TSO2 (Major), Ordnance Board, 1960-63; TSO2 (Major), Trials Establishment Guided Weapons, RA, 1963-65; postgraduate Guided Weapons Course, Royal Military College of Science, 1965-66; TSO1 (Lt. Col.), Royal Armament Research and Development Establishment, 1966-69; Assistant Director, Guided Weapons Trials (Col.), MOD Procurement Executive, 1970-73; Member (Col.), Ordnance Board, 1973-74; retired, 1974; self-employed holiday cottages proprietor, Scottish Manager, Blakes Holidays, 1976-93; Past President, Campbeltown Rotary Club. Recreations: wood-turning and manufacture of spinning wheels; creationism studies. Address: Kilchrist Castle, Campbeltown, Argyll PA28 6PH; T.-01586 553210.

Annand, David Andrew, DA, ARBS, JP. Sculptor; b. 30.1.48, Insch, Aberdeenshire; m., Jean; 1 s.; 1 d. Educ. Perth Academy; Duncan of Jordanstone College of Art, Dundee. Lecturer, Sculpture Department, Duncan of Jordanstone College of Art, Dundee, 1972-74; Art Department, St. Saviour's High School, Dundee, 1975-88; full-time sculptor, since 1988; RSA Latimer Award, 1976; RSA Benno Schotz Award, 1978; RSA Ireland Alloys Award, 1982; Scottish Development Agency Dundee Technology Park Competition, 1986, "Deer Leap", Sir Otto

Beit Medal, 1986; Royal Botanic Garden, Edinburgh "Ardea Cinerea", 1987; Winner, Almswall Road Sculpture Competition, Irvine Development Corporation, "The Ring", 1989; Winner, Perth High Street Sculpture Competition, Perth Partnership "Nae Day Sae Dark", 1989; Baxters of Speyside "Royal Stag" cast by Powderhall Bronze, 1993; Tranent Massacre Memorial bronze casting by Powderhall Bronze, 1995; Winner, competition to design sculpture for Lord Street, Wrexham, 1995, "Y Bwa" Civic Society Award, 1995; Winner, competition to design sculpture, Ashworth Roundabout, Blackpool, "Helter-skelter", 1995; Strathcarron Hospice composition, 1996; British High Commission, Hong Kong, "Three Cranes in Flight", 1997; Hamilton Town Square "Strongman", 1998. Recreations: music; bird watching; wine and food. Address: Pigscrave Cottage, The Wynd, Kilmany, Cupar, Fife KY15 4PT; T.-01382 330 714.

Annand, Louise Gibson, MBE, MA (Hons), AMA, DU. Artist; b. 27.5.15, Uddingston; m., 1, Alistair Matheson (deceased); 2, Roderick MacFarquhar (deceased). Educ. Hamilton Academy; Glasgow University. Teacher, primary and secondary schools, Glasgow, 1939-49; Assistant, Schools Museum Service, 1949-70; Museums Education Officer, 1970-80. Past Chairman: Scottish Educational Film Association (Glasgow Production Group); Glasgow Lady Artists Club Trust; National Vice-Chairman, Scottish Educational Media Association, 1979-84; President: Society of Scottish Women Artists, 1963-66 and 1980-85; Member, Royal Fine Art Commission for Scotland, 1979-86; Glasgow Society of Women Artists, 1977-79, 1988-91; Visiting Lecturer in Scottish Art, Regina University, 1982; Chairman, J.D. Fergusson Foundation, since 1982 (Trustee, since 1983); Member, Business Committee, General Council, University of Glasgow, 1981-85, 1988-91; Honorary Member, Saltire Society, since 1993; DUniv, Glasgow University, 1994; exhibited widely since 1945; produced numerous 16mm films, including the first on Charles Rennie Mackintosh, 1966. Recreations: mountaineering (Ladies Scottish Climbing Club). Address: (h.) 22 Kingsborough Gardens, Glasgow G12 9NJ; T.-0141-339 8956.

Annandale and Hartfell, 11th Earl of (Patrick Andrew Wentworth Hope Johnstone of Annandale and of That Ilk). Chief, Clan Johnstone; Baron of the Barony of the Lands of the Earldom of Annandale and Hartfell, and of the Lordship of Johnstone; Hereditary Steward, Stewartry of Annandale; Hereditary Keeper, Keys of Lochmaben Castle; Deputy Lieutenant, Dumfriesshire, since 1987; b. 19.4.41, Auldgirth, Dumfriesshire; m., Susan Josephine; 1 s.; 1 d. Educ. Stowe School; Royal Agricultural College, Cirencester. Member: Dumfriesshire County Council, 1970-75, Dumfries and Galloway Regional Council, 1975-85, Scottish Valuation Advisory Council, 1982, Solway River Purification Board, 1973-85; Underwriter, Lloyds, London, 1976. Address: (b.) House of Lords, London SW1.

Anstruther, Sir Ralph (Hugo), of that Ilk, 7th Bt. of Balcaskie and 12th of Anstruther, GCVO, MC, DL, BA. Equerry to the Queen Mother, since 1959, and Treasurer since 1961; b. 13.6.21. Educ. Eton; Magdalene College, Cambridge. Major (ret.), Coldstream Guards. Member, Queen's Bodyguard for Scotland (Royal Company of Archers); DL, Fife, 1960; DL, Caithness-shire, 1965. Address: Balcaskie, Pittenweem, Fife; Watten, Caithness.

Anthony, William Burns, FRICS. Chairman, Royal Institution of Chartered Surveyors in Scotland, since 1998; Building Manager, National Museums of Scotland, since 1988; b. 29.10.47, Edinburgh; m., Pamela; 1 s.; 1 d. Educ. Galashiels Academy; Daniel Stewarts College; Napier College. J&J Hall: Apprentice Quantity Surveyor, 1965-70, Assistant Quantity Surveyor, 1970-71; Senior Quantity Surveyor: John D. Hutchison and Partners, 1971-77, Kirkaldy District Council, 1977-78; Principal Quantity Surveyor, National Health Service, 1978-88. Recreation: curling. Address: (b.) Royal Museum of Scotland, Chambers Street, Edinburgh EH1 1JF; T.-0131-247 4157.

Anton, Alexander Elder, CBE, MA, LLB, LLD (Hon), FBA; b. 1922; m., Doris May Lawrence; 1 s. Educ. Aberdeen University. Solicitor, 1949; Lecturer, Aberdeen, 1953-59; Professor of Jurisprudence, Glasgow University, 1959-73; Honorary Professor, 1984, Aberdeen University; Member, Scottish Law Commission, 1966-82; UK Delegate to Hague Conference on Private International Law, 1964-82; Chairman, Scottish Rights of Way Society, 1988-92. Publications: Private International Law, 1967 and 1990; Civil Jurisdiction in Scotland, 1984. Recreation: hill-walking. Address: (h.) 5 Seafield Drive West, Aberdeen AB15 7XA.

Arbuthnot, Peter Geoffrey. Managing Director, Christie's Scotland Limited, since 1989; b. 18.9.50, London; m., Belinda Terry-Engell; 1 s.; 1 d. Educ. Stowe School; Trinity College, Cambridge. Research in Indian Archaeology, 1974-76; Specialist, Ethnographic Art, Christie's Auctioneers, London, 1976-80; Commodity Trader, E.D. and F. Man, 1980-83; Christie's in the City, 1983-88. Governor, Laurel Park School, Glasgow, since 1991. Recreations: squash; skiing; hockey; travel; public speaking. Address (b.) 164-166 Bath Street, Glasgow G2 4TB; T.-0141-332 8134.

Arbuthnott, 16th Viscount of (John Campbell Arbuthnott), KT, CBE, DSC, FRSE, FRSA, BGCOStJ, LLD. Lord Lieutenant, Kincardineshire, since 1977; b. 26.10.24; m.; 1 s.; 1 d. Educ. Fettes College; Gonville and Caius College, Cambridge. Served RNVR (Fleet Air Arm), 1942-46. Member, Countryside Commission for Scotland, 1967-71; Chairman, Red Deer Commission, 1969-75; Member, Aberdeen University Court, 1978-84; President, Scottish Landowners Federation, 1974-79; President, Royal Scottish Geographical Society, 1984-87; Chairman, Scottish Widows' Fund and Life Assurance Society, 1984-87; Lord High Commissioner to the General Assembly of the Church of Scotland, 1986, 1987; President, Royal Zoological Society of Scotland, 1976-96; President, Scottish Agricultural Organisation Society, 1980-83; President, Federation of Agricultural Cooperatives (UK), 1983-87; Deputy Chairman, Nature Conservancy Council, 1980-85, and Chairman, Scottish Committee, NCC; Chairman, Aberdeen and Northern Marts Ltd., 1986-91, Director, 1973-91; Director, Clydesdale Bank PLC, 1985-92 (Northern Area, 1975-85); Director, Britoil, 1988-90; Prior of Scotland, The Order of St. John, 1983-95; Member, Royal Commission on Historical Manuscripts, 1988-95; Member, BP Scottish Advisory Board, 1990-97. Address: (h.) Arbuthnott House, by Laurencekirk, Kincardineshire AB30 1PA.

Arbuthnott, Professor Sir John Peebles, PhD, ScD, FIBiol, HonFTCD, FRSA, FRSE, FIIB, FRCPath, HonFRCPSGlasg. Principal and Vice Chancellor, Strathclyde University, since 1991; Vice-Chairman, Committee of Vice-Chancellors and Principals; b. 8.4.39; m., Elinor Rutherford Smillie; 1 s.; 2 d. Educ. Glasgow University; Trinity College, Dublin. Assistant Lecturer, then Lecturer, Department of Bacteriology, Glasgow University, 1960-67; Fellow of the Royal Society, 1968-72; Senior Lecturer, Department of Microbiology, then Senior Lecturer, Department of Bacteriology, Glasgow University, 1972-75; Professor of Micriobiology, Trinity College, Dublin, 1976-88; Professor of Microbiology, Nottingham University, 1988-91. Member, Lister Institute; Member, Board, Glasgow Development Agency; Chairman, National Review of Allocation of Health Resources in Scotland, 1997-99. Recreations: bird-watching; attending soccer matches; golf. Address: (b.) Strathclyde University, Glasgow G1 1XQ; T.-0141-552 4400.

Archer, Gilbert Baird, DL. Chairman, Tods of Orkney Ltd, since 1970; Director (formerly Chairman), John Dickson & Sons Ltd; b. 24.8.42, Edinburgh; m., Irene Conn; 2 d. Educ. Melville College. Vice Convenor, George Watson's College, 1978-80; Governor, Fettes College, 1986-90; Director, Scottish Council of Independent Schools, 1988-91; Council Member, Governing Bodies Association of Independent Schools, 1988-91; Governor, Napier University, 1991-97; Governor, St. Columba's Hospice; Past President, Edinburgh Chamber of Commerce & Manufactures; Past Chairman, Scottish Chambers of Commerce; former Deputy President, Association of British Chambers of Commerce; Chairman, Edinburgh Common Purpose, 1991-94; Past Moderator, High Constabulary of the Port of Leith; Liveryman, Worshipful Company of Gunmakers, London; Master, The Company of Merchants of the City of Edinburgh. Recreations: fishing; shooting. Address: (b.) 12 Broughton Place, Edinburgh EH1 3RX; T.-0131-556 4518.

Archer, Professor John Stuart, BSc, PhD, FRSE, FEng. Principal and Vice-Chancellor, Heriot-Watt University, since 1997; b. 15.6.43, London; m., Lesley; 1 s.; 1 d. Educ. County Grammar School, Chiswick; City University, London; Imperial College of Science, Technology and Medicine. Trainee, ICI (Mond Division); Senior Research Engineer, Imperial Oil (Esso Canada), Calgary; Senior Petroleum Engineer, British Gas Corporation (Exploration Division); Manager Reservoir Studies, D and S Petroleum Consultants, London and Calgary; Director and Co-founder, ERC Energy Resources Consultants Ltd., London; Professor of Petroleum Engineering, Imperial College, London University; Pro Rector (Resources) and Deputy Rector, Imperial College of Science, Technology and Medicine. Director, Centre for Marine and Petroleum Technology; Advisory Editor, Kluwer and Elsevier; Non-Executive Director, LEEL (Lothian and Edinburgh Enterprise Ltd); Fellow, City and Guilds Institute; Distinguished Faculty Award, Society of Petroleum Engineers; Lubbock-Sambrook Award, Institute of Energy. Recreations: music; art; theatre; golf. Address: (b.) Heriot-Watt University, Riccarton, Edinburgh EH14 4AS; T.-0131-451 3360.

Archer, John William, BA (Hons). Chief Executive, Scottish Screen, since 1997; b. 19.9.53, Evesham; 3 s. Educ. Dean Close School, Cheltenham; University of Birmingham; University College, Cardiff. Researcher, Nationwide, 1975-77; Director, BBC TV, London: Writers and Places, Global Report, Omnibus; Producer, The Book Programme, Did You See...?; Editor, Saturday Review, A Week of British Art; Head of Music and Arts, BBC Scotland, 1989, including editing Edinburgh Nights; Executive Producer, The Bigger Picture, Billy Connolly's World Tour of Scotland/Australia; producing and directing Stevenson's Travels; BAFTA Award, best programme/series without a category for Did You See...?, 1983. Recreations: walking; tree planting; mountain biking; necessary gardening; novels. Address: (b.) 74 Victoria Crescent Road, Glasgow G12 9JN; T.-0141-302 1700.

Argyll, 12th Duke of, (Ian Campbell). Chief of Clan Campbell; Hereditary Master of the Royal Household, Scotland; Hereditary High Sheriff of the County of Argyll; Admiral of the Western Coast and Isles; Keeper of the Great Seal of Scotland and of the Castles of Dunstaffnage, Dunoon, and Carrick and Tarbert; b. 28.8.37; m. Iona Mary; 1 s.; 1 d. Address: Inverary Castle, Inverary, Argyll PA32 8XF.

Armistead, Major Norman. Scotland Secretary, Salvation Army, since 1998; b. 7.7.39, Bradford; m., Beryl Glenis Cox; 1 s.; 2 d. Engaged in editorial and pastoral work for 40 years. Address: (b.) 30 Rutland Square, Edinburgh EH1 2BW; T.-0131-221 9699.

Armour, Professor Sir James, CBE, PhD, FAMS, Dr hc Utrecht, DVM&S (Edin), FRCVS, FRSE. Emeritus Professor of Veterinary Parasitology, Glasgow University; Vice-Principal (Planning - External Relations), 1991-95; Dean, Faculty of Veterinary Medicine, 1986-91; Chairman, Glasgow Dental Hospital and School NHS Trust, since 1995; b. 17.9.29, Basra, Iraq; m., 1, Irene Morris (deceased); 2, Christine Strickland; 2 s.; 2 d. Educ. Marr College, Troon; Glasgow University. Colonial veterinary service, Nigeria, 1953-60; Research Scientist, Wellcome Ltd., 1960-63; Glasgow University: Research Fellow, 1963-67, Lecturer/Senior Lecturer, 1967-73, Reader, 1973-76. Chairman, Government Committee on Animal Medicines, 1987-95; Chairman, Editorial Board, In Practice (veterinary journal), 1980-90; Chairman, Governing Body, Institute of Animal Health, 1989-97; Member, Governing Body: Moredun Research Institute, Edinburgh, since 1997, Institute of Aquaculture, Stirling, since 1997. Awards: RCVS John Henry Steel Medal, Royal Agricultural Society Bledisloe Award, BVA Wooldridge Medal, Pfizer WAAVP Award, BVA Chiron Award. Publications: joint author of textbook on veterinary parasitology; editor, two books; 150 scientific articles. Recreation: golf. Address: (h.) Mokoia, 11 Crosbie Road, Troon, Ayrshire; T.-01292 314068.

Armour, Mary Nicol Neill, DA, RSA, RSW, RGI, LLD Glasgow (1980). Artist; b. 27.3.02, Blantyre; m., William Armour. Educ. Hamilton Academy; Glasgow School of Art. Elected ARSA, 1941; RSW, 1956; RSA, 1958; RGI, 1977; Honorary President: Glasgow School of Art, 1982; Royal Glasgow Institute of the Fine Arts, 1983; Vice President, Paisley Art Institute, 1983. Guthrie Award, RSA, 1937; Cargill Prize, RGI, 1972; Fellow, Paisley University, since 1989; Hon. Fellowship, Glasgow School of Art, 1993; Awarded Diploma PAI (Paisley Art Institute), 1995. Recreations: gardening; dress-making. Address: Priory Park Private Residential Home, 19 Main Road, Castlehead, Paisley PA2 6AJ; T.-0141-848 1718.

Armour, Robert Malcolm, MBA, LLB (Hons), DipLP, WS, NP. Company Secretary, British Energy plc, since 1995; formerly Director, Performance Development (1993-95) and Company Secretary (1990-95), Scottish Nuclear Limited; Director: British Nuclear Industry Forum, Quality Scotland Foundation, Lochside Insurance Limited, Electricity Association Limited, British Energy Trustees Limited, British Energy International Limited, Scottish Nuclear International Ltd.; b. 25.9.59, Edinburgh; m., Anne Ogilvie White. Educ. Daniel Stewart's and Melville College, Edinburgh; Edinburgh University. Solicitor, Haldanes McLaren and Scott, WS, Edinburgh, 1983-86; Partner, Wright, Johnston and MacKenzie, Edinburgh, 1987-90. Recreations: golf; curling. Address: British Energy plc, 10 Lochside Place, Edinburgh EH12 9DF.

Armstrong, Bryan. Editor: Annandale Observer, since 1994, Annandale Herald, since 1994, Moffat News, since 1994; b. 26.6.54, Chester. Educ. Annan Academy. Joined Dumfriesshire Newspaper Group, 1971, as apprentice/compositor; photographer, 1976-79; reporter, 1979-83; Group Assistant Editor, 1983-94. Recreations: cycling; greyhound racing; photography; music; travel. Address: (b.) 96 High Street, Annan DG12 5DW; T.-01461 202417.

Armstrong, Helen. Co-Founder and Director, M.E. Foundation, since 1994; b. 3.6.45, Lanarkshire; m., Findlay Armstrong; 1 s.; 1 d. Address: (b.) 8 Inverleith Gardens, Edinburgh EH3 5PU; T.-0131-478 7879.

Armstrong, Iain Gillies, LLB, DipLP. Clerk of Faculty, Faculty of Advocates, since 1995; b. 26.5.56, Edinburgh; m., Deirdre Elizabeth Mary Mackenzie; 1 s.; 1 d. Educ. Inverness Royal Academy; Glasgow University. Admitted to Faculty of Advocates, 1986. Address: (b.) Advocates Library, Parliament House, Edinburgh EH1 1RF; T.-0131-226 5071.

Arnold, Andy, MA (Hons), DipEd. Founder and Artistic Director, The Arches, Glasgow, since 1991; Theatre Director, since 1980; Community Artist and Cartoonist, since 1974; Teacher, since 1973; b. Southend-on-Sea. Artistic Director, Theatre Workshop, Edinburgh, 1980-85; Director, Bloomsbury Theatre, London, 1986-89; directing credits include: Metropolis: The Theatre Cut, Caligari, The Devils, The Crucible, Sexual Perversity in Chicago, I Licked a Slag's Deodorant; Freelance Director, The Battle of Stirling Bridge, Stirling Castle, 1997. Two Paper Boat awards; Spirit of Mayfest Award. Recreations: holidays; five-a-side football; Hibernian F.C.; golf. Address: (h.) The Arches, Midland Street, Glasgow G1 4PR; T.-0141-221 9736.

Arnold, James Edward, MBE, MA (Hon), BA, CertEd, FRIAS. Director, New Lanark Conservation Trust, since 1974; b. 16.3.45, Glasgow; m., Rose. Educ. Caludon Castle Comprehensive School; York University; London University. Recreations: New Lanark and life. Address: (b.) Mill Number Three, New Lanark, Lanark; T.-01555 661345.

Arnott, David Cleghorn, FILAM. Administrator, Scottish Association of Local Sports Councils; formerly Director of Leisure Services, Dunfermline District Council; Member: Scottish Sports Council, National Lottery Board – Sport and Sports Match Scotland Panel since 1995; b. 6.2.42, Hamilton; m., Jean McFarlane Lennox; 2 s.; 1 d. Educ. Woodside Secondary, Hamilton. Joined local government with Lanarkshire County Council, 1957. Past Chairman, Scottish Branch, Institute of Leisure and Amenity Management; Hon. Life Member, Scottish Association of Local Sports Councils. Recreations: football; golf; beach-combing. Address: (h.) 37 Donibristle Gardens, Dalgety Bay, Fife KY11 5NQ; T.-01368 820950.

Arnott, Ian Emslie, DA, DipTP, ARSA, RIBA, ARIAS. Consultant Architect, since 1994; b. 7.5.29, Galashiels. Educ. Galashiels Academy; Edinburgh College of Art. Flying Officer, RAF, 1955-57; Founding Partner, then Chairman, Campbell and Arnott, 1962-94; External Examiner, Dundee University, 1989-93; Assessor, Civic Trust Awards, since 1986. RSA Gold Medal for Architecture, 1981; nine Civic Trust Awards; one RIBA Award; two EAA Awards. Vice-Chairman, Saltire Society. Recreations: music; painting; reading; swimming; resting. Address: The Rink, Gifford, East Lothian EH41 4JD; T.-01620 810278.

Arnott, James Mackay, TD, BL, WS, SSC. Solicitor; Partner, MacRoberts, Glasgow and Edinburgh, since 1963; b. 22.3.35, Blackford, Perthshire; m., Jean Barbara Allan; 3 s. Educ. Merchiston Castle School, Edinburgh; Edinburgh University. National Service, RAF, 1957-60; TA, 1961-77. Council Member, Law Society of Scotland, 1983-85 (Convenor, Law Reform Committee); Secretary, Scottish Building Contract Committee. Recreation: cricket. Address: (b.) 152 Bath Street, Glasgow G2 4TB; T.-0141-332 9988; 27 Melville Street, Edinburgh EH3 7JF; T.-0131-226 2552.

Arnott, John Michael Stewart, BA. President, Scottish Arctic Club, 1995-98; Member, Council, Scottish Wildlife Trust, since 1995; b. 12.6.33; m., Lynne Gladstone-Millar; 1 s.; 1 d. Educ. Peterhouse, Cambridge. Pilot, RAF, 1952-54; Announcer, Producer, Editor Talks and Features, Edinburgh Manager, BBC Scotland, 1960-90; Member, 1982-92, Vice-Chairman, 1986-92, Countryside Commission for Scotland; Chairman, Isle of May Bird Observatory, 1980-85; Chairman, Fair Isle Bird Observatory Trust, 1983-85; Member: Committee for Scotland, Nature Conservancy Council, 1986-91, NCC Advisory Committee on Birds, 1990-91; Chairman, CCS Advisory Panel on Management of Mountain Areas, 1989-90; Member, National Parks of England and Wales Review Panel, 1990; President, Scottish Ornithologists' Club, 1984-87; Member: South East Regional Board, Scottish Natural Heritage, 1992-95, Board, Edinburgh Green Belt Trust, 1992-97. Sony Award for Radio Feature, 1985. Recreations: ornithology; hill-walking. Address: (h.) East Redford House, 133 Redford Road, Edinburgh EH13 0AS; T.-0131-441 3567.

Arnott, Kate, FIPD. Human Resource Consultant, since 1989; Chairman, Edinburgh's Telford College Board of Management, since 1997 (Member, since 1995); Lay Member, Employment Tribunal Service (Scotland); b. 13.1.43, Galashiels; m., Bert Arnott; 3 s.; 2 d. Educ. St. George's School for Girls, Edinburgh. Worked for Marks and Spencer and Harrods; Senior Personnel Officer, Ferranti (Scotland), 1966-69 and 1979-88. Scottish Board Member, Opportunity 2000; Chairman, Complaints Review Panel, Lothian Health Board. Recreations: music; reading; arts and crafts; trying to keep fit. Address: 14 West Savile Road, Edinburgh EH16 5NQ; T.-0131-667 6874.

Arnott, Professor Struther, CBE, BSc, PhD, ScD, DSc, FKC, FRSE, FRS. Principal and Vice-Chancellor, St. Andrews University, since 1986; b. 25.9.34, Larkhall; m., Greta Edwards; 2 s. Educ. Hamilton Academy; Glasgow University. King's College, London: Scientist, MRC Biophysics Research Unit, 1960-70, Demonstrator, Physics, 1960-67, Director of Postgraduate Studies in Biophysics, 1967-70; Purdue University, Indiana, USA: Professor of Molecular Biology, 1970, Head, Department of Biological Sciences, 1975-80, Vice-President for Research and Dean, Graduate School, 1980-86; Oxford University: Senior Visiting Research Fellow, Jesus College, 1980-81, Nuffield Research Fellow, Green College, 1985-86, Guggenheim Memorial Foundation Fellow, 1985. Recreations: birdwatching; botanizing. Address: (b.) College Gate, North Street, St. Andrews KY16 9AJ; T.-01334 462545.

Arshad, Rowena, MEd (Community Education). Director, Centre for Education for Racial Equality in Scotland (CERES), since 1994; Lecturer in Equity and Rights, since 1991; Member (first ever black woman Member), Scottish Trades Union Congress General Council, since 1997; b. 27.4.60, Brunei Town, Brunei; m., Malcolm Quarrie Parnell; 1 s.; 1 d. Educ. Methodist Girls School, Penang, West Malaysia; Moray House Institute of Education; Edinburgh University. Education and Campaigns Organiser, Scottish Education and Action for Development, 1985-88; Director, Edinburgh Multicultural Education Centre, 1988-90. Convenor, Educational Institute of Scotland Anti-Racist Committee; Member, Editorial Board, Scottish Affairs journal; Member, Advisory Committee, Centre for Scottish Public Policy. Author of numerous contributions to publications on equality. Recreations: keen reader of Scottish Highland history; active trade unionist; dogs and animal issues. Address: (b.) CERES, Moray House, Charteris Building, Room 5, Floor 2, Holyrood Road, Edinburgh EH8 8AQ; T.-0131-651 6371.

Arthur, Adrian, BL. Editor, The Courier, Dundee, since 1993; b. 28.9.37, Kirkcaldy; m., Patricia Mill; 1 s.; 2 d. Educ. Harris Academy, Dundee; St. Andrews University. Joined staff of People's Journal; through the editorial ranks of The Courier (Deputy Editor, 1978-93). Recreations: golf; travel; Rotary. Address: (b.) 80 Kingsway East, Dundee DD4 8SL; T.-01382 223131.

Arthur, Lt. General Sir Norman, KCB (1985); Lord Lieutenant, Stewartry of Kirkcudbright, Dumfries and Galloway Region; b. 6.3.31, London (but brought up in Ayrshire, of Scottish parents); m., Theresa Mary Hopkinson; 1 s.; 1 d.; 1 s. (deceased). Educ. Eton College; Royal Military Academy, Sandhurst. Commissioned Royal Scots Greys, 1951; commanded Royal Scots Dragoon Guards, 1972-74, 7th Armoured Brigade, 1976-77, 3rd Armoured Division, 1980-82; Director, Personal Services (Army), 1983-85; commanded Army in Scotland, and

Governor of Edinburgh Castle, 1985-88; retired, 1988; Honorary Colonel, Royal Scots Dragoon Guards, 1984-92; Col. Comdt. Military Provost Staff Corps, 1983-88; Honorary Colonel, 205 (Scottish) General Hospital, Territorial Army, 1988-93; Colonel, The Scottish Yeomanry, 1992-97; mentioned in Despatches, 1974. Officer, Royal Company of Archers; President, Scottish Conservation Projects Trust, 1989-93; Vice President, Riding for the Disabled Association, Edinburgh and the Borders, 1988-94; Chairman: Army Benevolent Fund, Scotland, since 1988, Leonard Cheshire Foundation, SW Scotland, since 1994; Member, Committee, Automobile Association, since 1990; humanitarian aid work, Croatia and Bosnia, since 1992; Member, British Olympic equestrian team (three-day event), 1960. Recreations: riding; country sports; country life; reading. Address: (h.) Newbarns, Dalbeattie, Kirkcudbrightshire DG5 4PY; T.-01556 630227.

Ashcroft, Professor Brian Kemp, BA (Hons), MA. Director, Fraser of Allander Institute, Strathclyde University, since 1989; Member, Secretary of State's Panel of Economic Consultants, since 1991; Member, Northern Ireland Economic Council, since 1995; b. 5.3.47, Stockton-on-Tees; m., Janet; 1 s.; 2 d. Educ. Stockton Grammar School; Lancaster University. Rock musician, 1962-65; Construction Industry: labourer, clerk, office manager, 1965-70; Lecturer, Glasgow Polytechnic, 1974-76; Strathclyde University: Lecturer/Senior Lecturer, 1976-89, Research Director, Fraser of Allander Institute, 1989. Publications: over 30 academic papers/books. Recreations: photography; jogging; trying to hide his English origins. Address: (b.) 100 Cathedral Street, Glasgow G4 0LN; T.-0141-552 4400.

Asher, Catherine Archibald, OBE, DUniv, BA, RGN, SCM, RNT. Chairman, National Board for Nursing, Midwifery and Health Visiting for Scotland, 1982-95; b. 6.7.33, Edinburgh. Educ. Woodside School, Glasgow; Edinburgh University; Open University. Ward Sister, Glasgow Royal Infirmary, 1956-61; Nurse Teacher, Senior Tutor, Principal Nursing Officer (Teaching), Glasgow Royal Infirmary School of Nursing, 1963-74; Director of Nurse Education, Glasgow Eastern College of Nursing and Midwifery, 1974-91; Acting Principal, Glasgow College of Nursing and Midwifery, 1991-95; Governor, University of Paisley, since 1996. Recreations: gardening; golf; swimming. Address: (h.) 68 Fifth Avenue, Glasgow G12 0AT; T.-0141-339 5072.

Asher, Professor R. E., BA, PhD, DLitt, FRSE, FRAS. Professor of Linguistics, Edinburgh University, 1977-93, Professor Emeritus and Honorary Fellow, Faculty of Arts, since 1993; b. 23.7.26, Gringley-on-the-Hill, Nottinghamshire. Educ. King Edward VI Grammar School, Retford; University College, London; University of London; University of Edinburgh. Assistant, Department of French, University College, London, 1951-53; Lecturer in Linguistics, then Lecturer in Tamil, School of Oriental and African Studies, London, 1953-65; joined Department of Linguistics, Edinburgh University, 1965; Dean, Faculty of Arts, 1986-89; Member, University Court, 1989-92; Vice-Principal, 1990-93; Curator of Patronage, 1991-93; Director, Centre for Speech Technology Research, 1994. Visiting appointments: Visiting Professor of Linguistics, University of Illinois, Urbana-Champaign, 1967; Visiting Professor of Tamil and Malayalam, Michigan State University, 1968; Visiting Professor of Linguistics, University of Minnesota, 1969; Chaire des Professeurs Etrangers, Collège de France, 1970; Subrahmaniya Bharati Fellow, Tamil University, Thanjavur, 1984-85; Visiting Professor, International Christian University, Tokyo, 1994-95; first occupant of Vaikom Muhammed Basheer Chair, Mahatma Gandhi University, Kottayam, Kerala, 1995-96. Medal, Collège de France, Paris, 1970; Gold Medal, Kerala Sahitya Akademi, India, 1983. Publications: A Tamil Prose Reader, 1971; Some Landmarks in the History of Tamil Prose, 1973; Me Grandad 'ad an Elephant! (translation), 1980; Towards a History of Phonetics (Co-Editor), 1981; Tamil, 1982; Studies on Malayalam Language and Literature, 1989; National Myths in Renaissance France: Francus, Samothes and the Druids, 1993; Scavenger's Son (translation), 1993; Atlas of the World's Languages (Co-Editor), 1994; Encyclopedia of Language and Linguistics (Editor-in-Chief), 1994; Concise History of the Language Sciences: from the Sumerians to the Cognitivists (Co-Editor), 1995; Malayalam, 1997; The Novels and Stories of Vaikom Muhammed Basheer, 1998. Address: (b.) Department of Linguistics, University of Edinburgh, Adam Ferguson Building, Edinburgh EH8 9LL; T.-0131-650 3484.

Ashford, Professor Michael Lawrence James, BSc, PhD. Professor of Pharmacology, University of Aberdeen, since 1995; b. 26.6.55, Aberdeen; m., Pamela Eileen Law; 1 s.; 3 d. Educ. Robert Gordon's College, Aberdeen; University of Aberdeen. MRC Training Fellowship Award, University of Nottingham, 1980-83; Department of Pharmacology, University of Cambridge: Demonstrator, 1983-88, Lecturer, 1988-95. Recreation: contemplation of alternative universes. Address: Department of Biomedical Sciences, Institute of Medical Sciences, Foresterhill, Aberdeen AB25 2ZD; T.-01224 273055.

Ashmore, Fionna Margaret, BA (Hons), FSA, FSAScot. Director, Society of Antiquaries of Scotland, since 1992; b. 21.5.50, London; m., P.J. Ashmore; 2 s.; 1 d. Educ. Oporto British School, Portugal; Convent of the Sacred Heart, Tunbridge Wells; University College, Cardiff; Glasgow University. Research on Portuguese Iron Age; archaeological indexer; Assistant Editor, Proceedings of the Society of Antiquaries of Scotland, 1978-90; Assistant Secretary, Cockburn Association, 1990-92. Recreations: reading; cinema; eating out; visiting buildings and archaeological sites. Address: (b.) Royal Museum of Scotland, Chambers Street, Edinburgh EH1 1JF; T.-0131-247 4115.

Ashworth, Bryan, MA, MD, FRCP(Lond), FRCP(Edin). Honorary Senior Lecturer (Medical History), St Andrews University, since 1997; Associate Lecturer, Society of Apothecaries (London), since 1998; Honorary Librarian, Royal College of Physicians of Edinburgh, 1982-91; Consultant Neurologist, Royal Infirmary and Western General Hospital, Edinburgh, and Senior Lecturer in Medical Neurology, Edinburgh University, 1971-92; b. 5.5.29, Oundle, Northants. Educ. Laxton School; Oundle School; St. Andrews University. National Service, Captain RAMC, Northern Nigeria, 1953-55; junior hospital posts, Manchester and Bristol; Wellcome-Swedish Travelling Research Fellow, Karolinska Hospital, Stockholm, 1965-66; Lecturer in Clinical Neurology, Manchester University, and Honorary Consultant Physician, Manchester Royal Infirmary, 1967-71; Chairman and Director (non-executive), Robert Bailey and Son, PLC, Stockport, since 1978. Publications: Clinical Neuro-ophthalmology, 2nd edition, 1981; Management of Neurological Disorders, 2nd edition, 1985; The Bramwells of Edinburgh, 1986. Recreations: writing; walking. Address: (h.) 13/5 Eildon Terrace, Edinburgh EH3 5NL; T.-0131-556 0547.

Ashworth, John Brian, OBE, FCA, CBIM. Former Vice Chairman, Seagram Distillers PLC (Managing Director, Chivas Brothers Ltd., 1974-93, and Seagram Distillers PLC, 1984-93); Chairman, Renfrewshire Enterprise Ltd.; Director, Scotch Whisky Heritage Centre Ltd; b. 2.9.36, Wakefield; m., Valerie; 2 s.; 1 d. Educ. Ackworth School; British College of Accountancy. Articled chartered accountancy, Leeds; Accountant, John Smiths Tadcaster Brewery Co. Ltd.; Commercial Director, Shaw Carpet Co. Ltd.; Founder/Managing Director, Crimpfil Ltd. Governor, Paisley University; Master, Keepers of the Quaich.

Recreations: golf; travel. Address: (b.) Woodside, Upper Colquhoun Street, Helensburgh; T.-01436 676050.

Atherton, Brian John, MCommH, FRSA, MMS, AHRIM, MIMgt. General Manager, Shetland Health Board, since 1990; b. 27.1.44, York; m., Margaret; 2 s. Educ. King's School, Pontefract; University of Liverpool. Civil Servant, 1966-71; various NHS posts, including District Planning Officer, Southmead Health Authority, 1983-86, General Administrator, Tayside Health Board, 1986-90. Trustee, Shetland Welfare Trust. Recreations: sailing; photography. Address: (b.) Brevik House, South Road, Lerwick ZE1 0RB; T.-01595 743062.

Atholl, 11th Duke of (John Murray); b. 19.1.29; m.; 2 s. 1 d. Succeeded to the title, 1996; lives in South Africa.

Atkinson, Professor David, BSc, PhD, FIBiol, CBiol, MIEEM, FRSA, MIPSS. Vice Principal (R. & D.), Scottish Agricultural College; b. 12.9.44, Blyth; m., Elisabeth Ann Cocks; 1 s.; 2 d. Educ. Newlands County Secondary Modern School; Hull University; Newcastle-upon-Tyne University. East Malling Research Station, Maidstone, 1969-85; Macaulay Institute for Soil Research, 1985-87; Macaulay Land Use Research Institute, 1987-88; Professor of Agriculture, Aberdeen University, and Head, Land Resources Department, Scottish Agricultural College, 1988-93; former Deputy Principal (R. &D.) and Dean, Edinburgh Centre, Scottish Agricultural College. Individual Member, BCPC Council, since 1994; Member, IEEM Council, since 1992. Recreations: music; reading thrillers; quotations. Address: (b.) SAC, West Mains Road, Edinburgh EH9 3JG.

Atkinson, Kate. Author; b. York; 2 children. Winner of several prizes for short stories, including the Ian St. James Award; Winner, 1995 Whitbread First Novel Award for Behind the Scenes at the Museum. Lives in Edinburgh.

Atkinson, Professor Michael David, MA, DPhil. Professor of Computational Science, St. Andrews University, since 1992; b. 4.5.46, Leeds; 2 s.; 2 d. Educ. Leeds Grammar School; Queen's College, Oxford. Lecturer, University College, Cardiff, 1970-82; Professor, Carleton University, Ottawa, 1982-92. Recreations: bridge; walking; music. Address: 146 North Street, St. Andrews KY16 9AF; T.-01334 478113.

Atkinson, Norman Keir, DipEd, FMA, AMA, FSA(Scot). Chairman, Angus Museums and Heritage Forum; Head of Support Services, Cultural Services, Angus Council, since 1996; b. 8.1.50, Arbroath; m., Noreen; 1 s; 1 d. Educ. Arbroath High; Dundee College of Education; Leicester University. Teacher, Angus County Council, 1972-75; Assistant Keeper, then Acting Keeper, Extension Services, Dundee Museum, 1975-77; District Curator, Angus District Council, 1977-96. Past President, Scottish Museums Federation; former Vice-Chairman, Scottish Museums Council. Recreations: football; archaeology; wildlife. Address: (b.) County Buildings, Forfar DD8 3WF; T.-01307 461460.

Atkinson, Valerie, MA (Hons). Deputy Head, News and Current Affairs, BBC Scotland, since 1997; b. 28.12.44, Glasgow; m., Ian Atkinson; 1 s.; 1 d. Educ. Hillhead High School, Glasgow; University of Glasgow. Awards: BAFTA Scotland, 1993, ISDD National Television Award, 1993, Industrial Society, 1994, Commission for Racial Equality Race in the Media Award, 1998. Trustee, National Galleries of Scotland, since 1998; Member, Scottish Office Constitution Group Expert Panel on Media Issues, since 1998. Address: (b.) BBC Current Affairs, Queen Margaret Drive, Glasgow G12 8DG.

Atwell, Brian Harvey. Chair, Marriage Counselling Scotland, 1994-98; Trustee, Sutherland Trust, since 1997; a Director, Confederation of Scottish Counselling Agencies, since 1995; Vice Convenor, Marriage Counselling Dumfries and Galloway, since 1994; b. 19.9.39, Glasgow; m., Ann Ramsay; 2 d. Educ. Trinity Academy, Edinburgh. Career civil servant, 1958-94; Industrial Counsellor, Forestry Commission, 1981-89; Marriage Counsellor, since 1977; Trainer, Scottish Association of Counselling, 1979-83; Member, Civil Service Training Advisory Committee, 1982-88. Recreations: jazz music; fly fishing; sailing. Address: (h.) Bartons House, Lockerbie Road, Dumfries DG1 3PG.

Audain, Irene, MA (Hons), DipInfoScience. National Development Officer, Scottish Out of School Care Network, since 1993; b. 10.7.56, Glasgow. Educ. University of Glasgow; University of Strathclyde. Has worked in voluntary sector for 20 years, developing childcare, community development work, campaigning on women's issues, housing rights and children's rights. Tutor in Women's Self-Defence and Adult Literacy; Youth Leader; Board Member: Scottish Childminding Association, Meadowside and Thornwood Housing Association. Recreations: learning British sign language; travel. Address: (b.) Floor 9, Fleming House, 134 Renfrew Street, Glasgow G3 6ST; T.-0141-331 1301.

Austin, Professor Brian, BSc, PhD, DSc, FRSA. Professor, Department of Biological Sciences, Heriot-Watt University; b. 5.8.51, Barnet; m., Dawn Amy; 1 d. Educ. Mount Grace School, Potters Bar; University of Newcastle-upon-Tyne. Research Associate, 1977-78; Senior Scientific Officer, 1978-84; Lecturer, 1984-89; Reader, 1989-92. Recreations: reading; writing; walking. Address: (b.) Heriot-Watt University, Riccarton, Edinburgh EH14 4AS; T.-0131-451 3452.

Austin, Juliet Leathes, BA (Hons). Headmistress, Kilgraston School, since 1993; b. 22.4.44, Reading; m., Anthony James Kirkpatrick Austin; 1 d. Educ. Downe House; Birmingham University. Downe House School, 1972-82, latterly as Head of English; Headmistress, Combe Bank School, 1982-93. Recreations: sailing; walking; painting. Address: (b.) Kilgraston School, Bridge of Earn, Perth PH2 9BQ; T.-01738 812257.

Axford, Nicola Dawn, BA (Hons). General Manager, Royal Lyceum Theatre Company, since 1995; b. 17.10.60, London; m., Prof. Ian Brown. Educ. Bradford University. Director, Big Bird Music Theatre, 1982-86; Administrator, Major Road Theatre Company, 1986-87; Drama Finance Officer, Arts Council of Great Britain, 1987-91; Business Manager, PW Productions Ltd., 1991-92; Administrator, Manchester City of Drama 1994 Ltd., 1993-94. Director: Royal Lyceum Theatre, Major Road Theatre Company; Member, Drama Panel, Scottish Arts Council, since 1997. Address: (h.) 30 Haddington Place, Edinburgh EH7 4AG; T.-0131-556 3987.

Azmy, Amir Fouad, FRCS (London, Glasgow and Edinburgh). Consultant Paediatric Surgeon, Royal Hospital for Sick Children, Glasgow, since 1980; Clinical Senior Lecturer, University of Glasgow, since 1980; b. 1.11.39, Egypt; m., Dr. F. S. Mohsen; 1 s.; 1 d. Educ. E in Shams University, Cairo. Registrar, Royal Hospital for Sick Children, Glasgow, Westminster Children's Hospital, London; Senior Registrar, Hospital for Sick Children, Great Ormond Street, London. Address: (h.) The Knowe, 301 Albert Drive, Pollokshields, Glasgow G41 5RP; T.-0141-201 0000.

B

Bader, Douglas, MA, FRSA, FIL. Rector, Perth Grammar School, since 1985; b. 22.11.41, Stirling; m., May Heather; 3 s. Educ. Larbert High School. Teacher of Modern Languages, High School of Glasgow, 1965-69; Principal Assistant, then Principal Teacher, Alloa Academy, 1969-74; Assistant Rector, Forfar Academy, 1974-79; Depute Rector, Montrose Academy, 1979-85. Member, Headteachers' Association of Scotland. Recreations: singing; basketball; canoeing. Address: (b.) Perth Grammar School, Gowans Terrace, Perth PH1 5AZ; T.-01738 620071.

Bagnall, John Michael, MA (Cantab), DipLib, MIInfSci. University Librarian, Dundee University, since 1987; b. 22.4.45, South Yorkshire. Educ. Mexborough Grammar School; Sidney Sussex College, Cambridge. Diploma in Librarianship, University College, London; Assistant Librarian and Sub-Librarian, Newcastle upon Tyne University. Recreations: music; bird-watching; languages. Address: University Library, Dundee DD1 4HN; T.-01382 344082.

Baikie, Fiona M., BA (Hons), FRSA, MIM. Principal and Chief Executive, Edinburgh's Telford College, since 1996; b. 15.11.44, Leicester; m., Jim (musician). Educ. John Neilson Institute, Paisley; Strathclyde University; Open University. Advertising and publishing assistant, 1965-69; Lecturer, then Senior Lecturer, Telford College, 1969-80; Head, Department of Commerce, Ayr College, 1980-82, Head, Department of Business Studies, 1982-88; Edinburgh's Telford College: Assistant Principal 1988-94, Vice Principal, 1994-96. Member, Board of Directors, Edinburgh Compact; Member, National Art Collections Fund. Recreations: languages and travel; collecting first editions; art. Address: (b.) Crewe Toll, Edinburgh EH4 2NZ; T.-0131-332 2491.

Bailey, Captain Ronald Richard. Master Mariner; Harbour Master, Clydeport, since 1997; b. 22.4.54, Guildford; 2 s. Educ. London Nautical School. Merchant Navy Officer, Mobil Shipping Company and Maersk Line, 1971-84; Assistant Harbour Master, then Harbour Master, Manchester Ship Canal, 1984-96. Former Director, Walk the Plank Charity. Recreations: golf; skiing; walking; travel. Address: (b.) Clydeport Operations Limited, Estuary Control, Campbell Street, Greenock PA16 8AW; T.-01475 726221.

Baillie, Ian David Hunter, CBE, CQSW. Director of Social Work, Church of Scotland Board of Social Responsibility, since 1990; Director, Social Care Association (Education), since 1987; Auxiliary Minister, United Reformed Church; b. 18.12.40, Dundee; m., Margaret MacCallum McFarlane; 3 d. Educ. Hutchesons Boys Grammar School. Eight years in life assurance; 30 years, to date, in social work; Member, Executive, International Christian Federation for Prevention of Alcoholism and Drug Addiction. Recreations: sport (watching); reading. Address: (b.) Charis House, 47 Milton Road East, Edinburgh EH15 2SR; T.-0131-657 2000.

Baillie, Professor John, MA, CA. Visiting Professor of Accountancy, Heriot-Watt University, Edinburgh, since 1989; Johnstone-Smith Professor of Accountancy, Glasgow University, 1983-88; Partner, Scott-Moncrieff Downie Wilson, since 1993; Partner, KPMG, 1978-92; b. 7.10.44; m., Annette Alexander; 1 s.; 1 d. Educ. Whitehill School. Convenor, Research Committee, Institute of Chartered Accountants of Scotland; member, various technical and professional affairs committees, Institute of Chartered Accountants of Scotland. Recreations: keeping fit; reading; music; golf. Address: (h.) The Glen, Glencairn Road, Kilmacolm, Renfrewshire; T.-Kilmacolm 3254.

Baillie, William James Laidlaw, CBE, PRSA, HRA, PPRSW, RGI, HRHA, HRWA, HFRBS, HBWS, HSSA, DAEdin, DLitt. President, Royal Scottish Academy, 1990-98; professional painter, since 1950; b. 19.4.23, Edinburgh; m. Helen Gillon; 1 s.; 2 d. Educ. Dunfermline High School; Edinburgh College of Art. Army Service (mainly Far East) 1942-47; Lecturer/Senior Lecturer in Drawing and Painting, Edinburgh College of Art, 1960-88; President, Royal Scottish Society of Painters in Water Colours, 1974-88; Royal Scottish Academy: Associate, 1968, Academician, 1979, Treasurer, 1980-90; 25 solo exhibitions in UK and abroad. Awards: 1980 EIS Award RSA, Cargill Award RGI, 1989 May Marshall Brown Award RSW, Sir William Gillies Award RSW; DLitt, Heriot Watt University, 1997. Recreations: music; travel. Address: 6A Esslemont Road, Edinburgh EH16 5PX; T.-0131-667 1538.

Bain, Aly. Fiddler; b. 1945, Lerwick. Co-founder, Boys of the Lough, 1972; Soloist; TV and radio anchorman.

Bain, Professor Andrew David, OBE, FRSE. Chairman of Trustees, Scottish Enterprise Pension Scheme, since 1995; Visiting Professor, Glasgow University, 1991-97; Board Member, Scottish Enterprise, 1991-97; Economic Consultant, since 1991; b. 21.3.36, Glasgow; m., Eleanor Riches; 3 s. Educ. Glasgow Academy; Cambridge University. Various posts, Cambridge University, 1959-67; Professor of Economics: Stirling University, 1967-77, Strathclyde University, 1977-84; Group Economic Advisor, Midland Bank, 1984-90. Member: Committee to Review the Functioning of Financial Institutions, 1977-80, Monopolies and Mergers Commission, 1980-81; Member, TEC National Council, 1994-97. Publications: The Control of the Money Supply, 1970; The Economics of the Financial System (2nd Edition), 1992. Address: (b.) Department of Economics, Glasgow University, Glasgow G12 8RT; T.-0141-330 6866.

Bain, Iain Andrew, MA. Editor and Proprietor, The Nairnshire Telegraph, since 1987; b. 25.2.49, Nairn; m., Maureen Beattie; 3 d. Educ. Nairn Academy; Aberdeen University. Joined The Geographical Magazine, 1974, Editor, 1981-87. Recreations: reading; writing; photography; golf. Address: (b.) 10 Leopold Street, Nairn IV12 4BG; T.-01667 453258.

Bain, Professor John, MD, FRCGP. Professor of General Practice, University of Dundee, since 1992; b. 18.8.40, Aberdeen. Educ. Inverurie Academy; University of Aberdeen. Principal in General Practice, Livingston; Professor of Primary Medical Care, University of Southampton. Chairman, Association of University Departments of General Practice; Adviser in Primary Care Research, Chief Scientist's Office, Scottish Office. Recreations: golf; hill-walking; photography. Address: (b.) Tayside Centre for General Practice, Kirsty Semple Way, Dundee DD2 4AD; T.-01382 632771.

Baird, Professor David Tennent, BA (Cantab), MB, ChB, DSc, FRCP Edin, FRCOG, FRS(Ed). Medical Research Council Professor of Reproductive Endocrinology, Edinburgh University, since 1985; Consultant Obstetrician and Gynaecologist, Simpson Memorial Maternity Pavilion, Edinburgh Royal Infirmary, since 1970; b. 13.3.35, Glasgow; m., Frances Lichtveld (m. dissolved); 2 s. Educ. Aberdeen Grammar School; Aberdeen University; Trinity College, Cambridge; Edinburgh University. After clinical training in endocrinology as well as obstetrics, spent three years (1965-68) as an MRC travelling Research Fellow at Worcester Foundation for Experimental Biology, Shrewsbury, Mass., USA, conducting research on reproductive endocrinology; Deputy Director, MRC Unit of Reproductive Biology, Edinburgh, 1972-77; Professor of

Obstetrics and Gynaecology, Edinburgh University, 1977-85; served on a number of national and international committees. Publications: four books on reproduction. Recreations: ski mountaineering; music; sport. Address: (b.) Department of Obstetrics and Gynaecology, Edinburgh University, Centre for Reproductive Biology, 37 Chalmers Street, Edinburgh EH3 9EW; T.-0131-229 2575.

Baird, Sheriff John A., LLB (Hons). Floating Sheriff based at Glasgow. Address: (b.): Sheriff Court House, 1 Carlton Place, Glasgow G5 9DA.

Baird, John Alexander, MD, FRCPsych, DCH. Consultant Forensic Psychiatrist, Glasgow, since 1993; b. 28.8.47, Edinburgh; m., Ann Easson; 3 s. Educ. Daniel Stewart's College, Edinburgh; Edinburgh University. Consultant Psychiatrist, State Hospital, Carstairs, 1981-85, Physician Superintendent, 1985-92. Standing Committee on Difficult Prisoners: Member, 1985-88, Chairman, 1988-91; Member, Parole Board for Scotland, 1992-94, and since 1998; Member, Advisory Committee on Prisoner Management, 1993-98. Recreation: hill walking. Address: (h.) 50 Munro Road, Jordanhill, Glasgow G13 1SF.

Baird, Susan, CBE, OStJ, JP, DUniv. Lord Provost of Glasgow, 1988-92; Convener, Economic and Industrial Development Committee, Glasgow City Council, since 1995; b. 26.5.40, Glasgow; m., George; 3 s.; 1 d. Educ. St. Mark's Secondary School, Glasgow. Worked in a city centre office; joined Labour Party, 1969; became Councillor for Parkhead, 1974; elected Bailie of the city, 1980; formerly: Convener, Manpower Committee, Vice-Convener, Parks and Recreation Committee. Address: (b.) City Chambers, George Square, Glasgow G2 1DU; T.-0141-287 2000.

Baker, Frances J.T., MBE, MSc, BA, RGN, OHNC, Cert Ed. Occupational Health Adviser, Lothian Occupational Health Research Project, since 1995; President, Federation of Occupational Health Nurses in the EU (FOHNEU); b. 29.4.34, Ayr; m., Alan; 1 s.; 1 d. Educ. Ayr Academy; London University (External); Manchester University. Casualty Staff Nurse, Ayr County Hospital; Sister, NCB, North Staffs; Lecturer, Senior Lecturer, Head of Health and Nursing Studies, Stoke on Trent Cauldon College, 1975-82; Senior Nursing Officer, British Gas Scotland, 1982-95. Member, National Board for Nursing, Midwifery and Health Visiting for Scotland, 1988-93. Publications: Role of Occupational Health Nurse in the Care of the Pregnant Woman at Work; Counselling Role of the Occupational Health Nurse. Recreations: opera and classical music; theatre; swimming; gardening; tapestry; reading. Address: (b.) Pardovan House, Linlithgow EH49 7RU.

Baker, Professor Michael John, TD, BA, BSc (Econ), DipM, CertITP (Harvard), DBA (Harvard), FCIM, F.SCOTVEC, FCAM, FRSA, FRSE, FAM, FSQA. Professor of Marketing, Strathclyde University, since 1971 (Deputy Principal, 1984-91); b. 5.11.35, Debden; m., Sheila; 1 s.; 2 d. Educ. Worksop College; Bede, Gosforth and Harvey Grammar Schools; Durham University; London University; Harvard University. Royal Artillery, 1956 (2nd Lt.); Richard Thomas & Baldwins (Sales) Ltd., 1958-64; Lecturer: Medway College of Technology, 1964-66, Hull College of Technology, 1966-68; FME Fellow, Harvard Business School, 1968-71; Member, Vice-Chairman and Chairman, SCOTBEC, 1973-85; Member, SSRC Management Committee, 1976-80; Dean, Strathclyde Business School, 1978-84; Marketing Education Group: Chairman, 1974-87, President, since 1987; Chairman, Institute of Marketing, 1987; Member: SHERT, 1983-96, UGC Business and Management Sub-Committee, 1986-89, Chief Scientist's Committee, since 1985, ESRC Research Resources Board, 1994-96; Governor, CAM; Chairman: Westburn Publishers Ltd, Scottish Management Projects Ltd. Publications: Marketing New Industrial Products; Market Development; Marketing (6th edition, 1996); The Marketing Book (Editor, 4th edition, 1999); The Role of Design in International Competitiveness; Marketing and Competitive Success; Dictionary of Marketing & Advertising (3rd edition, 1998); Research for Marketing; Perspectives on Marketing Management (Editor); Marketing: Theory & Practice (Editor, 3rd edition, 1996); Marketing Strategy and Management (2nd edition, 1992); Companion Encyclopedia of Marketing (2nd edition, 1999); The Marketing Manual, 1998; Product Strategy and Management, 1998. Recreations: sailing; gardening; travel. Address: (b.) Strathclyde University, 173 Cathedral Street, Glasgow G4 ORQ; T.-0141-552 4400.

Baker, Professor Michael John, BSc (Eng), ACGI, DIC, MICE, MIStructE, FSaRS. Professor of Safety Engineering, Aberdeen University, since 1991; b. 20.10.40, Oxford; m., Margaret Eleanor Lucas; 1 s.; 1 d. Educ. Leighton Park School, Reading; Imperial College of Science, Technology and Medicine, London. Civil Engineer, N.C.B., 1962-65; Research Assistant/Fellow, Imperial College, London, 1966-77; Lecturer in Structural Engineering, 1978-86, Reader in Structural Reliability, 1986-91. Vice-Chairman, Commission I, Comite Euro-International du Beton; Member of the Plenum, International Joint Committee on Structural Safety; Member, Research Strategy Board, Offshore Safety Division, Health and Safety Executive. Recreations: mountaineering; gardening. Address: (h.) 2 Thornton Place, Watson Street, Banchory, Kincardineshire AB31 5UB; T.-01330 825495.

Baker, Ray, CBE. Director, GEC Scotland Ltd.; Chairman: Fife Enterprise, Fife Industry Council, Fife European Vocational Training Partnership, Fife Education Industry – The Fife Partnership; Hon. President, Fife Area Board Young Enterprise; b. 15.10.26, Nuneaton. Educ. Lanchester and Dunchurch Colleges. Joined GEC, 1950; former Chairman: Fife Health Board, Fife College of Further and Higher Education, Association of Scottish Colleges, Youth Clubs Fife. Recreations: music; reading; gardening; walking. Address: (b.) Fife Enterprise, Kingdom House, Saltire Centre, Glenrothes, Fife KY6 2AQ; T.-01334 656200.

Baker, Professor Thomas Neville, BMet, PhD, DMet (Sheffield), DSc (Strathclyde), FIM, FInstP, CEng, CPhys. Professor, Department of Mechanical Engineering – Metallurgy and Engineering Materials Group, Strathclyde University; b. 11.1.34, Southport; m., Eileen May Allison. Educ. King George V School, Southport; Sheffield University. Research Metallurgist, Nelson Research Laboratories, English Electric Co., Stafford, 1958-60; Scientist, Project Leader, Tube Investments Research Laboratories, Hinxton Hall, Cambridge, 1961-64; Department of Metallurgy, Strathclyde University: SRC Research Fellow, 1965, Lecturer, 1966, Senior Lecturer, 1976, Reader, 1983, Professor, 1990, Professor of Metallurgy (1886 Chair), 1992, Vice Dean, School of Chemical and Materials Science, 1979-82, Head, Department of Metallurgy, 1986-87, Head, Division of Metallurgy and Engineering Materials, 1988-90; Committee Member, Institute of Metals, Metal Science Committee, 1980-94, Materials Technology Committee, since 1994, Process Science and Technology Committee since 1996; Chairman, Annual Conference on Metals and Materials, 1982-92. Publications: Yield, Flow and Fracture in Polycrystals (Editor), 1983; Titanium Technology in Microalloyed Steels (Editor), 1997; over 130 learned society publications. Recreations: music; literature; creating a garden. Address: (b.) Department of Mechanical Engineering, Strathclyde University, Glasgow; T.-0141-548 3101.

Baldwin, Professor Norma, BA (Hons), DipSocAdmin, MPhil. Professor of Child Care and Protection, University of Dundee, since 1995; Head, Department of Social Work, since 1996; Member, CCETSW Scottish Committee, since 1996; Member, Scottish Childcare Board; b. 21.5.39, Hull; 2 s. Educ. Malet Lambert, Hull; University of Manchester; London School of Economics; University of Warwick. Probation Officer, then Senior Probation Officer, Greater Manchester; Principal Officer, Warwickshire Social Services Department; Lecturer, Senior Research Fellow, Senior Lecturer, University of Warwick. Publications: The Power to Care in Children's Homes, 1990; Residents' Rights (Co-Author), 1993; Protecting Children: Promoting their Rights (Editor); Developing Neighbourhood Support and Child Protection Strategies (Co-author), 1998. Recreations: walking; gardening; theatre; music. Address: (b.) Department of Social Work, University of Dundee, Dundee DD1 4HN; T.-01382 344651.

Bale, Lesley Christine. Managing Director, Aberdeen Airport Ltd., since 1992; Director, Scottish Airports Ltd., since 1990; b. 14.4.59, Glasgow. Educ. Craigholme School, Glasgow; Strathclyde University. Deloitte Haskins & Sells (Glasgow), 1978-81; Coopers & Lybrand (Bermuda), 1981-83; Western International Financial Group (Bermuda): Vice-President, Treasurer and Director, 1983-87; Financial Controller, Prestwick Airport Ltd., 1988-90; Managing Director, Prestwick Airport Ltd., 1990-92. Alumnus of the Year, Strathclyde University, 1994; Scottish Young Business Achievement Award, 1996. Recreations: bridge; golf. Address: Aberdeen Airport Ltd., Dyce, Aberdeen AB21 7DU;T.-01224 725001.

Balekjian, Wahe Hagop, Dr (Law), Dr (pol sc), PhD. Honorary Senior Research Fellow, School of Law, Glasgow University, since 1990 (Reader in European Law, 1976-90, Head of Department, 1976-88); Visiting Titular Professor, University of Salzburg, Austria, since 1981; Titular Professor, European Faculty, Land Use Planning, Strasbourg, since 1982; Honorary Senior Research Fellow, School of Law, Glasgow University, since 1990; b. 2.10.24, Cairo; m., Eva Birgitta. Educ. College of Arts and Sciences, Cairo; Vienna University; Manchester University. Diploma, Hague Academy of International Law. Lecturer, Vienna University, 1957-73; Simon Research Fellow, Manchester University, 1963-65; Head of Department, European Studies, National Institute of Higher Education, Limerick, 1973-76. Publications: Legal Aspects of Foreign Investment in the EEC, 1967 (awarded Prize of European Communities, 1967); The Status of Unrecognised States in International Law (published in German, 1971). Recreations: hill-walking; piano playing; languages. Address: (b.) School of Law, The University, Glasgow G12 8QQ; T.-0141-339 8855, Ext. 5539.

Balfour of Burleigh, Lady (Janet Morgan), MA, DPhil, FRSAS. Writer; Company Director; b. 5.12.45, Montreal; m., Lord Balfour of Burleigh. Educ. Newbury County Girls' Grammar School; Oxford University; Sussex University; Harvard University. Member: Central Policy Review Staff, Cabinet Office, 1978-81, Board, British Council, since 1989; Special Adviser to Director-General, BBC, 1983-86; Chairman, Cable & Wireless Flexible Resource Ltd., 1993-97; Non-Executive Director: Cable & Wireless, W.H. Smith, 1989-95, Midlands Electricity, 1990-96, Scottish American Investment Co., since 1991, Scottish Oriental Smaller Companies Investment Trust, since 1994, The Scottish Life Assurance Company, since 1995, Nuclear Generation Decommissioning Fund Ltd, since 1996, New Medical Technologies plc, since 1997, Scottish Medical Research Fund, 1992-94; Member: Scottish Museums Council Development Resource, 1988-97, Ancient Monuments Board for Scotland, 1990-97, Book Trust Scotland, since 1992, Scottish Economic Council, 1993-95, Scottish Hospitals Endowment Research Trust, since 1992, Dorothy Burns Charity, since 1994; Chairman, Scotland's Book Campaign, 1994-96, Scottish Cultural Resources Access Network, since 1995; Trustee, Carnegie Endowment for the Universities of Scotland, since 1993. Publications: Diaries of a Cabinet Minister 1964-70 by Richard Crossman (4 volumes) (Editor); The Future of Broadcasting, (Co-Editor, 1982); Agatha Christie: a biography, 1984; Edwina Mountbatten: a life of her own, 1991. Recreations: music of Handel; sea bathing; pruning; ice skating out of doors.

Balfour of Burleigh, Lord, CEng, FIEE, FRSE, Hon. D Litt (Robert Gordon), Hon. DUniv (Stirling), Hon. FRIAS. Chairman, Capella Nova; Chancellor, Stirling University, 1988-98; Chairman, Advisory Board, Robert Gordon University Heritage Institute; b. 6.1.27, London. Educ. Westminster School, London. Graduate Apprentice, English Electric Company, 1951; various positions in manufacturing mangement; started English Electric's manufacturing operations in India as General Manager of new company in Madras, 1957-64; returned to Liverpool as General Manager; appointed General Manager, D. Napier & Son, before leaving the company in 1968; joined Bank of Scotland as a Director, 1968; Deputy Governor, Bank of Scotland, 1977-91. Forestry Commissioner, 1971-74; Chairman: Scottish Arts Council, 1971-80, Federation of Scottish Bank Employers, 1977-86, The Turing Institute, 1983-92, Scottish Committee, ABSA, 1988-94, United Artists Communications (Scotland) Ltd., until 1996; Director: Scottish Investment Trust plc, 1971-96, Tarmac plc, 1981-90, William Lawson Distillers Ltd., 1984-96, Television Educational Network, 1990-96, Edinburgh Book Festival, 1981-96 (Chairman, 1981-87); Member, British Railways (Scottish) Board, 1982-92; Treasurer: Royal Society of Edinburgh, 1989-94, Royal Scottish Corporation; President, Friends of Vellore; President, Franco-Scottish Society, 1985-96; Life Member and Trustee, 1990-96, John Muir Trust. Recreations: woodwork; hill-climbing; music. Address: House of Lords, London SW1A 0PW.

Balfour, Alastair. Managing Director, The Insider Group, since 1993; b. 15.6.47, Edinburgh; m., Anne Johnstone (second marriage); 2 s.; 3 d. Educ. Royal High School, Edinburgh. Trained as journalist with The Scotsman, 1966-68; became Industrial Reporter in Glasgow, 1974-78; joined Daily Record as Economics Correspondent, 1978-81; Business Editor, Sunday Standard, 1981-83; co-launched Scottish Business Insider, 1984; Editor, 1986-90; Editorial Director, until 1993. Member, Strathclyde Graduate Business School Council; Member, Scottish Advisory Board, FI Group PLC; Founder Member, The Entrepreneurial Exchange. Recreations: family; sailing. Address; (b.) 43 Queensferry Street Lane, Edinburgh EH2 4PF; T.-0131 535 5555; (h.) Kessogbank, 60 Glasgow Road, Blanefield, Stirlingshire G63 9BP; T.-01360 770750.

Balfour, 4th Earl of (Gerald Arthur James Balfour), JP; b. 23.12.25; m. Educ. Eton; HMS Conway. Member, East Lothian County Council, 1960-75; farmer. Address: (h.) The Tower, Whittingehame, Haddington EH41 4QA.

Balfour, Ian Leslie Shaw, MA, LLB, BD, PhD, SSC, NP. Solicitor (Consultant, Balfour & Manson) since 1955; b. 16.6.32, Edinburgh; m., Joyce Margaret Ross Pryde; 3 s.; 1 d. Educ. Edinburgh Academy; Edinburgh University. Qualified as Solicitor, 1955; commissioned, RASC, 1955-57; 1959-97: Partner, then Senior Partner, Balfour & Manson; Secretary, Oliver & Son Ltd., 1959-89; Fiscal to Law Society of Scotland, since 1981. Baptist Union of Scotland: President, 1976-77, Law Agent, 1964-97, Secretary, Charlotte Baptist Chapel, Edinburgh, since 1980, Secretary, Scottish Baptist College, since 1983; Secretary, Elba Housing Society Ltd., 1969-92; Council, Society for Computers and Law, 1988-92; Director, Edinburgh Medical Missionary Society. Recreations: gardening; home computing; lay preaching. Address: (h.) 38 Murrayfield Road, Edinburgh; T.-0131-337 2880.

Balfour, Peter Edward Gerald, CBE. President, Scottish Council (Development and Industry), 1985-92 (Chairman, 1978-85); Director, Royal Bank of Scotland, 1972-90;

Chairman, Charterhouse plc, 1985-91; b. 9.7.21, Woking; m., 1, Grizelda Ogilvy, 2, Diana Wainman; 3 s.; 2 d. Educ. Eton College. Served Scots Guards, 1940-54; joined William McEwan & Co., brewers, 1954; appointed Director, 1958; Director, Scottish Brewers, 1959; Scottish and Newcastle Breweries, 1961 (Chairman and Managing Director, 1970-83); Director and Vice Chairman, RBS Group, 1978. Recreations: farming; forestry. Address: (h.) Scadlaw House, Humbie, East Lothian; T.-01875 833252.

Balfour, William Harold St. Clair. Solicitor (retired); b. 29.8.34, Edinburgh; m., 1, Patricia Waite (m. dissolved); 1 s.; 2 d.; 2, Alice Ingsay McFarlane; 2 step. d. Educ. Hillfield, Ontario; Edinburgh Academy; Edinburgh University. Partner, Balfour & Manson, 1962-98; Clerk to Admission of Notaries Public, 1971-92; Prison Visiting Committee, 1965-70; Chairman, Basic Space Dance Theatre, 1980-86; Friends of Talbot Rice Art Centre, 1982-97, Garvald Trustees, since 1980, Wellspring Management, 1990-97. Recreations: sailing; walking; wine. Address: (h.) 11 Nelson Street, Edinburgh EH3 6LF; T.-0131-556 7298.

Ball, Derek William, MB, MRCPsych. Composer; Consultant Psychiatrist; b. 30.12.49, Letterkenny, Ireland; m., Marie Knox; 1 d. Educ. Kings Hospital, Dublin; Royal Irish Academy of Music; Trinity College, Dublin. Studied composition with Dr. Archie Potter; writes chamber and orchestral music; numerous performances in Dublin; pieces performed at festivals in Paris and Bordeaux. Founder Member, Association of Young Irish Composers; Secretary/Treasurer, Scottish Society of Composers. Address: (h.) Mazagon, 4 Glen Road, Lennoxtown G65 7JX.

Ball, Geoffrey A., FCA. Chairman, CALA plc (Group Managing Director, since 1974); b. 4.8.43, Bristol; m., Mary Elizabeth; 3 s.; 1 d. Educ. Cotham Grammar School, Bristol. Former Managing Director, Greencoat Properties Ltd.; non-executive Director: Standard Life Assurance Company; Scottish Mortgage & Trust p.l.c. Recreations: golf; music. Address: 26 Hermitage Drive, Edinburgh EH10 5BT; T.-0131-535 5200.

Ball, Graham Edmund, BDS, FDS, RCS (Eng), MHSM. Consultant in Dental Public Health, Fife, Borders and Lothian Health Boards, since 1995; Honorary Senior Lecturer in Dental Public Health, University of Edinburgh; Honorary Senior Lecturer, School of Biomedical Sciences, St Andrews University; b. 14.12.53; m., Carolyn Bowyer; 1 s.; 2 d. Educ. King Edward VI School, Southampton; Welsh National School of Medicine. Registrar, Oral and Maxillofacial Surgery, Portsmouth hospitals, 1979-81; Associate Specialist (part-time), Oral Surgery, Wessex Cardiothoracic Unit, 1982-84; general dental practice, 1984-88; Clinical Community Dental Officer, Orkney Health Board, 1988-91; Chief Administrative Dental Officer, Orkney Health Board, 1991-95. Recreations: sailing; walking. Address: (b.) Fife Health Board, Springfield House, Cupar, Fife; T.-01334 656200.

Ballantyne, Professor Colin Kerr, MA, MSc, PhD, FRSE, FRSA. Professor in Physical Geography, St. Andrews University, since 1994; b. 7.6.51, Glasgow; m., Rebecca Trengove; 1 s. Educ. Hutchesons' Grammar School; Glasgow University; McMaster University; Edinburgh University. Lecturer in Geography, St. Andrews University, 1980-89, Senior Lecturer in Geography and Geology, 1989-94. Gordon Warwick Award, 1987; Presidents' Medal, Royal Scottish Geographical Society, 1991; Newbigin Prize, Royal Scottish Geographical Society, 1992; Scottish Science Award, Saltire Society, 1996. Publications: The Quaternary of the Isle of Skye, 1991; The Periglaciation of Great Britain, 1994. Recreations: music; travel; mountaineering; skiing; writing. Address: (h.) Birchwood, Blebo Craigs, Fife KY15 5UF; T.-01334 850567.

Ballantyne, Fiona Catherine, MA, MCIM. Network Scotland Ltd.: Director since 1991, Chairman since 1997; Member, Board, Queen Margaret College, Edinburgh, since 1995; Director, Edinburgh Audience Development Initiative Ltd., since 1998; Member, Scottish Committee, Institute of Directors, since 1996; b. 9.7.50, Bristol; m., A. Neil Ballantyne. Educ. Marr College, Troon; Edinburgh University. Former Market Researcher and Market Research Manager; Research and Planning Manager, Thistle Hotels Ltd., 1975-77; Assistant Marketing Manager, Lloyds & Scottish Finance Group, 1977-79; Scottish Development Agency: Marketing Manager, Small Business Division, 1979-84, Head of Small Business Services, 1984-88, Director, Tayside and Fife, 1988-90; Managing Director, Ballantyne Mackay Consultants, since 1990; Vice-Chair: BBC Broadcasting Council for Scotland, 1991-96, Duncan of Jordanstone College of Art, 1988-94; Director, Edinburgh Healthcare Trust, 1994-96; Member, Board, Scottish Campaign for Learning,1997-98. Recreations: walking; swimming; tapestry; painting. Address: (b.) 2-8 Millar Crescent, Edinburgh EH10 5HW; T.-0131-447 9700.

Band, Thomas Mollison. Chairman: Perth Theatre Ltd., since 1995 (Director, since 1994), Andersons Enterprises Ltd., since 1994, Edinburgh Europa Ltd., 1994-98, Select Line Breaks Ltd., 1995-98; Governor: Edinburgh Telford College, 1990-98, Queen Margaret College, since 1995; b. 28.3.34, Aberdeen; m., Jean McKenzie Brien; 1 s.; 2 d. Educ. Perth Academy. Principal, Tariff Division, Board of Trade, London, 1969-73; Director (Location of Industry), Department of Industry, Glasgow, 1973-76; Assistant Secretary: (Industrial Policy), Scottish Economic Planning Department, 1976-78, (Housing), Scottish Development Department, 1978-82, (Finance), Scottish Office, 1982-84; Director, Historic Buildings and Monuments, Scottish Development Department, 1984-87; Chief Executive, Scottish Tourist Board, 1987-94; Member, Board of Management, Perth Housing Association, since 1993, Vice Chairman, since 1998. Recreations: gardening; skiing; shooting. Address: (h.) Heathfield, Pitcairngreen, Perthshire; T.-01738 583 403.

Banfill, Professor Phillip Frank Gower, BSc, PhD, CChem, FRSC. Professor of Construction Materials, Heriot-Watt University, since 1995; b. 20.3.52, Worthing; m., Patricia; 1 s.; 1 d. Educ. Lancing College; Southampton University; Liverpool University. Former Lecturer, Liverpool University. Publications: three books; 70 papers. Recreations: sailing; choral singing; bee-keeping. Address: (b.) Department of Building Engineering and Surveying, Heriot-Watt University, Riccarton, Edinburgh EH14 4AS; T.-0131-449 5111.

Banks, Iain. Novelist; b. 1954. Educ. schools in North Queensferry, Gourock, Greenock; Stirling University. Hitch-hiked through Europe, Scandinavia, Morocco, 1975, later worked for British Steel and IBM, and as a costings clerk in London. Books: The Wasp Factory, 1984; Walking on Glass, 1985; The Bridge, 1986; Consider Phlebas, 1987; Espedair Street, 1987; The Player of Games, 1988; Canal Dreams, 1989; Use of Weapons, 1990; The State of the Art, 1991; The Crow Road, 1992; Against a Dark Background, 1993; Complicity , 1993 (No. 1 bestseller in paperback); Feersum Endjinn, 1994; Whit, 1995; Excession, 1996; Song of Stone, 1997.

Bankowski, Professor Zenou Krzysztof, LLB. Professor of Legal Theory, University of Edinburgh, since 1993; b. 9.10.46, Germany. Educ. Becket School, Nottingham; Dundee University. Lecturer in Law, University College, Cardiff; successively Lecturer, Senior Lecturer, Reader, Edinburgh University. Recreation: athletics. Address: (h.) 76 Thirlestane Road, Edinburgh; T.-0131-447 4365.

Banks, Professor William McKerrell, BSc, MSc, PhD, CEng, FIMechE, FIM. Professor of Advanced Materials, Strathclyde University, since 1991; Director, Centre for Advanced Structural Materials; Member, IMechE and IOM Council; b. 28.3.43, Irvine; m., Martha Ruthven Hair; 3 s. Educ. Irvine Royal Academy; Strathclyde University. Senior Research Engineer, G. & J. Weir Ltd., 1966-70; Lecturer, Senior Lecturer, Reader, Professor, Strathclyde University, since 1970. Recreations: family; Bible teaching; gardening. Address: (h.) 19 Dunure Drive, Hamilton ML3 9EY; T.-01698 823730.

Bannister, John Roy, Clerk to the Scottish Traffic Commissioner, since 1987; b. 3.11.46, London; m., Jan; 1 s., 1 d. Educ. Edmonton County Grammar School. Department of Transport: London, 1965-72, 1984-87, Newcastle upon Tyne, 1972-83; Manager, International Road Freight Office, Newcastle upon Tyne, 1983-84. Recreations: home brewing/wine; foreign travel; railways. Address: (h.) 13 Warrender Court, North Berwick, East Lothian; T.-01620 894683.

Barbenel, Professor Joseph Cyril, BDS, BSc, MSc, PhD, LDS RCS(Eng), CBiol, FIBiol, CPhys, FInstP, CEng, FBES, FRSE. Professor, Bioengineering Unit, Strathclyde University, since 1982 (Head, Tissue Mechanics Division, since 1970); Vice-Dean (Research), Faculty of Engineering; b. 2.1.37, London; m., Lesley Mary Hyde Jowett; 2 s.; 1 d. Educ. Hackney Downs Grammar School, London; London Hospital Medical College; Queen's College, Dundee (St. Andrews University); Strathclyde University. Dental House Surgeon, London Hospital, 1960; National Service, RADC, 1960-61 (Lieutenant, 1960, Captain, 1961); general dental practice, London, 1963; student, 1963-67; Lecturer, Department of Dental Prosthetics, Dental School, Dundee, 1967-69; Senior Lecturer, Strathclyde University, 1970-82. Member, Administrative Committee, International Federation for Medical and Biological Engineering; Chancellor, International Faculty for Artificial Organs. Recreations: music; theatre. Address: (b.) University of Strathclyde, Bioengineering Unit, 106 Rottenrow, Glasgow G4 0NW; T.-0141-552 4400.

Barbour, John, BL. Senior Partner, Wright and Crawford Solicitors, Paisley, since 1984; b. 22.9.29, Barrhead; m., Martha Wallace; 1 d. Educ. Camphill School, Paisley; Glasgow University. Qualified as Solicitor, 1952; Partner, Wright and Crawford, 1960. Honorary Sheriff, Paisley; Elder, Bourock Church, Barrhead; Past Dean, Faculty of Procurators, Paisley; Past Chairman, Accord Hospice, Paisley; President, Paisley Burns Club; Past President, Paisley Rotary Club. Recreations: reading; walking; bowling. Address: (h.) 104 Paisley Road, Barrhead G78 1NW; T.-0141-881 3083.

Barbour, Very Rev. Robert Alexander Stewart, KCVO, MC, MA, BD, STM, DD, DipEd. Minister, Church of Scotland, since 1954; Chaplain, then Extra Chaplain to the Queen in Scotland, since 1976; b. 11.5.21, Edinburgh; m., Margaret Pigot; 3 s.; 1 d. Educ. Rugby School; Balliol College, Oxford; St. Mary's College, St. Andrews. Army (Scottish Horse), 1940-45, Territorial Army, 1947-54; Editorial Assistant, Thomas Nelson & Sons, 1948-49; Secretary, Edinburgh Christian Council for Overseas Students, 1953-55; Lecturer and Senior Lecturer in New Testament Language, Literature and Theology, New College, Edinburgh University, 1955-71; Professor of New Testament Exegesis, Aberdeen University, 1971-86; Master, Christ's College, Aberdeen, 1977-82; Prelate, Priory of Scotland, Order of St. John, 1977-93; Moderator, General Assembly of the Church of Scotland, 1979-80; Dean, Chapel Royal in Scotland, 1981-91;Honorary Secretary, Novi Testamenti Societas, 1970-77. Recreations: music; forestry; walking. Address: (h.) Old Fincastle, Pitlochry PH16 5RJ; T.-01796 473209.

Barcus, Shona, MBA, RGN, RMN, DipCPN. Chief Executive, Scottish Association for Mental Health, since 1996. Educ. Paisley Grammar School; Glasgow Caledonian University. Locality General Manager, Dumfries and Galloway Community Health NHS Trust, 1994-96; Nursing Services Manager, Dumfries and Galloway Community Services Unit, 1993-94; Dumfries and Galloway Mental Health Unit: Senior Nurse Strategic Planning, 1992-93, Clinical Nurse Manager, Community Psychiatric Nursing, 1986-92; Community Psychiatric Nurse, Greater Glasgow Health Board, Northern District, 1981-86. Member, Management Committee: Community Care Providers Scotland, Association of Chief Officers of Scottish Voluntary Organisations. Recreations: travel; music; reading; entertaining. Address: (b.) Cumbrae House, 15 Carlton Court, Glasgow G5 9JP; T.-0141-568 7000.

Barker, Alan. Music Director, The Scottish Ballet, since 1992; b. Australia. Educ. Melbourne University. Former Musical Director, New Zealand Ballet, and Artistic Director, New Zealand Opera; former Resident Conductor, Australian Ballet; joined American Ballet Theatre, 1978, as Associate Conductor, promoted to Principal Conductor, 1980; Music Director, Sacramento Ballet, 1987-90; Music Director, Pittsburgh Ballet Theatre, 1988-90; has conducted Royal Swedish Ballet, Royal Danish Ballet, National Ballet of Canada, Gothenburg Opera Ballet, and Birmingham Royal Ballet. Address: (b.) Scottish Ballet, 261 West Princes Street, Glasgow G4 9EE; T.-0141-331 2931.

Barker, Professor John Reginald, BSc, MSc, PhD, FBIS, FRSE. Professor of Electronics, Department of Electronics and Electrical Engineering, University of Glasgow, since 1985; b. 11.11.42, Stockport; m., Elizabeth Carol; 2 s.; 1 d. Educ. New Mills Grammar School; University of Edinburgh; University of Durham; University of Warwick. University of Warwick: SRC Personal Research Fellowship, 1969-70, Lecturer in Physics, 1970-84, Senior Lecturer, 1984-85; Affiliate Professor, Colorado State University, 1979-83; Distinguished Science Lecturer, Yale University, 1992; Irvine Lectures in Chemistry, St. Andrews, 1994; broadcasting: History of the Microchip, 1982; The Magic Micro Mission, 1983. Member, various SERC/DTI committees, 1987-93: Devices Committee, Electronic Materials Committee, National Committee for Superconductivity, Materials Commission, Molecular Electronics Committee (Chairman, 1990-93). Publications: over 190 scientific papers; Physics of Non-Linear Transport in Semi-conductors (Co-Author), 1979; Granular Nanoelectronics (Co-Author), 1991. Recreations: hill-walking; astronomy; reading; cooking. Address: (b.) Nanoelectronics Research Centre, Department of Electronics and Electrical Engineering, University of Glasgow, Glasgow G12 8QQ; T.-0141-330 5221.

Barker, Ralph Fraser, MA (Hons), DipEd. Rector, Alloa Academy, since 1995; b. 10.7.51, Edinburgh; m., Suzanne; 2 s.; 1 d. Educ. Royal High School, Edinburgh; Edinburgh University. Teacher of Mathematics, then Assistant Principal Teacher, Royal High School, 1974-81; Principal Teacher, Knox Academy, 1981-84; Assistant Head Teacher, then Depute Head Teacher, Queensferry High School, 1984-94. Recreation: public transport, especially buses. Address: (b.) Claremont, Alloa FK10 2EQ; T.-01259 214979.

Barlow, Professor (Arthur) John, PhD, DIC, BSc, ACGI, MIEE, CEng. Professor of Electronics, Glasgow University; b. 17.3.34, Nottinghamshire; m., Alma Marshall; 1 s.; 1 d. Educ. Nottingham High School; Imperial College. Turner and Newall Research Fellow, Imperial College, 1958-61; Glasgow University: Lecturer, 1961-66, Senior Lecturer, 1966-68, Reader, 1968-75. Address: (h.) 5 Auchencruive, Milngavie, Glasgow G62 6EE.

Barlow, Nevile Robert Disney, OBE, FRICS. Chartered Surveyor and Farmer; Member, Board, East of Scotland Water, since 1995; Member, East Region Board, Scottish Environmental Protection Agency, since 1996; b. 3.2.41, Bagshott, Surrey; m., Myfanwy Louise Kerr-Wilson; 3 s. Educ. Winchester College; Royal Agricultural College, Cirencester. Assistant Agent, Bathurst Estate, Cirencester, 1963-95; Resident Sub-Agent, Bletchingdon Park, 1966-67; Head Factor, National Trust for Scotland, 1986-91; Vice-President, Scottish Landowners' Federation, (Convener, 1991-94). Recreations: shooting; fishing; sailing; rowing. Address: The Park, Earlston TD4 6AB; T.-01896 849267.

Barltrop, Professor Nigel Douglas Philip, CEng, MSNAME, FICE, FRINA. Professor and Head of Department of Naval Architecture and Ocean Engineering, University of Glasgow, since 1995; b. 10.2.52, London; m., Suzanne Joyce; 1 s.; 2 d. Educ. Southgate School; Southampton University. Freeman Fox and Partners, 1973-77; W.S. Atkins, 1977-95. Publications: Fluid Loading on Fixed Offshore Structures (Joint Author), 1990; Dynamics of Fixed Marine Structures (Co-author), 1991; Floating Structures: A Guide for Design and Analysis (Editor), 1998. Recreations: hillwalking; Scottish country dancing. Address: James Watt Building, University of Glasgow, Glasgow G12 8QQ; T.-0141-330 4303.

Barnes, James David Kentish. Director, Dobbie Garden Centres PLC, since 1969; Director, National Trust for Scotland Trading Company, since 1998; Convener, National Trust for Scotland Gardens Committee, since 1996; b. 18.4.30, Chester; m., Susan Mary Harter; 1 s.; 1 d. Educ. Eton College; Royal Military Academy Sandhurst. Army 1948-57 (served Korea, Middle East and Germany); joined John Waterer Sons and Crisp (horticulture), 1957, Managing Director 1968-84; Owner and Managing Director, Dobbie and Co. Edinburgh, 1968-94. Member, Executive Committee, National Trust for Scotland. Address: (h.) Biggar Park, Biggar, Lanarkshire ML12 6JS; T.-01899 220185.

Barnet, James Paul, MA, LLB. Former Partner, Macbeth Currie & Co., Solicitors, now Consultant; Honorary Sheriff, Tayside Central and Fife, at Dunfermline; former Dean, Dunfermline District Society of Solicitors; b. 20.7.37, Darlington; m., Margaret Smart; 4 s. Educ. Dunfermline High School; Edinburgh University. Admitted as Solicitor, 1961. Council Member, Law Society of Scotland, 1985-88; Local Secretary, Scottish Garden City Housing Society Ltd.; Captain, Scottish Universities Golfing Society, 1980-81; President, Dunfermline Rotary Club, 1985-86. Recreations: golf; reading; quoting Dr. Johnson. Address: (h.) Bonnyton House, Dunfermline, Fife KY12 9HT; T.-Dunfermline 731011.

Barnett, Robert Hall, FIMI. Chairman, Barnetts Motor Group Ltd; b. 22.1.36, Dundee; m., Alison; 1 s.; 1 d. Educ. Morgan Academy. Dundee and President, Tayside Chamber of Commerce, 1992-93; President, Scottish Motor Trade Association, 1982-84. Recreations: golf; sailing; motorcycling. Address: (b.) Riverside Drive, Dundee; T.-01382 668622.

Barnicoat, Martin Kevin, ACIB. Scotland Director, Barclays Bank PLC, since 1998; b. 29.5.52, Truro, Cornwall; m., Judy Plumb; 1 d. Educ. Falmouth Grammar School; Bath University. Barclays Bank PLC: Credit Risk Assistant Director, 1989-91, Head of Pricing for UK Large Corporates, 1991-93, Credit Director for North and Central Wales, Shropshire and Hereford, 1993-95, Area Director for West Midlands, 1995-97. Recreations: golf; rugby; walking; music. Address: (h.) 1 Belhaven Place, Mearns Craig, Newton Mearns, Glasgow; T. (b.)-0141-207 2088.

Barr, David George Dryburgh, MB, ChB, FRCPEd, DCH. Consultant Paediatrician, Lothian Health Board, since 1971; part-time Senior Lecturer, Department of Child Life and Health, Edinburgh University, since 1977; Clinical Director for Medicine, Royal Hospital for Sick Children, Edinburgh, 1994-97; b. 14.2.36, Edinburgh; m., Anna Blair; 2 s.; 1 d. Educ. Daniel Stewart's College, Edinburgh; Edinburgh University. Senior Registrar, Royal Hospital for Sick Children, Edinburgh, 1965-69; Research Fellow, children's hospital, Zurich, Switzerland, 1969-70; Consultant Paediatrician, Edinburgh Northern and West Fife Hospitals, 1971-77; seconded to Ministry of Health and University of Riyadh, Saudi Arabia, 1980-83. Address: (b.) Royal Hospital for Sick Children, Sciennes Road, Edinburgh.

Barr, Sheriff Kenneth Glen, MA, LLB. Sheriff of South Strathclyde, Dumfries and Galloway, at Dumfries, since 1976; b. 20.1.41, Glasgow. Educ. Royal High School; Edinburgh University. Admitted Faculty of Advocates, 1964. Address: (b.) Sheriff's Chambers, Sheriff Court House, Dumfries DG1 2AN.

Barr, William James, OBE, CEng, FICE, FCIOB, FIMgt. Chairman and Chief Executive, Barr Holdings Limited (which includes Barr Limited, W. & J. Barr and Sons (Scotland) Limited, Alpha Crane Limited, Alpha Services Limited, Alpha Access Limited, Econospace Limited, Barr Quarries Limited, Barmix Concrete, Barr Construction, Barr Steel, Solway Precast, Solway Crane, Barr Homes, Barr Environmental, Barr Technical Services, Barr Construction Services); Chairman and Managing Director, Barr Leisure Limited; Chairman and Managing Director, Ice Hockey Services Ltd.; b. 12.3.39, Ayr; m., Marlean Ramage; 2 s.; 1 d. Educ. Girvan High School; Glasgow University; Paisley University. Chairman, Freeport (Scotland) Ltd; Chairman, Thomas Telford Services Ltd.; Member, Council and Executive, Institution of Civil Engineers; former Chairman, Glasgow and West of Scotland Association, Institution of Civil Engineers; Visiting Professor, Strathclyde University; former Chairman, Craigie College of Education; Chairman, Ayr College Board; Member, Court, Paisley University; Chairman, Ayr Locality Enterprise and Resources Trust; former Chairman, Ayrshire Hospice; Founder Chairman, Laigh Milton Viaduct Conservation Project; former Vice-Chairman, Enterprise Ayrshire; Past President, Ayr Chamber of Commerce; former Board Member, Ayrshire Chamber of Commerce and Industry; Past President, Association for Science and Education; Board Member, Ice Hockey Superleague; Member, AME Board. Recreations: the works of Robert Burns and Thomas Telford; walking; reading. Address: (h.) Harkieston, Maybole, Ayrshire, KA19 7LP; T.-01655 883123; (b.) Heathfield, Ayr KA8 9SL; T.-01292 281311.

Barrett, Professor Ann, MB, BS, FRCR, FRCP, MD. Professor of Radiation Oncology, Glasgow University, since 1986; Consultant, Royal Hospital for Sick Children, since 1986; President, European Society for Therapeutic Radiation Oncology, until 1999; b. 27.2.43, London; m., Adrian Bell; 1 s.; 2 d. Educ. Queen Elizabeth's Grammar School; St. Bartholomew's Hospital. Formerly Consultant in Radiotherapy and Oncology, Royal Marsden Hospital; Director, Beatson Oncology Centre, Glasgow, 1986-91; President, Scottish Radiological Society, 1995-97; Chairman, Scottish Standing Committee, RCR, 1994-97; Associate Editor, Medical and Paediatric Oncology. Former Member: MRC Molecular and Cell Medicine Board, Council, Royal College of Radiologists. Publications: Cancer in Childhood (Co-editor); Practical Radiotherapy Planning (Co-author). Recreations: walking; music; novels. Address: (b.) Beatson Oncology Centre, Western Infirmary, Glasgow; T.-0141-339 8822.

Barrie, Lesley, DPA, MHSM, DipHSM, MBIM. General Manager and Member, Tayside Health Board, 1993-97, retired; b. 20.9.44, Glasgow. Educ. Glasgow High School for Girls; Glasgow University. NHS administrative trainee, 1963-66; hospital management, 1966-77; District General Manager: Inverclyde District, 1977-81, Glasgow South East, 1981-83; Director Administrative Services, Glasgow Royal Infirmary, Glasgow Royal Maternity Hospital, Glasgow Dental Hospital, 1983-87; Unit General Manager, Stirling Royal Infirmary, 1987-91; General Manager and Member, Forth Valley Health Board, 1991-93. Hon. Lecturer, Dundee University; Children's Panellist, 1975-79; Chairman, Social Security Appeal Tribunals, 1978-90; Table Tennis Internationalist for Scotland, 1963-70; formerly National and International Secretary, Scottish Table Tennis Association. Recreations: table tennis; badminton; reading. Address: (b.) Gairdrum House, by Balbeggie, Perthshire.

Barron, Professor Laurence David, DPhil, BSc, MInstP, FRSE. Professor of Chemistry, Glasgow University, since 1984; b. 12.2.44, Southampton; m., Sharon Aviva Wolf; 1 s.; 1 d. Educ. King Edward VI Grammar School, Southampton; Northern Polytechnic, London; Lincoln College, Oxford. Post-doctoral research, Cambridge University, 1969-75; Ramsay Memorial Fellow, 1974-75; Glasgow University: Lecturer in Chemistry, 1975-80, Reader, 1980-84. Corday-Morgan Medal, Chemical Society, 1977; G.M.J. Schmidt Memorial Lecturer, Weizmann Institute of Science, 1984; F.L. Conover Memorial Lecturer, Vanderbilt University, 1987; Sir Harold Thompson Award, 1992; EPSRC Senior Fellow, 1995-2000. Publication: Molecular Light Scattering and Optical Activity, 1982. Recreations: water-colour painting; walking; music; radio-controlled model aircraft. Address: (b.) Chemistry Department, The University, Glasgow G12 8QQ; T.-0141-339 8855.

Barrow, Professor Geoffrey Wallis Steuart, MA (Hons), BLitt, DLitt, FBA, FRSE, FSA, FSA Scot, FRHistS, Hon. DLitt (Glasgow and Newcastle upon Tyne). Sir William Fraser Professor of Scottish History and Palaeography, Edinburgh University, 1979-92; b. 28.11.24, Headingley, Leeds; m., Heather Elizabeth Agnes Lownie; 1 s.; 1 d. Educ. St. Edward's School, Oxford; Inverness Royal Academy; St. Andrews University; Pembroke College, Oxford. Royal Navy and RNVR (Sub-Lieutenant), 1943-46; Lecturer in History, University College, London, 1950-61; Professor of Medieval History, Newcastle-upon-Tyne University, 1961-74; Professor of Scottish History, St. Andrews University, 1974-79. Member, Royal Commission on Historical Manuscripts, 1984-90; Royal Historical Society, Council, 1963-74; Joint Literary Director, 1964-74; Vice President, 1982-86; former Chairman: Council, Scottish History Society (President, 1973-77); President: Saltire Society, 1987-90, Scottish Record Society, 1993-97; Vice-President, Commission Internationale de Diplomatique. Publications: Feudal Britain, 1956; Acts of Malcolm IV, 1960; Robert Bruce, 1965 and 1988; Acts of William I, 1971; The Kingdom of the Scots, 1973; The Scottish Tradition (Editor), 1974; The Anglo-Norman Era in Scottish History, 1980; Kingship and Unity: Scotland 1000-1306, 1981; Scotland and its neighbours, 1992. Recreations: hill-walking; visiting graveyards; travel. Address: (h.) 12A Lauder Road, Edinburgh EH9 2EL; T.-0131-668 2173.

Barry, Professor (David) Andrew. Chair of Environmental Engineering, University of Edinburgh, since 1998; Director, Contaminated Land Assessment and Remediation Research Centre, University of Edinburgh; b. 19.4.58; m., Suellen Jill de Waard; 1 s.; 1 d. Educ. University of Queensland; Griffith University, Australia; Royal Melbourne Institute of Technology. Research Associate, Center for Environmental and Hazardous Materials Studies, Virginia Polytechnic Institute and State University, 1985-86; Postgraduate Research Soil Scientist, University of California, 1986-88; University of Western Australia: Lecturer in Subsurface Hydrology, Centre for Water Research, 1989-91, Senior Lecturer and Hydrology Group Leader, Department of Environmental Engineering, 1991-93, Associate Professor, Department of Environmental Engineering, 1994-98. Visiting Associate Professor, University of North Carolina, Chapel Hill, 1994; Visiting Scientist, Massachusetts Institute of Technology, 1996; Honorary Fellow, University of Western Australia, since 1998. Address: (b.) School of Civil and Environmental Engineering, University of Edinburgh, Edinburgh EH9 3JN; T.-0131-650 7204.

Barry, Stephen. Chief Executive, Festival City Theatres Trust, since 1997; Board Member, Scottish Ballet; Member, Dance Panel, Arts Council of England; b. 4.7.45, London; m., Jacqueline; 1 s.; 1 d. Educ. Marlborough College; University of Manchester. Trainee Director, Mermaid Theatre, 1968-69; Assistant Director, Yvonne Arnaud Theatre, 1969-71; Staff Producer, National Theatre, 1971-72; Director and Researcher, Cheltenham Everyman and Granada Television, 1972-74; Artistic Director: Harrogate Theatre, 1974-77, Perth, W. Australia, 1977-82, Redgrave Theatre, Farnham, 1982-86; Theatre Director, Theatre Royal, Bath, 1986-90. Recreations: reading; walking. Address: (b.) 13/29 Nicolson Street, Edinburgh EH8 9FT; T.-0131-662 1112.

Bartlett, Professor Christopher John, BA, PhD, FRHistS, FRSE. Emeritus Professor of International History, Dundee University (Head of Modern History Department, 1983-88); Member, Scottish Examination Board; b. 12.10.31, Bournemouth; m., Shirley Maureen Briggs; 3 s. Educ. Queen Elizabeth's Grammar School, Wimborne; University College, Exeter; London School of Economics. Assistant Lecturer, Edinburgh University, 1957-59; Lecturer, University of the West Indies, Jamaica, 1959-62; Lecturer, Queen's College, Dundee, 1962-68; Reader, Dundee University, 1968-78. Publications: Great Britain and Sea Power 1815-53; Castlereagh; The Long Retreat; The Rise and Fall of the Pax Americana; A History of Postwar Britain 1945-74; The Global Conflict 1880-1990; British Foreign Policy in the Twentieth Century; The Special Relationship since 1945; Defence and Diplomacy 1815-1914; The Annual Register 1987-97 (UK and Scotland chapters); Peace, War and the European Great Powers, 1814-1914. Address: (b.) Department of History, The University, Dundee.

Bartlett, Professor Robert John, MA, DPhil, FRHS, FBA, FSA. Professor of Mediaeval History, St. Andrews University, since 1992; b. 27.11.50, London; m., Honora Hickey; 1 s.; 1 d. Educ. Battersea Grammar School; Peterhouse, Cambridge; St. John's College, Oxford. Lecturer in History, Edinburgh University, 1980-86; Professor of Medieval History, University of Chicago, 1986-92. Publications: Gerald of Wales 1146-1223, 1982; Trial by Fire and Water: the medieval judicial ordeal, 1986; The Making of Europe, 1993. Recreations: walking; squash. Address: (b.) Department of Mediaeval History, St. Andrews University, St. Andrews KY16 9AL; T.-01334 463308.

Bastable, Arthur Cyprian, OBE, BSc, CEng, FIEE, FIMgt. General Manager, Ferranti plc, Dundee, 1958-86; Director, Ferranti Astron Ltd., 1983-86; Director, Ferranti Industrial Electronics Ltd., 1984-86; Deputy Chairman, Dundee Port Authority, 1981-92 (Member, since 1967, Convener, Corporate Planning Committee, 1975-92); b. 9.5.23, Kobe, Japan; m., Joan Cardwell; 1 s.; 1 d. Educ. St. Georges School, Harpenden; Manchester University. Joined Ferranti, 1950; President, Dundee & Tayside Chamber of Commerce, 1970-71 (Convener, Overseas Trade and Development, 1973-91); Member, Tayside Development Authority, 1972-75; Vice-Chairman, Board of Governors,

Dundee College of Technology, 1975-77; Member, Scottish Council, CBI, 1980; Member, Dundee Project Steering Committee, 1983-91; Director: Edinburgh Instruments Ltd., 1983-85; Taytec Ltd., 1985-88; Dundee and Tayside ITEC Ltd., 1985-88; Chairman, Tayside 1992 Committee, 1988-92. Recreations: sailing; skiing; ornithology. Address: (h.) Hunters Moon, 14 Lorne Street, Monifieth, Dundee DD5 4DU.

Baster, Jeremy, BA, MPhil, MRTPI. Director of Development and Planning, Orkney Islands Council, since 1996; b. 5.2.47, New York; m., Miriam Landor; 2 s.; 1 d. Educ. Leighton Park School, Reading; St. John's College, Oxford; University College, London. Early career in consultancy; Economist, Scottish Council (Development and Industry), 1975-80; Economist, Orkney Islands Council, 1980-85; Director of Economic Development, Orkney Islands Council, 1985-96. Director, Soulisquoy Printmakers Ltd.; Director, Orkney Enterprise. Address: (b.) Council Offices, School Place, Kirkwall KW15 1NY; T.-01856 3535.

Bateman, Malcolm, FCMA. Managing Director, Continental Tyres Ltd., since 1996, Financial Director, since 1986; Chairman, Continental UK Group Holdings, since 1993; Director, Continental Tyre Group, since 1986; Director, Contitech Power Transmission Systems, since 1995; b. 2.3.49, Welwyn Garden City; m., Lynda; 1 s.; 1 d. Educ. Dean Close School, Cheltenham. Recreations: golf; gardening; photography. Address: (b.) Newbridge, Midlothian EH28 8LG; T.-0131-333 2700.

Bateman, Meg (Vivienne Margaret), MA (Hons), PhD. Gaelic poet; b. 13.4.59, Edinburgh; 1 s. Educ. Mary Erskine School, Edinburgh; University of Aberdeen. Poetry collections: Orain Ghaoil (1990); Aotromachd is Dàin Eile (Lightness and Other Poems), (1997) shortlisted for Stakis Prize); translations of Gaelic poetry published in An Anthology of Scottish Women Poets, Gàir nan Clàrsach (The Harps' Cry). Address: (b.) Sabhal Mor Ostaig, Sleat, Isle of Skye IV44 0RQ; T.-01471 844 373.

Bateman, Richard Mark, BSc (Geol.), BSc (Biol.), PhD, FLS. Director of Science, Royal Botanic Garden Edinburgh, since 1997; Honorary Research Fellow, University of Edinburgh, since 1997; b. 27.5.58, Bradford; m., Orpah Susan Farrington. Educ. Francis Bacon School, St. Albans; University of Luton; Birkbeck College, University of London. Researcher, Quaternary Paleoenvironmental Unit, Rothamsted Experimental Station, 1977-84; Doctoral Researcher, Birkbeck College, University of London, 1984-88; Lindemann Research Fellow, Smithsonian Institution, 1988-91; Senior Research Fellow, University of Oxford, 1991-94; Principal Scientific Officer, Royal Botanic Garden Edinburgh/Royal Museum of Scotland, 1994-97. Council Member: Systematics Association, UK Systematics Forum; President's Award, Geological Society, 1988; Linnean Society Bicentenary Medal, 1994. Publications: 47 books and research papers; Editor, Smithsonian Series on Comparative Evolutionary Biology; 180 articles; 80 conference presentations. Recreations: natural history; golf; pontificating while drinking beer. Address: (b.) Royal Botanic Garden, 20a Inverleith Row, Edinburgh EH3 5LR; T.-0131-248 2957.

Bates, Professor David Richard, BA, PhD, FRHistS, FSA. Edwards Professor of Medieval History and Head, Department of History, University of Glasgow, since 1994; b. 30.4.45, Coventry; m., Helen Mary; 1 s.; 1 d. Educ. King Edward VI Grammar School, Nuneaton; University of Exeter. Research Assistant, Documents Section, Imperial War Museum, 1969-71; Fellow, University College, Cardiff, 1971-73; Lecturer, Senior Lecturer, Reader in History, 1973-94, Head of History and Welsh History, 1988-92, University of Wales, Cardiff. Member, Council, Royal Historical Society. Publications: Normandy Before 1066, 1982; A Bibliography of Domesday Book, 1986; William the Conqueror, 1989; Bishop Remigius of Lincoln 1067-1092, 1992; England and Normandy in the Middle Ages (Co-Editor), 1994; Contributor, The History Today Companion to British History; Conflict and Co-existence: Nationalism and Democracy in Modern Europe: Essays in Honour of Harry Hearder (Co-Editor), 1997; Regesta Regum Anglo-Normannorum: The Acta of William I 1066-1087, 1998; General Editor: The Medieval World series. Recreations: walking; music; reading; watching sport. Address: (b.) Department of History (Medieval History), University of Glasgow, Glasgow G12 8QQ; T.-0141-330 4511.

Bathgate, Gordon, BSc, CEng, FICE, FCIArb. Contracts Adviser, Scott Wilson Kirkpatrick & Co. (Scotland), since 1992; Chairman, Scottish Branch, Chartered Institute of Arbitrators, since 1997; b. 5.10.46, Edinburgh; m., Elizabeth Boddison; 1 s.; 1 d. Educ. Leith Academy; Heriot-Watt University. Graduate Trainee, Robert H. Cuthbertson & Partners, 1968-72; worked in local government, 1972-89; Regional Manager (Scotland), Reinforced Earth Company, 1989-92. Address: 6 Park Circus, Glasgow G3 6AX; T.-0141-332 2258.

Bauckham, Professor Richard John, MA, PhD. Professor of New Testament Studies, St. Andrews University, since 1992; b. 22.9.46, London. Educ. Enfield Grammar School; Clare College, Cambridge. Fellow, St. John's College, Cambridge, 1972-75; Lecturer in Theology, Leeds University, 1976-77; Lecturer in the History of Christian Thought, Manchester University, 1977-87, Reader, 1987-92; Fellow of the British Academy, 1998. Publications: Tudor Apocalypse; Jude, 2 Peter; Moltmann: Messianic Theology in the Making; The Bible in Politics; Jude and the Relatives of Jesus in the Early Church; The Theology of the Book of Revelation; The Climax of Prophecy; The Theology of Jurgen Moltmann. Recreations: walking; novels; poetry; gardening; sleeping. Address: (b.) St. Mary's College, St. Andrews KY16 9JU; T.-01334 462830.

Baughan, Mike, BEd. Chief Executive, Scottish Consultative Council on the Curriculum, since 1998; b. 11.6.44, Dumfries; m., Anna; 1 s.; 1 d. Educ. St. Joseph's College, Dumfries; Dundee University; Dundee College of Education. RAF; brief career in industrial banking; English Teacher, secondary schools, Dundee, 1971-75; Principal Teacher of Guidance then Assistant Rector, St. Saviour's High, Dundee, 1975-82; Churchill Fellow, 1977; Adviser in Education, Tayside Regional Council, 1982-87; Rector, Webster's High School, Kirriemuir, 1987-97; Development Fellow, Scottish Consultative Council on the Curriculum, 1997-98. Member, Ancient Monuments Board for Scotland; Secretary General, CIDREE, Member, Board, SCRAN; Member, various national education committees. Recreations: hillwalking; fishing; theatre; travel. Address: (b.) Gardyne Road, Broughty Ferry, Dundee DD5 1NY; T.-01382 455053.

Baverstock, John Browitt. President, Scottish Dairy Association, since 1997; b. 10.2.42, Blackpool; m., Brenda M. Slidders; 1 s.; 1 d. Educ. Kings School, Rochester; St. Andrews University. Senior buyer, Nestle UK Ltd. Recreations: golf; walking; gardening. Address: (b.) 46 Underwood Road, Paisley PA3 1TL.

Baxby, Keith, BSc, MB, BS, FRCS. Consultant Urological Surgeon, Tayside Health Board, since 1977; Honorary Senior Lecturer, Dundee University, since 1977; Editor, Urology News; b. 17.4.44, Sheffield. Educ. King Edward VII School, Sheffield; Durham University. House Officer, Royal Victoria Infirmary, Newcastle-upon-Tyne, 1968-69; Surgical Registrar, Newcastle University Hospitals, 1969-73; Northern Counties Kidney Fund Research Fellow, 1973-74; Senior Urological Registrar, Newcastle General Hospital, 1974-77; Visiting Professor of Urology, Louisiana

State University, 1981; WHO Fellow in Clinical Urodynamics, 1984. Recreations: deer-stalking; cycling. Address: (b.) Department of Urology, Royal Infirmary, Dundee; T.-01382 660111.

Baxter, Audrey Caroline, BA, DipACC. Managing Director, Baxters of Speyside Ltd.; b. 25.5.61; m., Colin McNiven. Educ. St. Leonard's School; Heriot-Watt University. International banking, Kleinwort Benson Ltd, London, 1983-87; Director, Corporate Planning, Baxters of Speyside, 1988-90. Address: (b.) W.A. Baxter and Sons Ltd, Fochabers, Moray.

Baxter, Brian Newland, BSc, MSc, PhD, CEng, FRINA, FIES. Marine Consultant; Visiting Professor, Department of Ship and Marine Technology, Strathclyde University, since 1980; b. London; m., Nadina McLeod; 2 d. Educ. King's College, Newcastle, Durham University. Scientific Officer, Royal Naval Scientific Service, 1948-50; Lecturer in Naval Architecture, King's College, Newcastle, 1950-57; Chief Representative, Bureau Veritas in the UK, 1957-62; Director, Yarrow & Co., Glasgow, 1962-79; Deputy Managing Director, Yarrow Shipbuilders, Glasgow, 1967-81; Director, British Shipbuilders Training and Education Co., 1981-84. President, Institution of Engineers and Shipbuilders in Scotland, 1979-81; Hon. Secretary, Seagull Trust, since 1984. Recreations: reading; writing; walking; golf. Address: (h.) Dunelm, Kilmacolm, RenfrewshirePA13 4DQ; T.-0150 587 2092.

Baxter, Jim. Footballer; b. 1939, Fife. Glasgow Rangers, 1960-64, later Sunderland and Nottingham Forest. Capped 34 times for Scotland.

Baxter, Mary Ross, MBE, MA, LRAM. Co-Ordinator, The Pushkin Prizes in Scotland; b. 23.9.27, Glasgow. Educ. Park School, Glasgow; Glasgow University. John Smith & Son, Booksellers, Glasgow, 1952-56; British European Airways, Glasgow Office, 1956-60; National Book League (now known as Book Trust), 1960-89; started the Scottish Office in 1961; former President, International PEN Scottish Centre. Honorary Member, Scottish Library Association. Recreations: music; books; home-decorating; cooking; gardening. Address: (h.) 18 Crown Terrace, Glasgow G12 9ES; T.-0141-357 0327.

Baxter, Peter R., DHE. Curator, Younger Botanic Garden, Benmore, since 1995; b. 30.6.58, Irvine; m.; 1 s.; 1 d. Address: (b.) Younger Botanic Garden, Benmore, Dunoon PA23 8QU.

Baxter, (William) Gordon, OBE, DL, LLD, DBA. President: W.A. Baxter & Sons Ltd., since 1994 (Chairman, 1970-94); b. 8.2.18, Fochabers, Moray; m., Ena E. Robertson; 2 s.; 1 d. Educ. Ashville College, Harrogate; Aberdeen University. ICI Explosives Ltd., 1940-45 (Research and Development Manager, various military projects); joined family business, 1946; Managing Director, 1947-71; Member, British Export Council Committee for Exports to USA, 1964-72; Member, North American Advisory Group, DTI, 1979-89; former Director, Grampian Regional Board, Bank of Scotland; President, Chartered Institute of Marketing: Northern Branch; Member of Council, Royal Warrant Holders Association, London; Hon. Fellow, Chartered Institute of Marketing; President, Scotland International. Recreations: fishing; tennis; cricket. Address: (h.) Speybank House, Fochabers, Moray; T.-01343 821234.

Bayliss, Anthony Paul, MB, ChB, FRCR, DMRD. Consultant Radiologist, Royal Aberdeen Hospitals NHS Trust; b. 7.2.44, Oldham; m., Margaret Anne; 3 s. Educ. Oldham Hulme Grammar School; St. Andrews University. Medical Intern., Mount Sinai Hospital, Minneapolis, 1969-70; House Officer, Ballochmyle Hospital, Ayrshire, 1970-71; Trainee Radiologist, Western Infirmary, Glasgow, 1971-75. Recreation: golf. Address: (h.) Middle Cottage, Mid Auguston, Peterculter, Aberdeen; T.-01224 735503.

Baynham, John William, CBE, Doctor honoris causa (Edinburgh), BSc, PhD, DIC. Chairman, Lothian Health Board, 1990-97; Chairman, Scottish Health Board Chairmen's Group, 1995-97; b. 20.1.29, Blantyre; m., Marie B. Friel; 1 d. Educ. Bathgate Academy; Aberdeen University; Imperial College, London. Scottish Agricultural Industries PLC, 1955-87, latterly as Agribusiness Director. Member, Lothian Health Board, 1987-90; Chairman, Board of Governors, Moray House Institute of Education, Heriot Watt University, 1991-95; Governor, Queen Margaret College, since 1995; Chairman, Salaries Committee, Conference of Scottish Centrally Funded Colleges, since 1997. Recreations: golf; grandchildren. Address: (h.) 2/18 Succoth Court, Succoth Park, Edinburgh EH12 6BZ; T.-0131-337 2813.

Bealey, Professor Frank William, BSc (Econ), DSc (Econ). Professor of Politics, Aberdeen University, 1964-90; b. 31.8.22, Bilston, Staffordshire; m., Sheila Hurst; 1 s.; 2 d. Educ. King Edward VI Grammar School, Stourbridge; London School of Economics. Seaman, Royal Navy, 1941-46; Extra-Mural Lecturer, Manchester University, 1951-52; Lecturer, Keele University, 1952-64; Temporary Lecturer, Birmingham University, 1958-59. Treasurer and founder Member, Society for the Study of Labour History, 1960-63; Convener, Committee for Social Science, Aberdeen University, 1970-74 and 1986-89; Fellow, Royal Historical Society, 1971; Editorial Board, Political Studies, 1975-83; Visiting Fellow, Yale University, 1980; Organiser, Parliamentary All-Party Group, Social Science and Policy, 1984-89; Trustee, Jan Hus Educational Foundation, since 1981; Co-ordinator: EC Tempus Project (Political Science, Czechoslovakia), 1990-93. Publications: Labour and Politics 1900-1906 (Co-author); Constituency Politics (Co-author); The Social and Political Thought of the British Labour Party; The Post Office Engineering Union; The Politics of Independence (Co-author); Democracy in the Contemporary State; Elements in Political Science (Co-author); A Dictionary of Political Science. Recreations: reading poetry; darts; eating and drinking; watching football and cricket. Address: (h.) 11 Viewforth Terrace, Edinburgh EH10 4LH.

Beastall, Graham Hedley, BSc, PhD, FRCPath. Top Grade Biochemist (Endocrinology), Glasgow Royal Infirmary, since 1981; Honorary Senior Lecturer, Glasgow University, since 1983; b. 11.12.47, Liverpool; m., Judith; 2 s. Educ. Liverpool Institute High School for Boys; Liverpool University. Lecturer in Biochemistry, Liverpool University, 1971-72; Lecturer in Steroid Biochemistry, Glasgow University, 1972-76; Senior Biochemist (Endocrinology), then Principal Biochemist (Endocrinology), Glasgow Royal Infirmary, 1976-81.Chairman, Association of Clinical Biochemists, since 1994; Chairman, Conference of Clinical Scientists Organisations, since 1996; Area Commissioner, Greater Glasgow Scout Council, 1980-88; Scottish Scout Council Programme and Training Co-ordinator, since 1995. Recreations: Scouting; gardening; sport. Address: (b.) Department of Clinical Biochemistry, Royal Infirmary, Glasgow G4 OSF; T.-0141-211 4632.

Beat, Janet Eveline, BMus, MA. Composer; Lecturer: Royal Scottish Academy of Music and Drama, 1972-96, Glasgow University since 1996; Artistic Director and Founder, Soundstrata (electro-acoustic ensemble); b. 17.12.37, Streetly. Educ. High School for Girls, Sutton Coldfield; Birmingham University. Freelance Orchestral Player, 1960s; Lecturer: Madeley College of Education, 1965-67, Worcester College of Education, 1967-71; founder Member and former Council Member, Scottish Society of Composers; a Director, Scottish Electro-Acoustic Music Association; wrote musical criticism for The Scotsman; G.D. Cunningham Award, 1962; her works have been performed throughout Scotland as well as in Switzerland, Germany, Poland, North America, South America, Greece, Australia, and Japan. Recreations: travel; reading; photography. Address: c/o Scottish Music Information Centre, 1 Bowmont Gardens, Glasgow, G12 9LR; T.-0141-334 6393.

Beath, Professor John Arnott, MA, MPhil. Professor of Economics, St. Andrews University, since 1991, and Head, School of Social Sciences; b. 15.6.44, Thurso; m., Dr. Monika Schroder. Educ. Hillhead High School; St. Andrews, London, Pennsylvania and Cambridge Universities. Research Officer, Department of Applied Economics, Cambridge University; Fellow, Downing College, Cambridge; Lecturer, then Senior Lecturer in Economics, Bristol University. Member, Research Priorities Board, Economic and Social Research Council. Publication: The Economic Theory of Product Differentiation. Recreations: gardening; golf; music. Address: (h.) Simonden, Ceres, Cupar KY15 5PP; T.-01334 858920.

Beattie, Alistair Duncan, MD (Hons), FRCPGlas, FRCPLond. Consultant Physician, Southern General Hospital, Glasgow, since 1976; Honorary Clinical Lecturer, Glasgow University, since 1977; b. 4.4.42, Laurencekirk; m., Gillian Margaret McCutcheon; 3 s.; 2 d. Educ. Paisley Grammar School; Glasgow University. Junior hospital appointments, Royal Infirmary and Western Infirmary, Glasgow, 1965-69; Department of Materia Medica, Glasgow University: Research Fellow, 1969-73, Lecturer, 1973-74; MRC Research Fellow, Royal Free Hospital, London, 1974-75. Honorary Treasurer, Medical and Dental Defence Union of Scotland. Recreations: golf; music. Address: (h.) 228 Queen Victoria Drive, Glasgow G13 1TN; T. 0141 959 7182.

Beattie, Bryan William, JP, BA. Chairman, Scottish Youth Theatre, since 1993; Chairman, Board of Governors, Eden Court Theatre, since 1996; Chairman, Cultural and Leisure Services Committee, Highland Council, since 1995; Board Member, Scottish Screen, since 1998; b. 3.5.60, Dundee. Educ. High School of Dundee; Stirling University. Director, Stirling Festival, 1984-86; established Stirling Writers Group, Stirling Youth Theatre; Arts Development Officer for Scotland, Scottish Council on Disability, 1986-87; Principal, Creative Services (arts consultancy), since 1992; Councillor, Highland Regional Council, 1994-96, and Highland Council, since 1995; Board Member, Ross and Cromarty Enterprise, since 1996; Member, University of Highlands and Islands Foundation; Fellow, RSA; author of plays for radio and theatre; broadcaster; columnist, Press and Journal; occasional acting. Recreations: music; books; sport; regular breathing; remembering family and friends' names. Address: (h.) Drumderfit, North Kessock, by Inverness, IV1 1XF; T.-01463 731596.

Beattie, Johnny. Comedian and entertainer; b. 1926, Glasgow. Established his career as principal comic in Robert Wilson's touring revue. Has appeared frequently in pantomime and in summer seasons at the Gaiety, Ayr.

Beattie, Professor Vivien Ann, MA (Hons), PhD, CA. Professor of Accountancy, University of Stirling, since 1997; Director of Research, Institute of Chartered Accountants of Scotland, since 1998; b. 9.5.58, Renfrew; m., John Stewart Beattie; 1 s. Educ. Renfrew High School; St. Andrews University. Student CA, Mann Judd Gordon, Chartered Accountants, Glasgow, 1980-83; Lecturer then Senior Lecturer, Portsmouth Polytechnic, 1983-86; Lecturer, Southampton University, 1987-93; Senior Lecturer then Reader, Stirling University, 1993-97. Recreations: hillwalking; tapestry; dogs. Address: (h.) 43 Menteith View, Dunblane FK15 0PD; T.-01786 825687.

Beaumont, Professor Paul Reid, LLB, LLM. Professor of European Union and Private International Law, University of Aberdeen, since 1995; b. 27.10.60, Hamilton; m., Marion; 1 s.; 1 d. Educ. Claremont High School, East Kilbride; Glasgow University; Dalhousie University, Canada. University of Aberdeen: Lecturer in Public Law, 1983-91, Senior Lecturer in Public Law, 1992-95. Academic and Scottish Co-ordinator, Lawyers Christian Fellowship; Company Secretary, Atholl Centre, Pitlochry. Author and editor of Several books. Recreations: golf; stamp collecting. Address: Faculty of Law, University of Aberdeen, Aberdeen AB24 3UB; T.-01224 272439.

Beaumont, Professor Phillip Barrington, BEcon (Hons), MEcon, PhD. Professor, Department of Management Studies, Glasgow University, since 1990 (Senior Lecturer, 1984-86, Reader, 1986-90); b. 13.10.49, Melbourne, Australia; m., Patricia Mary Ann McKinlay; 1 s. Educ. Camberwell High School, Melbourne; Monash University, Melbourne; Glasgow University. Research Fellow, then Lecturer, Glasgow University, 1976-84; Visiting Professor: Massachusetts Institute of Technology, Boston, 1982, McMaster University, 1986, Case Western Reserve University, 1988, Cornell University, 1990. Publications: Bargaining in the Public Sector, 1978; Safety at Work and the Trade Unions, 1981; Job Satisfaction in Public Administration, 1983; The Decline of Trade Union Organization, 1987; Change in Industrial Relations, 1990; Public Sector Industrial Relations, 1991; Human Resource Management, 1993; The Future of Employment Management, 1995. Recreations: tennis; badminton; cricket; shooting; fishing. Address: (b.) The University, Glasgow G12 8QQ; T.-0141-339 8855.

Beaumont, Professor Steven Peter, MA, PhD, CEng, MIEE, MIEEE. Professor of Nanoelectronics and Head, Department of Electronics and Electrical Engineering, Glasgow University; b. 20.2.52, Norwich; m., Joanne Mary; 1 s.; 2 d. Educ. Norwich School; Corpus Christi College, Cambridge University. Research Fellow, Glasgow University, 1978-83; Barr and Stroud Lecturer in Electronics, Glasgow University, 1983-86, Senior Lecturer, 1986-89; Director, Intellemetrics Ltd., 1982-90, Scot-Flow Dynamics Ltd., Institute for System Level Integration. Recreations: walking; crofting. Address: (h.) 13 Kelvinside Terrace South, Glasgow G20 6DW; T.-0141-330 5380.

Bechhofer, Professor Frank, MA. University Fellow, Edinburgh University; b. 10.10.35, Nurnberg, Germany; m., Jean Barbara Conochie; 1 s.; 1 d. Educ. Nottingham High School; Queens' College, Cambridge. Junior Research Officer, Department of Applied Economics, Cambridge University, 1962-65; Edinburgh University: Lecturer in Sociology, 1965-71, Reader in Sociology, 1971-87, Director, Research Centre for Social Sciences, 1984-97, Professor of Social Research, 1988-97. Address: (b.) Research Centre for Social Sciences, Old Surgeons' Hall, High School Yards, Edinburgh EH1 1LZ; T.-0131-650 6385.

Beckett, Rev. David Mackay, BA, BD. Minister, Greyfriars Tolbooth and Highland Kirk, Edinburgh, since 1983; b. 22.3.37, Glasgow; m., Rosalie Frances Neal; 2 s. Educ. Glenalmond; Trinity Hall, Cambridge; St. Andrews University. Assistant Minister, Dundee Parish Church (St. Mary's), 1963-66; Minister, Clark Memorial Church, Largs, 1966-83. Convener, Committee on Public Worship and Aids to Devotion, General Assembly, 1978-82; President, Church Service Society, 1986-88; Secretary, General Assembly Panel on Doctrine, 1987-95. Publication: The Lord's Supper, 1984. Address: (h.) 12 Tantallon Place, Edinburgh EH9 1NZ; T.-0131-667 8671.

Bedi, Tarlochan Singh, JP, MB, BS, FRCPsych, DPM. Consultant Psychiatrist and Honorary Clinical Senior Lecturer, Southern General Hospital, Glasgow, since 1980;

b. India; m., Dr. T.H. Ratani; 1 s. Educ. Poona University, India. Junior House Officer, Aga Khan Hospital, Nairobi; Senior House Officer, Glenside and Barrow Hospital, Bristol; Registrar, Coneyhill Hospital, Gloucester; Senior Registrar, Gartnavel and Southern General Hospital, Glasgow; Consultant Psychiatrist, Woodilee Hospital, Lenzie. Past President: Scottish Asian Action Committee, Glasgow; Indian Social and Cultural Association, Glasgow; Indian Graduates Society, Glasgow. Recreations: music; photography; culinary arts. Address: 156 Prestonfield, Milngavie G62 7QA; T.-0141-570 0734.

Beevers, Professor Clifford, BSc, PhD. Professor of Mathematics, Heriot Watt University, since 1993; b. 4.9.44, Castleford; m., Elizabeth Ann; 2 d. Educ. Castleford Grammar School; Manchester University. Senior Lecturer, 1985; Director, CALM, 1985. Past Chairman, Edinburgh Branch, British Retinitis Pigmentosa Society. Recreations: walking; jogging; music; theatre. Address: (b.) Department of Mathematics, Heriot Watt University, Riccarton, Edinburgh EH14 4AS; T.-0131-451 3233.

Begg, Anne, MA. MP (Labour), Aberdeen South, since 1997; b. 6.12.55, Forfar. Educ. Brechin High School; University of Aberdeen; Aberdeen College of Education. Teacher of English and History, Webster's High, Kirriemuir, 1978-88; Assistant Principal Teacher, then Principal Teacher of English, Arbroath Academy, 1988-97. Disabled Scot of the Year, 1988. Recreations: cinema; theatre; reading; public speaking. Address: (b.) House of Commons, London SW1A 0AA; T.-0171-219 2140.

Begg, David, BA (Hons). Chair of Transport, City of Edinburgh Council (Councillor, since 1986); Professor of Transport, Robert Gordon University; Non-Executive Director, BRB; Member, Government Advisory Panel on Transport White Paper; b. 12.6.56, Edinburgh. Educ. Portobello High School; Heriot-Watt University. Economic Researcher, PIEDA, 1979; management employee, BR, 1979-81; Lecturer in Economics, Napier University, 1981-91. Publications: articles on transport economics and local government finance. Recreations: golf; watching Hibernian F.C. Address: (b.) City Chambers, High Street, Edinburgh; T.-0131-529 3262.

Begg, Professor Hugh MacKemmie, MA, MA, PhD, DipTP, FRTPI, FRSA. Consultant Economist and Chartered Planner; part-time Reporter, Scottish Office Inquiry Reporters Unit; External Adjudicator, Scottish Enterprise; b. 25.10.41, Glasgow; m., Jane Elizabeth Harrison; 2 d. Educ. High School of Glasgow; St. Andrews University; University of British Columbia. Lecturer in Political Economy, St. Andrews University; Research Fellow, Tayside Study; Lecturer in Economics, Dundee University; Assistant Director of Planning, Tayside Regional Council; Visiting Professor, Technical University of Nova Scotia; Consultant, UN Regional Development Project, Egypt and Saudi Arabia; Consultant, Scottish Office Industry Department, Scottish Office Agriculture and Forestry Department; Head, School of Town and Regional Planning, Dundee University. Recreations: local history; hill walking; rugby. Address: (h.) 4 Esplanade, Broughty Ferry, Dundee; T.-01382 779642.

Begg, Ian McKerron, DA, FRIAS, FSA Scot. Architect (own practice), since 1983; b. 23.6.25, Kirkcaldy; 3 d. Educ. Kirkcaldy High School; Edinburgh College of Art. Partner, Robert Hurd & Partners, 1951-83; Interim Director, Edinburgh New Town Conservation Committee; Interim Director, Edinburgh Old Town Committee for Conservation and Renewal. Honorary Member, Saltire Society. Recreations: travel, particularly to Paris; supporting Scotland's identity. Address: Ravens'Craig, Plockton, Ross-shire IV52 8UB; T.-01599 544 265.

Begg, Norman Roderick Darroch, MA, LLB. Secretary, Aberdeen University, 1988-98; Director of Alumni Relations, since 1998; b. 23.12.41, London; m., Fiona Schofield; 3 d. Educ. Aberdeen Grammar School; Aberdeen University. Administrative Assistant, East Anglia University, 1964-66; Aberdeen University, since 1966: Administrative Assistant; Assistant Secretary; Registry Officer; Clerk to Senatus; Deputy Secretary. Member, Children's Panel, Grampian Region, 1984-87; Past Chairman, Aberdeen Studio Theatre Group; Director, Edinburgh Festival Fringe Society, 1980-83; Hon. Vice-President, Aberdeen Opera Company, since 1988. Recreation: amateur drama. Address: (b.) External Relations, Aberdeen University, Regent Walk, Aberdeen AB24 3FX.

Begg, Robert William, CBE (1977), DL, DUniv (Glas), MA, CA. Painter; b. 19.2.22; m., Sheena Margaret Boyd; 2 s. Educ. Greenock Academy; Glasgow University. Royal Navy, 1942-46 (Lt., RNVR) (Despatches). Consultant, Moores Rowland, 1987-95 (Partner, Mann Judd Gordon, Glasgow, 1951-86). Honorary Treasurer, Royal Philosophical Society of Glasgow, 1952-62; President, Royal Glasgow Institute of Fine Arts, 1987-90 (Honorary Treasurer, 1975-87); Member, Board of Governors, Glasgow School of Art, 1955-77 (Chairman, 1970-76); Trustee, National Galleries of Scotland, 1974-91 (Chairman, 1980-87); Member: Council, National Trust for Scotland, 1984-90 (Executive, 1985-90), Court, Glasgow University, 1986-90, Museums and Galleries Commission, 1988-91. Address: (h.) 3 Colquhoun Drive, Bearsden, Glasgow G61 4NQ; T.-0141-563 5705.

Begg, William Kirkwood, OBE. Chairman and Managing Director, Begg, Cousland Holdings Ltd.; Chairman, Begg Cousland & Co. Ltd.; b. 5.2.34; m., Thia St Clair; 2 s.; 1 d. Educ. Glenalmond College. Chairman, Scottish Advisory Committee on Telecommunications; Member, CBI SME Council; Privy Council Nominee to General Convocation, Strathclyde University; Director, Weavers' Society of Anderston; Founder Trustee, Dallas Benevolent Fund; Trustee, James Paterson's Trust; Vice Chairman, The Wise Group; Director, Commercially Wise Ltd.; Director, Merchants' House of Glasgow; former Member, Scottish Industrial Development Advisory Board; former Member, CBI Council for Scotland. Recreations: sailing; shooting; DIY. Address: (h.) 3 Mirrlees Drive, Glasgow G12 0SH.

Behan, Professor Peter Oliver, MB ChB, MD, DSc, FACP, FRCP (Glas), FRCP (Lond), FRCP (Ire). Consultant Neurologist, Greater Glasgow Health Board, since 1976; Professor of Neurology, Glasgow University; b. 8.7.35, Co. Kildare; m., Dr. Wilhelmina Behan; 2 s.; 1 d. Educ. Sir John Cass College, London; Leeds University Medical School. Demonstrator in Pathology, Cambridge University, 1965-66; Research Fellow in Psychiatry, Harvard University, 1966-67; Special Research Fellow, Oxford University, 1968-70; Lecturer in Neurology, then Senior Lecturer, then Reader, Glasgow University, from 1971. Patron, Motor Neurone Disease Association of Scotland; awarded Pattison Medal for contributions to neurology; International Dutch prize for study of fatigue states, 1995; Chief Editor, Journal of Neuroimmunology; papers and books on neurology; book on salmon and women (Co-author). Recreations: salmon fishing; Samuel Johnson. Address: (h.) 17 South Erskine Park, Bearsden, Glasgow; T.-0141-942 5713.

Belch, Professor Jill J. F., MB, ChB, FRCP, MD (Hons). Professor of Vascular Medicine and Biology, Dundee University, since 1993; Chairman, UK Forum on Angiology, since 1995; b. 22.10.52, Glasgow; m., Tom van der Ham; 1 s.; 3 d. Educ. Morrison's Academy, Crieff; University of Glasgow. University of Glasgow and Royal Infirmary: Research Fellow, 1980, Lecturer, 1984; University of Dundee and Ninewells Hospital: Senior

Lecturer, 1987, Reader, 1990. Medical Adviser, Raynaud's and Scleroderma Association. Publications: over 200 peer-reviewed articles in scientific journals. Recreations: family; skiing. Address: (b.) University Department of Medicine, Ninewells Hospital, Dundee DD1 9SY; T.-01382 632457.

Belch, Sir Ross, CBE (1972), LLD Strathclyde (1978), BSc, FRSE, FRINA, CBIM, CEng. Company Director; b. 13.12.20, London; m., 1, Janette Finnie Murdoch (deceased); 4 d.; 2, Dorothy West. Educ. Morrison's Academy, Crieff; Glasgow University. Lithgows Ltd.: Director and General Manager, 1954, Managing Director, 1964; Managing Director, Scott Lithgow Group, 1969-80; Member, Board, British Shipbuilders, 1977-79; President, Shipbuilders and Repairers National Association, 1974-76; Chairman: Irvine Development Corporation, 1985-90, Murray Hotels (Crieff) Ltd., Kelvin Travel Ltd.; President, Altnamara Shipping plc; Hon. President, Scottish Maritime Museum. Address: (h.) Westwinds, Greenock Road, Largs KA30 8RX; T.-01475 689855.

Belfall, David J., BA (Hons). Head, Housing and Area Regeneration Group, Scottish Office, since 1995; b. 26.4.47, Colchester; m., Lorna McLaughlan; 1 s.; 1 d. Educ. Colchester Royal Grammar School; St. John's College, Cambridge. Home Office, 1969-88 (Private Secretary to Permanent Under Secretary of State, 1973-74); Scottish Office, since 1988; Under Secretary, Police and Emergency Services, 1988-91, Health Policy and Public Health, 1991-95. Recreations: squash; badminton. Address: (b.) Scottish Office, Victoria Quay, Edinburgh EH6 6QQ.

Belhaven and Stenton, 13rd Lord (Robert Anthony Carmichael Hamilton); b. 27.2.27. Succeeded to title, 1961.

Bell, Alexander Scott, FFA, FPMI, DLitt. Group Managing Director, Standard Life Assurance Company, since 1988; b. 4.12.41, Falkirk; m., Veronica Jane Simpson; 2 s.; 1 d. Educ. Daniel Stewart's College, Edinburgh. Joined Standard Life, 1958; Director: Universities Superannuation Scheme Limited. Recreations: golf; travel. Address: (b.) 30 Lothian Road, Edinburgh, EH1 2DH; T.-0131-245 6011.

Bell, Sheriff Andrew Montgomery, BL. Sheriff of Lothian and Borders, at Edinburgh, since 1990 (Sheriff of Glasgow and Strathkelvin, at Glasgow, 1984-90); b. 21.2.40, Edinburgh; m., Ann Margaret Robinson; 1 s.; 1 d. Educ. Royal High School, Edinburgh; Edinburgh University. Solicitor, 1961-74; called to Bar, 1975; Sheriff of South Strathclyde, Dumfries and Galloway, at Hamilton, 1979-84. Address: (h.) 5 York Road, Edinburgh EH5 3EJ; T.-0131-552 3859.

Bell, Anne Rutherford, MA, MIPD. Head of Human Resources, Scottish Tourist Board, since 1996; b. 14.4.59, Carlisle. Educ. Annan Academy; Edinburgh University. Personnel Assistant, Hydro-Electric Board, 1984; Personnel Officer, Lothian Regional Council, 1987; Scottish Homes, 1988-96, latterly as Human Resources Development Manager. Recreations: travel; cinema; theatre. Address: (b.) 23 Ravelston Terrace, Edinburgh EH4 3EU.

Bell, Arthur J.A., CBE, BSc, MCIM, FRSA, FIDM. Chairman, Scotland Direct (Holdings) Ltd., and subsidiaries; Marketing Consultant; b. 6.10.46, Brechin; m., G. Susan Bell; 4 c. Educ. Royal High School, Edinburgh; Edinburgh University. Chair, New Lanark Housing Association; Vice Chair, New Lanark Conservation Trust; Director, Small Business Bureau; Editor, Small Business News; Member, Council, Institute of Direct Marketing; three times parliamentary candidate. Publication: Complete Edinburgh Pub Guide/A Flavour of Edinburgh (Co-author). Address: (b.) Scotland Direct (Holdings) Ltd., Thistle Mill, Biggar ML12 6LP; T.-01899 221001.

Bell, Colin John, MA (Hons), HonLLD (Aberdeen). Broadcaster; Journalist; Author; b. 1.4.38, London; m., Caroline Rose Bell; 1 s.; 3 d. Educ. St. Paul's School; King's College, Cambridge. Journalist, The Scotsman, 1960-62 and 1975-78; Journalist/Contributor, London Life, Sunday Times, Sunday Telegraph, Daily Mirror, Sunday Mail, etc.; Lecturer, Morley College, 1965-68; College Supervisor, King's College, Cambridge, 1968-75; Parliamentary candidate (SNP), West Edinburgh, 1979; European Parliamentary candidate (SNP), North East Scotland, 1979; Vice-Chairman, SNP, 1978-84; Campaign Director, Euro Election, 1984; a Senior Fellow, the 21st Century Trust, 1990; Rector, Aberdeen University, 1991-93. Publications: City Fathers, 1969; Boswell's Johnson, 1971; Scotch Whisky, 1985; Radical Alternative (Contributor), 1978; The Times Reports (Series) (Editor). Recreations: jazz; Scottish history. Address: (h.) Cockburnhill, Balerno, Midlothian.

Bell, Professor David Nevin Fraser, MA, MSc, PhD. Professor of Economics, Stirling University, since 1990; Research Director, Scottish Doctoral Programme in Economics; Member, Panel of Economic Advisers to Secretary of State for Scotland; b. 16.12.51, Inverness; 1 s.; 1 d. Educ. Dornoch Academy; Aberdeen University; London School of Economics; Strathclyde University. Lecturer, St. Andrews University, 1974-75; Research Fellow: Fraser of Allander Institute, Strathclyde University, 1975-83, Macroeconomic Modelling Bureau, Warwick University, 1983-85; Lecturer, Glasgow University, 1985-90. Recreations: golf; bird-watching; photography. Address: (b.) Department of Economics, Stirling University, Stirling FK9 4LA.

Bell, Donald Atkinson, BSc, PhD, FIMechE, CEng, MIEE, FBCS. Director, Marchland Consulting Ltd., since 1990 (Director, National Engineering Laboratory, 1983-90); b. 28.5.41, Belfast; m., Joyce Louisa Godber; 2 s. Educ. Royal Belfast Academical Institution; Queen's University, Belfast; Southampton University. National Physical Laboratory, Teddington, 1966-77; Electronics Applications Division, Department of Industry, 1978-82. Address: (b.) Marchland Consulting Ltd., 108 East Kilbride Road, Glasgow G76 8JF; T.-0141-644 2000.

Bell, George Armour, OBE, JP, BSc, MB, ChB. Former Chairman, Monklands and Bellshill Hospitals NHS Trust; Vice President, Tenovus-Scotland; b. 8.7.20, Bellshill; m., Elizabeth Davidson Porteous; 2 s. Educ. Bellshill Academy; Glasgow University. War Service, 609 Squadron – Normandy to Germany, SMO Prestwick, SMO Brize Norton, RAF. Retired General Practitioner, Bellshill; former Member, Lanarkshire Health Board; founder Chairman, Crime Prevention Panel, Bellshill and District; former Red Cross Detachment Medical Officer, Bellshill; founder Chairman, Community Council for Mossend; Honorary Medical Officer, Bellshill Bn., Boys Brigade; President, Bellshill Branch, Arthritis Care; Honorary Member, Rotary; Life Member, BMA; Life Member, RAF Association. Address: (h.) 16 Imlach Place, Parkside Gardens, Motherwell ML1 3FD.

Bell, Graham, MBChB, FRCS, ChM. Consultant Surgeon, Inverclyde Royal Hospital, since 1973; b. 9.8.36, Glasgow; 4 s. Educ. Kelvinside Academy; Glasgow University. Lecturer in Surgery, Department of Surgery, Glasgow Royal Infirmary, 1963-73. Recreations: golfing; fishing. Address: (h.) 11 Dalziel Drive, Glasgow G41 4JA; T.-0141-427 0233.

Bell, G. Susan, ACIS, FSA (Scot), MIDM. Founder Director, Scotland Direct (Holdings) Limited; Bell Lawrie of Biggar (Developments) Ltd.; Board Member, Scottish Centres; Board Member, SALVO; b. 31.8.46; m., Arthur J.A. Bell, CBE; 2 s.; 2 d. Educ. College of Commerce, Glasgow. Investment Analyst, Edinburgh, 1970-74;

Conservative Parliamentary candidate: Motherwell, 1970, Caithness & Sutherland, February 1974; Chairman, Conservative Candidates Association, 1971-74; joined Liberal Democrats, 1997; Member, Council, CBI Scotland, 1986-93; Board Member: Scottish Tourist Board, 1983-88, SCOTVEC, 1987-95, Southern General Hospital Trust, 1993-95; Member, Council, National Trust for Scotland, 1983-88; former Chair, Women into Business. Recreations: garden; reading. Address: (h.) Culter House, Coulter, Biggar; T.-01899 220064.

Bell, Robin, MA, MSc. Poet and Broadcaster; b. 4.1.45, Dundee; 2 d. Educ. Morrison's Academy, Crieff; St. Andrews University; Perugia University, Italy; Union College, New York; Columbia University, New York. Formerly: Director of Information, City University of New York, Regional Opportunity Program; Assistant Professor, John Jay College of Criminal Justice, City University of New York; Member, US Office of Education Task Force in Educational Technology; Audio-Visual Editor, Oxford University Press; Editor, Guidebook series to Ancient Monuments of Scotland; Secretary, Poetry Association of Scotland. Scottish Radio and Television Industries Award for Best Radio Feature, 1984; Sony Award, Best British Radio Documentary, 1985. Publications: The Invisible Mirror; Culdee, Culdee; Sawing Logs; Strathinver: A Portrait Album 1945-53; Collected Poems of James Graham, Marquis of Montrose (Editor); Radio Poems; The Best of Scottish Poetry; An Anthology of Living Scottish Poets (Editor); Bittersweet Within My Heart: collected poems of Mary Queen of Scots (Translator/Editor); Scanning the Forth Bridge. Address: (h.) The Orchard, Muirton, Auchterarder PH3 1ND.

Bellany, Dr. John, CBE (1994), RA; b. June, 1942, Port Seton; m., 1, Helen Margaret Percy; 2, Juliet Gray Lister (deceased); 3, for second time, Helen Margaret Bellany; 2 s.; 1 d. Educ. Cockenzie Public School; Preston Lodge, Prestonpans; Edinburgh College of Art; Royal College of Art, London. Lecturer in Fine Art, Winchester School of Art, 1969-73; Head, Faculty of Painting, Croydon College of Art, 1973-78; Visiting Lecturer in Painting, R.C.A., 1975-85; Lecturer in Fine Art, Goldsmiths College, London University, 1978-84; elected Fellow Commoner, Trinity Hall, Cambridge, 1988; lived and painted in Mexico, 1996; one-man exhibitions include: Arts Council touring show; Rosa Esman Gallery, New York; Christine Abrahams Gallery, Melbourne; Ikon Gallery, Birmingham; Walker Art Gallery, Liverpool; Roslyn Oxley Gallery, Sydney; National Portrait Gallery, London; Galerie Krikhar, Amsterdam; Fischer Fine Art, London; retrospective — Scottish National Gallery of Modern Art; Serpentine Gallery, London; Kimsthalle, Hamburg; Museum Ostral, Dortmund; Ruth Siegel Gallery, New York; Raab Gallery, Berlin; Fitzwilliam Museum, Cambridge; Kelvingrove Museum and Art Gallery (50th birthday tribute); Beaux Arts Gallery, Berkeley Square Gallery, London; Edinburgh Festival, 1997; elected ARA, 1987; RA, 1992; Hon. RSA, 1987; joint 1st prize, Athena International Award, 1985; honorary doctorates, Edinburgh University, 1996, Heriot-Watt University, 1998. Recreation: motoring around Europe in search of beauty.

Beltrami, Joseph, SSC, BL, NP. Solicitor/Advocate (Beltrami & Co.); b. 15.5.32, Rutherglen; m., Brigid D.; 3 s. Educ. St. Aloysius College, Glasgow; Glasgow University. Intelligence Corps, 1954-56 (Sgt.); qualified as Solicitor, 1956; specialised in criminal law; has instructed in more than 500 murder cases; closely associated with two cases of Royal Pardon; in first batch of Solicitor/Advocates to have rights of audience in High Court and Court of Criminal Appeal. Chairman, soccer testimonials: Jim Johnstone and Bobby Lennox, 1976; Danny McGrain, 1980. Publications: The Defender, 1980; Glasgow - A Celebration (Contributor), 1984; Tales of the Suspected, 1988; A Deadly Innocence, 1989. Recreations: bowls; soccer; snooker; writing; boxing. Address: (h.) 12 Valence Tower, Regents Gate, Bothwell, Lanarkshire; T.-01698 817841.

Benedetti, Giovanni. Chairman: Benedetti International Plc, Pendigo Ltd., Wallace Cameron & Co. Ltd., Wrap Film Systems Ltd., ProPac Ltd., GB Consulting and Management Services Ltd., KSS Supplies; Director, Prince's Scottish Youth Business Trust; b. 6.3.43, Italy; m., Francesca; 2 d. Arrived in Britain aged 11; worked in uncle's cafe until age of 19; started his own business with two dry-cleaning shops; opened his first factory in Ardrossan, 1970; company bought by BET, 1989. Recreations: skiing; sailing.

Benington, (Charles) Kenneth, BSc, PhD, CEng, FIMechE. Industrial Consultant, since 1996; b. 1.4.31, Belfast; m., Margaret Malcolm; 1 s.; 1 d. Educ. Dalriada Grammar School, Ballymoney; Queen's University, Belfast; Heriot-Watt University. Graduate apprentice and design engineer, Associated Electrical Industries Ltd., 1953-60; Assistant Chief Engineer, Trials, British Ship Research Association, 1960-63; Lecturer, Heriot-Watt University, 1963-72; Senior Engineer, Marine Industries Centre, Newcastle University, 1972-74; Brown Brothers & Co. Ltd.: Systems Manager, 1974-75; Technical Manager, 1975-77; Technical Director, 1977-80; Assistant Managing Director and Technical Director, 1980-81; Managing Director, 1981-86; Technical Director, Vickers Marine Engineering Division, 1986-88; Industrial Adviser to Secretary of State for Scotland, 1988-96; Member, Executive Committee, Scottish Employers' Association, 1984-86; Member, Board of Unilink, Heriot Watt University, 1987-90. Address: (h.) 4 Redfox Crescent, Penicuik, Midlothian EH26 0RQ.

Bennet, George Charters, BSc, MBChB, FRCS. Consultant Orthopaedic Surgeon, Royal Hospital for Sick Children, Glasgow, since 1982; b. 8.8.46, Edinburgh; m., Louise Spilsbury; 3 s. Educ. Holy Cross Academy; University of Edinburgh. Junior surgical posts, Edinburgh, Sheffield, London; orthopaedic training, Southampton, London, Oxford, Toronto. Honorary Consultant in paediatric orthopaedic surgery to Army. Books, chapters and scientific papers published on orthopaedic surgery and trauma in childhood. Recreations: rugby union; fishing; reading. Address: Department of Orthopaedic Surgery, Royal Hospital for Sick Children, Glasgow G3 8SJ; T.-0141-201 0275.

Bennet, Graham Alexander, OBE, QPM. Deputy Chief Constable, Fife, since 1991; b. 21.3.43, Insch. Educ. Aberlour High School. Joined Fife Constabulary, 1963; Assistant Chief Constable, 1987. Address: (b.) Police HQ, Detroit Road, Glenrothes, Fife KY6 2RJ.

Bennett, Professor David, BSc (Hons), BVetMed (Hons), PhD, DSAO, MRCVS. Professor and Head, Small Animal Clinical Studies, University of Glasgow, since 1996; Co-Head, Molecular Medicine and Therapeutics Unit, since 1996; RCVS Specialist in Small Animal Surgery, since 1986; b. 14.3.48, Ipswich; m., Carol Ann; 1 d. Educ. Northgate Grammar, Ipswich; Royal Veterinary College; University of London. Resident House Officer, Royal Veterinary College, 1972-74; Lecturer, Veterinary Surgery, University of Glasgow, 1974-81; Assistant in general practice, 1981-82; Senior Lecturer, 1982-1990, Reader in Comparative Rheumatology, 1990-96, University of Liverpool. Founder Member and Trustee, BVOA. Elanco Literary Award; Veterinary Drug Prize; Central Veterinary Society Centenary Award; BSAVA Simon Award; BEVA Silver Jubilee Prize; Honorary Member, Scottish Rheumatology Club. Publications: over 150 clinical and research publications. Recreations: hockey; gardening; restoring antique furniture and porcelain; bridge. Address :(b.) Department of Veterinary Clinical Studies, University of Glasgow Veterinary School, Bearsden Road, Bearsden, Glasgow G61 1QH; T.-0141-330 6959.

Bennett, David Andrew, MA, LLB, WS, NP. Partner, Bennett & Robertson, Solicitors, Edinburgh, since 1964; b. 27.3.38, Edinburgh; m., Marion Miller Park; 2 d. Educ. Melville College, Edinburgh; Fettes College, Edinburgh; Edinburgh University. Director, Jordan Group Ltd.; Member, Council, Law Society of Scotland, 1984-90. Session Clerk, Liberton Kirk, since 1975; Honorary Secretary, Scottish Hockey Association, 1973-82; Scottish Editor, Palmer's Company Law, since 1970, and Gore-Browne on Companies, since 1975. Recreations: most sports and arts. Address: (b.) 16 Walker Street, Edinburgh EH3 7NN; T.-0131-225 4001.

Bennett, Helen Margaret, PhD, FSA Scot. Crafts Director, Scottish Arts Council, since 1993; Group Director, Creative Arts, since 1996; Governor, Edinburgh College of Art, since 1992; b. 25.6.48, Newark; m., Philip Edwin Bennett; 1 d. Educ. Lilley and Stone High School for Girls, Newark; Exeter University; Edinburgh University. Edinburgh Common Purpose Graduate, 1996. Assistant Curator, Borough of Weston-super-Mare, 1969-71; Curator of Agricultural and Social History, Bristol City Museums, 1971-72; Research Assistant, Costume and Textiles, National Museum of Antiquities of Scotland, 1974-81; freelance arts administrator, 1984-88; Head of Crafts Division, Scottish Development Agency, 1989-91; freelance cultural consultant, 1991-93. Recreations: walking; gardening; textile crafts. Address: (b.) 12 Manor Place, Edinburgh EH3 7DD; T.-0131-226 6051.

Bennett, Robin Alexander George, MA, LLB, MSI. Solicitor, Bennetts, Cupar, since 1992; b. 6.6.40, Edinburgh; m., Mary Funk; 2 d. Educ. Hillhead High School, Glasgow; Glasgow University. Assistant: Harrisons and Crosfield, Malaysia and Brunei, 1965-78, Drummond Johnstone and Grosset, Cupar, 1978-80; Solicitor (Partner): Drummond Cook and Mackintosh, Cupar, 1980-90, Wallace and Bennett, 1990-92. Chairman, Tranquilliser Addiction Solicitors Group, 1988-90; Founder/Secretary, Scottish TSB Depositors Association, 1986; Chairman, Ceres and District Community Council, 1980-82 and 1993-98; Vice Convener, Scottish Legal Action Group, 1989-95; Honorary Sheriff, Cupar, since 1991. Recreations: hillwalking; water gardening. Address: (h.) Sandakan, Curling Pond Road, Ceres, Fife KY15 5NB; T.-01334 828452.

Bennett, William Walter, BSc, BPhil. Director of Social Work, Shetland, since 1991; b. 19.11.44; m., Christine; 1 s.; 2 d. Educ. Ashton-under-Lyne Grammar School; Edinburgh University; Exeter University. Social Worker and Team Leader, 1970-83; Adviser (Social Work), Scottish Office, 1983-88; Director, NCH in Scotland, 1988-91. Recreations: walking; fitness training; cricket; reading; wine. Address: (h.) Langside, Bridge End, Shetland ZE2 9LD; T.-01595 859275.

Bennie, Norma, DipCOT. Mental Welfare Commissioner, since 1994; Occupational Therapist, since 1968; b. 11.11.46, Beith; m., Ernest H. Bennie; 2 s.; 1 d. Educ. Spier's School, Beith; Glasgow School of Occupational Therapy. Occupational Therapist, Duke Street Hospital, Gartnavel Royal Hospital and Dykebar Hospital, 1968-1993; Service Manager for Mental Health, Dykebar Hospital, 1993-97; Community Care Development and Business Planning Manager, Renfrewshire Healthcare (NHS) Trust, 1997. Recreations: keep-fit; sailing. Address: (b.) Trust HQ, Dykebar Hospital, Paisley PA2 7DE; T.-0141-884 9052.

Bennie, Peter Fraser, MB, ChB, MRCPsych. Consultant Psychiatrist, Parkhead Hospital, Glasgow; b. 7.6.63, New Zealand. Educ. Dollar Academy; Glasgow University. Junior Doctors Committee: Member, UK Committee, 1990-98, Deputy Chairman, 1995-96, Chairman, 1996-97; Chairman, Scottish Committee, 1991-96, Chairman, UK Conference, 1995. Recreations: five a side football; cycling; hill-walking; theatre; cinema; eating and drinking well. Address: (b.) Parkhead Hospital, 83 Salamanca Street, Glasgow G32 5EX; T.-0141-211 8300.

Bennie, Robert William, BSc, CPFA. Director of Finance, Western Isles Council, since 1992; b. 19.8.56, Edinburgh. Educ. Melville College, Edinburgh; Linlithgow Academy; Heriot-Watt University. Trainee Accountant/Accounting Assistant, Falkirk District Council; Chief Technical Assistant, Aberconwy B.C.; Principal Accountant, Vale of White Horse D.C.; District Finance Officer, Hinckley and Bosworth B.C.; Deputy Treasurer, South Northamptonshire D.C. Recreations: mountaineering; rugby; running; music; reading. Address: (b.) Stornoway, Isle of Lewis HS1 2BW; T.-01851 703773, Ext. 230.

Benson, Bob, MSc, CQSW. Director, Disability Scotland, since 1997; m., Anne Houston. Educ. Stirling High School. Volunteer and Project Leader, Community Service Volunteers; Social Worker and Training Manager, Lothian and Fife; Senior Development Manager, Age Concern Scotland. Trustee, Scottish Disability Foundation; Trustee, Unemployed Voluntary Action Fund; Member, Board, Volunteer Development Scotland. Address: (h.) 7 Coltbridge Terrace, Edinburgh; (b.) Princes House, 5 Shandwick Place, Edinburgh EH2 4RG; T.-0131-229 8632.

Benson, Professor Gordon Mitchell, AADip, SADG, FRIAS, ARIBA. Architect; Partner, Benson and Forsyth; b. 5.10.44, Glasgow; 1 s. 1 d. Educ. Glasgow High School; Glasgow University and Architectural Association. Partner in private practice, since 1978; recent prize work includes Cowgatehead Library, Edinburgh, 1995, New Museum of Scotland (international competition), 1991; Chair of Architecture, Strathclyde University, 1986-90.

Benton, David Charles, RGN, RMN, BSc, MPhil. Chief Executive, National Board for Nursing, Midwifery and Health Visiting for Scotland, since 1998; b. 29.10.57, Torphins; m., (Elizabeth) Denise MacRae; 2 s.; 1 d. Educ. Elgin Academy; Robert Gordon's Institute of Technology; Dundee Institute of Technology; Highland College of Nursing and Midwifery. Staff Nurse then Charge Nurse (acute psychiatry and drug abuse services), Craig Duncan Hospital, Inverness; District Research Nurse, North East Essex Health Authority; Director of Quality and Nurse Advisor, Tower Hamlets Health Authority, subsequently East London and the City Health Authority, 1992-95; Regional Nurse Director, NHS Executive (Northern and Yorkshire), 1995-98. Visiting Professor of Nursing Policy, University of Northumbria, 1996; Member, ETA IOTA Chapter, Sigma Theta Tau. Dr George MacKenzie Award, 1983; Nursing Standard Leadership Award, 1993; Nursing Times 3M Award, 1994. Recreations: walking; taekwon-do. Address: (h.) 35 Whitehaugh Park, Peebles EH45 9DB; T.-0172 172 2735.

Berry, Professor Christopher Jon, BA, PhD. Professor of Political Theory, University of Glasgow, since 1995 (Head, Department of Politics, since 1998); b. 19.6.46, St. Helens; m., Christine Emma, 2 s. Educ. Upholland Grammar School; Nottingham University; London School of Economics. Lecturer, then Senior Lecturer, then Reader, Department of Politics, University of Glasgow. Publications: five books, many articles. Recreations: reading contemporary literature; walking. Address: (b.) Adam Smith Building, University of Glasgow, Glasgow G12 8RT; T.-0141-330 5064.

Berry, Graham, CA. Director of Finance and Administration, Scottish Arts Council, since 1989; b. 12.1.45, Edinburgh; 1 s.; 1 d. Educ. Royal High School, Edinburgh; CA Apprentice, Edinburgh, 1963-68; CA, Price Waterhouse, London, 1968-70; Divisional Chief Accountant, Trust House Forte, London, 1970-74;

Company Secretary, 1974-86: Scottish Film Council, Scottish Council for Educational Technology, Glasgow Film Theatre, Filmhouse Ltd., Scetlander Ltd.; Finance Officer, Stirling University, 1986-89. Recreations: mountaineering; photography. Address: (b.) Scottish Arts Council, 12 Manor Place, Edinburgh EH3 7DD; T.-0131-226 6051.

Berry, John, CBE (1968), DL (Fife) (1969), BA (Cantab), MA (Cantab), PhD (St. Andrews) Hon. LLD Dundee (1970), HonDSc St. Andrews (1991), FRSE (1936). Adviser and Consultant on environmental and wildlife conservation (retired); b. 5.8.07, Edinburgh; m., Hon. Bride Fremantle; 2 s.; 1 d. Educ. Ardvreck School, Crieff; Eton College; Trinity College, Cambridge. Salmon Research Officer, Fishery Board for Scotland, 1930-31; Biological Research Station, University College, Southampton: Research Officer, 1932-36; Director, 1936-39; Chief Press Censor for Scotland, 1940-44; Biologist and Information Officer, North of Scotland Hydro-Electric Board, 1944-49; Environment Conservation Adviser, 1944-89 (to South of Scotland Electricity Board, 1969-89, to Scottish Landowners Federation, 1984-87); Director of Nature Conservation in Scotland, 1949-67; consultancy work 1968-90. Honorary Life Member, Swiss League for Protection of Nature, 1946; founder Member (1948), International Union for Conservation of Natural Resources and first President, International Union Commission on Ecology; Member, Executive Board, International Waterfowl Research Bureau, 1963-72; Honorary Corresponding Member, Danish Natural History Society, since 1957; Vice-President and Honorary Life Fellow, Royal Zoological Society of Scotland, since 1959; Honorary Life Fellow: Wildfowl Trust, 1983; Glasgow Natural History Society, 1951; Member, Dundee University Court, 1970-78; Director, British Pavilion, Expo 71, Budapest; Member, Scottish Marine Biological Association, 1947-71 (Council, 1947-54 and 1957-66). Recreations: natural history (especially insects, water birds and fish); music. Address: (h.) The Garden House, Tayfield, Newport-on-Tay, Fife DD6 8HA; T.-01382 543118.

Berry, John Kyle, MBA, FCIBS. Head of Corporate Banking, European Regional Banks, National Australia Bank Group (including Clydesdale Bank PLC), since 1998; b. 7.10.50, Hamilton; m., Patricia Mary; 1 s.; 1 d. Educ. Duncanrig School, East Kilbride; Strathclyde Business School. Bank of Scotland: various posts, seconded to Shell UK Ltd. London Treasury Department, two years, establishment of HOBS, Societe Generale Scottish Representative, Director of Corporate Banking; Head of Corporate Banking, Clydesdale Bank; Head of Business Financial Services, Clydesdale Bank. Director, Forth Valley Enterprise. Recreations: golf; watching soccer; travel. Address: (b.) Clydesdale Bank Plc, 30 St. Vincent Place, Glasgow; T.-0141-223 2389.

Berry, William, MA, LLB, WS, NP. Senior Partner, Murray Beith Murray, WS, Edinburgh; Chairman, Scottish Life Assurance Co.; Director: Scottish American Investment Co. Plc, Fleming Continental European Trust Plc, Alliance Trust plc, Dawnfresh Seafoods Ltd., Inchcape Family Investments Ltd., and other companies; b. 26.9.39, Newport-on-Tay; m., Elizabeth Margery Warner; 2 s. Educ. Ardvreck, Crieff; Eton College; St. Andrews University; Edinburgh University. Interests in farming, forestry, etc. Depute Chairman, Edinburgh Festival Society, 1985-89; Member Council/Board, New Town Concerts Society Ltd. Performer in three records of Scottish country dance music. Recreations: music; shooting; forestry. Address: (b.) 39 Castle Street, Edinburgh EH2 3BH; T.-0131-225 1200.

Betts, Michael William, CBE, FCIT, FILog. Traffic Commissioner for Scotland, since 1992; Senior Traffic Commissioner, Great Britain, since 1996; b. 3.3.38, Bournemouth; m., Margaret Irene Lussi; 2 d. Educ. Hardye's School, Dorchester; Royal Military Academy, Sandhurst. Commissioned Royal Army Service Corps, 1957; Brigadier Logistics, British Army of the Rhine, 1987-90; Director of Movements (Army), Ministry of Defence, 1991-92; ADC to HM The Queen, 1990-92. Freeman, City of London, 1993; Freeman and Liveryman, Worshipful Company of Carmen, 1993. Recreations: sailing; skiing; bird-watching. Address: (b.) Scottish Traffic Area Office, Floor J, Argyle House, 3 Lady Lawson Street, Edinburgh EH3 9SE; T.-0131-529 8510.

Bevan, John Stuart, BSc (Hons), MBChB (Hons), MD, FRCP (Edin). Consultant Physician and Endocrinologist, Aberdeen Royal Infirmary, since 1991; Honorary Senior Clinical Lecturer, Aberdeen University, since 1991; Secretary, Clinical Committee, Society for Endocrinology, since 1997; Visiting Physician to Orkney Islands, since 1994; b. 18.9.53, Portsmouth; m., Sheena Mary; 2 s.; 2 d. Educ. Portsmouth Northern Grammar School; Dunfermline High School; Edinburgh University. Registrar in Endocrinology, Radcliffe Infirmary, Oxford, 1981-83; Medical Research Council Training Fellow in Endocrinology, Oxford, 1984-86; Senior Registrar in Medicine and Endocrinology, University Hospital of Wales, Cardiff, 1987-90; Assistant Editor, Clinical Endocrinology, since 1994; Trustee, Pituitary Foundation; Member, Specialist Advisory Committee in Endocrinology and Diabetes, since 1998. Publications: papers on clinical neuroendocrinology, particularly the treatment of human pituitary tumours. Recreations: cricket; guitar; ornithology. Address: (b.) Department of Endocrinology, Aberdeen Royal Infirmary, Ward 25, Foresterhill, Aberdeen AB25 2ZN; T.-01224 681818.

Beveridge, Crawford William, CBE, BSc, MSc. Chief Executive, Scottish Enterprise, since 1991; b. 3.11.45, Edinburgh; m., Marguerite Devoe; 1 s.; 1 d. Educ. Daniel Stewart's College; Edinburgh University; Bradford University Management Centre. Training Officer, Hewlett Packard, 1968; European Personnel Director, Digital, 1977; Vice President: Human Resources, Analog Devices, 1982, Corporate Resources, Sun Microsystems, 1985. Recreations: cooking; music; paperweights. Address: (b.) Scottish Enterprise, 120 Bothwell Street, Glasgow G2 7JP; T.-0141-248 2700.

Beveridge, John Mackenzie, BSc (Hons), MREHIS. Director, West Region, Scottish Environment Protection Agency, since 1995; Director of Public Affairs, Scottish Environment Protection Agency, since 1998; b. 27.2.53, Glasgow; m., Donna; 2 d. Educ. Camphill High School, Paisley; University of Strathclyde. Depute Director, Environmental Services, Argyll and Bute District Council, 1987-90; Director of Environmental Protection and Leisure Services, Dumbarton District Council, 1990-95. Royal Environmental Health Institute of Scotland: President, 1994-95, Member, Executive Council, since 1985. Director, Loch Lomond Steamship Company. Address: (b.) SEPA West, 5 Redwood Crescent, Peel Park, East Kilbride G75 5PP; T.-01355 574200.

Bewsher, Colonel Harold Frederick, LVO, OBE. Chairman, The Atlantic Salmon Trust, since 1995; Chairman, The Airborne Initiative (Scotland) Ltd., 1995-98; Brigadier, The Queen's Bodyguard for Scotland, since 1996 (Secretary, 1982-94); b. 13.1.29, Glasgow; m., Susan Elizabeth Cruickshank; 2 s. Educ. Merchiston Castle School; Royal Technical College; Glasgow University; Royal Military Academy, Sandhurst. Regular Army, The Royal Scots, 1949-72; Director-General, Scotch Whisky Association, 1973-94. Chairman: New Club, Edinburgh, 1981-82, Scottish Society for the Employment of Ex-Regular Soldiers, Sailors and Airmen, 1973-83; Freeman, City of London, 1992; Liveryman, Worshipful Company of Distillers, 1993. Recreations: outdoors — salmon fishing, field sports. Address: (b.) 33 Blacket Place, Edinburgh EH9 1RJ; T.-0131-667 4600.

Bicanic, Professor Nenad Josip Nikola, DiplIng, PhD. Regius Professor of Civil Engineering, since 1994, and Head of Department of Civil Engineering, University of Glasgow, since 1997; b. 6.9.45, Zagreb, Croatia; m., Jasna Babic; 1 s.; 1 d. Educ. University of Zagreb; University of Wales, Swansea. Structural Engineer, Zagreb, 1968-69; Consulting Engineer, Arnhem, Netherlands, 1969-72; Lecturer, Docent, Professor, University of Zagreb, 1972-83; Visiting Professor, University of Colorado, 1983-84; Lecturer, Senior Lecturer, Reader, Department of Civil Engineering, University of Wales, Swansea, 1985-94. President, AMAC-UK. Publication: Computational Modelling of Concrete Structures, 1990. Recreations: tennis; skiing; folk dancing. Address: (h.) 20 Ledcameroch Road, Bearsden G61 4AE; T.-0141-942 0711.

Biddulph, 5th Lord (Anthony Nicholas Colin). Interior Designer and Sporting Manager; b. 8.4.59; m., Hon. Sian Gibson-Watt; 2 s. Educ. Cheltenham; RAC, Cirencester. Recreations: shooting; design; fishing. Address: Address: (h.) Makerstoun, Kelso TD5 7PA; T.-01573 460 234.

Biggart, Thomas Norman, CBE (1984), WS, MA, LLB. Partner, Biggart Baillie & Gifford, Solicitors, Glasgow and Edinburgh, 1959-95; b. 24.1.30; m., Eileen Jean Anne Gemmell; 1 s.; 1 d. Educ. Morrison's Academy, Crieff; Glasgow University. Royal Navy, 1954-56 (Sub-Lt., RNVR). Law Society of Scotland: Council Member, 1977-86; Vice-President, 1981-82; President, 1982-83; President, Business Archives Council, Scotland, 1977-86; Member, Executive, Scottish Council (Development and Industry), 1984-94; Member: Scottish Tertiary Education Advisory Council, 1984-87, Scottish Records Advisory Council, 1985-91; Director: Clydesdale Bank, 1985-97; Independent Insurance Group, since 1986 (Chairman, 1989-93); Chairman, Beechwood, Glasgow, 1989-97; Trustee, Scottish Civic Trust, 1989-97; Member, Council on Tribunals (Chairman, Scottish Committee), 1990-98; Honorary Member, American Bar Association, 1982; OStJ, 1968. Recreations: golf; hill-walking. Address: (h.) Gailes, Kilmacolm, Renfrewshire PA13 4LZ; T.-0150 587 2645.

Bills, David James, BSc (For). Director General and Deputy Chairman, Forestry Commission, since 1995; b. 9.2.48, Australia; m., Michele Hartam-Ellis; 1 s.; 2 d. Educ. University of Tasmania; Australian National University. Research Scientist, Forest Research Institute (Australia); Department of Agriculture, Australian Government; various forestry positions, Associated Pulp and Paper Mills, becoming General Manager, North Forest Products (North Ltd.). Past President, National Association of Forest Industries, Australia; former Vice-President, Australian Forest Development Institute. Recreations: sailing; ski-ing; classic cars; music. Address: (h.) 17 Lansdowne Crescent, Edinburgh EH12 5EH; T.-0131-538 4926.

Binnie, Frank Hugh. Chief Executive, The Internet Society Scotland, since 1998; Senior Executives Career and Training Consultant, since 1997; Millennium Projects International Fundraiser, since 1998; former Chief Executive, The Caledonian Foundation; b. 1.3.50, Edinburgh; m., Fiona Margaret McLean Nicolson (née Hart); 4 s.; 1 d. Educ. Loughborough Grammar; De Montfort University. Design Management Trainee, Corahs Textiles, Leicester, 1970-73; Manufacturing Manager, Floreal Knitwear, Mauritius, 1973-76; Sales Manager, Kemptons Knitwear, Leicester, 1976-79; General Manager Design, Texport Unilever, 1979-82; Manufacturing Manager, Kilspindie Knitwear, 1982-85; Director and Company Secretary, Midlothian Enterprise, 1985-88; Managing Director, Perkins, Hodgkinson and Gillibrand (Coxmore plc), 1988-90; Chief Executive, Scottish Design (formerly Director, The Design Council Scotland), 1990-96. External Assessor, MBA, University of Westminster; Assessor, Management Course, De Montfort University; Member: Licensing Executive, Coutts Scottish Advisory Committee, Institute of Directors, Scottish Council Development and Industry, Guid Club; Visiting Professor in Engineering Design, Strathclyde University; Fellow, Chartered Society of Designers; Fellow, Royal Society of Arts, Design and Manufacturing; Chairman, Textile Institute Fashion, Product Design and Marketing Group. Recreations: yachting; running. Address: (b.) Binnie Consultancy, 6 Randolph Crescent, Edinburgh EH3 7TH; T.-07000 781169; (h.) 18 Fernlea, Bearsden, Glasgow G61 1NB.

Bird, Professor Colin C., MBChB, PhD, FRCPath, FRCPE, FRCSE, FRSE, FAMS. Dean, Faculty of Medicine, Edinburgh University, since 1995; b. 5.3.38, Kirkintilloch; m., Ailsa M. Ross; 2 s.; 1 d. Educ. Lenzie Academy; Glasgow University. McGhie Cancer Research Scholar, Glasgow Royal Infirmary, 1962-64; Lecturer in Pathology: Glasgow University, 1964-67, Aberdeen University, 1967-72; MRC Goldsmiths Travelling Fellow, Chicago, 1970-71; Senior Lecturer in Pathology, Edinburgh University, 1972-75; Professor and Head, Department of Pathology, Leeds University, 1975-86; Professor of Pathology and Head, Department of Pathology, Edinburgh University, 1986-95. Recreations: golf; hill walking; music. Address: (h.) 45 Ann Street, Edinburgh, EH4 1PL.

Bird, Jackie. Journalist; b. 31.7.62, Bellshill; 1 s.; 1 d. Educ. Earnock High School. Music/Film/Television Editor, Jackie Magazine; Radio News Reporter and Presenter, Radio Clyde; Reporter, Evening Times; Reporter, Sun; Reporter/Presenter, TVS; Presenter, Reporting Scotland. Patron, Glasgow Cat and Dog Home. Recreations: swimming; aerobics; running; music; animal welfare. Address; (b.) BBC, Queen Margaret Drive, Glasgow.

Birley, Tim(othy) Grahame, BSc(Eng), MSc, ACGI, FRTPI, FRICS, FRSA. Independent adviser on sustainable development and public policy, since 1995; b. 13.3.47, Kent; m., Catherine Anne; 1 s.; 2 d. Educ. Sir Roger Manwood's Grammar School; Imperial College, London University; Edinburgh University. Local government, 1965-71; academic appointments, 1973-81; Director, Energy and Environment Research, 1982-85; Scottish Office: Inquiry Reporter, 1985-87, Principal Inquiry Reporter, 1987-88, Deputy Director of Building, 1988-90, Head, Rural Affairs Division, 1990-95. Non-Executive Director, RPT (Scotland), 1989-91; Central Scotland Woodlands, 1991-92; Director, Centre for Human Ecology, Edinburgh University, 1995-96; Chair, Project Selection Panel, Millennium Forest for Scotland Trust, 1996-97; Board Member: Forward Scotland, Landwise, Friends of the Earth (Scotland); Vice-President, APRS. Recreation: family outings. Address: (b.) 6 Malta Terrace, Edinburgh EH4 1HR; T.-0131-332 3499.

Birnie, Professor George David, BSc, PhD. Senior Scientist, Beatson Institute for Cancer Research, 1969-99; Honorary Lecturer in Biochemistry, Glasgow University, since 1982; b. 8.8.34, Gourock; m., Jean Gray McCaig; 2 s.; 1 d. Educ. Gourock High School; Greenock High School; Glasgow University. Assistant Lecturer in Biochemistry, Glasgow University, 1959-60; Postdoctoral Fellow, McArdle Memorial Laboratory, University of Wisconsin, 1960-62; Scientist, Imperial Cancer Research Fund Laboratories, London, 1962-69. Kitchener Scholarship, 1952-56; Fulbright Travel Scholarship, 1960-62; US Public Health Service Fellowship, 1960-62; Member: Editorial Advisory Panel, Biochemical Journal, 1981-92, Editorial Board, Biochemical Journal, since 1992. Publications: Editor of five books, author of more than 140 papers. Deacon, Giffnock Congregational Church, 1980-91. Recreation: gardening.

Birss, Rev. Alan David, MA (Hons), BD (Hons). Minister, Paisley Abbey, since 1988; b. 5.6.53, Ellon; m., Carol Margaret Pearson. Educ. Glenrothes High School; St. Andrews University; Edinburgh University. Assistant

Minister, Dundee Parish Church (St. Mary's), 1978-80; Minister, Inverkeithing Parish Church of St. Peter, 1982-88. Secretary, Scottish Church Society; Member, Council, Church Service Society. Address: The Manse of Paisley Abbey, 15 Main Road, Castlehead, Paisley PA2 6AJ; T.-0141-889 3587.

Bishop, Professor Christopher Michael, MA (Oxon), PhD, FBCS. Professor of Computer Science, University of Edinburgh, since 1997; Senior Researcher, Microsoft Research, Cambridge, since 1997; b. 7.4.59, Norwich; m., Jennifer Mary; 2 s. Educ. University of Oxford; University of Edinburgh. AEA Technology, Culham Laboratory; Head of Applied Neurocomputing Centre, AEA Technology, Harwell Laboratory; Professor of Computer Science, Aston University, Birmingham. Recreations: flying light aircraft. Address: Artificial Intelligence, 5 Forrest Hill, Edinburgh EH1 2QL; T.-01223 744751.

Bisset, David W., ALA, MIInfSc, FSA (Scot), DEAB. Secretary, Scottish Esperanto Association, since 1997; Chairman: Architectural Heritage Society of Scotland (Strathclyde), since 1997, Esperanto Publicity Commission, since 1997; b. 8.8.38, Motherwell; m., Jean; 1 s.; 1 d. Educ. Dalziel High, Motherwell; University of Strathclyde. Librarian, Coatbridge Technical College, 1962-72; Head of Library Services, Bell College of Technology, Hamilton, 1972-95. Various positions within the Esperanto Movement in Scotland and Britain; Hon. Vice-President, Hamilton Civic Society. Recreations: cultural tourism; town walking; architectural history. Address: (h.) 47 Airbles Crescent, Motherwell ML1 3AP; T.-01698 263199.

Bissett-Johnson, Professor Alastair, LLB (Nottingham), LLM (Michigan), Barrister. Professor of Private Law, Dundee University, since 1991; b. Northumberland; m., 1, Dr. Winifred McPherson (deceased); 2, Ann Taylor. Educ. Royal Masonic School, Bushey. Assistant Lecturer, Sheffield University, 1963; Lecturer, Bristol University, 1963-67; Senior Lecturer, Monash University, Melbourne, 1968-71, Leicester University, 1971-76; Associate Professor, McGill University, Montreal, 1976-77; Professor, Dalhousie University, Halifax, Nova Scotia, 1977-90. Publications: Family Law in Australia (Co-author); Cases and Materials on Family Law (Co-author); Matrimonial Property Law in Canada (Co-author); The New Divorce Law (Co-author). Recreations: watercolour painting; music; food and wine. Address: (h.) 7 Shaftesbury Road, Dundee DD2 1HF; T.-01382 645264.

Black, Professor Antony, MA (Cantab), PhD (Cantab). Professor in Political Science, Dundee University, since 1994; Author; b. 23.6.36, Leeds; m., Aileen Pow; 4 s.; 1 d. Educ. Shrewsbury School; King's College, Cambridge. Assistant Lecturer, Department of Political Science, Queen's College, Dundee, 1963-66; Lecturer, Department of Political Science, Dundee University, 1967-80; Visiting Associate Professor, School of Government and Public Administration, The American University, Washington, DC, 1975-76. Publications: Monarchy and Community: political ideas in the later conciliar movement (1430-50); Council and Commune: the Council of Basle and the 15th-century heritage; Guilds and civil society in European political thought from the 12th century to the present; State, Community and Human Desire; Community in Historical Perspective (Editor); Political Thought in Europe, 1250-1450. Address: (b.) Department of Political Science, Dundee University, Dundee; T.-Dundee 344592.

Black, Rev. Archibald Tearlach, BSc. Chairman of Council, The Saltire Society, since 1997; retired Church of Scotland minister; b. 10.6.37, Edinburgh; m., Bridget Mary Baddeley; 2 s.; 1 d. Educ. Merchiston School; St. Andrews University; New College, Edinburgh. St. Andrew's Church, Calcutta, 1964-66; St. Columba's, Pont Street, London, 1966-68 (Assistant); Carstairs with Carstairs Junction, 1969-74; Chaplain, The State Hospital; Ness Bank Church, Inverness, 1974-97. Elected Member of Council, National Trust for Scotland, 1991-96, re-elected, 1997. Recreations: photography; the arts; the conservation and enrichment of all aspects of Scotland's natural and cultural heritage. Address: (h.) 16 Elm Park, Inverness IV2 4WN; T.-01463 230588.

Black, Elspeth Catherine, LLB, NP. Solicitor, since 1973; Honorary Sheriff, Dunoon, since 1997; b. 25.10.50, Kilmarnock; m., James Anthony Black; 1 s.; 1 d. Educ. Kilmarnock Academy; Glasgow University. Apprentice, then Assistant, Wright, Johnston and McKenzie, Glasgow, 1971-74; Assistant, Messers Wm. J. Cuthbert and Hogg, Fort William, 1974-75; Assistant, then Partner, Kenneth W. Pendreich and Co. Dunoon, 1975-87; Partner, Elspeth C. Black and Co., Dunoon and Anderson Banks and Co., Oban, Fort William and Balivanich, 1987-98; Partner, Corngall Black, Dunoon, since 1998; accredited Child Law Specialist. Honorary Solicitor to Scottish Amateur Swimming Association. Recreations: swimming coaching (Assistant Coach, Dunoon ASC); running/fitness training. Address: (b.) 63 Hillfoot Street, Dunoon; T.-01369 704777.

Black, Laurie, FRSA. Chairman, Taste of Scotland, since 1994; Chairman, Taste of Burns Country, since 1995; Joint Partner, Fouters Bistro, Ayr, since 1973; Vice-Chairman, Ayrshire Tourism Industry Forum; b. 10.7.48, West Germany; m., Fran; 1 s.; 1 d. Educ. Horley Secondary School; Bournemouth Technical College. Former policeman; left police, 1973, to open restaurant in Ayr. Member, Scottish Tourist Board working party on natural cooking of Scotland; Director: Taste of Scotland, since 1993, Ayrshire and Arran Tourist Board. Recreations: cooking; travel; walking; music; computing; wine; golf. Address: (b.) 2A Academy Street, Ayr; T.-01292 261391.

Black, Professor Robert, QC, LLB (Hons), LLM, FRSA, FRSE. Professor of Scots Law, Edinburgh University, since 1981; Temporary Sheriff, 1981-94; b. 12.6.47, Lockerbie. Educ. Lockerbie Academy; Dumfries Academy; Edinburgh University; McGill University, Montreal. Advocate, 1972; Lecturer in Scots Law, Edinburgh University, 1972-75; Senior Legal Officer, Scottish Law Commission, 1975-78; practised at Scottish bar, 1978-81; QC, 1987; General Editor, The Laws of Scotland: Stair Memorial Encyclopaedia, 1988-96 (formerly Deputy and Joint General Editor). Publications: An Introduction to Written Pleading, 1982; Civil Jurisdiction: The New Rules, 1983. Recreations: beer and books, not necessarily in that order. Address: (h.) 6/4 Glenogle Road, Edinburgh EH3 5HW; T.-0131-557 3571.

Black, Robert William, MA (Hons, Econ), MSc (Town Planning), MSc (Public Policy). Controller of Audit, Accounts Commission for Scotland, since 1995; b. 6.11.46, Banff; m., Doreen Mary Riach; 3 s.; 1 d. Educ. Robert Gordon's College, Aberdeen; Aberdeen University; Heriot-Watt University; Strathclyde University. Nottinghamshire County Council, 1971-73; City of Glasgow Corporation, 1973-75; Strathclyde Regional Council, 1975-85; Chief Executive: Stirling District Council, 1985-90, Tayside Regional Council, 1990-95. Fellow, Royal Statistical Society. Recreations: the outdoors and the arts. Address: (b.) 18 George Street, Edinburgh EH2 2QU.

Black, W.J. Murray, MBE, BSc, PhD, ARICS, FRAgS, JP. Honorary Senior Lecturer, Edinburgh University, since 1970; Farms Director, Edinburgh School of Agriculture, 1970-97; b. 26.7.35, Reading; m., Ann Warren; 3 d. Educ. Leighton Park School, Reading; Reading University; Durham University; College of Estate Management, Reading. Lecturer in Agriculture, Newcastle University, 1959-64; Principal Scientific Officer, Agricultural Institute, Dublin, 1964-70. Member: Farm Animal Welfare Council, London, 1988-97, NCCS (SNH) S.E. Scotland Regional

Board, 1991-96; Honorary Treasurer, British Society of Animal Science, since 1980; President, BSAS, 1995; Chairman of Governors, St. Margaret's School, Edinburgh, 1990-94. Publications: 45 scientific papers. Recreations: DIY houses and restoration of old cars; holidays in France. Address: Glenburnie, Boghall, Biggar Road, Edinburgh EH10 7OX; T.-0131-445 2247.

Black, William Scott, FCIBS, MBA. Director, Operations, UK Bank, Royal Bank of Scotland plc, since 1993; b. 8.3.48; m., Margaret Aitken; 1 s.; 1 d. Educ. Kelso High School; Strathclyde University Business School. Joined Royal Bank of Scotland plc, 1964; Treasurer, John Menzies plc, 1981-82; rejoined Royal Bank of Scotland plc, 1982; General Manager (Development), Royal Scottish Assurance, 1990-91; Assistant Director, Network, Royal Bank of Scotland plc, 1991-93. Recreations: golf; gardening; reading; keep fit. Address: (b.) 42 St. Andrew Square, Edinburgh EH2 2YE; T.-0131-523 2204.

Blackadder, Elizabeth, OBE, RA, RSA. Artist; b. 24.9.31, Falkirk. Educ. Falkirk High School; Edinburgh University; Edinburgh College of Art. Lecturer, School of Drawing and Painting, Edinburgh College of Art, 1962-66; first Scottish woman painter elected full member, Royal Academy and Royal Scottish Academy.

Blackford, Ian. Managing Director, BT Alex Brown, Scotland, since 1993; Hon. President, Paisley University; b. 14.5.61, Edinburgh; m., Mary; 1 s.; 2 d. Educ. Royal High School, Edinburgh. Assistant Fund Manager, Mercury Asset Managers, London, 1986-88; Analyst, Smith New Court, London, 1988-90; Director, Union Bank of Switzerland, London, 1990-93. SNP candidate, Ayr, General Election, 1997, Paisley South, by-election, 1997; elected Member, National Council, SNP; Member, SNP Cabinet with responsibility for social security and pensions. Recreations: reading; walking; rugby; football. Address: (h.) 25 Braid Road, Edinburgh; T.-0131-447 0778; (b.) 74-77 Queen Street, Edinburgh; T.-0131-243 4481.

Blackie, Alan John, BA, DipYCS. Director of Education and Community Services, East Lothian, since 1995; b. 6.6.48, Haddington; 2 d. Educ. Knox Academy, Haddington; Jordanhill College, Glasgow; Open University. Community Education Service, Dunbarton County Council/Strathclyde Regional Council, 1971-79; Community Education Officer, Castlebrae High School, Edinburgh, 1979-87; Education Officer, then Assistant Director of Education, Lothian, 1987-95. Former Chairman, Scottish Youth Work Forum; Chairman, Duke of Edinburgh's Award Advisory Committee (Scotland); Member, Scottish Community Education Council. Recreations: hill-walking; skiing. Address: (h.) Byre Court, East Saltoun, EH34 5ED; T.-01875 340083.

Blackie, Professor John Walter Graham, BA (Cantab), LLB. Professor of Law, Strathclyde University, since 1991 (Senior Lecturer in Scots Law, Edinburgh University, 1988-91, Lecturer, 1975-88); Director, Blackie & Son Ltd., publishers, 1970-93; Advocate, since 1974; b. 2.10.46, Glasgow; m., Jane Ashman. Educ. Uppingham School; Peterhouse, Cambridge; Harvard; Merton College, Oxford; Edinburgh University. Open Exhibitioner, Peterhouse, Cambridge, 1965-68; St. Andrews Society of New York Scholar, Harvard, 1968-69; practised at Scottish bar, 1974-75. Recreations: music; sailing. Address: (h.) 17 Parsonage Square, Glasgow G4 0TA.

Blackshaw, Alan, OBE, VRD. Management Consultant; Member, Cairngorms Partnership Board, since 1998 (Chair, Recreation Forum, since 1998); Academic Adviser, Highlands and Islands University Project, since 1998 (Chair, Tourism, Hospitality and Leisure Group); b. 7.4.33; m., 1, Jane Elizabeth Turner (m. dissolved); 1 d.; 2, Dr. Elspeth Paterson Martin; 1 s.; 2 d. Educ. Merchant Taylors' School, Crosby; Wadham College, Oxford (MA). Royal Marines (commissioned), 1954-56, and RM Reserve, 1956-76. Entered Home Civil Service, Ministry of Power, 1956; Principal Private Secretary to Minister of Power, 1967-69; Department of Energy: Under Secretary, 1974, Offshore Supplies Office, 1974-78 (Director-General, 1977-78), Coal Division, 1978-79; Consultant, N.C.B., 1979-86; Consultant Director, Strategy International, 1980-91; Member: Scottish Council Development and Industry, 1974-78, Scottish Sports Council, 1990-95, Scottish Natural Heritage, 1992-97 (Chairman: Task Force on Access, 1992-94, Audit Committee, 1995-97); Member, Adventure Activities Licensing Authority, since 1996; Director, Moray Badenoch and Strathspey Enterprise, since 1998; Patron, British Mountaineering Council, since 1979 (President, 1973-76); Chairman: Standing Advisory Committee on Mountain Training Policy, 1980-86 and since 1990, Sports Council's National Mountain Centre, Plas y Brenin, 1986-95, Mountaineering Committee, UIAA, (Berne, Switzerland), since 1990, Access and Conservation Working Group, UIAA, 1995-98, UK Mountain Training Board, 1991-94, Scottish National Ski Council, 1991-94, President, since 1994; Honorary Adviser, Mountaineering Council of Scotland, since 1995; Director, Paths for All Partnership, 1996-97; President, Ski Club of Great Britain, since 1997; Freeman, City of London; FRGS; FInstPet. Publication: Mountaineering, 1965. Recreations: mountaineering; skiing. Address: (h.) Rhu Grianach, Kingussie Road, Newtonmore PH20 1AY; T.-01540 673239.

Blackwood, Rev. Keith Thomas, BD, DipMin. Minister, Bearsden North Parish Church, since 1997; b. 29.5.69, Motherwell; m., Katrina Mary. Educ. Dalziel High School, Motherwell; University of Glasgow. Care Assistant, Church of Scotland Homeless Hostel, 1991-93. Recreations: golf; football. Address: 5 Fintry Gardens, Bearsden, Glasgow G61 4RJ; T.-0141-942 0366.

Blair, (Ann) Kay, MA (Hons). Managing Director, Business Perceptions; Marketing Columnist, The Scotsman, since 1990; Board Member, Scottish Legal Aid Board, since 1994; Non-Executive Director, Edinburgh Sick Children's NHS Trust, since 1994; b. 12.4.53, Edinburgh; m., William; 1 s.; 2 d. Educ. James Gillespie's High School for Girls; St. Andrews University; School of Slavonic and Eastern European Studies, London University. Journalist/ Researcher on Eastern Europe and Manager, Business Information Service, Financial Times, 1977-80; Marketing Information Manager, Scottish Development Agency, 1980-81. Recreations: skiing; cinema; travel. Address: (b.) 8 Winton Terrace, Edinburgh EH10 7AP; T.-0131-477 7477.

Blair, Anna Dempster, DPE. Writer and Lecturer; b. 12.2.27, Glasgow; m., Matthew Blair; 1 s.; 1 d. Educ. Hutchesons' Girls Grammar School, Glasgow; Dunfermline College. Novels: A Tree in the West; The Rowan on the Ridge; Short Stories: Tales of Ayrshire; Scottish Tales; The Goose Girl of Eriska; Seed Corn; social history: Tea at Miss Cranston's; Croft and Creel; More Tea at Miss Cranston's. Recreations: film-making; travel; reading; friendship. Address: (h.) 20 Barrland Drive, Giffnock, Glasgow G46 7QD; T.-0141-638 0676.

Blair, Frank. Director Scotland, Advisory Conciliation and Arbitration Service, since 1995; b. 18.4.48, Wishaw; m., Brenda; 2 s.; 1 d. Various posts, Department of Employment/Employment Service, 1967-82; ACAS Conciliator, 1982-91; Deputy Director Scotland, 1991-95. Recreation: golf. Address: (b.) 123 Bothwell Street, Glasgow; T.-0141-248 1400.

Blair, James Ballantyne, BL, InstAM (Dip). Honorary Sheriff, Grampian, Highland and Islands at Stonehaven, since 1989; b. 16.8.24, Dailly, Ayrshire; m., Margaret M.J. McCafferty (deceased); 2 s.; 2 d. Educ. Peebles High School; Edinburgh University. Post Office, Peebles, 1941-

44; Royal Signals, 1944-48 (GHQ (I) Signals, New Delhi, 1945-47); Sheriff Clerk's Offices, Edinburgh, Inverness, Peebles, Dingwall, Glasgow, 1948-73; Sheriff Clerk of Aberdeenshire at Aberdeen, 1973-82. Recreations: opera/operetta; reading (current affairs and law reports). Address: 41 Woodcot Park, Stonehaven AB39 2HG; T.-01569 762067.

Blair, John Samuel Greene, OBE (Mil), TD, KStJ, BA, Hon. DLitt (St. Andrews), ChM, FRCSEdin, FICS, D(Obst)RCOG. Reader, History of Medicine, St. Andrews University, since 1997 (Senior Lecturer, 1993-97); Honorary Senior Lecturer in Surgery, Dundee University, 1967-90; Member, Editorial Board, Vesalius, since 1994; b. 31.12.28, Wormit, Fife; m., Ailsa Jean Bowes, MBE; 2 s.; 1 d. Educ. Dundee High School; St. Andrews University (Harkness Scholar, 1946-50). National Service, RAMC, 1952-55; Tutor, Department of Anatomy, St. Salvator's College, St. Andrews, 1955; surgical and research training, Manchester, Dundee, Cambridge, London, 1957-65; Member, Court of Examiners, Royal College of Surgeons of Edinburgh, 1964-93; Consultant Surgeon, Perth Royal Infirmary, 1965-90; postgraduate Clinical Tutor, Perth, 1966-74; first North American Travelling Fellow, St. Andrews/Dundee Universities, 1971; Secretary, Tayside Area Medical Advisory Committee, 1974-83; Member, Education Advisory Committee, Association of Surgeons, 1984-88; Secretary, Perth and Kinross Division, British Medical Association, 1982-90; Member, Scottish Council and Chairman's Sub-Committee, BMA, 1985-89; Fellow of the BMA, 1990; Chairman, Armed Forces Committee, BMA, 1992-98; President: British Society for the History of Medicine, 1993-95, Scottish Society for the History of Medicine, 1990-93; Honorary Colonel (TA), RAMC; Member, Principal's Council, St Andrews University, since 1989; Elder, Church of Scotland; Hospitaller, Priory of Scotland, Order of St. John of Jerusalem; Mitchiner Lecturer, Army Medical Services, 1994. Publications: books on medical history and anatomy including the history of medicine at St. Andrews University, 1987, and the history of the RAMC, 1998. Recreations: golf; travel; bridge. Address: (h.) 143 Glasgow Road, Perth; T.-Perth 623739.

Blair, John Woodman, BA Oxon, LLB, WS. Senior Partner, Anderson Strathern WS, since 1992; b. 25.1.37, Edinburgh; m., Claire Ford; 1 s.; 2 d. Educ. Radley College; Brasenose College, Oxford; Edinburgh University. Partner then Senior Partner, Strathern and Blair WS until amalgamation with J. & F. Anderson, WS, 1992. Director, Edinburgh Fund Managers; Trustee, Royal Botanic Garden, Edinburgh. Recreation: gardening. Address: (b.) 48 Castle Street, Edinburgh EH2 3LX; T.-0131-220 2345.

Blair, Michael, FTS. Marketing Manager, Caledonian MacBrayne, since 1996; b. 5.12.43, Glasgow; m., Margaret; 1 d. Educ. Rothesay Academy. Merchant Navy, 1961-66; Assistant Tourist Officer, Glasgow Corporation, 1966-75; Tourist Officer, Cunninghame District Council, 1975-91; Director, Dunoon and Cowal Tourist Board, 1991-93; Director of Tourism, Bute and Cowal Tourist Board, 1993-96. Recreations: sailing; swimming. Address: (h.) 5 Eaglesham Terrace, Rothesay PA20 9HL; T.-01700 503211.

Blair, Robin Leitch, MB, ChB, FRCSEdin, FRCS(C), FACS. Head, Department of Otolaryngology, Ninewells Hospital and Medical School, Dundee, since 1984; Clinical Director of Otolaryngology, Dundee Teaching Hospitals NHS Trust; b. 28.11.45, Gourock; m., Elizabeth Anne Manson; 2 d. Educ. Greenock Academy; Edinburgh University; University of Toronto. House Surgeon, Royal Infirmary, Edinburgh; Lecturer, Department of Anatomy, Glasgow University; Assistant Professor, Department of Otolaryngology, University of Toronto. Address: (b.) Department of Otolaryngology, Ninewells Hospital and Medical School, Dundee DD1 9SY; T.-01382 660111, Ext. 32162.

Blair, Robin Orr, MA, LLB, WS. Partner, Turcan Connell WS, since 1997, Dundas & Wilson, 1967-97 (Managing Partner, 1976-83 and 1988-91); Director, Tullis Russell Group Ltd. Educ. Rugby School; St. Andrews University; Edinburgh University. Purse Bearer to the Lord High Commissioner to General Assembly of Church of Scotland. Address: (b.) Saltire Court, 20 Castle Terrace, Edinburgh, EH1 2EF; T.-0131-228 8111.

Blake, Professor Christopher, CBE, FRSE, MA, PhD. Chairman, Glenrothes Development Corporation, 1987-96; b. 28.4.26; m.; 2 s.; 2 d. Educ. Dollar Academy; St. Andrews University. Royal Navy, 1944-47; teaching posts, 1951-53; Assistant, Edinburgh University, 1953-55; Stewarts & Lloyds Ltd., 1955-60; Lecturer, then Senior Lecturer, St Andrews University, 1960-67; Dundee University: Senior Lecturer, then Professor of Economics, 1967-74; Bonar Professor of Applied Economics, 1974-88; Director, Alliance Trust plc, 1974-94; Director, William Low & Co. plc, 1980-90 (Chairman, 1985-90). Recreation: golf. Address: (h.) Westlea, 14 Wardlaw Gardens, St. Andrews, Fife, KY16 9DW.

Blakey, Rev. Ronald Stanton, MA, BD, MTh. Deputy Secretary, Department of Education, Church of Scotland, since 1981; Secretary, Assembly Council, from 1 Aug., 1988; b. 3.7.38, Glasgow; m., Kathleen Dunbar; 1 s. Educ. Hutchesons' Boys' Grammar School, Glasgow; Glasgow University. Minister: St. Mark's, Kirkconnel, 1963-67; Bellshill West, 1967-72; Jedburgh Old Parish with Edgerston and Ancrum, 1972-81. Member, Roxburgh District Council, 1974-80 (Chairman of Council, 1977-80); Religious Adviser, Border Television, 1973-81; Member, Borders Region Children's Panel, 1974-80; JP, 1974-80. Publication: The Man in the Manse, 1978. Recreation: collecting antiquarian books on Scotland. Address: (h.) 61 Orchard Brae Avenue, Edinburgh EH4.

Blanchflower, Brian William, BSc (Hons), PGCSE (Distinction). Rector, Lochgelly High School, Fife, since 1996; b. 8.1.56, Belfast; m., Karen Ann Simpson; 1 s.; 1 d. Educ. Dunfermline High School; University of Edinburgh; Moray House College of Education. Teacher of Mathematics and Geography, Inverkeithing High School, 1979-83; Assistant Principal Teacher of Geography, Buckhaven High School, 1983-84; Principal Teacher of Geography, Beath High School, 1984-87; Assistant Rector, 1987-90, Depute Rector, 1990-96, Lochgelly High School. Recreations: rugby; hill-walking. Address: (b.) Lochgelly High School, Station Road, Lochgelly, Fife KY5 8LZ; T.-01592 418000.

Blaxter, Professor John Harry Savage, MA (Oxon), DSc (Oxon), HonDUniv(Stirling), FIBiol, FRSE. Hon. Professor, Stirling University and St. Andrews University; Hon. Research Fellow, Scottish Association for Marine Science; b. 6.1.29, London; m., Valerie Ann McElligott; 1 s.; 1 d. Educ. Berkhamsted School; Brasenose College, Oxford. SO, then SSO, Marine Laboratory, Aberdeen, 1952-64; Lecturer, Zoology Department, Aberdeen University, 1964-69; PSO, 1969, SPSO, 1974, DCSO, 1985-91, Scottish Marine Biological Association, Oban; President, Fisheries Society of the British Isles, 1992-97 (Beverton Medal, 1998); Editor, Advances in Marine Biology, 1980-97; Editor, ICES Journal of Marine Science, 1991-97; Member, Editorial Board, Encyclopaedia of Ocean Sciences, since 1998. Recreations:golf; gardening. Address: (h.) Dems Lodge, Barcaldine, Oban PA37 1SF.

Bleiman, David, MA, MBA, MIPD. Assistant General Secretary (Scotland), Association of University Teachers, since 1982; Member, STUC General Council, since 1990;

Member, East of Scotland Water Authority, since 1998; b. 7.8.53, Cape Town; m., Maureen McGibbon; 1 s.; 1 d. Educ. Haberdashers' Aske's School; Christ's College and King's College, Cambridge. W.E.A. Tutor, 1978; General Secretary, Scottish Further Education Association, 1979-82. Publication: Labour and Scottish Nationalism (Co-author), 1980. Recreations:listening to German language programmes; birdwatching; wind-up gramophones. Address: (b.) 6 Castle Street, Edinburgh EH2 3AT; T.-0131-226 6694.

Bloomer, Keir, BA. Executive Director, Education and Community Services, Clackmannanshire, since 1996; b. 1.7.47, Glasgow; m., Jacquetta Megarry; 1 s.; 1 d. Educ. Greenock Academy; Cambridge University. Teacher, 1969-81; Depute General Secretary, Educational Institute of Scotland, 1981-84; Education Officer, then Depute Director of Education, Strathclyde Regional Council, 1984-95. Address: Lime Tree House, Alloa FK10 1EX; T.-01259 452435.

Bloxwich, Janet Elizabeth. Principal Bassoon, Orchestra of Scottish Opera, since 1980; b. 11.4.56, Brentwood; m., Alan J. Warhurst. Educ. Belfairs High School; Southend Technical College; Royal College of Music, London. Two years freelancing in London; on staff at Royal Scottish Academy, since 1997. Recreations: hillwalking; wood-turning; instrument repairs; cooking. Address: 91 Fotheringay Road, Pollokshields, Glasgow G41 4LH; T.-0141-423 2303.

Bluck, Professor Brian John, BSc, PhD, DSc, FRSE, FGS. Professor of Tectonics and Sedimentation, University of Glasgow, since 1989; b. 29.8.35, Bridgend, S. Wales; m., Barbra Mary; 1 s.; 1 d. Educ. Bridgend County Grammar; University College, Wales. Visiting Research Scholar, University of Illinois, USA, 1961; NATO Research Fellow, 1962; Assistant Lecturer, 1962, Reader, 1981, University of Glasgow. Awarded Keith Medal, Royal Society of Edinburgh, 1981; Lyell Fund, Geological Society of London, 1981; Saltire/Royal Bank of Scotland Award for contributions to geology in Scotland, 1991. Recreations: hill-walking; music; theatre. Address: (b.) Department of Geology and Applied Geology, University of Glasgow, Glasgow G12 8QQ; T.-0141-330 5447.

Boddy, Francis Andrew, MB, ChB, FRCPEdin, FFPHM, DPH. Department of Public Health, Glasgow University, since 1998; b. 1.3.35, York; m., Adele Wirszubska; 2 d. Educ. Prince Henry's Grammar School, Otley; Edinburgh University. Research Associate, New York City Department of Health; Senior Lecturer, Department of Community Medicine, Glasgow University; Director, Public Health Research Unit (formerly Social Paediatric and Obstetric Research Unit), Glasgow University, 1978-98. Honorary Secretary, Society for Social Medicine, 1982-87, Chairman, 1996; Convener, Scottish Affairs Committee, Faculty of Public Health Medicine, 1991-94. Publications on socio-medical and public health topics. Recreations: fishing; photography. Address: (b.) 1 Lilybank Gardens, Glasgow G12; T.-0141-330 5399.

Bolland, Alexander, QC (Scot),. BD, LLB; b. 21.11.50, Kilmarnock; m., Agnes Hunter Pate Moffat; 1 s.; 2 d. Educ. Kilmarnock Academy; St. Andrews University; Glasgow University. Admitted Faculty of Advocates, 1978; Captain, Army Legal Services, 1978-80; Standing Junior Counsel to Department of Employment in Scotland, 1988-92; QC (Scot), since 1992; Temporary Sheriff, since 1988; part-time Chairman, Industrial Tribunals, since 1992. Recreations: Hellenistics; walking; reading. Address: (h.) 60 North Street, St. Andrews, Fife; T.-01334 474599.

Bomont, Robert George, DUniv, BSc (Econ), IPFA, JP. University Secretary, Stirling University, 1973-95; General Commissioner of Income Tax, since 1977; b. 6.5.35, Preston; m., Marian; 1 s.; 2 d. Educ. Preston Grammar School; London University. Trainee and qualified accountant, Lancashire County Council, 1951-64; Assistant Finance Officer, Lancaster University, 1964-66; Accountant, then Accountant and Deputy Secretary, Stirling University, 1966-73. Member, Council of Management, Strathcarron Hospice. Recreations: golf; gardening; DIY. Address: (h.) Wester Ardoch, Feddal Road, Braco, by Dunblane, Perthshire.

Bonallack, Michael Francis, OBE. Secretary, Royal and Ancient Golf Club of St. Andrews, since 1983; b. 31.12.34. Address: (b.) St. Andrews, KY16 9JD.

Bond, Marj, DA, RSW, SSA. Painter; b. Renfrewshire; m., James A. Gray; 1 s.; 2 d. Educ. Paisley Grammar School; Glasgow School of Art. Teacher, Outer Hebrides and Inverness-shire until 1963; bringing up children; first one-woman show, Edinburgh, 1975; ran Fair Maids Gallery until 1988; paining full time since 1988; exhibited RSA, RSW and RA. Member, Dundee Printmakers Workshop. Recreations: music; gliding; collecting handmade paper. Address: Eden Cottage, Old Town, Gateside, Fife KY14 7SY; T.-01337 860569.

Bond, Professor Sir Michael R., MD, PhD, FRSE, FRCSEdin, FRCPsych, FRCPSGlas, DPM, DSc (Leics, Hon). Professor of Psychological Medicine, Glasgow University, 1973-98 (former Administrative Dean, Faculty of Medicine); b. 15.4.36, Balderton, Nottinghamshire; m., Jane; 1 s.; 1 d. Educ. Magnus Grammar School, Newark; Sheffield University. Former Vice-Principal, Glasgow University; Chairman, Head Injuries Trust for Scotland; Member, Council, St. Andrews Ambulance Association; Fellow, Royal Society of Arts; Knight Bachelor, 1995. Recreations: reading; music; painting. Address: (b.) Academic Centre, Gartnavel Royal Hospital, 1055 Great Western Road, Glasgow G12 0XH.

Bone, Professor (James) Drummond, MA. Vice-Principal, Glasgow University, since 1995; b. 11.7.47, Ayr; m., Vivian. Educ. Ayr Academy; Glasgow University; Balliol College, Oxford. Lecturer in English and Comparative Literary Studies, Warwick University; Lecturer and Senior Lecturer, English Literature, Glasgow University. Academic Editor and Advisory Editor, The Byron Journal; Editor, Romanticism. Recreations: music; skiing; Maseratis. Address: (h.) The Old Manse, Bow of Fife, Cupar, Fife.

Bone, Professor Thomas R., CBE, MA, MEd, PhD, FCCEA, FRSGS. Professor and Deputy Principal, Strathclyde University, until 1996 (Principal, Jordanhill College, 1972-92); b. 2.1.35, Port Glasgow; m., Elizabeth Stewart; 1 s.; 1 d. Educ. Port Glasgow High School; Greenock High School; Glasgow University; Jordanhill College. Teacher of English, Paisley Grammar School, 1957-62; Lecturer in Education: Jordanhill College, 1962-63, Glasgow University, 1963-67; Head of Education Department, Jordanhill College, 1967-71. Member, Dunning Committee, 1975-77; Chairman, Educational Advisory Council, IBA, 1985-88; Vice-Chairman: Scottish Examination Board, 1977-84; Scottish Tertiary Education Advisory Council, 1984-87; Chairman: Scottish Council for Educational Technology, 1981-87, Standing Conference on Studies in Education, 1982-84, Council for National Academic Awards Board for Organisation and Management, 1983-87, Council for National Academic Awards Committee for Teacher Education, 1987-89, General Teaching Council for Scotland, 1990-91; Member, Complaints Committee, Law Society of Scotland. Publication: School Inspection in Scotland, 1968; articles in journals. Recreation: golf. Address: (h.) 7 Marchbank Gardens, Ralston, Paisley.

Bonnar, Anne Elizabeth, MA. Director, Bonnar Keenlyside; Arts Management Consultant; b. 9.10.55, St. Andrews; m., Fernley Thompson; 2 s.; 2 d. Educ. Dumbarton Academy; Glasgow University; City University, London; Jordanhill College of Education. Theatre Manager, Young Vic Theatre, London, 1980; Director, Circuit, 1982, 1983; Press and Publicity, Mayfest, 1984, 1985; Publicity Officer, Citizens' Theatre, Glasgow, 1981-85; Arts Public Relations Consultant, 1985-86; General Manager, Traverse Theatre, 1986-91. Address: (b.) The Grange, Burntisland, Fife KY3 0AA; T.-01592 874478.

Bonnar, David James. Director (National Lottery), Scottish Arts Council, since 1994; b. 20.10.50, Dunfermline; m., Sally Elizabeth Armour; 2 s. Educ. Dunfermline High School. Royal Bank of Scotland, 1968-73; Theatre Royal, Glasgow, 1975-80; Theatre Royal, Newcastle upon Tyne, 1980-84; General Manager, Perth Repertory Theatre, 1984-94. Recreations: singing; gardening; opera; architecture. Address: (b.) Scottish Arts Council, 12 Manor Place, Edinburgh; T.-0131-226 6051.

Bonnington, Alistair James, LLB (Hons). Solicitor, BBC Scotland, since 1992; part-time Lecturer, University of Glasgow, since 1990; b. 28.5.52, Glasgow; m., Alison Margaret; 2 s.; 1 d. Educ. Hillhead High School, Glasgow; University of Glasgow. Apprentice, Biggart, Baillie and Gifford, Solicitors, Glasgow; pursued career in private practice, specialising in court work and media law. Secretary, Scottish Media Lawyers' Society. Publication: Scots Law for Journalists (Co-Author). Recreation: golf. Address: (b.) Broadcasting House, Queen Margaret Drive, Glasgow G12 8DG; T.-0141-338 2352.

Bonomy, Hon. Lord (Iain Bonomy). Senator of the College of Justice, since 1997; b. 15.1.46, Motherwell; m., Jan; 2 d. Educ. Dalziel High School; University of Glasgow. Apprentice Solicitor, East Kilbride Town Council, 1968-70; Solicitor, Ballantyne & Copland, 1970-83; Advocate, 1984-93; Queen's Counsel, 1993-96; Advocate Depute, 1990-93; Home Advocate Depute, 1993-96. Address: (b.) Parliament House, Edinburgh; T.-0131-225 2595.

Booker-Milburn, Sheriff Donald, BA, LLB. Sheriff of Grampian Highland and Islands, since 1983. Address: Sheriff Court House, The Castle, Inverness, IV2 3EG.

Boon, Nicholas, MA, BChir, MD, FRCPE. Consultant Cardiologist, Royal Infirmary of Edinburgh, since 1986; Honorary Senior Lecturer, University of Edinburgh, since 1986; b. 31.12.50, London; m., Anne Robertson; 2 d. Educ. Canford School, Dorset; Gonville and Caius College, Cambridge University; Middlesex Hospital Medical School, London. Lecturer and Senior Registrar in Cardiovascular Medicine, John Radcliffe Hospital, Oxford, 1983-86; Clinical Director, Royal Infirmary, Edinburgh, since 1996. Member: Council, British Cardiac Society, since 1994, Council, British Heart Foundation, since 1997. Author of scientific papers on heart disease; Co-Editor, Davidson's Principles and Practice of Medicine, 18th Edition. Recreations: golf; skiing. Address: Department of Cardiology, Royal Infirmary of Edinburgh, Edinburgh EH3 9YW; T.-0131-536 2004/6.

Borland, Marjorie Kirsteen, DA, RIBA, ARIAS, SpDip, FRTPI. Retired; Commissioner, Royal Fine Art Commission for Scotland, 1986-96; b. 13.1.25, Glasgow; m., John Charles Holmes, MC; 1 s.; 1 d. Educ. Westbourne School for Girls; Glasgow School of Architecture; School of Planning, London. Planner, London CC; Partner, Jack Holmes & Partners, Architects; Principal, The Jack Holmes Planning Group; Planning Consultant. Past Convener: RIAS Environment Committee, GIA Environment Committee. Address: (h.) Old Wing, Drumhead, Cardross G82 5EZ; T.-0138 984 1217.

Borley, Lester, CBE, DLitt, FRSGS, FTS, FRSA. Chairman: Icomos (UK), Cultural Tourism Committee; Council Member, Europe Nostra; Adviser, World Monuments Fund; b. 7.4.31, Pontardawe, S. Wales; m., Mary Alison Pearce; 3 d. Educ. Dover County Grammar School; Queen Mary College, University of London. Joined British Travel Association, London, 1955: Assistant to General Manager (USA), New York, 1956-61, Manager, Midwestern States (USA), Chicago, 1961-64, Manager, Australia, 1964-67, Manager, West Germany, Frankfurt, 1967-70; Chief Executive, Scottish Tourist Board, 1970-75; Chief Executive, English Tourist Board, 1975-83; Director, National Trust for Scotland, 1983-93; Secretary General, Europe Nostra, The Hague, 1992-96; Visiting Lecturer, Academia Istropolitana, Slovakia. Vice President, Edinburgh Film House; Trustee: Hopetoun House Trust, Cromarty Arts Trust. Recreations: gardening; visiting museums and galleries; reading social history; music. Address: (h.) 4 Belford Place, Edinburgh EH4 3DH; T.-0131-332 2364.

Borthwick, Alan Charles, LLB, NP. Partner, Brechin Tindal Oatts, Solicitors, Glasgow and Edinburgh, since 1983; b. 25.4.57, Glasgow; m., Sheila; 1 d. Educ. Glasgow Academy; Glasgow University. Brechin Robb, Solicitors, 1977-81; joined Tindal Oatts & Rodger, 1981. Member, Council, Law Society of Scotland, 1995-98; Board Member, Children's Hospice Association Scotland; a Trustee, Parents Oncology Support, Yorkhill. Recreations: golf; skiing; garden; family. Address: (b.) 48 St. Vincent Street, Glasgow G2 5HS; T.-0141-221 8012.

Borthwick of that Ilk, Lord (John Hugh Borthwick). 24th Lord Borthwick; Hereditary Falconer of Scotland to The Queen; b. 14.11.40; m.; 2 d. Educ. Gordonstoun; Edinburgh School of Agriculture. Address: (h.) Crookston, Heriot, Midlothian EH38 5YS.

Boswell, Sir Alexander, KCB, CBE, DL. Chairman, Scottish Veterans' Residences; Member, Scottish Advisory Committee, Army Benevolent Fund; President, Friends of St. Mary's, Haddington; b. 3.8.28, Malaya (of Scottish parents); m., Jocelyn Pomfret; 5 s. Educ. Merchiston Castle School; RMA, Sandhurst. Enlisted in Army, 1947; commissioned Argyll & Sutherland Highlanders, 1948; regimental appointments, 1949-58; Staff College, Camberley, 1959; Military Assistant (GSO 2) to GOC Berlin, 1960-62; Company Commander, then Second in Command 1 A & SH, Malaya and Borneo, 1963-65; Directing Staff, Staff College, Camberley, 1965-68; Commanding Officer, 1 A & SH, 1968-71; Colonel GS Army Strategic Command, 1971; Brigadier Commanding 39 Infantry Brigade, 1972-74; Chief of Staff, 1st British Corps, 1974-76; National Defence College, Canada, 1976-77; GOC 2nd Armoured Division, 1978-80; Director, Territorial Army and Cadets, 1980-82; GOC Scotland and Governor of Edinburgh Castle, 1982-85; Lieutenant Governor and Commander in Chief, Bailiwick of Guernsey, 1985-90. Address: c/o Bank of Scotland, 52 Shandwick Place, Edinburgh EH2 4SB.

Boswell, Lorne, BA. Scottish Secretary, Equity, since 1990; b. 9.1.59, Bridge of Allan; m., Noreen; 2 s.; 1 d. Freelance theatre worker and stage manager, 1981-89. Address: (b.) 114 Union Street, Glasgow G1 3QQ; T.-0141 248 2472.

Bouchier, Professor Ian Arthur Dennis, CBE, MB, ChB, MD, FRCP, FRCPEdin, FFPHM, Hon. FCP (SAf), FIBiol, FRSE, FRSA. Professor of Medicine, Edinburgh University, 1986-97 (now Emeritus Professor); b. 7.9.32, Cape Town, South Africa; m., Patricia Norma Henshilwood; 2 s. Educ. Rondebosch Boys High School; Cape Town University. Instructor in Medicine, School of Medicine, Boston University, 1964; London University: Senior Lecturer in Medicine, 1965; Reader in Medicine,

1970; Professor of Medicine, Dundee University, 1973-86. Member: Court, Dundee University, Council, Royal Society, Edinburgh, Medical Research Council; former Chief Scientist, Scotland; Past President, World Organization of Gastroenterology; former Dean, Faculty of Medicine and Dentistry, Dundee University; Past President, British Society of Gastroenterology. Publications: Clinical Skills (2nd edition), 1982; Gastroenterology (3rd edition), 1982; Gastroenterology: clinical science and practice (2nd edition), 1993. Recreations: music; history of whaling; cooking. Address: (h.) 8A Merchiston Park, Edinburgh EH10 4PN.

Boulton, Professor Geoffrey Stewart, FRS, FRSE, BSc, PhD, DSc, FGS. Regius Professor of Geology and Mineralogy, Edinburgh University, since 1986; Provost and Dean, Faculty of Science and Engineering, since 1994; b. 28.11.40, Stoke-on-Trent; m., Denise Bryers; 2 d. Educ. Longton High School; Birmingham University. Geological Survey of GB, 1962-64; University of Keele, 1964-65; Birmingham University, 1965-67; Water Supply Department, Kenya, 1968; University of East Anglia, 1968-81; Extraordinary Professor, University of Amsterdam, 1981-86. Kirk Bryan Award of the Geological Society of America, 1976; President, Quaternary Research Association, 1991-94; President, British Glaciological Society, 1989-91; President, Geological Society of Edinburgh, 1991-94; Member: Nature Conservancy Council for Scotland Science Board, 1991-92, Natural Environmental Research Council, 1993-98 (Chair, Earth Science and Technology Board, 1993-98), Royal Commission on Environmental Pollution, Scottish Higher Education Funding Council, since 1997, Scottish Association for Marine Science Council, since 1998, Royal Society Council, since 1997. Recreations: violin; mountaineering. Address: (b.) Department of Geology and Geophysics, University of Edinburgh, Grant Institute, Kings Buildings, West Mains Road, Edinburgh EH9 3JW.

Bovey, Keith S., BL. Solicitor, since 1951; President, Scottish CND; b. 31.7.27, Renfrew; m., Helen Cameron; 1 s.; 1 d. Educ. Paisley Grammar School; Glasgow University. Army, 1944-48. Publication: Misuse of Drugs, A Handbook for Lawyers. Address: (b.) 126 Morningside Road, Edinburgh EH10 4DT; T.-0131-452 8822.

Bowd, Nicholas John, CA. Director of Procurement, Scottish Office, since 1996; b. 3.4.45, Glasgow; m., Marjory; 2 d. Educ. High School of Glasgow; University of Glasgow. Qualified Assistant, Paterson & Steel CA, 1969; IBM UK, 1970-88 and 1991-95; IBM Europe (Paris), 1988-91; Motorola EICD (Swindon), 1996. Recreations: golf; rugby; football; personal investment; cars. Address: (b.) James Craig Walk, Edinburgh EH1 3BA; T.-0131-244 3504.

Bowdler, Timothy John, BSc, MBA. Chief Executive, Johnston Press plc; b. 16.5.47, Wolverhampton; m., Margaretha Eklund; 2 d. Educ. Wrekin College; Birmingham University; London Business School. Recreations: golf; tennis; skiing. Address: (b.) 53 Manor Place, Edinburgh EH3 7EG; T.-0131-225 3361.

Bowen, Edward Farquharson, TD, QC, LLB. Advocate; Sheriff Principal, Glasgow and Strathkelvin, since 1997; b. 1.5.45, Edinburgh; m., Patricia Margaret Brown; 2 s.; 2 d. Educ. Melville College, Edinburgh; Edinburgh University. Admitted Solicitor, 1968; Advocate, 1970; Standing Junior Counsel, Scottish Education Department, 1976; Advocate Depute, 1979-83; Sheriff of Tayside, Central and Fife, at Dundee, 1983-90; Partner, Thorntons WS, 1990-91; resumed practice at Scottish Bar; QC, 1992; Chairman (Part-time) Industrial Tribunals, 1995-97; Member, Criminal Injuries Compensation Board, 1996-97; Governor, Dundee Institute of Technology, 1987-90. Served RAOC TA/TAVR, 1964-80. Recreation: golf. Address: (b.) Sheriff's Chambers, Sheriff Court, 1 Carlton Place, Glasgow G5 9DA.

Bowler, David P., BA, MPhil, FSA Scot. Director, Scottish Urban Archaeological Trust, since 1993; b. 9.12.55, Southampton. Educ. McGill University, Montreal; Lincoln College, Oxford. Address: (b.) 55 South Methven Street, Perth PH1 5NX; T.-01738 622393.

Bowlt, Kenneth Stuart, BSc, FRICS. Chartered Surveyor; Member, Royal Institution of Chartered Surveyors Scottish Council, since 1990; b. 7.7.52, Nairn; m., Edith Bowman. Educ. Queen Victoria School, Dunblane; Edinburgh University. Voluntary Service Overseas, Zambia, 1975-80; set up Bowlts (chartered surveyors practice), 1991. Member, Royal Institution of Chartered Surveyors in Scotland Rural Practice Divisional Committee, since 1988, Divisional Council, since 1997; Secretary/Treasurer, West Ross Deer Management Group, since 1991; Member, Panel of Agricultural Arbiters, since 1998. Recreations: fishing; stalking; five-a-side football; keep fit. Address: (h.) Muirfield, 27 Forteath Avenue, Elgin; T.-01343 552088.

Bowman, Professor Adrian William, BSc (Hons), DipMathStat, PhD. Professor of Statistics, University of Glasgow, since 1995; b. 3.1.55, Ayr; m., Janet Edith Forster; 2 s.; 1 d. Educ. Prestwick Academy; Ayr Academy; University of Glasgow; University of Cambridge. Lecturer in Mathematical Statistics, University of Manchester, 1981-86; University of Glasgow: Lecturer in Statistics, 1986-90, Senior Lecturer in Statistics, 1990-92, Reader in Statistics, 1992-95. Publications: Applied Smoothing Techniques for Data Analysis, (Co-author), 1997; Statistical Problem Solving (Co-editor), 1999. Recreations: music, particularly singing. Address: (b.) Department of Statistics, University of Glasgow, Glasgow G12 8QQ; T.-0141-330 4046.

Bowman, (Bernard) Neil, LLB, NP. Consultant, formerly Senior Partner, Bowman Scottish Lawyers, Solicitors, Dundee and Forfar, 1984-98; b. 11.11.43, Dundee; m., Pamela Margaret Munro Wright; 2 d. Educ. High School of Dundee; Edinburgh University; St. Andrews University. Apprenticeship, Sturrock Morrison & Gilruth, Solicitors, Dundee, 1967-69; admitted Solicitor, 1969; Notary Public, 1970; assumed Partner, Gray Robertson & Wilkie (subsequently Bowman Gray Robertson and Wilkie, now Bowman) 1971. Secretary: Dundee Institute of Architects, 1970-96, Dundee Building Trades (Employers) Association, 1970-89, Dundee Construction Industry Group Training Association, 1970-93, Tayside Construction Safety Association, 1975-89; Joint Secretary, Local Joint Council for Building Industry, 1970-89, and Local Joint Apprenticeship Committee for the Building Industry, 1970-89; Clerk, Three United Trades of Dundee and to Mason Trade, Wright Trade and Slater Trade of Dundee, since 1970; Lord Dean of Guild of Guildry Incorporation of Dundee, 1987-90; first Lord President, Court of Deans of Guild of Scotland, 1989; Director, High School of Dundee, 1980-90; Chairman, High School of Dundee Scholarship Fund, 1987-90; Co-opted Member, Law Society of Scotland Committees — Public Relations and Conference, 1982-90, Complaints, 1987-90; Member: Working Party on "Corporate Conveyancing", 1989, School Age Team Sports Enquiry, 1989; Committee Member and National Selector, Scottish Cricket Union, 1974-83; Selector, 1990; President: Scottish Counties Cricket Board, 1981, Scottish Cricket Union, 1989. Recreations: cricketophile; breeding Highland cattle. Address: (b.) 27 Bank Street, Dundee; T.-01382 322267.

Bowman, Sheriff Pamela Margaret Munro, LLB, NP. All Scotland Sheriff; b. 1.8.44, Stirling; m., (Bernard) Neil Bowman; 2 d. Educ. Beacon School, Bridge of Allan, Stirling High School; Queens College, Dundee, St. Andrews University. Admitted Solicitor and Notary Public,

1967; Member, Scottish Legal Aid Board, 1994-97; Non-Executive Director, Angus NHS Trust, 1994-97. Recreations: theatre; literature; Highland cattle. Address: Newhouse of Balgavies, near Forfar, Angus, DD8 2TH; T.-01307 818258.

Bowman, Professor Emeritus William Cameron, BPharm, PhD, DSc, FIBiol, FRSE, FRSA, FRPharmS, HonFFARCS. Head, Department of Physiology and Pharmacology, Strathclyde University, 1966-87 and 1990-94; b. 26.4.30; m., Anne Wyllie Stafford; 1 s.; 1 d. Educ. London University. RAF (commissioned officer), 1955-57; Lecturer, then Reader in Pharmacology, London University, 1952-66. Dean, School of Pharmaceutical Sciences, Strathclyde University, 1974-77; Vice Principal, Strathclyde University, 1986-90; Visiting Professor: McGill University, Montreal; Cornell University, New York; Ohio Medical College. Member: Nomenclature Committee, BP Commission, 1964-67; Biology Committee, MOD, 1966-75; TCT and SEAR Sub-Committees, CSM, 1972-83; Biomedical Research Committee, SHHD, 1980-85; Chairman, Committee: British Pharmacological Society, 1981-84 (Foreign Secretary 1992-97), Heads of UK Pharmacology Departments, 1990-94; Member: Executive Committee, European Federation of Pharmacologists, 1991-96, Scottish Hospital Endowments Research Trust, since 1996; Secretary General, International Union of Pharmacology, 1994-98; Director, IUPHAR Media since 1997. Publications: Textbook of Pharmacology, 1968, 1980; Pharmacology of Neuromuscular Function, 1980, 1990; Dictionary of Pharmacology, 1986; many research articles in scientific journals. Address: Department of Physiology and Pharmacology, Strathclyde University, Glasgow G1 1XW; T.-0141-552 4400.

Bown, Professor Lalage Jean, OBE, MA (Oxon), DrUniv (Open University), DUniv (Paisley), Dr h.c. (Edinburgh), DUniv (Stirling), Hon. FITD, FRSA, FEIS, FRSE. Professor and Director, Department of Adult and Continuing Education, Glasgow University, 1981-92; Emeritus Professor from 1992, now Honorary Senior Research Fellow; Hon. Professor, Warwick University, 1992-97; Honorary Professorial Fellow, University of London Institute of Education, 1997-99; b. 1.4.27, Croydon. Educ. Wycombe Abbey School, Buckinghamshire; Cheltenham Ladies' College; Somerville College, Oxford. Resident Tutor: University College of the Gold Coast, 1949-55; Makerere University College, Uganda, 1955-59; successively Tutorial Advisor, Assistant Director, Deputy Director, Extra-Mural Department, Ibadan University, 1960-66 (Associate Professor, 1962-66); Director of Extra-Mural Studies and Professor Ad Personam, University of Zambia, 1966-70; Professor of Adult Education, Ahmadu Bello University, Nigeria, 1971-76; Commonwealth Visiting Professor, Edinburgh University, 1974; successively Professor of Adult Education and Dean of Education, Lagos University, 1977-80; Distinguished Visitor, Curtin University, Perth, Australia, 1995. Chair, Scottish Museums Council, 1993-96; Member: Board of Trustees, National Museums of Scotland, 1987-97, Council, Royal Society of Edinburgh, 1995-98; former Member, Commonwealth Standing Committee on Student Mobility and Higher Education Co-operation; former Member: Board, The British Council, Governing Body, Institute of Development Studies, Council, Scottish Poetry Library, Scottish Community Education Council; Past President: British Comparative and International Education Society, Development Studies Association; Vice-President, National Union of Townswomen's Guilds; former Vice-President, WEA; former Trustee, Womankind Worldwide; Vice-Chair, CODE Europe; President, British Association for Literacy in Development; Chair, Ethnological Research Centre, Edinburgh; Co-Chair, Scottish Somali Action; Member, Advisory Committee, WEA Scotland Oral History Project, since 1998. Publications: 10 academic books. Recreation: travel.

Bownes, Professor Mary, BSc, DPhil. Personal Chair of Developmental Biology, Edinburgh University, since 1994; b. 14.11.48, Drewsteignton; m., Michael J. Greaves; 1 d. Educ. Maldon Grammar School; Sussex University. Lecturer, Essex University; Lecturer, Senior Lecturer, Reader, Head of Institute of Cell and Molecular Biology, Edinburgh University. Publications: 100 research articles and reviews. Address: (b.) Institute of Cell and Molecular Biology, Edinburgh University, Darwin Building, Mayfield Road, Edinburgh EH9 3JR; T.-0131-650 5369.

Bowser of Argaty and the King's Lundies, David Stewart, JP, BA (Agric). Trustee, Scottish Forestry Trust, 1983-89 (Chairman, 1987); Member, Queen's Bodyguard for Scotland (Royal Company of Archers); Chairman, Scottish Council, British Deer Society, 1988-94; b. 11.3.26; m.; 1 s.; 4 d. Educ. Harrow; Trinity College, Cambridge. Captain, Scots Guards, 1944-47; Forestry Commissioner, 1974-82; President, Highland Cattle Society, 1970-72; Member, Perth County Council, 1954-61. Address: Auchlyne, Killin, Perthshire FK21 8RG.

Boxer, Professor David Howell, BSc, PhD. Professor of Biochemistry, Dundee University, since 1991, Head, Biochemistry Department, since 1988, Dean, Science and Engineering Faculty, since 1994; m., Dr. Maureen Boxer; 1 s.; 2 d. Educ. Aberdare Boys' Grammar School; Bristol University. Dundee University: Lecturer in Biochemistry, 1976, Senior Lecturer, 1985. Nuffield Research Fellow, 1983-84; Chairman, Biochemistry Biophysics Sub-Commitee, SERC, 1990-92. Recreations: travelling; skiing. Address: (b.) Department of Biochemistry, Medical Sciences Institute, Dundee University, Dundee DD1 4HN; T.-01382 344834.

Boyd, Alan Robb, LLB, BA, SSC, NP. Director, Public Sector Unit, McGrigor Donald, since 1997; b. 30.7.53, Glasgow; m., Frances Helen; 2 d. Educ. Irvine Royal Academy; Dundee University. Principal Solicitor, Shetland Islands Council, 1979-81; Principal Solicitor, Glenrothes Development Corporation, 1981-84; Legal Advisor, Irvine Development Corporation, 1984-87. Law Society of Scotland: Member, Council, 1985-97, Convener, Finance Committee, 1992-94, Vice-President, 1994-95, President, 1995-96; President, European Company Lawyers' Association, 1992-94. Recreations: golf; skiing; music. Address: (h.) 45 Craigholm Road, Ayr KA7 3LJ; T.-01292 262542.

Boyd, Colin David, QC, BA (Econ), LLB. Solicitor General for Scotland, since 1997; b. 7.6.53, Falkirk; m., Fiona Margaret MacLeod; 2 s.; 1 d. Educ. Wick High School; George Watson's College, Edinburgh; University of Manchester; University of Edinburgh. Solicitor, 1978-82; called to Bar, 1983; Advocate Depute, 1993-95; took Silk, 1995. Legal Associate, Royal Town Planning Institute. Publication: The Legal Aspects of Devolution (Contributor), 1997. Recreations: children; hill-walking; reading. Address: (b.) Crown Office, 25 Chambers Street, Edinburgh EH1 1LA; T.-0131-226 2626.

Boyd, Rev. Dr. Donald MacLeod, MB, ChB. Minister, Inverness Free Presbyterian Church of Scotland, since 1989 (Clerk, Northern Presbytery, since 1991); Church Tutor in Systematic Theology, since 1995; b. Glasgow; m., Elizabeth Schouten; 1 s.; 3 d. Educ. Glasgow Academy; Glasgow University. Southern General Hospital, 1978; Stobhill General Hospital, 1979; Vale of Leven Hospital, 1979; ordained Free Presbyterian Church of Scotland, 1983; Clerk of Religion and Morals Committee, 1984-92 and Convener, 1992-94; Deputy to Australia and New Zealand, 1988; Member, Churches Liaison Committee on AIDS, Highland Health Board, 1992-94; Member, Highland Regional Council Education Committee, 1994-96; Moderator of Synod of Free Presbyterian Church of Scotland, 1997-98. Publications: Popular History of the

Origins of the Free Presbyterian Church of Scotland, 1987; Free Presbyterians and the Requiem Mass, 1989. Recreations: reading; writing; gardening; walking; photography; British Sign Language; historical research. Address: 11 Auldcastle Road, Inverness IV2 3PZ; T.-01463 712872.

Boyd, Ian Mair, MSc, CA. Group Finance Director, The Weir Group PLC, since 1981; Director, Glasgow Income Trust plc, since 1990; Director, Inveresk PLC, since 1993; b. 4.9.44, Ayr; m., Theodora; 2 s.; 1 d. Educ. Ayr Academy; London Business School. The Weir Group PLC: Financial Controller International Division, 1975-78, Group Chief Accountant, 1978-81. Council Member, Institute of Chartered Accountants of Scotland, 1987-93; Chairman, Group of Scottish Finance Directors, 1990-91. Recreations: golf; hill-walking; fishing. Address: (b.) The Weir Group PLC, Cathcart, Glasgow G44 4EX; T.-0141-637 7111.

Boyd, Rev. Ian Robert, MA, BD, PhD. Minister, Netherlee Parish Church, since 1997; b. 29.11.61, Ayr; m., Dr. Carolyn Boyd; 2 s.; 1 d. Educ. Prestwick Academy; Glasgow University; Edinburgh University. Probationer Assistant Minister, Knightswood St. Margaret's, 1988-89; Minister, Perceton and Dreghorn, Irvine, 1989-92; post-graduate study, New College, Edinburgh University, 1992-96. Address: 532 Clarkston Road, Netherlee, Glasgow G44 3RT; T.-0141-637 2884.

Boyd, Joe, BSc (Hons), DipEd, MEd. Headteacher, St. David's High, Dalkeith, since 1997; Author, since 1989; b. 10.11.53, Ayr; m., Moira McCabe; 1 s.; 2 d. Educ. St. David's High, Dalkeith; University of St. Andrews; Moray House; University of Edinburgh. President, Students' Union, University of St. Andrews, 1975-76; teaching, various Lothian schools, including Beeslack High School, St. Augustine's High School, St. David's High School, 1977-97. Member, National Joint Working Party (Revised Higher Chemistry), 1987-90; seconded to SOEID, to work with HM Inspectorate, 1996-97; led Inservice workshops for teachers, 1983-97. Publications: co-author of 27 titles, including Understanding Science series, and Scottish Science 5-14. Recreations: cycling; hill-walking; football; sailing; skiing; reading. Address: (b.) St. David's High School, Abbey Road, Dalkeith, Midlothian; T.-0131-663 1961.

Boyes, John, MA (Hons). HM Chief Inspector of Schools; b. 20.5.43, Greenock; m., Margaret Anne Peat; 1 s.; 1 d. Educ. Greenock High School; Glasgow University. Teacher, Alloa Academy and Denny High School, 1967-74. Recreation: mixing metaphors. Address: (b.) Scottish Office Education and Industry Department, Greyfriars House, Gallowgate, Aberdeen; T.-01224 642544.

Boyle, Professor Alan Edward, MA, BCL. Professor of International Law, Edinburgh University, since 1994; Barrister, Middle Temple, since 1977; b. 28.3.53, Belfast; m., Caroline Patricia Tuckett. Educ. Royal Belfast Academical Institution; Pembroke College, Oxford University. Lecturer, Senior Lecturer, Reader, Queen Mary and Westfield College, London University, 1978-94; Visiting Professor, College of William and Mary, VA, 1987; Visiting Professor, University of Texas, 1988, 1994; Editor, International and Comparative Law Quarterly, since 1997. Publication: International Law and the Environment (Co-author), 1992. Recreations: gliding; walking; reading. Address: (b.) Faculty of Law, Edinburgh University, Old College, South Bridge, Edinburgh EH8 9YL; T.-0131-650 2019.

Boyle, Rt. Rev. Mgr. Hugh Noonan, PhL, STL, FSA Scot. Canon, Chapter of Metropolitan Cathedral Church of St. Andrew, Glasgow, since 1984; Chapter Secretary, since 1991; Prelate of Honour, since 1987; Archivist, Archdiocese of Glasgow, since 1973; b. 14.1.35, Glasgow. Educ. St. Aloysius' College, Glasgow; Glasgow University; Pontifical Scots College and Pontifical Gregorian University, Rome, 1956-63. National Service, RAF, 1954-56; ordained priest, Rome, 1962; Assistant Priest: St. Philomena's, Glasgow, 1963-66, St. Eunan's, Clydebank, 1966-76; Administrator, Metropolitan Cathedral Church of St. Andrew, Glasgow, 1983-92; Parish Priest, St. Leo's, Dumbreck, 1992-93; Chaplain, Bon Secours Convent Hospital, Glasgow, since 1995; Assistant Catholic Chaplain, Victoria Infirmary, Glasgow, since 1995; Archdiocese of Glasgow: Assistant Archivist, 1967-73; Chancellor, 1976-83. Editor, Catholic Directory for Scotland and Western Catholic Calendar, since issues of 1975; Member: Scottish Catholic Communications Commission, 1979-87; Scottish Catholic Heritage Commission, since 1981; Patron, Hutchesons' Hospital, since 1983. Recreations: music (listening); walking. Address: The Lindens, 36 Mansionhouse Road, Glasgow G41 3DW; T.-0141-649 9226.

Boyle, Iain Thomson, BSc (Hons), MB, ChB, FRCP, FRCP (London and Glasgow), FSA (Scot). Medical Advisor, University of Strathclyde, since 1991; Chairman: National Scientific Advisory Committee, Tenovus-Scotland, since 1997, Organising Committee, Glasgow 2000 National Philatelic Exhibition; Visiting Professor in Physiology/Pharmacology, University of Strathclyde, since 1994; b. 7.10.35, Glasgow; m., Elizabeth Johnston Carmichael; 1 s.; 2 d. Educ. Paisley Grammar School; Glasgow University. Lecturer in Medicine, Glasgow University and Glasgow Royal Infirmary, 1964-70; Hartenstein Research Fellow, Wisconsin University, 1970-72; Senior Lecturer in Medicine, Glasgow University and Glasgow Royal Infirmary, 1973-84; Reader in Medicine, Glasgow University and Glasgow Royal Infirmary, 1984-96. Chairman, Board of Management, Scottish Medical Journal, 1987-96; President, Bone and Tooth Society, 1994-96; Editor, Scottish Medical Journal, 1978-83; Co-Editor, Bone, 1983-93; Council Member, Royal College of Physicians and Surgeons, 1984-88; Secretary: Scottish Society for Experimental Medicine, 1984-88, Scottish Society of Physicians, 1984-88; President: Caledonian Philatelic Society, 1983-84, Association of Scottish Philatelic Societies, 1995-96, Harveian Society of Edinburgh, 1991; Vice President (Medical), Royal College of Physicians and Surgeons of Glasgow, 1992-94, and Hon. Librarian, since 1994. Fletcher Prize, Royal College of Physicians and Surgeons of Glasgow, 1973. Recreations: philately; Scottish social history; France and the French; angling; gardening; golf. Address: (h.) 7 Lochbrae Drive, High Burnside, Rutherglen, Glasgow G73 5QL.

Boyle, John Stirling, MA, DPA, FRSA. Director, Corporate Affairs, ScotRail, since 1994; b. 17.9.39, Paisley; m., Helen Dickson; 2 s.; 1 d. Educ. Camphill School, Paisley; Glasgow University. School Teacher, 1960-61; Reporter, Sunday Post, 1961-62; Technical Writer, Harland Engineering Company, 1962-64; Health Education Officer, Stirling County, 1964-66; Public Relations Officer, Heriot-Watt University, 1966-73; Director, External Relations, Scottish Council (Development and Industry), 1973-83; Director of Public Affairs (Scotland), British Rail, 1983-92; Director, Corporate Affairs (Scotland), British Railways Board, 1992-94. Recreation: motor cycling. Address (b.) Caledonian Chambers, 87 Union Street, Glasgow G1 3TA; T.-0141-335 4447.

Boyle, Sandy, DGA. Joint Deputy General Secretary, BIFU, since 1992; Member, STUC General Council, since 1992; b. 23.12.45, Falkirk; m., Elizabeth Ross Cockrill; 1 s.; 1 d. Educ. Falkirk High School. Civil Servant, 1964-92. Vice-President, Society of Civil and Public Servants; Deputy President, National Union of Civil and Public Servants (President, NUCPS, 1989-92); STUC: Chair, Home and International Committee, since 1996, Member, Finance and Strategy Committee. Recreations: trade union badge collector; music; reading; bridge; watching Falkirk F.C. Address: (b.) 146 Argyle Street, Glasgow G2 8BL; T.-0141-221 6475.

Bradford, Nicola Barbara, DL, LTCL. Partner, Kincardine House, since 1986; Suzuki Piano Teacher, since 1996; Vice Chairman, Children 1st, since 1997; b. 12.9.57, Prestwick; m., Andrew E. H. Bradford; 2 s.; 1 d. Educ. West Heath School, Kent; College of Occupational Therapy, Edinburgh. Occupational Therapist, Aberdeen, 1978-80. Board Member, North East Scotland Music School; Deputy Lieutenant, County of Aberdeenshire. Recreations: playing in a Scottish dance band; sailing; walking; gardening; charitable fundraising; Cocker spaniels. Address: Kincardine, Kincardine O'Neil, Aberdeenshire AB34 5AE; T.-013398 84225.

Bradley, Rev. Dr. Ian Campbell, MA, BD, DPhil. Writer and Broadcaster; Senior Lecturer in Practical Theology, St Andrews University; Member: Church of Scotland Panel on Worship, Liturgical Committee, Committee to Revise the Church Hymnary; b. 28.5.50, Berkhamsted; m., Lucy Patricia; 1 s.; 1 d. Educ. Tonbridge School, Kent; New College, Oxford; St. Andrews University. Research Fellow, New College, Oxford, 1971-75; Staff Journalist, The Times, 1976-82; ordained into Church of Scotland, 1990; Head, Religious Broadcasting, BBC Scotland, 1990-91. Publications: The Call to Seriousness, 1974; William Morris and his World, 1975; The Optimists, 1976; The Penguin Annotated Gilbert & Sullivan, 1980; The Strange Rebirth of Liberal Britain, 1982; Enlightened Entrepreneurs, 1986; The Penguin Book of Hymns, 1989; God is Green, 1990; O Love That Wilt Not Let Me Go, 1990; Marching to the Promised Land, 1992; The Celtic Way, 1993; The Power of Sacrifice, 1995; The Complete Annotated Gilbert and Sullivan, 1996; Columba, Pilgrim and Penitent, 1996; Abide with Me – the World of the Victorian Hymn, 1997; Celtic Christianity: Making Myths and Chasing Dreams, 1999. Recreations: music; walking; family; spas. Address: (b.) St Mary's College, South Street, St Andrews KY16 9JU; T.-01334 462840.

Bradley, John Russell, MA, LLB, DipLP, NP. Solicitor, Bird Semple, since 1989; b. 20.11.62, Glasgow; 3 s. Educ. Eastbank Academy, Glasgow; Glasgow University. Trainee, Wright & Crawford, Paisley, 1987-89; Bird Semple: Assistant, 1989-94, Associate, 1994-97. Recreations: hockey (not often enough); golf (mostly in the rough). Address: (b.) 27 Thistle Street, Edinburgh EH2 1BS; T.-0131-459 2345.

Brady, Paul A., BSc (Hons), PhD. Director of Finance, National Health Service in Scotland Management Executive; b. 28.7.49, Glasgow; 2 s.; 1 d. Educ. St. Mungo's Academy, Glasgow; University of Glasgow. Joined Scottish Office, 1974; posts in Industry, Police, and Energy areas, 1974-88; headed team advising on electricity privatisation, 1988-90; led on Higher Education reforms, 1991-92; Director of Policy, Scottish Higher Education Funding Council, 1992-93; Head, Finance Division (industry, transport and agriculture), Scottish Office, 1993-94; Director Finance and Planning, Scottish Enterprise, 1994-98. Recreations: walking; music; family. Address: (b.) Scottish Office Department of Health, St Andrew's House, Regent Road, Edinburgh EH1 3DG; T.-0131-244 3464.

Braid, Peter John, LLB (Hons), WS. Partner, The Morton Fraser Partnership, Solicitors, since 1985; Solicitor Advocate, since 1995; b. 6.3.58, Edinburgh; m., Heather McIntosh; 2 s. Educ. George Watson's College, Edinburgh; University of Edinburgh. Apprentice, 1980-82; has specialised in litigation since 1982, now concentrates on commercial litigation; acted for manufacturer in Lanark Blue Cheese case, 1995. Publications: articles on enforcement of judgements, food safety, the millennium bug. Recreations: golf; bridge. Address: (b.) 19 York Place, Edinburgh EH1 3EL; T.-0131-550 1100.

Braithwaite, Robert Barclay, BSc, CEng, FICE, MASCE. General Manager, Aberdeen Harbour Board, since 1990 (Assistant, then Deputy General Manager and Harbour Engineer, 1986-89); b. 17.2.48, Glasgow; m., Christine Isobel Ross; 2 s. Educ. Hutchesons' Boys' Grammar School; Strathclyde University. Graduate/Assistant Engineer, Rendel Palmer & Tritton, Consulting Civil Engineers, London, 1969-74; Deputy Harbour Engineer, 1974-75, Harbour Engineer, 1976-86, Aberdeen Harbour Board. Chairman, Aberdeen Maritime Museum Appeal; Council Member, Aberdeen Chamber of Commerce; Chairman, British Ports Association. Recreations: hill running; cycling; reading. Address: (b.) Harbour Office, 16 Regent Quay, Aberdeen AB11 5SS; T.-01224 597000.

Brand, David Allan, LLB (Hons), WS, NP. Solicitor; Senior Lecturer in Law, University of Dundee; Consultant, Thorntons WS, Dundee; b. 4.3.50, Dundee; 1 d. Educ. Grove Academy, Broughty Ferry; Dundee University. Former Member of Council, Law Society of Scotland; former Dean, Faculty of Procurators and Solicitors in Dundee. Recreations: all types of music; amateur operatics; theatre. Address: (b.) Department of Law, University of Dundee, Dundee DD1 4HN; T.-01382 223181.

Brand, Janet Mary Valentine, BA (Hons), DipTP, MRTPI. Senior Lecturer, Strathclyde University, since 1973 (Member of Senate, 1984-91 and since 1992; Member of Court, 1989-91; Convener, Programme of Opportunities for Women Committee, 1990-93); b. 19.4.44, Bath; 2 d. Educ. County High School for Girls, Brentwood; Exeter University. Local authority appointments in Departments of Planning, Essex County Council, London Borough of Barking and City of London, 1965-70; Senior Lecturer, South Bank Polytechnic, 1970-73. Specialist Assessor in Town and Country Planning and Landscape, HEFCE, since 1996. Recreations: the environment; gardening; family pursuits; travelling. Address: (b.) Department of Environmental Planning, Strathclyde University, 50 Richmond Street, Glasgow; T.-0141-548 3905/6.

Brannan, Micheline H., MA. Head, Civil Law Division, Scottish Office Home Department, since 1995; b. 23.10.54, Glasgow; m., Michael N. Brannan; 2 s. Educ. Hutchesons' Grammar School; St. Hilda's College, Oxford. Scottish Office: joined as administrative trainee, 1976, promoted to Principal, 1982, Industry Department for Scotland, 1982-84, Scottish Education Department, 1985-88, Home and Health Department Criminal Justice Group, 1989-95. Recreations: cycling; Jewish cultural activities. Address: (b.) Saughton House, Broomhouse Drive, Edinburgh; T.-0131-244 2258.

Breaks, Michael Lenox, BA, DipLib. University Librarian, Heriot-Watt University, since 1985; b. 12.1.45, Plymouth; m., Barbara Lawson; 1 s.; 1 d. Educ. St. George's College, Weybridge; Leeds University. Assistant Librarian: University College, Swansea, York University; Social Sciences Librarian, University College, Cardiff, 1977-81; Deputy Librarian, University College, Dublin, 1981-85. Chairman, JANET National User Group, 1991-93; Non-Executive Director, UKERNA, 1994-97; Member, SCONUL Executive Board, 1991-96; Member, SLIC Management Committee; Editor, New Review of Information Networking. Recreations: gardening; horse-riding; walking. Address: (h.) 2 Corrennie Gardens, Edinburgh EH10 6DG; T.-0131-451 3570.

Breen, James William, DPE. Deputy Chief Executive, Scottish Sports Council, since 1989; b. 1.7.53, Lennoxtown; m., Fiona; 2 d. Educ. Victoria Drive Secondary School, Glasgow; Jordanhill College, Glasgow. Assistant Director of Leisure Services, Motherwell District Council, 1986-89. Address: (b.) Caledonia House, South Gyle, Edinburgh EH12 9DQ; T.-0131-317 7200.

Breeze, David John, BA, PhD, FSA, PPSA Scot, FRSE, MIFA. Chief Inspector of Ancient Monuments, Scotland, since 1989; Visiting Professor, Department of Archaeology, Durham University, since 1993; Honorary Professor, Edinburgh University, since 1996; b. 25.7.44, Blackpool; m., Pamela Diane Silvester; 2 s. Educ. Blackpool Grammar School; Durham University. Inspector of Ancient Monuments, Scotland, 1969-88; Principal Inspector of Ancient Monuments, Scotland, 1988-89. Member: International Committee of the Congress of Roman Frontier Studies, since 1983, Council, Society of Antiquaries of London, 1984-86; Trustee, Senhouse Roman Museum, since 1985; Chairman: 1989 Hadrian's Wall Pilgrimage, British Archaeological Awards, since 1993; President, Society of Antiquaries of Scotland, 1987-90. Publications: The Building of Hadrian's Wall, The Army of Hadrian's Wall, Hadrian's Wall, and Roman Officers and Frontiers (all Co-author); Roman Scotland: a guide to the visible remains; Roman Scotland: some recent excavations (Editor); The Romans in Scotland (Co-author); The Northern Frontiers of Roman Britain; Roman Forts in Britain; Studies in Scottish Antiquity (Editor); Hadrian's Wall, a souvenir guide; A Queen's Progress, an introduction to the buildings associated with Mary Queen of Scots in Scotland; The Second Augustan Legion in North Britain; Service in the Roman Army (Co-editor); Invaders of Scotland (Co-author); Roman Scotland: Frontier Country; The Stone of Destiny: Symbol of Nationhood (Co-author). Recreations: reading; walking; swimming; travel. Address: (b.) Historic Scotland, Longmore House, Salisbury Place, Edinburgh, EH9 1SH; T.-0131-668 8724.

Bremner, Douglas, BSc (Hons). Regional Director, National Trust for Scotland (Lothians, Borders, Dumfries and Galloway Region), since 1989; b. 18.9.38, Glasgow; m., Vivien; 3 s. Educ. Aberdeen Grammar School; Aberdeen University. Whaling Inspector, Crown Agents, South Georgia; Warden, Malham Tarn Field Centre, Field Studies Council; National Trust for Scotland: Principal/Chief Ranger, Culzean Country Park, Chief Ranger, Scotland, Head of Interpretation/Presentation. NTS Assessor, Scottish Wildlife Trust. Recreations: natural history; walking; gardening; painting; sound recording. Address: (h.) 3 Bonaly Terrace, Colinton, Edinburgh EH13 0EL; T.-0131-441 4966.

Bremner, Ian, BSc, PhD, DSc. Deputy Director (Science), Rowett Research Institute, Aberdeen, since 1988; b. 19.2.39, Aberdeen; m., Kathleen Stewart; 3 s. Educ. Robert Gordon's College, Aberdeen; Aberdeen University. Senior Research Biochemist, Fisons Pharmaceuticals Ltd., Cheshire, 1964-65; SSO, Nutritional Biochemistry Department, Rowett Research Institute, 1967, PSO, 1974; Grade 6, Biochemistry Division, 1985. Member, Parent Committee, and Chairman, TEMA International: international symposia on trace elements in man and animals; Underwood Memorial Lecture, 1990. Address: (b.) Rowett Research Institute, Greenburn Road, Bucksburn, Aberdeen, AB21 9SB; T.-01224 716602.

Brett, Timothy Edward William, BSc (Hons), FHSM, DipHSM, GradIPM. General Manager, Tayside Health Board, since 1998; b. 28.3.49, Gravesend; m., Barbara Jane; 2 s; 1 d. Educ. Gravesend Grammar School for Boys; Bristol University. Unit Administrator, Plymouth General Hospital, 1981-85; Dundee General Hospitals Unit: Unit Administrator, 1985-87, Unit General Manager, 1987-93; Chief Executive, Dundee Teaching Hospitals, 1993-97. Recreations: hill-walking; squash; swimming; theatre; church activities. Address: (h.) Woodend Cottage, Hazelton Walls, Cupar KY15 4QL; T.-01382 632598.

Brett Young, Michael Jonathan, DL. Manager, East Sutherland Village Advisory Service, since 1986; Director: Voluntary Groups, East Sutherland, since 1996, Highland Advice and Information Network Ltd.; Deputy Lieutenant, Sutherland, since 1995; b. 18.10.37, Salisbury; m., Helen Dorothy Anne Barker; 2 s. Educ. Dartmouth. Royal Australian Navy, 1956-69; Sales and Marketing Manager, 1969-79; Senior Account Manager, 1979-84. Chairman, PR Committee, Retread Manufacturers Association, 1975-79; Executive Member, Community Organisations Group, Scotland, 1990-93; Chairman: East Sutherland Council of Social Service, 1991-94, East Sutherland Local Community Care Forum, since 1993; Executive Member, SSAFA, Sutherland; Chairman, Dornoch Cricket Club, since 1991. Recreations: cricket; naval history; music. Address: (h.) West Shinness Lodge, Lairg, Sutherland; T.-01549 402495.

Brettle, Raymond Patrick, BSc, MBChB, MD, FRCPEd. Consultant Physician, Regional Infectious Disease Unit, Western General Hospital, Edinburgh, since 1998; Reader in Medicine, University of Edinburgh, since 1995; b. 20.3.49, Halesowen; m., Helene Ferrier; 1 s.; 3 d. Educ. Halesowen Grammar School; Edinburgh University. Registrar, Hammersmith Hospital, London, 1977-79; Senior Registrar, City Hospital, Edinburgh, 1979-83; Fellow, Bowman Gray School of Medicine, Winston Salem, N. Carolina, 1982-83; Consultant, Regional Infectious Disease Unit, City Hospital, Edinburgh, 1983-98; Senior Lecturer, University of Edinburgh, 1983-95. Chairman, Medical Advisory Committee, Milestone House; Founder Member, British HIV Association. Recreations: computing; walking; DIY. Address: RIDU, Western General Hospital, Edinburgh, EH4 2XU; T.-0131-537 2841.

Brew, David Allan, BA, MSc. Assistant Secretary, Scottish Office, since 1990; b. 19.2.53, Kettering. Educ. Kettering Grammar School; Heriot-Watt University; Strathclyde University; European University Institute, Florence. Administration Trainee and HEO(D), Scottish Office, 1979-81; Administrator, DGV, Commission of the EC, 1981-84; Principal, Scottish Office, Glasgow, 1984-88, Edinburgh, 1988-90; Assistant Secretary, since 1990; Head: Electricity Privatisation Division, 1990-91, European Funds and Co-ordination Division, 1991-95, Sea Fisheries Division,1995-98; Cabinet Office, Constitution Secretariat, since 1998. Member, Court, Heriot-Watt University, 1985-91. Recreations: languages; music; film; gastronomy. Address (h.) Flat 4, 1 Dundas Street, Edinburgh, EH3 6QG; T.-0131-556 4692.

Bridgeford, Betty; CQSW. Director of Social Work, Perth and Kinross Council, since 1996; b. 2.1.37, Glasgow; m., Bob; 1 s.; 1 d. Educ. Perth Academy; Northern College, Dundee. Tayside Regional Council: unqualified Social Worker, 1971-75, seconded to Northern College, Dundee, 1978-80, Senior Social Worker, 1980-87, Assistant Area Fieldwork Manager (Perth and Kinross), 1987-89, District Manager (Perth and Kinross), 1991-93, Assistant Director (Perth and Kinross), 1993-96. Member, Board: Perth Housing Association, Dovetail Enterprises; Vice-Chair, Perth and Kinross Victim Support; Member, Scottish Task Force, Princess Royal Trust for Carers; Member, Executive, ADSW; Trustee, Bertha Trust. Recreations: reading; music; swimming; golf. Address: Perth and Kinross Council, Social Work Services, Rosslyn House, 32 Glasgow Road, Perth PH2 0PD; T.-01738 476701.

Bridges, Professor Roy Charles, BA, PhD, FRGS, FRHistS. Emeritus Professor of History, Aberdeen University; b. 26.9.32, Aylesbury; m., Jill Margaret Bridges; 2 s.; 2 d. Educ. Harrow Weald County Grammar School; Keele University; London University. Lecturer in History, Makerere University, Uganda, 1960-64; joined Aberdeen University, 1964; Head, History Department, 1977-82, 1985-88, 1990-94; Secretary, then Chairman, African Studies Group, 1966-94. Chairman, SEB Joint

Working Party on Higher and Post-Higher History, 1988-90; Council Member: Royal Historical Society, since 1995, Hakluyt Society, 1991-95, since 1998; Treasurer, Scottish Institute of Missionary Studies. Publications: Nations and Empires (Co-author), 1969; Africa in Times Atlas of World Exploration; Compassing the Vaste Globe of the Earth (Co-editor), 1996. Recreations: cricket; geology; gardening. Address: (b.) Department of History, King's College, Aberdeen, AB24 3FX; T.-Aberdeen 272456.

Brining, James Edward; MA (Cantab) (Hons). Artistic Director, TAG Theatre Co., since 1997; b. 10.6.68, Leeds. Educ. Leeds Grammar School; Girton College, Cambridge University. Formed Rendezvous Theatre Company 1989; Proteus Theatre Co.: Administrative Director, 1990, Artistic Director, 1992; Community Director, Orange Tree Theatre, Richmond, 1995. Recreation: playing football. Address: (h.) TAG Theatre Co., 18 Albion Street, Glasgow G1 1LH.

Brittain, Christopher Neil, MBA, MBChB, MRCGP, DRCOG, DFFP, DipIMC, RCS(Edin.), FRSocMed. Co-ordinator for Scotland, Sargent Cancer Care for Children, since 1997; b. 3.3.49, Birmingham; m., Rosemary; 1 s.; 1 d. Educ. Bishop Vesey's Grammar School, Sutton Coldfield; St. Andrews University; Dundee University; Heriot Watt University. Senior Partner, Anstruther Medical Practice, 1978-97. Chairman, British Association of Immediate Care, 1994-97; Director, Resuscitation Council UK, 1995-1997. Recreations; music; walking. Address: (b.) 158 South Street, St. Andrews KY16 9EG; T.-01334 470044.

Britton, Professor Celia Margaret, MA (Cantab), PhD. Carnegie Professor of French and Director, Centre for Francophone Studies, Aberdeen University, since 1991; b. 20.3.46, Stanmore, Middx. Educ. North London Collegiate School; New Hall, Cambridge. Temporary Lecturer in French, Kings College, London, 1972-74; Lecturer in French Studies, Reading University, 1974-91. Publications: Claude Simon: Writing The Visible, 1987; The Nouveau Roman: fiction, theory and politics, 1992; Claude Simon (Editor), 1993; Edouard Glissant and Postcolonial Theory, 1999; articles on French literature and cinema, French Caribbean literature. Address: (b.) Department of French, Aberdeen University, Old Aberdeen, AB9 2UB; T.-01224 272163.

Broadfoot, John Ledingham, BA, MEd. Rector, Kelvinside Academy, since 1998; b. 16.12.48, Glasgow; m., Cecilia; 1 s.; 2 d. Educ. Merchiston Castle School; Leeds University; Stirling University. Teacher of English, Kingston College, Jamaica, 1971-73; Assistant Principal Teacher, then Principal Teacher of English, Penicuik High School, 1973-78; Principal Teacher of English, Preston Lodge High School, East Lothian, 1978-87; Head of English, then Director of Studies, Strathallan School, Perthshire, 1987-98. Recreations: Scottish literature; theatre; mountaineering; sailing. Address: Kelvinside Academy, 33 Kirklee Road, Glasgow G12 OSW; T.-0141-357 3376.

Broadie, Professor Alexander, MA, PhD, DLitt, FRSE. Professor of Logic and Rhetoric, Glasgow University. Educ. Royal High School, Edinburgh; Edinburgh University; Balliol College, Oxford. Henry Duncan Prize Lecturer in Scottish Studies, Royal Society of Edinburgh, 1990-93; Gifford Lecturer, Aberdeen University, 1994. Publications: A Samaritan Philosophy, 1981; George Lokert: Late-Scholastic Logician, 1983; The Circle of John Mair, 1985; Introduction to Medieval Logic, 1987; Notion and Object, 1989; The Tradition of Scottish Philosophy, 1990; Paul of Venice: Logica Magna, 1990; Robert Kilwardby O.P.: on time and imagination, 1993; Introduction to Medieval Logic (2nd edition), 1993; The Shadow of Scotus, 1995; The Scottish Enlightenment: an anthology, 1997. Address: (b.) Philosophy Department, The University, Glasgow G12 8QQ; T.-0141-330 5692.

Brock, Professor David John Henry, BA (Oxon), PhD, FRCPath, FRSE, FRCPE. Professor of Human Genetics, Edinburgh University, since 1985; Director, Human Genetics Unit, Edinburgh University, since 1983; Chairman, Department of Medicine, Western General Hospital, 1994-97; b. 5.6.36, London; 4 s. Educ. Diocesan College, Cape Town; Cape Town University; Oxford University. Postdoctoral Fellow: Massachussets Institute of Technology, 1962-63; Harvard University, 1963-66; Oxford University, 1966-67; Senior Scientific Officer, ARC Animal Breeding Research Organisation, 1967-68; joined Edinburgh University as Lecturer in Human Genetics, 1968; appointed Reader, 1978. Address: (h.) Lagbeag, Little Dunkeld, Perthshire; T.-01350 727614.

Brockie, Rev. Colin Glynn Frederick, BSc (Eng), BD. Minister, Kilmarnock: Grange, since 1978; Clerk to Presbytery of Irvine and Kilmarnock, since 1992; Hon. Chaplain, 327 (Kilmarnock) Squadron, Air Training Corps, since 1978; b. 17.7.42, Westcliff on Sea; m., Barbara Katherine Gordon; 2 s.; 1 d. Educ. Musselburgh Grammar School; Aberdeen Grammar School; University of Aberdeen. Probationary year, Aberdeen: Mastrick, 1967-68; Minister, St. Martin's, Edinburgh, 1968-78. Recreations: billiards; photography; computing. Address: Grange Manse, 51 Portland Road, Kilmarnock, Ayrshire KA1 2EQ; T.-01563 525311.

Brockington, Professor John Leonard, MA, DPhil. Professor of Sanskrit, University of Edinburgh, since 1998 (Head, School of Asian Studies, since 1998); b. 5.12.40, Oxford; m., Mary Fairweather; 1 s.; 1 d. Educ. Mill Hill School; Corpus Christi College, Oxford. Lecturer in Sanskrit, 1965-82, Head, Department of Sanskrit, 1975-98, Senior Lecturer, 1982-89, Reader, 1989-98. Publications: The Sacred Thread, 1981; Righteous Rama, 1984; Hinduism and Christianity, 1992; The Sanskrit Epics, 1998. Recreation: gardening. Address: (b.) 7 Buccleuch Place, Edinburgh EH8 9LW; T.-0131-650 4174.

Brocklebank, Ted. TV Producer, Greyfriars Productions; b. 24.9.42, St. Andrews; 2 s. Educ. Madras College, St. Andrews. D.C. Thomson, Dundee, 1960-63; Freelance Journalist, 1963-65; Scottish TV, 1965-70; Grampian Television: Reporter, 1970-76, Head of News and Current Affairs, 1977-85, Head of Documentaries and Features, 1985-95. BAFTA Award for What Price Oil?; Radio Industries Club of Scotland Special Award (Documentary) for Tale of Two Cities; Norwegian Amanda award for eight-part series on world oil business, networked on Channel 4 and throughout USA on PBS; BMA Award for Scotland the Grave. Recreations: Trustee, St Andrews Preservation Trust; Board Member, Byre Theatre, St Andrews; Committee Member, Scottish Cancer Research Campaign. Address: (b.) Greyfriars Productions, Greyfriars Garden, St. Andrews KY16 9HG.

Brodie, Robert, CB, MA, LLB. Solicitor to Secretary of State for Scotland, 1987-98 (Deputy Solicitor, 1984-87); b. 9.4.38, Dundee; m., Jean Margaret McDonald; 2 s.; 2 d. Educ. Morgan Academy, Dundee; St. Andrews University; Queen's College, Dundee. Scottish Office: Legal Assistant, 1965; Senior Legal Assistant, 1970; Deputy Director, Scottish Courts Administration, 1975; Assistant Solicitor, Scottish Office, 1982. Chairman, Scottish Tourette Syndrome Support Group, 1993-98. Recreations: music; hill-walking. Address: (h.) 8 York Road, Edinburgh; T.-0131-552 2028.

Brodie, William, BSc, CBiol, MIBiol. Rector, Wallace High School, Stirling, since 1984; b. 16.9.37, Hamilton; m., Helen Bland; 1 s.; 1 d. Educ. Hamilton Academy; Glasgow University; Paisley College of Technology. Teacher, Wishaw High School, 1965-67; Principal Teacher of Biology, Hutchesons' Grammar School, Glasgow, 1967-74; Assistant Rector, Graeme High School, Falkirk, 1974-79;

Depute Rector, Kirkintilloch High School, 1979-81; Rector, Balfron High School, 1981-84. Recreations: golf; tennis; gardening. Address: (b.) Wallace High School, Dumyat Road, Stirling FK9 5HW; T.-01786 462166.

Brodie of Brodie, (Montagu) Ninian Alexander, DL, JP; b. 12.6.12, Forres; m., Helena Penelope Budgen (deceased); 1 s.; 1 d. Educ. Eton. Trained Webber-Douglas School of Dramatic Art, 1933-35; professional Actor and Director, occasional broadcasts, 1935-40; served with Royal Artillery, including North Africa and Italy, 1940-45; returned to stage, with occasional films and broadcasts, 1945-50; managed estate, market garden, etc., Brodie Castle, from 1950; transferred Brodie Castle and part of estate to National Trust for Scotland, 1979; voluntary work as guide etc., since 1980. Life Member, National Trust for Scotland. Recreations: shooting; hill-walking; collecting paintings. Address: (h.) Brodie Castle, Forres, Moray, IV36 0TE.

Bromage, Professor Niall R., BSc, PhD. Professor of Reproductive Physiology, University of Stirling, since 1994; Assistant Director, Institute of Aquaculture, since 1996; Editor, Aquaculture, since 1991; Technical Adviser, British Trout Association, since 1990; b. 4.7.42, Herts; m., Anne; 1 s.; 1 d. Educ. Welwyn Garden City Grammar School; University of Leicester. Lecturer, University of Aston, 1967-88; Lecturer, then Senior Lecturer, University of Stirling, 1988-94. Publications: author of books on intensive aquaculture, bacterial diseases of fish and broodstock management; over 200 scientific and trade articles. Recreation: squash. Address: (b.) University of Stirling, Stirling FK9 4LA; T.-01786 473171.

Broni, David Alexander Thomas, MBA, MIED. Senior Aftercare Executive, Locate in Scotland, since 1995; b. 25.10.57, Glasgow; m., Ann Frances; 1 s.; 1 d. Educ. St Mungo's Academy. Joined civil service, 1975; Manpower Services Commission, 12 years, Training Agency, 2 years, Scottish Office Industry Department, 2 years; Head of Secretariat, Scottish Enterprise, 4 years. Member, Institute of Economic Development; Member, Management Committee, Glasgow Quality Forum. Recreations: running; cycling; swimming; rugby; opera. Address: (b.) 120 Bothwell Street, Glasgow G2 7JP; T.-0141-228 2854.

Brooke, (Alexander) Keith, FRAgS. Director: Animal Diseases Research Association, now Moredun Foundation for Animal Health and Welfare, 1981-96, Scottish, English & Welsh Wool Growers Ld., 1988-95, Wigtownshire Quality Lamb Ltd., 1991-96; Member, Panel of Agricultural Arbiters appointed by Secretary of State for Scotland; b. 11.2.46, Minnigaff; m., Dilys K. Littlejohn; 1 s.; 3 d. Educ. George Watson's College, Edinburgh. President, Blackface Sheep Breeders Association, 1985-86, Hon. President, 1989-92; Director: Royal Highland and Agricultural Society of Scotland, 1986-93 and since 1994, Wallets Marts PLC, 1989-91; Chairman, Blackface Sheep Breeders' Development Board, since 1996; Member: Council for Awards of Royal Agricultural Societies, since 1997, Council, British Rouge de l'Ouest Sheep Society,1986-97 (Chairman, 1990-92, Treasurer, since 1993); former Member, Galloway Cattle Society, and Convener of Finance Committee. Address: (h.) Carscreugh, Glenluce, Newton Stewart, DG8 0NU; T.-01581 300334.

Brooks, James, BTech (Hons), MPhil, PhD, FRSC, CChem, FGS, FInstPet, AssocBIT. Senior Partner, Brooks Associates Glasgow, since 1986; Visiting Lecturer, Glasgow University, since 1978; Chairman/Director, Petroleum Geology '86 Limited, since 1985; b. 11.10.38, Co. Durham; m., Jan Slack; 1 s.; 1 d. Educ. University of Bradford. Research Scientist, British Petroleum, 1969-75; Senior Research Fellow, Bradford University, 1975-77; Research Associate/Section Head/Senior Scientist, British National Oil Corporation/Britoil PLC, 1977-86. Geological Society: Vice President, 1984-87, Secretary, 1987-90; Founder and Chairman, The Petroleum Group; AAPG Distinguished Achievement Award for service to petroleum geology and human need, 1993; AAPG Distinguished Lecturer to North America, 1989-90; Chairman, Shawlands Academy School Board, 1990-97; Church Secretary, Queen's Park Baptist Church, Glasgow; elected Member, Baptist Union of Scotland Council. Publications: 18 books; 85 research papers. Recreations:travel; reading; writing; sport (English soccer!); Christian work. Address: (h.) 10 Langside Drive, Newlands, Glasgow G43 2EE; T.-0141-632 3068.

Brooks, Patrick William, BSc, MB, ChB, DPM, FRCPsych. Former Senior Medical Officer, Scottish Office Department of Health; b. 17.5.38, Hereford. Educ. Hereford High School; Bishop Vesey's Grammar School, Sutton Coldfield; Edinburgh University. Royal Edinburgh and associated hospitals, including State Hospital, Carstairs, and Western General Hospital, Edinburgh: Senior House Officer, 1964-66; Registrar, 1966-69; Senior Registrar, 1969-74; Medical Officer, Scottish Home and Health Department, 1974-81. A founder Member, Edinburgh Festival Fringe Society, 1959 (Vice-Chairman, 1964-71); Chairman, Edinburgh Playhouse Society, 1975-81; Secretary, Lothian Playhouse Trust, 1981-83; Chairman, The Scottish Society. Recreations: opera; ballet; music; theatre; cinema; modern Scottish art; travel. Address: (h.) 11 Thirlestane Road, Edinburgh EH9 1AL.

Brooksbank, Morag Cranston, BMus, MA. Director, Scottish Music Information Centre, since 1999; b. 20.3.67, Ennerdale, Cumberland. Educ. Queen Elizabeth Grammar School, Penrith; Cardiff University; York University. Lecturer, Royal Forest of Dean College, 1989-90; Lecturer, Denstone College, 1990-91; Director, Wakefield Cathedral Girls' Choir, 1991-93; Lecturer, Performing Arts, Coventry University, 1993-99. Recreations: hillwalking; printmaking; gardening; lighthouses. Address: (b.) 1 Bowmont Gardens, Glasgow G12 9LR; T.-0141-334 6393.

Broome, Professor John, BA, MA, PhD. Professor of Philosophy, University of St. Andrews, since 1996; b. 17.5.47, Kuala Lumpur, Malaya; m., Ann; 1 s.; 1 d. Educ. Rugby School; Trinity Hall, Cambridge; Bedford College, London; Massachusetts Institute of Technology. Lecturer in Economics, Birkbeck College, London University, 1972-78; University of Bristol: Reader in Economics, 1979-92, Professor of Economics and Ethics, 1992-95. Publications: The Microeconomics of Capitalism, 1983; Weighing Goods, 1991; Counting the Cost of Global Warming, 1992. Recreation: sailing. Address: (b.) Department of Moral Philosophy, University of St. Andrews, St. Andrews, Fife KY16 9AL; T.-01334 462481.

Broster, Rev. David, BA, DipTh, CPS. Minister, Kilbirnie: St. Columba's, since 1983; Clerk, Ardrossan Presbytery, since 1989; b. 14.3.44, Liverpool; m., Margaret Ann Mercer; 2 d. Educ. Liverpool Institute High School; United Theological College, University of Wales; Open University. Ordained by Presbyterian Church of Wales, 1969; Minister, Park Place, Tredegar, Gwent, 1969-78; Clubmoor Presbyterian Church of Wales, Liverpool, 1978-83; Clerk, Association in East, Presbyterian Church of Wales, 1981-83; Moderator, Synod of Ayr, 1991-92; Secretary, Nan Stevenson Charitable Trust, since 1989. Chairman: Garnock Valley Victim Support, Moorpark School Board; Past Chairman, Garnock Valley Crime Prevention Panel; President, Garnock Valley Rotary. Recreations: computing; advanced driving; gardening; curling. Address: St. Columba's Manse, Kilbirnie, Ayrshire; T.-01505 683342.

Broun, Janice Anne, BA. Freelance journalist and author; b. 24.3.34, Tipton; m., Canon Claud Broun; 2 s.; 1 d. Educ. Dudley Girls High School; St. Anne's College, Oxford. Publications: Conscience and Captivity: Religion in Eastern

Europe, 1988; Prague Winter, 1988; Albania: Religion in a Fortress State, 1989; Bulgaria: Religion Denied, 1989; Romania: Religion in a Hardline State, 1989; six entries in Censorship: An International Dictionary, 1999; frequent contributions to Keston Institute publications. Recreations: swimming; cycling; music; art history; travel. Address: Martin Lodge, Ardross Place, Alness, Ross-shire, IV17 0PX; T.-01349 882442.

Brown, Alan. Chairman, Scottish Road Safety Campaign, since 1995; Head of Road Safety Branch, Scottish Office, since 1995; b. 9.5.47, Methil; m., Marion Dougal; 1 s.; 1 d. Educ. Buckhaven High School. Joined Scottish Office, 1965: posts in Education, Social Work Services, Transport, Local Government, and Criminal Justice. County Bird Recorder for East Lothian, 1983-89; Member: Lothian Birds Record Committee, 1983-96 and since 1998, Scottish Birds Record Committee, 1984-94 (Secretary, 1984-86), Council, Scottish Ornithologists Club, 1986-90, British Birds Rarities Committee, 1987-95. Recreations: birdwatching in the world's remote places (the ecstasy); supporting Hibernian FC (the agony); rock music; motor-cycling. Address: (b.) The Scottish Office, Victoria Quay, Edinburgh EH6 6QQ; T.-0131-244 0836.

Brown, Professor Alice, MA, PhD. Professor of Politics, University of Edinburgh, since 1997; Co-Director, Governance of Scotland Forum, since 1998; b. 30.9.46, Edinburgh; m., Alan James Brown; 2 d. Educ. Boroughmuir High School, Edinburgh; University of Edinburgh. Lecturer in Economics, University of Stirling, 1984; University of Edinburgh: Lecturer, Departments of Economics, Continuing Education and Politics, 1985-93, Senior Lecturer in Politics, 1993-97, appointed Head of Politics Department, 1995, appointed Head, Planning Unit, 1996, Personal Chair, 1997. Currently: Vice-Convener, Unit for the Study of Government in Scotland, Member, Neill Committee on Standards in Public Life; Council Member, Scottish Higher Education Funding Council; Member, Scottish Office Consultative Steering Group on Standing Orders and Procedures for the Scottish Parliament; Member, Advisory Group to Equal Opportunities Commission; Adviser on women's issues to Minister for Women; Board and Executive Member, Centre for Scottish Public Policy; Member, Scottish Committee, British Council; Member, Academic Advisory Panel, Hansard Society; Assistant Editor, Scottish Affairs journal; Member, Editorial Board, Edinburgh University Press; Member, Editorial Board, Scotland Forum; Member, Editorial Board, Talking Politics; founder Member, Scottish Gender Equality Research Network. Publications: A Major Crisis? (Joint Author), 1996; General Equality in Scotland (Joint Author), 1997; Politics and Society in Scotland (Joint Author), 1996; The Scottish Electorate (Joint Author), 1999. Recreations: reading; music; cooking. Address: Department of Politics, University of Edinburgh, 31 Buccleuch Place, Edinburgh EH8 9JT; T.-0131-650 4251.

Brown, Professor Alistair J.P., BSc, PhD. Professor of Molecular and Cell Biology, Aberdeen University, since 1998; b. 5.2.55; m., Carolyn Michie; 2 s. Educ. George Watson's College, Edinburgh; University of Aberdeen. Biotechnology Lecturer, Glasgow University, 1983-89; Aberdeen University: Biotechnology Lecturer, 1989-91, Senior Lecturer, 1992-96, Reader, 1996-98. Recreation: his sons, Myles and Cameron. Address: (b.) Institute of Medical Sciences, Foresterhill, Aberdeen AB25 2ZD; T.-01224 273183.

Brown, Alistair M. Director, Administrative Services, Scottish Office, since 1997; b. 1.3.57, Edinburgh; m., Sarah Thompson; 1 s.; 2 d. Educ. Linlithgow Academy. Scottish Office, since 1974; Personal Assistant to Chief Executive, S.D.A., 1987-89; Scottish Office Industry Department, 1989-93; Grade 5, 1993. Recreations: helping to bring up family; walking. Address: (b.) Scottish Office, Victoria Quay, Edinburgh EH6 6QQ; T.-0131-244 7692.

Brown, Allan, MA (Hons). Deputy Editor, Features, Sunday Times Scotland, since 1998 (Chief Feature Writer, since 1996, Columnist, since 1997); b. 12.1.67, Glasgow. Educ. Claremont High School, East Kilbride; University of Glasgow; University of Strathclyde. Press Officer, Glasgow 1990: Year of Culture, 1990; freelance work, 1990-93; Assistant, John Smith's Bookshop, Glasgow, 1994; News Sub-Editor, Scottish Sun, 1995; Sub-Editor, Sunday Times, 1996. Bank of Scotland Feature Writer of the Year, 1998-99; Scottish Journalist of the Year, 1998-99. Publication: Inside the Wicker Man – The Morbid Ingenuities, 1999. Recreations: whingeing; Glasgow Rangers FC. Address: (b.) 124 Portman Street, Glasgow G41 1EJ; T.-0141-420 5278.

Brown, Andrew Gibson, QPM. Chief Constable, Grampian Police, since 1998; b. 11.4.45, Kelso; m., Fiona; 1 s.; 1 d. Lothian and Borders Police: Detective Chief Superintendent, 1992-93, Assistant Chief Constable, 1993-98. Address: (b.) Police HQ, Queen Street, Aberdeen AB10 1ZA; T.-01224 386000.

Brown, Professor Charles Malcolm, BSc, PhD, DSc, FIBiol, FIBrew, FRSE. Professor of Microbiology, Heriot-Watt University, since 1979 (Head, Department of Biological Sciences, 1988-93; Dean of Science, 1993-95, Assistant Principal, 1994-95; Vice Principal, since 1995); b. 21.9.41, Gilsland; m., Diane Mary Bryant; 3 d. Educ. Houghton-le-Spring Grammar School; Birmingham University. Lecturer in Microbiology, Newcastle-upon-Tyne University, 1966-73; Senior Lecturer, Dundee University, 1973-79. Director, Microbiological Research Authority; Editor: Process Biochemistry, Journal of the Institute of Brewing. Recreations: music; walking. Address: (b.) Heriot-Watt University, Riccarton, Edinburgh EH14 4AS; T.-0131-449 5111.

Brown, Rev. Colin Campbell, BD. Minister, Darnley United Free Church, Glasgow, since 1979; Teacher (part-time) of Religious Education, Williamwood High School, Glasgow, since 1987; b. 30.8.54, Perth; m., Joyce; 1 s. Educ. Perth High School; University of Edinburgh; Moray House College of Education. Convener, United Free Church Youth Committee, 1985-89; Moderator, Presbytery of Glasgow and the West, 1990-91; Convener, Action of Churches Together in Scotland Education Group, 1992-94; Convener, United Free Church Ministry and Home Affairs Committee, since 1997; part-time Religious Education Teacher, Renfrew High School, 1980-87. Address: 2 Waukglen Drive, Southpark, Darnley, Glasgow G53 7UG; T.-0141-638 6101.

Brown, Professor Ewan, CBE, MA, LLB, CA, FRSA. Merchant Banker; Executive Director: Noble Grossart Ltd., since 1971; Chairman, Dunedin Income Growth Investment Trust Plc, Scottish Knowledge Plc; Director, TSB Bank Scotland plc; John Wood Group Plc; Noble Grossart Investments Ltd.; Stagecoach Holdings Plc; James Walker (Leith) Ltd.; b. 23.3.42, Perth; m., Christine; 1 s.; 1 d. Educ. Perth Academy; St. Andrews University. CA apprentice with Peat Marwick Mitchell, 1964-67. Honorary Professor in Finance, Heriot Watt University; Trustee, Carnegie Trust for the Universities of Scotland; Chairman, University Court, Heriot-Watt University; Master, The Company of Merchants of the City of Edinburgh, 1994-95; Lord Dean of Guild, City of Edinburgh, 1995-97; Council Member: Institute of Chartered Accountants of Scotland, 1988-91, Scottish Business School, 1974-80; Previous directorships: Scottish Transport Group, 1983-88, Scottish Development Finance, 1983-93, Pict Petroleum plc, 1973-95, Scottish Widows Bank plc, 1994-97; Governor, Edinburgh College of Art, 1986-89; Session Clerk, Mayfield Church, 1983-88.

Recreations: family; golf; skiing; Scottish watercolours; Mah Jongg. Address: (b.) 48 Queen Street, Edinburgh; T.-0131-226 7011.

Brown, Francis Henry, BA (Hons), MHSM, DipHSM. Chief Executive, Perth and Kinross Healthcare NHS Trust, since 1994; b. 17.4.47, Falkirk; m., Marion Muir Crawford; 2 s. Educ. Falkirk High School; Strathclyde University. Joined NHS as graduate trainee, 1975; various management/senior management posts, Borders Health Board, Ayrshire and Arran Health Board, 1977-94. Recreations: music; swimming; cycling; golf. Address: (b.) Perth Royal Infirmary, Taymount Terrace, Perth PH1 1NX; T.-01738 620540.

Brown, Gordon Lamont. Scottish Rugby International and British Lion; author and after-dinner speaker; ITV rugby commentator; Trustee, sole fund-raiser, Search M.E. charity (researching Chronic Fatigue Syndrome); b. 1.11.47, Troon; m., Linda; 1 s.; 1 d. Educ. Marr College, Troon. Bank clerk, British Linen Bank, 1965-71; Building Society Manager: Leicester Building Society, 1971-76, Bristol & West Building Society, 1976-97. Played for Scotland, 30 times; toured with British Isles Rugby Team ("Lions), New Zealand 1971, South Africa 1974, New Zealand 1977; holds world record for number of tries scored by a forward on a tour (eight). Publications: Broon from Troon (autobiography); Rugby is a Funny Game (rugby anecdotes). Recreation: golf. Address: (h.) 65 Bentinck Drive, Troon, Ayrshire; T.-01292 315125.

Brown, Hamish Macmillan, Hon.D.Litt (St Andrews). Author, Lecturer, Photographer and Mountaineer; b. 13.8.34, Colombo, Sri Lanka. Educ. several schools abroad; Dollar Academy. National Service, RAF, Middle East/East Africa; Assistant, Martyrs' Memorial Church, Paisley; first-ever full-time appointment in outdoor education (Braehead School, Fife); served many years on Scottish Mountain Leadership Board; has led expeditions world-wide for mountaineering, skiing, trekking, canoeing, etc. Publications: Hamish's Mountain Walk, 1979 (SAC award); Hamish's Groats End Walk, 1981 (Smith's Travel Prize shortlist); Time Gentlemen, Some Collected Poems, 1983; Eye to the Hills, 1982; Five Bird Stories, 1984; Poems of the Scottish Hills (Editor), 1982; Speak to the Hills (Co-Editor), 1985; Travels, 1986; The Great Walking Adventure, 1986; Hamish Brown's Scotland, 1988; Climbing the Corbetts, 1988; Great Walks Scotland (Co-author), 1989; Scotland Coast to Coast, 1990; Walking the Summits of Somerset and Avon, 1991; From the Pennines to the Highlands, 1992; The Bothy Brew & Other Stories, 1993; The Fife Coast, The Last Hundred, 1994; 25 Walks – Fife, 1995; Fort William and Glen Coe Walks, 1996; Exploring the Edinburgh to Glasgow Canal, 1997; Compendium: Hamish's Mountain Walks/Climbing the Corbetts, 1997; Fife in Focus, Photographs of the Fife Coast. Recreations: books; music; Morocco. Address: 26 Kirkcaldy Road, Burntisland, Fife, KY3 9HQ; T.-01592 873546.

Brown, Hilary Neilson, DipDomSc, DipEd. Chef/Proprietrix, La Potiniere, since 1975; b. 6.6.52, Glasgow; m., David Richard Brown. Educ. Hutchesons' Girls' Grammar School; Glasgow and West of Scotland College of Domestic Science; Jordanhill College of Education. Teacher, Bellarmine Secondary School, 1973-75. Michelin Star, since 1991; Egon Ronay Star, since 1985; AA Rosettes, since 1977. Publication: La Potiniere and Friends, 1990. Recreations: health and fitness; cinema; France. Address: (b.) La Potiniere, Gullane, East Lothian; T.-01620 843214.

Brown, Professor Ian James Morris, MA (Hons), MLitt, PhD, DipEd, FRSA. Playwright, since 1969; Professor of Drama, Queen Margaret College, Edinburgh, since 1995 (Head of Department, since 1996, Reader, 1994-95); Director, Scottish Centre for Cultural Management and Policy, since 1996; b. 28.2.45, Barnet; m., 1, Judith Sidaway; 2, Nicola Axford; 1 s.; 1 d. Educ. Dollar Academy; Edinburgh University; Crewe and Alasager College. Schoolteacher, 1967-69, 1970-71; Lecturer in Drama, Dunfermline College, 1971-76; British Council: Assistant Representative, Scotland, 1976-77, Assistant Regional Director, Istanbul, 1977-78; various posts, Crewe and Alsager College, 1978-86, latterly Leader, BA (Hons) Drama Studies; Programme Director, Alsager Arts Centre, 1980-86; Drama Director, Arts Council of Great Britain, 1986-94. British Theatre Institute: Vice Chairman, 1983-85, Chairman, 1985-87; Member, International Advisory Committee, O'Neill Theatre Center, since 1994; Chair, Scottish Society of Playwrights, 1973-75, 1984-87, since 1997; plays include Mother Earth, The Bacchae, Carnegie, The Knife, The Fork, New Reekie, Mary, Runners, Mary Queen and the Loch Tower, Joker in the Pack, Beatrice, First Strike, The Scotch Play, Bacchai, Wasting Reality. Recreations: theatre; sport; travel; cooking. Address: (b.) Queen Margaret College, Clerwood Terrace, Edinburgh EH12 8TS.

Brown, James Armour, RD, BL, FSA (Scot). Preceptor of Torphichen of the Priory of Scotland, Order of St. John of Jerusalem, since 1998; Partner, Kerr Barrie & Duncan (formerly Kerr, Barrie & Goss), Solicitors, Glasgow, 1957-91 (Consultant, 1991-93); b. 20.7.30, Rutherglen; m., Alexina Mary Robertson McArthur; 1 s. Educ. Rutherglen Academy; Glasgow University. National Service, Royal Navy, 1951-53; commissioned RNVR, 1952; served with Clyde Division, RNVR/RNR, 1953-72; Captain, 1972; Senior Reserve Supply Officer on staff of Admiral Commanding Reserves, 1973-76; Naval ADC to The Queen, 1975-76; Member, Suite of Lord High Commissioner to General Assembly of Church of Scotland, 1961-63; Session Clerk, Stonelaw Parish Church, Rutherglen, 1964-81; Member, Church of Scotland Committee on Chaplains to HM Forces, 1975-82 (Vice-Convener, 1979-82); Clerk, Incorporation of Bakers of Glasgow, 1964-89; Deacon, Society of Deacons and Free Preseses of Glasgow, 1978-80; Member, Glasgow Committee, Order of St. John of Jerusalem, since 1961 (Chairman, 1982-93, Honorary President, since 1995); Member, Chapter of the Priory of Scotland of the Order of St. John, since 1970; KStJ, 1975; Preceptor of Torphichen, Priory of Scotland, 1984-92; Chancellor, Priory of Scotland, 1992-97; Hon. Chairman, Orders and Medals Research Society (Scottish Branch), 1987- 91. Recreations: music; historical research. Address: (h.) 6 Arran Way, Bothwell, Glasgow G71 8TR; T.-01698 854226.

Brown, Rt. Hon. (James) Gordon. MA, PhD, MP. Chancellor of the Exchequer, since 1997; MP (Labour), Dunfermline East, since 1983; b. 20.2.51. Educ. Kirkcaldy High School; Edinburgh University. Rector, Edinburgh University, 1972-75; Temporary Lecturer, Edinburgh University, 1976; Lecturer, Glasgow College of Technology, 1976-80; Journalist and Current Affairs Editor, Scottish Television, 1980-83. Contested (Labour) South Edinburgh, 1979; Chairman, Labour Party Scottish Council, 1983-84; Opposition Chief Secretary to the Treasury, 1987; Shadow Minister for Trade and Industry, 1989. Publications: The Red Paper on Scotland (Editor), 1975; The Politics of Nationalism and Devolution (Co-Editor), 1980; Scotland: The Real Divide, 1983; Maxton, 1986; Where There is Greed, 1989. Recreations: reading and writing; football; golf; tennis. Address: 21 Ferryhills Road, North Queensferry, Fife.

Brown, J. Craig, BA, DipPE. International Team Manager and Technical Director, Scottish Football Association, since 1993; b. 1.7.40, Glasgow; 2 s.; 1 d. Educ. Hamilton Academy. Professional footballer: Rangers F.C., 1958-60, Dundee F.C., 1960-66, Falkirk F.C., 1966-68; Assistant Manager, Motherwell F.C., 1975-77; Manager, Clyde F.C.,

1977-86; Assistant National Coach and Under-21 Coach, 1986-93; Vice President, Union of European Football Trainers; Hon. Lecturer, Paisley University; Sports Photographers' Personality of the Year, 1996; City of Glasgow Sports Personality of the Year, 1997; Bells Manager of the Month, five occasions. Teacher of primary school subjects, Deputy Headteacher, Headteacher and Lecturer in Primary Education, 1963-86. Publication: Activity Methods in the Middle Years, 1975. Recreation: golf. Address: (b.) Scottish Football Association, 6 Park Gardens, Glasgow G3 7YF; T.-0141-353 3522.

Brown, Jenny, MA (Hons). Literature Director, Scottish Arts Council; b. 13.5.58, Manchester; m., Alexander Richardson; 3 s. Educ. George Watson's College; Aberdeen University. Assistant Administrator, Edinburgh Festival Fringe Society, 1980-82; Director, Edinburgh Book Festival, 1983-91; Presenter, Scottish Television book programmes, 1989-94; National Co-ordinator, Readiscovery Campaign, 1994-95; Commissioner, Press Complaints Commission, 1993-97. Address: (b.) Scottish Arts Council, 12 Manor Place, Edinburgh EH3 7DD.

Brown, Jock, MA (Cantab). General Manager, Football, Celtic F.C., 1997-98; b. 7.5.46, Kilmarnock; m., Ishbel; 3 d. Educ. Hamilton Academy; Sidney Sussex College, University of Cambridge. Journalist: Glasgow Herald, 1967, D.C. Thomson & Co. Ltd., 1967-68 and 1970-73; Assistant Secretary, Scottish Football League, 1968-70; Law Apprentice, Ballantyne & Copland, Solicitors, Motherwell, 1973-75, Solicitor, 1975-95; Director, Caledonian Television Ltd., 1993-95; Sports Law Consultant, Harper MacLeod, Solicitors, Glasgow, 1995-97; Sports Commentator: Scottish Television, 1980-90, BSkyB, 1989-95, BBC Scotland, 1990-97. Recreation: golf.

Brown, John Caldwell, DA, RSW. Painter; Lecturer (part-time): Edinburgh College of Art, since 1991, Leith School of Art, since 1991; b. 19.10.45, Irvine; m., Elizabeth Ann; 3 s. Educ. Ardrossan Academy; Glasgow School of Art. RSA Carnegie Travelling Scholarship and GSA Cargill Travelling Scholarship, 1968; Director of Art, Fettes College, 1971-86; Director of Art, Malvern College, 1986-88; Head of Art, Edinburgh Academy, 1988-97; solo exhibitions: GSA, 1970, Moray House, 1989, Torrance Gallery, 1992, Open Eye Gallery, 1996 and 1998, Duncan Miller Fine Art London, 1996 and 1997. James Torrance Award, RGI, 1970; Scottish Arts Club Award SAAC, 1993; Scottish Provident Award, 1993; Heinzel Gallery Award SAAC, 1994. Address: (h.) 92 Trinity Road, Edinburgh EH5 3JU; T.-0131-552 8676.

Brown, Professor John Campbell, BSc, PhD, DSc, FRAS, FRSE, FInstP. Astronomer Royal for Scotland, since 1995; Professor of Astrophysics, Glasgow University, 1984-96, Regius Chair of Astronomy, since 1996; Honorary Professor, Edinburgh University, since 1996, Aberdeen University, since 1997; b. 4.2.47, Dumbarton; m., Dr. Margaret I. Brown; 1 s.; 1 d. Educ. Dumbarton Academy; Glasgow University. Glasgow University Astronomy Department: Research Assistant, 1968-70, Lecturer, 1970-78, Senior Lecturer, 1978-80, Reader, 1980-84; Nuffield Fellow, 1983-84; Kelvin Medallist, 1983-86; DAAD Fellow, Tubingen University, 1971-72; ESRO/GROC Fellow, Space Research Laboratory, Utrecht, 1973-74; Visitor: Australian National University, 1975, High Altitude Observatory, Colorado, 1977; NASA Associate Professor, Maryland University, 1980; NSF Fellow, University of California at San Diego, 1984; Brittingham Professor, University of Wisconsin, 1987. SERC Solar System Committee, 1980-83; Council, Royal Astronomical Society, 1984-87, 1990-93 (Vice-President, 1986-87); Council, Royal Society of Edinburgh, since 1997; Member, International Astronomical Union, since 1976. Recreations: cycling; walking; painting; lapidary; conjuring; photography; woodwork. Address: (b.) Department of Physics and Astronomy, Glasgow University, Glasgow G12 8QW; T.-0141-330 5182.

Brown, John Souter, MA (Hons), MIPR. Head of Public Relations and Marketing, Glasgow City Council, since 1996; b. 15.10.48, Glasgow; m., Angela McGinn; 1 s.; 1 d. Educ. Kirkcaldy High School; Edinburgh University. Statistics and Information Officer, Lanark County Council, 1970-72; Senior Officer (Research, Planning Publicity), Manchester City Social Services Department, 1972-75; Press Officer, Strathclyde Regional Council, 1975-80; Journalist and Presenter, Scottish Television, 1980-82; Editor, What's Your Problem?, 1982-84; Ways and Means, 1984-86; Senior Producer (Politics), Scottish Television, 1986-91; North of Scotland TV Franchise Team, 1991; Managing Director, Lomond Television, 1992-93; Head of Public Relations, Strathclyde Regional Council, 1993-96; Chair, Volunteer Centre, Glasgow, since 1992; Director, Scottish Foundation, since 1990. Address: (b.) Public Relations and Marketing, City Chambers, George Square, Glasgow G2 1DU; T.-0141-287 0901.

Brown, Professor Kenneth Alexander, BSc, MSc, PhD, FRSE. Professor of Mathematics, Glasgow University; Vice-President, London Mathematical Society, 1997-99; b. 19.4.51, Ayr; m., Irene M.; 2 s. Educ. Ayr Academy; Glasgow University; Warwick University. Recreations: reading; running. Address: (b.) Mathematics Department, Glasgow University, Glasgow G12 8QW; T.-0141-330 5180.

Brown, Kenneth Graeme. National Field Manager, Muscular Dystrophy Group, since 1997 (Scottish Regional Director, since 1993); b. 28.8.58; Edinburgh; m., Norma. Educ. Daniel Stewart's College; Heriot Watt University. Scientific Officer, Moredun Institute; Liaison/Information Officer, Animal Diseases Research Association and ADRA Equine Research and Grass Sickness Fund; Fundraiser, National Schizophrenia Fellowship (Scotland). Recreations: fishing; model making; travel; rugby (spectating!). Address: (b.) 3rd Floor, Princes House, 5 Shandwick Place, Edinburgh EH2 4RG; T.-0131-221 0066.

Brown, Professor Kenneth J., BSc, PhD, FRSE. Professor in Mathematics, Heriot-Watt University, since 1993; b. 20.12.45, Torphins; m., Elizabeth Lobban; 1 s.; 2 d. Educ. Banchory Academy; Robert Gordon's College; Aberdeen University; Dundee University. Lecturer in Mathematics, Heriot Watt University, 1970-81, Senior Lecturer, 1981-91, Reader, 1991-93. Publications: 45 papers. Recreations: coaching athletics; reading. Address: (h.) 3 Highlea Grove, Balerno, Edinburgh EH14 7HQ; T.-0131-449 5314.

Brown, R. Iain F, MBE, MA, MEd, ABPsS, ChPsychol. Senior Lecturer, Department of Psychology, Glasgow University, since 1968; b. 16.1.35, Dundee; m., Catherine G. (qv); 2 d. Educ. Daniel Stewart's College, Edinburgh; St. Andrews University; Edinburgh University; Glasgow University. Education Department, Corporation of Glasgow; Department of Psychological Medicine, Glasgow University. National Training Adviser, Scottish Council on Alcohol, 1979-94; Member, Executive, Scottish Council on Alcohol, 1980-94 and since 1998; Chairman: Society for the Study of Gambling, London, 1987-92, European Association for the Study of Gambling, since 1992, Glasgow Council on Alcohol, since 1985, Confederation of Scottish Counselling Agencies, 1989-93; Member, Lead Body on Advice, Guidance, Counselling and Psychotherapy (UK), since 1992. Various publications, mainly on addictions, in scientific books and journals. Recreations: travel; music. Address: (h.) 13 Kirklee Terrace, Glasgow G12 0TH; T.-0141-339 7095.

Brown, Russell Leslie. MP (Labour), Dumfries, since 1997; b. 17.9.51, Annan; m., Christine Margaret Calvert; 2 d. Educ. Annan Academy. Employed by ICI for 23 years in variety of positions; Local Councillor, since 1986. Recreations: walking; sport, especially football. Address: (h.) 11 Great King Street, Dumfries DG1 1BA; T.-01387 247902.

Brown, Professor Sally, BSc, MA, PhD, FRSE. Professor of Education, Stirling University, since 1990; Deputy Principal, Stirling University, since 1996; b. 15.12.35, London; m., Professor Charles Brown (deceased); 2 s. Educ. Bromley High School GPDST; University College, London; Smith College, Massachusetts; Stirling University. Lecturer in College of Education, London, and College of Technology, Nigeria; University Lecturer, Nigeria; School Science Teacher, Helensburgh; University Researcher, Stirling; Research Adviser to Scottish Education Department; Director, Scottish Council for Research in Education, 1986-90. Publications: 120 (articles, monographs, books) on educational research and education generally. Recreations: squash; reading; music. Address: (b.) Department of Education, Stirling University, Stirling FK9 4LA.

Brown, Steven, LLB (Hons). Solicitor; Partner, McClure Naismith, since 1986; b. 20.11.56, Irvine; m., Carol Anne; 1 s. Educ. Irvine Royal Academy; University of Edinburgh. Trained with Kilgour McNeil & Syme, 1978-80; Assistant Solicitor, J&F Anderson, 1980-85. Chairman, Redwoods Caring Foundation. Recreations: family; computers; music; golf. Address: (b.) 49 Queen Street, Edinburgh EH2 3NH; T.-0131-220 1002.

Brown, Professor Stewart J., BA, MA, PhD, FRHistS. Professor of Ecclesiastical History, Edinburgh University, since 1988; Dean, Faculty of Divinity, since 1999; b. 8.7.51, Illinois; m., Teri B. Hopkins-Brown; 1 s.; 1 d. Educ. University of Illinois; University of Chicago. Fulbright Scholar, Edinburgh University, 1976-78; Whiting Fellow in the Humanities, University of Chicago, 1979-80; Assistant to the Dean, College of Arts & Sciences, and Lecturer in History, Northwestern University, 1980-82; Associate Professor and Assistant Head, Department of History, University of Georgia, 1982-88; Visiting Lecturer, Department of Irish History, University College, Cork, 1986; Editor, Scottish Historical Review, 1993-99. Publications: Thomas Chalmers and the Godly Commonwealth in Scotland, 1982 (awarded Agnes Mure Mackenzie Prize from Saltire Society); Scotland in the Age of the Disruption (Co-author), 1993; William Robertson and the Expansion of Empire (Editor), 1997; Religion, Politics and Culture in Ireland (Co-editor), 1999. Recreations: swimming; hill-walking. Address: (h.) 160 Craigleith Hill Avenue, Edinburgh EH4 2NB; T.-0131-343 1712.

Brown, William Alan, Master Mariner; Marine Superintendent, Scottish Fisheries Protection Agency, since 1997; b. 4.10.49, Edinburgh; m., Elizabeth Ann Connell; 1 s.; 1 d. Educ. Boroughmuir Secondary School; Leith Nautical College. Cadet to Second Officer, British and Commonwealth Shipping, 1967-77; Second Officer to Chief Officer, Fred. Olsen Lines, 1977-80; Scottish Fisheries Protection Agency (formerly DAFS), since 1980: Second Officer, then First Officer, then Commander. Address: (b.) Pentland House, 47 Robb's Loan, Edinburgh EH14 1TY.

Browne, Desmond. MP (Labour), Kilmarnock and Loudoun, since 1997; b. 22.3.52; m., 2 s. Educ. Glasgow University. Former Solicitor; admitted, Faculty of Advocates, 1993. Address: (b.) House of Commons, London SW1A 0AA.

Browning, Professor George Gordon, MD, ChB, FRCS(Ed.), FRCPS(Glas). Professor of Otolaryngology, Head and Neck Surgery, University of Glasgow, since 1991; Honorary Consultant Otolaryngologist, Glasgow Royal Infirmary, since 1978; Senior Consultant Otologist to British MRC Institute of Hearing Research, since 1992; b. 10.1.41, Glasgow; m., Annette; 1 s.; 2 d. Educ. Kelvinside Academy; University of Glasgow. Resident House Surgeon, Western Infirmary, Glasgow, 1964-65; West of Scotland General Surgical Training Scheme, 1965-70; West of Scotland Otorhinolaryngological Training Scheme, 1970-76; MRC Wernher-Piggot Travelling Fellow, Harvard University, 1976-77. Publications: Updated ENT (3rd Edition), 1994; Picture Tests in Otolaryngology (Co-Author), 1998; Clinical Otology and Audiology (2nd Edition), 1998; Otoscopy – A Structured Approach (Co-Author), 1995; over 80 scientific articles. President, Otorhinolaryngological Research Society UK, 1992-94; Chairman, British Society of Academics in Otolaryngology, UK, since 1995; Vice-Chairman, Specialist Advisory Committee in Otolaryngology, since 1997; President-Elect, Section of Otology, Royal Society of Medicine; Member, Post-Graduate Examining Boards, FRCS Edinburgh, since 1997, and FRCPS Glasgow, since 1987. Recreations: silversmithing; skiing; swimming. Address: (b.) Department of Otolaryngology, Glasgow Royal Infirmary University NHS Trust, 16 Alexandra Parade, Glasgow G31 2ER; T.-0141-211 4695.

Browning, Professor J. Robin, BA (Hons), FCIBS. Chief Executive, British Linen Bank; General Manager, Bank of Scotland, since 1986 (Divisional General Manager, 1983-86); b. 29.7.39, Kirkcaldy; m., Christine Campbell; 1 s.; 1 d. Educ. Morgan Academy, Dundee; Strathclyde University; Harvard Business School. Bank of Scotland: Assistant Management Accountant, 1971-74, Assistant Manager (Corporate Planning), 1974-77; British Linen Bank Ltd.: Manager, 1977-79, Assistant Director, 1979-81, Director, 1981-82; Assistant General Manager, Bank of Scotland, 1982-83. Former Member of Council, Chartered Institute of Bankers in Scotland, 1994-97; Deputy Chairman, Association for Payment and Clearing Services, 1994-97; Visiting Professor of Banking, University of Stirling. Recreations: curling; gardening; DIY enthusiast. Address: (b.) British Linen Bank Ltd., 4 Melville Street, Edinburgh EH3 7NZ; T.-0131-243 8301.

Brownlie, Alistair Rutherford, OBE, MA, LLB, SSC; b. 5.4.24, Edinburgh; m., Martha Barron Mounsey. Educ. George Watson's; Edinburgh University. Served as radio operator in 658 Air O.P. Squadron RAF, Europe and India; apprenticed to J. & R.A. Robertson, WS; qualified Solicitor, 1950; in private practice; Member, Committee on Blood Grouping (House of Lords); Solicitor for the poor, 1955-64, in High Court of Justiciary; Secretary, SSC Society, 1970-95, now Archivist; former Member, Council, Law Society of Scotland; Legal Aid Central Committee; Chairman, Legal Aid Committee, Scottish Legal Aid Board, 1986-90; founder Member, Past President, now Hon. Member, Forensic Science Society; Member, Vice-Chairman, Scottish Council of Law Reporting, 1975-97; Fellow, RSA; Elder, Church of Scotland and Congregational Union of Scotland. Publications: Drink, Drugs and Driving (Co-author); Crime Investigation: art or science (Editor); various papers on forensic science, criminal law and legal aid. Recreations: the pen, the spade, and the saw. Address: (h.) 8 Braid Mount, Edinburgh; T.-0131-447 4255.

Bruce, Alistair James, LLB, NP. Solicitor; Partner, Lows, Solicitors, Kirkwall, since 1985; b. 4.12.58, Perth; m., Jane; 2 s. Educ. Perth Academy; University of Dundee. Apprenticeship with A.C. Morrison and Richards, Advocates, Aberdeen, 1980-82; Assistant Solicitor, T.P. and J.L. Low, Kirkwall, 1982-85. Member, Council, Law Society of Scotland, 1996-98. President, Rotary Club of Kirkwall; Secretary: Orkney Arts Theatre, J.P. Advisory Committee for Orkney; Past President, Society of the Procurators of Orkney; Past Chairman, Family Mediation, Orkney. Recreations: golf; drama; St. Magnus Cathedral Choir. Address: (b.) 5 Broad Street, Kirkwall, Orkney; T.-01856 873151.

Bruce, David, MA, Chevalier de L'Ordre des Arts et des Lettres. Writer and Consultant; Director, Scottish Film Council, 1986-94; b. 10.6.39, Dundee; m., Barbara; 1 s.; 1 d. Educ. Dundee High School; Aberdeen Grammar School; Edinburgh University. Freelance (film), 1963; Assistant Director, Films of Scotland, 1964-66; Director, Edinburgh International Film Festival, 1965-66; Promotions Manager, Mermaid Theatre, London, 1966-67; Executive Officer, British Universities Film Council, 1967-69; joined Scottish Film Council as Assistant Director, 1969; Depute Director, SFC and Scottish Council for Educational Technology, 1977-86. Chairman, Mental Health Film Council, 1982-84; Chairman, Scottish Society for History of Photography, 1983-86; Chairman, Association of European Film Institutes, 1990-94. Various publications, including Scotland–the movie, 1996. Recreations: movies; music; photo-history. Address: (h.) Rosebank, 150 West Princes Street, Helensburgh G84 8BH.

Bruce, Fraser Finlayson, RD, MA (Hons), LLB, FSA(Scot). Regional Chairman, Industrial Tribunals for Scotland 1993-97 (Permanent Chairman, 1982-93); Solicitor, since 1956; b. 10.10.31, Kirkcaldy; m., Joan Gwendolen Hunter; 2 step-s. Educ. St. Andrews University. National Service, Royal Navy, 1956-58, commissioned Sub-Lieutenant, RNVR; Legal Assistant: Lanark County Council, 1958-60, Inverness County Council, 1960-66; Depute County Clerk: Argyll County Council, 1966-70, Inverness County Council, 1970-72; County Clerk, Inverness County Council, 1972-75; Joint Director of Law and Administration, Highland Regional Council, 1975-82; Temporary Sheriff, 1984-92. Served RNVR, 1956-76, retiring as Lieutenant-Commander RNR. Recreations: hill walking; Gaelic language; reading (in philosophy and naval/military history). Address: (h.) Drumdunan House, by Grantown-on-Spey PH26 3LG;T.-01479 873969.

Bruce, George, OBE (1984), MA, DLitt. Writer/Lecturer; b. 10.3.09, Fraserburgh; m., Elizabeth Duncan; 1 s.; 1 d. Educ. Fraserburgh Academy; Aberdeen University. Teacher, English Department, Dundee High School, 1935-46; BBC Producer, Aberdeen, 1946-56; BBC Talks (Documentary) Producer, Edinburgh, with special responsibility for arts programmes, 1956-70; first Fellow in Creative Writing, Glasgow University, 1971-73; Visiting Professor, Union Theological Seminary, Richmond, Virginia, and Writer in Residence, Prescott College, Arizona, 1974; Visiting Professor of English, College of Wooster, Ohio, 1976-77; Scottish-Australian Writing Fellow, 1982; E. Hervey Evans Distinguished Fellow, St. Andrews Presbyterian College, North Carolina, 1985; Vice-Chairman, Council, Saltire Society; Council Member, Advisory Council of the Arts in Scotland; Extra-Mural Lecturer, Glasgow, St. Andrews and Edinburgh Universities; Executive Editor, The Scottish Review, 1975-76; Honorary President, Scottish Poetry Library. Publications: Sea Talk, 1944; Selected Poems, 1947; Landscapes and Figures, 1967; Collected Poems, 1970; The Red Sky, 1985; Perspectives: poems 1970-86, 1987; Scottish Sculpture Today (Co-author), 1947; Anne Redpath, 1974; The City of Edinburgh, 1974; Festival in the North, 1975; Some Practical Good, 1975; A Scottish Postbag (Co-author), 1986; The Scottish Literary Revival, 1962 (Editor); Scottish Poetry Anthologies 1-6 (Co-Editor), 1966-72; The Land Out There, anthology (Editor), 1991. Recreation: visiting friends. Address: 25 Warriston Crescent, Edinburgh EH3 5LB; T.-0131-556 3848.

Bruce, Malcolm Gray, MA, MSc. MP (Liberal Democrat, formerly Liberal), Gordon, since 1983; Liberal Democrat Treasury Spokesman; b. 17.11.44, Birkenhead; 1 s.; 1 d. Educ. Wrekin College; St. Andrews University; Strathclyde University. Trainee Journalist, Liverpool Daily Post & Echo, 1966-67; Section Buyer, Boots the Chemist, 1968-69; Fashion Retailing Executive, A. Goldberg & Sons, 1969-70; Research and Information Officer, NESDA, 1971-75; Marketing Director, Noroil Publishing, 1975-81; Director, Aberdeen Petroleum Publishing; Editor/Publisher, Aberdeen Petroleum Report, 1981-83; Co-Editor, Scottish Petroleum Annual, 1st and 2nd editions; Called to the Bar (Gray's Inn), 1995. Vice Chairman, Political, Scottish Liberal Party, 1975-84; Rector, Dundee University, 1986-89. Recreations: reading; music; theatre; hill-walking; cycling; travel. Address: (b.) House of Commons, London, SW1A 0AA.

Bruce, Roderick Lawrence, LLB (Hons). Partner, Dickson Minto WS, since 1986; b. 8.3.48, Edinburgh; m., Jane; 1 s.; 3 d. Educ. Boroughmuir School; Edinburgh University. Partner, Dundas and Wilson CS, 1977-86. Recreations: golf; squash; skiing; theatre. Address: (b.) 11 Walker Street, Edinburgh EH3 7NE. T.-0131-225 4455.

Bruce, Professor Steve, BA, PhD. Professor of Sociology, Aberdeen University, since 1991; b. 1.4.54, Edinburgh; m., Elizabeth S. Duff; 1 s.; 2 d. Educ. Queen Victoria School, Dunblane; Stirling University. Variously Lecturer, Reader and Professor of Sociology, Queen's University of Belfast, 1978-91. Publications: author of numerous books on religion, and on the Northern Ireland conflict. Recreation: farming. Address: (b.) Department of Sociology, Aberdeen University, Aberdeen AB24 3QY; T.-01224 272761.

Bruce, Professor Victoria Geraldine, OBE, BA, MA, PhD, CPsychol, FBPsS, FRSE. Professor of Psychology, Stirling University, since 1992; Deputy Principal (Research), Stirling University, since 1995; b. 4.1.53; m., Professor A.M. Burton. Educ. Newcastle-upon-Tyne Church High School for Girls; Newnham College, Cambridge. Lecturer, then Reader, then Professor of Psychology, Nottingham University, 1978-92. Member, Economic and Social Research Council, 1992-96, and Chair, Research Programmes Board, 1992-96; Chair, SHEFC Research Policy Advisory Group, since 1998 President, European Society for Cognitive Psychology, 1996-98; Editor, British Journal of Psychology, since 1995; Chair, Psychology Panel for 1996 University Funding Councils' Research Assessment Exercise; Member, Scottish Higher Education Funding Council, since 1995. Publications: numerous papers and several books on visual perception and cognition. Recreations: dogs; walking; games. Address: (h.) The Mill House, Fintry, Stirlingshire G63 0YD; T.-01360 860 342.

Brunt, Professor Peter William, OBE, MD, FRCP(Lond), FRCP(Edin). Consultant Physician, Aberdeen Royal Infirmary, since 1970; Clinical Professor of Medicine, Aberdeen University, since 1996; Physician to The Queen in Scotland, since 1983; non-stipendiary Minister in Episcopal Church of Scotland; b. 18.1.36, Prestatyn; m., Marina Evelyn Anne Lewis; 3 d. Educ. Manchester Grammar School; King George V School; Liverpool University. Recreations: mountaineering; music. Address: (h.) 17 Kingshill Road, Aberdeen AB15 5JY; T.-Aberdeen 314204.

Bruntisfield, 2nd Baron (John Robert Warrender); b. 7.2.21; succeeded to title, 1993. Educ. Eton; Royal Military Academy, Sandhurst.

Bryan, Alan Charles, BSc, CEng, MICE, MIHTE. Head of Transportation, Fife Council, since 1995; b. 10.6.46, Stirling; m., Dorna; 3 s. Educ. High School of Stirling; Strathclyde University. Assistant Engineer. Transportation Engineer, De Leuw Chadwick, Edinburgh, 1974-75; Senior Engineer, Central Regional Council, 1975-76; Fife Regional Council: Principal Engineer (Transportation), 1976-81, Assistant Director of Engineering (Roads – Traffic and Transportation), 1981-89. Assistant Director of Engineering (Roads), 1990-95. Recreations: philosophy; hillwalking; swimming. Address: (h.) Norwood, 37 Kirkbank Road, Burntisland, Fife KY3 9HZ; T.-01592 872702.

Bryan, Pauline Christina. Director, Employee Counselling Service, since 1989; b. 3.1.50, London; partner Vincent Mills. Educ. St. Edward the Confessor School; Open University. Messenger, Daily Mirror; Secretary, National Labour Press, 11 years; Development Officer, Fabian Society, 1981-88; Secretary, Local Health Council, 1988-89. Publication: Winning Women's Votes, (Fabian Tract) 1985. Recreations: politics; music. Address: 120 Bath Street, Glasgow G2 2EN; T.-0141-332 9833.

Bryant, Anthony B., FRICS. Regional Director, Highlands, National Trust for Scotland, since 1986; b. 25.1.38; m., Jane E.A.; 1 s.; 1 d. Educ. Bryanston School. Trained as land agent, Chatsworth Estate, 1956-60, returning there 1964-69 after working for the Duchy of Cornwall; joined National Trust for Scotland as Depute Factor, 1969; Factor, 1976; Head Factor, 1984. Recreations: music; painting. Address: (b.) Abertarff House, Church Street, Inverness 1V1 1EU; T.-Inverness 232034.

Bryce, Professor Charles F.A., BSc, PhD, DipEdTech, EurBiol, CBiol, FIBiol, CChem, FRSC. Professor and Head, Department of Biological Sciences, Napier University, since 1983; b. 5.9.47, Lennoxtown; m., Maureen; 2 s. Educ. Lenzie Academy; Shawlands Academy; Glasgow University; Max Planck Institute, Berlin. Former Executive Editor, Computer Applications in the Biosciences; Member, EFB Task Group on Public Perceptions of Biotechnology; Chairman, EFB Working Party on Education; Adviser to the Committee on Science and Technology in Developing Countries (India); former Chairman, UK Deans of Science Committee; actively involved in quality audit and quality assessment in biomedical sciences in UK, Bangladesh and Zambia; Convener, UCAS Biology Panel. Recreations: competitive bridge; collecting wine. Address: (b.) Napier University, 10 Colinton Road, Edinburgh EH10 5DT; T.-0131-455 2525.

Bryce, Colin Maxwell, DA (Edin), CertEd, FCSD, FRSA. Dean, Faculty of Arts and Social Sciences, Napier University, since 1997; b. 14.9.45, Edinburgh; m., Caroline Joy; 2 s. Educ. Royal High School, Edinburgh; Edinburgh College of Art; Moray House College of Education. Art and Design Teacher, Portobello High School, 1968-75; Head of Art and Design, Wester Hailes Education Centre, 1975-85; Education Advisory Officer/Senior Education Officer/Director, The Design Council Scotland, 1985-90; Managing Director, Quorum Graphic Design, 1990-91; Principal, Hunter Maxwell Associates, 1991-92; Head, Department of Design, Napier University, 1992-97. Member, Society of High Constables of Edinburgh. Recreations: looking, listening, and talking. Address: (b.) Napier University, 10 Colinton Road, Edinburgh, EH10 5DT; T.-0131-455 2216.

Bryce, Professor Tom G.K., BSc, MEd, PhD, CPsychol. Professor, Department of Educational Studies, Faculty of Education, Strathclyde University, Jordanhill Campus, since 1993; Vice-Dean (Postgraduate Studies and Research), since 1997; b. 27.1.46, Glasgow; m., Karen Douglas Stewart; 1 s.; 1 d. Educ. King's Park Secondary School, Glasgow; Glasgow University. Teacher of Physics, Jordanhill College School, 1968-71; P.T. of Physics, King's Park Secondary School, 1971-73; part-time Lecturer in Psychology, Glasgow University, 1972-75; Open University Tutor, 1979-84; Lecturer, 1973, Head of Psychology, 1983, Head, Division of Education and Psychology, 1987-94, Jordanhill College of Education. Chairman, Editorial Board, Scottish Educational Review. Publications include: How to Assess Open-ended Practical Investigations in Biology, Chemistry and Physics, 1991. Recreations: moutaineering; badminton. Address: (b.) Jordanhill Campus, Southbrae Drive, Glasgow, G13 1PP; T.-0141-950 3220.

Bryden, Professor Ian Gordon, BSc, PhD, CEng, CPhys, MIMarE, MInstP. Professor and Head, School of Mechanical and Offshore Engineering, Robert Gordon University, since 1996; b. 12.9.58, Dumfries; m., Fiona Morag; 2 s.; 1 d. Educ. Lockerbie Academy; University of Edinburgh. Research Assistant, Heriot-Watt University; Research Engineer, BMT Ltd.; Lecturer, Heriot-Watt University; Senior Engineer, ICIT/IOE. Recreations: reading; cycling; music. Address: (b.) The Robert Gordon University, Schoolhill, Aberdeen AB10 1FR; T.-01224-262 301.

Bryden, Professor John Marshall, BSc (Hons), PhD, FRSA. Chair of Human Geography and Joint Director, Arkleton Centre for Rural Development Research, since 1995; Programme Director, Arkleton Trust, since 1980; Member, Land Reform Policy Group, Scottish Office, since 1997; b. 18.12.41, Perth; m., Elspeth Anderson Mowat (divorced); 2 s.; 2 d. Educ. Edinburgh Academy; Glasgow Academy; Wrekin College; University of Glasgow; University of the West Indies; University of East Anglia. Economist, Economic Planning Staff, Ministry of Overseas Development, 1965-67; Lecturer, Overseas Development Group, University of East Anglia, 1967-72; Regional Economic Adviser, Commonwealth Caribbean, 1968-70; Head, Land Development Division, Highlands and Islands Development Board, 1972-79; Research Director, Arkleton Trust (Research) Ltd., 1985-95. Visiting Professor, University of Guelph, Canada, 1994. Publications: Tourism Development, 1973; Agrarian Change in the Scottish Highlands (Co-author), 1976; Towards Sustainable Rural Communities, 1994; Rural Employment – An International Perspective (Co-author), 1997. Recreations: folk music; jazz; hillwalking; sailing. Address: University of Aberdeen, St. Mary's, Kings College, Aberdeen AB24 3UF; T.-01224 272352.

Brydon, Donald Lithgow, BSc, PhD, CChem, FRSC. Academic Co-ordinator, Scottish Borders Campus, Heriot-Watt University and Head, School of Textiles, since 1998; Vice Principal, Scottish College of Textiles, 1988-98; b. 13.12.40, Stirling; m., Sandra Elizabeth Lumsden; 1 s.; 1 d. Educ. Inverurie Academy; University of St. Andrews. Postdoctoral Fellow, Case Western Reserve University, Cleveland, Ohio, 1967-69; Research and Development, Organics and Fibres Divisions, latterly Project Manager, ICI, 1969-80. Publications: range of academic publications. Recreations: tennis; travelling; gardening. Address: (b.) Netherdale, Galashiels TD1 3HF; T.-01896 753351.

Bryson, Norval MacKenzie, MSc, DPhil, FFA. Deputy Group Managing Director and Group Finance Director, Scottish Provident; Non-Executive Director, Aberdeen Asset Management PLC; b. 22.1.49, Dundee; m., Pamela Judith Sallie; 1 s.; 2 d. Educ. High School of Dundee; St. Andrews University; Magdalen College, Oxford. Joined Scottish Provident, 1974. Former Member of Council, Faculty of Actuaries. Recreation: walking the dog. Address: (h.) Achmore, 1 Hillview Terrace, Corstorphine, Edinburgh EH12 8RA; T.-0131-334 2614.

Buccleuch, 9th Duke of, and Queensberry, 11th Duke of (Walter Francis John Montagu Douglas Scott), KT (1978), VRD, JP. Hon. Captain, RNR; Captain and President of the Council, Queen's Bodyguard for Scotland (Royal Company of Archers); Lord Lieutenant of Roxburgh, 1974-98, and of Ettrick and Lauderdale, 1975-98; b. 23.9.23, London; m., Jane McNeill, daughter of John McNeill, QC, Appin, Argyll; 3 s.; 1 d. Educ. Eton; Christ Church, Oxford. Served World War II, RNVR; MP (Conservative), Edinburgh North, 1960-73; PPS to the Scottish Office, 1961-64; Chairman, Royal Association for Disability and Rehabilitation, since 1978, and President, since 1993; President: Royal Highland and Agricultural Society of Scotland, 1969, St. Andrew's Ambulance Association, Royal Scottish Agricultural Benevolent

Institution, Scottish National Institution for War Blinded, Royal Blind Asylum and School, Galloway Cattle Society, East of England Agricultural Society, 1976, Commonwealth Forestry Association; President (Scotland), Malcolm Sargent Cancer Fund for Children; President, Royal Scottish Forestry Society, 1994-96; Chairman: Living Landscape Trust, since 1985, Buccleuch Heritage Trust, since 1986; Vice-President: Royal Scottish Society for Prevention of Cruelty to Children, Disablement Income Group Scotland, Disabled Drivers Motor Club, Spinal Injuries Association; Honorary President: Moredun Foundation for Animal Health, Scottish Agricultural Organisation Society; DL: Selkirk, 1955, Midlothian, 1960, Roxburgh, 1962, Dumfries, 1974; Chancellor, Most Ancient & Most Noble Order of the Thistle, since 1992; Chairman, Association of Lord Lieutenants, 1990-98. Recreations: travel; country sports; painting; photography; classical music. Address: Bowhill, Selkirk; T.-Selkirk 20732; and Drumlanrig Castle, Thornhill; T.-Thornhill 30248.

Buchan, 17th Earl of (Malcolm Harry Erskine); b. 4.7.30. Educ. Eton. Succeeded to title, 1984.

Buchan, Alexander Stewart, MB, ChB, FRCA. Consultant in charge of Obstetric Anaesthesia, Simpson Memorial Maternity Pavilion, Edinburgh, since 1988; b. 7.9.42, Aberdeen; m., Henrietta Young Dalrymple; 1 s. Educ. Loretto School; Edinburgh University. Anaesthetic training in Edinburgh, apart from work in Holland, 1972; appointed Consultant in NHS, 1975; Royal Infirmary, Edinburgh, Royal Hospital for Sick Children, and Princess Margaret Rose Orthopaedic Hospital. Publication: Handbook of Obstetric Anaesthesia, 1991. Recreations: sailing; fishing; golf. Address: (h.) 21 Chalmers Crescent, Edinburgh EH9 1TS; T.-0131-667 1127.

Buchan, Alistair. Chief Executive, Orkney Islands Council. Address: (b.) Council Offices, Kirkwall KW15 1NY. T.-01856 873535.

Buchan of Auchmacoy, Captain David William Sinclair, JP, KStJ. Chief of the Name of Buchan; b. 18.9.29; m., The Hon. Susan Blanche Fionodbhar Scott-Ellis; 4 s.; 1 d. Educ. Eton; Royal Military Academy, Sandhurst. Commissioned Gordon Highlanders, 1949; served Berlin, BAOR and Malaya; ADC to GOC-in-C, Singapore, 1951-53; retired 1955. Member, London Stock Exchange; Senior Partner, Messrs Gow and Parsons, 1963-72. Changed name from Trevor through Court of Lord Lyon King of Arms, 1949, succeeding 18th Earl of Caithness as Chief of Buchan Clan. Member: Queen's Body Guard for Scotland (Royal Company of Archers); The Pilgrims; Friends of Malta GC; Council, St. John's Ambulance, London; Governor, London Clinic; Vice-President, Bucks CCC; Member, Council for London, Order of St. John; Master, Worshipful Company of Borderers, 1992; President, Ellon Cricket Club. Address: Auchmacoy House, Ellon, Aberdeenshire AB41 8RB.

Buchan, Dennis Thorne, DA, RSA; b. 25.4.37, Arbroath; divorced; 1 s.; 1 d. Educ. Arbroath High School; Dundee College of Art; Patrick Allan Fraser College, Arbroath. Professional Member, Society of Scottish Artists, 1961-74; Lecturer in Painting, Duncan of Jordanstone College of Art, 1965-94; solo exhibitions: Douglas and Fowlis Gallery, Edinburgh, 1965, Saltire Society, 1974, Compass Gallery, Glasgow, 1975 and 1994; Traquair House, 1996. Keith Prize, RSA, 1962, Latimer Award, RSA, 1963, William McAuley Award, RSA, 1988; Gillies Bequest, RSA, 1991. Address: 8 Inchcape Road, Arbroath, Angus DD11 2DF; T.-01241 873080.

Buchanan, James Glen Stewart, MB, ChB, FRCGP, DCH, DRCOG. Chairman, Scottish Council on Alcohol, 1987-95; b. 11.6.24, Annan; m., Elizabeth Urquhart Macgregor; 2 s. Educ. Dumfries Academy; Edinburgh University. General Practitioner, Vale of Leven, 1958-87; Past President, Glasgow Psychosomatic Society. Recreations: hill-walking; fishing; reading. Address: (h.) Landalla Cottage, Glenisla, Blairgowrie, PH11 8PH; T.-01575 582318.

Buchanan, William Menzies, DA. Head of Fine Art, 1977-90, Acting Director, 1990-91, Deputy Director, 1991-92, Glasgow School of Art; b. 7.10.32, Caroni Estate, Trinidad, West Indies. Educ. Glasgow School of Art. Art Teacher, Glasgow, 1956-61; Exhibitions Officer, then Art Director, Scottish Arts Council, 1961-77. Chairman, Stills Gallery, Edinburgh, 1987-92; Member, Fine Art Board, Council for National Academic Awards, 1978-81. Publications: Scottish Art Review, 1965, 1967, 1973; Seven Scottish Painters catalogue, IBM New York, 1965; The Glasgow Boys catalogue, 1968; Joan Eardley, 1976; Mr Henry and Mr Hornel Visit Japan catalogue, 1978; Japonisme in Art (Contributor), 1980; A Companion to Scottish Culture (Contributor), 1981; The Stormy Blast catalogue, Stirling University, 1981; The Golden Age of British Photography (Contributor), 1984; The Photographic Collector (Contributor), 1985; Willie Rodger: A Retrospective (Contributor to catalogue), 1986; Scottish Photography Bulletin (Contributor), 1988; History of Photography (Contributor), 1989; Mackintosh's Masterwork (Editor), 1989; British Photography in the 19th Century (Contributor), 1989; The Art of the Photographer J. Craig Annan, 1992; Photography 1900 (Contributor), 1993; J. Craig Annan: selected texts and bibliography, 1994; Woven Image: Contemporary British Tapestry Catalogue (Contributor), 1996; Studies in Photography (Contributor), 1996; Charles Rennie Mackintosh: Art, Architecture and Design (CD Rom, General Editor), 1997. Recreations: gardening; cooking. Address: (h.) Allan Water School House, by Skelfhill, Hawick TD9 0PH; T.-01450 850311.

Buchanan-Jardine, Sir Andrew Rupert John, MC. Landowner; Deputy Lieutenant; b. 2.2.23, London; 1 s.; 1 d. Educ. Harrow; Royal Agricultural College. Joined Royal Horse Guards, 1941; served NW Europe; retired as Major, 1949. Joint Master, Dumfriesshire Foxhounds, 1950; JP. Recreation: country pursuits. Address: (h.) Dixons, Lockerbie, Dumfriesshire; T.-01576 202508.

Buchanan-Smith, Robin D., BA, ThM; b. 1.2.36, Currie, Midlothian; m., Sheena Mary Edwards; 2 s. Educ. Edinburgh Academy; Glenalmond; Cambridge University; Edinburgh University; Princeton Theological Seminary. Minister, Christ's Church, Dunollie, Oban, 1962-66; Chaplain: St. Andrews University, 1966-73, 8th Argylls, 1962-66, Highland Volunteer, 1967-69; British Council of Churches Preacher to USA, 1968; Commodore, Royal Highland Yacht Club, 1977-81; Member, Board of Directors, Scottish Television, 1982-96 (Chairman, Staff Trust, since 1993); Chancellor's Assessor, St. Andrews University, 1981-85; Chairman: Scotland's Heritage Hotels, 1988-91, Cross Trust, since 1989, Stray Theatre Company; Trustee: Carnegie Trust for the Universities of Scotland, since 1986, Scottish Orthopaedic Research Trust into Trauma, since 1992. Recreations: sailing; Scotland. Address: Isle of Eriska, Ledaig, Argyll PA37 1SD; T.-01631 720371.

Buck, Andrew Robin, BCom, CA. Managing Director, Abuckus Ltd., Dumfries, since 1979; Partner, DG Format, Dumfries, since 1985; Lecturer, University of Northumbria, Carlisle, since 1995; b. 6.2.44, Carlisle; m., Rowena Rosemary Morewood; 2 d. Educ. Bradfield College, Berkshire; Edinburgh University. Qualified CA with Wallace and Somerville, CA, Edinburgh 1967; Shell International Group, Philippines and Nigeria, 1967-73; Edward Bates Ltd., Edinburgh, 1974; Peat Marwick Mitchell & Co., Hong Kong, 1976-79. Member, Council, Institute of Chartered Accountants of Scotland, 1989-95 and since 1997 (Chairman, South West Area, 1991-95);

Chairman, Corporate Presentation Systems Ltd., 1989-94. Recreations: skiing; sailing. Address: 109 Irish Street, Dumfries DG1 2QU.

Buckland, Professor Roger, MA, MPhil. Professor of Accountancy, Aberdeen University, since 1993 (Head, Department of Accountancy, since 1993); b. 22.4.51, Sheffield; m., Dr. Lorna McKee; 2 d. Educ. Aston Woodhouse High School; Selwyn College, Cambridge. Research Fellow, York University; Lecturer, University of Aston. Publications: The Unlisted Securities Market; Finance for Growing Enterprises. Recreation: hot air balloon pilot; family. Address: (b.) Dunbar Street, Aberdeen AB24 3QY; T.-01224 272206.

Buckland, Professor Stephen T., BSc, MSc, PhD, CStat. Professor of Statistics, St. Andrews University, since 1993 (Head, Statistical Ecology Group, since 1995); b. 28.7.55, Dorchester; m., Patricia A. Peters; 1 d. Educ. Foster's School, Sherborne; Southampton University; Edinburgh University; Aberdeen University. Lecturer in Statistics, Aberdeen University, 1977-85; Senior Scientist, Tuna/Dolphin Program, Inter-American Tropical Tuna Commission, San Diego, 1985-87; Senior Consultant Statistician, Scottish Agricultural Statistics Service, 1988-93, Head, Environmental Modelling Unit, 1991-93. Publications: The Birds of North-East Scotland (Co-editor), 1990; Distance Sampling: estimating abundance of biological populations (Co-author), 1993. Recreations: natural history; walking; reading. Address: (b.) School of Mathematical and Computational Sciences, St. Andrews University, North Haugh, St. Andrews KY16 9SS; T.-01334 463787.

Buckley, Ernest Graham, MD, FRCPE, FRCGP. Director, Scottish Council for Postgraduate Medical and Dental Education, since 1993; b. 16.10.45, Oldham; m., Dr. Felicity Buckley; 2 s.; 1 d. Educ. Manchester Grammar School; Edinburgh University. General Practitioner, Livingston, 1974-93; Editor: British Journal of General Practice, 1982-90, Medical Education. Secretary, Association for the Study of Medical Education. Recreations: gardening; history; upholstery. Address: (b.) Hobart House, 80 Hanover Street, Edinburgh EH2 1JE; T.-0131-225 4365.

Budge, Keith Joseph, MA (Hons). Headmaster, Loretto School, since 1995; b. 24.5.57; m., Caroline Ann Gent; 2 s.; 1 d. Educ. Rossall School; University College, Oxford. Assistant Master, Eastbourne College, 1980-84; Marlborough College: Assistant Master, 1984-88 and 1989-91; Housemaster, Cotton House, 1991-95; Instructor in English, Stevenson School, Pebble Beach, CA, 1988-89. Recreations: hill-walking; trout fishing; gadgets; theatre. Address: (b.) Loretto School, Musselburgh, Midlothian EH21 7RE; T.-0131-653 4441.

Bulfield, Professor Grahame, PhD, FIBiol, FRSE. Director and Chief Executive, Roslin Institute (Edinburgh), since 1993; b. 12.6.41. Educ. Kings School, Macclesfield; Leeds University; Edinburgh University. Fullbright Fellow and NIH Postdoctoral Fellow, Department of Genetics, University of California, Berkeley, 1968-70; SRC Resettlement Fellow, 1970-71, and Research Associate, 1971-76, Institute of Animal Genetics, Edinburgh University; Lecturer and Convenor of Medical Genetics, Department of Genetics, Medical School and School of Biological Sciences, Leicester University, 1976-81; Head of Genetics Group, AFRC Poultry Research Centre, Roslin, 1981-86; Head of Gene Expression Group, 1986-88, and Head of Station and Associate Director, 1988-93, Edinburgh Research Station, Institute of Animal Physiology and Genetic Research. Hon. Fellow, 1981-90, and Hon. Professor, since 1990, Division of Biological Sciences, Edinburgh University; Non-Executive Director, Rosgen Ltd., since 1997; Chairman, Roslin Nutrition Ltd., since 1997; Non-Executive Director, Roslin Bio-Med, since 1998. Recreations: fell-walking; cricket. Address: (b.) Roslin Institute, Roslin, Midlothian EH25 9PS; T.-0131-527 4457.

Bulloch, Douglas, CQSW, MCC. Director of Social Work, East Ayrshire Council, since 1996; b. 5.2.51, Hamilton; m., Irene Waddell; 1 d. Educ. Hamilton Academy; Jordanhill College; University of Glasgow. Strathclyde Regional Council, 1976-95, Depute Director of Social Work (Community Care), East Ayrshire Council, 1995-96. Address: (b.) London Road Centre, London Road, Kilmarnock KA3 7BU; T.-01563 576020.

Bulloch, Janet, MA. Bank of England Agent for Scotland, since 1998. Educ. St. Andrews University. Career Bank of England official. Director, Right Track (Scotland) Ltd. Address: (b.) Bank of England, Agency for Scotland, 19 St. Vincent Place, Glasgow G1 2DT; T.-0141-221 7972.

Bunch, Antonia Janette, OBE, MA, FLA, FIInfSc, FSA Scot, FRSA. Freelance writer, editor, researcher; b. 13.2.37, Croydon. Educ. Notting Hill and Ealing High School; Strathclyde University. Assistant Librarian, Scottish Office; Librarian, Scottish Health Service Centre; Lecturer, Strathclyde University; Director, Scottish Science Library. Founding Chairman, Association of Scottish Health Sciences Librarians; Member: Standing Committee on Science and Technology Libraries, IFLA, 1987-91, Advisory Committee, British Library Science Reference and Information Service, 1987-96, Advisory Committee on Telematics for the Scottish Parliament, 1996-97. Publications: Libraries in Hospitals (Co-author), 1969; Hospital and Medical Libraries in Scotland: an Historical and Sociological Study, 1975; Health Care Administration: an Information Sourcebook, 1979. Recreations: gardening; music; travelling in Italy. Address: Dove Cottage, Garvald, Haddington, East Lothian EH41 4LL.

Buncle, Tom, BA, MA. Chief Executive, Scottish Tourist Board, since 1994; Board Member: Edinburgh Festival Council, Cairngorm Partnership, Scotland the Brand; b. 25.6.53, Arbroath; m., Janet; 2 s. Educ. Trinity College, Glenalmond; Exeter University; Sheffield University. Various overseas posts (North America, Europe, Asia), British Tourist Authority, 1978-91; International Marketing Director, Scottish Tourist Board, 1991-96. Recreations: wind-surfing; scuba diving; cycling; sailing; hill-walking, tennis. Address: (b.) Scottish Tourist Board, 23 Ravelston Terrace, Edinburgh EH4 3EU; T.-0131-332 2433.

Bundy, Professor Alan Richard, BSc, PhD, FRSA, FRSE, FAAAI. Professor, Head of Division of Informatics, Edinburgh University; b. 18.5.47, Isleworth; m., D. Josephine A. Maule; 1 d. Educ. Heston Secondary Modern School; Springgrove Grammar School; Leicester University. Tutorial Assistant, Department of Mathematics, Leicester University, 1970-71; Edinburgh University: Research Fellow, Metamathematics Unit, 1971-74, Lecturer, Department of Artificial Intelligence, 1974-84, Reader, 1984-87, Professorial Fellow, 1987-90. Editorial Board: Artificial Intelligence Journal, Journal of Automated Reasoning, AJ & Society Journal. Publications: Artificial Intelligence: An Introductory Course, 1978; The Computer Modelling of Mathematical Reasoning, 1983; The Catalogue of Artificial Intelligence Tools, 1984. Recreations: wine and beer making; walking; bridge. Address: (b.) Division of Informatics, Edinburgh University, 80 South Bridge, Edinburgh EH1 1HN; T.-0131-650 2716.

Burchell, Professor Brian, BSc (Hons), PhD, FRCPath, FRSEdin. Professor of Medical Biochemistry; Honorary Professor, St. Andrews University; b. 1.10.46, Bosworth; m., Ann; 1 s.; 1 d. Educ. King Edward VII Grammar School, Coalville; St. Andrews University. Lecturer in

Biochemistry: Loughborough University of Technology, 1974-75, Dundee University, 1976-78; Wellcome Trust Special Research Leave Fellow, 1978-80; Wellcome Trust Senior Lecturer in Biochemistry, Dundee University, 1980-88. Editor and Deputy Chairman, Editorial Board, Biochemical Journal. Publications: over 150 scientific papers and reviews. Recreation: golf. Address: (b.) Department of Molecular and Cellular Pathology, Ninewells Hospital and Medical School, Dundee DD1 9SY.

Burdon, Peter, MA (Cantab), FIA. Chief Executive, Glasgow Chamber of Commerce, since 1997; b. 15.5.47; m., Eileen; 4 s. Educ. Churchill College, University of Cambridge. Friends' Provident Life Office: Actuarial and User Management positions, 1968-79, User Liaison Manager, 1979-82, Manager, Unit Linked Department, 1982-85, Manager, Marketing Department, 1985-86; Deputy Managing Director, FS Assurance (transferred to Britannia Life, 1990), 1986-91; Managing Director, Britannia Life Limited, 1991-96; Marketing and Life Operations Director, Britannia Building Society, 1994-96. Member: UTA External Relations Committee, 1989-93, ABI Smaller Offices Committee, 1989-94, General Purposes Committee of the Associated Scottish Life Offices, 1991-96, Glasgow Discussion Group on Finance and Investment, 1986-96, Glasgow and West of Scotland Regional Committee, IOD, since 1996, Imperial Cancer Research Fund Scottish Advisory Committee, since 1994, Young Enterprise Scotland Business Adviser, since 1996, Court of Glasgow Caledonian University, since 1997, Glasgow Common Purpose Advisory Group, since 1997, Glasgow Exports Ltd., since 1997. Recreations: golf; squash; music. Address: (b.) Glasgow Chamber of Commerce, 30 George Square, Glasgow G2 1EQ; T.-0141-204 2121.

Burgon, Robert Douglas, BA, MLitt, APMI. Director and Secretary, Scottish & Northern Ireland Plumbing Employers' Federation, since 1988; Secretary and Pensions Manager, Plumbing Pensions (UK) Ltd., since 1988; b. 3.8.55, Haddington; m., Sheila Georgina Bryson. Educ. North Berwick High School; Heriot Watt University. SNIPEF: Assistant Industrial Relations Officer, 1978, Assistant to the Director, 1979, Secretary, 1983. Recreation: music (church organist). Address: (b.) 2 Walker Street, Edinburgh EH3 7LB; T.-0131-225 2255.

Burke, Professor Trevor, BDS, DDS, MSc, MDS, FDS, MGDS. Professor of Dental Primary Care, University of Glasgow, since 1996; Editor, Dental Update, since 1996; b. 23.8.46, Belfast; m., Maxine Burke; 1 s.; 3 d. Educ. Belfast Royal Academy; Queen's University, Belfast. Queen's University, Belfast Dental School, 1969-73; University of Manchester Dental School, 1973-75; part-time University of Manchester/part-time dental practice, 1975-92; Senior Lecturer in Dental Practice, University of Manchester, 1992-96. Publications: 120 in journals. Recreations: music; tennis. Address: Glasgow Dental School, 378 Sauchiehall Street, Glasgow G2 3JZ; T.-0141-211 9778.

Burley, Elayne Mary, BA (Hons). Head of Business Development, Napier University; b. 17.10.44, Cheshire; 2 s.; 1 d. Educ. Astley Grammar School for Girls; Leeds University. Leeds Polytechnic, 1966-68; Lecturer, Gordon Institute of Technology, Victoria, Australia, 1970-72; Lecturer, Open University in Scotland, 1972-84; Head of Training, Scottish Council for Voluntary Organisations, 1984-91. Member, Council, Rotary Club of Edinburgh. Recreations: golf; bridge; performing arts; walking on the beach; collecting blue and white china. Address: (b.) 74 Canaan Lane, Edinburgh; T.-0131-536 5686.

Burley, Lindsay, MB, ChB, FRCPE, FRCGP, MHSM. General Manager, Borders Health Board, since 1995; b. 2.10.50, Blackpool; m., Robin Burley. Educ. Queen Mary School, Lytham; University of Edinburgh. Lothian Health Board: Consultant Physician, Unit General Manager, Director of Planning and Development. Address: (b.) Newstead, Melrose, Roxburghshire TD6 9DB; T.-01896 825515.

Burnet, George Wardlaw, LVO, BA, LLB, WS, KStJ, JP. Lord Lieutenant, Midlothian, since 1992; Chairman, Caledonian Research Foundation, since 1988; b. 26.12.27, Edinburgh; m., Jane Elena Moncrieff; 2 s.; 1 d. Educ. Edinburgh Academy; Lincoln College, Oxford; Edinburgh University. Senior Partner, Murray Beith & Murray, WS, 1983-91; Chairman, Life Association of Scotland Ltd., 1985-93. Brigadier, Queen's Bodyguard for Scotland (Royal Company of Archers); former Midlothian County Councillor; Convenor, Church of Scotland Finance Committee, 1980-83; Hon. Fellow, Royal Incorporation of Architects in Scotland. Address: (h.) Rose Court, Inveresk, Midlothian EH21 7TD.

Burnett, Charles John, KStJ, DA, AMA, FSAScot, FHSS, MLitt. Ross Herald of Arms; Chamberlain, Duff House, Banff, since 1997; Curator of Fine Art, Scottish United Services Museum, Edinburgh Castle, 1985-96; Vice-President, Heraldry Society of Scotland, since 1986; Vice-Patron, Genealogical Society of Queensland, since 1986; b. 6.11.40, Sandhaven, by Fraserburgh; m., Aileen E. McIntyre; 2 s.; 1 d. Educ. Fraserburgh Academy; Gray's School of Art, Aberdeen; Aberdeen College of Education. Advertising Department, House of Fraser, Aberdeen, 1963-64; Exhibitions Division, Central Office of Information, 1964-68 (on team which planned British pavilion for World Fair, Montreal, 1967); Assistant Curator, Letchworth Museum and Art Gallery, 1968-71; Head, Design Department, National Museum of Antiquities of Scotland, 1971-85. Heraldic Adviser, Girl Guide Association in Scotland, since 1978; Librarian, Priory of the Order of St. John in Scotland, since 1987; Vice President, Society of Antiquaries of Scotland, 1992-95; Honorary Citizen of Oklahoma, 1989. Recreations: reading; visiting places of historic interest. Address: (h.) Seaview House, Portsoy, Banffshire, AB45 2RS; T.-01261 843378.

Burnett, James Murray, FRICS, DipTP. Partner, Donaldsons, Chartered Surveyors; b. 7.2.44, Edinburgh; m., Elizabeth Anne; 1 s.; 2 d. Educ. Boroughmuir School; Heriot-Watt University; Edinburgh College of Art. Joined Donaldsons in 1970, giving development consultancy advice for large shopping centres; became Partner, 1987. Vice-Chairman, Royal Institution of Chartered Surveyors in Scotland, 1992-93, Chairman, 1996-97. Recreations: golf; gardening. Address: (h.) 438 Lanark Road, Colinton, Edinburgh; T.-0131-441 2200.

Burnett, Robert Gemmill, LLB, SSC, NP. Solicitor, since 1972; b. 18.1.49, Kilmarnock; m., Patricia Margaret Masson; 1 s.; 2 d. Educ. George Heriot's School, Edinburgh; Edinburgh University. Apprentice, then Assistant, then Partner, Drummond Miller WS; Partner, Burnett Christie. Solicitor to General Teaching Council. Recreations: golf; gardening. Address: (b.) 53 George IV Bridge, Edinburgh; T.-031-225 3456.

Burnett, Rodney Alister, MB, ChB, FRCP, FRIPHH, FRCPath. Consultant Pathologist responsible for diagnostic services, University Department of Pathology, Western Infirmary, Glasgow, since 1985; b. 6.6.47, Congleton; m., Maureen Elizabeth Dunn; 2 d. Educ. Sandbach School; St. Andrews University. Lecturer in Pathology, Glasgow University, 1974-79; Consultant in administrative charge, Department of Pathology, Stobhill Hospital, Glasgow, 1979-85. Specialist Adviser, Royal Institute for Public Health and Hygiene, and Chairman, Board of Education and Examination for Anatomical Pathology Technology. Address: (h.) 134 Brownside Road, Cambuslang, Glasgow G72; T.-0141-641 3036.

Burnett, Rupert Gavin, BCom, CA, FCMA; b. 6.11.39, India; m., Elspeth Maclean; 2 s.; 1 d. Educ. George Watson's College; Edinburgh University; Harvard Business School. Procter & Gamble Ltd., 1963-65; Management Consultant, McLintock, Moores and Murray, 1965-68; Chartered Accountant, Arthur Young (latterly Ernst & Young), 1968-91, Partner, 1970; Honorary Professor, Stirling University, since 1991; Member, Council, Institute of Chartered Accountants of Scotland, 1990-96; Chairman, Glasgow & North Strathclyde Area Committee, 1992-95; CCAB Audit Practices Committee, 1986-91; Chairman, Church of Scotland Investors Trust; General Trustee, Church of Scotland; various non-executive directorships. Recreations: watching amateur rugby; wild brown trout fishing; croft; family. Address: (h.) 7 Ralston Road, Bearsden, Glasgow.

Burnett-Stuart of Crichie, George Slessor. Farmer and Landowner, since 1969; b. 3.1.48, Cobham; m., Patricia De Lavenne; 2 d. Educ. Winchester College; Bordeaux University. Elected Member, Council and Executive, National Trust for Scotland; Council Member: Stewart Society, Scottish Agricultural College; Past Chairman, Grampian Farming Forestry Wildlife Group;Treasurer, Friends of Grampian Stones. Recreations: kite-flying; travelling; tree-planting. Address: Crichie House, Stuartfield, Peterhead AB4 8DY; T.-01771 24202.

Burnie, Joan Bryson. Columnist, Daily Record, since 1987; b. 19.12.41, Glasgow; 1 s.; 1 d. Educ. Hutchesons' Girls' Grammar School. Filed pix, Herald; married; had children; freelanced; Contributing Editor, Cosmopolitan, 1977-81; You (Mail on Sunday), 1984-90; "Just Joan", Daily Record, since 1979; hacks around the air waves for BBC Radio 5 and BBC Scotland. Publications: Scotland The Worst; Post Bus Country. Recreations: lunch; walking dogs; gardening.

Burns, Elizabeth, OBE. Chief Executive, Volunteer Development Scotland, since 1983; 3 children. Educ. Edinburgh University. Former Teacher of Languages; has served on Government working groups and advisory groups at local, national and European levels; currently a Director: Scottish Council of Voluntary Organisations, Marriage Counselling Scotland; President, Centre European du Voluntariat; Member, Scottish Joint Working Group developing a new Compact between the Government and the Voluntary Sector; Member, Special Advisory Group on Active Citizenship, Ministry of Social Affairs, Baden-Wurttemberg; Member, Convention of Scottish Local Authorities' Working Group on the Voluntary Sector; Chair, UK Volunteering Forum. Address: (h.) 97b High Street, Tillicoultry FK13 6DL.

Burns, Dr. Harry J.G. Director of Public Health, Greater Glasgow Health Board. Address: (b.) Dalian House, PO Box 15329, 350 St. Vincent Street, Glasgow G3 8YZ.

Burns, Jessica Martha, BA (Hons), LLB, SSC. Chairman, Independent Tribunal Service, since 1992; special responsibility for tribunal training and District Chairman for Glasgow North, since 1998; b. 4.10.52, Dumfries; m., Bill Findlay; 2 d. Educ. Carlisle and County High School for Girls; Stirling University; Edinburgh University. Lecturer in Law, Glasgow University, 1983-85; Senior Lecturer, Faculty of Law, Aberdeen University, 1986-92. Member, Parole Board for Scotland, 1990-92; Member, Police Advisory Board for Scotland, 1988-92; Governor, Scottish Police College, 1988-92; Visiting Professor, School of Law, Maryland University, 1988. Recreations: relaxing with family; theatre; music; good company. Address: (b.) ITS, Wellington House, 134 Wellington Street, Glasgow G2 2XL; T.-0141-353 1441.

Burns, Rt. Rev. John Joseph, PhL, STh. Vicar General, Diocese of Motherwell, since 1992; Parish Priest, St. Bride's, Bothwell, since 1992; Vicar General for Pastoral Care and Planning, since 1992; b. 19.2.32, Rutherglen. Educ. Our Lady's High, Motherwell; St. Joseph's College, Dumfries; Gregorian University, Rome; Scots College, Rome. Assistant Priest, Motherwell Cathedral, 1956-65; Full-time Chaplain, Our Lady's High School, Motherwell, 1965-78; Resident at St. Brendan's, Motherwell, 1971-78; Diocesan Master of Ceremonies, 1956-81; Director of Religious Education, Diocese of Motherwell, 1978-85; Resident at Diocesan Centre, Motherwell, 1978-85; Parish Priest, St. Aidan's, Wishaw, 1983-92. Publications: series of Religious Education books for pupils and teachers, S1-S5, 1979-82. Recreations: general reading; walking; football. Address: St. Bride's, Fallside Road, Bothwell, Lanarkshire; T.-01698 852710.

Burnside, David Melville, LLB, NP. Senior Partner, Burnside Kemp Fraser, Solicitors, since 1989; b. 5.3.43, Dumfries; m., Gill; 3 s.; 2 d. Educ. Dumfries Academy; University of Edinburgh. Apprentice Solicitor, Melville & Lindesay W.S., Edinburgh, 1964-67; Assistant Solicitor: National Coal Board Legal Department, 1967-70, Clark & Wallace, Advocates, Aberdeen, 1970-71 (Partner, 1971-89); formed Burnside Advocates (later Burnside Kemp Fraser), 1989; acted for families in Chinook, Brent Spar and Cormorant Alpha helicopter crashes and Piper Alpha explosion (joint lead negotiator for Piper Alpha settlement); Member, Personal Injury Panel; certified by Law Society of Scotland as an employment law specialist; Treasurer, Employment Law Group; Past President: Aberdeen Bar Association, Junior Chamber, Aberdeen; Member, Board of Directors, Legal Defence Union. Recreations: family; music; theatre; tennis; skiing; following the Dons. Address: (b.) 4 Queens Terrace, Aberdeen AB10 1XL; T.-01224 624602.

Burnside, John. Writer; b. 19.3.55, Dunfermline. Scottish Arts Council Book Award, 1988, 1991, 1995; shortlisted for Forward Prize, 1992; Geoffrey Faber Memorial Prize, 1994; shortlisted for T.S. Eliot Prize, 1994; selected for New Generation Poets, 1994. Publications: poetry: The hoop, 1988; Common Knowledge, 1991; Feast Days, 1992; The myth of the twin, 1994; Swimming in the flood, 1995; A Normal Skin, 1997; fiction: The Dumb House, 1997. Address: (b.) c/o Jonathan Cape, Random House, 20 Vauxhall Bridge Road, London SW1V 2SA.

Burt, Gillian Robertson, MA (Hons), FRSA. Headmistress, Craigholme School, Glasgow, since 1991; b. 7.2.44, Edinburgh; m., Andrew Wallace Burt; 1 s.; 1 d. Educ. Mary Erskine School; Edinburgh University; Moray House College of Education. Teacher of Geography, Tabeetha Church of Scotland School, Jaffa, Israel, 1966-67; Teacher of Geography, Boroughmuir Secondary School, 1967-70; Head of Geography, St. Hilary's School, Edinburgh, 1970-71, 1976-86, Head of Careers, 1986-91 (merged with St. Margaret's School, 1983); Member, Governing Board, SCIS and of its Management Committee; Member, ISCO General Council and ISCO Scottish Council. Recreations: music; theatre; walking; cooking; foreign travel. Address: (b.) Craigholme School, 72 St Andrews Drive, Glasgow G41 4HS; T.-0141-427 0375.

Burt, Peter Alexander, MA, MBA, FCIBS. Group Chief Executive, Bank of Scotland, since 1996; b. 6.3.44, Nairobi; m., 3 s. Educ. Merchiston Castle School, Edinburgh; St Andrews University; University of Pennsylvania; Wharton School of Finance and Commerce. Joined Hewlett Packard Company, Palo Alto, 1968, as an Information Systems Analyst; joined Conversational Software Ltd., Edinburgh, as Marketing Director, 1970, and progressed to be Managing Director; Edward Bates & Sons Ltd., merchant bank, 1974-75; joined Bank of Scotland, 1975, as Executive Assistant, Special Duties; Assistant General Manager, 1979;

Divisional General Manager, 1984; Joint General Manager and Head, International Division, 1985; Treasurer and Chief General Manager, 1988; appointed to Board, 1995; Director, Bank of Western Australia, since 1995; Director, Bank of Wales PLC, since 1996. Address: (b.) The Mound, Edinburgh EH1 1YZ.

Burt, Professor Steven Leslie, BA, PhD, FRSA. Professor of Retail Marketing, University of Stirling, since 1998; Director, Institute for Retail Studies, University of Stirling, since 1999; b. 23.3.60, Chorley, Lancashire; m., Wendy Hayes; 2 s. Educ. Bolton School; Queen's College, Oxford University; University of Wales; University of Stirling. University of Stirling: Research Fellow then Lecturer then Senior Lecturer, 1984-98, Head, Department of Marketing, 1993-95, Acting Director, Institute for Retail Studies, 1993-96. President, European Association for Education and Research in Commercial Distribution. Recreation: watching Stirling Albion Football Club. Address: (b.) Department of Marketing, University of Stirling, Stirling FK9 4LA; T.-01786 467399.

Burton, Anthony Winston, OBE, BA (Hons). Managing Director, The Planning Exchange; b. 14.10.40, Leicester; 2 s.; 1 d. Educ. Wyggeston; Keele University. Chairman, Strategic Planning Society (Scotland); Director (Non-Executive): Consumers' Association, Scottish Greenbelt Company. Recreations: cooking; sailing. Address: (h.) 9 Marchmont Terrace, Glasgow G12 9LS; T.-0141-334 7697.

Burton, Lord (Michael Evan Victor Baillie). Landowner and Farmer; b. 27.6.24, Burton-on-Trent; m., 1, Elizabeth Ursula Foster Wise (m. diss., deceased); 2, Coralie Denise Cliffe; 2 s.; 3 d. (1 d. deceased). Educ. Eton; Army. Scots Guards, 1942 (Lt., 1943); Lovat Scouts, 1948; Member, Inverness County Council, 1948-75; JP, 1961-75; Deputy Lieutenant, Inverness, 1963-65; Executive Member, Scottish Landowners Federation, 1963-92; has served on numerous committees. Recreations: shooting, fishing and hunting (not much time); looking after the estate. Address: Dochgarroch Lodge, Inverness IV3 8JG; T.-01463 861252/861218.

Busby, John Philip, NDD, DA (Edin), RSW, ARSA, PPSSA; b. 2.2.28, Bradford; m., Joan; 1 s.; 2 d. Educ. Ilkley Grammar School; Leeds College of Art; Edinburgh College of Art. Lecturer in Drawing and Painting, Edinburgh College of Art, 1956-88; Founder Member, Society of Wildlife Artists; illustrated 30 books on natural history; author and illustrator: Birds in Mallorca, Drawing Birds, John Busby Nature Drawings, The Living Birds of Eric Ennion. Recreations: music; bird-watching; travel. Address: (h.) Easter Haining, Ormiston Hall, East Lothian EH35 5NJ; T.-01875 340512.

Bush, Paul Anthony, BEd, DipSC, FISC. Chief Executive, Scottish Swimming, since 1998; b. 11.6.57, Leicester; m., Katriona Christine. Educ. Gateway Sixth Form College, Leicester; Borough Road College; Moray House College. Professional Swimming Coach, Bradford and Leicester; Sports/Swimming Development Officer, Leeds City Council; Technical Director, Amateur Swimming Association; Assistant Head of Development, English Sports Council; Director, Sporting Initiatives Sports Marketing and Media Consultancy. Leicestershire County Swimming Coach; Swimming Team Manager, Olympic, World, European, Commonwealth Games; Chef de Mission, BOA, European Youth Olympics; Fellow, BISA; General Secretary, British Swimming Coaches Association; Member, English Sports Council Task Force – Young People and Sport; Event Director, World Cyclo Cross Championships, Leeds; school governor. Recreations: golf; walking the dogs; sport in general; travel. Address: (b.) Holmhills Farm, Cambuslang, Glasgow G72 8DT; T.-0141-641 8818.

Bush, Professor Peter Williams, BA, PhD, FRGS, FRSA. Vice-Principal, Glasgow Caledonian University, since 1989; b. 8.11.45, Liverpool; m., Judy; 1 s.; 1 d. Educ. St. Mary's College, Crosby, Liverpool; University College, London; Leeds University. Lecturer, Senior Lecturer, Principal Lecturer in Geography, Staffordshire University, 1970-81; Head, Department of Humanities, Glasgow College of Technology, 1981-84; Assistant Director, Glasgow Polytechnic, 1985-89. Chair, Scottish Advisory Committee on Credit and Access, 1993-96; Chair, Universities' Association for Continuing Education (Scotland), since 1996; Academic Auditor, Higher Education Quality Council, since 1993; Member: Board of Governors, St. Andrew's College of Education, 1987-95, Northern Ireland Higher Education Council, since 1993, Scottish Qualifications Authority, since 1997. Recreations: sports; music; travel. Address: (b.) Glasgow Caledonian University, Cowcaddens Road, Glasgow G4 0BA; T.-0141-331 3133.

Bushe, Frederick, OBE, RSA (1987), DA, DAE. Sculptor, since 1956; Founder Director, Scottish Sculpture Workshop, 1979-96; b. 1.3.31, Coatbridge; m., Fiona M.S. Marr; 1 d.; 3 s., 1 d. by pr. m. Educ. Our Lady's High School, Motherwell; Glasgow School of Art. Lecturer in Sculpture: Liverpool College of Education, 1962-69, Aberdeen College of Education, 1969-79; full-time Artist since 1979; established Scottish Sculpture Workshop and Scottish Sculpture Open Exhibition; exhibited in numerous one man and group exhibitions, since 1962. Recreations: music; cooking. Address: (h.) Rose Cottage, Lumsden, Huntly, Aberdeenshire AB54 4JJ; T.-01464 861394.

Busuttil, Professor Anthony, MD, FRCPath, FRCP(Glas), FRCPE, DMJ(Path). Regius Professor of Forensic Medicine, Edinburgh University, since 1987; Past Chairman, European Council for Legal Medicine; Honorary Consultant Pathologist, Royal Infirmary NHS Trust, since 1976; Police Surgeon, Lothian and Borders Police Force, since 1980; b. 30.12.45, Rabat, Malta; m., Angela; 3 s. Educ. St. Aloysius' College, Malta; Royal University of Malta. Junior posts, Western Infirmary, Glasgow; Lecturer in Pathology, Glasgow University. Address: (h.) 78 Hillpark Avenue, Edinburgh EH4 7AL; T.-0131-336 3241.

Bute, 7th Marquess of (John Colum Crichton-Stuart); b. 26.4.58; m.; 1 s.; 2 d. British Formula Three Champion, 1984; Formula One Ferrari Test Driver, 1985; JPS Lotus Grand Prix Driver, 1986; Works Driver for World Champion Sports Prototype Team Silk Cut Jaguar, 1988 (Joint Winner, Le Mans, 1988).

Butler, Vincent Frederick, RSA, RGI. Sculptor; b. 27.10.33, Manchester; m., Camilla Meazza; 2 s. Educ. Edinburgh College of Art; Accademia di Belle Arti, Milan. Tutor in English Language, British School, Milan, 1957-60; Head, Department of Sculpture, Ahmadu Bello University, Nigeria, 1960-63; Lecturer, Edinburgh College of Art, 1960-89. Recreations: paragliding; travel; languages. Address: (h.) 17 Dean Park Crescent, Edinburgh EH4 1PH; T.-0131-332 5884.

Butlin, Ron, MA, DipAECD. Poet and Novelist; b. 17.11.49, Edinburgh. Educ. Dumfries Academy; Edinburgh University. Writer in Residence, Lothian Region Education Authority, 1979, Edinburgh University, 1981, 1984-85; Scottish/Canadian Writing Exchange Fellow, University of New Brunswick, 1983-84; Writer in Residence for Midlothian, 1989-90; Writer in Residence, Craigmillar Literacy Trust. Publications: poetry: Stretto, 1976; Creatures Tamed by Cruelty, 1979; The Exquisite Instrument, 1982 (Scottish Arts Council Book Award); Ragtime in Unfamiliar Bars, 1985 (SAC Book Award, Poetry Book Society recommendation); prose: The Tilting Room (short stories), 1983 (SAC Book Award); The Sound of My Voice (novel), 1987; Blending In (play), 1989;

Histories of Desire (poetry), 1995; Mauritian Voices (Editor), 1996; Night Visits (novel), 1997; When We Jump We Jump High!, 1998. Recreations: music; travel. Address: (h.) 7 West Newington Place, Edinburgh EH9 1QT; T.-0131-667 0394.

Butter, Sir David Henry, KCVO, MC. Lord Lieutenant, Perth and Kinross, 1975-95; Landowner and Company Director; b. 18.3.20, London; m., Myra Alice Wernher; 1 s.; 4 d. Educ. Eton College; Oxford University. Served in World War II, 2nd Lt., Scots Guards, 1940; served in Western Desert, North Africa, Sicily and Italy (ADC to GOC 8th Army, 1944); Temporary Major, 1946; retired, 1948; Ensign, Queen's Bodyguard for Scotland (Royal Company of Archers); President, Highland TAVR, 1979-84; Member, Perth County Council, 1955-74; Deputy Lieutenant, Perthshire, 1956; Vice Lieutenant, Perthshire, 1960-71; Lord Lieutenant of County of Perth, 1971-75, of Kinross, 1974-75; Governor, Gordonstoun School, 1954-86. Recreations: golf; skiing; travel; shooting. Address: Cluniemore, Pitlochry, Perthshire; T.-01796 2006.

Butter, Professor Peter Herbert. Regius Professor of English Language and Literature, Glasgow University, 1965-86; b. 7.4.21, Coldstream; m., Bridget Younger; 1 s.; 2 d. Educ. Charterhouse; Balliol College, Oxford. Royal Artillery, 1941-46; Lecturer in English, Edinburgh University, 1948-58; Professor of English, Queen's University, Belfast, 1958-65. Secretary/Treasurer, International Association of University Professors of English, 1965-71. Publications: Shelley's Idols of the Cave, 1954; Francis Thompson, 1961; Edwin Muir, 1962; Edwin Muir: Man and Poet, 1966; Shelley's Alastor, Prometheus Unbound and Other Poems (Editor), 1971; Selected Letters of Edwin Muir (Editor), 1974; William Blake: Selected Poems (Editor), 1982; The Truth of Imagination: Uncollected Prose of Edwin Muir (Editor), 1988; Complete Poems of Edwin Muir (Editor), 1991. Recreations: gardening; book-collecting. Address: (h.) Ashfield, Prieston Road, Bridge of Weir, Renfrewshire PA11 3AW; T.-01505 613139.

Butterworth, Neil, MA, HonFLCM. Chairman, Scottish Society of Composers, since 1991; Music Critic, Times Educational Supplement, 1983-97; Broadcaster; b. 4.9.34, Streatham, London; m., Anna Mary Barnes; 3 d. Educ. Rutlish School, Surrey; Nottingham University; London University; Guildhall School of Music, London. Lecturer, Kingston College of Technology, 1960-68; Head, Music Department, Napier College, Edinburgh, 1968-87. Conductor: Sutton Symphony Orchestra, 1960-64, Glasgow Orchestral Society, 1975-83 and since 1989; Chairman: Incorporated Society of Musicians, Edinburgh Centre, 1981-86, Inveresk Preservation Society, 1988-95; Churchill Fellowship, 1975. Publications: Haydn, 1976; Dvorak, 1980; Dictionary of American Composers, 1983; Aaron Copland, 1984; Vaughan Williams, 1989; Neglected Music, 1991; Samuel Barber, 1996; The American Symphony, 1998; over 300 compositions. Recreations: autographs; collecting books and records; giant jigsaw puzzles. Address: (h.) 1 Roderick Place, West Linton, Peeblesshire EH46 7ES; T.-01968 661112.

Buxton, James Desmond, MA. Scottish Correspondent, Financial Times, since 1986; b. 20.8.47; m., Anna; 2 s. Educ. Eton College; Magdalene College, Cambridge. Evening Echo, Hemel Hempstead, 1969-72; Financial Times: joined 1972, foreign staff (Middle East and North East Africa), 1973-80; Rome Correspondent, 1980-86. Ischia Prize, Itlay, 1986. Recreations: travel; reading; genealogy; listening to music. Address: 23 Murrayfield Road, Edinburgh EH12 6EP.

Buxton, Paul Kenneth, MA (Cantab), MB, BChir, FRCP(C), FRCPEdin. Consultant Physician in Dermatology, Fife Health Board and Royal Infirmary, Edinburgh, since 1981; Member, Clinical Teaching Staff, Edinburgh University, since 1981; b. 28.2.36, Harrar, Ethiopia; m., Heather; 1 s.; 1 d. Educ. Trinity College, Cambridge; St. Thomas's Hospital, London. Dermatologist, Royal Jubilee Hospital, Victoria, BC, Canada, 1971-81. President, Fife Branch, BMA, 1986-87; Fellow, Royal Society of Medicine; Member, Ethical Committee, Fife Health Board; Member, Editorial Board, Ethics and Medicine. Publication: ABC of Dermatology. Recreations: seafaring; books; art; country pursuits. Address: (h.) Old Inzievar House, Dunfermline KY12 8HA; T.-01383 852424.

Buyers, Donald Morison, DA, RSW; b. 29.12.30, Aberdeen; m., Margaret; 1 s.; 1 d. Educ. Aberdeen Grammar School; Grays School of Art, Aberdeen. Art Therapist, 1953-58; Teacher of Art, 1961-64; Lecturer in Design Studies, Robert Gordon University, 1964-85; Visiting Lecturer, Grays School of Art, 1981-85. Address: (h.) 96 Gray Street, Aberdeen; T.-317717.

Byiers, Eric George, MA, DipTRP, FIMgt, MRTPI. Head, Economic Development Service, Fife Council, since 1995; b. 29.1.51, Aberdeen; m., Nicky. Educ. Aberdeen Grammar School; University of Aberdeen; University of Glasgow. Central Regional Council, 1975-80; Borders Regional Council, 1980-85; Fife Regional Council, 1985-95. Address: (b.) Fife House, North Street, Glenrothes; T,-01592 416294.

Byng, Jamie. Publisher and Joint Managing Director, Canongate Books, since 1994; b. 27.6.69, Winchester; m., Whitney Osborn McVeigh; 1 d. Educ. Winchester College; Edinburgh University. Recreations: tennis; cooking; "deejaying"; reading; drinking. Address: (b.) 14 High Street, Edinburgh EH1 1TE; T.-0131-557 5111.

Byrne, John. Dramatist and stage designer; b. 1940, Paisley. Plays include: The Slab Boys, Cuttin' A Rug, Still Life (trilogy); Normal Service; Cara Coco; television series: Tutti Frutti; Your Cheatin' Heart.

C

Cadell, Patrick Moubray, BA, FSA (Scot). Keeper of the Records of Scotland, since 1991; b. 17.3.41, Linlithgow; m., Sarah King (d. 1996); 2 s.; 1 d. Educ. Merchiston Castle School, Edinburgh; Cambridge University; Toulouse University. Information Officer, British Museum; Assistant Keeper, Department of MSS, British Museum; Keeper of Manuscripts, National Library of Scotland, 1983-90. Bailie, Abbey Court of Holyrood; Past President, West Lothian History and Amenity Society. Recreations: walking; the French language. Address: (b.) Scottish Record Office, HM General Register House, Edinburgh EH1 3YY; T.-0131-535 1312.

Cadell of Grange, William Archibald, DL, MA (Cantab), FRIAS, RIBA. Architect; Commissioner, Royal Fine Art Commission for Scotland; Trustee, Architectural Heritage Fund; b. 9.3.33, Aldershot; m., Mary-Jean Carmichael; 3 s. Educ. Merchiston Castle; Trinity College, Cambridge; Regent Street Polytechnic. Robert Matthew, Johnson Marshall and Partners; William A. Cadell Architects, 1968-95; DL, West Lothian, 1982; Former Member, Council, Executive, Buildings and Curatorial Committees, National Trust for Scotland; former Chairman, RIAS Conservation Working Group; former Chairman, West Lothian History and Amenity Society. Recreations: gardening; local history; theatre. Address: Grange, Linlithgow, West Lothian; T.-01506 842946.

Caddy, Professor Brian, BSc, PhD, CChem, MRSC. Professor of Forensic Science, Strathclyde University, since 1992; b. 26.3.37, Burslem, Stoke-on-Trent; m., Beryl Ashworth; 1 s.; 1 d. Educ. Longton High School, Stoke-on-Trent; Sheffield University. MRC Research Fellow, 1963-66; Strathclyde University: Lecturer in Forensic Science, 1966-77, Senior Lecturer in Forensic Science, 1977-92. Founder Member, European Network of Forensic Science Institutes. Publications: two books; over 90 papers/articles. Editor, Science and Justice (Forensic Science Society journal). Recreations: reading; painting; walking the dog; dining with friends; good food and wine. Address: (h.) 5 Kings Park, Torrance, Glasgow G64 4DX; T.-01360 622 358.

Caie, Professor Graham Douglas, MA, PhD. Professor of English Language, Glasgow University, since 1990; b. 3.2.45, Aberdeen; m., Ann Pringle Abbott; 1 s.; 1 d. Educ. Aberdeen Grammar School; Aberdeen University; McMaster University, Canada. Teaching Assistant, McMaster University, 1968-72; Amanuensis and Lektor, Copenhagen University, 1972-90. Chairman, Medieval Centre, Copenhagen University, 1985-90; Visiting Professor: McMaster University, 1985-86, Guelph University, 1989; Associate Fellow, Clare Hall, Cambridge, 1977-78; Chairman, Scottish Language Resource Centre; Member, English Panel: SQA, UCAS; Lead Assessor, SHEFC, TQA in English; Vice-President, Scottish Texts Society; Erasmus Academic Advisory Group (EU Commission); Secretary, European Society for the Study of English; Trustee, National Library of Scotland; Member, Council, Dictionary of Older Scottish Tongue; Convener, Friends of Glasgow University Library. Publications: Judgement Day II edition, The Theme of Doomsday in Old English Poetry; Beowulf; Bibliography of Junius XI MS; numerous articles. Address: (h.) 12B Upper Glenburn Road, Bearsden, Glasgow G61 4BW; T.-0141-943 1192.

Caimbeul, Aonghas Phàdraig, MA. Sgrìobhadair; Fear-naidheachd (òraidiche agus craoladair); r. Uibhist-a-Deas; p., Liondsaidh; 4 n. Foghlam: Ard-Sgoil an Obain; Oilthaigh Dhùn Eideann. Treis aig: A' Phàipear Bheag, BBC Rèidio, Grampian Telebhisean; Sgrìobhaiche an t-Sabhail Mhòir, 1990-92; Oraidiche an sin on uairsin; Crìosdaidh; ag obair air nobhal mòr'an-dràsda. Air foillseachadh: 2 leabhar bàrdachd; nobhal dheugairean; dà nobhal eile tighinn a-mach am bliadhna. Cuir-seachad: bhith ris an teachlach agus leughadh Tolstoy. Seòladh: Sabhal Mòr Ostaig, An Teanga, Slèite, an t-Eilein Sgitheanach; F.-01471 844373.

Cairns, Christopher, MA. Environment Correspondent, The Scotsman, since 1995; b. 11.3.61, Paisley; m., Marian Glen. Educ. St. Mungo's Academy; Glasgow University. The Buckinghamshire Advertiser, 1990-92; East Anglian Daily Times, 1992-94; freelance, 1994-95. Recreations: listening to jazz; hillwalking; golf; supporting Glasgow Celtic. Address: (b.) North Bridge, Edinburgh EH1 1YT; T.-0131-243 3366.

Cairns, Rev. John Ballantyne, LTh, LLB. Moderator, General Assembly of the Church of Scotland, 1999-2000; Parish Minister, Riverside Church, Dumbarton, since 1985; Chaplain to the Queen, since 1997; General Trustee of Church of Scotland, since 1995; b. 15.3.42, London; m., Dr. Elizabeth Emma Bradley; 3 s. Educ. Sutton Valence School, Kent; Bristol University; Edinburgh University. Messrs Richards, Butler & Co., Solicitors, City of London, 1964-68; Administrative Assistant, East Lothian County Council, 1968-69; Assistant Minister, St. Giles, Elgin, 1973-75; Minister, Langholm, Ewes and Westerkirk Parish Churches, 1975-85, also linked with Canonbie, 1981-85; Clerk, Presbytery of Annandale and Eskdale, 1980-82; Convener, Maintenance of the Ministry Committee and Joint Convener, Board of Ministry and Mission, Church of Scotland, 1984-88; Chairman, Judicial Commission of General Assembly, 1993-98; Convener, General Assembly Committee on Chaplains to Her Majesty's Forces, 1993-98; Moderator, Presbytery of Dumbarton, 1993-94; Chaplain to Moderator of General Assembly, 1995; Divisional Chaplain, Strathclyde Police. Publications: Keeping Fit for Ministry, 1988; Democracy and Unwritten Constitutions, 1989. Recreations: golf; curling. Address: (b.) High Street, Dumbarton, G82 1NB; (h.) 5 Kirkton Road, Dumbarton G82 4AS.

Cairns, Joyce Winifred, ARSA, RSW, MA (RCA), DA, ATC. Artist; Lecturer in Drawing and Painting, Grays School of Art, Robert Gordon's University, Aberdeen, since 1976; b. 21.3.47, Haddington; m., Captain Robert K.H. Cunningham. Educ. Mary Erskine School for Girls; Gray's School of Art; Goldsmiths College, University of London; Royal College of Art. Visiting Lecturer: Glasgow School of Art, Duncan of Jordanstone College of Art, Dundee; Fellow, Gloucester College of Art and Design; Scottish Arts Council: Member, Art Committee, 1986-89, Member, Awards Panel, 1981-83 and 1987-90; President, Aberdeen Artists Society, 1985-88; Board Member, Peacock Printmakers, since 1993; solo exhibitions: Compass Gallery, Glasgow, 1980, ESU, Edinburgh, 1981, Peacock Printmakers, Aberdeen, 1981, Art Space Galleries, Aberdeen, 1984, Perth Museum and Art Gallery, 1986, 369 Gallery, Edinburgh, 1986, Third Eye Gallery, Glasgow, 1987, Talbot Rice Gallery, University of Edinburgh, 1991, Peacock Gallery, Aberdeen, 1991, Odette Gilbert Gallery, London, 1991, Kirkcaldy Art Gallery and Museum, 1992, An Lanntair, Stornoway, 1992, Lamont Gallery, 1993, Elektra Fine Art, Toronto, Roger Billcliffe Gallery, Glasgow, 1995, Rendezvous Gallery, Aberdeen, 1998; work in public collections; numerous awards and prizes. Recreations: swimming; reading. Address: 5 New Pier Road, Footdee, Aberdeen AB11 5DR; T.-01224 575331.

Cairns, Robert, MA, DipEd. Chairman, East of Scotland Water, since 1998; Member, City of Edinburgh Council, since 1995 (Convener, Planning Committee, since 1995); b. 16.7.47, Dundee; 2 s. Educ. Morgan Academy; Edinburgh University; Moray House College of Education. Assistant Editor, Scottish National Dictionary, 1969-74;

Parliamentary candidate (Labour), North Edinburgh, 1973, February 1974; Teacher, James Gillespie's High School, 1975-96; Member, City of Edinburgh District Council, 1974-95 (Convener, Planning and Development Committee, 1986-95); Board Member: Old Town Renewal Trust, Old Town Community Development Project; Queen's Hall; Canongate Youth Project; Member, Historic Buildings Council. Recreations: gardening; theatre. Address: (h.) 70 Ratcliffe Terrace, Edinburgh; T.-0131-667 1741.

Cairns, Professor Robert Alan, BSc, PhD, FInstP, FRSE. Professor, School of Mathematical and Computational Sciences, St. Andrews University, since 1991 (Reader, 1985-91); b. 12.3.45, Glasgow; m., Ann E. Mackay. Educ. Allan Glen's School, Glasgow; Glasgow University. Lecturer in Applied Mathematics, St. Andrews University, 1970-83; Senior Lecturer, 1983-85; Consultant, UKAEA Culham Laboratory, since 1984. Committee Member, Plasma Physics Group, Institute of Physics, 1981-84; Member, SERC Laser Committee, 1990-93; Member, SERC Atomic and Molecular Physics Sub-Committee, 1990-93; Member, Editorial Board, Plasma Physics, 1983-85; Editor, Journal of Plasma Physics, since 1995. Publications: Plasma Physics, 1985; Radiofrequency heating of plasmas, 1991. Recreations: music (listening to and playing recorder and baroque flute); golf; hill-walking. Address: (b.) School of Mathematical and Computational Sciences, St. Andrews University, North Haugh, St. Andrews, Fife KY16 9SS; T.-01334 463707.

Caithness, 20th Earl of (Malcolm Ian Sinclair), PC; b. 3.11.48; m.; 1 s.; 1 d. Educ. Marlborough; Royal Agricultural College, Cirencester. Succeeded to title, 1965; Paymaster General and Minister of State, HM Treasury, 1989-90; Minister of State, Foreign and Commonwealth Office, 1990-92; Department of Transport, 1992-94.

Calder, Angus Lindsay, MA, DPhil. Writer; b. 5.2.42, Sutton, Surrey; m., 1, Jennifer Daiches; 1 s.; 2 d.; 2, Catherine Kyle; 1 s. Educ. Wallington County Grammar School; Kings College, Cambridge. Lecturer in Literature, Nairobi University, 1968-71; Visiting Lecturer, Chancellor College, Malawi University, 1978; Reader and Staff Tutor in Arts, Open University in Scotland, 1979-93; Visiting Professor of English, University of Zimbabwe, 1993; Distinguished Visiting Scholar, University of Waikato, 1995; Member, Board of Directors, Royal Lyceum Theatre Company, 1984-96; Editorial Board, Wasafiri; Member, Panel of Judges, Saltire Society Scottish Book of the Year Award, 1983-97; Eric Gregory Award for Poetry, 1967. Publications: The People's War: Britain 1939-1945, 1969 (John Llewellyn Rhys Memorial Prize); Revolutionary Empire, 1981 (Scottish Arts Council Book Award); The Myth of the Blitz, 1991; Revolving Culture: notes from the Scottish Republic, 1994 (SAC Book Award); Waking in Waikato (poems), 1997. Recreations: curling; cricket. Address: (h.) 15 Spittal Street, Edinburgh EH3 9DY; T.-0131-229 8196.

Calder, Finlay, OBE. Grain Exporter; b. 20.8.57, Haddington; m., Elizabeth; 1 s.; 1 d. Educ. Daniel Stewart's and Melville College. Played rugby for Scotland, 1986-90; captained Scotland, 1989; captained British Isles, 1989. Recreation: work! Address: (b.) Alexander Inglis & Son Ltd., Meadow Stores, Ormiston, Tranent, East Lothian; T.-01875 616161.

Calder, George D., BA (Hons), LLB, MIPD. Senior Civil Servant, Scottish Office, since 1987; b. 20.12.47, Edinburgh; m., Kathleen Bonar; 2 d. Educ. George Watson's College; Pembroke College, Cambridge; Edinburgh University. Department of Employment, 1971-73; European Commission, 1973-76; HM Treasury, 1976-79; Manpower Services Commission Scotland, 1979-83; MSC Director for Northern England, 1983-85; MSC Director for Scotland, 1985-87. Recreations: hill-walking; football; country; writing; book collecting. Address: (b.) 1-577, Victoria Quay, Edinburgh; T.-0131-244 0246.

Calder, Jenni, BA, MPhil. Freelance Writer; Head of Scotland and The World Initiative, National Museums of Scotland, Edinburgh, since 1987; b. 3.12.41, Chicago, Illinois; 1 s.; 2 d. Educ. Perse School for Girls, Cambridge; Cambridge University; London University. Freelance writer, 1966-78; taught and lectured in Scotland, England, Kenya and USA; Lecturer in English, Nairobi University, 1968-69; Education Officer, Royal Scottish Museum, 1978-87. Publications: Chronicles of Conscience: a study of George Orwell and Arthur Koestler, 1968; Scott (with Angus Calder), 1969; There Must be a Lone Ranger: the Myth and Reality of the American West, 1974; Women and Marriage in Victorian Fiction, 1976; Brave New World and Nineteen Eighty Four, 1976; Heroes: from Byron to Guevara, 1977; The Victorian Home, 1977; The Victorian Home from Old Photographs, 1979; RLS, A Life Study, 1980; The Robert Louis Stevenson Companion (Editor), 1980; Robert Louis Stevenson and Victorian Scotland (Editor), 1981; The Strange Case of Dr Jekyll and Mr Hyde (Editor), 1979; Kidnapped (Editor), 1981; Catriona (Editor), 1981; The Enterprising Scot (Editor), 1986; Island Landfalls (Editor), 1987; Bonny Fighters: The Story of the Scottish Soldier, 1987; Open Guide to Animal Farm and Nineteen Eighty Four, 1987; The Wealth of a Nation (Editor), 1989; St. Ives, a new ending, 1990; Scotland in Trust, 1990; Treasure Islands (Editor), 1994; Mediterranean (poems, as Jenni Daiches), 1995; The Nine Lives of Naomi Mitchison, 1997; Robert Louis Stevenson (Editor), 1997. Recreations: music; films; walking the dog. Address: (h.) 31 Station Road, South Queensferry, West Lothian; T.-0131-331 1287.

Calder, Robert Russell, MA. Critic, Philosophical Writer, Historian of Ideas, Poet, Freelance Journalist, Book Reviewer; b. 22.4.50, Burnbank. Educ. Hamilton Academy; Glasgow University; Edinburgh University. Co-Editor, Chapman, 1974-76 and since 1988; Editor, Lines Review, 1976-77; Theatre Critic and Feature Writer, Scot, 1983-86; books: A School of Thinking, 1995; Narcissism, Nihilism, Simplicity (Editor), 1992; poetry: Il Re Giovane, 1976, Ettrick & Annan, 1981; Serapion, 1996. Recreations: music - opera singing; jazz piano. Address: (h.) 23 Glenlee Street, Burnbank, Hamilton ML3 9JB; T.-01698 824244.

Calderwood, Sir Robert, Kt. Chairman, Greater Glasgow Health Board, 1993-97; Chief Executive, Strathclyde Regional Council, 1980-92; b. 1.3.32; m., Meryl Anne; 3 s.; 1 d. Educ. William Hulme's School, Manchester; Manchester University (LLB Hons). Town Clerk: Salford, 1966-69, Bolton, 1969-73, Manchester, 1973-79. Director, Glasgow Garden Festival 1988 Ltd., 1985-88; Chairman, Strathclyde Buses Ltd., 1989-93; Member: Parole Board for England and Wales, 1971-73, Society of Local Authority Chief Executives, 1974-92 (President, 1989-90), Scottish Consultative Committee, Commission for Racial Equality, 1981-88; Director, European Summer Special Olympic Games 1990 (Strathclyde) Ltd., 1989-90; Member, Council, Industrial Society, 1983-92; Director: GEC (Scotland) Ltd., since 1991, Scottish Opera, 1991-96 (Deputy Chairman, 1991-96); Member: Employers' Panel, Industrial Tribunals in Scotland, 1992-98, Local and Central Government Relations Research Committee, Joseph Rowntree Foundation, 1992-97; Director, Quality Scotland Foundation, 1991-92; Honorary Patron, Scottish Overseas Aid, 1993-98; Honorary Member, The Incorporation of Coopers, Trades House of Glasgow, since 1994; Member, Court of Governors, Glasgow Caledonian University, 1994-96. Hon. Fellow, IWEM, 1992. Recreations: theatre; watching rugby; interested in United Nations activities. Address:(h.) 6 Mosspark Avenue, Milngavie, Glasgow G62 8NL.

Caldwell, David Cleland, SHNC, MA, BPhil. Secretary, The Robert Gordon University, since 1984; b. 25.2.44, Glasgow; m., Ann Scott Macrae; 1 s.; 1 d. Educ. George Watson's College, Edinburgh; St. Andrews University; Glasgow University. Warwick University: Lecturer in Politics, 1969-76, Administrative Assistant, 1976-77, Assistant Registrar, 1977-80; Registry Officer, Aberdeen University, 1980-84. Member: Warwick District Council, 1979-80, Grampian Regional Council, 1983-84; Parliamentary candidate (Labour), North East Fife, 1983; Member, Aberdeen Grammar School Council, 1983-88 (Chairman, 1985-88); Member, St. Andrews University Court, 1986-94 (Convener, Audit Commitee, 1990-94); Member, Board of Management, and Convener, Finance Committee, Moray College, since 1995; Director, Viscom (Aberdeen) Ltd., 1992-97 (Chairman, 1994-95); Director, RGIT Ltd., since 1997. Address: (b.) The Robert Gordon University, Schoolhill, Aberdeen AB10 1FR; T.-01224 262010.

Caldwell, David Hepburn, MA, PhD, FSAScot. Curator in Charge of the Scottish Medieval Collections, Royal Museum of Scotland; b. 15.12.51, Kilwinning, Ayrshire; m., Margaret Anne McGovern; 1 s.; 2 d. Educ. Ardrossan Academy; Edinburgh University. Joined staff, National Museum of Antiquities, 1973. Publications: The Scottish Armoury, 1979; Scottish Weapons and Fortifications, 1981; Scotland's Wars and Warriors, 1998. Recreation: travelling. Address: (h.) 3 James Park, Burntisland, Fife KY3 9EW; T.-872175.

Caldwell, Sheila Marion, BA (Hons), ARSGS. Member, Council, Royal Scottish Geographical Society; b. England; m., Major Robert Caldwell, TD. Educ. Tunbridge Wells Grammar School; University College, London. Founder/Principal, Yejide Girls' Grammar School, Ibadan, Nigeria; first Principal, Girls' Secondary (Government) School, Lilongwe, Malawi; Depute Head, Mills Grammar School, Framlingham, Suffolk; Head, St. Columba's School, Kilmacolm, 1976-87; Treasurer, Secondary Heads' Association, Scotland, 1984-87; Public Affairs Liaison, Glasgow Association of Women Graduates. Recreations: travel; art history and architecture; music, opera and ballet; cooking. Address: (h.) 27 Oxford Road, Renfrew PA4 0SJ; T.-0141-886 2296.

Callander, Alexander Dougal, BA (Oxon), LLB, WS. Solicitor (retired); Honorary Sheriff at Stirling, 1991; b. 10.3.26, Doncaster; m., Mona Patricia Meldrum; 1 s.; 2 d. Educ. Winchester College; Magdalen College, Oxford University; Edinburgh University. Director, James Dougall and Sons (refactories industry), 1952-62; Mathie Macluckie and Lupton, Solicitors, Stirling: Assistant, 1962, Partner, 1963, retired 1994. Recreations: hillwalking; fishing; golf. Address: (h.) Coldon, Port of Menteith, Stirling FK8 3RD; T.-01877 385275.

Callison, Fiona Margaret, MA, MIPR; Head of Corporate Affairs: Scotland, Railtrack, since 1994; b. 11.9.64, Aberdeen; m., Stuart Callison; 1 s. Educ. Breadalbane Academy, Aberfeldy; University of Glasgow. Adviser to Rt. Hon. Dr. David Owen, MP, Leader, SDP, 1986-87; Graduate Management Trainee, Burton Group, 1987-88; External Liaison Officer, Federation of Civil Engineering Contractors, 1988-89; Public Affairs Adviser, International E & P Division, Sun Co. Inc., 1989-92; Parliamentary Lobbyist (freelance), 1992-93. Member, Board, North Glasgow College. Recreations: domestic engineering and motherhood; gardening; politics. Address: 2nd Floor, Buchanan House, 58 Port Dundas Road, Glasgow G4 0LQ; T.-0141-335 2061.

Calman, Professor Sir Kenneth Charles, KCB 1996, MD, PhD, FRCP, FRCS, FRSE. Vice-Chancellor and Warden, Durham University, since 1998; Chief Medical Officer, Department of Health, 1991-98; Chief Medical Officer, Scottish Home and Health Department, 1989-91; b. 25.12.41, Glasgow; m., Ann; 1 s.; 2 d. Educ. Allan Glen's School, Glasgow; Glasgow University. Lecturer in Surgery, Western Infirmary, Glasgow, 1968-72; MRC Clinical Research Fellow, London, 1972-73; Professor of Oncology, Glasgow University, 1974-84; Dean of Postgraduate Medicine, 1984-89. Recreations: golf; jogging; gardening; cartoons; sundials. Address: (h.) 585 Anniesland Road, Glasgow; T.-0141-954 9423.

Cameron, Alasdair, FSA Scot. Farmer and Crofter; b. 12.6.44, Dingwall; m., Jeannette Benzie; 2 d. Educ. Dingwall Academy. Hon. President, Black Isle Farmers Society; Former Vice-Chairman, Crofters Commission; Member: Scottish Farm and Countryside Educational Trust, Highlands and Islands Forum, Scottish Agricultural Arbiters Association, Northern Counties Valuators Association, Scottish Vernacular Buildings Working Group, Historic Farm Buildings UK; Past Chairman: Highland Farming and Forestry Advisory Group, Dingwall Round Table. Recreations: photography; industrial archaeology; local history; the countryside. Address: Wellhouse Farm, Black Isle, Muir of Ord, Ross-shire IV6 7SF; T.-01463 870416.

Cameron, Alastair Ian, BA (Hons). Co-ordinator, Scottish Churches Housing Agency, since 1994; b. 3.4.53, Dundee; m., Mary Jane Elton; 2 s.; 1 d. Educ. Glasgow Academy; Lenana School, Nairobi; University of Kent at Canterbury; Manchester Polytechnic; Stirling University; Heriot-Watt University. Industrial Relations Officer, TBA Industrial Products, Rochdale, 1977-79; Neighbourhood Worker, Rochdale Metropolitan Council, 1980-85; Development Worker, Edinburgh Council for the Single Homeless, 1985-92; Housing Strategy Manager, Wester Hailes Partnership, 1992-94. Member, Religious Society of Friends. Recreations: raising children; traditional music; cycling; allotment gardening. Address: 3 Esplanade Terrace, Edinburgh EH15 2ES.

Cameron, Allan John, MBE, DL, JP. Farmer and Landowner, since 1947; b. 25.3.17, Edinburgh; m., Elizabeth Vaughan-Lee; 2 s.; 2 d. Educ. Harrow; Royal Military College. Regular officer, Queen's Own Cameron Highlanders, 1936-47 (ret. Major); Member: Ross and Cromarty County Council, 1955-75 (Chairman, Education Committee, 1962-75), Ross and Cromarty District Council, since 1975 (Convener, since 1991); former Commissioner: Red Deer Commission, Countryside Commission for Scotland; former Member, BBC Council for Scotland; President: Royal Caledonian Curling Club, 1963, International Curling Federation, 1965-69. Recreations: curling; golf; shooting; fishing; gardening. Address: (h.) Allangrange, Munlochy, Ross and Cromarty IV8 8NZ; T.-014638 11249.

Cameron, Rt. Rev. Andrew Bruce. Bishop of Aberdeen and Orkney, Scottish Episcopal Church, since 1992; b. 2.5.41, Glasgow; m., Elaine Cameron; 2 s. Educ. Eastwood Secondary School; Edinburgh Theological College. Curate, Helensburgh and Edinburgh, 1964-70; Chaplain, St. Mary's Cathedral, Edinburgh, 1970-75; Diocesan and Provincial Youth Chaplain, 1969-75; Rector, St. Mary's Church, Dalmahoy, and Anglican Chaplain, Heriot Watt University, 1975-82; Churches Development Officer, Livingston Ecumenical Parish, 1982-88; Rector, St. John's Episcopal Church, Perth, 1988-92; Convener, Mission Board, Scottish Episcopal Church, 1988-92. Recreations: music; theatre; various sports; gardening. Address: (b.) Diocesan Centre, 39 Kings Crescent, Aberdeen AB24 3HP; T.-01224 636653; (h.) Bishop's House, Ashley House, Ashley Gardens, Aberdeen, AB10 6RQ; T.-01224 208142.

Cameron, Colin. Head of Production, BBC Scotland, since 1997; b. 30.3.50; m., Christine Main; 2 s. Educ. Glasgow Academy; Duke of York School, Nairobi; Polytechnic of

Central London. Journalist, Current Affairs, BBC Scotland, 1973-76; Film Director, That's Life, 1976-77; Producer/Director, Everyman and Heart of the Matter, 1977-85; Editor, Brass Tacks, BBC North, 1985-88; Head of Documentary Features, BBC Television, 1988-91; Head of Television, BBC Scotland, 1991-96. Advisor, Glasgow Common Purpose; RTS International Current Affairs Award, 1984; UN Association Media Peace Prize, 1984. Recreations: dinghy sailing; cycling; hillwalking; cinema; Scottish art. Address: (b.) BBC Scotland, Queen Margaret Drive, Glasgow, G12 8DG; T.-0141-338 2424.

Cameron, David Roderick Simpson, RIBA, ARIAS, MRTPI, FSA Scot. Architect/Planner; Urban Design Consultant, Broad and Hughes Architects, since 1997; Director, AUi Ltd., since 1998; Director, Central Bucharest Consortium Ltd., since 1998; Associate, Impart Studio, since 1998; Convener, Historic Burghs Association of Scotland (Steering Committee), since 1993; Chairman, Sir Patrick Geddes Memorial Trust, since 1991; b. 2.6.41, Inverness; m., Filitsa Boulton; 1 s.; 2 d. Educ. Angusfield and George Watson's College; Edinburgh College of Art; Newcastle University. Architect, Rowand Anderson, Kininmonth and Paul, 1968-71; Conservation Officer, Edinburgh Corporation and Edinburgh District Council, 1971-83; Depute Executive Director of Planning, City of Edinburgh District Council, 1983-96; European Union, ECOS Project Manager (of Edinburgh and Berlin team) for revival of Kazimierz quarter of Krakow, Poland, 1993-95; Principal, Chambers Design, 1996-97; Chairman, The Saltire Society, 1990-95; Convener: Saltire Performing Arts Committee, 1991-94, Saltire Planning and Environment Committee, 1995-98, Scottish Environment and Amenity Link, 1996-97; Secretary: Saltire Arts and Crafts in Architecture Award Panel, 1987-94, Saltire Housing Award Panel, 1974-83; Hon. Secretary, Edinburgh Architectural Association, 1972-75, and Editor, EAA Review, 1980-84; Member: International Society of City and Regional Planners, since 1987, Executive Committee, Scottish Society of Directors of Planning, 1988-96, Council, Clan Cameron Association, since 1988, and Vice-President, since 1995; Convener, Charles Cameron Conservation Campaign, 1994-98; Council, National Trust for Scotland, since 1994, Grants Council, Scottish Community Foundation, since 1996, Scottish Homes Advisory Group on Physical Quality, 1996-98. Recreations: art; fishing; Hillman Imp car; Scottish and Greek heritage. Address: (b.) 9 South College Street, Edinburgh EH8 9AA; T.-0131-668 1942.

Cameron, Younger of Lochiel, Donald Angus, MA, FCA, DL. Director, J. Henry Schroder & Co. Limited, since 1984; President, Highland Society of London, 1994-97; b. 2.8.46, London; m., Lady Cecil Kerr; 1 s. 3 d. Educ. Harrow; Christ Church, Oxford. 2nd Lieutenant, Queen's Own Cameron Highlanders (TA), 1966-68; Chartered Accountant, 1971. Vice-Lieutenant, Lochaber, Inverness, Badenoch and Strathspey. Address: (h.) Achnacarry, Spean Bridge, Inverness-shire.

Cameron of Lochiel, Colonel Sir Donald (Hamish), KT (1973), CVO, TD, JP. 26th Chief of the Clan Cameron; Lord Lieutenant, County of Inverness, 1971-86; Chartered Accountant; b. 12.9.10; m., Margaret Gathorne-Hardy; 2 s.; 2 d. Educ. Harrow; Balliol College, Oxford. Lt.-Col. commanding: Lovat Scouts, 1944-45; 4/5th Bn. (TA), Queen's Own Cameron Highlanders, 1955-57; Colonel, 1957 (TARO); Vice-Chairman, Royal Bank of Scotland, 1969-80; Chairman: Culter Guard Bridge Holdings Ltd., 1970-76, Scottish Widows Life Assurance Society, 1964-67; President: Scottish Landowners Federation, 1979-84, Royal Highland and Agricultural Society of Scotland, 1971, 1979, 1987; Member, Scottish Railways Board (Chairman, 1959-64). Address: (h.) Achnacarry, Spean Bridge, Inverness-shire.

Cameron, Rt. Rev. Douglas M. Bishop of Argyll and the Isles, since 1993; b. 23.3.35, Natal; m., Anne Patricia Purnell; 2 d. Educ. Eastwood Grammar School; Edinburgh Theological College; University of the South, Sewanee, Tennessee. Curate, Christ Church, Falkirk, 1962-65; Priest, Papua New Guinea, 1965-74, Archdeacon, 1972-74; Rector: St. Fillan's and St. Hilda's, Edinburgh, 1974-88, St. Mary's, Dalkeith, and St. Leonard's, Lasswade, 1988-92; Canon and Synod Clerk, Diocese of Edinburgh, 1990-92; Dean of Edinburgh, 1991-92. Recreations: hill-walking; music; cooking. Address: (b.) The Pines, Ardconnel Road, Oban PA34 5DR; T.-01631 566912.

Cameron, Professor Dugald, DA, FCSD, FRSA. Director, Glasgow School of Art, since 1991; Hon. Professor, Glasgow University, since 1993; Companion, Royal Aeronautical Society, 1996; Director, Squadron Prints, since 1977; Industrial Design Consultant, since 1965; b. 4.10.39, Glasgow; m., Nancy Inglis. Educ. Glasgow High School; Glasgow School of Art. Industrial Designer, Hard Aluminium Surfaces Ltd., 1962-65; Visiting Lecturer, Glasgow School of Art, 1963-70; Head of Product Design, Glasgow School of Art, 1970-82; Head of Design, 1982-91. Member: Engineering Advisory Committee, Scottish Committee, Council of Industrial Design, since 1966, Industrial Design (Engineering) Panel and 3D Design Board, CNAA, since 1978, Scottish Committee of Higher Education, Design Council; commission RAFVR (T), 1974. Publications: Glasgow's Own (a history of 602 City of Glasgow Squadron, Royal Auxiliary Air Force), 1987; Glasgow's Airport, 1990. Recreations: railways; flying (lapsed private pilot). Address: (h.) Achnacraig, Skelmorlie, Ayrshire.

Cameron, Duncan Inglis, OBE, JP, BL, DUniv, CA, FRSGS. Director of Administration and Secretary, Heriot-Watt University, 1965-90; b. 26.8.27, Glasgow; m., Elizabeth Pearl Heron; 2 s.; 1 d. Educ. Glasgow High School; Glasgow University. RAF, 1945-48; CA apprentice, Alfred Tongue & Co., 1948-51; Qualified Assistant, Cooper Brothers & Co., 1951-52; Assistant Accountant, Edinburgh University, 1952-65; Commonwealth Universities Administrative Fellow, 1972. President, Edinburgh Junior Chamber of Commerce, 1962-63; Governor, Keil School, Dumbarton, 1967-85; Chairman of Council, Royal Scottish Geographical Society, 1983-88 (Trustee, since 1973); Governor, Scottish College of Textiles, 1991-98; Chairman, Bioscot Ltd., 1983-84; Chairman, Edinburgh Conference Centre Ltd., 1987-90; Director, Heriot-Watt Computer Application Services Ltd., 1987-90; Chairman, SCOT Innovation and Development Ltd., 1991-98; Member: Universities Central Council on Admissions, 1967-90, Directing Group, Programme on Institutional Management in Higher Education, OECD, Paris, 1986-90, Executive Committee, Federated Superannuation System for Universities, since 1988, Executive Committee, Scottish Norwegian Business Forum, 1991-96, Board of Management, Petroleum Science and Technology Institute, 1989-93; Chairman, Edinburgh Society of Glasgow University Graduates, 1984-85; Session Clerk, St. Ninian's Church, Corstorphine, 1969-96; Convener, Finance Committee, Action of Churches Together in Scotland, 1993-96; Vice-Convener, Personnel Committee, Church of Scotland, since 1996; Honorary Fellow, Royal Scottish Geographical Society, 1989; Honorary Doctor, Heriot-Watt University, 1991; Officer of the Royal Norwegian Order of St. Olav, 1979. Recreations: travel; photography. Address: (h.) 11 The Hermitage, 1 Kinellan Road, Edinburgh EH12 6ES; T.-0131 346 4454.

Cameron, Brigadier Ewen Duncan, OBE. Deputy Director, National Trust for Scotland, since 1998; b. 10.2.35, Bournemouth; m., Joanna Margaret Hay; 2 d. Educ. Wellington College; Royal Military Academy, Sandhurst. Commissioned The Black Watch, 1955; DS, The Staff College, 1972-75; Commanding Officer, 1st Bn., The

Black Watch, 1975-78; Commander, Royal Brunei Armed Forces, 1980-82; Indian College of Defence Studies, Delhi, 1983; Divisional Brigadier, Scottish Division, 1984-86; Director of Administration and Personnel, National Trust for Scotland, 1986-98. Member, Queen's Bodyguard for Scotland (Royal Company of Archers). Recreations: opera; bridge; bird-watching; travel; gardening. Address: (h.) The Old Manse, Arngask, Glenfarg, Perthshire PH2 9QA; T.-01577 830394.

Cameron, Professor Iain Thomas, BSc (Hons), MA (Cantab), MD (Edin), MRCOG, MRACOG. Regius Professor, Obstetrics and Gynaecology, Queen Mother's Hospital, Glasgow; b. 21.2.56, Flixton; m., Heidi D. Wade; 1 s.; 1 d.; 2 d by pr. m. Educ. Hutton Grammar School; Edinburgh University. Research Fellow, Department of Obstetrics and Gynaecology, Edinburgh University, 1982-84; Lecturer and Registrar, 1984-86; Clinical Research Fellow, Monash University, 1986-88; Senior Registrar, Royal Women's Hospital, Melbourne, 1988-89; Lecturer, Cambridge University, 1989-92. Recreation: solo piping. Address: (b.) Department of Obstetrics and Gynaecology, The Queen Mother's Hospital, Glasgow G3 8SJ; T.-0141-201 0567.

Cameron, Sheriff Ian Alexander, MA, LLB. Sheriff of Grampian, Highland and Islands, at Wick, Dornoch and Stornoway, since 1993; b. 5.11.38, Elgin; m., Dr. Margaret Anne Innes; 1 s. Educ. Elgin Academy; Edinburgh University; Aberdeen University. Partner, Stewart and McIsaac, Solicitors, Elgin, 1962-86; Sheriff at Edinburgh, 1987-93. Recreation: travel. Address: Braemoray, Elgin, IV30 2NJ; T.-01343 542731; 19/4 Damside, Dean Village, Edinburgh, EH4 3BB; T.-0131-220 1548.

Cameron, James, BSc (Hons), PhD. Head Teacher, Kilchuimen Academy, Fort Augustus, since 1992; b. 29.1.47, Fraserburgh; m., Jo; 2 s.; 2 d. Educ. Peterhead Academy; University of Aberdeen; Aberdeen College of Education. Research Chemist, Courtaulds Ltd., Coventry, 1972-76; Teacher: Robert Gordon's College, Aberdeen, 1977-79, Peterhead Academy, 1979-83; Principal Teacher (Chemistry), Dyce Academy, Aberdeen, 1983-89; Assistant Head Teacher, Northfield Academy, Aberdeen, 1989-92. Recreations: walking; DIY; caravanning; reading. Address: Kilchuimen Academy, Station Road, Fort Augustus; T.-01320 366296.

Cameron, Professor Rev. James Kerr, MA, BD, PhD, FRHistS. Professor of Ecclesiastical History, St. Andrews University, 1970-89; b. 5.3.24, Methven; m., Emma Leslie Birse; 1 s. Educ. Oban High School; St. Andrews University; Hartford Theological Seminary, Hartford, Connecticut. Ordained as Assistant Minister, Church of the Holy Rude, Stirling, 1952; appointed Lecturer in Church History, Aberdeen University, 1955; Lecturer, then Senior Lecturer in Ecclesiastical History, St. Andrews University, 1956-70; Dean, Faculty of Divinity, 1978-83. President: Ecclesiastical History Society, 1976-77, British Sub-Commission, Commission Internationale d'Histoire Ecclesiastique Comparee, 1979-92; Vice-President, International Association for Neo-Latin Studies, 1979-81; Co-Editor and Contributor, Theologische Realenzyklopädie (Vol. 17 onwards). Publications: Letters of John Johnston and Robert Howie, 1963; First Book of Discipline, 1972; Contributor to: Acta Conventus Neo-Latini Amstelodamensis, 1973; Advocates of Reform, 1953; The Scottish Tradition, 1974; Renaissance and Renewal in Christian History, 1977; Reform and Reformation: England and the Continent, 1979; Origins and Nature of the Scottish Enlightenment, 1982; A Companion to Scottish Culture, 1981; Humanism in Renaissance Scotland, 1990; The Impact of Humanism on Western Europe, 1990. Recreation: gardening. Address: (h.) Priorscroft, 71 Hepburn Gardens, St. Andrews KY16 9LS; T.-01334 473996.

Cameron, J. Gordon, MA, LLB, DipLP, WS, NP. Partner, Stuart & Stuart WS, since 1987; b. 15.11.57, Edinburgh; m., Deborah Jane; 1 s.; 1 d. Educ. George Watson's College; Aberdeen University. Joined Stuart & Stuart WS as assistant, 1985. Hon. Secretary and Treasurer, Royal Celtic Society. Recreations: hill-walking; cycling; keep-fit; fell-running; photography; foreign travel. Address: (b.) 23 Rutland Street, Edinburgh EH1 2RN; T.-0131-228 6449.

Cameron, John Bell, CBE, FRAgricS, AIAgricE. Chairman, British Railways (Scottish) Board, 1988-93 (Member, 1988-94); Director, South West Trains, since 1995; Chairman, Scottish Beef Council, since 1997; Farmer, since 1961; b. 14.6.39, Edinburgh; m., Margaret Clapperton. Educ. Dollar Academy. Vice President, National Farmers' Union, 1976-79, President, 1979-84; Member, Agricultural Praesidium of EEC, 1979-84; Chairman, EEC Advisory Committee for Sheepmeat, 1982-90; Chairman, World Meats Group, (IFAP), since 1983; Chairman, Board of Governors, Dollar Academy, since 1985; Chairman, United Auctions Ltd., since 1985; Member, Board of Governors, Macaulay Land Use Research Institute, since 1987; honorary doctorate of technology, Napier University, 1998. Long Service Award, Royal Observer Corps. Recreations: flying; shooting; travelling. Address: (h.) Balbuthie Farm, by Leven, Fife; T.-01333 730210.

Cameron, (John Roderick) Hector, LLB, NP. Solicitor; Director, Telecom Service Centres Ltd.; Director, McColl McGregor Ltd.; b. 11.6.47, Glasgow; m., Rosemary Brownlee; 1 s.; 1 d. Educ. High School of Glasgow; Friends School, Wigton; St. Andrews University. Admitted Solicitor, 1971; Partner, Bishop, Milne Boyd & Co., 1973; Chairman, Glasgow Junior Chamber of Commerce, 1981; Managing Partner, Bishop & Co., 1985; Partner, Dorman Jeffrey & Co., 1990; Director, Merchants House of Glasgow, 1986; Director, Glasgow Chamber of Commerce, 1987. Recreations: reading; sailing; golf. Address: (h.) 2 Lancaster Crescent, Glasgow G12 0RR.

Cameron, Rev. Dr. John Urquhart, BA, BSc, PhD, BD, ThD. Minister, Parish of Broughty Ferry, since 1974; b. 10.6.43, Dundee; m., Jill Sjoberg; 1 s.; 1 d. Educ. Falkirk High School; St. Andrews University; Edinburgh University; University of Southern California. Marketing Executive, Beechams, London, 1969-73; Assistant Minister, Wellington Church, Glasgow, 1973-74; Chaplain, Royal Naval Reserve, 1976-81; Marketing Consultant, Pergamon Press, Oxford, 1977-81; Religious Education Department, Dundee High School, 1980-87; Sports Journalist and Travel Writer, Hill Publications, Surrey, since 1981; Physics Department, Dundee College of Further Education, 1987-95; Moderator, Presbytery of Dundee, 1993-94; Chaplain, Royal Caledonian Curling Club, 1980-95; Chaplain, Black Watch ACF, since 1994. National and international honours in both summer and winter sports, 1960-85; sports scholarship, University of Southern California, 1962-64. Recreations: golf; skiing; curling. Address: St. Stephen's Manse, 33 Camperdown Street, Broughty Ferry; T.-01382 477403.

Cameron of Lochbroom, Lord (Kenneth John Cameron), Life Baron (1984), PC (1984), MA (Oxon), LLB, QC, FRSE, Hon. FRIAS. Senator of the College of Justice, since 1989; Chairman, Royal Fine Art Commission for Scotland; b. 11.6.31, Edinburgh; m., Jean Pamela Murray; 2 d. Educ. Edinburgh Academy; Corpus Christi College, Oxford; Edinburgh University. Advocate, 1958; Queen's Counsel, 1972; President, Pensions Appeal Tribunal for Scotland, 1976; Chairman, Committee of Investigation Under Agricultural Marketing Act 1958, 1980; Advocate Depute, 1981; Lord Advocate, 1984; Hon.

Bencher, Lincoln's Inn; Hon. Fellow, Corpus Christi College, Oxford. Recreations: fishing; sailing. Address: (h.) Stoneyhill House, Musselburgh.

Cameron, Sheriff Lewis, MA, LLB. Solicitor, since 1962; Sheriff of South Strathclyde Dumfries and Galloway at Hamilton, since 1994, at Dumfries, 1988-94; b. 12.8.35, Glasgow; m., Sheila Colette Gallacher; 2 s.; 2 d. Educ. St. Aloysius College; Blairs College; St. Sulpice, Paris; Glasgow University. RAF, 1954-56; admitted Solicitor, 1962. Member, Legal Aid Central Committee, 1970-80; Legal Aid Secretary, Airdrie, 1978-87; Chairman, Social Security Appeal Tribunals, 1983-88; Dean, Airdrie Society of Solicitors, 1984-85; Tutor, Strathclyde University, 1981-88; Treasurer, Monklands Victim Support Scheme, 1983-88; Chairman: Dumfries and Galloway Family Conciliation Service, 1988-92, Dumfries and Galloway, Scottish Association for the Study of Delinquency, 1988-92; Member, Scotland Committee, National Children's Homes; Trustee, Oscar Marzaroli Trust; Chairman, PHEW. Address: (b.) Sheriff Court House, Beckford Street, Hamilton.

Cameron, Professor Peter Duncanson, LLB, PhD. Professor of International Energy Law and Policy, University of Dundee, since 1997; b. 21.6.52, Hamilton. Educ. High School of Stirling; Dundee University. Lecturer in Jurisprudence, University of Dundee, 1977-86; Director, Institute of Energy Law, University of Leiden, Netherlands, 1986-97. Member, Council, International Bar Association Energy Law Section. Publications: Nuclear Energy Law After Chernobyl; Property Rights and Sovereign Rights: The Case of North Sea Oil. Recreation: jogging. Address: (b.) University of Dundee, Park Place, Dundee DD1 4HN; T.-01382 344300.

Cameron, Roy, QPM. Chief Constable, Lothian and Borders Police. Address: (b.) Fettes Avenue, Edinburgh EH4 1RB. Tel.: 0131-311 3131.

Cameron, Thomas Anthony (Tony). Head of Food and Agriculture, Scottish Office, since 1992; b. 3.2.47; m., Elizabeth Christine Sutherland; 2 s. Educ. Stranraer High School. Department of Agriculture and Fisheries for Scotland, 1966; Private Secretary to Deputy Under Secretary of State, Scottish Office, 1972, to Permanent Under Secretary of State, 1973-74; HEO(D), DAFS, 1974-77; Principal, DAFS, 1977-82; Assistant Secretary, DAFS, 1982-87; Scottish Office Finance Division, 1987-92; Member, Duke of Edinburgh's Sixth Commonwealth Study Conference, Australia. Recreations: reading; mountaineering; cycling. Address: Scottish Office Agriculture and Fisheries Department, Pentland House, 47 Robb's Loan, Edinburgh; T.-0131-244 6032.

Cameron-Jones, Professor Margot, MA, MEd, FRSA. Professor of Teacher Education, Edinburgh University, since 1998; b. 11.1.39, Isle of Man; m., Richard John; 1 s. Educ. St. Winifred's School, Llanfairfechan; University of Edinburgh. Schoolteacher, Edinburgh; Research Fellow, University of Dundee; Lecturer, Head of Department and Professor, Moray House College of Education, Heriot-Watt University. Address: (b.) Faculty of Education, Edinburgh University, Holyrood Road, Edinburgh EH8 8AQ; T.-0131-651 6160.

Campbell, Alan Grant, LLB. Chief Executive, Aberdeenshire Council, since 1995; b. 4.12.46, Aberdeen; m., Susan Black; 1 s.; 2 d. Educ. Aberdeen Grammar School; Aberdeen University. Various legal appointments, Aberdeen County Council, 1968-75; Grampian Regional Council: Assistant Director of Law and Administration, 1975-79, Depute Director, 1979-84, Director of Law and Administration, 1984-91, Chief Executive, 1991-95. Recreations: cycling; gardening. Address: Woodhill House, Westburn Road, Aberdeen AB16 5GB; T.-01224 665400.

Campbell, Alastair James, LLB. Partner, Mitchells Roberton, Solicitors, since 1985; Clerk and Treasurer, Royal Faculty of Procurators in Glasgow, since 1994; b. 29.12.48, Glasgow; m., Pamela Crichton; 3 s. Educ. Merchiston Castle School, Edinburgh; University of Strathclyde. Qualified as Solicitor, 1972; Partner, Mackenzie Roberton & Co. (later Mitchells Roberton), 1975. Secretary, National Burns Homes, Mauchline, Ayrshire, since 1976. Recreations: golf; tennis; curling. Address: (b.) George House, 36 North Hanover Street, Glasgow G1 2AD; T.-0141-552 3422.

Campbell of Airds, Alastair Lorne, OStJ. Chief Executive, Clan Campbell, since 1984; Archivist, Inveraray Castle, since 1984; H.M. Unicorn Pursuivant of Arms, Court of the Lord Lyon, since 1987; b. 11.7.37, London; m., Mary-Ann Campbell-Preston; 3 s.; 1 d. Educ. Eton; R.M.A., Sandhurst. Regular Army, 1955-63 (commissioned Argyll and Sutherland Highlanders); Reid Pye and Campbell, 1963-71 (Managing Director, 1970-71); Waverley Vintners Ltd., 1972-83 (Marketing Director, 1972, Managing Director, 1977). Member: Queen's Bodyguard for Scotland (Royal Company of Archers), Chapter of Scottish Priory, Order of St John; FSA Scot; Patron, Armorial and Heraldry Society of Australasia; Chairman, Advisory Committee on Tartan to the Lord Lyon; Member, Council, National Trust for Scotland; Honorary Research Fellowship, University of Aberdeen, 1996. Publications: Two Hundred Years — The Highland Society of London; The Life and Troubled Times of Sir Donald Campbell of Ardnamurchan. Recreations: painting; fishing; walking. Address: (h.) Inverawe Barn, Taynuilt, Argyll PA35 1HU; T.-0186 62 207.

Campbell, Professor Alexander George Macpherson, MB, ChB, FRCPEdin, DCH. Emeritus Professor of Child Health, Aberdeen University; b. 3.2.31, Glasgow; m., Sheila Mary Macdonald; 1 s.; 2 d. Educ. Dollar Academy; Glasgow University. Paediatric Registrar, Royal Hospital for Sick Children, Edinburgh, 1959-61; Senior House Officer, Hospital for Sick Children, London, 1961-62; Assistant Chief Resident, Children's Hospital of Philadelphia, 1962-63; Fellow in Paediatric Cardiology, Hospital for Sick Children, Toronto, 1963-64; Fellow in Fetal and Neonatal Physiology, Nuffield Institute for Medical Research, Oxford, 1964-66; Lecturer in Child Health, St. Andrews University, 1966-67; Assistant, then Associate Professor of Paediatrics, Yale University School of Medicine, 1967-73; Professor of Child Health, Aberdeen University, 1973-92. Recreation: golf. Address: (h.) 34 Woodburn Crescent, Aberdeen; T.-01224 319152.

Campbell, Alexandra Speir, MPhil, MB, ChB, FRCSEd, FRCSGlasg, LLB (Hons), DFM. Secretary, Royal College of Surgeons of Edinburgh, since 1996; b. 9.4.53, Dumfries. Educ. Ayr Academy; Glasgow University; London University. Junior hospital doctor, 1977-85; Consultant in Accident and Emergency, 1985-88; Medical and Dental Defence Union of Scotland, 1988-96, latterly as Senior Medical Adviser. Surgeon Lieutenant Commander, Royal Naval Reserve, 1986-93; private pilot's licence, 1989. Recreations: cookery; gardening; travel; reading. Address: (b.) Royal College of Surgeons of Edinburgh, Nicolson Street, Edinburgh; T.-0131-527 1600.

Campbell, Alison Rigg, MA. Director, Scottish Housing Associations Charitable Trust, since 1992; b. 20.8.50, Paisley; m., Niall; 3 s. Educ. Cumnock Academy; University of St. Andrews. Scottish Office, 1972-77; Action on Smoking and Health, 1987-91. Secretary, Church and Nation Committee, Church of Scotland, 1991-96; Committee Member: Scottish Refugee Council, Edinburgh Youth Homes; Director, Edinburgh Academy. Recreations: going to school functions; getting out of town. Address: (b.) 38 York Place, Edinburgh EH1 3HU; T.-0131-556 5777.

Campbell, Alistair Bromley, OBE. Farmer; Agricultural Consultant and Valuer; Chairman of Council, Scottish Conservation Projects Trust, 1984-97; b. 23.6.27, Charing, Kent; m., Rosemary Pullar (deceased); 1 s.; 2 d. Educ. Tonbridge School. Training in agriculture, 1944-47; self-employed Farmer, 1948-81; Agricultural Consultant, Arbiter, Valuer, 1968-81; Agricultural Adviser and Valuer, South of Scotland Electricity Board, 1972-81; Vice-Chairman, Countryside Commission for Scotland, 1972-81 (Member from 1969); Member: Secretary of State's Panel of Agricultural Arbiters, 1968-81, Scottish Land Court, 1981-92; Chairman, Executive Committee of Council of Management, Strathcarron Hospice, Denny; former Council Member, British Trust for Conservation Volunteers (Chairman, Scottish Regional Committee, 1975-84); Church Warden, St. Mary's Episcopal Church, Dunblane, since 1960; Honorary Vice-President and a Director, Doune and Dunblane Agricultural Society; former Convener, Legal Committee, NFU of Scotland; General Commissioner of Income Tax, since 1971; Chairman, Scottish Executive Committee, Association of Agriculture, 1980-86; Vice-President and Treasurer, SFACET. Recreations: work; shooting; enjoying countryside; farming. Address: (h.) Grainston Farm, Kilbryde, Dunblane, Perthshire FK15 9NF; T.-01786 823304.

Campbell, Catherine, JP, BSc, BA (Hons), MSc. Educational Psychologist; Member, Scottish Milk Marketing Board, 1981-92; Chairman, Cumbernauld "I" Tech, 1984-88; b. 10.1.40, Glasgow; m., John Campbell; 2 s.; 1 d. Educ. Notre Dame High School; Glasgow University; Open University; Strathclyde University. Teacher of Mathematics, 1962-68; Member: Cumbernauld and Kilsyth District Council, 1969-78, Cumbernauld Development Corporation, 1975-84. Jubilee Medal, 1977; CACDP (stage 3 sign language). Recreations: promotion of equal opportunities for deaf people; cooking; homecrafts. Address: (h.) 10 Westray Road, Cumbernauld G67 1NN; T.-0123 67 24834.

Campbell, Christopher Robert James, LLB (Hons). Regional Managing Partner, Garretts/Dundas and Wilson, since 1997; Managing Partner, Dundas and Wilson, since 1996; b. Edinburgh; m., Kay; 1 s.; 1 d. Educ. Daniel Stewart's and Melville College; University of Edinburgh. Joined Dundas and Wilson, 1980: Assistant Solicitor, 1982, Partner, 1987, Partner in Charge of Glasgow Office, 1991, Deputy Managing Partner, 1995. Honorary Professor of Commercial Law, University of Glasgow. Recreations: golf; music; football. Address: (b.) Saltire Court, 20 Castle Terrace, Edinburgh EH1 2EN; T.-0131-228 8000.

Campbell, Colin MacIver, MA (Hons). National Secretary, Scottish National Party, since 1997 (Defence Spokesman, since 1995); Member, Renfrewshire Council, since 1995; b. 31.8.38, Ralston, Paisley; m., Evelyn; 3 s. Educ. Paisley Grammar School; Glasgow University; Jordanhill College of Education. Teacher: Hillhead High School, 1961-63, Paisley Grammar School, 1963-67; Principal Teacher, Greenock Academy, 1967-73; Depute Head Teacher, Westwood Secondary, 1977-89; Tutor (part-time), Strathclyde University Senior Studies Institute, 1995-98. General Election Candidate: 1987, 1992, 1997; Euro Candidate: 1989, 1994. Elder, Church of Scotland; Former Chairman, Kilbarchan Civic Society and Kilbarchan Community Council; Convener, Kilbarchan SNP; Past Convener, Renfrew West SNP. Recreation: military history. Address: (h.) Braeside, Shuttle Street, Kilbarchan PA10 2PR.

Campbell, David Ross, CMIM, FInstD. Chairman, Health Education Board for Scotland, since 1995; Deputy Chairman, Enterprise Ayrshire, since 1990; Chairman and Director of a number of private companies; b. 27.9.43, Glasgow; m., Moira. Educ. Whitehill Senior Secondary School, Glasgow; James Watt Memorial College, Greenock. Officer, Merchant Navy, 1961-68; Sales Executive, 1968-69; various management positions, George Outram & Co. Ltd., 1969-73; Managing Director, Scottish & Universal Newspapers Ltd., 1974-84; Executive Director, Scottish & Universal Investments Ltd.; Chief Executive, Clyde Cablevision Ltd., 1982-84; Chairman and Chief Executive, West Independent Newspapers Ltd., 1984-94; Chairman, Saltire Holdings Ltd., 1991-93. Past President: Scottish Newspaper Proprietors Association, Glasgow Chamber of Commerce; Liveryman and Freeman, City of London; Regional Chairman, PSYBT. Recreations: golf; theatre; reading. Address: (h.) Summerlea, Summerlea Road, Seamill KA23 9HP.

Campbell, Donald. Writer; b. 25.2.40, Wick; m., Jean Fairgrieve; 1 s. Educ. Boroughmuir High School, Edinburgh. Playwright, essayist, lyricist and poet; stage plays include: The Jesuit, 1976; The Widows of Clyth, 1979; Blackfriars Wynd, 1980; Till All The Seas Run Dry, 1981; Howard's Revenge, 1985; Victorian Values, 1986; The Fisher Boy and the Honest Lass, 1990; The Ould Fella, 1993; also active as writer and director in a number of community projects; script co-ordinator, The Dundee Mysteries, Dundee Rep; poetry includes: Rhymes 'n Reasons, 1972; Blether, 1979; Selected Poems: 1970-1990, 1990; other work includes: A Brighter Sunshine (theatre history), 1983, Playing for Scotland (theatre history), 1996, four television plays, 50 radio programmes; Fellow in Creative Writing, Dundee University, 1987-89; William Soutar Fellow, Perth, 1991-93; awards include: three Fringe Firsts; Silver Medal, 1983 New York Radio Festival for A Clydebuilt Man; Radio Industries Club Award for The Miller's Reel, 1987. Address: (h.) 85 Spottiswoode Street, Edinburgh EH9 1BZ; T.-0131-447 2305.

Campbell, Donald McKechnie, MA (Hons), BA. Headteacher, Islay High School, since 1997; Member, West Region Board, Scottish Environment Protection Agency, since 1996; Member, BBC Scotland Gaelic Advisory Committee, since 1995; Crofter; b. 3.8.55, Glasgow; m., Fiona; 1 s.; 1 d. Educ. Clydebank High School; University of Glasgow; Open University. Assistant Teacher, Bearsden Academy, 1978-82; Tiree High School: Principal Teacher, 1982-93, Depute Head Teacher, 1993-97; Member, Argyll and Bute District Council, 1988-94. Recreations: cinema; theatre; keeping fit. Address: (h.) Schoolhouse, Lennox Street, Port Ellen, Isle of Islay, Argyll PA42 7BW; T.-01496 302579.

Campbell, Doris Margaret, MD, FRCOG. Senior Lecturer in Obstetrics and Gynaecology and Reproductive Physiology, Aberdeen University, since 1984; part-time secondment to Centre for Learning and Professional Development, University of Aberdeen; b. 24.1.42, Aberdeen; m., Alasdair James Campbell; 1 s.; 1 d. Educ. Aberdeen High School for Girls; Aberdeen University. Resident house officer posts, Aberdeen, 1967-69; Research Fellow, Aberdeen University, 1969-73; Registrar in Obstetrics and Gynaecology, Aberdeen Hospitals, 1973-74; Lecturer in Obstetrics and Gynaecology and Physiology, Aberdeen University, 1974-84. Former Member, Scottish Women's Hockey Council. Recreations: bridge; badminton; guiding. Address: (h.) 77 Blenheim Place, Aberdeen; T.-01224 639984.

Campbell, Douglas I., BSc (Psych). Head of PR and Marketing, East Ayrshire Council, since 1995; b. 4.10.64, Kilwinning; m., E.A. McMurrich. Educ. Ardrossan Academy; Stirling University. Assistant Tourism Officer, Stirling District Council, 1986-89; Manager, Ayrshire Valleys Tourist Board, 1989-90; Public Relations Officer, Kilmarnock and Loudoun District Council, 1990-95. Recreation: squash. Address: (b.) Council HQ, London Road, Kilmarnock KA3 7BU; T.-01563 576165.

Campbell, Elizabeth (Libby), OBE, RGN, RM, MSc. Executive Director, Nursing and Quality, West Lothian NHS Trust, since 1993 (Director of Nursing, 1989-93); National Chairman, National Association of Theatre Nurses; b. 9.8.50, Dundee. Educ. Mary Erskine School for Girls, Edinburgh; Edinburgh University. Assistant, then Deputy, Director of Nursing Services, Bangour General Hospital, West Lothian, 1985-89. Former Member, UK Central Council for Nurses, Midwives and Health Visitors. Recreations: singing; travelling; Munro bagging; music. Address: (h.) 8 Fettes Row, Edinburgh EH3 6SE.

Campbell, Wing Commander George, MBE, SBStJ, DL, MIMgt; b. 24.11.22, Renton; m., Marion T.H. Halliday; 1 s.; 1 d. Educ. Vale of Leven Academy. Joined RAF, 1941; served in UK, India, Burma, Malaya, Singapore; demobilised, 1946, and continued in Royal Air Force Voluntary Reserve (Training Branch), serving with Air Training Corps; formed 2319 (Vale of Leven) Squadron, 1956; appointed to Wing Staff, Glasgow, and Western Wing, 1973; promoted to Wing Commander, 1978; retired, 1983; attended Bisley as competitor, coach, and team captain for 48 years; Vice Chairman, 602 City of Glasgow Squadron, Royal Auxiliary Air Force Squadron Museum; Chairman: 912 Squadron ATC, Duke of Edinburgh Award (County Co-ordinating Committee); Elder, Church of Scotland; County Representative, Royal Air Forces Benevolent Fund; Director, Dumbartonshire Branch, British Red Cross, 1983-92; Past President, Dumbarton Rotary Club; Past Chairman, RNLI, Dumbarton Branch. Address: (h.) Valeview, Comley Bank, Oxhill, Dumbarton; T.-Dumbarton 763700.

Campbell of Croy, Baron (Gordon Thomas Calthrop Campbell), PC (1970), MC and Bar. Consultant, oil industry, 1975-94; Director, Alliance and Leicester Building Society and Chairman of its Scottish Board, 1975-94; Chairman, Stoic Insurance Services, 1979-93; b. 8.6.21; m.; 2 s.; 1 d. Educ. Wellington. Commissioned, Regular Army, 1939; RA, 1942 (Major); wounded and disabled, 1945; entered HM Foreign Service, 1946 and served in the Foreign Office, at the UN, in the Cabinet Office (Private Secretary to the Secretary of the Cabinet) and in the Embassy in Vienna; MP (Conservative), Moray and Nairn, 1959-74; Government Whip, 1961-62; Lord Commissioner of the Treasury and Scottish Whip, 1962-63; Parliamentary Under-Secretary of State, Scottish Office, 1963-64; Secretary of State for Scotland, 1970-74; Chairman, Scottish Committee, International Year of Disabled, 1981; Partner, Holme Rose Estate and Farms; Trustee, Thomson Foundation, since 1980; Chairman: Advisory Committee on Pollution of the Sea, 1987-89, Scottish Council of Independent Schools, 1976-80; Vice Lord Lieutenant of Nairnshire, since 1988; President, Anglo-Austrian Society, since 1991. Address: (h.) Holme Rose, Cawdor, Nairnshire.

Campbell, Hugh Hall, QC, BA (Hons), MA (Oxon), LLB (Hons), FCIArb. Queen's Counsel, since 1983; b. 18.2.44, Glasgow; m., Eleanor Jane Hare; 3 s. Educ. Glasgow Academy; Trinity College, Glenalmond; Exeter College, Oxford; Edinburgh University. Called to Scottish Bar, 1969; Standing Junior Counsel to Admiralty, 1976. Recreations: carnival, wine, music. Address: (h.) 12 Ainslie Place, Edinburgh EH3 6AS; T.-0131-225 2067.

Campbell, Rev. Iain Donald, MA, BD, MTh. Minister, Back Free Church of Scotland, Isle of Lewis, since 1995; Editor, The Monthly Record of the Free Church of Scotland, since 1996; b. 20.9.63, Stornoway; m., Anne M. Davidson; 2 s.; 1 d. Educ. Nicolson Institute, Stornoway; University of Glasgow; Free Church College. Minister, Snizort Free Church, Isle of Skye, 1988-95; Editor, The Instructor (Free Church of Scotland youth magazine), 1990-96. Publications: In Thy Likeness, 1990; Heart of the Gospel (Editor), 1995. Recreations: reading; walking. Address: Free Church Manse, Vatisker, Isle of Lewis HS2 0LN; T.-01851 820317.

Campbell, Sir Ian, CBE, OStJ, VRD, JP. Deputy Chairman, Heath (Scotland) Ltd., 1987-95; Chairman, Select Assured Properties PLC, 1989-96; Director, Hermiston Securities, since 1990; b. 3.2.23, Edinburgh; m., Marion Kirkhope Shiel; 1 d. Educ. Daniel Stewart's College, Edinburgh. Royal Navy, 1942-46; Royal Naval Reserve, 1946-64 (retired with rank of Commander); John Line & Sons, 1948-61 (Area Manager, West of England); Managing Director, MacGregor Wallcoverings Ltd., 1965-77; Finance Director, Scottish Conservative Party, 1977-89. Director, Travel System Ltd., 1987-90; Councillor, City of Edinburgh, 1984-88; Member, Transport Users Consultative Committee for Scotland, 1981-87; Freeman, City of Glasgow, 1991. Recreations: golf; vintage cars; water colour painting. Address: (h.) Merleton, 10 Boswall Road, Edinburgh EH5 3RH; T.-0131-552 4825.

Campbell, Sir Ilay Mark, Bt, MA (Oxon). Director, High Craigton Farming Co.; b. 29.5.27, Edinburgh; m., Margaret Minette Rohais Anderson; 2 d. Educ. Eton; Christ Church, Oxford. Christie's: Scottish Agent, 1968, Joint Scottish Agent, 1973-92, Chairman, 1978-96; Honorary Vice-President, Scotland's Garden Scheme; Trustee: Crarae Gardens Charitable Trust, since 1978, Tree Register of the British Isles, since 1988; Trustee, Church Buildings Renewal Trust (Glasgow), Chairman, 1993-98; Past President, Association for the Protection of Rural Scotland; former Convener, Church of Scotland Committee on Artistic Matters; Member, Historic Buildings Council for Scotland, 1989-98; Member, Gardens Committee, and Argyll, Lochaber and Western Isles Regional Committee, National Trust for Scotland; former Scottish Representative, National Arts Collection Fund. Recreations: heraldry; genealogy; collecting heraldic bookplates. Address: (h.) Crarae Lodge, Inveraray, Argyll PA32 8YA; T.-01546 86274/370.

Campbell, James Hugh, BL. Senior Partner, Bird Semple Fyfe Ireland, WS, 1987-91, Consultant until 1993; b. 13.11.26, Old Kilpatrick; m., Iris Burnside Hercus; 2 s.; 1 d. Educ. Bearsden Academy; Glasgow University. Bird Son & Semple: Partner, 1952-65, then Senior Partner, 1965-73; Senior Partner, Bird Semple Crawford Herron, 1973-87. Member, Council, Law Society of Scotland, 1986-95 (President, 1991-92); President, Glasgow Juridical Society, 1952; Deacon, Incorporation of Wrights in Glasgow, 1980-81; Honorary Member, Royal Faculty of Procurators, Glasgow. Recreations: music; reading; golf. Address: (h.) 24 Woodvale Avenue, Giffnock, Glasgow G46 6RQ; T.-041-638 2630.

Campbell, John Ivor, FCCA. Director of Financial Services, Scottish Borders Council, since 1995; b. 23.8.51, Galashiels; m., Sheila; 2 d. Educ. Kelso High School. Roxburgh County Council, 1970-75; Borders Regional Council, 1975-84; Chief Accountant, Fife Regional Council, 1984-86; Depute Director of Finance, Glenrothes Development Corporation, 1986-88; Director of Finance, Roxburgh District Council, 1988-96. Past President, Scottish Branch, Association of Chartered Certified Accountants; Member, ACCA International Assembly, since 1997; Treasurer, Scottish Borders Tourist Board, since 1989. Address: (b.) Council Headquarters, Newtown St. Boswells, Melrose, TD6 0SA; T.-01835 824000.

Campbell, Melfort Andrew. Director, IMES Group and Industrial and Marine Engineering Services Ltd.; Director, Grampian Enterprise Ltd.; Member, CBI Scottish Council, since 1989; b. 6.6.56, Exeter; m., Lucy Jane Nickson (Hon. Mrs); 3 d. Educ. Ampleforth College. Joined Water Weights Ltd., 1979; Managing Director, since 1985; founded IMES Ltd., 1993. Member, Queen's Bodyguard for

Scotland (Royal Company of Archers). Recreations: rugby; cricket; fishing; shooting. Address: (h.) Mains of Altries, Maryculter, Aberdeen AB12 5GN; T.-01224 734381.

Campbell, Rev. Neil Gregor, BA, BD. Minister, Bargrennan with Penninghame St. John's Church, Newton Stewart, since 1989; Chaplain, Penninghame Prison; b. 5.5.61, Brighton; m., Elizabeth Sharp; 2 s.; 1 d. Educ. George Watson's College; Edinburgh University. Assistant Minister, Palmerston Place Church, Edinburgh, 1987-89. Publications: Penninghame St. John's 1841-1991; Prayers for Today's World (Contributor), 1993; Penninghame – the story of a parish, 1998. Address: (h.) The Manse, York Road, Newton Stewart DG8 6HH; T.-01671 402259.

Campbell, Neil Martin, MA, BSc, RMN, RGN, DPSN. Board General Manager (Chief Executive), Dumfries and Galloway Health Board, since 1996; b. 9.11.57; m., Debra Ann; 3 s.; 1 d. Educ. St. Dominic's Comprehensive School; De La Salle Grammar School; Liverpool John Moores University; University of Manchester; University of Lancaster. Divisional Manager, Liverpool Priority Services Unit, 1987-89; Director of Operations, North Mersey Community NHS Trust, 1989-91; Co-ordinator for Priority Services, Mersey Regional Health Authority, 1991-93; Director for Service Development and Commissioning, South Cheshire Health Authority, 1993-96. Address: (b.) Grierson House, The Crichton, Bankend Road, Dumfries DG1 4ZG; T.-01387 272701.

Campbell, Niall Gordon, BA. Under Secretary, Civil and Criminal Law Group, Scottish Office Home Department: since 1997 (Social Work Services Group, 1989-97); b. 9.11.41, Peebles; m., Alison M. Rigg; 3 s. Educ. Edinburgh Academy; Merton College, Oxford. Entered Scottish Office 1964; Assistant Secretary, 1978; various posts in Scottish Education Department and Scottish Development Department. Address (h.) 15 Warriston Crescent, Edinburgh.

Campbell, Robert Craig, BSc, MCIM. Policy Director, National Farmers' Union of Scotland, since 1996; Chief Economist, Scottish Council (Development and Industry), 1988-96; b. 29.4.47, Glasgow; m., Elizabeth Helen C.; 2 d. Educ. Glasgow Academy; St. Andrews University. Scottish Council: Research Executive, 1970-77, Research Director, 1977-84, Director, Overseas Projects Unit, 1984-86, Policy Research Director, 1986-88. Recreation: angling. Address: (b.) The Rural Centre, West Mains, Ingliston, Newbridge EH28 8LT.

Campbell, (Robert) Mungo (McCready), BA, MPhil, FRSA. Deputy Director, Hunterian Art Gallery, University of Glasgow, since 1997; b. 8.10.59, Newcastle upon Tyne; m., Teresa Margaret Green. Educ. Royal Grammar School, Newcastle upon Tyne; University of Durham; University of Glasgow. Assistant Keeper, National Gallery of Scotland, Edinburgh, 1987-97; Member, Scottish Arts Council New Directions and Visual Arts Committees. Recreations: walking my dog; cooking good food; eating good food. Address: (b.) Hunterian Art Gallery, 82 Hillhead Street, Glasgow G12 8QQ; T.-0141-330 4735.

Campbell, Rev. Roderick D.M., TD, BD, FSA Scot. Minister, Mearns Parish Church, 1979-97; Vice Chairman, Greater Glasgow Health Board, 1994-96 (Member, 1989-96); Chairman: Greater Glasgow Drug Action Team, 1995-97, Victoria Infirmary NHS Trust, 1997-99; Chaplain, 3rd (Volunteer) Battalion The Royal Highland Fusiliers; Staff Chaplain, TA Army HQ, Scotland, since 1997; Locum Minister, Ruchazie Parish Church, since 1997; b. 1.8.43, Glasgow; m., Susan Norman; 2 d. Educ. Daniel Stewart's College, Edinburgh; Arbroath High School; Jordanhill College of Education; New College, Edinburgh University. Teacher, Technical Subjects, Glasgow, Tanzania and London, 1967-70; Associate Minister, St. Andrew's, Nairobi, 1975-78; Chieftain, Caledonian Society of Kenya, 1978; founder Member, Undugu Society of Kenya, 1975; Chairman, Institute of Advanced Motorists (Kenya), 1977-78. Convener, Lodging House Mission, Glasgow Presbytery, 1981-86; Convener, National Church Extension Committee, Church of Scotland, 1987-89; Deacon, Incorporation of Barbers, Trades House, Glasgow, 1992-93. Recreations: swimming; horse-riding; hill-walking; fishing. Address: 22 Greenlaw Road, Newton Mearns, Glasgow G77 6ND; T.-0141 639 7328.

Campbell, Professor Thomas, BSc (Hons), PhD, CEng, FIMechE, MSAE, MCIBSE, MInstE, FRSA. Head, Department of Environment, and Professor, Glasgow Caledonian University, since 1993; Director: Kelvin International, since 1996, Score Environment Limited, since 1996; b. 19.12.51, Glasgow; m., Fiona; 3 s. Educ. Bellahouston Academy; University of Strathclyde. Design Engineer, GEC Reactor Equipment Ltd., 1977-80; Senior Lecturer, 1980-87, Reader, 1987-89, Glasgow Caledonian University; Royal Society Industrial Fellow, Kelvin Diesels, 1989-91. Recreations: athletics; swimming; hill-walking; sailing. Address: (b.) Department of Environment, Glasgow Caledonian University, 70 Cowcaddens Road, Glasgow G4 0BA; T.-0141-331 3520/013552 72041.

Campbell, (Walter) Menzies, CBE (1987), QC, MA, LLB. MP (Liberal Democrat), North East Fife, since 1987; Advocate, since 1968; Queen's Counsel, since 1982; Member, Select Committee on Defence, since 1992; Member, Parliamentary Assembly of CSCE, until 1997; Member, North Atlantic Assembly, since 1989; Party Spokesman on Defence and Sport, until 1997, Foreign Affairs, Defence and Europe, since 1997; b. 22.5.41, Glasgow; m., Elspeth Mary Urquhart. Educ. Hillhead High School, Glasgow; Glasgow University; Stanford University, California. President, Glasgow University Union, 1964-65; took part in Olympic Games, Tokyo, 1964; AAA 220-yards champion, 1964, 1967; Captain, UK athletics team, 1965, 1966; 1966 Commonwealth Games, Jamaica; UK 100-metres record holder, 1967-74. Advocate Depute, 1977-80; Standing Junior Counsel to the Army in Scotland, 1980-82. Parliamentary candidate (Liberal): Greenock and Port Glasgow, February, 1974, and October, 1974, East Fife, 1979, North East Fife, 1983; Chairman, Scottish Liberal Party, 1975-77; Member: UK Sports Council, 1965-68; Scottish Sports Council, 1971-81; Chairman, Royal Lyceum Theatre, Edinburgh, 1984-87; Member, Broadcasting Council for Scotland, 1984-87. Recreations: all sports; music; theatre. Address: (b.) House of Commons, London SW1A 0AA; T.-0171-219 4446.

Campbell, William Kilpatrick, MA (Hons). Director, Mainstream Publishing, since 1978; Director, Edinburgh Book Festival, since 1992; b. 1.3.51, Glasgow; m., Marie-France Callie; 2 d. Educ. Kilmarnock Academy; Edinburgh University. Postgraduate research, Universities of Edinburgh and California; world travel, 1975; Publications Manager, Edinburgh University Student Publications, 1976-78. Publications: Alternative Edinburgh (Co-Editor), 1972; Another Edinburgh, 1976. Recreations: soccer; tennis; rugby; wine; books; people. Address: (b.) 7 Albany Street, Edinburgh EH1 3UG; T.-0131-557 2959.

Campbell-Gibson, Lt.Comdr. R.N. (Ret.) Hugh Desmond. Member, Executive and Finance Committees, Scotland's Gardens Scheme; b. 18.8.24; m., Deirdre Wilson; 2 s.; 1 d. Educ. Royal Naval College, Dartmouth. Naval cadet, 1937-41; served Royal Navy, 1941-60; war service convoy duties, Atlantic and Mediterranean; farmed Glenlussa, by Campbeltown, 1960-68; farmed and ran hotel, Dunmor, Seil, Argyll, 1969-83; now manages family woodlands at Melfort. Recreations: gardening; skiing. Address: (h.) Tighnamara, Melfort, Kilmelford, Argyll; T.-Kilmelford 224.

Campion, Nigel Henry, QFSM, MIFireE. Firemaster, Fife Fire and Rescue Service, since 1996; b. 12.5.45, Leicester; m., Kathryn; 1 s.; 1 d.; 2 step d. Formerly with Leicestershire Fire and Rescue Service. Recreations: keep fit; walking; reading. Address: (b.) Fire and Rescue Service Headquarters, Strathore Road, Thornton, Kirkcaldy KY1 4DF; T.-01592 774451.

Campsie, Alistair Keith, SDA. Author, Journalist and Piper; b. 27.1.29, Inverness; m., Robbie Anderson; 2 s.; 1 d. Educ. West Sussex High School; Lanark Grammar School; West of Scotland College of Agriculture. Inspector of Agriculture, Sudan Government Service, 1949; Cocoa Survey Officer, Nigeria, 1951; experimental staff, National Institute of Agricultural Engineering (Scotland), 1953; Country Editor, Weekly Scotsman, 1954; Sub-Editor, Verse Writer, Scottish Daily Mail, 1955; Founder Editor, East African Farmer and Planter, 1956; Chief Sub-Editor, Weekly Scotsman, 1957; designed and appointed first Editor, Geneva Weekly Tribune, 1958; Chief Feature Writer, Scottish Daily Mail, 1959; Columnist, Science Correspondent and Senior Writer, Scottish Daily Express, 1962-73; founded The Piper's Press, 1988; two Scottish Arts Council writer's bursaries; two SAC publisher's awards. Publications: Poems and a Pibroch (with Hugh MacDiarmid), 1972; By Law Protected, 1976; The MacCrimmon Legend or The Madness of Angus Mackay, 1980; We Bought a County Pub (under pen-name Alan Mackinnon), 1984; Perfect Poison, 1985; Pibroch: the tangled Web (radio series), 1985; Dundas or How They Murdered Robert Burns (play), 1987; The Clarinda Conspiracy, 1989; The True Story of the Ball of Kirriemuir, 1989; Cary Grant Stopped Me Smoking, 1991; Hunt Down a Prince, 1994; Burns, The Political Prisoner (in press); The MacCrimmon Scam (in press). Recreations: bagpipes (playing and composing); good whisky; self-important people. Address: Sunnybrook, Main Street, St. Cyrus, Kincardineshire DD10 0BA; T.-01674 850586.

Canavan, Dennis, BSc (Hons), DipEd. MP (Labour), Falkirk West, since 1983; b. 8.8.42, Cowdenbeath. Educ. St. Bride's and St. Columba's Schools, Cowdenbeath; Edinburgh University. Principal Teacher of Mathematics, St. Modan's High School, Stirling, 1970-74; Assistant Head, Holyrood High School, Edinburgh, 1974; Leader, Labour Group, Stirling District Council, 1974; MP, West Stirlingshire, 1974-83; Chair: Scottish Parliamentary Labour Group, 1980-81, PLP Northern Ireland Committee, 1989-97; Member: Foreign Affairs Select Committee, 1982-97, British–Irish Inter-Parliamentary Body, since 1992, International Development Select Committee, since 1997. Founder and Convener, All Party Parliamentary Scottish Sports Group, since 1987; Honorary President, Milton Amateurs Football Club. Recreations: marathon running; hill-walking; fishing; swimming; football (former Scottish Universities football internationalist). Address: (b.) Constituency Office, 37 Church Walk, Denny FK6 6DF; T.-01324 825922.

Canavan, Sheriff Vincent Joseph, LLB. Sheriff of South Strathclyde, Dumfries and Galloway at Hamilton, since 1987; b. 13.12.44. Address: (b.) Sheriff Court House, Beckford Street, Hamilton ML3 6AA.

Candlish, Kenneth Henry, BL, JP, DL. Retired Solicitor; Deputy Lieutenant, Berwickshire; b. 22.8.24, Edinburgh; m., Isobel Robertson-Brown; 2 d. Educ. George Watson's; Edinburgh University. Depute County Clerk, West Lothian, 1951-64; County Clerk, Berwickshire, 1964-75. Recreations: photography; wine-making; music. Address: (h.) The Elms, Duns, Berwickshire; T.-Duns 883298.

Canning, Very Rev. Bernard John Canon, FSA Scot. Parish Priest, St. John the Baptist's, Port Glasgow, since 1996; Paisley Diocesan Archivist, since 1983; b. 30.3.32, Derry. Educ. St. Eugene's Boys' School, Derry; St. Columb's College, Derry; St. Kieran's College, Kilkenny. Ordained Priest for the Diocese of Paisley, 1956; Assistant: St. James's, Renfrew, 1956-68, St Fergus', Paisley, 1968-74, St Laurence's, Greenock, 1974-87; Parish Priest: Christ the King, Howwood, and Our Lady of Fatima, Lochwinnoch, 1987-95, St James's, Paisley, 1995-96. Hon. Canon, Paisley Cathedral Chapter, 1989; Member, Editorial Board, The Parish Magazine & Journal, Glasgow, 1962-74; first Press Officer, Paisley Diocese, 1964-88; Member, Board of Governors, National Catholic Press Office, 1968-87. Publications include: Joy and Hope: St. Fergus', Paisley, 1971; A Building from God: St James's, Renfrew 1877-1977, 1977; Padraig H. Pearse and Scotland, 1979; Irish-born Secular Priests in Scotland 1829-1979, 1979; Adventure in Faith: St Ninian's, Gourock 1880-1980, 1980; The Living Stone: St Aloysius', Springburn 1882-1982, 1982; Instruments of His Work : Little Sisters of the Poor, Greenock 1884-1984, 1984; St. Mungo's, Ladyburn, Greenock 1935-1985, 1985; The Charleston Story: St Charles', Paisley, 1986; Bishops of Ireland 1870-1987, 1989; St. Fillan's, Houston 1841-1991, 1991; St. Mary's, Paisley 1891-1991, 1991; The Poor Sisters of Nazareth & Derry 1892-1992, 1992; St Colm's Church, Kilmacolm, 1992; Bishop Neil Farren, Bishop of Derry 1893-1980, 1993; St John the Baptist Parish, Port Glasgow, 1846-1946, 1996. Recreation: historical research. Address: (b.) St. John's, 23 Shore Street, Port Glasgow PA14 5HD; T.-01475 741139.

Cannizzo, Jeanne Elizabeth, PhD, MA, BA, FSA(Scot). Anthropologist and Museum Curator; Senior Lecturer, University of Edinburgh, since 1998; b. 12.12.47, Fond du Lac, Wisconsin, USA (Canadian citizen); m., David Alexander Tetlow Stafford. Educ. University of Washington; University of Toronto, University of Wisconsin. Associate Curator, Royal Ontario Museum, 1987; Lecturer, University of Edinburgh, 1994. Exhibitions: O Caledonia, Scottish National Portrait Gallery, 1999; David Livingstone and the Victorian Encounter with Africa, National Portrait Gallery, London, and RSA, Edinburgh, 1996; Into the Heart of Africa, Toronto, 1989. Member, Council, Cockburn Association; Member, Ancient Monuments Board. Recreations: writing for radio; opera. Address: (b.) Department of Social Anthropology, Adam Ferguson Building, University of Edinburgh EH8 9LL; T.-0131-650 6860.

Cannon, Steven, MA (Hons). Secretary, Aberdeen University, since 1998; b. 19.12.57, Keighley; m., Joyce. Educ. St. Bedes Grammar School, Bradford; Dundee University. Administrative Assistant, then Admissions Officer, Warwick University, 1983-86; Financial and Administration Manager, Warwick University Science Park, 1986-88; Financial Manager, Ninewells Hospital and Medical School, Dundee, 1988-93; College Secretary, Duncan of Jordanstone College of Art, 1993-94; Deputy Secretary, Dundee University, 1994-96; Secretary to the Council and Director of Finance and Central Services, Scottish Higher Education Funding Council, 1996-98. Recreations: family interests; golf; cricket; music. Address: (b.) Scottish Higher Education Funding Council, Donaldson House, 97 Haymarket Terrace, Edinburgh EH12 5HD.

Cantley, Maurice, OBE, BSc, PhD. Director, Highlands and Islands Enterprise, since 1991; b. 6.6.37, Cambuslang; m., Rosalind Diana Jones; 2 d. Educ. Bedford Modern and Bristol Grammar; Bristol University. Unilever Ltd., 1961-67; McCann Erickson Advertising, London, 1967-76; Director of Recreation and Tourism, Tayside Regional Council, 1976-82; Head of Tourism, HIDB, 1982-85; Marketing Director, Highlands and Islands Development Board, 1985-91. Chairman, Association of Directors of Recreation, Leisure and Tourism, 1980-82; Hon. Education Officer, Society of Cosmetic Chemists of GB, 1963-66.

Recreations: driving north of Ullapool; natural history; hill-walking. Address: (h.) Oldshorebeg, Kinlochbervie, Sutherland IV27 4RS; T.-01971 521257.

Caplan, Hon. Lord (Philip Isaac Caplan), MA, LLB, LLD(Hon), QC. Senator of the College of Justice, since 1989; b. 24.2.29, Glasgow; m., Joyce Stone (2nd m.); 2 s.; 2 d. Educ. Eastwood School; Glasgow University. Solicitor, 1952-56; called to Bar, 1957; Standing Junior Counsel to Accountant of Court, 1964-70; Chairman, Plant Varieties and Seeds Tribunal, Scotland, 1977-79; Sheriff of Lothian and Borders, at Edinburgh, 1979-83; Sheriff Principal of North Strathclyde, 1983-88; Member, Sheriff Courts Rules Council, 1984-88; Commissioner, Northern Lighthouse Board, 1983-88; Chairman, Scottish Association for the Study of Delinquency, 1985-89, Hon. Vice President, 1990; Member, Advisory Council on Messengers at Arms and Sheriff Officers, 1987-88; Chairman, Scottish Association of Family Conciliation Services, 1989-94, Honorary President, since 1994; Chairman, James Powell UK Trust. FRPS (1988), AFIAP (1985). Recreations: photography; bridge; music; reading. Address: (b.) Court of Session, Parliament House, Edinburgh.

Capperauld, Ian, MB, ChB, DObst, RCOG, FRCSEdin, FRCSGlas, FRCSEng. Consultant Surgeon, since 1962; Medical Director, Huntly Nursing Home, since 1981; Member, Lothian Health Board, since 1981; b. 23.10.33, New Cumnock; m., Wilma Hyslop Young; 2 s. Educ. Cumnock Academy; Glasgow University; Edinburgh University. Served as Major, RAMC, 1959-69 (Consultant Surgeon); former Executive Director, Research and Development, Ethicon Ltd. Recreations: fishing; shooting. Address: (h.) The Old Mill House, Dalkeith EH22 2AQ; T.-0131-663 2469.

Carbery, Emeritus Professor Thomas Francis, OBE, KSG, FRSA, MSc, PhD, DPA. Former Professor, Strathclyde Business School, Strathclyde University; Member, Board of Directors, Energy Action Scotland, since 1996; Member, Data Protection Tribunal, since 1985; b. 18.1.25, Glasgow; m., Ellen Donnelly; 1 s.; 2 d. Educ. St. Aloysius' College, Glasgow; Glasgow University; Scottish College of Commerce. Cadet navigator/meteorologist, RAF, 1943-47; civil servant, 1947-61; Lecturer, then Senior Lecturer, Scottish College of Commerce, 1961-64; Strathclyde University: Senior Lecturer in Government-Business Relations, 1964-75, Head, Department of Office Organisation, 1975-79, Professor of Office Organisation, 1979-85, Professor of Business Information, 1985-88; part-time Professor of Marketing, 1988-90. Member: Independent Broadcasting Authority, 1970-79, Broadcasting Complaints Commission, 1981-86, Royal Commission on Gambling, 1975-77, Transport Users Consultative Committee (Chairman, Scottish TUCC), 1975-81, Press Council, 1987-90, Scottish Consumer Council (latterly Vice-Chairman), 1976-84; Chairman, Scottish Transport Research Group, 1983-87; Member, Scottish Legal Aid Board, 1986-92; Chairman, South of Scotland Consumers Committee/Office of Electricity Regulation, 1990-95; Member, Church of Scotland Committee on Higher Education, 1986-87; Chairman, Strathclyde University Inter-denominational Chaplaincy Committee, 1981-87; Joint Editor, Bulletin of Society for Co-operative Studies, 1967-95; Chairman, Scottish Catholic Communications Commission; Member, Scottish Catholic Education Commission, 1980-93. Recreations: conversation; watching television; spectating at association football; very bad golf. Address: (h.) 24 Fairfax Avenue, Glasgow, G44 5AL; T.-0141-637 0514.

Cardownie, Steve. Member, Edinburgh City Council (Convenor, Recreation Committee); Director, International Arts Exchange, Street Life Ltd., Scot-Slav Ltd.; b. 1.6.53, Leith; m.; 2 s. Educ. Leith Academy; Telford College. Civil service; National Executive Committee Member, CPSA, five years; Industrial Tribunal Member, 16 years; Councillor, Edinburgh, 10 years; Director: Edinburgh International Festival Council, Edinburgh Festival Theatre, Royal Lyceum Theatre, Traverse Theatre, Edinburgh Science Festival. Recreations: hill-walking; running; Heart of Midlothian FC; theatre; reading; fine wines and ale sampling. Address: (b.) City Chambers, High Street, Edinburgh; T.-0131-529 3266.

Cargill, Kenneth George, MA, LLB. Head of News and Current Affairs, BBC Scotland, since 1994; b. 17.2.47, Arbroath; m., Una Gallacher. Educ. Arbroath High School; Edinburgh University. BBC TV Scotland: Researcher, Current Affairs, 1972; Reporter, Current Account, 1973; Film Director, Public Account, 1978; Producer, Current Account, 1979, Agenda, 1981, People and Power (London), 1983; Editor of the day, Reporting Scotland, 1983; Editor, Scotland 2000, 1986-87; Deputy Editor, News and Current Affairs, Television, 1984-88; Head of TV News, Current Affairs and Sport, 1988-94. Publication: Scotland 2000 (Editor), 1987. Recreations: passive gardening and active consumption of Havana cigars, malt whisky and books on UK and US politics. Address: (b.) Broadcasting House, Queen Margaret Drive, Glasgow G12 8DG; T.-0141-338 2250.

Carlyle, Robert, OBE. Actor and Director. Trained, RSAMD; Duncan Macrae Memorial Prize for Scots verse. Credits include: (film) The Full Monty, Carla's Song, Trainspotting, Riff Raff (European film of the year), Priest, Plunkett and MacLeane, Ravenous; (television) Hamish Macbeth (title role); (theatre) Twelfth Night, Cuttin' A Rug, Othello; as Director of Rain Dog Theatre Company: Wasted, One Flew Over the Cuckoo's Nest (Paper Boat Award), Conquest of the South Pole, Macbeth (Paper Boat Award).

Carmichael, Iain. Chief Executive, Lanarkshire Development Agency; m., Angie; 2 d. Formerly: Scottish Regional Manager, Kellock Ltd. (part of Bank of Scotland Group), Executive Director, Clydesdale Enterprise Trust, Director of Finance and Administration and Company Secretary, Lanarkshire Development Agency, 1991-96. Address: (b.) New Lanarkshire House, Strathclyde Business Park, Bellshill ML4 3AD; T.-01698 745454.

Carmichael, Peter, CBE, DSc; b. 26.3.33, Dunblane; m., June; 2 s.; 4 d. by pr. m. Educ. McLaren High School, Callander; Glasgow University. Design engineer, Ferranti Ltd., Edinburgh, 1958-65; Hewlett-Packard, South Queensferry: Project Leader, 1965-67, Production Engineering Manager, 1968-73, Engineering Manager, 1973-75, Manufacturing Manager, 1975-76, Division General Manager, 1976-82, Joint Managing Director, 1980-82; Scottish Development Agency: Director, Small Business and Electronics, 1982-88, Group Director East, 1988-89. Former Chairman, Esmee Fairbairn Economic Institute. Address: (h.) 86 Craiglea Drive, Edinburgh; T.-0131-447 6334; Marchbank Cottage, Ballantrae, Ayrshire; T.-0146 5831355.

Carmichael of Carmichael (Richard John). 26th Baron of Carmichael, since 1980; 30th Chief of Name and Arms of Carmichael, since 1981; Chartered Accountant; Farmer; b. 1.12.48, Stamford; m., Patricia Margaret Branson; 1 s.; 2 d. Educ. Hyton Hill Preparatory School; Kimbolton School; Coventry College of Technology. Audit Senior, Coopers and Lybrand, Tanzania, 1972; Audit Manager, Granger Craig Tunnicliffe, Tauranga, New Zealand, 1974; ACA, 1971; FCA, 1976; Factor/Owner, Carmichael Estate, 1980; Director: Carmichael Heritage Leisure Ltd., World Orienteering Co. Ltd., Scottish Orienteering 6-Day Event Co. Ltd.; claims family titles: Earldom of Hyndford, Viscountcies of Inglisberry and Nemphlar, and Lordship Carmichael of Carmichael. Member, Research and Operations Committee, Standing Council of Scottish

Chiefs; Chairman, Clyde Valley Tourism Group; New Zealand Orienteering Champion, 1977; International Controller, International Orienteering Federation, 1994. Recreations: orienteering; skiing; Clan Carmichael Association. Address: Carmichael House, Carmichael, by Biggar, Lanarkshire ML12 6PG; T.-01899 308336.

Carmichael, Professor Stuart, BVMS, MVM, DSAO. Professor of Veterinary Clinical Studies, University of Glasgow, since 1999; Director, Small Animal Hospital, since 1996; b. 6.7.55, Dumbarton; m., Lesley; 1 s.; 1 d. Educ. Clydebank High School; Glasgow University. Lecturer in Veterinary Surgery, Glasgow University, 1981-89; Royal Veterinary College, London: Lecturer in Small Animal Surgery, 1991, Director of Small Animal Hospital, 1992, Senior Lecturer, 1994; Senior Lecturer, University of Glasgow Veterinary School, 1996-99. British Small Animal Veterinary Association Simon Award, 1996; Chairman, British Veterinary Orthopaedic Association. Address: (b.) University of Glasgow Veterinary School, Bearsden Road, Bearsden, Glasgow G61 1QH.

Carnegy-Arbuthnott, David, TD, DL, LLD, CA. Landowner; b. 17.7.25, London; m., Helen Adamson Lyell; 2 s.; 2 d. Educ. Stowe. Emergency commission, The Black Watch, 1944-47; Chartered Accountant, 1953; in practice, Dundee, 1956-86; TA, 1955-69; Brevet Colonel, 1969; Hon. Colonel, 1st Bn., 51st Highland Volunteers (TA), 1980-89; Deputy Lieutenant, County of City of Dundee, 1973-89, Angus, since 1989; Member, Queen's Bodyguard for Scotland (Royal Company of Archers), since 1959; Governor: Dundee College of Education, 1985-87, Northern College of Education, 1987-91; President, Dundee Chamber of Commerce, 1971-72; Member of Court, Dundee University, 1977-85; Convener, Standing Committee, Scottish Episcopal Church, 1987-92; Trustee, Scottish Episcopal Church, since 1992. Recreations: shooting; country pursuits. Address: (h.) Meadowburn, Balnamoon, Brechin, Angus DD9 7RH; T.-01356 660273.

Carnegy of Lour, Baroness (Elizabeth Patricia), DL. Life Peer, since 1982; Member, Council and Finance Committee, Open University, 1984-96; Member, Court, St. Andrews University, 1991-96; b. 28.4.25. Educ. Downham School. Cavendish Laboratory, Cambridge, 1943-46; Girl Guides Association: Training Adviser for Scotland, 1958-62 and for Commonwealth HQ, 1963-65; co-opted Angus County Council Education Committee, 1967-75; Councillor, Tayside Regional Council, 1974-82; Chairman, Education Committee, 1976-82; Chairman, Working Party on Professional Training in Community Education Scotland, 1975-77; Commissioner, Manpower Services Commission, 1979-82, and Chairman, Committee for Scotland, 1980-83; Member, Scottish Economic Council, 1980-92; President for Scotland, Girl Guides Association, 1979-89; Member, Scottish Council for Tertiary Education, 1979-84; Chairman, Scottish Council for Community Education, 1980-88; Honorary Sheriff, 1969-84; Deputy Lieutenant, 1988; Fellow, Royal Society of Arts, 1987; Honorary LLD: Dundee University, 1991, University of St. Andrews, 1997; Honorary DUniv, Open University, 1998. Address: (h.) Lour, Forfar, Angus DD8 2LR; T.-01307 82 237.

Carr, Isabel Anne, BA. Scottish Director, YWCA, since 1992; b. 23.6.54, Gifford. Educ. Berwickshire High School; Edinburgh University; Jordanhill College of Education. Rhodesia Ministry of Education, 1976; Lothian Regional Council Community Education, 1978-80; Church of Scotland Board of World Mission and Unity, Pakistan, 1981-85; Area Secretary, South Scotland, Christian Aid, 1985-92. Address: (b.) 7 Randolph Crescent, Edinburgh EH3 7TH; T.-0131-225 7592.

Carr, John Roger, CBE, JP, FRICS. Chairman, Countryside Commission for Scotland, 1985-92 (Member, since 1979); Member, Macaulay Land Use Research Institute, 1987-97; Director, UK 2000 Scotland, 1990-93; Vice President, FWAG Scotland, since 1993; b. 18.1.27, Ackworth, Yorkshire; m., Cathrine Elise Dickson-Smith; 2 s. Educ. Ackworth & Ayton (Quaker) School. Royal Marines, 1944-47; Gordon Highlanders TA, 1950-55; Factor, Walker Scottish Estates Co., Ballater; Factor, subsequently Director and General Manager, Moray Estates Development Co., Forres; former Convenor, Scottish Recreational Land Association; former Council Member, Scottish Landowners Federation; former District Councillor, Moray. Recreations: most country pursuits. Address: (b.) Goosehill, Invererne Road, Forres, Moray IV360DZ; T.-01309 671320.

Carrie, Professor Allan Stewart, PhD, MSc, BSc (Eng), FIEE, SMIEEE, CEng, FRSA. Professor of Manufacturing Systems, Department of Design, Manufacture and Engineering Management, University of Strathclyde, since 1987; b. 7.5.42, Glasgow; m., Marie; 2 s. Educ. Fettes College, Edinburgh; Paisley College of Technology (University of London external degree); University of Birmingham. Babcock & Wilcox, Renfrew: Student Apprentice, 1960-63, Graduate Engineer, 1963-64, Methods Engineer, 1964-65; Industrial Engineer, Northern Electric, Montreal, 1966-67; University of Strathclyde: Lecturer, 1968-79, Senior Lecturer, 1979-85, Reader, 1985-87. Recreation: Scottish country dancing. Address: (b.) University of Strathclyde, 75 Montrose Street, Glasgow G1 1XJ; T.-0141-548 2894.

Carroll, Professor Robert Peter, MA, PhD. Professor of Hebrew Bible and Semitic Studies, Department of Theology and Religious Studies, Glasgow University, since 1991 (Dean, Faculty of Divinity, 1991 94); Senate Asesssor on University Court, 1996-2000; b. 18.1.41, Dublin; m., Mary Anne Alice Stevens; 2 s.; 1 d. Educ. High School, Dublin; Trinity College, Dublin University; Edinburgh University. After postgraduate degree, worked as swimming pool attendant, barman, brickie's mate, secondary school teacher; Glasgow University: Assistant Lecturer in Semitic Languages, 1968, Lecturer in Old Testament Language and Literature, 1969, Senior Lecturer in Biblical Studies, 1981; Reader, 1986. Publications: When Prophecy Failed, 1979; From Chaos to Covenant, 1981; Jeremiah: A Commentary, 1986; Jeremiah (JSOT Guide), 1989; Wolf in Sheepfold, 1991; The Bible (Co-Editor), 1997. Recreations: cinema; day-dreaming; writing imaginary books in my head. Address: (h.) 5 Marchmont Terrace, Glasgow G12 9LT; T.-0141-339 0440.

Carruthers, John, MBE, HND. Chief Executive, Metcom Ltd., since 1988; Chairman, Scottish Industries Training and Management Services, since 1982; b. 5.11.38, Clackmannan; m., Catherine; 3 s. Educ. Alloa Technical and Commercial School; Stow College of Engineering. Marine Engineering Trainee, Royal Dockyards; Engineering Officer, Ben Line; Training Manager, Harland Engineering; Executive Director, Training, Metcom. Chairman, Apex Scotland; Chairman, Scottish Offender Employment Forum. Recreations: mountaineering; sailing; skiing. Address: (h.) 35 Victoria Street, Alloa FK10 2AZ; T.-01259 213670.

Carson, James Grant, MA, DipEd, FSAScot. Chairman, Scottish National Committee, English-Speaking Union in Scotland, since 1996; b. Isle of Fetlar, Shetland; m., Catherine Nisbet; 1 s.; 1 d. Educ. John Watson's; Fettes College, Edinburgh; Trinity College, University of Cambridge. Former Depute Rector, Jordanhill School. Leader, ESU Pupil Exchanges to USA, 1975-94; ESU Debates Convenor; Member, Chorus: Edinburgh Festival, Scottish Opera; Director of plays and operas; Hon. President, Greenock Burns Club, 1986. Recreations:

gardening; bridge; reading; travel; food; wine. Address: 23 Atholl Crescent, Edinburgh EH3 8HQ; T.-0131-229 1528.

Carter, Christopher John, BA (Hons), PhD, MRTPI, FRSA. Higher Education Consultant; b. 5.2.41, Capel, Surrey; m., Ann Fisher Prince; 1 s.; 1 d. Educ. Ottershaw School, Chertsey, Surrey; Birmingham University; Glasgow University. Town Planning Assistant, Cumbernauld Development Corporation, 1963-64 and 1967-68; Visiting Lecturer in Geography, Brock University, St. Catharines, Ontario, 1968-69; Lecturer/Senior Lecturer in Planning, Glasgow School of Art, 1969-76; Principal Lecturer in Planning, Coventry (Lanchester) Polytechnic, 1976-78; Senior Lecturer/Head, Department of Town and Regional Planning, Duncan of Jordanstone College of Art, 1978-81; Vice Principal, Duncan of Jordanstone College of Art, 1981-93, Acting Principal, 1993-94; Director, Duncan of Jordanstone College and Deputy Principal, Dundee University, 1994-97. Winner, RTPI Prize, 1970. Member: Board of Governors, Dundee Institute of Technology, 1989-91; Scottish Committee, Universities Funding Council, 1989-92; Scottish Higher Education Funding Council, 1992-93; Member: Board of Governors, Northern College, 1994-95, Board of Management, Elmwood College, since 1997. Publications: Innovations in Planning Thought and Practice at Cumbernauld New Town 1956-62; The Designation of Cumbernauld New Town (case study) (Co-author). Recreations: skiing; running; photography; music. Address: (h.) Etchachan, 12A Deshar Road, Boat of Garten, Inverness-shire PH24 3BN; T.-01479 831732.

Carter, Professor Sir David Craig, MB, ChB, MD, FRCSEdin, FRCSGlas, FRCPEdin, FRCSIre (Hon), FACS (Hon), FRACS (Hon), LLD (Hon), FRSEd, DSc (Hon), LLD (Hon). Chief Medical Officer (Scotland), since 1997; Surgeon to the Queen in Scotland, 1993-97; b. 1.9.40, Penrith; m., Ilske; 2 s. Educ. St. Andrews University. Lecturer in Clinical Surgery, Edinburgh University, 1969-74; 12-month secondment as Lecturer in Surgery, Makerere University, Kampala, Uganda, 1972; Senior Lecturer in Surgery, Edinburgh University, 1974-79;12-month secondment as Associate Professor of Surgery, University of California, 1976; St. Mungo Professor of Surgery, Glasgow University, 1979-88; Honorary Consultant, Glasgow Royal Infirmary, 1979-88; Regius Professor of Surgery, Edinburgh University, 1988-97; Honorary Clinical Consultant, Edinburgh Royal Infirmary, 1988-97. Former Council Member, Royal College of Surgeons of Edinburgh; former Member, Broadcasting Council for Scotland; former Chairman, Scottish Council for Postgraduate Medical and Dental Education; former Co-editor, British Journal of Surgery; Member, Medical Advisory Committee, Higher Education Funding Council, 1994-97; Non-executive Director, Lothian Health Board, 1994-97; President, Surgical Research Society, Association of Surgeons (Great Britain and Ireland), 1996-97. Moynihan Prize, 1973; James IV Association of Surgeons Travelling Fellow, 1975. Recreations: golf; music. Address: (b.) University Department of Surgery, Royal Infirmary, Edinburgh EH3 9YW; T.-0131-536 3812.

Carter, Roger, MBE, BSc, PhD, FTS, MTMS. Director, International Tourism Research Group, Napier University, Edinburgh, since 1997; Managing Partner, Tourism Enterprise and Management; b. 8.12.45, Dorking; m., Dee; 3 s. Educ. Dorking County Grammar School; Birmingham University; Strathclyde University. Transport Development Unit, Strathclyde University, 1970; Leader, Research Unit, Greater London and SE Sports Council, 1970-71; Director of Research and Planning, Scottish Tourist Board, 1971-82; Director, Heart of England Tourist Board, 1982-90; Chief Executive, Edinburgh Tourist Board, 1990-96. Recreation: reading. Address: (b.) ITRG at New Craig, Napier University, Craighouse Campus, Craighouse Road, Edinburgh EH10 5LG; T.-0131-455 6216; (b.) TEAM, 1/1 Liddesdale Place, Edinburgh EH3 5JW; T.-0131-557 5867.

Carty, Matthew John, MB, ChB, FRCSEdin, FRCPSGlas, FRCOG. Consultant Obstetrician and Gynaecologist, Southern General Hospital, Glasgow, since 1977; b. 8.3.42, Hamilton; m., Caroline Martin; 2 s.; 2 d. Educ. St. Aloysius College, Glasgow; Glasgow University. Lecturer in Midwifery, Nairobi University, Kenya, 1970-71; Lecturer in Midwifery, Glasgow University, 1972-77. Recreation: golf. Address: (h.) 31 Monreith Road, Newlands, Glasgow; T.-0141-632 1033.

Casely, (Frederick) Gordon (Polson), OStJ, FSAScot, MIPR. Head of Communications, Aberdeenshire Council, since 1995; Hon. Vice-President, Lonach Highland and Friendly Society, since 1990; b. 29.6.43, Glasgow; m., Valerie Ann Thomas; 1 s. Educ. Hutchesons' Boys Grammar School. Reporter, D.C. Thomson & Co. Ltd., Dundee, Aberdeen and Elgin, 1966-68; Feature Writer, Evening Express, Aberdeen, 1968-73; Public Relations Officer, Greater Glasgow Passenger Transport Executive, 1973-78; public affairs posts in banking, electricity and energy industries, 1978-95 (Assistant Director, CBI Scotland, 1988-91). Founder Member, Heraldry Society of Scotland, 1977; Press Officer, Commonwealth Games Council for Scotland, 1989-93; Member: Scottish Commonwealth Games Team, Auckland, 1990, Guild Burgess of Aberdeen, 1992; President, Aberdeen Welsh Society, 1997-98. Recreations: travelling by bike; promoting heraldry; competing in veteran athletics; remembering 1745. Address: (h.) 45 Beaconsfield Place, Aberdeen AB15 4AB; T.-01224 647927.

Cash, John David, CBE, BSc, MB, ChB, PhD, FRCPath, FRCPGlas, FRCPE, FRCSEdin. National Medical and Scientific Director, Scottish National Blood Transfusion Service, 1979-96; Honorary Professor, Department of Medicine, Edinburgh University, 1987-96; Non-Executive Director, National Institute of Biological Standards and Control, since 1996; b. 3.4.36, Reading; m., Angela Mary Thomson; 1 s.; 1 d. Educ. Ashville College, Harrogate; Edinburgh University. Edinburgh and South East Scotland Blood Transfusion Service: Deputy Director, 1969, Regional Director, 1974. President, Royal College of Physicians of Edinburgh, 1994-98; Adviser in Blood Transfusion, WHO. Recreations: fishing; gardening. Address: 1 Otterburn Park, Edinburgh EH14 1JX.

Cassidy, Anthony (Tony) F., BSc (Hons). Chief Executive, Renfrewshire Enterprise, since 1991; b. 17.11.44, Kilbarchan; m., Laura Jane; 2 s. Educ. Glasgow University. Lecturer, Mechanical Engineering, Glasgow University, 1969-72; British Council official: India, 1972-76, Japan, 1976-81, France, 1983-84; Director, Japan/Asia, Locate in Scotland, 1984-91. Address: (b.) 27 Causeyside Street, Paisley PA1 1UL; T.-0141-848 0101.

Cassidy, Professor James, MB, ChB, MSc, MD, FRCP (Glasgow, Edinburgh). Professor of Oncology, University of Aberdeen, since 1994; Consultant Oncologist, Aberdeen Royal Hospital NHS Trust, since 1994; b. 28.8.58, Lennoxtown; m., Penelope Jane; 2 s.; 1 d. Educ. St. Mirin's Academy, Paisley; University of Glasgow. General Training, Wales and Scotland MRCP (UK), 1985; Lecturer in Oncology, University of Edinburgh. Member, Board of Governors, ICRF. Recreations: soccer, cycling; music. Address: (b.) Institute of Medical Sciences, Foresterhill, Aberdeen; T.-01224 681818, Ext. 53019.

Cassidy, Peter D., MA, CQSW, DipSW, MBA. Director of Social Work Services, Aberdeen City Council, since 1995; b. 14.12.48, Dundee; m., Patricia; 3 d. Educ. Lawside Academy, Dundee; Edinburgh University; Dundee University. Lothian Region: Social Worker, Edinburgh, 1974-77, Senior Social Worker, Midlothian, 1977-82, Area Manager, West Lothian, 1982-88; Depute Director then Senior Depute Director, Fife Region, 1988-95. President, Association of Directors of Social Work, 1998; Convener,

Directors of Social Work, since 1997; Chair, British Agencies for Adoption and Fostering, since 1997. Recreations: golf; swimming; photography; music; reading; family. Address: (b.) St. Nicholas House, Broad Street, Aberdeen AB10 1BY; T.-01224 522529.

Cates, Professor Michael Elmhirst, MA, PhD. Professor of Natural Philosophy, University of Edinburgh, since 1995; b. 5.5.61, Bristol. Educ. Clifton College; Trinity College, University of Cambridge. Research Fellow, Trinity College, University of Cambridge, 1985-89; Cavendish Laboratory, Cambridge: Royal Society University Research Fellow, 1988-89, University Assistant Lecturer, 1989-92, University Lecturer, 1992-94. Maxwell Medal and Prize, Institute of Physics, 1991; Prix Franco-Britannique de l'Academie des Sciences, Paris, 1994. Publications: 150 publications in scientific journals. Recreations: hill-walking; painting. Address: (b.) Department of Physics and Astronomy, University of Edinburgh, Kings Buildings, Edinburgh EH9 3JZ; T.-0131-650 5296.

Catto, Professor Graeme R.D., MB, ChB (Hons), MD (Hons), DSc, FRCP, FRCPE, FRCPGlas, FRSE. Chief Scientist, NHS in Scotland, since 1997; Vice-Principal since 1995, Professor in Medicine and Therapeutics since 1988, Aberdeen University; Honorary Consultant Physician/Nephrologist, since 1977; Vice Chairman, Aberdeen Royal Hospitals NHS Trust, since 1992; Chairman, Robert Gordon's College; b. 24.4.45, Aberdeen; m., Joan Sievewright; 1 s.; 1 d. Educ. Robert Gordon's College; Aberdeen University. Research Fellow/ Lecturer/Senior Lecturer/Reader in Medicine, Aberdeen University, 1970-88; Harkness Fellow of Commonwealth Fund of New York, 1975-77 (Fellow in Medicine, Harvard Medical School and Peter Bent Brigham Hospital, Boston); Dean, Faculty of Clinical Medicine, Aberdeen University, 1992-98; Member, Scottish Higher Education Funding Council, since 1996; Member, General Medical Council, Education and Standards Committee, since 1994; Treasurer, Academy of Medical Sciences, since 1998. Recreations: curling; fresh air; France. Address: (b.) Department of Medicine, Aberdeen University, Foresterhill, Aberdeen AB9 2ZB; T.-01224 681818.

Cawdor, 7th Earl of (Colin Robert Vaughan Campbell); b. 30.6.62; m., Lady Isabella Stanhope. Succeeded to title, 1993. Educ. Eton; St. Peter's College, Oxford. Address: Cawdor Castle, Nairn.

Cawthra, David Wilkinson, CBE, BSc, FEng, FICE, CBIM. Principal, Cawthra & Co; b. 5.3.43, Halifax; m., Maureen Mabel Williamson; 1 s.; 1 d. Educ. Heath Grammar School, Halifax; Birmingham University. Mitchell Construction Company Ltd., 1964-73; Tarmac Construction Ltd., 1973-79; Balfour Beatty Ltd., 1979-91; Chief Executive, The Miller Group Limited, 1992-94. Member, NEDO Construction Industry Sector Group, 1990-92; Vice-President, Institution of Civil Engineers, since 1996. Recreations: hill-walking; American history. Address: (b.) 68 Ravelston Dykes, Edinburgh EH12 6HF; T.-0131-337 2155.

Chalmers, David Watson Penn. Director and Deputy Chief Executive, Dunfermline Building Society, since 1995; b. 28.4.46, Dundee; m., Jacky; 1 d. Educ. Harris Academy, Dundee. Joined Dunfermline Building Society, 1968. Director, South Fife Enterprise Trust Ltd.; Member, Committee of Management, Kingdom Housing Association Ltd.; Member, Mortgage Practitioners Panel, Council of Mortgage Lenders; Chairman, Committee of Management, Dundee Employment and Aftercare Project; Trustee, Scottish Housing Association's Charitable Trust; Director, Business Enterprise Scotland. Recreations: golf; chess; hill-walking; running. Address: (b.) Caledonia House, Carnegie Avenue, Dunfermline KY11 5PJ; T.-01383 627727.

Chalmers, Professor Ian Donald, BSc, PhD, CEng, MInstP, FIEE, SMIEEE. Professor, Department of Electronic and Electrical Engineering, Strathclyde University, since 1988; b. 4.6.40, London; 1 s.; 1 d. Educ. Montrose Academy; Dundee Technical College; Strathclyde University. CEGB Research Fellow, 1968-73; Lecturer, Department of Electrical Engineering, Strathclyde University, 1973-83, Senior Lecturer, 1983-86, Reader, 1986-88, Professor, 1988. Publications: 100 research papers. Address: (b.) Royal College Building, 204 George Street, Glasgow G1 1XW.

Chalmers, Rev. John Pearson, BD. Depute General Secretary, Department of Ministry, Church of Scotland, since 1995; Vice Chairman, Board of Governors, Donaldson's College, since 1991; b. 5.6.52, Bothwell; m., Elizabeth; 2 s.; 1 d. Educ. Marr College; Strathclyde University; Glasgow University. Minister, Renton Trinity, 1979-86; Clerk, Dumbarton Presbytery, 1982-86; Minister, Palmerston Place, Edinburgh, 1986-95. Recreations: golf; bee-keeping. Address: (b.) 121 George Street, Edinburgh EH2 4YN; T.-0131-225 5722.

Chalmers, Patricia, MA (Hons). Councillor, Glasgow District Council, 1982-96; b. Glasgow; m., Walter Scott Chalmers; 1 s.; 2 d. Educ. Rothesay Academy; Glasgow University. Member, Board, Tron Theatre, since 1992; a Director, Glasgow Cultural Enterprises Ltd., since 1991, Executive Member, Glasgow Building Preservation Trust, since 1991; Chair: West End Festival, Alexander Greek Thomson Trust; Trustee, Scottish Civic Trust; Hon. Vice-President, Four Acres Charitable Trust; Member, Church Buildings Renewal Trust, since 1998. Recreations: conservation; work; the arts. Address: (h.) 92 Southbrae Drive, Glasgow G13 1TZ; T.-0141-959 3131.

Chamberlain, Rt. Rev. Canon Neville, BA, MA. Episcopal Bishop of Brechin, since 1997; b. 1939. Educ. Nottingham University; Oxford University. Deacon, 1963; ordained Priest, 1964; Curate, St. Paul's, Birmingham, 1963-64; Priest-in-Charge, St. Michael's, Birmingham, 1964-69; Rector, Deer Creek Parish, USA, 1967-68; Vicar, St. Michael's Anglican Methodist Church, 1969-72; Executive Secretary, Lincoln Social Responsibility Commission, 1974-82; Canon and Prebend, Lincoln Cathedral, 1979; Rector, St. John the Evangelist, Edinburgh, 1982-97. Address: (b.) St. Paul's Cathedral, 1 High Street, Dundee DD1 1TD; T.-01382 229230.

Chambers, Ernest George Wilkie, MBA, BSc (Hons). Chief Executive, West of Scotland Water Authority; b. 10.5.47, Dundee; m., Jeanette; 1 s.; 1 d. Educ. Harris Academy, Dundee. Assistant Engineer, East of Scotland Water Board and Lower Clyde Water Board, 1969-75; Strathclyde Regional Council Water Department: Area Engineer (Renfrew), 1975-79, Divisional Operations Engineer, Lower Clyde Division, 1979-84, Assistant Divisional Manager, 1984-86, Assistant Director (Operations & Maintenance), 1986-88; Director, 1988-94; Director, Strathclyde Water Services, 1994-95. National President, Institution of Water Officers, 1996-97; President, Scottish Area, Association of Water Officers, 1991-92. Recreations: DIY; gardening. Address: (b.) 419 Balmore Road, Glasgow G22 6NU; T.-0141-355 5177.

Chambers, Fergus Allan, MHCIMA. Director, Catering and Domestic Care Services, Glasgow City Council, since 1995; b. 20.1.56, Glasgow; m., Ruth Elizabeth; 1 s.; 1 d. Educ. Uddingston Grammar School; Glasgow College of Food Technology. Various posts, commercial catering group, 1977-82; Business Development Manager, Sutcliffe Catering, 1982-86; General Manager, Moccomat UK, 1986-88; Depute Director, Strathclyde Regional Council/Catering Direct, 1988-95. Trustee and Honorary Secretary, Hospitality Industry Trust of Scotland; Chairman, Industry Dinner Committee; Member, Executive Committee,

Association of Civic Hosts. Recreations: golf; DIY. Address: (h.) 24 Clydeford Drive, Kylepark, Uddingston, Glasgow G71 7DJ; T.-01698 813814 (h.); 0141-353 9130 (b.).

Chapman, Francis Ian, CBE, FRSA, CIMgt, DLitt (Hon). President, Scottish Radio Holdings PLC, since 1996 (Chairman, 1972-96); Deputy Chairman, Guinness Publishing, since 1997 (Chairman, 1991-96); President, SAS Guinness Media, Paris, since 1996; Chairman, Radio Trust PLC, since 1997; b. 26.10.25, St. Fergus, Aberdeenshire; m., Marjory Stewart Swinton; 1 s.; 1 d. Educ. Shawlands Academy, Glasgow; Ommer School of Music. War Service: RAF air crew cadet, 1943-44; National Service coal mines, 1945-47. William Collins: trainee, 1947, Sales Representative, New York Branch, 1951, General Sales Manager, London, 1955, appointed to main operating Board as Group Sales Director, 1960; appointed to Board, William Collins (Holdings) Ltd. as Joint Managing Director, 1967; Deputy Chairman, William Collins (Holdings) Ltd., 1976; Chairman, William Collins Publishers Ltd., 1979; Chairman and Chief Executive, William Collins PLC, 1981-89; Chairman, Hatchards Ltd., 1976-89; Pan Books Ltd.: Board Member, 1962-84, Chairman, 1971-73; Chairman, Harvill Press Ltd., 1976-89; Board Member, Book Tokens Ltd., 1981-95; Member, Governing Council, SCOTBIC, since 1983; Board Member, IRN Ltd., 1983-85; President, Publishers Association, 1979-81; Trustee, Book Trade Benevolent Society, since 1982; Board Member, Scottish Opera Theatre Royal Ltd., 1974-79; Director, Stanley Botes Ltd., 1985-89; Non-Executive Director, Guinness PLC, 1986-91; Joint Chairman and Chief Executive, Harper and Row, New York, 1987-89; Director, United Distillers PLC, 1988-93; Chairman and Managing Director, Chapmans Publishers Ltd., 1989-94; Deputy Chairman, Orion Publishing Group, 1993-94. Scottish Free Enterprise Award, 1985; Hon. DLitt, Strathclyde, 1990. Recreations: golf; swimming; music; grandchildren. Address: (b.) Radio Clyde, Clydebank Business Park, Clydebank.

Chapman, Professor John N., MA, PhD, FInstP, FRSE. Professor, Physics and Astronomy, Glasgow University, since 1988; b. 21.11.47, Sheffield; m., Judith M.; 1 s.; 1 d. Educ. King Edward VII School, Sheffield; St. John's College and Fitzwilliam College, Cambridge. Research Fellow, Fitzwilliam College, Cambridge; Lecturer, Glasgow University. Publication: Quantitative Electron Microscopy (Co-Editor). Recreations: photography; walking; squash. Address: (b.) Department of Physics and Astronomy, Glasgow University, Glasgow G12 8QQ; T.-0141-330 4462.

Chapman, Professor Robert, BSc, PhD, CPhys, FInstP. Professor of Physics, since 1993, and Head, Department of Electronic Engineering and Physics, since 1996, University of Paisley; b. 10.8.41, Holytown; m., Norma Gilchrist Hope; 3 d. Educ. Bellshill Academy; University of Glasgow. UKAEA Research Fellow, AWRE, Aldermaston, and AERE, Harwell, 1966-70; University of Manchester: Lecturer, 1970-75, Senior Lecturer, 1975-87, Reader in Physics, 1987-93; Head, Department of Physics, University of Paisley, 1993-96. Recreations: walking; gardening; listening to music. Address: (b.) Department of Electronic Engineering and Physics, University of Paisley, Paisley PA1 2BE; T.-0141-848 3600.

Chapman, Robert Sutherland, MB, ChB (Hons), FRCP(Glas), FRCP(Edin), FRCP(Lond). Consultant Dermatologist, Stobhill NHS Trust and Greater Glasgow Health Board; Clinical Senior Lecturer, Glasgow University, since 1973; b. 4.6.38, Cults, Aberdeenshire; m., Dr. Rosalind S. Slater (deceased); 2 s.; 1 d. Educ. Turriff Academy; Aberdeen University. House Officer, Aberdeen Royal Infirmary; Research Fellow, Department of Materia Medica and Therapeutics, Aberdeen University; Registrar and Senior Registrar in Dermatology, Aberdeen Hospitals; Senior Registrar in Dermatology, Middlesex Hospital and St. John's Hospital for Diseases of the Skin, London. Recreations: gardening; hill-walking. Address: (h.) 4 Seafield Avenue, Bearsden, Glasgow G61 3LB; T.-0141-942 8993.

Chapman, Professor Stephen Kenneth, BSc, PhD, CChem, MRSC. Professor of Chemistry, since 1996; b. 12.5.59, Newcastle upon Tyne; m., Karen; 1 s.; 2 d. Educ. Lakes School, Windermere; University of Newcastle. NATO Research Fellow, Massachusetts Institute of Technology, Cambridge, Mass., USA, 1983-85; Department of Chemistry, Edinburgh University: Lecturer, 1986, Senior Lecturer, 1992, Reader, 1995. Publications: 110 scientific publications. Recreations: watching sport; gardening; playing with my children. Address: (b.) Department of Chemistry, University of Edinburgh, West Mains Road, Edinburgh EH9 3JJ; T.-0131-650 4760.

Chart, Helga, RSW, DA. Artist; b. 31.8.44, Edinburgh; m., Bert Robertson; 1 s. Educ. Trinity Academy, Edinburgh; Edinburgh College of Art. Art Teacher, Craigmount High School, Edinburgh, 1971-79; Lecturer in Art and Design, Edinburgh's Telford College, 1983-96. Council Member, Royal Scottish Society of Painters in Watercolours; Council Member, Scottish Artists and Artist Craftsmen. RSA Stuart Award, 1967; RSA City of Edinburgh Award, 1985; SSA IBM Award, 1985; RSW Council Award, 1998. Recreations: gardening; birdwatching. Address: (h.) 19 Dalrymple Crescent, The Grange, Edinburgh EH9 2NX; T.-0131-667 1150.

Chatterji, Professor Monojit, BA, MA, PhD. Bonar Professor of Applied Economics, Dundee University, since 1989 (Head, Department of Economic Studies, 1993-97); Associate Dean, Faculty of Arts and Social Sciences, Dundee University, since 1995; Member, Advisory Group, BBC World Service; b. 15.1.51, Bombay; m., Anjum Rahmatulla; 1 s.; 2 d. Educ. Cathedral School, Bombay; St. Columba's, Delhi; Elphinstone College, Bombay; Christ's College, Cambridge. Recreations: tennis; cinema; history; theology. Address: (b.) Department of Economics, Dundee University, Dundee; T.-01382 344371.

Cheetham, Professor Juliet, OBE, MA. Social Work Commissioner, Mental Welfare Commission for Scotland; National Co-ordinator, SHEFC Contract Research Staff Initiative, 1996-97; Professor and Director, Social Work Research Centre, Stirling University, 1986-95; b. 12.10.39, Jerusalem; m., Christopher Paul Cheetham; 1 s.; 2 d. Educ. St. Andrews University; Oxford University. Probation Officer, Inner London, 1959-65; Lecturer in Applied Social Studies and Fellow of Green College, Oxford University, 1965-86. Member: Committee of Enquiry into Working of the Abortion Act; Northern Ireland Human Rights Commission; Commission of Racial Equality; Social Security Advisory Committee; Council for National Academic Awards; Economic and Social Research Council. Recreation: canal boats. Address: (b.) Peffermill House, 91 Peffermill Road, Edinburgh EH16 5UX.

Chester, Richard Waugh, ARAM, GRSM, ARCM, FRSA. Director, National Youth Orchestra of Scotland, since 1987; b. 19.4.43, Hutton Rudby; m., Sarah Chapman-Mortimer; 1 s.; 2 d. Educ. The Friends' School, Great Ayton; Huddersfield University; Royal Academy of Music. Flautist: BBC Northern Ireland, 1965, Royal Scottish National Orchestra, 1967; Conductor; Teacher; Examiner. Chairman, Glasgow Festival Strings; Member, Scottish Arts Council (Chairman, Music Committee); Treasurer, European Federation of National Youth Orchestras; Member, Board, World Youth Orchestra Conference and World Federation of Amateur Orchestras; Governor, St. Mary's Music School, Edinburgh. Recreations: tennis; swimming; good food. Address: (h.) Milton of Cardross,

Port of Menteith, Stirling FK8 3JY; T.-01877 385634; (b.) National Youth Orchestra of Scotland, 13 Somerset Place, Glasgow G3 7JT; T.-0141-332 8311.

Chesworth, Air Vice Marshal George Arthur, CB, OBE, DFC. Lord-Lieutenant of Moray, since 1994; b. 4.6.30; m.; 1 s. (deceased); 2 d. RAF, 1948-84; Chief Executive, Glasgow Garden Festival, 1985-98.

Cheyne, Rev. Professor Alexander Campbell, MA (Hons), BLitt, BD, HonDLitt (Memorial University, Newfoundland). Professor of Ecclesiastical History, Edinburgh University, 1964-86; Principal, New College, Edinburgh, 1984-86; Moderator, Edinburgh Presbytery, Church of Scotland, 1987-88; Hon. President, Scottish Church History Society, since 1998; b. 1.6.24, Errol, Perthshire. Educ. Kirkcaldy High School; Edinburgh University; Oriel College, Oxford; New College, Edinburgh; Basel University, Switzerland. National Service (Instructor, Army School of Education), 1946-48; Glasgow University: Assistant Lecturer, 1950-51, Lecturer in History, 1951-53; Lecturer in Ecclesiastical History, Edinburgh University, 1958-64. Carnegie Scholar, 1948-50; Aitken Fellow, 1956-57; Visiting Professor, Wooster College, Ohio, 1973; Chalmers Lecturer (Trinity College, Glasgow, and Christ's College, Aberdeen), 1976-80; Visiting Fellow, Wolfson College, Cambridge, 1979; Burns Lecturer, Knox College, Dunedin, New Zealand, 1980; Lee Lecturer, 1993; President, Scottish Church History Society, 1986-89. Publications: The Transforming of the Kirk: Victorian Scotland's Religious Revolution, 1983; The Practical and the Pious: Essays on Thomas Chalmers 1780-1847 (Editor), 1985; The Ten Years' Conflict and the Disruption, 1993; Studies in Scottish Church History, 1998; contributions to: Reformation and Revolution: Essays presented to Hugh Watt, 1967; introduction to Movements of Religious Thought in Britain during the Nineteenth Century, 1971; The Westminster Confession in the Church Today, 1982; The Bible in Scottish Life and Literature, 1988; In Divers Manners, 1990; Christ, Church and Society: essays, 1993; Dictionary of Scottish Church History and Theology, 1993; William Robertson Smith: Essays in Reassessment, 1995; From Disruption to Diversity: Edinburgh Divinity 1846-1996, 1996; Oxford Dictionary of the Christian Church, 1997. Recreation: classical music. Address: (h.) 12 Crossland Crescent, Peebles EH45 8LF; T.-01721 722288.

Chezeaud, Jacques-Marcel, BA (Hons). Rector, St. Joseph's College, Dumfries, since 1994; b. 16.8.52, Bourges, France; m., Joan I. Campbell; 1 s.; 1 d. Educ. Lycee Alain Fournier, France; Orleans University; Stirling University. Foreign language assistant, Wallace Hall and Sanquhar Academies, 1974-75; manager, wine trade, 1979-80; Teacher, English/French, Biggar High School and St. Mary's Academy, Bathgate, 1980-82; Principal Teacher, Modern Languages, Our Lady's High School, Broxburn, 1982-85; Depute Rector, St. Columba's High School, Perth, 1985-91; Depute Head, St. David's High School, Dalkeith, 1991-94. Member, Executive Committee, Scottish Association for Language Teaching. Recreations: long-distance running; reading; good food and wines. Address: (b.) St. Joseph's College, Craigs Road, Dumfries DG1 4UU; T.-01387 252893.

Chiappelli, Marco Luigi Autimio, CA. Finance Director, Johnston Press plc, since 1980; b. 27.8.44, Glasgow; m., Jane Geddes McLaughlin; 2 d. Educ. Lourdes Senior Secondary School, Glasgow. Indentured Student, Aikman & Glen, CA, Glasgow (later Alexander Sloan), 1963-69; qualified as CA, 1969; Audit Senior, then Audit Manager, Alexander Sloan, 1969-74; joined F. Johnston & Co. Ltd. (later Johnston Press plc), as Company Secretary, 1974. Chairman, Group of Scottish Finance Directors; Board of Governors, St. Margaret's School, Edinburgh, 1995; Finance Director of the Year, 1995. Recreations: golfing; tennis; travel; music. Address: (b.) 53 Manor Place, Edinburgh EH3 7EG; T.-0131-225 3361.

Chick, Jonathan Dale, MA (Cantab), MB, ChB, MPhil, FRCPE, FRCPsych. Consultant Psychiatrist, Royal Edinburgh Hospital, since 1979; part-time Senior Lecturer, Edinburgh University, since 1979; b. 23.4.45, Wallasey; m., Josephine Anna; 2 s. Educ. Queen Elizabeth Grammar School, Darlington; Corpus Christi College, Cambridge; Edinburgh University. Posts in Edinburgh teaching hospitals, 1971-76; scientific staff, MRC Unit for Epidemiological Studies in Psychiatry, 1976-79. Adviser, WHO, Department of Transport; awarded Royal College of Psychiatrists Research Medal and Prize. Publication: Drinking Problems (Co-author). Recreations: wheels, reels, spiels and stichomythia.

Chirnside, Peter Huett, BSc (Hons). National Co-ordinator, Tear Fund, since 1979; Chairman, Scottish Mission Secretaries Fellowship, since 1984; Member, Scottish Lausanne Committee, since 1995; b. 27.12.49, Lancaster; m., Fiona; 1 s.; 1 d. Educ. Silcoates School, Wakefield; University of Dundee. Teacher of Biology, Mackie Academy, 1973-79. Address: (b.) Challenge House, 29 Canal Street, Glasgow G4 0HD.

Chisholm, Professor Derrick Mackenzie, BDS, PhD, FDSRCPS(Glas), FDSRCS(Edin). Boyd Professor of Dental Surgery, University of Dundee, since 1978 (Honorary Consultant in Oral Medicine and Pathology, since 1978, Director, School of Dental Hygiene, since 1992); b. 27.3.40, Glasgow; m., June Romayne Race; 1 step-s.; 1 step-d. Educ. Hillhead High School; University of Glasgow. Clinical Research Assistant in Oral Medicine, 1966-68; University of Glasgow: Lecturer in Oral Medicine and Pathology, 1968-76, Senior Lecturer in Oral Medicine and Pathology, 1976-78; University of Dundee: Dean of Dentistry, 1982-89, Deputy Principal, 1989-91; Vice-Principal, 1991-92. Visiting Professor of Oral Pathology, University of Illinois, USA, 1970-72. Publications: Salivary Glands in Health and Disease, 1975; Introduction to Oral Medicine, 1978. Recreations: gardening; reading; music. Address: Bruckley House, St. Andrews, Fife KY16 9YF; T.-01334 838375.

Chisholm, Duncan Douglas, MB, ChB, FRCPsych, DPM, DPsychother. Consultant Child and Adolescent Psychiatrist, Department of Child and Family Psychiatry, Royal Aberdeen Children's Hospital, since 1975; Clinical Senior Lecturer, Department of Mental Health, Aberdeen University, since 1975; b. 8.10.41, Grantown-on-Spey; m., Rosemary Galloway Doyle; 2 d. Educ. Grantown Grammar School; Aberdeen University. Pre-registration House Officer, Aberdeen, 1965-66; post-registration Senior House Officer/Registrar, Royal Cornhill Hospital and Ross Clinic, Aberdeen, 1966-70; Senior Registrar in Child and Adolescent Psychiatry, 1970-75 (including one-year sabbatical, Clarke Institute of Psychiatry, Toronto, 1973-74). Vice-President, Family Mediation Grampian; Academic Secretary, Scottish Child and Adolescent Section, Royal College of Psychiatrists, 1994-97. Recreations: reading; chess; crosswords; literature, history and culture of Scotland and Scottish Highlands; golf. Address: (h.) Figurettes, 6 Crombie Road, Westhill, Aberdeenshire AB32 6PN; T.-01224 749197.

Chisholm, Duncan Fraser, JP. Managing Director, Duncan Chisholm & Sons Ltd., Inverness, since 1979; b. 14.4.41, Inverness; m., Mary Rebecca MacRae; 1 s.; 1 d. Educ. Inverness High School. Member, Inverness District Council, 1984-92; Member, Board of Governors, Eden Court Theatre, Inverness, 1984-88; President, Inverness and Highland Chamber of Commerce, 1983-84 (Vice-President, 1982-83); Member, Highland TAVRA Committee, 1988-92; Vice-Chairman, Inverness, Loch Ness and Nairn Tourist Board, 1988-96; President, Clan Chisholm Society, 1978-

89; Chairman, Inverness Town Twinning Committee, 1992-98; Member, Management Committee: Highland Export Club, since 1998, Inverness Town Management, since 1997. Recreations: swimming; music; painting. Address: (b.) 47-51 Castle Street, Inverness; T.-01463 234599.

Chisholm, Duncan John, FRICS. Assessor and Electoral Registration Officer for Fife (previously for Fife Regional Council), since 1990; b. 22.1.53, Musselburgh; m., Ann Thomson; 1 s.; 1 d. Educ. Trinity Academy, Edinburgh. Apprentice Surveyor, Midlothian County Assessor, 1970-74; Valuer, Midlothian County Assessor, 1974-75; Valuer, Senior Valuer, Divisional Assessor, Lothian Regional Assessor, 1975-89. Recreations: golf; music; eating; real ale. Address (b.) Fife House (03), North Street, Glenrothes, Fife; T.-Glenrothes 414141.

Chisholm, Malcolm. MP (Labour), Edinburgh North and Leith (formerly Edinburgh Leith), since 1992; Parliamentary Under-Secretary of State, Scottish Office (Minister for Local Government and Transport) 1997 (resigned over cuts); b. 7.3.49; m.; 2 s.; 1 d. Former teacher. Address: (b.) House of Commons, London, SW1A 0AA.

Chisman, Neil, MA, FCCA, FCT. Finance Director, Stakis PLC, since 1989; b. 1.3.47, Southend on Sea; m., Elizabeth Gausden; 1 s.; 1 d. Educ. Preston Manor County Grammar School, Wembley; Fitzwilliam College, University of Cambridge. British Leyland, 1968-70; Mars, 1970-72; BBC, 1972-75; Twinlock, 1975-76; Arabian Construction Co., Abu Dhabi, 1976-77; Abu Dhabi Petroleum Co., 1977-81; Coopers & Lybrand, 1981-85; University of Surrey, 1985-88; Underwoods PLC, 1988-89. Member, Financial Reporting Council. Recreations: work; family; bridge; history. Address: (b.) 3 Atlantic Quay, York Street, Glasgow G2 8JH; T.-0141-304 1038.

Chiswick, Derek, MB, ChB, MPhil, FRCPsych. Honorary Senior Lecturer in Forensic Psychiatry, Edinburgh University; Consultant Forensic Psychiatrist, Edinburgh Healthcare NHS Trust; b. 7.1.45, Hampton, Middlesex; m., Ann Williams; 3 d. Educ. Preston Manor County School, Wembley; Liverpool University. Parole Board for Scotland: Member, 1983-88, Vice-Chairman, 1984-88; Member, Home Office Advisory Board on Restricted Patients, 1991-97. Recreation: relaxing with family. Address: (h.) 6 St. Catherine's Place, Edinburgh EH9 1NU; T.-0131-667 2444.

Christian, Professor Reginald Frank, MA (Hons) (Oxon). Professor of Russian and Head of Department, St. Andrews University, 1966-92, now Emeritus Professor; b. 9.8.24, Liverpool; m., Rosalind Iris Napier; 1 s.; 1 d. Educ. Liverpool Institute High School; Queen's College, Oxford. RAF, 1943-46 (aircrew), flying on 231 Sqdn. and 6 Atlantic Ferry Unit (Pilot Officer, 1944); Foreign Office (British Embassy, Moscow), 1949-50; Lecturer and Head of Russian Department, Liverpool University, 1950-55; Senior Lecturer, then Professor of Russian and Head of Department, Birmingham University, 1955-66; Visiting Professor: McGill University, Montreal, 1961-62, Institute of Foreign Languages, Moscow, 1964-65; Dean, Faculty of Arts, St. Andrews University, 1975-78; Member, University Court, 1971-73, 1981-85. President, British Universities Association of Slavists, 1967-70; Member, International Committee of Slavists, 1970-75; Honorary Vice-President, Association of Teachers of Russian; Member, UGC Arts Sub-Committee on Russian Studies. Publications: Russian Syntax (with F.M. Borras), 1959 and 1971; Korolenko's Siberia, 1954; Tolstoy's War and Peace: A Study, 1962; Russian Prose Composition (with F.M. Borras), 1964 and 1974; Tolstoy: A Critical Introduction, 1969; Tolstoy's Letters, edited, translated and annotated, 1978; Tolstoy's Diaries, edited, translated and annotated, 1985 and 1994. Recreations: violin; fell-walking; formerly association football. Address: (h.) Culgrianach, 48 Lade Braes, St. Andrews, Fife; T.-01334 474407; Scioncroft, Knockard Road, Pitlochry; T.-01796 472993.

Christie, Professor Andrew John McPhedran, BAcc, CA, ATII. Co-owner (with wife, Barbara), Stenton Gallery; Professor, Heriot-Watt University; Partner, Arthur Andersen (Chartered Accountants), 1983-98; b. 17.7.50, Glasgow; m., Barbara Isabel Tait; 2 s. Educ. Hillhead High School, Glasgow; Glasgow University. Member of Council, ICAS; Governor, Edinburgh College of Art. Recreations: golf; skiing. Address: (b.) Heriot-Watt University, Edinburgh EH14 4AS; T.-0131-449 5111.

Christie, Campbell, CBE, DLitt. General Secretary, Scottish Trades Union Congress, 1986-98; Visiting Professor, Glasgow Caledonian University; Honorary Professor, Glasgow University; b. 23.8.37, Carsluith, Kirkcud-brightshire; m., Elizabeth Brown Cameron; 2 s. Educ. Albert Senior Secondary School, Glasgow; Woolwich Polytechnic, London. Civil Servant, Department of Health and Social Security, 1954-72; National Officer, then Deputy General Secretary, Society of Civil and Public Servants, 1972-86. Member, EU Economic and Social Committee; Director: Wildcat Theatre Company, Mining (Scotland) Ltd.; Board Member: Falkirk Royal Infirmary Hospital Trust, Scottish Enterprise, British Waterways, Falkirk Football and Athletic Club; Chairman, Lothian Trade Union and Community Resource Centre. Address: (h.) 31 Dumyat Drive, Falkirk; T.-01324 624555.

Christie, Fergus John Francis, MA, LLB. Solicitor; Partner, Burnett Christie, since 1993; b. 8.5.61, Edinburgh; m., Liesa Spiller; 1 s. Educ. Scotus Academy, Edinburgh; University of St. Andrews; University of Edinburgh. Assistant-Partner, Drummond Miller, 1985-93. Secretary, Edinburgh Bar Association, 1991-98, Vice-President, since 1998; Secretary,St. Andrews Children's Society. Recreations: golf; antiques. Address: 53 George IV Bridge, Edinburgh; T.-0131-225 3456.

Christie, John, MTheol, DipEd. Director of Education, Scottish Borders Council, since 1995; Non-Executive Director: Scottish Consultative Council on the Curriculum, since 1995; Health Education Board for Scotland, 1991-97; b. 25.12.53, Edinburgh; m., Katherine; 2 d. Educ. Daniel Stewart's College; St. Andrews University; Edinburgh University; Moray House College of Education. Teacher, 1977-83; Principal Assistant, Stockport MBC, 1983-85; Assistant Director of Education, then Depute Director of Education, Tayside Regional Council, 1985-95. Hon. Treasurer, Association of Directors of Education in Scotland. Recreation: house-building. Address: (b.) Council HQ, Newtown St. Boswells TD6 0SA; T.-01835 825095.

Christie, Robert Johnstone Stevenson, BSc (Hons), FRSA. Scottish Secretary, Professional Association of Teachers, since 1989; b. 7.8.46, Edinburgh; m., Anne Elisabeth Fraser Macleod; 3 d. Educ. Grangemouth High School; Paisley College of Technology; Jordanhill College of Education; Glasgow University. Chemist, British Petroleum Chemicals Ltd., 1964-68; Principal Teacher of Physics, Tain Royal Academy, 1976-88. Recreations: family; music; history; sailing. Address: (b.) 4/6 Oak Lane, Edinburgh EH12 6XH; T.-0131-317 8282.

Chrystie, Kenneth, LLB (Hons), PhD. Partner, McClure Naismith, since 1971; Chairman, Hugh Fraser Foundation, 1988; President, Royal Glasgow Institute of the Fine Arts, since 1997; b. 24.11.46, Glasgow; m., Mary; 1 s.; 2 d. Educ. Duncanrig Senior Secondary; University of Glasgow; University of Virginia. Joined McClure Naismith, 1968. Founder Member and Director, Intellectual Property Lawyers Organisation; Member, DTI Committees, Arbitration Law Reform. Publications: contributor to Encyclopedia of Scots Law, Labour Law Handbook and other legal publications. Recreations: golf; curling; tennis. Address: (b.) 292 St. Vincent Street, Glasgow G2 5TQ; T.-0141-204 2700.

Clapham, David Charles, LLB, SSC. Solicitor (Principal, private practice, since 1984); Temporary Sheriff, since 1998; Secretary, Glasgow, Argyll and Bute and Dunbartonshire Local Valuation Panel, since 1996; part-time Chairman, Social Security Appeal Tribunals, since 1992; Director, Legal Defence Union; b. 16.10.58, Giffnock; m., Debra Harriet Samuels; 1 s.; 2 d. Educ. Hutchesons' Boys' Grammar School, Glasgow; Strathclyde University. Legal apprenticeship, 1979-81; admitted Solicitor, 1981; admitted Notary Public, 1982; founded own legal practice, 1984; Tutor, Strathclyde University, 1984-92; part-time Lecturer, Glasgow University, 1991-94; Secretary, Strathclyde Region Local Valuation Panel, 1988-96; Glasgow Bar Association: Secretary, 1987-91, Vice President, 1991-92, President, 1992-93; Secretary, Scottish Law Agents Society, 1994-97; Senior Vice President, Eastwood Rotary Club. Recreations: reading; collecting books; cycling. Address: (b.) 79 West Regent Street, Glasgow G2 2AW; T.-0141-332 5537.

Clark, Alastair Trevor, CBE (1976), LVO (1974), MA (Oxon), AMA, FSA Scot, FRSSA. Barrister (Middle Temple); Member, Race Relations Assessors Panel, Scottish Sheriff Courts, since 1983; b. 10.6.23, Glasgow; m., Hilary Agnes Mackenzie Anderson. Educ. Giffnock Academy; Glasgow Academy; Edinburgh Academy; Magdalen College, Oxford; Inns of Court (Middle Temple); Ashridge Management College. War service, Queen's Own Cameron Highlanders and Royal West African Frontier Force, Nigeria, India and Burma, 1942-46; Administrative Branch, HM Colonial Service (later HMOCS): Nigeria, 1949-59 (Secretary to Cabinet, Northern Region; Senior District Officer), Hong Kong, 1960-72 (Director of Social Welfare; Deputy and Acting Director of Urban Services; Acting Chairman Urban Council; Clerk of Councils; Principal Assistant Colonial Secretary, etc.), Western Pacific, 1972-77 (Chief Secretary Western Pacific High Commission; Deputy and Acting Governor, Solomon Islands); retired, 1977; Vice-President, Hong Kong Scout Association, 1965-72; Joint Founder, HK Outward Bound School; Honorary Secretary, St. John's Cathedral Council, 1963-72; USA State Department Country Leader Fellowship to USA, 1972; Selector, Voluntary Service Overseas, 1978-80; Leverhulme Trust Grant, 1979-81; Chairman, Scottish Museums Council, 1981-84 and 1987-90; Member, Council, National Trust for Scotland, 1981-84 and 1987-90; Member, Museums Association Council, 1983-86 and 1990-94; Member, Edinburgh International Festival Council, 1980-86 and 1990-94; Vice-Chairman, Committee of Area Museum Councils, 1983-84; Member, Secretary of State's Museums Advisory Board, 1983-85; Trustee, National Museums of Scotland, 1985-87; a Director, Royal Lyceum Theatre Company, 1982-84; Member: Lothian Health Board, 1981-89, City of Edinburgh District Council, 1980-88, Court of Directors, Edinburgh Academy, 1979-84; a Governor, Edinburgh Filmhouse, 1980-84 and since 1987; Member, National Museums of Scotland Charitable Trust, since 1987; Member, Almond Valley Heritage Trust, since 1990 (Vice Chairman, since 1993); Trustee, Stirling Smith Art Gallery and Museum, since 1993; Volunteer Guide, Royal Museum of Scotland, since 1993. Publication: A Right Honourable Gentleman — Abubakar from the Black Rock, 1991. Recreations: music; books; theatre; netsuke; cartophily. Address: (h.) 11 Ramsay Garden, Edinburgh EH1 2NA; T.-0131-225 8070.

Clark, Alex. Member, Board of Directors, Arran Theatre and Arts Trust; Trustee: James Milne Memorial Trust, Hugh MacDiarmid Memorial Trust, Scottish Working People's History Trust; b. 2.1.22, Larkhall; m., Jessie Beveridge McCulloch; 1 s.; 1 d. Educ. Larkhall Academy. Grain miller, 1936-39; coal miner, 1939-53; political organiser, 1953-69; Scottish and Northern Ireland Secretary, British Actors Equity Association, 1969-84; created the post of STUC Arts Officer, 1985-87; founder Member, Boards, Scottish Youth Theatre, Scottish Theatre Company, Royal Lyceum Theatre Company; Glasgow Jazz Festival, Mayfest (Founder and Honorary President); also served on Boards of Pitlochry Festival Theatre and Cumbernauld Theatre Company, Scottish Ballet, Scottish Opera, Glasgow Film Theatre; Member: Scottish Arts Council's Review Committee on Scottish Theatre Company, 1987, Working Party on a National Theatre for Scotland, 1987, STUC Entertainment and Arts Committee, 1975-94. Lord Provost's Award for services to the city of Glasgow, 1987; Winner, ABSA-Goodman & Reed Elsevier Award for Services to the Arts, 1994. Recreations: reading; music; theatre; walking; gardening. Address: (h.) Ponfeigh, 8 Strathwhillan, Brodick, Isle of Arran.

Clark, Alistair Campbell, MA, LLB, WS. Formerly Senior Partner, Blackadder, Reid, Johnston (formerly Reid, Johnston, Bell & Henderson), Solicitors, Dundee; Honorary Sheriff, Tayside Central & Fife, since 1986; Chairman, Dovetail Enterprises, since 1993; Trustee, Dundee Disabled Children's Association, since 1993; Chairman, Scottish Conveyancing and Executry Services Board, since 1996; Member, Nominations Committee, Scottish Enterprise Tayside, since 1998; b. 4.3.33, Dundee; m., Evelyn M. Clark; 3 s. Educ. Grove Academy, Broughty Ferry; St. Andrews University. Dean, Faculty of Procurators and Solicitors in Dundee, 1979-81, Hon. Life Member, since 1991; President, Law Society of Scotland, 1989-90 (Council Member, since 1982); founder Chairman, Broughty Ferry Round Table; Founder President, Claverhouse Rotary Club, Dundee. Recreations: family; travel; erratic golf. Address: (b.) 34 Reform Street, Dundee; T.-01382 229222.

Clark, Amanda Jane, MHCIMA. Chief Executive, Taste of Scotland, since 1995; b. 15.9.62, Hong Kong; 1 s.; 2 d. Educ. Craigholme School, Glasgow; Napier University. Director of Sales, The George Hotel, Edinburgh, 1986; Sales, The Howard Hotel, Edinburgh, 1990; Marketing Executive, Taste of Scotland, 1994. Recreations: hillwalking; swimming. Address: (b.) Taste of Scotland, 33 Melville Street, Edinburgh EH3 7JF; T.-0131-220 1900.

Clark, Barbara E., MA, DipG. Assistant General Secretary, Scottish Secondary Teachers' Association, since 1997; b. 13.3.46, Stirling; m., John; 1 s.; 1 d. Educ. St. Modan's High School; University of Glasgow; Notre Dame College; Moray House. Alva Academy: Teacher of English, 1968-69 and 1979-85, A.P.T. Guidance, 1969-70 and 1985-90, P.T. Guidance, 1970-73; Guidance Development Officer, Central Region, 1990-93; P.T. Guidance, Bo'ness Academy, 1993-97; Education Liaison Officer, Children's Panel, 1995-96. Member, General Teaching Council, 1992-97; Vice-President then President, S.S.T.A., 1993-97. Recreations: reading; theatre; music; walking; art; travel. Address: (h.) 16 Lothian Crescent, Causewayhead, Stirling FK9 5SB; T.-01786 462968.

Clark, David Findlay, OBE, DL, MA, PhD, CPsychol, FBPsS, ARPS. Deputy Lieutenant, Banffshire, since 1992; Consulting Clinical Psychologist; former Director, Area Clinical Psychology Services, Grampian Health Board; Clinical Senior Lecturer, Department of Mental Health, Aberdeen University; b. 30.5.30, Aberdeen; m., Janet Ann Stephen; 2 d. Educ. Banff Academy; Aberdeen University. Flying Officer, RAF, 1951-53; Psychologist, Leicester Industrial Rehabilitation Unit, 1953-56; Senior, then Principal Clinical Psychologist, Leicester Area Clinical Psychology Service, and part-time Lecturer, Leicester University and Technical College, 1956-66; WHO short-term Consultant, Sri Lanka, 1977; various lecturing commitments in Canada and USA, since 1968. Honorary

Sheriff, Grampian and Highlands; former Governor, Aberdeen College of Education; Member, Grampian Children's Panel, 1970-85; Safeguarder (in terms of Social Work Scotland Act), since 1985; Past Chairman, Clinical Division, British Psychological Society. Publications: Help, Hospitals and the Handicapped, 1984; One Boy's War, 1997; book chapters and technical articles. Recreations: photography; sailing; chess; guitar playing; painting and drawing; golf; hill-walking. Address: (h.) Glendeveron, 8 Deveron Terrace, Banff AB45 1BB; T.-01261 812624.

Clark, David McNair, MA, BD. General Director, Scripture Union Scotland, since 1996; b. 26.2.48, Glasgow. Educ. Hutchesons' Grammar School; University of Glasgow. Principal Teacher of Geography, Kelso, 1975; Church of Scotland Minister, Airdrie, 1989. Recreations: outdoor pursuits – cycling and running. Address: (h.) 39 Blairbeth Road, Burnside, Glasgow G73 4JF; T.-0141-634 4256.

Clark, Derek John, BMus (Hons), DipMusEd (Hons), DRSAMD. Head of Music, Scottish Opera, since 1997; b. 22.8.55, Glasgow; m., Heather Fryer; 1 d. Educ. Dumbarton Academy; Royal Scottish Academy of Music and Drama; University of Durham; London Opera Centre. Debut as professional accompanist, 1976; joined music staff, Welsh National Opera, 1977, conducting debut 1982; Guest Conductor, Mid Wales Opera, 1989-92; Guest Coach and Conductor, Welsh College of Music, 1990-97; Conductor, South Wales Opera, 1994-96; Guest Coach, RSAMD, since 1997; arranger/composer since late 1980s including radio and television; musicals for young people: The Mowgli Musical, The Witch of Mawddwy; operas for young people: Hardlock House, The Forest Child. Silver Medallist, Worshipful Company of Musicians, 1976. Recreation: reading. Address: (b.) Scottish Opera, 39 Elmbank Crescent, Glasgow G2 4PT; T.-0141-248 4567.

Clark, Professor Frank, CBE, MHSM, DipHSM. Director, Strathcarron Hospice, since 1996; Honorary Professor, University of Stirling, since 1997; Visiting Professor, Glasgow Caledonian University, since 1993; Board Member, New Lanarkshire Ltd., since 1994; Member, Council of Management, Scottish Partnership Agency, since 1998; Chairman, Scottish Hospices Forum, since 1998; Director, b. 17.10.46, Aberdeen; m., Linda Margaret; 2 d. Educ. Aberdeen Academy. Greater Glasgow Health Board: Assistant District Administrator, 1977-81, District General Administrator, 1981-83; Lanarkshire Health Board: Director of Administrative Services, 1983-84, Secretary, 1984-85; General Manager, Lanarkshire Health Board, 1985-96; Chairman, Scottish Health Board General Managers Group, 1993-95 (Vice-Chairman, 1995-97). Recreations: reading; music; gardening; driving; swimming; DIY; poetry. Address: (b.) Strathcarron Hospice, Randolph Hill, Denny FK6 5HJ; T.-1324 826222.

Clark, Graham M. BSc, PhD, CChem, FRSC, FIMgt, FRSA. Principal, Falkirk College of Further and Higher Education, since 1992; b. 2.8.41, Dumfries; m., Linda A.; 3 d. Educ. George Watson's College, Edinburgh; Edinburgh University. Research Fellow, Hull University, 1966-67; Lecturer, Huddersfield Polytechnic, 1967-79; Head of Applied Science, North East Surrey College of Technology, 1980-85; Deputy Director, Nene College, Northampton, 1986-89; Principal, Angus College of Further Education, 1990-92. Editor, Thermal Analysis Reviews and Abstracts, 1986-93. Recreations: golf; hill walking; UK philately. Address: (b.) Falkirk College of Further and Higher Education, Grangemouth Road, Falkirk FK2 9AD; T.-01324 403203.

Clark, Guy Wyndham Nial Hamilton, JP, DL. Deputy Lieutenant, Renfrewshire, since 1987; Managing Director (Glasgow), Murray Johnstone Private Investors Ltd., since 1997; b. 28.3.44; m., Brighid Lovell Greene; 2 s.; 1 d. Educ. Eton. Commd. Coldstream Guards, 1962-67; Investment Manager, Murray Johnstone Ltd., Glasgow, 1973-77; Partner, R.C. Greig & Co. (Stockbrokers), Glasgow, 1977-86; Director, Greig, Middleton & Co. Ltd., 1986-97. Member, Executive Committee, Erskine Hospital; Chairman, JP Advisory Committee, since 1991. Recreations: hunting; shooting; fishing; racing. Address: (h.) Braeton, Inverkip PA16 0DU; T.-01475 520 619.

Clark, John Kenneth, BA (Hons), MA. Glasspainter; b. 1.12.57, Dumbarton. Educ. Dumbarton Academy; Glasgow School of Art. Commissions include: Cafe Gandolfi, Glasgow (Saltire Award); Paisley Abbey (Saltire Award); Heaton Memorial Window, Ledbury; Lockerbie Memorial Window; Queens Park Synagogue, Glasgow; Beirut Hostages Windows, Broxted; St Petrus Worms — Herrnsheim; St. Konrad, Amberg-Ammersricht; University of Strathclyde Bicentenary Windows; Oakshaw Trinity, Paisley; Pibroch Windows, The Piping Centre, Glasgow; Millennium Window for Glasgow Cathedral. Address: (h.) 11A Maxwell Drive, Glasgow G41 5DR; T.-0141-429 0987.

Clark, Karen, MA (Hons). Presenter, BBC Radio Scotland, since 1990; b. 11.10.58, Carlisle; m., Dr. Iain Hutchison; 2 s. Educ. Grange Academy, Kilmarnock; University of Edinburgh; University College, Cardiff. News Reporter, Radio Tay, 1981-82; News Reporter, Presenter, Consumer Programme, Radio Forth, 1982-83; News Reporter, LBC, 1984-85; Editor, Capital Radio, 1985-88; Producer, Good Morning Scotland, 1989-90; Presenter: Good Morning Scotland, Newsdrive, 1990-94; The Slice, since 1994, Now You're Talking, since 1997, Radio Scotland. New York Radio Society Award for coverage of London hurricane, 1987. Recreations: fishing; fitness; my family. Address: (b.) BBC Scotland, Beechgrove Terrace, Aberdeen AB15 5ZT; T.-01224 625233.

Clark, M. Lynda, QC. MP (Labour), Edinburgh Pentlands, since 1997. Admitted Advocate, 1977; called to English Bar, 1988; contested Fife North East (Labour), 1992. Address: (b.) House of Commons, London, SW1A 0AA.

Clark, Pamela Ann Dean, LLB (Hons). Head of Policy, The Highland Council; b. 18.10.60, Inverness. Educ. Lossiemouth High School; Edinburgh University; Aberdeen College of Education. Welfare Benefits Adviser, Central Regional Council; Legal Services Adviser, Citizens Advice Scotland; Director, Tenant Participation Advisory Service; Executive Director, Highland Community Care Forum. Former Member: Scottish Homes Board, Scottish Homes Advisory Committee on Housing Information and Advice, Commission on the Future of the Voluntary Sector in Scotland; Member, Scottish New Deal Advisory Task Force. Recreations: Irish wolfhound; swimming; cinema. Address: (h.) 8 Burnfarm Cottages, Killen, Avoch, Ross-shire.

Clark, Susan M. BSc, MBA, SecDip. Director of Corporate Affairs, ScottishPower, since 1995; b. Chesterfield; m., Richard Roberts. Educ. Manchester University; Heriot Watt University. Joined ScottishPower 1992. Recreation: hill-walking. Address: ScottishPower, 1 Atlantic Quay, Glasgow G2; T.-0141-636 4560.

Clarke, Alan, BSc, MSc. Chief Executive, Aberdeen and Grampian Tourist Board, since 1997; b. 10.4.51, Lurgan, Northern Ireland; m., Mary; 1 d. Educ. Lurgan College; University of Ulster; University of Strathclyde. Northern Ireland Tourist Board, 1974-77; Gwent County Council, 1979-85; Head of Tourism, Devon Tourism, 1985-90; Director, Marketing and Membership, Edinburgh Tourist Board/Edinburgh and Lothians Tourist Board, 1990-97. Recreations: watching sport; gardening; photography; watercolours. Address: (b.) 27 Albyn Place, Aberdeen AB101 YL; T.-01224 288800.

Clarke, (Christopher) Michael, BA (Hons), FRSA. Keeper, National Gallery of Scotland, since 1987; b. 29.8.52, York; m., Deborah Clare Cowling; 2 s.; 1 d. Educ. Felsted School, Essex; Manchester University. Art Assistant, York City Art Gallery, 1973-76; Research Assistant, British Museum, 1976-78; Assistant Keeper in charge of prints, Whitworth Art Gallery, Manchester, 1978-84; Assistant Keeper, National Gallery of Scotland, 1984-87. Visiting Fellow, Yale Center for British Art, 1985. Publications include: The Tempting Prospect; A Social History of English Watercolours; The Arrogant Connoisseur (Co-Editor); Richard Payne Knight; Lighting Up the Landscape – French Impressionism and its Origins; Corot and the Art of Landscape; Eyewitness Art – Watercolours; Corot, Courbet und die Maler von Barbizon (Co-Editor). Recreations: listening to music; tennis; golf. Address: (b.) National Gallery of Scotland, The Mound, Edinburgh EH2 2EL; T.-0131-556 8921.

Clarke, Eric Lionel. MP (Labour), Midlothian, since 1992; b. 9.4.33, Edinburgh; m., June; 2 s.; 1 d. Educ. Holy Cross Academy; W.M. Ramsey Technical College; Esk Valley Technical College. Coal miner, 1949-77; General Secretary, NUM Scottish Area, 1977-89; County Councillor, Midlothian, 1962-74; Regional Councillor, Lothian, 1974-78. Recreations: fly fishing; gardening; carpentry. Address: (h.) 32 Mortonhall Park Crescent, Edinburgh; T.-0131-654 1585.

Clarke, Professor Joseph Andrew, BSc, PhD. Professor, Environmental Engineering, University of Strathclyde, since 1991; Director, Energy Systems Research Unit, since 1987; President, International Building Performance Simulation Association, since 1994; b. 6.3.52, Glasgow; m., Kathryn Ann Clarke; 1 s.; 2 d. Educ. Whitehill Senior Secondary School; University of Strathclyde. SERC (now EPSRC) Research Fellow, 1977-79; SERC Senior Research Fellow, 1979-83; SERC Advanced Research Fellow, 1983-87; Personal Professorship, 1987; Director: Environmental Engineering, 1991, Energy Systems and the Environment MSc, 1988. Royal Society Esso Energy Award, 1989. Publication: Energy Simulation in Building Design, 1985. Recreation: running. Address: (b.) ESRU, Department of Mechanical Engineering, University of Strathclyde, Glasgow G1 1XJ; T.-0141-548 3986.

Clarke, Kevin John, BA. Secretary, University of Stirling, since 1995; b. 8.3.52, Reading; m., Linda Susan Stewart; 2 d. Educ. Presentation College, Reading; University of Stirling. Scientific Officer, British Library Lending Division, 1975-77; Administrative Assistant, Loughborough University, 1977-83; Assistant Registrar, University of Newcastle upon Tyne, 1983-85; Clerk to the Senatus Academicus, 1985-89, Deputy Secretary, 1989-95, University of Aberdeen. Recreations: music; hill-walking; gardening. Address: (b.) University of Stirling, Stirling FK9 4LA; T.-01786 467018.

Clarke, Martin Peter; Editor-in-Chief, Scottish Daily Record and Sunday Mail Ltd., since 1998; b. 26.8.64, Dartford. Educ. Bristol University. Various positions, Daily Mail, 1986-95; News Editor, The Mirror, 1995; Editor: Scottish Daily Mail, 1995-97, The Scotsman, 1997-98. Recreations: football; newspapers. Address: (b.) Daily Record, 40 Anderston Quay, Glasgow G3 8DA; T.-0141-248 7000.

Clarke, Owen J., CBE. Chairman, Scottish Ambulance Service, since 1997; b. 15.3.37, Edinburgh; m., Elizabeth; 2 s.; 1 d. Educ. Portobello High School, Edinburgh. Head of Inland Revenue, North of England, 1988-90; Head of Inland Revenue, Scotland, 1990-97. Director, Friends of Craigmillar, since 1994. Recreations: jogging; golf; hill-walking. Address: (h.) dyngarth, Redholm Park, North Berwick EH39 4RA; T.-01620 892623.

Clarke, Peter, CBE, BSc, PhD, LLD (Hon), CChem, FRSC, DEd(Hon), FInstPet. President, Association for Educational and Training Technology, 1993-95; Chairman, Industrial Training Centre, Aberdeen, 1989-95; b. 18.3.22, Mansfield; m., Ethel; 2 s. Educ. Queen Elizabeth's Grammar School, Mansfield; University College, Nottingham. Principal, Robert Gordon's Institute of Technology, Aberdeen, 1970-85. Chairman: Scottish Vocational Education Council, 1985-91, Aberdeen Enterprise Trust, 1984-92; President, Association of Principals of Colleges, 1980-81; Member, Science and Engineering Research Council, 1978-82; Trustee, Gordon Cook Foundation, since 1988 (Chairman, since 1997). Recreations: walking; gardening. Address: (h.) Dunaber, 12 Woodburn Place, Aberdeen, AB15 8JR; T.-01224 311132.

Clarke, Professor Roger John, ALCM, BA, BTech, MSc, PhD, CEng, MIEE, MIEEE. Professor of Electronic Engineering, Heriot Watt University, since 1989; b. 1.10.40, Ewell, Surrey; m., Yvonne Clarke; 1 s. Educ. Gravesend Grammar School; Loughborough University. Development Engineer, STC Ltd., Woolwich, 1962-64; Research Associate, then Lecturer in Electrical Engineering, Loughborough University, 1964-86; Reader in Electrical Engineering, Heriot Watt University, 1986-89. Recreations: gardening; playing the cello; Shakespeare. Address: (b.) Department of Computing and Electrical Engineering, Heriot Watt University, Riccarton, Edinburgh EH14 4AS; T.-0131-451 3323.

Clarke, Rt. Hon. Thomas, CBE, JP. Minister for Film and Tourism; MP (Labour), Monklands West, since 1983; Shadow Secretary of State for Scotland, 1992-93; b. 10.1.41, Coatbridge. Educ. Columba High School, Coatbridge. Former Assistant Director, Scottish Council for Educational Technology; Provost of Monklands, 1975-82; Past President, Convention of Scottish Local Authorities; MP, Coatbridge and Airdrie, 1982-83; author, Disabled Persons (Services Consultation and Representation) Act, 1986; elected four times to Shadow Cabinet; director, amateur film, Give Us a Goal. Recreations: films; walking; reading. Address: (h.) 37 Blairhill Street, Coatbridge ML5 1PG; T.-01236 600800.

Clarkson, Professor Euan Neilson Kerr, MA, PhD, DSc, FRSE. Professor of Palaeontology, University of Edinburgh, since 1998 (Reader, 1981-98); b. 9.5.37; m., Cynthia; 4 s. Educ. Shrewsbury School; Emmanuel College, University of Cambridge. University of Edinburgh: Assistant Lecturer, 1963-65, Lecturer, 1965-78, Senior Lecturer, 1978-81, Director of Studies, 1967-73 and since 1995, Associate Dean, Science Faculty, 1978-81; many university committees. Trustee, Natural History Museum, 1987-92. President: Edinburgh Geological Society, 1983-87, Palaeontological Association, since 1998; Clough Medal, 1993; Keith Medal, 1994. Publications: Invertebrate Palaeontology and Evolution; 80 scientific articles. Recreations: classical music; hillwalking; writing; painting; wine. Address: (b.) Department of Geology and Geophysics, University of Edinburgh, West Mains Road, Edinburgh EH9 3JW.

Clarkson, Graeme Andrew Telford, LLB. Senior Partner, Baird & Company, Solicitors, Kirkcaldy, since 1990; b. 6.9.53, Fraserburgh; m., Moira; 3 s. Educ. High School of Dundee; Aberdeen University. Law Apprentice, Allan MacDougall & Co., Edinburgh; Assistant, Ranken & Reid, Edinburgh; Assistant, then Partner, Baird & Company. Past Chairman, Kirkcaldy Round Table; Council Member, Law Society of Scotland. Address: (b.) 2 Park Place, Kirkcaldy Fife; T.-01592 268608.

Cleall, Charles, MA(Wales), BMus(Lond), ADCM, FRCO(CHM), GTCL, LRAM, HonTSC. Author and Writer; Tutor in Speech-Training, Scottish Congregational College, and Scottish Churches' Open College, Napier

University; b. 1.6.27, Heston, Middlesex; m., Mary Turner; 2 d. Educ. Hampton School, Middlesex; Trinity College of Music; London University; Jordanhill College of Education, Glasgow; University College of North Wales. Organist and Choirmaster, St. Luke's, Chelsea, 1945-46; Command Music Adviser to Royal Navy, Plymouth Command (Instr. Lieut., RN) 1946-48; Professor of Solo Singing and Voice Production, and of ear-training and of choral repertoire, Trinity College of Music, London, 1949-52; Choral Scholar, Westminster Abbey, 1949-52; Organist and Choirmaster, Wesley's Chapel, City Road, London, 1950-52; Conductor, Morley College Orchestra, 1950-52; Conductor, Glasgow Choral Union, 1952-54; BBC Music Assistant, Midland Region, 1954-55; Music Master, Glyn County School, Ewell, 1955-66; Conductor, Aldeburgh Festival Choir, 1957-60; Organist and Choirmaster: St. Paul's, Portman Square, W1, 1957-61, Holy Trinity, Guildford, 1961-65; Lecturer in Music, The Froebel Institute, Roehampton, 1967-68; Adviser in Music, London Borough of Harrow, 1968-72; Northern Divisional music specialist, HM Inspectorate of Schools in Scotland, 1972-87; Editor, Journal, Ernest George White Society, 1983-88; has given many lectures on singing and choir training. Limpus Fellowship Prizeman, Royal College of Organists; International Composition Prizeman, Cathedral of St. John the Divine, New York. Publications: Voice Production in Choral Technique, 1955/1970; The Selection and Training of Mixed Choirs in Churches, 1960; Sixty Songs from Sankey, 1960 and 1966; John Merbecke's Music for the Congregation at Holy Communion, 1963; Music and Holiness, 1964; Plainsong for Pleasure, 1969; Authentic Chanting, 1969; A Guide to Vanity Fair, 1982; Walking round the Church of St. James the Great, Stonehaven, 1993; scores of articles and book reviews. Recreations: writing; reading; natural history; walking. Address: (h.) 10 Carronhall, Stonehaven, Aberdeen AB39 2QF.

Clements, Professor John Barklie, BSc, PhD, FRSE. Professor of Virology, Glasgow University, since 1995; b. 14.3.46, Belfast. Educ. Belfast Royal Academy; Queen's University, Belfast. Research Fellow, California Institute of Technology, 1971-73; joined Institute of Virology, Glasgow University, 1973; Cancer Research Campaign Travelling Fellow, Department of Biochemistry and Molecular Biology, Harvard University, 1983; Council Member, Society for General Microbiology, 1984-88; Member, MRC Physiological Systems and Disorders Board, 1990-94; Chairman, Grants Committee B, PMIB, 1992-94; Member, Clinical and Biomedical Research Committee, Scottish Home and Health Department, 1990-93. Recreations: walking; golf; music. Address: (b.) Institute of Virology, Glasgow University, Glasgow; T.-0141-330 4027.

Clemson, Gareth, BMus (Auckland), BMus (Edinburgh). Composer; teaches violin and piano at home since retiring in 1994 ; b. 1.10.33, Thames, New Zealand; m., Thora Clyne; 2 s.; 1 d. Educ. St. Peter's School, New Zealand; King's College, New Zealand; Auckland University; Edinburgh University. Music teaching, New Zealand, Edinburgh and West Lothian, 1960-75; String Teacher, West Lothian, 1975-85, Fife Region, since 1985; lessons in composition from Thomas Wilson, 1963-65; chamber works including Nexus I and II, Waters of Separation, The Singing Cat, Invocation; broadcasts, New Zealand and Scotland; recent compositions, Trumpet in the Dust, Blackbird, General Reid's Garb of Old Gaul, two versions (piano and orchestral); Flight of the Kiwi; Pandura (orchestral); Pandura Turning (viola and piano); Rounding the Score (chamber ensemble); Six Repartitions for Solo Viola. Recreations: reading, photography; cats. Address: (h.) Tillywhally Cottage, Milnathort, Kinross-shire KY13 7RN; T.-Kinross 864297.

Clerk of Penicuik, Sir John Dutton, 10th Bt, CBE (1966), VRD, FRSE, JP. Lord Lieutenant of Midlothian, 1972-92; Commodore RNR (Retd); b. 30.1.17; m.; 2 s.; 2 d. Educ. Stowe. Lieutenant, Queen's Bodyguard for Scotland (Royal Company of Archers). Address: (h.) Penicuik House, Penicuik, Midlothian EH26 9LA.

Clifford, Nigel Richard, MA (Cantab), DipInstM, DipCAM, MBA, FIMgmt, FRSA. Chief Executive, Glasgow Royal Infirmary University NHS Trust, since 1994; b. 22.6.59, Emsworth; m., Jeanette; 2 s.; 1 d. Educ. Portsmouth Grammar School; Downing College, Cambridge; Strathclyde University. British Telecom, 1981-92, latterly as Head of Business Strategy, BT Mobile Communications. Founding Trustee, Herald Foundation for Women's Health. Recreations: family life; walking; swimming; running. Address: (b.) 84 Castle Street, Glasgow, G4 0SF; T.-0141-211 4924.

Clifford, Timothy Peter Plint, BA, AMA, LLD, FRSA, FSAScot. Director, National Galleries of Scotland, since 1984; b. 26.1.46; m., Jane Olivia Paterson; 1 d. Educ. Sherborne; Perugia University; Courtauld Institute, London University. Manchester City Art Galleries: Assistant Keeper, Department of Paintings, 1968-72, Acting Keeper, 1972; Assistant Keeper, Department of Ceramics, Victoria and Albert Museum, London, 1972-76; Assistant Keeper, British Art, Department of Prints and Drawings, British Museum, London, 1976-78; Director, Manchester City Art Galleries, 1978-84. Chairman, International Committee for Museums of Fine Art (ICOM), 1980-83; Member, Museums and Galleries Commission, 1983-88; Member, Board, British Council, 1987-92; Member, Executive Committee, Scottish Museums Council; Vice President, Turner Society, 1984-86 and since 1989; Vice-President, Frigate Unicorn Preservation Society, since 1987; British Institute of Management's Special Award, 1991; Member, Ateneo Veneto (Italy), since 1997. Cavaliere all'Ordine del Merito della Repubblica Italiana, since 1988; Member, Advisory Council, Friends of Courtauld Institute, since 1990; President, NADFAS, since 1996 (Vice-President, 1990-96); Trustee, the former Royal Yacht Britannia, since 1998. Recreations: shooting; bird-watching; entomology. Address: (b.) National Galleries of Scotland, The Mound, Edinburgh, EH2 2EL.

Clinkenbeard, Janette, MB, ChB, FRCGP, DRCOG. Vice-Chairman, Scottish Council, Royal College of General Practitioners, since 1991; General Practitioner, since 1981; b. 11.2.44, Glasgow; m., William Clinkenbeard; 2 s.; 1 d. Educ. Rutherglen Academy; Glasgow University. Member, UK Council, RCGP, 1990-91, 1992-95, Chairman, SES Faculty, 1990-93. Recreations: music; sport; reading. Address: Riccarton Practice, Heriot Watt University, Edinburgh; T.-0131-451 3010.

Clinkenbeard, Rev. William Ward, BSEE, BD, STM. Minister, Carrick Knowe Parish Church, Edinburgh; b., 25.8.37, Nebraska, USA; m., Janette McKay Hunter; 2 s.; 1 d. Educ. Lincoln High School; University of Nebraska; McCormick Theological Seminary; Glasgow University; Yale University. Design Engineer, General Dynamics Corporation; Parish Minister, Wood River Presbyterian Church. Publications: The Contemporary Lesson; Full on the Eye (Co-author); Mind the Gap. Address: (h.) 40A Harlaw Road, Balerno EH14 7AX; T.-0131-449 6984.

Clive, Eric McCredie, MA, LLB, LLM, SJD. Visiting Professor, Faculty of Law, Edinburgh University, since 1999; b. 24.7.38, Stranraer; m., Kay McLeman; 1 s.; 2 d. Educ. Stranraer Academy; Stranraer High School; Universities of Edinburgh, Michigan, Virginia. Lecturer, Senior Lecturer, Reader, Professor of Scots Law, Faculty of Law, Edinburgh University, 1962-81; Commissioner, Scottish Law Commission, 1981-98. Publications: The Law of Husband and Wife in Scotland (4th edition), 1997; legal articles. Address: (h.) 14 York Road, Edinburgh EH5 3EH; T.-0131-552 2875.

Closier, Michael John. Group Chief Executive, Scottish Exhibition and Conference Centre, since 1992; Non Executive Director, Greater Glasgow and Clyde Valley Tourist Board, since 1993; b. 15.2.47, London; m., Anne-Marie; 1 s. 1 step-d. Educ. Lanchester Polytechnic. Managing Director, Compuser Ltd.; Technical Director, Centronics Ltd.; Managing Director, Bix Ltd.; Director, Peerless Control Systems. Member: IoD, CBI, EVA, ICCA, Advisory Committee, Glasgow Common Purpose; Past Chair, NAEH. Recreations: fell walking; gardening; opera; cooking. Address: SECC, Glasgow G3 8YW; T.-0141-275 6210.

Clouting, David Wallis, BDS, MSc, LDSRCS (Eng), DDPH. Community Dental Services Manager, Borders Community Health Services NHS Trust, since 1995; b. 29.3.53, London; m., Dr. Margaret M.C. Bacon; 3 s.; 1 d. Educ. Leyton County High School for Boys; University College Hospital Dental School, London; Institute of Dental Surgery, London; Joint Department of Dental Public Health, London Hospital Medical College and University College. Senior Dental Officer for Special Needs, East and North Hertfordshire Health Authorities, 1983-90; Chief Administrative Dental Officer, Borders Health Board, 1990-95. Recreations: amateur radio; DIY; swimming; hill walking; sailing. Address: (b.) Borders Community Health Services NHS Trust, Clinical Services Directorate, Tweed Road, Galashiels TD1 3EB; T.-01896 758895.

Clow, Robert George Menzies. Chairman (since 1979) and Managing Director (1969-94), John Smith & Son (Glasgow) Ltd.; b. 27.1.34, Sian, Shensi, North China; m., Katrina M. Watson. Educ. Eltham College, London. Interned by Japanese as a child; National Service, RAF; trained as a bookseller, Bumpus London; worked in Geneva; joined John Smith & Son (Glasgow), 1960. Founded, with others, The New Glasgow Society, 1965 (Chairman 1967, 1968); worked for 12 years in rehabilitating St. Vincent Crescent, Glasgow, as founder member, St. Vincent Crescent Area Association; Secretary, First Glasgow Housing Association, since 1978; Director, St. Vincent Crescent Buildings Preservation Trust; restored Aiket Castle, 1976-79 (winner of an Europa Nostra Merit Award, 1989; National Trust for Scotland: elected to Council 1978 and 1991, Executive, 1980-90; Executive Member, Committee, Strathclyde Building Preservation Trust, 1986; appointed to Architectural Heritage Fund Executive, 1989. Recreations: farming; bee keeping; opera; restoring old houses; swimming; skiing; reading on holiday. Address: Aiket Castle, Dunlop, Ayrshire; T.-(b.) 0141-221 7472.

Clyde, The Rt. Hon. The Lord (James John Clyde), PC, Baron (Life Peer), DUniv (Edin), DUniv (Heriot-Watt), DLitt (Napier), BA (Oxon), LLB. Lord of Appeal in Ordinary, since 1996; Senator of the College of Justice, since 1985; b. 29.1.32, Edinburgh; m., Ann Clunie Hoblyn; 2 s. Educ. Edinburgh Academy; Corpus Christi College, Oxford; Edinburgh University. Called to Scottish Bar, 1959; QC, 1971; Advocate Depute, 1973-74; Chancellor to Bishop of Argyll and the Isles, 1972-85; a Judge of the Courts of Appeal of Jersey and Guernsey, 1979-85; Chairman: Medical Appeal Tribunal, 1974-85, Committee of Investigation for Scotland on Agricultural Marketing, 1984-85, Scottish Valuation Advisory Council, 1987-96 (Member, since 1972); Member, UK Delegation to CCBE, 1978-84 (Leader, 1981-84); Chairman of the Inquiry into the removal of children from Orkney, 1991-92. Trustee and Manager, St. Mary's Music School, 1976-93; Trustee, National Library of Scotland, 1978-94; Director, Edinburgh Academy, 1979-88; Vice-President, Royal Blind Asylum and School, since 1987; President, Scottish Young Lawyers' Association, 1988-97; Chairman, St. George's School for Girls, 1989-97; Governor, Napier Polytechnic of Edinburgh, 1989-93; Chancellor's Assessor and Vice Chairman, Court, Edinburgh University, 1993-97; Chairman, Scottish Valuation and Rating Council, since 1996. Recreations: music; gardening. Address: (h.) 12 Dublin Street, Edinburgh, EH1 3PP.

Clydesmuir, 3rd Baron (David Ronald Colville); b. 8.4.49; m.; 2 s.; 2 d. Educ. Charterhouse. Succeeded to title, 1996.

Clyne, Rev. Douglas Roy, BD. Minister, Old Parish Church, Fraserburgh, since 1973; b. 9.11.41, Inverness; m., Annette Taylor; 1 s. Educ. Inverness High School; Aberdeen University. Accountancy, Inverness County Council and Highland Printers Ltd.; studied for ministry; Assistant Minister, Mastrick Parish Church, Aberdeen. Address: (b.) Old Parish Church Manse, 97 Saltoun Place, Fraserburgh AB43 9RY; T.-01346 518536.

Coats, Sir William David, Kt, DL, HonLLD (Strathclyde), 1977. Chairman, Coats Patons PLC, 1981-86; Deputy Chairman, Clydesdale Bank PLC, 1985-93; b. 25.7.24, Glasgow; m., The Hon. Elizabeth L.G. MacAndrew; 2 s.; 1 d. Educ. Eton College. Joined J. & P. Coats Ltd., 1948, as management trainee; held various appointments and became a Director, 1957; appointed Director, Coats Patons PLC, on its formation, 1960; Deputy Chairman, 1979. Recreations: golf; shooting. Address: (h.) The Cottage, Symington, Ayrshire KA1 5QG.

Cobbe, Professor Stuart Malcolm, MA, MD, FRCP. Professor of Medical Cardiology, Glasgow University, since 1985; b. 2.5.48, Watford; m., Patricia Frances; 3 d. Educ. Royal Grammar School, Guildford; Cambridge University. Training in medicine, Cambridge and St. Thomas Hospital, London; qualified, 1972; specialist training in cardiology, National Heart Hospital, London, and John Radcliffe Hospital, Oxford; research work, University of Heidelberg, 1981; Consultant Cardiologist and Senior Lecturer, Oxford, 1982-85. Recreation: walking. Address: (b.) Department of Medical Cardiology, Queen Elizabeth Building, Royal Infirmary, Glasgow G31 2ER; T.-0141-221 4722.

Cochran, Hugh Douglas, BA (Oxon), LLB. Advocate in Aberdeen, since 1958; b. 26.4.32, Aberdeen; m., Sarah Beverly Sissons; 4 s.; 2 d. Educ. Loretto; Trinity College, Oxford; Edinburgh University. Partner: Cochran & Macpherson, 1958-80, Adam, Cochran, 1980-93; Member, Grampian Health Board, 1980-88; Chairman, Castlehill Housing Association, 1974-83. Secretary, Aberdeen Association for the Prevention of Cruelty to Animals, 1972-96; Registrar, Diocese of Aberdeen and Orkney, since 1984. Recreations: cycling; collecting stamps; archaeology. Address: 15 Golden Square, Aberdeen AB10 1WF; T.-Aberdeen 644333.

Cochrane of Cults, 4th Baron (Ralph Henry Vere Cochrane), DL; b. 20.9.26; m.; 2 s.; succeeded to title, 1990. Educ. Eton; King's College, Cambridge. Address: Cults, Cupar, KY15 5RD.

Cockburn, David William, LLB, WS, NP. Partner, Archibald Campbell and Harley WS, since 1970; b. 4.2.43, Peebles; m., Evelyn; 1 d. Educ. Peebles High School; Edinburgh University. Apprentice, Glasgow Corporation, 1964-66; Assistant: Breeze Paterson and Chapman, Glasgow, 1966-69, Archibald Campbell and Harley, WS, 1969-70; lectures widely on commercial property and planning law. Recreations: sports; hillwalking. Address: (b.) 37 Queen Street, Edinburgh EH2 1JX; T.-0131-220 3000.

Cockburn, Professor Forrester, CBE, MD, FRCPGlas, FRCPEdin, FRCPCH (Hon), DCH. Emeritus Professor and Senior Research Fellow, Department of Child Health, Royal Hospital for Sick Children, Yorkhill, Glasgow; formerly Samson Gemmell Professor of Child Health, Glasgow University; b. 13.10.34, Edinburgh; m., Alison Fisher

Grieve; 2 s. Educ. Leith Academy; Edinburgh University. Early medical training, Edinburgh Royal Infirmary, Royal Hospital for Sick Children, Edinburgh, and Simpson Memorial Maternity Pavilion, Edinburgh; Research Fellow in Paediatric Metabolic Disease, Boston University; Visiting Professor, San Juan University, Puerto Rico; Nuffield Fellow, Institute for Medical Research, Oxford University; Wellcome Senior Research Fellow, then Senior Lecturer, Department of Child Life and Health, Edinburgh University. Publications: a number of textbooks on paediatric medicine, neonatal medicine, nutrition and metabolic diseases. Recreation: sailing. Address: (b.) University Department of Child Health, Royal Hospital for Sick Children, Yorkhill Glasgow, G3 8SJ; T.-0141-201 0236.

Cockburn, James Masson Thomson, BSc (Hons), CEng, FICE, FIWEM, FIWO. Managing Director, Water Services, North of Scotland Water Authority; b. 22.1.47, Aberdeen; m., Avril; 2 s. Educ. Robert Gordon's College; Dundee University. Assistant Engineer, East of Scotland Water Board, 1969-75; Assistant Divisional Manager (Dundee), Department of Water Services, Tayside Regional Council, 1975-76; Assistant Director, Department of Water and Sewerage, Dumfries and Galloway Regional Council, 1976-79; Depute Director, Department of Water Services, Grampian Regional Council, 1979-88; Director of Water Services, Grampian Regional Council, 1988-95. Past President, Scottish Section, Institution of Water Engineers and Scientists; Member of Council, Institution of Water and Environmental Management, 1987-91; President, Scottish Area Institution of Water Officers, 1994-95; Secretary, Scottish Association of Directors of Water and Sewerage, 1989-96; Chairman, Scottish Association of Directors of Water and Sewerage Services, 1995-96. Recreations: hill-walking; sailing; skiing; curling; Rotary. Address: (b.) North of Scotland Water Authority, Cairngorm House, Beechwood Park North, Inverness IV2 3ED; T.-01463 245427.

Cocker, Douglas, DA, ARSA, FRBS. Sculptor; b. 23.3.45, Alyth, Perthshire; m., Elizabeth Filshie; 2 s.; 1 d. Educ. Blairgowrie High School; Duncan of Jordanstone College of Art, Dundee. SED Travelling Scholar, Italy and Greece, 1966; RSA Andrew Carnegie Travelling Scholar, 1967; RSA Benno Schotz Award, 1967; Greenshields Foundation (Montreal) Fellowship, 1968-69 (studies in New York and Greece); RSA Latimer Award, 1970; Arts Council of GB Award, 1977; East Midlands Arts Award, 1979; Scottish Arts Council Major Bursary, 1989; Lecturer in Sculpture, Grays School of Art, Aberdeen, 1982-90; Essex Fine Art Fellowship, 1991-92; Visiting Artist: Newcastle Polytechnic, Duncan of Jordanstone College of Art, Edinburgh College of Art, Glasgow Art College and Tyler University, Philadelphia. Numerous solo and group exhibitions; various major public commissions. Recreations: reading; travel; sport. Address: (h.) Lundie Mill, Lundie, Angus DD2 5NW.

Cockhead, Peter, BSc (Econ), MA, MSc, MRTPI. Director of Planning and Strategic Development, Aberdeen City Council, since 1995; Chairman, Scottish Society of Directors of Planning, since 1997; b. 1.12.46, Beckenham; m., Diana; 2 s.; 1 d. Educ. Beckenham Grammar School; London School of Economics; University of Witwatersrand, South Africa; University of Edinburgh. Lecturer: University of Witwatersrand, 1970-71, University of Edinburgh, 1973-74; Consultant: OECD, Paris, 1974, Percy Johnson-Marshall and Associates, Edinburgh, 1974-75; Grampian Regional Council: Assistant Director of Planning, 1975-83, Depute Director of Planning, 1983-90, Regional Planning Manager, 1990-95. Recreations: hillwalking; swimming; squash; family. Address: (h.) 158 Midstocket Road, Aberdeen AB15 5HT; T.-01224 522270.

Cocozza, Mario G., BSc (Econ). Director of Corporate Services, East Dunbartonshire Council, since 1997; b. 11.1.51, Glasgow. Educ. St. Thomas Aquinas School, Glasgow; University of London. Strathclyde Regional Council, 1975-95 (with specific responsibilities for issues within the Glasgow division, including Chair, Citywatch CCTV Initiative); East Dunbartonshire Council: Interim Clerk, 1995, Assistant Chief Executive, 1995. Director, Centre for Contemporary Arts, Glasgow. Recreations: reading; walking. Address: (b.) Tom Johnston House, Civic Way, Kirkintilloch G66 4TJ; T.-0141-578 8000.

Coffey, Daniel, JP. Councillor, East Ayrshire; Provost, Kilmarnock and Loudoun District, 1992-96; SNP Group Leader and Leader of the Opposition: Strathclyde Regional Council, 1994-96, East Ayrshire Council, since 1995; b. 19.7.54, Kilmarnock. Educ. St. Joseph's, Kilmarnock. SNP Group Leader: Kilmarnock and Loudoun District, 1988-92, Strathclyde Regional Council, 1986-90; Member, Justices Committee, East Ayrshire; Member, European Committee of the Regions; Bureau Member and Treasurer, European Alliance Group; Convener, Convention of Scottish Local Authorities SNP Group, 1992-96; Member, SNP National Executive, National Council and National Assembly; SNP Depute Spokesperson, Europe and Foreign Affairs; Convener, Association of Nationalist Councillors; Treasurer: Kilmarnock FC Supporters Association, Kilmarnock FC Supporters Travel Club; Hon. President: Burns Federation, Kilmarnock Amateur Operatic Society. Recreations: football supporter; marathon runner; Burns. Address: (h.) 7 Craufurdland Road, Kilmarnock, KA3 2HT; T.-01563 531916; (b.) East Ayrshire Council, London Road Centre, London Road, Kilmarnock KA3 7BU; T.-01563 576055.

Cogdell, Professor Richard John, BSc, PhD, FRSE. Hooker Professor of Botany, Glasgow University, since 1993; b. 4.2.49, Guildford; m., Barbara; 1 s.; 1 d. Educ. Royal Grammar School, Guildford; Bristol University. Post-doctoral research, USA, 1973-75; Botany Department, Glasgow University, 1975-94, now Institute of Biomedical and Life Sciences. Recreations: cricket; aerobics; Scottish dancing; theatre. Address: (b.) Division of Biochemistry and Molecular Biology, Glasgow University, Glasgow G12 8QQ; T.-0141-330 4232.

Coggins, Professor John Richard, MA, PhD, FRSE. Professor of Enzymology and Director of Research, Institute of Biomedical and Life Sciences, Glasgow University, since 1998; b. 15.1.44, Bristol; m., Dr. Lesley F. Watson; 1 s.; 1 d. Educ. Bristol Grammar School; Queen's College, Oxford; Ottawa University. Post-doctoral Fellow: Biology Department, Brookhaven National Laboratory, New York, 1970-72, Biochemistry Department, Cambridge University, 1972-74; Biochemistry Department, Glasgow University: Lecturer/Senior Lecturer/Professor, 1974-95; Director, Graduate School of Biomedical and Life Sciences, Glasgow University, 1995-97; Head, Division of Biochemistry and Molecular Biology, Glasgow University, 1997-98. Chairman: Molecular Enzymology Group, Biochemical Society, 1982-85, Biophysics and Biochemistry Committee, SERC, 1985-88; Managing Director, Biomac Ltd., 1988-94; Member, DTI-Research Councils Biotechnology Joint Advisory Board, 1989-94; Member of Council, AFRC, 1991-94; Biochemistry Adviser to UFC, 1989-92; Member of Council, Hannah Research Institute, since 1994; Governing Member, Caledonian Research Foundation, since 1994; Chairman, HEFC Research Assessment Panel for Biochemistry, 1995-96. Recreations: sailing; travelling. Address: (b.) Research Office, IBLS, West Medical Building, Glasgow University, Glasgow G12 8QQ; T.-0141-330 5267.

Cohen, Professor Anthony Paul, BA, MSc (SocSc), PhD, FRSE. Professor of Social Anthropology, Edinburgh University, since 1989; Provost of Law and Social Sciences,

Dean, Social Sciences, Edinburgh University, since 1997; Convener, Scottish Forum for Graduate Education, 1996-98; b. 3.8.46, London; m., Dr. Bronwen J. Cohen; 3 s. Educ. Whittingehame Collge, Brighton; Southampton University. Assistant Professor, Queen's University, Kingston, Ontario, 1970-71; Lecturer/Senior Lecturer in Social Anthropology, Manchester University, 1971-89. Publications: The Management of Myths; The Symbolic Construction of Community; Whalsay: Symbol, Segment and Boundary in a Shetland Island Community; Self Consciousness: an alternative anthropology of identity; Belonging (Editor); Symbolising Boundaries (Editor); Humanising the City? (Co-Editor); Questions of Consciousness (Co-Editor). Recreations: occasional thinking; music; novels. Address: (b.) 55 George Square, Edinburgh EH8 9JH; T.-0131-650 4089.

Cohen, Cyril, OBE, JP, FRCPEdin, FRCPGlas. Honorary Fellow, Dundee University; retired Consultant Physician, Geriatric Medicine, and Hon. Senior Lecturer, Geriatric Medicine, Dundee University; Chairman, Angus Community Care Forum; b. 2.11.25, Manchester; m., Dr. Sarah E. Nixon; 2 s. Educ. Manchester Central High School; Victoria University, Manchester. Embarked on career in geriatric medicine, 1952. Past President, Forfarshire Medical Association; former Chairman, Advisory Group on Health Education for Elderly People, Health Education Board for Scotland; former Member/Chairman, Angus District and Tayside Area Medical Committees; Secretary/Chairman, Tayside Area Hospital Medical Services Committee; Member, Scottish and UK Central Committee, Hospital Medical Services, and Chairman, Geriatric Medicine Sub-committee; Past Chairman, Scottish Branch, British Geriatric Society (former Council Member); Member, Panel on Nutrition of the Elderly, COMA; Honorary Vice-President, Dundee and District Branch, British Diabetic Association; Life Member, Manchester Medical Society; former Member, Chief Scientist's Committee for Research on Equipment for the Disabled and Health Services Research Committee; Chairman, Angus Access Panel; Director, Angus Community Care Charitable Trust; Director, Angus Care and Repair; Member, Angus Joint Planning Group, Care in the Community; Member, Angus SVQ Management Committee; Chairman, Radio North Angus (Hospital Radio); former Member, Brechin and Forfar School Councils, Forfar Academy School Board and Central Committee on Primary Education; Secretary, Aberlemno Community Council; Vice-Chairman, Angus Association of Voluntary Organisations and Member, Brechin Day Care Centre Committee; former Director, Scottish Hospital Advisory Service; Past President, Montrose Burns Club and Brechin Arts Guild; Member, League of Friends, Forfar Hospitals; Past Chairman, Angus Care of the Elderly Group. Publications: many on geriatric medicine and care of the elderly. Recreations: photography; short walks; being at home. Address: (h.) Mansefield, Aberlemno, Forfar DD8 3PD; T.-0130-783 259.

Cohen, George Cormack, MA, LLB. Advocate; b. 16.12.09, Glasgow; m., Elizabeth Wallace; 1 s.; 1 d. Educ. Kelvinside Academy, Glasgow; Glasgow University. Admitted to Faculty of Advocates, 1935; Sheriff of Caithness at Wick, 1944-51; Sheriff of Ayrshire at Kilmarnock, 1951-55; Sheriff of Lothians and Peebles at Edinburgh, 1955-66. Recreations: gardening; travel. Address: (h.) 37B Lauder Road, Edinburgh EH9 1UE; T.-0131-668 1689.

Cohen, Patricia Townsend Wade, BSc, PhD. Head of Molecular Biology and Special Appointments Scientist, Medical Research Council Protein Phosphorylation Unit, Department of Biochemistry, Dundee University; b. 3.5.44, Worsley, Lancashire; m., Professor Philip Cohen (qv); 1 s.; 1 d. Educ. Bolton School; University College, London. Postdoctoral Research Fellow, Department of Medical Genetics, Washington University, Seattle, USA, 1969-71; Department of Biochemistry, Dundee University: Science Research Council Fellowship, 1971-72, Research/Teaching Fellow (part-time), 1972-83, Lecturer (part-time), 1983-90, Senior Lecturer, 1990-91, Reader, 1995. Publications: 120 papers and reviews in scientific journals. Recreations: reading; skiing; golf. Address: (h.) Inverbay II, Invergowrie, Dundee DD2 5DQ; T.-01382 562328.

Cohen, Professor Sir Philip, BSc, PhD, FRS, FRSE, FRSA. Royal Society Research Professor, University of Dundee, since 1984 and Director, Wellcome Trust Building, since 1997; Honorary Director, Medical Research Council Protein Phosphorylation Unit, since 1990; b. 22.7.45, London; m., Patricia Townsend Wade (qv); 1 s.; 1 d. Educ. Hendon County Grammar School; University College, London. Science Research Council/NATO postdoctoral Fellow, Department of Biochemistry, University of Washington, 1969-71; Dundee University: Lecturer in Biochemistry, 1971-78, Reader in Biochemistry, 1978-81, Professor of Enzymology, 1981-84. Publications: 380 papers and reviews, one book. Recreations: bridge; golf; natural history. Address: (h.) Inverbay II, Invergowrie, Dundee; T.-01382 562328.

Coid, Donald Routledge, MSc, BMedSci, BM, BS, FRACMA, FAFPHM, FRCPEdin, FFPHM, FRIPHH. Consultant in Health Services Research, Department of Epidemiology, Dundee University, since 1998; Chief Administrative Medical Officer and Director of Public Health, Tayside Health Board, since 1994; b. 13.6.53, Wallingford; m., Susan Kathleen Ramus Crocker; 3 d. Educ. Bromley Grammar School for Boys; Harrow County School for Boys; Nottingham University; London University. Field Medical Officer, Royal Flying Doctor Service of Australia, 1979-80; Medical Officer, Community Health Services, Western Australia, 1981-82; Regional Director of Public Health, Eastern Goldfields, Western Australia, 1982-85; Medical Superintendent, Kalgoorie Regional Hospital, 1984-85; Fife Health Board: Consultant in Public Health, 1985-92; Assistant General Manager, 1992-93. Recreations: golf; singing; cricket; piano. Address: (h.) 90 Hepburn Gardens, St. Andrews KY16 9LN; T.-01334 472710.

Cole-Hamilton, Arthur Richard, CBE, BA, CA, FIB(Scot). Non-Executive Director, Stakis plc (former Chairman); b. 8.5.35, Kilwinning; m., Prudence Ann; 1 s.; 2 d. Educ. Ardrossan Academy; Loretto School; Cambridge University. Partner, Brechin Cole-Hamilton & Co., CA, 1962-67; various appointments, Clydesdale Bank, 1967-82; appointed Chief Executive, 1982, Director, 1984; retired, 1992. Former Council Member, Institute of Chartered Accountants of Scotland (Chairman, Finance and General Purposes Committee, 1981-85); Chairman, Committee of Scottish Clearing Bankers, 1991-92; President, Institute of Bankers in Scotland, 1988-90; former Chairman, Scottish Council (Development and Industry); Director, Glasgow Chamber of Commerce, 1985-91; Trustee: National Galleries of Scotland, 1986-96, Princess Royal Trust for Carers; former Chairman, General Committee, Royal and Ancient Golf Club of St Andrews. Recreation: golf. Address: (h.) 26 Lady Margaret Drive, Troon KA10 7AL; T.-01292 311338.

Cole-Hamilton, Professor David John, BSc, PhD, CChem, FRSC, FRSE. Irvine Professor of Chemistry, St. Andrews University, since 1985; b. 22.5.48, Bovey Tracey; m., Elizabeth Ann Brown; 2 s.; 2 d. Educ. Haileybury and ISC; Hertford; Edinburgh University. Research Assistant, Temporary Lecturer, Imperial College, 1974-78; Lecturer, Senior Lecturer, Liverpool University, 1978-85. Sir Edward Frankland Fellow, Royal Society of Chemistry, 1984-85; Corday Morgan Medallist, 1983; President: Chemistry Section, British Association for the Advancement of Science, 1995, Chemistry Sectional Committee, Royal

Society of Edinburgh, 1993-95; Vice President, Royal Society of Chemistry, Dalton Council, 1996-99. Museums and Galleries Commission Award for Innovation in Conservation, 1995 (runner-up); Royal Society of Chemistry Award, 1998. Address: (b.) Department of Chemistry, The Purdie Building, St. Andrews, Fife KY16 9ST; T.-01334 463805.

Collier, H. Bruce, DCA, MITSA. Director of Community Protection, South Ayrshire Council, since 1995; b. 24.5.46, Dumbarton; m., Margaret; 3 d. Educ. Clydebank High School. Director, Department of Consumer and Trading Standards, Strathclyde Regional Council, 1991-95. Chairman, Association of Petroleum and Explosives Acts Administration, 1973; Chairman, Institute of Trading Standards Scotland, 1986; Director, European Inter-Regional Institute of Consumer Affairs; former Chair, Irvine CAB; Vice-Chairman, Scottish Consumer Council; Council Member, Institute of Trading Standards Administration. Recreations: reading; walking. Address: (b.) South Ayrshire Council, County Buildings, Wellington Square, Ayr KA7 1DR; T.-01292 612429.

Collingham, Lynne, LLB (Hons), DipLP. Associate Solicitor, Andrew MacAllan and Son, Glasgow, since 1992; Secretary/Treasurer, Scottish Sunday School Union for Christian Education, since 1993; b. 1.4.67, Glasgow; m., Douglas; 1 s. Educ. Woodfarm High School; University of Glasgow. AJ&A Graham Solicitors, Glasgow, 1990-92. Address: (b.) 236 Stonelaw Road, Burnside, Glasgow; T.-0141-613 1787.

Collins, Professor David John, BEd, MSc, AdDipCouns, PhD. Chair of Sport and Head, Department of Physical Education, Sport and Leisure, University of Edinburgh, since 1998; accredited sport psychologist working with athletes, since 1984; b. 31.12.53, Forest of Dean, Gloucester; divorced; 1 s.; 2 d. Educ. Royal Liberty School, Romford, Essex; Borough Road College, University of London. Officer, Royal Marines; Teacher of PE and Mathematics, public, state and special schools; Senior Lecturer in Movement Studies, St. Mary's College, Twickenham; Visiting Professor, Pennsylvania State University; Senior Lecturer then Reader then Professor, Manchester Metropolitan University. Member, British Olympic Association's Psychology Steering Group. Publications: five books; over 70 scientific publications. Recreations: outdoor pursuits; martial arts; training; curry. Address: University of Edinburgh, Cramond Road North, Edinburgh EH4 6JD; T.-0131-312 6001.

Collins, Dennis Ferguson, MA, LLB, WS, FRPSL. Senior Partner, Carlton Gilruth, Solicitors, Dundee (retired); Honorary Sheriff; b. 26.3.30, Dundee; m., Elspeth Margaret Nicoll; 1 s.; 1 d. Educ. High School of Dundee; St. Andrews University. Part-time Lecturer in Scots Law, St. Andrews University, then Dundee University, 1960-79; Agent Consulaire for France in Dundee, 1976-97; Hon. Secretary, Dundee Society for Prevention of Cruelty to Children, 1962-90; Treasurer, Dundee Congregational Church, since 1966; Past President, Dundee and District Philatelic Society; Past President, Association of Scottish Philatelic Societies; Dean, Faculty of Procurators and Solicitors in Dundee, 1987-89. Recreations: Chinese postal history; gardening; Sherlock Holmes pursuits; travelling in France. Address: (h.) Stirling House, Craigiebarn Road, Dundee DD4 7PL; T.-01382 458070.

Collins, Jeffrey Hamilton, DSc, FEng, FRSE, CPhys, FIEE, FIEEE, Hon. DEng (Napier). Specialist Adviser to the Principal and Vice-Chancellor, Napier University, 1994-97; b. 22.4.30, Luton; m., Sally; 2 s. Educ. Royal Grammar School, Guildford; University of London. Lecturer, then Senior Lecturer, University of Glasgow, 1957-66; Research Engineer, Stanford University, USA, 1966-68; Director of Physical Sciences, Rockwell International, California, 1968-70; Research Professor, Professor of Industrial Electronics, Professor of Electrical Engineering, University of Edinburgh, 1970-84; Director of Automation and Robotics Research Institute, and Professor of Electrical Engineering, University of Texas at Arlington, 1987-90; Senior Technical Specialist, Lothian Regional Council, Edinburgh, and Chairman, Edinburgh Parallel Computing Centre, 1991-93. Hewlett Packard Europhysics Prize, 1979. Publications: 192 articles in science and engineering journals. Recreations: gardening; music; croquet; tennis. Address: (h.) 28 Muirfield Park, Gullane EH31 2DY; T.-01620 843006.

Collins, Kenneth Darlingston, BSc (Hons), MSc. Member (Labour), European Parliament, since 1979; b. 12.8.39, Hamilton; m., Georgina Frances Pollard; 1 s.; 1 d. Educ. St. John's Grammar School; Hamilton Academy; Glasgow University; Strathclyde University. Steelworks apprentice, 1956-59; University, 1960-65; Planning Officer, 1965-66; WEA Tutor, 1966-67; Lecturer: Glasgow College of Building, 1967-69, Paisley College of Technology, 1969-79; Member: East Kilbride Town and District Council, 1973-79, Lanark County Council, 1973-75, East Kilbride Development Corporation, 1976-79; Chairman, NE Glasgow Children's Panel, 1974-76; European Parliament: Deputy Leader, Labour Group, 1979-84, Chairman, Environment Committee, 1979-84 and since 1989 (Vice-Chairman, 1984-87), Socialist Spokesman on Environment, Public Health and Consumer Protection, 1984-89; Fellow, Royal Scottish Geographical Society; Hon. Fellow, Chartered Institute of Water and Environment Management; Hon. Senior Research Fellow, Department of Geography, Lancaster University; Member, Advisory Committee, European Public Policy Institute, Warwick University; Director, Institute for European Environmental Policy, London; Fellow, Industry and Parliament Trust; Chairman, Central Scotland Countryside Trust. Recreations: music; boxer dogs; cycling. Address: (b.) 11 Stuarton Park, East Kilbride G74 4LA; T.-013552 37282.

Collins, Kenneth E., MPhil, PhD, MRCGP. Hon. President, Glasgow Jewish Representative Council, since 1998 (President, 1995-98); b. 23.12.47, Glasgow; m., Irene Taylor; 1 s.; 3 d. Educ. High School of Glasgow; Glasgow University. General medical practitioner in Glasgow, since 1976; Medical Officer, Newark Lodge, Glasgow, since 1978; Research Associate, Wellcome Unit for the History of Medicine, Glasgow University. Past Chairman, Glasgow Board of Jewish Education. Publications: Aspects of Scottish Jewry, 1987; Go and Learn: International Story of the Jews and Medicine in Scotland, 1988; Second City Jewry, 1990. Address: (h.) 3 Glenburn Road, Giffnock, Glasgow G46 6RE.

Colquhoun of Luss, Captain Sir Ivar (Iain), 8th Bt, JP, DL. Honorary Sheriff; Chief of the Clan; b. 4.1.16; m.; 1 s. (deceased); 1 d. Educ. Eton.

Coltart, George John Letham, CStJ, TD, MA, MSc, CEng, MICE; b. 2.2.29, Edinburgh; m., Inger Christina Larsson; 1 s.; 1 d. Educ. George Watson's College, Edinburgh; Royal Military Aademy, Sandhurst; King's College, Cambridge; Cornell University, USA. Commissioned, Royal Engineers, 1949; Captain, Adjutant, 23 Engineer Regiment, 1957-58; Staff College, Camberley, 1962; DAA & QMG 5 Bde, 1963-65; OC 51 Field Squadron, 1965-66; transferred to Reserve, 1966; Senior Lecturer in Civil Engineering, Heriot-Watt University, 1966-91 (Deputy Head of Department, 1987-90). Convener, Edinburgh and Heriot-Watt Universities Joint Military Education Committee, 1988-91; Commanding Officer, Edinburgh and Heriot-Watt UOTC, 1971-74; TA Colonel, Lowlands, 1975-80; Chairman, Lowland TAVRA, 1987-90; Priory Secretary, Most Venerable Order of St John of Jerusalem, 1991-96. Recreations: reserve forces; forestry;

DIY. Address: Napier House, 8 Colinton Road, Edinburgh EH10 5DS; T.-0131-447 6314.

Coltrane, Robbie, DA. Actor/Director; b. 31.3.50, Glasgow. Educ. Trinity College, Glenalmond; Glasgow School of Art. Film credits: Subway Riders, 1979, Balham Gateway to the South, 1980, Britannia Hospital, 1981, Scrubbers, 1982, Krull, 1982, Ghost Dance, 1983, Chinese Boxes, 1984, The Supergrass, 1984, Defense of the Realm, 1985, Revolution, 1985, Caravaggio, 1985, Absolute Beginners, 1985, Mona Lisa, 1985, Eat the Rich, 1987, The Fruit Machine, 1987, Slipstream, 1988, Bert Rigby, You're a Fool, 1988, Danny Champion of the World, 1988, Let It Ride, 1988, Henry V, 1988, Nuns on the Run, 1989, Perfectly Normal, 1989, Pope Must Die, 1990, Oh What A Night, 1991, Adventures of Huck Finn, 1992, Goldeneye, 1995, Buddy, 1996, Montana, 1997, Frogs for Snakes, 1997, Message in a Bottle, 1998; theatre credits: The Bug, 1976, Mr Joyce is Leaving, 1978, The Slab Boys, 1978, The Transfiguration of Benno Blimpie, 1978, The Loveliest Night of the Year, 1979-80, Dick Whittington, 1979, Snobs and Yobs, 1980, Yr Obedient Servant (one-man show), 1987, Mistero Buffo (one-man show), 1990; television credits include: roles in several The Comic Strip Presents productions, lead role in Tutti Frutti (BBC Scotland), Alive and Kicking, 1991, Coltrane in a Cadillac, 1992, Cracker, 1993, 1994, 1995, Ebbtide, 1996, Coltrane's Planes and Automobiles, 1997. Recreations: vintage cars; sailing; painting; reading; movies. Address: c/o CDA, 19 Sydney Mews, London SW3 6HL.

Colville of Culross, 4th Viscount (John Mark Alexander Colville, QC); b. 19.7.33; m.; 1 s.; 4 s. by pr. m. Educ. Rugby; New College, Oxford. Barrister; Minister of State, Home Office, 1972-74; Director, Securities and Futures Authority, 1987-93; Chairman: Mental Health Act Commission, 1983-88, Alcohol Education and Research Council, 1984-90, Parole Board, 1988-92; UK Representative, UN Human Rights Commission, 1980-83; Member, UN Working Group on Disappeared Persons, 1980-84 (Chairman, 1981-84); Special Rapporteur on Human Rights in Guatemala, 1983-86; Member, UN Human Rights Committee, since 1996; reports on Prevention of Terrorism Act and Northern Ireland Emergency Powers Act, 1986-93.

Colvin, David, CBE, DSH. Chair, SACRO; Governor, St Columba's Hospice; Scottish Correspondent, Action on Child Exploitation, since 1995; b. 31.1.31, Glasgow; m., Elma; 2 s.; 3 d. Educ. Whitehill School, Glasgow; Glasgow University; Edinburgh University. Probation Officer, Glasgow, 1955-60; Psychiatric Social Worker, Scottish Prison Service, 1960-61; Crichton Royal Hospital, Dumfries, 1961-65; Family Service Unit, Paisley, 1965-66; Adviser in Social Work, then Chief Adviser in Social Work, Scottish Office, 1966-91; Director of Social Work, Shetland, 1991. Former Chair, Dumfries Constituency Labour Party; former Chair, Scottish Marriage Council; Governor, National Institute for Social Work, 1981-91; Scottish Secretary, British Association of Social Workers, 1992-96; Scottish Chair, NCH Action for Children, 1992-97. Recreations: mountaineering; encouragement of fine arts. Address: (h.) The Studio, 53 Windsor Place, Edinburgh EH15 2AF; T.-0131-468 0087.

Comins, David, MA, PGCE. Rector, The Glasgow Academy, since 1994; b. 1.3.48, Scarborough; m., (Christine) Anne Speak; 1 s.; 2 d. Educ. Scarborough Boys' High School; Downing College, Cambridge. Assistant Maths Teacher: Mill Hill School, 1971-75, Strathallan School, 1975-76, Glenalmond College, 1976-80; Head of Maths, then Director of Studies, Glenalmond College, 1980-89; Deputy Head, Queen's College, Taunton, 1989-94. Winston Churchill Fellow, 1981. Recreations: mountaineering; ballet; crosswords; music. Address: (h.) 11 Kirklee Terrace, Glasgow G12 OTH; T.-0141-357 1776.

Comley, David John, BSc, PhD, FIH. Director of Housing, Glasgow City Council, since 1988; b. 25.4.50, Carshalton. Educ. Ashlyns School, Berkhamsted; Birmingham University. Housing Management Trainee, then District Housing Manager, Dudley Metropolitan Borough, 1976-80; District Housing Manager, then Assistant Director, then Depute Director, Glasgow City Council, since 1980. Adviser to COSLA, since 1988. Recreations: jazz; classical music; saxophone; hill walking; literature; cinema; theatre. Address: (b.) Wheatley House, 25 Cochrane Street, Glasgow, G1 1HZ.

Conboy, William Morgan, MA (Oxon), FRSA. Principal, Newbattle Abbey College, since 1993; b. 8.5.31, Edinburgh; m., Irene; 1 s.; 1 d. Educ. Royal High School; Ruskin College and Jesus College, Oxford. Assistant Research Officer, Institute of Economics and Statistics, Oxford University, 1966-69; Staff Tutor, Economics and Industrial Relations, Oxford University, 1969-79; Vice Principal, Ruskin College, Oxford, 1979-94; Acting Principal, Newbattle Abbey College, 1990-93; National President, WEA, 1991-97. Recreations: choral singing; golf. Address: (h.) Principal's Flat, Newbattle Abbey College, Dalkeith EH22 3LL.

Conn, Stewart. Poet and playwright; b. 1936, Glasgow, brought up Kilmarnock. Educ. Glasgow University. Author of numerous stage plays, including The Burning, Herman, The Aquarium, By the Pool, Clay Bull; television work includes The Kite, Bloodhunt; recent poetry includes In the Kibble Palace, The Luncheon of the Boating Party, At the Aviary, In the Blood; Stolen Light; his production of Carver (by John Purser) won Gold Medal Award, International Radio Festival, 1991; left BBC, 1992.

Connarty, Michael, BA, DCE. MP (Labour), Falkirk East, since 1992; Chairman, Scottish Parliamentary Labour Party Group, 1998-99; Chairman, All-Party Group for Chemical Industries; Member, House of Commons Information Select Committee; Board Member, Parliamentary Office of Science and Technology; b. 3.9.47, Coatbridge; m., Margaret Mary; 1 s.; 1 d. Educ. Stirling University; Jordanhill College of Education; Glasgow University. Member, Scottish Executive, Labour Party, 1981-92; Chair, Labour Party Scottish Local Government Committee, 1988-90; Member: Convention of Scottish Local Authorities, 1980-90 (Depute Labour Leader, 1988-90), Stirling District Council, 1977-90 (Council Leader, 1980-90); Vice-Chair, Socialist Educational Association, 1983-85; Council Member, Educational Institute of Scotland, 1984-85; Founding Secretary, Labour Coordinating Committee (Scotland); Vice-Chairman, Scottish MAP, since 1988; Scottish Task Force Leader on Skills and Training in Scotland and Youth and Students, 1995-97; Member, Select Committee on the Parliamentary Commissioner for Administration, 1995-97; Chair, Economy, Industry and Energy Committee, Scottish PLP Group, 1993-97; Scottish Co-ordinator, Labour Crime and Drugs Campaign, 1993-97; PPS to Tom Clarke, MP, 1987-88; Secretary, PLP Science and Technology Comittee, 1992-97; Member, European Directives Committee on Agriculture, Environment and Health and Safety, 1993-96. Recreations: family; hill-walking; reading; music; Falkirk FC; Bo'ness United FC. Address: (b.) 47 Bo'ness Road, Grangemouth FK3 8AP; T.-01324 474832.

Connal, Robert Craig, LLB(Hons). Solicitor, since 1977; Partner, McGrigor Donald, since 1980; Solicitor Advocate, since 1996; b. 7.7.54, Brentwood; m., Mary Ferguson Bowie; 2 d. Educ. Hamilton Academy; University of Glasgow. Apprentice, Brown, Mair, Gemmill & Hislop, 1975-77; Assistant, McGrigor Donald, 1977-1980. Council Member, Royal Faculty of Procurators in Glasgow, 1995-98; Member, Thorntonhall Community Council (Chairman, Planning Committee), since 1997. Publications: Contributor, Stair Memorial Encyclopedia; many articles in press and professional journals. Recreations: rugby referee; gardens (but not gardening). Address: (b.) Pacific House, 70 Wellington Street, Glasgow G2 6SB; T.-0141-248 6677.

Connell, Douglas Andrew, LLB, NP, WS, FRSA. Joint Senior Partner, Turcan Connell WS; Member: Scottish Arts Council, 1994-97, Edinburgh Festival Council, since 1997; Chairman, Lottery Committee, Scottish Arts Council, 1994-97; b. 18.5.54, Callander; m., Marjorie Elizabeth; 2 s. Educ. McLaren High School; Edinburgh University. Qualified as a solicitor, 1976; admitted as a Writer to the Signet, 1976; President, Scottish Young Lawyers Association, 1975-76; Tutor in Scots Law, Edinburgh University, 1974-76; Partner, Dundas and Wilson, 1979-97. Member, Revenue Committee, Law Society of Scotland, 1979-92; Trustee, Pushkin Prizes in Scotland; Patron, National Galleries of Scotland; Fellow, Royal Society of Arts; Chairman, Edinburgh Book Festival, 1991-95. Recreations: books; travel; good food. Address: (b.) Saltire Court, 20 Castle Terrace, Edinburgh EH1 2EF; T.-0131-228 8111.

Connelly, David, MA (Oxon), FSAScot. Trustee and Secretary, Buildings of Scotland Trust, since 1990; b. 23.2.30, Halifax; m., Audrey Grace Salter; 1 s.; 1 d. Educ. Heath Grammar School, Halifax; Queen's College, Oxford. Colonial Administrative Service, Tanganyika, 1954-62; Assistant Secretary, St. Andrews University, 1962-63; Principal, Commonwealth Relations Office, 1963-64; First Secretary, British High Commission, New Delhi, 1964-66; Principal, Scottish Office, 1966-73; Assistant Secretary, 1973-87; Director, Historic Buildings and Monuments, Scotland, 1987-90; Chairman, Cockburn Conservation Trust, Edinburgh, 1990-96. Recreations: opera; literature; history; architecture; walking the hills; country life. Address: c/o Royal Bank of Scotland plc, 36 St. Andrew Square, Edinburgh EH2 2YB.

Connolly, Billy. Stand-up comedian; actor; television presenter; b. 24.11.42; m. 1., Iris (m. dissolved) 1 s.; 1 d.; 2, Pamela Stephenson; 3 d. Welder, Clyde shipyards; began showbusiness career with Gerry Rafferty as The Humblebums; first solo concert, 1971; has toured throughout the world with stand-up comedy shows; television: Androcles and the Lion, Head of the Class (USA), Billy (USA), Billy Connolly's World Tour of Scotland (Scottish BAFTA: Best Entertainment Programme), Down Among the Big Boys (Scottish BAFTA: Best Drama), The Bigger Picture (Scottish BAFTA: Best Arts Programme), The Life and Crimes of Deacon Brodie, Billy Connolly's World Tour of Australia, Return to Nose and Beak (Comic Relief special), Billy Connolly: A Scot in the Arctic; films: Absolution, Bullshot, Water, The Big Man, Treasure Island (Muppet movie), Mrs Brown, Still Crazy, The Changeling, PAWS, The Debt Collector, The Boon Dock Saints, Ship of Fools; appeared with Scottish Opera in Die Fledermaus; theatre: wrote The Red Runner, performed in The Beastly Beatitudes of Blathazar B; videos: Live at Hammersmith, Bite Your Bum (Music Week and Record Business Award, 1981), Hand-picked By Billy Connolly, 25 BC, Billy and Albert, An Audience with Billy Connolly, Billy Connolly Live, Live '94, World Tour of Scotland (Two Bites of), World Tour of Australia, Two Night Stand; gold disc for album Pick of Billy Connolly, 1982; UK No. 1 hit with D.I.V.O.R.C.E.; books: Gullible's Travels, 1982, Billy Connolly's World Tour of Australia, 1996. Address: c/o Tickety-boo, The Boat House, Crabtree Lane, London SW6 6TY.

Connolly, Liz, BA (Hons), MBA. Chief Executive, Enterprise Ayrshire, since 1999; b. 21.11.58, Glasgow. Educ. Our Lady and St. Francis School, Glasgow; Strathclyde University. Media Planner, J.F. Green Associates, 1981-83; Marketing and Economic Research, SDA, 1983-91; Planning Executive in Policy Planning Unit, S.E. National, 1991-92; Head of Strategy then Director of Strategy, LDA, 1992-98. Member, Court, Paisley University. Recreations: music; theatre; keep fit; socialising. Address: (b.) 17/19 Hill Street, Kilmarnock KA3 1HA; T.-01563 526623.

Connon, Joyce Blair. Scottish Secretary, Workers Educational Association, since 1992; b. 11.6.47, Edinburgh; m., Neil Connon; 1 s.; 1 d. W.E.A. Tutor Organiser, Lothian, 1988; District Secretary, South-East Scotland, 1989. Recreations: reading; theatre; walking. Address: (b.) W.E.A., Riddle's Court, 322 Lawnmarket, Edinburgh EH1 2PG; T.-0131-226 3456.

Connor, Professor James Michael, MD, DSc, BSc (Hons), MB, ChB (Hons), FRCP. Professor of Medical Genetics and Director, West of Scotland Regional Genetics Service, since 1987 (Wellcome Trust Senior Lecturer and Honorary Consultant in Medical Genetics, Glasgow University, 1984-87); b. 18.6.51, Grappenhall, England; m., Dr. Rachel A.C. Educ. Lymm Grammar School, Cheshire; Liverpool University. House Officer, Liverpool Royal Infirmary; Resident in Internal Medicine, Johns Hopkins Hospital, USA; University Research Fellow, Liverpool University; Instructor in Internal Medicine, Johns Hopkins Hospital, USA; Consultant in Medical Genetics, Duncan Guthrie Institute of Medical Genetics, Yorkhill, Glasgow. Publications: Essential Medical Genetics (Co-author), 1984 (5th edition, 1996); Principles and Practice of Medical Genetics (Co-Editor), (3rd edition, 1996); various articles on aspects of medical genetics. Recreations: windsurfing; mountaineering. Address: (h.) East Collarie Farm, by Fenwick, Ayrshire; T.-Fenwick 600790.

Considine, John, MA, MEd. Rector, Inverness Royal Academy, since 1993; President, Highland Secondary Headteachers Association, since 1997; Director, Highlands and Islands Arts; b. 26.11.50, Glasgow; m., Hellen L. Campbell; 1 s.; 2 d. Educ. St. Aloysius College; Glasgow University. Teacher: St. Margaret Mary's, Glasgow, 1973, Inverness High, 1974, Millburn Academy, Inverness, 1976; Principal Teacher, then Assistant Rector, Charleston Academy, Inverness, 1978-88; Depute Rector, Woodmill High, Dunfermline, 1988-93. Member, Inverness College Board of Management, and Chair, College Personnel Sub-Committee. Recreations: hill-walking; running; squash. Address: (b.) Inverness Royal Academy, Culduthel Road, Inverness; T.-01463 222884.

Constable, Alan W., BSc (Hons), CertEd. Rector, Morgan Academy, Dundee, since 1987; b. 30.8.46, Blairgowrie; m., Irene M.; 2 s. Educ. Blairgowrie High School; Heriot Watt University, Edinburgh; Moray House College, Edinburgh. Design Engineer, 1970-71; Teacher/Principal Teacher/Assistant Headteacher, 1972-83; HMI Technology, Scottish Education Department, 1983-84; Depute Rector, Montrose Academy, 1984-86. Recreations: golf; hockey. Address: (b.) Morgan Academy, Forfar Road, Dundee DD4 7AY; T.-01382 438700.

Conti, Rt. Rev. Mario Joseph, STL, PhL, DD, FRSE. Bishop of Aberdeen, since 1977; Member, Pontifical Council for the Promotion of Christian Unity, Rome, since 1984; Member, International Commission for English in the Liturgy, 1978-87; b. 20.3.34, Elgin. Educ. St. Marie's Convent; Springfield School, Elgin; Blairs College, Aberdeen; Scots College, Pontifical Gregorian University, Rome. Ordained priest, Rome, 1958; Curate, St. Mary's Cathedral, Aberdeen, 1959-62; Parish Priest, St. Joachim's, Wick and St. Anne's, Thurso, 1962. Commendatore, Order of Merit, Italian Republic; President-Treasurer, SCIAF, 1977-85; President, National Liturgy Commission, 1978-86; Chairman, Scottish Catholic Heritage Commission; President, Commission for Christian Doctrine and Unity, since 1986; first Convener, Central Council, ACTS, 1990; Co-Moderator, Joint Working Group of the World Council of Churches and the Roman Catholic Church, since 1996; Member, Pontifical Commission for the Cultural Heritage of the Church, since 1994; Knight Commander of the Holy Sepulchre, 1989; Conventual Chaplain Ad Honorem, Knights of Malta, 1991, Principal Chaplain to British Association of the Order, since 1995. Recreations: music; art. Address: Bishop's House, 3 Queen's Cross, Aberdeen AB15 4XU; T.-01224 319154.

Convery, Sheriff Daniel. Sheriff of Glasgow and Strathkelvin. Address: (b.) Sheriff Court House, 1 Carlton Place, Glasgow, G5 9DA.

Convery, Francis, ARSA. Head of Painting, Grays School of Art, Aberdeen, since 1997; b. 12.2.56, Paisley; 2 d. Educ. St. Mirin's Academy, Paisley; Edinburgh College of Art. Part-time Lecturer, Edinburgh College of Art, 1984-86. Solo exhibitions: Edinburgh University Festival Hall, 1984, Mercury Gallery, Edinburgh, 1984, Andrew Grant Gallery, Edinburgh College of Art, 1988; The Scottish Gallery, Edinburgh, 1991 and 1995, Art Wise, British Airways, Aberdeen Airport, 1998; exhibited in numerous group exhibitions, Britain and internationally; work in public collections; President, Aberdeen Artists Society, 1996; Member, Selection and Arrangements Committee, Royal Scottish Academy, 1998; Consultant and Adviser, Art Wise, 1997. Address: Bridgend Farm, Glassel, by Banchory, Aberdeenshire AB31 4DV; T.-013398 82794.

Conway, Rt. Rev. Mgr. Michael Joseph, BA, MSc (Econ). Rector, Scotus College, since 1993; Prelate of Honour, since 1988; b. 5.3.40, Newry. Educ. St. Colman's College, Newry; St. Kieran's College, Kilkenny; University College, Dublin; London School of Economics. St. James's, Coatbridge, 1963-65; St. David's, Plains, Airdrie, 1965-66; St. Theresa's, Newarthill, 1966-69; St. Monica's, Coatbridge, 1975-77; Catholic Chaplain, Glasgow University, 1977-93; Member, Task Force, Lanarkshire Health Board, 1994-97. Recreations: golf; hill-walking; reading; listening to music. Address: (b.) Scotus College, 2 Chesters Road, Bearsden, Glasgow G61 4AG; T.-01698 458770.

Cook, Ian David, RI, RSW. Artist; b. 2.3.50, Paisley; m., Elaine Hall; 2 s.; 1 d. Educ. Camphill High School; Glasgow School of Art. Travelling scholarships to Spain and North Africa, and awards for research in Central Africa and Indian reservations of N.W. United States. Recreations: historical research; literature; horticulture. Address: (h.) 3 Falside Road, Paisley PA2 6JZ; T.-0141-884 3062.

Cook, Rt. Hon. Robin. MP (Labour), Livingston, since 1983 (Edinburgh Central, 1974-83); Foreign Secretary; b. 28.2.46. Formerly: Opposition Spokesman on Trade and Industry; Opposition Spokesman on Health and Social Security. Address: (b.) House of Commons, London, SW1A 0AA.

Cooke, Professor David John, BSc, MSc, PhD, CPsych, FBPsS. Professor of Forensic Psychology, Glasgow Caledonian University, since 1992; Head of Forensic Clinical Psychology, Greater Glasgow Community and Mental Health Services NHS Trust, since 1984; Glasgow University: Honorary Lecturer, since 1984, Honorary Senior Research Fellow, since 1989, Visiting Professor, since 1997; b. 13.7.52, Glasgow; m., Janet Ruth Salter; 2 d. Educ. Larbert High School; St. Andrews University; Newcastle-upon-Tyne University; Glasgow University. Clinical Psychologist, Gartnavel Royal Hospital, 1976-83; Cropwood Fellow, Institute of Criminology, Cambridge University, 1986. Recreations: sailing; opera; cooking. Address: (b.) Douglas Inch Centre, 2 Woodside Terrace, Glasgow G3 7UY; T.-0141-211 8016.

Cooke, Nicholas Huxley, MA (Oxon), FRSA. Director, Scottish Conservation Projects, since 1984; b. 6.5.44, Godalming, Surrey; m., Anne Landon; 2 s.; 3 d. Educ. Charterhouse School; Worcester College, Oxford. Retail management, London, 1967; chartered accountancy training, London, 1968-71; British International Paper, London, 1972-78; Director (Scotland), British Trust for Conservation Volunteers, 1978-84. Member: Policy Committee, Scottish Council for Voluntary Organisations; Board Member: Youthlink Scotland, Dundee Waste and Environment Trust, Falkirk Environment Trust; Chair, NTO Steering Group, SCVO; Member, Scottish Committee, European Year of the Environment, 1987-88. Recreations: fishing; walking; photography; outdoor conservation work. Address: (b.) Balallan House, 24 Allan Park, Stirling FK8 2QG; T.-01786 79697.

Cooke, Professor Timothy, MD, FRCS, MB, ChB. St. Mungo Professor of Surgery, Glasgow University, since 1989; Honorary Consultant Surgeon, Royal Infirmary, Glasgow; b. 16.9.47, Liverpool; m., Lynn; 1 s.; 1 d. Educ. Birkenhead Institute; Liverpool University. Surgical training, Liverpool University, 1973-79; Lecturer in Surgery, Southampton University, 1980-83; Senior Lecturer and Honorary Consultant Surgeon, Charing Cross & Westminster Medical School, 1983-86; Senior Lecturer and Honorary Consultant Surgeon, Liverpool University and Royal Liverpool and Broadgreen Hospitals, 1986-89. Hunterian Professor, Royal College of Surgeons of England. Publications: numerous scientific articles about cancer research. Recreations: playing wide range of indoor and outdoor sports; lifetime supporter, Liverpool FC. Address: (b.) University Department of Surgery, Royal Infirmary, Glasgow G31 2ER; T.-0141-211 4870.

Coombs, Professor Graham H., BSc, PhD, FRSE. Professor of Biochemical Parasitology, Glasgow University, since 1996; b. 22.9.47, Coventry; m., Isabel; 1 d. Educ. King Henry VIII School, Coventry; University College, London. Research Fellow, University of Kent, 1972-74; Lecturer, Department of Zoology, Glasgow University, 1974-86, Senior Lecturer, 1986-88, Reader, 1988-90, Professor, 1990-96, Head, Department of Zoology, 1991-94. Recreation: golf. Address: (b.) Infection and Immunity, Joseph Black Building, Glasgow University, Glasgow G12 8QQ; T.-0141-330 4777.

Cooper, Rev. David, BA, MPhil. Superintendent Minister, Edinburgh and Forth Circuit, since 1992; Secretary to Synod of Methodist Church in Scotland, since 1995; b. 6.11.49, Seaham; m., Veronica; 3 s.; 1 d. Educ. Bede Grammar School for Boys, Sunderland; University of Manchester; Hartley Victoria Methodist College. Minister: Morpeth Circuit, Newcastle District, 1977, Lerwick, North Roe and North Isles Circuit, Shetland District, 1980, Witney and Faringdon Circuit, Oxford and Leicester District, 1985. World Council of Churches Scholarship, University of Ghana, 1976-77. Recreation: music. Address: (b.) Central Hall, Tollcross, Edinburgh EH3 9BP; T.-0131-229 7937.

Cooper, Sheena M.M., MA. Rector, Aboyne Academy and Deeside Community Centre; b. 7.3.39, Bellshill. Educ. Dalziel High School, Motherwell; Glasgow University. Teacher of History, Dalziel High School, Motherwell, 1962-68; Lecturer in History, Elizabeth Gaskell College of Education, Manchester, 1968-70; Woman Adviser, then Assistant Rector, Montrose Academy, 1970-76; Rector, John Neilson High School, Paisley, 1976-83. Member: Council for Tertiary Education in Scotland, 1979-83, Scottish Examination Board, 1984-92, Scottish Vocational Education Council, 1985-88, Religious Advisory Council, BBC, 1980-91, Broadcasting Council for Scotland, 1991-96, Scottish Higher Education Funding Council, 1995-98; President, Education Section, British Association for Advancement of Science, 1978-79. Recreations: walking; skiing. Address: (b.) Aboyne Academy and Deeside Community Centre, Aboyne; T.-01339 86222, Ext. 207.

Cope, Professor Peter Anthony, BSc, DipEd, DPSE, PhD. Professor of Education, University of Stirling, since 1998 (Director of Initial Teacher Education, since 1993); b. 29.8.48, Hitchin; m., Catherine Morrison; 3 d. Educ. Hitchin Boys' Grammar School; University of Aberdeen. Research Fellow, Strathclyde University; Teacher, Berwickshire High School; Lecturer/Senior Lecturer, University of Stirling. Recreations: traditional music, especially fiddle playing. Address: Institute of Education, University of Stirling, Stirling; T.-01786 467611.

Copland, Rt. Rev. Mgr. John Forbes. Prelate of Honour to His Holiness the Pope; Vicar General R.C. Diocese of Aberdeen, since 1979; Provost of Cathedral Chapter, since 1996; Parish Priest, St. Thomas', Keith, since 1974; b. 26.12.20, Glenlivet. Educ. Tombae R.C. School; Blairs College Junior Seminary; Gregorian University, Rome; St. Peter's, Glasgow; St Joseph's, London. Ordained Priest, 1946; Curate: St. Peter's, Aberdeen, 1946, St Mary's Cathedral, Aberdeen, 1948; Parish Priest: Church of Annuniciation, Portsoy, 1951, St Andrew's, Braemar, 1964, St Joseph's, Woodside, Aberdeen, 1968. Chairman, Portsoy Improvement Association, 1954-64; Group Scoutmaster, Portsoy, 1952-64; Area Chairman, O.A.P.'s Association, 1958-64; Member: Aberdeenshire Education Committee, 1964-74, Grampian Education Committee, 1974-86; Chairman and Founder Member, Braemar Mountain Rescue Association, 1965-66; Founder Member, Aberdeen Cyrenians, 1970; President, Keith Initiative, since 1990. Recreations: hill-walking; stone polishing; photography. Address: (h.) St. Thomas' Rectory, Chapel Street, Keith, Banffshire AB55 5AL; T.-01542 882352.

Coppock, Emeritus Professor John Terence, CBE, MA, PhD, FBA, FRSE. Secretary and Treasurer, Carnegie Trust for the Universities of Scotland, since 1986; Emeritus Professor of Geography, Edinburgh University; b. 2.6.21, Cardiff; m., Sheila Mary Burnett (deceased); 1 s.; 1 d. Educ. Penarth County School; Queens' College, Cambridge. Civil Servant, 1938-47 (Lord Chancellor's Department, Ministry of Works, Customs and Excise); War Service, Army, 1939-46 (Commissioned, 1941); Departmental Demonstrator, Department of Geography, Cambridge University, 1949-50; University College, London: Assistant Lecturer, 1950-52, Lecturer, 1952-64, Reader, 1964-65; Ogilvie Professor of Geography, Edinburgh University, 1965-86. Institute of British Geographers: Vice-President, 1971-73, President, 1973-74; Vice-President: Royal Scottish Geographical Society, since 1975, British Academy, 1985-87. Recreations: walking; natural history; listening to music. Address: (b.) Carnegie Trust for the Universities of Scotland, Cameron House, Abbey Park Place, Dunfermline KY12 7PZ; T.-01383 622148.

Corcoran, Professor Cornelius David, MA, MLitt(Oxon). Professor of English, University of St. Andrews, since 1996; b. 23.9.48, Cork; m., Gillian Anne Jeffs; 3 s. Educ. Austin Friars, Carlisle; St. Edmund Hall, Oxford; Wolfson College, University of Oxford. Lecturer, then Senior Lecturer in English, University of Sheffield; Professor, University of Wales, Swansea. Publications include: Seamus Heaney, 1986; English Poetry since 1940, 1993; After Yeats and Joyce, 1997. Address: University of St. Andrews, St. Andrews KY16 9AL.

Cormack, John James Callender, MD, FRCPE, FRCGP. General Medical Practitioner; Apothecary to HM Household at the Palace of Holyroodhouse, since 1991; Chairman, Corstorphine Trust, since 1995; b. 21.2.34, Edinburgh; m., Joy Mackenzie Gourlay; 1 s.; 2 d. Educ. Edinburgh Academy; Edinburgh University. House Officer, Grenfell Mission, Canada, 1960-61; Medical Officer, CCAP Mission Hospital, Nyasaland, 1961-62; Principal in general practice, Corstorphine, since 1964; part-time Lecturer, Department of General Practice, Edinburgh University, 1966-76; Member, Panel of Examiners, Royal College of General Practitioners, 1971-82. Elder (former Joint Session Clerk), Corstorphine Old Parish Church; Hon. Librarian and Trustee, Royal Medical Society. Publications: Practice – Clinical Management in General Practice (Co-editor); Teaching General Practice (Co-editor). Recreations: cycling; walking; painting; Scottish history. Address: (b.) Ladywell Medical Centre, Ladywell Road, Edinburgh EH12 7TB; T.-0131-334 3602.

Corner, David John, BA (Oxon), FRHS. Secretary, St. Andrews University, since 1991; Honorary Lecturer, Department of Mediaeval History, St. Andrews University, since 1991; b. 24.10.47, Birmingham; m., Carol Ann; 2 s. Educ. King Edward VI Grammar School, Aston, Birmingham; Worcester College, Oxford. Prize Fellow, Magdalen College, Oxford, 1972-75; Lecturer, Department of Mediaeval History, St. Andrews University, 1975-91. Governor, Newbattle Abbey College, since 1991; President, St. Andrews Association of University Teachers, 1985-88. Recreations: cinema; sport. Address: St. Andrews University, College Gate, North Street, St. Andrews KY16 9AJ; T.-01334 462549.

Corner, Douglas Robertson, FCIBS. Director, Adam and Company PLC, since 1997; b. 19.5.44, Glasgow; m., Alice Cairns; 1 s.; 1 d. Educ. Duncanrig Secondary School, East Kilbride. Clydesdale Bank PLC (latterly as General Manager, Banking), 1969-95; Head of Human Resources and Consultant to Venture Capital Division, Murray Johnstone Ltd., 1995-97. Director: Quarriers Homes; Director, Glasgow International Jazz Festival (Chairman, Management Committee); Director: Eurogarden Ltd., Hairmyres and Stonehouse Hospitals NHS Trust. Recreations: golf; collecting Scottish contemporary painting. Address: (b.) 238 West George Street, Glasgow G2 4DY; T.-0141-226 4848.

Cornish, Melvyn David, BSc, PGCE. Deputy Secretary, Edinburgh University, since 1991; b. 29.6.48, Leighton Buzzard; m., Eileen Joyce Easterbrook; 1 s.; 1 d. Educ. Cedars Grammar School, Leighton Buzzard; Leicester University. Chemistry Teacher, Jamaica and Cumbria, 1970-73; Administrator, Leicester Polytechnic, 1973-78; Senior Administrative Officer, Assistant Secretary, Director of Planning, Edinburgh University, 1978-91. Recreations: walking; photography; travel; family. Address: (b.) Old College, South Bridge, Edinburgh; T.-0131-650 2136.

Cornwell, Professor John Francis, PhD, BSc, DIC, ARCS, FRSE. Professor of Theoretical Physics, St. Andrews University, since 1979 (Chairman, Physics Department, 1984-85); b. 28.1.37, London; m., Elizabeth Margaret Burfitt; 2 d. Educ. Ealing Grammar School; Imperial College, London. Lecturer in Applied Mathematics, Leeds University, 1961-67; St. Andrews University: Lecturer in Theoretical Physics, 1967-73, Reader, 1973-79. Publications: Group Theory in Physics, three volumes, 1984, 1989; Group Theory and Electronic Energy Bands in Solids, 1969. Recreations: sailing; hill-walking; tennis; badminton; golf. Address: (b.) Department of Physics and Astronomy, St. Andrews University, North Haugh, St. Andrews, Fife KY16 9SS; T.-01334 476161.

Cornwell, Professor Keith, BSc, PhD, DEng, FIMechE. Professor, Department of Mechanical and Chemical Engineering and Director of Quality, Heriot-Watt University; b. 4.4.42, Abingdon; m., Sheila Joan Mott; 1 s.; 1 d. Educ. City University, London. Research Fellow, then Lecturer, Middlesex Polytechnic; Lecturer, Head of Department, Dean of Engineering, Heriot-Watt University. Secretary, UK Committee on Heat Transfer. Publications: The Flow of Heat; numerous journal papers. Recreations: classic cars; hillwalking. Address: (h.) Strathview, Templar Place, Gullane EH39 2AH.

Corrie, John Alexander. Member (Conservative), European Parliament for Worcestershire and South Warwickshire, since 1994; Chief Whip, Conservatives in Europe; farms family farm in Galloway; Council Member, Royal Agricultural Society of England, since 1992; b. 1935; m.; 1 s.; 2 d. Educ. Kirkcudbright Academy; George Watson's College, Edinburgh; Lincoln Agricultural College, New Zealand. Nuffield Farming Scholar, 1972; National Chairman, Scottish Young Conservatives, 1964; MP (Conservative): Bute and North Ayrshire, 1974-83, Cunninghame North, 1983-87; PPS to Secretary of State for Scotland, 1979-81; introduced Private Member's Bill to reduce upper limit on abortion, 1979; Member: European Assembly, 1975-76 and 1977-79, Council of Europe, 1983-87, Western European Union (Defence Committee), 1983-87; Senior Instructor, British Wool Board, Agricultural Training Board, 1970-74; elected to Council, Belted Galloway Cattle Society, 1978; Chairman, Scottish Transport Users Consultative Committee, 1988-94; Vice Chairman, Central Transport Consultative Committee, 1988-94; Industrial Fellowship with Conoco and Du Pont, USA, 1987; awarded Wilberforce Plaque for Humane Work, 1981. Publications: Forestry in Europe; Fish Farming in Europe; The Importance of Forestry in the World Today; Towards a Community Rural Policy (Co-author). Address: (h.) Park of Tongland, Kirkcudbright DG6 4NE.

Corsar, Charles Herbert Kenneth, LVO, OBE, TD, JP, DL, MA. Farmer, since 1953; Secretary for Scotland, Duke of Edinburgh's Award, 1966-87; b. 13.5.26, Edinburgh; m., The Honourable Dame Mary Corsar, DBE, FRSE (qv) ; 2 s.; 2 d. Educ. Merchiston Castle; King's College, Cambridge. Commissioned, The Royal Scots TA, 1948; commanded 8/9 Bn.,The Royal Scots TA, 1964-67; Edinburgh and Heriot-Watt Universities OTC, 1967-72; TA Colonel, 1972-75; Hon. ADC to The Queen, 1977-81; Honorary Colonel, 1/52 Lowland Volunteers, 1975-87; Chairman, Lowland TA and VR Association, 1984-87; Zone Commissioner, Home Defence, East of Scotland; County Councillor, Midlothian, 1958-67; Deputy-Lieutenant, Midlothian; Vice President, The Boys Brigade, 1970-91 and President, Edinburgh Bn., Boys Brigade, 1969-87 (Hon. President, Edinburgh Bn.,1987-98); Chairman, Scottish Standing Conference of Voluntary Youth Organisations, 1973-78; Governor: Merchiston Castle School, Clifton Hall School; Chairman: Wellington List D School, 1978-84, Earl Haig Fund Scotland, 1984-90; Secretary, Royal Jubilee and Princes' Trusts (Lothian and Borders); Member, Scottish Sports Council, 1972-75; Elder, Church of Scotland, since 1956. Recreations: gardening; bee-keeping; shooting. Address: (h.) Burg, Torloisk, Ulva Ferry, Isle of Mull PA74 6NH; T.-01688 500289; 11 Ainslie Place, Edinburgh EH3 6AS; T.-0131-225 6318.

Corsar, Kenneth, MA (Hons), MEd (Hons), FRSA. Director of Education, Glasgow City Council, since 1995; b. 16.7.46, Clackmannan; m., Mary Massie; 2 s. Educ. Alloa Academy; St. Andrews University; Glasgow University. Teacher, Principal Teacher of Classics, 1970-75; Education Officer, Senior Education Officer, Divisional Education Officer, Strathclyde Regional Council, 1975-90; Divisional Education Officer, Depute Director of Education, Strathclyde Regional Council, 1990-95. Vice-President, Association of Directors of Education in Scotland, 1992-93, President, 1993-94. Recreations: golf; calligraphy. Address: (b.) India Street, Glasgow; T.-0141-287 6710; (h.) 9 Eaglesfield Crescent, Strathaven, Lanarkshire; T.-01357 520817.

Corsar, The Hon. Dame Mary Drummond, DBE (1993), FRSE, MA; b. 8.7.27, Edinburgh; m., Colonel Charles H.K. Corsar (qv); 2 s.; 2 d. Educ. Westbourne, Glasgow; St. Denis, Edinburgh; Edinburgh University. Chairman, Women's Royal Voluntary Service, 1988-93; Chairman, Scotland, WRVS, 1981-88; Midlothian Girl Guides: Secretary, 1951-66, County Commissioner, 1966-72; Deputy Chief Commissioner, Girl Guides Scotland, 1972-77; Member: Parole Board for Scotland, 1982-89; Executive Committee, Trefoil Centre, since 1975; Visiting Committee, Glenochil Detention Centre, 1976-94; Management Committee, Church of Scotland Youth Centre, Carberry, 1976-82; Governor, Fettes College; Member of Convocation, Heriot Watt University; Chairman, TSB Foundation for Scotland, 1994-95. Recreation: hill-walking. Address: (h.) Burg, Torloisk, Ulva Ferry, Isle of Mull PA74 6NH; T.-0168 8500289.

Cosgrove, Hon. Lady (Hazel Josephine Aronson), QC, LLB, LLD. Senator of the College of Justice in Scotland, since 1996; b. 12.1.46, Glasgow; m., John A. Cosgrove; 1 s.; 1 d. Educ. Glasgow High School for Girls; Glasgow University. Advocate at Scottish Bar, 1968-79; Sheriff: Glasgow and Strathkelvin at Glasgow, 1979-83, Lothian and Borders at Edinburgh, 1983-96; Temporary Judge, Court of Session and High Court, 1992-96; Past Chairman, Mental Welfare Commission for Scotland. Recreations: swimming; walking; opera; foreign travel. Address: (b.) Parliament House, Edinburgh EH1 1RQ; T.-0131-225 2595.

Cosgrove, Stuart, PhD. Head of Programmes (Scotland, Wales and Northern Ireland), Channel Four Television, since 1997; b. Perth. Educ. Hull University. Lecturer, film and television; cultural critic; Media Editor, NME; contributor, The Face, The Guardian, The Observer, Arena; regular presenter, The Late Show, BBC TV; joined Channel Four after period as independent producer; appointed Senior Commissioning Editor, then Controller of Arts and Entertainment, before returning to Scotland. Recreation: supporter of St Johnstone F.C.

Costley, William James McCreadie. Owner: Costley and Costley Hoteliers Limited, Airclose Limited; Chairman, Kilmarnock Football Club, since 1997; b. 1.5.52, Dumfries; m., Catherine; 2 s. Educ. Prestwick Public School; Prestwick Academy; Ayr College. Trainee Chef, Turnberry Hotel; Head Chef: Caledonian Hotel, Ayr, Chapeltoun House Hotel, Stewarton; Executive Chef, Hospitality Inn, Irvine; Costley & Costley Hoteliers Limited: bought Highgrove House Hotel, 1988, Lochgreen House, 1990, Cochrane Inn, Gatehead, Brig O'Doon House, Alloway, 1996-97. Recreations: food; eating out; football. Address: Lochgreen Courtyard, Monktonhill Road, Troon KA10 7EN; T.-01292 313343.

Cotter, Elizabeth Faith, LLB. Solicitor; Partner, Stewarts and Murdochs, since 1997; b. 11.9.43, Motherwell; m., James Logan Millar Cotter; 2 s.; 1 d. Educ. Westbourne School; Glasgow University. Stewarts Nicol McCormick, 1966-68; Motherwell and Wishaw District Council, 1968-69; Director, Motherwell Times Ltd., 1966-84; Partner, Bellshill Speaker, 1966-84; Partner, Stewarts Nicol D. & J. Hill, 1984-97. Part-time Commissioner, Mental Welfare Commission for Scotland. Recreations: reading; gardening; fishing; antiques. Address: (b.) 1 Royal Bank Place, Buchanan Street, Glasgow G1 3AA; T.-0141-248 8810.

Cotton, Andrew, BA, MA (Cantab). Head of Acquisition Finance, Clydesdale Bank Plc, since 1997; b. 10.5.65, Nantwich; m., Christine Martin; 2 step-s. Educ. Alsager Comprehensive School; Fitzwilliam College, Cambridge University. Royal Navy (reaching rank of Lieutenant); qualified CA with KPMG, Edinburgh; joined acquisition finance team, Clydesdale Bank, 1996. Recreations: walking; football; sailing. Address: (b.) 150 Buchanan Street, Glasgow G1 2HL; T.-0141-223 2762.

Coulsfield, Hon. Lord (John Taylor Cameron), QC, BA, LLB. Senator of the College of Justice, since 1987; b. 24.4.34, Dundee; m., Bridget Deirdre Sloan. Educ. Fettes College; Corpus Christi College, Oxford; Edinburgh University. Admitted to Faculty of Advocates, 1960; Queen's Counsel, 1973; Lecturer in Public Law, Edinburgh

University, 1960-64; Advocate Depute, 1977-80; Keeper of the Advocates Library, 1977-87; Chairman, Medical Appeal Tribunals, 1985-87; Judge of the Appeal Courts of Jersey and Guernsey, 1986-87; Scottish Judge, Employment Appeal Tribunal, 1992-96.

Coulthard, William George, LLB. Solicitor, since 1971; Honorary Sheriff, since 1988; b. 13.3.48, Whitehaven; m., Fiona Jane McQueen; 1 s.; 2 d. Educ. Glasgow Academy; Glasgow University. Partner in legal firm, since 1974; Dean, Faculty of Procurators, Stewartry of Kirkcudbright, 1986-88; Chairman, Castle Douglas High School Board, 1990-94; President, Castle Douglas Rotary Club, 1995. Recreations: golf; swimming; jogging. Address: (h.) Netherby, Castle Douglas DG7 1BA; T.-01556 502965.

Couper, Jean, BSc, MIMgt. Chairman, Scottish Legal Aid Board, since 1998; Member, Health Education Board for Scotland, since 1994; Director, Catalyst Consulting, since 1995; b. 31.8.53, Kilmarnock; m., John Anderson Couper; 1 s.; 1 d. Educ. Kilmarnock Academy; University of Glasgow. Production Engineer and Foundry Manager, Glacier Metal Co. 1974-79; Materials Manager, Levi Strauss, 1979-81; Management Consultant: Arthur Young, 1982-87, Price Waterhouse, 1987-95; Vice-Chairman, Wise Group, 1988-96; Vice Chairman, Heatwise Glasgow Ltd., 1988-96.National President, Junior Chamber Scotland, 1983; Senator, Junior Chamber International. Recreations: gardening; skiing. Address: Lismore, 13 Otterburn Drive, Giffnock, Glasgow G46 6PZ; T.-0141-571 7657.

Courtney, Professor James McNiven, BSc, PhD, Dr sc nat, ARCST, EurChem, CChem, FRSC, FIM. Professor, Bioengineering Unit, Strathclyde University, since 1989 (Reader, 1986-89, Senior Lecturer, 1981-86); Tenured Professor, International Faculty for Artificial Organs, since 1992; Secretary/Treasurer, International Society for Artificial Organs, since 1994; b. 25.3.40, Glasgow; m., Ellen Miller Courtney; 2 s.; 1 d. Educ. Whitehill Senior Secondary School; Royal College of Science and Technology; Strathclyde University. Rubber technologist: MacLellan Rubber Ltd., Glasgow, 1962-65, Uniroyal Ltd., Dumfries, 1965-66; Lecturer, Bioengineering Unit, Strathclyde University, 1969-81. Recreation: football supporter (Glasgow Rangers). Address: (b.) Strathclyde University, Bioengineering Unit, 106 Rottenrow, Glasgow; T.-0141-548 3349.

Cousin, (David) Alastair (Henry), BVMS, MRCVS, DBR, JP. Senior Partner, veterinary practice, Kintyre, since 1972; Honorary Sheriff, Campbeltown Sheriff Court, since 1990; b. 19.4.44, Kincardine on Forth; m., Anne Macleod; 1 s.; 1 d. Educ. Balfron High School; Glasgow University; Liverpool University. Veterinary practice, Campbeltown: Veterinary Assistant, 1966, Junior Partner, 1972, Senior Partner, 1982. Former Commodore, Campbeltown Sailing Club, 1995. Recreations: sailing; shooting; gardening; music. Address: (h.) Southpark, Kilkerran Road, Campbeltown; T.-01586 553108.

Coutts, Alister William, DQS, BA, MBA, MSc, PhD, FRICS, FCIOB, FIMgt. Director of Property and Architectural Services, The Highland Council, since 1998; Tutor, Open University, since 1992; b. 21.12.50, Aberdeen; m., Sheelagh Anne; 1 s.; 2 d. Educ. Robert Gordon's College, Aberdeen; University of Abertay, Dundee; Open University; University of Hong Kong; Heriot-Watt University. Armour and Partners, Chartered Quantity Surveyors: Assistant Quantity Surveyor, 1969-71, Quantity Surveyor, 1975-76; Senior Quantity Surveyor, Anderson Morgan Associates, Chartered Surveyors, 1976-78; Professional Officer, Public Works Department, Hong Kong Government, 1978-81; Project Co-ordinator, Hong Kong Mass Transit Railway Corporation, 1981-89; Project Management and Development Director, DCI (Holdings) Ltd., 1989-93; Director of Operations, Fife Healthcare NHS Trust, 1993-98. President, Scottish Football Association Referees (Angus and Perthshire), 1994-96. Recreations: soccer referee; hillwalking. Address: (h.) Mo Tien, 29 Lady Nairne Drive, Perth PH1 1RF; T.-01738 633694.

Coutts, Rev. Fred, MA, BD. Hospital Chaplain, Aberdeen Royal Hospitals NHS Trust; Healthcare Chaplaincy Training Officer (Scotland), since 1997; b. 13.1.47, Forfar; m., Mary Lawson Fraser Gill; 2 s.; 1 d. Educ. Brechin High School; Dollar Academy; St. Andrews University; Edinburgh University. Assistant Minister, Linwood Parish Church, 1972-74; Minister: Buckie North, 1974-84, Mastrick, Aberdeen, 1984-89. Chairman: Buckie Community Council, 1981-83, Moray Firth Community Radio Association, 1982-83. Recreations: music; photography; computing. Address: 9A Millburn Street, Aberdeen, AB11 6SS; T.-01224 583805.

Coutts, Herbert, SBStJ, AMA, FMA, FSAScot. Acting Director of Recreation, Edinburgh City Council, since 1988; City Curator, Edinburgh City Museums and Art Galleries, 1973-96, Head of Museums and Galleries, 1996-97, Head of Heritage and Arts, 1997-98; b. 9.3.44, Dundee; m., Angela E.M. Smith; 1 s.; 3 d. Educ. Morgan Academy, Dundee. Assistant Keeper of Antiquities and Bygones, Dundee City Museums, 1965-68; Keeper, 1968-71; Superintendent, Edinburgh City Museums, 1971-73; Vice-President, Museum Assistants Group, 1969-70; Member: Government Committee on future of Scotland's National Museums and Galleries, 1979-80; Council, Museums Association, 1977-78, 1987-88; Council, Society of Antiquaries of Scotland, 1981-82; Board, Scottish Museums Council, 1985-88; Museums Adviser, COSLA, 1985-90; Member, Paxton House Trust, since 1988; Member, East Lothian Community Development Trust, since 1989; External Examiner, St. Andrews University, 1994-97. Member, Board, Museums Training Institute, since 1995; Contested Angus South (Lab), 1970; major projects include: City of Edinburgh Art Centre, Museum of Childhood extension, People's Story Museum, City Art Centre extension. Publications: Ancient Monuments of Tayside; Tayside Before History; Edinburgh: an illustrated history; Huntly House; Lady Stair's House; The Pharaoh's Gold Mask; Gold of the Pharaohs (Editor); Dinosaurs Alive! (Editor); Sweat of the Sun — Gold of Peru (Editor); Golden Warriors of the Ukrainian Steppes (Editor); StarTrek – the exhibition (Editor); Quest for a Pirate (Editor); Gateway to the Silk Road – Relics from the Han to the Tang Dynasties from Xi'an, China (Editor); Faster, Higher, Stronger – The Story of the Olympic Movement (Editor). Recreations: family; gardening; opera; writing; reading; walking. Address: (h.) Kirkhill House, Queen's Road, Dunbar EH42 1LN; T.-01368 63113.

Coutts, John R.T., BSc, PhD. Reader in Biochemistry, IBLS, Glasgow University, since 1996; b. 10.7.41, Dundee; m., Marjory R.B.; 1 s.; 2 d. Educ. Morgan Academy, Dundee; St. Andrews University. Dundee University: Research Fellow in Obstetrics and Gynaecology, 1966-69, Honorary Lecturer in Obstetrics and Gynaecology, 1969-70; Lecturer, then Senior Lecturer, Glasgow University, 1970-87; Reader, Reproductive Medicine, Glasgow University, 1987-96. Publications: The Functional Morphology of the Human Ovary (Editor); many journal articles. Recreation: bowling. Address: (h.) 7 Spence Street, Glasgow G20 0AW; T.-0141-579 6553.

Coutts, T(homas) Gordon, MA, LLB, QC, FCIArb. Queen's Counsel, since 1973; b. 5.7.33, Aberdeen; m., Winifred K. Scott; 1 s.; 1 d. Educ. Aberdeen Grammar School; Aberdeen University. Advocate, 1959; Chairman, Industrial Tribunals, 1972; Chairman, Medical Appeal Tribunals, 1984; Vice President (Scotland), VAT and Duties Tribunals, since 1996; Temporary Judge, Court of

Session, 1991; Member, Panel of Arbitrators, CIArb, 1995. Recreations: travel; stamp collecting. Address: (h.) 6 Heriot Row, Edinburgh.

Cowan, Sheriff Annella Marie, LLB (Hons), MSc. Sheriff of Grampian Highland and Islands at Aberdeen since 1997; b. 14.11.53, Sheffield; m., James Temple Cowan (marriage dissolved). Educ. Elgin Academy; University of Edinburgh. Admitted Solicitor, 1978; Procurator Fiscal Depute, 1978-86; seconded to Scottish Law Commission, 1984-86; admitted Faculty of Advocates, 1987; Sheriff, Tayside Central and Fife at Stirling, 1993. Recreation: equestrianism. Address: Sheriff's Chambers, Sheriff Court, Aberdeen AB10 1WP; T.-01224 648316.

Cowan, Brigadier Colin Hunter, CBE, MA, FRSA, CEng, MICE. Chief Executive, Cumbernauld Development Corporation, 1970-85; b. 16.10.20, Edinburgh; m., 1, Elizabeth Williamson (deceased); 1 s. (deceased); 1 s.; 1 d.; 2, Mrs Janet Burnett. Educ. Wellington College; Trinity College, Cambridge. Commissioned, Royal Engineers, 1940; service in India and Burma, Royal Bombay Sappers and Miners, 1942-46; staff and regimental appointments, UK and Malta, 1951-60; commanded Field Engineer Regiment, Germany, 1960-63; Defence Adviser, UK Mission to UNO, New York, 1964-66; Chief Staff Officer to Engineer-in-Chief (Army), Ministry of Defence, 1966-68; Brigadier, Engineer Plans (Army), Ministry of Defence, 1968-70. Recreations: hill-walking; photography; music. Address: (h.) Flat 11, Varrich House, 7 Church Hill, Edinburgh EH10 4BG; T.-0131-447 9768.

Cowan, David Lockhart, MB, ChB, FRCSEdin. Consultant Otolaryngologist, City Hospital, Royal Hospital for Sick Children and Western General Hospital, Edinburgh, since 1974; Honorary Senior Lecturer, Edinburgh University; b. 30.6.41, Edinburgh; m., Eileen M. Masterton; 3 s.; 1 d. Educ. George Watson's College, Edinburgh; Trinity College, Glenalmond; Edinburgh University. Scottish Representative, Council, British Association of Otolaryngologists. Publications: Logan Turner's Diseases of the Ear, Nose and Throat (Co-author); Paediatric Otolaryngology (Co-author). Recreations: golf; all sport. Address: (h.) Kellerstane House, Gogar Station Road, Edinburgh EH12 9BS; T.-0131-339 0293.

Cowan, Professor Edward James, MA. Professor of Scottish History, Glasgow University, since 1993; b. 5.2.44, Edinburgh; widower; 1 s.; 2 d. Educ. Dumfries Academy; Edinburgh University. Lecturer in Scottish History, Edinburgh University, 1967-79; Professor of History and Chair of Scottish Studies, University of Guelph, Ontario, 1979-93. Recreations: hill-walking; Scottish folk music. Address: (b.) 9 University Gardens, Glasgow G12 8QH.

Cowan, Rev. Gordon Leith. Former Moderator, United Free Church of Scotland; Minister, Leith: Ebenezer UF Church of Scotland, since 1987; Presbytery Clerk, since 1992; b. 2.8.39, Glasgow; m., Agnes Allan Copeland; 2 s.; 2 d. Educ. Whitehill Senior Secondary School, Glasgow; Glasgow University; UF Congregational College, Edinburgh. Former Apprentice CA and book-keeper; Minister: Cumnock St. Andrews UF Church, 1968-76, Glasgow Wynd, 1976-87. Children's Panel Member, 1972-87. Recreations: genealogy; Scotland; watching athletics. Address: (h.) 14 Wardie Crescent, Edinburgh EH5 1AG; T.-0131-552 2349.

Cowan, John Mervyn, TD, MCIBS. Lt. Col. (Retd), RA/TA; Chairman: Earl Haig Fund (Scotland), since 1993, Royal Artillery Association Scottish Region, since 1991; Chairman, The Sandilands Trust, since 1994; b. 13.2.30, Oban; m., Marion Neilson Kidd; 1 s.; 2 d. Educ. Oban High School. National Bank of Scotland, National Commercial Bank of Scotland, Royal Bank of Scotland, 1946-90 (retired); TA commission, 1963; commanded 207 (Scottish) Battery RA(V), 1980-82; J.S.L.O., HQ Scotland, 1982-90; Member, RA Council for Scotland; Trustee, 445 and City of Edinburgh RA Regimental Trusts. Recreations: travel; charitable works; sport. Address: (h.) 43 Hunter Grove, Bathgate EH48 1NN; T.-01506 655784.

Cowan, Margaret Morton (Lady Cowan), MA, JP. Member, Executive and Highland Committees and of Council, National Trust for Scotland; Member, Scottish Committee, British Council, since 1991; b. 4.11.33, Newmilns; m., Sir Robert Cowan ; 2 d. Educ. St. George's School for Girls, Edinburgh; Edinburgh University. British Petroleum Company, 1955-59; Teacher, West Midlands Education Authority, 1965-76; Consultant and Lecturer in Use of Language, Hong Kong, 1976-81; Convener, Highland Festival, 1992-97; Member, Justice of the Peace Committee, Inverness, since 1985. Address: (h.) The Old Manse, Farr, Inverness-shire IV1 2XA; T.-01808 521209.

Cowe, Alan Wilson, MA, LLB. Secretary and Clerk, Church of Scotland General Trustees, since 1964; b. 9.8.38, Kelso; m., Agnes Cunningham Dick. Educ. Dunfermline High School; Edinburgh University. Law apprentice, Simpson Kinmont & Maxwell, WS, Edinburgh; Assistant to Secretary, Church of Scotland General Trustees, 1963-64. Recreations: running; hill-walking; theatre; jazz. Address: (b.) 121 George Street, Edinburgh EH2 4YR; T.-0131-225 5722.

Cowe, Andrew. Chief Executive, North Lanarkshire Council. Address: (b.) PO Box 14, Civic Centre, Motherwell, ML1 1TW.

Cowie, Alan, PGCE. Editor, Current Affairs, Grampian Television, since 1998; b. 28.4.48, Aberdeen; m., Evelyn; 2 d. Educ. Aberdeen Grammar School; Central College, London; Jordanhill College of Education, Glasgow. Teacher, Glasgow, 1971-72; Reporter/Presenter, Radio Scotland, 1972-75; joined Grampian Television as News Reporter, 1975; Programme Editor, 1988. Burgess, City of Aberdeen. Recreations: Scottish art; music; fishing. Address: (b.) Queen's Cross, Aberdeen; T.-01224 846560.

Cowie, Elspeth Elizabeth, MBA. National Organiser, Traditional Music and Song Association of Scotland, since 1996; traditional singer, since 1980; folk club organiser and concert promoter, since 1993; b. 16.2.54, Lanark. Educ. Hamilton Academy; Napier University. Retail management, 1972-82; Northsound Radio, Aberdeen: Production Assistant, 1982-83, PA to Managing Director, 1983-86;Assistant Director Finance/Administration, Penumbra, 1986-93; Assistant Director Administration, Alzheimer Scotland, 1993-96; Director and Company Secretary, Rockville Communications Ltd., since 1994; Director, Hallside Management Ltd., since 1997; recordings of traditional music and song, since 1987. Trustee: New Makars Trust, North East Scotland Heritage Trust. Recreations: singing; percussion; reading; sewing; current affairs. Address: (b.) 3 Rockville Terrace, Bonnyrigg EH19 2AG.

Cowie, Professor John McKenzie Grant, BSc, PhD, DSc, CChem, FRSC, FRSE. Professor of Chemistry of Materials, Heriot-Watt University, since 1988; Chairman, British High Polymer Research Group, 1990-98; Chairman, Macro Group UK, 1995-98; b. 31.5.33, Edinburgh; m., Agnes Neilson Campbell; 1 s.; 1 d. Educ. Royal High School, Edinburgh; Edinburgh University. Assistant Lecturer, Edinburgh University, 1956-58; Research Officer, National Research Council of Canada, Ottawa, 1958-67; Lecturer, Essex University, 1967-69; Senior Lecturer, Stirling University, 1969-73; Professor of Chemistry, Stirling University, 1973-88. Staff Assessor, Bangladesh Agricultural College; Chairman, Scottish Spinal Cord Injury Association, 1991-94; Hon. President, Scottish Council on Disability (Stirling District); Vice Chairman,

Scottish Council on Disability, 1989-90; Hon. President, Stirling Association of Voluntary Services. Recreations: reading; painting; listening to music. Address: (h.) Traquair, 50 Back Road, Dollar, Clackmannanshire; T.-Dollar 742031.

Cowie, Julian Martin, BA, CPFA, ACIS, IRRV. Director for Corporate Finance, Dumfries and Galloway Council, since 1995; b. 5.1.52, Castlerea, Eire; m., Anne Marie; 2 s.; 1 d. Educ. St. Joseph's College, Dumfries; Heriot-Watt University. Trainee Accountant, Midlothian CC, 1973-74; Assistant Accountant, Lothian Health Board, 1974-76; Accountant, Lothian RC, 1976-77; Senior Accountant, Fife RC, 1977-79; Chief Accountant, Dumfries and Galloway RC, 1979-85; Depute Director of Finance, Nithsdale District Council, 1985-92; Director of Financial Services, Annandale and Eskdale District Council, 1992-95. Address: (b.) Council Offices, English Street, Dumfries DG1 2DD; T.-01387 260000.

Cowie, Hon. Lord (William Lorn Kerr Cowie), MA (Cantab), LLB (Glas). Senator of the College of Justice in Scotland, 1977-94; Botswana Court of Appeal, 1995-98; b. 1.6.26, Glasgow; m., Camilla Henrietta Grizel Hoyle; 2 s.; 2 d. Educ. Fettes College, Edinburgh; Clare College, Cambridge; Glasgow University. RNVR, 1944-47 (Sub. Lt.); Member, Faculty of Advocates, 1952; QC, 1967. Scottish rugby internationalist, 1953. Recreation: fishing. Address: (h.) 20 Blacket Place, Edinburgh; T.-0131-667 8238.

Cowley of Innerwick, Col. Victor Charles Vereker, TD, JP, DL. Land Owner; b. 4.4.18, Glasgow; m., Moyra McClure; 1 s.; 2 d. Educ. St. Mary's, Melrose; Merchiston Castle School. Young master printer, 1937; commissioned, RATA, 1939; served France, North Africa, Sicily, Italy, Burma, Indo China; Col. Depute CRA 51st Highland Division; Chairman, Brownlie Scandrett and Graham Ltd. (retired 1960); Vice Convener, East Lothian County Council, 1973; Regional Councillor, Lothian, 1975; Commissioner of Income Tax, East Lothian, 1965-87. Recreations: shooting; golf. Address: Crowhill, Innerwick, Dunbar EH42 1QT; T.-01368 840279.

Cox, Derek, MBChB, MRCP(UK). Director of Public Health, Shetland Health Board, since 1990; b. 29.7.45, Glasgow. Educ. Hutchesons' Boys Grammar School; Glasgow University. Research Fellow, Cardiology, Glasgow University; Senior House Officer/Registrar in Cardiology, Glasgow Royal Infirmary; Medical Officer/Senior Medical Officer, Falkland Islands Government Medical Department; Registrar, General Surgery, Bignold Hospital, Wick; GP, Walls, Shetland. Address: (h.) 29 Burgh Road, Lerwick, Shetland ZE1 0LA; T.-01595 696466.

Cox, Gilbert Kirkwood, MBE, DL, JP. Retired General Manager Scotland, Associated Perforators & Weavers Ltd.; Director/Trustee, Airdrie Savings Bank, since 1987 (President, 1996-98); b. 24.8.35, Chapelhall, Airdrie; m., Marjory Moir Ross Taylor; 2 s.; 1 d. Educ. Airdrie Academy. National Coal Board, 1953-63; David A. McPhail & Sons Ltd., 1963-68; D.A. Monteith Holdings, 1968-71. Deputy Lieutenant, Lanarkshire; Chair, Board of Management, Coatbridge College; founder Member and Past President, Monklands Rotary Club; Member, Scottish Kidney Research Fund. Recreations: golf; gardening; walking. Address: (h.) Bedford House, Commonhead Street, Airdrie ML6 6NS; T.-01236 763331.

Cox, Sheriff Principal Graham Loudon, QC, MA, LLB, Sheriff Principal of South Strathclyde Dumfries and Galloway, since 1993; b. 22.12.33, Newcastle-upon-Tyne; m., Jean Nelson; 3 c. by pr. m. Educ. Hamilton Academy; Grove Academy; Edinburgh University. Army 1956-61 (latterly Major, Directorate of Army Legal Services); called to the Bar, 1962; Advocate-Depute, 1966-68; Sheriff of Tayside Central and Fife, at Dundee, 1968-93; QC, 1993; Secretary, Sheriffs' Association, 1987-91, President, 1991-93; Honorary Vice-President, Scottish Association for the Study of Delinquency, since 1996; Vice-Chairman, Northern Lighthouse Board, since 1997. Recreations: skiing; golf; restoration of decaying property. Address: (h.) Crail House, Crail, Fife; T.-01333 450270.

Cox, Richard Anthony Victor, MA, PhD. Lecturer in Celtic Studies, Aberdeen University, since 1996; Secretary, Scottish Gaelic Texts Society, since 1996; b. 31.5.54, Croydon. Educ. Rugby School; Cambridge Tutors (Croydon); Glasgow University. Editorial Assistant, Historical Dictionary of Scottish Gaelic, Glasgow University, 1985-91; Honorary Lecturer, Department of Gaelic, Glasgow University, 1982-91, 1995-96; Writer/Researcher, 1991-95. Publications: Brìgh nam Facal – Faclair Ur don Bhun-sgoil (dictionary); articles in academic journals. Address: (b.) Department of Celtic, Taylor Building, Aberdeen University, Aberdeen AB24 3UB; T.-01224 272544.

Cox, Roy Frederick. Managing Director, A. Richardson & Son Ltd., since 1983; Chairman, Sense Scotland, since 1992; b. 4.11.49, Leicester; m., Elizabeth; 2 s.; 2 d. Educ. New Parks Boys' School; Leicester Polytechnic College. Engineering apprentice; hosiery mechanic; builder. Past President, Rotary Club of Clydebank. Recreations: golf; skiing; football. Address: (b.) 34 Old Mill Road, Duntocher, Clydebank G81 6BX; T.-01389 872436.

Craig, Emeritus Professor Gordon Younger, BSc, PhD, CGeol, FRSE. Emeritus Professor of Geology, Edinburgh University, since 1984; Trustee, Dynamic Earth Charitable Trust, since 1995; b. 17.1.25, Milngavie; m., Mary Thornton; 2 s.; 2 step s.; 1 step d. Educ. Hillhead High School; Bearsden Academy; Glasgow University; Edinburgh University. Joined Edinburgh University as Lecturer, 1947; James Hutton Professor of Geology, 1967-84; Visiting Professor, University of Colorado, 1958-59, UCLA, 1959, 1965; Leverhulme Fellow, ANU, Canberra, 1978; Distinguished Foreign Scholar, Mid-America State Universities, 1980; Green Professor, University of British Columbia, 1977, Texas Christian University, 1994; President: Edinburgh Geological Society, 1967-69, International Commission on the History of the Geological Sciences, 1984-89; Clough Medal, Edinburgh Geological Society, 1987; History of Geology Division Award, Geological Society of America, 1990. Publications: Geology of Scotland (Editor), 1991 (3rd ed.); James Hutton: The Lost Drawings (Co-author), 1977; A Geological Miscellany (Co-author), 1982. Recreations: golf; gardening. Address: (h.) 14 Kevock Road, Lasswade, Edinburgh EH18 1HT; T.-0131-663 8275.

Craig, Rev. Maxwell Davidson, MA, BD, ThM. General Secretary, Action of Churches Together in Scotland, since 1990 (Minister, St. Columba's Parish Church, Bridge of Don, Aberdeen, 1989-91); Chaplain to the Queen in Scotland, since 1986; b. 25.12.31; m., Janet Margaret Macgregor; 1 s.; 3 d. Educ. Oriel College, Oxford; Edinburgh University. National Service, 1st Bn., Argyll and Sutherland Highlanders (2nd Lt.), 1954-56. Assistant Principal, Ministry of Labour, 1957-61; Private Secretary to Parliamentary Secretary, 1959-61; left London and civil service to train for ministry of Church of Scotland, 1961; ThM, Princeton, 1965; Minister, Grahamston Parish Church, Falkirk, 1966-73; Minister, Wellington Church, Glasgow, 1973-89; Convener, Church and Nation Committee, Church of Scotland, 1984-88; Chairman: Falkirk Children's Panel, 1970-72, Hillhead Housing Association Ltd., 1975-89; Member, Strathclyde Children's Panel, 1973-86. Recreations: hill-walking; choral singing. Address: (h.) 9 Kilbryde Crescent, Dunblane, Perthshire FK15 9BA; T.-01786 823147.

Craig, Robert, BA, MA, ALA. Director, Scottish Library Association, since 1984, and Scottish Library and Information Council, since 1991; b. 2.7.43, Hamilton; m., Ann Beaton; 1 s.; 1 d. Educ. Dalziel High School; Strathclyde University. Depute County Librarian, Lanark County Council, 1974-75; Principal Education Librarian, Glasgow Division, Strathclyde Regional Council, 1975-79; Lecturer, Strathclyde University, 1979-84. Publications: Scottish Libraries (Editor); Lights in the Darkness (Co-Editor); Scotland 1939 (Co-author); Scotland 1945 (Co-author). Recreations: reading; gardening; football. Address: (b.) Scottish Centre for Information and Library Services, 1 John Street, Hamilton ML3 7EU; T.-01698 458888.

Craig, Robert Harvey, RD, CA. Chartered Accountant in professional practice 1955-97; Honorary Sheriff, North Strathclyde at Campbeltown, since 1986; b. 18.12.29, Campbeltown; m., Marion Caldwell; 1 s.; 1 d. Educ. Campbeltown Grammar School; Glasgow University. Admitted to Institute of Chartered Accountants of Scotland, 1953; Fleet Air Arm, 1953-55; later commanded a Naval Reserve minesweeper; Director, Loch Fyne Oysters Ltd. and various companies. Recreations: sailing; skiing. Address: (h.) Ferndean, Campbeltown, Argyll, PA28 6EN; T.-01586 552495; (b.) T.-01586 551781.

Craik, Sheriff Roger George, QC (Scot). Sheriff of Lothian and Borders, at Edinburgh, since 1984; b. 22.11.40.

Cramb, Rev. Erik McLeish, LTh. National Co-ordinator, Scottish Churches Industrial Mission; b. 26.12.39, Glasgow; m., Elizabeth McLean; 2 s.; 3 d. Educ. Woodside Secondary School, Glasgow; Glasgow University and Trinity College. Minister: St. Thomas' Gallowgate, Glasgow, 1973-81, St. Paul's United Church, Kingston, Jamaica, 1981-84, Yoker, Glasgow, 1984-89; Organiser for Tayside, Scottish Churches International Mission, 1989-97. Socialist; Member, Iona Community; Chairman, Church Action on Poverty. Recreation: supports Partick Thistle. Address: (h.) 65 Clepington Road, Dundee DD4 7BQ; T.-01382 458764.

Cramond, Ronald Duncan, CBE (1987), MA, FIMgt, FSA (Scot). Chairman, Scottish Greenbelt Foundation (formerly Strathclyde Greenbelt Company), since 1992; Secretary, Intellectual Access Trust, since 1995; b. 22.3.27, Leith; m., Constance MacGregor (deceased); 1 s.; 1 d. Educ. George Heriot's School; Edinburgh University. Commissioned Royal Scots, 1950; entered War Office, 1951; Private Secretary to Parliamentary Under Secretary of State, Scottish Office, 1956; Principal, Department of Health for Scotland, 1957; Mactaggart Fellow, Glasgow University, 1962; Haldane Medallist in Public Administration, 1964; Assistant Secretary, Scottish Development Department, 1966; Under Secretary, 1973; Under Secretary, Department of Agriculture and Fisheries for Scotland, 1977. Deputy Chairman, Highlands and Islands Development Board, 1983-88; Member, Scottish Tourist Board, 1985-88; Trustee: National Museums of Scotland, 1985-96, Cromarty Arts Trust, 1988-91, Bo'ness Heritage Trust, 1989-97, Scottish Civic Trust, 1988-95; Vice President, Architectural Heritage Society of Scotland, 1989-94; Chairman, Scottish Museums Council, 1990-93; Commissioner, Countryside Commission for Scotland, 1988-92. Recreations: golf; hill-walking; testing a plastic hip. Address: (b.) Scottish Greenbelt Foundation, 375 West George Street, Glasgow G2 4LW.

Crampsey, Robert A. McN., MA (Hons), ARCM. Freelance Broadcaster and Writer; b. 8.7.30, Glasgow; m., Dr. Veronica R. Carson; 4 d. Educ. Holyrood School, Glasgow; Glasgow University; London University (External). RAF, 1952-55 (demobilised in rank of Flt. Lt.); Head of History Department, St. Aloysius College, Glasgow, 1967-71; Assistant Head Teacher, Holyrood Secondary School, 1971-74; Rector, St. Ambrose High School, Coatbridge, 1974-86. Winner, Brain of Britain, BBC, 1965; Churchill Fellow, 1970; semi-finalist, Mastermind, 1972-73; BBC Sports Commentator. Publications: History of Queen's Park FC; Puerto Rico; The Manager; The Scottish Footballer; The Edinburgh Pirate (Arts Council Award); The Run Out; Mr Stein (a biography); The Young Civilian; The Glasgow Golf Club 1787-1987; The Empire Exhibition; The Somerset Cricket Quiz Book; The Surrey Cricket Quiz Book; Ranfurly Castle Golf Club — a centenary history; The Official Centenary History of the Scottish Football League; Scottish Railway Connections; The King's Grocer - a Life of Sir Thomas Lipton. Recreations: travel; things Hispanic; listening to and playing music; cricket. Address: (h.) 15 Myrtle Park, Glasgow G42; T.-0141-423 2735.

Cranston, Colin. Firemaster, Lothian and Borders. Address: (b.) Brigade Headquarters, Lauriston Place, Edinburgh, EH3 9DE.

Cranstoun of That Ilk and Corehouse, David Alexander Somerville, TD, MA, MSc, PhD, DL. Cereal Specialist, SAC, since 1982; National List Trials Officer, ESCA, since 1973; Member, Queen's Bodyguard for Scotland (Royal Company of Archers); b. 19.12.43, Washington DC; m., Dr. Iur M.M. Glättli; 2 s. Educ. Winchester College; Trinity College, Oxford. Director, Scottish Quality Cereals; Hon. Director: Lord Roberts Workshops (Edinburgh), Scottish Union Jack Association. Commissioned Queens Own Lowland Yeomanry (TA), 1964, Lt. Col., 1982; Comd District Specialist Training Team, 1988, TA Col Lowlands, 1990; Recreation: forestry. Address: (h.) Corehouse, Lanark ML11 9TQ.

Craven, Professor Alan James, MA, PhD, FInstP, CPhys. Professor of Physics, University of Glasgow, since 1998; b. 18.4.47, St. Helens; m., Rosalind; 1 s.; 1 d. Educ. Prescot Grammar School; Emmanuel College, Cambridge University. Cavendish Laboratory, Cambridge: Research Student, 1969-75, Post-doctoral Research Assistant, 1975-78; Department of Physics and Astronomy, University of Glasgow: Lecturer, 1978-89, Senior Lecturer, 1989-91, Reader in Physics, 1991-98. Address: Department of Physics and Astronomy, University of Glasgow, Glasgow G12 8QQ; T.-0141-330 5892.

Crawford, Allan James, MA, LLB, SSC. Solicitor, since 1971; Senior Court Partner, Cochran, Sayers, Cook; Solicitor Advocate, since 1994; Part-time Tutor in Civil Advocacy, University of Strathclyde, since 1990; Temporary Sheriff; b. 9.6.46, Glasgow; m., Patricia; 1 s.; 2 d. Educ. King's Park School, Glasgow; University of Glasgow. Law apprenticeship, Maclay, Murray, Spens, 1969-71; joined Cochran, Sayers, Cook, Solicitors, 1971, Partner, 1974. Recreations: music; opera; tennis; badminton. Address: (b.) 33a Gordon Street, Glasgow G1 3PQ; T.-0141-248 5961.

Crawford, Barbara Elizabeth, MA (Hons), PhD. Lecturer in Medieval History, St. Andrews University, since 1972; Member, Royal Commission on Ancient and Historical Monuments of Scotland, since 1995; Chair, Treasure Trove Advisory Panel for Scotland, since 1994; b. 5.4.40, Barnsley; m., Robert M.M. Crawford; 1 s. Educ. Queen Margaret's School; St. Andrews University. Carnegie Senior Scholarship, 1968; Temporary Lecturer, Department of History, Aberdeen University, 1969; elected Fellow, Society of Antiquaries London, 1973, Fellow Society of Antiquaries of Scotland, 1964, Member Norwegian Academy of Science and Letters, 1997. Publication: Scandinavian Scotland, 1987. Recreations: exploring areas of Viking settlement in Scotland and North Atlantic. Address: (h.) Kincaple Cottage, St. Andrews KY16 9SH.

Crawford, Professor Dorothy H., MBBS, PhD, MD, DSc, FRCPath. Professor of Medical Microbiology, University of Edinburgh, since 1997; b. 13.4.45, Glasgow; m., Dr. W.D.

Alexander; 2 s. Educ. St. Thomas's Hospital Medical School. Senior Lecturer then Reader, Royal Post-graduate Medical School, London, 1985-90; Professor of Medical Microbiology, London School of Hygiene and Tropical Medicine, 1990-97. Address: (b.) University of Edinburgh Medical School, Teviot Place, Edinburgh EH8 9AG; T.-0131-650 3142.

Crawford, Professor Robert, MA, DPhil. Professor of Modern Scottish Literature, School of English, St. Andrews University, since 1995; Associate Director, St. Andrews Scottish Studies Institute, since 1993; Poetry Editor, Polygon, since 1991; Poet and Critic; b. 23.2.59, Bellshill; m., Alice Wales; 1 s.; 1 d. Educ. Hutchesons' Grammar School, Glasgow; Glasgow University; Balliol College, Oxford. Snell Exhibitioner & Carnegie Scholar, Balliol College, Oxford, 1981-84; Elizabeth Wordsworth Junior Research Fellow, St. Hugh's College, Oxford, 1984-87; British Academy Postdoctoral Fellow, Department of English Literature, Glasgow University, 1987-89; Lecturer in Modern Scottish Literature, School of English, St. Andrews University, 1989-95. Former Co-Editor, Verse Magazine. Publications: The Savage and the City in the Work of T.S. Eliot, 1987; A Scottish Assembly, 1990; Sharawaggi (Co-author), 1990; About Edwin Morgan (Co-Editor), 1990; Other Tongues: young Scottish poets in English, Scots and Gaelic (Editor), 1990; The Arts of Alasdair Gray (Co-Editor), 1991; Devolving English Literature, 1992; Talkies, 1992; Reading Douglas Dunn (Co-Editor), 1992; Identifying Poets, 1993; Liz Lochhead's Voices (Co-Editor), 1993; Twentieth Century Literature of Scotland: a selected bibliography, 1995; Talking Verse (Co-Editor), 1995; Masculinity, 1996; Penguin Modern Poets 9 (Co-Author), 1996; Robert Burns and Cultural Authority (Editor), 1997; Launch-site for English Studies: Three Centuries of Literary Studies at the University of St. Andrews (Editor), 1997; Impossibility, 1998; The Scottish Invention of English Literature (Editor), 1998; The Penguin Book of Poetry from Britain and Ireland since 1945 (Co-Editor), 1998. Recreation: quietness. Address: (b.) School of English, St. Andrews University, St. Andrews, KY16 9AL; T.-01334 476161, Ext. 2666.

Crawford, 29th Earl of, and Balcarres, 12th Earl of (Robert Alexander Lindsay), KT, PC, DL. Premier Earl of Scotland; Head of House of Lindsay; b. 5.3.27; m., Ruth Beatrice Meyer; 2 s.; 2 d. Educ. Eton; Trinity College, Cambridge. Grenadier Guards, 1945-49; MP (Conservative), Hertford, 1955-74, Welwyn and Hatfield, February to September, 1974; Opposition Front Bench Spokesman on Health and Social Security, 1967-70; Minister of State for Defence, 1970-72; Minister of State for Foreign and Commonwealth Affairs, 1972-74; Chairman, Lombard North Central Bank, 1976-80; Director, National Westminster Bank, 1975-88; Director, Scottish American Investment Co., 1978-88; Vice-Chairman, Sun Alliance & London Insurance Group, 1975-91; President, Rural District Councils Association, 1959-65; Chairman, National Association of Mental Health, 1963-70; Chairman, Historic Buildings Council for Scotland, 1976-83; Chairman, Royal Commission on Ancient and Historical Monuments of Scotland, 1985-95; First Crown Estate Commissioner, 1980-85; Deputy Lieutenant, Fife; Chairman, National Library of Scotland, since 1990; Lord Chamberlain to HM Queen Elizabeth The Queen Mother, since 1992. Address: (h.) Balcarres, Colinsburgh, Fife KY9 1HL.

Crawford, Robert Caldwell. Composer; b. 18.4.25, Edinburgh; m., Alison Braedine Orr; 1 s.; 1 d. Educ. Melville College, Edinburgh; Keswick Grammar School; Guildhall School of Music, London. Freelance Composer and Critic until 1970; BBC Music Producer, 1970-85; Chairman, Music Advisory Committee for Sir James Caird's Travelling Scholarships Trust, 1978-93. Recreations: carpentry; hill-walking; gardening; beekeeping. Address: (h.) 12 Inverleith Terrace, Edinburgh EH3 5NS; T.-0131-556 3600.

Crawford, Robert Hardie Bruce, JP. Leader, Perth and Kinross Council, since 1995; b. 16.2.55, Perth; m., Jacqueline; 3 s. Educ. Kinross High School; Perth High School. Civil servant, Scottish Office, since 1974; Chairman, Perth and Kinross Recreation Facilities Ltd; Member: Perthshire Tourist Board, Scottish Enterprise Tayside, Perth College. Recreations: watching Dunfermline Athletic; family. Address: (h.) 12 Douglas Crescent, Kinross; T.-01577 863531.

Crawford, Professor Robert MacGregor Martyn, BSc, DocSciNat (Liege), FRSE, FInstBiol. Professor of Plant Ecology, St. Andrews University, since 1977; b. 30.5.34, Glasgow; m., Barbara Elizabeth Hall; 1 s. Educ. Glasgow Academy; Glasgow University; Liege University; Moscow University. Lecturer, then Reader in Botany, St. Andrews University; Past President, Edinburgh Botanical Society; Editor, Flora. Publications: Studies in Plant Survival, 1989; Disturbance and Recovery in Arctic Lands, 1997. Recreations: languages; music; photography. Address: (b.) Sir Harold Mitchell Building, The University, St. Andrews, KY16 9AJ; T.-01334 463370.

Crawford, Ronald Lyndsay, MA, BLitt, Dr h.c., Commander of the Polish Order of Merit, 1989 (Gold Medal, 1982). Secretary, Committee of Scottish Higher Education Principals, since 1993; Secretary, Committee of Scottish University Principals, since 1988; b. 31.1.39, Paisley; m., Evelyn Ewing Knox; 2 s. Educ. Paisley Grammar School; Glasgow University; University of Freiburg. Editor, educational publishing, 1961-63; Strathclyde University: Administrative Assistant, 1963-67, Assistant, then Senior Assistant Registrar, 1967-73, Secretary to Court, 1973-81, Academic Registrar, 1981-93. Honorary Citizen, Lodz, Poland; President, Scottish-Polish Cultural Association, 1985-92. Recreations: fishing; boating; music. Address: (b.) COSHEP, St. Andrew House, 141 West Nile Street, Glasgow G1 2RN; T.-0141-353 1880.

Crawford, Rudy, BSc (Hons), MBChB, FRCS (Glas), FFAEM. Consultant in Accident and Emergency Care, Royal Infirmary, Glasgow, since 1990; Honorary Clinical Senior Lecturer, Glasgow University, since 1991; b. 5.5.49, Glasgow; m., Jane Crawford; 1 s.; 1 d. Educ. Glasgow University. Temporary Lecturer in Anatomy, Glasgow University; general surgery training; specialist training in accident and emergency medicine and surgery, Glasgow and Aberdeen; formerly member of offshore specialist team providing medical support for North Sea oil emergencies; founder Member and Local Project Director, Scottish Trauma Audit Group; Vice Chairman, Council, St. Andrew's Ambulance Association; Member, Scottish Management Efficiency Group Working Party on Accident and Emergency Services. Recreations: karate; running; photography; travel; Rotary International. Address: (b.) Accident and Emergency Department, Royal Infirmary, Glasgow G4 0SF; T.-0141-211 5166.

Crawford, Thomas, MA. Hon. Reader in English, Aberdeen University, since 1985; b. 6.7.20, Dundee; m., Jean Rennie McBride; 1 s.; 1 d. Educ. Dunfermline High School; Edinburgh University; University of Auckland. University of Auckland: Lecturer in English, 1953-60, Senior Lecturer, 1960-62, Associate Professor, 1963-65; Lecturer in English, Edinburgh University, 1965; Commonwealth Research Fellow, Hamilton, Ontario, 1966; Senior Lecturer in English, then Reader, Aberdeen University, 1967-85; Warnock Fellow, Yale University, various times, since 1978. Past President, Association for Scottish Literary Studies; former Editor, Scottish Literary Journal. Publications: Burns: a study of the poems and songs, 1960; Scott, 1965; Scott, selected poems (Editor),

1972; Love, Labour, and Liberty, 1976; Society and the Lyric, 1980; Boswell, Burns and the French Revolution, 1990; Correspondence of James Boswell and William Johnson Temple 1756-1795, Vol I. (Editor), 1997; Boswell in Scotland and Beyond (Editor), 1997. Recreations: walking and rambling; music. Address: (h.) 34 Summerhill Terrace, Aberdeen AB15 6HE; T.-01224 331764.

Crawley, David Jonathan, MA (Oxon). Head, Schools Group – Scottish Office Education and Industry Department, since 1998; b. 6.5.51, Barnet; m., Anne Anderson; 1 s.; 2 d. Educ. Chichester High School; Christ Church, Oxford. Scottish Office, 1972-81; Department of Energy, 1981-84; Assistant Secretary, Scottish Education Department, 1984-87; Principal Private Secretary to Secretary of State for Scotland, 1987-89; Assistant Secretary, Scottish Home and Health Department, 1989-90; Counsellor, UK Permanent Representation to European Communities, Brussels, 1990-94; Head, Private Finance Unit, Scottish Office, 1995-97; Head, Constitution Group Recreations: family; walking; gardening. Address: (b.) Functions Division, 1997-98. Recreations: family; walking; gardening. Address: (b.) Scottish Office, Victoria Quay, Edinburgh EH6 6QQ; T.-0131-244 7108.

Crean, Gerard Patrick, PhD, FRCPE, FRCPG, FRCPI; President, Scottish Fiddle Orchestra; Former Consultant Physician, Ross Hall Hospital, Glasgow; Consultant Physician and Physician-in-charge, Gastro-Intestinal Centre, Southern General Hospital, Glasgow, 1967-92; b. 1.5.27, Courtown Harbour, County Wexford; m., Janice Dodds Mathieson; 1 s.; 2 d. Educ. Rockwell College, Cashel, County Tipperary; University College, Dublin. House appointments, Mater Misericordiae Hospital, Dublin, Western General Hospital, Edinburgh and Edinburgh Royal Infirmary; Registrar, then Senior Registrar, Western General Hospital, Edinburgh; Member, scientific staff, Medical Research Council Clinical Endocrinology Unit, Edinburgh; Honorary Lecturer, Department of Therapeutics, Edinburgh University; Visiting Professor in Physiology, Pennsylvania University. Clarke Prize, Edinburgh Pathological Club; contributed to several textbooks. Past President, British Society of Gastroenterology. Recreations: fiddle playing; traditional music; history of Antarctic exploration; golf. Address: (h.) St. Ronan's, Duchal Road, Kilmacolm PA13 4AY.

Cresser, Professor Malcolm Stewart, PhD, DIC, BSc, ARCS, FRSC, CChem, CBiol, FIBiol. Professor of Plant & Soil Science, Aberdeen University, since 1989; b. 17.4.46, London; m., Louise Elizabeth Blackburn; 1 s.; 2 d. Educ. St. Ignatius College, Tottenham; Imperial College, London. Lecturer, Senior Lecturer, Reader, Department of Soil Science, Aberdeen University, 1970-89; awarded 11th SAC Silver Medal, 1984. Publications: Solvent Extraction in Flame Spectroscopic Analysis; Flame Spectrometry in Environmental Chemical Analysis; Environmental Chemical Analysis (Co-author); Acidification of Freshwaters (Co-author); Soil Chemistry and its Applications (Co-author). Recreations: painting; drawing; gardening. Address: (b.) Department of Plant and Soil Science, Cruickshank Building, Old Aberdeen AB24 3UU; T.-01224 272259.

Cresswell, Lyell Richard, BMus (Hons), MusM, PhD. Composer; b. 13.10.44, Wellington, New Zealand; m., Catherine Mawson. Educ. Victoria University of Wellington; Toronto University; Aberdeen University. Music Organiser, Chapter Arts Centre, Cardiff; Forman Fellow, Edinburgh University, 1980-82; Canadian Commonwealth scholarship, 1969-70; Dutch Government bursary, 1974-75; Ian Whyte Award, 1978; APRA Silver Scroll, 1979; Cramb Fellow, Glasgow University, 1982-85. Address: (h.) 4 Leslie Place, Edinburgh EH4 1NQ; T.-0131-332 9181.

Crichton, David, MA (Hons). Chief Executive, Lothian and Edinburgh Enterprise Ltd. (LEEL), since 1998; b. 14.10.55, Bridge of Allan; m., Pat; 2 s. Educ. Larbert High School; Edinburgh University. Industrial Economist, SDA, Glasgow, 1979-84; Director, Firn Crichton Roberts Ltd., 1984-89; Head of Projects, SDA, Edinburgh, 1989-91; Director of Projects, LEEL, 1991-98; Director, Alba Centre, Livingston, 1998. Address: (b.) LEEL, Apex House, 99 Haymarket Terrace, Edinburgh EH12 5HD; T.-0131-313 4000.

Crichton, Robin, FRAI. Film Producer and Director, since 1961; b. 14.5.40, Bournemouth; m., Trish Dorrell; 3 d. Educ. Sherborne; Paris; Edinburgh. Built Scotland's first independent film studio, 1968; started film training scheme, now Napier University M.A., 1970; founded first animation studio in Scotland; managed first independent outside broadcast unit in Scotland; Founder Member: Scottish ACTT Committee, Scottish Film Archive; former UK Vice-Chair and Scottish Chair, Independent Programme Producers' Association; former Co-ordinator, Working Party, Scottish Screen; co-initiated Annual Co-production Conference; organised Scottish stand at international TV television markets; Churchill Fellowship, 1990 (to study models for Scottish Screen); Co-production Consultant to various European broadcasters and producers; Project Leader, Eureka Audiovisual Federation; Director, Scottish Screen Locations; Consultant Programme Buyer, Gaelic Television Committee. Publications: Sara; The Curious Case of Santa Claus; Christmas Mouse. Recreations: dancing; gardening; DIY. Address: (b.) Edinburgh Film Productions, by Penicuik, Midlothian EH26 9LT; T.-01968 672131.

Critchlow, Howard Arthur, BDS, FDSRCS(Eng), FDSRCPS(Glas). Consultant Oral Surgeon (Honorary Senior Lecturer), Glasgow Dental Hospital, Stobhill General Hospital and Royal Hospital for Sick Children, Glasgow, since 1976; b. 22.4.43, Littleborough; m., Avril; 1 s.; 1 d. Educ. Nottingham High School for Boys; Sheffield University. General dental practice, Sheffield; oral surgery training post, Sheffield, Southampton, Odstock and Newcastle. Chairman, Greater Glasgow Health Board Dental Ethical Committee. Recreations: gardening; hill-walking; running. Address: (b.) Glasgow Dental Hospital and School, 378 Sauchiehall Street, Glasgow G2 3JZ; T.-0141-211 9600.

Croall, Alastair Menzies, LLB. Chief Executive, Scottish Borders Council, since 1995; b. 18.12.46, Kirkcaldy; m., Pauline; 3 s. Educ. Kirkcaldy High School; Edinburgh University. Worked with Roxburgh County Council, Moray and Nairn Joint County Council, Ross and Cromarty County Council; joined Borders Regional Council, 1975; appointed Depute Chief Executive and Solicitor to the Council, 1986. Recreations: walking; rugby; reading. Address: (b.) Council Headquarters, Newtown St. Boswells, Melrose, TD6 0SA; T.-01835 825055.

Croan, Sheriff Thomas Malcolm, MA, LLB. Sheriff of North Strathclyde at Kilmarnock, since 1983; b. 7.8.32, Edinburgh; m., Joan Kilpatrick Law; 1 s.; 3 d. Educ. St. Joseph's College, Dumfries; Edinburgh University. Admitted to Faculty of Advocates, 1956; Standing Junior Counsel, Scottish Development Department, 1964-65 and (for highways work), 1967 69; Advocate Depute, 1965-66; Sheriff of Grampian, Highland and Islands at Banff and Peterhead, 1969-83. Recreation: sailing. Address: (h.) Overdale, 113 Bentinck Drive, Troon.

Croft, Trevor Anthony, BSc, DipTRP, MRTPI, ARSGS, FRSA. Director, The National Trust for Scotland, since 1997; b. 9.6.48, Bradford; m., Janet Frances Halley; 2 d. Educ. Belle Vue Boys Grammar School, Bradford; Hull University; Sheffield University. Senior Assistant Planning Officer, N. Ireland Government, 1971-72; Assistant

Planning Officer, Countryside Commission for Scotland, 1972-75; Physical Planning Officer, Office of the President, Malawi Government, 1976-78; Parks Planning Officer, Department of National Parks and Wildlife, Malawi Government, 1978-82; Planning Officer, then Head of Policy Research, then Regional Director, then Deputy Director/Director of Countryside, National Trust for Scotland, 1982-96; Member, Forestry Commission, South Conservancy Regional Advisory Committee, 1987-90. Chairman, Dunfermline Branch, Royal Scottish Geographical Society, 1993-96. Recreations: sailing; travel; photography; equestrian vaulting; hill-walking. Address: (h.) Glenside, Tillyrie, Milnathort, Kinross KY13 7RW; T.-01577 864105.

Crofton, Sir John Wenman, KB, MA, MD, Dr h.c. Bordeaux, FRCP, FRCPE, Hon FRSE; b. 27.3.12, Dublin; m., Eileen Chris Mercer, MBE; 2 s.; 3 d. Educ. Tonbridge; Sidney Sussex College, Cambridge. Professor of Respiratory Diseases, Edinburgh University, 1952-77; Dean, Faculty of Medicine, 1963-66; Vice-Principal, 1969-70; President, Royal College of Physicians of Edinburgh, 1973-76; Vice-Chairman, Scottish Committee, Chest, Heart and Stroke Association, 1976-90; Chairman: Scottish Health Education Co-ordinating Committee, SHHD, 1981-86, Tobacco and Health Committee, International Union Against Tuberculosis and Lung Disease, 1984-88; Edinburgh Medal for Science and Society, 1995. Recreations: history; music; mountàins. Address: (h.) 13 Spylaw Bank Road, Edinburgh EH13 0JW; T.-0131-441 3730.

Crofts, Roger Stanley, BA, MLitt, CertEd, FRSA. Chief Executive, Scottish Natural Heritage, since 1991; Visiting Professor in Environmental Management, Royal Holloway, London University; Honorary Professor in Geography, University of Aberdeen; b. 17.1.44, Leicester; m. Lindsay Manson; 1 s.; 1 d. Educ. Hinckley Grammar School; Liverpool University; Leicester University. Research Assistant in Geography: Aberdeen University, 1966-72, University College, London, 1972-74; entered Scottish Office, 1974; Senior Research Officer, 1974-78; Principal Research Officer, 1978-84; Assistant Secretary, Highlands and Tourism Division, Industry Department, 1984-88; Assistant Secretary, Rural Affairs Division, Scottish Development Department, 1988-91. Member, Council: World Commission on Protected Areas (Europe), National Trust for Scotland, Scottish Association of Marine Science. Recreations: gardening; choral singing; hill-walking; wildflower photography. Address: (h.) 6 Old Church Lane, Duddingston Village, Edinburgh EH15 3PX; T.-0131-661 7858.

Cromartie, 5th Earl of (John Ruaridh Grant Mackenzie). Chief of the Clan Mackenzie; b. 12.6.48; m.; 2 s. Explosives Engineer. Publication: Selected Climbs in Skye, 1982. Address: Castle Leod, Strathpeffer, IV14 9AA.

Cromarty, Professor John Alfred, BSc, MSc (Pharmacol), MSc (ClinPharm), CertEd, MRPharmS. Professor of Clinical Pharmacy, The Robert Gordon University, Aberdeen, since 1993; National Specialist in Clinical Pharmacy (Scotland), since 1993; Honorary Consultant Clinical Pharmacist, Dundee Teaching Hospitals NHS Trust; Honorary Clinical Pharmacist, Grampian Health Board, Grampian Healthcare NHS Trust, Aberdeen Royal Hospitals NHS Trust; b. 26.8.51, Kirkwall; m., Evelyn McKenzie; 2 d. Educ. Kirkwall Grammar School; Heriot Watt University; Strathclyde University; Aberdeen College of Education; Aberdeen University. Staff Pharmacist/Lecturer, Oldham AHA/University of Manchester, 1979-80; Principal Pharmacist, North West Thames RHA, 1980-81; Principal Pharmacist/Senior Lecturer, North West Thames RHA/London University, 1981-89; Director, Post Qualification Education for Pharmacists in Scotland/Senior Lecturer, Strathclyde University, 1989-93; Member: National Pharmaceutical Advisory Committee, since 1994, Scottish Intercollegiate Guidelines Network, since 1995, Royal Pharmaceutical Society of Great Britain Working Group on Getting Research into Pharmacy Practice, since 1998, Clinical Resource and Audit Group Implementation Sub-Group, since 1998, Scottish Office Steering Group on Public Involvement in Primary Care, since 1998, Stonehaven and District Community Council, since 1996. Recreations: wine; natural history; rugby (spectating); poetry. Address: (b.) Clinical Pharmacy Practice Unit, School of Pharmacy, The Robert Gordon University, Schoolhill, Aberdeen AB10 1FR; T.-01224 262540.

Crompton, Professor David William Thomasson, MA, PhD, ScD, FIBiol, FRSE. John Graham Kerr Professor of Zoology, Glasgow University, since 1985; b. 5.12.37, Bolton; m., Effie Mary Marshall; 1 s.; 2 d. Educ. Bolton School; Sidney Sussex College, Cambridge. National Service, commission, King's Own Royal Regiment, 1957; Assistant in Research, Cambridge University, 1963-68; Fellow, Sidney Sussex College, 1964-85; Vice-Master, 1981-83; Lecturer in Parasitology, Cambridge University, 1968-85; Joint Editor, Parasitology, 1972-82; Adjunct Professor, Division of Nutritional Sciences, Cornell University, New York, since 1981; Aquatic Life Sciences Committee, Natural Environment Research Council, 1981-84; Director, Company of Biologists Ltd., since 1985; Member, WHO Expert Committee on Parasitic Diseases, since 1985; Scientific Medal, Zoological Society of London, 1977; Head, WHO Collaborating Centre for soil-transmitted helminthiases, Glasgow University; Chairman, Company of Biologists Ltd. Recreations: mountain walking; fishing; books; bull terriers. Address: (b.) Institute of Biomedical and Life Sciences, Glasgow University, Glasgow, G12 8QQ; T.-0141-330 5395; (h.) Melrose Cottage, Tyndrum, Perthshire FK20 8SA; T.-01838-400 203.

Crompton, Graham Kenneth, MB, ChB, FRCPE, FCCP. Consultant Physician, Lothian Health, since 1969; Senior Lecturer in Medicine and Respiratory Medicine, Edinburgh University, since 1969; b. 14.2.35, Salford; m., 1, Dorothy Margaret Graham (deceased); 2 s.; 2, Jane Anne Robertson (née Harrison). Educ. Salford Grammar School; Edinburgh University. Appointed Consultant Physician, 1969; Director of Studies, Faculty of Medicine, 1977-88; Member: Medical Advisory Committee, Asthma Society, 1981-88, Faculty of Medicine Admission Committee, Edinburgh University, since 1994, National Asthma Campaign Therapy Task Force, since 1991; President: British Thoracic Society 1994-95, Scottish Thoracic Society, 1994-96. Publications: Diagnosis and Management of Respiratory Diseases; chapters in 14 medical text books; author or co-author of over 200 scientific publications. Recreation: watching sport; fishing. Address: (h.) 14 Midmar Drive, Edinburgh EH10 6BU; T.-0131-447 1022.

Crook, Eunice Campbell, BSc, MBA. Director, The British Council, Scotland, since 1996; b. 24.11.50; m., Philip Crook. Educ. Campbeltown Grammar School; Glasgow University; Jordanhill College of Education. Teacher, Scotland, Seychelles and Botswana, 1972-85; British Council: Finance Division, 1985-90, Director Glasgow/International Arts Officer Scotland, 1990-94; study leave, 1994-96. Recreations: performing arts; travel; bridge. Address: (b.) 3/4 Bruntsfield Crescent, Edinburgh EH10 4HD; T.-0131-447 4716.

Crookall, Simon Philip. Chief Executive, Royal Scottish National Orchestra, since 1997; b. 1.10.60, Macclesfield. Educ. Nantwich and Acton Grammar School; King's College, Cambridge. Academic Assistant/Assistant to Principal/Front of House Manager, Royal Scottish Academy of Music and Drama, Glasgow, 1983-89; General Manager, Queen's Hall, Edinburgh, 1989-95; General

Manager, Royal Scottish National Orchestra, 1995-96. Recreations: singing as soloist for Council for Music in Hospitals; Chorusmaster, Haddo House Choral and Operatic Society, Aberdeen; Member, Order of St. John. Address: (b.) RSNO Centre, 73 Claremont Street, Glasgow G3 7JB; T.-0141-225 3550.

Crosbie, William, BSc(Hons). Headteacher, Castlebrae Community High School, since 1991; b. 14.8.50, Dumbarton; m., Rosemary; 1 s.; 1 d. Educ. Clydebank High School; University of Glasgow; Moray House College of Education. Teacher of Chemistry, Greenfaulds High School, Cumbernauld, 1973-76; Assistant Principal Teacher of Science, Holy Rood R.C. High School, Edinburgh, 1976-78; Castlebrae High School, Edinburgh: Principal Teacher of Chemistry, 1978-87, Assistant Headteacher, 1987-89, Depute Headteacher, 1989-91. Scottish Teacher of the Year, 1993; Scottish Schools Ethos Award, 1997. Recreations: golf; cinema; swimming. Address: (b.) 2a Greendykes Road, Edinburgh EH16 4NY; T.-0131-661 1282.

Crosby, William Scott, CBE (1982), BL. Lawyer; b. 31.7.18, Hawick; m., Margaret Elizabeth Bell; 3 s. Educ. Hawick High School; Edinburgh University. Army Service, 1939-46; Croix de Guerre, 1945; acted as Brigade Major 152 Brigade, 1945; Former Senior Partner, Storie, Cruden & Simpson, Advocates, Aberdeen; Chairman, Grampian Health Board, 1973-82; President, Society of Advocates in Aberdeen, 1984-85. Recreations: golf; swimming; walking; gardening. Address: (h.) 16 Golf Place, Aboyne AB34 5GA; T.-013398 85357.

Crosfield, Rev. Canon George Philip Chorley, OBE, MA (Cantab). Provost, St. Mary's Cathedral, Edinburgh, 1970-90; Hon. Canon, St. Mary's Cathedral, since 1991; b. 9.9.24, London; m., Susan Mary Jullion; 1 s.; 2 d. Educ. George Watson's College, Edinburgh; Selwyn College, Cambridge. Royal Artillery, 1942-46 (Captain); Priest, 1952; Assistant Curate: St. David's, Pilton, Edinburgh, 1951-53, St. Andrew's, St. Andrews, 1953-55; Rector, St. Cuthbert's, Hawick, 1955-60; Chaplain, Gordonstoun School, 1960-68; Canon and Vice-Provost, St. Mary's Cathedral, Edinburgh, 1968-70. Recreations: gardening; walking; carpentry. Address: (h.) 21 Biggar Road, Silverburn, near Penicuik EH26 9LQ; Tel.-01968 676607.

Cross, Professor Rod, BSc(Econ), BPhil. Professor of Economics, University of Strathclyde, since 1991; b. 27.3.51, Wigan. Educ. Wigan Grammar School; London School of Economics; University of York. Research Assistant, University of Manchester, 1972-74; Temporary Lecturer, Queen Mary College, University of London, 1974-75; Lecturer, University of St. Andrews, 1975-91. Adviser to Governor, Polish National Bank, 1990-92; Occasional Member, H.M. Treasury Academic Panel. Publications: Economic Theory and Policy in the UK, 1982; Unemployment Hysteresis and the Natural Rate Hypothesis (Editor), 1988; The Natural Rate of Unemployment, 1995. Recreations: hillwalking; rugby league and union, fiction. Address: (b.) Department of Economics, University of Strathclyde, Curran Building, 100 Cathedral Street, Glasgow G4 0LN; T.-0141-548 3855.

Crowe, David T., LLB, WS, NP. Solicitor, since 1969; Partner, Andrew Haddon & Crowe, W.S., Hawick, since 1971; Temporary Sheriff, since 1984; Chairman, Social Security Appeals Tribunal, since 1991; b. 9.8.45, Kilmarnock; m., Agi Pusztai; 1 s.; 3 d. Educ. Royal Academy, Irvine; University of Edinburgh. Hospital Administrator, Hôpital Protestante, Dabou, Ivory Coast, W. Africa, 1969-71. Former Dean, Faculty of Procurators for Roxburghshire; Treasurer, Temporary Sheriffs Association. Author: The Shrieval Vade Mecum; The Scottish Courts Companion. Recreations: music; transport; gardening; family. Address: (b.) 3 Oliver Place, Hawick TD9 9BG; T.-01450 372738.

Crowe, Frank Richard, LLB, NP. Deputy Crown Agent, since 1999; Regional Procurator Fiscal, South Strathclyde, Dumfries and Galloway, 1996-99; Procurator Fiscal, Hamilton, 1996-99; Solicitor Advocate; 15.3.52, Kirkcaldy; m., Alison Margaret Purdom; 2 d. Educ. Kirkcaldy High School; Royal High School, Edinburgh; University of Dundee. Law Apprentice, North of Scotland Hydro-Electric Board, 1973-75; Procurator Fiscal Depute: Dundee, 1975-78, Glasgow 1978-81; Senior Legal Assistant, Crown Office, 1981-83; Senior Depute Procurator Fiscal, Edinburgh 1983-87; Senior Depute i/c Crown Office Fraud Unit, 1987-88; Assistant Solicitor i/c High Court Unit, Crown Office, 1988-91; Procurator Fiscal, Kirkcaldy, 1991-96. Member: Management Committee, Lothian Victim Support Scheme, 1983-89, Training Advisory Committee, Victim Support Scotland, since 1994, Council, Law Society of Scotland, since 1996. Recreations: golf; cycling; racing; music. Address: (b.) Crown Office, 25 Chambers Street, Edinburgh EH1 1LA; T.-0131-226 2626.

Crowe, Victoria Elizabeth, MA (RCA), ARSA, RSW. Artist, Painter and Printmaker; b. 8.5.45, Kingston-on-Thames; m., Michael Walton; 1 s. (deceased); 1 d. Educ. Ursuline Convent Grammar School, London; Kingston College of Art; Royal College of Art. Part-time Lecturer, Drawing and Painting, Edinburgh College of Art, 1968-98; solo exhibitions: Scottish Gallery, Edinburgh, 1970, 1973, 1977, 1982, 1995, 1998; Thackeray Gallery, London, 1983, 1985, 1987, 1989, 1991, 1994, 1999; Bruton Gallery, Bath and Leeds, 1989, 1993, 1998; Corrymella Scott, Newcastle, 1997; exhibited throughout Europe and USA with Artists for Nature Foundation; work in public collections. Recreation: travel. Address: (h.) Bank House, Main Street, West Linton, Peeblesshire EH46 7EE.

Crowe, William J.J., BSc (Hons). Chief Executive, Scottish Salmon Growers Association, since 1988; b. 2.8.47, Edinburgh; m., Susan A.C. Knott; 1 s.; 1 d. Educ. High School of Glasgow; Aberdeen University. Address: (b.) Drummond House, Scott Street, Perth PH1 5EJ; T.-01738 635420.

Crowther, John Alexander, MBChB, FRCS(Eng), FRCS(Glas). Consultant Otorhinolaryngologist, Victoria Infirmary, Glasgow, since 1990; b. 8.3.56, Glasgow; m., Sally-Ann Crowther; 1 s.; 2 d. Educ. Kelvinside Academy, Glasgow; Dundee University. Trained in Dundee, Nottingham, Oxford and Glasgow; developed subspecialty interest in otology, neuro otology and skull base surgery at University of Michigan. Recreations: golf; skiing; squash; football. Address: Department of Otolaryngology, Victoria Infirmary, Langside, Glasgow G42; T.-0141-201 5289.

Crowther, Professor Margaret Anne, BA, PhD, FRHS, FRSE. Professor of Social History, University of Glasgow, since 1994; Chairman, Scottish Records Advisory Council, since 1995; b. 1.11.43, Adelaide, South Australia; m., John McCauley Crowther; 1 s. Educ. Walford Grammar School; Adelaide University; Oxford University. Publications: The Workhouse System, 1981; On Soul and Conscience, 1988. Recreation: gardening. Address: (b.) Department of Economic and Social History, University of Glasgow, Glasgow G12 8QQ; T.-0141-330 5991.

Cruickshank, Alastair Harvey, LLB, WS, NP, DL. Solicitor and Partner, Condies, Solicitors, Perth, since 1967; b. 10.8.43, Perth; m., Moira E. Pollock (deceased); 2 s. Educ. Perth Academy; Edinburgh University. Apprentice, then Assistant, Shepherd & Wedderburn, WS, Edinburgh, 1964-67; Assistant, then Partner, Condie Mackenzie & Co. (now Condies), since 1967. Registrar, Diocese of Brechin, since 1974; Member, Perth Society of High Constables. Recreations: hill-walking; sailing; chamber music, opera and classical music generally. Address: (b.) 2 Tay Street, Perth PH1 5LJ; T.-01738 440088.

Cruickshank, Alistair Booth, MA, FRSGS, FRCGS; b. 3.8.31, Dumfries; m., Sheena Carlin Brown; 2 s.; 1 d. Educ. High School of Stirling; Glasgow University; Georgia University. RAF, 1956-58; Glasgow University, 1958-61; Nottingham University, 1961-65; Glasgow University, 1965-86. Director, Royal Scottish Geographical Society, 1986-96; ordained Auxiliary Minister, Church of Scotland, 1991; Deputy Lieutenant, County of Clackmannan, since 1991. Recreations: fly fishing; peoples and places.

Crummy, Helen Murray, MBE, DLitt, DL, JP; b. 10.5.20, Edinburgh; m., Larry Crummy; 3 s. Educ. James Clark's School. Co-Founder Member and Organising Secretary, 23 years, Craigmillar Festival Society; served on Morris Committee (Housing and Social Work); former Member: Scottish Council for Community Education, Scottish Arts Council Development Committee, various Gulbenkian committees, DHSS Appeals Tribunal, Lothian Regional Council Education Advisory Committee. Recreations: writing; historical research; reading; gardening. Address: (h.) 4 Whitehill Street, Newcraighall, Musselburgh EH21 8RA; T.-0131-669 7344.

Crump, Professor John, BDS, BA, PhD. Professor and Director, Scottish Centre for Japanese Studies, since 1997; President, British Association for Japanese Studies, since 1998; b. 2.8.44, Leeds; m., Taeko Midorikawa; 2 d. Educ. Emanuel School; London University; Sheffield University. Dental Surgeon until 1973; research at University of Tokyo, 1973-75, and University of Sheffield, 1975-78; Senior Lecturer, University of York, 1978-96. Publications include: The Origins of Socialist Thought in Japan; State Capitalism; Non-market Socialism in the 19th and 20th Centuries; Hatta Shuzo and Pure Anarchism in Japan. Recreations: walking the hills; keeping fit; revolutionary thought. Address: (b.) University of Stirling, Stirling FK9 4LA; T.-01786 466085.

Cubie, Andrew, LLB (Hons), NP, WS, FRSA. Senior Partner, Fyfe Ireland WS, since 1994; Chairman, Bird Semple Fyfe Ireland WS, 1991-94; b. 24.8.46, Northallerton; m., Dr. Heather Ann Cubie; 1 s.; 2 d. Educ. Dollar Academy; Edinburgh University. Partner, Fyfe Ireland & Co., WS, 1971; non-executive Director of Murray VCT3 PLC and a number of private companies; Chairman of Governors, George Watson's College; Chairman, RNLI Scotland; Member, UK and Eire Committee of Management, and Deputy Chairman, Fund-Raising Committee, RNLI; Chairman: Scotland's Health at Work, W.S. Society Education and Training Committee; Member, Napier University Court; Member, Ministerial Action Group on Standards in Scottish Schools; Member, Independent Commission on Local Government and the Scottish Parliament and the Consultative Steering Group on the Scottish Parliament; former Chairman, CBI Scotland. Recreation: sailing. Address: (b.) Orchard Brae House, 30 Queensferry Road, Edinburgh EH4 2HG; T.-0131-343 2500.

Cullen, Paul B., QC, LLB. Solicitor-General for Scotland, 1995-97. Address: (b.) Advocates' Library, Parliament House, Edinburgh EH1 1RF.

Cullen, Rt. Hon. Lord (William Douglas Cullen), PC, LLD, DUniv, FRSE, HonFEng. Lord Justice Clerk, since 1997; Senator of the College of Justice, since 1986; b. 18.11.35, Edinburgh; m., Rosamond Mary Downer; 2 s.; 2 d. Educ. Dundee High School; St. Andrews University (MA); Edinburgh University (LLB). Called to the Scottish Bar, 1960; QC, 1973; Advocate-Depute, 1977-81; Chairman: Inquiry into the Piper Alpha Disaster, 1988-90, Inquiry into the Shootings at Dunblane Primary School, 1996. Member, Royal Commission on the Ancient and Historical Monuments of Scotland, 1987-97; Member, Napier University Court, since 1996; Chairman: Cockburn Association, 1984-86, Board of Governors, St. Margaret's School, Edinburgh, since 1994. Recreations: gardening; natural history. Address: (b.) Court of Session, Parliament House, Edinburgh; T.-0131-240 6732.

Culliven, John. Provost, Perth and Kinross Council, since 1996; b. 6.2.37, Glasgow; m., Sheila Elizabeth Grant MacKenzie; 4 s. Regional Councillor, since 1989. Recreations: bagpipes; horse-riding. Address: (h.) Craigmhor, Calvine, Pitlochry; T.-01796 483 250.

Cumming, Lt. Col. Alaistair Michael, OBE. Regimental Secretary to The Highlanders (Seaforth, Gordons and Camerons), since 1995; Commandant, Queen's Own Highlanders Battalion Army Cadet Force; b. 22.12.41, Singapore; m., Hilary Katharine Gray; 2 d. Educ. Bradfield College, Berkshire. Cadet, RMA Sandhurst, 1960-61; commissioned into The Gordon Highlanders, 1962; Major/Company Commander, Northern Ireland, 1976-77; Major/Staff Officer, Edinburgh, 1978-79; Battalion Second in Command, Hong Kong, 1980-81; Major/Staff Officer, Londonderry, 1982-84; Lt. Col.: Commander Ground Liaison Team, Germany, 1985-88; Naval and Military Attache, British Embassy, Poland, 1989-92; Commander Support Weapons Wing, Netheravon, 1992-95. Recreations: cricket; golf; tennis; shooting; skiing. Address: (b.) RHQ, The Highlanders, Cameron Barracks, Inverness IV2 3XD.

Cumming, Alexander James, MA (Hons), CIMA, IPFA. Chief Executive, Aberdeen Royal Hospitals NHS Trust, since 1994; b. 7.3.47, Aberdeen; m., Margaret Callan; 1 s.; 2 d. Educ. Fordyce Academy; Robert Gordon's College; Aberdeen University. VSO, 1968-70; Accountant, Company Secretary, Chief Accountant, 1970-75; joined Grampian Health Board, 1975. Chairman, Langstane Housing Association. Address: (b.) Foresterhill House, Ashgrove Road West, Aberdeen; T.-01224 681818.

Cumming, Allan David, BSc, MBChB, MD, FRCP. Senior Lecturer in Medicine, University of Edinburgh, since 1989; Consultant Physician, Royal Infirmary of Edinburgh, since 1989; Director of Undergraduate Medical Education and Associate Dean (Teaching), University of Edinburgh Medical School, since 1998; b. 12.2.51, Buenos Aires, Argentina; m., Lindsay Galloway; 1 s.; 1 d. Educ. Dundee High School; Nairn Academy; Boroughmuir High School; Edinburgh University. House Officer Posts, Royal Infirmary of Edinburgh, 1975-76; Registrar: Medical Unit, Bangour General Hospital 1977-79, Renal Medicine, Royal Infirmary of Edinburgh, 1980-84; Clinical Research Fellow, University of Western Ontario, Canada, 1985-86; Lecturer/Senior Registrar, Medicine, Royal Infirmary of Edinburgh, 1987-89. Chairman, Healthy Volunteers Research Ethics Committee, Lothian Health. Publications: 51 papers in journals; 13 book chapters. Recreations: golf; curling; music; more golf. Address: Department of Renal Medicine, Royal Infirmary NHS Trust, Lauriston Place, Edinburgh EH3 9YW; T.-0131-536 2307.

Cumming, Eric Alexander, MIMgt, AInstAM, FSA (Scot). Principal, Scottish Court Service HQ, since 1995; b. 9.5.54, Glasgow; m., Isabel Rodger. Educ. Albert Senior Secondary School; Glasgow College of Commerce. Entered Scottish Court Service (Sheriff Clerk's Branch), 1972; posts in Glasgow, Nairn, Ayr, Dumbarton; Depute Clerk of Session and Justiciary, 1983; Sheriff Clerk, Ayr, 1990-92; Deputy Principal Clerk of Justiciary, 1992-95. Recreations: Clyde steamers; reading; naval history. Address: (b.) Hayweight House, 23 Lauriston Street, Edinburgh; T.-0131 221 6822.

Cumming, Robert Currie, BL, FCIBS, ACIB, FRCSEdin (Hon.), FRSGS; b. 21.5.21, Strathaven; m., Mary Jean McDonald Crombie. Educ. Hutchesons' Grammar School, Glasgow; Glasgow University. Former Executive Director, Royal Bank of Scotland Group PLC and Royal Bank of Scotland PLC; Chairman, English Speaking Union —

Scotland, 1984-90; Trustee, Royal Scottish Geographical Society. Recreations: fishing; golf; walking. Address: (h.) 3 Succoth Park, Edinburgh EH12 6BX; T.-0131-337 1910.

Cummings, John Andrew, BA, MA. Headmaster, Keil School, since 1993; b. 15.5.49, Eastbourne; m., Claire; 1 s.; 1 d. Educ. Eastbourne Grammar School; University of Kent; London University. Assistant Master: Glasgow Academy, 1975-80, Tonbridge School, Kent, 1980-89; Melbourne Grammar School, Australia, 1985; Head of English and Drama/Head of Sixth Form, Wycliffe College, 1989-93. Recreations: reading; theatre; hill-walking; tennis. Address: (b.) Keil School, Helenslee Road, Dumbarton G82 4AL; T.-01389 762003.

Cunningham, David Kenneth, BEd, MEd (Hons), FRSA. Head Teacher, Hillhead High School, Glasgow, since 1993; b. 19.4.48, Saltcoats; m., Marion S. Shedden; 2 d. Educ. Ardrossan Academy; Glasgow University; Jordanhill College of Education. Principal Teacher of English, North Kelvinside Secondary, 1976-80; Assistant Head Teacher, Garthamlock Secondary, 1980-82; Adviser in English, Dunbarton Division, 1982-90, Education Officer (Acting), 1989-90; Inspector, Quality Assurance Unit, Strathclyde Regional Council, 1990-93; Member, Board, Glasgow Area, Young Enterprise Scotland; Executive Member, National Council, Headteachers Association of Scotland; UCAS Standing Committee, since 1997. Publications: Reading for 'S' Grade English, 1988. Recreations: various sports; reading; photography; travel; family. Address: (h.) 7 Waterfoot Road, Newton Mearns, Glasgow; T.-0141-639 3367.

Cunningham, Professor Ian M.M., CBE, FRSE, FIBiol, FRAgS, Hon. Assoc. RCVS, Bsc, PhD. Chairman, National Trust for Scotland; General Council Assessor, Court, Edinburgh University; Director, Edinburgh Technopole Co. Ltd; b. 30.9.25, Kirknewton; m., Agnes Whitelaw Frew. Educ. Lanark Grammar School; Edinburgh University. Assistant Economist, West of Scotland Agricultural College, 1946-47; Lecturer in Agriculture, Durham School of Agriculture, 1947-50; Lecturer, then Senior Lecturer, Edinburgh University, 1950-68; Director, Hill Farming Research Organisation, 1968-80; Professor of Agriculture, Glasgow University, and Principal, West of Scotland Agricultural College, 1980-87. Member: Farm Animal Welfare Council, Hill Farming Advisory Committee, Scotland; Chairman, Board, Macaulay Land Use Research Institute, 1987-95; George Hedley Memorial Award for services to the sheep industry; Massey Ferguson Award for services to British agriculture; Sir William Young Award for services to livestock production in Scotland; Hon. Assoc., RCVS. Address: (h.) 5 The Bridges, Peebles EH45 8BP.

Cunningham, Very Rev. Monsignor John, JCD. Parish Priest, St. Patrick's Greenock, since 1992; Chairman, Roman Catholic Scottish National Tribunal, 1986-92; Papal Chaplain, since 1994; Vicar General, Diocese of Paisley, since 1997; b. 22.2.38, Paisley. Educ. St. Mary's College, Blairs, Aberdeen; St. Peter's College, Cardross; Scots College and Gregorian University, Rome. Assistant Priest, Our Lady of Lourdes, Bishopton, 1964-69; Professor of Canon Law, St. Peter's College, Cardross and Newlands (Glasgow), 1967-81; Advocate of the Roman Catholic Scottish National Tribunal, 1970-82; Assistant Priest, St. Columba's, Renfrew, 1974-86; Vice-President, RC Scottish National Tribunal, 1982-86. Address: 5 Orangefield Place, Greenock PA15 1YX; T.-01475 720223.

Cunningham, (Robert) Grahame. Divisional Director, Edinburgh Chamber of Commerce and Enterprise, since 1996; Chief Executive, Edinburgh Business Development Ltd., since 1996; Divisional Director, Edinburgh International Trade, since 1997; b. 8.1.44, Edinburgh; m., Elaine Macfie; 3 s.; 1 d. British Transport Hotels, 1963-66 (Trainee Manager); United Biscuits Group of Companies, 1966-87, latterly General Manager (London and Midlands); Assistant Director, EVENT Enterprise Trust, Edinburgh, 1987, which merged with Leith Enterprise Trust, 1992, subsequently Director of Operations in new Capital Enterprise Trust. Director, Edinburgh Community Trust; Director, Edinburgh Business Loan Fund Ltd.; partner in own business, Cunningham & Co. Recreations: golf; renovating classic cars; tennis; motor racing. Address: (h.) 16 Dean Park Crescent, Edinburgh EH4 1PH; T.-0131-315 3302.

Cunningham, Robert Ritchie, MA (Hons). Rector, Inverness High School, since 1991; Director, Inverness and Nairn Enterprise, since 1998; b. 22.5.53, Stirling; m., Linda; 2 s. Educ. Lenzie Academy; University of Glasgow. Teacher of Geography, Cumbernauld High School, 1977-80; Principal Teacher of Geography, John Neilson High School, Paisley, 1980-84; Field Development Officer, Scottish Examination Board, 1984-86; Adviser in Social Subjects, Highland Region, 1986-91. Publications: author or co-author of over 20 publications, mostly on geography for schools. Recreations: Rotary; writing; playing with my children. Address: (b.) Inverness High School, Montague Row, Inverness IV3 5DZ; T.-01463 233586.

Cunningham, Roseanna, MP. MP (SNP), Perth, since 1995; b. 27.7.51, Glasgow. Educ. University of Western Australia. SNP Research Department, 1977-79; law degree, Edinburgh University; Trainee Solicitor, Dumbarton District Council, 1983-84; Solicitor, Dumbarton, 1984-86; Solicitor, Glasgow, 1986-89; called to the Scottish Bar, 1990. Recreations: folk festivals; reading; cinema; cats; novice hill-walker. Address: (b.) House of Commons, Westminster, London, SW1A 0AA.

Cunningham-Jardine, Ronald Charles. Lord Lieutenant, Dumfries, since 1991; Farmer; b. 19.9.31, Edinburgh; m., Constance Mary Teresa Inglis; 1 s.; 1 d. Educ. Ludgrove; Eton; Royal Military Academy, Sandhurst. Royal Scots Greys (retired as Captain), 1950-58. Recreations: all country sports. Address: (h.) Fourmerkland, Lockerbie, Dumfriesshire DG11 1EH; T.-01387 810226.

Cupples, Dorothy May, MA, BSc, FRSGS; a Vice-President, Royal Scottish Geographical Society, since 1975; b. 29.4.12, Glasgow; m., James Barclay Glen; 1 step-s.; 1 step-d. Educ. Albert Road Academy; Laurel Bank School; Glasgow University; Jordanhill College, Glasgow. Teacher of Mathematics and Botany for 36 years (35 at Laurel Bank School). Member, Antique and Fine Arts Society. Recreations: golf; hill-walking; motoring. Address: 2 Kennedy Court, Braidholm Crescent, Giffnock, Glasgow G46 6HQ; T.-0141-638 5680.

Currie, Eleanor Jean, MA, DipSecEd. Director of Education, East Renfrewshire Council, since 1995; b. 1.6.50, Ayr; m., Robert L. Currie. Educ. Cumnock Academy; Glasgow University; Jordanhill College. Teacher/Principal Teacher of Modern Studies; seconded to Consultative Committee on the Curriculum; Principal Office (Staffing), then Education Officer (Renfrew Division), then Senior Education Officer (Dumbarton Division), then Divisional Assistant Director of Education (Dumbarton Division), Strathclyde Regional Council. Recreations: keep fit exercising; walking; travel. Address: (b.) Eastwood Park, Rouken Glen Road, Giffnock, G46 6UG; T.-0141-557 3430.

Currie, Rev. Ian Samuel, MBE, BD. Minister, Oakshaw Trinity Church, Paisley, since 1991; b. 14.8.43, Glasgow; m., Jennifer; 1 s.; 1 d. Educ. Bellahouston Academy; Trinity College; University of Glasgow; Minister: Blairhill Dundyvan Church, Coatbridge, 1975-80, St John's Church, Paisley, 1980-91. Chair, Victim Support Scotland, 1993-98;

Director, Wynd Centre, Paisley. Recreation: chess. Address: (b.) Oakshaw Trinity Church Office, 6 School Wynd, Paisley PA1 2DB; T.-0141-887 4647.

Currie, Ken. Painter; b. 1960, North Shields. Educ. Paisley College; Glasgow School of Art. Worked on two films about Glasgow and Clyde shipbuilding, 1983-85; specialises in political realism, including a series of murals for the People's Palace Museum, Glasgow, on the socialist history of the city.

Curtis, Professor Adam Sebastian Genevieve, MA, PhD. Professor of Cell Biology, Glasgow University, since 1967; Director, Centre for Cell Engineering, since 1996; b. 3.1.34, London; m., Ann Park; 2 d. Educ. Aldenham School; Kings College, Cambridge. University College, London: Honorary Research Assistant, 1957-62, Lecturer in Zoology, 1962-67. Director, Company of Biologists Ltd., since 1961; Governor, Westbourne School, 1985-90; Council Member, Royal Society of Edinburgh, 1983-86; President, Society of Experimental Biology, 1991-93; Editor, Scottish Diver magazine, 1978-91, and since 1994; Editor-in-Chief, Experimental Biology Online, since 1996; President, Scottish Sub-Aqua Club, 1972-76. Recreations: sports diving; gardening. Address: (h.) 2 Kirklee Circus, Glasgow G12 OTW; T.-0141-339 2152.

Curtis, Professor David James, BSc, PhD, FZS, CBiol, FIBiol. Professor of Biology, Paisley University, 1990-97 (Visiting Professor, since 1997); Tutor in Biology and Psychology, Open University, since 1973; Ecologist; b. 5.4.45, Liverpool; m., Margaret Angela Lacey; 2 d. Educ. St. Mary's College, Crosby; Liverpool University. Lecturer in Biology, Paisley College of Technology, 1970-81; Senior Lecturer in Biology, Paisley College of Technology, 1981-90; edited five books, written many scientific papers and reports; organised international conferences about environmental conservation; Hon. Secretary, Scottish Environmental Education Council and Director, Scottish Environmental Information Network for Education, 1983-91; Co-Director, Scottish Chough Study Group, 1988-93; Founding Co-Director, European Forum on Birds and Pastoralism, 1988-93; Board Member, Clyde River Purification Board, 1984-92; Member, Species Survival Commission (Steppe and Grassland Birds), IUCN - World Conservation Union, since 1992. Recreations: motor-caravanning; walking; bird-watching; jogging. Address: (b.) Department of Biological Sciences, Paisley University, High Street, Paisley PA1 2BE; T.-0141-848 3119.

Cuschieri, Professor Sir Alfred, MD, ChM, FRCSEd, FRCSEng, FIBiol, MD Liverpool Univ (Hon), FRCSI (Hon), FRCPSGlas (Hon). Professor and Head, Department of Surgery, Dundee University, since 1976; b. 30.9.38, Malta; m., Dr. M.P. Holley; 3 d. Educ. St. Aloysius College; Royal University of Malta; Liverpool University. Lecturer/Senior Lecturer/Reader in Surgery, then Professor of Surgery, Liverpool University. Recreations: fishing; music. Address: (h.) Denbrae Mill, Strathkinness Low Road, St Andrews, Fife KY16 9TY; T.-01334 475046.

Cusine, Professor Douglas James, LLB. Professor, Department of Conveyancing and Professional Practice of Law, Aberdeen University, since 1990; Member: Council, Law Society of Scotland, since 1988, Lord President's Advisory Council on Messengers-at-Arms and Sheriff Officers, since 1989; Member, UK Delegation to CCBE, since 1997; Honorary Sheriff, since 1994; b. 2.9.46, Glasgow; m., Marilyn Calvert Ramsay; 1 s.; 1 d. Educ. Hutchesons' Boys' Grammar School; Glasgow University. Solicitor, 1971; Lecturer in Private Law: Glasgow University, 1974-76, Aberdeen University, 1977-82; Senior Lecturer, 1982-90. Publications: Marine Pollution: Law and Practice (Co-Editor), 1980; Cases and Materials in Commercial Law (Co-Editor), 1987; A Scots Conveyancing Miscellany (Editor), 1987; New Reproductive Techniques: a legal perspective, 1988; Law and Practice of Diligence (Co-author), 1989; Reproductive Medicine and the Law (Co-Editor), 1990; Standard Securities, 1990; Missives (Co-Author), 1993; Requirements of Writing (Co-Author), 1995; various articles on medico-legal issues and conveyancing. Recreations: swimming; walking; bird-watching. Address: (b.) Aberdeen University, Taylor Building, Regent Walk, Old Aberdeen AB24 3UB.

Cuthbert, Thomas Paterson, MA (Hons), MEd. Regional Manager (Scotland), Lantra (National Training Organisation), since 1993; b. 20.12.57, Dunfermline; m., Margaret; 1 s.; 2 d. Educ. Queen Anne High School, Dunfermline; Edinburgh University. British Universities Soccer Internationalist, 1980. Teacher, Alloa Academy, 1981-87; Research and Development Officer, Scottish Vocational Education Council, 1987-88; Project Development Officer, Fife Education Department, 1989-91; Business Development and Training Manager, Scottish Association of Master Bakers, 1991-93. Recreations: sport, including football, tennis and golf; current affairs; cinema; collecting classic Westerns; reading history. Address: (b.) The Rural Centre, West Mains, Ingliston, Newbridge, Midlothian, EH28 8NZ; T.-0131-472 4131.

Cuthbertson, Iain, MA (Hons), FRSAMD. Actor; b. 4.1.30. Educ. Glasgow Academy; Aberdeen Grammar School; Aberdeen University. General Manager/Director of Productions, Citizens' Theatre, Glasgow, 1962-65; Associate Director, Royal Court Theatre, London, 1965; Director, Perth Theatre, 1967-68; sometime Administrator, Playhouse Theatre, Nottingham; stage performances include title roles in Armstrong's Last Goodnight (Citizens'), The Wallace (Edinburgh Festival), Serjeant Musgrave's Dance (Royal Court), Sutherland's Law (TV series); 1,500 broadcasts; TV work includes Budgie, Charles Endell Esq.; premiere of A Drunk Man Looks at the Thistle, set to music and dance; Hon. LLD, Aberdeen University; former Board Member, Scottish Theatre Company; former Hon. President, SCDA; Visiting Stage Director and Tutor, Royal Scottish Academy of Music and Drama. Recreations: countryside; sailing. Address: (b.) Janet Welch, Personal Management, 46 The Vineyard, Richmond, Surrey TW10 6AN.

Cuthbertson, Ian Jardine, LLB, NP, MIPA, MSPI, FInstD. Solicitor, Notary Public and Licensed Insolvency Practitioner; Partner, Dorman, Jeffrey, Solicitors, Glasgow and Edinburgh, since 1979; b. 8.5.51, Glasgow; m., Sally Jane; 1 s.; 2 d. Educ. Jordanhill College School, Glasgow; Glasgow University. Apprenticeship, Messrs Boyds; admitted as Solicitor, 1974; Partner, Messrs Boyds, 1978; jointly founded firm of Dorman Jeffrey & Co., 1979. Recreations: watching football and rugby. Address: (b.) Madeleine Smith House, 6/7 Blythswood Square, Glasgow; T.-0141-221 9880; Saltire Court, Castle Terrace, Edinburgh; T.-0131-228 8000.

Cuthbertson, Rev. Malcolm, BA, BD (Hons). Minister, Easterhouse: St. George's and St. Peter's Church of Scotland, since 1984; Non-Executive Director, Glasgow Dental Hospital and School NHS Trust, since 1995; b. 3.4.56, Glasgow; m., Rena Fennel; 1 s.; 2 d. Educ. Grangemouth High School; Stirling University; Aberdeen University. Probationer Assistant, Crown Court Church, London, 1983-84. Recreations: eating out; reading theology. Address: 2 Lochdochart Road, Glasgow G34 0PZ; T.-0141-773 2667.

Cuthell, Rev. Thomas Cuthbertson, MA, BD. Minister, St. Cuthbert's Parish Church, Edinburgh, since 1976; b. 18.2.41, Falkirk. Educ. Bo'ness Academy; University of Edinburgh. Assistant Minister, St. Giles Cathedral,

Edinburgh; Minister, North Church, Uphall. Recreations: travel; music; sailing. Address: St. Cuthbert's Parish Church, 5 Lothian Road, Edinburgh EH1 2EP; T.-0131-229 1142.

Cutler, Timothy Robert (Robin), CBE, BSc, DSc. Forestry Consultant; b. 24.7.34, India; m., Ishbel W.M.; 1 s.; 1 d. Educ. Banff Academy; Aberdeen University. Colonial Forest Service, Kenya, 1958-64; New Zealand Government Forestry, 1964-90, latterly Chief Executive, New Zealand Ministry of Forestry; Director General, Forestry Commission, 1990-95. Recreations: tennis; golf; travel. Address: 14 Swanston Road, Edinburgh EH10 7BB; T.-0131-445 5437.

Cywinski, Professor Robert, BSc, PhD, CPhys, MInstP, FRSA. Professor of Physics (Magnetism), School of Physics and Astronomy, University of St. Andrews, since 1995; Director, St. Andrews Centre for Advanced Materials, since 1996; b. 18.4.52, Huddersfield; 1 d. Educ. Huddersfield New College; University of Manchester; University of Salford. Postdoctoral Research Assistantship, Department of Physics, Imperial College, London, 1976-77; Australian Research Grants Committee Research Fellow, Department of Physics, Monash University, Australia, 1977-80; Senior Scientific Officer, Neutron Division, ISIS, Rutherford Appleton Laboratory, Oxfordshire, 1980-85; Lecturer in Physics, J. J. Thomson Physical Laboratory, University of Reading, 1985-95. UK Delegate and Vice Chairman, European Neutron Scattering Association; Member, Physics College, UK Engineering Physical Sciences Research Council; Member, Neutron Scattering Group Committee, Institute of Physics; Member, European Spallation Source Science Working Group Muon Subcommittee; Chairman, Institut Laue Langevin (Grenoble) Magnetic Structures College, Scientific Council; Member, Board of Governors, Dollar Academy. Publications: Neutron Scattering at a Pulsed Source (Co-Editor); over 130 publications on magnetism, superconductivity, neutron beam science, and muon spin relaxation in international scientific journals. Recreations: photography; music; literature. Address: (b.) School of Physics and Astronomy, University of St. Andrews, St. Andrews, KY16 9SS; T.-01334 463108.

Czerkawska, Catherine Lucy, MA (Hons); MA (postgraduate). Novelist and Dramatist; b. 3.12.50, Leeds; m., Alan Lees; 1 s. Educ. Queen Margaret's Academy, Ayr; St. Michael's Academy, Kilwinning; Edinburgh University; Leeds University. Wrote and published two books of poety (White Boats and a Book of Men); taught EFL in Finland and Poland for three years; returned to Scotland to work as Community Writer in Fife; thereafter, full-time freelance writer working on radio, television and stage plays; author, Shadow of the Stone and The Golden Apple; Pye Radio Award for Best Play of 1980, O Flower of Scotland; Scottish Radio Industries Club Award, 1983, for Bonnie Blue Hen; Wormwood, produced by Traverse Theatre, Edinburgh, 1997. Recreations: travel; films; local history; swimming; genealogy. Address: c/o Peters Fraser and Dunlop, 5th Floor, The Chambers, Chelsea Harbour, Lots Road, London, SW10 0XF; T.-0171-376 7676.

D

Daglish, James Francis Stephen, BSc (Hons). Group Chief Executive, Tullis Russell & Co. Ltd., since 1992; b. 16.5.42; m., 4 children. Educ. King Edward VII School, Sheffield; Acklam Hall, Middlesbrough; St. Andrews University. Graduate Trainee, Stoneywood Mill, Aberdeen; Project Leader, Devon Valley Mill, Exeter; Tullis Russell: Sales Research Assistant, 1966, Salesman, Industrial Papers, 1969, Marketing Research Manager, 1972, Marketing Manager, 1976, UK Sales Director Designate, 1981, UK Sales Director, 1982, Sales and Marketing Director, 1985, Deputy Managing Director, 1988; Managing Director, 1989. Chairman, Association of Manufacturers of Printings and Writings, 1988; President, International Cast Coated Association, 1993; Vice Chairman, Real Art Paper Manufacturers Association, since 1993; President, Paper Federation of Great Britain, 1998; Member, CEPI Board, 1998. Recreations: golf; gardening; music; walking. Address: (b.) North Cardsknolls, Rameldry Mill Bank, Kingskettle, Fife KY15 7TY.

Daiches, Professor David, CBE, MA (Edin), DPhil (Oxon), Hon. DLitt (Edinburgh, Glasgow, Sussex, Brown, Guelph), Docteur de l'Universite (Sorbonne), DUniv (Stirling), Dottore in Lettere (Bologna). Writer; b. 2.9.12, Sunderland; m., Isobel J. Mackay (deceased); 1 s.; 2 d. Educ. George Watson's College, Edinburgh; Edinburgh University; Balliol College, Oxford. Professor of English, Cornell University, 1946-51; University Lecturer in English and Fellow of Jesus College, Cambridge, 1951-61; Professor of English, Sussex University, 1961-77; Director, Institute for Advanced Studies in the Humanities, Edinburgh University, 1980-86. President, Saltire Society, 1981-87, now Hon. President; Past President, Association for Scottish Literary Studies. Publications: numerous works of criticism and biography, including A Critical History of English Literature; Robert Burns; Sir Walter Scott and His World; The Paradox of Scottish Culture; God and the Poets (Gifford Lectures, 1983); A Weekly Scotsman and Other Poems. Recreations: music; talking. Address: (h.) 22 Belgrave Crescent, Edinburgh EH4 3AL.

Daiches, Lionel Henry, MA, LLB. Queen's Counsel, since 1956; Fellow, International Academy of Trial Lawyers, since 1976; b. 8.3.11, Sunderland; 2 s. Educ. George Watson's College, Edinburgh; Edinburgh University. Solicitor, Scotland, 1936-39; Army service, 1940-46, including Judge Advocate-General's Branch, Central Mediterranean Forces, North Africa and Italy (including Anzio Beachhead); Advocate, Scots Bar, 1946; QC Scotland, 1956; broadcaster on television and radio. Publication: Russians at Law, 1960.

Dalby, Martin, BMus, ARCM. Composer; freelance music/recording producer; Chairman, Composers' Guild of Great Britain, 1995-98; b. 25.4.42, Aberdeen; m., Hilary. Educ. Aberdeen Grammar School; Royal College of Music. Music Producer, BBC Radio 3, 1965-71; Cramb Research Fellow in Composition, Glasgow University, 1971-72; Head of Music, BBC Scotland, 1972-91; Executive Music Producer, BBC Scotland, 1991-93. Recreations: flying; railways; bird-watching; hill-walking. Address: (h.) 23 Muirpark Way, Drymen, near Glasgow G63 ODX; T.-01360 660427.

Dale, Brian Graeme, LLB, WS, NP. Partner, Brooke & Brown, WS, Dunbar, since 1974; b. 20.11.46, London; m., Judith Gail de Beaufort Franklin; 4 s.; 2 d. Educ. Bristol Grammar School; Aberdeen University. Shepherd & Wedderburn, WS, Edinburgh, 1968-70; Stuart & Stuart WS, Edinburgh, 1970-85; Diocese of Edinburgh, Scottish Episcopal Church: Treasurer, since 1995, Secretary, 1974-90, Registrar, 1974; Honorary Secretary, Abbeyfield Society (Dunbar) Ltd. Recreations: music; armchair sport; singing; family life. Address: (h.) 5 The Doon, Spott, Dunbar, East Lothian; T.-Dunbar 862059.

Dale, Professor John Egerton, BSc, PhD, FRSE, FIBiol. Emeritus Professor of Plant Physiology, Edinburgh University, since 1993; b. 13.2.32, London; m., Jacqueline Joyce Benstock; 1 s.; 2 d. Educ. City of London School; Kings College, London. Plant Physiologist, Empire Cotton Growing Corporation, Uganda, 1956-61; Edinburgh University: Lecturer in Botany, then Reader, 1961-85, Professor of Plant Physiology, 1985-93, Head, Division of Biological Sciences, 1990-93. Secretary, Society for Experimental Biology, 1974-79; Secretary General, Federation of European Societies of Plant Physiology, 1978-84; Trustee, Peter Potter Gallery, since 1994; Convener, Conservation Stategy Committee, Scottish Wildlife Trust (Member, Council, since 1997). Publications: 100 papers on growth of leaves and related topics. Recreations: the arts; travel; gardening. Address: (h.) The Old Bothy, Drem, North Berwick, EH39 5AP; T.-01620 850394.

Dalhousie, Earl of (Simon Ramsay), KT, GCVO, GBE, MC, LLD. Lord Lieutenant, County of Angus, 1967-89; Lord Chamberlain to Queen Elizabeth, the Queen Mother, 1965-92; Chancellor, Dundee University, 1977-92; b. 17.10.14, London; m., Margaret Elizabeth Mary Stirling; 3 s.; 2 d. Educ. Eton; Christ Church, Oxford. Major, 4/5 Black Watch TA; served overseas, 1939-45 (prisoner); MP, Forfar, 1945-50; Conservative Whip, 1946-48; Governor-General, Federation of Rhodesia and Nyasaland, 1957-63. Address: (h.) Brechin Castle, Brechin, Angus; T.-0135-62 2176.

Dalkeith, Earl of (Richard Walter John Montagu Douglas Scott). Deputy Chairman, Independent Television Commission, 1996-98; Member, Millennium Commission, since 1994; b. 14.2.54; m., Lady Elizabeth Kerr; 2 s.; 2 d. Son and heir of 9th Duke of Buccleuch (qv). Address: (h.) Dabton, Thornhill, Dumfriesshire.

Dallas, Garry, BA (Hons), DipTP, MSc, MRTPI. Executive Director, Development Services, Clackmannanshire Council, since 1995; b. 15.8.59, Kirkcaldy; m., Ruth. Educ. Glenrothes High School; Strathclyde University; Heriot-Watt University. Planning Officer, Principal Planner, Planning Manager, Property Development Manager, Head of Planning and Property Development, Clackmannan District Council, 1983-95. Founding Director, Alloa Tower Building Preservation Trust. Recreations: motor sports; swimming; golf; heritage site visits. Address: (b.) Clackmannanshire Council, Greenfield, Alloa FK10 2AD; T.-01259 452180.

Dalrymple, Sir Hew (Fleetwood) Hamilton-, 10th Bt (created 1697), KCVO, 1985 (CVO, 1974). Lord Lieutenant, East Lothian, since 1987; Captain General, Queen's Bodyguard for Scotland (Royal Company of Archers); Gold Stick for Scotland, since 1996; b. 9.4.26; m., Lady Anne-Louise Mary Keppel; 4 s. Educ. Ampleforth; Staff College, Camberley, 1957. Commissioned Grenadier Guards, 1944; DAAG HQ 3rd Division, 1958-60; Regimental Adjt., Grenadier Guards, 1960-62; retired, 1962; Vice-Chairman, Scottish & Newcastle Breweries, 1983-86 (Director, 1967-86); Chairman, Scottish American Investment Co., 1985-91 (Director, 1967-94); DL, East Lothian, 1964; JP, 1987. Address: Leuchie, North Berwick, East Lothian; T.-North Berwick 2903.

Dalrymple, Professor John Francis, BA, PhD, MInstP, CPhys, FSS. Computing Devices Professor of Quality Management and Director, Centre for Management Quality Research, RMIT (leave of absence from Stirling University); Director, Scottish Quality Management Centre,

Stirling University, 1990-97; Governor, BMT Quality Assurance Ltd., 1990-97; b. 18.9.49, Rosyth; 1 s.; 3 d. Educ. St. Andrew's High School, Kirkcaldy; Stirling University; Strathclyde University. Research Fellow, then Lecturer, Department of Applied Physics, Strathclyde University, 1974-79; Lecturer, Senior Lecturer, Head, Department of Management Science, Stirling University, 1979-92; Member, Strathclyde Region Children's Panel, since 1977; Chairman, Scottish Association of Children's Panels, 1983-88. Publications: 100 papers and presentations. Recreations: skiing; walking; reading; swimming. Address: (b.) Management Science, Faculty of Management, Stirling University, Stirling FK9 4LA; T.-01786 467360.

Dalrymple-Hamilton, Christian Margaret, MBE, DL; b. 20.9.19, Devon. Former President: Wigtownshire Girl Guides, Wigtownshire Branch British Red Cross Society. Address: (h.) Cladyhouse, Cairnryan, Stranraer, Wigtownshire.

Dalrymple Hamilton, North John Frederick, OBE, TD, MA (Hons), DL. Farmer and Estate Manager; b. 7.5.50, Edinburgh; m., Sally Anne How; 2 s.; 1 d. Educ. Eton College; Aberdeen University. Scottish and Newcastle Breweries, 1972-82; certificate of farming practice, East of Scotland College of Agriculture, 1982-84; farming of Bargany Estate, since 1984. TA Commission, 1967-95; Member, Queen's Bodyguard for Scotland; Deputy Lieutenant for Ayrshire; President, RBL(S), Maybole Branch. Address: (h.) Houdston, Girvan, Ayrshire KA26 9PH.

Dalyell, Kathleen Mary, MA, FRSAS; Administrator, The Binns; Member, Ancient Monuments Board for Scotland, since 1989; Member, Royal Fine Art Commission for Scotland, since 1992; Director, Heritage Education Trust, since 1987; Director, Weslo Housing Association, since 1994; Director, Carmont Settlement Trust, since 1997; b. 17.11.37, Edinburgh; m., Tam Dalyell; 1 s.; 1 d. Educ. Convent of Sacred Heart, Aberdeen; Edinburgh University; Craiglochart Teacher Training College. Teacher of History, St. Augustine's Secondary School, Glasgow, 1961-62; James Gillespie's High School for Girls, Edinburgh, 1962-63; Member, Historic Buildings Council for Scotland, 1975-87; Member, Lady Provost of Edinburgh's Delegation to China, 1987; Member, National Committee of Architectural Heritage Society for Scotland, 1983-89 (Vice-Chair, 1986-89); Chairman, Bo'ness Heritage Trust, 1988-93; Trustee, Paxton Trust, 1988-92. Recreations: reading; travel; hillwalking; chess. Address: The Binns, Linlithgow EH49 7NA; T.-01506 83 4255.

Dalyell, Tam. MP (Labour), Linlithgow (formerly West Lothian), since 1962; Weekly Columnist, New Scientist, since 1987; b. 9.8.32, Edinburgh; m., Kathleen Wheatley; 1 s.; 1 d. Educ. Edinburgh Academy; Harecroft; Eton; King's College, Cambridge; Moray House, Edinburgh. National Service, Scots Greys; Teacher, Bo'ness Academy, 1957-61; Deputy Director of Studies, Ship-School Dunera, 1961-62; Member, Public Accounts Committee, 1962-66; PPS to R.H.S. Crossman, 1964-70; Vice-Chairman, Parliamentary Labour Party, 1974-76; Member, European Parliament, 1975-78; Member: National Executive Committee, Labour Party, 1986-87, Advisory Council on Biological Sciences, Edinburgh University; a Vice-President, Research Defence Society; Hon. Doctor of Science, Edinburgh University, 1994; Hon. Doctor, City University, London, 1998. Publications: Case for Ship Schools, 1959; Ship-School Dunera, 1961; Devolution: the end of Britain?, 1978; A Science Policy for Britain, 1983; One Man's Falklands, 1983; Misrule, 1987; Dick Crossman: a portrait, 1989. Address: (h.) The Binns, Linlithgow EH49 7NA; T.-0506-83 4255.

Dane, Graham Charles, BSc, BA, MEd, MIL, MInstP, CPhys. Principal Teacher of Physics, St. Augustine's High School, Edinburgh, since 1983; b. 19.7.50; m., Margaret Coupar; 1 s.; 1 d. Educ. St. Andrews University. Teacher of Science, Merksworth High School, Paisley, 1973-75; Information Scientist, The Electricity Council, London, 1975-77; Teacher of Physics, Forrester High School, Edinburgh, 1978-80; Assistant Principal Teacher of Science, Deans Community High School, Livingston, 1980-83. Elected Member, General Teaching Council for Scotland (Convener, Committee on Exceptional Admission to the Register); holder of numerous trade union positions, mainly in the EIS (Member, Executive Council, EIS); Member, Board, SCRE, 1992-98; Chair, Currie Community Council; Vice-Chair, Socialist Educational Association Scotland; Governor, Donaldson's College. Recreations: learning new things; meeting people he likes; enjoying the arts. Address: (h.) 25 Thomson Road, Edinburgh EH14 5HT.

Daniels, Peter William, MA. Chief Executive, East Renfrewshire Council, since 1995; b. 8.6.49, Wishaw; m., Anne M.S. Smith; 3 s.; 1 d. Educ. Brandon High School, Motherwell; Dalziel High School, Motherwell; Glasgow University; Jordanhill College of Education, Glasgow. Lecturer in Public Administration, Bell College of Technology, Hamilton, 1972-75; Personal Assistant to Chief Executive, Renfrew District Council, 1975-81; Assistant Chief Executive, Leicester City Council, 1981-83; Chief Executive, Clydesdale District Council, 1983-95. Member, East Kilbride District Council, 1979-81; Member, Scottish Records Advisory Council, since 1998. Recreations: Motherwell Football Club; classical music; playing clarinet. Address: (b.) East Renfrewshire Council, Eastwood Park, Rouken Glen Road, Giffnock, East Renfrewshire G46 6UG; T.-0141-577 3010.

Dareau, Margaret Grace, MA. Senior Editor and Editorial Director, Dictionary of the Older Scottish Tongue, since 1984; b. 11.3.44, Dumfries; m., Michel Dareau; 1 s.; 2 d. Educ. Annan Academy; Edinburgh University. Research Assistant on Middle English Dialects Atlas, 1967; Kennedy Scholarship to study linguistics, MIT, 1967; began work at Dictionary of Older Scottish Tongue, 1968; Editor, Concise Scots Dictionary, 1976-77, 1980-84; Glossary Editor, Edinburgh Encyclopedia of Language and Linguistics. Recreation: horse riding. Address: (h.) The Old Manse, Howgate, Penicuik EH26 8QB; T.-01968 673028.

Darling, Alistair Maclean, LLB. Secretary of State for Social Security, since 1998; Chief Secretary to the Treasury, 1997-98; MP (Labour), Edinburgh Central, since 1987; Member, Faculty of Advocates, since 1984; b. 28.11.53, London; m., Margaret Vaughan; 1 s.; 1 d. Educ. Loretto School; Aberdeen University. Solicitor, 1978-83; Advocate, since 1984; Member: Lothian Regional Council, 1982-87, Lothian and Borders Police Board, 1982-87; Governor, Napier College, 1985-87. Address: (b.) 78 Buccleuch Street, Edinburgh; T.-0131-662 0123.

Darling, Ian Marshall, FRICS. Chairman, Royal Institution of Chartered Surveyors in Scotland, 1997-98; Director, Chesterton Scotland, since 1996; b. 16.4.45, Perth; m., Kate; 1 s.; 1 d. Educ. Perth Academy; London University (College of Estate Management). Qualified as a Chartered Surveyor, 1968; Partner, Bell Ingram, 1974; Managing Partner, 1987. Member, Council, British Trust for Ornithology; Member, Scottish Committee, RSPB; President, Scottish Ornithologists' Club. Recreations: nature conservation; ornithology. Address: (b.) 36 Castle Street, Edinburgh EH2 3HT; T.-0131-226 4791.

Darwent, Rt. Rev. Frederick Charles, LTh (Hon), JP. Bishop of Aberdeen and Orkney, 1978-92; b. 20.4.27, Liverpool; m., 1, Edna Lilian Waugh (deceased); 2 d.; 2, Roma Evelyn Fraser. Educ. Warbreck School, Liverpool;

Ormskirk Grammar School; Wells Theological College, Somerset. Followed a banking career, 1943-61; War Service, Far East, 1945-48; ordained Deacon, 1963, Priest, 1964, Diocese of Liverpool; Curate, Pemberton, Wigan, 1963-65; Rector: Strichen, 1965-71, New Pitsligo, 1965-78, Fraserburgh, 1971-78; Canon, St. Andrew's Cathedral, Aberdeen, 1971; Dean of Aberdeen and Orkney, 1973-78. Recreations: amateur stage (acting and production); calligraphy; music. Address: (h.) 107 Osborne Place, Aberdeen AB25 2DD; T.-01224 646497.

Das, Sachinandan, MB, BS, FRCR, DMRT. Consultant in administrative charge, Ninewells Hospital, Dundee, and Head, University Department, Dundee University, since 1987, Clinical Director, 1991-98; Chairman, Area Oncology Committee, since 1987; Council Member, Scottish Radiological Society, since 1987; Regional Postgraduate Education Advisor in Radiotherapy and Oncology, since 1987; b. 1.8.44, Cuttack, India; m., Dr. Subhalaxmi; 1 s.; 1 d. Educ. Ravenshaw Collegiate School; SCB Medical College, Cuttack, India; Utkal University. Senior House Officer in Radiotherapy, Plymouth General Hospital, 1969-70; Registrar in Radiotherapy and Oncology, then Senior Registrar, Mersey Regional Centre for Radiotherapy, Liverpool, 1970-77; Member: Standing Scottish Committee, National Medical Consultative Committee, Scottish Paediatric Oncology Group, Joint Radiological Safety Committee, Radiation Hazards Sub-Committee, Unit Medical and Dental Advisory Committee. Recreations: hill-walking; table tennis; reading. Address: (h.) Grapevine, 42 Menzieshill Road, Dundee DD2 1PU; T.-Dundee 642915.

Datta, Dipankar, MB, BS, FRCPGlas. Consultant Physician (with special interest in gastroenterology), 1975-97; Honorary Senior Clinical Lecturer and Clinical Sub-Dean, Glasgow University; Chairman, Scottish India Forum; Founder Director, Scottish Overseas Aid; b. 30.1.33, Chittagong, India; m., Dr. J.B. Datta; 1 s.; 1 d. Educ. Calcutta University. Former Vice Chairman, UN Association, Glasgow; former Chairman, Overseas Doctors' Association, Scottish Division; former Chairman, British Medical Association, Lanarkshire; former Member, Central Executive Committee, Scottish Council, United Nations Association; former Member, Lanarkshire Health Board; former Member, Scottish Council, British Medical Association; former Member, Executive Committee, Scottish Council, Royal Commonwealth Society for the Blind; former Member, Senate, Glasgow University; Member, General Medical Council; Chairman, South Asia Voluntary Enterprise. Recreations: reading - history, economics and international politics. Address: (h.) 9 Kirkvale Crescent, Newton Mearns, Glasgow G77 5HB; T.-0141-639 1515.

Datta, Pradip Kumar, MS, FRCS(Edin), FRCS(Eng), FRCS(Ire), FRCS(Glas). Consultant Surgeon, Caithness General Hospital, since 1980; b. 14.5.40, Calcutta, India; m., Swati; 1 s. Educ. St. Aloysius High School, Visakhapatnam, India; Andhra University, Visakhapatnam, India. Surgical Registrar: Hope Hospital, Salford, Poole General Hospital, Plymouth General Hospital, Royal Cornwall Hospital, Truro; Senior Surgical Registrar, Whittington Hospital, London; Surgical Tutor, Royal College of Surgeons of Edinburgh. Visiting Lecturer: University Sains Malaysia, 1997, National University of Singapore, 1998. Recreations: playing squash; fly-fishing. Address: (h.) Garvyk, 17 Newton Avenue, Wick KW1 5LJ; T.-01955 605050.

Davenport, Professor John, BSc, MSc, PhD, DSc, FIBiol, FZS, FRSE. Director, University Marine Biological Station, Millport, since 1991; Professor of Marine Biology, London University; b. 12.2.46; m., Julia Ladner; 2 d. Educ. Bablake School, Coventry; London University; Southampton University; University of Wales. Demonstrator in Marine Biology, University of Wales at Bangor, 1970-72; Researcher, NERC Unit of Marine Invertebrate Biology, 1972-83 (promoted Principal Scientific Officer, 1980); Lecturer, then Senior Lecturer, School of Animal Biology, University of Wales at Bangor, 1983-88; Reader in Marine Biology, School of Ocean Sciences, Marine Sciences Laboratories, Menai Bridge, 1988-91. Publications: Animal Osmoregulation (Co-Author), 1981; Environmental Stress and Behavioural Adaptation, 1985; Animal Life at Low Temperature, 1992. Recreations: skiing; sailboarding; swimming; birding. Address: (b.) University Marine Biological Station, Isle of Cumbrae KA28 0EG.

Davidson, Alan Ingram, ChM, FRCSEdin, DObstRCOG. Consultant Surgeon, Aberdeen Royal Infirmary, since 1974; Honorary Senior Lecturer in Surgery, Aberdeen University, since 1974; b. 25.3.35, Aberdeen; m., Margaret Elizabeth Mackay; 1 s.; 1 d. Educ. Robert Gordon's College, Aberdeen; Aberdeen University. House Officer, Aberdeen Royal Infirmary, 1959-60; National Service, Royal Army Medical Corps, 1960-62; Lecturer, Department of Pathology, Aberdeen, 1963-64; Registrar and Senior Registrar, Aberdeen Royal Infirmary, 1964-74. Recreations: gardening; watching TV; music. Address: (h.) 20 Hillview Road, Cults, Aberdeen; T.-Aberdeen 867347.

Davidson, Hon. Lord (Charles Kemp Davidson), MA, LLB, FRSE. Chairman, Scottish Law Commission, 1988-96; Senator of the College of Justice, 1983-96; Deputy Chairman, Boundaries Commission for Scotland, 1985-96; b. 13.4.29, Edinburgh; m., Mary Mactaggart; 1 s.; 2 d. Educ. Fettes College, Edinburgh; Oxford University; Edinburgh University. Advocate, 1956; QC (Scot), 1969; Keeper, The Advocates Library, 1972-77; Vice Dean, Faculty of Advocates, 1977-79; Dean, 1979-83; Procurator to the General Assembly of the Church of Scotland, 1972-83; Chairman, National Health Service Tribunal for Scotland, 1970-83. Address: (h.) 22 Dublin Street, Edinburgh EH1 3PP; T.-0131-556 2168.

Davidson, Professor Colin William, BSc, DipER, PhD, CEng, FIEE, FRSA. Consulting Engineer; b. 18.9.34, Edinburgh; m., Ranee M.N. Cleland; 2 d. Educ. George Heriot's School; Edinburgh University. Lecturer, Edinburgh University, 1956-61; Electronics Engineer, Nuclear Enterprises (GB) Ltd., 1961-64; Lecturer, Heriot-Watt College/University, 1964-67; Associate Professor, Chulalongkorn University, Bangkok, 1967-68; Heriot-Watt University: Senior Lecturer, 1968-85, Professor of Electrical Engineering, 1985-88, Dean of Engineering, 1976-79 and 1984-87, Head of Department, 1979-87. Member, Lothian Regional Council, 1990-94; Vice-President, Institution of Electrical Engineers, 1990-93, 1995-98; Liveryman, Worshipful Company of Engineers, City of London; Member, Engineering Council Senate and Board for Engineers' Regulation, 1996-98. Recreation: sailing (Royal Highland Yacht Club). Address: (h.) 20 East Barnton Avenue, Edinburgh EH4 6AQ; T.-0131-336 5806.

Davidson, Professor Donald Allen, BSc, PhD, FRSE. Professor of Environmental Science, Stirling University, since 1991; b. 27.4.45, Lumphanan; m., Caroline E. Brown; 1 s.; 2 d. Educ. Robert Gordon's College, Aberdeen; Aberdeen University; Sheffield University. Lecturer, St. David's University College, Wales, 1971-76; Lecturer, Senior Lecturer, Reader, Strathclyde University, 1976-86; Reader, Stirling University, 1986-91. Member, Terrestrial Sciences Committee, Natural Environmental Research Council. Publications include: The Evaluation of Land Resources, 1992; many papers. Recreations: exploring the countryside; real ale. Address: (b.) Department of Environmental Science, Stirling University, Stirling FK9 4LA; T.-01786 467840.

Davidson, Duncan Lewis Watt, BSc (Hons), MB, ChB, FRCPEdin. Consultant Neurologist, Tayside Health Board, since 1976; Honorary Senior Lecturer in Medicine, Dundee University, since 1976; b. 16.5.40, Kingston, Jamaica; m., Dr. Anne V.M. Maiden; 4 s.; 1 d. Educ. Knox College, Jamaica; Edinburgh University. House Officer, Senior House Officer, Registrar and Senior Registrar posts in medicine and neurology, Edinburgh, 1966-75; Peel Travelling Fellowship, Montreal, 1973-74; MRC clinical scientific staff, MRC Brain Metabolism Unit, Edinburgh, 1975-76. Recreations: gardening; photography. Address: (h.) Brooksby, Queens Terrace, St. Andrews, Fife; T.-01334 76108.

Davidson, Euan, LLB(Hons). Director, Clydeport plc, since 1994; b. 8.7.58, Bellshill; m., 1, Elspeth Robertson (divorced); 2, Dawn Gaw; 1 s.; 1 d. Educ. Hutchesons' Grammar School, Glasgow; University of Glasgow. Wright, Johnston and Mackenzie, Solicitors, Glasgow: Apprentice, 1979, Solicitor, 1981, Partner, 1985, Managing Partner, 1991-94; Clydeport plc: Director and Secretary, 1994, Corporate Services Director, 1996, Operations Director, 1997; Member of Council, British Ports Association; Session Clerk, Cairngryffe Parish Church. Recreations: hillwalking; gardening. Address: (b.) 16 Roberston Street, Glasgow G2 8DS; T.-0141-221 8733.

Davidson, Professor Fraser Paul, LLB, PhD, MCIArb. Alexander Stone Professor of Commercial Law, Glasgow University, since 1997; b. 10.7.54, Dundee; m., Fiona. Educ. Lawside Academy, Dundee; University of Dundee; University of Edinburgh. University of Dundee: Lecturer, 1978-90, Senior Lecturer, 1990-94. Recreation: chocolate. Address: School of Law, University of Glasgow, Glasgow G12 8QQ.

Davidson, Ian Graham, MA (Hons). MP (Labour and Co-op), Glasgow Pollok, since 1997 (Glasgow Govan 1992-97); Secretary, Tribune Group; Secretary, Trade Union Group; b. 8.9.50, Jedburgh; m., Morag Mackinnon; 1 s.; 1 d. Educ. Jedburgh Grammar School; Galashiels Academy; Edinburgh University; Jordanhill College of Education. Chairman, Strathclyde Education Committee, 1990-92; Chairman, COSLA Education Committee, 1990-92. Address: (b.) Constituency Office, 1829 Paisley Road West, Glasgow G52 3SS; T.-0141-883 8338.

Davidson, Rev. Ian Murray Pollock, MBE, MA, BD. Minister, Allan Park South Church and Church of the Holy Rude, Stirling, 1985-94; Chairman, General Trustees, Church of Scotland, since 1993; b. 14.3.28, Kirriemuir; m., Isla; 2 s. Educ. Montrose Academy; St. Andrews University. National Service, 1949-51; Minister: Crieff North and West Church (St. Andrew's), 1955-61, Grange Church, Kilmarnock, 1961-67, Cambuslang Old Church, 1967-85; Convener, Maintenance of the Ministry Committee and Board, Church and Ministry Department, 1981-84; General Trustee, since 1975. Publications: At the Sign of the Fish (history of Cambuslang Old Parish Church), 1975; A Guide to the Church of the Holy Rude. Recreations: travel; photography; reading; writing. Address: (h.) 13/8 Craigend Park, Edinburgh EH16 5XX; T.-0131-664 0074.

Davidson, John F., MB, ChB, FRCPEdin, FRCPath. Consultant Haematologist, Glasgow Royal Infirmary, 1969-98; b. 11.1.34, Lumphanan; m., Laura G. Middleton; 1 s.; 1 d. Educ. Robert Gordon's College, Aberdeen; Aberdeen University. Surgeon Lt., RN; Registrar in Medicine, Aberdeen Royal Infirmary; Research Registrar in Medicine, then Senior Registrar in Haematology, Glasgow Royal Infirmary; Honorary Clinical Senior Lecturer, Glasgow University; Honorary Consultant Haematologist, Strathclyde University. Secretary, British Society for Haematalogy, 1983-86; President, British Society for Haematology, 1990-91; Chairman: BCSH Haemostasis and Thrombosis Task Force, 1986-81, Steering Committee NEQAS in blood coagulation, 1986-91; Member, Council, Royal College of Pathologists, two terms; Secretary, Joint Committee on Haematology, Royal College of Pathologists and Royal College of Physicians; Chairman, UK Joint Working Group on Quality Assurance. Editor, Progress in Fibrinolysis, Volumes I to VII; Chairman, International Committee on Fibrinolysis, 1976-84; Co-Editor in Chief, Fibrinolysis, 1986-96. Recreation: gardening. Address: (h.) Craigiebank, 20 Roman Road, Bearsden, Glasgow; T.-0141-942 3356.

Davidson, John Knight, OBE, MD, FRCP (Edin), FRCP (Glas), FRCR, (Hon) FACR, (Hon) FRACR. Consultant Radiologist; expert adviser on bone disease in compressed air and diving medicine; b. 17.8.25, Edinburgh; m., Edith E. McKelvie; 2 s.; 1 d. Educ. George Watson's Boys College, Edinburgh; Edinburgh University. Adviser in Bone Disease in Divers MRC, Aberdeen, US Navy, 1970-92; Non Executive Director, Yorkhill NHS Trust, 1993-95; Member, Council, Medical and Dental Defence Union, 1971-95; Chairman, Health Policy, Council, Scottish Conservative and Unionist Association, 1991-95; Member, BBC Medical Advisory Group, 1988-95; Consultant Radiologist in Administrative Charge, Western Infirmary and Gartnavel General, Glasgow, 1967-90; Royal College of Radiologists: Member, Council, 1984-87, Chairman, Examining Board, 1976-79, Scottish Committee, 1985-89; Member, Council, Royal Glasgow Institute of Fine Arts, 1978-88; Deputy President, Glasgow and Renfrewshire, British Red Cross Society, 1988-93; Honorary Fellow: Royal Australian College of Radiology, 1981, Scottish Radiological Society, 1990, American College of Radiology, 1992, Medical and Dental Defence Union, Scotland, 1995; Honorary Fellow and Medallist, International Skeletal Society, 1995; Rohan Williams Professor, Australasia, 1977; Aggarwal Memorial Oration, India, 1988. Editor, Aseptic Necrosis of Bone and numerous publications. Recreations: golf; painting; bridge; meeting people; skiing. Address: (h.) 15 Beechlands Avenue, Netherlee, Glasgow G44 3YT; T.-0141-637 0290.

Davidson, Julie Wilson. Writer and Broadcaster; Freelance Contributor to radio, television, books, newspapers and magazines, since 1981; b. 11.5.43, Motherwell; m., Harry Reid (qv); 1 d. Educ. Aberdeen High School for Girls. Trainee Journalist, D.C. Thomson Ltd., Dundee, 1961-64; Feature Writer and Sub-Editor, Aberdeen Press & Journal, 1964-67; The Scotsman: Feature Writer, 1967-77, Columnist, 1977-81; Columnist, The Herald, 1995-97; Television Critic, The Herald, 1981-95. Columnist/Critic of the Year, Scottish Press Awards, 1985; Critic of the Year, Scottish Press Awards, 1988-89-92-94-95; Canada Travel Award, 1992. Recreations: reading; walking; travelling; lunching. Address: (h.) 15 Albion Buildings, Ingram Street, Glasgow; T.-0141-552 8403.

Davidson, Sheriff Richard Alexander, LLB, NP. Sheriff of Tayside Central and Fife at Dundee, since 1994; b. 3.11.47, Lennoxtown; m., Shirley Margaret Thomson; 1 s.; 1 d. Educ. Oban High School; Glasgow University. Apprentice Solicitor, 1969-72; Assistant Solicitor, 1972-76; Partner, Tindal Oatts, 1976-94. Member, Glasgow and North Argyll Legal Aid Committee, 1984-89. Address: (b.) Sheriff Courthouse, West Bell Street, Dundee.

Davidson, Professor Robert, MA, BD, DD, FRSE. Moderator, General Assembly of the Church of Scotland, 1990-91; Professor of Old Testament Language and Literature, Glasgow University, 1972-91; Principal, Trinity College, Glasgow, 1981-91; b. 30.3.27, Markinch, Fife; m., Elizabeth May Robertson; 4 s.; 4 d. Educ. Bell-Baxter School, Cupar; St. Andrews University. Lecturer in Biblical Studies, Aberdeen University, 1953-60; Lecturer in Hebrew and Old Testament Studies, St. Andrews University, 1960-66; Lecturer/Senior Lecturer in Old Testament, Edinburgh University, 1966-72. Publications: The Bible Speaks, 1959;

The Old Testament, 1964; Geneses 1 - 11, 1973; Genesis 12 - 50, 1979; The Bible in Religious Education, 1979; The Courage to Doubt, 1983; Jeremiah Volume 1, 1983; Jeremiah Volume 2, Lamentations, 1985; Ecclesiastes, Song of Songs, 1986; Wisdom and Worship, 1990; A Beginner's Guide to the Old Testament, 1992; Go by the Book, 1996; The Vitality of Worship, 1998. Recreations: music; gardening. Address: (h.) 30 Dumgoyne Drive, Bearsden, Glasgow G61 3AP; T.-0141-942 1810.

Davidson, William Keith, CBE, JP; b. 20.11.26, Glasgow; m., Dr. Mary W.A. Davidson; 1 s.; 1 d. Educ. Coatbridge Secondary School; Glasgow University. Medical Officer, 1st Bn., RSF, 1950; Maj. 2 i/c 14 Field Ambulance, 1950-51; Medical Officer, i/c Holland and Belgium, 1952; General Medical Practitioner, 1953-90; Chairman: Glasgow Local Medical Committee, 1971-75, Scottish General Medical Services Committee, 1972-75; Member, Scottish Council on Crime, 1972-75; Fellow, BMA, 1975; Deputy Chairman, General Medical Services Committee (UK), 1975-79; Member, Scottish Medical Practices Committee, 1968-80; Chairman: Scottish Council, BMA, 1978-81, Scottish Health Services Planning Council, 1984-89; Member, Scottish Health Services Policy Board, 1985-89; Vice President, BMA, since 1983; Hon. President, Glasgow Eastern Medical Society, 1984-85; Member, General Medical Council, 1984-94; Fellow, Royal College of General Practitioners, since 1980; Member, Greater Glasgow Health Board, 1989-91; Chairman: Strathclyde Aids Forum, 1990-93, Greater Glasgow Health Board Aids Forum, 1990-93, Greater Glasgow Health Board Drugs & Alcohol Forum, 1990-93, Chryston High School Board, 1995-97; Elder, Church of Scotland, since 1956; Session Clerk, Stepps Parish Church, 1983-97. Recreation: gardening. Address: (h.) Dunvegan, Hornshill Farm Road, Stepps, Glasgow G33 6DE; T.-0141-779 2103.

Davidson, William Powell, MREHIS, MInstWM, MILAM. Head of Environmental Health, Dumfries and Galloway Council; Chairman, Scottish Food and Drugs Co-ordinating Committee, since 1991; b. 28.8.48, Paisley; m., Elizabeth Ann Davidson; 1 s. Educ. Camphill Senior Secondary School, Paisley; Langside College, Glasgow; Bell College, Hamilton. Trainee, then Assistant Sanitary Inspector, Renfrew County Council, 1966-71; Sanitary Inspector, Paisley Burgh Council, 1971-72; Assistant District Sanitary Inspector, Perth and Kinross Joint County Council, 1972-75; Area Environmental Health Officer, Argyll and Bute District Council, 1975-76; Regional Manager, Ciba Geigy Public Hygiene Project, Saudi Arabia, 1976-77; Senior Environmental Health Officer, Perth and Kinross District Council, 1977-79; Depute Director of Environmental Health, Stewartry District Council, 1979-82; Director of Environmental Health & Leisure Services, Stewartry District Council, 1982-96. Recreations: golf; gardening; travel; jogging. Address: (b.) Environmental Health Department, Cannonwalls, High Street, Kirkcudbright.

Davie, Ivor Turnbull, MB, ChB, FRCA, FRCPE, HonFCPS. Consultant Anaesthetist, Western General Hospital, Edinburgh, since 1971; Honorary Senior Lecturer, Edinburgh University, since 1979; Lecturer, Central Midwives Board (Scotland), since 1974; b. 23.2.35, Edinburgh; m., Jane Elizabeth Fleischmann; 1 s.; 1 d. Educ. Royal High School, Edinburgh; Edinburgh University. Member, Board of Examiners, Faculty of Anaesthetists, Royal College of Surgeons of England and Royal College of Anaesthetists, 1978-91; President, Edinburgh and East of Scotland Society of Anaesthetists, 1990-91; Tutor, Faculty of Anaesthetists, 1979-87; Regional Educational Adviser, Royal College of Anaesthetists, 1988-95; Member, Editorial Board, British Journal of Obstetrics and Gynaecology, 1980-84; Visiting Medical Officer, Westmead Centre, Sydney, NSW, 1983. Address: (h.) 26 Kingsburgh Road, Edinburgh EH12 6PZ; T.-0131-337 1117.

Davies, Adrian Hartley Kemp, BA(Econ), CQSW, MPhil, MBA. Director, Glasgow Council on Alcohol, since 1992; b. 7.8.47, Birkenhead; m., Anne; 2 s.; 1 d. Educ. Ellesmere College, Shropshire; University of Manchester; University of Aberdeen; University of Strathclyde. Simon Worker, Simon Community, Liverpool, 1969-71; Trainee Social Worker, Cheshire Social Services Department, 1971-72; Group Leader, St. Mungo Community, London, 1972-74; professional social work training, Aberdeen, 1974-76; Senior Social Worker, Helping Hand Organisation, Manchester, 1976-79; Lecturer, Alcohol Studies Centre, Paisley College of Technology, 1979-83; Hostels Co-ordinator and Depute Housing Manager, Glasgow City Council Housing Department, 1983-92. Recreations: hill-walking; swimming; history. Address: (b.) 9th Floor, Elmbank Chambers, 289 Bath Street, Glasgow G2 4JL; T.-0141-226 3883.

Davies, Alan Graham, LLB(Hons), Dip. Legal Practice. Solicitor in private practice since 1983, Partner, since 1987; Council Member, Law Society of Scotland, since 1996; b. 4.2.59, Perth; m., Fiona; 2 s.; 1 d. Educ. Perth Grammar School; University of Edinburgh. Chair, People United for Supported Housing; accredited family law mediator. Recreations: squash; golf; football (President, Methven Amateur F.C.). Address: (b.) 25 South Methven Street, Perth; T.-01738 620451.

Davies, Professor Alun Millward, BSc, MB, ChB, PhD. Professor of Developmental Neurobiology, St. Andrews University, since 1993; b. 2.8.55, Tredegar. Educ. Pontllanfraith Grammar School; Liverpool University; London University. Lecturer, Middlesex Hospital Medical School, London, 1982-83; Lecturer, then Senior Lecturer, then Reader in Neurobiology, St. George's Hosital Medical School, London, 1983-93. Recreations: playing piano and harpsichord; sailing; scuba diving. Address: (b.) Bute Medical Building, St. Andrews University, St. Andrews KY16 9TS; T.-01334 63219.

Davies, David Somerville, FTCL, ARCM. Conductor, flautist, composer; Artistic Director, Paragon Ensemble Scotland, since 1980; b. 13.6.54, Dunfermline. Educ. Dunfermline High School; Royal Scottish Academy of Music and Drama; Edinburgh University; Marseille Conservatoire. Assistant Principal Flute, Scottish National Orchestra, 1975-80; Principal Flute, Scottish Opera, 1980-85; Freelance Conductor: Edinburgh International Festival, France, Germany, Iceland, Italy, Luxembourg, Spain, Switzerland, BBC Scottish Symphony Orchestra, Royal Liverpool Philharmonic Orchestra, Royal Scottish National Orchestra, Scottish Chamber Orchestra, Ulster Orchestra; RSAMD: Head of Woodwind, since 1991, Head of Orchestral Studies, since 1997. Recordings: two volumes of world premiere recordings of Scottish contemporary music, 1991, 1993; one volume of works by MacKenzie with RSNO, 1997. Awards: Clutterbuck Scholarship; Performing Rights Society/Scottish Society of Composers Award for services to contemporary Scottish music; Sir James Caird Scholarship; Scottish Arts Council Music Award; Scottish International Education Trust Award; Tovey Memorial Prize. Recreations: computing; gardening; photography; reading. Address: (b.) 20 Renfrew Street, Glasgow G2 3BW; T.-0141-332 9903.

Davies, Professor Sir Graeme John, Kt, BE, MA, PhD, ScD, FEng, FRSE. Principal and Vice-Chancellor, Glasgow University, since 1995; b. 7.4.37, New Zealand; m., Florence; 1 s.; 1 d. Educ. Mt. Albert Grammar School, Auckland; University of Auckland; Cambridge University. Junior Lecturer, University of Auckland, 1960-62; Lecturer, Cambridge University, 1962-77; Professor of Metallurgy, Sheffield University, 1978-86; Vice-Chancellor, Liverpool University, 1986-91; Chief Executive: Universities Funding Council, 1991-93, Higher Education Funding Council for England, 1992-95. Hon. LLD, Liverpool, 1991; Hon.

FRSNZ, 1993; Hon. DMet, Sheffield, 1995; Hon. DSc, Nottingham, 1995; Hon. FTCL, 1995; FIMechE; FIM; FRSA; CBIM; DL, Merseyside, 1989-93; Hon. DEng, Manchester Metropolitan University, 1996. Recreations: bird-watching; golf; The Times crossword. Address: (b.) Glasgow University, Glasgow G12 8QQ; T.-0141-330 5995.

Davies, Ivor, MA, DipEd, PhD. Director of Planning, Scottish Sports Council, since 1975, and Director, Lottery Sports Fund, since 1994; b. Scotland. Educ. Edinburgh University. Founded and developed Department of Geography, Lakehead University, Thunder Bay, Ontario, and became first Chairman of Department. Member, Board, European Association for Sport Management; Member, Grants Council, Caledonian Foundation. Recreations: sport; music. Address: (b.) Caledonia House, South Gyle, Edinburgh EH12 9DQ; T.-0131-339 9000.

Davies (a.k.a. Glasse-Davies), Professor R. Wayne, MA, PhD, ScD. Robertson Professor of Biotechnology, Glasgow University, since 1989; b. 10.6.44, Cardiff; m., Victoria Glasse; 3 s.; 2 d. Educ. Queen Elizabeth's Hospital, Bristol; St. John's College, Cambridge. Research Fellow, University of Wisconsin, 1968-71; H3 Professor, Universität zu Köln, FRG, 1971-77; Lecturer, University of Essex, 1977-81; Senior Lecturer, UMIST, 1981-83; Vice-President, Scientific and Research Director, Allelix Biopharmaceuticals, Toronto, 1983-89; Neuropa Ltd.: Founding Director, 1996, CEO, 1997. Recreations: poetry and literature; cello; skiing. Address: (b.) Robertson Laboratory of Biotechnology, Institute of Biomedical and Life Sciences, Glasgow University, 54 Dumbarton Road, Glasgow G11 6NU.

Davies, Trevor John, BA. Independent Television Producer, since 1981; b. 23.1.44, London; lives with Elaine Pidgeon; 1 step-s.; 1 step-d. Educ. University of Leicester. General Secretary, Scottish Union of Students, 1968; Secretary, Open University in Scotland, 1969-74; Assistant Director, Scottish Council of Social Service, 1974-78; Freelance Journalist and Broadcaster, 1978-85; credits include: Producer, The Big Day, Glasgow, 1990; Executive Producer, Hamish MacBeth; Producer, Bombay Blue. Councillor, Edinburgh Town Council, 1971-75; Parliamentary Candidate, 1974; Councillor, Lothian Region Council, 1974-78; Chair: Scottish Volleyball Association, 1979-83, Edinburgh Central Citizens' Advice Bureau, 1980-84; Vice-Chair, Edinburgh Council of Social Service, 1982-84; Director and Vice-Chair, Wester Hailes Community Enterprises, 1983-91; Scottish Convener and UK Council Member, Independent Programme Producers Association, 1988-91; Governor, Scottish Film Council, 1990-95; Chair, Scottish Screen Industry Project, 1991-94. Recreations: jazz; gardening. Address: (b.) 10 Scotland Street, Edinburgh EH3 6PS; T.-0131-557 4580.

Davis, Alan Angus, BSc (Hons). Manager, BBC Scottish Symphony Orchestra, since 1992; b. 7.2.58, Glasgow. Educ. Queen Anne High School, Dunfermline; Aberdeen University. Publicity and Publications Assistant, The Poetry Society, 1981-82; Marketing Officer, Incorporated Society of Musicians, 1982-84; freelance administrator, 1984-92. Council Member, Society for the Promotion of New Music; Director, Chamber Group of Scotland. Recreations: cooking; gardening; American literature. Address: (b.) Broadcasting House, Queen Margaret Drive, Glasgow G12; T.-0141-338 2606.

Davis, Christine A.M., CBE, MA, DipEd. Chairman, Scottish Agricultural Wages Board, since 1995 (Member, since 1990); Member, Secretary of State's Panel on Public Appointments; Chairman, Scottish Legal Aid Board, 1991-98; b. 5.3.44, Salisbury; m., Robin John Davis; 2 d. Educ. Perth Academy; Ayr Academy; St. Andrews University; Aberdeen University; Aberdeen College of Education. Teacher of History and Modern Studies, Cumbernauld High School and High School of Stirling, 1967-69; joined Dunblane Town Council and Perth and Kinross Joint County Council, 1972; undertook research in Canada on Ontario Hydro and small claims in Ontario courts, 1977-78; Chairman, Electricity Consultative Council for North of Scotland, 1980-90; Member: North of Scotland Hydro Electric Board, 1980-90, Scottish Economic Council, 1987-95, Scottish Committee of the Council on Tribunals, 1989-95; Clerk, Britain Yearly Meeting, Society of Friends (Quakers), 1991-95; a President, Council of Churches for Britain and Ireland, 1990-92; Trustee, Quaker Tapestry at Kendal Ltd, Joseph Rowntree Charitable Trust. Recreations: embroidery; bird-watching; walking. Address: (h.) 24 Newton Crescent, Dunblane, Perthshire FK15 ODZ; T.-Dunblane 823226.

Davis, Gerry. Journalist/Public Relations Consultant, since 1970; TV Producer and Presenter, since 1989; Media Training Provider, since 1991; b. 7.10.35, Glasgow; m., June Imray; 1 s.; 1 d. Educ. Shawlands Academy, Glasgow; Strathclyde University. Trainee analytical chemist, ICI; pharmaceutical chemist; actor; television continuity announcer/programme presenter/reporter, BBC Radio Scotland. Former Radio Reporter of the Year/Presenter of the Year. Recreation: holidaying. Address: (b.) Davis Media, 10 Wellwood Terrace, Cults, Aberdeen AB15 9JA; T.-01224 862330.

Davis, Margaret Thomson. Novelist; b. Bathgate; 2 s. Educ. Albert Secondary School. Worked as children's nurse; Red Cross nurse; short story writer; novelist; author of autobiography, The Making of a Novelist; novels include The Breadmakers, A Baby Might Be Crying, A Sort of Peace, The Prisoner, The Prince and the Tobacco Lords, Roots of Bondage, Scorpion in the Fire, The Dark Side of Pleasure, A Very Civilised Man, Light and Dark, Rag Woman Rich Woman, Daughters and Mothers, Wounds of War, A Woman of Property, A Sense of Belonging, Hold Me Forever, Kiss Me No More,A Kind of Immortality, Burning Ambition. Committee Member: International PEN (Scottish Branch); Society of Authors; Lecturer in Creative Writing; Honorary President, Strathkelvin Writers Club. Recreations: reading; travelling; being with friends.

Davison, Timothy Paul, BA (Hons), MHSM, DipHSM, MBA, MPH. Chief Executive, Greater Glasgow Community and Mental Health Services NHS Trust, since 1994; b. 4.6.61, Newcastle upon Tyne; m., Hilary Williamson; 1 s. Educ. Kenton School, Newcastle upon Tyne; Stirling University; Glasgow University. Appointments in Stirling Royal Infirmary, Royal Edinburgh Hospital, Glasgow Royal Infirmary, 1984-90; Sector General Manager, Gartnavel Royal Hospital, 1990-91; Unit General Manager, Mental Health Unit, Glasgow, 1991-92, Community and Mental Health Unit, Glasgow, 1992-94. Recreations: tennis; military and political history. Address: (b.) Gartnavel Royal Hospital, 1055 Great Western Road, Glasgow G12 0XH; T.-0141-211 3782.

Dawson, James Ronald, FRICS, MIPS. Honorary Secretary, Royal Institution of Chartered Surveyors in Scotland, since 1997; Director, Institution of Planning Supervisors, since 1996; b. 28.5.41, Glasgow; m., Marion; 1 s.; 1 d. Educ. High School of Glasgow; Stow College of Building, Glasgow. Apprentice Quantity Surveyor, 1958-63; Partner, Robert H. Soper & Co., 1965-72; Founding Partner, Robertson and Dawson, Edinburgh and Galashiels, since 1972; Chairman, RICS in Scotland, 1992-93. President, Edinburgh Junior Chamber of Commerce, 1974-75; Captain, Ward XXIII, Society of High Constables of Edinburgh, 1992. Recreations: hill-walking; golf; opera. Address: (b.) 6 Manor Place, Edinburgh; T.-0131-225 2219.

Dawson, Professor John Alan, BSc, MPhil, PhD, MIPDM. Professor of Marketing, Edinburgh University, since 1990; Visiting Professor, Escuela Superior de

Administración y Dirección de Empresas (ESADE), Barcelona; b. 19.8.44, Hyde; m., Jocelyn Barker; 1 s.; 1 d. Educ. Lady Manners School, Bakewell; University College, London; Nottingham University. Lecturer, Nottingham University; Lecturer, Senior Lecturer, Reader, St. David's University College, Wales; Fraser of Allander Professor of Distributive Studies, Stirling University; Visiting Lecturer, University of Western Australia; Visiting Research Fellow, Australian National University; Visiting Professor: Florida State University, Chuo University. Chairman, National Museums of Scotland Retailing Ltd. Publications: Evaluating the Human Environment, 1973; Man and His World, 1975; Computing for Geographers, 1976; Small-Scale Retailing in the UK, 1979; Marketing Environment, 1979; Retail Geography, 1980; Commercial Distribution in Europe, 1982; Teach Yourself Geography, 1983; Shopping Centre Development, 1983; Computer Methods for Geographers, 1985; Retailing in Scoland 2005, 1988; Evolution of European Retailing, 1988; Retailing Environments in Developing Countries, 1990; Competition and Markets, 1992. Recreations: sport; writing. Address:(b.) Edinburgh University, 50 George Square, Edinburgh; T.-0131-650 3828.

Dawson, Patricia, MBA, DipLSc/Nursing, RGN, RNMD. Director, Scottish Association of Health Councils, since 1994; b. 14.7.56, Edinburgh; m., David; 1 d. Educ. James Gillespie's High School; Queen Margaret College, Edinburgh; Napier University, Edinburgh. Various nursing posts, 1974-94; Co-founder and former Chairperson, Scottish Society of Anaesthetic and Recovery Nurses; Former Chairperson, Balgreen Out of School Care Club. Recreations: gardening; swimming; reading; holidays in Greece. Address: (b.) Scottish Association of Health Councils, 24a Palmerston Place, Edinburgh EH12 5AL; T.-0131-220 4101.

Dawson, Professor Patrick, BSocSc, PhD. Salvesen Chair of Management, University of Aberdeen, since 1997; m., Susan Thomson; 2 s.; 1 d. Educ. Colston School; Southampton University. Research Fellow, University of Surrey, 1984-86; Lecturer: University of Edinburgh, 1986-88, University of Adelaide, 1988-91; Honorary Principal Fellow, University of Wollongong, 1991; Senior Lecturer, University of Adelaide, 1991-97. Publications: Organizational Change: A Processual Approach, 1994; Technology and Quality: Change in the Workplace, 1994. Recreations: hill-walking; music. Address: Fullwood, Grampian Terrace, Torphins AB31 4JS; T.-013398 82384.

Dawson, Hon. Lord (Thomas Cordner Dawson), QC (Scot), LLB. Senator of the College of Justice in Scotland, since 1995; b. 14.11.48; m., 2 s. Educ. Royal High School of Edinburgh; Edinburgh University. Advocate, 1973; QC, 1986; Lecturer, Dundee University, 1971-74; Advocate Depute, 1983-87; Solicitor-General for Scotland, 1992-95. Address: Court of Session, Parliament House, Parliament Square, Edinburgh, EH1 1RQ.

Dawson Scott, Robert, MA, MLitt. Arts Editor, The Scotsman, since 1997; b. 24.7.56, London; 3 d. Educ. Oxford University; Strathclyde University. Recreations: skiing; hill-walking. Address: (b.) 20 North Bridge, Edinburgh EH1 1YT; T.-0131-225 2468.

Deakins, Professor David Arthur, BSc(Econ.), BA(Bus. Studs.), MA(Bus. Econ.), FRSA. Renfrewshire Enterprise Professor of Enterprise Development, University of Paisley, since 1994; b. 5.1.50, Cheshire; m., June Patricia Eglen; 1 s.; 2 d. Educ. Sutton Secondary Modern Boys' School; University of London (External Degree); University of Essex. Lecturer: Rothenham College of Technology, 1975-81, Chelmsford College of Further Education, 1981-88, University of Central England, Birmingham, 1988-94. Vice-President, Institute for Small Business Affairs. Publications: Enterpreneurship and Small Firms, 1996; Entrepreneurship in the Nineties, 1997. Recreations: cycling; walking; mountain biking. Address: (b.) Paisley Enterprise Research Centre, University of Paisley, Paisley PA1 2BE; T.-0141-848 3933.

Deane, Robert Fletcher, MB, ChB, MSc, FRCSEdin, FRCSGlas. Consultant Urological Surgeon, since 1971; President, British Association of Urological Surgeons, 1998-2000; b. 25.3.38, Glasgow; m., Sylvia Alison Yuill; 3 s. Educ. Hillhead High School, Glasgow; Glasgow University. Consultant Urologist, Western Infirmary, Glasgow, since 1971; Senior Consultant Surgeon to Family Planning Association, Glasgow; Member, Specialist Advisory Committee (Urology); Founder, Board of Intercollegiate Specialty Board in Urology. Publication: Urology Illustrated. Recreations: golf; music. Address: (h.) 27 Bellshaugh Lane, Glasgow G12 0PE; T.-0141-334 8102.

Deans, Rev. Graham Douglas Sutherland, MA, BD(Hons), MTh (Oxon) (award pending). Parish Minister, St. Mary's Parish Church, Dumfries, since 1987; b. 15.8.53, Aberdeen; m., Marina Punler. Educ. Mackie Academy, Stonehaven; University of Aberdeen; Westminster College, University of Oxford. Assistant Minister, Craigsbank Parish Church, Corstorphine, 1977-78; Parish Minister, Denbeath with Methilhill, 1978-87. Depute Clerk and Treasurer, Presbytery of Kirkcaldy, 1981-87; Chaplain, Randolph Wemyss Memorial Hospital, 1980-87; Moderator, Presbytery of Dumfries and Kirkcudbright, 1994-95; Convener: Committee on Glebes, 1991-92, Committee on Music and Worship, 1993-96, Committee on the Maintenance of the Ministry, since 1997 (Member, since 1991, Vice-Convener, 1991-96); Conductor, Dumfries and Kirkcudbright Presbytery Choir, 1994-96; Member, Assembly Committee on Probationers, 1991-97, Maintenance of the Ministry Committee, 1991-98; Member, Board of Ministry, since 1998; Member, Ministry Support Committee, since 1998; Member, Executive Committee, Hymn Society of Great Britain and Ireland, since 1993. Publications: A History of Denbeath Church, 1980; Children's Addresses in the Expository Times, 1983. Recreation: music. Address: (h.) 47 Moffat Road, Dumfries DG1 1NN; T.-01387 254873.

Deans, Joyce Blair, MBE, DUniv, BArch, PPRIAS, RIBA, ACIArb, FRSA. Architect; President, Royal Incorporation of Architects in Scotland, 1991-93 (first woman President); b. 29.1.27, Glasgow; m., John Albert Gibson Deans; 2 s.; 2 d. Educ. Laurel Bank School for Girls; University of Strathclyde. Re-entered profession as Assistant, private practice, 1968; appointed Associate, 1972; established own practice, 1981; elected Member, Council: Glasgow Institute of Architects, 1975-90 (first female President, 1986-88), Royal Incorporation of Architects, 1979-95; first female Vice President, Royal Incorporation of Architects in Scotland, 1986-88; Member, Building Standards Advisory Committee, 1987-96; Chairman, BSAC (Research), 1988-96; Chairman, Scottish Construction Industry Group, since 1996 (Member, since 1991); Director: Cairn Housing Association, since 1988, Glasgow West Conservation Trust, since 1987; Governor: Laurel Bank (now Laurel Park) School for Girls since 1981, Glasgow School of Art, 1986-98; Member, Court, Strathclyde University, since 1992 Deputy Chairman of Court (Estates), since 1993; elected Vice President, Royal Institute of British Architects, 1993-95; Member: RIBA Council, since 1993, Patrick Geddes Award Panel, since 1993; Industrial Assessor (Architecture), SHEFC, 1994-95; External Examiner, Part 3, since 1994; Hon. DUniv (University of Strathclyde), 1996. Recreations: gardening; golf; walking; reading; theatre. Address: 11 South Erskine Park, Bearsden, Glasgow G61 4NA; T.-0141-942 6795.

Deans, Leslie George, LLB, NP. Chairman, Heart of Midlothian PLC, since 1996; Senior Partner, Leslie Deans & Co., Solicitors, since 1986; b. 10.8.51, Edinburgh. Educ.

George Watson's, Edinburgh; Edinburgh University. Professional life as practising solicitor; with C.P. Robinson acquired controlling interest in Heart of Midlothian, 1994. Recreations: cycling; bridge; travel; fine wines. Address: (b.) Tynecastle Stadium, Gorgie Road, Edinburgh; T.-0131-200 7200.

Deans, Mungo Effingham, BSc(Econ), LLB. Regional Adjudicator, Immigration Appellate Authority, since 1996; b. 25.5.56, Lytham St. Annes; m., Kathryn Atkinson; 3 s. Educ. Fettes College, Edinburgh; London School of Economics; University of Edinburgh. Admitted as Solicitor, 1981; Lecturer, Department of Law: Napier University, 1981-82, Dundee University, 1983-96; Chairman: Social Security Appeal Tribunals, 1989, Disability Appeal Tribunals, 1992; Immigration Adjudicator, 1994. Publication: Scots Public Law, 1995. Recreations: Scottish history; fine art. Address: (b.) Immigration Appellate Authority, 5th Floor, Portcullis House, 21 India Street, Glasgow G2 4PZ; T.-0141-221 3489.

Deary, Professor Ian John, BSc, PhD, MBChB, FRCPE, AFBPSS, CPsychol, MRCPsych. Professor of Differential Psychology, University of Edinburgh, since 1995; b. 17.5.54, Carluke; m., Ann Marie Barclay; 1 s.; 2 d. Educ. Hamilton Academy; University of Edinburgh. House Officer, Royal Informary of Edinburgh, 1983-84; Senior House Officer in Psychiatry, Maudsley Hospital, London, 1984-85; Department of Psychology, University of Edinburgh: Lecturer, 1985-90, Senior Lecturer, 1990-92, Reader, 1992-95. President-Elect, International Society for the Study of Individual Differences; Executive Committee Member, European Association of Personality Psychology; Distinguished International Affiliate, Laboratory for the Cross-Cultural Study of Individual Differences, University of Haifa, Israel. Publications: Personality Traits (Co-author); editor of two books on personality; over 100 refereed scientific papers, principally on human cognitive ability and personality. Recreations: saxophone; lyric-writing; late Victorian novels; English Romantic composers; Motherwell F.C. Address: (b.) Department of Psychology, University of Edinburgh, 7 George Square, Edinburgh EH8 9JZ; T.-0131-650 3452.

Deerin, Chris. Scottish Political Editor, Daily Record, since 1998; b. 9.9.73, Stirling. Educ. St. Modan's High School, Stirling; Napier University. Reporter, Stirling Observer; Political Reporter, Scottish Daily Mail; Political Correspondent, Scotland on Sunday. Recreation: humbly seeking the truth. Address: (b.) Anderston Quay, Glasgow G3 8DA; T.-0141-248 7000.

DeFelice, Hilda, BA (Hons). Headteacher, St. Luke's High School, Barrhead, since 1993; b. 16.2.49, Glasgow; m. Gordon Herriot; 1 s.; 1 d. Educ. Holyrood Secondary School, Glasgow; Strathclyde University. Teacher, 1973-76; Assistant Principal Teacher, 1976-79; Principal Teacher, 1979-86; Assistant Head Teacher, St. Ninian's High School, Giffnock, 1986-90; Depute Head Teacher, St. Bride's High School, East Kilbride, 1990-93. Recreations: reading; guitar; music. Address: (b.) St. Luke's High School, Springfield Road, Barrhead, G78 2SG; T.-0141-577 2400.

Delahunt, Jim, BA. Presenter, Scotsport, Extra Time, Football First, Scottish Television, since 1998; Columnist, Sunday Herald, since 1999; Columnist, The Scottish Farmer, since 1983; b. 10.5.62, Irvine; m., Marina Livingston. Educ. St. Andrews Academy, Saltcoats; Glasgow Caledonian University. Reporter, Kilmarnock Free Press; Reporter, West Sound; Editor, Daily Winner; Night News Editor, Radio Clyde; Sub-Editor, The Sunday Times; Sub-Editor, Reporter then Presenter, Scottish Television. Deputy FOC, STV Chapel, NUJ. Recreations: horse-racing; amateur jockey. Address: Scottish Television, Cowcaddens, Glasgow; T.-0131-300 3734.

De La Rue, Professor Richard Michael, BSc(Eng), MASc, PhD, FIEE, FRSE, SMIEEE. Professor of Optoelectronics, University of Glasgow, since 1986; b. 15.5.45, Reading, Berkshire; m., Barbara; 1 s.; 1 d. Educ. Forest Grammar School, Winnersh, Berkshire; University College, London; University of Toronto. University of Glasgow, Department of Electronics and Electrical Engineering: Lecturer, 1971, Senior Lecturer, 1982, Reader, 1985. Visiting Lecturer, Tohoku University, Japan, 1980; Consultant, Bell Labs, Murray Hill, NJ, 1978; Visiting Researcher, Communications Research Laboratories, Tokyo, Japan, 1997-98. Recreations: climbing; skiing; walking; cinema; theatre; concerts; cycling; wine-tasting. Address: (b.) Department of Electronics and Electrical Engineering, University of Glasgow, Glasgow G12 8QQ; T.-0141-330 4793/5220.

Della Sala, Professor Sergio F., MD, PhD. Chair of Psychology, Aberdeen; b. 23.9.55, Milan. Senior Neurologist, Milan teaching hospital; Head, Neuropsychology Unit, Veruno, Italy. Address: (b.) King's College, Aberdeen University, Aberdeen.

Demarco, Professor Richard, OBE, RSW, SSA, Hon. FRIAS, FRSA, DA, Hon. DFA, ACA, Hon. LLD (Dundee). Artist and Writer; Director, Richard Demarco Gallery, since 1966; b. 9.7.30, Edinburgh; m., Anne Muckle. Educ. Holy Cross Academy, Edinburgh; Edinburgh College of Art. National Service, KOSB, 1954-56; Art Master, Duns Scotus Academy, Edinburgh, 1957-67; Vice-Chairman, Board, Traverse Theatre Club, 1963-67; Director, Sean Connery's Scottish International Education Trust, 1972-73; Member: Board of Governors, Carlisle School of Art, 1970-74, Edinburgh Festival Society, 1971-86; Contributing Editor, Studio International, 1982-84; External Assessor, Stourbridge College of Art, 1988-90; Artistic Director, European Youth Parliament, since 1993; Professor of European Cultural Studies, Kingston University, since 1993; Director, Demarco European Art Foundation, since 1993; Trustee, Kingston-Demarco European Cultural Foundation, since 1993; Honorary Member, Scottish Arts Club; Elected Member, L'Association International des Critiques D'Art (AICA), 1994. Awards: Gold Order of Merit, Polish People's Republic; Chevalier de L'Ordre Des Arts Et Des Lettres; Order of Cavaliere Della Republica d'Italia; Scottish Arts Council Award for services to Scotland's visual arts, 1975; Medal, International Theatre Institutes of Great Britain and Poland, 1992; Honorary Doctorate, Atlanta College of Art, 1993; Arts Medal, Royal Philosophical Society of Glasgow, 1995; appointed Commander, Military and Hospitaller Order of St. Lazarus of Jerusalem, 1996. Publications: The Road to Meikle Seggie; The Artist as Explorer; A Life in Pictures; Kunst=Kapital: The Adam Smith Lecture, 1995; Honouring Colmcille, 1997. Recreation: walking "The Road to Meikle Seggie".

Dempsey, John, JP, CEng, MICE, MIBC. Chartered Civil Engineer, since 1963; Provost, East Dunbartonshire Council, since 1995; b. 24.11.35, Lennoxtown; 1 d. Educ. St. Machans, Lennoxtown; St. Ninian's High School, Kirkintilloch. District Councillor, Strathkelvin DC, 1980-95. Address: (b.) Tom Johnston House, Kirkintilloch, Glasgow G66; T.-0141-578 8000.

Dempster, Alastair Cox, FCIBS. Chairman, Scottish Community Foundation, since 1996; b. 22.6.40, Glasgow; m., Kathryn; 2 s. Educ. Paisley Grammar School. Royal Bank of Scotland, 1955-62; various managerial appointments, Scotland, Hong Kong, New York, 1962-81; AGM, International Division, Royal Bank of Scotland, 1981-86; Director of Commercial Banking and International/ Executive Director, TSB Scotland plc, 1986-91; TSB Bank Channel Islands Ltd.: Chief Executive, 1991-92; Deputy Chairman, 1992-96; Chief Executive, TSB Bank Scotland, 1992-98. Chairman, Committee of Scottish

Clearing Bankers, 1993-95; President, Chartered Institute of Bankers in Scotland, 1995-97; Member, Scottish Council Development and Industry and Executive Committee, 1992-98; Convener, Heriot Watt Audit Committee; Member, Heriot Watt University Court; Director, Scottish Homes, 1994-98; Director: Office of the Banking Ombudsman, Scottish Financial Enterprise; Director, Aberforth Split Level Trust plc; Member, Board of Governors, Edinburgh College of Art; Member, Scottish Hospital Endowment Research Trust. Recreations: golf; tennis; bridge. Address: (h.) Dalshian, 8 Harelaw Road, Edinburgh EH13 0DR; T.-0131-441 5202.

Denholm, Alastair Kennedy, FUniv, FCIBS, FInstP; b. 27.9.36, Glasgow; m., Rosalind Murray Hamilton;. Educ. Hutchesons' (Boys) Grammar School. Clydesdale Bank PLC, 1953-91; Managing Director, Quality Management Advisers (Scotland), 1992-98; Director, The Prince's Scottish Youth Business Trust, since 1985; Vice Chairman, Central College of Commerce, since 1991; Governor, Hutchesons' Grammar School, since 1996; Director, Merchants House of Glasgow; Lay Member, Audit Registration Committee, Institute of Chartered Accountants of Scotland, since 1995; Director, Glasgow Bute Benevolent Society, since 1980; Director, Glasgow Native Benevolent Society, since 1991; Treasurer, Action for Disaster, since 1973; Chairman, Chartered Institute of Bankers in Scotland, Glasgow, 1987-88; Director, Glasgow Chamber of Commerce, 1994-97; Treasurer and Elder, Williamwood Parish Church of Scotland, since 1962; District Governor Elect, Rotary District 1230, 1998-99; HOEC Treasurer, Rotary International World Conference 1997, 1996-98. Recreations: golf; curling; Rotary. Address: (h.) Whitley, 28 Milverton Road, Whitecraigs, Glasgow G46 7JN; T.-0141-638 2939.

Denholm, James Allan, CBE, CA, FRSA. Director, William Grant & Sons Ltd., 1975-96; Director, Scottish Mutual Assurance Society, since 1987 (Deputy Chairman, since 1992); Director, Scottish Cremation Society Limited, since 1980; Director, Abbey National plc, 1992-97; b. 27.9.36, Glasgow; m., Elizabeth Avril McLachlan, CA; 1 s.; 1 d. Educ. Hutchesons Boys Grammar School, Glasgow; Institute of Chartered Accountants of Scotland. Apprenticed, McFarlane Hutton & Patrick, CA, Glasgow (Sir William McLintock prizeman); Chief Accountant, A. & W. Smith & Co. Ltd., Glasgow, 1960-66; Secretary, William Grant & Sons Ltd., 1968-96; Chairman, East Kilbride Development Corporation, 1983-94 (Member, since 1979). Council Member, Institute of Chartered Accountants of Scotland, 1978-83, 1989-93 (President, 1992-93); Director and Treasurer, Glasgow YMCA, 1966-79; Chairman, Glasgow Junior Chamber of Commerce, 1972-73; Elder, New Kilpatrick Parish Church, since 1971; Visitor of the Incorporation of Maltmen in Glasgow, 1980-81; President, The Deacons' Association of Glasgow, 1994-95; Preses, The Weavers' Society of Anderston, 1994-95; Collector, Society of Deacons and Free Preseses of Glasgow, 1997-98; President, 49 Wine and Spirit Club of Scotland, 1983-84; Trustee, Scottish Cot Death Trust; Fellow, Society of Antiquaries of Scotland, since 1987; Deacon Convener, The Trades House of Glasgow, 1998-99; Fellow, Royal Society for the Encouragement of Arts, Manufactures and Commerce, 1993. Recreations: shooting; golf. Address: (h.) Greencroft, 19 Colquhoun Drive, Bearsden, Glasgow G61 4NQ; T.-0141-942 1773.

Denholm, John Clark, MA (Hons), MIPA. Chairman, Leith Advertising Agency Ltd., since 1995; Chairman, One to One Direct Communications Ltd., since 1990; b. 10.9.50, Chesterfield; m., Julia; 1 s.; 1 d. Educ. Buckhaven High School; St. Andrews University. Product Manager, The Boots Company, Nottingham, 1972-76; Brand Manager, Scottish & Newcastle Breweries, 1976-80; Account Director, Hall Advertising, Edinburgh, 1980-84. Recreation: golf. Address: (b.) The Canon Mill, Canon Street, Edinburgh; T.-0131-557 5840.

Denney, Alan Alexander, National Officer Scotland, Institution of Professionals, Managers and Specialists (IPMS), since 1990; b. 25.1.57, Stirling; m., Jacqueline May; 2 s.; 1 d. Educ. Plaistow Grammar School; East Ham College of Technology. Civil Service (Department of Trade), 1975-78; Institution of Professionals, Managers and Specialists (formerly IPCS), since 1979. Address: (b.) 18 Melville Terrace, Stirling FK8 2NQ; T.-01786 465999.

Dennis, Richard Benson, PhD, BSc. Managing Director, Edinburgh Instruments Ltd.; Director, Edinburgh Sensors Ltd.; Founder, Mütek GmbH, West Germany; b. 15.7.45, Weymouth; m., Beate Stamm; 2 d. Educ. Weymouth Grammar School; Reading University. SRC Postdoctoral Fellow, Reading; Guest Fellow, Freiburg University, 1968-70; Lecturer/Senior Lecturer, Heriot-Watt University, 1970-91; Alexander von Humboldt Fellow, Munich University, 1976-78; Treasurer, UK Laser and Electro-Optic Trade Association; Council Member, Scottish Consultative Committee on the Curriculum, 1991-94; Chairman, Balerno High School Board, 1990-94; Joint Winner, Department of Industry EPIC Award (Education in Partnership with Industry and Commerce), 1982. Recreations: bridge; sport. Address: (b.) Edinburgh Instruments Ltd., Riccarton, Currie, Edinburgh; T.-0131-449 5844.

Dennis, Roy, MBE. Wildlife Consultant/Ornithologist; Specialist, species recovery projects, UK and overseas; crofter, since 1985; b. 4.5.40; m., Marina MacDonell; 2 s.; 1 d. Educ. Price's School. Migration Research Assistant, UK Bird Observatories, 1958-59; Warden, Lochgarten Osprey Reserve, 1960-63; Warden, Fair Isle Bird Observatory, 1963-70; Highland Officer, RSPB, 1971-87, Regional Officer (North Scotland), 1987-91; Main Board Member, Scottish Natural Heritage, 1992-97; Director, Cairngorms Partnership, 1995-97. Publications: Ospreys and Speyside Wildlife; Birds of Badenoch and Strathspey; Puffins; Ospreys; Peregrine Falcons; Divers; The Loch; Golden Eagles. Recreations: travel; photography; cross-country skiing; bird-watching. Address: Inchdryne, Nethybridge, Invernessshire PH25 3EF; T.-01479 831 384.

Denniston, Rev. David William, BD, DipMin. Minister, North Church, Perth, since 1996; b. 23.4.56, Glasgow; m., Jane Ross; 2 s.; 1 d. Educ. Hutchesons' Boys Grammar School, Glasgow; University of Glasgow. Minister: Ruchazie Parish Church, Glasgow, 1981-86, Kennoway, Fife, 1986-96. Recreations: hill-walking; fishing; music. Address: (h.) 127 Glasgow Road, Perth PH2 0LU; T.-01738 625728.

Denny, Margaret Bertha Alice, OBE, DL, BA (Hons), PhD. Member, Council and Executive Committee, National Trust for Scotland, since 1974 (Vice President, 1981-91); b. 30.9.07, Chatham; m., Edward Leslie Denny. Educ. Dover County School; Bedford College for Women, London University. Entered Civil Service as Principal, Ministry of Shipping, 1940; Assistant Secretary, 1946; Under Secretary, 1957; Governor, Bedford College; Member: Scottish Advisory Council for Civil Aviation, 1958-67, Western Regional Hospital Board, 1960-74, Scottish Committee, Council of Industrial Design, 1961-71, General Advisory Council, BBC, 1962-66, General Nursing Council, Scotland, 1963-78, Board of Management, State Hospital, Carstairs, 1966-76; Vice-Chairman, Argyll and Clyde Health Board, 1974-77; County Commissioner, Girl Guides, Dunbartonshire, 1958-68; DL, Dunbartonshire, since 1973; Officer, Order of Orange Nassau, 1947. Recreations: gardening; needlework; music. Address: (h.) Dalnair House, Croftamie, Glasgow G63 0EZ; T.-01360 660106.

Deregowski, Professor Jan Bronislaw, BSc, BA, PhD, DSc, FBPsS, FRSE. Professor of Psychology, Aberdeen University, since 1986 (Reader, 1981-86); b. 1.3.33, Pinsk, Poland; m., Eva Loft Nielsen; 2 s.; 1 d. Educ. London University. Lecturer, then Senior Lecturer, Aberdeen University, 1969-81. Publications: Illusions, Patterns and Pictures: a cross-cultural perspective; Distortion in Art; Perception and Artistic Style (Co-author). Address: (b.) Department of Psychology, King's College, Old Aberdeen AB9 2UB; T.-Aberdeen 272247.

Dervaird, Hon. Lord (John Murray), MA (Oxon), LLB (Edin), FCIArb. Dickson Minto Professor of Company Law, Edinburgh University, since 1990, Dean, Faculty of Law, 1994-96; b. 8.7.35, Stranraer; m., Bridget Jane Godfrey; 3 s. Educ. Stranraer schools; Edinburgh Academy; Corpus Christi College, Oxford; Edinburgh University. Advocate, 1962; QC, 1974; Law Commissioner (part-time), 1979-88; Senator of the College of Justice, 1988-89; Chairman, Scottish Council for International Arbitration, since 1989; Council Member, London Court of International Arbitration, since 1990; Trustee, David Hume Institute, since 1992; Member, ICC Committee on Business Law, Paris, since 1992; Chairman, BT Scottish Ensemble, since 1988; Member: City Disputes Panel, since 1994, Panel of Arbitrators, International Centre for Settlement of Investment Disputes, since 1998; Hon. President, Advocates' Business Law Group, since 1988; Chairman, Edinburgh Wigtownshire Association, since 1997. Publications: Stair Encyclopaedia of Scots Law (Contributor); articles on legal and ornithological subjects. Recreations: farming; gardening; bird-watching; music; curling. Address: (h.) Auchenmalg House, Auchenmalg, Glenluce, Wigtownshire.

Devereux, Alan Robert, CBE, DL, CEng, MIEE, CBIM. Chairman, Scottish Ambulance Service NHS Trust, 1995-97; Founder, Quality Scotland Foundation; International Director, Gleneagles PLC, since 1990; Director, Scottish Mutual Assurance Society, since 1976; b. 18.4.33, Frinton-on-Sea; m., 1, Gloria Alma Hair (deceased); 1 s.; 2, Elizabeth Tormey Docherty. Educ. Colchester School; Clacton County High School; Mid Essex Technical College. Marconi's Wireless Telegraph Company: apprentice, 1950-55, Standards Engineer, 1955-56; Technical Production Manager, Halex Division, British Xylonite Company, 1956-58; Technical Sales Manager, SPA Division, Sanitas Trust, 1958-65; General Manager, Dobar Engineering, 1965-67; various managerial posts, Norcros Ltd., 1967-69; Group Managing Director, Scotcros Ltd., 1969-78; Deputy Chairman, Scotcros Ltd., 1978-80. CBI: Chairman, Scotland, 1977-79 (Deputy Chairman, 1975-77), Council Member, 1972-84, Member, President's Advisory Committee, 1979; UK Regional Chairman, 1979; Chairman, Small Industries Council for Rural Areas of Scotland, 1975-77; Member, Scottish Development Agency, 1977-83; Chairman: Scottish Tourist Board, 1980-90, Glasgow City Mission; Director, Children's Hospice Association for Scotland; Scottish Free Enterprise Award, 1978; Deputy Lieutenant, Renfrewshire, since 1985. Recreations: work; amateur radio; reading. Address: (h.) South Fell, 24 Kirkhouse Road, Blanefield, Glasgow G63 9BX; T.-0360 770464.

Devine, Bernard. Chief Executive, North Ayrshire Council. Address: (b.) Cunninghame House, Irvine, KA12 8EE.

Devine, John, FRICS, IRRV. Member, Lands Tribunal for Scotland, since 1991; b. 23.10.29, Glasgow; m., Agnes Susan McLaughlin; 2 s.; 1 d. Educ. St. Mary's College, Blairs, Aberdeen; Glasgow College of Technology; College of Estate Management. Apprentice and qualified assistant, Thomas Binnie & Hendry, Chartered Valuation Surveyors, 1947-57; Senior Valuer, Fife County Council's Assessor's Department, 1957-62; Partner, then Senior Partner, Graham & Sibbald, Chartered Surveyors, 1962-91. Member: Board of Management, Fife College of Further and Higher Education, 1992-98, Scottish Valuation and Rating Council, since 1996. Recreation: golf. Address: (h.) 80 Milton Road, Kirkcaldy KY1 1TP; T.-01592 264806.

Devine, Rt. Rev. Joseph, PhD. Bishop of Motherwell, since 1983; b. 7.8.37, Glasgow. Educ. St. Mary's College, Blairs, Aberdeen; St. Peter's College, Cardross; Pontifical Scots College, Rome. Ordained Priest, Glasgow, 1960; Private Secretary to Archbishop of Glasgow, 1964-65; Assistant Priest, St. Robert Bellarmine, Glasgow, 1965-67; St. Joseph's, Helensburgh, 1967-72; on staff, St. Peter's College, Cardross, 1967-74; Assistant Chaplain, Catholic Chaplaincy, Glasgow University, 1974-77; nominated Titular Bishop of Voli, and Auxiliary Bishop to Archbishop of Glasgow, 1977. Vice-Convener, Central Council, ACTS; President, Catholic Communications Commission. Recreations: reading; watching sport. Address: (b.) Diocesan Centre, Coursington Road, Motherwell ML1 1PW; T.-01698 269114.

Devine, Professor Thomas Martin, BA, PhD, DLitt, FRHistS, FRSE, FBA. University Research Professor in Scottish History and Director, Research Institute of Irish and Scottish Studies, Aberdeen University, since 1998; b. 30.10.46, Motherwell; m., Catherine Mary Lynas; 2 s. of whom 1 deceased; 3 d. Educ. Our Lady's RC High School, Motherwell; Strathclyde University. Strathclyde University: Lecturer, then Senior Lecturer and Reader, Department of History, 1969-88 (Head of Department, 1990-92), Dean, Faculty of Arts and Social Sciences, 1993-94, Deputy Principal, 1994-97, Professor of Scottish History, 1988-98, Director of Research Centre in Scottish History, 1994-98; Visiting Professor, University of Guelph, Canada, 1983 and 1988 (Adjunct Professor in History, since 1988); Adjunct Professor in History, University of North Carolina; Governor, St. Andrews College of Education, 1990-94. Joint Founding Editor, Scottish Economic and Social History, 1980-84. British Academy/Leverhulme Trust Senior Research Fellow, 1992-93; Trustee, National Museums of Scotland, since 1995; Winner: Senior Hume Brown Prize, 1977, Agnes Mure MacKenzie Prize, Saltire Society, 1992, Henry Duncan Prize, Royal Society of Edinburgh, 1995. Publications: The Tobacco Lords, 1975; Lairds and Improvement in Enlightenment Scotland, 1979; Ireland and Scotland 1600-1850 (Co-Editor), 1983; Farm Servants and Labour in Lowland Scotland 1770-1914, 1984; A Scottish Firm in Virginia 1767-77, 1984; People and Society in Scotland 1760-1830 (Co-Editor), 1988; The Great Highland Famine, 1988; Improvement and Enlightenment (Editor), 1989; Conflict and Stability in Scottish Sociey (Editor), 1990; Irish Immigrants and Scottish Society in the Eighteenth and Nineteenth Centuries (Editor), 1991; Scottish Emigration and Scottish Society, 1992; Scottish Elites, 1993; The Transformation of Rural Scotland, 1994; Clanship to Crofters' War, 1994; Industry, Business and Society in Scotland since 1700 (Co-Editor), 1994; Glasgow: I, Beginnings to 1830, 1995; St. Mary's, Hamilton: a social history; Exploring the Scottish Past, 1995; Scotland in the Twentieth Century (Co-Editor), 1996; Eighteenth Century Scotland: New Perspectives (Co-Editor), 1998. Recreations: walking and exploring the Hebrides; watching skilful football; travelling in Italy. Address: (b.) Research Institute of Irish and Scottish Studies, Aberdeen University, King's College, Old Aberdeen.

de Vink, Peter Henry John, BComm. Managing Director, Edinburgh Financial and General Holdings Ltd., since 1978; b. 9.10.40, Amsterdam; m., Julia Christine (Krista) Quarles van Ufford; 1 s.; 1 d. Educ. Edinburgh University. National Service, Dutch Army, 1961-63; Edinburgh University, 1963-66; Ivory and Sime Investment Managers, 1966-78, latterly as Director. Address: (b.) 7 Howe Street, Edinburgh EH3 6TE; T.-0131-225 6661; (h.) Huntly Cot, Temple, Midlothian EH23 4TS; T.-01875 830345.

Dewar, The Rt Hon. Donald Campbell, PC, MA, LLB. Secretary of State for Scotland, since 1997; MP (Labour), Glasgow Anniesland, since 1997 (MP, Garscadden, 1978-96); b. 21.8.37, Glasgow; 1 s.; 1 d. Educ. Glasgow Academy; Glasgow University. Practised as Solicitor in Glasgow; MP, Aberdeen South, 1966-70; PPS to Tony Crosland, 1967; Chairman, Select Committee on Scottish Affairs, 1980-81; Member, Scottish front bench team, 1981-83; elected to Shadow Cabinet, 1984; Opposition Spokesman on Scottish Affairs, 1983-92, Social Security, 1992-95; Opposition Chief Whip, 1995-97; Privy Councillor, 1996. Address: (h.) 23 Cleveden Road, Glasgow G12; T.-0141-334 2374.

Dewar, Douglas, MA (Hons), CA. Finance Director, Scottish Airports Ltd., since 1992; b. 18.6.47, Glasgow; m., Nancy; 1 s.; 1 d. Educ. High School of Glasgow; Glasgow University. Arthur Young McClelland Moores; Scotish Co-ordinated Investments Ltd.; Scottish Express Ltd. (Finance Director); Stansted Airport Ltd. (Finance Director). Address: (b.) Scottish Airports Ltd., St. Andrews Drive, Glasgow Airport, Glasgow PA3 2SW; T.-0141-848 4298.

Dewar, Ian McGregor, CA. Senior Partner, PricewaterhouseCoopers, Edinburgh, since 1995; b. 21.8.46, Helensburgh; m., Avril; 2 s. Educ. Hutchesons' Grammar School, Glasgow. Qualified as CA, 1969; joined Price Waterhouse, Glasgow, 1969, Partner, 1979. Past President, Junior Chamber, Scotland. Recreations: golf; shooting. Address: (b.) 58 Albany Street, Edinburgh EH1 3QR; T.-0131-557 9900.

Dewar, Lawrence, MBE. Chief Executive, Scottish Grocers' Federation, since 1980; b. 12.1.36, Blackford; m., Nancy Kelly; 2 s.; 2 d. Educ. Dunfermline High School. Grocer of the Year, 1967; President, Scottish Grocers' Federation, 1975; Member, Board, SCOTBEC, 1981-85; Member, Sector Sector Board 5, SCOTVEC, 1986-97; Recreations: golf; reading; TV. Address: (h.) 222/224 Queensferry Road, Edinburgh EH4 2BN.

Dewar-Durie, Andrew Maule. Chairman, Allied Distillers Ltd., since 1997; Chairman, CBI Scotland, since 1997; b. 13.11.39; Bath; m., Marguerite Kottulinsky; 2 s.; 1 d. Educ. Wellington College. Regular soldier, Argyll and Sutherland Highlanders, 1958-68, retiring with rank of Captain; Export Representative to Senior Export Director, White Horse Distillers, 1968-83; International Sales Director, Long John International, 1983-87; James Burrough Distillers: International Sales Director, 1987-89, Managing Director, 1990; Chief Executive Officer, James Burrough Ltd., 1990-91, Managing Director, 1991-92; Managing Director, Allied Distillers Ltd., 1992-97. Deputy Lieutenant, Dunbartonshire, since 1996; CBI Scotland: Council Member, 1993, Vice Chairman, 1996; Non-Executive Director, Dumyat Investment Trust PLC, since 1995; Director, Scotch Whisky Association, since 1992; Keeper of the Quaich, since 1989, Master, since 1992; Liveryman, Worshipful Company of Distillers, since 1986; Council Member, Gin and Vodka Association of GB, since 1997; Member, Scottish Business Forum, since 1998. Recreations: tennis; rough shooting; sailing; theatre; cinema. Address: Finnich Malise, Croftamie, West Stirlingshire G63 0HA; T.-0136 066 0257.

Dewing, Irene Isabel Joan, DL; b. 21.9.36, Inverness; m., William Beresford Dewing; 2 d. Educ. Heatherley, Inverness. Deputy Lieutenant. Address: (h.) The Hollies, Kildary, Rossshire; T.-01862 842204.

Dhillon, Bal Jean, BMedSci, FRCS(Glas), FRCS(Edin), FRCOphth. Consultant Ophthalmic Surgeon, Edinburgh, since 1991; b. 21.7.59; m., Alethaea; 2 s.; 2 d. Educ. Gateway Boys' Grammar School; Nottingham University. Registrar, Edinburgh and Singapore, 1988-90. Publication: The Child's Eye. Recreations: travel; writing. Address: (h.) 25 Granby Road, Edinburgh EH16 5NP; T.-0131-667 2686.

Dhir, Professor Ravindra Kumar, OBE. Professor of Concrete Technology, University of Dundee, since 1990; b. 3.11.35, Nakodar, Jallandhar, Punjab, India; m., Bharti; 3 d. Educ. Arya High School, Nakodar.; University of Durham; University of Sheffield. Came to UK, 1954; Labourer; Management Trainee; University of Dundee: Lecturer, Civil Engineering, 1972, Senior Lecturer, 1978, Reader in Concrete Technology, 1988, Director, Concrete Technology Unit, since 1988. Honorary Fellow, Institute of Concrete Technology. Address: (h.) 265 Perth Road, Dundee DD2 1JP; T.-01328 344347; (b.) Department of Civil Engineering, University of Dundee, Dundee DD1 4HN; T.-01328 667396.

Diani, Professor Mario, PhD. Professor of Sociology, Strathclyde University, since 1996; b. 29.5.57, Cuorgne, Italy; m., Silvia N. Fargion; 1 s. Educ. Liceo Classico Botta, Ivrea, Italy; University of Milan; University of Turin. Lecturer in Sociology, Bocconi University of Milan, 1987-93; Senior Lecturer in Sociology, University of Pavia, 1993-96. Publications: Studying Collective Action (Co-author), 1992; Green Networks, 1995; Social Movements (Co-Author), 1998. Recreations: classical music; movies; mountaineering; cycling. Address: (h.) 74 Thirlestane Road, Edinburgh EH9 1AR; T.-0131-466 0365.

Dick, David, OBE, DIC, CEng, FIEE. H.M. Managing Director, Clerkington Publishing Co. Ltd., since 1998; Lay Inspector of Fire Services for Scotland, 1994-98; b. 20.3.29, Edinburgh; m., Muriel Elsie Margaret Buchanan; 5 d. Educ. Boroughmuir School, Edinburgh; Heriot-Watt College, Edinburgh; Imperial College, London. Electrical Engineer, North of Scotland Hydro-Electric Board, 1951-54; Lecturer, Dundee College of Technology, 1954-60; Head, Department of Electrical Engineering, Coatbridge Technical College, 1960-64; Depute Principal, Napier College of Science and Technology, Edinburgh, 1964-69; Principal, Stevenson College of Further Education, Edinburgh, 1969-87. Manpower Services Commission: Chairman, Lothian District Manpower Committee, 1981-82, Member, Lothian and Borders Area Manpower Board, 1982-85; Member and Chairman, various committees: Scottish Technical Education Council, Scottish Business Education Council, 1969-87; Member and Chairman, Fire Services Examination Board (Scotland), 1968-86; Member, Construction Industry Training Board, 1976-85; Member: Electrical Engineering Services Committee, CITB, 1976-88, General Convocation, Heriot-Watt University, Edinburgh, 1970-73; Past Chairman, Scottish Committee, Institution of Electronic and Radio Engineers; former Honorary President, Edinburgh and District Spastics Association. Publications: Capital Walks in Edinburgh – The New Town, 1994; Street Biographies of the Royal Burgh of Haddington, 1997; Who was Who on the Royal Mile, Edinburgh, 1997; Who was Who in Dunbar Street Names, 1998. Recreations: music (flute); gardening; writing historical biographies. Address: (h.) West Lodge, Clerkington, near Haddington, East Lothian.

Dick, James, OBE, BA, DMS. Director of Social Work, The Highland Council, since 1986; b. 19.5.39, Kirkcaldy; m., Isabel; 1 d. Educ. Buckhaven High School; Schumacher High School, Ontario; Jordanhill College; Open University; RGIT. Probation Officer, Edinburgh, 1967; Child Care Officer, Moray and Nairn, 1969; Area Team Leader, Perth and Kinross, 1971; Principal Social Work Officer, Selkirk County Council, 1973; Divisional Officer, Child Care, Borders Regional Council, 1975; Divisional Officer, Grampian Regional Council, 1975; Highland Regional Council: Senior Depute Director of Social Work, 1985, Director of Social Work, since 1986. Past President, Association of Directors of Social Work. Recreations: golf; gardening; reading; bowls. Address: (b.) Kinmylies Building, Leachkin Road, Inverness IV3 6NN; T.-01463 703444.

Dick, Jill (Gillian Avril). Director: Scottish Cultural Press, since 1992, Scottish Children's Press, since 1995; b. 9.4.49, Croydon; 3 s. Educ. Croham Hurst School, South Croydon. Variety of positions with Aberdeen University Press for 10 years, until its collapse at the death of Robert Maxwell. Recreations: crosswords; reading; walking; good food and drink. Address: (b.) Unit 14, Leith Walk Business Centre, 130 Leith Walk, Edinburgh EH6 5DT; T.-0131-555 5950.

Dick, Rev. John Hunter Addison, MA, MSc, BD. Parish Minister, Aberdeen: Ferryhill, since 1982; Vice-Convener, Church of Scotland Board of Parish Education, since 1997; b. 27.12.45, Dunfermline; 3 s. Educ. Dunfermline High School; Edinburgh University. Research Assistant, Department of Geography, Edinburgh University, 1967-70; Senior Tutor, Department of Geography, Queensland University, 1970-78; student of divinity, 1978-81; Assistant Minister, Edinburgh: Fairmilehead, 1981-82. Governor, Robert Gordon's College, since 1994. Recreations: music; bowls. Address: Ferryhill Manse, 54 Polmuir Road, Aberdeen AB11 7RT; T.-01224 586933.

Dickie, Bobbie, MSc, CQSW, DipOT, DipComCare, LRCCO. Executive Director Housing and Social Services, Clackmannanshire Council, since 1995; b. 18.11.43, Glasgow; m., Greig Stobo; 1 d. Educ. The Academy, Hamilton; Stirling University; Glasgow University; Suffolk College. Team Leader, Child Protection, NSPCC, London, 1973-78; Children and Family work, St. Albans Social Services, 1978-81; Central Region: Team Manager, Learning Disabilities, 1981-89; Principal Professional Officer, Disabilities, 1989-93; Head of Service, Adult Care, 1993-95. Recreations: travel; motoring; gardening; DIY. Address: (b.) Limetree House, Castle Street, Alloa FK10 1EX; T.-01259 452416.

Dickinson, Professor Harry Thomas, BA, DipEd, MA, PhD, DLitt, FRHistS, FRSE. Professor of British History, Edinburgh University, since 1980; Professor of British History, Nanjing University, since 1987; b. 9.3.39, Gateshead; m., Jennifer Elizabeth Galtry; 1 s.; 1 d. Educ. Gateshead Grammar School; Durham University; Newcastle University. Teacher of History, Washington Grammar School, 1961-64; Earl Grey Fellow, Newcastle University, 1964-66; History Department, Edinburgh University: Assistant Lecturer, 1966-68, Lecturer, 1968-73, Reader, 1973-80; Associate Dean (Postgraduate), 1992-96; Convener, Senatus PGS Committee, since 1998; Visiting Professor, Nanjing University, China, 1980-83-87-94; Fulbright Scholar, 1973; Huntington Library Fellowship, 1973; Folger Shakespeare Library Fellowship, 1973; Winston Churchill Fellow, 1980; Leverhulme Award, 1986-87; Ahmanson Fellowship, UCLA, 1987; Anstey Lecturer, University of Kent, 1989; Douglas Southall Freeman Professor, University of Richmond, Virginia, 1987; Chairman, Publications Committee, Historical Association, 1991-94; Vice-President: Royal Historical Society, 1991-95, Historical Association, 1995-97 (Deputy President, 1997-98); Member, Humanities Committee, CNAA, 1991-93; National Auditor, Higher Education Quality Council, 1993-95; Team Assessor, History, TQA, SHEFC, 1995-96; Member, Marshall Aid Commonwealth Commission, 1987-96; Member, QAA History Subject Benchmarking Committee, 1998-99; Editor, History. Publications: Bolingbroke; Walpole and the Whig Supremacy; Liberty and Property; British Radicals and the French Revolution; The Correspondence of Sir James Clavering; Politics and Literature in the 18th Century; The Political Works of Thomas Spence; Caricatures and the Constitution 1760-1832; Britain and the French Revolution; The Politics of the People in Eighteenth-century Britain; Britain and the American Revolution; many pamphlets, essays and reviews. Recreations: reading; films. Address: (h.) 44 Viewforth Terrace, Edinburgh EH10 4LJ; T.-0131-229 1379.

Dickinson, Professor Keith William, BSc, MEng, PhD, CEng, MICE, FIHT. Assistant Principal, Academic Development, Napier University, since 1997; b. 17.9.48, Liverpool; m., Dorothy Mills; 1 s.; 1 d. Educ. Ormskirk Secondary School; Sheffield Polytechnic; University of Sheffield.Senior Lecturer and Director, Transport Engineering Research Unit, Napier Polytechnic, 1986-90; Napier University: Head, Civil & Transportation Engineering, 1990-94, Dean, Faculty of Engineering, 1994-97. Recreations: walking; travelling; fishing; drawing. Address :(b.) Napier University, Craighouse Campus, Craighouse Road, Edinburgh EH10 5LG; T.-0131-455 6000/1.

Dickson, Alastair Ronald. Senior Partner, Dickson Minto WS, since 1985; b. 16.1.51, Glasgow; m., Josephine; 2 s.; 1 d. Educ. Glenalmond College; Edinburgh University. Trained, Dundas & Wilson, 1971-73; Maclay, Murray & Spens, 1973-76; Dundas & Wilson, 1976-85 (Partner, from 1985); Founding Partner, Dickson Minto WS, 1985. Recreations: golf; squash; hill-walking. Address: (b.) 11 Walker Street, Edinburgh EH3 7NE; T.-0131-225 4455.

Dickson, Captain Alexander Forrest, OBE, RD, FRIN. Commissioner of Northern Lighthouses, 1979-96; b. 23.6.20, Edinburgh; m., Norma Houston; 3 s.; 2 d. Educ. George Watson's; Leith Nautical College. Apprentice, P. Henderson and Co., 1936-39; Royal Navy service in destroyers, 1939-45; Lecturer, Leith Nautical College, 1945-49; Shell International Marine Co. Ltd., 1949-79 (Director Operations, 1968-79). Honorary Sheriff, Perth. Recreations: fishing; gardening; golf. Address: (h.) Birchburn, Kenmore, Perthshire; T.-018873 283.

Dickson, Campbell S., MA, DipEd. Rector, Nairn Academy, since 1987; b. 25.11.44, Edinburgh; 2 s. Educ. Boroughmuir High School, Edinburgh; Edinburgh University. Teacher of Modern Languages, Dunfermline High School, 1968-71; Principal Teacher of Modern Languages, Golspie High School, 1971-79; Assistant Rector, Banff Academy, 1979-82; Depute Rector, Lochaber High School, 1982-87. Member, Scottish Central Committee on Modern Languages, 1977-80. Address: (b.) Nairn Academy, Duncan Drive, Nairn IV12 4RD; T.-01667 453700.

Dickson, Professor James Holms, BSc, MA, PhD, FLS, FRSE. Professor of Archaeobotany and Plant Systematics, Glasgow University, since 1998 (Reader in Botany, 1993-98); b. 29.4.37, Glasgow; m. Camilla A. Lambert, 1 s.; 1 d. Educ. Bellahouston Academy; University of Glasgow; University of Cambridge. Fellow, Clare College, University of Cambridge, 1963-70; Lecturer then Senior Lecturer in Botany, University of Glasgow, 1970-93. Leader, Trades House of Glasgow Expedition to Papua, New Guinea, 1987; Consultant, Britoil, Glasgow Garden Festival, 1988; currently working on plant remains found with 5,300 year old Tyrolean Iceman. Neill Medallist, Royal Society of Edinburgh, 1996; twice Past President, Glasgow Natural History Society; Past President, Botanical Society of Scotland. Publications: three books, including Wild Plants of Glasgow; many papers on Scottish flora, Ice Age plants, archaeo-botany. Address: (b.) Graham Kerr Building, Glasgow University; T.-0141-330 4364.

Dickson, Leonard Elliot, CBE, MC, TD, DL, BA (Cantab), LLB. Retired Solicitor; b. 17.3.15, Edinburgh; m., Mary Elisabeth Cuthbertson; 1 s.; 1 d. Educ. Uppingham; Magdalene College, Cambridge; Glasgow University. 1st Bn., Glasgow Highlanders HLI, 1939-46; former Senior Partner, Dickson, Haddow & Co., Solicitors, Glasgow (retired, 1985); Clerk, Clyde Lighthouses Trust, 1953-65; Secretary, Glasgow Society of Sons of Clergy, 1953-83; serving Officer, TA, 1939-55 (Lt. Col. commanding 1st Bn., Glasgow Highlanders, 1952-55); Chairman, Lowland TAVR, 1968-70; Member, Glasgow Executive Council,

NHS, 1956-74 (Vice Chairman, 1970-74). Recreations: travel; gardening. Address: (h.) Bridge End, Gartmore, Stirling FK8 3RR; T.-01877 382 220.

Dickson, Sheriff Robert Hamish, LLB, WS. Sheriff of South Strathclyde, Dumfries & Galloway at Airdrie, since 1988; b. 19.10.45, Glasgow; m., Janet Laird Campbell; 1 s. Educ. Glasgow Academy; Drumtochty Castle; Glenalmond; Glasgow University. Solicitor, Edinburgh, 1969-71, and Glasgow, 1971-86; Partner, Brown Mair Gemmill & Hislop, Solicitors, Glasgow, 1973-86; appointed floating Sheriff of South Strathclyde, Dumfries & Galloway at Hamilton, 1986. Publication: Medical and Dental Negligence, 1997. Recreations: golf; music; reading. Address: (b.) Airdrie Sheriff Court, Airdrie; T.-Airdrie 751121.

Diggory, Robert, MD, FRCS, FRCS(Edin). Consultant Surgeon, Victoria Hospital, Kirkcaldy and St. Andrews Memorial Hospital, since 1993; b. 5.3.53. Educ. Liverpool College; Dundee University. Recreations: historic motor racing. Address: (h.) Royal Terrace, Falkland, Fife; T.-(b.) 01592 643355.

Dillon, J. Shaun H., DRSAM (Comp), FSA Scot. Professional Musician; Composer, Oboist and Teacher of Woodwind; b. 30.12.44, Sutton Coldfield. Educ. Berwickshire High School; Fettes College; Royal Scottish Academy of Music; Guildhall School of Music. Studied composition with Frank Spedding and Edmund Rubbra; awarded prize for composition for Leicestershire Schools Orchestra, 1965; commissions from various bodies, including Scottish Amateur Music Association; Instructor of Woodwind: Edinburgh Corporation, 1967-72, Aberdeen Corporation (latterly Grampian Region), 1972-81; Freelance Musician, since 1981; sometime Director of Music, St. Mary's Cathedral, Aberdeen; two suites of Airs and Graces for strings published; Secretary, Association of Instrumental and Vocal Specialists, 1975-78. Recreations: reading, especially history, literature; crosswords; playing flute (badly) in ceilidh bands. Address: (b.) 34 Richmond Street, Aberdeen AB25 4TR; T.-01224 630954.

Dilworth, Rt. Rev. Gerard Mark, OSB, MA, PhD, FRHistS, FSA Scot. Abbot, Fort Augustus Abbey, 1991-98, now Emeritus; Titular Abbot of Iona, since 1998; b. 18.4.24. Educ. St. Andrew's School, Edinburgh; Fort Augustus Abbey School, Invernessshire; Oxford University; Edinburgh University. Fort Augustus Abbey School: Senior Modern Languages Master, 1956-59, Headmaster, 1959-72; Parish Priest, Fort Augustus, 1974-79; Editor, The Innes Review, 1979-84; Keeper, Scottish Catholic Archives, Edinburgh, 1979-91. Publications: The Scots in Franconia, 1974; George Douglas: priest and martyr, 1987; Scottish Monasteries in the Late Middle Ages, 1995. Address: (b.) The Abbey, Fort Augustus, Inverness PH32 4DB; T.-01320 366232.

Dingwall-Fordyce Andrew. Convener, Scottish Landowner's Federation, since 1997; b. 22.2.57, Liverpool; m., Lucinda Williams; 1 s.; 2 d. Educ. Rugby School; Scottish Agricultural College, Aberdeen. Runs mixed agricultural estate in Aberdeenshire; Member, Banff and Buchan Valuation Appeal Committee; Chairman, Game Conservancy in Scotland, 1993-97; Trustee, Roland Sutton Trust; President, Highland Gundog Club; Past Treasurer and President, New Deer Agricultural Association. Council Member, Scottish Agricultural College. Recreations: golf; tennis; shooting; bridge; skiing. Address: Brucklay, Maud, Peterhead; T.-01771613 263.

Divers, Catherine, SHND, ICFM. Fundraising Co-ordinator, Scotland, Arthritis Research Campaign, since 1998; b. 25.4.50, Dundee; m., Al; 2 s.; 1 d. Educ. secondary schools in India and Central America; Dundee College of Further Education. Training Co-ordinator, government-funded training schemes; Assessor and Verifier, Royal Society of Arts; PA to Appeals Director for Scotland, Arthritis and Rheumatism Council for Research, 1995-98. Address: (b.) 140 High Street, Lochee, Dundee DD2 3BZ; T.-01382 400911.

Dixon, Professor Geoffrey Richard, BSc, PhD, FIHort, FIBiol, CBiol. Professor of Horticulture, University of Strathclyde; independent international consultant, specialising at the interface between biotechnology, horticulture, plant pathology, education; Director, GreenGene International; formerly Head of Horticulture, Director, Scottish Horticultural Advisory Service, SAC; b. 13.6.42, London; m., Kathleen Hilda Edwards; 1 s.; 1 d. Educ. Pewley County School, Guildford; Wye College, University of London. Plant Pathologist, National Institute of Agricultural Botany, Cambridge, 1968-78; Head, Horticulture Division and Chairman, Crop Production and Protection Group, and Senior University Lecturer, Aberdeen School of Agriculture, 1978-87; Chairman, Education and Research Commission, International Society for Horticultural Research; Chairman, International Clubroot Working Group; Visiting Professor, Mansourah University, Egypt; Honorary Professor, Von Humboldt University, Berlin; Senior Research Scholar, University of Wisconsin; Visiting Lecturer, University of Horticulture, Budapest; Vice-Chairman, Education and Training Committee; former Chairman, Scottish Branch, Institute of Horticulture; Member, Examinations Board, Royal Horticultural Society; created Freeman Citizen of Glasgow and Member; Incorporation of Gardeners of Glasgow; Member of the Master Court; Liveryman, Worshipful Company of Fruiterers of the City of London; Chairman, Agricultural Sciences Committee, Institute of Biology. Wain Fellowship, BBSRC; Nuffield Foundation Fellowship, European Community Erasmus Programme Co-ordinator. Publications: Vegetable Crop Diseases; Plant Pathogens and their control in Horticulture; 200 scientific papers. Recreations: gardening; photography; travel; hill-walking. Address: (h.) Helenton Mote, Symington, by Ayr KA1 5PP; T.-01563 830251.

Dixon-Carter, Clare, OBE. Vice-Chairman, Board of Trustees, British Red Cross Society; b. 18.9.38, London. Educ. Moira House School, Eastbourne. Technical staff, EMI; hotel management, 1959-65; Assistant Regional Organiser for Scotland, World Worldlife Fund, 1969-77; joined Invernessshire Branch, British Red Cross Society, 1965; Branch Director, 1979-86; awarded Voluntary Medical Service Medal, 1983; BRCS Badge of Honour for distinguished service and life membership of society, 1986; Scottish Central Council Branch: Vice-Chairman, 1986-90, Chairman, 1990-97. Recreations: photography; travel; music. Address: (h.) Easter Balnabaan, Drumnadrochit, Invernessshire IV3 6UX; T.-01456 450310.

Dobie, Margaret G.C., OBE, MA, DipSocStud. Hon. Vice President, Scottish Association for the Study of Delinquency; Chair, Dumfries & Galloway Valuation Appeal Panel, since 1987; Member, Polmont Young Offenders' Institution Visiting Committee, since 1992; b. Galloway; m., James T.J. Dobie; 3 s. Educ. Benedictine Convent, Dumfries; Dumfries Academy; Edinburgh University. Medical Social Worker; Chair, Dumfries and Galloway Regional Children's Panel, 1971-77; Social Worker, Child Guidance Service, Dumfries; National Secretary, Scottish Association for the Study of Delinquency, 1982-87; Member, Broadcasting Council for Scotland, 1987-91; Chair, Dumfries and Galloway Children's Panel Advisory Committee, 1982-89; Chair, Children's Panel Advisory Group, 1985-88. Recreations:travel; tennis; reading. Address: (h.) 8 New Abbey Road, Dumfries DG2 7ND; T.-01387-254 595.

Dobie, Rev. Rachel Jean Wayland, LTh. Minister, Broughton, Glenholm, Kilbucho linked with Skirling, linked with Stobo, Drumelzier linked with Tweedsmuir; b. 17.8.42, Forres; m., Kirkpatrick H. Dobie; 1 s.; 1 d. Educ. Dumfries Academy; Jordanhill College; Edinburgh University. Primary schoolteacher, 1963-80; Auxiliary Minister, Dalbeattie with Urr, 1990-93; Church of Scotland Sunday School Adviser, 1976-86; Reader, 1982-90; Chair, Marriage Guidance, Dumfries, 1984-86; Member, General Assembly Youth Education Committee, 1985-93; Vice-Convener, General Assembly Board of Parish Education 1993-97; Hon. Secretary, Church Service Society; Contributor to BBC religious broadcasting. Publication: Time Together, 1981. Recreations: music; fine arts. Address: (h.) The Manse, Broughton, Biggar ML12 6HQ; T.-01899 830331.

Docherty, Michael. Executive Director (Enterprise Resources) and Depute Chief Executive, South Lanarkshire Council; b. 12.1.52, Glasgow; m., Linda; 2 s.; 1 d. Educ. St. Mungo's Academy, Glasgow. Trainee Accountant, Electricity Board, 1971-74; Accountancy Assistant, Coatbridge Town Council, 1974-75; Accountant, Monklands District Council, 1975-77, Stirling District Council, 1977-79; Senior Accountant, Monklands District Council, 1979-82; Principal Accountant, Renfrew District Council, 1982-84; Depute Director of Finance, Motherwell District Council, 1984-91; Director of Finance, Hamilton District Council, 1991-92; Chief Executive, Hamilton District Council, 1992-96. Recreations: running; reading; hill-walking. Address: (b.) Montrose House, 154 Montrose Crescent, Hamilton ML3 6LL.

Docker, Chris. Executive Secretary, Voluntary Euthanasia Society of Scotland, since 1992; Founder, International Drugs Consensus Working Party, 1993; Director, Living Will and Values History Project, since 1996; b. 29.1.53, Birmingham. Educ. Bishop Veseys Grammar School; Glasgow University (Masters in Law and Ethics in Medicine). Worked in publishing (human rights) and marketing before embarking on campaigning career. Member, Mensa; Award Winner, Natural Death Centre, 1996. Publications: Departing Drugs; Beyond Final Exit; and contributions to other books. Address: (b.) 17 Hart Street, Edinburgh EH1 3 RN; T.-0131-556 4404.

Dodd, Raymond Henry, PhD, MA, BMus, ARAM. Cellist and Composer; b. 31.3.29; m., Doreen Joyce; 1 s.; 1 d. Educ. Bryanston School; Royal Academy of Music; Worcester College, Oxford. Music Master, Sedbergh School, 1951-55; Aberdeen University: Lecturer in Music, 1956, Senior Lecturer in Music, 1971-91, Head of Department, 1981-88; Visiting Professor of Music, Wilson College, USA, 1972-73. Various orchestral, vocal and chamber music compositions; awarded Szymanowski Medal, Polish Ministry of Art and Culture, 1982. Address: (h.) 14 Giffordgate, Haddington, East Lothian EH41 4AS; T.-01620 824618.

Dodds, Alistair Bruce, MA (Hons), MBA, FIPD. Director of Corporate Services, The Highland Council, since 1998; b. 23.8.53, Kelso; m., Joan N. Aitken; 1 d. Educ. Glenrothes High School; Edinburgh University; Strathclyde University; Dundee University. Assistant Director of Personnel, Fife Regional Council, 1988; Depute Director of Manpower Services, Highland Regional Council, 1991; Director of Personnel Services, The Highland Council, 1995. Recreations: Scottish contemporary art; watching rugby; golf; walking dog. Address: Highland Council, Glenurquhart Road, Inverness IV3 5NX; T.-01463 702845.

Doig, Ian, CPFA, FCCA. Scottish Director, Chartered Institute of Public Finance and Accountancy (CIPFA); Secretary, Local Authority (Scotland) Accounts Advisory Committee, since 1986; Director, FSF LTD.; b. 25.11.45, Glasgow; m., Barbara; 1 d. Educ. Alva and Alloa Academies; Strathclyde University. Address: (b.) CIPFA Scotland, 8 North West Circus Place, Edinburgh EH3 6ST; T.-0131-220 4316.

Doig, John. Violinist; Leader, Orchestra of Scottish Opera, since 1991; Founder and Artistic Director, Scottish Bach Consort, since 1994. b. 2.8.58, Helensburgh. Educ. Holyrood School, Glasgow; St. Mary's Music School, Edinburgh. BBC Symphony Orchestra, 1975-78; Principal First Violin, BBC Philharmonic Orchestra, 1979-81; Co-Leader, Orchestra of Scottish Opera, 1981-83 and 1986-88; Guest Leader, Scottish Chamber Orchestra, 1988-90. President, Scottish Bach Society. Recreations: horse riding; swimming; country walks. Address: (h.) Endrick Mews, Killearn G63 9ND; T.-01360 550588.

Doig, P. Michael R., MA (Hons), FRSA. Head Teacher, Cumbernauld High School, since 1992; b. 2.5.48, Glasgow; m., Catherine; 2 s. Educ. High School of Glasgow; Glasgow University. Teacher/Assistant Principal Teacher/Principal Teacher of Modern Languages, 1972-81; Assistant Head Teacher, Hermitage Academy, Helensburgh, 1981-85; Depute Head Teacher, Kirkintilloch High School, 1985-92. Member, National Council, Headteachers' Association of Scotland; Editor, Scottish Headlines. Recreations: music; golf; current affairs. Address: (b.) Cumbernauld High School, Ring Road, S. Carbrain, Glasgow G67 2UF; T.-01236 725511.

Donachie, Professor William David, BSc, PhD, MAcadEurop, FRSE. Professor of Bacterial Genetics, Edinburgh University, since 1993; b. 27.4.35, Edinburgh; m.,Millicent Masters, BS, MS, PhD; 1 s. Educ. Dunfermline High School; Edinburgh University. Assistant Lecturer in Genetics, Edinburgh University, 1958-62; Research Associate in Biochemical Sciences, Princeton University, 1962-63; Lecturer in Genetics, Edinburgh University, 1963-65; Scientific Staff, MRC Molecular Genetics Unit, London and Edinburgh, 1965-74; Senior Lecturer/Reader in Molecular Biology, Edinburgh University, 1974-93. Publications: 83 research papers. Recreations: drawing; natural history; T'ai Chi. Address: (b.) Institute of Cell and Molecular Biology, Edinburgh University, Darwin Building, King's Buildings, Mayfield Road, Edinburgh EH9 3JR; T.-0131-650 5354.

Donald, Colin Dunlop, BA (Cantab), LLB, DUniv, FRSA, DL. b. 24.7.34, Strathaven; m., Theresa Ann Gilliland; 2 s.; 1 d. Educ. Cargilfield; Rugby; Gonville and Caius College, Cambridge; Glasgow University. National Service, 1953-55, 2nd Lt., The Cameronians (Scottish Rifles); Partner and latterly Consultant, McGrigor Donald, Solicitors, Glasgow, 1966-94; Vice-President, National Trust for Scotland; Deputy Chairman, Universities Superannuation Scheme Ltd.; Trustee: Lloyds, TSB Foundation for Scotland; Director, TSB Bank Scotland plc; a Deputy Lieutenant of Stirling and Falkirk. Recreations: golf and other outdoor sports. Address: (h.) 33 Park Terrace, Stirling FK8 2JS; T.-01786 473565.

Donald, George Malcolm, RSA, RSW, DA, ATC, MEd. Lecturer, Edinburgh College of Art; Director, Centre for Continuing Studies, ECA; b. 12.9.43, Ootacamund, South India; 1 s.; 1 d. Educ. Robert Gordon's College; Aberdeen Academy; Edinburgh College of Art; Hornsey College of Art; Edinburgh University. Joined Edinburgh College of Art as Lecturer, 1969; Visiting Lecturer, five Faculties of Art in India, 1979; Visiting Professor: University of Central Florida (Art, 1981, Drawing and Anatomy, 1985), Strasbourg, 1986, Belgrade, 1987, Sechuan Fine Art Institute, China, 1989, Chinese Academy of Fine Art, 1994; Latimer Award, RSA, 1970; Guthrie Award, RSA, 1973; Scottish Arts Council Bursary, 1973; RSA Gillies Bequest Travel Award to India, 1978; SAC Travel and Study Award, Indiana, 1981; RSA Gillies Prize, 1982; RSW Mary Marshall Brown Award, 1983; RGI Cargill Award, 1987; former Council Member, Printmakers Workshop (Edinburgh); one man shows: Florida, 1985, Helsinki, 1985, Edinburgh Festival, 1985, Belgrade, 1987, Florida, 1987, Edinburgh, 1988, 1990, London, 1992-94, Edinburgh 1993-

94-95-98. Address: (h.) Bankhead, by Duns, Berwickshire TD11 3QJ; T.-01361 883014.

Donald, Hugh R. LLB (Hons), WS. Chief Executive, Shepherd and Wedderburn, since 1994; b. 5.11.51, Edinburgh; m., M. Grace Donald; 1 s.; 1 d. Educ. Melville College, Edinburgh; Edinburgh University. Shepherd and Wedderburn: legal training, 1973-75, Assistant Solicitor, 1975-77, Partner, since 1977. Chairman, Family Mediation Scotland. Recreations: family; church; gardening. Address: Saltire Court, 20 Castle Terrace, Edinburgh EH1 2ET; T.-0131-228 9900.

Donald, Rev. Peter Harry, MA, PhD, BD. Minister, Leith St. Serf's Parish Church, since 1991; b. 3.2.62, Edinburgh; m., Brigid Mary McNeill; 1 s.; 1 d. Educ. George Watson's College; Gonville and Caius College, University of Cambridge; University of Edinburgh. Scouloudi Research Fellow, Institute of Historical Research, University of London, 1986-87; Probationer Assistant, St. Michael's Church, Edinburgh, 1990-91. Hon. Secretary, Scottish Church History Society; Board Member, Faith and Order Commission. Publication: An Uncounselled King: Charles I and the Scottish Troubles 1637-1641, 1990. Recreations: golf; swimming; racquet sports; piano; singing; walking; family. Address: 1 Denham Green Terrace, Edinburgh EH5 3PG; T.-0131-552 4059.

Donaldson, Rev. David, MA, BD (Hons), DipEd. Minister, Duddingston Kirk, Edinburgh, since 1990; b. 6.7.43, Glasgow; m., Jean Lacey; 1 s.; 3 d. Educ. Glasgow Academy; Glasgow University. Missionary, Church of Scotland, Taiwan, 1969-75; Minister: St. David's Bathgate, 1975-83, Whitfield, Dundee, 1983-90. Convener, Diaconate Committee, Church of Scotland, 1990-95. Recreations: tennis; badminton. Address: (h.) Duddingston Manse, 5 Old Church Lane, Edinburgh EH15 3PX; T.-0131-661 4240.

Donaldson, Professor Gordon Bryce, MA, PhD, FInstP, FRSE. Honorary Editor, Superconductor Science and Technology, since 1998; Professor of Applied Physics and Head of Department, Strathclyde University, 1993-98; b. 10.8.41, Edinburgh; m., Christina Martin; 1 s.; 1 d. Educ. Glasgow Academy; Christ's College, Cambridge. Cavendish Laboratory, Cambridge, 1962-65; Lecturer in Physics, Lancaster University, 1966-75; Strathclyde University: Lecturer, 1976, Senior Lecturer, 1978; Visiting Scientist and Fulbright Scholar, University of California, 1975; Visiting Professor, University of Virginia, 1981; Chairman, Institute of Physics Low Temperature Group, 1990-93; DTI/SERC Coordinator for National Superconductivity Programme, 1990-93. Address: (b.) Department of Physics and Applied Physics, Strathclyde University, Glasgow G4 ONG.

Donaldson, Professor Iain Malcolm Lane, BSc, MB, ChB, MA, FRCPE, MRCP. Professor of Neurophysiology, Edinburgh University, since 1987; b. 22.10.37; m.; 1 s. Educ. Edinburgh University. House Physician and Surgeon, Research Fellow, Honorary Lecturer, Honorary Senior Registrar, Departments of Medicine and Surgical Neurology, Edinburgh University, 1962-69; Anglo-French Research Scholarship, University of Paris, 1969-70; Research Officer, University Laboratory of Physiology, Oxford, 1970-79; Fellow and Tutor in Medicine, St. Edmund Hall, Oxford, 1973-79; Professor of Zoology, Hull University, 1979-87; Emeritus Fellow, St. Edmund Hall, Oxford, since 1979. Recreation: studying the past. Address: (b.) Department of Neuroscience, Edinburgh University, Appleton Tower, Crichton Street, Edinburgh EH8 9LE.

Donaldson, James Andrew, BDS, BA, DFM. Principal in general dental practice; b. 28.2.57, Glasgow; m., Patricia H. Winter; 1 s.; 3 d. Educ. Coatbridge High School; Dundee University; Open University; Glasgow University. Dental Adviser, British Antarctic Survey, 1986-97; Member: National Council, General Dental Practitioners Association, since 1989, Scottish General Dental Services Committee, 1991-93, Aberdeen District Council, 1984-86, Grampian Regional Council, 1986-88; Director, "Open Wide" Dental Courses. Recreations: golf; skiing; football. Address: (h.) Ellon Castle, Ellon, AB41 9QN; T.-01358 721865.

Donaldson, Marion. Fashion Designer; b. 1944, Glasgow. Trained as primary school-teacher; with husband, founded fashion company, mid-1960s.

Donaldson, William, MA, PhD. Writer, Researcher, Traditional Musician; b. 19.7.44, Fraserburgh. Educ. Fraserburgh Academy; Aberdeen University. Publications: Popular Literature in Victorian Scotland, 1986; The Jacobite Song, 1988; The Language of the People, 1989. Recreation: piobaireachd. Address: (b.) 13 Mile End Avenue, Aberdeen.

Donegan, Kate. Governor, HM Prison and Institution, Cornton Vale, since 1996; b. 21.4.53, Newport on Tay; m., Chris Donegan; 2 s. Educ. Kirkcaldy High School. Assistant Governor: Cornton Vale, 1977-84, Barlinnie Prison, 1984-87; Deputy Governor: Reading Prison, 1987-89; Deputy Governor, Perth Prison, 1989-91; Head, Operational Manpower, Planning Unit, 1991-93; seconded to Staffing Structure Review Team, 1993-94; Deputy Governor, Barlinnie Prison, 1994-95; Deputy Chief Inspector of Prisons, 1995-96. Recreations: gardening; reading; computing. Address: (b.) HM Prison and YOI, Cornton Vale, Cornton Road, Stirling FK9 5NU; T.-01786 832591.

Donnachie, Ian, MA, MLitt, PhD, FRHistS, FSA (Scot). Senior Lecturer in History, since 1985, Staff Tutor, since 1970, Director, Centre for Scottish Studies, Open University in Scotland; b. 18.6.44, Lanark. Educ. Lanark Grammar School; Glasgow University; Strathclyde University. Research Assistant, Galloway Project, Strathclyde University, 1967-68; Lecturer in Social Studies: Napier Polytechnic, 1968-70, Deakin University, Victoria, 1982; Visiting Fellow: Deakin University, Victoria and Sydney University, NSW, 1985; Hon. Lecturer, Dundee University, since 1998; Vice-Chairman, Scottish Brewing Archive; Consultant: SHEFC, HEFCE, QAA; Member: Universities Association for Continuing Education (Scotland); Conference Secretary, Economic and Social History Society of Scotland. Publications include: A History of the Brewing Industry in Scotland; Industrial Archaeology in the British Isles (jointly); Scottish History 1560-1980 (jointly); That Land of Exiles: Scots in Australia (jointly); Forward! Labour Politics in Scotland 1888-1988 (Co-Editor); A Companion to Scottish History from the Reformation to the Present (jointly); The Manufacture of Scottish History (Co-editor); Historic New Lanark: the Dale and Owen Industrial Community since 1785 (Co-author); Studying Scottish History, Literature and Culture; Modern Scottish History: 1707 to the present (Co-Editor). Recreations: walking; cycling; eating; drinking. Address: (b.) 10 Drumsheugh Gardens, Edinburgh EH3 7QJ; T.-0131-226 3851.

Donnelly, Dougie, LLB. Broadcaster; b. 7.6.53, Glasgow; m., Linda; 3 d. Educ. Hamilton Academy; Strathclyde University. Presenter, BBC Television Sport, since 1978: Grandstand, World Championship snooker and bowls, golf, Sportscene, Match of the Day; Mid-Morning Show, Alubm Show, Radio Clyde, 1976-92; Columnist, Evening Times; after-dinner speaker, conference and seminar host. Recreations: sport; travel; reading; good food and wine. Address: (b.) David John Associates, 6 Victoria Crescent Road, Glasgow G12 9DB; T.-0141-357 0532

Donnison, Professor David. Honorary Research Fellow, Glasgow University; Visiting Professor, Warwick University; b. 19.1.26. Lecturer: Manchester University,

1950-53, Toronto University, 1953-55; London School of Economics and Political Science: Reader, 1956-61, Professor, 1961-69; Director, Centre for Environmental Studies, London, 1969-75; Chairman, Supplementary Benefits Commission, 1975-80; Professor of Town and Regional Planning, Glasgow University, 1980-90. Address: (b.) Glasgow University, Glasgow G12 8RT.

Donohoe, Brian H. MP (Labour), Cunninghame South, since 1992; b. 10.9.48, Kilmarnock; m., Christine; 2 s. Educ. Irvine Royal Academy; Kilmarnock Technical College. Secretary, Irvine and District Trades Council, 1973-81; Chair: North Ayrshire and Arran LHC, 1977-79, Cunninghame Industrial Development Committee, 1975-79; former full-time trade union official (NALGO). Recreation: gardening. Address: (h.) 5 Greenfield Drive, Irvine, Ayrshire; T.-01294 274419.

Donovan, Professor Robert John, BSc, PhD, CChem, FRSC, FRSE. Professor of Chemistry, Edinburgh University, since 1979; b. 13.7.41, Nantwich; m., Marion Colclough; 1 d. Educ. Sandbach School; University College of Wales, Aberystwyth; Cambridge University. Research Fellow, Gonville and Caius College, 1966-70; Edinburgh University: Lecturer in Physical Chemistry, 1970-74, Reader in Chemistry, 1974-79. Member: Physical Chemistry Panel, Science & Engineering Research Council, 1977-80, Management Committee, SERC Synchrotron Radiation Source, Daresbury, 1977-80, SERC Synchroton Radiation Facility Committee, 1979-84; Chairman, SERC Laser Facility Committee, 1989-92; Member, SERC Science Board, 1989-92; Chairman, Facilities Commission, SERC, 1993-94; awarded Corday-Morgan Medal and Prize, Royal Society of Chemistry, 1975; Member: Faraday Council, Royal Society of Chemistry, 1981-83, 1991-93, Royal Society of Edinburgh Council, since 1996; Tilden Prize, Royal Society of Chemistry, 1995. Recreations: hill-walking; skiing; sail-boarding; cross-country riding. Address: (b.) Department of Chemistry, Edinburgh University, West Mains Road, Edinburgh EH9 3JJ; T.-0131-650 4722.

Doran, Frank, LLB(Hons). MP (Labour), Aberdeen Central, since 1997; b. 13.4.49; 2 s. Educ. Leith Academy; University of Dundee. Solicitor, 1977-87; MP (Labour), Aberdeen South, 1987-92; Co-ordinator, National Trade Union Political Fund Ballot Campaign, 1993-96. Address: (b.) House of Commons, London SW1A 0AA; T.-0171-219 3000.

Dorman, Arthur Brian, LLB, FIMgt. Solicitor; Senior Partner, Glasgow, Dundas and Wilson CS; b. 21.6.45, Glasgow; 1 s.; 1 d. Educ. Hillhead High School; Glasgow University. Recreation: occasional golf. Address: (b.) Madeleine Smith House, 6/7 Blythswood Square, Glasgow G2 4AD; T.-0141-221 9880.

Dorward, David Campbell, MA, GRSM, LRAM. Composer, since 1944; Music Producer, BBC, 1962-91; b. 7.8.33, Dundee; m., Janet Offord; 1 s.; 2 d. Educ. Morgan Academy, Dundee; St. Andrews University; Royal Academy of Music. Teaching, 1960-61; Freelance, 1961-62. Arts Adviser, Lamp of Lothian Collegiate Trust, since 1967; Member, Scottish Arts Council, 1972-78; Consultant Director, Performing Right Society, 1985-90; Patron's Fund Award, 1958; Royal Philharmonic Prizewinner, 1958; compositions include four string quartets, two symphonies, four concertos, Tonight Mrs Morrison (one-act opera), A Christmas Carol (musical), and incidental music for TV, radio, film and stage. Recreations: photography; computers; walking in the country. Address: (h.) Dovecot House, Preston Road, Prestonpans EH32 9JZ; T.-01875 810 512.

Dorward, David Keay, CPFA. Director of Finance, Dundee City Council, since 1995; Depute Director of Finance, Tayside Regional Council, since 1993; Chief Financial Policy Officer, Tayside Regional Council, since 1986; b. 24.5.54, Dunfermline; m., Gail; 3 d. Educ. Kinross High School; Perth High School; Perth College of Further Education; Dundee College of Commerce; Glasgow College of Technology. Director: Dundee Energy Recycling Limited, Dundee Small Business Finance. Recreations: supporting Dundee United; golf; bowls; listening to music. Address: (h.) 4 Norrie Street, Broughty Ferry, Dundee; T.-01382 739006; (b.) T.-01382 433359.

Dorward, David Philip, MA (Hons), LLB; b. 10.4.31, Dundee; m., Joy Stewart; 2 s. Educ. Dundee High School; St. Andrews University. Joined St. Andrews University as Administrative Assistant, 1959; successively Assistant Secretary, Deputy Secretary, Secretary; retired; Honorary Sheriff, Tayside, Central and Fife at Cupar, since 1995. Publications: Scottish Surnames; Scotland's Place-Names; Dundee, Names, People and Places. Recreations: music; golf; gardening; walking; European travel. Address: (h.) 7 Drumcarrow Crescent, Strathkinness, Fife KY16 9XT; T.-0133 485630.

Douglas, Alan. Journalist and Broadcaster; b. 16.10.51, Dundee; m., Viv Lumsden (qv); 2 d. Educ. Forfar Academy. Local newspapers, 1970-74; BBC Local Radio Reporter and Producer, 1974-78; Reporter/Presenter, BBC TV Scotland, 1978-89; freelance broadcaster and journalist, BBC TV and Radio, corporate and Scottish TV (co-presenting The Home Show with his wife); Partner, The Broadcasting Business (media consultancy); Motoring Columnist, Glasgow Evening Times; Member: Guild of Motoring Writers, Association of Scottish Motoring Writers. Recreations: cars; walking; eating; drinking. Address: 9 Lethington Road, Glasgow G46 6TA.

Douglas, Rev. Andrew Morrison, MA. Clerk to the Presbytery of Aberdeen, since 1995; b. 23.2.30; b. Orange, Australia; m., Margaret Rennie; 2 s.; 2 d. Educ. Robert Gordons College, Aberdeen; University of Aberdeen. Minister: Lochcraig, Fife, 1957-62, Bon Accord St Paul's, Aberdeen, 1963-72, Southesk, Brechin, 1972-77, High Church Hilton, Aberdeen, 1977-95. Recreations: golf; gardening; choral singing. Address: (b.) Aberdeen Presbytery Office, c/o Mastrick Parish Church, Greenfern Road, Aberdeen AB16 6TR; T.-01224 690494.

Douglas, Rev. Colin Rutherford, MA, BD, STM. Minister, Livingston Ecumenical Parish, since 1987; b. 10.4.42, Leven; Educ. Loretto School; University of St. Andrews; University of Edinburgh; Union Theological Seminary, New York. Scottish Schoolboys Half-mile Champion, 1960. Address: 27 Heatherbank, Ladywell, Livingston EH54 6EE; T.-01506 432326.

Douglas, David Pringle, DipTP, MRTPI. Chief Executive, Scottish Borders Enterprise, since 1990; b. 13.5.39, Edinburgh; m., Diane; 1 s.; 1 d. Local government, 1957-86; Material International, USA, 1986-87; Roger Tym & Partners, Glasgow, 1987-90. Recreations: golf; walking. Address: (b.) Bridge Street, Galashiels TD1 1SW; T.-01896 758991.

Douglas, Gavin Stuart, RD, QC, MA, LLB; b. 12.6.32. Educ. South Morningside School; George Heriot's School; Edinburgh University. Qualified as Solicitor, 1955; National Service, Royal Navy; admitted to Faculty of Advocates, 1958; Sub-editor (part-time), The Scotsman, 1957-61; Member, Lord Advocate's Department in London, (as Parliamentary Draftsman) 1961-64; returned to practice at Scots Bar, 1964; Counsel to Scottish Law Commission, 1965-96; Hon. Sheriff, 1965-71; a Chairman of Industrial Tribunals, 1966-78; Counsel to Secretary of State for Scotland under Private Legislation Procedure (Scotland) Act 1936, 1969-1975, Senior Counsel under that Act since 1975; Member, Lothian Health Board, 1981-85; Editor, Session Cases, seven volumes, 1976-82; Temporary Sheriff, since 1990. Recreations: golf; skiing. Address: (b.) Parliament House, Parliament Square, Edinburgh EH1 1RF.

Douglas, Sheriff Neil. Sheriff of North Strathclyde at Paisley. Address: (b.) Sheriff Court House, 106 Renfrew Road, Paisley, PA3 4DD.

Douglas, Professor Neil James, MD, FRCP. Professor of Respiratory and Sleep Medicine, Edinburgh University; Director, Scottish National Sleep Laboratory; Dean, Royal College of Physicians of Edinburgh; Consultant Physician, since 1983; b. 28.5.49, Edinburgh; m., Dr. Sue Galloway; 1 s.; 1 d. Educ. Dundee High School; Trinity College, Glenalmond; St. Andrews University; Edinburgh University. Lecturer in Medicine, Edinburgh University, 1974-83; MRC Travelling Fellow, University of Colorado, 1980-81. Recreations: fishing; gardening; eating. Address: (b.) Respiratory Medicine Unit, Department of Medicine, Royal Infirmary, Lauriston Place, Edinburgh EH3 9YW; T.-0131 536 3252.

Douglas, Sadie Naomi, MBE. Administrative Director, Scottish Civic Trust, 1983-93; b. Huddersfield; m., Alexander Douglas (deceased); 1 s. Educ. Longley Hall, Huddersfield; Huddersfield Technical College. Worked with Oxfam, 1966-70; Organising Secretary, Facelift Glasgow, 1970-73; Trust Secretary, Scottish Civic Trust, 1973-83. Member: Countrywide Holiday Association (Past President, Glasgow CHA Club), Scottish Countryside Activities Council; Chairman, West Kilbride Amenity Society. Recreation: voluntary work. Address: (h.) Hillhouse, Ardneil Avenue, West Kilbride, Ayrshire KA23; T.-01294 822465.

Douglas-Home, Lady (Lavinia) Caroline, DL, FSA Scot. Estate Factor, Douglas and Angus Estates, 1960-95; Trustee, National Museum of Antiquities of Scotland, 1982-85; Deputy Lieutenant, Berwickshire, since 1983; b. 11.10.37 (daughter of Baron Home of the Hirsel, KT, PC). Educ. privately. Woman of the Bedchamber (Temporary) to Queen Elizabeth the Queen Mother, 1963-65; Lady-In-Waiting (Temporary) to HRH Duchess of Kent, 1966-67. Recreations: fishing; reading; antiquities. Address: (h.) Heaton Mill House, Cornhill-on-Tweed, Northumberland; T.-01890 882303.

Douglas Miller, Andrew, BA. Managing Director, Jenners Princes Street Edinburgh Ltd., since 1996; b. 29.9.63, Edinburgh; m., Helen Bateman; 2 s. Educ. Harrow School; City of London Polytechnic. Jenners Princes Street Edinburgh Ltd.: General Manager, 1993, Merchandise Director, 1994. Address: 48 Princes Street, Edinburgh EH2 2YJ.

Dover, Sir Kenneth James, MA, DLitt, Hon.LLD (St. Andrews, Birmingham), Hon.LittD (St. Andrews, Bristol, London, Liverpool, Durham), Hon.DHL (Oglethorpe), FRSE, FBA. Chancellor, St. Andrews University, since 1981; b. 11.3.20, Croydon; m., Audrey Ruth Latimer; 1 s.; 1 d. Educ. St. Paul's School, London; Balliol College, Oxford; Merton College, Oxford. Fellow and Tutor, Balliol College, Oxford, 1948-55; Professor of Greek, St. Andrews, 1955-76; President, Corpus Christi College, Oxford, 1976-86. Served in Royal Artillery, 1940-45; President, Hellenic Society, 1971-74; President, Classical Association, 1975; President, British Academy, 1978-81; Foreign Honorary Member, American Academy of Arts and Sciences, since 1979; Foreign Member, Royal Netherlands Academy, since 1979; Honorary Fellow, Balliol, Corpus Christi and Merton Colleges, Oxford. Recreations: gardening; historical linguistics. Address: (h.) 49 Hepburn Gardens, St. Andrews, Fife KY16 9LS; T.-01334 473589.

Dow, Professor Alexander Carmichael, MA, PhD. Professor and Head, Department of Economics, Glasgow Caledonian University, since 1989; b. 28.8.46; m., Sheila Christine; 2 d. Educ. Perth Academy; St. Andrews University; Simon Fraser University; University of Manitoba. Research Officer, Commonwealth Secretariat; Lecturer and Assistant Professor, University of Toronto; Lecturer, Stirling University. Recreations: curling; travel. Address: (b.) Department of Economics, Glasgow Caledonian University, Cowcaddens Road, Glasgow G4 0BA; T.-0141-331 3310.

Dow, Alister, CA, FCMA. Chief Executive, Scottish Motor Trade Association, since 1992; Managing Director, Scottish Motor Show Ltd., since 1995; Managing Director, Scotsure Insurance Company, since 1993; Director, Ivory and Sime Optimum Trust PLC, since 1989; b. Cupar; m., Jacqueline; 2 d. Educ. Bell Baxter High School; Edinburgh University. Cost and Management Accountant, Ethicon Ltd., Edinburgh; Financial Director, Operations Director, Managing Director, Devro Ltd., Glasgow; Chairman, Forth Investments PLC, Edinburgh, and Hibernian Football Club, Edinburgh. Recreations: golf; hill-walking; Rotary; amateur operatics; gardening. Address: (h.) 23 Victoria Place, Stirling FK8 2QT; T.-01786 475995.

Dow, Rear-Admiral Douglas Morrison, CB, DL. Director, The National Trust for Scotland, 1992-97; b. 1.7.35; m., Felicity Margaret Mona Napier; 2 s.; Educ. George Heriot's School; BRNC Dartmouth. Joined RN, 1952; served Staff of C-in-C Plymouth, 1959-61; HMS Plymouth, 1961-63; RN Supply Sch., 1963-65; Staff of Comdr FEF, 1965-67; HMS Endurance, 1968-70; BRNC Dartmouth, 1970-72; Cdr 1972; Assistant Director, Officer Appointments (S), 1972-74; Sec to Comdr British Navy Staff, Washington, 1974-76; HMS Tiger, 1977-78; NDC Latimer, 1978-79; Captain 1979; CSO(A) to Flag Officer Portsmouth, 1979; Sec to Controller of Navy, 1981; Captain, HMS Cochrane, 1983; Commodore, HMS Centurion, 1985; RCDS, 1988; Rear Admiral, 1989; Director General, Naval Personal Services, 1989-92. Vice-Chairman, George Heriot's Trust, since 1996. Recreations: rugby union; fly fishing; shooting; golf; gardening. Address: (h.) Tor Lodge, 1 Eskbank Terrace, Dalkeith, Midlothian EH22 3DE.

Dow, Professor Sheila Christine, MA (Hons), PhD. Professor in Economics, Stirling University, since 1996; Director, MSc in Banking and Finance; b. 16.4.49, Dumfries; m., Professor Alexander Dow; 2 d. Educ. Hawick High School; St. Andrews University; University of Manitoba; McMaster University; Glasgow University. Overseas Office, Bank of England, 1970-72; Economist, then Senior Economist, Department of Finance, Government of Manitoba, 1973-77; Lecturer, then Reader, Department of Economics, Stirling University, 1979-96. Publications: Macroeconomic Thought, 1985; Financial Markets and Regional Economic Development, 1990; Money Matters (Co-author), 1982; Money and the Economic Process, 1993; The Methodology of Macroeconomic Thought, 1996. Recreations: travel; various sports. Address: (b.) Department of Economics, Stirling University, Stirling FK9 4LA; T.-01786 467474.

Dowds, Stephen, BSc (Hons), FEIS. Rector, Lochaber High School; b. 2.4.53, Saltcoats; m., Myna J. Dowds; 2 d. Educ. Adrossan Academy; Glasgow University; Edinburgh University. Instructor, Faskally Outdoor Centre, Pitlochry; Teacher of Biology, Dingwall Academy; Culloden Academy: Principal Teacher of Biology, Assistant Rector. Recreations: hillwalking and mountaineering; musician. Address: (h.) 1 Corran Gardens, Onich, by Fort William, Lochaber; T.-01855 821573.

Downes, Robert, DipTP, BPhil. Director, Scottish Enterprise, since 1998; Director, Scottish Business, Scottish Enterprise, 1997-98 (Director, Industry and Skills, 1994-97); b. 10.8.51, Belfast; m., Pauline; 2 s. Educ. Portora Royal School, Enniskillen; Dundee University; Duncan of

Jordanstone College of Art, Dundee. Local government, 1976-82; Dundee Project, 1982-84; SDA, 1984-87; Director: North East, SDA, 1987-90, Conran Roche Planning, London, 1990-92; independent consultant, 1992-93; Chief Executive, Dumfries and Galloway Enterprise, 1993-94; Director, Scottish and International Operations, Scottish Enterprise, 1994; Advisor, Ulster Community Conference and Flax Trust, Belfast, since 1994; part-time Lecturer, Glasgow University, since 1997; Director: Wise Group, Glasgow, since 1997, Emerging Business Trust, Belfast, since 1996, Ulster Community Investment Trust, Belfast, since 1995; Member, President's Executive Committee, National Council for Urban Economic Development, Washington D.C., since 1996; Member, Senate, Windsor Meeting, since 1998. Recreations: running; cycling; live music; travelling; films; pub crack; Jim Thompson novels; journalists' biographies; Kelvin walkway. Address: (h.) 57 Hughenden Lane, Hyndland, Glasgow G12 9XN; T.-0141-338 6124.

Downie, Rev. Alan Frew Munro, MA, BD. Parish Minister, St. Mungo's, Alloa, since 1996; b. 17.11.46, Uddingston; m., Margaret Elizabeth Moore; 2 s.; 2 d. Educ. Hamilton Academy; Langside College; University of Glasgow. Trainee Underwriter, 1964-68; Probationer Assistant Minister: Largs St. Columba's, 1976-77; Minister, Dun l/w Hillside, 1977-96. Area Chaplain, Clackmannanshire Scouts. Recreations: hillwalking; curling; music. Address: (h.) 37a Claremont, Alloa FK10 2DG; T.-01259 213872.

Downie, Professor Robert S., MA, BPhil, FRSE. Professor of Moral Philosophy, Glasgow University, since 1969 (Stevenson Lecturer in Medical Ethics, 1984-88); b. 19.4.33, Glasgow; m., Eileen Dorothea Flynn; 3 d. Educ. High School of Glasgow; Glasgow University; Queen's College, Oxford. Tutor, Worcester College, Oxford, 1958-59; Glasgow University: Lecturer in Moral Philosophy, 1959-68, Senior Lecturer, 1968-69; Visiting Professor: Syracuse University, New York, 1963-64, Dalhousie University, Nova Scotia, 1976. Publications: Government Action and Morality, 1964; Respect for Persons, 1969; Roles and Values, 1971; Education and Personal Relationships, 1974; Caring and Curing, 1980; Healthy Respect, 1987; Health Promotion: models and values, 1990; The Making of a Doctor, 1992; Francis Hutcheson, 1994; The Healing Arts: an Oxford illustrated anthology, 1994; Palliative Care Ethics, 1996; Medical Ethics, 1996. Recreation: music. Address: (b.) Department of Philosophy, Glasgow University G12 8QQ; T.-0141-339 8855.

Dowse, Pauline Hazel, GMusRNCM, PPRNCM, PGDipRNCM. Principal Cellist, Royal Scottish National Orchestra, since 1989; b. 10.3.63, Chelmsford; m., Dr. Peter Argondizza; 1 d. Educ. Chelmer Valley High School; Colchester Institute; Royal Northern College of Music, Banff School of Fine Arts, Banff, Alberta, Canada. Co-Principal Cellist, English National Opera Orchestra, 1988. Address: (h.) 38 Hallydown Drive, Jordanhill, Glasgow G13 1UF; T.-0141-954 9346.

Doyle, Professor Christopher John, BA, MSc. Head: Management Division, since 1997, Applied Economics and Agricultural Systems Department, since 1989, Scottish Agricultural College, Auchincruive; Adjunct Professor of Agricultural Economics, Glasgow University, since 1989; Vice Dean (Education), 1991-94, and Professor of Agricultural Economics, since 1994, Scottish Agricultural College, Auchincruive; b. 21.8.48, Sale, Cheshire; m., Alice; 1. d. Educ. St. Ambrose College, Cheshire; Keele University; Newcastle upon Tyne University. Departmental Demonstrator in Agricultural Economics, Oxford University, 1972-76; Research Officer, Centre for Agricultural Strategy, Reading University, 1976-79; Principal Scientific Officer, Institute for Grassland and Animal Production, 1979-86; Senior Economist, Ruakura Research Centre, MAF, New Zealand, 1987; Principal Scientific Officer, Institute for Grassland and Animal Production, 1988-89. Publications: 100 scientific papers and publications. Recreations: languages; foreign travel; modern history; theatre. Address: (b.) Scottish Agricultural College, Auchincruive, Ayr KA6 5HW; T.-01292 525053.

Doyle, Rev. David Wallace, MA(Hons), BD(Hons). Minister, St. Mary's Parish Church, Motherwell, since 1987; b. 12.4.48, Glasgow; m., Alison W. Britton; 1 s.; 1 d. Educ. High School of Glasgow; University of Glasgow; Corpus Christi, University of Cambridge. Assistant Minister, East Kilbride Old Parish Church, 1973-74; Minister, Tulliallan and Kincardine Parish Church, Fife, 1977-87. Recreations: music, gardening. Address: (h.) Manse of St. Mary's, 19 Orchard Street, Motherwell ML1 3JE; T.-01698 263472.

Doyle, Rev. Ian Bruce, MA, BD, PhD. Pastoral Assistant, Palmerston Place Church, Edinburgh, 1991; General Secretary, Department of National Mission, 1989-91; b. 11.9.21, Methil, Fife; m., Anne Watt Wallace; 2 s. Educ. Buckhaven High School; St. Andrews University; New College, Edinburgh. Served with Church of Scotland Huts, Germany, 1945-46; Assistant to Rev. D.P. Thomson, Evangelist, 1946; Minister: St. Mary's, Motherwell, 1946-60, Eastwood, Glasgow, 1960-77; Convener: Home Mission Committee, 1970-74, Home Board, 1974-77; Secretary, Department of Home Mission, 1977-84; Joint Secretary, Department of Ministry and Mission, 1984-89; General Secretary, Board of National Mission, 1989-91; Secretary, Prison Chaplaincies Board, 1977-91; Member, STV Religious Advisory Board, 1976-86. Publications: This Jesus; Reformation and Revolution (Contributor); The Word for All Seasons (Contributor); Local Church Evangelism (Contributor); D.P.: a memoir of Dr. D.P. Thomson. Recreation: reading. Address: (h.) 21 Lygon Road, Edinburgh; T.-0131-667 2697.

Doyle, Roberta, BA. Director of Marketing and Press, Scottish Opera, since 1992; b. 5.1.60, Glasgow; m., Mahmut Cemal Öztürk. Educ. Notre Dame High School, Glasgow; University of Strathclyde. Marketing Manager, Citizens' Theatre, 1986; Director of Marketing and Press, Scottish Ballet, 1990. Chair, Clyde Unity Theatre Co.; Board Director, Anatomy Performance Co; Vice-Chair, Theatrical Management Association Marketing Committee. Recreations: theatre; film; travel; riding. Address: (b.) Scottish Opera, 39 Elmbank Crescent, Glasgow G2 4PT; T.-0141-248 4567.

Draper, Professor Paul Richard, BA, MA, PhD. Walter Scott and Partners Professor of Finance, University of Edinburgh, since 1997; b. 28.12.46, Hayes; m., Janet Margaret; 1 s.; 1 d. Educ. Exeter, Reading and Stirling Universities. Lecturer: St. Andrews and Edinburgh Universities; Professor of Finance, Strathclyde University, 1986-97 (Head, Department of Accounting and Finance, 1990-95, Vice Dean, Strathclyde Business School, 1993-97). Publication: Scottish Financial Sector (Co-author), 1988; Investment Trust Industry in the UK, 1989. Recreations: renovating country cottages; home computing. Address: (h.) 19 Upper Gray Street, Newington, Edinburgh; T.-0131-667 4087.

Drewry, James Michael, FITSA, DCA. Director of Environmental and Consumer Services, City of Edinburgh Council, since 1996; b. Hexham. Trained, Northumberland County Council; Inspector of Weights and Measures, Cheshire County Council; Senior Assistant Chief Trading Standards Officer, Humberside County Council, 1976-79; County Consumer Protection Officer, Durham County Council, 1980-89; Director of Trading Standards, Lothian Regional Council, 1989-96. Past Chairman, Institute of Trading Standards Administration; Chairman, Prosafe (Product Safety Enforcement Forum of Europe); President, European Consumer Product Safety Association; Adviser,

Convention of Scottish Local Authorities. Recreations: squash; golf; travel. Address: (b.) Chesser House, 500 Gorgie Road, Edinburgh EH11 3YJ; T.-0131-469 5454.

Drummond, Humphrey, MC. Writer and Farmer; Proprietor and Managing Director, The Historical Press; b. 18.9.22, Old Buckenham, Norfolk; m., Cherry Drummond, 16th Baroness Strange; 3 s.; 3 d. Educ. Eton; Trinity College, Cambridge. Captain, 1st Mountain Regiment; former General Secretary, Council for Preservation of Rural Wales; Welsh Representative, National Trust; Chairman, Society of Authors (Scotland), 1976-82. Publications: Our Man in Scotland; The Queen's Man; The King's Enemy; Falconry For You; Falconry; Balkan Assault; Nazi Gold. Recreations: mechanical musical instruments; pre-Raphaelitism. Address: Megginch Castle, Errol, Perthshire; T.-01821 642 222.

Drummond, Rev. John Whiteford, MA, BD. Minister, Rutherglen West Parish Church, since 1986; b. 27.6.46, Glasgow; m., Barbara S. Grant; 1 s.; 3 d. Educ. Bearsden Academy; University of Glasgow. Probationer Assistant, St. Francis-in-the-East Church, Bridgeton, 1970-71; Ordained Assistant, King's Park Parish Church, Glasgow, 1971-73; Minister, Linwood Parish Church, 1973-86. Recreations: reading; television; family. Address: (h.) 12 Albert Drive, Rutherglen G73 3RT; T.-0141-569 8547.

Drummond, Rev. Norman Walker, MA, BD. BBC National Governor and Chairman, Broadcasting Council for Scotland, since 1994; Chairman, BBC Children in Need Board of Trustees; Minister, Kilmuir and Stenscholl, Isle of Skye, since 1996; Headmaster, Loretto School, 1984-95; b. 1.4.52, Greenock; m., Lady Elizabeth Kennedy; 3 s.; 2 d. Educ. Merchiston Castle School; Fitzwilliam College, Cambridge; New College, Edinburgh. Chaplain to the Forces, 1976-82; Depot, The Parachute Regiment and Airborne Forces, 1977-78; 1st Bn., The Black Watch (Royal Highland Regiment), 1978-82; Chaplain, Fettes College, 1982-84; Chaplain to Her Majesty the Queen in Scotland; Member, Queen's Bodyguard for Scotland (Royal Company of Archers); Past President: Victoria League for Overseas Students in Scotland, Edinburgh Bn., Boys' Brigade; Governor: Gordonstoun School, Aiglon College, Switzerland; former Member, Scottish Committee for Imperial Cancer Research; Trustee, Foundation for Skin Research; former Member, Scottish Committee, Duke of Edinburgh's Award Scheme; former Member, Court, Heriot-Watt University; former Chairman, Musselburgh and District Council of Social Services. Publications: The First Twenty Five Years (the official history of the Black Watch Kirk Session); Mother's Hands. Recreations: rugby football; cricket; golf; curling; traditional jazz. Address: BBC Scotland, Broadcasting House, Queen Margaret Drive, Glasgow G12 8DG; T.-0141 338 2835.

Drummond, Sheriff Thomas Anthony Kevin, LLB, QC. Sheriff, Glasgow and Strathkelvin, since 1997; Joint Chairman, Institute of Chartered Accountants of Scotland, since 1993; b. 3.11.43, Howwood, Renfrewshire; m., Margaret Evelyn Broadley; 1 d. (1 d. deceased). Educ. St. Mirin's Academy, Paisley; Blairs College, Aberdeen; Edinburgh University. Admitted, Faculty of Advocates, 1974; Advocate Depute, 1985-90; Member, Firearms Consultative Committee, 1989-97; Member, Criminal Injuries Compensation Board, 1990-96; Home Advocate Depute, 1996-97. Publications (legal cartoons): The Law at Work; The Law at Play; Great Defences of Our Time. Recreations: fishing; shooting. Address: (h.) Pomathorn House, Penicuik, Midlothian; T.-01968 674064.

Drury, John Kenneth, MBChB, PhD, FRCS. Consultant, General Surgeon, Victoria Infirmary NHS Trust, since 1986 (Clinical Director, General Surgery, since 1993); b. 23.1.47; m., Gillian Gilmore; 1 s.; 1 d. Educ. Paisley Grammar School; University of Glasgow. Research Fellow, Department of Physiology, University of Glasgow, 1973-76; West of Scotland Surgical Training Scheme, 1976-86. Committee Member, RNLI; Member: Vascular Society of Great Britain, European Society for Vascular and Endovascular Surgery. Recreations: sailing; golf; local art. Address: (b.) Department of Surgery, Victoria Infirmary NHS Trust, Glasgow G42 9TY; T.-0141-201 5464.

Dry, Philip John Seaton, LLB. Partner, Biggart Baillie, Solicitors, since 1972; President, Law Society of Scotland, 1998-99; b. 21.4.45, Lincolnshire; m., Joyce Christine Hall; 1 s.; 1 d. Educ George Watson's College; Greenock Academy; Glasgow University. Apprenticeship with Biggart Lumsden & Co., 1966-68; Assistant Solicitor, 1968-70; Director: Westscot Homes PLC and Westscot Homes II PLC, Fyfe Chambers (Glasgow) Ltd.; Council Member, Law Society of Scotland; Member, Post Office Users' Council for Scotland, 1995-98; Director, Glasgow Renfrewshire Society. Recreations: sailing; the garden; opera; swimming; travel. Address: (b.) Dalmore House, 310 St. Vincent Street, Glasgow G2 5QR; T.-0141-228 8000.

Drysdale, Thomas Henry, LLB, WS. Solicitor; Partner, Shepherd & Wedderburn, WS, Edinburgh, since 1967 (Managing Partner, 1988-94); b. 23.11.42, Buchlyvie; m., Caroline Shaw; 1 s.; 2 d. Educ. Cargilfield; Glenalmond; Edinburgh University. Chairman, Edinburgh Solicitors Property Centre, 1981-88; Deputy Keeper of Her Majesty's Signet, 1991-98. Recreations: skiing; walking; reading; amateur photography. Address: (b.) Saltire Court, 20 Castle Terrace, Edinburgh EH1 2ET; T.-0131-228 9900.

Dudgeon, Alexander (Sandy) Stewart, MA, CA. Managing Director, Martin Currie Unit Trusts Ltd.; b. 16.10.57, Edinburgh; m., Jennifer J.K. Waddell; 2 s.; 1 d. Educ. Trinity College, Glenalmond; Aberdeen University. Recreations: racing; farming; squash; golf; bridge. Address: (h.) 8 Cluny Drive, Edinburgh EH10 6DW; T.-0131-229 5252.

Dudley Edwards, Owen, BA, FRHistS, FSA (Scot). Reader in History, Edinburgh University; b. 27.3.38, Dublin; m., Barbara Balbirnie Lee; 1 s.; 2 d. Educ. Belvedere College, Dublin; University College, Dublin; Johns Hopkins University, Baltimore. Visiting Lecturer in History, University of Oragon, 1963-65; Assistant Lecturer in History, Aberdeen University, 1966-68; Lecturer in History, Edinburgh University, 1968-79; Visiting Lecturer, California State University of San Francisco, 1972-73; Visiting Associate Professor, University of South Carolina, 1973; Sir David Owen Evans Lecturer, University College of Wales, Aberystwyth, 1987; Journalist and Broadcaster, notably for Irish Times, 1959-95, and BBC, since 1969; contributor to various journals, especially The Scotsman, Scottish Affairs; Life Member: American Historical Association, Organisation of American Historians, Royal Medical Society (Edinburgh University), Royal Lyceum Theatre Club; External Examiner: Queen's University, Belfast, Bradford University, Manchester University, Sorbonne, University College Cardiff, Oxford University; Chair, Edinburgh University Settlement, since 1996; Member, Editorial Board, Journal of American Studies, since 1995; Chair, Council, Roman Catholic Parish of St Albert the Great, Edinburgh, 1986-89, 1995-98; Hon. Vice-President, Scottish Homosexual Rights Association (and successor organisation), 1977-97. Publications: Celtic Nationalism (with Gwynfor Evans, Ioan Rhys and Hugh MacDiarmid), 1968; The Sins of Our Fathers - Roots of Conflict in Northern Ireland, 1970; The Mind of an Activist - James Connolly, 1971; P.G. Wodehouse - a Critical and Historical Essay, 1977; Burke and Hare, 1980; The Quest for Sherlock Holmes: a Biographical Study of Arthur Conan Doyle, 1982; Eamon de Valera, 1987; Macaulay (Historians on Historians), 1988; The Edinburgh Festival, 1990; City of 1000 Worlds — Edinburgh in Festival, 1991; as Editor/Contributor: 1916 - The Easter Rising (with Fergus

Pyle), 1968; Conor Cruise O'Brien Introduces Ireland, 1969; James Connolly: Selected Political Writings (with Bernard C. Ransom), 1973; Scotland, Europe and the American Revolution (with George Shepperson), 1976; Christmas Observed (with Graham Richardson), 1981; Edinburgh (with Graham Richardson), 1983; A Claim of Right for Scotland, 1989; The Fireworks of Oscar Wilde, 1989; A. Conan Doyle: The Exploits of Brigadier Gerard, 1991; The Oxford Sherlock Holmes (General Editor), 1993; The Complete Brigadier Gerard, 1995. Address: (b.) Department of History, Edinburgh University, 50 George Square, Edinburgh, EH8 9JY.

Duff, John Hume, MA (Cantab), MA (Edin), DipEd (Oxon). Rector, Kelvinside Academy, 1980-98, retired; Chairman, HMC (Scottish Division), 1996; b. 24.4.40, Edinburgh. Educ. St. Mary's School, Melrose; Edinburgh Academy; Corpus Christi College, Cambridge; Edinburgh University; Brasenose College, Oxford. Housemaster and Head of History Department, Kelly College, Tavistock, Devon, 1967-80. Major, TA; Governor, Wellbeck College, since 1996. Recreations: squash rackets; skiing; hill-walking; foreign travel. Address: (h.) 1 Devonshire Terrace, Glasgow G12 0XE; T.-0141-334 1254.

Duff, Thomas Alexander Vaughan, BSc (Hons), DipArch, RIBA, ARIAS, AKH. Partner, Law and Dunbar-Nasmith, Architects, since 1988; b. 20.3.55, Kirkcudbright; m., Lorraine Marie; 3 s. Aberdeen Grammar School; Forres Academy; Scott Sutherland School of Architecture, Aberdeen. Architect, since 1980 (projects include rehabilitation of Fort George, Inverness and Sunninghill Park, Windsor); Managing Partner, Hilger LDN, Wiesbaden, Germany, 1993-98. Recreations: family; golf; German language and culture. Address: (b.) St. Leonards Road, Forres IV36 0DN; T.-01309 673221.

Duffin, Stuart, DA, RE, ARSA. Studio Workshop Manager, Glasgow Print Studio, since 1989; b. 13.6.59. Educ. Gray's School of Art, Aberdeen. Member of staff, Glasgow Print Studio, 1984; SAC award to study and travel in Italy, 1987; exchange visit to Semej Print Workshop, Moscow, 1992; solo exhibitions: Glasgow Print Studio, 1995, Gallery of Jerusalem Print Workshop, 1998. Arts Adviser, Moor Fire Productions. Address: (b.) Glasgow Print Studio, 22 King Street, Glasgow G1 5QP; T.-0141-552 0704.

Duffty, Paul, MB, ChB, FRCP, FRCPE, FRCPCH, LMCC. Consultant Paediatrician, since 1982; Senior Lecturer in Child Health, Aberdeen University, since 1982; b. 1.9.46, Leeds; m., Lesley Marjory Macdonald; 2 d. Educ. Leeds Central High School; Aberdeen University. Lecturer in Child Health, Aberdeen University, 1972-75; Trainee in General Practice, Aberdeen, 1975-76; Lecturer in Child Health, Aberdeen University, 1976-78; Fellow in Neonatology, Toronto University, 1978-80; Staff Paediatrician, Hospital for Sick Children, Toronto, and Assistant Professor, Toronto University, 1980-82. Recreations: hill-walking; cross-country skiing; philately. Address: (h.) 13 Louisville Avenue, Aberdeen; T.-01224 317072.

Duffus, Professor Carol Margaret, BSc, MS, PhD, DIC, DSc, FRSE. Director Management Development, Scottish Agricultural College and Professor, Crop Science and Technology, since 1997; b. Belfast; m., John Henderson Duffus; 2 d. Educ. Victoria College, Belfast; Queens's University, Belfast; University of Michigan, Ann Arbor, USA; Imperial College, London; University of Edinburgh. Lecturer in Biochemistry, School of Molecular Sciences, University of Warwick, 1966; Lecturer, University of Edinburgh and East of Scotland College of Agriculture, 1968; Scottish Agricultural College: Head, Agricultural Biochemistry Department, 1987, Head, Crop Sciences Division, 1990. Hon. Senior Lecturer, Institute of Ecology and Resource Management, University of Edinburgh; Member: Scottish Natural Heritage, South East Regional Board, Scientific Advisory Committee, 1990-97, Law Society of Scotland Complaints Committee, 1993-95; President, Association of Applied Biologists, 1999-2000. Publications: Carbohydrate Metabolism in Plants (Co-Author), 1984; Toxic Substances in Crop Plants (Co-Author), 1991. Recreations: gardening; chamber music; golf. Address: (b.) Scottish Agricultural College, King's Buildings, West Mains Road, Edinburgh EH9 3JG; T.-0131-535 4060.

Duffus, George McKay, FREHIS. Director of Environmental and Consumer Protection, Aberdeen City Council, since 1995; b. 10.7.45, Aberdeen; m., Patricia; 2 s. Educ. Aberdeen Grammar School. Corporation of City of Aberdeen, 1964-79; City of Aberdeen District Council, 1979-96. Recreations: walking; reading; listening to music. Address: (b.) Environmental and Consumer Protection Department, St. Nicholas House, Broad Street, Aberdeen; T.-01224 522210.

Duffus, John Henderson, BSc, PhD, DSc, CBiol, MIBiol, CChem, FRSC. Director, Edinburgh Centre for Toxicology (EdinTox). Educ. Arbroath High School; Edinburgh University; Heriot-Watt University. Research Fellow: Warwick University, 1965-67, Edinburgh University, 1967-70; Lecturer, Heriot-Watt University, 1970-80; Senior Lecturer in Environmental Toxicology, Heriot-Watt University, 1980-97; Hon. Fellow in Public Health Sciences, Edinburgh University, since 1997; WHO Consultant, Toxicology and Chemical Safety, since 1981; Member, UK Department of the Environment Advisory Committee on Hazardous Substances, since 1991; Titular Member, IUPAC Commission on Toxicology, since 1991, Chair, since 1997; Member, RSC Committee on Environment, Health and Safety. Publications: Environmental Toxicology, 1980; Environmental Toxicology and Ecotoxicology, 1986; Magnesium in Mitosis and the Cell Cycle (Co-author), 1987; Yeast: A Practical Approach (Co-Editor), 1988; The Toxicology of Chemicals, Series 1, Carcinogenicity, Vol III, Vol IV (Co-Editor/Author), 1991-93; Toxic Substances in Crop Plants (Co-Editor/Author), 1991; Cancer and Workplace Chemicals, 1995; Carcinogenicity of Inorganic Substances (Chief Editor/Author), 1997. Address: (b.) Edinburgh Centre for Toxicology, 43 Mansionhouse Road, Edinburgh EH9 2JD.

Duffy, Mgr. Francis. Former Vicar General to RC Bishop of Galloway; Resident Chaplain, Nazareth House, Kilmarnock, since 1992; b. 15.10.14, Edinburgh. Educ. Holy Cross Academy, Edinburgh; Blairs College, Aberdeen; Pontifical Scots College, Rome; Gregorian University, Rome. Ordained Priest (Rome), 1938; Curate, Ayr, 1939-41; Professor, Blairs College, Aberdeen, 1941-55; parish work in various towns, since 1955; Monsignor, since 1972. RC Religious Adviser, Scottish Television, 1958-78; Member, Dumfries Education Committee, 1963-72; Composer of congregational Church music and hymns. Address: Nazareth House, 23 Hill Street, Kilmarnock KA3 1HG.

Duffy, Graham Woodburn. Partner, Graphic Partners Design Consultants, since 1971; Director: Edinburgh Chamber of Commerce, since 1992, Scottish Design, since 1994; Fellow, Royal Society of Arts; b. 19.6.42, Edinburgh; m., Rosemary Jean; 1 s.; 1 d. Educ. Royal High School, Edinburgh; Heriot Watt College/Edinburgh College of Art. Andrew Grant Scholar, Edinburgh College of Art, 1961-63; Graphic Designer, Pillans and Wilson, 1963-67; Graphic Designer/ Typographer, Forth Studios, 1967-68; self-employed Design Consultant, 1969-71. Recreations: masters rowing; skiing; English literature; music; theatre; film. Address: (b.) 179 Canongate, Edinburgh; T.-0131-557 3558.

Duffy, Professor John Alastair, BSc, PhD, DSc, CChem, FRSC. Professor of Chemistry, Aberdeen University, since 1996; Quality Assessor for Scottish Higher Education Funding Council, 1993-94; b. 24.9.32, Birmingham; m., Muriel F.L. Ramsay; 1 s.; 1 d. Educ. Solihull School, Warwickshire; Sheffield University. Research Chemist, Albright & Wilson, Oldbury, 1958-59; Lecturer in Inorganic Chemistry, Wolverhampton Polytechnic, 1959-61; Senior Lecturer in Inorganic Chemistry, NE Wales Institute, 1961-65; Lecturer, Senior Lecturer, Reader in Chemistry, Aberdeen University, 1966-96; Assessor in Inorganic Chemistry for Ordinary and Higher National Certificates and Diplomas in Scotland, 1971-82; Consultant to Schott Glaswerke, Mainz, West Germany, 1984-86; Past Chairman, NE Scotland Section, Royal Society of Chemistry. Publications: General Inorganic Chemistry, 1966; Bonding Energy Levels and Bands in Inorganic Solids, 1990. Recreations: 20th-century opera; music. Address: (h.) 35 Beechgrove Terrace, Aberdeen AB15 5DR; T.-01224 641752.

Duffy, John Charles, BSc, MSc, CStat. Research Manager, Chief Scientist Office, Scottish Office Department of Health, since 1996; b. 6.3.49, Glasgow; m., Rosemary Clare Arthur; 2 s.; 1 d. Educ. St. Andrew's High School, Kirkcaldy; Edinburgh University; Reading University. Lecturer, Department of Statistics, Edinburgh University, and Non-Clinical Scientist, Medical Research Council, 1970-89; Senior Lecturer, Department of Statistics, Edinburgh University, 1990-96; Director, Statistics and Information, Alcohol Research Group, Edinburgh University, 1990-96. Hon. Secretary, Association of University Teachers (Scotland), 1992-96; President, Association of University Teachers (Scotland), 1988-90. Recreations: reading; music; computers; puzzles; conversation. Address: (b.) Scottish Office Department of Health, St. Andrew's House, Edinburgh EH1 3DG; T.-0131-244 2254.

Duffy, Sheila Sinclair, MA. Women's Editor, Radio Clyde, since 1973; Freelance Journalist, since 1967; b. 6.8.46, Silloth, Cumberland; m., Paul Young; 2 d. Educ. St. Joseph's, Nicosia; Boroughmuir School, Edinburgh; Edinburgh University. Auxiliary nurse, Edinburgh Royal Infirmary, 1965-66; croupier, Edinburgh night club, 1966-67; graduate trainee, Scottish Television, 1967-68; Reporter, Scottish Television, 1968-73; Presenter, Dateline Early/Edinburgh Film Festival programmes/Moneywise; Member, Visiting Committee, Glenochil Young Offenders Institution, since 1995. Glenfiddich Food Writer Award, 1986; Member, Scottish Genealogy Society. Recreations: children; husband; genealogy; cooking; reading; cake decorating; walking; sampler embroidery. Address: c/o Young Casting Agency, 7 Beaumont Gate, Glasgow; T.-0141-339 5180.

Dukes, Professor Paul, BA (Cantab), MA, PhD. Professor of History, Aberdeen University, since 1988; b. 5.4.34, Wallington; m., Rosemary Mackay; 1 s.; 1 d. Educ. Wallington County Grammar School; Cambridge University. Advisory Editor, History Today. Publications: several books on aspects of Russian, American, European and world history. Recreations: hill-walking; travel. Address: (b.) History Department, Aberdeen University, Aberdeen; T.-01224 272465.

Dun, Thomas Dixon Connochie. Farmer; Hon. Secretary, Royal Highland Agricultural Society, since 1995; Hon. President, North Country Cheviot Sheep Society, since 1970; b. 16.8.30, Selkirk; m., Jacqueline Joan Bruce; 3 s.; 1 d. Educ. Dollar Academy; Edinburgh Agriculture College. Farming, since 1953. Chairman, Royal Highland Agricultural Society, 1992-93, Director, 1972-94; President, North Country Cheviot Sheep Society, 1967-68; Council Member, National Sheep Association, since 1960; winner, George Hedley Memorial Award, 1991. Recreations: horse-racing; rugby. Address: Nether Brotherstone, Heriot, Midlothian EH38 5YS; T.-01875 835225.

Dunbar, Sir Archibald Ranulph, MA, DipAgric (Cantab), DTA (Trin). Retired; b. 8.8.27, London; m., Amelia M.S. Davidson; 1 s.; 2 d. Educ. Wellington College; Pembroke College, Cambridge. Military Service, Cameron Highlanders (attached Gordon Highlanders), 1945-48; Imperial College of Tropical Agriculture, Trinidad, 1952-53; Agricultural Officer, Colonial Service, Uganda (later Overseas Civil Service, Uganda) 1953-70; Landowner, Duffus Estate, Elgin, since 1970. Honorary Sheriff, Sheriff Court District of Moray, since 1989; Knight of Honour and Devotion, Sovereign Military Order of Malta, 1989. Recreations: swimming; railways; model railways; military models. Address: (h.) The Old Manse, Duffus, Elgin, Moray; T.-01343 830270.

Dunbar, Sheriff Ian Duncan, LLB. Floating Sheriff, based in Kirkcaldy, since 1998; Partner, Miller Hendry, Solicitors, 1990-98; b. 31.10.48, Dundee; m., Susan Young. Educ. Lawside Academy, Dundee; Queens College, Dundee/St. Andrews University. Law apprentice, Soutar Reid & Mill, Dundee, 1969-71; Assistant Solicitor, Sneddon Campbell & Munro, Perth, 1971-72, Partner, 1972-85; merged to form Miller Sneddon, 1985, Partner, 1985-90; merged to form Miller Hendry, 1990. President, Law Society of Scotland, 1993-94. Recreations: golf; rugby; cooking; wine. Address: (h.) Craigrownie, Forgandenny Road, Bridge of Earn, Perth PH2 9HA; T.-01738 812255.

Dunbar, John Greenwell, MA, FSA, FSA Scot, HonFRIAS. Secretary, Royal Commission on the Ancient and Historical Monuments of Scotland, 1978-90; b. 1.3.30, London; m., Elizabeth Mill Blyth. Educ. University College School, London; Balliol College, Oxford. joined staff, Royal Commission on the Ancient and Historical Monuments of Scotland, 1953; Member, Ancient Monuments Board for Scotland, 1978-90. Publications: The Historic Architecture of Scotland, 1966; Accounts of the Masters of Works, Volume 2 (1616-1649), (Joint Editor), 1982; Sir William Burrell's Northern Tour, 1997. Address: (h.) Paties Mill, Carlops, by Penicuik, Midlothian EH26 9NF; T.-01968 660250.

Dunbar, Lennox Robert, DA, ARSA. Head of Printmaking, Grays School of Art, since 1987; Painter and Printmaker; b. 17.5.52, Aberdeen; m., Jan Storie; 2 s.; 1 d. Educ. Aberdeen Grammar School; Grays School of Art. Part-time Lecturer, 1975-82; Etching Technician, Peacock Printmakers, 1978-82; Education Officer, Peacock Printmakers, 1982-86; appointed Lecturer in Painting and Printmaking, Grays School of Art, 1986; Visiting Lecturer, Duncan of Jordanstone College of Art, Dundee, and Newcastle University; Visiting Artist/Tutor, Louisiana State University; participated in many group and one-man exhibitions; numerous awards including Latimer Award, 1978, Guthrie Award, 1984, Shell Expro Premier Award, 1991 and 1993; work in many private and public collections.

Dunbar, Morrison Alexander Rankin, KStJ, FCIOB, FFB, FBIM, FRSAMD, FRSA. Chairman: Royal Scottish Academy of Music and Drama Trust, since 1992, Westbourne Music, since 1998; b. 27.4.29, Glasgow; m., Sally Joan Sutherland; 2 s.; 1 d. Educ. Belmont House; Gresham House. Managing Director, Morrison Dunbar Ltd. Builders, 1957-81. President: Scottish Building Contractors Association, 1968, Scottish Building Employers Federation, 1975, Building Employers Confederation, 1980, Builders Benevolent Institution, 1987; Lord Dean of Guild, Merchants House of Glasgow, 1991-93; Chairman: Epilepsy Association of Scotland, 1990-93, Royal Scottish Academy of Music and Drama, 1987-91, Royal Scottish National Orchestra, 1993-97; Trustee, University of Strathclyde Foundation; Member, Trades House of

Glasgow. Recreations: music; art galleries; golf. Address: (h.) 18 Devonshire Terrace Lane, Glasgow G12 9XT; T.-0141-357 1289.

Dunbar-Nasmith, Professor Emeritus Sir James Duncan, CBE, BA, DA, RIBA, PPRIAS, FRSA, FRSE. Chairman, Scottish Civic Trust; Vice-President, Europa Nostra; Partner, Law and Dunbar-Nasmith, Architects, Edinburgh and Forres since 1957; b. 15.3.27, Dartmouth. Educ. Lockers Park; Winchester College; Trinity College, Cambridge; Edinburgh College of Art. Lt., Scots Guards, 1945-48; ARIBA, 1954; President: Edinburgh Architectural Association, 1967-69, Royal Incorporation of Architects in Scotland, 1971-73; Member, RIBA Council, 1967-73 (Vice-President and Chairman, Board of Architectural Education, 1972-73); Council, ARCUK, 1976-84, Board of Education, 1976-88 (Vice Chairman, 1977); Professor and Head, Department of Architecture, Heriot-Watt University and Edinburgh College of Art, 1978-88; Member: Royal Commission on Ancient and Historical Monuments of Scotland, 1972-96, Ancient Monuments Board for Scotland, 1969-82 (interim Chairman, 1972-73), Historic Buildings Council for Scotland, 1966-93; Trustee, Architectural Heritage Fund, Theatres Trust, 1983-95; Member, Edinburgh New Town Conservation Committee; Deputy Chairman, Edinburgh Festival Society, 1981-85. Recreations: music; theatre; skiing; sailing. Address: (b.) 16 Dublin Street, Edinburgh EH1 3RE; T.-0131-556 8631.

Duncan, Sheriff Agnes Lawrie Addie, LLB. Sheriff of Glasgow and Strathkelvin, since 1982; b. 17.6.47. Admitted Solicitor, 1969; called to the Scottish Bar, 1976.

Duncan, Professor Alan James, BSc (Hons), MS, PhD, CPhys, FInstP, FRSE. Professor of Experimental Physics, University of Stirling, since 1998; b. 4.11.38, North Berwick; m., Helen Irene Thompson; 1 s.; 1 d. Educ. North Berwick High School; St. Andrews University; Stanford University. Research Officer, Tube Investments, 1961-63; International Research and Development Company Ltd., 1963-65; Research Assistant, Stanford University, 1965-70; Stirling University: Lecturer in Physics, 1970-89, Reader in Physics, 1989-98. Chairman, Scottish Branch, Institute of Physics, 1983-85; Member, Atomic, Molecular and Optical Physics Committee, Institute of Physics, 1990-93. UK National Physical Laboratory Metrology Prize, 1998. Recreations; reading; swimming. Address: (h.) 13 Newton Crescent, Dunblane FK15 0DZ; T.-01786 822806.

Duncan, Professor Archibald Alexander McBeth, MA, FBA, FRSE, FRHistS. Emeritus Professor of Scottish History, Glasgow University, 1962-93, currently Honorary Research Fellow; b. 17.10.26, Pitlochry; m., Ann Hayes Sawyer; 2 s.; 1 d. Educ. George Heriot's School, Edinburgh; Edinburgh University; Balliol College, Oxford. Lecturer: Balliol College, 1950-51, Queen's University, Belfast, 1951-53, Edinburgh University, 1953-61; Leverhulme Fellow, 1961-62; Clerk of Senate, Glasgow University, 1978-83; Dean of Faculties, Glasgow University, since 1988. Publications: Scotland, The Making of the Kingdom; revised 3rd edition of W.C. Dickinson's Scotland from Earliest Times to 1603; Regesta Regum Scottorum, v., The Acts of Robert I 1306-29, 1988; edition of John Barbour's The Bruce, 1997. Recreation: swimming. Address: (h.) 17 Campbell Drive, Bearsden, Glasgow G61 4NF: T.-0141-942 5023.

Duncan, Geoffrey Cheyne Calderhead, BL. Lord Dean of Guild, Merchants House of Glasgow, 1993-95; b. 6.10.29, Whitecraigs, Glasgow; m., Lorna Dowling (deceased); 1 s.; 1 d. Educ. Belmont House School; Glasgow Academy; Glasgow University. Partner, Aitken, Hamilton & Duncan, 1951-70; Partner, Kerr, Barrie & Duncan, 1970-91; Chairman, Glasgow Junior Chamber of Commerce, 1963-64; Director, The Girls' School Company Ltd., 1964-90 (Chairman, 1977-90); Chairman, St. Columba's School, 1972-83; Director, The West of Scotland School Company Ltd., 1972-92 (Chairman, 1989-92); Member: Board of Management, Glasgow South Western Hospitals, 1964-69, Clyde River Purification Board, 1969-75; Director, Glasgow Chamber of Commerce, 1972-92; Chairman, Glasgow Post Office Advisory Committee, 1974-84; Member, Post Office Users' National Council, 1974-87; Chairman: Post Office Users' Council for Scotland, 1984-87, Advisory Committee on Telecommunications for Scotland, 1984-87; Director, The Merchants' House of Glasgow, since 1982; Trustee, Ferguson Bequest Fund, 1987-97; Member: Executive Committee, Abbeyfield Quarrier's Society (now Abbeyfield Strathgryffe Society), 1981-97 (Chairman, 1988-96), Council of Management, Quarrier's Homes, 1985-93; Director, The Scottish Cremation Society Ltd. (Chairman, since 1993); Member, Iona Cathedral Management Board, 1990-93; Director, Iona Abbey Ltd., 1993-96; Chairman, Renfrewshire Valuation Appeal Panel, since 1993; General Commissioner for Income Tax, since 1994; Patron and Member, Executive Committee, Royal Incorporation of Hutcheson's Hospital, since 1995; Patron, Unity Enterprise, 1997. Recreations: golf; gardening; photography. Address: (h.) Mid Clevans, Bridge of Weir, Renfrewshire PA11 3HP; T.-01505 612566.

Duncan, Professor James Lindsay, BVMS, PhD, MRCVS. Professor in Veterinary Parasitology, Glasgow University, since 1987; b. 26.2.41, Law, Carluke; m., Helen M.; 1 s.; 1 d. Educ. Wishaw High School; Glasgow University. Veterinary Practice, UK, and clinical teaching posts, Kenya, 1964-70; Glasgow University: Research Fellow, Department of Veterinary Parasitology, 1970-76, Lecturer, 1976-79, Senior Lecturer, 1979-82, Reader, 1982-87; Vice-Dean, Faculty of Veterinary Medicine, 1994-96; Consultant, international animal health agencies and multinational pharmaceutical companies; Co-author of several textbooks. Recreations: farming; gardening; music. Address: (h.) Eastfield of Wiston, Biggar, Lanarkshire; T.-Lamington 270.

Duncan, James Wann, MBE, Hon. LLD, JP, MIMFT. Rector's Assessor, University of Dundee, 1992-98; former Vice-Chairman, Tayside Health Board (Convener, General Purposes Committee); Convener, Personnel and Accommodation Sub-Committee, Management Committee, Common Services Agency for the Scottish Health Service; retired Senior Chief Maxillofacial Technician, Dundee Royal Infirmary; b. 14.7.25, Dundee; m., Hilda Mackenzie Gray; 3 d. Educ. Stobswell Secondary School; Dundee College of Technology. Former Convener, Property Equipment Supplies Committee, General Board of Management, Dundee General Hospitals; former Vice-Convener, General Purposes Committee, General Board of Management, Dundee Northern Hospitals; former Member, Dundee Town Council (Senior Magistrate); former Convener: Dundee Art Galleries and Museums Committee, Further Education Committee, Dundee Police Committee; former Member, Board of Governors, Scottish Police College; Member, Dundee District Council, 1974-77 (Convener, Planning and Development Committee); Chairman, Dundee City Labour Party, 1960-62; former Member, Scottish Council, SDP; former Scottish Representative, National Committee for Dental Technicians, USDAW; former Member, STUC Health and Social Services Committee; former Member, University of Dundee Court. Recreations: golf; gardening; DIY. Address: (h.) 13 Clive Road, Downfield, Dundee DD3 8LP; T.-01382 825488.

Duncan, Robert Alexander, BCom, CA. Director UK Bus, Firstgroup PLC, since 1997; b. 31.5.50, Aberdeen; m., Gail; 2 d. Educ. Robert Gordon's College, Aberdeen; Edinburgh University. Qualified CA, Coopers and Lybrand, Glasgow; Audit Manager, Brussels, four years; various finance positions; Finance Director, Grampian Transport; Managing

Director GRT Bus Group; Regional Director North, First Group PLC. Director, Auris Limited. Recreations: golf; fishing; cycling; art and antique hunting. Address: 395 King Street, Aberdeen; T.-01224 650114.

Duncan, William, BSc (Hons), GradIPM, PhD. Executive Secretary, Royal Society of Edinburgh, since 1985; Executive Secretary, RSE Scotland Foundation, since 1996; Secretary to Trustees, Scottish Science Trust, 1997-98; b. 6.12.50, Edinburgh. Educ. Linlithgow Academy; Edinburgh University. Greater London Council, 1975-78; Lothian Regional Council, 1978-85. Recreations: contemporary music; opera. Address: (b.) 22/24 George Street, Edinburgh EH2 2PQ; T.-0131-240 5000.

Duncan Millar, James, LVO, psc. Managing Partner, A&J Duncan Millar, Remony Estate, since 1986; Commissioner, Deer Commission for Scotland, since 1996; b. 5.4.48, Aberfeldy; m., Susan Ferrier Marshall; 1 s.; 1 d. Educ. Loretto School; RMA Sandhurst. Commissioned, The Black Watch, 1968-86; Army Staff College, Camberley, 1982. Member, Kenmore and District Community Council. Recreation: downhill skiing. Address: Remony, Aberfeldy, Perthshire PH15 2HR.

Dundas, Ronald Edgar, MA (Hons). Chief Financial Editor, The Herald, since 1993; b. 11.7.42, Glasgow; widowed; 1 s.; 1 d. Educ. Hutchesons' Grammar School, Glasgow; St. Salvators College, St. Andrews University. Glasgow Herald: Sub-Editor, 1964, Leader Writer, 1965, Chief Leader Writer, 1967, Business Editor, 1973. Conservative candidate: Greenock, 1966, Glasgow Kelvingrove, 1970; Chairman, East Renfrewshire Conservative Association, 1971-73. Address: (b.) The Herald, 195 Albion Street, Glasgow; T.-0141-552 6255.

Dundas-Bekker, Althea Enid Philippa, DL. Deputy Lieutenant, Midlothian, since 1991; b. 4.11.39, Gorebridge; m., Aedrian Ruprecht Bekker (deceased); 2 d. Secretarial work abroad, in London, and with the National Trust for Scotland; inherited Arniston House, 1970, and restoring ever since. National Trust for Scotland: Member, Council, Curatorial Committee, Regional Committee; Commissioner, Royal Commission on Historical Manuscripts; Trustee: Arniston Village Improvement Trust, Scottish Businessman's Achievement Award Trust; Member, Historic Buildings Council for Scotland. Recreation: Scottish history; Scottish songs; walking dogs. Address: (h.) Arniston House, Gorebridge, Midlothian EH23 4RY; T.-01875 830238.

Dundee, 12th Earl of (Alexander Henry Scrymgeour). Hereditary Royal Standard-Bearer for Scotland; b. 5.6.49; m.; 1 s.; 3 d. Educ. Eton; St. Andrews University. Address: Farm Office, Birkhill, Cupar, Fife.

Dundonald, 15th Earl of (Iain Alexander Douglas Blair); b. 17.2.61; m., Marie Beatrice Louise Russo; 2 s.; 1 d. Educ. Wellington College; Royal Agricultural College, Cirencester. Company Director; Hon. Chilean Consul to Scotland. Recreations: marine and rural environment; rural housing; Scottish affairs. Address: Lochnell Castle, Ledaig, Argyll.

Dunion, Kevin Harry, MA (Hons), MSc, FRSA. Director, Friends of the Earth Scotland, since 1991; b. 20.12.55, Bridge of Allan; m., Linda Dunion (qv); 2 s. Educ. St. Andrew's High School, Kirkcaldy; St. Andrews University; Edinburgh University. HM Inspector of Taxes, 1978-80; Administrator, Edinburgh University Students Association, 1980-84; Scottish Campaigns Manager, Oxfam, 1984-91. Editor, Radical Scotland, 1982-85; Chair: Scottish Education and Action for Development, 1990-92, Friends of the Earth International, since 1996 (Treasurer, 1993-96), Scottish Environmental Forum; Member: Secretary of State's Advisory Group on Sustainable Development, Lord Provost's Commission on Sustainable Development for Edinburgh, Scottish Council for Voluntary Organisations Policy Committee, Centre for Scottish Public Policy Advisory Committee. Publication: Living in the Real World: An International Role for Scotland's Parliament. Address: (b.) Bonnington Mill, 72 Newhaven Road, Edinburgh EH6 5QG; T.-0131-554 9977.

Dunion, Linda M., BSc (Soc Sci). Assistant Director, Age Concern Scotland; formerly Director, Scottish Down's Syndrome Association; b. 15.9.56, Perth. Educ. Morrisons Academy Girls' School, Crieff; Edinburgh University. Administrator, Scottish War on Want; Councillor, Edinburgh District Council; formerly Director, SEAD (Scottish Education and Action for Development). Council Member, Scottish Civic Assembly. Address: 113 Rose Street, Edinburgh EH2 3DT.

Dunlop, Alastair Barr, OBE (1989), FRICS. Deputy Chairman, Lothians Ethics of Medical Research Committee, since 1984; General Commissioner for Income Tax, since 1991; b. 27.12.33, Calcutta; m., Catriona C.L.H. MacLaurin; 1 s.; 1 d. Educ. Radley. Member, British Schools Exploring Society Expedition, Arctic Norway, 1950. National Service, 1952-54 (active service, Malaya: 2nd Lt., 1st Bn., RWK); commerce, City of London, 1954-58; agricultural student, 1959-61; Land Agent, Inverness, 1962-71 (Partner, Bingham Hughes & Macpherson); Joint Founding Director, Martin Paterson Associates Ltd., 1971; ecology studies, Edinburgh University, 1973-74. Member, Lothian Health Board, 1983-91 (Vice-Chairman, 1989-91); Scottish Member, RICS Committee for Wilson Report on Financial Institutions, 1973-74; Chairman: Edinburgh and Borders Branch, RICS, 1977, Paintings in Hospitals Scotland; Life Member, Institute of Directors; Past President, Edinburgh South Conservative Association; Chairman: South Edinburgh Conservative Association, 1980-84 and 1992-99, Central and South, Scottish Conservative and Unionist Association, 1985-88, Edinburgh Branch, World Wildlife Fund, 1982-96; elected Member, Council, National Trust for Scotland, 1992-97. Recreations: golf; skiing; fine arts. Address: 46 Dick Place, Edinburgh EH9 2JB; T.-0131-667 5343.

Dunlop, Eileen. Children's Writer; b. 13.10.38, Alloa; m., Antony Kamm (qv). Educ. Alloa Academy; Moray House College. Publications: Robinsheugh, 1975; A Flute in Mayferry Street, 1976; Fox Farm, 1978; The Maze Stone, 1982 (SAC Book Award); Clementina, 1985 (SAC Book Award); The House on the Hill, 1987 (commended, Carnegie Medal); The Valley of Deer, 1989; Finn's Island, 1991; Tales of St. Columba, 1992; Green Willow's Secret, 1993; Finn's Roman Fort, 1994; Tales of St. Patrick, 1995; Castle Gryffe, 1995; Waters of Life, 1996; The Ghost by the Sea, 1997; Co-author, with Antony Kamm: Scottish Verse to 1800, 1985; A Book of Old Edinburgh, 1983; Warrior's Bride, 1998. Recreations: reading; gardening; theatre. Address: (h.) 46 Tarmangie Drive, Dollar FK14 7BP; T.-01259 742007.

Dunlop, Sheriff William, LLB. Sheriff of North Strathclyde, since 1995; b. 7.3.44, Glasgow; m., Janina Marthe; 1 s.; 2 d. Educ. High School of Glasgow; Glasgow University. Solicitor, 1968-84; called to Scottish Bar, 1985. Address: (b.) Sheriff Court, Castlehill, Campbeltown, PA28 6AN; T.-01586 552503.

Dunmore, 12th Earl of (Malcolm Kenneth Murray); b. 17.9.46; m.; 1 s.; 1 d. Succeeded to title, 1995; lives in Australia.

Dunn, Bill, BA. Chief Executive, Ayr Locality Enterprise Resource Trust (ALERT), since 1988; b. 26.2.48, Ayr; m., Sheila; 2 s.; 2 d. Educ. Ayr Academy; Strathclyde University. Transport Manager, National Freight Corporation/British (later Scottish) Road Services, 1970-73;

Administrator, Ayrshire Joint Police Committee, 1973; Internal Audit Department, British Steel Corporation, Glasgow, 1973-81; Garnock Valley Task Force: Project Co-ordinator, 1981-83, Business Development Consultant, 1983-84; Managing Director, Development Executive, 1984-88. Recreations: family; golf; football; music; DIY; model railways. Address: (b.) 16 Smith Street, Ayr KA7 1TD; T.-01292 264181.

Dunn, Professor Douglas Eaglesham, BA, FRSL, Hon.LLD (Dundee, 1987), Hon.DLitt (Hull, 1995). Professor and Head, School of English, St. Andrews University, since 1991, and Director, St. Andrews Scottish Studies Institute, since 1993; b. 23.10.42, Inchinnan. Educ. Renfrew High School; Camphill Senior Secondary School, Paisley; Hull University. Books of poems: Terry Street, 1969, The Happier Life, 1972, Love or Nothing, 1974, Barbarians, 1979, St. Kilda's Parliament, 1981, Elegies, 1985, Selected Poems, 1986, Northlight, 1988, Dante's Drum-Kit, 1993; Secret Villages (short stories), 1985; Boyfriends and Girlfriends (short stories), 1995; Andromache (translation), 1990; Poll Tax: The Fiscal Fake, 1990; Editor: Choice of Lord Byron's Verse, 1974, The Poetry of Scotland, 1979, A Rumoured City: New Poets from Hull, 1982; Two Decades of Irish Writing: a Critical Survey, 1975; The Essential Browning, 1990; Scotland: an anthology, 1991; Faber Book of Twentieth Century Scottish Poetry, 1992; Oxford Book of Scottish Short Stories, 1995; author of plays, and TV films using commentaries in verse. Gregory Award, 1968; Somerset Maugham Award, 1972; Geoffrey Faber Memorial Prize, 1975; Hawthornden Prize, 1982; Whitbread Award for Poetry and Whitbread Book of the Year Award, 1985; Cholmondeley Award, 1989. Honorary Visiting Professor, Dundee University, 1987; Fellow in Creative Writing, St. Andrews University, 1989-91; Honorary Fellow, Humberside College, 1987. Address (b.) School of English, St. Andrews University, St. Andrews KY16 9AL.

Dunn, James Clark. Motoring Correspondent, The Scotsman, since 1986; b. 11.7.51, Dunfermline; m., Margaret; 1 s.; 1 d. Educ. Dunfermline High School; Napier University. Alloa Advertiser, 1970-74; Home Counties Newspapers, 1974-75; PR, SSEB, 1975-84. UK Motoring Writer of the Year, 1990. Publications: David Coulthard the Flying Scot; David Coulthard In the Wheeltracks of Legends. Recreations: sailing; fishing; classic cars. Address: (h.) 3 Thorniewood Gardens, Uddingston G71 6NQ; T.-0131-243 3212.

Dunne, John Joseph, MA (Hons), MPhil, PhL, AFBPsS, CPsychol. Consultant Clinical Psychologist and Head, Community Clinical Psychology Service, Central Scotland Healthcare NHS Trust; Honorary Senior Lecturer in Psychology, Stirling University, since 1994; Honorary Clinical Senior Lecturer, Department of Nursing Studies, University of Glasgow, since 1996; Honorary Fellow, Edinburgh University, since 1984; b. 31.8.42, Kirkcaldy; m., Marie Anne Cecile. Educ. Blairs College, Aberdeen; Gregorian University, Rome; St. Andrews University; Edinburgh University. Clinical Psychologist, Royal Edinburgh Hospital, 1977-81; Senior Clinical Psychologist (Primary Care), Dedridge and Craigshill Health Centres, Livingston, 1981-85; Honorary Lecturer in Psychology, Stirling University, 1986-94 (Director, Macmillan Nursing Research Project, 1987-91). Member: Scottish Office Home & Health Department's National Panel for the Care of the Dying and Bereaved in Scotland, 1992-96, steering group for establishment of BACUP (Scotland), since 1995, working group to develop guidelines in palliative and cancer care, 1993, Advisory Group to "Partnership in Cancer Care"; Consultant in Clinical Psychology, Cancer Relief Macmillan Fund, since 1993. Address: (b.) Community Clinical Psychology Service, Department of Psychology, Stirling University, Stirling; T.-01786 467680.

Dunnett, Dorothy, OBE. Writer, since 1960; Portrait Painter, since 1950; b. 25.8.23, Dunfermline; m., Sir Alastair M. Dunnett; 2 s. Civil Service: Assistant Press Officer, Scottish Government Departments, Edinburgh, 1940-46, Executive Officer, Board of Trade, Glasgow, 1946-55; Trustee for the Secretary of State for Scotland, Scottish National War Memorial, 1962-96; Non-Executive Director, Scottish Television p.l.c., 1979-92; Fellow, Royal Society of Arts, since 1986; Trustee, National Library of Scotland, since 1986; Board, Edinburgh Book Festival, 1990-95. Publications (novels): Game of Kings, 1961; Queens' Play, 1964; The Disorderly Knights, 1966; Dolly and the Singing Bird, 1968; Pawn in Frankincense, 1969; Dolly and the Cookie Bird, 1970; The Ringed Castle, 1971; Dolly and the Doctor Bird, 1971; Dolly and the Starry Bird, 1973; Checkmate, 1975; Dolly and the Nanny Bird, 1976; King Hereafter, 1982; Dolly and the Bird of Paradise, 1983; Niccolo Rising, 1986; The Spring of the Ram, 1987; The Scottish Highlands (Co-author), 1988; Race of Scorpions, 1989; Moroccan Traffic, 1991; Scales of Gold, 1991; The Unicorn Hunt, 1993; To Lie with Lions, 1995; Caprice and Rondo, 1997; Contributor, Scottish Short Stories, anthology, 1973, and A Scottish Childhood, anthology, 1998. Recreations: travel; medieval history; opera; orchestral music; ballet. Address (h.) 87 Colinton Road, Edinburgh EH10 5DF; T.-0131-337 2107.

Dunnett, Major G.T., TD. Lord-Lieutenant of Caithness, since 1995; b. 8.3.29; m.; 3 s. Educ. Wick High School; Archbishop Holgate's Grammar School, York.

Dunning, Norman Moore, BA (Oxon), CQSW. Director, Enable, since 1991; b. 15.4.50, Crewe; m., Diana Mary; 2 s. Educ. Sandbach School; Jesus College, Oxford; Manchester University. Probation Officer, City of Manchester and Salford, 1973-75; Social Worker, NSPCC, 1975-77; Leader, RSSPCC Overnewton Centre, Glasgow, 1978-87; Divisional Manager (East and North Scotland), RSSPCC, 1987-91. Recreations: running; cycling; swimming. Address: (h.) 7 The Ness, Dollar, Clackmannshire; T.-01259 43354.

Dunrossil Viscount (John William Morrison), CMG, JP, MA, KStJ. Lord Lieutenant, Western Isles, since 1993; Consultant, Bank of Bermuda, since 1989; Director, International Registries Inc., since 1993; b. 22.5.26, London; m., Diana; 3 s.; 3 d. Educ. Fettes College; Oriel College, Oxford. RAF (Pilot), 1945-48 and 1951; HM Diplomatic Service, 1951-88; served in Australia, East Pakistan, South Africa; International Maritime Consultative Organization, 1968-70; Counsellor and Head of Chancery, Ottawa, 1970-74; Counsellor, Brussels, 1975-78; High Commissioner: Fiji and Tuvalu, 1978-82, Barbados, 1982-83; Governor, Bermuda, 1983-88. Recreation: music. Address: (h.) Dunrossil House, Clachan Sands, Lochmaddy, Isle of North Uist HS6 5AY; T.-01876 500 213.

Dunsire, Thomas, MA, LLB, WS. Partner, then Consultant, J. & J. Milligan, WS, Edinburgh (now Morton, Fraser & Milligan, WS), 1951-90; b. 16.11.26, Rangoon, Burma; m., Jean Mary. Educ. Morrison's Academy, Crieff; Edinburgh University. Royal Navy; Solicitor and WS, 1950. Chairman, Governors, Morrison's Academy, 1984-96. Recreations: formerly rugby, football, golf and cricket. Address: (h.) 40 Liberton Brae, Edinburgh.

Durie, Roy Ross, FRICS, FSVA, MIMgt. A Senior Partner, Ryden, Edinburgh, since 1979; Chairman, Ryden Plant & Machinery Ltd., since 1989; b. 11.5.48, Edinburgh; m., Dorothy; 1 s.; 3 d. Educ. Edinburgh Academy; Britannia Royal Naval College, Dartmouth. Royal Navy Officer (Lt. R.N.), 1966-72; Surveyor, Ryden, Edinburgh, 1974-79. Chairman, Chamber Developments Ltd.; Director, Edinburgh Chamber of Commerce; Governor: Stewarts Melville School, Mary Erskine School; Elder, St. Giles, Edinburgh; Past Chairman, ISVA, Scotland. Recreations:

walking; swimming; sailing; skiing; golf; rugby. Address: (b.) Ryden, 46 Castle Street, Edinburgh EH2 3BN; T.-0131-225 6612.

Durrani, Professor Tariq Salim, BSc (Hons), MSc, PhD, FIEE, FEng, FIEEE, FRSE. Professor, Department of Electronic and Electrical Engineering, Strathclyde University, since 1986; b. 27.10.43, Amraoti, India; m., Clare Elizabeth; 1 s.; 2 d. Educ. Marie Colaco High School, Karachi; Engineering University, Dacca; Southampton University. Research Fellow, Southampton University, 1970-76; joined academic staff, Strathclyde University, 1976, Chairman, Department of Electronic and Electrical Engineering, 1986-90, Deputy Principal, 1990-91; Special Advisor, IT, since 1983; Director, Scottish Electronics Technology Group; President, IEEE Signal Processing Society, 1993-94; Chair: IEEE Periodicals Council, 1996-98, Management Committee, IT Associate Companies Scheme (ITACS). Publications: six books; over 250 technical research papers. Recreation: playing occasional golf badly. Address: (b.) Department of Electronic and Electrical Engineering, Strathclyde University, Glasgow; T.-0141-548 2883.

Durward, William Farquharson, MB, ChB, FRCP(Edin), FRCP(Glas). Consultant Neurologist, Greater Glasgow and Lanarkshire Health Boards, since 1977; Honorary Clinical Senior Lecturer in Neurology, Glasgow University, since 1978; Director, Cloburn Quarry Co. Ltd.; b. 16.9.44, Kilmarnock; m., Ann Roy Paterson; 1 s.; 1 d. Educ. Kilmarnock Academy; Glasgow University; Boston University. Employed by NHS, since 1968; specialist training grades, 1969-77. Recreations: walking; reading; railway conservation. Address: (h.) Overdale, 20 South Erskine Park, Bearsden, Glasgow G61 4NA; T.-0141-942 3143.

Duthie, Sir Robert (Robin) Grieve, CBE (1978), CA, LLD, CBIM, FRSA, FRIAS, DTech (Napier). Chairman, Neill Clerk Group plc, since 1993; Director, Royal Bank of Scotland plc, since 1978, British Assets Trust plc, since 1977, Devol Engineering Ltd., since 1993; Member, Board of Governors, Beatson Institute for Cancer Research, since 1989; Vice Chairman, BP Advisory Board Scotland, since 1990; b. 2.10.28, Greenock; m., Violetta Noel Maclean; 2 s.; 1 d. Educ. Greenock Academy. Apprentice Chartered Accountant, Thomson Jackson Gourlay and Taylor, CA, 1946-51; joined Blacks of Greenock, 1952; appointed Managing Director, 1962; Chairman, Black & Edgington, 1972-83. Chairman, Inverkip Society, 1966; Director, Greenock Chamber of Commerce, 1966; Member, Clyde Port Authority, 1971-83 (Chairman, 1977-80); Chairman, Scottish Development Agency, 1979-88; Chairman, Britoil PLC, 1988-90; Director, Greenock Provident Bank, 1969-75 (Chairman, 1975); Member, Scottish Telecommunications Board, 1972-77; Council Member, Institute of Chartered Accountants of Scotland, 1973-78; Member: East Kilbride Development Corporation, 1976-78, Strathclyde Region Local Valuation Appeal Panel, 1976-83; CBI Tax Liaison Officer for Scotland, 1976-79; Chairman, Made Up Textile Association of Great Britain, 1972; Member: British Institute of Management Scottish Committee, 1976, Glasgow and West of Scotland Committee, Scottish Council (Development and Industry), 1975-79; Chairman, Greenock Club, 1972; Captain, Greenock Cricket Club, 1960-61; Commissioner, Queen Victoria School, Dunblane, 1972-89; Commissioner, Scottish Congregational Ministers Pension Fund, since 1973; Member, Scottish Economic Council, 1980-96; Member of Council, Royal Caledonian Curling Club, 1984-88; Treasurer, Nelson Street EU Congregational Church, Greenock, since 1970. Awarded Honorary Degree of Doctor of Laws, Strathclyde University, 1984. Recreations: curling; golf. Address: (h.) Fairhaven, 181 Finnart Street, Greenock, PA16 8JA; T.-01475 722642.

Dutton, Rory N., BSc(Agr). Director, Scottish Crofters Union, since 1998; b. 3.4.61, Dundee; m., 2 d. Educ. Blairgowrie High School; Edinburgh University; North of Scotland College of Agriculture, Aberdeen. Agricultural Adviser, Scottish Agricultural College, Forfar; Agricultural Consultant, Smiths Gore Farm Management Ltd., Dumfries; Agricultural Project Officer, Highlands and Islands Development Board; Highlands and Islands Enterprise: Development Manager (Land Resources), Marketing Manager; Business Support Manager, Business Information Source Ltd., Inverness. Address: (b.) Scottish Crofters Union, Old Mill, Broadford, Isle of Skye IV49 9AQ; T.-01471 822529.

Du Vivier, Paul Eastwood, FIMgt. Chief Executive, Scottish Fisheries Protection Agency, since 1995; b. 24.5.45, Bath; m., Diana Rochsoles Robertson; 1 s.; 2 d. Educ. Malvern College; Britannia Royal Naval College, Dartmouth. Service at sea, 1965-88; in command, HMS Maxton, 1974-76, HMS Achilles, 1980-81; service in MoD Naval Secretary's Department, 1977-79, Naval Plans, 1981-84; BRNC Dartmouth, 1984-86; HMS Dryad, 1989-91; Board President, Admiralty Interview Board, 1991; Director, Joint Maritime Operational Training Staff, 1991-94; Chief of Staff to Flag Officer Scotland, Northern England and Northern Ireland, 1994-95; Member, Institute of Directors; Selected Naval Member, Lowland TAVRA. Recreation: sport (golf). Address: (b.) Pentland House, 47 Robb's Loan, Edinburgh EH14 1TY; T.-0131-244 6059.

Duxbury, Professor Geoffrey, BSc, PhD, CPhys, FInstP, FRSE. Professor, Chemical Physics, Strathclyde University; b. 6.11.42, Blackburn; m., Mary R.; 1 s.; 1 d. Educ. Cheadle Hulme School; Sheffield University. Junior Research Fellow, National Physical Laboratory, 1967-69; Research Assistant, Research Associate, Lecturer in Chemical Physics, Bristol University, 1970-80; Senior Lecturer/Reader, Strathclyde University, 1981-86. Marlow Medal, Faraday Division, Royal Society of Chemistry, 1975. Address: (b.) Department of Physics and Applied Physics, Strathclyde University, Glasgow, G4 0NG; T.-0141-548 3271.

Dyer, James A.T., MB, ChB (Hons), FRCPsych. Medical Commissioner, Mental Welfare Commission for Scotland, since 1991, and Director, since 1993; b. 31.12.46, Arbroath; m., Suzanne Whitaker; 2 s.; 1 d.; 1 step-s.; 2 step d. Educ. Bo'ness Academy; Robert Gordon's College, Aberdeen; Aberdeen University. Trainee General Practitioner, Skene, Aberdeenshire, 1971-72; junior clinical appointments, then Senior Registrar in Psychiatry, Royal Edinburgh Hospital, 1972-77; Scientific Officer, MRC Unit for Epidemiological Studies in Psychiatry, Edinburgh, 1977-80; Consultant Psychiatrist, Royal Edinburgh Hospital, 1981-91; Treasurer, Scottish Division, Royal College of Psychiatrists; Member, Medical Action for Global Security. Recreations: walking; reading; family. Address: (b.) 37 Lauder Road, Edinburgh EH9 1UE; T.-0131-667 2479.

Dykes, Kenneth, BA, MEd, DipTechEd. Headteacher, Barrhead High School, since 1996; b. 18.1.55, Glasgow; m., Helen; 3 s. Educ. Cumbernauld High School; Strathclyde University; Stirling University; Open University. Kilsyth Academy, 1976-87; Claremont High School, 1987-88; Strathclyde Regional Council, 1988-93; Garthamlock Secondary School, 1993-96. Member, Barrhead Crime Prevention Panel. Recreations: church; DIY; completing doctorate. Address: (h.) 3 Birkwood Place, Mearnskirk, Newton Mearns, Glasgow G77 5FW; T.-0141-639 5164.

E

Eagles, John Mortimer, MBChB, MPhil, FRCPsych. Consultant Psychiatrist, Royal Cornhill Hospital, Aberdeen, since 1985; Honorary Senior Lecturer in Mental Health, Aberdeen University, since 1985; b. 21.10.52, Newport-on-Tay; m., Janette Isobel Rorke; 2 d. Educ. Bell-Baxter High School, Cupar; Aberdeen University; Edinburgh University. Resident House Officer posts, Aberdeen, 1977-78; Senior House Officer/Registrar in Psychiatry, Royal Edinburgh Hospital, 1978-82; Lecturer, Department of Mental Health, Aberdeen University, 1982-85; Psychiatric Tutor for trainee psychiatrists, Aberdeen, 1987-92. Chairman, North-East Regional Postgraduate Medical Education Committee, 1990-95. Recreations: cricket; golf; travel; reading. Address: (h.) 41 Binghill Park, Milltimber, Aberdeenshire AB13 0EE; T.-01224 732434.

Eassie, Lord (Ronald Mackay). Senator of the College of Justice, since 1997; b. 1945; m.; 1 s. Educ. Berwickshire High School; St. Andrews University; Edinburgh University. Admitted, Faculty of Advocates, 1972; QC, 1986. Address: Parliament House, Parliament Square, Edinburgh EH1 1RQ.

Eastmond, Clifford John, BSc, MD, FRCP, FRCPE. Clinical Director of Medicine, since 1995, and Consultant Rheumatologist, since 1979, Aberdeen Royal Hospitals NHS Trust; Clinical Senior Lecturer, Aberdeen University, since 1979; b. 19.1.45, Ashton-under-Lyne; m., Margaret Wadsworth; 2 s.; 1 d. Educ. Audenshaw Grammar School; Edinburgh University. House Officer posts, Edinburgh, one year; moved to Liverpool for further training, subsequently to Rheumatism Unit, Leeds. Elder, Church of Scotland. Recreations: skiing; hill-walking; music; shooting. Address: (h.) The Rowans, Skene, Aberdeenshire AD32 6YP; T.-01224 790370.

Easton, Lorna, MA, MSc. Director of UK Marketing, Scottish Tourist Board; b. 8.8.60, Hawick. Educ. Hawick High School; Edinburgh University; Strathclyde University. Economic Development, Central Regional Council, 1984-87, Lothian Regional Council, 1987-90; joined Scottish Tourist Board, 1990. Governor, Eden Court Theatre. Address: (b.) Scottish Tourist Board, Thistle House, Beechwood Park North, Inverness IV2 3ED; T.-01463 716996.

Easton, Sir Robert William Simpson, CBE (1980), DUniv, CEng, FIMechE, FIMarE, FRINA. Director, Caledonian MacBrayne Ltd., since 1997; Chairman, Clydeport Pension Trust; Chairman, GEC Scotland, since 1990; Chancellor, University of Paisley, since 1993; b. 30.10.22, Glasgow; m., Jean Fraser; 1 s.; 1 d. Educ. Govan High School, Glasgow; Royal Technical College, Glasgow. Apprentice, Marine Engineer, 1939-51; Manager, Yarrow & Co. Ltd., 1951-65; Yarrow Shipbuilders Ltd.: Director, 1965-70, Deputy Managing Director, 1970-77, Managing Director, 1977-91; Main Board Director, Yarrow & Co. Ltd., 1971-77; Chairman: Yarrow Shipbuilders Ltd., 1979-94, GEC Naval Systems, 1991 94; Chairman, Clyde Port Authority, 1983-93; Director: Supermarine Consortium Ltd., 1986-94, Glasgow Development Agency, 1990-94, West of Scotland Water Board, 1993-95; Vice-President, Clyde Shipbuilders Association, 1972-79; Freeman, City of London, 1982; Council Member, RINA, 1983; Trustee, Seagull Trust, 1984; Director, Merchant House of Glasgow, 1994; Member, Incorporation of Hammermen, 1989; Past President, Institute of Welding; President, Institute of Engineers and Shipbuilders, Scotland, since 1997. Recreations: sailing; golf; walking; family. Address: (h.) Springfield, Stuckenduff Road, Shandon, Argyllshire G84 8NW; T.-01436 820 677.

Easton, Robin Gardner, OBE, MA, DipEd. Rector, The High School of Glasgow, since 1983; b. 6.10.43, Glasgow; m., Eleanor Mary McIlroy; 1 s.; 1 d. Educ. Kelvinside Academy; Sedbergh School; Christ's College, Cambridge; Wadham College, Oxford. Teacher of French and German, Melville College, Edinburgh, 1966-72; Housemaster and Deputy Head, French Department, Daniel Stewart's and Melville College, 1972-78; Head, Modern Languages, George Watson's College, 1979-83. Elder, Church of Scotland. Recreations: watching rugby; tennis; hill-walking; visiting ancient monuments. Address: (h.) 21 Stirling Drive, Bearsden, Glasgow G61 4NU; T.-0141-943 0368.

Eastwood, Martin Anthony, MB, MSc, FRCPE. Honorary Librarian, Royal College of Physicians of Edinburgh; retired Gastroenterologist; b. 7.8.35, Hull; m., Jenny; 3 s.; 1 d. Educ. Minster Grammar School, Southwell; Edinburgh University. Publications: papers on physiology of the colon and nutrition; History of Western General Hospital Edinburgh (Co-Author), 1995; Principles of Human Nutrition, 1996. Address: (h.) Hill House, North Queensferry KY11 1JJ.

Eccles, Alexander Charles William Anderson, RD—, BA, LLB, WS. Temporary Sheriff, since 1984; part-time Chairman, Social Security Appeals Tribunals, since 1985, and Rent Assessment Committee, since 1975; part-time Chairman, Industrial Tribunals, since 1991; b. 8.1.33, Newcastle upon Tyne; m., Judith Margaret Hardy; 2 s.; 2 d. Educ. Loretto; Gonville and Caius College, Cambridge; Edinburgh University. National Service, 1951-53 (commissioned HLI); TA, Royal Scots, 1953-59; qualified Solicitor and WS, 1960; Assistant with various firms and local authorities, 1960-68; Partner, J.L. Anderson & Co., Solicitors, Cupar, Kinross, Glenrothes and Cowdenbeath, 1968-84. Lt. Cdr., RNR, 1966-85; Rugby Blue, Edinburgh University (played for Scottish Universities and Durham County). Recreations: rugby; squash; reading military history. Address: (h.) Ringwood House, 33A High Street, Auchtermuchty, Fife.

Eckford, James Millar, OBE, FCIS, FHSM, FIM, FRSA. Health Management Consultant; Executive Chairman, Carstairs Patient Advocacy Service; Chairman: Ayrshire Careers Partnership Ltd., Dalmellington and District Conservation Trust; Member, Board, Ayr College; Member, Board, East Ayshire Employment Initiative; District Secretary, Rotary District 1230; b. 8.7.36, Leith; m., Joan Miller. Educ. George Heriot's School, Edinburgh. District Administrator, East Fife District, Fife Health Board, 1974-79; Board Secretary, Forth Valley Health Board, 1979-85; Board General Manager, Ayrshire and Arran Health Board, 1985-95. Recreations: Rotary; bowling; fishing; curling; Ayr United. Address: (h.) 22 Abbots Way, Doonfoot, Ayr KA7 4EY; T.-01292 442323.

Eddie, Rev. Duncan Campbell, MA (Hons), BD (Hons). Minister, Old Cumnock: Crichton West linked with St. Ninian's, since 1992; b. 17.2.63, Fraserburgh; m., Dr. Carol Buchanan; 1 s. Educ. Mackie Academy, Stonehaven; Aberdeen University; Edinburgh University. Assistant Minister, Edinburgh, 1990-91. Recreations: music; reading. Address: 46 Ayr Road, Cumnock KA18 1DW; T.-01290 420119.

Edge, David Owen, BA, MA, PhD, FRSE, FRAS, FRSA. Reader Emeritus in Science Studies, since 1992, Edinburgh University; b. 4.9.32, High Wycombe; m., Barbara Corsie; 2 s.; 1 d. Educ. Aberdeen Grammar School; Leys School, Cambridge; Gonville and Caius College, Cambridge. Assistant Physics Master, Perse School, Cambridge; Producer, Science Unit, Talks Department, BBC Radio, London, 1959-66; Senior Fellow, Society for the Humanities, and Senior Research Associate, Science, Technology and Society Program, Cornell University, 1973; Reader in Science Studies, Edinburgh University, 1979-92.

Scottish HQ Adviser for Students, Scout Association, 1966-85; President (Past Chairman), Scout & Guide Graduate Association; Circuit Steward, Methodist Church, Edinburgh and Forth Circuit, 1983-86; Editor, Social Studies of Science, since 1971; Member: various CNAA panels and committees, since 1972, Edinburgh University Court, 1983-86, DQA Auditing Team, HEQC, 1991-93, ABRC Working Party on Peer Review, 1990-91; Chair, Board of Science Policy Support Group, 1989-93; President, Society for Social Studies of Science (4S), 1985-87. John Desmond Bernal Prize, 1993; Fellow, American Association for the Advancement of Science, 1989; Fellow, Royal Society of Edinburgh, 1992. Publications: Astronomy Transformed (Co-author), 1976; Science in Context (Co-Editor), 1982. Recreations: hill-walking; music; watching sport - especially soccer and baseball. Address: (h.) 25 Gilmour Road, Edinburgh EH16 5NS; T.-0131-667 3497.

Edgeler, Ian George, MIMgt. Director of Corporate Services, Royal Botanic Garden Edinburgh, since 1993; b. 2.12.49, Gravesend; m., Jane; 4 s. Educ. Springhead School; Britannia Royal Naval College, Dartmouth. Joined Royal Navy as Cadet Seaman Officer, 1968; specialised as aircrew (Observer), 1976; flying and specialist operations posts; promoted to Commander, 1988; retired from Royal Navy, 1993. Recreations: amateur gardener and exhibitor; travel; family pursuits. Address: (b.) Royal Botanic Garden Edinburgh, 20a Inverkeith Row, Edinburgh EH3 5LR; T.-0131-248 2877.

Edward, Judge David Alexander Ogilvy, CMG, QC, MA, LLD, FRSE. Judge of the Court of Justice of the European Communities, since 1992 (Judge of the Court of First Instance, 1989-92); Advocate, since 1962; b. 14.11.34, Perth; m., Elizabeth Young McSherry; 2 s.; 2 d. Educ. Sedbergh School; University College, Oxford (Hon. Fellow, 1995); Edinburgh University. National Service, RNVR, 1956-57 (Sub-Lt.); Clerk, Faculty of Advocates, 1967-70, Treasurer, 1970-77; President, Consultative Committee, Bars and Law Societies of the European Community, 1978-80; Salvesen Professor of European Institutions, Edinburgh University, 1985-89 (Hon. Professor, since 1990); Member: Law Advisory Committee, British Council, 1974-88, Panel of Arbitrators, International Centre for Settlement of Investment Disputes, 1981-89; Chairman, Continental Assets Trust plc, 1986-89; Director, Adam & Company plc, 1984-89; Director, Harris Tweed Association Ltd., 1985-89; Specialist Adviser to House of Lords Select Committee on the European Communities, 1985-88; Trustee: National Library of Scotland, 1966-95, Industry and Parliament Trust, since 1995, Carnegie Trust for the Universities of Scotland, since 1995, Hopetoun Foundation (Chairman, Hopetoun House Preservation Trust, 1988-92); President, Franco-Scottish Society, since 1996; Hon. President, Scottish Council for International Arbitration; President, Johnson Society, 1995-96. Hon. Bencher, Gray's Inn, 1992; Hon. LLD: Edinburgh University,1993, Aberdeen University, 1997, Napier University, 1998. Address: (h.) 32 Heriot Row, Edinburgh EH3 6ES; (b.) EC Court of Justice, L-2925 Luxembourg; T.-00-352-43032203.

Edward, Ian, MA, LLB. Consultant, Ledingham Chalmers, Solicitors, Aberdeen, since 1997; b. 3.9.35, Aberdeen; m., Marguerite Anne Leiper (deceased); 2 s.; 1 d. Educ. Robert Gordon's College, Aberdeen; University of Aberdeen; Fitzwilliam College, University of Cambridge. HM Colonial Service (District Officer, Northern Rhodesia), 1959-63; C. & P. H. Chalmers, Solicitors, Aberdeen (now Ledingham Chalmers): Legal Assistant, Partner, Senior Partner, 1963-97. Part-time Chairman of Employment Tribunals, since 1997; Chairman, Scottish Motor Neurone Disease Association; Trustee, Grampian Hospitals Art Trust; Archivist, Royal Aberdeen Golf Club. Recreations: golf; gardening. Address: (b.) 17 Golden Square, Aberdeen; T.-01224 408428.

Edwards, Frederick Edward, LVO, RD, DUniv, MUniv, FIMgt. President, Volunteer Development Scotland, since 1993; b. 9.4.31, Liverpool; 2 s.; 1 d. Educ. St. Edward's College, Liverpool; Glasgow University. Midshipman to Second Officer, Alfred Holt & Co., 1948-57; awarded Perm. Commn. RNR, 1953; Lt.-Cmdr., 1963; Reserve Decoration, 1972; Clasp, 1982; Management Trainee, Morgan Crucible Group, 1957-60; Probation Service, Liverpool, 1960-69; Director of Social Work: Joint County Council of Moray and Nairn, 1969-75, Grampian Region, 1975-76, Strathclyde Regional Council, 1976-93; Visiting Professor of Social Administration and Social Work, Glasgow University, 1988-93; Trustee, New Lanark Conservation Trust, since 1993; President, Disability Scotland, since 1995; Member: Board, East Region SEPA, 1996, Council, Scottish Wildlife Trust, 1994; Chairman, Capability Scotland, 1997. Awarded Hon. Doctorate, Paisley University, 1993. Recreations: hill-walking; natural history; Scottish country dancing. Address: (h.) Gardenfield, Ninemileburn, by Penicuik EH26 9LT; T.-01968 674566.

Edwards, George Lowden, CEng, MIMechE, MIEE, FIM, FInstPet, FRSA. Chairman, GPC Scotland; Associate, Smythe Dorward Lambert; Director: Network Scotland Limited, European Editions Ltd, SSK Conferences and Events; Trustee: Scottish Civic Trust, William Thyne Trust; b. 6.2.39, Kirriemuir; m., Sylvia Izatt; 1 d. Educ. Webster's Seminary, Kirriemuir; Dundee Institute of Technology. Production Engineer, Burroughs Machines Ltd., Cumbernauld, 1961-64; Development Division, Scottish Council (Development and Industry), Edinburgh, 1964-67; General Manager, GR Designs Ltd., Perth, 1967-68; London Director, Scottish Council (Development and Industry), 1968-78; Manager, Public Affairs Scotland, Conoco (UK) Ltd., Aberdeen, 1978-83; Manager, Public Affairs, Conoco (UK) Ltd., London, 1983-85; Head of Corporate Affairs, Clydesdale Bank PLC, 1988-96. Recreations: music; travel; food and wine. Address: (h.) 1 Back Dean, Ravelston Terrace, Edinburgh EH4 3UA.

Edwards, Gordon, MA, CPFA. Director of Finance, Aberdeen City Council, since 1996; b. 1.4.56, Aberdeen; m., Diane; 2 d. Educ. Aberdeen Grammar School. Assistant Director of Finance, Grampian Regional Council, 1991-96. Address: (b.) Town House, Broad Street, Aberdeen AB10 1AH.

Edwards, Neil, DMS, DCA, MITSA. Head of Trading Standards, Fife Council, since 1996; b. 6.10.45, Wrexham, N. Wales. Educ. Yale High School, Wrexham; Liverpool Polytechnic. Inspector of Weights and Measures, Denbighshire CC, 1967-74; Area Officer, Department of Trading Standards, Clywd CC, 1974-78; retail management, Italy, 1978-81; Trading Standards Officer, Durham CC, 1981-83; Principal Trading Standards Officer, West Midlands CC, 1983-86; Depute Director of Trading Standards, Dumfries and Galloway RC, 1986-88; Director of Trading Standards and Consumer Protection, Fife Regional Council, 1988-96. Recreation: sport. Address: (b.) Fife House (03), North Street, Glenrothes, Fife KY7 5LT; T.-01592 416353.

Edwards, Rob (Robert Philip), MA. Consultant, New Scientist, since 1994; Freelance Journalist, since 1980; Television Producer, since 1990; b. 13.10.53, Liverpool; m., Fiona Grant Riddoch; 2 d. Educ. Watford Boys Grammar School; Jesus College, University of Cambridge. Organiser, Scottish Campaign to Resist the Atomic Menace, 1977-78; Campaigns Organiser, Shelter (Scotland), 1978-80; Research Assistant to Robin Cook M.P., 1980-83; Freelance Journalist, writing for Social Work Today, The Scotsman, New Statesman, 1980-89; Environment Editor, Scotland on Sunday, 1989-94; Correspondent, The Guardian and Columnist, Edinburgh Evening News, 1989-94; Freelance Journalist, writing for New Scientist, Scotland on Sunday,

The Scotsman, The Observer etc., since 1994; Member, Scottish Advisory Council, World Wildlife Fund; various media awards. Publications: Co-author of three books, including Still Fighting for Gemma, 1995. Recreations: music; opera; mountains. Address: 53 Nile Grove, Edinburgh EH10 4RE; T.-0131-447 2796.

Edwards, Susan Spencer, MA (Oxon), DipHistArt, ACIS. Administrator, National Galleries of Scotland, since 1990; b. 25.8.46, London. Educ. Paddington & Maida Vale High School for Girls; Lady Margaret Hall, Oxford. Early career teaching; Tutor-Counsellor, Open University, 1977-80; joined North of Scotland College of Agriculture; Secretary and Treasurer, 1982-90. Publication: Biographical Dictionary of Scottish Painters. Recreations: clarinet; calligraphy; riding; cooking; theatre. Address: (b.) 13 Heriot Row, Edinburgh EH3 6HP; T.-0131-556 8921.

Eglinton and Winton, 18th Earl of (Archibald George Montgomerie); b. 27.8.39; m.; 4 s. Educ. Eton. Succeeded to title, 1966.

Eilbeck, Professor John Christopher, BA, PhD, FIMA, FRSE. Professor, Department of Mathematics, Heriot-Watt University, since 1986 (Head of Department, 1984-89, Dean of Science, since 1998); b. 8.4.45, Whitehaven; 3 s. Educ. Whitehaven Grammar School; Queen's College, Oxford; Lancaster University. Royal Society European Fellow, ICTP, Trieste, 1969-70; Research Assistant, Department of Mathematics, UMIST, Manchester, 1970-73; Heriot-Watt University: Lecturer, Department of Mathematics, 1973-80, Senior Lecturer, 1980-85, Reader, 1985-86; Long-term Visiting Fellow, Center for Nonlinear Studies, Los Alamos National Laboratory, New Mexico, 1983-84. Publications: Rock Climbing in the Lake District (Co-author), 1975; Solitons and Nonlinear Wave Equations (Co-author), 1982. Recreation: mountaineering. Address: (b.) Department of Mathematics, Heriot-Watt University, Riccarton, Edinburgh EH14 4AS; T.-0131-451 3220.

Elder, Derek Ian, BSc, CEng, MICE, FRSA. Deputy Chief Executive, Scottish Financial Enterprise, since 1996; Member, Board, Advanced Management Programme in Scotland, since 1997; Member, Board, Scottish Environment Protection Agency, West Region, since 1997; b. 11.7.54, Lennoxtown; divorced; 1 s.; 1 d. Educ. Allan Glen's School, Glasgow; Paisley College of Technology. Apprentice, Crouch and Hogg Consulting Engineers, Glasgow, 1972-75; Strathclyde Regional Council, 1975-78; Scottish Development Agency, 1981-90; Dumbartonshire Enterprise, 1991-94; Director, Strathkelvin Development Company, 1991-94; Assistant Director, CBI Scotland, 1994-97. Member, Board of Academic Standards, Faculty of Business, Bell College of Technology; Member, Executive Committee, Association of European Finance Centres. Recreations: reading; travel; computers; family. Address: (h.) 51 Orchard Brae Avenue, Edinburgh EH4 2HR.

Elder, Dorothy-Grace. Columnist, Scotland on Sunday, Scottish Daily Express, and Daily Express; Television Scriptwriter and Producer; m., George Welsh; 1 s.; 2 d. D.C. Thomson newspapers; Glasgow Herald as reporter, news feature writer, leader writer; TV and radio news, BBC Scotland; feature writer and columnist, Scottish Daily News Co-operative; freelance feature writer and columnist, Sunday Mail; productions for Scotland and the network, BBC and Scottish TV. Trustee, Yorkhill Children's Fund, Royal Hospital for Sick Children; Member, ACHE UK Committee (opposing child pornography); Oliver Award winning columnist, 1995-96; British Reporter of the Year, UK Press Awards, 1996-97; SNP Candidate, Scottish Parliament, 1998. Address: Scotland on Sunday, 20 North Bridge, Edinburgh EH1 1YT.

Elders, Rev. (Iain) Alasdair, MA, BD. Minister, Broughton St. Mary's Parish Church, Edinburgh, since 1992; b. 17.4.39, Sunderland; m., Hazel Stewart Steven; 1 s.; 1 d. Educ. Daniel Stewart's College, Edinburgh; Edinburgh University. Assistant Minister: Edinburgh: St. Andrew's, 1961-63, Edinburgh: High (St. Giles Cathedral), 1963-65; Minister, Cumbernauld: Abronhill (church extension charge), 1965-73; Minister, Edinburgh: Broughton McDonald, 1973-92; Secretary, Cumbernauld Council of Churches, 1967-72; Chairman: Council of East End Churches of Edinburgh, 1978-82, New Town Community Council, 1986-89 and since 1992; Scout Commissioner, 1966-90; Secretary, East End Churches Together, since 1989; Vice-Chairman, Edinburgh and East of Scotland Society for the Deaf, 1978-97; Moderator, Edinburgh Presbytery, 1994. Address: Broughton St. Mary's Manse, 103 East Claremont Street, Edinburgh EH7 4JA; T.-0131-556 7313.

Elgin, 11th Earl of, and Kincardine, 15th Earl of, (Andrew Douglas Alexander Thomas Bruce), KT (1981), DL, JP; 37th Chief of the Name of Bruce; Lord Lieutenant of Fife, since 1987; Lieutenant, Queen's Bodyguard for Scotland (Royal Company of Archers); President, Royal Scottish Automobile Club; b. 17.2.24; m., Victoria Usher; 3 s.; 2 d. Educ. Eton; Balliol College, Oxford. President, Scottish Amicable Life Assurance Society, 1975-94; Chairman, National Savings Committee for Scotland, 1972-78; Member, Scottish Postal Board, 1980-96; Lord High Commissioner, General Assembly, Church of Scotland, 1980-81; Grand Master Mason of Scotland, 1961-65; President, Royal Caledonian Curling Club, 1968-69; Hon. LLD, Dundee, 1977, Glasgow, 1983. Address: (h.) Broomhall, Dunfermline KY11 3DU.

Eliott of Redheugh, Margaret Frances Boswell. Chief of Clan Elliot; Chairman, Elliot Clan Society and Sir Arthur Eliott Memorial Trust; b. 13.11.48; m., 1, Anthony Vaughan-Arbuckle (deceased); 1 s.; 1 d.; 2, Christopher Powell Wilkins. Educ. Hatherop Castle School. Address: Redheugh, Newcastleton, Roxburghshire.

Ellington, Marc Floyd, DL. Baron of Towie Barclay; Laird of Gardenstown and Crovie; Deputy Lieutenant, Aberdeenshire, since 1984; b. 16.12.45; m., Karen Leigh; 2 d. Member: British Heritage Commission (representing Scottish Tourist Board), Historic Buildings Council for Scotland, Heritage Lottery Fund Committee for Scotland; Vice-President, Buchan Heritage Society; Chairman: Grampian Regional Council Tourism Task Force, 1992-96, Heritage Press (Scotland), Soundcraft Audio; Director: Gardenstown Estates Ltd., Heritage Sound Recordings; Director, Grampian Enterprise Ltd., 1992-96; Communications, Tourism and Heritage Consultant. Saltire Award, 1973; Civic Trust Award, 1975; European Architectural Heritage Award, 1975; SBStJ; FSA. Recreations: sailing; historic architecture; art collecting; music. Address: Towie Barclay Castle, Auchterless, Turriff, Aberdeenshire AB53 8EP; T.-01888 511347.

Elliot, Alison Janet, MA, MSc, PhD. Convener, Church and Nation Committee, Church of Scotland, since 1996; Vice-Convener, ACTS Commission on Justice, Peace, Social and Moral Issues, since 1995; Member, Central Committee, Conference of European Churches, since 1997; b. 27.11.48, Edinburgh; m., John Christian Elliot; 1 s.; 1 d. Educ. Bathgate Academy; Edinburgh University; Sussex University. Research Associate, Department of Linguistics, Edinburgh University, 1973-74; Lecturer in Psychology, Lancaster University, 1974-76, Edinburgh University, 1977-85; Member, Church of Scotland's Committee on Church and Nation, since 1988; Elder, Greyfriars Kirk, Edinburgh. Publication: Child Language, 1981. Recreations: music; cookery. Address: (b.) Church of Scotland Offices, 121 George Street, Edinburgh EH2 4YN; T.-0131-225 5722.

Elliot, Frances Mary, MB, ChB, DRCOG, DCH. Medical Director, Fife Healthcare NHS Trust; Principal in general practice, 1987-98; Non-executive Member, Board, HEBS, since 1996; b. 13.4.60, Edinburgh; m., John Gordon Elliot. Educ. St. Columba's High School, Dunfermline; Glasgow University. Hon. Secretary, Fife Local Medical Committee, 1990-97; Member, BMA Scottish Council, 1994-97. Recreations: hill-walking; cycling; swimming; photography. Address: (h.) 10 Durie Vale, Windygates, Leven KY8 5EF; T.-01333 351509.

Elliot, Sir Gerald Henry; b. 24.12.23, Edinburgh; m., Margaret Ruth Whale; 2 s.; 1 d. Educ. Marlborough College; New College, Oxford. Chairman: Christian Salvesen PLC, 1981-88, Scottish Provident Institution, 1983-89, Scottish Arts Council, 1980-86, Prince's Scottish Youth Business Trust, 1987-94; Vice Chairman, Scottish Business in the Community, 1987-89; Trustee, National Museums of Scotland, 1987-91; Member of Court, Edinburgh University, 1984-93; Chairman: Scottish Unit Managers Ltd., 1984-88, Martin Currie Unit Trusts, 1988-90; Chairman, Forth Ports Authority, 1973-79; Chairman, Scottish Opera, 1987-92; Chairman of Trustees, David Hume Institute, 1985-95; Chairman, Institute of Directors, Scottish Division, 1989-92; Trustee and Director, Edinburgh Festival Theatre, 1995-98; Member, Court of Regents, Royal College of Surgeons, since 1990; President, UN50 Scotland, 1994-95; Fellow, Royal Society of Edinburgh, since 1977; Honorary Consul for Finland in Edinburgh and Leith, 1957-89; Hon. d.h.c., Edinburgh University, 1989; Hon. LLD, Aberdeen University, 1991. Address: (b.) 8 Howe Street, Edinburgh EH3 6TD; T.-0131-220 3739.

Elliot, John. Farmer; Vice Chairman, British Wool Marketing Board and Member for Southern Scotland; b. 29.5.47, Duns, Berwickshire; m., Joan Kathleen Wight; 1 s.; 1 d. Educ. St. Mary School, Melrose; Edinburgh Academy. Nuffield Scholar, US and Canada, 1982. Recreations: spectator sports; reading; writing; agriculture. Address: Roxburgh Mains, Kelso TD5 8NJ.

Elliot, Robert John, LLB, WS. Solicitor; Chairman, Scottish Committee, Council on Tribunals, since 1998; Deputy Keeper of W.S. Society, since 1999; b. 18.1.47, Edinburgh; m., Christine; 1 s.; 1 d. Educ. Loretto School; Edinburgh University. Partner, Lindsays WS, since 1973; President, Law Society of Scotland, 1997-98. Recreations: golf; Scottish country dancing; detective novels; argument. Address: (b.) 11 Atholl Crescent, Edinburgh EH3 8HE; T.-0131-229 1212.

Elliott, Professor Alex, BA, PhD, DSc, CPhys, FInstP, FIPEM. Director, West of Scotland Health Boards' Department of Clinical Physics and Bioengineering, since 1990 (Clinical Director, Laboratory Medicine and Clinical Physics, since 1996); Professor of Clinical Physics, Glasgow University, since 1991; b. 1.2.49, Edinburgh; m., Barbara; 2 d. Educ. Trinity Academy, Edinburgh; Stirling University; Glasgow University. Temporary Lecturer, Nuclear Medicine Unit, Strathclyde University, 1974-75; Lecturer in Nuclear Medicine, Middlesex Hospital Medical School, 1975-77; Principal Physicist, Department of Nuclear Medicine, St. Bartholomew's Hospital, London, 1977-81; Chief Physicist, Western Infirmary/Gartnavel General Hospital, Glasgow, 1981-90. Publications: 200 papers and presentations. Recreations: cycling; orienteering; squash. Address: (b.) 22 Western Court, 100 University Place, Glasgow G12 8SQ; T.-0141-211 2948.

Elliott, Rev. Gavin John, MA, BD. Minister, Biggar Kirk, since 1995; Convenor, Sub-Saharan Africa Committee, Board of World Mission, Church of Scotland, since 1995; b. 12.6.50, Perth; m., Rachel Ann Jones; 2 s.; 2 d. Educ. Perth Academy; Aberdeen University. Minister, Carntyne Old, 1976-82; Missionary, United Church of Zambia, 1982-89; Minister, South Uist, 1989-95. WCC Delegate to WCC Assembly, 1998. Recreations: hill-walking; music. Address: 61 High Street, Biggar ML12 6DA; T.-01899 220227.

Elliott, Professor Robert F., BA (Oxon), MA. Professor of Economics, Aberdeen University, since 1990; b. 15.6.47, Thurlow, Suffolk; m., Susan Elliott Gutteridge; 1 s. Educ. Haverhill Secondary Modern School, Suffolk; Ruskin College and Balliol College, Oxford; Leeds University. Joined Aberdeen University, 1973, as Research Fellow, then Lecturer; Chair, Review of Area Cost Adjustment commissioned by Department of the Environment; acted as Consultant to numerous public and private sector organisations, including Megaw Committee of Inquiry into Civil Service Pay, the EEC Commission, HM Treasury OECD, Highlands and Islands Development Board, on issues of pay and employment. Publications: books on Pay in the Public Sector, 1981; Incomes Policies, Inflation and Relative Pay, 1981; Incomes Policy, 1981; Unemployment and Labour Market Efficiency, 1989; Labour Market Analysis, 1990. Recreations: music; reading; golf. Address: (h.) 11 Richmondhill Place, Aberdeen AB15 5EN; T.-01224 314901.

Elliott, Hon. Lord (Walter Archibald Elliott), QC, MC, BL. President, Lands Tribunal for Scotland, 1971-92; Chairman, Scottish Land Court, 1978-92; Ensign, Queen's Bodyguard for Scotland (Royal Company of Archers); b. 6.9.22, London; m., Susan Isobel MacKenzie Ross; 2 s. Educ. Eton College; Edinburgh University. 2nd Bn., Scots Guards, 1943-45 (Staff Captain, 1947); Advocate and at the Inner Temple, Barrister-at-Law, 1950; QC (Scotland), 1963; conducted Edinburgh ring road inquiry, 1967. Publications: Us and Them: a study of group consciousness, 1986; Esprit de Corps, 1995. Recreations: gardening; shooting. Address: (h.) Morton House, 19 Winton Loan, Edinburgh EH10 7AW; T.-0131-445 2548.

Ellis, Charles William, OBE, BA (Hons), LLD. Chairman, Grampian Health Board, 1982-89; Member, Whitley Council for Professions Allied to Medicine, 1987-89; b. 15.11.21, Horsham, Sussex; m., Maureen Patricia Radley; 1 s.; 3 d. Educ. Oxted County School; University College London. Indian Army and Royal Artillery, 1941-64; completed degree in modern history, 1964-66 (begun in 1940-41); Junior Lecturer to Head, School of Social Studies, Robert Gordon's Institute of Technology, Aberdeen, 1966-85. Councillor, City of Aberdeen, 1971-75 (Convener, Education Committee, 1974-75); Councillor, Grampian Regional Council, 1974-78 (Leader, Labour Group). Recreations: International affairs; family; genealogy. Address: (h.) 78 Kirk Brae, Cults, Aberdeen AB15 9QQ; T.-Aberdeen 861581.

Ellis, Richard Tunstall, OBE, TD, DL, MA, LLB, LLD (Hon); b. 6.9.18, Liverpool; m., Jean Bruce Maitland Porter (deceased); 2 s.; 2 d. Educ. Merchant Taylors School, Crosby; Silcoates School, Wakefield; Aberdeen University. Captain, Royal Signals, 1939-45 (POW, Germany); Partner, Paull & Williamsons, Advocates, Aberdeen, 1949-83, Senior Partner, 1970-83; Chairman: Trustee Savings Bank Scotland, 1983-86, TSB Scotland p.l.c., 1986-89; Director, TSB Group p.l.c., 1986-89; Chairman, Board of Governors, Dunfermline College of Physical Education, 1964-67; Governor, Aberdeen College of Education, 1969-75; Member: Scottish Board, Norwich Union Insurance Society, 1973-80, Aberdeen Board, Bank of Scotland, 1972-82, Aberdeen University Court, 1984-93, Council, National Trust for Scotland, 1984-89; Chairman, Scottish Division, Institute of Directors, 1988-89. Recreations: golf; hill-walking; skiing. Address: (h.) 18 Rubislaw Den North, Aberdeen AB15 4AN; T.-01224 316680.

Ellison, Rosemary E. H., LRAM, DipRAM. Member, Scottish Chamber Orchestra, since 1982; Violin Teacher: Royal Scottish Academy of Music Junior School, since

1993, St. Mary's Music School, Edinburgh, since 1996; b. 29.7.40, Sherborne, Dorset. Educ. Sherborne School for Girls, Dorset; Royal Academy of Music, London. Bath Festival/Menuhin Festival Orchestra, 1966-76; staff, Yehudi Menuhin School, 1964-72; Academy of St. Martin in the Fields, 1972-82. Director: Scottish Chamber Orchestra, since 1985, Queens Hall Co. Edinburgh, since 1985. Recreations: skiing; hillwalking; gardening. Address: 12 St. Bernard's Row, Edinburgh EH4 1HW.

Elphinstone, 19th Lord (Alexander Mountstuart Elphinstone); b. 15.4.80. Succeeded to title, 1994.

Elson, Stephen, BA, AMA, FMA, FSA Scot. Head of Buildings and Museum Services, National Museums of Scotland, since 1990; b. 7.5.49, Burton on Trent; m., Nicola Eddy; 1 s.; 1 d. Educ. Burton on Trent Grammar School; University of Leeds. Museum Curator, University of Strathclyde, 1973-75; Depute Keeper of Decorative Art, Glasgow Museums and Art Galleries, 1975-79; Director, Scottish Craft Centre, 1979-81; Director, North of England Museums Service, 1981-90. Recreations: music; painting; reading. Address (b.) Chambers Street, Edinburgh EH1 1JF; T.-0131-247 4152.

Embrey, John Derek, FCA, MCT. Director, Nimrod House Ltd., since 1994; b. 14.7.45, Shrewsbury; m., Carol Anne. Educ. Bishop Vesey's School. Finance Director, Dawson International PLC, 1983-94; Member, Investment Committee, Carnegie Trust for the Universities in Scotland. Recreations: equestrian activities; theatre. Address: (b.) Nimrod House, Muckhart, Dollar, Clackmannanshire FK14 7JN.

Emmanuel, Professor Clive Robert, BSc (Econ), MA, PhD, ACIS. Professor of Accounting and Director of CIFA; Adjunct Professor, Deakin University, Australia, since 1997; b. 23.5.47; m.; 1 s.; 2 d. Educ. UWIST; Lancaster University; UCW, Aberystwyth. Steel Company of Wales, Port Talbot, 1964-68; Lecturer, Lancaster University, 1974-78; Senior Lecturer, then Reader, UCW, Aberystwyth, 1978-87; Associate Professor, University of Kansas, 1980-82. Address: (b.) Department of Accounting and Finance, Glasgow University, Glasgow.

Emslie, Donald, BEd (Hons). Managing Director, Broadcasting, Scottish Media Group; b. Aberdeen; m., Sarah Gardner; 2 d. Educ. Inverness High School. Commercial Director, Scottish Television; Sales Controller, TV MM; Account Director, TV MM; Sales Director, Time Exchange; Deputy Chairman and Chief Executive, Grampian Television. Address: (b.) Scottish Media Group PLC, Cowcaddens, Glasgow G2 3AZ.

Emslie, Rt. Hon. Lord (George Carlyle), MBE, PC, LLD, FRSE. Lord Justice General of Scotland, 1972-89; Lord President of the Court of Session, 1972-89; b. 6.12.19, Glasgow; m., Lilias Ann Mailer Hannington (deceased); 3 s. Educ. High School of Glasgow; Glasgow University. Commissioned A. & S.H., 1940; served War of 1939-45 (Despatches), North Africa, Italy, Greece, Austria, 1942-46; p.s.c. Haifa, 1944; Brigade Major (Infantry), 1944-46; Advocate, 1948; Advocate-Depute (Sheriff Courts), 1955; QC (Scotland), 1957; Sheriff of Perth and Angus, 1963-66; Dean, Faculty of Advocates, 1965-70; Senator of the College of Justice, 1970-72; Chairman, Scottish Agricultural Wages Board, 1969-73; Member, Council on Tribunals (Scottish Committee), 1962-70; Hon. Bencher, Inner Temple, 1974, and Inn of Court of N. Ireland, 1981; PC, 1972; Baron (Life Peer), created 1980. Recreation: golf. Address: (h.) 47 Heriot Row, Edinburgh EH3 6EX; T.-0131-225 3657.

Emslie, Hon. (George) Nigel (Hannington), QC. Dean, Faculty of Advocates, since 1997; b. 17.4.47. Admitted, Faculty of Advocates, 1972. Address: (b.) Faculty of Advocates, Advocates' Library, Parliament House, Edinburgh EH1 1RF; T.-0131-260 5658.

Emslie-Smith, Donald, OStJ, MD (Hons), FRCP, FRCPEdin, FSA Scot. Honorary Fellow, Dundee University (Reader in Medicine, 1971-87, Head, Department of Medicine, 1986-87); Honorary Consultant Physician (Cardiologist), Tayside Health Board, 1961-87; b. 12.4.22, Aberdeen; m., Ann Elizabeth Milne; 1 s.; 1 d. Educ. Trinity College, Glenalmond; Aberdeen University. House Physician, Aberdeen Royal Infirmary; RAFVR (Medical Branch), UK and Middle East; Registrar in Cardiology, Dundee Royal Infirmary; Edward Wilson Memorial Research Fellow, Baker Institute, Melbourne; Tutor and Senior Registrar in Medicine, Royal Postgraduate Medical School and Hammersmith Hospital, London; Senior Lecturer in Medicine, St. Andrews University. Member for Scotland, Executive Committee, Association of Physicians of Great Britain and Ireland, 1977-80; Chairman, British Cardiac Society, 1987; President, Harveian Society of Edinburgh, 1986-87, Harveian Orator, 1987. Publications: Textbook of Physiology (Co-author and Editor) (8th to 11th editions); Accidental Hypothermia, 1977. Recreations: fly-fishing; dinghy-sailing; music; painting. Address: (b.) University Department of Medicine, Ninewells Hospital and Medical School, Dundee DD1 9SY; T.-01382 660111.

Engeset, Jetmund, FRCSE, FRCSG. Consultant Surgeon, Grampian Health Board, since 1987; Surgeon to the Queen in Scotland, since 1985; b. 22.7.38.

Entwistle, Professor Noel James, BSc, PGCE, PhD, FilDr (h.c.), FBPsS. Bell Professor of Education, Edinburgh University, since 1978; Director, Centre for Research on Learning and Instruction, since 1978; b. 26.12.36, Bolton; m., Dorothy Bocking; 1 d. Educ. King's School, Ely; Sheffield University; Aberdeen University. Teacher, Rossall School, Fleetwood, 1961-64; Research Fellow, Aberdeen University, 1964-68; Department of Educational Research, Lancaster University: Lecturer, 1968, Senior Lecturer, 1971, Professor, 1972. Editor: British Journal of Educational Psychology, 1975-79, Higher Education, 1993-98. Recreations: reading; walking; golf. Address: (b.) 10 Buccleuch Place, Edinburgh EH8 9JT; T.-0131-650 4333.

Entwistle, Raymond Marvin, FCIB. Managing Director, Adam & Company Group Plc, since 1993; b. 12.6.44, Croydon; m., Barbara Joan Hennessy; 2 s.; 1 d. Educ. John Ruskin Grammar School. Several managerial appointments with Lloyds Bank. Governor, Edinburgh College of Art; Chairman, Fruit Market Gallery, Edinburgh; Non-executive Director: John Davidson (Holdings) Ltd, 1992-96, JW International Plc., 1995-96. Recreations: golf; shooting; fishing; antiques. Address: (b.) 22 Charlotte Square, Edinburgh EH2 4DF; T.-0131-225 8484.

Erdal, David Edward, MA, MBA. Director, Tullis Russell & Co. Ltd. (Chairman, 1985-96); Chairman: Job Ownership Ltd., Baxi Partnership Ltd., Tayburn Ltd.; Director, China Heartland Fund; b. 29.3.48, Umtali, Zimbabwe; 1 s.; 1 d. Educ. Glenalmond; Brasenose College, Oxford; Harvard Business School. English Language Teacher, London, 1972-74; Tianjin Foreign Language Institute, People's Republic of China, 1974-76; joined Tullis Russell, 1977. Trustee, Baxi Partnership; Fellow, Royal Society of Arts. Recreations: sailing; skiing; reading. Address: (h.) West Court, Hepburn Gardens, St Andrews KY16 9LN; T.-01334 473724.

Erickson, Professor John, MA, FRSE, FBA, FRSA. Honorary Fellow, Centre for Defence Studies, Edinburgh University; b. 17.4.29, South Shields; m., Ljubica; 1 s.; 1 d. Educ. South Shields High School; St. John's College, Cambridge. Research Fellow, St. Antony's College, Oxford; Lecturer, Department of History, St. Andrews University; Lecturer/Reader, Department of Government,

Manchester University; Reader/Professor, Defence Studies, Edinburgh University. President, Association of Civil Defence and Emergency Planning Officers, until 1984; Visiting Professor, Yale University, 1987; Hon. Fellow, Aerospace Academy of Ukraine, 1995. Publications: The Soviet High Command, 1962; The Road to Stalingrad, 1975; The Road to Berlin, 1984; Soviet Ground Forces, An Operational Assessment, 1986; Barbarossa, The Axis and the Allies (Editor and Contributor), 1994; The Soviet Armed Forces, 1918–1992: Research Guide to Soviet Forces (jointly), 1996; The Russian General Staff 1716-1998, forthcoming. Recreation: model-making. Address: (b.) 13 Ravelston House Road, Edinburgh EH4 3LP; T.-0131-650 4263.

Eriksen, Gunn; b. 28.12.56, Grimstad, Norway; m., Fred Brown. Educ. Grimstad, Norway; tutored in ceramics by Rolf Tiemroth. Worked as ceramicist in Norway and Scotland; exhibited ceramics and weaving in Norway; since 1980 has run Altnaharrie Inn with Fred Brown; various awards, including maximum ratings in Good Food Guide, AA Restaurant Guide, Egon Ronay etc. Recreations: reading; sailing; skiing; design. Address: (b.) Altnaharrie Inn, Ullapool IV26 2SS; T.-01854 633230.

Ermarth, Professor Elizabeth Deeds, BA, MA, PhD. Saintsbury Professor of English Literature, Edinburgh University, since 1994; b. 30.11.39, Denver, Colorado; m., Professor Thomas Vargish; 1 s. Educ. Carleton College, Minn.; University of California at Berkeley; University of Chicago. Taught at Northwestern University, Illinois, 1969-71; Dartmouth College, New Hampshire, 1972-74; Reed College, Oregon, 1974-78; University of Maryland, Baltimore, 1979-94 (Presidential Research Professor, 1991-95); Fullbright Senior Fellow and Overseas Fellow, Churchill College, Cambridge, 1992-93. Publications: numerous works of cultural history and theory, including: The English Novel in History, 1840-1895; Sequel to History: Postmodernism and the Crisis of Representational Time; George Elliot; Realism and Consensus in the English Novel. Recreations: visual arts; music; hiking; travel. Address: (b.) English Department, Edinburgh University, David Hume Tower, George Square, Edinburgh, EH8 9JX; T.-0131-650 3612/3618; (h.) T.-0131-447 0617.

Erroll, 24th Earl of (Merlin Sereld Victor Gilbert Hay). Hereditary Lord High Constable of Scotland; b. 20.4.48; m.; 2 s.; 2 d. Educ. Eton; Trinity College, Cambridge. Succeeded to title, 1978.

Erskine, Donald Seymour, DL, FRICS. Factor and Director of Estates, National Trust for Scotland, 1961-89; b. 28.5.25, London; m., Catharine Annandale McLelland; 1 s. 4 d. Educ. Wellington College. RA (Airborne), 1943-47 (Captain); Pupil, Drumlanrig Estate, 1947-49; Factor, Country Gentlemen's Association, Edinburgh, 1950-55; Factor to Mr A.L.P.F. Wallace, 1955-61. Member, Queen's Bodyguard for Scotland (Royal Company of Archers); Deputy Lieutenant, Perth and Kinross; Elder and General Trustee, Church of Scotland. Recreations: golf; shooting; singing. Address: (h.) Cleish House, Cleish, Kinrossshire KY13 7LR; T.-01577 850232.

Ervine, Professor David Alan, BSc, PhD, CEng, MICE, MCIWEM, MASCE. Professor of Water Engineering, University of Glasgow, since 1997; b. 9.4.49, Rathfriland, N. Ireland; m., Elizabeth; 1 s. Educ. Banbridge Academy; Queen's University, Belfast. Assistant Lecturer, Queen's University, Belfast, 1973-75; Babtie Group, Consulting Engineers, Glasgow, 1975-78; Lecturer, University of Edinburgh, 1978-79; joined University of Glasgow 1979: Lecturer then Senior Lecturer. Former Chair, Scottish Hydraulics Study Group; James Forrest Medal and James Watt Medal, Institution of Civil Engineers. Recreations: jogging; dinner parties; Glasgow Rangers; visiting USA; writing. Address: Department of Civil Engineering, University of Glasgow, Glasgow G12 8LT; T.-0141-330 5210.

Eva, David, BCom, CPFA. Director of Finance, Shetland Health Board, since 1974; b. 2.12.42, Romford; m., Marina; 2 s. Educ. Merchant Taylors; University of Liverpool. Auditor, Halifax Borough Council; Zetland County Council: Assistant County Treasurer, Depute County Treasurer. Past President, Shetland Rotary Club; Treasurer, Lerwick Methodist Church. Recreations: bird-watching; record collecting; foreign travel. Address: (b.) Brevik House, South Road, Lerwick, Shetland ZE1 0RB; T.-01595 696767.

Evans, David Pugh, ARCA, RSA, RSW; paints in Edinburgh; b. 20.11.42, Gwent. Educ. Newbridge Grammar School; Newport College of Art; Royal College of Art. Lecturer, Edinburgh College of Art, 1965-68; Fine Art Fellow, York University, 1968-69; Lecturer, Edinburgh College of Art, since 1969; travelled and painted throughout USA, 1975; solo exhibitions: Marjorie Parr Gallery, London; Mercury Gallery, London; York University; Fruitmarket Gallery, Edinburgh; Open Eye Gallery, Edinburgh. Address: (h.) 17 Inverleith Gardens, Edinburgh EH3 5PS; T.-0131-552 2329.

Evans, James, MBE, RD, DL, BSc, CEng, FRINA, MIMechE. Managing Director: Thomas Evans (Berwick) Ltd.; Consultant Naval Architect, since 1990; b. 9.5.33, South Shields; m., Patricia Alexena Kerr; 1 s.; 2 d. Educ. Merchiston Castle School; Kings College, Durham. Apprenticeship, 1950-56; Royal Navy, 1956-58; YARD, 1958-63; UKAEA, 1963-68; RNR, 1956-80 (retired as Captain (E) RNR); Member, Eyemouth Burgh Council, 1972-75; Berwickshire County Council; Chairman, Berwickshire District Council; Managing Director, Eyemouth Boat Building Co. Ltd., 1988-90; Deputy Lieutenant, Berwickshire, since 1978; Chairman: Berwick Freemen's Guild, since 1975, Fishing Boat Builders Association, 1979-90, Berwickshire District Council, 1980-96; Lord President, Court of Deans of Guild Scotland, 1994-95. Awarded Silver Medal, Nuclear Engineering Society, 1962; Hon ADC, The Queen, 1979-80. Address: (h.) Makore, Northburn View, Eyemouth, Berwickshire; T.-Eyemouth 50231.

Eveling, Stanley, BA, BPhil. Fellow, Edinburgh University; Playwright; b. 4.8.25, Newcastle upon Tyne; m., Kate Howell; 2 s.; 2 d. Educ. King's College, Durham University; Lincoln College, Oxford. Recreations: golf; tennis; going abroad. Address: (b.) 30 Comely Bank, Edinburgh EH4 1AJ.

Everett, Peter, BSc (Hons), SPMB. Director: Scottish Hydro-Electric, since 1989, Forth Ports Authority, since 1989, Edinburgh Java Trust plc, since 1995, Ramco Energy Ltd., since 1993; b. 24.9.31, London; m., Annette Patricia Hyde; 3 s.; 1 d. Educ. George Watson's College; Edinburgh University. Royal Engineers, 1953-55 (2nd Lt.); joined Shell International Petroleum Company, 1955; Managing Director: Brunei Shell Petroleum Co. Ltd., 1979-84, Shell UK Exploration and Production, 1985-89; retired, 1989. Honorary Professor, Heriot Watt University, 1989. Recreation: golf. Address: (h.) Cluain, Castleton Road, Auchterarder, Perthshire PH3 1JW.

Ewing, David John, MA, MD, FRCP(Ed). Senior Medical Officer, Scottish Office Department of Health; b. 27.8.40, London; m., E. Anne Bellamy; 2 d. Educ. Dulwich College; Jesus College, Cambridge; Guy's Hospital, London. Lecturer in Medicine, Edinburgh University, 1970-80; Wellcome Trust Senior Lecturer in Medicine, Edinburgh University, and Hon. Consultant Physician, Lothian Health Board, 1980-91. Castelli-Pedroli Prize, 1987, European Association for the Study of Diabetes. Recreations:

walking; reading; cathedral and church architecture. Address: (b.) Scottish Office Department of Health, St. Andrew's House, Edinburgh EH1 3DE.

Ewing of Kirkford, Lord (Harry Ewing), DL. Deputy Lord Lieutenant, Fife, since 1995; Joint Chair, Scottish Constitutional Convention, 1987-96; b. 20.1.31; m., Margaret; 1 s.; 1 d. MP (Labour), Stirling and Falkirk Burghs, 1971-74, Stirling, Falkirk and Grangemouth, 1974-83, Falkirk East, 1983 92; Under Secretary of State for Scotland, 1974-79; Opposition Spokesman on Scottish Affairs, 1979-83, UK Trade and Industry, 1983-84, Scottish Affairs, 1984-87; Chairman, Ewing Inquiry into availability of housing for wheelchair disabled, since 1993; Chairman, Scottish Disability Foundation, since 1994; Member, Council of Europe, 1987-92; Opposition Spokesman on Transport and Scottish Affairs, House of Lords, since 1992; Hon. Doctorate, Stirling University, 1998. Address: (h.) Gowanbank, 45 Glenlyon Road, Leven KY8 4AA.

Ewing, Margaret Anne, MA, BA (Hons). MP (Moray), since 1987; Parliamentary Leader, SNP, since 1987; b. 1.9.45, Lanark; m., Fergus Stewart Ewing. Educ. Biggar High School; Glasgow University; Strathclyde University; Jordanhill College. Schoolteacher, 1968-74 (Principal Teacher of Remedial Education, St. Modan's, Stirling, 1972-74); SNP MP (East Dunbartonshire), 1974-79; Freelance Journalist, 1979-81; Co-ordinator, West of Scotland CSS Scheme, 1981-87. Recreations: gardening; reading; arts in general. Address: (h.) Burns Cottage, Tulloch's Lane, Tulloch's Brae, Lossiemouth, Moray IV31 6QY; T.-0134381 3218/2222.

Ewing, Winifred Margaret, MA, LLB, NP. Member (SNP), European Parliament, since 1975; President, European Free Alliance; President, Scottish National Party; b. 10.7.29, Glasgow; m., Stewart Martin Ewing; 2 s.; 1 d. Educ. Queen's Park School; Glasgow University. Solicitor, since 1952; former Secretary and President, Glasgow Bar Association; President, Soroptimist Club (Glasgow), 1966; MP (SNP), Hamilton, 1967-70, Moray and Nairn, 1974-79; Doctor, Open University; Doctor of Laws, Glasgow University. Recreations: walking; reading; painting; swimming. Address: (h.) Goodwill, Miltonduff, Elgin IV30 3TL.

F

Fair, James Stuart, CBE, MA, LLB, WS, LLD. Solicitor; formerly Senior Partner, Thorntons, WS, Dundee; Honorary Sheriff and Temporary Sheriff; b. 30.9.30, Perth; m., Anne Lesley Cameron; 2 s.; 1 d. Educ. Perth Academy; St. Andrews University; Edinburgh University. Past Chairman: University Court, Dundee, Review Committee, Perth Prison, Dundee Port Authority, Dundee Teaching Hospitals NHS Trust; Past President: Dundee and Tayside Chamber of Commerce & Industry, Dundee Choral Union; former Member, Scottish Solicitors' Discipline Tribunal; former Member, Committee on Medical Ethics, Ninewells Hospital and Medical School, Dundee; former Clerk, Commissioners of Inland Revenue (Dundee District); Trustee, Sir James Caird's Travelling Scholarship Trust; Chairman, Dundee Incubator Company; Hon. Doctor of Laws, Dundee University. Address: (h.) Beechgrove House, 474 Perth Road, Dundee DD2 1LL.

Fairbairn, Alasdair Chisholm, MA (Hons). Chief Executive, Sea Fish Industry Authority, since 1997; b. 23.1.40, Calcutta, India; m., Henriette Tichelman; 2 s.; 1 d. Educ. Trinity College, Glenalmond; Corpus Christi College, Cambridge. Managing Director, Conimex BV, Netherlands, 1975-78; Reckitt and Colman plc: Chief Manager, Planning and Evaluation, 1978-80, Regional Director, 1980-84; Director, LR Overseas Ltd., 1984-91; Chief Executive, Potato Marketing Board, 1991-97. Address: (b.) 18 Logie Mill, Logie Green Road, Edinburgh EH7 4HG; T.-0131-558 3331.

Fairbairn, The Hon. Mrs Elizabeth, BA. Chairman: Edinburgh New Town Conservation Committee, Lothian Housing Association, Live Music Now! Scotland; Trustee, Scottish National War Memorial; Council Member, The Cockburn Association; President, Clan Mackay Society; b. 21.6.38; 3 d. Address: 38 Moray Place, Edinburgh EH3 6BT; T.-0131-225 2724.

Fairgrieve, Brian David, OBE, DL, MB, ChB, FRCSEd. Deputy Lieutenant, Falkirk and Stirling Districts; General Surgeon, Falkirk Royal Infirmary, 1960-87; b. 21.2.27, Glasgow. Educ. Glasgow Academy; Glasgow University. RMO, 2/6th Gurkha Rifles, 1952-54; initial medical training, Western Infirmary, Glasgow, Stobhill General Hospital, Killearn Hospital; Area Scout Commissioner, 21 years; President, Forth Valley Area Scout Council; Past President, Rotary Club of Falkirk; Lecturer and Examiner, Scotish Police College; Member, Council, St. Andrew's Ambulance Association; former Director, Incorporated Glasgow Stirlingshire & Sons of the Rock Society; Hon. Vice President, Grangemouth Rugby Club; awarded Silver Wolf, 1983, and OBE, 1986, for services to International Scouting. Recreations: photography; travel. Address: (h.) 19 Lyall Crescent, Polmont, Falkirk FK2 0PL; T.-01324 715449.

Fairgrieve, James Hanratty, DA, ARSA, RSW. Painter; Senior Lecturer in Drawing and Painting, Edinburgh College of Art, since 1968; b. 17.6.44, Prestonpans; m., Margaret D. Ross; 2 s.; 1 d. Educ. Preston Lodge Senior Secondary School; Edinburgh College of Art. Postgraduate study, 1966-67; Travelling Scholarship, Italy, 1968; President, SSA, 1978-82; exhibited in Britain and Europe, since 1966. Recreation: angling. Address: (h.) Burnbrae, Gordon, Berwickshire; T.-Gordon 357.

Fairhead, Nigel Derek, FCA. Director of Finance, National Trust for Scotland, since 1991; b. 17.10.52, Malaya; m., Morag McGregor; 1 s.; 1 d. Educ. Brighton College; Hendon College. Trained with Spain Brothers & Co., Kent; qualified as a chartered accountant, 1976; Price Waterhouse, Paris, 1978-79; Marcus Hazelwood, Cheltenham, 1979-81; joined National Trust for Scotland, 1981; Executive Member, Scottish Charity Finance Directors' Group, since 1996; Member, Standard Life Ethical Unit Trust Committee. Address: (b.) 5 Charlotte Square, Edinburgh EH2 4DU; T.-0131-226 5922.

Fairley, Janet Christine, PhD, MPhil, BA (Hons). Elected Fellow, Institute of Popular Music, Liverpool University, 1998; Director, Edinburgh Book Festival, 1995-97; Hon. Fellow, Institute of Latin American Studies, 1989-97; b. 16.3.49, Birkenhead; 1 s.; 2 d. Taught, Catholic University, Temuco, Chile, 1971-73; Leverhulme Research Fellow, 1992; British Council-Andes Foundation Visiting Professor in Musicology, University of Chile, 1994; Editorial Board, Popular Music Journal, Cambridge University Press, since 1988; Editorial team, New Grove Dictionary of Music and Musicians, 1998; freelance journalist since late 1980s; freelance broadcaster, since 1989, producing arts programmes (Presenter, Earthbeat, 1989-93); music critic, Folk Roots, Classic CD, Gramophone; numerous academic publications; contributor, Rough Guide to World Music; UK Chair, International Vice-Chair, International Association for the Study of Popular Music, 1985-92. Recreations: yoga; Latin tango and flamenco dancing; tennis; swimming; reading; singing; music; theatre; film. Address: (h.) 7A Cluny Gardens, Edinburgh EH10 6BE.

Fairlie, Andrew Patrick. Executive Chef, One Devonshire Gardens, Glasgow; b. 21.11.63, Perth; m., Gillian Laird Ashley; 2 d. Educ. Perth Academy; Westminster Hotel School, London. Began apprenticeship aged 15 at Station Hotel, Perth; Chef de Partie, Boodles, London; studied with Michael Guererd, Eugene-les-Bains, S.W. France; worked in establishments in Paris (Hotel de Crillion), French Alps, Sydney and East Africa, and aboard Royal Scotsman train; Senior Sous Chef, Ritz, London; worked in Adare Manor, S. Ireland; Head Chef, Disneyland Hotel, Euro Disney, Paris. Winner, first Michael Roux Scholarship, 1985; Scottish Chef of the Year 1996; Member, Academie Culinaire de France; awarded Michelin Star, 1996, 1997. Recreation: hill-walking. Address: (b.) One Devonshire Gardens, Glasgow G12 0UX; T.-0141-339 2001.

Fairlie of Myres, David Ogilvy, MBE. Landowner; b. 1.10.23, Edinburgh; m., Jane Bingham-Newland. Educ. Ampleforth College, York; Oriel College, Oxford. Officer, Royal Signals, Europe, Ceylon, Singapore, Java, Malaya, Korea, SHAPE Paris; retired, 1959; Fife Area Scouts: President, former County Commissioner; former Cupar District Commissioner for Scouts; awarded Silver Acorn and Silver Wolf; DL, Fife; JP; Member, Queen's Bodyguard for Scotland; Knight Commander with Star of the Equestrian Order of the Holy Sepulchre of Jerusalem, Lieutenant of Scotland. Publication: Fairlie of that Ilk. Recreations: genealogy; photography; bee-keeping. Address: Myres Castle, Auchtermuchty, Cupar, Fife KY14 7EW.

Fairlie, Peter James Morrison. Director, The Macallan Distillers Ltd., since 1996; Director, Highland Distillers Brands Ltd., since 1998; Member, Scottish Tourist Board, 1995-98; b. 18.12.57, Bridge of Allan; m., Anne (Louise) Moon; 1 s.; 1 d. Educ. Strathallan School. Glenturret Distillery Ltd., 1977-96 (Managing Director, 1989-96).Vice Chairman, Association of Scottish Visitor Attractions, 1988-94; Member, Scottish Sports Council, 1990-93; Member, Scottish Tourist Board Seasonality Working Group, 1994-97; Member, Board of Governors, Strathallan School, since 1994. Recreations: squash (Internationalist, 1980-87); golf; skiing; angling. Address: (b.) The Macallan Distillers Ltd., West Kinfauns, Perth PH2 7XZ; T.-01738 443777.

Fairweather, Andrew Burton, OBE, TD, BA, MIMgt. General Secretary, Abbeyfield Society for Scotland, since 1991; b. 26.2.31, Edinburgh; m., Elizabeth Brown; 3 s. Educ. Royal High School, Edinburgh; Edinburgh University; Open University. Clerical Officer, HM Customs and Excise, 1949; Executive Officer: Accountant of Court for Scotland, 1949, Department of Health for Scotland, 1951 (Secretary, Scottish Medical Practices Committee, 1954-58); Higher Executive Officer, Department of Health for Scotland and Scottish Development Department, 1958, Senior Executive Officer, Scottish Development Department, 1965 (Secretary, Rent Assessment Panel for Scotland, 1965-67); Principal: Chief Administrative Officer, Civil Service College, Edinburgh, 1970, Scottish Economic Planning Department, 1972, Scottish Development Department, 1974 (Secretary, Local Government Staff and Property Commissions, 1974-77), Scottish Office Central Services, 1981; Senior Principal, Scottish Office Central Services, 1982. Rifle Brigade, RAEC; Royal Scots (TA) and Royal Corps of Transport (TA); Commanding Officer, 495 Liaison Unit (BAOR), Royal Corps of Transport (TA), 1977-81; Colonel, Regular Army Reserve of Officers, 1982. Address: (h.) 127 Silverknowes Gardens, Edinburgh.

Fairweather, Clive Bruce, OBE. HM Chief Inspector of Prisons for Scotland, since 1994; b. 21.5.44, Edinburgh; m., Ann; 1 s.; 1 d. Commanding Officer: Scottish Division Depot, 1984-87, 1st Bn., King's Own Scottish Borderers, 1987-89; Divisional Colonel, The Scottish Division, 1991-94. Address: (b.) Scottish Office, St. Andrews House, Edinburgh; T.-0131-244 8481.

Fairweather, Henry, MA. Group Personnel and Services Director, Scottish and Newcastle plc, since 1986; Independent Director, Havelock Europa plc, since 1991; Non-executive Director, Western General Hospitals NHS Trust, since 1994; b. 16.7.46, Edinburgh; m., Lesley; 2 s. Educ. Edinburgh Academy; St. Andrews University. Scottish and Newcastle, since 1969. Director, Edinburgh Academy; FIPD. Recreations: squash; golf. Address: (b.) 111 Holyrood Road, Edinburgh EH8 8YS; T.-0131-556 2591.

Fairweather, Rev. Ian C.M., MA (Hons), BD. Associate Minister, Glasgow Cathedral, 1985-90; b. 7.3.20, Glasgow; m., Joan Margaret Dickinson. Educ. Hutchesons' Boys' Grammar School, Glasgow (Dux); Glasgow University. Professor of Philosophy, Scottish Church College, Calcutta, and Murray College, Sialkot, 1945-47; Minister, Perceton & Dreghorn Parish Church, 1948-63; Lecturer in Religious Studies and Religious Education, Jordanhill College of Education, 1964-82. Church of Scotland Representative, General Teaching Council for Scotland, 1983-91; Hon. Fellow, New College, Edinburgh, 1984-85. Publications: The Quest for Christian Ethics: an inquiry into ethics and Christian ethics (Co-author); Religious Education (Co-author). Recreation: gardening. Address: (h.) 86 Whittingehame Court, 1300 Great Western Road, Glasgow G12 0BH.

Falconer, Alexander. Member (Labour), Mid Scotland and Fife, European Parliament, since 1984; b. 1.4.40, Dundee; m., Margaret Cavell Aldridge; 1 s.; 1 d. Educ. St. John's Junior Secondary School, Dundee. Former foundry worker; Royal Navy stoker, 1959-68; Rosyth Dockyard, 1969-84; Shop Steward, TGWU, 1970-84; Chair, Fife Federation of Trades Councils. Address: (b.) 25 Church Street, Inverkeithing, Fife KY11 1LH; T.-01383 419330.

Falconer, Professor Kenneth John, MA, PhD (Cantab), FRSE. Professor in Pure Mathematics, St. Andrews University, since 1993; b. 25.1.52, Middlesex; m., Isobel Jessie Nye; 1 s.; 1 d. Educ. Kingston Grammar School; Corpus Christi College, Cambridge. Research Fellow, Corpus Christi College, Cambridge, 1977-80; Lecturer, then Reader, Bristol University, 1980-93; Visiting Professor, Oregon State University, 1985-86. Publications: The Geometry of Fractal Sets; Fractal Geometry — Mathematical Foundations and Applications; Techniques in Fractal Geometry; Unsolved Problems in Geometry (Co-author); 70 papers. Recreations: hill-walking and long distance walking (National Committee Member, Long Distance Walkers Association, 1987-92, and Editor of its magazine Strider). Address: (h.) Lumbo Farmhouse, St. Andrews, Fife; T.-01334 478507.

Falconer, Lake. Solicitor (retired); b. 21.10.27, Oban; m., Winifred Margaret Payne; 2 s. Educ. Oban High School; Glasgow University. RAF, 1946-48; qualified Solicitor, 1951; Partner, then Senior Partner, D.M. MacKinnon & Co., WS, Oban, 1953-89; Council Member, Law Society of Scotland, 1980-90; Vice President, 1985-86; Dean, Oban Faculty of Solicitors, 1983-86; Honorary Sheriff of North Strathclyde at Oban, since 1988; Chairman, Oban Social Security Appeal Tribunal, 1957-97; Commodore, Royal Highland Yacht Club, 1974-77; Chairman and Depute Launching Authority, Oban Lifeboat, 1972-97; Chairman, North Argyll District Scout Council, since 1982; Session Clerk, Kilmore and Oban Church of Scotland, 1974-93; President, Oban Burns Club, 1995-98. Recreation: enjoying his grandchildren. Address: (h.) Birkhill, Glenmore, Oban PA34 4PG; T.-01631 562940.

Falkland, 15th Viscount (Lucius Edward William Plantagenet Cary). Premier Viscount of Scotland on the Roll; b. 8.5.35, London; 2 s.; 3 d. (1 deceased). Educ. Wellington College; Alliance Francaise, Paris. Formerly journalist, theatrical agent, chief executive of international trading company; entered Parliament, 1984 (SDP), 1987 (Liberal Democrats); Deputy Chief Whip, House of Lords, for Liberal Democrats, since 1987; Culture, Sport and Media Spokesman, since 1994. Recreations: golf; motor-cycling; cinema. Address: (b.) House of Lords, London SW1.

Fallick, Professor Anthony Edward, BSc, PhD, FRSE, FRSA. Professor of Isotope Geosciences, University of Glasgow, since 1996; Head of Isotope Geosciences Unit, Scottish Universities Research and Reactor Centre, East Kilbride, since 1986; b. 21.4.50, Chatham; Educ. St. Columba's High School, Greenock; University of Glasgow. Research Fellow: McMaster University, Canada, 1975-78, University of Cambridge, 1978-80; Research Fellow, Lecturer, Reader, Professor, Scottish Universities Research and Reactor Centre, East Kilbride, since 1980. Address: (b.) S.U.R.R.C., Rankine Avenue, East Kilbride, Glasgow G75 0QF; T.-0141-339 8564.

Fallon, Edward Brian. Member, City of Edinburgh Council, since 1995; Deputy Chairman, Labour Group; Convener: General Purposes and Consumer Services Committee, and Lothian Valuation Joint Board, since 1996; b. 10.11.47, Edinburgh; m., Jennifer Mary; 1 s.; 1 d. Educ. St. Anthony's School, Edinburgh; Napier College; Edinburgh School of Building and Crafts. Elected, Lothian Regional Council, 1982, Deputy Leader, 1990-96, and Chair, General Purposes Committee, 1986-96; Convener, Protective Services Committee, COSLA, 1990-96; Vice-President, ECOSA; Hon. Vice-President, ITSA; Deputy Chair, LACOTS. Recreations: golf; football; rugby; reading; swimming. Address: (b.) City Chambers, High Street, Edinburgh, EH1 1YJ; T.-0131-529 3271.

Fannin, A. Lorraine, BA (Hons), DipEd. Director, Scottish Publishers Association, since 1987; Member, British Council Publishers Committee; Council Member, Institute of Publishing; b. Belfast; m., Nigel Fannin; 2 s.; 1

d. Educ. Victoria College, Belfast; Queen's University, Belfast; Reading University. Teacher of Modern Languages, Henley-on-Thames and Edinburgh; owned children's bookshop, 1979. Recreations: theatre; gardening; antique-hunting; reading. Address: (b.) 137 Dundee Street, Edinburgh EH11 1BG; T.-0131-228 6866.

Farley-Sutton, Captain Colin David, RN, CEng, FIMechE, DL. Independent Consulting Engineer, retired; Deputy Lieutenant, Caithness, since 1986; b. 20.12.31, Rugby; m., Sheila Wilson Baldwin; 2 s.; 2 d. Educ. Rugby College of Technology and Arts; RN Engineering College, Plymouth; RN College, Greenwich. Royal Navy, 1950-82 (Captain Superintendent, HMS Vulcan, Dounreay, 1980-82). President, Caithness Branch, Red Cross, 1991-97. Address: (h.) Shepherd's Cottage, Lynegar, Watten, Caithness KW1 5YJ; T.-01955 621697.

Farmer, Sir Tom, CBE, KCSG. Chairman and Chief Executive, Kwik-Fit Holdings PLC, since 1984; b. 10.7.40, Edinburgh; m., Anne Drury Scott; 1 s.; 1 d. Educ. Holy Cross Academy. Address: (b.) 17 Corstorphine Road, Edinburgh; T.-0131-337 9200.

Farquhar, Caroline McAra Barclay Murray, MBE, MBA. Chief Executive, Right Track, since 1984; b. 10.12.54, Airdrie; m., James. Educ. Coatbridge High School; Strathclyde University. Civil Servant, DHSS, 1972-75; Scheme Consultant, Community Industry, 1975-77; Detached Youth Worker, Torran Road Project, 1977-79; Project Manager, Project Fullemploy, 1979-84. Chair, STAG (Support Training Action Group); Director, Careers Partnership; Executive Member, Education Business Partnership; Member, Glasgow Learning Alliance; Member, Scottish Office Beattie Committee; Member, European Parliament Social Inclusion Commission. Publication: Altered Perspectives – A Review of Special Needs Training in Scotland. Recreations: walking; painting watercolours; tapestry; cross stitch; eating out. Address: (b.) 3rd Floor, Brook Street Studios, 60 Brook Street, Glasgow G40 2AB; T.-0141-556 1991.

Farquhar, Charles Don Petrie, JP, DL. Member, Dundee City Council (Chairman, Leisure Services Committee); b. 4.8.37, Dundee; 2 d. Educ. Stobswell Secondary School; Dundee Trades College; NCLC. Time-served engineer; elected Dundee Corporation, 1965; former Magistrate and Chairman of various Committees; served Royal Engineers (TRG NCO); Supervisory Staff, Plant Engineering Division, NCR; elected Dundee District Council, 1974; Lord Provost and Lord Lieutenant, City of Dundee District, 1975-77; Past Chairman, Tayside and Fife Committee for Employment of Disabled People. Recreations: fresh-water angling; numismatics; DIY; pool; golf; bowls. Address: (h.) 2 Killin Avenue, Dundee DD3 6EB.

Farquhar, Gavin Blair, LLB (Hons), DipLP. Partner, Ledingham Chalmers, Solicitors, since 1988; b. 16.3.59, Salisbury, S. Rhodesia; m., Shirley Innes. Educ. Waterford Kamhlaba, Swaziland; Aberdeen University. Standard Chartered Bank; Assistant Solicitor then Partner, C&PH Chalmers. Recreations: hillwalking; travel; motorcycling. Address: (b.) 5 Melville Crescent, Edinburgh; T.-0131-200 1030.

Farquhar, Margaret, LLD, JP. Lord Provost of Aberdeen, until May 1999; Lord Lieutenant of Aberdeen, until May 1999; b. 14.3.30, Aberdeen; m., Councillor W. Farquhar (deceased); 1 s.; 1 d. Educ. Ruthrieston Secondary School, Aberdeen; Webster's College, Aberdeen. Elected as a Councillor, 1971; held various Convenerships; Hon. President, Grampian Girls' Brigade, since 1988; former Board Member, Grampian Enterprise Ltd. Hon. LLD, University of Aberdeen, 1996; Hon. LLD, Robert Gordon University, 1998. Recreations: bowling; television; driving; working with elderly and young. Address: (b.) Town House, Aberdeen AB10 1LP; T.-01224 522514.

Farquhar, William John, OBE, MA, DSA, FHSM. Secretary, Clinical Resource and Audit Group, NHS in Scotland, 1989-98; b. 29.5.35, Maud, Aberdeenshire; m., Isabel Henderson Rusk; 4 s. Educ. Peterhead Academy; Aberdeen University; Manchester University. National Administrative Trainee, Scottish Health Service; Hospital Secretary, Whitehaven Hospital, Cumberland; Deputy Secretary and Treasurer, West Cumberland Hospital Management Committee; Regional Staff Officer, South-Eastern Regional Hospital Board; Deputy Secretary, Eastern Regional Hospital Board; Lothian Health Board: District Administrator, South Lothian District, then Administrator, Operational Services. Secretary, Scottish Health Service Planning Council, 1985-89; Director, Planning Unit, Scottish Home and Health Department, 1987-90; Secretary, Scottish Health Service Advisory Council, 1989-93; Council of Europe Medical Fellowship, 1988; Elder, Colinton Parish Church; Vice-Convener, Church of Scotland Board of National Mission, 1991-94; Convener, Health Care Advisory Group, Board of World Mission, since 1991; Member, Executive Committee, Crossroads, Edinburgh. Recreations: gardening; walking. Address: (h.) Craigengar, 7 Harelaw Road, Colinton, Edinburgh EH13 0DR; T.-0131-441 2169.

Farquharson, Angus Durie Miller, OBE, DL, MA, FRICS. Lord Lieutenant of Aberdeenshire, since 1998; Vice Lord Lieutenant, 1987-98 (DL, 1984); b. 27.3.35, Haydon Bridge; m., Alison Mary Farquharson of Finzean; 2 s.; 1 d. Educ. Trinity College, Glenalmond; Downing College, Cambridge. Chartered Surveyor, Estate Factor, Farmer and Forester; Council Member, Scottish Landowners Federation, 1980-88; Member: Regional Advisory Committee, Forestry Commission, 1980-94; Red Deer Commission, 1986-92; Nature Conservancy Committee for Scotland, 1986-91; NE Committee, SNH, 1991-94; Hon. President, Kincardine/ Deeside Scouts; Director, Lathallan School; Elder and General Trustee, Church of Scotland. Recreations: gardening; shooting; walking; local history; nature conservation. Address: (h.) Finzean House, Finzean, Banchory, Aberdeenshire, AB31 6NZ; T.-01330850 229.

Farquharson, Captain Colin Andrew, JP, DL, FRICS. Lord Lieutenant of Aberdeenshire, 1987-98; Chartered Surveyor and Land Agent, since 1953; b. 9.8.23; m., 1, Jean Sybil Mary Hamilton (deceased, 1985); 2 d.; 1 d. deceased; 2, Clodagh, JP, DL, widow of Major Ian Houldsworth of Dallas, Morayshire; 3 step s.; 2 step d. Educ. Rugby. Grenadier Guards, 1942-48; ADC to Field Marshal Sir Harald Alexander (Earl Alexander of Tunis), 1945; Member, Board of Management, Royal Cornhill Hospitals, 1962-74; Director, MacRobert Farms (Douneside), 1971-87; Chairman, Gordon Local Health Council, 1975-81; Member, Grampian Health Board, 1981-89; DL, Aberdeenshire, 1966; Vice Lord Lieutenant, Aberdeenshire, 1983-87; Member, Queen's Bodyguard for Scotland (Royal Company of Archers), since 1964. Recreations: shooting; fishing; farming. Address: Whitehouse, Alford, Aberdeenshire AB33 8DP.

Farquharson, Sir James Robbie, KBE, BSc, CEng, FICE. Upland farmer, since 1965; b. 1.11.03, Kirriemuir; m., Agnes Binny Graham; 2 s. Educ. Websters High School, Kirriemuir; Royal Technical College, Glasgow; Glasgow University. Trainee Civil Engineer, LMS Railway, 1923-25; Civil Engineer, Kenya and Uganda Railway, 1925-37; Tanganyika Railway: Assistant to General Manager, 1937-41, Chief Engineer, 1941-45, General Manager, 1945-48; Deputy General Manager and Chief Engineer, East African Railways and Harbours, 1948-52; General Manager: Sudan Railways, 1952-57, East African Railways and Harbours, 1957-61; Assistant Crown Agent and Engineer-in-Chief, Crown Agents, 1961-65. Fellow, Scottish Council

Development and Industry; Former Member, Executive Committee, Scottish Council Development and Industry; undertook missions to Nigeria, Malawi, Jordan and Philippines for Overseas Development Administration; advised African Development Bank on transport matters. Publication: Tanganyika Transport, 1945. Recreation: farming in retirement. Address: (h.) Kinclune, Kirriemuir, Angus DD8 5HX; T.-01575 574710.

Farquharson, Kenneth James (Kenny), MA (Hons), DipJour. Scottish Political Editor, The Sunday Times, since 1998; b. 8.5.62, Dundee; m., Caron Stoker; 2 s. Educ. Lawside R.C. Academy, Dundee; University of Aberdeen; University College, Cardiff. Industry Reporter, Coventry Evening Telegraph, 1985-88; Scotland on Sunday: Investigative Reporter, 1989-93, Political Editor, 1993-97; Political Editor, Daily Record, 1997-98. Director, Scottish European Aid, 1993-94; Founder, Scottish Parliamentary Press Association. Publication: Restless Nation (Co-author), 1996. Recreations: cooking; architecture; Scottish writing and painting. Address: (b.) 124 Portman Street, Glasgow G41 1EJ; T.-0141-420 1000.

Farrell, Sheriff James Aloysius, MA, LLB. Sheriff of Lothian and Borders, since 1986; b. 14.5.43, Glasgow; m., 1, Jacqueline Allen (divorced); 2, Patricia McLaren; 2 d. Educ. St. Aloysius College; Glasgow University; Dundee University. Admitted to Faculty of Advocates, 1974; Advocate-Depute, 1979-83; Sheriff: Glasgow and Strathkelvin, 1984-85, South Strathclyde, Dumfries and Galloway, 1985-86. Recreations: sailing; cycling; hill-walking. Address: (b.) Sheriff's Chambers, Edinburgh; T.-0131-225 2525.

Farrell, William John. Secretary, Board of Stewardship and Finance, Church of Scotland, since 1993; b. 10.5.35, Glasgow; m., Mary Elizabeth Kelly. Educ. Whitehill School; Glasgow Technical College. Church of Scotland Elder and Reader. Recreations: walking; swimming; reading; joking. Address: (b.) 121 George Street, Edinburgh; T.-0131-225 5722.

Farrington, Dennis Joseph, BSc, DPhil, LLM, FRSA. Deputy Secretary and Clerk to the Court, Stirling University, since 1995; b. 13.8.47, Ellesmere Port; m., Julia Baverstock; 1 s.; 1 d. Educ. Ellesmere Port County Grammar School; University of Kent; University of Ulster. Civil Service, 1972-81: Customs and Excise, 1972-73, Northern Ireland Office, 1973-78, HM Stationery Office, 1978-81; Personnel Officer, Hull University, 1981, Administrative Secretary, 1986; Deputy Secretary and Registrar, Stirling University, 1986-95. Secretary, Conference of University Administrators, 1982-88; Chairman, Cancer Research Campaign, Stirling, 1987-91. Publications: Universities and the Law (Co-author), 1990; The Law of Higher Education, 1994, 2nd edition, 1998; Going to University, 1996. Recreations: DIY; home computing. Address: (b.) Stirling University, Stirling FK9 4LA; T.-01786 467017.

Fass, Rev. Michael J., MA. Director, Partners in Economic Development Ltd., since 1992; b. 22.6.44, Sonning, Berks; m., Iola Mary Ashton; 1 s.; 2 d. Educ. Eton College; Trinity College, Cambridge; IMD, Lausanne. Served C Squadron (Berkshire Yeomanry) Berkshire and Westminster Dragoons (TA), 1963-68; worked in industry at Hays Wharf, Miles Druce-GKN, and DTI's Small Firms Service; Director, West Lothian Enterprise Ltd., 1983-92. Director, Prince's Scottish Youth Business Trust, 1989-97; NSM Priest in Charge, Collegiate Church of St. Matthew, Rosslyn Chapel, Roslin (Scottish Episcopal Church, since 1997; Vice Chairman, Industrial Christian Fellowship and Presiding Moderator, Christians in Secular Ministry, 1998-99. Publication: The Vital Economy, Integrating Training and Enterprise (Co-Author). Address: 60 Braid Road, Edinburgh EH10 6AL.

Faulkner, Professor Douglas, WhSch, PhD, DSc, RCNC, FEng, FRINA, FIStructE, FRSA, FSNAME. President, Institution of Engineers and Shipbuilders in Scotland,1995-97; Head, Department of Naval Architecture and Ocean Engineering, Glasgow University, 1973-95; Emeritus Professor, now; b. 29.12.29, Gibraltar; m., Isobel Parker Campbell; 3 d. Educ. Sutton High School, Plymouth; HM Dockyard Technical College, Devonport; Royal Naval College, Greenwich. Aircraft carrier design, 1955-57; production engineering, 1957-59; structural research, NCRE Dunfermline, 1959-63; Assistant Professor of Naval Construction, RNC, Greenwich, 1963-66; Structural Adviser to Ship Department, Bath, 1966-68; Naval Construction Officer attached to British Embassy, Washington DC, 1968-70; Member, Ship Research Committee, National Academy of Sciences, 1968-71; Research Associate and Defence Fellow, MIT, 1970-71; Structural Adviser, Ship Department, Bath, and Merrison Box Girder Bridge Committee, 1971-73; UK Representative, Standing Committee, International Ship Structures Congress, 1973-85; Member, Marine Technology Board, Defence Scientific Advisory Council; Expert Assessor: Lord Donaldson's Assessment (Derbyshire), 1995, Department of Transport (re. Derbyshire survey), 1996. Awarded: David W. Taylor Medal; William Froude Medal; Peter the Great Medal. Recreations: hill-walking; music; croquet; GO. Address: (h.) 4 Murdoch Drive, Milngavie, Glasgow G62 6QZ; T.-0141-956 5071.

Fawkes, Robert, BSc, BA (Hons), Headteacher, Park Mains High School, Erskine, since 1995; b. 17.7.50; m., Margaret Ann; 2 s. Educ. Knightswood Secondary School; Glasgow University. Teacher, North Kelvinside; Principal Teacher of Guidance, Cranhill Secondary School; Principal Teacher of Mathematics, Waverley Secondary School; Assistant Headteacher, Cathkin High School; Depute Headteacher, Waverley Secondary School; Headteacher, Blantyre High School. Recreations: squash; hillwalking. Address: (b.) Park Mains High School, Barrhill Road, Erskine PA8 6EY; T.-0141-812 2801.

Fearn, Professor David Ross, BSc, PhD, FRSE. Professor of Applied Mathematics, University of Glasgow, since 1993 (Head, Department of Mathematics, since 1997); b. 11.2.54, Dundee; m., Elvira D'Annunzio; 1 s.; 1 d. Educ. Grove Academy, Dundee; University of St. Andrews; University of Newcastle upon Tyne. Research Associate: Florida State University, 1979-80, University of Cambridge, 1980-85; University of Glasgow: Lecturer, 1985-90, Senior Lecturer, 1990-92, Reader, 1992-93. Member, Board of Governors, Morrison's Academy, Crieff. Recreations: walking; gardening; DIY. Address: (b.) University Gardens, Glasgow G12 8QW; T.-0141-330 5417.

Fearon, Brian Joseph, BSSc, MA, DipASocStud. Director of Social Services, East Dunbartonshire Council, since 1995; b. 8.11.48, Belfast; m., Roseanne; 1 s.; 2 d. Educ. St. Mary's CBS Grammar School, Belfast; Queens University, Belfast; Sheffield University; Middlesex University. Social Worker, LB of Waltham Forest, 1973-75; Senior/Assistant Principal Social Worker, Eastern Health and Social Services Board, N. Ireland, 1975-79; Principal Social Worker (Field Work), Northern Health and Social Services Board, 1979-80; Central Regional Council, 1980-95, latterly as Head of Child Care. Member, Northern Ireland Supplementary Benefits Commission, 1978-80. Publications: Cost of Caring; In Defence of the Welfare State; Social Work and Citizenship. Recreation: golf. Address: (b.) 2-4 West High Street, Kirkintilloch G66 1AD; T.-0141-775 9000.

Fedak, Professor Michael A., BA, MA, PhD. Professor, School of Environmental and Evolutionary Biology, University of St. Andrews, since 1996; b. 22.4.43, New Jersey; m., Wendy Brown; 1 s.; 1 d. Educ. Rutgers University; Duke University. Research Associate, Duke

University; Lecturer, Harvard University; Biologist (Principal Scientific Officer), Natural Environment Research Council, 1979-96. Address: (b.) Sea Mammal Research Unit, Gatty Marine Laboratory, University of St. Andrews, St. Andrews, Fife KY16 8LB; T.-01334 462630.

Fee, Kenneth, MA, FRCS. Editor, Scots Independent, since 1985; b. 14.7.31, Glasgow; m., Margery Anne Dougan; 3 s.; 1 d. Educ. Gourock High School; Hamilton Academy; Glasgow University. President, Glasgow University SRC and Scottish Union of Students; Editor, Gum, Ygorra and GU Guardian; sometime in military intelligence; Sub-Editor, Glasgow Herald; Strathclyde Publishing Group; itinerant teaching; Member, Scottish Executive, NASUWT, 1983-98; various SNP branch, constituency and national offices, since 1973. Publication: How to Grow Fat and Free. Recreations: chess; gastronomy; campaigning. Address: (h.) 157 Urrdale Road, Dumbreck G41 5DG; T.-0141-427 0117.

Fenton, Professor Emeritus Alexander, CBE, MA, BA, DLitt, HonDLitt (Aberdeen), FRSE, FSA, FRSGS, HRSA, FSA Scot. Director, European Ethnological Research Centre, since 1989; Honorary Professor of Antiquities to Royal Scottish Academy, since 1996; b. 26.6.29, Shotts; m., Evelyn Elizabeth Hunter; 2 d. Educ. Turriff Academy; Aberdeen University; Cambridge University. Senior Assistant Editor, Scottish National Dictionary, 1955-59; part-time Lecturer, English as a Foreign Language, Edinburgh University, 1958-60; National Museum of Antiquities of Scotland: Assistant Keeper, 1959-75, Deputy Keeper, 1975-78, Director, 1978-85; part-time Lecturer, Department of Scottish History, Edinburgh University, 1974-80; Research Director, National Museums of Scotland, 1985-89; Chair of Scottish Ethnology and Director, School of Scottish Studies, Edinburgh University, 1990-94; Honorary Fellow, School of Scottish Studies, since 1969; Foreign Member: Royal Gustav Adolf Academy, Sweden, since 1978, Royal Danish Academy of Sciences and Letters, since 1979; Honorary Member: Volkskundliche Kommission fur Westfalen, since 1980, Hungarian Ethnographical Society, since 1983; Jury Member, Europa Prize for Folk Art, 1975-95; President, Permanent International Committee, International Secretariat for Research on the History of Agricultural Implements; President, Scottish Vernacular Buildings Working Group; President, Scottish Country Life Museums Trust; Secretary and Trustee, Friends of the Dictionary of the Older Scottish Tongue; Secretary and Trustee, Scotland Inheritance Fund; Co-Editor: Tools and Tillage, since 1968, The Review of Scottish Culture, since 1984. Publications: The Various Names of Shetland, 1973, 1977; Scottish Country Life, 1976 (Scottish Arts Council Book Award); The Diary of a Parish Clerk (translation from Danish), 1976; The Island Blackhouse, A Guide to the Blackhouse at 42 Arnol, Lewis, 1978 (re-issued, 1989); A Farming Township, A Guide to Auchindrain, the Museum of Argyll Farming Life, 1978; The Northern Isles, Orkney and Shetland, 1978 (Dag Stromback Award); The Rural Architecture of Scotland (Co-author), 1981; The Shape of the Past 1, 1985; If All The World Were a Blackbird (translation from Hungarian), 1985; The Shape of the Past II, 1986; 'Wirds an' Wark 'e Seasons Roon on an Aberdeenshire Farm, 1987; Country Life in Scotland, Our Rural Past, 1987; Scottish Country Life, 1989; The Turra Coo, 1989; Cruiters...or Twenty Buchan Tales, 1995. Recreation: languages. Address: (b.) European Ethnological Research Centre, National Museums of Scotland, Chambers Street, Edinburgh, EH1 1JF; T.-0131-2247 4086.

Fenton, Professor George Wallace, MB, FRCPEdin, FRCPLond, FRCPsych, MRCP, DPM. Emeritus Professor of Psychiatry, University of Dundee, since 1996; Consultant in Neuropsychiatry, Kathleen May Trust, since 1996; b. 30.7.31, Londonderry, Northern Ireland; m., Nini Hodgson; 1 s. Educ. Ballymena Academy; Queen's University of Belfast. Lecturer, Academic Department of Psychiatry, Middlesex Hospital, London, 1962-66; Senior Lecturer, Institute of Psychiatry, University of London, 1967-75; Maudsley Hospital, London: Consultant Psychiatrist, Professorial Unit, 1967-75, Consultant Neurophysiologist, 1968-75; Professor and Head, Department of Mental Health, Queen's University of Belfast, 1976-83; Professor and Head, Department of Psychiatry, University of Dundee, 1983-96. Publications: numerous on clinical neurophysiology and neuropsychiatry. Recreations: sailing; history; literature; drama. Address: Invergowrie House, Dundee DD2 1UA; T.-01382 668224.

Fenton, Gordon Perring, MCIBS, MIPR. Secretary, Committee of Scottish Clearing Bankers, since 1998; b. 18.1.48, Perth; m., Margaret Elizabeth; 2 s.; 1 d. Educ. Perth High School. Royal Bank of Scotland, 1965-98: Dundee; Perth; London; Houston, Texas; Head Office, Edinburgh, latterly Head of Sponsorship and Community Programme. Committee Member: Association for Business Sponsorship of the Arts, Sportsmatch. Recreations: reading; foreign travel; tennis. Address: Drumsheugh House, 38 Drumsheugh Gardens, Edinburgh EH3 7SN; T.-0131-473 7770.

Fenwick, Hubert Walter Wandesford. Architectural Historian and Lecturer; Chairman, Royal Martyr Church Union; b. 17.7.16, Glasgow. Educ. Huntley School, New Zealand; Royal Grammar School, Newcastle-upon-Tyne. Architectural student; qualified, 1950; office of Ian G. Lindsay, then Lorimer & Matthew, Edinburgh; gave up architectural career, 1958; RIBA Examiner for Scotland in History of Architecture, until post abolished; Assistant Secretary and PRO, Scottish Georgian Society, 1960-65; Council Member, Cockburn Association, 1966; Scottish Editor, Church Illustrated, 1959-64; Editor and Manager, Edinburgh Tatler and Glasgow Illustrated, 1966-67; regular contributor to Scots Magazine, 25 years, and other journals. Publications: Architect Royal; Auld Alliance; Scotland's Historic Buildings; Scotland's Castles; Chateaux of France; Scotland's Abbeys and Cathedrals; View of the Lowlands; Scottish Baronial Houses. Recreations: foreign travel; architectural history; sketching and photography (for own books and articles); gardening. Address: The Priory, Pittenweem, Fife KY10 2LJ; T.-013333 311 453.

Ferguson, Professor Allister Ian, BSc, MA, PhD, FInstP, CPhys. Professor of Photonics, Strathclyde University, since 1989; Technical Director, Institute of Photonics, University of Strathclyde, since 1996; Managing Director, Microlase Optical Systems Ltd.; b. 10.12.51, Aberdeen; m., Kathleen Ann Challenger. Educ. Aberdeen Academy; St. Andrews University. Lindemann Fellow, Stanford University, 1977-79; SERC Research Fellow, St. Andrews, 1979-81; SERC Advanced Fellow, Oxford, 1981-83; Junior Research Fellow, Merton College, Oxford, 1981-83; Lecturer, then Senior Lecturer, Southampton University, 1983-89. Fellow: Royal Society of Edinburgh, since 1993, Institute of Physics, Optical Society of America. Address: (b.) Department of Physics and Applied Physics, Strathclyde University, Glasgow, G4 0NG; T.-0141-548 3359.

Ferguson, Charles, LLB(Hons), NP. Solicitor; Senior Partner, Charles Ferguson & Co.; Solicitor Advocate; writer and broadcaster of legal programmes, Scot FM; b. 19.7.63, Glasgow; 4 s.; 2 d. Educ. University of Dundee. Chairman, Hamilton South Conservative and Unionist Party; Election Agent, Conservative and Unionist Party. Address: (b.) 43 Quarry Street, Hamilton ML3 7AH; T.-01698 285885.

Ferguson, David Joseph. Board Secretary, National Board for Nursing, Midwifery and Health Visiting for Scotland, since 1993; b. 7.8.55, Edinburgh; m., Margaret; 1 d. Educ. George Watson's College, Edinburgh; University of Dundee. Executive Officer, The Scottish Office, 1974-81; Senior Administrator, National Board for Nursing,

Midwifery and Health Visiting for Scotland, 1982-92. Recreations: music; reading; cinema; football; walking; spending time with family. Address: (b.) 22 Queen Street, Edinburgh EH2 1NT; T.-0131-247 6619.

Ferguson, Duncan John, MA, MEd, FSA (Scot). Rector, Plockton High School, since 1992; Director, Skye and Lochalsh Local Enterprise Company, since 1993; Chair, Highland Secondary Headteachers' Association, since 1998; b. 26.2.53; m., Catriona; 1 s.; 1 d. Educ. Keil School; University of Glasgow. Teacher of Classics, Albert Secondary School, Glasgow, 1976-79; Head of Classics, Lochgilphead High School, Argyll, 1979-86; Depute Headteacher, Tobermory High School, Mull, 1986-92. Schoolteacher Fellow, British School at Rome, March and April, 1992; part-time Lecturer in Scottish History, Continuing Education Departments, Glasgow and Aberdeen Universities; Evening Class Tutor in Gaelic; Trustee, Catherine MacKichan Trust; ceilidh compere; five times Winner, National Mod traditional storytelling trophy; Chair, BBC Gaelic Advisory Committee, 1992-95; Gaelic world activist, currently Vice-Chair, CLI; Member, Gaelic Broadcasting Committee; Church Elder. Recreations: family archaeological rambles; family holidays in Auvergne; Irish literature and drama; passionate interest in Scottish culture; French wine; Italian food; Bibliophile. Address: (h.) Aros, Achmore, by Stromeferry, Ross-shire.

Ferguson, J. Colin, MA (Hons), DipEd. Headteacher, Alness Academy, Ross-shire, since 1997; b. 4.12.48, Galashiels; m., Doreen; 1 s.; 1 d. Educ. Galashiels Academy; Edinburgh University; Moray House College. Teacher of Geography, Alva Academy, 1972-77; Principal Teacher of Geography, Alness Academy, 1977-87; Assistant Headteacher, Fortrose Academy, 1987-93; Depute Headteacher, Alness Academy, 1993-97. President: Fortrose and Rosemarkie Bowling and Tennis Club; Former President, Ross-Sutherland Rugby Club. Recreations: hillwalking; tennis; golf; reading; creative writing. Address: Alness Academy, Dalmore, Alness, Ross-shire IV17 0UY; T.-01349 883341.

Ferguson, James Murray, BSc (Econ), MPhil, DipEd, FCIS, FIPM, FBIM, FSA Scot; b. 21.4.28, Almondbank, Perthshire; m., Moira McDougall, BA; 2 d. Educ. Perth Academy; London University; Edinburgh University; Dundee University; Moray House College of Education. Military Service, 1946-79: full-time, Army Emergency Reserve, Territorials, T&AVR, Regular Army Reserve of Officers (final rank of Major); variety of business appointments, mainly in insurance, investment and finance, 1952-64; lectureships in range of management subjects, various higher educational establishments, 1965-76; Principal, Elmwood College, Fife, 1976-82; Principal, Aberdeen College of Commerce, 1982-90; Principal and Chief Executive, Aberdeen College, 1990-93. Governor: Further Education Staff College, Coombe Lodge, Bristol, 1982-87, Aberdeen College of Education, 1983-87. Recreations: sporting: badminton, tennis, hill-walking; non-sporting: reading, writing, public speaking, local history studies. Address: (h.) Crosslands, Meethill Road, Alyth PH11 8DE; T.-Alyth 2701.

Ferguson, Joan P.S., MBE, MA, ALA, FRCPEdin. Hon. Secretary, Scottish Genealogy Society, since 1960; b. 15.9.29, Edinburgh. Educ. George Watson's Ladies College; Edinburgh University. Scottish Central Library, 1952-66; Librarian, Royal College of Physicians of Edinburgh, 1966-94. Member, Scottish Records Advisory Council, 1987-93; Compiler: Scottish Newspapers, Scottish Family Histories; Contributor, Companion and New Companion to Scottish Culture. Recreations: genealogy; gardening; reading. Address: (h.) 21 Howard Place, Edinburgh EH3 5JY; T.-0131-556 3844.

Ferguson, Professor Michael Anthony John, BSc (Hons), PhD. Professor of Molecular Parasitology, Department of Biochemistry, Dundee University, since 1994; b. 6.2.57, Bishop Auckland; m., Dr. Maria Lucia Sampaio Guther; 1 s. Educ. St. Peters School, York; UMIST; London University. Research Associate, Rockefeller University, New York, 1982-85; Research Assistant, Oxford University, 1985-88; Lecturer, then Reader, Dundee University, 1988-94. FRSE; Colworth Medal, 1991; Howard Hughes International Research Scholar. Address: (b.) Department of Biochemistry, Dundee University, Dundee DD1 4HN; T.-01382 229595.

Ferguson, Rev. Ronald, MA, BD, ThM. Minister, St. Magnus Cathedral, Orkney, since 1990 (Leader, Iona Community, 1981-88); Columnist, The Herald, since 1997; b. 27.10.39, Dunfermline; m., Cristine Jane Walker; 2 s.; 1 d. Educ. Beath High School, Cowdenbeath; St. Andrews University; Edinburgh University; Duke University. Journalist, Fife and Edinburgh, 1956-63; University, 1963-71; ordained Minister, Church of Scotland, 1972; Minister, Easterhouse, Glasgow, 1971-79; exchange year with United Church of Canada, 1979-80; Deputy Warden, Iona Abbey, 1980-81. Publications: Geoff: A Life of Geoffrey M. Shaw, 1979; Grace and Dysentery, 1986; Chasing the Wild Goose, 1988; The Whole Earth Shall Cry Glory (Co-Editor), 1985; George MacLeod, 1990; Daily Readings by George MacLeod (Editor), 1991; Black Diamonds and the Blue Brazil, 1993; Love Your Crooked Neighbour, 1998; plays: Every Blessed Thing, 1993, Orkneyinga, 1997; poetry: Pushing the Boat Oot (Contributor), 1997. Recreation: supporting Cowdenbeath Football Club. Address: (h.) Cathedral Manse, Berstane Road, Kirkwall, Orkney KW15 1NA; T.-01856 3312.

Ferguson, William James, OBE, FRAgS. Farmer, since 1954; Chairman, Aberdeen Milk Company; former Vice Chairman, Scottish Agricultural College; Director, Hannah Research Institute, since 1995; Vice Lord Lieutenant, Aberdeenshire; b. 3.4.33, Aberdeen; m., Carroll Isobella Milne; 1 s.; 3 d. Educ. Turriff Academy; North of Scotland College of Agriculture. National Service, 1st Bn., Gordon Highlanders, 1952-54, serving in Malaya during the emergency. Former Director, Rowett Research Institute, Aberdeen; former Member, Scottish Country Life Museums Trust Ltd. Recreations: golf; field sports. Address: Rothiebrisbane, Fyvie, Turriff, Aberdeenshire AB53 8LE; T.-01651 891 213.

Fergusson of Kilkerran, Sir Charles, 9th Bt; b. 10.5.31; m., Hon. Amanda Mary Noel-Paton; 2 s.

Fergusson, Professor David Alexander Syme. MA, BD, DPhil. Professor of Systematic Theology, Aberdeen University, since 1990; b. 3.8.56, Glasgow; m., Margot McIndoe; 2 s. Educ. Kelvinside Academy; Glasgow University; Edinburgh University; Oxford University. Assistant Minister, St. Nicholas Church, Lanark, 1983-84; Associate Minister, St. Mungo's Church, Cumbernauld, 1984-86; Lecturer, Edinburgh University, 1986-90. Chaplain to Moderator of the General Assembly, 1989-90. Publications: Bultmann, 1992; Christ, Church and Society, 1993; The Cosmos and the Creator, 1998; Community, Liberalism and Christian Ethics, 1998. Recreations: football; golf; jogging. Address: 44 Ashley Road, Aberdeen AB10 6RJ; T.-01224 583817.

Ferrier, Professor Robert Patton, MA (Cantab), BSc, PhD, FInstP, FRSE. Professor of Natural Philosophy, Glasgow University, since 1973; b. 4.1.34, Dundee; m., Valerie Jane Duncan; 2 s.; 1 d. Educ. Morgan Academy, Dundee; Queen's College, Dundee, St. Andrews University. Scientific Officer, AERE Harwell, 1959-61; Research Associate, Massachusetts Institute of Technology, 1961-62; Senior Research Assistant, Cavendish Laboratory, Cambridge, 1962-65; Fellow, Fitzwilliam College,

Cambridge, 1964-73; Assistant Director of Research, Cavendish Laboratory, Cambridge, 1965-71; Lecturer in Physics, Cambridge University, 1971-73; Guest Scientist, IBM Research Division, California, 1972-73. Member, Physics Committee, SERC, 1979-82 (Chairman, Semiconductor and Surface Physics Sub-Committee, 1979-82). Recreations: tennis; reading crime novels; garden and house maintenance. Address: Department of Physics and Astronomy, The University, Glasgow G12 8QQ; T.-0141-330 5388.

Fewson, Professor Charles Arthur, BSc, PhD, FRSE, FIBiol. Professor and Director, Institute of Biomedical and Life Sciences, Glasgow University, since 1994; b. 8.9.37, Selby, Yorkshire; m., Margaret C.R. Moir; 2 d. Educ. Hymers College, Hull; Nottingham University; Bristol University. Research Fellow, Cornell University, New York, 1961-63; Department of Biochemistry, Glasgow University: Assistant Lecturer, 1963-64, Lecturer, 1964-68, Senior Lecturer, 1968-79, Reader, 1979-82; Titular Professor, 1982-94. Address: (h.) 39 Falkland Street, Glasgow G12 9QZ; T.-0141-339 1304.

Field, Christopher David Steadman, MA, DPhil, ARCM. Hon. Fellow, Faculty of Music, Edinburgh University; b. 27.4.38, Frimley; m., Elizabeth Ann. Educ. Winchester College Choir School; Radley College; New College, Oxford. Lecturer in Music, St. Andrews University, 1974-76, Senior Lecturer, 1976-87; Senior Lecturer in Music, Edinburgh University, 1987-95, Dean, Faculty of Music, 1993-95; Associate Director, Scottish Early Music Consort, 1979-98; Member, Governing Board, RSAMD, 1973-82; Hon. Music Adviser, Scottish Arts Council, since 1996. Recreation: gardening. Address: (h.) 2 Maynard Road, St. Andrews KY16 8RX.

Fife, 3rd Duke of (James George Alexander Bannerman Carnegie); b. 23.9.29; m., Hon. Caroline Cecily Dewar (m. diss.); 1 s.; 1 d. Educ. Gordonstoun. National Service, Scots Guards, Malaya, 1948-50; Royal Agricultural College; Clothworkers' Company and Freeman, City of London; President, ABA, 1959-73; Vice Patron, ABA, 1973-94; Ships President, HMS Fife, 1964-87; a Vice-Patron, Braemar Royal Highland Society; a Vice-President, British Olympic Association. Address: Elsick House, Stonehaven, Kincardineshire AB39 3NT.

Findlay, A.F. (Sandy). Chairman, Hewden Stuart Plc; Chairman, Graham Group plc; Director, Motherwell Bridge Group Ltd.; b. 19.5.36, Mintlaw; m., Marty; 2 d. Educ. Peterhead Academy; Robert Gordon's Technical College. Design/development engineer; Atlas Copco, 1963-69; joined Hewden Stuart Plc, 1969, and worked through the ranks to main board; main board, since 1982. Recreations: golf; gardening; grand-children. Address: (h.) Pitfour, 1 Leewood Park, Dunblane FK15 0NX.

Findlay, Alastair Donald Fraser, MA. Chief Executive, North of Scotland Water Authority, since 1995; Trustee, Lloyds TSB Foundation for Scotland, since 1998; b. 3.2.44, Perth; m., Morag Cumming Peden; 1 s.; 3 d. Educ. Pitlochry High School; Kelso High School; Edinburgh University. Assistant Principal, DAFS, 1966-70; Private Secretary to Joint Parliamentary Under Secretary, Scottish Office, 1970-71; Principal, 1971-74; on loan to Diplomatic Service as First Secretary (Agriculture and Food), The Hague, 1975-78; Assistant Secretary, Higher Education, SED, 1979-82; Fisheries Division, 1982-85, Livestock Products Division, 1985-88, DAFS; Under Secretary, Scottish Office Industry Department, 1988-93; Fisheries Secretary, Scottish Office Agriculture and Fisheries Department, 1993-95. Recreations: golf; walking; watching rugby and football. Address: (b.) North of Scotland Water Authority, Cairngorm House, Beechwood Park North, Inverness IV2 3ED; T.-01463 245424.

Findlay, Professor Allan, MA, PhD. Professor of Geography, University of Dundee, since 1994; b. 2.10.54, Glasgow; m., Anne; 2 s. Educ. Jordanhill College School; Aberdeen University; Durham University. Lecturer, University of Glasgow, 1979-90; Research Associate, International Labour Office, 1987; Senior Lecturer, University of Glasgow, 1991-94. Board member, Tear Fund UK, since 1996; Board Member, ESRC, since 1998. Publications: Population and Development, 1987; The Arab World, 1994. Recreations: hill-walking; cycling. Address: Department of Geography, University of Dundee, Dundee DD1 4HN.

Findlay, Donald Russell, QC, LLB (Hons), MPhil, FRSA. Advocate, since 1975; Vice-Chairman, Glasgow Rangers FC; Lord Rector, St. Andrews University; Newspaper Columnist; Writer; Broadcaster; b. 17.3.51, Cowdenbeath; m., Jennifer E. Borrowman. Educ. Harris Academy, Dundee; Dundee University; Glasgow University. Sometime Lecturer in Commercial Law, Heriot-Watt University. Recreations: Glasgow Rangers FC; Egyptology; archaeology; wine; ethics; travelling first class. Address: (b.) Advocates Library, Parliament House, Parliament Square, Edinburgh EH1 1RF; T.-0131-226 2881.

Findlay, Johan, JP. Honorary Sheriff, since 1995; b. 30.9.52, Ayr; m., David Gibson Findlay; 2 s.; 2 d. Educ. St. Joseph's Convent, Girvan. Member, Criminal Justice Forum, since 1996; Chairman, Dumfries Branch, Scottish Association for the Study of Delinquency, since 1993; Chairman: Nithsdale Justices Committee, 1991-98, Dumfries and Galloway Justices Committee, 1997-98; Chairman, Training Committee of the District Courts Association, 1995-96; President, Lockerbie Little Theatre, 1990-96. Publications: Handbook for Justices of the Peace (Co-editor and Co-author); All Manner of People (history of the JP in Scotland); co-producer of video on use of court interpreters. Recreations: books; theatre. Address: (h.) The Birks, Watchhill Road, Lochmaben, Dumfries DG11 1RX; T.-01387 810911.

Findlay, Richard Martin, LLB, NP. Entertainment Law Partner, Tods Murray WS, Edinburgh, since 1990; b. 18.12.51, Aberdeen. Educ. Gordon Schools, Huntly; Aberdeen University. Trained, Wilsone & Duffus, Advocates, Aberdeen; Legal Assistant, Commercial Department, Maclay Murray & Spens, Glasgow and Edinburgh, 1975-78; Partner, Ranken & Reid SSC, Edinburgh, 1979-90. Member: International Association of Entertainment Lawyers, International Entertainment and Multimedia Law and Business Network, International Bar Association, BAFTA, The Writers' Guild, Scottish Media Lawyers Society, Business in the Arts Placement Scheme; Associate, Theatrical Management Association; Trustee, Peter Darrell Trust; Managing Editor, i2i (The Business Journal of the International Film Industry); Company Secretary: Edinburgh Capital Group Limited, Edinburgh Arts and Entertainment Limited, French Film Festival Ltd., Edinburgh International Jazz and Blues Festival, Italian Film Festival, Arts Research and Development Scotland, Great Distribution Ltd, Moonstone International Ltd.. Recreations: music; theatre; opera; cinema. Address: (b.) 66 Queen Street, Edinburgh EH2 4NE; T.-0131-226 4771.

Fink, Professor George, MB, BS, MD, MA, DPhil, FRCPE, FRSE. Director, MRC Brain Metabolism Unit, since 1980; Honorary Professor, Edinburgh University, since 1984; b. 13.11.36, Vienna; m., Ann Elizabeth; 1 s.; 1 d. Educ. Melbourne High School; Melbourne University; Hertford College, Oxford. House Officer appointments, Royal Melbourne and Alfred Hospitals, 1961-62; Demonstrator and Lecturer, Department of Anatomy, Monash University, 1963-64; Nuffield Dominions Demonstrator, Oxford, 1965-67; Senior Lecturer, Monash University, 1968-71; University Lecturer, Oxford, 1971-80; Official Fellow and Tutor in Physiology and Medicine,

Brasenose College, Oxford, 1974-80. Member of Council, European Neuroscience Association, 1980-82, since 1994; President, European Neuroendocrine Association 1991-95; Chairman, EU Biomed Assessment Panel, 1991-96. Publications: Neuropeptides: Basic and Clinical Aspects (Co-Editor), 1982; Neuroendocrine Molecular Biology (Co-Editor), 1986; Neuropeptides: a Methodology (Co-Editor); 340 papers. Recreations: skiing and squash. Address: (b.) MRC Brain Metabolism Unit, Department of Pharmacology, Edinburgh University, 1 George Square, Edinburgh EH8 9JZ; T.-0131-650 3548.

Finlay, Robert Derek, BA, MA, FInstD, MCIM. Chairman, Dawson International PLC, since 1995; b. 16.5.32, London; m., Una Ann Grant; 2 s.; 1 d. Educ. Kingston Grammar School; Emmanuel College, Cambridge. Lt., Gordon Highlanders, 1950-52; Mobil Oil Co. UK, 1953-61; Associate, Principal, Director, McKinsey & Co., 1961-79; Managing Director, H.J. Heinz Co. Ltd., 1979-81; Senior Vice-President, World HQ, H.J. Heinz Co., 1981-93. Recreations: tennis; rowing; music; theatre. Address: (h.) Grantully Castle, by Aberfeldy, PH15 2EG.

Finlayson, Niall Diarmid Campbell, OBE, MBChB, PhD, FRCP, FRCSE. Consultant Physician, Royal Infirmary of Edinburgh, since 1973; Registrar, Royal College of Physicians of Edinburgh, since 1997; b. 21.4.39, Georgetown, Guyana; m., Dale Kristin Anderson; 1 s.; 1 d. Educ. Loretto School, Musselburgh; Edinburgh University. Lecturer in Therapeutics, Edinburgh University, 1966-69; Assistant Professor of Medicine, Cornell University Medical College, New York Hospital, USA, 1970-72. Recreations: history; music. Address: (b.) Royal Infirmary of Edinburgh, Lauriston Place, Edinburgh EH3 9YW; T.-0131-536 2178.

Finlayson, Robert William, LLB, BCom, CA, ATII. Managing Partner, Edinburgh, Ernst & Young, since 1991; Director, Ernst &Young Financial Management Ltd., since 1989; b. 16.12.49, Glasgow; m., Jennifer Catherine; 2 s.; 1 d. Educ. Glasgow Academy; Edinburgh University. Touche Ross, Glasgow, 1972-75; Arthur Young: Glasgow, 1976-77, Edinburgh, 1977-79, Birmingham, 1979-82 (Tax Manager/Tax Partner), Edinburgh, since 1982 (Head of Tax, Office Managing Partner). Member, Scottish Committee, Wooden Spoon Society; Chairman, Wooden Spoon Society "BT Pay to Play" Scheme. Recreations: golf; sailing; skiing; hill-walking. Address: (b.) Ernst & Young, Ten George Street, Edinburgh EH2 2DZ; T.-0131-226 6400.

Finn, Anthony, MA (Hons), FEIS (1997). Rector, St. Andrew's High School, Kirkcaldy, since 1988; Teachers' Representative, National Committee for the Staff Development of Teachers; former Governor, Moray House Institute of Education; b. 4.6.51, Irvine; m., Margaret Caldwell. Educ. St. Joseph's Academy, Kilmarnock; Glasgow University. Teacher, Principal Teacher, Assistant Head Teacher, Depute Head Teacher, Acting Head Teacher, St. Andrew's Academy, Saltcoats, 1975-88. Member: General Teaching Council (Convener, Education Committee); Member, Catholic Education Commission for Scotland; Assessor, Teacher Education, Scottish Higher Education Funding Council, 1994-95; Chair, Fife Secondary Head Teachers Association, until 1997; Member, Steering Group for Scottish Qualification for Headship. Recreations: sport; travel; literature; current affairs. Address: (h.) 1 Blair Place, Kirkcaldy KY2 5SQ; T.-01592 640109.

Finnie, James Ross, CA. Member, Inverclyde Council, since 1995 (Member, Inverclyde District Council, 1977-96); Ross Finnie & Co., Chartered Accountants; Chairman, Systems Reliability Scotland Ltd., Finance Director, Buko Holdings Ltd.; Director, Mico Ltd; b. 11.2.47, Greenock; m., Phyllis Sinclair; 1 s.; 1 d. Educ. Greenock Academy. Member, Executive Committee, Scottish Council (Development and Industry), 1976-87; Chairman: Scottish Liberal Party, 1982-86, Scottish Liberal Democrats General Election Campaign, 1997. Address: (h.) 91 Octavia Terrace, Greenock PA16 7PY; T.-01475 631495.

Firth, Professor William James, BSc, PhD, CPhys, FInstP, FRSE. Professor of Physics, Strathclyde University (Head, Department of Physics and Applied Physics, 1990-93); b. 23.2.45, Holm, Orkney; m., Mary MacDonald Anderson; 2 s. Educ. Perth Academy; Edinburgh University; Heriot-Watt University. Lecturer to Reader, Physics, Heriot-Watt University, 1967-85. Fellow, Optical Society of America. Recreation: sports (Edinburgh University Hockey Blue, 1967-68). Address: (b.) John Anderson Building, 107 Rottenrow, Glasgow G4 0NG.

Fisher, Archie. Folk singer, guitarist, composer, broadcaster; b. 1939, Glasgow. First solo album, 1966; presenter, Travelling Folk, BBC Radio; Artistic Director, Edinburgh International Folk Festival, 1988-92.

Fisher, Gregor. Actor (television, theatre, film). Credits include (BBC TV): Rab C. Nesbitt series (leading role), Naked Video series, Scotch and Wry, Para Handy. Best Actor award, Toronto Festival, for One, Two, Three.

Fisher, Kenneth Holmes, BA, ACIS, MCIM, DipABCC. Depute Principal, North Glasgow College, since 1987; b. 19.3.41, Glasgow. Educ. Hillhead High School, Glasgow. Administrative appointments, Colvilles Ltd., 1957-67; Lecturer and Senior Lecturer, Anniesland College, Glasgow, 1967-75; Head: Department of Business Studies, Cumbernauld College, 1975-80, Department of Commerce, Anniesland College, Glasgow, 1980-86. Address: (b.) 110 Flemington Street, Glasgow G21 4BX; T.-0141-558 9001.

Fitzgerald, Professor Alexander Grant, BSc, PhD, DSc, CPhys, FInstP, FRSE. Head, Department of Applied Physics and Electronic and Mechanical Engineering and Professor of Analytical Electron Microscopy, Dundee University, since 1992; b. 12.10.39, Dundee; m., June; 1 s.; 2 d. Educ. Perth Academy; Harris Academy; St. Andrews University; Cambridge University. Research Fellow, Lawrence Berkeley Laboratory, University of California; Lecturer, Senior Lecturer, Reader, Professor, Dundee University. Publications: 136 conference and journal papers; book: Quantitative Microbeam Analysis (Co-editor). Recreations: swimming; golf. Address: (b.) Department of Applied Physics and Electronic and Mechanical Engineering, Dundee University, Dundee, DD1 4HN; T.-01382 344553.

Fitzgerald, Maren L., LLB, MICFM. National Organiser, Scotland, RNLI; b. 20.4.47, Glasgow; 2 s. Educ. Glasgow High School for Girls; Glasgow University. Appeal Director, Strathcarron Hospice, 1989-92; Director of Fundraising, Scottish Medical Research Fund, 1992-94; Administrator, Scottish Hospital Endowments Research Trust, 1993-94; Depute Campaign Director, Children 1st, 1994-96. Member, Business Committee, General Council, Glasgow University, 1982-92, and Convenor, Social Affairs Committee of the Business Committee, 1988-92; Trustee, University of Glasgow Trust, 1989-97. Recreation: golf. Address: (b.) Bellevue House, Hopetoun Street, Edinburgh EH7 4ND; T. 0131-557 9171.

Fitzsimons, Sheriff J.T. Sheriff of North Strathclyde. Address: (b.) Dumbarton Sheriff Court, Sheriff Court House, Church Street, Dumbarton, G82 1QR.

Flanagan, Andrew, BAcc, CA. Chief Executive, Scottish Media Group, since 1997; b. 15.3.56, Glasgow; m., Ginni; 1 s.; 1 d. Educ. Hillhead High School; Glasgow University. Trainee Accountant, Touche Ross, 1976-79; Senior Auditor, Price Waterhouse, Brussels, 1979-81; Manager of

Financial Control, ITT Inc., Brussels, 1981-86; Finance Director, PA Consulting, London, 1987-91; Group Finance Director, BIS Group, London, 1991-93; Group Finance Director, then Managing Director, Scottish Television, 1993-97. Recreations: golf; skiing. Address: (b.) Cowcaddens, Glasgow G2 3PR; T.-0141-300 3089.

Fleck, Professor James, MA, BSc, MSc. Chair of Organisation of Industry and Commerce, University of Edinburgh, since 1996; Director, University of Edinburgh Management School, since 1996; b. 18.7.51, Kano, Nigeria; m., Heather Anne Morrison; 2 s.; 3 d. Educ. Perth Academy; University of Edinburgh; Manchester University. Engineer, MK-Shand, Invergordon, 1974-75; Computer Programmer, CAP Limited, London, 1976; Research Fellow and Lecturer, Technology Policy Unit, University of Aston, 1980-85; Lecturer in Operations Management, Heriot-Watt University, 1985-86; Lecturer, then Senior Lecturer, Department of Business Studies, University of Edinburgh, 1986-96. Joseph Lister Lecturer for the Social Sciences, British Association for the Advancement of Science, 1995-96. Publications: Expertise and Innovation – Information Technology Strategies in the Financial Services Sector (Joint Author), 1994; Exploring Expertise (Joint Editor), 1998. Recreations: reading; DIY; windsurfing; eating out. Address: (h.) Grange Park House, 38 Dick Place, Edinburgh EH9 2JB; T.-0131-667 3176.

Fleetwood, Gordon, LLB, NP, WS. Partner, Fleetwood & Robb, Solicitors, since 1986; Solicitor-Advocate, since 1994; b. 3.10.51, Elgin; m., Jean Arthur; 2 d. Educ. Elgin Academy; University of Edinburgh. Recreations: fishing; curling. Address: (b.) 11 Queensgate, Inverness IV1 1DF; T.-01463 226232.

Fleming, Alistair, BSc. Chairman, Scottish Council for Educational Technology, since 1994; Chief Executive, Forth Ports PLC, since 1996; Non-Executive Director, Edinburgh International Conference Centre; Member, Court, Napier University; b. 31.3.44, Glasgow; m., Sandra; 1 s.; 2 d. Educ. Shawlands Academy; Strathclyde University. Corpus Christi Petrochemicals/ICI America, 1975-80; Britoil, 1980-87; General Manager of Projects, BP Exploration, 1987-89; Managing Director, Eurotunnel, 1990; Director, The Weir Group, 1991-96. Address: (b.) Forth Ports PLC, Tower Place, Leith, Edinburgh EH6 7DB; T.-0131-554 6473.

Fleming, Archibald Macdonald, MA, BCom, PhD, FRSA. Director of Continuing Education, Strathclyde University, since 1987 (Director, Management Development Programmes, Strathclyde Business School, 1984-87); Lecturer, Department of Information Science, Strathclyde University, since 1968; Consultant on Management Training and Development, since 1970; b. 19.6.36, Glasgow; m., Joan Moore; 1 s.; 1 d. Educ. Langholm Academy; Dumfries Academy; Edinburgh University. W. & T. Avery, 1961-63; IBM (UK) Ltd., 1963-64; Sumlock Comptometer Ltd., 1964-68; Consultancies: Scottish Co-operative Wholesale Society, 1969, Hotel and Catering Industry Training Board, 1971, Scottish Engineering Employers Association, 1973. Member: Strathclyde Children's Panel, Committee on Food Processing Opportunities in Scotland, Scottish Council (Development and Industry), Vice-President, Royal Philosophical Society of Glasgow, since 1998, International Vocational Education and Training Association, Church of Scotland Education Committee, American Association of Adult and Continuing Education; Vice-Chairman, Universities Council for Adult and Continuing Education (Scotland), since 1990. Publication: Collins Business Dictionary (with B. McKenna). Recreation: reading, observing and talking on Scotland and the Scots. Address: (b.) 40 George Street, Glasgow G1 1QE.

Fleming, Professor George, BSc, PhD, FEng, FRSE, FICE, MIWEM. Professor of Civil Engineering, Strathclyde University, since 1985, and Managing Director of Envirocentre, since 1995; Vice President, Institution of Civil Engineers; b. 16.8.44, Glasgow; m., Irene Fleming; 2 s.; 1 d. Educ. Knightswood Secondary School, Glasgow; Strathclyde University; Stanford University, California. Research Assistant, Strathclyde University, 1966-69, Stanford University, 1967; Senior Research Hydrologist, Hydrocomp International, California, 1969-70; Research Associate, Stanford University, 1969-70; Director and Vice President, Hydrocomp International, Palo Alto and Glasgow, 1970-79; Lecturer, then Senior Lecturer, then Reader in Civil Engineering, Strathclyde University, 1971-85; Visiting Professor, University of Padova, Italy, since 1980; Vice Dean, Engineering Faculty, Strathclyde University, 1984-87. Member, Scottish Exports Forum. Publications: Computer Simulation in Hydrology, 1975; The Sediment Problem, 1977; Deterministic Models in Hydrology, 1979. Recreations: farming; fishing; food. Address: (b.) John Anderson Building, 107 Rottenrow, Glasgow G4 0NG; T.-0141-553 4169.

Fleming, Sheriff Grahame R, QC. Sheriff of Lothian and Borders, since 1993; b. 13.2.49. Address: (b.) Linlithgow Sheriff Court, Sheriff Court House, High Street, Linlithgow, EH49 7EQ.

Fleming, Maurice. Editor, The Scots Magazine, 1974-91; b. Blairgowrie; m., Nanette Dalgleish; 2 s.; 1 d. Educ. Blairgowrie High School. Trained in hotel management before entering journalism; worked on various magazines; has had five full-length plays performed professionally, as well as one-act plays by amateurs; founder Member: Traditional Music and Song Association of Scotland, Scottish Poetry Library; Chairman, Blairgowrie, Rattray and District Civic Trust; Past Chairman, Blair in Bloom. Publications: The Scots Magazine — A Celebration of 250 Years (Co-Editor); The Ghost O' Mause and Other Tales and Traditions of East Perthshire; Old Blairgowrie and Rattray; The Real Macbeth and Other Stories from Scottish History. Recreations: theatre; reading; bird-watching; enjoying the countryside; folksong and folklore. Address: (h.) Craigard, Perth Road, Blairgowrie; T.-Blairgowrie 873633.

Fleming, Tom, CVO, OBE. Actor and Director; b. 29.6.27, Edinburgh. Professional theatre debut, 1945, in company led by Edith Evans; Co-Founder, Edinburgh Gateway Company, 1953; joined Royal Shakespeare Company at Stratford upon Avon, 1962, and played several classical roles, including Prospero, Brutus, Cymbeline, Buckingham and Kent; toured with RSC in USSR, USA and Europe, 1964; Director and Founder, Royal Lyceum Theatre Company, 1965; there played title role in Galileo; Director, Scottish Theatre Company, 1982-87; awarded Roman Szlydowski Prize for his production of The Thrie Estaites, Warsaw, 1986; TV work includes portrayals of Robert Burns, William Wallace, Jesus of Nazareth, Henry IV, Weir of Hermiston, and Sir John Reith; films include Mary, Queen of Scots, King Lear, Meetings with Remarkable Men; Radio and television commentator, including Coronation, Silver Jubilee celebrations, Cenotaph service since 1965, VE and VJ Day 50th anniversaries, funeral of Diana, Princess of Wales; Hon. Member, Saltire Society, Royal Scottish Pipers' Society, Scottish Arts Club. Publications: So That Was Spring; Miracle at Midnight; Voices Out of the Air (Editor); It's My Belief; BBC Book of Memories; A Scottish Childhood, Volume II (Contributor); Hon. doctorate, Heriot-Watt University; FRSAMD.

Fletcher, Sheriff Michael John, LLB. Sheriff of South Strathclyde Dumfries & Galloway at Dumfries, since 1994; b. 5.12.45, Dundee; m., Kathryn Mary; 2 s. Educ. High School of Dundee; St. Andrews University. Solicitor, 1968-94. Recreations: golf; gardening.

Fletcher, Professor Roger, MA, PhD, FIMA, FRSE. Professor of Optimization, Department of Mathematics, Dundee University, since 1984; b. 29.1.39, Huddersfield; m., Mary Marjorie Taylor; 2 d. Educ. Huddersfield College; Cambridge University; Leeds University. Lecturer, Leeds University, 1963-69; Principal Research Fellow, then Principal Scientific Officer, AERE Harwell, 1969-73; Senior Research Fellow, then Senior Lecturer, then Reader, Dundee University, 1973-84. Publications: Practical Methods of Optimization, 2nd edition, 1987. numerous others. Recreations: hill-walking; music; bridge. Address: (h.) 43 Errol Road, Invergowrie, Dundee DD2 5BX; T.-01382 562452.

Flett, Ian Stark, CBE (1984), MA, MEd, ABPS; b. 26.1.20, Aberdeen; m., Moyra. Educ. Aberdeen Grammar School; Aberdeen University; Aberdeen College of Education. RAF, Signals and Intelligence Branch, 1940-46; Teacher, Aberdeen, 1947-49; Adviser, Durham, 1949-54; Assistant Education Officer, Lancashire, 1954-59; Deputy, 1959-63; Deputy Education Officer, City of Hull, 1963-66; Member, Dalegacy Institute of Education, Hull University, 1963-66; Director of Education, Fife, 1966-85; General Secretary, Association of Directors of Education in Scotland, 1975-85; President, 1979-80; Adviser to Association of County Councils, 1970-74; Principal Adviser, Convention of Scottish Local Authorities, 1975-84; Member: Consultative Committee on the Curriculum, 1977-87, General Teaching Council, 1976-84; Governor, Craiglockhart College of Education, 1977-83; Chairman: Scottish Association of Educational Management and Administration, 1981-84, Scottish Centre for Tuition of the Disabled, 1980-89, National Association for Gifted Children Scotland, 1985-93. Publication: The Years of Growth 1945-75, 1989. Recreations: music; gardening. Address: (h.) 5 Townsend Place, Kirkcaldy, Fife KY1 1HB; T. 01592 260279.

Flett, James. JP. Honorary Sheriff, Lothians and Borders; Past Chairman, City of Edinburgh Valuation Appeal Committee; b. 26.1.17, Findochty; m., Jean Walker Ross; 1 s. Educ. Findochty Public School; Heriot-Watt University; Royal Military College, Sandhurst. Commissioned Seaforth Highlanders; Chief Official, Royal Burgh of Linlithgow (retired). Governor, West Lothian Educational Trust; former Member, JP Advisory Committee; former Member, Scottish Home Department Interviewing Committee at Edinburgh Prisons; former Member, West Lothian Licensing Board. Recreations: gardening; travel; walking. Address: (h.) Craigenroan, Linlithgow, West Lothian; T.-Linlithgow 842344.

Flint, Professor David, TD, MA, BL, CA. Professor of Accountancy, Glasgow University, 1964-85 (Vice-Principal, 1981-85); b. 24.2.19, Glasgow; m., Dorothy Mary Maclachlan Jardine; 2 s.; 1 d. Educ. High School of Glasgow; Glasgow University. Royal Signals, 1939-46 (Major; mentioned in Despatches); Partner, Mann Judd Gordon & Company, Chartered Accountants, Glasgow, 1951-71; Lecturer (part-time), Glasgow University, 1950-60; Dean, Faculty of Law, 1971-73. Council Member, Scottish Business School, 1971-77; Institute of Chartered Accountants of Scotland: President, 1975-76, Vice-President, 1973-75, Convener, Research Advisory Committee, 1974-75 and 1977-84, Convener, Working Party on Future Policy, 1976-79, Convener, Public Sector Committee, 1987-89, Convener, Taxation Review and Research Sub-Committee, 1960-64; Trustee, Scottish Chartered Accountants Trust for Education, 1981-87; Member: Management Training and Development Committee, Central Training Council, 1966-70, Management and Industrial Relations Committee, Social Science Research Council, 1970-72 and 1978-80, Social Sciences Panel, Scottish Universities Council on Entrance, 1968-72; Chairman, Association of University Teachers of Accounting, 1969; Member, Company Law Committee, Law Society of Scotland, 1976-85; Scottish Economic Society: Treasurer, 1954-62, Vice-President, 1977-88, Hon. Vice-President, since 1988; Member, Commission for Local Authority Accounts in Scotland, 1978-80; President, European Accounting Association, 1983-84. Publication: Philosophy and Principles of Auditing, 1988. Recreation: golf. Address: (h.) 16 Grampian Avenue, Auchterarder, Perthshire PH3 1NY; T.-01764 663978.

Flitsch, Professor Sabine Lahja, Diplom, MA, DPhil, MRSC, CChem. Professor of Protein Chemistry, University of Edinburgh, since 1998; b. 10.10.58, Münster, Germany; m., Professor N.J. Turner; 2 s. Educ. Schillergymnasium. Münster; University of Münster; Oxford University. Demonstrator, University of Exeter, 1988-89; Lecturer, University of Oxford, 1989-95. Address: Weir Building, King's Buildings, Edinburgh EH9 3JY.

Flockhart, (David) Ross, OBE, BA, BD; b. 20.3.27, Newcastle, NSW, Australia; m., Pamela Ellison Macartney; 3 s.; 1 d.; 1 d. (deceased). Educ. Knox Grammar School, Sydney; Sydney University; Edinburgh University. Royal Australian Engineers, 1945-46; Chaplain to Overseas Students, Edinburgh, 1955-58; Parish Minister (Church of Scotland), Northfield, Aberdeen, 1958-63; Warden, Carberry Tower, Musselburgh, 1963-66; Lecturer and Senior Lecturer, School of Community Studies, Moray House College of Education, 1966-72; Director, Scottish Council for Voluntary Organisations, 1972-91. Member: Scottish Arts Council, 1976-82, Court, Stirling University, since 1989, Council, National Trust for Scotland; former Trustee and Vice-Chairman, Community Development Foundation. Recreations: bee-keeping; sailing. Address: (h.) Longwood, Humbie, East Lothian EH36 5PN; T.-01875 833208.

Florey, Professor Charles du Ve, MD, MPH, FFCM, FRCPE. Professor of Epidemiology and Public Health, Dundee University, since 1983. Instructor, Assistant Professor, Yale University, 1963-69; Member, Scientific Staff, MRC, 1969-71; Senior Lecturer, then Reader, then Professor, St. Thomas's Hospital Medical School, 1971-83; Member, Committee on Data Protection, 1976-78; Chairman, Commissioning Group, Health Technology Assessment. Publications: Introduction to Community Medicine; Methods for Cohort Studies of Chronic Airflow Limitation; The Pocket Guide to Grant Applications. Address: (b.) Department of Epidemiology and Public Health, Ninewells Hospital and Medical School, Dundee DD1 9SY; T.-01382 632124.

Flowerdew, Stuart Alan, LLB(Hons), DipLP, NP. Solicitor; Associate, John MacRitchie & Co., SSC, Peterhead, since 1997; Secretary and Treasurer, Faculty of Solicitors in Peterhead and Fraserburgh, since 1993; b. 5.2.67, Kings Lynn; m., Natalie Anne Lamb. Educ. Forres Academy; University of Dundee. Trainee/Assistant, Miller Hendry, Perth, 1989-92; Assistant: Stewart and Watson, Peterhead, 1992-94, Masson & Glennie, Peterhead, 1994-96. Recreation: cricket. Address: (b.) The Townhouse, Broad Street, Peterhead; T.-01779 478877.

Flynn, Mary Theresa, DA, RSW. Artist; b. 30.11.23, Selkirk. Educ. Galashiels Academy; Edinburgh College of Art. Teacher of Art, Fife, Edinburgh and Glasgow schools (retired as Principal Teacher of Art, John Paul Academy, Glasgow, 1984); regular contributor to RSA, RSW, RGI and SSWA/SAAC; elected membership to SSWA (later SAAC), 1962; elected membership to RSW, 1969. Recreations: extensive travel; theatre (particularly ballet); historical reading. Address: 6 Roseberry Crescent, Edinburgh EH12 5JP; T.-0131-346 0993.

Follett, Professor Georgina Louise Patricia, MDes, FRSA, FCSD. Head, School of Design, Duncan of Jordanstone College, since 1993; b. 16.7.49, London; m.,

Adrian Franklin; 1 s.; 1 d. Educ. Channing School; Royal College of Art. Course Leader, Sir John Cass College, 1979-88; Acting Head, Grays School of Art, 1988-93; Jeweller (exhibitions include one woman show, Jewellery Gallery, Victoria and Albert Museum). Founding Member, IDEAS; Member, Steering Group, Dundee by Design; Member, Council, Chartered Society of Designers (Chair, Education Group); Member, Scottish Higher Education Funding Council (Chair, Quality Assessment Committee); Member, Board of Directors, Crawford Arts Centre, St. Andrews. Recreations: gardening; drawing; reading. Address: University of Dundee, Perth Road, Dundee DD1 4HT; T.-01382 345289.

Foot, Professor Hugh Corrie, BA, PhD, FBPsS. Professor of Psychology, Strathclyde University, since 1992; b. 7.6.41, Northwood, Middx; m., Daryl M.; 1 s.; 1 d. Educ. Durham University; Queen's College, Dundee. Research Fellow, Dundee University, 1965-68; University of Wales Institute of Science and Technology: Lecturer, 1968-77, Senior Lecturer, 1977-88; Reader, University of Wales College of Cardiff, 1989-91. Recreations: tennis; hill walking. Address: Department of Psychology, Strathclyde University, 40 George Street, Glasgow, G1 1QE; T.-0141-552 4400, Ext. 2580.

Footman, Raymond Alan, BA, DipEd. Director, Communications and Public Affairs, University of Edinburgh; b. 19.5.39, London; m., Els; 1 s. Educ. Kirkham Grammar School; University of Wales. College of Estate Management; Committee of Vice Chancellors and Principals of UK Universities; University of Edinburgh, since 1977. Former Chair, Standing Conference of University Information Officers; founding Member and former Chair, European Universities Information and PR Association; Chair, Board of Trustees of Council for Advancement and Support of Education (CASE) Europe; Member, Board of Trustees, CASE International; Association of Commonwealth Universities Travelling Fellowship, 1982. Publication: Boosting University Income (contributor). Recreations: theatre; skiing. Address: University of Edinburgh Centre, 7-11 Nicolson Street, Edinburgh EH8 9BE; T.-0131-650 2249.

Forbes, Alexander Douglas, MA, LLB. Chairman, Scottish Friendly Assurance Society Ltd., since 1996; Consultant (formerly Partner), Robertson Paul (Solicitors), Glasgow; b. 18.2.37, Glasgow; m., Rachel Mary; 1 s.; 2 d. Educ. High School of Glasgow; Glasgow University. Solicitor, since 1964; Board Member, Scottish Friendly Assurance, since 1980. Recreations: curling; angling; walking. Address: (h.) 29 Tannoch Drive, Milngavie, Glasgow G62 8AR; T.-0141-956 3561.

Forbes, Professor Charles Douglas, DSc, MD, MB, ChB, FRCP, FRCPGlas, FRCPEdin, FRSA, FRSE. Professor of Medicine, Dundee University, and Honorary Consultant Physician, Dundee Teaching Hospitals NHS Trust, since 1987; b. 9.10.38, Glasgow; m., Janette MacDonald Robertson; 2 s. Educ. High School of Glasgow; Glasgow University. Assistant Lecturer in Materia Medica, Glasgow University; Lecturer in Medicine, Makerere, Uganda; Registrar in Medicine, Glasgow Royal Infirmary; Reader in Medicine, Glasgow University; Fellow, American Heart Association; Fullbright Fellow; Director, Regional Haemophilia Centre, Glasgow. Recreation: gardening. Address: (h.) East Chattan, 108 Hepburn Gardens, St. Andrews KY16 9LT; T.-01334 472428.

Forbes, David Fraser, LLB (Hons). Regional Officer, Scottish Health Visitors' Association/UNISON; b. 11.4.56, Glasgow; m., Isabel Hamilton; 3 d. Educ. Greenock Academy; Edinburgh University. Porter, Royal Edinburgh Hospital, and Senior Shop Steward, NUPE, 1978-87; Diploma in Accountancy, Stirling University, 1987-88. Address: (b.) Douglas House, 60 Belford Road, Edinburgh, EH4 3UQ.

Forbes, Sheriff John Stuart, MA, LLB. Sheriff of Tayside, Central and Fife, at Dunfermline, since 1980; b. 31.1.36.

Forbes, 22nd Lord (Nigel Ivan Forbes), KBE (1960), JP, DL. Premier Lord of Scotland; Chairman, Rolawn Ltd., 1975-98; b. 19.2.18; m., Hon. Rosemary Katharine Hamilton-Russell; 2 s.; 1 d. Educ. Harrow; Sandhurst. Retired Major, Grenadier Guards; Representative Peer of Scotland, 1955-63; Minister of State, Scottish Office, 1958-59. Member: Scottish Committee, Nature Conservancy, 1961-67, Aberdeen and District Milk Marketing Board, 1962-72, Sports Council for Scotland, 1966-71; Chairman, River Don District Board, 1962-73; President: Royal Highland and Agricultural Society of Scotland, 1958-59, Scottish Scout Association, 1970-88; Chairman, Scottish Branch, National Playing Fields Association, 1965-80; Deputy Chairman, Tennant Caledonian Breweries Ltd., 1964-74. Address: (h.) Balforbes, Alford, Aberdeenshire AB33 8DR; T.-019755 62516.

Forbes, Ronald Douglas, ARSA. Artist; Head of Painting, Duncan of Jordanstone College of Art, since 1995; b. 22.3.47, Braco; m., Sheena Henderson Ball; 1 s.; 2 d. Educ. Morrison's Academy, Crieff; Edinburgh College of Art. Leverhulme Senior Art Fellow, Strathclyde University, 1973-74; Head of Painting, Crawford School of Art, Cork, Ireland, 1974-78; Artist in Residence, Livingston, 1978-80; Scottish Arts Council Studio Residence Bursary, Amsterdam, 1980; Lecturer, Glasgow School of Art, 1979-83; Director, Master Fine Art postgraduate studies, Duncan of Jordanstone College of Art, University of Dundee, 1983-95; Artist in Residence, University of Tasmania Hobart Centre for the Arts. First Prize, first Scottish Young Contemporary Exhibition, 1967; RSA Guthrie Award, 1979; Scottish Arts Council Award for Film-making, 1979; Highland Society of London Award, Royal Scottish Academy, 1996. Recreations: cinema; theatre; gardening. Address: (h.) 13 Fort Street, Dundee DD2 1BS; T.-01382 641498.

Ford, Gordon J.W., BA, DipEd. Headmaster, Broughton High School, since 1993;' b. 1.5.52, Inverkeithing; m., Audrey; 1 s.; 2 d. Educ. Kirkcaldy High School; Knox Academy; Stirling University. Teacher of History, Modern Studies, 1974-87; Assistant Headteacher, Greenhall High School, 1987-89; Depute Headteacher: Ainslie Park High School, 1989-91, Armadale Academy, 1991-93. Publication: Timetabling Explained. Recreations: coaching rugby; tennis; music; tai chi. Address: (b.) Broughton High School, Carrington Road, Edinburgh EH4 1EG; T.-0131-332 7805.

Ford, Professor Ian, BSc, PhD. Professor of Biostatistics and Director, Robertson Centre for Biostatistics, Glasgow University, since 1991; b. 4.2.51, Glasgow; m., Carole Louise Ford; 1 s. Educ. Hamilton Academy; Glasgow University. Visiting Lecturer, University of Wisconsin, Madison, 1976-77; Lecturer, then Senior Lecturer, Reader and Personal Professor, Glasgow University, since 1977. Publications: 80 papers. Recreations: gardening; travel. Address: (b.) Robertson Centre for Biostatistics, Boyd Orr Building, Glasgow University, Glasgow; T.-0141-330 4744.

Ford, James Allan, CB, MC. Author; b. 10.6.20, Auchtermuchty; m., Isobel Dunnett; 1 s.; 1 d. Educ. Royal High School, Edinburgh; Edinburgh University. Employment Clerk, Ministry of Labour, 1938-39; Executive Officer, Inland Revenue, 1939-40; Captain, The Royal Scots, 1940-46 (POW, Far East, 1941-45); Executive Officer, Inland Revenue, 1946-47; Department of Agriculture for Scotland, 1947-66 (Assistant Secretary,

1958); Registrar General for Scotland, 1966-69; Under Secretary, Scottish Office, 1969-79. Trustee, National Library of Scotland, 1981-91. Publications (novels): The Brave White Flag, 1961; Season of Escape, 1963; A Statue for a Public Place, 1965; A Judge of Men, 1968; The Mouth of Truth, 1972. Recreation: gardening. Address: (h.) 6 Hillpark Court, Edinburgh EH4 7BE; T.-0131 336 5398.

Ford, James Angus, OBE, MB, ChB, FRCPEdin, FRCPGlas, FRCP (Lond), FRCPCH, DCH. Consultant Paediatrician, since 1975; Chairman: Scottish Joint Consultants Committee, National Medical Advisory Committee; Member, General Medical Council and Professional Conduct Committee; b. 5.11.43, Arbroath; m., Dr. Veronica T. Reid. Educ. Kelvinside Academy; Glasgow University. House appointments: Glasgow Royal, Southern General, Stobhill, Belvidere; Registrar/Senior Registrar, Stobhill; Consultant appointments: Rutherglen Maternity Hospital, Royal Hospital for Sick Children, Glasgow; Territorial Army: six years, 6/7th Bn., Cameronians (Scottish Rifles), Captain; BMA: former Chairman, Scottish Council, Chairman, Hospital Junior Staff Committee (Scotland), Deputy Chairman, HJSC (UK), Member of Council (Scottish and UK), Member, Joint Consultants Committee (Scottish and UK). Recreation: gardening. Address: (h.) 20 Ralston Road, Bearsden, Glasgow; T.-0141-942 4273.

Ford, John Noel Patrick, CStJ, FInstD. Director of Administration and Finance, Scottish Civic Trust, since 1993; Regional Chairman, Glasgow, Princes Scottish Youth Business Trust, since 1993; Chairman, Glasgow Committee, Order of St. John, since 1993; Trustee, New Lanark Conservation Trust, since 1994; b. 18.12.35, Surbiton; m., Roslyn Madeleine Penfold; 2 s.; 2 d. Educ. Tiffin School, Kingston on Thames. Retired, 1992, as Chairman, Scotland and Northern Ireland, and Marketing Director, OCS Group Ltd. Deacon, Incorporation of Masons of Glasgow, 1985-86; Deacon Convener, Trades House of Glasgow, 1991-92; Governor, Hutchesons' Educational Trust, since 1986; General Commissioner of Inland Revenue, Glasgow North. Recreations: golf and sport in general; gardening. Address: (b.) 42 Miller Street, Glasgow G1 1DT; T.-0141 221 1466.

Ford, Margaret, MA, MPhil. Chairman, Lothian Health Board, since 1997; Managing Director, Eglinton Management Centre. Address: (b.) 148 The Pleasance, Edinburgh EH8 9RS.

Forrest, Professor Sir (Andrew) Patrick (McEwen), Kt (1986), BSc, MD, ChM, FRCS, FRCSEdin, FRCSGlas, DSc (Hon), LLD (Hon), FACS (Hon), FRACS (Hon), FRCSCan (Hon), FRCR (Hon), FIBiol, FRSE. Professor Emeritus, Edinburgh University; b. 25.3.23, Mount Vernon, Lanarkshire; m., 1. Margaret Beryl Hall (deceased); 1s.; 1d.; 2. Margaret Anne Steward; 1 d. Educ. Dundee High School; St. Andrews University. House Surgeon, Dundee Royal Infirmary; Surgeon Lieutenant, RNVR; Mayo Foundation Fellow; Lecturer and Senior Lecturer, Glasgow University; Professor of Surgery, Welsh National School of Medicine; Regius Professor of Clinical Surgery, Edinburgh University; Visiting Scientist, National Cancer Institute, USA; Associate Dean of Clinical Studies, International Medical College, Malaysia; Chief Scientist (part-time), Scottish Home and Health Department, 1981-87; Chairman, Working Group, Breast Cancer Screening, 1985-86; President: Surgical Research Society, 1974-76, Association of Surgeons of Great Britain and Ireland, 1988-89; Lister Medal, Royal College of Surgeons of England, 1987; Member, Kirk Session, St. Giles Cathedral. Publications: Prognostic Factors in Breast Cancer (Co-author), 1968; Principles and Practice of Surgery (Co-author), 1985; Breast Cancer: the decision to screen, 1990. Recreations: sailing; golf. Address: (h.) 19 St. Thomas Road, Edinburgh EH9 2LR; T.-0131-667 3203.

Forrest, Peter, ATI. Chief Executive, Dawson International PLC, since 1998, Main Board Director, since 1994; Managing Director, Todd & Duncan Ltd., Kinross, since 1991; b. 2.5.38, Dewsbury; m., Evelyn Margaret; 3 s. Educ. Batley Grammar School; Huddersfield College of Textiles. Yorkshire textile industry, 1959-70; founded and become Managing Director, Dundee Fabrics Ltd., 1971-76; Dundee Fabrics taken over, 1976, continuing as MD until 1980, also joining board of Courtaulds Northern Weaving Division; Operations Director, Legler Industria Tessile, Italy, 1980-91. Recreations: sailing; walking; classical music. Address: (h.) Whinfield House, Kinross KY13 7AU.

Forrest, Robert Jack, OBE, FRAgS, DL. Director, Royal Highland & Agricultural Society of Scotland, 1979-95 (Hon. Treasurer, 1985-88, Chairman, 1989-90, Hon. Secretary 1991-95); Director, Scottish Agricultural College, since 1996; b. 4.1.39, Duns; m., Jennifer McCreath; 2 s.; 1 d. Educ. Loretto School; East of Scotland College of Agriculture. Director, Robert Forrest Ltd. (Farmers), since 1960, Chairman since 1986; President, British Simmental Cattle Society, 1983-84; President, Scottish Agricultural Arbiters Association, 1993-94; Vice Chairman, Scottish Agricultural Benevolent Institution, 1991; Director, Scottish Borders Enterprise, 1994-98; Director, Scottish SPCA, since 1998; Elder, Bonkyl Church. Address: (h.) Preston, Duns, Berwickshire TD11 3TQ; T.-01361 882826.

Forrester, Rev. Professor Duncan Baillie, MA (Hons), BD, DPhil. Dean, Faculty of Divinity, New College, Edinburgh, since 1996 (Principal, 1986-96) and Professor of Christian Ethics and Practical Theology, since 1978; Church of Scotland Minister; b. 10.11.33, Edinburgh; m., Rev. Margaret McDonald; 1 s.; 1 d. Educ. Madras College, St. Andrews; St. Andrews University; Chicago University; Edinburgh University. Part-time Assistant in Politics, Edinburgh University, 1957-58; Assistant Minister, Hillside Church, Edinburgh, and Leader of St. James Mission, 1960-61; as Church of Scotland Missionary, Lecturer and then Professor of Politics, Madras Christian College, Tambaram, South India, 1962-70; ordained Presbyter, Church of South India, 1962; part-time Lecturer in Politics, Edinburgh University, 1966-67; Chaplain and Lecturer in Politics, Sussex University. Member, WCC Faith and Order Commission, 1983-96; President: Society for Study of Theology, 1991-93, Society for Study of Christian Ethics, 1991-94. Publications: Caste & Christianity, 1980; Encounter with God (Co-author), 1983; Studies in the History of Worship in Scotland (Co-Editor), 1984; Christianity and the Future of Welfare, 1985; Theology and Politics, 1988; Just Sharing (Co-author), 1988; Beliefs, Values and Policies, 1989; Worship Now Book II (Co-editor), 1989; Theology and Practice (Editor), 1990; The True Church and Morality, 1997; Christian Justice and Public Policy, 1997. Recreations: hill-walking; reading; listening to music. Address: (h.) 25 Kingsburgh Road, Edinburgh, EH12 6DZ; T.-0131-337 5646.

Forrester, Frederick Lindsay, MA (Hons), DipEd, FEIS. Depute General Secretary, Educational Institute of Scotland, since 1992; b. 10.2.35, Glasgow; 1 s.; 1 d. Educ. Victoria Drive Senior Secondary School, Glasgow; Glasgow University; Jordanhill College of Education. Teacher of English, Glasgow secondary schools, 1962-64; Teacher of English and General Studies, Coatbridge Technical College, 1964-67; Assistant Secretary, Educational Institute of Scotland, 1967-75, Organising Secretary, 1975-92. Recreations:walking; cycling; swimming; foreign travel. Address: (h.) 2/6 East Farm of Gilmerton, Edinburgh EH17 8TQ; T.-0131 672 1638.

Forrester, Ian Stewart, QC, MA, LLB, MCL. Honorary Visiting Professor in European Law, Glasgow University, since 1991; Member, European Advisory Board, Tulane University Law School, since 1992; b. 13.1.45, Glasgow; m., Sandra Anne Therese Keegan; 2 s. Educ. Kelvinside

Academy, Glasgow; Glasgow University; Tulane University of Louisiana. Admitted to Faculty of Advocates, 1972; admitted to Bar of State of NY, 1977; called to Bar, Middle Temple, 1996. Maclay, Murray & Spens, 1968-69; Davis Polk & Wardwell, 1969-72; Cleary Gottlieb Steen & Hamilton, 1972-81; established independent chambers, Brussels, 1981; Co-Founder, Forrester & Norall, 1981 (Forrester Norall & Sutton, 1989), practising before European Commission and Courts. Chairman: British Conservative Association, Belgium, 1982-86, European Trade Law Association, since 1989 ; author of numerous papers on European law; Member, European Committee of British Invisibles; Elder, St. Andrew's Church of Scotland, Brussels. Recreations: politics; wine; cooking; restoring old houses.

Forrester, Professor John V., MD (Hons), FRCS(Ed), FRCOphth, FRCS(G). Cockburn Professor of Ophthalmology, since 1984; Editor, British Journal of Ophthalmology, since 1992; b. 11.9.46, Glasgow; m., Anne Gray; 2 s.; 2 d. Educ. St. Aloysius College, Glasgow; Glasgow University. Various hospital appointments, Glasgow, 1971-78; MRC Travelling Fellow, Columbia University, New York, 1976-77; Consultant Ophthalmologist, Southern General Hospital, 1979-83; Spinoza Professor, University of Amsterdam, 1997. Recreation: family. Address: (b.) Department of Ophthalmology, Aberdeen University, Aberdeen AB9 2ZD; T.-01224 681818.

Forrester, Rev. Margaret Rae, MA, BD. Minister, St. Michael's, Edinburgh, since 1980; b. 23.11.37, Edinburgh; m., Duncan B. Forrester; 1 s.; 1 d. Educ. George Watson's Ladies' College; Edinburgh University and New College. Assistant Pastor, Tambaram, Madras; Minister, Telscombe Cliffs URC, Sussex; Assistant Minister, St. George's West, Edinburgh; Chaplain, Napier College, Edinburgh. Convener, Board of World Mission and Unity, Church of Scotland, 1992-96. Recreation: gardening. Address: 25 Kingsburgh Road, Edinburgh EH12 6DZ; T.-0131-337 5646.

Forsyth of That Ilk, Alistair Charles William, JP, KHS, FSCA, FSA Scot, FInstPet, CStJ. Baron of Ethie; Chief of the Name and Clan of Forsyth; b. 7.12.29; m., Ann Hughes; 4 s. Educ. St. Paul's School; Queen Mary College, London. Company Director; CStJ, 1982; KHS, 1992; Freeman of the City of London; Liveryman of the Scriveners Company. Recreations: Scottish antiquities. Address: (h.) Ethie Castle, by Arbroath, Angus DD11 5SP.

Forsyth, Bill. Film Director and Script Writer; b. 1947, Glasgow. Films include: Gregory's Girl, 1981, Local Hero, 1983, Comfort and Joy, 1984, Housekeeping, 1988, Breaking In, 1990, Being Human, 1993. BAFTA Awards: Best Screenplay, 1982, Best Director, 1983.

Forsyth, Janice, MA (Hons). Broadcaster; b. Glasgow. Educ. Glasgow High School for Girls; Glasgow University. Presenter, Janice Forsyth Show, Working Lives (Radio Scotland), Artists' Question Time (Radio 3); TV includes: Filmnight (C4), Don't Look Down, NB and Festival Cinema (all Scottish); Columnist, Scotsman/Scotland on Sunday. Board Member, Giant Productions. Recreations: cinema; travel; theatre.

Forsyth, Rt. Hon. Sir Michael (Bruce), PC, Kt, MA. MP (Conservative), Stirling, 1983-97; Secretary of State for Scotland, 1995-97; Director, Robert Fleming & Co. Ltd.; b. 16.10.54, Montrose; m., Susan Jane; 1 s.; 2 d. Educ. Arbroath High School; St. Andrews University. National Chairman, Federation of Conservative Students, 1976; Member, Westminster City Council, 1978-83; Member, Select Committee on Scottish Affairs; Parliamentary Private Secretary to the Foreign Secretary, 1986-87; Chairman, Scottish Conservative Party, 1989-90; Parliamentary Under Secretary of State and Minister of State, Scottish Office, 1987-92; Minister of State, Department of Employment, 1992-94; Minister of State, Home Office, 1994-95. Recreations: mountaineering; astronomy; gardening. Address: (h.) Na Lagan, Aberfoyle, Stirling FK8 3TJ.

Forsyth, Roderick Hugh (Roddy). Journalist; b. 22.9.53, Lennoxtown; m., Marian Charlotte Reilly; 2 d. Educ. Allan Glen's School, Glasgow. Journalist, D.C. Thomson & Co., 1972-74; Scottish Daily News, 1975; Editor, Carnoustie Times, 1976-77; Editor, What's On in Glasgow, 1978-79; Editor, Clyde Guide, 1979-80; Journalist, Glasgow Herald, 1980-81; Sunday Standard, 1982-83; freelance, since 1983; Scottish Football Correspondent: The Times, 1988-93, Daily and Sunday Telegraph, since 1993, BBC Radio Sport, since 1983, RTE Ireland, since 1988, Ireland on Sunday, since 1996. Publications: The Only Game, 1990; Fields of Green, 1996; Blue and True, 1996.

Forteviot, 4th Baron (John James Evelyn Dewar). Member, Queen's Bodyguard for Scotland (Royal Company of Archers); b. 5.4.38. Educ. Eton. Black Watch (RHR), 1956-58. Address: (h.) Aberdalgie House, Perth.

Forty, Professor Arthur John, CBE, BSc, PhD, DSc, LLD, DUniv, FRSE. Principal and Vice-Chancellor, Stirling University, 1986-94; b. 4.11.28, Shrivenham; m., Alicia Blanche Hart Gough; 1 s. Educ. Headlands School, Swindon; Bristol University. RAF, 1953-56; Senior Scientist, Tube Investments Ltd., 1956-58; Lecturer, Bristol University, 1958-64; founding Professor of Physics, Warwick University, 1964-86; Pro-Vice-Chancellor, Warwick Univ., 1970-86; Member, Physics and Materials Science Committees, SERC, 1970-74; Member: UGC, 1982-86 (Vice-Chairman, 1985-86), Computer Board, Universities and Research Councils, 1982-85 (Chairman, 1988-91); Chairman, Committee of Scottish University Principals, 1990-92; Member, British Library Board, 1987-94; Chairman, Information Systems Committee, UFC, 1991-92; Hon. Fellow and Chairman, EPCC, Edinburgh University, 1994-97; Member, Board of Trustees, National Library of Scotland, since 1995; author of "Forty Report" on future facilities for advanced research computing. Recreations: dinghy sailing; gardening. Address: (h.) Port Mor, St. Fillans, Perthshire PH6 2NF.

Foster, Alan, MA, MEd, MBA, PhD, MICFM, FRSA. Chief Executive, Scottish Council on Alcohol, since 1997; b. 2.4.50, St. Andrews; m., Elizabeth Jessie Margaret Denham; 3 d. Educ. Kirkcaldy High School; Lancaster Royal Grammar School; Edinburgh, Dundee and Glasgow Universities. Lothian Regional Council Department of Education, 1979-83; Save the Children Fund, 1983-89; Chief Executive, Glasgow and West of Scotland Society for the Blind, 1989-97. Recreations: sailing; hill-walking; cricket; opera; running (slowly). Address: (b.) 166 Buchanan Street, Glasgow G1 2NH.

Foster, Elizabeth. BA, MSc, MBA. Director, Family Mediation Scotland, since 1997; b. Glasgow; 1 d. Educ. Albert Secondary School, Glasgow; Strathclyde University; Glasgow University. Research Officer, National Children's Bureau, 1979-83; Projects Manager, Aberlour Child Care Trust, 1983-86; Assistant Divisional Director, Save the Children, 1986-96. Recreations: walking; skiing; sailing; reading; music; films. Address: (b.) 127 Rose Street South Lane, Edinburgh EH2 4BB; T.-0131-220 1610.

Foster, John, CBE, FRICS, FRTPI, RIBA, ARIAS, FRSA. President, Ramblers Association (Scotland); b. 13.8.20, Glasgow; m., Daphne Househam. Educ. Whitehill School, Glasgow; Royal Technical College, Glasgow. Surveyor with private firm in Glasgow, 1937; Air Ministry during War; Assistant Planning Officer: Kirkcudbright County Council, 1945-47, Holland Joint Planning Committee, Lincolnshire, 1947-48; Deputy County Planning Officer,

Holland County Council, 1948-52; Deputy Planning Officer, Peak Park Planning Board, 1952-54; Director: Peak District National Park Board, 1954-68, Countryside Commission for Scotland, 1968-85. Honorary Vice-President, Countrywide Holidays Association; Honorary Fellow, Royal Scottish Geographical Society; Member, Executive Committee, Scottish Council for National Parks; Honorary Member and Past Vice Chairman, Commission on National Parks and Protected Areas, World Conservation Union; Hon. Member, European Federation of Nature and National Parks; Vice-Chairman, Heritage Unit Advisory Board, Robert Gordon University, Aberdeen; Life Member, National Trust for Scotland; George Waterston Memorial Award, 1991; Hon. Fellow, Robert Gordon University. Recreations: walking; swimming; photography; philately; reading; travel. Address: (h.) Birchover, Ferntower Road, Crieff PH7 3DH; T.-01764 652336.

Foster, Professor John Odell, MA, PhD. Professor of Applied Social Studies, Paisley University, since 1981; b. 21.10.40, Hertford; m., Renee Prendergast; 1 d. Educ. Guildford Grammar School; St. Catherine's College, Cambridge. Postdoctoral Research Fellow, St. Catherine's College, Cambridge, 1965-68; Lecturer in Politics, Strathclyde University, 1966-81. Secretary, Scottish Committee, Communist Party of Britain, since 1988. Publications: Class Struggle and the Industrial Revolution, 1974; Politics of the UCS Work-In, 1986; Track Record: the Caterpillar Occupation, 1988; Paying for the Piper (Co-author), 1996. Recreation: hill-walking. Address: (h.) 845 Govan Road, Glasgow G51.

Foulds, Emeritus Professor Wallace Stewart, CBE, MD, ChM, FRCS, FRCSGlas, DO, Hon. FRCOphth, Hon. DSc (Strathclyde), Hon. FRACO, Hon. FCMSA. Emeritus Professor of Ophthalmology, Glasgow University; Visiting Professor, National University of Singapore and Singapore National Eye Centre; b. 26.4.24, London; m., Margaret Holmes Walls; 1 s.; 2 d. Educ. George Watson's Boys College, Edinburgh; Paisley Grammar School; Glasgow University. RAF Medical Branch, 1946-49; training posts, Moorfields Eye Hospital, London, 1952-54; Research Fellow, Institute of Ophthalmology, London University, and Senior Registrar, University College Hospital, London, 1954-58; Consultant Ophthalmologist, Addenbrookes Hospital, Cambridge, 1958-64; Tennent Professor, Glasgow University, 1964-89; Honorary Lecturer, Cambridge University and Research Fellow, London University, 1958-64; Past President: Ophthalmological Society of UK, Faculty of Ophthalmologists; Past Chairman, Association for Eye Research; Founder President, Royal College of Ophthalmologists. Recreations: sailing; diving; DIY; natural history. Address: Kinnoul Place, 68 Dowanside Road, Glasgow G12 9DL; T.-0141-334 2463.

Foulis, Alan Keith, BSc, MD, MRCPath, FRCP(Ed). Consultant Pathologist, Royal Infirmary, Glasgow, since 1983; b. 25.5.50, Glasgow; m., Anne Don Martin; 1 s.; 1 d. Educ. Glasgow Academy; Glasgow University. Trained in pathology, Western Infirmary, Glasgow, following brief flirtation with surgery at Aberdeen Royal Infirmary; C.L. Oakley Lecturer, Pathological Society, Oxford, 1987; Bellahouston Medal, Glasgow University, 1987; R.D. Lawrence Lecturer, British Diabetic Association, Manchester, 1989. Publications: research papers on diseases of the pancreas. Recreations: choral and Leider singing; walking; cycling; arctophilia; natural history. Address: (h.) 32 Tannoch Drive, Milngavie, Glasgow; T.-0141-956 3092.

Foulkes, George, JP, BSc. Parliamentary Under-Secretary of State, Department for International Development; MP (Labour and Co-operative), Carrick, Cumnock and Doon Valley, since 1979; b. 21.1.42, Oswestry; m., Elizabeth Anna; 2 s.; 1 d. Educ. Keith Grammar School; Haberdashers' Aske's School; Edinburgh University. Opposition Spokesman on Foreign Affairs, 1984-92, Defence, 1992-93, Overseas Development, 1994-97. President, Scottish Union of Students, 1964-66; Director: European League for Economic Co-operation, 1967-68, Enterprise Youth, 1968-73, Age Concern Scotland, 1973-79; Chairman: Lothian Region Education Committee, 1974-79, Education Committee, COSLA, 1975-79; Rector's Assessor, Edinburgh University, 1968-71; Treasurer, Parliamentarians for Global Action. Recreations: boating; watching football (Heart of Midlothian and Ayr United). Address: (h.) 18A Ewenfield Road, Ayr KA7 2QB; T.-01292 265776.

Fourman, Professor Michael Paul, BSc, MSc, DPhil. Professor of Computer Systems, Edinburgh University, since 1988; b. 12.9.50, Oxford; m., Jennifer Robin Head; 2 s.; 1 d. Educ. Allerton Grange, Leeds; Bristol University; Oxford University. Junior Research Fellow, Wolfson College, Oxford, 1974-78; J.F. Ritt Assistant Professor of Mathematics, Columbia University NY, 1976-82; Department of Electrical & Electronic Engineering, Brunel University: Research Fellow, 1983-86, Hirst Reader in Integrated Circuit Design, 1986, Professor of Formal Systems, 1986-88. Recreations: cooking; sailing. Address: (b.) Informatics Department, Edinburgh University, 2 Buccleuch Place, Edinburgh EH8 9LW; T.-0131-650 4416.

Fowkes, Professor Francis Gerald Reid, MB, ChB, PhD, FRCPE, FFPHM. Professor of Epidemiology, Edinburgh University, since 1994; Director, Wolfson Unit for Prevention of Peripheral Vascular Diseases, since 1989; Hon. Consultant Public Health Medicine, since 1985; b. 9.5.46, Falkirk; 1.s.; 1 d. Educ. George Watson's College, Edinburgh; Edinburgh University. Senior Lecturer, University of Wales, 1980-85; Reader/Professor, Edinburgh University, since 1985. Address: (b.) Department of Public Health Sciences, Edinburgh University, Teviot Place, Edinburgh EH8 9AG; T.-0131-650 3220.

Fowler, Agnes Isobel, BSc, FRSAMD. Director of Finance and Administration, Royal Scottish Academy of Music and Drama; b. 13.2.42, Glasgow; m., William M. Fowler; 2 s.; 1 d. Educ. Jordanhill College School; Glasgow University. Governor, Associated Board, Royal Schools of Music. Recreations: hill-walking; swimming; gardening; Church. Address: (h.) Hillside, 7 Main Street, Drymen, Glasgow; T.-01360 660009.

Fowlie, Hector Chalmers, OBE, MB, ChB, FRCPEdin, FRCPsych, DPM. Retired Consultant Psychiatrist; Member of Court, Abertay University, Dundee; b. 21.6.29, Dundee; m., Christina N.M. Walker; 2 s.; 1 d. Educ. Harris Academy, Dundee; St. Andrews University. House Officer, Maryfield Hospital, Dundee, and Perth Royal Infirmary; Registrar, Dundee Royal Mental Hospital; Lecturer, Department of Psychiatry, Medical School, Dundee University; Consultant Psychiatrist and Deputy Physician Superintendent, Gartnavel Royal Hospital, Glasgow; Physician Superintendent, Royal Dundee Liff and Strathmartine Hospitals; Consultant Psychiatrist, Tayside Health Board. Vice-Chairman, Mental Welfare Commission for Scotland, 1984-89; sometime Vice-Chairman, Parole Board for Scotland; Member, Tayside Health Board; Council of Europe Scholar; Consultant, WHO; Past Chairman: Dundee Association for Mental Health, Dundee Healthcare NHS Trust. Recreations: reading; walking. Address: (h.) 21 Clepington Road, Dundee; T.-01382 456926.

Fox, Andrew John Arthur, MA. General Manager, H. M. Frigate Unicorn, since 1994; b. 1.5.53, Bristol; m., Lyubov Mikhailovna Yampolskaya; 1 s. Educ. Dundee High School; University of Aberdeen. Assistant Collector of Taxes, Dundee and London, 1977-78; Teacher of English, Invergordon Academy, 1979-80; Information Worker, Dundee Association for Social Services, 1985-86; H.M. Frigate Unicorn: Curator, 1987-90, Project Supervisor,

1992-94. Publications: three books of poetry. Recreations: writing; reading; swimming. Address: (b.) H. M. Frigate Unicorn, Victoria Dock, Dundee DD1 3JA; T.-01382 200900.

Fox, Christopher Howard Christian, MRAC, ARICS. Chartered Surveyor and Director (Estates), Scottish Greenbelt Company, since 1996; b. 13.1.41, Whitehaven; m., Caroline Jane Porter; 1 s.; 1 d. Educ. Fettes College, Edinburgh; Royal Agricultural College, Cirencester. Assistant Land Agent: W.H. Cooke & Arkwright, Chartered Surveyors, Hereford, 1963-69, Nature Conservancy Council, Edinburgh, 1969-73; Area Land Agent, North Scotland, Nature Conservancy Council, 1973-83; Senior Land Agent (Scotland), Nature Conservancy Council, 1983-91; Regional Director: South West Scotland, Nature Conservancy Council for Scotland, 1991-92, South West Region, Scottish Natural Heritage, 1992-96. Director, Scottish Agricultural College, Auchincruive, 1991-94; Member, Advisory Committee, Scottish Agricultural College. Recreations: country sports; contemporary Scottish painters; music. Address: (h.) 3 Brandon Terrace, Edinburgh EH3 5EA; T.-0131-557 4481.

Fox, Professor Keith Alexander Arthur, BSc (Hons), MB, ChB, FRCP. Duke of Edinburgh Professor of Cardiology, Edinburgh University, since 1989; Honorary Consultant Cardiologist, Royal Infirmary of Edinburgh; b. 27.8.49, Salisbury, Rhodesia; m., Aileen E.M.; 1 s.; 1 d. Educ. Falcon College; Edinburgh University. Assistant Professor of Medicine, Washington University School of Medicine, 1980-85; Senior Lecturer in Cardiology and Consultant Cardiologist, University Hospital of Wales College of Medicine, 1985-89. Address: (b.) Department of Cardiology, Royal Infirmary of Edinburgh, Lauriston Place, Edinburgh EH3 9YW; T.-0131 536 2743.

Fraile, Emeritus Professor Medardo, PhD. Writer; Emeritus Professor in Spanish, Strathclyde University, since 1985; b. 21.3.25, Madrid; m., Janet H. Gallagher; 1 d. Educ. Madrid University. Teacher of Spanish language and literature, Ramiro de Maeztu Secondary School, Madrid, 1956-64; Assistant in Spanish, Southampton University, 1964-67; Strathclyde University: Assistant Lecturer in Spanish, 1967-68, Lecturer, 1968-79, Reader, 1979-83, Personal Professor, 1983-85. Travelling Scholarship for authors, 1954; Premio Sesamo for short story writing, 1956; literary grant, Juan March Foundation, 1960; Book of the Year award, 1965; La Estafeta Literaria Prize for short stories, 1970; Hucha de Oro Prize for short stories, 1971; research grant, Carnegie Trust, 1975; Ibanez Fantoni Prize for journalism, 1988. Publications: El Weir de Hermiston by R.L. Stevenson (Translator), 1995; short stories translated into eight languages (Complete Short Stories, Madrid, 1991); five books for children; a novel; books of essays and literary criticism; contributor to periodicals in many countries. Recreations: swimming; walking. Address: (h.) 24 Etive Crescent, Bishopbriggs, Glasgow G64 1ES; T.-0141-772 4421.

Frame, John Neil Munro, LLB. Director: Stocktrade, The Caledonian Foundation; Trustee, The Sportsman's Charity; b. 8.10.46, Edinburgh; m., Susan Macmillan; 2 s.; 2 d. Educ. Edinburgh University. Recreations: jogging slowly downhill; golfing erratically; reading profusely; reading my daughters' Brian Jacques' books. Address: 30 Murrayfield Road, Edinburgh EH12 6ER; T.-0131-346 0077.

Frame, Roger Campbell Crosbie, CA. Secretary, Royal Scottish Society of Painters in Water Colours, since 1986; Secretary, Glasgow Eastern Merchants and Tradesmen's Society, since 1983; Treasurer, Glasgow Group of Artists, 1983-88; b. 7.6.49, Glasgow; m., Angela M. Evaristi; 2 s.; 1 d. Educ. Glasgow Academy. Qualified CA, 1973; formed Frame & Co., CA, 1976. Deacon, Incorporation of Coopers of Glasgow, 1985-86; Secretary, Glasgow Eastern Merchants and Tradesmen Society, 1983-98; Hon. Fellowship, Glasgow University, 1998. Recreations: clay pigeon shooting; art. Address: (h.) Dunglass, 56 Manse Road, Bearsden, Glasgow G61 3PN; T.-0141-942 9178.

France, Anthony James, MA, MB, BChir, FRCP. Consultant Physician, Dundee Teaching Hospitals, since 1989; Honorary Senior Lecturer, Dundee University, since 1989; b. 5.4.54, London; m., Rosemary; 1 s.; 2 d. Educ. Perse School, Cambridge; Magdalene College, Cambridge; St. Thomas' Hospital, London. Qualified 1978; specialises in management of HIV infection, communicable diseases and respiratory medicine. Recreations: photography; gardening; decorating an old house. Address: (b.) King's Cross Hospital, Clepington Road, Dundee DD3 8EA; T.-01382 660111.

France, Professor Peter, MA, PhD, FBA. Professor of French, Edinburgh University, 1980-90, Endowment Fellow, since 1990; b. 19.10.35, Londonderry; m., Sian Reynolds; 3 d. Educ. Bradford Grammar School; Magdalen College, Oxford. Fellow, Magdalen College, Oxford, 1960-63; Lecturer, then Reader in French, Sussex University, 1963-80; French Editor, Modern Language Review, 1979-85; President: British Comparative Literature Association, since 1992, International Society for the History of Rhetoric, 1993-95. Publications: Racine's Rhetoric, 1965; Rhetoric and Truth in France, 1972; Poets of Modern Russia, 1982; Diderot, 1982; Rousseau: Confessions, 1987; Politeness and its Discontents, 1992; New Oxford Companion to Literature in French, 1995; Translator: An Anthology of Chuvash Poetry, 1991, Gennady Aygi: Selected Poems, 1997. Address: (b.) 60 George Square, Edinburgh EH8 9JU; T.-0131-650 8417.

Francis, David, MA. Artistic Director, Edinburgh Folk Festival, since 1996; Traditional Music Co-ordinator, Scottish Arts Council, since 1997; Folk Musician, since 1983; Dance Teacher; b. 14.9.54, Dumfries; m., Mairi Campbell. Educ. Dumfries Academy; University of Aberdeen. Former Librarian, Printer, Publisher, Radio Researcher and Presenter; albums, with The Cast: The Winnowing, 1993; Colours of Lichen, 1996; Founder Member, Scottish Traditions of Dance Trust. Recreations: food; conversation; listening to anything except folk music. Address: 34 Prince Regent Street, Edinburgh EH6 4AT; T.-0131-554 3092.

Francis, John Michael, BSc, ARCS, PhD, DIC, FRSGS, FRSE, FRZSS. Senior Policy Adviser, Home Department, Scottish Office, since 1995; b. 1.5.39, London; m., Eileen; 2 d. Educ. Gowerton Grammar School, near Swansea; Imperial College of Science and Technology, London University. CEGB Berkeley Nuclear Laboratories, 1963-70; Director, Society, Religion and Technology Project, Church of Scotland, 1970-74; Senior Research Fellow, Heriot-Watt University, 1974-76; Principal, Scottish Development Department, 1976-81; Assistant Secretary, Scottish Office, 1981-84, and 1992-95; Director – Scotland, Nature Conservancy Council, 1984-91, then Chief Executive, Nature Conservancy Council for Scotland. Consultant, World Council of Churches, 1971-83; Chairman, SRT Project, Church of Scotland, 1979-94; Member: Oil Development Council for Scotland, 1973-76, Advisory Committee for Scotland, Nature Conservancy Council, 1973-76, Council, National Trust for Scotland, 1984-92; Chairman, Edinburgh Forum, 1986-92; Professional Member, World Future Society, Washington DC, since 1992; Member: John Muir Trust, since 1994, British Association for the Advancement of Science; UK Representative, Millennium Project, United Nations University; Trustee, Society, Religion and Technology Project Trust, since 1998. Publications: Scotland in Turmoil, 1972; Changing Directions, 1973; Facing Up to Nuclear Power, 1976; The Future as an Academic Discipline, 1975; The Future of Scotland, 1977; North Sea

Oil and the Environment (Jointly), 1992; contributions to scientific journals. Recreations: theatre; hill-walking; ecumenical travels. Address: (h.) 49 Gilmour Road, Newington, Edinburgh EH16 5NU; T.-0131-667 3996.

Franklin, Ian Maxwell, BSc, MB, ChB, FRCP (Lond, Glasg, Edin), FRCPath, PhD. Professor of Transfusion Medicine, Glasgow University, since 1996; National Medical and Scientific Director, Scottish National Blood Transfusion Service, since 1997; Honorary Consultant, Bone Marrow Transplant Unit, Glasgow Royal Infirmary; b. 6.9.49, London; m., Dr. Anne Christine Bush; 1 s.; 1 d. Educ. Owen's Boys School, Islington; Leeds University; University College London Medical School. MRC Research Training Fellow, University College London Medical School, 1977-80; Consultant Haematologist, Queen Elizabeth Hospital, Birmingham, 1982-92; Director of Haematology, Central Birmingham Health Authority, 1989-91; Director, Glasgow and West of Scotland Blood Transfusion Service, 1996-97; Consultant-in-Administrative Charge, Bone Marrow Transplant Unit, Glasgow Royal Infirmary, 1992-97; Co-Editor, Blood Reviews. Scientific Secretary, British Society for Haematology, 1995-98; Chairman, Working Party on Relationship Between Blood Banks and Bone Marrow Transplant Units, Council of Europe, 1995-96; author of various papers. Recreations: sailing; cycling; eating and drinking; music. Address: (b.) Department of Medicine, Glasgow University, Royal Infirmary, 10 Alexandra Parade, Glasgow; T.-0141-211 1202.

Franks, Peter, AGSM. Principal Trumpet, Scottish Chamber Orchestra, since 1984; Trumpet Teacher, Royal Scottish Academy of Music and Drama, since 1989; b. 22.4.58, Aylesbury; m., Maureen Hilary Rutter; 1 s.; 1 d. Educ. Aylesbury Grammar School; Guildhall School of Music and Drama. Sub-principal Trumpet, Scottish Chamber Orchestra, 1981-84. Address: 29 West Bankton Place, Murieston West, Livingston EH54 9ED; T.-01506 415514.

Fransman, Professor Martin, BA, MA, PhD. Professor of Economics, University of Edinburgh, since 1996; Director, Institute for Japanese-European Technology Studies, since 1988; b. 17.4.48, Johannesburg; m., Tamar Ludwin; 1 s.; 2 d. Educ. University of the Witwatersrand; University of Sussex. Lecturer: University of Swaziland, 1971-77, University of London, 1977-78; University of Edinburgh: Lecturer, 1978-86, Reader, 1987-96. Publications: The Market and Beyond, 1990 (Masayoshi Ohira Prize, 1991); Japan's Computer and Communications Industry, 1995. Recreations: hill-walking; foreign travel; music; cinema. Address: (b.) Institute for Japanese-European Technology Studies, University of Edinburgh, 25 Buccleuch Place, Edinburgh EH8 9LN; T.-0131-650 4060.

Franz, Rev. Kevin Gerhard, MA, BD, PhD. General Secretary, Action of Churches Together in Scotland, since 1999; Chairman, Perth and Kinross Association of Voluntary Service, since 1995; b. 16.6.53, St. Andrews; m., Veda; 1 s.; 1 d. Educ. Bell-Baxter High School, Cupar; University of Edinburgh. Assistant Curate, St. Martin and St. Luke, Edinburgh, 1979-83; Rector, St. John, Selkirk, 1983-90; St. Ninian's Cathedral, Perth: Provost, 1990-99, Canon, 1999. Recreations: travel in Eastern Europe; watching rugby. Address: (b.) Scottish Churches House, Kirk Street, Dunblane FK15 0AJ; T.-01786 823588.

Fraser, Alan Alexander, BSc (Hons), MBChB, MRCPsych. Consultant Psychiatrist, Southern General Hospital, Glasgow, since 1987; Honorary Clinical Senior Lecturer in Psychiatry, Glasgow University, since 1988; Visiting Consultant: Langside Priory Hospital, Glasgow Nuffield Hospital, Bon Secours Hospital, Glasgow; b. 17.10.55, Kilbirnie. Educ. Spier's School, Beith; Glasgow University. Address: (h.) 65 Dowanside Road, Glasgow G12 9DL; T.-0141-357 2283.

Fraser, Alan William, BSc, PhD. Rector, Arbroath High School, since 1995; b. 12.3.47, Forres; m., Edith; 1 s.; 2 d. Educ. Forres Academy; Aberdeen University. Teacher, Buckhaven High, Kirkcaldy High; Assistant Rector, Montrose Academy, 1985-88; Depute Rector, Webster's High School, Kirriemuir, 1988-95; served on a number of national science committees and projects. Publication: Starting Science. Recreations: hill-walking; sports; music; church work. Address: (h.) High Croft, Usan Road, Ferryden, Montrose; T.-01674 671879.

Fraser, Alan William, MA (Hons). Head, Enterprise and Tourism Division, Scottish Office Education and Industry Department, since 1993; b. 17.12.51, Lennoxtown; m., Joan; 2 s.; 1 d. Educ. Daniel Stewart's College; Banff Academy; Aberdeen University. Entered Scottish Office, 1973; Assistant Secretary to Inquiry into UK Prison Services, 1978-79; Private Secretary to Minister of State, 1979-81; secondment to Aberdeen District Council, 1981-82; Head, New Towns Branch, IDS, 1982-85; Manager, Scottish Office Efficiency Unit, 1985-88; Head, Industrial Policy and Technology Division, SOID, 1988-91; Principal Private Secretary to Secretary of State for Scotland, 1991-93. Recreations: hill-walking; skiing; wind-surfing. Address; (b.) Scottish Office Education and Industry Department, Victoria Quay, Edinburgh EH6 6QQ; T.-0131-244 7588.

Fraser, Callum George, BSc, PhD, FAACB. Clinical Director of Biochemical Medicine, Ninewells Hospital and Medical School, since 1983; Honorary Senior Lecturer, Dundee University, since 1983; Honorary Senior Lecturer, St. Andrews University, since 1988; b. 3.1.45, Dundee; m., Stella Sim; 2 d. Educ. Dunfermline High School; Perth Academy; Aberdeen University. Postdoctoral Fellow, National Research Council of Canada, 1969-70; Lecturer in Chemical Pathology, Aberdeen University, and Honorary Biochemist, Grampian Health Board, 1970-75; Chief Clinical Biochemist, Flinders Medical Centre, South Australia, 1975-83; Honorary Senior Lecturer, then Honorary Associate Professor, Flinders University of South Australia, 1975-83. Former Chairman, Education Division, International Federation of Clinical Chemistry; former Member, Commission on Teaching of Clinical Chemistry, International Union of Pure and Applied Chemistry. Recreations: sailing; gardening; reading; travel. Address: (b.) Directorate of Biochemical Medicine, Ninewells Hospital, Dundee DD1 9SY; T.-01382 660111.

Fraser, Sir Campbell, FRSE, BCom, DUniv, DL, LLD, CBIM. Chairman, Tandem Computers Ltd., 1987-97; Non-Executive Director, Bridgewater Paper Ltd., since 1985; Chairman, Riversoft Ltd., since 1997; b. 2.5.23, Dunblane; m., Myar McLaren (deceased); 2 d. Educ. McLaren High School, Callander; Dundee School of Economics; University of Glasgow; McMaster University. Economist, Raw Cotton Commission; Staff, Economist Intelligence Unit; many positions with Dunlop Holdings (Chairman, 1978-83); Non-Executive Director, Morgan Crucible; Chairman, Scottish Television, 1975-91; Non-Executive Director, 3 i's; Non-Executive Director, B.A.T. Industries Ltd.; Non-Executive Director, British Petroleum PLC and associated companies; Past President, Confederation of British Industry; Chairman: Wells Fargo's International Advisory Council, Barkers (Scotland) Ltd., Tandem Inc. International Advisory Council (Director, Tandem Inc.); Trustee: The Economist, Institute of Hepatology; Governor, N.I.E.S.R.; Visiting Professor: University of Stirling, University of Strathclyde; Chairman, Business School, Strathclyde University. Recreations: watching Dundee F.C.; reading history; writing. Address: (h.) Pine Lodge, 23 Doune Road, Dunblane FK15 9AT; T.-0181-660 1703.

Fraser, Sir Charles Annand, KCVO, WS, DL. Partner, W. & J. Burness, 1956-92 (retired); former Chairman, Adam and Company PLC; former Director: British Assets Trust PLC, Scottish Television PLC, Scottish Business in the Community, Stakis PLC; b. 16.10.28, Humbie, East Lothian; m., Ann Scott-Kerr; 4 s. Educ. Hamilton Academy; Edinburgh University. Purse Bearer to Lord High Commissioner to General Assembly of Church of Scotland, 1969-88; served on Court, Heriot-Watt University, 1972-78; Council Member, Law Society of Scotland, 1966-72; Chairman, Lothian & Edinburgh Enterprise, 1991-94. Recreations: gardening; skiing; piping. Address: (h.) Shepherd House, Inveresk, Midlothian; T.-0131-665 2570.

Fraser, Charles (Charlie) William Simpson, LLB, DipLP, NP. Partner, Burnside Kemp Fraser, Solicitors, since 1990; b. 10.5.62, Bellshill. Educ. Perth High School; Aberdeen University. James and George Collie, Solicitors, Aberdeen: trained, 1984-86, Assistant, 1986-89; Associate, Burnside Kemp Fraser, 1989-90. Recreations: football; golf; actor/singer/director; travelling the world. Address: (h.) 116 Brighton Place, Aberdeen AB10 6SU; T.-01224 310764.

Fraser, David James, MA, MHSM, MIPD. Chief Executive, North Ayrshire and Arran NHS Trust, since 1993; b. 1.7.52, Fraserburgh; m., Anne; 1 s. Educ. Peterhead Academy; Aberdeen University. Peat Marwick Mitchell & Co., City of London, 1974-75; Scottish Health Service Management Training Scheme, 1975-77; Lothian Health Board, 1977-93. Recreations: gardens; photography; opera. Address: (b.) Crosshouse Hospital, Kilmarnock KA2 0BE; T.-01563 572230.

Fraser, Hugh Donald George, MBE, QPM, DipSM, OStJ, FBIM, MIPM, MIIRSM. Councillor, City of Edinburgh Council, for Balerno ward, since 1996; Honorary Secretary, Scottish Chamber of Safety, since 1979; former Senior Assistant Secretary, Heriot-Watt University; b. Edinburgh; m., Margaret Jane Stothard; 1 s.; 2 d. War Service, RAF Aircrew, 1939-45 (Pilot); Edinburgh City Police, 1941-71; Chief Superintendent, Research and Planning Branch, Home Office, London, 1966-68; Deputy Commandant, Scottish Police College, 1968-71. Honorary Secretary, Edinburgh and District Spastic Association, 14 years; Member: Edinburgh Accident Prevention Council, Lothian Retirement Committee; Member, Lothian Regional Council, 1982-96. Recreations: Burns' enthusiast; work with senior citizens; jogging; the theatre. Address: (h.) 181 Braid Road, Edinburgh EH10 6JA; T.-0131-447 1270.

Fraser, James Edward, CB, MA (Aberdeen), BA (Cantab), FSA (Scot). Assistant Local Government Boundary Commissioner for Scotland, since 1997; Secretary of Commissions for Scotland, 1992-94; b. 16.12.31, Aberdeen; m., Patricia Louise Stewart; 2 s. Educ. Aberdeen Grammar School; Aberdeen University; Christ's College, Cambridge. Royal Artillery, 1953-55 (Staff Captain, "Q", Tel-El-Kebir, 1954-55); Assistant Principal, Scottish Home Department, 1957-60; Private Secretary to Permanent Under-Secretary of State, Scottish Office, 1960-62; Private Secretary to Parliamentary Under-Secretary of State, Scottish Office, 1962; Principal, 1962-69: SHHD, 1962-64, Cabinet Office, 1964-66, HM Treasury, 1966-68, SHHD, 1968-69; Assistant Secretary: SHHD, 1970-76, Scottish Office Finance Division, 1976; Under Secretary, Local Government Finance Group, Scottish Office, 1976-81, Scottish Home and Health Department, 1981-91. President: Scottish Hellenic Society, Edinburgh and Eastern Scotland, 1987-93, Aberdeen Grammar School Former Pupils' Club, 1997-98 (Hon. Vice-President, since 1998). Recreations: reading; music; walking; Greece, ancient and modern; DIY. Address: (h.) 59 Murrayfield Gardens, Edinburgh EH12 6DH; T.-0131-337 2274.

Fraser, Sheriff James Owen Arthur, MA, LLB. Sheriff of Grampian, Highland and Islands, since 1984; b. 9.5.37. Solicitor, 1967-84. Address: (b.) Sheriff Court House, Ferry Road, Dingwall, IV15 9QX.

Fraser, Jeremy William, LLB (Hons), DipLP, NP. Solicitor; Legal Adviser and Company Secretary, TSB Bank Scotland plc, since 1990; b. 2.5.62, Inverness; m., Claudia Bölling; 2 s.; 1 d. Educ. Alloa Academy; Edinburgh University. Lindsay Duncan & Black WS; Lloyds Bowmaker Ltd. Recreations: hockey; squash; golf; hill-walking. Address: (b.) 120 George Street, Edinburgh; T.-0131-225 4555.

Fraser, John A., DipEd, DipPhysEd. Rector, Mearns Academy, since 1993; b. 3.6.52, Inverness; m., Moira; 2 s.; 1 d. Educ. Kingussie High School; Jordanhill College of Education. P.E. Teacher, Northfield Academy; Principal Teacher of Guidance, Northfield Academy; Assistant Head Teacher, Hazlehead Academy; Depute Rector, Mearns Academy. Recreation: sport. Address: (b.) Mearns Academy, Laurencekirk AB30 1AJ; T.-01561 378817.

Fraser, John A.W., MA, FEIS, JP, DL. Deputy Lieutenant for Shetland, since 1985; b. 9.11.28, Lerwick; m., Jane Ann Jamieson; 2 s. Educ. Anderson Educational Institute; Edinburgh University; Moray House College of Education. Education Officer, RAF, 1950-52; Teacher, Baltasound Junior Secondary School, 1952-54; Head Teacher: Haroldswick Primary School, 1954-59, Aith Junior High School, 1959-66, Scalloway Junior High School, 1966-88. Former Member, National Council, EIS; Chairman, Scalloway Development Association; Member, Shetland Valuation Appeals Committee; Director, Scalloway Waterfront Trust; General Commissioner of Income Tax. Recreations: genealogy; travel; gardening. Address: (h.) Broadwinds, Castle Street, Scalloway, Shetland; T.-01595 880644.

Fraser, Kit, BA. Presenter, Newsdrive, Radio Scotland, since 1997; b. 3.12.51, Giffnock; m., Fiona Morrison; 2 s. Educ. Kingussie High School; University of Stirling. Entered journalism with D.C. Thomson (worked on The People's Journal, Sunday Post, Dundee Courier); joined BBC on setting up of BBC Highland, Inverness; Radio Scotland: Producer, 1978-88, Reporter, 1988-97, occasional Presenter, Good Morning Scotland. Publications: Christie Boy, father's autobiography (Editor). Recreations: five-a-side football; golf; real ale. Address: c/o Newsroom, BBC Scotland, Queen Margaret Drive, Glasgow G12 8DG.

Fraser, Lindsey M., BA (Hons), PGCE. Executive Director, Scottish Book Trust, since 1991; b. 15.8.61, Edinburgh. Educ. George Watson's College; York University; Froebel Institute, London. Manager, Heffers Children's Bookshop, Cambridge, 1986-91. Recreations: reading; music. Address: (b.) Scottish Book Trust, Scottish Book Centre, 137 Dundee Street, Edinburgh EH11 1BG; T.-0131-229 3663.

Fraser, Lady Marion Anne, LT, MA, LRAM, ARCM, LLD, DUniv (Stirling). Chairman, Scottish International Piano Competition, since 1995; Chair, Scottish Association of Mental Health, since 1995; b. 17.10.32, Glasgow; m., Sir William Kerr Fraser; 3 s.; 1 d. Educ. Hutchesons' Girls' Grammar School; University of Glasgow; RSAMD. Lord High Commissioner to General Assembly of the Church of Scotland, 1994; Her Majesty's High Commissioner to the General Assembly of the Church of Scotland, 1995. Formerly Director: RGI, Scottish Opera, Laurel Bank School; Founder Chairman, Friends of the RSA; Director, St. Mary's Music School; Chair: Board, Christian Aid, 1990-97; Trustee, Scottish Churches Architectural Heritage Trust; President, Scotland's Churches' Scheme, 1997; Member, Sponsoring Group, Churches' Enquiry into Unemployment and the Future of Work, 1995-97.

Recreations: family and friends; people and places. Address: (h.) Broadwood, Edinburgh Road, Gifford, East Lothian EH41 4JE; T.-01620 810 319.

Fraser, Professor Patricia, MA, PhD. Aberdeen Asset Management Professor of Finance and Investment Management, University of Aberdeen, since 1995; b. 30.6.43, Arbroath; m., Finlay McRae Fraser; 3 s. Educ. Arbroath High School; University of Dundee. Lecturer in Financial Economics, Dundee University, 1989-94; Senior Lecturer in Finance, University of Stirling, 1994-95; Houblon-Norman Fellow, Bank of England, 1992. Visiting Professor: University of Tasmania, since 1993, University of Western Australia, since 1993. Recreations: reading; travel; walking; conversation with friends. Address: (b.) Department of Accountancy, University of Aberdeen, Dumbar Street, Aberdeen AB24 3QY; T.-01224 272210.

Fraser of Carmyllie, Lord (Peter Fraser), PC, QC. Minister of State, Department of Trade and Industry, 1995-97; b. 29.5.45; m., 1 s.; 2 d. MP (Conservative), Angus South, 1979-83, Angus East, 1983-87; Solicitor-General for Scotland, 1982-89; Lord Advocate, 1989-92; Minister of State, Scottish Office, 1992-95.

Fraser, Robert Dunbar, MA (Hons), MIMgt. Rector, Kirkcaldy High School, since 1989; b. 30.11.45, Dingwall; m., Annice; 2 s.; 2 d. Educ. Dingwall Academy; Aberdeen University. Depute Rector, Culloden Academy, 1979-84; Rector, Keith Grammar School, 1984-89. Recreations: sports; golf; DIY; being with family. Address: (h.) Elphinstone Lodge, 77 Hepburn Gardens, St. Andrews, Fife.

Fraser, Shannon Marguerite, MA, PhD, PIFA, FSAScot. Director, Council for Scottish Archaeology, since 1998; b. San Francisco. Educ. Point Grey Secondary School, Vancouver; Lomond School, Helensburgh; University of Glasgow; University of Leicester; Universita Italiana, Stranieri, Perugia. Archaeological fieldwork in Dorset, Lincolnshire, Cambridgeshire, Northamptonshire, Perthshire, Dumfriesshire, 1986-94; doctoral research, 1991-96; Property Management Planner, National Trust for Scotland, 1996-98. Recreations: writing; hillwalking; language study; travel. Address: (b.) c/o National Museums of Scotland, Chambers Street, Edinburgh EH1 1JF; T.-0131-247 4119.

Fraser, Sheriff Simon William Hetherington, LLB, NP. Sheriff of North Strathclyde at Dumbarton, since 1989; b. 2.4.51, Carlisle; m., Sheena Janet; 1 d. Educ. Glasgow Academy; Glasgow University. Solicitor, 1973; Partner, Flowers & Co., Solicitors, Glasgow, 1976-89; Temporary Sheriff, 1987-89. Glasgow Bar Association: Secretary, 1977-79, President, 1981-82. Recreations: watching cricket, and Partick Thistle. Address: (b.) Sheriff Court, Church Street, Dumbarton; T.-01389 63266.

Fraser, William Alexander Elrick, OStJ, JP. Provost, Inverness District Council, 1992-96; Councillor, since 1962; b. 19.8.27, Inverness; m., Margaret Elizabeth; 2 s.; 2 d. Educ. Inverness Royal Academy. Past President: Inverness Round Table, Inverness Rotary, Inverness Master Butchers, Inverness Amateur Swimming Club, Highland District Swimming Association; former Chairman: Inverness Harbour Trust, Governors of Eden Court Theatre; Director: Highland Hospice Ltd., Highland Prospect Ltd., Highland Opportunity Ltd., Inverness and Loch Ness Horizons Ltd.; Patron, Inverness Sea Cadets; Hon. President, Inverness Opera Company, Inverness Festival Association, Inverness Tattoo Committee; Past President, Scottish Accident Prevention Council; Chairman, Princes Scottish Youth Business Trust, Highland Area; Chairman, Seagull Trust; Chairman, Provost Smith Memorial Trust; Vice Chairman, Caledonian Leisure Ltd.; Hon. Treasurer, Clan Fraser Society. Address: (h.) Balwearie, Drummond Road, Inverness IV2 4NA; T.-01463 233345.

Fraser, Professor William Douglas, BSc, MSc, PhD, FRICS. Professor and Head, Department of Land Economics, Paisley University, since 1986; b. 3.1.40, Edinburgh. Educ. Edinburgh Academy; London University; Strathclyde University. Partner, Bingham, Hughes and Macpherson, Chartered Surveyors, Inverness, 1970-72; Lecturer: Department of Land Economics, Paisley College, 1972-83, Centre for Property Valuation and Management, City University, London, 1983-86. Publication: Principles of Property Investment and Pricing, 1984. Recreations: climbing; gardening. Address: (b.) Department of Land Economics, Paisley University, High Street, Paisley PA1 2BE; T.-0141-848 3450.

Fraser, Professor William Hamish, MA, DPhil, FRHistS. Professor of History, Strathclyde University (Dean, Faculty of Arts and Social Studies, 1987-93); b. 30.6.41, Keith; m., Helen Tuach; 1 d. Educ. Keith Grammar School; Aberdeen University; Sussex University. Lecturer in History, Strathclyde University, 1966-77. Publications: Trade Unions and Society 1850-1880, 1973; Workers and Employers, 1981; The Coming of the Mass Market, 1982; Conflict and Class: Scottish Workers 1700–1838, 1988; People and Society in Scotland 1830–1914, 1990; Glasgow 1830–1914 (Co-author), 1996; Alexander Campbell and the Search for Socialism, 1996. Recreations: hill-walking; skiing. Address: (h.) 112 High Station Road, Falkirk FK1 5LN; T.-01324 622868.

Fraser, Sir William Kerr, GCB (1984), LLD, FRSE. Chancellor, Glasgow University, since 1996; Chairman, Royal Commission on the Ancient and Historical Monuments of Scotland, since 1995; b. 18.3.29; m., Lady Marion Fraser, LT (qv); 3 s.; 1 d. Educ. Eastwood Secondary School; Glasgow University. RAF, 1952-55; various posts in Scottish Office, 1955-88, including Permanent Under Secretary of State, Scottish Office, 1978-88; Principal and Vice Chancellor, Glasgow University, 1988-95. Director, Scottish Mutual Assurance plc; Chairman, Scottish Inheritance Fund; Governor, Caledonian Research Foundation. Address: (h.) Broadwood, Edinburgh Road, Gifford, East Lothian EH41 4JE; T.-01620 810 319.

Frazer, Rev. Richard Ernest, BA, BD, SBStJ. Minister, St. Machar's Cathedral, Old Aberdeen, since 1993; b. 20.11.57, Stirling; m., Katherine Tullis Sinclair; 2 s.; 1 d. Educ. Doncaster Grammar School; University of Newcastle upon Tyne; University of Edinburgh. Assistant Minister, St. Giles Cathedral, Edinburgh, 1985-87; Minister, Schoharie, Breakabeen, N. Bleheim, New York, USA, 1987-88; Minister, Cargill-Burrelton with Collace, 1988-93. Publication: A Collace Miscellany: a History of the Parish of Collace (Co-Editor and Contributor), 1992. Recreations: family; walking; squash; timber construction. Address: (b.) St. Machar's Cathedral, The Chanonry, Old Aberdeen AB24 1RQ; T.-01224 485988.

Freeman, James Martin, BSc, MSc, DipEduc. Rector, Lawside R.C. Academy, Dundee, since 1986; b. 7.11.34; m., Mary Agnes; 2 s.; 1 d. Educ. St. Anthony's, Edinburgh; University of Edinburgh; University of East Anglia. Chemistry Teacher, Broughton Secondary School, Edinburgh, 1963-65; Chemistry Teacher/Depute Head, Makerere College School, Kampala, 1966-69; Lecturer in Education, Makerere University, Kampala, 1969-73; Principal Teacher, Gracemount High School, 1974-76; Assistant Headteacher, Liberton High School, Edinburgh, 1976-82; Depute Headteacher, Holy Rood High School, Edinburgh, 1982-86. Recreations: walking; theatre; sport. Address: (b.) West School Road, Dundee DD3 8RT; T.-01382 436100.

Freer, Professor John Henry, BSc, MSc, PhD. Professor of Bacterial Toxinology, Glasgow University, since 1986; Deputy Director, Institute of Biomedical and Life Sciences; b. 17.11.36, Kasauli, India; m., Jocelyn Avril Williams; 4 d. Educ. Durham University; Nottingham University; Birmingham University. Lecturer in Microbiology, New South Wales University, Australia, 1962-65; New York University Medical Centre: Associate Research Scientist, then Assistant Professor, Microbiology, 1965-68; Senior Lecturer, Microbiology Department, Glasgow University, 1968-82; Reader in Microbiology, 1982-86; Editor-in-Chief, Journal of General Microbiology, 1990-95. Publications: Bacterial Protein Toxins (Joint Editor), 1988; Sourcebook of Bacterial Protein Toxins, 1991; 100 scientific articles. Address: (b.) West Medical Building, Glasgow University, Glasgow, G12 8QQ.

French, William Allan, DL, BSc, MSc, CEng, FIM, FIEE, FIBF. Associate Principal, Falkirk College of Further and Higher Education, since 1986; Depute Lieutenant, Stirling and Falkirk Districts, since 1994; Director, Careers Central Ltd., since 1995; b. 30.12.41, Falkirk; m., Joyce; 2 d. Educ. George Watson's College, Edinburgh; Strathclyde University. Scientific Officer, UKAEA, Dounreay; Production Manager, British Aluminium Co. Ltd., Falkirk; Lecturer, Napier College, Edinburgh; Head, Department of Industrial Engineering, Falkirk College of Technology. Secretary, Forth Valley Area Scout Association; District Scout Commissioner; founder Area Chairman, Central Scotland Round Table; Past President, Larbert Rotary Club. Recreations: golf; bridge; bowling; scouting; rotary; music. Address: (b.) Falkirk College of Further and Higher Education, Falkirk FK2 9AD; T.-01324 403210.

Frew, Rev. Michael William, BSc, BD. Parish Minister, Carluke: St. John's, since 1991; b. 16.5.51, Edinburgh; m., Margaret; 3 s.; 1 d. Educ. Broughton Senior Secondary; University of Edinburgh. Parish Minister: Alloa West; Organiser for Evangelism, Church of Scotland Department of National Mission. Recreations: cycling; walking; football. Address: 18 Old Bridgend, Carluke, Lanarkshire ML8 4HN; T.-01855 772259.

Friel, Professor Edward J. Chief Executive, Greater Glasgow and Clyde Valley Tourist Board, since 1997; Broadcaster and Writer; b. 20.9.41, Londonderry; m., Eleanor; 3 s. Educ. Northern Ireland. Northern Ireland Tourist Board: Director, North America, Chief Executive, 1991; Director, Marketing and Public Relations, Scottish Opera; Proprietor, Eddie Friel Associates, since 1992; Chief Executive, Greater Glasgow Tourist Board and Convention Bureau, 1983-97. Former Chairman: Theatre Royal, Glasgow 1990 Marketing; former Member, Board of Directors, Scottish Opera; a Director, Glasgow Chamber of Commerce, Scottish National Youth Orchestra, Glasgow Centre for Contemporary Arts; Visiting Professor, Scottish Hotel School, Strathclyde University; Governor, Glasgow Caledonian University; Fellow, Royal Society of Arts; Fellow, Tourism Society. Recreations: golf; music; theatre; opera. Address: (b.) 11 George Square, Glasgow G2 1DY; T.-0141-566 4001.

Friend, James, MA, MB, ChB, FRCPEdin. Consultant in Thoracic Medicine, Grampian Health Board, since 1973; Clinical Reader in Medicine and Therapeutics, Aberdeen University, since 1996; b. 2.6.38, Edinburgh; m., Elizabeth; 1 s.; 2 d. Educ. Edinburgh Academy; Gonville and Caius College, Cambridge; Edinburgh University. Hospital posts in Edinburgh and Oxford; Dorothy Temple Cross Fellowship, Seattle, 1971-72; British Thoracic Society: Council Member, 1983-91, Treasurer, 1984-91, President, 1998; Chairman, Grampian Action on Smoking and Health, 1989-97. Recreation: the Scottish hills. Address: (b.) Aberdeen Royal Infirmary, Aberdeen AB25 2ZN.

Frier, Brian Murray, BSc (Hons), MD, FRCP (Edin), FRCP (Glas). Consultant Physician, Royal Infirmary, Edinburgh, since 1987; part-time Reader in Medicine, Edinburgh University, since 1995; b. 28.7.47, Edinburgh; m., Dr. Isobel M. Wilson; 1 d. Educ. George Heriot's School, Edinburgh; Edinburgh University. Medical Registrar, Ninewells Hospital, Dundee, 1974-76; Research Fellow in Diabetes and Metabolism, Cornell University Medical Centre, The New York Hospital, 1976-77; Senior Medical Registrar, Royal Infirmary, Edinburgh, 1978-82; Consultant Physician, Western Infirmary and Gartnavel General Hospital, Glasgow, 1982-87. R.D. Lawrence Lecturer, British Diabetic Association, 1986; Governor, George Heriot's Trust, Edinburgh, 1988-94. Publication: Hypoglycaemia and Diabetes: clinical and physiological aspects, 1993; publications on diabetes and hypoglycaemia. Recreations: appreciation of the arts; ancient and modern history. Address: (h.) 100 Morningside Drive, Edinburgh EH10 5NT; T.-0131-447 1653.

Frith, Professor Simon, BA, MA, PhD, FRSA. Director, John Logie Baird Centre, since 1987, and Professor of English Studies, since 1988, University of Strathclyde; Director, ESRC Media Economics and Media Culture Programme, since 1995; b. 25.6.46, England. Educ. Leys School, Cambridge; Balliol College, University of Oxford; University of California, Berkeley. Lecturer, then Senior Lecturer in Sociology, University of Warwick, 1972-87; Rock Critic, Sunday Times, 1982-86; Pop Critic, Observer, 1987-91; Chair of Judges, Mercury Music Prize. Publications: Sound Effects, 1981; Art into Pop, 1987; Music for Pleasure, 1988; Performing Rites, 1996. Recreations: music; reading; walking. Address: (b.) John Logie Baird Centre, University of Strathclyde, Glasgow G1 1XH; T.-0141-553 4150.

Frizzell, Edward W. MA (Hons). Chief Executive, Scottish Prison Service, since 1991; Board Member, Quality Scotland Foundation, since 1991; b. 4.5.46, Paisley; m., Moira Calderwood; 2 s.; 1 d. Educ. Paisley Grammar School; Glasgow University. Scottish Milk Marketing Board, 1968-73; Scottish Council (Development and Industry), 1973-76; DAFS, Scottish Office, 1976-78; First Secretary, Fisheries, Office of the UK Permanent Representative to European Communities, Brussels (Foreign and Commonwealth Office), 1978-82; Assistant Secretary (Grade 5), Scottish Education Department, Higher Education Division, 1982-86; Scottish Office Finance Division, 1986-89; Director, Locate in Scotland, Scottish Office Industry Department (Grade 4), 1989-91. Address: (b.) Calton House, 5 Redheughs Rigg, Edinburgh, EH12 9HW; T.-0131-244 8522.

Frizzell, Rev. Robert Stewart, BD. Minister, Wick Old Parish Church, since 1998; Chaplain, Army Cadet Force, Queen's Own Highlanders Battalion, since 1993; Chaplain, Caithness General Hospital, Wick, since 1991; b. 24.6.34, Motherwell; m., Elizabeth Brown; 2 d. Educ. Bellshill Academy; University of Glasgow. Ordained 1961; Minister: Vale of Leven; Kirkintilloch; Partick Anderson Church, Glasgow; Balshagray Parish Church, Broomhill, Glasgow. Recreations: touring with car; grandchildren; foreign holidays. Address: (h.) Old Parish Manse, Miller Avenue, Wick, Caithness; T.-01955 604252.

Frutin, Bernard Derek, MBE, FRSA, MInstPkg. Inventor; Chairman and Managing Director: Rocep Lusol Holdings Ltd., since 1973, Rocep Pressure Packs Ltd., since 1987; b. 7.2.44, Glasgow; 3 d. Educ. Kelvinside Academy, Glasgow. Winner of nine international innovator awards since 1989, including John Logie Baird and British Institute of Packaging Environmental Awards; Innovator of the Year, 1989 (Institute of Packaging); Finalist, 1992 Prince of Wales Award. Recreations: sailing; skiing; fine food; listening to music. Address: (b.) Rocep Lusol Holdings

Ltd., Rocep Business Park, Kings Inch Road, Deanpark, Renfrew PA4 8XY; T.-0141-885 2222.

Fry, Professor Stephen C., BSc, PhD, FRSE. Professor of Plant Biochemistry, Edinburgh University, since 1995; b. 26.11.53, Sheffield; m., Verena Ryffel; 3 d. Educ. Thornbridge School, Sheffield; Leicester University. Postdoctoral Research Fellow, Cambridge University, 1978-79; Royal Society Rosenheim Research Fellow, Cambridge University, 1979-82; Senior Research Associate, University of Colorado, 1982-83; Lecturer in Botany, then Reader in Plant Biochemistry, Edinburgh University, 1983-95. President's Medal, Society for Experimental Biology, 1988. Publication: The Growing Plant Cell Wall: Chemical and Metabolic Analysis, 1988. Recreations: hill-walking; paper chromatography. Address: (b.) Division of Biological Sciences, Edinburgh University, King's Buildings, Mayfield Road, Edinburgh EH9 3JH; T.-0131-650 5320.

Fullarton, John Hamilton, ARIAS, DipTP. Consultant Architect and Town Planner; b. 21.2.31, Dalry, Ayrshire; m., Elvera Peebles; 1 s. Educ. Dalry High School; Glasgow School of Art; Royal Technical College, Glasgow; Edinburgh College of Art. Architect with local authorities before joining Scottish Office, 1964; Superintending Architect, Scottish Development Department, 1970-78; Head of New Towns, Construction Industry Division, Scottish Economic Planning Department, 1978-79; Director of Technical Services, Scottish Special Housing Association, 1979-89. Research Fellowship, Urban Planning, Edinburgh College of Art, 1966-67. Publication:Waverley Park Conservation Study, 1977. Address: (h.) 7 Queens Crescent, Edinburgh EH9 2AZ; T.-0131-667 5809.

Fulton, Rev. John Oswald, BSc, BD. General Secretary, United Free Church of Scotland, since 1994; b. 9.7.53, Glasgow; m., Margaret P.; 1 d. Educ. Clydebank High School; Glasgow University. Ordained as minister, 1977; Minister, Croftfoot U.F. Church, Glasgow, 1977-94. Recreations: reading; gardening; photography. Address: (b.) 11 Newton Place, Glasgow G3 7PR; T.-0141-332 3435.

Fulton, Rikki, OBE, DLitt, DArts. Actor; b. 15.4.24, Glasgow; m., Kate Matheson. Educ. Whitehill Secondary School. Invalided out of RNVR as Sub-Lt., 1945; began professional career broadcasting with BBC in Glasgow; Presenter, BBC Showband, London, 1951-55; appeared in numerous pantomimes and revues with Howard & Wyndham from 1955, including Five Past Eight shows; television work including Scotch & Wry (creator, Rev. I.M. Jolly) and starring roles in The Miser and A Winter's Tale; films including The Dollar Bottom, Gorky Park, Local Hero, Comfort and Joy and The Girl in the Picture. Scottish TV Personality of the Year, 1963 and 1979; Best Light Entertainment Performance of the Year, 1969 and 1983; President's Award, Television and Radio Industries Club, 1988; Lifetime Achievement Award, BAFTA Scotland, 1993. Recreations: bridge; chess; reading; music (listening and piano); writing; painting.

Fulton, William Francis Monteith, BSc, MD (Hons), MB, ChB, FRCP, FRCPGlas, FRCPEdin. Reader, Department of Materia Medica, Glasgow University, 1977-84; Consultant Physician, Stobhill General Hospital, Glasgow, 1958-84; b. 12.12.19, Aberdeen; m., Dr. Frances I. Melrose; 1 s.; 1 d. Educ. Bryanston School, Dorset; Glasgow University. Resident Physician and Surgeon, Western Infirmary, Glasgow, 1945-46; National Service, Merchant Navy, 1946-48 (Ship's Surgeon); joined National Health Service, 1950; Research Assistant, Cardiology, Edinburgh University, 1952-53; Senior Lecturer, Department of Materia Medica, Glasgow University, 1958-77; Senior Fellow, Cardiology, Johns Hopkins Hospital, Baltimore, 1963-64; Foundation Professor of Medicine, Nairobi University, 1967-72. Publications: The Coronary Arteries, 1965; Modern Trends in Pharmacology and Therapeutics, 1967. Address: (h.) Woodhill, Braemar AB35 5XX; T.-0133 97 41239.

Fulton, Sheriff William J. Sheriff of Grampian, Highland and Islands at Inverness. Address: (b.) The Castle, Inverness, IV2 3EG.

Furley, Professor Peter Anthony, MA, DPhil. Professor of Biogeography, University of Edinburgh, since 1997; b. 5.8.35, Gravesend; m., Margaret Brenda Dunlop; 1 s.; 3 d. Educ. Gravesend Grammar School; Brasenose College, Oxford University. Tutor, Oxford; University of Edinburgh: Lecturer, 1962, Senior Lecturer, 1975; Professor of Ecology, University of Brasilia, Brazil, 1976; Reader in Tropical Biogeography and Soils, 1989. Publications: Geography of the Biosphere, 1983; Nature and Dynamics of Forest–Savanna Boundaries, 1992; The Forest Frontier – Brazilian Roralma, 1994. Recreations: travel; hillwalking. Address: Department of Geography, University of Edinburgh, Drummond Street, Edinburgh EH8 9XP; T.-0131-650 2517/2523.

Furnell, Professor James R.G., MA (Hons), DCP, PhD, LLB, FBPsS, DipLP. Consultant Clinical Psychologist (Child Health), Forth Valley Health Board, since 1980; Advocate (called to Scottish Bar, 1993); Chartered Clinical and Forensic Psychologist; Honorary Fellow, Edinburgh University, since 1987; b. 20.2.46, London; m., Lesley Anne Ross; 1 s.; 1 d. Educ. Leighton Park Society of Friends School, Reading; Aberdeen University; Glasgow University; Stirling University; Dundee University. Clinical Psychologist, Royal Hospital for Sick Children, Glasgow, 1970-72; Senior Clinical Psychologist, Forth Valley Health Board, 1972-80. Member: National Consultative Committee of Scientists in Professions Allied to Medicine, 1984-87 (Secretary, Clinical Psychology Sub-Committee), Forth Valley Health Board, 1984-87; Chairman, Division of Clinical Psychology, British Psychological Society, 1988-89; Visiting Professor, Caledonian University, since 1996. Recreations: flying; cross-country skiing. Address: (h.) Glensherup House, Glendevon, by Dollar, Perthshire FK14 7JY; T.-01259 781234.

Furness, Professor Raymond Stephen, BA, MA, PhD. Professor of German, St. Andrews University, since 1984; b. 25.10.33, Builth Wells; m., Janice Fairey; 1 s.; 2 d. Educ. Welwyn Garden City Grammar School; University College, Swansea. Modern Languages Department, University of Manchester Institute of Science and Technology; Department of German, Manchester University. Publications: Expressionism; Literary History of Germany 1890-1945; Wagner and Literature; A Companion to Twentieth Century German Literature; An Introduction to German Literature 1871-1989; The Dedalus Book of German Decadence. Recreation: sleeping. Address: (h.) The Dirdale, Boarhills, St. Andrews KY16 8PP; T.-01334 88469.

Furness, Col. Simon John, DL. Landowner; Vice Lord Lieutenant, Berwickshire, since 1990; b. 18.3.36, Ayton. Educ. Charterhouse; RMA, Sandhurst. Commissioned Durham Light Infantry, 1956, 2nd Lt.; served Far East, UK, Germany; active service, Borneo, Northern Ireland; retired, 1978; Deputy Colonel (Durham) The Light Infantry, 1989-93. Member, Executive, National Trust for Scotland, 1986-96; Chairman: Berwickshire Civic Society, since 1996, Eyemouth Museum Trust, since 1981. Recreations: field sports; gardening. Address: The Garden House, Netherbyres, Eyemouth, Berwickshire TD14 5SE; T.-01890 750337.

Furness, William Arthur, BA, MSc. Chair, Scottish Council Foundation; Chair, Scottish Water and Sewerage Customers Council; Chair, Internet Society for Scotland; b.

6.9.45, London. Educ. St. Benedict's Abbey School, Ealing; Exeter University; London University. Various posts within BT. Vice-President, Edinburgh Chamber of Commerce; Director, Edinburgh Science Festival; Executive Committee Member, Scottish Council Development and Industry. Recreations: travel; dogs; reading; art. Address: 26 Moray Place, Edinburgh EH3 6DA.

Fyfe, Andrew, MA (Hons). Executive Director, Glasgow Alliance, since 1998; b. 26.6.54, Glasgow; m., Louise Drummond; 2 d. Educ. Hutchesons', Glasgow; Glasgow University. Research Assistant, Strathclyde University, 1975-78; Senior Development Officer, Govanhill Housing Association, 1978-81; Director, Shettleston Housing Association, Glasgow, 1982-89; Scottish Homes: Director Strategic Development, 1989-92, Director Operations, 1992-97; Managing Director, Glasgow and North Clyde, 1997-98; Member, Glasgow 1999 Festival Company; Chairman, Scottish Federation of Housing Associations, 1987-89. Address: (b.) 39 St Vincent Place, Glasgow G1 2ER; T.-0141-572 1300.

Fyfe, Maria, BA (Hons). MP, Glasgow Maryhill, since 1987; Chair, Labour Backbench Committee on International Development, since 1997; Member, Council of Europe, since 1997; Member, British-Irish Parliamentary Body, since 1997; Chair, Scottish All-Party Parliamentary Group on Children, since 1996; b. 25.11.38, Glasgow; 2 s. Educ. Notre Dame High School, Glasgow; Strathclyde University. Glasgow District Councillor, 1980-87; Senior Lecturer, Central College of Commerce, 1977-87; Member, Scottish Executive Committee, Labour Party, 1981-87; Opposition Spokesperson on Women, 1988-91; Scottish Affairs Spokesperson, 1992-95. Address: (b.) House of Commons, London, SW1A 0AA; T.-0171-219 4430; 0141-945 1495.

G

Gage, Anthea Dominique Juliet, SSA, RSW. Artist; Teacher of Art and Design, Royal High School, Edinburgh, since 1980; b. 21.3.56, Edinburgh. Educ. Edinburgh College of Art; Craiglockhart College of Education. Work exhibited throughout Scotland. Recreations: cycling; kite flying. Address: (h.) 16/8 Craighouse Gardens, Edinburgh EH10 5TX.

Gage, Edward Arthur, MBE, RSW, PPSA, DA. Artist; b. 28.3.25, Gullane, East Lothian; m., Valerie Alexandra; 1 s.; 2 d. Educ. Royal High School, Edinburgh; Edinburgh College of Art. Served Scots Guards and Royal Scots, 1943-47; Staff Officer, India and Malaya, 1945-47; designer of stage sets and illustration work (drawing especially for Radio Times), 1952-68; Art Master, Fettes College, Edinburgh, 1951-68; Visiting Lecturer, Edinburgh College of Art, 1958-75; Art Critic, The Scotsman, 1966-95; Senior Lecturer, Napier University, 1968-86; President, Society of Scottish Artists, 1960-64. Solo exhibitions: Scottish Gallery, Edinburgh, 1964, 1971, 1974, 1979, 1983, 1986, Peter Potter, Haddington, 1976, 1978, Macaulay Gallery, Stenton, 1982, 1985, Ancrum Gallery, 1988, 1990; work in public and private collections. Publication: The Eye in the Wind – Scottish painting since 1945, 1977. Recreations: swimming; classical music. Address: (h.) 6 Hillview, Edinburgh EH4 2AB; T.-0131-332 6670.

Gage, Simon Martin, BSc, MSc, PhD. Research Physicist, University of Edinburgh, since 1985; Events Manager, since 1990, and Director, since 1994, Edinburgh International Science Festival; b. 18.5.62, London; m., Sarah Price; 1 d. Educ. Ivybridge Comprehensive School; University of Bristol; University of Dundee; University of Edinburgh. Publications: author of science books for children, including Light and Illusion Activity Pack. Recreations: cycle touring; classical music; walking on hot coals and other demonstrations of unusual scientific principles. Address: (b.) Edinburgh International Science Festival, 149 Rose Street, Edinburgh EH2 4LS; T.-0131-220 3977.

Galbraith, Professor Roderick Allister McDonald, BSc, PhD (Cantab), CEng, MRAeS. Head of Aerospace Engineering, Glasgow University, since 1989; b. 4.8.47, Lowmoor, England; m., Lynn Margaret Fraser. Educ. Greenock High School; James Watt Memorial College; Paisley College of Technology; Cambridge University. Apprentice Draughtsman/Engineer, Scott's Shipbuilding & Engineering Co. Ltd., 1964-72; Department of Aerospace Engineering, Glasgow University: joined 1975; Reader, 1989, Professor, 1992. Publications: over 100 reports and publications on aerodynamics. Recreations: sailing; walking. Address: (b.) Department of Aerospace Engineering, Glasgow University, Glasgow G12 8QQ; T.-0141-330 5295.

Galbraith, Samuel Laird, BSc, MBChB, MD, FRCSGlas. MP (Labour), Strathkelvin and Bearsden, since 1987; Parliamentary Under-Secretary of State, Scottish Office (Minister for Health, the Arts and Children); Neurosurgeon; b. 18.10.45. Address: (b.) House of Commons, London, SW1A 0AA.

Galea, Paul, MD (Malta), DCH, FRCP(Glas), FRCPCH. Consultant Paediatrician and Neonatologist, Royal Hospital for Sick Children and Royal Maternity Hospital, Glasgow, since 1983; b. 8.10.50, Rabat, Malta; m., Irene. Educ. Royal University of Malta. Recreations: gardening; DIY, classical music. Address: (h.) 30 Garngaber Avenue, Lenzie, Glasgow G66 4LL; T.-0141-776 6031.

Gallacher, Tom. Writer; b. 16.2.34, Alexandria. Stage plays: Our Kindness to 5 Persons, 1969; Mr Joyce is Leaving Paris, 1971; Revival, 1972; Three to Play, 1972; Schellenbrack, 1973; Bright Scene Fading, 1973; The Only Street, 1973; Personal Effects, 1974; A Laughing Matter, 1975; Hallowe'en, 1975; The Sea Change, 1976; A Presbyterian Wooing (adapted from Pitcairne's The Assembly), 1976; The Evidence of Tiny Tim, 1977; Wha's Like Us - Fortunately!, 1978; Stage Door Canteen, 1978; Deacon Brodie (adapted from Stevenson and Henley), 1978; Jenny, 1979; Natural Causes, 1980; The Parole of Don Juan, 1981; The Treasure Ship (adapted from Brandane), 1982; Renée Houston Rehearses her Life, 1995; Of Time and Loss, 1997. Publications: (fiction): Hunting Shadows, 1981; Apprentice, 1983; Journeyman, 1984; Survivor, 1985; The Jewel Maker, 1986; The Wind on the Heath, 1987; The Stalking Horse, 1989; Gainful Perjury, 1990; The Last of Zenda, 1996; Remembering Clare and Herald Stories, 1997. Address: (b.) 25 Linn Walk, Garelochhead, Dunbartonshire G84 0DS.

Gallagher, Jim, BSc, MSc. Head, Local Government and Europe Group, Scottish Office, since 1998; b. 23.9.54, Clydebank; m., Una Green; 1 s.; 2 d. Educ. St. Aloysius College, Glasgow; Glasgow University; Edinburgh University. Administration Trainee, Scottish Office, 1976; Private Secretary to Minister for Home Affairs and Environment, 1980-82; Principal, Criminal Justice Division, 1982-86; Secretary, Scottish Office Management Group, 1986-88; Head, Urban Policy Division, 1988-89; Private Secretary to successive Secretaries of State for Scotland, 1989-91; Director (Human Resources), Scottish Prison Service, 1991-96; Head, Local Government Finance, 1996-98. Address: (b.) Scottish Office, Victoria Quay, Edinburgh; T.-0131-244 5505.

Gallagher, Sister Maire T., CBE, MA (Hons), MEd, FScotVec, DCE, FSQA. Retired Headteacher; Sister of Notre Dame Religious Congregation, since 1959; b. 27.5.33, Glasgow. Educ. Notre Dame High School, Glasgow; Glasgow University; Notre Dame College of Education. Principal Teacher of History, Notre Dame High School, Glasgow; Lecturer in Secondary Education, Notre Dame College of Education; Headteacher, Notre Dame High School, Dumbarton, 1974-87; Chairman, Scottish Consultative Council on the Curriculum, 1987-91 (Member, Consultative Committee on the Curriculum, since 1976). Member, Executive, Secondary Heads Association (Scottish Branch), 1976-83; Coordinator, Christian Life Movement Groups, West of Scotland; Fellow, Scottish Qualifications Authority, 1997. Recreations: reading; dress-making; bird-watching. Address: (h.) Sisters of Notre Dame, 67 Moorpark Avenue, Penilee, Glasgow G52 4ET; T.-0141 810 4214.

Gallie, Philip Roy, TEng, MIPlantE. Vice-Chairman, Scottish Conservative and Unionist Party, 1995-97; MP (Conservative), Ayr, 1992-97; business advisor; b. 3.6.39, Portsmouth; m., Marion Wands. Educ. Dunfermline High School; Kirkcaldy Technical College. Apprenticeship, H.M. Dockyard, Rosyth, 1955-60; Merchant Navy, 1960-64; electricity industry, 1964-92. Recreations: sports; politics. Address: (b.) 35 Auchentrae Crescent, Ayr; T.-01292 619350.

Galloway, George. MP, Glasgow Kelvin, since 1997; MP, Glasgow Hillhead, 1987-97; Senior Vice-Chair, Parliamentary Labour Party Foreign Affairs Committee; b. 16.8.54, Dundee; 1 d. Educ. Harris Academy, Dundee. Production Worker, Michelin Tyres, 1974; Dundee Labour Party Organiser, 1977; General Secretary, War on Want, 1983. Chairman, Scottish Labour Party, 1981-82; Member, Scottish Labour Party Executive Committee, 1974-84; Founder and first General Secretary, Trade Union Friends of Palestine, 1979. Recreations: football; music; films. Address: (b.) House of Commons, Westminster, London; T.-0171-219 6940.

Galloway, Janice. Writer; b. 2.12.56, Saltcoats. Educ. Ardrossan Academy; Glasgow University. Variety of paid and unpaid work, including 10 years' teaching English in Ayrshire; music criticism for Glasgow Herald, The Observer, Scotland on Sunday; fiction writing, including two collections of short stories and two novels; Co-Editor, New Writing Scotland, 1990-92. Publications: The Trick Is To Keep Breathing, 1990; Blood, 1991; Foreign Parts, 1994; Where You Find It, 1996; Staged work: The Trick is to Keep Breathing; Fall. Song cycle: Clara (Co-Writer); Monster, for orchestra and voices (Co-Writer).

Galloway, Michael Peter, BSc (Hons), MA, MRTPI. Director of Planning and Transportation, Dundee City Council, since 1997; b. 12.5.57, Aberfeldy; m., Joyce; 1 d. Educ. Perth Academy; Dundee University; Oxford Brookes University. Glasgow District Council: Planning Assistant, 1980-82, Planning Officer, 1982-84; Principal Planning Officer: London Borough of Lewisham, 1984-88, Manchester City Council, 1988-89; Assistant Chief Planning Officer, Glasgow City Council, 1989-91; Director, Crown Street Regeneration Project, 1991-97. Recreations: painting; travel; sailing; scuba diving. Address: (b.) Tayside House, Crichton Street, Dundee DD1 3RB; T.-01382 433610.

Galloway, 13th Earl of (Randolph Keith Reginald Stewart); b. 14.10.28; m.; succeeded to title, 1978. Educ. Harrow. Address: Senwick House, Brighouse Bay, Borgue, Kirkcudbrightshire, DG6 4TP.

Gamble, Alan James, LLB(Hons), LLM, Advocate. Full-time Chairman, Independent Tribunal Service, Glasgow, since 1993; Deputy Social Security and Child Support Commissioner, Edinburgh, since 1994; b. 29.4.51, Glasgow; m., Elizabeth Waugh; 2 s.; 1 d. Educ. High School of Glasgow; University of Glasgow; Harvard Law School, USA. Law Apprentice, 1974-76; admitted to Faculty of Advocates, 1978; Lecturer, then Senior Lecturer in Law, University of Glasgow, 1976-93. Bible Teacher, Christian Brethren Assemblies; Trustee, Interlink, and other charitable trusts; Dr J. McCormick Prize, 1972; Harkness Fellow, 1972-74. Publications: Contributor, Stair Memorial Encyclopedia; articles in legal journals. Recreations: reading; hill-walking. Address: (b.) Wellington House, 134-136 Wellington Street, Glasgow G2 2XL; T.-0141-353 1441.

Gamble, Kevin George Alfred, BEng. Executive Director, Weir Group PLC, since 1995; b. 1.9.47, Liverpool: m., Marie-Luise Paganetty; 2 s.; 1 d. Educ. Liverpool College; University of Liverpool. Stewarts & Lloyds, Bilston, Staffs, 1965-1970; Stone Manganese Marine Ltd., 1970-82; G.E.C. Turbine Generators Ltd., Rugby, 1982-88; Managing Director, Express Lift Co. Ltd., Northampton, 1988-92; Executive Director, Senior Engineering Group plc, 1992-95. Director, Northamptonshire Training and Enterprise Council, 1989-94. Recreations: tennis; family; garden. Address: (b.) Weir Group plc, 149 Newlands Road, Cathcart, Glasgow G44 4EX; T.-0141-308 2006.

Gammell, James Gilbert Sydney, MBE, CA; b. 4.3.20, Camberley; m., Susan Patricia Bowring; 5 s.; 1 d. Educ. Winchester College. Major, Grenadier Guards, Second World War; Partner, Ivory & Sime, 1949, Chairman, 1974-85; former Director, Bank of Scotland, Standard Life. Recreation: farming. Address: (h.) Foxhall, Kirkliston, West Lothian EH29 9ER; T.-0131-333 3275.

Gane, Professor Christopher H.W., LLB. Professor of Scots Law, University of Aberdeen, since 1994 (Dean, Faculty of Law, since 1995); b. 1.12.49, Jedburgh; m., Christine Mary; 2 s. Educ. Jedburgh Grammar School; Hawick High School; Edinburgh University; Université d' Aix en Provence. Lecturer in Law, University of Reading, 1974-77; Lecturer in Scots Law, University of Edinburgh, 1977-80; University of Lancaster: Lecturer in Law, 1980-87, Senior Lecturer in Law, 1987-90; University of Sussex: Senior Lecturer in Law, 1990-92, Professor of Law, 1992-94. Visiting Professor in Criminal Law, University of Antwerp, 1991-92; University of Notre Dame: Associate Professor of Law (Adjunct), 1987-92, Professor of Law (Adjunct), 1992-94; Honorary Sheriff of Grampian, Highland and Islands. Publications: A Casebook on Scottish Criminal Law (Co-author), 1980; Criminal Procedure in Scotland – Cases and Materials (Co-author), 1983; Sexual Offences, 1992; Criminal Procedure Systems in the European Community (Joint Author), 1993; Human Rights and the Administration of Justice (Co-author), 1997; contributor of numerous chapters and articles. Recreations: reading; music; cinema; playing guitar. Address: (b.) Faculty of Law, University of Aberdeen, Aberdeen AB24 3UB; T.-01224 273689.

Garbutt, David Charles Gemmell, QPM, GradIPD. HM Director, Scottish Police College, since 1998; HM Assistant Inspector of Constabulary for Scotland, Edinburgh, 1997; b. 16.8.45, Harthill; m., Moira Murdoch; 1 s.; 1 d. Educ. College of Commerce, Hull; Napier, Edinburgh. Joined Edinburgh City Police, 1964; transferred to Kingston upon Hull, 1967; returned to Edinburgh, 1970; promoted Chief Superintendent, 1987, as Divisional Commander, West Lothian; promoted Assistant Chief Constable, Lothian and Borders Police, 1991; appointed Deputy Chief Constable, Grampian Police, 1992. Recreations: hill-walking; cycling; curling. Address: (b.) Tulliallan Castle, Kincardine, Alloa FK10 4BE; T.-01259 732000.

Garden, Neville Abbot. Broadcaster; Writer and Lecturer on musical and media matters; b. 13.2.36, Edinburgh; m., Jane Fowler; 1 s., 1 d.; 3 d. by pr. m. Educ. George Watson's College, Edinburgh. Reporter, Sub-Editor, Feature Writer, Evening Dispatch, 1953-63; Daily Columnist and Music Critic, Edinburgh Evening News, 1963-64; Senior Feature Writer, Scottish Daily Express, 1964-78; Presenter, Good Morning Scotland, BBC Radio Scotland, 1978-90, Queen Street Garden, 1990-93; Music Critic and Columnist, Sunday Standard, 1981-83; Music Writer, Scotland on Sunday, since 1988; Conductor: Edinburgh Grand Opera, seven years; Edinburgh Ballet Theatre, nine years. Publication: Bloomsbury Good Music Guide.

Garden, Ralph, MA, FFA. Chief Executive, Scottish Office Pensions Agency, since 1998; b. 21.4.50, Aberchirder; 2 s.; 1 d. Educ. Robert Gordon's College; Aberdeen University. Scottish Widows, 1972-96 (various posts, finally as Executive Director, Client Services); Government Actuary's Department, 1997-98. Member, Council, Faculty of Actuaries; Chairman, Education Committee, Faculty and Institute of Actuaries. Recreations: golf; curling; hillwalking; tennis. Address: (b.) St. Margaret's House, 151 London Road, Edinburgh; T.-0131-244 3211.

Gardiner, Iain Derek, FRICS. Chartered Surveyor, since 1957; Consultant, Souter & Jaffrey, Chartered Surveyors (Senior Partner, 1986-95); b. 22.12.33, Glasgow; m., Kathleen Elizabeth Johnson; 2 s.; 1 d. Educ. Hutcheson's Grammar School, Glasgow; Royal Technical College, Glasgow. Trainee and Assistant Quantity Surveyor, John H. Allan & Sons, Glasgow, 1950-57; National Service, Royal Engineers, 1957-59; Souter & Jaffrey, Inverness: Quantity Surveyor, 1959-63, Partner, 1963-86. Past Chairman, Royal Institution of Chartered Surveyors in Scotland; Chairman: Inverness Area, RICS in Scotland, 1969-70, Quantity Surveyors Committee, RICS in Scotland, 1989-90, Friends of Eden Court Theatre, 1981-82, Inverness Area Scout

Council. Recreations: swimming; travel; cookery. Address: (h.) 77 Stratherrick Road, Inverness IV2 4LL; T.-01463 235607.

Gardiner, John Ronald, BL, WS, NP. Senior Partner, Brodies W.S, Solicitors, since 1992 (Partner, since 1964); b. 25.10.38, Rangoon; m., Aileen Mary Montgomery; 1 s.; 1 s. (deceased); 1 d. Educ. Fettes College; University of Edinburgh. Admitted Solicitor, 1963; admitted Writer to the Signet, 1964; Partner, Brodie Cuthbertson & Watson W.S. (now Brodies W.S.), 1964; Notary Public, 1966. Governor, Fettes Trust, 1986-96; Member, Rent Assessment Panel for Scotland, 1973-97; Hon. Secretary: Standing Council of Scottish Chiefs, 1970-72, Salmon and Trout Association (Scottish Branch), 1971-84. Recreations: fishing; shooting; golf; gardening. Address: (b.) 15 Atholl Crescent, Edinburgh EH3 8HA; T.-0131-228 3777.

Gardner, Angela Joy, BSc (Hons). Independent Public Affairs Consultant, AJ Enterprises, since 1994; b. 16.9.62, Wolverhampton; m., Andrew Ronald Gardner; 1 d. Educ. Codsall High School; UMIST. BP Chemicals Ltd., South Wales and Grangemouth, 1984-90; BP Schools Link Officer, 1985-90; Senior Public Affairs Officer, BP, 1990-94. Member, General Teaching Council for Scotland, since 1990. Address: (h.) 72 Craigcrook Road, Edinburgh EH4 3PN; T.-0131-336 5164.

Gardner, Dianne Alicia, BA (Hons). Headmistress, Wellington School, Ayr, since 1988; b. 15.9.47, Wolverhampton; m., John W. Gardner. Educ. Ounsdale School; Liverpool University. Museum Assistant, 1969-71; Teacher of History, 1971-72; Head of History, then Senior Mistress, Wellington School, 1972-88. Recreations: painting; gardening. Address: (b.) Carleton Turrets, Ayr KA7 2XH; T.-01292 269321.

Gardner, James, BSc. Rector, Dunblane High School, since 1989; b. 3.2.41, Glasgow; m., Margaret Catherine; 1 s.; 1 d. Educ. Allan Glen's School, Glasgow; Glasgow University; Strathclyde University. Teacher of Mathematics, Allan Glen's School, 1968-76; Principal Teacher of Mathematics, Cranhill Secondary, Glasgow, 1976-80; Assistant Head Teacher, Dunoon Grammar School, 1980-84; Depute Rector, Wallace High School, Stirling, 1984-89. Member, British Antarctic Survey, 1963-66. Recreations: climbing; skiing; orienteering; chess; golf. Address: (b.) Dunblane High School, Highfields, Dunblane; T.-01786 823823.

Garland, Harry Mitchell, MBE, CQSW, FBIM. Chairman, Secretary of State's Advisory Committee on Scotland's Travelling People, since 1987; b. 7.7.28, Aberdeen; m., Phyllis Sandison; 1 s.; 1 d. Educ. Rockwell Academy, Dundee; Robert Gordon's College, Aberdeen; Moray House College, Edinburgh; Edinburgh University. Probation Officer/Senior Probation Officer/Principal Probation Officer, 1958-69; Depute Director of Social Work, Aberdeen and Kincardine Counties, 1969-73; Director of Social Work: Paisley Burgh, 1973-74, Western Isles, 1974-78, Central Region, 1978-86. Chairman, National Association of Probation Officers in Scotland, 1968-69; President, Association of Directors of Social Work, 1983; Member, Forth Valley Health Board, 1986-90. Recreations: voluntary work; church; golf; walking. Address: (h.) 7 Cromarty View, Nairn IV12 4HX; T.-01667 453684.

Garner, John Angus McVicar, MB, ChB, DRCOG, DCH, FRCGP. Principal in general practice, since 1980; Past Chairman, Scottish General Medical Services Committee; British Medical Association: Vice Chairman, Scottish Council, Member, Council; Vice Chairman, Medical and Dental Defence Union of Scotland; Treasurer, General Medical Services Defence Fund Ltd.; b. 4.9.50, London; m., Catherine Lizbeth; 1 s.; 1 d. Educ. Eltham College; Edinburgh University. Lothian Local Medical Committee: Secretary, 1986-89, Chairman, 1991-92; Member: General Medical Services Committee, since 1989, National Medical Advisory Committee, 1989-95. Recreations: amphibians and photographing fungi. Address: (h.) 25 Murrayfield Avenue, Edinburgh EH12 6AU; T.-0131-337 6120.

Garrick, Sir Ronald, FEng, FRSE. Managing Director and Chief Executive, The Weir Group Plc, since 1982; b. 21.8.40; m.; 2 s.; 1 d. Non-Executive Director, Scottish Power, Shell UK; Member, Scottish Economic Council. Address: (b.) Weir Group PLC, 149 Newlands Road, Glasgow, G44 4EX.

Garrity, Rev. Thomas Alan Whiteway, BSc, BD, MTh. Minister, Auld Kirk of Ayr, since 1982; b. 13.7.43, Glasgow; m., Elizabeth Caroline Whiteford; 2 d. Educ. Allan Glen's School; University of Glasgow; University of Edinburgh. Minister, Fraserburgh South, 1971-82. Director, Bridge Projects; Chairman, Mathieson House. Recreations: golf; photography; woodwork; travel. Address: 58 Monument Road, Ayr; T.-01292 262580.

Garrod, Professor Neil, BSc (Hons), PhD, ACIS. Professor of Financial Analysis and Head, Department of Accounting and Finance, Glasgow University, since 1993; b. 7.6.54; m., Sonja Gortnar; 1 s.; 1 d. Educ. Guthlaxton Upper School, Wigston; Manchester Institute of Science and Technology. Lecturer in Business Finance, University College of Wales, Aberystwyth, 1979-87; Associate Professor, Graduate Management Institute, Union College, New York, 1987-89; Senior Lecturer in Accounting and Finance, University of Wales, Bangor, 1989-90, Royal Insurance Professor of Finance and Accounting, 1990-93. Recreation: running. Address: (b.) Department of Accounting and Finance, Glasgow University, Glasgow G12 8LE; T.-0141-339 8855, Ext. 5426.

Garrod, Professor Simon Christopher, MA, PhD. Professor of Cognitive Psychology, University of Glasgow, since 1991; Deputy Director, ESRC Human Communicator Research Centre, since 1989; b. 19.11.47, London; 1 s.; 1 d. Educ. Bradfield College, Berkshire; Oxford University; Princeton University. Lecturer, then Reader, Psychology, University of Glasgow. Member, ESRC Grants Board and Centres Board, 1989-95; Member, Government's Technology Foresight Panel in Information Technology, Electronics and Communications. Publications: Understanding Written Language (Co-author); Language Processing (Editor); articles in psychology and communication. Recreations: mountaineering; fishing. Address: (h.) 11 Crown Gardens, Glasgow G12 9EZ; T.-0141-334 8120.

Gaskin, Professor Maxwell, DFC (and bar), MA. Jaffrey Professor of Political Economy, Aberdeen University, 1965-85; b. 18.11.21, Liverpool; m., Brenda Stewart; 1 s.; 3 d. Educ. Quarry Bank School, Liverpool; Liverpool University. War Service, RAF, 1941-46; Lecturer and Senior Lecturer in Economics, Glasgow University, 1951-65; Head, Department of Political Economy, Aberdeen University, 1965-81; Economic Consultant to Secretary of State for Scotland, 1965-87; Member, Scottish Agricultural Wages Board, 1972-90; Chairman: Foresterhill and Associated Hospitals Board, 1972-74, Flax and Hemp and Retail Bespoke Tailoring Wages Councils, 1978-93; Member, Civil Engineering EDC, 1978-84; Chairman, Section F, British Association, 1978-79; President, Scottish Economic Society, 1981-84; Fellow, Royal Economic Society. Publications: The Scottish Banks: A Modern Survey, 1965; North East Scotland: A Survey of its Development Potential (Co-author), 1969; Economic Impact of North Sea Oil on Scotland (Co-author), 1978; Employment in Insurance, Banking and Finance in Scotland, 1980; The Political Economy of Tolerable

Survival (Editor), 1981. Recreations: music; gardening. Address: (h.) Westfield, Ancrum, Roxburghshire TD8 6XA; T.-018353 830237.

Gaston, Rev. Arthur Raymond Charles, MA, BD. Secretary for Staffing, Board of World Mission, Church of Scotland, since 1993; Secretary, Presbytery of Europe, since 1997; Secretary for Staffing, Church of Scotland Board of World Mission, 1993-98; b. 25.5.36, Atherstone; m., Evelyn Wilson Mather; 1 s.; 2 d. Educ. The Gordon Schools, Huntly; Aberdeen University. Teacher of Mathematics, 1961-62; Principal of theological college in Madagascar, 1962-67; Missionary with London Missionary Society, 1967-69; Minister, Sauchie Parish Church, 1969-75, Dollar with Muckhart with Glendevon, 1975-89, Scottish Church, Knox's Chapel, Geneva, 1989-93. Recreations: water colour painting; walking; choral singing; wildlife. Address: (h.) 137 Newhaven Road, Edinburgh EH6 4NP; T.-0131-554 6579.

Gautam, Prasanna Chandra, MBBS (Hon), MRCP (UK), FRCPEdin; FRCPGlas, FRIPHH. Consultant Physician, since 1989; Clinical Senior Lecturer in Medicine, Medical School, Aberdeen, since 1989; b. 3.4.45, Nepal; m., Leela Mani; 1 s.; 1 d. Educ. Padmodaya High School, Kathmandu; Bangalore Medical College, India. Registrar in Cardiology, Liverpool, 1981-84; Registrar in Geriatric Medicine, Liverpool, 1984-86; Senior Registrar in General Medicine and Geriatrics, 1986-89. Former Chairman, Nepalese Doctors Association (UK); former Executive Member, Scottish Branch, BGS. Publications: several books in Nepali; publications on hypothermia, cardiac problems in the elderly, and urinary incontinence. Recreations: chess; travelling; gardening; walking. Address: (b.) Department of Medicine for the Elderly, Woodend Hospital, Aberdeen; T.-01224 663131, Ext. 56319.

Gavin, Anthony John, BSc, DipEd. Head Teacher, St. Margaret's Academy, Livingston, since 1993; Member, Strategy Group, Higher Still Development Programme Scotland; b. 11.10.41, Perth; m., Charlotte Duffy; 2 d. Educ. Perth Academy; St. Andrews University. Teacher, St. Andrew's High School, Kirkcaldy, 1964-71; Principal Teacher/Assistant Headteacher, St. David's High School, Dalkeith, 1971-77; Depute Headteacher, St. Augustine's High School, Edinburgh, 1977-79; Headteacher, St. Saviour's High School, Dundee, 1979-93; TVEI Adviser Scotland, 1986-90. Member, Scottish Community Education Council, since 1993; Chair, Catholic Headteachers' Association of Scotland, 1994-96. Recreations: music; golf. Address: (h.) 5 Colinton Court, Glenrothes KY6 3PE; T.-01592 743462.

Gavin, Derek, FRICS, IRRV. Chartered Surveyor, since 1971; Executive Director, Stirling Enterprise Park and Stirling Enterprise, since 1984; Board Director: Stirling Business Links Ltd., Business Enterprise Scotland Ltd.; b. 12.12.46, Perth; m., Terry; 1 s. Educ. Perth Academy; College of Estate Management. Trainee Surveyor, Bell Ingram, Perth, 1964-69; Management Surveyor, Scottish Industrial Estates Corporation, Glasgow, 1969-72; Valuation Surveyor, Bell Ingram, Perth, 1972-77; Estates Property Manager, Central Regional Council, 1977-84. Recreations: curling; golf. Address: (b.) John Player Building, Players Road, Stirling; T.-01786 463416.

Gavin, Kevin George, MA (Hons), DipEd. Director of Education, The Moray Council, since 1995; b. 4.7.48, Aberdeen; m., Jessie M.C. Connell; 1 d. Educ. Aberdeen Academy; Aberdeen University; Aberdeen College of Education. Assistant Head Teacher, Silverwood Primary School, Kilmarnock, 1974-77; Head Teacher, Monkton Primary School, 1977-80; Adviser in Primary Education: Grampian, 1980-83, Strathclyde, 1983-85; HM Inspector of Schools, 1985-90; Chief Adviser, Strathclyde Regional Council Education Department, 1990-95. Recreations: walking; food and drink; motor-cycling. Address: (h.) Monymusk, Benslie Village, by Kilwinning, KA13 7QY.

Gawthrop, Professor Peter John, MA, DPhil, MIEE, MInstMC, CEng, EurIng. Wylie Professor of Mechanical Engineering, Glasgow University, since 1987; b. 10.3.52, Seascale; 2 d. Educ. Whitehaven Grammar School; Queen's College, Oxford. W.W. Spooner Research Fellow, New College, Oxford; Lecturer, then Reader, Sussex University. Recreation: hill-walking. Address: (b.) Department of Mechanical Engineering, James Watt Building, Glasgow University, Glasgow G12 8QQ; T.-0141-339 8855.

Gemmell, Curtis Glen, BSc, PhD, MIBiol, FRCPath. Reader and Head of Academic Department of Bacteriology, Glasgow University; Honorary Bacteriologist, Greater Glasgow Health Board, since 1976; Director, Scottish MRSA Reference Laboratory; b. 26.8.41, Beith, Ayrshire; m., Anne Margaret; 2 d. Educ. Spier's School, Beith; Glasgow University. Glasgow University: Assistant Lecturer, 1966-68, Lecturer, 1968-69; Paisley College of Technology: Lecturer, 1969-71, Senior Lecturer, 1971-76; Glasgow University: Senior Lecturer, 1976-90, Reader, 1990-94; Visiting Assistant Professor, University of Minnesota, Minneapolis, 1979-80. Recreations: gardening; golf. Address: (h.) Sunninghill, 19 Lawmarnock Crescent, Bridge of Weir PA11 3AS; T.-Bridge of Weir 613350.

Gemmell, Gavin John Norman, CA. Senior Partner, Baillie, Gifford & Co., since 1989 (Partner, since 1967); Chairman, Toyo Trust Baillie Gifford Ltd., since 1989; Deputy Chairman, Scottish Widows Fund & Life Assurance Society, since 1995; Director: Guardian Baillie Gifford Ltd., since 1990, LEEL, since 1995, SFE, since 1998; b. 7.9.41, Edinburgh; m., Kathleen Fiona Drysdale; 1 s.; 2 d. Educ. George Watson's College. Qualified CA, 1964; joined Baillie, Gifford & Co., 1964; Chairman, Standing Committee, Scottish Episcopal Church, since 1997; Member, Court, Heriot Watt University, since 1993. Recreations: golf; foreign travel. Address: (b.) 1 Rutland Court, Edinburgh EH3 8EY; T.-0131-222 4000.

Gemmell, William Ruthven, LLB, WS. Partner, Murray Beith Murray WS, since 1987; Director, Inchcape Family Investments Ltd., Lawshare Ltd., Association of Solicitor Investment Managers, and other companies; b. 4.4.57; m., Fiona Elizabeth Watson; 1 s.; 1 d. Educ. Loretto; Edinburgh University; Aberdeen University. Apprentice at Law, Brodies WS, 1979-82; Trainee Accountant, Arthur Young CA, 1983-85; Solicitor, Murray Beith Murray WS, 1985-87. Law Society of Scotland: Chairman, Investor Protection Committee, since 1992, Council Member, since 1993; Member, Financial Services Tribunal, since 1993. Address: (b.) 39 Castle Street, Edinburgh EH2 3BH; T.-0131-225 1200.

Gemmill, Robert, MA, FIMC. Member, Business Committee, General Council, Glasgow University, 1987-98, Assessor of the General Council on the University Court, 1990-98, and Co-opted Court Member, since 1998; b. 20.2.30; m., 1, Anne MacMurchy Gow (deceased); 2, Elisabeth Mary MacLennan; 2 s.; 1 d. Educ. High School of Glasgow; Glasgow University. Manufacturing management, Procter & Gamble Ltd., 1953-56; Management Consultant, PA Management Consultants Ltd., 1956-85. Played rugby football for Glasgow High School FP, Northumberland, Cheshire, Barbarians and Scotland, 1950-51. Recreations: golf; travel; music. Address: (h.) 123 Fotheringay Road, Glasgow G41 4LG; T.-0141-423 1860.

Gennard, Professor John, BA (Econ), MA (Econ), FIPM. Professor of Human Resource Management, Strathclyde University, since 1981; b. 26.4.44, Manchester; m., Florence Anne Russell; 1 s.; 1 d. Educ. Hulme Grammar School for Boys; Sheffield University; Manchester University. Research Officer, Industrial Relations

Department, then Lecturer in Industrial Relations, London School of Economics, 1968-81. Publications: The Reluctant Militants (Co-author), 1972; Financing Strikers, 1978; Industrial Relations and Job Security, 1979; The Closed Shop in British Industry, 1984; A History of the National Graphical Association, 1990; A History of the Society of Graphical and Allied Trades, 1995; Employee Relations, 1997. Recreations: football; swimming; politics; trade unions; food and drink. Address: (h.) 4 South Avenue, Carluke, Lanarkshire; T.-01555 51361.

Gent, William, OBE. H.M. Commissioner (part-time), Mental Welfare Commission for Scotland, since 1996; b. 3.3.44, Crawcrook, Co. Durham; m., Audrey Charlton; 1 s.; 1 d. Educ. Hookergate Grammar School. Staff Nurse/Deputy Charge Nurse, Prudhoe Hospital, 1965-66; Charge Nurse, Balderton Hospital, 1966-69; Nursing Officer, Earls House Hospital, 1969-73; Royal Scottish National Hospital: Senior Nursing Officer, 1973-85, Director of Nursing, 1985-93, Director of Nursing and Quality and Executive Board Member, 1993-94; Clinical Director, Central Scotland Health Care Trust, 1994-99. Member, NBS, 1983-93, UKCC, 1988-93. Recreations: reading; walking; DIY; caravanning. Address: (h.) 5 Murdiston Avenue, Callander, Perthshire; T.-01877 330990.

George, John Charles Grossmith, FSAScot, FHS. Kintyre Pursuivant of Arms, since 1986; b. 15.12.30, London; m., Margaret Mary Maria Mercedes Weld. Educ. Ampleforth. Lt., Hertfordshire Yeomanry, 1951-54; films and television advertising, 1952-62; College of Arms, 1962-72; Earl Marshal's Liaison Officer with the Churchill family, 1965; Green Staff Officer, Prince of Wales's Investiture, 1969; Garioch Pursuivant, 1976. Chairman, Philbeach Light Opera Society, 1961-63; Vice President, BBC "Mastermind" Club, 1979-81; Knight of Obedience, Sov. Mil. Ord. of Malta; Commander, Ord. Pro Merito Melitensi; Knight Constantinian Order of St. George. Publications: The Puffin Book of Flags, 1975; The French Heralds (paper), 1985; numerous historical articles. Recreations: English light opera and musical comedies; hagiographies; sports. Address: (h.) Flat 15, 1 New Cut Rigg, Craighall Road, Edinburgh EH6 4QR; T.-0131-551 3900.

George, Judith Wordsworth, MA (Oxon), PhD. Deputy Scottish Director, The Open University, since 1984; b. 26.8.40, Bradford; 2 d. Educ. Heath Grammar School, Halifax; Somerville College, Oxford. Tutor in Philosophy, St. Andrews University; Lecturer in History of Fine Art, Manchester University; Tutor in Classics, Open University; Senior Counsellor, Open University in Scotland. Recreations: gardening; classical music; hill-walking. Address: (b.) 10 Drumsheugh Gardens, Edinburgh EH3 7QJ; T.-0131-549 7130.

George, Professor William David, MB, BS, FRCS, MS. Professor of Surgery, Glasgow University, since 1981; b. 22.3.43, Reading; 1 s.; 3 d. Educ. Henley Grammar School; London University. Lecturer in Surgery, Manchester University, 1973-77; Senior Lecturer in Surgery, Liverpool University, 1977-81. Member, National Committees, British Association of Surgical Oncology and Surgical Research Society. Recreations: veteran rowing; golf. Address: (b.) University Department of Surgery, Western Infirmary, Glasgow G11 6NT; T.-0141-211 2166.

Gerber, Pat, MA (Hons). Writer, since 1982; Lecturer (part-time), Glasgow University, since 1985; b. 17.3.34, Glasgow; m., Cyril Gerber; 3 s.; 2 d. Educ. St. Leonard's School; Glasgow University. Publications: The Stone of Destiny; Maiden Voyage; several plays. Recreations: reading; travel; swimming; tennis; hill-walking; sailing; cars; sewing; music. Address: (h.) 6 Golf Road, Clarkston, Glasgow G76 7LZ; T.-0141-638 2269.

Gerrard, John Henry Atkinson, MBE, FRIAS, DA (Edin), MA (Cantab), FRSA, FSA(Scot). Technical Director, Scottish Civic Trust, since 1984; b. 15.9.34, Leicester; m., Dr. Margaret Mackay. Educ. Abbotsholme; Corpus Christi College, Cambridge; Edinburgh College of Art. Assistant Architect: Sheffield Corporation, 1961-63, Planning Department, Oxford City Council, 1965-68; Assistant Director, Scottish Civic Trust, 1968-84. Recreation: travelling hopefully. Address: (b.) The Tobacco Merchant's House, 42 Miller Street, Glasgow G1 1DT; T.-0141-221 1466.

Gerrie, Ian Stewart. Director, Inland Revenue Scotland, since 1997; b. 1.12.45, Aberdeen. Director, Inland Revenue North West, 1993-97. Address: (b.) Clarendon House, 114-116 George Street, Edinburgh EH2 4LH.

Gerson, Jack Barton. Dramatist and Novelist; b. 31.7.28, Glasgow; 1 d. Educ. Hillhead High School, Glasgow. RAF, two years; worked in advertising and cinema distribution, 1949-59; writing full-time since 1959; won BBC Television Play Competition, 1959, for Three Ring Circus; has written more than 100 hours of television drama; created two series, The Regiment and The Omega Factor; 14 radio plays; novels include Whitehall Sanction, Assassination Run, Treachery Game, The Back of the Tiger, Deaths Head Berlin, The Evil Thereof, The Fetch. Recreations: cinema; reading; swimming; Caribbean Islands; sleeping in front of television set. Address: (b.) The Agency, 24 Pottery Lane, Holland Park, London W11 4LZ.

Gerstenberg, Frank Eric, MA (Cantab), PGCE, FRSA. Principal, George Watson's College, Edinburgh, since 1985; b. 23.2.41, Balfron; m., Valerie MacLellan; 1 s.; 2 d. Educ. Trinity College, Glenalmond; Clare College, Cambridge; London University. Assistant Master, Kelly College, Tavistock, 1963-67; Housemaster and Head of History, Millfield School, 1967-74; Headmaster, Oswestry School, 1974-85. Recreations: skiing; sailing; travelling; music. Address: (h.) 27 Merchiston Gardens, Edinburgh EH10 5DD; T.-0131-337 6880.

Gerver, Professor Elisabeth, BA (Hons), MA, PhD. Professor and Director of Continuing Education, University of Dundee, 1990-97; b. 15.4.41, Winnipeg; m., Dr. David Gerver (deceased); 1 s.; 1 d. Educ. Wolfville High School, Nova Scotia; Dalhousie University, Canada; Toronto University; King's College, London. Lecturer in Communications, Newcastle upon Tyne Polytechnic, 1968-69; part-time staff, Open University, 1971-84; Lecturer in Communication, Queen Margaret College, Edinburgh, 1974-83; Director: Scottish Community Education Microelectronics Project, Glasgow, 1981-82, Scottish Institute of Adult and Continuing Education, 1983-90. Member, Council: Scottish Community Education Council, 1979-83, BBC Continuing Education Advisory Council, 1983-86; Vice-President, European Bureau of Adult Education, 1986-90; Executive Member, Universities Association for Continuing Education, 1992-97; Governor, Queen Margaret College, 1985-88; Member: Board, Tayside Education Business Partnership, 1992-96, IBA Educational Advisory Council, 1988-90, Education Panel, Research Assessment Exercise, 1992 and 1996, Post-Qualification Education Board for Pharmacists (Scotland), 1996-98. Publications: Computers and Adult Learning, 1984; Humanising Technology, 1985; Strategic Women: how do they manage in Scotland? (Co-author), 1991. Recreations: travel; the performing arts; hill-walking; sailing. Address: (h.) 65 Magdalen Yard Road, Dundee DD2 1AL; T.-01382 566794.

Gibb, Alexander Russell. Director and General Manager, Royal Mail Scotland and Northern Ireland, since 1996; b. 19.9.46, Motherwell; m., Elizabeth Ann Watney. Educ. Wishaw High School. Management Trainee, Post Office, 1965; Assistant Controller, Royal Mail, 1968; Assistant

Head Postmaster, Oxford, 1976; Head Postmaster, Aberdeen, 1984; Operations Controller, Scotland, Royal Mail, 1986; Operations Director, Scotland, Royal Mail, 1992. Director, Quality Scotland Foundation; Chairman, Head Postmaster Fellowship, Scotland; President, Post Office Sports Association (Scotland and Northern Ireland). Recreations: sport; walking; family; travel. Address: (b.) 102 West Port, Edinburgh EH3 9HS; T.-0131-228 7400.

Gibb, Andrew Thomas Fotheringham, LLB (Hons), SSC, NP. Solicitor, since 1972; Chairman and Head, Family Law Team, Balfour & Manson, Edinburgh, since 1995; b. 17.8.47, Perth; m., Patricia Anne Eggo; 2 s. Educ. Perth Academy; University of Edinburgh. Qualified 1971; joined Balfour & Manson, 1972: Partner, 1975. Solicitor, Educational Institute of Scotland, since 1983; President, Law Society of Scotland, 1990-91 (Member, Council, 1981-93); Joint Editor, Family Law Bulletin. Recreations: music; golf. Address: (b.) 58 Frederick Street, Edinburgh EH2 1LS.

Gibb, Francis. General Manager, Common Services Agency. Address: (b.) Trinity Park House, South Trinity Road, Edinburgh, EH5 3SE.

Gibb, George Frederick Cullen, MA, LLB. Consultant to Messrs Marshall Wilson, Solicitors, Falkirk, since 1997; Honorary Sheriff at Falkirk, since 1987; b. 19.3.33, Edinburgh; m., Inga Mary Grieve; 1 s.; 2 d. Educ. George Heriot's School, Edinburgh; Edinburgh University. Messrs Marshall Wilson, Solicitors: Partner, 1964, Senior Partner, 1990. Recreations: golf; music; bowls; reading. Address: (h.) 85 Muirhead Road, Larbert, Stirlingshire; T.-01324 562713.

Gibbons, John Ernest, PhD, DipArch, DipTP, ARIBA, ARIAS, FSA(Scot), FRSA. Director of Building and Chief Architect, Scottish Office, since 1984; b. 20.4.40, Halesowen; m., Patricia Mitchell; 1 s.; 2 d. Educ. Oldbury Grammar School; Birmingham School of Architecture, Aston University; Edinburgh University. Lecturer, Birmingham School of Architecture and Aston University, 1962-65; Research Fellow, Architecture Research Unit, then Lecturer in Architecture, Edinburgh University, 1966-72; Principal, Architect's Division, Scottish Development Department, 1972-78; Visiting Research Scientist, CSIRO, Melbourne, 1975; Assistant Director, Building Directorate, SDD, 1978; Deputy Director, Scottish Office Building Directorate, 1982-84. Member, Council: EAA and RIAS, 1977-80, ARCUK, since 1984; Assessor, Design Council, 1984-88. Address: (h.) Crichton House, Pathhead, Midlothian EH37 5UX; T.-01875 320085.

Gibbs, Lavinia. Trustee, National Galleries of Scotland, 1986-98; Member: Brodick Country Park Committee, since 1980, Ayrshire and Arran Health Council, since 1994; b. 7.6.39, London; m., Stephen Gibbs; 2 s.; 1 d. Educ. Heathfield, Ascot; Ipswich Civic College. Librarian, Courtauld Institute of Art, London, 1960-66; Child Care Officer/Social Worker, Royal Borough of Kensington and Chelsea, 1968-73; Representative for Norfolk, National Art Collections Fund, 1968-73; Member, Council, National Trust for Scotland, 1975-80, and Curatorial Committee, 1982-92. Recreation: gardening. Address: (h.) Dougarie Lodge, Isle of Arran KA27 8EB; T.-0177 084 0229.

Gibbs, Ronald Percy, OBE. President, Phab Scotland, since 1992 (Chairman, 1984-92); a Director, Handicabs (Lothian), since 1985; Convener, History Section, The Cramond Association, since 1983; b. 1.6.21, London; m., Margaret Eleanor Dean; 3 s.; 1 d. Educ. Owen's School, Islington. Ministry (later Department) of Transport, 1938-81; set up the Ports Office for Scotland in Edinburgh, 1973, and remained Head of that Office until retiral in 1981. Recreations: transport and communications; music; Scottish and industrial history; photography. Address: (h.) 13 Inveralmond Drive, Edinburgh EH4 6JX; T.-0131-312 6034.

Gibbs, Stephen Cokayne, Director, Vaux Group PLC, since 1970; b. 18.7.29, Hertingfordbury, England; m., Lavinia Bacon; 2 s.; 1 d. Educ. Eton College. Served with KRRC (60th Rifles), 1947-49; TA, service with QVR (TA), 1951-63: Lt., 1951, Captain, 1956, Major, 1958; Port Line Ltd., 1949-62: Assistant Manager, 1957, London Manager, 1959; Charles Barker PLC, 1962-87: Director, 1962, Deputy Chairman, 1982-87. National Trust for Scotland: Member, Executive, since 1987 and Council, 1991-96; Member: TUCC for Scotland, 1992-97, Red Deer Commission, since 1993; Chairman: Association of Deer Management Groups, since 1994, Isle of Arran District Salmon Fishery Board, since 1990. Recreations: shooting; fishing. Address: The Estate Office, Dougarie, Isle of Arran KA27 8EB; T.-01770 840259.

Gibson, Edgar Matheson, MBE, TD, DL, DA. Deputy Lieutenant, Orkney, since 1976; Honorary Sheriff, Grampian, Highlands and Islands, since 1992; full-time professional artist since 1990; b. 1.11.34, Kirkwall; m., Jean McCarrick; 2 s.; 2 d. Educ. Kirkwall Grammar School; Gray's College of Art, Aberdeen. National Service, 1958-60; TA and TAVR service to 1985 with Lovat Scouts, reaching Lt. Col.; Battalion Second in Command, 2/51 Highland Volunteers, 1973-76; Joint Services Liaison Officer for Orkney, 1980-85; Cadet Commandant, Orkney Lovat Scouts ACF, 1979-86, Honorary Colonel, since 1986; Member, Orkney Health Board, since 1991; Vice Chairman, Italian Chapel Preservation Committee, since 1994; Hon. President: Society of Friends of St. Magnus Cathedral, since 1994, Orkney Craftsmen's Guild, since 1997 (Chairman, 1962-82); President, Orkney Branch, SSFA and FHS, since 1997 (Chairman, 1990-97); Chairman: St. Magnus Cathedral Fair Committee, since 1982, Northern Area, Highland TA&VR Association, 1987-93. Recreation: whisky tasting. Address: (h.) Transcona, New Scapa Road, Kirkwall, Orkney; T.-0856 2849.

Gibson, Rev. Henry Montgomerie, MA, BD, PhD. Minister, The High Kirk, Dundee, since 1979; b. 11.6.36, Wishaw; m., Dr. Anne Margaret Thomson; 1 s. Educ. Wishaw Academy; Hamilton Academy; Glasgow University. Assistant Minister, Glasgow Cathedral, 1960; Minister: Carmunnock Parish Church, Glasgow, 1961-71, Aberfeldy, 1971-79; Convener, Church of Scotland Working Party on Alcohol and Drugs, 1975-81; Moderator, Dundee Presbytery, 1996-97. Recreations: reading; table tennis (occasionally); steam locomotives. Address: High Kirk Manse, 6 Adelaide Place, Dundee DD3 6LF; T.-Dundee 322955.

Gibson, Ian Ford, BSc, BA(Hons). Headteacher, Woodfarm High School, Thornliebank, since 1995; b. 16.4.49, Girvan; m., Marion. Educ. Hamilton Academy; University of Glasgow; Open University. Teacher of Mathematics: Hamilton Grammar, 1972-74, Earnock High, Hamilton, 1974-80; Barrhead High: Principal Teacher of Mathematics, 1980-85, Assistant Head Teacher, 1985-91, Depute Head Teacher, 1991-95. Recreations: bowling; gardening. Address: (b.) Woodfarm High School, Robslee Road, Thornliebank, Glasgow G46 7HG; T.-0141-577 2600.

Gibson, Ian Robert Lusk, MA, DipHSM. Regional Director, Scotland and Northern Ireland, Macmillan Cancer Relief, since 1996; b. 15.5.53, Kilmarnock; m., Rosemary Margaret Copland. Educ. Dollar Academy; Edinburgh University. Commissioning Administrator, Crosshouse Hospital, Ayrshire, 1978-79; Assistant Administrator, Stobhill Hospital, Glasgow, 1979-83; Administrator, Western General Hospital, Edinburgh, 1983-86; Assistant General Manager, Royal Infirmary of Edinburgh, 1986-89;

Civil Servant, 1989-90; Operations Director, Mediguard Services, 1990-92; Regional Director, Scottish Ambulance Service, 1992-96. Trustee, Edinburgh Cyrenians, since 1993. Recreations: golf; tennis; skiing; hill-walking; gardening; foreign languages. Address: (b.) 9 Castle Terrace, Edinburgh; T.-0131-229 3276.

Gibson, John Alan, MB, ChB, MD, FRCGP, FRSMed, DObstRCOG, CBiol, FIBiol, FLS, FZS, FRGS, FRMS, FGS, FSA (Scot). Senior Honorary Secretary, British Medical Association, since 1979; Chairman, Scottish Natural History Library, since 1974; Editor, the Scottish Naturalist, since 1972; b. 15.5.26, Kilbarchan; m., Dr. Mary M. Baxter; 1 d. Educ. Lindisfarne School; Paisley Grammar School; Glasgow University. Family doctor, village of Kilbarchan; Hon. Secretary, Renfrewshire Division, BMA, 1957-95; last Secretary, Renfrewshire Local Medical Committee; first Secretary, Argyll and Clyde Area Medical Committee; Member, Central Council, Central Ethical Committee, Scottish Council and Scottish GMS Committee, BMA; Past President, West of Scotland Branch, BMA; Hon. President, Renfrewshire Division, BMA; Fellow, Royal Society of Medicine; Life Fellow, Royal College of General Practitioners; Scottish Representative and Vice-President, Society for the Bibliography of Natural History; Scientific Meetings Secretary, Vice-President and Hon. Member, Society for the History of Natural History; Chairman: Friends of Glasgow University Library, Scottish Natural History Trust; former Chairman, Clyde Area Branch, Scottish Wildlife Trust; President, Renfrewshire Natural History Society; Secretary and Honorary Life Member, Scottish Society for the Protection of Birds; Scientific Fellow, Zoological Society of London; Life Fellow: RSPB, Royal Zoological Society of Scotland; Chairman, Clyde Bird Club; Honorary President, Kintyre Bird Club; former Secretary and Life Fellow, Royal Physical Society of Edinburgh; Gold Medal, Scottish Society for the Protection of Birds, 1967; Queen's Silver Jubilee Medal, 1977; Fellowship, BMA, 1982. Publications: Mammals of West of Scotland; Birds of Clyde Area; Atlas of Clyde Vertebrates; Regional Bibliography of West of Scotland Vertebrates; Bibliography of Scottish Vertebrate Zoology; 300 scientific papers, books and reports on Scottish natural history, 1939-98. Recreations: natural history; golf (Royal Troon). Address: (h.) Foremount House, Kilbarchan PA10 2EZ; T.-01505 702419.

Gibson, John Sibbald. Author (Scottish history); b. 1.5.23, Barrhead; m., Moira Helen Gillespie; 1 s.; 1 d. Educ. Paisley Grammar School; Glasgow University. Army Service, 1941-46 (Lieut., 1 Commando); returned to Glasgow University; joined administrative grade, Civil Service, 1947 and served in Scottish Office until 1985, retiring as Under Secretary. Vice Chairman, Saltire Society, since 1995. Publications: Ships of the '45; Deacon Brodie; The Thistle and the Crown; Playing the Scottish Card; The Jacobite Threat; Summer Hunting A Prince; Lochiel of the '45; Edinburgh in the '45. Recreation: writing on historical themes. Address: (h.) 28 Cramond Gardens, Edinburgh EH4 6PU; T.-0131-336 2931.

Gibson, Martin. Principal Timpanist, Royal Scottish National Orchestra, since 1980; Lecturer in Timpani, Royal Scottish Academy of Music and Drama, since 1980; b. 11.2.56, Newcastle-upon-Tyne; separated; 1 s.; 1 d. Educ. Tynemouth High School; Royal College of Music, London. Member, National Youth Orchestra of Great Britain, 1970-73; freelance musician, London, 1976-78; Principal Timpanist, English Northern Philharmonia (Opera North), 1978-80. Director, Royal Scottish National Orchestra Society Limited, since 1995; Examiner, Guildhall School of Music, 1983; Tutor, National Youth Orchestra of Scotland, 1990, 1993; Panel Member, Shell/LSO Scholarship, 1992; Tutor, Northern Junior Philharmonic Orchestra, 1997; Lecturer, National Association of Percussion Teachers, 1998. Fellow, Royal Society of Musicians. Recreation: golf. Address: (h.) 9 School Wynd, Kinross KY13 7EJ.

Gibson, Robert Irvine, MA(Hons). Rector, Eastwood High School, since 1995; b. 14.8.47, Ayr; m., Elizabeth; 1 s.; 2 d. Educ. John Neilson Institution, Paisley; University of Glasgow. Teacher, Paisley Grammar School; Principal Teacher, then Assistant Headteacher, Woodfarm High School; T.R.I.S.T. Co-ordinator, Renfrew Division, Strathclyde Council; Depute Headteacher, Greenock High School. Member, Mearns Parish Kirk Trust. Address: (b.) Eastwood High School, Capelrig Road, Newton Mearns G77 6NQ; T.-0141-577 2200.

Gibson, Sheriff William Erle, BA, LLB. Sheriff, since 1989; b. 30.8.34, Glasgow; m., Anne; 1 s.; 2 d. Educ. Dollar Academy; Trinity Hall, Cambridge; Glasgow University. Solicitor in Glasgow, 1961-89; Clerk to General Commissioners of Taxes, City of Glasgow, 1968-89; Clerk to General Council, Glasgow University, 1976 86. Member, European Ethical Review Committee, since 1976. Recreations: golf; fishing; piping; hill-walking; the family. Address: (h.) 7A Briarwell Road, Milngavie, Glasgow; T.-0141-956 2770.

Giegerich, Professor Heinz Joachim, MA, PhD. Professor of English Linguistics, University of Edinburgh, since 1997; b. 4.12.52, Aachen, Germany. Educ. Gymnasium Eschweiler, Germany; Johannes Gutenberg Universität, Mainz. Department of English Language, University of Edinburgh: Lecturer, 1979-92; Reader, 1992-97. Publications: Metrical Phonology and Phonological Structure, 1985; English Phonology, 1992; Lexical Strata in English, 1999. Address: (b.) Department of English Language, University of Edinburgh, George Square, Edinburgh EH8 9JX; T.-0131-695 3628.

Gifford, Professor Thomas Douglas MacPharlain, MA, PhD, FRSE. Head, Department of Scottish Literature, University of Glasgow, since 1994; Honorary Librarian of Abbotsford (Walter Scott's Library), since 1993; b. 14.7.40; m., Anne Tait Gifford; 3 d. Educ. Hillhead High School; University of Glasgow; Baliol College, University of Oxford. Lecturer then Senior Lecturer, University of Strathclyde, 1967-86; University of Glasgow: Senior Lecturer, 1986, Reader, 1990, Professor and Chair of Scottish Literature, 1995. Publications: James Hogg; Neil Gunn and Lewis Grassic Gibbon; History of Scottish Literature – The Nineteenth Century (Editor), 1988; History of Scottish Women's Writing (Co-editor) 1998. Address: (h.) 9 Shielhill, Ayr KA7 4SY; T.-01292 443360.

Gilbert, George, DA, RSW. Painter; Partner, Courtyard Gallery, since 1994; b. 12.9.39, Glasgow; m., Lesley Johnston; 3 s. Educ. Victoria Drive Secondary School, Glasgow; Glasgow School of Art. Teacher of Art, Aberdeenshire, Glasgow, Fife, 1963-89; painter (exhibited widely), since 1963. Elected: RSW, 1973 (Council Member, 1994-98); SAAC, 1991, PAI, 1992. Artstore Award, 1992; Gillies Award (RSW), 1993. Recreations: walking; reading; music; the arts. Address: 44 Marketgate South, Crail, Fife KY10 3TL; T.-01333 450797.

Gilbert, Leo Howard. National Director, Apostleship of the Sea, since 1997; National Secretary, Apostleship of the Sea (Scotland), since 1985; b. 21.5.20, Shaftesbury; m., Catherine; 3 s. Educ. village school, Storrington, Sussex. Royal Navy, 1940-46; Clyde RNR, 1946-85. Recreations: soccer; cricket. Address: (b.) 937 Dumbarton Road, Glasgow G14 9UF; T.-0141-339 6657.

Gilchrist, Archibald, OBE, MA. Vice-Chairman, Scottish Friendly Assurance Society Ltd. (Director, since 1988); b. 17.11.29, Glasgow; m., Elizabeth Jean; 2 s.; 1 d. Educ. Loretto School; Pembroke College, Cambridge. Barclay Curle & Co. Ltd., 1954-64; Brown Bros. & Co. Ltd., 1964-

72; Govan Shipbuilders Ltd., 1972-79; Vosper Pte Ltd., Singapore, 1980-86; Director, Caledonian MacBrayne Ltd., 1990-97; Director, RMJM Ltd., 1988-98. Recreations: shooting; fishing; golf. Address: (h.) 35 Barnton Avenue, Edinburgh EH4 6JJ; T.-0131-336 4288.

Gilchrist, Bernard, MBE, MA (Hons) (Oxon); b. 20.5.19, Manchester; m., Jean W. Gregory; 2 s.; 1 d. Educ. Manchester Grammar School; Queen's College, Oxford. Tanganyika: Forest Officer, HM Colonial/Overseas Civil Service, 1942-62 (Conservator of Forests, 1960), Conservator of Forests, Tanganyika/Tanzania Government Service, 1962-65; Chief Executive, Scottish Wildlife Trust, 1965-85. Recreations: countryside; natural history; hill-walking; photography. Address: (h.) 9 Murrayfield Gardens, Edinburgh EH12 6DG; T.-0131-337 3869.

Gilchrist, Stewart Kerr, BSc (Hons), DMS, MIMgt, MIMBM. Executive Director (Housing and Technical Resources), South Lanarkshire Council, since 1997; b. 17.2.49, Glasgow; m., Jean; 1 s.; 1 d. Educ. Renfrew High School; Camphill Secondary School, Paisley; Heriot-Watt University; Glasgow College of Technology. Lanarkshire County Council: Management Trainee, 1971, Maintenance Co-ordinator, 1973; Strathclyde Regional Council: Co-ordination and Development Manager, 1975, Assistant Head of Building and Works, 1980, Depute Director, Building and Works, 1986, Senior Depute Director, Building and Works, 1988, Director of Building and Works, 1994; Director of Technical Services, South Lanarkshire Council, 1995. Scottish Secretary, Association of Direct Labour organisations. Recreations: family; church; gardening. Address: (b.) Council Offices, Almada Street, Hamilton ML3 0AA'; T.-01698 454406.

Gilchrist, Thomas, BSc, PhD, CChem, FRSC. Managing Director, Giltech Ltd., since 1984; b. 18.6.36, Ayr; m., Fiona Christina Brown; 2 d. Educ. Ayr Academy; Glasgow University. Assistant Lecturer in Chemistry, Glasgow University, 1961-62; Research Chemist: Canadian Industries Ltd., Quebec, 1962-64, ICI Ltd., Stevenston, Ayrshire, 1964-69; Strathclyde University: Lecturer in Bioengineering, 1969, Head, Division of Artificial Organs, Bioengineering Unit, 1972, Senior Lecturer in Bioengineering, 1975-84. Recreations: golf; curling. Address: (h.) The Lodge, 67 Midton Road, Ayr KA7 2TW; T.-Ayr 266088.

Giles, Cecilia Elspeth, CBE, MA. Member, Rail Users Consultative Committee for Scotland, 1989-97; b. Dumfries. Educ. Queen Margaret's School, Yorkshire; Edinburgh University. Administrative staff, Khartoum University, 1956-57; joined Administrative staff, Edinburgh University, 1957; Assistant Secretary, Edinburgh University, 1972-87; Committee of Vice-Chancellors and Principals' Administrative Training Officer (seconded part-time), 1983-85. President, Edinburgh University Graduates' Association, 1989-91, Member, Executive Committee and Editorial Committee, since 1987; Member, Business Committee, General Council, Edinburgh University, 1988-93, Convener, Constitutional Sub-Committee, 1991-93; Member, Church of Scotland Board of Stewardship and Finance, 1986-93, Vice Convener 1990-93; Member, Church of Scotland Assembly Council, 1993-96. Publication: Scotland for the Tourist (Co-author). Recreations: entertaining friends, family and godchildren; theatre. Address: (b.) Graduates' Association, 5 Buccleuch Place, Edinburgh EH8 9LW.

Gill, Hon. Lord (Brian Gill), MA, LLB, PhD, Hon. LLD (Glas). Senator of the College of Justice in Scotland, since 1994; Chairman, Scottish Law Commission; b. 25.2.42; m.; 5 s.; 1 d. Educ. St. Aloysius College; Glasgow University; Edinburgh University. Advocate, 1967; Advocate-Depute, 1977-79; Standing Junior Counsel: Foreign and Commonwealth Office (Scotland), 1974-77, Home Office (Scotland), 1979-81, Scottish Education Department, 1979-81; QC, 1981; called to the Bar, Lincoln's Inn, 1991; Keeper, Advocates' Library, 1987-94. Address: (b.) Court of Session, Parliament House, Parliament Square, Edinburgh, EH1 1RQ.

Gill, Professor Roger William Thomas, BA (Hons), BPhil, MA, PhD, AFBPsS, FIPD, FIMgt, FRSA, CPsychol. Director, Research Centre for Leadership Studies, The Leadership Trust, and Visiting Professor of Business Administration (Human Resource Management), Strathclyde University Graduate Business School, since 1992; b. 3.10.45, Cumbria; 1 s.; 1 d. Educ. Merchant Taylors' School, Crosby; St. Peter's College, Oxford; Liverpool University; Bradford University. English Electric, 1967-68; Inbucon/AIC Management Consultants, 1969-71; Personnel Manager, De La Rue, 1971-72; Manpower Manager, Associated Weavers, 1972-74; Lecturer, Bradford University Management Centre, 1974-78; Assistant Professor, State University of New York at Binghamton, 1979-82; Managing Director, Roger Gill & Associates, Singapore, 1982-90; Regional Manager (Asia), PA Consulting Group, Singapore, 1990-91. Publications: numerous articles and research reports. Recreations: music; theatre; food and wine; reading; doing nothing. Address: (h.) Craigmarloch Cottage, Kilmacolm PA13 4SE; T.-01505 874386.

Gillespie, Ed. Chief Executive Officer, Grampian Enterprise, since 1998; b. 7.2.45, Greenock; m., Winnie. Paper industry: Management Trainee, Foreman/PA, Superintendent, Production Manager, Mill Manager, General Manager, Director. Recreations: sailing; wine. Address: (h.) Muiryfold, Newmachar, Aberdeenshire; T.-01651 863484.

Gillespie, Morag Helen, MSc. Director, Scottish Low Pay Unit, since 1989; b. 9.10.55, Inverness. Educ. Ayr Academy; Glasgow Caledonian University. Clerical/Executive Officer, Civil Service, 1972-86; Welfare Rights Worker, Rights Office, Fife, 1986-87; Senior Welfare Rights Officer, Central Regional Council, 1987-89. Member: Broadcasting Council for Scotland, Engender, Advisory Board, Scottish Poverty Information Unit. Address: (b.) 24 Sandyford Place, Glasgow G3 7NG; T.-0141-221 4491.

Gillespie, Professor Thomas Alastair, BA, PhD, FRSE. Professor of Mathematical Analysis, University of Edinburgh, since 1997; b. 15.2.45, Torrance; m., Judith Anne Nelmes; 2 s.; 1 d. Educ. Glasgow Academy; University of Cambridge; University of Edinburgh. Lecturer, 1968-87, Senior Lecturer, 1987-92, Reader in Mathematics, 1992-97, University of Edinburgh; Visiting Professor, Indiana University, 1973-74, 1983-84. Recreations: gardening; making music; jogging. Address: (b.) Department of Mathematics and Statistics, James Clerk Maxwell Building, Edinburgh EH9 3JZ; T.-0131-650 5081.

Gillingham, Professor John, CBE, MBE(Mil), FRSE, FRCSEng, FRCSEdin, FRCPEdin, MD(Hon), Thessaloniki, FRACS(Hon), FRCSI(Hon), FCMSA(Hon). Member, Court of Regents, Royal College of Surgeons of Edinburgh; Professor Emeritus, Department of Surgical Neurology University of Edinburgh; Foundation Professor of Surgical Neurology, Kind Saud University, Saudi Arabia, 1983-85; Honorary Consultant Neurosurgeon, St. Bartholomew's Hospital, since 1980; b. 15.3.16, Dorchester, Dorset; m., Judy; 4 s. Educ. Hardy's School, Dorset; St. Bartholomew's Hospital Medical College, London University. House Officer posts, St. Bartholomew's; Lieutenant, RAMC, Military Hospital for Head Injuries, Oxford, 1940-41; Surgeon (later o/c Major), No. 4 Mobile Neurosurgery Unit, North African Desert and Italy, 1942-45; St. Bartholomew's Hospital: Senior Registrar, 1946-47, Senior Registrar, Neurosurgery Unit, 1957; Senior Lecturer, then Reader, then Professor of Surgical Neurology, Edinburgh University, 1950-79; Consultant Neurosurgeon, Royal Infirmary of Edinburgh and Western General Hospital, Edinburgh; Consultant Neurosurgeon to the Army in Scotland, 1970-83; Hon. President, World Federation of Neurosurgical Societies, 1979; President, Royal College of Surgeons of Edinburgh, 1979-82; Publications: Head Injuries (Editor); Stereotactic Surgery; sixty papers on stereotactic surgery, head and spinal injuries, epilepsy, postgraduate training and education. Recreations: sailing; landscape gardening (cactus). Address: Easter Park House, Easter Park Drive, Barnton Avenue, Edinburgh EH4 6SN; T.-0131-336 3528.

Gillies, Anne Lorne, MA, PhD, PGCE, LRAM, Drhc. Singer and Writer, since 1962; Lecturer in Gaelic, University of Strathclyde, 1995-98; Member, National Executive, Scottish National Party, since 1996, SNP Spokesperson on Arts, Broadcasting and Gaelic; b. 21.10.44, Stirling; 1 s.; 2 d. Educ. Oban High School; Edinburgh University; London University; Jordanhill College of Education; Glasgow University. Singer: TV, radio, concert, recital, theatre, recording; writer: scripts, children's books, novels, articles, autobiography, songs; education/ community development: teacher, resource development; National Education Officer, Comunn na Gaidhlig, 1988-90, Arts Development Officer, Govan Initiative Ltd., 1991-93; Producer and Writer, Scottish Television 1993-95. Recreation: married bliss. Address: (h.) 54 Terregles Avenue, Glasgow G41 4LX.

Gillies, Norman Neil Nicolson, BA, MIMgt, FRSA. Director, Sabhal Mor Ostaig, since 1988; b. 1.3.47, Flodigarry, Isle of Skye; m., Jean Brown Nixon; 1 s.; 2 d. Educ. Portree High School; Strathclyde University; Open University. College Secretary, Sabhal Mor Ostaig, 1983-88; Director: Skye and Lochalsh Enterprise Ltd., Sabhal Mor Ostaig (Developments) Ltd., Canan Ltd, UHI Ltd.; Member: Barail (Centre for Highlands and Islands Policy Studies); Leirsinn Research Centre; University of the Highlands and Islands Academic Council; Gaelic Broadcasting Committee; Gaelic Television Training Trust. Recreations: reading; broadcasting; family. Address: (h.) Innis Ard, Ardvasar, Isle of Skye IV45 8RU; T.-01471 844 281.

Gillies, Rev. Dr. Robert Arthur, BD, PhD. Rector, St. Andrew's Episcopal Church, St. Andrews, since 1991; b. 21.10.51, Cleethorpes; m., Elizabeth; 3 s. Educ. Barton-upon-Humber Grammar School; Edinburgh University; St. Andrews University. Medical Laboratory Technician, 1968-72; Curate: Christ Church, Falkirk, 1977-80, Christ Church Morningside, and Chaplain, Napier College, 1980-84; Chaplain, Dundee University, 1984-90. Hon. Lecturer, Department of Philosophy, Dundee University, 1985-95. Publications: A Way for Healing, 1995; Informing Faith, 1996; Healing: Broader and Deeper, 1998. Recreations: family; garden; Scotland's mountains. Address: St. Andrew's Rectory, Queen's Terrace, St. Andrews, Fife KY16 9QF; T.-01334 473344.

Gillies, Valerie, MA, MLitt, FSAScot. Poet; b. 4.6.48, Edmonton, Canada; m., William Gillies; 1 s.; 2 d. Educ. Edinburgh University; University of Mysore, S. India. Writer to the School, Boroughmuir High School and Edinburgh Academy; Radio and Television Scriptwriter; Poet to Borders Festival; Writer in Residence, Duncan of Jordanstone College of Art and Dundee District Libraries; Writer in Residence, East Lothian and Midlothian District Libraries; Writer in Residence, Edinburgh University; Senior Arts Worker (Hospital Arts), Artlink. Publications: Each Bright Eye; Bed of Stone; Tweed Journey; The Chanter's Tune; The Ringing Rock; St. Kilda Song. Recreations: whippet-racing; field-walking; Taichi; swimming. Address: (h.) 67 Braid Avenue, Edinburgh EH10 6ED; T.-0131-447 2876.

Gillies, Professor William, MA (Edin), MA (Oxon). Professor of Celtic, Edinburgh University, since 1979; b. 15.9.42, Stirling; m., Valerie; 1 s.; 2 d. Educ. Oban High School; Edinburgh University; Corpus Christi College, Oxford; Dublin University. Dublin Institute for Advanced Studies, 1969-70; Lecturer, Edinburgh University, 1970-79; Fellow, Royal Society of Edinburgh, 1990. Director, SNDA Ltd. Recreations: walking; gardening; music. Address: (h.) 67 Braid Avenue, Edinburgh EH10 6ED.

Gillis, Charles Raphael, MD, FRCP(Glas), FFCM, FFPHM. Director: West of Scotland Cancer Surveillance Unit, since 1973, WHO Collaborating Centre; Honorary Clinical Senior Lecturer, Glasgow University, since 1973; Honorary Professor, Glasgow University, since 1997; b. 23.10.37, Glasgow; m., Judith Ann Naftalin; 1 s.; 1 d. Educ. High School of Glasgow; Glasgow University. Lecturer in Epidemiology and Preventive Medicine, then Senior Lecturer and Honorary Consultant Epidemiologist, Glasgow University, 1965-73. Past Chairman: Cancer Education Co-ordinating Group of the UK and Republic of Ireland, West of Scotland Oncological Organisation. Address: (b.) University Department of Public Health, Lilybank Gardens, Glasgow G12 8RZ.

Gilloran, Alan James, MA PhD. Head of Department, Management and Social Sciences, Queen Margaret College, Edinburgh, since 1996; Sociologist; b. 7.6.56, Edinburgh; m., Barbara; 1 s.; 1 d. Educ. Daniel Stewart's College, Edinburgh; University of Edinburgh. Researcher, Wester Hailes Representative Council; Research Assistant, Moray House; Research Associate, Edinburgh University; Research Fellow, University of Edinburgh; Lecturer in Sociology and Social Policy, University of Stirling; Senior Lecturer in Sociology and Social Policy, Queen Margaret College, Edinburgh. Publications: eleven academic articles; book chapters; five funded research reports. Recreations: badminton; wine; travel. Address: (b.) Queen Margaret College, Clerwood Terrace, Edinburgh EH12 8TS; T.-0131-317 3606.

Gilmour, Colonel Sir Allan Macdonald, KCVO, OBE, MC (and Bar), DSC (USA); b. 23.11.16, Edinburgh; m., Jean Wood; 3 s.; 1 d. Educ. Cargilfield, Edinburgh; Winchester College; Trinity College, Oxford. Commissioned Seaforth Highlanders, 1939; served War in Middle East, Sicily and NW Europe; Regimental and Staff appointments, 1945-69, including Instructor, Staff College, Quetta, and Chief of Staff, Ghana Armed Forces; Member, Sutherland County Council, 1970; Member, Highland Health Board, 1974 (Chairman, 1982-84); DL, Sutherland, 1969; Lord Lieutenant of Sutherland, 1972-96; Member, Highlands and Islands Development Consultative Council, 1980-88; Chairman: Sutherland District Council, 1974-78, East Sutherland Council of Social Service, 1972-76; Member: Board, Scottish National Orchestra Society, 1976-86, Highland Regional Council, 1976-96; President, Highland Territorial & Auxiliary Reserve Association, 1988-91; Chairman, Highland River Purification Board, 1994-96. Recreation: fishing. Address: (h.) Invernauld, Rosehall, Lairg, Sutherland; T.-0154 984 204.

Gilmour, Andrew Parr, BSc (Hons). Rector, Rothesay Academy, since 1983; b. 26.4.46, Glasgow; m., Elizabeth Morrison MacPherson; 1 s.; 2 d. Educ. Allan Glen's School, Glasgow; Glasgow University. Teacher of Chemistry, Allan Glen's School, 1969; Dunoon Grammar School: Principal Teacher of Chemistry, 1972, Assistant Rector, 1975; Depute Head Teacher, Mearns Castle High School, 1981. Recreations: golf; badminton; rugby (spectating nowadays); swimming; cycling; windsurfing; gardening. Address: (h.) Millford, 34 Mount Stuart Road, Rothesay, Isle of Bute; T.-Rothesay 503336.

Gilmour, Douglas Graham, BSc (Hons), MB, ChB, MD, FRCS. Consultant Vascular Surgeon, Glasgow Royal Infirmary, since 1983; b. 15.4.47, Glasgow; m., Evelyn Jean; 2 s.; 2 d. Educ. Kelvinside Academy, Glasgow; Glasgow University. House Surgeon/Physician, then Senior House Officer/Registrar in Surgery, Western Infirmary, Glasgow, 1971-77; Glasgow Royal Infirmary: Senior Registrar in Surgery, 1977-80, Senior Lecturer (Honorary Consultant) in Surgery, 1980-83. Recreations: family; golf; skiing; sailing. Address: (b.) Vascular Surgery Department, Royal Infirmary, Glasgow; T.-0141-211 4772.

Gilmour, John, DL, MFH. Farmer; b. 15.7.44, Edinburgh; m., Valerie Jardine Russell; 2 s.; 2 d. Educ. Eton; Aberdeen College. Captain, FFY/SH (TA); Member, Queen's Bodyguard for Scotland (Royal Company of Archers); Hon. Col. FFY/SH (TA); Trustee and Director, The Moredun Foundation; Chairman, Scottish Farm Venison. Recreations: fishing; reading. Address: Balcormo Mains, Leven, Fife; T.-01333 360229.

Gilmour, John Andrew George, MA, LLB, NP. Solicitor; Marketing Consultant; Honorary Sheriff at Dumbarton, since 1991; b. 17.11.37, Balloch; m., Roma Aileen; 3 d. Educ. Morrison's Academy, Crieff; Edinburgh University. Partner, McArthur Brown Robertson; Partner, McArthur Stanton; President, Strathclyde Junior Chamber of Commerce, 1973; Director, Dumbarton Enterprise Trust, since 1985; Dean, Faculty of Dunbartonshire Solicitors, 1988-90; Law Society accredited Liquor Licensing Specialist, 1993. Recreations: sport; music; gastronomy. Address: (h.) Cramond Cottage, 19 East Lennox Drive, Helensburgh; T.-01436 675057.

Gilmour, Col. Sir John Edward, 3rd Bt, DSO, TD, JP, BA. Lord Lieutenant of Fife, 1980-87; b. 24.10.12, Edinburgh; m., Ursula Mabyn Wills; 2 s. Educ. Eton College; Trinity Hall, Cambridge; Dundee School of Economics. Served with Fife and Forfar Yeomanry, 1939-45; served on Fife County Council, 1951-61; MP (Conservative), East Fife, 1961-79; Chairman, Conservative Party in Scotland, 1965-67; Lord High Commissioner, General Assembly, Church of Scotland, 1982, 1983. Recreation: gardening. Address: (h.) Montrave, Leven, Fife, KY8 5NY; T.-Leven 426159.

Gilmour, William McIntosh, OStJ, BL. Honorary Sheriff, Dumbarton; Lawyer; b. 9.3.23, Newcastle-upon-Tyne; m., Elinor Adams. Educ. Hillhead High School; Cally House, Gatehouse of Fleet; Glasgow University. Early experience with legal firms in Glasgow; became Partner, latterly Senior Partner, in firm in Dunbartonshire; now retired; former Dean, Faculty of Solicitors in Dunbartonshire; founder Member and Past President, Clydebank Rotary Club; Past Deacon, Society of Deacons and Free Presces; former Chairman for Dunbartonshire, Order of St. John; Member, Incorporation of Gardeners (Glasgow Trades House). Recreations: dog-walking (formerly, motor sport). Address: (h.) 65 Killermont Road, Bearsden, Glasgow; T.-0141-942 0498.

Gimblett, Sheriff Margaret, MA. Sheriff, Glasgow and Strathkelvin, since 1995; b. 24.9.39, Perth; m., Iain; 1 s.; 1 d. Educ. St. Leonards, St. Andrews; University of Edinburgh; University of Glasgow. Retail Management, John Lewis Partnership, London, until 1970; Partner, Russel and Aitken, Solicitors, 1972-95; Temporary Sheriff, 1994-95; Churchill Fellow. Recreations: gardening; tourism. Address: (b.) Glasgow Sheriff Court, Carlton Place, Glasgow G5 9DA; T.-0141-429 8888.

Gimingham, Professor Charles Henry, OBE, BA, PhD, ScD, FRSE, FIBiol. Regius Professor of Botany, Aberdeen University, 1981-88; b. 28.4.23, Leamington; m., Elizabeth Caroline Baird; 3 d. Educ. Gresham's School, Holt, Norfolk; Emmanuel College, Cambridge. Research Assistant, Imperial College, London, 1944-45; Department of Botany, Aberdeen University: Assistant, 1946-48, Lecturer, 1948-61, Senior Lecturer, 1961-64, Reader, 1964-69, Professor, since 1969, Head of Department, 1981-88; Member: Scottish Committee of Nature Conservancy, 1966-69, Scottish Advisory Committee, Nature Conservancy Council, 1970-80, Countryside Commission for Scotland, 1980-92; President, Botanical Society of Edinburgh, 1982-84; Vice-Chairman, NE Regional Board, Nature Conservancy Council for Scotland, 1991-92; Member: NE Regional Board, SNH, 1992-96, Science Advisory Committee, SNH, since 1996, Board of Management, Hill Farming Research Organisation, 1981-87, Governing Body, Aberdeen College of Education, 1981-87, Council of Management, Macaulay Institute for Soil Research, 1983-87, Board of Management, Macaulay Land Use Research Institute, 1987- 90; British Ecological Society: Joint Secretary, 1956-61, Vice-President, 1962-64, Joint Editor, Journal of Ecology, 1975-78, President, 1986-87. Publications: Ecology of Heathlands, 1972; Introduction to Heathland Ecology, 1975; Lowland Heathland Management Handbook, 1992. Recreations: hill-walking; photography; history and culture of Japan. Address: (h.) 4 Gowanbrae Road, Bieldside, Aberdeen.

Gimson, George Stanley, QC (Scot); b. 1915. Educ. High School of Glasgow; Glasgow University. Advocate, 1949; QC, 1961; Sheriff Principal: Aberdeen, Kincardine and Banff, 1972-74, Grampian, Highland and Islands, 1975-82; Member, Edinburgh Central Hospitals Board, 1960-70 (Chairman, 1964-70); Director, SNO Society Ltd., 1962-80; Trustee, National Library of Scotland, 1963-76; Chairman: Pensions Appeals Tribunals, Scotland, 1971-95, RSSPCC, Edinburgh, 1972-76, Scottish Far-East P.O.W. Association, since 1996; Hon. LLD, Aberdeen, 1981. Address: (h.) 16 Royal Circus, Edinburgh EH3 6SS.

Girdwood, Professor Ronald Haxton, CBE, MB, ChB (Hons), MD, PhD, FRCPEd, FRCP, FRCPI, FRCPath, Hon. FACP, Hon. FRACP, FRSE. President, Royal College of Physicians of Edinburgh, 1982-85; Chairman, Scottish National Blood Transfusion Association, 1980-95; b. 19.3.17, Arbroath; m., Mary Elizabeth Williams; 1 s.; 1 d. Educ. Daniel Stewart's College, Edinburgh; Edinburgh University; Michigan University. Army service, RAMC, UK and India, 1942-46, successively as Lt., Captain, Major and Lt.-Col. (when posted to Burma); Lecturer, then Senior Lecturer, Reader in Medicine, Edinburgh University, 1946-62; Research Fellow, Michigan University, 1948-49; Consultant Physician, Edinburgh Royal Infirmary, 1950-82; Professor of Therapeutics and Clinical Pharmacology, Edinburgh University, 1962-82 (Dean, Faculty of Medicine, 1975-79); President, Edinburgh University Church of Scotland Society, 1938-39; Elder, Kirk of the Greyfriars, since 1955; Chairman, Scottish Group, Nutrition Society, 1961-62; President, British Society for Haematology, 1963-64; Chairman, Executive Committee, Edinburgh and SE Scotland Blood Transfusion Association, 1970-95; Member, UK Committee on Safety of Medicines, 1972-83; Chairman, Medico-Pharmaceutical Forum, 1985-87; President, University of Edinburgh Graduates' Association, 1991-92; Member, Board of Governors, St. Columba's Hospice, 1985-97; Suniti Panja Gold Medal, Calcutta School of Tropical Medicine, 1980; given the Freedom of Sirajgunj, Bangladesh, 1984; Oliver Memorial Award for services to blood transfusion, 1991. Publications: Travels with a Stethoscope, 1991; editor of four medical books and more than 300 medical papers. Recreations: writing; photography. Address: (h.) 2 Hermitage Drive, Edinburgh EH10 6DD; T.-0131-447 5137.

Glasby, Michael Arthur, BM, BCh, MA, MSc (Oxon), MA (Cantab), CBiol, MIBiol, FICS, FRCS (Edin), FRCS (Eng). Reader in Experimental Neurology, Edinburgh University, since 1997; b. 29.10.48, Nottingham; m., Celia M.E. Robinson. Educ. High Pavement Grammar School,

Nottingham; Christ Church, Oxford; Oxford Medical School. Senior Scholar and Assistant Tutor in Physiology, Christ Church, Oxford, 1971-76; Surgeon, Harefield Hospital Transplant Trust, 1981-83; Fellow and Lecturer in Anatomy, New Hall, Cambridge, 1983-87; Lecturer in Anatomy, Royal College of Surgeons of England, 1984-87; joined Edinburgh University as Lecturer, 1987; Reader in Anatomy, 1992-97. Editor, anatomy textbook for surgeons and physiology textbook for surgeons; numerous articles. Recreations: golf; Latin and Greek literature; music; beekeeping; wine. Address: (b.) Department of Clinical Neurosciences, Edinburgh University, Western General Hospital, Crewe Road, Edinburgh EH4 2XU; T.-0131-537 2905.

Glasgow, 10th Earl of (Patrick Robin Archibald Boyle). Television Director/Producer; b. 30.7.39; m., Isabel Mary James; 1 s.; 1 d. Educ. Eton; Paris University. Sub.-Lt., RNR, 1959-60; Producer/Director, Yorkshire TV, 1968-70; freelance Film Producer, since 1971; created Kelburn Country Centre (leisure park), 1977, and now manages this and Kelburn Estate. Address (b.) Kelburn Castle, Fairlie, Ayrshire KA29 0BE; T.-01475 568685.

Glasier, Anna, MB, ChB, BSc, FRCOG, MD. Director, Lothian Health Board Family Planning and Well Woman Services, since 1990; Senior Lecturer, Department of Obstetrics and Gynaecology, Edinburgh University, since 1990; Consultant Gynaecologist, Lothian Health Board, since 1989; b. 16.4.50, Salisbury. Educ. Lord Digby's School, Sherborne. Clinical Research Scientist, Medical Research Council Centre for Reproductive Biology, Edinburgh, 1989-90. Recreations: ski mountaineering; sailing. Address: (b.) 18 Dean Terrace, Edinburgh EH4 1NL; T.-0131-332 7941.

Glass, Alexander, OBE, MA, DipEd. Rector, Dingwall Academy, 1977-97; b. 1.6.32, Dunbar; m., Edith Margaret Duncan Baxter; 3 d. Educ. Dunbar Grammar School; Edinburgh University; Heidelberg University; University of Aix-en-Provence. Teacher of Modern Languages, Montrose Academy, 1958-60; Special Assistant Teacher of Modern Languages, Oban High School, 1960-62; Principal Teacher of Modern Languages, Nairn Academy, 1962-65; Principal Teacher of French and Assistant Rector, Perth Academy, 1965-72; Rector, Milne's High School, Fochabers, 1972-77. Chairman, COSPEN; former President, Highland Secondary Headteachers' Association; former Chairman, Highland Region Working Party for Modern Languages; former Chairman, Children's Panel Chairmen's Group; former Chairman, Highland Children's Panel; Reader, Church of Scotland; Licentiate, Auxiliary Ministry, Church of Scotland; Scottish Community Drama Association: Divisional Secretary/Festival Organiser, Highland Division, Member, General Council; former Chairman and Secretary, Scottish Secondary Schools' Travel Trust; Member, Highland Health Council; Member, Church of Scotland Education Committee; Member, Church of Scotland Board of Social Responsibility. Churchill Fellow, 1991. Recreations: amateur drama; foreign travel; Rotary. Address: (h.) Craigton, Tulloch Avenue, Dingwall IV15 9TU; T.-01349 863258.

Glass, Colin Howard, BSc (Hons), DipInstM. Chief Executive Officer, Watson and Philip plc, since 1996; Non Executive Director, Oasis Stores PLC, since 1998; Member, CBI Governing Council, since 1998; b. 21.1.57, Manchester; m., Sarah; 2 s.; 2 d. Educ. Leeds University. Boots Company PLC; Burton Group PLC; Dixons Group PLC. Recreation: sport. Address: (b.) Watson and Philip, Strathtay House, Dundee.

Glass, Douglas James Allan, MB, ChB. General Practitioner, Ballater, since 1987; Apothecary to HM Household, Balmoral, since 1988; Partner in farm (D.L. Glass), since 1982; b. 8.10.53, Dinnet, Aboyne; m., Suzanne; 1 s.; 3 d. Educ. Aboyne Academy; Banchory Academy; Aberdeen University. Junior House Officer, 1977-78; Senior House Officer, 1978-79; General Practitioner Trainee, 1979-80; General Practice, Australia and New Zealand, 1980-81; General Practice Principal, Peterhead, 1981-87. Church Elder. Recreations: dry stane dyking; golf; snooker; football. Address: (h.) Deecastle, Dinnet, Aboyne, Aberdeenshire; T.-013397 55686.

Glasser, Lesley Scott Dent, MBE, BA (Cantab), PhD, DSc, CChem, FInstP, CPhys, FRSE. Director, SATRO North Scotland, 1986-98; Managing Director, Satrosphere, since 1989; b. 19.5.32, Grimsby; m., Professor Fredrick Paul Glasser; 1 s.; 2 d. Educ. Wintringham Grammar School; Newnham College, Cambridge; Aberdeen University. Research Fellow, Lecturer, Senior Lecturer, Reader, Aberdeen University Department of Chemistry, 1958-85. President, ASE Scotland, 1996; Secretary, UK Crystallographic Council, 1978-82; Trustee, National Museums of Scotland; Member, Council, Royal Society of Edinburgh, and Convenor, Links with Young People Committee; Member, Council, British Association for the Advancement of Science; Chairman, Scottish Branch, Institute of Physics, 1995-97; Kelvin Medal and Prize, Institute of Physics, 1998. Recreation: gardening. Address: (b.) SATRO North Scotland, Marischal College, Aberdeen; T.-01224 273161.

Glen, Alexander Iain Munro, MB, ChB, FRCPsych, FRCP (Glas), DPM. Hon. Senior Lecturer, Aberdeen University, since 1986; Research Director, Highland Psychiatric Research Foundation; Member (SNP), Highland Council; Member, SNP National Council; Chairman, Aviemore Partnership; b. 25.5.30, Glasgow; m., Dr. Evelyne Glen; 2 s.; 2 d. Educ. Albert Road Academy, Glasgow; Glasgow Academy; Glasgow University. National Service as Surgeon Lt., RNVR, 3rd Frigate Squadron, Far East, 1955-57; Research Fellow, Psychiatry, Glasgow University, 1964-68; Medical Research Council: Clinical Psychiatry Unit, 1968-72, Brain Metabolism Unit, Research Fellow, Pharmacology, Edinburgh University, 1972-81. Recreations: politics; poetry; Scotland. Address: (h.) Dalnavert Community Co-operative, Dalnavert, by Kincraig PH21 1NG; T.-0154 04 347.

Glen, Charles Noel, BL, NP. Solicitor; Honorary Sheriff at Dumbarton, since 1990; b. 25.12.35, Airdrie; m., Muriel; 3 s. Educ. Vale of Leven Academy; Glasgow University. Solicitor, since 1956; Partner, Ritchie, Wilson and Glen, 1965-75; Senior Partner: McArthur Brown Ritchie and Co., 1975-85, McArthur Stanton, since 1985. Dunbartonshire County Secretary, SSAFA; Past President, Rotary Club of Dumbarton. Recreations: music; theatre. Address: (h.) Kincraig, 1 Kilmahew Drive, Cardross, Dumbarton; T.-01389 841706.

Glen, Duncan Munro. Writer and Lecturer; Sole Owner, Akros Publications, since 1960; b. 11.1.33, Cambuslang; m., Margaret Eadie; 1 s.; 1 d. Educ. West Coats, Cambuslang; Edinburgh College of Art. Book Designer, London; Lecturer in Typography; Editor, Robert Gibson & Co. Ltd.; Lecturer, then Senior Lecturer, then Head of Graphic Design, Lancashire Polytechnic; Professor and Head, Department of Visual Communication, Nottingham Trent University (Emeritus Professor); Member, Council for Academic Awards, 1979-89; Editor: Akros, poetry magazine, 1-51, ZED 2 0, 1-11, Scottish Poetry Library Newsletter. Author and editor of many books including Hugh MacDiarmid and The Scottish Renaissance, Selected Essays of Hugh MacDiarmid, In Appearances: Poems, The Autobiography of a Poet, Makars' Walk, The Poetry of the Scots, Selected Poems 1965-1990, Hugh MacDiarmid: Out of Langholm and Into the World; A Nation in a Parish; Four Scottish Poets; Splendid Lanarkshire; New Selected Poems, 1987-96; Illustrious Fife: literary, historical and architectural pathways and walks. Recreation: walking. Address: (h.) 33 Lady Nairn Avenue, Kirkcaldy, Fife KY1 2AW; T.-01592 651522.

Glen, Eric Stanger, MB, ChB, FRCSGlas, FRCSEdin. Consultant Urological Surgeon, Walton Urological Teaching and Research Centre, Southern General Hospital, Glasgow; Honorary Clinical Senior Lecturer, Glasgow University; Member, Surgical Examination Panel, Royal College of Physicians and Surgeons of Glasgow; b. 20.10.34, Glasgow; m., Dr. Patricia. Educ. Glasgow University. Pre-Consultant posts, Western and Victoria Infirmaries, Glasgow; Ship Surgeon, Royal Fleet Auxiliary. Medical Director, Continence Resource Centre and Helpline for Scotland; Past Chairman, Area Medical Committee; Founder and former Secretary, International Continence Society; Founder, Urological Computing Society; Member, Historical Committee, European Association of Urology. Publications: chapters in books; papers on urodynamics, urology and computing. Recreations: travel; writing; computer applications. Address: (h.) 9 St. John's Road, Pollokshields, Glasgow G41 5RJ; T.-0141-423 0759.

Glen, Norman MacLeod, CBE, TD, MA, JP. Former Member, Dumbarton District Council, 1975-96; b. 22.12.11, Glasgow; m., Dr. Janet M.S. Glen (deceased); 2 s.; 2 d. Educ. Glasgow Academy; Glasgow University. Retail trade as Buyer, Director and Managing Director, John Glen & Co. Ltd., Glasgow, 1932-74; War Service, six years; TA (mostly 474 HAA Regt RA), 1938-56 (Lt. Colonel, 1954-56); Parliamentary candidate (Liberal), 1945, (Conservative), 1951, 1955, 1959, 1964, 1966 and By-Election, Woodside, 1962; elected, Helensburgh Town Council, 1966 (last Provost of Helensburgh, 1970-75); Member, Dunbartonshire County Council, 1966-75; Elder, West Kirk of Helensburgh. Recreation: walking. Address: (h.) Flat 11, Queen's Court, Helensburgh G84 7AH; T.-01436 673497.

Glen, Robbie, BA, FIMgt. After Dinner Speaker and Event Management Consultant, since 1996 (Partner, Glen Enterprises and Kintra Consultants); Governor, H.M. Institution, Cornton Vale, 1994-96; b. 31.5.46, Hamilton; m., Elspeth Reyburn; 2 d. Educ. Hamilton Academy; Strathclyde University. Assistant Governor: Polmont Borstal, 1969, Longriggend Remand Institution, 1972; Deputy Governor, Edinburgh Prison, 1976; seconded to Prison HQ Admin Branch, 1979; Governor: Castle Huntly Borstal, 1981, Dungavel Prison, 1984; seconded to Prisons Inspectorate, 1986; returned to Dunvagel, 1987, transferred to Prisons HQ Operations Branch; Deputy Governor/Acting Governor, Barlinnie Prison, 1991. Barker, Variety Club of Great Britain; Member: Stars of Scotland for Cerebral Palsy, Lord's Taverners. Recreations: golf; reading; writing; speaking; holidaying on Arran. Address: (b.) 22 Lochaber Road, Strathaven, Lanarkshire ML10 6HZ; T.: 01357 522531.

Glen, William Hamish. Artistic Director, Dundee Rep, since 1992; b. 20.12.57, Edinburgh; m., Denise Maria Winford. Educ. Edinburgh Academy. ASM, Traverse Theatre, 1979-81; Trainee Director, Tron Theatre, 1986-87, Associate Director, 1988-89; Artistic Director, Winged Horse, 1990-92; worked as freelance director in Lithuania and Finland. Address: (b.) Tay Square, Dundee; T.-01382 227684.

Glenarthur, 4th Baron (Simon Mark Arthur), Bt, DL, MCIT, FRAeS. DL, Aberdeenshire, since 1987; Consultant: British Aerospace PLC, since 1989, Hanson PLC, since 1989, Imperial Tobacco Ltd., since 1996; Deputy Chairman, Hanson Pacific Ltd., 1994-97; Director: Millennium Chemicals Inc., since 1996, Whirly Bird Services Ltd., since 1995; b. 7.10.44; m.; 1 s.; 1 d. Educ. Eton. Retired Major, 10th Royal Hussars (PWO); Helicopter Captain, British Airways, 1976-82; a Lord in Waiting, 1982-83; Parliamentary Under Secretary of State: Department of Health and Social Security, 1983-85, Home Office, 1985-86; Minister of State: Scottish Office, 1986-87, Foreign and Commonwealth Office, 1987-89. Chairman, St. Mary's Hospital, Paddington, NHS Trust, 1991-98, British Helicopter Advisory Board, since 1992, European Helicopter Association, since 1996; President, National Council for Civil Protection, since 1991; Member (Brigadier), Queen's Bodyguard for Scotland (Royal Company of Archers); Scottish Patron, The Butler Trust, since 1994. Address: (b.) House of Lords, London SW1A 0PW.

Glennie, John Ellis, FCCA, CIPFA. Chief Executive, Borders General Hospital NHS Trust, since 1995; b. 28.9.48, Keith; 2 s; 1 d. Educ. Keith Grammar School. Joined NHS as a trainee accountant, Aberdeen, 1966, and progressed through a number of posts to become Director of Finance, Darlington Health Authority, 1982; Director of Finance, Information and Computing, Central Manchester Health Authority, 1985-91; Director of Finance, then Deputy Chief Executive/Director of Operations, Central Manchester Healthcare NHS Trust, 1992-95. National Treasurer, Healthcare Financial Management Association. Address: (b.) Borders General Hospital NHS Trust, Melrose TD6 9BS; T.-01896 754333.

Gloag, Ann. Executive Director, Stagecoach Holdings plc; b. 10.12.42. Educ. Perth High School. Nursing, 1960-80; Founding Partner, Stagecoach, 1980. Address: (b.) Charlotte House, 20 Charlotte Street, Perth PH1 5LL.

Gloag, Matthew Irving. Director, Highland Distillers Ltd., since 1971; b. 1.12.47, Perth; m., Dilly Moon; 2 d. Chairman, Scottish Licensed Trade Association, 1984-85 and 1995-96. Address: (b.) West Kinfauns, Perth PH2 7EF; T.-01738 440000.

Glover, Professor David Moore, BA, PhD, FRSE. Professor of Molecular Genetics, Dundee University, since 1989; Director, Cancer Research Campaign Cell Cycle Group, since 1989; b. 28.3.48, Chapeltown. Educ. Broadway Grammar School, Barnsley; Fitzwilliam College, Cambridge. Postdoctoral Fellow, Stanford University, California, 1972-75; Imperial College, London, 1975-89, latterly as Head, Biochemistry Department. Publications: 140 scientific papers; two books; Editor, 18 books. Address: (b.) CRC Laboratories, Medical Sciences Institute, Dundee DD1 4HN; T.-01382 344793.

Glover, Rev. Robert Lindsay, BMus, BD, ARCO. Minister, Chalmers Memorial, Cockenzie and Port Seton, since 1997; b. 21.7.45, Watford; m., Elizabeth Mary Brown; 2 s.; 2 d. Educ. Langholm Academy; Dumfries Academy; Glasgow University. Minister: Newton Parish, near Dalkeith, 1971-76, St. Vigeans Parish, Arbroath, 1976-85, Knox's, Arbroath, 1982-85, St. George's West, Edinburgh, 1985-97. Recreations: music (organ, piano, accordion); caravanning; following Heart of Midlothian FC; reading. Address: Braemar Villa, 2 Links Road, Port Seton, Prestonpans, East Lothian EH32 0HA.

Glover, Sue, MA. Writer; b. 1.3.43, Edinburgh; m., John Glover; 2 s. Educ. St. George's School, Edinburgh; Montpellier University; Edinburgh University. Original drama and other scriptwriting for radio, television and theatre; theatre productions include: The Seal Wife, Edinburgh Festival, 1980; An Island in Largo, Byre Theatre, 1981; The Bubble Boy, Glasgow Tron, 1981; The Straw Chair, Traverse Theatre, 1988; Bondagers, Traverse Theatre, 1991 (winner, 1990 LWT Plays on Stage Award); Sacred Hearts, 1994; Artist Unknown, 1996; television work includes: The Spaver Connection; Mme Montand and Mrs Miller; Dear Life; televised version of The Bubble Boy won a silver medal, New York Film and Television

Festival, and a merit, Chicago International Film Festival, 1983. Publications: The Bubble Boy, 1991; Bondagers (Made in Scotland), 1995; Bondagers and The Straw Chair, 1997. Recreations: house and garden. Address: Castlefield Cottage, Castlebank Road, Cupar, Fife; T.-Cupar 653664.

Godden, Anthony John, BSc (Hons), FRSH, AIHE. Principal, West Lothian College, since 1987; b. 26.3.46, Swansea; m., Kelly; 1 s.; 1 d. Educ. Dynevor Grammar School; North East London Polytechnic; Open University. Lecturer, Bridgnorth College of Further Education, 1970-73; Social Tutor, Airedale and Wharfedale College of Further Education, 1973-75; Warden, Mildmay Hall, and Head, Section of General Studies and Information Sciences, Essex Institute of Higher Education, 1975-78; Assistant Inspector, Kent County Council Education Department, 1978-82; Principal, Gainsborough College of Further Education, 1982-86. Knight Commander of the Holy Sepulchre of Jerusalem; Chairman, Almond Housing Association, Livingston, 1993-98. Recreations: armchair sport; theatre; guitar; travel. Address: (b.) West Lothian College, Marjoribanks Street, Bathgate EH48 1QJ; T.-01506 634300.

Godden, Tony Richard Hillier, CB, BSc (Econ). Secretary, Friends of the Royal Scottish Academy, since 1988; b. 13.11.27, Barnstaple; m., Marjorie Florence Snell; 1 s.; 2 d. Educ. Barnstaple Grammar School; London School of Economics. Commissioned, RAF Education Branch, 1950; entered Civil Service, 1951; first appointed to Colonial Office; Private Secretary to Parliamentary Under Secretary of State, 1954-55; seconded to Cabinet Office, 1957-59; joined Scottish Home Department, 1961; Assistant Secretary, Scottish Development Department, 1964; Under Secretary, 1969; Secretary, Scottish Economic Planning Development, 1973-80; Secretary, Scottish Development Department, 1980-87. Member: The Council on Tribunals and its Scottish Committee, 1988-94, Advisory Board on Ancient Monuments, 1990-95. Address: 9 Ross Road, Edinburgh EH16 5QN.

Godfray, Martin Francis, BSc, CChem, FRSC, MChemA. Consultant Scientist and Microscopist; Public Analyst, Official Agricultural Analyst and Scientific Adviser, Lothian, Borders and Highland Regional Councils and Orkney and Shetland Islands Councils, 1980-96; b. 10.5.45, Barry, Glamorgan; m., Heather Jean; 1 s.; 2 d. Educ. Barry Boys Grammar Technical School; Birmingham University. Deputy Public Analyst and Deputy Agricultural Analyst, London Boroughs of Southwark, Greenwich, Islington and Tower Hamlets, 1973-80. Address: (b.) 27 Burnbrae, Edinburgh, EH12 8UB; T.-0131-339 1212.

Godfrey, Professor Alan Dearn, BA (Hons), FCCA. Professor of Accounting and Head, Department of Finance and Accounting, Glasgow Caledonian University; b. 12.5.46, Falkirk; 1 s.; 1 d. Educ. Falkirk High School; Strathclyde University. Financial Consultant, Engineering Services Ltd., 1972-76; Lecturer, then Senior Lecturer, Glasgow College, 1976-88; Depute Head of Department, then Acting Head of Department, Glasgow Polytechnic, 1988-93. Recreations: music; golf. Address: (b.) Department of Finance and Accounting, Glasgow Caledonian University, Glasgow G4 0BA; T.-0141-331 3361.

Godfrey, Andrew Paul, CA. Regional Managing Partner, Scottish Region, Grant Thornton, since 1998; b. 12.8.53, Edinburgh; m., Irene; 2 s. Educ. Morrison's Academy; Edinburgh University. Joined Grant Thornton Glasgow Office, 1982; Office Managing Partner, 1998; Head of Growth and Development, Grant Thornton (sits on National Management Board). Recreation: keen member of Dunblane and Gleneagles Golf Clubs. Address: (b.) 112 West George Street, Glasgow G2 1QF.

Godman, Norman. MP (Labour), Greenock and Inverclyde (formerly Greenock and Port Glasgow) since 1983; b. 11.4.38; m. Educ. Hull University; Heriot-Watt University. Former teacher. Address: (b.) House of Commons, London, SW1A 0AA.

Gold, Lex. Director, Scottish Chambers of Commerce; Director, Caledonian MacBrayne; Director, Scotlander Ltd; b. 14.12.40, Rigside; m., Eleanor; 1 s.; 1 d. Educ. Lanark Grammar School. Sub-Editor, Daily Record; professional footballer; joined Civil Service, Glasgow, 1960; Inland Revenue, two years, Civil Service Department, four years, Home Office, 21 years, Training Agency, three years; former Managing Director, Scottish Enterprise; former Director, CBI Scotland; former Chairman, Hibernian Football Club Ltd. Address: (b.) 152 Morrison Street, Edinburgh EH3 8EB.

Goldberg, Professor Sir Abraham, KB, MD, DSc, FRCP, FRCPEdin, FRCPGlas, FRSE. Regius Professor of the Practice of Medicine, Glasgow University, 1978-89; Founder President, Faculty of Pharmaceutical Medicine of Royal Colleges of Physicians of UK, 1989; b. 7.12.23, Edinburgh; m., Clarice Cussin; 2 s.; 1 d. Educ. Sciennes School, Edinburgh; George Heriot's School, Edinburgh; Edinburgh University. House Physician, Royal Hospital for Sick Children, Edinburgh, 1946-47; RAMC, 1947-49 (granted rank of honorary Major on discharge); Nuffield Research Fellow, UCH Medical School, London, 1952-54; Eli Lilly Travelling Fellow in Medicine (MRC), Department of Medicine, Utah University, 1954-56; Glasgow University: Lecturer in Medicine, 1956-59, Titular Professor of Medicine, 1967-70, Regius Professor of Materia Medica, 1970-78. Chairman, Grants Committee 1, Clinical Research Board, MRC, 1973-77; Member, Chief Scientist's Committee, SHHD, 1977-83; Chairman, Biomedical Research Committee, SHHD, 1977-83; Editor, Scottish Medical Journal, 1962-63; Chairman, Committee on Safety of Medicines, 1980-86; Fitzpatrick Lecturer, Royal College of Physicians, London, 1988; Goodall Memorial Lecturer, Royal College of Physicians and Surgeons of Glasgow, 1989; City of Glasgow Lord Provost's Award, 1988. Publications: Disorders of Porphyrin Metabolism (Co-Author), 1987; Recent Advances in Haematology (Joint Editor), 1971; Clinics in Haematology "The Porphyrias" (Co-Author), 1980. Recreations: medical history; literature; writing; walking; swimming. Address: (h.) 16 Birnam Crescent, Bearsden, Glasgow G61 2AU.

Goldie, Annabel MacNicoll, DL, LLB, NP. Deputy Lord Lieutenant, Renfrewshire, since 1993; Scottish Conservative Party: Deputy Chairman, 1995-97, Chairman, March-July 1997, Deputy Chairman, 1997-98, Deputy Leader, since 1998; Director, Prince's Scottish Youth Business Trust, since 1994; b. 27.2.50, Glasgow. Educ. Greenock Academy; Strathclyde University. Solicitor in private practice, since 1978. Elder, Church of Scotland; Member, West of Scotland Advisory Board, Salvation Army; Member, Strathclyde University Court. Recreations: weeding; walking; dogs; swimming. Address: (h.) Levernholm, Gledstane Road, Bishopton PA7 5AU; T.-0141-331 1333.

Goldstraw, C. Wendy, BSc(SocSci), DBA, MIPD. Regional General Manager, Post Office Counters Ltd., since 1993; b. 8.2.50, Edinburgh; m., Brian. Educ. Preston Lodge High School; University of Edinburgh. Joined Post Office as Graduate Trainee, 1971; various junior/middle management roles; District Manager, Post Office Counters Ltd., Edinburgh, 1986. Member, Accounts Commission for Scotland; Member, Scottish Post Office Board. Recreations: travel; cooking; theatre. Address: (b.) The Athenaeum, Nelson Mandela Place, Glasgow G2 1BT; T.-0141-353 7000.

Good, John Russell. Secretary, Royal Highland and Agricultural Society of Scotland, since 1981; b. 9.8.41, Kirkcudbright; m., Muriel Law Bathgate; 2 s.; 1 d. Joined RHASS, 1967. Address: (b.) Royal Highland Centre, Ingliston, Edinburgh EH28 8NF.

Goodall, Alexander, OBE, MA (Hons). Principal, Wester Hailes Education Centre, since 1982; b. 25.8.38, Dolphinton, Peebles-shire; 1 s.; 1 d. Educ. Portobello High School; Edinburgh University; Moray House College of Education. Teacher of History, Niddrie Marischal Secondary School, 1961-64; Education Officer, Teso College, Uganda, 1964-69; Preston Lodge High School: Principal Teacher of History, 1969-74, Assistant Head Teacher, 1974-78; Depute Principal, Wester Hailes Education Centre, 1978-82. Editor, Scottish History Teaching Review. Publication: Economics and Development (Co-author). Recreations: trout angling; rubber bridge. Address: (b.) 5 Murrayburn Drive, Edinburgh; T.-0131-442 2201.

Goodall, Oscar Ronald, RSW, DA. Painter; Educationalist; b. 30.6.24, Adelaide, Australia; m., Janet M. Wylie; 1 s.; 1 d. Educ. Perth Academy; Dundee College of Art. RAFVR Bomber Command (Air Crew); part-time teaching, Bell Baxter High School, Fife; Principal Teacher, Glenwood High, Glenrothes; Arts Council Lecturer; Adviser in Art/Design for Clackmannan then Central Region; Member, SED Committee on the Curriculum; Co-Founder, Dollar Summer School and Dollar Civic Trust; Member, Dollar and Muthill Community Councils. Exhibited widely in oil, water colour, acrylic and pastel; paintings in public and private collections. Recreations: conservation; gardening; discussion; good company; travel. Address: Oakfield, 27 Drummond Street, Muthill, Perthshire; T.-01764 681367.

Gooday, Professor Graham W., BSc, PhD, FRSE, FIBiol. Professor of Microbiology, Aberdeen University, since 1984; b. 19.2.42, Colchester; m., Margaret A. Mealing; 1 s.; 2 d. Educ. Hove Grammar School for Boys; Bristol University. VSO, Sierra Leone, 1964; Research Fellowships: Leeds University, 1967, Glasgow and Oxford Universities, 1969; Lecturer, Senior Lecturer, Reader, Aberdeen University, 1972-84; Honorary Professorial Fellow, Rowett Research Institute, 1992; Member: Aquatic Life Sciences Committee, NERC, 1984-87, Council, Society for General Microbiology, 1976-80; British Mycological Society: Member, Council, 1974-77, President, 1993, Centenary Fellow, 1996; awarded first Fleming Lectureship, Society for General Microbiology, 1976. Recreation: open countryside. Address: (b.) Department of Molecular and Cell Biology, Institute of Medical Sciences, University of Aberdeen, Aberdeen AB25 2ZD; T.-01224 273147.

Goodman, Professor Anthony Eric, MA (Oxon), BLitt (Oxon), FRHistS. Professor of Medieval and Renaissance History, Edinburgh University, since 1993; b. 21.7.36, London; m., Jacqueline; 1 d. Educ. Selhurst Grammar School, Croydon; Magdalen College, Oxford. Joined staff, Edinburgh University, 1961. Secretary, Edinburgh Branch, Historical Association, since 1975. Publications: The Loyal Conspiracy, 1971; A History of England from Edward II to James I, 1977; The Wars of the Roses, 1981; A Traveller's Guide to Medieval Britain (Co-author), 1986; The New Monarchy, 1471-1534, 1988; John of Gaunt, 1992. Address: (h.) 23 Kirkhill Gardens, Edinburgh EH16 5DF; T.-0131-667 5988.

Goodlad, Professor Robina, MA (Hons), MPhil. Professor of Housing Studies, University of Glasgow, since 1998; b. 16.8.50, Lerwick; m., Peter D. Taylor; 2 d. Educ. Anderson Educational Institute, Lerwick; Aberdeen University; Glasgow University. Worked for Planning Exchange; Director, Tenant Participation Advisory Service, 1980-84; Lecturer then Senior Lecturer, University of Glasgow, 1984-98. Labour Candidate, Orkney and Shetland, 1979 and 1983. Publications: six books; many articles and book chapters. Address: (b.) Department of Urban Studies, University of Glasgow, 25 Bute Gardens, Glasgow; T.-0141-330 4516.

Goodman, Professor Timothy Nicholas Trewin, BA, MSc, DPhil, FRSE. Professor of Applied Analysis, Dundee University, since 1994; b. 29.4.47, London; m., Choo-Tin; 3 d. Educ. Judd School; St. John's College, Cambridge; Warwick University; Sussex University. Teacher, VSO, 1973; Teacher, Singapore, 1974-75; Lecturer, Universiti Sains Malaysia, 1975-79; Lecturer, Dundee University, 1979-90; Professor Texas A&M University, 1990-91; Reader, Dundee University, 1992-94. Recreations: walking; Scottish country dancing; music. Address: (b.) Department of Mathematics, Dundee University, Dundee; T.-01382 344488.

Goodsman, James Melville, CBE. Chairman, Michael Fraser & Co. Ltd; Director, ICP Ltd.; Consultant, Democracy International Ltd.; b. 6.2.47, St. Andrews; m., Victoria Smitherman. Educ. Elgin Academy. Conservative Party Agent, 1968-80; Deputy Central Office Agent, North West Area, 1980-84; Assistant Director (Community Affairs), CCO, 1984-89; Head, Community and Legal Department, CCO, 1989-90; Director, Conservative Party in Scotland, 1990-93; Chairman, Edinburgh Morayshire Club, 1996-97. Recreations: golf; Church music; gardening. Address: (b.) The Old Schoolhouse, Collessie, Fife KY15 7UU; T.-01337 810745.

Goodwin, Michael David, OBE, FIMgt. Managing Director, Electrical Contractors' Association of Scotland (SELECT) since 1991; The Director, Scottish Joint Industry Board, since 1993; Director: Scottish Electrical Contractors' Insurance, since 1991, Electrical Engineering Training Foundation, National Electrotechnical Training; Trustee, Scottish Electrical Training Trust, since 1991; b. 18.1.40, Colombo; m., Anne Dundas, nee Finlay; 2 s.; 2 d. Educ. Stowe School; Britannia Royal Naval College, Dartmouth. Graduated as full career commission officer, Royal Navy, 1960; NATO appointments, 1980-86; retired as Commander, 1988; Assistant Director, Administration, Information and Settlement Division, International Stock Exchange, 1988-91. Recreations: tennis; theatre; music; reading; clay shooting; swimming. Address: (b.) Bush House, Bush Estate, Midlothian EH26 0SB; T.-0131-445 5577.

Goodwin, Michael J., BSc, DipEd. Headteacher, Prestwick Academy, since 1998; b. 17.9.45, Aberdeen; m.; 1 s.; 1 d. Educ. High School of Glasgow; Glasgow University; Makerere University College, Uganda. Headteacher, Carrick Academy, 1990-97. Address: Prestwick Academy, Newdyke Road, Prestwick KA9 2LB.

Gordon, Alasdair Maclean, MA, LLB; Honorary Sheriff at Kilmarnock, since 1989; Chairman, The Ayrshire Hospice, since 1983; b. 13.7.31, Aberdeen; m., Sally M.S. Millar; 3 s.; 2 d. Educ. Ayr Academy; University of Glasgow. Solicitor in general practice, 1955-96. Member, Council, Law Society of Scotland, 1982-85; Secretary: Kilmarnock Burns Club, 1975-90, Kilmarnock Retail Trades Association, 1962-96, Kilmarnock and District Arts Guild, 1969-94; Treasurer, Albino Fellowship, 1979-96. Recreations: music; hillwalking; golf; ancient history. Address: (h.) 7 St. Leonard's Road, Ayr KA7 2PR; T.-01292 283039.

Gordon, Donald Neil, MA, LLB, WS, NP, MSI, TEP. Partner, Carltons, Solicitors, since 1979; Senior Tutor, Diploma in Legal Practice, University of Dundee, since 1994; Vice Dean, Faculty of Procurators and Solicitors in Dundee, since 1997; b. 30.3.51, Aberdeen; m., Alison Mary

Whyte; 1 s.; 1 d. Educ. Robert Gordon's College, Aberdeen; University of Aberdeen; University of Edinburgh. Law Apprenticeship, Edinburgh, 1973-75; Assistant Solicitor, Carlton & Reid, Dundee, 1975-79. WS, 1975; Notary Public, 1975; Chairman, Dundee Citizens Advice Bureau, 1996; Honorary French Consul, Dundee, 1996; Secretary, Abertay Rotary Club, 1995; Treasurer, Dundee Orchestral Society, since 1978; Past Chairman, High School of Dundee Parents Association. Recreations: music; gardening. Address: (b.) 30 Whitehall Street, Dundee DD1 AAL; T.-01382 200111.

Gordon, Professor George, MA (Hons), PhD. Director of Academic Practice, Strathclyde University, since 1987; b. 14.11.39, Edinburgh; m., Jane Taylor Collins; 2 d. Educ. George Heriot's School; Edinburgh University. Edinburgh University: Vans Dunlop Scholar, 1962-64, Demonstrator, 1964-65; Strathclyde University: Assistant Lecturer, 1965-66, Lecturer, 1966-80, Dean, Faculty of Arts and Social Studies, 1984-87; served on SUCE and SCE Geography Panels, SCOVACT, and General Teaching Council for Scotland; Convener, Publications Committee, Royal Scottish Geographical Society; Vice President, British Association for the Advancement of Science, 1991-97; former Member, General Assembly of Open University; Member, Senate, Strathclyde University; Governor, Jordanhill College of Education, 1982-93 (Chairman, 1987-93). Publications: Regional Cities of the UK 1890-1980 (Editor), 1986; Perspectives of the Scottish City (Editor), 1985; Scottish Urban History, 1983; The Making of Scottish Geography (Co-Author), 1984; Settlement Geography, 1983; Urban Geography (Co-Author), 1981; Scottish Urban History (Co-Editor), 1983; Settlement Geography (Co-Author), 1983. Recreations: theatre-going; watching sport. Address: (b.) Centre for Academic Practice, Strathclyde University, 50 George Street, Glasgow; T.-0141-548 2637.

Gordon, George, MB, ChB, FRCSE, FRCOG. Consultant Obstetrician and Gynaecologist, Dumfries and Galloway, since 1969; b. 4.9.36, Markinch, Fife; m., Rosemary Gould Hutchison; 1 s.; 1 d. Educ. Bell Baxter School; Edinburgh University. Senior Registrar, Western General Hospital, Edinburgh, 1966-69; Chairman, Scottish Confidential Enquiry into Maternal Mortality; Member, Central Midwives Board for Scotland, 1978-84; Examiner, FRCS Edinburgh, MRCOG and DRCOG London; Clinical Director, Local Acute and Maternity Hospitals Trust; Honorary Secretary, Dumfries and Stewartry Division, BMA, 1975-87; Fellow of BMA. Recreations: music; Scottish literature; golf; gardening. Address: (b.) Dumfries and Galloway Royal Infirmary, Bankend Road, Dumfries DG1 4AP.

Gordon, Sheriff Gerald Henry, CBE, QC, MA, LLB, PhD, LLD. Sheriff of Glasgow and Strathkelvin, since 1978; Temporary Judge, Court of Session and High Court of Justiciary, since 1992; b. 17.6.29, Glasgow; m., Marjorie Joseph; 1 s.; 2 d. Educ. Queen's Park Senior Secondary School; Glasgow University. Advocate, 1953; Procurator Fiscal Depute, Edinburgh, 1960-65; Edinburgh University: Head, Department of Criminal Law and Criminology, 1965-72, Personal Professor of Criminal Law, 1969-72, Dean, Faculty of Law, 1970-73, Professor of Scots Law, 1972-76; Sheriff of South Strathclyde, Dumfries and Galloway, at Hamilton, 1976-77; Member: Interdepartmental Committee on Scottish Criminal Procedure, 1970-77, Committee on Criminal Appeals and Miscarriages of Justice, 1995-96. Publications: Criminal Law of Scotland, 1967, 1978; Renton & Brown's Criminal Procedure (Editor), 1972, 1983, 1996. Recreations: Jewish studies; coffee conversation; swimming. Address: (b.) Sheriff Court, Glasgow; T.-0141-429 8888.

Gordon, Giles Alexander Esme, FRSL. Director, Curtis Brown Ltd., Literary Agents, since 1995; b. 23.5.40, Edinburgh; m., 1, Margaret Anna Eastoe (deceased); 1 s.; 1 s. (deceased); 1 d.; 2, Maggie McKernan; 2 d. Educ. Edinburgh Academy; Edinburgh College of Art. Trainee Publisher, Oliver & Boyd, Edinburgh, 1959-63; Advertising Manager, Secker & Warburg, 1963-64; Editor, Hutchinson, 1964-66; Plays Editor, Penguin Books, 1966-67; Editorial Director, Victor Gollancz, 1967-73; Literary Agent, Anthony Sheil Associates, later Sheil Land Associates, 1973-95. C. Day Lewis Fellow in Writing, KCL, 1974-75; Secretary and Chairman, Society of Young Publishers; Member: Literature Panel, Arts Council, 1968-72; Committee of Management, Society of Authors; Committee, Association of Authors' Agents; Council, RSL, 1992-94; Committee, Authors Club, since 1992; Lecturer: Tufts University in London, 1970-74, Hollins College, London, 1983-86; Theatre Critic: Spectator, London Daily News, Drama; Books Columnist, The Times, 1993-95; Editor, Drama; Editor, Bloomsbury Classics Short Stories, since 1995, Clarion Tales, since 1996; Member, Committee, Society of Authors in Scotland, 1997-99. Publications: Pictures from an Exhibition, 1970; The Umbrella Man, 1971; About a Marriage, 1972; Girl with Red Hair, 1974; Factions (Co-Editor), 1974; Walter and the Balloon (Co-Author), 1974; Beyond the Words (Editor), 1975; Farewell, Fond Dreams, 1975; Prevailing Spirits (Editor), 1976; 100 Scenes from Married Life, 1976; Members of the Jury (Co-Editor), 1976; You Always Remember the First Time (Co-Editor), 1976; A Book of Contemporary Nightmares (Editor), 1977; Enemies, 1977; The Illusionist, 1978; Modern Scottish Short Stories (Co-Editor), 1978; Ambrose's Vision, 1980; Shakespeare Stories (Editor), 1982; English Short Stories 1940-80 (Editor), 1982; Best Short Stories (Co-Editor, annually), 1986-95; English Short Stories: 1900 to the present (Editor), 1988; The Twentieth Century Short Story in English: a bibliography (Editor), 1989; Aren't We Due a Royalty Statement?, 1993; The Best of Best Short Stories 1986-95 (Co-Editor), 1995; Scotland from the Air, 1996. Recreations: theatre; opera; walking; travelling; eating; drinking; book collecting. Address: 6 Ann Street, Edinburgh EH4 1PJ; T.-0131-332 1993.

Gordon, Graeme Henry, OBE, DUniv. Chairman, Scottish Environment Protection Agency, West Region, since 1998 (Member, Main Board, since 1995); Trout Farmer, since 1965; b. 11.9.30, London; m., Kirsten Ahlefeldt-Laurvig; 1 s.; 3 d. Educ. Kings College, Wimbledon; Royal Military Academy, Sandhurst. Army Officer, 1951-54 (Royal Tank Regiment and 22 SAS Regiment); Engineer and Manager, grain mill, 1955-65. Convener, NFUS Fish Farm Committee; Chairman, British Trout Association; President, European Trout and Salmon Federation; Chairman, Scottish Quality Trout; Convener, Scottish Landowners Federation, 1993-96. Recreation: country life. Address: (h.) Kenmure Kennels, New Galloway DG7 3RZ; T.-01644 420348.

Gordon of Strathblane, Lord (James Stuart Gordon), CBE, DLitt., DUniv, MA (Hons). Chairman, Scottish Radio Holdings, since 1996; Director, Johnston Press plc, since 1996, The AIM Trust plc, since 1996; Chairman, Scottish Tourist Board, since 1998; Member, BP Scottish Advisory Board, since 1990; Trustee, National Galleries of Scotland, since 1998; b. 17.5.36, Glasgow; m., Anne Stevenson; 2 s.; 1 d. Educ. St. Aloysius College, Glasgow; Glasgow University (President of the Union, 1958-59). Political Editor, STV, 1965-73; Managing Director, Radio Clyde, 1973-96; Chief Executive, Scottish Radio Holdings, 1991-96; Member, Court, Glasgow University, 1984-97; Chairman, Advisory Group on Listed Sports Events on Television, 1997-98; Winner, Observer Mace Debating Tournament, 1957; Sony Special Award for Services to Radio, 1984. Chairman, Scottish Exhibition Centre, 1983-89; Member, Scottish Development Agency, 1981-90.

Recreations: his children; genealogy; golf. Address: (b.) Scottish Radio Holdings, Clydebank Business Park, Clydebank, Glasgow G81 2RX; T.-0141-565 2202.

Gordon, Canon Kenneth Davidson, MA. Rector, St. Devenick's Episcopal Church, Bieldside, Aberdeen, since 1971; Synod Clerk, Diocese of Aberdeen and Orkney, since 1996; Warden of Lay Readers, Diocese of Aberdeen and Orkney, since 1978; b. 27.12.35, Edinburgh; m., Edith Jessica Newing; 2 s. Educ. George Heriot's School, Edinburgh; Edinburgh University; Tyndale Hall, Bristol. Curate, St. Helens Parish Church, Lancashire, 1960-66 (with charge of St. Andrew's Mission Church, 1962-66); Vicar, St. George the Martyr's Parish Church, Bolton, 1966-71; Examining Chaplain to Bishop of Aberdeen and Orkney, 1978-86; Canon, St. Andrew's Cathedral, Aberdeen, since 1981. Representative, Scottish Episcopal Church, Church Pastoral Aid Society. Address: The Rectory, Bieldside, Aberdeen AB15 9AP; T.-01224 861552.

Gordon, Robert, QFSM, AIFireE. Firemaster, Highland and Islands Fire Brigade, since 1995; b. 21.11.42, Nairn; m., Pamela; 1 s.; 1 d. Educ. Nairn Academy; Inverness Technical College. Joined Northern Fire Brigade, 1964; Highland and Islands Fire Brigade, since 1983. Queen's Fire Service Medal, 1995; Chairman, Appliances, Equipment and Uniform Committee, Chief and Assistant Chief Fire Officers Association District No. 7 (Scotland); Member, National AEU Committee. Recreations: sailing; golf; painting and sketching; vegetable gardening; running. Address: (b.) 16 Harbour Road, Inverness IV1 1TB; T.-01463 227000.

Gordon, Robert Smith Benzie, MA. Head, Constitution Group, Scottish Office, since 1997; b. 7.11.50, Aberdeen; m., Joyce Cordiner; 2 s.; 2 d. Educ. Gordon Schools, Huntly; Aberdeen University. Joined Scottish Office, 1973; Principal, Scottish Development Department, 1979-85; Principal Private Secretary to Secretary of State for Scotland, 1985-87; Assistant Secretary: Department of Agriculture and Fisheries, 1988-90, Management, Organisation and Industrial Relations Division, Scottish Office, 1990-91; Director, Administrative Services, 1991-97. Address: (b.) Victoria Quay, Edinburgh EH6 6QQ; T.-0131-244 7937.

Gordon, Professor William Morrison, MA, LLB, PhD, FRSE. Douglas Professor of Civil Law, Glasgow University, since 1969; Solicitor (non-practising), since 1956; b. 3.3.33, Inverurie; m., Isabella Evelyn Melitta Robertson; 2 s.; 2 d. Educ. Inverurie Academy; Robert Gordon's College, Aberdeen; Aberdeen University. National Service, Royal Navy, 1955-57; Assistant in Jurisprudence, Aberdeen University, 1957-60; Glasgow University: Lecturer in Civil Law, 1960-65, Senior Lecturer in Law, 1965-69 (and Sub-Dean of Faculty); Dean of Faculty, 1974-76. Elder and, until 1998, Session Clerk, Jordanhill Parish Church; Literary Director, The Stair Society, 1985-98. Publications: Studies in Transfer of Property by Traditio, 1970; Scottish Land Law, 1989; Stair Society Miscellany III, 1992; European Legal History (2nd Ed.), (with others), 1994. Recreation: golf. Address: (b.) School of Law, Stair Building, University, Glasgow G12 8QQ; T.-0141-339 8855, Ext. 5387.

Gordon-Duff-Pennington, Patrick Thomas, OBE, DL. Chairman, Deer Commission for Scotland, 1993-98; b. 12.1.30, London; m., Phyllida Rosemary; 4 d. Educ. Eton; Trinity College, Oxford. Farmed in Dumfriesshire, 1959-82; Hon. President, Scottish NFU, 1981-83; Convenor, Scottish Landowners Federation, 1988-91; DL, Cumbria; Vice-President, Field Studies Council.

Gordon-Gillies (nee McCall-Smith), Anne Bethea, MA, LLB. Advocate; Honorary Sheriff of South Strathclyde, Dumfries and Galloway, at Lanark, since 1960; b. 12.4.22, Lochgilphead, Argyll; m., Sheriff Principal M.G. Gillies, T.D., Q.C. (d. 1997). Educ. Sherborne School for Girls, Dorset; Edinburgh University. Served in WAAF, until 1946; called to Scottish Bar, 1951; married, 1954. Member, Valuation Appeal Panel, Strathclyde, 1974-88. Recreations: gardening; cats. Address: (h.) The Coach House, Broadgait, Gullane, East Lothian EH31 2DH; T.-01620 842971.

Goring, Rev. Iain McCormick, BSc, BD. Minister, Callander Kirk, since 1985; b. 22.7.50, Edinburgh; m., Janet Page; 2 s.; 1 d. Educ. Dunfermline High School; University of Edinburgh. Minister, Lochwood Parish Church, Easterhouse, Glasgow, 1977-85. Address: (h.) The Manse, Aveland Park Road, Callander, Perthshire FK17 8EN; T.-01877 330097.

Gorman, Brian, MA. Vice President, Commonwealth Youth Exchange Council, since 1999; Board Member, Suspect Culture Theatre Co., since 1998; b. 31.10.51, Wishaw. Educ. Our Lady's High School, Motherwell; University of Glasgow; Jordanhill College. Teacher, Columba High School, Coatbridge, 1974-76; Principal Teacher of Modern Studies, St. John's High, Dundee, 1976-78; Group Travel Manager, Cotter Tours, Glasgow, 1978-84; Director, English-Speaking Union (Scotland), 1984-93; Chairman, Suspect Culture Theatre Co., 1994-98. Recreations: theatre; debating. Address: (h.) 4/5 Guardianswood, Murrayfield, Edinburgh EH12 6PG; T.-0131-346 1327.

Gorman, Professor Daniel Geelan, BSc, PhD, DSc, CEng, FIMechE. CPhys, MInstP. Professor of Mechanical Engineering, Aberdeen University, since 1995; b. 9.8.47, Bellshill; m., Dr. June Neilson; 1 s.; 1 d. Educ. Holy Cross High School, Hamilton; Strathclyde University. Honeywell Ltd., 1968-69; E. Scragg & Sons Ltd., 1969-74; PhD student, 1974-77; Trinity College, Dublin, 1977-80; University of Limerick, 1980-81; Queen Mary and Westfield College, London, 1981-89; Robert Gordon University, 1989-95; Editor-in-Chief, Machine Vibration, 1991-95. Recreations: golf; motor cars. Address: (h.) The Linns, Catterline, Stonehaven, Kincardineshire AB39 2UL; T.-01569 750273.

Gorrie, Donald Cameron Easterbrook, OBE, MA, JP. MP (Liberal Democrat), Edinburgh West, since 1997; Leader, Liberal Democrat Group: City of Edinburgh Council, 1995-97, City of Edinburgh District Council, 1980-96, Lothian Regional Council, 1974-96; b. 2.4.33, India; m., Astrid Salvesen; 2 s. Educ. Hurst Grange, Stirling; Oundle School; Corpus Christi College, Oxford. Schoolmaster: Gordonstoun School, 1957-60, Marlborough College, 1960-66; Scottish Liberal Party: Director of Research, 1969-71, Director of Administration, 1971-75; Edinburgh Town Councillor, 1971-75. Director, 'Edinburgh Translations'; Member, Board: Queens Hall, Lothian Association of Youth Clubs, Edinburgh Youth Cafe, Diverse Attractions, Castle Rock and Lothian Housing Associations; former Member, Board: Edinburgh Festival, Scottish Chamber Orchestra, Royal Lyceum Theatre Company; former Scottish native record holder, 880 yards. Address: (h.) 9 Garscube Terrace, Edinburgh EH12 6BW; T.-0131-337 2077.

Gossip, Michael A.J., OBE, JP, BL. Honorary Sheriff, Dunoon, since 1989, and Campbeltown, since 1997; Clerk, Presbytery of South Argyll, since 1996; b. 27.4.33, Edinburgh; m., Margaret; 1 s.; 2 d. Educ. George Watson's Boys' College, Edinburgh; Edinburgh University. Legal Assistant, Midlothian County Council, 1955-57; Dumfries County Council: Senior Legal Assistant, 1957-60, Depute County Clerk, 1960-71; Argyll County Council: Depute County Clerk, 1971-72, County Clerk, 1972-75; Chief Executive, Argyll and Bute District Council, 1974-96.

Recreations: bowls; gardening. Address: (h.) Tigh-na-Coille, Ardrishaig, Argyll PA30 8EP; T.-01546 603454.

Gotts, Iain McEwan, DipLE, DipTP, FRICS, MRTPI. Director, DTZ Pieda Consultancy, since 1997; b. 26.2.47, Glasgow; m., Pamela; 1 s.; 2 d. Educ. Jordanhill College School, Glasgow; Paisley College of Technology; Heriot-Watt University/Edinburgh College of Art. Trainee Surveyor, British Rail Property Department, Glasgow, 1965-68; further education, 1968-72; Surveyor/Land Economist, Wright & Partners, Edinburgh, 1972-76; Chief Executive, Pieda plc, 1976-97. Governor, Stewart's Melville College and Mary Erskine School, since 1992. Recreations: music; golf; rugby. Address: (b.) 28 Drumsheugh Gardens, Edinburgh EH3 7RN; T.-0131-225 5737.

Gow, Alistair Martin, MBA, BSc, FICE, FIHT. Director of Transportation and Property, Argyll and Bute Council, since 1995; b. 17.4.47, Glasgow; m., Rosalind; 2 d. Educ. Hyndland Secondary School, Glasgow; Glasgow University. Argyll County Council, 1969-74; City of Glasgow, 1974-75; Strathclyde Regional Council, 1975-95. Elder, Church of Scotland. Recreations: sailing; hill-walking; reading. Address: (h.) Oakbank, Churchill Wood, Inverneill, Ardrishaig, Argyll PA30 8ES; T.-01546 606222.

Gow, Sir (James) Michael, GCB, DL (Edinburgh), FSAScot. President, Royal British Legion Scotland, 1986-96; President, Earl Haig Fund (Scotland), 1986-96, Vice-President, since 1996; Vice-President, Officers' Association Scotland, since 1986 (President, 1985-86); Vice-President, Scottish Institution for the War Blinded, since 1986; b. 3.6.24; m., Jane Emily Scott; 1 s.; 4 d. Educ. Winchester College. Enlisted, Scots Guards, 1942; commissioned, 1943; served NW Europe 1944-45, Malayan Emergency, 1949; Equerry to the late HRH Duke of Gloucester, 1952-53; Brigade Major, 1955-57; Regimental Adjutant, Scots Guards, 1957-60; Instructor, Army Staff College, 1962-64; Command, 2nd Bn Scots Guards, Kenya and England, 1964-66; GSO1, HQ London District, 1966-67; Command, 4th Guards Brigade, 1968-69; Imperial Defence College, 1970; Brigadier General Staff (Int.) HQ, BAOR and Assistant Chief of Staff, G2 HQ, Northag, 1971-73; GOC 4th Div., BAOR, 1973-75; Director of Army Training, 1975-78; General Officer Commanding, Scotland, Governor of Edinburgh Castle, 1979-80; Commander-in-Chief, BAOR and Commander, Northern Army Group, 1980-83 (awarded die Plakette des deutschen Heeres); ADC Gen. to the Queen, 1981-84; Commandant, Royal College of Defence Studies, 1984-86. Colonel Commandant: Intelligence Corps, 1973-86, Scottish Division, 1979-80; Ensign, Queen's Body Guard for Scotland, (Royal Company of Archers); UK Member, Eurogroup US Tour, 1983; UK Kermit Roosevelt Lecturer, USA, 1984; Vice President: Queen Victoria School, Dunblane, 1979-80, Royal Caledonian Schools, Bushey, since 1980; County Commissioner, British Scouts, W. Europe, 1980-83 (Silver Acorn); Elder, Church of Scotland, since 1988; President, National Association of Sheltered Employment, since 1993; Freeman: City of London, 1980, State of Kansas, USA, 1984; Freeman and Liveryman, Painters' and Stainers' Company, 1980. Publications: Trooping the Colour: A History of the Sovereign's Birthday Parade by the Household Troops, 1989; Jottings in a General's Notebook, 1989; General Reflections, 1991. Recreations: sailing; music; travel; reading. Address: (h.) 18 Ann Street, Edinburgh EH4 1PJ; T.-0131-332 4752.

Gow, Sheriff Neil, QC (Scot). Sheriff of South Strathclyde at Ayr, since 1976; b. 24.4.32; m., Joanna; 1 s. Educ. Merchiston Castle School, Edinburgh; Glasgow University; Edinburgh University. Advocate, 1957-76.

Gow, Professor Neil A.R., BSc, PhD. Professor, Department of Molecular and Cell Biology, University of Aberdeen, since 1983; b. 30.11.57, Tezpur, India; m., Ann; 2 s.; 1 d. Educ. Madras College, St. Andrews; Perth Academy; University of Edinburgh; University of Aberdeen. Postdoctoral Fellow, National Jewish Hospital/University of Colorado, Denver, 1982-83; Lecturer, then Senior Lecturer, then Reader, University of Aberdeen. Awards from British Society for Medical Mycology, British Mycological Society (Berkeley Award), Society for General Microbiology (Fleming Award); Saltire Society. Address: Institute of Medical Sciences, Foresterhill, Aberdeen AB25 2ZD; T.-01224 273179.

Grace, Professor John, BSc, PhD, FIBiol, FRSE. Professor of Environmental Biology, Edinburgh University, since 1992; b. 19.9.45, Northampton; m., Elizabeth Ashworth; 2 s.; 1 d. Educ. Bletchley Grammar School; Sheffield University. Lecturer, then Reader in Ecology, Edinburgh University, 1970-92. Co-Editor, Functional Ecology, 1986-99; Technical Editor, International Society for Biometeorology, 1983-98; Member, Terrestrial Life Sciences Committee, Natural Environment Research Council, 1986-89; Council Member, British Ecological Society, since 1983. Publications: Plant Response to Wind, 1977; Plants and their Atmospheric Environment (Co-Editor), 1981; Plant-atmosphere Relationships, 1983. Recreations: hill-walking; cycling; fishing; bridge. Address: (h.) 25 Craiglea Drive, Edinburgh EH10 5PB; T.-0131-447 3030.

Grace, Paul Henry, BSc, FFA. Managing Director and Actuary, Scottish Equitable Policyholders Trust Ltd., since 1994; b. 25.9.38, Bletchley; m., Aileen Anderson; 1 d. Educ. Bedford Modern School; St. Andrews University. Joined Scottish Equitable as Actuarial Trainee, 1960; joined Zurich Life Assurance Co. as Actuary and Life Manager, 1965; rejoined Scottish Equitable, 1980. President, Faculty of Actuaries, 1996-98. Publication: Introduction to Life Assurance, 1988. Recreations: golf; gardening. Address: Edinburgh Park, Edinburgh EH12; T.-0131-549 3013.

Graham, Rev. A. David M., BA, BD. Minister, Rosemount Parish Church, Aberdeen, since 1990; b. 17.7.40, Tralee; m., Mary A. Taylor; 2 s.; 1 d. Educ. Wesley College, Dublin; Methodist College, Belfast; Queen's University, Belfast; Glasgow University. Assistant, South Leith Parish; Secretary for Christian Education, Scottish National Council of YMCAs; Minister, Anderston Parish, Glasgow; Warden, Iona Abbey; Minister, Rutherford Parish, Aberdeen. Recreations: jogging; climbing. Address: 22 Osborne Place, Aberdeen AB2 4DA; T.-01224 648041.

Graham. Rev. Alasdair Giffen, BD, Dip. Ministry. Minister, Arbroath West Kirk, since 1990; Part-time Chaplain, Arbroath Infirmary; b. 20.4.54, Lanark; m., Joan Janet Forsyth; 1 d. Educ. Gordon Schools, Huntly; Kirkcaldy High School; University of Glasgow. Probationary Assistant, Mastrick Church, Aberdeen, 1980-81; Minister, Redgorton and Stanley Churches, Perthshire, 1981-86; Chaplain, HM Prison, Perth; Minister, St Margaret's Church, Arbroath, 1986-90. District Scout Chaplain; Chaplain, Angus Training Group. Recreations: time with family; badminton; swimming. Address: (h.) 1 Charles Avenue, Arbroath DD11 2EY; T.-01241 872244.

Graham, Professor David I., MB, ChB, PhD, FRCPath, FRCPS, FRSE. Professor of Neuropathology, Glasgow University, since 1983; b. 20.7.39, Glasgow; m., Joyce; 1 s.; 1 d. Educ. Penarth County Grammar School; Welsh National School of Medicine, Cardiff. Registrar, Western Infirmary, Glasgow, 1965-68; Lecturer, Department of Neuropathology, Glasgow, 1968-72; Fogarty Fellow, Laboratory of Neuropathology, Philadelphia, 1972-74; Senior Lecturer, Glasgow, 1974-83. Publications: several books; 300 papers. Recreations: hill-walking; music. Address: (b.) Department of Neuropathology, Institute of Neurological Sciences, Southern General Hospital, Govan Road, Glasgow G51 4TF; T.-0141-201 2113.

Graham, Lord Donald, BSc, MBA. Director of Information Technology, Adam & Company plc, since 1991; Director: Fruit Market Gallery, since 1992, KDCL Ltd., Property Developers, since 1992, Children's Music Foundation, since 1995; b. 28.10.56, Salisbury, Southern Rhodesia; m., Bridie; 1 s.; 3 d. Educ. St. Andrews College, South Africa; St. Andrews University; INSEAD. Recreations: piping; music. Address: (b.) Adam & Company plc, 22 Charlotte Square, Edinburgh EH2 4DF; T.-0131-225 8484.

Graham, Elspeth Forbes, MA, PhD. Senior Lecturer in Geography, St. Andrews University, since 1997; Member, Local Government Boundary Commission for Scotland, since 1994; b. 7.2.50, Edinburgh; 1 s.; 1 d. Educ. George Watson's Ladies College, Edinburgh; St. Andrews University; Durham University. Visiting Lecturer, University of Minnesota, 1979-80. Publications: Postmodernism and the Social Sciences (Co-editor), 1992; research papers on population policies and issues. Recreations: horse-riding; Celtic music. Address: (b.) Department of Geography, St. Andrews University, St. Andrews KY16 9ST; T.-01334 463908.

Graham, Professor Gordon, MA, MA, PhD. Regius Professor of Moral Philosophy, University of Aberdeen, since 1996; Director, Aberdeen Centre for Philosophy, Technology and Society, since 1996; b. 15.7.49, Belfast; 1 s.; 1 d. Educ. Methodist College, Belfast; University of St. Andrews; University of Durham. Lecturer in Moral Philosophy, University of St. Andrews, 1975-95; Director, St. Andrews University Music Centre, 1991-95. Publications: Historical Explanation Reconsidered, 1983; Politics in its Place – A Study of Six Ideologies, 1986; Contemporary Social Philosophy, 1988; Living the Good Life – An Introduction to Moral Philosophy, 1990; The Idea of Christian Charity – A Critique of Some Contemporary Conceptions, 1990; With Strings and Pipe – Essays in Church Music (Editor), 1994; Ethics and International Relations, 1996; The Shape of the Past – A Philosophical Approach to History, 1997; Philosophy of the Arts – An Introduction to Aesthetics, 1997; The Internet – A Philosophical Inquiry, 1999. Recreation: hillwalking. Address: (b.) Department of Philosophy, University of Aberdeen, Aberdeen AB24 3UB; T.-01224 272372.

Graham, Ian, BSc(Econ) (Hons), DipEdTech (CNAA). Principal, John Wheatley College, Glasgow, since 1992; b. 26.6.51, Devizes. Educ. Queen Victoria School, Dunblane; London Universty (External). Lecturer/Senior Lecturer, Reid Kerr College, Paisley, 1975-86; Head of Department, Clydebank College, 1986-88; Further Education Officer, Strathclyde Regional Council, 1988-89; HM Inspector of Schools, 1989-90; Assistant Director of Education (FE), Strathclyde Region, 1990-92. Fellow, Royal Society of Arts; Fellow, Institute of Personnel and Development; Member, Board: Scottish Community Education Council, Association of Scottish Colleges; Chair, West of Scotland Colleges' European Partnership. Recreations; reading; cinema; foreign travel; admiring Burmese cats. Address: (b.) 1346 Shettleston Road, Glasgow G32 9AT; T.-0141-778 2426.

Graham, John James, OBE, MA, MUniv (Aberdeen), FEIS. Joint Editor, The New Shetlander, 1956-98; b. 12.7.21, Lerwick; m., Beryl Smith; 3 s.; 2 d. Educ. Lerwick Central Secondary School; Edinburgh University. RAF Training Command, 1941-44, Bomber Command, 1944-46; Principal Teacher of English, Anderson Educational Institute, Lerwick, 1950-66; Headmaster: Lerwick Central Secondary School, 1966-70, Anderson High School, Lerwick, 1970-82; Member: Consultative Committee on the Curriculum, 1976-80, Broadcasting Council for Scotland, 1981-84; President, Shetland Folk Society. Publications: A Grammar and Usage of the Shetland Dialect (Co-author); Northern Lights (Joint Editor); The Shetland Dictionary; Shadowed Valley (novel); Strife in the Valley (novel); Four Centuries of Education in Shetland; A Shetland Anthology (Co-Editor). Recreations: local history; golf. Address: (h.) 10 Reform Lane, Lerwick, Shetland; T.-Lerwick 3425.

Graham, John Michael Denning, LLB (Hons), NP, FRSA. Solicitor and Notary Public, since 1970; Senior Partner, Paterson Roberson & Graham, since 1971; Senior Tutor in Law, Glasgow University; Director, John Smith & Son (Glasgow) Ltd.; Non Executive Director, West Glasgow Hospitals University NHS Trust; b. 7.9.44, Kirkintilloch; m., Christina Jeanne Sinclair; 2 s. Educ. Royal Belfast Academical Institution; Queen's University, Belfast. Chairman: Rent Assessment Committee, Glasgow, since 1983, Child Support Appeal Tribunal, since 1993, Social Security Appeal Tribunal, since 1995; Governor, Glasgow Caledonian University. Recreations: tennis; golf; hang-gliding. Address: (b.) 12 Royal Crescent, Glasgow G3 7SL; T.-0141-353 0550.

Graham, John Murdo, DipCom, FEIS. Retired Schoolmaster; Honorary Sheriff of Grampian, Highland and Islands at Stornoway; b. 1.5.36, Stornoway; m., Murdina; 3 s.; 1 d. Educ. Nicolson Institute, Stornoway; Scottish College of Commerce; Jordanhill College of Education. Nicolson Institute, Stornoway: Assistant Teacher, 1959-68, Principal Teacher of Business Studies and Economics, 1968-72, Assistant Rector, 1972-88. Member, North of Scotland Electricity Consumers' Committee, since 1992; Member, Social Security Appeal Tribunals, since 1982; Member, Social Security Disability Appeal Tribunals; Member, Council, Educational Institute of Scotland, 1975-85; Elder and Honorary Congregational Treasurer, Stornoway Free Church; General Trustee and Member, Finance, Law and Advisory Committee, Free Church of Scotland. Recreations: angling; gardening. Address: (h.) 25 Goathill Road, Stornoway, Isle of Lewis HS1 2NL; T.-01851 703469.

Graham, John Strathie, BA. Secretary and Head of Scottish Office Agriculture, Environment and Fisheries Department, since 1998; b. 27.5.50, Edinburgh; m., Anne Graham; 2 s.; 1 d. Educ. Edinburgh Academy; Corpus Christi College, Oxford. Joined Scottish Office, 1972; Principal, Scottish Economic Planning Department, 1976; Assistant Secretary, Industry Department for Scotland, 1982; Private Secretary to Secretary of State, 1983; Assistant Secretary: Planning Division, Scottish Development Department, 1985, Finance Division 1, 1990; Under Secretary, Local Government Group, 1991; Principal Finance Officer, 1996. Recreations: exploring Scotland; listening to music. Address: (b.) Victoria Quay, Edinburgh EH6 6QQ.

Graham, Keith H.R., LLB, WS. Principal Clerk, Scottish Land Court, since 1982; b. 29.5.47, Edinburgh; m., Patricia; 2 d. Educ. George Watson's College; Edinburgh University. Apprenticeship, Davidson & Syme, WS, 1968-70; private practice, 1970-72; Legal Assessor, Scottish Land Court, 1972-82. Publication: The Scottish Land Court: Practice and Procedure. Address: (b.) 1 Grosvenor Crescent, Edinburgh EH12 5ER; T.-0131-225 3595.

Graham, Professor Neil Bonnette, BSc, PhD, CChem, FRSC, FIM, FRSE. Professor in Chemical Technology, Strathclyde University, 1973-97; Emeritus Professor in Chemistry, since 1997; b. 23.5.33, Liverpool; 1 s.; 3 d. Educ. Alsop High School, Liverpool; Liverpool University. Research Chemist, Research Scientist, Canadian Industries Ltd., MacMasterville PQ, Canada, 1956-67; Assistant Group Head, then Group Head, Polymer Chemistry, ICI, Runcorn, Cheshire. Member: Advisory Committee on Dental and Surgical Materials, 1980-86; Expert Advisor to the Secretary of State on Active Medical Implants, since 1993; sometime member of various committees, Society of Chemical Industry, Royal Society of Chemistry and Plastics and Rubber Institute; Member, International Editorial Boards, Biomedical Polymers; Founder and Technical Director, Polysystems Ltd., 1980-90; Governor and Trustee, Keil School; Trustee, James Clerk Maxwell Trust. Recreations: music; walking. Address: (b.) Strathclyde University, Department of Pure and Applied Chemistry, Thomas Graham Building, 295 Cathedral Street, Glasgow G1 1XL; T.-0141-548 2133.

Graham, Sir Norman William, Kt (1971), CB (1961), MA, DLitt (Heriot-Watt), DUniv (Stirling), FRSE; b. 11.10.13, Dundee; m., Catherine Mary Strathie; 2 s.; 1 d. Educ. High School of Glasgow; Glasgow University. Assistant Principal, Department of Health for Scotland, 1936; Principal, Ministry of Aircraft Production, 1941; Principal Private Secretary to Minister, 1944; Assistant Secretary, Department of Health for Scotland, 1945; Under Secretary, 1956; Secretary, Scottish Education Department, 1964-73.

Graham, Lieutenant General Sir Peter, KCB, CBE, DLitt. Chairman, Regimental Trust Fund, The Gordon Highlanders, since 1986; Chairman, The Gordon Highlanders Museum Management Committee, since 1994; b. 14.3.37; m., Dr Alison Mary Morren; 3 s. Educ. Fyvie Village School, Aberdeenshire; Hall School, Hampstead; St. Paul's School, London; RMA Sandhurst. Commissioned The Gordon Highlanders, 1956; regimental appointments, Dover, Germany, Scotland, Kenya, 1957-62; HQ Highland Brigade, 1962-63; Adjutant 1 Gordons, Kenya, Edinburgh, Borneo (Despatches), 1963-66; Staff Captain, HQ 1 Br Corps, 1966-67; Australian Staff College, 1968; Company Commander, 1 Gordons, Germany, 1969-70; Brigade Maj., HQ 39 Brigade, Northern Ireland, 1970-72; 2nd i/c, 1 Gordons, Ulster, Singapore, 1972-74; Military Assistant to Adjutant General MoD, 1974-75; CO, 1 Gordons, Scotland, Ulster, 1976-78; COS, HQ 3 Armoured Division, Germany, 1978-82; Comd UDR, Ulster (Despatches), 1982-84; Canadian National Defence College, Ontario, 1984-85; Deputy Military Secretary, MoD, 1985-87; GOC Eastern District, 1987-89; Commandant RMA, Sandhurst, 1989-91; GOC Army in Scotland and Governor, Edinburgh Castle, 1991-93. Colonel, The Gordon Highlanders, 1986-94; Member, Royal Company of Archers, since 1985. Publications: The Gordon Highlanders Pipe Music Collection (Co-author), 1983 and 1985; DLitt, Robert Gordon University, 1996. Recreations: stalking; hill-walking; shooting; reading; pipe music; gardening under my wife's directions. Address: (b.) The Gordon Highlanders Museum, Viewfield Road, Aberdeen AB1 7XH; T.-01224 311200.

Graham, Riddell, BSc, MTS. Chief Executive, Scottish Borders Tourist Board, since 1996, Director, 1990-96; b. 13.2.54, Galashiels; m., Sandra; 1 s. Educ. Galashiels Academy; Edinburgh University. Borders Regional Council, 1976-83, latterly as Assistant Tourist Officer; joined Scottish Borders Tourist Board, 1983, as Assistant Director of Tourism. Recreations: mountain biking; watching rugby. Address: (b.) Shepherds Mill, Whinfield Road, Selkirk; T.-01750 20555.

Graham, Ronald Cairns, CBE, MB, ChB, DipSocMed, FRCP, FFCM. Honorary Senior Lecturer, Dundee University, since 1969; b. 8.10.31, Airdrie; m., Christine Fraser Osborne; 2 s.; 1 d. Educ. Airdrie Academy; Glasgow University. Deputy Medical Superintendent, Edinburgh Royal Infirmary; Assistant Senior Administrative Medical Officer, South-Eastern Regional Hospital Board; Eastern Regional Hospital Board: Deputy Senior Administrative Medical Officer, Senior Administrative Medical Officer; Tayside Health Board: Chief Administrative Medical Officer, 1973-85, General Manager, 1985-93. Recreation: fishing. Address: (h.) 34 Dalgleish Road, Dundee; T.-Dundee 455426.

Graham, Thomas. MP (Labour), Renfrewshire West, since 1997 (Renfrew West and Inverclyde, 1987-97); b. 5.12.43; m.; 2 s. Former engineer. Address: (b.) House of Commons, London, SW1A 0AA.

Graham, Rev. William Peter, MA, BD. Clerk, Edinburgh Presbytery, since 1993; b. 24.11.43, Edinburgh; m., Isabel Arnot Brown; 2 s. Educ. George Watson's College, Edinburgh; Edinburgh University. Assistant Minister, Dundee (St. Mary's) Parish Church, 1966-68; Minister, Chirnside Parish Church, 1968-93, Bonkyl & Preston, 1973-93, Edrom-Allanton, 1978-93; Clerk, Duns Presbytery, 1982-93; Convener, General Assembly's Nomination Committee, 1990-93; Vice-Convener, Committee on Education for Ministry, 1996-98; Vice-Convener, Board of Ministry, 1998-99. Recreations: golf; theatre; reading. Address: (b.) 10 Palmerston Place, Edinburgh EH12 5AA; T.-0131-225 9137.

Graham-Bryce, Ian James, DPhil, BA, MA, BSc, FRSC, CChem, FRSE, FRSA. Principal and Vice-Chancellor, Dundee University, since 1994; b. 20.3.37; m., Anne Elisabeth Metcalf; 1 s.; 3 d. Educ. William Hulme's Grammar School, Manchester; University College, Oxford. Lecturer, UCNW, Bangor, 1961-64; Senior Scientific Officer, Rothamsted Experimental Station, 1964-70; Senior Research Officer, ICI Plant Protection Division, Berks, 1970-72; Imperial College of Science and Technology: Special Lecturer in Pesticide Chemistry, Department of Zoology and Applied Entomology, 1970-72, Visiting Professor, 1976-79, Governor, since 1985; Rothamsted Experimental Station: Head, Department of Insecticides and Fungicides, 1972-79, Deputy Director, 1975-79; Director, East Malling Research Station, 1979-86; Cons. Director, Commonwealth Bureau of Horticulture and Plantation Crops, 1979-86; Head, Environmental Affairs Division, Shell Internationale Petroleum Maatschappij BV, 1986-94. Society of Chemical Industry, London: President, 1982-84, Member, Council, 1969-72, 1974-89, Hon. Secretary, Home Affairs, 1977-80; President: Association of Applied Biologists, 1988, British Crop Protection Council, since 1996; Member, NERC, 1989-96 (Chairman, Polar Sciences Committee, 1995-96); Convener, Committee of Scottish Higher Education Principals, since 1998; Member, Board of Directors, Educational Counselling Service, British Council, 1996-98; Member, Board of Directors, Quality Assurance Agency for Higher Education (Chairman, Scottish Advisory Committee), 1997-98. Publications: Physical Principles of Pesticide Behaviour, 1980; papers on soil science, plant nutrition, crop protection and environmental matters. Recreations: music (especially opera); sport. Address: (b.) Dundee University, Dundee DD1 4HN.

Grahame, David Currie, MA (Hons). Executive Director, LINC Scotland, since 1993; b. 10.12.53, Hawick. Educ. Langholm Academy; Lockerbie Academy; St. Andrews University. Hotelier and company director, 1980-87; Small Business Consultant, 1987-90; Area Manager, Princes Scottish Youth Business Trust, 1990-91; Head of Business Development, Glasgow Opportunities Enterprise Trust, 1991-93; Founding Director, LINC Scotland (National Business Angels Network). Recreations: music; classic cinema; food and wine. Address: (b.) 30 George Square, Glasgow G2 1BB; T.-0141-221 3321.

Grainger, John McGregor Leighton, MBE, FTS. Chief Executive, Perthshire Tourist Board, since 1982; b. 3.9.43, Aberdeen; m., Kathleen; 1 s. (deceased); 2 d. Assistant Tourist Officer, Aberdeen Town Council, 1959-67; Tourism Manager: Dunbar Town Council, 1967-69, Perth Tourist Association, 1969-74; Senior Tourist Officer, Tayside Regional Council, 1974-82. Recreations: fishing; hill-walking. Address: (b.) Lower City Mills, West Mill Street, Perth PH1 5QP; T.-01738 627958.

Grains, Florence Barbara, OBE, JP. Member, Shetland Islands Council, since 1986; Director, Shetland Careers Service; former Chairman, Shetland Health Board; b. 2.11.32, Shetland; m., Alistair M. Grains; 4 s. Educ. Whiteness School, Shetland; Lerwick FE Centre. Retired Sub-postmaster, Whiteness, Shetland. Chairman, Alting Debating Society; Trustee, Shetland Amenity Trust; Chairman, Shetland Branch, Post Office Users Council for Scotland; Member, Shetland Area Licensing Board; Trustee, Walls and District Agricultural Society; Supervisor, Whiteness and Weisdale Playgroup; GCSL, 1st Whiteness/Weisdale; Chairman, Foula Electricity Trust; Member, Aith Lifeboat Branch Committee. Address: (h.) Hoove, Whiteness, Shetland; T.-01595 84 243.

Grant, Donald Blane, CBE, TD, LLD, CA; b. 8.10.21, Dundee; m., Lavinia Margaret Ruth Ritchie; 3 d. Educ. Dundee High School. Royal Artillery, 1939-46 (retired as Major); Partner, Thomson, McLintock & Co., 1950-86. Chairman, Tayside Health Board, 1984-91; Chairman: Scottish Legal Aid Board, 1986-91, Mathew Trust, Caird Travelling Scholarships Trust. Recreations: golf; fishing; shooting; gardening. Address: (h.) 24 Albany Road, Broughty Ferry, Dundee DD5 1NT.

Grant, Dr. Douglas, TD, FRSE, FSA Scot; b. 6.1.18; m., Enid Whitsey; 3 s. Educ. George Watson's College; University of St. Andrews. Lt.-Col., RA (served W. Africa and staff), 1939-46; Scottish Widows Fund, 1936-39; Director: Oliver and Boyd Ltd., 1947-67, Edinburgh C. of C., 1952-56, New Education Ltd., 1962-66, Bracken House Publications Ltd., 1963-67, Sprint Productions Ltd., 1963-80, E. & S. Livingston Ltd., 1963-67, Darien Press Ltd., 1963-68, R. & R. Clark Ltd., 1963-80, Port Seton Offset Printers Ltd., 1965-75, T. & A. Constable Ltd., 1965-75, British Journal of Educational Psychology, 1970-91, Pindar (Scot) Ltd., 1986-89, Macdonald Lindsay (Printers) Ltd., 1988-89; Chairman: Scottish Journal of Theology Ltd., 1948-91, Robert Cunningham & Sons Ltd., 1952-76, Hunter and Foulis Ltd., 1963-75, Port Seton Offset Printers Ltd., 1965-75, Multi Media (AU) Services Ltd., 1967-75, Church of Scotland Publications Committee, 1971-76, Scottish Academic Press Ltd., 1969-91, Scottish International Review Ltd., 1970-75, Handsel Press Ltd., 1975-91, Scottish Academic Press (Journals) Ltd., 1976-91, Clark Constable Printers Ltd., 1978-89; Consultant Editor, Scottish Academic Press, since 1991. Trustee, The Lodge Trust (Natural History), 1949-85, Darling (Ogilby) Investment Trust, 1955-78, Kilwarlin Trust, since 1964, Esdaile Trust, since 1975, Society for the Benefit of Sons and Daughters of the Clergy of the Church of Scotland, since 1990; Committee Member: Scottish Council of Law Reporting, 1948-93 (Consultant, since 1993), Police Dependents' Trust (Lothian and Borders Police), since 1956, NEDO, 1968-75, New College University of Edinburgh Finance Board, since 1970, University of Edinburgh Court, 1972-84, Scottish Arts Council, 1975-79; President: Edinburgh Master Printers' Association, 1962-64, Edinburgh Bookseller Society, 1977-80, Edinburgh Amateur Angling Club, 1978-80; Honorary Fellow, Edinburgh Geological Society, 1992; Hon. DLitt, University of St. Andrews, 1986. Address: Flat G, The Lodge, 2 East Road, North Berwick, East Lothian EH39 4HN; T.-01620 894972.

Grant, (Helen) Rae. Party Administrator, Scottish Liberal Democrats, since 1989; b. 17.12.40, Edinburgh; m., James Sturrock Grant; 2 d. Educ. Boroughmuir High School; Torphichen Commercial College. Party Secretary, 1974-89. Recreations: reading; swimming; walking. Address: (b.) 4 Clifton Terrace, Edinburgh EH12 5DR; T.-0131-337 2314.

Grant, Ian David, CBE, FRAgS. Scottish Crown Estate Commissioner, since 1996; b. 28.7.43, Dundee; m., Eileen May Louisa Yule; 3 d. Educ. Strathallan School; East of Scotland College of Agriculture. Chairman, EEC Cereals Working Party, 1982-88 and International Federation of Agricultural Producers, Grains Committee, 1984-90; President, NFU of Scotland, 1984-90; Director: Scottish Hydro Electric, East of Scotland Farmers Ltd., NFU Mutual Insurance Society Ltd., Clydesdale Bank PLC, 1989-97, Scottish Exhibition Centre; Member: Scottish Council, CBI, 1984-96, Board, British Tourist Authority, 1990-98, Scottish Economic Council, 1993-97; Chairman, Scottish Tourist Board, 1990-98 (Member, 1988-90); Vice President, Royal Smithfield Club. Recreations: shooting; swimming; music. Address: (h.) Leal House, Alyth PH11 8JQ. Tel.: 01828 632695.

Grant, Ian Faulconer Heathcoat, JP, DL. Managing Director, Glenmoriston Estates Limited; Director, Pacific Assets Trust PLC, Royal Bank of Scotland PLC, Royal Bank of Scotland Group plc, Banco Santander S.A., Holland Pacific Fund N.V., Grandom International Limited, Dransfield Holdings Limited; Trustee, Bartlett Trusts (USA); b. 3.6.39, Singapore; m., Sally; 1 s.; 3 d. Educ. Cargilfield; Sedbergh; Liverpool College of Commerce. ICI Ltd., 1957-62; various positions, Jardine Matheson & Co. Ltd., Hong Kong, 1962-73, culminating in directorship on Main Board. Address: (b.) Glenmoriston Estates Ltd., Glenmoriston, near Inverness; T.-01320 351202.

Grant, Major James MacAlpine Gregor, TD, NDA, MRAC. Landowner and Farmer, since 1961; b. 18.2.38, Nakuru, Kenya; m., Sara Marjory, DL; 3 d. Educ. Eton; Royal Agricultural College, Cirencester. National Service, Queen's Own Cameron Highlanders, 1957-58; TA with 4/5th Queen's Own Cameron Highlanders; Volunteers with 51st Highland Volunteers. Address: Roskill House, Munlochy, Rossshire IV8 8PA; T.-01463 811207.

Grant, James Shaw, CBE, LLD, FRSE, FRAgS, MA. Author; b. 22.5.10, Stornoway; m., Catherine Mary Stewart. Educ. Nicolson Institute, Stornoway; Glasgow University. Editor, Stornoway Gazette, 1932-63; Governor, Pitlochry Festival Theatre, 1954-84 (Chairman, 1971-83); Member, Crofters Commission, 1955-78 (Chairman, 1963-78); Director, Grampian TV, 1969-80; Member: Highlands and Islands Development Board, 1970-82, Scottish Advisory Committee, British Council, 1972-94; Chairman, Harris Tweed Association Ltd., 1972-84; Member, Council, National Trust for Scotland, 1979-84; Governor, Eden Court Theatre, 1980-96 (Vice Chairman, 1987-96); author of plays: Tarravore, The Magic Rowan, Legend is Born, Comrade the King. Publications: Highland Villages, 1977; Their Children Will See, 1979; The Hub of My Universe, 1982; Surprise Island, 1983; The Gaelic Vikings, 1984; Stornoway and the Lews, 1985; Discovering Lewis and Harris, 1987; Enchanted Island, 1989; A Shilling for Your Scowl, 1992; Morrison of the Bounty, 1997. Address: (h.) Ardgrianach, Inshes, Inverness; T.-Inverness 231476.

Grant, Professor John Paxton, LLB, LLM. Professor, School of Law, Glasgow University, since 1988 (Dean, Faculty of Law and Financial Studies, 1985-89 and 1992-96); b. 22.2.44, Edinburgh; m., Elaine E. Sutherland. Educ. George Heriot's School, Edinburgh; Edinburgh University; Pennsylvania University. Lecturer, Faculty of Law: Aberdeen University, 1967-71, Dundee University, 1971-74; Senior Lecturer, Department of Public International Law, Glasgow University, 1974-88; Visiting Professor: Saint Louis University School of Law, 1981, Northwestern School of Law, Lewis and Clark College, 1984, 1986, 1998. Editor, The Juridical Review, since 1988. Publications: Independence and Devolution (Editor), 1976; The Impact of Marine Pollution: Law and Practice (Joint Editor), 1980; The Encyclopaedic Dictionary of International Law (Joint General Editor), 1985; Legal Education 2000 (Joint Editor), 1988; English–Estonian Law Glossary (Joint Editor), 1993; English for Lawyers (Joint Editor), 1995. Recreations: walking; travelling. Address: (h.) 87 Warrender Park Road, Edinburgh EH9 1EW; T.-0131-229 7705.

Grant, Lesley Dunbar, MBE, MA; b. Banchory. Educ. Banchory Academy; Aberdeen University; Aberdeen College of Education. Former teacher/head teacher; Past Chairman, Northern Area, Scottish Conservative and Unionist Association; former Councillor, Dean of Guild and Hon. Treasurer, Banchory Town Council; former Handicap Adviser and Selector, Scottish Ladies Golf Association; former Member, Scottish Sports Council; Elder, Banchory-Ternan East Church. Recreations: current affairs; travel; caring; some holes of golf. Address: (h.) Ordeans, Arbeadie Terrace, Banchory AB31 5TN; T.-01330 822782.

Grant, Very Rev. Malcolm Etheridge, BSc (Hons), BD (Hons). Provost and Rector, Cathedral Church of S. Andrew, Inverness; b. 6.8.44, Maidstone; m., Katrina Russell Nuttall; 1 s.; 1 d. Educ. Dunfermline High School; Edinburgh University; Edinburgh Theological College. Assistant Curate: S. Mary's Cathedral, Glasgow, 1969-72, Grantham Parish Church, in charge of Church of the Epiphany, Earlesfield, 1972; Team Vicar, Earlesfield, Grantham Team Ministry, 1972-78; Priest-in-charge, S. Ninian's, Invergordon, 1978-81; Provost and Rector, Cathedral Church of S. Mary the Virgin, Glasgow, 1981-91; Examining Chaplain to Bishop of Moray, Ross and Caithness, 1979-81; Member, Highland Region Education Committee, 1979-81; Rector, S Paul's, Strathnairn, and Priest-in-charge, S Mary's-in-the-Fields, Culloden, 1991-97. Address: 15 Ardross Street, Inverness IV3 5NS; T.-01463 233535.

Grant, Sir (Matthew) Alistair, DL, FRSE. Governor, Bank of Scotland, since 1998; Chairman, Scottish and Newcastle plc, since 1997; b. 6.3.37, Haddington; m., Judith Mary Grant; 2 s. ; 1 d. Educ. Woodhouse Grove School, Yorkshire. Unilever, 1958-63; J. Lyons, 1963-65; Connell May & Steavenson, 1965-68; Marketing Director, Fine Fare Ltd., 1968-72; Managing Director, Oriel Foods Ltd., 1973-77; Managing Director of companies which formed Argyll Group, 1977-86; Deputy Chairman, Chief Executive, Chairman, Argyll Group, 1986-97. Chairman, Biotechnology and Biological Sciences Research Council, 1996-98; Ordinary Director, Bank of Scotland; Non-Executive Director, Scottish & Newcastle PLC; Visiting Professor, Strathclyde University; Trustee: National Museums of Scotland, National Heritage Memorial Fund; Regent, Royal College of Surgeons, Edinburgh; Chairman, Lamp of Lothian Collegiate Trust; Deputy Lieutenant of East Lothian, since 1997. Recreations: fishing; painting; reading; music. Address: (b.) Bank of Scotland, The Mound, Edinburgh EH1 1YZ.

Grant, Professor Nigel Duncan Cameron, MA, MEd, PhD, FRSE. Professor of Education, Glasgow University, 1978-95, now Emeritus Professor; b. 8.6.32, Glasgow; m., Valerie Keeling Evans; 1 s.; 1 d. Educ. Inverness Royal Academy; Glasgow University. Teacher of English, Glasgow secondary schools, 1957-60; Lecturer in Education, Jordanhill College of Education, 1960-65; Lecturer in Educational Studies, then Reader, Edinburgh University, 1965-78. Past Chairman and President, British Comparative and International Education Society; former Executive Member, Comparative Education Society in Europe; Past Chairman: Scottish Educational Research Association, Scottish Universities Council for Studies in Education; Educational Consultant, Comann Sgoiltean Da-Chananach Ghlaschu; Member: Executive Committee, Advisory Council for the Arts in Scotland, Editorial Board, Comparative Education; Trustee, Urras Foghlam na Gaidhlig; Member, Scottish Constitutional Steering Committee; Hon. President, Glasgow Educational Colloquium. Publications: Soviet Education, 1964; Society, Schools and Progress in Eastern Europe, 1969; Education and Nation-Building in the Third World (Editor and Co-Author), 1971; A Mythology of British Education (Co-Author), 1974; Scottish Universities: The Case for Devolution (Co-Author), 1976; Patterns of Education in the British Isles (Co-Author), 1977; The Crisis of Scottish Education, 1982. Recreations: theatre; music; poetry; natural history; languages; art; travel; calligraphy.

Grant, Professor Peter Mitchell, PhD, CEng, FIEE, FIEEE, FRSE, FEng. Professor of Electronic Signal Processing, Edinburgh University, since 1987; b. 20.6.44, St. Andrews; m., Marjory Renz; 2 d. Educ. Strathallan School; Heriot-Watt University; Edinburgh University. Publications: Digital Communications (Co-Author), 1997; Signal Processing and Coding (Co-Author), 1988. Address: (b.) Department of Electrical Engineering, Edinburgh University, Edinburgh EH9 3JL; T.-0131-650 5569.

Grant, Richard Anthony, BSocSc, MSc. Head of Housing Division 2, Scottish Office Development Department, since 1997; Head of Division, Land Use and Crofting, Scottish Office Agriculture and Fisheries Department, 1991-97; b. 12.6.48, Leicester; m., Jacqueline Claire; 1 s.; 1 d. Educ. Loughborough College School; Birmingham University; Strathclyde University. Research Officer/Senior Research Officer, Scottish Education Department and Scottish Development Department, 1969-75; Principal Research Officer, Housing Research Unit, Scottish Development Department, 1975-77; Principal, Sports Policy Branch, Scottish Education Department, 1977-79; Principal Research Officer, Housing and Urban Renewal Research Unit, Scottish Development Department, 1979-85; Principal: Land Use and Conservation Branch, Department of Agriculture and Fisheries, 1986-89, NHS Management Executive, 1989-91. Recreations: cycling; hill-walking; cross-country skiing. Address: (b.) RG1/73, Victoria Quay, Leith, Edinburgh; T.-0131-224 5511.

Grant of Dalvey, Sir Patrick Alexander Benedict, 14th Bt, FSA Scot, LLB. Chieftain of Clan Donnachy; Company Director; b. 5.2.53; m.; 2 s. Educ. Glasgow University. Former deerstalker and inshore fisherman.

Grant of Rothiemurchus, John Peter, DL. Landowner; b. 22.10.46, Rothiemurchus; m., Philippa; 1 s.; 2 d. Educ. Gordonstoun. Chairman and Director, Scot Trout Limited, 1989-95; Past Chairman, Highland Region, Forestry, Farming and Wildlife Advisory Group; Patron, Highland Hospice; Vice-President, Scottish Landowners' Federation, since 1991; Deputy Lieutenant, Districts of Lochaber, Inverness, Badenoch and Strathspey, since 1986; Member: Council, National Trust for Scotland, 1990-95, Native Woodlands Advisory Panel to the Forestry Commission, since 1993, National Access Forum, since 1993, Cairngorm Partnership, since 1995; Chairman, Tourism and Enivronment Task Force, 1995-98; President, Royal Zoological Society of Scotland, since 1996. Recreations: skiing; shooting. Address: (b.) Doune of Rothiemurchus, by Aviemore; T.-01479 810647.

Grant Peterkin, Brigadier Anthony Peter, OBE, BA. Army Officer, since 1967; Army Director of Manning and Career Management, since 1996; Landowner; b. 6.7.47, London; m., Joanna Young; 1 s.; 1 d. Educ. Ampleforth College; University of Durham; University of Madras. Commissioned into Queen's Own Highlanders, 1967: service in Middle East, Germany, Northern Ireland, Belize, Hong Kong and India; ADC to CGS; Command of 1st Bn. Queen's Own Highlanders, Belize and Germany, 1987-89; Higher Command and Staff Course, Camberley, 1991; Military Adviser to UN Mission, Iraq and Kuwait, 1991; Commander, 24 Airmobile Brigade, 1993-94; Royal College of Defence Studies, 1995. Recreation: travelling off the beaten track in Indochina. Address: (h.) Grange Hall, Forres, Morayshire; T.-0171-727 5399.

Grantham, Michael, BSc (Hons), FRICS. Secretary and Chief Executive, Crofters Commission, since 1992; b. 9.3.43, Sunderland; m., Jacqueline; 1 d. Educ. Bede School; Glasgow University. Research Assistant, University of

Queensland, Australia; Chartered Surveyor, private practice, Glasgow; Lands Officer, Scottish Office Department of Agriculture, Glasgow, Shetland, Lanarkshire; Principal Agricultural Officer, Scottish Office DAFS; Estate Factor, Historic Scotland. Recreations: first iconoclastic Jewish Secretary of the Croftres Commission, is fond of his wife, his daughter, listening to jazz, making useful and useless things out of leather, and training dogs. Address: 4/6 Castle Wynd, Inverness IV2 3EQ; T.-01463 663450.

Gray, Adam, OBE, NDA, NDD, FRAgS. Farmer; b. 6.8.29, Borgue, Kirkcudbright; m., Elaine West Russell; 3 s. Educ. George Watson's Boys College; West of Scotland Agricultural College. Nuffield Scholar, 1955; Past President, Stewartry NFU; Member, NFU Council; Director: Royal Highland & Agricultural Society (Honorary Vice-President, 1994-95), Scottish Milk Marketing Board, 1981-94; former Council Member, British Simmental Cattle Society; former Chairman: SW Scotland Grassland Society, Kirkcudbright District Council, UK Milk Publicity Council; Past President, Scottish Agricultural Arbiters Association; former Director, Scottish Pride Ltd.; Honorary President, Stewartry Agricultural Society; Governor, West of Scotland Agricultural College, 1980-86; Governor, Hannah Research Institute; Secretary, Kirkcudbright Burns Club; Past President: Kirkcudbright Rotary Club. Awarded OBE, 1994, FRAgS, 1997. Publications: Borgue Academy; White Gold?; A Scots Agricultural Glossary. Recreations: rugby; local history. Address: (h.) Ingleneuk, Borgue, Kirkcudbright; T.-01557 870 250.

Gray, Alasdair. Artist and Writer; b. 28.12.34, Glasgow; m., Morag McAlpine; 1 s. Educ. Whitehill Senior Secondary School; Glasgow Art School. Part-time Art Teacher, 1958-62; Scene Painter, 1963-64; has since lived by drawing, painting, writing; Glasgow People's Palace has a collection of his portraits and cityscapes; extant murals: Palacerigg nature reserve, Cumbernauld; Abbots House local history museum, Dunfermline. Publications: novels: Lanark; 1982 Janine; The Fall of Kelvin Walker; Something Leather; McGrotty and Ludmilla; A History Maker; Poor Things; Mavis Befrage; short story collections: Unlikely Stories, Mostly; Lean Tales (this last also containing work by Jim Kelman and Agnes Owens); Ten Tales Tall and True; Five Glasgow Artists (an exhibition catalogue); Saltire Self-Portrait No. 4; Why Scots Should Rule Scotland (1992 and 1997), Working Legs, a play for people without them; editing The Anthology of Prefaces, 1999; Scottish National Library has a collection of his unpublished plays and other material. Recreations: reading; talking to friends; drinking; walking.

Gray, Alexander, OBE, MA, LLB, DUniv, FSA Scot. Honorary Sheriff, Dumbarton; b. 6.5.12, Glasgow; m., Margaret; 2 s. Educ. Hillhead High School; Glasgow University; Edinburgh University. Town Clerk, Cove and Kilcreggan, 1948-67; Queen's Coronation Medal, 1953; Dean, Faculty of Procurators, Dumbarton, 1972; Clerk of Peace, Dunbartonshire, 1974; Law Society of Scotland Charity Work Award, 1998. Fundraiser, Glasgow University Centre for Rheumatic Diseases. Recreations: archaeology; Gaelic; arthritis charity. Address: (h.) (h.) Borraichill, 116 Frederick Crescent, Port Ellen, Isle of Islay PA42 7BQ.

Gray, Alistair B., BA, CA. Managing Director, Ortak Jewellery Limited, since 1990; Board Member, Highlands and Islands Enterprise, since 1997; b. 14.6.58, Kirkwall, Orkney; m., Linda; 3 s.; 1 d. Educ. Kirkwall Grammar School; Heriot-Watt University. Chartered Accountant, Arthur Young, Edinburgh, 1979-84. Address: Hatston, Kirkwall, Orkney KW15 1RW; T.-01856 872224.

Gray, 22nd Lord (Angus Diarmid Ian Campbell-Gray); b. 3.7.31; m.; 1 s.; 3 d. by pr. m. Address: Airds Bay House, Taynuilt, Argyll, PA35 1JR.

Gray, Charles Ireland, CBE, FRSA, JP. Chair, Education, North Lanark Council; b. 25.1.29, Gartcosh; m., Catherine; 3 s.; 2 d. Educ. Coatbridge High School. Local government, since 1958; Leader, Strathclyde Regional Council, 1986-92 (Depute Leader, 1978-86); former Director, Scottish Exhibition and Conference Centre; former Member: Scottish Enterprise Board, East Kilbride Development Corporation, Scottish Development Agency, Clyde Port Authority; former Vice-Chairman, Planning Exchange; former UK Vice-President, European Committee of Regions. Recreations: music; reading; local government. Address: (b.) Civic Centre, Motherwell ML1 1TW.

Gray, David, DipArch (Aberdeen), RIBA, FRIAS, DipTP (Strath). Director of Architectural and Related Services, Strathclyde Regional Council, 1991-95; b. 2.10.37, Aberdeen; m., Margaret Ross Allen Gordon; 1 s.; 2 d. Educ. Robert Gordon's College; Scott Sutherland School of Architecture; Strathclyde University. Apprentice architect/architect, Aberdeen, 1956-62; architect, Lanark County Council, 1962-66; architect/planner, East Kilbride Development Corporation, 1966-67; Group Leader/ Assistant County Architect, then Depute County Architect, Renfrew County Council, 1967-75; Strathclyde Regional Council: Area Architect (Renfrew Division), 1975-76, Depute Director (Renfrew/Dumbarton/Argyll), 1976-78, Depute Director (Glasgow Division), 1978-87, Senior Depute Director, 1987-91. Past President, Association of Chief Architects of Scottish Local Authorities; Chairman, Investigations Committee, Royal Incorporation of Architects in Scotland. Recreations: sport; theatre; gardening. Address: (h.) 73A Broomfield Avenue, Newton Mearns, Glasgow G77 5JR; T.-0141-639 4366.

Gray, Ethel Marian, CBE, JP, MA, LLD, DUniv, FEIS. Patron, LEAD (Scotland), since 1997 (Board Member, and Chairman, Advisory Committee, 1987-95); Patron and Board Member, LEAD Telematics, since 1995; b. 19.4.23, Glasgow; m., George Deans Gray (deceased). Educ. Hutchesons' Girls Grammar School; Paisley Grammar School; Glasgow University. Teacher of English, 1946-52; Lecturer in English and Drama, Jordanhill College, 1952-63; Founding Principal, Craigie College of Education, Ayr, 1963-75; Director, Scottish Adult Literacy Agency, 1976-79; Chairman, National Book League Scotland, 1977-81; Convener, Adult Access to Education, Scottish Institute of Adult and Continuing Education, 1988-89 (President of Institute, 1984-87); Vice-Chairman, Board of Governors, The Queen's College, Glasgow, 1980-88; Chairman, Education Project for Older People, Age Concern Scotland, 1982-85; Member of Court, Chairman of Staffing Committee and Joint Faculty Staff Review Board, Heriot-Watt University, 1979-84; Adviser in Adult Education, IBA, 1983-88; Member: Scottish Tertiary Education Advisory Council, 1984-87, Scottish Advisory Committee, British Council, 1968-89, STV Education Advisory Committee, 1981-92, Scottish Community Education Council, 1979-85 (Chairman, Communications and Technology Group and Chairman, Management Committee, Micro-Electronics Project), Crawford Commission on Radio and Television Coverage, 1973-75, Committee of Enquiry on the Police, 1977-79, Consultative Committee on the Curriculum, 1965-71. Recreations: reading; travelling; theatre. Address: (h.) Flat 5, Varrich House, 7 Church Hill, Edinburgh EH10 4BG; T.-0131-447 5403.

Gray, George Bovill Rennie, OBE. Farmer; Chairman, G.B.R. Gray Ltd.; Trustee, Scottish Society for Crop Research, Invergowrie; a Director, Cruden Foundation; b. 5.3.20, Edinburgh; m., Anne Constance Dale; 4 s.; 2 d. Educ. Clayesmore, Dorset; Edinburgh and East of Scotland College of Agriculture. A Director, West Cumberland

Farmers, 1955-85; Member, Moredun Foundation, 1958-97; Member, Pig Industry Development Authority, 1958-68; Chairman, Oxford Farming Conference, 1972; Member, Agricultural and Veterinary Sub-Committee, UGC, 1972-82; Lothian Regional Councilor, 1974-82. Address: Smeaton-Hepburn, East Linton EH40 3DT; T.-01620 860275.

Gray of Contin, Lord (Hamish Gray), PC, DL. Business and Parliamentary Consultant, since 1986; b. 28.6.27, Inverness; m., Judith W. Brydon; 2 s.; 1 d. Educ. Inverness Royal Academy. Queen's Own Cameron Highlanders, 1945-48; Director, family and other private companies, 1949-70; MP, Ross and Cromarty, 1970-83; Government Whip, 1971-74; Opposition Spokesman on Energy, 1975-79; Minister of State for Energy, 1979-83; Minister of State for Scotland, 1983-86; Spokesman for Government in Lords for Scotland, Employment and Energy, 1983-86. Non-Executive Director, Dove Energy Ltd.; Non-Executive Chairman, Union Advertising Agency Ltd.; Non-Executive Director, Allied Deals Capital Ltd.; Vice President, Neighbourhood Energy Action (President, Energy Action Scotland), Scottish Association of Youth Clubs; Lord Lieutenant, Invernessshire, since 1996. Recreations: golf; cricket; hill-walking; reading. Address: (h.) Achneim House, Flichity, Invernessshire IV2 6XE.

Gray, James Allan, MB, ChB, FRCPEdin. Principal Medical Officer, Scottish Widows' Fund, Edinburgh, 1990-97; President, British Society for the Study of Infection, 1989-91; b. 24.3.35, Bristol; m., Jennifer Margaret Newton Hunter; 1 s. (deceased); 2 d. Educ. St. Paul's School, London; Edinburgh University. House Surgeon and Physician posts, Edinburgh and Middlesbrough; Short Service Commission, RAF Medical Branch, 1960-63; Senior House Officer, Research Fellow and Registrar posts, Edinburgh, 1965-67; Registrar, Bristol Royal Infirmary, 1967-68; Senior Registrar, Royal Free Hospital (Department of Infectious Diseases), London, 1968-69; Consultant in Communicable Diseases, City Hospital, Edinburgh, 1969-95; Assistant Director of Studies (Medicine), Edinburgh Post-Graduate Board, 1976-84; Honorary Senior Lecturer, Department of Medicine, Edinburgh University, 1992-95; Fellow, Royal Medical Society (Senior President, 1958-59); Founder Editor, Res Medica, 1957-58; Assistant Editor, Journal of Infection, 1979-86. Publications: Antibacterial Drugs Today (Co-author), 1983; Infectious Diseases (Co-author), 1984, 1992, new edition 1998. Recreations: hill-walking; pottery collecting; photography. Address: (h.) St. Andrews Cottage, 15 Lauder Road, Edinburgh EH9 2EN; T.-0131-667 4124.

Gray, Professor James Robertson, OBE, BSc, FRSGS, DipActMaths, FFA, FIMA, CMath, FSS. Professor and Head, Department of Actuarial Mathematics and Statistics, Heriot-Watt University, 1971-89 (now Emeritus); b. 21.2.26, Dundee; m., Catherine McAulay Towner. Educ. High School of Dundee; Edinburgh University. Actuarial Trainee, Scottish Life Assurance Company, 1947-49; St. Andrews University: Lecturer in Mathematics, 1949-50, Lecturer in Statistics, 1950-62, Senior Lecturer in Statistics (also Head of Department), 1962-71; Heriot-Watt University: established first Department of Actuarial Science in UK; Dean, Faculty of Science, 1978-81; Council Member, Faculty of Actuaries, 1969-87 (Vice President, 1983-87); Vice-Chairman, Scottish Examination Board, 1984-90 (Convener of Examinations Committee, 1982-90); former Member, Council, Royal Scottish Geographical Society and former Convener, Lecture Committee; former Vice-Chairman, Scottish Universities Council on Entrance; Past Chairman: Scottish Branch, Institute of Mathematics and Its Applications, Edinburgh Branch, Royal Statistical Society. Recreations: golf; hill-walking; bridge; music; Probus. Address: (h.) Green Gables, 9 Cammo Gardens, Edinburgh EH4 8EJ; T.-0131-339 3330.

Gray, John William Reid, MA, LLB, Advocate; b. 24.12.26, Aberdeen. Educ. Aberdeen Grammar School; Aberdeen University. Resident Magistrate, Uganda, 1954-62; Temporary Procurator-Fiscal Depute, Glasgow, 1962-63; Lecturer in Private Law, Queen's College, Dundee, then Dundee University, 1964-84; Warden, Airlie Hall, 1966-75; Member of Senate, 1971-75. Fellow, Saltzburg Seminar, 1964. Publications: articles in legal journals; The Administration of Justice Act. 1982. Address: (h.) Rhynuie, 41 Golf Road, Ballater, Aberdeenshire AB35 5RS. T.-013397 55656.

Gray, Michael Maxwell, OBE, DL. Senior Vice President, Global Development, Sykes Europe Ltd.; b. 5.5.47, Galashiels; m., Trish; 2 s. Educ. Galashiels Academy. Joined McQueen as management trainee, 1964; management buy-out, 1976; acquired by Sykes, 1997; Board Member, Scottish Enterprise; Director, Caledonian Foundation. Recreations: rugby; cricket; golf; reading. Address: (b.) Sykes Europe Ltd., Nether Road, Galashiels TD1 3HE; T.-01896 754866.

Gray, Muriel, BA (Hons). Broadcaster; Joint Managing Director, Ideal World Productions; b. Glasgow. Educ. Glasgow School of Art. Worked as an illustrator; then as a designer with National Museum of Antiquities; was member of rock band, The Family Von Trapp; had own show with Radio Forth; was frequent presenter on Radio 1; co-presented The Tube, Channel 4; had own arts programme, The Works, Tyne Tees; own music programme, Studio 1, Border TV; presented Casebook Scotland, BBC Scotland; Frocks on the Box, Thames TV; Acropolis Now, ITV; presented The Media Show, Channel 4; Co-Producer and Presenter, Walkie Talkie, Channel 4; first woman Rector, Edinburgh University; Producer/Presenter/Director, The Munro Show, Scottish TV; Producer/Presenter, Art is Dead...Long Live TV!, Channel Four; The Golden Cagoule, BBC; Ride On. Publications: The First Fifty; The Trickster (novel); Furnace (novel). Recreation: being in the Scottish Highlands — gets grumpy and miserable if can't be up a mountain every few weeks. Address: (b.) St. Georges Studios, 93-97 St. Georges Road, Glasgow G3 6JA.

Gray, Professor Peter Michael David, MA, DPhil, FBCS. Professor, Department of Computing Science, Aberdeen University, since 1989; b. 11.2.40, Abingdon; m., Doreen F. Ross; 1 s.; 1 d. Educ. Abingdon School; Queens' College, Cambridge; Jesus College, Oxford. Systems Analyst, Plessey Co., Poole, 1966-68; Research Fellow, Computer Research Group, Aberdeen University, 1968-72; Lecturer in Computing Science, Aberdeen University, 1972-84; Visiting Associate Professor, University of Western Ontario, 1985; Senior Lecturer, 1985-89. Reader, Church of Scotland. Publication: Logic, Algebra and Databases. Recreation: croquet. Address: (b.) Department of Computing Science, King's College, Aberdeen, AB24 3UE; T.-01224 272292.

Gray, Professor Robert Hugh, BSc (Econ), MA (Econ), FCA, FCCA, FRSA. Mathew Professor of Accounting and Information Systems, Dundee University, since 1990; b. 1.4.52, Manchester; 2 s. Educ. De La Salle College, Salford; Hull University; Manchester University. Qualified as accountant with KPMG Peat Marwick, 1976; Lecturer, Lancashire Polytechnic, UCNW Bangor, University of East Anglia; Editor, Social and Environmental Accounting; Director, Centre for Social and Environmental Accounting Research. Publications: over 100 articles; various books including Accounting for the Environment; The Greening of Accountancy; Accounting and Accountability. Recreations: golf; sailing; rock music. Address: (b.) Department of Accountancy and Business Finance, Dundee University, Dundee DD1 4HN; T.-01382 344789.

Gray, Sir William (Stevenson), Kt (1974), JP, BL, DL, HonLLD (Strathclyde), HonLLD (Glasgow), FRSA. Solicitor and Notary Public, since 1958; b. 3.5.28, Glasgow; m., Mary Rodger; 1 s.; 1 d. Educ. Hillhead High School, Glasgow; Glasgow University. Chairman: Scottish Special Housing Association, 1966-72, Clyde Tourist Association, 1972-75, Scotland West Industrial Promotion Group, 1972-75, WPHT Scotland Ltd. (formerly World of Property Housing Trust Scottish Housing Association Ltd.), 1974-98, Irvine New Town Development Corporation, 1974-76, Scottish Development Agency, 1975-79, The Oil Club, since 1975, Research Trust for Institute of Neurological Sciences, 1978-94, Glasgow Independent Hospital Ltd., 1982-89, Webtec Industrial Technology Ltd., 1984-91, Barrell Selection Ltd., since 1987, Norcity Homes PLC, 1988-95, Gap Housing Association Ltd., 1988-97, Gap Housing Association (Ownership) Ltd., 1988-98, Clan Homes plc, since 1988, Manchester Village Homes plc, 1989-97, Norhomes plc, 1989-97, Norcity II Plc, 1989-96, Paragon Group, since 1990, Home Partners Plus Plc, 1991-95, Paragon Protected Growth, since 1993, Norcity III and IV plc, since 1993, Clan FM Ltd., since 1997. Member: Lower Clyde Water Board, 1971-72, National Trust for Scotland, 1971-72, Scottish Opera Board, 1971-72, Executive, Scottish Council (Development and Industry), 1971-75, Convention of Royal Burghs, 1971-75, Clyde Port Authority, 1972-75, Scottish National Orchestra Society, 1972-75, Advisory Council for Energy Conservation, 1974-84, Scottish Economic Council, 1975-83, Central Advisory Committee on JPs, 1975-97, Glasgow Advisory Committee on JPs, 1975-97, Third Eye Centre, 1984-91 (Chairman, 1975-84), Hodgson Martin Ltd. Advisory Board, 1988-94, Dermalase Ltd., 1989-91; Vice President: Charles Rennie Mackintosh Society, since 1974, Glasgow Citizens' Theatre, since 1975 (Member, Board of Directors, 1970-75), Strathclyde Theatre Group, 1975-86, Scottish Association for Care and Resettlement of Offenders, 1982-86 (Chairman, 1975-82); Governor, Glasgow School of Art, 1961-75; Patron: Scottish Youth Theatre, 1978-86, Scottish Pakistani Society, since 1984; Member: Court, Glasgow University, 1972-75, Council, Strathclyde University Business School, 1978-88, Glasgow Corporation, 1958-75 (Chairman, Property Management Committee, 1964-67); Treasurer, City of Glasgow, 1971-72; Lord Provost and Lord Lieutenant of the City of Glasgow, 1972-75. Recreations: sailing; theatre. Address: (b.) 13 Royal Terrace, Glasgow G3 7NY; T.-0141-332 8877.

Green, Geoffrey, MA, PhD. Proprietor and Managing Director, T. & T. Clark Ltd., Professional and Academic Publishers, since 1991; b. 22.8.47, Bradford; m., Ellen Hughes; 1 s.; 1 d. Educ. Bootham School, York; University of Edinburgh. Director, T. & T. Clark Ltd., 1975 (Managing Director, 1990). Address: (b.) 59 George Street, Edinburgh EH2 2LQ; T.-0131-225 4703.

Green, Kenneth Malcolm, BSc, MIChemE, CEng. Group Chief Executive, Meconic PLC, since 1997; Managing Director, Macfarlan Smith Ltd., since 1997; b. 28.10.44, Chesterfield; m., Sheila; 1 s. Educ. Henry Cavendish School, Derby; University of Salford. Davy Power Gas, 1967-69; Laporte PLC, 1969-84; SCM Chemicals Ltd., 1984-88; Laporte PLC, 1988-96. Recreations: ballet; opera; gardening. Address: 10 Wheatfield Road, Edinburgh EH11 2QA; T.-0131-313 1416.

Green, Malcolm Robert, MA, DPhil. Member, City of Glasgow Council (Convener, Education Committee; Member: Arts and Culture Committee, Policy and Resources Committee, Roads and Transportation Committee); Lecturer in Roman History, Glasgow University, 1967-98; b. 4.1.43, Leicester; m., Mary Margaret Pratley; 1 s.; 2 d. Educ. Wyggeston Grammar School, Leicester; Magdalen College, Oxford. Formerly Member, Strathclyde Regional Council: Chairman, Environment Committee; Chairman, Education Committee, 1982-90; Chairman, Education Committee, Convention of Scottish Local Authorities, 1978-90. Address: (b.) City Chambers, George Square, Glasgow G2 1DU.

Green, Professor Roger Philip Hywel, MA, BLitt. Professor of Humanity (Latin), since 1995, and Head, Department of Classics, since 1997, University of Glasgow; b. 14.6.43, High Wycombe; m., Anne Mary Perry; 1 s.; 1 d. Educ. Royal Grammar School, High Wycombe; Balliol College, University of Oxford. University of St. Andrews: Assistant Lecturer, 1967-70, Lecturer, 1970-92, Senior Lecturer, 1992-94, Reader, 1994-95. Former Secretary, International Association of Neo-Latin Studies. Publications include: The Works of Ausonius, 1991; Augustine on Christian Teaching, 1997. Recreations: walking; cycling; rail travel; birdwatching; gardening; music; architecture. Address: (b.) Department of Classics, University of Glasgow, Glasgow G12 8QQ; T.-0141-330 4276.

Greene, John Gerald, MA, PhD, FBPsS. Registrar, Board of Examiners in Clinical Psychology, British Psychological Society; Clinical Lecturer, Glasgow University; b. 10.3.38, Glasgow; m., Dr. Elisabeth Rose Hamil; 2 s.; 2 d. Educ. St. Aloysius College, Glasgow; Glasgow University. Clinical Tutor, Glasgow University Master of Applied Science degree in Clinical Psychology, 1976-95; Chairman, National (Scotland) Scientific Consultative Committee on Clinical Psychological Services, 1985-87; Secretary and Treasurer, Scottish Branch Committee, Division of Clinical Psychology, 1977-81. Publications: The Social and Psychological Origins of the Climacteric Syndrome, 1984; Clinical Psychology in the Scottish Health Service (Co-author), 1984. Recreations: music; tennis; skiing. Address: (b.) The Medical Centre, 1 High Street, Neilston, Glasgow G78 3HJ.

Greene, John Henderson, MA, LLB. Former Partner, MacRoberts, Solicitors, Glasgow, Edinburgh and London; b. 2.6.32, Kilmarnock; m., Catriona McGillivray Scott; 1 s. Educ. Merchiston Castle School, Edinburgh; Edinburgh University. Assistant: Joseph Kirkland & Son, Solicitors, Saltcoats, 1958-60, MacRoberts, Solicitors, 1960 (appointed Partner, 1961); Law Society of Scotland: former Vice-Convener, Company Law Committee, former Member, Bankruptcy and Liquidation Committee; former Council Member, Royal Faculty of Procurators, Glasgow; founder Chairman, Troon Round Table, 1964; Captain, Royal Troon Golf Club, 1989-90; Elder, Portland Church, Troon; President, Glasgow Ayrshire Society, 1985-86, 1993-94, 1998-99; Vice-Chairman, Ayrshire and Arran Health Board. Publication: Law and Practice of Receivership in Scotland (Co-Author). Recreations: golf; gardening. Address: (h.) Silvertrees, 7 Lady Margaret Drive, Troon KA10 7AL; T.-Troon 312482.

Greening, Andrew Peter, BSc, MBChB, FRCPE. Consultant Physician, Western General Hospital, Edinburgh, since 1984; part-time Senior Lecturer, University of Edinburgh, since 1984; b. 10.10.48, London; m., Rosemary Jean Renwick; 2 s. Educ. George Watson's College, Edinburgh; University of Edinburgh. House Officer and Senior House Officer posts, Edinburgh, 1973-75; Registrar, Senior Registrar, MRC Training Fellow posts, St. Bartholomew's and Hammersmith Hospitals and Royal Postgraduate Medical School, London, 1975-82. Director, Scottish Adult Cystic Fibrosis Service, Western General Hospital, Edinburgh, since 1992; Associate Editor, Thorax and Respiratory Medicine, since 1990; Member, Grants Committees: Chest, Heart and Stroke Association, British Lung Foundation (Chair), Cystic Fibrosis Trust. International Lecturer on asthma and cystic fibrosis; Member, Scottish, British, European and American Thoracic Societies. Address: (b.) Western General Hospital, Edinburgh EH4 2XU.

Greenman, Professor Jonathan Vaughan, BA, MA, PhD. Professor of Mathematics and Its Applications, Stirling University, since 1990; b. 3.3.39, Cardiff; m., Barbara Phyllis; 2 s. Educ. Kingston Grammar School; Cambridge University. Harkness Scholar, University of California, Berkeley; Department of Physics, MIT; Stanford Research Institute, California; Department of Mathematics, Essex University; Tutor, Open University; Senior Analyst, Corporate Planning, British Petroleum plc; Industry Analyst, Centre for Global Energy Studies. Recreations: cinema; walking; travel. Address: (b.) Department of Mathematics, Stirling University, Stirling, FK9 4LA; T.-01786 467460.

Greenshields, David, MA, DipEd. Headteacher, Uddingston Grammar School, since 1997; b. 24.7.49, Bellshill; 2 d. Educ. Biggar High School; University of Edinburgh; Moray House College. History Teacher, Lanark Grammar, 1971; Assistant Principal Teacher, Social Subjects, Auchmuty High, Fife, 1973; Assistant Principal Teacher, Guidance, Lanark Grammar, 1974; various posts, Uddingston Grammar School, since 1978. Recreation: supporter of Heart of Midlothian F.C. Address: (b.) Uddingston Grammar School, Station Road, Uddingston G71 7BS; T.-01698 327400.

Greensted, Professor Christopher Stanford, BSc, MSc. Director, Strathclyde Graduate Business School, since 1986; Chair, UK Association of Business Schools, 1996-98; Chair, EQUAL (European Business Schools Association), 1997-2000; b. 10.9.41, Leeds; m., Candace Helen; 1 s.; 1 d.; 1 s. by pr. m. Educ. Cranbrook School, Kent; Sir John Cass College, London; Strathclyde University. Chemist in pharmaceuticals, 1960-65; operational research/consultancy in food industry, 1966-68; appointed Lecturer in OR, Strathclyde, 1969, then in Accounting and Finance, 1974; was part-time Director of yacht chandlery company, eight years. RNR officer, eight years. Publications: three books; several articles on business statistics and management development. Recreations: sailing; golf; theatre and concerts. Address: (h.) 18 Carrick Drive, Glasgow, G32 0RW; T.-0141-778 9120.

Greer, Professor Ian Andrew, MB, ChB, MD (Glas), MRCP(UK), FRCP(Glas), MFFP, MRCOG, MAE. Muirhead Professor and Head, Department of Obstetrics and Gynaecology, Glasgow University, since 1991; Honorary Consultant Obstetrician and Gynaecologist, Glasgow Royal Infirmary and Glasgow Royal Maternity Hospital, since 1991; b. 16.4.58, Glasgow. Educ. Allan Glen's School, Glasgow; Glasgow University. Registrar in General Medicine, Glasgow Royal Infirmary; Registrar in Obstetrics and Gynaecology, Glasgow Royal Maternity Hospital and Glasgow Royal Infirmary; Lecturer in Obstetrics and Gynaecology, Edinburgh University; Clinical Research Scientist/Consultant Obstetrician and Gynaecologist, MRC Reproductive Biology Unit, Edinburgh. MRCOG Gold Medal; Blair-Bell Lectureship, Royal College of Obstetricians and Gynaecologists 1989; Travelling Fellowship, RCOG, 1989; Watson Prize Lecture, Royal College of Physicians and Surgeons of Glasgow, 1990. Address: (b.) Department of Obstetrics and Gynaecology, Glasgow University, Glasgow Royal Infirmary, Glasgow G31 2ER; T.-0141-552 8316.

Gregory, David Richard Monro, MBE, LLB. Director, Margaret Blackwood Housing Association, since 1978; Director, Scottish Trust for the Physically Disabled, since 1978; b. 31.8.39, Bournemouth; m., Jill Alison; 1 s.; 2 d. Educ. Marlborough College; University of Aberdeen. Royal Navy, 1957-72 (Fighter Pilot, invalided following flying accident); legal apprenticeship/Solicitor, Burnett and Reid, Aberdeen and W. & J. Burness, Edinburgh, 1975-78. Member, Boards of Management: Disability Scotland, Lothian Centre for Integrated Living, Disabled Persons Housing Services (Lothian), Ownership Options (Scotland). Recreations: sea canoeing; photography. Address: (h.) 32 Midmar Gardens, Edinburgh EH10 6DZ; T.-(b.) 0131-317 7227.

Greig, Rev. Alan, BSc, BD. Minister, Kintore Parish Church, since 1992; b. 19.11.51, Helensburgh; m., Ruth D. Evans; 2 s. Educ. Coatbridge High School; University of Strathclyde; University of Edinburgh. Probationer Minister, Northfield Parish, Aberdeen, 1976-77; Minister, Hurlford Reid Memorial Church, Ayrshire, 1977-83; Church of Scotland Missionary working with United Church of Zambia, 1983-92. Recreations: swimming; cycling; walking. Address: 6 Forest Road, Kintore, Inverurie AB51 0XG; T.-01467 632219.

Greig, Christopher George, BSc, PhD. Non-Executive Chairman: William Grant & Sons Ltd., PPL Therapeutics plc; Non-Executive Director, Robert Wiseman Dairies plc; m., Anne; 1 s.; 2 d. Educ. Harris Academy; St. Andrews University; London University. Invergordon Distillers Group PLC, 1966-94 (Managing Director, 1983-94); Director (Non-Executive): Simpsons Malt Ltd., Belhaven Brewery Group plc, Edinburgh Green Belt Trust, Scottish Quality Cereals, Heriot Watt Trading, Canongate Technology Ltd., The Airborne Initiative (Scotland) Ltd.; Director: Scotch Whisky Association, C.G. (Farms) Ltd., Mosszone Ltd; Trustee, Scottish Civic Trust. Address: (h.) North Mains, Ormiston, East Lothian EH35 5NG; T.-01875 613721.

Greig, G. Andrew, MA. Author; b. 23.9.51, Bannockburn. Educ. Waid Academy, Anstruther; Edinburgh University. Full-time writer, since 1979; Writer-in-Residence, Glasgow University, 1979-81; Scottish-Canadian Exchange Fellow, 1981-82; Writer-in-Residence, Edinburgh University, 1993-94; climbed on Himalayan expeditions. Publications: six volumes of poetry including Men on Ice, Surviving Passages, The Order of the Day, Western Swing; two mountaineering books; novels: Electric Brae, Return of John Macnab; When They Lay Bare. Recreations: climbing; fishing; music. Address: Stirling's Dairy, 2 Brewery Close, South Queensferry; T.-0131-331 2535.

Grier, Arnold Macfarlane, MB, ChB, FRCSEdin. Consultant Ear, Nose and Throat Surgeon, Highland Health Board, since 1962; National Vice-President, Scottish Association for the Deaf; b. 5.9.21, Musselburgh; m., Elisabeth J. Kluten; 2 s.; 1 d. Educ. Musselburgh Grammar School; Edinburgh University. Recreations: gardening; aviculture; painting. Address: (h.) Elmbank, 68 Culduthel Road, Inverness; T.-Inverness 234682.

Grier, Scott, OBE, MA, CA, MCIT. Chairman: Loganair Limited, Scottish Tanning Industries Limited; b. 7.3.41, Kilmacolm; m., Frieda Gardiner; 2 s. Educ. Greenock High School; Glasgow University. Apprenticed, Grahams Rintoul & Co., 1962-66; Accountant, Ardrossan Harbour Company Ltd./Clydeport, from 1967; various posts, Loganair, since 1976; Director: Glasgow Chamber of Commerce, since 1990, Caledonian MacBrayne Limited, since 1996; Chairman: Bridge of Weir Leather Co. Ltd., Andrew Muirhead & Son Ltd., W. J. & W. Lang Ltd., NCT Leather Ltd., since 1997, Garston Leather Ltd., since 1998; Governor, Scottish Sports Aid Foundation, since 1993; Member, Scottish Tourist Board, 1992-98; Recreations: golf; philately. Address: (h.) Lagavulin, 15 Corsehill Drive, West Kilbride, KA23 9HU; T.-01294 823138.

Grieve, Professor Andrew Robert, DDS, BDS, FDS RCSEd. Professor of Conservative Dentistry, since 1980, Dean of Dentistry, 1993-97, Dundee University; Consultant in Restorative Dentistry, since 1980; b. 23.5.39, Stirling; m., Frances M. Ritchie; 2 d. Educ. Perth Academy; St. Andrews University. Junior hospital appointments and general dental practice, 1961-63; Lecturer in Operative Dental Surgery and Dental Therapeutics, St. Andrews

University, 1963-65; Lecturer in Conservative Dentistry, Birmingham University, 1965; appointed Senior Lecturer and Consultant in Restorative Dentistry, Birmingham Area Health Authority (Teaching), 1975. Member, Dental Council, Royal College of Surgeons of Edinburgh, 1983-88; President: British Society for Restorative Dentistry, 1986-87, Royal Odonto-Chirurgical Society of Scotland, 1994-95 (Council Member, 1985-88); Chairman: Tayside Area Dental Advisory Committee, 1987-90, Legislation Committee, General Dental Council, since 1994 (Member, since 1989). Recreations: hill-walking; travel in France and study of French language and culture. Address: (b.) The Dental School, The University, Dundee DD1 4HN; T.-01382 26041.

Grieve, John. Actor; b. 14.6.24, Glasgow. Trained, Royal Scottish Academy of Music and Drama (James Bridie Gold Medallist), followed by five full seasons, Citizens' Theatre, Glasgow; also appeared in Guthrie's production of The Anatomist, Citizens', 1968; numerous other performances on the Scottish stage, including leading roles in The Bevellers, The Flouers o' Edinburgh, The Good Soldier Schweik, Twelfth Night; television work includes The Vital Spark, Oh Brother, Doctor at Sea, New Year shows; numerous appearances in pantomime; appeared with Scottish Theatre Company in Waiting for Godot and The Thrie Estaites.

Grieve, Professor Robert, MA, PhD, CPsych, FBPsS. Professor of Psychology, Edinburgh University, since 1987; b. 2.8.44, Bathgate; m., Anne; 1 s.; 2 d. Educ. Edinburgh University. Lecturer in Psychology, St. Andrews University; Senior Lecturer in Psychology, then Associate Professor of Psychology, University of Western Australia. Address: (b.) Department of Psychology, Edinburgh University, 7 George Square, Edinburgh EH8 9JZ; T.-0131-650 3441.

Grieve, Hon. Lord (William Robertson Grieve), VRD (1958), QC (Scot), MA, LLB. Senator of the College of Justice in Scotland, 1972-88; Chairman, Board of Governors, St. Columba's Hospice, since 1983; b. 21.10.17, Glasgow; m., Lorna St. John Benn (deceased); 1 s.; 1 d. Educ. Glasgow Academy; Sedbergh School; Glasgow University. Served with Royal Navy as an RNVR officer, 1939-45; Advocate, Scots Bar, 1947; QC, 1957; Sheriff Principal, Renfrew and Argyll, 1964-72; Judge of Appeal, Jersey and Guernsey, 1971-72; Procurator, Church of Scotland, 1968-72; Chairman, Governors, Fettes Trust, 1978-86. President, Glasgow University Union, 1938. Recreations: golf; painting. Address: (h.) 20 Belgrave Crescent, Edinburgh EH4 3AJ; T.-0131-332 7500.

Griffith, Richard Jeremy, MA (Cantab), DipArch (Cantab), RIAS. Director, Edinburgh New Town Conservation Committee, since 1994; b. 18.3.47, London. Educ. Malvern Boys College; St. John's College, Cambridge. Choral Scholar, 1966-69; RIBA, 1974; International Centre for Conservation and Restoration of Monuments, 1977; Listed Buildings Case Officer, Greater London Council's Historic Buildings Division, 1979-86; Senior Statutory Officer, English Heritage, London Region, 1986-94. Member, Council, Cockburn Association. Recreations: travel; music; skiing. Address: (b.) 13a Dundas Street, Edinburgh EH3 6QG; T.-0131-557 5222.

Griffiths, Nigel. Minister for Competition and Consumer Affairs, 1997-98; MP (Labour), Edinburgh South, since 1987; Opposition Spokesman on Consumer Affairs, 1989-97; Vice President, Institute of Trading Standards Administration, since 1994; b. 20.5.55; m., Sally McLaughlin. Educ. Hawick High School; Edinburgh University; Moray House College of Education. Secretary, Lothian Devolution Campaign, 1978; Rights Adviser, Mental Handicap Pressure Group, 1979-87; City of Edinburgh District Councillor, 1980-87 (Chairperson, Housing Committee); Member: Edinburgh Festival Council, 1984-87, Edinburgh Health Council, 1982-87; Executive Member, Edinburgh Council of Social Service, 1984-87; Member, Wester Hailes School Council, 1981; Executive Member, Scottish Constitutional Convention (Chair, Finance Committee). Recreations: travel; live entertainment; badminton; hill-walking; rock-climbing; architecture; reading; politics. Address: (h.) 30 McLaren Road, Edinburgh EH9 2BN; T.-0131-667 1947.

Griffiths, Professor Peter Denham, CBE, BSc, MD, LRCP, MRCS, FRCPath, FRCP(Edin), FIMgt, FRSA. Emeritus Professor of Biochemical Medicine, Dundee University (Vice-Principal, 1979-85, Dean of Medicine and Dentistry, 1985-89); Director and Trustee, Scottish Hospitals Endowment Research Trust, 1994-98; b. 16.6.27, Southampton; m., Joy Burgess; 3 s.; 1 d. Educ. King Edward VI School, Southampton; Guy's Hospital, London University. House appointments, Guy's Hospital, 1956-57; Junior Lecturer in Physiology, Guy's Hospital, 1957-58; Registrar and Senior Registrar, Guy's and Lewisham Hospitals, 1958-64; Consultant Pathologist, Harlow Hospitals Group, 1964-66; Senior Lecturer in Clinical Chemistry/Honorary Consultant, St. Andrews University, then Dundee University, 1966-68. Member, General Medical Council, 1986-93; President, 1987-89, and sometime Chairman of Council, Association of Clinical Biochemists; Consultant, Tayside Health Board, 1986-89; former Director, Dundee Repertory Theatre. Recreations: music; domestic activities. Address: (h.) 52 Albany Road, West Ferry, Dundee DD5 1NW; T.-01382 776772.

Grimble, Professor Michael John, BSc, MSc, PhD, DSc, BA, CEng, FIEE, FInstMC, FIMA, FIEEE. Professor of Industrial Systems, University of Strathclyde, since 1981; Technical Director, ISC, since 1988; b. 30.10.43, Grimsby; m., Wendy; 1 s.; 1 d. Educ. Armstrong Street School, Grimsby; University of Birmingham. Design Engineer, GEC Electrical Projects, and seconded, Imperial College of Science and Technology, 1971-74; Senior Design Engineer, GEC Electrical Projects Limited, 1974-75; Senior Lecturer then Reader in Control Systems, Sheffield City Polytechnic, 1975-81. Awarded IEE Heaviside Premium, 1978, Coopers Hill War Memorial Prize Medal, 1979, Honeywell International Medal, 1991. Recreations: theatre; reading; family; travel and sightseeing; eating out. Address: (b.) University of Strathclyde, ICC, Graham Hills Building, 50 George Street, Glasgow G1 1QE; T.-0141-548 2378.

Grimmond, Iain William, BAcc (Hons), CA. Director of Finance, Erskine Hospital for Disabled Ex-Servicemen and Women, since 1981; b. 8.8.55, Girvan; m., Marjory Anne Gordon Chisholm; 1 s.; 2 d. Educ. Hutchesons' Boys Grammar School; Glasgow University. Trainee CA, Ernst & Whinney, Glasgow, 1976-79; Assistant Treasurer, Erskine Hospital, 1979-81. Elder, Giffnock South Parish Church. Recreations: golf; football; reading. Address: (h.) 9 Wemyss Avenue, Crookfur, Newton Mearns, Glasgow G77 6AR; T.-0141-639 4894.

Grimson, Dermot, FRSA. Director, Rural Forum, since 1987; Chairman, UK Rural Development Network; Member: National Rural Partnership, BBC Rural Advisory Committee, SCVO Policy Committee, Equal Opportunities Commission for Scotland Advisory Committee, Scottish Social Inclusion Network, Board of Rural Development Ltd., Investors in People Recognition Panel; b. 22.5.52, Glasgow. Educ. Kelvinside Academy; Glasgow School of Art. Planner, Renfrew District Council; Planner, Banff and Buchan District Council. Former Member of Banff and Buchan Health Council; Past Chairman, Buchan Countryside Group; former Secretary, Banff and Buchan Constituency Labour Party; Past Chairman, Perth Civic Trust. Address: (h.) 10 St. John's Place, Perth; T.-01738 630014.

Grinyer, Professor John Raymond, MSc, FCA. Professor of Accountancy and Business Finance, Dundee University, since 1976 and Deputy Principal, since 1997 (Head, Department of Accountancy and Business Finance, 1976-90, Dean, Faculty of Law, 1984-85 1991-1993); b. 3.3.35, London; m., Shirley Florence Marshall; 1 s.; 2 d. Educ. Central Park Secondary Modern School, London; London School of Economics. London Electricity Board, 1950-53; National Service, RAMC, 1953-55; Halifax Building Society, 1955-56; Martin Redhead & Co., Accountants, 1956-60; Hope Agar & Co., Chartered Accountants, 1960-62; Kemp Chatteris & Co., Chartered Accountants, 1962-63; Lecturer, Harlow Technical College, 1963-66; City of London Polytechnic, 1966-71; Cranfield School of Management, 1971-76; Chairman, British Accounting Association, 1980-81 and 1990, and Scottish Representative, 1984-93. Recreations: golf; dinghy sailing; Member, Royal Tay Yacht Club. Address: (b.) The University, Dundee DD1 4HN; T.-Dundee 344192 or 345560.

Grinyer, Professor Peter Hugh, MA (Oxon), PhD. Emeritus Professor, since 1993, and Professorial Fellow, St. Andrews University; b. 3.3.35, London; m., Sylvia Joyce Boraston; 2 s. Educ. Balliol College, Oxford; London School of Economics. Senior Managerial Trainee, Unilever Ltd., 1957-59; Personal Assistant to Managing Director, E.R. Holloway Ltd., 1959-61; Lecturer and Senior Lecturer, Hendon College of Technology, 1961-64; Lecturer, The City University, London, 1965-69; The City University Business School: Senior Lecturer and Co-ordinator of Research, 1969-72, Reader, 1972-74, Professor of Business Strategy, 1974-79; Esmee Fairbairn Professor of Economics (Finance and Investment), St. Andrews University, 1979-93; Chairman, Department of Economics, 1979-85; Vice-Principal, 1985-87 (Acting Principal, 1986); Chairman, Department of Management, 1987-89; Chairman: St. Andrews Management Institute, 1989-96, St. Andrews Strategic Management Ltd.; Member, Sub-Committee on Management and Business Studies, University Grants Committee, 1979-85; Consultant to NEDO on Sharpbenders Project, 1984-86; Visiting Professor, New York University; Non-Executive Director: Glenrothes Enterprise Trust, 1983-86, John Brown plc, 1984-86, Don Bros. Buist plc (now Don and Low (Holdings) Ltd.) 1985-91, Ellis and Goldstein plc, 1987-88; Chairman (non-executive), McIlroy Coates, 1991-95; Member, Scottish Legal Aid Board, since 1992; Erskine Fellow, University of Canterbury, New Zealand, 1994. Recreations: mountain walking; golf; listening to music. Address: (b.) University of St. Andrews, Department of Management, St Katherine's West, The Scores, St. Andrews KY16 9AL; T.-01334 462871.

Grossart, Sir Angus McFarlane McLeod, CBE, LLD, FRSE, DL, MA, CA. Advocate; Merchant Banker; Vice Chairman, Royal Bank of Scotland, since 1996; Chairman, Scottish Daily Record and Sunday Mail, since 1998; Director: Hewden Stuart plc, since 1988, Edinburgh US Tracker Trust, Edinburgh Fund Managers PLC, since 1983 (Deputy Chairman), Mirror Group PLC, since 1998, Noble Grossart Limited, since 1969 (Chairman), The Scottish Investment Trust PLC, since 1973 (Chairman); b. 6.4.37, Glasgow; m., Gay Kerr Dodd; 1 d. Educ. Glasgow Academy; Glasgow University. CA, 1962; Advocate, Scottish Bar, 1963-69; Managing Director, Noble Grossart Ltd., since 1969; Chairman of the Trustees, National Galleries of Scotland, 1988-97; former Scottish Editor, British Tax Encyclopaedia and British Tax Review. Recreations: golf; decorative arts. Address: (b.) 48 Queen Street, Edinburgh EH2 3NR; T.-0131-226 7011.

Grosset, Alan George, MA, LLB, WS, NP. Partner, Alex. Morison & Co., WS; b. 18.1.42, Edinburgh; 1 s.; 1 d. Educ. Royal High School, Edinburgh; Edinburgh University. Law Society of Scotland "Troubleshooter" from inception of scheme, until 1987; Council Member, W.S. Society; President, Scottish Lawn Tennis Association, 1983-84; Council Member, Lawn Tennis Association, 1980-89; first Chairman, Scottish Sports Association, 1984-90; Vice-Chairman, Scottish Sports Council, since 1994 (Member since 1984); Captain, Duddingston Golf Club, 1992-94; Founder Member, Scottish Branch, Society for Computers and Law; first Secretary, British Sports Forum, 1991-95; Vice Chairman, Confederation of British Sport. Recreations: golf; tennis; squash. Address: (b.) 68 Queen Street, Edinburgh; T.-0131-226 6541.

Grosz, David Peter, BA (Hons). Chairman, Ramblers' Association, since 1998 (Vice Chairman, 1995-98); b. 2.4.39, London. Educ. Wyggeston Boys' Grammar School, Leicester; Nottingham University; School of Education, Leicester University. School Teacher, Leicester, 1962-78, West Lothian, 1978-84. Member: RA National Executive Committee, since 1983, Board of Directors, Scottish Rights of Way Society, 1984-92, Council, National Trust for Scotland, 1989-94; Chairman: Friends of New Lanark, 1985-89, Ramblers' Association Scottish Council, 1985-96; Founding Member and Committee Member, Scottish Council for National Parks, 1991-95. Recreations: walking; reading; campaigning with passion for public access and countryside conservation. Address: (h.) 57 Harburn Avenue, Deans, Livingston EH54 8NH; T.-01506 410493.

Groves, C. Arthur, JP. Chairman: Borders Region Valuation Panel, 1991-94, Justices Committee, Ettrick and Lauderdale, 1984-94, General Inland Revenue Commissioners, since 1983; b. 28.11.24, London. Educ. Raine's Foundation, London. Selkirk Town Council, 1961-75 (Hon. Treasurer); former Selkirk County Councillor (Chairman, Finance Committee). Recreation: equestrian activities. Address: (h.) 24 Hillview Crescent, Selkirk TD7 4AZ; T.-01750 21126.

Grundy, John Douglas, BMus (Hons), LTCL. Director of Music, St. Mary's Music School, since 1996; Musical Director, Edinburgh Grand Opera, since 1995; Patron, Australian Intervarsity Choral Association, since 1988; b. 6.4.52, Eastwood, England; partner: Clare Powne. Educ. Annie Holgate Technical Grammar School; Edinburgh University. Teacher, Fettes College, 1976-82; Director of Music: Dollar Academy, 1982-84, Edinburgh Festival Productions Scottish Theatre Company, Sydney Philharmonia; Artistic Director, Australian Opera and Ballet Orchestra; Director, St. Andrew's Cathedral Festival, Sydney; Principal Teacher, University of St. Andrews. Recordings of Australian music: Sounds Australia. Recreations: cycling; sailing; woodwork. Address: (b.) St. Mary's Music School, Coates Hall, 25 Grosvenor Crescent, Edinburgh EH12 5EL; T.-0131-538 7766.

Guest, Andrew, MA, Director, Scottish Sculpture Trust, since 1990; b. 8.11.51, Edinburgh; m., Elizabeth Cuthbert; 1 s.; 1 d. Educ. Charterhouse School; University of St. Andrews; University of Edinburgh. Museum Assistant, Geffrye Museum, 1975-77; Interpretive Projects Officer, Montgomery Canal, 1980-83; Exhibitions Officer, Smith Art Gallery and Museum, Stirling, 1983-90. Publications: Platform for Partnership (Editor), 1990; The City is a Work of Art - Glasgow, 1994; The City is a Work of Art - Edinburgh, 1996. Address: (h.) 2 Coltbridge Terrace, Edinburgh EH12 6AE; T.-0131-337 1021.

Guest, Peter David. Chairman: Lineplan Ltd., Perth, since 1992, Powerplan (Scotland), Ltd., since 1994, Epilepsy Association of Scotland, since 1996; b. 25.10.39, Solihull; m., Kathleen Althea Ward; 1 s.; 3 d. Educ. King Edward's School, Birmingham; College of Advanced Technology, Birmingham. Sales Director, Bonar Long Ltd., Dundee, 1982; Vice-President, National Industri, Norway, 1985; Managing Director, E.B. Power Projects Ltd., 1985; Deputy Managing Director, Nitran, Dundee, 1989. Member, Court of Governors, Abertay University Dundee. Recreations:

fishing; shooting. Address: (h.) The Well, Kirkinch, by Meigle, Blairgowrie, Perthshire PH12 8SL; T.-01828 640790.

Guild, Ivor Reginald, CBE, FRSE, MA, LLB, WS; b. 2.4.24, Dundee. Educ. Cargilfield; Rugby; New College, Oxford; Edinburgh University. Director: Fulcrum Investment Trust, Scottish Oriental Smaller Companies Trust PLC; former Partner, Shepherd & Wedderburn, WS; former Procurator Fiscal to the Lyon Court. Recreations: golf; genealogy. Address: (b.) Saltire Court, 20 Castle Terrace, Edinburgh, EH1 2ET; T.-0131-225 8585.

Guild, Stuart Alexander, TD, BL, WS, NP. Writer to the Signet, since 1950; Senior Partner, Guild and Guild WS, 1958-89; b. 25.1.24, Edinburgh; m., Fiona Catherine MacCulloch; 1 s.; 2 d. Educ. Edinburgh Academy; George Watson's College, Edinburgh; Queen's University, Belfast; Edinburgh University. Royal Artillery, 1942-47; Territorial Army (RA), 1947-65; County Cadet Commandant, Lothian Bn., ACF, 1967-69 (Hon. Lt-Col.); Honorary Treasurer, 1976-91, Shooting Convener, 1969-94, and Vice Chairman, 1995-98, Army Cadet Force Association (Scotland), 1969-94; Member: Council, Army Cadet Force Association, 1976-91 (now Hon. Vice President), Royal Artillery Council of Scotland, 1982-84 and 1985-93; President, Lothian & Peebles Home Guard Rifle Association, 1980-91; Member, Lowland TAVRA, 1967-99; Vice-President, Lothian Smallbore Shooting Association, 1985-92; Governor, Melville College Trust, 1976-91 (now Hon. Governor); Chairman, Sandilands Memorial Trust, 1980-94; Assistant, The Company of Merchants of the City of Edinburgh, 1972-75; Vice-Convener, Mary Erskine School for Girls, 1973-75. Recreations: golf; target shooting; photography. Address: (h.) 7 Lockharton Gardens, Edinburgh EH14 1AU.

Gulliver, Stuart, BSc (Econ). Chief Executive, Glasgow Development Agency, since 1991; b. 10.1.42, Sheffield; m., Barbara McKewan; 3 s.; 1 d. Educ. Firth Park Grammar School; London School of Economics. Research Fellow in Economics, Leeds University; Senior Lecturer, Leeds Polytechnic; commercial development, Warrington New Town Development Corporation; Regional Director, Scottish Development Agency. Visiting Professor in Economic and Social Research, Glasgow University. Recreations: cricket; tennis; watching football; music, especially modern jazz; theatre. Address: (b.) Atrium Court, 50 Waterloo Street, Glasgow G2 6HQ; T.-0141-204 1111.

Gunn, Alexander MacLean, MA, BD. Minister, Aberfeldy with Amulree and Strathbraan with Dull and Weem, since 1986; b. 26.2.43, Inverness; m., Ruth T.S.; 1 s.; 1 d. Educ. Edinburgh Academy; Beauly; Dingwall Academy; Edinburgh University and New College. Parish Minister: Wick St. Andrews and Thrumster, 1967-73; Member, Caithness Education Committee, 1968-73; Parish Minister, Glasgow St. David's Knightswood, 1973-86; Convener: Church of Scotland Rural Working Group, 1988-90, General Assembly's Presbytery Development Committee, 1990-92, General Assembly's Mission and Evangelism Resource Committee, 1992-95; Interim Convener, Board of National Mission, 1996. Chairman, Breadalbane Academy School Board, 1989-92 and since 1996. Address: The Manse, Taybridge Terrace, Aberfeldy PH15 2BS; T.-01887 820656.

Gunn, Iain Gillies, MB, ChB, FRCS(Glas), FRCSEd. Consultant Surgeon, Dr. Gray's Hospital, Elgin, since 1986; b. 28.5.51, Glasgow; m., Norma MacMillan; 1 s.; 1 d. Educ. Hutchesons' Boys' Grammar School, Glasgow; Glasgow University. Senior Registrar, Glasgow Royal Infirmary, 1982-86. Recreations: classic cars; skiing; running. Address: Ach-na-Muilne, Sheriffmill, Elgin, Moray; T.-01343 547447.

Gurney, Professor Alison Marion, BSc, PhD, CBiol, FIBiol. W.C. Bowman Chair of Pharmacology, University of Strathclyde, since 1995; b. 30.7.57, Ayr. Educ. Prestwick Academy; Aberdeen University; University College London. Research Fellow, California Institute of Technology, USA, 1983-85; United Medical and Dental Schools, St. Thomas's Hospital, London: Lecturer in Pharmacology, 1985-91, Senior Lecturer in Pharmacology, 1991-95, Reader in Pharmacological Sciences, 1995. Sandoz Prize, British Pharmacological Society, 1991; Conference Science Medal, Royal Pharmaceutical Society of Great Britain, 1992; Susan Tucker Prize, St. Thomas's Health District, 1993. Address: Department of Physiology and Pharmacology, Institute for Biomedical Sciences, 27 Taylor Street, Glasgow G4 0NR; T.-0141-548 4119.

Guy, Professor John Alexander, MA, PhD, FRHistS. Professor of Modern History, since 1991, and Head, School of History and International Relations, 1992-94, St. Andrews University; Provost, 1994-97, and Vice-Principal, 1996-97, St. Leonard's College; b. 16.1.49, Australia; m., Rachel Hooper; 1 s.; 1 d. Educ. King Edward VII School, Lytham; Clare College, Cambridge. Research Fellow, Selwyn College, Cambridge, 1970-73; Assistant Keeper of Public Records, Public Record Office, London, 1973-78; Visiting Lecturer in British History, University of California, Berkeley, 1977; History Department, Bristol University, 1978-90; British Academy Marc Fitch Research Reader, 1987-89; John Hinkley (Visiting) Professor, Johns Hopkins University, Baltimore, 1990; Richard L. Turner Professor of Humanities, and Professor of History, University of Rochester, 1990-91. Publications: The Cardinal's Court; The Public Career of Sir Thomas More; Law and Social Change in British History (Co-Editor); The Court of Star Chamber and its Records to the Reign of Elizabeth I; Christopher St. German on Chancery and Statute; Reassessing the Henrician Age (Co-Author); The Complete Works of Thomas More, Vol. X (Co-Editor); Tudor England; The Tudors and Stuarts (Co-Author); The Reign of Elizabeth I; The Tudor Monarchy. Address: School of History, St. Andrews University, College Gate, St. Andrews KY16 9AJ.

Guy, Roger Robert, MSc, PhD, CEng, MICE. Director for Environment and Infrastructure, Dumfries and Galloway Council, since 1995; b. 8.8.47. Educ. Westminster City School; Imperial College, London University; Manchester University. Research Fellow, Edinburgh University, 1972; South West of Scotland Water Board, 1973; Dumfries County Council, 1974; Dumfries and Galloway Regional Council, 1975: Assistant Director (Transportation), 1987, Director Roads and Transportation, 1991. Henrici Medal, 1967; Unwin Medal, 1968. Recreation: outdoor pursuits. Address: (b.) Militia House, Council Offices, Dumfries DG1 2DD; T.-01387 260100.

Gwilt, George David, MA, FFA, FBCS. Director: European Assets Trust NV, since 1979, Scottish Mortgage & Trust plc, 1983-98, Hodgson Martin Ltd., since 1989, Edinburgh Festival Society Ltd., 1989-95; b. 11.11.27, Edinburgh; m., Ann Sylvester; 3 s. Educ. Sedbergh; St. John's College, Cambridge. Standard Life, 1949-88, latterly as Managing Director; President, Faculty of Actuaries, 1981-83; Trustee, South of Scotland TSB, 1966-83; Member: Younger Committee on Privacy, 1970-72, Monopolies and Mergers Commission, 1983-87; Convener, Scottish Poetry Library, since 1988. Recreations: flute playing; squash. Address: (h.) 39 Oxgangs Road, Edinburgh EH10 7BE; T.-0131-445 1266.

H

Haddington, 13th Earl of (John George Baillie-Hamilton); b. 21.12.41; m.; 1 s.; 2 d. Succeeded to title, 1986. Educ. Ampleforth. Address: Mellerstain, Gordon, Berwickshire, TD3 6LG.

Hadley, Geoffrey, MBE, BSc (Hons), PhD. Honorary Senior Lecturer, Aberdeen University, since 1985; Consultant Microbiologist, since 1985; b. 7.2.32, Stoke-on-Trent; m., Margaret Murison; 3 d. by pr. m. Educ. Longton High School; Birmingham University. Research Fellow, Nottingham University, 1956-58; Lecturer, Glasgow University, 1958-60; Lecturer, then Senior Lecturer, Aberdeen University, 1960-85; seconded to University of Malaya, 1967-68; Member, Aberdeen County Council, 1973-75, Grampian Regional Council, 1974-94; Convener, Grampian Regional Council, 1986-90; British Mycological Society: Chairman of Publications, since 1985, Editor, Mycologist, Vice-President, 1987; Chairman, Aberdeen Civic Society; Chairman, Grampian Heart Campaign, 1991-96; Member, Management Committee, Hanover (Scotland) Housing Association. Recreations: classical music; home brewing and wine-making; cricket; cycling; DIY. Address: (h.) 74 Don Street, Old Aberdeen, Aberdeen AB24 1UU; T.-01224 494472.

Hadley, Ruth, MCGB. Chef; b., 18.4.49, Liverpool; m., Anthony; 1 s.; 1 d. Educ. Holly Lodge High School for Girls, Liverpool. Taste of Scotland Restaurant of the Year, 1989; Macallan Scottish Restaurant of the Year, 1993. Address: The Cross, Kingussie; T.-01540 661166.

Hafren, Paul Anthony, BA(Hons), MA, MBA. Depute Principal, Inverness College, since 1996; b. 22.9.55, London; m., Jane; 1 s. Educ. Chatham House Grammar School, Ramsgate; University of Bristol; University of East Anglia; South Bank University. Secondary Teacher: Gloucester, 1979-80, East Devon College, 1980-84, Norfolk College, 1984-89, Stafford College, 1989-96. Executive Officer, National Association of Student Services. Recreations: mountaineering; kayaking; skiing; windsurfing. Address: (b.) 3 Longman Road, Longman South, Inverness IV1 1SA; T.-01463 256039.

Hagart-Alexander of Ballochmyle, Sir Claud, Bt, DL, JP, BA, CEng, MInstMC. Vice Lord-Lieutenant, Ayrshire and Arran, 1983-98; b. 6.1.27, Peking; m., Hilda Etain Acheson; 2 s.; 2 d. Educ. Sherborne; Corpus Christi College, Cambridge. Address: (h.) Kingencleugh House, Mauchline, Ayrshire KA5 5JL; T.-01290 550217.

Haggart, David Ballantine, JP, MA. Writer and Broadcaster; b. 15.3.34, Dundee; m., Gwendolen Hall; 3 s. Educ. Aberdeen Grammar School; Aberdeen University. National Service, Band of Royal Corps of Signals, 1956-58; Teacher, Perth and Kinross County Council, 1958-59; Youth Employment Officer, City of Aberdeen, 1959-63; Head of Careers Service, Aberdeen University, 1963-92; Member: Justices' Committee, Aberdeen, since 1976, Justice of the Peace Advisory Committee, since 1991; Chairman: Ferryhill Community Council, 1976-82, Castlehill Housing Association, 1991-94, Aberdeen and NE Scotland Music Festival, 1982-84; Director, Grampian Community Care Charitable Trust, since 1998; Writer and Producer, educational television programmes, including The Interview (Royal Television Society award); Editor, Current Vacancies, 1986-93; Columnist, Prospects Today, Evening Express; regular radio broadcasts, mainly on religious programmes; Presenter, Sunday Best, Northsound Radio, since 1981, Producer, since 1988. Recreations: music; motoring; local history. Address: (h.) 24 Polmuir Road, Aberdeen AB11 7SY; T.-01224 584176.

Haggart, Mary Elizabeth, OBE; b. 8.4.24, Leicester; m., Rt. Rev. A.I.M. Haggart. Educ. Wyggeston Grammar School for Girls, Leicester; Leicester Royal Infirmary and Children's Hospital. Leicester Royal Infirmary: Staff Nurse, 1947-48, Night Sister, 1948-50, Ward Sister, 1950-56, Night Superintendent, 1956-58, Assistant Matron, 1958-61; Assistant Matron, Brook General Hospital, London, 1962-64; Matron, Dundee Royal Infirmary and Matron Designate, Ninewells Hospital, Dundee, 1964-68; Chief Nursing Officer, Board of Managements, Dundee General Hospitals and Ninewells Hospital, 1968-73; Chief Area Nursing Officer, Tayside Health Board, 1974-82; President, Scottish Association of Nurse Administrators, 1972-77; Member: Scottish Board, Royal College of Nursing, 1965-70, General Nursing Council for Scotland, 1965-70 and 1978-82; Chairman, Scottish Board of Nursing Midwifery and Health Visiting, 1980-83; Member: Standing Nursing and Midwifery Committee, 1971-74 (Vice Chairman, 1973-74), Action on Smoking and Health Scotland, 1978-82 (Chairman, Working Party, Smoking and Nurses); Governor, Dundee College of Technology, 1978-82; Honorary Lecturer, Department of Community Medicine, Dundee University and Medical School, 1980-82; Member: Management Committee, Carstairs State Hospital, 1982-92, United Kingdom Central Council for Nursing Midwifery and Health Visiting, 1980-82, Scottish Hospital Endowments Research Trust, 1986-96. Recreations: walking; music; travel. Address: (h.) 14/2 St. Margaret's Place, Edinburgh EH9 1AY.

Haggarty, George, MA (Hons), DipEd. Rector, St. John's R.C. High School, Dundee, since 1992; b. 20.12.48, Glasgow; m., Eileen; 3 d. Educ. St. Mary's College, Blairs, Aberdeen; University of Glasgow; Jordanhill College of Education. Teacher, St. Augustine's Secondary, Glasgow, 1972-75; Assistant Principal Teacher, St. Margaret Mary's Secondary, Glasgow, 1975-76; Principal Teacher (History), St. Margaret's High, Airdrie, 1976-82; Assistant Headteacher, Taylor High, Motherwell, 1982-87; Depute Headteacher, Holy Rood High, Edinburgh, 1987-92. President, Glasgow University Catholic Society, 1970-71; Convener of Debates, Glasgow University Union, 1971-72. Recreations: hillwalking; running; reading; badminton; music. Address: (h.) 7 Cambustay Gardens, Broughty Ferry, Dundee DD5 2SR; T.-01382 778697.

Haggarty, William McLaughlan, TD, BL. Solicitor, since 1950; Consultant, Mathie-Morton Black & Buchanan, Ayr; Honorary Sheriff, South Strathclyde, Dumfries and Galloway; b. 22.2.26, Glasgow; m., Olive Dorothy Mary Speirs; 1 s.; 1 d. Educ. High School of Glasgow; Glasgow University. War Service, Merchant Navy, 1943-47; Chairman, National Insurance Tribunal, North and South Ayrshire, 1963-88; Lt. Col. Commanding 264 (Scottish) Regiment, Royal Corps of Transport (TA), 1966; Dean, Ayr Faculty of Solicitors, 1982; Governor, Craigie College of Education, Ayr, 1983-91. Recreations: golf; travel; gardening. Address: (b.) 4 Alloway Place, Ayr; T.-01292 263549.

Haig, Andrew James Newton, BSc, PhD, CBiol, FIBiol, FCIWEM. Regional Scientist, Scottish Environment Protection Agency (West Region), since 1996; b. 2.4.47, London; m., Barbara Mary Jackson; 1 s.; 1 d. Educ. King's School, Bruton; London University; Leeds University. Research Assistant, Leeds University Wellcome Marine Laboratory, 1968-71; Clyde River Purification Board: Marine Biologist, 1971-74, Assistant Marine Survey Officer, 1974-75, Marine Survey Officer, 1975-89, Assistant Director, 1989-92, Depute Director (Chief Scientist), 1992-96. Member, Scottish Council, Institute of Biology, 1978-81; Consultant/Adviser, World Health Organisation, Copenhagen 1978, Lisbon 1978, Athens 1979; NATO Invited Specialist, Lisbon 1977; Member, Fish Farming Advisory Committee, since 1994.

Recreations: natural history; gardening; music. Address: (b.) SEPA West, 5 Redwood Crescent, Peel Park, East Kilbride, Glasgow G74 5PP; T.-01355 574200.

Haig of Bemersyde, The Earl (George Alexander Eugene Douglas), OBE, DL, MA, ARSA, KStJ. Painter; b. 15.3.18, London; 1 s.; 2 d. Educ. Cargilfield; Stowe School; Christ Church, Oxford. 2nd Lt., Royal Scots Greys, 1938; retired on account of disability, 1951 (rank of Captain); attended Camberwell School of Arts and Crafts; paintings in many public and private collections; served Second World War; taken prisoner, 1942; Member, Royal Fine Art Commission for Scotland, 1958-61; Chairman, SE South East Scotland Disablement Advisory Committee, 1960-73; Trustee, Scottish National War Memorial, 1961-96; Trustee, National Galleries of Scotland, 1962-72; Member, Scottish Arts Council, 1968-74; Past Chairman, Royal British Legion Scotland; President: Earl Haig Fund Scotland/Royal British Legion Scotland, 1980-86, Scottish Branch, Officers Association, 1978-95, Scottish Craft Centre, 1952-73; Vice President, Scottish National Institution for War Blinded and of Royal Blind Asylum, since 1960. Recreations: fishing; shooting. Address: (h.) Bemersyde, Melrose TD6 9DP; T.-018352 2762.

Haines, Gerald, MA. Rector, Keith Grammar School, since 1989; b. 28.7.38, Glamorgan; m., Avril Esther Shearer; 1 s.; 1 d. Educ. Eastwood Senior Secondary, Glasgow; Glasgow University. Teacher of English, Cumbernauld High School, 1964-69; Principal Teacher of English, then Assistant Head Teacher, Lossiemouth High School, 1969-78; Depute Rector, Keith Grammar School, 1978-89. Recreations: bridge; gardening; golf. Address: (b.) School Road, Keith AB55 5ES; T.-01542 882461.

Halcrow, James George, MA, BMus (Hons), DipEd. Director of Education and Community Services, Shetland Islands Council, since 1996 (Director of Education, Shetland Islands Council, 1992-96); b. 28.2.45, Lerwick; m., Anne; 2 d. Educ. Anderson Educational Institute, Lerwick; Edinburgh University. Teacher of Music, Royal High School, Edinburgh, 1970-71; Principal Teacher of Music, Anderson High School, Lerwick, and part-time County Music Organiser, 1971-74; Shetland Islands Council: Adviser in Music, 1974-89, Home/School Adviser, 1989-92. Chairman, Association of Music Advisers in Scotland, 1988-90; Convenor, Music Panel, Scottish Examination Board, 1991. Recreations: performing music; DIY. Address: (b.) Education Office, Schlumberger Base, Gremista Industrial Estate, Lerwick ZE1 0PX; T.-01595 744303.

Haldane of Gleneagles, James Martin, MA, CA, FRSA. 28th Laird of Gleneagles; Partner, Chiene & Tait, CA, since 1989; Director: Scottish Life Assurance Co., since 1990, Investors Capital Trust PLC, since 1995, Stace Barr Angerstein PLC, Shires Investment plc, since 1996; Chairman, Queen's Hall (Edinburgh) Ltd., since 1987; b. 18.9.41, Edinburgh; m., Petronella Victoria Scarlett; 1 s.; 2 d. Educ. Winchester College; Magdalen College, Oxford. Partner, Arthur Young, 1970-89. Chairman, Scottish Chamber Orchestra, 1978-85; Chairman, Craighead Investments PLC, 1982-90; Trustee, D'Oyly Carte Opera Trust, 1985-92; Treasurer, Queen's Bodyguard for Scotland (Royal Company of Archers), since 1992; Member: Council, Edinburgh Festival Society, 1985-89, Northern and Scottish Board, Legal and General Assurance Co., 1984-87, Council, National Trust for Scotland, 1992-97, Court, Stirling University, since 1997. Recreations: music; golf. Address: (h.) Gleneagles, Auchterarder PH3 1PJ; T.-01764 682 388.

Haldane, Professor John Joseph, BA, PGCE, BA, PhD, Hon LLD, FRSA, FRSE. Professor of Philosophy, St. Andrews University, since 1994; Director, Centre for Philosophy and Public Affairs, St. Andrews University, since 1988; b. 19.2.54, London; m., Hilda Marie Budas; 2 s.; 2 d. Educ. St. Aloysius College, Glasgow; Wimbledon School of Art; London University. Art Master, St. Joseph's Grammar School, Abbey Wood, 1976-79; Lecturer in Moral Philosophy, St. Andrews University, 1983-90, Reader, 1990-94; Member, Editorial Board: The Philosophical Quarterly, since 1984, Environmental Values, Ethical Perspectives, Medieval Philosophy and Theology, Philosophical Explorations, Journal of Medical Ethics, Journal of Philosophy of Education, American Journal of Jurisprudence, Cambridge Studies in Philosophy, Innes Review. Fellow: Royal Society of Arts, Royal Society of Edinburgh. Recreations: reading; photography; gardening; art. Address: (b.) Department of Moral Philosophy, St. Andrews University, St. Andrews KY16 9AL; T.-01334 462488.

Haldane, Scott Thomas, BA, CA. Director of Finance, Greater Glasgow Health Board, since 1997; b. 4.10.59, Glasgow; m., Jacqueline; 2 s. Educ. Uddingston Grammar; Stirling University. Chief Accountant, Denholm World Travel, 1984-87; Finance Director, Bell Travel Ltd., 1987-91; Regional Finance Director (Scotland), Erskine House PLC, 1991-93; Director of Finance, Edinburgh Sick Children's NHS Trust, 1993-96; Director of Finance, West Lothian NHS Trust, 1996-97. Chairman, National Finance Training Steering Group; Chairman, Healthcare Financial Management Association Scottish Branch. Recreations: golf; football; jogging. Address: (h.) 14 Manse Avenue, Bothwell G71 8PQ; (b.) Greater Glasgow Health Board, Dalian House, 350 St. Vincent Street, Glasgow; T.-0141-201 4612.

Hale, Professor Bob, BA, BPhil. Professor of Metaphysical Philosophy, University of Glasgow, since 1995; British Academy Research Reader, since 1997; b. 4.5.45, Aldershot; m., Maggie; 2 s.; 1 d. Educ. Woking County Grammar School for Boys; University of Bristol; University of Oxford. Part-time Lecturer in Philosophy, University of Nottingham; Lecturer in Philosophy, University of Lancaster; Lecturer then Reader in Logic and Metaphysics, University of St. Andrews. Publications: Abstract Objects, 1987; Reading Putnam, 1994; Blackwell Companion to Philosophy of Language (Co-Author), 1997. Recreations: film; theatre; music; reading; hill-walking. Address: (b.) Department of Philosophy, University of Glasgow, Glasgow G12 8QQ; T.-0141-330 5173.

Haley, Christopher Simon, BSc, PhD. Head, Division of Genetics and Biometry, Roslin Institute, since 1995; b. 3.5.55, Rickmansworth; m., Sara Knott; 2 s.; 1 d. Educ. Royal Grammar School, Guildford; University of Birmingham. Post-doctoral Scientist, University of Birmingham, 1980-84; Senior Scientific Officer, Animal Breeding Research Organisation, then Institute of Animal Physiology and Genetics Research, Edinburgh, 1984-91; Principal Scientific Officer, Institute of Animal Physiology and Genetics Research, then Roslin Institute, 1991-95. Recreations: children; cooking; eating; gardening; walking; Morgan sports cars. Address: (b.) Roslin Institute, Roslin, Midlothian EH25 9PS; T.-0131-527 4200.

Halford-MacLeod, Col. (ACF), Retired Lt. Col. Aubrey Philip Lydiat, MA (Hons), late Black Watch (RHR); retired Army Officer; Schools Liaison Officer (Scotland), Army HQ Scotland; Director, Round Tower Ltd., since 1993; b. 28.4.42, Bagdad; m., Alison Fiona Brown; 2 s.; 1 d. Educ. Winchester College; RMA Sandhurst; Magdalen College, Oxford. Commissioned into Black Watch, 1962; Lt., 1964; Capt., 1968; Maj., 1975; Lt. Col., 1985; appointed Commanding Officer, Glasgow and Strathclyde Universities OTC, 1985; Chief of Staff, The Scottish Division, 1988; UK Liaison Officer (as Colonel), US European Command Stuttgart, 1991; SO1 G1 Action and Support Team (Demob Cell), Army HQ Scotland, 1992; Commandant, The Black Watch ACF Battalion, 1993.

Recreations: walking the dogs; shooting; fishing; opera; model soldiers; curling; country dancing. Address: (b.) Craigiehall, Edinburgh EH30 9TN; T.-0131-310 2190; (h.) Westview, 28 Skene Street, Strathmiglo KY14 7QL; T.-01337 860715/868930.

Halford-MacLeod, Aubrey Seymour, CMG, CVO, MA (Oxon); b. 15.12.14, Birmingham; m., Giovanna M. Durst; 3 s.; 1 d. Educ. King Edward's School, Birmingham, and abroad; Magdalen College, Oxford. HM Diplomatic Service, Third Secretary, Foreign Office, 1937; Bagdad, 1939; Office of Minister of State, Algiers, 1943; reopened Embassy, Rome, 1944; Secretary, Advisory Council Italy, and Political Adviser to Allied Control Commission, 1943-46; PPS to Permanent Under Secretary, Foreign Office, 1946-49; Deputy Secretary-General, Council of Europe, 1949-52; Tokyo, 1953-55; Libya, 1955-57; Kuwait, 1957-59; Munich, 1959-65; Ambassador to Iceland, 1966-70. Director, Scottish Opera, 1972-77; President, Scottish Society for Northern Studies, 1972-75; Vice-President, Clan MacLeod Society of Scotland, 1973-77; Adviser, Scottish Council (Development and Industry), 1970-77. Recreations: fishing; ornithology. Address: (h.) Mulag House, North Harris, Western Isles HS3 3AB; T.-Harris 2054.

Hall, Diana M., MA(Hons), DipEdTech. Depute Principal, Central College of Commerce, since 1996; b. 22.5.49, Glasgow; m., J.C. Russell Hall; 1 s.; 2 step-d. Educ. Glasgow High School for Girls; University of Glasgow; Jordanhill College of Education; Dundee College of Education. English Teacher: Eastwood High School, 1971, St. George's School, Switzerland, 1974, King's Park Secondary, 1975; Lecturer then Senior Lecturer in English and General Studies, Cardonald College, 1976; joined Central College of Commerce, 1987: Staff Development and Equality Officer, Head of Staff and Learner Services, Vice Principal, Staff Development Officer (on secondment), Scottish Wider Access Programme, West of Scotland, 1989-91. Recreations: reading; walking. Address: (b.) 300 Cathedral Street, Glasgow G1 2TA; T.-0141-552 3941.

Hall, Professor Graham Stanley, BSc, PhD, FRSE. Professor of Mathematics, University of Aberdeen, since 1996; b. 5.9.46, Warrington; 1 s.; 1 d. Educ. Boteler Grammar School, Warrington; University of Newcastle upon Tyne (Earl Grey Memorial Fellow, 1971-73); Lecturer in Mathematics, University of Aberdeen, since 1973 (Senior Lecturer, 1982, Reader, 1990, Head of Department, 1992-95). Publication: General Relativity (Co-Editor), 1996. Recreation: music (playing piano); sport. Address: (b.) Department of Mathematical Sciences, University of Aberdeen, Aberdeen AB24 3UE; T.-01224 272748.

Hall, Jacqueline, MA (Hons), DMS, DipM, MSc. Executive Director, Gordon Enterprise Trust, since 1990; b. 17.1.65, Aberdeen. Educ. Bankhead Academy, Aberdeen; Napier University; Aberdeen University; Robert Gordon's University. Executive Officer, Civil Service, 1986-87; Assistant Director, Moray Enterprise Trust, 1987-90. Scottish Young Career Woman of the Year, 1991; Member: Board, Grampian Young Enterprise Scotland; Committee Member, Institute of Directors, Aberdeen; Advisor, Young Enterprise Scotland. Recreations: scuba diving; running; swimming; aerobics; reading; salmon fishing. Address: (b.) Thainstone Business Centre, Inverurie, Aberdeenshire AB51 5TB; T.-01467 621166.

Hall, James Firth, Comendador O.M. (Portugal), Medhalha de Vasco da Gama (Portugal), OStJ. Honorary Consul of Portugal (Scotland), since 1973; retired Chartered Surveyor; b. 1.12.27, Edinburgh; m., Helen Davidson Smith. Educ. George Watson's Boys College. Senior Partner, D.M. Hall & Son, 1966-88; former Member, Valuation Appeal Committee; Fellow, Royal Institution of Chartered Surveyors; Member, Institute of Revenues, Ratings and Valuation; Member, International Real Estate Federation. Recreations: golf; sailing; shooting. Address: 25 Bernard Street, Edinburgh EH6 6SH.

Hall, Rev. Keith Ferrier, BD(Hons). Minister, Dundee Parish Church (St. Mary's), since 1994; Chaplain, Dundee High School, since 1994; b. 20.10.55, Arbroath; m., Amilia Elaine Donaldson; 2 s.; 1 d. Educ. Arbroath High School; University of St. Andrews. Minister: Blairgowrie, St. Mary's South, 1981-87, Alloa Parish, St. Mungo's, 1987-94. Recreations: family; gardening; golf; theatre. Address: (b.) Dundee Parish Church (St. Mary's), Nethergate, Dundee DD1 4DG; T.-01382 226271.

Hall, Professor Peter Anthony, BSc, PhD, MD, MRCPath. Professor of Cellular Pathology, Dundee University, since 1993; b. 2.2.58, Italy. Educ. Tunbridge Wells Technical School; London University. Lecturer in Pathology, London University; Research Fellow, Imperial Cancer Research Fund; Senior Lecturer, Royal Postgraduate Medical School; Professor of Histopathology, London University; Purser Lecturer, Trinity College, Dublin, 1996; Visiting Professor, Columbia University, New York, 1997. Publications: over 160 scientific papers, reviews and editorials. Recreation: walking. Address: (b.) Department of Molecular and Cellular Pathology, Dundee University, Dundee DD1 9SY; T.-01382 632169.

Hall, William, CBE, DFC, FRICS. Honorary Sheriff, Paisley, since 1974; b. 25.7.19, Paisley; m., Margaret Semple Gibson; 1 s.; 3 d. Educ. Paisley Grammar School. Pilot, RAFVR, 1939-45 (Despatches); Senior Partner, R. & W. Hall, Chartered Surveyors, Paisley, 1949-79; Chairman, Royal Institution of Chartered Surveyors in Scotland, 1971; Member: Valuation Advisory Council, 1970-80, Lands Tribunal for Scotland, 1971-91, Lands Tribunal for England and Wales, 1979-91; Executive Member, Erskine Hospital, since 1976. Recreation: golf. Address: (h.) Windyridge, Brediland Road, Paisley PA2 9HF.

Hall, (William) Douglas, OBE (1985), BA, FMA; b. 9.10.26, London; m., 1, Helen Elizabeth Ellis (m. diss.); 1 s.; 1 d.; 2, Matilda Mary Mitchell. Educ. University College School, Hampstead; University College and Courtauld Institute of Art, London University, 1948-52. Intelligence Corps, 1945-48 (Middle East); Manchester City Art Galleries: Keeper, Rutherston Collection, 1953-58, Keeper, City Art Gallery, 1958-59, Deputy Director, 1959-61; Keeper, Scottish National Gallery of Modern Art, 1961-86. Recreations: music; travel; gardening; wall-building. Address: (h.) Wellgate, Morebattle, Roxburghshire TD5 8QN; T.-01573 440687.

Halliburton, Ian Scott. Director, Bell Lawrie Investment Management; b. 30.1.43, Huddersfield; m., Anne Whitaker; 1 s.; 1 d. Educ. Royal High School, Edinburgh; Royal Scottish Academy of Music and Drama. General banking training, Royal Bank of Scotland, 1961-63; RSAMD, 1963-66; professional actor, 1967-70; sales consultant, 1970-71; insurance broker, 1971-78. Director, Enterprise Music Scotland. Recreations: hill-walking; listening to music; supporting the arts. Address: (h.) 259 Garrioch Road, Glasgow G20 8QZ; T.-0141-946 5426.

Halliday, James, MA, MLitt, JP. Chairman, Scots Independent Newspapers; b. 27.2.27, Wemyss Bay; m., Olive Campbell; 2 s. Educ. Greenock High School; Glasgow University. Teacher: Ardeer FE Centre, 1953, Kildonan Secondary School, Coatbridge, 1954-56, Uddingston Grammar School, 1956-58, Dunfermline High School, 1958-67; Lecturer in History, Dundee College of Education, 1967-79; Principal Lecturer in History, 1979-87. Chairman, Scottish National Party, 1956-60; Parliamentary candidate: Stirling and Falkirk Burghs, 1955 and 1959, West Fife, 1970. Publications: World in Transformation — America; Scotland The Separate; A Concise History of Scotland; 1820: The Radical War; Story of Scotland (Co-author). Recreations: reading; folk music; football spectating. Address: (h.) 72 Fintry Place, Broughty Ferry, Dundee DD5 3BH.

Halliday, John Dixon, BA, PhD. Headmaster, Rannoch School, since 1997; b. 24.6.55, Wantage; m., Anna Salvesen; 2 s.; 1 d. Educ. Abingdon School; Exeter University; Robinson College, Cambridge University. University Lecturer, University of Passau, Germany; Freelance Translator, Cambridge; Head of German, Merchiston Castle School, Edinburgh; Head of Modern Languages, Sedbergh School (Housemaster, Evans House). Recreations: music; sport; reading political philosophy. Address: Rannoch School, Rannoch, by Pitlochry, Perthshire PH17 2QQ; T.-01882 632332.

Halliday, Rt. Rev. Robert Taylor, MA, BD. Bishop of Brechin, 1990-96; b. 7.5.32, Glasgow; m., Dr. Gena M. Chadwin; 1 d. Educ. High School of Glasgow; Glasgow University; Trinity College, Glasgow; Episcopal Theological College, Edinburgh. Deacon, 1957; Priest, 1958; Assistant Curate, St. Andrew's, St. Andrews, 1957-60, St. Margaret's, Newlands, Glasgow, 1960-63; Rector, Holy Cross, Davidson's Mains, Edinburgh, 1963-83; External Lecturer in New Testament, Episcopal Theological College, Edinburgh, 1963-74; Canon, St. Mary's Cathedral, Edinburgh, 1973-83; Rector, St. Andrew's, St. Andrews, 1983-90; Tutor in Biblical Studies, St. Andrews University, 1984-90. Recreations: walking; reading; gardening. Address: 28 Forbes Road, Edinburgh EH10 4ED; T.-0131-221 1490.

Halling, Professor Peter James, BA, PhD, FRSE. Robertson Professor of Bioprocess Technology, Strathclyde University, since 1996; b. 30.3.51, London. Educ. Calday Grammar School; Churchill College, Cambridge; Bristol University. Postdoctoral Fellow, University College, London, 1975-78; Research Scientist, Unilever Research, Bedford, 1978-83; Professor of Biocatalyst Science, Strathclyde University, 1990-96. Recreation: orienteering. Address: (h.) 34 Montague Street, Glasgow G4 9HX; T.-0141-552 4400.

Halliwell, Professor Francis Stephen, MA, DPhil(Oxon). Professor of Greek, University of St. Andrews, since 1995; b. 18.10.53, Wigan; m., Helen Ruth Gainford; 2 s. Educ. St. Francis Xavier's, Liverpool; Worcester College, University of Oxford. Lecturer in Classics and Drama, Westfield College, London, 1980-82; Fellow in Classics, Corpus Christi College, University of Cambridge, 1982-84; Lecturer, Senior Lecturer, Reader in Classics, University of Birmingham, 1984-95; Visiting Professor in Classics, University of Chicago, 1990; Visiting Faculty Fellow, University of California at Riverside, 1993; Visiting Professor, University of Rome, 1998. Publications: various books on Greek literature and philosophy. Recreations: music; golf. Address: (b.) Department of Greek, Swallowgate, University of St. Andrews, St. Andrews KY16 9AL; T.-01334 462617.

Halls, Michael, FREHIS, FRSH, MInstWM. Hon. Secretary, International Federation of Environmental Health (President, 1996-98); b. 6.12.39, Galashiels; m., Sheila; 1 s.; 1 d. Educ. Galashiels Academy; Heriot-Watt. Trainee Burgh Surveyor, Galashiels Town Council, 1959-63; Additional Public Health Inspector, Thame Urban District Council, 1963-64; Galashiels Town Council: Assistant Burgh Surveyor and Sanitary Inspector, 1964-68, Depute Burgh Surveyor, 1968-71, Burgh Surveyor, 1971-75; Director of Environmental Services, Ettrick and Lauderdale District Council, 1975-96. Last Honorary Secretary, Scottish Institute of Environmental Health, 1978-83; President, Royal Environmental Health Institute of Scotland, 1984-85. Recreation: golf; philately; wine-making/drinking; music; eating; photography. Address: (h.) Eastfield, 16 Abbotsford Road, Galashiels TD1 3DS; T.-01896 752624.

Hamblen, Professor David Lawrence, MB, BS, PhD, FRCS, FRCSEdin, FRCSGlas. Professor of Orthopaedic Surgery, Glasgow University, since 1972; Chairman, Greater Glasgow Health Board, since 1997; Honorary Consultant in Orthopaedic Surgery, Greater Glasgow Health Board, since 1972; Visiting Professor to National Centre for Training and Education in Prosthetics and Orthotics, Strathclyde University, since 1981; Hon. Consultant Orthopaedic Surgeon to Army in Scotland; b. 31.8.34, London; m., Gillian; 1 s.; 2 d. Educ. Roan School, Greenwich; London University. The London Hospital, 1963-66; Teaching Fellow in Orthopaedics, Harvard Medical School/Massachusetts General Hospital, 1966-67; Lecturer in Orthopaedics, Nuffield Orthopaedic Centre, Oxford, 1967-68; Senior Lecturer in Orthopaedics/Honorary Consultant, Edinburgh University/South East Regional Hospital Board, 1968-72. Member, Chief Scientist Committee and Chairman, Committee for Research on Equipment for Disabled, 1983-90; Chairman, Journal of Bone and Joint Surgery, since 1995 (Member, Editorial Board, 1978-82 and 1985-89); Secretary and Treasurer, JBJS Council of Management, 1992-95; Member, Physiological Systems Board, Medical Research Council, 1983-88; President, British Orthopaedic Association, 1990-91 (Chairman, Education Sub-Committee, 1986-89); Non-Executive Director, West Glasgow Hospitals University NHS Trust, 1994-97. Recreation: golf. Address: (b.) Greater Glasgow Health Board, Dalian House, 350 St Vincent Street, Glasgow G3 8YZ.

Hamer-Hodges, David William, MS, FRCS, FRCSE. Consultant Surgeon, Western General Hospital, Edinburgh, since 1979; Honorary Senior Lecturer, Edinburgh University, since 1979; b. 17.10.43, Portsmouth; m., Gillian Landale Kelman; 3 s.; 1 d. Educ. Portsmouth Grammar School; University College London. Senior Registrar, Aberdeen Teaching Hospitals; Research Fellow, Harvard Medical School; Resident Surgical Officer, St. Mark's Hospital, London. Address: (b.) 38 India Street, Edinburgh; T.-0131-226 5720.

Hamill, J., CB. Secretary, Scottish Office Home Department. Address: (b.) Saughton House, Broomhouse Drive, Edinburgh, EH11 3XD.

Hamill, Sir Patrick, Kt (1984), QPM, OStJ, BA. Chief Constable of Strathclyde, 1977-85; b. 29.4.30, Clydebank; m., Nellie Gillespie; 4 s.; 1 d. Educ. St. Patrick's High School, Dumbarton. Joined Dunbartonshire Constabulary, 1950, and rose through the ranks until promoted Chief Superintendent, 1970; transferred to City of Glasgow Police, 1972; appointed Assistant Chief Constable, 1974; joined Strathclyde Police, 1975, and attended the Royal College of Defence Studies, 1976; President, Association of Chief Police Officers (Scotland), 1982-83, Honorary Secretary and Treasurer, 1983-85; Member, Board of Governors: St. Aloysius College, Glasgow, 1983-90, St. Andrew's College of Education, Bearsden, 1987-88.

Hamilton, Alex. Writer of fiction; b. 14.4.49, Glasgow. Publications: Three Glasgow Writers, 1976; Gallus, Did You Say?, 1982; Abdul the Tobacco Curer, forthcoming; The Formulae, forthcoming; many articles, songs, stories, reviews, broadcasts, audio and videotapes. Recreations: language; literature; music; theatre. Address: (h.) 12 Woodlands Drive, Glasgow G4 9EH; T.-0141-339 2258.

Hamilton, Alexander Macdonald, CBE, JP, MA, LLB. Former Vice Chairman: Royal Bank of Scotland Group plc, Royal Bank of Scotland plc; b. 11.5.25, Motherwell; m., Catherine; 2 s.; 1 d. Educ. Hamilton Academy; Glasgow University. Former Senior Partner, subsequently Consultant, McGrigor Donald, Solicitors, Glasgow; former

Member, Council, Law Society of Scotland, now Convener, Insolvency and Diligence Sub Committees; President of the Society, 1977-78; former Member, Court House Committee, Royal Faculty of Procurators of Glasgow; Past President, Glasgow Juridical Society; former Chairman, Scottish Committee, The Scout Association; Secretary, Cambuslang Old Parish Church; former Vice-Chairman and Legal Adviser, Cambuslang Community Council. Recreations: sailing; golf. Address: (h.) 30 Wellshot Drive, Cambuslang; T.-0141-641 1445.

Hamilton, 15th Duke of, (Angus Alan Douglas Douglas-Hamilton), MA, CEng, MIMechE, FBIS. Premier Peer of Scotland; Hereditary Keeper of Palace of Holyroodhouse; b. 13.9.38; m., Sarah Scott (deceased); 2 s.; 2 d. Educ. Eton; Balliol College, Oxford. Joined RAF, 1956; Flt.-Lt., 1963; flying instructor, 1965; Instrument Rating Examiner, 1966; invalided, 1967; Senior Commercial Pilot, 1968; Test Pilot, Scottish Aviation, 1971-72; Knight of St. John, 1974, Prior for Scotland, 1975-82; Patron, British Airways Pipe Band, 1977; Member: European Community Sub-Committee on Energy and Transport, 1975-77, Queen's Bodyguard for Scotland (Royal Company of Archers), since 1976, Royal Scottish Pipers Society, 1977, Piobaireachd Society, 1979, Council, Cancer Research Campaign, 1978; Honorary Air Commodore, No. 2 (City of Edinburgh) Maritime Headquarters Unit, R.Aux.AF, 1982-93. Publication: MARIA R, 1991. Address: (b.) Lennoxlove, Haddington, East Lothian, EH41 4NZ; T.-0162 082 3720; (h.) Archerfield, by Dirleton, East Lothian EH39 5HQ; T.-0162 085 0298.

Hamilton, Hon. Lord (Arthur Campbell Hamilton), BA (Oxon), LLB (Edin). Senator of the College of Justice, since 1995; b. 10.6.42, Glasgow; m., Christine Ann; 1 d. Educ. High School of Glasgow; Glasgow University; Worcester College, Oxford; Edinburgh University. Advocate, 1968; Standing Junior Counsel to Scottish Development Department, 1975-78, Inland Revenue (Scotland), 1978-82; Queen's Counsel, 1982; Advocate Depute, 1982-85; Judge of the Courts of Appeal of Jersey and of Guernsey, 1988-95; President, Pensions Appeal Tribunals for Scotland, 1992-95. Recreations: hill-walking; fishing; music; history. Address: (b.) Parliament House, Edinburgh EH1 1RQ; T.-0131-225 2595.

Hamilton, Christine M., MA. Depute Director, Cultural and Leisure Services, Glasgow City Council, since 1997; b. 9.8.54, Hamilton. Educ. Kirkcaldy High School; Harris Academy, Dundee; Glasgow University; City University, London (Diploma, Arts Administration). House Manager, Citizens' Theatre, Glasgow; Administrator: 7:84 Theatre Company, Tag Theatre Company; Arts Officer, Scottish Trades Union Congress; Depute Director and Director, Planning and Development, Scottish Arts Council, 1991-97. Recreations: arts; hill-walking; swimming. Address: (b.) 37 High Street, Glasgow G1 1LX.

Hamilton, Gordon MacMillan, MB, ChB, DFM, MPhil, CLEM. Medical Director, Glasgow University Health Service, since 1989; Hon. Senior Lecturer, Glasgow University, since 1989; Branch Medical Officer and Council Member, Glasgow and Renfrewshire Branch, British Red Cross, since 1992; b. 6.2.54, Motherwell. Educ. Glasgow University. Various hospital appointments, 1977-89. Past Chairman, Friends of the S.N.O.; Member, Glasgow Art Club. Recreations: tennis: squash; keep-fit; art; antiques; music. Address: (b.) University Health Service, Glasgow University, 63 Oakfield Avenue, Glasgow G12 8LP; T.-0141-330 4538.

Hamilton, Ian Robertson, QC (Scot), BL, LLD (Hon); b. 13.9.25, Paisley; m., Jeannette Patricia Mari Stewart; 1 s.; 1 s., 2 d. by pr. m. Educ. John Neilson School, Paisley; Allan Glen's School, Glasgow; Glasgow University; Edinburgh University. RAFVR, 1944-48; called to Scottish Bar, 1954, and to Albertan Bar, 1982; Founder, Castle Wynd Printers, Edinburgh, 1955; Advocate Depute, 1962; Director of Civil Litigation, Republic of Zambia, 1964-66; Hon. Sheriff of Lanarkshire, 1967; retired from practice to work for National Trust for Scotland and later to farm in Argyll, 1969; returned to practice, 1974; Sheriff of Glasgow and Strathkelvin, May-December, 1984; returned to practice. Chief Pilot, Scottish Parachute Club, 1979-90; Student President, Heriot-Watt University, 1990-96; Rector, Aberdeen University, 1994-96. University of Aberdeen, 1997: LLD (Hon), Hon Research Fellow. Publications: No Stone Unturned, 1952; The Tinkers of the World, 1957 (Foyle award-winning play); A Touch of Treason, 1990; The Taking of the Stone of Destiny, 1991; A Touch More Treason, 1993. Recreation: motor-biking. Address: (h.) Lochnaheithe, North Connel, Argyll PA37 1QX; T.-01631 710 427.

Hamilton, Rev. Ian William Finlay, BD, LTH, ALCM, AVCM. Minister, Nairn Old Parish Church, since 1986; b. 29.11.46, Glasgow; m., Margaret McLaren Moss; 1 s.; 2 d. Educ. Victoria Drive Senior Secondary School, Glasgow; University of Glasgow and Trinity College. Employed in banking, then music publishing; ordained, Alloa North Parish Church, 1978. Moderator, Presbytery of Inverness, 1990-91; Member: General Assembly Parish Re-appraisal Committee, 1994-97, General Assembly Maintenance of the Ministry Committee, since 1995; has participated in five pulpit exchanges, Reformed Church, New Jersey, USA; Presenter, Reflections (Grampian TV), Crossfire (Moray Firth Radio). Publications: Reflections from the Manse Window; Second Thoughts; They're Playing My Song; Take Four!; A Century of Christian Witness; several children's talks published in The Expository Times; regular contributor to Manse Window page in People's Friend. Recreations: music (piano and organ); writing; broadcasting on radio and television. Address: (h.) Nairn Old Parish Manse, 3 Manse Road, Nairn IV12 4RN; T.-01667 452203.

Hamilton, John Patterson, QPM, BA (Hons), MBA, BSc. Chief Constable, Fife Constabulary, since 1996; b. 27.1.44, Belfast; m., Patricia; 1 s.; 1 d. Educ. Templemore Avenue School, Belfast; Open University. RUC (latterly as Chief Superintendent 1963-90); Assistant Chief Constable, Greater Manchester Police, 1990-96; seconded to National Criminal Intelligence Service, Home Office (Deputy Director General), 1994-96. Address: (b.) Police HQ, Detroit Road, Glenrothes, Fife; T.-01592 418888.

Hamilton, Loudon Pearson, CB (1987), MA (Hons). Chairman: Scottish Food Quality Certification Company since 1995, Scottish Agricultural and Rural Development Centre, since 1992, Hanover (Scotland) Housing Association, since 1998; b. 12.1.32, Glasgow; m., 1, Anna Mackinnon Young (deceased); 2, Rosemary Hutton; 2 s. Educ. Hutchesons Grammar School, Glasgow; Glasgow University. National Service, RA, 1953-55 (2nd Lt.); Inspector of Taxes, Inland Revenue, 1956-60; Assistant Principal, Department of Agriculture and Fisheries for Scotland, 1960; Private Secretary to Parliamentary Under Secetary of State for Scotland, 1963-64; First Secretary, Agriculture, British Embassy, Copenhagen and The Hague, 1966-70; Assistant Secretary, Department of Agriculture and Fisheries for Scotland, 1973-79; Principal Establishment Officer, Scottish Office, 1979-84; Secretary, Scottish Office Agriculture and Fisheries Department, 1984-92. Chairman, Corstorphine Trust, 1990-95. Address: (h.) 8a Dick Place, Edinburgh EH9 2JL; T.-0131-667 5908.

Hamilton, Thomas Banks, BAcc, CA. Chairman and Chief Executive, Ashbourne PLC, since 1988; European President, Sun Healthcare Group Inc., since 1997; b. 22.11.55, Glasgow; 3 s.; 1 d. Educ. Glasgow Academy; Glasgow University. Director, West Highland Way PLC; Chairman, Bon Secours Health Systems Ltd. Recreations:

hill-climbing; golf; painting; drawing. Address: (b.) Sun House, 58 West Regent Street, Glasgow G2 2QZ; T.-0141-331 2222.

Hamilton-Grierson, Philip John, OBE, MA. Chairman, Raigmore NHS Trust; Director, Investors in People Scotland Ltd., A1 Welders Ltd., Made in Scotland Ltd.; b. 10.10.32, Inveresk; m., Pleasaunce Jill Cardew; 1 s.; 2 d. Educ. Rugby School; Corpus Christi College, Oxford. Contracts Manager, Bristol Aircraft Ltd.; Economic Adviser, Joseph Lucas Industries Ltd.; Secretary to Liberal Parliamentary Party; Director, Gallaher Ltd. Fellow, Royal Society of Arts. Recreations: hill-walking; tennis; music. Address: Pitlundie, North Kessock, Rossshire IV1 1XG; T.-01463 731392.

Hammerton, Professor Desmond, OBE, BSc, CBiol, FIBiol, FIWEM, FIMgt, FRSE. Visiting Professor, Department of Biology, Paisley University; b. 17.11.29, Wakefield, Yorkshire; m., Jean Taylor; 2 s.; 2 d. Educ. Harrow Weald County School; Birkbeck College, London University. Assistant Biologist, Metropolitan Water Board, 1953-55; Research Biologist, Bristol Waterworks, 1955-58; Principal Assistant, Lothians River Purification Board, 1958-62; Director, Hydrobiological Research Unit, Khartoum University, 1962-71; Deputy Director, Clyde River Purification Board, 1971-74, Director, 1975-94; Consultant, World Health Organisation, 1977-90; Member: Aquatic Life Sciences Grants Committee, Natural Environment Research Council, 1975-79, Marine Pollution Monitoring Management Group and its Steering Committee, 1974- 91, Steering Committee for the Development of Environmental Quality Objectives and Standards, Department of Environment, 1981-94, Scottish Council, Institute of Biology, 1973-76; elected to Committee of Environment Division, Institute of Biology, 1977 (Chairman, Environment Division, 1980-82), Terrestrial and Freshwater Sciences Committee, Natural Environment Research Council, 1985-89, Court, University of Paisley, Advisory Committee on Sites of Special Scientific Interest, 1995-98, Board, Institute of Offshore Engineering, Heriot-Watt University, since 1995, West Regional Board, Scottish Environmental Protection Agency, since 1996; Chairman, Scottish Council, Institute of Biology, 1995-97. Recreations: chess; tennis; hill-walking. Address: (h.) Mansefield Lodge, Ancaster Square, Callander, Stirling FK17 8BL; T.-01877 330105.

Hampson, Stephen F., MA, BPhil. Under Secretary, Scottish Office, since 1993; b. 27.10.45, Grimsby; m., Gunilla Brunk; 1 s.; 1 d. Educ. The Leys School, Cambridge; University College, Oxford. Lecturer, Department of Political Economy, Aberdeen University, 1969-71; Economist, National Economic Development Office, 1971-75; Economic Adviser, Scottish Office, 1975-78 and 1982-84; First Secretary, British High Commission, New Delhi, 1978-81; Assistant Secretary, Scottish Office, 1984-93. Recreations: hill-walking; theatre. Address: (h.) Glenelg, Park Road, Kilmacolm, Renfrewshire; T.-Kilmacolm 872615.

Hankey, Maurice S., BSc, PhD. Director, Scottish Landowners Federation, since 1996; b. 3.7.54, Newcastle upon Tyne; m., Catherine; 1 s.; 1 d. Educ. Royal Grammar School, Newcastle upon Tyne; Wye College, London; Newcastle upon Tyne University. Specialist Adviser, East of Scotland College of Agriculture, 1978-80; Lecturer, Newcastle upon Tyne University, 1980-83; farming, 1983-90; Land Use Specialist, Scottish Landowners Federation, 1992-96. Member, Scottish Agricultural Wages Board. Recreations: landscape gardening; computing; rural interests. Address: (b.) Scottish Landowners Federation, 25 Maritime Street, Edinburgh EH6 5PW; T.-0131-555 1031.

Hanley, Clifford. Writer and Performer; b. 28.10.22, Glasgow; m., Anna Clark (deceased); 1 s.; 2 d. Educ. Eastbank Academy, Glasgow. Journalist, since 1940; Novelist, since 1957; Songwriter; Broadcaster; Member: Scottish Arts Council, 1965-72, Inland Waterways Advisory Council, 1970-73; Writer in Residence, York University, Toronto, 1979-80. Publications: Dancing in the Streets; Love from Everybody; The Taste of Too Much; Nothing but the Best; The System; The Redhaired Bitch; It's Different Abroad; The Italian Gadget; The Chosen Instrument; The Scots; Another Street, Another Dance; History of Scotland. Recreations: music; talk.

Hannaford, Professor Philip Christopher, MD, MBChB, FRCGP, MFFP, DRCOG, DCH. Grampian Health Board Professor of Primary Care, since 1997; Director, RCGP Centre for Primary Care Research and Epidemiology, since 1997; b. 1.7.58, London; m., Dr. Anne Carol Gilchrist; 1 s.; 1 d. Educ. Aberdeen Grammar School; Aberdeen University. GP training, Sheffield, 1982-85; research training posts, RCGP Manchester Research Unit, 1986-94; Principal, general practice, Manchester, 1986-92; Director, RCGP Manchester Research Unit, 1994-97. Publications: Evidence Guided Prescribing of the Pill (Co-editor); over 50 contributions on contraception, cardiovascular disease, HRT in scientific journals. Recreations: children; walking; music. Address: (b.) Department of General Practice and Primary Care, Foresterhill Health Centre, Westburn Road, Aberdeen; T.-01224 663123.

Hannay of Kirkdale and That Ilk, Ramsay William Rainsford., BA (Hons); b. 15.6.11, India; m., Margaret Wiseman (deceased); 1 s.; 1 d. Educ. Winchester College; Trinity College, Cambridge (Hons. degree in Law). Called to the English Bar and practised in the Bankruptcy Court; called up for service in the Forces, 1939; commissioned, HLI; served throughout the War in Europe, with a short spell in USA and Canada; demobilised with rank of Major; Legal Assistant, then Assistant Solicitor, Board of Trade, 1946-64; Honorary Sheriff, Stewartry of Kirkcudbright; Member, Queen's Bodyguard for Scotland (Royal Company of Archers); President, Dumfries and Galloway Boy Scouts Association; Chief of the Clan Hannay; President, Drystane Walling Association of Great Britain. Recreations: sailing; shooting; fishing. Address: (h.) Cardoness Cottage, Gatehouse-of-Fleet, Kirkcudbrightshire; T.-01557 840286.

Hanson, William Stewart, BA, PhD, FSA, FSA Scot. Senior Lecturer in Archaeology, Glasgow University, since 1990; b. 22.1.50, Doncaster; m., Lesley Macinnes; 1 d. Educ. Gravesend Grammar School; Manchester University. Lecturer in Archaeology, Glasgow University, 1975; Chairman: Scottish Field School of Archaeology, 1982-89, Scottish Archaeological Link, 1990-96; Member, Executive Committee, Council for British Archaeology, 1989-98; President, Council for Scottish Archaeology, 1989-96; Vice-President, Council for British Archaeology, 1995-98; Director, large-scale archaeological excavations at several sites in Scotland and northern England, including complete excavation of the Roman Fort at Elginhaugh, Dalkeith; recipient, Glenfiddich Living Scotland Award, 1987. Publications include: Agricola and the conquest of the north; Rome's north-west frontier: the Antonine Wall (Co-Author); Scottish archaeology: new perceptions (Co-Editor); papers and articles. Recreations: tennis; film. Address: (h.) 4 Victoria Road, Stirling FK8 2RH; T.-01786 465506.

Happs, John Henderson, MA (Hons). Head Teacher, Mainholm Academy, Ayr, since 1994; b. 1.9.47, Irvine; m., Jean; 4 s.; 1 d. Educ. Irvine Royal Academy; Glasgow University; Jordanhill College. Teacher of English/Principal Teacher of English, Ravenspark Academy, 1970-80; Assistant Head Teacher/Depute Head Teacher/Acting Head Teacher, Kilwinning Academy, 1980-94. Recreations: caravanning; music; reading; computing; playing with grand-daughter. Address: (b.) Mainholm Academy, Mainholm Road, Ayr KA8 0QQ; T.-01292 267300.

Hardie, Alison Isabel, DipJour. Scottish Political Correspondent, The Scotsman, since 1998; b. 8.7.68, Glasgow. Educ. Lenzie Academy; Napier. Reporter, Peeblesshire News; Reporter, Evening Express, Aberdeen; Deputy News Editor, News Team International, Birmingham; Reporter, Daily Mail; Reporter, The Herald. Recreations: reading; pop trivia; sleeping late; quietly detesting Glasgow Rangers. Address: (b.) 20 North Bridge, Edinburgh EH1 3RN; T.-0131-225 2468.

Hardie, The Rt. Hon The Lord (Andrew Rutherford Hardie), QC (Scot). Lord Advocate, since 1997; b. 8.1.46, Alloa; m., Catherine Storrar Elgin; 2 s.; 1 d. Educ. St. Modan's High School, Stirling; Edinburgh University. Enrolled Solicitor, 1971; Member, Faculty of Advocates, 1973; Advocate Depute, 1979-83; Dean, Faculty of Advocates, 1994-97. Address: (b.) Crown Office, 25 Chambers Street, Edinburgh EH1 1LA.

Hardie, Donald Graeme, KStJ, TD, JP, FIM. Director, Hardie Polymers Ltd., since 1976; Director, Ronaash Ltd., since 1988; Chairman, Scottish Supply Base; b. 23.1.36, Glasgow; m., Rosalind Allan Ker (divorced); 2 s. Educ. Blairmore and Merchiston Castle. Commissioned 41st Field Regiment RA, 1955; Battery Commander 277 (Argyll & Sutherland Highlanders) Regiment RA (TA), 1966; Commanding Officer GSVOTC, 1973; TA Col. Lowlands, 1976; TA Col. DES, 1980; TA Col. Scotland, 1985; ACF Brigadier Scotland, 1987. UTR Management Trainee, 1956-59; F.W. Allan & Ker, Shipbrokers, 1960-61; J. & G. Hardie & Co. Ltd., since 1961 (currently Managing Director); Director, Gilbert Plastics Ltd., 1973-76. Lord Lieutenant, Dunbartonshire, since 1990; Hon. Col. 105 Regiment RA(V); Hon. Col. Glasgow & Lanarkshire ACF; Vice President, ACFA Scotland; Keeper, Dumbarton Castle, since 1996; Chairman, RA Council of Scotland; Chieftain, Balloch Games; President, SSAFA, Dunbartonshire; President, Scout Council, Dunbartonshire Area; President, Girl Guides of Dumbarton; President, Argyll and Lennox Boys Brigade; Chairman, Duke of Edinburgh Co-ordinating Committee; Trustee, Tullochan Trust. Recreations: skiing; sailing; shooting; fishing. Address: (h.) Dun Ruadh, Gartocharn, Dunbartonshire G83 8SB.

Hardie, Sir Douglas Fleming, CBE, LLD, Hon. FRIAS. Chairman, Edward Parker & Co. Ltd., since 1960; Non-Executive Chairman, DDS Medicines Research Ltd. (Contract Clinical Research), since 1997; b. 26.5.23, Dundee; m., Dorothy Alice Warner; 2 s.; 1 d. Educ. Trinity College, Glenalmond. Trooper, 58 Training Regt., RAC, 1941; commissioned RMA Sandhurst, 1942, 1 Fife & Forfar Yeomanry Flamethrowing Tank Regt., NW Europe, 1942-46 (Despatches), Major. Director, Dayco Rubber (UK) Ltd., 1956-86; Chairman, CBI Scotland, 1976-78; Director: Clydesdale Bank plc, 1981-92, The Alliance Trust plc, 1982-93, The Second Alliance Trust plc, 1982-93, Alliance Trust (Finance) Ltd., 1982-93, SECDEE Leasing, 1982-93, Alliance Trust (Nominees) Ltd., 1982-93; Chairman, A.G. Scott Textiles, 1985-87; Deputy Chairman, Scottish Development Agency, 1978-91; Chairman, Grampian Television PLC, 1989-93; Member: CBI Grand Council, London, 1976-85, Scottish Economic Council, 1977-91; Councillor, Winston Churchill Memorial Trust, 1985-98; Vice Chairman, Prince's Scottish Youth Business Trust, 1987; Past President, Dundee Rotary Club; Vice-President, Fife & Forfar Yeomanry Regimental Association; Deacon Convener, Nine Incorporated Trades of Dundee, 1951-54; Elder, Dundee Parish Church (St. Mary's). Recreations: golf; fishing. Address: (h.) 6 Norwood Terrace, West Park, Dundee DD2 1PB.

Hardie, William Dunbar, MBE, MA, BA, MUniv. Writer and Entertainer; b. 4.1.31, Aberdeen; m., Margaret Elizabeth Simpson; 1 s.; 1 d. Educ. Robert Gordon's College, Aberdeen; Aberdeen University; Sidney Sussex College, Cambridge. Administrative Assistant, then Assistant Secretary, NE Regional Hospital Board; District Administrator, North District, Grampian Health Board; Secretary, Grampian Health Board, 1976-83. Co-Writer and performer, Scotland The What? (comedy revue); Writer, Dod'N'Bunty column, Aberdeen Evening Express. Recreations: reading; TV-watching; film and theatre-going; sport; avid and totally biased follower of Aberdeen's football team, Scotland's rugby team, and England's cricket team. Address: (h.) 50 Gray Street, Aberdeen AB10 6JE; T.-01224 310591.

Harding, Professor Dennis William, MA, DPhil, FRSE. Abercromby Professor of Archaeology, University of Edinburgh, since 1977; b. 11.4.40. Educ. Keble College, University of Oxford. Assistant Keeper, Department of Antiquities, Ashmolean Museum, University of Oxford, 1965; Lecturer in Celtic Archaeology, University of Durham, 1966 (Senior Lecturer, 1975); Dean, Faculty of Arts, 1983-86, Vice-Principal, 1988-91, University of Edinburgh. Member, S.A.A.S. Studentships Committee, since 1982 (Chairman, since 1997); Trustee, Urras Nan Jursachan, since 1985. Address: (h.) Department of Archaeology, The Old High School, Infirmary Street, Edinburgh EH1 1LT; T.-0131-650 2364.

Hare Duke, Rt. Rev. Michael Geoffrey, BA, MA, DD. Bishop of St. Andrews, Dunkeld and Dunblane, 1969-94 (retired); Chairman, Age Concern Scotland, since 1994; b. 28.11.25, Calcutta; m., Grace Lydia Frances Dodd; 1 s.; 3 d. Educ. Bradfield College; Trinity College, Oxford; Westcott House, Cambridge. Sub-Lt., RNVR, 1944-46; Deacon, 1952; Priest, 1953; Curate, 1952-56; Vicar, Bury, 1956-62; Pastoral Director, Clinical Theology Association, 1962-64; Vicar, St. Paul's Daybrook and Officiating Chaplain, E. Midlands District HQ, 1964-69. Chairman, Scottish Association for Mental Health; Member, Anglican Communion Peace and Justice Network, Convener, 1992-94. Publications: The Caring Church (Co-author); First Aid in Counselling (Co-author); Understanding the Adolescent; The Break of Glory; Freud; Good News; Stories Signs and Sacraments of the Emerging Church; Praying for Peace, reflections on the Gulf crisis; Hearing the Stranger. Recreations: walking; writing; broadcasting. Address: (h.) 2 Balhousie Avenue, Perth PH1 5HN; T.-01738 622642.

Hargreave, Timothy Bruce, MB, MS, FRCSEdin, FRCS, FEB (Urol). Consultant Urological Surgeon and Clinical Director, Surgical Services, Western General Hospital, Edinburgh, since 1978; b. 23.3.44, Lytham; m., Molly; 2 d. Educ. Harrow; University College Hospital, London University. Senior Registrar: Western Infirmary, Glasgow, University College Hospital, London; Medical Officer, Paray Mission Hospital, Lesotho. Publications: Diagnosis and Management of Renal and Urinary Disease; Male Infertility (Editor); Practical Urological Endoscopy; The Management of Male Infertility. Recreation: skiing. Address: (h.) 20 Cumin Place, Edinburgh.

Harkess, Ronald Dobson, OBE, BSc, MS, PhD, NDA, CBiol, MIBiol, FRAgS, FRSA. Agricultural Scientist and Consultant; b. 11.7.33, Edinburgh; m., Jean Cuthbert Drennan (deceased); 2 d. Educ. Royal High School, Edinburgh; Edinburgh University; Cornell University. Senior Fison Research Fellow, Nottingham University, 1959-62; Assistant Grassland Adviser, West of Scotland Agricultural College, Ayr, 1962-72; Senior Agronomist, 1972-86; Technical Secretary, Council, Scottish Agricultural Colleges, 1986-90, Company Secretary, 1987-90; Company Secretary, Scottish Agricultural College, 1990-91; Assistant Principal, Scottish Agricultural College, 1991-93. Member, Earn Community Council, since 1997;

Chairman, Friends of Perth Festival of the Arts, since 1997; President, Perth Philatelic Society, since 1997. Recreations: amateur radio; philately; gardening. Address: (h.) Friarton Bank, Rhynd Road, Perth PH2 8PT; T.-01738 643435.

Harkness, Very Rev. James, CB, OBE, MA, FRSA, OStJ. Dean of the Chapel Royal in Scotland, since 1996; Moderator, General Assembly of the Church of Scotland, 1995-96; Chaplain to The Queen; b. 20.10.35, Thornhill; m., Elizabeth Anne; 1 s.; 1 d. Educ. Dumfries Academy; Edinburgh University. Assistant Minister, North Morningside Parish Church, 1959-61; Chaplain: KOSB, 1961-65, Queen's Own Highlanders, 1965-69; Singapore, 1969-70; Deputy Warden, RAChD, 1970-74; Senior Chaplain, Northern Ireland, 1974-75; 4th Division, 1975-78; Staff Chaplain, HQ BAOR, 1978-80; Assistant Chaplain, Scotland, 1980-81; Senior Chaplain, 1st British Corps, 1981-82; BAOR, 1982-84; Deputy Chaplain General, 1985-86; Chaplain General to the Forces, 1987-95. QHC, 1982-95; General Trustee, Church of Scotland, since 1996; Chairman, Carberry Board; Member, Committee on Chaplains to HM Forces, since 1997; Member, Board of World Mission, since 1997; President, Army Cadet Force Association Scotland; Hon. Chaplain to BLESMA, Royal British Legion Scotland; Patron, St. Mary's Music School, Edinburgh, Napier University. Recreations: walking; reading; watching sport. Address: (h.) 13 Saxe-Coburg Place, Edinburgh EH3 5BR; T.-0131-343 1297.

Harlen, Professor Wynne, OBE, MA (Oxon), MA (Bristol), PhD, FRSA. Director, Scottish Council for Research in Education, since 1990; Visiting Professor, Liverpool University, since 1990; b. 12.1.37, Swindon; 1 s.; 1 d. Educ. Pate's Grammar School for Girls, Cheltenham; St. Hilda's College, Oxford; Bristol University. Teacher/Lecturer, 1958-66; Research Associate, Bristol University School of Education, 1966-73; Research Fellow, Project Director, Reading University, 1973-77; Research Fellow, Centre for Science Education, King's College, London, 1977-84; Sidney Jones Professor of Science Education, Liverpool University, 1985-90. Chair, Children in Scotland Early Years Forum, 1991-95; Member, Secretary of State's Working Party on the Development of the National Curriculum in Science, 1987-88; President, British Educational Research Association, 1993-94. Publications: 33 books, and contributions to 39 others; 136 papers. Recreations: concerts; opera; hill-walking. Address: (h.) 26 Torphin Road, Colinton, Edinburgh EH13 0HW; T.-0131-441 6130.

Harper, Professor Alexander Murray, MB, ChB, MD (Hons). Emeritus Professor of Surgical Research, and Honorary Senior Research Fellow, Glasgow University, since 1996; Honorary Consultant Clinical Physiologist, Greater Glasgow Health Board, since 1970; b. 31.5.33, Glasgow; m., Charlotte Maria Fossleitner; 2 s.; 1 d. Educ. Hutchesons' Grammar School; Glasgow University. House Physician and Surgeon, Southern General Hospital and Glasgow Royal Infirmary, 1957-58; McIntyre Research Scholar in Clinical Surgery, Glasgow Royal Infirmary, 1958-60; Scientific Assistant, Medical Research Council, 1960-63; Wellcome Senior Research Fellow in Clinical Science and Honorary Lecturer in Surgery, Glasgow University, 1963-68; Glasgow University: Senior Lecturer in Surgery and Surgical Physiology, 1968-69, Reader, 1969-81; Professor of Surgical Research, 1981-96. Editor in Chief, Journal of Cerebral Blood Flow and Metabolism, 1981-89; Editor, Cerebrovascular and Brain Metabolism Reviews, 1989-96; David Patey Prize, Surgical Research Society, 1966; H.G. Wolff Award, American Association for Study of Headache, 1968; Gold Medal, British Migraine Association, 1976; Honorary Fellow, American Heart Association (Stroke Council), 1980. Recreations: fishing; contract bridge; gardening. Address: (b.) Wellcome Surgical Institute, Glasgow University, Garscube Estate, Bearsden Road, Glasgow G61 1QH; T.-0141-330 5826.

Harper, Anne Courage. Business Consultant, since 1992; Director, Art in Partnership, since 1991; b. 17.9.50, Kumasi, Ghana; m., H.W. (Harry) Bawden (deceased); 2 step-s.; 1 step-d. Educ. Aberdeen High School for Girls; University of Aberdeen; University College London. Manager, British Petroleum, 1974-92; Manager, External Affairs, BP in Scotland, 1991-92. Lay Member, H.M. Inspectorate of Schools, since 1993; Member, Scottish Churches Industrial Mission, since 1993; Member, Executive, Scottish Council of the European Movement, since 1993; Member, General Teaching Council for Scotland, since 1995; President, Scottish Oil Club, 1996-98; Vice Chairman, Conservative Group for Europe, since 1998. Recreations: gardening; politics; hillwalking. Address: (h.) 2F1, 5 Randolph Place, Edinburgh EH3 7TQ; T.-0131-226 6475.

Harper, Rev. Anne J. McInroy, BD, STM, MTh, Cert.Soc.Psych. Chaplain, Glasgow Royal Infirmary University NHS Trust, since 1990; b. 31.10.49, Glasgow. Educ. Camphill Senior Secondary School, Paisley; Glasgow University; Union Theological Seminary, New York. Graduate Fellow, Union Theological Seminary, and Assistant Minister, 2nd Presbyterian Church, New York City, 1974-75; research, Church history and liturgics, Glasgow University, 1975-78; Assistant Minister, Abronhill Church, Cumbernauld, 1978-79; Christian Education Field Officer, Church of Scotland Department of Education, 1979-84; Minister, Linthouse St. Kenneth's Parish Church, 1984-90. Holder (first woman), The Scots Fellowship awarded by Union Theological Seminary, New York, 1974. Address: The Chaplain's Office, Glasgow Royal Infirmary, Glasgow G4 0SF; T.-0141-211 4000.

Harper, Professor David John, BSc(Hons), PhD, CEng, FBCS. Head, School of Computer and Mathematical Sciences, The Robert Gordon University, Aberdeen, since 1993; b. 28.2.52, Melbourne; m., Morna G. Stewart; 1 s. Educ. Blackburn South High School, Victoria, Australia; Monash University; Jesus College, University of Cambridge. Analyst/Programmer, Lincoln Agricultural College, New Zealand; Research Scientist, Commonwealth Scientific and Industrial Research Organisation, Melbourne; Lecturer, Department of Computer Science, University College, Dublin; Lecturer, Department of Computing Science, University of Glasgow. Recreations: shooting; fishing; skiing; sailing; hill-walking. Address: (b.) The Robert Gordon University, S.C.M.S., St. Andrew Street, Aberdeen AB25 1HG; T.-01224 262706.

Harper, Rev. David Little, BSc, BD (Hons). Minister, St. Meddan's Church, Troon, since 1979; b. 31.10.47, Moffat; m., Janis Mary Clark; 2 s. Educ. Morton Academy, Thornhill; Dumfries Academy; Edinburgh University. Assistant Minister, Cumbernauld St. Mungo's, 1971-72; first Minister, New Erskine Parish Church, 1972-79. Moderator, Presbytery of Ayr, 1991-92; Member, Scottish Advisory Committee, Independent Broadcasting Authority, 1974-79; Scottish Member, Religious Advisory Panel, IBA, 1978-79. Recreations: golf; hill-walking; swimming. Address: St. Meddan's Manse, 27 Bentinck Drive, Troon, Ayrshire KA10 6HX; T.-01292 311784.

Harper, Douglas Ross, BSc, MD, FRCSEdin, FRCSEng, FRCSGlas. Consultant Surgeon, since 1976, Medical Director, since 1994, Falkirk and District Royal Infirmary NHS Trust; Examiner: Royal College of Surgeons of Edinburgh, since 1979, Royal College of Surgeons of Glasgow, since 1987; Honorary Senior Lecturer, Department of Clinical Surgery, Edinburgh University, since 1976; b. 16.2.40, Aberdeen; m., Dorothy Constance Wisely; 1 s.; 3 d. Educ. Aberdeen Grammar School; Aberdeen University. House Officer, Registrar and Fellow in Vascular Surgery, Aberdeen Royal Infirmary, 1967-73; Senior Registrar, Edinburgh Royal Infirmary, 1973-76. Elder, Bridge of Allan Chalmers Church of Scotland.

Recreations: hill-walking; geology; woodwork. Address: (h.) 142 Henderson Street, Bridge of Allan, Stirling FK9 4HF; T.-01786 832242.

Harper, Edward James, MA, BMus, ARCM, LRAM. Composer, since 1957; Reader in Music, Edinburgh University, since 1990; Director, New Music Group of Scotland, 1973-91; b. 17.3.41, Taunton; m., Dorothy Caroline Shanks. Educ. King Edward VI School, Guildford; Royal College of Music, London; Christ Church, Oxford. Main works as a Composer: Piano Concerto, 1971; Bartok Games, 1972; Ricercari in Memoriam Luigi Dallapiccola, 1975; Fanny Robin (chamber opera), Chester Mass, 1979; Clarinet Concerto, 1981; Hedda Gabler (opera, commissioned for Scottish Opera), 1985; Fantasia V (for chamber orchestra), 1985; The Mellstock Quire (chamber opera), 1987; Homage to Thomas Hardy (baritone and orchestra), 1990; The Fiddler of the Reels (str. orch.), 1993; And Winds Austere and Pure (choir and piano duet), 1993; Psalm 150 (unacc. choir), 1996; Trio (cl., cello, piano), 1997. Address: (h.) 7 Morningside Park, Edinburgh EH10 5HD; T.-0131-447 5366.

Harper, George, MA, DipTP, MRTPI. Director of Development and Environment Services, Argyll and Bute Council, since 1996; b. 21.3.51, Perth; m., Katherine; 1 s.; 1 d. Educ. Perth Academy; Aberdeen University; Heriot-Watt University (Diploma, Town and Country Planning). Planner, Dundee Corporation, 1972-75; Planner/Senior Planner, Tayside Regional Council, 1975-88; Depute Director of Planning, Argyll and Bute District Council, 1988-90; Director of Planning, Development and Tourism, Argyll and Bute District Council, 1990-96. Director, Strathclyde Building Preservation Trust. Recreations: hill-walking; football; golf; gardening; family. Address: (b.) Kilmory Castle, Lochgilphead, Argyll; T.-01546 604225.

Harper, John Ross, CBE, MA, LLB. Senior Partner, Ross Harper & Murphy and Harper Macleod, Solicitors, since 1962; b. 20.3.35, Glasgow; m., Ursula; 2 s.; 1 d. Educ. Hutchesons' Boys' Grammar School; Glasgow University. Parliamentary Commissioner; Professor of Law, Strathclyde University; Past President: Law Society of Scotland, Scottish Conservative & Unionist Association, International Bar Association; former Chairman, Society of Scottish Conservative Lawyers; former Parliamentary candidate (Conservative), Hamilton and West Renfrewshire; Chairman: Mining (Scotland) Ltd., Scottish Coal Company; Member, Board of Trustees, National Galleries of Scotland; Trustee, Strathclyde Foundation Board. Publications: Glasgow Rape Case; My Client My Lord; A Practitioner's Guide to the Criminal Courts; Fingertip Criminal Law; Rates Revaluation; Devolution; New Unionism; Scotland '97; Referendums are Dangerous. Recreations: angling; bridge. Address: (b.) The Ca'd'oro, 45 Gordon Street, Glasgow, G1 3PE; T.-0141-221 8888; (h.) 23 Clabon Mews, Cadogan Square, London SW1X 0EG.

Harper, Robin C. M., MA, DipGC, FRSA. Speaker, formerly Convenor, Scottish Green Party, since 1995; Teacher, since 1962; b. 4.8.40, Thurso; m., Jenny Helen Carter Brown. Educ. St. Marylebone Grammar School; Elgin Academy; Aberdeen University. Teacher Braehead School, Fife, 1964-68; Education Officer, Kenya, 1968-70; Musician/Actor, 1971; Boroughmuir High School: Assistant Principal Teacher, Modern Studies, 1972-85, Assistant Principal Teacher, Guidance, since 1985. Musical Director, Theatre Workshop, Edinburgh, 1972-75; President, Edinburgh Classical Guitar Society, 1980-90; Member, Lothian Children's Panel, 1985-88; Member, Lothian Health Council, 1993-97; President, EIS Edinburgh Local Association, 1990-91; Co-ordinator, Duke of Edinburgh's Award Scheme, since 1998. Recreations: music; walking; photography; travel; theatre. Address: 11 Greenbank Terrace, Edinburgh EH10 6ER; T.-0131-447 1843.

Harris, Rev. John William Forsyth, MA. Minister, Bearsden South Church, since 1987; b. 10.3.42, Hampshire; m., Ellen Lesley Kirkpatrick Lamont; 1 s.; 2 d. Educ. Merchant Taylors' School, London; St. Andrews University; New College, Edinburgh. Ordained Assistant, St. Mary's Church, Haddington, 1967-70; Minister: St. Andrew's Church, Irvine, 1970-77, St. Mary's Church, Motherwell, 1977-87. Convener: Scottish Churches' Christian Aid Committee, 1986-90, Scottish Christian Aid Committee, 1990-98, Scottish Television's Religious Advisory Committee, since 1990; Vice-Convener, Board of World Mission, since 1996; Member: Jubilee 2000 Scottish Coalition Steering Group, since 1997, Board of Christian Aid, 1990-98, Executive, Church and Nation Committee, 1985-91, Executive, Scottish Churches Council, 1986-90; Moderator, Dumbarton Presbytery, 1994-95. Fencing Blue, St. Andrews and Edinburgh; Scottish Fencing Team, 1963-66. Recreations: Cruban walking and holiday home in Kintyre. Address: 61 Drymen Road, Bearsden, Glasgow G61 2SU; T.-0141-942 0507.

Harris, Marshall James, DPA. Director, Scottish Educational Trust for United Nations and International Affairs, since 1986; b. 14.3.28, Edinburgh; m., Matilda Currie Main; 2 s.; 1 d. Educ. Armadale Secondary; Glasgow University. Accountancy, pre-1958; Scottish National Officer, UN Association, 1958-86; Secretary, Scottish Standing Committee for Voluntary International Aid. Former Liberal and Alliance candidate. Recreations: reading; member of Rotary, Liberal International and Royal Institute of International Affairs. Address: (h.) Hopetoun, Charlotte Street, Brightons, Falkirk; T.-01324 715203.

Harris, Paul Anthony, MA(Hons). Writer, since 1967; b. 22.7.48, Dartford. Educ. Bradford Grammar School; Elgin Academy; University of Aberdeen. Pirate Radio, 1969-71; Publisher, 1967-85; Publishing Consultant, 1985-97; Journalist (Foreign Correspondent), 1990-97. Lecturer, Cunard World University Programme; British Press Award (Bosnia), 1992. Publications: 28 books including: When Pirates Ruled the Waves, 1968, The Garvie Trial, 1969, Dictionary of Scottish Painters, 1990, Somebody Else's War, 1992, Cry Bosnia, 1995. Recreations: photography; travel. Address: (h.) Whittingehame House, Haddington EH41 4QA; T.-01368 850369.

Harris, Professor William Joseph, BSc, PhD. Professor and Chair of Genetics, University of Aberdeen, since 1987; b. 17.11.44, Dundee; m., Linda; 2 s.; 1 d. Educ. Lawside Academy, Dundee; St. Andrews University. Lecturer in Biochemistry, University of Aberdeen, 1969-78; Inveresk Research International, Musselburgh: Manager, In Vitro Toxicology, 1978-80, Head, Biotechnology, 1980-86; Research Director, Bioscot Ltd., Edinburgh, 1986-87; Technical Director, Biotechnology Investments, Cogent Ltd., 1980-86; Co-founder and Managing Director, Scotgen Ltd., 1987-92; Chief Scientific Officer, Scotgen Biopharmaceutical Inc., 1992-94. Publications: 65 papers; two books; 15 book chapters. UK Endeavour Prize, 1968; DTI SMART Award, 1986; DTI SMART Stage 1 Award 1988, 1989; DTI SMART Stage 2 Award, 1989. Recreations: golf; travel; pubs. Address: 18 Queen Street, Carnoustie DD7 7AB; T.-01241 853900.

Harrison, Professor Bryan Desmond, CBE, BSc, PhD, FRS, FRSE, Hon. DAgric. Emeritus Professor of Plant Virology, Dundee University, since 1997 (Professor of Plant Virology, 1991-96); b. 16.6.31, Purley, Surrey; m., Elizabeth Ann Latham-Warde; 2 s.; 1 d. Educ. Whitgift School, Croydon; Reading University. Agricultural Research Council Postgraduate Research Student, 1952-54; Scientific Officer, Scottish Horticultural Research Institute, 1954-57; Senior and Principal Scientific Officer, Rothamsted Experimental Station, 1957-66; Scottish Horticultural Research Institute/Scottish Crop Research Institute: Principal Scientific Officer, 1966, Senior Principal

Scientific Officer (Individual Merit), 1969, Deputy Chief Scientific Officer (Individual Merit), 1981; Head, Virology Department, 1966-91; Foreign Associate, US National Academy of Science; Honorary Professor, Department of Biochemistry and Microbiology, St. Andrews University, since 1987; Honorary Research Professor, Scottish Crop Research Institute, since 1991; Honorary Visiting Professor, Dundee University, 1987-91; Past President, Association of Applied Biologists. Recreation: gardening. Address: (b.) Scottish Crop Research Institute, Invergowrie, Dundee DD2 5DA.

Harrison, Professor Richard T., BA, PhD. Professor of Management Studies and Director, Centre for Entrepreneurship, University of Aberdeen, since 1998; b. 15.4.55, Belfast; m., Sharon; 2 s.; 1 d. Educ. Campbell College, Belfast; Queen's University of Belfast. Research Officer, Northern Ireland Economic Council, 1981-85; Lecturer in Business Economics, Queen's University of Belfast, 1985-89; University of Ulster: Lecturer/Senior Lecturer in Applied Economics, 1989-91, Professor of Management Development, 1991-97, Professor of Strategy and Organisation Development, 1997-99. Editor, Venture Capital – An International Journal of Entrepreneurial Finance; former Board Member, Northern Ireland Software Industry Federation; Member: British Academy of Management, American Academy of Management. Publications: author of books on economics of shipbuilding, regional policy, informal venture capital. Recreations: fly fishing; jazz; contemporary fiction. Address: (b.) Department of Management Studies, University of Aberdeen, Aberdeen AB24 3QY; T.-01224 272712.

Harrison, Professor Robert Graham, BSc (Hons), PhD, FRSE. Professor of Physics, Heriot-Watt University, since 1987; b. 26.2.44 Oxford; m., Rowena Indrania; 1 s.; 1 d. Educ. Wanstead High School; London University. Postgraduate and postdoctoral research, Royal Holloway College, London, and Culham Laboratories, UKAEA, 1966-72; Lecturer, Bath University; joined Physics Department, Heriot-Watt University. Publications: 200 scientific publications, including editorship of five books. Address: (b.) Physics Department, Heriot-Watt University, Riccarton, Currie, Edinburgh EH14 4AS; T.-0131-449 5111.

Harrison, Sydney, OBE. Proprietor, Paisley and Renfrewshire Gazette Group, 1963-87; Chairman, James Paton Ltd., Printers, 1970-87; Editor, Scot, 1981-87; b. 13.4.13, Glasgow; m., Joan Morris. Educ. Whitehill School, Glasgow. Journalist, various newspapers, 1927-37; Sub-Editor, Glasgow Herald, 1938-39; Army, 1939-46 (Lt.-Col., 1944); Editor, Scottish Field, 1946-63; Director, Scottish Counties Newspapers, 1950-63; Councillor, 4th District, Renfrewshire, 1956-67; Member, Council of Industrial Design, Board of Trade, 1955-65; Honorary Member, Scottish PEN; Past President: Paisley Burns Club, Rotary Club of Paisley. Recreations: curling; motoring; caravanning; travel. Address: (h.) 17 Stanley Drive, Brookfield, Renfrewshire PA5 8UF; T.-01505 320634.

Harrower, Neil, Scottish Director, International Voluntary Service, since 1986; b. 28.8.59, Falkland, Fife; m., Beverly Wainwright; 1 s. Educ. Inverness Royal Academy; University of Aberdeen. Address: (b.) 7 Upper Bow, Edinburgh EH1 2JN; T.-0131-226 6722.

Hart, Morag Mary, JP, DL, RGN, RSCN. Deputy Lieutenant, Dunbartonshire, since 1989; Director, Scotsell Ltd., since 1982; b. 19.4.39, Glasgow; m., Tom Hart; 1 s.; 1 d. Educ. Westbourne School for Girls, Glasgow. Sick Children's Hospital, Glasgow, 1956-59; Western General Hospital, Edinburgh, 1960-62. County Commissioner, Dunbartonshire Girl Guides, 1982-90; Chairman, Dunbartonshire Area Scouts, since 1994; Member, The Guide Association Council for Scotland, since 1996. Recreations: reading; gardening; walking. Address: (h.) 18 Campbell Drive, Bearsden, Glasgow G61 4NE; T.-0141-942 1216.

Hart, Professor Robert Albert, BA (Hons), MA. Professor of Economics, Stirling University, since 1986; b. 7.1.46, Hartlepool; m., Shirley; 3 d. Educ. Hartlepool Grammar School; Liverpool University. Economics Lecturer, Aberdeen University, 1969-73, Leeds University, 1974-75; Senior Lecturer, Strathclyde University, 1976-80; Senior Research Fellow, Science Centre, Berlin, 1980-86; Head, School of Management, Stirling University, 1991-94. Recreations: walking; reading; drinking beer. Address: (b.) Department of Economics, Stirling University, Stirling FK9 4LA; T.-01786 467471.

Hart, Professor Susan Jane Ritchie, BA (Hons), PhD, DipMRS. Professor of Marketing, Strathclyde University, since 1998; b. 18.7.60, Edinburgh; 1 s.; 1 d. Educ. Bearsden Academy; Strathclyde University. Universite de Technologie de Compiegne, 1982-83; Procter and Gamble PLC, 1983-84; Research Assistant/Lecturer/Senior Lecturer, Department of Marketing, Strathclyde University, 1984-93; Professor of Marketing, Heriot-Watt University, 1993-95; Professor of Marketing, Stirling University, 1995-98. Publications: Marketing and Competitive Success (Co-Author); New Product Development, 1996; papers. Recreations: hill-walking; skiing. Address: (b.) Department of Marketing, Strathclyde University, Glasgow; T.-0141-548 4927.

Hart, Thomas, MA, LLB. Chair, Scottish Transport Studies Group, since 1994; Editor, Scottish Transport Review, since 1998; Vice President, Scottish Association for Public Transport, since 1976; Lecturer, Department of Economic and Social History, Glasgow University, 1965-98, Honorary Research Fellow, since 1998; b. 15.11.39, Kilmarnock; m., Ellen Elizabeth Jones; 2 s. Educ. Spiers School, Beith; Glasgow University. Consultant on transport and environmental issues, since 1990; Founder Member and Secretary, Scottish Transport Studies Group; Founder Member, Scottish Railway Development Association (Secretary, 1962-67, Vice Chairman, 1967-72); Chairman, Scottish Association for Public Transport, 1972-76; Member, Board, TRANS*form* Scotland, since 1997. Recreations: walking; travel; gardening. Address: (h.) Birchfield, Kings Road, Beith, Ayrshire KA15 2BN; T.-01505 502164.

Harte, Professor Ben, BA, MA, PhD(Cantab), FRSE. Professor of Metamorphism, Edinburgh University, since 1991; b. 30.5.41, Blackpool; m., Angela Elizabeth; 1 s.; 2 d. Educ. Salford Grammar School; Trinity College, Cambridge University. Lecturer/Reader, Edinburgh University, 1965-91; Guest Research Investigator, Carnegie Institution of Washington, 1974-75; Visiting Associate Professor, Yale University, 1982; Visiting Research Fellow, University of Cape Town, 1990. Address: (b.) Department of Geology and Geophysics, King's Buildings, Edinburgh EH9 3JW; T.-0131-650 8528.

Hartley, Clive, BA, DipTP, MRTPI. Chief Executive, Dumfries and Galloway Tourist Board, since 1996; b. 20.4.47; m, Joyce Walker. Educ. Nelson Secondary Technical School; Hull University; Central London Polytechnic. Assistant Research Officer, Countryside Commission for England and Wales; Research Officer, Department of the Environment; Principal Planning Officer, Dumfries and Galloway Regional Council; Depute Director of Economic Development, Dumfries and Galloway Regional Council; Director of Tourism, Dumfries and Galloway Tourist Board. Past President: Galloway Mountaineering Club, Dumfries and Galloway Architectural and Engineering Society. Recreations: hill-walking; gardening; natural history; photography. Address: (b.) 64 Whitesands, Dumfries DG1 2RS; T.-01387 245550.

Hartley, Graeme Edward, BA. Deputy Director, Royal Institution of Chartered Surveyors in Scotland, since 1990; b. 9.4.61, Edinburgh; m., Lee Adams Rankine; 1 s. Educ. Perth High School; Napier University. Dundee Chamber of Commerce, 1983-85; Electrical Contractors' Association of Scotland, 1985-90. Member, Scottish Building Contract Committee, since 1986. Recreations: golf; running: X-C skiing. Address: (b.) 9 Manor Place, Edinburgh EH3 7DN; T.-0131-225 7078.

Hartley, Keith Scott, BA, MA. Assistant Keeper, Scottish National Gallery of Modern Art, since 1979; b. 27.1.49, Evesham. Educ. Prince Henry's Grammar School, Evesham; St. Catherine's College, University of Oxford; Courtauld Institute; University of London; Freie Universität, W. Berlin. Curator of numerous exhibitions, and author of corresponding catalogues, including: Scottish Art Since 1900, 1989, Otto Dix, Tate Gallery, 1992, The Romantic Spirit in German Art 1790-1990, 1994. A Director, Art in Partnership (Scotland). Recreations: travel; reading. Address: (b.) Scottish National Gallery of Modern Art, Belford Road, Edinburgh EH4 3DR; T.-0131-624 6328.

Hartnett, Frank Ernest Lawrence, OBE, BSc (Econ), CertEd, DipEdTech. General Manager, Grampian Health Board, since 1991; b. 3.9.40, Alton; m., 1, Catherine Mary Adams (deceased); 2, Louisa MacAllan; 1 s.; 1 d. Educ. Lord Wandsworth College; London University; Southampton University; Sussex University. Head, Economics Department, Cheshunt Grammar School; commissioned RAF, 1965; lead role in achieving organisational change in RAF training, 1972-75; involved in fast jet operations, RAF Germany, 1975-78; introduction of Tornado into RAF, 1978-81; OFFR and aircrew selection, 1982; OC Trg WG, RAF Hereford, 1982-85; OC Admin WG, RAF Cosford, 1985-87; Grampian Health Board: General Manager, Maternity and Child Health, 1987-89, General Manager, Mental Health, 1989-91. Recreations: hill-walking; shooting; badminton. Address: (b.) Summerfield House, 2 Eday Road, Aberdeen AB15 6RE; T.-01224 404000.

Harvey, Professor Alan L., BSc, PhD, MBA, CBiol, FIBiol. Director, Strathclyde Institute for Drug Research, since 1988; Professor in Physiology and Pharmacology, Strathclyde University, since 1986; b. 23.6.50, Glasgow. Educ. Hutchesons', Glasgow; Strathclyde University. Lecturer in Physiology and Pharmacology, Strathclyde University, 1974-83; Senior Lecturer, 1983-86. British Pharmacological Society Sandoz Prize, 1983; British Pharmaceutical Conference Science Award, 1983. Publications: Toxicon (Editor); Snake Toxins, 1991; Advances in Drug Discovery Techniques, 1998. Address: (b.) Department of Physiology and Pharmacology, Strathclyde University, Glasgow, G1 1XW; T.-0141-553 4155.

Harvey, Jake, DA, RSA. Sculptor and Lecturer; Acting Head of Sculpture, Edinburgh College of Art; b. 3.6.48, Kelso; m., Anne Penelope; 1 s.; 2 d. Educ. Kelso High School; Edinburgh College of Art. Benno Schotz Sculpture Prize, RSA, 1976; Macaulay Prize, RSA, 1996; Hugh MacDiarmid Memorial Sculpture, 1982-85; William Gillies Bursary, 1989; RSA, 1989; has shown in many solo and group exhibitions; major retrospective exhibition, Talbot Rice Gallery, 1993; commissions include: Hugh MacDiarmid Memorial Sculpture, 1982, Newcraighall Mining Sculpture, 1987, Poacher's Tree, 1991, Motherwell Heritage Centre Sculpture, 1996, Sculpture for Hunterian Museum, Glasgow, 1996; residency, Iwate Art Festival, Japan, 1998; exhibits with Art First, Cork Street, London. Recreation: fishing. Address: (h.) Maxton Cross, Maxton, St. Boswells, Roxburghshire; T.-01835 822650.

Harvey, Rev. William John, BA (Hons), BD (Hons). Staff Member, Craighead Institute, Glasgow; Minister, Church of Scotland, since 1964; Leader, The Iona Community, 1988-95; b. 17.5.37, Glasgow; m., Isabel Mary Douglas; 2 s.; 2 d. Educ. Fettes College, Edinburgh; Oxford University; Glasgow University. National Service, Argyll & Sutherland Highlanders, 1956-58; Ordained Assistant, Govan Old Parish Church, 1964-66; Member, Gorbals Group Ministry, 1963-71; Minister, Laurieston-Renwick Parish Church, Glasgow, 1968-71; Warden, Iona Abbey, 1971-76; Minister: Raploch Parish Church, Stirling, 1976-81, Govan Old Parish Church, 1981-88. Member, Church of Scotland Committee on Church and Nation, 1978-86; Kerr Lecturer, Glasgow University, 1987. Recreations: reading; history; bread and wine-making; sea-bird watching. Address: (h.) 501 Shields Road, Glasgow G41 2RF; T.-0141-429 3774.

Harvey-Jamieson, Rodger Ridout, TD, LLB, MBA, WS. Partner, Murray Beith Murray WS, since 1973; b. 30.6.47, Edinburgh; m., Alison; 1 s.; 1 d. Educ. Edinburgh Academy; Edinburgh University. Trustee, Seagull Trust; Director, Fruitmarket Gallery; Member, Queen's Bodyguard for Scotland (Royal Company of Archers). Recreations: sailing; scuba diving; archery. Address: (b.) 39 Castle Street, Edinburgh EH2 3BH.

Haslett, Professor Christopher, BSc (Hons), MBChB (Hons), FRCP Edin, FRCP Lond. Professor of Respiratory Medicine, Edinburgh University, and Director, The Rayne Laboratories, since 1990; Honorary Consultant Physician, Lothian Health Board, since 1990; Chairman, Department of Medicine, Royal Infirmary, since 1995; Visiting Professor, Department of Medicine, Royal Postgraduate Medical School, since 1990; b. 2.4.53, Chester; m., Jean Margaret; 1 s.; 1 d. Educ. Wirral Grammar School; Edinburgh University Medical School. House Physician, Department of Medicine, Royal Infirmary, Edinburgh, 1977-87; Rotating Medical Registrar, Ealing Hospital and Hammersmith Hospital, London, 1980-82; MRC Travelling Fellow, National Jewish Hospital, Denver, Colorado, 1982-85; MRC Senior Clinical Fellow and Senior Lecturer, Department of Medicine, Royal Postgraduate Medical School, Hammersmith Hospital, London, 1986-90. Vice-Chairman, National Asthma Campaign Research Committee; Member, MRC Molecular and Cellular Medicine Board; Member and Vice Chairman, MRC Systems "A" Grants Committee; Secretary, Lung Injury Section, European Respiratory Society. Recreation: rugby union. Address: (b.) Respiratory Medicine Unit, Department of Medicine, Royal Infirmary, Edinburgh EH3 9YW; T.-0131-229 2477.

Hassan, Gerrard Lewis, MA (Hons). Director, Centre for Scottish Public Policy, since 1998; b. 21.3.64, Dundee; m., Rosemary Catherine Ilett. Educ. Rockwell High School, Dundee; Glasgow University. Advice and Information Worker, Tayside Regional Council, 1983-87; Parliamentary Researcher for Mike Watson, MP, 1993-94; Equal Opportunities Officer, Save the Children Fund, 1994-95; Press Officer, Citizens Advice Scotland, 1995-97; Policy Officer, Scottish Association for Mental Health, 1997-98. Organiser: Scottish Nexus Group, 1997-98, Remaking Scotland, 1997, The New Scotland, 1998. Publications: The New Scotland; Scotland's Parliament: lessons for Northern Ireland, 1998. Recreations: cats; talking politics, collecting Frank Sinatra records. Address: (h.) 29 Moray Place, Glasgow G41 2BL; T.-0141-423 3114.

Hastings, Gavin, OBE, DUniv (Paisley). Former rugby player; Managing Director, Hastings International; b. 1962, Edinburgh. Educ. George Watson's College, Edinburgh; Paisley University; Cambridge University. 61 Scotland Caps, 1986-95 (20 as Captain); 3 World Cups, 1987, 1991, 1995; 2 British Lions Tours: 1989, Australia, 3 Tests, 1993, New Zealand (Captain), 3 Tests; Marketing Consultant, Hastings International.

Hastings, Professor Gerard Bernard, BSc, PhD. Director, Centre for Social Marketing, Department of Marketing, Strathclyde University, since 1987; Head, Department of Marketing; Member, Board, SACRO; b. 5.10.54, Ilkley; 3 s. Educ. St. Michael's College, Leeds; Newcastle upon Tyne Polytechnic; Strathclyde University. Recreations: hill-walking; travel; books. Address: (b.) Department of Marketing, Strathclyde University, 173 Cathedral Street, Glasgow G4 0RQ; T.-0141-552 4400.

Hathorn, (Alexander) Michael, CA, CPFA. Managing Partner, Scott-Moncrieff, since 1990; Chairman, Moore Stephens (UK), Ltd., since 1991; Chairman, Baillie Gifford Shin Nippon plc; b. 5.6.48, Peterborough; m., Deborah Christian; 2 s.; 1 d. Educ. Stranraer High School; Sedbergh. Joined Scott-Moncrieff Thomson-Shiells, CA (later Scott-Moncrieff), 1967: qualified 1972, Partner, 1974. Financial Advisor, Edinburgh International Festival; Trustee and Treasurer, Age Concern Scotland. Recreations: art; music. Address: (b.) 17 Melville Street, Edinburgh EH3 7PH; T.-0131-473 3500.

Hatwell, Anthony, DFA(Lond). Sculptor; Head, School of Sculpture, Edinburgh College of Art, 1969-90; b. 21.6.31, London; m., Elizabeth; 2 d. Educ. Dartford Grammar School; Slade School of Fine Art; Borough Polytechnic; Bromley College of Art. Some exhibitions: Scottish Arts Council Edinburgh Festival Exhibition, 1978; British Sculpture in the 20th Century, Whitechapel Gallery, 1981; Built in Scotland exhibition in Edinburgh, Glasgow, and London, 1983; Slade Postgraduate Scholarship, 1956; Boise Travelling Scholarship, 1957; Assistant to Henry Moore, 1958; Member, London Group, 1959-69 (Vice-President, 1961-63); works in collections of Scottish National Gallery of Modern Art, Arts Council of GB, Scottish Arts Council and private collections. Address: (h.) 4 North Street, Belhaven, Dunbar, East Lothian.

Haughan, Barbara, LLB. Director of Support Services, East Ayrshire Council, since 1995; b. 27.8.51, Glasgow; m., Alistair. Educ. Hamilton Academy; University of Glasgow. Legal Apprentice, Sutherland County Council, 1972-74; Legal Apprentice and Legal Assistant, Ayr Burgh, 1974-75; Kyle and Carrick District Council: Legal Assistant and Senior Legal Assistant, 1975-79, Assistant Director of Administration, 1979-90, Assistant Chief Executive, 1990-95. Address: (b.) East Ayrshire Council, Council Headquarters, London Road, Kilmarnock KA3 7BU; T.-01563 576061.

Havenga, Frances Mary, MBE, MIEx. Chairman, Tayside Health Board, since 1997; b. 14.2.43, Forfar; m., Henry Lucas Havenga. Educ. Webster's High School; Bruce's Business College. Wright Dental Group: joined 1962, Export Manager, 1974-84, Export Director, 1984-97. Former Director: Millner's Dental Suppliers Ltd., South Africa, P. Grant Smith Ltd., South Africa, P. Grant Smith Ltd., Zimbabwe. Past President, Dundee and Tayside Chamber of Commerce and Industry; formerly: Chairman, Tayside Export Forum, Board Member, Glenrothes Development Corporation, Member, Social Security Appeals Tribunal, President, Soroptimist International of Dundee; Chairman, Kirriemuir Golf Club, since 1994. Recreations: reading; travel; golf (lapsed!). Address: (b.) Gateway House, Technology Park, Dundee DD2 1TP; T.-01382 424026.

Havergal, Giles Pollock, OBE, MA, DLitt (Glasgow, Strathclyde), DDra, FRSE. Director, Citizens Theatre, Glasgow, since 1969; b. 9.6.38, Edinburgh. Educ. Harrow; University of Oxford. Director, Palace Theatre, Watford, 1964-69. Awarded St. Mungo Prize, Glasgow, 1995. Address: (b.) Citizens Theatre, Gorbals, Glasgow G5 9DS; T.-0141-429 5561.

Hawkins, Anthony Donald, BSc, PhD, FSA Scot, FRSE. Director of Fisheries Research for Scotland, since 1987; Honorary Professor, Aberdeen University; b. 25.3.42, Dorset; m., Susan Mary; 1 s. Educ. Poole Grammar School; Bristol University. Entered Scottish Office as Scientific Officer, Marine Laboratory, Aberdeen, 1965; Senior Scientific Officer, 1969, Principal Scientific Officer, 1972, Senior Principal Scientific Officer, 1978, Deputy Chief Scientific Officer, 1983; Deputy Director of Fisheries Research for Scotland, 1983; conducts research into behaviour and physiology of fish; awarded A.B. Wood Medal, Institute of Acoustics, 1978; Chairman, The Green Wedge. Publications: books on fish physiology and aquarium systems. Recreations: reading; angling; soccer; breeding whippets. Address: (b.) Marine Laboratory, PO Box 101, Victoria Road, Torry, Aberdeen; T.-01224 876544.

Hay, Francis (Frank) Walker Christie, OBE, DL, MA (Hons). Deputy Lieutenant, Banffshire, since 1988; Honorary Sheriff, Banff, since 1992; Vice-President, Aberdeen, Banff and Kincardine Area, Royal British Legion Scotland; b. 20.3.23, Aberdeen; m., Margaret Anne Castel; 2 s.; 1 d. Educ. Robert Gordon's College, Aberdeen; Aberdeen University. Commissioned into Reconnaissance Corps, 1943; gazetted Captain, 1947; Teacher of History, 1950-58; Special Assistant, Turriff Academy, 1958-63; Principal Teacher of History, Breadalbane Academy, Banff Academy, 1963-74; Assistant Rector, Banff Academy, 1974-88; Member, Banffshire Education Committee, 1961-75. Recreations: furniture making; Banff Choral Society. Address: (h.) 11 Fife Street, Banff AB45 1JB; T.-01261 812285.

Hay, Ian, FCIBS, FRSA, FSAE. Chief Executive, Scottish Association of Master Bakers, since 1989; b. 31.8.39, Aberdeen; m., Amelia Robertson; 3 s.; 1 d. Educ. Ellon Academy. Thirty years with Clydesdale Bank PLC, including senior positions as General Manager London and Regional Director with responsibilities for East of Scotland; appointed Chief Executive, Craft Bakery Training Organisation, 1993; Chairman, Scottish Council of National Training Organisations; Member: Board of Management, Scottish Qualifications Authority, Board, NTO National Council, Employment Tribunal Panel. Recreations: golf; football; reading; complementary medicine. Address: (b.) 4 Torphichen Street, Edinburgh EH3 8JQ; T.-0131-229 1401.

Hay, J. Iain, FRICS, IRRV. J. Iain Hay, Chartered Surveyors, since 1992; Director, KDCL Ltd., since 1992; b. 17.7.44, Ayr; m., Elizabeth; 2 d. Educ. Kelvinside Academy. Thomas Binnie & Hendry, Chartered Surveyors, 1962-66; Dunbarton County Assessors Office, 1966-69; Bovis Homes, 1969-70; Senior Surveyor, Millar Macrae and Stewart, 1970-72, Partner, 1972-86; Partner, Knight Frank & Rutley, 1986-91 (Consultant, 1991-93); Director, Montrose Estates (1982) Ltd., 1986-93; Chairman, Royal Institution of Chartered Surveyors in Scotland, 1993-94; Past President, Property Agents International. Recreations: golf; gardening. Address: (h.) Castle House, Drymen, Glasgow; T.-01360 660550.

Hay, James Taylor Cantlay, MBE, BSc (Hons), DTech, FInstPet, SPE, AAPG. Oil and Gas Consultant; Chairman, Scottish Sub-sea Technology Group, since 1991; Director, Midmar Energy Ltd., since 1998; b. 13.6.35, Huntly; m., Mary Gordon Davidson; 1 s.; 2 d. Educ. Banchory Academy; Aberdeen University. Geologist, Iraq Petroleum Co. Ltd., Iraq, 1958-66; Head of Geology, Abu Dhabi Petroleum Co. Ltd., Abu Dhabi, 1967-71; Lecturer in Geology, Aberdeen University, 1971-74; Senior Production Geologist, Burmah Oil, London, 1974-76; various management roles, BNOC, Aberdeen and Glasgow, 1977-80; General Manager: BNOC/Britoil, Aberdeen, 1980-87, BP Exploration, Aberdeen, 1988-91. Recreations: golf;

shooting. Address: (h.) 67 Fountainhall Road, Aberdeen; T.-01224 645955.

Hay, Michael James, BSc (Hons), DipEd. Head Teacher, Tynecastle High School, since 1987; b. 8.3.47, Newport Pagnell; m., Rosalind Margaret Gibling; 1 s.; 1 d. Educ. Perth Academy; Edinburgh University. Teacher of Mathematics, Royal High School, 1968-71; Principal Teacher of Mathematics: John Watson's School, 1971-73, Leith Academy, 1973-79; Assistant Head Teacher, Penicuik High School, 1979-83; Depute Head Teacher, Tynecastle High School, 1983 87. Recreations: music (organist and choirmaster); hill-walking; recreational computing. Address: (b.) Tynecastle High School, McLeod Street, Edinburgh EH11 2NJ; T.-0131-337 3488.

Hay, Sheriff Principal Robert Colquhoun, CBE, MA, LLB, WS. Sheriff Principal of North Strathclyde, 1989-98; b. 22.9.33, Glasgow; m., Olive Black; 2 s.; 2 d. Educ. Edinburgh University. Legal practice, 1956-63, 1968-76; Depute Procurator Fiscal, 1963-68; Chairman, Industrial Tribunals (Scotland), 1976-81, President, 1981-89; Commissioner of Northern Lights, since 1989, Chairman, 1992-93; Member, Sheriff Court Rules Council, 1990-95, Chairman, 1993-95; Commissioner for Clan Hay, since 1995. Address: (b.) Sheriff Principal's Chambers, Sheriff Court House, St. James Street, Paisley PA3 2HW; T.-0141-887 5291.

Hay, Robert King Miller, BSc, MSc, PhD, FIBiol. Director, Scottish Agricultural Science Agency, since 1990; b. 19.8.46, Edinburgh; m., Dorothea Harden Vinycomb; 2 s.; 1 d. Educ. Forres Academy, Moray; Aberdeen University; University of East Anglia. AFRC Research Fellow, Edinburgh University, 1971-74; Lecturer in Crop Production: University of Malawi, 1974-76, Edinburgh University, 1976-77; Lecturer in Environmental Sciences, Lancaster University, 1977-82; Leverhulme European Fellow, Agricultural University of Norway, 1981; Head of Plant Sciences, Scottish Agricultural College, Ayr, 1982-90; British Council Research Fellow, University of Western Australia, 1989; Visiting Scientist, McGill University, Montreal, 1997. Publications: Environmental Physiology of Plants; Chemistry for Agriculture and Ecology; Introduction to the Physiology of Crop Yield; Volatile Oil Crops (Editor); Science Policies in Europe: Unity and Diversity (Editor); Science and the Scottish Parliament (Editor); Annals of Botany (Editor); 60 scientific papers. Recreations: walking; Nordic skiing; mending walls; music; Scotland. Address: (h.) 16 Polton Road, Lasswade EH18 1AA.

Hay, Professor Robert Walker, BSc, PhD, CChem, FRSC, FRSE. Professor of Chemistry, St. Andrews University, since 1988; b. 17.9.34, Stirling; m., Alison Laird; 1 s.; 3 d. Educ. Stirling High School; Glasgow University. Assistant Lecturer, Glasgow University, 1959; subsequently worked at Esso Research; Lecturer, Senior Lecturer and Reader, Victoria University, Wellington, New Zealand, 1961; Reader, Stirling University, 1971; Professor, Stirling University, 1984; Pro Dean of Science (Graduate Studies), 1993-96; Governor, Morrisons Academy, Crieff. Publications: Bioinorganic Chemistry, 1984; numerous scientific papers. Recreations: walking; travel; gardening; reading. Address: (b.) School of Chemistry, St. Andrews University, St. Andrews KY16 9ST; T.-01334 463827.

Haythornthwaite, Professor Josephine Angela, BA, PhD, FLA, FInstInfSc. Chief Librarian, Glasgow Caledonian University, since 1989; b. 24.6.38, Leamington Spa. Educ. St. Margaret's School, Ludlow, Strathclyde University. Began career as librarian, 1962; Depute Librarian, Glasgow College of Technology, 1971-78; Lecturer: Strathclyde University, 1978-82, Loughborough University, 1983-89. Publications: Distance Education in Library and Information Studies (Co-author); Business Information Maze; Scotland in the Nineteenth Century. Recreations: theatre; music; cooking; entertaining; travel. Address: (b.) Glasgow Caledonian University, Cowcaddens Road, Glasgow G4 OBA; T.-0141-331 3860.

Hazel, George McLean, BSc, MSc, PhD, CEng, MICE, MCIT, MIHT. Director of City Development, City of Edinburgh Council, since 1996; b. 27.1.49, Dunfermline; m., Fiona Isabella Gault; 1 s.; 2 d. Educ. Dunfermline High School; Heriot-Watt University; Cranfield Institute of Technology. Transportation Engineer: City of Edinburgh Corporation, five years, Lothian Regional Council, four years; Lecturer, Senior Lecturer, Head of Department and Professor, Napier College/Polytechnic/University, 11 years; Director, Oscar Faber TPA, three years; Director of Transportation, Lothian Regional Council, two years; Royal Academy of Engineers Visiting Professor, Heriot-Watt University; Visiting Professor, Napier University. Member, Secretary of State for Scotland's Advisory Group on Sustainable Development; Chairman: Edinburgh and East of Scotland Association, Institution of Civil Engineers, Institution of Highways and Transportation (Central and Southern Scotland Branch). Recreations: golf; gardening; music; vintage cars. Address: (h.) 7 Glenlockhart Valley, Edinburgh EH14 1DE.

Heading, Robert Campbell, BSc, MD, FRCPE, FRCP. Consultant Physician, Edinburgh Royal Infirmary, since 1975; Reader in Medicine, Edinburgh University, since 1992; b. 3.7.41, Stepps, Lanarkshire; m., Patricia Mary Goldie; 2 s.; 1 d. Educ. Birkenhead School; King Edward's School, Birmingham; Edinburgh University. Address: (h.) 20 Frogston Road West, Edinburgh EH10 7AR; T.-0131-445 1552.

Heald, Professor David Albert, BA, ACMA. Professor of Accountancy, Aberdeen University, since 1990; Specialist Adviser: Treasury and Civil Service Committee, House of Commons, since 1989, Scottish Affairs Committee, House of Commons, 1980-81, 1983, 1993-96; b. 25.9.47, York; m., Yvonne Duncan. Educ. Nunthorpe Grammar School, York; Leicester University; Jordanhill College. Accountant, Raleigh Industries, 1969-70, British Steel Corporation, 1971-72; Lecturer in Economics, Glasgow College of Technology, 1972-78; Lecturer in Economics, later in Management Studies, Glasgow University, 1978-90. Labour Parliamentary candidate, Roxburgh, Selkirk and Peebles, 1979. Publications: several books, including: Making Devolution Work; Financing Devolution within the UK: a study of the lessons from failure; Public Expenditure: its defence and reform; Financing a Scottish Parliament: options for debate; and numerous articles on topics such as public expenditure, government accounting, privatisation and the Private Finance Initiative. Recreations: theatre; cinema; everything French; squash; boating on the Moray Firth. Address: (b.) Department of Accountancy, Aberdeen University, Edward Wright Building, Aberdeen, AB24 3QY; T.-01224 272213.

Healy, Brendan John Patrick. Chief Executive, St. Andrew's Ambulance Association, since 1995; b. 25.3.46, Dublin; m., Catherine; 1 s.; 2 d. Educ. Britania Royal Naval College. Specialised in naval aviation; Joint Service Defence College, 1987; Commanding Officer, Royal Naval Air Station, Prestwick, 1990-93. Recreations: golf; philately; travel. Address: (b.) St. Andrew's House, 48 Milton Street, Glasgow G4 0HR.

Heaney, (Alison) Jane, BEd. Teacher of Physical Education, since 1975; General Commissioner of Taxes, since 1994; Member, Scottish Sports Council, since 1996; b. 25.3.53, Inverness; m., Robert J. Heaney, JP, FRICS; 1 s.; 1 d. Educ. St. Leonards School for Girls, St. Andrews; Dunfermline College of Physical Education. Teacher of Physical Education, 1975-78; Partner in catering business, 1978-81; Director of property development company, 1985-

90; Partner in farming business, since 1980; Teacher of Physical Education, since 1993. Secretary, Dalkeith and District Pony Club, 1995-96; President, Scottish Lacrosse Association, 1994-96. Recreations: golf; tennis; sailing; skiing; interior design; cooking; gardening. Address: (h.) Pogbie House, Humbie, East Lothian EH36 5PN; T.-01875 833 332.

Hearne, John Michael, BMus, MMus. Publisher (Longship Music); Freelance Composer and Professional Singer; Conductor and Copyist; b. 19.9.37, Reading; m., Margaret Gillespie Jarvie. Educ. Torquay Grammar School; St. Luke's College, Exeter; University College of Wales, Aberystwyth. Teaching, Rugeley, Staffordshire, 1959-60; Warehouseman/ Driver, Torquay, 1961-64; Teaching: Tonlistarskoli Borgarfjardar, Iceland, 1968-69, UCW Aberystwyth, 1969-70; Lecturer, Aberdeen College of Education, 1970-87. Composer, vocal, instrumental and incidental music: BBC commission for BBCSSO, 1990 (trumpet concerto); McEwen Commission, Glasgow University, 1979; A Legend of Margaret, commissioned to celebrate 150th anniversary of St. Margaret's School, Aberdeen, 1996; Member, John Currie Singers; Awarded Radio Forth Trophy, 1985, for most outstanding work on Edinburgh Festival Fringe; joint winner, Gregynog Composers' Award for Wales, 1992. Chorus Manager, Aberdeen International Youth Festival, since 1978; Chairman: Scottish Music Advisory Committee, BBC, 1986-90, Gordon Forum for the Arts, 1991-94; Conductor, Stonehaven and District Choral Society; Past Chairman, Scottish Society of Composers; Member: Executive Committee, Composers' Guild GB, Board, National Youth Choir of Scotland; Winner, Gregynog Composres' Award for Wales, 1998; Conductor, Inverurie Choral Society; Warden, Performers and Composers Section, Incorporated Society of Musicians, 1999. Recreations: motoring and travel (1954 Daimler Roadster). Address: (h.) Smidskot, Fawells, Keith-Hall, Inverurie AB51 OLN; T.-01651 882 274.

Heatly, Sir Peter, CBE, DL, BSc, CEng, FICE. Chairman, Peter Heatly & Co. Ltd., since 1958; b. 9.6.24, Edinburgh; m., Mae Calder Cochrane. Educ. Leith Academy; Edinburgh University. Structural Designer, Redpath Brown & Co. Ltd., 1946; Lecturer in Civil Engineering, Edinburgh University, 1948. Chairman: Scottish Sports Council, 1975-87, Commonwealth Games Federation, 1982-90, International Diving Committee, 1984-88; Master, Edinburgh Merchant Company, 1988-90; awarded Honorary Doctorate, Edinburgh University, 1992, Queen Margaret College, 1994; Honorary Doctorate, Stirling University, 1998. Recreations: swimming; gardening; travel. Address: (h.) Lanrig, Balerno, Edinburgh EH14 7AJ; T.-0131-449 3998.

Hector, Gordon Matthews, CMG, CBE (OBE, 1955), MA (Oxon). Honorary Vice President, The St. Andrew Society; b. 9.6.18, Aberdeen; m., Dr. Mary Forrest Gray; 1 s.; 2 d. Educ. St. Mary's School, Melrose; Edinburgh Academy; Lincoln College, Oxford. HM Colonial Administrative Service and Overseas Civil Service, 1946-66: District Commissioner, Kenya, Secretary, Kenya Road Authority, Secretary to Government of Seychelles, 1952-55, Acting Governor, 1953, Deputy Resident Commissioner and Government Secretary, Basutoland (now Lesotho), 1956-64, Deputy British Government Representative, Lesotho, 1965-66; Aberdeen University: Clerk to University Court, 1967, Deputy Secretary, 1976-80; Secretary to Assembly Council, General Assembly of Church of Scotland, 1980-85. Fellow, Commonwealth Fund, 1939; Burgess of Guild, Aberdeen; Chairman, West End Community Council, Edinburgh, 1986-89; Court of Directors, Edinburgh Academy, 1967-75; Chairman: Great North of Scotland Railway Association, 1990-92, Scottish Council, Victoria League, 1983-88; Member, sometime Chairman, Board of Managers, Oakbank List D School, 1969-90. Recreations: town and country walking; railways ancient and modern; grandchildren. Address: (h.) 4 Montgomery Court, 110 Hepburn Gardens, St. Andrews KY16 9LT; T.-01334 473784.

Hedderwick, Alexander Mark. Managing Director, Adam & Company Investment Management, since 1989; Director, Adam & Company Group PLC, since 1992; b. 13.12.48. Hedderwick Borthwick, Stockbrokers, 1969-73; Langton Underwriting Agents, Lloyds, 1973-84. Recreations: family; gardening; bee-keeping. Address: (b.) 22 Charlotte Square, Edinburgh EH2 4DF; T.-0131-225 8484.

Hedderwick, Mairi Crawford, DA (Edin). Illustrator, Writer and Public Speaker; b. 2.5.39, Gourock; 1 s.; 1 d. Educ. St. Columba's School, Kilmacolm; Edinburgh College of Art; Jordanhill College of Education. Publications: for children: Katie Morag series, Peedie Peebles series, Carpenter MacPheigh; for adults: An Eye on the Hebrides, Highland Journey. Recreations: a day outside ending round a table with friends, food and wine.

Heggie, Professor Douglas Cameron, MA, PhD, FRAS, FRSE. Professor of Mathematical Astronomy, Edinburgh University, since 1994; b. 7.2.47, Edinburgh; m., Linda Jane Tennent; 2 d. Educ. George Heriot's School, Edinburgh; Trinity College, Cambridge. Research Fellow, Trinity College, Cambridge, 1972-76; Lecturer in Mathematics, Edinburgh University, 1975-85, Reader, 1985-94; Council Member, Royal Astronomical Society, 1982-85; President, Commission 37, International Astronomical Union, 1985-88; Member, Board of Editors, Monthly Notices of the RAS, since 1994. Publications: Megalithic Science; scientific papers on dynamical astronomy. Recreations: family life; walking; music. Address: (b.) Edinburgh University, Department of Mathematics and Statistics, King's Buildings, Edinburgh EH9 3JZ; T.-0131-650 5035.

Heilig, James Leedom, BSc. Chief Executive, Low & Bonar PLC, since 1995; b. 9.10.35, United States; m., Susie; 2 s.; 1 d. Educ. Oregon State University. Background in sales and marketing; former Vice-President – Operations, Flexible Packaging Group, James River Corporation, Cincinnati, Ohio; joined Low & Bonar Group, 1992; became C.E.O. and President of Group's North American operations and member of Group Board. Recreations: golf; travel; reading. Address: (b.) Bonar House, Faraday Street, Dundee DD1 9JA; T.-01382 818171.

Heller, Martin Fuller Vernon, FRSAMD. Actor, since 1947; b. 20.2.27, Manchester; m., Joyce Allan; 2 s.; 4 d. Educ. Rondebosch Boys High School, Cape Town; Central School of Speech Training and Dramatic Art, London. Compass Players, 1948-52; repertory seasons and/or individual productions at following Scottish theatres: St. Andrews Byre, Edinburgh Gateway, Glasgow Citizens' (eight seasons), Edinburgh Royal Lyceum, Edinburgh Traverse, Dundee Repertory, Perth Repertory, Pitlochry Festival; Founder/Artistic Director, Prime Productions; extensive television and radio work; Member: Scottish Arts Council, 1975-82 (latterly Chairman, Drama Committee), Board, Pitlochry Festival Theatre; Governor, Royal Scottish Academy of Music and Drama, 1982-94. Recreations: politics; history; listening to music. Address: (h.) 54 Hermiston, Currie, Midlothian EH14 4AQ; T.-0131-449 4055.

Helms, Professor Peter Joseph, MB, BS, PhD, FRCP, FRCPCH. Professor of Child Health, Aberdeen University, since 1991; Consultant Paediatrician, since 1982; b. 26.6.47, Melbourne; m., Kathleen Mary; 1 s.; 3 d. Educ. Wimbledon College; Royal Free Hospital School of Medicine; London University. SHO, Hospital for Sick Children, Great Ormond Street, 1976; Lecturer in Paediatrics, Charing Cross Hospital Medical School, 1977-

78; Research Fellow, Institute of Child Health, London, 1978-81, National Heart and Lung Institute, London, 1981-82; Senior Lecturer, Institute of Child Health, 1982-91; Honorary Consultant Paediatrician, Hospital for Sick Children, Great Ormond Street, 1982-91. Recreations: music; hill-walking; European history. Address: (b.) Department of Child Health, Foresterhill, Aberdeen, AB25 2ZD; T.-01224 404461.

Henderson, Andrew Kerr, MB, ChB, FRCP. Consultant Physician, Lorn and the Islands District General Hospital, Oban; Honorary Clinical Senior Lecturer, Glasgow University; b. 1.3.46, Hawick; m., Doreen Innes Wilkinson; 1 s.; 2 d. Educ. Glasgow Academy; Glasgow University. Medical Registrar, Western Infirmary, Glasgow; Medical Registrar/Senior Registrar, Glasgow Royal Infirmary. Chairman, Counties Branch, Scottish Schoolboys' Club. Recreations: gardening; hill-walking. Address: (h.) Birkmoss, North Connel, Argyll; T.-01631 710379.

Henderson, Douglas Mackay, CBE, BSc, FLS, FRSE, VMH. Queen's Botanist in Scotland, since 1987; b. 30.8.27, Blairgowrie; m., Julia Margaret Brown; 1 s.; 2 d. Educ. Blairgowrie High School; Edinburgh University. Scientific Officer, Department of Agriculture, Scotland, 1948-50; Research Botanist, Royal Botanic Garden, Edinburgh, 1950-70; Curator, Royal Society of Edinburgh, 1978-87; Secretary, International Association of Botanical Gardens, 1969-81; Regius Keeper, Royal Botanic Garden, Edinburgh, 1970-87; Honorary Professor, Edinburgh University, since 1982; Administrator, Inverewe Garden, National Trust for Scotland, 1987-92; Council Member, National Trust for Scotland, since 1993; Secretary, Help the Aged Highland Committee. Recreations: natural history; painting; sailing; cooking. Address: (h.) Larachan, 54 Lonemore, Gairloch, Ross-shire IV21 2DB; T.-01445 2391.

Henderson, Elizabeth Kidd, MA (Hons), MEd (Hons). Governor, Glasgow Academy; Headmistress, Westbourne School, 1970-88; b. 25.5.28, Dunfermline. Educ. Dunfermline High School; Edinburgh University; St. Andrews University. Mathematics Teacher, Morrison's Academy, Crieff; Second Master, Mathematics, Dundee High School; Principal Teacher of Mathematics, Aberdeen High School; former Secretary, Mathematics Panel, Scottish Examination Board; President, Scottish Area, Secondary Heads Association; former Member, Church of Scotland Education Committee; President, Glasgow Mathematical Association; Chairman, Community Council. Publication: Modern Mathematics for Schools (Co-author). Recreations: walking; golf. Address: (h.) 16 George Reith Avenue, Glasgow G12 0AN; T.-0141-334 8545.

Henderson, Hamish Scott, MA, Hon.LLD, Hon.DUniv, Dr.h.c., DLitt. Lecturer/Research Fellow, School of Scottish Studies, Edinburgh University, since 1952 (Honorary Fellow, since 1988); b. 11.11.19, Blairgowrie; m., Felicity Schmidt; 2 d. Educ. Blairgowrie High School; Dulwich College; Downing College, Cambridge University. Wartime: Intelligence Officer, 51st Highland Division and other Infantry Divisions, Egypt, Libya, Tunisia, Sicily, Italy; mentioned in Dispatches, 1945; District Secretary, WEA, 1947-49; Assistant to Alan Lomax in folklore collection and editing, 1950-51; first translator of Gramsci into English. Publications: Elegies for the Dead in Cyrenaica, 1948 (Somerset Maugham Award, 1949); Ballads of World War II (published by Lili Marlene Club of Glasgow), 1947; Alias MacAlias (anthology of essays), 1992; The Armstrong Nose: selected letters, 1996; Gramsci's Prison Letters, 1996. Recreations: writing; singing; song-writing. Address: (h.) 20 Melville Terrace, Edinburgh; T.-0131-667 5143.

Henderson, James. Registrar of Companies for Scotland, since 1992; b. 22.11.48, Kilmarnock; m., Patricia Mazs; 2 d. Educ. Kilmarnock Academy. Joined the Queen's and Lord Treasurer's Remembrancer, 1967; Department of Trade and Industry, 1981; became Companies House DTI's first agency, 1988. Recreations: bowls; rugby (spectating); reading; gardening. Address: (b.) 37 Castle Terrace, Edinburgh EH1 2EB; T.-0131-535 5855.

Henderson, James Gunn, MBE. Editor, Northern Times, 1975-96; b. 10.7.31, Wick; m., 1, Catherine Maclean (deceased); 2 d.; 2, Christine Mackay; 4 s. Educ. Wick High School. Reporter, John O'Groat Journal, 1948-53; Scottish Daily Express: Reporter, 1953-60, Deputy Chief, Edinburgh, 1960-65, Deputy News Editor, Glasgow, 1965-69, News Features Editor, Glasgow, 1969-75.Trustee, Moray Firth Radio Charity, Highland Community Foundation. Recreation: reading newspapers. Address: (h.) Littleferry, Golspie, KW10 6TD; T.-01408 633548.

Henderson, John Gunn, BA, FRSA. Head of Private Finance Unit and Assistant Director of Finance, Scottish Office, since 1997; b. 29.5.53, Edinburgh; m., Caroline; 1 s.; 2 d. Educ. Broughton Secondary, Edinburgh; Open University. Scottish Development Department, 1970-78; Department of Agriculture and Fisheries for Scotland, 1978-85; Scottish Development Department, Trunk Roads Division, 1985-88; Scottish Office Education and Industry Department, 1988-97 (Head, Further Education Funding Unit, 1992-97). Recreations: reading; gardening; beachcombing. Address: (b.) Scottish Office, Victoria Quay, Edinburgh EH6 6QQ; T.-0131-244 7497.

Henderson, Major Richard Yates, TD, JP, BA (Oxon), LLB. Lord Lieutenant, Ayrshire and Arran, since 1991; b. 7.7.31, Nitshill; m., Frances Elizabeth Chrystal; 3 s. (inc. 1 s. dec.); 1 d. Educ. Rugby; Hertford College, Oxford; Glasgow University. Royal Scots Greys, 1950-52; TA Ayrshire (ECO) Yeomanry, 1953-69 (Major); Deputy Lieutenant, Ayrshire and Arran, 1970-90; Partner, Mitchells Roberton, Solicitors, 1958-90, Consultant, 1991-92. Brigadier, Queen's Bodyguard for Scotland (Royal Company of Archers); President, Lowland TAVRA, since 1996; Hon. Colonel, Ayrshire Yeomanry Sqn., Scottish Yeomanry, 1992-97; Honorary Sheriff, South Strathclyde Dumfries and Galloway at Ayr, since 1997. Recreations: shooting; tennis; golf. Address: (h.) Blairston, by Ayr; T.-01292 441601.

Henderson, Stewart Alexander, RIBA, FRIAS. Director, Parkman Scotland Ltd.; b. 18.1.47, Glasgow; 1 s.; 1 d. Educ. Falkirk High School; Glasgow School of Art. Private practice, Glasgow; Principal Architect, Stewartry District; Depute Director of Architectural Services, Stornoway; Chief Architect, Clydesdale District; Chief Architect, Scottish & Newcastle; Executive Director of Property Services, Edinburgh District Council; Director of Property Services, City of Edinburgh Council. Recreations: shooting; stalking; fishing. Address: (b.) Parkman Scotland Ltd., 38 Henderson Row, Edinburgh EH3 5DN.

Henderson, Thomas Wilson. Former Director, John Turnbull & Sons Ltd., Hawick; Member, Scottish Borders Council, since 1995 (formerly Member, Ettrick and Lauderdale District Council, and Provost of Selkirk); b. 28.9.41, Selkirk; m., Catherine Helen Herbert; 2 s. Educ. Selkirk Public School; Selkirk High School; Scottish College of Textiles; Paisley College of Technology. Served apprenticeship as dyer with George Roberts & Co. Ltd., Selkirk, 1957-61; Dyer, Grays Carpets, Ayr, 1961-70; Assistant Manager, John Turnbull & Sons Ltd., Hawick, 1978-83; involved in management buy-out, 1983; Member, Selkirk Town Council, 1973-75; Corporate Member, Society of Dyers and Colourists; holder of various offices, Transport and General Workers Union, since 1970; Organiser, Scottish National Party, Ayr Constituency, 1967-70. Recreations: hill-walking; horse-riding; reading; folk music; jazz; football; cricket. Address: (h.) Triglav, 29 Shawpark Crescent, Selkirk; T.-01750 20821.

Henderson-Howat, David Barclay, BSc, MA, MBA. Chief Conservator, Forestry Commission, Scotland, since 1996; b. 23.1.54, Trinidad; m., Jean Buchanan-Smith; 1 s.; 3 d. Educ. Abingdon School; University of Edinburgh; Magdalene College, University of Cambridge; University of Strathclyde. Scottish Office, 1976-79; Personal Assistant to Chief Executive, Scottish Development Agency, 1979-80; Harvesting and Marketing Manager, Thetford Forest, 1980-84; Forest Manager, Shiselweni Forest, Swaziland, 1984-86; Forest District Manager, Aberfoyle, Perthshire, 1986-90; Forestry Commission Headquarters, 1990-96. Member, Lamancha, Newlands and Kirkurd Community Council, 1992-95. Recreations: walking; sailing. Address: (b.) Forestry Commission, 231 Corstorphine Road, Edinburgh EH12 7AR; T.-0131-314 6162.

Hendron, Frances, MA (Cantab). Director, Celtic Film and Television Association, since 1994. Educ. St. Michael's High School, Lurgan; Newnham College, Cambridge. Address: (b.) 1 Bowmont Gardens, Glasgow G12 9LR; T.-0141-342 4947.

Hendry, Alan. Editor: John O'Groat Journal, since 1988, Caithness Courier, since 1988; b. 26.3.62, Wick; m., Yvonne; 2 s. Educ. Wick High School; Aberdeen College of Commerce. Address: (b.) 42 Union Street, Wick, Caithness KW1 5ED; T.-01955 604242.

Hendry, Professor Alan, BSc (Hons), PhD, CEng, FIM, MInstP, CPhys, FRSA. Dean, Faculty of Engineering, Strathclyde University; b. 29.1.47, Ochiltree; m., Jean Carey Kerr; 1 s.; 1 d. Educ. Cumnock Academy; Strathclyde University. Postdoctoral Research Associate, Newcastle University, 1971-75; Research Officer, Midlands Region, CEGB, 1975-76; Lecturer in Metallurgy and Assistant Director, Wolfson Research Group for High Strength Materials, Newcastle University, 1976-85; Strathclyde University: Reader in Ceramics, 1985-88, Professor of Metallurgy and Engineering Materials, since 1988, Head of Department of Metallurgy and Engineering Materials, 1990-96; Vice-Dean (Engineering), 1996-97. President, Scottish Association for Metals, 1990-92; Member, Materials Commission, SERC, 1989-92, Materials College, EPSRC, since 1994; Member, International Academy of Ceramics; Allan B. Dove Medal, Wire Assoc. Int., 1993. Address: (h.) Ardleven, 23 Campbell Drive, Bearsden, Glasgow G61 4NF; T.-0141-942 3169.

Hendry, Professor Arnold William, BSc, PhD, DSc, FICE, FIStructE, FRSE. Professor Emeritus, University of Edinburgh, since 1988; President, Scottish Association for Public Transport; b. 10.9.21, Buckie; m., 1, Sheila Mary Cameron Roberts; 2, Elizabeth Lois Alice Inglis; 1 s.; 1 s. deceased; 1 d. Educ. Buckie High School; Aberdeen University. Civil Engineer, Sir Wm. Arrol & Co. Ltd., Glasgow, 1941-43; Lecturer, University of Aberdeen, 1943-49; Reader, King's College, University of London, 1949-51; Professor of Civil Engineering and Dean, Faculty of Engineering, University of Khartoum, 1951-57; Professor of Building Science, University of Liverpool, 1957-63; Professor of Civil Engineering, University of Edinburgh, 1964-88. Member, Transport Committee, Cockburn Association. Publications: eight books; over 150 papers on structural engineering. Recreations: walking; reading; travel. Address: (h.) 146/6 Whitehouse Loan, Edinburgh EH9 2AN; T.-0131-447 0368.

Hendry, Joy McLaggan, MA (Hons), DipEd. Editor, Chapman Magazine, since 1972; Writer; Writer-in-Residence, Stirling District Council, 1991-93; b. 3.2.53, Perth; m., Ian Montgomery. Educ. Perth Academy; Edinburgh University. Former teacher; Co-Editor, Chapman, 1972-76, Sole Editor, since 1976; Deputy Convener, Scottish Poetry Library Association, 1983-88; Convener, Committee for the Advancement of Scottish Literature in Schools; Member AdCas; Scottish National Theatre Steering Committee; Campaign for a Scottish Assembly; Member, Drama Committee, Scottish Arts Council; writes poetry; gives lectures and talks and performances of poetry and song; radio critic, The Scotsman, 1988-97; theatre reviewer. Publications: Scots: The Way Forward; Poems and Pictures by Wendy Wood (Editor); The Land for the People (Co-Editor); Critical Essays on Sorley MacLean (Co-Editor); Critical Essays on Norman MacCaig (Co-Editor); Gang Doun wi a Sang (play); radio: The Wa' at the Warld's End, Radio 3 (play); A Many-Faceted Thing (Memory), Radio 4 (major 4-part series). Recreations: going to theatre; cinema; reading. Address: 4 Broughton Place, Edinburgh EH1 3RX; T.-0131-557 2207.

Hendry, Professor Leo Brough, MSc, MEd, PhD, DLitt, FBPS, FECSS. Professor of Education, Aberdeen University, since 1989, and Visiting Professor in Health Psychology, Norwegian University of Science and Technology, Trondheim; b. 12.11.35, Glasgow; m., Philomena Walsh; 2 d. Educ. Hermitage Academy, Helensburgh; Jordanhill College of Education, Glasgow; Bradford University; Leicester University; Aberdeen University. School Teacher in Scottish and English schools, including two posts as Head of Department, 1957-64; Lecturer in Education and Physical Education, College of St. Mark and St. John's, Chelsea, London University Institute, 1964-66; Head of Human Movement Studies, Trinity and All Saints' Colleges, Leeds University Institute, 1966-71; Lecturer in Education, then Senior Lecturer, Aberdeen University, 1971-88; Head, Education Department, 1988-94; Member, Scottish Council for Research in Education, 1983-86. Publications: School, Sport, Leisure: three dimensions of adolescence, 1978; Adolescents and Leisure, 1981; Growing Up and Going Out, 1983; Personality and Performance in Physical Education and Sport (Co-Author), 1974; Physical Education in England (Co-Author), 1976; Towards Community Education (Co-Author), 1980; The Nature of Adolescence (Co-Author), 1990; Young People's Leisure and Lifestyles (Co-Author), 1993; Educating for Health (Co-Author), 1995; New Perspectives on Youth Disaffection (Co-Author), 1997; Growing Up, Speaking Out (Co-author), 1998; book chapters; research articles. Recreations: golf; writing; broadcasting; presenting papers at international conferences. Address: (b.) Centre for Educational Research, Department of Sociology, Aberdeen University, Aberdeen AB9 2UB; T.-01224 272731.

Hendry, Stephen, MBE. Professional snooker player; b. 13.1.69; m., Mandy. Youngest-ever Scottish Amateur Champion (aged 15); has won 64 major titles worldwide; youngest player to attain No. 1 ranking; youngest player to win World Championship, 1990; World Champion six times; UK Champion, five times; Masters Champion, six times. Address: (b.) Cuemasters Ltd., Kerse Road, Stirling, FK7 7SG; T.-01786 462634.

Henley, Professor John Sebastian, BSc(Eng), PhD. Professor of International Management, University of Edinburgh Management School, since 1996; b. 5.4.43, Malvern; m., Sarah J. Sieley; 2 d. Educ. King Edward's School, Birmingham; University College, London; London School of Economics. Personnel Officer, Glaxo Laboratories, 1966-68; Lecturer, Industrial Relations Department, London School of Economics, 1968-72; Lecturer, Faculty of Commerce, University of Nairobi, 1972-75; joined Department of Business Studies, University of Edinburgh, 1975. Publications: co-author of three books; editor of two books; author of over 50 academic papers. Recreations: gardening; theatre; opera; sailing. Address: (b.) University of Edinburgh Management School, 50 George Square, Edinburgh EH8 9JT; T.-0131-650 3814.

Henley, Rt. Rev. Michael Harry George, CB. Bishop of St. Andrews, Dunkeld and Dunblane, since 1995; b. 16.1.38; m.; 2 d.

Henry, Sheriff A.C., MA, LLB. Sheriff of Glasgow and Strathkelvin, at Glasgow. Admitted, Faculty of Advocates, 1969. Address: (b.) Sheriff Court House, 1 Carlton Place, Glasgow, G5 9DA.

Henry, Captain Michael Charles, RN (Rtd.), DL. Deputy Lieutenant, Dunbartonshire, since 1989; Director, Merchants House of Glasgow, 1990-96; b. 4.6.28, London; m., Nancie Elma Nicol; 2 s.; 3 d. Educ. Royal Naval College, Dartmouth. Naval career, Cadet to Captain, 1942-78; submarine specialist; commanded HM Submarines Seraph, Trump and Resolution, Britain's first Polaris submarine; fired first British missile, Cape Canaveral, and conducted first deterrent patrol, 1968; commanded 10th (Polaris) Submarine Squadron, Faslane, and Queen's Harbour Master, Clyde, 1972-74; commanded HMS Hampshire, 1975-76; Director of Naval Operations and Trade, 1976-78; Marine Manager, British National Oil Corporation, Aberdeen, 1978-80; Naval Regional Officer Scotland and Northern Ireland, Glasgow, 1980-90. Recreation: sailing. Address: (h.) Aldavhu, Garelochhead, Helensburgh G84 0EL; T.-01436 810533.

Henshelwood, James, JP, FISMM, MCIM, MInstM, AMNI. Director, Glasgow Building Preservation Trust, since 1982; Member, St. John Association of Scotland; Member, Central Advisory Committee on Justices of the Peace; b. 18.2.22, Glasgow; m., Mavis Irene Watson (deceased); 3 s.; 2 d. Educ. Allan Glen's School; Whitehill Senior Secondary School; Royal Technical College, Glasgow. Joined Merchant Navy as cadet, 1938, and "swallowed the anchor" in 1953 as Master Mariner; Special Services, RNR; Independent Councillor, Johnstone, 1966-69 (Burgh Treasurer); President, Chartered Institute of Marketing, West of Scotland Branch; Past Chairman, Nautical Institute, West of Scotland; Governor, RNLI; Vice-Chairman, Scottish Pre-Retirement Council; Past President, Glasgow Bute Benevolent Society; former Director, Glasgow Chamber of Commerce; former Captain, Bute Golf Club. Recreations: golf; sailing; walking. Address: (h.) 72 Globe Court, Calderwood, East Kilbride, Glasgow G74 3QZ; T.-013552 38851.

Herald, Sheriff John Pearson, LLB, NP, SSC. Sheriff of North Strathclyde at Greenock and Rothesay, since 1992; b. 12.7.46, Glasgow; m., Catriona; 1 d. Educ. Hillhead High School, Glasgow; Glasgow University. Partner, Carlton Gilruth, Solicitors, Dundee, 1970-91; Depute Town Clerk, Newport-on-Tay, 1970-75; Member, Angus Legal Aid Committee, 1970-79, Secretary, 1979-87; Member, Legal Aid Central Committee, 1981-87; Temporary Sheriff, 1984-91; part-time Chairman, Industrial Tribunals, 1984-91. Chairman, Dundee Citizens Advice Bureau, 1972-79 and 1982-91; President, Rotary Club of North Fife, 1989. Recreations: football; golf; reading. Address: (b.) Sheriff Court House, Nelson Street, Greenock; T.-01475 787073.

Herbert, Professor Rodney Andrew, BSc, PHD, CBiol, FIBiol. Professor of Microbiology, Dundee University, since 1992; b. 27.6.44, York; m., Helen Joyce Macpherson Millard; 2 s. Educ. Archbishop Holgate's Grammar School, York; Bradford University; Aberdeen University. Research Fellow, Edinburgh University, 1970-71; Lecturer/Reader in Microbiology, Dundee University, 1971-92. General Secretary, Society for General Microbiology, 1989-94; President, Society for Applied Microbiology, 1997-99; Senior Visiting Scientist: British Antarctic Survey, 1976-77, Ross Sea, Antarctica, 1982-83. Recreations: music; walking; gardening. Address: (b.) Department of Biological Sciences, Dundee University, Dundee DD1 4HN; T.-Dundee 23181, Ext. 4262.

Herd, James Peter, MBE, WS, NP. Consultant, Beveridge, Herd & Sandilands, WS, Kirkcaldy (Partner, 1951-97); Honorary Sheriff, Kirkcaldy, 1987-97; b. 18.5.20, Kirkcaldy; m., Marjory Phimister Mitchell; 3 s.; 2 d. Educ. Edinburgh Academy; St. Andrews University; Edinburgh University. Army Service as Major, Black Watch, UK and South East Asia, 1939-46; Local Director, Royal Insurance Group, 1951-97; Trustee, Kirkcaldy and District Trustee Savings Bank, 1952-83; Director: Kirkcaldy Ice Rink Limited, 1982-88, Kirkcaldy Abbeyfield Society, 1970-92. Recreations: curling; gardening. Address: (b.) 1 East Fergus Place, Kirkcaldy, Fife KY1 1XT; T.-01592 261616.

Herd, John Downie, BL, NP, FRSA. Managing Director, Scottish Prudential Investment Association Ltd., since 1984; Director, Chairman, Dunfermline Building Society; Chairman, Accord Hospice; b. 23.3.34, Paisley; m., Morag; 1 s.; 1 d. Educ. Paisley Grammar School; Glasgow University. Partner, McFadyen-Semple, Solicitor, Paisley, 1960; resigned partnership to become Consultant (position still held), 1984; Director, Paisley Building Society, 1981 – became Edinburgh & Paisley, latterly Dunfermline Building Society; various other non-executive directorships. Regional Chairman, Princes Scottish Youth Business Trust. Recreations: reading; Rotary; travel; gardening. Address: (h.) Rydale, South Avenue, Paisley PA2 7SP; T.-0141-884 7744.

Herdman, John Macmillan, MA (Hons), PhD (Cantab), DipTh. Writer, since 1963; b. 20.7.41, Edinburgh. Educ. Merchiston Castle School, Edinburgh; Magdalene College, Cambridge. Creative Writing Fellow, Edinburgh University, 1977-79; Scottish Arts Council bursaries, 1976, 1982, 1998; Scottish Arts Council Book Awards, 1978 and 1993; Hawthornden Writer's Fellowship, 1989 and 1995; William Soutar Fellowship, 1990-91. Publications: Descent, 1968; A Truth Lover, 1973; Memoirs of My Aunt Minnie/ Clapperton, 1974; Pagan's Pilgrimage, 1978; Stories Short and Tall, 1979; Voice Without Restraint: Bob Dylan's Lyrics and Their Background, 1982; Three Novellas, 1987; The Double in Nineteenth Century Fiction, 1990; Imelda and Other Stories, 1993; Ghostwriting, 1996; Cruising (play), 1997. Recreations: reading; walking; listening to music. Address: (h.) Roselea, Bridge of Tilt, Blair Atholl, Perthshire; T.-01796 481437.

Heron, Garth McAllen Drennan, BA, FIPM, FRSA. Managing Partner, Garth Heron Search and Consultancy, since 1995; b. 21.5.49, Belfast; m., Louise Dick; 1 s.; 1 d. Educ. Friend's School, Lisburn; Queen's University, Belfast; Strathclyde University. Personnel Officer, United Dominions Trust Ltd., 1971-73; Personnel Manager: Alcan Aluminium Ltd., 1973-76, Bourns Ltd., Fife, 1976-78; Personnel Director, Honeywell Ltd., Bracknell, 1978-87; General Manager, Personnel Division, Clydesdale Bank, 1987-93; Personnel Director, United Distillers, 1993-95. Elder, Cramond Kirk. Recreations: family; church; sports; cinema. Address: (b.) 4 Wemyss Place, Edinburgh EH3 6DH.

Herron, Very. Rev. Andrew, ATCL, MA, BD, LLB, DD, LLD. Moderator, General Assembly of Church of Scotland, 1971; b. 29.9.09, Glasgow; m., Joanna Fraser Neill; 4 d. Educ. Strathbungo H.G. School; Albert Road Academy; Glasgow University and Trinity College. Minister: Linwood, 1936-40, Houston and Killellan, 1940-59; Clerk, Glasgow Presbytery, 1959-81. Baird Lecturer, 1985; William Barclay Lecturer, 1989. Publications: Record Apart, 1972; Guide to the General Assembly, 1976; Guide to Congregational Affairs, 1979; Guide to the Presbytery, 1982; Kirk by Divine Right, 1985; Guide to the Ministry, 1987; Guide to Ministerial Income, 1987; The Law and Practice of the Kirk, 1950; Minority Report, 1990; Inter Alia, 1995. Address: (h.) 36 Darnley Road, Glasgow G41 4NE; T.-0141-423 6422.

Hetherington, Professor Emeritus (Hector) Alastair, Dhc (Lille), MA, Hon. Fellow RIAS. Emeritus Professor in Media Studies, Stirling University, since 1987; b. 31.10.19, Llanishen, Glamorgan; m., 1, Miranda; 2 s.; 2 d.; 2, Sheila; 1 step s.; 2 step d. Educ. Corpus Christi College, Oxford. Army, 1940-46; Glasgow Herald, 1946-50; The Guardian, 1950-75 (Foreign Editor, 1953-56, Editor, 1956-75); BBC Scotland, 1976-79; Director, Scotquest (film company), 1982-89; Chairman, The Scott Trust (owners, The Guardian and Manchester Evening News), 1984-89; various films for Channel Four. Publications: Guardian Years, 1981; News, Newspapers and Television, 1985; Perthshire in Trust, 1988; News in the Regions, 1989; Highlands and Islands, a generation of progress, 1990; Cameras in the Commons, 1990; Inside BBC Scotland 1975-1980, 1992; A Walker's Guide to Arran, 1995. Recreation: hill-walking. Address: (h.) 38 Chalton Road, Bridge of Allan FK9 4EF; T.-01786 833316.

Hewitt, Professor David S., MA, PhD, FRSE. Professor in Scottish Literature, Aberdeen University, since 1994 (Reader, 1991-94); b. 22.4.42, Hawick; m., Angela Catherine Williams; 1 s.; 1 d. Educ. Melrose Grammar School; George Watson's College, Edinburgh; Edinburgh University; Aberdeen University. Aberdeen University: Assistant Lecturer in English, 1964, Lecturer, 1968, Senior Lecturer, 1982; Treasurer, Association for Scottish Literary Studies, 1973-96; Editor-in-Chief, Edinburgh Edition of the Waverley Novels, 1984; President, Edinburgh Sir Walter Scott Club, 1988-89; Fellow, Royal Society of Edinburgh, 1990; Elder, Cathedral Church of St. Machar, Old Aberdeen; Managing Editor, New Writing Scotland, 1983-86. Publications: Scott on Himself (Editor), 1982; Literature of the North, 1983; Scott and His Influence, 1984; Longer Scottish Poems, Vol. 2 1650-1830, 1987; Scottish in Carnival, 1993; The Antiquary, 1995; Northern Visions, 1996; The Edinburgh Edition of the Waverley Novels: A Guide for Editors, 1996; Redgauntlet, 1997. Address: (b.) Department of English, Aberdeen University, Aberdeen AB24 3UB; T.-01224 273777.

Heys, Steven Darryll, BMedBiol, MB, ChB, MD, PhD, FRCS(Glas), FRCS(Ed), FRCS(Eng). Director, Surgical Nutrition and Metabolism Unit, Aberdeen University, since 1995; Reader in Surgery, Aberdeen University, since 1996; Consultant Surgeon, Aberdeen Royal Infirmary, since 1992; Honorary Research Fellow, Rowett Research Institute, since 1992; b. 5.7.56, Accrington; m., Margaret Susan Proctor; 2 s.; 1 d. Educ. St. Mary's College, Blackburn; Aberdeen University Medical School. House Officer/SHO, Surgery, Aberdeen Royal Infirmary, 1981-84; Registrar, Grampian Health Board, 1984-87; Wellcome Research Training Fellow, Rowett Research Institute, 1987-89; Lecturer in Surgery, Aberdeen University, 1989-92; Senior Lecturer, 1992-96. Examiner in Surgery, Royal College of Surgeons of Glasgow; External Examiner in Surgery, Royal College of Surgeons of England. Publications: numerous scientific papers on aspects of breast cancer, oncology, nutrition and metabolism; book chapters on nutrition, metabolism, oncology. Recreations: karate; hill-walking; golf. Address: (b.) University Medical Buildings, Foresterhill, Aberdeen AB9 2ZD.

Heywood, Barry Keith, MA, LLB. Regional Procurator Fiscal, Dundee, since 1991; b. 24.7.46, Oldham; m., Mary A.; 1 s.; 1 d. Educ. Kirkcaldy High School; Edinburgh University. Procurator Fiscal Depute, Ayr, 1971-77, Glasgow, 1977-78; Procurator Fiscal, Wick, 1978-83; Assistant Procurator Fiscal, Glasgow, 1983-86; Procurator Fiscal, Inverness, 1986-91. Recreations: walking; Roman and Byzantine history; "railway buff". Address: (b.) Caledonian House, Greenmarket, Dundee DD1 1QX.

Hickman, Richard Michael, BA (Hons), MA, DipTP, MRTPI. Chief Inquiry Reporter, since 1997; b. 30.4.42, Beckenham; m., Sandie Randall; 3 s; 1 d. Educ. Kingswood School, Bath; London School of Economics; University of British Columbia. Work in town and country planning for London County Council, Greater London Council, Lower Mainland Regional Planning Board (British Columbia), Scottish Development Department; Scottish Office Inquiry Reporters Unit, since 1979. Hon. Visiting Fellow, Department of Planning and Housing, Edinburgh College of Art. Recreations: walking; cycling; sailing; skiing. Address: (b.) 2 Greenside Lane, Edinburgh EH1 3AG; T.-0131-244 5644.

Higgins, Sheriff Colin Kirk, LLB. Sheriff of North Strathclyde at Paisley, since 1990; b. 9.11.45, Slough; m., Anne Marie McMahon; 1 s.; 2 d. Educ. St. Patrick's High School, Coatbridge; Glasgow University. Law Apprentice, Coatbridge, 1967-69; Legal Assistant, Coatbridge, 1969-70; Legal Assistant, James Bell & Sons, 1970-73; Partner, Bell, Russell & Co., 1973-90. Dean, Airdrie Society of Solicitors, 1989-90. Recreations: reading; travel; tennis; theatre. Address (b.) Court House, St. James' Street, Paisley; T.-041-887 5291.

Higgs, Professor Peter Ware, BSc, MSc, PhD, FRS, FRSE, FInstP, DSc (Hon). Professor of Theoretical Physics, Edinburgh University, 1980-96; b. 29.5.29, Newcastle-upon-Tyne; m., Jo Ann Williamson; 2 s. Educ. Cotham Grammar School, Bristol; King's College, London. Postdoctoral Fellow, Edinburgh University, 1954-56, and London University, 1956-58; Lecturer in Mathematics, University College, London, 1958-60; Lecturer in Mathematical Physics, then Reader, Edinburgh University, 1960-80. Hughes Medal, Royal Society, 1981; Rutherford Medal, Institute of Physics, 1984; James Scott Prize, Royal Society of Edinburgh, 1993; Paul Dirac Medal and Prize, Institute of Physics, 1997; High Energy and Particle Physics Prize, European Physical Society, 1997. Recreations: music; walking; swimming. Address: (h.) 2 Darnaway Street, Edinburgh EH3 6BG; T.-0131-225 7060.

Hill, Ann. Chief Executive, Scottish School Board Association, since 1990; Chief Executive, Furbie Foundation within Scottish School Board Association, since 1999; b. 18.7.50, Lerwick; m., David Malcolm Hill; 1 s.; 3 d. Educ. Lerwick Central Public School. Founder and first President, Scottish School Board Association. Chairman: Dumfries High School Board, Mouswald School Board; Author of "Bella", The Shetland Times. Recreations: bridge; reading; cooking; entertaining; family. Address: (h.) Mouswald House, Mouswald, Dumfries DG1 4LT; (b.) Newall Terrace, Dumfries DG1 1LW; T.(h.)-01387 830638.

Hill, Professor Malcolm, PhD. Professor of Social Work, University of Glasgow, since 1996; Director, Centre for the Child and Society, since 1995; b. 18.9.46, London; m., Dr. Wan Ying Hill; 1 s.; 1 d. Educ. Latymer Upper School, Hammersmith; St. Edmund Hall, Oxford; University of London; University of Edinburgh. Social Worker, 1968-79; Researcher, 1979-84; Lecturer, 1985-93; Senior Lecturer, 1993-96. Publications: books on adoption, child care, family support, social work and the EC, teenagers, middle childhood, children and society. Recreations: bridge; gardening; swimming. Address: (b.) Lilybank House, Bute Gardens, Glasgow G12 8RT; T.-0141-330 4056.

Hill, Robin (Edward), LLB, PhD. Editor, Life and Work, the Magazine of the Church of Scotland, since 1994; b. 7.3.64, Glasgow; m., Ailsa Kerr McPhee; 1 s.; 1 d. Educ. Hyndland Secondary School, Glasgow; Glasgow University; St. Andrews University. Honorary Research Assistant, Department of Politics and International Relations, University of Aberdeen 1986-89; Researcher, Department of International Relations, University of St. Andrews, 1990-91; Alumnus Relations Officer, University of St. Andrews, 1991-94. Recreations: family life; mandolins; fair trading; studying terrorism. Address: (b.)

Church of Scotland, 121 George Street, Edinburgh EH2 4YN; T.-0131-225 5722.

Hill, Professor William George, BSc, MS, PhD, DSc, FRSE, FRS. Professor of Animal Genetics, Edinburgh University, since 1983; b. 7.8.40, Hemel Hempstead; m., C. Rosemary Austin; 1 s.; 2 d. Educ. St. Albans School; London University; University of California; Iowa State University; Edinburgh University. Edinburgh University: Assistant Lecturer, 1965-67, Lecturer, 1967-74, Reader, 1974-83, Head, Department of Genetics, 1989-90, Institute of Cell, Animal and Population Biology, 1990-93, and Division of Biological Sciences, 1993-98; Visiting Research Associate, Iowa State University, 1967-68-69-72; Visiting Professor: University of Minnesota, 1966, Iowa State University, 1978, North Carolina State University, 1979, since 1985; Consultant Geneticist: Cotswold Pig Development Co., since 1965, Holstein Friesian Society, 1978-98; Editor, Genetical Research, since 1996; Member: AFRC Animals Research Grant Board, 1986-92, Director's Advisory Group, AFRC Animal Breeding Research Organisation, 1982-86, AFRC Institute of Animal Physiology and Genetics Research, 1986-93, Governing Council, Roslin Institute, since 1994, Council, Royal Society, 1993-94, Commonwealth Scholarships Commission, since 1998. Recreations: farming; bridge. Address: (h.) 4 Gordon Terrace, Edinburgh EH16 5QH; T.-0131-667 3680.

Hillan, Professor Edith Margaret, PhD, MSc, MPhil, DipLSc, RGN, RSCN, RM. Professor of Midwifery, University of Glasgow, since 1998; b. 26.6.58, Johnstone; m., Professor J. Stewart Aitchison; 2 s. Educ. Paisley Grammar School; Queen Margaret College; University of Strathclyde; University of Glasgow. Sister, Midwifery/Research, Royal Maternity Hospital, Glasgow, 1980-83; University of Glasgow: SODoH Research Fellow, Department of Nursing Studies, 1983-86, Lecturer, Department of Nursing Studies, 1986-92, Senior Lecturer, Nursing and Midwifery Studies, 1992-98. Member, Council, Royal College of Midwives, since 1998; Trustee, Iolanthe Midwifery Research Trust, since 1997. Recreations: good wine, food and conversation. Address: Nursing and Midwifery School, University of Glasgow, Glasgow G12 8QQ; T.-0141-330 4053.

Hillhouse, Sir (Robert) Russell, KCB, FRSE. Permanent Under-Secretary of State, Scottish Office, 1988-98; b. 23.4.38, Glasgow; m., Alison Fraser; 2 d. Educ. Hutchesons' Grammar School, Glasgow; Glasgow University. Entered Home Civil Service as Assistant Principal, Scottish Education Department, 1962; Principal, 1966; HM Treasury, 1971; Assistant Secretary, Scottish Office, 1974; Scottish Home and Health Department, 1977; Principal Finance Officer, Scottish Office, 1980; Under-Secretary, Scottish Education Department, 1985; Secretary, 1987. Recreation: making music.

Hillier, Professor Stephen Gilbert, BSc, MSc, PhD, DSc, FRCPath. Professor, Department of Obstetrics and Gynaecology, Edinburgh University, since 1994, Director, Reproductive Medicine Laboratory, since 1985 and Director, Graduate School of Life Sciences, since 1997; b. 16.1.49, Hillingdon; m., Haideh; 2 d. Educ. Hayes County Grammar School; Leeds University; Welsh National School of Medicine. Postdoctoral Research Fellow, National Institutes of Health, USA, 1976-78; Research Scientist, University of Leiden, 1978-82; Senior Lecturer: Reproductive Biochemistry, RPMS, London University, 1982-85, Department of Obstetrics and Gynaecology, Edinburgh University, 1985-94. Member: Interim Licensing Authority for Human Fertilisation and Embryology, 1987-91, Human Fertilisation and Embryology Authority, 1990-96; 1991 Society for Endocrinology Medal. Publications: Ovarian Endocrinology, 1991; Scientific Essentials of Reproductive Medicine, 1996. Recreations: fly-fishing; walking. Address: (b.) Edinburgh University Centre for Reproductive Biology, 37 Chalmers Street, Edinburgh EH3 9EW; T.-0131-229 2575.

Hillman, John Richard, BSc, PhD, HonDSc, CBiol, FIBiol, FLS, FIM, FIHort, FRSA, FRSE. Director, Scottish Crop Research Institute, since 1986; Visiting Professor, Dundee University, Edinburgh University and Glasgow University; Deputy Chairman, Mylnefield Research Services Ltd.; b. 21.7.44, Farnborough, Kent; m., Sandra Kathleen Palmer; 2 s. Educ. Chislehurst and Sidcup Grammar School; University of Wales. Assistant Lecturer, 1968, and Lecturer, 1969, Physiology and Environmental Studies, Nottingham University; Lecturer, 1971, Senior Lecturer, 1977, Reader, 1980, Professor of Botany, 1982, Glasgow University; Chairman, Agriculture, Natural Resources and Environment Sector Panel, UK Technology Foresight Programme, 1994-95, Agriculture, Horticulture and Forestry Sector Panel, 1995-97. Recreations: landscaping; building renovations; horology; reading. Address: (b.) Scottish Crop Research Institute, Invergowrie, Dundee DD2 5DA; T.-01382 562731.

Hills, Professor Sir Graham (John), PhD, DSc, FRSE, Hon DSc (Lodz, Southampton, Lisbon), Hon. LLD (Glasgow, Waterloo and Strathclyde), DUniv (Paisley). National Governor for Scotland, BBC, 1989-94; Principal and Vice-Chancellor, Strathclyde University, 1980-91; b. 9.4.26, Leigh-on-Sea; m., 1, Brenda Stubbington; 2, Mary Jane McNaughton; 1 s.; 3 d. Educ. Westcliff High School for Boys; Birkbeck College and Imperial College, London University. Lecturer in Physical Chemistry, Imperial College, 1949-62; Professor of Physical Chemistry, Southampton University, 1962-80; Visiting Professor, University of Western Ontario, 1968; Visiting Professor and National Science Foundation Fellow, Case-Western Reserve University, Ohio, 1968-69; Visiting Professor, Buenos Aires University, 1976; Member, Advisory Council on Science and Technology, 1987-93; (Non-Executive) Member, Scottish Post Office Board, since 1986; Non-Executive Director, Scottish Enterprise, 1988-94; Fellow, Birkbeck College; Fellow, Royal Scottish Academy of Music and Drama; Honorary Fellow, Chartered Society of Designers, 1996; Fellow, University of East London; Director, Glasgow Chamber of Commerce, since 1981; President: Friends of Glasgow Cathedral, 1987-95, Society of Chemical Industry, 1991-93; Chairman, Quarriers Homes, 1992-97; Commander Insignia: Order of Merit of Polish People's Republic, Royal Norwegian Order of Merit. Publications: Reference Electrodes, 1961; Polarography, 1964. Recreations: music; crofting; European politics. Address: 1 Holm Burn Place, Inverness IV1 2WT.

Hind, Archie. Novelist and Playwright; b. 1928. Author, The Dear Green Place, 1966.

Hine, Professor Harry Morrison, MA, DPhil (Oxon). Scotstarvit Professor of Humanity, St. Andrews University, since 1985; b. 19.6.48, Portsmouth; m., Rosalind Mary Ford; 1 s.; 1 d. Educ. King Edward's School, Birmingham; Corpus Christi College, Oxford. P.S. Allen Junior Research Fellow, Corpus Christi College, 1972-75; Lecturer in Humanity, Edinburgh University, 1975-85. Editor (Joint), The Classical Review, 1987-93. Publications: An Edition with Commentary of Seneca, Natural Questions, Book Two, 1981; Studies in the Text of Seneca's Naturales Quaestiones, 1996; L. Annaei Senecae Naturales Quaestiones (Editor), 1996. Recreations: walking; reading. Address: (h.) 33 Drumcarrow Road, St. Andrews, Fife KY16 8SE; T.-01334 474459.

Hird, David Forbes, CA. General Manager, Forth Valley Health Board, since 1993; b. 11.5.43, Aberdeen; m., Irene; 1 s.; 2 d. Educ. Robert Gordon's College, Aberdeen; Aberdeen University. Range of finance posts in NHS, since 1966; District Finance Officer, East Fife District, 1974,

North Lothian District, 1979; Director of Finance, Forth Valley Health Board, 1984. Recreation: curling. Address: (b.) 33 Spittal Street, Stirling FK8 1DX; T.-01786 457248.

Hirst, Sir Michael William, LLB, CA, FRSA. Chairman, Scottish Conservative and Unionist Party, 1993-97; b. 2.1.46, Glasgow; m., Naomi Ferguson Wilson; 1 s.; 2 d. Educ. Glasgow Academy; Glasgow University. Partner, Peat Marwick Mitchell & Co., Chartered Accountants, until 1983; Director of and Consultant to various companies; contested: Central Dunbartonshire, February and October, 1974, East Dunbartonshire, 1979; MP (Conservative), Strathkelvin and Bearsden, 1983-87; Member, Select Committee on Scottish Affairs, 1983-87; Parliamentary Private Secretary, Department of Energy, 1985-87; Vice-Chairman, Scottish Conservative Party, 1987-89; President, Scottish Conservative and Unionist Association; Chairman, Scottish Conservative Candidates Association, 1978-81; Hon. Secretary, British Diabetic Association; Chairman, The Park School Educational Trust; Member, Court, Glasgow Caledonian University; Director, Children's Hospice Association Scotland; Member, Executive Committee, Princess Louise Scottish Hospital, Erskine; Elder, Kelvinside Hillhead Parish Church. Recreations: golf; hill-walking; skiing. Address: (h.) Glentirran, Kippen, Stirlingshire FK8 3JA.

Hislop, William Stuart, BSc, MBChB, FRCP, FACG. Consultant Physician, Royal Alexandra Hospital, Paisley, since 1982; b. 27.2.48, Edinburgh; m., Dr. Linda J. Hislop; 1 s.; 3 d. Educ. Dundee High School; Kilmarnock Academy; Glasgow University. Junior House Officer, Stobhill Hospital and Southern General Hospital, 1973-74; Western Infirmary, Glasgow: Senior House Officer, 1974-76, Medical Registrar, 1976-77; Senior Registrar, Ninewells Hospital, Dundee, 1977-82. Recreations: walking; cycling; gardening; cricket; music (country and western). Address: (b.) Ross Hall Hospital, 221 Crookston Road, Glasgow G52 3NQ; T.-0141-810 3151.

Hitchman, Professor Michael L., BSc, DPhil, CChem, FRSC, FRSA, FRSE. Young Professor of Chemistry, Strathclyde University, since 1984; b. 17.8.41, Woburn, Bedfordshire; m., Pauline J. Thompson; 1 s.; 2 d. Educ. Stratton Grammar School, Biggleswade; Queen Mary College and King's College, London University; University College, Oxford. Assistant Lecturer in Chemistry, Leicester Regional College of Technology, 1963-65; Junior Research Fellow, Wolfson College, Oxford, 1968-70; ICI Postdoctoral Research Fellow, Physical Chemistry Laboratory, Oxford University, 1968-70; Chief Scientist, Orbisphere Corporation, Geneva, 1970-73; Staff Scientist, Laboratories RCA Ltd., Zurich, 1973-79; Lecturer, then Senior Lecturer, Salford University, 1979-84; Strathclyde University: Chairman, Department of Pure and Applied Chemistry, 1986-89, Vice-Dean, Faculty of Science, 1989-92; Honorary Professor, Taiyuan University of Technology, China, since 1994; Editor, Advanced Materials CVD, since 1995. Royal Society of Chemistry: Chairman, Electro-analytical Group, 1985-88, Treasurer, Electrochemistry Group, 1984-90; Member, Chemistry and Semiconductor Committees, Science and Engineering Research Council; Member, since 1985, Chairman, 1989-92, International Advisory Board, EUROCVD; Medal and Prize, British Vacuum Council, 1993. Publications: Ring-disk Electrodes (Co-Author), 1971; Measurement of Dissolved Oxygen, 1978; Chemical Vapor Deposition (Co-Editor), 1993. Recreations: humour; cooking; eating; rambling; losing weight. Address: (b.) Department of Pure and Applied Chemistry, Strathclyde University, 295 Cathedral Street, Glasgow G1 1XL; T.-0141-548 2793.

Hobsbaum, Professsor Philip Dennis, MA, PhD, DLitt, LRAM, LGSM. Poet and Critic; Professor of English Literature, Glasgow University, 1985-97, and Honorary Professorial Research Fellow, since 1997; b. 29.6.32, London; m., Rosemary Phillips. Educ. Belle Vue Grammar School, Bradford; Downing College, Cambridge; Sheffield University. Lecturer in English, Queen's University, Belfast, 1962-66; Lecturer, Senior Lecturer, Reader in English Literature, Glasgow University, 1966-85; Chairman of writers' groups in London, 1955-59, Belfast, 1962-66, Glasgow, 1966-75. Publications: A Group Anthology (Co-Editor), 1963; The Place's Fault, 1964; In Retreat, 1966; Coming Out Fighting, 1969; Ten Elizabethan Poets (Editor), 1969; A Theory of Communication, 1970; A Reader's Guide to Charles Dickens, 1972; Women and Animals, 1972; Tradition and Experiment in English Poetry, 1979; A Reader's Guide to D.H. Lawrence, 1981; Essentials of Literary Criticism, 1983; A Reader's Guide to Robert Lowell, 1988; Wordsworth: Selected Poetry and Prose (Editor), 1989; Channels of Communication (Co-editor), 1992; Metre, Rhythm and Verse Form, 1996; over 100 articles in learned journals; over 1,000 book reviews. Recreations: walking the dog; playing the piano. Address: (h.) 10 Oban Drive, Glasgow G20 6AF; T.-0141 946 6653.

Hodge, Robin Mackenzie, BA (Hons). Publisher, The List magazine, since 1985; b. Edinburgh. Educ. Edinburgh Academy; Clifton College, Bristol; Durham University. Certificat Europeen en Administration de Projects Culturels (Bruxelles). Director, Canongate Publishing Ltd., 1981-84; restoration of 16th-century buildings around Tweeddale Court, Edinburgh Old Town, 1981-88; founded The List, 1985. Address: (b.) 14 High Street, Edinburgh EH1 1TE; T.-0131-558 1191.

Hogg, Lt. Col. Colin Grant Ogilvie, DL. King's Own Scottish Borderers (KOSB), since 1962; Regimental Secretary, since 1991; b. 6.12.43, Glasgow; m., Cynthia Rose Mackenzie; 2 d. Educ. St. Mary's Preparatory School; Merchiston Castle School. Commissioned into KOSB, 1965; service with 1st Battalion in Aden, Hong Kong, Borneo, BAOR, Berlin, Northern Ireland; Deputy Assistant Adjutant General, HQ of 1st Armoured Division, Germany, 1981-83; on directing staff, Royal Military Academy, Sandhurst, 1983-84; Commanding Officer, 2nd Battalion, 52 Lowland Volunteers, 1985-88; SOI, Foot Guards and Infantry Manning and Records Office, 1988-91; retired from active list, 1991; Honorary Colonel of the Lothian and Border Army Cadet Force, since 1997. Member: Queen's Bodyguard for Scotland, since 1986, Ancient Order of Mosstroopers; Chairman, Borders Branch, SSAFA, since 1993; Member, Board, South of Scotland Youth Awards Scheme, since 1994; Chairman, Roxburgh and Berwickshire Conservative and Unionist Association, 1995-98; Governor: Oxenfoord Castle School, 1986-93, St. Mary's School, Melrose, 1994-98; Vice President, Jedburgh Branch, Royal British Legion Scotland, since 1994; Member, National Council, Royal British Legion Scotland, since 1998; Deputy Lieutenant, Roxburgh, Ettrick and Lauderdale, since 1995. Recreations: foxhunting; shooting; all equestrian events. Address: (h.) Mounthooly, Jedburgh TD8 6TJ; T.-01835 863368.

Hogg, Ian Alisdair Lawrence, MA, CA. Secretary, Scottish Rugby Union, since 1983; b. 13.6.40, Edinburgh; m., Louise; 1 s.; 1 d. Educ. George Watson's College; Edinburgh University. Chartered Accountant, 1961-78; Treasurer, Scottish Rugby Union, 1978-83. Recreations: rugby; cricket. Address: (b.) Scottish Rugby Union, Murrayfield, Edinburgh EH12 5PJ; T.-0131-346 5000.

Hogg of Cumbernauld, Lord (Norman), MP, Cumbernauld and Kilsyth, 1983-97 (MP, East Dunbartonshire, 1979-83); Lord High Commissioner, General Assembly of the Church of Scotland, 1998; Hon. President, YMCA Scotland, since 1998; b. 12.3.38, Aberdeen; m., Elizabeth M. Christie. Educ. Ruthrieston Secondary School, Aberdeen. Local Government Officer, Aberdeen Town Council, 1953-67; District Officer, NALGO, 1967-79; Member: Transport Users Consultative

Committee for Scotland, 1977-79, Select Committee on Scottish Affairs, 1979-82; Scottish Labour Whip, 1982-83; Chairman, Scottish Parliamentary Labour Group, 1981-82; Deputy Chief Opposition Whip, 1983-87; Scottish Affairs Spokesman, 1987-88; Member, Public Accounts Committee, 1991-92. Recreation: music. Address: House of Lords, Westminster, London SW1A 0PW; T.-0171-219 3000.

Hogwood, Professor Brian Walter, BA, PhD. Professor of Politics, Department of Government, Strathclyde University, since 1991; b. 29.6.50, Glasgow; m., Patricia Brearey. Educ. Hamilton Academy; Glenrothes High School; Keele University. Economics Sub-Editor, Cambridge University Press, 1974-75; appointed Lecturer in Politics, Strathclyde University, 1975; Senior Lecturer, 1985; Reader, 1988. Recreations: cooking; computing; cross-country running. Address: (b.) Department of Government, Strathclyde University, McCance Building, 16 Richmond Street, Glasgow; T.-0141-552 4400, Ext. 2919.

Holland, Professor John, BSc, MBA, PhD. Professor of International Finance and Banking, since 1996, Head, Department of Accounting and Finance, since 1997, and Director of Postgraduate Studies, since 1990, University of Glasgow; b. 16.6.47; m., Janet Laurie; 1 s.; 1 d. Educ. Ullathorne Grammar School, Coventry; Aston University; University of Liverpool. Research Fellow, London Guildhall University, 1972-75; Lecturer, University of Bath, 1975-79; Lecturer, 1979-85, Senior Lecturer, 1986-95, University of Glasgow. Publications: many publications on international financial management, banking, corporate communication and fund management. Recreations: walking; theatre; eating out. Address: (b.) Department of Accounting and Finance, University of Glasgow, 65-71 Southpark Avenue, Glasgow G12 8LE; T.-0141-330 4136.

Holloway, Most Rev. Richard Frederick, BD, STM, DUniv (Strathclyde), DD (Aberdeen), FRSE. Gresham Professor of Divinity, since 1997; Bishop of Edinburgh, since 1986; Primus of the Scottish Episcopal Church, since 1992; b. 26.11.33; m., Jean Elizabeth Kennedy; 1 s.; 2 d. Educ. Kelham Theological College; Edinburgh Theological College; Union Theological Seminary, New York. Curate, St. Ninian's, Glasgow, 1959-63; Priest-in-charge, St. Margaret and St. Mungo's, Glasgow, 1963-68; Rector, Old St. Paul's, Edinburgh, 1968-80; Rector, Church of the Advent, Boston, Mass, 1980-84; Vicar, St. Mary Magdalen's, Oxford, 1984-86. Recreations: running; long-distance walking; reading; going to the cinema; listening to music. Address: (h.) 3 Eglinton Crescent, Edinburgh EH12 5DH.

Holmes, George Dennis, CB (1979), FRSE, FICfor. Forestry Consultant, since 1987; b. 9.11.26, Conwy; m., Sheila Rosemary; 3 d. Educ. John Bright's School, Llandudno; University of Wales, Bangor. Forestry Commission, 1948-86 (Director General, 1976-86). Recreations: fishing; golf. Address: (h.) 7 Cammo Road, Barnton, Edinburgh EH4 8EF; T.-0131-339 7474.

Holmes, Professor Peter Henry, BVMS, PhD, MRCVS. Professor of Veterinary Physiology, University of Glasgow, since 1982; Vice-Principal (Research), since 1997; b. 6.6.42, Cottingham, Yorkshire; m., Ruth Helen; 2 d. Educ. Beverley Grammar School, Yorkshire; University of Glasgow. Joined staff of University of Glasgow Veterinary School, Department of Veterinary Physiology, 1966. Member, Court, University of Glasgow, 1991-95; served on committees of ODA (DfID), BVA, UFAW; Chairman, Internation Programme Against African Trypanosomiasis. Recreations: hillwalking; tennis; cycling. Address: (b.) Research and Enterprise, No. 10 The Square, University of Glasgow, Glasgow G12 8QQ; T.-0141-330 3836.

Home, 15th Earl of (David Alexander Cospatrick Douglas-Home), CVO, CBE. Chairman, Morgan Grenfell (Scotland), since 1986; b. 20.11.43; m.; 1 s.; 2 d. Educ. Eton; Christ Church, Oxford. Succeeded to title, 1995. Address: The Hirsel, Coldstream, Berwickshire.

Home Robertson, John David. MP (Labour), East Lothian, since 1983 (Berwick & East Lothian, 1978-83); b. 5.12.48, Edinburgh; m., Catherine Brewster; 2 s. Educ. Ampleforth College; West of Scotland Agricultural College. Farmer; Member: Berwickshire District Council, 1974-78, Borders Health Board, 1975-78; Chairman, Eastern Borders Citizens' Advice Bureau, 1976-78; Member, Select Committee on Scottish Affairs, 1979-83; Chairman, Scottish Group of Labour MPs, 1983; Scottish Labour Whip, 1983-8 4; Opposition Front Bench Spokesman on Agriculture, 1984-87, on Scotland, 1987-88, on Agriculture, 1988-90; Member, Select Committee on Defence, 1990-97; Member, British-Irish Parliamentary Body, since 1993; Parliamentary Private Secretary to Dr Jack Cunningham, since 1997; established Paxton Trust, 1988; Edinburgh Direct Aid convoys to Bosnia, 1994 and 1995 (HGV driver); Observer, elections in Sarajevo, 1996. Address: (b.) House of Commons, Westminster, London, SW1A OAA.

Homfray, John L., MBE, TD, FCA. Director, Iona Abbey Ltd., since 1993; b. 5.8.16, Darjeeling, India; m., Elizabeth M. Shand; 2 s.; 1 d. Educ. Sherborne. Captain, RA 80 Field Regiment, 1940-45 (mentioned in Despatches); Director, Clyde Shipping Co. Ltd., Glasgow, 1948-81; Deputy Lieutenant, Dunbartonshire, 1975-90; Chairman, Iona Cathedral Trust Management Board, 1982-92; Lt. Col., City of Glasgow Artillery, RATA, 1953-57; Director, Glasgow Aged Seamen Relief Fund, 1980-98; Director, Sailors Orphan Society of Scotland, 1980-98. Recreation: travelling. Address: (h.) Ardballachan, Bracklinn Road, Callander, Perthshire; T.-01877 330256.

Hood, James. MP (Labour), Clydesdale, since 1987; b. 16.5.48, Lesmahagow; m., Marion; 1 s.; 1 d. Educ. Lesmahagow High School; Nottingham University. Local councillor, 1973-87; official of NUM, 1973-87; Leader, Nottingham striking miners, 1984-85; Chairman, Miners' Parliamentary Group, 1991-92; former Chairman, All-Party Group on ME; Chairman, European Legislation Select Committee; Member, Defence Select Committee; Convenor, Scottish Labour Group of MPs Home Affairs Committee; sponsor of three Private Members' Bills on under-age drinking and a Bill on ME. Address: (b.) House of Commons, London SW1A 0AA; T.-0171-219 4585.

Hood, Professor Neil, FRSE, MA, MLitt. Professor of Business Policy, Department of Marketing, Strathclyde University, since 1979; Director, Strathclyde International Business Unit, since 1992; b. 10.8.43, Wishaw; m., Anna Watson Clark; 1 s.; 1 d. Educ. Wishaw High School; Glasgow University. Research Fellow, Scottish College of Textiles, 1966-68; Lecturer/Senior Lecturer, Paisley College of Technology, 1968-78; Economic Adviser, Scottish Economic Planning Department, 1979; Director: Locate in Scotland, 1987-89, Employment and Special Initiatives, SDA, 1989-90; Visiting Professor: International Business, University of Texas, Dallas, 1981, Institute of International Business, Stockholm School of Economics, since 1982; Director, Euroscot Meat Exports Ltd., 1981-85; Economic Consultant to Secretary of State for Scotland, 1980-87; Director, Scottish Development Finance Ltd., 1984-90 and 1993-96; Chairman, Scottish Equity Partnership, since 1998; Chairman, Scottish Technology Fund, since 1997; Investment Adviser, Castleforth Fund Managers, 1984-87; Director, LIFE Ltd., 1984-86; Board Member, Irvine Development Corporation, 1985-87; Director: Prestwick Holdings PLC, 1986-87, Lamberton (Holdings) Ltd., 1989-92, GA (Holdings) Ltd., 1990-92, Shanks and McEwan PLC, 1990-94, I & S UK Smaller

Companies Trust plc, 1993-98, I & S Trustlink Ltd., 1994-97, Kwik-Fit plc, since 1991, Grampian Holdings plc, since 1993; Corporate Adviser, Scottish Power, since 1989; Chairman, John Dickie Group Ltd., since 1995; Director, FI Group plc, since 1997; Deputy Chairman, British Polythene Industries plc, since 1998; President, European International Business Association, 1985-86. Publications: Industrial Marketing — A Study of Textiles (Co-Author), 1970; Chrysler UK: A Corporation in Transition (Co-Author), 1977; The Economics of Multinational Enterprise (Co-Author), 1979; European Development Strategies of US Multinationals Located in Scotland (Co-Author), 1980; Multinationals in Retreat: The Scottish Experience (Co-Author), 1982; Multinational Investment Strategies in the British Isles (Co-Author), 1983; Industry, Policy and the Scottish Economy (Co-Editor), 1984; Transnational Corporations in the Textile Industry (Co-Author), 1984; Foreign Multinationals and the British Economy (Co-Author), 1987; Strategies in Global Competition (Co-Editor), 1987; Scottish Financial Sector (Co-Author), 1988; Marketing in Evolution (Co-Editor), 1996; Transition in Baltic States: Microlevel Studies (Co-Editor), 1997; Multinational Corporate Evolution and Subsidiary Development (Co-Editor), 1998. Recreations: swimming; reading; gardening. Address: (h.) 95 Mote Hill, Hamilton ML3 6EA; T.-01698 424870.

Hook, Professor Andrew Dunnet, MA, PhD. Bradley Professor of English Literature, Glasgow University, since 1979; b. 21.12.32, Wick; m., Judith Ann (deceased); 2 s.; 1 d. (deceased). Educ. Wick High School; Daniel Stewart's College, Edinburgh; Edinburgh University; Manchester University; Princeton University. Edinburgh University: Assistant Lecturer in English Literature, 1961-63, Lecturer in American Literature, 1963-70; Senior Lecturer in English, Aberdeen University, 1970-79; Chairman, Committee for Humanities and Member, Committee for Academic Affairs, CNAA, 1987-92; Chairman: Scottish Universities Council on Entrance English Panel, 1986-92, Universities and Colleges Admissions Service English Panel, since 1995; Member: Scottish Examination Board, 1984-92, Scottish Qualifications Authority English Panel, since 1996; President, Eighteenth-Century Scottish Studies Society, 1990-92. Publications: Scotland and America 1750-1835, 1975; American Literature in Context 1865-1900, 1983; Scott's Waverley (Editor), 1971; Charlotte Brontë's Shirley (Editor, with Judith Hook), 1974; Dos Passos: A Collection of Critical Essays (Editor), 1974; The History of Scottish Literature II, 1660-1800 (Editor), 1987; Scott Fitzgerald, 1992; The Glasgow Enlightenment (Co-Editor), 1995. Recreations: theatre; opera; catching up on reading. Address: (b.) Department of English Literature, Glasgow University, Glasgow G12 8QQ; T.-0141-339 8855, Ext. 4226.

Hooper, Ian Ross, BA. Depute Director (Resources), National Museums of Scotland, since 1989; Director, Museum of Scotland Project, since 1990; b. 26.5.49, Edinburgh; m., Julie Ellen Vaughan; 1 s.; 1 d. Educ. Hornchurch Grammar School; University of East Anglia. Administrator, Department of the Environment, 1973-89; seconded to English Heritage, 1984-85, responsible for historic buildings policy. Recreations: historic buildings; hill-walking; golf. Address: (b.) Royal Museum of Scotland, Edinburgh EH1 1JF; T.-0131-225 7534.

Hooper, Professor Martin Leslie, MA, PhD, FRCPE, FRSE. Professor of Molecular Pathology, University of Edinburgh, since 1996; b. 1.3.47, Walsall. Educ. Queen Mary's School, Walsall; University of Cambridge. MRC Research Scholar, MRC Laboratory of Molecular Biology, University of Cambridge, 1968-71; EMBO Research Fellow, Centre de Génétique Moléculaire, Gif-sur-Yvette, 1972-73; Research Fellow, Institute of Genetics, Glasgow, 1973-80; University of Edinburgh: Senior Lecturer in Experimental Pathology, 1980-90, Reader, Department of Pathology, 1990-96. Co-recipient, Margaret MacLellan Award, Tenovus Scotland, 1996. Recreations: walking; watching cricket; opera. Address: (b.) Sir Alastair Currie CRC Laboratories, Molecular Medicine Centre, Western General Hospital, Edinburgh EH4 2XU; T.-0131-651 1071.

Hope, Colin John Filshill, OStJ, BA, FCII, FCIS, FCIT, FBIM, MCIM, DipM. Director, Merchants House of Glasgow, 1981-87, 1988-94, 1995; Governor, Glasgow Educational and Marshall Trust, since 1986; b. 24.6.24, Dullatur; m., Jean Calder Douglas; 1 s.; 2 d. Educ. Glasgow High School; Glasgow Academy; Open University. RAF, 1942-47; joined Stenhouse & Partners, 1947; appointed Director, 1949; served in many capacities, including Managing Director, Stenhouse International; joined Norman Frizzell Scotland Ltd. as Managing Director, 1974; additionally Director, Norman Frizzell UK Ltd., 1976-81; Director, G.T. Senior, 1981-83 (Consultant, 1983-85); a Director, Glasgow Chamber of Commerce, 1979-88. Member: Scottish Consumer Council, 1979-85, Electricity Consultative Council for Scotland, 1979-87, General Convocation, Strathclyde University, 1980-90, Council, Insurance Ombudsman Bureau, 1981-94, Glasgow Airport Consultative Committee, since 1984; Governor, Keil School, 1986-91; former Chairman, Scottish Transport Users Consultative Committee; Member: Air Transport Committee, Association of British Chambers of Commerce, 1986-90, South of Scotland Electricity Consultative Committee, 1990-91; Director, Glasgow Native Benevolent Association, 1988-91 and since 1992 (Chairman, 1997-98); Member, Dumbartonshire Committee, Order of St. John, 1987-93. Address: (h.) Omaha, 4 Munro Drive East, Helensburgh G84 9BS; T.-01436 673091.

Hope of Craighead, Rt. Hon. Lord (James Arthur David Hope), PC. A Lord of Appeal in Ordinary, since 1996; Chancellor, Strathclyde University, since 1998; b. 27.6.38, Edinburgh; m., Katharine Mary Kerr; 2 (twin) s.; 1 d. Educ. Edinburgh Academy; Rugby School; St. John's College, Cambridge (BA); Edinburgh University (LLB); Hon. LLD, Aberdeen (1991), Strathclyde (1993), Edinburgh (1995). National Service, Seaforth Highlanders, 1957-59; admitted Faculty of Advocates, 1965; Standing Junior Counsel to Inland Revenue, 1974-78; QC, 1978; Advocate Depute, 1978-82; Chairman, Medical Appeal Tribunal, 1985-86; Legal Chairman, Pensions Appeal Tribunal, 1985-86; Dean, Faculty of Advocates, 1986-89; A Senator of the College of Justice, Lord Justice General of Scotland, and Lord President of the Court of Session, 1989-96. President, The Stair Society, 1993; Hon. Professor of Law, Aberdeen, 1994; Baron (Life Peer), 1995. Publications: Gloag and Henderson's Introduction to Scots Law (Joint Editor, 7th edition, Assistant Editor, 8th and 9th editions); Armour on Valuation for Rating (Joint Editor, 4th and 5th editions); (Contributor) Stair Memorial Encyclopaedia of Scots Law. Address: (h.) 34 India Street, Edinburgh EH3 6HB; T.-0131-225 8245.

Hope, William, MA. Rector, Elgin High School, since 1978; b. 26.9.43, Scotland; m., Patricia Miller. Educ. Dalbeattie High School; Kirkcudbright Academy; Edinburgh University; Jordanhill College of Education. Alloa Academy: Assistant Teacher, Principal Teacher of Guidance; Assistant Rector, Lochaber High School. Chairman, Moray Branch, UNICEF; Vice Chairman, Elgin and District Branch, Macmillan Cancer Relief; President: Forres St. Lawrence Cricket Club, North of Scotland Cricket Association. Recreations: umpiring hockey and cricket; fishing; public speaking. Address: (b.) Elgin High School, High School Drive, Elgin, Moray; T.-01343 545181.

Hopkins, Professor David William, BSc, PhD. Professor, Department of Environmental Science, University of Stirling, since 1999; b. 12.3.63, London; m., Claire Louise; 2 s.; 1 d. Educ. Manchester Polytechnic; University of

Newcastle upon Tyne. Postdoctoral Research Associate, University of Newcastle, 1988-90; Lecturer then Senior Lecturer, University of Dundee, 1990-99. Erskine Visiting Fellow, University of Canterbury, Christchurch, New Zealand, 1998. Recreation: fatherhood. Address: University of Stirling, Stirling FK9 4LA.

Horden, Professor John Robert Backhouse, MA, MLitt, DHL, FSA, FSA Scot, FRSL. Professor Emeritus of Bibliographical Studies, Stirling University; b. Warwickshire; m., Aileen Mary Douglas (deceased); 1 s. Educ. Oxford University; Cambridge University; Heidelberg University; Sorbonne; Lincoln's Inn. Former Director: Centre for Bibliographical Studies, Stirling University, Institute of Bibliography and Textual Criticism, Leeds University; former Tutor and Lecturer in English Literature, Christ Church, Oxford; Visiting Professorial appointments, Universities of Pennsylvania State, Saskatchewan, Erlangen-Nurnberg, Texas at Austin, Munster; Editor, Dictionary of Scottish Biography, since 1982; Cecil Oldman Memorial Lecturer, 1971; Marc Fitch Prize for Bibliography, 1979. Publications: Francis Quarles: A Bibliography of his Work to 1800, 1953; Francis Quarles' Hosanna and Threnodes (Editor), 1960; Annual Bibliography of English Language and Literature (Editor), 1967-75; English and Continental Emblem Books (22 vols.) (Editor), 1968-76; Art of the Drama, 1969; George Wither's Emblemes (Editor), 1973; Dictionary of Concealed Authorship, Vol. 1 (Editor), 1980; initiator and first editor, Index of English Literary Manuscripts, 11 volumes, 1980-97; Everyday Life in Seventeenth-Century England, 1974; Techniques of Bibliography, 1977; John Freeth: Political Ballad Writer and Inn Keeper, 1985; Bibliographia (Editor), 1992; Francis Quarles' Emblemes and Hieroglyphikes (Co-Editor), 1993. Recreations: golf (represented England, Warwickshire, Oxford, Cambridge); music; painting. Address: (b.) Department of English Studies, Stirling University, Stirling FK9 4LA.

Horn, David Bowes, BSc, PhD, CChem, FRSC, FRCPath, CBiol, FIBiol, FRSE; b. 18.8.28, Edinburgh; m., Shirley Kay Riddell; 2 d. Educ. Daniel Stewart's College, Edinburgh; Heriot-Watt University, Edinburgh; Edinburgh University. Senior Grade Biochemist: Vale of Leven Hospital, Alexandria, 1956, Queen Elizabeth Hospital, Birmingham, 1959; Biochemist, Royal Victoria Infirmary, Newcastle-upon-Tyne, and Honorary Lecturer, Department of Clinical Biochemistry, Newcastle-upon-Tyne University, 1959; Head, Department of Clinical Chemistry, Western General Hospital, Edinburgh, 1966-87; Honorary Senior Lecturer in Clinical Chemistry, Edinburgh University, 1966-87. Past Chairman: Scottish Region, Association of Clinical Biochemists (former Member, ACB National Council), Scientific Services Advisory Group Clinical Chemistry Sub-Committee; Royal Society of Chemistry Representative, Mastership in Clinical Biochemistry Examination Board, 1973-88. Recreations: computation; gardening; walking. Address: (h.) 2 Barnton Park, Edinburgh EH4 6JF; T.-0131-336 3444.

Horne, Allan Maxwell, BL. Solicitor (retired); Honorary Sheriff, Elgin, since 1981; b. 24.2.17, Brora; m., Margaret Ross; 1 d. Educ. Elgin Academy; Edinburgh University. Royal Artillery, 1940-46: commissioned 128th Field Regiment, 51st (H) Division, served as Air Observation Pilot, 1945-46, demobilised with rank of Captain; Legal Assistant, Inverness, 1946-49; Partner, Grigor & Young, Solicitors, Elgin, 1949-83, retiring as Senior Partner; Burgh Prosecutor, Elgin, 1950-75. Recreation: golf. Address: (h.) Melford, 11 Fleurs Place, Elgin; T.-Elgin 542833.

Horne, Rev. Archibald Sinclair. Minister, Reformed Presbyterian Church of Scotland, since 1955; Secretary and Lecturer, Scottish Reformation Society, since 1964; b. 9.3.27, Port Seton; m., Margaret Robertson Paterson; 2 s.; 1 d. Educ. Preston Lodge Secondary; London Bible College (External Student); New College, University of Edinburgh. Publications: Torchbearers of the Truth, 1966; In the Steps of the Covenanters, 1974. Recreations: golf; gardening; photography; producing video films. Address: (b.) Magdalene Chapel, 41 Cowgate, Edinburgh EH1 1EE; T.-0131-220 1450.

Horner, Professor Robert Malcolm Wigglesworth, CEng, BSc, PhD, MICE, MIM. Professor of Engineering Management, since 1986 and Chair, School of Engineering and Physical Sciences, since 1997, Dundee University; Atlantic Power and Gas Ltd.: Non-executive Director, since 1991, Director, Research and Development, 1993-97; Chairman, Winton Caledonian Ltd., 1995-97; b. 27.7.42, Bury; m., Beverley Anne Wesley; 1 s.; 1 d. Educ. The Bolton School; University College, London. Civil Engineer, Taylor Woodrow Construction Ltd., 1966-77; Lecturer, Senior Lecturer, Head, Department of Civil Engineering, Dundee University, 1977-91; Managing Director, International Maintenance Management, 1996-97. Founder Chairman, Dundee Branch, Opening Windows on Engineering; Winner, CIOB Ian Murray Leslie Award, 1980 and 1984; Director, Dundee Rep., since 1991; Member, Council, National Conference of University Professors, 1989-93; Director, Scottish International Resource Project, 1994-95; Member: Technology Foresight Construction Sector Panel, since 1994, British Council Advisory Committee on Science and Engineering, since 1994; Chairman, Friends of St. Paul's Cathedral, 1993-95. Recreations: squash; gardening. Address: (h.) Westfield Cottage, 11 Westfield Place, Dundee DD1 4JU; T.-01382 225933.

Hornibrook, John Nevill, OBE, VRD, FEng, FIChemE. Chairman, Awarding Body for Vocational Qualifications for the Chemical and Pharmaceutical Industries; Member, Court, Waste Management Centre, University of Paisley; b. 25.10.28, Gerrards Cross, Buckinghamshire; m., Dr. (Norma) Gillian Newbury; 2 d. Educ. Wellington College; Birmingham University. Various industrial appointments at home and overseas; Roche Products, Dalry, 1972-93, Divisional Director, 1981-93. Former Chairman, Enterprise Ayrshire; a former Director, Renfrewshire Healthcare NHS Trust. Recreations: sailing; gardening. Address: (h.) Cruachan, West Glen Road, Kilmacolm PA13 4PN; T.-01505 873265.

Horobin, John Charles, BSc, PhD. Head of Conference and Group Services, St. Andrews University, since 1989; Director, British Universities Accommodation Consortium Ltd.; b. 13.2.45, Long Eaton; m.; 2 s.; 2 d. Educ. Long Eaton Grammar School; King's College, London University; Durham University. Tutor-Organiser, WEA, Plymouth and West Devon, 1971-74; Assistant Director of Adult Education, St. Andrews University, 1974-89. Address: (b.) Residence and Business Services, St. Andrews University, 79 North Street, St. Andrews KY16 9AJ; T.-01334 462520.

Horsburgh, Sheriff John Millar Stewart, QC. Sheriff of Lothian and Borders, at Edinburgh, since 1990; b. 15.5.38. Admitted to Scots Bar, 1965. Address: (b.) Sheriff Court House, 27 Chambers Street, Edinburgh, EH1 1LB.

Houlihan, Professor Dominic Francis Joseph, BSc, PhD. Professor in Zoology, since 1992, Head, Department of Zoology, 1993-98, Dean and Vice-Principal, Faculty of Science and Engineering, since 1998, University of Aberdeen; b. 2.8.45, London; m., Margaret Swanston Catto; 2 s.; 1 d. Educ. St. Bonaventure's Grammar School, London; University of Bristol. Lecturer, 1970-84, Senior Lecturer, 1984-87, Reader, 1987, Personal Chair in Zoology, 1992, University of Aberdeen; Ciba-Geigy Senior Research Fellow, CNRS. Laboratory, Strasbourg, 1983-84; Visiting Professor, University of Naples, 1987; Member, SERC, AFRC, BBSRC. Grant Awarding Committees;

Senate Assessor to University Court, since 1996; External Examiner, undergraduate degree programmes, PhD, DSc. Publications: over 100 publications in scientific journals on animal physiology; seven reviews on protein metabolism in animals. Address: (b.) Department of Zoology, University of Aberdeen, Tillydrone Avenue, Aberdeen AB24 2TZ; T.-01224 272393.

Housden, Stuart David, BSc (Zoology). Director Scotland, RSPB, since 1993; b. 24.6.53, Croydon; m., Catherine Juliet Wilkin; 3 d. Educ. Selhurst Grammar School; Royal Holloway College, London University. Freshwater biologist, Thames Water, 1976; RSPB: Species Investigation Officer, 1977-79, Parliamentary Officer, 1979-82, Manager — Government Unit, 1982-85, Head, Conservation Planning Department, 1985-90, Head, Conservation Planning, 1990-93. Member, Cairngorms Partnership Board, 1995-97; Churchill Fellow, 1992. Publications: Important Bird Areas in the UK (Co-Editor); numerous articles. Recreations: ornithology; travel; rugby football; politics; work. Address: (b.) Dunedin House, 25 Ravelston Terrace, Edinburgh EH4 3TP.

Houslay, Professor Miles Douglas, BSc, PhD, FRSE, FRSA, FIBiol, CBiol. Gardiner Professor of Biochemistry, Glasgow University, since 1984; b. 25.6.50, Wolverhampton; m., Rhian Mair; 2 s.; 1 d. Educ. Grammar School, Brewood, Stafford; University College, Cardiff; King's College, Cambridge; Cambridge University. ICI Research Fellow and Fellow, Queens' College, Cambridge, 1974-76; Lecturer, then Reader in Biochemistry, UMIST, 1976-82; Selby Fellow, Australian Academy of Science, 1984; Colworth Medal, Biochemical Society of Great Britain, 1984; Honorary Research Fellow, California Metabolic Research Foundation, since 1981; Editor in Chief, Cellular Signalling; Deputy Chairman, Biochemical Journal, 1984-89; Editorial Board, Biochimica Biophysica Acta; Member: Committee, Biochemical Society, 1982-85, Research Committee, British Diabetic Association, 1986-91; Chairman, Grant Committee A, Cell and Disorders Board, Medical Research Council, 1989-92; Member: Scientific and Medical Grant Committee, Scottish Home and Health Department, 1991-94, Advisory Board for External Appointments, London University, 1990-92, HEFC RAE Basic Medical and Dental Sciences Panel, since 1996, Wellcome Trust BMB Grant Panel, since 1996; Chairman, British Heart Foundation Project Grant Panel; Member, British Heart Foundation Chairs and Programme Grant Panel, since 1997; Trustee, British Heart Foundation, since 1997. Publication: Dynamics of Biological Membranes; over 300 scientific papers. Address: (b.) Department of Biochemistry, Glasgow University, Glasgow G12 8QQ; T.-0141-330 5903.

Housley, Edward, MB, ChB, FRCPEdin, FRCP. Consultant Physician, Edinburgh Royal Infirmary, since 1970; Honorary Senior Lecturer, Department of Medicine, Edinburgh University, since 1970; Medical Specialist, Armed Forces Scotland, since 1975; Consultant Physician to the Army in Scotland, since 1998; b. 10.1.34, Chester, USA; 1 d. Educ. Mundella Grammar School, Nottingham; Birmingham University. Postgraduate training, Department of Medicine, Birmingham University and McGill University, Montreal. Recreation: crossword puzzles. Address: (h.) 6 Kew Terrace, Edinburgh, EH12 5JE.

Houston, Anne C., CQSW. Director, ChildLine Scotland, since 1994; b. 28.8.54, Glasgow. Educ. Bishopbriggs High School; Strathclyde University. Social Worker, Intermediate Treatment Officer, Team Leader, Southampton Social Services Department, 1980-86; Project Manager/Tutor, Richmond Fellowship, Glasgow, 1986-90; Counselling Manager, Childline Scotland, 1990-94. Council Member, Stepfamily Scotland; Board Member, Children in Scotland; Member, Advisory Council, Scottish Child Law Centre; Member, Advisory Committee, Prisoner Management. Recreations: reading; music; swimming; gardening; animals. Address: (b.) 18 Albion Street, Glasgow G1 1LH; T.-0141-552 1123.

Houston, Major General David, CBE. Lord Lieutenant of Sutherland, since 1991; b. 24.2.29; m.; 2 s. Educ. Latymer Upper School. Military Attaché and Commander, British Army Staff, Washington, 1977-79; HQ UKLF, 1979-80; President, Regular Commissions Board, 1980-83.

Houston, Rev. Dr. Graham Richard, BSc (Hons), BD (Hons), MTh, PhD. Executive Director, National Bible Society of Scotland, since 1998; b. 3.5.50, Glasgow; m., Irene Elizabeth Robertson; 1 s.; 2 d. Educ. Hutchesons' Boys' Grammar School, Glasgow; Strathclyde University; Aberdeen University. Assistant, project, Govan, 1972-73; Assistant Minister, Palmerston Place Church, Edinburgh, 1976-77; Minister: Kildonan and Loth Church, Sutherland, 1978-82, Letham St. Mark's Church, Perth, 1982-90; Chaplain, Heriot-Watt University, 1990-98. Publications: Prophecy Now, 1989; Virtual Morality, 1998. Recreations: squash; golf. Address: (h.) 3 Ramsay Place, Penicuik, Midlothian EH26 9JS; T.-01968 672752.

Houston, John, OBE, RSA, RSW, RGI. Artist; b. 1.4.30, Buckhaven; m., Elizabeth V. Blackadder. Educ. Buckhaven High School; Edinburgh College of Art. Travelling scholarship to Italy, 1953-54; started teaching, Edinburgh College of Art, 1955; elected: Associate, Royal Scottish Academy, 1964, Academician, 1972; Depute Head, School of Drawing and Painting, Edinburgh College of Art, 1982-89. Guthrie Award, RSA, 1964; Cargill Prize, Royal Glasgow Institute of Fine Arts, 1965, 1988; Lothians Award, RSA, 1982; Sir William Gillies Prize, RSW, 1990. Recreations: golf; fishing; travel. Address: (h.) 57 Fountainhall Road, Edinburgh EH9 2LH; T.-0131-667 3687.

Houstoun, Andrew Beatty, OBE, MC, JP, DL. Vice President, Scottish Landowners Federation, 1984-98; b. 15.10.22, Cranleigh; m., Mary Elizabeth Spencer-Nairn; 4 s. Educ. Harrow. Regular Army, 1941-56; retired as Major, 1st The Royal Dragoons; farming, Angus and Perthshire, since 1956; commanded Fife and Forfar Yeomanry/Scottish Horse (TA), 1962-65; retired Brevet Col. and Lt. Col, 1965; Angus County Councillor, 1966-75 (Vice Chairman, Education Committee); Convener, Scottish Landowners Federation, 1979-82; Chancellor's Assessor, Dundee University Court, 1981-92; Vice Lord Lieutenant, Angus, since 1986. Address: Kirkhill, Lintrathen, Kirriemuir, Angus DD8 5JH; T.-01575 560228.

Howard, Professor Ian, MA (Hons), ARSA. Professor of Fine Art, Duncan of Jordanstone College of Art, Dundee, since 1986; b. 5.11.52, Aberdeen; m., Ruth D'Arcy; 2 d. Educ. Aberdeen Grammar School; Edinburgh College of Art; Edinburgh University. Travelling scholarship to Italy, 1976; part-time Lecturer in Painting, Gray's School of Art, Aberdeen, 1977 (appointed full-time, 1980); Scottish Arts Council Award, 1979, Bursary, 1985-86; numerous one-man and group exhibitions; appointed to Faculty of Fine Art, British School at Rome. Recreations: reading; music; cooking. Address: (b.) School of Fine Art, Duncan of Jordanstone College of Art, University of Dundee, Dundee; T.-01382 345227.

Howard, Philip, MA (Hons) (Cantab), MLitt. Artistic Director, Traverse Theatre, Edinburgh, since 1996; b. 27.5.63, York. Educ. Ampleforth College, York; Girton College, Cambridge; St. Andrews University. Assistant Director, Royal Court Theatre, London, 1988-90; Director, National Gaelic Youth Theatre, Isle of Benbecula, 1989-92. Director, Tosg Gaelic Theatre Company, since 1996. Address: (b.) Traverse Theatre, Cambridge Street, Edinburgh, EH1 2ED; T.-0131-228 3223.

Howat, Angus John, MA. Minister, Campbeltown, Tarbert and Islay Free Church, since 1996; Assistant Clerk, General Assembly, Free Church of Scotland, since 1998; b. 5.8.44, Monifieth; m., Irene Agnes Gardner Bickerton; 3 d. Educ. Daniel Stewart's College, Edinburgh; Edinburgh University; Strathclyde University; Free Church College. Assistant Librarian, Ayr Public Library, 1966-71; Depute County Librarian, Moray and Nairn, 1971-75; Principal Librarian, Moray District Council at Elgin, 1975-85; Temporary Assistant Librarian, Free Church College, 1988-90; Minister, Campbeltown Free Church, 1990-96. Publication: Churches of Moray (Joint Author). Recreations: family history; walking. Address: Free Church Manse, Kilberry Road, Tarbert PA29 6XX; T.-01880 820134.

Howatson, William, MA (Hons). Freelance journalist, since 1996; b. 22.1.53, Dumfries; m., Hazel Symington Paton; 2 d. Educ. Lockerbie Academy; Edinburgh University. Press and Journal: Agricultural Editor, 1984-96, Leader Writer, 1990-96. Chairman, Guild of Agricultural Journalists, 1995; Member, Scottish Water and Sewerage Customers Council, since 1995; Member, Angus College Board of Management, since 1996; Member, Health Education Board for Scotland, since 1997; Member, East Area Board, Scottish Natural Heritage, since 1997; Vice Chairman, St. Cyrus Community Council, since 1997; Non Executive Director, Angus NHS Trust, 1998. Columnist of the Year, Bank of Scotland Press Awards, 1992. Publication: Farm Servants and Labour in Lowland Scotland, 1770-1914 (Contributor). Recreations: gardening; hillwalking; reading; Scottish history. Address: (h.) Rosefield, Beach Road, St. Cyrus, Montrose; T.-01674 850340.

Howe, Professor Emeritus Jim (James) Alexander Macgregor, MA, PhD, FAAAI, FAISB. Professor Emeritus, Edinburgh University, and Hon. Fellow, Faculty of Science and Engineering, since 1997; b. 7.7.37, Glasgow; m., Nan Harvie Bell; 1 s.; 2 d. Educ. Kelvinside Academy, Glasgow; St. Andrews University; Cambridge University. Senior Assistant in Research, Laboratory of Experimental Psychology, Cambridge University, 1964-66; Edinburgh University: Research Fellow, Lecturer, Senior Lecturer, Reader, Department of Artificial Intelligence, 1967-85; Professor of Artificial Intelligence, 1985-97; Head, Department of Artificial Intelligence, 1978-96; Founder Director, Conversational Software Ltd., 1969-73; Founder and Chairman, Artificial Intelligence Applications Institute, Edinburgh University, since 1984; Governor, Scottish Council for Educational Technology, 1981-84; Chairman, Society for the Study of Artificial Intelligence and the Simulation of Behaviour, 1982-85; Chairman, Alvey Directorate's IKBS Advisory Group, 1983-88; Chairman, SERC/DTI Systems Engineering – Committee A, 1988-91; Member, Ordnance Survey Science and Technology Advisory Committee, 1987-92; Member, Court, Edinburgh University, 1994-97. Publications: contributor to 60 books and journals. Recreations: skiing; curling; gardening; golf. Address: (h.) 26 Essex Road, Edinburgh, EH4 6LJ; T.-0131-339 5390.

Howie, Andrew Law, CBE, FRAgrS. Chairman: Robert Howie & Sons, since 1982, Scottish Milk Ltd., 1994-95; b. 14.4.24, Dunlop; m., Joan Duncan; 2 s.; 2 d. Educ. Glasgow Academy. Joined Robert Howie & Sons, 1941; War Service, RN; became Director, 1965; President, Scottish Compound Feed Manufacturers, 1968-70 and 1983-85; President, Compound Animal Feed Manufacturers National Association, 1971-72; Director, Scottish Corn Trade, 1976-78; Vice-President/Feed, UK Agricultural Supply Trade Association, 1980-81; Chairman, Scottish Council, UKASTA, 1985-87; Director, Scottish Milk Marketing Board, 1980-94 (Chairman, 1982-94); Member, CBI Scottish Council, 1989-95. Recreations: golf; gardening. Address: (h.) Newmill House, Dunlop, Kilmarnock KA3 4BQ; T.-01560 484936.

Howie, Professor John Garvie Robertson, CBE, MD, PhD, FRCPE, FRCGP. Professor of General Practice, Edinburgh University, since 1980; b. 23.1.37, Glasgow; m., Elizabeth Margaret Donald; 2 s.; 1 d. Educ. High School of Glasgow; Glasgow University. Registrar, Laboratory Medicine, Western Infirmary, Glasgow, 1962-66; General Practitioner, Glasgow, 1966-70; Lecturer/Senior Lecturer in General Practice, Aberdeen University, 1970-80; Member: Biomedical Research Committee, SHHD, 1977-81, Health Services Research Committee, SHHD, 1982-86, Chief Scientist Committeee, SHHD, 1987-97, Committee on the Review of Medicines, 1986-91. Publication: Research in General Practice. Recreations: golf; gardening; music. Address: (h.) 4 Ravelrig Park, Balerno, Midlothian EH14 7DL; T.-0131-449 6305.

Howie, Professor John Mackintosh, CBE, MA, DPhil, DSc, FRSE. Regius Professor of Mathematics, St. Andrews University, 1970-97; b. 23.5.36, Chryston, Lanarkshire; m., Dorothy Joyce Miller; 2 d. Educ. Robert Gordon's College, Aberdeen; Aberdeen University. Assistant in Mathematics, Aberdeen University, 1958-59; Assistant, then Lecturer in Mathematics, Glasgow University, 1961-67; Senior Lecturer in Mathematics, Stirling University, 1967-70; visiting appointments:Tulane University, 1964-65, State University of New York at Buffalo, 1969-70, University of Western Australia, 1968, Monash University, 1979, Northern Illinois University, 1988, University of Lisbon, 1996; Dean of Science, St. Andrews University, 1976-79. President, Edinburgh Mathematical Society, 1972-73; Vice-President, London Mathematical Society, 1984-86 and 1990-92; Convener, SCEEB Mathematics Panel, 1970-73; Chairman, Scottish Central Committee on Mathematics, 1975-81; Member, Committee to Review Examinations (Dunning Committee), 1975-77; Chairman, Governors, Dundee College of Education, 1983-87; Keith Prize, Royal Society of Edinburgh, 1979-81; Chairman, Committee to review Fifth and Sixth Years (Howie Committee), 1990-92. Publications: An Introduction to Semigroup Theory, 1976; Automata and Languages, 1991; Fundamentals of Semigroup Theory, 1995; papers in mathematical journals. Recreations: music; gardening. Address: (b.) Mathematical Institute, St. Andrews University, North Haugh, St. Andrews, KY16 9SS; T.-01334 463746.

Howie, Professor Peter William, MD, FRCOG, FRSE, FRCP (Glas). Professor of Obstetrics and Gynaecology, Dundee University, since 1981 (Deputy Principal, Dundee University, since 1996, Dean, Medicine and Dentistry, 1990-93); b. 21.11.39, Aberdeen; m., Anne Jardine Quigg; 1 s.; 1 d. Educ. High School of Glasgow; Glasgow University. Astor Foundation Research Fellow, Royal College of Pathologists, 1970-71; Lecturer, then Senior Lecturer, Department of Obstetrics and Gynaecology, Glasgow University, 1971-78; Clinical Consultant, Medical Research Council Reproductive Biology Unit, Edinburgh, 1978-81. Recreations: golf; music. Address: (h.) 8 Travebank Gardens, Monifieth, Angus DD5 4ET; T.-01382 534802.

Howie, William Forbes, DL, JP, BSc, CEng, MIEE, BA. Justice of the Peace, since 1974; Deputy Lieutenant, Stirling and Falkirk District, since 1981; General Commissioner of Income Tax, since 1983; b. 13.8.20, Falkirk; m., Janet M. Campbell; 2 s.; 1 d. Educ. Falkirk High School; Glasgow University; Open University. RAF, during Second World War (demobbed as Flight Lieutenant); Managing Director, Thomas Laurie & Co. Ltd., 1956-81; appointed Chairman, Children's Panel Advisory Committee, Falkirk, 1970; Chairman, Supplementary Benefit Appeal Tribunal, Stirling and Falkirk, 1973-88; Past Chairman, Forth Valley Scouts; former Session Clerk St. Andrews Church, Falkirk; set up Stirling and District Amateur Football Association, 1951 (its first Secretary); set up Falkirk Section, Scottish Wildlife

Trust, 1984. Recreations: golf; bowls; colour photography; gardening; wildlife. Address: 12 Gartcows Crescent, Falkirk FK1 5QH; T.-Falkirk 24128.

Howison, John Andrew, BSc, MSc, CEng, MICE, ACIArb. Deputy Chief Engineer, Roads Directorate, Scottish Office Industry Department, since 1992; b. 12.8.46, Ruislip; m., Teresa Maria; 2 s.; 2 d. Educ. Surbiton Grammar School; Edinburgh University; Heriot Watt University. Edinburgh Corporation, 1968-70; Livingston Development Corporation, 1970-73; Department of Environment/Department of Transport/Scottish Office, since 1973. Address: (b.) Victoria Quay, Edinburgh; T.-0131-244 7204.

Howson, Peter. Painter; b. 1958, London. Studied, Glasgow School of Art, 1975-77. Official artist, Gulf War.

Hoy, William. Director of Communications, Scottish Homes, since 1992; b. 23.4.50, Dalkeith; m., Sheena; 2 s.; 1 d. Educ. Dalkeith High School; Esk Valley College. Scottish Office: Information Officer, 1978-82, Senior Information Officer, 1982-90, Principal Information Officer, 1990-92. Recreations: golf; gardening; art; reading. Address: (h.) 5 New Meadowspott, Eskbank, Midlothian; T.-0131-663 5986.

Ho-Yen, Darrel Orlando, BMSc (Hons), MBChB, MD, FRCPath. Consultant Microbiologist, Raigmore Hospital, Inverness, since 1987; Director, Scottish Toxoplasma Reference Laboratory, since 1987; Honorary Clinical Senior Lecturer, Aberdeen University, since 1987; b. 1.5.48; m., Jennifer Nicholls; 2 s. Educ. Dundee University. Ninewells Hospital and Medical School, Dundee, 1974-83; Regional Virus Laboratory, Ruchill Hospital, Glasgow, 1983-87. Publications: Better Recovery from Viral Illnesses; Diseases of Infection (Co-Author); Unwind; Human Toxoplasmosis (Co-Author); Climbing Out; Ticks (Co-author). Address: (b.) Microbiology Department, Raigmore Hospital, Inverness IV2 3UJ; T.-01463 704206.

Hubbuck, Professor John Reginald, BA (Cantab), MA, DPhil (Oxon), FRSE, FRSA, CMath, FIMA. Professor of Mathematics, Aberdeen University, since 1978; b. 3.5.41, Girvan; m., Anne Neilson; 1 s.; 1 d. Educ. Manchester Grammar School; Queens' College, Cambridge; Pembroke College, Oxford. Fellow: Gonville and Caius College, Cambridge, 1970-72, Magdalen College, Oxford, 1972-78; President, Edinburgh Mathematical Society, 1985-86. Recreation: hill-walking. Address: (h.) 8 Fonthill Terrace, Aberdeen AB11 7UR; T.-01224 588738.

Hudson, Christopher Sydney, DSO (and Bar), FInstM, CIPD; b. 1.8.16, Tunbridge Wells; m., Ruth Julia Risse; 1 d. Educ. privately, in Switzerland. Army Service, Royal Fusiliers and SOE, 1940-45 (Lt.-Col.); Control Commission for Germany (British and US Sectors), 1946-53; Personnel Manager in overseas companies, Shell International Petroleum Co., Israel, Trinidad, Congo, Algeria; seconded to International Labour Organisation, Geneva, 1966; Executive in charge of Personnel, Training and Industrial Relations, Bank of Scotland, 1968-80. Croix de Guerre with Palme. Recreations: golf; swimming. Address: (h.) 4 Sarazen Court, Deer Park, Livingston EH54 8SW; T.-01506 432572.

Hudson, Rev. Eric Vallance, LTh. Minister, Westerton Fairlie Memorial Church, since 1990; b. 22.2.42, Glasgow; m., Lorna Mary Miller; 1 s.; 1 d. Educ. Paisley Grammar School; Wollongong High School, NSW; Christ's College, Aberdeen and Aberdeen University. Sub-Editor, D.C. Thomson & Co. Ltd., Dundee, 1961-66; Student Assistant, West Kirk of St. Nicholas, Aberdeen, 1966-69; Senior Assistant Minister, New Kilpatrick Parish Church, Bearsden, 1971-73; Minister, Kintore Parish Church, 1973-78; Religious Programmes Officer, Scottish Television, 1978-89; Convener, Association of Bearsden Churches, since 1997; Member: Religious Advisory Committee, Radio Clyde, Church of Scotland Board of Social Responsibility, since 1997; Moderator, Dumbarton Presbytery, 1998-99. Address: 3 Canniesburn Road, Bearsden, Glasgow G61 1PW.

Huggins, Martin, MA, FRSA. Co-Founder and Principal, Edinburgh School of English, since 1969; b. 11.4.39, Edinburgh; m., 1, Astrid Chalmers Watson (m. diss.); 2 d.; 2, Margot Learmond. Educ. George Watson's College; Edinburgh University. Chairman, Scottish Craftsmanship Association, 1977-84; Governor, Edinburgh College of Art, 1980-92; Director, Edinburgh Chamber of Commerce, 1982-86; Chairman, ARELS, 1984-86; Member, British Council Recognition Advisory Committee, 1984-86; Chairman, Board of Governors, Edinburgh College of Art, 1990-92; President, Scottish Arts Club, 1990-92; Assistant, Masters Court, Edinburgh Merchant Company, 1992-95; Trustee, Hospitalfield Trust, since 1994. Recreations: music; travel; lunching at the Arts Club. Address: (h.) 13 Ainslie Place, Edinburgh EH3 6AS; T.-0131-226 1246.

Hughes, Rev. Clifford Eryl, MA, BD, CertEd. Minister, St. Mary's Parish Church, Haddington, since 1993; b. 16.12.36, Newport, S. Wales; m., Kathleen Mackenzie Craig; 1 s.; 1 d. Educ. Dulwich College, London; King's College, University of Cambridge; New College, University of Edinburgh. Teacher, Hurst Grange School, Stirling; Headmaster, Beaconhurst School, Bridge of Allan; Headmaster, Loretto Junior School. Professional singer (opera, concert hall, radio and television performances). President, Haddington Rotary Club, 1998. Recreations: listening to and reviewing music. Address: St. Mary's Manse, 21 Sidegate, Haddington EH41 4BZ; T.-01620 823109.

Hughes, Professor John, BSc, CEng, FIMechE, FISPO. Professor and Director, National Centre for Prosthetics and Orthotics, Strathclyde University, since 1972; b. 20.4.34, Renfrew; m., Margaret Scoular Crichton; 2 d. Educ. Camphill School; Strathclyde University. Worked in shipbuilding and engineering, 1950-63; Strathclyde University: Lecturer in Mechanical Engineering Design, 1963-67, Senior Lecturer, Bioengineering Unit, 1967-72; Past President, International Society for Prosthetics and Orthotics. Recreations: golf; gardening. Address: (b.) Strathclyde University, Curran Building, 131 St. James' Road, Glasgow G4 OLS; T.-0141-552 4049.

Hughes, Professor Michael David. Professor of Management, University of Stirling, since 1989; b. 8.2.47, London; m., Ewa Maria Helinska-Hughes; 1 s.; 2 d. Educ. Farnborough Grammar School; Brunel University. Address: (b.) Department of Management and Organization, University of Stirling, Stirling FK9 4LA; T.-01786 467309.

Hughes of Woodside, Lord (Robert Hughes). MP (Labour), Aberdeen North, 1970-97; Life Peer; b. 3.1.32; m.; 2 s.; 3 d. Educ. Powis Secondary School, Aberdeen; Robert Gordon's College, Aberdeen; Benoni High School, Transvaal; Pietermaritzburg Technical College, Natal. Engineering apprenticeship, South African Rubber Company, Natal, 1949-54; draughtsman, C.F. Wilson & Co., Aberdeen, 1954-70; Member, Aberdeen City Council, 1962-71; Chairman, Aberdeen City Labour Party, 1961-69; Member, Select Committee on Scottish Affairs, 1971; Opposition Junior Spokesman on Scottish Affairs, 1972-74; Parliamentary Under Secretary of State, Scottish Office, 1974-75; Chairman, Select Committee on Scottish Affairs, 1981; Opposition Junior Spokesman on Transport, 1981-83; Opposition Principal Spokesman on Agriculture, 1984-85, on Transport, 1985-87; Member, General Medical Council, 1976-79; Chairman: Anti Apartheid Movement, 1976-94, Action for Southern Africa (ACTSA), since 1994; Vice-Convenor, Scottish Group, Labour MPs, 1989; Convenor,

Scottish Group of Labour MPs, 1990-91; Member, Select Committee on Scottish Affairs, 1992-97. Address: (b.) House of Lords, London.

Hughes, Tom, LLB, CA, ATII, MSPI, FPC. Partner, Gerber Landa and Gee CAs, since 1976; Area Chairman, North Strathclyde Committee, Institute of Chartered Accountants of Scotland; Vice Chairman, Partick Thistle Football Club, since 1998; b. 24.2.52, Glasgow. Educ. St. Mungo's Academy; Glasgow University. Member, Council, Institute of Chartered Accountants of Scotland. University blue, soccer; represented British Universities at soccer; former Queen's Park footballer. Publications: Scottish Insolvency Case Book (Editor); Impecunias (Editor). Recreations: football; tennis; travel. Address: (b.) Gerber, Landa and Gee, 11 Newton Terrace, Glasgow G3 7PJ; T.-0141-221 7446.

Hughes, Rt. Hon. Lord (William Hughes), PC (1970), CBE (1956), DL, LLD. Company Director; b. 22.1.11, Dundee; m., Christian Clancher Gordon (deceased); 2 d. Educ. Balfour Street School; Dundee Technical College. ARP Controller, Dundee, 1939-43; Armed Forces, 1943-46 (commissioned 1944, demobilised as Captain, 1946, served India, Labuan and Burma); Member, Dundee Town Council, 1933-36 and 1937-61; City Treasurer, 1946-47; Lord Provost, 1954-60; Chairman, Eastern Regional Hospital Board, 1948-60; Member: Court, St. Andrews University, 1954-63, Council, Queen's College, Dundee, 1954-63, Committee on Civil Juries, 1958-59, Committee to Inquire into Registration of Title to Land, 1960-62, North of Scotland Hydro Electric Board, 1957-64, Scottish Transport Council, 1960-64; Chairman: Glenrothes Development Corporation, 1960-64, East Kilbride Development Corporation, 1975-82, Royal Commission on Legal Services in Scotland, 1976-80; Joint Parliamentary Under Secretary of State for Scotland, 1964-69; Minister of State for Scotland, 1969-70 and 1974-75; President, Scottish Federation of Housing Associations, 1975-93; Member, Council of Europe and Western European Union, 1976-87; Hon. Member, Council of Europe, since 1987. Recreation: gardening. Address: (h.) The Stables, Ross, Comrie, Perthshire; T.-01764 670557.

Hughes, William Young, CBE. Chairman and Chief Executive, Grampian Holdings plc, 1985-98 (Chief Executive, 1976-85); Chairman, Aberforth Smaller Companies Trust PLC, since 1990; Treasurer, Scottish Conservative Party, 1993-98 (Deputy Chairman, 1989-92); Director, Central Scotland Healthcare NHS Trust, 1994-97; b. 12.4.40, Milnrow, Lancaster; m., Anne Macdonald Richardson; 2 s.; 1 d. Educ. Firth Park Grammar School, Sheffield; Glasgow University; Strathclyde University; Heriot-Watt University. Partner, R. Gordon Drummond, 1966-70; Managing Director, MSJ Securities Ltd., 1970-76. Chairman, CBI Scotland, 1987-89; Member, Governing Council, Scottish Business in the Community. Recreations: Member, Glenbervie Golf Club.

Hughes Hallett, Professor Andrew Jonathan, BA (Hons), MSc (Econ), DPhil, FRSA. Professor of Economics, Strathclyde University, since 1989; Research Fellow, Centre for Economic Policy Research, since 1985; Consultant to World Bank, European Commission, UN, IMF, since 1986; Professor and Fulbright Fellow, Princeton University, 1992-94; Jean Monet Professor, since 1996; b. 1.11.47, London; m., Claudia; 2 s.; 1 d. Educ. Radley College; Warwick University; LSE; Oxford University. Lecturer in Economics, Bristol University, 1973-77; Associate Professor, Erasmus University, Rotterdam, 1977-85; David Dale Professor, Newcastle University, 1985-89. Publications: four books; 145 papers. Address: (b.) 100 Cathedral Street, Glasgow G4 0LN; T.-0141-552 4400.

Hughes Hallett, David John, FRICS. Director, Scottish Wildlife Trust, 1989-98; Main Board Member, Scottish Environment Protection Agency, since 1995; b. 19.6.47, Dunfermline; m., Anne Mary Wright; 2 s.; 1 d. Educ. Fettes College; Reading University. Chartered Surveyor, rural practice, 1966-76; Land Use Adviser, then Director, Scottish Landowners' Federation, 1976-89. Chairman, Royal Institution of Chartered Surveyors in Scotland, 1988-89; Member, Policy Committee, Scottish Council for Voluntary Organisations. Recreations: sailing; cycling; singing. Address: (h.) 8 Crosswood Crescent, Balerno, Edinburgh EH14 7HS; T.-0131-449 2244.

Hughson, A.V. Mark, MD, MB, ChB, FRCPsych, DPM. Consultant Psychiatrist, Leverndale Hospital, Glasgow, since 1990; Honorary Clinical Senior Lecturer, Glasgow University, since 1991; b. 12.3.47, Edinburgh; m., Joan Scally; 2 s. Educ. George Watson's College, Edinburgh; Glasgow University. Recreations: playing the organ (not too badly); skiing (badly). Address: (h.) 1 Cleveden Gardens, Glasgow G12 0PU; T.-0141-334 2473.

Hukins, Professor David William Lawrence, PhD, DSc, CPhys, FInstP, FIPEM, FRSE. MacRobert Professor of Physics, University of Aberdeen, since 1994; Honorary Medical Physicist, Aberdeen Royal Hospitals NHS Trust, since 1994; Managing Director, Aubec R&D Ltd., since 1998; Honorary Research Affiliate, Forsyth Dental Center, Boston, MA, USA, since 1990; b. 3.2.47; Ashford; m., Celia Elizabeth; 2 s. Educ. Ashford Grammar School; Queen Mary College, University of London; King's College, University of London. Research Associate, Purdue University, IN, USA, 1971-73; Research Assistant, University of Oxford, 1973-74; University of Manchester, Department of Medical Biophysics: Lecturer, 1974-80, Senior Lecturer, 1980-91, Reader, 1991-94; Graduate Education Co-ordinator, Faculty of Medicine, University of Manchester, 1993-94. Volvo Prize, International Society for the Study of the Lumbar Spine, 1979; Thomas Stephen Prize, Medical Engineering Division, Institution of Mechanical Engineers, 1998; Member, Scientific Sub-committee, Arthritis Research Campaign, since 1998; Honorary Scientific Advisor, Manchester and Salford Back Pain Centre, 1993-96. Publications: X-Ray Diffraction by Disordered and Ordered Systems, 1981; Editor/Co-editor of five books on connective tissues, calcified tissues and back pain. Recreations: hillwalking; gardening; skiing. Address: (b.) Department of Bio-medical Physics and Bio-Engineering, University of Aberdeen, Foresterhill, Aberdeen AB25 2ZD; T.-01224 681818, Ext. 53495.

Hull, John Hewett, FRSE, BSc (Hons), MSc, CGeol, FGS. Assistant Director, British Geological Survey, and Senior Officer in Scotland, 1982-94; Head, Geological Survey of Scotland, N. Ireland and Northern England, 1982-85; b. 18.6.34, Manchester; m., Peggy Dunning. Educ. Manchester Central Grammar School; Birmingham University. H.M. Geological Survey of Great Britain, 1958-65; Natural Environment Research Council, 1966-94; Hon. Research Fellow, Edinburgh University; Vice-President, Edinburgh Geological Society, 1993-97. Publications: numerous books, professional papers and maps. Recreations: sport; visual arts; music. Address: (h.) 14 Laverockdale Park, Colinton, Edinburgh EH13 0QE; T.-0131-441 7563.

Hume, Sir Alan (Blyth), Kt, CB, MA; b. 5.1.13, Broxburn; m., Marion Morton Garrett; 1 s.; 1 d. Educ. George Heriot's School, Edinburgh; Edinburgh University. Scottish Office: entered, 1936, Under Secretary, Scottish Home Department, 1957-59, Assistant Under Secretary of State, 1959-62, Under Secretary, Ministry of Public Building and Works, 1963-64, Secretary, Scottish Development Department, 1965-73. Chairman: Ancient Monuments Board for Scotland, 1973-81, Edinburgh New Town Conservation Committee, 1975-90. Recreations: golf; fishing. Address:(h.) 12 Oswald Road, Edinburgh EH9 2HJ; T.-0131-667 2440.

Hume, John Robert, OBE, BSc, ARCST, FSA, FSA Scot, Hon FRIAS. Chief Inspector of Historic Buildings, Historic Scotland; Member, Inland Waterways Amenity Advisory Council, since 1974; Member, Industrial Archaeology Sub-Committee, English Heritage, since 1985; Honorary Life President, Seagull Trust, since 1994 (Chairman, 1978-93); Trustee, Scottish Maritime Museum,1983-98; Honorary Vice-President, Association for Industrial Archaeology; b. 26.2.39, Glasgow; m., Catherine Hope Macnab; 4 s. Educ. Hutchesons' Boys' Grammar School; Glasgow University; Royal College of Science and Technology. Assistant Lecturer, Lecturer, Senior Lecturer in Economic History, Strathclyde University, 1964-91. Member, Ancient Monuments Board for Scotland, 1981-84; Director, Scottish Industrial Archaeology Survey, 1978-84. Publications: The Industrial Archaeology of Glasgow; The Industrial Archaeology of Scotland; as Co-Author: Workshop of the British Empire: Engineering and Shipbuilding in the West of Scotland; Beardmore: the History of a Scottish Industrial Giant; The Making of Scotch Whisky; A Bed of Nails: a History of P. MacCallum & Sons Ltd.; Shipbuilders to the World: a History of Harland and Wolff; Steam Entertainment; Historic Industrial Scenes: Scotland; Industrial History in Pictures: Scotland; Glasgow's Railway Stations. Recreations: photography; reading. Address: (h.) 28 Partickhill Road, Glasgow G11 5BP.

Hume, Krystyna D., BSc. Head Teacher, St. Serf's School, Edinburgh, since 1992; b. 2.10.43, Edinburgh; m., Bill Hume; 2 s. Educ. James Gillespie's High School for Girls; Edinburgh University. Teacher of Mathematics: Portobello Secondary School, 1966-74 (Housemistress, 1970-74), St. Serf's School, 1981-92. Recreations: reading; going to the theatre and concerts; listening to music. Address: (b.) St. Serf's School, 5 Wester Coates Gardens, Edinburgh EH12 5LT; T.-0131-337 1015.

Hume, Professor Robert, BSc, MBChB, PhD, FRCP(Edin), FRCPCH. Professor of Developmental Medicine, Dundee University; Consultant Paediatrician and Honorary Consultant in Biochemical Medicine, Dundee Teaching Hospitals NHS Trust; b. 5.4.47, Edinburgh; m., Shaena Finlayson Blair; 2 d. Educ. Dalkeith High School; Edinburgh University. MRC Fellow, Department of Biochemistry, Edinburgh University, 1975-78; Lecturer, Department of Child Life and Health, Edinburgh University, 1978-80; Senior Lecturer, Department of Child Life and Health, Edinburgh University, 1980-92. Medical and Dental Defence Union of Scotland Specialist Advisor. Address: (b.) Centre for Research into Human Development, Departments of Child Health, Obstetrics and Gynaecology, Ninewells Hospital and Medical School, Dundee DD1 9SY; T.-01382 660111.

Humfrey, Professor Peter Brian, BA, MA, PhD. Professor of Art History, University of St. Andrews, since 1995; b. 9.4.47, Cyprus; m., Margaret Zarina; 2 s. Educ. Cranleigh School, Surrey; Trinity College, Dublin; Courtauld Institute of Art, London. Lecturer in Art History, University of St. Andrews, 1977; Senior Visiting Fellow, Center for Advanced Studies in the Visual Arts, National Gallery of Art, Washington D.C., 1986; Fellow, Harvard Center for Italian Renaissance Studies, Villa I Tatti, Florence, 1987, 1991; Member, Institute for Advanced Study, Princeton, 1988. Publications: Cima da Conegliano, 1983; The Altarpiece in Renaissance Venice, 1993; Painting in Renaissance Venice, 1995; Lorenzo Lotto, 1997. Address: (b.) School of Art History, University of St. Andrews, St. Andrews KY16 9AL; T.-01334 462400.

Humphrey, James Malcolm Marcus, CBE, DL, OStJ, MA, FRICS. Member, Aberdeenshire Council, since 1995 (Member, Grampian Regional Council, 1974-94); Deputy Lieutenant, Aberdeenshire, since 1989; Alternate Member, European Committee of the Regions; Non-Executive Director, Grampian Healthcare NHS Trust; b. 1.5.38, Montreal, Canada; m., Sabrina Margaret Pooley; 2 s.; 2 d. Educ. Eton College; Oxford University. Conservative Parliamentary candidate, North Aberdeen, 1966, Kincardine and Deeside, 1991; Council Member, National Farmers Union of Scotland, 1968-73; Member, Aberdeen County Council, 1970-75 (Chairman of Finance, 1973-75); Grampian Regional Council, 1974-78: Leader of the Council, Chairman of Finance, Leader, Conservative Group; Grand Master Mason of Scotland, 1983-88; former Chairman, Clinterty Agricultural College Council; Member, Queen's Bodyguard for Scotland (Royal Company of Archers); Chairman, North of Scotland Board, Eagle Star Group, 1973-91. Recreations: shooting; fishing; photography. Address: (h.) Dinnet, Aboyne, Aberdeenshire.

Hunter, A. Colin J., BA. Head Teacher, Tiree High School, since 1985; b. 26.9.47, Falkirk; m., June Sinclair Stark; 2 s.; 1 d. Educ. Falkirk High School; Stirling University. Entered teaching, 1972; Teacher, Falkirk High School and Forres Academy; Principal Teacher of Biology, Whitfield High School, Dundee; Depute Head Teacher, Auchtercairn Secondary School, Gairloch. Recreations: gardening; golf; walking. Address: (h.) Cornaigmore Schoolhouse, Isle of Tiree, Argyll PA77 6XA; T.-01879 220556.

Hunter, Allison Carnegie. Director of Organisation, Scottish National Party, since 1990; b. 8.1.42, Glasgow; m., Ian James Hunter; 1 s.; 2 d. Educ. Pollokshields Senior Secondary School; Jordanhill College of Education. Schoolteacher, 1961-65 and 1971-90. Recreations: cooking; reading; music. Address: (h.) 4 Tantallon Road, Shawlands, Glasgow G41 3BX; T.-0141-649 1093.

Hunter, Andrew Reid, BA (Hons), PGCE. Headmaster, Merchiston Castle School, Edinburgh, since 1998; b. 28.9.58, Nairobi, Kenya; m., Barbara G.; 2 s.; 1 d. Educ. Kenton College, Nairobi; Aldenham School, Elstree; University of Manchester; St. Luke's College, Exeter. Westbrook Hay Preparatory School, 1978-79; Worksop College, 1983-91 (Housemaster, 1987-91); Bradfield College, 1991-98 (Housemaster, 1992-98). Former Chairman, Public Schools Hockey Festival, Oxford; Committee Member, Public Schools Lawn Tennis Association. Recreations: reading; attending theatre; former men's county player, tennis, squash and hockey. Address: Castle Gates, Merchiston Castle School, Colinton, Edinburgh EH13 0PU; T.-0131-312 2202.

Hunter, Archibald Sinclair, DL, CA. Senior Partner, Scotland, KPMG; b. 20.8.43, Glasgow; m., Pat; 2 s.; 1 d. Educ. Queen's Park School, Glasgow. Trained with Mackie & Clark, CA, Glasgow; qualified as CA, 1966; joined Thomson McLintock, 1966; Partner, 1974; UK Board, 1992-96; Latin American Board, since 1995; President, Institute of Chartered Accountants of Scotland, 1997-98; Member, Council, Scotbic. Recreations: golf; swimming; walking. Address: (b.) 24 Blythswood Square, Glasgow G2 4QS; T.-0141-226 5511.

Hunter, Christopher G.W., MA, FNI, MRIN. Principal, Glasgow College of Nautical Studies, since 1991; b. 8.10.42, Bristol; m., Irene Mary; 3 d. Educ. Pangbourne College. Seafaring career, Deck Officer to Master, 1960-77; Fleet Training Manager/Deputy Personnel Manager, Cunard Shipping Services Ltd., 1978-84; Principal, National Sea Training College, Kent, 1984-91. Vice-Chairman, Merchant Navy Training Board; Chairman, Thistle Education and Consultancy Ltd.; Chairman, Adelphi Management Company Ltd.; Vice Chairman, West of Scotland Ports Welfare Committee; Chairman, The Gorbals Initiative. Recreation: family. Address: (b.) 21 Thistle Street, Glasgow G5 9XB; T.-0141-565 2550.

Hunter, Colin M., MB, ChB, DRCOG, FRCGP. Chairman, Scottish Council, Royal College of General Practitioners, since 1996; Hon. Secretary, N.E. Scotland Faculty, RCGP, 1989-96; Hon. Fellow, Association of Managers in General Practice, since 1996; b. 28.4.58, Stirling. Educ. High School of Stirling; Aberdeen University. Principal in general practice, Skene Medical Group, 1986; Teaching Fellow, Aberdeen University, 1988; first member, RCGP in Scotland, to attain Fellowship of Royal College by Assessment, 1993; Sally Irvine Lecture, Glasgow, 1996. Recreations: hill-walking; singing. Address: The Langdales, 1 Craigston Gardens, Westhill, Aberdeen AB32 6NL; T.-01224 742594.

Hunter, Professor Geoffrey, BSc, PhD, CChem, FRSC. Professor of Chemistry, Dundee University, since 1993, and Head, Department of Chemistry, since 1990; b. 28.6.43, Co. Durham; m., Jacqueline; 1 d. Educ. Stanley Grammar School; Sheffield University; Newcastle-upon-Tyne University. Research Fellow, Simon Fraser University, Vancouver, 1967; Scientific Officer, Atomic Energy Research Establishment, Harwell, 1968; Lecturer, Dundee University, 1969, Senior Lecturer, 1988; Visiting Fellow, Princeton University, 1980, 1982; Visiting Professor, University of Victoria, 1986; Gast Professor, University of Vienna, 1994. Publications: author/co-author of more than 100 publications. Recreation: sailing. Address: (b.) Chemistry Department, Dundee University, Dundee DD1 4HN.

Hunter, George Alexander, OBE (1980), CStJ. Secretary, Commonwealth Games Council for Scotland, since 1978; Founder Governor, Scottish Sports Aid Foundation, since 1980; Member, Edinburgh City Council, since 1992; b. 24.2.26, Edinburgh; m., Eileen Elizabeth. Educ. George Watson's College, Edinburgh. Served with Cameronians, seconded to 17th Dogara Regiment, Indian Army, 1944-47 (Captain); Lawson Donaldson Seeds Ltd., 1942-82 (Director, 15 years); Secretary, Scottish Amateur Rowing Association, 1948-78 (President, 1978-84); Adviser, Sports Aid Foundation, since 1979; Treasurer, Commonwealth Games Council for Scotland, 1962-78; Member, Scottish Sports Council, 1976-84 (Chairman, Games and Sports Committee, 1976-84); Chairman, Scottish Standing Conference for Sport, 1977-84. Address: (h.) 1 Craiglockhart Crescent, Edinburgh EH14 1EZ; T.-0131-443 2533.

Hunter, James, MA (Hons), PhD. Writer, Historian, Journalist and Broadcaster; Member, Scottish Tourist Board; Member, Northern Areas Board, Scottish Natural Heritage; b. 22.5.48, Duror, Argyll; m., Evelyn; 1 s.; 1 d. Educ. Oban High School; Aberdeen University; Edinburgh University. Former Director, Scottish Crofters Union; former Chairman, Skye and Lochalsh Enterprise. Publications: The Making of the Crofting Community, 1976; Skye: The Island, 1986; The Claim of Crofting, 1991; Scottish Highlanders: A People and their Place, 1992; A Dance Called America: The Scottish Highlands, the United States and Canada, 1994; On the Other Side of Sorrow: Nature and People in the Scottish Highlands, 1995; Glencoe and the Indians, 1996. Address: (b.) Rowanbrae, Kiltarlity, Beauly IV4 7HT; T.-01463 741644.

Hunter, Professor John Angus Alexander, OBE, BA, MD, FRCPEdin. Grant Professor of Dermatology, Edinburgh University, since 1981; b. 16.6.39, Edinburgh; m., Ruth Mary Farrow; 1 s.; 2 d. Educ. Loretto School; Pembroke College, Cambridge; Edinburgh University. Research Fellow, Institute of Dermatology, London, 1967; Registrar, Department of Dermatology, Edinburgh Royal Infirmary, 1968-70; Exchange Research Fellow, Department of Dermatology, Minnesota University, 1968; Lecturer, Department of Dermatology, Edinburgh University, 1970-74; Consultant Dermatologist, Lothian Health Board, 1974-80; Member: Executive Committee of Investigative Group, British Association of Dermatologists, 1974-76; Executive Committee, British Association of Dermatologists, 1977-79; SEC, Scottish Dermatological Society, 1980-82; Specialist Advisory Committee, (Dermatology), Joint Committee on Higher Medical Training, 1980-87 (Chairman, 1986-90); Medical Appeal Tribunal, since 1982; Scottish Committee for Hospital Medical Services, 1983-85; President: Section of Dermatology, Royal Society of Medicine, 1993-94, Scottish Dermatological Society, 1994-97, British Association of Detmatologists, 1998-99. Publications: Common Diseases of the Skin (Co-author); Clinical Dermatology (Co-author); Skin Signs in Clinical Medicine (Co-author). Recreations: music; gardening; tropical fish; golf. Address: (h.) Leewood, Rosslyn Castle, Roslin, Midlothian EH25 9PZ; T.-0131-440 2181.

Hunter, Kirk John, MA (Hons). Secretary, Scottish Dairy Association, since 1989; b. 1.12.54, Glasgow; m., June Wilson. Educ. George Heriots School; Dundee University. Graduate Trainee, SSEB, 1977-79; Trade Association Executive, Thomson McLintock, Glasgow, 1980-83; Commercial Officer, Metal Trades Confederation, London and Glasgow, 1983-86; Peat Marwick McLintock, Glasgow, 1986-89. Recreations: golf; gardening; cycling. Address: (h.) 18 Ravelston Road, Bearsden, Glasgow G61 1AW; T.-0141-942 3799.

Hunter, Sir Laurence Colvin, Kt, MA, DPhil, FRSE. Professor of Applied Economics, Glasgow University, since 1970; b. 8.8.34, Glasgow; m., Evelyn Margaret Green; 3 s.; 1 d. Educ. Hillhead High School, Glasgow; Glasgow University; University College, Oxford. Assistant Lecturer, Manchester University, 1958-59; 2nd Lt., RAEC, 1959-61; Walgreen Postdoctoral Fellow, University of Chicago, 1961-62; joined Glasgow University as Lecturer, 1962; Vice-Principal, 1982-86; Director: External Relations, 1987-90, Business School since 1996. Council Member, ACAS, 1974-86; Chairman, Police Negotiating Board, since 1986; Council Member, Economic and Social Research Council, 1989-92; Editor, Scottish Journal of Political Economy, 1966-97; President, Scottish Economic Society, 1993-96. Recreations: golf; painting; curling. Address: (h.) 23 Boclair Road, Bearsden, Glasgow G61 2AF; T.-0141-563 7135.

Hunter, Mark S. Managing Director, Chesterton Scotland Ltd., Edinburgh, since 1993; Director, Northern Retail Property Fund, since 1994; b. 2.11.51, Newcastle upon Tyne; m., Rosalind (deceased); 1 s.; 2 d. Educ. Rugby School; Royal Agricultural College, Circencester. Weatherall, Green and Smith, London; Chestertons, London; Associate Director, Conrad Ritblat, Glasgow; Associate Director, Leavers, Edinburgh; Joint Founder/Chairman, Conroy Hunter, Edinburgh. Trustee, Young Musicians Trust. Recreations: music; opera; fishing; shooting; wine; Scottish art; family. Address: (b.) 36 Castle Street, Edinburgh EH2 3HT; T.-0131-226 4791.

Hunter, Michael William, FRICS. Regional Director West, The National Trust for Scotland, since 1992; b. 1.6.44, Glasgow; m., Olive; 1 s.; 1 d. Educ. Eastwood High School, Glasgow; College of Estate Management. Assistant Factor, Viscount Cowdray, Dunecht Estates, Aberdeenshire; Senior Assistant Factor, J. T. Sutherland, Chartered Surveyors, Brechin; Regional Factor, The National Trust for Scotland: Pitmedden House, Ellon, then West Regional Office, Glasgow. Recreations: walking; country life; rugby. Address: (b.) West Regional Office, Greenbank House, Clarkston, Glasgow G76 8RB; T.-0141-616 2266.

Hunter, Mollie. Writer; b. 30.6.22, Longniddry; m., Thomas McIlwraith; 2 s. Educ. Preston Lodge School. Freelance Journalist, until 1960; Past Chairman, Society of Authors in Scotland; writer of various types of fiction (fantasy, historical novels, "realism") for children of varying age groups; 30 titles published, including Talent Is Not Enough, on the craft of writing for children; travelled extensively (Australia, New Zealand, Canada, USA); Lecturer on writing for children; Writer-in-Residence, Dalhousie University, Halifax, Canada, on two occasions; awarded Arbuthnot Lectureship, 1975, and Carnegie Medal, 1975. Recreations: reading; gardening; music. Address: Rose Cottage, 7 Mary Ann Court, Inverness IV3 5BZ; T.-01463 713914.

Hunter, Richard J. A., BA, CA. Group Finance Director, The Edrington Group Ltd., since 1994; Finance Director, Robertson and Barr, since 1988; b. 11.5.55, Glasgow; m., Christine; 1 s.; 2d. Educ. Kelvinside Academy; Glenalmond College; Strathclyde University. Qualified CA, Arthur Young McClelland Moores, 1978; joined Edrington Group, 1981. Member, Council, Institute of Chartered Accountants of Scotland, since 1998. Recreations: sailing; fishing; golf. Address: (b.) 106 West Nile Street, Glasgow G1 2QX.

Hunter, Russell. Actor; b. 18.2.25, Glasgow. Former shipyard worker; began acting as an amateur; made professional debut with Glasgow Unity Theatre, 1947; appeared in repertory with Edinburgh Gateway, Edinburgh Traverse and Glasgow Citizens'; acted with the RSC, Bristol Old Vic and at the Old Vic, London; played title role in The Servant o' Twa Maisters, 1965, opening production of Edinburgh Civic Theatre Company; played The Pope in Galileo, also at Royal Lyceum; played The Gravedigger in Hamlet, Assembly Hall, Edinburgh Festival; took title role in Cocky, one-man play, 1969; played Jock, solo play, 1972.

Hunter, Thomas Blane, BA. Chief Executive Officer, Sports Division, 1984-98; b. 6.5.61, Irvine. Educ. Cumnock Academy; University of Strathclyde.

Hunter, William, MA. Columnist, The Herald, retired 1996; b. 16.8.31, Paisley; m., Mo (deceased); 1 s.; 1 d. Educ. Paisley Grammar School; Glasgow University. Publications: The Saints; Bell the Cage!; Dear Happy Ghosts. Recreation: weeding. Address: (h.) 233 Fenwick Road, Glasgow; T.-0141-638 1323.

Hunter, William Hill, CBE, CA, JP, DL. Partner, McLay, McAlister & McGibbon, CA, 1946-91, Consultant, since 1991; Director, J. & G. Grant, Glenfarclas Distillery, 1966-92; b. 5.11.16, Cumnock; m., Kathleen Cole; 2 s. Educ. Cumnock Academy. Enlisted as private, RASC, 1940; commissioned Royal Artillery, 1941; Staff Captain, Middle East, 1944-46; Director: Abbey National Building Society (Scottish Advisory Board), 1966-86, City of Glasgow Friendly Society, 1966-88 (President, 1980-88); Member: CBI Scottish Council, 1978-84, Institute of Directors West of Scotland Committee, 1980-91; President: Renfrew West and Inverclyde Conservative and Unionist Association, since 1972, Scottish Young Unionist Association, 1958-60, Scottish Unionist Association, 1964-65; contested (Unionist), South Ayrshire, 1959 and 1964; Hon. Treasurer, Quarrier's Homes, 1972-94 (Chairman, 1991-94); Hon. Financial Advisor, Erskine Hospital, since 1981; Session Clerk, Kilmacolm Old Kirk, 1972-77; Chairman: Salvation Army Advisory Board in Strathclyde, 1982-93, Salvation Army Housing Association Scotland Ltd., 1986-91; admitted to Distinguished Order of Auxiliary Service of Salvation Army, 1981; Deacon Convener, Trades House of Glasgow, 1986-87; Honorary Vice President, Royal Scottish Agricultural Benevolent Institution, since 1994; Honorary President, Friends of Glasgow Botanic Gardens, since 1994. Recreations: gardening; golf; swimming; music. Address: (h.) Armitage, Kilmacolm PA13 4PH; T.-0150587 2444.

Hunter Blair, Francis, JP. Hill Farmer; Vice-President and Past Chairman, Galloway Cattle Society of Great Britain and Ireland; b. 29.10.30, Lincoln; m., Joyce Adeline Mary Graham; 4 s.; 1 d. Educ. Royal Naval College, Dartmouth; West of Scotland Agricultural College. President, Stewartry Branch, National Farmers' Union of Scotland, 1968-69; Council Member, NFU of Scotland, 1969-70; Vice President, Royal Highland and Agricultural Society of Scotland, 1987; several periods of office as Secretary and President, local agricultural shows; Past Chairman, Carsphairn Community Council; Elder and Session Clerk, Carsphairn Kirk. Recreations: country pursuits; reading. Address: Marbrack, Carsphairn, Castle Douglas, Stewartry of Kirkcudbright; T.-Carsphairn 207.

Hunter Blair, James, DL. Landowner and Forester; b. 18.3.26, Ayr. Educ. Eton; Oxford. Scots Guards, 1944-48; University, 1948-50; merchant bank, London, 1951-53; managed family estate, since 1953. Past President, Royal Scottish Forestry Society; former Vice-President, Royal Highland Society; Past Chairman, Historic Houses Association for Scotland; Trustee, National Galleries of Scotland; Member, Historic Buildings Council for Scotland. Recreations: shooting; fishing; going to the opera. Address: Blairquhan, Maybole, Ayrshire; T.-01655 770239.

Hunter Gordon, Nigel, MA, FCA, ATII. Managing Partner, Ernst & Young, Highlands and Islands, since 1993; b. 2.9.47, Camberley; m., Linda; 2 s. Educ. Ampleforth College; St. Andrews University. Secretary, Highlands and Islands Area Group, CBI; Member, Scottish Council, Institute of Directors, 1992-98. Recreations: skiing; gardening. Address: (b.) Moray House, 16 Bank Street, Inverness IV1 1QY; T.-01463 237581.

Huntly, 13th Marquess of (Granville Charles Gomer Gordon). Premier Marquess of Scotland; Chief, House of Gordon; b. 4.2.44; m.; 1 d.; 1 s., 2 d. by pr. m. Address: Aboyne Castle, Aberdeenshire, AB34 5JP.

Huq, Mohammed Mozammel, BA(Hons), MA, MLitt, PhD. Senior Lecturer in Economics, since 1990, and Associate Director, Developing Countries Research Unit, since 1991, University of Strathclyde; President, North Bengal College, Kakina, Lalmonirhat, Bangladesh, since 1994; b. 29.11.40, Kakina, Bangladesh; m., Kumkum; 1 s.; 1 d. Educ. Kakina M.R.M. High School; Carmichael College, Rangpur; University of Rajshahi, Bangladesh; University of Glasgow. Lecturer in Economics, Rajshadi College (University of Rajshadi), then Associate Professor of Economics, M.C. College (University of Chittagong), Bangladesh; postgraduate research, University of Glasgow; returned to Bangladesh, 1974, as Researcher; Researcher, David Livingstone Institute of Overseas Development Studies, University of Strathclyde, 1976-87; Senior Research Fellow (on secondment), Centre for Development Studies, University of Ghana, 1982-84; Lecturer in Economics, University of Strathclyde, 1987. President, North Bengal College, Bangladesh; Chairman, Third World Science, Technology and Development Forum UK; President, Scottish Asian Action Committee. Publications: author of several books and co-editor of two books. Recreations: tennis; bridge. Address: (b.) Department of Economics, University of Strathclyde, Glasgow G4 0LN; T.-0141-548 3863.

Hurford, Professor James Raymond, BA, PhD. Professor of General Linguistics, Edinburgh University, since 1979; b. 16.7.41, Reading; m., Sue Ann Davis; 2 d. Educ. Exeter School; St. John's College, Cambridge; University College, London. Assistant Professor, Department of English, University of California, Davis, 1968-71; Lecturer, then Senior Lecturer, Department of Linguistics, Lancaster University, 1972-79. Publications: Language and Number: the emergence of a cognitive system; Semantics: a coursebook (Co-author); The Linguistic Theory of Numerals; Grammar: a student's guide. Address: (b.) Edinburgh University, Edinburgh EH8 9YL.

Hurman, David Charles, MBChB, DTM&H, DMRT, FRCR, HonMD (Manitoba). Consultant in Clinical

Oncology, Aberdeen Royal Hospitals NHS Trust (Head of Department, since 1991); Visiting Consultant, Shetland Health Board, since 1988; Clinical Senior Lecturer, Aberdeen University, since 1988; b. 9.2.52, London; m., Dr. Dorothy Elizabeth McMurray; 1 s.; 1 d. Educ. Ashford County Grammar School; Liverpool University. Pre-registration and junior medical posts, Southport General Infirmary and Christiana Hartley Maternity Hospital, 1975-77; Medical Officer, Trans-Borneo Expedition, 1978; Mersey Regional Centre for Radiotherapy and Oncology, Clatterbridge Hospital, Bebington, 1979-86; Clinical Research Fellow, Cross Cancer Institute and University of Alberta, 1986-87; Senior Medical Officer, International Scientific Support Trust Expedition to Java and Kalimantan, 1994; Expert Adviser and Honorary Consultant, Bhaktapur Cancer Care Centre, Kathmandu, Nepal, since 1995. Recreations: foreign travel; football; cricket; hills and mountains; rock music. Address: (h.) 85 Cairnfield Place, Aberdeen AB15 5LX; T.-01224 638411.

Hurst, Professor Andrew, CGeol, FGS. Professor of Production Geoscience, Aberdeen University, since 1992; b. 5.9.53, Stoke-on-Trent; m., Liv Christiansen; 1 s.; 1 d. Educ. Cheadle Grammar School; Aberdeen University; Reading University. Geologist, Norway, 1981-82; Senior Geologist, Norway, 1982-90; Senior Geologist, Unocal UK, 1990-91; Advising Geologist, Unocal UK, 1991-92. Executive Editor, Sedimentary Geology; William Smith Fund Award, Geological Society of London, 1993; Chief Editor, Petroleum Geoscience; editor of five books. Recreations: squash; music; natural history. Address: (b.) Department of Geology and Petroleum Geology, King's College, Aberdeen AB24 3UE; T.-01224 273713.

Hurst, Nigel Peter, BSc, MBBS, FRCP (Edin), PhD. Consultant Rheumatologist, since 1989; Senior Lecturer, University of Edinburgh, since 1990; b. 29.4.46, London; m., Susan F. Hurst; 2 s.; 2 d. Educ. Eastbourne College; Bristol University; St. Mary's Hospital Medical School, London. Professional training in London, University Hospital of Wales and Edinburgh; research and clinical posts in Edinburgh and Adelaide; Consultant Rheumatologist and Clinical Senior Lecturer, Adelaide, 1983-89. Publications in fields of cell biochemistry and pharmacology, rheumatology and health economics. Recreations: occasional sailor, hillwalker and dilettante. Address: (h.) Fairnielaw House, Athelstaneford; T.-01620 880607/0131-537 1806.

Hurtado, Professor Larry Weir, BA, MA, PhD. Professor of New Testament Language, Literature and Theology, Faculty of Divinity, Edinburgh University, since 1996; b. 29.12.43, Kansas City; m., Shannon Hunter; 1 s.; 2 d. Educ. Case Western Reserve University. Pastor, North Shore Assembly of God, Illinois, 1971-75; Assistant Professor of New Testament, Regent College, Vancouver BC, 1975-78; Professor of Religion, University of Manitoba, Winnipeg, 1978-96. Address: (b.) New College, Mound Place, Edinburgh EH1 2LX; T.-0131-650 8920.

Hutcheon, Rev. Douglas John. Superintendent, Baptist Union of Scotland, since 1993; b. 27.7.38, Buckie; m., Helen Smith; 2 s.; 2 d. Educ. Buckie High School; Milnes High School, Fochabers; Bible Training Institute. Bank of Scotland, 1953-57; Minister of the Baptist Church, since 1962. Recreations: reading; hill-walking; watching football; music. Address: (b.) 14 Aytoun Road, Glasgow G41 5RT; T.-0141-423 6169.

Hutcheson, Rev. Norman McKenzie, MA, BD. Minister, Dalbeattie and Urr Parish Churches; Convener, Europe Committee, Board of World Mission, Church of Scotland, since 1998; b. 11.10.48, Leven; m., Elizabeth; 2 d. Educ. Hillhead High School, Glasgow; Glasgow University; Edinburgh University. Minister, St. Andrews, Kirkcaldy, 1973-88. Recreations: photography; travel; reading. Address: (h.) 36 Mill Street, Dalbeattiew DG5 4HE; T.-01556 610029.

Hutchins, Michael John Patrick, FCIB. Director UK Retail Banking, Royal Bank of Scotland Plc, since 1995; b. 19.4.44, Sale; m., Rosemary Isabelle; 1 s.; 2 d. Educ. Burnage Grammar School, Manchester. Career banker with William Deacon's Bank, Williams & Glyns Bank and Royal Bank of Scotland; Manager of a group of bank branches in Sheffield and Nottingham; a senior manager, International Division, running North of England and Midlands area; a branch area manager covering Cheshire and Derbyshire; Local Director, Yorkshire and North East of England; ran all branch banking operations in North of England and Midlands from Manchester, as Director; moved to Edinburgh in 1995. Director: Royal Scottish Assurance, Royal Bank of Scotland Unit Trust Management, Royal Exchange Theatre (Manchester). Recreations: all sports; theatre. Address: (b.) Royal Bank of Scotland, PO Box 31, 42 St. Andrew Square, Edinburgh; T.-0131-556 8555.

Hutchinson, Peter, PhD, FIFM. Assistant Secretary, North Atlantic Salmon Conservation Organization, since 1986; b. 26.5.56, Glasgow; m., Jane MacKellaig; 1 s.; 1 d. Educ. Queen Elizabeth's Grammar School, Blackburn; Edinburgh University. Project Co-ordinator, Surface Water Acidification; Research Biologist: Institute of Terrestrial Ecology, Edinburgh University; Member, Consular Corps in Edinburgh and Leith, since 1991. Recreations: golf; squash; rugby union; angling. Address: (h.) 3 St. Ronan's Terrace, Morningside, Edinburgh.

Hutchison, David, MA, MLitt. Senior Lecturer in Communication Studies, Glasgow Caledonian University, since 1975; b. 24.9.44, West Kilbride; m., Pauleen Frew; 2 d. Educ. Ardrossan Academy; Glasgow University. Tutor/Organiser, WEA (West of Scotland), 1966-69; Teacher, Reid Kerr College, Paisley, 1969-71; Lecturer in Communication Studies, Glasgow College of Technology, 1971-75; Member, West Kilbride District Council, 1970-75 (Chairman, 1972-75); Governor, Scottish Film Council, 1987-95; Member, General Advisory Council, BBC, 1988-96; author of play, Deadline, Pitlochry Festival Theatre, 1980. Publications: The Modern Scottish Theatre, 1977; Headlines: the Media in Scotland (Editor), 1978; Media Policy, 1998; various articles/chapters. Recreations: walking; swimming; the arts. Address: (b.) Department of Language and Media, Caledonian University, Cowcaddens Road, Glasgow G4 OBA; T.-0141-331 3255.

Hutchison, Ian Somerville, OBE, JP. Member, East Renfrewshire Council; Member: Historic Buildings Council for Scotland, since 1983, Renfrewshire Valuation Appeals Committee, Management Committee, Renfrewshire Enterprise, Scottish Council Development and Industry Executive; Delegate to COSLA, since 1975 (Vice-President, 1979-82); Managing Director, Timbertection Ltd., since 1973; Director, The Planning Exchange; Vice Chairman, Scottish Housing Planning Council; b. 10.4.28, Glasgow; m., Aileen Wallace; 2 s.; 2 d. Educ. Hutchesons' Boys' Grammar School. Former Member: Eastwood District Council, Renfrew County Council, First (Eastwood) District Council, Scottish Valuation Advisory Council. Recreations: gardening; fishing. Address: (h.) 39 Hazelwood Avenue, Newton Mearns, Glasgow G77 5QT; T.-0141-639 2186.

Hutchison, John Charles, JP, BSc, CEng, FICE, FIHT, FIES. Lochaber Area Manager, The Highland Council, since 1995; b. 23.7.47, Edinburgh; m., Christine; 1 s.; 2 d. Educ. Leith Academy; Heriot-Watt University. Student Apprentice, Redpath Brown and Co., Edinburgh, 1965-69; Graduate Engineer, Redpath Dorman Long, Bedford, 1969-71; Inverness County Council, Skye: Assistant Engineer, 1971-72, Senior Resident Engineer, 1972-75; Highland Regional Council, Lochaber: Sub-Divisional Engineer,

1975-78, Divisional Engineer, 1978-96. Honorary Sheriff, since 1994. Recreations: singing; walking; reading; Scottish culture; Europe; land. Address: (b.) Lochaber House, High Street, Fort William PH33 6EL; T.-01397 703881.

Hutchison, Sir Peter Craft, Bt, CBE, FRSE. Chairman, Forestry Commission, since 1994; formerly Chairman, Hutchison & Craft Ltd., Insurance Brokers; b. 5.6.35, London; m., Virginia Colville; 1 s. Educ. Eton; Magdalene College, Cambridge. National Service, Royal Scots Greys (2nd Lt.); Northern Assurance Co. (London); Director of various companies; Past Chairman, Ailsa Shipbuilding Co. Ltd.; Director, Stakis plc, 1979-91; Board Member, Scottish Tourist Board, 1981-87; Vice Chairman, British Waterways Board, 1988-97; Chairman, Board of Trustees, Royal Botanic Garden, Edinburgh, 1985-94; Chairman, Loch Lomond and Trossachs Working Party, 1991-93; Deacon, Incorporation of Hammermen of Glasgow, 1984-85. Recreations: plant hunting; gardening; calligraphy. Address: (h.) Broich, Kippen, Stirlingshire FK8 3EN; T.-01786 870317.

Hutton, Alasdair Henry, OBE, TD. Chairman, Calchou Electronics; Writer and Broadcaster; Writer and Narrator, Edinburgh Military Tattoo and other public events; Member, Social Security Advisory Committee; Scottish Trustee, Community Service Volunteers; Senior Consultant, Career Associates, Scotland; Chairman, Disease Prevention Organisation; Member, Kelso and Jedburgh Advisory Committee, Scottish Borders Enterprise; Member, International Relations Committee, Law Society of Scotland; b. 19.5.40, London; m., Deirdre Mary Cassels (see Deirdre Mary Hutton); 2 s. Educ. Dollar Academy; Brisbane State High School. Journalist, The Age, Melbourne, 1959-61, Aberdeen Journals, 1962-64; Broadcaster, BBC, 1964-79; Member, European Parliament, 1979-89. Member, Queen's Bodyguard for Scotland (Royal Company of Archers); Former 2ic, 15th (Scottish Volunteer) Bn., The Parachute Regiment; Vice-President, Kelso Branch, Royal British Legion; Elder, Kelso North Church of Scotland; Patron ROKPA; Vice-Chairman and Life Member, John Buchan Society; Life Member, Edinburgh Sir Walter Scott Club; Fellow, Industry and Parliament Trust; Honorary President, Scottish Association of CB Clubs; Patron, Kelso Laddies' Association; Member, Ancient Order of Mosstroopers; Honorary Chairman, Hawick Conservative Club; European Adviser, Scottish Police College and Isle of Man Parliament. Address: (b.) Rosebank, Shedden Park Road, Kelso, TD5 7PX; T.-01573 224369.

Hutton, Deirdre Mary. Vice-Chairman, National Consumer Council, since 1997; Chairman: Scottish Consumer Council, since 1991, Rural Forum, since 1992, Personal Investment Authority Ombudsman Council, since 1997 (Member, Personal Investment Authority Consumer Panel, 1994-98); Non-Executive Director: Financial Services Authority, since 1998, Borders Health Board, since 1997, Edinburgh Theatres Ltd., since 1997; b. 15.3.49, Haddington; m., Alasdair Hutton (qv); 2 s. Educ. Sherborne School for Girls; secretarial college. Research Assistant, Glasgow Chamber of Commerce, 1976-81; seconded to Scotland is British Campaign and Scotland Says No Campaign during devolution referendum, 1979; Founder Chairman, Enterprise Music Scotland Ltd. Recreations: music; reading. Address: (h.) Rosebank, Shedden Park Road, Kelso TD5 7PX; T.-01573 224368.

Hutton, V. Rosemary S., MA, PhD, FRAS, FRSE. Honorary Fellow, Department of Geology and Geophysics, University of Edinburgh, since 1990; b. 22.10.25, Dundee. Educ. Harris Academy, Dundee; University of St. Andrews; University of London. Research Physicist, British Jute Trade Research Association, Dundee, 1949-53; Lecturer in Physics, University of Ghana, Accra, 1954-62; Senior Lecturer/Reader in Physics, Ahmadu Bello University, Zaria, Nigeria, 1963-67; Associate Professor of Physics, University of Ibadan, Nigeria, 1968-69; University of Edinburgh: Lecturer in Geophysics, 1969-73, Senior Lecturer, 1973-82, Reader, 1982-90. Former Member of several international scientific committees; guest lectureships at universities and research institutes in Russia, Australia, Italy and India. Publications: over 60 articles in international scientific journals. Recreations: video photography; gardening. Address: (h.) Kerfield Grange, Innerleithen Road, Peebles EH45 8BG; T.-01721 720376.

Hutton, William Riddell, BDS. Dentist, since 1961; Honorary Sheriff, since 1996; b. 22.10.38, Glasgow; m., Patricia Margaret Burns; 1 s.; 1 d. Educ. Hamilton Academy; Glasgow University Dental School. International Grenfell Association, Newfoundland and Labrador, 1961-64; General Practice, Lanark, since 1964; Member, Secretary and Chairman, Lanarkshire Local Dental Committee, 1964-94; Member and Chairman, Lanarkshire Area Dental Committee, 1975-94. Recreations: music; golf; hillwalking; travel. Address: (h.) St. Anthony, 9 Braedale Road, Lanark ML11 7AW; T.-01555 662927.

Hyslop, A. Graeme, BA (Hons), MSc, TQ(FE), FRSA. Principal, Langside College, Glasgow, since 1999; b. 23.3.53, Glasgow; m., Aileen; 1 d. Educ. High School of Glasgow; Glasgow Caledonian University; Glasgow University; Strathclyde University. Car Park Attendant, 1979-80; College Lecturer, 1980-88; Further Education Officer, Strathclyde Regional Council, 1988-91; Depute Principal, Langside College, Glasgow, 1991-98. Board Member, Castlemilk Economic Development Agency; Board Member, Continuing Education Gateway. Recreations: sport (football, squash, golf); reading; cinema. Address: (b.) 50 Prospecthill Road, Glasgow G42 9LB; T.-0141-649 4991.

Hyslop, John Michael, OBE, FInstD, FInstPet, FIM. Chairman, Brown and Root AOC (part of the Halliburton Group); b. 31.8.37, Pontypridd; m., Marjorie Lorraine Rowe; 1 s. Educ. Pontypridd Grammar School; Glamorgan Technical College. Former Managing Director and Chairman, AOC International; Director, Fairhaven International plc, 1988-93; former Managing Director, OGC International plc; Grampian Industrialist of the Year, 1991; elected FRSA, 1993. Recreations: game shooting; rugby; golf; country pursuits. Address: (b.) Alba Gate, Stoneywood Park, Dyce, Aberdeen AB21 7HW; T.-01224 770033.

I

Ibbett, Professor Roland Norman, BSc, MSc, PhD, FRSE, CEng, FBCS. Professor of Computer Science, Edinburgh University, since 1985, Vice-Principal, since 1994; b. 21.6.41, Burton upon Trent; m., Janet; 3 s.; 3 d. Educ. Burton upon Trent Grammar School. Lecturer in Computer Science, Manchester University, 1967-75, Senior Lecturer, 1975-82, Reader, 1982-85. Chairman, Conference of Professors and Heads of Computing, 1993-95. Publications: two books; 50 papers. Recreations: gardening; DIY; listening to music. Address: (b.) Division of Informatics, Edinburgh University, King's Buildings, Edinburgh EH9 3JZ; T.-0131-650 5119.

Idiens, Dale, BA, DipEd. Depute Director (Collections) and Keeper, Department of History and Applied Art, National Museums of Scotland; b. 13.5.42, Prestatyn. Educ. Wycombe High School, High Wycombe; Leicester University. Royal Scottish Museum, Department of Art and Archaeology: Assistant Keeper in Charge of Ethnography, 1964, Deputy Keeper, 1979, Keeper, 1983. Address: (b.) Royal Museum, Chambers Street, Edinburgh; T.-0131-225 7534.

Iles, Paul Raymond, MPhil, FRSA. Theatrical Manager; Associate Director, Scottish Centre for Cultural Management and Policy, Queen Margaret College, Edinburgh; Trustee, The Theatres Trust; Director, Scottish Actors' Studio Ltd.; Chairman, Gloria Theatre Ltd.; Trustee, Centre for the Study of Theatre and Opera Trust, Ltd.; Member, Scottish Arts Council (Chairman, Dance Committee); b. 11.4.52. Educ. Kimbolton School; Glasgow University. Concurrently: General Manager, Watermill Theatre, Newbury, Business Manager, 69 Theatre Company at the Manchester Royal Exchange, Finance Officer, Oxford Playhouse Company, 1973-76; in Australia: General Manager, Nimrod Theatre of Sydney, 1976-79, State Theatre Company, Adelaide Festival Centre, 1980-82, Producer, North Queensland Theatre Company, 1982-86; General Manager, Blackpool Grand Theatre, 1988-92; founding General Manager, Edinburgh Festival Theatre, 1992-96. Address: (h.) 47 Thistle Street, Edinburgh EH2 1DY; T.-0131-225 2499.

Ingle, Professor Stephen James, BA, MA (Econ), DipEd, PhD. Professor of Politics (and Head, Politics Department), Stirling University; b. 6.11.40, Ripon; m., Margaret Anne; 2 s.; 1 d. Educ. The Roan School, London; Sheffield University; Wellington University, NZ. Commonwealth Scholar, 1964-67; Lecturer in Politics, Hull University, 1967-80; Senior Lecturer, 1980-91; Head of Department, 1985-90. Secretary, Political Studies Association, 1988-89; Member, East Yorkshire Health Authority, 1985-90; Visiting Research Fellow, Victoria University of Wellington, 1993. Publications: Socialist Thought in Imaginative Literature, 1979; Parliament and Health Policy, 1981; British Party System, 1987, 1989; George Orwell: a political life, 1993. Recreations: reading; music; hill-walking. Address: (b.) Department of Politics, Stirling University, Stirling FK9 4LA; T.-01786 467593.

Inglis, George Finlay, CA. Director of Finance and Administration, Scottish Tourist Board, since 1988; b. 2.1.46, Edinburgh; m., Catherine; 1 s.; 1 d. Educ. Royal High School, Edinburgh. Recreations: sport; literature; good wine; good food. Address: (h.) 67 Hillpark Avenue, Edinburgh EH4 7AL; T.-0131-336 2338.

Inglis, Ian Brownlie, LLB, FCIBS, FRSA, WS. Director: Bank of Scotland Treasury Services PLC, since 1997, Ivory & Sime UK Smaller Companies Trust plc, since 1992, The Edinburgh Investment Trust plc, since 1997, Murray Ventures Investment Trust PLC, since 1998; Member, Scottish Regional Advisory Group, London Stock Exchange, since 1994; b. 6.2.41, Carluke; m., Eleanor McLuckie Taylor; 2 d. Educ. Lanark Grammar School; University of Edinburgh. Apprentice Clerk, Clerk, Apprentice Solicitor, Royal Bank of Scotland, 1957-66; Shepherd & Wedderburn WS: Apprentice Solicitor, 1966-67, Assistant Solicitor, 1967-68, Partner, 1968-98. Recreations: golf; walking. Address: (h.) 10 Brechin Drive, Polmont, Falkirk FK2 0YH; T.-01324 713775.

Inglis, Professor Emeritus James Alistair Macfarlane, CBE (1984), MA, LLB. Emeritus Professor, Glasgow University; Professor of Conveyancing, Glasgow University, 1979-93; Professor of Professional Legal Practice, Glasgow University, 1984-93; Partner, McClure, Naismith, Anderson & Gardiner, Solicitors, Glasgow, 1956-93; Honorary Member, Court of Patrons, Royal College of Physicians and Surgeons of Glasgow, since 1995; b. 24.12.28, Kilmarnock; m., Mary Elizabeth Howie; 2 s.; 3 d. Educ. Kilmarnock Academy; Fettes College; St. Andrews University; Glasgow University. Qualified as Solicitor, 1952; Member: Board of Management, Victoria and Leverndale Hospitals, 1964-74, Greater Glasgow Health Board, 1975-83; President, Rent Assessment Panel for Scotland, 1976-87; Chairman, Glasgow Hospitals Auxiliary Association, since 1985; Dean, Royal Faculty of Procurators in Glasgow, 1989-92; Convener, Ad Hoc Committee, Church of Scotland, into Legal Services of Church, 1978-79; Session Clerk, Caldwell Parish Church, since 1963; General Trustee, Church of Scotland, since 1994. Address: (h.) Crioch, Uplawmoor, Glasgow; T.-01505 850315.

Inglis, John, RSW, FSA(Scot), DA. Painter and Lecturer; b. 27.7.53, Glasgow; m., Heather; 2 s.; 2 d. Educ. Hillhead High School; Gray's School of Art. Travelling scholarships to Italy, 1976; Member, Dundee Group, 1979-84; one-man exhibitions: Aberdeen, 1976 and 1977; Glasgow, 1980; Skipton, 1981; Aberdeen Hospitals, 1989; Alloa Museum, 1989; Smith Art Gallery, Stirling, 1993; Illinois, USA, 1997. Scottish Arts Council Award, 1981; RSA Keith Prize, 1975; SAC Bursary, 1982; RSA Meyer Oppenheim Prize, 1982; RSW EIS Award, 1987; SAC Grant, 1988; May Marshall Brown Award, 1994. Address: (h.) 21 Hillview Road, Larbert, Stirlingshire; T.-01324 558891.

Ingram, Adam. Minister of State for Northern Ireland, since 1997; MP (Labour), East Kilbride, since 1987; b. 1.2.47, Glasgow; m., Maureen McMahon. Educ. Cranhill Senior Secondary School. Programmer/analyst, 1965-1970; systems analyst, 1970-77; full-time union official, 1977-87; Councillor, East Kilbride District Council, 1980-87 (Leader of the Council, 1984-87); PPS to Neil Kinnock, Leader of the Opposition, 1988-92; Labour Opposition Spokesperson on Social Security, 1993-95, Science and Technology, 1995-97; JP. Recreations: fishing; cooking; reading. Address: (b.) House of Commons, London SW1A 0AA; T.-0171-219 4093.

Ingram, Professor David Stanley, BSc, PhD, MA, ScD, FLS, FIBiol, FIHort, FRCPEd, FRSE. Botanist and Plant Pathologist; Regius Keeper (Director), Royal Botanic Garden, Edinburgh, 1990-98; Visiting Professor, Glasgow University, since 1991; Hon. Professor, Edinburgh University, since 1991; Honorary Professor of Horticulture, Royal Horticultural Society, since 1995; Professor, Napier University, since 1998; President: British Society for Plant Pathology, International Congress of Plant Pathology; b. 10.10.41, Birmingham; m., Alison W.; 2 s. Educ. Yardley Grammar School, Birmingham; Hull University; Cambridge University. Research Fellow, Glasgow University, 1966-68, Cambridge University, 1968-69; Senior Scientific Officer, Unit of Developmental Botany, Cambridge, 1969-74; Lecturer, then Reader in Plant Pathology, Botany Department, Cambridge University, 1974-90; Fellow (also

Tutor, Dean and Director of Studies in Biology), Downing College, Cambridge, 1974-90; author of several books and many papers in learned journals. Recreations: gardening; literature; film; theatre; music; travel. Address: (h.) 65 Dublin Street, Edinburgh EH3 6NS.

Ingram, Greig Webster, MA. Rector, High School of Stirling, since 1994; b. 20.11.47, Burnhervie; m., Patricia Annette Miller. Educ. Mackie Academy, Stonehaven; Aberdeen University; Aberdeen College of Education. Teacher of Modern Studies and History, 1970-74; Principal Teacher of Modern Studies, St. Margaret Mary's Secondary, Glasgow, 1974-84; Assistant Head Teacher, Eastbank Academy, Glasgow, 1984-89, Depute Head Teacher, 1989-94. Recreations: reading; music; travel; running; soccer. Address: (b.) Ogilvie Road, Stirling FK8 2PA; T.-01786 472451.

Ingram, Hugh Albert Pugh, BA (Cantab), PhD (Dunelm). Chairman, Council, Scottish Wildlife Trust, since 1996 (Vice-Chairman, Conservation and Science, 1982-87); b. 29.4.37, Rugby; m., Dr. Ruth Hunter; 1 s.; 1 d. Educ. Lawrence Sheriff School, Rugby; Rugby School; Emmanuel College, Cambridge; Hatfield College, Durham. Demonstrator in Botany, University College of North Wales, Bangor, 1963-64; Staff Tutor in Natural Science, Department of Extra-Mural Studies, Bristol University, 1964-65; Lecturer, then Senior Lecturer in Botany (Ecology), Dundee University, 1966-97; Editor, Journal of Applied Ecology, 1991-97; Member: Executive Committee, Scottish Field Studies Association, since 1989, Museums and Galleries Commission Working Party on the non-national museums of Scotland, 1984-86; Trustee, National Museums of Scotland, 1987-94. Publications: numerous scientific research papers on hydrological aspects of the ecology of peat bogs and other mires. Recreations: music (clarinet, piano); literature; rural history; hill-walking. Address: Johnstonfield, Dunbog, Cupar, Fife KY14 6JG.

Ingram, Professor Malcolm David, BSc, PhD, DSc, CChem, FRSC. Professor of Chemistry, Aberdeen University, since 1993; b. 18.1.39, Wallasey; m., Lorna Hardman; 1 s.; 1 d. Educ. Oldershaw Grammar School; Liverpool University. Aberdeen University: Lecturer in Physical Chemistry, 1965-78, Senior Lecturer in Chemistry, 1978-90, Reader, 1990-93. Chairman, Aberdeen and North of Scotland Section, Royal Society of Chemistry, 1990-93. Publications: 170 in scientific journals. Recreations: gardening; foreign travel. Address: (b.) Department of Chemistry, Aberdeen University, Aberdeen AB9 2UE; T.-01224 272905.

Innes, Andrew, MBChB, MD, MRCP, FRCP(Glas), FRCP(Edin). Consultant Physician/Nephrologist, Crosshouse Hospital, Kilmarnock, since 1994; b. 29.7.56, Inverness; m., Nora; 1 s.; 2 d. Educ. Dingwall Academy; University of Aberdeen. Medical Registrar, Aberdeen teaching hospitals; Senior Medical Registrar, City Hospital, Nottingham; Clinical Research Fellow, Centre de Rein Artificiel, Tassin, France. Address: (b.) Crosshouse Hospital, Kilmarnock KA2 0BE; T.-01563 577358.

Innes, James, BSc, CEng, FICE, FIHT. Director of Roads and Chief Road Engineer, Scottish Office Development Department, since 1995; Visiting Professor of Civil Engineering, Strathclyde University, since 1992; Chairman, Scottish Construction Clients' Forum, since 1995; b. 7.8.44, Helmsdale; m., June Pearson; 1 s.; 1 d. Educ. Woodside Secondary School, Glasgow; Strathclyde University. Lanark County Council, 1966-67; Inverness County Council, 1967-73; Scottish Development Department, 1973-84; Department of Transport (Superintending Engineer), 1984-85; Assistant Chief Road Engineer, Scottish Office Industry Department, 1985-88; Deputy Chief Road Engineer, Scottish Office Industry Department, 1988-95. Recreations: golf; foreign travel. Address: (b.) 3-H 31 Victoria Quay, Edinburgh EH6 6QQ; T.-0131-244 0626.

Innes, Professor John, BCom, PhD, CA, FCMA. Professor of Accountancy, University of Dundee, since 1991; b. 11.7.50, Edinburgh; m., Ina. Educ. George Watson's College; University of Edinburgh. Student Accountant and Staff Auditor, KPMG, 1972-75; International Operational Auditor, Uniroyal Inc., 1975-78; Lecturer and Senior Lecturer in Accounting, University of Edinburgh, 1978-91; Canon Foundation Visiting Research Fellow, 1992-93. Publication: various books including Handbook of Management Accounting, 1998. Recreation: tennis. Address: Department of Accountancy and Business Finance, University of Dundee, Dundee DD1 4HN; T.-01382 344197.

Innes, Norman Lindsay, OBE, BSc, PhD, DSc, FIBiol, FRSE. Agricultural Research Consultant; b. 3.5.34, Kirriemuir; m., Marjory Niven Farquhar; 1 s.; 1 d. Educ. Websters High School, Kirriemuir; Aberdeen University; Cambridge University. Senior Cotton Breeder: Sudan, 1958-66, Uganda, 1966-71; Head, Cotton Research Unit, Uganda, 1972; National Vegetable Research Station, Wellesbourne: Head, Plant Breeding Section, 1973-84, Deputy Director, 1977-84; Scottish Crop Research Institute: Deputy Director, 1986-94, Head, Plant Breeding Division, 1984-89; Honorary Lecturer, then Honorary Professor, Birmingham University, 1973-84; Governing Board Member, International Crops Research Institute for Semi-Arid Tropics, India, 1982-88; Honorary Professor, Dundee University, 1988-95; Governing Board Member, International Potato Centre, Peru, 1988-95, Chairman, 1991-95; Vice-President, Association of Applied Biologists, 1990-92, President, 1993-94; Governing Council Member, since 1996, Chairman: since 1997, International Centre of Insect Physiology and Ecology, Kenya, British Association of Plant Breeders, 1982-84; Member, Oxfam Council of Trustees, 1982-85. Recreations: golf; photography; travel. Address: (b.) Scottish Crop Research Institute, Invergowrie, Dundee DD2 5DA; T.-01382 562731.

Innes of Edingight, Sir Malcolm Rognvald, KCVO, MA, LLB, WS, KStJ. Lord Lyon King of Arms, since 1981; Secretary to Order of the Thistle, since 1981; b. 25.5.38, Edinburgh; m., Joan Hay; 3 s. Educ. Edinburgh Academy; Edinburgh University. Carrick Pursuivant, 1958; Marchmont Herald, 1971; Lyon Clerk and Keeper of the Record, 1966; Member, Queen's Bodyguard for Scotland (Royal Company of Archers); President, Scottish Heraldry Society. Recreation: shooting. Address: (b.) Court of the Lord Lyon, HM New Register House, Edinburgh; T.-0131-556 7255.

Inverarity, James Alexander (Sandy), CBE, FRSA, FRAgS, CA. Farmer and Landowner; Chairman: Scottish Agricultural College, 1990-98, Scottish Agricultural Securities Corporation, plc, since 1987; President, Scottish Farm and Countryside Educational Trust, 1990-98; b. 17.9.35; m., Jean; 1 s.; 2 d. Educ. Loretto School. President, National Farmers Union of Scotland, 1970-71; Member: Eggs Authority, 1971-74, Farm Animal Welfare Council, 1978-88, Panel of Agricultural Arbiters, since 1983, Governing Body, Scottish Crop Research Institute, 1984-97, Dairy Produce Quota Tribunal for Scotland, 1984-85; Director, United Oilseed Producers Ltd., 1985-97 (Chairman, 1987-97). Recreations: shooting; curling. Address: Cransley, Fowlis, Dundee DD2 5NP; T.-01382 580327.

Ireland, Dr Kenneth, OBE, DUniv, BL, FRSA, FTS. Consultant, Hanover Fine Arts (Edinburgh); b. 17.6.20, Edinburgh; m., Moira Lamb; 2 s. Educ. Edinburgh Academy; Edinburgh University. Law Apprentice, Steedman Ramage & Co., WS, Edinburgh, 1938-41; War service: Royal Artillery, L. Bdr., 1941-42, Intelligence

Corps, WO II, 1942-46; Lt. (TA), 1948-52; General Manager: Park Theatre, Glasgow, 1946-49, Pitlochry Festival Theatre, 1951-52; Pitlochry Festival Society Ltd.: General Manager and Secretary, 1953-57, Festival Director and Secretary, 1957-83 (retired, 1984); Board Member, Scottish Tourist Board, 1966-69; Chairman, Tourist Association of Scotland, 1967-69; Deputy Chairman, Scottish Tourist Consultative Council, 1977-83; ESU Scotland Thyne Scholarship, 1970; Bill Heron Trophy, 1981 (first recipient for services to tourism). Recreations: foreign travel; drama; music; art; literature. Address: (h.) 10 Ravelston Rise, Edinburgh EH4 3LH; T.-0131-346 2292.

Ireland, Sheriff Ronald David, QC, HonLLD. Sheriff Principal, Grampian, Highland and Islands, 1988-93; b. 13.3.25, Edinburgh. Educ. George Watson's College, Edinburgh; Balliol College, Oxford (Scholar); Edinburgh University. Advocate, 1952; Clerk, Faculty of Advocates, 1957-58; Professor of Scots Law, Aberdeen University, 1958-71; QC, 1964; Dean, Faculty of Law, Aberdeen University, 1964-67; Chairman, Board of Management, Aberdeen General Hospitals, 1964-71; Sheriff, Lothian and Borders at Edinburgh, 1972-88; Director, Scottish Courts Administration, 1975-78. Address: (h.) 6A Greenhill Gardens, Edinburgh EH10 4BW.

Irons, James Fraser, BSc(Hons), CEng, FICE, FIHT. Director of Roads, Transport and Architectural Services, Perth and Kinross Council, since 1996; Chairman, Society of Chief Officers of Transportation in Scotland, since 1997; b. 25.6.47, Dundee; m., Frances Heron; 1 s.; 1 d. Educ. Morgan Academy, Dundee; University of Dundee. Graduate Engineer, Perth and Kinross Council, 1969-75; Senior Engineer, Dundee Corporation, 1975-76; Project Engineer, Government of Bahrain, 1976-78; Tayside Regional Council: Senior Engineer, 1978-85, Principal Engineer, 1985-88, Assistant Director of Roads and Transport, 1988-91, Depute Director of Roads and Transport, 1991-96. Recreations: golf; squash; hillwalking. Address: 65 Bay Road, Wormit, Fife; T.-01382 541223.

Irons, Norman MacFarlane, CBE, DL, DLitt, DUniv, Hon. FRCSE, CEng, MIMechE, MCIBSE, JP. Lord Provost and Lord Lieutenant of the City of Edinburgh, 1992-96; Partner, Building Services Consulting Engineers, since 1993; b. 4.1.41, Glasgow; m., Anne Buckley; 1 s.; 1 d. Held various posts as Consulting Engineer; founded own practice, 1983. SNP Member, City of Edinburgh District Council, 1976-96. Recreation: rugby football. Address: (h.) 141 Saughtonhall Drive, Edinburgh EH12 5TS; T.-0131-337 6154.

Ironside, Leonard, JP. Member, Aberdeen City Council, since 1995 (Convener, Social Work Committee); Deputy Leader of the Council; Chairman, Aberdeen International Youth Festival), since 1996; Director: Foxlane Special Needs Garden Centre, Crown St. Day Centre, Voluntary Service, Aberdeen, Grampian Food Resource Centre Ltd; Patron, Grampian Special Olympics for Handicapped; Commonwealth Professional Wrestling Champion, since 1981; Athletics Coach, Bon Accord (Special Needs); appointed Justice of the Peace, 1997; b. Aberdeen; m., Wendy; 2 d. Educ. Hilton Academy, Aberdeen. Member, Grampian Regional Council, 1982-96; Inspector, contributions agency, DHSS, since 1990; former Chairman, Grampian Initiative; won Commonwealth Professional Wrestling Championship at Middleweight, 1979; lost Championship, 1981; regained title, 1981; gained European Lightweight title, 1985, relinquished title, 1989; Grampian Ambassador for services to industry, 1996; awarded Scottish Sports Council Rosebowl for services to disabled sports; former Director: Grampian Enterprise Ltd., Scottish Sub-Sea Technology Group; Member: Grampian Racial Equality Commission, Aberdeen Sports Council. Recreations: yoga teacher; also plays tennis, squash, badminton; cycling. Address: (h.) 42 Hillside Terrace, Portlethen, Kincardineshire; T.-Aberdeen 780929.

Irvine of Lairg, Baron (Alexander Andrew Mackay Irvine), PC. Lord High Chancellor of Great Britain, since 1997; b. 23.6.40; m.; 2 s. Educ. Inverness Academy; Hutchesons' Boys' Grammar School, Glasgow; Glasgow University; Christ's College, Cambridge. Called to the Bar, Inner Temple, 1967; QC, 1978; a Recorder, 1985-88; Deputy High Court Judge, 1987-97.

Irvine, Hugh McLelland; Chairman, A. McLelland and Son Ltd., since 1984 (Director, since 1964); Chairman, Caledonian Cheese Company, since 1995; Chairman, IMG Foods Ltd.; b. 13.9.37, Ayr; m., Agnes Wilson Forbes; 2 s.; 1 d. (deceased). Educ. Ayr Academy. National Service, RAF, 1956-58; became fourth generation in family business, A. McLelland and Son, 1955; Chairman, Islay Creamery Co. 25 years; Chairman, Scottish Cheese Factors Association, 25 years; international cheese judge, since 1972. Recreations: golf and, hopefully, now travel. Address: (h.) Trynlaw House, Symington, Ayrshire; T.-(b.) 0141-552 2962.

Irvine, Joseph Andrew, BSc. Head Teacher, Brae High School, since 1988; b. 18.6.44, Lerwick; m., Ishbel; 2 s. Educ. Anderson Educational Institute, Lerwick; Aberdeen University. Teacher of Maths/Science, Lerwick Central School, 1967-68; Teacher of Maths, Assistant Principal Teacher, Principal Teacher, Anderson High School, 1968-84; Field Officer, Shetland Islands Council, 1984-88. Chairman: Northern Sports Development Trust, Shetland Recreational Trust. Recreations: sailing; photography. Address: (b.) Brae High School, Brae, Shetland ZE2 9QG; T.-01806 522 370.

Irvine-Fortescue, James William, MA (Hons), CA, JP, DL, KLJ, FSA Scot; b. 7.6.17, Wilmslow; m., Margaret Guise Yates; 3 s.; 1 d. Educ. Aberdeen Grammar School; Edinburgh Academy; Aberdeen University. War Service: Royal Army Pay Corps, 1940-46, service in India and Ceylon, 1942-46 (Major and Staff Paymaster); JP and Magistrate, Kincardineshire, 1957; Member, Kincardine County Council, 1952-73; Commissioner of Income Tax, County of Kincardine, 1957-92; Chairman: Lower Deeside District Council, 1964-73, Grampian Region Valuation Appeal Committee, 1975-90. President, Deeside Field Club, 1981-86; a Vice President, Royal Society for Asian Affairs, 1983-88; Past President, Auchinleck Boswell Society; Past Chairman, Aberdeen Music Festival. Recreations: family history research; foreign travel. Address: (h.) Kingcausie, Maryculter, Kincardineshire AB12 5FR; T.-01224 732224.

Irving, George Livingston, MSc, CSW, MIM. Director of Social Work, North Ayrshire Council, since 1996; Vice President, Association of Directors of Social Work, since 1998; Board Member, Scottish Association for the Care and Resettlement of Offenders, since 1997; Honorary Lecturer, Caledonian University, since 1990; b. 11.11.41, Glasgow; m., Dorothy; 1 s.; 1 d. Educ. Whitehill Secondary School, Glasgow; University of Strathclyde. Residential Social Worker, Approved School Service, 1964-68; Social Worker, Paisley Town Council, 1968-70; Senior Social Worker/Area Officer, Ferguslie Park, Paisley, 1970-72; Director, Community Development Project, Paisley, 1972-75; Divisional Organiser (Ayr Division), Strathclyde Region, 1975-86; District Social Work Manager: Glasgow North West, 1986-90, North Ayrshire, 1990-96. Representative, European Children's Trust (Romanian Orphanage Trust); six years voluntary child care work in Romania. Recreations: bowling; hill-walking; art; grandchildren. Address: (b.) Elliott House, Redburn Estate, Kilwinning Road, Irvine KA12 8TB; T.-01294 317723/5.

Irving, Gordon, MA (Hons). Writer, Journalist and Broadcaster; b. 4.12.18, Annan; m., Elizabeth Dickie (deceased). Educ. Dumfries Academy; Edinburgh University. Staff Journalist, Daily Record, Edinburgh and Glasgow; Reuters' News Agency, London; TV Guide, Scotland; The Viewer, Scotland; Freelance Writer/Journalist, since 1964; Travel Correspondent, UK and overseas media; Scotland Correspondent, Variety, New York. Publications: Great Scot! (biography of Sir Harry Lauder); The Good Auld Days; The Solway Smugglers; The Wit of the Scots; The Wit of Robert Burns; The Devil on Wheels; Brush Up Your Scotland; Annie Laurie; Take No Notice and Take No More Notice! (World's Funniest Signs); The First 200 Years (Story of Dumfries and Galloway Royal Infirmary); 90 Glorious Years (Story of the King's Theatre, Glasgow). Recreations: making video films of personal travels; collecting trivia; researching Scottish music-hall history; fighting bumbling bureaucrats; reading all the Sunday broadsheets; surfing the World Wide Web on Internet. Address: (h.) 36 Whittingehame Court, Glasgow G12 OBG; T.-0141-357 2265.

Irving, Margaret Anne, MB, ChB, FRIPHH, FRCPCH. Consultant Paediatrician, Child Health, Dumfries and Galloway Community HS Trust; b. 28.4.43, Glasgow; m., Dr John Bruce Irving; 2 s.; 1 d. Educ. Bathgate Academy; Glasgow University. Registrar in Bacteriology, Western Infirmary, Glasgow; Principal in general practice, Ayrshire; CMO in Child Health, Salford Health Authority; Senior Clinical Medical Officer in Child Health, Dumfries & Galloway Health Board; Medical Adviser to Regional Adoption and Fostering Panel; Chairman, Scottish Medical Group, British Agencies for Adoption and Fostering, 1990-93. Recreations: gardening; opera. Address: (h.) Bonshaw Tower, Kirtlebridge, Lockerbie, Dumfriesshire DG11 3LY; T.-01461 500256.

Irwin, Professor David George, MA, PhD, FSA, FRSA. Professor Emeritus, History of Art, Aberdeen University (Professor and Head of Department, 1970-96); b. 24.6.33, London; m., Francina Sorabji; 1 s.; 1 d. Educ. Holgate Grammar School, Barnsley; Queen's College, Oxford (Exhibitioner); Courtauld Institute of Art, London University. Lecturer in History of Fine Art, Glasgow University, 1959-70; Past President, British Society for 18th Century Studies; former Council Member, Walpole Society; former Member, Art Panel, Scottish Arts Council; Member, Editorial Board, British Journal of 18th Century Studies; Committee Member: Aberdeen Art Gallery, Architectural Heritage Society of Scotland; elected Member, International Association of Art Critics; won Laurence Binyon Prize, Oxford, 1956. Publications: English Neoclassical Art; Paul Klee; Visual Arts, Taste and Criticism; Designs and Ornaments of Empire Style; Winckelmann, Writings on Art; John Flaxman, Sculptor, Illustrator, Designer; Neoclassicism; Scottish Painters, At Home and Abroad, 1700 to 1900 (with Francina Irwin). Recreations: travel; painting. Address: (b.) Department of History of Art, King's College, Old Aberdeen, Aberdeen AB24 3UG; T.-01224 272458.

Isaacs, Professor Neil William, BSc, PhD, FRSE. Joseph Black Professor of Protein Crystallography, University of Glasgow, since 1989; b. 11.6.45, Brisbane, Australia; m., Margaret; 3 d. Educ. St. Patrick's College, Brisbane; University of Queensland. Research Assistant, University Chemical Laboratories, Cambridge, 1969-72; IBM Research Fellow, University of Oxford, 1972-75; IBM World Trade Research Fellow, IBM T.J. Watson Research Center, New York, 1976; Research Fellow, University of York, 1977-78; NH and MRC Senior Research Fellow, St. Vincent's Institute of Medical Research, Melbourne, 1978-88. Publications: over 80 in scientific literature on molecular structures. Recreations: walking; gardening; reading. Address: (h.) Eastwood, Shore Road, Cove, Helensburgh G84 0NA; T.-01436 842901.

Ivory, Brian Gammell, MA (Cantab), CA, FRSA. Chairman, Highland Distillers plc, since 1994; b. 10.4.49, Edinburgh; m., Oona Mairi MacPhie Bell-Macdonald (see Oona Mairi MacPhie Ivory); 1 s.; 1 d. Educ. Eton College; Magdalene College, Cambridge. CA apprentice, Thomson McLintock, 1971-75; joined Highland Distillers, 1976, became Director, 1978, Managing Director, 1988, Group Chief Executive, 1994; Director, Matthew Gloag and Son Ltd., 1987, Chairman, since 1994; Director, Orpar SA, since 1990; Director, Remy Cointreau SA, since 1991; Member, Scottish Arts Council, 1983-92 (Vice-Chairman, 1988-92); Member, Arts Council of GB, 1988-92; Chairman, The Piping Centre, since 1996; CIMgt, 1997; Member, Queen's Bodyguard for Scotland (Royal Company of Archers). Recreations: the arts; farming; hill-walking. Address: (h.) Brewlands, Glenisla, by Blairgowrie, Perthshire, PH11 8PL; 12 Ann Street, Edinburgh, EH4 1PJ; (b.) West Kinfauns, Perth PH2 7XZ; T.-01738 440000.

Ivory, Oona Mairi MacPhie, DL, MA (Cantab), ARCM, FRSA. Professional Musician; former Chairman, Scottish Ballet; Governor, Royal Scottish Academy of Music and Drama; Trustee, The Piping Trust; Founder Director, The Piping Centre; Deputy Lieutenant, City of Edinburgh; b. 21.7.54, Ayr; m., Brian Gammell Ivory (qv); 1 s.; 1 d. Educ. King's College, Cambridge; Royal Scottish Academy of Music and Drama; Royal Academy of Music. Recreations: visual and performing arts; wild places; sailing. Address: (h.) Brewlands, Glenisla, by Blairgowrie, Perthshire PH11 8PL; 12 Ann Street, Edinburgh EH4 1PJ.

Izat, Alexander John Rennie, MA. Chairman: United Auctions (Scotland) Ltd., since 1992, Moredun Research Institute, since 1995, Shires Income Trust, since 1996; Partner, John Izat & Partners (Farmers), since 1975; Director: Glasgow Investment Managers, since 1990, Moredun Foundation, since 1992, Shires Smaller Companies Trust, since 1997, Pentlands Science Park Ltd.; b. 14.7.32, London; m., Frederica Ann McNiel; 1 s.; 2 d. Educ. Glenalmond; Oriel College, Oxford. Partner, Williams de Broe & Co., Stockbrokers, 1955-75; farming at Balliliesk and Naemoor, 1975-87; farming at High Cocklaw, since 1987; former Member, Council, Scottish NFU; Director, Moredun Scientific Ltd., 1992-97; Past President, Fife and Kinross NFU and Kinross Agricultural Association; Director, Royal Highland Agricultural Society, 1985-97 (Hon. Treasurer, 1992-96); Member, Council, Glenalmond College, 1975-95 (Chairman, Committee of Council, 1989-95); President, Northern Area, Suffolk Sheep Society, 1989-91. Address: (b.) High Cocklaw, Berwick-upon-Tweed TD15 1UZ; T.-01289 86591.

Izod, Professor (Kenneth) John, BA (Hons), PhD. Professor of Screen Analysis, Stirling University, since 1998; Dean, Faculty of Arts, 1995-98; Senior Lecturer, Department of Film and Media Studies, 1978-98; b. 4.3.40, Shepperton; m., Irene Chew Geok Keng (divorced 1994); 1 s.; 1 d. Educ. Prince Edward School, Harare City, Zimbabwe; Leeds University. Clerk articled to Chartered Accountant, 1958-63; Projectionist, mobile cinema unit, 1963; Lecturer in English, New University of Ulster, 1969-78; former Governor, Scottish Film Council; Chairman, Stirling Film Theatre, 1982-89 and 1991-92; Member, National Film and Video Forum, since 1994. Publications: Reading the Screen, 1984; Hollywood and the Box Office 1895-1986, 1988; The Films of Nicolas Roeg, 1991; Introduction to Television Documentary (Co-Author). Address: (b.) Film and Media Studies, University, Stirling FK9 4LA; T.-01786 473171.

J

Jack, Alister William. Vice Chairman, Scottish Conservative and Unionist Party, since 1997 (Scottish Conservative Party Spokesman on Industry and Economic Affairs); Managing Director, Aardvark Self Storage Limited, since 1995; b. 7.7.63, Dumfries; m., Ann Hodgson; 1 s.; 2 d. Educ. Trinity College, Glenalmond. Knight Frank, 1983-86; Director, Field and Lawn (Marquees) Ltd., since 1986. Governor, St. Mary's School, Melrose; Member, Executive Board, Scottish Conservative Party; Parliamentary Candidate, Tweeddale, Ettrick and Lauderdale, 1997 General Election; Prospective Parliamentary Candidate, Tweeddale, Ettrick and Lauderdale, 1999 Scottish General Election. Recreations: field sports; golf; sailing; skiing. Address: (b.) 70 Albion Road, Edinburgh EH7 5QZ; T.-0131-652 2121.

Jack, David, BSc (Agric), DipAgric (Cantab), ARAgS. Honorary President, National Farmers Union of Scotland, 1996-97; Chairman, Scottish Quality Cereals Ltd., since 1994; Vice-Chairman, H-GCA, Cereals R. & D. Committee, 1992-98; b. 9.8.32, Peterhead; m., Isabell Cowie; 2 s.; 2 d. Educ. Aberdeen Grammar School; Aberdeen University; Cambridge University. Farmer in Aberdeenshire; Member, Council, NFU of Scotland, 1988-97; Convener, Cereals Committee, 1990-96. Recreations: golf; music. Address: Jackstown, Rothienorman, Inverurie, Aberdeenshire AB51 8UR; T.-01467 671205.

Jack, Professor Robert Barr, CBE, MA, LLB. Senior Partner, McGrigor Donald, Solicitors, Glasgow, Edinburgh and London, 1990-93 (Partner, 1957-93); Professor of Mercantile Law, Glasgow University, 1978-93; b. 18.3.28; m., Anna Thorburn Thomson; 2 s. Educ. Kilsyth Academy; High School of Glasgow; Glasgow University. Admitted a Solicitor in Scotland, 1951; Member, Scottish Law Commission, 1974-77; Scottish Observer, Department of Trade's Insolvency Law Review Committee, 1977-82; Member, Council for the Securities Industry, 1983-85; Lay Member, Council of the Stock Exchange, 1984-86; Independent Member, Board, Securities and Futures Authority (formerly Securities Association), 1986-94; Board Member, Securities and Investments Board, 1994-97; Chairman, Review Committee on Banking Services Law, 1987-89; Member: Panel on Takeovers and Mergers, since 1992, Financial Law Panel, since 1993; Chairman: Brownlee plc, Timber Merchants, Glasgow, 1984-86 (Director, 1974-86); Joseph Dunn (Bottlers) Ltd., Soft Drink Manufacturers, Glasgow, since 1983; Director: Bank of Scotland, 1985-96, Scottish Metropolitan Property plc, 1980-98 (Deputy Chairman, 1991-98), Scottish Mutual Assurance plc, 1987-98 (Chairman, 1992-98), Clyde Football Club Ltd., 1980-96, Gartmore Scotland Investment Trust PLC, since 1991, Glasgow Development Agency, 1992-97; President, Scottish National Council of YMCAs, 1983-98 (Chairman, 1966-73); Governor, Hutchesons' Educational Trust, Glasgow, 1978-87 (Chairman, 1980-87); Chairman, The Turnberry Trust, since 1983; Member, Scottish Higher Education Funding Council, 1992-96; Governor, Beatson Institute for Cancer Research, since 1989. Publications: lectures and articles on various aspects of company law, the statutory regulation and self-regulation of the City, and banking and insolvency law. Recreations: golf; music; hopeful supporter of one of Scotland's less fashionable football teams; a dedicated lover of the Isle of Arran. Address: (h.) 50 Lanton Road, Lanton Park, Newlands, Glasgow G43 2SR; T.-0141-637 7302.

Jack, Professor Ronald Dyce Sadler, MA, PhD. Professor of Scottish and Medieval Literature, Edinburgh University, since 1987; b. 3.4.41, Ayr; m., Kirsty; 2 d. Educ. Ayr Academy; Glasgow University; Edinburgh University. Department of English Literature: Assistant Lecturer, 1965, Lecturer, 1968, Reader, 1978, Associate Dean, Faculty of Arts, 1971-73; Visiting Professor, Virginia University, 1973-74; Director, Universities Central Council on Admissions, 1988-94 (Member, 1973-76); Pierpont Morgan Scholar, British Academy, 1976; Advising Editor: Scotia, 1980-96, Scottish Literary Journal, since 1996; Member, Scottish Universities Council on Entrance, since 1981; Governor, Newbattle Abbey College, 1984-89; Beinecke Fellow, Yale, 1992; Visiting Professor, Strathclyde University, 1993; Lynn Woods Neag Distinguished Visiting Professor of British Literature, University of Connecticut, 1998. Publications: Robert MacLellan's Jamie the Saxt (Co-Editor), 1970; Scottish Prose 1550-1700, 1972; The Italian Influence on Scottish Literature, 1972; A Choice of Scottish Verse 1560-1660, 1978; The Art of Robert Burns (Co-Author), 1982; Sir Thomas Urquhart, The Jewel (Co-Author), 1984; Alexander Montgomerie, 1985; Scottish Literature's Debt to Italy, 1986; The History of Scottish Literature, Volume 1, 1988; Patterns of Divine Comedy, 1989; The Road to the Never Land, 1991; Of Lion and of Unicorn, 1993; The Poems of William Dunbar, 1997; The Mercat Anthology of Early Scottish Literature (Co-Editor). Address: (b.) Department of English Literature, Edinburgh University, David Hume Tower, George Square, Edinburgh EH8 9JX.

Jackson, Anthony Arthur, MA, MSc, FICDDip, MIED, AIEMgt. Senior Lecturer, School of Town and Regional Planning, Dundee University, since 1991; Founding Partner, St. Andrews Economic Services, 1986; b. 18.6.46, London; m., Alicia; 3 d. Educ. Westminster City School; Gonville and Caius College, Cambridge; Reading University. Agricultural Economist, Malawi Government, 1968-71; St. Andrews University: Stanley Smith Senior Fellow, 1971-73, Lecturer in Economics, 1973-91; FAO/FFHC Food and Nutrition Consultant, Malawi Government, 1973-76; Warning Officer, 1975-81, and Sector Scientific Adviser, UKWMO, 1981-91; Editor, Journal of Institute of Civil Defence, 1982-89; Group Leader, Conservative Group, Fife Regional Council, 1982-86; Director: Claverhouse Group, since 1992, Byre Theatre, 1980-89; Home Office Civil Defence Medal, 1990. Recreations: theatre; cricket; philately. Address: (h.) Creinch, Peat Inn, by Cupar, Fife KY15 5LH; T.-01334-840275.

Jackson, Eileen. Author; b. 18.4.26, Bristol; m., John Tunnard Jackson; 3 d. Short story/article writer, 1935-74; novels, since 1974; first novel, published USA, 1976, UK, 1978; 21 novels in over 65 editions and 10 languages; pseudonyms: Helen May, Linda Comer, Elizabeth Warne; also publishes as Eileen Jackson; President, Strathclyde Writers, since 1985; Lecturer. Recreations: reading; book collecting; swimming; golf; travel. Address: (h.) Girvan Lodge, Blairquhan, Maybole, Ayrshire KA19 7QP; T.-01655 770639.

Jackson, Jack, BSc (Hons), PhD, FIBiol, CIBiol. HM Staff Inspector of Schools with responsibility for science subjects; b. 31.5.44, Ayr; m., Sheilah Margaret Fulton; 1 s.; 3 d. Educ. Ayr Academy; Glasgow University; Jordanhill College of Education. Demonstrator, Zoology Department, Glasgow University, 1966-69; Lecturer in Zoology, West of Scotland Agricultural College, 1969-72; Assistant Teacher of Biology, Cathkin High School, 1972-73; Principal Teacher of Biology, Ayr Academy, 1973-83. Senior Examiner and Setter, Scottish Examination Board, 1978-83; Director, Board, Scottish Youth Theatre, 1979-82; Member: Scottish Council, Institute of Biology, 1980-83, School Board, Balerno High School, since 1989. Recreations: family life; gardening; hill-walking; conservation. Address: (b.) HM Inspector of Schools' Office, Saughton House, Broomhouse Drive, Edinburgh EH11 3XD; T.-0131-244 8324.

Jackson, Jim, OBE, BA. Executive Director, Alzheimer Scotland – Action on Dementia, since 1994; b. 10.2.47, Bradford; m., Jennifer; 1 s.; 1 d. Educ. Stand Grammar School; West Ham College of Technology; Open University. Playleader, 1969-72; Community Development Worker, 1972-77; Principal Assistant, Community Services and Development, Wirral, 1977-81; Consultant, Home Office Voluntary Services Unit, 1981-84; Assistant Director, Scottish Council for Voluntary Organisations, 1984-93; Director, Alzheimer's Scotland, 1993-94. Recreations: hill-walking; modern jazz. Address: (b.) 22 Drumsheugh Gardens, Edinburgh, EH3 7RN; T.-0131-243 1453.

Jackson, Professor Michael Herbert, BA, PhD, CBiol, MIBiol, FRSH, FRSA, MREHIS, MIEH. Professor and Head, Division of Environmental Health, Strathclyde University; b. 17.7.40, Hornchurch; m., Diana Evans; 2 d. Educ. Nantwich and Acton Grammar School; Open University; Strathclyde University. Lecturer, Senior Lecturer, Reader in Environmental Health, Strathclyde University, 1977-93; previously public health inspector and environmental health officer; Editor-in-Chief, International Journal of Environmental Health Research; Member, Commission on Environment and Health, 1996-97. Recreations: gardening; reading; holidaying. Address: (b.) Department of Civil Engineering, Strathclyde University, John Anderson Building, Glasgow G4 0NG; T.-0141-548 3437.

Jackson, Professor Michael Peart, BA, MA, GradIPM. Senior Deputy Principal, Stirling University, since 1991; b. 1.7.47, Oldham; m., Sylvia; 1 s.; 1 d. Educ. Hulme Grammar School, Oldham; Hull University. Lecturer and Senior Lecturer in Sociology, Professor of Human Resource Management, Stirling University. JP; author of 12 books on industrial relations and employment policy. Address: (b.) Deputy Principal's Office, Stirling University, Stirling; T.-01786 467013.

Jackson, Philip, LLB. Reporter Manager for West Scotland, since 1996; b. 3.12.50, Glasgow; m., Miriam E. Levy; 1 s.; 2 d. Educ. Allan Glen's School, Glasgow; University of Glasgow. Assistant Reporter, Glasgow Corporation, 1974; Area Reporter: Strathclyde Region (Hamilton), 1976, Glasgow South West, 1988; Divisional Reporter, Strathclyde South, 1994. Recreations: cinema; calligraphy; history. Address: (b.) Merchant Exchange Building, 4th Floor, 10/20 Bell Street, Glasgow G1 1LG; T.-0141-567 7957.

Jackson, Robert Penman, MIBM. Director, Dundee Contract Services, Dundee City Council, since 1996; b. 2.4.47, Dunfermline; m., Helen Paxton; 1 s.; 1 d. Educ. Beath Senior High School, Cowdenbeath; Napier College of Science and Technology, Edinburgh. RSAS Diploma. Burgh Surveyor and Sanitary Inspector, Lochgelly Town Council, 1971-75; Assistant Director of Technical Services, Dunfermline District Council, 1975-84; Director of Public Works, City of Dundee District Council, 1984-96. Honorary Secretary, Lochgelly Old Folks' Reunion Committee. Recreation:golf. Address: (b.) 353 Clepington Road, Dundee; T.-Dundee 434729.

Jackson, Ronald William, LLB. Director of Legal Administrative and Property Services, Perth and Kinross Council, since 1995; Member, Policy Committee, Society of Directors of Administration, since 1979; Member, Competition Joint Committee, CIPFA, since 1990; b. 31.7.49, Dundee; m., Morag; 2 d. Educ. Dundee High School; Dundee University. Banff and Buchan District Council: Depute Director of Administration and Legal Services, 1975-79; Director of Administration and Legal Services and Joint Chief Officer, 1979-89; Depute Director of Corporate Services, Fife Regional Council, 1989-95. Recreations: golf; skiing. Address: (b.) PO Box 77, 2 High Street, Perth PH1 5PH; T.-01738 475101.

Jago, Beryl Germaine, MBE, BSc, PGCE. Chairman, Dumfries and Galloway Arts Festival, since 1990; b. 10.7.41, Leeds; m., John Christopher Jago; 1 s.; 1 d. Educ. Leeds Girls' High School; Leeds College of Technology; Leeds University; London Institute of Education. Teacher of Chemistry: Manchester High School for Girls, 1963-66, Lawnswood High School, Leeds, 1966-67; Principal Teacher of Chemistry, Hammersmith County School, London, 1968-70; Teacher of Chemistry, Dumfries High School, 1978-81; Violin Teacher, Dumfries and Galloway Council, 1981-96. Member, Lockerbie Quartet; Member, Solway Sinfonia. Address: (h.) Mansefield, Torthorwald, Dumfries DG1 3QA; T.-01387 750284.

James, David Nicholas Henderson, MA (Cantab). Chairman, State Hospitals Board for Scotland, since 1997; b. 30.12.32, Simla, India; m., Beverly Ann Catherine; 2 s.; 1 d. Educ. Ardvreck and Loretto Schools; Peterhouse, Cambridge University. Former Director, Ciba-Geigy PLC; General Manager, St. Andrews Links Trust, 1992-97. Recreation: golf; fishing; skiing; shooting. Address: Lynedale House, West Linton, Peeblesshire EH46 7HB; T.-01968 660440.

James, David Sheard, MB, ChB, DipEd, DCH, DPM, FRCPsych, FRCP (Glas). Consultant Child Psychiatrist, Royal Hospital for Sick Children, Glasgow, since 1971; Honorary Clinical Senior Lecturer, Child and Adolescent Psychiatry, Glasgow University, since 1991; b. 19.2.39, Harrogate; m., Hilary; 1 s.; 2 d. Educ. Warwick School; Sheffield University. Paediatrics, Sheffield Children's Hospital; Registrar in Psychiatry, Mapperley Hospital, Nottingham; Research Registrar, United Sheffield Hospitals; Senior Registrar, Child Psychiatry, Birmingham Children's Hospital and Charles Burns Clinic. Publication: Families Without Hope (Co-Author), 1975. Recreations: motor vehicles; model railway. Address: (h.) Waterside, Lochlibo Road, Uplawmoor, Glasgow G78 4AA; T.-01505 850269.

James, Professor Keith, BSc, PhD, DSc, FIBiol, FRCPath, FRSE. Professor of Immunology, Edinburgh University, since 1991; b. 15.3.38, Cumbria; m., Valerie Spencer Jubb; 3 s. Educ. Whitehaven Grammar School; Birmingham University. Research Fellow, Birmingham University, 1962-64; Research Assistant, University of California, 1964-65; Senior Lecturer, Edinburgh University, 1965-77, Reader, 1977-91; Past Chairman, Treasurer, Education Secretary and Trustee, British Society for Immunology; Secretary General, International Union of Immunological Societies; serves on the editorial board of a number of journals. Publications: Introducing Immunology (Co-Author); numerous scientific papers. Recreations: hill-walking; photography. Address: (h.) 23 Crosswood Crescent, Balerno, Edinburgh EH14 7LX; T.-0131-449 5583.

James, Mary Charlotte, BA (Hons). Headmistress, St. Leonards School, St. Andrews, since 1988; b. 2.4.44, Bilston, Staffs; m., Lawrence Edwin James; 2 s. Educ. St. Leonards School; York University; St. Anne's College, Oxford. Head of History, Casterton School, Kirkby Lonsdale, 1979-84; Headmistress, Queen Ethelburga's School, Harrogate, 1984-88. Chairman, Demarco European Cultural Initiative, since 1997; Member, Scottish Council, ISCO, since 1988; SCIS: Member, Governing Board, Member, Working Party on Marketing and PR, since 1996. Recreations: reading; cooking; walking; sleeping. Address: St. Leonards House, St. Andrews, Fife; T.-01334 472126.

James, Stuart, BA, FLA, MIInfSc, FRSA. Librarian, Paisley University, since 1989; b. 17.3.44, Borehamwood; m., Gillian Margaret Buckman; 1 s.; 1 d. Educ. Bushey

Grammar School; Birmingham University. Leeds City Libraries, 1965-69; Northampton Development Corporation, 1970-71; Irvine Development Corporation (Librarian/ Information Specialist), 1971-78; Depute Librarian, Paisley College, 1978-89. Editor, Library Review; Editor, Reference Reviews; Convenor, Scottish Academic Libraries Co-operative Training Group, 1987-92; Member, Council of Polytechnic Librarians Executive Committee, 1991-93; Honorary Secretary, Library Association Cataloguing and Indexing Group, 1992-97; Chairman, Cataloguing and Indexing Group in Scotland; Chairman, Information for Scotland Conference Steering Group, since 1993; Member, British Library National Bibliographic Service Advisory Board, 1995-97; Chairman, Open Learning Foundation Library and Learning Support Group, since 1997; Chairman, European Association of Distance Teaching Universities, Libraries and Learning Support Working Group, since 1998. Recreations: history of aviation; reading; book collecting. Address: (b.) Library, Paisley University, High Street, Paisley PA1 2BE; T.-0141-848 3750.

James, Professor (William) Philip (Trehearne), CBE, MA, MD, DSc, FRCP, FRCPEdin, FRSE, MFPHM. Director, Rowett Research Institute, Aberdeen, since 1982; Research Professor, Aberdeen University, since 1983; b. 27.6.38, Liverpool; m., Jean Hamilton Moorhouse; 1 s.; 1 d. Educ. Bala School, North Wales; Ackworth School, Yorkshire; University College, London. Senior House Physician, Whittington Hospital, London, 1963-65; Clinical Research Scientist, Medical Research Council Tropical Metabolism Research Unit, Kingston, Jamaica, 1965-68; Harvard Research Fellow, Massachusetts General Hospital, 1968-69; Wellcome Trust Research Fellow, MRC Gastroenterology Unit, London, 1969-70; Senior Lecturer, Department of Human Nutrition, London School of Hygiene and Tropical Medicine, and Honorary Consultant, UCH, 1970-74; Assistant Director, MRC Dunn Nutrition Unit, and Honorary Consultant Physician, Addenbrooke's Hospital, Cambridge, 1974-82. Sir David Cuthbertson Lecturer; Van den Berghs & Jurgens Reporting Award; Amos Memorial Lecturer; Sir Thomas Middleton Memorial Lecturer; Sir Stanley Davidson Memorial Lecturer; Minshull Lecture; Member, COMA and its Sub-Committees; Chairman, Panel on Novel Foods; Member: Nutrition Task Force; Advisory Committee on Novel Foods and Processes; Chief Executive's Research Advisory Group, Scottish Higher Education Funding Council; President, National Food Alliance; WHO Committee on Nutrition Policy, 1989; FAO Commission on National Energy Needs, 1987-88; Department of Health Task Force on Obesity, 1994; Royal College of Physicians of Edinburgh Working Party on Management of Obesity in the NHS, 1994-96; Association of Professors of Human Nutrition, since 1994; International Task Force on Obesity Management, since 1995; Planning Group, European Young Nutrition Leadership Courses, since 1994; European Panel for European Heart Foundations' Analysis of Cardiovascular Risk, since 1994; Member: EC Scientific Committee for Food, 1992-95, World Cancer Research Fund International Panel on Diet and Cancer, since 1994, EC Scientific Steering Committee, since 1997; Adviser, European Directors of Agricultural Research on Diet and Health, since 1995; Chairman, UN Commission on Global Nutrition for the 21st Century, since 1997; author: WHO report on nutrition and European health, FAO book on human energy requirements; editor, textbook on human nutrition and dietetics, 1992. Address: (b.) Rowett Research Institute, Greenburn Road, Bucksburn, Aberdeen AB21 9SB; T.-01224 712751.

Jameson, John, CBE, QFSM, CIMgt, AIFireE. Firemaster, Strathclyde Fire Brigade, since 1991; b. 12.4.46, Chapelhall; m., Helen Mulvey; 1 s.; 1 d. Educ. St. Aloysius and St. Patrick's High School, Coatbridge. Lanarkshire Fire Brigade, 1965-70; Glasgow Fire Service, 1970-75; Strathclyde Fire Brigade: joined 1975, Assistant Firemaster, 1987-88, Deputy Firemaster, 1988-91. Fire Brigade Long Service and Good Conduct Medal, 1985; Strathclyde Regional Council Medal for Bravery, 1987; Churchill Fellowship, 1983. Recreations: historic buildings; golf. Address: (b.) Fire Headquarters, Bothwell Road, Hamilton ML3 0EA.

Jameson, John Valentine McCulloch, OBE, JP, DL, BSc, FRICS. Senior Partner, G.M. Thomson & Co., Chartered Surveyors, since 1970; b. 5.10.33, Twynholm, Stewartry of Kirkcudbright; m., Mary Irene Butters; 1 s.; 2 d. Educ. Rugby School; College of Estate Management (External). Commissioned 4/7 Royal Dragoon Guards, 1952-54; Shell Petroleum Co., London, 1954-57; Richard Costain (Canada) Ltd., Toronto, 1958-64. Member and Bailie, Gatehouse-of-Fleet Town Council, 1970-75; Member, Dumfries and Galloway Regional Council, 1974-94: Chairman, Finance Committee, 1974-83, Convener, 1983-90; Chairman: Dumfries and Galloway Tourist Association, 1978-82, Royal Institution of Chartered Surveyors in Scotland, 1981-82; Council Member, National Trust for Scotland, 1980-84; Chairman, Dumfries & Galloway Enterprise Co. Ltd., 1993-94; Chairman, West of Scotland Water, 1995-98; Treasurer, Anwoth and Girthon Kirk Session. Recreations: golf; shooting; squash; hill-walking. Address: (h.) Laghead, Gatehouse-of-Fleet; T.-01557 814389.

Jameson, Brigadier Melville Stewart, CBE. Producer, Edinburgh Military Tattoo, since 1995; b. 17.7.44, Clunie; m., Sarah Amy Walker Munro; 2 s. Educ. Glenalmond; RMA, Sandhurst. Commissioned into Royal Scots Greys, 1965; served with regiment in Germany, Northern Ireland, Cyprus, Middle East and Edinburgh (where, in 1971, regiment amalgamated with 3rd Carbiniers to form Royal Scots Dragoon Guards); following tour as Chief of Staff 52 Lowland Brigade, commanded Royal Scots Dragoon Guards, 1986-88, at Tidworth; posted as Instructor to Joint Service Defence College Greenwich; Colonel PB17 on Military Secretary's staff, Ministry of Defence; Command, 51 Highland Brigade, 1994-96 based in Perth. Member, Royal Company of Archers; Honorary Colonel: Aberdeen University OTC, The Scottish Yeomanry. Recreations: shooting; gardening; polo; music (Highland bagpipes). Address: (b.) Tattoo Office, 32 Market Street, Edinburgh EH1 1QB; T.-0131-225 4783.

Jamie, Kathleen, MA. Writer; b. 13.5.62, Johnstone. Educ. Currie High School; Edinburgh University. Publications: The Way We Live; The Autonomous Region; The Queen of Sheba; The Golden Peak.

Jamieson, George, LLB (Hons), DipLP. Solicitor, since 1985; Examiner, Society of Messengers-at-Arms and Sheriff Officers, since 1995; b. 21.8.61, Paisley. Educ. Paisley Grammar School; Strathclyde University. Trainee Solicitor, Hart, Abercrombie, Caldwell and Co., Paisley, 1984-86; Walker Laird, Paisley: Assistant Solicitor, 1986-89, Partner, since 1990. Council Member, Paisley Sheriff Court District, Law Society of Scotland, since 1997. Publication: Parental Responsibilities and Rights, 1995. Address: (b.) 9 Gilmour Street, Paisley PA1 1DG; T.-0141-887 5271.

Jamieson, Rev. Gordon David, MA, BD. Minister, Barnhill St. Margaret's Parish Church, Dundee, since 1986; b. 1.3.49, Glasgow; m., Annette; 1 s.; 1 d. Educ. Hamilton Academy; Edinburgh University. Assistant Minister, Tron Moredun, Edinburgh, 1973-74; Minister: Schaw Kirk, Drongan, 1974-79, Elie Parish Church, linked with Kilconquhar and Colinsburgh Parish Church, 1979-86; Vice-Convener, Committee on the Maintenance of the Ministry, 1993-95; Interim Convener, Church of Scotland Board of Ministry, 1995-96. Address: The Manse, Invermark Terrace, Broughty Ferry, Dundee DD5 2QU; T.-01382 779278.

Janes, Derek Charles, MA, AMA. Support Services Manager, Heritage and Arts, City of Edinburgh Council Recreation Department, since 1998; with Edinburgh City Museums, since 1985; b. 24.3.48, Bristol; m., Diane; 1 s.; 1 d. Educ. Bristol Grammar School; George Watson's College; Edinburgh University. Lancaster City Museum, 1969-71; Assistant Curator, Bury County Borough Museum and Art Gallery, 1972-74; Keeper of Social History, Bury Metropolitan Borough Museum, 1974-76; Senior Keeper, Social History, Coventry City Council Herbert Art Gallery, 1976-84. Publication: Lancaster. Recreations: garden; house; music; towns; reading. Address: (b.) City Art Centre, 2 Market Street, Edinburgh EH1 1DE. T.-0131-529 3951.

Jardine, Sir (Andrew) Rupert (John) Buchanan-, 4th Bt, MC, DL. Landowner; b. 2.2.23; m., Jane Fiona Edmonstone (m. diss.); 1 s.; 1 d. Educ. Harrow; Royal Agricultural College. Retired Major, Royal Horse Guards; Joint Master, Dumfriesshire Foxhounds, 1950; Deputy Lieutenant, Dumfriesshire, 1978. Address: (h.) Dixons, Lockerbie, Dumfriesshire.

Jardine, Ian William, BSc, PhD. Director of Strategy and Operations (East), Scottish Natural Heritage; b. 22.5.59, Edinburgh; m., Anne Daniel; 3 s. Educ. Royal High School, Edinburgh; Durham University; Leeds University. Joined Scottish Office, 1984; worked in various departments, including Scottish Development and Industry Departments; Private Secretary to Ian Lang MP; involved in setting-up of urban partnership initiatives and management of Castlemilk Partnership; joined Scottish Natural Heritage, 1992. Recreations: acting; gardening; natural history. Address: (b.) Battleby, Redgorton, Perth PH1 3EW; T.-01738 444177.

Jardine, Leslie Thomas, LLB. Director for Community Resources, Dumfries and Galloway Council, since 1995; b. 4.6.49, Dumfries; m., Angela; 1 s. Educ. Dumfries Academy; Glasgow University. Law apprentice, then Legal Assistant, Dumfries County Council, 1972-75; Policy Planning Assistant, then Regional Public Relations Officer, then Director of Economic Development, Dumfries and Galloway Regional Council, 1985-96. Solicitor. Recreation: riding. Address: (b.) 118 English Street, Dumfries; T.-01387 260070.

Jarnecki, Liam, BSc (Hons). Director, National Union of Students Scotland, since 1998; b. 10.7.68, Taplow. Educ. Desborough School; North East London Polytechnic. North East London Polytechnic Student Union President, 1991-92; Member, National Executive Committee, National Union of Students, 1992-93; freelance researcher/journalist, 1993-95; Development and Training Officer, National Union of Students Scotland, 1995-98. Recreations: football (qualified referee); promotion of European music and culture. Address: (b.) 26 Rutland Street, Edinburgh EH1 2AN; T.-0131-221 1966.

Jarvie, Sheriff Elizabeth, QC. Sheriff of Lothian and Borders at Edinburgh. Address: Sheriff Court House, 27 Chambers Street, Edinburgh EH1 1LB.

Jarvie, Professor Grant, BEd, MA, PhD. Chair of Sports Studies, University of Stirling, since 1997; President, British Society of Sports History, since 1996; b. 7.11.55, Motherwell. Educ. John Watson's School, Edinburgh; University of Exeter; Queen's University; University of Leicester. Secondary School Teacher, 1979-81; Lecturer/Senior Lecturer, Leeds Polytechnic, 1982-86; Lecturer/Senior Lecturer, University of Warwick (Director, Warwick Centre for the Study of Sport, Chairman, Physical Education Department), 1986-95; Chair/Head of Sport and Leisure Studies, Moray House Institute, Heriot-Watt University, 1995-97. Publications: Class, Race and Sport in South Africa's Political Economy, 1985; Highland Games: The Making of the Myth, 1991; Sport, Racism and Ethnicity (Editor), 1991; Scottish Sport in the Making of the Nation: Ninety-Minute Patriots? (Co-editor), 1994; Sport and Leisure in Social Thought, Revised 1st Ed., 1995 and Revised 2nd Ed., 1999 (Co-author); Sporting Worlds: A Critical Perspective (Co-author), 1999; Sport, Scotland and the Scots (Co-editor), 1999; Sport in the Making of Celtic Cultures (Editor), 1999; numerous book chapters and journal articles. Recreations: squash; hillwalking. Address: Department of Sports Studies, University of Stirling, Stirling FK9 4LA; T.-01786 466490.

Jarvie, Norman Dobson, MB, ChB, FRCGP, FRCP(G), DObstRCOG. General Practitioner, Crieff; b. 31.3.36, Glasgow; m., Dr. Anne Jarvie; 2 s.; 1 d. Educ. Rutherglen Academy; Glasgow University. Medical Officer to Crieff Hospital, Ardvreck School, Morrison's Academy and Crieff Hydro; Chairman, Local Medical Committee, Perth and Kinross Division, 1978-80; President, Perth and Kinross Division, BMA, 1980; Chairman, Scottish Association of General Practitioner Community Hospitals, 1981-85; General Practitioner Tutor, Dundee University; Chairman, Scottish Council, Royal College of General Practitioners, 1987-90; Provost, East Scotland Faculty, RCGP, 1987-90; Chairman, National Medical Advisory Committee, 1990-95; Chairman, Area Drug and Therapeutics Committee, Tayside Health Board, 1994-97. Recreations: skiing; sailing; golf. Address: (b.) Craggan, Victoria Terrace, Crieff PH7 4AD; T.-01764 652067.

Jarvis, Geoffrey, FRIAS. Architectural Consultant; b. 9.1.28, London; m., Rosalind Bailey; 2 s.; 2 d. Educ. Kelvinside Academy; Glasgow Academy; Glasgow School of Architecture. Worked for two years in Philadelphia and New York (Marcel Breuer); returned to Glasgow, setting up in private practice; Consultant to National Trust for Scotland, 1972-87; principal works include Culzean Country Park Centre; Clan Donald Centre, Skye; Chatelherault, Hamilton; Edinburgh Castle Visitor Reception Feasibility Study; Past Chairman, Glasgow Tree Lovers' Society; Founder, former Honorary Secretary and Chairman, New Glasgow Society; Co-Founder and Vice-Chairman, Clyde Fair International, 1972-73; Co-founder, Clydebuilt, 1991; RIBA national award, Regenerating Scotland Award, three Europa Nostra Diplomas of Merit; two Civic Trust Awards; Founder and Vice Chair, Clyde Heritage Trust; Founder Director, Clyde Festival Gardens 1999 Ltd. Recreations: travel and sight-seeing; local and Scottish history; Glasgow; family. Address: (b./h.) Manse Brae, Baldernock, Milngavie G62 6HA; T.-0141-956 3899.

Jarvis, Professor Paul Gordon, PhD, Fil dr, FRS (London), FRSE, FRS (Uppsala), FIBiol, FIChFor. Professor of Forestry and Natural Resources, Edinburgh University, since 1975; b. 23.5.35, Tunbridge Wells; m., Margaret Susan Gostelow; 1 s.; 2 d. Educ. Sir Anthony Brown's School, Brentwood; Oriel College, Oxford. PhD study, Sheffield University, 1957-60; Postdoctoral Fellow, NATO, Institute of Plant Physiology, Uppsala University, 1960-62; Fil dr, Uppsala University, 1963; Senior Lecturer in Plant Physiology, Royal College of Agriculture, Uppsala; Aberdeen University: Lecturer in Botany, 1966-72, Senior Lecturer, 1972-75. Council Member, Society for Experimental Biology, 1977-80, President, 1993-95; Commissioner, Countryside Commission for Scotland, 1976-78; Council Member, National Trust for Scotland, since 1987; Trustee, John Muir Trust, since 1989; Member, Governing Body, Scottish Crops Research Institute, 1977-86; Co-Founder and Sectional Editor, Plant, Cell and Environment; present interests: environmental change, biodiversity, forest ecology and carbon sequestration; serves on various editorial and review boards. Recreations: hill-walking; gardening; growing trees. Address: (h.) Belmont, 47 Eskbank Road, Dalkeith, Midlothian EH22 3BH; T.-0131-663 8676.

Jasinski, Alfons B., RSW, DA. Principal Teacher of Art/Design, since 1989; b. 14.9.45, Falkirk; m., Ann Conlan; 1 s.; 2 d. Educ. St. Modan's High School, Stirling; Edinburgh College of Art. Began teaching in Balwearie High School, Kirkcaldy, 1969. One man exhibitions: Loomshop, 1971, 1974, 1976, 1980, 1982, 1990, 1992; Kirkcaldy Art Gallery, 1975; The Scottish Gallery, 1976, 1986; Cornerstone, Dunblane, 1976; Gallery 22, Cupar, 1976; Portfolio 4, Linlithgow, 1984; many mixed exhibitions; work in private and public collections. Latimer Award, RSA, 1975. Recreations: caravanning; distance running. Address: 15 Normand Road, Dysart, Kirkcaldy KY1 2XN; T.-01592 652505.

Jaspan, Andrew, BA (Hons). Editor, Sunday Herald, since 1999; b. 20.4.53, Manchester; m.; 2 s. Educ. Beverley Grammar School; Manchester University. Founder Editor, New Manchester Review, 1977-80; Sub-Editor, Daily Telegraph and Daily Mirror, Manchester, 1980; Journalists in Europe Fellowship, Paris, 1981; Late News Editor, Times (London), 1982-85; Assistant News Editor, Sunday Times (London), 1985-88; Editor, Sunday Times Scotland, 1988-89; Editor, Scotland on Sunday, 1989-94; Editor, The Scotsman, 1994-95; Editor, The Observer, 1995-96; Publisher and Managing Director, The Big Issue, 1996-98. Address: (b.) 195 Albion Street, Glasgow G1 1QP.

Jasper, Professor David, MA (Cantab), MA (Oxon), BD, PhD. Dean of Divinity and Professor of Literature and Theology, University of Glasgow, since 1998; b. 1.8.51, Stockton; m., Alison Elizabeth Collins; 3 d. Educ. Dulwich College; Jesus College, Cambridge; St. Stephen's House, Oxford; Durham University. Curate of Buckingham (Anglican), 1976-79; Chaplain and Fellow, Hatfield College, Durham, 1979-87; Principal, St. Chad's College, Durham, 1988-91; Senior Lecturer then Reader, University of Glasgow, 1991-98; Director, Centre for Literature and Theology, University of Glasgow, 1991-99. Publications: six books, most recently The Sacred and Secular Canon in Romanticism, 1999. Recreations: reading; photography; walking. Address: Department of Theology and Religious Studies, University of Glasgow, Glasgow G12 8QQ; T.-0141-330 4405.

Jauhar, Pramod, MB, BS, DPM, FRCPsych. Consultant Psychiatrist, since 1981; Clinical Director, since 1995; H.M. Medical Commissioner, Mental Welfare Commission for Scotland, since 1998; b. 15.3.48, Agra, India; m., Pamela; 2 s.; 1 d. Educ. St. Xavier School, Jaipur, India; Armed Forces Medical College, Pune, India. General professional training in pyschiatry, Charing Cross Hospital, London, 1974-77; higher professional training, St. Thomas's Hospital, London, 1977-79; Consultant Pyschiatrist, St. Brendan's Hospital, Bermuda, 1979-81; Honorary Clinical Senior Lecturer, Glasgow, since 1981. Publications: contributions on pyschiatry and substance misuse in medical journals. Recreations: golf; travel. Address: (h.) 7 Dalziel Drive, Glasgow G41 4JA; T.-0141-427 1187.

Jauncey of Tullichettle, Lord (Charles Eliot Jauncey), PC. Lord of Appeal in Ordinary, 1988-96; Senator of the College of Justice in Scotland, 1979-88; b. 8.5.25; m., Sarah Camilla Cathcart; 2 s.; 2 d. Educ. Radley; Christ Church, Oxford; Glasgow University. Advocate, 1949; Kintyre Pursuivant of Arms, 1955; QC, 1963; Sheriff Principal of Fife and Kinross, 1971. Member, Historic Buildings Council for Scotland, 1971-92. Recreations: fishing; shooting; bicycling; genealogy. Address: (h.) Tullichettle, Comrie, Perthshire PH6 2HU; T.-01764 670349.

Jeeves, Professor Malcolm Alexander, CBE, MA, PhD (Cantab), Hon. DSc (Edin), FBPsS, FRSE. President, Royal Society of Edinburgh, since 1996 (Vice-President, 1990-93); Professor of Psychology, St. Andrews University, since 1969; b. 16.11.26, Stamford, England; m., Ruth Elisabeth Hartridge; 2 d. Educ. Stamford School; St. John's College, Cambridge University. Lt., 1st Bn., Sherwood Foresters, BAOR, 1945-48; Exhibitioner, St. John's College, Cambridge, 1948-52; research and teaching, Cambridge and Harvard Universities, 1952-56; Lecturer, Leeds University, 1956-59; Professor and Head, Department of Psychology, Adelaide University, 1959-69 (Dean, Faculty of Arts, 1963-64); Member: Council, SERC, 1985-89, Neuroscience and Mental Health Board, MRC, 1985-89, Council, Royal Society of Edinburgh, 1985-88 (Vice President, 1990-93); Director, Medical Research Council Cognitive Neuroscience Research Group, 1983-88; Vice-Principal, St. Andrews University, 1981-85; Chairman, Executive Committee, International Neuropsychological Symposium, 1986-91; Editor-in-Chief, Neuropsychologia, 1990-93; Cairns Memorial Lecturer, Australia, 1986; New College Lecturer, University of NSW, 1987. Honorary Sheriff, Fife, since 1986. Publications: Analysis of Structural Learning (Co-Author); Psychology Survey No. 3 (Editor); Experimental Psychology: An introduction for biologists; The Effects of Structural Relations upon Transfer (Co-Author); Thinking in Structures (Co-Author); Behavioural Science and Christianity (Editor); Free to be Different (Co-Author); Psychology and Christianity: The View Both Ways; The Scientific Enterprise and Christian Faith; Psychology: Through the eyes of faith (Co-Author); Mind Fields; Human Nature at the Millennium; Science, Life and Christian Belief (Co-author). Recreations: walking; music; fishing. Address: (b.) Department of Psychology, St. Andrews University, St. Andrews KY16 9JU; T.-01334 76161.

Jeffares, Professor Alexander Norman, AM, MA, PhD, DPhil, Ddel'U, DLitt, FAHA, FRSE, FRSL, FRSA. Professor of English Studies, Stirling University, 1974-86; Honorary Professor, since 1987; Managing Director, Academic Advisory Services Ltd.; Director, Colin Smythe Ltd.; b. 11.8.20, Dublin; m., Jeanne Agnes Calembert; 1 d. Educ. The High School, Dublin; Trinity College, Dublin; Oriel College, Oxford. Lecturer in Classics, Trinity College, Dublin, 1943-45; Lector in English, Groningen University, 1946-48; Lecturer in English Literature, Edinburgh University, 1949-51; Professor of English Language and Literature, Adelaide, 1951-56; Professor of English Literature, Leeds, 1957-74. Secretary, Australian Humanities Research Council, 1954-57; Honorary Fellow, Australian Academy of Humanities; Founding Chairman, Association for Commonwealth Literary and Language Studies, 1966-68 (Honorary Life Fellow); Founding Chairman, International Association for Study of Anglo-Irish Literature, 1968-70 (Honorary Life President, since 1973); Member, Scottish Arts Council (Chairman, Literature Committee, 1977-83, Vice Chairman, 1980-84); Member, Arts Council of GB, 1980-84; Chairman, National Book League Scotland, 1985-87, Book Trust Scotland, 1987-89; Board Member, Book Trust, 1987-89; President, International PEN, Scottish Centre, 1986-89; Vice-President, Royal Society of Edinburgh, 1988-89; Vice-Chairman, Muckhart Community Council, 1979-86; Chairman of Judges, McVitie Prize, 1988-91. Publications: Yeats: Man and Poet; Seven Centuries of Poetry; The Scientific Background (Co-Author); A Commentary on the Poems of Yeats; A Commentary on the Plays of Yeats (Co-Author); History of Anglo-Irish Literature; Restoration Drama; New Commentary on Poems of Yeats; Brought up in Dublin (poems); Brought up to Leave (poems); An Irish Childhood (Co-Editor); A Jewish Childhood (Co-Editor); Yeats: a new biography; Yeats's Poems; Yeats's Vision; Yeats: the love poems; Always Your Friend (Co-Editor); Swift, the selected poems; Joycechoyce (Co-Editor); Ireland's Women (Co-Editor); Collins Dictionary of Quotations (Co-Editor); Images of Imagination (essays); Victorian Love Poems; Pocket History of Irish Literature; Irish Love Poems; The Irish Literary Movement; The Shadowy Rose. Recreations: drawing; painting; restoring old houses. Address: (h.) Craighead Cottage, Fife Ness, Crail, Fife; T.-01333 450898.

Jeffcoat, Marilyn Annette, BCom, FCCA. Chairman, D.M. Vaughan & Co. Ltd., Accountants; Member of Court, Napier University, since 1990; Commissioner, Mental Welfare Commission, since 1992; b. 7.4.47, Birmingham; 5 s.; 1 d. Educ. Erdington Grammar School, Birmingham; Edinburgh University. Worked in investment management, tax accountancy and audit with Baillie Gifford, Ivory & Sime, and Coopers & Lybrand until 1978, qualifying as a certified accountant in 1976; public practice since 1979. Convener, One Parent Families, Scotland; Director, St. Mary's Cathedral Workshop Ltd.; Treasurer: Society of Scottish Artists, St. Mary's Episcopal Cathedral, Edinburgh, Royal Scottish Country Dance Society; Administrator, Mendelssohn on Mull Festival; Trustee, Scottish Hospital Trust. Recreations: theology; mathematics; dance. Address: (b.) 10 Gloucester Place, Edinburgh; T.-0131-225 8282.

Jeffery, Professor Jonathan, MA, BSc, DPhil, DSc, CChem, FRSC, CBiol, FIBiol, FRSA, FRSE. Professor of Biochemistry, Aberdeen University, since 1983; b. 29.7.35, Liverpool; m., Christa Torriano-Williams; 2 d. Educ. Liverpool Institute High School; Jesus College, Oxford University. Research Biochemist, ICI, 1962-66; Aberdeen University: Lecturer in Chemical Pathology, 1966-72, Lecturer in Biochemistry, 1972-74, Senior Lecturer in Biochemistry, 1974-83. Recreations: country walks; some interest in theatre, visual arts and music. Address: (b.) Department of Molecular and Cell Biology, Aberdeen University, Marischal College, Aberdeen, AB10 1YS; T.-01224 272000.

Jeffery, Patricia Margaret, MA, MA, PhD. Professor of Sociology, University of Edinburgh, since 1996; b. 25.3.47, Leamington Spa; 2 d. Educ. King's High School for Girls, Warwick; Newnham College, Cambridge University. University of Edinburgh: Lecturer and Research Fellow in Social Anthropology, 1973-77, Lecturer/Reader in Sociology, 1978-96; Visiting Fellow, Indian Social Institute, 1982-83; Institute of Economic Growth, 1990-91. Publications: Migrants and Refugees, 1975; Frogs in a Well, 1979; Labour Pains and Labour Power (Co-author), 1989; Don't Marry Me to a Plowman (Co-author), 1996; Population, Gender and Politics (Co-author), 1997. Recreations: hillwalking; chamber concerts. Address: (b.) Department of Sociology, University of Edinburgh, 18 Buccleuch Place, Edinburgh EH8 9LN; T.-0131-650 4001.

Jeffery, Professor Roger, BA, MSc, PhD. Professor of Sociology of South Asia, since 1997; b. 5.12.47, Hampstead; 2 d. Educ. Harrow Weald CGS; Churchill College, Cambridge University. University of Edinburgh: Lecturer then Senior Lecturer, 1972-97; Visiting Fellow, Delhi School of Economics, 1975-76; Indian Social Institute, 1982-83; Institute of Economic Growth, 1990-91; Convenor, Centre for South Asian Studies, since 1993. Publications: The Politics of Health in India, 1988; Labour Pains and Labour Power (Co-author), 1989; Don't Marry Me to a Plowman (Co-author), 1996; Population, Gender and Politics (Co-author), 1997. Recreations: hillwalking; badminton; chamber music. Address: (b.) Department of Sociology, University of Edinburgh, 18 Buccleuch Place, Edinburgh EH8 9LN; T.-0131-650 4001.

Jeffreys-Jones, Professor Rhodri, BA (Wales), PhD (Cantab), FRHistS. Professor of American History, Edinburgh University, since 1997; b. 28.7.42, Carmarthen; m., Mary Fenton; 2 d. by pr. m. Educ. Ysgol Ardudwy; University of Wales; Cambridge University; Michigan University; Harvard University. Tutor: Harvard, 1965-66, Fitzwilliam College, Cambridge, 1966-67; Assistant Lecturer, Lecturer, Senior Lecturer, Reader, Edinburgh University, 1967-97; Fellow, Charles Warren Center for the Study of American History, Harvard, 1971-72; Canadian Commonwealth Visiting Fellow and Visiting Professor, University of Toronto, 1993. Publications: Violence and Reform in American History; American Espionage: From Secret Service to CIA; Eagle Against Empire: American Opposition to European Imperialism 1914-82 (Editor); The Growth of Federal Power in American History (Joint Editor); The CIA and American Democracy; North American Spies (Joint Editor); Changing Differences: Women and the Shaping of American Foreign Policy, 1917-1994; Eternal Vigilance? – 50 years of the CIA (Joint Editor). Recreations: snooker; vegetable gardening. Address: (b.) Department of History, Edinburgh University, William Robertson Building, George Square, Edinburgh EH8 9JY; T.-0131-650 3773/3780.

Jenkins, Robin, MA. Novelist; b. 11.9.12. Author of: So Gaily Sings the Lark, Happy for the Child, The Thistle and the Grail, The Cone-Gatherers, Guests of War, The Missionaries, The Changeling, Some Kind of Grace, Dust on the Paw, The Tiger of Gold, A Love of Innocence, The Sardana Dancers, A Very Scotch Affair, The Holy Tree, The Expatriates, A Toast to the Lord, A Far Cry from Bowmore, A Figure of Fun, A Would-be Saint, Fergus Lamont, The Awakening of George Darroch, Just Duffy, Poverty Castle, Willie Hogg, Leila, Lunderston Tales, Matthew and Sheila. Address: (h.) Fairhaven, Toward, Dunoon PA23 7UE.

Jennett, Professor Bryan, MD, FRCS. Professor of Neurosurgery, Glasgow University, 1968-91 (Dean, Faculty of Medicine, 1981-86); Member, Court, Glasgow University, 1987-91; b. 1.3.26, Twickenham, Middlesex; m., Professor Sheila Jennett; 3 s.; 1 d. Educ. King's College, Wimbledon; King George V School, Southport; Liverpool University. Lecturer in Neurosurgery, Manchester University; Rockefeller Travelling Fellow, University of California; Hunterian Professor, Royal College of Surgeons of England. Member: Medical Research Council, 1979-83, Chief Scientist Committee, Scotland; Rock Carling Fellow. Publications: Epilepsy After Non-Missile Head Injuries; Introduction to Neurosurgery; High Technology Medicine - Benefits and Burdens. Recreations: writing; cruising under sail. Address: (h.) 83 Hughenden Lane, Glasgow G12 9XN.

Jennings, James, OBE, JP. Member, North Ayrshire Council, since 1996 (Chair, Social Work Committee); Former Convener, Strathclyde Regional Council; Honorary Sheriff, Kilmarnock, since 1991; Chairman, Police Negotiating Board, since 1990; b. 18.2.25; m., 1, Margaret Cook Barclay (deceased); 3 s.; 2 d.; 2, Margaret Mary Hughes, JP; 2 d. Educ. St. Palladius School, Dalry; St. Michael's College, Irvine. Steel industry, 1946-79. Member: Ayr County Council, 1958, Strathclyde Regional Council, 1974 (Vice-Convener, 1982-86); Chairman: Ayr CC Police and Law Committee, 1964-70, Ayrshire Joint Police Committee, 1970-75, North Ayrshire Crime Prevention Panel, 1970-82, Police and Fire Committee, Strathclyde Regional Council, 1978-82; contested Perth and East Perthshire, 1966; Vice-President, St. Andrew's Ambulance Association; Patron, Association of Youth Clubs in Strathclyde; Honorary President: Scottish Retirement Council, Princess Louise Scottish Hospital (Erskine Hospital); Honorary Vice-President: SNO Chorus, Royal British Legion Scotland (Dalry and District Branch); JP, Cunninghame, 1969 (Chairman, Cunninghame Justices Committee, since 1974); Vice-Chairman, Official Side, Police Negotiating Board, 1984-86, Chairman, 1986-88; Chairman, Garnock Valley Development Executive, since 1988; Freeman of North Ayrshire, since 1997. Recreation: local community involvement. Address: (h.) 4 Place View, Kilbirnie KA25 6BG; T.-Kilbirnie 3339.

Jennings, Kevin, MB, FRCP. Consultant Cardiologist, Aberdeen Royal Infirmary, since 1983; b. 9.3.47, Charleville, Eire; m., Heather; 2 s.; 1 d. Educ. Downside; St. Bartholomew's Hospital, London. Registrar: King's College Hospital, London, London Chest Hospital; Senior Registrar, Freeman Hospital, Newcastle-upon-Tyne.

Recreations: theatre; ballet; golf; windsurfing. Publication: Acute Cardiac Care. Address: 58 Rubislaw Den South, Aberdeen AB15 4AY; T.-Aberdeen 311466.

Jensen-Butler, Professor Christopher Nigel, BA, PhD. Professor, Department of Economics, University of St. Andrews, since 1996; b. 5.6.45, Derby. Educ. Bemrose School, Derby; University College, University of Durham. University of Aarhus, Denmark: Assistant Professor, 1969-72, Associate Professor, 1972-87, Department of Geography, Associate Professor, Department of Mathematics, 1987-91, Associate Professor, Department of Political Science, 1991-95; Professor of Urban and Regional Planning, Department of Geography, University of St. Andrews, 1995-96; Guest Professor, University of Lisbon, 1987. Publication: European Cities in Competition (Co-Editor), 1997. Recreations: sailing; hill-walking; classical music. Address: (b.) Department of Economics, University of St. Andrews, Castlecliffe, The Scores, St. Andrews, Fife KY16 9AL; T.-01334 478074.

Jessamine, Rev. Alistair Lindsay, MA, BD. Minister of Dunfermline Abbey, since 1991; b. 17.6.49, Hill of Beath; m., Eleanor Moore. Educ. Beath High School, Cowdenbeath; University of Edinburgh. Assistant Minister, Newlands South Parish Church, Glasgow, 1978-79; Minister, Rankin Parish Church, Strathaven linked with Chapelton, 1979-91; Chaplain: HM Prison, Dungavel, 1979-91, RAF Pitreavie Castle, 1991-95; Moderator, Presbytery of Dunfermline, 1993-94. Recreations: travel; cooking; golf. Address: Abbey Manse, 12 Garvock Hill, Dunfermline, Fife KY12 7UU; T.-01383 721022.

Jessop, Sheriff Alexander Smethurst, MA, LLB. Sheriff at Aberdeen, since 1990; b. 17.5.43, Montrose; m., Joyce Isobel Duncan; 2 s.; 1 d. Educ. Montrose Academy; Fettes College; Aberdeen University. Partner, Campbell, Middleton, Burness and Dickson, Montrose; Procurator Fiscal Depute, Perth, 1976-78; Assistant Solicitor, Crown Office, 1978-80; Senior Assistant Procurator Fiscal, Glasgow, 1980-84; Regional Procurator Fiscal, Aberdeen, 1984-87, Glasgow, 1987-90. Member, Scottish Legal Aid Board; External Examiner, Aberdeen University. Recreation: golf (Captain, Royal Montrose Golf Club). Address: (b.) Sheriff Court House, Aberdeen AB9 1AP; T.-01224 648316.

Johnson, Professor Christopher William, MA, MSc, DPhil, CEng, FBCS. Personal Chair in Computing Science, Glasgow University, since 1997; b. 15.4.65, Edinburgh; m., Fionnuala Muireann; 2 s. Educ. Verulam School, St. Albans; Trinity College, Cambridge. Lecturer in Computing Science, University of York, 1991-94; Senior Lecturer in Computing Science, University of Glasgow, 1994-97. Chair, IFIP Working Group 13.5 (Human Error and Systems Development). Publications: over 90 papers and articles. Winner, 1998 Systems Safety Award. Recreation: running. Address: (b.) Department of Computing Science, University of Glasgow, Glasgow G12 8QQ; T.-0141-330 6053.

Johnson, David (Charles), MA, BA, PhD. Composer; Musical Historian; Cellist, McGibbon Ensemble, since 1979; 27.10.42, Edinburgh; 1 s. Educ. Aberdeen University; St. John's College, Cambridge. Research Fellow in Scottish Music, Napier University, 1995; Tutor, Edinburgh University Music Faculty, 1988-94; awarded Scottish Arts Council composer's bursary, 1992-93; compositions include four operas, an orchestral suite, chamber music, songs, a piano concerto, church music. Publications: Music and Society in Lowland Scotland, 1972; Scottish Fiddle Music in the 18th Century, 1984; contributions to the New Grove Dictionary of Music, 1981; The Scots Cello Book, 1990; Stepping Northward, 1991; 12 Preludes and Fugues, 1995. Address: (h.) 8 Shandon Crescent, Edinburgh EH11 1QE. T.-0131-337 4621.

Johnson, Ian M., BA, FLA, MIInfSc, MIMgt. Head, School of Information and Media, Robert Gordon University, Aberdeen, since 1989; Chairman: Heads of Schools and Departments Committee, British Association for Information and Library Education and Research, 1997-2000; b. 17.3.45, Sheffield; m., Jean Trevena. Educ. King Edward VII School, Sheffield; Liverpool College of Commerce; Leeds Polytechnic. Sheffield City Libraries, 1962-74; Department of Education and Science (Office of Arts and Libraries), 1970-72 (on secondment); Rotherham M.B. Council, 1974-78; College of Librarianship Wales, 1978-89. Chairman, Professional Board, International Federation of Library Associations and Institutions, 1993-95; Chairman, Library Association Personnel Training and Education Group, 1994-95; Member, Library Association Council, since 1996; Chairman, EUCLID, 1998-2001. Recreations: theatre; cinema; travel. Address: (b.) Garthdee Road, Aberdeen AB10 7QE.

Johnson, Professor Keith Jack, BSc, PhD, MRCPath. Professor of Genetics, University of Glasgow, since 1995; b. 17.5.55, Dorset; m., Margot Ross; 1 s.; 1 d. Educ. Brockenhurst Grammar School, Hants; University of Dundee. Charing Cross and Westminster Medical School: Lecturer, 1989-93, Senior Lecturer, 1993-95. Recreations: golf; crosswords. Address: (b.) Division of Molecular Genetics, Anderson College, 56 Dumbarton Road, Glasgow; T.-0141-330 5101.

Johnston, Hon. Lord (Alan Charles Macpherson), BA (Hons) (Cantab), LLB. Senator of the College of Justice, since 1994; Queen's Counsel (1980); b. 13.1.42, Stirling; m., Anthea Jean Blackburn; 3 s. Educ. Edinburgh Academy; Loretto School; Jesus College, Cambridge; Edinburgh University. Advocate, 1967; Standing Junior Counsel, Scottish Home and Health Department, 1972; Advocate Depute, 1978-82; Chairman: Industrial Tribunal, 1982-85, Medical Appeal Tribunal, 1985-89; Treasurer, Faculty of Advocates, 1977-89, Dean, Faculty of Advocates, 1989-93. Publication: Introduction to Law of Scotland 7th Edition (Joint Editor). Address: (h.) 3 Circus Gardens, Edinburgh; T.-0131-225 1862.

Johnston, Sheriff Alexander Graham, LLB, BA. Sheriff of Glasgow and Strathkelvin, at Glasgow, since 1985 (Grampian, Highland and Islands, 1982-85); b. 16.7.44.

Johnston, Alistair, BSc (Hons). Rector, Kelso High School, since 1975; b. 2.5.39, Stirling; m., Elizabeth; 2 s.; 1 d. Educ. High School of Stirling; Glasgow University. Teacher, George Heriot's School, 1962-65; Principal Teacher of Physics, Galashiels Academy, 1965-71; Depute Rector, Banff Academy, 1971-75. Past President, Headteachers' Association of Scotland. Recreations: gardening; walking; sailing; skiing; golf. Address: (b.) Kelso High School, Bowmont Street, Kelso TD5 7EG; T.-01573 224444.

Johnston, Frederick Patrick Mair, CBE, FRSA, MA. Chairman, Johnston Press plc (formerly F. Johnston & Co. Ltd.), since 1973; Director, TSB Bank Scotland plc, since 1996; b. 15.9.35, Edinburgh; m., Elizabeth Ann Jones; 2 s. Educ. Morrison's Academy, Crieff; Lancing College, Sussex; New College, Oxford. Editorial Department, Liverpool Daily Post and Echo, 1959; Assistant Secretary, The Times Publishing Co. Ltd., 1960; Company Secretary, F. Johnston & Co. Ltd., 1969. Chairman, Central Scotland Manpower Committee, 1976-83; Member, Press Council, 1974-88; President, Scottish Newspaper Proprietors' Association, 1976-78; Treasurer, Society of Master Printers of Scotland, 1981-86; President, The Newspaper Society, 1989-90; Director, Scottish Mortgage & Trust plc, since 1991; Chairman, Edinburgh Book Festival, since 1996; Director, Press Association Ltd., since 1997. Recreations: reading; travelling. Address: (b.) 53 Manor Place, Edinburgh EH3 7EG; T.-0131-225 3361.

Johnston, Geoffrey Edward Forshaw, LLB, CA. Managing Director, Arbuckle, Smith and Company, since 1972; Chairman, Scottish Chambers of Commerce, since 1996; Non-executive Director, Scottish Friendly Assurance Society Ltd., since 1996; b. 20.6.40, Burton-Wirral, England; m., Elizabeth Anne Lockhart; 2 d. Educ. Loretto School, Musselburgh; University of St. Andrews. Wilson Stirling & Co. CA, 1959-65; Arbuckle Smith Group, since 1965: Director, 1968, management buy-out, 1984. Honorary Consul for Belgium, Scotland West and Northern Islands, 1989-95; National Chairman, British International Freight Association, 1990-91; President, Glasgow Chamber of Commerce, 1994-95; Member, Scottish Valuation and Rating Council, since 1981; Governor, Lomond School; Director, Central College of Commerce. Recreations: sailing; skiing; hillwalking; golf. Address: (h.) Upper Dunard, Station Road, Rhu, Dunbartonshire G84 8LW; T.-01436 820563.

Johnston, George Bonar, DA, RSW. Artist; b. 14.6.33, Edinburgh; m., Margaret; 1 s.; 1 d. Educ. Bathgate Academy; Edinburgh College of Art. Teacher, 1955-56; Army Officer, 1956-58; Teacher, 1958-59; Lecturer, 1959-66; Art Adviser, Tayside Region, 1966-91. Paintings in private and public collections in Scotland, England, France, North America, Canada. Recreations: fly fishing; reading. Address: 10 Collingwood Crescent, Barnhill, Dundee DD5 2SX; T.-01382 779857.

Johnston, George Hermiston, Dip., Youth and Community Work. Chief Executive, Youthlink Scotland, since 1992; Chairman, Scottish Youth Work Partnership; b. 22.11.36. Director, Clermiston Centre and Youth Secretary, Edinburgh YMCA, 1964-70; General Secretary, Belfast YMCA, 1970-74; Training Officer, Northern Ireland Association of Youth Clubs, 1974-76, Director, 1976-92. Past President, European Confederation of Youth Clubs. Recreations: photography; music; walking; art. Address: (b.) YouthLink Scotland, Central Hall, West Tollcross, Edinburgh EH3 9BP; T.-0131-229 0339.

Johnston, Grenville Shaw, OBE, TD, KCSG, DL, CA. Chartered Accountant, since 1968; Vice Lord Lieutenant of Moray, since 1996; Territorial Army Officer, 1964-89 (Lt. Col.); b. 28.1.45, Nairn; m., Marylyn Jean Picken; 2 d. Educ. Blairmore School; Fettes College. Qualified in Edinburgh with Scott Moncrieff Thomson & Sheills; Thomson McLintock & Co., Glasgow, 1968-70; joined family firm, W.D. Johnston & Carmichael, Elgin, 1970; Senior Partner, 1975. Commanding Officer, 2nd 51st Highland Volunteers, 1983-86; Hon. Col., 3rd Highland Volunteers, 1997; Knight Commander, Order of St. Gregory, 1982, for work for Pluscarden Abbey; OBE for services to Territorial Army; Chairman, Grampian Committee, Royal Jubilee Trusts, 1982-91; Member, Cairngorm Recreation Trust Ltd.; Vice Chairman, Gordonstoun School; Junior Vice President, Institute of Chartered Accountants of Scotland; Trustee and Council Member: Queens Own Highlanders, The Highlanders; Trustee, National Museums of Scotland, since 1998. Recreations: shooting; fishing; hockey; golf; skiing; singing (tenor). Address: (h.) Spynie Kirk House, Spynie, By Elgin, Moray IV30 3XJ.

Johnston, Ian Alistair, CB, PhD, BSc, CIMgt, FIPD, FRSA. Principal, Glasgow Caledonian University, since 1998; Honorary Treasurer, Industrial Society, since 1990; Board Member, University for Industry, since 1998; Director, Qualifications for Industry, since 1995; b. 2.5.44, Watlington, Oxford; m., Mary Bridget Lube; 1 s.; 1 d. Educ. High Wycombe Royal Grammar School; Birmingham University. Department of Employment: Assistant Principal, 1969, Principal, 1974; First Secretary (Labour Attaché), British Embassy, Brussels, 1975-77; Director, Advisory Conciliation Arbitration Service, 1978-82; Finance Director (Under Secretary) then Chief Executive/Director General (Deputy Secretary), Manpower Services Commission, 1983-95; Deputy Principal, Sheffield Hallam University, 1995-98. Member, High Level Expert Advisory Group on Education and Training Strategy, European Commission; Assessor, National Advisory Council on Education and Training Targets, 1992-95; writes on public sector management and applying IT to learning. Recreations: bird watching; travel; tennis; armchair rugby. Address: (b.) Glasgow Caledonian University, Cowcaddens Road, Glasgow G4 0BA; T.-0141-331 3113.

Johnston, Professor Ian Alistair, BSc, PhD, FRSE. Chandos Professor of Physiology, Director, Gatty Marine Laboratory and Head, School of Environmental and Evolutionary Biology, St. Andrews University, since 1985; b. 13.4.49, Barking, Essex. Educ. Addey and Stanhope Grammar School, London; Hull University. NERC Postdoctoral Research Fellow, Bristol University, 1973-75; Lecturer in Physiology, St. Andrews University, 1976-84; Reader, 1984-85; Visiting Senior Lecturer, Department of Veterinary Physiology, Nairobi University, 1981; Visiting Scientist, British Antarctic Survey base, Signy Island, South Orkneys, 1983-84; Council Member, NERC; Chairman, NERC Marine Science and Technology Board; Director, Company of Biologists; awarded Scientific Medal, Zoological Society of London. Recreations: photography; walking; reading. Address: (b.) School of Environmental and Evolutionary Biology, St. Andrews University, St. Andrews KY16 8LB; T.-01334 463440.

Johnston, Jim A., MA. Headteacher, Farr High School, since 1991; b. 11.9.50, Lerwick; m., Jenny Mackay; 1 d. Educ. Anderson Educational Institute; Aberdeen University; Aberdeen College of Education. Farr High School: Assistant Teacher of English, 1973-75, Principal Teacher of English, 1975-77, Depute Head, 1977-91. Company Secretary, Tongue and Farr Sports Association Ltd., since 1991; founding Chairman, Scottish Peat and Land Development Association (Caithness Branch); Chairman, Bettyhill, Strathnaver and Altnaharra Community Council, 1977-88. Publications: A Future for Peat, 1981; Tongue and Farr, 1984, Gleannan am Fraoch, 1988; The Best of the Bard (Editor), 1987; Recreations: journalism; photography; crofting; reading; hillwalking. Address: (h.) Vaila, Bettyhill, by Thurso, Caithness KW14 7SS; T.-01641 521302.

Johnston, Joyce Sara Ramsay, BA, MEd. Principal, Fife College of Further and Higher Education, Kirkcaldy, since 1996; b. Brisbane, Australia. Educ. Knightswood School, Glasgow; University of Strathclyde; University of Edinburgh. Tourism Research, Australia, 1970-80; Education Administration, Dundee College, 1980-83; Depute Principal, Glenrothes College, 1983-89; Principal, Anniesland College, Glasgow, 1989-92; H.M.I., Scottish Office Education and Industry Department, 1992-96. Recreations: reading; gardening; cinema. Address: (b.) St. Brycedale Avenue, Kirkaldy KY1 1EX; T.-01592 268591.

Johnston, Professor Marie, BSc, PhD, DipClinPsych, FBPsS, CPsychol, FRSE. Professor in Psychology, St. Andrews University, since 1992; b. 6.7.44, Aberdeen; m., Derek Johnston. Educ. High School for Girls, Aberdeen; Aberdeen University; Hull University. Research Officer, Oxford University, 1971-77; Lecturer, Senior Lecturer, Reader, Royal Free Hospital School of Medicine, 1977-90; Reader, Professor of Psychology, St. Andrews University, since 1990; Honorary Clinical Psychologist, Tayside and Fife Health Boards, since 1991; first Chair, Section of Health Psychology, British Psychological Society; Past President, European Health Psychology Society. Recreation: gardening. Address: (b.) School of Psychology, St. Andrews University, St. Andrews KY16 9JU; T.-01334 62060.

Johnston, Peter William, MA, LLB, FRSA. Chief Executive and Secretary, Institute of Chartered Accountants of Scotland, since 1989; b. 8.2.43, Peebles; m., Patricia Sandra; 1 s.; 1 d. Educ. Larbert High School; Glasgow University. Partner, MacArthur & Co., Solicitors, Inverness, 1971-76; Procurator Fiscal Service, 1976-89. Recreations: music; languages; sailing. Address: (b.) 27 Queen Street, Edinburgh, EH2 1LA; T.-0131-225 5673.

Johnston, Robin Alexander, BSc, MB, BCh, BAO, MD, FRCS (Edin). Consultant Neurosurgeon, since 1985 (of Queen Elizabeth National Spinal Injury Unit, since 1992); Honorary Clinical Senior Lecturer, Glasgow University, since 1990; b. 30.3.49, Belfast; m., Ann. Educ. Belfast Royal Academy; Queens University, Belfast. Various surgical posts, UK, 1974-77; neurosurgical training, Belfast, Dallas, Glasgow, 1977-85. Address: (b.) Institute of Neurological Sciences, Southern General Hospital, Glasgow; T.-0141-201 2021.

Johnston, Thomas Lothian, MA, PhD, DL, FRSA, FRSE, CIMgt, FIPD, DrHC, DEd, LLD, DUniv, DLitt, FEIS. President, Royal Society of Edinburgh, 1993-96; Chairman, Scottish Committee, Royal Society of Arts, 1991-95; b. 9.3.27, Whitburn; m., Joan Fahmy; 2 s.; 3 d. Educ. Hawick High School; Edinburgh University; Stockholm University. Served RNVR (Sub. Lieut.), 1944-47; Lecturer in Political Economy, Edinburgh University, 1953-65; Professor of Economics, Heriot-Watt University, 1966-76; Vice-Chancellor, Heriot-Watt University, 1981-88; industrial relations arbitrator and mediator; Chairman, Manpower Services Committee for Scotland, 1977-80; Member, Scottish Economic Council, 1977-91; Chairman, Enquiry into Staff Representation, London Clearing Banks, 1978-79; Member, Review Committee, New Zealand Universities, 1987; Scottish Chairman, Industry Year, 1986, and Industry Matters, 1987-89; Trustee, National Galleries of Scotland, 1989-95; academic appointments in other countries: University of Illinois, 1957, 1962-63, Queen's University, Canada, 1965, Western Australian Institute of Technology, 1979, Visiting Professor, International Institute for Labour Studies, Geneva, 1973. Publications: Collective Bargaining in Sweden, 1962; Economic Expansion and Structural Change, 1963; The Structure and Growth of the Scottish Economy (Co-Author), 1971; Introduction to Industrial Relations, 1981; translations from Swedish. Recreations: gardening; walking. Address: (h.) 14 Mansionhouse Road, Edinburgh EH9 1TZ; T.-031-667 1439.

Johnston, Very Rev. William Bryce, MA, BD, DD, DLitt. Minister, Colinton Parish Church, 1964-91; Chaplain to The Queen in Scotland, 1981-91, Extra Chaplain, since 1991; b. 16.9.21, Edinburgh; m., Ruth Margaret Cowley; 1 s.; 2 d. Educ. George Watson's College, Edinburgh; Edinburgh University. Chaplain to the Forces, 1945-49; Minister: St. Andrew's Church, Bo'ness, 1949-55, St. George's Church, Greenock, 1955-64; Chaplain, HM Prison, Greenock, 1959-64; Convener, General Assembly Committees: Adult Christian Education, 1970-72, Church and Nation, 1972-76, Inter-Church Relations, 1979-81, Judicial Commission, 1986-91; Moderator of the General Assembly, 1980; Cunningham Lecturer, New College, 1968-71; Visiting Lecturer in Social Ethics, Heriot-Watt University, 1966- 88; Member, Broadcasting Council for Scotland, 1983-87. Publications: translations of Karl Barth and John Calvin; Ethics and Defence (Contributor). Recreations: organ music; bowls. Address: (h.) 15 Elliot Road, Edinburgh EH14 1DU; T.-0131-441 3387.

Johnston, William John, BSc (Hons), DipEd(Tech). Rector, Aberdeen Grammar School, since 1987; b. 17.8.47, Kilmarnock; m., Katie Mary Maclean; 3 d. Educ. Spier's School, Beith; Glasgow University. Marketing Assistant, ICI Silicones, 1969-70; Teacher: Cranhill Secondary, 1971-73, Perth High School, 1973-75; Assistant Principal Teacher, Glenrothes High School, 1975-78; Principal Teacher, Millburn Academy, 1978-81; Assistant Rector, Kingussie High School, 1981-84; Depute Rector, Culloden Academy, 1984-87. Address: (b.) Aberdeen Grammar School, Skene Street, Aberdeen; T.-01224 642299.

Johnstone, Professor Eve Cordelia, MB, ChB, MD, FRCP, FRCPsych, DPM. Professor of Psychiatry and Head, Department of Psychiatry, University of Edinburgh, since 1989; b. 1.9.44, Glasgow. Educ. Park School, Glasgow; University of Glasgow. Junior posts in Glasgow hospitals; Lecturer in Psychological Medicine, University of Glasgow, 1972-74; Member of Scientific Staff, Medical Research Council, Clinical Research Centre, Northwick Park, 1974-89. Member of Council, Medical Research Council. Publications: four books on psychiatric illness; over 200 papers on biological psychiatry. Address: (b.) Royal Edinburgh Hospital, Morningside Park, Edinburgh.

Johnstone, Sir Raymond, CBE, BA, CA. Director, RJ KILN PLC, since 1995; Director, Lomond Underwriting plc (Chairman, since 1993); Chairman: Historic Buildings Council for Scotland, since 1995, The Nuclear Generation Decommissioning Fund Limited, since 1996, The Nuclear Trust, since 1996, Patrons of the National Galleries of Scotland, since 1995; b. 27.10.29, London; m., Susan Sara; 5 step s.; 2 step d. Educ. Eton; Trinity College, Cambridge. Investment Analyst, Robert Fleming & Co. Ltd., London, 1955-60; Partner (CA), Brown, Fleming & Murray (later Whinney Murray & Co.), 1960-68; Director: Dominion Insurance Co. Ltd., 1973-95 (Chairman, 1978-95); Scottish Financial Enterprise, 1986-91 (Chairman, 1989-91); Summit Group PLC (Chairman, 1989-98); Murray Income PLC, since 1989; Murray International PLC, since 1989; Murray Smaller Markets PLC, since 1989; Murray Ventures PLC, since 1984; Murray Enterprise PLC, since 1989; Chairman, Murray Johnstone Ltd., 1984-91 (Managing Director, 1968-88); Chairman, Forestry Commission, 1989-94; Chairman, Murray Split Capital Trust PLC, 1991-98; Director, Scottish Amicable Life Assurance Society, 1971-97 (Chairman, 1983-85); Chairman, 1982-86, Hon. President, 1986-97, Scottish Opera. Recreations: fishing; shooting; opera; farming. Address: (h.) Wards, Gartocharn, Dunbartonshire G83 85B.

Johnstone, Professor William, MA (Hons), BD, DLitt. Professor of Hebrew and Semitic Languages, Aberdeen University, since 1980; Minister, Church of Scotland, since 1963; b. 6.5.36, Glasgow; m., Elizabeth M. Ward; 1 s.; 1 d. Educ. Hamilton Academy; Glasgow University; Marburg University. Lecturer in Hebrew and Semitic Languages, Aberdeen University, 1962-72, Senior Lecturer, 1972-80, Dean, Faculty of Divinity, 1983-87; President, Society for Old Testament Study, 1990. Recreation: alternative work. Address: (h.) 37 Rubislaw Den South, Aberdeen AB15 4BD; T.-Aberdeen 316022.

Jolliffe, Professor Ian, BSc, DPhil. Professor of Statistics, Aberdeen University, since 1992; b. 22.12.45, Isle of Wight; m., Jean Peddar; 1 s.; 1 d. Educ. Sandown Grammar School; Sussex University. Lecturer, then Senior Lecturer, Kent University; visiting positions, Dalhousie University, University of Guelph. Recreations: running; dinghy sailing; folk music. Address: (b.) Department of Mathematical Sciences, Aberdeen University, King's College, Aberdeen, AB24 3UE; T.-01224 272611.

Jonathan, Professor Ruth Madeline, BA(Hons), PGCE, MA, PhD. Professor of Educational Theory and Policy (Personal Chair), University of Edinburgh, since 1993; b. 25.6.41. Educ. Arnold High School, Blackpool; Universities of Liverpool, Sorbonne, Leicester. To 1979, teacher and teacher trainer for French, Russian and EFL in Finland, E. Africa and England; from 1980, lecturer and researcher in Educational Theory and Philosophy, Edinburgh University; Founding Director, Graduate School in Social and Political Studies, Edinburgh University, 1993-99; Chair, SUCSE, 1988-92; Chair, Philosophy of Education Society GB, 1989-92, now Life Vice-President; Member, GTC;

Member, SCCC, 1992-96; many publications, including recent monograph Illusory Freedoms: Liberalism Education and the Market, 1997. Recreations: home and family (sole parent of son and two daughters); friends; gardening; chamber music; travel. Address: University of Edinburgh, South Bridge, Edinburgh; T.-0131-650 6323.

Jones, Professor Barry Thomas, BSc, PhD. Professor of Psychology, University of Glasgow, since 1996; b. 13.6.45, Normanby, Yorkshire; m., Anne Pilkington Sargeant; 2 s. Educ. Eston Grammar School; Durham University. SRC Postgraduate Student in Psychology, Edinburgh University; Lecturer in Psychology, St. Andrews University; Glasgow University: Lecturer then Senior Lecturer in Psychology. Editor, Portman Group's Quarterly Review of Alcohol Research. Recreations: hill-walking; sailing; music. Address: 43 Rowallan Gardens, Broomhill, Glasgow G11 7LH; T.-0141-579 1617.

Jones, Carole A., BA (Hons). Senior Reporter/Presenter, BBC Scotland, since 1996; b. 27.10.65, Dorchester. Educ. Largs Academy; University of Strathclyde. Westsound Radio, Ayr, 1989-90; Northsound Radio, Aberdeen, 1991-92; Radio Clyde, Glasgow, 1992-94; Border Television, Carlisle, 1994-95; joined BBC Scotland, 1995. Recreations: dining out (mostly); reading (always); gym (occasionally); dog walking (always). Address: (b.) Broadcasting House, Queen Margaret Drive, Glasgow; T.-0141-338 2444.

Jones, Professor Charles, MA, BLitt, FRSE. Forbes Professor of English Language, Edinburgh University, since 1990; b. 24.12.39, Glasgow; m., Isla Shennan. Educ. St. Aloysius College, Glasgow; Glasgow University. Lecturer in Linguistics, Hull University, 1964-67; Lecturer, Department of English Language, Edinburgh University, 1967-78; Professor of English Language, Durham University, 1978-90. Convenor, Scots Language Resource Centre Association, 1993-95; former Council Member, Saltire Society (Convenor, Education Committee); Member, Edinburgh University Court, 1993-96. Publications: An Introduction to Middle English; Phonological Structure and the History of English; Grammatical Gender in English; A History of English Phonology; A Treatise on the Provincial Dialect of Scotland (Editor); Historical Linguistics (Editor); A Language Suppressed; The Edinburgh History of the Scots Language (Editor). Recreation: breeding Soay sheep. Address: (h.) Laggan Cottage, Faladam, Midlothian, EH37 5SU; T.-01875 833 652.

Jones, Professor Hamlyn Gordon, MA (Cantab), PhD, FIHort. Professor of Plant Ecology, University of Dundee, since 1997; Honorary Research Professor, Scottish Crop Research Institute, Dundee, since 1998; b. 7.12.47, Kuala Lumpur, Malaysia; m., Amanda Jane Corry; 2 d. Educ. St. Lawrence College, Ramsgate; St. John's College, University of Cambridge; Australian National University, Canberra. Research Fellow, St. John's College, Cambridge, 1973-76; Researcher, Plant Breeding Institute, Cambridge, 1972-76; Lecturer in Ecology, University of Glasgow, 1977-78; Leader of Stress Physiology Group, East Malling Research Station, Kent, 1978-88; Director, Crop Science Research and Head of Station, Horticulture Research International, Wellesbourne, Warwick; Special Professor, University of Nottingham, 1991-97; Honorary Professor, University of Birmingham, 1995-98. Publications: Plants and Microclimate, 1983/1992; joint editor of four other books; on editorial board of six scientific journals. Recreations: squash; tennis; mountains; lounging. Address: (b.) Department of Biological Sciences, University of Dundee, Dundee DD1 4HN; T.-01382 344720.

Jones, Professor Huw, BA, MA. Professor of Geography and Dean, Faculty of Arts and Social Sciences, Dundee University; b. Llanidloes; 2 s. Educ. Newtown Boys Grammar School, Powys; University College of Wales, Aberystwyth. Editor, International Journal of Population Geography. Address: (b.) Department of Geography, Dundee University, Dundee DD1 4HN; T.-01382-344 427.

Jones, Keith Greig, LLB. Head of Law and Administration (North Division), Aberdeenshire Council, since 1996; b. 10.9.48, Edinburgh; m., Margaret. Educ. Aberdeen Grammar School; Aberdeen University. Various appointments in private legal practice, 1969-75; joined Law and Administration Department, Kincardine and Deeside District Council, 1975: Director of Legal Services and Depute Chief Executive, 1985-97. Trustee: Grampian Transport Museum Trust, Kinneff Old Church Preservation Trust, 1979-97. Address: (b.) St. Leonard's, Sandyhills Road, Banff.

Jones, Mark Ellis Powell, MA, FSA, FSA Scot. Director, National Museums of Scotland, since 1992; b. 5.2.51, Bogota; m., Dr. A.C. Toulmin; 2 s.; 2 d. Educ. Eton College; Oxford University; London University. Assistant Keeper of Coins and Medals, British Museum, 1974-90; Keeper of Coins and Medals, 1990-92. Founding Director, Scottish Cultural Resources Access Network (SCRAN); President, Fédération Internationale de la Médaille; Member, Royal Mint Advisory Committee; President, British Art Medal Society. Address: (h.) 39 Regent Street, Portobello, Edinburgh EH15 2AY; T.-0131-657 3335.

Jones, Professor Peter (Howard), MA, FRSE, FRSA, FSA Scot. Professor of Philosophy, University of Edinburgh, 1984-98; Director, Institute for Advanced Studies in the Humanities, since 1986; b. 18.12.35, London; m., Elizabeth Jean Roberton; 2 d. Educ. Highgate School; Queens' College, Cambridge. Regional Officer, The British Council, London, 1960-61; Research Scholar, University of Cambridge, 1961-63; Assistant Lecturer in Philosophy, Nottingham University, 1963-64; University of Edinburgh: Lecturer in Philosophy, 1964-77, Reader, 1977-84; Visiting Professor of Philosophy: University of Rochester, New York, 1969-70, Dartmouth College, New Hampshire, 1973, 1983, Carleton College, Minnesota, 1974, Oklahoma University, 1978, Baylor University, 1978, University of Malta, 1993; Distinguished Foreign Scholar, Mid-America State Universities, 1978; Visiting Fellow, Humanities Research Centre, Australian National University, 1984; Calgary Institute for the Humanities, 1992; Lothian Lecturer, 1993; Gifford Lecturer, University of Aberdeen, 1994-95; Loemker Lecturer, Emory University, 1996; Trustee: National Museums of Scotland, since 1987, University of Edinburgh Development Trust, 1990-98, Morrison's Academy, Crieff, 1984-98, Fettes College; Founder Member, The Hume Society, 1974. Publications: Philosophy and the Novel, 1975; Hume's Sentiments, 1982; A Hotbed of Genius, 1986; Philosophy and Science in the Scottish Enlightenment, 1988; The Science of Man in the Scottish Enlightenment, 1989; Adam Smith Reviewed, 1992. Recreations: opera; chamber music; the arts; architecture. Address: (b.) Institute for Advanced Studies in the Humanities, Hope Park Square, Edinburgh EH8 9NW; T.-0131-650 4671.

Jones, Philip Neville, MMS(Dip), EuroIE, MIMgt. Depute Chief Executive, Dumfries and Galloway Council, since 1995 (Head of Corporate Business, since 1995, Council Monitoring Officer, since 1997); Clerk to Children's Panel Advisory Committees, since 1996; b. 8.6.51; m., Jacqueline Fiona; 3 s. Educ. Kelsterton College, Deeside. Productivity Services Officer, Unilever, Port Sunlight, 1976-80; Dumfries and Galloway Regional Council: Assistant Regional Management Services Officer, 1980-86, Assistant Director Information Technology, 1986-89, Corporate Business Manager, 1989-96. Recreations: golf; gardening; walking. Address: Council Offices, English Street, Dumfries; T.-01387 260025.

Jones, Raymond J. Chief Executive, Royal Highland and Agricultural Society of Scotland, since 1998; b. 30.9.47,

Birmingham; m., Jean; 2 s.; 1 d. Educ. Lordswood; Harper Adams Agricultural College. Alfa-Laval; Unilever; Managing Director, LI Ireland, 1990-92; Regional Managing Director, Diverseylever, 1992-98. Recreations: walking; sailing. Address: (b.) Royal Highland Centre, Ingliston, Edinburgh EH28 8NF; T.-0131-335 6200.

Jones, Trevor, CPSA, FCCA, ACIS, MIMgt. General Manager, Lothian Health Board, since 1995; b. 23.12.50, Penshaw, Co. Durham; m., Hazel Oliver. Entered NHS, 1978; Northern Regional Health Authority; South Manchester Health Authority; Waltham Forest Health Authority; Chief Executive, Forest Healthcare NHS Trust, 1991-95. Recreations: golf; squash; Durham CCC; Sunderland AFC. Address: (b.) Lothian Health Board, 148 Pleasance, Edinburgh EH8 9RS; T.-0131-536 9001.

Jones, Rev. William Gerald, MA, BD, ThM. Minister, Kirkmichael with Straiton St. Cuthbert's, since 1985; Moderator, Presbytery of Ayr, 1997-98; b. 2.11.56, Irvine; m., Janet Blackstock. Educ. Dalry High School; Garnock Academy, Kilbirnie; Glasgow University; St. Andrews University; Princeton Theological Seminary, Princeton, New Jersey. Assistant Minister, Glasgow Cathedral, 1983-85. Freeman Citizen of Glasgow, 1984; Member, Incorporation of Gardeners of Glasgow, 1984; Convener, Administration Committee, Presbytery of Ayr, 1988-91; Member, Presbytery of Ayr ad hoc Committee on Doctrine and Worship, since 1998; Member: General Assembly Panel on Worship, 1987-91, Council, Church Service Society, 1986-98, Committee to Nominate the Moderator of the General Assembly, 1988-92 and since 1998, Societas Liturgica, since 1989; AssChLJ (Assistant Chaplain, Order of St. Lazarus of Jerusalem), 1995; Member, Society for Liturgical Study, since 1995. Publications: Prayers for the Chapel Royal in Scotland, 1989; Worshipping Together (Contributor), 1991; Common Order (Contributor), 1994. Recreations: music; liturgies; reading; writing. Address: The Manse, Kirkmichael, Maybole, Ayrshire KA19 7PJ; T.-01655 750286.

Jordan, Professor James Redmon, DipEE, DIC, MSc, PhD, FRSA, FIEE, FInstMC, CEng. Professor of Electronic Instrumentation and Head, Department of Electronics and Electrical Engineering, University of Edinburgh, since 1994; b. 5.6.38, Isleworth, Middlesex; m., Dr. Elizabeth Jordan; 2 d. Educ. Twickenham College of Technology; Imperial College; University of Surrey; University of Bradford. Student apprenticeship, EMI Electronics Ltd.; engineering experience of machine tool control and analogue computers, three years; research and teaching; Lecturer then Senior Lecturer, Department of Electrical Engineering, University of Edinburgh; EPSRC Information Technology Senior Fellow, then Professorial Fellow. Chairman, Management Board, Institute for System Level Integration; Director, Edinburgh Research and Innovation Ltd. Recreations: appreciating the visual arts; studying natural systems; reading poetry; playing classical and jazz piano. Address: (b.) The King's Buildings, Edinburgh EH9 3JL; T.-0131-650 5595.

Joseph, Professor John E., BA, MA, PhD, FRSA. Professor of Applied Linguistics and Head, Department of Applied Linguistics, University of Edinburgh, since 1997; b. 30.10.56, Monroe, Michigan, USA; m., Jeannette; 2 s. Educ. Monroe High School, Michigan; University of Michigan, Ann Arbor. Lecturer in Linguistics, Université Paul Valéry, Montpellier, France, 1980-81; Assistant then Associate Professor of French and Italian, Oklahoma State University, 1981-85; Visiting Associate Professor of French, University of Maine, 1986; Assistant, then Associate Professor of French and English Linguistics, University of Maryland at College Park, 1986-93; University Fellow, National Endowment for the Humanities, 1993; Camargo Foundation Fellow, Cassis, France, 1993; Professor of English Language and Linguistics and Head, Department of of English, University of Hong Kong, 1993-96. Publications: Eloquence and Power, 1987; Ideologies of Language (Co-Author), 1990; Linguistic Theory and Grammatical Description (Co-Author), 1991. Recreations: playing piano; reading literature and philosophy; theatre; concerts; swimming. Address: (b.) Department of Applied Linguistics, University of Edinburgh, Edinburgh EH8 9LN; T.-0131-650 3497.

Jowitt, Professor Paul William, PhD, DIC, BSc(Eng), ACGI, CEng, FICE. Professor of Civil Engineering Systems, Heriot-Watt University, since 1987 (Head, Civil Engineering Department, 1989-91; Head, Civil and Offshore Engineering, since 1991); Editor, Civil Engineering Systems, since 1985; b. 3.8.50, Doncaster; m., Jane Catriona Urquhart; 1 s.; 1 d. Educ. Maltby Grammar School; Imperial College. Lecturer in Civil Engineering, Imperial College 1974-86 (Warden, Falmouth Hall, 1980-86); Director, Tynemarch Systems Engineering Ltd., 1984-91 (Chairman, 1984-86). Recreations: painting; Morgan 3-wheelers; restoring old houses. Address: (h.) 14 Belford Mews, Edinburgh EH4 3BT; T.-0131-225 7583.

Jung, Roland Tadeusz, BA, MA, MB, BChir, MD, MRCS, LRCP, MRCP, FRCPEdin, FRCPLond. Consultant Physician (Specialist in Endocrinology and Diabetes), since 1982; Honorary Professor, Dundee University; Director, Research and Development for Tayside NHS Consortium, since 1997; b. 8.2.48, Glasgow; m., Felicity King; 1 d. Educ. St. Anselm's College, Wirral; Pembroke College, Cambridge; St. Thomas Hospital and Medical School, London. MRC Clinical Scientific Officer, Dunn Nutrition Unit, Cambridge, and Honorary Senior Registrar, Addenbrooke's Hospital, Cambridge, 1977-79; Senior Registrar in Endocrinology and Diabetes, Royal Postgraduate Medical School, Hammersmith Hospital, London, 1980-82; Clinical Director of General Medicine, Dundee Teaching Hospitals Trust, 1991-94. Publication: Endocrine Problems in Oncology (Co-Editor), 1984; Colour Atlas of Obesity, 1990. Recreation: gardening. Address: (b.) Diabetes Centre, Ninewells Hospital and Medical School, Dundee; T.-Dundee 660111.

Justice, David Brian, BSc. Chairman and Chief Executive Officer, Quality Scotland Foundation, since 1997; b. 1.7.35, Tain; m., Marion; 2 s. Educ. Boroughmuir Senior Secondary School; Edinburgh University. General Manager, Rank Hovis McDougal, 1959; IBM Scotland, 1962-71; General Manager, IBM Banking Systems, London, 1971-73; Manager IBM Scottish Branch, 1973-76; Industry Systems, IBM Europe Headquarters, 1976-80; Regional Operations Manager, IBM London, 1980-85; Public Sector Manager, IBM Scotland, 1985-90; Chief Executive Officer, Quality Scotland Foundation, 1990-97. Recreations: golf; wine. Address: 13 AbercrombyPlace, Edinburgh EH3 6LB; T.-0131-556 2333.

K

Kamm, Antony, MA. Author; b. 2.3.31, London; m., Eileen Dunlop (qv). Educ. Charterhouse; Worcester College, Oxford. Editorial Director, Brockhampton Press, 1960-72; Senior Education Officer, Commonwealth Secretariat, 1972-74; Managing Editor (Children's Books), Oxford University Press, 1977-79; Consultant to UNESCO and other international organisations, 1963-76; part-time Lecturer in Publishing Studies, Stirling University, 1988-95; Chairman, Children's Book Group, The Publishers Association, 1963-67, and of Children's Book Circle, 1963-64; played cricket for Middlesex, 1952. Publications include: Collins Biographical Dictionary of English Literature, 1993; The Romans: an Introduction, 1995; Wallace, Bruce, and the War of Independence, 1996; Scotland in Roman Times, 1998; several anthologies. Address: (h.) 46 Tarmangie Drive, Dollar FK14 7BP; T.-01259 742007.

Kane, Jack, OBE, JP, DL, Dr hc (Edin). Honorary Vice-President, Age Concern Scotland, since 1986; Honorary President: Workers Educational Association (SE Scotland), Craigmillar Festival Society, Jack Kane Centre; b. 1.4.11, Addiewell, Midlothian; m., Anne Murphy; 1 s.; 2 d. Educ. Bathgate Academy. Librarian, 1937-55; War Service, Royal Artillery, 1940-46; District Secretary, Workers Educational Association (SE Scotland), 1955-76; Chairman, South of Scotland Electricity Consultative Council, 1977-80; Chairman, Board of Trustees, National Galleries of Scotland, 1975-80; Councillor, Edinburgh, 1938-75 (Bailie, 1947-51, Lord Provost, 1972-75). Recreations: reading; writing.

Kane, Patrick Mark, MA (Hons). Writer and Broadcaster; b. 10.3.64, Glasgow; m., Joan McAlpine; 1 d. Educ. St. Ambrose RC Secondary, Coatbridge; Glasgow University. Worked in London as a freelance writer; returned to Scotland to start professional music career with brother Gregory; achieved Top 10 and Top 20 singles and albums successes with Hue and Cry, 1987-89; Columnist, The Herald; TV arts presenter; former Rector, Glasgow University. Recreations: being with family; listening to music; reading abstruse social theory.

Kaut-Howson, Helena, MA. Theatre and Opera Director, since 1969; Artistic Director, Communicado Theatre Company, since 1999; b. Lvov, Poland; m., Richard G. Howson; 1 s. Educ. Polish State Theatre Academy; Royal Academy of Dramatic Art, London; University of Warsaw, Poland. Company member, Polish State Theatre; Lecturer, University of Tel-Aviv; Staff Director, London Academy of Music and Dramatic Art; worked extensively as freelance director; Artistic Director, Theatr Clwyd, Wales. Associate, Royal Academy of Dramatic Art. Awards: Best Production: Liverpool Echo, 1992, Manchester Evening News, 1996, and 1997, TMA, 1995; Peter Brook Award, 1994. Recreations: travel; swimming; walking. Address: 2 Hill Street, Edinburgh EH2 3YZ; T.-0131-624 4040.

Kay, Stefan George, OBE, BSc, CEng, FIMechE, CIMgmt, FRSA. Group Managing Director, Inveresk PLC, since 1989; Non-Executive Director, Dunedin Enterprise Investment Trust PLC, since 1995; b. 25.7.44, Peebles; m., Helen Eugenia; 2 d. Educ. Holy Cross Academy; Heriot-Watt University. Graduate Trainee, Production Superintendent, Chief Chemist, Thames Board Ltd., 1967-73; Production Manager, Dexter Ltd., Berwickshire, 1973-78; Mill MD, St. Regis Paper Co. Ltd., Berkshire and Devon, 1979-88. Past President, Paper Federation of Great Britain; awarded paper industry Gold Medal, 1996; Chairman, Environment Committee, Confederation of European Paper Industries; Honorary President, Students' Association and Member, Court, Heriot-Watt University. Recreations: railway history; classical music. Address: (b.) Inveresk PLC, Group HQ, Kilbagie Mills, Alloa FK10 4AF; T.-01259 455000.

Kay, William, MA. Freelance Broadcaster/Writer/Producer; b. 24.9.51, Galston, Ayrshire; m., Maria Joao de Almeida da Cruz Dinis; 1 s.; 2 d. Educ. Galston High School; Kilmarnock Academy; Edinburgh University. Producer, Odyssey series, Radio Scotland; produced about 40 documentaries on diverse aspects of working-class oral history; Writer/Presenter, TV documentaries, including Miners, BBC Scotland; Presenter, Kay's Originals, Scottish TV. Commandeur d'Honneur, Commanderie du Bontemps de Medoc et des Graves; won Australasian Academy of Broadcast Arts and Sciences Pater award, 1987, 1988; Medallist, International Radio Festival of New York, 1990-92; Sloan Prize for writing in Scots, 1992; Wine Guild of UK 1994 Houghton Award, for Fresche Fragrant Clairettis; Winner: Heritage Society Award, 1995, Wines of France Award, 1996. Publications: Odyssey: Voices from Scotland's Recent Past (Editor); Odyssey: The Second Collection (Editor); Knee Deep in Claret: A Celebration of Wine and Scotland (Co-author); Made in Scotland (poetry); Jute (play for radio); Scots — The Mither Tongue; They Fairly Mak Ye Work (for Dundee Repertory Theatre); Lucky's Strike (play for radio); The Dundee Book. Recreations: the weans; languages; films; Dundee United. Address: (h.) 72 Tay Street, Newport on Tay, Fife DD6 8AP.

Kaye, Professor Stanley Bernard, BSc, MD, FRCP (Glas, Edin, Lond). CRC Professor of Medical Oncology, University of Glasgow, since 1986; b. 5.9.48, Leeds; m., Anna; 2 s.; 1 d. Educ. Roundhay School, Leeds; Charing Cross Hospital Medical School; University of London. Junior hospital posts, London, 1972-80; Staff Specialist, Sydney, Australia, 1980; Senior Lecturer, Department of Medical Oncology, Glasgow, 1981-85. Chairman of scientific/clinical committees, Cancer Research Campaign, European Organisation for Research and Treatment of Cancer. Publications: 280 peer-reviewed papers relating to cancer therapy. Recreations: various sports, including tennis, golf and football. Address: (b.) Department of Medical Oncology, Garscube Estate, Glasgow G61 1BD; T.-0141-330 4884.

Kayne, Steven Barry, PhD, MBA, LLM, BSc, MRPharmS, FCPP, DAgVetPharm, LFHom(Pharm), MPS(NZ), ACNZP, MIPharmM, MBIM. Consultant Homoeopathic and Veterinary Pharmacist; medical journalist; b. 8.6.44, Cheltenham Spa; m., Sorelle; 2 s. Educ. Westcliff High School; Aston University; Strathclyde University; Glasgow University; University of Wales. Lecturer; Visiting Lecturer, University of Strathclyde School of Pharmacy; Pharmacy Tutor to UK Faculty of Homoeopathy; Member: Academic Board, UK Faculty of Homoeopathy; Council, British Homoeopathic Association; Pharmacy Practice Adjudication Panel, British Pharmaceutical Conference; Government Advisory Board on Homoeopathic Registration; Homoeopathic Research Committee; Pharmaceutical Advisor, Epilepsy Association Scotland. Publication: Homoeopathic Pharmacy, 1997; People are Pets (Co-author), 1998. Recreations: walking in Spey Valley; watching rugby; photography. Address: (h.) 79 Milverton Road, Whitecraigs, Giffnock, Glasgow; T.-0141-638 3216.

Keane, Sheriff Francis Joseph, PhL, LLB. Sheriff of Tayside, Central and Fife, at Kirkcaldy, since 1993; b. 5.1.36, Broxburn; m., Lucia Corio Morrison; 2 s.; 1 d. Educ. Blairs College, Aberdeen; Gregorian University, Rome; Edinburgh University. Partner, McCluskey, Keane & Co., 1959; Procurator Fiscal Depute, Perth, 1961, Edinburgh, 1963; Senior PF Depute, Edinburgh, 1971; Senior Legal Assistant, Crown Office, Edinburgh, 1972; Procurator

Fiscal, Airdrie, 1976; Regional Procurator Fiscal, South Strathclyde, Dumfries and Galloway, 1980; Sheriff of Glasgow and Strathkelvin, 1984-93; Sheriff of Lothians and Borders, 1993-98; President, Procurators Fiscal Society, 1982-84. Recreations: music; tennis; walking; painting. Address: (b.) Sheriff Court House, Whytescauseway, Kirkcaldy KY1 1XQ; T.-01592 260171.

Keane, Rev. Martin C., BA, BD. Minister, Lossiemouth United Free Church of Scotland, since 1989; Clerk to Presbytery of the North, United Free Church of Scotland, since 1998; b. 6.3.64, Glasgow; m., Margaret Adams; 1 s.; 2 d. Educ. Govan High School, Glasgow; Glasgow College of Technology; University of Glasgow. Address: 49 James Street, Lossiemouth, Moray.

Keane, Professor Simon Michael, MA, LLB, PhD, CA. Professor of Accountancy, Glasgow University, since 1983; b. 8.4.35, Glasgow; m., Mary; 1 d. Educ. St. Aloysius College; Glasgow University. Investigating Accountant, Admiralty, 1965-67; Lecturer, Glasgow College of Commerce, 1967-69; Glasgow University: Lecturer, 1969-81, Reader, 1981-83. Publications: Efficient Market Hypothesis, 1980; Stock Market Efficiency, 1983. Recreations: golf; painting. Address: (b.) 67 Southpark Avenue, Glasgow G12; T.-0141-339 8855.

Kearney, Sheriff Brian, MA, LLB. Sheriff of Glasgow and Strathkelvin, since 1977; b. 25.8.35.

Kearns, Mary Elizabeth, LLB(Hons), DipLP, DipTA. Consultant, Brodies W.S., Solicitors, since 1997 (Partner, 1995-97); Accredited Employment Law Specialist, since 1995; Solicitor Advocate, since 1995; b. 25.4.61, London; m., Dr. Patrick Kearns; 2 s.; 2 d. Educ. St. Georges School, Harpenden, Hertfordshire; University of Edinburgh. Trainee Solicitor, W. & J. Burness W.S., Edinburgh, 1986-88; Brodies W.S., Edinburgh: Assistant Solicitor, 1988-93, Associate, 1993-95. Nominated by Secretary of State for Scotland to General Teaching Council for Scotland, 1995; Scottish Representative, Employment Lawyers' Association, 1996; Member, Scottish Council on Bioethics. Recreation: hill-walking. Address: (b.) 15 Atholl Crescent, Edinburgh EH3 8HA; T.-0131-228 3777.

Kee, Professor A. Alistair, MA, BD, STM, PhD, DLitt. Professor of Religious Studies, Edinburgh University; b. 17.4.37, Alexandria; m., Anne Paterson; 1 s.; 1 d. Educ. Clydebank High School; Glasgow University; Union Theological Seminary, New York. Lecturer: University College of Rhodesia, 1964-67, Hull University, 1967-76; Glasgow University: Senior Lecturer, then Reader (Head, Department of Religious Studies, 1976-88); Visiting Professor: Augusta College, Georgia, 1982-83, Dartmouth College, New Hampshire, 1990,1995; Director, SCM Press Ltd.; delivered Jaspers Lectures, Ripon Hall, Oxford, 1975; Ferguson Lectures, Manchester University, 1986. Publications: The Way of Transcendence; A Reader in Political Theology; Constantine Versus Christ; Being and Truth; Domination or Liberation; The Roots of Christian Freedom; Marx and the Failure of Liberation Theology; From Bad Faith to Good News. Address: (b.) Department of Theology and Religious Studies, Edinburgh University, New College, Mound Place, Edinburgh EH1 2LX; T.-0131-650 8953.

Keeble, Professor Neil Howard, BA, DPhil, DLitt, FRHistS. Professor of English, Stirling University, since 1995; b. 7.8.44, London; m., Jenny Bowers; 2 s.; 1 d. Educ. Bancroft's School, Woodford Green; St. David's College, Lampeter; Pembroke College, Oxford. Foreign Lektor, Department of English, University of Aarhus, Denmark, 1969-72; Lecturer in English, Aarhus, 1972-74; Lecturer in English, Stirling University, 1974-88; Reader in English, Stirling University, 1988-95. Publications: Richard Baxter: Puritan Man of Letters; The Literary Culture of Nonconformity in later seventeenth-century England; The Autobiography of Richard Baxter (Editor); The Pilgrim's Progress (Editor); John Bunyan: Coventicle and Parnassus (Editor); A Handbook of English and Celtic Studies in the United Kingdom and the Republic of Ireland (Editor); The Cultural Identity of Seventeenth-Century Woman (Editor); Lucy Hutchinson, Memoirs of the Life of Colonel Hutchinson (Editor); Calendar of the Correspondence of Richard Baxter (Co-Compiler). Recreations: books and book-collecting; films; the Midi; gardening. Address: Duncraggan House, Airthrey Road, Stirling FK9 5JS; T.-01786 473758.

Keen, Richard Sanderson, LLB (Hons). Queen's Counsel; b. 29.3.54, Rustington; m., Jane Carolyn Anderson; 1 s.; 1 d. Educ. King's School, Rochester; Dollar Academy; Edinburgh University (Beckman Scholar). Admitted to Faculty of Advocates, 1980; Standing Junior Counsel in Scotland to DTI, 1986-93; QC, 1993; Chairman, Appeals Committee, Institute of Chartered Accountants of Scotland. Recreations: golf; skiing; shooting; opera. Address: (b.) Parliament House, Parliament Square, Edinburgh; T.-0131-226 5071; (h.) The Castle, Elie, Fife; 39 Ann Street, Edinburgh.

Keenan, Thomas Gibson. Executive Director, Social Work and Housing Services, Inverclyde Council, since 1998; b. 18.11.54; m., Carol Keenan. Educ. Holy Cross High School; Strathclyde University; Bell College of Technology. Clerical Officer, Strathclyde Regional Council, 1975; Lanarkshire Health Board, 1978-81; Motherwell District Council, 1981-88; Kyle and Carrick District Council: Depute Director of Housing, 1988, Head of Housing, 1991; Director of Housing and Customer Services, Inverclyde Council, 1996. Chair, Association of Chief Housing Officers; Member, Management Committee, Clyde Housing Association. Recreations: football; golf; reading current affairs. Address: (b.) Inverclyde Council, Wallace Place, Greenock; T.-01475 712502.

Keighley, Brian Douglas, MB, ChB, FRCGP. General Practitioner Principal, Balfron, since 1975; Chairman, Scottish General Medical Services Committee (BMA), 1995-98; Chairman, Joint Committee on Postgraduate Training for General Practice; b. 21.5.48, Glasgow; m., Ruth Patricia Maguire; 2 s. Educ. Glasgow Academy; Glasgow University. House Officer, Law Hospital, Stobhill Hospital, 1972-73; SHO, Robroyston Hospital, 1973; SHO, Falkirk Royal Infirmary, 1974; Trainee GP, Balfron, 1974. Member: GMSC (UK) since 1992, General Medical Council, since 1994, Scottish Council for Postgraduate Medical and Dental Education (Chairman, Audit Committee), BMA Scottish Council, BMA Council, National Medical Advisory Committee. Publication: Guide to Postgraduate Medical Education, 1996. Recreations: reading; politics; angling; jogging; squash. Address: (h.) Hector Cottage, Banker's Brae, Balfron G63 0PY; T.-01360 440520.

Keir, Professor Hamish Macdonald, BSc, PhD, DSc, CBiol, FIBiol, CChem, FRSC, FRSE. Professor of Biochemistry, Aberdeen University, 1968-96 (Vice-Principal, 1982-84); Vice-Chairman, Governors, Macaulay Land Use Research Institute, since 1987; b. 5.9.31, Moffat; m., 1, Eleanor Campbell; 1 s.; 2 d.; 2, Linda Gerrie; 2 d.; 3, Evelyn Cook. Educ. Ayr Academy; Glasgow University; Yale University. Hon. Secretary, The Biochemical Society, 1970-77, Chairman, 1986-89; Member, Cell Board, Medical Research Council, 1970-74; Scottish Home and Health Department, BRC, 1974-78; Ethical and Research Committees, Grampian Health Board; Science and Engineering Research Council (Biology), 1980-84; University Grants Committee (Biology), 1984-90; Royal Society — British National Committee for Biochemistry, 1986-90; Board of Governors: North of Scotland College of Agriculture, 1976-91, Longridge Towers School, since

1988; Tenovus — Scotland, Grampian Region, 1980-86; Committees of the International Union of Biochemistry, 1974-82; Chairman: Natural Environment Research Council, Institute of Marine Biochemistry, 1969-84, Universities of Scotland Purchasing Consortium, 1988-96, Board of Governors, Rowett Research Institute, 1989-93; President, European Union of Societies for Experimental Biology, 1989-96; European Science Foundation, since 1989; President, Council, Federation of European Biochemical Societies, 1980-83; Member, Executive, Ross, Skye and Inverness West Conservative and Unionist Association, since 1996. Recreations: piano; politics; travel. Address: (b.) Institute of Medical Sciences, University of Aberdeen, Aberdeen AB25 2ZD; T.-01224 273121; (h.) Dundalachie, The Black Isle, Ross and Cromarty IV10 8TB; T.-01381 621239.

Kelbie, Sheriff David, LLB (Hons); Sheriff of Grampian, Highland and Islands, at Aberdeen and Stonehaven, since 1986 (North Strathclyde, at Dumbarton, 1979-86); b. 28.2.45, Inverurie; m., Helen Mary Smith; 1 s.; 1 d. Educ. Inverurie Academy; Aberdeen University. Passed Advocate, 1968; Associate Lecturer, Heriot-Watt University, 1971-76; Secretary, Scottish Congregational College, 1974-82; Member, UK/Ireland Committee of Christian Aid, 1986-90; Member, Scottish Christian Aid Committee, 1986-95; Editor, Scottish Civil Law Reports, 1996-98. Recreations: sailing; reading; music. Address: (h.) 38 Earlspark Drive, Bieldside, Aberdeen.

Kellas, Professor James Grant, MA, PhD, FRHistS. Professor in Politics, Glasgow University, since 1984; b. 16.5.36, Aberdeen; m., Norma Rennie Craig; 2 s.; 1 d. Educ. Aberdeen Grammar School; Aberdeen University; London University. Tutorial Fellow in History, Bedford College, London University, 1961-62; Assistant in History, Aberdeen University, 1962-64; Glasgow University: Lecturer in Politics, 1964-73; Senior Lecturer, 1973-77, Reader, 1977-84. Member, Study of Parliament Group. Publications: Modern Scotland, 1968, 1980; The Scottish Political System, 1973, 1975, 1984, 1989; The Politics of Nationalism and Ethnicity, 1991, 1998. Recreations: mountaineering; music. Address: (b.) Department of Politics, Glasgow University, Glasgow G12 8RT; T.-0141-339 8855.

Kelly, Barbara Mary, CBE, DL, LLD, DipEd. President, Rural Forum Scotland; Member, Broadcasting Council for Scotland; Member, Board, Scottish Natural Heritage (Chair, South West Region); Member, Scottish Advisory Board, BP plc; Chairman, Architects' Registration Board; Director, Scottish Post Office Board; Convenor, Priority Fund Areas; Director, Clydesdale Bank plc; Convener, Millennium Forest for Scotland Trust; Trustee, Caledonian Foundation; Partner in dairy farming enterprise; b. 27.2.40, Dalbeattie; m., Kenneth A. Kelly; 1 s.; 2 d. Educ. Dalbeattie High School; Kirkcudbright Academy; Moray House College. Past Chairman, Scottish Consumer Council; former Member: Scottish Economic Council, National Consumer Council, Scottish Enterprise Board, Scottish Tourist Board, Priorities Board, MAFF; former Vice-Chairman, SWRI; Duke of Edinburgh's Award: former Chairman, Scottish Advisory Committee and former Member, UK Advisory Panel; former EOC Commissioner for Scotland; Past Chairman, Dumfries and Galloway Area Manpower Board, Manpower Services Commission. Recreations: painting; music. Address: (h.) Barncleugh, Irongray, Dumfries DG2 9SE; T.-01387 730210.

Kelly, Lt. Col. John Lewis, MBE, BSc(Hons). Regimental Secretary, Royal Highland Fusiliers, since 1997; b. 9.7.50, Glasgow; m., Alison; 1 s.; 1 d. Educ. Allan Glen's School, Glasgow; Glasgow University. Regular Army Officer, Royal Highland Fusiliers, 1974-97. Deputy Commandant, Glasgow and Lanark Battalion ACF; City and Guilds Insignia Award. Recreation: keeping the house up and the garden down. Address: (b.) 518 Sauchiehall Street, Glasgow G2 3LW; T.-0141-332 5639.

Kelly, Professor John Shearer, BSc, MB ChB, PhD, MA, FRSE, FRCPE. Professor of Pharmacology, University of Edinburgh, since 1985; Director, Fujisawa Institute of Neuroscience, since 1992; b. 3.3.37, Edinburgh; m., E. Anne Wilkin; 1 s.; 1 d. Educ. George Heriot's School, Edinburgh; University of Edinburgh. House Physician, Western General Hospital, Edinburgh, 1962; House Surgeon, Royal Hospital for Sick Children, Edinburgh, 1963; University of Edinburgh, Department of Pharmacology: Assistant Lecturer, 1963-65, Lecturer, 1965-68; McGill University, Canada: Wellcome Post-doctoral Fellow, Department of Research in Anaesthesia, 1967-68, Canadian Medical Research Council Scholar and Assistant Professor, Departments of Research in Anaesthesia and Physiology, 1968-71; IBRO Research Fellow, University of Geneva, 1970; MRC Scientific Staff, Department of Pharmacology, Cambridge, 1971-79; Fellow of King's College, Cambridge and Lecturer in Pharmacology and Neurobiology, 1976-79; Professor and Chairman, Pharmacology, St. George's Hospital Medical School, London, 1979-85. Publications: 121 papers on neuroscience; 59 book chapters; 207 abstracts. Recreations: Japan; classical music; Scottish restaurants; sailing; Scottish outdoors. Address: (b.) Department of Neuroscience, 1 George Square, Edinburgh EH8 9JZ; T.-0131-650 3519.

Kelly, Michael, CBE (1983), OStJ, JP, BSc(Econ), PhD, LLD, DL, FCIM. Public Relations Consultant, since 1984; Honorary Vice-President, Children 1st, since 1996 (Chairman, Royal Scottish Society for the Prevention of Cruelty to Children, 1987-96); Secretary, Scottish Industry Forum, since 1995; Member, National Arts Collection Fund, since 1990; Columnist, The Scotsman; b. 1.11.40, Glasgow; m., Zita Harkins; 1 s.; 2 d. Educ. St. Joseph's College, Dumfries. Assistant Lecturer in Economics, Aberdeen University, 1965-67; Lecturer in Economics, Strathclyde University, 1967-80; Lord Provost of Glasgow, 1980-84; Rector, Glasgow University, 1984-87; Director, Drumkinnon Development Company; British Tourist Authority Medal for services to tourism, 1984; Robert Burns Award from University of Old Dominion, Virginia, for services to Scottish culture, 1984; Scot of the Year, 1983; Radio Scotland News Quiz Champion, 1986, 1987; Radio Scotland Christmas Quiz Champion, 1987; Honorary Mayor of Tombstone, Arizona; Kentucky Colonel, 1983. Publications: Paradise Lost: the struggle for Celtic's soul, 1994; London Lines: the capital by underground, 1996. Recreations: philately; golf. Address: (b.) 50 Aytoun Road, Pollokshields, Glasgow G41 5HE.

Kelly, Patrick Joseph, BSc, CEng, MICE. Scottish Officer, Public Services, Tax and Commerce Union, since 1986; Treasurer, STUC General Council; Director, Lothian and Edinburgh Enterprise, since 1992; b. 26.10.50, Glasgow; m., Rhona; 1 s.; 3 d. Educ. St. Mungo's Academy, Glasgow; Glasgow University. Civil Engineer, Central Regional Council, 1973-86; full-time trade union official, since 1986. Member, Executive, European Federation of Agricultural Workers; Member, Management Committee, War on Want. Recreations: golf; sailing; football. Address: (b.) 6 Hillside Crescent, Edinburgh EH7 5DZ; T.-0131-556 0407.

Kelly, Robert Fraser, MA (Hons). Rector, Berwickshire High School, since 1998; b. 8.11.47, Glasgow; m., Norma; 2 d. Educ. Knightswood Secondary School, Glasgow; University of Glasgow; Jordanhill College of Education. Teacher of Modern Languages, Allan Glen's School, Glasgow, 1971-76; Assistant Principal Teacher, Hamilton Grammar School, Hamilton; Ballerup High School, East Kilbride: Principal Teacher, 1978-88, Assistant Head, 1988-94, Depute Head, 1994-97. Recreations: hillwalking;

gardening; reading. Address: Berwickshire High School, Duns, Berwickshire TD11 3QQ; T.-01361 883710.

Kelly, Tom. Chief Officer, Association of Scottish Colleges, since 1996; b. 4.5.49, Loughborough. Educ. Hinckley Grammar School; Clare College, Cambridge. Home Civil Service, 1970-96; Head, Higher Education Division, Scottish Office, 1992-96. Address: (b.) Argyll Court, Castle Business Park, Stirling FK9 4TY; T.-01786 892100.

Kelman, James. Novelist; b. 1946, Glasgow. Works include: The Busconductor Hines; A Chancer; Greyhound for Breakfast; A Disaffection; How Late It Was How Late (Booker Prize, 1994).

Kelnar, Christopher J.H., MA, MD, FRCP, FRCPCH, DCH. Consultant Paediatric Endocrinologist, Royal Hospital for Sick Children, Edinburgh, since 1983; Senior Lecturer, Department of Child Life and Health, Edinburgh University, since 1983; b. 22.12.47, London; m., Alison; 1 s.; 2 d. Educ. Highgate School, London; Trinity College, Cambridge; St. Bartholomew's Hospital, London. Research Fellow, Paediatric Endocrinology, Middlesex Hospital, London, 1979-81; Senior Registrar, Hospital for Sick Children, Great Ormond Street, London, and Tutor, Institute of Child Health, London, 1981-83. Publications: The Sick Newborn Baby, 1981 (3rd edition, 1995); Childhood and Adolescent Diabetes, 1995; Growth Disorders, 1998; chapters and papers on paediatric endocrinology. Recreations: music; gardening. Address: (b.) Royal Hospital for Sick Children, Sciennes Road, Edinburgh EH9 1LF; T.-0131-536 0000.

Kelso, David Elliot, BSc, MEd, FIPD. HM Chief Inspector, Scottish Office Education and Industry Department; b. 25.3.45, Glasgow; m., Dorothy Louise Christie; 1 s.; 2 d. Educ. St. Joseph's College, Dumfries; Edinburgh University; Glasgow University; Dundee University. Personnel Officer, Singer (UK) Ltd., Clydebank, 1968-69; Personnel Manager, Rank Organisation, Kirkcaldy, 1969-71; Lecturer in Management, Glasgow College, 1971-73; Senior Lecturer, Dundee College of Commerce, 1973-76; Head, Department of Commerce and Business Studies, Falkirk College, 1976-83; Assistant Principal, 1983-85; HMI, 1985. Recreations: running; esperanto; hill-walking. Address: (h.) Lomond, St. Mary's Drive, Dunblane, Perthshire; T.-01786 822605.

Kemp, Alexander, LLB (Hons), DipLP, NP. Solicitor; Partner, Burnside Kemp Fraser, since 1994; b. 8.2.59, London; m., Myra; 2 s.; 2 d. Educ. Robert Gordon's College; The Perse School; Aberdeen University. Solicitor in Aberdeen, since 1983; Partner, Philip and Kemp, 1987-94; Secretary, Legal Groups, offshore oil industry disasters, Chinook, 1986, Piper Alpha, 1988, Brent Spar, 1990, Cormorant Alpha, 1992; accredited Specialist in Employment Law; Member, Assessment Committee for Personal Injury Panel. Recreations: golf; music. Address: 4 Queen's Terrace, Aberdeen AB10 1XL; T.-01224 624602.

Kemp, Professor Alexander George, MA (Hons). Professor of Economics, Aberdeen University, since 1983; Member, Energy Advisory Panel to UK Minister of Energy, since 1993; b. Blackhall, Drumoak, Aberdeenshire. Educ. Robert Gordon's College, Aberdeen; Aberdeen University. Economist, Shell International Petroleum, London, 1962-64; Lecturer in Economics, Strathclyde University, 1964-65; Lecturer, then Senior Lecturer, then Reader, Aberdeen University, 1966-83. Specialist Adviser to House of Commons Select Committee on Energy, 1980-92; Member, Energy Advisory Panel to UK Minister for Energy. Publications: 150 books and papers on petroleum economics. Address: (b.) Department of Economics, King's College, Aberdeen AB24 3QY.

Kemp, Arnold, MA. Editor, The Herald, 1981-94; b. 15.2.39; 2 d. Educ. Edinburgh Academy; Edinburgh University. Sub-Editor: The Scotsman, 1959-62, The Guardian, 1962-65; The Scotsman: Production Editor, 1965-70, London Editor, 1970-72, Deputy Editor, 1972-81. Publication: The Hollow Drum, 1993. Recreations: music; reading; theatre.

Kemp, Professor Peter Anthony, BSc(Hons), MPhil, DPhil. Professor of Housing and Urban Studies, University of Glasgow, since 1996; Director, ESRC Centre for Housing Research, since 1996; b. 25.12.55, Romford; 2 d. Educ. University of Southampton; University of Glasgow; University of Sussex. Researcher, SHAC (London Housing Aid Centre), 1983-85; Research Fellow, ESRC Centre for Housing Research, University of Glasgow, 1985-87; Lecturer in Housing Studies, University of Salford, 1987-90; Joseph Rowntree Professor of Housing Policy and Director, Centre for Housing Policy, University of York, 1990-95. Publications include: The Private Provision of Rented Housing, 1988; Tax Incentives and the Revival of Private Renting, 1991; Housing and Social Policy, 1990; Single Homeless People, 1993; Managing Social Housing, 1993; Housing Benefit: an appraisal, 1992; A Comparative Study of Housing Allowances, 1997. Recreation: cycling. Address: (b.) Department of Urban Studies, University of Glasgow, 25 Bute Gardens, Glasgow G12 8RS; T.-0141-330 3665.

Kempton, Rodney Alistair, MA, BPhil, CStat. Director, Biomathematics and Statistics Scotland (formerly Scottish Agricultural Statistics Service), since 1986; b. 2.7.46, London; m., Annelise; 2 s.; 1 d. Educ. Chislehurst and Sidcup Grammar School; Wadham College, Oxford. Rothamsted Experimental Station, Harpenden, 1970-76; Head, Statistics Department, Plant Breeding Institute, Cambridge, 1976-86. President, British Region, International Biometric Society, 1994-96. Recreations: hill-walking; cycling. Address: (b.) BioSS, The King's Buildings, Edinburgh University, Edinburgh EH9 3JZ; T.-0131-650 4902.

Kendell, Robert Evan, CBE, MD, FRCP, FRCPsych. President, Royal College of Psychiatrists; Chief Medical Officer, Scottish Office Home and Health Department, 1991-96; b. 28.3.35, Rotherham; m., Ann Whitfield; 2 s.; 2 d. Educ. Mill Hill School; Cambridge University; King's College Hospital Medical School. Visiting Professor, University of Vermont College of Medicine, 1969-70; Reader in Psychiatry, Institute of Psychiatry, London University, 1970-74; Professor of Psychiatry, Edinburgh University, 1974-91, and Dean, Faculty of Medicine, 1986-90. Gaskell Medal, Royal College of Psychiatrists, 1967; Paul Hoch Medal, American Psychopathological Association, 1988; Marcé Society Medal, 1994; Fellow, Royal Society of Edinburgh, 1993; Honorary Fellow: Royal College of Surgeons of Edinburgh, since 1995, Royal College of Physicians and Surgeons of Glasgow, since 1995. Publications: The Classification of Depressive Illnesses, 1968; The Role of Diagnosis in Psychiatry, 1975; Companion to Psychiatric Studies (Editor), 1983, 1988, 1993. Recreations: walking up hills; overeating. Address: (h.) 3 West Castle Road, Edinburgh EH10 5AT.

Kendle, Professor Keith Emery, BPharm (Hons), PHD, MRPharmS. Professor of Clinical Pharmacy, Robert Gordon University, since 1992; b. 24.8.41, Hetton-Le-Hole. Educ. Houghton Le Spring Grammar School; School of Pharmacy, London University. Endocrinologist,. then Deputy Head of Endocrinology, BDH Research Ltd.; Senior Lecturer, Robert Gordon's Institute of Technology. Recreations: hill-walking; music. Address: (b.) School of Pharmacy, Robert Gordon University, Schoolhill, Aberdeen; T.-01224 262537.

Kennedy, Alison Louise, BA (Hons). Writer; b. 22.10.65, Dundee. Educ. High School of Dundee; Warwick University. Community Arts Worker, 1988-89; Writer in Residence, Project Ability, 1989-94; Writer in Residence, Hamilton/East Kilbride Social Work Department, 1990-92; fiction critic for Scotsman, etc.; Booker Prize Judge, 1996; five S.A.C. book awards; Saltire Best First Book Award; Saltire Best Book Award; John Llewellyn Rees/Mail on Sunday Prize; listed, Sunday Times Best of Young British Novelists; Encore Award; Festival Fringe First; Social Work Today Award. Publications: Night Geometry; Garscadden Trains; Looking for the Possible Dance; Now That You're Back; So I Am Glad; Original Bliss; The Life and Death of Colonel Blimp (essay); The Audition (play); Stella Does Tricks (film); Delicate (performance piece). Recreations: cinema; clarinet; fencing.

Kennedy, (Alistair James) Spencer, MA, LLB, SSC, NP. Partner, Balfour & Manson, since 1991; b. 3.5.45, Dumfries; m., Joan Margaret Whitelaw. Educ. Royal High School of Edinburgh; Edinburgh University. Estate Duty Office, 1965-68; Connell & Connell, 1968-70; Nightingale & Bell, SSC, 1970-90; Past President, Society of Solicitors in the Supreme Courts of Scotland. Recreations: hill-walking; horticulture. Address: (b.) 58 Frederick Street, Edinburgh EH2 1LS; T.-0131-200 1240.

Kennedy, Professor Angus Johnston, MA, PhD, Officier dans l'Ordre des Palmes Academiques. Stevenson Professor of French Language and Literature, Glasgow University; b. 9.8.40, Port Charlotte; m., Marjory McCulloch Shearer; 2 d. Educ. Bearsden Academy; Glasgow University. Glasgow University: Assistant Lecturer in French, 1965, then Lecturer, Senior Lecturer, Reader; former Secretary, British Branch, International Arthurian Society. Publications: books on Christine de Pizan. Address: (b.) French Department, Glasgow University, Glasgow; T.-0141-339 8855.

Kennedy, Professor Arthur Colville, CBE, MD, FRCP(Lond), FRCPE, FRCP(Glas), FRCPI, FRSE, FACP(Hon.), FRACP (Hon.). Consultant Physician, Royal Infirmary, Glasgow, 1959-88; Muirhead Professor of Medicine, Glasgow University, 1978-88; President, Royal College of Physicians and Surgeons of Glasgow, 1986-88; b. 22.10.22, Edinburgh; m., Agnes White Taylor; 1 s. (deceased); 2 d. Educ. Whitehill School, Glasgow; Glasgow University. Medical Officer, RAFVR, 1946-48; junior NHS posts, 1948-57; Lecturer in Medicine, Glasgow University, 1957; Senior Lecturer, 1961; Reader, 1966; Titular Professor, 1969; responsible for establishment of Kidney Unit, Glasgow Royal Infirmary, 1959; Chairman, MRC Working Party in Glomerulonephritis, 1976-88; Member, Executive Committee, National Kidney Research Fund, 1976-83; Expert Adviser to WHO on Renal Disease; Adviser to EEC on Nephrology in Developing Countries; Chairman, Professional and Linguistic Assessments Board (PLAB), GMC, 1987-89; President: Royal Medico-Chirurgical Society of Glasgow, 1971-72, European Dialysis and Transplant Association, 1972-75, Scottish Society of Physicians, 1983-84, Harveian Society of Edinburgh, 1985; Member: Greater Glasgow Health Board, 1985-89, General Medical Council, 1989-92; President, British Medical Association, 1991-92. Recreations: gardening; walking; reading; photography. Address: (h.) 16 Boclair Crescent, Bearsden, Glasgow G61 2AG; T.-0141-942 5326.

Kennedy, Charles Peter, MA (Hons). MP (SLD, formerly SDP), Ross, Cromarty and Skye, since 1983, Ross, Skye and Inverness West, since 1997; Liberal Democrat Spokesman on Agriculture and Rural Affairs, since 1997; b. 25.11.59, Inverness. Educ. Lochaber High School, Fort William; Glasgow University; Indiana University. President, Glasgow University Union, 1980-81; Winner, British Observer Mace for Student Debating, 1982; Journalist, BBC Highland, Inverness, 1982; Fulbright Scholar, Indiana University (Bloomington Campus), 1982-83. Chairman, SDP Council for Scotland, 1986-88; SDP Spokesman on Health and Social Services, and Scotland, 1983-87; Alliance Election Spokesman, Social Security, Jan.-June, 1987; Member, Select Committee on Social Services, 1985-87; SLD Interim Joint Spokesman, Social Security, 1988; SLD Spokesman, Trade and Industry, 1988-89; President, Liberal Democrats, 1989-94; Liberal Democrat Spokesman: Health, 1989-92, Europe, 1992-97; Member: Select Committee on House of Commons Televising, 1988, Standards and Privileges Committee, since 1997. Recreations: reading; writing. Address: (b.) House of Commons, London SW1A 0AA; T.-0171-219 5090.

Kennedy, Garfield. Chief Executive, Gosh Films (formerly Garfield Kennedy Company), since 1984; b. 21.8.51, Belfast; m., Carrie Rolls; 2 d. Educ. Coleraine Academical Institution; Edinburgh University. Reporter, Radio Forth, 1975; Television Researcher, Granada TV, 1975-78; Associate Producer, Anglia TV, 1978-81; Television Producer/Director, TVS, responsible for four series of science series, The Real World, 1981-84; Producer and Director, The Garfield Kennedy Company, 1984-97. Science Writer of the Year, 1988. Recreations: cycling; skiing; hill-walking. Address: (b.) 420 Sauchiehall Street, Glasgow G2 3JD; T.-0141-353 0456.

Kennedy, Professor Gavin, BA, MSc, PhD, FCIM. Professor, Edinburgh Business School, Heriot-Watt University; Managing Director, Negotiate Ltd., Edinburgh; b. 20.2.40, Collingham, Yorkshire; m., Patricia Anne; 1 s.; 2 d. Educ. London Nautical School; Strathclyde University. Lecturer: Danbury Management Centre, NE London Polytechnic, 1969-71, Brunel University, 1971-73. Lecturer, National Defence College, Latimer, 1972-74; Senior Lecturer in Economics, Strathclyde University, 1973-83; Professor, Defence Finance, Heriot-Watt University, 1983-86. Publications: Military in the Third World, 1974; Economics of Defence, 1975; Bligh, 1978 (Yorkshire Post Book of the Year, 1979); Death of Captain Cook, 1978; Burden Sharing in NATO, 1979; Mathematics for Innumerate Economists, 1982; Defence Economics, 1983; Invitation to Statistics, 1983; Everything is Negotiable, 1984; Negotiate Anywhere, 1985; Macro Economics, 1985; Superdeal, 1985; The Economist Pocket Negotiator, 1987; Captain Bligh: the man and his mutinies, 1988; Do We Have A Deal?, 1991; Simulations for Training Negotiators, 1993; The Perfect Negotiation, 1993; Negotiation, 1994; Local Pay Bargaining, 1995; The Negotiate Trainer's Manual, 1996; Practical Negotiation Works, 1996; Kennedy on Negotiation, 1997; The New Negotiating Edge, 1998. Recreation: reading. Address: (h.) 99 Caiyside, Edinburgh; T.-0131-445 7778.

Kennedy, Rev. Gordon, BSc, BD. Church of Scotland Minister, New Cumnock Parish Church, Ayrshire, since 1993; b. 15.9.63, England. Educ. Crookston Castle Secondary; University of Strathclyde; University of Glasgow. Graduate Civil Engineer, Strathclyde Regional Council, 1985-89; Probationer Assistant, Bearsden North Parish Church, 1992-93. Address: 37 Castle, New Cumnock, Ayrshire KA18 4AG; T.-01290 338296.

Kennedy, Gordon Philip, MA (Hons), MPhil, MBA, MRTPI, MIED. Director, Corporate Development, Glasgow Development Agency, since 1993; b. 30.5.57, Glasgow. Educ. St. Mungo's Academy; Glasgow University; Strathclyde University. Planning Assistant, Clydebank District Council, 1982-85; Industrial Economist, Scottish Development Agency, 1985-91; Glasgow Development Agency: Head of Strategic Projects,1991, Head of Corporate Strategy, 1991-93. Recreations: cinema; theatre; eating out. Address: (b.) Atrium Court, 50 Waterloo Street, Glasgow G2; T.-0141-242 8284.

Kennedy, Professor Peter Graham Edward, MB, BS, MPhil, MLitt, PhD, MD, DSc, FRCPath, FRCPLond, FRCPGlas, FRSE. Burton Professor of Neurology and Head of Department, Glasgow University, since 1987; Consultant Neurologist, Institute of Neurological Sciences, Southern General Hospital, Glasgow, since 1986; b. 28.3.51, London; m., Catherine Ann; 1 s.; 1 d. Educ. University College School, London; University College, London; University College Medical School. Medical Registrar, University College Hospital, 1977-78; Hon. Research Assistant, MRC Neuroimmunology Project, University College, London, 1978-80; Research Fellow, Institute of Virology, Glasgow University, 1981; Registrar and Senior Registrar, National Hospital for Nervous Diseases, London, 1981-84; Assistant Professor of Neurology, Johns Hopkins University School of Medicine, 1985; "New Blood" Senior Lecturer in Neurology and Virology, Glasgow University, 1986-87. BUPA Medical Foundation "Doctor of the Year" Research Award, 1990; Linacre Medal and Lectureship, Royal College of Physicians of London, 1991; T.S. Srinivasan Endowment Lecturer and Gold Medal, 1993; Fogarty International Scholar, NIH, USA, 1993-94; Associate Editor, Journal of Neurovirology; Member: Medical Research Advisory Committee, Multiple Sclerosis Society, Association of Physicians Great Britain and Ireland, Association of British Neurologists; Fellow of the Academy of Medical Sciences. Publications: Infections of the Nervous System (Co-Author); numerous papers on neurology, neurovirology and neurobiology. Recreations: reading and writing; music; astronomy; tennis; walking in the country; philosophy. Address: (b.) Institute of Neurological Sciences, Southern General Hospital, Glasgow G51; T.-0141-201 2474.

Kennedy, Peter Norman Bingham, TD, CA, DL; b. 11.10.42; 4 d. Educ. Rugby. Qualified as CA, 1967; Managing Director, Gartmore Scotland Ltd., 1988-96; Chairman, BFS Income and Growth Trust plc; Director, Ivory and Sime Optimum Income Trust PLC and Ritchie Baird and Barclay Ltd.; Member, Board, West of Scotland Water Authority; Chairman, River Doon Fishery Board, since 1980; Deputy Lieutenant, Ayrshire and Arran. Address: (h.) Doonholm, Ayr.

Kennedy, Professor Robert Alan, BA, PhD, FBPsS, FRSE. Professor of Psychology, University of Dundee, since 1972; b. 1.10.39, Stourbridge; m., Elizabeth Wanda; 1 s. Educ. King Edward VI Grammar School, Stourbridge. Senior Tutor then Lecturer in Psychology, University of Melbourne, 1963-65; Lecturer in Psychology: Queen's College, University of St. Andrews, University of Dundee, 1965-72; Senior Lecturer in Psychology, University of Dundee, 1972. Member, Psychology Committee, Social Science Research Council (UK), 1980-82; Committee Member, Experimental Psychology Society, 1984-88; Member, Scientific Affairs Board, British Psychological Society, 1986-88; Member, MRC Neuropsychology Sub-committee, 1982-89; Editorial Board: Acta Psychologica, 1980-88, Psychological Research, 1978-88; Founder Member, European Conference on Eye Movements, since 1980; Convener, Scottish Group of Professors of Psychology, 1985-91; Governor, Dundee College of Education, 1974-78; Member of Court, University of Dundee, 1976-80 and since 1990; Convener, University Research Committee, 1994-97. Publications: Studies in Long-Term Memory (Co-author); The Psychology of Reading. Recreations: hill-walking; playing the piano. Address: (b.) Psychology Department, University of Dundee, Dundee DD1 4HN; T.-01382 344622.

Kennedy, William Michael Clifford, BA, CA. Chairman, Adam and Company Group PLC, since 1998; Chairman, Havelock Europa PLC, since 1998; Director, Scottish Life Assurance Co., since 1976; b. 29.10.35, Edinburgh; m., Judith Victoria Gibb; 1 s.; 1 d. Educ. Edinburgh Academy; Rugby School; Merton College, Oxford University. Qualified as CA in Edinburgh; London, 1963-64: Joseph Sebag & Co., Kleinwort Benson Ltd.; Partner, Martin Currie & Co., CA, Edinburgh, 1965 (firm incorporated, 1985); Martin Currie Ltd.: Joint Managing Director, 1989, Chief Executive, 1991, Chairman and CEO, 1992, retired 1996. Former Financial Adviser to Royal Scottish Academy. Recreations: golf; shooting; fishing; music. Address: (h.) Oak Lodge, Inveresk, Midlothian EH21 7TE; T.-0131-665 8822.

Kent, Roger Williamson, CBE, CQSW, DipAppSocStud. Co-opted Member, East Lothian Education Committee; b. 27.12.31, Portsmouth; m., Angela Mary; 1 d. Educ. Royal Naval College, Dartmouth; London University; Newcastle University. Royal Navy, 1945-61; approved schools, 1962-64; social worker, 1964-73; Director: Social Services, Doncaster, 1973-79, Social Work, Lothian Region, 1979-89, Waverley Care Trust, 1989-95; Convener, Scottish Council for Voluntary Organisations, 1990-96. Commissioner for Scotland, CRE, 1989-93. Recreations: watching cricket; walking dog. Address: (h.) Strawfields, Foulden, Berwickshire TD15 1UH.

Kerby, Nigel Wells, BSc, PhD, CBiol, FBiol. Managing Director, Mylnefield Research Services Ltd., since 1993; b. 5.4.53, Anglesey; m., Marigold; 1 s. Educ. Sedburgh School; United World College of the Atlantic; Leeds University. SERC Fellowship, Leeds University, 1979-82; AFRC Fellowship, Dundee University, 1982-90; Lecturer in Microbiology, Dundee University, 1990-93; Hon. Lecturer, Dundee University. Member, Institute of Directors, Institute of Advanced Motorists. Recreations: gardening; flying kites; wine; golf. Address: (b.) Mylnefield Research Services Ltd., Invergowrie, Dundee, DD2 5DA; T.-01382 568568.

Kermack, Sheriff Stuart Ogilvy, BA (Oxon), LLB (Glas). Sheriff of Tayside, Central and Fife, at Forfar, Perth, Arbroath, and Dundee, 1971-93; b. 9.7.34, Edinburgh; m., Barbara Mackenzie; 3 s.; 1 d. Educ. Glasgow Academy; Jesus College, Oxford; Glasgow University. Called to Scottish Bar, 1958. Address: (h.) 23 South Learmonth Gardens, Edinburgh; T.-0131-332 1898; 1 Linshader, Isle of Lewis; T.-01851 621201.

Kernohan, Robert Deans, OBE, MA. Journalist, Writer and occasional Broadcaster; b. 9.1.31, Mount Vernon, Lanarkshire; m., Margaret Buchanan Bannerman; 4 s. Educ. Whitehill School, Glasgow; Glasgow University; Balliol College, Oxford. RAF, 1955-57; Editorial Staff, Glasgow Herald, 1957-67 (Assistant Editor, 1965-66, London Editor, 1966-67); Director-General, Scottish Conservative Central Office, 1967-71; Freelance Journalist and Broadcaster, 1972; Editor, Life and Work, The Record of the Church of Scotland, 1972-90. Chairman, Federation of Conservative Students, 1954-55; Conservative Parliamentary candidate, 1955, 1959, 1964; Member: Newspaper Panel, Monopolies and Mergers Commission, 1987-99, Ancient Monuments Board for Scotland, 1990-97, Broadcasting Standards Council, 1994-97, Broadcasting Standards Commission, 1997-99; Chairman, Scottish Christian Conservative Forum, 1991; HM Inspector of Constabulary for Scotland (Lay Inspector), 1992-95; Director, Handsel Press Ltd; Trustee, Carberry Tower; Elder, Cramond Kirk, Edinburgh. Publications: Scotland's Life and Work, 1979; William Barclay, The Plain Uncommon Man, 1980; Thoughts through the Year, 1985; Our Church, 1985; The Protestant Future, 1991; The Road to Zion, 1995. Recreations: rugby-watching; travel; pontification. Address: (h.) 5/1 Rocheid Park, Edinburgh EH4 1RP; T.-0131-332 7851.

Kerr, Sheriff B.A., QC, BA, LLB. Sheriff of Glasgow and Strathkelvin at Glasgow. Admitted to Faculty of Advocates, 1973. Address: (b.) Sheriff Court House, 1 Carlton Place, Glasgow, G5 9DA.

Kerr, Brian Alexander, BSc, CA. Director, Scottish Development Finance, since 1995; Director, Bathgate Investment Fund; b. 27.8.61, Gourock; m., Vicky Beal. Educ. Greenock Academy; Strathclyde University. CA, Ernst and Young, Glasgow and London, 1989-93; joined Scottish Development Finance (venture capital arm of Scottish Enterprise), 1993. Recreations: golf; curling; travel; food and wine. Address: (b.) 120 Bothwell Street, Glasgow G2 7JP; T.-0141-228 2392.

Kerr, David Alexander, MC, TD, JP, DL; b. 30.9.16, Inverkip; m., Elizabeth Phoebe Coxwell Cresswell; 1 s.; 1 d. Educ. Canford School. Joined Westburn Sugar Refineries Ltd., Greenock, 1936; joined 5/6 Bn., Argyll & Sutherland Highlanders, 1936; mobilised, 1939, serving in France, Belgium, North Africa, Italy, Palestine and Syria; MC, 1945; mentioned in Despatches; Territorial Decoration, 1948; returned to Westburn, 1946; Technical Director, 1949; Refinery Director, 1955; Joint Managing Director, 1960; Managing Director, 1967; Chairman, 1972; Director, The Sankey Sugar Company Ltd., 1965; Managing Director, Maubre Sugars Ltd., 1972; Director, Tate & Lyle Refineries Ltd., 1976-79; retired, 1979. County Commissioner, County of Renfrew Scout Association, 1964-70, County Chairman, 1971-73; Area President, 1976-93; Chief Commissioner for Scotland, 1977-81; Honorary Vice President, since 1981; a County Vice President, Renfrewshire Guide Association. Recreations: garden; philately; photography. Address: (h.) Whitefarland, 88 Octavia Terrace, Greenock PA16 7PY; T.-01475 631980.

Kerr, Douglas J., JP. Convenor, Edinburgh City Council Licensing Board, since 1996, and of City Licensing Committee, 1995-97; b. 9.1.57, Perth. Educ. Perth High School. Vice-Chair, Edinburgh District Council Planning Committee, 1990-96. Recreations: cricket; golf; football; skiing. Address: (b.) City Chambers, High Street, Edinburgh EH1 1YJ; T.-0131-529 3279.

Kerr, Rev. Fergus Gordon Thomson, OP, STM, MA, DD. Honorary Senior Lecturer in Theology, University of Edinburgh, since 1995; Editor, New Blackfriars, since 1995; b. 16.7.31, Banff. Educ. Banff Academy; University of Aberdeen. Flying Officer, Royal Air Force, 1953-55; entered Order of Preachers, 1956; ordained Priest, 1962; Prior, Blackfriars, Oxford, 1969-78; Prior, Blackfriars, Edinburgh, 1992-98; Member, Theology Faculty, University of Oxford, 1978-86; President, Catholic Theological Association of Great Britain, 1990-92; Stanton Lecturer, University of Cambridge, 1995; Member, Editorial Board, Modern Theology, Innes Review. Publications: Theology after Wittgenstein, 1986; Immortal Longings, 1997. Recreation: reading. Address: (h.) Blackfriars, 25 George Square, Edinburgh EH8 9LD; T.-0131-650 0901.

Kerr, Finlay, MB, ChB, DObsRCOG, FRCPEdin, FRCPGlas. Consultant Physician, Raigmore Hospital, Inverness, since 1976; Honorary Senior Lecturer, Aberdeen University, since 1976; Board Director, Highland Hospice, 1985-90 (Chairman, Board of Directors, 1985-87); Chairman, Area Medical Committee, 1993-96; b. 8.8.41, Edinburgh; m., Margaret Ann Carnegie Allan; 1 s.; 2 d. Educ. Keil School; Glasgow University. House Physician and Surgeon, Western Infirmary, Glasgow; House Physician, Ruchill Hospital, Glasgow; House Surgeon, Queen Mother's Hospital, Glasgow; Senior House Officer, Western Infirmary, Glasgow; Fellow, University of Southern California; Lecturer in Medicine, then Senior Registrar in Medicine, Edinburgh Royal Infirmary. Recreations: sailing; windsurfing; skiing; golf. Address: (h.) The Birks, 2 Drummond Place, Inverness.

Kerr, Rev. Philip John, PhB, STL. Parish Priest, Our Lady and St. Ninian, Bannockburn, and Sacred Heart, Cowie; R.C. Chaplain, Stirling University; Lecturer in Systematic Theology, Scotus College, Bearsden, 1993-96; b. 23.4.56, Edinburgh. Educ. Holy Cross Academy; St. Augustine's High School, Edinburgh; Scots College and Gregorian University, Rome. Assistant Priest, St. Francis Xavier's, Falkirk, 1980-82; Lecturer in Systematic Theology, St. Andrew's College, Drygrange, 1982-86; Vice-Rector and Lecturer in Systematic Theology, Gillis College, Edinburgh, 1986-93. Recreations: classical music; walking. Address: Catholic Presbytery, Quakerfield, Bannockburn FK7 8HJ; T.-01786 812249.

Kerr, Robert James, MA (Hons), PhD. Rector, Peebles High School, since 1986; b. 14.6.47, Jedburgh; m., Isobel Grace Atkinson; 2 s.; 1 d. Educ. Kelso High School; Edinburgh University. Assistant Teacher, Lochaber High School, 1973-75; Assistant Principal Teacher of Geography, Forrester High School, 1976-77; Principal Teacher of Geography, Douglas Ewart High School, 1977-82; Assistant Rector, Elgin High School, 1982-85; Depute Rector, Forres Academy, 1985-86. Chairman, "Higher Still" Specialist Group in PSE, 1994-97. Recreations: fishing; rugby supporter; hill-walking/mountaineering; mountain biking; ornithology; skiing; travel. Address: (h.) Enniskerry, Eshiels, Peebles EH45 8NA; T.-01721 722131.

Kerr, Professor William John Stanton, BDS, FDS, RCSEdin, MDS, FFD, RCSIrel, DOrthRCS, FDS RCPS Glas, DDS. Professor of Orthodontics, Glasgow Dental Hospital and School, since 1993; Honorary Consultant in Orthodontics, since 1978; b. 12.7.41, Belfast; m., Marie-Francoise; 1 d. Educ. Campbell College, Belfast; Queen's University, Belfast. Address: (b.) Glasgow Dental Hospital and School, 378 Sauchiehall Street, Glasgow G2 3JZ; T.-0141-211 9665.

Kerrigan, Herbert Aird, QC, MA, LLB (Hons); b. 2.8.45, Glasgow; 1 s. Educ. Whitehill School, Glasgow; Aberdeen University; Keele University; Hague Academy. Admitted to Faculty of Advocates, 1970; Lecturer in Criminal Law and Criminology, Edinburgh University, 1969-73; Lecturer in Scots Law, Edinburgh University, 1973-74; Member, Longford Commission, 1972; Church of Scotland: Elder, 1967 (now at Greyfriars Tolbooth and Highland Kirk), Reader, 1969, elected Member, Assembly Council, 1981-85; called to the English Bar (Middle Temple), 1990; joined Chambers of Edmund Lawson, QC, 1991; appointed QC in Scotland, 1992. Publications: An Introduction to Criminal Procedure in Scotland, 1970; Ministers for the 1980s (Contributor), 1979; The Law of Contempt (Contributing Editor), 1982; The Law of Sport (2nd edition) (Contributor), 1995. Recreation: travel. Address: (h.) 20 Edinburgh Road, Dalkeith, Midlothian EH22 1JY; T.-0131-660 3007.

Kettle, Ann Julia, MA, FSA, FRHistS, FRSA. Senior Lecturer, Mediaeval History, University of St. Andrews, since 1964; b. 2.8.39, Orpington. Educ. Lewes Grammar School; St. Hugh's College, Oxford. University of St. Andrews: Hebdomadar, 1991-94, Dean of Arts, since 1998; President, Association of University Teachers (Scotland), 1994-96; Member, Scottish (Garrick) Committee of National (Dearing) Committee of Inquiry into Higher Education, 1996-97; Member, Scottish Higher Education Funding Council, since 1997. Address: (b.) Department of Mediaeval History, University of St. Andrews, St. Andrews KY16 9AL; T.-01334 463317.

Khan, Anvar (nee Anwar Begum Khan). Writer; Journalist; Broadcaster; Columnist, The Herald, since 1998; b. 13.7.67, Glasgow. Educ. Laurel Bank School, Glasgow. Broadcasting: Presenter, Citizen Khan, Scottish Television, 1997; Presenter, The Slice, BBC Radio Scotland, 1997; BBC Radio 4 Columnist and Presenter, The Afternoon Shift, 1997; Presenter and Reporter, Scottish Reporters, Scottish Television, 1999; newspapers: Feature Writer and Diarist: The Herald, The Scotsman, Scottish Daily Mail;

The Herald, 1993-96: Diary Editor, Fashion Editor, Style Editor, Beauty Editor; Columnist, The Scotsman, 1997. Trained opera singer. UK Press Gazette Feature Writer of the Year, 1994. Address: (b.) The Herald, 195 Albion Street, Glasgow G1 1PQ; T.-0141-576 4082.

Kidd, Professor Cecil, BSc, PhD, FIBiol, FRSA. Professor of Physiology (part-time), Aberdeen University, since 1997; Regius Professor of Physiology, 1984-97; b. 28.4.33, Shotley Bridge, Co. Durham; m., Margaret Winifred; 3 s. Educ. Queen Elizabeth Grammar School, Darlington; King's College, Newcastle-upon-Tyne; Durham University. Demonstrator in Physiology, King's College, Newcastle-upon-Tyne; Lecturer/Senior Lecturer/Reader in Physiology, Senior Research Associate in Cardiovascular Studies, Leeds University. Recreations: squash; gardening. Address: (b.) Department of Biomedical Sciences, Medical School, Foresterhill Campus, Aberdeen University, Aberdeen AB25 2ZD; T.-01224 273005/6.

Kidd, David Hamilton, LLB, LLM, WS, NP. Partner, Biggart Baillie, since 1978; Solicitor Advocate, since 1994; b. 21.9.49, Edinburgh; m., Geraldine Stephen; 2 s.; 1 d. Educ. Edinburgh Academy; Edinburgh University. Recreations: cycling; skiing; hill-walking. Address: (b.) 7 Castle Street, Edinburgh EH2 3AP; T.-0131-226 5541.

Kidd, Mary Helen (May), JP, MA. National Chairman, Scottish Women's Rural Institutes, 1993-96; Member: Scottish Consumer Council, 1991-96, Advisory Board and Council, Scottish Agricultural College, since 1991, Women's National Commission, 1993-98; m., Neil M.L. Kidd; 2 s. Educ. Brechin High School; Edinburgh University. Partner in family farming business; former Member, WNC International Committee; Member: MAFF Consumer Panel, Committee, Associated Countrywomen of the World. Recreations: playing piano and organ; creative writing. Address: (h.) Holemill of Kirkbuddo, Forfar, Angus DD8 2NQ; T.-01307 820 318.

Kiddie, Charles, BSc (Hons). Rector, Perth High School, since 1993; b. 3.4.49, Dundee; m., Esther Linda Power; 2 s. Educ. Harris Academy, Dundee; Aberdeen University; University of Kansas; Dundee College of Education. Teacher, Forfar Academy; Principal Teacher, Breadalbane Academy, Aberfeldy; Assistant Head Teacher, Whitfield High School, Dundee; Adviser in Social Subjects, Tayside Regional Council; Rector, Auchterarder High School. Recreations: family; ice hockey. (b.) Perth High School, Oakbank Road, Perth; T.-01738 628271/2.

Kilbey, Professor Brian John, BSc, PhD, DSc, FRSE. Professor of Molecular Parasitology, University of Edinburgh, since 1998; b. 1.3.36, London; m., Sarah; 1 s.; 3 d. Educ. Tottenham Grammar School; University College London. Reader, Genetics, University of Edinburgh, 1975-98. Visiting Professor, University of Rochester, NY, USA, 1987-88. Address: (b.) Faculty of Science and Engineering, Weir Building, King's Buildings, Edinburgh EH9 3JY.

Killham, Professor Kenneth Stuart, BSc, PhD, FAAM, FIPSS. Established Chair of Soil Science, Aberdeen University, since 1995 (Head, Department of Plant and Soil Science, since 1996); Chairman, UK Soil Science Advisory Committee, since 1997; Vice-Chairman, Remedios Ltd., since 1999; b. 1.3.57, Formby; m., Pauline. Educ. Merchant Taylors School, Crosby; Sheffield University. Visiting Scientist, University of California, Berkeley, 1981-83; Lecturer in Soil Microbiology, Aberdeen University, 1983-90; Reader in Soil Microbiology, Aberdeen University, 1990-93. Publications: Soil Ecology; Soil Chemistry – Theory and Applications. Recreation: sailing. Address: (b.) University of Aberdeen, St. Machar Drive, Aberdeen AB24 3UU; T.-01224 272260.

Killick, Roger John, BSc, MBA, MA, PhD, CBiol, MIBiol. Secretary, Scottish Crop Research Institute, since 1988; b. 27.5.45, London; m., E. Marion Smith; 1 s.; 1 d. Educ. Purley County Grammar School for Boys; London University; Birmingham University; Dundee University; Leicester University. Research Geneticist, Scottish Plant Breeding Station, 1969-82; Assistant to Director, Scottish Crop Research Institute, 1982-88. Recreations: hill-walking; watching ballet. Address: (h.) Hilltops, 19 Sidlaw Terrace, Birkhill, Dundee DD2 5PY; T.-01382 580396.

Kilpatrick, Lord (Robert Kilpatrick), MD, FRCP(Edin), FRCP, FRCPS(Glas), HonFRCS, HonFRCP(Dub), HonFRCS(Edin). Chairman, Scottish Hospital Endowment Research Trust, since 1996; b. 29.7.26, Wemyss; m., Elizabeth Forbes; 2 s.; 1 d. Educ. Buckhaven High School; Edinburgh University. House Officer, Senior House Officer, Registrar, Edinburgh, 1949-54; Lecturer and Senior Lecturer, Sheffield University, 1955-66; Professor of Clinical Pharmacology, Sheffield University, 1966-75; Professor of Clinical Pharmacology and Medicine, Leicester University, 1975-89; President, General Medical Council, 1989-95; President, British Medical Association, 1997-98; Hon. Degrees: DrHc (Edin), LLD (Dundee), DSc (Hull), DSc (Leics), LLD (Sheff). Recreation: golf. Address: (h.) 12 Wester Coates Gardens, Edinburgh EH12 5LT; T.-0131-337 7304.

Kilshaw, David Andrew George. Solicitor, since 1979; Chairman, Borders Health Board, since 1993; b. 18.3.53, Glencoe; 3 s. Educ. Keil School, Dumbarton. Traineeship, Brunton Miller, Solicitors, Glasgow, 1975-80; Solicitor, Borders Regional Council, 1980-83; Partner, Cullen Kilshaw Solicitors, Galashiels and Melrose, since 1983. Safeguarder, Borders Region Children's Panel, since 1987. Recreations: golf; fishing; walking; self-improvement. Address: (b.) 27 Market Street, Galashiels; T.-01896 758311.

Kimbell, Professor David Rodney Bertram, MA, DPhil, LRAM, FRSA. Professor of Music, Edinburgh University, since 1987 (Professor of Music, St. Andrews University, 1979-87); b. 26.6.39, Gillingham, Kent; m., Ingrid Else Emilie Lübbe; 1 s.; 2 d. Educ. Dartford Grammar School; Kent College, Canterbury; Worcester College, Oxford. Lecturer in Music, Edinburgh University, 1965-78. Publication: Verdi in the Age of Italian Romanticism, 1981; Italian Opera, 1991. Address: (h.) 3 Bellevue Crescent, Edinburgh EH3 6ND; T.-0131-556 5480.

Kinane, Professor Denis Francis, BDS, PhD, FDSRCS, FDSRCPS. Professor of Periodontology and Oral Immunology, since 1996; Consultant in Periodontology/Restorative Dentistry, since 1992; b. 29.1.57, Edinburgh; m., Celina Alice Scott; 1 s.; 2 d. Educ. St. Augustine's High School, Edinburgh; University of Edinburgh. Lecturer, Dundee University, 1984-87; Senior Lecturer, University of Glasgow, 1988-95. President, Periodontal Research Group, International Society of Periodontology, 1998. Wilfred Fish Prize, 1998. Publications: 80 papers; 12 chapters; three books. Recreations: running; tennis. Address: (h.) 24 Victoria Park Gardens North, Glasgow G11 7EJ; T.-0141-357 0506.

Kincraig, Hon. Lord (Robert Smith Johnston), QC (Scot), BA (Hons), LLB. Senator of the College of Justice in Scotland, 1972-88; Chairman, Parole Review Body for Scotland; b. 10.10.18, Glasgow; m., Margaret Joan Graham (deceased); 1 s.; 1 d. Educ. Strathallan; St. John's College, Cambridge; Glasgow University. Member, Faculty of Advocates, 1942; Advocate-Depute, 1953-55; QC (Scot), 1955; contested (Unionist), Stirling and Falkirk Burghs, General Election, 1959; Home Advocate Depute, 1959-62; Sheriff of Roxburgh, Berwick and Selkirk, 1964-70; Dean, Faculty of Advocates, 1970-72. Recreations: gardening;

golf. Address: (h.) Westwood Cottage, Southfield Farm, Longniddry EH32 0PL; T.-01875 853583.

King, Professor Bernard, MSc, PhD, FIWSc, CBiol, FIBiol. Principal and Vice-Chancellor, University of Abertay, Dundee, since 1992; b. 4.5.46, Dublin; m., Maura Antoinette Collinge; 2 d. Educ. Synge St. Christian Brothers School, Dublin; College of Technology, Dublin; University of Aston in Birmingham. Research Fellow, University of Aston, 1972-76; Dundee Institute of Technology, 1976-91: Lecturer, Senior Lecturer, Head, Department of Molecular and Life Sciences, Dean, Faculty of Science; Assistant Principal, Robert Gordon Institute of Technology/Robert Gordon University, 1991-92. Director, Dundee Healthcare Trust; Governor, Unicorn Preservation Society; Chairman, Committee of Principals of Scottish Centrally-Funded Colleges; Director, Scottish Enterprise Tayside; Governor, Scottish Crop Research Institute. Recreations: reading; music; sailing. Address: (h.) 11 Dalhousie Place, Arbroath, DD11 2BT; T.-01382 308012.

King, Elspeth Russell, MA, FMA.Director, Smith Art Gallery and Museum, Stirling, since 1994; b. 29.3.49, Lochore, Fife. Educ. Beath High School; St. Andrews University; Leicester University. Curator, People's Palace, Glasgow, 1974-91, with responsibility for building up the social history collections for the city of Glasgow; Director, Dunfermline Heritage Trust, 1991-94; responsible for restoration of, and new displays in, Abbot House. Publications include: The Thenew Factor: the hidden history of women in Glasgow, 1993; Blind Harry's Wallace by Hamilton of Gilbertfield (Editor), 1998; Address: (b.) Smith Art Gallery and Museum, Dumbarton Road, Stirling FK8 2RQ; T.-01786 471917.

King, Geoffrey Harry, MA (Oxon), DPhil. Vice-Principal (Resources), Queen Margaret College; b. 25.8.46, Swindon; m., Deborah Anne King; 2 d. Educ. Commonweal Grammar School, Swindon; Balliol College, Oxford; Sussex University. Research Manager, Unilever, 1972-74; Lecturer in Analytical Chemistry, Dorset Institute of Higher Education, 1974-77; Programme Manager, Renewable Energy Research and Development, Energy Technology Support Unit, 1977-83; Manager, Energy Efficiency Demonstration Scheme, 1983-87; Business Planning Manager, Thames Water Authority, 1987-89; Business Services and Market Testing Manager, NRA, 1989-95; Director of Projects, SEPA, 1995-97. Recreations: railways; walking; listening to music; sailing. Address: (h.) 43 Grange View, Linlithgow EH49 7HY; T.-01506 846108.

King, Robert Lees Lumsden. Secretary: Post Office Users' Council for Scotland, since 1988, Scottish Advisory Committee on Telecommunications, since 1988; b. 23.3.49, Peebles; m., Yvonne Mary Black. Educ. Leith Academy. Department of Agriculture and Fisheries for Scotland, 1966-70; Department of Environment, 1970-72; Forestry Commission, 1972-79; Nature Conservancy Council, 1979-88. Recreations: country life; shooting; reading; travel. Address: (b.) 2 Greenside Lane, Edinburgh EH1 3AH; T.-0131-244 5576.

King, Steve. Composer/Music Educationalist; Musician in Residence, Heriot-Watt University, since 1998; Viola Player, Scottish Chamber Orchestra, since 1984; b. 4.12.56, Waltham Cross; 2 s. Educ. Queen Eleanor Grammar School; Royal Northern College of Music. Co-Principal, Icelandic Symphony Orchestra, 1979-82. Address: (h.) 8 Hopeward Mews, Dalgety Bay KY11 5TB; T.-01383 821187.

King, Thomas Robertson, BL. Director, Corporate Affairs, Standard Life Assurance Company, since 1996; b. 29.6.41, Edinburgh; m., Sheila; 2 d. Educ. Lasswade Senior Secondary; University of Edinburgh. Joined Standard Life, 1967: Sales Manager, South of England, 1973, General Manager (Marketing), 1985, Director, 1992. Recreation: golf. Address: (b.) Standard Life House, 30 Lothian Road, Edinburgh EH1 2DH; T.-0131-245 0324.

Kingarth, Lord (Hon. Derek Emslie). Senator of the College of Justice, since 1997; b. 21.6.49. Educ. Cambridge University; Edinburgh University. Advocate, 1974; Advocate Depute 1985-1988. Address: Parliament Square, Edinburgh EH1 1RQ.

Kinnaird, Alison, MBE, MA, FGE. Glass Engraver and Artist; Clarsach Player; b. 30.4.49, Edinburgh; m., Robin Morton; 1 s.; 1 d. Educ. George Watson's Ladies College; Edinburgh University. Freelance glass artist, since 1971; exhibitions in Edinburgh, 1978, 1981, 1985, in London, 1988, 1995; work in many public and private collections; professional musician, since 1970; has produced three LPs as well as film and TV music; served on Council, Scottish Craft Centre, 1974-76; Council, SSWA, 1975-76; Member: BBC Scottish Music Advisory Committee, 1981-84, BBC Broadcasting Council for Scotland, 1984-88, SAC Crafts Commitee, 1993-96; awarded: SDA/CCC Craft Fellowship, 1980, Glass-Sellers of London Award, 1987, MBE, for services to music and art, 1997. Recreations: children; cooking; garden. Address: (h.) Shillinghill, Temple, Midlothian EH23 4SH; T.-01875 830328.

Kinnis, William Kay Brewster, PhD, FRSA. Solicitor and Notary Public; Consultant Lawyer with Stewarts & Murdochs, Solicitors, Glasgow, since 1995; Director, East Neuk Properties Ltd., Kilrymont Properties Ltd., Culdee Properties Ltd., Madras Properties Ltd.; b. 5.1.33, St. Andrews; m., Agnes Inglis Erskine, MA; 2 d. d. Educ. Hamilton Academy; Glasgow University; London University (External). Partner: MacArthur Stewart & Orr, Solicitors, Oban and Lochgilphead, 1959-62; Town Clerk and Burgh Chamberlain, Lochgilphead, 1960-62; Partner, Murdoch Jackson, Solicitors, Glasgow, 1963-92; Senior Partner: Miller Jackson, Solicitors, Lenzie, 1982-92, Cannon, Orpin & Murdochs, 1992-95; Council Member, Member, Royal Faculty of Procurators, 1980-83; Governor, Baillie's Institution, 1983-94. Choral Scholar, Glasgow University, 1954-58; Choirmaster, Lochgilphead Parish Church, 1959-62; Reader, Church of Scotland, since 1960; Member, Church of Scotland Board of Practice and Procedure (Vice-Convener) and Law Committee (Convener), since 1990. Recreations: choral singing; swimming; reading; travel. Address: (b.) Royal Bank Place, Glasgow G1 3AA; T.-0141-248 8810.

Kinnoull, 15th Earl of (Arthur William George Patrick Hay); b. 26.3.35; m.; 1 s.; 3 d. Educ. Eton. Chartered Land Agent; succeeded to title, 1938; former Conservative Spokesman on Aviation, House of Lords; Past President, National Council on Inland Transport.

Kinross, Lord (Christopher Patrick Balfour), LLB, WS. Solicitor, since 1975; b. 1.10.49, Edinburgh; m., Susan Jane Pitman; 2 s. Educ. Eton College; Edinburgh University. Member, Royal Company of Archers, Queen's Bodyguard for Scotland; James IV Association of Surgeons. Recreations: off-road motorsport; shooting. Address: (b.) Taylor Kinross Legal Partnership, 27 Stafford Street, Edinburgh; T.-0131-623 1997.

Kinsman, Stewart Hayes, BSc, FRICS. Chief Executive, Hanover (Scotland) Housing Association Ltd., since 1979; Chairman, Scottish Federation of Housing Associations, since 1998; b. 18.9.43, Burntisland, Fife; 1 s.; 1 d. Educ. Kirkcaldy High School; Heriot-Watt University. Chartered Surveyor, 1966-71; Estates and Buildings Officer, Stirling University, 1971-76; Regional Manager, Hanover Housing Association (GB), 1976-79. Trustee, SHACT (Scottish Housing Associations' Charitable Trust). Recreations: sailing; wines; natural environment. Address: (b.) 36 Albany Street, Edinburgh EH1 3QH; T.-0131-557 0598.

Kintore, 13th Earl of (Michael Canning William John Keith); b. 22.2.39; m.; 1 s.; 1 d. Educ. Eton; Royal Military Academy, Sandhurst. Address: The Stables, Keith Hall, Inverurie, AB51 0LD.

Kirk, David, MA, BM, BCh, DM, FRCS (Eng), FRCS-RCPS (Glas), FRCS Edin). Consultant Urological Surgeon, Greater Glasgow Health Board, since 1982; Honorary Professor, Glasgow University, since 1995; b. 26.5.43, Bradford; m., Gillian Mary Wroot; 1 s.; 2 d. Educ. King Edwards School, Birmingham; Balliol College, Oxford; Oxford University Clinical Medical School. Resident House Physician and House Surgeon, Radcliffe Infirmary, Oxford; University Demonstrator, Oxford; clinical surgical posts, Oxford and Bristol; Arris and Gale Lecturer, Royal College of Surgeons (England), 1980-81; rotating surgical Registrar appointment, Sheffield; academic surgical research, Sheffield University; Senior Registrar in General Surgery, then in Urology, Bristol; Honorary Clinical Lecturer, Glasgow University, 1984-95. Secretary/Treasurer, 1983-85, Chairman, 1985-88, Scottish Urological Oncology Group; Council Member: Urology Section, Royal Society of Medicine, 1984-87, British Association of Urological Surgeons, 1988-91; Chairman: Prostate Forum, 1991-94, Intercollegiate Board in Urology, 1994-97; Specialist Adviser in Urology, National Medical Advisory Committee (Scottish Office). Recreations: skiing; hill-walking; classical music. Address: (h.) Woodend, Prospect Road, Dullatur, Glasgow G68 0AN; T.-01236 720778.

Kirk, Professor David, BSc (Hons), MPhil, FIFST, MHCIMA. Head, Department of Business and Consumer Studies, Queen Margaret College, since 1991; b. 30.7.45, Stockport; m., Helen Kathleen; 2 s. Educ. New Mills Grammar School; University of Reading; University of Surrey. Food Technologist, International Stores; Research Fellow, University of Surrey; Lecturer, Polytechnic of the South Bank; Senior/Principal Lecturer, Sheffield City Polytechnic. Publications: Environmental Management for Hotels; Kitchen Planning and Management; The Design and Operation of Catering Equipment. Recreations: music; gardening. Address: (b.) Clerwood Terrace, Edinburgh EH12 8TS; T.-0131-317 3000.

Kirk, Professor Gordon, MA, MEd, FRSA, PhD. Dean, Faculty of Education, Edinburgh University, since 1998; Principal, Moray House Institute of Education, 1981-98; Vice-Convener, General Teaching Council, since 1992; b. 8.5.38, Dunfermline; m., Jane D. Murdoch; 1 s.; 1 d. Educ. Camphill Secondary School, Paisley; Glasgow University. Lecturer in Education, Aberdeen University, 1965-74; Head, Education Department, Jordanhill College of Education, 1974-81; Member, Munn Committee on the Curriculum of the Secondary School, 1974-77; Chairman: Educational Broadcasting Council, Scotland, 1985-91, Scottish Council for Research in Education, 1984-92; Member: General Teaching Council for Scotland, since 1984, Consultative Committee on the Curriculum, 1984-91, Council for National Academic Awards, 1979-93; Vice-Convener, Committee of Scottish Higher Principals, 1993-94. Publications: Scottish Education Looks Ahead (Assistant Editor), 1969; Curriculum and Assessment in the Scottish Secondary School, 1982; Moray House and Professional Education (Editor), 1985; The Core Curriculum, 1986; Teacher Education and Professional Development, 1988; Handbook of Educational Ideas and Practices (Associate Editor), 1990; Scottish Education and the European Community (Editor), 1992; 5-14: Scotland's National Curriculum (Editor), 1994; Moray House and Change in Higher Education (Editor), 1995; Professional Issues in Education series (Co-Editor). Recreations: walking; golf; bridge. Address: (h.) Craigroyston, Broadgait, Gullane, East Lothian; T.-01620 843299.

Kirk, James, MA, PhD, DLitt, FRHistS, FRSE. Reader in Scottish History, Glasgow University, since 1990; b. 18.10.44, Falkirk. Educ. Stirling High School; Edinburgh University. Lecturer in Scottish History, Glasgow University, 1972-89; Senior Lecturer, 1989-90; David Berry Prize, Royal Historical Society, 1973; Wolfson Award, 1977; British Academy Major Research Awards, 1989-96; ESRC Research Award, 1993-95. President, Scottish Church History Society, 1989-92; Hon. Secretary: Scottish Record Society, since 1973, Scottish Society for Reformation History, 1980-90; Member, Council, Scottish History Society, 1989-93; Scottish Section Editor, Royal Historical Society, Annual Bibliography of British and Irish History; an Associate Editor, The New Dictionary of National Biography, 1998. Publications: The University of Glasgow 1451-1577, 1977; Records of the Synod of Lothian and Tweeddale, 1977; The Second Book of Discipline, 1980; Stirling Presbytery Records, 1981; Visitation of the Diocese of Dunblane, 1984; Patterns of Reform, 1989; Humanism and Reform (Editor), 1991; The Books of Assumption of the Thirds of Benefices: Scottish Ecclesiastical Rentals at the Reformation, 1995; Scotland's History (Editor), 1995; The Medieval Church in Scotland (Editor), 1995; Her Majesty's Historiographer, 1996; Calendar of Scottish Supplications to Rome 1447-1471, vol. 5 (Editor), 1997; Contributor to: Encyclopedia of the Reformed Faith, 1992, Dictionary of Scottish Church History and Theology, 1993, The Oxford Encyclopedia of the Reformation, 1996. Recreations: living in Wester Ross; viticulture. Address: (h.) Woodlea, Dunmore, Stirlingshire FK2 8LY; T.-01324 831240.

Kirk, William, CPFA. Director of Finance, South Lanarkshire Council, since 1995; Treasurer, Strathclyde Fire Board, since 1995; Treasurer, Lanarkshire Joint Valuation Board, since 1995; b. 21.8.50, Holytown; m., Eleanor; 2 d. Educ. Hamilton Academy. Lanarkshire County Council, 1968-75; Hamilton District Council, 1975-96. Recreations: sport; reading. Address: (b.) Council Offices, Almada Street, Hamilton; T.-01698 454530.

Kirkhill, Lord (John Farquharson Smith); b. 7.5.30; m.; 1 step d. Lord Provost of Aberdeen, 1971-75; Minister of State, Scottish Office, 1975-78; Chairman, North of Scotland Hydro-Electric Board, 1979-82; Delegate, Parliamentary Assembly, Council of Europe, and W.E.U., since 1987. Address: (h.) 3 Rubislaw Den North, Aberdeen, AB15 4AL; T.-01224 314167.

Kirkness, Professor Colin Mainland, BMedBiol, MBChB, FRCS(Edin), FRCS (Glas), FRCOphth. Tennent Professor of Ophthalmology, Glasgow University, since 1991; President, European Board of Ophthalmology; Secretary, EUPO; Vice-President, Royal College of Ophthalmologists; b. 4.5.49, Kirkwall. Educ. Fraserburgh Academy; Aberdeen University. Resident Surgical Officer and Senior Resident, Moorfields Eye Hospital, London, 1980; Lecturer, 1983, Senior Lecturer and Director, 1989, Pocklington Eye Transplant Unit, Institute of Ophthalmology, London; Honorary Consultant, Moorfields Eye Hospital, 1987. Publications: books on ophthalmology; papers. Address: (b.) Tennent Institute, Upper Ground Floor, Gartnavel Hospital, Glasgow G12 0YN; T.-0141-211 2000, Ext. 2640.

Kirkpatrick, William, BSc. Rector, Blairgowrie High School, since 1995; b. 5.8.46, Kirkcaldy; m., Jenifer; 1 s. Educ. Kirkcaldy High; University of Edinburgh. Teacher of Physics, Kirkcaldy High School; Principal Teacher of Physics: Kirkland High School, Kirkcaldy High School; Assistant Head Teacher, Auchmuty High; TVEI Co-ordinator then Senior Adviser, Fife Region; Depute Rector, Auchmuty High. Address: (b.) Beeches Road, Blairgowrie PH10 6PW; T.-01250 873445.

Kirkwood, Archy, BSc. MP (Liberal Democrat), Roxburgh and Berwickshire, since 1983; Chairman, Social Security Select Committee, since 1997; Commissioner, House of

Commons; b. 22.4.46, Glasgow; m., Rosemary Chester; 1 s.; 1 d. Educ. Cranhill School; Heriot-Watt University. Solicitor, Notary Public; Aide to Sir David Steel, 1971-75, 1977-78; Liberal Spokesman on Health and Social Services, and on Social Security, 1985-87; Alliance Spokesman on Overseas Development, 1987; Liberal Spokesman on Scotland, 1987-88; Social and Liberal Democrat Convener on Welfare, Health and Education, 1988-89; Liberal Democrat Deputy Chief Whip, and Spokesman on Welfare and Social Security, 1989-92, Community Care, 1994-97. Trustee, Joseph Rowntree Reform Trust, since 1985. Recreations: music; photography. Address: (b.) House of Commons, London SW1A 0AA.

Kirkwood, Hon. Lord (Ian Candlish Kirkwood). Senator of the College of Justice, since 1987; b. 8.6.32. Advocate, 1957; QC, 1970. Address: (b.) Court of Session, Parliament House, Edinburgh, EH1 1RQ.

Kirkwood, Ralph C., BSc, PhD, FRSE, FIBiol. Reader in Biology, Strathclyde University, since 1981; b. 6.7.33, Glasgow; m., Mair Enid; 3 s. Educ. Jordanhill College School, Glasgow; Glasgow University; University of Wales, Aberystwyth. Lecturer, Botany Department, West of Scotland Agricultural College, 1959-64; Strathclyde University: Lecturer, Biology Department, 1964-72, Senior Lecturer, 1972-81; Member, Advisory Committee, Scottish Agricultural College; Member, West Areas Board and Scientific Advisory Committee, S.N.H. Publications: Target sites for herbicide action (Editor); Clean Technology and the Environment (Co-Editor). Recreations: sailing; photography; natural history; walking. Address: (b.) Department of Bioscience and Biotechnology, Royal College Building, Strathclyde University, Glasgow, G1 1XW; T.-0141-548 3624.

Kirwan, Frank, BA, MA. Director Privilege Insurance, since 1997; Chairman, Crystal Media Group, since 1997; Visiting Professor, University of Strathclyde, since 1997; Member, Accounts Commission, since 1995; Director, Underwriter Insurance, since 1998; Honorary Fellow, Edinburgh University, since 1998; b. 16.7.52, Dublin; m., Moira; 1 s.; 1 d. Educ. Colaiste Mhuire, Dublin; Trinity College, University College, Dublin. Economic and Social Research Institute, 1974-76; Strathclyde University, 1976-81; Lund University, 1981-82; Fraser of Allander Institute, 1983-84; Scottish Development Agency, 1984-88; Royal Bank of Scotland, 1988-97. Recreation: gardening. Address: (h.) Gateside House, Hill Road, Gullane EH31 2BE.

Kitchen, John Philip, MA, BMus, PhD (Cantab), FRCO, LRAM. Senior Lecturer in Music, Edinburgh University, since 1987; Harpsichord Consultant, Royal Scottish Academy of Music and Drama; Concert Organist, Harpsichordist, Pianist; b. 27.10.50, Airdrie. Educ. Coatbridge High School; Glasgow University; Cambridge University. Lecturer in Music, St. Andrews University, 1976-87; Harpsichoridst/Organist, Scottish Early Music Consort, 1977-98; BBC and commercial recordings; music reviewer; Organist, Old St. Paul's Episcopal Church, Edinburgh. Recreations: more music; entertaining. Address: (b.) Faculty of Music, Alison House, 12 Nicolson Square, Edinburgh EH8 9DF; T.-0131-650 2432.

Klein, Bernat, CBE, FCSD, Hon. FRIAS; b. 6.11.22, Senta, Yugoslavia; m., Margaret Soper; 1 s.; 2 d. Educ. Senta, Yugoslavia; Bezalel School of Arts and Crafts, Jerusalem; Leeds University. Designer: Tootal, Broadhurst, Lee, 1948-49, Munrospun, Edinburgh, 1949-51; Chairman and Managing Director, Colourcraft, 1952-62; Managing Director, Bernat Klein Ltd., 1962-66; Chairman and Managing Director: Bernat Klein Design Ltd., 1966-81, Bernat Klein Ltd., 1982-92. Member: Design Council, 1962-68, Royal Fine Art Commission for Scotland, 1981-87. Publications: Eye for Colour, 1965; Design Matters, 1975. Recreations: tennis; reading. Address: High Sunderland, Galashiels; T.-01750 20730.

Kleinpoppen, Professor Hans, DiplPhysicist, Chart Phys, Dr re nat & habil, FInstPhys, FRAS, FRSA, FRSE, Fellow, American Physical Society. Professor of Experimental Physics, Stirling University, 1968-96, Professor Emeritus, since 1996; b. 30.9.28, Duisburg, Germany. Educ. Giessen University; Heidelberg University; Tuebingen University. Visiting Fellow, Colorado University, 1967; Visiting Associate Professor, Columbia University, New York, 1968; Stirling University: Head, Physics Department, 1970-72, Director, Institute of Atomic Physics, 1975-81, Head, Unit of Atomic and Molecular Physics, School of Natural Sciences, since 1989. Visiting Professor, Bielefeld University, since 1979; Visiting Fellow, Fritz Haber Institut, Max Planck Gessellschaft, since 1991. Co-Director, three International Summer Schools; Chairman, several national and international Conferences on Atomic Physics; Hans Kleinpoppen Symposium held in honour of research at Stirling University, Italy, 1998. Publications: editor of 13 books; research papers; articles in many journals; monograph series on physics of atoms and molecules (Co-Editor). Address: (b.) Unit of Atomic and Molecular Physics, Stirling University, Stirling.

Knight, Alanna, FSA Scot. Novelist; b. Co. Durham; m., Alistair Knight; 2 s. Educ. Jesmond High School. Writing career began, 1965; novels: Legend of the Loch, 1969 (RNA First Novel Award), The October Witch, 1971, This Outward Angel, 1971, Castle Clodha, 1972, Lament for Lost Lovers, 1972, The White Rose, 1974, A Stranger Came By, 1974, The Wicked Wynsleys, 1977; historical novels: The Passionate Kindness, 1974, A Drink for the Bridge, 1976, The Black Duchess, 1980, Castle of Foxes, 1981, Colla's Children, 1982, The Clan, 1985; Estella, 1986; detective novels: Enter Second Murderer, 1988, Blood Line, 1989, Deadly Beloved, 1989, Killing Cousins, 1990, A Quiet Death, 1991, To Kill A Queen, 1992; The Evil that Men Do, 1993, The Missing Duchess, 1994, Inspector Faro and the Edinburgh Mysteries, 1994, The Bull Slayers, 1995; Murder by Appointment, 1996; Inspector Faro's Second Casebook, 1996; The Coffin Lane Murders, 1998; crime novels: the Sweet Cheat Gone, 1992, This Outward Angel, 1994; Angel Eyes, 1997; plays: The Private Life of R.L.S., 1973, Girl on an Empty Swing, 1977; non-fiction: The Robert Louis Stevenson Treasury, 1985; RLS in the South Seas, 1986, Bright Ring of Words (Co-Author), 1994; radio short stories, plays and documentaries. Recreations: walking; reading; painting. Address: (h.) 24 March Hall Crescent, Edinburgh EH16 5HL; T.-0131-667 5230.

Knill-Jones, Jennifer Gillian, MB, BS, LRCP, MRCS, MRCPsych. Consultant Psychiatrist, since 1986; b. 15.8.36, Stockton-on-Tees; 3 d. Educ. Sutton High School; St. Bartholomew's Hospital Medical School. House Officer posts, Luton and Dunstaple Hospital, Elizabeth Garrett Anderson Hospital, London, St. Bartholomew's Hospital, London; Clinical Assistant, Gartnavel Royal Hospital, Glasgow; Senior Registrar in Psychiatry, Greater Glasgow Health Board. Recreations: walking; Scottish country dancing. Address: (b.) Parkhead Hospital, Salamanca Street, Glasgow G32; T.-0141-211 8300.

Knops, Professor Robin John, BSc, PhD, FRSE. Professor of Mathematics, Heriot-Watt University, Edinburgh, since 1971 (Vice Principal, 1988-95; Special Adviser to the Principal, 1995-97); b. 30.12.32, London; m., Margaret; 4 s.; 2 d. Educ. Nottingham University. Nottingham University: Assistant Lecturer in Mathematics, 1956-59, Lecturer in Mathematics, 1959-62; Newcastle-upon-Tyne University: Lecturer in Applied Mathematics, 1962-68, Reader in Continuum Mechanics, 1968-71; Head, Department of Mathematics, Heriot-Watt University, 1971-83; Visiting Professor: Cornell University, 1967 and 1968;

University of California, Berkeley, 1968; Pisa University, 1974; Ecole Polytechnique Federale Lausanne, Switzerland, 1980; Royal Society of Edinburgh: Council Member, 1982-92, Executive Committee Member, 1982-92, Meetings Secretary, 1982-87, Chief Executive Editor, Proceedings A, 1982-87, Curator, 1987-92; President: Edinburgh Mathematical Society, 1974-75, International Society for the Interaction of Mechanics and Mathematics, 1991-95 (Vice-President, since 1995); Editor, Applied Mathematics and Mathematical Computation, 1990-97; Convener, Executive Committee, International Centre for Mathematical Sciences, Edinburgh, since 1996. Publications: Uniqueness Theories in Linear Elasticity (Co-author), 1971; Theory of Elastic Stability (Co-author), 1973. Recreations: walking; reading. Address: (b.) Lord Balerno Building, Heriot-Watt University, Edinburgh EH14 4AS; T.-0131-451 3363.

Knott, David G., DHE, MIHort. Curator, Dawyck Botanic Garden, since 1992; b. 28.2.60, Edinburgh. Educ. Perth Grammar School; Royal Botanic Garden, Edinburgh. National Trust for Scotland: Branklyn Garden, Perth, Threave Garden, Castle Douglas; Longwood Gardens, Pennsylvania, USA; Royal Botanic Garden, Edinburgh; Brodick Castle Garden, Isle of Arran; Castle Kennedy Garden, Stranraer; Logan Botanic Garden. Recreations: photography; natural history; hillwalking; golf. Address: Dawyck Botanic Garden, Stobo, Peebles EH45 9JU; T.-01721 760254.

Knowler, Professor John T., PhD, CBiol, FIBiol. Head, School of Biological and Biomedical Sciences, Glasgow Caledonian University, since 1990; b. 19.10.42, Whitstable; m., Susan Penelope; 2 d. Educ. Canterbury Technical School; Glasgow University. Insecticide and pharmaceutical industries, 1962-69; pre-doctoral research, 1969-72; post-doctoral research, 1972-73; Lecturer then Senior Lecturer, Biochemistry, Glasgow University, 1973-90. Publications: 75 papers, 11 chapters in academic books, two authored books. Recreations: bird-watching and other aspects of natural history; gardening. Address: (b.) School of Biological and Biomedical Sciences, Glasgow Caledonian University, Cowcaddens Road, Glasgow G4 0BA; T.-0141-331 3210.

Knox, Col. Sir Bryce Muir, KCVO, MC (and Bar), CStJ, TD, BA (Cantab); b. 4.4.16, Edinburgh; m., Patricia Mary Dunsmuir; 1 s.; 1 d. Educ. Stowe; Trinity College, Cambridge. County of Ayr: Deputy Lieutenant, 1953, Vice Lieutenant, 1970-74, Ayrshire and Arran Lord Lieutenant, 1974-91; Chairman, W. & J. Knox Ltd., Kilbirnie, 1970-78; Vice-Chairman, Lindustries Ltd., 1979 (Director, 1953-79); served with Ayrshire (ECO) Yeomanry, 1939-45, North Africa and Italy (CO, 1953-56, Hon. Col., 1960-71); Honorary Colonel, Ayrshire Yeomanry Squadron, Queen's Own Yeomanry, 1971-77; Member, Queen's Bodyguard for Scotland (Royal Company of Archers), since 1974; President, Royal Highland Agricultural Society of Scotland, 1990-91. Publications: brief historical notes of the Ayrshire Yeomanry; History of the Eglinton Hunt. Recreation: country sports. Address: (h.) Martnaham Lodge, by Ayr KA6 6ES; T.-01292 560204.

Knox, Jack, RSA, RGI, RSW, HonFRIAS. Painter; b. 16.12.36, Kirkintilloch; m., Margaret K. Sutherland; 1 s.; 1 d. Educ. Lenzie Academy; Glasgow School of Art; André Lhôte Atelier, Paris. Lecturer in Drawing and Painting, Duncan of Jordanstone College of Art, 1965-81; Head of Painting Studios, Glasgow School of Art, 1981-92. Solo exhibitions: Scottish Gallery, Edinburgh; Richard Demarco Gallery, Edinburgh; Serpentine Gallery, London; Buckingham Gallery, London; Civic Arts Centre, Aberdeen; retrospective – Fruit Market Gallery, Edinburgh, Third Eye Centre, Glasgow, touring to Aberdeen, Inverness Dundee; Kelvingrove Art Gallery and Museum, Glasgow; Open Eye Gallery, Edinburgh; many mixed exhibitions internationally; work in numerous private collections. Member, Scottish Arts Council, 1974-79; Member, Trustees Committee, Scottish National Gallery of Modern Art, 1975-82; Trustee, National Galleries of Scotland, 1982-87; Secretary, Royal Scottish Academy, 1990-91; Many awards, most recently, Maude Gemmell Hutchison Prize, RSA, 1998. Books illustrated: The Scottish Bestiary, by George Mackay Brown, 1986; La Pontinière, by David and Hilary Brown. Address: 31 North Erskine Park, Bearsden, Glasgow G61 4LY; T.-0141-942 6629.

Knox, John, BA, BD. General Secretary, YMCA Scotland, since 1992; b. 28.1.35, Larne, Co. Antrim; m., Patricia Ringland; 1 s.; 1 d. Educ. Larne Grammar School; Queen's University, Belfast; Edgehill College; London University. Methodist Minister, Dublin, Donegal and Belfast, 1959-69; General Secretary, Methodist Youth Department, Ireland, 1969-78; Associate Secretary, Irish Council of Churches, 1978-82; Chief Officer, Scottish Standing Conference of Voluntary Youth Organisations, 1982-92. Recreations: gardening; mountain walking; music. Address: (b.) 11 Rutland Street, Edinburgh EH1 2AE; T.-0131-228 1464.

Knox, William. Author and Journalist; b. 20.2.28, Glasgow; m., Myra Ann McKill; 1 s.; 2 d. Educ. Eastwood School. Deputy News Editor, Evening News, Glasgow, 1957; Scottish Editor, Kemsley Newspapers, Glasgow, 1957-60; News Editor, Scottish Television, 1960-62; Freelance Author and Broadcaster, since 1962; author of more than 60 books, including novels of crime, sea and adventure: most recent novel, Death Bytes, 1998; awarded Police Review Award for best novel of British police procedures, 1987 (The Crossfire Killings); Presenter Crime Desk, STV, 1977-88; William Knox Collection established Boston University, USA; Past President and Honorary Member, Association of Scottish Motoring Writers; former Member, Scottish Committee, Society of Authors; Past President, Eastwood Rotary Club; Honorary Editor, Scottish Lifeboat, RNLI; Fellow, Paul Harris Foundation, Rotary International, 1989. Recreations: motoring; photography; dogs. Address: (h.) 55 Newtonlea Avenue, Newton Mearns, Glasgow G77 5QF.

Knox, William James. Member, Council, ACAS, since 1992; President, Rotary Club of Greenock, 1995-96; Member, Executive, Scottish Council Development and Industry, 1995-97; Member, Council, Scottish Bowling Association, since 1995; UK Employment Spokesman, Federation of Small Businesses; b. 4.8.44, Glasgow; m., Ann May; 1 d. Educ. Greenock High School; Reid Kerr College, Paisley. Partner, A.F. McPherson & Co., Builders and Merchants, since 1962; Board Member, Scottish National Federation of Building Trade Employers, 1970-79; Member, Social Security Tribunal, 1978-84; Director, Morton Football and Athletic Club, 1986-89; Chairman, Morton Development Club, 1986-89; Member: Board of Directors, Greenock Arts Guild, since 1993, Executive, Scottish Constitutional Convention, 1989-90; Chairman: UK Federation of Small Businesses, 1989-92, Inverclyde Megawatt Festival, 1994-95. Recreations: football; bowling; photography; canals. Address: (h.) 3 Moorfield Road, Gourock PA19 1DD; T.-01475 633327.

Kocienski, Professor Philip Joseph, PhD, FRSC, FRSE, FRS. Regius Professor of Chemistry, University of Glasgow, since 1997; b. 23.12.46, Troy, New York, USA; m., Joanna; 1 s.; 2 d. Educ. Columbia High School; Brown University. Lecturer, Leeds University, 1977-85; Professor, Southampton University, 1985-97. President, Perkin Division, Royal Society of Chemistry. Tilden Medal and Simonsen Medal, Royal Society of Chemistry. Recreations: 20th century Eastern European music and literature. Address: Department of Chemistry, University of Glasgow, Glasgow G12 8QQ; T.-0141-330 3716.

Kuenssberg, Nicholas Christopher, BA (Hons) (Oxon), FCIS, FInstD, CIMgt, FRSA. Chairman: Stoddard International PLC, since 1997, GAP Group Ltd., since 1996, Institute of Directors, Scotland, since 1997, Non-executive Director: Standard Life Assurance Company, since 1988, Baxi Partnership Ltd., since 1996, Bio-Logic Remediation Ltd., since 1997, Sanmex International plc, since 1998; Member: Advisory Group to Secretary of State on Sustainable Development, since 1996, Scottish Legal Aid Board, since 1996; b. 28.10.42, Edinburgh; m., Sally Robertson; 1 s.; 2 d. Educ. Edinburgh Academy; Wadham College, Oxford. Director, J. & P. Coats Ltd., 1978-91; Chairman, Dynacast International Ltd, 1978-91; Director, Coats Patons plc, 1985-91; Director, Coats Viyella plc, 1986-91; Managing Director, Dawson International plc, 1994-95 (Managing Director, Premier Brands, 1991-94); Non-executive Director: Bank of Scotland West of Scotland Board, 1984-88, ScottishPower plc, 1984-97; Chairman: David A. Hall Ltd., 1997-98, Association for Management Education and Training in Scotland, 1996-98; Visiting Professor, Strathclyde Business School, 1988-91. Recreations: languages; opera; travel; sport. Address: (b.) 6 Cleveden Drive, Glasgow, G12 0SE.

Kuenssberg, Sally, BA, DipAdEd. Chairman, Scottish Children's Reporter Administration, since 1995; Non-Executive Director, Yorkhill NHS Trust, since 1993; b. 30.7.43, Edinburgh; m., Nicholas; 1 s.; 2 d. Educ. St Leonard's School; University of Oxford. Language Teaching, Europe and South America, 1966-78; Partner, Heatherbank Press, Milngavie, 1981-90; Children's Panel Training Organiser, Department of Adult and Continuing Education, University of Glasgow, 1990-95. Adult Literacy Tutor, 1979-83; Member, Children's Panel, Glasgow, 1984-90. Address: (b.) SCRA, Ochil House, Springkerse Business Park, Stirling FK7 7XE.

Kyle, David Justice. Director, Board, British Deer Society, since 1997 (Chairman, N.E. Scotland Branch, since 1995); Higher Scientific Officer, International Feed Resources Unit, Rowett Research Institute, since 1991 (currently Deputy Quality Assurance Manager for the Institute); b. 12.2.58, St. Andrews; m., Carol Elizabeth. Educ. Bell Baxter School, Cupar. Scientific Officer, Scottish Office Agriculture and Fisheries Department, Rowett Research Institute, Aberdeen, 1981-89; Red Deer Research Unit, Macaulay Land Use Research Organisation, Glensaugh Research Station, Kincardineshire, 1989-91; Churchill Fellow, 1997. Recreations: deer welfare; politics; theatre; classical music. Address: Skene Croft, Glenfarquhar, Auchinblae, Aberdeenshire AB30 1TS; T.-01561 320665.

Kyle, James, CBE, DSc, MCh, FRCS. Chairman, Raigmore Hospital NHS Trust, Inverness; b. 26.3.25, Ballymena, Northern Ireland; m., Dorothy Elizabeth Galbraith; 2 d. Educ. Ballymena Academy; Queen's University, Belfast. Scholarship to Mayo Clinic, USA, 1950; Tutor in Surgery, Royal Victoria Hospital, Belfast, 1952; Lecturer in Surgery, Liverpool University, 1957; Senior Lecturer in Surgery, Aberdeen University, 1959-60, and Surgeon, Aberdeen Royal Infirmary, 1959-89. Member, Grampian Health Board, 1973-77, Chairman, 1989-93; Chairman, Scottish Committee for Hospital Medical Services, 1976-79; elected Member, General Medical Council, since 1979; Chairman: Scottish Joint Consultants Committee, 1984-89, Representative Body, British Medical Association, 1984-87; President, Aberdeen Medico-Chirurgical Society, 1989-90; Examiner: Belfast, Dublin, Dundee, Edinburgh, Sydney, University of West Indies; Burgess of Aberdeen. Publications: Peptic Ulcer; Pye's Surgical Handicraft; Crohn's Disease; Scientific Foundations of Surgery. Recreations: Fellow, Royal Philatelic Society, London; licensed radio amateur, GM4 CHX. Address: (h.) 7 Fasaich, Gairloch IV21 2BD; T.-01445 712398.

Kyle, Peter McLeod, MBChB, FRCS(Edin), FRCS(Glas), FRCOphth. Consultant Ophthalmologist, Southern General Hospital NHS Trust, since 1982 (Clinical Director of Ophthalmology, since 1995); Honorary Clinical Senior Lecturer, Glasgow University, since 1985; Member, Medical Appeal Tribunals, Scotland, since 1986; Member, General Optical Council; b. 19.8.51, Rutherglen; m., Valerie Anne Steele; 1 s.; 2 d. Educ. High School of Glasgow; Glasgow University. Lecturer in Ophthalmology, Glasgow University, 1980-84. Convener, Ophthalmology Sub-committee, Royal College of Physicians and Surgeons of Glasgow; Member, Opthalmology Specialist Advisory Board, Royal College of Surgeons of Edinburgh. Recreations: walking; skiing. Address: (h.) 36 Sutherland Avenue, Glasgow; T.-0141-427 4400; The Stables, Earlsferry, Fife; T.-01333 330647.

Kynoch, George Alexander Bryson, BSc. Non-Executive Chairman: Silvertech International plc, London Marine Group Ltd., Muir Matheson Ltd., Benson Construction Ltd.; Non-Executive Director: P.S.L. Holdings Ltd., Midmar Energy Ltd., W.M.L. Group PLC; MP (Conservative), Kincardine and Deeside, 1992-97; Parliamentary Under Secretary of State for Scotland – Minister for Industry and Local Government, 1995-97; b. 7.10.46, Keith; m., Dr. Rosslyn Margaret McDevitt; 1 s.; 1 d. Educ. Cargilfield School, Edinburgh; Glenalmond College, Perth; Bristol University. Plant Engineer, ICI Ltd., Nobel Division, 1968-71; G. and G. Kynoch PLC, 1971-92, latterly as Group Executive Director; Non-Executive Director: Kynoch Group PLC, Aardvark Clear Mine Ltd., 1992-95; Member, Aberdeen and District Milk Marketing Board, 1988-92; Director, Moray Badenoch and Strathspey Local Enterprise Co. Ltd., 1991-92; Chairman, Scottish Woollen Publicity Council, 1983-90; President, Scottish Woollen Industry, 1990-91; Vice Chairman, Northern Area, Scottish Conservative and Unionist Association, 1991-92. Recreations: golf; skiing; travel. Address: (h.) Newton of Drumduan, Dess, Aboyne, Aberdeenshire AB34 5BD.

L

Lacy, Rev. David William, BA, BD. Minister, Henderson Parish Church, Kilmarnock, since 1989; Vice Convener, General Assembly Business Committee, since 1996; Member, Judicial Commission of General Assembly; b. 26.4.52, Inverness; m., Joan Stewart Roberston; 1 s.; 1 d. Educ. Aberdeen Grammar School; High School of Glasgow; University of Strathclyde; University of Glasgow and Trinity College. Assistant Minister, St. George's West, Edinburgh, 1975-77; Minister, Knightswood: St. Margaret's, Glasgow, 1977-89. Chaplain, "U" Division, Strathclyde Police; Chaplain, Kilmarnock College. Recreations: sailing; snooker; choral singing. Address: 52 London Road, Kilmarnock, Ayrshire KA3 7AJ; T.-01563 523113.

Laidlaw, Bruce, ACIS. Administrative Secretary, Royal Scottish Academy, since 1995; b. 11.7.45, Edinburgh; m., Sandra; 1 s.; 1 d. Educ. Royal High School; Napier College, Edinburgh. Assistant Secretary, Cranston London Hotels Co. Ltd., 1963-65; public service, Edinburgh City, 1966-74; Elections Officer, Lothian Regional Council, 1975-79; public service, Lothian Regional Council, 1980-95. Chairman, MS Therapy Centre, Lothian. Recreations: fishing; skiing. Address: (b.) Royal Scottish Academy, The Mound, Edinburgh EH2 2EL; T.-0131-225 6671.

Laidlaw, Professor Emeritus James Cameron, MA, PhD. Emeritus Professor of French, Aberdeen University (Professor of French, 1975-92); Honorary Fellow, Arts Faculty, Edinburgh University; b. 3.3.37, Ecclefechan; m., Elizabeth Fernie Bosomworth; 1 s.; 2 d. Educ. George Watson's College, Edinburgh; Edinburgh University; Trinity Hall, Cambridge. Research Fellow, Trinity Hall, Cambridge, 1961-63; Lecturer in Medieval French, Queen's University, Belfast, 1963-65; University Assistant Lecturer (from 1969 University Lecturer) in French, and Fellow, Trinity Hall, Cambridge, 1965-74; Visiting Fellow, Gonville and Caius College, Cambridge, 1986-87; Visiting Professor, Victoria University of Wellington, New Zealand, 1990-91; Vice-Principal, Aberdeen University, 1984-86. Member Arts Sub-Committee, University Grants Committee, 1980-89; Adviser in Modern Languages, Universities Funding Council, 1989-91; Honorary Secretary, Modern Humanities Research Association, 1961-67; Chevalier des palmes académiques. Publications: The Future of the Modern Humanities (Editor), 1969; The Poetical Works of Alain Chartier, 1974; Alain Chartier: poemes, 1988. Recreations: walking; cycling. Address: (h.) Orchard Walls, Traquair, Innerleithen EH44 6PU; T.-01896 831227.

Laing, Anne Katherine, LLB, NP. Senior Partner, P.H. Young & Co., Solicitors, since 1990; b. 18.1.54, Galashiels. Educ. Grangemouth High School; University of Dundee. Peter Young, Bo'ness: Apprenticeship, Assistant, Partner, 1980, took over business in 1983, sole practitioner until 1990. Honorary Sheriff, Tayside Central and Fife; Director (Past President), Central Scotland Chamber of Commerce; Director/Board Member, Forth Valley Enterprise, since 1993; Director, Careers Central Limited, since 1995 (Chair, since 1997). Recreations: gym; gardening; travel; food and wine. Address: (b.) 54 South Street, Bo'ness EH51 826166.

Laing, David Kemlo, LLB. Managing Partner, Ledingham Chalmers, since 1996; b. 17.6.53, Aberdeen; m., Marina Maclean; 2 d. Educ. Robert Gordon's College, Aberdeen; University of Edinburgh. Clark and Wallace, Aberdeen, 1974-76; C. & P. H. Chalmers, Aberdeen, 1976-78, Partner, 1978-90; Partner, Ledingham Chalmers, 1991. Recreations: music; outdoors. Address: (b.) 1 Golden Square, Aberdeen AB10 1HA; T.-01224 408510.

Laing, The Hon. Mark Hector, MA. Managing Director, Simmers of Edinburgh, since 1996; Member, Executive Council, Scottish Business in the Community; Chairman, Friends of Craigmillar; b. 22.2.51, London; m., Susanna Crawford; 1 s.; 2 d. Educ. Eton College; Cambridge University. United Biscuits p.l.c., 1972-96: Factory Director, Glasgow, 1985; Production Director, McVities, 1988; Managing Director, Simmers Biscuits, 1990. Recreations: walking; gardening; fishing; shooting. Address: (b.) Simmers of Edinburgh Ltd., 90 Peffermill Road, Edinburgh EH16 5UU; T.-0131-661 3384.

Lally, Patrick James, OStJ, LLD, JP, HRGI, FRSA. Rt. Hon. Lord Provost of the City of Glasgow and Lord Lieutenant, City of Glasgow, until May 1999; Commandeur, Ordre National du Merite (France); Chairman, Greater Glasgow and Clyde Valley Tourist Board, since 1996; Director, Glasgow Cultural Enterprises, since 1988; b. Glasgow; m., Margaret Beckett McGuire; 2 s. Elected, Corporation of Glasgow, 1966-75 (Deputy Leader, 1972-75); elected City of Glasgow Council, 1975-77, and 1980-96; City Treasurer, 1984-86; Leader, City of Glasgow District Council, 1986-92 and 1994-96; Chairman, Greater Glasgow Tourist Board, 1989-96; Director, Glasgow International Jazz Festival; Hon. Director, Chinese Peoples Association for Friendship with Foreign Countries; Hon. Member, Royal Glasgow Institute of Fine Arts; Hon. Member, Rotary International; Hon. Citizen, Dalian, China. Recreations: enjoying the arts; reading; watching TV; football. Address: (b.) City Chambers, George Square, Glasgow; T.-0141-287 4201.

Lamb, Rev. A. Douglas, MA, FSA (Scot). Parish Minister, Dalry: St. Margaret's, since 1973; Convener, Mission and Evangelism Resource Committee, Board of National Mission, Church of Scotland, since 1995; b. 9.11.36, Glasgow; m., Jean A. Beattie; 3 s.; 1 d. Educ. Hermitage School, Helensburgh; Glasgow University; Princeton Seminary. Assistant Minister: First Presbyterian, Philadelphia, Airdrie West; Parish Minister, Unst (Shetland). Recreations: hill-walking; history; continental travel. Address: St. Margaret's Manse, Dalry KA24 4DA; T.-01294 832234.

Lamb, Professor Joseph Fairweather, MB, ChB, BSc, PhD, FRCPEdin, FRSE. Honorary Professor; Chandos Professor of Physiology, St. Andrews University, 1969-93; Chairman, Save British Science Society, 1986-97; b. 18.7.28, Brechin; m., 1, Olivia Jane Horne; 3 s.; 1 d.; 2, Bridget Cecilia Cook; 2 s. Educ. Brechin High School; Edinburgh University. National Service, 1947-49; House Surgeon, Dumfries Royal Infirmary, 1955-56; House Physician, Eastern General Hospital, Edinburgh, 1956; Research Scholar, then Lecturer, Edinburgh University, 1957-61; Lecturer, then Senior Lecturer, Glasgow University, 1961-69; Editor, Journal of Physiology, 1968-74; Senior Secretary, Physiological Society, 1982-85; Chairman, Gas Greed campaign, 1994-95; Governor, Rowett Research Institute, since 1998; Chairman and Founder, Save British Science, 1986-97. Publication: Essentials of Physiology, 1980. Recreations: boat-building; sailing; amateur radio. Address: (h.) Kenbrae, 23 Millbank, Cupar KY15 5DP.

Lambie, David, BSc (Hons), DipEd, FEIS. Chairman, Development Committee and Member, Management Committee, Cunninghame Housing Association, since 1992; Member, Board, Galloway Training Association Ltd., since 1997; MP (Labour), Cunninghame South, 1970-92; b. 13.7.25, Saltcoats; m., Netta Merrie; 1 s.; 4 d. Educ. Ardrossan Academy; Glasgow University; Geneva University. Teacher, Glagow Corporation, 1950-70. Secretary, All Party Committee for Energy Studies, 1980-92; chaired Select Committee on Scottish Affairs, 1981-87; UK Member, Council of Europe and Western European Union, 1987-92; Chairman, PLP Aviation Committee,

1988-92; Chairman, Saltcoats Labour Party, 1992-96. Recreation: watching junior football. Address: (h.) 11 Ivanhoe Drive, Saltcoats, Ayrshire KA21 6LS; T.-01294 464843.

Lammie, Neil Robertson, FCCA. Director of Finance and Executive Board Member, Ayrshire and Arran Health Board, since 1992; b. 4.11.41, Ayr; m., Winnie; 2 s.; 1 d. Educ. Marr College, Troon. Treasurer, Fife Health Board, 1979-85; Treasurer, Ayrshire and Arran Health Board, 1985-91. Recreations: sport in general, rugby union and golf in particular. Address: (b.) Boswell House, 10 Arthur Street, Ayr KA7 2QJ.

Lamont, Colin C., MA, PhD. Headteacher, Ross High School, Tranent, since 1989; b. 6.10.44, Glasgow; m.; 2 s. Educ. Robert Gordon's College, Aberdeen; Aberdeen University; Edinburgh University. Teacher, Merchiston Castle School, Edinburgh; Principal Teacher, Robert Gordon's College, Aberdeen; Adviser in English, Renfrew Division, Strathclyde; Headteacher, Gracemount High School, Edinburgh. Address: (b.) Ross High School, Well Wynd, Tranent, East Lothian EH33 2EQ; T.-01875 610433.

Lamont, Rev. Stewart Jackson, BSc, BD. Minister, Church of Scotland, since 1972; Freelance Journalist and Broadcaster (Religious Affairs Correspondent, Glasgow Herald), since 1980; Parish Minister, Kinning Park, Glasgow, since 1991; b. 8.1.47, Broughty Ferry; m., Larisa V. Gaidakova. Educ. Grove Academy, Broughty Ferry; St. Andrews University. General Council Assessor, St. Andrews University Court, 1970-82; Producer, BBC Religious Department, 1972-80; Freelance Radio and Television Presenter and Producer, 1980-91; part-time Minister, Abernyte, 1980-82. Publications: The Third Angle, 1978; Is Anybody There?, 1980; Religion and the Supernatural (Co-Author), 1985; Religion Inc. (Scientology), 1986; Scotland 2000 (BBC TV, 1987; Church and State, 1989; In Good Faith, 1989; The Swordbearer: John Knox, 1991; Glasgow Herald Book of Glasgow (Contributor); St. Andrews Rock, 1993; Life of St. Andrew, 1997. Winner, Scottish Schools Debating Competition, 1965; President of the Union, St. Andrews, 1969. Recreations: cooking; music; foreign travel. Address: Apartment 9, 10 Mavisbank Gardens, Glasgow G51 1HG; T.-0141-427 2191.

Lamont, William David Dawson, CA, IRRV. Head of Revenues, Finance Service, The Highland Council, since 1996; b. 14.11.49, Irvine; m., Eleanor; 1 s.; 1 d. Educ. Irvine Royal Academy; Institute of Chartered Accountants of Scotland (Glasgow University). Alexander Sloan & Company, Glasgow, 1966-73; Depute Burgh Chamberlain, Royal Burgh of Irvine, 1973-75; Depute Director of Finance, Argyll & Bute District Council, 1975-90; Director of Finance, Argyll & Bute District Council, 1990-96. Recreations: family; travel; music; Rotary. Address: (b.) The Highland Council, Glenurquhart Road, Inverness IV3 5NX; T.-01463 702404.

Lamont-Brown, Raymond, MA, AMIET, MJS, FSA (Scot). Author and Broadcaster; Lecturer, Centre for External Services, St. Andrews University, 1978-98, Centre for Continuing Education, Dundee University, 1988-98; Founder, Japan Research Projects, since 1965; b. 20.9.39, Horsforth, Leeds; m., Dr. Elizabeth Moira McGregor. Educ. Wheelwright Grammar School, Dewsbury; Bradford Technical College; SOAS; Nihon Daigaku, Japan. Honorary Secretary/Treasurer, Society of Authors in Scotland, 1982-89; Past President, St. Andrews Rotary Club; Vice-Chairman, St. Andrews Community Council, 1988-91; Chairman, Arthritis Care Liaison Committee (Central, Fife and Tayside), 1991-97; Member, Council, Arthritis Care, 1991-97. Publications: 50 published books, including Discovering Fife; Phantoms of the Sea; The Life and Times of Berwick-upon-Tweed; The Life and Times of St. Andrews; Royal Murder Mysteries; Scottish Epitaphs; Scottish Superstitions; Scottish Traditions and Festivals; Famous Scots; Scottish Witchcraft; Around St. Andrews; Scottish Folklore; Kamikaze: Japan's Suicide Samurai; Scotland of 100 Years Ago; Kempeitai: Japan's Dreaded Military Police; Edward VII's Last Loves; Tutor to the Dragon Emperor. Address: (h.) 11 Seabourne Gardens, Broughty Ferry, Dundee DD5 2RT; T.-01382 732032.

Lamprell-Jarrett, Peter Neville, KCSG, KCHS, PPIAAS, FIAS, FFB, FSA(Scot), FRSA. Retired Partner, Archard & Partners, Architects and Surveyors; b. 23.6.19, Margate; m., Kathleen Furner; 1 s.; 1 d. Educ. Vernon House Preparatory School; Cliftonville College. Architectural Assistant, LCC (later GLC) Housing Department, 1947-49; Deputy Controller of Works, Land Settlement Association, 1950-54; President, Incorporated Association of Architects and Surveyors, 1967-68; Kt. Commander: Equestrian Order Holy Sepulchre of Jerusalem, 1974, Pontifical Order of St. Gregory the Great, 1975; responsible for design of many Catholic schools and churches; Freeman, City of London; Life Vice President, London Caledonian Catholic Association; Past Chairman, Archdiocese of Westminster Catholic Parents and Electors Association; Liveryman, Worshipful Company of Wheelwrights, since 1978. Recreations: painting; walking; fishing; classical music. Address: (h.) Carrick House, Carrick Castle, by Lochgoil, Argyll PA24 8AF; T.-Lochgoilhead 703394.

Landale, Sir David William Neil, KCVO, DL. Chairman, Malcolm Sargent Fund in Scotland, since 1996; b. 27.5.34, London; m., (Norah) Melanie; 3 s. Educ. Eton College; Balliol College, Oxford (MA). Black Watch, Royal Highland Regiment, 1952-54; Jardine Matheson & Co. Ltd., 1958-75, served in Hong Kong, Thailand, Taiwan and Japan (Director, 1967-75); Director, Matheson & Co. Ltd., 1975; Secretary and Keeper of the Records, Duchy of Cornwall, 1987-93; Member, Royal Company of Archers, Queen's Bodyguard for Scotland, since 1966. Recreations: all countryside pursuits; theatre; reading (history). Address: (h.) Dalswinton, Dumfries; T.-01387 740 208/279.

Lander, Ronald, OBE, BSc, Comp. IEE, FScotvec, FSQA. Chairman and Managing Director: Scotlander plc, since 1985, Scetlander Ltd., since 1986; Director, Picardy Television Ltd., since 1998; Chairman, Newstel Information Ltd., since 1998; b. 5.8.42, Glasgow; m., Elizabeth Stirling; 2 s. Educ. Allan Glen's School; Glasgow University. Chairman and Managing Director, Lander Grayburn & Co. Limited, 1970-83; Deputy Managing Director, Lander Alarm Company (Scotland) Limited, 1975-79; Managing Director, Lander Alarms Limited and Lander Alarms (Scotland) Limited, 1979-85; Chairman, Lander & Jess Limited, 1983-87; Director, Centre for Entrepreneurial Development, Glasgow University, 1985-88. Member, CBI Scottish Council, 1977-83, 1984-90 and since 1992; (founding) Chairman, CBI Scotland's Smaller Firms' Working Group, 1977-80; founding Chairman, Entrepreneurial Exchange, 1995-96; founder Member, CBI Industrial Policy Committee, London, 1978-86; Chairman, CBI Scotland Smaller Firms' Committee, 1993-95; Chairman, Scottish Fire Prevention Council, 1979-80; Member, Glasgow University Appointments Committee, since 1979; CBI Representative, Home Office/CBI/TUC Joint Committee on Prison Industries, 1980-87; Industrial Member, Understanding British Industry, Scotland, 1981-89; Member, Council, Scottish Business School, 1982-87; Director, British Security Industry Association Council, 1984-85; Governor, Scottish Sports Aid Foundation, 1985-88; Vice-Chairman, CBI Scotland Education and Training Committee, 1986-87; Member: Kincraig Committee (review of parole system and related matters), 1987-89, Manpower Services Committee for Scotland (later the Training Agency), 1987-88; founder Chairman, Local Employer Network (LENS) Scottish Co-ordinating Committee, 1987; Chairman, CBI Scotland Education and

Training Committee, 1987-89; Director, SCOTVEC, 1987-93; Member, CBI Business/Education Task Force (the Cadbury Report), 1988; Member, Scottish Consultative Council on the Curriculum, 1988-91; Vice-Convener, Scottish Education/Industry Committee, 1988-91; founder Member, Glasgow Action, 1985; Member, Secretary of State for Scotland's Crime Prevention Committee, 1984-87; Companion IEE, 1986; Board Member, Glasgow Development Agency, since 1991; Visiting/Honorary Professor, Glasgow University, since 1991; National Judge, National Training Awards, 1989-92. Address: (b.) Scotlander plc, 1 Atlantic Quay, Broomielaw, Glasgow, G2 8JE; T.-0141 226 5611.

Lane, Professor David Philip, BSc, PhD, FRSE, FRS, FRCPath. Professor of Molecular Oncology, Department of Biochemistry, Dundee University, since 1990; Director, Cancer Research Campaign Cell Transformation Group, since 1990; Gibb Fellow, Cancer Research Campaign, since 1990; b. 1.7.52, London; m., Professor Ellen Birgitte Lane (qv); 1 s.; 1 d. Educ. John Fisher School, Purley; University College, London. Lecturer in Zoology, then Lecturer in Biochemistry, Imperial College, London; Principal Scientist, Imperial Cancer Research Fund, South Mimms. Publications: (book) Antibodies, a laboratory manual; 200 articles. Recreations: walking; tennis; motor bikes. Address: (b.) CRC Laboratories, Dundee University, Dundee DD1 4HN; T.-01382 344982.

Lane, Professor Ellen Birgitte, BSc, PhD, FRSE. Cox Professor of Anatomy and Cell Biology, Dundee University, since 1991; Director, Cancer Research Campaign Cell Structure Research Group, since 1990; b. 24.12.50, Welwyn Garden City; m., David Philip Lane (qv); 1 s.; 1 d. Educ. Withington Girls' School, Manchester; University College, London. Research Assistant, Imperial College of Science and Technology, 1975-77, University College, 1977-78, Cold Spring Harbour Laboratories, New York, 1978-80; Imperial Cancer Research Fund, 1980-90; ICRF Clare Hall Laboratories, 1985-90. Publications: scientific papers in cell biology and cancer research. Address: (b.) CRC Laboratories, Department of Anatomy and Physiology, MSI/WTB Complex, Dundee University, Dundee DD1 5EH; T.-01382 344883.

Lang, Lt.-Gen. Sir Derek, KCB (1967), DSO (1944), MC (1941), DL; b. 7.10.13, Guildford; 1 s.; 1 d. Educ. Wellington College; RMC, Sandhurst. Director of Army Training, 1964-66; GOC-in-C, Scottish Command, and Governor of Edinburgh Castle, 1966-69. President, Army Cadet Force Association (Scotland), 1974-86. Recreations: golf; fishing; shooting; music. Address: (h.) Templeland, Kirknewton, Midlothian EH27 8DJ; T.01506 883211.

Lang of Monkton, Baron (Ian Bruce Lang), DL, PC, OStJ, BA. President of the Board of Trade, 1995-97; Life Peer; President, Association for the Protection of Rural Scotland, since 1998; Deputy Lieutenant, Ayrshire and Arran, since 1998; Company Directorships including: CGU plc, Marsh & McLennan Inc., Murray Ventures Investment Trust plc, Second Scottish National Trust plc; b. 27.6.40, Glasgow; m., Sandra Caroline Montgomerie; 2 d. Educ. Lathallan School; Rugby School; Sidney Sussex College, Cambridge. MP (Conservative) Galloway and Upper Nithsdale, 1983-97 (Galloway, 1979-83); Member, Select Committee on Scottish Affairs, 1979-81; Honorary President, Scottish Young Conservatives, 1982-84; Trustee, Glasgow Savings Bank and West of Scotland TSB, 1969-82; Lord Commissioner of HM Treasury, 1983-86; Scottish Whip, 1981-83; Vice-Chairman, Scottish Conservative Party, 1983-87; Parliamentary Under Secretary of State, Scottish Office, 1986-87, and at Department of Employment, 1986; Minister of State, Scottish Office, 1987-90; Secretary of State for Scotland, 1990-95. Member, Queen's Bodyguard for Scotland (Royal Company of Archers), since 1974; Insurance Broker and Company Director, 1962-81. Address (b.) House of Lords, Westminster, London SW1A OPW.

Langford, Professor David Anthony, FCIOB, MSc, MPhil, MIMgt, FRSA. Barr Professor of Construction, Strathclyde University, since 1991; b. 6.5.50, Notingham; m., Victoria; 1 d. Educ. Barstable School, Basildon; Bristol Polytechnic; Aston University; Cranfield School of Management. MSc Course Director, Department of Building Technology, Brunel University, 1975; Director of Postgraduate Studies, Bath University, 1987. Address: (b.) Department of Civil Engineering, Strathclyde University, Glasgow G4 0NG; T.-0141-552 4400.

Langley, Crawford James, LLB (Hons), DPA, ACIS, NP. Director of Legal and Corporate Services, Aberdeen City Council, since 1995; Advocate in Aberdeen; b. 21.11.51, Glasgow; m., Janette Law Hamilton. Educ. Bellahouston Academy, Glasgow; Glasgow University. Legal apprentice, Corporation of Glasgow, 1973-75; various legal posts, Strathclyde Regional Council, 1975-89, Principal Solicitor, 1984-89; Depute Director of Law and Administration, Tayside Regional Council, 1989-91; Director of Law and Administration, Tayside Regional Council, 1991-95. Assistant Area Commissioner, Scout Association. Recreations: travel; gardening. Address: (h.) Canouan, Eassie, Angus DD8 1SG; T.-Glamis 518.

Lansdowne, 8th Marquess of (George John Charles Mercer Nairne Petty-Fitzmaurice); b. 27.11.12; 2 s.; 1 d. Minister of State for Colonial Affairs, 1962-64, for Commonwealth Relations, 1963-64. Address: Meikleour House, Perthshire, PH2 6EA.

Larkin, Professor Maurice John Milner, MA, PhD. Professor of Modern European History, Edinburgh University, since 1976; b. 12.8.32, Harrow on the Hill; m., Enid Thelma Lowe; 1 s.; 1 d. Educ. St. Philip's Grammar School, Birmingham; Trinity College, Cambridge. Assistant Lecturer, then Lecturer, Glasgow University, 1958-65; Lecturer, then Senior Lecturer, then Reader, Kent University, 1965-76. Publications: Gathering Pace: Continental Europe 1870-1945, 1969; Church and State after the Dreyfus Affair, 1974; Man and Society in Nineteenth-Century Realism, 1977; France since the Popular Front, 1988; Religion, politics and preferment in France since 1890, 1995. Recreations: bird-watching; music; films. Address: (b.) History Department, Edinburgh University, Edinburgh EH8 9JY; T.-0131-650 3754.

Last, Professor Frederick Thomas, DSc, ARCS, SHM. Applied Biologist; Honorary Professor, Institute of Ecology and Resource Management, Edinburgh University, since 1972; b. 5.2.28, Wembley; m., Pauline Mary Cope; 2 s. Educ. Haberdashers' Aske's Hampstead School; Imperial College of Science and Technology, London. Rothamsted Experimental Station, Herts, 1950-61; Chief Plant Pathologist to Government of Sudan, 1956-58; Head, Mycology and Bacteriology, Glasshouse Crops Research Institute, Sussex, 1961-69; Visiting Professor, Pennsylvania State University, 1969-70; Member of Directorate, Institute of Terrestrial Ecology, Midlothian, 1970-86; Commissioner, Red Deer Commission, 1981-86; Visiting Professor, Agriculture and Environmental Science, Newcastle upon Tyne University, 1986-94; Chairman, Advisory Committee on Sites of Special Scientific Interest, 1992-96; Chairman, Tree Advice Trust, since 1993; Advisor, Chongqing Institute of Environmental Science, since 1993; Board Member, Scottish Natural Heritage, since 1996; Member, Joint Nature Conservation Committee, since 1996. Publications: Tree Physiology and Yield Improvement (Joint Editor), 1976; Land and its Uses, Actual and Potential: An Environmental Appraisal (Joint Editor), 1986; Acidic Deposition, Its Nature and Impacts

(Joint Editor). Recreations: gardening; philately; travelling. Address: (h.) Furuly, Seton Mains, Longniddry, East Lothian EH32 0PG; T.-01875 852102.

Lathe, Professor Richard Frank, BSc, Dr. ès Sci. Professorial Fellow, Edinburgh University, since 1989; b. 23.4.52, London; m., Margaret. Educ. Edinburgh University; Universite Libre de Bruxelles. Assistant Scientific Director, Transgene SA, Strasbourg; Principal Scientific Officer, ABRO, Edinburgh; Professor of Genetics/Genetic Engineering, University of Strasbourg; Director/Scientific Director, Ecole Superieure de Biotechnologie de Strasbourg. Publications: more than 100 scientific papers. Recreations: guitar; squash. Address: (b.) King's Buildings, West Mains Road, Edinburgh EH9 3JQ; T.-0131-650 5890.

Lauderdale, 17th Earl of (Patrick Francis Maitland), BA (Hons) (Oxon). Company Director; b. 17.3.11, Walsall; m., Stanka Lozanitch; 2 s.; 2 d. Educ. Lancing College; Brasenose College, Oxford. Journalist, Fleet Street, 1934-39; War Correspondent, Poland, 1939; Balkans/Danubian Correspondent, The Times, 1939-41; War Correspondent, the Pacific, News Chronicle, 1941-43; Foreign Office, 1943-45; Editor, The Fleet Street Letter Service, 1945-51; MP (Conservative), Lanark, 1951-59; Peer, since 1968; Chairman, Lords Committee on Energy, 1974-79; Founder/Deputy Chairman, Parliamentary Group for Energy Studies, since 1983; Guardian, Shrine of Our Lady of Walsingham, since 1955 (now Emeritus); Chairman, Parliamentary 'Church in Danger' Group, 1988-95; Hereditary Bearer of the National Flag of Scotland. Recreations: reading; travel; pilgrimages to St. Mary's, Haddington.

Laughlin, Patrick D., MA (Hons). Chief Executive, Kingdom of Fife Tourist Board, since 1998; b. 23.4.61, Edinburgh; m., Alison. Educ. Perth High School; University of Edinburgh. Tourist Officer, Crieff and District Tourist Association, 1983-86; Depute Director, Perthshire Tourist Board, 1986-97. Chairman, Scottish Association of Tourist Officers, since 1997. Recreations: road running; travel. Address: (b.) Haig House, Balgonie Road, Markinch KY7 6AQ; T.-01592 750066.

Laurenson, Arthur Bruce, OBE, FRSA. Consultant; Chairman, Shetland Catch Ltd., since 1992; b. 22.7.31, Lerwick; m., Janet S. Mullay; 2 d. Educ. Anderson High School. Crofter, 1947-64; Assistant Clerk and Treasurer, 1964-1968, then General Manager and Clerk, 1972-91, Lerwick Harbour Trust; Consultant, since 1991. Honorary Sheriff; Member, Lerwick Lifeboat Committee. Recreations: crofting; breeding Shetland ponies; gardening. Address: (h.) Vatnagarth, 2 Lovers Loan, Lerwick, Shetland ZE1 0BA; T.-01595 692799.

Laurenson, James Tait, FCA. Chairman, Erskine Stewart's Melville Governing Council; Non-Executive Director: I & S UK Smaller Companies Trust plc, since 1983, Hiscox Harrison Ltd., since 1992, Frizzell Bank, Ltd., since 1996, Fidelity Special Values plc, since 1994, Finsbury Income & Growth Investment Trust plc, since 1996; Chairman, Nippon Assets Investments SA, since 1983; b. 15.3.41, Farnborough; m., Hilary Josephine; 1 s.; 3 d. Educ. Eton College; Magdalene College, Cambridge. Ivory & Sime PLC: joined 1968; Partner, 1970; Director, 1975; left 1983; Managing Director, Tayburn Design Group Limited, 1983-84 (Chairman, 1984-88); Managing Director, Adam & Company Group plc, 1984-93. Recreations: spending time with the family; gardening. Address: (h.) Hill House, Kirknewton, Midlothian EH27 8DR; T.-01506 881990.

Laurie, Thomas, OBE, FRICS. Senior Partner, Keillor Laurie Martin Partnership, since 1991; b. 11.11.38, Wishaw; m., Jennifer Rose Dunthorne; 1 s.; 2 d. Educ. Hamilton Academy; Glasgow Technical College. Partner, Robert H. Soper & Co., Cumbernauld, 1964-77; Sole Principal, Thomas Laurie Associates, Cumbernauld and Glasgow, 1977-90. Founder Member, Cumbernauld Theatre Group, 1961; Board Member: Cottage Theatre, Cumbernauld, 1964-72, Traverse Theatre, 1972-76 (Chairman); Chairman, WASPS; Member: Drama Panel, Scottish Arts Council, 1973-82, SAC, 1976-82. Recreations: traditional singing; all forms of art appreciation; hill-walking. Address: (h.) 21 Dunglass Avenue, Glasgow G14 9ED; T.-0141-959 4025.

Laver, Professor John David Michael Henry, MA (Hons), DipPh, PhD, DLitt, FBA, FRSE, FRSA, FIoA. Professor of Phonetics, Edinburgh University, since 1985; b. 20.1.38, Nowshera, Pakistan; m., Sandy Hutcheson; 3 s.; 1 d. Educ. Churcher's College, Petersfield; Edinburgh University. Assistant Lecturer, then Lecturer in Phonetics, Ibadan University, 1963-66 (Exchange Lecturer, Edinburgh University, 1964-65); Edinburgh University: Lecturer, then Senior Lecturer in Phonetics, 1966-80, Reader in Phonetics, 1980-84, Director, Centre for Speech Technology Research, 1984-89, Vice Principal, 1994-97; Visiting Assistant Professor, Department of Linguistics, University of California, 1971; Visiting Research Fellow, Macquarie University, Sydney, 1982; Information Technology Fellowship, Edinburgh, 1983-84; President, International Phonetic Association, 1991-95; Vice-President, Royal Society of Edinburgh, 1996-99; Member, Council, British Academy, 1998-2001; Chairman, Humanities Research Board, British Academy, 1994-98. Publications: Communication in Face to Face Interaction (Joint Editor), 1972; Phonetics in Linguistics (Joint Editor), 1973; Voice Quality, 1979; The Phonetic Description of Voice Quality, 1980; The Cognitive Representation of Speech (Joint Editor), 1981; The Prospect of Future Speech Technology (Co-Author), 1987; Proceedings of the European Conference on Speech Technology (Co-Editor), 1987; Aspects of Speech Technology (Co-Editor), 1988; The Gift of Speech, 1991; Principles of Phonetics, 1994; Menschen und ihre Stimmen (Co-Author), 1994; The Handbook of Phonetic Sciences (Co-Editor), 1997. Address: (b.) Institute for Advanced Studies in the Humanities, University of Edinburgh, 8 Hope Park Square, Edinburgh EH8 9NW; T.-0131-650 2088.

Laverock, Edward, MA, LLB. Retired Solicitor; b. 21.10.19, Dunlop; m., Helen Moffat Harriet Mackison; 1 s.; 1 d. Educ. Hutchesons' Grammar School, Glasgow; Glasgow University. Partner, J. & W. Buchan, Peebles, 1945-86 (Senior Partner, 1954-86); Town Clerk, Peebles, 1948-75; Procurator Fiscal, Peeblesshire, 1949-76. Honorary Sheriff, since 1983. Address: (h.) Craigmount, Bonnington Road, Peebles; T.-01721 720314.

Law, Derek, MA, FLA, FIInfSc, FKC. Librarian and Director of Information Strategy, University of Strathclyde, since 1998; b. 19.6.47, Arbroath; m., Jacqueline Anne; 2 d. Educ. Arbroath High School, George Watson's College, Edinburgh; University of Glasgow. Assistant Librarian, St. Andrews University, 1970-77; Sub Librarian, Edinburgh University, 1977-81; Librarian, Erskine Medical Library, 1981-83; Director of Automation, Edinburgh University Library, 1983-84; King's College, London: Librarian, 1984-93, Director of Information Services, 1993-98. Member, Libraries and Information Commission; Treasurer, International Federation of Library Associations. Barnard Prize for Informatics, 1993. Publications: Royal Navy in World War Two; The Battle of the Atlantic; Networking and the Future of Libraries. Address: (b.) Andersonian Library, University of Strathclyde, Curran Building, 101 St. James' Road, Glasgow G4 0NS; T.-0141-552 3701.

Law, Professor Robin C. C., BA, PhD, FRHS. Professor of African History, University of Stirling, since 1993; b. 7.8.44, Chester. Educ. Southend-on-Sea High School;

Balliol College, University of Oxford; Centre of West African Studies, Birmingham. Research Assistant in African History, University of Lagos, Nigeria, 1966-69; Research Fellow in West African History, University of Birmingham, 1970-72; University of Stirling: Lecturer in History, 1972-78, Senior Lecturer, 1978-83, Reader, 1983-93. Editor, Journal of African History, 1974-82, 1991-95. Publications: The Oyo Empire c.1600-c.1836, 1977; The Horse in West African History, 1980; The Slave Coast of West Africa, 1550-1750, 1991; The Kingdom of Allada, 1997. Address: (b.) Department of History, University of Stirling, Stirling FK9 4LA; T. 01786 833772.

Lawrence, Professor Andrew, BSc, PhD, FRAS. Regius Professor of Astronomy, Edinburgh University, since 1994; b. 23.4.54, Margate; partner, Debbie Ann Capel; 2 s.; 1 d. Educ. Chatham House Grammar School, Ramsgate; Edinburgh University; Leicester University. Exchange Scientist, Massachusetts Institute of Technology, 1980-81; Senior Research Fellow, Royal Greenwich Observatory, 1981-84; Research Assistant, then SERC Advanced Fellow, School of Mathematical Sciences, Queen Mary College, London, 1984-89; Lecturer, Physics Department, Queen Mary and Westfield College, London, 1989-94. Publications: over 60 in learned journals. Recreations: painting electrons and teasing publishers; acting. Address: (b.) Institute for Astronomy, Edinburgh University, Royal Observatory, Blackford Hill, Edinburgh.

Lawrie, Frank James. Director of Heritage Policy, Historic Scotland, since 1991; Member, Board of Management, Buildings of Scotland Trust; Trustee, Rainbow Sports Trust; Assessor, Railway Heritage Trust; Assessor, Edinburgh Old Town Renewal Trust; b. 30.10.45, Edinburgh; m., Ann Macamon Kerr; 2 s.; 1 d. Educ. Royal High School, Edinburgh. Executive Officer, Department of Agriculture and Fisheries for Scotland, 1964-70; Higher Executive Officer, Scottish Office Finance Division, 1970-78; Senior Executive Officer, 1978-81; Principal, Department of Agriculture and Fisheries for Scotland, 1981-88; Deputy Director, Historic Buildings and Monuments, Scotland, 1988-91. Recreations: railway archaeology; cricket; golf. Address: (b.) Longmore House, Salisbury Place, Edinburgh EH9 1SH; T.-0131 668 8727.

Lawrie, Nigel Gilbert, BSc, PhD. Head Teacher, Port Glasgow High School, since 1985; Member, Board of Management, Scottish Qualifications Authority, since 1997; b. 2.6.47, Edinburgh; m., Janet Clark Warnock; 1 d. Educ. Bearsden Academy; Strathclyde University. Chemistry Teacher, Hermitage Academy, Helensburgh, 1972-75; Principal Teacher of Chemistry, Dunoon Grammar School, 1975-81; Assistant Head Teacher, Garnock Academy, 1981-84; Depute Head Teacher, Castlehead High School, Paisley, 1984-85. Member, National Council, Headteachers' Association of Scotland, since 1991, Vice-President, 1997-98; Member: Scottish Examination Board, 1994-97, Board, SCOTVEC, 1995-97, Board, SQA, since 1997. Recreations: reading; gardening; football. Address: (b.) Port Glasgow High School, Marloch Avenue, Port Glasgow; T.-01475 705921.

Lawson, Alexander Adamson Hutt, MD, FRCPEdin. Consultant Physician, Fife Health Board, 1969-95; Honorary Senior Lecturer, Edinburgh University, 1979-95; Medical Member and Chairman, War Pensions Appeal Tribunal, Scotland, since 1979; b. 30.7.37, Dunfermline; m., Barbara Helen Donnet; 3 s.; 1 d. Educ. Dunfermline High School; Edinburgh University. Consultant Member, Clinical Teaching Staff, Faculty of Medicine, Edinburgh University, 1971-95; Postgraduate Tutor in Medicine, West Fife, 1973-81; Medical Assessor, General Medical Council, since 1982; Member, Fife Health Board, 1981-91 (Vice-Chairman, 1989-91); President: Scottish Society of Physicians, 1989-90, West Fife Medical Society, 1982-83; Life Trustee: Carnegie Dunfermline Trust and Carnegie United Kingdom Hero Fund, since 1980 (Vice Chairman, 1995-98, Chairman, since 1998), Carnegie United Kingdom Trust, since 1983; Member: Committee of Safety, Efficacy and Adverse Reactions of Drugs (Committee, Safety of Medicines, DHSS, London), 1982-84, Specialist Advisory Committee (UK) HCMT - General (Internal) Medicine, 1984-88; UK Representative to European Union of Medical Specialties, Monospecialty Committee for General Medicine, 1986-95. Publications: Common Acute Poisonings; Acute Poisoning in Principles and Practice of Medicine; Toxicology and Drug Monitoring in Chemical Diagnosis of Disease; scientific papers. Address: (h.) 16 Green Wood, Kinross, Tayside KY13 7FG; T.- Kinross 865193.

Lawson, Isobel. Director/Company Secretary, Stepping Stones in Scotland, since 1988; b. Paisley; 2 d. Training and consultancy, voluntary sector childcare/education development; local government officer. Director, Scottish Council for Voluntary Organisations; Member, Executive Committee, Scottish Early Years Forum. Address: (b.) 55 Renfrew Street, Glasgow G2 3BD; T.-0141-331 2828.

Lawson, John Philip, BSc, FEIS. Chairman, Scottish Youth Hostels Association, since 1980; Headteacher, St. Joseph's School, Linlithgow, 1974-94; b. 19.8.37, Bathgate; m., Diana Mary Neal. Educ. St. Mary's Academy, Bathgate; Edinburgh University; Moray House College of Education. Teacher, West Lothian, 1962-94; held various offices in the Educational Institute of Scotland, including President, West Lothian Local Association and Chairman, Lothian Regional Executive; Member, West Lothian Children's Panel, 1972-81; Member, SYHA National Executive, since 1966; Vice-Chairman, SYHA, 1975-80; awarded: Richard Schirrmann Medal by German Youth Hostels Association, 1988, Gezel van de Rugzak, Flemish Youth Hostels Association, 1993; a Director, Scottish Rights of Way Society Ltd., since 1979; a Director, Gatliff Hebridean Hostels Trust, since 1988; President, West Lothian Headteachers Association, 1986-88; President, Federation of Youth Hostels Associations in the European Community, since 1990; First Vice-President, International Youth Hostel Federation, 1994-98. Recreations: hill-walking; music; reading. Address: (h.) Ledmore, Carnbee, Anstruther KY10 2RU; T.-01333 720312.

Lawson, Rev. Kenneth Charles, MA. Tutor-Organiser, Department of Parish Education, Church of Scotland, since 1984; Director, Ecumenical Spirituality Programme, Scottish Churches Open College, since 1991; b. 24.12.34, Agadir, Morocco; m., Mary Elizabeth Anderson; 3 s. Educ. Royal High School, Edinburgh; Preston Lodge School; Stranraer High School; Edinburgh University. Assistant Minister, Brechin Cathedral; Sub-Warden, St. Ninian's Training Centre, Crieff; Minister: Paisley South, Cumbernauld St. Mungo. Recreations: walking; reading; painting. Address: (b.) Scottish Churches Open College, 18 Inverleith Terrace, Edinburgh EH3 5NS; T.-0131-332 0343.

Lawson, Lilian Keddie, BSc (Hons), MBA. Director, RNID Scotland, since 1993; b. 23.2.49, Pittenweem; m., John McDonald Young, OBE; 2 d. Educ. Donaldson's School, Edinburgh; Mary Hare Grammar School, Newbury; Edinburgh University; Strathclyde University. Administrative Assistant, progressing to Head of Administration, British Deaf Association, 1981-92; Manager, Sign Language Interpreting Services, Strathclyde Regional Council, 1992-93. Publication: Words in Hand (Co-Author), 1984. Recreations: gardening; her children. Address: (b.) 9 Clairmont Gardens, Glasgow G3 7LW; T.-0141-332 0343.

Lawson, Rev. Ronald George, MA, BD. Minister, Wellpark Mid Kirk, Greenock, since 1988; b. 9.9.33, Glasgow; m., Beryl Read; 2 s.; 1 d. Educ. Allan Glen's School, Glasgow; University of Glasgow. Probationer, St.

Martin's, Port Glasgow, 1961-63; Minister: Perceton and Dreghorn, Irvine, Ayrshire, 1964-76, St. Andrew's, Dumbarton, 1976-88. Chaplain to various schools, and in industry, hospital, police. Recreations: walking; reading. Address: 101 Brisbane Street, Greenock PA16 8PA; T.-01475 721741.

Laybourn, Professor Peter John Robert, MA (Cantab), PhD, FIEE, FRSE. Professor of Electronic Engineering, Glasgow University, since 1985; b. 30.7.42, London; m., Ann Elizabeth Chandler; 2 d. Educ. William Hulme's Grammar School; Bristol Grammar School; Clare College, Cambridge. Research Assistant, Leeds University, 1963-66; Research Fellow, Southampton University, 1966-71; Lecturer, then Senior Lecturer, then Reader, Glasgow University, 1971-85; Honorary Editor, IEE Proceedings: Optoelectronics. Recreations: sailing; boat-building; plant collecting. Address: (h.) Ashgrove, Waterfoot Row, Thorntonhall, Glasgow; T.-0141-644 3992.

Lazaroff, Rosalin, BMus; Principal Second Violin, Royal Scottish National Orchestra, since 1989; b. 23.1.64, Brisbane, Australia. Educ. Brisbane State High School; Queensland Conservatorium of Music; University of Tasmania. Address: (b.) 73 Claremont Street, Glasgow G3 7JB; T.-0141-632 0567.

Lazarowicz, Mark, MA, LLB, DipLP. Advocate; b. 8.8.53. Educ. St. Andrews University; Edinburgh University. Member, Edinburgh District Council, 1980-96: Leader of the Council, 1986-93, Chairperson, Labour Group, 1993-94; Deputy Leader, COSLA Labour Group, 1990-93; Vice-Chairperson, 1988-89, Chairperson, 1989-90, Scottish Labour Party; Founder Member and Board Member, Centre for Scottish Public Policy, since 1990; Vice-Chairperson, Edinburgh International Conference Centre Ltd., 1992-93; Chairperson, Edinburgh Tourist Board, 1993-94. Address: (h.) 17 Bellevue Place, Edinburgh; T.-0131-556 4438.

Leach, Professor Donald, CBE, BSc, CMath, FIMA, CPhys, MInstP, CEng, MBCS, FRSA. Interim Chief Executive, Edinburgh's Lifelong Learning Partnership, since 1998; Vice-Convenor, One Parent Families Scotland, since 1998; b. 24.6.31, Croydon; m., June Valentine Reid (deceased); 2 s.; 1 d. Educ. John Ruskin Grammar School, Croydon; London University (External). Pilot Officer, Navigator, RAF, 1951-53; Physicist, British Jute Trade Research Association, Dundee, 1955-65; Technical Director, A.R. Bolton & Co. Ltd., Edinburgh, 1965-66; Napier College: Lecturer and Senior Lecturer in Mathematics, 1966-68, Head, Department of Mathematics and Computing, 1968-74, Assistant Principal/Dean, Faculty of Science, 1974-85; Principal, Queen Margaret College, Edinburgh, 1985-96. Member, South-Eastern Regional Hospital Board, 1969-74, and Lothian Health Board, 1977-81; Member: Scottish Health Service Information Processing and Computer Systems Advisory Group, 1979-86, Computer Steering Committee (Chairman), 1981-86; Institute of Mathematics: Council Member, 1978-81, Chairman, Scottish Branch, 1980-83, Member, Joint IMA-Royal Society of London Mathematical Education Committee, 1981-84; Council for National Academic Awards: Member, various boards, 1975-79, Science Technology and Society Board, 1979-82 (Chairman, 1981-82), Committee for Scotland, 1987-92; Chairman: Science Technology and Society Association, 1982-85, Mathematics and Computing Course Committees, SCOTEC/SCOTBEC, 1981-85; Hon. Secretary, Committee of Principals and Directors of Scottish Central Institutions (COPADOCI), 1985-88, Chairman, 1988-92; Member: Council for Professions Supplementary to Medicine, since 1985, Executive, Scottish Council (Development and Industry), since 1987, Board of Directors, Edinburgh Chamber of Commerce, 1991-98 (President of the Chamber, 1996-98), Council, World Association for Cooperative Education, 1991-97, Board of Directors, Higher Education Quality Council, 1992-96, Board of Directors, Capital Enterprise Trust, since 1993; President, Leith Chamber of Commerce, 1994-96; Honorary Fellow, Society of Chiropodists and Podiatrists, 1991; Liberal candidate, West Edinburgh, 1959, East Fife, 1961; Labour candidate, West Perthshire, 1970. Recreations: badminton; walking; skiing; cooking. Address: (h.) 18 Rothesay Terrace, Edinburgh EH3 7RY; T.-0131-226 7166.

Lean, Professor Michael E. J., MA, MD, FRCP (Edin), FRCPS (Glas). Professor of Human Nutrition, University of Glasgow, since 1992; Honorary Consultant Physician, Glasgow Royal Infirmary, since 1990; b. 16.3.52, Chester; m., Annie S. Anderson; 3 s.; 2 d. Educ. Glenalmond; Downing College, Cambridge; St. Bartholomews Medical School. RHO, 1976-77; Registrar, Aberdeen Royal Infirmary, 1977-80; MRC Clinical Scientist, Dunn Nutrition Laboratory, Cambridge, 1980-84; Senior Registrar in General Medicine, Diabetes and Endocrinology, Aberdeen Royal Infirmary, 1984-89; Senior Lecturer, Department of Human Nutrition, University of Glasgow. Director, Health Education Board for Scotland, since 1995. Author of books and papers on diabetes, obesity and nutrition. Recreations: Scottish fiddling; violin making; hill running; mountains. Address: (h.) Hatton Castle, Newtyle, Blairgowrie PH12 8UN; T.-01828 650404.

Lederer, Peter J, OBE. Managing Director, Gleneagles Hotels plc, since 1987; General Manager, The Gleneagles Hotel, since 1983; Director, Guinness Enterprises, since 1987; Board Member, Scottish Tourist Board; b. 30.11.50; m., Marilyn Ruth MacPhail. Four Seasons Hotels, Canada, 1972-79; Vice President, Wood Wilkings Ltd., Toronto, 1979-81; General Manager, Plaza Group of Hotels, Toronto, 1981-83. Chairman, Tourism Training Scotland; Chairman, Hospitality Industry Trust Scotland; Freeman, City of London; Member, Advisory Scottish Council for Education and Training Targets; FHCIMA; Master Innholder. Recreations: Matthew and Mark; TVR. Address: (b.) The Gleneagles Hotel, Auchterarder, Perthshire PH3 1NF; T.-01764 662231.

Ledger, Philip Stevens, CBE, FRSE, HonLLD (Strathclyde), MA, MusB, FRCM, HonRAM, FRNCM, HonGSM, FRCO, DUniv (Birmingham). Principal, Royal Scottish Academy of Music and Drama, since 1982; b. 12.12.37, Bexhill-on-Sea; 1 s.; 1 d. Educ. Bexhill Grammar School; King's College, Cambridge. Master of the Music, Chelmsford Cathedral, 1962-65; East Anglia University: Director of Music, 1965-73, Dean, School of Fine Arts and Music, 1968-71; Conductor, Cambridge University Musical Society, 1973-82; Director of Music and Organist, King's College, Cambridge, 1974-82; President: Royal College of Organists, 1992-94, Incorporated Society of Musicians, 1994-95; Chairman, Committee of Principals of Conservatoires, 1994-98; Editor, Anthems for Choirs 2 and 3; Composer/Editor, Six Carols with Descants. Publication: The Oxford Book of English Madrigals (Editor). Recreations: swimming; theatre. Address: (b.) Royal Scottish Academy of Music and Drama, 100 Renfrew Street, Glasgow G2 3DB; T.-0141-332 4101.

Ledingham, Professor Iain McAllan, MD(Hons), FRCS(Ed), FRCP(Ed, Glas), FInstBiol, FCCM, FRSE. Professor of Medical Education, Faculty of Medicine, Dentistry and Nursing, University of Dundee, since 1995; Honorary Consultant Physician, Dundee Teaching Hospitals NHS Trust, since 1995; b. 26.2.35, Glasgow; m., Eileen; 3 s. Educ. King's Park Senior Secondary, Glasgow; Central School, Aberdeen; University of Glasgow. Early training in surgery/trauma/intensive care; MRC Senior Research Fellow in hyperbaric medicine; first UK Professor of Intensive Care Medicine, University of Glasgow, 1980; Chair, Intensive Therapy Unit, Western Infirmary, Glasgow, 1985; Foundation Chair, Department of Emergency and Critical Care Medicine, Faculty of

Medicine and Health Sciences, United Arab Emirates University, 1988 (Dean, FMHS, 1989). First Chair, Intensive Care Society, UK; President: European Shock Society, European Society of Intensive Care Medicine; Bellahouston Medal, University of Glasgow; La Médaille de la Ville de Paris. Recreations: jogging; hill-walking; gardening; music; reading; woodworking; occasional bad golf. Address: (b.) Clinical Skills Centre, Ninewells Hospital and Medical School, Dundee DD1 9SY; T.-01382 632615.

Lee, Professor Clive Howard, MA, MLitt (Cantab). Professor of Historical Economics, Aberdeen University, since 1991; Convener of Council, since 1994; b. 21.4.42, Leeds; m., Christine Ann. Educ. West Leeds High School; Fitzwilliam College, Cambridge. Assistant Lecturer to Professor, Aberdeen University, since 1966. Publications include: The British Economy since 1700: A Macroeconomic Perspective, 1986; British Regional Employment Statistics 1841-1971, 1979; Scotland and the United Kingdom: The Economy and the Union in the Twentieth Century, 1995; New History of Aberdeen (Co-Editor). Recreations: watching and playing football; gardening. Address: (b.) Department of Economics, Aberdeen University, Regent Walk, Aberdeen; T.: 01224 272198.

Lee, Professor Michael Radcliffe, MA, DM, DPhil (Oxon), FRCP, FRCPE, FRSE. Emeritus Professor of Clinical Pharmacology, Edinburgh University; b. 21.11.34, Manchester; m., Judith Ann Horrocks; 1 s.; 1 d. Educ. Manchester Grammar School; Brasenose College, Oxford. Beit Memorial Fellow for Medical Research; Lecturer in Medicine, Oxford University; Lecturer in Medicine, St. Thomas's Hospital Medical School; Medical Director, then Managing Director, Weddel Pharmaceuticals Ltd.; Senior Lecturer in Clinical Pharmacology, Leeds University. Publications: books on medicine and hypertension. Recreations: gardening; walking; old trains; old books. Address: (h.) 112 Polwarth Terrace, Edinburgh EH11 1NN; T.-0131-337 7386.

Lees, James George Grahame, MA, LLB, NP. Partner, McLean & Stewart, Solicitors, Dunblane, since 1974; Vice Chairman, Judicial Commission, Church of Scotland; b. 22.6.46, Perth; m., Hazel Margaret Raffan; 1 s.; 2 d. Educ. Dundee High School; St. Andrews University; Edinburgh University. Solicitor, J. & F. Anderson, WS, Edinburgh, 1969-72; Solicitor, McLean & Stewart, Solicitors, Dunblane, since 1972. Elder, Dunblane Cathedral Church of Scotland. Recreations: walking; photography; fishing. Address: (h.) Northbank, St. Margaret's Drive, Dunblane, FK15 ODP; T.-Dunblane 822928.

Lees, Martin McArthur, MD, FRCP(Edin), FRCS(Ed), FRCOG. Consultant Obstetrician and Gynaecologist, Royal Infirmary and Simpson Memorial Maternity Pavilion, Edinburgh, since 1969; Senior Lecturer (part-time), in Obstetrics and Gynaecology and Director of Studies, University of Edinburgh Medical School; b. 24.4.35; m., Maureen Yetton. Educ. Aberdeen Grammar School; University of Aberdeen. Postgraduate training, Royal Infirmary of Aberdeen, Royal Infirmary and Simpson Maternity Pavilion, Edinburgh; Research Fellow, University of Edinburgh; lately Regional Adviser in Obstetrics and Gynaecology, Royal College of Obstetricians and Gynaecologists; Member, Board of Management and Council, Medical and Dental Defence Union of Scotland; Regional Adviser in Gynaecology, Royal College of Surgeons of Edinburgh; lately Chairman, Area Division of Obstetrics and Gynaecology, Lothian Health Board; Inspector, Human Fertilisation and Embryology Authority; Social Convener and Member of Council, Royal College of Physicians of Edinburgh; National Adviser, National Counselling Service for Sick Doctors; Examiner: University of Edinburgh, University of London, Royal College of Obstetricians and Gynaecologists, Royal College of Surgeons of Edinburgh; lately Examiner, University of Dundee, University of Glasgow, Royal College of Obstetricians and Gynaecologists; Past President, Edinburgh Obstetrical Society; Past President, Harveian Society of Edinburgh. Recreations: music; ornithology; reading. Address: (b.) Simpson Memorial Maternity Pavilion, Lauriston Place, Edinburgh EH3 9YW; T.-0131-536 2582.

Lefevre, Frank Hartley, MA, LLB, NP. Solicitor and Advocate in Aberdeen, since 1959; Senior Partner, Lefevre Litigation, since 1988; Chairman, Quantum Claims Compensation Specialists Ltd., since 1988; b. 4.12.34, Aberdeen; m., Hazel Gray; 1 s.; 2 d. Educ. Robert Gordon's College, Aberdeen; Aberdeen University. Commenced legal practice, 1959; set up, 1988, Britain's first no-win no-fee professional compensation company. Treasurer, Aberdeen Society of Advocates, 1994, President 1995; Past President, Grampian Squash Racquets Association (now Honorary President); accredited by the Law Society of Scotland as specialist in employment law, 1993, and as solicitor/mediator, 1995; part-time Chairman, Industrial Tribunals (Scotland), 1996; Member, Council, Royal Aberdeen Golf Club, 1993-95. Recreations: squash; golf; music. Address: (h.) Braco Lodge, 11 Rubislaw Den North, Aberdeen; T.-01224 317170.

Leggat, (John) Brian, WS. Partner, since 1973, and Head of Education Group, since 1996, Dundas and Wilson CS; b. 29.7.48; m., Iona Aitken; 1 s.; 1 d. Educ. Edinburgh Academy; University of Edinburgh. Trainee, Lindsay, Duncan and Black, 1969-71; Assistant Solicitor, Dundas and Wilson, 1971-73; Head of Commercial Property Group, 1983-93; Chairman of Partnership, 1993-96. Member, IPF Scottish Education Committee. Recreations: rugby; golf; curling; sailing; horse-riding, music. Address: (b.) Saltire Court, 20 Castle Terrace, Edinburgh; T.-0131-228 8000.

Leggate, Peter James Arthur, JP, FRICS. Chartered Surveyor, since 1967; Chairman, Lowland Insurance Brokers Ltd.; Director: Isla Mines Ltd., James Gammell & Son Ltd., Ptarmigan International Capital Trust Plc, Cheviot Investments Ltd.; b. 17.10.43; m., Jennifer Susan Gammell; 1 s.; 1 d. Educ. Wrekin College. Qualified as Chartered Surveyor, 1967; Kenneth Ryden & Partners, 1967-70; P.G. Matineau, Jedburgh, 1970-72; Founder, P.J. Leggate & Co., Edinburgh, 1973 (Sole Principal, since 1979). Recreations: horses; sailing; skiing. Address: (h.) Greenlawdean House, Greenlaw, Berwickshire, TD10 6XP.

Leiper, Joseph, MA, DipEd, ACII. Rector, Oldmachar Academy, since 1983; elected Vice Convener, Business Committee, General Council, Aberdeen University, 1997; b. 13.8.41, Aberdeen; m., Moira Taylor; 2 d. Educ. Aberdeen Grammar School; Aberdeen University. Inspector, Commercial Union Assurance, until 1967; Aberdeen University, 1967-72; Aberdeen College of Education, 1971-72; Teacher of English, since 1972. Recreation: sailing. Address: (b.) Oldmachar Academy, Jesmond Drive, Bridge of Don, Aberdeen AB2 8ZJ; T.-01224 820887.

Leishman, Brian Archibald Scott, MBE. Consultant, Edinburgh Military Tattoo (Business Manager, 1978-97); b. 16.9.36; 1 s.; 1 d. Educ. Fettes College, Edinburgh. Retired Regular Army Officer; commissioned The Cameronians (Scottish Rifles); re-badged King's Own Scottish Borderers; service in the Arabian Gulf, East Africa and Europe; Italian Staff College, 1971-73; Assistant Defence Attache, British Embassy, Rome, 1974-76; Ticketing Consultant, XIII Commonwealth Games in Edinburgh, 1986; Board Member, Edinburgh International Jazz and Blues Festival; Founder Member, Edinburgh Capital Group (Edinburgh Entertains). Recreations: sailing; music; photography. Address: (h.) 61 Northumberland Street, Edinburgh EH3 6JQ; T.-0131-557 0187.

Leishman, Marista Muriel, MA, FRSA. Senior Partner, The Insite Consultancy for Management and Training; b. 10.4.32, Beaconsfield; m., Murray Leishman; 1 s.; 3 d. Educ. St. George's School, Ascot; St. Andrews University. First Head of Education, National Trust for Scotland, 1979-86; two National Training Awards recognising Insite's innovatory training programmes and disabled access initiatives. Recreations: music; painting; writing; hill-walking. Address: 9/23 St. Leonard's Crag, Edinburgh EH8 9SP; T.-0131-667 1246.

Leishman, Mark Murray. Secretary and Head of Corporate Affairs, BBC Scotland; b. 4.3.62, Perth. Educ. Firrhill High School, Edinburgh; Napier College, Edinburgh. Press and PR, National Trust for Scotland, 1979-81; Reporter, United News Service, 1982-84; Reporter, Fife Free Press, Kirkcaldy, 1986-87; Chief Reporter, Radio Forth/Tay, 1987-88; Reporter, Radio Clyde, 1988-90; Reporter, Political Correspondent, Sunday Times, 1990-93; Presenter, Good Morning Scotland, BBC Scotland, 1993-95. Recreations: fishing; running; golf; gym work; reading; cinema; music. Address: (h.) 34 Polwarth Street, Glasgow G12 9TX.

Leitch, Donald H., DMS, MHCIMA, FCFA. Principal, Glasgow College of Food Technology, since 1998 (Depute Principal, 1991-98); b. 2.4.48, Glasgow; m., Mary B.; 2 s. Educ. Hyndland Senior Secondary School; Langside College, Glasgow; Glasgow College of Technology. Catering management, Health Service, 1967-70; Depute Catering Officer, Glasgow University, 1970-74; Lecturer then Senior Lecturer, Glasgow College of Food Technology, 1974-85; Head of Department, Cambuslang College, Glasgow, 1985-91. Past Chairman, Scottish Division, Cookery and Food Association. Recreations: hill-walking; gardening. Address: (b.) 230 Cathedral Street, Glasgow G1 2TG; T.-0141-552 3751.

Leitch, Iain Douglas Cameron Muil, JP, BSc, MRCVS. Honorary Sheriff, since 1997; b. 28.3.32, Glasgow; m., Kathleen Mae Nicholson; 1 s.; 2 d. Educ. Hillhead High School; Edinburgh University; Royal (Dick) School of Veterinary Studies. Partner, general veterinary practice, 1956-92. Former Council Member, British Veterinary Association. Recreations: gardening; hillwalking; DIY; golf; curling; swimming; wood carving; painting; bowling; kirk session. Address: (h.) Caline, Haulkerton Wood, Laurencekirk AB30 1DZ; T.-01561 377287.

Lenman, Professor Bruce Philip, MA (Aberdeen), MLitt, LittD (Cantab), FRHistSoc. Professor of Modern History, St. Andrews University, since 1992 (formerly Reader in Modern History); b. 9.4.38, Aberdeen. Educ. Aberdeen Grammar School; Aberdeen University; St. John's College, Cambridge. Assistant Professor, Victoria University, Canada, 1963; Lecturer in Imperial and Commonwealth History, Queen's College, Dundee (St. Andrews University), 1963-67; Lecturer, Dundee University, 1967-72; United College, St. Andrews: Lecturer, Department of Modern History, 1972-78, Senior Lecturer, 1978-83; British Academy Fellow, Newberry Library, Chicago, 1982; John Carter Brown Library Fellow, Brown University, Providence, RI, 1984; Harrison Professor, College of William & Mary, VA, 1988-89; Mayers Fellow, Huntington Library, CA, 1997; Bird Professor, Emory University, Atlanta, GA, 1998. Publications: Esk to Tweed, 1975; An Economic History of Modern Scotland 1660-1976, 1977 (Scottish Arts Council Award); The Jacobite Risings in Britain 1689-1746, 1980 (Scottish Arts Council Award); Scotland 1746-1832, 1981; The Jacobite Clans of the Great Glen 1650-1784, 1984; The Jacobite Cause, 1986; The Jacobite Threat (Co-Author), 1990; The Eclipse of Parliament, 1992; Editor, Chambers Dictionary of World History, 1993. Recreations: golf; tennis; Scottish country dancing. Address: (b.) Department of Modern History, St. Andrews University, St. Andrews KY16 9AL; T.-01334 476161.

Leonard, Professor Thomas, BSc, ARCS, MSc, PhD. Chair of Statistics, Professor of Mathematics and Statistics, University of Edinburgh, since 1995; Director, University of Edinburgh Statistical Laboratory, since 1996; statistical expert witness in legal cases, since 1985; b. 24.3.48, Plympton; 2 d. Educ. Sutton High School, Plymouth; Imperial College, London; University College, London. Predoctoral Research Fellow, American College Testing Program, Iowa City, 1971, 1972; Co-Founder and Lecturer, Department of Statistics, University of Warwick, 1972-80 (Co-Founder, MORSE degree, 1975); Senior Medical Statistician, Queen's University, Kingston, Ontario, 1978; Associate Professor, Mathematics Research Center, University of Wisconsin-Madison, 1979-86; Associate, then full Professor, Department of Statistics, University of Wisconsin-Madison, 1979-96. Publications: Statistical Inference, Data Analysis and Robustness (Co-Author), 1983; Bayesian Methods (Co-Author), 1998; 60 papers in scientific journals. Recreations: chess (Edinburgh Premier League Team Champion, 1996); football supporter (Green Bay Packers, Newcastle United). Address: (b.) Department of Mathematics and Statistics, University of Edinburgh, The King's Buildings, Mayfield Road, Edinburgh EH9 3JZ; T.-0131-650 8569.

Leonard, Wilfred. Member, Island Policy Committee, Scottish Accident Prevention Council; Honorary President, Harris Local Supporters Network (promoting jobs in Harris); b. 9.5.12, Humberton, Brafferton, Yorkshire; m., Margaret Ross (deceased); 1 s.; 2 d. Educ. Brafferton Church of England School. Staffordshire County Police, 1935-67 (retired in rank of Inspector); Member, Inverness County Council, 1973-74; Past Chairman: Harris District Council, South Harris Agricultural Society, Harris Council of Social Service; former Member: Highlands and Islands Consultative Council; Highlands and Islands Manpower Board, MSC; Member, Western Isles Islands Council, 1974-86 (Chairman, Planning and Development, 1980-86). Recreation: gardening. Address: (h.) Cnoc-Na-Ba, Finsbay, Isle of Harris, T.-01859 530 232.

Leslie, Professor Frank Matthews, JP, BSc, PhD, DSc, FIMA, FInstP, FRSE, FRS. Professor of Mathematics, Strathclyde University, since 1982; Chairman, British Liquid Crystal Society, 1987-91; b. 8.3.35, Dundee; m., Ellen Leitch Reoch; 1 s.; 1 d. Educ. Harris Academy; Queen's College, Dundee; Manchester University. Assistant Lecturer, Manchester University, 1959-61; Research Associate, MIT, USA, 1961-62; Lecturer, Newcastle University, 1962-68; Visiting Assistant Professor, Johns Hopkins University, USA, 1966-67; Strathclyde University: Senior Lecturer, 1968-71, Reader, 1971-79, Personal Professor, 1979-82; Consultant, DERA Malvern; Annual Award, British Society of Rheology, 1982; Sykes Gold Medal, St. Andrews University, 1996; G.W. Gray Medal, British Liquid Crystal Society, 1997. Recreations: golf; hill-walking. Address: (b.) Department of Mathematics, Strathclyde University, Livingstone Tower, 26 Richmond Street, Glasgow G1 1XH; T.-0141-548 3655.

Leslie, John, MRPharmS. Chairman, Orkney Health Board, since 1991; b. 1.1.35, Kirkwall; m., Evelyn MacGillivray; 1 s. Educ. Kirkwall Grammar School; Robert Gordon's Institute of Technology, Aberdeen. Member, NHS Executive Council for Orkney, 1968-74; Chairman, Kirkwall Chamber of Commerce, 1973-74; Member, Orkney Health Board, 1979-85 and since 1987. Past President, Kirkwall Rotary Club. Recreations: participating in amateur music and drama groups; simple electronics/computing. Address: (h.) Failte, Bignold Park Road, Kirkwall, Orkney; T.-01856 874002.

Leslie, Martin Rowley Melville, CVO, FRICS. Chartered Surveyor (semi-retired); Factor to Her Majesty Queen Elizabeth the Queen Mother, since 1975; Honorary Secretary and Factor to Queen Elizabeth Castle of Mey Trust, since 1996; President, Aberdeen Angus Cattle Society of Great Britain and Ireland, 1999-2000; b. 12.8.32, Malawi, Central Africa; m., Catriona Bridget Macdonald; 1 s.; 2 d. Educ. King's School, Canterbury; Royal Dick Veterinary College, Edinburgh University; College of Estate Management (correspondence course). National Service, Seaforth Highlanders and Argyll and Sutherland Highlanders (2nd Lt.), 1951-53; TA, 11th Bn., Seaforth Highlanders (retired as Captain), 1953-67; Pupil Factor, Moray Estates Development Company, Forres, 1959-60; Assistant Factor, Fairburn Estates, Conan and Gairloch Estates, Ross-shire, 1960-62; 1962-79: Factor to Welbeck Estates Company, Langwell and Braemore, Caithness and Ross-shire, Factor to Achentoul Estate Company, Achentoul, Sutherland and Ross-shire; Factor to Her Majesty the Queen, Balmoral Estates, Aberdeenshire, 1979-95. Field Trial Panel Judge for Hunt, Point and Retrieve Breeds (dogs), since 1972; Member, Deer Committee, Highland Committee of Scottish Land Owners Federation, 1972-92; Member, Deer and Uplands Committee, Scottish Landowners' Federation, 1992-96; Aberdeen Angus Cattle Society: Member, Council, 1993-95, Junior Vice President, 1997-98, Senior Vice President, 1998-99; Member, Skye District Salmon Fisheries Board, since 1996 (Chairman, since 1998); Skye District Salmon Fisheries Board Representative on Association of Scottish District Salmon Fisheries Board, since 1997. Recreations: country sports; German shorthaired pointers; reading. Address: Redcliff, Portree, Isle of Skye IV51 9DH; T.-01478 612014.

Lessels, Norman, CBE, CA. Director, Standard Life Assurance Company (Chairman, 1988-98); Director: Scottish Eastern Investment Trust PLC, Robert Wiseman Diaries PLC, Cairn Energy; b. 2.9.38, Edinburgh; m., Christine Stevenson; 1 s. Educ. Edinburgh Academy. Partner, Ernst & Whinney, until 1980; Partner, Chiene & Tait, CA, until 1998; President, Institute of Chartered Accountants of Scotland, 1987-88. Recreations: golf; music; bridge. Address: (b.) 50 Lothian Road, Edinburgh EH3 9BY; T.-0131-475 3000.

Lester, Andrew, BArch, RIBA, ARIAS. Partner, Aitken and Turnbull Architects, since 1986; Board Member, Scottish Society for Autistic Children; b. 15.6.49, Glasgow; m., Kate; 1 s.; 2 d. Educ. High School of Dundee; Heriot-Watt University. Architect, Sir Basil Spence, Glover and Ferguson, Edinburgh; Architect, Forgan and Stewart, Edinburgh; Architect, Aitken and Turnbull, Duns. Member, Executive Committee, Scottish Society for Autistic Children, since 1982. Recreations: football supporter; amateur dramatics; opera. Address: (h.) Wellfield Cottage, Preston Road, Duns, Berwickshire TD11 3DZ; T.-01361 883445.

Levein, Charles Peter Alexander, MA, PhD, FRSGS. Chief Research Officer, Scottish Office, since 1988; b. 16.5.40, Devonport; 1 s.; 2 d. Educ. Dunfermline High School; Edinburgh University. Demonstrator, Geography Department, Edinburgh University; Research Officer, Central Planning Research Unit, Scottish Development Department; Senior Research Officer, WC Scotland Planning Team; Principal Research Officer, Scottish Office Urban Deprivation Unit; Senior Principal Research Officer, Scottish Office. Recreations: golf; bowls; theatre. Address: (h.) 45 The Wynd, Dalgety Bay, Fife; T.-01383 822952.

Leven and Melville, Earl of (Alexander Robert Melville). Lord Lieutenant of Nairn, since 1969; b. 13.5.24, London; m., Susan Steuart-Menzies; 2 s.; 1 d. Educ. Eton. Coldstream Guards, 1942-52 (retired as Captain); ADC to Governor General of New Zealand, 1951-52; Convener, Nairn County Council, 1970-74. Chairman of Governors, Gordonstoun School, 1971-89; President, British Ski Federation, 1981-85. Address: (h.) Glenferness House, Nairn IV12 5UP; T.-01309 651202.

Leven, Allan McPherson, LLB, NP, WS. Partner, Gray Muirhead WS, Edinburgh, since 1990; b. 2.4.52, Dundee. Educ. Montrose Academy; University of Dundee. With Gray Muirhead WS throughout career. Recreations: singing; the arts; hillwalking. Address: (b.) 33 York Place, Edinburgh EH1 3HS; T.-0131-556 7122.

Leven, Marian Forbes, DA, RSW. Artist; b. 25.3.44, Edinburgh; m., Will Maclean; 2 s.; 1 d. Educ. Bell-Baxter School, Cupar; Gray's School of Art, Aberdeen. Teacher of Art, 1967-84 (with breaks for family); exhibited RSA, RGI, RSW, SSA, AAS; work in private and public collections. Noble Grossart Painting Prize, 1997. Address: (h.) Bellevue, 18 Dougall Street, Tayport, Fife DD6 9JD; T.-01382 552219.

Levinthal, Terrence Scott, BES, DipUD, FSAScot. Secretary, The Cockburn Association (Edinburgh Civic Trust), since 1992; Member, National Transport Forum for Scotland; Member, Edinburgh Environment Partnership; Board Member, Cockburn Conservation Trust; b. 9.12.61, Winnipeg. Educ. University of Waterloo; Heriot-Watt/Edinburgh College of Art. Investigator, Royal Fine Art Commission for Scotland, 1988-92. Recreations: hill-walking, skiing, cycling and other outdoor pursuits; the arts; woodworking. Address: (b.) Trunk's Close, 55 High Street, Edinburgh EH1 1SR; T.-0131-557 8686.

Levison, Rev. Mary Irene, BA, BD, DD. Minister of the Church of Scotland (retired); (Extra) Chaplain to the Queen in Scotland, since 1991; Vice-President, St. Leonard's School, since 1996; b. 8.1.23, Oxford; m., Rev. Frederick Levison. Educ. St. Leonard's School, St. Andrews; Oxford University; Edinburgh University. Administrative Assistant, Scottish Home Department, 1943-46; Deaconess, Church of Scotland, Musselburgh, 1954-58; Tutor, St. Colm's College, 1958-61; Assistant Chaplain, Edinburgh University, 1961-64; Assistant Minister, St. Andrew's and St. George's Church and Chaplain to the retail trade, Edinburgh, 1978-83; Moderator, Edinburgh Presbytery, 1988. Publication: Wrestling with the Church, 1992. Recreations: gardening; music; travel. Address: (h.) 2 Gillsland Road, Edinburgh EH10 5BW; T.-0131-228 3118.

Levy, Professor Roger P., BA (Hons), MPhil, PhD. Head, School of Public Administration and Law, Robert Gordon University, since 1991; b. 14.12.50, London. Educ. Southgate Technical College; Leicester University; Glasgow University; McGill University. Tutor in Government, Glasgow University, 1974-75; Lecturer in Public Administration, Bell College, 1975-79; worked in Canada, 1979-83; Education Development Officer, Scottish Civil Liberty Trust, Glasgow, 1983; Lecturer/Senior Lecturer in Public Administration, Glasgow Polytechnic, 1983-91. Publications (books): A Guide to Civil Liberties in Scotland (Co-Author), 1980; Young People and the Law (Co-Author), 1985; Scottish Nationalism at the Crossroads, 1990; numerous book chapters and articles. Address: (b.) Robert Gordon University, School of Public Administration and Law, 352 King Street, Aberdeen AB24 5BN; T.-01224 262900.

Lewis, Andrew Douglas Fyfe, MBA, FInstD. Director, The Goldcrest Company (UK) Ltd., since 1982; b. 11.2.43, Aberdeen; m., Cathrine Diana; 1 s.; 1 d. Educ. Fettes College, Edinburgh; University of Aberdeen; Robert Gordon University. Trainee, Ernst & Young, 1963; Trawler Manager, Associated Fisheries PLC, 1964-68; Director, Trawling Division, John Lewis & Sons Limited, 1969-72; Director, Trawling Scotland, Associated Fisheries PLC, 1972-82. Honorary Consul, Federal Republic of Germany, since 1976; Chairman, Northsound Local Commercial

Radio, Aberdeen, since 1979; President, Aberdeen Chamber of Commerce; Board of Governors, Robert Gordon University, since 1993; Chairman, National Art Collections Fund, Grampian Area, since 1994; Board, North of Scotland Water Authority, since 1995. Cross of the Order of Merit of Federal Republic of Germany. Recreations: Scottish art; tennis; running; reading biographies; work; listening to music. Address: The Glebe House, Kirkton of Durris, Kincardineshire AB31 6BQ; T.-01330 844 414.

Lewis, Gareth Llewellyn, ARICS. Factor, Buccleuch Estates, Langholm, since 1992; Member, Deer Commission for Scotland, since 1996; Member, Annan District Salmon Fisheries Board, since 1992; b. 13.1.54, Nairobi, Kenya; m., Barbara Anne. Educ. Trinity College, Glenalmond. Assistant Land Agent, J. M. Clark and Partners, Cumbria and Northumberland, 1975-83; Defence Land Agent, Ministry of Defence, Otterburn, Northumberland, 1984-92. Chairman: Esk and Liddle Improvement Association, Eskdalemuir Deer Management Group. Recreations: shooting; fishing; beekeeping. Address: (h.) Park House, Canonbie, Dumfriesshire; T.-013873 71482.

Lewis, John Ivor, MSc, CEng, FIEE. Director, United Distillers and Vintners, since 1998; Managing Director, Operations, United Distillers, 1992-97; b. 24.2.45, Shrewsbury; m., Karolyn Richards; 1 s.; 1 d. Educ. Adams Grammar School, Shropshire; Birmingham University; INSEAD. With Rolls Royce for 10 years; Management Consultancy, 1972-81; J. C. Bamford Excavators, 1981-85; Rover Cars, 1985-91; Director, Gleneagles Hotels. Member, Council, CBI Scotland; Member, Council, and Treasurer, Scotch Whisky Association; Member, Board, Scottish Natural Heritage; Member, Management Committee, Keepers of the Quaich. Recreations: shooting; riding; photography; reading. Address: (h.) 21 Rothesay Terrace, Edinburgh; T.-0131-519 2306.

Lewis, Penelope Frances, BSc(Hons). Head of Fundraising and Sponsorship, Scottish Opera, since 1992; b. 7.7.58; m., Roy Lewis; 1 s.; 1 d. Educ. Kendal High School; University of Edinburgh. Worked in tourism in Italy, 1980-86; Scottish Development Agency (Locate in Scotland and Tourism Departments), 1986-89; Commercial Manager, Scottish Chamber Orchestra, 1989-92. Founder Committee Member, West of Scotland Businesswomen's Club. Recreations: spending time with the family; hill-walking; gardening; going to the theatre. Address: (b.) Scottish Opera, 39 Elmbank Crescent, Glasgow G2 4PT; T.-0141-248 4567.

Liddell, Colin. Partner, Liddell Thomson, Management Consultants; b. 28.8.47, Falkirk; m., Sheena Wood Mackay. Educ. Denny High School. Journalist, Johnston Newspaper Group, 1964-69; Editor, Linlithgow Journal & Gazette, 1968-69; Journalist, Scotsman Publications, 1969-77; Senior Press Officer, Scottish Development Agency, 1977-82; PR Director, then Chief Executive, Charles Barker Scotland, 1982-86; Public Affairs Director, United Distillers, 1986-93; Corporate Communications Director, Scottish Power plc, 1993-95. Non-Executive Director: Falkirk F.C., Billcliffe Gallery; Advisory Director, Scotland the Brand. Recreations: golf; gardening; football. Address: (b.) 225 West George Street, Glasgow G2 2ND.

Liddell, David, BSc (Hons), DipSW. Director, Scottish Drugs Forum, since 1993 (Co-ordinator, since 1986); b. 1957, Kingston. Educ. Riddlesdown School; Sheffield University; Edinburgh University. Project Worker, Bristol Cyrenians and Dublin Simon Community; Researcher, Queen Charlotte's Hospital, London; Biochemist, Children's Hospital, Dublin; Youth Worker, Dublin Committee for Travelling People; Field Worker, Standing Conference on Drug Abuse. Publications: Drug Problems in Edinburgh District, 1987 (Co-author); Drugfax (Co-author), 1991; Drug Use in Scotland (Co-author). Recreations: travel; cycling; working on allotment. Address: (b.) Shaftsbury House, 5 Waterloo Street, Glasgow, G2 6AY.

Liddell, Faith Ann, MA(Hons), DEML. Director, Edinburgh Book Festival, since 1997; b. 9.4.65, Lanark. Educ. Dalkeith High School; University of Aberdeen; Napier University. Box-Office Manager, Traverse Theatre, 1989-90; Press and Publicity Officer, Royal Lyceum Theatre, 1990-91; Marketing and Press Manager, Edinburgh Festival Fringe, 1992-94; Press Officer, Edinburgh Book Festival, 1995; Freelance Arts and Events Manager, since 1995. Recreations: literature; theatre; film; travel. Address: (b.) The Book Centre, 137 Dundee Street, Edinburgh EH11 1BG; T.-0131-228 5444.

Liddell, Helen Lawrie, BA. Minister of State, Scottish Office, since 1998; Economic Secretary to the Treasury, 1997-98; MP (Labour), Airdrie and Shotts (formerly Monklands East), since 1994; b. 6.12.50, Coatbridge; m., Dr. Alistair H. Liddell; 1 s.; 1 d. Educ. St. Patrick's High School, Coatbridge; Strathclyde University. Head, Economic Department, STUC, 1971-76; Economics Correspondent, BBC, 1976-77; Scottish Secretary, Labour Party, 1977-88; Scottish Daily Record and Sunday Mail Ltd.: Director of Personnel and Public Affairs, 1988-91, Director of Corporate and Public Affairs, 1991-92; Chief Executive, Business Venture Programme, 1993-94; Labour Candidate, East Fife, 1974. Publication: Elite, 1990. Address: (b.) House of Commons, London SW1A 0AA; T.-0171-219 3000.

Liddle, Robert Christie, CA. Consultant (former Partner), Robb Ferguson CA; Secretary, Scottish Artists Benevolent Association, since 1993; b. 2.8.33, Hamilton; m., Elizabeth Jean Smith; 2 s.; 1 d. Educ. Hamilton Academy. Partner, Russ Ferguson & Maclennan, CA, 1958. Recreations: travel; bowling. Address: (b.) 5 Oswald Street, Glasgow G1 4QR; T.-0141-248 7411.

Lidgate, Professor David, BEng, PhD, CEng, FIEE, FInstE. Professor and Head, Department of Electrical and Electronic Engineering, Napier University, since 1994; b. 11.7.46, Gosforth; m., Janet; 2 d. Educ. Royal Grammar School, Newcastle upon Tyne; Liverpool University. Research Engineer, A. Reyrolle & Co. Ltd., 1965-75; Lecturer, UMIST, 1975-88; Head, School of Engineering, Greenwich University, 1988-94. Member, Electricity Consumers Committee for Southern Scotland, 1994-97. Recreations: genealogy; model railways. Address: (b.) 219 Colinton Road, Edinburgh EH14 1DJ; T.-0131-455 4361.

Lilley, Professor David Malcolm James, FRSE. Professor of Molecular Biology, Dundee University, since 1989; b. 28.5.48, Colchester; m., Patricia Mary; 2 d. Educ. Gilberd School, Colchester; Durham University. Joined Biochemistry Department, Dundee University, 1981; awarded: Colworth Medal by Biochemical Society, 1982, Gold Medal of G. Mendel, Czech Academy of Sciences, 1994, Gold Medal of V. Prelog in Stereochemistry, ETH, Zurich. Publications: 200 scientific papers. Recreation: foreign languages. Address: (b.) Department of Biochemistry, Dundee University, Dundee DD1 4HN; T.-01382 344243.

Lillico, William Allan, MREHIS, MInstWM. Director of Protective Services, Scottish Borders Council, since 1996; b. 8.3.45, Galashiels; m., Doreen Ann; 2 d. Educ. Galashiels Academy; Napier College, Edinburgh. Burgh of Galashiels: Trainee Burgh Surveyor/Sanitary Inspector, 1964-68, Junior Assistant Burgh Surveyor/Sanitary Inspector, 1968-71, Assistant Burgh Surveyor/Sanitary Inspector, 1971-72, Depute Burgh Surveyor/Sanitary Inspector, 1972-75; Ettrick and Lauderdale District Council: Area Inspector, Technical Services Department, 1975-76, Depute Director of Environmental Services, 1976-96. Member, Ettrick and Lauderdale Crime Prevention Panel. Recreation: golf.

Address: (b.) Protective Services Department, Scott House, Sprouston Road, Newton St. Boswells TD6 0QD; T.-01835 825111.

Lindsay, Frederic, MA (Hons). Writer; b. 12.8.33, Glasgow; m., Shirley; 1 s.; 3 d. Educ. North Kelvinside Senior Secondary School; Glasgow University; Jordanhill College; Edinburgh University. Worked as library assistant, teacher, lecturer; since becoming full-time writer in 1979, has published six novels: Brond, 1984, Jill Rips, 1987, A Charm Against Drowning, 1988, After the Stranger Came, 1992, Kissing Judas, 1997, A Kind of Dying, 1998; has written plays for Scottish Youth Theatre; radio plays for children; adapted Brond as serial for Channel 4. Former Chair, Society of Authors in Scotland; former Vice-President, PEN Scotland; former Member, Scottish Arts Council, Literature Committee. Recreations: cinema; theatre; television; reading; walking in the Pentlands. Address: (h.) 2a Hopelands Road, Silverburn, Penicuik EH26 9LH; T.-01968 678498.

Lindsay, James Kerr, MA. Manager, Scottish Fisheries Museum Trust Ltd., since 1989; b. 13.7.34, Dundee; m., Dorothy Pattullo; 1 s.; 1 d. Educ. Morgan Academy, Dundee; St. Andrews University. Production Controller/Finishing Manager, Alex. Pirie & Sons, 1958-66; Head of Fisheries Division, Highlands and Islands Development Board, 1966-89. Governor, Unicorn Preservation Society, Dundee; Council Member, Scottish Museums Council, Edinburgh. Recreations: ornithology; chess. Address: (h.) 5 St. Ayles Crescent, Anstruther, Fife; T.-01333 310028.

Lindsay, 16th Earl of (James Randolph Lindesay-Bethune). Chairman, Scottish Salmon Growers Association Ltd., since 1998; Chairman, RSPB Scotland, since 1998 (Council Member, RSPB UK); Board Member, Cairngorms Partnership, since 1998; Non-Executive Director, United Auctions (Scotland) plc, since 1998; Member, Secretary of State's Advisory Group on Sustainable Development, since 1998; Member, UK Round Table on Sustainable Development Sub-Group, since 1998; Member, Scottish Power Environment Forum, since 1998; Chairman, Assured British Meat Ltd., since 1997; Member, Select Committee on European Community Affairs: Environment, Public Health and Consumer Protection Sub-Committee, since 1997; b. 19.11.55; m., Diana Mary Chamberlayne-Macdonald. Educ. Eton; Edinburgh University; University of California, Davis. Lord in Waiting (Government Whip), 1995; Parliamentary Under Secretary of State, Scottish Office, 1995-97; Green Ribbon political award, 1995. Address: (h.) Lahill, Upper Largo, Fife KY8 6JE.

Lindsay, John. Chief Executive, East Lothian Council. Address: Council Buildings, Court Street, Haddington, EH41 3HA.

Lindsay, Professor John Gordon, BSc, PhD. Professor of Medical Biochemistry, Glasgow University, since 1992; b. 9.8.45, Birkenhead; m., Joan Cameron Barr; 2 s. Educ. Bellshill Academy; Glasgow University. Lecturer in Biochemistry, then Senior Lecturer, then Reader, Glasgow University, 1973-92. Fulbright Scholar, 1979-80; Editorial Adviser, Biochemical Journal; 110 publications in learned journals. Recreations: playing and coaching cricket; golf; classical music. Address: (b.) Division of Biochemistry and Molecular Biology, Institute of Biomedical and Life Sciences, Glasgow University, Glasgow G12 8QQ; T.-0141-330 4720.

Lindsay, John Maurice, CBE, TD, DLitt, HonFRIAS. Consultant, Scottish Civic Trust (Director, 1967-83); b. 21.7.18; m., Aileen Joyce Gordon; 1 s.; 3 d. Educ. Glasgow Academy; Scottish National Academy of Music. Drama Critic, Scottish Daily Mail, 1946-47; Music Critic, The Bulletin, 1946-60; Border Television: Programme Controller, 1961-62, Production Controller, 1962-64, Features Executive and Chief Interviewer, 1964-67. Atlantic-Rockefeller Award, 1946; Editor: Scots Review, 1949-50, The Scottish Review, 1975-85; Member, Historic Buildings Council for Scotland, 1976-87; Secretary-General, Europa Nostra, 1983-91; Council Member, Association of Scottish Literary Studies, 1983-94, President, 1988-90; Trustee: New Lanark Conservation Trust, 1985-94, National Heritage Memorial Fund, 1980-84; HonDLitt, Glasgow, 1982. Publications: poetry: The Advancing Day, 1940; Perhaps To-morrow, 1941; Predicament, 1942; No Crown for Laughter: Poems, 1943; The Enemies of Love: Poems 1941-45, 1946; Selected Poems, 1947; Hurlygush: Poems in Scots, 1948; At the Wood's Edge, 1950; Ode for St. Andrew's Night and Other Poems, 1951; The Exiled Heart: Poems 1941-56, 1957; Snow Warning and Other Poems, 1962; One Later Day and Other Poems, 1964; This Business of Living, 1969; Comings and Goings: Poems, 1971; Selected Poems 1942-72, 1973; The Run from Life, 1975; Walking Without an Overcoat, Poems 1972-76, 1977; Collected Poems, 1979; A Net to Catch the Winds and Other Poems, 1981; The French Mosquitoes' Woman and other diversions and poems; Requiem for a Sexual Athlete; Collected Poems 1940-90; On the Face Of It: Collected Poems, Vol. 2; News of the World: Last Poems; Speaking Likenesses: A Postscript; prose: Pocket Guide to Scottish Culture; The Scottish Renaissance; The Lowlands of Scotland: Glasgow and the North; Robert Burns: The Man, His Work, The Legend; Dunoon: The Gem of the Clyde Coast; The Lowlands of Scotland: Edinburgh and the South; Clyde Waters: Variations and Diversions on a Theme of Pleasure; The Burns Encyclopedia; Killochan Castle; By Yon Bonnie Banks: A Gallimaufry; Environment: A Basic Human Right; Portrait of Glasgow; Robin Philipson; History of Scottish Literature; Lowland Scottish Villages; Francis George Scott and the Scottish Renaissance; The Buildings of Edinburgh (Co-Author); Thank You For Having Me: A Personal Memoir; Unknown Scotland (Co-Author); Castles of Scotland: A Constable Guide; Count All Men Mortal: The Story of the Scottish Provident Institution; Victorian and Edwardian Glasgow; An Illustrated Guide to Glasgow; The Comic Poems of William Tennant (Co-Editor); Edinburgh Past and Present (Co-Author); The Youth and Manhood of Cyril Thornton (Editor); The Scottish Dog (Co-Author); A Pleasure of Gardens (Co-Author); The Scottish Quotation Book (Co-Author); The Music Quotation Book (Co-Author); The Theatre and Opera Lover's Quotation Book (Co-Author); The Burns Quotation Book (Co-Author); The Chambers Guide to Good Scottish Gardens (Co-Author). Recreations: music; walking. Address: (h.) 7 Milton Hill, Milton, Dumbarton G82 2TS; T.-Dumbarton 762655.

Lindsay, Margaret R., OBE, MA, MSc. Director, The Centre for Residential Child Care, since 1994; b. 27.6.48, Glasgow; m., William G. Lindsay; 2 s.; 1 d. Educ. Jordanhill College School; Glasgow University; Strathclyde University. Social Worker: Glasgow Child Guidance Service, 1971-73, Strathclyde Regional Council, 1975-83; Supervisor, Youth Training Scheme in Caring Skills, Orkney Islands Council, 1983-85; Counsellor, Barnardo's Scottish Adoption Advice Service, 1982-83; Project Leader, Barnardo's Fred Martin Project, Glasgow, 1985-89; Director of Services to People with Learning Disabilities, Archdiocese of Glasgow Social Services Centre, 1989-92; Assistant Director, NCH Action for Children Scotland, 1992-94; Independent Consultant in Community Care, 1992-94. Publications: books and articles on adoption, learning disability, respite care, advocacy and child residential services. Recreations: creative writing; cycling; walking. Address: (h.) 49 Morven Road, Bearsden, Glasgow G61 3BY; Y.-0141-942 7560.

Lindsay, Ranald Bruce, LLB(Hons), DipLP, NP. Solicitor-Advocate, since 1993; Solicitor, since 1986; b.

18.3.62, Bellshill; m., Jennifer Vesey; 1 s.; 1 d. Educ. Wishaw High; University of Glasgow. Trained with Bishop & Co., Glasgow, 1984-86; qualified as first Solicitor Advocate in both civil and criminal law, 1993; established own practice, 1994. Recreations: reading; films; history; computing; getting away from it all. Address: (b.) Lindsay Solicitors, 33 Buccleuch Street, Dumfries DG1 2AB; T.-01387 259236.

Lindsay, Stephen James. Regimental Secretary, The Black Watch (RHR), since 1997; b. 2.3.40, London; m., Ann Powell; 3 s.; 1 d. Educ. Eton College; Royal Military Academy, Sandhurst. Commissioned into The Black Watch, 1959; commanded Royal Guard, Balmoral, 1978; Commanding Officer, 1st Bn., 51st Highland Volunteers, 1984-86; retired in rank of Lt. Col., 1995. Recreations: piping; painting. Address: (b.) Balhousie Castle, Perth PH1 5HR; T.-01738 441784.

Lingard, Joan Amelia. Author; b. Edinburgh; 3 d. Educ. Bloomfield Collegiate School, Belfast; Moray House College of Education, Edinburgh. Member, Scottish Arts Council, 1980-85; Chair, Society of Authors in Scotland, 1980-84; a Director, Edinburgh Book Festival, since 1994; first novel published, 1963; has also written plays for TV, including 18-part series, Maggie, adapted from quartet of teenage books; novels: Liam's Daughter, 1963; The Prevailing Wind, 1964; The Tide Comes In, 1966; The Headmaster, 1967; A Sort of Freedom, 1968; The Lord on our Side, 1970; The Second Flowering of Emily Mountjoy, 1979; Greenyards, 1981; Sisters By Rite, 1984; Reasonable Doubts, 1986; The Women's House, 1989; After Colette, 1993; Dreams of Love and Modest Glory, 1995; 40 children's books. Recreations: reading; walking; travelling. Address: (b.) David Higham Associates, 5-8 Lower John Street, Golden Square, London W1R 4HA.

Lingard, Robin Anthony, MA, FTS. Independent Consultant; b. 19.7.41, Enfield; m., Margaret; 2 d. Educ. Felsted School; Emmanuel College, Cambridge. Joined Ministry of Aviation, 1963; Private Secretary to Joint Parliamentary Secretary, Ministry of Technology, 1966-68; appointments, Department of Industry, DTI, etc., to 1984; Head, Enterprise Unit, Cabinet Office, 1984-85; Head, Small Firms and Tourism Division, Department of Employment, 1985-87; full-time Board Member, Highlands and Islands Development Board, 1988-91; Director of Training and Social Development, Highlands and Islands Enterprise, 1991-93; Project Director, University of the Highlands and Islands Project, 1993-97. Member, Scottish Tourist Board, 1988-92; Chairman, Prince's Trust Committee for Highlands, Western Isles and Orkney; Member, Management Board, Prince's Trust and Royal Jubilee Trusts, 1989-95; Chairman, Youth Link Scotland, since 1997; Chairman, BBC Scotland Appeals Advisory Committee. Recreations: watching birds; walking; reading; aviation history; dinghy sailing. Address: (h.) Kinnairdie House, Dingwall IV15 9LL; T.-01349 61044.

Linklater, Professor Karl Alexander, BVM&S, PhD, CBiol, FIBiol, FRAgS, FRCVS. Vice Principal and Professor, Scottish Agricultural College, since 1997; (Member, Veterinary Products Committee, since 1990); a Director, The Moredun Foundation, since 1991; Director, Vet CPD, since 1991; b. 1.9.39, Stromness, Orkney; m., Margaret Carr Gibb; 1 s.; 1 d. Educ. Robert Gordon's College, Aberdeen; Edinburgh University. General veterinary practice, Tarland, Aberdeenshire, 1962-66; North of Scotland College of Agriculture, Aberdeen, 1966-67; Royal (Dick) School of Veterinary Studies, Edinburgh University, 1967-73; East of Scotland College of Agriculture, St. Boswells, 1973-86; Director, SAC Veterinary Services, 1986-97. President: Sheep Veterinary Society, 1983-85, British Veterinary Association, 1996-97, Association of Veterinary Teachers and Research Workers (Scotland), 1988-90, Scottish Branch, British Veterinary Association, 1992-94, Scottish Metropolitan Division, BVA, 1979-80; Alan Baldry Award, 1982. Recreations: sport; gardening; sheep breeding. Address: (h.) Bridge Park, Old Bridge Road, Selkirk TD7 4LG; T.-01750 20571.

Linklater, Magnus Duncan. Journalist; Chairman, Scottish Arts Council, since 1996; b. 21.2.42, Harray, Orkney; m., Veronica Lyle; 2 s.; 1 d. Educ. Eton College; Cambridge University. Reporter, Daily Express, Manchester, 1965-66; London Evening Standard: Diary Reporter, 1966-67, Editor, Londoner's Diary, 1967-69; Sunday Times: Editor, Spectrum, 1969-72, Editor, Colour Magazine, 1972-75, News Editor/Features Editor, 1975-83; Managing Editor, The Observer, 1983-86; Editor, London Daily News, 1986-87; Editor, The Scotsman, 1988-94; Chairman, Edinburgh Book Festival, 1994-96; Presenter, Eye to Eye, Radio Scotland, 1994-97; Columnist, The Times and Scotland on Sunday. Publications: Hoax: the Howard Hughes-Clifford Irving Affair (Co-Author); Jeremy Thorpe: A Secret Life (Co-Author); The Falklands War (with Sunday Times Insight team); Massacre — the story of Glencoe; The Fourth Reich — Klaus Barbie and the Neo-Fascist Connection (Co-Author); Not With Honour — the inside story of the Westland Affair (Co-Author); For King and Conscience — John Graham of Claverhouse, Viscount Dundee (Co-Author); Anatomy of Scotland (Co-Editor); Highland Wilderness; People in a Landscape. Honorary Doctor of Arts, Napier University; Honorary Doctor of Law, Aberdeen University. Recreations: book-collecting; fishing. Address: (h.) 5 Drummond Place, Edinburgh EH3 6PH; T.-0131-557 5705.

Linklater of Butterstone, Baroness (Veronica Linklater). Founder and Executive Chairman, The New School, Butterstone, since 1991; President, Society of Friends of Dunkeld Cathedral, since 1989; Trustee, Esmée Fairbairn Charitable Trust, since 1991; b. 15.4.43, Meikleour, Perthshire; m., Magnus Duncan Linklater (qv); 2 s.; 1 d. Educ. Cranborne Chase; Sorbonne; University of Sussex; University of London. Child Care Officer, London Borough of Tower Hamlets, 1967-68; Co-Founder, Visitors Centre, Pentonville Prison, 1971-77; Governor, three Islington schools, 1970-85; Prison Reform Trust Winchester Prison Project, 1981-82; Founder, Administrator, Consultant, Butler Trust, 1983-87 (Trustee, since 1987); JP, Inner London, 1985-88; Co-ordinator, Trustee, Vice Chairman, Pushkin Prizes (Scotland), since 1989; Member, Children's Panel, Edinburgh South, 1989-97; Committee Member, Gulliver Award for the Performing Arts in Scotland, 1990-96; Patron, Sutherland Trust, since 1993; Trustee, Young Musicians Trust, 1993-97; Candidate (Liberal Democrat), Perth & Kinross By-Election, 1995; Director, Maggie Keswick Jencks Cancer Caring Centres Trust, since 1997; Life Peer, since 1997. Recreations: music; theatre; gardening. Address: (h.) 5 Drummond Place, Edinburgh EH3 6PH; T.-0131-557 5705.

Linkston, Alexander Millar, IPFA. Chief Executive Officer, West Lothian Council, since 1996; b. 13.12.49, Bathgate; m., Margaret Cuddihy; 2 d. Educ. Lindsay High School, Bathgate; Glasgow College of Commerce. Joined West Lothian County Council as trainee accountant, 1965. Recreations: horse riding; swimming; Rotary. Address: (b.) West Lothian Council, West Lothian House, Livingston EH54 6QG; T.-01506 777141.

Linlithgow, 4th Marquess of (Adrian John Charles Hope); b. 1.7.46; m.; 1 s.; 1 d.; 2 s. by pr. m.; succeeded to title, 1987. Educ. Eton. Stockbroker. Address: Hopetoun House, South Queensferry, West Lothian, EH30 9SL.

Lisgo, John, BSc (Econ) (Hons), DipEd (Hons). Principal, Jewel and Esk Valley College, Edinburgh, since 1986 (Lauder Technical College, Dunfermline, 1983-86); b. 8.7.40, Seaham, Durham; m., Norma Ranson Peel; 1 s. Educ. Ryhope School, Sunderland; London School of

Economics and Political Science; Durham University. Assistant Teacher of History and Mathematics, Boldon Secondary School, 1962-63; Assistant Lecturer in Economics, then Liaison Officer for Adult Education, Monkwearmouth College of Further Education, 1963-72; Stevenson College of Further Education: Senior Lecturer in Social Studies, 1972-75, Head, Department of Language and Social Studies, 1975-80, Assistant Principal, 1980-83. Board Member: JEVCEL, Craigmillar Opportunities Trust, Midlothian Enterprise, Dalkeith Community Business. Recreation: swimming. Address: (b.) 24 Milton Road East, Edinburgh EH15 2PP; T.-0131-660 1010.

Lishman, Professor Joyce, MA (Oxon), PhD, DipSW. Head, School of Applied Social Studies, Robert Gordon University, since 1993; m., Dr. J.R. Lishman; 1 s.; 1 d. Educ. Normanton Girls High School; St. Hilda's College, Oxford University; Edinburgh University; Aberdeen University. Social Worker/Senior Social Worker, Departments of Child and Family Psychiatry, Edinburgh; Research Assistant/Research Fellow, Aberdeen University; Editor, Research Highlights Series; Malcolm Sargent Social Worker, Royal Aberdeen Children's Hospital; Lecturer/Senior Lecturer, RGIT; Lead Assessor, Quality Assessment of Social Work, 1995-96. Publications: Handbook of Theory for Practice; Teachers in Social Work (Editor); Communication in Social Work; The Role of Volunteer Coordinators in the Provision of Care (Co-Author); Research Highlights in Social Work series (General Editor). Recreations: family and friends; music; theatre; reading; cycling; swimming. Address: (b.) School of Applied Social Studies, The Robert Gordon University, Kepplestone Annexe, Queen's Road, Aberdeen AB9 2PG; T.-01224 263201.

Lister-Kaye, Sir John, 8th Bt. of Grange, DUniv. Naturalist, Author, Lecturer; Member, International Committee, World Wilderness Foundation, since 1984; President, Scottish Wildlife Trust, since 1996; Vice President, Association for the Preservation of Rural Scotland, since 1998; b. 8.5.46; m., 1, Lady Sorrel Deirdre Bentinck; 1 s.; 2 d.; 2, Lucinda Anne Law. Educ. Allhallows School. Founded Field Studies Centre, Highlands, 1970; founder Director, Aigas Trust, 1979; Director, AigasQuest Ltd., 1997; Chairman, Scottish Committee, RSPB, 1985-92; Member, Committee for Scotland, NCC, 1989-90; NW Regional Chairman, Scottish Natural Heritage, 1992-96; Honorary Doctorate, University of Stirling, 1995. Publications: The White Island, 1972; Seal Cull, 1979; The Seeing Eye, 1980; One for Sorrow, 1994; Ill Fares the Land, 1995. Address: (h.) House of Aigas, Beauly, Inverness-shire IV4 7AD.

Lithgow, Sir William (James), 2nd Bt. of Ormsary, DL, LLD, CEng, FRINA, CBIM. Industrialist; Farmer; Chairman, Lithgows Limited, since 1959 (Director, since 1956); b. 10.5.34; m., 1, Valerie Helen Scott (deceased); 2, Mary Claire Hill; 2 s.; 1 d. Educ. Winchester College. Chairman, Hunterston Development Company Limited, 1987 (Director, since 1971); Director: Lithgows Limited, Lithgows Pty Limited; Chairman, Scott Lithgow Drydocks Ltd., 1967-78; Vice-Chairman, Scott Lithgow Ltd., 1968-78; Chairman, Western Ferries (Argyll) Ltd., 1972-85; Director, Bank of Scotland, 1962-86. Member: British Committee, Det Norske Veritas, 1966-92, Greenock District Hospital Board, 1961-66, General Board (Royal Society Nominee), Nat. Physical Lab., 1963-66; Honorary President, Students Association, and Member, Court, Strathclyde University, 1964-69; Member: Executive Committee, Scottish Council Development and Industry, 1969-85, Scottish Regional Council, CBI, 1969-76, Clyde Port Authority, 1969-71, West Central Scotland Plan Steering Committee, 1970-74, Board, National Ports Council, 1971-78, Scottish Milk Marketing Board, 1979-83; Chairman, Iona Cathedral Trustees Management Board, 1979-83; Council Member, Winston Churchill Memorial Trust, 1979-83; Member, Queen's Body Guard for Scotland (Royal Company of Archers), 1964; Fellow, Scottish Council Development and Industry; Honorary President: West Renfrewshire Battalion Boys' Brigade, Mid-Argyll Agricultural Society. Recreations: rural life; invention; photography. Address: (b.) PO Box 7, Lochgilphead, Argyll PA31 8JH; T.-01880 770700.

Little, David Irving, BSc (Hons), DMS, CEng, MICE, MCIWEM. Engineering Services Director, West of Scotland Water, since 1995; b. 6.12.43, Glasgow; m., Margo Forrest Little Hood; 2 d. Educ. Allan Glen's School, Glasgow; Strathclyde University. Assistant Area Engineer (Operations), Glasgow Corporation Water Department, 1963-69; Engineer/Principal Engineer New Works, Lower Clyde Water Board, 1970-87; Strathclyde Regional Council Water Department: Reservoir Engineer, 1978-82, Operations Engineer, Lower Clyde Division, 1982-84, Assistant Director (Resources and Planning), 1984-87, Area Director, New Works/Engineering Services Manager, 1987-95. Recreations: golf; reading. Address: (h.) 10 Balmerino Place, Bishopbriggs, Glasgow G64 1LW; T.-0141-772 8451.

Little, Professor John Anthony, BSc, MSc, MBA, PhD, CEng, MICE, CGeol, FGS. Assistant Principal, since 1997, and Dean, Faculty of Engineering, Paisley University; Professor and Head, Department of Civil, Structural and Environmental Engineering, 1992-96; Associate Dean, Faculty of Engineering, 1993-97; b. 24.11.48, Catterick; m., Gail; 1 s.; 2 d. Educ. Chatham House Grammar School, Ramsgate; University of Wales; Durham University; City University; Edinburgh University. Research engineer, construction industry, 1972-76; Senior Lecturer, Hatfield Polytechnic, 1976-86; Lecturer/Senior Lecturer, Heriot-Watt University, 1986-92. Chairman, Scottish Geotechnical Group, since 1992; Co-ordinator, Scotland Science Engineering and Technology, 1996; Member, Women into Science and Engineering Scotland Committee, since 1996. Address: (b.) Paisley University, High Street, Paisley PA1 2BE; T.-0141-848 3250.

Little, Keith, MB, ChB, MD, FRCP, FRCSEdin, FFAEM. Consultant in Accident and Emergency Medicine, Edinburgh Royal Infirmary; b. 26.4.43, Yeadon, Yorkshire; 2 s.; 2 d. Educ. Dalbeattie High School; Dumfries Academy; Edinburgh Medical School. First posts in Edinburgh; moved to Derby as a Registrar in Accident and Emergency Medicine; Consultant, Chester Royal Infirmary, 1974-78. Past President, British Association for Accident and Emergency Medicine; President, Faculty of Accident and Emergency Medicine. Publication: Accident and Emergency Resuscitation (Co-Author). Recreations: golf; tennis. Address: (b.) Accident and Emergency Department, Royal Infirmary, Edinburgh; T.-0131-536 4007.

Little, Tom (Thomas J.J.), MA (Hons). Education Correspondent, The Scotsman, since 1997; b. 27.11.66, Dumfries; m., Claire Phillips Little. Educ. Dumfries Academy; Glasgow University. Dumfriesshire Newspapers; Depute Editor, East Lothian Courier; Edinburgh Evening News; Health Reporter, Daily Record. Recreations: football; rugby; pub gossip. Address: (b.) 20 North Bridge, Edinburgh EH1 1 YT; T.-0131-243 3695.

Littlejohn, Professor David, BSc, PhD, CChem, FRSC, FRSE. Professor of Analytical Chemistry, Strathclyde University, since 1988; b. 1.5.53, Glasgow; m., Lesley Shaw MacDonald; 1 d. Educ. Duncanrig Secondary School, East Kilbride; Strathclyde University. Technical Officer, ICI Petrochemicals Division, Wilton, Middlesborough, 1978-80; Lecturer/Senior Lecturer in Chemistry, Strathclyde University, 1981-88. Awarded 15th SAC Silver Medal by Royal Society of Chemistry, 1987; joint Editor in Chief, Talanta, International Journal of Pure and Applied Analytical Chemistry, 1989-91. Publications: 150 research papers, 10 reviews, one book. Address: (b.) Department of Pure and Applied Chemistry, Strathclyde University, 295 Cathedral Street, Glasgow G1 1XL; T.-0141-548 2067.

Littlejohn, Doris, JP, BL, DUniv, CBE. President, Employment Tribunals (Scotland), since 1991; b. 19.3.35, Glasgow; m., Robert; 3 d. Educ. Queen's Park School, Glasgow; University of Glasgow. Solicitor in private practice in Stirling until 1977; Chairman, Industrial Tribunals, until 1988, Regional Chairman, until 1991. Member of Court, University of Stirling; Non-Executive Director, Stirling Royal Infirmary; Member, Human Genetics Advisory Commission; former Member: Broadcasting Council for Scotland, General Advisory Committee, BBC. Address: (b.) Central Office of the Industrial Tribunals, Eagle Building, 215 Bothwell Street, Glasgow G2 7TS; T.-0141-204 0730.

Littlejohn, Robert King, MA (Aberdeen), MA (Sussex), MIPD. Registrar, Royal College of Physicians and Surgeons of Glasgow, since 1996; b. 17.3.46, Aberdeen; m., Anna; 1 s.; 2 d. Educ. Morrison's Academy, Crieff; Aberdeen University; Moray House College; Sussex University. Administrative (Education) Officer, RAF, 1969-96 including: Directorate of Air Staff Briefing and Co-ordination, 1987-90; Officer Commanding Administration Wing, RAF Leeming, 1990-93; Head of RAF Resettlement Service, 1993-96; retired in rank of Wing Commander. Recreations: golf; hill-walking; opera; Aberdeen FC. Address: (b.) 232-242 St. Vincent Street, Glasgow G2 5RJ; T.-0141-221 6072.

Littlejohn, William Hunter, RSA, RSW, RGI; b. 16.4.29, Arbroath. Educ. Arbroath High School; Dundee College of Art. Art teaching in Angus schools, 1953-56; Art teaching, Arbroath High School, 1956-66; Gray's School of Art, Aberdeen: Lecturer, 1966-72, Head of Painting, then Head of Fine Art, 1972-86; retired from teaching, 1986. Address: (h.) 16 Colvill Place, Arbroath DD11 1RB; T.-01241 874402.

Livesay, Admiral Sir Michael Howard, KCB, CIMgt. President, Royal British Legion Scotland, since 1996; President, Earl Haig Fund Scotland, since 1996; Non-Executive Director, Scottish Nuclear, since 1993; Commissioner, Northern Lighthouse Board, since 1994 (Chairman, 1997); b. 5.4.36, Middlesbrough; m., Sally House; 2 d. Educ. Acklam Hall Grammar School; Britannia Royal Naval College. Joined Royal Navy, 1952; Commissioned 1957; Aircraft Direction Specialist, 1959; served HM Ships: Loch Alvie, Hermes, Aisne, Victorious; in command, HMS Hubberston, 1966; promoted Commander, 1970 and in command HMS Plymouth; promoted Captain, 1975; Captain, Fishery Protection and Mine Counter Measures at South Queensferry; first Commanding Officer, HMS Invincible, 1980; Director, Naval Warfare, 1982; promoted Rear Admiral, 1984; Flag Officer, Sea Training, 1984-86; Assistant Chief of Naval Staff, 1986-89; promoted Vice Admiral, 1989; Flag Officer, Scotland and Northern Ireland, 1989-91; promoted Admiral, 1991; Second Sea Lord and Chief of Naval Personnel, 1991-93; retired from RN 1993. Member, Council, Thistle Foundation. Recreations: fishing; golf; gardening; reading; outdoor sports. Address: c/o Naval Secretary, Victory Building, HM Naval Base, Portsmouth PO1 3LS.

Livingstone of Bachuil, Alastair, MA, LLB, FSA Scot. Baron of Bachuil; b. 1.9.14, Blantyre, Nyasaland; m., Valerie Collins; 2 s.; 3 d. Educ. Loretto School; Edinburgh University; Cambridge University. Sudan Political Service, 1938-40; 1940-43: commissioned into West Yorkshire Regiment in Khartoum, later Brigade Intelligence Officer, 9th Indian Infantry Brigade, active service in Eritrea and Western Desert; seconded to Palestine Government as Assistant District Commissioner, 1943-47; Executive, Iraq Petroleum Company Ltd., 1948-73. Chairman, Lismore Community Council, 1977-80; Member, Convention of the Baronage of Scotland; Hereditary Keeper of the Pastoral Staff of Saint Moluag; Past Chairman, 1745 Association; Co-Editor, Muster Roll of Prince Charles Edward Stuart's Army, 1746. Recreations: genealogy; Scottish history; country pursuits. Address: (h.) Bachuil, Isle of Lismore, Argyll; T.-01631 760 256.

Livingstone, Andrew Hugh, BSc (Hons), DipEd. Rector, St. Columba's School, Kilmacolm, since 1987; b. 7.12.44, Campbeltown; m., 1, Christine Margaret Henderson (deceased), 2, Alison Brown Reid; 1 s.; 1 d. Educ. Campbeltown Grammar School; University of Aberdeen; University of Glasgow; Jordanhill College of Education. High School of Glasgow, 1968-70; Principal Teacher, Mathematics, Paisley Grammar School, 1970-79; Assistant Rector, Williamwood High School, 1979-83; Depute Rector, Paisley Grammar School, 1987. Recreations: golf; bridge; walking; skiing. Address: (h.) Nithsdale, Lyle Road, Kilmacolm; T.-01505 872404.

Livingstone, Bill (William). Editorial Director, Dunfermline Press Group, since 1997; Chairman, Guild of Editors (Scotland), 1994-96; Life Trustee, Carnegie Dunfermline and Hero Fund Trusts, since 1991; b. 23.7.44, Dunfermline; m., Margaret Stark; 2 s.; 2 d. Educ. Dunfermline High School. Entire career with Dunfermline Press Group: Editor, Dunfermline Press, 1984-96. Elder, St. Paul's Parish Church, Dunfermline; Hon. Vice-President, Dunfermline and District Bn., Boys' Brigade. Address: (b.) Pitreavie Business Park, Dunfermline, Fife KY11 5QS; T.-01383 728201.

Livingstone, George, MA, DipEd, MEd, FEIS. Vice-Dean, Faculty of Education, University of Strathclyde, since 1994; b. 19.5.38, Tranent; m., Jean Laidlaw Ritchie; 2 s. Educ. Preston Lodge; Edinburgh University; Glasgow University. Teacher/Head of Department, primary and secondary schools, East Lothian and Tanzania, 1960-67; Head Teacher, Glendinning School, Galashiels, 1967-70; Hamilton College of Education: Lecturer/Research Officer, 1970-78, Head of Department, 1978-83; Jordanhill College of Education: Senior Lecturer, 1983-90, Course Director, 1990-94. President, Association of Lecturers in Colleges of Education in Scotland, 1982-86; Member, General Teaching Council for Scotland, 1986-98 (Convener, Supply Committee, Vice-Convener, Exceptional Admissions Committee); Chairman, S.J.N.C. (F.E.), 1988-92; Selector, Glasgow District Rugby Union, 1988-94. Publications: Co-author three series of books for children; Scotland – Still a Half-educated Nation (Co-author), 1986. Recreations: rugby union; walking; literature. Address: (h.) 1 Scott Grove, Hamilton; T.-01698 429756.

Livingstone, Ian Lang, OBE, BL, NP. Chairman: Lanarkshire Health Board, since 1993, Lanarkshire Development Agency, since 1991, Board, Motherwell College, 1989-97; Consultant Solicitor, since 1989; b. 23.2.38, Hamilton; m., Diane; 2 s. Educ. Hamilton Academy; Glasgow University. Qualified as Solicitor, 1960; Partner, Senior Partner, Ballantyne & Copland, Solicitors, Motherwell, 1962-86; Chairman and Director, family property investment and development company, since 1987. Former Chairman, Motherwell Football Club; Member, Dalziel High School Board; Governor, David Livingstone Memorial Trust; Elder, St. Mary's Parish Church, Motherwell. Recreations: walking; football; music. Address: (h.) 223 Manse Road, Motherwell ML1 2PY; T.-01698 253750.

Lloyd, Professor Ian John, LLB, LLM, PhD. Professor of Information Technology Law, University of Strathclyde, since 1996; b. Barrow in Furness. Educ. St. Ninian's High School, Kirkintilloch; Strathclyde University; Exeter University. Lecturer, University of Aberdeen; University of Strathclyde: Lecturer, Senior Lecturer, Reader. Publication:

Information Technology Law (second edition); The Data Protection Act 1998. Recreations: golf; following Celtic Football Club. Address: (b.) 173 Cathedral Street, Glasgow G4 0RQ; T.-0141-548 3291.

Lloyd, Ivor Graham, BA, DipLib, MLib, ALA. Head of Information Services, University of Abertay Dundee, since 1996; b. 28.10.50, Edinburgh; m., Rosemary; 1 s.; 1 d. Educ. Ainslie Park Secondary School, Edinburgh; University of Strathclyde; University of Wales. Assistant Librarian, Kirkcaldy Technical College, 1975-76; Subject Librarian, Duncan of Jordanstone College of Art, 1976-84; Depute Chief Librarian, Dundee College of Technology, 1984-89; Chief Librarian, University of Abertay Dundee, 1989-96. Recreations: golf; gardening. Address: (b.) University of Abertay Dundee, Bell Street, Dundee; T.-01382 308866.

Lloyd-Jones, Glyn Robin, MA, BA. Author and Novelist; President, Scottish PEN International, since 1997; Co-ordinator, Scottish Forum for Development Education in Schools (SFDES), since 1996; b. 5.10.34, London; m., Sallie Hollocombe; 1 s.; 2 d. Educ. Blundell's School, Tiverton; Selwyn College, Cambridge University; Jordanhill College of Education. Teaching in Scottish secondary schools; Director, Curriculum Development Centre, Clydebank; English-Speaking Union Thyne Travel Scholarship to America, 1974; President, Scottish Association of Writers, 1981-86; Adviser, Education Department, Dunbartonshire, 1972-89; radio drama: Ice in Wonderland, 1992 (winner, Radio Times new drama script award); Rainmaker, 1995. Publications: children's: Where the Forest and the Garden Meet, 1980; novels: Lord of the Dance (Winner, BBC/Arrow First Novel Competition, 1983); The Dreamhouse, 1985; Fallen Angels, 1992; education books: Assessment: From Principles to Action, 1985; How to Produce Better Worksheets, 1985; non-fiction: Argonauts of the Western Isles, 1989. Recreations: mountaineering; sea-kayaking; photography; chess. Address: (h.) 26 East Clyde Street, Helensburgh G84 7PG; T.-01436 672010.

Lo, Professor Kwok Lun, MSc, PhD, CEng, FIEE. Professor of Power Systems, Strathclyde University, since 1989; Visiting and Consultant Professor to several overseas universities, since 1987; power systems consultant, since 1970; b. 23.6.43; m., Dr. K.K.N. Lo; 2 s. Educ. St. Joseph's College, Hong Kong; UMIST. Began career with South Wales Switchgear Ltd., Central Electricity Generating Board, South Wales Electricity Board; joined Department of Electrical Engineering, Paisley College of Technology, 1971; joined Strathclyde University, 1977, as Lecturer, then Senior Lecturer, then Reader; author/co-author of more than 200 technical publications. Recreations: swimming; walking. Address: (b.) Department of EEE, Royal College, 204 George Street, Strathclyde University, Glasgow; T.-0141-552 4400, Ext. 2169.

Lochhead, Liz. Poet and Playwright; b. 1947, Motherwell. Educ. Glasgow School of Art. Combined teaching art and writing for eight years; became full-time writer after selection as first holder, Scottish/Canadian Writers' Exchange Fellowship, 1978; former Writer in Residence, Tattenhall Centre, Chester. Publications include: Memo for Spring, Islands, Grimm Sisters, Dreaming of Frankenstein, True Confessions; plays include: Blood and Ice, Dracula, Same Difference, Sweet Nothings, Now and Then, True Confessions, Mary Queen of Scots Got Her Head Chopped Off, The Big Picture.

Locke, Alasdair James Dougall, MA. Chairman, Abbot Group PLC, since 1992; b. 29.8.53, Aldershot; m., Kathleen Anne; 2 s. Educ. Uppingham School, Rutland; Wadham College, Oxford University. Assistant Vice President: Citibank N. A., 1974-78, Oceanic Finance Corporation, 1978-81; Vice President, American Express Leasing Corporation, 1981-83; Director, Henry Ansbacher and Co., Ltd., 1983-87; Deputy Chairman, Kelt Energy PLC, 1987-91. Member, OSO Advisory Board. Recreations: shooting; golf; skiing. Address: (b.) Minto Drive, Altens, Aberdeen AB12 3LW; T.-01224 299600.

Lockett, Patrick Gordon, CA. Director, James Finlay PLC; Chairman, Gartmore SNT PLC, since 1998; Director, Murray Ventures Investment Trust PLC, since 1998; b. 3.5.46, Glasgow; m., Erica; 1 s.; 1 d. Educ. Wellington College, Berkshire; Harvard Business School. Partner, Whinney Murray & Co., 1979; Partner, Ernst & Young, 1979-95. Director, Cumbernauld Development Corporation, 1989-97. Recreations: field sports; tennis; travel. Address: (h.) Swindridgemuir, Dalry, Ayrshire; T.-01294 832079.

Lockhart, Sheriff Brian Alexander, BL. Sheriff, Glasgow and Strathkelvin, since 1981; b. 1.10.42, Ayr; m., Christine Ross Clark; 2 s.; 2 d. Educ. Glasgow Academy; Glasgow University. Partner, Robertson Chalmers and Auld, Solicitors, 1967-79; Sheriff, North Strathclyde, at Paisley, 1979-81; Member, Parole Board for Scotland; Secretary, Sheriffs' Association. Recreations: fishing; golf; squash; family. Address: (h.) 18 Hamilton Avenue, Glasgow G41; T.-0141-427 1921.

Lockhart, Brian Robert Watson. MA (Hons), DipEd. Headmaster, Robert Gordon's College, Aberdeen, since 1996; b. 19.7.44, Edinburgh; m., Fiona Anne Sheddon; 1 s.; 2 d. Educ. George Heriot's School, Edinburgh; Aberdeen University. Teacher of History and Economic History, George Heriot's School, 1968-72; Principal Teacher of History, 1972-81; Deputy Rector, High School of Glasgow, 1981-96. Headteachers' Association of Scotland: Member, Council, 19988-98, Member, Executive, 1989-94; Co-Chair, Universities and Colleges Admissions Service Scottish Standing Committee; Member, Higher Still Implementation Group. Recreations: reading biographies; sport; films; politics. Address: (h.) 80 Gray Street, Aberdeen AB10 6JE; T.-01224 315776.

Lockhart of the Lee, Angus Hew; b. 17.8.46, Dunsyre; m., Susan Elizabeth Normand; 1 s.; 1 d. Educ. Rannoch School, Perthshire; North of Scotland College of Agriculture. Recognised as Chief of the Name Lockhart, 1957; Owner and Manager, Lee and Carnwath Estates; Member, Standing Council of Scottish Chiefs. Recreations: shooting; skiing. Address: (h.) Newholm, Dunsyre, Lanark ML11 8NQ; T.-01968 682254.

Lockhart, Peter. Solicitor, since 1978; Partner, Lockharts Solicitors, Ayr, since 1982; Member, Council, Law Society of Scotland, since 1997; b. 24.2.54, Ayr; m., Carol; 1 s.; 2 d. Educ. Gordonstoun School; Ayr Academy; Glasgow University. Apprenticeship with Joseph Mellicks, Glasgow; Court Assistant, Messrs Gair and Gibson, Solicitors, Falkirk, 1978-79; joined family firm, Lockhart Solicitors, Ayr and Kilmarnock, 1979. Broadcaster, West Sound, Ayr, 1988-92. Recreations: fishing; walking; swimming; music. Address: (b.) 1 Barns Street, Ayr KA7 1XB; T.-01292 265045.

Lockhead, Moir, OBE, IEng, MCIT, MIRTE. Deputy Chairman and Chief Executive, First Group plc; b. 25.4.45, Sedgefield; m., Audrey; 3 s.; 1 d. Educ. West Cornforth Secondary School; Darlington Technical College; Middlesborough Polytechnic. Former Head of Engineering, Strathclyde Passenger Transport Executive; joined Grampian Regional Transport as General Manager, 1985; Executive Chairman, GRT Bus Group PLC, 1989. Address: (b.) 395 King Street, Aberdeen AB24 5RP; T.-01224 650102.

Lockley, Stephen Randolph, BSc, CEng, MICE, FICT, MIHT, DipTE. Transport Consultant, since 1997; b. 19.6.43, Manchester; m., Angela; 2 d. Educ. Morecambe

Grammar School; Manchester University. Highway and Planning Engineer, Lancashire County Council, 1964-72; Transportation and Planning Engineer, Lanarkshire County Council, 1972-75; Strathclyde Regional Council: Principal Engineer (Transportation), 1975-77, Depute Director of Policy Planning, 1977-80, Principal Executive Officer, 1980-86; Director General, Strathclyde Passenger Transport Executive, 1986-97. Address: 64 Townhead Street, Strathaven, Lanarkshire ML10 6DJ; T.-01357 529395.

Lodge, Professor Raymond Anthony, BA, PhD. Professor of French Language and Linguistics, University of St. Andrews, since 1995; b. 12.7.42, Leeds; m., Janet Mary Martin; 2 s.; 1 d. Educ. Pudsey Grammar School; University of Manchester. Lecturer then Senior Lecturer in French, University of Aberdeen, 1967-84; Professor of French, University of Newcastle upon Tyne, 1984-95. Publication: French: From Dialect to Standard, 1993. Recreation: singing. Address: (b.) French Department, University of St. Andrews, St. Andrews KY16 9AJ; T.-01334 463636.

Logan, Alec, MB, ChB, FRCGP. Founding Editor, Hoolet (Scottish magazine, Royal College of General Practitioners); Deputy Editor, British Journal of General Practice, since 1997; b. 18.11.59, Bellshill; m., Janice Crofts; 2 s. Educ. Hutchesons' Grammar School; Glasgow University. Medical Officer, Royal Navy, 1980-88; GP, Wishaw, since 1988. Recreations: sailing; reading; music. Address: (h.) 47 Orchard Street, Motherwell ML1 3JE; T.-01698 258201.

Logan, Andrew, SDA, NDA, FIHort. Farmer; Director, Scottish Nuclear Stock Association, 1983-98; Chairman, Dorward Gray Ltd.; Chairman, Scotfruit, since 1997; b. 24.3.40, Cupar; m., M.L. Fleming; 3 s.; 1 d. Educ. Strathallan School; Edinburgh School of Agriculture. Director: Fifegro, 1973-79, Elba, 1979-84, Central Farmers, 1974-83; Chairman, Soft Fruit and Field Vegetable Committee, Scottish NFU, 1979-83; Member, Scottish Agricultural Development Council, 1983-86; Governor: Scottish Crop Research Institute, 1986-97, National Vegetable Research Station, 1977-87, Strathallan School, since 1986; Director, East of Scotland Growers, 1987-89; Member, Horticultural Development Council, 1986-92; Member, Home Grown Cereals Authority Research and Development Committee, 1987-89; Director, Scotfresh, 1984-89; Governor, Institute of Horticultural Research, 1987-89; Member, Scottish Agricultural Research and Development Advisory Council, 1987-90; Director, Futursky, since 1988; Director, Top Hat Holdings, since 1989; Council Member, Scottish Agricultural Organisation Society, 1991-97. Recreations: skiing; golf. Address: (h.) Tarvit Home Farm, Cupar, Fife; T.-Cupar 652808.

Logan, Jimmy. Actor/Manager; Comedian; b. 4.4.28, Glasgow. One of five children who appeared on stage as The Logan Family; toured as an accordionist, juvenile lead and comedian's feed; for many years starred in Five Past Eight (summer revue) and numerous pantomimes; wrote and produced Lauder (one-man show); nine appearances at Royal performances.

Logan, Rev. Robert James Victor, MA, BD. Minister, Abdie and Dunbog linked with Newburgh, since 1998; Minister, Crown Church, Inverness, 1970-98; b. 8.6.38, Kilmarnock; m., Catherine Steel Young. Educ. Dundee High School; St. Andrews University; Edinburgh University. Assistant Minister, Auld Kirk of Ayr, 1962-64; Minister, Newton Parish Church, Dalkeith, 1964-70; Member, Church Boundaries' Commission, 1974-75; Clerk: Synod of Moray, 1972-75, Synod of the Southern Highlands, 1976-92, Inverness Presbytery, 1980-96; Convener, Nomination Committee, General Assembly, 1979-82; Chairman, successful group applying for franchise to operate Moray Firth Radio, 1979-81. Publication: The Lion, The Pit and the Snowy Day. Recreations: classical music; opera; bridge; reading history. Address: (h.) 2 Guthrie Court, Cupar Road, Newburgh, Fife KY14 6HA; T.-01337 840275.

Logan, Rt. Rev. Vincent, DipRE. Roman Catholic Bishop of Dunkeld, since 1981; b. 30.6.41, Bathgate. Educ. Blairs College, Aberdeen; St. Andrew's College, Drygrange. Ordained Priest, 1964; Assistant Priest, St. Margaret's, Edinburgh, 1964-66; Corpus Christi College, London, 1966-67; Chaplain, St. Joseph's Hospital, Rosewell, Midlothian, 1966-67; Adviser in Religious Education, Archdiocese of St. Andrews and Edinburgh, 1967; Parish Priest, St. Mary's, Ratho, 1977-81; Vicar Episcopal for Education, Edinburgh, 1978. Address: Bishop's House, 29 Roseangle, Dundee DD1 4LS; T.-01382 224327.

Logan, (William) Bruce, BA (Cantab), LLB, NP, WS. Partner, Burness, Solicitors, since 1969; b. 7.9.41, Forfar; m., Jennifer Mary; 3 d. Educ. Fettes College, Edinburgh; Cambridge University; Edinburgh University. Director: Art in Partnership Scotland Ltd, Scottish Rights of Way Society Ltd. Recreations: music; contemporary art; cycling; walking. Address: (b.) 50 Lothian Road, Festival Square, Edinburgh EH3 9WJ; T.-0131-473 6000.

Logie, John Robert Cunningham, MB, ChB, PhD, FRCS(Eng), FRCS(Edin), FRCS(Glas). Consultant General Surgeon, Inverness Hospitals, since 1981; Member, Council, Royal College of Surgeons of Edinburgh, since 1991; b. 9.9.46, Aberdeen; m., Sheila C. Will. Educ. Robert Gordon's College, Aberdeen; Trinity College, Glenalmond; Aberdeen University. House Officer, then Senior House Officer, then Lecturer, Department of Surgery, then Senior Registrar, Aberdeen Royal Infirmary. Recreations: rugby refereeing; garden; railways; ornamental waterfowl. Address: (h.) The Darroch, Little Cantray, Culloden Moor, Inverness IV1 5EG; T.-01463 792090.

Logie, Professor Robert Howie, BSc, PhD, CPhyschol, FBPsS, FRSA. Anderson Professor of Psychology, University of Aberdeen, since 1998 (Head, Department of Psychology, since 1997); b. 23.3.54, Ajmer, India; m., Elizabeth; 2 s. Educ. Aberdeen Academy; University of Aberdeen; University College, London. Researcher, MRC Applied Psychology Unit, Cambridge, 1980-86; University of Aberdeen: Lecturer in Psychology, 1987, Senior Lecturer, 1992, Personal Professor, 1995. Publications: over 100 including 12 authored or edited books, notably Visuo Spatial Working Memory, 1995. Dorothy Hodgkin Lecturer, British Association for the Advancement of Science, 1995. Recreation: choral singing. Address: William Guild Building, Old Aberdeen AB24 2UB; T.-01224 272241.

Logue, James, CEng, FIMechE, MIMgt. Business Development Manager, Scot-Train Ltd., since 1997; Personnel Director, ScotRail Railways Ltd., 1994-97; Board Member, Institution of Mechanical Engineers, since 1990; b. 13.5.39, Glasgow; m., Pamela; 1 s.; 2 d. Educ. St. Mungo's, Glasgow; Stow College, Glasgow. ScotRail: Area Engineer, 1978-89, Quality Programmes Manager, 1989-92, Retail Manager, 1992-94; Chairman, IMechE Railway Division, Scottish Branch. Recreations: golf; DIY; car maintenance; socialising. Address: (h.) 1 Linnhe Avenue, Bishopbriggs, Glasgow G64 1HG; T.-0141-563 6598.

Longmore, Alexander Bryan George, MA, LLB. Deputy Lieutenant, Inverness, since 1998; Honorary Sheriff, Inverness, since 1992; General Commissioner of Inland Revenue, Inverness 1st, since 1992; b. 30.4.35, Evanton; m., Leonella Lucia; 2 s. Educ. Robert Gordon's College, Aberdeen; University of Aberdeen. Assistant Trust Officer, The National Trust Co. Ltd., Toronto, Canada, 1958-60; Teacher of English, European School, Parma, Italy, 1960-61; Solicitor, Anderson Shaw and Gilbert, Inverness (retired as Senior Partner, 1995, Consultant, since 1995). Chairman, Inverness Civic Trust; Past Chairman, Highland Italian Circle. Recreations: gardening; walking; theatre; reading. Address: 25 Midmills Road, Inverness IV2 3NZ; T.-01463 235236.

Lonie, James William Laing, MA. Head of Arts and Cultural Heritage Division, Scottish Office Education and Industry Department; b. 21.6.41, Falkirk; m., Nuala Clare Ward. Educ. Falkirk High School; Edinburgh University; Gonville and Caius College, Cambridge. HM Treasury, 1967-76; joined Scottish Office, 1976. Recreations: music; walking; languages. Address: (b.) 1-A21, Education and Industry Department, Victoria Quay, Edinburgh, EH6 6QQ; T.-0131-244 0341.

Lord, Geoffrey, OBE, MA, AIB, FRSA. Founder Trustee, The ADAPT Trust, since 1992; Trustee, National Youth Orchestra of Scotland, since 1998; Hon. Secretary, Edinburgh Voluntary Organisations Trust, since 1997; b. 24.2.28, Rochdale; m., Jean; 1 s.; 1 d. Educ. Rochdale Grammar School; Bradford University. Midland Bank Ltd., 1946-58; Greater Manchester Probation and After-Care Service, 1958-76 (Deputy Chief Probation Officer, 1974-76); Secretary and Treasurer, Carnegie UK Trust, 1977-93; Vice-President, Selcare Trust; Chairman, Pollock Memorial Missionary Trust; Honorary Fellow, Manchester Metropolitan University, 1987; Former Trustee and Chairman, HomeStart UK; Chairman, The Unemployed Voluntary Action Fund, 1990-95; Past President, Centre for Environmental Interpretation. Publications: The Arts and Disabilities, 1981; Interpretation of the Environment, 1984. Recreations: the arts; philately; walking; enjoying life. Address: (h.) 9 Craigleith View, Edinburgh.

Lord, John, BA, FRSA. Founder, John Lord Associates, strategy, economic development and organisation change consultants, since 1997; b. 15.4.52, Bristol; m., Wendy; 2 s.; 1 d. Educ. Australia; Woking County Grammar School; Kingston College of Further Education; Warwick University. Freelance journalist and writer; Administrative Trainee, Department of Employment; Area Manager, Training Agency, 1989-90; Chief Executive, Enterprise Ayrshire, 1990-93; Director Strategy, Scottish Enterprise, 1993-96; Director, EDAW Consultants, 1996-97. Publication: The Floating Harbour – A Landscape History of Bristol City Docks. Recreations: architectural history; football; the arts. Address: (b.) 13 Ormonde Avenue, Glasgow G44 3QU.

Lord, Jonathan Christopher, MA. Secretary, Royal Scottish Automobile Club, since 1991; b. 29.4.53, Alverstoke; m., Angela Phillips; 1 s. Educ. Dollar Academy; St. Andrews University. Ministry of Defence (Naval), 1975-76; Royal Scottish Automobile Club, since 1976; Member, RAC British Motor Sports Council, since 1991; RAC Rallies Committee, since 1982; FIA Observer for International Rallies; RACMSA Steward; Clerk of the Course, RSAC International Scottish Rally, since 1982; Standing Joint Committee of RAC, AA and RSAC: Joint Secretary, 1986, Member, since 1991; Secretary, RSAC (Motor Sport) Limited, since 1982; Secretary to the Vestry, St. Bride's Episcopal Church, Glasgow, since 1991. Recreations: music (especially choral singing); cricket; motor sport; following Dunfermline Athletic FC. Address: (h.) 11 Melrose Gardens, Glasgow G20 6RB; T.-0141-946 5045.

Lorimer, A. Ross, MD, FRCP, FRCPGlas, FRCPEdin. Honorary Professor, Glasgow University; Consultant Physician and Cardiologist, Glasgow Royal Infirmary, since 1970; b. 5.5.37, Bellshill; m., Fiona Marshall; 3 s. Educ. Uddingston Grammar School; High School of Glasgow; Glasgow University. Recreations: reading; walking. Address: (b.) Department of Cardiology, Royal Infirmary, Glasgow.

Lorimer, Thomas Aitken (Ken), FFCS, BEd, MInstAM, FIMgt. Chief Executive, Hansel Foundation, since 1998; Chief Executive, Hansel Alliance, since 1998; b. 17.5.54, Mauchline; m., Susan; 2 d. Educ. Belmont Academy, Ayr; Ayr Academy; Ayr College; Craigie College of Education; Strathclyde University. Joined Ayr County Council, 1971, transferred to Strathclyde Regional Council, 1975, held administrative and public relations appointments with both; Hansel Village: General Administrator,1985; General Manager, 1992. Scottish Chair, UK Council Member, Director, Association for Residential Care. Recreations: music; theatre/cinema; literature; badminton. Address: (b.) Hansel Village, Symington, Ayrshire KA1 5PU; Y.-01563 830340.

Lothian, Sheriff Andrew, MA, LLB. Sheriff of Lothian and Borders at Edinburgh. Advocate, 1968. Address: (b.) Sheriff Court House, 27 Chambers Street, Edinburgh, EH1 1LB.

Lothian, Professor Niall, BA, CA, FRSA. Professor, Graduate School of Business, Heriot-Watt University, since 1996; b. 27.2.48, Edinburgh; m., Carol Miller; 1 s.; 1 d. Educ. Daniel Stewart's College, Edinburgh; Heriot-Watt University. Lecturer, Senior Lecturer, Professor and Head, Department of Accountancy and Finance, Heriot-Watt University, 1973-96; Visiting Professor: IMEDE, Lausanne, 1979-80, INSEAD, Fontainebleau, since 1984; Consultant, United Nations Industrial Development Organisation, Vienna, since 1980; President, Institute of Chartered Accountants of Scotland, 1995-96. Publications: Accounting for Inflation: Issues and Managerial Practices, 1978; Audit Quality and Value for Money, 1983; How Companies Manage R. & D., 1984; Corporate Performance Indicators, 1987. Address: (b.) Graduate School of Business, Heriot-Watt University, PO Box 807, Riccarton, Edinburgh EH14 4AT; T.-0131-451 3090.

Lothian, 12th Marquess of (Peter Francis Walter Kerr), KCVO, DL; b. 8.9.22, Melbourne, near Derby; m., Antonella Newland; 2 s.; 4 d. Educ. Ampleforth College, York; Christ Church, Oxford. Parliamentary Under Secretary, Ministry of Health, 1964; Parliamentary Under Secretary, Foreign and Commonwealth Office, 1970-72; Lord in Waiting, 1972-73; Lord Warden of the Stannaries, 1977-83. Knight of Malta; Lieutenant, Queen's Bodyguard for Scotland; Chairman of Council, Scottish Branch, British Red Cross, 1973-83. Recreation: music. Address: Ferniehirst Castle, Jedburgh, Roxburghshire; T.-01835 864021/0835 862872.

Loudon, Alasdair John, LLB, NP, WS. Senior Partner, Loudons WS, Edinburgh, since 1992; President, Edinburgh Bar Association, 1996-98; b. 7.4.56, Edinburgh; m., Mary V.; 2 s.; 1 d. Educ. Edinburgh Academy; Dundee University. Apprentice, Tods, Murray and Jamieson, WS, 1978-80; Qualified Assistant, Warner & Co., 1980-82, Partner, 1982-92; founded Loudons WS, 1992; accredited as specialist in family law. Recreations: golf (Bruntsfield Links and Luffness New); football (Heart of Midlothian supporter). Address: (b.) 29 St. Patrick Square, Edinburgh; T.-0131-662 4193.

Loudon, John Alexander, LLB, NP, SSC. Partner, Dundas & Wilson CS (formerly of MacRoberts); specialist in Liquor Licensing Law; b. 5.12.49, Edinburgh; m., Alison Jane Bruce Laird; 2 s. Educ. Edinburgh Academy; Dundee University. Apprenticeship, Tindal, Oatts and Roger, Solicitors, Glasgow. Former Member, Council, Law Society of Scotland; Secretary, Scottish Division, British Hospitality Association; Legal Adviser, Scottish Decorators Federation; Vice President, SSC Society; High Constable, City of Edinburgh Ward XV. Recreations: children;

shooting; stalking; skiing; occasional use of a mountain bike and even more occasional golf. Address: (b.) Dundas & Wilson CS, Saltire Court, 20 Castle Terrace, Edinburgh EH1 2EN.

Loudon, John Bruce, MB, ChB, FRCPsych, DPM. Consultant Psychiatrist, Royal Edinburgh Hospital, since 1978; Principal Medical Officer (part-time, on secondment), Department of Health, Scottish Office, since 1997; Honorary Senior Lecturer, Department of Psychiatry, Edinburgh University; b. 12.8.43, Edinburgh; m., Susan Mary Lay; 3 s. Educ. Edinburgh Academy; Edinburgh University. Clinical Director, General Psychiatry, Royal Edinburgh Hospital, 1991-94; Head, Mental Health Service, Edinburgh Healthcare NHS Trust, 1994-96. Address: (b.) Andrew Duncan Clinic, Morningside, Edinburgh EH10 5HF; T.-0131-537 6452.

Lovat, 18th Lord (Simon Fraser); b. 13.2.77. Educ. Harrow; Edinburgh University. Succeeded to title, 1995.

Love, Frances Mary. Director, Marriage Counselling Scotland, since 1987; Tutor and Lecturer, Scottish Human Relations and Counselling Course, since 1986; Organisational Consultant, SIHR, since 1986; b. 2.7.38, Edinburgh; m., James Love; 1 d. Educ. Broughton Secondary School. Edinburgh Public Library Service; voluntary playleader, Edinburgh Toddlers Playcentres; Pre-School Playgroup Association: playgroup supervisor, fieldworker, Scottish Adviser; General Secretary, Pre-School Playgroups Association; Executive Officer/Company Secretary, Scottish Council for Opportunities in Play Experience (SCOPE). Member, Management Board, Scottish Council of Voluntary Organisations; Member, Executive Committees, Scottish Child & Family Alliance and Scottish Council for Single Parents; Member, Council, Stepfamily Scotland. Recreations: gardening; reading; theatre; dress-making. Address: (b.) 105 Hanover Street, Edinburgh EH2 1DJ; T.-0131-225 5006.

Love, Robert Malcolm, MA (Hons), FRSAMD. Former Controller of Drama, Scottish Television; b. 9.1.37, Paisley. Educ. Paisley Grammar School; Glasgow University; Washington University, St. Louis. Actor and Director, various repertory companies, including Nottingham Playhouse, 1962-65; Producer, Thames TV, 1966-75, including Public Eye, Van Der Valk; freelance Producer, 1976-79, including Thames TV, LWT, Seacastle Film Productions, Scottish TV. Awards including: Commonwealth Festival, New York TV and Film Festival, Chicago Film Festival, BAFTA Scotland, nominated for International Emmy, New York, 1982; productions for Scottish include Taggart, High Road, Doctor Finlay, McCallum. Governor, RSAMD, since 1994; Member, Scottish Arts Council, since 1994. Recreations: literature; music; theatre; travel.

Lovelace, 5th Earl of (Peter Axel William Locke King); b. 26.11.51; m.; succeeded to title, 1964. Address: Torridon House, Torridon, IV22 2HA.

Low, Alistair James, BSc, FFA. Director, Scottish Widows Fund, since 1984; b. 2.8.42, Dundee; m., Shona Wallace; 2 s.; 1 d. Educ. Dundee High School; St. Andrews University. Recreations: golf; skiing; bridge. Address: (h.) Thornfield, Erskine Loan, Gullane, East Lothian.

Low, Bet, ARSA, RSW, RGI. Freelance Artist; b. 27.12.24, Gourock. Educ. Greenock Academy; Glasgow School of Art; Hospitalfield College of Art. Joined Unity Theatre Company, set designing etc., 1946; exhibited in international exhibition, Warsaw, 1954; co-founder and exhibitor, first open-air exhibition on railings at Botanic Gardens, Glasgow; worked part-time as art therapist, early 60s; Co-Founder and Co-Director, New Charing Cross Gallery, Glasgow, 1963-68; major retrospective exhibition, Third Eye Centre, 1985; exhibited widely in Britain and Europe and recently in Hong Kong. Recreations: reading; opera; Glasgow Art Club; beach-combing; just pottering. Address: 53 Kelvinside Gardens, Glasgow G20 6BQ; T.-0141-946 1377.

Low, Cuthbert Whyte Fraser, FFA, AIA, FPMI. President, Faculty of Actuaries, since 1998; Chairman, Fraser Low Actuarial Consultancy Ltd., since 1997; b. 6.6.43, Glasgow; m., Jennifer Jean; 1 s.; 1 d. Educ. Merchiston Castle School, Edinburgh. Scottish Mutual Assurance Society, 1961-72; Chief Actuarial Officer, Sedgwick Group, 1972-89; Director, W.F. Corroon Ltd., 1990-96. President, Society of Pension Consultants, 1986-88; Master, Worshipful Company of Actuaries, 1995-96. Recreations: golf; tennis; swimming; dancing; bridge. Address: 4B Belford Park, Edinburgh EH4 3DP; T.-0131 332 9132.

Low, Eur Ing. Sir James (Richard) Morrison-, 3rd Bt, DL, DFH, CEng, MIEE. Director, Osborne & Hunter Ltd., Glasgow, 1956-89; b. 3.8.25; m., Ann Rawson Gordon; 1 s.; 3 d. Educ. Ardvreck; Harrow; Merchiston; Faraday House, London. Royal Corps of Signals, 1943-47 (Captain). President, Electrical Contractors Association of Scotland, 1982-84; Director, National Inspection Council of Electrical Installation Contractors, 1982-88 (Chairman, Scottish Committee, 1982-88); Chairman, Electrical Industry Liaison Committee, 1986-88; Chairman, Fife Area Scout Council, 1966-84; Chairman, Cupar Branch, East Fife Conservative Association, 1965-78; Trustee, TSB, 1960-80; President, Elecrical Contractors Association of Scotland, 1982-84; DL, Fife, 1978.

Low, William, CBE, LLD, JP. Chairman, Dundee Heritage Trust, 1986-96; b. 12.9.21, Dundee; m., Elizabeth Ann Stewart Sime; 2 s. Educ. Merchiston Castle School, Edinburgh. Chairman: Don & Low (Holdings) Ltd., 1975-89, UBI Scotland, 1984-89, European Association for Textile Polyolefins, 1982-85, British Polyolefin Association, 1971-73 and 1978-79; President, Dundee & Tayside Chamber of Commerce & Industry, 1973-74; Chairman, Scottish Enterprise Tayside, 1991-94. Past President, Scottish Lawn Tennis Association; Provost, Burgh of Kirriemuir, 1973-75; appointed Fellow, Scottish Council (Development & Industry), 1989. Recreations: shooting; fishing; golf; gardening. Address: (h.) Herdhill Court, Kirriemuir, Angus DD8 5LG; T.-01575 572215.

Lowden, Professor Gordon Stuart, MA, LLB, CA. Director, Dundee and London Investment Trust PLC, since 1981; b. 22.5.27, Bangkok; m., Kathleen; 2 s.; 1 d. Educ. Dundee High School; Strathallan School; St. John's College, Cambridge; St. Andrews University. Trained with Moody Stuart & Robertson, CA, Dundee; became Partner, 1959; part-time Lecturer/Senior Lecturer, Dundee University, 1955-83; Honorary Professor, Department of Accountancy and Business Finance, Dundee University, since 1987; Member, Board of Governors, Strathallan School; Honorary Sheriff, since 1991; former Chairman, Dundee Port Authority; Past President, Institute of Chartered Accountants of Scotland. Recreations: golf; watching rugby; bridge. Address: (h.) 169 Hamilton Street, Barnhill, Dundee DD5 2RE; T.-01382 778360.

Lowe, Professor Gordon Douglas Ogilvie, MB, ChB, MD, FRCPEdin, FRCPGlas, FRCPLond. Professor of Vascular Medicine, Glasgow University, since 1993; Consultant Physician, Glasgow Royal Infirmary, since 1985; Co-Director, West of Scotland Haemophilia Centre, since 1987; b. 2.1.49, London; m., Ann Harvie; 1 s.; 1 d. Educ. Dundee High School; St. Andrews University. House Officer, Royal Infirmary and Maryfield Hospital, Dundee, 1972-73; Senior House Officer, City Hospital, Nottingham, 1973-74; Registrar, Royal Infirmary, Glasgow, 1974-77;

Lecturer, Glasgow University, 1978-85, Senior Lecturer, 1985-92, Reader, 1992-93. Past President, British Society for Haemostasis and Thrombosis. Publications: editor of books and author of publications on thrombosis and bleeding disorders. Recreations: travel; railways; gardening. Address: (b.) Department of Medicine, Royal Infirmary, Glasgow G31 2ER; T.-0141-211 5412.

Lowe, Janet, BA (Hons), MBA, MIPD. Principal, Lauder College, Dunfermline, since 1996; b. 27.9.50, South Normanton; m., Donald Thomas Stewart. Educ. Swanwick Hall Grammar School; Hull University; Dundee University. Immigration Officer, Home Office, 1973-76; Personnel Assistant, Hull University, 1976-80; Administrator, Lothian Region Social Work Department, 1980-82; Napier University: Examinations Officer, Personnel Officer, Assistant Academic Registrar, 1982-88; Secretary and Registrar, Duncan of Jordanstone College of Art, 1988-93; Depute Principal, Lauder College, 1993-96. Member: Scottish Consultative Council on the Curriculum, since 1995, Board of Management, Scottish Further Education Unit, since 1993; Member, Board, Scottish Enterprise, since 1998. Recreations: travel; literature; outdoor pursuits. Address: (b.) Lauder College, Halbeath, Dunfermline KY11 5DY; T.-01383 845002.

Lowe, Martin John Brodie, BSc, PhD. Secretary to Edinburgh University, since 1990; b. 10.4.40, Dorking; m., Janet MacNaughtan; 3 s.; 1 d. Educ. Dunfermline High School; St. Andrews University. British Council Officer, with service in Tanzania and South India, 1965-69; Strathclyde University: Administrative Assistant, 1969-71, Assistant Registrar, 1971-73, Secretary to Senate, 1973-81; Secretary and Registrar, St. Andrews University, 1981-89. National Council, Voluntary Service Overseas, 1976-83; Honorary Secretary, then Chairman, Glasgow and West of Scotland VSO Committee, 1973-81; Hon. Secretary, Royal Scottish Pipers' Society, since 1997. Recreations: piping; hill-walking; family interests. Address: (b.) Old College, South Bridge, Edinburgh EH8 9YL; T.-0131-650 2143.

Löwenhardt, Professor John, MA, PhD. Director, Institute of Central and East European Studies, University of Glasgow, since 1997; Alexander Nove Professor, University of Glasgow, since 1997; b. 22.8.47, Almelo, Netherlands. Educ. Erasmus Lyceum, Almelo; University of Amsterdam. Lecturer then Senior Lecturer, University of Amsterdam, 1976-86; Reader, University of Leiden, 1986-97. Member, Editorial Board, Europe-Asia Studies, since 1997. Publications: The Soviet Politburo, 1982; The Reincarnation of Russia, 1995; Party Politics in Postcommunist Russia (Editor), 1998. Address: (b.) ICEES, University of Glasgow, Bute Gardens, Glasgow G12 8RS; T.-0141-330 4579.

Lowrie, Patricia Joan, BSc, MBA, FRSA. Dean, Faculty of Education and Depute Director, Craigie Campus, University of Paisley, since 1997; b. 5.3.41, Southport; m., Robert Brown Lowrie (deceased); 2 s. Educ. Bradford Girls Grammar School; Nottingham University; Keele University; Jordanhill College of Education. Teacher of Mathematics: Manchester, 1961-63, Bristol, 1963-65, Billingham, Teesside, 1965-68; Lecturer/Senior Lecturer in Mathematics, Middleton St. George College of Education, 1968-71; Schools Adviser, Blackburn, 1971-73; Teacher of Mathematics: Malaysian Government, 1973-75, Ayr Divison, 1980-84; SCOTVEC: External Moderator/ Education Officer, 1984-86, Assistant Director, 1986-88; Vice-Principal, Craigie College of Education, 1988-93; Associate Dean, Faculty of Education, University of Paisley, 1993-97. Scottish Council for Educational Technology: Governor, 1990, Vice-Chairman, 1991-96; Scottish Representative, National Council for Educational Technology, 1991-96; Member, Board of Management, Kilmarnock College, since 1992; Member, COSHEP Staff Development Co-ordinating Committee, since 1994; Member, Board of Management, Ayrshire Careers Partnership, since 1995; Scottish Qualifications Authority: Member, Board of Management, Vice Convenor, Higher National Qualifications Committee, Member, Finance, Planning and General Purposes Committee, since 1997. Recreations: hillwalking; gardening; music; reading. Address: (b.) Craigie Campus, Ayr KA8 0SR; T.-01292 886201.

Lucas, Adrian. Chief Executive, Scottish Ambulance Service, since 1999. Address: (b.) National Headquarters, Tipperlinn Road, Edinburgh EH10 5UU; T. 0131-446 7000.

Luckhurst, Timothy Colin Harvey, MA (Cantab). Deputy Editor, The Scotsman, since 1998; b. 8.1.63, Sheffield; m., Dorothy Anne; 1 s.; 2 d. Educ. Peebles High School; Robinson College, University of Cambridge. Research Assistant to Donald Dewar, MP, 1985-87; BBC News and Current Affairs, 1988-96: Producer, Today programme, Producer, Washington D.C., Reporter, Jordan, Israel, Kuwait, Iraq during Gulf War, Assistant Editor, Radio 5 Live; Editor, News Programmes, BBC Scotland. Parliamentary Candidate (Labour), Roxburgh and Berwickshire, 1987. Recreations: playing guitar; supporting Partick Thistle; reading. Address: (h.) 26 Hamilton Drive, Glasgow G12 8DS; T.-0141-357 5833.

Ludlam, Christopher A., BSc (Hons), MB, ChB, PhD, FRCP, FRCPath. Consultant Haematologist, Edinburgh Royal Infirmary, since 1980; Director, Edinburgh Haemophilia Reference Centre, since 1980; part-time Reader in Medicine, Edinburgh University, since 1997; b. 6.6.46, Edinburgh. Educ. Edinburgh University. MRC Research Fellow, 1972-75; Senior Registrar in Haematalogy, University Hospital of Wales, Cardiff, 1975-78; Lecturer in Haematology, University of Wales, 1979. Address: (b.) Department of Haematology, Royal Infirmary, Edinburgh; T.-0131-536 2122.

Lumsden of Cushnie, David Gordon Allen d'Aldecamb, MA (Cantab), FSA (Scot). Garioch Pursuivant of Arms, since 1986; Chairman, Castles of Scotland Preservation Trust, since 1985; President, 1745 Association and Scottish Military History Society, since 1991; b. 25.5.33, Quetta, Baluchistan, Empire of India. Educ. Allhallows, Devon; Bedford School; Jesus College, Cambridge. London Scottish TA; Executive, British American Tobacco, 1959-82; Director: Heritage Porcelain Ltd., Heritage Recordings Ltd.; Member of Lloyds, since 1985; Co-Founder, Scottish Historic Organs Trust, 1991; Member, Council, Royal Stuart Society; Convenor, Monarchist League of Scotland, 1993; Knight of Malta Honour and Devotion, 1980; Knight of Justice Sacred Military Constantinian Order of St George, 1978; Patron, Aboyne Highland Games, since 1999. Recreations: shooting; polo; rowing; sailing; architectural history; Scottish history; heraldry. Address: Keithick House, Coupar Angus, Blairgowrie PH13 9NF; T.-01828 670532.

Lumsden, Iain C., MA, FFA. Group Finance Director and Appointed Actuary, Standard Life Assurance Company, since 1990; b. 6.6.46, Perth; m., Rosemary; 1 s.; 1 d. Educ. Exeter College, Oxford University. Standard Life, since 1967. Address: (b.) 30 Lothian Road, Edinburgh EH1 2DH; T.-0131 225 2552.

Lumsden, James Alexander, MBE, TD, MA, LLB, DL. Director, Bank of Scotland, 1958-85; Director, Scottish Provident Institution, 1968-85; b. 24.1.15, Arden, Dunbartonshire; m., Sheila Cross; 3 s. Educ. Cargilfield School, Edinburgh; Rugby School; Corpus Christi College, Cambridge; Glasgow University. Territorial Army, 1937-46; Partner, Maclay Murray & Spens, Solicitors, Glasgow and Edinburgh, 1947-82; Director of certain Investment Trust companies managed by Murray Johnstone Ltd., 1967-85; Director, Burmah Oil, 1957-76; Member, Queen's Body

Guard for Scotland (Royal Company of Archers), 1963; Commissioner of Income Tax, County of Dumbarton, 1964-90; Member, Committee on Company Law, 1960-62; Fellow, Law Society of Scotland. Recreations: shooting; fishing; other country pursuits. Address: (h.) Bannachra, by Helensburgh, Dunbartonshire G84 9EF; T.-01389 850653.

Lumsden, Professor Keith Grant, MA, PhD, FRSE. Professor and Director, Edinburgh Business School, Heriot-Watt University; b. 7.1.35, Bathgate; m., Jean Baillie MacDonald; 1 s. Educ. Bathgate Academy; Edinburgh University; Stanford University, California. Instructor, Department of Economics, then Assistant Professor, Graduate School of Business, Stanford University, 1960-67; Research Associate, Stanford Research Institute, 1965-71; Director, Stanford University Conference: NDTE, 1966, RREE, 1968; Associate Professor, Graduate School of Business, Stanford University, 1968-75; Visiting Professor of Economics, Heriot-Watt University, 1969-70; Director: Economics Education Project, 1969-74, Behavioral Research Laboratories, 1970-72, Capital Preservation Fund Inc., 1971-75, Nielsen Engineering Research Inc., 1972-75; Member, American Economic Association Committee on Economic Education, 1978-81; Academic Director, Sea Transport Executive Programme (STEP), since 1979; Professor of Economics, Advanced Management College, Stanford University, since 1971; Affiliate Professor of Economics, INSEAD, France; Member: Economics Education 14-16 Project, Manchester University, Advisory Council, David Hume Institute, since 1984, Board of Directors, Hewlett Packard Ltd., 1982-92; Henry Villard Award, Economics America, 1994. Publications: The Free Enterprise System, 1963; The Gross National Product, 1964; International Trade, 1965; Microeconomics: A Programmed Book, 1966; Macroeconomics: A Programmed Book, 1966; New Developments in the Teaching of Economics (Editor), 1967; Excess Demand and Excess Supply in World Tramp Shipping Markets, 1968; Recent Research in Economics Education (Editor), 1970; Basic Economics: Theory and Cases, 1973; Efficiency in Universities: The La Paz Papers (Editor), 1974; Economics Education in the United Kingdom, 1980; Economics: a distance learning study programme, 1991. Recreations: tennis; deep sea sports fishing. Address: (h.) 40 Lauder Road, Edinburgh EH9 1UE.

Lumsden, Vivien Dale Victoria, DSD, CDS. Television Presenter, since 1984; b. 22.11.52, Edinburgh; m., Alan Douglas (qv); 1 s.; 1 d. Educ. James Gillespie's High School for Girls, Edinburgh; RSAMD. Full-time mother, 1975-82; AA Traffic News Reporter, 1982-84; BBC Scotland: Breakfast Newsreader, 1984-85, Reporting Scotland Presenter, 1985-89, Garden Party, 1988; joined Scottish TV as Presenter, Scotland Today, 1989; also presented chat show, Telethon, BAFTA Awards, Business Game, Home Show. Trustee, Parents Oncology Support Yorkhill. Address: (b.) Broadcasting Business, 9 Lethington Road, Glasgow.

Lumsden, William Hepburn Russell, DSc, MD, DTM, DTH, FIBiol, FRCPEdin, FRSE. Scientific and Medical Writer; b. 27.3.14, Forfar; m., Pamela Kathleen Bartram; 2 s.; 1 d. (deceased). Educ. Queen Elizabeth's Grammar School, Darlington; Glasgow University; Liverpool University. MRC Fellow in Tropical Medicine, 1938-41; active service, Malaria Field Laboratories, RAMC, 1941-46; Yellow Fever (subsequently East African Virus) Research Institute, Entebbe, 1947-57; Director, East African Trypanosomiasis Research Organisation, Tororo, 1957-63; Lecturer, Department of Bacteriology, Edinburgh University Medical School, 1963-64; Senior Lecturer, Department of Animal Health, Royal (Dick) School of Veterinary Studies, Edinburgh University, 1964-68; Visiting Professor, Toronto University, 1968; Professor of Medical Protozoology, London School of Hygiene and Tropical Medicine, London University, 1968-79; Senior Editor, Advances in Parasitology, 1978-82; Member: Council, Royal Society of Tropical Medicine and Hygiene, 1969-73, 1974-77, Council, Royal Zoological Society of Scotland, 1967-68, Expert Advisory Panel on Parasitic Diseases (Trypanosomiasis), WHO, 1962-84, Trypanosomiasis Panel, Ministry of Overseas Development, 1973-79, International Malaria Review Teams, Bangladesh, 1978, Nepal, 1979, Sri Lanka, 1980; Editing Secretary, Berwickshire Naturalists' Club, 1988-91. Publications: Techniques with Trypanosomes, 1973; Biology of the Kinetoplastida (Editor), 1976 and 1979. Recreation: hill-walking. Address: (h.) 16A Merchiston Crescent, Edinburgh EH10 5AX; T.-0131-229 2702.

Lunan, Charles Burnett, MD, FRCOG, FRCS. Consultant Obstetrician, Royal Maternity Hospital, Glasgow, since 1977; Consultant Gynaecologist, Royal Infirmary, Glasgow, since 1977; b. London; m., Helen Russell Ferrie; 2 s.; 1 d. Educ. High School of Glasgow; Glasgow University. Lecturer, Obstetrics and Gynaecology, Aberdeen University, 1973-75; Senior Lecturer, University of Nairobi, 1975-77; WHO Consultant, Family Planning Programme, Bangladesh, 1984-85. Treasurer, 1982-90, Vice-President, 1990-91, President, Royal Medico-Chirurgical Society of Glasgow, 1991-92; Secretary, Glasgow Obstetrical and Gynaecological Society, 1978-82, Vice President, since 1998.Recreations: gardening; photography; hill-walking. Address: (h.) 1 Moncrieff Avenue, Lenzie, Glasgow G66 4NL; T.-0141-776 3227.

Lunney, James Thomas, LLB, NP. Full-time Chairman, Independent Tribunal Service, since 1995; Director, Paisley Hammermen Society, since 1990; b. 24.7.54, Glasgow; m., Patricia Anne Lunney, BDS; 2 d. Educ. St. Mirin's Academy, Paisley; Strathclyde University. Apprentice to Pattison & Sim, Solicitors, Paisley, 1979-81; Assistant, 1981-83, Partner, 1983-95; part-time Chairman, Independent Tribunal Service, 1992-95. Recreations: golf; reading; architecture; skiing; motor-cycling. Address: (b.) Wellington House, 134-136 Wellington Street, Glasgow G2 2XL.

Lunny, Sheriff William Francis, MA, LLB. Sheriff of South Strathclyde, Dumfries and Galloway, since 1984; b. 10.12.38. Advocate, 1977. Address: (b.) Sheriff Court House, Beckford Street, Hamilton, ML3 6AA.

Lusby, John David, MEd, BA. Rector, Buckhaven High School, since 1997; b. 23.10.50, Wales; m., Hazel Ann; 2 s.; 1 d. Educ. Kirkton High School; Jordanhill College; Dundee University. Teacher, 1971-74; Youth Tutor, 1975-76; Principal Teacher of Guidance, 1976-82; Assistant Head Teacher, 1982-84; TVEI Co-ordinator, 1986-89; Rector, Arbroath Academy, 1989-97. Board, Angus College, 1990-97. Recreations: cycling; music; reading. Address: (h.) 11 Lawside Road, Dundee DD3 6BP; T.-01382 229496.

Luscombe, Rt. Rev. Lawrence Edward, ChStJ, MA, MPhil, PhD, LLD, DLitt, CA, FRSA, FSA Scot. Primus of the Scottish Episcopal Church, 1985-90, and Bishop of Brechin, 1975-90; b. 10.11.24; m., Dr. Doris Morgan (deceased); 1 d. Educ. Kelham College; King's College, London; Dundee University. Indian Army, 1942-47; Major; Chartered Accountant, 1952; Partner, Galbraith Dunlop & Co. (later Watson and Galbraith), CA, 1953-63; Curate, St. Margaret's, Glasgow, 1963-66; Rector, St. Barnabas', Paisley, 1966-71; Provost, St. Paul's Cathedral, Dundee, 1971-75. Honorary Canon, Trinity Cathedral, Davenport, Iowa, since 1983; Member, Education Committee, Renfrew County Council, 1967-71; Chairman, Governing Body: Glenalmond College, 1986-94; President, Old Glenalmond Club, since 1998; Chairman, Governing Body, Edinburgh Theological College, 1985-90; Governor: Lathallan School, Dundee College of Education; Chairman, Inter-Anglican Finance Committee, 1989-93; Member, Tayside Health Board, 1989-93; Honorary Research Fellow, Dundee

University, since 1993; Member, Court, Corporation of Sons of the Clergy. Address: (h.) Woodville, Kirkton of Tealing, by Dundee DD4 0RD; T.-01382 380331.

Lyall, Fiona Jane, MBE, DL, MB, ChB, DPH. Family Doctor, Laurencekirk, since 1959; Director, Grampian Television PLC, since 1980; Non-Executive Director: Aberdeen Royal Hospitals NHS Trust, since 1992, Templehill Community Council, since 1990; Deputy Lieutenant, Kincardineshire, since 1985; b. 13.4.31, Inverness; m., Dr. Alan Richards Lyall; 1 s.; 1 d. Educ. Inverness Royal Academy; Aberdeen University. Former Member, Laurencekirk Burgh Council; former Kincardine County and Grampian Regional Councillor; Member: Grampian Health Board, 1974, and Kincardine & Deeside Health Council, 1974, Children's Panel Advisory Committee, 1974, Grampian Valuation Appeals Committee, Prince's and Royal Jubilee Trust for Grampian; Treasurer, Action Research for Crippled Child; Trustee, Kincardineshire Silver Jubilee Trust, since 1985. Recreations: skiing; riding; golf. Address: Melrose Bank, Laurencekirk AB30 1AL; T.-01561 377220.

Lyall, Ian Alastair, DSC, VRD, DL, FICS; b. 16.3.17, Bangor, Co. Down; m., Eileen Patricia Bennet; 1 d. Educ. Hillhead High School, Glasgow; College of Nautical Studies, Glasgow. Chairman and Managing Director, Roxburgh Henderson & Co. Ltd., 1967-80; Director: British & Burmese Steam Navigation Co. Ltd., 1971-80, Henderson Line Ltd., 1971-80; President, Glasgow Chamber of Commerce, 1978-79; retired Lt. Commander, RNR, 1963. Recreations: sailing; fishing; shooting. Address: (h.) 21 Chapelacre, Helensburgh G84 7SH; T.-01436 673976.

Lyall, Michael Hodge, MB, ChB, ChM, FRCSEdin. Consultant Surgeon, Tayside Health Board, since 1975; Honorary Senior Lecturer, Dundee University, since 1975; b. 5.12.41, Methilhill, Fife; m., Catherine B. Jarvie; 3 s. Educ. Buckhaven High School; St. Andrews University. President, Tayside Division, Ileostomy Association of Great Britain; Past President, North Fife Rotary Club. Recreation: computing. Address: (h.) 26 Linden Avenue, Newport on Tay, Fife DD6 8DU.

Lyddon, William Derek Collier, CB, DLitt, BA (Arch), DipTP, FRTPI, FRSGS. Acting Chairman, Edinburgh Old Town Renewal Trust; Chief Planner, Scottish Development Department, 1967-85; b. 17.11.25, Loughton, Essex; m., Marian Louise Kaye Charlesworth; 2 d. Educ. Wrekin College; University College, London. Depute Chief Architect Planner, Cumbernauld Development Corporation; Chief Architect Planner, Skelmersdale Development Corporation. President, International Society of City and Regional Planners, 1981-84; Chairman, The Planning Exchange, 1992-95. Address: (h.) 31 Blackford Road, Edinburgh EH9 2DT; T.-0131-667 2266.

Lyell, 3rd Baron (Charles Lyell), Bt. Parliamentary Under-Secretary of State, Northern Ireland Office, 1984-89; b. 27.3.39. Educ. Eton; Christ Church, Oxford. Scots Guards, 1957-59; CA; Opposition Whip, 1974-79; Government Whip, 1979-84; Member, Queen's Bodyguard for Scotland (Royal Company of Archers); DL, Angus, 1988. Address: (h.) Kinnordy House, Kirriemuir, Angus.

Lyle, David Angus, MA, LLB, NP, SSC, FCIS, FIMgt, FInstD, FIAM, FRSA. Consultant, Solicitor, and Chartered Company Secretary, in private practice, since 1993; b. 7.9.40; m., Dorothy Ann Clark; 1 s.; 3 d. Educ. George Watson's College, Edinburgh; Edinburgh University. Account Executive, Advertising Agencies, London; Indentured, Edinburgh Corporation; Solicitor, Lloyds and Scottish Finance Ltd., Edinburgh; Depute County Clerk, East Lothian County Council; Director of Administration and Law, Dumfries and Galloway Regional Council; Agency Secretary, Scottish Development Agency; Director/Company Secretary, Scottish Enterprise. Recreations: shooting; golf; bridge. Address: (b.) The Caledonian Suite, St Andrew House, 141 West Nile Street, Glasgow G1 2RN; T.-0141-333 1119.

Lynch, Alexander McKay, ACMA, MCIT. Deputy Managing Director/Finance Director, ScotRail, since 1994; b. 6.10.49, Greenock; m., Christina Keenan; 2 d. Educ. St. Columba's High School, Greenock; Central College of Commerce and Distribution, Glasgow. BR management posts, since 1976. Hon. President, Railway Staff Association, Scotland. Recreations: youth football; TV; music. Address: (b.) Caledonian Chambers, 87 Union Street, Glasgow G1 3TA; T.-0141-335 4180.

Lynch, Professor Michael, MA, PhD, FRHistS, FRSE, FSAScot. Sir William Fraser Professor of Scottish History, University of Edinburgh, since 1992; Chairman, Ancient Monuments Board for Scotland, since 1996; President, Society of Antiquaries of Scotland, since 1996; b. 15.6.46, Aberdeen. Educ. Aberdeen Grammar School; University of Aberdeen; University of London. Lecturer, Department of History, University College, Bangor, 1971-79; Department of Scottish History, University of Edinburgh: Lecturer, 1979-88, Senior Lecturer, 1988-92. Chairman, Historical Association Committee for Scotland, since 1992; Editor, The Innes Review, 1984-92. Publications: Edinburgh and the Reformation, 1981 (SAC Literary Award); The Early Modern Town in Scotland, 1986; The Scottish Medieval Town, 1987; Mary Stewart: Queen in Three Kingdoms, 1988; Scotland: A New History, 1991 (SAC Literary Award); The Reign of James VI, 1999. Address: (b.) Department of Scottish History, University of Edinburgh, 17 Buccleuch Place, Edinburgh EH8 9LN; T.-0131-650 4030.

Lyon, Robert Alexander, MA, CA, CMA. Dean, Faculty of Law and Accountancy, Dundee University, since 1994; Member, Council, Institute of Chartered Accountants of Scotland, since 1994; Non-Executive Director, Dundee Teaching Hospitals NHS Trust, since 1993; b. 18.2.48, Dundee. Educ. Morgan Academy, Dundee; Dundee University. CA student, Dundee, 1969-73; Senior Accountant, Peat, Marwick, Mitchell & Co., USA, Germany, Scotland, 1973-76; Lecturer, then Senior Lecturer, Dundee University, since 1976. Address: (b.) Faculty of Law and Accountancy, Dundee University, Dundee DD1 4HN; T.-01382 344195.

Mac/Mc

McAllion, John, MA (Hons). MP (Lab), Dundee East, since 1987; b. 13.2.48, Glasgow; m., Susan Jean; 2 s. Educ. St. Augustine's Secondary, Glasgow; St. Andrews University. Teacher, History and Modern Studies, St. Saviour's Secondary, Dundee, 1973-78, Social Studies, Balgowan List D School, Dundee, 1978-82; Research Assistant to Bob McTaggart, MP, 1982-86; Regional Councillor, 1984-87; Convener, Tayside Regional Council, 1986-87. Member, Scottish Executive, Labour Party, 1986-88; Senior Vice Chairperson, Dundee Labour Party, 1986, 1987. Recreations: football; reading; music. Address: (h.) 3 Haldane Street, Dundee DD3 0HP; T.-01382 200329.

McAlpine, Joan, MA (Hons). Columnist and Feature Writer, Sunday Times, since 1996; b. 28.1.64, Gourock; m., Pat Kane (qv); 2 d. Educ. St. Columba's RC Comprehensive, Greenock; James Watt Further Education College, Greenock; Glasgow University; City University, London. Reporter, Greenock Telegraph, The Scotsman; Feature Writer, Columnist, The Scotsman, 1992-95; joined Daily Record as Feature Writer and Columnist, 1995. Publications: A Time to Rage (Co-author), 1994; The Best of The Scotsman (Contributor), 1995. Recreations: spending time with my children; reading. Address: (b.) Sunday Times, 124 Portman Street, Kinning Park, Glasgow G41 1EJ; T.-0141-420 1000.

McAlpine, Thomas, BSc, CEng, MIEE. Business Consultant; b. 23.9.29, Motherwell; m., Isobel Lindsay; 2 s.; 1 d. Educ. Dalziel High School, Motherwell; Strathclyde University. National Service, REME, 1952-54 (2nd Lt.); Chief Engineer, Belmos Co. Ltd., Bellshill, 1954-58; Chief Development Engineer, Mine Safety Appliances, Glasgow, 1958-62; Managing Director: Rowen Engineering Co. Ltd., Glasgow, 1962-71, Chieftain Industries PLC, Livingston, 1971-85. Former Executive Vice Chairman Administration, Scottish National Party (former Vice President, SNP); Parliamentary candidate, Clydesdale (Lanark), 1974, 1979, 1983, Dumfries, 1987; District Councillor, Clydesdale, 1988-96, now South Lanarkshire Councillor. Recreations: when young, played rugby, swimming and tennis. Address: (h.) 9 Knocklea Place, Biggar, Lanarkshire ML12 6DZ; T.-01899 220423.

McAndrew, Nicolas, CA. Chairman, Murray Johnstone Ltd., since 1992; Deputy Chairman, Burn Stewart Distillers PLC, since 1991; Chairman, Martin Currie Smaller Companies Investment Trust PLC; Chairman, Guinness Flight Extra Income Trust PLC; Board Member, North of Scotland Water Authority, since 1995; b. 9.12.34, London; 2 s.; 1 d. Educ. Winchester College. National Service (The Black Watch) commission, 1953-55; articled clerk, Peat Marwick Mitchell, 1955-61; qualified CA, 1961; S.G. Warburg & Co. Ltd., Merchant Bankers, 1962-78; became Chairman, Warburg Investment Management Ltd., and Director, Mercury Securities Ltd.; Managing Director, N.M. Rothschild & Sons Ltd., Merchant Bankers, 1979-88. Master, Worshipful Company of Grocers, 1978-79; Board Member, Highlands and Islands Enterprise, 1993-97. Recreations: fishing; shooting; golf. Address: (h.) Kilcoy Castle, Killearnan, Muir of Ord, Ross-shire IV6 7RX; T.-01463 871 393.

McArdle, Professor Colin S., MD, FRCS, FRCSEdin, FRCSGlas. Professor of Surgery, University of Edinburgh, Western General Hospital, Edinburgh, since 1996; b. 10.10.39, Glasgow; m., June M.C. Merchant; 2 s.; 1 d. Educ. Jordanhill College School; Glasgow University. Senior Registrar in General Surgery, Western Infirmary, Glasgow, 1972-75; Consultant Surgeon: Victoria Infirmary, Glasgow, 1975-78, Glasgow Royal Infirmary, 1978-80; University Department of Surgery, Glasgow Royal Infirmary, 1981-96. Address: (h.) 6 Collylinn Road, Bearsden, Glasgow.

McArdle, Harry John, BSc (Hons), PhD, MIBiol, CBiol. Head, Division of Nutrition, Pregnancy and Development, Rowett Research Institute, since 1997; Honorary Reader in Biomedical Sciences, University of Aberdeen, since 1996; b. 4.1.53, Glasgow; m., Karen Ann. Educ. St. Augustine School, Edinburgh; St. Andrews University. Raines Research Fellow, University of Western Australia; Senior Scientist, Murdoch Institute for Research into Birth Defects, Melbourne, Australia, 1985-90; Lecturer/Senior Lecturer, Department of Child Health, University of Dundee, 1990-96. Recreations: hillwalking; horse riding; skiing. Address: (b.) Rowett Research Institute, Bucksburn, Aberdeen AB21 9SB; T.-01224 716628.

MacArthur, Rev. Allan Ian, BD, JP. Minister, Lochcarron Parish, 1973-98; District Councillor, 1984-96; b. 22.5.28, Marvig, Isle of Lewis; m., Effie Macleod; 1 s.; 6 d. Educ. Nicolson Institute, Stornoway; Glasgow University and Trinity College. Meteorologist, Air Ministry and Falkland Islands Dependencies Survey, Antarctica; teaching; Minister of Religion and Presbytery Clerk. Member, Crofters Commission, 1984-90. Address: 220 Croft Road, Lochcarron IV54 8YD; T.-01520 722278.

McArthur, Archibald Roderick, CPFA. Director of Finance, Perth and Kinross Council, since 1995; b. 1.3.51, Greenock; m., Marilyn; 2 d. Educ. Greenock Academy. Trainee Accountant, Greenock Town Council, 1969; Accountant, Tayside Regional Council, 1975; Perth and Kinross District Council: Management Accountant, 1978, Depute Director of Finance, 1981, Director of Finance, 1992. Recreations: member of Blairgowrie Golf Club; supporter, St. Johnstone F.C. Address: (b.) Council Building, 2 High Street, Perth PH1 5PH; T.-01738 475501.

McArthur, Christine Louise, RSW, RGI. Artist; b. 14.3.53, Lennoxtown; separated; 2 d. Educ. Lenzie Academy; Glasgow School of Art. Travelling bursary, 1975, 1976; Arts Council Award, 1980; Lauder Award, Glasgow Society of Women Artists; N. S. MacFarlane Award, Royal Glasgow Institute of Fine Arts; elected Member, RGI, 1990; elected Member, RSW, 1995; exhibits widely Scotland and London. Address: 17 Grosvenor Terrace, Glasgow G12 0TB; T.-0141-339 4998.

McArthur, Douglas B., BSc (Hons). Managing Director, Radio Advertising Bureau, since 1992; Chairman, JICRIT Ltd.; Director, RAJAR Ltd.; Chairman, Strategic Marketing Scotland Ltd; b. 17.3.51, Dundee; m., Elizabeth M.A.; 3 d. Educ. Kirkton High School, Dundee; Glasgow University. Marketing management roles, Proctor and Gamble, Scottish & Newcastle, Campbell's Soups Ltd., Radio Clyde; marketing and advertising consultancy roles with Hall Advertising and Baillie Marshall Advertising. Director, Drumchapel Opportunities Ltd.; Member, Scottish Arts Council (Chairman, Drama Committee, 1989-94); Director, Balgray Communications Group Ltd. and subsidiaries, 1984-92; Fellow: Radio Academy, CAM Foundation. Recreations: swimming; music; visual arts; drama.

Macarthur, Edith. Actress; b. Ardrossan, Ayrshire. Educ. Ardrossan Academy. Began career, 1948, with Wilson Barrett Company, then Perth Repertory, Gateway Theatre Company, Citizens' Theatre, Glasgow, Bristol Old Vic, Royal Shakespeare Company, Ochtertyre Theatre, Royal Lyceum Theatre Company, West End; television work includes The Borderers, Sunset Song, Weir of Hermiston, Sutherland's Law, Take the High Road, Dr. Finlay, Hamish Macbeth; Taggart; Golden Wedding; nominated for Scottish BAFTA award in The Long Roads, 1993; recent stage appearances: solo-performance play, Marie of Scotland, Jamie the Saxt and The Thrie Estates for the Scottish

Theatre Company at Edinburgh Festivals and Warsaw International Festival, 1986, Judith Bliss in Hay Fever, Royal Lyceum Theatre, 1987, Charley's Aunt, Death of a Salesman, Royal Lyceum, 1988, Daphne Laureola, Pygmalion, Pride and Prejudice, Pitlochry Festival Theatre, 1988; The Cherry Orchard, Royal Lyceum, 1989; The Cherry Orchard, The Circle, Arsenic and Old Lace, Pitlochry, 1990; Driving Miss Daisy, Perth, 1991; Cinderella, Glasgow and Edinburgh, 1990, 1991; Good, Glasgow and Edinburgh, 1992; Long Day's Journey into Night, Dundee, 1994 (TMA/Martini Best Actress nomination); The Prime of Miss Jean Brodie, London, 1994-95; The Flou'ers o' Edinburgh; On Golden Pond; Long Day's Journey into Night, Pitlochry Festival Theatre, and tour, 1996; Widows, Traverse Theatre, and tour, 1997. Recreations: music; books.

McArthur, George, OBE. Chairman, Scottish Churches Housing Agency, since 1993; Convener: Edinburgh Peace and Justice Resource Centre, since 1992; b. 22.7.30, Edinburgh; m., Margaret Moffat Wilson; 1 s.; 1 d. Educ. Leith Academy. Missionary (youth worker), Church of Scotland, South Africa, 1956-71; Official Correspondent for Church of Scotland's List D schools, 1972-77; involved in formation of Kirk Care Housing Association Ltd., 1973, becoming its first Director, 1978, retired, 1992. Chairman, Council, Scottish Federation of Housing Associations, 1984-86; a Vice-President, Churches National Housing Coalition, 1995. Recreations: golf; supporting Hibernian F.C.; walking; reading. Address: (h.) 3 Craigcrook Road, Edinburgh EH4 3NQ; T.-0131-477 0312.

McArthur, John Duncan, BSc (Hons), MB, ChB (Hons), DM, FRCPGlas, MRCP, FRCPEdin. Consultant Physician and Cardiologist, Western Infirmary and Gartnavel General Hospital, Glasgow, since 1978; Honorary Clinical Senior Lecturer, Glasgow University, since 1978; b. 7.1.38, Hamilton; m., Elizabeth A. Bowie; 2 s.; 1 d. Educ. Hamilton Academy; Glasgow University. Junior doctor, Royal Infirmary, Glasgow, and in Ayrshire, 1963-67; St. Colm's College, Edinburgh, 1967-68; Missionary, Church of Scotland, working as Cardiologist at Christian Medical College Hospital, Vellore, India, 1968-73; Senior Registrar, Glasgow Teaching Hospitals, 1974-78. Elder, Killermont Parish Church; Council Member, Interserve, Scotland. Recreations: DIY; gardening. Address: (h.) 8 Durness Avenue, Bearsden, Glasgow, G61 2AQ; T.-0141-563 9068.

McAteer, Charles, MA, BA (Hons). Rector, Dumfries Academy, since 1995; Minutes Secretary, Headteachers' Association of Scotland; b. 5.5.50, Glasgow; m., Anne Neil; 1 s.; 3 d. Educ. Our Lady's High School, Motherwell; Edinburgh University; Jordanhill College; Strathclyde University. Teacher of English, St. Augustine's High School, Edinburgh, 1972-74; Principal Teacher of English, St. Kentigern's Academy, W. Lothian, 1974-83; Depute Rector, Moffat Academy, 1983-88; Rector, Dalbeattie High School, 1988-95. Recreations: squash; indoor football; reading; walking; film; family. Address: (b.) Dumfries Academy, Academy Street, Dumfries, DG1 1DD; T.-01387 252846.

Macaulay, Rev. Donald, OBE, JP. Former Minister, Park, Isle of Lewis; former Convener, Western Isles Council; b. 25.2.26, Great Bernera; m., Catherine Macleod; 3 s.; 3 d. Educ. Great Bernera School; Aberdeen University. Several years a fisherman; Member: Ross and Cromarty County Council, 1969-75, Lewis District Council, 1969-75, COSLA Policy Committee, 1975-82; Director, Western Isles Enterprise. Recreations: fishing; travel; local history; silviculture. Address: Garymilis, Great Bernera, Isle of Lewis; T.-01851 612341.

MacAulay, Professor Emeritus Donald, MA, BA, DipGenLing. Professor of Celtic, Glasgow University, 1991-96; b. 21.5.30, Isle of Lewis; m., Ella Murray Sangster; 1 s.; 1 d. Educ. Nicolson Institute, Stornoway; Aberdeen University; Cambridge University. Lecturer in English Language, Edinburgh University, 1957-60; Lecturer in Irish and Scottish Gaelic, Trinity College, Dublin, 1960-63; Lecturer in Applied Linguistics, Edinburgh University, 1963-67; Senior Lecturer in Celtic, then Reader in Celtic, Aberdeen University, 1967-91. Publications: Seobhrach as a' Chlaich; Nua-bhardachd Ghaidhlig; The Celtic Languages. Recreations: poetry; living. Address: (b.) 7 Ledcameroch Park, Bearsden Glasgow G61 4AT; T.-0141-942 9801.

Macaulay of Bragar, Rt. Hon. Lord (Donald Macaulay), QC; b. 1933. Advocate, 1963; QC (Scot), 1975; Life Peer, since 1989. Address: (b.) Advocates' Library, Parliament House, Edinburgh, EH1 1RF.

MacAulay, Fred. Comedian; Television and Radio Presenter. Presenter, The Fred MacAulay Show, BBC Radio Scotland; television includes: Presenter, Life According to Fred; Co-host, New Year Live; Co-host, series and World Cup special, McCoist and MacAulay; Co-host, The 11 O'Clock Show; Team Captain, The Best Show in the World...Probably; Team Captain, Bring Me the Head of Light Entertainment; Team Captain, A Game of Two Halves; Presenter, Comedy Rules; Presenter, Now You See It; theatre: Bad and Crazy in a Jam.

McAveety, Frank (Francis), BA (Hons). Leader, Glasgow City Council, since 1997; Councillor, since 1995 (Convenor, Arts and Culture Committee); Councillor, Glasgow District Council, 1988-96; b. 27.7.62, Glasgow; m., Anita Mitchell; 1 s.; 1 d. Educ. All Saints Secondary School, Glasgow; Strathclyde University; St. Andrew's College, Bearsden. Director: Citizens' Theatre, Glasgow, Glasgow Jazz Festival Board; Chairperson, Glasgow North Co-operative Party. Recreations: labour history; record collecting; football. Address: (h.) 156 Glenbuck Avenue, Robroyston, Glasgow G33 1LW; T.-0141-558 1341.

McAvoy, Peter, BA (Hons). Rector, Crieff High School, since 1997; b. 14.10.57, Paisley; m., Anne; 1 s.; 1 d. Educ. St. Mirin's Academy, Paisley; Paisley College of Technology; Jordanhill College of Education. Teacher, Renfrewshire, 1979-85; Principal Teacher of Modern Studies, Dundee, 1985-90; Assistant Headteacher, Dundee, 1990-91; Adviser, Social Subjects, Tayside, 1991-94; Headteacher, Islay High School, 1994-97. Recreations; football; reading; gardening. Address: (h.) 25 Kinnordy Terrace, Dundee; T.-01382 454056.

McAvoy, Thomas McLaughlin. Government Whip, Comptroller of Her Majesty's Household, since 1997; MP (Labour and Co-operative), Glasgow Rutherglen, since 1987; b. 14.12.43, Rutherglen; m., Eleanor Kerr; 4 s. Member, Strathclyde Regional Council, 1982-87; Opposition Whip, 1990-93. Address: (b.) House of Commons, London SW1A 0AA.

McBryde, Professor William Wilson, LLB, PhD, LLD, FRSE. Professor of Scots Law, Dundee University, since 1987, Deputy and Vice Principal, 1991-94; Solicitor, since 1969; b. 6.7.45, Perth; m., Joyce Margaret Gossip; 1 s; 2 d. Educ. Perth Academy; Edinburgh University. Apprentice and Assistant, Morton, Smart, Macdonald & Milligan, WS, Edinburgh, 1967-70; Court Procurator, Biggart, Lumsden & Co., Glasgow, 1970-72; Lecturer in Private Law, Glasgow University, 1972-76; Member, Scottish Law Commission Working Party on Contract Law, since 1975; Senior Lecturer in Private Law, Aberdeen University, 1976-87; Specialist Parliamentary Adviser to House of Lords Select Committee on the European Communities, 1980 83; Member: Scottish Consumer Council, 1984-87, Scottish Advisory Committee on Arbitration, since 1986; Director, Scottish Universities' Law Institute, 1989-95; Honorary Sheriff, Tayside, Central and Fife, at Dundee, since 1991;

Member, DTI Working Party on Rights in Security over Moveables, since 1994. Recreations: walking; photography. Address: (b.) Faculty of Law, Dundee University, Dundee DD1 4HN; T.-01382 23181.

McBurnie, Gavin John, MB, ChB, MBA, DRCOG, MHSM. Director, Primary Care, Fife Health Board, since 1994; b. 9.9.59, Edinburgh; m., Doreen Elizabeth; 3 s. Educ. Royal High School, Edinburgh; Glasgow University; Edinburgh University. Junior doctor, 1982-86; general medical practitioner, 1986-91; Assistant Director, Strategic Planning and Contracts, 1993-94. Recreations: rugby union; r. and b. Address: (h.) 25 Ferryfield, Cupar, Fife; T.-01334 656572.

McCabe, Primrose Smith, CA. Senior Partner, The McCabe Partnership, since 1987; b. 21.9.40, Gorebridge; m., Ernest McCabe. Educ. Ayr Academy. Trained with Stewart Gilmour, Ayr; qualified as CA 1963; joined Romanes & Munro, Edinburgh, 1964; progressed through manager ranks to Partner, Deloitte Haskins & Sells, 1981-87; set up own practice, Linlithgow, 1987; moved practice to Edinburgh, 1997. Member, Accounts Commission, 1988-92; Non-Executive Director: Dunfermline Building Society, 1990, Northern Venture Trust plc, 1995; Institute of Chartered Accountants of Scotland: Member, Council, since 1988, first Convener, GP Committee, 1990, Vice President, 1992-94, President, 1994-95; Honorary Treasurer, Hospitality Industry Trust Scotland, 1994; Fellow, SCOTVEC, 1994. Recreation: walking her three dogs. Address: (b.) The McCabe Partnership, 56 Palmerston Place, Edinburgh EH12 5AY; T.-0131-225 6366.

McCabe, Thomas. Leader, South Lanarkshire Council, since 1995; Vice-Convener, Strathclyde Joint Police Board; Leader, Hamilton District Council, 1992-96; Member: Lanarkshire Development Agency Board, Labour Party Scottish Executive; b. 28.4.54, Hamilton. Educ. St. Martin's Secondary; Bell College of Technology. Senior shop steward, Hoover Ltd., 1974-93; welfare rights officer, since 1993. Recreations: walking; reading; gardening; cinema. Address: (b.) South Lanarkshire Council, Council Offices, Almada Street, Hamilton ML3 0AA; T.-01698 454192.

McCafferty, Rev. Allan, BSc, BD (Hons). Minister, Kirkwall East Church, since 1993; b. 19.1.67, Motherwell. Educ. Garrion Academy, Wishaw; Glasgow University; Edinburgh University. Probationer Minister, Holy Trinity Church, Bridge of Allan, 1991-93. Recreations: choral singing; hill-walking. Address: East Church Manse, Thoms Street, Kirkwall KW15 1PF; T.-01856 875469.

McCaffrey, Rev. Kenneth, BEd, DTheol, DAREd. Parish Priest, St. Mungo's, Alloa, since 1995; Convenor, Joint Prison Chaplaincies Board, since 1997; b. 27.5.47, Glasgow. Educ. St. Thomas Aquinas Secondary School, Glasgow; Manchester University; St. Patrick's College, Thurles, Eire. Ordained priest, 1982; Assistant Priest, St. Ninian's, Dundee, 1982-86; Parish Priest, St. John's, Alva, 1986-95. Chaplain, Glenochil Prison. Recreations: soccer; reading. Address: 25 Mar Street, Alloa FK10 1HR; T.-01259 212486.

McCall, Frances, MBE. Board Member, Scottish Homes, since 1988; Member, Management Committee, Calvay Housing Co-operative, since 1984; b. 2.7.37, Glasgow; m., Thomas McCall; 2 s.; 1 d. Educ. St. Columba of Iona School; Notre Dame College. Recreations: grand-children; voluntary work. Address: (h.) 45 Calvay Road, Barlanark, Glasgow G33 4RQ; T.-0141-771 4294.

McCall, Professor James, BSc, MEd, PhD, CPsychol, AFBPsS, FRSA. Professor, Department of Educational Studies, Strathclyde University, since 1993; b. 14.7.41, Kilmarnock; m., Mary Elizabeth Stuart Maclean; 3 s. Educ. Kilmarnock Academy; Glasgow University; Aberdeen University; Jordanhill College of Education. Teacher of Science, Hillhead High School, Glasgow; Principal Teacher of Physics, Queen's Park Secondary School, Glasgow; Lecturer in Educational Psychology, Aberdeen College of Education; Jordanhill College of Education: Head, Psychology Department, Vice Principal, 1983-92, Acting Principal, 1992-93, Dean, Faculty of Education, 1993-97; Member: Board of Governors, Glasgow School of Art, 1986-98, CNAA Committee on Teacher Education, 1989-92, General Teaching Council for Scotland, 1992-97. Publications: Techniques for the Assessment of Practical Skills in Foundation Science, 1983; Techniques for Assessing Process Skills in Practical Science, 1988; Teacher Education in Europe, 1990; How to assess open-ended practical investigations in Biology, Chemistry and Physics, 1991; Partnership and Co-operation in Teacher Education, 1997. Recreations: bridge; golf. Address: (b.) Jordanhill Campus, Strathclyde University, Southbrae Drive, Glasgow G13 1PP; T.-0141-950 3366.

McCall, Kathleen Mary, DL, LRAM. Deputy Lieutenant for Borders Region, District of Tweeddale, since 1988; Patron, Borders Branch, British Red Cross Society, since 1998; b. 20.2.33, Karachi; m., J.A.G. McCall, CMG. Educ. Calder Girls' School, Seascale; Royal Scottish Academy of Music and Drama. Held various teaching posts; voluntary offices with Red Cross in Nigeria. Recreations: music; walking; the arts. Address: (h.) Burnside, West Linton EH46 7EW; T.-01968 660488.

McCall Smith, Professor Alexander, LLB, PhD. Professor, Faculty of Law, Edinburgh University; Author; b. 24.8.48, Zimbabwe; m., Dr. Elizabeth Parry; 2 d. Publications: (non-fiction): Law and Medical Ethics (Co-Author); Butterworth's Medico-Legal Encyclopaedia (Co-Author); Scots Criminal Law (Co-Author); The Duty to Rescue (Co-Author); The Criminal Law of Botswana; Forensic Aspects of Sleep (Co-Author); fiction: Children of Wax; Heavenly Date; numerous books for children. Recreation: wind instruments. Address: (h.) 16A Napier Road, Edinburgh EH10 5AY; T.-0131-229 6083.

MacCallum, Alasdair Norman, BSc (Hons). Chief Executive, Don & Low Ltd., since 1986; Director, Hamish Morison Ltd., Vico Properties PLC; Chairman, Joseph Johnston & Sons Ltd.; b. 27.1.36, Connel, Argyll; m., Helga Diana; 1 s.; 1 d. Educ. Keil School; Glasgow University. National Service Commission, Royal Artillery; Unilever, six years; Culter Guard Bridge Paper Co. Ltd., seven years; Devro Ltd. (Production Director, Managing Director), 14 years; Baxters of Fochabers (Managing Director), one year. Chairman: Montrose Harbour Trust, CBI Scotland, 1991-93, New South Mills Ltd.; Member, Board, North of Scotland Water Authority; Chairman, Scottish Crop Research Institute. Recreations: angling; shooting; gardening; theatre; music; reading. Address: (h.) Inverossie, Rossie Braes, Montrose DD10 9TJ; T.-01674 673013.

MacCallum, Professor James Richard, BSc, PhD, DSc, CChem, FRSC, FRSE. Professor of Polymer Chemistry, St. Andrews University (Vice-Principal, 1992-96); Pro-Principal, since 1997; b. 3.5.36, Kilmartin; m., Eleanor Margaret Thomson; 2 s.; 1 d. Educ. Dumfries Academy; Glasgow University. Technical Officer, ICI Fibres Division, 1961-62; ICI Research Fellow, Aberdeen University, 1962-63; Lecturer, St. Andrews University, 1964; Master, United College, 1988-92. Recreation: golf. Address: (h.) 9 Cairnsden Gardens, St. Andrews, Fife; T.-01334 473152.

MacCallum, Neil Robb. Poet, Critic and Editor; Editor, Lallans, 1996-99; Preses, Scots Language Society, 1993-95; b. 15.5.54, Edinburgh. Educ. Firrhill High School; Napier College, Edinburgh. Lothian Health Board, 1973-87; Edinburgh City Councllor, 1977-80; Assistant National Secretary, SNP, 1980-81, National Secretary, 1981-86; Arts Columnist, Scots Independent, 1991-98; Editor, Scots

Glasnost, 1991-95; Committee Member, Scottish Poetry Library, 1989-95; Vice-Convener, Scots Language Resource Centre, 1993-95. Publications: Report of the SNP Commission of Inquiry (Editor), 1984; Portrait of a Calvinist, 1991; Mak It New (Co-Editor), 1995; Sing Frae the Hert, (Editor), 1996, A Stern's Licht, 1999. Recreations: reading; theatre; fitness and weight-training; running. Address: (h.) 18 Redford Avenue, Edinburgh EH13 0BU; T.-0131-441 3724.

Maccallum, Professor Norman Ronald Low, BSc, PhD, CEng, FIMechE. Emeritus Professor, Honorary Research Fellow, Department of Mechanical Engineering, Glasgow University; b. 18.2.31, Walston, Lanarkshire; m., Mary Bentley Alexander; 1 s.; 2 d. Educ. Allan Glen's School, Glasgow; Glasgow University. Assistant in Mechanical Engineering, Glasgow University, 1952-55; National Service, Royal Navy, 1955-57 (final rank: Sub-Lt.); Lecturer in Mechanical Engineering, Glasgow University, 1957-61; Performance Engineer, Rolls-Royce Ltd. (Scottish Group), 1961-62; Lecturer in Mechanical Engineering/ Senior Lecturer/Reader/Professor, Glasgow University. Chairman, Glasgow Panel, IMechE. Joint Session Clerk, Trinity St. Paul's Church, Cambuslang. Recreation: singing. Address: (h.) 43 Stewarton Drive, Cambuslang, Glasgow G72 8DQ.

McCalman, Ian Alister, MA (Hons). President, Educational Institute of Scotland, 1997-98; Member, STUC Education Committee, 1997-98; b. 26.4.42, Elgin; m., Gilllian; 1 s.; 1 d. Educ. Elgin Academy; Aberdeen University; Jordanhill College. Research in history, Balliol College, Oxford, 1964-67; Lecturer in History, Aberdeen University, 1967-70; Teacher in Glasgow, 1970-97; Teacher of History and Modern Studies, 1970-86, of Learning Support, 1986-97. Recreations: reading; cinema. Address: (h.) 18 Mossgiel Road, Glasgow G43 2DF.

McCann, Fergus John, MBA, CA. Chairman and Managing Director, Celtic plc; b. Stirling; moved to Canada 1963 to work for Touche Ross & Co.; financial executive posts: Cott Beverages (Canada) Ltd., Distillers Corporation Seagrams Limited, Pretty Polly Canada Ltd.; founded International Golf Inc., Montreal, 1973; President, World Golf Management Ltd., Bermuda, 1982-87; joined Board, Celtic Football Club, 1994. Address: (b.) Celtic Plc, Celtic Park, Glasgow G40 3RE.

McCann, James Aloysius, MA, LLB. Solicitor and Notary Public; a founding Director, Legal Defence Union in Scotland, 1987, Chairman, since 1990; b. 14.8.39, Glasgow; m., Jane Marlow; 3 s.; 1 d. Educ. St. Mungo's Academy, Glasgow; Glasgow University. Former Member, Legal Aid Central Committee; Dean, Faculty of Dunbartonshire Solicitors, 1986-88; Convenor for Law Society PQLE Advocacy Training Courses, 1983-91; Senior Tutor (Professional Legal Practice), Glasgow University, 1981-91; Member, Law Society of Scotland Legal Aid Committee, 1987-97; Reporter, Scottish Legal Aid Board (Co-opted Member, Criminal Applications Committee, 1987-93); appointed Honorary Sheriff at Dumbarton, 1990; commission as Temporary Sheriff, 1991. Recreations: sailing/windsurfing; chess; music. Address: (b.) 499 Kilbowie Road, Clydebank G81 2AX.

McCann, Michael. National Officer (Scotland), Public and Commercial Services Union; b. 2.1.64, Glasgow; m., Tracy Anne; 1 s.; 1 d. Educ. St. Andrew's R. C. High School, East Kilbride. Overseas Development Administration, 1982-92; Civil and Public Services Association, 1992-98. Recreations: Celtic Football Club; music; golf. Address: (b.) 6 Hillside Crescent, Edinburgh EH7 5DY; T.-0131-556 0407.

McCann, Peter Toland McAree, CBE (1977), OStJ, DL, JP, BL. Solicitor and Notary Public, since 1947; b. 2.8.24, Glasgow; m., Maura Eleanor Ferris; 1 s. Educ. St. Mungo's Academy, Glasgow; Glasgow University. Councillor, Corporation of Glasgow, 1961-75; River Bailie, 1962; Magistrate, 1963-66; Police Judge, 1967-74; JP, since 1967; Lord Lieutenant, 1975-77; Lord Provost, City of Glasgow District, 1975-77; Depute Lieutenant, since 1977; Chairman, St. Thomas More Society for Lawyers, 1960; Chairman, McCann Committee for Provision of Secondary Education for Physically Disabled Children, 1968; Disabled Scot, 1973; awarded two Golden Swords from HRH Prince Fawaz of Saudi Arabia, 1977-78; awarded Silver and Golden Swords from City of Jeddah, 1975-78; awarded Medal of King Faisal of Saudi Arabia, 1976. Recreations: music; history; model railways; collecting model cars and model soldiers. Address: (h.) Craig En Ross, 31 Queen Mary Avenue, Crosshill, Glasgow G42 8DS.

McCarthy, James, BSc, FRZSS (Hon). Lecturer/Conservation Consultant; b. 6.5.36, Dundee; m.; 2 s.; 1 d. Educ. Harris Academy, Dundee; Aberdeen University; University of East Africa, Kampala. Military Service, 1954-56 (Royal Marines, commissioned Black Watch, seconded King's African Rifles); Leverhulme Scholar, Makerere College, Kampala, 1959-61; Assistant Conservator of Forests, Tanzania, and Lecturer in Forest Ecology, Forest Training School, 1961-63; Deputy Regional Officer (North England), Nature Conservancy, 1963-69; Deputy Director (Scotland), Nature Conservancy Council, 1975-91; Member, Board, Scottish Natural Heritage. Churchill Fellow, USA, 1976; Nuffield/ Leverhulme Fellow, 1988. Recreation: cross-country skiing. Address: (h.) 6a Ettrick Road, Edinburgh; T.-0131-229 1916.

McClatchie, Colin James Stewart, BSc (Econ) (Hons), MCIM. General Manager, News International Newspapers in Scotland, since 1995; b. 1.1.49, Belfast; m., Claire McConaghy; 2 d. Educ. Coleraine Academical Institution; Queen's University, Belfast. Senior management positions, Thomson Regional Newspapers, Belfast, Newcastle, Reading, Edinburgh, 1971-84; Circulation/Marketing Director, Scottish Daily Record and Sunday Mail Ltd., 1984-94 (and Managing Director, Maxwell Free Newspapers Ltd., 1990-93); Marketing Consultant, 1995. Chairman, Newspaper Press Fund, 1998-2000; Committee Member, Institute of Directors, West of Scotland Branch. Recreations: family; golf; theatre. Address: (b.) 124 Portman Street, Glasgow G41 1EJ; T.-0141-420 5101.

McClellan, John Forrest, MA, Hon. FDIT. Director, Scottish International Education Trust, since 1986; Member, Management Committee, Hanover (Scotland) Housing Association, since 1986; b. 15.8.32, Glasgow; m., Eva Maria Pressel; 3 s.; 1 d. Educ. Aberdeen Grammar School; Aberdeen University. 2nd Lt., Gordon Highlanders and Nigeria Regiment, Royal West African Frontier Force, 1954-56; entered Civil Service, 1956; Assistant Principal, Scottish Office, 1956-59; Private Secretary to Permanent Under Secretary of State, Scottish Office, 1959-60; Principal, Scottish Office, 1960-68; Civil Service Fellow, Glasgow University, 1968-69; Assistant Secretary, Scottish Office, 1969-77; Under Secretary, Scottish Office, 1977-85. Publication: Then A Soldier (novel), 1991. Recreations: gardening; walking. Address: (h.) 7 Cumin Place, Edinburgh EH9 2JX; T.-0131 667 8446.

McClelland, Professor John Ferguson, CBE, CIMgt, FRSA, FRSE. Global Chief Industrial Officer, Philips B.V.; Visiting Professor and Fellow, Paisley University, since 1993; b. 27.3.45, Glasgow; m., Alice; 1 d. Educ. North Kelvinside School; Glasgow College. South of Scotland Electricity Board, 1963-68; IBM Corporation, 1968-95; Controller, Greenock Manufacturing, 1977, European Director of Operations, 1980, European Manufacturing Controller, 1983, Director of Manufacturing, Greenock, 1987, Director of UK Manufacturing, 1992, Vice President,

Worldwide Manufacturing, 1994; Digital Corporation, 1995-98, V.P. Worldwide Manufacturing, 1997; former Chairman, Judging Panel, Quality Scotland Excellence Award; Chairman: Higher Education Funding Council's Quality Assessment Committee, CBI UK Technology and Innovation Committee. Recreations: golf; football; gardening.

McClements, Rev. Duncan Elliott, MA (Hons), BD (Hons), MTh. Parish Minister, Falkirk Grahamston United, since 1976; Clerk, Falkirk Presbytery, since 1989; Convener, Committee on Ecumenical Affairs, Church of Scotland,1994-98; b. 28.8.40, Glasgow; m., Dorothy Jean Easton; 1 s.; 1 d. Educ. Daniel Stewart's College; Edinburgh University. Assistant Minister, Carrick Knowe Parish, Edinburgh, 1965-66; Parish Minister, Hurlford Reid Memorial, 1967-76. Sometime Chairman, Kirk Care Housing Association. Recreations: gardening; reading; watching sport; Rotary. Address: 30 Russel Street, Falkirk FK2 7HS; T.-01324 624461.

McClure, Judith, MA (Oxon), DPhil, FRSA, FSAScot. Head, St. George's School, Edinburgh, since 1994; Chairman, Scottish Region, 1995-98, and Member, Council, Girls' Schools Association; b. 22.12.45, Stockton; m., Dr. Roger Collins. Educ. Newlands Grammar School, Middlesbrough; Somerville College, Oxford. Sir Maurice Powicke Research Fellow, Lady Margaret Hall, Oxford, 1976-77; Lecturer in Medieval Latin and Medieval History, Liverpool University, 1977-79; Lecturer in History, Oxford University (Jesus, Somerville and Worcester Colleges), 1979-81; Teacher and Head of Department in History and Politics, School of St. Helen & St. Katherine, Abingdon, 1981-84; Deputy Head, Kingswood School, Bath, 1984-87; Head, Royal School, Bath, 1987-93. Member: Court, University of Bath, 1989-92, General Convocation, Heriot Watt University, since 1994, Board of Governors, Clifton Hall School, since 1995, Governing Body, Scottish Council of Independent Schools, since 1995, Management Committee, since 1998. Publication: Bede: The Ecclesiastical History (Co-author), 1994. Recreations: reading; using a computer; travelling. Address: (b.) St. George's School for Girls, Garscube Terrace, Edinburgh EH12 6BG; T.-031-332 4575.

McCluskey, Baron (John Herbert McCluskey), LLD (Dundee). Senator of the College of Justice in Scotland, since 1984; Life Peer, since 1976; b. 12.6.29, Glasgow; m., Ruth Friedland; 2 s.; 1 d. Educ. St. Bede's Grammar School, Manchester; Holy Cross Academy, Edinburgh; Edinburgh University; MA, LLB. Admitted Faculty of Advocates, 1955; Standing Junior Counsel to Ministry of Power (Scotland), 1963; Advocate-Depute, 1964-71; QC (Scot), 1967; Chairman, Medical Appeal Tribunals for Scotland, 1972-74; Sheriff Principal of Dumfries and Galloway, 1973-74; Solicitor General for Scotland, 1974-79. Chairman, Scottish Association for Mental Health, 1985-94; Independent Chairman: Scottish Football League Compensation Tribunal, SFA Appeals Tribunal; Reith Lecturer, BBC, 1986; Editor, Butterworth's Scottish Criminal Law and Practice series. Publications: Law, Justice and Democracy, 1987; Criminal Appeals, 1992. Recreations: tennis; pianoforte. Address: (b.) Court of Session, Parliament House, Edinburgh EH1 1RF; T.-0131-225 2595.

McCluskey, Mary, DCE. Artistic Director, Scottish Youth Theatre, since 1992; freelance Theatre Director/Drama Tutor, since 1985; b. 16.9.54, Glasgow. Educ. West Senior High School, Garden City, Michigan, USA; Hamilton College of Education; Royal Scottish Academy of Music and Drama. President, Hamilton College of Education SRC, 1975-76; Teacher, Glenlee Primary, Hamilton, 1976-79; Assistant Stage Manager, Dundee Repertory Theatre, 1980-81; YOP Supervisor, Community Projects Agency (East End), 1981-83; YTS Training Officer, Community Projects Agency (South East), 1983-85; Associate Director, Scottish Youth Theatre, 1989-91; Education Officer, Royal Shakespeare Company, 1991-92. Adapted: Wee MacGreegor, Wee MacGreegor Enlists, Medea. Recreations: theatre; films; books; visiting historic sites. Address: (b.) Scottish Youth Theatre, Sixth Floor, Gordon Chambers, 90 Mitchell Street, Glasgow G1 3NQ; T.-0141-221 5127.

McCoist, Alistair (Ally) Murdoch, MBE. Footballer, Kilmarnock F.C. (formerly Glasgow Rangers); b. 24.9.62, Bellshill; m., Allison; 3 s. Educ. Hunter High School. Debut for St. Johnstone aged 16; signed for Sunderland, 1981; joined Rangers, 1983; became club's leading goal-scorer, August 1997 (421 goals); 57 caps for Scotland, since 1986; Member, Scotland squad, 1990 World Cup Finals, 1992 European Championships; regular contributor to Question of Sport, BBC TV; chat-show host, McCoist and MacAulay, BBC Scotland. Scottish Sports Personality of the Year, 1992; Scottish Sports Writers' Player of the Year, 1992. Recreations: reading autobiographies; listening to music; playing pranks on his team-mates. Address: (b.) Carnegie Sports International Ltd., 4 Redheughs Rigg, South Gyle, Edinburgh EH12 9DQ; T.-0131-317 7773.

McColgan, Elizabeth. Athlete; b. 24.5.64, Dundee; m., Peter Conor McColgan. Educ. University of Alabama. Commonwealth Games Gold medallist (10,000 metres), 1986; Silver medallist, World Cross-Country Championships, 1987; Olympic Games Silver medallist (10,000 metres), 1988; Silver medallist, World Indoor Championships, 1989; Gold medallist (10,000 metres) and Bronze medallist (3,000 metres), Commonwealth Games, 1990; Winner, 1996 London Marathon.

McColl, James Hamilton, MBE, NDH, SDH, SHM. Freelance Horticulturalist; b. 19.9.35, Kilmarnock; m., Billie; 1 s.; 1 d. Educ. Kilmarnock Academy; West of Scotland Agricultural College. Staff Member, WSAC, Auchincruive, Ayr, 1956-59; Assistant Head Gardener, Reading University Botanic Garden, 1959-61; Horticultural Adviser/Lecturer, Shropshire Education Authority, 1961-67; Horticultural Adviser: MAFF, Leicestershire, Northants and Rutland, 1967-73, North of Scotland College of Agriculture, 1973-78; former PRO, Morrison Bowmore Distillers Ltd.; Co-Presenter, The Beechgrove Garden, BBC TV Scotland, 1978-89, since 1994. Recreations: golf; music; rugby. Address: (h.) Ayrshire House, Oldmeldrum, Aberdeenshire; T.-01651 873955.

McComb, Professor (William) David, BSc, MSc, PhD, CPhys, FInstP. Professor of Statistical Physics, Edinburgh University, since 1997; b. 31.10.40, Belfast; m., Doyleen M. McLeod; 3 d. Educ. Methodist College, Belfast; Queens University, Belfast; Manchester University. Senior Scientific Officer, Theoretical Physics Division, AERE, Harwell; Edinburgh University: Lecturer in Engineering Science, Lecturer in Physics, Reader in Physics. Publications: The Physics of Fluid Turbulence, 1990; Dynamics and Relativity, 1999. Recreations: reading; gardening; listening to music. Address: (b.) Department of Physics and Astronomy, King's Buildings, Edinburgh University, Edinburgh.

McConnell, Bridget Mary, MA (Hons), DIA, MEd. Director, Cultural and Leisure Services, Glasgow City Council, since 1998; b. 28.5.58, Lennoxtown; m., Jack Wilson McConnell (qv); 1 s.; 1 d. Educ. St. Patrick's High School, Kilsyth; Our Lady's High School, Cumbernauld; St. Andrews University; Dundee College of Commerce; Stirling University. Curator, Doorstep Gallery, Fife Regional Council, 1983-84; Arts Officer, Stirling District Council, 1984-88; Principal Arts Officer, The Arts in Fife, Fife Regional Council, 1988-96; Service Manager, Community Services, Fife Council, 1996-98. Conference

Co-ordinator, Fourth International Conference in Adult Education and the Arts, St. Andrews, 1995; External Verifier, SCOTVEC Arts and Leisure Management Courses, 1990-97; Member, Board, Workshop and Artists Studio Provision Scotland (WASPS) Ltd, 1985-90; Chair, Scottish Youth Dance Festival, 1993-96 (Founder Member, 1988); Chair, Scottish Local Authority Arts Officers Group, 1993-96 (Founder Member, 1991); Vice Chair, Scottish Arts Lobby (SALVO), 1995-97; Member, Scottish Arts Council Combined Arts Committee, 1988-94; Arts Adviser to COSLA, since 1997; Awards: British/American Arts Association/University of Minnesota Fellowship, 1987. Publications: Modernising Britain: Creative Futures (Co-Author), 1997; conference papers on arts and adult education. Recreations: walking; playing piano; swimming; reading. Address: (b.) 37 High Street, Glasgow G1 1LX; T.-0141-287 5058.

McConnell, Charles Stephen, BA (Hons), MPhil. Chief Executive, Scottish Community Education Council, since 1993; Secretary General, International Association for Community Development; b. 20.6.51, Harrogate. Educ. Huyton Hill School, Ambleside; Granby Park School, Harrogate; City of Birmingham Polytechnic; Paisley College of Technology. Community Educator; Lecturer in Community Studies, Clydebank Technical College; Action Researcher, Community Education, Scottish Local Government Unit; Lecturer in Community Education, Dundee College of Education; Senior Policy Development Officer, National Consumer Council; Development Director, Action Resource Centre; Public and European Affairs Director, Community Development Foundation; former Labour Party Parliamentary candidate. Publications: Community Worker as Politiciser of the Deprived; Deprivation, Participation and Community Action; Community Education and Community Development; Post 16 — Developments in Continuing Education in Scotland; Classroom Commercials — business sponsorship of education; Consumer Action and Community Development; Community Development — the European dimension; A Citizen's Europe; Promoting Community Development in Europe; Community Development and Urban Regeneration; Community Education: The Making of an Empowering Profession. Recreations: fell-walking; reading political biography. Address: (b.) Rosebery House, 9 Haymarket Terrace, Edinburgh EH12 5EZ; T.-0131-313 2488.

McConnell, Jack Wilson, BSc, DipEd. Chief Executive, Public Affairs Europe Limited; b. 30.6.60, Irvine; m., Bridget (qv); 1 s.; 1 d. Educ. Arran High School; Stirling University. Mathematics Teacher, Lornshill Academy, 1983-92; General Secretary, Scottish Labour Party, 1992-98; Member, Stirling District Council, 1984-93, Council Leader, 1990-92, Treasurer, 1988-92, Chair, Leisure and Recreation Committee, 1986-87, Equal Opportunities Committee, 1986-90; President, 1980-82, Hon. President, 1984-85 and 1991-93, Stirling University Students Association; Executive Member, Scottish Constitutional Convention, 1990-98; Deputy President, NUS Scotland, 1982-83; Chair, Board of Directors, Stirling Windows Ltd., 1988-92; Member, Labour Party Scottish Executive Committee, 1989-92; Parliamentary candidate, Perth and Kinross, 1987. Publication: Proposals for Scottish Democracy, 1989. Recreations: golf; swimming; cinema; music. Address: (h.) 10a Argyll Avenue, Stirling FK8 1UL; T.-01786 479470.

McConnell, Rodger Raymond, FRICS, MBA. Director of Physical and Economic Regeneration, Glasgow City Council, since 1998; Chairman, General Practice Division, Royal Institution of Chartered Surveyors in Scotland, 1996; b. 13.5.47, Bellshill; m., Rosalind; 3 s.; 1 d. Educ. Our Lady's High School, Motherwell; College of Estate Management; Glasgow University. Trainee Valuer, District Valuer's Office, Glasgow, 1966-71; Senior Assistant, Richard Ellis, 1971-75; Strathclyde Regional Council: Assistant Head of Estates, 1975-78, Depute Director of Estates, 1978-91; City Estates Surveyor, Glasgow District Council, 1992-95; Director of Property Services, Glasgow City Council, 1995-98; Member, Association of Chief Estates Surveyors and Property Managers in Local Government. Recreations: family activities; following sport; theatre. Address: (b.) Tontine Building, 20 Trongate, Glasgow G1 5EY; T.-0141-287 8400.

McConnell, Walter Scott, OBE, FRPharmS, PhC. Community Pharmacist, since 1962; Vice Chairman, Ayrshire and Arran Community Health Care Trust; b. 7.4.36, Kilmarnock; m.; 1 s.; 3 d. Educ. Kilmarnock Academy; Royal Technical College, Glasgow. Former Chairman, Pharmaceutical General Council (Scotland). Recreations: curling; golf. Address: (h.) 27 Mauchline Road, Hurlford, Kilmarnock KA1 5AB; T.-01563 525393.

McCormack, Ian Andrew. Editor, West Highland Free Press, since 1976; b. 5.2.48, Kilmarnock; 2 d. Educ. Kilmarnock Academy. Trainee Journalist, Evening Times, Glasgow, 1965, Kilmarnock Standard, 1966-67; Reporter, Glasgow Herald, 1968-69; joined West Highland Free Press, 1975. Address: (b.) Broadford, Isle of Skye; T.-01471 822464.

McCormack, Jean Elizabeth Wallace, DL. Provost, Perth and Kinross District Council, 1992-96; b. 13.6.38, Duundee; m., Peter McCormack; 1 s.; 1 d. Educ. Harris Academy, Dundee; Dundee College of Education. Address: Grangeside, Grange Road, Errol, Perth PH2 7SR

MacCormick, Professor (Donald) Neil, MA, LLD, Hon. LLD (Uppsala), Hon.LLD (Saarland), Hon.LLD (Queen's University, Ontario), FRSE, FBA. Vice-Principal, 1997-2000, and Regius Professor of Public Law, Edinburgh University, since 1972; b. 27.5.41, Glasgow; m., 1, Karen (Caroline) Rona Barr (m. diss.); 3 d.; 2, Flora Margaret Britain. Educ. High School of Glasgow; Glasgow University; Balliol College, Oxford. Lecturer in Jurisprudence, Queen's College, Dundee, 1965-67; Fellow, Balliol College, Oxford, 1967-72; Oxford University: CUF Lecturer, 1968-72, Pro-Proctor, 1970-71; Dean, Faculty of Law, Edinburgh University, 1973-76 and 1985-88; Senate Assessor, University Court, 1982-85; Provost, Faculty Group of Law and Social Sciences, 1993-97; Member, Broadcasting Council for Scotland, 1985-89; Vice President: International Association for Legal and Social Philosophy, 1991-95, Royal Society of Edinburgh, 1991-94; Member, Economic and Social Research Council, since 1995; Member, Scottish Examination Board, 1994-97. President, Oxford Union, 1965; Executive Member, Scottish National Party, 1978-81, Council Member, 1978-84 and 1989-97; Foreign Member, Finnish Academy of Science. Publications: as author or editor, books on philosophy of law, political philosophy, etc. Address: (h.) 19 Pentland Terrace, Edinburgh EH10 6AA; T.-0131-447 7945.

McCormick, John, MA, MEd. Controller, BBC Scotland, since 1992; b. 24.6.44; m., Jean Frances Gibbons; 1 s.; 1 d. Educ. St. Michael's Academy, Irvine; Glasgow University. Former schoolteacher; joined BBC as Education Officer, 1970; Senior Education Officer, Scotland, 1975-82; Secretary and Head of Information, BBC Scotland, 1982-87; Secretary of BBC, 1987-92. Chairman, Edinburgh International Film Festival, since 1996; Hon. Joint Chairman, BAFTA Scotland, since 1992; Lay Member, Court, University of Strathclyde, since 1996; Board Member, Scottish Screen, since 1997; Member, Scottish Business Forum, since 1998. Recreations: theatre; cinema; biography; newspapers. Address: (b.) Broadcasting House, Queen Margaret Drive, Glasgow, G12 0TT; T.-0141-339 8844.

McCormick, John St. Clair, MB ChB, FRCSEd. Medical Director, Dumfries and Galloway Royal Infirmary NHS Trust, since 1994; Consultant Surgeon, Dumfries and Galloway Royal Infirmary, since 1979; Director of Standards, Royal College of Surgeons of Edinburgh, since 1997; b. 20.9.39, Sherborne; m., Fiona Helen McLean; 2 s. Educ. St. Paul's Cathedral Choir School; University of Edinburgh. Consultant Surgeon, Dunfermline and West Fife Hospital, 1974-79. Recreation: fishing. Address: Dumfries and Galloway Royal Infirmary, Bankend Road, Dumfries DG1 4AP; T.-01387 246246, Ext. 3113.

McCormick, John William Penfold, BSc, PhD. Chairman, Scottish Association for Public Transport, since 1988; Information Technology Manager, Weir Pumps Ltd., since 1979; b. 9.6.46, Renfrew; m., Linda M.L.; 1 d. Educ. Paisley Grammar School; Glasgow University. Research Fellow, Glasgow University, 1971-74; computer management, since 1975. Recreations: hill-walking; transport; music. Address: (b.) 5 St. Vincent Place, Glasgow G1 2HT; T.-0141-639 3697.

McCormick, Julie Elizabeth, LLB (Hons), DipLP, NP. Solicitor; Membership Secretary, Scottish Young Lawyers Association; Member, Admissions Committee, Law Society of Scotland; b. 10.12.71, Farnborough, Kent. Educ. John Paul Academy, Glasgow; Strathclyde University. Joined Allan McDougall & Co, SSC, as trainee Solicitor, 1994; Qualified Solicitor, since 1996. Recreations: cinema; theatre; Celtic music; food and drink. Address: (b.) 3 Coates Crescent, Edinburgh EH3 7AL; T.-0131-225 2121.

McCosh, Professor Andrew Macdonald, BSc, DBA, HonMBA, CA. Professor of Finance Emeritus and University Fellow, Edinburgh University, since 1995; b. 16.9.40, Glasgow; m., Anne; 3 d. Educ. Edinburgh Academy; Edinburgh University; Harvard University. Associate Professor of Accounting, University of Michigan, 1964-71; Research Assistant, Visiting Professor of Business Administration, Harvard Business School, 1964-75; Professor of Management Accounting, Manchester Business School, 1971-85; Professor of the Organisation of Industry and Commerce, Edinburgh University, 1986-95; Director, The Lexington Mutual Funds, New York, USA, since 1996. Recreations: mountaineering; fishing; golf. Address: (b.) Department of Business Studies, William Robertson Building, 50 George Square, Edinburgh EH8 9JY; T.-0131-650 3801.

McCourt, Arthur David, BSc (Hons). Chief Executive, Highland Council, since 1995; b. 11.7.47, Newburgh, Fife; m., Jan; 1 d. Educ. Bell-Baxter High School, Cupar; Edinburgh College of Art; Heriot-Watt University. Various posts with Northumberland County Council, Central Regional Council, Stirling District Council; Assistant Chief Executive, Tayside Regional Council, 1990-93. Recreation: mountaineering. Address: (b.) Glenurquhart Road, Inverness IV3 5NX; T.-01463 702838.

McCreadie, Robert Anderson, LLB, PhD, Advocate; b. 17.8.48, St. Andrews. Educ. Madras College, St. Andrews; Edinburgh University; Christ's College, Cambridge. Lecturer, Dundee University, 1974-78, Edinburgh University, 1978-93; called to Scottish Bar, 1992; Standing Junior Counsel, Department of Transport, 1994-95, Scottish Home and Health Department, 1995; Member: Scottish Consumer Council, 1977-82, Social Security Appeal Tribunals, 1987-92; Labour Parliamentary Candidate, Edinburgh South, 1983; joined Scottish Liberal Party, 1985; Parliamentary Candidate: Livingston, 1987, Glasgow Central, 1989, Edinburgh South, 1992; Vice Chairman, Scottish Liberal Democrats, 1988-92; Executive Committee, Scottish Constitutional Convention, 1989-82; Chairman, Scottish Legal Action Group, 1980-82; Fellow, British-American Project, 1985. Publication: You and Your Rights: An A to Z Guide to the Law in Scotland, 1984 (Joint Editor). Recreations: music; Scottish history; walking. Address: (h.) 40 Marchmont Crescent, Edinburgh EH9 1HG; T.-0131-667 1383.

McCreadie, Robin G., DSc, MD, FRCPsych. Director of Clinical Research, Crichton Royal Hospital, Dumfries, since 1982; b. 21.2.42, Troon; 2 d. Educ. Ayr Academy; Glasgow University. Lecturer in Psychological Medicine, Glasgow University; Consultant Psychiatrist, Gartnavel Royal Hospital, Glasgow. Recreations: hill-walking; all things Italian. Address: (b.) Crichton Royal Hospital, Dumfries; T.-01387 255301.

McCrone, Alasdair Iain, DDA. Artistic Director, Mull Theatre, since 1995; b. 21.10.59, Glasgow; m., Alicia Hendrick. Educ. Dalziel High School, Motherwell; Glasgow University; Royal Scottish Academy of Music and Drama. Freelance actor, 1984-90; twice toured Highlands with one-man plays; directed The Vanek Plays (Havel) as part of Glasgow's 1990 celebrations; Drama Director, Banff and Buchan Council, 1991-92 and 1993; Director, Mull Little Theatre, 1992-93; resigned, 1994, to resume freelance work; appeared as Stan Laurel, Laurel and Hardy; re-appointed to Mull Theatre, 1995; directing credits include: The Road to Mecca, The Bend, Not About Heroes, Speed-The-Plow, Whisky Galore, Death and the Maiden, all for Mull Theatre; Columcille, Stray Theatre; Highland Voices, Traverse Theatre; Whisky Galore, Royal Lyceum, Perth Theatre. Recreations: golf; cycling; rail travel; Gaelic choir; reading; walking; messing about in boats. Address: (h.) Thornliebank, Argyll Terrace, Tobermory, Isle of Mull; T.-01688 302602.

McCrone, Iain Alistair, CBE (1987), SDA. Farmer and Company Director; b. 29.3.34, Glasgow; m., Yvonne Findlay; 4 d. Educ. Glasgow Academy; Trinity College, Glenalmond; West of Scotland Agricultural College. Farming on own account, since 1956; Managing Director, McCrone Farmers Ltd., since 1958; began fish farming, 1968; Director: Highland Trout Co. (now Marine Harvest McConnell), Otter Ferry Salmon Ltd., since 1974; Member: Fife Regional Council, 1978-82; Parliamentary candidate (Conservative), Central Fife, 1979, Council, National Farmers Union of Scotland, 1977-82, Board, Glenrothes Development Corporation, 1980-96, Fife Health Board, 1983-91; Nuffield Farming Scholar, 1966; President, Scottish Conservative and Unionist Association, 1985-87. Recreations: golf; rugby (spectator). Address: (h.) Cardsknolls, Markinch, Fife KY7 6LP; T.-01337 830267.

McCrone, Professor Robert Gavin Loudon, CB, MA, MSc, PhD, Hon.LLD, FRSE. Visiting Professor, Department of Business Studies, since 1994, and Hon. Fellow of the Europa Institute, since 1992, Edinburgh University; Deputy Chairman, Royal Infirmary of Edinburgh NHS Trust, since 1994; Board Member, Scottish Opera, 1992-98; b. 2.2.33, Ayr; m., Alexandra Bruce Waddell (deceased); 2 s.; 1 d. Educ. St. Catharine's College, Cambridge; University of Wales; Glasgow University. Fisons Ltd., 1959-60; Lecturer in Economics, Glasgow University, 1960-65; Fellow, Brasenose College, Oxford, 1965-70; Consultant, UNESCO, 1964; Member, NEDC Working Party on Agricultural Policy, 1967-68; Adviser, House of Commons Select Committee on Scottish Affairs, 1969-70; Senior Economic Adviser, Scottish Office, 1970-72; Under Secretary, 1972-80; Secretary, Industry Department for Scotland, 1980-87; Secretary, Scottish Office Environment Department, 1987-92; Chief Economic Adviser, Scottish Office, 1972-92. Member, Economic and Social Research Council, 1986-89, Council, Royal Economic Society, 1977-82, Council, Scottish Economic Society, 1982-91, Advisory Committee, Inquiry into Implementation of Constitutional Reform, 1995-97, National Review of Resources Allocation in the NHS in Scotland, since 1998. Publications: The Economics of Subsidising Agriculture, 1962; Scotland's Economic

Progress 1951-60, 1963; Regional Policy in Britain, 1969; Scotland's Future, 1969; Housing Policy in Britain and Europe (Co-Author), 1995; European Monetary Union and Regional Development, 1997. Recreations: music; walking. Address: (b.) Department of Business Studies, Edinburgh University, 50 George Square, Edinburgh EH8 9JY; T.-0131 650 4603.

McCrorie, Ian, BSc. Chorusmaster, Scottish Festival Singers, since 1991; Assistant Rector, Greenock Academy, since 1975; b. 6.5.41, Greenock; m., Olive Simpson Bolton; 2 s. Educ. Greenock Academy; Glasgow University. Founded Toad Choir, Greenock, which appeared in numerous BBC Songs of Praise programmes; this choir became the nucleus of the Scottish Philharmonic Singers (1976-91); Organist and Choirmaster, Mid Kirk of Greenock, 1964-93; conducted at Festivals in France and Poland, took SPS to Israel and the London Proms, and prepared the choir for leading conductors; Member, Greenock Presbytery, and Panel on Worship, General Assembly; Past President and Convener of Cruising, now Review Editor, Clyde River Steamer Club; author of numerous books and articles on Clyde and West Highland steamers. Recreations: as above! Address: (h.) 72 Newton Street, Greenock; T.-01475 726689.

McCrossan, Margaret B.P., MA, CPFA. Executive Director, Resource Services, Inverclyde Council, since 1998; b. 12.1.61, Helensburgh; m., Bill; 1 s. Educ. Braidfield High School; University of Glasgow. Joined Strathclyde Regional Council as Trainee Accountant, 1981; qualified, 1986; joined Inverclyde Council as Director of Finance, 1995. Recreations: golf; travel. Address: (b.) Department of Finance, Municipal Buildings, Greenock PA15 1LX; T.-01475 712201.

McCue, William, OBE (1982), LRAM, ARAM. Bass Singer; b. 17.8.34, Allanton, Shotts; m., Patricia Carrick; 1 d. Educ. Calderhead High School; Royal Scottish Academy of Music; Royal Academy of Music. Began professional singing career in 1960; his work has included opera, oratorio, recital, concert, cabaret, pantomime and stage musical, radio and TV; has travelled throughout the world, making numerous visits to USA, Canada, USSR, Iceland, Europe and Israel; has made various recordings of Scots songs and Negro spirituals; Director, Scottish Singers Company; Honorary Life Member, Saltire Society; former Member, Scottish Arts Council. Recreations: watching all sport; listening to all kinds of music; gardening; escaping to the Scottish countryside.

McCulloch, Andrew Grant, LLB, BSc(Soc Sci). Partner, Drummond Miller WS, since 1979; b. 10.2.52, Edinburgh; m.; 1 s.; 1 d. Educ. Glasgow Academy; Edinburgh University. Trained, then Assistant, Drummond & Co., 1974-79; Partner, since 1979; Member, Council, Law Society of Scotland, since 1987, President of Society, 1996-97; Solicitor Advocate, since 1992; Temporary Sheriff, since 1991. President, Grange Sports Club, 1990-92. Recreations: golf; cricket; wine. Address: (b.) 31/2 Moray Place, Edinburgh; T.-0131-226 5151.

McCulloch, Ian, DA, ARSA. Painter and Printmaker; b. 4.3.35, Glasgow; m., Margery Palmer; 2 s. Educ. Eastbank Academy; Glasgow School of Art. Elected Member, Society of Scottish Artists, 1964; elected Associate, Royal Scottish Academy, 1989; paintings in many private and public collections; numerous one-man and group exhibitions; 1st prize, Stirling Smith Biennial, 1985; winner, Glasgow International Concert Hall Mural Competition, 1989-90; Fine Art Fellow, Strathclyde University, since 1994. Address: (h.) 51 Victoria Road, Lenzie, Glasgow G66 5AP; T.-0141-776 1053.

McCulloch, Professor James, BSc, PhD. Professor of Neuroscience, Glasgow University, since 1988; b. 7.4.51, Irvine; m., Mailis Christina; 2 s. Educ. Spiers School, Beith; Glasgow University. Lecturer, 1978-86, Reader, 1986-88, Glasgow University; Editor, Journal of Cerebral Blood Flow and Metabolism, since 1997. Publications: four books; 200 scientific papers. Recreations: squash; golf; skiing. Address: (b.) Glasgow University, Bearsden Road, Glasgow, G61 1QH; T.-0141-330 5828.

McCulloch, John David, CA, DL. Deputy Lieutenant, Midlothian, since 1992; Clerk to Church of Scotland Presbytery of Lothian, since 1994; Chartered Accountant, since 1963; b. 5.4.37, Edinburgh; m., Cicely Blackett; 2 s.; 2 d. Educ. Belhaven Hill, Dunbar; Marlborough College. Address: (h.) Auchindinny House, Penicuik EH26 8PE; T.-Penicuik 672943.

McCulloch, Margery Palmer, BA, MLitt, PhD, LRAM. University teacher and writer; m., Ian McCulloch; 2 s. Educ. Hamilton Academy; London University; Glasgow University. Convener, Glasgow Branch, Saltire Society. Publications: The Novels of Neil M. Gunn: a critical study, 1987; The Man Who Came Back: short stories and essays by Neil M. Gunn, 1991; Edwin Muir: poet, critic and novelist, 1993. Recreation: music. Address: (h.) 51 Victoria Road, Lenzie, Glasgow G66 5AP; T.-0141-776 1053.

McCulloch, Tony, BSc, MEd, MA, FRSA. Rector, Charleston Academy, Inverness, since 1991; b. 12.12.50, Glasgow; m., Anne C.; 1 s.; 1 d. Educ. St. Pius Secondary, Glasgow; University of Ulster; Edinburgh University; Open University. Taught in Glasgow, Cumbernauld, Edinburgh, and Armadale (formerly Depute Rector, Armadale Academy, West Lothian). Recreations: traditional music; mandolin. Address: (b.) Charleston Academy, Kinmylies, Inverness; T.-01463 234324.

McCunn, Archibald Eddington, OBE, BSc (Hons), CEng, MIMechE, FIMgt. Board Member, Scottish Greenbelt Foundation; b. 27.5.27, Motherwell; m., Olive Isobel Johnston; 1 s.; 1 d. Educ. Dalziel High School; Strathclyde University. Engineering Management, Colvilles Ltd. BSC, 1952-64; Senior Consultant, Inbucon/AIC, 1964-67; Divisional Chairman, Stenhouse Industries, 1967-71; Divisional Chairman/Consultant, Grampian Holdings plc, 1971-89; Board Member, Highlands and Islands Development Board, 1985-89; Director: A.E. McCunn Consultants Ltd., 1985-95; Chairman, Craftpoint Ltd., 1986-91; Director, McConnell Salmon Ltd., 1990-94; Vice Chairman and Trustee, Argyll and Bute Countryside Trust, 1990-95; Hon. Vice-President, Scottish Salmon Growers Association, 1990-95; Board Member: State Hospital, 1992-96, Scottish Natural Heritage (South West), 1992-97. Recreations: painting; music; writing; cycling; gardening. Address: (h.) 2 McIntosh Way, Motherwell ML1 3BB; T.-01698 253500.

McDaid, Professor Seamus, CA, MBA. Vice Principal, University of Paisley, since 1997; Non-Executive Director, Renfrewshire Healthcare NHS Trust; b. 23.7.52, Glasgow; m., Alice; 2 d. Educ. St. Mungo's Academy; Glasgow University; Strathclyde University. Qualified as CA, 1974; trained with Wylie & Bisset, CA; worked for Coopers & Lybrand; joined Glasgow College as Lecturer, 1976; Senior Lecturer, 1980, Head, Department of Finance and Accounting, 1987; Dean, Faculty of Business, Glasgow Caledonian University, 1992. Recreations: football; badminton. Address: (b.) University of Paisley, Paisley PA1 2BE; T.-0141 848 3000.

McDevitt, Professor Denis Gordon, DSc, MD, FRCP, FRCPI, FRCPEd, FFPM, FRSE. Professor of Clinical Pharmacology, Dundee University Medical School, since 1984, and Dean, Faculty of Medicine, Dentistry and Nursing, 1994-97; Honorary Consultant Physician, Tayside Health Board, since 1984; Civil Consultant in Clinical Pharmacology, RAF, since 1987; Member, General Medical

Council, since 1996; b. 17.11.37, Belfast; m., Anne McKee; 2 s.; 1 d. Educ. Campbell College, Belfast; Queen's University, Belfast. Assistant Professor of Medicine and Consultant Physician, Christian Medical College, Ludhiana, North India, 1968-71; Senior Lecturer in Clinical Pharmacology and Consultant Physician, Queen's University Medical School, 1971-76; Merck International Fellow in Clinical Pharmacology, Vanderbilt University, Nashville, Tennessee, 1974-75; Reader in Clinical Pharmacology, Queen's University Medical School, 1976-78; Professor of Clinical Pharmacology, Queen's University of Belfast and Consultant Physician, Belfast Teaching Hospitals, 1978-83. Chairman, Clinical Section, British Pharmacological Society, 1985-88 (Secretary, 1978-82); Member, Medicines Commission, 1986-95; President, Association of Physicians of Great Britain and Ireland, 1987-88. Recreations: golf; classical music. Address: (h.) 1 Godfrey Street, Barnhill, Dundee DD5 2QZ.

McDiarmid, Donald, BL, NP, DL. Consultant, Stewart and Bennett, Solicitors, Dunoon, since 1993 (Partner, 1959-93); Tutor, Glasgow University Department of Law, since 1997; b. 16.11.33, Glasgow; m., Audrey Mary McIntosh; 2 d. Educ. Dunoon Grammar School; Loretto School; Glasgow University. Recreations: gardening; tapestry; researching and lecturing on murders with local interest. Address: (h.) Pembroke, 77 Hunter Street, Kirn, Dunoon PA23 8SR; T.-01369 702304.

MacDonald, Rev. Alex J., MA. Minister, Buccleuch and Greyfriars Free Church, Edinburgh, since 1993; b. 17.3.49, Kinbrace, Sutherland; m., Evelyn; 2 s.; 2 d. Educ. Golspie High School; Edinburgh University; Free Church College. Minister, Bishopbriggs Free Church, 1973-83; Chaplain, Woodlee Mental Hospital, 1973-78; Clerk, Training of the Ministry Committee, 1978-83; Minister, Bon Accord Free Church, Aberdeen, 1983-93; Free Church Chaplain/ Lecturer, Northern College, 1983-93; Supervisor, Free Church Youth Camps, 1987-98. Convener: Youth Committee, Free Church, 1993-94, Public Questions Committee, Free Church, 1994-97; Religious Representative, Edinburgh City Council Education Committee. Publications: Love Minus Zero, 1989; Creation in Crisis?, 1992. Recreations: song writing; hillwalking; playing football; Bob Dylan, Tolkien and C. S. Lewis freak. Address: 14 Gilmour Road, Edinburgh EH16 5NT; T.-0131-667 4651.

McDonald, Very Rev. Alexander, BA, CMIWS. Moderator of the General Assembly, Church of Scotland, 1997-98; General Secretary, Department of Ministry, Church of Scotland, since 1988; b. 5.11.37, Bishopbriggs; m., Essdale Helen McLeod; 2 s.; 1 d. Educ. Bishopbriggs Higher Grade School; Whitehill Senior Secondary School, Glasgow; Glasgow University and Trinity College. RAF, 1954-56; Management in timber trade: 1952-54, 1956-58; motor trade, 1958-62; student, 1962-68; Minister: St. David's Bathgate, 1968-74, St. Mark's, Old Hall, Paisley, 1974-88. Trustee, Scottish Television Staff Trust; wide range of involvement with Boys' Brigade in Scotland, Scottish Spastics, mentally handicapped children, ACCORD, Christian Aid and many others; President, Glasgow Bn., Boys' Brigade; Patron, Friends of Carronvale Boys' Brigade; regular broadcaster. Recreations: reading; walking; fishing. Address: Church of Scotland, 121 George Street, Edinburgh EH2 4YN; T.-0131-225 5722.

McDonald, Alexander John. Breed Secretary, Galloway Cattle Society, since 1990; b. 12.6.39, Fochabers. Educ. Milnes High School. RAF, 1958-90. Editor and Publsher, The Galloway Journal. Recreations: country pursuits; photography. Address: (b.) 15 New Market Street, Castle Douglas DG7 1HY; T.-01556 502753.

Macdonald, Alister Gordon, BSc, PhD, DSc. Reader in Physiology, Aberdeen University, since 1984; b. 25.1.40, London; m., Jennifer; 1 s.; 2 d. Educ. Boys' High School, Trowbridge, Wiltshire; Bristol University. University of East Anglia, 1963-69; joined Aberdeen University as Lecturer in Physiology, 1969. Publications: Physiological Aspects of Deep Sea Biology, 1975; Effects of High Pressure on Biological Systems, 1993. Recreations: hill-walking; badminton; music; Scottish country dancing. Address: (b.) Department of Biomedical Sciences, c/o Zoology Building, Tillydrone Avenue, Aberdeen AB24 2TZ; T.- Aberdeen 272399.

MacDonald, Allan, MA. Managing Director: MNE Television, since 1989, Corrodale Ltd., since 1988; (first) Chairman, CRANN Ltd; (first) Chairman, Federation of TAC, REALT, CRANN and Breton TV (independent sector for film/TV/radio in Celtic countries); b. 11.6.53, Eriskay; m., Marion Margaret; 1 d. Educ. St. Vincent's College, Langbank; Blairs College, Aberdeen; Glasgow University. Senior Producer, BBC Highland, Inverness; Senior Producer/Manager, BBC Radio Nan Eilean, Stornoway; Manager, BBC Highland, Inverness; Television Producer, BBC Scotland, Glasgow; Head of Gaelic Television, Grampian TV, 1992-94. Member, Board of Management, Lews Castle College, 1992-95. Address: (h.) 39 Hughenden Gardens, Hyndland, Glasgow G12 9YH.

Macdonald, Angus David, MA (Hons) (Cantab), DipEd. Headmaster, Lomond School, Helensburgh, since 1986; Chairman, Clan Donald Lands Trust; b. 9.10.50, Edinburgh; m., Isabelle Marjory Ross; 2 d. Educ. Portsmouth Grammar School; Cambridge University; Edinburgh University. Assistant Teacher, Alloa Academy, 1972-73; Assistant Teacher, Edinburgh Academy, 1973-82 (Exchange Teacher, King's School, Parramatta, NSW, 1978-79); George Watson's College, Edinburgh: Principal Teacher of Geography, 1982, Deputy Principal, 1982-86. Recreations: outdoor recreation; sport; piping; gardening. Address: 8 Millig Street, Helensburgh, Argyll; T.-01436 679204.

MacDonald, Very Rev. Canon Bernard Gordon. Parish Priest, St. Mary's, Fochabers, since 1997; b. 25.12.24, Dufftown. Educ. Blairs College, Aberdeen; St. Edmund's, Herts. Curate, St. Mary's, Aberdeen, 1948-54; Parish Priest: Holy Family, Mastrick, 1954-61, St. Lawrence's, Dingwall, and St. Joseph's, Invergordon, 1961-79, St. Ninian's, Inverness, 1979-89, St. Anne's, Thurso, and St. Joachim's, Wick, 1989-97. Recreations: English literature; bowling; golf; art. Address: St Mary's, 22 South Street, Fochabers IV32 7ED; T.-01343 820 285.

MacDonald, Calum Alasdair, PhD. MP (Labour), Western Isles, since 1987; Parliamentary Under-Secretary of State, Scottish Office, since 1997; b. 7.5.56, Stornoway. Address: (b.) House of Commons, London, SW1; T.-071-219 4609.

MacDonald, Professor Caroline Mary, BSc, PhD, CBiol, FIBiol. Assistant Principal, since 1997, and Professor and Head, Department of Biological Sciences, Paisley University, 1992-97; b. 4.9.51, Edinburgh; m., Alastair MacDonald; 2 d. Educ. Glasgow High School for Girls; Glasgow University. Lecturer/Senior Lecturer, Strathclyde University, 1983-92; Chairman, European Society for Animal Cell Technology, 1994-97 (Secretary and Treasurer, 1991-94); Chief Editor, Genetic Engineer and Biotechnologist; Member, Executive Committee, and Secretary, Heads of University Biological Sciences. Recreations: family; gardening; travel. Address: (b.) Department of Biological Sciences, Paisley University, High Street, Paisley PA1 2BE; T.-0141-848 3607.

MacDonald, Colin Cameron, BA. Under Secretary, Principal Establishment Officer, Scottish Office; b. 13.7.43, Glasgow; m., Kathryn Campbell; 1 s.; 1 d. Educ. Allan Glen's School; Strathclyde University. Scottish Development Department: Research Officer, Research Services, 1967-70, Senior Research Officer, Research

Services, 1970-71, Principal Research Officer, Central Planning Research Unit, 1971-75; Senior Principal Research Officer, Scottish Office Central Research Unit, 1975-81; Chief Research Officer, 1981-88; Assistant Secretary, Housing, 1988-91. Non-Executive Director, TSB Bank Scotland PLC, 1994-98. Recreations: tennis; fishing; music. Address: (b.) 16 Waterloo Place, Edinburgh EH1 3DN; T.-0131-244 3938.

Macdonald, David Robert, BSc (Hons), MBA. Director, Locate in Scotland; former Chief Executive, Enterprise Ayrshire; b. 10.4.51, Edinburgh; m., Mary Anne Turner; 2 d. Educ. Daniel Stewart's College, Edinburgh; University of Stirling; University of Strathclyde. Research Assistant, University of Dundee, 1974; Economic Analyst, West Midlands County Council, 1975-77; Head of Industrial Projects, Government of Papua New Guinea, 1978-81; Senior Economist, West Midlands County Council, 1982; Industrial Economist, Project Executive and Head of Service Industries, Scottish Development Agency, 1983-85; Director, Glasgow Action, 1985-91; Director, Glasgow Development Agency, 1991-93. Recreations: cycling; skiing; MGs; youth church; family. Address: (b.) Locate in Scotland, 120 Bothwell Street, Glasgow.

MacDonald, Rev. Donald, MA, BD. Minister, Free Church of Scotland, Carloway, Isle of Lewis, since 1964; Clerk, Free Western Synod, since 1974; b. 6.3.38, Glasgow; m., Mary Etta Macleod. Educ. Nicolson Institute, Stornoway; Aberdeen University; Free Church College; Edinburgh University. Served in Vancouver, Canada, 1970, Livonia, USA, 1991-92; Moderator, General Assembly of the Free Church of Scotland, 1992. Recreations: book collecting; music; gardening; hillwalking. Address: Free Church Manse, Carloway, Isle of Lewis HS2 9AG; T.-01851 643208.

MacDonald, Professor Donald Gordon, RD**, BDS, PhD, FRCPath, FDSRCPS(G). Professor of Oral Pathology, Glasgow University, since 1991; Consultant Oral Pathologist, Glasgow Dental Hospital, since 1974; b. 5.7.42, Glasgow; m., Emma Lindsay Cordiner; 2 s. Educ. Kelvinside Academy, Glasgow; Glasgow University. Assistant, then Lecturer, Glasgow University, 1964-69; Visiting Associate Professor in Oral Pathology, University of Illinois, 1969-70; Lecturer, Senior Lecturer, Reader in Oral Medicine and Pathology, Glasgow University, 1970-91; Editor, Glasgow Dental Journal, 1969-75; Honorary Consultant Forensic Odontologist, Strathclyde Police, since 1976; Vice President, Association of Head and Neck Oncologists of Great Britain, 1987-90; President, British Society for Oral Pathology, 1988-91; Vice Dean, Dental Faculty, RCPSGlas, since 1998; Commodore, Royal Naval Reserves, 1995-97. Recreations: golf; curling. Address: (h.) 2 Dougalston Gardens South, Milngavie, Glasgow; T.-0141-956 2075.

MacDonald, Donald John, BSc. Rector, Nicolson Institute, Stornoway, since 1989; b. 25.5.39, Glasgow; 1 s.; 2 d. Educ. Hill's Trust School, Glasgow; Lionel School, Lewis; Govan High School, Glasgow; Glasgow University; Jordanhill College of Education. Teacher of Science, Govan High School; Principal Teacher of Physics: Kirkwall Grammar School, Govan High School; Assistant Head, Linwood High School; Depute Rector, Dingwall Academy; Assistant Divisional Education Officer, Highland Region; Rector, Thurso High School, 1980-89. Address: (b.) Springfield Road, Stornoway PA87 2PZ.

MacDonald, Professor Donald Murray, MB, ChB, FRCS(Edin), Dip.Theol. Moderator, Free Church of Scotland, 1997; Professor of Apologetics and Practical Theology, Free Church College, Edinburgh, since 1997; b. 16.1.44, Kildonan, Sutherland; m., Joan; 1 s.; 3 d. Educ. Golspie Senior Secondary School; Edinburgh University. Medical and surgical training posts, Edinburgh area, 1967-73; Medical Superintendent, Lakhnadon Christian Hospital, Seoni District, India, 1973-88; divinity training, Free Church College, 1988-90; Minister Bishopbriggs Free Church of Scotland, 1990-97. Address: (b.) Free Church College, The Mound, Edinburgh EH1 2LS; T.-0131-226 5286.

Macdonald, Rev. Finlay Angus John, MA, BD, PhD. Principal Clerk, General Assembly of the Church of Scotland; b. 1.7.45, Watford; m., Elizabeth Mary Stuart; 2 s. Educ. Dundee High School; St. Andrews University. Assistant Minister, Bo'ness Old Kirk, 1970-71; Minister, Menstrie Parish Church, 1971-77; Junior Clerk and Treasurer, Stirling and Dunblane Presbytery, 1973-77; Minister, Jordanhill Parish Church, Glasgow, 1977-96; Convener, General Assembly Board of Practice and Procedure, 1988-92; Convener, General Assembly Business Committee, 1989-92; Depute Clerk, General Assembly, 1993-96. Recreations: music; hill-walking; reading; gardening. Address: (b.) 121 George Street, Edinburgh EH2 4YN; T.-0131-225 5722.

Macdonald, Fiona Margaret Taylor, LLB, NP. Solicitor, since 1981; Member, Western Isles Health Board, since 1993; b. 14.4.56, Glasgow; m., Norman Lewis Macdonald; 1 s. Educ. Hillpark Secondary School; Dundee University. Solicitor, Inverclyde District Council, 1981-83; Solicitor, Bird Semple & Crawford Heron, Stornoway, 1983-89; Solicitor, Western Isles Islands Council, 1989-98. Member, Council, Law Society of Scotland, 1992-96. Recreation: founder member, Goathill Ceilidh Band. Address: (h.) Valasay, Goathill Crescent, Stornoway HS1 2TA; T.-01851 70 6364.

Macdonald, Gibson Torbett. Conservative Group Leader, South Ayrshire Council; b. 21.1.33; m., Muirkirk; m., Mary Hastings Logan Lambie; 1 s.; 1 d. Educ. Kilmarnock Academy. National President, Junior Chamber Scotland; Executive Vice President, Junior Chamber International; Chairman, Ayr Branch, Ayr Conservative Association; Chairman, Ayr Conservative Constituency; Town Councillor, Royal Burgh of Ayr; District Councillor, Kyle and Carrick District (Provost, 1984-88 and 1992-96; held Convenership of Planning, Employment and Policy and Resources Committees); Chairman, Culzean Country Park Joint Committee; Member, COSLA Planning and Town Twinning Committees. Treasurer, Ayrshire Decorative and Fine Arts Society; Past President, Ayr Town Twinning Association; Secretary, Franco Scottish Society (Ayrshire); President, Ayr Chamber of Commerce, 1990-92; Dean of Guildry, 1991-92; Vice-President, Ayrshire Chamber of Commerce and Industry, since 1993. Recreations: bowling; bridge; computing; philately. Address: (h.) 14 Belmont Avenue, Ayr KA7 2JN.

Macdonald, 8th Baron, (Godfrey James Macdonald of Macdonald). Chief of the Name and Arms of Macdonald; b. 28.11.47; m., Claire Catlow; 1 s.; 3 d. Address: (h.) Kinloch Lodge, Isle of Skye.

Macdonald of Tradeston, Lord (Gus Macdonald), CBE. Minister for Business and Industry, Scottish Office, since 1998; Television Journalist; b. 20.8.40, Larkhall; m., Teen; 2 d. Educ. Allan Glen's School, Glasgow. Marine engineer, Stephens, Linthouse, 1955-62; Circulation Manager, Tribune, 1963-65; Journalist, The Scotsman, 1965-67; World in Action, Granada, 1967-75; successively Head of Current Affairs, Head of Regional Programmes, Head of Features, Granada, 1975-82; C4 Viewers Ombudsman, Right to Reply, 1982-88; Scottish Television: Director of Programmes, 1986-90, Managing Director, 1990-96; Chairman, Scottish Television, subsequently Scottish Media Group plc, 1996-98; BAFTA Awards: Best Factual Series, 1973; Lifetime Achievement Award, 1997; Scottish Business Elite Awards: Business Leader of the Year, Chairman of the Year, 1997; founder Chairman, Edinburgh

International Telvision Festival, 1976; Visiting Professor, Film and Media Studies, Stirling University, 1985-98; Chairman, Edinburgh International Film Festival, 1993-96; Governor, National Film and Television School, 1986-97; Member, Boards: Scottish Screen, 1997, British Film Institute, 1997-98; Chairman, Cairngorms Partnership, 1997-98; Chairman, Taylor and Francis Group plc, 1997-98. Recreations: words; music; pictures; sports; hills.

Macdonald, Hugh Robert Nichol, BMus, MLitt, ARCO. Director, BBC Scottish Symphony Orchestra, since 1997; b. 11.10.48, Haddington; m., Elizabeth Jane Boase; 1 s.; 1 d. Educ. Royal High School of Edinburgh; Edinburgh University; Royal College of Music; Amsterdam University. Assistant Lecturer in Music, Hitchin College, 1971-72; Lecturer in Musicology, School of Scottish Studies, Edinburgh University, 1974-75; Assistant Lecturer in Music, Chinese University of Hong Kong, 1976-79; Lecturer in Music, Stirling University, 1979-85; Music Producer (Radio), BBC Scotland/Radio 3, 1985-88; Producer, BBC Scottish Symphony Orchestra, 1988-91; Head of Music, BBC Scotland, 1991-97. Address: (b.) BBC Scotland, Queen Margaret Drive, Glasgow G12 8DG; T.-0141-338 2606.

Macdonald, Ian Hamish, OBE, FCIBS, CIMight; b. 30.12.26, Inverness; m., Patricia Lace; 1 d. Educ. Inverness Royal Academy; Inverness Technical High School. RAFVR, 1944; Queen's Own Cameron Highlanders, 1945 (Hon. Captain, 1948); Mercantile Bank, 1948-59; The Hongkong and Shanghai Banking Corporation: Manager, 1959-72, General Manager, India, 1972-73, General Manager International, 1973-80, Executive Director, 1980-83; Chairman, Hongkong Bank of Canada, 1981-83; Chief General Manager, TSB Scotland, 1983-86, and TSB Scotland PLC, 1986-87; Director, TSB Group PLC, 1986-87; Director, Scottish Power PLC, 1987-92; Chairman, Clairmont PLC, 1987-91, First Edinburgh Homes PLC, 1988-92, EFM Dragon Trust, 1987-92, Scottish Council Foundation, 1983-92; Director, Macdonald Orr, 1987-93, TSB Northern Ireland PLC, 1987-92, Morgan Grenfell Scotland Ltd., 1987-91, AIB Group Northern Ireland PLC, 1992-96; Member, Court, Edinburgh University, 1989-92; former Chairman, Clan Donald Lands Trust. Recreations: fishing; golf; bridge. Address: (h.) Minewood Cottage, 11 Abercromby Drive, Bridge of Allan, FK9 4EA.

Macdonald, Professor Ian Robert, MA, PhD. Senior Vice-Principal, and Professor in Spanish, Aberdeen University, since 1991; b. 4.5.39, The Hague; m., Frances Mary; 3 s. Educ. Whitgift School; St. Andrews University. United Steel Cos. Ltd., 1961-64; research student, 1964-65; Lecturer, then Senior Lecturer, Aberdeen University, 1965-90. Recreations: walking; digging; carpentry. Address: (h.) 47 North Deeside Road, Peterculter, Aberdeenshire; T.-01224 732284.

McDonald, Sheriff Iona Sara, MA, LLB, NP. Solicitor, since 1980; Partner, Mathie Morton Black and Buchanan, Ayr, since 1984; Temporary Sheriff (all Scotland jurisdiction), since 1994; Honorary Sheriff, Ayr Sheriff Court, since 1997; b. 18.11.54; m., Colin Neale McDonald; 1 s.; 1 d. Educ. Cumnock Academy; Glasgow University. Apprentice Solicitor, Cannon Orpin and Co., Glasgow, 1978-80; joined Mathie Morton Black and Buchanan, Ayr, 1980. Safeguarder; Reporter to the Court and Curator Ad Litem in adoption hearings. Address: (b.) Mathie Morton Black and Buchanan, 4 Alloway Place, Ayr KA7 2AD; T.-01292 263549.

McDonald, Rev. James Ian Hamilton, MA, BD, MTh, PhD, FEIS. Honorary Fellow, Edinburgh University, since 1998; Reader in Christian Ethics and New Testament Studies, Edinburgh University, 1992-98; b. 7.2.33, Stonehouse; m., Jenny Paterson Fleming. Educ. Rutherglen Academy; Glasgow University; Edinburgh University. Parish Minister, Johnstone West; Baird Research Fellow in Christian Education; Lecturer in Religious Education, Moray House, Edinburgh; Lecturer in Christian Ethics and Practical Theology, then Senior Lecturer in Christian Ethics and New Testament, Edinburgh University; Associate Dean, Faculty of Divinity, 1991-94; Head, Department of Christian Ethics, since 1995; Convener, Church of Scotland Education Committee, 1985-89; Honorary President, Scottish Church Theology Society, 1997. Recreations: walking; reading; painting. Address: (b.) New College, Mound Place, Edinburgh EH1 2LX; T.-0131-650 8923.

McDonald, Professor Janet B.I., MA, FRSE, FRSAMD, FRSA. Professor of Drama, Glasgow University, since 1979; b. 28.7.41, Netherlee, Renfrewshire; m., Ian James McDonald; 1 d. Educ. Hutchesons' Girls' Grammar School; Glasgow University. Member: Governing Body, Royal Scottish Academy of Music and Drama, 1979-94, Academic Council, since 1994, Board, Citizens' Theatre, 1979-82 and since 1989 (Chair, since 1991); Member, Glasgow University Court, 1991-94; Council Member, Royal Society of Edinburgh, since 1994; Chairman: Drama and Theatre Board, Council for National Academic Awards, 1981-85, Standing Committee of University Departments of Drama, 1982-85, Drama Committee, Scottish Arts Council, 1985-88; Chair, Creative and Performing Arts Committee, CNAA, 1989-91. Address: (b.) Gilmorehill Centre for Theatre, Film and Television, University of Glasgow; T.-0141-330 5162.

Macdonald, John. Editor, Inverness Courier, since 1991; b. 6.4.45, Haddington; m., Jean Nimmo; 1 d. Educ. Dunbar Grammar School. Reporter, Haddingtonshire Courier, 1961-65; Assistant Editor, Barrow News series, 1965-68; Editor, Linlithgow Journal & Gazette, 1968-73; Editor, Lincolnshire Chronicle, 1973-75; Chief Sub-Editor, Farmers Weekly, 1975-77; Senior Editor, Reader's Digest, 1977-82; Executive Editor, Telegraph Sunday Magazine, 1982-86; Sub-Editor, The Times, 1986-89; Editor, Northern Scot, 1989-91. Publications: Great Battlefields of the World; Great Battles of World War II; Great Battles of the American Civil War. Recreations: military history; photography; travel. Address: (b.) 12-14 Seafield Road, Inverness IV1 1SG; T.-01463 233059.

Macdonald, Father John Angus, STB, MA, MLitt. Parish Priest, Fort William, and R.E. Adviser, Diocese of Argyll and the Isles, since 1991; Member: Scottish Catholic Education Commission,1993-96, Rural Forum Action Network for Scotland, since 1997; Commissioner for South Argyll, Argyll Islands and Southern Isles, Crofters Commission, 1992-98; Treasurer, Burns–Gaelic Trust, since 1997; b. 6.12.45, Askernish, South Uist. Educ. Daliburgh J.S. School; St. Mary's College, Blairs; Royal Scots College, Spain (Comillas University); Aberdeen University. Ordained, 1970; Curate, 1970-72; Staff, St. Mary's College, Blairs, 1972-83, Depute Rector, 1978-83; Administrator, St. Mary's, Arisaig, 1983-85; Parish Priest: St. Mary's, Bornish, 1985-87, St. Peter's, Daliburgh, 1987-91. School Board Member, Fort William R.C. School, since 1991; Editor, Crann, Aberdeen University Celtic Society magazine, 1974-78; Spanish language translator for Concilium, 1981-90; Member: Western Isles Islands Council Education Committee, 1985-91, Gaelic Advisory Committee, BBC, 1986-90, Western Isles Health Board, 1989-92. Recreations: music; reading; local and church history; hill-walking; languages; DIY. Address: (h.) St. Mary's, Belford Road, Fort William PH33 6BT; T.-01397 702174.

MacDonald, Major-General John Donald, CB, CBE, DL. General Secretary, Royal British Legion Scotland, and The Earl Haig Fund Scotland; b. 5.4.38; m., Mary Warrack; 1 s.; 2 d. Educ. George Watson's College, Edinburgh; RMA, Sandhurst; RMCS, Shrivenham; DSSC, India; National Defence College, Latimer. Commissioned King's Own

Scottish Borderers, 1958, RASC, 1963, Royal Corps of Transport, 1976-78; Commander, Armd. Division Transport Regiment, BAOR, 1978-80 (Lt.-Col.); Exchange Instructor, Australian Army Cmd. and Staff College, 1980-82; Head of Personnel and Logistics, Armd. Division, BAOR, 1983-86 (Col.); Head of Personnel and Officer for Human Resources, MoD, London, 1987-88; Distribution and Transport Director, 1 Br Corps, BAOR, 1988-91 (Brigadier); Director General, Transport and Movement (Distribution), Army, 1991-93 (Major-General). FCIT; FILDM. Recreations: travel; music; art; rugby (internationalist); athletics (internationalist); golf; skiing. Address: (b.) New Haig House, Logie Green Road, Edinburgh EH7 4HR.

Macdonald, Kenneth, LLB. Education and Science Correspondent, BBC Scotland, since 1993; b. 11.7.57, Paisley; m., Alyson Mitchell; 1 d. Educ. Paisley Grammar School. Reporter: St. Andrews Citizen, 1978-81, Fife Leader, 1981; Broadcaster: West Sound, 1981-82, Radio Tay, 1982; BBC Radio Scotland: Broadcaster, 1982-84, Reporter, Dundee, 1984-89, Executive Producer, 1989-93; Senior Assistant, Editorial Policy, BBC Policy and Planning Unit, London, 1991-92. BBC Alexander Onassis Bursary, 1988; Honorary President, Scottish Association of Geography Teachers. Recreations: music; history; laughter. Address: (b.) Broadcasting House, Queen Margaret Drive, Glasgow G12 8DG; T.-0141-339 8844.

MacDonald, Margo. Freelance journalist and broadcaster; b. Hamilton; m., Jim Sillars; 1 step s.; 2 d.; 1 step-d. Educ. Hamilton Academy; Dunfermline College. Teacher, 1963-65; barmaid and mother, 1965-73; Member of Parliament, 1973-74; Broadcaster/Writer, 1974-78; Director, Shelter, Scotland, 1978-81; Radio Forth: Broadcaster, 1981-83, Editor, Topical Programmes, 1983-85; political and current affairs broadcasting as reporter/presenter, 1985-91; former Chief Executive, Network Scotland.

Macdonald, Professor Murdo, MA, PhD, LCAD, FRSA. Professor of History of Scottish Art, University of Dundee, since 1997; b. 25.1.55, Edinburgh. Educ. Hammersmith College of Art; University of Edinburgh. Commissioning Editor, Polygon Books, 1982-94; freelance art school and university lecturing, 1986-90; freelance Art Critic (mainly for The Scotsman), 1987-92; Editor, Edinburgh Review, 1990-94; Lecturer and Adviser in Scottish Studies, Centre for Continuing Education, University of Edinburgh, 1990-97. Trustee, Sir Patrick Geddes Memorial Trust. Publications: papers on Sir Patrick Geddes; Scottish Art (in press). Recreation; hill-walking. Address: Department of History, University of Dundee, Dundee DD1 4HN; T.-01382 344516.

Macdonald, Rev. Professor Murdo Ewen, MA, BD, DD (St. Andrews), DD (McGill University). Emeritus Professor, Trinity College, Glasgow University; b. 28.8.14, Isle of Harris; 2 s. Educ. Sir Edward Scott School, Harris; Kingussie Secondary School; St. Andrews University. Minister, Portree, Isle of Skye, 1939-40; Chaplain to 4th Camerons, 1940-42; Chaplain to 2nd Paras, 1942; wounded and taken prisoner, North Africa, and spent rest of War in Germany (acted as Chaplain to American Air Force); awarded Bronze Star; Pollock Lecturer in Preaching, Canada; Syme Lecturer in Theology and Preaching, Lutheran Colleges, USA; Ferrie Lecturer in Preaching and Theology, Australia. Publications: Vitality of Faith; Need to Believe; Call to Obey; Crisis of Belief; Call to Communicate; Lost Provinces of Religion; Padre Mac, The Man from Harris. Address: (h.) 68 Lauderdale Gardens, Glasgow, G12 9QW; T.-041-334 2087.

MacDonald, Norman Hamilton, FRSA, FSAScot. Chairman, The 1745 Association, 1991-97; President, Clan Donald Society of Edinburgh, since 1993; President, Edinburgh Gaelic Choir, 1995-97; b. 4.3.33, Edinburgh; m., Morag Young McKenzie. Educ. Royal High School, Edinburgh. RAF, 1953-55; accountancy, 1955-63; S.E. Regional Hospital Board, 1963-67; Edinburgh Corporation, later Edinburgh District Council, 1967-91 (retired). Editor, Clan Donald Magazine. Publications: histories of MacDonalds of Glengarry and Keppoch; two cassette recordings of Gaelic and Scots songs. Address: (h.) Ceapach, 8 Ethel Terrace, Edinburgh EH10 5NB: T.-0131-447 3970.

Macdonald, Norman Malcolm. Writer and Dramatist; b. 24.7.27, Thunder Bay, Canada; m., Mairi F. Educ. Nicolson Institute; Newbattle Abbey College. New Zealand Air Force, 1949-57; journalism and administration at various periods; Administrator and Writer, Fir Chlis (Gaelic theatre company), 1978-80; Secretary and Writer in Residence, Sabhal Mor Ostaig Gaelic College, 1982-83. Publications: Calum Tod (novel); An Sgaineadh (novel); Fad (poetry); Bathach Chaluim, Anna Chaimbeul, The Catechist, The Brahan Seer, Sublime Savage, Aimhreit Aignis, The Teuchtar's Tale, Or an Amadain, Ordugh na Saorsa, Beul Nam Breug (plays); Call Na h'Iolaire, Clann-Nighean a Sgadain (historical); The Shutter Falls (television); Portrona Community Play, 1996. Recreation: walking. Address: 14 Tong, Isle of Lewis.

Macdonald, Peter Cameron, DL, SDA. Vice-President, Scottish Landowners' Federation, since 1990 (Convener, 1985-88); Farmer, 1961-96; Director, J. Dickson & Son, Gunmakers, since 1968, Chairman, since 1997; b. 14.12.37, Edinburgh; m., Barbara Helen Drimmie Ballantyne; 2 step-s. Educ. Loretto; East of Scotland College of Agriculture. Council Member: Scottish Landowners Federation, since 1976, Blackface Sheepbreeders Association, 1970-74; Member, Forth River Purification Board, 1979-87; Director, Royal Highland and Agricultural Society of Scotland, 1985; Deputy Lieutenant, West Lothian, since 1987. Recreations: fishing; shooting; golf. Address: Waterheads, Eddleston, Peeblesshire EH45 8QX; T.-01721 730229.

Macdonald, Rhoda Mairi, MA. Head of Gaelic, Scottish Television, since 1991; b. 18.10.58, Stornoway. Educ. Nicolson Institute, Stornoway; Glasgow University; Jordanhill College. Freelance Television Presenter, 1979-88; Scottish Television: Researcher, 1988, Programme Executive, Gaelic, 1989. Director, Scottish Television Enterprises. Recreations: reading; cinema; cooking. Address: (b.) Scottish Television, Cowcaddens, Glasgow G2 3PR; T.-0141-332 9999.

McDonald, Hon. Lord (Robert Howat McDonald), MC (1944), MA, LLB. Senator of the College of Justice in Scotland, 1973-89; b. 15.5.16, Paisley; m., Barbara Mackenzie. Educ. John Neilson Institution, Paisley; Glasgow University. Admitted Solicitor, 1938; KOSB, 1939-46 (mentioned in Despatches); admitted, Faculty of Advocates, 1946; QC (Scot), 1957; Sheriff of Ayr and Bute, 1966-71; Member, Criminal Injuries Compensation Board, 1964-71; Chairman: Mental Welfare Commission for Scotland, 1964-83, General Nursing Council for Scotland, 1970-73. Address: (h.) 5 Doune Terrace, Edinburgh EH3 6EA.

Macdonald, Roderick, BSc(Agri), MSc. Member, Scottish Land Court, since 1986; b. 6.2.27, Benbecula; m., Elizabeth MacLeod; 3 d. Educ. Portree High School; Aberdeen University; Michigan State University, USA. Bayer Agriculture, 1952-54; Lands Division, Department of Agriculture and Fisheries for Scotland, 1954-67 and 1972-86, latterly as Assistant Chief; Head, Land Development Division, Highlands and Islands Development Board, 1967-72; appointed Gaelic Speaking Member, Scottish Land Court, 1986; Trustee and Surveyor, Glebes Committee, Church of Scotland, since 1994; Secretary, Highland Fund, since 1993. Recreations: golf; fiddle playing; fishing. Address: 19 Cherrytree Loan, Balerno, Edinburgh; T.-0131-449 3600.

Macdonald, Rt. Rev. Mgr. Roderick, STL. Parish Priest, Glencoe/Kinlochleven, since 1990; Delegate to Diocesan Administrator, since 1996; b. 4.11.25, Mallaig. Educ. Blairs College, Aberdeen; Gregorian University, Rome. Assistant, St. Columba's Cathedral, Oban, 1950-56, St. Peter's, Daliburgh, South Uist, 1956-58; Parish Priest: St. Mun's, Glencoe, 1958-62, St. Kieran's, Campbeltown, 1962-69, St. Mun's, Dunoon, 1969-90. Address: (b.) St. Mun's, Ballachulish, Argyll PA39 4JG; T.-01855 811203.

Macdonald, Vice-Admiral Sir Roderick (Douglas), KBE (1978). Painter; b. 25.2.21, Java; m., 1, Joan Willis (m. diss.); 2 s.; 1 s. deceased; 2, Mrs Pamela Bartosik (nee Bowman). Educ. Fettes (Captain, Scottish Schoolboys' rugby, 1937-38). Entered Royal Navy, 1939; served at sea throughout War, 1939-45: Norway, Battle of Atlantic, Malta convoys, Indian Ocean, Normandy and East Coast convoys; Comd. six HM ships, one minesweeper and two frigate squadrons; Cyprus (Despatches, 1957); Commander, Naval Forces Borneo, 1965 (CBE); Captain of the Fleet, 1970; COS to C-in-C, Naval Home Command, 1973-76; ADC to The Queen, 1975; COS to Comdr., Allied Naval Forces Southern Europe, 1976-79. Chieftain, Skye Highland Games; President, Skye Piping Society; Fellow, Nautical Institute (Vice-President, 1976-85); Trustee and Executive, Clan Donald Lands Trust; President, Inverness Sea Cadets Unit; own exhibitions, Naples, Edinburgh (2), London (5). Publication: The Figurehead, 1993. Recreations: sailing; Highland bagpipe, gardening. Address: (h.) Ollach, Braes, Skye IV51 9LJ.

MacDonald, Professor Ronald, BA, MA, PhD. Professor of International Finance, Strathclyde University, since 1993; b. 23.4.55, Glasgow. Educ. Falkirk High School; Heriot Watt University; Manchester University. Midland Bank Fellow in Monetary Economics, Loughborough University, 1982-84; Lecturer in Economics, Aberdeen University, 1984-88; Senior Lecturer, 1988-89; Robert Fleming Professor of Finance and Investment, Dundee University, 1989-93; Visiting Professor, Queen's University, Canada, 1988, University of New South Wales, Australia, 1989, European University Institute, Florence; Visiting Scholar, International Monetary Fund, Washington DC, since 1991; Consultant to the European Commission. Publications: Floating Exchange Rates; International Money: theory evidence and institutions (Co-Author); five co-edited books; over 100 journal articles. Recreations: music; photography; hill-walking. Address: (b.) Department of Economics, Strathclyde University, Glasgow, G4 0LN; T.-0141-548 3861.

McDonald, Sheena Elizabeth, MA. Television and Radio Broadcaster/Producer. Educ. George Watson's Ladies' College; Edinburgh University; Bristol University. BBC Radio Scotland, 1978-81; Scottish Television, 1981-87; Radio Presenter: The World At One, The World This Weekend, Beyond the Millennium, Mediumwave, BBC Radio; Television Presenter: Channel 4 News, House to House, McLibel, Midnight Special, Power and the People, Right to Reply, Channel 4 Television. Address: (b.) Curtis Brown, 28/9 Haymarket, London SW1Y 4SP.

MacDonald, Professor Simon Gavin George, MA, PhD, FInstP, FRSE; b. 5.9.23, Beauly, Inverness-shire; m., Eva Leonie Austerlitz; 1 s.; 1 d. Educ. George Heriot's, Edinburgh; Edinburgh University. Junior Scientific Officer, Royal Aircraft Establishment, Farnborough, 1943-46; Lecturer in Physics, St. Andrews University, 1948-57; Senior Lecturer in Physics: University College of the West Indies, 1957-62, St. Andrews University, 1962-67; Dundee University: Senior Lecturer in Physics, 1967-73, Professor of Physics, 1973-88, Dean of Science, 1970-73, Vice-Principal, 1974-79, Head, Department of Physics, 1979-85; Chairman, Statistics Committee, Universities Central Council on Admissions, 1989-93; Member, Scottish Universities Council on Entrance, 1969-82 (Vice-Convener, 1973-77, Convener, 1977-82); Chairman, Technical Committee, UCCA, 1979-83; Deputy Chairman, UCCA, 1983-89; Chairman, Board of Directors, Dundee Repertory Theatre, 1975-89. Publications: Problems and Solutions in General Physics; Physics for Biology and Premedical Students; Physics for the Life and Health Sciences. Recreations: bridge; golf; fiction writing. Address: (h.) 7A Windmill Road, St Andrews KY16 9JJ; T.-01334 478014.

McDonald, Thomas, MA. Headteacher, All Saints Secondary School, Glasgow, since 1998; b. 28.7.53, Helensburgh; m., Carol; 2 s. Educ. St. Patrick's High School, Dumbarton; University of Glasgow; Jordanhill College. Teacher of Modern Languages, St. Patrick's High School, Dumbarton, 1976-82; Principal Teacher of Modern Languages, St. Andrew's High School, Clydebank, 1982-89; Assistant Head Teacher, St. Mungo's Academy, Glasgow, 1989-96; Depute Head Teacher, Bellarmine R.C. Secondary School, Glasgow 1996-98. Address: (b.) 21 Scotsburn Road, Glasgow G21 3HX; T.-0141-558 1241.

McDonald, William, JP, CA. Bursar, The Carnegie Trust for the Universities of Scotland, since 1990; b. 9.11.29, Perth; m., Anne Kidd Laird McDonald; 1 s.; 1 d. Educ. Perth Academy. RAF, 1952-54; Secretary, South Mills and Grampian Investment, Dundee, 1957-62; The Company of Merchants of the City of Edinburgh: Chamberlain, 1962-90, Secretary, 1971-90; Clerk and Treasurer, Incorporation of Guildry in Edinburgh, 1975-90; Joint Secretary, Scottish Council of Independent Schools, 1978-90. Scout Association: Deputy Chief Commissioner of Scotland, 1977-79, Hon. Treasurer, Scotland, 1989-93, Chairman, UK Finance Sub-Committee, 1993-98, Hon. Treasurer, European Scout Region (Geneva), since 1995; Member, High Constables of Edinburgh, since 1982; Chairman: Scottish Environmental and Outdoor Education Centres, 1987-92, Lothian Valuation Appeal Committee, since 1995. Recreations: Scout Association; bridge. Address (h.) 1/3 Wyvern Park, The Grange, Edinburgh EH9 2JY; T.-0131-662 4145.

McDonald, Very Rev. William James Gilmour, MA, BD, Hon. DD (Edinburgh); b. 3.6.24, Edinburgh; m., Patricia Watson; 1 s.; 2 d. Educ. Daniel Stewart's College; Edinburgh University; Gottingen University. Royal Artillery and Indian Artillery, 1943-46; Parish Minister, Limekilns, 1953-59; Minister, Mayfield Parish Church, Edinburgh, 1959-92; Convener, Assembly Council, 1984-87; Moderator, General Assembly of Church of Scotland, 1989-90. Chaplain, Edinburgh Merchant Company; Chaplain, National Trust for Scotland; Hon. Chaplain, Loretto School; Warrack Lecturer, 1993-95; Turnbull Trust Preacher, Melbourne, 1993-94. Address: (h.) 7 Blacket Place, Edinburgh EH9 1RN; T.-0131-667 2100.

MacDonell of Glengarry, Air Cdre. Aeneas Ranald Donald, CB, DFC. 22nd Chief of Glengarry; Member, Standing Council of Scottish Chiefs; Trustee, Clan Donald Lands Trust; Trustee, Finlaggan Trust; b. 15.11.13, Baku, Russia; m., 1, Diana Dorothy Keane; 2 s.; 1 d.; 2, Lois Eirene Frances Streatfeild; 1 s.; 1 d. Educ. Hurtspierpoint College; Royal Air Force College, Cranwell. RAF Officer, 1931-64; seconded to Fleet Air Arm, 1935-37; Flying Instructor, 1938-39; Air Ministry; Officer Commanding Spitfire Squadron during Battle of Britain; POW, Germany, 1941-45; Chief Flying Instructor, RAF College, Cranwell; Air Attache, Moscow, 1956-58; Director of Management and Work Study, Ministry of Defence, 1960-64; retired from RAF; Construction Industry Training Board, 1967-72; Head, Commercial Department, Industrial Society, 1972-76; Partner, John Courtis & Partners, Management Selection Consultants; finally retired and moved to

Scotland, 1981. Honorary President, Ross and Cromarty Branch, Soldiers', Sailors' and Airmen's Families Association, 1983-86. Recreation: bird watching. Address: (h.) Elonbank, 23 Castle Street, Fortrose, Ross-shire IV10 8TH; T.-01381 620121.

Macdonell, Hamish Alasdair, BA (Hons). Political Editor, Scottish Daily Mail, since 1998; b. 5.1.68, Inverness. Educ. Fettes College, Edinburgh; University of York. Reporter, Yorkshire Evening Press, 1990-94; freelance journalist, Africa and Australia, 1994-95; Press Association: Parliamentary Reporter, 1995-97, Scottish Political Editor, 1997-98. Recreations: golf; fishing. Address: 24b Albany Street, Edinburgh EH1 3QB; T.-0141-553 4600.

McDonnell, Michael Anthony, BD, DipCE, FIRSO. Road Safety Manager (Scotland), ROSPA, since 1990; Secretary, Scottish Accident Prevention Council, since 1990; b. 13.5.55, Bellshill; m., Rosemary Boyle; 1 s. Educ. St. Patrick's High School, Coatbridge; Hamilton College of Education; Chesters College, Glasgow. Strathclyde Regional Council, 1976-81, 1982-83, 1988-90, latterly as Assistant Road Safety Training Officer. Recreations: football; golf; cinema. Address: (b.) Slateford House, 53 Lanark Road, Edinburgh EH14 1TL; T.-0131-455 7457.

McDougall, Professor Bonnie S., BA, MA, PhD. Professor of Chinese, Edinburgh University, since 1990; b. 12.3.41, Sydney; m., A. Hansson; 1 s. Educ. University of Sydney. Lecturer in Chinese, University of Sydney; Nuffield Fellow, London University; Visiting Lecturer, Harvard University; editor, translator and teacher, Peking; Professor of Modern Chinese, University of Oslo. President, British Association of Chinese Studies. Recreations: reading; travelling. Address: (b.) School of Asian Studies, Edinburgh University, 8 Buccleuch Place, Edinburgh EH8 9LW; T.-0131-650 4227.

McDougall, Douglas Christopher Patrick, MA. Investment Manager; Senior Partner, Baillie Gifford & Co., since 1989; Chairman, Investment Management Regulatory Organisation, since 1997; b. 18.3.44, Edinburgh; m., Hon. Carolyn Griffiths; 2 d. Educ. Edinburgh Academy; Christ Church, Oxford. Baillie Gifford & Co.: joined, 1965; Partner, 1969; Chairman: Association of Investment Trust Companies, 1995-97, Institutional Fund Managers Association, 1993-95; Director: Baillie Gifford Japan Trust, since 1989, Pacific Horizon Trust, since 1993, Provincial Insurance, 1989-94; Member, Investments Committee, Cambridge University. Address: (b.) 1 Rutland Court, Edinburgh EH3 8EY; T.-0131-222 4000.

MacDougall, James Taylor, CBE; b. 14.5.30, Perth; m., Fiona; 1 d. Educ. Perth Academy; St. Andrews University (University College, Dundee).. Admitted as a Solicitor, 1953; National Service, commissioned Royal Armoured Corps (3 Royal Tank Regiment), 1953-55; private practice/local government, 1955-59; Procurator Fiscal Depute at Dumfries, 1959-69; Procurator Fiscal: at Elgin, 1969-76, at Dumfries, 1976-93 (including Kirkcudbright, 1987-93); Honorary Sheriff at Dumfries, since 1995. Recreations: fishing; shooting; colour photography. Address: (h.) Wheatyards, Torthorwald, Dumfries DG1 3QE; T.-01387 750683.

MacDougall, John William, JP, FIIM. Convener, Fife Council, since 1996; Leader of Administration, Fife Regional Council, 1987-96; Trustee, St. Andrews Links Trust; Member, Court, St. Andrews University; b. 8.12.47, Dunfermline; m., Catherine; 1 s.; 1 d. Educ. Templehall Secondary Modern; Rosyth Dockyard College; Fife College; Glenrothes College. Vice-President/Treasurer, Assembly of European Regions; Member, COSLA International Affairs Committee; former Board Member: Glenrothes Development Corporation, Fife Enterprise Company; Founder Member and Chairman, East of Scotland European Consortium. Recreations: DIY; sport. Address: (b.) Fife House, North Street, Glenrothes, Fife; T.-01592 414141, Ext. 6209.

McDougall, Peter. Screenwriter; b. 1947, Greenock. Television and film work includes: Just Another Saturday, 1974 (Prix Italia); Elephant's Graveyard, 1976; Just A Boy's Game, 1979; Shoot for the Sun, 1985; Down Where The Buffalo Go, 1988; Down Among The Big Boys, 1993.

MacDougall, Robert Hugh, MB, ChB, DMRT, FRCS, FRCR, FRCPEdin. Clinical Director, Department of Clinical Oncology, Western General Hospitals, Edinburgh, and Honorary Senior Lecturer in Clinical Oncology, Edinburgh University, since 1986; Honorary Senior Lecturer, St. Andrews University; b. 9.8.49, Dundee; m., Moira Jean Gray; 1 s.; 2 d. Educ. High School of Dundee; St. Andrews University; Edinburgh University. Demonstrator in Anatomy, St. Andrews University; Registrar in Surgery, Aberdeen Royal Infirmary; Lecturer in Clinical Oncology, Edinburgh University; Consultant Radiotherapist and Oncologist, Tayside Health Board. Recreation: reading. Address: (b.) Department of Clinical Oncology, Western General Hospital, Edinburgh.

McDowall, Linda, MA. Chief Executive, East Kilbride Business Centre, since 1993; Member: Lanarkshire Health Board, since 1995, New Lanarkshire Ltd., since 1996; Director, EKBC, since 1997; b. 29.1.55, Glasgow; m., Colin McDowall. Educ. Glenwood Secondary School; Glasgow University. Entered civil service, 1977; joined Motherwell Enterprise Development Co., 1989. Panel Member, Investors in People (Scotland) Ltd. Recreations: swimming; keep-fit; sailing; skiing. Address: (b.) PO Box 1, James Watt Building, Scottish Enterprise Technology Park, East Kilbride G75 0NS; T.-01355 238456; Platthorn Road, East Kilbride G74 1NW; T.-01355 245096.

McDowall, Stuart, CBE, MA. Local Government Boundary Commissioner for Scotland, since 1982; b. 19.4.26, Liverpool; m., Margaret B.W. Gyle; 3 s. Educ. Liverpool Institute; St. Andrews University. Royal Air Force, 1944-47; Lecturer then Senior Lecturer in Economics, St. Andrews University, 1961-91; Deputy Chairman, Central Arbitration Committee, 1976-96; Master, United College of St. Salvator and St. Leonard, St. Andrews University, 1976-80; Member: Monopolies and Mergers Commission, 1985-90, Restrictive Practices Court, 1993-96; Chairman, Fife Healthcare NHS Trust, 1994-96; Secretary, Scottish Economic Society, 1970-76. Recreations: golf; gardening; music. Address: (h.) 10 Woodburn Terrace, St. Andrews, Fife KY16 8BA; T.-01334 473247.

MacDowell, Professor Douglas Maurice, MA, DLitt, FRSE, FBA. Professor of Greek, Glasgow University, since 1971; b. 8.3.31, London. Educ. Highgate School; Balliol College, Oxford. Schoolmaster, 1954-58; Manchester University: Assistant Lecturer, 1958-61, Lecturer, 1961-68, Senior Lecturer, 1968-70, Reader, 1970-71; Visiting Fellow, Merton College, Oxford, 1969; President, Glasgow Centre, Classical Association of Scotland, 1973-75, 1977-79, 1982-84, 1988-90; Chairman, 1973-76, and Vice President, since 1976, Scottish Hellenic Society; Chairman, Council, Classical Association of Scotland, 1976-82. Publications: Andokides: On the Mysteries, 1962; Athenian Homicide Law, 1963; Aristophanes: Wasps, 1971; The Law in Classical Athens, 1978; Spartan Law, 1986; Demosthenes: Against Meidias, 1990; Aristophanes and Athens, 1995; Antiphon and Andocides (Co-author), 1998. Address: (b.) Department of Classics, Glasgow University, Glasgow G12 8QQ.

McEachran, Colin Neil, QC, MA, LLB, JD. QC, since 1981; b. 14.1.40, Glasgow; m., Kathrine Charlotte; 2 d. Educ. Glenalmond College; Merton College, Oxford;

Glasgow University; University of Chicago. Advocate, since 1968; Advocate Depute, 1974-77; QC, 1981; Member, Scottish Legal Aid Board, 1990-98; President, Pension Appeal Tribunal Scotland; Chairman, Commonwealth Games Council for Scotland. Recreations: target shooting; hill-walking. Address: 13 Saxe Coburg Place, Edinburgh; T.-0131-332 6820.

McEwan, Angus Maywood, BA (Hons), RSW. Artist; Lecturer (part-time) in Art and Design, Dundee College, since 1997; b. 19.7.63, Dundee; m., Wendy Ann Bell McEwan. Educ. Carnoustie High School; Duncan of Jordanstone College of Art. Elizabeth Greenshields Foundation Award, Canada, 1987, 1990; RSA Latimer Award, 1995; scholarship to China, 1996; solo exhibitions: Riverside Gallery, Stonehaven, 1990, Tolquhon Gallery, Aberdeenshire, 1992, Gallery 41, Edinburgh, 1994, Royal Scottish Academy, 1996, Leith Gallery, 1997, Le Mur Vivant Fine Art, London, 1997; many mixed and group exhibitions; work in public and private collections. Recreations: art; photography; reading; walking dog; enjoying life. Address: (h.) 7 Glenleven Drive, Wormit, Newport on Tay, Fife DD6 8NA; T.-01382 542314.

McEwan, Leslie J., JP, MA, DipSA, DipSW. Director of Social Work, City of Edinburgh Council, since 1996; b. 26.2.46; m., Catherine; 2 s. Educ. Dundee University; Edinburgh University. Midlothian, East Lothian and Peebles: Child Care Officer, Children's Department, 1967-69, Social Worker, 1969-71, Senior Social Worker, 1971-74, Social Work Advisor, 1974-75; Lothian Regional Council: Divisional Director of Social Work, Midlothian, 1975-80, West Lothian, 1980-85, Depute Director of Social Work, 1985 90, Senior Depute Director of Social Work, 1990-95; Director of Social Work, 1995-96. Recreations: fly-fishing; golf; woodturning. Address: (h.) 1 Esk Glades, Dalkeith, Midlothian EH22 1BZ.

McEwan, M. Shirley Ramsay, MBE, MBChB, FRSocMed. Medical Practitioner; Chairman/Medical Administrator, SHARP (Scottish Heart and Arterial Risk Prevention), since 1988; Senior Research Fellow, University Department of Medicine, Ninewells Hospital, Dundee, since 1995; part-time Specialist, Lipid Clinic, Dundee Teaching Hospitals Trust, since 1996; b. 18.11.35, Perth. Educ. Perth Academy; St. Andrews University. House Surgeon, Dundee Royal Infirmary, 1960-61; House Physician, Kings Cross Hospital, Dundee, 1961; House Surgeon, Craigtoun Maternity Hospital, 1961-62; Trainee General Practitioner, Innerleithen, 1962-63; Assistant General Practitioner, Glasgow, 1963; Principal General Practitioner: Perth, 1963-67, Dundee, 1967-71; Senior Partner, General Practitioner, Dundee, 1971; Principal General Practitioner, Dundee, 1991-95. President, Forfarshire Medical Association, 1998-99. Publication: Coronary Risk Factors Revisited (Co-Editor). Recreations: gardening; reading; swimming; skating; travel; music. Address: (h.) Craig Duich, 4 Golspie Terrace, Broughty Ferry, Dundee DD5 2PW; T.-01382 77510.

McEwan, Sheriff Robin Gilmour, QC, LLB, PhD. Sheriff of Ayr, since 1988 (of Lanark, 1982-88); Temporary Judge, Court of Session and High Court of Justiciary, since 1991; b. 12.12.43, Glasgow; m., Sheena McIntyre; 2 d. Educ. Paisley Grammar School; Glasgow University. Faulds Fellow in Law, Glasgow University, 1965-68; admitted to Faculty of Advocates, 1967; Standing Junior Counsel, Department of Energy, 1974-76; Advocate Depute, 1976-79; Chairman, Industrial Tribunals, 1981; Member, Scottish Legal Aid Board, 1989-96. Publications: Pleading in Court, 1980; A Casebook on Damages (Co-author), 1983; Contributor to Stair Memorial Encyclopaedia of the Laws of Scotland, 1986. Recreations: formerly: football, boxing; skating; now: golf, tennis. Address: (b.) Sheriff Court, Ayr KA7 1DR; T.-Ayr 268474.

McEwan, Roy James, BSc (Econ), DAARL, FRSA. Managing Director, Scottish Chamber Orchestra, since 1993; Member, Board: Association of British Orchestras, since 1993, Scottish Music Information Centre, since 1994; Member, Scottish Arts Council Combined Arts Committee, since 1993; b. 12.5.51, Dumfries. Educ. Dumfries High School; Carlisle Grammar School; London School of Economics; Polytechnic of Central London. House Manager, St. George's Theatre, London, 1977-78; Manager, Whitechapel Art Gallery, 1978-79; Administrator, then Director, MacRobert Arts Centre, Stirling, 1979-91; Director of Arts Development, North West Arts Board, Manchester, 1991-93. Chairman, Federation of Scottish Theatres, 1988-91; Member, Drama Committee, Scottish Arts Council, 1991. Address: (b.) 4 Royal Terrace, Edinburgh EH7 5AB.

McEwen, Professor James, MB, ChB, FRCP (Glasgow), FFPHM, FFOM, DIH. Henry Mechan Professor of Public Health, Glasgow University, since 1989; Consultant in Public Health Medicine, Greater Glasgow Health Board; President, Faculty of Public Health Medicine, Royal College of Physicians UK; b. 6.2.40, Stirling; m., Elizabeth May Archibald; 1 s.; 1 d. Educ. Dollar Academy; St. Andrews University. Lecturer in Industrial Medicine, Dundee University; Senior Lecturer in Community Medicine, Nottingham University; Chief Medical Officer, The Health Education Council; Professor of Community Medicine, King's College, University of London. Recreations: church; gardening. Address: (b.) 2 Lilybank Gardens, Glasgow G12 8RZ. T.-0141-330 5013.

McEwen, John, MB, ChB, PhD, FRCPE, FFPM. Managing Director, DDS Medicines Research Ltd., since 1998 (Medical Director, DDS, 1983-98); Honorary Professor, Dundee University, since 1995; Honorary Consultant, Tayside Health Board, since 1984; b. 11.4.43, Uddingston; m., Veronica Rosemary Iverson; 1 s.; 1 d. Educ. Ecclesfield Grammar School; St. Andrews University. Resident Physician/Surgeon, Dundee Hospitals, 1966-67; Lecturer in Therapeutics, Dundee University, 1969-75; Visiting Fellow in Clinical Pharmacology, Vanderbilt University, Tennessee, 1972-74; Head of Clinical Pharmacology, Hoechst, UK, 1975-82. Recreations: keyboard instruments; hill-walking; choral singing. Address: (h.) 1 Osborne Place, Dundee DD2 1BE; T.-Dundee 641060.

McFadden, Jean Alexandra, CBE, JP, DL, MA, LLB. Member, Glasgow City Council; (Convener, 1995-96, Convener, Labour Group, since 1995, Convener, Social Strategy Committee, since 1996); Lecturer in Law, Strathclyde University; b. 26.11.41, Glasgow; m., John (deceased). Educ. Hyndland Secondary School; Glasgow University; Strathclyde University. Principal Teacher of Classics, Strathclyde schools, 1967-86; entered local government as Member, Cowcaddens Ward, Glasgow Corporation, 1971; Glasgow District Council: Member, Scotstoun Ward, 1984, Chairman, Manpower Committee, 1974-77, Leader: Labour Group, 1977-86, and 1992-94, Council, 1980-86, and 1992-94, Treasurer, 1986-92; Vice Lord Lieutenant, City of Glasgow, 1980-92; President, COSLA, 1990-92; Convener, Scottish Local Government Information Unit, since 1984; Member, Board, Scottish Development Agency, 1989-91, GDA, since 1992; Chairman, Mayfest, 1983-97; Member, Secretary of State's Health Appointments Advisory Committee, since 1994. Recreations: cycling; theatre; walking; golf; West Highland terriers. Address: (h.) 16 Lansdowne Crescent, Glasgow G20 6NG; T.-0141-334 3522.

McFadden, John Alexander Crawford, MA, LLB. Solicitor; b. 11.9.36, Dunoon; m., Patricia Mary Thompson; 1 s. 2 d. Educ. Robert Gordon's College, Aberdeen; Aberdeen University. Solicitor in private practice, since 1962; Honorary Sheriff Substitute at Dumfries, since 1995.

Recreation: reading. Address: (h.) Braeside, 54 Moffat Road, Dumfries DG1 1NY; T.-01387 253077.

Macfadyen, Hon. Lord (Donald James Dobbie Macfadyen), LLB, FCIArb. Senator of the College of Justice; b. 8.9.45, Glasgow; m., Christine Balfour Gourlay Hunter; 1 s.; 1 d. Educ. Hutchesons' Grammar School, Glasgow; Glasgow University. Advocate, 1969; Standing Junior Counsel, Department of Agriculture and Fisheries for Scotland, 1977-79, Scottish Home and Health Department, 1982-83; Advocate-Depute, 1979-82; QC, 1983; part-time Chairman, Medical Appeal Tribunals, 1989-95; Vice-Dean, Faculty of Advocates, 1992-95; Temporary Judge, Court of Session, 1994-95. Address: (h.) 66 Northumberland Street, Edinburgh EH3 6JE; T.-0131-556 6043.

McFadyen, Thomas, MB, ChB. Director of Medical Services, Erskine Hospital, since 1978; b. 30.11.39, Glasgow. Educ. Allan Glen's School; Glasgow University. Appointments, Glasgow Royal Infirmary, Law Hospital, Carluke and Royal Alexandra Infirmary, Paisley. Recreation: golf. Address: (h.) Tigh-Na-Coille, Erskine Hospital, Bishopton PA7 5PU; T.-0141-812 7555.

McFall, John, BSc (Hons), BA, MBA. Parliamentary Under Secretary of State, Northern Ireland Office, since 1998; MP (Labour), Dumbarton, since 1987. Serves on: Information Committee, Parliamentary and Scientific Committee, Executive Committee – Parliamentary Group for Energy Studies; Treasurer, British/Hong Kong Group; Vice Chairman, British/Italian Group; Joint Secretary, British/Peru Group; Secretary, Retail Industry Group; Member, Roads Study Group; Treasurer, Scotch Whisky Group; Hon. Secretary, Parliamentary and Scientific Committee; formerly Opposition Whip with responsibility for Foreign Affairs, Defence and Trade and Industry (resigned post at time of Gulf War); former Deputy Shadow Secretary of State for Scotland. Recreations: jogging; reading; golf. Address: (b.) House of Commons, Westminster, London.

MacFarlane, Professor Alistair George James, CBE, PhD, DSc, MA, ScD, FIEE, FEng, FRS, FRSE. Principal and Vice Chancellor, Heriot-Watt University, 1989-96; Chairman, Scottish Council for Research in Education, 1993-98; Chairman, Scottish Library and Information Council, 1994-98; b. 1931, Edinburgh; m., Nora; 1 s. Educ. Hamilton Academy; Glasgow University. Metropolitan-Vickers Electrical Company Ltd.: Electronic Engineer, Radar and Servo Division, Group Leader, Moving Target Indication and Receiver Laboratories; Lecturer, Electrical Engineering, Queen Mary College, London University, 1959 (Reader, 1965); UMIST: Reader in Control Engineering, 1966, Professor, 1969; Cambridge University: Chair, Engineering, 1974, Head, Information Engineering Division, Fellow, Selwyn College, 1974 (Vice-Master, 1980-88); Non-Executive Director, BNFL plc, since 1994; Member, BT Advisory Forum in Scotland, 1996-98; former Consultant Editor, International Journal of Control. Past Member: SERC Computer Board, Joint Policy Committee for National Facilities for Advanced Research Computing, Advisory Committee on Safety of Nuclear Installations. American Society of Mechanical Engineers Centennial Medal, 1980; Sir Harold Hartley Medal, Institute of Measurement and Control,1982; IEE Achievement Medal, 1992; IEE Faraday Medal, 1993.

Macfarlane, Rev. Alwyn James Cecil, BA, MA; b. 14.6.22, Edinburgh; m., Joan Cowell Harris; 1 s.; 1 d. Educ. Cargilfield School, Edinburgh; Rugby School; New College, Oxford; New College, Edinburgh. Captain, 6th Black Watch, North Africa, Italy and Greece, 1940-45; entered Ministry, Church of Scotland, 1951; Minister: Fodderty and Strathpeffer, 1952-59, St. Cuthbert's Church, Edinburgh (Associate), 1959-63, Portobello Old, Edinburgh, 1963-68, Newlands (South), Glasgow, 1968-85; Associate Minister, The Scots' Church, Melbourne, 1985-88. Chaplain to The Queen in Scotland; Member, The Queen's Household in Scotland. Recreations: photography; travel. Address: 4/9 Belhaven Place, Edinburgh.

McFarlane, Sheriff C.W., QC, LLB. Sheriff of Glasgow and Strathkelvin at Glasgow. Address: (b.) Sheriff Court House, 1 Carlton Place, Glasgow, G5 9DA.

MacFarlane, Professor Colin John, BSc, CEng, FRINA, FIMarE, FRSA. Lloyd's Register Professor of Subsea Engineering, Strathclyde University, since 1986; Governor, Centre for Advanced Maritime Studies, since 1988; b. 4.3.50, Inverkip; m., Sheila Gardner; 1 s.; 1 d. Educ. Uddingston Grammar School; Strathclyde University. P&O Steam Navigation Company and Three Quays Marine Services, 1973-80; BP Engineering (specialist naval architect), 1981-86. Recreations: family; reading; gardening. Address: (b.) Strathclyde University, Department of Ship and Marine Technology, 100 Montrose Street, Glasgow; T.-0141-548 3304.

Macfarlane of Bearsden, Lord, (Norman (Somerville) Macfarlane), KT, DL, FRSE, HRSA, HRGI, Hon.FRIAS, Hon.FScotvec, Hon.FRCPSGlas, Hon. LLD (Strathclyde, 1986; Glasgow, 1988; Glasgow Caledonian, 1993; Aberdeen, 1995), DUniv (Stirling, 1992); Dr. h.c. (Edinburgh, 1992). Chairman, Macfarlane Group (Clansman) PLC, 1973-98 (Managing Director, 1973-90); Honorary Life President, United Distillers (Chairman, 1987-96); b. 5.3.26; m., Marguerite Mary Campbell; 1 s.; 4 d. Educ. High School of Glasgow. Commissioned, Royal Artillery, 1945, served Palestine, 1945-47; founded N.S. Macfarlane & Co. Ltd., 1949 (became Macfarlane Group (Clansman) PLC, 1973); Underwriting Member of Lloyd's, since 1978; Chairman: The Fine Art Society PLC, since 1976, American Trust PLC, since 1984 (Director, since 1980), Guinness PLC, 1987-89 (Joint Deputy Chairman, 1989-92); Deputy Chairman, Clydesdale Bank PLC, 1993-96 (Director, 1980-96); Director: General Accident Fire and Life Assurance Corporation plc, 1984-96, Edinburgh Fund Managers plc, since 1980, Glasgow Chamber of Commerce, 1976-79; Member: Council, CBI Scotland, 1975-81, Board, Scottish Development Agency, 1979-87; Chairman, Glasgow Development Agency, 1985-92; Vice-Chairman, Scottish Ballet, 1983-87 (Director, since 1975); Director, Scottish National Orchestra, 1977-82; Lord High Commissioner, General Assembly of Church of Scotland, 1992-93); President, Royal Glasgow Institute of the Fine Arts, 1976-87; Member, Royal Fine Art Commission for Scotland, 1980-82; Scottish Patron, National Art Collection Fund, since 1978; Governor, Glasgow School of Art, 1976-87; Trustee: National Heritage Memorial Fund, 1984-97, National Galleries of Scotland, since 1986; Director, Third Eye Centre, 1978-81; Chairman, Governors, High School of Glasgow, 1979-92; Member, Court, Glasgow University, 1979-87; President: Stationers' Association of GB and Ireland, 1965, Company of Stationers of Glasgow, 1968-70, Glasgow High School Club, 1970-72; Honorary President, Charles Rennie Mackintosh Society, since 1988; Hon. Fellow, Glasgow School of Art, since 1993; knighted, 1982; created a Life Peer, 1991; created Knight of the Thistle, 1996. Recreations: golf; cricket; theatre; art. Address: (b.) Macfarlane Group (Clansman) PLC, Sutcliffe Road, Glasgow, G13 1AH; (h.) 50 Manse Road, Bearsden, Glasgow G61 3PN.

Macfarlane, Professor Peter Wilson, BSc, PhD, FBCS, FESC, FRSE. Professor of Electrocardiology, Glasgow University, since 1995; b. 8.11.42, Glasgow; m., Irene Grace Muir; 2 s. Educ. Hyndland Senior Secondary School, Glasgow; Glasgow University. Glasgow University: Assistant Lecturer in Medical Cardiology, 1967, Lecturer, 1970, Senior Lecturer, 1974, Reader, 1980, Professor, 1991; President, 5th International Congress on Electrocardiology, Glasgow, 1978; Chairman, 15th and 18th Annual

Conferences, International Society of Computerized Electrocardiology, 1990, 1993; Author/Editor, 14 books. Recreations: watching football; running half-marathons; playing violin. Address: (h.) 12 Barrcraig Road, Bridge of Weir PA11 3HG; T.-01505 614443.

Macfarlane, Ray, MA, LLB, MBA, NP, FRSA. Managing Director, Operations, Scottish Enterprise, since 1996; Director: BT Scotland, Scottish Institute of Sport; m., John Macfarlane; 1 d. Educ. Spier's School, Beith; University of Glasgow. Solicitor, McGrigor Donald; Principal Solicitor and Project Manager, Scottish Development Agency; Director: Corporate Affairs and Property, Scottish Borders Enterprise, Network Services, Scottish Enterprise. Director: Quality Scotland, Scottish Development Finance, Scottish Screen. Address: (b.) 120 Bothwell Street, Glasgow G2 7UP; T.-0141-248 2700.

MacFarlane, Professor Thomas Wallace, DDS, DSc, FRSE, FRCPath, FDSRCPSGlas, FDS RCSEdin. Professor of Oral Microbiology, Glasgow University, since 1991; Honorary Consultant in Oral Microbiology; Dean of the Dental School, since 1995; b. 12.12.42, Glasgow; m., Nancy McEwan Fyfe; 1 s. Educ. Hyndland Senior Secondary School; Glasgow University. Assistant Lecturer, Dental Histology and Pathology, 1966-69; trained in Medical Microbiology and Histopathology, Glasgow Royal Infirmary; Lecturer in Oral Medicine and Pathology, 1969-77; organised and ran the diagnostic service in Oral Microbiology, Glasgow Dental Hospital and School; Senior Lecturer in Oral Medicine and Pathology and Consultant in Oral Microbiology, 1977; Reader in Oral Medicine and Pathology, 1984-91; Head, Department of Oral Sciences, 1992-95. Recreations: music; reading; painting; walking. Address: (b.) Glasgow Dental Hospital and School, 378 Sauchiehall Street, Glasgow G2 3JZ; T.-0141-211 9701.

McFarlane, William Stewart, CA; b. 26.3.33, Glasgow; m., Sandra; 1 d. Educ. High School of Glasgow. Trained as Chartered Accountant, Wilson Stirling (now Touche, Ross & Co.), Glasgow; Parlane McFarlane CA, 1957-58; National Service (Second Lieutenant, Royal Corps of Signals),. 1959-60; Partner, McFarlane, Son & Co., CA, 1961-62 (merged with Dickson, McFarlane & Robinson, CA, 1963-84, merged with Wylie & Bisset, CA, since 1985). Member, Council, Institute of Chartered Accountants of Scotland, 1971-76, Institute's representative, directorate of Glasgow Chamber of Commerce, 1970-88; President, Glasgow Chamber of Commerce, 1990-92; Past Finance Convener, Scottish Golf Union; Past Treasurer, Scottish Squash Rackets Association; Captain, Association of Golf Club Secretaries, 1980; Director, The Laurel Park School Co. Ltd.; Past Deacon, Incorporation of Masons of Glasgow; Past President, Rotary Club of Charing Cross. Recreations: golf; curling; swimming; squash. Address: (b.) 135 Wellington Street, Glasgow G2 2XE; T.-0141-248 3904.

Macfarlane Smith, William Holmes, BSc, PhD, CBiol, MIBiol, FIMgt. Head of Scientific Liaison and Information Services, Scottish Crop Research Institute, since 1995; b. 23.4.42, Newcastle upon Tyne; m., Daphne Henderson; 3 s. Educ. Aberdeen Grammar School; Dundee High School; Aberdeen University; Reading University. Post-doctoral research, University of Dundee, 1971-72; Rothwell Plant Breeders (Shell Nickerson): Barley Breeder, Senior Barley Breeder, Head of Barley Breeding Team, Technical Manager, 1972-78; Scottish Plant Breeding Station (subsequently Scottish Crop Research Institute): Rape and Swede Breeder, Head of Brassica Department, Leader, Commercial Brassica Breeding, 1978-95. Director, Dundee High School; Chairman, Dundee High School Patrons' Association; Trustee, Dundee High School Trust Fund; Past President, Dundee High School Old Boys Club; Junior Vice-President, Dundee Rotary Club. Recreations: golf; hillwalking; photography. Address: (h.) 42 Holly Road, Broughty Ferry, Dundee DD5 2LZ; T.-01382 739148.

McGarry, Gerald William. MD, FRCS(Glas), FRCS(Ed), FRCS(ORLHNS). Consultant Otolaryngologist, Head and Neck Surgeon, since 1995; Honorary Senior Lecturer, University of Glasgow, since 1995; b. 30.1.62, Glasgow; m., Carol; 3 s. Educ. St. Augustine's Secondary School, Glasgow; Glasgow University. Senior Registrar in Otolaryngology: Glasgow Rotational Scheme, 1992, Royal Brisbane Hospital, Australia, 1993; Locum Consultant Otolaryngologist, Glasgow Royal Infirmary, 1994. MATTUS Tutor; Council Member, Otorhinolaryngological Society; Member, Medical Appeals Tribunal. Recreations: mountaineering; aviation. Address: Department of Otolaryngology, Royal Infirmary, Glasgow G31 2ER; T.-0141-211 4330.

McGeoch, Duncan J., BSc, PhD, FRSE. Director, Medical Research Council Virology Unit, Glasgow, since 1995; Honorary Professor, Glasgow University, since 1996. Educ. Hutchesons' Grammar School; Glasgow University. Jane Coffin Childs Memorial Fund Fellow, Department of Microbiology and Molecular Genetics, Harvard Medical School, 1971-73; Researcher, Division of Virology, Department of Pathology, University of Cambridge, 1973-76; Staff Member, MRC Virology Unit, Glasgow, since 1976. Fleming Award, Society for General Microbiology, 1980; Editor, Journal of General Virology, 1984-87, Editor-in-Chief, 1988-92. Address: (b.) MRC Virology Unit, Church Street, Glasgow G11 5JR.

McGeough, Professor Joseph Anthony, FRSE, BSc, PhD, DSc, CEng, FIMechE, FIEE. Regius Professor of Engineering, Edinburgh University, since 1983; Honorary Professor, Nanjing Aeronautical and Astronautical University, China, since 1991; Visiting Professor: University Federico II of Naples, 1994, Glasgow Caledonian University, 1997-2000; b. 29.5.40, Kilwinning; m., Brenda Nicholson; 2 s.; 1 d. Educ. St. Michael's College; Glasgow University; Aberdeen University. Research Demonstrator, Leicester University, 1966; Senior Research Fellow, Queensland University, Australia, 1967; Research Metallurgist, International Research and Development Co. Ltd., Newcastle-upon-Tyne, 1968-69; Senior Research Fellow, Strathclyde University, 1969-72; Lecturer in Engineering, Aberdeen University, 1972-77 (Senior Lecturer, 1977-80, Reader, 1980-83). Honorary Vice-President, Aberdeen University Athletic Association, since 1981; Chairman: Edinburgh and S.E. Scotland Panel, IMechE, 1988-92, Scottish Branch, IMechE, 1993-95; Member, Engineering Research Board, AFRC, 1992-94; Editor, Journal of Processing of Advanced Materials, 1991-94; CIRP Editor, Journal of Materials Processing Technology, since 1991; Editor, Proceedings of International Conference on Computer-Aided Production Engineering, since 1986. Publications: Principles of Electrochemical Machining, 1974; Advanced Methods of Machining, 1988. Recreations: gardening; golf; athletics. Address: (h.) 39 Dreghorn Loan, Colinton, Edinburgh EH13 ODF; T.-0131-441 1302.

McGettrick, Professor Andrew David, BSc, PhD, FRSE, FIEE, FBCS, CEng. Head, Computer Science Department, since 1996, Professor of Computer Science, Strathclyde University, since 1984; b. 15.5.44, Glasgow; m., Sheila Margaret Girot; 5 s.; 1 d. Educ. St. Aloysius College, Glasgow; Glasgow University; Cambridge University. Lecturer, then Reader, then Professor, Strathclyde University, since 1969; Editor, Addison Wesley's International Computer Science series; Chairman, IEE Safety Critical Systems Committee; Chairman, UK Computer Science Professors Conference, 1991-93. Publications: four books as author, three books edited. Recreations: running; golf; squash. Address: (b.)

Strathclyde University, Glasgow G1 1XH; T.-0141-548 3589.

McGettrick, Professor Bartholomew John, OBE, FRSAMD, KCHS, DHLitt, FRSA, BSc (Hons), MEd (Hons), Silver Palm of Jerusalem (1996). Honorary Professor, Glasgow University; Dean (designate), Faculty of Education; Principal, St. Andrew's College of Education, since 1985; Member: Scottish Consultative Council on the Curriculum, since 1988 (Deputy Chairman, since 1991), General Teaching Council for Scotland, since 1986, various CNAA committees; Chairman, Committee on Assessment 5-14; b. 16.8.45, Glasgow; m., Elizabeth Maria McLaughlin; 2 s.; 2 d. Educ. St. Aloysius' College, Glasgow; Glasgow University. Teacher and Head, Department of Geography, St. Aloysius' College, Glasgow, 1968-72; Educational Psychologist, Scottish Centre for Social Subjects, 1972-75; Assistant Principal, then Vice-Principal, Notre Dame College of Education (latterly St. Andrew's College of Education), 1975-85. Chairman, Catholic Education Commission for Scotland, 1981-87; Chair, "Higher Still" Task Group – Staff Development; Member: Council for Educational Technology, 1982-86, SCOTVAC, 1984-88; Chairman, Committee of Principals of Colleges of Education, 1990-92; President, Association Catholique Internationale des Institutions de Sciences de L'Education, 1995-97; Chairman, Board of Governors, St. Aloysius' College, Glasgow; Chairman of Governors, Clifton Hall School, Edinburgh; Governor: Kilgraston School, Craighalbert Centre; Chairman, Governors, Craighead Institute; Member, International Committee for the Education of Teachers; Vice Chair: Educational Broadcasting Council for Scotland, Advisory Group on Sustainable Development; Chairman, Education for Sustainable Development Group; Chairman, Scottish Council for Independent Schools, since 1997; Chairman, Committee of Scottish Higher Education Principals in Scotland (COSHEP) Staff Development Committee, since 1997. Recreations: sports (golf, rugby). Address: (h.) 174 Carmunnock Road, Glasgow G44 5AJ; T.-0141-637 8112.

McGhee, Professor Charles N.J., MB, BSc (Hons), FRCS(G), FRCOphth, FRSA. Professor of Ophthalmology, Dundee University, since 1996; Honorary Consultant Ophthalmic Surgeon, Ninewells Hospital and Medical School, Dundee, since 1996; b. 26.1.59, Motherwell; m., J. Jane Oliver-McGhee. Educ. Our Lady's High School, Motherwell; Glasgow University. Junior medical posts, Glasgow and Eidnburgh before ophthalmology training in Southern General Hospital and Tennant Institute of Ophthalmology, Glasgow, 1986-93; sub-specialty training in corneal diseases, Lions Eye Institute, Perth, Australia, 1991-92; Consultant Ophthalmologist and Honorary Professor of Ocular Therapeutics, Sunderland Eye Infirmary, 1993-96. President, British Excimer and Keratorefractive Laser Society, 1994-97; Privy Council appointment to General Optical Council, since 1996. Publications: Excimer Lasers in Ophthalmology (textbook); many scientific articles. Recreations: art; photography; travel; architectural restoration; guitar. Address: (b.) Department of Ophthalmology, Ninewells Hospital and Medical School, Dundee DD1 9SY; T.-01382 632714.

McGhee, Owen Reid, DipMS, DipIEng. Chief Executive, Young Enterprise Scotland, since 1994; b. 5.8.38, Glasgow; m., Helen Scott Anderson; 2 s. Educ. Whitehill Senior Secondary School; University of Strathclyde. Industrial Engineer: Honeywell Controls, 1962-65, Gourock Ropework Co., 1965-67; IBM UK Ltd., Greenock: Personnel Manager, Materials Manager, Manufacturing Manager, 1967-92; Development Director, Quality Scotland Foundation, 1992-94. Award, on Vellum, Royal Humane Society; Gold Award, Young Enterprise. Recreations: rowing (represented Scotland, 1960 and 1972), music; cooking; hill-walking; canoeing; windsurfing. Address: The White Cottage, Torr Road, Bridge of Weir PA11 3BE; T.-01505 612161.

McGhie, Hon. Lord (James Marshall), QC, LLB (Hons). Queen's Counsel, since 1983; Chairman, Scottish Land Court; President, Lands Tribunal for Scotland, since 1996; b. 15.10.44, Perth; m., Ann M. Cockburn; 1 s.; 1 d. Educ. Perth Academy; Edinburgh University. Advocate-Depute, 1983-86; part-time Chairman, Medical Appeal Tribunals, 1987-92; Member, Criminal Injuries Compensation Board, 1992-96. Address: (b.) 1 Grosvenor Crescent, Edinburgh; T.-0131-225 3595.

McGibbon, David Campbell, FCMA, DipMS, FBIM. Finance Director and Company Secretary, Grampian Holdings plc, since 1984; Director (Non-Executive), Paladin Resources plc, since 1994; Chairman, Stock Exchange Regional Advisory Group, Scotland, since 1995; b. 3.12.47, Airdrie; m., Anne Ferguson; 2 d. Educ. Coatbridge High School; Glasgow College of Technology. Accountancy posts, 1967-78; joined Grampian Holdings plc as Group Accountant, 1978; Group Financial Controller, 1983-84. Past Chairman, Group of Scottish Finance Directors. Recreation: golf. Address: (b.) Stag House, Castlebank Street, Glasgow G11 6DY; T.-0141-357 2000.

McGillivray, Rev. (Alexander) Gordon, MA, BD, STM; b. 22.9.23, Edinburgh; m., Winifred Jean Porter; 2 s.; 2 d. Educ. George Watson's Boys' College, Edinburgh; Edinburgh University; Union Theological Seminary, New York. Royal Artillery, 1942-45; Assistant Minister, St. Cuthbert's Parish Church, Edinburgh; Minister: Waterbeck Church, 1951-58, Nairn High Church, 1958-73; Clerk, Presbytery of Edinburgh, 1973-93; Clerk, General Assembly of Church of Scotland, 1971-94, retired. Recreations: golf; theatre. Address: 7 Greenfield Crescent, Balerno, Midlothian EH14 7HD; T.-0131-449 4747.

McGillivray, Elizabeth Norma, LLB (Hons), NP. Solicitor; part-time University Lecturer; b. 16.1.48, Perth; m., Robert Gordon McGillivray. Educ. Grove Academy, Broughty Ferry; Dundee University. Partner, Bowmans Solicitors, Dundee, since 1985; part-time Tutor, Dundee University, 1984-92, part-time Lecturer, since 1989. Member, Council, Law Society of Scotland and various committees and working parties; Member, Board of Management, Angus College; Founder Chairman, Tayside Cancer Support Group; Member, Local Committee, National Trust for Scotland. Recreations: music; walking; reading. Address: (h.) Lochtyknowe, Carnoustie, Angus; T.-01241 854887.

McGinlay, Alan Douglas, BSc. Head Teacher, Hillpark Secondary School, since 1994; b. 14.4.50, Glasgow; m., Lynn; 1 s.; 1 d. Educ. Queen's Park Secondary School; Glasgow University. Assistant Head Teacher, then Depute Head and Acting Head, James Hamilton Academy, 1984-91; Head Teacher, Govan High School, 1991-94. Address: (b.) 36 Cairngorm Road, Glasgow G43 2XA; T.-0141-637 1071.

McGinley, Alan Peter, BA (Hons). Scotland Manager, Carers National Association, since 1994; b. 8.4.60, Glasgow; m., Barbara; 2 d. Educ. Holy Cross High School, Hamilton; University of Strathclyde. Community Worker, Strathclyde Regional Council, Airdrie, 1986; Development Officer (Lanarkshire), Age Concern Scotland, 1990; Scotland Co-ordinator, Carers National Association, 1994. Member, Policy Committee, Scottish Council of Voluntary Organisations. Recreations: song writing; acting/directing. Address: (b.) 162 Buchanan Street, Glasgow G1 2LL; T.-0141-333 9495.

McGirr, Professor Emeritus Edward McCombie, CBE, BSc, MD, DSc (Hon.), FRCP, FRCPEdin, FRCPGlas, FFCM, FACP (Hon.), FRSE; b. 15.6.16, Hamilton; m.,

Diane Curzon Woods (deceased); 1 s.; 3 d. Educ. Hamilton Academy; Glasgow University. RAMC, 1941-47, including posts as graded physician and specialist in medicine ; appointments in University Department of Medicine, Glasgow Royal Infirmary, 1947-78, latterly Muirhead Chair of Medicine, Glasgow University, and Physician in charge of wards, Glasgow Royal Infirmary; Dean, Faculty of Medicine, Glasgow University, 1974-81; Administrative Dean and Professor of Administrative Medicine, Glasgow University, 1978-81; Emeritus Professor, Glasgow University, since 1981 (Dean of Faculties, 1992-94); President, Royal College of Physicians and Surgeons of Glasgow, 1970-72; Chairman, Scottish Health Service Planning Council, 1978-84; Honorary Physician to the Army in Scotland, 1975-81; Chairman, Scottish Council for Postgraduate Medical Education, 1979-85; sometime Member: Greater Glasgow Health Board, National Radiological Protection Board, General Nursing Council for Scotland, National Board for Nursing, Midwifery and Health Visiting; Past President, Royal Medico-Chirurgical Society of Glasgow; Chairman, Scottish Council for Opportunities for Play Experience (SCOPE), 1985-87; Chairman, Clyde Estuary Amenity Council, 1986-90. Recreations: reading; curling. Address: (h.) Anchorage House, Bothwell, by Glasgow G71 8NF; T.-01698 852194.

McGlynn, Archie Smith, BA (Hons), MPhil, DipComm. HM Chief Inspector of Schools, Eastern Division, since 1997; Director, HMI Audit Unit, since 1992; b. Tarbert, Argyll; m., Leah Sutherland Ross; 1 s.; 1 d. Educ. Tarbert Secondary School; Campbeltown Grammar School; Strathclyde University; Glasgow University. Industry and commerce, 1962-64 and 1966-67; Teacher in schools and further/higher education colleges, 1964-69; Depute Principal, Glenrothes College, 1969-75; HM Inspector of Schools, 1976-87; HM Chief Inspector of Schools, since 1987. Recreations: hedgehog preservation; following Fife Flyers. Address: (b.) Room G1-1, Saughton House, Broomhouse Drive, Edinburgh EH11 3XD.

McGlynn, Rt. Rev. Lord Abbot (James Aloysius) Donald, OCSO, STL, SLJ. Monk, Order of Cistercians of Strict Observance, since 1952; Abbot of Nunraw, since 1969; b. 13.8.34, Glasgow. Educ. Holyrood School, Glasgow; St. Bernardine's School, Buckinghamshire; Gregorian University, Rome. President: Scottish Council of Major Religious Superiors, 1974-77, British Isles Regional Council of Cistercian Abbeys, 1980-84; Chairman, Union of Monastic Superiors, 1985-89; Official Roman Catholic Visitor to the General Assembly, Church of Scotland, 1976 and 1985; Commandeur Ecclesiastique, Military & Hospitaller Order of St. Lazarus of Jerusalem, 1985; Patron, Friends of the Beatitudes, Madras; Patron, Haddington Pilgrimage of St. Mary & the Three Kings. Recreations: iconography; farm work; computer printing. Address: Sancta Maria Abbey, Nunraw, Garvald, Haddington EH41 4LW; T.-0162 083 0223.

McGougan, Donald, CPFA. Director of Finance, City of Edinburgh Council, since 1995; Director, Edinburgh Military Tattoo, since 1995; b. 26.12.50; Glasgow; m., Mandy; 1 s.; 1 d. Educ. Hermitage Academy, Helensburgh. Trainee Accountant, Midlothian County Council, 1971; Professional Assistant, City of Edinburgh District Council, 1975; Falkirk District Council: Principal Assistant, 1979, Depute Director of Finance, 1981; Depute Director of Finance, City of Edinburgh District Council, 1987. Recreations: family; golf; football. Address: (b.) Council Headquarters, George IV Bridge, Edinburgh EH1 1UQ; T.-0131-469 3005.

McGowan, Professor David Alexander, MDS, PhD, FDSRCS, FFDRCSI, FDSRCPSG. Professor of Oral Surgery, Glasgow University, since 1977 (Dean of Dental Education, 1990-95); Consultant Oral Surgeon, Greater Glasgow Health Board, since 1977; b. 18.6.39, Portadown, Co. Armagh; m., Margaret Vera Macaulay; 1 s.; 2 d. Educ. Portadown College; Queen's University, Belfast. Oral surgery training, Belfast and Aberdeen, 1961-67; Lecturer in Dental Surgery, Queen's University, Belfast, 1968; Lecturer, then Senior Lecturer and Deputy Head, Oral and Maxillofacial Surgery, London Hospital Medical College, 1968-77. Postgraduate Adviser in Dentistry, Glasgow University, 1977-90; Chairman, Dental Committee, Scottish Council for Postgraduate Medical Education, 1980-90; Dean, Dental Faculty, and Member of College Council, Royal College of Physicians and Surgeons of Glasgow, 1989-92; Member and Vice-Chairman of Executive, General Dental Council; Member, Court, Glasgow University, 1995-99; Chairman, National Dental Advisory Committee; Member, EC Advisory Committee on training of dental practitioners; former Council Member, British Association of Oral and Maxillofacial Surgeons. Recreations: sailing; music. Address: (b.) Department of Oral Surgery, Glasgow Dental Hospital and School, 378 Sauchiehall Street, Glasgow G2 3JZ; T.-0141-211 9700.

McGowan, Ian David, MA, PhD. Director, Centre for Publishing Studies, Stirling University, since 1988, and Senior Lecturer in English Studies, since 1992; Member, Scottish Arts Council, and Chairman, Literature Committee, 1993-97; b. Glasgow. Educ. Pembroke College, Oxford. Joined Stirling University as Lecturer in English Studies, 1973. Member and Chairman, Grants to Publishers Panel, 1985-97, Chairman, Grants to Magazines Panel, 1992-97, Scottish Arts Council; Member, Executive Committee, Book Trust Scotland, 1986-93; Trustee, Arts Trust of Scotland. Publications: The Restoration and the Eighteenth Century; Charles Dickens: Little Dorrit; Journey to the Hebrides; articles and chapters. Address: (b.) Centre for Publishing Studies, Stirling University, Stirling FK9 4LA; T.-01786 473171.

McGowan, Ian Duncan, BA. Librarian, National Library of Scotland, since 1990; b. 19.9.45, Liverpool; m., Elizabeth Ann Weir; 2 d. Educ. Liverpool Institute; Exeter College, Oxford. Assistant Keeper, National Library of Scotland, 1971-78; Keeper (Catalogues and Automation), 1978-88; Secretary of the Library, 1988-90; President, Scottish Library Association, 1998. Address: (b.) National Library of Scotland, George IV Bridge, Edinburgh EH1 1EW; T.-0131-226 4531.

McGowan, Sheriff John, LLB. Sheriff of Glasgow and Strathkelvin; b. 15.1.44, Kilmarnock; m., Elise Smith; 2 s. Educ. St. Joseph's Academy, Kilmarnock; Glasgow University. Admitted Solicitor, 1967; Temporary Sheriff, 1986-93; Council Member, Law Society of Scotland, 1982-85. Recreations: golf; tennis; curling; listening to music. Address: (h.) 19 Auchentrae Crescent, Ayr; T.-01292 260139; (b.) Sheriff Court House, 1 Carlton Place, Glasgow; T.-0141-429 8888.

McGowan, Neal L., DipTechEd. Head Teacher, Gracemount High School, Edinburgh, since 1997; b. 12.5.63, Edinburgh. Educ. Musselburgh Grammar School; Moray House College of Education. Teacher, Assistant Principal Teacher, Principal Teacher, all of CDT; Depute Head Teacher, Selkirk High School. Publications: three books on technological studies. Recreation: golf. Address: (b.) Gracemount High School, Lasswade Road, Edinburgh EH16 6TZ; T.-0131-664 7440.

McGown, Archibald M, OStJ. Director, Scottish Pre-Retirement Council, since 1987; b. 15.11.33, Paisley; m., Janet Robertson; 1 s.; 2 d. Educ. Rutherglen Academy. Managing Director, Elvestead Canned Meat Co. Ltd., 1976-86. Chairman, Royal Scottish Automobile Club, 1992-94. Recreations: curling; bowling. Address: (b.) Alexandra House, 204 Bath Street, Glasgow G2 4HL; T.-0141-332 9427.

McGrail, Frank Robert, MA (Hons), DipEd. Head Teacher, Drummond Community High School, Edinburgh, since 1995; b. 7.2.52, Edinburgh; 2 d. Educ. St. Augustine's High School, Edinburgh; Edinburgh University. Teacher of History, then Principal Teacher of History; Assistant Head, Tynecastle High, Edinburgh; Depute Head, Craigmount High, Edinburgh. Recreations: swimming; walking; adventure sports; theatre; cinema. Address: (b.) 41 Bellevue Place, Edinburgh EH7 4BS; T.-0131-556 2651.

McGrath, John. Playwright; Theatre, Film and TV Director; Artistic Director, 7:84 Theatre Company (Scotland), 1973-88; Producer/Director, Freeway Films, since 1982; Director, Moonstone International, since 1997; b. 1.6.35, Birkenhead; m., Elizabeth MacLennan; 2 s.; 1 d. Educ. Alun Grammar School, Mold, Clwyd; St. John's College, Oxford. Playwright (more than 40 plays produced professionally in UK and abroad); Writer of film screenplays for feature films and TV plays; Director in theatre and TV; Poet and Songwriter; plays for theatre including Events While Guarding the Bofors Gun, The Cheviot, The Stag and the Black, Black Oil, Blood Red Roses, Border Warfare, John Brown's Body, Watching for Dolphins, The Wicked Old Man, The Last of the MacEachans, The Four Estaites. Visiting Judith E. Wilson Fellow, Cambridge, 1979 and 1989; recent film and television productions: Border Warfare, John Brown's Body, The Dressmaker, Mairi Mhor, Carrington, Half the Picture, Ma Vie en Rose. Publications: A Good Night Out (lectures); The Bone Won't Break; many plays, including 6-Pack, Six Plays for Scotland (1996). Address: (b.) Freeway Films, 67 George Street, Edinburgh EH2 2JG; T.-0131-225 3200.

McGrath, Professor John Christie (Ian), BSc, PhD. Regius Professor of Physiology, Glasgow University, since 1991; Co-Director, Clinical Research Initiative in Heart Failure, since 1994; Head of Division, Department of Neuroscience and Biomedical Systems, Institute of Biomedical and Life Sciences; b. 8.3.49, Johnstone; m., Wilma Nicol; 1 s.; 1 d. Educ. John Neilson Institution, Paisley; Glasgow University. Glasgow University: Research Fellow in Pharmacology and Anaesthesia, 1973-75, Lecturer, 1975-83, Senior Lecturer, 1983-88, Reader, 1988-89, Titular Professor, 1987-91. Sandoz Prizewinner, British Pharmacological Society, 1980; Pfizer Award for Biology, 1983. Recreations: running; politics; travel. Address: (b.) Institute of Physiology, Glasgow University, Glasgow; T.-041-330 4483.

McGrath, Tom. Playwright and Poet; b. 1940, Rutherglen. Educ. Glasgow University. Founder Editor, International Times, 1966-67; Musical Director, Great Northern Welly Boot Show; Director, Third Eye Centre, Glasgow, 1974-77; plays include: Laurel and Hardy, 1976, The Hardman, 1977.

McGregor, Rev. Alistair Gerald Crichton, QC, BD, BA, LLB, WS. Minister, North Leith Parish Church, Edinburgh, since 1987; Temporary Sheriff, 1984-87; b. 15.10.37, Sevenoaks, Kent; m., Margaret Dick Lees or McGregor; 2 s.; 1 d. Educ. Charterhouse; Pembroke College, Oxford; Edinburgh University. Solicitor; Advocate; QC; former Standing Junior Counsel to Queen's and Lord Treasurer's Remembrancer, to Scottish Home and Health Department and to Scottish Development Department; Past Chairman, Discipline Committee, Potato Marketing Board; former Clerk, Rules Council, Court of Session; former Tutor in Scots Law, Edinburgh University; former Chairman, Family Care; Director, Apex (Scotland) Ltd; Chairman, Drug Prevention Group. Publication: Obscenity (Co-Author). Recreations: squash; tennis; swimming; travel; cinema. Address: (h.) 22 Primrose Bank Road, Edinburgh EH5; T.-0131-551 2802.

McGregor, Bill, MA, MEd. Rector, James Hamilton Academy, Kilmarnock, since 1989; b. 14.2.44, Kilmarnock; m., Elspeth Barbara Greene; 1 s.; 1 d. Educ. Kilmarnock Academy; Glasgow University. Teacher, Assistant Rector, Depute Rector, Mainholm Academy, Ayr, 1968-89. Publications: bus histories. Recreations: photography (transport); writing. Address: (h.) 25 Blackburn Drive, Ayr KA7 2XN; T.-01292 282043.

MacGregor, Professor Bryan Duncan, BSc, MSc, PhD, DipSurv, MRTPI, ARICS. MacRobert Professor of Land Economy, Aberdeen University, since 1990; b. 16.10.53, Inverness; m., Nicola; 2 twin d. Educ. Inverness Royal Academy; Edinburgh University; Heriot Watt University; Cambridge University; College of Estate Management. Lecturer, Department of Land Management, Reading University, 1981-84; Lecturer, Department of Town and Regional Planning, Glasgow University, 1984-87; Deputy, then Property Research Manager, Prudential Portfolio Managers, 1987-90. Recreations: hill-walking; football; literature; music; thinking. Address: (b.) Department of Land Economy, St. Mary's, King's College, Aberdeen University, Aberdeen AB24 3UF; T.-01224 272356.

Macgregor, Rt. Rev. Gregor, MA, BD (Hons). Bishop of Moray, Ross and Caithness, since 1994; b. 17.11.33, Glasgow; m., Elizabeth Jean; 1 s.; 3 d. Educ. Hutchesons' Boys Grammar School, Glasgow; St. Andrews University. Deaconed and priested, 1977; St. Michael's, Elie, 1978-81; St. Luke's, Glenrothes, 1981-86; St. James', Dollar, 1986-90; St. Luke's, Wester Hailes, 1991-93. Recreations: hill-walking; rugby. Address: (b.) 11 Kenneth Street, Inverness IV3 5NR; T.-01463 226255.

MacGregor of MacGregor, Brigadier Sir Gregor, 6th Bt. 23rd Chief of Clan Gregor; b. 22.12.25; m., Fanny Butler; 2 s. Educ. Eton. Commissioned, Scots Guards, 1944; commanding 1st Bn., Scots Guards, 1966-69; Col. Recruiting, HQ Scotland, 1971; Lt.-Col. commanding Scots Guards, 1971-74; Defence and Military Attache, British Embassy, Athens, 1975-78; Comdr., Lowlands, 1978-80; Grand Master Mason of Scotland, 1988-93; Member, Queen's Bodyguard for Scotland (Royal Company of Archers). Address: (h.) Bannatyne, Newtyle, Blairgowrie, Perthshire; T.-01828 650 314.

McGregor, Iain. Honorary Secretary, SABRE (Scotland Against Being Ruled By Europe); b. 19.3.37, Stirling. Educ. Selkirk High School; Kelso High School. Army Service, REME; International Trade Exhibitions Publicist, London; Editor, BIPS International Photo-Feature Agency; Journalist, Fleet Street and provinces; Writer and Lecturer in Journalism, Asia, Europe, North America; Founding Director, Institute for Christian Media (Canada); Editor, The Patriot for Scotland; Editor and Publisher, Social Credit International; Scotland Representative, European Anti-Maastricht Alliance; Council Member, Heritage Society of Scotland. Recreations: local history; travel; music; theatre; film; books. Address: (h.) 8 Baileyfield Road, Edinburgh EH15 1DL.

Macgregor, Janet Elizabeth, OBE, BSc, MB, ChB, MD, FRCPath, FRCOG. Former Director, Harris Birthright Research Centre, Aberdeen University; b. 12.1.20, Glasgow; m., Professor A.G. Macgregor (deceased); 3 s.; 1 d. Educ. Bearsden Academy; Glasgow University. Captain, RAMC, 1943-45; Medical Officer, Maternity and Child Welfare, Glasgow, Sheffield and Edinburgh, 1946-59; Research Fellow, Department of Obstetrics and Gynaecology, Aberdeen University, 1960-66; Medical Assistant, Grampian Health Board, 1966-73; appointed Senior Lecturer, Aberdeen University, 1973. Member, Cytology Sub-Committee, Royal College of Pathologists, 1980-82; Chairman and President, British Society for Clinical Cytology, 1977-83; former Member, Medical Advisory Committee, Women's National Cancer Control

Campaign; Member, IARC (WHO) Study Group on Cervical Cancer, 1978-84; Fellow, International Academy of Cytology, since 1963. Address: (h.) Ardruighe, Clachan, Isle of Seil, Argyll; 22 Ovington Square, London, SW3 1LR.

Macgregor, Jimmie, MBE, DA. Radio and Television Presenter; Author; Lecturer. Educ. Springburn Academy; Glasgow School of Art. Forefront of British folk revival for more than 20 years; countless radio and TV appearances, tours in Britain and abroad; more than 20 albums recorded; own daily radio programme, Macgregor's Gathering, for more than 10 years; regular TV series on long-distance walks; various books on folk song and the outdoors; has written theme music for TV and radio, illustrated books; gives regular lectures and slide shows; Life Member, RSPB, Scottish Wildlife Trust, Friends of Loch Lomond; President, Friends of River Kelvin; Vice-President, Scottish Conservation Projects and Scottish Youth Hostels Association; twice Scot of the Year; Hon. Fellow, Royal Zoological Society of Scotland. Recreations: collecting paintings, pottery, glass, furniture; the outdoors; wildlife; hill-walking; theatre; art; music; antiques; old cars; anything and everything Scottish.

McGrenary, Thomas Joseph, OBE, BSc (Hons). Principal, Cumbernauld College, since 1985; b. 12.2.39, Hamilton; m., Marlyn; 4 s. Educ. Our Lady's High School, Motherwell; University of Strathclyde. Research Scientist: Ministry of Aviation, General Electric Company; Lecturer, Aberdeen Technical College; Senior Lecturer, Glasgow College of Food Technology; Further Education Officer, Strathclyde Regional Council; Depute Principal, Ayr College. Recreations: sport; reading (non-fiction). Address: (h.) 42 Buchanan Drive, Rutherglen G73 3PE; T.-(b.) 01236 731811.

McGrigor, Captain Sir Charles Edward, 5th Bt. Life Vice-President, RNLI; Member, Queen's Bodyguard for Scotland (Royal Company of Archers); a Deputy Lieutenant, Argyll and Bute; b. 5.10.22; m., Mary Bettine (eldest daughter of the late Sir Archibald Edmonstone, 6th Bt. of Duntreath); 2 s.; 2 d. Educ. Eton. Joined Army, 1941; Rifle Brigade, North Africa, Italy, Austria (mentioned in Despatches); ADC to Duke of Gloucester, 1945-47.

McGuire, Anne, MP, MA (Hons). MP (Labour), Stirling, since 1997; Parliamentary Private Secretary to Secretary of State for Scotland, since 1997; Assistant Government Whip (Scotland), since 1998; b. 26.5.49, Glasgow; m., Len McGuire, JP, CA; 1 s.; 1 d. Educ. Our Lady and St. Francis School, Glasgow; University of Glasgow; Notre Dame College of Education. Development Officer, Community Service Volunteers, 1984-88; National Officer, CSU, 1988-93; Depute Director, Scottish Council for Voluntary Organisations, 1993-97. Address: (b.) 38 Forth Crescent, Stirling FK8 1LG; T.-01786 446515.

McGuire, Edward, ARCM, ARAM. Composer; b. 15.2.48, Glasgow. Educ. Junior Department, RSAMD; Royal Academy of Music, London; State Academy of Music, Stockholm. Won National Young Composers Competition, 1969; Rant selected as test piece for 1978 Carl Flesch International Violin Competition; Proms debut, 1982, when Source performed by BBC SSO; String Quartet chosen for 40th Anniversary Concert, SPNM, Barbican, 1983; featured composer, Park Lane Group series, Purcell Room, 1993, Bath International Guitar Festival, 1996, Proms, 1997; International Viola Congress, 1998; frequent commissions and broadcasts including Euphoria (EIF/Fires of London), Songs of New Beginnings (Paragon Ensemble), Quintet II (Lontano), Peter Pan (Scottish Ballet), A Glasgow Symphony (NYOS), The Loving of Etain (Paragon Opera), Trombone Concerto (Aix-en-Provence Festival), plays flute with and writes for Whistlebinkies folk group. Address: c/o Scottish Music Information Centre, 1 Bowmont Gardens, Glasgow G12 9LR; T.-0141-334 6393.

McGurk, John C. Editor, Scotland on Sunday, since 1997; b. 12.12.52, Edinburgh; m., Karen Ramsay; 1 s.; 1 d. Educ. Tynecastle Secondary School, Edinburgh. Deputy Editor, Sunday Mail, 1987-89; Editor, Sunday Sun, Newcastle-upon-Tyne, 1989-91; Deputy Editor, Daily Record, 1991-94; Editor, Evening News, 1994-97. Runner Up, UK Regional Editor of the Year, 1991. Recreation: paying for children. Address: (b.) 20 North Bridge, Edinburgh EH1 1YT; T.-0131-225 2468.

McHaffie, Rev. Robin Dunlop, BD (Hons). Minister, Linton, Morebattle and Hownam, Yetholm, since 1991; b. 12.7.48, Glasgow; m., Hazel Wallace Lyons; 3 d. Educ. Bishopbriggs High School; Whitehill Secondary School; Glasgow University. Insurance Trainee, Management Trainee, Templeton Carpets; Publicity Manager, Philips Welding; Minister: Calton Mission, Kinning Park Church. Past Chair, Churches Together Through Garden Festival and Year of Culture. Address: (b.) The Manse, Kirk Yetholm, Kelso TD5 8PF; T.-01573 420308.

McHardy, Stuart Andrew, MA (Hons), FSAScot. Director, Scots Language Resource Centre, Perth, since 1993; Chairman, Pictish Arts Society; Lecturer on Scottish History and Folklore; b. 19.4.47, Dundee; m., Sandra Davidson; 1 s. Educ. Morgan Academy, Dundee; Edinburgh University. Formerly worked in advertising and marketing and as professional musician, writer, broadcaster, journalist and poet. Publications: Strange Secrets of Ancient Scotland; Tales of Whisky and Smuggling; The Wild Haggis an the Greetin-Faced Nyaff. Recreations: music; hill-walking. Address: (h.) 52 Brunswick Street, Edinburgh EH7 5HY.

McIldowie, James Robert, MA, LLB, NP. Solicitor, since 1962; Honorary Sheriff, since 1986; b. 24.9.37, Crieff; m., Isabella Junor (June) Anderson; 2 d. Educ. Morrison's Academy, Crieff; Edinburgh University. Apprentice and Assistant in Edinburgh; joined McLean & Stewart, Dunblane and Callander, 1962; became a Partner, 1963; now Senior Partner. Accredited Expert in Agricultural Law; former Secretary and Treasurer, Highland Pony Society. Recreations: golf; music; theatre; all sports. Address: (b.) 51-53 High Street, Dunblane, Perthshire; T.-01786 823217.

McIlvanney, William. Novelist and Poet; b. 1936, Kilmarnock. Educ. Kilmarnock Academy; Glasgow University. Teacher (Assistant Rector (Curriculum), Greenwood Academy, Irvine, until 1975); Creative Writing Fellow, Strathclyde University, 1972-73; author of Remedy is None, 1966 (joint winner, Geoffrey Faber Memorial Award, 1967), A Gift from Nessus, 1968 (Scottish Arts Council Publication Award, 1969), Docherty, 1975 (Whitbread Award for Fiction, 1975), Laidlaw, 1977, The Papers of Tony Veitch, 1983, The Big Man, 1985, Strange Loyalties, 1990; three books of poetry: The Longships in Harbour, 1970, Weddings and After, 1983, In Through the Head, 1985; Surviving the Shipwreck (essays and collected journalism), 1991.

McIlwain, Alexander Edward, CBE, MA, LLB, SSC, WS. Retired Solicitor, formerly Senior Partner, Leonards, Solicitors, Hamilton; Honorary Sheriff, South Strathclyde, Dumfries and Galloway, at Hamilton, since 1981; b. 4.7.33, Aberdeen; m., Moira Margaret Kinnaird; 3 d. Educ. Aberdeen Grammar School; Aberdeen University. Commissioned, Royal Corps of Signals, 1957-59; Burgh Prosecutor then District Prosecutor, Hamilton, 1966-76; Dean, Society of Solicitors of Hamilton, 1981-83; Chairman, Legal Aid Central Committee, 1985-87; President, Law Society of Scotland, 1983-84; Member: Central Advisory Committee for Scotland on Justices of the Peace, 1986-96; Lanarkshire Health Board; The Scout Council (UK); Honorary Member, American Bar

Association; Chairman, Lanarkshire Scout Area, 1981-91; Chairman, Hamilton Sheriff Court Project, 1990-94; Temporary Sheriff, since 1984; President, Temporary Sheriffs Association, since 1994; Member: Criminal Injuries Compensation Appeal Panel, Judicial Studies Committee. Publications: Time Costing and Time Recording (in collaboration); Supporting Victims in the Criminal Justice System. Recreations: work; gardening. Address: (h.) 7 Bothwell Road, Uddingston, Glasgow; T.-01698 813368.

Macinnes, Professor Allan Iain, MA, PhD, FRHistS. Burnett-Fletcher Professor of History, University of Aberdeen, since 1993 (Head, Department of History, since 1998); b. 26.11.49, Inverness; widower. Educ. Oban High School; University of St. Andrews; University of Glasgow. University of Glasgow: Lecturer in Scottish History, 1973-89, Senior Lecturer in Scottish History, 1989-93, Director, Postgraduate School of Scottish Studies, 1992-93; Head, Department of History and Economic Affairs, Aberdeen University, 1994-97. Membership Secretary and Executive Member, Council, Scottish History Society, 1988-93; Member, Company of Scottish History Ltd., since 1987; Member, Scottish Committee on the History of Parliament, since 1991; Member, Editorial Committee for the History of the Scottish Parliament, since 1991; Scottish Referee, North Carolina Colonial Records Project, 1991-94; Medieval or Later Rural Settlement Advisory Group, Historic Scotland, since 1992; Historical Consultant, BBC Scotland, Gaelic and Features Television, 1993-98; Founder and Joint Promoter, Doctoral Programme in History, Aberdeen and University of Northern Carolina at Charlotte, since 1994; Member, Steering Committee, History at Universities Defence Group, since 1995; Member, Steering Committee, Irish and Scottish Academic Initiative, 1995-97 (Chair, 1995-96); Chair, Scottish Land Commission, 1996-98; Member, Advisory Panel, Scottish Parliamentary Records Project, University of St. Andrews, since 1997; Joint Founder (Chair, Steering Committee), Northern European Historical Research Network, 1997; Associate Editor, New Dictionary of National Biography for Scottish nobles and gentry, since 1998. Fletcher Jones Fellow of the Huntington Library, San Marino, California, 1993; Frank Watson Prize in Scottish History, University of Guelph, 1997. Publications: Charles I and the Making of the Covenanting Movement, 1625-41, 1991; Clanship, Commerce and the House of Stuart, 1603-1788, 1996; published extensively on covenants, clans and clearances. Recreations: five-a-side football; supporting Hibernian; hillwalking; listening to music – especially jazz; drinking malt whisky. Address: Department of History, University of Aberdeen AB25 3RX; T.-01224 272453.

MacInnes, Hamish, OBE, BEM, DUniv. Writer and Designer; b. 7.7.30, Gatehouse of Fleet. Educ. Gatehouse of Fleet. Mountaineer with numerous expeditions to Himalayas, Amazon and other parts of the world; Deputy Leader, 1975 Everest SW Face Expedition; film Producer/Advisor/safety expert, with Zinnemann, Connery, Eastwood, Putnam, etc.; Advisor, BBC TV live outside broadcasts on climbing; author of 20 books on travel and adventure, including two autobiographies and fiction; designed the first all-metal ice axe, Terodactyl ice climbing tools, the MacInnes stretchers; Founder, Search and Rescue Dog Association; Honorary Member, Scottish Mountaineering Club; former President, Alpine Climbing Group; world authority on mountain rescue; Doctor of Laws (Hons), Glasgow University; Hon. DSc: Heriot Watt University, Aberdeen University; Doctor of the University, University of Stirling, 1997; President, Guide Dogs Adventure Group; past Leader, Glencoe Mountain Rescue Team. Recreations: as above. Address: (h.) Glencoe, Argyll; T.-0855 811258.

McInnes, Sheriff John Colin, QC, BA (Hons) (Oxon), LLB (Edin), HonLLD (St. Andrews), DL. Advocate; Sheriff, Tayside, Central and Fife, since 1974; Deputy Lieutenant for Fife, since 1997; b. 21.11.38, Cupar, Fife; m., Elisabeth Mabel Neilson; 1 s.; 1 d. Educ. New Park School, St. Andrews; Cargilfield School, Edinburgh; Merchiston Castle School, Edinburgh; Brasenose College, Oxford; Edinburgh University. 2nd Lt., 8th Royal Tank Regiment, 1956-58; Lt., Fife and Forfar Yeomanry, Scottish Horse, TA, 1958-64; Advocate, 1963; Director, R. Mackness & Co. Ltd., 1963-70; Chairman, Fios Group Ltd., 1970-72; Parliamentary candidate (Conservative), Aberdeen North, 1964; Tutor, Law Faculty, Edinburgh University, 1965-72; in practice, Scottish Bar, 1963-73; Sheriff of Lothian and Peebles, 1973-74. Member, St. Andrews University Court, 1983-91; Chairman, Fife Family Conciliation Service, 1988-90; Member and Vice-President: Security Service Tribunal, since 1989, Intelligence Services Tribunal, since 1994; President, The Sheriffs' Association, 1995-97; Member: Scottish Criminal Justice Forum, since 1996, Judicial Studies Committee, since 1996. Publication: Divorce Law and Practice in Scotland, 1990. Recreations: fishing; shooting; hill-walking; skiing; photography. Address: (h.) Sheriff Court, Tay Street, Perth PH2 8NL.

McInnes, Professor William McKenzie, MSc, PhD, CA, FRSA. Professor of Accounting, since 1994, and Head, Department of Accounting, Finance and Law, since 1995, Stirling University; Vice-Dean, Faculty of Management, 1996-97; b. 24.5.42, Hawick; m., Christine Mary; 1 s.; 1 d. Educ. George Watsons College, Edinburgh; Durham University; Glasgow University. Management Accountant, IBM (UK) Ltd., 1966-68; Lecturer, Kirkcaldy Technical College, 1968-70; Audit Senior, Coopers and Lybrand, Bermuda, 1970-72; Senior Lecturer, Newcastle upon Tyne Polytechnic, 1974-76; Lecturer, then Senior Lecturer, Strathclyde University, 1976-91; Director of Research, Institute of Chartered Accountants of Scotland, 1992-93; SHEFC Team Leader for Quality Assessment of Finance and Accounting, 1995-96; Elder, Cadder Parish Church. Recreations: golf; tennis; music. Address: (b.) Department of Accounting, Finance and Law, Stirling University, Stirling FK9 4LA; T.-01786 467280.

McIntosh, Rev. Colin George, MA, BD (Hons). Minister, Dunblane Cathedral, since 1988; b. 5.4.51, Glasgow; m., Linda Mary Henderson; 2 d. Educ. Govan High School; Glasgow University. Assistant Minister, Corstorphine, Edinburgh, 1975-76; Minister, St. John's-Renfield Church, Glasgow, 1976-88. Chairman, Leighton Library Trustees; Chairman, Society of Friends of Dunblane Cathedral. Recreations: gardening; music; reading. Address: (h.) Cathedral Manse, The Cross, Dunblane FK15 0AQ.

McIntosh, David Bainbridge, MA, MHSM, FIPD. Founder and Director, Bainbridge McIntosh International Management Consultants; b. 28.10.46, Oxford; m., Judith Mary Mitchell; 4 d. Educ. Edinburgh Academy; Christ Church, Oxford; London School of Economics. Industrial Relations Adviser, Coats Patons (UK) Ltd., 1972-73; Personnel Manager: J. & P. Coats (UK) Ltd., 1974-79, J. & P. Coats Ltd., 1979-81; Mill Manager: Comphanhia De Linha Coats & Clark LDA Portugal, 1981-84, Hilos Cadena SA Colombia, 1984-87; Director, Scottish Health Service Management Development Group, 1987-90; General Manager, Scottish National Blood Transfusion Service, 1990-96; former Chairman, Scotland, The Association for Quality in Health Care; former Member, Broadcasting Council for Scotland. Recreations: golf; sailing; skiing; squash; fishing. Address: 6 Oswald Court, Oswald Road, Edinburgh EH9 2HY.

Macintosh, Farquhar, CBE, MA, DipEd, DLitt, Dr. hc (Edinburgh), FEIS, FScotvec, FSQA. Chairman: Sabhal Mor Ostaig, since 1991, Education Executive Committee, Royal Blind School, since 1994, Gaelic Education Action Group, since 1994, European Movement (Scotland), since 1996; b. 27.10.23, Isle of Skye; m., Margaret M. Inglis; 2 s.;

2 d. Educ. Portree High School; Edinburgh University; Glasgow University; Jordanhill College of Education. Taught, Greenfield Junior Secondary School, Hamilton, Glasgow Academy and Inverness Royal Academy; Headmaster: Portree High School, Oban High School; Rector, Royal High School, Edinburgh, 1972-89; Member, Highlands and Islands Development Consultative Council and Convener, Education Sub-Committee, 1965-82; Chairman: Jordanhill Board of Governors, 1970-72, BBC Secondary Programme Committee, 1972-80, Scottish Examination Board, 1977-90, School Broadcasting Council for Scotland, 1981-85; Vice-Chairman, School Broadcasting Council for UK, 1984-86; Chairman, Scottish Association for Educational Management and Administration, 1979-82; Member, Court, Edinburgh University, 1976-91; Governor, St. Margaret's School, since 1989 (and Vice-Chairman of Governors, 1996-98), Royal Blind School, Edinburgh, since 1990; Member, Board of Directors and Foundation, University of the Highlands and Islands Project, since 1997; Gaelic Correspondent, Weekly Scotsman, 1953-57. Recreations: hill-walking; travel; Gaelic. Address: 12 Rothesay Place, Edinburgh EH3 7SQ; T.-0131-225 4404.

McIntosh, Professor Francis George, BSc, MSc, CEng, MIEE, FRSA. Professor of Electronic and Electrical Engineering, Robert Gordon University, since 1984 (Assistant Principal and Dean of Science and Technology, since 1988); b. 19.3.42; 1 d. Previously Head, School of Electronic and Electrical Engineering, RGIT. Register of advisors, IEE accreditation; Member, COSHEP Research Advisory Group, Scottish Higher Education Funding Council Executive Research Advisory Group. Address: (b.) Robert Gordon University, Schoolhill, Aberdeen AB10 1FR; T.-01224 262020.

McIntosh, Gordon, BSc, CAS. Director of Economic Development, Aberdeen City Council, since 1996; Director, Aberdeen Exhibition and Conference Centre, since 1997; b. 10.8.56; m., Lesley; 2 s.; 1 d. Educ. Keith Grammar School; Glasgow University; Aberdeen University. KPMG (Thomson McLintock), Chartered Accountants, 1979-84; Grampian Regional Council, 1984-96. Chairman, Scottish Local Authorities Economic Development Officers; Member, Scottish Export Forum; Past Chairman, Aberdeen and St. John Mountain Rescue Association; President, Junior Chamber. Recreations: mountaineering; angling; golf. Address: (b.) Economic Development Department, Aberdeen City Council, 74-76 Spring Garden, Aberdeen AB25 1GN; T.-01224 522020.

McIntosh, Iain Redford. Sculptor; b. 4.1.45, Peterhead; m., Freida; 2 d. Educ. Peterhead Academy; Gray's School of Art. Recreation: sculpture. Address: (h.) 53 Kilrymont Road, St. Andrews, Fife.

McIntosh, Professor Jean Barbara, PhD, BSc, SRN, CMB, FRCN. Professor of Community Nursing Research, Glasgow Caledonian University, since 1993; Non-Executive Director, Greater Glasgow Community and Mental Health Services NHS Trust, since 1994; b. 16.8.44, Fulmer; m., Dr. James R.B. McIntosh; 2 s. Educ. Watford Girls' Grammar School; LSE; University College Hospital, London. Former student nurse and staff nurse; Research Fellow, Aberdeen University, 1972-76; Senior Nurse Research, Greater Glasgow Health Board, 1981-88; Reader, then Professor, Glasgow Caledonian University, since 1989. Publications: two books; numerous papers. Recreations: hill-walking; gardening; classical music. Address: (b.) Department of Nursing and Community Health, Glasgow Caledonian University, 70 Cowcaddens Road, Glasgow G4 0BA; T.-0141-331 3461.

Macintosh, Joan, CBE (1978), MA (Oxon), LLD (Hon., Dundee and Strathclyde), DUniv. (Stirling); b. 23.11.19. Chairman, Scottish Consumer Council, 1975-80; Vice-Chairman, National Consumer Council, 1976-84; Lay Observer for Scotland, 1982-89; Chairman, Scottish Child Law Centre, 1989-92; Member: Council, Victim Support Scotland, 1992-96, Commission, Scottish Constitutional Convention, 1993-95; Hon. President, Scottish Legal Action Group; Member, Auchterarder District Community Council. Address: (h.) Wynd End, Auchterarder, Perthshire PH3 1AD.

McIntosh, Professor Neil, FRCP, FRCPE, FRCPCH, DSc (Med). Professor of Child Life and Health, University of Edinburgh, since 1987; Consultant Paediatrician, Royal Hospital for Sick Children, Edinburgh, since 1987; Consultant Neonatologist, Simpson Memorial Maternity Pavilion, Edinburgh, since 1987; b. 21.5.42, London; 2 s.; 1 d. Educ. Lower School of John Lyon, Harrow; University College Hospital, London. Senior Registrar, University College Hospital and Whittington Hospital, London, 1973-78; Fellow in Paediatric Endocrinology, University of California, 1974-75; Consultant Paediatrician, St. George's Hospital, London, 1978-87; Senior Lecturer, St. George's Hospital Medical School, London, 1978-87; Neonatologist to British Army, since 1980; Visiting Professor to Harvard University, Boston, USA, 1997-98. Publication: Textbook of Paediatrics (Co-editor), 1993. Address (b.) 20 Sylvan Place, Edinburgh EH9 1UW; T.-0131-536 0801.

McIntosh, Neil William David, CBE, ACIS, FIPM, FRSA. Convener, Scottish Council for Voluntary Organisations; Chairman, National Companies Implementation Group; Head, COSLA Consultancies; b. 30.1.40, Glasgow; m., Marie Elizabeth Lindsay. Educ. King's Park Senior Secondary School, Glasgow. O. and M. Trainee, Honeywell Controls Ltd., Lanarkshire, 1959-62; O. and M. Assistant, Berkshire, Oxford and Reading Joint Management Services Unit, 1962-64; O. and M. Officer, Stewarts and Lloyds Ltd., Lanarkshire, 1964-66; Senior O. and M. Officer, Lanark County Council, 1966-69; Establishment/O. and M. Officer, Inverness County Council, 1969-75; Personnel Officer, Highland Regional Council, 1975-81; Director of Manpower Services, Highland Regional Council, 1981-85; Clerk, Dumfries Lieutenancy, 1985; Chief Executive, Dumfries and Galloway Regional Council, 1985-92; Chief Executive, Strathclyde Regional Council, 1992-96.

McIntosh, Peter William, BA, FIMgt. Assistant Principal, Robert Gordon University, since 1988, and Dean, Faculty of Management, since 1988; b. 9.4.51, Dunfermline; m., Christine; 1 s.; 1 d. Educ. Dunfermline High School; Strathclyde University. Lecturer in Economics, Strathclyde University, 1974-75; Lecturer in Business Studies, Bell College, Hamilton, 1975-78; Lecturer, Senior Lecturer, Head of Department and Dean, Faculty of Professional Studies, Napier Polytechnic, 1978-88. Recreations: sport; music; travel. Address: (b.) Faculty of Management, Robert Gordon University, Garthdee Road, Aberdeen; T.-01224 263552.

McIntosh, Robert, BSc, PhD, FICF. Chief Executive, Forest Enterprise, since 1997; b. 6.10.51, Edinburgh; m., Elizabeth Ann. Educ. Linlithgow Academy; Edinburgh University. Joined Forestry Commission, 1973: District Manager, Research Scientist, Operations Director. Recreations: shooting; farming; fishing. Address: (b.) 231 Corstorphine Road, Edinburgh EH12 7AT; T.-0131-314 6456.

Macintosh, Robert Macfarlan, MA, LLB. Solicitor; Chairman, Rent Assessment Committee, Glasgow, since 1966; Honorary Sheriff Substitute, Dumbarton, since 1975; b. 16.6.17, Dumbarton; m., Ann McLean Kelso; 1 s. Educ. Dumbarton Academy; George Watson's College, Edinburgh; Glasgow University. Qualified as Solicitor, 1949; Local Secretary, Dumbarton Legal Aid Committee, 1950-84; Dean, Faculty of Procurators, Dumbarton, 1973; Chairman: Dunbartonshire Rent Tribunal, 1960, Glasgow

Rent Tribunal, 1974; Clerk to Commissioners of Income Tax, East and West Dunbartonshire, since 1973; President, Dumbarton Burns Club; President, Cardross Golf Club. Recreation: golf. Address: (h.) Ardmoy, Peel Street, Cardross, Dunbartonshire.

McIntosh, Stewart, BA (Hons). Journalist; b. 7.5.48, Glasgow; m., Marion; 2 d. Educ. Rutherglen Academy; Strathclyde University. Assistant Secretary, STUC, 1976-79; Education Officer, GMB, 1979-83; Freelance Researcher/Reporter, BBC Scotland, 1983-87; Freelance Journalist and Writer, since 1987. UK Property Writer of the Year, 1997. Recreations: athletics; mountain biking; Rioja; Tennent's Bar; Spain. Address: (b.) 29 Cleveden Road, Glasgow G12 0PQ; T.-0141-334 8475.

McIntyre, Alasdair Duncan, CBE, BSc, DSc, FRSE, FIBiol, FRSA. Chairman: Marine Forum for Environmental Issues, 1990-98, Atlantic Frontier Environmental Forum, since 1996, Buckland Foundation, since 1994; President, Sir Alister Hardy Foundation for Ocean Science, since 1992; Emeritus Professor of Fisheries and Oceanography, Aberdeen University, since 1986; b. 17.11.26, Helensburgh; m., Catherine Helen; 1 d. Educ. Hermitage School, Helensburgh; Glasgow University. Senior Principal Scientific Officer in charge of environmental team, Marine Laboratory, Aberdeen, 1973-79; Deputy Director, Department of Agriculture and Fisheries for Scotland, Marine Laboratory, Aberdeen, 1979-83; Director of Fisheries Research for Scotland, 1983-86; Co-ordinator, UK Fisheries Research and Development, 1986; President, Estuarine and Coastal Sciences Association, 1992-95; Member, Research Board, Scottish Natural Heritage, 1992-96; Editor, Fisheries Research. Hon. doctorate, Stirling University, 1997. Recreations: reading; food and wine; walking. Address: (h.) 63 Hamilton Place, Aberdeen AB15 5BW; T.-01224 645633.

McIntyre, Archibald Dewar, CBE, MB, ChB, DPH, FFCM, FRCPE, DIH, DTM&H; b. 18.2.28, Dunipace; m., Euphemia Hope Houston; 2 s.; 2 d. Educ. Falkirk High School; Edinburgh University. Senior Medical Officer, Overseas Civil Service, Sierra Leone; Depute Medical Officer of Health, Stirling County Council; Depute Secretary, Scottish Council for Postgraduate Medical Education; Senior Medical Officer, Scottish Home and Health Department; Principal Medical Officer, Scottish Home and Health Department, 1977-93. Recreations: gardening; photography. Address: (h.) Birchlea, 43 Falkirk Road, Linlithgow EH49 7PH; T.-01506 842063.

Macintyre, Iain Melfort Campbell, QHS, MB, ChB, MD, FRCSE, FRCPE, FSA (Scot). Consultant Surgeon, Edinburgh, since 1979; Director of Education, Royal College of Surgeons, Edinburgh, since 1997; Chairman, Edinburgh Postgraduate Board for Medicine, since 1995; Surgeon to the Queen in Scotland, since 1997; b. 23.6.44, Glasgow; m., Tessa Lorna Mary Millar; 3 d. Educ. Daniel Stewart's College, Edinburgh; Edinburgh University. Lecturer in Surgery, Edinburgh University, 1974-78; Visiting Professor, University of Natal, 1978-79; Council of Europe Travelling Fellow, 1986; Member: Council, Royal College of Surgeons of Edinburgh, since 1991, National Medical Advisory Committee, 1992-95. Recreations: Scottish history; photography; flying light aircraft; skiing; sailing. Address: (b.) Department of Surgery, Western General Hospital, Edinburgh; T.-0131-537 1549.

McIntyre, Rev. Mgr. John, MA (Hons), STL, PhL, DipEd. Parish Priest, St. Bridget's, Baillieston, since 1995; Member, Scottish Catholic Heritage Commission, since 1981; b. 12.11.37, Airdrie. Educ. St. Aloysius College, Glasgow; Gregorian University, Rome; Glasgow University; Jordanhill College of Education. Ordained to priesthood, Rome, 1961; Assistant, St. Monica's, Coatbridge, 1962-63; student, 1963-68; staff, St. Vincent's College, Langbank, 1968-69, St. Mary's College, Blairs, Aberdeen, 1969-86 (Rector, 1985-86); Parish Priest, St. Bride's, East Kilbride, 1986-89; Rector, Scots College, Rome, 1989-95. Bradley Medal, Glasgow University, 1967. Publication: Scotland and the Holy See, 1982. Recreations: English literature; bird-watching; history. Address: 15 Swinton Road, Baillieston, Glasgow G69 6DT; T.-0141-771 1058.

McIntyre, Very Rev. Professor John, CVO, MA, BD, DLitt, DD, DHL, Dr hc, FRSE. Professor of Divinity, Edinburgh University, 1956-86; Honorary Chaplain to The Queen in Scotland, 1974-86 (Extraordinary Chaplain, since 1986); Dean of the Order of the Thistle, 1974-89; b. 20.5.16, Glasgow; m., Jessie Brown Buick; 2 s.; 1 d. Educ. Bathgate Academy; Edinburgh University. Ordained, 1941; Locum Tenens, Parish of Glenorchy and Inishail, 1941-43; Minister, Fenwick, Ayrshire, 1943-45; Hunter Baillie Professor of Theology, St. Andrew's College, Sydney University, 1946-56; Principal, St. Andrew's College, 1950-56, Hon. Fellow, since 1991; Principal Warden, Pollock Halls of Residence, Edinburgh University, 1960-71; Acting Principal and Vice-Chancellor, Edinburgh University, 1973-74, 1979; Principal, New College, and Dean, Faculty of Divinity, 1968-74; Moderator, General Assembly of the Church of Scotland, 1982; Convener, Board of Education, Church of Scotland, 1983-87; former Council Member (1980-86) and Vice President (1983-86), Royal Society of Edinburgh. Publications: St. Anselm and his Critics, 1954; The Christian Doctrine of History, 1957; On the Love of God, 1962; The Shape of Christology, 1966; Faith, Theology and Imagination, 1987; The Shape of Soteriology, 1992; Theology after the Storm, 1997; The Shape of Pneumatology, 1997. Recreation: travel. Address: (h.) 22/4 Minto Street, Edinburgh EH9 1RQ; T.-0131-667 1203.

Macintyre, Lorn, BA (Hons), PhD. Freelance Writer; b. 7.9.42, Taynuilt, Argyll; m., Mary. Educ. Stirling University; Glasgow University. Novelist and Short Story Writer; publications include Cruel in the Shadow, The Blind Bend and Empty Footsteps in Chronicles of Invernevis Series. Recreations: Scottish country dancing; nightjars; the paranormal. Address: (h.) Priormuir, by St. Andrews, Fife; T.-01334 476428.

McIntyre, Major Robert George. Salvation Army Officer, since 1967 (Divisional Commander for East Scotland Division); b. 15.10.44, Glasgow; m., Isobel Laird. Educ. Woodside Senior Secondary School; Stow College of Engineering. Commanded Salvation Army churches in Scotland, 21 years; Divisional Youth Secretary, 1984-87; Church Growth Consultant, 1991-98. Recreations: piano; brass banding; reading; computing; watching all sports. Address: 5 East Adam Street, Edinburgh EH8 9TF; T.-0131-662 3300.

Macintyre, Professor Sally, OBE, FRSE, BA, MSc, PhD. Director, Medical Research Council Medical Sociology Unit, since 1983; Honorary Professor, Glasgow University, since 1991; b. 27.2.49, Edinburgh; m., Dr. Guy Muhlemann. Educ. Durham, London and Aberdeen Universities. Research Fellow, Aberdeen University, 1971-75; Researcher, MRC Medical Sociology Unit, Aberdeen, 1975-83. Fellow, Royal Society of Medicine; Hon. Member, Faculty of Public Health Medicine. Recreations: skiing; hill-walking; climbing. Address: (b.) MRC Medical Sociology Unit, 6 Lilybank Gardens, Glasgow G12 8QQ; T.-0141-357 3949.

MacIver, Alistair. President, Scottish Crofters Union, 1995-97; Chairman, Caithness and Sutherland Constituency Labour Party, 1985-97; Branch Secretary, General, Municipal and Boilermakers' Union, since 1971; b. 13.5.30, Brora. Educ. Lairg Senior School. Member: Rogart Community Council, since 1982, Sutherland Council on Alcohol, 1990-96. Recreations: reading; indoor bowling.

Address: (h.) Elcama, Inchcape, Rogart IV28 3UD; T.-01408 641373.

MacIver, Donald John Morrison, MA (Hons). Education Adviser, Western Isles Council, since 1989; b. 12.11.42, Stornoway; m., Alice Macleod; 1 s. Educ. Nicolson Institute; Aberdeen University. Teacher of Gaelic, 1968-73; Principal Teacher of Gaelic, Nicolson Institute, 1973-89. President, An Comunn Gaidhealach, 1985-90; former Director, National Gaelic Arts Project; former Member, Gaelic Books Council; Director, Acair Publishing Co.; former Editor, Sruth (newspaper of An Comunn Gaidhealach). Publications: Gaelic Oral Composition; Gaelic Language Practice; Gaelic O-Grade Interpretation; Sgriobh Seo; Feuch Seo; Feuch Freagairt; Faic Is Freagair; Camhanaich; Eadar Peann Is Paipear; Coinneach Odhar; Grian is Uisge; Co Rinn E?; A'Chlach; Bonaidean is Breacain. Recreations: writing (prose and poetry); computing; reading poetry; gardening; Coronation Street. Address: (h.) 32 Goathill Road, Stornoway, Isle of Lewis PA87 2NL; T.-01851 702582.

MacIver, Ian, BSc, DipEd, MSc, PhD. Principal, Coatbridge College, since 1989; b. 25.11.38, Stornoway; m., Anne Maureen Ramsay; 3 s.; 2 d. Educ. Nicolson Institute, Stornoway; Portree High School; Glasgow University. Secondary school teacher, 1962-64; studied and taught, University of Alberta, University of Chicago, and York University, Toronto, 1964-73; returned to Scotland and held posts, Langside College, 1973-74, Jordanhill College, 1975-76, James Watt College, 1977-82, Anniesland College, 1982-89. Elder, Free Church of Scotland. Recreations: distance running; reading; loafing. Address: (b.) Coatbridge College, Kildonan Street, Coatbridge ML5 3LS; T.-01236 422316.

Maciver, Sheriff K. M. Sheriff of Glasgow and Strathkelvin. Address: Sheriff Court House, 1 Carlton Place, Glasgow, G5 9DA.

MacIver, Matthew M., MA, MEd, FRSA. Depute Registrar (Education), General Teaching Council for Scotland, since 1998; b. 5.7.46, Isle of Lewis; m., Katrina; 1 s.; 1 d. Educ. Nicolson Institute, Stornoway; Edinburgh University; Moray House College. History Teacher, 1969-72; Principal Teacher of History, Craigmount High School, 1972-80; Assistant Rector, Royal High School, 1980-83; Depute Head Teacher, Balerno High School, 1983-86; Rector, Fortrose Academy, 1986-89; Rector, Royal High School, Edinburgh, 1989-98. Chairman: Gaelic Broadcasting Committee, Highlands and Islands Educational Trust; Winston Churchill Travelling Fellowship, 1998. Recreation: Gaelic culture. Address: (h.) 21 Durham Road, Edinburgh EH15 1NY; T.-0131-669 5029.

McKain, Bruce, LLB (Hons). Law Correspondent, The Herald, since 1978; b. 23.6.48, Dundee; m., Helen Murray Lennox, 2 s. Educ. Madras College, St. Andrews; Edinburgh University. Joined D.C. Thomson, 1970; Weekly News, Manchester and London; Peterborough Evening Telegraph; Radio Clyde; Aberdeen Evening Express. Publication: Scots Law for Journalists (Co-author). Recreations: golf; football (watching); cinema; reading. Address: (b.) 10 George Street, Edinburgh; T.-0131-200 8171.

McKay, Alexander, BSc (Hons), CertEd. Head of Education, Fife Council, since 1995; b.11.9.49, Buckie; m., Jennifer; 1 s. Educ. Fordyce Academy; Banff Academy; Aberdeen University; Aberdeen College of Education. Teacher, Perth Academy, 1972-76; Assistant Principal Teacher, Ellon Academy, 1976-78; Principal Teacher, Elgin High School, 1978-81; secondment to Scottish Curriculum Development Service as Munn-Dunning Development Officer (Mathematics) for Northern Division, 1981-83; General Adviser, Fife Regional Council, 1983-90; Chief Adviser, Fife Regional Council, 1990-93; Assistant Director of Education, Fife Regional Council, 1993-95. Recreations: cricket; walking; reading; jogging and trying to keep fit; holidays with family. Address: (b.) Fife House, North Street, Glenrothes KY7 5LT; T.-01592 414141.

Mackay, Angus Victor Peck, OBE, MA, BSc (Pharm), PhD (Cantab), MB, ChB, FRCPsych, FRCP (Ed), TPsych. Physician Superintendent and Clinical Director, Argyll and Bute Hospital, and MacKintosh Lecturer in Psychological Medicine, Glasgow University, since 1980; Hon. Senior Lecturer, Department of Psychology, St. Andrews University; Medical Director, Argyll & Bute NHS Trust; Chairman, National Mental Health Reference Group; Psychiatric Representative, Committee on Safety of Medicines, DHSS, since 1983; b. 4.3.43, Edinburgh; m., Elspeth M.W. Norris; 2 s.; 2 d. Educ. George Heriot's School, Edinburgh; Edinburgh University; Churchill and Trinity Colleges, Cambridge. MRC Research Fellow, Cambridge; Member, senior clinical staff, MRC Neurochemical Pharmacology Unit, Cambridge, with appointment as Lector in Pharmacology, Trinity College (latterly, Deputy Director of Unit). Deputy Chairman, Health Services Research Committee of the Chief Scientist for Scotland; Chairman: Scottish Working Group on Mental Illness, Research and Clinical Section of Royal College of Psychiatrists (Scotland); Member: Research Committee, Mental Health Foundation, Scottish Executive, Royal College of Psychiatrists. Recreations: rowing; sailing; rhododendrons. Address: (h.) Tigh an Rudha, Ardrishaig, Argyll; T.-01546 603272.

McKay, Bob, BA (Hons), DipEd. Director of Education, Perth and Kinross Council, since 1995; President, Association of Directors of Education, 1995-96; b. 2.11.43, Glasgow; m., Norma; 1 s.; 1 d. Educ. St. Mungo's Academy, Glasgow; Strathclyde University. Teacher, Principal Teacher, Assistant Headteacher, 1969-85 (mainly at St. Augustine's Secondary, Glasgow, first Strathclyde Community School); seconded to regional headquarters to promote community school concept, 1985-86; Education Officer, Dunbarton Division, 1986-88; Assistant Director of Education, Strathclyde Regional Council, 1988-91; Senior Depute Director, Tayside Regional Council, 1991-95. Publication: Contemporary Britain (textbook). Recreations: theatre; music; art; reading; Spain and things Spanish; sport. Address: (b.) Education Offices, Blackfriars, Perth; T.-01738 476201.

McKay, Sheriff Colin Graham, MA, LLB. Sheriff of North Strathclyde at Oban, since 1990; b. 20.1.42. Solicitor, 1966; private practice, 1966-90.

MacKay, Colin Hinshelwood, MA (Hons), FSA Scot. Partner, Colin MacKay Associates; Broadcaster and Writer; b. 27.8.44, Glasgow; m., Olive E.B. Brownlie; 2 s. Educ. Kelvinside Academy, Glasgow; Glasgow University; Jordanhill College of Education. Reporter/Presenter: Border Television Ltd., 1967-70, Grampian Television Ltd., 1970-73; Political Editor, Scottish Television PLC, 1973-92 (Presenter, Ways and Means, 1973-86), Parliamentary Lobby Correspondent, 1985-95; recent programmes include: People and Power and Sunday Morning (BBC Radio Scotland); Talk-In Sunday (Radio Clyde); Westminster File (Border TV); Eikon (Scottish TV); General Assembly (BBC TV/Radio); contributions to BBC World Service, Radio 4, Radio 5 Live; ITV Commentator: Papal Visit to Scotland, 1982, CBI Conference, Glasgow, 1983. Winner, Observer Mace, 1967 (British Universities Debating Championship); Member, two-man British Universities Canadian Debating Tour, 1967; Commonwealth Relations Trust Bursary to Canada, 1981; Member, Scottish Arts Council, 1988-94; BT Scottish Radio News Broadcaster of the Year, 1997. Publications: Kelvinside Academy: 1878-1978, 1978; The Scottish

Dimension in Central and Eastern Canada, 1981. Recreations: music (especially opera); reading; writing.

McKay, Colin Ian, LLB (Hons). Legal and Policy Adviser, Enable (Scottish Society for the Mentally Handicapped), since 1989; Member, Mental Welfare Commission for Scotland, since 1996; b. 21.8.59, Dundee; m., Allison Brisbane; 1 s.; 1 d. Educ. North Berwick High School; Edinburgh University. Legal Trainee/Legal Assistant, 1982-86; Assistant Solicitor, Lothian Regional Council, 1986-88. Norman McEwan Award. Publications: The Care Maze (Co-author); Sex, Laws and Red Tape; Invisible Citizens (Editor). Address: (b.) 6th Floor, 7 Buchanan Street, Glasgow G1 3HL; T.-0141-226 4541.

Mackay, David J., BA, ACIB. Area Manager, Scotland, Midland Bank plc, since 1998; b. 4.5.58, Edinburgh; m., Carole; 2 s.; 1 d. Educ. Scotus Academy, Edinburgh; Napier University. Joined Midland Bank 1980. Address: (b.) 76 Hanover Street, Edinburgh EH1 1HQ; T.-0131-456 3256.

Mackay, David James, FCIM, FILT. Chief Executive, John Menzies PLC, since 1997; b. 20.5.43, St. Andrews; m., Jane; 1 s.; 1 d. Educ. Kirkcaldy High School; Bradford University; Edinburgh University; Companion, Institute of Management, 1998; FCIT, 1993. Various posts in John Menzies PLC from Transport Manager in Northern Ireland in 1965 to Assistant Regional Director, Southern and London in 1973; returned to Edinburgh as Operations Director, 1978; Managing Director – Wholesale, 1984. Recreations: golf; walking. Address: 108 Princes Street, Edinburgh EH2 3AA; T.-0131-225 8555.

Mackay, David Johnstone, BA, ACIB. Area Manager, Midland Bank plc, since 1998; b. 4.5.58; m., Carole; 2 s.; 1 d. Educ. Scotus Academy; Napier University. Joined Midland Bank, 1980: appointments in Manchester, Liverpool, Sheffield, London, Nottingham, Chesterfield, Glasgow; Managing Director, Griffin Credit Services Ltd., 1997-98. Recreations: golf, walking and that sort of thing. Address: (b.) 76 Hanover Street, Edinburgh EH2 1HQ; T.-0131-456 3256.

McKay, David Sutherland. Director, SETG Ltd., since 1984; Chairman, Lanarkshire Quality Forum; b. 28.8.38, Wick; m., Catherine Margaret; 2 d. Educ. Wick High School; Robert Gordon's College. Apprenticeship in control engineering; Design Engineer, British Oxygen Co.; joined Honeywell Control Systems as Design Engineer; appointed Technical Director, 1983; Director and General Manager, JVC Manufacturing UK Ltd., 1988-98. Member, Bell College Management Board; Member, Scottish Electronic Forum; Visiting Professor, Strathclyde University. Recreation: gardening; DIY. Address: (h.) Green Garth, Nethan Glen, Crossford ML8 5QU; T.-Crossford 309.

Mackay, Professor David William, OBE, CBiol, FIBiol, FIWEM, FBIM, MIFM. Regional Director (North), Scottish Environment Protection Agency, since 1996; Visiting Professor, Institute of Aquaculture, Stirling University, since 1992; Board Member, Scottish Marine Biological Association, since 1991; b. 6.4.36, Stirling; m., Maureen. Educ. High School of Stirling; Strathclyde University; Paisley College. Experimental Officer, Freshwater Fisheries Laboratory, Pitlochry; Freshwater Biologist, then Marine Survey Officer, Clyde River Purification Board; Principal Environmental Protection Officer, Government of Hong Kong; Depute Director, Clyde River Purification Board; Head of Environmental Services, Ove Arup and Partners, Hong Kong; General Manager and Clerk, North East River Purification Board, Aberdeen; Chief Officer, North East River Purification Board. Vice President and Secretary, Scottish Anglers National Association, 1970-89. Recreations: farming; fishing. Address: (b.) SEPA, North Region Headquarters, Graesser House, Fodderty Way, Dingwall, IV15 9XB; T.-01349 862021.

Mackay, Donald George, MA PhD. Honorary Research Fellow, Aberdeen University, since 1990; b. 25.11.29; m., Elizabeth Ailsa Barr; 2 s.; 1 d. Educ. Morgan Academy, Dundee; St. Andrews University; Aberdeen University. Assistant Principal, Scottish Home Department, 1953; Assistant Private Secretary to Secretary of State for Scotland, 1959-60; Assistant Secretary, Royal Commission on the Police, 1960-62; Secretary, Royal Commission on Local Government in Scotland, 1966-69; Assistant Secretary, Scottish Development Department, 1969-79; Assistant Secretary, 1980-83, Under Secretary, 1983-85, Department of Agriculture and Fisheries for Scotland; Under Secretary, Scottish Development Department, 1985-88. Member, Scottish Agricultural Wages Board, 1991-97. Publication: Scotland's Rural Land Use Agencies, 1995. Recreation: hill walking; photography; music. Address: (h.) 38 Cluny Drive, Edinburgh EH10 6DX; T.-0131-447 1851.

MacKay, Professor Sir Donald Iain, MA, FRSE, FRSGS. Chairman, DTZ Pieda Consulting, since 1976; Chairman, Grampian Holdings, since 1998; Honorary Professor, Heriot-Watt University, since 1982; b. 27.2.37, Kobe, Japan; m., Diana Marjory Raffan; 1 s.; 2 d. Educ. Dollar Academy; Aberdeen University. Professor of Political Economy, Aberdeen University, 1971-76; Professor of Economics, Heriot-Watt University, 1976-82; Chairman, Scottish Enterprise, 1993-97; Director, Highland Distilleries; Vice President, Scottish Association of Public Transport; Member, Scottish Business Council; Economic Consultant to Secretary of State for Scotland; Governor, National Institute of Economic and Social Research; Chairman, Edinburgh Business School Ltd. Recreations: tennis; bridge. Address: (h.) Newfield, 14 Gamekeepers Road, Edinburgh; T.-0131-336 1936.

Mackay, Donald John, MA, FRSA, FIMgt. Chairman, Highland Communities NHS Trust, 1994-96; Chief Executive, Harris Tweed Association, 1982-93; b. 8.6.30, North Uist; m., Rhona MacLeod; 3 d. Educ. Portree High School; Aberdeen University; London University. District Commissioner and Private Secretary/Aide de Camp to Governor, Sierra Leone, 1954-58; Scottish Agricultural Organisation Society, 1958-61; AEA, Dounreay, 1961-63; British Aluminium, 1964-65; Director, An Comunn Gaidhealach, 1965-70; Primary Division, British Aluminium, 1970-82. Member, Red Deer Commission, 1966-74; Member, Highland Disablement Committee, 1970-91, Chairman, 1991-94; Member: Highland Area Group, Scottish Council, 1971-93, North of Scotland Electricity Council, 1981-84; Secretary, CBI Highland Area Group, 1978-87, Chairman, 1988-91; Member: HIDB Consultative Council, 1978-81, 1988-91, Nature Conservancy Council Scottish Advisory Committee, 1979-86; MSC Chairman, Highlands & Islands, 1981-88; Member, Executive Committee, Scottish Council, 1982-93; Chairman: CNAG, 1984-86, Albyn Housing Society, 1979-83; Director, Fearann Eilean Iarmain, 1972-91; Member, Industrial Tribunal Panel, since 1986; Deputy Chairman, Sabhal Mor Ostaig, 1981-85; Member: Highland River Purification Board, 1981-83, Highland Health Board, 1991-93. Recreations: sailing; shooting; fishing; Gaelic. Address: (h.) Kildonan, Teandalloch, Beauly, by Inverness.

Mackay of Drumadoon, Rt. Hon. Lord (Donald Sage Mackay), QC, LLB, LLM. Life Peer; former Lord Advocate; b. 30.1.46; m., 1 s.; 2 d. Educ. George Watson's; University of Edinburgh; University of Virginia. Called to Scottish Bar, 1976.

MacKay, Donald Stewart, BA, DipPE, AUPE. Director of Education, Midlothian, since 1996; b. 18.4.50, Edinburgh; 2 s. Educ. Firrhill Secondary, Boroughmuir Secondary, Edinburgh; Moray House College of Education; Open University. Teacher/Assistant Head Teacher/Headteacher, Fife; Curriculum Development Officer, Fife; Advisor in Primary Education, Lothian; Assistant Director of

Education, Lothian. Recreations: skiing; football. Address: (b.) Fairfield House, 8 Lothian Road, Dalkeith EH22 3ZG; T.-0131-270 7500.

Mackay, Rev. Canon Douglas Brysson. Rector, Church of the Holy Rood, Carnoustie, since 1972; Synod Clerk, Diocese of Brechin, since 1981; Canon, St. Paul's Cathedral, Dundee, since 1981; Tutor, Primary Care, Tayside Centre for General Practice; b. 20.3.27, Glasgow; m., Catherine Elizabeth; 2 d. Educ. Possil Senior Secondary School; Edinburgh Theological College. Precentor, St. Andrew's Cathedral, Inverness, 1958; Rector, Gordon Chapel, Fochabers, 1961 (also Priest-in-Charge, St. Margaret's Church, Aberlour, 1964); Canon, St. Andrew's Cathedral, Inverness, 1965; Synod Clerk, Diocese of Moray, Ross, Caithness, 1965; Honorary Canon, St. Andrew's Cathedral, Inverness, 1972; Convenor of Youth, Moray Diocese, 1965; Brechin Diocese: Convenor, Social Service Board, 1974, Convenor, Joint Board, 1974, Convenor, Administration Board, 1982, Synod Clerk, 1981; Honorary Canon, St Paul's Cathedral, Dundee, 1998; Chairman, Truth and Unity Movement, 1980-87. President: British Red Cross, Carnoustie, 1974-82, British Legion, Carnoustie, 1981; Vice-Chairman, Carnoustie Community Care, 1981; Chairman, Carnoustie Community Council, 1979-81; President, Carnoustie Rotary Club, 1976; Joint Founder and Vice Chairman, Carnoustie Community Care; Carnoustie Citizen of the Year, 1998. Recreations: golf; snooker; reading; music. Address: Balmore House, 24 Philip Street, Carnoustie DD7 6EB.

Mackay, Lt. Col. Hugh David Ruthven. Secretary to the Trustees, Scottish National War Memorial, since 1997; b. 29.12.28, Blackheath, Kent; m., Suzanne Dimoline; 3 d. Educ. Epsom College; Royal Military Academy, Sandhurst. Served in the Highland Light Infantry and Royal Highland Fusiliers, 1949-68; Adjutant, 1st Bn., HLI, Cyprus and Germany, 1956-58; Nigerian Military Forces, 1958-60; Instructor, Royal Canadian School of Infantry, 1962-64; Commander, Edinburgh/Heriot Watt Universities OTC, 1974-77; Abbey Life Assurance Co., Broker Division, 1972-80; Skandia Life Assurance Co. Ltd., 1982-93, latterly as Regional Director Scotland. Chairman, Perth and Kinross Conservative Association, 1990-93; Hon. Treasurer, Scottish Conservative and Unionist Association, 1994-96; Chairman, Supervisory Board, BLESMA Home, Crieff, 1993-96. Recreations: current affairs; history; antiques; walking. Address: (b.) Scottish National War Memorial, The Castle, Edinburgh EH1 2YT; T.-0131-310 5130.

Mackay, Ian Lindsay. Collector Scotland, H.M. Customs and Excise, since 1998; b. 31.8.43, Belfast; m., Carol; 1 s.; 1 d. Educ. Worthing School. Deputy Collector, Northern Ireland, 1993; Deputy Collector, Anglia, 1996. Address: (b.) 44 York Place, Edinburgh EH1 3JW; T.-0131-469 7300.

Mackay, Ian Munro, BCom, CA. Principal, Mackay & Co., Chartered Accountants, Golspie and Dornoch, since 1979; Honorary Sheriff, Dornoch Sheriff Court, since 1985; b. 14.9.47, Brora; m., Maureen; 2 s.; 2 d. (1 d. deceased). Educ. Golspie High School; Edinburgh University. Trained as CA in Edinburgh, qualifying in 1973; has worked in the profession since, spending three years in United Arab Emirates, returning to UK in 1979 to set up own practice. Auditor, Treasurer, Secretary of several local charities and sporting organisations; Secretary, Dornoch Curling Club; Past President, Sutherland Curling Province; Treasurer, Brora Ice Rink Club. Recreations: curling; local history; holidays in France or USA; garden; following most sports. Address: (h.) 4 Sutherland Road, Dornoch, Sutherland; T.-01862 810333.

Mackay, James Alexander, MA, DLitt. Author and Journalist; Numismatic and Philatelic Correspondent, Financial Times, since 1972; b. 21.11.36, Inverness; m., Renate Finlay-Freundlich. Educ. Hillhead High School, Glasgow; Glasgow University. Lt., RA Guided Weapons Range, Hebrides, 1959-61; Assistant Keeper, Department of Printed Books, British Museum, in charge of philatelic collections, 1961-71; returned to Scotland as a full-time Writer, 1972; Editor-in-Chief, IPC Stamp Encyclopedia, 1968-72; Columnist on antiques, Financial Times, 1967-72, philately and numismatics, 1972-85; Editor: the Burns Chronicle, 1978-91, The Burnsian, 1986-89; Consultant Editor: Coin News, since 1992, Stamp and Coin Mart, since 1995, International Stamp and Exhibition News, since 1996; Trustee, James Currie Memorial Trust, since 1987, Burns-Gaelic Trust, since 1992; Secretary, West of Scotland Numismatic Society, since 1993; Publisher of books on philately and postal history; author of 170 books on aspects of the applied and decorative arts, numismatics, philately, postal history; Scottish books include Robert Bruce, King of Scots, 1974; Rural Crafts in Scotland, 1976; Scottish Postmarks, 1978; The Burns Federation 1885-1985, 1985; The Complete Works of Robert Burns, 1986; The Complete Letters of Robert Burns, 1987; Burnsiana, 1988; Burns-Lore of Dumfries and Galloway, 1988; Burns at Ellisland, 1989; Scottish Post Offices, 1989; Burns A-Z, 1990; Kilmarnock, 1992; Burns, a biography, 1992 (Saltire Prize); Vagabond of Verse, 1995; William Wallace Brave Heart, 1995; Land o' Burns, 1996; Allan Pinkerton, The Eye Who Never Slept, 1996; Michael Collins, 1996; Sounds out of Silence, a life of Alexander Graham Bell, 1996; Under the Gum, 1997; Little Boss: a life of Andrew Carnegie, 1997; The Man who Invented Himself: a life of Sir Thomas Lipton, 1998; I Have Not Yet Begun to Fight: a life of John Paul Jones, 1998. Recreations: travel; languages; music (piano-playing); photographing post offices. Address: (h.) 67 Braidpark Drive, Glasgow G46 6LY; T.-0141-633 5422.

Mackay of Clashfern, Lord (James Peter Hymers), Baron (1979), PC (1979), FRSE, Hon. FRICE, FRCOG. Lord High Chancellor of Great Britain, 1987-97; Chancellor, Heriot Watt University, since 1991; b. 2.7.27, Edinburgh; m., Elizabeth Gunn Hymers; 1 s.; 2 d. Educ. George Heriot's School, Edinburgh; Edinburgh University. Lecturer in Mathematics, St. Andrews University, 1948-50; Major Scholar, Trinity College, Cambridge, in Mathematics, 1947, taken up, 1950; Senior Scholar, 1951; BA (Cantab), 1952; LLB Edinburgh (with distinction), 1955; admitted, Faculty of Advocates, 1955; QC (Scot), 1965; Standing Junior Counsel to: Queen's and Lord Treasurer's Remembrancer, Scottish Home and Health Department, Commissioners of Inland Revenue in Scotland; Sheriff Principal, Renfrew and Argyll, 1972-74; Vice-Dean, Faculty of Advocates, 1973-76; Dean, 1976-79; Lord Advocate of Scotland, 1979-84; a Senator of the College of Justice in Scotland, 1984-85; a Lord of Appeal in Ordinary, 1985-87. Part-time Member, Scottish Law Commission, 1976-79; Hon. Master of the Bench, Inner Temple, 1979; Fellow, International Academy of Trial Lawyers, 1979; Fellow, Institute of Taxation, 1981; Director, Stenhouse Holdings Ltd., 1976-77; Member, Insurance Brokers' Registration Council, 1977-79; a Commissioner of Northern Lighthouses, 1975-84; Hon. LLD: Edinburgh, 1983, Dundee, 1983, Strathclyde, 1985, Aberdeen, 1987, Cambridge, 1989, Birmingham, 1990, University of India Law School, 1994, Bath, 1996, Leicester University, 1996; Hon. DCL: Newcastle, 1990, Oxford, 1998; Hon. Doctor of Laws, College of William and Mary, 1989; Hon. Fellow, Institution of Civil Engineers, 1988; Hon. Fellow, Trinity College, Cambridge, 1989; Hon. Fellow, Royal College of Surgeons, Edinburgh, 1989; Hon. Fellow, Royal College of Physicians of Edinburgh, 1990; Hon. Fellow, Royal College of Obstetricians and Gynaecologists, 1996; Fellow, American College of Trial Lawyers, 1990. Recreation: walking. Address: House of Lords, London, SW1A 0PW.

Mackay, John, TD, MA, FRSGS, FInstD. Chairman, Earl Haig Fund Scotland; Chairman, Scotland the Brand Judging Panel; Member, Scottish Rugby Union Business

Development Board; Member, Committee, Army Benevolent Fund Scotland; b. 14.9.36, St. Andrews; m., Barbara Wallace; 1 s.; 2 d. Educ. Madras College; Dunfermline High School; Kircaldy High School; Edinburgh University. Lieutenant, 1st East Anglian Regiment, 1959-63; Territorial Army, 1964-86: Colonel, Royal Engineers (Postal and Courier); Royal Mail, 1963-96: Director, Philately, 1979-84, Chairman, Scottish Post Office Board, 1988, Operations Director, UK, 1991-92, Director and General Manager, Scotland and Northern Ireland, 1986-96. President, Lord's Taverners Scotland, 1994-98; Chairman, Scottish Premier Rugby Limited, 1996-97; Chairman, Scottish Business in the Community Executive Council, 1995-98; Chairman, Edinburgh Common Purpose, 1995-96; Board Member, Quality Scotland, 1991-98; Board Member, Scottish Business in the Community, 1993-98; Member, Quality Assessment Committee, Scottish Higher Education Funding Council, 1994-96. Recreations: golf; watching cricket and rugby; reading; walking dog; convivial company. Address: (h.) Kinrymont, 8 Damside, Dean Village, Edinburgh EH4 3BB; T.-0131-226 2512.

MacKay, John, OBE, MB, ChB, FRCGP. Retired General Medical Practitioner; Member, General Medical Council; Member, Scottish National Board for Nursing, Midwifery and Health Visiting; b. 24.7.26, Glasgow; m., Matilda MacLennan Bain; 2 s.; 2 d. Educ. Govan High School; Glasgow University. Junior House Doctor, Victoria Infirmary and Southern General Hospital, Glasgow, 1949; Ship's Surgeon, 1950; Assistant in General Practice, Govan, 1951-52 (Principal, since 1953); Member, Board of Management, Glasgow South West Hospitals, prior to 1973; Tutor, University Department of General Practice, Glasgow; part-time Medical Referee, Scottish Home and Health Department; Honorary Life Manager, Govan Weavers Society; Member, Scottish General Medical Services Committee. Recreations: angling; golf; gardening. Address: (h.) Moorholm, Barr's Brae, Kilmacolm, Renfrewshire PA13 4DE; T.-Kilmacolm 3234.

MacKay, John Angus, MA, FRSA. Director, Gaelic Broadcasting Fund, since 1991; Board Member, Highlands and Islands Enterprise, 1991-97; Director, Comunn Na Gaidhlig, since 1985; Chairman, Gaelic Television Training Trust; Board Member, Gaelic Arts Agency; b. 24.6.48, Shader, Stornoway; m., Maria F.; 4 s. Educ. Nicolson Institute; Aberdeen University; Jordanhill College. Aberdeen Circulation Rep., D.C. Thomson, 1970-71; Jordanhill College, 1971-72; Teacher, 1972-77; Field Officer, then Development Officer, then Senior Administrative Officer, HIDB, 1977-85. Chairman: Gaelic Youth Radio Trust, Sabhal Mor Ostaig, 1987-91; Director, Acair. Recreations: reading; skiing; swimming; running. Address: (h.) Druimard, Arnol, Isle of Lewis; T.-01851 71479.

McKay, John Henderson, CBE (1987), DL, JP, BA (Hons), PhD, Dr h.c. (Edinburgh). Chairman: Scottish Working Peoples' History Trust, since 1992, Edinburgh Quartet Trust, since 1996; Hon. Vice-President, St. Andrew Society, since 1989; Hon. President, Scottish Craftsmanship Association, since 1987; Patron, Scotland Yard Adventure Centre, since 1988; b. 12.5.29, Kirknewton; m., Catherine Watson Taylor; 1 s.; 1 d. Educ. West Calder High School; Open University. Labourer and Clerk, Pumpherston Oil Co. Ltd., 1948-50; National Service, Royal Artillery, 1950-52; Customs and Excise, 1952-85; Lord Provost of Edinburgh, 1984-88. Vice President, Royal Caledonian Horticultural Society, 1984-88 and 1993-96, Secretary and Treasurer, 1988-93; Convener, Business Committee, General Council, Edinburgh University, 1992-96; General Council Assessor, Edinburgh University Court, since 1996. Recreations: gardening; reading; listening to music. Address: (h.) 2 Buckstone Way, Edinburgh EH10 6PN; T.-0131-445 2865.

MacKay of Ardbrecknish, Rt. Hon Lord (John Jackson MacKay), PC, DL, BSc, DipEd, JP. Life Peer, since 1991; Opposition Spokesman on Constitutional Affairs, since 1997; b. 15.11.38, Lochgilphead; m., Sheena Wagner; 2 s.; 1 d. Educ. Dunoon Grammar School; Campbeltown Grammar School; Glasgow University; Jordanhill College of Education. Member: Oban Town Council, 1969-74, Argyll Water Board, 1969-74; Principal Teacher of Mathematics, Oban High School, 1969-79; MP for Argyll, 1979-83, for Argyll & Bute, 1983-87; Parliamentary Private Secretary to Secretary of State for Scotland, 1982; Parliamentary Under Secretary of State, Scottish Office, 1982-87; Chief Executive, Scottish Conservative Party, 1987-90; Chairman, Sea Fish Industry Authority, 1990-93; Member, Select Committee on the European Communities, 1992-93; Lord in Waiting (Government Whip in the House of Lords), 1993-94; Under Secretary of State, Department of Transport, January-July, 1994; Minister of State, Social Security, 1994-97. Recreation: fishing. Address: (h.) Innishail, 51 Springkell Drive, Pollokshields, Glasgow G41 4EZ.

McKay, Rev. Johnston Reid, MA (Glasgow), BA (Cantab). Senior Producer, Religious Programmes, BBC, since 1987; b. 2.5.42, Glasgow. Educ. High School of Glasgow; Glasgow University; Cambridge University. Assistant Minister, St. Giles' Cathedral, 1967-71; Church Correspondent, Glasgow Herald, 1968-70; Minister, Bellahouston Steven Parish Church, 1971-78; frequent Broadcaster; Governor, Paisley College; Minister, Paisley Abbey, 1978-87; Editor, The Bush (newspaper of Glasgow Presbytery), 1975-78; Chairman, Scottish Religious Advisory Committee, BBC, 1981-86; Stanley Mair Lecturer on Preaching, Glasgow University, 1995. Publications: From Sleep and From Damnation (with James Miller), 1970; Essays in Honour of William Barclay (Joint Editor), 1976; Through Wood and Nails, 1982; This Small Pool, 1996. Recreations: good music and bad golf. Address: (b.) 41 Stakehill, Largs KA30 9NH; T.-01475 672960.

MacKay, Professor Norman, CBE, MD, FRCP(Glas), FRCP(Edin), FRCS(Edin), FRCGP, FCPSP, FACP(Hon), FRACP(Hon), FAMS, FAMM, FRCS(Eng), FRCS(I), FRCP(I), FCPSBangl., FCCP(Hon). Dean of Postgraduate Medicine and Professor of Postgraduate Medical Education, Glasgow University, since 1989; Consultant Physician, Victoria Infirmary, Glasgow, since 1974; President, Royal College of Physicians and Surgeons of Glasgow, 1994-97; b. 15.9.36, Glasgow; m., Grace Violet McCaffer; 2 s.; 2 d. Educ. Govan High School; Glasgow University. Honorary Secretary: Royal College of Physicians and Surgeons of Glasgow, 1973-83, Standing Joint Committee, Scottish Royal Colleges, 1978-82, Conference of Royal Colleges and Faculties in Scotland, 1982-91; Speciality Adviser in Medicine, West of Scotland Committee of Postgraduate Medical Education, 1982-89; President, Royal Medico-Chirurgical Society of Glasgow, 1982-83; Member, Area Medical Committee, Greater Glasgow Health Board, 1987-89; President, Southern Medical Society, 1989-90. Address: (b.) Department of Postgraduate Medical Education, 124 Observatory Road, Glasgow G12 8UZ; T.-0141-330 5273.

Mackay, Peter, CB. Director, British Linen Bank; Member, Board, Scottish Natural Heritage, since 1997; Member, Court, Napier University; Member, Monopolies and Mergers Commission, since 1996; Trustee, Scottish Maritime Museum; Visiting Professor, Strathclyde Graduate Business School; b. 6.7.40, Arbroath; m., Sarah Holdich; 1 s.; 2 d. Educ. Glasgow High School; St. Andrews University. Teacher, New South Wales, Australia, 1962-63; Private Secretary to Secretaries of State for Scotland, 1973-75; Director for Scotland, Manpower Services Commission, 1983-85; on secondment from Scottish Office to Department of Employment, London, 1985; Under Secretary, Scottish Education Department (Further and Higher Education, Arts and Sport), 1987-89;

Secretary and Chief Executive, Scottish Office Industry Department, 1990-95; Executive Director, Advanced Management Programme in Scotland, 1995-97. Recreations: Scotland; high altitudes and latitudes; dinghy sailing; sea canoeing; tennis. Address: (h.) 6 Henderland Road, Edinburgh EH12 6BB; T.-0131-337 2830.

McKean, Professor Charles Alexander, BA, FRSA, FSA Scot, HonFRIBA, Hon FRIAS. Professor of Architectural History, Dundee University; Secretary, Royal Incorporation of Architects in Scotland, 1979-94; b. 16.7.46, Glasgow; m., Margaret Yeo; 2 s. Educ. Fettes College; Bristol University. RIBA: Secretary, London Region, 1968-76, Secretary, Eastern Region, 1972-79, Secretary, Community Architecture, 1976-79; Architectural Correspondent, The Times, 1977-83; Trustee, Thirlestane Castle, 1982-92; author of architectural guides to Edinburgh, Dundee, Stirling, London, Cambridge, Moray, Central Glasgow, Banff and Buchan; General Editor, RIAS/Landmark Trust Guides to Scotland. Publications: The Scottish Thirties; Edinburgh: Portrait of a City; Claim! Recreations: books; glasses; gardens; stately homes. Address: (b.) Department of History, Dundee University, Perth Road, Dundee DD1 4HN; T.-01382 345738.

McKechin, Ann, LLB, DipLP. Solicitor, since 1983; Secretary, Strathkelvin Association of Solicitors, since 1992; b. 22.4.61, Johnstone. Educ. Paisley Grammar School; Strathclyde University. Partner, Pacitti Jones, Solicitors, since 1991 (Associate, 1987-91). Secretary, Glasgow Kelvin Labour Party, 1995-98; Scottish Representative, World Development Movement, since 1998. Recreations: art history; Scottish country dancing; music. Address: (b.) Pacitti Jones, 64 Townhead, Kirkintilloch, Glasgow G66 1NZ; T.-0141-777 8899.

McKee, Graham Hamilton, BSc, BPhil. Chief Executive, Scottish Enterprise Tayside, since 1994; b. 11.9.51; m., Pilar; 1 s.; 2 d. Educ. Hutchesons' Grammar School, Glasgow; Glasgow University; Newcastle-upon-Tyne University. Assistant Planner, Burnley Borough Council, 1975-77; Scottish Development Agency, 1977-91, latterly as Regional Manager; Director Economic Development, Scottish Enterprise Tayside, 1991-93. Recreation: family. Address: (b.) Scottish Enterprise Tayside, Enterprise House, 45 North Lindsay Street, Dundee DD1 1HT; T.-01382 223100.

McKee, Professor (James Clark St. Clair) Sean, BSc, MA, PhD, DSc, FIMA, CMath, FRSE. Professor of Mathematics, Strathclyde University, since 1988; b. 1.7.45, Belfast. Educ. George Watson's College, Edinburgh; St. Andrews University; Dundee University; Oxford University. NCR Research Fellow, 1970-72; Lecturer in Numerical Analysis, Southampton University, 1972-75; Fellow, Hertford College, Oxford, 1975-86; Professor of Industrial Mathematics, Strathclyde University, and Consultant Mathematician, Unilever Research, 1986-88. Member, Council: IMA, ECMI; President, Scottish Branch, Institute of Mathematics and Its Applications; Member, IMA Programmes Committee. Publications: 100 papers; Industrial Numerical Analysis (Co-Editor), 1986; Vector and Parallel Computing (Co-Editor), 1989; Artificial Intelligence in Mathematics (Co-Editor), 1994. Recreations: climbing Munros; golf; theatre; running conferences. Address: (b.) Department of Mathematics, Strathclyde University, Glasgow G1 1XH; T.-0141-552 4400.

McKeganey, Professor Neil Patrick, BA, MSc (Econ), PhD. Professor of Drug Misuse Research, University of Glasgow, since 1997; Director, Centre for Drug Misuse Research, University of Glasgow, since 1994; b. 25.4.55, Sussex. Educ. Thomas Bennet School, Crawley; University of Sussex; University of London; University of Aberdeen. Member, Prevention Working Group, Advisory Council on Misuse of Drugs; Member, Executive, Society for the Study of Addiction; Member, Greater Glasgow Drug Action Team. Publications: AIDS Drugs and Sexual Risk: Lives in the Balance, 1992; Sex Work in the Streets: Prostitutes and their Clients, 1996; over 100 academic articles and articles for newspapers and magazines. Recreation: his two children, Rebecca and Gabriel; Formula One racing; cinema. Address: (b.) 11 Professor Square, Glasgow G12 8QG; T.-0141-330 3616.

McKellar, Kenneth, BSc. Singer, Composer, Writer; b. 23.6.27, Paisley. Gave first concert in local hall, aged 13; continued singing while at school, university and during his first two years working in forestry; has made numerous records of classical and popular music; numerous tours, especially in Australia and New Zealand; has appeared a number of times at the London Palladium.

McKellar, Peter Archibald, LLB (Hons). Finance Director, Clydeport plc, since 1995; b. 28.5.65, Glasgow; m., Kathleen Scarlett; 1 s. Educ. Daniel Stewart's and Melville College, Edinburgh; Edinburgh University. J.P. Morgan, Investment Bank, New York and London, 1986-88; EFT Group PLC, Corporate Finance Division, 1988-89; London and Edinburgh Trust plc, 1989-90; Co-Founder, Barry McKellar Ltd., 1990-95; Non-Executive Director, Red Lemon Studios Ltd. Recreations: golf; shooting; swimming. Address: (b.) 16 Robertson Street, Glasgow G2 8DS; T.-0141-221 8733.

McKenna, Rosemary, CBE, DCE, JP. MP (Labour), Cumbernauld and Kilsyth; b. 8.5.41, Kilmacolm; m., James Stephen McKenna; 3 s.; 1 d. Educ. St. Augustine's Secondary School, Glasgow; St. Andrew's College, Bearsden. Taught in various primary schools, 1974-93; Leader of Council, Cumbernauld and Kilsyth, 1984-88, Provost 1988-92, Leader of Council, 1992-94; former Member, North Lanarkshire Council; former Policy Board Member: Local Government Management Board, Local Government International Bureau; former Member, Board, Scottish Enterprise; Member, Executive, Scottish Constitutional Convention; Immediate Past President, Convention of Scottish Local Authorities. Recreations: reading; cooking. Address: (b.) House of Commons, London SW1A 0AA.

MacKenzie, Angus Alexander, CA. Chartered Accountant, since 1955; b. 1.3.31, Nairn; m., Catherine; 1 d. Educ. Inverness Royal Academy; Edinburgh University. National Service, RAF, 1955-57; in private practice as CA Assistant in Edinburgh, 1957-59, Inverness, 1959-61; commenced in practice on own account, 1961; Chairman, Highland Group, Riding for the Disabled Association. Recreations: shooting; stalking; hill-walking; gardening. Address: (h.) Tigh an Allt, Tomatin, Inverness-shire; T.-01808 511270.

Mackenzie, Anne, MA (Hons). Broadcaster and Journalist; b. Stornoway, Isle of Lewis; m., Neil McConaghy; 1 s. Educ. Nicolson Institute, Stornoway; Glasgow University. Reporter, News Presenter, Political/Current Affairs Presenter, Grampian TV, 1981-95 (Presenter, North Tonight, Crossfire, We The Jury, etc.); Presenter, BBC Scotland, Glasgow, 1995-97 (Good Morning Scotland, Reporting Scotland, Campaign Scotland, election/devolution specials); Reporter/Presenter, Here and Now, BBC London, 1996; Presenter, Westminster Live, The World Tonight, Breakfast with Frost, BBC London, since 1998. Recreations: gardening; antiques; history; old movies.

MacKenzie, Archibald MacIntosh, DL. Vice Lord Lieutenant, Dunbartonshire, since 1990; b. 3.6.33, Inveraray; m., Margaret Young Ritchie; 1 s.; 1 d. Educ. Hermitage School, Helensburgh. Assistant Chief Constable, British Transport Police, 1982-92; Vice-President and Member, Executive Committee, Royal National Lifeboat

Institution (Chairman, Dumbarton Branch); Convenor, Scottish Lifeboat Council; Chairman, Scottish Lifeboat Executive Committee, 1990-96; Member, Committee of Management, Royal National Lifeboat Institution; Director, Dunbartonshire Branch, British Red Cross, 1992-95; Member, Loch Lomond Rescue Committee; Non-Executive Director, Lomond Health Trust; Chairman, 2319 Sqd. ATC Committee; Elder, Church of Scotland. Recreations: sailing; golf; reading; classical music. Address: (h.) Millerston, 10 Boghead Road, Dumbarton; T.-Dumbarton 763654.

MacKenzie, Archie Michael. Editor, Scottish Field, since 1994; Consultant Editor, Oban Times, since 1994; m. 1, Christine Anne Davidson (deceased); 2, Jill Bell Clapham. Educ. St. Columba's R. C. School; Oban High School. Oban Times: Junior Reporter, Senior Reporter; Editor: Argyllshire Advertiser, Campbeltown Courier, Scottish World magazine. Recreations: music; Gaelic; walking; sailing. Address: North Werber Place, Edinburgh T.-0131-551 2942; The Mains, Oban.

Mackenzie, Major Colin Dalzell, MBE, MC, DL. Vice Lieutenant, Inverness-shire, 1986-95; b. 23.3.19, Fawley; m., Lady Anne Fitz Roy; 1 s.; 3 d. Educ. Eton; RMC, Sandhurst. Page of Honour to King George V, 1932-36; joined Seaforth Highlanders, 1939; ADC to Viceroy of India, 1945-46; Deputy Military Secretary to Viceroy of India, 1946-47; retired, 1949; TA, 1950-56; Inverness County Council, 1949-52; Director, various companies. Recreation: reading. Address: (h.) Farr House, Inverness, IV1 2XB.

Mackenzie, Sheriff Colin Scott, DL, BL, NP. Sheriff of Grampian Highland and Islands, at Lerwick and Kirkwall, since 1992; b. 7.7.38, Stornoway; m., Christeen E.D. MacLauchlan. Educ. Nicolson Institute; Fettes College; Edinburgh University. Procurator Fiscal, Stornoway, 1969-92; Burgh Prosecutor, Stornoway, 1971-75; JP Fiscal, 1971-75; Deputy Lieutenant and Clerk to Lieutenancy of the Western Isles, 1975-92; Vice Lord Lieutenant of Islands Area, Western Isles, 1984-92; Founder President, Stornoway Flying Club, 1970; Founding Dean, Western Isles Faculty of Solicitors; elected Council Member, Law Society of Scotland, 1985-92; Convener, Criminal Law Committee, 1991-92; Elder, Church of Scotland, since 1985; Member, Board of Social Responsibility, Church of Scotland, 1990-96; Convener, Assembly Study Group on Young People and the Media, 1991-93; author of article on Lieutenancy, Stair Memorial Encyclopaedia of Law of Scotland, 1987; President, Stornoway Rotary Club, 1977; President, Lewis Pipe Band. Recreation: fishing. Address: (h.) Park House, Matheson Road, Stornoway, Lewis; Middlebank, Bells Road, Lerwick, Shetland.

MacKenzie, Professor Donald, BSc, PhD. Professor of Sociology, University of Edinburgh, since 1992; b. 3.5.50, Inverness; m., Caroline Bamford; 1s.; 1 d. Educ. Golspie High School; University of Edinburgh. University of Edinburgh: Lecturer in Sociology, 1975-88, Reader in Sociology, 1988-92. Visiting Professor of the History of Science, Harvard University, 1997. Co-winner, U.S. Navy Prize in Naval History, 1989; American Sociological Association Merton Award, 1993; Society for Social Studies of Science Fleck Prize, 1993. Publication: Knowing Machines, 1996. Recreations: cycling; walking; chess. Address: (b.) Department of Sociology, 18 Buccleuch Place, Edinburgh EH8 9LN; T.-0131-650 3980.

McKenzie, Graham. Director, Centre for Contemporary Arts, Glasgow, since 1997; b. 14.8.58, Glasgow. Educ. Renfrew High School; Heriot Watt University. Social Worker, 1978-88; freelance writer, arts critic, playwright, 1988-90; Principal Arts Officer, South East, Glasgow City Council, 1990-97. Five plays produced for stage, three for radio. Recreation: improvised music. Address: (b.) 350 Sauchiehall Street, Glasgow G2; T.-0141-332 7521.

MacKenzie, Hugh D., MA (Hons), FEIS, JP, FRSA. Headteacher, Craigroyston Community High School, 1972-93; Director, Craigroyston Curriculum Project, since 1980; b. 29.5.33, Edinburgh; m., Helen Joyce; 1 s.; 1 d. Educ. Royal High School; Edinburgh University; Moray House College of Education, Edinburgh. Education Officer, RAF, 1956-58; Assistant Teacher, Niddrie Marischal Junior Secondary School and Falkirk High School, 1958-62; Principal Teacher: Broxburn Academy, 1962-64, Liberton High School, 1964-70; Deputy Headteacher, Craigmount High School, 1970-72; Scottish Representative, Northern Regional Examination Board, 1973-88; Vice Chairman, Lothian Regional Consultative Committee, 1984-87; a Director, Royal Lyceum Theatre, Edinburgh, since 1985, Scottish Community Education Council, 1985-88; President, Royal High School Rugby Club; President and Founder Member, Edinburgh Golden Oldies Rugby Club. Publication: Craigroyston Days, 1995. Recreations: rugby; squash; golf; ornithology; philately; jazz. Address: (h.) 3 Beechwood Mains, Edinburgh.

MacKenzie, Ian Kenneth, OBE, JP. Chairman, Red Deer Commission, 1984-92; Chairman, Highlands and Islands Development Consultative Council, 1988-91; Landowner; b. 1.3.31, Nairn; m., Margaret Vera Matheson; 2 s.; 2 d. Educ. Inverness Royal Academy. Member, Secretary of State's Panel of Arbiters; Director, Royal Highland and Agricultural Society of Scotland, 1980-84. Recreation: field sports. Address: Leanach House, Culloden Moor, Inverness IV1 2EJ.

Mackenzie, Rev. Ian Murdo. Church of Scotland Minister; Writer, Broadcaster, Organist; b. b. 3.8.31, Fraserburgh; m., Elizabeth Alice Whitley; 1 s.; 1 d. Educ. Strichen School; Fettes College; Edinburgh University. Assistant Organist, St. Giles Cathedral, 1952-58; Editor, The Student, Sooth and Breakthrough; Founder Member, Telephone Samaritans Scotland, 1960; Columnist, Edinburgh Evening Dispatch; Conductor, Calton Singers; Music Organiser, Iona Abbey; Assistant Minister, St. Giles, 1960-62; Founder, Edinburgh University CND, 1962; Scottish Secretary, Student Christian Movement, 1962-63; Assistant General Secretary, Student Christian Movement, 1963-64; Secretary, University Teachers Group, 1963-65; Religious Adviser and Executive Producer, Religious Programmes, ABC TV, 1964-68; LWT, 1968-69; conceived and produced From Inner Space, Looking for an Answer, Don't Just Sit There, Question '68, Roundhouse; Religious Columnist, The Times, 1966-68; Minister, Peterhead Old Parish Church, 1969-73; Presenter, For Christ's Sake and What The Religious Papers Say, Grampian TV; Chairman, Scottish Religious Panel, IBA, 1970-72; Head of Religious Programmes, BBC Scotland, 1973-89; conceived Eighth Day, Voyager, Angles, Gates to Space, The Quest; Writer/Presenter, He Turned Up, Channel Four, 1990; Baird Lectures on Church Music, 1990; Presenter/Improviser on hymns and other programmes, Radio Scotland. Publications: Tunes of Glory; Vision and Belief; various papers, articles and essays. Recreations: attending concerts, cathedrals, and newsagents; driving with majestic care and attention; writing novels; wondering about God; preaching about wondering. Address: (h.) 1 Glenan Gardens, Helensburgh, Dunbartonshire, G84 8XT; T.-01436 673429.

MacKenzie, Kenneth, MB, ChB, FRCA, DRCOG. Chairman, Scottish Committee for Hospital Medical Services, 1995-98; Clinical Director, Anaesthesia, Ayr Hospital, since 1993; b. 13.1.48, Paisley; m., Anne Scott; 1 s.; 1 d. Educ. Paisley Grammar School; Glasgow University. Consultant Anaesthetist, Ayrshire and Arran Health Board; Honorary Medical Officer, Western Meeting Club. Recreation: golf; reading. Address: (h.) Arden, Maidens Road, Turnberry KA26 9LS; T.-01655 331239.

MacKenzie, Kenneth, MBChB, FRCS. Consultant Otolaryngologist, Head and Neck Surgeon, Glasgow Royal

Infirmary, since 1989; Honorary Senior Lecturer, University of Glasgow, since 1989; b. 26.11.54, Greenock; m., Karin; 2 s.; 2 d. Educ. Greenock Academy; University of Dundee. Senior Registrar in Otorhinolaryngology, Glasgow Rotational Scheme, 1984-89. Honorary Otorhinolaryngologist to University of Strathclyde; Otorhinolaryngologist, Royal Scottish Academy of Music and Drama. Publication: Case Presentations in Otolaryngology (Co-Author), 1992. Recreations: golf; sailing; Rugby Union. Address: Department of Otolaryngology Head and Neck Surgery, Royal Infirmary, Glasgow G31 2ER; T.-0141-211 4742.

MacKenzie, Kenneth John, CB, MA, AM. Secretary and Head of Department, Scottish Office Development Department, since 1998; b. 1.5.43, Glasgow; m., Irene Mary Hogarth; 1 s.; 1 d. Educ. Birkenhead School, Cheshire; Pembroke College, Oxford; Stanford University, California. Assistant Principal, Scottish Home and Health Department, 1965-70; Private Secretary to Joint Parliamentary Under Secretary of State, Scottish Office, 1969-70; Principal: General Register Office, 1970, Regional Development Division, Scottish Office, 1970-73, Scottish Education Department, 1973-77; Civil Service Fellow: Downing College, Cambridge, 1972, Department of Politics, University of Glasgow, 1974-75; Principal Private Secretary to Secretary of State for Scotland, 1977-79; Assistant Secretary: Scottish Economic Planning Department, 1979-83, Scottish Office Finance Division, 1983-85; Principal Finance Officer, Scottish Office, 1985-88; Under Secretary, Scottish Home and Health Department, 1988-91; Scottish Office, Agriculture and Fisheries Department: Under Secretary, 1991-92, Secretary, 1992-95; Head Economic and Domestic Secretariat, Cabinet Office, 1995-97; Head, Constitution Secretariat, Cabinet Office, 1997-98. Member, Agriculture and Food Research Council, 1992-94; Member, Biotechnology and Biological Sciences Research Council, 1994-95. Recreations: amateur dramatics (Member, Edinburgh Civil Service Dramatic Society); church activities (Elder, St Cuthbert's Parish Church, Edinburgh). Address: (b.) Scottish Office Development Department, Victoria Quay, Edinburgh EH6 6QQ; T.-0131-244 0759.

Mackenzie, Rory Donald, BEd, MEd. Headteacher, Balerno High School, since 1995; b.10.10.48, Edinburgh; m., Agnes; 1 d. Educ. Edinburgh Rudolf Steiner School; Telford College; Stevenson College; Edinburgh University. Teacher of English, James Gillespie's High School; APT, Guidance, Craigroyston High School; PT, Guidance, Deans Community High School; Assistant Headteacher, Blackburn Academy; Depute Headteacher, Broxburn Academy. Recreations: apart from my young daughter: golf; holidays; gardening; football. Address: (b.) 5 Bridge Road, Balerno EH14 7AQ; T.-0131-477 7788.

Mackenzie, Ruth, OBE. General Director, Scottish Opera, since 1997; b. 1957. Educ. London, Paris and Cambridge. Editor's Assistant, Time Out, 1980-81; Fellow in Theatre, Bradford University, 1982-84; Artistic Director, Bradford Multicultural Festival, 1983; Drama Officer, Arts Council of GB, 1984-86; Head of Strategic Planning, South Bank Centre, 1986-90; Executive Director, Nottingham Playhouse, 1990-97. Board Member, London International Festival of Theatre; Member, Lottery Panel and Touring Panel, Arts Council of England; Director, New Millennium Experience Company Ltd. Address: (b.) Scottish Opera, 39 Elmbank Crescent, Glasgow G2 4PT; T.-0141-248 7646.

McKenzie Smith, Ian, OBE, RSA, PRSW, LLD, FSA (Scot), FMA; b. 3.8.35; m., Mary Rodger Fotheringham; 2 s.; 1 d. Educ. Robert Gordon's College, Aberdeen; Gray's School of Art, Aberdeen; Hospitalfield College of Art, Arbroath. Teacher of Art, 1960-63; Education Officer, Council of Industrial Design, Scottish Committee, 1963-68; Director, Aberdeen Art Gallery and Museums, 1968-89; City Arts and Recreation Officer, City of Aberdeen, 1989-96. Work in permanent collections: Scottish National Gallery of Modern Art, Scottish Arts Council, Arts Council of Northern Ireland, Contemporary Art Society, Aberdeen Art Gallery and Museums, Glasgow Art Gallery and Museums, Abbot Hall Art Gallery, Kendal, Hunterian Museum, Glasgow, Nuffield Foundation, Carnegie Trust, Strathclyde Education Authority, Lothian Education Authority, Royal Scottish Academy, Department of the Environment, City Art Centre, Edinburgh, Perth Art Gallery, IBM, Robert Fleming Holdings; Member, Scottish Arts Council, 1970-77; Member, Scottish Museums Council, 1980-87; President, RSW, since 1988; Deputy President, RSA, 1990-91, Treasurer, 1990, Secretary, since 1991; Governor: Edinburgh College of Art, 1976-88, The Robert Gordon University, 1989-95; Member, National Heritage Scottish Group, since 1977; National Trust for Scotland: Member, Curatorial Committee, since 1991, Member of Council, since 1995, Member, Buildings Committee, since 1998; Commissioner, Museums and Galleries Commission, since 1997; FSS; FRSA. Address: (h.) 70 Hamilton Place, Aberdeen AB15 5BA; T.-01224 644531.

Mackenzie-Stuart, Lord (Alexander John Mackenzie-Stuart); b. 18.11.24; m., Anne Burtholme Millar; 4 d. Educ. Fettes College; Sidney Sussex College, Cambridge; Edinburgh University (LLB). Admitted Faculty of Advocates (Scottish Bar), 1951; Honorary Keeper, Advocates' Library, 1969; Sheriff-Principal of Aberdeen, Kincardine and Banff, 1971; Senator of the College of Justice, 1972; Judge of the Court of Justice of the European Communities, 1973; elected President of the Court, 1984; retired from Court of Justice, 1988; since retirement, Woodrow Wilson Center for International Scholars, Washington; lectures on Community Law and other matters in UK and Europe; international arbitration; Honorary Doctorates: Stirling, Exeter, Edinburgh, Glasgow, Aberdeen, Cambridge, Birmingham; Prix Bech for services to Europe, 1989; Honorary Bencher, Middle Temple, King's Inn, Dublin; created Life Baron, 1988, as Lord Mackenzie-Stuart of Dean; FRSE; President: British Academy of Experts, 1989-92, European Movement (Scotland). Publication: A French King at Holyrood, 1995. Address: (h.) 7 Randolph Cliff, Edinburgh EH3 7TZ; T.-0131-225 1089.

McKeown, James Patrick, LLB, DipLP, NP. Solicitor; b. 17.3.59, Coatbridge; m., Pamela Mary; 2 s.; 1 d. Educ. Aberdeen University. Assistant, Esslemont & Cameron, Aberdeen, 1983-85; Company Secretary, Sysdrill Ltd., 1985-86; Assistant, C. & D. Mactaggart, 1986, appointed Partner, 1987; Chairman, Social Security Appeal Tribunal. Vice-Chairman, Scottish Liberal Democrats, Argyll and Bute, 1990-97; former Vice President, Scottish Young Lawyers Association. Recreations: politics; travel. Address: (b.) Castlehill, Campbeltown, Argyll PA28 6AR; T.-01586 552317.

McKerrell of Hillhouse, Charles James Mure. Baron of Dromin; Hereditary Keeper of Cashel; Hereditary Niadh Nask (ancient Gaelic Irish Knightly Order); OSt.J; Knight Order of St. Michael of the Wing; Knight Commander, Order of Polonia Restituta; Knight Grand Cross of Justice Order of St. Lazarus of Jerusalem; Knight Grand Cross of the Patriarcal Order of St Ignatius of Antioch; Honorary Captain, Canadian Bush Pilots' Squadron; recognised as McKerrell of Hillhouse and Head of the Name by Lord Lyon, 1973, and as 15th Head of the Name by Chief Herald of Ireland 1974; b. 2.1.41; m., May Weston Cochrane, Niadh Nask, DLJ, FSA (Scot). Educ. Cranleigh. Chancellor to The Mac Carthy Mor, Prince of Desmond, Head of the Royal House of Munster; Chancellor of the Niadh Nask. FSA (Scot); Vice-Chairman, International Commission for Orders of Chivalry; founder Member, Heraldry Society of Ireland; Council Member, The Nobility of Desmond.

Address: (h.) Magdalene House, Lochmaben, Dumfries DG11 1PD; T.-01387 810439.

McKerrell, Douglas Gordon, LLB. Partner: Kidstons & Co., Solicitors, Glasgow, since 1992, Maclay Murray and Spens, 1976-92; b. 18.8.44, Edinburgh; m., Elizabeth Anne (Lizanne) Brown; 3 s.; 1 d. Educ. Royal High School, Edinburgh; High School of Glasgow; Glasgow University. After training and qualifying, spent several years in private practice in London and Glasgow; Tutor/Senior Tutor, Finance and Investment, Diploma in Legal Practice, Glasgow University, 1980-89; Chairman, Rent Assessment Panel for Scotland, 1980-89; Scottish Representative, UK Committee, UNICEF, 1985-88; Chairman: Scottish Music Information Centre, 1990-93, Scottish SPCA, 1988-93; Director, Scottish International Piano Competition; Secretary, Children's Music Foundation in Scotland; Trustee, Scottish Musicians' Benevolent Fund; Board Member, Edinburgh International Film Festival. Publication: The Rent Acts: A Practitioner's Guide, 1985. Recreations: music; theatre; cinema; collecting records. Address: (b.) 1 Royal Bank Place, Buchanan Street, Glasgow; T.-0141-221 6551.

MacKessack-Leitch, Hilda Jane Marshall. Deputy Lieutenant, Moray, since 1993; Elgin Local Organiser, WRVS, since 1976; b. 4.9.40, Rothes; m., 1, Dr. Ernest V. C. Dawson (deceased); 2, David C. MacKessack-Leitch; 2 s. Educ. Elgin Academy. Past County Commissioner, The Guide Association, Moray; Past Chairman, Cancer Research Campaign Committee, Elgin and District. Recreations: cooking; walking; reading; music. Address: (h.) Inchstelly House, Alves, Elgin, Moray IV30 3UY. T.-01343 850203.

Mackey, Professor James Patrick, PhD, LPh, BD, STL, DD, BA. Thomas Chalmers Professor of Theology, Edinburgh University, since 1979; b. 9.2.34; m., Hanorah Noelle Quinlan; 1 s.; 1 d. Educ. Mount St. Joseph College, Roscrea; National University of Ireland; Pontifical University, Maynooth; Queen's University, Belfast; Oxford University; London University; Strasbourg University. Lecturer in Philosophy, Queen's University, Belfast, 1960-66; Lecturer in Theology, St. John's College, Waterford, 1966-69; Associate Professor and Professor of Systematic and Philosophical Theology, San Francisco University, 1969-79; Visiting Professor: University of California, Berkeley, 1974, Dartmouth College, New Hampshire, 1989; Member, Centre for Hermeneutical Studies, Berkeley, 1974-79; Dean, Faculty of Divinity, Edinburgh University, 1984-88, Associate Dean and Director of Graduate School, 1995-98; Editor, Studies in World Christianity (international journal), since 1995. Publications: The Modern Theology of Tradition, 1962; Life and Grace, 1966; Tradition and Change in the Church, 1968; Contemporary Philosophy of Religion, 1968; Morals, Law and Authority (Editor), 1969; The Church: Its Credibility Today, 1970; The Problems of Religious Faith, 1972; Jesus: The Man and the Myth, 1979; The Christian Experience of God as Trinity, 1983; Religious Imagination (Editor), 1986; Modern Theology: A Sense of Direction, 1987; New Testament Theology in Dialogue, (Co-Author), 1987; Introduction to Celtic Christianity, 1989; The Cultures of Europe: the Irish contribution, 1993; Power and Christian Ethics, 1994. Recreations: yachting; rediscovery of original Celtic culture of these islands. Address: (h.) 10 Randolph Crescent, Edinburgh EH3 7TT; T.-0131-225 9408.

McKichan, Duncan James, OBE, BL. Solicitor (former Senior Partner, Maclay Murray & Spens); Honorary Consul for Canada, 1986-92; Dean, Royal Faculty of Procurators in Glasgow, 1983-86; b. 28.7.24, Wallington, Surrey; m, Leila Campbell Fraser; 2 d. Educ. George Watson's College, Edinburgh; Solihull School; Downing College, Cambridge; Glasgow University. Royal Navy, 1943-46; qualified as Solicitor, 1950. Recreations: gardening; walking; sailing; skiing. Address: (h.) Invermay, Queen Street, Helensburgh; T.-01436 674778.

Mackie, Michael James, BMedBiol, MBChB, MD, FRCP, FRCPath. Consultant Haematologist, since 1981; Area Director, Haematology Services, 1991-93; b. 17.11.48, Aberdeen; 1 s.; 1 d. Educ. Robert Gordon's College, Aberdeen; Aberdeen University. Junior appointments in Aberdeen and Canada; Consultant and Senior Lecturer, Liverpool University, 1981-86; Consultant Haematologist, Western General Hospital, Edinburgh, since 1986; Director, Clinical Services, 1998. Recreation: squash. Address: (b.) Department of Haematology, Western General Hospital, Crewe Road, Edinburgh; T.-0131-537 1902.

MacKie, Professor Rona McLeod, MD, DSc, FRCP, FRCPGlas, FRCPLond, FRCPath, FRSE, FInstBiol. Professor of Dermatology, Glasgow University, since 1978; Honorary Consultant Dermatologist, Greater Glasgow Health Board, since 1978; b. 22.5.40, Dundee; m., Sir James Black; 1 s.; 1 d. Educ. Laurelbank School, Glasgow; Glasgow University. Registrar, Department of Dermatology, Western Infirmary, Glasgow, 1970-71; Lecturer in Dermatology, Glasgow University, 1971-72; Consultant Dermatologist, Greater Glasgow Health Board, 1972-78. Publications: textbooks and papers on skin cancer. Recreations: opera; gardening; skiing. Address: Department of Dermatology, Glasgow University, Glasgow G11 6NU; T.-0141-339 8855, Ext. 4006.

McKiernan, Professor Peter, BA, MA, PhD, MIM, FBAM, FRSA. Professor of Strategic Management, St. Andrews University, since 1992; b. 28.12.53, Accrington; m., Morna; 1 s.; 1 d. Educ. Preston Catholic College; Lancaster University; Surrey University. Former M.D. of mechanical engineering company; Lecturer in Management, St. Andrews University; Senior Lecturer in Strategic Management, Warwick University. Publications: Sharpbenders; Strategies of Growth; Inside Fortress Europe; Historical Evolution of Strategic Management. Recreations: cricket; poetry. Address: (b.) Department of Management, St. Andrews University KY16 9AL; T.-01334 462795.

McKillop, Professor James Hugh, BSc, MB, ChB, PhD, FRCP, FRCR. Muirhead Professor of Medicine, Glasgow University, since 1989; Honorary Consultant Physician, Glasgow Royal Infirmary, since 1982; b. 20.6.48, Glasgow; m., Caroline A. Oakley; 2 d. Educ. St. Aloysius' College, Glasgow; Glasgow University. Hall Fellow in Medicine, then Lecturer in Medicine, Glasgow University, 1974-82; Postdoctoral Fellow, Stanford University Medical Center, California, 1979 and 1980; Senior Lecturer in Medicine, Glasgow University, 1982-89. Watson Prize Lectureship, Royal College of Physicians and Surgeons of Glasgow, 1979; Harkness Fellowship, Commonwealth Fund of New York, 1979-80; Robert Reid Newall Award, Stanford University, 1980; Honorary Treasurer, Scottish Society of Experimental Medicine, 1982-87; Honorary Secretary, British Nuclear Cardiology Group, 1982-87; Symposium Editor, Scottish Medical Journal, 1984-93; Council Member, British Nuclear Medicine Society, 1985-94 (Hon. Secretary, 1988-90, President, 1990-92); Editor, Nuclear Medicine Communications, 1989-98; Congress President, European Association of Nuclear Medicine, 1997, Member, Executive Committee, 1995-98, Chairman, Education Committee, since 1998; Chairman, Administration of Radioactive Substances Advisory Committee, Department of Health, since 1996 (Vice Chairman, 1989-95); Member, National Medical Advisory Committee, 1995-98; Specialty Adviser on Nuclear Medicine, SODOH, since 1998; Vice-President, Nuclear Medicine Section, Union Europeene Medecines Specialistes. Recreations: music (especially opera); history; football. Address: (b.) University Department of Medicine, Royal Infirmary, Glasgow G31 2ER; T.-0141-211 4675.

MacKinlay, Gordon Alexander, MB, BS, LRCP, FRCS(Ed), FRCS(Eng). Senior Lecturer in Clinical Surgery, University of Edinburgh, since 1980; Consultant Surgeon, Royal Hospital for Sick Children, Edinburgh, since 1980; Director of Surgery, Edinburgh Sick Children's NHS Trust, since 1992; b. 25.4.46, Dunfermline; m., Genevieve Anne Bailey; 1 s.; 2 d. Educ. Tiffin School, Kingston-upon-Thames; Charing Cross Hospital Medical School; London University. House Physician, then Senior House Officer appointments, Charing Cross Hospital; Senior House Officer: Royal Hospital for Sick Children, Edinburgh, 1973, Hospital for Sick Children, Great Ormond Street, London, 1973-74; Registrar in General Surgery, Wycombe General Hospital, 1974-76; Senior Registrar, Paediatric Surgical Units, Edinburgh, 1976-80; Senior Medical Officer then Consultant, Red Cross Children's Hospital Cape Town, 1977-78; Senior Paediatric Surgeon, Tawam Hospital, Abudhabi, 1982-83. Member, United Kingdom Children's Cancer Study Group; Director, Scottish Children's Tumor Register. Recreations: skiing; travel. Address: (h.) Marhaba, Johnsburn Park, Balerno EH14 7NA, T.-0131-449 5979; (b.) Royal Hospital for Sick Children, Sciennes Road, Edinburgh EH9 1LF, 0131-536 0662.

McKinlay, Margaret Elizabeth, BSc (Hons). Director, Scottish Gas, since 1997; b. 30.7.51, Edinburgh. Educ. George Watson's Ladies' College; Edinburgh University. Department of Energy, 1977-90; Chief Executive, Electricity Pool of England and Wales, 1990-94; Head of Compliance, British Gas PLC, 1994-97; Head of Quality and Customer Service, Centrica PLC, 1997. Address: (b.) Granton House, 4 Marine Drive, Edinburgh EH3 6SS; T.-0131-559 5222.

McKinlay, Peter, MA (Hons). Chief Executive, Scottish Homes, since 1991; Chairman, The Wise Group, since 1998; Board Member, The Cairngorms Partnership, since 1998; Chairman, Tomorrow's Company in Scotland, since 1998; Director, St. Mary's Cathedral Workshop, since 1994; b. 29.12.39, Campbeltown; m., Anne Thomson; 2 s.; 1 d. Educ. Campbeltown Grammar School; Glasgow University. Assistant Postal Controller, GPO HQ, Edinburgh; Assistant Principal, PS to Secretary, Scottish Development Department; Principal, Housing, SDD; Principal Private Secretary to Rt. Hon. Bruce Millan, Minister of State; Principal, Local Government Finance; Assistant Secretary, Finance; Assistant Secretary, Industry Department for Scotland; Director, Scottish Prison Service, 1988-91. Non-Executive Director, D.S. Crawford; Badminton Blue, Glasgow University; Member, National Executive, First Division Association, 1977-80. Recreations: reading; gardening; family; friends. Address: (b.) Thistle House, 91 Haymarket Terrace, Edinburgh EH12 5HE; T.-0131-313 0044.

McKinney, Alan. National Director, Scottish Decorators' Federation; Secretary, National Specialist Contractor Council (Scottish Committee); Director of Organisation and Headquarters, Scottish National Party, 1977-90; b. 16.10.41, Glasgow; m., Elma; 1 s.; 1 d. Educ. Brechin High School. Time-served refrigeration engineer before entering politics full-time as National Organiser, SNP, 1977; former Election Agent, Dundee East; former elected Member, NEC. Played football for Brechin City. Recreation: golf. Address: (b.) 222 Queensferry Road, Edinburgh EH4 2BN; T.-0131-343 3300.

McKinnon, David Douglas, BSc, FFA, CMath, FIMA. Director, General Manager and Actuary, Scottish Mutual Assurance Society, 1982-90, Director, 1981-91, Director, Scottish Mutual Assurance plc, 1992-96; b. 18.7.26, Larbert; m., Edith June Kyles; 1 s.; 2 d. Educ. High School of Stirling; Glasgow University. Faculty of Actuaries: Fellow, since 1951, President, 1979-81; Member of Council, International Actuarial Association, 1972-89 and Secretary for the UK, 1975-89; Member, Investment Advisory Committee, Glasgow University Court, since 1982; Chairman, Associated Scottish Life Offices, 1988-90; Member, Board of Association of British Insurers, 1988-90; Session Clerk, Larbert West Church, 1968-87; Vice-Chairman, Church of Scotland Trust, 1984-89, Chairman, 1991-96; Member, Church of Scotland Assembly Council, 1987-96; Director: Church of Scotland Insurance Company Ltd., since 1992, Scotsure Insurance Company Ltd., 1992-97; Member, Trinity College (Glasgow) Financial Board, 1977-97; President, Falkirk and District Battalion, The Boys' Brigade, 1972-77. Recreations: music; gardening. Address: (h.) 4 Carronvale Road, Larbert, Stirlingshire FK5 3LZ; T.-01324 562373.

Mackinnon, Donald McDougall, CEng, MIW, LCG. Chairman, Scottish Inland Waterways Association, since 1981; President, Forth and Clyde Canal Society, since 1986; b. 14.11.29, Glasgow; m., Regine; 1 s.; 2 d. Educ. Hillhead High School; Stow College, Glasgow; London University. Lecturer in Welding Technology and Metallurgy, 1955-78; Senior Lecturer in Welding and Heavy Fabrication, 1978-81; Depute Head, Department of Fabrication, 1981-82; Head, Department of Fabrication and Heating, Ventilation and Refrigeration, 1982-91. Vice-President, Scottish Maritime Heritage Association; Member: Forth and Clyde Canal Local Plan Working Group, Forth and Clyde Canal Local Plan Advisory Committee, Marine Safety Agency Inland Waterway Committee. Address: (h.) 8 Kelvin Way, Kirkintilloch, Glasgow G66 1BX; T.-0141-776 3812.

MacKinnon, Major John Farquhar, MC, DL, JP; b. 27.1.18, Melbourne; m., Sheila Pearce (deceased); 1 s.; 1 d. (deceased); 2, Mrs Anne Swann. Educ. Geelong, Australia; Corpus Christi College, Cambridge (MA). Army, Queen's Own Cameron Highlanders, 1939-46 (Major); twice wounded; Middle East, 1940-41; ADC, Governor General, Union of South Africa, 1942; Staff, UK, 1943-46 (left service due to wounds); Staff TA, 1949-54; ICI Ltd., 1949-73, Regional Manager; Secretary, British Field Sports Society, Berwickshire, 1974-80; Elder, Kirk of Lammermuir; JP, 1966; Deputy Lieutenant, Berwickshire, since 1987. Recreation: fishing. Address: (h.) Craigie Lodge, Longformacus, by Duns, Berwickshire; T.-Longformacus 890251.

Mackintosh, Hugh Robertson, OBE, MSocSc. Director, Barnardo's Scotland, since 1991; b. 10.12.47, Blair Atholl. Educ. Pitlochry High School; University of Bristol; University of Birmingham. Caldecott Community Kent (latterly as a Director), 1970-76; Assistant Director: Barnardo's, London, 1976-81, Barnardo's Scotland, 1981-91. Elder, Church of Scotland. Recreations: golf; fly-fishing; curling; bowling. Address: (b.) 235 Corstorphine Road, Edinburgh EH12 7AR; T.-0131-334 9893.

Mackintosh, Simon, MA, LLB, WS. Partner, Turcan Connell, WS, since 1997; Director, MacPhie of Glenbervie Ltd., since 1993; Board Member, Edinburgh Book Festival, since 1996; b.2.2.57, Wisbech; m., Catriona; 2 s.; 1 d. Educ. Edinburgh Academy; Glenalmond; Magdalene College, Cambridge University; Edinburgh University. W. & J. Burness: Apprentice, 1980-82, Assistant Solicitor, 1982-85; secondment, Boodle Hatfield, 1983; Partner, W. & J. Burness, 1985-97. Member, Tax Law Committee and Trust Law Committee, Law Society of Scotland; Council Member, International Academy of Estate and Trust Law. Recreations: gardening; golf; rugby. Address: (b.) Saltire Court, 20 Castle Terrace, Edinburgh EH1 2EF; T.-0131-228 8111.

McLachlan, Alastair Stevenson, MA (Hons). Rector, Lornshill Academy, Alloa, since 1988; b. 7.8.40, Glasgow; m., Anne Rutherford; 1 s.; 1 d. Educ. High School of Glasgow; Glasgow University. Recreations: family; golf; after-dinner speaking; singing. Address: (b.) Lornshill

Academy, Tullibody Road, Alloa FK10 2ES; T.-01259 214331.

Maclachlan, Alistair Andrew Duncan, BA (Hons), FRSA. Rector, Forres Academy, since 1982; b. 14.3.46, Perth; m., Alison M.S. Love; 2 s. Educ. Perth Academy; Strathclyde University. Teacher in various schools, 1969-71; Principal Teacher of Economics and Business Studies, 1971-74; Assistant Rector, Keith Grammar School, 1974-78; Depute Rector, Elgin High School, 1978-82; Member, SCCC. Secretary and Treasurer, Keith Agricultural Show, 1972-82; Past Chairman, Elgin Squash Club; Chairman, Moray Swing Band. Recreations: keeping fit; reading; music. Address: (h.) 82 Duncan Drive, Elgin, Moray IV30 2NH; T.-Elgin 542193.

Maclagan, Ian, LLB, FSAScot. Partner, Macbeth and Maclagan, Solicitors, Rothesay, since 1970; b. 21.5.43, Rothesay; m., Marjorie; 1 s. Educ. Rothesay Academy; George Watson's College; Edinburgh University. Solicitor in private practice, since 1967; Hon. Sheriff of North Strathclyde at Rothesay; Dean, Faculty of Solicitors in Bute. Trustee, Bute Museum; Past President, Buteshire Natural History Society. Recreations: walking; local history; archaeology; reading. Address: (b.) 34 Castle Street, Rothesay, Bute; T.-01700 503157.

McLaren, Bill. Rugby Union Commentator, BBC; b. 16.10.23. Played wing forward for Hawick; had trial for Scotland but forced to withdraw because of illness; became reporter on local newspaper; first live radio broadcast, Glasgow v. Edinburgh, 1953; former teacher of physical education.

MacLaren, Iain Ferguson, MB, ChB, FRCSEdin, FRCS, FRCP Edin. Consultant Surgeon, Royal Infirmary, Edinburgh, 1974-92; b. 28.9.27, Edinburgh; m., Dr. Fiona Barbara Heptonstall; 1 s.; 1 d. Educ. Edinburgh Academy; Fettes College; Edinburgh University. Captain, RAMC, Egypt, 1950-52; Surgical Registrar, Royal Hospital for Sick Children, Edinburgh, 1956-58; Senior Surgical Registrar, Royal Infirmary, 1959-63 and 1964-67; Fellow in Surgical Research, Hahnemann Medical College and Hospital, Philadelphia, 1963-64; Consultant Surgeon, Deaconess Hospital, Edinburgh, 1967-85; Vice-President, Royal College of Surgeons of Edinburgh, 1983-86 (Council Member, 1977-83 and 1987-94); Fellow, Royal Medical Society (Honorary Treasurer, 1979-85); Chairman, Royal Medical Society Trust, since 1985; Honorary Pipe-Major, Royal Scottish Pipers' Society, 1959-62; Honorary Secretary: Harveian Society of Edinburgh, 1968-87, Aesculapian Club, since 1978; Hon. Secretary, Royal College of Surgeons of Edinburgh, 1972-77; Secretary, Edinburgh University General Council, 1993-97; Chairman: Professional and Linguistic Assessments Board, General Medical Council, since 1996, Clan MacLaren Society, 1968-91; Chieftain, Clan Labhran, 1991. Recreations: music; the study of military history; all aspects of Scottish culture. Address: (h.) 3 Minto Street, Edinburgh EH9 1RG; T.-0131-667 3487.

McLatchie, Cameron, CBE, LLB. Chairman and Chief Executive, British Polythene Industries, formerly Scott & Robertson PLC, since 1988; Deputy Chairman, Scottish Enterprise, since 1997; b. 18.2.47, Paisley; m., Helen Leslie Mackie; 2 s.; 1 d. Educ. Boroughmuir School, Edinburgh; Largs High School; Ardrossan Academy; Glasgow University. Whinney Murray & Co., Glasgow, 1968-70; Thomas Boag & Co. Ltd., Greenock, 1970-75; Chairman and Managing Director, Anaplast Ltd., Irvine, 1975-83; this company purchased by Scott & Robertson. Recreations: bridge; golf. Address: (b.) 96 Port Glasgow Road, Greenock; T.-01475 501000.

McLaughlan, Ian, BA, DipHE. Secretary for Scotland, The Boys' Brigade, since 1996; b. 31.8.54, Motherwell; m., Ann Hutchison; 2 s. Educ. Wishaw Secondary School; YMCA George Williams College (in association with University of Kent at Canterbury). Heavy engineering industry with Lanarkshire Welding Co. Ltd., Terex Ltd., BSC Fullwood Foundaries, 1970-88; Training and Development Officer, The Boys' Brigade, Dumfries and Galloway and Scottish Borders, 1988-96. Vice-Chair, Newton Primary School Board; Member: Stirling North Christian Aid Committee, YouthLink Scotland Chief Officers' Group, Route '98 Trainee Project Committee. Recreations: reading; cycling; hillwalking. Address: (b.) Scottish Headquarters, Carronvale House, Larbert FK5 3LH; T.-01324 562008.

McLaughlin, Mary, MA. Head Teacher, Notre Dame High School, Glasgow, since 1990; b. 18.8.48, Glenboig; m., William J. McLaughlin; 1 d. Educ. St. Patrick's High School, Coatbridge; Glasgow University; Notre Dame College of Education. Principal Teacher of Modern Languages, St. Margaret's High, Airdrie; Assistant Head Teacher, Taylor High School, New Stevenston. Recreations: reading; music; cycling; walking. Address: (b.) 160 Observatory Road, Glasgow G12 9LN; T.-0141-339 3015.

Maclay, Baron (Joseph Paton Maclay), 3rd Baron; Bt. Deputy Lieutenant, Renfrewshire, since 1986; Director, Altnamara Shipping Plc, since 1994; Group Marketing Executive, Acomarit Group, since 1993; Commissioner, Northern Lighthouse Board, since 1996; b. 11.4.42; m., Elizabeth Anne Buchanan; 2 s.; 1 d. Educ. Winchester; Sorbonne. Managing Director: Denholm Maclay Co. Ltd., 1970-83, Denholm Maclay (Offshore) Ltd., Triport Ferries (Management) Ltd., 1975-83; Deputy Managing Director, Denholm Ship Management Ltd., 1982-83; Director: Milton Shipping Co. Ltd., 1970-83, Marine Shipping Mutual Insurance Company, 1982-83; President, Hanover Shipping Inc., 1982-83; Director: British Steamship Short Trades Association, 1978-83, North of England Protection and Indemnity Association, 1976-83; Chairman, Scottish Branch, British Sailors Society, 1979-81; Vice-President, Glasgow Shipowners & Shipbrokers Benevolent Association, 1982-83; President, Glasgow Shipowners and Shipbrokers Benevolent Association, 1998-99; Director, Denholm Ship Management (Holdings) Ltd., 1991-93. Address: (h.) Duchal, Kilmacolm, Renfrewshire.

McLay, Louisa Mary, MA. Headmistress, Fernhill School, Rutherglen, since 1992; b. 14.8.45, Glasgow; m., Dr. Arthur McLay. Educ. Notre Dame High School; Glasgow University. Primary Teacher, 1966-73; Fernhill School: Teacher of English, French, History, 1973-76, Principal Teacher of English, 1976-94, Deputy Headmistress, 1978-92. Recreations: music; gardening. Address: (b.) Fernhill School, Fernbrae Avenue, Burnside, Rutherglen, Glasgow; T.-0141-634 2674.

MacLean, Rev. Andrew Thomas, BA, BD. Parish Minister, St. Andrew's, Port Glasgow, since 1993; b. 1.2.50, Abadan, Iran; m., Alison Douglas Blair; 1 s.; 1 d. Educ. Bearsden Academy; Clydebank Technical College; Stirling University; Edinburgh University. Co-operative Insurance Society, 1967-70; Partner, Janus Enterprises, 1970-72; Probationer, Loanhead, 1979-80; Minister, Aberdeen Stockethill, 1980-85; Chaplain, Strathclyde University, 1985-93. Member, Church of Scotland Board of Practice and Procedure, since 1995; Convener, Church of Scotland Board of Social Responsibility, 1989-93; Moderator, Greenock Presbytery, 1997-98. Recreations: sound recording; photography; parachuting; desk top publishing. Address: St. Andrew's Manse, Barr's Brae, Port Glasgow PA14 5QA; T.-01475 741486.

McLean, Angus, BL, SSC. Solicitor; Honorary Sheriff, Argyll (Dunoon); b. 26.10.12, Kilmartin, Argyll; m., Celia Jane Oliver; 1 s.; 1 d. Educ. Dunoon Grammar School; Glasgow University. Solicitor (Corrigall Ritchie & McLean,

Dunoon), 1935; Royal Artillery, 1940-46; seconded Indian Army, 1942, Major (DAAG), 1945. Member, Council, Law Society of Scotland, 1950-74 (Vice President, 1964); Past President, Dunoon Business Club and Dunoon Rotary Club. Publications: History of Dunoon; Place Names of Cowal. Recreations: local history; travel; gardening. Address: (h.) 21 Ravelston Dykes, Edinburgh EH4 3JE; T.-0131-332 4774.

Maclean of Dunconnel, Sir Charles (Edward), Bt; b. 31.10.46; m.; 3 d. Educ. Eton; New College, Oxford. Publications: The Wolf Children; The Watcher; Island on the Edge of the World; Scottish Country; Romantic Scotland; The Silence. Address: (h.) Strachur House, Cairndow, Argyll PA27 8BX.

MacLean, Charles Hector, BL, AE, DL. Former Senior Partner, Montgomerie & Co., Solicitors, Glasgow; Chairman, Association for Relief of Incurables in Glasgow and West of Scotland, 1964-94; Deputy Lieutenant, County of Renfrew, since 1987; b. 9.12.13, Glasgow; m., Rachael Malcolm Hutchesson; 2 s.; 2 d. Educ. Canford School; Glasgow University. Commissioned, 602 Squadron Auxiliary Air Force, 1936; mobilised, 1939; severely wounded, 1940, as Flt. Commander in Battle of Britain; released in rank of Wing Commander, 1945; re-commissioned as wing Commander, RAuxAF to raise and command 3602 Fighter Control Unit. Member, Committee, Earl Haig Fund Scotland, 1965-94; Vice President, Officers Association, Scottish Branch, 1983-97; Address: (h.) 71 Lochwinnoch Road, Kilmacolm, Renfrewshire.

Maclean, Christian. Manager, Floris Books, since 1976; b. 14.2.50, Edinburgh; m., Astrid; 2 s.; 1 d. Educ. Rudolf Steiner School. Treasurer, Scottish Publishers Association; Director, Scottish Book Source. Address: (b.) 15 Harrison Gardens, Edinburgh; T.-0131-337 2372.

MacLean, Colin R., BSc (Hons), DipEd, MSc. Chief Statistician, Scottish Office Education and Industry Department, since 1996; Chief Professional Officer (Statistics), Scottish Office, since 1997; b. 22.5.51, Dundee; m., Ilse; 2 s.; 1 d. Educ. Forfar Academy; Edinburgh University. Teacher of Mathematics, Edinburgh, 1973-79; Education Adviser (Microelectronics/Computing), Lothian Regional Council, 1980-85; HM Inspector of Schools, 1985-96. Recreations: gardening; swimming; travel; playing computer games with my children. Address: (b.) 1-A75, Victoria Quay, Edinburgh; T.-0131-244 0302.

Maclean, Sir Donald, FCOptom. Ophthalmic Optician, since 1952; Chairman, Ayrshire Medical Support Ltd.; Chairman, Bell Hollingworth Ltd; b. Annan; widower; 1 s.; 1 d. Educ. Morrison's Academy, Crieff; Heriot-Watt, Edinburgh. Ophthalmic Optician in Edinburgh, Newcastle, Perth and now Ayr; Chairman, Ayrshire Local Optical Committee, 1986-88; former Member, Transport Users Local Consultative Committee; Chairman, Ayr Constituency Conservative Association, 1971-75; Chairman, West of Scotland Area Council, Scottish Conservative Association, 1977-78-79; President, Scottish Conservative and Unionist Association, 1983-85; Scottish Conservative Party: Deputy Chairman, 1985-89, Vice Chairman, 1989-91; Chairman, Carrick, Cumnock and Doon Valley Conservative Association, since 1998; Dean of Guildry, Ayr Guildry, 1993-95; Elder, Church of Scotland; Past President, West Highland Steamer Club; Liveryman of the Worshipful Copany of Spectacle Makers; Freeman, City of London. Recreations: photography; reading. Address: (b.) 59 Newmarket Street, Ayr KA7 1LL.

MacLean, Sheriff Hector Ronald. Sheriff of Lothian and Borders, at Linlithgow, since 1988; b. 6.12.31. Advocate, 1959. Address: (b.) Sheriff Court House, Court Square, Linlithgow, EH49 7EQ.

McLean, Jack, DA, MSIAD. Freelance Writer and Broadcaster; b. 10.8.43, Irvine. Educ. Allan Glen's School; Edinburgh College of Art; Jordanhill College. Art Teacher in Glasgow for many years; The Scotsman, 1977-81; Glasgow Herald, 1981-97; The Scotsman, 1997-98; Scotland on Sunday, since 1997; Radio Clyde, 1982-85; BBC Scotland Art Critic and Adviser, 1991-95; Presenter, The Jack McLean Talk Show, Scottish Television. Columnist of the Year, British Press Awards, 1985; Recipient of several Scottish Press Awards. Publications: The Bedside Urban Voltaire; More Bedside Urban Voltaire; The Sporting Urban Voltaire; City of Glasgow; Hopeless But Not Serious; Earthquake. Recreations: collecting art; dressing; cooking; public houses.

McLean, James Angus, BA, LLB, WS. Partner, Burness, since 1974; b. 25.4.47, Gosforth; m., Carol Inglis; 1 s.; 2 d. Educ. Dunoon Grammar School; Fettes College; Sidney Sussex College, Cambridge; Edinburgh University. Solicitor, 1972. Member, High Constables of Edinburgh; Member, Scottish Lawyèrs European Group; Member, various committees, Law Society of Scotland. Recreations: swimming; cycling; theatre. Address: (b.) 50 Lothian Road, Festival Square, Edinburgh EH3 9WJ.

McLean, John David Ruari, CBE, DSC, Croix de Guerre. Typographer and Author; b. 10.6.17, Minnigaff; m., Antonia Maxwell Carlisle (deceased); 2 s.; 1 d. Educ. Dragon School, Oxford; Eastbourne College. Royal Navy, 1940-45; Tutor in Typography, Royal College of Art, 1948-51; Typographic Adviser, Hulton Press, 1953-60; The Observer, 1960-62; Art Editor, The Connoisseur, 1962-73; Founder-Partner, Rainbird, McLean Ltd., 1951-58; Founder Editor, Motif, 1958-67; Honorary Typographic Adviser to HM Stationery Office, 1966-80; Senior Partner, Ruari McLean Associates Ltd., 1960-81; Trustee, National Library of Scotland, 1981. Publications include: Modern Book Design, 1958; Victorian Book Design and Colour Printing, 1963; Magazine Design, 1969; Jan Tschichold, Typographer, 1975; The Thames & Hudson Manual of Typography, 1980; Benjamin Fawcett, Engraver and Colour Printer, 1988; Edward Bawden, war artist, and his letters home 1940-45 (Editor), 1989; Nicolas Bentley drew the pictures, 1990; Typographers on Type (Editor), 1995; Jan Tschichold: a life in typography, 1997; True to Type, 1999. Recreations: used to enjoy sailing and acquiring books. Address: (h.) Pier Cottage, Carsaig, Mull PA70 6HD; T.-01681 704 216.

Maclean, John Robert, DL; b. 24.5.51, Lossiemouth; m., Veronica Mary Lacy Hulbert-Powell; 1 s.; 2 d. Educ. Milton Abbey School. Commissioned into Queen's Own Highlanders, 1971; left Army, 1978, and returned home to farm via Royal Agricultural College, Cirencester; Deputy Lieutenant, County of Moray, since 1987; Member, Royal Company of Archers (Queen's Bodyguard for Scotland), since 1987; Chairman, Elgin Branch, Earl Haig Fund. Recreations: shooting; field sports. Address: (h.) Westfield House, near Elgin, Moray.

Maclean of Duart, Major The Hon. Sir Lachlan, DL. Major, Scots Guards retired; 28th Chief of Clan Maclean; b. 25.8.42.

MacLean, Rev. Marjory Anne, LLB, BD, DipLP. Depute Secretary, Board of Practice and Procedure, and Depute Clerk, General Assembly of Church of Scotland, since 1998; Minister, Stromness Parish Church, 1992-98; b. 11.6.62, Forfar. Educ. Forfar Academy; Edinburgh University. Trainee to Qualified Solicitor, T.P. & J.L. Low, Kirkwall, 1985-87; Probationer to Assistant Minister, Fairmilehead Parish Church, Edinburgh, 1990-92. Company Member, St. Magnus Festival, Orkney. Recreations: chamber singing; indifferent golf. Address: (b.) 121 George Street, Edinburgh EH2 4YN; T.-0131-240 2240.

McLean, Miller Roy, MA, LLB, NP, FCIB (Scotland). Director, Group Legal and Regulatory Affairs and Group Secretary, The Royal Bank of Scotland plc, since 1994; Director, Adam and Company PLC, since 1998; Vice Chairman, Banco Santander, Portugal, since 1993; b. 4.12.49, Scotland; m., Anne Charlotte Gourlay; 1 s.; 1 d. Educ. Vale of Leven Academy; Glasgow University; Edinburgh University. The Royal Bank of Scotland Group plc: Assistant Secretary, 1982-83, Secretary, 1983-88; The Royal Bank of Scotland plc: Secretary, 1985-88, Group Secretary, 1988-90, Assistant Director, Legal and Administration, 1990-91, Director, Legal and Regulatory Affairs, 1991-94. Corporate Fellow and Chairman, Council and Management Committee, Industry and Parliamentary Trust. Recreations: golf; gardening; reading. Address: (b.) 42 St. Andrew Square, Edinburgh EH2 2YE; T.-0131-523 2223.

McLean, Pauline, MA (Hons), DipJour. Arts and Media Correspondent, BBC Scotland, since 1997; b. 13.1.69, Glasgow. Educ. Notre Dame High School, Dumbarton; Glasgow University; University of Wales. Dumbarton Reporter; Evening Times, Glasgow; Western Mail, Cardiff; BBC Scotland. Recreations: cinema; live music; theatre. Address: (b.) BBC Scotland, Queen Margaret Drive, Glasgow G12 9DG; T.-0141-338 2793.

MacLean, Hon. Lord (Ranald Norman Munro MacLean), BA, LLB, LLM. Senator of the College of Justice, since 1990; Queen's Counsel, since 1977; b. 18.12.38, Aberdeen; m., Pamela Ross (m. dissolved); 2 s.; 1 d. Educ. Inverness Royal Academy; Fettes College, Edinburgh; Cambridge University; Edinburgh University; Yale University. Advocate, 1964; Advocate Depute, 1972-75; Advocate Depute (Home), 1979-82; Member, Secretary of State for Scotland's Criminal Justice Forum, since 1996; Member, Parole Board for Scotland, since 1998; Chairman of Governors, Fettes College, since 1996. Recreations: hill-walking; swimming. Address: (h.) 38 Royal Terrace, Edinburgh EH7 5AH.

McLean, Professor Sheila Ann Manson, LLB, MLitt, PhD, FRSE, FRCP(Edin), FRSA. International Bar Association Professor of Law and Ethics in Medicine, University of Glasgow, since 1990; Director, Institute of Law and Ethics in Medicine, since 1985; b. 20.6.51, Glasgow; m., Alan McLean (divorced). Educ. Glasgow High School for Girls; University of Glasgow. Area Reporter to Children's Panel, 1972-75; School of Law, University of Glasgow: Lecturer, 1975-85, Senior Lecturer, 1985-90. Previously: Member, Broadcasting Council for Scotland, Member, Scottish Higher Education Funding Council, Chair, Steering Group, Review of the Professions Supplementary to Medicine Act (Department of Health appointment), Member, Scottish Office Working Group on the Confidentiality of Personal Health Information at the Interface Between Medical and Social Services, Vice-Chair, Multi-Centre Research Ethics Committee (Scotland), Secretary of State Appointee to the United Kingdom Central Council for Nursing, Midwifery and Health Visiting; currently: Chair, Scottish Criminal Cases Review Commission, Chair, Scottish Office Steering Group on Female Offenders, Member, Review Body on Doctors' and Dentists' Remuneration, has been appointed by Department of Health to review the consent provisions of the Human Fertilisation and Embryology Authority, Member, UK Xenotransplantation Interim Regulatory Authority, Member, Audit Committee, International Association of Medical Law, Member, Informal Advisory Group to the Data Protection Registrar on Biotechnology, Member, Policy Advisory Committee, Nuffield Council on Bioethics, Member, Selection Panel for the Broadcasting Council for Scotland. Publications: monographs: Medicine, Morals and the Law, 1983; A Patient's Right to Know: Information Disclosure, the Doctor and the Law, 1989; The Case for Physician Assisted Suicide, 1997; Old Law, New Medicine, 1998; edited books: Legal Issues in Medicine, 1981; Human Rights: From Rhetoric to Reality, (Co-Editor), 1986; The Legal Relevance of Gender (Joint Editor), 1988; Legal Issues in Human Reproduction, 1989; Law Reform and Human Reproduction, 1992; Compensation for Personal Injury: An International Perspective, 1993; Law Reform and Medical Injury Litigation, 1995; Law and Ethics in Intensive Care, 1996; Death, Dying and the Law, 1996; Contemporary Issues in Law, Medicine and Ethics, 1996. Recreations: music; reading; playing guitar; singing. Address: School of Law, University of Glasgow, Glasgow G12 8QQ; T.-0141-330 5577.

McLean, Una. Actress; b. 1930, Strathaven. Trained, Royal Scottish Academy of Music and Drama; professional debut, Byre, St. Andrews, 1955 ; pantomime debut, Mother Goose, 1958; joined Citizens' Theatre, Glasgow, 1959; appeared in Five Past Eight revue, 1960s; many television appearances.

Maclean, Professor William James, DA, RSA, RGI, RSW, FSA Scot. Professor of Fine Art, Duncan of Jordanstone College, University of Dundee; b. 12.10.41, Inverness; m., Marian Forbes Leven; 2 s.; 1 d. Educ. Inverness Royal Academy; HMS Conway; Grays School of Art, Aberdeen. Postgraduate and Travel Scholarship, Scottish Education Trust Award, Visual Arts Bursary, Scottish Arts Council; Benno Schotz Prize; one-man exhibitions in Rome, Glasgow, Edinburgh and London; group exhibitions in Britain, Europe and North America; represented in private and public collections including Arts Council, British Museum, Scottish National Gallery of Modern Art, Fitzwilliam Museum, Cambridge, and Scottish museum collections. Address: (h.) Bellevue, 18 Dougall Street, Tayport, Fife.

MacLeary, Alistair Ronald, MSc, DipTP, FRICS, FRTPI, FBIM, FRSA. Honorary Fellow, Commonwealth Association of Surveying and Land Economy; Member, Lands Tribunal for Scotland; MacRobert Professor of Land Economy, Aberdeen University, 1976-89 (Dean, Faculty of Law, 1982-85); b. 12.1.40, Glasgow; m., Claire Leonard; 1 s.; 1 d. Educ. Inverness Royal Academy; College of Estate Management; Heriot-Watt University; Strathclyde University. Assistant Surveyor, Gerald Eve & Co., Chartered Surveyors, 1962-65; Assistant to Director, Murrayfield Real Estate Co. Ltd., 1965-67; Assistant Surveyor and Town Planner/Partner, Wright & Partners, 1967-76; seconded to Department of the Environment, London, 1971-73; Member: Committee of Inquiry into the Acquisition and Occupancy of Agricultural Land, 1977-79, Home Grown Timber Advisory Committee, Forestry Commission, 1981-87; Chairman, Board of Education, Commonwealth Association of Surveying and Land Economy, 1981-90; President, Planning and Development Division, Royal Institution of Chartered Surveyors, 1984-85; Editor, Land Development Studies, 1986-90; Member, Natural Environment Research Council, 1988-91. Recreations: shooting; golf. Address: (h.) St. Helen's, St. Andrew's Road, Ceres, Fife KY15 5NQ; T.-01334 828862.

McLeary, Bernard, MA. Director of Education Services, Inverclyde Council, since 1995; b. 29.10.51, Greenock; m., Anne Marie; 2 d. Educ. St. Columba's High School; University of Glasgow; Notre Dame College of Education. Teacher, Principal Teacher, Assistant Head Teacher, St. Stephen's High School, 1973-84; Education Adviser, Dunbarton Division, 1984-88; Education Officer: Dunbarton Division, 1988-90, Argyll and Bute, 1990-93, Glasgow Division, 1993-95. Chairman, Working Groups on Curriculum and Special Needs; consultant to national organisations on educational matters. Recreations: collecting books on Russia; keeping fit; theatre and arts. Address: (b.) Department of Education Services, 105 Dalrymple Street, Greenock PA15 1HT; T.-01475 712824.

MacLeay, Very Rev. John Henry James, MA. Dean of Argyll, since 1987; Rector, St. Andrew's, Fort William, since 1978, retiring 1999; Canon, St. John's Cathedral, Oban, since 1980; b. 7.12.31, Inverness; m., Jane Speirs Cuthbert; 1 s.; 1 d. Educ. St. Edmund Hall, Oxford. Ordained Deacon, 1957; Priest, 1958; Curate: St. John's, East Dulwich, 1957-60, St. Michael's, Inverness, 1960-62; Rector, St. Michael's, Inverness, 1962-70; Priest-in-Charge, St. Columba's, Grantown-on-Spey and St. John's, Rothiemurchus, 1970-78. Recreations: fishing; reading; visiting churches and cathedrals. Address: St. Andrew's Rectory, Parade Road, Fort William PH33 6BA; T.-01397 702979.

MacLehose of Beoch, Baron (Crawford Murray MacLehose), KT (1983), GBE (1976), KCMG (1971), KCVO (1975), DL, Hon. LLD (York, 1983, Strathclyde, 1984). Director, National Westminster Bank, 1982-88; Chairman, School of Oriental and African Studies, 1983-91; Chairman, Scottish Trust for the Physically Disabled and Margaret Blackwood Housing Association, 1983-91; Life Peer; 16.10.17; m.; 2 d. Educ. Rugby; Balliol College, Oxford. Served Second World War (Lt., RNVR); joined Foreign Service, 1947; Governor and C-in-C, Hong Kong, 1971-82. Address: (h.) Beoch, Maybole, Ayrshire.

McLeish, Henry Baird. MP (Labour), Fife Central, since 1987; Minister of State, Scottish Office (Minister for Home Affairs, Local Government and Devolution), since 1997; b. 15.6.48; m.; 1 s.; 1 d. Educ. Buckhaven High School, Methil; Heriot-Watt University. Former Research Officer and Planning Officer in local government; former Member, Kirkcaldy District Council and Fife Regional Council (Leader, 1982-87); Scottish Front Bench Spokesman for Education and Employment, 1988-89, for Employment and Training, 1989-92; Shadow Scottish Minister of State, 1992-94; Shadow Minister of Transport, 1994-95; Shadow Minister for Health, 1995-97. Recreations: reading; history; life and work of Robert Burns; malt whisky; Highlands and Islands. Address: House of Commons, London SW1A 0AA.

McLellan, Rev. Andrew Rankin Cowie, MA, BD, STM. Minister, St. Andrew's and St. George's, Edinburgh, since 1986; b. 16.6.44, Glasgow; m., Irene L. Meek; 2 s. Educ. Kilmarnock Academy; Madras College, St. Andrews; St. Andrews University; Glasgow University; Union Theological Seminary, New York. Assistant Minister, St. George's West, Edinburgh, 1969-71; Minister: Cartsburn Augustine, Greenock, 1971-80, Viewfield, Stirling, 1980-86; Member, Inverclyde District Council, 1977-80; Tutor, Glasgow University, 1978-82; Chaplain, HM Prison, Stirling, 1982-85; Convener, Church and Nation Committee, General Assembly, 1992-96; Chairman, Scottish Religious Advisory Committee, BBC, since 1996. Publication: Preaching for these People, 1997. Recreations: sport; travel; books. Address: 25 Comely Bank, Edinburgh EH4 1AJ; T.-031-332 5324.

McLellan, Douglas Richard, MD, FRCPath, DipFM. Consultant Pathologist, Victoria Infirmary, Glasgow, since 1989; Honorary Senior Lecturer, Glasgow University, since 1989; b. 13.6.55, Glasgow; m., Caitriona; 3 s. Educ. High School of Glasgow; Glasgow University. Registrar in Pathology, Southern General Hospital, Glasgow, 1978-81; Honorary Senior Registrar in Neuropathology (MRC Head Injury Project), Institute of Neurological Sciences, Glasgow, 1981-84; Senior Registrar in Pathology, Western Infirmary, Glasgow, 1984-89. Recreations: bibliomania; Celtology. Address: (h.) 8 Calderwood Road, Newlands, Glasgow G43 2RP.

McLellan, James Alexander, LLB. Chief Executive, Argyll and Bute Council, since 1995 (Director of Administration, Argyll and Bute District Council, 1978-95); b. 23.12.50, Lochgilphead; m., Alexis; 2 s.; 1 d. Educ. Keil School; Glasgow University. Recreations: fishing; gardening. Address: (b.) Kilmory, Lochgilphead, Argyll PA31 8RT; T.-01546 602127.

McLellan, Robert (Bob), BSc, PhD, CEng, MICE, MAPM, FIHT, MIAT, ACIArb. Director of Roads, Angus Council, since 1995; b. 18.5.61, Dunoon; m., Christine; 1 s. Educ. Belmont Academy, Ayr; Strathclyde University. Lothian Regional Council: Graduate Engineer, 1982-87, Works Engineer, 1987-88, Works Manager, 1988-90, Sub-Regional Engineer, 1990-92, Divisional Roads Manager, 1992-93, Assistant Director of Transportation, 1993-95. UK Representative, Construction Industry Standing Conference for NVQ/SVQ Development in Areas of Transport Planning and Project Administration; Chair, Funding/Procurement Group, Society of Chief Officers for Transportation in Scotland; Committee Member, Dundee Area Branch and East of Scotland, Institution of Civil Engineers; Committee Member, Association of Municipal Engineers (Scottish Division). Publication: Bituminous Mixtures in Construction (Contributor). Recreations: travel; golf; football; books; visiting/ researching tall structures. Address: (b.) County Buildings, Market Street, Forfar DD8 3WR; T.-01307 473276.

MacLennan, Professor Alexander Hope, BSc, PhD, PGCE, CChem, FRSC. Director of Corporate Communications, University of Paisley, since 1996; b. 17.3.53, Glasgow; m., Alison. Educ. Bellahouston Academy; Paisley College of Technology. Research and Development Chemist, CIBA Geigy, 1979; Development Chemist, Glaxo, 1983; Paisley College: Lecturer in Organic Chemistry, 1985, CATS Co-ordinator, Credit Accumulation and Transfer Scheme, 1990, Director, CATS Unit, 1991; Director of CATS and Continuing Education, University of Paisley, 1993; Head, Department of Continuing Education, 1995. Recreations: golf; curling; wine. Address: (b.) University of Paisley, Paisley PA1 2BE; T.-0141-848 3730.

MacLennan, David Peter Hugh, LLB (Hons), WS, NP. President, Scottish Law Agents Society, since 1995; Secretary, Edinburgh Legal Dispensary, since 1988; Member, Advisory Council on Messengers-at-Arms and Sheriff Officers, since 1993; b. 6.9.47, Edinburgh; m., Joan Isobel; 2 s.; 1 d. Educ. Edinburgh Academy; Edinburgh University. Apprentice Solicitor/Assistant Solicitor, 1969-73; admitted as a Solicitor, 1971; Assistant Solicitor/ Partner, Balfour & Manson, Edinburgh, since 1973; Solicitor to the Society of Messengers-at-Arms and Sheriff Officers; Elder, Gorgie Parish Church, and Member, Edinburgh Presbytery; Director, Edinburgh City Mission; Member, Westray Buildings Preservation Trust; Honorary Member, Clan Gregor Society. Recreations: hill-walking; swimming; cycling; genealogy; enjoying the county of Sutherland. Address: (b.) 54-66 Frederick Street, Edinburgh EH2 1LS; T.-0131-200 1215.

Maclennan, Professor Duncan, CBE, MA, MPhil. Mactaggart Professor of Land Economics and Finance, Glasgow University; Director, ESRC Cities Programme; Member, Board, Scottish Homes; Member, Glasgow Alliance; Adviser, Joseph Rowntree Foundation; Trustee, David Hume Institute; Member, Glasgow Alliance; Adviser, HM Treasury; b. 12.3.49, Glasgow; 1 s.; 1 d. Educ. Allan Glen's Secondary School; Glasgow University. Lecturer in Applied Economics, Glasgow University, 1974-76; Lecturer in Political Economy, Aberdeen University, 1976-78; Lecturer in Applied Economics, Glasgow University, 1979-82; Regents Professor, University of California at Berkeley, 1996. Address: (b.) Department of Urban Studies, 25 Bute Gardens, Glasgow; T.-0141-330 4615.

Maclennan, Rt. Hon. Robert Adam Ross, PC. MP (Lib. Dem.), Caithness, Sutherland and Easter Ross; Liberal Democrat Spokesman on Constitutional Affairs, National Heritage and Broadcasting; Barrister-at-Law; b. 26.6.36,

Glasgow; m., Helen Cutter Noyes; 2 s.; 1 d. Educ. Glasgow Academy; Balliol College, Oxford; Trinity College, Cambridge; Columbia University, New York. Parliamentary Private Secretary to Secretary of State for Commonwealth Affairs, 1967; Opposition Spokesman on Scottish Affairs and Defence, 1970; Parliamentary Under-Secretary of State, Department of Prices and Consumer Protection, 1974-79; Opposition Spokesman on Foreign Affairs, 1979; Member, Public Accounts Committee, since 1979; Founder Member, SDP, 1981; Parliamentary Spokesman on Agriculture, 1981, Home Affairs, 1983, Economic Affairs, 1987; elected Leader, SDP, 1987; President, Liberal Democrats, 1994-98. Recreations: music; theatre; visual arts. Address: (b.) House of Commons, London SW1A 0AA; T.-0171-219 6553.

MacLeod, Ally; b. 1931, Glasgow. Played for Third Lanark, St. Mirren, Blackburn, Hibernian, Ayr United; Manager, Ayr United, Aberdeen, Motherwell, Airdrie, Queen of the South; led Scotland to World Cup, Argentina, 1978.

MacLeod, Andrew Kenneth, BA. Head, New Deal and Adult Training Division, Scottish Office Education and Industry Department; b. 28.3.50, Elgin; m., Sheila Janet; 2 d. Educ. Fettes College, Edinburgh; St. John's College, Oxford. Nuffield College, Oxford, 1971-74; National Economic Development Office, 1974-78; Economic Adviser, Manpower Services Commission, Office for Scotland, 1978-83; Economic Adviser/Principal, Scottish Office, 1983-90; Head, Fisheries Division III, 1990-91; Chief Executive, Scottish Fisheries Protection Agency, 1991-95. Address: (b.) Victoria Quay, Leith, Edinburgh EH6 6QQ; T.-0131-244 0812.

Macleod, Anne Colleen, MBChB. Associate Specialist in Dermatology, Raigmore NHS Trust, since 1985; Poet; b. 11.10.51, Perthshire; m., James M. Macleod; 1 s.; 3 d. Educ. Inverness Royal Academy; Aberdeen University.Publications (poetry): Standing by Thistles, 1997; Just the Caravaggio, 1998. Recreations: yoga; music; art. Address: (h.) Rowan Wood, Upper Raddery, Fortrose IV10 8SW.

MacLeod, Archibald, OBE, NDA, NDD. Member: Scottish Advisory Committee, RSPB, 1993-98, Red Deer Commission, 1989-95; b. 23.3.28, Kames, Argyll; m., Sheena Fleming Ferguson; 2 s.; 1 s deceased. Educ. Greenock High School; West of Scotland Agricultural College. Research Assistant, West of Scotland Agricultural College, 1949-53; Officer-in-Charge, Lephinmore Research Farm, Hill Farming Research Organisation, 1953-56; Senior Adviser (North Argyll), West of Scotland Agricultural College, 1956-66; Head of Advisory Services, Argyll Area, 1966-86. Chairman, Crofters Commission, 1986-89; Past President: Oban Rotary Club, Oban Speakers Club; founder Chairman, West Cowal YFC; Honorary Vice-President, Lorn Agricultural Society. Recreations: curling; gardening; reading. Address: (h.) Drimfern, 4 Hazel Gardens, Toward, Dunoon PA23 7SW.

MacLeod, Calum Alexander, CBE, MA, LLB, LLD. Chairman: Grampian Television, since 1993, Grampian Health Board, since 1993, Britannia Building Society, since 1994, Abtrust Scotland Investment Company PLC, since 1986, Albyn of Stonehaven Ltd., since 1973; Deputy Chairman: Scottish Eastern Investment Trust plc, since 1988, Scottish Media Group plc, since 1997; Director: Bradstock Group PLC, since 1994, Macdonald Hotels plc, since 1995, Scotia Holdings PLC, since 1997; North Board Member, Bank of Scotland, since 1980; b. 25.7.35, Stornoway; m., Elizabeth M. Davidson; 2 s.; 1 d. Educ. Nicolson Institute; Glenurquhart High School; Aberdeen University. Partner, Paull & Williamsons, Advocates, Aberdeen, 1964-80; Member, White Fish Authority, 1973-80; Member: North of Scotland Hydro-Electric Board, 1976-84, Highlands and Islands Development Board, 1984-91; Chancellor's Assessor, Aberdeen University, 1979-90; Chairman of Governors, Robert Gordon's College, 1981-94; Chairman, Scottish Council of Independent Schools, 1991-97; Trustee, Carnegie Trust for the Universities of Scotland, since 1997. Recreations: golf; motoring; hill-walking; reading; music. Address: (b.) Grampian Television, Queen's Cross, Aberdeen AB15 4XJ; T.-01224 846600.

Macleod, Rev. Professor Donald, MA. Professor of Systematic Theology, Free Church College, since 1978; Editor, The Monthly Record, 1977-90; Vagrant Preacher, since 1978; b. 24.11.40, Ness, Isle of Lewis; m., Mary Maclean; 3 s. Educ. Nicolson Institute, Stornoway; Glasgow University; Free Church College. Ordained Guy Fawkes Day, 1964; Minister: Kilmallie Free Church, 1964-70, Partick Highland Free Church, Glasgow, 1970-78. Recreations: dreaming about cricket, fishing and gardening; Gaelic music.

Macleod, Donald Angus David, MB, ChB, FRCS Edin, FRCPEdin, DipSpMed, FISM. Consultant General Surgeon, since 1976; b. 4.3.41, Selkirk; m., Lucile Janette Kirkpatrick; 1 s.; 2 d. Educ. Gordonstoun; Edinburgh University. Chairman, Lothian Health Board Basic Surgical Training Committee, 1986-91; Director of Studies (Surgery), Edinburgh Postgraduate Board for Medicine, 1976-86; Chairman: Scottish Committee, Medical Commission for Accident Prevention, 1980-85, West Lothian Medical Staff Committee, 1986-89; Member, West Lothian Unit Management Team, 1987-89; Hon. Medical Adviser, Scottish Rugby Union, since 1969; Member, International Rugby Football Board Medical Advisory Committee, since 1978; Vice-Chairman, Medical Advisory Committee, 13th Commonwealth Games, Scotland, 1984-86; Chairman, Sports Medicine and Sports Science Consultative Group, Scottish Sports Council, 1990-93; Associate Post Graduate Dean, Lister Post Graduate Institute, since 1993; Councillor, Royal College of Surgeons of Edinburgh, since 1992; Chairman, Intercollegiate Board for General Surgery, UK and Ireland, 1995-98, Intercollegiate Basic Surgical Training and Examinations Committee, UK and Ireland, 1996-99; Intercollegiate Academic Board for Sport and Exercise Medicine, UK and Ireland, 1998-2002; awarded Robert Atkins Award for services to sports medicine, 1992; Honorary Professor of Sports Medicine, Aberdeen University, since 1998. Recreation: orienteering. Address: (h.) The Haining, Woodlands Park, Livingston, West Lothian EH54 8AT.

MacLeod, Donald Ian Kerr, RD—, MA, LLB, WS. Partner, Shepherd & Wedderburn, WS, since 1964; b. 19.4.37, Edinburgh; m., Mary St. Clair Bridge; 1 s.; 2 d. Educ. Aberdeen Grammar School; Aberdeen University; Edinburgh University. Apprentice, MacPherson & Mackay, WS, 1957-60; Assistant, Shepherd & Wedderburn, 1960-64; Solicitor in Scotland to HM Customs and Excise and Department for Education and Employment, since 1970, and Health and Safety Executive, since 1974. Lt.-Cdr. RNR (Retd.); Member, Court of Session Rules Council; Governor, Rannoch School; Church Elder. Recreations: hockey; golf; walking. Address: (b.) Saltire Court, Castle Terrace, Edinburgh EH1 2ET; T.-0131-228 9900.

Macleod, Duncan, DA, RSW. Teacher; Artist; b. 5.4.52, Glasgow; 1 s.; 1 d. Educ. Clydebank High School; Glasgow School of Art; Jordanhill College of Education. Teacher of Art, secondary schools, since 1975; work exhibited nationwide and in private and public collections. Torrance Memorial Award; Member, Scottish Arts Council Lecturers Panel. Recreation: environmental preservation. Address: (h.) 13 Miltonhill, Milton, by Dumbarton G82 2TS; T.-01389 761248.

MacLeod, Duncan James, CBE. Director, Scottish Provident Institution, since 1976; b. 1.11.34, Edinburgh; m., Joanna Bibby; 2 s.; 1 d. Educ. Eton College. Partner, Brown, Fleming and Murray, Glasgow (now Ernst and Young), 1960; Managing Partner, Ernst and Whinney, Glasgow, 1985-89; Director: Harry Ramsden Plc, since 1989, Motherwell Bridge Holdings Ltd., since 1990, Hunterston Development Co. Ltd., since 1983, Macleod Hotels Ltd., since 1960, de Jersey Co. Ltd., since 1991. Recreations: golf; shooting; fishing. Address: Monkredding House, Kilwinning; T.-01294 552336.

Macleod, Rev. Duncan Macaskill, MA. Minister, Knox Free Church, Perth, since 1996; b. 15.11.54, Stornoway; m., Morag Cunningham; 1 s.; 2 d. Educ. Nicolson Institute, Stornoway; Aberdeen University and College of Education. Teacher of Gaelic, Daliburgh, South Uist, 1977-79; Principal Teacher of Gaelic, Paible, North Uist, 1979-80; Minister, Helmsdale Free Church, Sutherland, 1983-96; part-time Adult Learners Gaelic Tutor, University of Dundee, since 1998. Chairman, BBC Gaelic Advisory Committee, since 1997; Editor, Gaelic Pages, Free Church Monthly Record, since 1992. Recreations: Gaelic media/culture; watching football (long-suffering supporter of Partick Thistle F. C.); swimming (still learning). Address: 25 Wilson Street, Perth PH2 0EX; T.-01738 626515.

Macleod, George Norman, CA, JP. Sole practitioner, chartered accountant practice, Stornoway, since 1984; Honorary Sheriff, Stornoway; b. 12.11.36, Stornoway; m., Dena; 3 s. Educ. Nicolson Institute, Stornoway; Glasgow University. Financial Accountant, Lonsdale and Bartholomew Ltd., London, 1962-65; Financial Controller: Standard Plumbing Ltd., Nassau, Bahamas, 1965-74, Lewis Offshore Ltd., Stornoway, 1975-84. Recreations: choral singing; reading. Address: (h.) 25 Urquhart Gardens, Stornoway HS1 2TX; T.- (h.) 01851 703850; (b.) 01851 704476.

McLeod, Iain Alasdair. Assistant Director of Finance, Scottish Office, since 1995; b. 28.9.44, Glasgow. Educ. Allan Glen's School. Ministry of Social Security, 1968-70; Department of Trade and Industry, 1970-75; Scottish Office, SEPD, Glasgow, 1975-78; Glasgow District Council (on secondment), 1978-80; Scottish Development Department, 1980-85; Scottish Office Finance Group, since 1985. Address: (b.) Victoria Quay, Edinburgh EH6 6QQ.

MacLeod, Professor Iain Alasdair, BSc, PhD, CEng, FICE, FIStructE. Professor of Structural Engineering, Strathclyde University, since 1981; b. 4.5.39, Glasgow; m., Barbara Jean Booth; 1 s.; 1 d. Educ. Lenzie Academy; Glasgow University. Design Engineer, Crouch and Hogg, Glasgow, 1960-62; Assistant Lecturer in Civil Engineering, Glasgow University, 1962-66; Design Engineer, H.A. Simons Ltd., Vancouver, 1966-67; Structural Engineer, Portland Cement Association, Illinois, 1968-69; Lecturer in Civil Engineering, Glasgow University, 1969-73; Professor and Head, Department of Civil Engineering, Paisley College of Technology, 1973-81; Chairman, Scottish Branch, Institution of Structural Engineers, 1985-86; Vice-President, Institution of Structural Engineers, 1989-90; Member, Standing Committee on Structural Safety, 1989-97. Recreations: climbing; sailing. Address: (b.) Department of Civil Engineering, Strathclyde University, 107 Rottenrow, Glasgow; T.-0141-548 3275.

McLeod, Ian, RSW, DA. Artist; Tutor in Drawing and Painting (part-time), Glenrothes College, since 1994; b. 27.6.39, Port Glasgow; m., Mary N. B. Rintoul; 1 s.; 1 d. Educ. Kirkcaldy High School; Burntisland Secondary School; Edinburgh College of Art; Regent Road Institute for Adult Education; Moray House Institute of Education. Welder, Burntisland Shipbuilding Co., Fife, 1954-61; Teacher of Art, Auchmuty High School, Fife, 1967-90; 10 one-man exhibitions; various Scottish Arts Council exhibitions including: Scottish Realism: Bellany, Crozier, Gillon, McLeod and Moffat, 1971, Facts and Fantasy, 1972, Expressionism in Scottish Painting, 1977; over 50 group exhibitions; work in private and public collections. Elected: SSA, 1968, GLA, 1978, RSW, 1996. Vice Chairman, Burntisland Community Council. Recreations: people; books; all kinds of music, especially popular 30s and 40s; watching his daughter on her pony and his wife on her horse; left-wing politics; detesting New Labour; hoping for an independent Scotland in his lifetime; gentle hillwalking; watching his son and his friends playing football. Address: (h.) 33 Craigkennochie Terrace, Burntisland, Fife KY3 9EN; T.-01592 873440.

Macleod, Ian Buchanan, BSc, MB, ChB, FRCSEdin. Honorary Secretary, Royal College of Surgeons of Edinburgh, 1993-96; Consultant Surgeon, Royal Infirmary, Edinburgh, 1969-93; Honorary Senior Lecturer, Department of Clinical Surgery, Edinburgh University, 1969-93; Surgeon to the Queen in Scotland, 1987-93; b. 20.5.33, Wigan; m., Kathleen Gillean Large; 1 s.; 1 d. Educ. Wigan Grammar School; Edinburgh University. House Surgeon and House Physician, Royal Infirmary, Edinburgh, 1957-59; National Service, RAMC, Malaya, Singapore, Nepal, 1959-61; appointments, Department of Clinical Surgery, Edinburgh University and Royal Infirmary, Edinburgh, since 1961. Editor, Journal, Royal College of Surgeons of Edinburgh, 1982-87. Publications: Principles and Practice of Surgery (Co-author), 1985, 1989, 1995; Farquharson's Text Book of Operative Surgery (Contributor), 1986; Companion to Medical Studies (Contributor), 1981, 1985. Recreations: golf; photography. Address: (h.) Derwent House, 32 Cramond Road North, Edinburgh EH4 6JE; T.-0131-336 1541.

Macleod, Iseabail Campbell, MA. Editorial Director, Scottish National Dictionary Association Ltd., since 1986; b. 27.5.36, Glasgow. Educ. Clydebank High School; Lenzie Academy; Glasgow University. Teacher, 1958-64; Editorial Assistant, Europa Publications, 1965-66; Editor of bilingual dictionaries, Collins, Glasgow, 1966-74; Dictionaries Editor, Editorial Director, W. & R. Chambers, Edinburgh, 1974-77. Publications: Pocket Guide to Scottish Words, 1986; Pocket Scots Dictionary (Co-Editor), 1988; Scots Thesaurus (Co-Editor), 1990; Concise English-Scots Dictionary (Co-Editor), 1993; Scots School Dictionary (Co-Editor), 1996; Edinburgh Pocket Guide, 1996. Recreations: hill-walking; cooking; languages; music. Address: (h.) 11 Scotland Street, Edinburgh EH3 6PU; T.-0131-556 5683.

MacLeod, Professor James Summers, LLM, CA, FTII. Professor, Department of Accountancy, Edinburgh University, since 1986; Member, Scottish Industrial Development Advisory Board, since 1996; Chairman, Martin Currie High Income Trust PLC; Director, Invesco Geared Opportunities Trust PLC; b. 3.8.41, Dumfries; m., Sheila Stromier; 2 s.; 1 d. Educ. Dumfries Academy; Glasgow University. Lecturer, Edinburgh University, 1965-68; Lecturer, Heriot Watt University, 1968-71; joined Arthur Young (now Ernst & Young), 1971; Partner, Ernst & Young, Edinburgh, 1973-98. Publications: Taxation of Insurance Business (Co-author), 3rd edition, 1992; 200 papers. Recreations: bridge; music; reading. Address: (h.) 2 Bonaly Road, Edinburgh; T.-0131-441 4144.

MacLeod of MacLeod, John. 29th Chief of Clan MacLeod; b. 10.8.35; m.; 1 s.; 1 d. Educ. Eton. Address: Dunvegan Castle, Isle of Skye.

Macleod, John Alasdair Johnston, DL, FRCGP, DCH, DObsRCOG. General Practitioner, North Uist, since 1973; Secretary, Western Isles Local Medical Committee (GP), 1977-91; Deputy Lieutenant, Western Isles, since 1979; b. 20.1.35, Stornoway; m., Lorna Jean Ferguson; 2 s.; 1 d. Educ. Nicolson Institute; Keil School; Glasgow University.

National Service, Royal Navy, 1957-59; hospital posts, Glasgow and London, 1963-73; Non-Executive Director, Olscot Ltd., 1969-93; trainer in general practice, 1975-95; Visiting Professor, Department of Family Medicine, University of North Carolina, 1985; Member, World Organisation of National Colleges Academique of Family Practice, since 1989 (Member, WONCA World Group "Recruitment for Rural Practice", since 1992); Member, General Practitioner Writers Association, since 1986. Member, Committee of North Uist Highland Gathering; Fellow, Royal Society of Medicine; Admiralty Surgeon and Agent, 1974-91; author of papers and articles, singly and jointly, on aspects of isolated practice. Recreations: boating; horticulture; photography; time-sharing. Address: (h.) Tigh-Na-Hearradh, Lochmaddy, Isle of North Uist HS6 5AE; T.-01876 500224.

Macleod, John Francis Matheson, MA, LLB, NP. Solicitor in Inverness, 1959-94; b. 24.1.32, Inverness; m., Alexandra Catherine; 1 s. Educ. Inverness Royal Academy; George Watson's College; Edinburgh University. Solicitor, Fife County Council, 1957-59; in private practice, 1959-94; Parliamentary candidate (Liberal): Moray and Nairn, 1964, Western Isles, 1966; Chairman, Highland Region, Scottish Liberal Party, until 1978; former Vice-Chairman, Broadcasting Council for Scotland; Dean, Faculty of Solicitors of the Highlands, 1988-91; Chairman, Crofters Commission, 1978-86; Member, Council, Law Society of Scotland, 1988-92; Chairman of Council, Gaelic Society of Inverness, 1996-97; Vice-Chairman, National Trust for Scotland's Culloden Advisory Committee. Address: (h.) Bona Lodge, Aldourie, Inverness; T.-01463 751327.

Macleod, John Murray, MA (Hons). Writer at large; Columnist, The Herald, since 1991; b. 15.4.66, Kilmallie, Inverness-shire. Educ. Jordanhill College School, Glasgow; James Gillespie's High School, Edinburgh; Edinburgh University. Freelance journalist and broadcaster, since 1988; Scottish Journalist of the Year, 1991; Young Scottish Journalist of the Year, 1991-92; Commended, Columnist of the Year, 1992; Commended, Feature Writer of the Year, 1996; Columnist of the Year, UK Press Gazette Regional Newspaper Awards, 1996. Publications: No Great Mischief If You Fall – The Highland Experience, 1993; Highlanders – A History of the Gael, 1996; Dunasty – The Stuarts 1560-1807, 1999. Recreations: applied Free Presbyterianism; tennis; poaching; meeting the boat; not going to the pub. Address: (h.) Twin Peaks, Scott Road, Harris, Western Isles HS3 3DL; T.-01859 50 2187.

MacLeod, Lorne Buchanan, BA, CA. Head of Network Operations, Highlands and Islands Enterprise; b. 13.4.63, Oban. Educ. Oban High School; University of Strathclyde. Trainee Chartered Accountant, Ernst and Whinney, Inverness, 1983-87; Highlands and Islands Development Board, 1987-92; Chief Executive, Skye and Lochalsh Enterprise, 1992-98. Member: An Comunn Gaidhealach, Scottish Crofters Union, Talisker Quality Awards Trust. Recreations: hillwalking; sailing; Gaelic music and culture. Address: (b.) Bridge House, 20 Bridge Street, Inverness: T.-01463 234 171.

MacLeod, Professor Emeritus Malcolm, MD (Hons), FRCPEdin. Professor Emeritus in Renal Medicine, Aberdeen University; b. 9.12.16, Glasgow; m., Elizabeth Shaw Ritchie; 1 s. Educ. Nicolson Institute, Stornoway; Aberdeen University. Military Service, Africa, India, SE Asia, 1940-46 (Medical Specialist, RAMC); Lecturer, Senior Lecturer, Reader in Medicine, 1947-80; Personal Professor in Renal Medicine, Aberdeen University, 1981; Honorary Consultant Physician, Aberdeen Royal Infirmary, 1955-82 and Honorary Consultant in charge, Medical Renal Unit, 1966-82; President, Scottish Society of Physicians, 1980. Recreation: natural history. Address: (h.) 76 Hamilton Place, Aberdeen AB15 5BA; T.-01224 635537.

McLeod, Professor Malcolm Donald, MA, BLitt (Oxon), FRSE. Director, Hunterian Museum and Art Gallery, Glasgow University, since 1990; Chairman, Scottish Museums Council, since 1996; Trustee, The Hunterian Collection, London, since 1998; b. 19.5.41, Edinburgh; m., I.V. Barry; 2 s.; 1 d. Educ. Birkenhead School; Hertford and Exeter Colleges, Oxford. Research Assistant, Institute of Social Anthropology, Oxford, 1964-65; Lecturer, Sociology Department, University of Ghana, 1967-69; Assistant Curator, Museum of Archaeology and Ethnology, Cambridge, 1969-74; College Lecturer and Director of Studies, Magdalene and Girton Colleges, Cambridge, 1969-74; Fellow, Magdalene College, 1972-74; Keeper of Ethnography, British Museum, 1974-90; Honorary Lecturer, Department of Anthropology, UCL, 1976-81; Honorary Lecturer, Department of Archaeology, University of Glasgow, since 1992. Publications: The Asante, 1981; Treasures of African Art, 1981; Ethnic Sculpture (Co-author), 1985; Jacob Epstein Collector (Co-author), 1989. Address: (h.) Tweediemill, Sandford, Strathaven ML10 6PL.

Macleod, Mary Elizabeth, LLB (Hons), DipLP, NP. Depute Solicitor of the Church of Scotland, since 1995; b. 23.12.63, Stornoway. Educ. Nicolson Institute, Stornoway; Edinburgh University. Trainee Solicitor, Anderson, Shaw and Gilbert, Inverness, 1986-88; Assistant: Morton, Fraser and Milligan, WS, Edinburgh, 1988-90, Skene, Edwards and Garson, W. S., Edinburgh, 1990-92, Campbell, Smith, Edinburgh, 1992-95. Recreations: travel; music; reading. Address: (b.) 121 George Street, Edinburgh EH2 4YN; T.-0131-225 5722.

Macleod, Murdoch, MBE, JP. Honorary Sheriff; b. 11.8.32, Shawbost, Isle of Lewis; m., Crisybil; 1 s.; 1 d. Educ. Nicolson Institute, Stornoway. Ross and Cromarty Council: Highways Department, 1955-57, Education Department, 1957-65; Stornoway Town Council: Town Clerk's Department, 1965-68, Town Clerk, 1968-75; General Manager, Secretary and Treasurer, Stornoway Pier and Harbour Commission, 1975-96. Former Deputy Chairman, Transport Users Consultative Committee for Scotland; Past Chairman, District Courts Association; Chairman, Western Isles Justices Committee; former Member, Council, British Ports Asssociation; former Chairman, Scottish Port Members, British Ports Association; former Deputy Chairman, British Ports Federation; Director, Western Isles Development Fund Ltd.; Honorary President, Lewis Pipe Band; former Member, British Airways Consumer Council for Highlands and Islands; Trustee, Scottish Hydro Electric Community Trust; Chairman, League of Friends, Stornoway Hospitals and Homes. Recreation: reading. Address: (h.) 46 Barony Square, Stornoway, Isle of Lewis; T.-01851 703024.

MacLeod, Sheriff Principal Norman Donald, QC, MA, LLB. Sheriff Principal of Glasgow and Strathkelvin, 1986-97; b. 6.3.32, Perth; m., Ursula Jane Bromley; 2 s.; 2 d. Educ. Mill Hill School; George Watson's Boys College; Edinburgh University; Hertford College, Oxford. Called to the Bar, 1956; District Officer and Crown Counsel, Colonial Service, East Africa, 1957-63; at the Bar, 1963-67; Sheriff at Glasgow, 1967-86. Recreation: rustic pursuits. Address: (h.) Calderbank, Lochwinnoch, Renfrewshire.

McLeod, Norman Duff, FCCA. Group Finance Director, Low & Bonar PLC, since 1990; b. 2.8.51, Dundee; m., Alison; 1 s.; 1 d. Educ. Grove Academy, Dundee. Henderson & Loggie, CAs, Dundee, 1968-77; Bonar Long Ltd., 1977-84, latterly as Finance Director and Company Secretary; Low & Bonar PLC, since 1984. Recreation: golf. Address: (b.) Bonar House, Faraday Street, Dundee, DD1 9JA; T.-01382 818171.

MacLeod, Peter, MCIBS. Retired Banker; yachting journalist; Honorary Sheriff, Oban, since 1988; b. 9.6.33, Ruaig, Isle of Tiree; m., Jean MacDonald Buchanan; 2 s. Educ. Oban High School. Served as Captain, Royal Signals, AER; joined Royal Bank of Scotland, 1949; Bank Manager: Tobermory, Kinlochleven, Wick, Oban. Past Commodore, Royal Highland Yacht Club. Publication: History of Royal Highland Yacht Club, 1881-1986. Recreations: sailing; island wandering; impromptu ceilidhs; beachcombing. Address: (h.) The Wheelhouse, Ganavan, Oban, Argyll; T.-01631 563577.

MacLeod, Rev. Roderick, MA (Hons), BD, PhD (Edin), PhD (Open). Minister, Cumlodden, Lochfyneside and Lochgair, Argyll, since 1985; b. 24.6.41, Lochmaddy. Educ. Paible Secondary School; Portree High School; Edinburgh University. Minister, Berneray, North Uist, 1966-85; Member: Western Isles Islands Council, 1974-82, Western Isles Health Board, 1975-79; Clerk, Uist Presbytery, 1981-85; Mackinnon Memorial Lecturer, Cape Breton College, 1979; Visiting Scholar, Harvard Divinity School, 1981; Editor, Gaelic Supplement, Life and Work, since 1980; Depute Clerk, Presbytery of South Argyll, since 1995; President, Scottish Gaelic Texts Society, since 1996; Founder, Cruisgean (Gaelic newspaper); author of several Gaelic books; writes and broadcasts on Highland affairs in Gaelic and English. Recreations: walking; shinty. Address: Furnace, Inveraray, Argyll, PA32 8XU.

Macleod, Rev. William, BSc, ThM. Minister, Portree Free Church, since 1993; b. 2.11.51, Stornoway; m., Marion; 2 s.; 1 d. Educ. Aberdeen University; Free Church College; Westminster Seminary. Minister, Partick Free Church, Glasgow, 1976-93. Editor, Free Church Foundations. Chairman, Portree High School Board. Recreations: gardening; fishing; reading. Address: (h.) Portree Free Church Manse, Staffin Road, Portree, Isle of Skye; T.-01478 612678

McLernan, Sheriff Kieran Anthony, KCHS, MA, LLB. Sheriff of Grampian Highlands and Islands at Banff and Peterhead, since 1991; b. 29.4.41, Wemyss Bay; m., Joan Doherty; 1 s.; 3 d. Educ. St. Aloysius College, Glasgow; Glasgow University. Solicitor, 1965-91; Temporary Sheriff, 1986-91; Tutor, Glasgow University, 1987-91. Recreations: golf; hockey; skiing. Address: (h.) Peockstone Farm, Lochwinnoch, Renfrewshire; T.-01505 842128.

McLetchie, David William, LLB (Hons), WS. Solicitor, since 1976; elected Leader, Scottish Conservative Parliamentary Candidates, since 1998; b. 6.8.52, Edinburgh; m., 1, Barbara Gemmell Baillie (deceased); 1 s.; 2, Sheila Elizabeth Foster. Educ. George Heriot's School; Edinburgh University. Solicitor, Tods Murray WS, 1976-80; Partner, Tods Murray WS, since 1980. President, Scottish Conservative and Unionist Association, 1994-97. Recreations: golf; football (Heart of Midlothian); rock and pop music. Address: (h.) 13 Keith Crescent, Edinburgh EH4 3NH; T.-0131-332 4691.

McLuskie, Norman Cardie, CA. Deputy Chief Executive, UK Bank, Royal Bank of Scotland, since 1998; Group Executive Director, Royal Bank of Scotland, since 1992; b. 23.8.44, Uddingston; m., Anne Gibb; 1 s.; 2 d. Educ. Kings Park School, Glasgow. Qualified with Touche Ross & Co., 1969; various senior executive positions; joined Royal Bank of Scotland plc as Management Accountant, 1982; appointed: Assistant General Manager, Group Management and Cost Accounting, 1985, Group Controller, Management Accounting, 1986, Assistant Director, Finance, 1988. Director, Tesco Personal Finance Ltd., RBS Cards Ltd.; Chairman: BACS Ltd, RoyScot Financial Services Limited, RBS Advanta; Deputy Chairman, APACS; Deputy Chairman, Tesco Personal Finance; Chairman, RBS Cards Ltd. Recreations: golf; travel. Address: (b.) 42 St. Andrew Square, Edinburgh EH2 2YE; T.-0131-523 2415.

McMahon, Hugh Robertson, MA (Hons). Member (Labour), European Parliament, Strathclyde West, since 1984; b. 17.6.38, Saltcoats; m., Helen Paterson Grant; 1 s.; 1 d. Educ. Stevenston High School; Ardrossan Academy; Glasgow University. Schoolteacher in Ayrshire (Largs High, Stevenston High, Irvine Royal Academy, Mainholm Academy); Assistant Head, Ravenspark Academy, 1971-84. Vice-Chair, EP Social Affairs, Employment and Working Environment Committee, 1992-94; Member, Social Affairs, Fisheries and Transport Committees; Chair, EP Delegation with Norway, 1989-92; currently Member, Delegation with Czechoslovakia. Recreation: golf. Address: (b.) Euro Office, 9 Low Road, Paisley PA2 6AQ.

MacMahon, Rev. Janet P.H., BD, MSc, LCST, LLCM. Chaplaincy Co-ordinator, Southern General Hospital, Glasgow, since 1992; b. 31.5.44, Glasgow; m.., Professor M.K.C. MacMahon (qv); 1 s.; 1 d. Educ. Glasgow High School for Girls; Glasgow University; Glasgow School of Speech Therapy. Senior Speech Therapist, 1965-80; Chief Speech Therapist, Greater Glasgow Health Board, 1980-82; Senior Speech Therapist, Scottish Council for Spastics, 1983-85; Assistant Minister, Cairns Church, Milngavie, and Govan Old Church, 1989-90; Research and Development Officer in special educational needs, Department of Education, Church of Scotland, 1990-92. Publications include: Walk in God's Ways, 1993. Recreations: reading crime novels; watching TV soaps. Address: (h.) 6 Jubilee Gardens, Bearsden, Glasgow G61 2RT; T.-0141-942 3671.

MacMahon, Professor Michael Kenneth Cowan, BA, PhD, DipLing. Professor of Phonetics, Glasgow University, 1977-97; b. 7.8.43, Winchester; m., Rev. Janet P.H. MacMahon (qv); 1 s.; 1 d. Educ. Hymers College, Hull; Durham University; Gottingen University; Glasgow University; Reading University. Lecturer in Phonetics and Linguistics, Jordanhill College, Glasgow, 1966-72; Lecturer in Linguistics and Phonetics, 1972-83, Lecturer in English Language, 1983-87, Senior Lecturer in English Language, 1987-97, Glasgow University. Member, Council, International Phonetic Association; Member, Executive Committee, Henry Sweet Society; Archivist and Secretary, British Association of Academic Phoneticians. Publications include: Basic Phonetics. Recreations: singing; flute-playing. Address: (h.) 6 Jubilee Gardens, Bearsden, Glasgow G61 2RT; T.-0141-942 3671.

MacMahon, Peter, BSc (Hons). Assistant Editor (Politics), formerly Scottish Political Editor, The Scotsman, since 1995; b. 31.7.59, Dublin; m., Seonag MacKinnon; 2 s.; 1 d. Educ. St. Augustine's High School, Edinburgh; St. Andrews University. Reporter, Cambrian News Agency, Cardiff; Reporter, Northampton Chronicle and Echo; Political Correspondent, Central Press Features, Westminster; Political Correspondent, Daily Star; Westminster Editor, Scotland on Sunday; Political Editor, Sunday Mirror. Recreations: music; sport. Address: (b.) 20 North Bridge, Edinburgh EH1 1YT; T.-0131-225 2468.

McManus, James John, LLB, PhD. Scottish Prisons Complaints Commissioner, since 1994; Honorary Senior Research Fellow, University of Dundee, since 1994; b. 23.6.50, Cleland; m., Catherine MacKellaig; 1 s.; 4 d. Educ. Our Lady's High School, Motherwell; University of Edinburgh; University of Dundee. Tutor, University of Edinburgh, 1972-74; Lecturer, University of Wales, 1974-76; Lecturer, then Senior Lecturer, University of Dundee, 1976-94. Member, Parole Board for Scotland, 1987-94; Expert Adviser, Council of Europe, since 1993; Chair, Dundee Legal Advice Association, since 1992. Publication: Prisons Prisoners and the Law, 1994. Recreations: golf; cycling. Address: (b.) Government Buildings, Broomhouse Drive, Edinburgh EH11 3XA; T.-0131-244 8423.

McManus, Professor John, DSc, PhD, ARCS, DIC, FRSE, CGeol, MIEnvSci. Professor of Geology, St.

Andrews University, since 1993 (Reader, 1988-93); Honorary Director, Tay Estuary Research Centre, 1979-92; b. 5.6.38, Harwich; m., J. Barbara Beveridge; 2 s.; 1 d. Educ. Harwich County High School; Imperial College, London University. Assistant, then Lecturer, St. Andrews University, 1964-67; Lecturer, Senior Lecturer, Reader, Dundee University, 1967-88; UNESCO Representative, International Commission on Continental Erosion, 1980-84 and 1986; Member: Scottish Natural Heritage East Areas Board and Scientific Advisory Committee, Secretary of State's Committee on Waste Discharges into the Marine Environment; President, Estuarine and Brackish Water Sciences Association, 1995-98; Member, Eden Estuary Nature Reserve Management Committee; former Treasurer, British Sedimentological Research Group; Consultant on Coastal Erosion and Protection to four Regional Councils; Executive Editor, Transactions of the Royal Society of Edinburgh, Earth Sciences, 1988-95; Associate Editor, Continental Shelf Research. President: Cupar Choral Association, 1968-78, Cupar Amateur Opera, 1979-91. Recreations: music; bird-watching; swimming; stamp collecting. Address: (b.) School of Geography and Geology, Purdie Building, St. Andrews University, St. Andrews, Fife KY16 9ST.

McManus, Rev. Matthew Francis. Parish Priest, Kilwinning; b. 22.9.40, Rutherglen. Educ. Sacred Heart High School, Girvan; St. Andrew's College, Drygrange. Ordained, 1965, Assistant Priest, St. Margaret's, Ayr; Parish Priest, New Cumnock, Kirkconnel and Sanquhar, 1976-81, Kirkcudbright, 1981-88; Chairman: Dumfries and Galloway Local Health Council, 1985-87, Castle Douglas District CAB, 1984-87, Stewartry Council of Voluntary Service, 1985-88, Stewartry School Council, 1985-87; Member, Scottish Consumer Council, 1983-90; Convenor, Association of Scottish Local Health Councils, 1983-92; Complaints Reporter, Law Society of Scotland, 1985-97; Secretary, Association of Vocations Directors of Scotland, 1987-96; Member, Ayrshire and Arran Health Council, 1988-97; Non-Executive Director, Ayshire and Arran Health Board, since 1996; Member, North Ayrshire Education Committee, since 1996; Vice Chair, Minerva Housing Association, since 1996. Address: St. Winin's, St. Winning's Lane, Kilwinning KA13 6EP; T.-Kilwinning 552276.

McMaster, Brian John, CBE. Director and Chief Executive, Edinburgh International Festival, since 1991; b. 9.5.43. General Administrator, subsequently Managing Director, W.N.O., 1976-91. Address: (b.) 21 Market Street, Edinburgh, EH1 1BW.

McMath, Katherine Sally, MCSP. Scottish Chief Commissioner, The Guide Association, since 1997; b. 29.10.53, Edinburgh; m., Robert Patrick John McMath; 1 s.; 1 d. Educ. Lansdowne House School, Edinburgh; School of Physiotherapy, Royal Infirmary, Edinburgh. Chartered Physiotherapist. County Commissioner, West Lothian Guide Association, 1990-96; Scottish Guide Public Relations Adviser, 1987-90. Recreations: choral singing; music; badminton; tennis. Address: (b.) Scottish Guide HQ, 16 Coates Crescent, Edinburgh EH3 7AH; T.-0131-226 4511.

McMicking, Major David John, LVO, MSc. Consultant, Human Resources/Sporting, since 1986; b. 29.4.39, Jerusalem; m., Janetta; 1 s.; 1 d. Educ. Eton; RMA, Sandhurst; Strathclyde University. Career soldier, Black Watch, rising to rank of Major; left Army, 1973; executive positions, John Menzies Holdings Ltd., 1973-86; family farming interests, since 1996. Extra Equerry, Queen Elizabeth The Queen Mother; Chairman, Officers Association Scotland; Earl Haig Fund: Chairman, North, South and East Scotland, for 15 years an Executive Member and Chairman, Investment Committee; Secretary, Friends of St. Andrew's, Jerusalem. Recreation: field sports. Address: (b.) 10 Albert Terrace, Edinburgh EH10 5EA; T.-0131-447 6192.

McMillan, Rev. Andrew, BA, BD. Minister, United Free Church of Scotland, Knightswood, Glasgow, since 1982; Hospital Chaplain, Drumchapel Hospital, since 1995; Convenor, Ethics and Current Affairs Committee, since 1995; b. 28.9.45, Bridge of Allan; m., May Henrietta Sloan; 2 s.; 1 d. Educ. Braidfield Secondary School, Clydebank; University of Aberdeen. Home Missionary, Boddam, near Peterhead, 1970-73; Student Pastor, Woodside Congregational Church, Aberdeen, 1974-78; Minister, Bannockburn United Free Church, 1978-82. Vice-Chairman, Kirk Care Housing Association. Recreations: swimming; hillwalking. Address: 1 Swallow Gardens, Glasgow G13 4QD; T.-0141-959 7158.

Macmillan, Angus. Chief Executive, Western Isles Tourist Board; b. 3.12.55, Ness, Isle of Lewis; m., Isabel; 3 d. Educ. Govan High School, Glasgow. Address: (b.) 4 South Beach, Stornoway HS1 2XY; T.-01851 701818.

MacMillan of MacMillan and Knop, George Gordon, MA (Cantab). Chief of Clan MacMillan; Deputy Lieutenant, Renfrewshire; b. 20.6.30, London; m., (Cecilia) Jane Spurgin; 2 s. Educ. Aysgarth School; Eton; Trinity College, Cambridge. Schoolmaster, Wellington College, 1953-63; Lecturer, Trinity College, Toronto, 1963-64; Lecturer, Bede College, Durham, 1965-74. Owner, small historic house with gardens and woods open to the public. Address: (h.) Finlaystone, Langbank, Renfrewshire PA14 6TJ; T.-01475 540285.

Macmillan, Very Rev. Gilleasbuig Iain, MA, BD. Minister, St. Giles', The High Kirk of Edinburgh, since 1973.

MacMillan, Hector. Playwright; b. 1929, Glasgow. Plays include: The Rising, 1970; The Sash, 1973.

Macmillan, Iain Alexander, CBE, LLD, BL. Sheriff of South Strathclyde, Dumfries and Galloway, at Hamilton, 1981-92; b. 14.11.23, Oban; m., Edith Janet McAulay; 2 s.; 1 d. Educ. Oban High School; Glasgow University; Scottish Commercial College. RAF (France, Germany, India), 1944-47; Solicitor (Sturrock & Co., Kilmarnock), 1952-81; Council Member, Law Society of Scotland, 1964-79 (President, 1976-77); Chairman: Lanarkshire Branch, Scottish Association for the Study of Delinquency, 1986-92, Chairman, Victim Support East Ayrshire; President: Temporary Sheriffs Association, 1993-94, Glasgow Ayrshire Society. Recreations: golf; music. Address: (h.) 2 Castle Drive, Kilmarnock, Ayrshire; T.-01563 525864.

McMillan, Iain Macleod, FCIB, FCIBS, FFA, FIMgt, FRSA. Director, CBI Scotland, since 1995; Member, Board, Scottish Qualifications Authority; Chairman, Higher Still Employment and Training Group; Member, Scottish Advisory Board, Equal Opportunities Commission; b. 25.4.51, Glasgow; m., Guiseppina; 3 s. Educ. Bearsden Academy. Trainee Banker, 1970-76; TSB Group plc: Manager, 1976-89, Senior Manager, 1989-93; Assistant Director, CBI Scotland, 1993-95. Publications: Manufacturing Matters (Co-Author), 1994; The Challenge for Government in Scotland (principal author), 1996, Scottish Manufacturing: a shared vision (Co-author), 1997; Business and Parliaments – Partners for Prosperity (Co-author), 1998. Recreations: squash; walking. Address: (b.) Beresford House, 5 Claremont Terrace, Glasgow G3 7XT; T.-0141-332 8661.

McMillan, James, OBE, BSc (Hons). Managing Director: Consafe Group, since 1985, Safe Service Group, since 1998, Prosafe Companies in UK; b. 7.5.47, Kilwinning; m., Elizabeth; 3 d. Educ. Queens Park Secondary School, Glasgow; Strathclyde University. Technical Apprentice,

Rolls Royce, Hillington, 1967-70; Product Engineer/ Assistant Chief Engineer, GEC-Elliott Controls, 1972-75; Hydraulics Engineer, Sperry Vickers, 1975-78; Sales and Technical Director, Speyside Engineering (Aberdeen), 1978-82; Managing Director, Consafe (UK) Ltd., 1982-85, management buy-out, 1985, merged with Prosafe ASA, 1998. Recreations: golf; tennis. Address: (h.) Belmont House, Belmont Brae, Stonehaven; T.-01224 406600.

MacMillan, James Loy, BMus, PhD. Composer and Conductor; Affiliate Composer, Scottish Chamber Orchestra, since 1990; Artistic Director, Philharmonia Music of Today Season; Artistic Director, Royal Scottish National Orchestra, since 1998; b. 16.7.59, Kilwinning; m., Lynne; 1 s.; 2 d. Educ. Cumnock Academy; Edinburgh University; Durham University. Principal compositions: The Confession of Isobel Gowdie, London Proms, 1990; Busqueda, Edinburgh International Festival, with Diana Rigg, 1990; featured composer, Musica Nova, 1990, Huddersfield Contemporary Music Festival, 1991; Veni, Veni, Emmanuel, percussion concerto for Evelyn Glennie, London Proms, 1992; Visitatio Sepulchri, one act opera, Mayfest, 1993; Ines de Castro, for Scottish Opera, Edinburgh International Festival, 1996; The World's Ransoming, for orchestra and cor anglaise, 1996; Cello Concerto, 1996; Symphony : Vigil, 1997; featured composer, Edinburgh International Festival, 1993; recording of Tryst and The Confession of Isobel Gowdie by BBC SSO won Gramophone Award, contemporary music category, 1993; Seven Last Words, BBC TV, 1994; Raising Sparks, 1997, for chamber ensemble; String Quartet: Why Is This Night Different?, 1988; featured composer, Raising Sparks Festival, South Bank Centre, London, 1997 (South Bank Show Award for Classical Music, 1997); Evening Standard Classical Music Award, 1997 for Outstanding Artistic Achievement for Symphony: Vigil and Raising Sparks Festival. DUniv, (Paisley); DLitt (University of Strathclyde); FRASMD; HonFRIAS.

McMillan, John Boyd, BSc. Rector, Invergordon Academy, since 1986; b. 16.12.41, Irvine; m., Kathleen Miller (deceased); 2 s. Educ. Irvine Royal Academy; Glasgow University; Jordanhill College of Education. Mathematics Teacher: Irvine Royal Academy, 1964-67, Gloucester School, Hohne, 1967-72, Invergordon Academy, 1972-74; Principal Teacher of Mathematics, Thurso High School, 1974-82; Assistant Rector, Alness Academy, 1982-86; In-Service Training Co-ordinator, HRC, Inverness, 1986; Chairman, Highland Education Industry Liaison Committee, 1990-91; President: Highland Secondary Heads Association, 1988-90, Invergordon Highland Gathering, Highland Family History Society. Football Blue. Recreations: gardening; public speaking; genealogy; sailing; photography. Address: (b.) Invergordon Academy, Academy Road, Invergordon IV18 0LD; T.-0349 852362.

Macmillan, Professor (John) Duncan, MA, PhD, FRSA, HRSA. Professor of the History of Scottish Art, Edinburgh University; Curator, Talbot Rice Gallery and University Collections, Edinburgh University, since 1979; Hon. Keeper of Portraits, Royal College of Surgeons, Edinburgh; Art Critic, The Scotsman; b. 7.3.39, Beaconsfield; m., Vivien Rosemary Hinkley; 2 d. Educ. Gordonstoun School; St. Andrews University; London University; Edinburgh University. Lecturer, then Senior Lecturer, then Reader, Department of Fine Art, Edinburgh University. Chairman, Torvean Project. Recreation: walking. Address: (h.) 20 Nelson Street, Edinburgh; T.-0131-556 7100.

McMillan, Joyce Margaret, MA (Hons), DipEd. Journalist and Arts Critic; Theatre Critic and Columnist, The Scotsman, since 1998; b. 29.8.52, Paisley. Educ. Paisley Grammar School; St. Andrews University; Edinburgh University. Theatre Reviewer, BBC Radio Scotland and The Scotsman, 1979-81; Theatre Critic, Sunday Standard, 1981-83; Radio Critic, The Herald, 1983-95; Scottish Theatre Critic, The Guardian, 1984-93; Scotland on Sunday: Social/Political Columnist, 1989-97, Theatre Critic, 1993-97; Arts/Political Columnist, The Herald, 1997-98. Chair, NUJ Freelance Branch, Edinburgh; Member, National Executive Committee, NUJ, London; Chair, Scottish Constitutional Commission, 1994; Executive Member, Helsinki Citizens' Assembly, Prague. Publications: The Traverse Story, 1963-88, 1988; Charter for the Arts in Scotland, 1992. Recreations: food; drink; films; music; talking politics. Address: 8 East London Street, Edinburgh, EH7 4BH; T.-0131-557 1726.

McMillan, Lorraine Anne, BSc (Hons), MBA. Chief Executive, Renfrewshire Enterprise, since 1999; b. 12.8.61, Johnstone; m., Ian Stuart McMillan; 1 s.; 1 d. Educ. Glasgow University; Strathclyde University. Barr and Stroud, 1982-89; Scottish Development Agency, 1989-91; Dunbartonshire Enterprise, 1991-99. Address: (b.) Spectrum House, Clydebank Business Park, Clydebank G81 2DR; T.-0141-848 0101.

McMillan, Michael Dale, BSc, LLB, NP. Managing Partner, Burnett & Reid, Solicitors, Aberdeen; Partner, Macdonalds Sergeants, Solicitors, East Kilbride and Glasgow, 1971-92; b. 15.2.44, Edinburgh; m., Isobel Ross Mackie; 2 s.; 1 d. Educ. Edinburgh Academy; Edinburgh University. Secretary: East Kilbride Chamber of Commerce, 1971-86, East Kilbride Chamber of Trade, 1971-92; Member, East Kilbride Development Corporation, 1979-84; Secretary, Pilgrim Legal Users' Group, 1985-92; Captain, East Kilbride Golf Club, 1979; Chairman, Strathaven Academy School Board, 1991-92; President, East Kilbride Burns Club, 1989-91; Captain, Inchmarlo Golf Club (Banchory), 1997-99; Vice-President, Deeside Musical Society, 1998-99. Recreations: golf; sailing; skiing. Address: (h.) Belnies, Strachan, Banchory, Aberdeenshire AB31 6LU; T.-01330 850249.

McMillan, William Alister, BL. Solicitor, since 1955; b. 19.1.34, Ayr; m., Elizabeth Anne; 3 d. Educ. Strathallan; Glasgow University. Clerk of the Peace, County of Ayr, 1974-75; Honorary Sheriff, Ayr; Governor, Strathallan School. Recreations:sailing; golf; philately. Address: (h.) Afton Lodge, Mossblown, by Ayr; T.-01292 520 710.

Macmillan, Very Rev. William Boyd Robertson, MA, BD, HonLLD (Dundee), Hon. DD (Aberdeen). Minister, Dundee Parish Church (St. Mary's), 1978-93; Extra Chaplain to The Queen in Scotland, since 1997 (Chaplain in Ordinary to The Queen, 1988-97); President, Scottish Church Society, 1993-97; b. 3.7.27, Keith; m., Mary Adams Bisset Murray. Educ. Royal High School, Edinburgh; Aberdeen University. Royal Navy, 1946-48; Aberdeen University, 1948-54 (President, SRC, 1953-54); Minister: St. Andrew's Church, Bo'ness, 1955-60, Fyvie Parish Church, 1960-67, Bearsden South Church, 1967-78. Convener, Board of Practice and Procedure, 1984-88, and of Business Committee, 1985-88, General Assembly, Church of Scotland; Moderator, General Assembly, 1991-92; Chaplain, City of Dundee District Council, 1978-93; Freeman of Dundee, 1991; Prelate, Order of St. John of Jerusalem (Scotland), 1993-96; Chairman of Directors, High School of Dundee, 1993-96; Chairman, The Murray Home for Scottish Veterans, 1994-96; Trustee, Scottish National War Memorial, since 1994; Committee Member, Royal Society for the Relief of Indigent Gentlewomen of Scotland, since 1994. Recreations: golf; reading. Address: (h.) 3/5 Craigend Park, Edinburgh EH16 5XY.

McMurdo, Professor Marion Elizabeth Taylor, MBChB, MD, FRCPEdin, FRCPGlas. Professor of Ageing and Health, University of Dundee, since 1997; Honorary Consultant, Medicine for the Elderly, Dundee Healthcare Trust, since 1997; b. 16.11.55, Glasgow; m., Dr. Grant L. Hutchison. Educ. Marr College, Troon; University of Dundee. Deputy Medical Director, Drug Development

(Scotland) Ltd., 1984-86; Lecturer in Geriatric Medicine, University of Dundee, 1986-88, Senior Lecturer/Reader in Ageing and Health, 1988-97. Member, Biomedical and Therapeutics Committee, Chief Scientist Office, since 1997; British Geriatrics Society Regional Training Adviser, since 1993. Recreations: golf; swimming; hill-walking; photography. Address: Department of Medicine, Ninewells Hospital and Medical School, Dundee DD1 9SY; T.-01382 632436.

Macnab of Macnab, Hon. Mrs, DL. Honorary Vice President, Scotland's Gardens Scheme, since 1991 (Chairman, 1983-91); Chairman, East Fife Members' Centre, National Trust for Scotland, 1995-98; Member, Executive Committee, National Trust for Scotland, 1991-96; President, Central and North Fife Preservation Society; Deputy Lieutenant, Fife, since 1992; b. 6.6.36, Edinburgh; m., J.C. Macnab of Macnab (qv); 2 s.; 2 d. Address: (h.) Leuchars Castle Farmhouse, Leuchars, St. Andrews KY16 0EY; T.-01334 838777.

Macnab of Macnab, James Charles — The Macnab. Senior Consultant, Hill Samuel Investment Services Ltd., 1982-92, now retired; 23rd Chief, Clan Macnab; b. 14.4.26, London; m., Hon. Diana Mary Anstruther-Gray (see Hon. Mrs. Macnab of Macnab); 2 s.; 2 d. Educ. Radley College; Ashbury College, Ottawa. Served, RAF and Scots Guards, 1944-45; Lt., Seaforth Highlanders, 1945-48; Assistant Superintendant and Deputy Superintendant, Federation of Malaya Police Force, 1948-57; Captain, Seaforth Highlanders (TA), 1960-64; managed family estate and farms, 1957-82; County Councillor, Perth and Kinross Joint County Council, 1964-75; District Councillor, Perth, 1961-64; JP, 1968-86; Member: Central Regional Council, 1978-82, Queen's Bodyguard for Scotland (Royal Company of Archers). Address: (h.) Leuchars Castle Farmhouse, Leuchars, St. Andrews KY16 0EY; T.-01334 838777.

Macnair, Terence Crawford, LLB, NP. Solicitor, since 1967; Director, Argyll and the Islands Enterprise Company, since 1996; Honorary Sheriff, North Strathclyde, since 1988; b. 16.12.42, Kingston, Jamaica; m., Ishbel Ross Hunter; 1 s. Educ. High School of Glasgow; Glasgow University. Town Clerk, Lochgilphead, 1970-75; Partner, MacArthur Stewart & Orr, 1970-81; Senior Partner, MacArthur Stewart, since 1981; Assistant Clerk, Tarbert Harbour Authority, since 1970; Clerk, Awe District Salmon Fishery Board, since 1979; President, Oban Rotary Club, 1988-89; Past Chairman, Oban Tennis and Squash Club; Secretary/Treasurer, Oban and District Licensed Trade Association, since 1977; Chairman, North Argyll Development Agency, since 1994. Recreations: tennis; squash; golf; curling; bridge; music. Address: (b.) Boswell House, Oban; T.-01631 562215.

McNally, Rt. Rev. Anthony Joseph. Rector, Gillis College, Edinburgh, since 1987; Vicar General, Archdiocese of St. Andrews and Edinburgh, since 1985; b. 27.5.32, Edinburgh. Educ. Blairs College, Aberdeen; Seminaire St. Sulpice, Paris. Ordained Priest, 1955; Assistant Priest, Methil, Fife, 1955-63; Missioner, Calabar and Bauchi Province, Nigeria, 1963-67; Assistant Priest, Bonnybridge, 1967-72; Parish Priest, Burntisland, 1972-80, St. Peter's, Morningside, 1980-85; Parish Priest, Musselburgh, and Vicar General, Archdiocese, 1985; Parish Priest, St. Columba's, Edinburgh, since 1993. Recreations: reading; walking. Address: (b.) St. Columba's, 9 Upper Gray Street, Edinburgh EH9 1SN.

McNaught, Brian, BSc (Hons), FRSA. Rector, Garnock Academy, Kilbirnie, since 1993; b. 30.3.50, Dumfries; m., Judith Park; 3 d. Educ. Lockerbie Academy; Glasgow University. Mathematics Teacher, Annan Academy; Stranraer Academy: Principal Teacher of Mathematics, Assistant Rector; Depute Rector, Beath High School, Cowdenbeath. Recreations: angling; sea fishing; shooting. Address: (h.) 74 Greenock Road, Largs; T.-01505 682685.

McNaught, Peter Cairn, MA, MLitt, DUniv, FRSA. Principal, Craigie College of Education, Ayr, 1976-87; b. 29.5.25, Glasgow; m., Else Kristine Sandvad; 1 s.; 1 d. Educ. Hutchesons' Boys' Grammar School, Glasgow; Glasgow University. Teacher, Queen's Park and Hutchesons' Boys' Grammar Schools, Glasgow, 1952-58; Lecturer in English, Moray House College of Education, Edinburgh, 1958-60; Principal Lecturer in English, Aberdeen College of Education, 1960-61; Moray House College of Education: Senior Assistant Principal, 1961-70, Vice-Principal, 1970-75. Vice-Chairman, Scottish Council for the Validation of Courses for Teachers; Member, General Teaching Council for Scotland; Vice-Chairman, West Sound; Chairman, STV Education Committee; Member, STV Staff Trust; Visiting Professor in English Studies, Strathclyde University, 1988; Director, Wider Access Programme, 1988-1992; Chairman, Committee of College of Education Principals, 1984-86. Address: (h.) 1a Victoria Drive, Troon KA10 6EN; T.-01292 312200.

McNaughton, John Ewen, OBE, JP, FRAgS. Chairman, Scotch Quality Beef & Lamb Association, 1981-97; Vice President, Royal Highland and Agricultural Society of Scotland, 1997-98; Member: British Wool Marketing Board, since 1975, Panel of Agricultural Arbiters, 1973-98, Red Deer Commission, 1975-92; Member, Scottish Beef Council, since 1997; b. 28.5.33, Edinburgh; m., Jananne Ogilvie Honeyman; 2 s.; 2 d. Educ. Cargilfield; Loretto. Born and bred a hill sheep farmer; after a short spell in America, began farming at Inverlochlarig with father; served on Council, NFU of Scotland; Elder, Church of Scotland. Recreations: yachting; stalking. Address: Inverlochlarig, Balquhidder, Lochearnhead, Perthshire FK19 8PH; T.-01877 384 232.

Macnaughton, Professor Sir Malcolm Campbell, MD, LLD, FRCPGlas, FRCOG, FFFP, FRSE, FSLCOG (Hon.), FACOG (Hon.), FRCA (Hon.), FRACOG (Hon.). Vice President, Royal College of Midwives; Professor of Obstetrics and Gynaecology, Glasgow University, 1970-90; b. 4.4.25, Glasgow; m., Margaret-Ann Galt; 2 s.; 3 d. Educ. Glasgow Academy; Glasgow University. RAMC, 1949-51; Lecturer in Obstetrics and Gynaecology, Aberdeen University, 1957-61; Senior Lecturer, St. Andrews University, 1961-66; Consultant, Eastern Regional, 1966-70. Member: Chief Scientist Committee, SHHD, Biomedical Research Committee and Health Service Research Committee, SHHD, MRC Grant Committee and Cell Systems Board, MRC, Scientific Committee, Hospital Recognition Committee, RCOG; President: RCOG, 1984-87, British Fertility Society, 1993-95; Chairman: Scottish Perinatal Mortality Advisory Group, SCOTMEG Working Party on Accident and Emergency Services in Scotland. Recreations: walking; fishing; curling. Address: (h.) 15 Boclair Road, Bearsden, Glasgow G61 2AF; T.-0141-942 1909.

McNay, W. Gordon, OBE, DL, JP, BL; b. 11.12.25, Wishaw; m., Margaret C. MacKay. Educ. Wishaw High School; Glasgow University. Depute Town Clerk, Burgh of Airdrie, 1952-53; Senior Depute Town Clerk, Burgh of Motherwell and Wishaw, 1953-63; Town Clerk, Burgh of East Kilbride, 1963-75; Chief Executive, East Kilbride District Council, 1975-88. Deputy Lieutenant, Lanarkshire; Honorary Freeman, East Kilbride District. Recreations: golf; photography; philately. Address: (h.) Solbakken, 17 Kibblestane Place, Strathaven ML10 6EL; T.-01357 520889.

MacNeacail, Aonghas. Writer (poetry, journalism, scriptwriting for TV, film and radio, librettoes); b. 7.6.42, Uig, Isle of Skye; m., Gerda Stevenson (qv); 1 s. Educ. Portree High School; Glasgow University. Writing fellowships: Sabhal Mor Ostaig, 1977-79, An Comunn Gaidhealach, 1979-81, Ross and Cromarty District Council, 1988-90, Glasgow and Strathclyde Universities, 1993-95, Sabhal Mor Ostaig, 1995-98; tours to Ireland, Germany, North America, Japan, Israel, etc.; opera librettoes for Alasdair Nicolson and William Sweeney; songs for Capercaillie, Phil Cunningham; art with Simon Fraser, Kenny Munro, Diane MacLean; short-listed, Paul Hamlyn Foundation Award for Poets, 1997; Stakis Award, Scottish Writer of the Year, 1997. Publications: books: An Seachnadh, 1986; Rock-Water, 1990; Oideachadh Ceart, 1996; poems widely anthologised. Recreations: newsprint; red wine; thinking about walking. Address: (h.) The Rock, Carlops, Peeblesshire EH26 9NF; T.-01968 661058.

McNee, Sir David Blackstock, Kt, QPM, FBIM, FRSA, KStJ. President, National Bible Society of Scotland, 1983-96; Non-Executive Director and Adviser to a number of public limited companies; b. 23.3.25; m., Isabella Clayton Hopkins (deceased); 1 d. Educ. Woodside Senior Secondary School, Glasgow. Joined City of Glasgow Police, 1946; Deputy Chief Constable, Dunbartonshire Constabulary, 1968; Chief Constable: City of Glasgow Police, 1971-75, Strathclyde Police, 1975-77; Commissioner, Metropolitan Police, 1977-82. Honorary Vice-President, Boys' Brigade, since 1980; Vice-President, London Federation of Boys Clubs, since 1982; Patron, Scottish Motor Neurone Association, 1982-97; Freeman, City of London, 1977; President, Glasgow City Committee, Cancer Relief, 1987-92. Recreations: fishing; golf; music.

McNee, Ian. Member, Parole Board for Scotland, since 1989 (Chairman, since 1995); b. 22.4.32, Edinburgh; m., Betty; 1 s.; 1 d. Educ. Boroughmuir School. Former Managing Director, now Chairman, MacDonald Lindsay Pindar PLC. Member, Lothian Region Children's Panel, 1972-88, Chairman, 1985-88; Past President, Edinburgh Master Printers; Past Captain, Kingsknowe Golf Club. Recreation: golf. Address: (h.) 16 Camptoun, Drem, East Lothian, EH39 5BA; T.-01620 880 631.

MacNee, Professor William, MB, ChB, MD(Hons), FRCP(Glas), FRCP(Edin). Professor of Respiratory and Environmental Medicine, Edinburgh University; Visiting Professor, Department of Biological Sciences, Napier University; Honorary Consultant Physician, Lothian Health Board, since 1987; Clinical Director, Respiratory Medicine Unit, 1992-98; Head, Cardiovascular-Thoracic Service, Royal Infirmary of Edinburgh; b. 18.12.50, Glasgow; m., Edna Marina Kingsley; 1 s.; 1 d. Educ. Coatbridge High School; Glasgow University. House Physician/House Surgeon, Glasgow and Paisley, 1975-76; SHO/Registrar in Medicine, Western Infirmary/Gartnavel Hospitals, Glasgow, 1976-79; Registrar in Respiratory Medicine, City Hospital, Edinburgh, 1979-80; MRC Research Fellow/Honorary Registrar, Department of Respiratory Medicine, Royal Infirmary, Edinburgh, 1980-82; Lecturer, Department of Respiratory Medicine, City Hospital, Edinburgh, 1982-83; Senior Registrar, Respiratory Medicine/Medicine, Lothian Health Board, 1983-87; MRC Research Fellow, University of British Columbia, Vancouver, 1985-86; Senior Lecturer in Respiratory Medicine, 1987-93; Reader in Medicine, Edinburgh University, 1993-97. Council Member, Scottish Thoracic Society, 1990-93; Hon. Secretary, British Lung Foundation (Scotland); Chairman, British Lung Foundation Grants Committee. Recreations: music; sport. Address: (b.) Department of Medicine, Royal Infirmary, Lauriston Place, Edinburgh EH3 9XW; T.-0131-536 3254.

Macneil of Barra, Ian Roderick, BA, LLB, FSA Scot. Wigmore Professor of Law, Northwestern University, Chicago, since 1980; b. 20.6.29, New York City; m., Nancy C. Wilson; 2 s.; 1 d. Educ. Scarborough School; University of Vermont; Harvard University. Lt., AUS, 1951-53; Commissioned Officer, USAR, 1950-67; practised law, 1956-59; Member, Cornell Law School Faculty, 1959-72, 1974-80; Visiting Professor, University College, Dar es Salaam, 1965-67, Duke Law School, 1971-72; Professor of Law and Member, Centre for Advanced Studies, Virginia University, 1972-74; Visiting Fellow, Centre for Socio-Legal Studies, Wolfson College, Oxford, 1979, and Edinburgh University Faculty of Law, 1979, 1987; Visiting Professor, Harvard University, 1988-89; Guggenheim Fellow, 1978-79. Member, Standing Council of Scottish Chiefs; Member, Grange Association Committee; author of numerous books and articles. Recreations: walking; reading; historical studies. Address: (h.) Kisimul Castle, Isle of Barra HS9; T.-Castlebay 300; 95/6 Grange Loan, Edinburgh EH9 2ED; T.-0131-667 6068.

McNeil, Neil, MB, ChB, DPH, DPA, FFCM, FFPHM, MREHIS. Consultant in Public Health Medicine/Director of Community Medicine/Unit Medical Officer/District Medical Officer, Lanarkshire Health Board, 1976-92; Honorary Senior Clinical Lecturer/Honorary Clinical Lecturer, Department of Public Health, Glasgow University, 1976-92; b. 4.6.31, Glasgow; m., Florence Ward Butterworth; 2 s.; 1 d. Educ. Govan High School; Glasgow University. SHO, Senior Resident, House Physician and House Surgeon, Western Infirmary, Glasgow, 1956-58; Hall Fellow, Glasgow University, 1958-60; Registrar, Western Infirmary, Glasgow, 1960-61; Divisional Medical Officer of Health, City of Glasgow, 1962-65; Principal Lecturer in Health Education and Medical Officer, Jordanhill College, Glasgow, 1965-68; Medical Officer of Health, North-East Hampshire, and Honorary Consultant, Aldershot, 1968-69; Medical Officer, Scottish Home and Health Department, 1969-73; Honorary Lecturer, Departments of Materia Medica and Community Medicine, Glasgow University, 1973-74; Consultant Epidemiologist, Communicable Diseases (Scotland) Unit, Ruchill Hospital, 1973-74; Senior Medical Officer, Scottish Home and Health Department, 1974-76. Dr. MacKinlay Prize in Public Health and Preventive Medicine, Glasgow University, 1962. Publications on community medicine, environmental medicine, public health, immunisation and infectious disease control. Recreations: tennis; photography; natural history; Gaelic language and culture; Scottish history and archaeology. Address: (h.) Claddach, 25 Waterfoot Road, Newton Mearns, Glasgow G77 5RU.

McNeill, James Walker, QC. Advocate, since 1978; b. 16.2.52, Dunoon; m., Katherine Lawrence McDowall; 2 s.; 1 d. Educ. Dunoon Grammar School; Sidney Sussex College, Cambridge; Edinburgh University. QC, 1991; Standing Junior Counsel, Department of Transport in Scotland, 1984-88, Inland Revenue, 1988-91. Member of Council, Scottish Universities Law Institute. Recreations: music; hill-walking; golf; sailing; travel. Address: (b.) Advocates' Library, Parliament House, Edinburgh EH1 1RF; T.-0131-226 5071.

McNeill, Robert John, BA (Hons), MSc, MPhil, FInstD, FIMgt. Deputy Director, Scottish Prison Service, responsible for Regime Development, since 1996; Chief Executive, SACRO, 1991-96; b. 7.7.45, Belfast; m., Margaret Alison McCartney; 1 s.; 2 d. Educ. Annadale Grammar School, Belfast; Queen's University, Belfast; Open University; Edinburgh University. Probation Officer, Northern Ireland Probation Service, 1972-73; Governor, N.I. Prison Service, 1973-80, Scottish Prison Service, 1980-85; Depute Director, SACRO, 1985-91. Non-Executive Director, International Federation of Settlements; Cropwood Fellow, Institute of Criminology, Cambridge University, 1985; Associate, Centre for Law, Edinburgh University; Associate Lecturer, Glasgow Caledonian University, 1998. Recreations: fly fishing; golf. Address: (b.) Calton House, 5 Redheughs Rigg, Edinburgh EH12 9HW.

McNeill, Sheriff Peter Grant Brass, PhD, MA (Hons), LLB, QC. Formerly Sheriff of Lothian and Borders at Edinburgh; b. 3.3.29, Glasgow; m., Matilda Farquhar Rose; 1 s.; 3 d. Educ. Hillhead High School, Glasgow; Morrison's Academy, Crieff; Glasgow University. Law apprentice, Biggart Lumsden & Co., Glasgow, 1952-55; Carnegie Fellowship, 1955; Faulds Fellowship, 1956-59; Scottish Bar, 1956; Honorary Sheriff Substitute of Lanarkshire, and of Stirling, Clackmannan and Dumbarton, 1962; Standing Junior Counsel to Scottish Development Department (Highways), 1964; Advocate Depute, 1964; Sheriff of Lanarkshire, subsequently of Glasgow and Strathkelvin, at Glasgow, 1965-82; Temporary Sheriff, 1996-98; President, Sheriffs' Association, 1982-85; Chairman: Council, Stair Society, 1990-98, Scottish Legal History Group, 1990-97 Publications: Balfour's Practicks (Editor), 1962-63; An Historical Atlas of Scotland c. 400 - c. 1600 (Co-Editor), 1975; Adoption of Children in Scotland, 1982, 2nd ed., 1986; Atlas of Scottish History to 1707 (Co-Editor), 1996. Recreations: legal history; gardening; book-binding. Address: (h.) 31 Queensferry Road, Edinburgh EH4 3HB.

McNeilly, Professor Alan S., BSc, PhD, DSc, FRSE. Deputy Director, MRC Reproductive Biology Unit, Edinburgh, since 1998, Acting Director, 1996-98; b. 10.2.47, Birmingham; m., Judy; 1 s.; 3 d. Educ. Handsworth Grammar School, Birmingham; Nottingham University; Reading University; Edinburgh University. Research Lecturer, Department of Reproductive Medicine, St. Bartholomew's Hospital, London, 1971-75; Visiting Professor, University of Manitoba, Canada, 1975-76; Research Scientist, MRC Reproductive Biology Unit, Edinburgh, since 1976, Deputy Director, since 1986. Recreations: walking; golf; orienteering; bee-keeping; gardening. Address: (b.) 37 Chalmers Street, Edinburgh EH3 9EW; T.-0131-229 2575.

McNicoll, Professor Iain Hugh, BA, PhD, FRSA. Professor of Applied Economics, Strathclyde University, since 1987; Senior Research Advisor, Fraser of Allander Institute, since 1991; b. 24.6.51, Glasgow; m. Educ. St. Mungo's Academy, Glasgow; Stirling University. Leverhulme Research Fellow, Industrial Science, Stirling University, 1974-76; Lecturer, Business Studies, Edinburgh University, 1976-79; Fellow/Senior Fellow, Director of Research, Acting Director/Director, Fraser of Allander Institute, 1979-89. Publications: two books; 15 monographs; 60 academic journal and book articles. Recreations: hi-fi; golf; astronomy. Address: (b.) Department of Economics, Strathclyde University, 100 Cathedral Street, Glasgow G4 0LN; T.-0141-552 4400.

MacNish, Alastair J.H., FCCA, MIPD. Chief Executive, South Lanarkshire Council, since 1995; b. 4.2.47, Greenock; m., Jean Ferguson Bell; 1 s.; 2 d. Educ. Gourock High School. Chief Auditor, Renfrew County Council, 1973-75; Principal Accountant, then Assistant Director of Education, then Depute Director of Social Work, Strathclyde Regional Council, 1975-95. Recreations: golf; curling; bridge. Address: (b.) South Lanarkshire Council, Regional Offices, Almada Street, Hamilton ML3 0AA; T.-01698 454208.

McNiven, David Martin. Songwriter, Music Director and Producer, Composer, Actor; b. 4.11.45, Glasgow; m., Angela Rew; 1 s.; 2 d. Educ. High School of Glasgow; Royal Scottish Academy of Music and Drama. Traverse Theatre Company, 1970-73; Young Lyceum, 1974-76; Mickery Theatre, 1976; Oxford and Cambridge Shakespeare Company, 1977-78; Wildcat, 1978-83; Royal Lyceum, 1987-88; various TV comedy series for ITV and BBC, since 1983, including Naked Video, Rab C. Nesbitt, The Baldy Man, etc.; Vice-Chairman, Board, Wildcat Stage Productions; three albums for Decca Records; Edinburgh Festival Fringe First Award for Hot Burlesque, 1981; Partnership, McNivensent Music. Recreations: walking to New Orleans; photography.

Macniven, Duncan, TD, MA, MLitt. Head of Police, Fire and Emergencies Group, Scottish Office, since 1997; b. 1.12.50, Edinburgh; m., Valerie Clark (see Valerie Macniven); 2 d. Educ. Melville College, Edinburgh; Aberdeen University. Graduate trainee, Scottish Office, 1973-78, Principal, 1978-86, Assistant Secretary, 1986-90; Deputy Director, Historic Scotland, 1990-95; Head of Police Division, Scottish Office, 1995-97. Recreations: walking; skiing; Scottish dancing; swimming; cycling; exploring; Scottish history. Address: (b.) Saughton House, Broomhouse Drive, Edinburgh; T.-0131-244 2127.

Macniven, Valerie Margaret, MA (Hons). Head of Division, Scottish Office Home Department, since 1996; b. 14.1.51, Perth; m., Duncan Macniven (qv); 2 d. Educ. Aberdeen High School for Girls; Edinburgh University. Scottish Office, 1973-82 and since 1987. Elder, Church of Scotland. Recreations: Scottish country dancing; tennis; travel. Address: (b.) James Craig Walk, Edinburgh EH1 3BA; T.-0131-244 5434.

McNulty, Des, BA. Member, Glasgow City Council, since 1995 (Chair, Glasgow Healthy City Partnership); Chair, Glasgow 1999 Festival Company Limited, since 1996; b. 28.7.52, Stockport. Educ. St. Bede's College Manchester; University of York. Senior Lecturer in Sociology, Glasgow Caledonian University; Member, Strathclyde Regional Council, 1990-96 (responsibility for dealing with issues associated with local government reorganisation and for organising the 1994 Strathclyde Water Referendum); Vice Chair, Policy and Resources Committee, Glasgow City Council, 1995-98; Member of Court, University of Glasgow; Deputy Chair, The Wise Group; Non-Executive Director, Greater Glasgow Health Board. Address: (b.) City Chambers, George Square, Glasgow G2 1DU; T.-0141-287 0478.

McOwan, Rennie, DUniv, FSA Scot. Writer and Broadcaster; b. Stirling; m., Agnes Mooney; 3 s.; 1 d. Educ. Alva Academy. Reporter, Stirling Journal; Sub-Editor, Kemsley Newspapers, Daily Record; Public Relations, Roman Catholic Church; Sub-Editor, Features Writer, Scotsman Publications; Assistant Publicity Secretary, National Trust for Scotland; now: Scottish Book Trust Lecturer under Writers in Schools and Writers in Public schemes; Guest Lecturer, Film and Media Studies, Stirling University; Contributor to newspapers and magazines in Britain and overseas; radio and TV scripts and research; Writres Guild Golden Eagle award for access campaigning and writing about Scottish subjects, 1997. Publications: Light on Dumyat; The White Stag Adventure; The Day the Mountain Moved; Robert Burns for Beginners; St. Andrew for Beginners; Magic Mountains; Walks in the Trossachs and the Rob Roy Country; The Green Hills; Kilchurn Castle: a history; contributed to: Walking in Scotland; Poetry of the Scottish Hills; Speak to the Hills; Wild Walks; The Story of Scotland; Discover Scotland; Great Walks, Scotland; Classic Coastal Walks of Britain; On Foot Through History. Recreations: mountaineering; Scottish history and literature. Address: 7 Williamfield Avenue, Stirling FK7 9AH; T.-01786 461316.

McPartlin, Sheriff Noel, MA, LLB. Sheriff of Grampian, Highland and Islands, at Elgin, since 1985; b. 25.12.39.

McPhail, Angus William, MA (Oxon). Headmaster, Strathallan School, since 1993; b. 25.5.56, Ipswich; m., Elizabeth Hirsch; 2 s.; 1 d. Educ. Abingdon School; University College, Oxford. Overseas Department, Bank of England, 1978-82; Assistant Master, Glenalmond College, 1982-85; Head of Economics and Housemaster, Sedbergh School, 1985-93. Recreations: cricket; golf; walking; music;

theatre. Address: (h.) Strathallan School, Forgandenny, Perth PH2 9EG; T.-01738 812546.

Macphail, Sheriff Iain Duncan, QC, MA (Hons), LLB. Sheriff of Lothian and Borders at Edinburgh, since 1995; b. 24.1.38; m., Rosslyn Graham Lillias Hewitt; 1 s.; 1 d. Educ. George Watson's College; Edinburgh University; Glasgow University. Admitted Faculty of Advocates, 1963; practice, Scottish Bar, 1963-73; Faulds Fellow in Law, Glasgow University, 1963-65; Lecturer in Evidence and Procedure, Strathclyde University, 1968-69, Edinburgh University, 1969-72; Standing Junior Counsel to Scottish Home and Health Department and Department of Health and Social Security, 1971-73; Extra Advocate-Depute, 1973; Sheriff of Glasgow and Strathkelvin (formerly Lanarkshire), 1973-81; Sheriff of Tayside, Central and Fife at Dunfermline and Alloa, 1981-82; Sheriff of Lothian and Borders at Linlithgow, 1982-88, at Edinburgh, 1988-89. Member, Scottish Law Commission, 1990-94; Chairman, Scottish Association for the Study of Delinquency, 1978-81; Hon. LLD, Edinburgh, 1992. Publications: Evidence, 1987; Sheriff Court Practice, 1988. Address: (b.) Sheriff Court House, 27 Chambers Street, Edinburgh EH1 1LB; T.-0131-225 2525.

Macphail, Madeline, BSc, DipEd. Board Member, Scottish Tourist Board, since 1997; Board Member, Thurso College, since 1994; Chair, Assynt Care Ltd., since 1990; Member, National Transport Forum for Scotland, since 1997; b. 23.5.39, Dundee; m., Pat Macphail; 1 s.; 1 d. Educ. Morgan Academy, Dundee; Queen's College, Dundee, St. Andrews University. Teacher of Mathematics, Glasgow and Lanark; Tourism operator. Recreations: reading; walking. Address: (h.) 216 Clashmore, Stoer, by Lairg IV27 4JQ; T.-01571 855295.

McPhee, George, MBE, BMus, FRCO, DipMusEd, RSAM, Hon. FRSCM. Visiting Professor of Organ, St. Andrews University; Chairman, Paisley International Organ Festival; Organist and Master of the Choristers, Paisley Abbey, since 1963; President, Incorporated Society of Musicians, 1999-2000; b. 10.11.37, Glasgow; m., Margaret Ann Scotland; 1 s.; 2 d. Educ. Woodside Senior Secondary School, Glasgow; Royal Scottish Academy of Music and Drama; Edinburgh University. Studied organ with Herrick Bunney and Fernando Germany; Assistant Organist, St. Giles' Cathedral, 1959-63; joined staff, RSAMD, 1963; Conductor, Scottish Chamber Choir, 1971-75; Conductor, Kilmarnock and District Choral Union, 1975-84; since 1971, has completed 12 recital tours of the United States and Canada; has been both Soloist and Conductor with Scottish National Orchestra; numerous recordings and broadcasts; has taken part in numerous music festivals as Soloist; Adjudicator; Examiner, Associated Board, Royal Schools of Music; Special Commissioner, Royal School of Church Music; Silver Medal, Worshipful Company of Musicians; Honorary Doctorate, University of Paisley. Recreations: golf; walking. Address: (h.) 17 Main Road, Castlehead, Paisley PA2 6AJ; T.-0141-889 3528.

McPherson, Alastair, MA, MSc, MCIT. Managing Director, ScotRail, since 1997; b. 6.7.51, Glasgow. Educ. Kings Park Secondary School, Glasgow; Glasgow University; Birmingham University. Local Government Officer, 1974-77; Tyne and Wear Passenger Transport Executive, 1977-90; National Express Group, 1990-97 (formerly Commercial Director, National Express Ltd.). Recreation: architecture; history. Address: (b.) Caledonian Chambers, 87 Union Street, Glasgow G1 3TA; T.-0141-335 4500.

Macpherson, Sheriff Alexander Calderwood, MA, LLB. Sheriff of South Strathclyde, Dumfries and Galloway, at Hamilton, since 1978; b. 14.6.39.

Macpherson, Archibald (Archy) Cameron, MA, LLB, NP, FSA Scot. Law Lecturer, Department of Building, Heriot-Watt University, since 1979; Chairman, Royal Celtic Society; b. 23.10.27, Edinburgh; m., Christina Cameron. Educ. Clunie and Blairgowrie High; St. Andrews University; Edinburgh University; Moray House College; Jordanhill College. Ferguson Reekie and Kilgour, WS; various posts in education; Tait and Crichton WS; Clerk of Court, Edinburgh Burgh Court; Macpherson and Black; Lecturer in Law, Glasgow College of Building, 1979-92; Lecturer in Law, Glasgow Caledonian University, 1990-92. Editor, Creag Dhubh, 1968-92; former Tutor, College of Estate Management, National Extension College. Publications: Contributor (as Gilleasbuig MacMhuirich) to Garim and Carn; The Scottish Building Regulations, first and second editions, (Contributor). Recreations: Gaelic language and culture (ar cànain 's ar ceòl); creative writing; poetry writing; screen writing; reading; foreign travel, especially Portugal. Address: (h.) Bath House, Trinity Crescent, Edinburgh EH5 3EE; T.-0131-552 2230.

Macpherson, Archie. Sports broadcaster and journalist; b. 1935, Glasgow. Former headmaster; football commentator, BBC Scotland, until 1990; reported Olympic Games, 1984 and 1988, for BBC network; author of Action Replays, 1991.

McPherson, Duncan James, CBE, DL, MA, SDA. Farmer; Deputy Lieutenant, Ross and Cromarty; Member, Highland Council; formerly Convener, Highland Regional Council; b. 29.10.30, Santos, Brazil; m., Vivian Margaret; 1 s.; 1 d. Educ. Robert Gordon's College, Aberdeen; Aberdeen University. Member, Cromarty Town Council, 1964-75, Ross and Cromarty County Council, 1972-75; Fellow, Scottish Council (Development and Industry), since 1990; former Member, Board, Scottish Natural Heritage; President, Rosemarkie Golf Club. Recreations: golf; curling; formerly rugby (Scottish trialist, 1951-56). Address: Cromarty Mains, Cromarty, Ross-shire; T.-01381 600 232.

Macpherson, Rev. Duncan James, BSc(Eng), BD. Minister, Annan Old Parish Church, since 1997; b. 26.4.67, Hardgate; m., Jillian Margaret. Educ. Glasgow Academy; Glasgow University. Associate and Youth Minister, Christ Church, Bermuda; part-time Ordained Assistant, Canonbie with Langholm and Westerkirk. Recreations: volleyball; squash; diving; kite flying; singing; drumming. Address: 12 Plumdon Park, Annan DG12 6EY; T.-01461 201405.

McPherson, James Alexander Strachan, CBE, MA, BL, LLB, FSA Scot, JP. Lord Lieutenant, Grampian Region (Banffshire), since 1987; Consultant, formerly Senior Partner, Alexander George & Co., Solicitors, Macduff; Honorary Sheriff, Grampian, Highland and Islands at Banff, since 1972; b. 20.11.27, Wormit, Fife; m., Helen Marjorie Perks, MA; 1 s.; 1 d. Educ. Banff Academy; Aberdeen University. Member, Macduff Town Council and Banff County Council, 1958-75; Provost of Macduff, 1972-75; Convener, Banff County Council, 1970-75; Member: Grampian Health Board, 1974-82, Post Office Users National Council for Scotland, 1976-80, Police Advisory Board for Scotland, 1974-86, Grampian Regional Council, 1974-90; Chairman, Public Protection Committee, 1974-86; Governor, Scottish Police College, 1974-86; Chairman, Banff and Buchan JP Advisory Committee, since 1987; Member, Scottish Solicitors Discipline Tribunal, 1990-94; Vice President, Highland Territorial and Reserve Forces Association; Member, Aberdeen University Court, 1993-97. Recreations: reading; sailing; swimming. Address: (h.) Dun Alastair, 126 Gellymill Street, Macduff; T.-Macduff 832377.

Macpherson of Drumochter, Lord (James) Gordon Macpherson), 2nd Baron, JP, FRES, FRSA, FZS. Chairman and Managing Director, Macpherson, Train &

Co. Ltd., since 1964; Chairman, A.J. Macpherson & Co. Ltd., since 1973; b. 22.1.24; m., 1, Dorothy Ruth Coulter (deceased); 2 d.; 1 s. deceased; 2, Catherine MacCarthy; 1 s.; 2 d. Educ. Loretto; Wells House, Malvern. RAF, 1939-45; Member, Council, London Chamber of Commerce, 1952-73; Chief, Scottish Clans Association of London, 1972-74; Chairman, Macpherson Clan Association, 1963-64; Life Managing Governor, Royal Scottish Corporation; Freeman, City of London. Address: (h.) Kyllachy, Tomatin, Inverness-shire.

Macpherson, John Hannah Forbes, CBE, OStJ, CA, DUniv. Lord Dean of Guild, Glasgow; Chairman of Court, University of Glasgow; b. 23.5.26, Glasgow; m., Margaret Graham Roxburgh; 1 s. Educ. Glasgow Academy; Merchiston Castle School, Edinburgh. Royal Naval Volunteer Reserve, 1943; Apprentice CA, Wilson Stirling & Co., 1947 (qualified, 1949); Partner, Wilson Stirling & Co. (subsequently Touche Ross & Co.), 1956-86; Chairman: Glasgow Junior Chamber of Commerce, 1965, Scottish Mutual Assurance Society, 1971, Scottish Industrial Estates Corporation, 1972, Irvine Development Corporation, 1976, TSB Scotland plc, 1984, Glasgow Development Agency, 1990; President, Glasgow Chamber of Commerce, 1980; Director: Scottish Metropolitan Property plc, 1986, TSB Group plc, 1985; Deputy Chairman, Hill Samuel Bank Ltd., 1991; Director, PCT Group plc, 1992; Governor, Merchiston Castle School, 1988; Member, Charity Appeals Committee for Prince and Princess of Wales Hospice; Director, Glasgow Native Benevolent Society. Recreations: travel; gardening; reading. Address: (h.) 16 Collylinn Road, Bearsden, Glasgow; T.-0141-942 0042.

McPherson, Malcolm Henry, LLB. Solicitor (Henderson Boyd Jackson); b. 22.5.54, Edinburgh; m., Fiona Sutherland Hogg; 1 s.; 3 d. Educ. George Watson's College, Edinburgh; Edinburgh University. Apprentice, Henderson & Jackson, WS, 1975-77; Partner, 1978; Managing Partner, 1982; development of commercial practice, 1982-86; merged with Wilson Pyle & Co., WS, Allan Dawson Simpson & Hampton, WS, Boyd Jameson, WS. Lay Member, ICAS Investigation Committee. Recreations: shooting; sailing; golfing. Address: (b.) 19 Ainslie Place, Edinburgh EH3 6AU; T.-0131-226 6881.

Macpherson, Peter, FRCP, FRCR, DTCD, FLS. Emeritus Consultant Neuroradiologist, Institute of Neurological Sciences; President: British Society of Neuroradiologists, 1990-92, Botanical Society of the British Isles, 1991-93; b. 10.10.25, Inveraray; m., Agnes Cochrane Davidson; 4 d. Educ. Inveraray Grammar School; Keil School, Dumbarton; Anderson College, Glasgow. House Surgeon, Royal Infirmary, Stirling; Junior Hospital Medical Officer, Robroyston Hospital, Glasgow; Chest Physician, Argyll; Registrar/Senior Registrar, Western Infirmary, Glasgow. Commodore, Oban Sailing Club, 1958-60; President, Glasgow Natural History Society, 1979-81 and 1983-86; Honorary Secretary, Botanical Society of the British Isles, Committee for Scotland, 1977-95, Chairman, since 1995; Plant Recorder for Lanarkshire, since 1978; Elder, Church of Scotland, since 1957. Recreations: natural history; sailing. Address: (h.) Ben Alder, 15 Lubnaig Road, Glasgow; T.-0141-632 0723.

Macpherson of Cluny (and Blairgowrie), The Honourable Sir William, KB (1983), TD, MA. 27th Hereditary Chief of the Clan Macpherson (Cluny-Macpherson); b. 1.4.26; m., Sheila McDonald Brodie; 2 s.; 1 d. Educ. Summer Fields, Oxford; Wellington College; Trinity College, Oxford. Scots Guards, 1944-47 (Captain); 21st Special Air Service Regiment (TA), 1951-65 (Lt.-Col. Commanding, 1962-65); Honorary Colonel, 21st SAS, 1983-91. Called to the Bar, Inner Temple, 1952; Queen's Counsel, 1971-83; Recorder of the Crown Court, 1972-83; Member, Senate and Bar Council, 1979-83; Bencher, Inner Temple, 1978; Judge of the High Court of Justice (of England and Wales), Queen's Bench Division, 1983-96; Honorary Member, Northern Circuit, since 1987. Member, Queen's Bodyguard for Scotland (Royal Company of Archers), since 1976, Brigadier, 1989; Vice President, Royal Scottish Corporation; President, Highland Society of London, 1991-94. Recreations: golf; fishing; rugby football; archery. Address: (h.) Newton Castle, Blairgowrie, Perthshire PH10 6SU.

Macquaker, Donald Francis, CBE, MA (Oxon), LLB. Partner, T.C. Young & Son, Writers, Glasgow, 1957-93; retired Director, Lithgows Limited; b. 21.9.32, Stair; m., Susan Elizabeth Finlayson; 1 s.; 1 d. Educ. Winchester College; Trinity College, Oxford; Glasgow University. Greater Glasgow Health Board: Chairman, Finance and General Purposes Committee, 1974-83, Chairman, 1983-87; Chairman, Scottish Health Service Common Services Agency, 1987-91; former Member, Board of Management, Glasgow Royal Maternity Hospital and Associated Women's Hospitals (latterly Vice-Chairman); Director, Prince and Princess of Wales Hospice, Glasgow, 1991-94; Chairman, Western Meeting Club (Ayr Racecourse), since 1996. Recreations: shooting; fishing; gardening. Address: (h.) Blackbyres, by Ayr; T.-0292 441088.

MacQueen, Professor Hector Lewis, LLB (Hons), PhD, FRSE. Professor of Private Law, Edinburgh University, since 1994; Director, David Hume Institute, Edinburgh, since 1991; b. 13.6.56, Ely; m., Frances Mary Young; 2 s.; 1 d. Educ. George Heriot's School, Edinburgh; Edinburgh University. Lecturer, Senior Lecturer, Reader, all in Law, Edinburgh University, 1979-94; Visiting Professor, Cornell University, 1991; Visiting Professor, Utrecht University, 1997; Secretary, Scottish Historical Review, since 1986; Editor, Hume Papers on Public Policy, since 1993; Editor, Edinburgh Law Review, since 1996; Scottish Representative, European Contract Commission, since 1995. Publications: Common Law and Feudal Society in Medieval Scotland; Studying Scots Law; Copyright, Competition and Industrial Design. Recreations: Scotland; cricket; walking; reading. Address: (b.) Faculty of Law, Edinburgh University, Edinburgh EH8 9YL; T.-0131-650 2060.

MacQueen, Professor Emeritus Jack (John), MA (Glasgow), MA (Cantab), Hon DLitt, FRSE. Professor Emeritus, Edinburgh University, since 1988; b. 13.2.29, Springboig; m., Winifred W. MacWalter; 3 s. Educ. Hutchesons' Boys Grammar School; Glasgow University; Christ's College, Cambridge. RAF, 1954-56 (Pilot Officer, Flying Officer); Assistant Professor of English, Washington University, St. Louis, Missouri, 1956-59; Edinburgh University: Lecturer in Medieval English and Scottish Literature, 1959-63, Masson Professor of Medieval and Renaissance Literature, 1963-72; Director, School of Scottish Studies, 1969-88; Professor of Scottish Literature and Oral Tradition, 1972-88; Endowment Fellow, 1988-92. Publications: St. Nynia, 1961, 1990; Robert Henryson, 1967; Ballattis of Luve, 1970; Allegory, 1970; Progress and Poetry, 1982; Numerology, 1985; Rise of the Historical Novel, 1989; Scotichronicon III and IV (with W. MacQueen), 1989; Scotichronicon I and II (with W. MacQueen), 1993; Scotichronicon V and VI (with W. MacQueen and D.E.R. Watt), 1995; Oxford Book of Scottish Verse (with T. Scott), 1966; A Choice of Scottish Verse 1470-1570 (with W. MacQueen), 1972; Humanism in Renaissance Scotland (Co-Author), 1990. Recreations: walking; occasional archaeology; music; astronomy. Address: (h.) Slewdonan, Damnaglaur, Drummore, Stranraer DG9 9QN.

McQueen, James Donaldson Wright, MA, PhD, ARSGS. Food Industry Analyst and Consultant; Honorary Research Fellow, Department of Geography and Topographic Science, University of Glasgow; Council Member, Royal

Scottish Geographical Society; b. 14.2.37, Dumfries; m., Jean Evelyn Brown; 2 s.; 1 d. Educ. King's Park School, Glasgow; Glasgow University. Assistant Lecturer, Department of Geography, Glasgow University, 1960-61; Junior Manager, Milk Marketing Board (England and Wales), 1961-62; Scottish Milk Marketing Board, 1963-89 (Deputy Managing Director, 1985-89); Chief Executive, Scottish Dairy Trade Federation (latterly Scottish Dairy Association), 1989-95. Member: CBI Scottish Council, 1987-89, CBI National Council, 1991-94. Recreations: golf; gardening; photography. Address: (h.) Ormlie, 53 Kingston Road, Bishopton, Renfrewshire PA7 5BA; T.-Bishopton 862380.

McQueen, William Robert James, BSc, MA, MBA. Head, Transport Division, Scottish Office, since 1995; b. 19.4.51, Widnes; m., Maureen Frances Hall; 2 d. Educ. Kirkham Grammar School; London University; University of California; Strathclyde University. Social Science Research Council, 1973-74; joined Scottish Office, 1974. Recreations: tennis; skiing; music. Address: (b.) Victoria Quay, Edinburgh EH6 6QQ; T.-0131-244 0862.

McQuillin, Robert, BSc, MSc, MInstPet, FGS, FRSE. Managing Director, Hydrocarbon Management International Ltd., since 1991; Senior Consultant, R. McQuillin & Associates, since 1990; b. 28.5.35, Cumbria; m., Angela; 2 s. Educ. White House School, Brampton; Durham University; London University. British Geological Survey: Staff Geophysicist, 1957-66; set up offshore geophysical exploration of UK shelf, 1966-73; Head, Marine Geophysics Unit, 1973-85, Deputy Director, Marine Surveys, Hydrocarbons and Geothermal Energy Division, 1983-85; Britoil: Chief Geophysicist, 1985-88, Chief Scientist and Deputy Exploration Manager, 1986-88; Scientific Adviser, BP NW Europe, Exploration and Production, 1988-89; Oil Industry Consultant, 1990-91. Former Vice-President, Geological Society of London and of Geological Society of Edinburgh. Publication: An Introduction to Seismic Interpretation (principal author), 1986. Recreations: wine and food; good hotels; golf; history of art of china. Address:(b.) HMI Ltd., 94 Liberton Drive, Edinburgh EH16 6NR; T.-0131-664 2193.

MacRae, Rev. Angus, MA, DipTh. Minister, Kilwinning Free Church of Scotland, since 1992; Moderator, Glasgow Free Presbytery, since 1998; Vice Convenor, Free Church Youth Committee, since 1998; b. 11.9.67, Glasgow; m., Dr. Ann Sheila Macrae; 1 s.; 2 d. Educ. Nicolson Institute, Stornoway; Edinburgh University; Free Church College, Edinburgh. Recreations: playing and reading with his children; Scotland's hills; music and poetry in English and Gaelic. Address: Free Church Manse, 57 Dalry Road, Kilwinning KA13 7HN; T.-01294 552163.

Macrae, John Grant, CA, CPFA, FRSA. Partner in charge Public Sector Practice, KPMG; b. 9.11.50, Glasgow; m., Inez; 1 s.; 2 d. Educ. Melville College. Former Convener, ICAS Public Sector Committee; Member, ICAS Accounting Standards Committee; former Chairman, Scottish Branch, CIPFA. Recreations: skiing; golf; walking. Address: (b.) Saltire Court, 20 Castle Terrace, Edinburgh EH1 2EG; T.-0131-222 2000.

MacRae, Kenneth. Chief Executive, Student Awards Agency for Scotland, since 1994; b. 4.11.39, Kirkintilloch; m., Elizabeth Marjorie. Joined Board of Trade, 1960; transferred to Scottish Office, 1973; various posts, Industry Department for Scotland, 1973-84; Principal, Scottish Development Department Housing Division, 1984-86; Assistant Secretary, Scottish Education Department, 1986-94. Recreations: motor racing (voluntary senior official); gardening. Address: (b.) Gyleview House, 3 Redheughs Rigg, Edinburgh EH12 9HH; T.-0131-244 5867.

Macrae, Col. Sir Robert Andrew Alexander Scarth, KCVO, MBE (1953). Lord Lieutenant of Orkney, 1972-90; Farmer; b. 14.4.15; m., Violet Maud MacLellan (d., 1997); 2 s. Educ. Lancing; RMC, Sandhurst. Commissioned Seaforth Highlanders, 1935; active service, BEF 1940 (PoW, 1940-45), NW Europe, 1945 (Despatches, 1945), Korea, 1952-53, East Africa, 1953-54; retired from Army, 1968; farming in Orkney, since 1967; Councillor, Orkney CC, 1970-74; Orkney Islands Council, 1974-78; Vice-Chairman, Orkney Hospital Board, 1971-74; Orkney Health Board, 1974-79; Honorary Sheriff, Grampian Highlands and Islands, 1974; JP, 1975; Freedom of Orkney, 1990. Recreations: sailing; gardening (watching the cabbages being blown out to sea). Address: (h.) Grindelay, Orphir, Orkney KW17 2RD.

McSorley, George Joseph, JP, MInstM, MCIM, MInstAM. Chief Executive, Unity Enterprise Ltd., since 1991; Director, Notre Dame Centre, since 1995; Member Scottish Office Beattie Committee, since 1998; b. 4.1.50, Glasgow; m., Anne Maria Leslie; 2 d. Educ. St Mary's College, Blairs, Aberdeen. Formerly: Civil Servant, Department of Employment, Personnel Manager, Community Industry, Glasgow, Area Manager, Community Industry Lower Clyde, District Manager, Social Services, Archdiocese of Glasgow. Formerly: Chair, Children's Panel Advisory Sub-Committee, Inverclyde, Vice Chair, Management Committee, Citizens Advice Bureau, Largs, Secretary, Largs Community Council, Chair, Christian Aid Largs, Chair, National Commission for Pastoral and Social Care. Recreations: family; reading; travel; ecumenical activities. Address: (h.) 34 Springkell Drive, Glasgow G41 4EZ; T.-(b.) 0141-849 0400.

McSwan, Malcolm, OBE, CA. Chairman, Adaptive Engineering Group Ltd., since 1995; Proprietor, Knapp Tree Farm; Chairman, Hearing Enhancement PLC, since 1996; b. 31.8.39, Glasgow; m., Juliet Cowper-Jackson; 2 s. Educ. Royal High School, Edinburgh. Recreations: renovation; trees. Address: (h.) Millhill House, Inchture, Perthshire; T.-01828 686019.

MacSween, Iain MacLean, BA (Econ), MPhil. Chief Executive, Scottish Fishermen's Organisation, since 1982; b. 20.9.49, Glasgow; m., Jean Gemmill Martin; 3 s.; 1 d. Educ. Knightswood Secondary School; Strathclyde University; Glasgow University. Fisheries Economics Research Unit, 1973-75; Department of Agriculture and Fisheries for Scotland, 1975-77; Scottish Fishermen's Organisation, since 1977; President, European Federation of Fishermen's Organisations. Address: (b.) 601 Queensferry Road, Edinburgh EH2 6EA; T.-0131-339 7972.

MacSween, Professor Roderick Norman McIver, BSc, MD, FRCPGlas, FRCPEdin, PRCPath, FRSE, FIBiol. Professor of Pathology, Glasgow University, since 1984; Honorary Consultant Pathologist, Western Infirmary, Glasgow, since 1970; President, Royal College of Pathologists, since 1996; Chairman, Academy of Medical Royal Colleges, since 1998; b. 2.2.35, Kinloch, Lewis; m., Marjory Pentland Brown; 1 s.; 1 d. Educ. Inverness Royal Academy; Glasgow University. Honorary Fellow, South African Society of Pathologists, 1982; Otago Savings Bank Visiting Professor, Otago University, 1983; Hans Popper Lecturer in Liver Pathology, Columbia University College of Physicians and Surgeons, New York, 1988; Henry Moon Lecturer, University of California, San Francisco, 1993; Basil Morson Lecturer, British Society of Gastroenterology, 1995; President, Royal Medico-Chirurgical Society of Glasgow, 1978-79; President, International Academy of Pathology, British Division, 1988-90; Editor, Histopathology (Journal), 1985-96. Publications: Muir's Textbook of Pathology, 13th edition (Co-Editor); Pathology of the Liver, 3nd edition (Co-Editor); Recent Advances in Histopathology, Nos. 11-17; Recent Advances in Hepatology, No. 1. Former Captain, Dunaverty and

Machrihanish Golf Clubs. Recreations: golf; gardening; opera; hill-walking; more golf! Address: (b.) University Department of Pathology, Western Infirmary, Glasgow G11 6NT; T.-0141-211 2233.

MacTaggart, Kenneth Dugald, BA, PhD. Directory of Strategy, Highlands and Islands Enterprise, since 1995; b. 15.4.53, Glasgow; m., Caroline McNicholas; 2 d. Educ. Allan Glen's School, Glasgow; Glasgow University; Paisley College; Aston University. Economic research, Aston University, 1976-80; Editor, Export Times, London, 1980-84; Editor, Property International, London and Bahrain, 1984-87; Director, Inc Publications, London, 1987-88; Senior Economist, HIDB, 1988-91. Recreations: hill-walking; piano; photography. Address: (h.) The Sutors, 28 Broadstone Park, Inverness IV2 3LA; T.-01463 233717.

MacVicar, Angus, MA, DUniv. Author; b. 28.10.08, Argyll; m., Jean Smith McKerral (deceased); 1 s. Educ. Campbeltown Grammar School; Glasgow University. Reporter, Campbeltown Courier, 1931-33; Freelance Author; Army Service, 1940-45 (Captain, RSF); Freelance Author, Journalist, Radio and TV Scriptwriter; published 78 books, including adult novels, children's novels, adult and children's non-fiction, plays; Honorary Sheriff-Substitute, Argyll, 1965; Doctorate, Stirling University, 1985. Recreations: golf; gardening; amateur drama. Address: (h.) Achnamara, Southend, Campbeltown, Argyll PA28 6RW; T.-01586 830228.

McVicar, George Christie, DipMusEd, RSAM; Hon.FTSC. Chairman, Scottish Amateur Music Association, 1982-95; b. 17.3.19, Dumbarton. Educ. Dumbarton Academy; Royal Scottish Academy of Music and Drama. Teacher of Music, Dunbartonshire Schools, 1946-54; Lecturer in Music, Moray House College of Education, 1954-56; Adviser in Music to Stirlingshire and subsequently Central Region, 1956-79. Former Adjudicator Member, British Federation of Music Festivals; Examiner, Trinity College of Music, 1979-91; Hon. Vice President, Scottish Amateur Music Association, since 1995. Publications: The Saltire Scottish Song Book (formerly Oxford Scottish Song Book); Saltire Two-Part Scottish Song Book; The New Scottish Song Book. Address: (h.) 22 Queen Street, Stirling FK8 1HN; T.-01786 72074.

McVie, John, BL, WS, NP. Retired Solicitor; Honorary Sheriff-Substitute, Lothian and Borders; b. 7.12.19, Edinburgh; m., Lindsaye Woodburn Mair; 1 s.; 1 d. Educ. Royal High School; Edinburgh University. Captain, 7/9th Bn., The Royal Scots, 1940-46 (Signal Officer, North West Europe); mentioned in Despatches; Town Clerk, Royal Burgh of Haddington, 1951-75. Address: (h.) Ivybank, Haddington, East Lothian; T.-0162-082 3727.

MacWalter, Ronald Siller, BMSc (Hons), MB, ChB (Hons), MRCP(UK); FRCP(Edin); FRCP (Glas). Consultant Physician in General Medicine, Ninewells Hospital, Dundee, since 1997; Consultant Physician in Medicine for the Elderly, Royal Victoria Hospital, Dundee, 1986-97; Honorary Senior Lecturer in Medicine, Dundee University, Ninewells Hospital, Dundee, since 1986; b. 14.12.53, Broughty Ferry; m., Sheila Margaret Nicoll; 2 s. Educ. Harris Academy, Dundee; Dundee University. Registrar in Medicine and Haematology, Department of Clinical Pharmacology, Ninewells Hospital, Dundee; Senior Registrar in General Medicine and Geriatric Medicine, Nuffield Department of Medicine, John Radcliffe Hospital, Oxford. Publication: Aids to Clinical Examination.

McWilliam, James, OBE, MA (Hons), DipEd. Rector, Lochaber High School, 1970-88; Chairman, Highland Health Board, 1983-91; b. 4.10.27, Portsoy, Banffshire; m., Helen C. Brodie; 3 d. Educ. Fordyce Academy, Banffshire; Glasgow University. Teacher of English, Calderhead School, Shotts, 1951; National Service (Royal Army Education Corps), 1951-53; Teacher, Coatbridge High School, 1953; Special Assistant, Beath High School, Cowdenbeath, 1958; Principal Teacher of English, Campbeltown Grammar School, 1961-70. Member, Highland Health Board, since 1978 (Chairman, Practitioners' Committee, 1981); Honorary Sheriff, Grampian, Highlands and Islands, since 1978; Past President: Lochaber Rotary Club, Lochaber EIS, Highland Secondary Headteachers Association. Recreations: music; TV; golf (occasionally). Address: (h.) 19 Seafield Street, Portsoy, Banff; T.-01261 843148.

McWilliam, Rev. Thomas Mathieson, MA, BD. Minister, Contin Parish, Ross-shire, since 1997; b. 12.11.39, Glasgow; m., Patricia Jane Godfrey; 1 s.; 1 d. Educ. Eastwood Secondary School; Glasgow University; New College, Edinburgh. Assistant Minister, Auld Kirk of Ayr, 1964-66; Minister: Dundee St. David's North, 1966-72, East Kilbride Greenhills, 1972-80, Lylesland Parish Church, Paisley, 1980-97; Convener, Youth Education Committee, General Assembly, 1980-84; Moderator, Paisley Presbytery, 1985-86; Convener, Board of Practice and Procedure, General Assembly, 1992-96. Recreations: walking; reading; gardening; bowling. Address: (h.) Contin Manse, Contin, Strathpeffer IV14 9ES; T.-01997 421380.

M

Maan, Bashir Ahmed, JP, MSc, DL, FRSA; b. 22.10.26, Maan, Pakistan; 1 s.; 3 d. Educ. D.B. High School, Quila Didar Singh; Punjab University. Involved in the struggle for creation of Pakistan as a student, 1943-47; organised rehabilitation of refugees from India in Maan and surrounding areas, 1947-48; emigrated to UK and settled in Glasgow, 1953; Founder Secretary, Glasgow Pakistan Social and Cultural Society, 1955-65 (President, 1966-69); Member, Executive Committee, Glasgow City Labour Party, 1969-70; Vice-Chairman, Glasgow Community Relations Council, 1970-75; Member, Glasgow Corporation, 1970-75 (Magistrate, City of Glasgow, 1971-74; Vice-Chairman, then Chairman, Police Committee, 1971-75); Member, National Road Safety Committee, 1971-74 and Scottish Accident Prevention Committee, 1971-75; Member, BBC Immigrant Programmes Advisory Committee, 1972-80; Convenor, Pakistan Bill Action Committee, 1973; contested East Fife Parliamentary seat, February 1974; President, Standing Conference of Pakistani Organisations in UK and Eire, 1974-77; Police Judge, City of Glasgow, 1974-75; Member: City of Glasgow District Council, 1975-84, Glasgow City Council, since 1995 (Bailie, since 1996); Deputy Chairman, Commission for Racial Equality, 1977-80; Member, Scottish Gas Consumers Council, 1978-81; Bailie, City of Glasgow, 1980-84; Member, Greater Glasgow Health Board, 1981-92; Deputy Lieutenant, Glasgow, since 1982; Hon. Research Fellow, Glasgow University, 1988-91; Founder Chairman, Scottish Pakistani Association, 1984-91, and since 1994; Judge, City of Glasgow District Courts, 1968-97; Chairman, Strathclyde Community Relations Council, 1986-93 and 1994-96; Member, BBC General Advisory Council, 1992-95; a Governor, Jordanhill College of Further Education, 1987-91; Chairman, Mosque Committee, Islamic Centre, Glasgow, 1986-91. Publication: The New Scots. Recreations: golf; reading. Address: (h.) 8 Riverview Gardens, Glasgow G51 8EL; T.-0141-429 7689.

Macara, (John David) Murray, LLB, SSC, NP. Solicitor, since 1973; Solicitor Advocate, since 1993; b. 22.7.49, Glasgow; m., Elaine; 1 d. Educ. Loretto School; Glasgow University. Apprentice and Assistant, McGrigor Donald & Co., 1970-73; Beltrami & Co., Solicitors, since 1973, Partner, since 1975. Recreations: golf; hockey; travel. Address: (b.) 93 West Nile Street, Glasgow G1 2FH; T.-0141-221 0981.

Machin, Professor George Ian Thom, MA, DPhil, FRHistS. Professor of British History, Dundee University, since 1989, Head, Department of Modern History, 1992-95; b. 3.7.37, Liverpool; m., Dr. Jane Margaret Pallot; 2 s. Educ. Silcoates School, near Wakefield; Jesus College, Oxford. Research Student and Tutor, Oxford University, 1958-61; Assistant Lecturer, then Lecturer in History, Singapore University, 1961-64; Lecturer in Modern History, St. Andrews University, 1964-67; Lecturer, then Senior Lecturer, then Reader, Dundee University, 1967-89; Course Tutor, Open University in Scotland, 1971-82. Member, History Panel, Scottish Universities Council on Entrance, 1990-94; Observer, Scottish Examination Board, 1991-94; Universities' Member, History Panel, Scottish Qualifications Authority, since 1997 (Scottish Examination Board, 1996-97); sometime External Examiner, Universities of Cambridge, St. Andrews, Aberdeen, Hull, Leicester, Sussex, Stirling; Treasurer, Abertay Historical Society, 1966-73; Treasurer, Dundee Branch, Historical Association, 1981-92, President, 1992-95; Elder, Church of Scotland, since 1981. Publications: The Catholic Question in English Politics 1820 to 1830, 1964; Politics and the Churches in Great Britain 1832 to 1868, 1977; Politics and the Churches in Great Britain 1869 to 1921, 1987; The Liberal Governments 1905-15, 1991; Disraeli, 1995; Churches and Social Issues in Twentieth Century Britain, 1998. Recreations: the arts; hill-walking; photographing historic sign-posts. Address: (h.) 50 West Road, Newport-on-Tay, Fife DD6 8HP; T.-01382 543371.

Mack, Douglas Stuart, MA, PhD, FRSE. Reader, Stirling University, since 1994; General Editor, Association for Scottish Literary Studies, 1980-90; General Editor, Stirling/South Carolina Edition of James Hogg, since 1990; President, The James Hogg Society, since 1982; b. 30.1.43, Bellshill; m., Wilma Stewart Grant; 2 s. Educ. Uddingston Grammar School; Glasgow University; Stirling University. Research Assistant, National Library of Scotland, 1965-66; Assistant Librarian: St. Andrews University, 1966-70, Stirling University, 1970-86; Lecturer, Stirling University, 1986-94. Editor of various books by James Hogg and Sir Walter Scott. Recreations: watching Hamilton Accies; sailing on paddle steamers. Address: (h.) 2 Law Hill Road, Dollar FK14 7BG; T.-Dollar 742452.

Mack, Jimmy, MBE. Broadcaster and Journalist; Presenter, The Jimmy Mack Show, Radio Clyde 2, since 1990; b. 26.6.34, Greenock; m., Barbara; 1 s.; 1 d. Educ. Lenzie Academy; Bathgate Academy. Insurance Inspector, Guardian Royal Exchange Assurance Co., 1956-70; Producer and Presenter, various programmes, BBC Radio Medway, Kent, 1970-79; Presenter, Radio 1 Club, BBC Radio 1, 1967-70; Presenter, The Early Show, Night Ride, Junior Choice, BBC Radio 2, 1971-76; Producer, You and Yours, Woman's Hour, In Britain Now, BBC Radio 4, 1977-78; Presenter: The Jimmy Mack Show and Jimmy Mack's Old Gold, BBC Radio Scotland, 1979-89, Top Club and Best Years of Their Lives, Grampian TV, 1980-84, Scotland Today, Scottish TV, 1984-85, I Believe You Believe, BBC TV, 1986. Television and Radio Industries Club of Scotland Award for best live radio programme, 1986; MBE, for services to charity in Scotland, 1996. Patron, Scottish Motor Neurone Disease Association. Publication: Jimmy Mack Show Book, 1984. Recreation: photography. Address: (b.) Radio Clyde, Clydebank Business Park, Glasgow G81 2RX; T.- 0141-565 2200.

Mack, Thomas Angus, MBE, DL, MRPharmS. Proprietor Pharmacist, since 1963; b. 20.9.30, Menstrie; m., Lynne; 2 d. Educ. Alva Academy; Heriot-Watt University. After five years in retail pharmacy management opened own retail pharmacy in Tillicoultry. Scout Leader, Menstrie Scout Group, 1953-95 (District Commissioner 1964-85); Scout Awards: Medal of Merit, 1963, Silver Acorn, 1980, Silver Wolf, 1990. Recreations: mountaineering; skiing; canoeing; gardening; photography. Address: (h.) 36 Middleton, Menstrie, Clackmannanshire FK11 7HD; T.-01259 761465.

Mackie, Dugald Mabon, MA, FRSA. Secretary to University Court, University of Glasgow, since 1996; b. 26.12.52, Ayr. Educ. Ayr Academy; University of Edinburgh. Administrative Assistant: Didsbury College of Education, 1974-76, University of Aston, 1976-80; University of Strathclyde: Faculty Officer, 1980-89, Deputy Registrar, 1989-92; Secretary, Scottish Higher Education Funding Council, 1992-96; Board Member, New Opportunities Fund, since 1998. Recreations: mountaineering; gardening; railways. Address: (b.) University of Glasgow, Glasgow G12 8QQ; T.-0141-330 4246.

Mackie of Benshie, Baron (George Yull Mackie), CBE, DSO, DFC, LLD. Farmer; Liberal Democrat Spokesman, House of Lords, on Devolution, Agriculture, Scotland, Industry; Member, Council of Europe and Western European Union, 1986-96; b. 10.7.19, Aberdeen; m., 1, Lindsay Lyall Sharp; 1 s. (deceased); 3 d.; 2, Mrs Jacqueline Lane. Educ. Aberdeen Grammar School; Aberdeen University. Bomber Command and Air Staff, 1944. Contested South Angus, 1959; Vice-Chairman

(Organisation), Scottish Liberal Party, 1959-64; MP (Liberal), Caithness and Sutherland, 1964-66; Chairman, Scottish Liberal Party, 1965-70; contested Caithness and Sutherland, 1970; contested NE Scotland, European Parliamentary Election, 1979; Member, EEC Scrutiny Committee (D), House of Lords; Executive, Inter-Parliamentary Union; Chairman: Caithness Glass, 1966-84, Industrial Appeal Committee, Pitlochry Festival Theatre, 1979, Angus Committee, Salvation Army, 1976-84; Rector, Dundee University, 1980-83; Director, Scottish Ballet, 1986-88. Address: (h.) Benshie Cottage, Oathlaw, by Forfar, Angus.

Mackie, Joyce Grant, BA (Hons), DipCE, DL. Vice-President, National Trust for Scotland, since 1988; Partner, farming business, since 1963; b. 7.5.40, Forfar; m., Bruce Stephen Mackie; 2 s.; 2 d. Educ. St. Margaret's School for Girls, Aberdeen; Moray House College of Education. Teacher, Dalmilling School, Ayr, 1961-63. National Trust for Scotland: Member, Council, 1974-79, 1985-90, Member, Executive Committee, 1976-86; former Member, Aberdeen Committee, Scottish Children's League (RSSPCC); Trustee, David Gordon Memorial Trust, since 1977; Director, Lathallan Preparatory School, Montrose, since 1979, Chairman, since 1990; Member, Council, Glenalmond College, since 1991; Member, Church of Scotland Nomination Committee, 1985-88; former Member, Executive Committee, Aberdeen University Quincentenary Campaign. Recreations: gardening; art; Scotland. Address: (h.) Balquhindachy, Methlick, Ellon, Aberdeenshire AB41 7BY; T.-01651 806373.

Mackie, Maitland, CBE, BSc, MA, LLD. Farmer; Owner, Mackie's; Chairman: Farmdata, Grampian Enterprise Ltd; Chairman, Scottish Agricultural College; former Director, Rowett Research Institute and Rowett Research Services; Member, Priorities Board for Agricultural Research; b. 21.9.37, Aberdeen; m., Dr. Halldis Mackie; 1 s.; 2 d. Educ. Aberdeen Grammar School; Aberdeen University. Former Chairman, Food and Animal Committees, Agricultural and Food Research Council; former Chairman, Farm Assured Scotch Livestock; former Chairman, Scottish Pig Industry Initiative; former Vice-President, National Farmers Union of Scotland; Recreations: skiing; sailing; Norway. Address: Westertown, Rothienorman, Aberdeenshire; T.-01467 671466.

Mackie, Marie Watson-Watt, MA (Hons), EdB (Dip). National Chairman, Scottish Women's Rural Institutes, 1987-93; Chairman, Borders Arts Network; Non-Executive Director, Borders Community Health NHS Trust; b. Kilmarnock; m., Alex. O. Mackie, MA (Hons), FSA Scot. Educ. Kilmarnock Academy; Glasgow University. County Federation Chairman, SWRI, Roxburghshire, 1975-81; National Vice-Chairman, SWRI, 1981-87; Member, Women's National Commission, 1987-89; former Executive Member, Scottish Institute of Adult Education; Producer, Lecturer and Adjudicator, amateur drama; Chairman, Roxburghshire Drama Association; Britain in Bloom Judge, 1975-84; SWRI Delegate to ACWW Hague conference, 1992; Member: Borders Enterprise Focus on Community Sustainability Steering Group, 1993, Council, Scottish Association of Young Farmers Clubs, 1987-94, Council, Rural Forum (Scotland), 1987-90; Chairman, House Management Committee, Sue Ryder Home (Borders), since 1998; Member, Community Sub-Group, Borders Environmental Education Forum. Recreations: interior design; 19th-century pottery; Samoyed dogs; enjoying the countryside of Scotland; art and architecture. Address: (h.) Linton Downs, Kelso, Roxburghshire.

Maddox, Professor Christopher Edward Ralph, BSc, PhD, CBiol, MIBiol, DipManEd. Assistant Principal (Welfare), Heriot Watt University, since 1998; Principal, Scottish College of Textiles, Galashiels, 1988-98 (Vice Principal, Queen Margaret College, Edinburgh, 1983-88); Professor, Heriot-Watt University, since 1991; b. 21.11.40; m., Janet; 2 s. Educ. Priory School, Shrewsbury; Birmingham University. MRC Research Fellow, Warwick University, 1965-66; Senior Lecturer, Luton University, 1966-67; Senior Lecturer, then Principal Lecturer, then Assistant Dean of Studies, Manchester Metropolitan University, 1967-77; Head, Department of Molecular and Life Sciences, University of Abertay, 1977-83. Member: SCOTEC Committees for Biology and Medical Laboratory Sciences, 1978-83, Council, Scottish Branch, Institute of Biology, 1979-82, CNAA Combined Studies Board, 1983-87, CNAA Health Studies Committee, 1987-89, Health Visiting Joint Committee, UK Central Council for Nursing, Midwifery and Health Visiting, 1983-88; Director: Scottish Borders Enterprise Company, since 1990, SCOT Innovation & Development, since 1992, Higher Education Statistics Agency, since 1993; Member, Scottish Examination Board, 1992-97. Recreations: reading; watching sports. Address: (b.) Heriot-Watt University, Galashiels TD1 3HF; T.-01896 753351.

Magee, William F., LLB. Secretary, Accounts Commission for Scotland, since 1995; b. 25.1.50, Glasgow; m., Helen McCann; 2 s. Educ. St. Aloysius College, Glasgow; Glasgow University. Legal work with various Scottish local authorities; Depute Director of Administration, Edinburgh District, 1984-88; Director of Administration and Legal Services, Central Region, 1988-95. Past Chairman, Society of Directors of Administration in Scotland; Governor, RSAMD. Recreations: music; golf. Address: (b.) 18 George Street, Edinburgh; T.-0131-477 1234.

Maguire, Francis Thomas, PHB, LLB. Solicitor Advocate; Thompsons, Glasgow, since 1987 (Thompsons, Edinburgh, 1981-87); b. 4.10.55, Glasgow; m., Fiona Macdonald; 3 s. Educ. St. Vincent's College, Langbank; Gregorian University, Rome; St. Mary's College, Blairs; Aberdeen University. Apprentice, McLachlan & McKenzie, Edinburgh, Robin Thompson & Partners, Edinburgh; Assistant Solicitor, Robin Thompson & Partners; Salaried Partner, Thompsons; Equity Partner, Thompsons. Executive Member, Society of Solicitor Advocates; Member, Personal Injury Panel, Law Society of Scotland; Member, Steering Committee, Piper Alpha Trade Union Group; Legal Adviser, STUC. Recreations: sailing; windsurfing; mountain biking; jogging; insurance companies. Address: (b.) Berkeley House, 285 Bath Street, Glasgow G2 4HQ; T.-0141-221 8840.

Maguire, Sheriff John, PhD, LLB, QC. Sheriff Principal, Tayside, Central and Fife, since 1990; b. 30.11.34, Kirkintilloch; m., Eva O'Hara; 2 s.; 2 d. Educ. St. Ninian's High School, Kirkintilloch; St. Mary's College, Blairs; Pontifical Gregorian University, Rome; Edinburgh University. Standing Junior Counsel, Ministry of Public Buildings and Works, 1962-68; Sheriff at Airdrie, 1968-73; Sheriff at Glasgow, 1973-90; Secretary, Sheriffs Association, 1982-87, President, 1988-90. Co-Founder and Chairman, PHEW, 1985-90; Chairman, Northern Lighthouse Board, 1995-97. Recreations: reading; thinking about doing the garden. Address: (b.) Sheriff Principal's Chambers, Perth Sheriff Court, Tay Street, Perth; T.-01738 620546.

Magnusson, Magnus, KBE (Hon.), MA (Oxon), FRSE, FRSA, FSA Scot. Writer and Broadcaster; Chairman, Scottish Natural Heritage, since 1992; b. 12.10.29, Reykjavik, Iceland; m., Mamie Baird; 1 s.; 3 d. Educ. Edinburgh Academy; Jesus College, Oxford. Reporter, Scottish Daily Express; Features Writer, The Scotsman; Co-Presenter, Tonight, BBC TV, 1964-65; Presenter: Chronicle, Cause for Concern, Checkpoint, All Things Considered, Mainly Magnus, BC - The Archaeology of the Bible Lands, Living Legends, Vikings!, Mastermind; Rector, Edinburgh University, 1975-78.

Magnusson, Sally Anne, MA (Hons). Presenter, Reporting Scotland, BBC, since 1998; Presenter, Breakfast News (formerly Breakfast Time), BBC, since 1985; Presenter, Songs of Praise, BBC, since 1983; b. 11.10.55, Glasgow; m., Norman Stone; 4 s.; 1 d. Educ. Laurel Bank School; Edinburgh University. Reporter, The Scotsman, 1979-81; News/Feature Writer, Sunday Standard, 1981-83; Reporter, Current Account, BBC Scotland, 1983, Presenter, Sixty Minutes, BBC, 1983-84; Presenter, London Plus, BBC, 1984-85. Feature Writer of the Year, Fraser Scottish Press Awards, 1982. Publications: The Flying Scotsman, 1981; Clemo-A Love Story, 1984; A Shout in the Street, 1990. Address: (b.) c/o Curtis Brown, 28/29 Haymarket, London SW1; T.-0171-396 6600.

Mahmood, Tahir Ahmed, MB, BSc, DObstRCP, MD, MRCOG, FRCP(Ireland); MFFP. Consultant Obstetrician and Gynaecologist, Forth Park Hospital, Kirkcaldy, since 1990; Clinical Senior Lecturer, Obstetrics and Gynaecology, Aberdeen University, since 1990; Senior Lecturer, School of Biological and Medical Sciences, St. Andrews University, since 1995; Clinical Senior Lecturer, University of Edinburgh, since 1996; b. 7.10.53, Pakistan; m., Aasia Bashir; 2 s. Educ. King Edward Medical College, Lahore, Punjab University. Member, Scottish Hospital Staffing Review Committee, sub-speciality of obstetrics and gynaecology, 1986-88; Member, Minimal Invasive Surgery Subgroup and Clinical Resource Management — Procurement Group for Acute Unit, Fife, 1991-92; Ethicon RCOG Travelling Fellowship, 1991; Member, Senate, Aberdeen University, since 1992; Hon. Secretary, Northern Obstetrical and Gynaecological Society, since 1993; Member, Area Medical Committee, Fife, since 1993, Chairman, since 1995; Member, Council, Royal College of Obstetricians and Gynaecologists, since 1994, and of Scottish Executive Council, since 1994. Recreations: squash; jogging; reading; history; walking. Address: (b.) Forth Park Hospital, 30 Bennochy Road, Kirkcaldy, Fife; T.-01592 643355.

Main, Rt. Rev. Professor Alan, TD, MA, BD, STM, PhD. Professor of Practical Theology, Christ's College, Aberdeen, since 1980; Moderator, General Assembly, Church of Scotland, 1998-99; b. 31.3.36, Aberdeen; m., Anne Louise Swanson; 2 d. Educ. Robert Gordon's College, Aberdeen; University of Aberdeen; Union Theological Seminary, New York. Minister, Chapel of Garioch Parish, Aberdeenshire, 1963-70; Chaplain, University of Aberdeen, 1970-80; Chaplain, 153(H) Artillery Support Regiment, RCT(V), 1970-92; Provost, Faculty of Divinity, Aberdeen University, 1990-93; Master, Christ's College, Aberdeen, since 1992. Moderator: Garioch Presbytery, 1969-70, Aberdeen Presbytery, 1984-85; Adviser in Religious Broadcasting, Grampian Television, 1976-86; Chairman: Grampian Marriage Guidance, 1977-80, Cruse, 1981-84. Recreations: music, golf; beekeeping. Address: (h.) Kirkfield, Barthol Chapel, Inverurie AB51 8TD.

Main, Professor Brian G.M., BSc, MBA, MA, PhD. Professor of Economics, Edinburgh University, since 1991 b. 24.8.47, St. Andrews; m., June Lambert; 2 s.; 1 d. Educ. Buckhaven High School; St. Andrews University; University of California, Berkeley. Lecturer, then Reader in Economics, Edinburgh University, 1976-87; Professor of Economics and Chairman, Department of Economics, St. Andrews University, 1987-91. Recreation: fishing. Address: (b.) Department of Economics, Edinburgh University, George Square, Edinburgh EH8 9JY; T.-0131-650 8361.

Main, Carol B.L.D., BA. Director, National Association of Youth Orchestras, since 1979; Scottish Director, Live Music Now, since 1984; Classical Music Editor, The List, since 1985; b. 21.12.58, Kirkcaldy; 1 d. Educ. Kirkcaldy High School; Edinburgh University. Freelance music critic, mainly with Scotsman. Board Director: Edinburgh Festival Fringe Society, Enterprise Music Scotland. Address: (b.) 14 Lennox Street, Edinburgh EH4 1QA; T.-0131 332 2110.

Main, Professor Kirkland, ARSA, RSW, DA, FEIS. Professor, Heriot-Watt University, since 1998; Head, School of Drawing and Painting, Edinburgh College of Art (Deputy Principal, 1991-97); b. 1.7.42, Edinburgh; m., Geraldine Francis; 1 d. Educ. Daniel Stewart's College; Edinburgh College of Art. Assistant to Vice Principal, Edinburgh College of Art, 1980-83 (Governor, 1979-85); Member, Central Institutions Staffs Salaries Committee, 1977-81; Member, Scottish Joint Negotiating Committee, Further Education, 1982-87; Chairman, Association of Lecturers in Scottish Central Institutions, 1982-86.

Main, Sir Peter (Tester), ERD, MD, LLD (Hon.), FRCPE, CIMgt; b. 21.3.25, Aberdeen; m., 1, Margaret Tweddle (deceased); 2 s.; 1 d.; 2, May Heatherington McMillan. Educ. Robert Gordon's College; Aberdeen University. House Surgeon, Aberdeen Royal Infirmary, 1948-49; Captain, RAMC, 1949-51; Medical Officer with Field Ambulance (Suez), 1956; Lt. Col., RAMC (AER), retired 1964; general practice, 1953-57; The Boots Co. PLC: joined Research Department, 1957; Director of Research, 1968; Managing Director, Industrial Division, 1979; Director, 1973-85, Vice Chairman, 1980-81, Chairman, The Boots Co. PLC, 1982-85; Director: Scottish Development Agency, 1986-91, W.A. Baxter & Sons Ltd., 1985-91. Member, National Economic Development Council, 1984-85; Chairman, Committee of Inquiry into Teachers' Pay and Conditions, Scotland, 1986; Governor, Henley Management College, 1983-86. Recreations: fishing; Scottish music. Address: Ninewells House, Chirnside, Duns, Berwickshire TD11 3XF; T.-01890 818191.

Main, Lt. Col. William. Divisional Commander, West Scotland, Salvation Army; b. 15.7.35, Edinburgh; m., Sylvia Ann; 3 s.; 1 d. Educ. David Kilpatrick School, Leith. Entered Salvation Army Training College, London, 1960; served for 20 years on Corps work before serving on Youth Work and Finance; appointed Leader, Salvation Army in Ireland, 1987; moved to East Midlands; returned to Glasgow, 1995. Recreations: reading; golf. Address: (b.) 4 Buchanan Court, Cumbernauld Road, Stepps, Glasgow G33 6HZ; T.-0141-779 5000.

Mair, Alexander, MBE (1967). Governor, Robert Gordon's College, Aberdeen, since 1988; b. 5.11.22, Echt; m., Margaret Isobel. Educ. Skene Central School; School of Accountancy, Glasgow. Company Secretary, Grampian TV, 1961-70; appointed Director, 1967; Director and Chief Executive, 1970-87. President, Aberdeen Chamber of Commerce, 1989-91; Chairman: Aberdeen International Football Festival, 1988-91, Oil Industry Community Fund, since 1993, RGIT Limited, 1989-98. Recreations: golf; skiing; gardening. Address: (h.) Ravenswood, 66 Rubislaw Den South, Aberdeen AB15 4AY; T.-01224 317619.

Mair, Alistair S.F., MBE, DL, BSc, FIMgt. Chairman, since 1991, Managing Director, since 1977, Caithness Glass Ltd.; Chairman, CBI Scotland, 1989-91, and Member, CBI Council, 1985-97; President, British Glass Manufacturers Confederation; b. 20.7.35, Drumblade; m., 1, Anne Garrow (deceased); 2, Mary Bolton; 4 s.; 1 d. Educ. Robert Gordon's College, Aberdeen; Aberdeen University. Rolls Royce, Glasgow, 1957-71: graduate apprentice, PA to General Manager, Production Control Manager, Product Centre Manager; RAF, 1960-62 (short-service commission, Technical Branch); Managing Director, Caithness Glass Ltd., 1971-75; Marketing Director, Worcester Royal Porcelain Co., 1975-76. Non-Executive Director: Grampian Television, since 1986, Crieff Hydro Ltd., since 1994 (Chairman, since 1996); Governor, Morrison's Academy, Crieff, since 1985 (Chairman, since 1996); Commissioner,

Queen Victoria School, Dunblane, 1992-97; Member, Aberdeen University Court, since 1993, Convener, Finance and Estates Committee, since 1998; Chairman, Crieff Auxiliary Association (Richmond House); Patron, Perth and Kinross Association of Voluntary Services, since 1994; Honorary President, Duke of Edinburgh Award, Perth and Kinross, since 1993. Recreations: reading; history; O.U. student; gardening; walking; current affairs. Address: (h.) Woodend, Madderty, Crieff PH7 3PA; T.-01764 683210.

Mair, Professor Douglas, FRSA. Professor, Department of Economics, Heriot-Watt University, Edinburgh, since 1993; b. 3.6.39, Arbroath; m., Ishbel Fraser; 2 s.; 1 d. Educ. Arbroath High School; St. Andrews University. Ford Motor Company, 1960-63; Scottish Council (Development and Industry), 1963-67; joined Heriot-Watt University, 1967. Recreation: golf. Address: (b.) Department of Economics, Heriot-Watt University, Riccarton, Edinburgh EH14 4AS; T.-0131-451 3491.

Mair, Henry. Poet; b. 4.3.45, Kilmarnock; m., Etta; 1 s.; 1 d. Educ. St. Joseph's High School, Kilmarnock. Originator, 1972, and Secretary, Scottish National Open Poetry Competition; guest, USSR Writers' Union, 1980. Publications: I Rebel, 1970; Alone I Rebel, 1974; Flowers in the Forest, 1978; The Prizewinners, 1987. Address: (h.) 42 Tollerton Drive, Irvine, Ayrshire; T.-Irvine 76381.

Mair, William Wallace, MA, MBA, FRSA. Secretary, Faculty of Actuaries in Scotland, since 1974; b. 19.6.49, Bellshill; m., Sandra Cunningham; 1 s.; 1 d. Educ. Uddingston Grammar School; Glasgow University; Edinburgh University. Assistant Secretary, Royal Institution of Chartered Surveyors, 1969-72; Secretary, Scottish National Federation of Building Trades Employers, 1972-73. Recreations: badminton; cricket; hill-walking; cycling; photography. Address: (b.) Maclaurin House, 18 Dublin Street, Edinburgh EH1 3PP.

Maitland, Peter Salisbury, BSc, PhD, FRSE. Independent Consultant in Freshwater Ecology, since 1986; Visiting Professor, Glasgow University, since 1997; Secretary, Scottish Freshwater Group, since 1968; Member, SEPA South East Regional Board, since 1996; b. 8.12.37, Glasgow; m., Kathleen Ramsay; 1 s.; 2 d. Educ. Bearsden Academy; Glasgow University. Lecturer in Zoology, Glasgow University, 1959-67; Senior Scientific Officer, Nature Conservancy, 1967-70; Principal Scientific Officer, Institute of Terrestrial Ecology, 1970-86; Senior Lecturer in Ecology, St. Andrews University, 1978-82. Royal Society of Edinburgh Fellowship, 1980; Neill Medal, 1993; Freshwater Biological Association Fellowship, 1996. Publications: eight books; 200 scientific papers. Recreations: wildlife conservation; fish-keeping; gardening; walking; music. Address: (h.) Nether Sunnyside, Gladshot, Haddington EH41 4NR; T.-01620 823691.

Maitland-Carew, The Hon. Gerald Edward Ian, DL; b. 28.12.41, Dublin; m., Rosalind Averil Speke; 2 s.; 1 d. Educ. Harrow School. Army Officer, 15/19 The Kings Royal Hussars, 1960-72; looked after family estates, since 1972; Member, Royal Company of Archers; Chairman, Lauderdale Hunt; Chairman, Lauderdale and Galawater Branch, Royal British Legion Scotland; Deputy Lieutenant, Ettrick and Lauderdale and Roxburgh, 1989; elected Member, Jockey Club, 1989; Chairman, Musselburgh Racecourse, 1993; Member, Border Area, TA Committee; Vice Chairman, International League for the Protection of Horses, 1993; President, Border Rifle League, 1994; Chairman, Gurkha Welfare Trust of Scotland, 1996; Racecourse Steward at Ayr, Kelso, Newcastle, Cheltenham and Newmarket. Recreations: racing; hunting; shooting. Address: (h.) Thirlestane Castle, Lauder, Berwickshire; T.-01578 722 254.

Maizels, Professor Rick, BSc, PhD. Professor of Zoology, Edinburgh University, since 1995; Head, Institute of Cell, Animal and Population Biology, since 1997; b. 14.5.53, London. Educ. University College London. MRC Scientific Staff, NIMR, Mill Hill, 1979-83; Lecturer, Reader and Professor, Department of Biology, Imperial College, London, 1983-95. Address: (b.) Ashworth Laboratories, Edinburgh University EH9 3JT; T.-0131-650 5511.

Makin, Keith, BSc, MSc, DipSocAdmin, CQSW, MInstM, FRSA. Director of Social Services, Dumfries and Galloway Council, since 1995; b. 22.4.53, Luton; m., Margaret Louise; 1 s.; 2 d. Educ. Kingsbury Grammar School, Dunstable; Cardiff University; Manchester University; Birmingham University. Social Worker, Cheshire County Council, 1975-80; Senior Social Worker, Oxfordshire, 1980-83; Team Manager/Operations Manager, Warwickshire, 1983-89; Divisional Director, Northumberland, 1990-93; Depute Director, then Director of Social Work, Dumfries and Galloway Regional Council, 1994-95. Executive Committee Member, Association of Directors of Social Work. Recreations: fishing; driving; music; cookery; sailing. Address: (b.) Grierson House, The Crichton, Bankend Road, Dumfries DG1 4ZH.

Malcolmson, Peter, OBE, JP, CQSW. Councillor, Shetland Islands Council (Chairman, Education Committee); former Director of Social Work, Shetland Islands Council; b. 27.7.39, Lerwick; m., Grace Eleanor Robson; 2 s.; 2 d. Educ. Anderson High School, Lerwick; Moray House College, Edinburgh. Social Worker, 1963-90. Recreations: voluntary social work; guizing and sailing Viking Longship. Address: (h.) Skersund, Upper Sound, Lerwick, Shetland Isles ZE1 0SU.

Malik, Hanzala Shaheed, JP, BSc. Member, Glasgow City Council, since 1995; Chair, West of Scotland Community Relations Council, since 1995; Chair, Ethnic Minority Respite Care Project, since 1995; Chair, North West Advisory Council, since 1995; Chair, Woodlands Education Trust, since 1996; b. 26.11.56, Glasgow; m., Haleema Sadia; 1 s.; 1 d. Educ. North Kelvinside Secondary School; Clydebank College; Paisley University. Strathclyde Police Special Constable, 1975-76; Strathclyde Police Traffic Warden, 1976-82; Manager, Dhool Farms Ltd, 1982-87; Financial Consultant, Allied Dunbar Plc, 1987-88; Director, Azad Video Link Ltd, 1988-92. Glasgow City Council: Member, Education Committee (Vice-Convener), Policy and Resources (Budget and Financial Monitoring) Sub-committee; Member, Equality Committee (and Gay and Lesbian Issues Working Group and Race Working Group); Finance Committee; Housing Committee; Licensing Committee; Social Strategy Committee (and Community Councils Sub Committee); Social Work Committee (and Care Planning Sub Committee); Committee Member: Queens Cross Housing Association, Charing Cross Housing Association; Director, Queens Cross Workspace; Member, North West Action Group; Member, Scottish Pakistani Friends Society. Recreations: badminton; charity work; cooking; football; gardening; overseas travel; philately; swimming. Address: (b.) Glasgow City Chambers, George Square, Glasgow G2 1DU; T.-0141-287 7041.

Mallinson, Edward John Harold, MPharm, FRPharmS, FIMgt, FRSH. Chief Administrative Pharmaceutical Officer, Lanarkshire Health Board, since 1984; b. 15.3.50, Bingley; m., Diana Gray; 2 d. Educ. Bradford Grammar School; Bradford University. Staff Pharmacist (Ward Pharmacy Services), Bradford Royal Infirmary, 1973-78; District Pharmaceutical Officer, Perth and Kinross District, 1978-83. Chairman, Scottish Chief Administrative Pharmaceutical Officers' Group, 1990-92, and since 1997; Royal Pharmaceutical Society of Great Britain: Hon. Secretary, Bradford & District Branch, 1978, Hon. Secretary, Dundee & Eastern Scottish Branch, 1979-83, Hon. Secretary and Treasurer, Lanarkshire Branch, since

1984; Member of Council, Royal Society of Health, 1992-96, Honorary Treasurer, 1996; Vice Chairman and Secretary, Pharmaceutical Group, Royal Society of Health, 1986-89; Chairman, Strathclyde Police/Lanarkshire Health Board Drug Liaison Committee, 1985-91; Member, General Synod, Scottish Episcopal Church, 1986-95; Honorary Treasurer, Comunn Gaidhlig na h-Eaglais Easbaigich; Honorary Treasurer, Affirming Apostolic Order, 1993-98; Secretary, Lanarkshire Branch, British Institute of Management, 1989-91, Chairman, 1991-94. Recreations: genealogy; Gaelic language and culture; walking and cooking. Address: (h.) Malden, North Dean Park Avenue, Bothwell, Glasgow G71 8HH; T.-01698 852973.

Mallon, Con. Chief Executive, East Dunbartonshire Council. Address: (b.) Tom Johnston House, Civic Way, Kirkintilloch, G66 4TJ.

Malone, Wilson, CA, MPhil. Head, Industrial Assistance Division, Scottish Office Education and Industry Department, since 1994; b. 20.6.55, Glasgow; m., Anna Tunn; 1 s. Educ. Hillhead High school; Glasgow Technical College; Glasgow University. CA trainee, 1975-79; Accountant, John G. Kincaid & Co., 1980-82; Civil Servant, since 1983; Deputy Director, Locate in Scotland, 1988-94. Recreations: sailing; music. Address: (b.) Meridian Court, 5 Cadogan Street, Glasgow G2 6AT; T.-0141-242 5801.

Mann, Professor David George, BSc, PhD. Senior Principal Research Scientist, Royal Botanic Garden, Edinburgh, since 1996; Hon. Professor, Glasgow University, since 1996; b. 25.2.53, Romford, Essex; m., Lynn Barbara; 1 s.; 1 d. Educ. Brentwood School; Bristol University. Edinburgh University: Demonstrator, 1978-81, Lecturer, 1981-90, Director of Studies, 1989-90; Deputy Regius Keeper (Deputy Director), Royal Botanic Garden, Edinburgh, 1990-96. Member, Council, International Society for Diatom Research; G.W. Prescott Award, 1991, 1997. Publications: editor/author of 70 papers and books. Recreations: classical piano; drawing and painting. Address: (b.) Royal Botanic Garden, Inverleith Row, Edinburgh EH3 5LR; T.-0131-552 7171.

Mann, Gordon Laurence, DipTP, MRTPI. Managing Director, The Crichton Trust; b. 28.4.48, Dundee. Director of Planning, Shetland Islands Council, 1980-87; Director of Physical Planning, Dumfries and Galloway Regional Council, 1987-96; Chief Planning Officer, Dumfries and Galloway Council, 1996-97. Address: (b.) Grierson House, The Crichton, Dumfries DG1 4ZE; T.-01387 247544.

Manning, Professor Aubrey William George, OBE, BSc, DPhil, FInstBiol, Dr (h c) (Toulouse), FRSE. Professor of Natural History, Division of Biological Sciences, Edinburgh University, 1973-97, Professor Emeritus, since 1997; b. 24.4.30, London; m.; 3 s., inc. 2 by pr. m. Educ. Strode's School, Egham; University College, London; Merton College, Oxford. Research, 1951-54; National Service, Royal Artillery, 1954-56; Lecturer, then Reader in Zoology, Edinburgh University, 1956-73; Secretary-General, International Ethological Committee, 1971-79; President: Association for the Study of Animal Behaviour, 1981-84, Biology Section, British Association for the Advancement of Science, 1993; Member: Scottish Advisory Committee, Nature Conservancy Council, 1982-89, Advisory Committee on Science, NCC, 1985-89; Chairman of Council, Scottish Wildlife Trust, 1990-96; Trustee, National Museums of Scotland, since 1997. Association for the Study of Animal Behaviour Medal, 1998; Member, Wellcome Trust Population Studies Panel, since 1996; Dobzhansky Memorial Award, Behavioural Genetics Association, 1996. Publication: An Introduction to Animal Behaviour, 5th edition, 1998; research papers in biological journals. Recreations: woodland conservation; walking; architecture. Address: (h.) The Old Hall, Ormiston, East Lothian; T.-Pencaitland 340536.

Mansfield and Mansfield, 8th Earl of (William David Mungo James Murray), JP, DL; b. 7.7.30; m., Pamela Joan Foster; 2 s.; 1 d. Educ. Eton; Christ Church, Oxford. National Service, Malayan Campaign; called to Bar, Inner Temple, 1958; Barrister, 1958-71; Member, British Delegation to European Parliament, 1973-75; Minister of State, Scottish Office, 1979-83; Minister of State, Northern Ireland Office, 1983-84; Director: General Accident Fire and Life Assurance Corporation Ltd., 1972-79, and 1985-98; The American Trust Ltd., since 1985; Pinneys of Scotland Ltd., 1985-89; Ross Breeders Ltd., 1989-90; Hon. President, St. Andrews Society of Glasgow, 1972-92; President, Royal Scottish Country Dance Society, since 1977; Hon. Member, RICS; First Crown Estate Commissioner, 1985-95. Address: (h.) Scone Palace, Perthshire PH2 6BE.

Manson, Alexander Reid, CBE, SDA, FRAgS. Farmer; Member, Meat and Livestock Commission, 1986-95; General Commissioner of Income Tax, since 1991; Director, National Animal Data Centre, 1992-95; b. 2.9.31, Oldmeldrum; m., Ethel Mary Philip; 1 s.; 2 d. Educ. Robert Gordon's College; North of Scotland College of Agriculture. Member, Oldmeldrum Town Council, 1960-65; founder Chairman, Aberdeen Beef and Calf Ltd., 1962; Past President, Scottish Agricultural Organisation Society Ltd.; Chairman, Buchan Meat Producers Ltd., 1982-92; Past President, Federation of Agricultural Cooperatives; Member, Williams Committee of Enquiry, 1989; Member, EU Beef Advisory Committee, 1986-96. Recreations: golf; bird-watching. Address: (h.) Kilblean, Oldmeldrum, Inverurie AB51 ODN; T.-01651 872226.

Manson, Frank, MA, MIOSH, MIIRSM. Managing Director, Registers of Scotland, since 1996; b. 18.3.50, Lerwick; m., Mary. Educ. Anderson Educational Institute, Lerwick; Edinburgh University. HM Inspector of Factories, Health and Safety Executive, 1976-80; Technical Executive, BP Detergents International, 1980-84; Production Controller, William Moir Ltd., 1984-85; Business Development Manager, Unisys Corporation, 1985-89; Management Consultant, 1989-92; Assistant Director of Property, Tayside Region, 1992-96; Head of Central Services, Angus Council, 1995-96. Recreations: reading; walking; rugby. Address: (b.) Meadowbank House, 153 London Road, Edinburgh; T.-0131-479 3615.

Manson, Richard U., MCIH. General Manager, State Hospital, Carstairs, since 1990; b. 2.5.51, Glasgow; m., Barbara; 2 s.; 1 d. Educ. Shawlands Academy; Glasgow College of Commerce; Glasgow College of Building. District Housing Manager, then Management Auditor, Glasgow District Council, 1979-87; Operations Director, Quality Street Ltd., 1987-89; Managing Director, Homesense Ltd., 1989-90. Address: (b.) State Hospital, Carstairs, Lanark ML11 8RP; T.-01555 840293.

Mar and Kellie, Earl of (James Thorne Erskine). Estate Worker; Scottish Liberal Democrat Peer; b. 10.3.49, Edinburgh; m., Mary Irene; 1 step s.; 4 step d. Educ. Eton; Moray House College of Education; Inverness College. Community Service Volunteer, York, 1967-68; Youth and Community Worker, Craigmillar, 1971-73; Social Worker, Sheffield, 1973-76, Grampian Region, 1976-78; Social Worker, Prison Social Worker, Community Service Supervisor, Highland Region, 1979-87; Builder, Kincardine, 1990-92; Project Worker, SACRO, Falkirk, 1992-93; Royal Auxiliary Air Force Regiment, 1979-85; Royal Naval Auxiliary Service, 1985-88; Chairman, Strathclyde Tram Inquiry, 1996; Parliamentary Commissioner, Burrell Collection (Lending) Inquiry, 1997. Recreations: canoeing; hill-walking; boat building; Alloa

Tower. Address: House of Lords, London, SW1A 0PW; Erskine House, Clackmannan FK10 4JF.

Maran, Professor Arnold George Dominic, MB, ChB, MD, FRCS, FACS, FRCP, FRCS (Eng), FDS (Hon). Professor of Otolaryngology, Edinburgh University, since 1988; President, Royal College of Surgeons; Consultant Surgeon, Royal Infirmary and City Hospital, Edinburgh, since 1974; b. 16.6.36, Edinburgh; m., Anna; 1 s.; 1 d. Educ. Daniel Stewart's College; Edinburgh University; University of Iowa. Trained in Otolaryngology in Edinburgh and America; former Consultant Otolaryngologist, Tayside Health Board, and Professor of Otolaryngology, West Virginia University. Fifteen Visiting Professorships to foreign universities; Honorary Fellowship, Royal College of Surgeons of South Africa, and Royal College of Surgeons of Hong Kong. Publications: six books and 150 scientific papers. Recreations: golf; music; travel. Address: (h.) 27 Learmonth Terrace, Edinburgh EH4 1NZ; T.-0131-332 0055.

Marjoribanks, Gerald Brian, BA, LRAM, ALAM. Controller (UK Regions), Independent Television Commission, previously Independent Broadcasting Authority, since 1983; b. 22.7.42, Falkirk; m., Kathleen; 2 s.; 2 d. Educ. Falkirk High School; Edinburgh College of Speech and Drama; Open University. Sports Presenter, Sportsreel, Sportscene, Sportsound, BBC Scotland, 1966-83; Lecturer in Drama, Notre Dame College of Education, 1967-79; Co-ordinator of Learning Resources, Dunfermline College of Physical Education, 1979-80; Head of Public Relations, Cumbernauld Development Corporation, 1980-83. Recreations: drama adjudication; badminton; photography. Address: (h.) 11 Majors Place, Falkirk FK1 5QS.

Marjoribanks, Sir James Alexander Milne, KCMG (1965), MA. HM Diplomatic Service, 1934-71; b. 29.5.11, Edinburgh; m., Sonya Patricia Stanley de Brandon (deceased); 1 d. Educ. Edinburgh Academy; Edinburgh University; Strasbourg University. Served in Peking, Hankow, Marseilles, Jacksonville, New York, Bucharest, Canberra, Luxembourg, Bonn, Brussels, London; Assistant Under-Secretary of State, Foreign Office, 1962-65; Ambassador to European Communities, 1965-71. Director, Distillers PLC, 1971-76; Member, Edinburgh University Court, 1976-80; Governing Member, Caledonian Research Foundation; Chairman, Scotland in Europe, 1979-91; Member, Committee for European Community Cultural Co-operation. Recreation: hill-walking.

Markland, John A., MA, PhD, ACIS. Chief Executive, Fife Council, since 1995; b. 17.5.48, Bolton; m., Muriel Harris; 4 d. Educ. Bolton School; Dundee University. Demographer, Somerset County Council, 1974-76; Senior Professional Assistant, Tayside Regional Council; Personal Assistant to Chief Executive, then Assistant Chief Executive, then Chief Executive, Fife Regional Council, 1979-95; Chairman, Forward Scotland Ltd.; Chairman, Secretary of State's Advisory Group on Sustainable Development; Director, Going for Green; Director, Fife Enterprise; Clerk to Lord Lieutenant of Fife. Recreations: climbing Scotland's Munros; cycling. Address: (b.) Fife House, North Street, Glenrothes, Fife; T.-01592 413999.

Marks, Frederick Charles, OBE, MA, LLB, FIMgt. Commissioner for Local Administration in Scotland (Local Government Ombudsman); Local Government Adjudicator; Vice Chairman, Queen Margaret Hospital, Dunfermline, NHS Trust; b. 3.12.34, Bellshill; m., Agnes M. Bruce; 3 s.; 1 d. Educ. Wishaw High School; Glasgow University. Depute Town Clerk, Dunfermline, 1963-68; Town Clerk, Hamilton, 1968-75; Chief Executive, Motherwell, 1974-83; General Manager, Scottish Special Housing Association, 1983-89; Deputy Chairman, Local Government Boundary Commission for Scotland, 1989-94. Address: (b.) 23 Walker Street, Edinburgh EH3 7HX; T.-0131-225 5300.

Marnoch, Hon. Lord (Michael Stewart Rae Bruce), QC (Scot), MA, LLB. Senator of the College of Justice, since 1990; b. 26.7.38; m., Alison M. Stewart; 2 d. Educ.; Loretto; Aberdeen University. Advocate, 1963; QC, 1975; Standing Counsel to Department of Agriculture and Fisheries for Scotland, 1973; to Highlands and Islands Development Board, 1973; Advocate-Depute, 1983-86; Member, Criminal Injuries Compensation Board, 1986-89. Chairman for Scotland, Salmon and Trout Association, 1989-94. Recreations: golf; fishing. Address: (b.) Parliament House, Edinburgh; T.-0131-225 2595.

Marnoch, Derek George, MBE, BSc, ACMA. Chief Executive, Aberdeen Chamber of Commerce, since 1983; b. 30.10.35, Aberdeen; m., Kathleen Howard (deceased); 3 s. Educ. Aberdeen Grammar School; Aberdeen University. Recreation: golf. Address: (h.) Fairways, The Drive, Edzell, Brechin, Angus DD9 7XX.

Marquis, Alistair Forbes, BA, MEd, DipCE, FCollP. Chairman, Scottish Committee of The Boys' Brigade, since 1991; elected Representative, UK Brigade Executive for East Lowland District, since 1989; Scottish Member, UK Management Committee, since 1991; Hon. Vice President: The Scout Association, The Scottish Council, since 1996; b. 13.1.50, Glasgow; m., Margaret Jarvie Greenlees; 1 d. Educ Queen's Park Secondary School; Jordanhill College, Glasgow; Open University; Edinburgh University. Teacher/Assistant Head Teacher/Head Teacher; HM Inspector of Schools, 1989. Member, Scottish Committee on Special Educational Needs, 1985-88; Chairman, Lanthorn Community Complex Management Committee, 1979-82; SFA Football Referee, 1972; Church of Scotland Elder; Member, Rotary International. Recreations: gardening; reading; walking. Address: (h.) 39 Bankton Drive, Murieston, Livingston EH54 9EH; T.-01506 414406.

Marr, Colin. Theatre Director, Eden Court Theatre, since 1997; b. 3.4.66, Glasgow; m., Nicky; 2 d. Educ. Hutcheson's Grammar School; University of Edinburgh; Open University. Hall Manager, Queen's Hall, Edinburgh, 1988-92; Theatre and Commercial Manager, Traverse Theatre, Edinburgh, 1992-97. Address: (b.) Bishop's Road, Inverness IV3 5SA; T.-01463 239841.

Marr, Derek Shepherd, QFSM, FIFireE. Firemaster, Tayside Fire Brigade, since 1990; Secretary, Scottish Chief & Assistant Chief Fire Officers Association, since 1991; b. 6.7.48, Arbroath; m., Edna; 1 s.; 1 d. Educ. Arbroath High School. Joined fire service, 1967. Chairman, Tayside Fire Liaison Panel; COSLA Adviser to Protective Services Committee; Council Member, Chief & Assistant Chief Fire Officers Association. Recreations: reading; golf. Address: (b.) Fire Brigade Headquarters, Blackness Road Dundee.

Marr, Douglas, MA, MEd. Rector, Banchory Academy, since 1995; b. 7.2.47, Aberdeen; m., Alison; 1 d. Educ. Aberdeen Grammar School; University of Aberdeen. Teacher of History, Hilton Academy, Aberdeen, 1970-71; Assistant Principal Teacher of History, Aberdeen Grammar School, 1971-76; Principal Teacher of History, Hilton Academy, Aberdeen, 1976-81; Assistant Rector, Kemnay Academy, 1981-84; Depute Rector, The Gordon Schools, Huntly, 1984-87; Headteacher: Hilton Academy, 1987-88, St. Machar Academy, Aberdeen, 1988-95. Publication: Leisure Education and Young People's Leisure (Co-Author), 1988. Recreations: squash; suffering at the hands (and feet) of Aberdeen F. C. Address: (b.) Banchory Academy, Schoolhill, Banchory AB31 5TQ; T.-01330 823357.

Marr, Norman G., CStJ, DipArch, ARIBA, FRIAS. Consultant Architect/Planner; Director of Planning and

Development, Kincardine and Deeside District Council, 1975-92; b. 19.5.37, Aberdeen. Educ. Aberdeen Grammar School; Scott Sutherland School of Architecture, Aberdeen. Architectural Assistant, Aberdeen County Council, 1961-66; Senior Research Assistant, Corporation of the City of Aberdeen, Town Planning Department, 1967-69 (Principal Development Assistant, 1970-75). Organist and Choirmaster, Denburn Parish Church, Aberdeen, since 1956; Secretary, Scottish Federation of Organists, 1970-92 (President, 1993-94); Cross Bearer, Priory of the Order of St. John in Scotland, and Member, Aberdeen Committee of the Order; Member, Church of Scotland Property Commission; Vice-Chairman, Friends of St. Machar's Cathedral, Aberdeen, and Friends of the Kirk of St. Nicholas, Aberdeen. Recreations: organ playing/building; swimming; long-distance running; hill-walking; books; entertaining. Address: (h.) 63 Devonshire Road, Aberdeen, AB10 6XP; T.-01224 322937.

Marrian, Ian Frederic Young, MA, CA. Deputy Chief Executive and Secretary, Institute of Chartered Accountants of Scotland, since 1994 (Director of Education, since 1981); b. 15.11.43, Kilwinning; m., Moira Selina McSwan; 1 s.; 2 d. Educ. Royal Belfast Academical Institution; Queens University, Belfast; Edinburgh University. Qualified as CA, 1969; Deloitte Haskins & Sells: audit practice, Rome, 1969-72, London, 1972-73, Audit Partner, Edinburgh, 1973-78, Technical Partner, London, 1978-81. Recreations: gardening in the grand scale; wines. Address: (h.) Bowerhouse, Dunbar EH42 1RE; T.-0131-247 4815.

Marsh, Professor John Haig, BA, MEng, PhD, CEng, FIEE, FRSA. Professor of Optoelectronic Systems, University of Glasgow, since 1996; Non-executive Director, Compound Semiconductor Technologies Ltd., since 1999; b. 15.4.56, Edinburgh; m., Anabel Christine Mitchell. Educ. Glasgow Academy; Cambridge University; Liverpool University; Sheffield University. University of Sheffield: Research Fellow, 1980-83, Research Scientist, 1983-86; Department of Electronics and Electrical Engineering, University of Glasgow: Lecturer, 1986-90, Senior Lecturer, 1990-94, Reader, 1994-96. Director, NATO Advanced Study Institute, Glasgow, 1990; Member, IEE Professional Group E13 (Optical Devices and Systems), 1988-94; Founding Chair, Scottish Chapter, IEEE/LEOS, 1996-98; Vice President, LEOS, 1999. Publications: Waveguide Optoelectronics (Co-editor); 290 papers. Recreations: walking; Treasurer, Woodland Methodist Church; cooking; music; malt whisky. Address: Department of Electronics and Electrical Engineering, University of Glasgow, Glasgow G12 8QQ; T.-0141-330 4790.

Marshall, David. MP (Labour), Glasgow Shettleston, since 1979; b. 1941. Address: (b.) House of Commons, London, SW1A 0AA.

Marshall, Enid Ann, MA, LLB, PhD, Assoc. RICS, ACIArb, FRSA, Solicitor. Reader, Scots Law Research Unit, Stirling University, since 1994; Editor, Scottish Law Gazette, since 1983; Chairman, Social Security Appeal Tribunal, Stirling and Falkirk, since 1984; b. 10.7.32, Boyndie, Banffshire. Educ. Banff Academy; Bell-Baxter School, Cupar; St. Andrews University. Apprentice Solicitor, 1956-59; Lecturer in Law, Dundee College of Technology, 1959-72; Lecturer, then Senior Lecturer, then Reader in Business Law, Stirling University, 1972-94. Departmental Editor, Arbitration Section, Journal of Business Law, since 1976. Publications: General Principles of Scots Law; Scottish Cases on Contract; Scottish Cases on Agency; Scottish Cases on Partnerships and Companies; Scots Mercantile Law; Gill on Arbitration; Charlesworth and Morse Company Law (Scottish Editor); Notes on the Law of Property in Scotland (Editor, 3rd edition); M.C. Oliver's Company Law (10th, 11th, 12th editions). Recreations: veganism; animal welfare. Address: (h.) 24 Easter Cornton Road, Stirling FK9 5ES; T.-Stirling 478865/467285.

Marshall, Professor Ian Howard, MA, BD, PhD (Aberdeen), BA (Cantab), DD (Asbury). Professor of New Testament Exegesis, Aberdeen University, since 1979; b. 12.1.34, Carlisle; m., Joyce Elizabeth (deceased); 1 s.; 3 d. Educ. Aberdeen Grammar School; Aberdeen University; Cambridge University; Göttingen University. Assistant Tutor, Didsbury College, Bristol; Methodist Minister, Darlington; Lecturer, then Senior Lecturer and Reader in New Testament Exegesis, Aberdeen University. Publications: Kept by the Power of God; Luke: Historian and Theologian; The Origins of New Testament Christology; New Testament Interpretation (Editor); The Gospel of Luke; I Believe in the Historical Jesus; The Epistles of John; Acts; Last Supper and Lord's Supper; Biblical Inspiration; 1 and 2 Thessalonians; Jesus the Saviour; 1 Peter; Philippians; The Acts of the Apostles; Witness to the Gospel (Co-Editor). Address: (b.) Department of Divinity with Religious Studies, King's College, Aberdeen AB24 3UB; T.-01224 272388.

Marshall, Janet Ann, ALA. Vice-Chairman, Scottish Society for the Prevention of Cruelty to Animals, since 1993; b. 3.7.47, Inchinnan; m., Allan W. Marshall; 2 s. Educ. John Neilson Institution, Paisley; Strathclyde University. Glasgow Public Libraries, 1965-67; Children's Librarian, 1969-73; School Librarian, 1973-75; Senior Education Resources Librarian, 1975-79; Farmer, 1979-92. Member, East Ayrshire Children's Panel. Recreation: gardening. Address: (h.) Silverhill Farm, Dunlop, Kilmarnock KA3 4BN; T.-01560 484807.

Marshall, Professor Mary Tara, OBE, MA, DSA, DASS. Director, Dementia Services Development Centre, Stirling University; b. 13.6.45, Darjeeling, India. Educ. Mary Erskine School for Girls; Edinburgh University; London School of Economics; Liverpool University. Child Care Officer, London Borough of Lambeth, 1967-69; Social Worker, Personal Service Society, Liverpool, 1970-74; Research Organiser, Age Concern, Liverpool, 1974-75; Lecturer in Social Studies, Liverpool University, 1975-83; Director, Age Concern Scotland, 1983-89. Board Member, Edinvar Housing Association; Governor, Centre for Policy on Ageing; Governor, PPP Healthcare Medical Trust; Member: Journal of Dementia Care Advisory Board, Health and Social Care in the Community Editorial Advisory Board, Royal Commission on Long-term Care of the Elderly. Publications: I Can't Place This Place At All: Working with people with dementia and their carers, 1996; The State of Art in Dementia Care, 1997. Recreations: photography; bird-watching. Address: (b.) Dementia Services Development Centre, Stirling University, Stirling FK9 4LA; T.-01786 467740.

Marshall, Maud Evelyn, MA (Hons), MSc, MRTPI. Chairperson, Building Standards Advisory Committee; Chairperson, Lottery Capital Committee, Scottish Arts Council; Member, Scottish Arts Council; Director, WiseStart Ltd.; Trustee, The Lighthouse; b. 24.1.50, Glasgow. Educ. Park School, Glasgow; Edinburgh University; Swiss Federal Institute of Technology; Strathclyde University. Managing Director, South and West, Scottish Homes. Recreations: skiing; music; travel. Address: (b.) St. James House, 25 St. James Street, Paisley PA3 2HQ; T.-0141-842 3209.

Marshall, Rosalyn Adela, BSc (Hons), FCCA. Vice Principal (Strategic Planning and Development), Queen Margaret College, since 1997; Member, Accounts Commission for Scotland, since 1997; b. 22.7.54, Dundee. Educ. High School of Dundee; Dundee University. Financial Accountant, Lothian Regional Council, 1976-79; Development Officer, Lothian Health Board, 1979-81;

Edinburgh District Council: Administrative Officer, 1982-85, Principal Officer (Financial Incentives), Department of Economic Development and Estates, 1985-86; Financial Controller, Graphic Partners, Edinburgh, 1986-92; Assistant Principal, Administration and Finance, Queen Margaret College, 1992-97. Adviser, Business in the Arts. Recreations: golf; theatre; art; travel. Address: (b.) Queen Margaret College; Edinburgh EH12 8TS; T.-0131-317 3207.

Marshall, Thomas Graham, LLB, WS, FCIArb. Solicitor; Partner, Bishop and Robertson Chalmers, Edinburgh, since 1988; Solicitor Advocate, since 1995; b. 2.4.57, Kilmacolm; m., Anne Gibson; 3 s.; 1 d. Educ. Loretto School; Dundee University. Collector of Taxes, 1980-81; Law Apprentice, then Assistant Solicitor, Bishop & Co., Glasgow, 1982-86; Senior Assistant, Bishop and Robertson Chalmers, Glasgow, 1986-88. Secretary, Eurocopy Complainers Advisory Group, 1991-95; Fellow, Chartered Institute of Arbitrators, since 1993; Chair, Dunfermline East Constitutency Labour Party, since 1992. Publications: The Scots Dimension to Cross Border Litigation (Contributor), 1996. Recreations: family; Fife Opera; cricket (Largo C.C.). Address: (b.) 22 Ainslie Place, Edinburgh EH3 6AJ; T.-0131-220 3355.

Martin, Daniel, MA, BSc, PhD, FRSE, CMath, FIMA. Honorary Lecturer in Mathematics, Glasgow University, since 1980; b. 16.4.15, Carluke. Educ. High School of Glasgow; Glasgow University. Lecturer in Mathematics, Royal Technical College, Glasgow, 1938-47; Scientific Officer, Air Navigation Section, Royal Aircraft Establishment, Farnborough, 1941-45; Lecturer/Senior Lecturer in Mathematics, Glasgow University, 1947-80; Snell Visitor to Balliol College, Oxford, 1975-76. President: Glasgow Mathematical Association, 1958-59, Edinburgh Mathematical Society, 1960-61; former Assessor, Church of Scotland's selection schools for candidates for the Ministry. Publications: Solving Problems in Complex Numbers, 1968; An Introduction to Vector Analysis (Reviser), 1970; Manifold Theory: an introduction for mathematical physicists, 1991. Recreations: theology; local history; Gaelic. Address: (b.) Department of Mathematics, Glasgow University, Glasgow G12 8QW; T.-0141-339 8855, Ext. 6537.

Martin, David McLeod, DA, RSW, RGI. Painter; b. 30.12.22, Glasgow; m., Isobel Agnes Fowlie Smith; 4 s. Educ. Govan High School; Glasgow School of Art; Jordanhill College of Education. RAF, 1942-46. Principal Teacher, Hamilton Grammar School, 1973-83; retired early to paint full-time; exhibits regularly in Scotland; exhibited RA, 1984; numerous group shows; one man shows, Glasgow, Edinburgh, Perth, Greenock, Newcastle, Stenton, London; former Vice President, RSW. Address: (h.) The Old Schoolhouse, 53 Gilmour Street, Eaglesham, Glasgow G76 0LG.

Martin, David Weir, BA (Econ), MA. Member (Labour), European Parliament, for Lothians, since 1984; Vice-President, European Parliament, since 1989; b. 26.8.54, Edinburgh; m., Margaret Mary Cook; 1 s.; 1 d. Educ. Liberton High School; Heriot-Watt University; Leicester University. Worked as stockbroker's assistant and animal rights campaigner; became Lothian Regional Councillor, 1982; Vice-President, Mobile Projects; Director, St. Andrew Animal Fund; Rapporteur, Intergovernmental Conferences. Publications: Bringing Common Sense to the Common Market — A Left Agenda for Europe; European Union and the Democratic Deficit; Europe — An Ever Closer Union; Towards a Wider, Deeper, Federal Europe; Maastricht in a Minute; 1996 and all that; A Partnership Democracy for Europe. Recreations: soccer; reading. Address: (b.) 4 Lothian Street, Dalkeith EH22 1DS.

Martin, Donald, MA. Editor, Evening Express, Aberdeen, since 1997; b. 23.4.64, Glasgow. Educ. Bishopbriggs High School; Glasgow University. Assistant Editor/Deputy Editor, Thames Valley Newspapers; Launch Editor, Edinburgh and Lothians Post; Editor, Thames Valley Free Newspapers; Production Editor/Chief Sub, Reading Evening Post; Deputy Editor, Cambridge Evening News; Editor, North West Evening Mail. Recreations: golf; football; sailing. Address: (b.) Aberdeen Journals Ltd., Lang Stracht, Mastrick, Aberdeen AB15 6DP; T.-01224 690222.

Martin, Professor Ged, BA, MA, PhD, FRHistS. Professor of Canadian Studies, Edinburgh University, since 1983; Past President, British Association for Canadian Studies; b. 22.5.45, Hornchurch; m., Ann Barry. Educ. Royal Liberty School, Romford; Magdalene College, Cambridge. Research Fellow, Magdalene College, Cambridge, 1970-72, Australian National University, 1972-77; Lecturer, then Statutory Lecturer, University College, Cork, 1977-83. Canadian High Commissioner's Award for Service to British-Canadian Relations, 1989. Publications: ten books, including Canada's Heritage in Scotland (Co-author), 1989. Recreations: reading and writing history; music; talking to cats. Address: (b.) 21 George Square, Edinburgh EH8 9LD; T.-0131-650 4129, Ext. 6801.

Martin, Graham Dunstan, MA, BLitt, GradCertEd. Writer; Senior Lecturer, Edinburgh University, since 1982; b. 21.10.32, Leeds; m., 1, Ryllis Daniel; 2 s.; 1 d.; 2, Anne Crombie; 2 s. Educ. Leeds Grammar School; Oriel College and Linacre College, Oxford. Schoolteacher, 1956-65; Assistant Lecturer, then Lecturer, in French, Edinburgh University, 1965-82. Publications: (philosophy) Language, Truth and Poetry, 1975; The Architecture of Experience 1981, Shadows in the Cave, 1990; (novels) Giftwish, 1980; Catchfire, 1981; The Soul Master, 1984; Time-Slip, 1986; The Dream Wall, 1987; Half a Glass of Moonshine, 1988; poems and poetry translations. Recreations: music; jazz; walking; good food; the Celtic past. Address: (b.) French Department, Edinburgh University, 60 George Square, Edinburgh EH8 9JU; T.-0131-650 8409.

Martin, Rev. Iver, BSc, DipTheol. Minister, Bon Accord Free Church, Aberdeen, since 1997; b. 29.6.57, Grantown on Spey; m., Mairi Isabel Macdonald; 2 s.; 4 d. Educ. Camphill High School, Paisley; Robert Gordon's Institute of Technology; Free Church College. National Semiconductor (UK) Ltd.: Graduate Process Engineer, 1980, Senior Engineer, 1983; European Process Engineer, Lam Research Corporation Ltd., 1985; European Product and Sales Engineer, Silicon Glen Technology, 1987-90; own company, Solus (UK) Ltd., 1990-92; Assistant Minister, Stornoway Free Church, 1995-97. Recreations: cycling; reading; music. Address: 77 Forest Avenue, Aberdeen; T.-01224 324630.

Martin, Rev. James, MA, BD, DD. Minister, High Carntyne, Glasgow, 1954-87; b. 21.1.21, Motherwell; m., Marion Gordon Greig; 2 d. Educ. Dalziel High School, Motherwell; Glasgow University. Minister, Newmilns West Church, 1946-54; Convener, Publications Committee, General Assembly, 1978-83 and Board of Communications, 1983-87; Bruce Lecturer, Trinity College, 1960-64. Publications: Did Jesus Rise from the Dead?; The Reliability of the Gospels; Letters of Caiaphas to Annas; Suffering Man, Loving God; The Road to the Aisle; People in the Jesus Story; A Plain Man in the Holy Land; Listening to the Bible; William Barclay: A Personal Memoir; My Friend Bobby; It's You, Minister; It's My Belief; Travels in the Holy Land; God-Collared; William Barclay in a Nutshell; You Can't Be Serious; A Parish Minister's Hats; More About Bobby; Grit for the Road of Life. Recreations: football; tennis; conversation. Address: 9 Magnolia Street, Wishaw; T.-01698 385825.

Martin, John, Chairman and Founder, The John Martin Group, since 1964; b. 5.6.36; m., Vera; 2 s. First franchise, Volvo, 1969; biggest Datsun dealer in Edinburgh, 1970s; added Rolls-Royce, Aston Martin, Bentley, BMW, Lotus, Honda, Nissan, Peugot, Vauxhall franchises, 1980s; acquired bodyshops; awarded Chrysler, Jeep, Mitsubishi, Daihatsu, Suzuki, Lexus, Skoda franchises, 1990s. Rolls-Royce Distributor of the Year, 1993; Automotive Management Marketing Award, 1997; Motor Trader Top Marketing Award, 1998. Recreation: classic cars. Address: The John Martin Group, 6 Bankhead Drive, Edinburgh EH11 4DJ; T.-0131-442 1000.

Martin, John Sharp Buchanan, BSc. Head of Transport and Planning Group, Scottish Office, since 1998; b. 7.7.46, West Kilbride; m., Catriona Meldrum; 1 s.; 1 d. Educ. Bell-Baxter High School, Cupar; St. Andrews University. Assistant Principal, 1968-73; Private Secretary to Parliamentary Under Secretary of State, 1971-73; Principal, 1973-79; Rayner Scrutinies, 1979-80; Assistant Secretary, Highlands and Tourism Division, 1980-84; Housing Division 1, 1984-89; Transport and Local Roads Division, 1989-92; Under Secretary, School Education and Sport, 1992-98. Recreations: tennis; cricket; golf; philately. Address: (b.) Victoria Quay, Leith, Edinburgh; T.-0131-244 0629.

Martin, Michael John. Deputy Speaker of the House of Commons, since 1997; MP (Labour), Glasgow Springburn, since 1979; Chairman, Scottish Grand Committee, since 1987; b. 3.7.45, Glasgow; m., Mary McLay; 1 s.; 1 d. Educ. St. Patrick's Boys' School, Glasgow. Member, Glasgow Corporation, 1973-74, and of Glasgow District Council, 1974-79. Member, Speaker's Panel of Chairmen, since 1987; Fellow, Parliament and Industry Trust; Member, College of Piping. Recreations: hill-walking; studying history of Forth and Clyde Canal; listening to pipe band music. Address: (h.) 144 Broomfield Road, Glasgow G21 3UE; T.-0141-558 2975.

Martin, Robert (Roy) Logan, QC, LLB. Advocate, since 1976; Barrister, since 1990; b. 31.7.50, Glasgow; m., Fiona Frances Neil; 1 s.; 2 d. Educ. Paisley Grammar School; Glasgow University. Solicitor, 1973-76; Member, Sheriff Courts Rules Council, 1981-84; Standing Junior Counsel, Department of Employment (Scotland), 1983-84; Advocate-Depute, 1984-87; admitted to Bar of New South Wales, 1987; Queen's Counsel, 1988; called to the Bar, Lincoln's Inn, 1990; Chairman (part-time), Industrial Tribunals, 1990-96; Chairman, Scottish Planning, Local Government and Environmental Bar Group, 1991-96; Chairman, Police Appeals Tribunal, since 1997. Affiliate, Royal Incorporation of Architects in Scotland, 1995; Honorary Secretary, The Wagering Club, 1982-91. Recreations: shooting; skiing; modern architecture; vintage motor cars. Address: (h.) Kilduff House, Athelstaneford, East Lothian EH39 5BD; T.-01620 880202.

Martin, Professor Roderick, MA, DPhil, DLitt. Professor of Organizational Behaviour, Glasgow University, since 1992 (Director, Glasgow University Business School, 1992-96); b. 18.10.40, Lancaster; 1 s.; 2 d. Educ. Royal Grammar School, Lancaster; Balliol College, Oxford; University of Pennsylvania; Nuffield College, Oxford. Lecturer, York University, 1964-66; Lecturer in Sociology, Oxford University, 1966-69; Fellow and Tutor in Politics and Sociology, Trinity College, Oxford, 1969-84; Professor of Industrial Sociology, Imperial College, London, 1984-88; Fellow, Templeton College, Oxford, 1988-91. Member, ESRC Research Grants Board, 1987-91. Publications: eight books, including Bargaining Power, 1992. Recreations: reading; listening to music. Address: (b.) 55-59 South Park Avenue, Glasgow G12 8LF; T.-0141-330 5410.

Martin, Ruth Rosemary, LLB, DipLP, NP, SSC. Partner, Digby Brown Solicitors, since 1997; Council Member, Law Society of Scotland, since 1997; b. 5.10.67, Edinburgh. Educ. George Watson's College; University of Edinburgh. Digby Brown: Assistant, 1991-94, Associate, 1995-97. Address: (b.) 7 Albyn Place, Edinburgh EH2 4NG; T.-0845 273 23 23.

Martin, Professor Ursula Hilda Mary, MA, PhD, CEng, FRSA. Professor, School of Mathematical and Computational Sciences, University of St Andrews, since 1992; b. 3.8.53, London. Educ. Cambridge University. Lecturer, London University, 1978-81; Visiting Professor, University of Illinois, 1981-83; Lecturer, Manchester University, 1983-87; Reader, then Professor, London University, 1987-92. Address: (b.) School of Mathematical and Computational Sciences, Computer Science Division, University of St Andrews, North Haugh, St. Andrews KY16 9SS; T.-01334 463252.

Martin-Bates, Robert Stuart, BL. Honorary Sheriff, Perth, since 1989; b. 8.5.21, Perth; m., Ursula Louise Sarena Peter; 2 s. Educ. Glenalmond College; Edinburgh University. Served in Royal Navy, 1941-46; private practice as solicitor in Perth and Pitlochry, 1948-90; Burgh Prosecutor, Crieff, 1960-74; Depute Burgh Prosecutor, Perth, 1963-74. Member and Past Moderator, Perth Society of High Constables, since 1957; Past President, Society of Solicitors of the City and County of Perth; Member: Committee, Perth Model Lodging House Association, 1950-85 (Chairman, 1968-85), Committee, Perthshire & Kinrosshire Society for the Blind, 1979-89, including three years as Chairman, now Hon. Vice-President. Recreations: golf; gardening; reading. Address: (h.) Immeriach, Glencarse, Perth PH2 7NF; T.-01738 860284.

Marwick, George Robert, SDA, JP. Lord Lieutenant for Orkney, 1997 (Vice Lieutenant, 1995, Deputy Lieutenant, 1976); Chairman, Swannay Farms Ltd., since 1972; Chairman, Campbeltown Creamery (Holdings) Ltd., 1974-90; b. 27.2.32, Edinburgh; m., 1, Hanne Jensen; 3 d.; 2, Norma Gerrard. Educ. Port Regis; Bryanston; Edinburgh School of Agriculture. Councillor, local government, 1968-78; Vice-Convener, Orkney County Council, 1970-74, Convener, Orkney Islands Council, 1974-78; Chairman, North of Scotland Water Board, 1970-73; Member, Scottish Agricultural Consultative Panel, 1972-98 (formerly Winter Keep Panel, 1964-72); Director, North Eastern Farmers Ltd., 1968-98;, Member: Countryside Commission for Scotland, 1978-86, Council, National Trust for Scotland, 1979-84. Recreations: shooting; tennis; motor sport. Address: (h.) Swannay House, by Evie, Orkney; T.-01856 721365.

Mason, Christopher Michael, MA, PhD, JP. Chairman, Clyde Maritime Trust Ltd., since 1991; Member, City of Glasgow Council, since 1995; b. 8.3.41, Hexham; m., Stephanie Maycock; 2 d. Educ. Marlborough College; Magdalene College, Cambridge. Lecturer in Politics, Glasgow University, 1966-93; Alliance candidate, Glasgow, European Elections, 1984; Liberal Democrat candidate in General Elections, Glasgow Hillhead, 1992, Eastwood, 1997; Chairman, Scottish Liberal Party, 1987-88; Member, Strathclyde Regional Council, 1982-96; Leader, Strathclyde Liberal Democrat Group, 1986-96; Member, Scottish Constitutional Convention, 1989-97. Publication: Effective Management of Resources: The International Politics of the North Sea, 1979. Recreation: sailing. Address: (h.) 2 Holyrood Crescent, Glasgow G20 6HJ; T.-0141-339 2840.

Mason, Professor Sir David Kean, KB, CBE, BDS, MD, FRCS, FDS, FRCPath, Hon. DSc, Hon. DChD, Hon. LLD, Hon. FFD, Hon. FDS, Hon. FRCS. President, General Dental Council, 1989-94; Honorary Consultant Dental Surgeon, since 1965; b. 5.11.28, Paisley; m., Judith Armstrong; 2 s.; 1 d. Educ. Paisley Grammar School; Glasgow Academy; St. Andrews University; Glasgow University. RAF Dental Branch, 1952-54; Registrar in Oral

Surgery, Dundee, 1954-56; Senior Lecturer in Dental Surgery and Pathology, Glasgow University, 1964-67; Professor of Oral Medicine, Glasgow University, 1967-92 (Dean of Dental Education, 1980-90); Chairman, National Dental Consultative Committee, 1976-80; Member: Medicines Commission, 1976-80, Dental Committee, MRC, 1973-83, Physiological Systems Board, MRC, 1976-80, GDC, 1976-93, Dental Strategy Review Group, 1980-81, Dental Review Working Party, UGC, 1986-87, WHO Expert Committee on Oral Health, since 1991; Convener, Dental Council, RCPSGlas, 1977-80; John Tomes Prize, RCS England, 1979; Colyer Prize RCS England, 1993; Honorary Member, British Dental Association, 1993; Honorary Member, American Dental Association, 1994. Publications: Salivary Glands in Health and Disease (Co-Author); Introduction to Oral Medicine (Co-Author); Self Assessment: Manuals I and II (Co-Editor); Oral Manifestations of Systemic Disease. Recreations: golf; tennis; gardening; enjoying the pleasure of the countryside. Address: (h.) Greystones, Houston Road, Kilmacolm, Renfrewshire; T.-Kilmacolm 2001.

Mason, Derek Stevens, CBE (1986), JP, FRICS, FFB. Partner, John Baxter, Dunn and Gray, Chartered Quantity Surveyors, since 1970; Chairman, Hutchesons' Educational Trust (Governor, since 1972); Chairman, West Glasgow Hospitals University NHS Trust, 1996-97; b. 21.5.34, Glasgow; m., Jeanette M. Mason, OBE, JP; 2 s.; 1 d. Educ. Allan Glen's School, Glasgow; Royal Technical College (part-time). RICS: Chairman, West of Scotland Junior Sub-Branch, 1965-66, Chairman, Scottish Junior Branch, 1966-67, Chairman, Scottish Branch, Faculty of Building, since 1994; Councillor, Glasgow Corporation, 1970 and 1972-75, Glasgow District Council, 1974-84 (Deputy Leader, Conservative Group, 1977-80, Bailie, 1977-80); Chairman, Glasgow Sports Promotion Council, 1977-80 (Hon. Vice-President, since 1980); Preceptor, Hutchesons' Hospital, 1978-80; JP, since 1977; Past Deacon, Incorporation of Masons of Glasgow; Chairman, Scottish Special Housing Association, 1981-89; Member: Merchants House of Glasgow, SCOTVEC Council, 1993-97, Glasgow Eastern Merchants Association, Incorporation of Tailors of Rutherglen, Incorporation of Wrights in Glasgow; Elder, Newlands South Church of Scotland. Recreations: reading; current affairs; watching football. Address: (h.) 45 Ayr Road, Glasgow G46 6SP; T.-0141-571 1245.

Mason, Douglas C., BSc. Member, Glenrothes Development Corporation, 1985-96; Parliamentary Research Assistant, 1979-97; Freelance Journalist, since 1977; b. 30.9.41, Dunfermline. Educ. Bradford Grammar School; St. Andrews University. Conservative Party Organising Secretary, 1969-77; Member: Fife County Council, 1967-70, Kirkcaldy District Council, 1974-88, Scottish Housing Advisory Committee, 1978-80; contested Central Fife, General Election, 1983; Convener, General Council Business Committee, St. Andrews University. Domestic Policy Adviser, Adam Smith Institute, since 1984. Publications: Allocation and Transfer of Council Houses (Co-Author), 1980; The Qualgo Complex, 1984; Revising the Rating System, 1985; Room for Improvement, 1985; University Challenge, 1986; Time to Call Time, 1986; Ex Libris, 1986; Expounding the Arts, 1987; Licensed to Live, 1988; Pining for Profit, 1988; A Home for Enterprise, 1989; Privatizing the Posts, 1989; Wiser Councils and Shedding a Tier, 1989; Wood for the Trees, 1991; City in the Mist (Co-Editor), 1995. Recreations: books; music. Address: (h.) 84 Barnton Place, Glenrothes, Fife; T.-01592 758766.

Mason, John Kenneth, BA (Oxon), MPhil. Head of Industrial Policy, The Scottish Office, since 1996; b. 26.6.56, Chichester; m., Alison Margaret Cruickshanks; 1 s.; 2 d. Educ. Chichester High School; Hertford College, Oxford; University College, London. Kent County Council, 1980-85; Department of Environment, 1985-90; Scottish Office, 1990-94; Registers of Scotland, 1994-96. Recreations: photography; gardening. Address: (b.) Meridian Court, 5 Cadogan Street, Glasgow G2 6AT; T.-0141-242 5537.

Mason, Professor Emeritus John Kenyon French, CBE, MD, LLD, FRCPath, DMJ, FRSE. Regius Professor of Forensic Medicine, Edinburgh University, 1973-85; b. 19.12.19, Lahore; m., Elizabeth Latham (deceased); 2 s. Educ. Downside School; Cambridge University; St. Bartholomew's Hospital. Regular Officer, Medical Branch, RAF, following War Service; Consultant in charge, RAF Department of Aviation and Forensic Pathology, 1957-73. President, British Association in Forensic Medicine, 1981-83; Swiney Prize in Jurisprudence, 1978. Publication: Forensic Medicine for Lawyers, 3rd Edition; Law and Medical Ethics, 4th Edition (Co-Author); Medico-legal Aspects of Reproduction and Parenthood, 2nd Edition; Human Life and Medical Practice. Address: (h.) 66 Craiglea Drive, Edinburgh EH10 5PF; T. 0131-447 2301.

Massie, Allan Johnstone, BA, FRSL. Author and Journalist; b. 16.10.38, Singapore; m., Alison Langlands; 2 s.; 1 d. Educ. Drumtochty Castle; Trinity College, Glenalmond; Trinity College, Cambridge. Schoolmaster, Drumtochty Castle, 1960-71; taught EFL, 1972-75; Creative Writing Fellow, Edinburgh University, 1982-84, Glasgow and Strathclyde Universities, 1985-86; Editor, New Edinburgh Review, 1982-84; Fiction Reviewer, The Scotsman, since 1975; Television Critic, Sunday Standard, 1981-83 (Fraser of Allander Award, Critic of the Year, 1982); Sports Columnist, Glasgow Herald, 1985-88; Columnist: Daily Telegraph, Daily Mail, The Scotsman, Sunday Times. Publications: (novels): Change and Decay in all around I see; The Last Peacock; The Death of Men (Scottish Arts Council Book Award); One Night in Winter; Augustus; A Question of Loyalties; The Sins of the Father; Tiberius; The Hanging Tree; Shadows of Empire; Caesar; These Enchanted Woods; The Ragged Lion; King David; Antony; (non-fiction): Muriel Spark; Ill Met by Gaslight; The Caesars; Portrait of Scottish Rugby; Colette; 101 Great Scots; Byron's Travels; Glasgow; Edinburgh; (as Editor): Edinburgh and the Borders in Verse; (radio play): Quintet in October; (plays): The Minstrel and the Shirra; First-Class Passengers. Recreations: reading; watching rugby, cricket, racing; walking the dogs. Address: (h.) Thirladean House, Selkirk, TD7 5LU; T.-Selkirk 20393.

Masson, Alastair H.B., BA, MB, ChB, FRCSEdin, FRCA; b. 30.1.25, Bathgate; m., Marjorie Nan Paisley-Whyte; 3 s.; 1 d. Educ. Bathgate Academy; Edinburgh University. Consultant Anaesthetist, Edinburgh Royal Infirmary (retired); Visiting Professor of Anesthesiology, South Western Medical School, Dallas, Texas, 1962-63. President: Scottish Society of Anaesthetists, 1978-79, British Society of the History of Medicine, 1989-91; Honorary Archivist, Royal College of Surgeons, Edinburgh; President, Scottish Society of the History of Medicine, 1984-87. Publication: Portraits, Paintings and Busts in the Royal College of Surgeons of Edinburgh, 1995. Recreations: golf; hill-walking; music; travel. Address: (h.) 28 Beechmount Park, Edinburgh.

Masterman, Eileen Mary, MA (Hons), ACIArb. Director, Royal Institution of Chartered Surveyors in Scotland, since 1992; Member, Committee of Investigation for Great Britain, since 1995; Member, Extra Parliamentary Panel, since 1996; b. Spennymoor, Co. Durham; m., Norman A. Fiddes; 2 d. Educ. St. Anthony's School for Girls, Sunderland; Dundee University. Research Assistant, Dundee University, 1976-80; Investigator and Complaints Examiner, Commissioner for Local Administration in Scotland, 1980-90; Advocates' Clerk/Business Manager, Faculty of Advocates, 1990-92. Member, Building Standards Advisory Committee, 1994-97; Director, Edinburgh Chamber of Commerce, 1994-97. Recreations:

food; friends; fresh air. Address: (b.) 9 Manor Place, Edinburgh EH3 7DN; T.-0131-225 7078.

Masters, Christopher, BSc (Hons), PhD, AKC. Executive Chairman Designate, Aggreko plc, since 1997; b. 2.5.47, Northallerton; m., Gillian Mary Hodson; 2 d. Educ. Richmond School; King's College, London; Leeds University. Shell Research BV/Shell Chemicals UK Ltd., 1971-77; joined Christian Salvesen as Business Development Manager, 1979; transferred to Christian Salvesen Inc., USA, 1982, as Director of Planning; Managing Director, Christian Salvesen Seafoods, 1983; Managing Director, Industrial Services Division, 1985; appointed a Director, Christian Salvesen PLC, 1987; Chief Executive, Christian Salvesen PLC, 1989-97; Chairman, Young Enterprise Scotland, 1994-97; Chairman, Quality Assessment Committee of Higher Education Funding Council, 1991-95; Member, Scottish Higher Education Funding Council, since 1995, Chairman, since 1998; Non-Executive Director: British Assets Trust, since 1989, Scottish Widows, since 1991, Scottish Chamber Orchestra Trust, since 1993; Vice Chairman, Scottish Opera, since 1996. Recreations: wines; music. Address: (b.) Aggreko plc, 121 West Regent Street, Glasgow G2 2SD; T.-0141-225 5900.

Mather, Professor Alexander Smith, BSc, PhD, FRSGS. Professor of Geography, University of Aberdeen, since 1995 (Head, Department of Geography, since 1998); b. 17.9.43, Aberdeenshire. Educ. Peterhead Academy; Aberdeen Grammar School; University of Aberdeen. Reader in Geography, University of Aberdeen, 1995-98; Editor, Scottish Geographical Magazine, 1987-94; Editor, Land Use Policy, since 1998. Publications: Land Use, 1986; Global Forest Resources, 1990; Environmental Resources (Co-author), 1995. Recreation: hill-walking. Address: (b.) Department of Geography, University of Aberdeen, Aberdeen AB24 3UF; T.-01224 272354.

Matheson, Alexander (Sandy), OBE, FRPharmS, MRSH, DL, JP. Chairman, Western Isles Health Board (Member, since 1973; Vice-Chairman, 1991-93); b. 16.11.41, Stornoway; m., Irene Mary Davidson, BSc, MSc; 2 s.; 2 d. Educ. Nicolson Institute, Stornoway; Robert Gordon's Institute of Technology, Aberdeen. Chairman, Stornoway Pier and Harbour Commission, since 1991 (Member, since 1968); Member, Stornoway Trust Estate, since 1967 (Chairman, 1971-81); Chairman: Stornoway Branch, RNLI, Western Isles Development Fund, since 1972; Member, Stornoway Town Council, 1967-75; Provost of Stornoway, 1971-75; Member: Ross and Cromarty County Council, 1967-75, Western Isles Islands Council, 1974-94 (Chairman, Development Services, 1974-80, Vice-Convener, 1980-82, Convener, 1982-90); President, Islands Commission of the Conference of Peripheral Maritime Regions of Europe, 1987-91 and 1993-94; Honorary Sheriff, since 1972; Vice Lieutenant, Western Isles Islands Area; Director, Harris Tweed Authority; Chairman, Roderick Smith Ltd., Stornoway. Address: (h.) 33 Newton Street, Stornoway, Isle of Lewis; T.-01851 702082.

Matheson, Allen Short, CBE, FRIBA, PPRIAS, MRTPI. Retired Partner, Matheson Gleave Partnership; b. 28.2.26, Egypt; m., Catherine Anne; 2 s. Educ. George Watson's College; Edinburgh College of Art. Past President, Royal Incorporation of Architects in Scotland; Past Chairman, Scottish Construction Industry Group; former Vice-Chairman, Board of Governors, Glasgow School of Art; former Director, Glasgow Chamber of Commerce; former Member, Royal Fine Art Commission for Scotland; Past Chairman, Joint Standing Committee of Architects, Surveyors and Building Contractors. Address: (h.) 11 Spence Street, Glasgow G20 0AW; T.-0141-946 5670.

Matheson, John Alexander, MA, MBA, CPFA. Chairman, Scottish Branch, Chartered Institute of Public Finance and Accountancy, 1998-99; Member, Board of Management, Edinburgh's Telford College, since 1998; Finance Director, Lothian Primary Care NHS Trust, since 1999; b. 23.6.55, Dingwall; m., Judith; 1 s.; 1 d. Educ. Invergordon Academy; Heriot-Watt University; Edinburgh University. Finance Director, Edinburgh Healthcare NHS Trust, 1994-99. Recreation: hill-walking; golf. T.-0131-537 9514.

Matheson, Lindsay S.G., MA, MLitt. Rector, Madras College, St. Andrews, since 1997; b. 2.10.44, Edinburgh; m., Katherine R.; 2 d. Educ. Otago Boys' High School, Dunedin; George Watson's, Edinburgh; St. Andrews University; Oxford University. History Teacher, Banff Academy, 1970-72; Principal Teacher of History, Lochaber High School, 1972-80; Assistant Rector, Inverurie Academy, 1980-85; Rector, Milne's High School, Fochabers, 1985-97. Recreations: cycling; golf; bridge. Address: (h.) 52 Largo Road, St. Andrews, Fife; T.-01334 472744.

Matheson, Susan Margaret Graham, BSc (Soc Sci). Chief Executive, Sacro, since 1996; b. 6.6.49, Tarbert, Harris; 1 d. Educ. St. George's School for Girls, Edinburgh; Edinburgh University. Antique dealer, 1971-73; Research Officer, then Senior Research Officer, Scottish Office Central Research Unit, 1973-88; Director, Family Mediation Scotland, 1988-96. Publications: several Government research reports and other publications. Recreation: skiing. Address: (b.) 31 Palmerston Place, Edinburgh EH12 5AP.; T.-0131-226 4222.

Mathews, Very Rev. Canon Eugene Joseph, JCL. Parish Priest of Girvan, since 1982; b. 2.9.21, Dumfries. Educ. St. Joseph's College, Dumfries; Blairs College, Aberdeen; Scots College, Rome; St. Peter's College, Bearsden; Gregorian University, Rome. Ordained Priest, St. Andrew's Cathedral, Glasgow, 1946; Curate, St. Mary's, Saltcoats, 1949-56; Parish Priest: Kirkconnel, 1956-63, Maybole, 1963-67, Kilbirnie, 1967-73, St. Michael's, Kilmarnock, 1973-82. Publications: Counting My Blessings; Counting My Joys. Recreation: reading. Address: 17 Harbour Street, Girvan KA26 9AJ; T.-01465 713331.

Mathewson, David Carr, BSc, CA. Merchant Banker; Director, Noble Grossart Limited, since 1989; b. 26.7.47, Broughty Ferry; m., Jan McIntyre; 1 s.; 1 d. Educ. Daniel Stewart's College, Edinburgh; St. Andrews University. Deloitte Haskins & Sells, Edinburgh, 1968-72; Williams Glyn & Co., London, 1972-75; Nedbank Group, South Africa, 1976-86; Noble Grossart Limited, since 1986; Director, Rodime plc, since 1992, Edinburgh US Tracker Trust plc, since 1998, Martin Currie High Income Trust plc, since 1998; Director of various private companies. Recreations: family interests; golf; skiing; athletics. Address: (b.) 48 Queen Street, Edinburgh EH2 3NR; T.-0131-226 7011.

Mathewson, George Ross, CBE, BSc, PHD, MBA, LLD, FRSE, CEng, MIEE, CIMgt, FCIBS. Group Chief Executive, Royal Bank of Scotland Group plc, Royal Bank of Scotland plc, since 1992; Director, Strategic Planning and Development, Royal Bank of Scotland Group plc, Royal Bank of Scotland plc, since 1987; Director: Scottish Investment Trust Ltd., since 1981, Citizens Financial Group, since 1989, Direct Line Group Ltd., since 1990; b. 14.5.40, Dunfermline; m., Sheila Alexandra Graham Bennett; 2 s. Educ. Perth Academy; St. Andrews University; Canisius College, Buffalo, New York. Assistant Lecturer, St. Andrews University, 1964-67; Systems Engineer (various positions), Bell Aerospace, Buffalo, New York, 1967-72; ICFC: Executive in Edinburgh Area Office, 1972-81, Area Manager, 1974-79, Director and Assistant General Manager, 1979-81; Chief Executive, Scottish Development Agency, 1981-87. Recreations: tennis; skiing;

geriatric rugby; golf; business. Address: (h.) 29 Saxe Coburg Place, Edinburgh EH3 5BP.

Mathieson, David Grant, BSc (Hons). Head Teacher, Ayr Academy, since 1997; b. 17.4.51, Irvine; m., Carol Margaret; 1 s. Educ. Girvan Academy; Glasgow University; Jordanhill College of Education. Grange Academy, Kilmarnock: Assistant Teacher of Physics, 1974-80, Assistant Principal Teacher of Science, 1980-84; Principal Teacher of Physics, Shawlands Academy, Glasgow, 1984-90; Girvan Academy: Assistant Head Teacher, 1990-93, Depute Head Teacher, 1993-97. Recreations: athletics; gardening; rugby. Address: (b.) 7 Fort Street, Ayr KA7 1HX; T.-01292 261562.

Mathieson, Derek, MA (Hons), DipEd. Headteacher, Stewarton Academy, since 1994; b. 21.2.48, Falkirk; m., Lynne; 3 s. Educ. Graeme High School, Falkirk; Edinburgh University; Glasgow University. High School of Glasgow; Marr College, Troon; Kilwinning Academy; Belmont Academy, Ayr; Stewarton Academy. Recreation: golf. Address: (b.) Cairnduff Place, Stewarton KA3 5QF; T.-01560 482342.

Mathieson, John George, CBE, TD, DL, BL, WS. Retired Solicitor; Chairman, Thorntons, WS, Tayside, 1990-97; b. 15.6.32, Argyll; m., Shirley Bidder; 1 s.; 1 d. Educ. George Watson's College, Edinburgh; Glasgow University. Territorial Army, 1951-86: Commanding Officer The Highland Regiment RA, TA Colonel for Highlands, Honorary Colonel 105 Regiment RA(TA), Chairman, Highlands TA Association; ADC TA, the Queen, 1975-80. Scottish Director, Woolwich Building Society, 1975-96; Chairman: Independent Tribunal Service, 1992, Arbroath Branch, Royal British Legion and Earl Haig Fund; Deputy Lieutenant, Angus, 1977; Chairman: Scottish Solicitors Discipline Tribunal, 1986-92, Royal Artillery Council for Scotland; Honorary President, Angus Bn., Boys' Brigade; Elder, Colliston Parish Church. Recreations: shooting; golf; gardening. Address: (h.) Willanyards, Colliston, Arbroath, Angus; T.-01241 890286.

Matthew, Alan Stuart, LLB. Solicitor, since 1980; b. 9.12.56, Dundee; m., Eileen; 2 d.. Educ. Morgan Academy, Dundee; University of Dundee. Apprentice Solicitor, J. R. Stevenson and Marshall, Dunfermline, 1978-80; Solicitor: Clark Oliver, Arbroath and Forfar, 1982-84, Messrs Burns Veal and Gillan (later Burns Veal), Dundee, 1984-85; Partner: Burns Veal, 1985-98, Partner, Miller Hendry (incorporating Burns Veal), since 1998. Director, Solicitors Financial Services Ltd., since 1990; Member, Council, Law Society of Scotland, since 1997; Member, Council, Faculty of Solicitors and Procurators in Dundee, since 1997; External Examiner in Professional Ethics, University of Dundee, since 1998. Recreations: rugby; hillwalking; after dinner speaking. Address: (b.) 13 Ward Road, Dundee DD1 1LU; T.-01382 200000.

Matthews, Baird, BL. Solicitor in private practice, since 1950; Honorary Sheriff, Kirkcudbright and Stranraer; b. 19.1.25, Newton Stewart; m., Mary Thomson Hope; 2 s.; 1 d. Educ. Douglas Ewart High School; Edinburgh University. Commissioned, Royal Scots Fusiliers, 1944; demobilised as Captain, 1st Bn., 1947; Partner, A. B. & A. Matthews, Solicitors, Newton Stewart; Clerk to General Commissioners of Income Tax, Stranraer and Newton Stewart Districts, from 1952; Burgh Prosecutor, Newton Stewart, from 1968; Depute Procurator Fiscal for Wigtownshire, 1970; Chairman, Board of Local Directors, General Accident Fire and Life Assurance Corporation, 1988; Director, Newcastle Building Society (Scottish Board), 1991; Dean of Faculty of Stewartry of Kirkcudbright Solicitors, 1979; Dean of Faculty of Solicitors of the District of Wigtown, 1983; Chairman, Appeals Tribunal, 1984; President, Newton Stewart Golf Club 1996 (Centenary Year). Recreations: golf; curling. Address: (b.) Bank of Scotland Buildings, Newton Stewart, Wigtownshire; T.-01671 404100.

Matthews, Herbert Eric, MA (Oxon), BPhil (Oxon). Professor of Philosophy, Aberdeen University, since 1995 (Head, Department of Philosophy, 1989-96); b. 24.10.36, Liverpool; m., Hellen Kilpatrick Matthews; 2 s. Educ. Liverpool Institute High School for Boys; St. John's College, Oxford. Lecturer, Department of Logic, Aberdeen University, 1963; Reader in Philosophy, 1993. Publications: numerous articles in learned journals; translations of works of German philosophy; The Philosophy of Thomas Reid (Editor); Philosophy and Health Care (Editor); Twentieth Century French Philosophy. Recreations: cinema; reading; walking; cycling. Address: (b.) Department of Philosophy, Aberdeen University, Aberdeen AB24 3UB; T.-01224 272367.

Matthews, Hugh, QC, LLB. Sheriff of Glasgow and Strathkelvin at Glasgow. Admitted, Faculty of Advocates, 1979. Address: (b.) Sheriff Court House, 1 Carlton Place, Glasgow, G5 9DA.

Matthews, Professor John Burr Lumley, MA, DPhil, FRSE, FRSA. Secretary, The Scottish Association for Marine Science, since 1988; Honorary Professor, University of Stirling, since 1984; b. 23.4.35, Isleworth; m., Jane Rosemary; 1 s.; 2 d. Educ. University of Warwick; St. John's College, Oxford University. Research Scientist, Oceanographic Laboratory, Edinburgh, 1961-67; Senior Lecturer, later Professor, Department of Marine Biology, University of Bergen, Norway, 1967-84; Visiting Professor, University of British Columbia, Canada, 1977-78; Deputy Director, Dunstaffnage Marine Laboratory, 1984-88; Director, NERC Dunstaffnage Marine Laboratory and Scottish Association for Marine Science, 1988-94. Deputy Chairman, South West Regional Board, Scottish Natural Heritage, 1994-97. Recreations: cross-country skiing; gardening (chopping and sawing). Address: (h.) Grianaig, Rockfield Road, Oban PA34 5DH; T.-01631 562734.

Matthews, Professor Keith, MBChB, MD, PhD, MRCPsych. Professor of Psychiatry, University of Dundee, since 1997; b. 9.5.62, Kirkcaldy; m., Christine; 1 s.; 1 d. Educ. Beath High School, Cowdenbeath; Aberdeen University; Darwin College, Cambridge University. Lecturer in Mental Health, Aberdeen University; Wellcome Trust Research Fellow, Cambridge University; Professor of Psychiatry and Behavioural Sciences, Wolverhampton University. Address: (b.) Ninewells Medical School, Dundee DD1 9SY; T.-01382 632121.

Matthews, Peter A.H., LLB, WS, NP. Solicitor, since 1977; Senior Partner, A.B. & A. Matthews, since 1997; b. 30.12.54, Dumfries; m., Mary Josephine; 2 d. Educ. Edinburgh Academy; Edinburgh University. Tods Murray & Jamieson, WS, Edinburgh, 1975; Shepherd & Wedderburn, WS, Edinburgh, 1977; A.B. & A. Matthews, since 1979. Dean, Wigtown District Faculty of Solicitors. Recreations: sailing; cycling; hill-walking; scuba-diving. Address: (b.) Bank of Scotland Buildings, Newton Stewart DG8 6EG; T.-01671 404100.

Maver, Professor Thomas Watt, BSc (Hons), PhD, FInstE, FRSA, HonFRIAS. Professor of Computer Aided Design, Department of Architecture and Building Science, and Director of the Graduate School, Strathclyde University, since 1982 (Head of Department, 1983-85, 1988-91, Vice-Dean, Faculty of Engineering, since 1993); b. 10.3.38, Glasgow; m., Avril Elizabeth Cuthbertson; 2 d. Educ. Eastwood Secondary School; Glasgow University. Special Research Fellow, Engineering Faculty, Glasgow University, 1961-67; Strathclyde University: Research Fellow, School of Architecture, 1967-70, Director, Architecture and Building Aids Computer Unit, Strathclyde, since 1970; Visiting Professor: Technical University

Eindhoven, Universiti Sains Malaysia, University of Rome (La Sapienza); Past Chairman, Design Research Society; Royal Society Esso Gold Medal, 1989; Founder, CAAD Futures and ECAADE. Recreation: experiencing Europe. Address: (h.) 8 Kew Terrace, Glasgow G12 0TD; T.-0141-339 7185.

Mavor, Professor John, BSc, PhD, DSc(Eng), Hon. DSc (Greenwich), Hon. DSc (City), FRSE, FEng, FIEEE, CEng, FIEE, CPhys, FInstP. Principal and Vice-Chancellor, Napier University, since 1994; b. 18.7.42, Kilwinning; m., Susan Christina; 2 d. Educ. Bromley Technical High School; City University; London University. AEI Research Laboratories, London, 1964-65; Texas Instruments Ltd., Bedford, 1968-70; Emihus Microcomponents Ltd., Glenrothes, 1970-71; Edinburgh University: joined 1971, first holder, Lothian Chair of Microelectronics, 1980-86, Head, Department of Electrical Engineering, 1984-89, Chairman, School of Engineering, 1987-89, Dean, Faculty of Science & Engineering, 1989-94, Chair of Electrical Enginering, 1986-94. Recreations: steam railways; hill-walking. Address: (b.) Napier University, Craiglockhart Campus, 219 Colinton Road, Edinburgh EH14 1DJ; T.-0131-455 4600.

Mavor, Ronald Henry Moray, CBE, MB, ChB, FRCP(Glas); b. 13.5.25, Glasgow; m., Sigrid Bruhn (m. diss.); 1 s.; 1 d.; 1 d. deceased. Educ. Glasgow University. In medical practice, 1948-57; Drama Critic, The Scotsman, 1957-65; Director, Scottish Arts Council, 1965-71; Professor and Head, Department of Drama, University of Saskatchewan, 1977-90; Deputy Chairman, Edinburgh Festival, 1975-81. Author of plays: The Keys of Paradise, Aurelie, Muir of Huntershill, The Partridge Dance, A Private Matter, The Quartet, A House on Temperance, The Grand Inquisitor; also Dr Mavor and Mr Bridie (biography). Address: (h.) 19 Falkland Street, Glasgow G12 9PY; T.-0141-339 3149.

Maxton, John Alston. BA (Oxon), DipEd (Oxon). MP (Labour), Glasgow Cathcart, since 1979; b. 5.5.36, Oxford; m., Christine Elspeth; 3 s. Educ. Lord Williams Grammar School, Thame; University College, Oxford. Lecturer in Social Studies, Hamilton College of Education, before entering Parliament; Chairman, Association of Lecturers in Colleges of Education in Scotland, 1974-78; Member, Scottish Select Committee, 1980-83, Public Accounts Committee, 1983-84; Opposition Treasury and Scottish Whip, 1984-85; Opposition Scottish Front Bench Spokesperson on Health, Local Government and Transport, 1985-87, on Industry and Local Government Finance, 1987-92; Member: National Heritage Select Committee, Speaker's Panel of Chairmen. Recreations: listening to jazz (Director, Glasgow International Jazz Festival); running. Address: (h.) 37 Larch Grove, Hamilton ML3 8NF; T.-01698 458473.

Maxwell, Donald, MA. Professional Singer; b. 12.12.48, Perth; m., Alison Jayne Norman; 1 d. Educ. Perth Academy; Edinburgh University. Former Teacher of Geography; since 1976, professional Singer with British opera companies and orchestras; Principal Baritone, Scottish Opera, 1978-82; Principal Baritone, Welsh National Opera, 1982-85; guest appearances, BBC Proms, Edinburgh Festival, Royal Opera House, London, Vienna, Paris, Milan, Tokyo, New York, Buenos Aires – notably as Falstaff; comedy – The Music Box with Linda Ormiston. Recreation: railways. Address: (b.) c/o 39 Colinhill Road, Strathaven, Lanarkshire.

Maxwell, Gordon Stirling, MA, FSA, FSA Scot, FRSE. Archaeologist and Author; b. 21.3.38, Edinburgh; m., Kathleen Mary King; 2 d. Educ. Daniel Stewart's College, Edinburgh; St. Andrews University. Investigator (Archaeological), Royal Commission on the Ancient and Historical Monuments of Scotland, 1964-86; Head of Field Survey, RCAHMS, 1986-91, Head of Archaeology, 1991-95; President, Society of Antiquaries of Scotland, 1993-96; Hon. Professor, School of History, University of St. Andrews, since 1997. Publications: Rome's North-West Frontier: The Antonine Wall (Co-author), 1983; The Impact of Aerial Reconnaissance on Archaeology (Editor), 1983; The Romans in Scotland, 1989; A Battle Lost: Romans and Caledonians at Mons Graupius, 1990; A Gathering of Eagles, 1998; The Cleaven Dyke, 1998. Recreations: archaeology; gardening; aviation; Scottish literature. Address: (h.) Micklegarth, 72A High Street, Aberdour, Fife KY3 0SW; T.-01383 860796.

Maxwell, Ingval, DA, RIBA, FRIAS, FSA Scot. Director, Technical Conservation Research and Education, Historic Scotland, since 1993; b. 28.5.44, Penpont; m., Susan Isabel Maclean; 1 s.; 1 d. Educ. Dumfries Academy; Duncan of Jordanstone College of Art, Dundee. Joined Ministry of Public Buildings and Works as Architect, 1969; Area Architect, then Principal Architect, Ancient Monuments Branch, 1972-85; Assistant Director of Works, Historic Scotland, 1985-93; RIBA Research Award, 1970-71; RIAS Thomas Ross Award, 1988; Chairman, Scottish Vernacular Buildings Working Group, 1990-94; Chairman: Scottish Conservation Forum in Training and Education, since 1994, Scottish Stone Liaison Group, since 1997; Member, RIAS Conservation Working Group; Member, European Commission Cost Action C5, since 1996. Publications: Historic Scotland International Lime Conference Proceedings (Co-Editor), 1995; Building Materials of the Scottish Farmstead, 1996; Historic Scotland Traditional Building Materials Conference Proceedings (Co-Editor), 1997. Recreations: photography; astronomy; aircraft; buildings. Address: (h.) 135 Mayfield Road, Edinburgh EH9 3AN.

Maxwell, (Thomas) Fordyce, MBE. Diary Editor, Columnist, Agricultural Editor, The Scotsman, since 1989; b. 21.8.45, Northumberland; m., Liz (Elizabeth Duncan); 1 s.; 1 d. Educ. Berwick Grammar School; Harper Adams Agricultural College. Farming News, 1967-69; The Scotsman: Assistant Agricultural Editor, 1969-75, Agricultural Editor, 1975-77; farming/freelance, 1977-89; rejoined The Scotsman, 1989. Seaton Award, 1992; author of three books. Recreations: family; gardening; reading. Address: (b.) 20 North Bridge, Edinburgh; T.-0131-243 3323.

Maxwell, Professor Thomas Jefferson, OBE, BSc, PhD, CBiol, FIBiol, FRSE, FRSGS. Director, Macaulay Land Use Research Institute, since 1987 and Chief Executive, Macaulay Research and Consultancy Services, since 1994; Honorary Research Professor, Aberdeen University; b. 7.10.40, Aspatria, Cumbria; m., Christine Patrick Speedie; 1 s.; 1 d. Educ. Silcoates School, Wakefield; Edinburgh University. Specialist Animal Production Adviser, East of Scotland College of Agriculture, 1967-70; Research Scientist, then Head, Animal Production Department, Hill Farming Research Organisation, 1970-87. Recreations: reading; hill-walking; gardening. Address: (b.) Macaulay Land Use Research Institute, Craigiebuckler, Aberdeen.

Maxwell-Irving, Alastair Michael Tivey, BSc, CEng, MIEE, MIMgt, FSAScot. Antiquarian and Archaeologist; b. 1.10.35, Witham, Essex; m., Esther Mary Hamilton, MA, LLB. Educ. Lancing College; London University; Stirling University. General Electric Company, 1957; English Electric Company, 1960; Assistant Factor, Annandale Estates, 1966; Weir Pumps Ltd., 1970-91; founder Member and Secretary, 1975-78, Central Scotland Branch, British Institute of Management. Publications: Genealogy of the Irvings of Dumfries, 1965; The Irvings of Bonshaw, 1968; The Irvings of Dumfries, 1968; Lochwood Castle, 1968; Early Firearms and their Influence on the Military and Domestic Architecture of the Borders, 1974; Cramalt Tower: Historical Survey and Excavations, 1977-79, 1982;

Borthwick Castle: Excavations 1979, 1982; Andrew Dunlop (Clockmakers' Company 1701-32), 1984; Hoddom Castle: A Reappraisal of its Architecture and Place in History, 1989; Lochwood Castle, 1990; The Castles of Buittle, 1991; Lockerbie Tower, 1992; Torthorwald Castle, 1993; Scottish Yetts and Window Grilles, 1994; The Tower-Houses of Kirtleside, 1997; Kenmure Castle, 1997. Recreations: architecture and history of the Border towers of Scotland; archaeology; family history and genealogy; Florence and the art and architecture of Tuscany; horology; heraldry; photography; gardening. Address: (h.) Telford House, Blairlogie, Stirling FK9 5PX.

Maxwell-Scott, Dame Jean (Mary Monica), DCVO (1984). Lady in Waiting to Princess Alice, Duchess of Gloucester, since 1959; b. 8.6.23. VAD Red Cross Nurse, 1941-46; great-great-great grand-daughter of Sir Walter Scott. Address: (h.) Abbotsford, Melrose, Roxburghshire TD6 9BQ.

May, David Jeans, MA (Hons). Rector, Craigie High School, Dundee, since 1990; b. 28.12.45, Aberdeen; m., Anne Elizabeth Raeside Eastop; 1 s.; 1 d. Educ. Robert Gordon's College, Aberdeen; Aberdeen University; Jordanhill College of Education. Teacher, St. Columba's, Gourock, 1973-74; Assistant Principal Teacher of Social Subjects, Castlehead High, Paisley, 1974-78; Principal Teacher of Modern Studies/Economics, Grange Secondary, Glasgow, 1978-84; Assistant Head Teacher, Dunoon Grammar School, 1984-87; Deputy Rector, Montrose Academy, 1987-90. Convener, SEB Modern Studies Panel; Member: Secretary of State for Scotland's Working Group on Environmental Education, Steering Committee, Scottish Office Education and Industry Department Improving School Effectiveness Project. Recreations: hill-walking; golf; gardening. Address: (h.) Evanston, Lamondfauld Lane, Hillside, Montrose DD10 9HY; T.-0167 4830673.

May, Douglas James, LLB. Queen's Counsel, since 1989; b. 7.5.46, Edinburgh. Educ. George Heriot's; Edinburgh University. Advocate, 1971; Temporary Sheriff, since 1990; Social Security Commissioner, Child Support Commissioner, since 1993; Parliamentary candidate (Conservative), Edinburgh East, 1974, Glasgow Cathcart, 1983. Recreations: golf (Captain: Scotland Universities Golfing Society, 1990-91, Merchants of Edinburgh Golf Club, 1997); photography (ARPS, 1997, President, Edinburgh Photographic Society); travel. Address: 23 Melville Street, Edinburgh; T.-0131-225 2201.

May, Malcolm Stuart, BA, BD, STM, CQSW. Chief Officer, Dundee Voluntary Action, since 1979; b. 9.9.40, Isle of Shapinsay, Orkney; m., Alison Wood; 1 s.; 1 d. Educ. Kilmarnock Academy; The Gordon Schools, Huntly; Hamilton Academy; Queen's University, Belfast; Glasgow University; Union Theological Seminary, New York. Assistant Minister, The Old Kirk, West Pilton, Edinburgh, 1966-68; staff, Iona Community, Glasgow, 1968-72; social work training, 1972-73; Training Officer, Scottish Council for Voluntary Organisations, 1973-78. Member, Board of Management, Dundee College; Non-Executive Director, Tayside Health Board, 1994-98. Recreations: reading; choral singing; hill-walking. Address: (b.) Kandahar House, 71 Meadowside, Dundee DD1 1EN.

Meek, Brian Alexander, OBE, JP. Columnist, The Herald; Chairman, Conservative Group, City of Edinburgh Council, since 1995; b. 8.2.39, Edinburgh; m., Frances C. Horsburgh; 1 s.; 1 d. Educ. Royal High School, Edinburgh; Edinburgh Secretarial College. Joined Scotsman Publications as trainee, then Sub-Editor, Features Writer; transferred to Express Newspapers as Feature Writer, Leader Writer and Rugby Correspondent; elected, Edinburgh Corporation, 1969; Leader, Conservative Group, 1970-72; elected as Bailie, 1972; Convener, Lothian Regional Council, 1982-86; Member, Edinburgh District Council, 1992-96; Vice-President, Scottish Conservative and Unionist Association, 1989-92. Address: (b.) City of Edinburgh Council, City Chambers, High Street, Edinburgh EH1 1YJ; T.-0131-529 4953.

Meek, David, MA, MEd. Rector, Queen Anne High School, Dunfermline, since 1997; b. 20.7.54, Bonnybridge; m., Sheena Flora Meek; 2 s. Educ. Falkirk High School; Glasgow University. Teacher, Renfrew High School; Assistant Principal Teacher, Vale of Leven Academy; Principal Teacher of English, then Assistant Head Teacher, Boclair Academy; Inspector, Quality Assurance Unit, Strathclyde; Rector, Portree High School. Address: (b.) Broomhead, Dunfermline, Fife KY12 0PQ.

Meek, Professor Donald Eachann MacDonald, MA (Cantab), MA, PhD (Glas), FRHistS. Professor of Celtic, Aberdeen University, since 1993; b. 16.5.49, Glasgow, brought up in Tiree; m., Rachel Jane Rogers; 2 d. Educ. Oban High School; Glasgow University; Emmanuel College, Cambridge. Lecturer, Senior Lecturer and Reader in Celtic, Edinburgh University, 1979-92. Assistant Editor, Historical Dictionary of Scottish Gaelic, Glasgow University, 1973-79; Honorary Secretary, Gaelic Society of Glasgow, 1974-79; Member, Gaelic Advisory Committee to Broadcasting Council for Scotland, 1976-78 and of Gaelic Panel, National Bible Society of Scotland, since 1978; President, Edinburgh and Lothians Baptist Association, 1992-93; Clerk and Treasurer, Board of Celtic Studies (Scotland), since 1994; Editor, Gaelic Bible, 1992 edition and later revisions; a General Editor, Dictionary of Scottish Church History and Theology, 1993; Vice-President, Scottish Church History Society; lay preacher. Publications: books include Mairi Mhor nan Oran, 1977, second edition 1998; The Campbell Collection of Gaelic Proverbs and Proverbial Sayings, 1978; Island Harvest: A History of Tiree Baptist Church, 1988; Sunshine and Shadow: the story of the Baptists of Mull, 1991; A Mind for Mission: essays (Editor), 1992; Tuath is Tighearna: Poetry of the Clearances and the Land Agitation (Editor), 1995; numerous articles on Gaelic and Highland themes. Recreations: family activities; getting to know the Highlands. Address: (h.) 50 Dunecht Road, Westhill, Aberdeenshire AB32 6RH; T.-01224 742668.

Mehta, Phiroze Sorabji, BSc (Hons), BSc(Eng), MSc, CEng, MIMechE, FIDiagE, FRSA. Senior Lecturer in CAD, Glasgow Caledonian University, since 1986; b. 9.10.44, Bombay; m., Margaret Jane Bowie; 2 s.; 1 d. Whessoe Ltd.: Design Engineer, 1970-75, Senior Design Engineer, 1975-78; Senior Design Engineer, Nuclear Design Department, Babcock Power Ltd., 1978-84; Senior Lecturer in Engineering Design, University of Central England, Birmingham, 1984-86. Member, Organising Committee and University Representative Member, Conference on Education and Training in Finite Element Analysis; SQA External Verifier; Institution of Mechanical Engineers: Member, Professional Interview Panel, Treasurer, Glasgow Panel, Academic Liaison Officer; Academic Liaison Officer, Institution of Mechanical Incorporated Engineers; Board Member, Scottish Qualifications Authority; Member, National Qualifications Committee; Director, SPTC; Secretary, Bearsden Academy PTA; Open University Tutor. Recreations: theatre; concerts; music. Address: (h.) 8 Dumgoyne Drive, Bearsden, Glasgow G61 3AP; (b.) Department of Engineering, Glasgow Caledonian University, Glasgow G4 0BA.

Meldrum, Angus Alexander, BSc, DIA. Managing Director, Tennent Caledonian Breweries Ltd., since 1992; Director, Bass Ireland Ltd., since 1981; Director, Maclay's Brewery & Co. Ltd., since 1992; Managing Director, J.G. Thomson Ltd. (Wines and Spirits Merchants), since 1981; Director, Tennents Ireland Ltd. (Dublin), since 1981; Director, Bass Export Ltd., 1990-94; b. 7.11.45, Stornoway; m., Anne-Marie; 1 s. Educ. Kingussie School; Edinburgh

University; Bath University Management School. Joined Bass plc, London, 1971; Tennent Caledonian Breweries Ltd., 1978; Brands Marketing Director, Bass Brewers Ltd., Burton-on-Trent, 1990-92. President, Brewers Association of Scotland, 1992-94; Council Member, UK Brewers Society, 1992-94. Recreations: fishing; shooting; sport. Address: (b.) Wellpark Brewery, 161 Duke Street, Glasgow G31 1JD; T.-0141-552 6552.

Meldrum, James, MA. Registrar General for Scotland, since 1994; b. 9.8.52, Kirkintilloch. Educ. Lenzie Academy; Glasgow University. Administration Trainee/HEO (Admin), Scottish Office, 1973-79; Principal grade posts, Scottish Economic Planning Department, Scottish Development Department, Scottish Office Personnel Division, 1979-86; Deputy Director, Scottish Courts Administration, 1986-91; Head, Investment Assistance Division, Scottish Office Industry Department, 1991-94. Address: (b.) New Register House, Edinburgh EH1 3YT; T.-0131-334 0380.

Mellows, Susan Mary, BSc, PhD, DIC. Academic Registrar, Strathclyde University, since 1993; b. 20.1.44, Brackley, Northants. Educ. Brackley High School; Edinburgh University; Imperial College, London. Kodak Ltd., 1966-67; Science and Engineering Research Council, London, 1970-85; YARD Ltd., Glasgow, 1985-90 (Manager, System Dynamics and Underwater Engineering Group); joined Strathclyde University, 1990, as Deputy Registrar. Recreations: hill-walking; other outdoor activities; books; music. Address: (b.) John Anderson Campus, Strathclyde University, Glasgow G1 1XG; T.-0141-552 4400, Ext. 2002.

Melville, Ian Dunlop, MB, ChB, FRCPGlas, FRCPLond. Consultant Neurologist, Institute of Neurological Sciences, Glasgow, 1965-88; Honorary Clinical Lecturer, Glasgow University, 1968-88; b. 9.11.27, Glasgow; m., Eliza Duffus; 1 s.; 3 d. Educ. Shawlands Academy; Glasgow University. RAF Medical Branch; Medical Registrar, Glasgow Royal Infirmary; Academic Registrar, National Hospital for Nervous Diseases, London; Clinical Research Fellow, Medical Research Council, London; Senior Medical Registrar, Glasgow. Artist Member, Committee, Paisley Art Institute; Editor, Bulletin of Royal College of Physicians and Surgeons, Glasgow. Recreations: golf; photography; watercolour painting. Address: (h.) 9 Mirrlees Drive, Glasgow G12 OSH; T.-0141-339 7085.

Mennie, Alastair Douglas, LLB, PhD, FSA Scot. Academic and practising lawyer; b. 2.10.57, Aberdeen. Educ. Aberdeen University; Edinburgh University. Advocate, since 1982; Part-time Lecturer in Law, 1987-92; Professor of Law, ESADE Business School, Barcelona, 1992-94; Professor of Law, Abat Oliba University Centre, Barcelona, since 1994; Visiting Professor: Toulouse University, 1994, Aarhus University, 1996-97, Belgrano University, Buenos Aires, 1997; Guest Lecturer at various universities including Universities of Paris II, Bologna and Asuncion; Visiting Scholar, Cornell Law School, 1997; Director of Studies, Hague Academy of International Law, 1997. Publications: Domicile Flowcharts, 1991; numerous articles in British and foreign law journals. Recreations: visiting prehistoric sites; viewing modern art exhibitions. Address: (h.) 25 Panmure Place, Edinburgh EH3 9HP; T.-0131-229 5604.

Mennie, William Patrick, BL, NP, IAC. Partner, Grigor & Young, Solicitors, Elgin and Buckie, since 1964 (Senior Partner, since 1984); b. 11.10.37, Elgin; m., Patricia Leslie Bogie; 2 s.; 1 d. Educ. Elgin Academy; Edinburgh University. Solicitor, 1960; Honorary Sheriff at Elgin, since 1993; accredited by Law Society of Scotland as a specialist in agricultural law; Secretary, Malt Distillers Association of Scotland. Recreation: game shooting. Address: (h.) Innesmill, Urquhart, Elgin; T.-01343 842643.

Menzies, Duncan A.Y., QC, MA (Oxon), LLB. Queen's Counsel, since 1991; b. 28.8.53, Edinburgh; m., Hilary Weston; 2 s. Educ. Edinburgh Academy; Cargilfield; Glenalmond; Wadham College, Oxford; Edinburgh University. Advocate, 1978; Standing Junior Counsel to The Admiralty, 1984-91; accredited mediator, 1992; Temporary Sheriff, 1996-97; Advocate Depute, since 1998; Chairman, Scottish Planning, Local Government and Environmental Bar Group, 1997. Parliamentary Candidate, Midlothian, 1983, Edinburgh Leith, 1987; founder, Scottish Wine Society, 1976. Recreations: shooting; golf; wines. Address: (h.) Leaston House, Humbie, East Lothian; T.-01875 833219.

Menzies, George Macbeth, BA, LLB. Consultant Partner, Turcan Connell Solicitors, since 1997; formerly with Burness Solicitors; b. 18.4.43, Edinburgh; m., Patricia Mary; 1 s.; 2 d. Educ. Edinburgh Academy; Corpus Christi College, Oxford; Edinburgh University. Past Chairman, North British Steel Group (Holdings) PLC; Non-Executive Director, Cairn Petroleum Oil & Gas Ltd., 1986-88; Chairman, Fruitmarket Gallery, 1984-88; President, Edinburgh Academical Football Club, 1990-92; Chairman, Endeavour Training (Scotland) Ltd., 1983-97; Director, Scottish Council (Development and Industry), since 1990; Director, Greencastle Farming Plc, since 1995. Recreations: walking; contemporary arts; rugby. Address: (b.) Saltire Court, 20 Castle Terrace, Edinburgh EH1 2EF.

Menzies, Gordon, MA (Hons), DipEd. Independent Producer (retired Head of Educational Broadcasting, BBC Scotland); b. 30.7.27, Logierait, Perthshire; m., Charlotte; 2 s.; 1 d. Educ. Breadalbane Academy, Aberfeldy; Edinburgh University. Producer/Director, Who Are the Scots?, 1971, The Chiel Amang Us, 1974, Ballad Folk, 1975, History Is My Witness, 1976, Play Golf with Peter Alliss, 1977, Scotch and Wry, 1978-79, Two Views of Burns, 1979, Barbara Dickson in Concert, 1981-84-86, The World of Golf, 1982, The Celts, 1987, Play Better Golf with Peter Alliss, 1989, Scotch and Wry Hogmanay, 1980-91; Editor, The Afternoon Show, 1981-85; Play Snooker with Dennis Taylor, 1990; Play Bridge with Zia, 1991. Publications: Who Are the Scots?, 1971; The Scottish Nation, 1972; History Is My Witness, 1976; Play Golf, 1977; The World of Golf, 1982; Scotch and Wry, 1986; Double Scotch and Wry, 1988; Play Better Golf, 1989. Recreations: golf; snooker; curling; theatre. Address: (h.) 8 Ingleside, Lenzie, Glasgow G66 4HN.

Menzies, John Maxwell. Life President, John Menzies PLC (Chairman, 1952-97); b. 13.10.26; m., Patricia Eleanor Dawson; 4 d. Educ. Eton. Lt., Grenadier Guards; Member, Berwickshire County Council, 1954-57; Director: Scottish American Mortgage Co., 1959-63, Standard Life Assurance Co., 1960-63, Vidal Sassoon Inc., 1969-80, Gordon & Gotch plc, 1970-85, Atlantic Assets Trust, 1973-88, Ivory and Sime Enterprise Capital PLC (formerly Independent Investment Co. plc), 1973-96 (Chairman, 1983-96), Fairhaven International, 1980-88, Rocky Mountains Oil & Gas, 1980-85, Ivory & Sime plc, 1980-83, Personal Assets PLC, 1981-92, Bank of Scotland, 1984-94, Guardian Royal Exchange, 1985-96, Malcolm Innes & Partners Ltd., since 1989. Life Vice President, NewstrAid Benevolent Institution (Trustee, 1974-95, President, 1968-74, Newsvendors' Benevolent Institution); Member: Royal Company of Archers, Queen's Bodyguard for Scotland, Board of Trustees, National Library of Scotland, since 1991. Recreations: farming; shooting; reading; travel. Address: (b.) 108 Princes Street, Edinburgh EH2 3AA; T.-0131-225 8555.

Menzies, Neil Graham Finlay, BSc, FRSA. Corporate Adviser; Scottish Adviser to Chemical Industries Association; b. 14.10.41, Meiklour; m., Lorna; 2 d. Educ. Lower School of John Lyon, Harrow; St. Andrews University. Voluntary Service Overseas, Nigeria, 1964-66;

ICI, 1966-93, lately Scottish Affairs Adviser; Deputy Chairman, Scottish Water and Sewerage Customers Council; Member, Executive, Scottish Council Development and Industry; Director, Royal Lyceum Theatre Company; Member, Investors in People Recognition Panel for Scotland; Lay Member, Scottish Office, Education Department, HM Inspectorate; Non-Executive Director, Scottish Ambulance Service. Address: (h.) 13 Northumberland Street, Edinburgh EH3 6LL; T.-0131-557 4321.

Mercer, John, MA, DipEd. Headmaster, Belmont House School, since 1972; b. 11.8.40, Glasgow; m., Eileen Margaret; 2 s.; 1 d. Educ. Eastwood Senior Secondary School; Glasgow University; Jordanhill College of Education. Teacher of English/History, Mossvale Secondary School, Paisley, 1962-66; Head Teacher of English, Belmont House School, 1966-72. Elder and Session Clerk, Mearns Parish Kirk; President, Eastwood Rotary Club, 1986-87. Recreations: golf; skiing; walking; reading; palaeontology. Address: (b.) Belmont House School, Newton Mearns, Glasgow G77 5DU; T.-0141-639 2922.

Mercer, Roger James, MA, FSA, FRSE, FSA Scot, MIFA. Secretary, Royal Commission for the Ancient and Historical Monuments (Scotland); b. 12.9.44, Hertfordshire; m., Susan; 1 s.; 1 d. Educ. Harrow County Grammar School; Edinburgh University. Inspector of Ancient Monuments, AM Division, Department of the Environment, London, 1969-74; Lecturer and Reader, Department of Archaeology, Edinburgh University, 1974-89. Treasurer, Society of Antiquaries of Scotland, 1977-87; Vice President: Society of Antiquaries of Scotland, 1988-91, Prehistoric Society, 1987-91, Council for British Archaeology, 1991-94. Recreations: music; reading; learning. Address: (b.) RCAHMS, John Sinclair House, 16 Bernard Terrace, Edinburgh EH8 9NX.

Merchant, Bruce Alastair, OBE, LLB. Solicitor; Partner, South, Forrest, Mackintosh & Merchant, Inverness, since 1971; Deputy Chairman, Accounts Commission for Scotland; b. 17.5.45, Edinburgh; m., Joan Isobel Sinclair Hamilton; 1 s.; 2 d. Educ. Inverness Royal Academy; Aberdeen University. Council Member, Law Society of Scotland, 1982-88 (Convener, Guarantee Fund Committee, 1984-87, Convener, Finance Committee, 1987-88); Member: Highland Health Board, 1981-91, Board of Management for Inverness Hospitals, 1971-74, Inverness Local Health Council, 1975-81; Dean, Faculty of Solicitors of the Highlands, 1994-96. Address: (h.) 3 Crown Circus, Inverness; T.-01463 239980.

Merrylees, Andrew, BArch, DipTP, RSA, RIBA, FRIAS, FCSD, FRSA. Honorary Professor of Architecture, University of Dundee, since 1998; Consultant, Merrylees and Robertson, since 1997; b. 13.10.33, Newmains; m., Maie Crawford; 2 s.; 1 d. Educ. Wishaw High School; University of Strathclyde. Sir Basil Spence, Glover and Ferguson: joined 1957, Associate, 1968, Partner, 1972; set up Andrew Merrylees Associates (now Merrylees and Robertson), 1985. Member: Advisory Council for the Arts in Scotland; Visiting Tutor: Strathclyde University, Dundee University. RIBA Bronze Medal; Saltire Award; Civic Trust Award; Art in Architecture Award; RSA Gold Medal; SCONUL Award. Recreations: architecture; painting; cooking. Address: (b.) Quadrant, 17 Bernard Street, Edinburgh EH6 6PW; T.-0131-555 0688.

Meston, Professor Michael Charles, MA, LLB, JD. Professor of Scots Law, Aberdeen University, 1971-96; b. 13.12.32, Aberdeen; m., Dorothea Munro; 2 s. Educ. Robert Gordon's College, Aberdeen; Aberdeen University; Chicago University. Lecturer in Private Law, Glasgow University, 1959-64; Aberdeen University: Senior Lecturer in Comparative Law, 1964-68, Professor of Jurisprudence, 1968-71; Dean, Faculty of Law, 1970-73 and 1988-91; Honorary Sheriff, Grampian Highland and Islands, since 1972; Temporary Sheriff, since 1993; Vice Principal, Aberdeen University, 1979-82; Trustee, National Museum of Antiquities of Scotland, 1982-85; Governor, Robert Gordon's College, Aberdeen, until 1997; Member, Grampian Health Board, 1985-91; Non-Executive Director, Aberdeen Royal Hospitals NHS Trust, 1992-97. Publications: The Succession (Scotland) Act 1964; The Matrimonial Homes (Family Protection) (Scotland) Act 1981; The Scottish Legal Tradition, 1991. Recreations: golf; photography. Address: (h.) 4 Hamilton Place, Aberdeen AB15 4BH; T.-Aberdeen 641554.

Metcalfe, Professor Ian Saxley, BSc (Eng), MA, PhD, ACGI, MIChemE, CEng, MRSC, CChem. Professor of Chemical Engineering, University of Edinburgh, since 1997; b. 7.8.61, Stockton. Educ. Grange School, Stockton-on-Tees; Imperial College; Princeton University. Imperial College, Department of Chemical Engineering: Lecturer, 1987-96, Senior Lecturer, 1996-97. Royal Scholarship, Imperial College, 1979; Hinchley Medal, Institution of Chemical Engineers, 1982; Esso Education Award, 1989; ICI Fellowship, 1993; Imperial College Award for Excellence in Teaching, 1996. Publication: Chemical Reaction Engineering: A First Course, 1997. Address: (b.) Department of Chemical Engineering, University of Edinburgh, Edinburgh EH9 7LJ; T.-0131-650 8553.

Michels, David Michael Charles, FHCIMA. Chief Executive, Stakis plc, since 1991; b. 8.12.46, London; m., Michele; 1 s.; 1 d. Educ. Hendon College. Sales and Marketing Manager: Grand Metropolitan Hotels, Ladbroke Leisure; Managing Director: Ladbroke Leisure, Ladbroke Hotels; Executive Vice President, Hilton International; Non Executive Director: Aberforth, Split Level Trust PLC. DLitt, Caledonian. Address: (b.) 3 Atlantic Quay, York Street, Glasgow G2 8JH; T.-0141-204 4321.

Michie, Professor David Alan Redpath, OBE, RSA, RGI, RWA, DA, FRSA. Professor, Heriot Watt University, 1988-90; Head, School of Drawing and Painting, Edinburgh College of Art, 1982-90; b. 30.11.28, St. Raphael, France; m., Eileen Anderson Michie; 2 d. Educ. Hawick High School; Edinburgh College of Art. Travelling Scholarship, Italy, 1954-55; Lecturer, Grays School of Art, Aberdeen, 1957-61; Lecturer, Edinburgh College of Art, 1961 (Vice Principal, 1974-77). President, Society of Scottish Artists, 1961-63; Member: General Teaching Council for Scotland, 1975-80, Court, Heriot-Watt University, 1979-82, Council, British School at Rome, 1980-85, Museums and Galleries Commission, 1991-96; Guthrie Award, RSA, 1964; David Cargill Prize, RGI, 1977; Lothian Region Award, 1977; Sir William Gillies Award, 1980; RGI Prize, 1990; Cornelissen Prize, RWA, 1992; one-man exhibitions, Mercury Gallery, London, eight times, 1966-96, Lothian Region Chambers, 1977, The Scottish Gallery, 1980, 1994, 1998, Loomshop Gallery, Lower Largo, 1981, 1987, Mercury Gallery, Edinburgh, 1986; Baarn and Amsterdam, 1991; Visiting Professor, Faculty of Art Studio Department, UCLA, Santa Barbara, 1992. Address: (h.) 17 Gilmour Road, Edinburgh EH16 5NS.

Michie, Donald, MA (Oxon), DPhil (Oxon), DSc (Oxon), Hon. DSc (NCAA), Hon. DSc (Salford), Hon. DUniv (Stirling). Scientific Worker, since 1949; Treasurer, Human-Computer Learning Foundation, since 1995; b. 11.11.23, Rangoon; m., Jean Hayes; 2 s.; 2 d. Educ. Rugby School; Oxford University. War Service, F.O., Bletchley Park, 1942-45; Research Associate, London University, 1952-58; Edinburgh University: Senior Lecturer, Reader, in Surgical Science, 1958-65, Director, Experimental Programming Unit, 1965-67, Professor of Machine Intelligence, 1967-84; Founder and first Director, Turing Institute, Glasgow, 1984-86, Chief Scientist, 1986-92. Pioneer Award, International Embryo Transfer Society (jointly), 1988; Achievement Award, Institution of Electrical Engineers, 1995. Publications: The Creative Computer (Co-author), 1984; Machine Intelligence and Related Topics, 1982; On Machine Intelligence, 1986. Recreation: travel. Address: (h.) 6 Inveralmond Grove, Edinburgh EH4 6RA; T.-0131-336 3826.

Michie, (Janet) Ray. MP (Lib. Dem.), Argyll and Bute, since 1987; b. 4.2.34; m.; 3 d. Educ. Aberdeen High School for Girls; Lansdowne House School, Edinburgh; Edinburgh School of Speech Therapy. Former Area Speech Therapist, Argyll and Clyde Health Board. Address: (b.) House of Commons SW1A 0AA.

Micklem, Professor Henry Spedding, MA, DPhil (Oxon). Freelance Musician and Lecturer; Professor of Immunobiology, Edinburgh University, 1980-92, Emeritus, since 1992; b. 11.10.33, Oxford; m., 1, Lisel Ruth Thomas (deceased); 3 s.; 1 d.; 2, Damaris Manson. Educ. Rugby School; Oriel College, Oxford. Scientific Staff, Medical Research Council; Research Fellow, Institut Pasteur, Paris; Academic Staff, Department of Zoology, Edinburgh University; Visiting Professor, Department of Genetics, Stanford University; Visiting Fellow, Department of Pathology, New York University Medical School. Address: (h.) 1 Dryden Place, Edinburgh, EH9 1RP; T.-0131-667 5618.

Micklem, Rosalind, BA (Hons), PGCE, MPhil. Principal, Cardonald College, since 1997; b. 7.6.56, Surrey. Educ. St. Paul's Girls' School, London; Oxford University; Leicester University; London University. Lecturer, North Oxfordshire Technical College, 1979-84; Education Officer, Northants and Hounslow, 1985-89; Vice Principal, Enfield College, 1989-95; Deputy Principal, Wirral Metropolitan College, 1995-97. Address: (b.) Cardonald College, 690 Mosspark Drive, Glasgow G52 3AY; T.-0141-883 6151.

Middleton, Robert, OBE, JP, Hon. DLitt, HonLLD. Member, Aberdeen City Council, since 1995 (Chair of Finance, since 1997); b. 28.7.32, Aberdeen; m., Audrey Ewen; 2 s. Educ. Aberdeen Grammar School. Started apprenticeship with Post Office Telephones, 1948; Aberdeen Town Council: elected, 1961, appointed Magistrate, 1963, Chairman of Magistrates, 1965-66, Chairman, Education Committee, 1966-69; Chairman, Labour Party in Scotland, 1986-87; contested Banffshire as Labour candidate, 1966; contested Aberdeen South, 1974 (twice) and 1983; elected, Grampian Regional Council, 1975 (Convener, 1990-95); President, North Sea Commission of the Conference of Peripheral Maritime Regions, 1992-95. Publications: North Sea Brose; Grampian Homeland. Recreations: golf; reading; writing not very good poetry; travel; bridge; bowls. Address: (h.) 9 Stronsay Avenue, Aberdeen AB15 6HX; T.-01224 313366.

Midgley, Professor John Morton, OBE, BSc, MSc, PhD, CChem, FRSC, FRPharmS. Professor of Pharmaceutical and Medicinal Chemistry, Strathclyde University, since 1984 (Chairman and Head of Department, 1985-90); b. 14.7.37, York; m., Jean Mary Tillyer; 2 s. Educ. Nunthorpe Grammar School, York; Manchester University; London University. Demonstrator, Manchester University, 1959-61; Assistant Lecturer, School of Pharmacy, London University, 1962-65; Research Associate, Massachusetts Institute of Technology, 1965-66; Lecturer, then Senior Lecturer, School of Pharmacy, London University, 1965-83; Member: Committee on the Review of Medicines, 1984-92, British Pharmacopoeia Commission, since 1985, Committee on the Safety of Medicines, since 1990, European Panal of Experts on Human Medicines, since 1995, Council of Royal Pharmaceutical Society of GB, 1991-92, Science and Engineering Research Council Pharmacy Panel, since 1985; UK Delegation to European Pharmacopoeia Commission, since 1998; Vice-Chairman, Chemistry, Pharmacy and Standards Sub-Committee, CSM, since 1990. Recreations: fly fishing; fisheries management; training labradors; gardening; music. Address: (b.) Strathclyde University, Department of Pharmaceutical Sciences, Royal College, 204 George Street, Glasgow G1 1XW; T.-0141-552 4400, Ext. 2125.

Milburn, Professor George Henry William, PhD, CChem, FRSC, FBIM, Dr (h.c.), FRSA. Head, Department of Applied Chemical and Physical Sciences, Napier University, since 1973; Reseach Adviser/Research Professor, since 1998; b. 25.11.34, Wallasey; m., Jean Muriel; 1 s.; 1 d. Educ. Wallasey Grammar School; Leeds University. Short service commission, Royal Corps of Signals, 1959-63; Staff Demonstrator, Leeds University, 1963-66; Research Fellow, Sydney University, 1967-68; Senior Scientific Officer, Agricultural Research Council, 1968-69; Lecturer, Plymouth Polytechnic, 1969-70; Senior Lecturer, Sheffield Polytechnic, 1970-73.Convener, Committee of Scottish University Heads of Chemistry Departments, 1994-97; Honorary Doctorate, Technical University, Budapest, 1988; Silver Star Laureate, Poland, 1996. Publications: more than 50 scientific publications including a textbook on crystal structure analysis. Recreations: golf; bridge; photography. Address: (h.) 9 Orchard Court, Longniddry, East Lothian; T.-01875 853228.

Mill, Douglas Russell, LLB, BA, MBA, WS, NP. Secretary, Law Society of Scotland, since 1997; b. 3.1.57, Paisley; m., Christine; 2 s.; 1 d. Educ. Paisley Grammar School; Glasgow University. Former Depute Director, Centre for Professional Legal Studies, Strathclyde University; former Partner, MacFarlane Young & Co., Solicitors, Paisley; former Member, Council, Law Society of Scotland. Publication: Successful Practice Management, 1992. Recreations: golf; rugby. Address: (h.) 110 Caiyside, Edinburgh EH10 7HR; T.-0131-445 7483.

Millan, Rt. Hon. Bruce, PC, CA. European Commissioner, 1989-95; b. 5.10.27, Dundee; m., Gwendoline May Fairey; 1 s.; 1 d. Educ. Harris Academy, Dundee. MP, Glasgow Craigton, 1959-83, Glasgow Govan, 1983-88; Parliamentary Secretary for the RAF, 1964-66; Parliamentary Secretary, Scottish Office, 1966-70; Minister of State, Scottish Office, 1974-76; Secretary of State for Scotland, 1976-79; Opposition Spokesman on Scottish Affairs, 1979-83. Address: (h.) 1 Torridon Avenue, Glasgow G41 5LA; T.-0141-427 6483.

Millan, Professor Charles Gordon, MA, PhD, FRSA. Professor of French, Strathclyde University, since 1991; Chairman, Department of Modern Languages, since 1994; Vice-Dean, Faculty of Arts and Social Sciences, since 1995; b. 25.9.46, Kirkcaldy; m., Margaret Anne Robbie; 1 s.; 1 d. Educ. Kirkcaldy High; Merrywood Grammar, Bristol; Edinburgh University. Temporary Lecturer, Edinburgh University, 1970-71; Teacher, Broughton High School, 1972-76; Strathclyde University, since 1976; Director, Languages for Business Unit, since 1990 (Languages for Export Award, 1994). Publications include: Pierre Louÿs ou le Culte de l'Amitié, 1979; Stéphane Mallarmé, Poésies (jointly), 1983; A Throw of the Dice: The Life of Stéphane Mallarmé, 1994. Recreations: cinema; reading. Address: (b.) Livingstone Tower, Richmond Street, Glasgow G1 1XH; T.-0141-552 4400.

Millan, William Robert, LLB, NP. Director of Central Services, Scottish Borders Council, since 1995; Clerk to the JP Advisory Committee, since 1993; Clerk of the Peace (Scottish Borders Commission Area), since 1996; Clerk to the Licensing Board and District Court, since 1996; b. 17.8.52, Glasgow; m., Margaret Hamilton McCulloch; 1 s.; 1 d. Educ. Hillhead High School; Glasgow University. Bannatyne, Kirkwood, France & Co., Writers, Glasgow, 1973-75; Senior Legal Assistant, Cumnock and Doon

Valley District Council, 1975-79; Roxburgh District Council: Depute Director of Administrative and Legal Services, 1979-86, Director of Administrative and Legal Services, 1986-96, Chief Executive, 1993-96. Recreations: reading; DIY; gardening; skiing; badminton; golf; photography. Address: (b.) Council Headquarters, Newtown St. Boswells, Melrose TD6 0SA.

Millar, Professor Alan, MA, PhD. Professor of Philosophy, Stirling University, since 1994; b. 14.12.47, Edinburgh; m., Rose-Mary Marchand; 1 s. Educ. Edinburgh University; Cambridge University. Stirling University: Lecturer in Philosophy, 1971, Senior Lecturer, 1991, Head, Department of Philosophy, 1988-94. Member, Postgraduate Studentship Selection Committee, Student Awards Agency for Scotland; former Convener, Religious Studies Panel, Scottish Universities Council on Entrance; awarded Mind Association Research Fellowship, 1996-97; Visiting Fellow, Clare Hall, Cambridge, 1997. Publications: Reasons and Experience, 1991; articles in the philosophy of mind, epistemology, philosophy of religion, history of ethics. Recreations: reading; walking; films; cooking. Address: (b.) Stirling University, Stirling FK9 4LA; T.-01786 467555.

Millar, Bob, MA, CA. Director of Corporate Development, Miller Homes, since 1997; b. 30.3.50, Edinburgh; m., Sandra; 1 s.; 1 d. Educ. George Heriot's School; Edinburgh University. Chartered Accountant, Touche Ross; Financial Accountant, Bredero UK Ltd., Castle Rock Housing Association; Head of Registration, Housing Corporation; Director of Strategy, Scottish Homes. Address: (b.) Miller House, 18 South Groathill Avenue, Edinburgh EH4 2LW.

Millar, Douglas Andrew Terris. Deputy Director, Scottish Chambers of Commerce, since 1997; Non-Executive Director, Scottish Television (Regional) Ltd., since 1998; b. 18.6.55, Dunfermline. Educ. Queen Anne High School, Dunfermline; Aberdeen College of Commerce. Civil Servant, Scottish Office, 1972-97, latterly Head of Film, Broadcasting and Gaelic Policy Branch, Education and Industry Department. Elder, Dunfermline Abbey. Recreations: youth work; football. Address: (b.) Conference House, The Exchange, 152 Morrison Street, Edinburgh EH3 8EB; T.-0131-477 8025.

Millar, Graeme Stewart, BSc (Hons), MRPharmS. Chairman, Common Services Agency, National Health Service in Scotland, since 1998; Chairman, Royal Pharmaceutical Society in Scotland, since 1998; Chairman, Southern Scotland Electricity Consumers' Committee, since 1996; b. 20.2.55, Edinburgh; m., Fay; 3 s. Educ. Boroughmuir Senior Secondary School, Edinburgh; Heriot-Watt University. Director, Graeme Millar Chemist's Ltd., 1979-94; Member, Lothian Health Board, 1984-93; Chairman: Scottish Pharmaceutical General Council, 1988-94, Edinburgh Sick Children's NHS Trust, 1993-99, Scottish NHS Trust Chairman's Group, 1996-98; Secretary, Lothian NHS Endowment Investment Advisory Committee; Director, Scottish Community Foundation; Court Member, Merchant Company of Edinburgh; Member, Governing Council, Erskine Stewart's Melville. Recreations: golf; rugby. Address: 2 Campbell Avenue, Edinburgh EH12 6DS; T.-0131-337 0608.

Millar, Helen Jean, MA, FRSA. Chairman, Rail Users Consultative Committee for Scotland; Deputy Lieutenant, City of Glasgow; Member, Glasgow Local Health Council; Member, Multi Centre Research Ethics Committee for Scotland; Vice Chairman, Consumer Congress; Member, UK Central Council for Nurses; b. 10.10.31, Glasgow; 3 s.; 2 d. Educ. Craigholme School, Glasgow; Glasgow University. Chairman, Consumers in European Community Group, 1988-91; Chairman, Consumer's Committee for Scotland, 1980-89; Member and Vice-Chairman, Scottish Consumer Council, 1979-87; Chairman, Strathclyde Children's Panel, 1979-81; Member, Advisory Committee on Novel Foods, 1991-98; Member, Air Users Council, 1991-98; Vice-Chairman, New Glasgow Society, 1980-87; former Lecturer in charge, Children's Panel Training, Glasgow University; Founder Member, Board, Tron Theatre Club, Glasgow. Recreations: theatre; arts in general; Glasgow; arguing. Address: (h.) 33 Aytoun Road, Glasgow G41; T.-0141-423 4152.

Millar, Henry Rankin, MB, ChB, BMedBiol (Hons), FRCPsych. Consultant Psychiatrist, Royal Cornhill Hospital, Aberdeen, since 1991; b. 23.4.47, Aberdeen; m., Frances Morgan; 3 d. Educ. Aberdeen Grammar School; Aberdeen University. House Officer, Aberdeen Royal Infirmary, 1972-73; Junior Fellow in Community Medicine and Honorary Senior House Officer in Medicine, Aberdeen University and Aberdeen Royal Infirmary, 1973-74; Senior House Officer/Registrar in Psychiatry, Royal Edinburgh Hospital, 1975-77; Senior Registrar and Lecturer, Dundee Psychiatric Services and Dundee University, 1977-80; Consultant Psychiatrist, Southern General Hospital, Glasgow, 1980-91. Recreation: walking. Address: (h.) Failte, Quarryhill, Mid Auguston, Peterculter, Aberdeen AB14 0PP.

Millar, Professor Keith, BA, PhD, CPsychol, FBPsS. Professor of Behavioural Science, Medical Faculty, Glasgow University, since 1988; b. 27.6.50, Dundee; m., Dr. Margaret Elspeth Reid; 1 step s. Educ. Dundee High School; Stirling University; Dundee University. Research Scientist, MRC Applied Psychology Unit, Cambridge, 1976-79; Lecturer, Department of Psychiatry, University Hospital and Medical School, Nottingham, 1979-84; Senior Lecturer, Behavioural Sciences Group, Medical Faculty, Glasgow University, 1984-88. Publications: papers and edited book on topics relating psychology to medicine. Recreations: reading; travelling; hill-walking; procrastination. Address: (h.) 33 West Chapelton Crescent, Bearsden, Glasgow G61 2DE; T.-0141-942 4978.

Millar, Peter Carmichael, OBE, MA, LLB, WS. Chairman, Medical Appeal Tribunals, since 1991, and of Pension Appeal Tribunals, since 1992; b. 19.2.27, Glasgow; m., Kirsteen Lindsay Carnegie; 2 s.; 2 d. Educ. Aberdeen Grammar School; Glasgow University; St. Andrews University; Edinburgh University. Royal Navy, 1944-47; Partner, W. & T.P. Manuel, WS, 1954-62; Partner, Aitken Kinnear & Co., WS, 1963-87; Partner, Aitken, Nairn WS, 1987-92; Clerk, Society of Writers to HM Signet, 1964-83; Deputy Keeper of Her Majesty's Signet, 1983-91; Chairman: Church of Scotland General Trustees, 1973-85, Mental Welfare Commission for Scotland, 1983-91. Recreations: golf; hill-walking; music. Address: (h.) 25 Cramond Road North, Edinburgh EH4 6LY.

Millar, Rev. Peter William, MA, BD, MTh. Minister, Church of Scotland, since 1970; Warden, Iona Abbey, 1995-98; b. 24.5.43, Edinburgh; m., Dr. Dorothy Somerville; 2 s.; 1 d. Educ. George Heriot's School, Edinburgh; Edinburgh University; Princeton University; Chicago University. Parish Minister, 1970-76; Priest, Church of South India, 1976-88; Director, Ecumenical Retreat Centre, 1989-94. Publications: Letters from Madras, 1988; Words from the Cross, 1989; Set Free, 1989; Prayers from a Columban House, 1990; Notes for a Pilgrim, 1991; Pilgrim Guide to Iona, 1997; Prayers from Iona, 1998. Recreations: walking; writing; travelling. Address: (h.) 59 Braid Avenue, Edinburgh EH10 6EB.

Millar, William Mungall. Editor, Scottish Business Insider, since 1996; b. 13.12.50, Falkirk; 2 s.; 1 d. Address: (b.) 43 Queensferry Street Lane, Edinburgh EH2 4PF; T.-0131-535 5512.

Miller, Professor Alan, LLB (Hons), NP. Visiting Professor of Law, specialising in human rights, Strathclyde University, since 1996; Director, Scottish Human Rights

Centre; practising Solicitor; b. 9.4.52, Irvine; m., Brenda; 2 s.; 2 d. Educ. Ardrossan Academy; Edinburgh University. Admitted as practising Solicitor, 1984; published draft Bill of Rights for Scotland, 1992. Secretary, Common Cause. Recreation: time with family. Address: (b.) Scottish Human Rights Centre, 146 Holland Street, Glasgow G2 4NG; T.-0141-332 5960.

Miller, Professor Alan, BSc, PhD, CPhys, FInstP, FRSE, FIEEE (USA). Professor of Semiconductor Physics and Head, School of Physics and Astronomy, St. Andrews University, since 1993; Professor of Physics and Electrical Engineering, University of Central Florida, since 1989; b. 5.6.49, Dunfermline; m., Susan Linklater; 3 d. Educ. Gibraltar Grammar School; Edinburgh University; Bath University. Research Fellow, Heriot-Watt University, 1974-79; Visiting Assistant Professor, North Texas University, 1979-81; Senior Principal Scientific Officer, Royal Signals and Radar Establishment, Malvern, 1981-89. Editor, Optical and Quantum Electronics, and of Cambridge Studies in Modern Optics (series of monographs); Chairman, Committee of Scottish Professors of Physics; Chairman, Scottish Chapter, Lasers and Electro-Optics Society. Publications: Nonlinear Optics in Signal Processing (Editor); Nonlinear Optical Materials and Devices for Applications in Information Technology (Editor); Laser Sources and Applications (Editor); 150 research papers. Address: (b.) Department of Physics and Astronomy, North Haugh, St. Andrews KY16 9SS; T.-01334 463122.

Miller, Alan Douglas, LLB (Hons), DipLP. Principal Reporter, Scottish Children's Reporter Administration, since 1995; b. 30.11.59, Edinburgh; m., Alison; 1 s.; 2 d. Educ. Stewart's/Melville College, Edinburgh; Edinburgh University. Assistant/Area Reporter, Strathclyde, 1985-90; Regional Reporter, Dumfries and Galloway, 1990-95; Secretary, Association of Children's Reporters, 1990-93. Associate Member, Iona Community; Elder, Church of Scotland. Address (b.): Ochil House, Springkerse Business Park, Stirling FK7 7XE; T.-01786 459500.

Miller, Alastair Robert John Dunlop, BSc, MAg, NDA, FRAgS. Farmer; Chairman, Scotfresh (1997) Ltd.; b. 5.3.37, Tranent; m., Margaret Eileen Lees-Brown; 3 d. Educ. Edinburgh Academy; Rugby; Edinburgh University; Purdue University, USA. Scottish Horticulture Medal; Fellow, Royal Agricultural Societies. Recreations: golf; travel. Address: (h.) Ferrygate, North Berwick, East Lothian.

Miller, Professor Andrew, MA, BSc, PhD, FRSE, FIBiol. Principal and Vice-Chancellor, University of Stirling, since 1994; b. 15.2.36, Kelty, Fife; m., Rosemary S.H. Fyvie; 1 s.; 1 d. Educ. Beath High School; Edinburgh University. Assistant Lecturer in Chemistry, Edinburgh University, 1960-62; Postdoctoral Fellow, CSIRO, Melbourne, and Tutor in Chemistry, Ormond College, Melbourne University, 1962-65; Staff Scientist, MRC Laboratory of Molecular Biology, Cambridge, 1965-66; Lecturer in Molecular Biophysics, Oxford University and (from 1967) Fellow, Wolfson College, 1966-83 (Honorary Fellow, since 1994); on secondment as first Director, European Molecular Biology Laboratory, Grenoble Antenne, France, 1975-80. Committee Member: British Biophysical Society, 1972-74, SERC Synchrotron Radiation Facility Committee, 1979-82, Biological Sciences Committee, 1982-85, Neutron Beam Research Committee, 1982-85; Council Member, Institut Laue-Langevin, 1981-85; Member: MRC Joint Dental Committee, 1984-86, UGC Biological Sciences Committee, 1985-89; (part-time) Director of Research, European Synchrotron Radiation Facility, Grenoble, 1986-91; Member: Advisory Board, AFRC Food Research Institute, 1985, UFC Advisory Groups on Biological Sciences and Pre-clinical Medicine, 1989, Scientific Council, Grenoble University, 1989; Vice-Dean of Medicine, Edinburgh University, 1991-93; Professor of Biochemistry, Edinburgh University, 1984-94; Vice-Principal, Edinburgh University, 1993-94; Director, Scottish Knowledge plc, since 1997; Member, Minister of Education's Action Group on Standards in Scottish Schools, since 1997; Member, Council, Royal Society of Edinburgh, since 1997. Address: (b.) University of Stirling, Stirling FK9 4LA.

Miller, Bill, BSc, DipTP. Member, European Parliament, Glasgow, since 1994; b. 22.7.54, Gartocharn; 1 s.; 1 d. Educ. Paisley Technical College; Kingston Polytechnic. Strathclyde Regional Councillor, 1986-94. Recreations: ties; records; Kilmarnock F.C. Address: 9 Chisholm Street, Glasgow G1 5HA; T.-0141-552 2234.

Miller, Brian, BSc (Hons). Rector, Dalziel High School, Motherwell, since 1990; b. 4.1.51, Glasgow; m., Margaret; 1 s.; 1 d. Educ. High School of Glasgow; Strathclyde University. Teacher of Mathematics, 1974-77; Assistant Principal Teacher, 1977-80; Principal Teacher, 1980-84; Assistant Head Teacher, Cranhill Secondary School, Glasgow, 1984-86; Depute Head Teacher, Stonelaw High School, Glasgow, 1986-90. Recreation: bowls. Address: (b.) Crawford Street, Motherwell ML1 3AG.

Miller, Rev. Charles W., MA. Chaplain, Royal Dundee Liff Hospital, since 1980; b. 4.2.26, Kinross; m., Isabella Russell Stewart, MA; 3 s. Educ. St. Mary's School, Dunblane; McLaren High School, Callander; Aberdeen University; St. Andrews University. Assistant Minister, Auld Kirk of Ayr, 1953-54; Minister: Torthorwald, Dumfries, 1953-59, Munro Church, Rutherglen, 1959-65, Cruden, Aberdeenshire, 1965-72, Anstruther Parish Church, 1972-80, Fowlis Easter and Liff Parish Church, 1980-94; former Convener: Overseas Committee, Dumfries Presbytery; Church and Nation and Social Responsibility Committees, Aberdeen Presbytery; Social Responsibility Committee, St. Andrews Presbytery; Church of Scotland Pulpit Supply Agent (Dundee and Tayside); Member, Scottish Churches Consultative Committee on Road Safety; Institute of Advanced Motorists: Member, Governing Council, 1962-95, elected Fellow, since 1996, Founder Member and President, Institute's Groups Association in Scotland. Recreations: caravanning; swimming; landscape painting; hospital radio broadcasting. Address: Palm Springs, Parkside, Auchterhouse, Dundee DD3 0RF; T.-01382 320407.

Miller, Sheriff Colin Brown, LLB, SSC. Sheriff for South Strathclyde, Dumfries and Galloway, since 1991; b. 4.10.46, Paisley; m., Joan Elizabeth Blyth; 3 s. Educ. Paisley Grammar School; Glasgow University. Partner, McFadyen & Semple, Solicitors, Paisley, 1971-91; Council Member, Law Society of Scotland, 1983-91 (Convener, Conveyancing Committee, 1986-89; Convener, Judicial Procedure Committee, 1989-91; Chairman, Working Party on Rights of Audience in Supreme Courts, 1990-91); Dean, Faculty of Procurators in Paisley, 1991. Recreations: Clyde steamers; railways; photography; travel. Address: (b.) Ayr Sheriff Court, Wellington Square, Ayr; T.-01292 268474.

Miller, Sir Donald John, DSc, DUniv, BSc, FEng, FIMechE, FIEE, FRSE. Chairman, Premium Trust; Chairman, National Cycle Network Steering Committee; b. 9.2.27, London; m., Fay G. Herriot; 1 s.; 2 d. Educ. Banchory Academy; Aberdeen University. Metropolitan-Vickers, 1947-53; British Electricity Authority, 1953-55; Preece Cardew & Rider (Consulting Engineers), 1955-66; Chief Engineer, North of Scotland Hydro-Electric Board, 1966-74; SEEB: Director of Engineering, 1974, appointed Deputy Chairman, 1979; Chairman, Scottish Power, 1982-92. Chairman, Power Division, IEE, 1977. Recreations: gardening; walking; sailing. Address: (h.) Puldohran, Gryffe Road, Kilmacolm, Renfrewshire; T.-Kilmacolm 3652.

Miller, Hugh Craig, BSc, MB, ChB, FRCPEdin. Consultant Cardiologist, Edinburgh Royal Infirmary, since 1975; b. 7.4.42, Edinburgh; m., Isobel Margaret; 1 s.; 1 d. Educ. George Watson's College; Edinburgh University. Registrar, Edinburgh Royal Infirmary, 1969-72; Senior Registrar, Brompton Hospital, London, 1972-75; Research Fellow, Duke University, North Carolina, 1973-74; Fulbright Scholar. Recreations: skiing; sailing. Address: (h.) 12 Dick Place, Edinburgh; T.-0131-667 4235.

Miller, Professor Hugh Graham, OBE, BSc, PhD, DSc, FICFor, FIBiol, FRSE, FRSA. Professor and Head, Department of Forestry, Aberdeen University, since 1984; b. 22.11.39, Ndola, Zambia; 1 s.; 1 d. Educ. Kaptagat School, Kenya; Strathallan School; Sutton High School; Aberdeen University. Joined Department of Peat and Forest Soils, Macaulay Institute for Soil Research, 1986. Awarded Institute of Foresters Silvicultural Prize, 1974; selected for International Union of Forest Research Organization's Scientific Achievement Award, 1981; President, Institute of Chartered Foresters, 1994-96; OBE, 1996. Recreation: curling. Address: (b.) Department of Forestry, Aberdeen University, St. Machar Drive, Aberdeen AB9 2UD; T.-01224 272666.

Miller, Ian George Tweedie, BSc, AFIMA, MBCS, CEng, FRSA. Principal, North Glasgow College, since 1990; Chairman, Skill (Scotland), since 1992; b. 5.8.42, Hamilton; m., Una; 1 s.; 1 d. Educ. George Heriot's, Edinburgh; Heriot Watt University. Research Assistant, Hatfield Polytechnic; Lecturer, Computer Science, Strathclyde University; Director, Computer Centre, Paisley College; Depute Principal, Stevenson College. Recreations: golf; bowling. Address: (b.) 110 Flemington Street, Glasgow G21 4BX; T.-0141-558 9001.

Miller, Rev. Ian Hunter, BA, BD. Minister, Bonhill, since 1975; b. 30.5.44, Johnstone; m., Joan Elizabeth Parr; 2 s. Educ. Johnstone High School; Glasgow University; Open University. Travel agent, latterly Branch Manager, A.T. Mays, 1962-69; Assistant Minister, Renfrew Old Kirk, 1974-75. Moderator, Dumbarton Presbytery, 1985-87 (Convener, Presbytery Planning and Re-adjustment); Non-executive Director, Lomond Healthcare NHS Trust. Recreations: golf; badminton; music; drama. Address: Bonhill Manse, 1 Glebe Gardens, Bonhill, Alexandria G83 9HR; T.-Alexandria 53039.

Miller, Ian James, MA, LLB. Secretary and Academic Registrar, Napier University, Edinburgh, since 1987; Director, Edinburgh Healthcare NHS Trust, since 1995; Governor, Morrison's Academy, Crieff, since 1998; b. 21.10.38, Fraserburgh; m., Sheila Mary Hourston; 1 s.; 2 d. Educ. Fraserburgh Academy; Aberdeen University; Edinburgh University. Private legal practice, 1963-68; Senior Legal Assistant, Inverness County Council, 1968-70; Depute County Clerk, then County Clerk, Ross and Cromarty County Council, 1970-75; Chief Executive, Inverness District Council, 1975-77; Director of Law and Administration, Grampian Regional Council, 1977-84; Director, Kildonnan Investments Ltd., Aberdeen, 1984-87. Recreations: golf; curling. Address: (b.) 219 Colinton Road, Edinburgh EH14 1DJ; T.-0131-455 4603.

Miller, Dr. Jack Elius, OBE, JP, OStJ, FRCGP. Director, The Medical Insurance Agency Ltd., since 1978; b. 7.3.18, Glasgow; m., Ida Warrens. Educ. Hillhead High School; Glasgow University. General Medical Practitioner in Glasgow (retired); Captain, Royal Army Medical Corps, 1944-46; Chairman (founder Member), Glasgow Marriage Guidance Council, 1956-61 (Hon. Vice-President, since 1961); Hon. Vice-President, Scottish Marriage Guidance Council, since 1967; Chairman: Scottish General Medical Services Committee, 1969-72, Association of Jewish Ex-Servicemen and Women of Scotland, 1952-61 and 1964-68; President, Glasgow Jewish Representative Council, 1969-72; Member, Council, BMA, 1964-81 (National Treasurer, 1972-81; Gold Medallist, 1982); Freeman, City of London; Member, Board of Deputies of British Jews, 1979-88; Vice-President, Prince and Princess of Wales Hospice, since 1981; Co-Chairman, Scottish Jewish Archives Committee, since 1986; Chairman, Scottish Health Authorities Review of Priorities for the Eighties and Nineties, 1985-87. Publications: Glasgow Doctors' Handbook (three editions); Sharpen report. Recreations: travel; reading; communal affairs. Address: (h.) 38 Fruin Court, Fruin Avenue, Newton Mearns, Glasgow G77 6HJ; T.-0141-639 7869.

Miller, James, CBE (1986), MA, FCIOB, FCIArb, CBIM. Chairman, since 1970, Managing Director, 1970-91, The Miller Group Ltd. (formerly James Miller & Partners); Director, British Linen Bank Ltd., since 1983 (Chairman, since 1997); Member, Scottish Advisory Board, British Petroleum, since 1990; Chairman, Court, Heriot-Watt University, 1990-96; Director, Bank of Scotland, since 1993; Chairman, Royal Scottish National Orchestra, since 1997; b. 1.9.34, Edinburgh; m., 1, Kathleen Dewar (deceased); 2, Iris Lloyd-Webb; 1 s.; 3 d. Educ. Edinburgh Academy; Harrow School; Balliol College, Oxford. National Service, Royal Engineers. James Miller & Partners Ltd.: joined, 1958, appointed Director, 1960; Scottish Representative, Advisory Committee to the Meteorological Services, 1980-92; Chairman, Federation of Civil Engineering Contractors, 1985-86, President, 1990-93; Deacon Convener, Incorporated Trades of Edinburgh, 1974-77; President, Edinburgh Chamber of Commerce, 1981-83; Assistant, 1982-85, Treasurer, 1990-92, Master, 1992-94, Merchant Company of Edinburgh. Recreation: shooting. Address: (b.) The Miller Group Ltd., Miller House, 18 South Groathill Avenue, Edinburgh EH4 2LW; T.-0131-315 6000.

Miller, James David Frederick, CBE, DUniv(Stirling, Paisley), MA (Cantab), CIMgt, FIPD, FRSA. Chairman: SQA (Scottish Qualifications Authority), since 1996, University of Stirling Court, since 1992, Wolverhampton and Dudley Breweries PLC, since 1992, Fairbridge Scotland, since 1998; Vice-Chairman, Forth Valley Enterprise, since 1996; Director: J. and J. Denholm Ltd., since 1997, Edinburgh Military Tattoo Ltd., since 1990, Scottish Life Assurance Company, since 1995; b. 5.1.35, Wolverhampton; m., Saffrey Blackett Oxley; 3 s. (1 deceased); 1 d. Educ. Emmanuel College, Cambridge; London School of Economics. National Service, Argyll and Sutherland Highlanders (commissioned South Staffords); Council Member, Outward Bound Limited; Member, Court, Stirling University, 1978-84; Vice-Chairman, Royal National Orchestra; Director, Edinburgh Academy, 1985; Member, CBI Employee Involvement Panel; Governor, Scottish College of Textiles, 1989. Recreations: gardening; golf; walking. Address: (h.) Blairuskin Lodge, Kinlochard, Aberfoyle, by Stirling FK8 3TP; T.-01877 387 249.

Miller, Professor James Edward, MA, PhD. Professor, Department of Linguistics, University of Edinburgh, since 1997; b. 6.9.42, Falkirk; m., Margaret Stewart Johnstone; 3 s. Educ. Bathgate Academy; University of Edinburgh. Department of Linguistics, University of Edinburgh: Assistant Lecturer, 1967-70, Lecturer, 1970-85, Senior Lecturer, 1985-87, Reader, 1987-97. Publication: Spontaneous Spoken Language – Syntax and Disguise, 1998. Address: Department of Linguistics, Adam Ferguson Building; 40 George Square, Edinburgh EH8 9LL; T.-0131-650 3961.

Miller, Rev. John Stewart Abercromby Smith, MA, BD, STM. Minister, Morningside United Church, Edinburgh, 1980-97; Pastoral Associate, St Ninian's, Corstorphine, since 1997; b. 3.5.28, Gibraltar; m., Lorna Vivien Fraser; 1 s.; 1 d. Educ. Lanark Grammar School; Edinburgh University; Union Theological Seminary, New York. Assistant Minister, St. Giles' Cathedral, Edinburgh, 1953-

54; Minister: St. Andrew's, Hawick, 1954-59, Sandyhills, Glasgow, 1959-67, Mortlach and Cabrach, Banffshire, 1967-75, North Morningside, Edinburgh, and Morningside Congregational Church, 1975-80; Visiting Instructor, Columbia Theological Seminary, Georgia, 1986; Honorary Associate Minister, Peachtree Presbyterian Church, Atlanta, 1986; Moderator, Edinburgh Presbytery, 1996-97. Recreations: reading; listening to music; exploring Britain. Address: (h.) 54 Hayfield, East Craigs, Edinburgh EH12 8UH; T.-0131 339 0537.

Miller, Josephine L., BA, BMus, MLitt. Course Leader, BA (Scottish Music), Royal Scottish Academy of Music and Drama, since 1996; Lecturer in Scottish Music and Ethnomusicology, since 1989; freelance musician, researcher and teacher; b. 1.10.62, Carluke; m., Steven Sutcliffe; 1 s. Educ. Kirkcudbright Academy; RSAMD; Glasgow University; Edinburgh University. Provision of teaching materials and teacher support for Scottish music in schools; freelance singer and fiddler; Lecturer in Traditional Arts, Glasgow Arts Centre, 1990-92. Publications: music transcriptions for Come Gie's A Sang, 1995; The Music of Scotland (teacher support package). Recreations: gardening; walking; reading. Address: (b.) RSAMD, 100 Renfrew Street, Glasgow G2 3DB.

Miller, Keith Manson, BSc (Hons), DipMS. Chief Executive, Miller Group, since 1994; b. 19.3.49, Edinburgh. Educ. Loretto; Heriot-Watt University; Glasgow University. Managing Director: Miller Mining, 1976-90, Miller Developments, 1990-94. Director, Aberforth Smaller Companies Trust PLC. Recreations: sailing; skiing. Address: (b.) Miller Group Ltd., 18 South Groathill Avenue, Edinburgh EH4 2LW; T.-0131-315 6000.

Miller, Professor Kenneth, LLB, LLM, PhD. Professor of Law, Strathclyde University, since 1992; Vice-Dean (Academic), Strathclyde Business School; b. 11.12.51, Paisley; m., Margaret Macleod. Educ. Paisley Grammar School; Strathclyde University; Queen's University, Canada. Lecturer in Law, then Senior Lecturer, Strathclyde University, 1975-91; Deputy General Editor, Stair Memorial Encyclopaedia of the Laws of Scotland, 1990-96; Member, Employment Law Committee, Law Society of Scotland. Publications: Employment Law in Scotland (Co-Author); Property Law (Co-Author); Law of Health and Safety at Work in Scotland. Recreations: reading; golf; theatre. Address: (b.) Law School, Strathclyde University, 173 Cathedral Street, Glasgow; T.-0141-552 4400.

Miller, Marshall William, BA, CA. Partner, Deloitte and Touche, Glasgow, since 1985; b. 10.5.54, Glasgow; m., Jill; 1 s.; 1 d. Educ. Hutchesons' Grammar School; University of Strathclyde. Joined Touche Ross, Glasgow, 1974, following international and London secondments became Partner, 1985; Partner in Charge, Glasgow Office, since 1986. Member, Council, Institute of Chartered Accountants. Recreations: golf; tennis; skiing. Address: (b.) 39 St. Vincent Place, Glasgow G1 2QQ; T.-0141-304 5640.

Miller, Sir Ronald Andrew Baird, CBE (1985), CA, DSc. former Chairman, Dawson International PLC; b. 13.5.37, Edinburgh. Non-Executive Director: Aggreko PLC, Securities Trust of Scotland PLC, Quality Assurance Agency for Higher Education; Chairman, Court, Napier University. Address: (b.) 7 Doune Terrace, Edinburgh EH3 6DY.

Miller, Professor Timothy John Eastham, PhD, BSc, FIEE, CEng, FIEEE, FRSE. Lucas Professor in Power Electronics, Glasgow University, since 1986; b. 25.9.47, Wigan; m., Janet Ann; 3 d. Educ. Atlantic College; Glasgow University; Leeds University. Research Fellow, Department of Electrical and Electronic Engineering, Leeds University, 1973-77; joined Corporate Research and Development Center, General Electric, NY, 1979, Manager, Power Electronics Control Program, 1983-86; appointed GEC Titular Professor in Power Electronics, Glasgow University, 1986. Publications: five textbooks and reference book; 100 papers. Ten patents. Recreation: racing cyclist. Address: (b.) Department of Electronics and EE, Glasgow University, Glasgow G12 8LT; T.-0141-330 4922.

Miller, Professor William L., MA, PhD, FBA, FRSA. Edward Caird Professor of Politics, Glasgow University, since 1985; b. 12.8.43, Glasgow; m., Fiona Thomson; 2 s.; 1 d. Educ. Aberdeen Grammar School; Royal High School, Edinburgh; Edinburgh University; Newcastle University. Formerly Lecturer, Senior Lecturer and Professor, Strathclyde University; Visiting Professor, Virginia Tech., Blacksburg, Virginia, 1983-84; also taught at Universities of Essex and Cologne; frequent Contributor to Press and TV; Member, Editorial Boards: Electoral Studies, Political Studies. Publications: Electoral Dynamics, 1977; The End of British Politics?, 1981; The Survey Method in the Social and Political Sciences, 1983; Elections and Voters, 1987; The Quality of Local Democracy, 1988; How Voters Change, 1990; Media and Voters, 1991; Alternatives to Freedom, 1995; Political Culture in Contemporary Britain, 1996; Values and Political Change in Postcommunist Europe, 1998. Address: (b.) Department of Politics, Glasgow University G12 8RT; T.-0141-339 8855.

Milligan, Eric. Lord Provost and Lord Lieutenant, City of Edinburgh, since 1996; b. 27.1.51, Edinburgh; m., Janis. Educ. Tynecastle High School; Napier College of Commerce and Technology. Edinburgh District Councillor, 1974-78; Lothian Regional Councillor, 1978-96; Chairman, Finance Committee, 1980-82, 1986-90; President, COSLA, 1988-90; Convener, Lothian Regional Council, 1990-96; City of Edinburgh Councillor, since 1995; awarded Chevalier dans l'Ordre National du Merite, 1996. Address: (b.) City Chambers, High Street, Edinburgh EH1 1YJ.

Milligan, Hon. Lord (James George Milligan). Senator of the College of Justice, since 1988; b. 10.5.34. Advocate, 1959; QC, 1972; Advocate Depute, 1971-78; Chairman, Medical Appeal Tribunal (Scotland), 1979-88. Address: (b.) Court of Session, Parliament House, Edinburgh EH1 1RQ.

Mills, Harold Hernshaw, CB, BSc, PhD. Chairman, Edinburgh World Heritage Trust; Chairman, Land Trust; Governor, Queen Margaret University College, Edinburgh; Trustee, Scottish Maritime Museum; Board Member, Home in Scotland; b. 2.3.38, Greenock; m., Marion Elizabeth Beattie. Educ. Greenock High School; Glasgow University. Cancer Research Scientist, Roswell Park Memorial Institute, Buffalo, New York, 1962-64; Lecturer, Chemistry Department, Glasgow University, 1964-69; Principal, Scottish Home and Health Department, 1970-76; Assistant Secretary: Scottish Office, 1976-81, Privy Council Office, 1981-83, Scottish Development Department, 1983-84; Under Secretary, Scottish Development Department, 1984-88; Principal Finance Officer, Scottish Office, 1988-92; Secretary, Scottish Office Environment Department, 1992-95; Secretary and Head of Department, Scottish Office Development Department, 1995-98. Address (h.) 21 Hatton Place, Edinburgh EH9 1UB; T.-0131-667 7910.

Mills, Ian Thomas, BSc, MPhil, MIMgt. Director of Education and Leisure Services, East Dunbartonshire Council, since 1995; b. 20.5.48, Hamilton; m., Margaret; 2 d. Educ. Dalziel High School, Motherwell; Glasgow University; Strathclyde University. Chemistry Teacher, Dalziel High School, Motherwell, 1970-75; Senior Housemaster, Lanark Grammar School, 1975-78; Assistant Head Teacher, then Depute Head Teacher, Carluke High School, 1978-85; Area Education Officer, Perth and Kinross, 1985-91; Assistant Director of Education, Tayside Regional Council, 1991-95. Adviser to Scottish Arts Council; Church of Scotland Elder; Past President, Rotary Club of Perth St. Johns; Vice Chair, Scottish Amateur

Music Association. Recreations: music; family-based activities; various sports (curling, walking). Address: (b.) Department of Education, Boclair House, 100 Milngavie Road, Bearsden G61 2TQ; T.-0141-942 9000.

Mills, Thomas, BEd, CBiol, MIBiol, MIM. Head Teacher, St. Patrick's High School, Coatbridge, since 1996; b. 17.2.47, Lennoxtown; m., Janice Alexis; 1 s.; 1 d. Educ. St. Mungo's Academy; St. Andrew's College; Paisley University. Teacher of Biology, John Bosco Secondary School, 1974-77; A.P.T., Biology, Lourdes Secondary School, 1977-83; Principal Teacher of Biology, Our Lady and St. Francis Secondary School, 1983-87; Assistant Head Teacher, Our Lady's High School, Motherwell, 1987-92; Depute Headteacher, John Ogilvie High School, Hamilton, 1992-96. Recreations: keep-fit; DIY; music; caravanning. Address: (b.) St. Patrick's High School, Muiryhall Street, Coatbridge ML5 3NN; T.-01236 426191.

Milne, Alastair David, OBE, FRSE, PhD, MSc, BSc, CEng, FIEE, SMIEEE. Managing Director, Wolfson Microelectronics Ltd., since 1984; b. 8.11.42, Edinburgh; m., Rosemary C.; 1 s.; 2 d. Educ. George Watson's College; Heriot-Watt University; Bristol University. Research Fellow, Bristol University, Edinburgh University; Director, Wolfson Microelectronics Institute. Vice-President, Royal Society of Edinburgh. Recreations: climbing; sailing; skiing. Address: (h.) 17 Napier Road, Edinburgh; T.-0131-229 2161.

Milne, Brian, MB, ChB, FRCOG. Consultant Gynaecologist and Obstetrician, Raigmore Hospital NHS Trust, Inverness, since 1978; Clinical Senior Lecturer, Aberdeen University, since 1978; b. 9.1.42, Elgin; m., Mary I.B.; 2 s. Educ. Keith Grammar School; Aberdeen University. House Officer and Senior House Officer appointments, Aberdeen Royal Infirmary; Registrar appointments, Raigmore Hospital, Inverness and Southern General Hospital, Glasgow; Senior Registrar, Obstetrics and Gynaecology, Leicester Royal Infirmary, 1974-78. Recreations: golf; curling. Address: (h.) Muirfield House, 28 Muirfield Road, Inverness; T.-01463 222134.

Milne, Colin McLeod, LLB. Regional Chairman of Employment Tribunals, since 1994; b. 14.3.47, Glasgow; m., Margaret; 1 s.; 1 d. Educ. Kilmarnock Academy; Glasgow University. Partner, Wright Johnston & Mackenzie, Solicitors, Glasgow, until 1991; appointed Chairman of Industrial Tribunals, 1991, Regional Chairman, 1994. Address: (b.) Central Office of Employment Tribunals, Eagle Building, 215 Bothwell Street, Glasgow G2 7TS; T.-0141-204 0730.

Milne, George, BSc (Hons), MEd, MBA. Headteacher, Peterhead Academy since 1991; b. 4.6.49, Aberdeen; m., Elizabeth Kerr; 2 s.; 1 d. Educ. Aberdeen Grammar School; Aberdeen University. Maths Teacher, 1972-81; Principal Teacher of Maths, Peterhead Academy, 1981-84; Assistant Head Teacher, then Depute Head, Mintlaw Academy, 1984-91. Recreations: Rotary activities; golf; reading. Address: (b.) Peterhead Academy, Prince Street, Peterhead AB42 1SY; T.-01779 472231.

Milne, John Alexander, BA, BSc (Hons), PhD. Deputy Director and Head, Ecology and Animal Science Group, Macaulay Land Use Research Institute; b. 22.11.43, Edinburgh; m., Janet Erskine; 1 s. Educ. Edinburgh Academy; Edinburgh University; London University; Open University. Deputy Editor, Grass and Forage Science; Address: (b.) Craigiebuckler, Aberdeen AB9 2QJ.

Milne, Professor John Sim, BSc (Hons), CEng, FIMechE, FRSA. Professor Emeritus, University of Abertay, Dundee, since 1996 (Professor of Mechatronics, 1993-96); b. 22.6.36, Arbroath; m., Isabella Paton; 2 s. Educ. Arbroath High School; Strathclyde University. Lecturer, then Senior Lecturer in Mechanical Engineering, Dundee Institute of Technology, 1958-93. Principal Assessor for Higher Still courses; Adviser for Construction and Technology Working Curriculum Working Group, University of the Highlands and Islands Project; Consultant on Mechatronics for the Scottish Qualifications Authority; co-author of two textbooks and invited contributor to two engineering reference books. Recreations: cycling; hill-walking. Address: (h.) 45 Monymusk Road, Arbroath DD11 2BZ; T.-01241 873988.

Milne, Robert Hughes, MBE, JP. Managing Director, Aberdeen Fish Curers and Merchants Association Ltd., since 1987 (Chief Executive/Secretary, 1983-87); b. 4.6.39, Pittenweem. Educ. Waid Academy, Anstruther. Assistant Chief Fisheries Advisor, then Regional Officer, Herring Industry Board, 1962-73; Development Officer/Secretary, then Secretary General, Scottish Federation of Fishermen's Co-operatives Ltd., Fishing Co-operative Trading (Scotland) Ltd. and Fishing Co-operatives (Manufacturing) Ltd., 1973-83. Served, European Community Social Problems Fisheries Committee, European Community Advisory Committee on Fisheries and Association of European Agricultural and Fisheries Co-operatives, 1973-83; Member: Isle of Man Government's Commission of Inquiry, 1982-83, Sea Fish Industry Authority Research and Development Committee and Sea Fish Training Council, since 1983; Secretary, Scottish Fish Merchants Federation Ltd., since 1984. Burgess of Guild, City of Aberdeen. Recreations: gardening; church activities. Address: (b.) South Esplanade West, Aberdeen AB9 2FJ; T.-01224 897744.

Milner, Professor A.D., MA, DipPsych, PhD, FRSE. Professor of Neuropsychology, St. Andrews University, since 1990 (Dean, Faculty of Science, 1992-94, Head, School of Psychology, 1994-97); b. 16.7.43, Leeds. Educ. Bradford Grammar School; Lincoln College, Oxford. Research Worker, Institute of Psychiatry, London, 1966-70; Lecturer, then Senior Lecturer, St. Andrews University, 1970-85, Reader, 1985-90. Publications: The Neuropsychology of Consciousness (Editor); The Visual Brain in Action, 1995; Comparative Neuropsychology (Editor), 1998. Address (b.) Psychological Laboratory, St. Andrews University, St. Andrews KY16 9JU; T.-01334 462065.

Milton, Ian Murray, MCIM. Chairman, Milton Hotels Ltd.; Director, Nevis Range Development Company PLC; b. 25.7.45, Glasgow; m., Ann; 1 s.; 3 d. Educ. Lochaber High School; Scottish Hotel School, Glasgow. Began Milton Hotels with brother, 1965. Recreations: golf; skiing; computing. Address: (b.) Milton Hotels Ltd., North Road, Fort William PH33 6TG; T.-01397 703139.

Minto, Brian J. L., CA, ATII, FRSA. Senior Partner, Minto Finnie Parsons Turnbull, Chartered Accountants; Vice-Chairman, Scottish Qualifications Authority; b. 10.8.42, Lanark; m., Margot Morris; 1 s.; 1 d. Educ. Arbroath High School. Apprentice CA, 1959-64; Scottish Malt Distillers Ltd., 1967-70. Chairman, Scottish Fisheries Museum, Anstruther; Director, Dundee College. Recreations: golf; walking; photography. Address: (b.) 164 South Street, St. Andrews; T.-01334 478150.

Minto, 6th Earl of (Gilbert Edward George Lariston Elliot-Murray-Kynynmound), OBE (1986), JP. Brigadier, Queen's Bodyguard for Scotland (Royal Company of Archers); President, Scottish Council on Alcohol, since 1988; Vice Lord-Lieutenant, Roxburgh, Ettrick and Lauderdale, since 1992; former Convenor, Borders Regional Council; b. 19.6.28; m., 1, Lady Caroline Child-Villiers (m. diss.); 1 s.; 1 d.; 2, Mary Elizabeth Ballantine (deceased); 3, Mrs Caroline Larlham. Educ. Eton; Sandhurst. Former Captain, Scots Guards. Address: (h.) Minto, Hawick.

Mirodan, Vladimir, DipDiz, MA, PhD, DGGB, FRSA. Director of Drama, Royal Scottish Academy of Music and Drama, since 1996; Vice-Chair, Directors' Guild of Great Britain, since 1992; Member, Drama Committee, Scottish Arts Council; Director, Citizens' Theatre Ltd.; Member, Drama Panel, Hong Kong CAA; Member, Directors' Training Council, 1990-98; b. 29.7.51, Bucharest; m., Barbara Berkery; 1 s. Educ. St. Sava, Bucharest; Drama Centre, London; Royal Holloway College, London University. Artistic Director, Attitude Theatre Company, 1978-85; Director, New End Theatre, London, 1981-83; Director, School of Performance, Rose Bruford College, 1989-94; Director, MA/MFA, Middlesex University, 1995-96; Director, Royal Academy of Dramatic Art, Webber-Douglas Academy, Drama Centre London, Royal Holloway College, London University. Publication: The Balkan Cook Book. Recreation: horse-riding. Address: (b.) RSAMD, 100 Renfrew Street, Glasgow G2 3DB; T.-0141-332 4101.

Misra, Prem Chandra, BSc, MBBS, DPM (RCP&S, Edin and Glas), FAGS. Consultant Psychiatrist, Parkhead Hospital; Clinical Senior Lecturer, Glasgow University, since 1976; b. 24.7.41, Lucknow, India; m., Sandhya; 1 s.; 2 d. Educ. KK Degree College and King George's Medical College, Lucknow, India; Lucknow University. Rotating Intern, King George's Medical College Hospital, Lucknow, 1967; Demonstrator, Department of Human Physiology, Lucknow University, 1967; Resident Senior House Officer, General Medicine and Geriatrics, Wigan and Leigh Group of Hospitals, 1968-69; Resident House Surgeon, General Surgery, Wigan Royal Infirmary, 1968-69; Resident House Physician, General Medicine, Whelley Hospital, Wigan, 1969-70; Resident Senior House Officer in Psychiatry, then Resident Registrar in Psychiatry, Bolton District General Hospital, 1970-73; Senior Psychiatric Registrar (Midland Area Consultant Training Scheme), Hollymoor Hospital, Birmingham, 1973-76; Consultant Psychiatrist, Solihull Area Health Authority, 1976; appointed Consultant Psychiatrist, Glasgow Royal Infirmary and Duke Street Hospital, 1976; Consultant in Charge, Acorn Street Day Hospital, 1979; Deputy Physician Superintendent, Gartloch and Parkhead Hospitals, Glasow, 1984-92. President, Indian Association of Strathclyde, since 1981; Member, Executive Committee: Strathclyde Community Relations Council, 1981-85, Scottish Council for Racial Equality, 1982; Member: Social and Welfare Committee, CRC, for Ethnic Groups and Vietnam Refugees, 1982, Board of Directors, Scottish Refugee Council, since 1995; Secretary, Division of Psychiatry, Eastern District of Glasgow, 1980-94; President, British Society of Medical and Dental Hypnosis (Scotland), 1987-89; Member: Executive Committee, British Society of Research on Sex Education, International Scientific Committee on Sexuality and Handicap, International Advisory Board of Israel Society of Clinical and Experimental Hypnosis, International Committee of Sexologists, Society for the Advancement of Sexual Health; Executive Committee Member, European Society of Hypnosis; Justice of the Peace; awarded Ludwika Bierkoskigo Medal by Polish Medical Association for "outstanding contributions in the prevention and treatment of disabilities". Publications: Modern Trends in Hypnosis; research papers. Address: (b.) Parkhead Hospital, 81 Salamanca Street, Glasgow G31 5BA; T.-0141-211 8300.

Mitcalfe, Kirsteen, BA. Deputy Lieutenant of Moray, since 1991; Member, Gordonstoun School Board of Governors, 1982-94; b. 23.7.36, Edinburgh; m., Hugh Mitcalfe; 4 d. Educ. Oxenfoord Castle School; Open University. Recreations: skiing; tennis; reading. Address: (h.) Milton Brodie, Forres, Moray IV36 0UA; T.-01343 850281.

Mitchell, Rev. Alexander Bell, DipTechEd, BD. Minister, St. Leonard's Church, Dunfermline, since 1981; b. 28.6.49, Baillieston; m., Elizabeth Brodie; 1 s.; 2 d. Educ. Uddingston Grammar School; New College, Edinburgh. Assistant Minister, Dunblane Cathedral, 1979-81. Recreations: golf; hill-walking. Address: 12 Torvean Place, Dunfermline KY11 4VY; T.-01383 721054.

Mitchell, Anne Clouston, MA (Hons). Principal, St. Margaret's School, Edinburgh, since 1994; b. 24.2.46, Aberdeen. Educ. Lossiemouth High School; Elgin Academy; Aberdeen University. Assistant Teacher of English, Kirkcaldy and Lossiemouth; Teacher of English as a Foreign Language, Germany; Teacher of English/Assistant Housemistress, St. Leonards School; Principal Teacher of English, North Berwick High School and Balerno High School; Assistant Headteacher, then Depute Head, Dunbar Grammar School; seconded as Lothian Region Arts Co-ordinator. Co-author, Heinemann Core English Series. Recreations: theatre; reading; gardening. Address: (h.) 22 Cedar Drive, Port Seton EH32 0SN; T.-01875 815187.

Mitchell, Colin Malcolm, BSc, CBiol, MIBiol, MIMgt. Headteacher, Dumfries High School, since 1990; b. 11.6.50, Paisley; m., Pamela Margaret; 2 s. Educ. Forrester Secondary School, Edinburgh; Heriot Watt University. Teacher of Science/Biology, then Principal Teacher of Biology, Craigroyston High School, Edinburgh; Assistant Headteacher, then Depute Headteacher, Maxwelltown High School, Dumfries. Deputy team leader, Moffat Mountain Rescue Team; Chairman: Dumfries Group, Scottish Wildlife Trust, Dunscore Community Council. Recreations: mountaineering; bird-watching. Address: (b.) Dumfries High School, Marchmont, Dumfries DG1 1PX.

Mitchell, Rev. Duncan Ross, BA (Hons), BD (Hons). Minister, St. Andrews Church, West Kilbride, since 1980; b. 5.5.42, Boddam, Aberdeenshire; m., Sandra Brown; 2 s.; 1 d. Educ. Hyndland Senior Secondary School, Glasgow; Strathclyde University; Glasgow University. Worked in insurance industry, four years; Minister, Craigmailen UF Church, Bo'ness, 1972-80; Convener, Assembly Youth Committee, UF Church, 1974-79; Member: Scottish Joint Committee on Religious Education, 1974-79, Multilateral Conversation in Scotland, 1976-79, Board of Social Responsibility, Church of Scotland, 1983-86;Ardrossan Presbytery: Convener, World Mission and Unity, 1984-88, Convener, Stewardship and Finance, 1988-91; Convener, General Assembly Board of World Mission and Unity, Local Involvements Committee, and Executive Member of the Board, 1987-92; Church of Scotland Delegate to Council of Churches for Britain and Ireland Assembly; Moderator, Ardrossan Presbytery, 1992-93. Recreations: cycling; supporting Partick Thistle; writing poetry and short stories. Address: St. Andrew's Manse, 7 Overton Drive, West Kilbride; T.-01294 823142.

Mitchell, Professor Falconer, BCom, CA. Professor of Management Accounting, Edinburgh University; b. 24.11.50, Stirling; m., Maureen Wilson; 2 s. Educ. High School of Stirling; Edinburgh University. Audit apprenticeship, KPMG Edinburgh; Lecturer in Accounting, Heriot Watt University; Lecturer, Senior Lecturer, Edinburgh University. Canon Foundation in Europe Visiting Fellow, 1990-91. Recreations: bowling; gardening; reading; travel. Address: (b.) Department of Accounting, Edinburgh University, George Square, Edinburgh EH8 9JY; T.-0131-650 8340.

Mitchell, George Edward, FCIBS. General Manager, Bank of Scotland, since 1994; b. 7.4.50, Edinburgh; m., Agnes; 3 d. Educ. Forrester High School, Edinburgh. Bank of Scotland, since 1966. Recreations: football; tennis; family. Address: (b.) Bank of Scotland, Teviot House, 41 South Gyle Crescent, Edinburgh EH12 9DR; T.-0131-317 5700.

Mitchell, Gordon K., DA, ARSA, RSW, RGI. Artist; b. 16.11.52, Edinburgh; m., Deirdre; 1 s.; 3 d. Educ. Royal High School; Edinburgh College of Art. Former Art

Teacher (Deputy Headmaster, St. Serf's School, 1986-89); elected: SSA, 1977, SAAC, 1990 (President, 1993-96), RSW, 1996, ARSA, 1998, RGI, 1998. served on council of SSA, SAAC, RSW, SABA; exhibited widely at home and abroad; work in public and private collections. Prizes include: RSA Student Prize; Borders Biennial Competition; Scottish Drawing Competition; Mayfest Award. Recreations: current affairs; golf. Address: 4A Randolph Cliff, Edinburgh EH3 7TZ; T.-0131-225 9550.

Mitchell, Iain Grant, QC, LLB (Hons), FSA Scot, FRSA. Queen's Counsel, since 1992; Temporary Sheriff, 1992-97; Honorary Secretary, Scottish Conservative and Unionist Association, 1993-98, Scottish Conservative and Unionist Party, since 1998; b. 15.11.51, Edinburgh. Educ. Perth Academy; Edinburgh University. Called to Scottish Bar, 1976; Past President, Diagnostic Society of Edinburgh; former Vice-President, Edinburgh University Conservative Association; Conservative candidate, Falkirk West, General Election, 1983, Kirkcaldy, General Election, 1987, Cumbernauld and Kilsyth, General Election, 1992, Dunfermline East, General Election, 1997; Chairman, Trust for an International Opera Theatre of Scotland; Vice-Chairman, Scottish Baroque Ensemble Ltd.; Member: Scottish Committee, Royal Institute of International Affairs, Executive Committee of European Movement (Scottish Council); Vice-Chairman, Scottish Lawyers' European Group; Member, Scottish Committee, Society for Computers and Law. Recreations: music and the arts; photography; cinema; walking; history; travel; writing; finding enough hours in the day. Address: (b.) Advocates Library, Parliament House, High Street, Edinburgh; T.-0131-226 5071.

Mitchell, Sheriff J.K., LLB. Sheriff of Glasgow and Strathkelvin at Glasgow. Advocate, 1979. Address: (b.) Sheriff Court House, 1 Carlton Place, Glasgow, G5 9DA.

Mitchell, (John) Angus (Macbeth), CB, CVO, MC, LLD(Hon), (Dundee), DUniv (Stirling). b. 25.8.24, Ootacamund, India; m., Ann Williamson; 2 s.; 2 d. Educ. Marlborough College; Brasenose College, Oxford. Royal Armoured Corps (Captain), 1943-46; Scottish Office, 1949-84; Principal Private Secretary to Secretary of State for Scotland, 1958-59; Under Secretary, Social Work Services Group, 1969-74; Secretary, Scottish Education Department, 1976-84. Order of Orange-Nassau, 1946; Chairman, Scottish Marriage Guidance Council, 1965-69; Vice-Convener, Scottish Council of Voluntary Organisations, 1986-91; Member, Commission for Local Authority Accounts in Scotland, 1985-89; Chairman of Court, Stirling University, 1984-92; Chairman, Scottish Action on Dementia, 1986-94; Member, Historic Buildings Council for Scotland, 1988-94; Co-ordinator, Recording Scottish Graveyards Project, since 1992; Secretary, Greyfriars Kirkyard Trust. Publications: Scottish Office Ministers 1885-1985; Procedures for the Reorganisation of Schools in England, 1986. Recreations: old Penguins; gravestones; family history. Address: (h.) 20 Regent Terrace, Edinburgh EH7 5BS; T.-0131-556 7671.

Mitchell, John Logan, QC, LLB (Hons). Queen's Counsel, since 1987; Advocate Depute, 1981-85; b. 23.6.47, Dumfries; m., Christine Brownlee Thomson; 1 s.; 1 d. Educ. Royal High School, Edinburgh; Edinburgh University. Called to Bar, 1974; Standing Junior Counsel to Forestry Commission; Standing Junior Counsel, Department of Agriculture and Fisheries. Past President, Royal High School F.P. Club. Recreations: running; golf. Address: (h.) 17 Braid Farm Road, Edinburgh; T.-031-447 8099.

Mitchell, Jonathan James, BA, LLB, QC. Deputy Social Security Commissioner, since 1995; Advocate, 1979; Queen's Counsel, since 1992; Temporary Sheriff, 1988-95; b. 4.8.51, Edinburgh; m., Melinda McGarry; 1 s.; 1 d. QC, 1992. Publication: Eviction and Rent Arrears, 1995. Address: (h.) 30 Warriston Crescent, Edinburgh; T.-0131-557 0854.

Mitchell, Louise C., MA. Director, Glasgow Royal Concert Hall, since 1996; b. 12.8.56, London. Educ. Lady Margaret School, London; St. Andrews University; City University, London. Assistant Manager, Scottish Baroque Ensemble, 1979-81; Concerts Manager, London Sinfonietta, 1982-87; Assistant Director, Edinburgh International Festival, 1989-91; Music Programme Manager, Barbican Centre, 1992-94; Concerts Director, London Philharmonic Orchestra, 1994-96. Committee Member, International Society for Contemporary Music; Trustee, Microtonal Arts Trust; Chair, Scottish Music Information Centre; Member, Music Committee, Children's Hospice Association in Scotland. Recreations: travel; food and wine. Address: (b.) 2 Sauchiehall Street, Glasgow G2 3NY; T.-0141-332 6633.

Mitchell, Professor Emeritus Ross Galbraith, MD, FRCPEdin, FRCPCH, DCH. Professor of Child Health, Dundee University, 1973-85, now Emeritus; b. 18.11.20; m., June Phylis Butcher; 1 s.; 3 d. Educ. Kelvinside Academy, Glasgow; Edinburgh University. Surgeon Lt., Royal Naval Volunteer Reserve, 1944-47; junior medical posts, Edinburgh, Liverpool and London, 1947-52; Rockefeller Research Fellow in Physiology, Mayo Clinic, USA, 1952-53; Lecturer in Child Health, St. Andrews University, 1952-55; Consultant Paediatrician, Dundee Teaching Hospitals, 1955-63; Professor of Child Health, Aberdeen University, 1963-72. Chairman: Editorial Board, Mac Keith Press, 1980-95, Scottish Advisory Council on Child Care, 1966-68; Dean, Faculty of Medicine and Dentistry, Dundee University, 1978-81; Chairman, Aberdeen Association of Social Service, 1971-72; President: Scottish Paediatric Society, 1982-84, Harveian Society of Edinburgh, 1982-83; Member, General Medical Council, 1983-85; Vice-Chairman, Scottish Child and Family Alliance, 1985-92. Recreations: fishing; gardening; languages. Address: (h.) Craigard, Abertay Gardens, Broughty Ferry, Dundee DD5 2RR; T.-01382 776983.

Mitchison, Professor John Murdoch, ScD, FRS, FRSE. Professor Emeritus and Honorary Fellow, Edinburgh University (Professor of Zoology, 1963-88); b. 11.6.22; m., Rosalind Mary Wrong; 1 s.; 3 d. Educ. Winchester College; Trinity College, Cambridge. Army Operational Research, 1941-46; Research Scholar, then Fellow, Trinity College, Cambridge, 1946-54; Lecturer, then Reader in Zoology, Edinburgh University, 1953-62; Member, Edinburgh University Court, 1971-74, 1985-88; Dean, Faculty of Science, 1984-85; Member: Academia Europaea, Scottish Marine Biological Association, 1961-67; Executive Committee Member, International Society for Cell Biology, 1964-72; Member: Biological Committee, SRC, 1972-75, Royal Commission on Environmental Pollution, 1974-79, Science Board, SRC, 1976-79, Working Group on Biological Manpower, DES, 1968-71, Advisory Committee on Safety of Nuclear Installations, Health and Safety Executive, 1981-84; President, British Society for Cell Biology, 1974-77. Publication: The Biology of the Cell Cycle. Address: (h.) Great Yew, Ormiston, East Lothian EH35 5NJ; T.-Pencaitland 340530.

Mitchison, Professor Emeritus Rosalind Mary, Hon DLitt, HonDUniv, FRSE, FRHistS, MA. Professor of Social History, Edinburgh University, 1981-86; b. 11.4.19, Manchester; m., J.M. Mitchison (qv); 1 s.; 3 d. Educ. Channing School, Highgate; Lady Margaret Hall, Oxford. Assistant Lecturer, Manchester University, 1943-46; Tutor, Lady Margaret Hall, Oxford, 1946-47; Assistant: Edinburgh University, 1954-57, Glasgow University, 1962-63; Lecturer, Glasgow University, 1966-67; Lecturer, then Reader, Edinburgh University, 1967-81. President, Scottish History Society, 1981-84. Publications: Agricultural Sir John, 1962; A History of Scotland, 1970; British Population Change since 1860, 1977; Life in Scotland, 1978; Lordship to Patronage: Scotland 1603-1745, 1983; Sexuality and Social Control: Scotland 1660-1780 (Co-Author), 1989; Coping with destitution: poverty and relief in Western Europe, 1991. Recreation: walking. Address: (h.) Great Yew, Ormiston, East Lothian EH35 5NJ; T.-Pencaitland 340530.

Mithen, Dallas Alfred, CB, BSc, FICFor. President, Institute of Chartered Foresters, 1984-86; Chairman, Forestry Training Council, 1984-92; b. 5.11.23; m., 1, Peggy Clarke (deceased); 2, Avril Teresa Dodd; 1 s.; 1 d. Educ. Maidstone Grammar School; University College of North Wales, Bangor. Fleet Air Arm, 1942-46; joined Forestry Commission as District Officer, 1950; Deputy Surveyor, New Forest, and Conservator, SE (England), 1968-71; Senior Officer, Scotland, 1971-75; Head, Forest Management Division, Edinburgh, 1975-76; Commissioner for Harvesting and Marketing, Forestry Commission, 1977-83. Trustee, Central Scotland Countryside Trust, 1985-97; President, Forestry Section, BAAS, 1985. Recreations: swimming; walking; gardening. Address: (h.) 12 Stanehead Park, Biggar, South Lanarkshire ML12 6PU; T.-01899 221 308.

Mochrie, Ronald George. Deputy Chief Executive/Support Services Director, Scottish SPCA, since 1988; b. 10.8.36, Bonnybridge; m., Helen Joan Farquhar; 1 s.; 1 d. Educ. Denny High School; Falkirk Technical College. Company Secretary/Accountant, Gilbert Plastics Ltd., 1974-77; Secretary and Treasurer, Glasgow and West of Scotland SPCA, 1977-87. Leader Trainer, The Scout Association. Recreations: gardening; walking; photography. Address: (b.) Braehead Mains, 603 Queensferry Road, Edinburgh EH4 6EA.

Moffat, Alistair Murray, MA (Hons), MPhil. Managing Director, Scottish Television Enterprises, since 1993 (Director of Programmes, 1990-93); b. 16.6.50, Kelso; m., Lindsay Thomas; 1 s.; 2 d. Educ. Kelso High School; St. Andrews University; Edinburgh University; London University. Ran Edinburgh Festival Fringe, 1976-81; Arts Correspondent/Producer/Controller of Features, Scottish Television. Publications: The Edinburgh Fringe, 1978; Kelsae — A History of Kelso from Earliest Times, 1985; Remembering Charles Rennie Mackintosh, 1989. Recreations: sleeping; supporting Kelso RFC. Address: (b.) Scottish Television, Cowcaddens, Glasgow G2 3PR.

Moffat, Douglas William John, LLB, WS. Partner, Tods Murray, WS, since 1974; b. 3.10.47, Castle Douglas; 1 s.; 1 d. Educ. The Edinburgh Academy; Edinburgh University. Scottish Secretary, British Council of Shopping Centres; Member: British Council of Offices; Member, Investment Property Forum. Recreations: cricket (SCU Committee Member); golf; squash; shooting; hillwalking. Address: (b.) 66 Queen Street, Edinburgh EH2 4NE; T.-0131-226 4771.

Moir, Dorothy Carnegie, MB, ChB, MD, FFPHM, FRCP, DipMgt. Chief Administrative Medical Officer/Director of Public Health, Lanarkshire Health Board, since 1994; Community Medicine Specialist, since 1979; Honorary Senior Clinical Lecturer in Public Health, Aberdeen University; Honorary Senior Clinical Lecturer, Department of Public Health, Glasgow University; b. 27.3.42, Aberdeen; m., Alexander D. Moir; 3 s. Educ. Albyn School for Girls, Aberdeen; Aberdeen University. Research Fellow in Therapeutics and Pharmacology, 1966-69; Lecturer in Community Medicine, 1970-79; Chief Administrative Medical Officer/Director of Public Health, Forth Valley Health Board, 1988-94. Address: (b.) 14 Beckford Street, Hamilton ML3 0TA.

Moir, Rev. Ian Andrew, MA, BD. Church of Scotland Adviser for Urban Priority Areas, since 1991; Minister, Old Kirk of Edinburgh, 1983-91; b. 9.4.35, Aberdeen; m., Elizabeth; 3 s. Educ. Aberdeen Grammar School; Aberdeen University. Sub-Warden, St. Ninian's Training Centre, Crieff, 1959-61; Superintendent, Pholela High School, Natal, 1962-73; Assistant Secretary, Church of Scotland Overseas Council, 1974-83. Recreations: walking; golf. Address: (h.) 47 Millersneuk Drive, Lenzie G66 5JE.

Molana, Professor Hassan, BA, MA, PhD. Professor of Economics, Dundee University, since 1993; b. 16.5.53, Tehran. Educ. Southampton University; Essex University. Research Assistant, Essex University; Research Officer, Southampton University; Lecturer, then Senior Lecturer, Glasgow University; Senior Lecturer, Dundee University. Recreation: classical music. Address: (b.) Department of Economics, Dundee University DD1 4HN; T.-01382 344375.

Molchanov, Professor Ilya, PhD, DrRerNatHabil. Professor of Applied Probability, University of Glasgow, since 1998; b. 18.8.62, Penza, Russian Federation; m., Nadya; 1 d. Educ. School No. 145, Kiev, Ukraine; Kiev State University. Assistant Professor, Kiev Technology Institute, 1987-92; Research Fellow: TU Bergakademie Freiberg, Germany, 1992-94, CWI Amsterdam, 1994-95; Lecturer/Reader, University of Glasgow, 1995-98. Publications: two books. Associate Editor: Metrika; Journal of Statistical Computation and Simulation. Recreations: hill-walking; badminton. Address: Department of Statistics, University of Glasgow, Glasgow G12 8QW; T.-0141-330 5141.

Mole, George Alexander (Sandy). President, National Farmers Union of Scotland, 1996-97; Vice-Chairman, Coastal Grains Ltd., since 1994; Vice-Chairman, Scottish Agricultural and Rural Centre Ltd, since 1992; b. 7.6.43, Duns; m., Jean Mitchell; 1 s.; 2 d. Educ. St. Mary's, Melrose; Merchiston Castle. NFU of Scotland: President, Mid and East Berwick; Chairman, AFRC Cereal Consultative; Convener, Cereals Committee; Member: EEC Commission Cereals Advisory Committee, Home Grown Cereals Authority R. & D. Committee, Institute of Brewing Cereal Publicity. Recreations: golf; shooting. Address: Greenburn, Reston, Eyemouth TD14 5LP.

Mollison, Professor Denis, ScD. Professor of Applied Probability, Heriot-Watt University, since 1986; Trustee, John Muir Trust, since 1986 (Co-Founder,1983); b. 28.6.45, Carshalton; m., Jennifer Hutton; 1 s.; 3 d. Educ. Westminster School; Trinity College, Cambridge. Research Fellow, King's College, Cambridge, 1969; Lecturer in Statistics, Heriot-Watt University, 1973. Elected Member of Council, National Trust for Scotland, 1979-84; Chairman, Mountain Bothies Association, 1978-94. Address: (h.) The Laigh House, Inveresk, Musselburgh EH21 7TD; T.-0131-665 2055.

Molloy, Daniel Frances. Provost, Midlothian Council, since 1996; Member, Edinburgh and Lothians Tourist Board, since 1996; b. 16.10.52, County Donegal; m., Mara; 1 s.; 1 d. Educ. St. Connells School, Co. Donegal. Member, Lothian Health Board, 1979-87; Convener, Midlothian District Council, 1992-96; Chairman, Midlothian Tourism Association, 1988-96. Recreations: reading; walking in the countryside. Address: (h.) 57 Woodburn Bank, Dalkeith EH22 2HP; T.-0131-663 2120.

Moncreiff, 5th Baron (Harry Robert Wellwood Moncreiff), Bt; b. 4.2.15; m., Enid Marion Watson Locke (deceased); 1 s. Educ. Fettes College, Edinburgh. Lt.-Col. (Hon.), RASC (retired). Address: (h.) Tulliebole Castle, Fossoway, Kinross-shire.

Moncur, Charles C., MA (Hons), MIPR. Director, Scottish Business Crime Centre; b. 22.3.41, Aberdeen; m., Sheila; 2 d. Educ. Culter School; Aberdeen University. Economic Analyst, ICI, Harrogate, 1969-72; Economic Adviser, Scottish Office Industry Department, 1972-85; Senior

Planning Officer, BP Exploration, Aberdeen, 1985-88; Manager Community Affairs, BP Exploration, Glasgow, 1988-92; Manager Public Affairs Scotland, British Petroleum Co. plc, 1992-95. Formerly: Member, Executive Council, Scottish Business in the Community, Member, Executive Council, Scottish Council Development and Industry, Board of Management, Marine Biological Research Station, Millport, Advisory Committee, UBI Scotland; Chairman, Commission on Scottish Education, 1994-96. Recreations: golf; football. Address: (h.) 60 Cammo Gardens, Barnton, Edinburgh EH4 8HF; T.-0131-339 5219.

Mone, Rt. Rev. John Aloysius. Bishop of Paisley, formerly Titular Bishop of Abercorn and Auxiliary Bishop of Glasgow; b. 22.6.29, Glasgow. Educ. Holyrood Secondary School; Seminaire St. Sulpice and Institut Catholique, Paris. Ordained Priest, 1952; Assistant: St. Ninian's, Knightswood, Glasgow, 1952-75, Our Lady and St. George, Glasgow, 1975-79; Parish Priest, St. Joseph's, Tollcross, Glasgow, 1979-84. Scottish President, Scottish Catholic Marriage Care; Chairman, Scottish Catholic International Aid Fund, 1975-77; President, National Justice and Peace Commission, 1987-96; President, National Social Care Commission since 1996; President/Treasurer, Scottish Catholic International Aid Fund, since 1985. Address: (b.) Cathedral House, 8 East Buchanan Street, Paisley PA1 1HS.

Monelle, Raymond, MA, BMus, PhD, ARCM. Writer on music; Reader in Music, Edinburgh University; b. 19.8.37, Bristol; 2 d. Educ. Bristol Grammar School; Pembroke College, Oxford; Royal College of Music. Publication: Linguistics and Semiotics in Music, 1992. Address: (h.) 80 Marchmont Road, Edinburgh EH9 1HR.

Money, Neil, Chief Executive, Caithness and Sutherland Enterprise Co. Ltd., since 1996; b. 1.7.43, Wolverhampton; m., Diana Bryan; 1 s. 3 d. Address: (b.) Tollemache House, High Street, Thurso, Caithness KW14 8AZ; T.-01847 805208.

Monro of Langholm, Rt. Hon The Lord (Hector), PC, AE, DL, JP, FRAgS, MP (Conservative), Dumfries, 1964-97; Under Secretary of State, Scottish Office, 1992-95; Privy Councillor, since 1995; Farmer; b. 4.10.22, Edinburgh; m., 1, Lady (Anne) Monro (deceased); 2 s.; 2, Lady (Doris) Monro. Educ. Canford School; Cambridge University; Dundee School of Economics. RAF, 1941-46; Royal Auxiliary Air Force, 1946-53, Honorary Air Commodore, since 1981, Inspector General since 1990; Member, Dumfries County Council, 1952-67 (Chairman, Planning Committee and Joint Police Committee); Scottish Conservative Whip, 1967-70; Lord Commissioner, HM Treasury, 1970-71; Minister of Health and Education, Scottish Office, 1971-74; Opposition Spokesman on Scottish Affairs, 1974-75, Sport, 1974-79; Minister of Sport and Rural Affairs, 1979-81; Member: Nature Conservancy Council, 1982-91, Area Executive, NFU, 1964-97, Council, National Trust for Scotland, 1983-92; Vice-President, Scottish Rugby Union, 1975, President, 1976-77; Member, Queen's Bodyguard for Scotland (Royal Company of Archers); President: NSRA, 1987-92, ACU, 1983-90. Recreations: rugby; golf; flying; vintage cars; country sports. Address: (h.) Williamwood, Kirtlebridge, Lockerbie, Dumfriesshire; T.-01461 500213.

Montagu-Smith, Group Captain Arthur, DL, RAF (Retd); b. 17.7.15; m., Elizabeth Hood Alexander; 1 s.; 1 d. Educ. Whitgift School; RAF Staff College. Commissioned RAF, 1935; Adjutant 99 Squadron, 1938-39; served Second World War, European Theatre, North Africa and Mediterranean; Flt. Cdr., 264 Squadron, 1940, and 221 Squadron, 1941; OC 248 Squadron, 1942-43; Battle of Britain Gold Rosette, 1940; mentioned in Despatches, 1942; Deputy Director, RAF Training, USA (Washington), 1944; OC 104 Wing, France, 1945; Hon. ADC, Governor, N.I., 1948-49; Air Adviser, New Delhi, 1949-50; RAF Representative, Chiefs of Staff Committee, UN, New York, 1951-53; HM Air Attache, Budapest, 1958-60; retired at own request, 1961; Regional Executive, Small Industries Council and Scottish Development Agency, 1962-80; Member, Elgin District Council, 1967-75; Member, Moray TAFA, 1961-68; Director, Elgin and Lossiemouth Harbour Company, 1966-90; Deputy Lieutenant, Morayshire, 1970-91; Hon. County Representative, Moray and Nairn, RAF Benevolent Fund, since 1964; Chairman, Elgin and Lossiemouth Scottish SPCA, 1971-82; Past President, Victoria League, Moray and Nairn; Past Chairman, Moray Association of Youth Clubs. Recreations: outdoor interests; travel; animal welfare. Address: (h.) Woodpark, by Elgin, Moray IV30 3LF; T.-0134 384 2220.

Monteith, W. Graham, MA, BD, BPhil, PhD. Chairman, Disability Scotland, since 1998; Honorary Scottish Secretary, Student Christian Movement, since 1997; b. 14.11.46, Glasgow; m., Edna Jean Little. Educ. Ross High School; Edinburgh University; York University. Assistant Minister, St. Andrew, Drumchapel; Minister: Berwick-upon-Tweed, Wallace Green; Minister, Hoy and Walls linked with Flotta, Orkney. Director: Capability Scotland, Handicabs (Lothian), Artlink Lothian. Publication: Disability: Faith Acceptance, 1987. Recreations: music; travel. Address: 20/3 Grandfield, Edinburgh EH6 4TL; T.-0131-552 2564.

Montgomery, Sir (Basil Henry) David, 9th Bt, JP, DL. Lord Lieutenant, Perth and Kinross, since 1995; Chairman, Forestry Commission, 1979-89; b. 20.3.31.

Montgomery, David Andrew, MA, CertEd. Chief Executive, East Ayrshire Council, since 1995; b. 22.10.46, Irvine; 2 s.; 1 d. Educ. Irvine Royal Academy; Glasgow University; Jordanhill College of Education. Teacher, Principal Teacher, Assistant Head Teacher, 1969-81; Strathclyde Regional Council: Principal Officer (Teacher Staffing), 1982-84; Education Officer, 1984-86; Assistant Director of Education, then Depute Director of Education, then Senior Depute, 1986-95. Recreations: photography; aviation. Address: (b.) Council Headquarters, London Road, Kilmarnock KA3 7BU; T.-01563 576002.

Montgomery, Iona Allison Eleanor, BA (Hons), RSW. Artist; Lecturer (part-time): Edinburgh College of Art, since 1997, Grays School of Art, since 1994; b. 14.4.65, Glasgow. Educ. Boclair Academy; Glasgow School of Art; Tamarind Institute, University of New Mexico. Exhibited widely in UK, Europe, USA and Japan, since 1989; solo exhibitions: Edinburgh 1989, Glasgow, 1990, Jedburgh, 1992, Vienna, 1993; work in numerous public collections; Alexander Graham Munro Award, RSW, 1990; Lauder Award, 1991, Lady Artists Club Trust Award, 1992, Cross Trust Bursary, 1994, Glasgow District Council Bursary, 1995; elected, RSW, 1991. Recreations: walking; music; film; travel. Address: (h.) Flat 2/3, 171A Maryhill Road, Glasgow G20 7XL; T.-0141-332 9512.

Montrose, 8th Duke of (James Graham), OStJ. Brigadier, Queen's Bodyguard for Scotland (Royal Company of Archers), since 1986 (Member, since 1965); b. 6.4.35; m., Catherine Elizabeth MacDonell; 2 s.; 1 d. Educ. Loretto. President, Royal Highland and Agricultural Society, 1997-98; Council Member, National Farmers' Union of Scotland, 1982-84, 1987-90. Address: (h.) Buchanan, Drymen, Glasgow.

Moonie, Lewis George, MB, ChB, DPM, MRCPsych, MSc, MFCM. MP (Labour), Kirkcaldy, since 1987; b. 25.2.47, Dundee; m., Sheila Burt; 2 s. Educ. Nicolson Institute, Stornoway; Grove Academy, Dundee; St. Andrews University. A variety of junior and senior medical posts, 1970-87, latterly Consultant in Public Health

Medicine, Fife Health Board. Member: Fife Regional Council, 1982-86, Social Services Select Committee, 1987-88, Treasury Select Committee, 1989-90; Opposition Front-Bench Spokesman on Technology, 1990-92, Science and Technology, 1992-94, Industry, since 1994, National Heritage Spokesman on Broadcasting, 1995-97. Address: (b.) 25 High Street, Kirkcaldy, Fife; T.-01592 201873.

Moore, Andrew F., BL. Director, SCIENTIA (Scottish Chapter, International Society for Business Education and Scotland's Europe House); Interim Chief Executive, Fife Chamber of Commerce; b. 5.12.39, Leven; m., Anne MacGregor; 2 s.; 1 d. Educ. Buckhaven High School; Edinburgh University. Examiner, Estate Duty Office, Edinburgh, 1958-63; Assistant, then Depute Secretary, Scottish Council for Commercial Education, 1963-73; Depute Chief Officer, Scottish Business Education Council, 1973-80; Chief Officer, SCOTBEC, 1980-86; seconded to Stirling University, 1987-89; Director: Scottish Chambers of Commerce, 1989-95, Chinese Enterprise Management Development Programmes, 1989-94. Governor, Scottish Council for Educational Technology, 1976-84; Director, Filmhouse, Edinburgh, 1980-85; British Association for Commercial and Industrial Education: Honorary Treasurer, 1979-81, Honorary Secretary, 1966-80; President: International Society for Business Education, 1993-97, Pedagogical Committee, International Society for Business Education and Member, ISBE/SIEC Executive, since 1980; Member, Scottish Council for Research in Education, 1984-87; Hon. Secretary, Scottish Students' Song Book Committee Ltd., 1980-93; Session Clerk, Scoonie Kirk, Leven, 1982-92; President, Leven YMCA 1972-95; Member: Council, Association of British Chambers of Commerce; Executive Committee, Scottish Business in the Community; Executive Committee, Scottish Council (Development & Industry); Forces Resettlement Committee for Scotland, 1989-95; RNIB Alwyn House Advisory Committee, 1994; Director: Fife Enterprise, 1994, North of Scotland European Partnership, 1994, Fife Careers Ltd., 1996; Chairman, Economic Affairs, Fife Chamber of Commerce, 1995-97; Chairman, Finance Committee, Glenrothes College; Chairman, Steering Group on Health Promotion in SMEs, 1995; Director: Centre for Europe, 1995, QTAC, since 1997; Member, Board of Management, Fife College of Further and Higher Education, since 1997. Recreations: golf; foreign travel. Address: (h.) Annandale, Linksfield Street, Leven, Fife; T.-01333 422644.

Moore, David Arthur, MB, BS, DPH, DIH, DTM&H, FFOM. Chairman, Scottish Council on Alcohol, since 1995; b. 5.2.40, South Shields; m., Susan Thomley; 1 s.; 2 d. Educ. Jarrow Grammar School; Durham University. Consultant Occupational Physician, Hon. Clinical Teacher, Edinburgh University. Recreations: yachting; books; music. Address: (h.) 94 Murrayfield Gardens, Edinburgh EH12 6DJ; T.-0131-346 0861.

Moore, George, LLB (Hons). Solicitor and Solicitor Advocate; Joint Senior Partner, Hamilton Burns Moore, since 1973; b. 7.11.47, Kilmarnock; m., Ann Beattie; 2 s.; 1 d. Educ. High School of Glasgow; Glasgow University. Member, Glasgow and North Argyll Legal Aid Committee, 1979; Reporter to Scottish Legal Aid Board, 1986; part-time Chairman, Industrial Tribunals in Scotland, 1986; Member, Sheriff Court Rules Council, 1987. Recreations: tennis; golf; windsurfing. Address: (b.) 13 Bath Street, Glasgow G2 1HY; T.-0141-353 2121.

Moore, Malcolm Robert, LLB. Assistant Chief Executive, South Lanarkshire Council, since 1998; b. 15.11.48, Lennoxtown; m., Betty; 1 s.; 1 d. Educ. Broxburn Academy; Edinburgh University. Law Apprentice, Leonards, Solicitors, 1970-73; Solicitor, Burgh of Hamilton, 1973-75; Legal Manager, then District Solicitor, then Director of Corporate Services, Hamilton District Council, 1974-96; Director of Legal Services, South Lanarkshire Council, 1995-98. Recreations: photography; walking; reading; cinema. Address: (b.) Town House, Cadzow Street, Hamilton; T.-01698 452020.

Moore, Michael, MA, CA. MP (Liberal Democrat), Tweeddale, Ettrick and Lauderdale, since 1997; Member, House of Commons Scottish Select Committee, since 1997; b. 3.6.65. Educ. Strathallan School; Jedburgh Grammar School; Edinburgh University. Manager, Corporate Finance practice, Coopers and Lybrand. Recreations: jazz; films; walking; golf. Address: (b.) House of Commons, London SW1A 0AA.

Moore, Rev. William Haisley, MA. Secretary for Scotland, Boys Brigade, 1990-96; b. 9.7.35, Donaghadee; m., Geraldine Ann Moorhead; 1 s.; 2 d. Educ. Bangor Grammar School; Magee University College, Londonderry; Dublin University; Presbyterian College, Belfast. Chaplain to the Forces, attached Royal Highland Fusiliers, 1966-70; Minister, Church of Scotland, 1970-90. Convener, Church of Scotland Youth Education Committee. Recreations: golf; gardening. Address: (h.) Loughaghery, 17 Shawpark Crescent, Selkirk TD7 4EX; T.-01750 22566.

Moorhouse, John Edwin, DL (Edinburgh). Chairman, Nobel Exhibition Trust, Lime and Associates, Jane Moore Trust;; b. 7.10.41, Stone, Staffs; m., Susan; 2 s.; 2 d. Educ. Bridlington School. With Royal Dutch/Shell Group of companies, 1963-94; Shell UK, 1963-94; Director, Scottish Business in the Community, 1990-98. Recreations: music; theatre. Address: (b.) 4 Oxford Terrace, Edinburgh EH4 1PX; T.-0131-343 3777.

Moorhouse, Professor Robert Gordon, MA, PhD, FRSE, FRAS, ChP, FInstP. Honorary Senior Research Fellow, Glasgow University, since 1994; Theoretical Physicist; b. 14.3.26, Huddersfield; m., Peggy Gee; 1 s. Educ. Huddersfield College; Cambridge University; Birmingham University. Glasgow University, 1950-61; Rutherford-Appleton Laboratory, 1961-67; Glasgow University, 1967-94 (Emeritus Professor, since 1994). Publication: The Pion-Nucleon System, 1973. Recreation: history. Address: (b.) Department of Physics and Astronomy, Glasgow University, Glasgow G12 8QQ; T.-0141-330 5160.

Moos, Khursheed Francis, OBE, MB, BS, BDS, FRCSEdin, FDS RCS (Eng, Edin), FDS RCPS (Glas). Consultant Oral and Maxillofacial Surgeon; Honorary Professor, Glasgow University; Chairman, Intercollegiate Board in Oral and Maxillofacial Surgery; b. 1.11.34, London; m., Katharine Addison; 2 s.; 1 d. Educ. Dulwich College; Guy's Hospital, London; Westminster Hospital. National Service, RADC, Lt., 1959, Capt., 1960; Registrar in Oral Surgery, Mount Vernon Hospital, Middlesex, 1966-67; Senior Registrar, Oral Surgery, University of Wales, Cardiff, 1967-69; Consultant Oral Surgeon, S. Warwicks and Coventry Hospitals, 1969-74; Consultant Oral and Maxillofacial Surgeon, Canniesburn Hospital, Glasgow, since 1974; Dean, Dental Faculty, Royal College of Physicians and Surgeons of Glasgow, 1992-95; Chairman, Intercollegiate Examination Board in oral and maxillofacial surgery, 1995-98; Civilian Consultant to Royal Navy, since 1976; President: Cranio-facial Society of Great Britain, 1994-95, British Association of Oral and Maxillofacial Surgeons, 1991-92; Down Surgical Prize, 1988; Colyer Medal, Royal College of Surgeons of England, 1997. Publications include contributions to books and various papers. Recreations: music; natural history; philately; Eastern philosophy; gardening. Address: (h.) 43 Colquhoun Street, Helensburgh, Dunbartonshire G84 9JW; T.-01436 673232.

Moray, Earl of (Douglas John Moray Stuart), BA, FRICS. Chairman, Moray Estates Development Co., since 1974; b. 13.2.28, Johannesburg; m., Malvina Dorothea Murray; 1 s.; 1 d. Educ. Hilton College, Natal; Trinity

College, Cambridge. Address: (h.) Doune Park, Doune, Perthshire.

Morbey, Gillian, OBE, BA (Hons), RGN. Director, Sense Scotland, since 1989; Trustee, Family Fund, since 1996; b. 11.6.53, Glasgow; m., Jeremy Morbey; 1 s.; 1 d. Educ. Williamwood High School; Strathclyde University. Nursing career within NHS; first Development Officer, Sense Scotland, 1985. Past Chairperson, West of Scotland Branch, Scottish Association for the Deaf; Chairperson, Glasgow Council of Voluntary Services, 1994-97. Recreations: supporter of Worldwide Fund for Nature; reading; music; walking. Address: (b.) 45 Finnieston Street, Clydeway Centre, Glasgow G3 8JU; T.-0141-564 2444.

Morgan, Alasdair, MP, MA, BA. MP (SNP), Galloway and Upper Nithsdale, since 1997; Vice President, Scottish National Party; Member, Select Committee for Trade and Industry; b. 21.4.45, Aberfeldy; m., Anne Gilfillan; 2 d. Educ. Breadalbane Academy, Aberfeldy; Glasgow University. SNP: National Treasurer, 1983-90, Senior Vice-Convener, 1990-91, National Secretary, 1992-97. Recreation: hill-walking. Address: (h.) Nether Cottage, Crocketford, Dumfries.

Morgan, David Ivor, MA (Hons), LLB, NP. Regional Chairman of Employment Tribunals (Scotland), since 1997; Member, Panel of Chairmen, Reserve Forces Appeal Tribunal, since 1997; b. 7.12.36, Giffnock; m., Diane Scott; 1 s.; 1 d. Educ. Hutchesons Grammar School; Aberdeen Grammar School; Aberdeen University. Assistant Solicitor, 1961-64; Partner, Davidson and Garden, Advocates in Aberdeen, 1964-89; full-time Chairman of Employment Tribunals (Scotland), 1989-97. Burgess, City of Aberdeen. Recreations: hill-walking; fishing. Address: (b.) Atholl House, 84-88 Guild Street, Aberdeen; T.-01224 593137.

Morgan, Edwin (George), OBE, MA, Hon. DLitt (Loughborough, Glasgow, Edinburgh), Hon.DUniv (Stirling, Waikato); Hon. MUniv (Open). Freelance Writer (Poet, Critic, Translator), since 1980; Emeritus Professor of English, Glasgow University, since 1980; Honorary Professor, University College of Wales, Aberystwyth, since 1990; b. 27.4.20, Glasgow. Educ. Rutherglen Academy; High School of Glasgow; Glasgow University. War Service, Royal Army Medical Corps, 1940-46; Glasgow University: Assistant Lecturer in English, 1947, Lecturer, 1950, Senior Lecturer, 1965, Reader, 1971, Titular Professor, 1975; Visiting Professor of English, Strathclyde University, 1987-90; received Cholmondeley Award for Poets, 1968; Hungarian PEN Memorial Medal, 1972; Scottish Arts Council Book Awards, 1968, 1973, 1977, 1978, 1983, 1985, 1988, 1991, 1992; Saltire Society and Royal Bank Scottish Literary Award, 1983; Soros Translation Award (New York), 1985; Order of Merit, Republic of Hungary, 1997. Publications: (poetry): The Vision of Cathkin Braes, 1952, Beowulf, 1952, The Cape of Good Hope, 1955, Poems from Eugenio Montale, 1959, Sovpoems, 1961, Collins Albatross Book of Longer Poems (Editor), 1963, Starryveldt, 1965, Emergent Poems, 1967, Gnomes, 1968, The Second Life, 1968, Proverbfolder, 1969, Twelve Songs, 1970, The Horseman's Word, 1970, Scottish Poetry 1-6 (Co-Editor), 1966-72; Glasgow Sonnets, 1972, Wi the Haill Voice, 1972, The Whittrick, 1973, From Glasgow to Saturn, 1973, Fifty Renascence Love-Poems, 1975, Rites of Passage, 1976, The New Divan, 1977, Colour Poems, 1978, Platen: Selected Poems, 1978, Star Gate, 1979, Scottish Satirical Verse (Editor), 1980, Poems of Thirty Years, 1982, Grafts/Takes, 1983, Sonnets from Scotland, 1984, Selected Poems, 1985, From the Video Box, 1986, Themes on a Variation, 1988; Tales from Limerick Zoo, 1988; Collected Poems, 1990; Hold Hands Among the Atoms, 1991; Sweeping Out the Dark, 1994; Collected Translations, 1996; Virtual and Other Realities, 1997; prose: Essays, 1974, East European Poets, 1976, Hugh MacDiarmid, 1976, Twentieth Century Scottish Classics, 1987; Nothing Not Giving Messages, 1990; Crossing the Border, 1990; Evening Will Come They Will Sew The Blue Sail, 1991; plays: The Apple-Tree, 1982; Master Peter Pathelin, 1983; Cyrano de Bergerac, 1992. Address: (h.) 19 Whittingehame Court, Glasgow G12 0BG; T.-0141-339 6260.

Morgan, Leslie, DMS, DPE, FILAM, MIM. Managing Director, Slainte Mhath; b. 7.8.53, Perth; m., Jill; 1 s.; 1 d. Educ. Perth Academy; Jordanhill College; Glasgow College of Technology. Sports Officer, Magnum Leisure Centre, Irvine; Deputy Manager, Bishopbriggs Sports Centre; Manager, Spectrum Leisure Centre, Co. Durham; Chief Leisure Officer, Wear Valley District Council; Director of Leisure and Economic Development, Wear Valley D.C.; Chief Executive, Moray District Council; General Manager, Hoskyns Forres BPD (first Business Process Management Centre in Europe). British Leisure Personality of the Year, 1990. Recreations: basketball; skiing; squash. Address: (h.) The Orchard Dyke, near Forres, Moray IV36 0TF; T.-01309 641364.

Morgan, Tom, CBE, DL, NDD, CDD; b. 24.2.14, Aberdeenshire; m., Mary Montgomery McLauchlan (deceased); 2 s. Educ. Longside School; North and West of Scotland Colleges of Agriculture. Unigate PLC, 38 years (Regional Director, Scotland); Councillor, City of Edinburgh Corporation, 1954-71, City of Edinburgh District Council, 1977-84; City Treasurer, 1968-71; Lord Provost and Lord Lieutenant, 1980-84; Chairman, Edinburgh Military Tattoo and Edinburgh International Festival, 1980-84. Recreations: golf; gardening. Address: (h.) 400 Lanark Road, Edinburgh EH13 0LX; T.-0131-441 3245.

Morison, Hugh, MA, DipEd. Director General, Scotch Whisky Association, since 1994; b. 22.11.43, Bognor Regis; m.; 2 d. Educ. Chichester High School for Boys; St. Catherine's College, Oxford. Assistant Principal, Scottish Home and Health Department, 1966-69; Private Secretary to Minister of State, Scottish Office, 1969-70; Principal: Scottish Education Department, 1971-73, Scottish Economic Planning Department, 1973-79 (seconded to Offshore Supplies Office, Department of Energy, 1974-75); Assistant Secretary, Scottish Economic Planning Department, 1979-82; Gwilym Gibbon Research Fellow, Nuffield College, Oxford, 1982-83; Assistant Secretary, Scottish Development Department, 1983-84; Under Secretary, Scottish Home and Health Department, 1984-88, Scottish Office Industry Department, 1988-93; Non-Executive Director, Weir Group PLC, 1988-93; Member, Health Appointments Advisory Committee (Scotland), since 1995; Member, Executive Committee, Barony Housing Association, since 1996. Publications: The Regeneration of Local Economies, 1987; Dauphine (Co-Author), 1991. Recreations: hill-walking; archaeology; literature. Address: (b.) Scotch Whisky Association, 20 Atholl Crescent, Edinburgh, EH3 8HF; T.-0131-222 9201.

Morkis, Jerzy Tomasz, BSc. Editor, Fife Free Press, since 1993; b. 29.9.56, Leven; m., Judith Anne Spencer; 1 s.; 1 d. Educ. Buckhaven High School; Stirling University. Joined Fife Free Press Group, 1978; Chief Reporter, East Fife Mail, 1982; Editor, East Fife Mail, 1990. Trustee, T.S. Murray Award; Member, Media and Communication Programme Committee, Fife College. Recreations: tennis; reading; travel. Address: (b.) 23 Kirk Wynd, Kirkcaldy KY1 1EP; T.-01592 261451.

Morrice, Graeme. Leader, West Lothian Council; b. 23.2.59, Edinburgh. Educ. Broxburn Academy; Napier University. Recreations: music; art; reading. Address: (h.) 39 Burnside Road, Uphall, Broxburn EH52 5DE; T.-01506 853266.

Morrice, Ken, MD, DPM, FRCPsych. Poet and Writer, since 1965; Psychiatrist, since 1956; b. 14.7.24, Aberdeen; m., Norah Thompson; 1 s.; 2 d. Educ. Robert Gordon's College; Aberdeen University. Hon. Fellow, Aberdeen University Mental Health Department. Publications: Crisis Intervention; Studies in Community Care; seven volumes of poetry; numerous papers; short stories. Recreations: golf; walking; TV. Address: (h.) 30 Carnegie Crescent, Aberdeen; T.-Aberdeen 310136.

Morris, Alistair Lindsay, LLB, DipLP. Solicitor; Director, Sinclair Osborne Financial Services Ltd., since 1987; Partner, Pagan Osborne Services Ltd.; Partner, Pagan Osborne; Partner, Pagan Macbeth; b. 30.7.58, Dunfermline; m., Sandra Willins; 2 s. Educ. Queen Anne High School, Dunfermline; Aberdeen University. Council Member, Law Society of Scotland, since 1992, Convenor, Professional Practice Committee, 1996-98, Convener, Insurance Committee, since 1998. Recreations: motor sport; football; rugby. Address: (b.) 83 Market Street, St. Andrews, KY16 9NX; T.-01334 475001.

Morris, Arthur MacGregor, MA, MB, BChir, FRCSEdin, FRCSEng, LRCP. Consultant Plastic Surgeon, Dundee Teaching Hospitals, since 1975; Honorary Senior Lecturer in Surgery, Dundee University, since 1975; b. 6.5.41, Heswall; m., Victoria Margaret Whitaker; 1 s.; 1 d. Educ. Dulwich College; Cambridge University; Guy's Hospital. House Officer, 1965-66; Anatomy Demonstrator, Newcastle, 1966-67; Rotating Surgical Trainee in Surgery, Bristol, 1967-69; Research Registrar, then Casualty Registrar, Guy's Hospital, 1969-71; Plastic Surgery Registrar, Canniesburn Hospital, Glasgow, 1972; Plastic Surgery Senior Registrar, Bangour General Hospital and Royal Hospital for Sick Children, Edinburgh, 1972-75. Chairman, Scottish Council, BMA; Deputy Chairman, Scottish Joint Consultants Committee. Publications: Complications of Plastic Surgery (book); papers. Recreations: golf; curling; photography; bee-keeping; gardening; fishing. Address: (b.) Plastic Surgery Unit, Ninewells Hospital, Dundee; T.-01382 660111.

Morris, Professor Arthur Stephen, BA, MA, PhD. Professor, Department of Geography, Glasgow University; b. 26.12.36, Broadway, Worcestershire; m., Estela C.; 1 s.; 1 d. Educ. Chipping Campden; Exeter College, Oxford University; University of Maryland; University of Wisconsin. Instructor/Assistant Professor, Western Michigan University, 1964-67; Lecturer, Senior Lecturer, Reader, Glasgow University; Visiting Professor: Central University of Venezuela 1976-77, CEPEIGE, Quito, 1980, Colegio Mexiquense, Mexico, 1987. Publications: South America; Latin America. Recreations: gardening; music; sailing. Address: (h.) The Old Manse, Shandon, near Helensburgh; T.-0141-339 8855.

Morris, Professor Christopher David, BA, DipEd, MIFA, FSA, FSA Scot, FRHistS, FRSE. Professor of Archaeology, Glasgow University, since 1990; b. 14.4.46, Preston; m., Dr. Colleen E. Batey. Educ. Queen Elizabeth's Grammar School, Blackburn; Durham University; Oxford University. Assistant Lecturer, Hockerill College of Education, Bishops Stortford, 1968-72; Lecturer, then Senior Lecturer in Archaeology, 1972-88, Reader in Viking Archaeology, 1989-90, Durham University. Member: Ancient Monuments Board for Scotland, since 1990, Court, University of Glasgow. Recreations: classical music; opera; theatre; walking. Address: (b.) Department of Archaeology, Gregory Building, Lilybank Gardens, Glasgow University, Glasgow G12 8QQ; T.-0141-339 8855, Ext. 5690/4422.

Morris, James, CBE, BSc. Chief Executive, Scottish Society for the Prevention of Cruelty to Animals, since 1991; President, Scottish Area, Royal Air Forces Association, since 1991; Chairman, ATC Council for Scotland and NI, 1995-97; President, Scottish Union Jack Association, since 1995; b. 8.7.36, Kirkcaldy; m., Anna W. Provan; 3 s. Educ. Kirkcaldy High School; Edinburgh University. Entered RAF, 1957; commanded No. 201 Squadron, 1975-77; commanded RAF Kinloss, 1981-84; Director Operational Requirements (Air), 1986-89; Air Officer, Scotland and Northern Ireland, 1989-91 (Air Vice Marshal); HM Commissioner, Queen Victoria School, since 1995. Recreations: sailing; curling. Address: (b.) Braehead Mains, 603 Queensferry Road, Edinburgh EH4 6EA; T.-0131-339 0222.

Morris, James Shepherd, RSA, RIBA, FRIAS, ALI. Principal, Morris and Steedman, Architects and Landscape Architects, since 1956; Hon. Treasurer, Royal Scottish Academy, since 1992; b. 22.8.31, St. Andrews; m., Eleanor Kenner Smith; 2 s.; 1 d. Educ. Daniel Stewart's College, Edinburgh; Edinburgh School of Architecture; University of Pennsylvania. Lt., Royal Engineers, 1957-59. Member, Council: RIAS and Edinburgh Architectural Association, 1969-71, Cockburn Association, Edinburgh; Convenor, Fellowship Committee, RIAS, 1985-87; Trustee, Museum of Antiquities, 1980-86; Member, Arts Council of GB, 1973-80; Vice Chairman, Scottish Arts Council, 1976-80; Member, Management Committee, Traverse Theatre; ARSA, 1975; RSA, 1989; two RIBA awards for Scotland; British Steel Award; 10 Civic Trust awards. Recreations: painting; golf; skiing; tennis. Address: (b.) 38 Young Street, Edinburgh EH2 4JD; T.-0131-226 6563.

Morris, Jean Daveena Ogilvy, CBE, MA, MEd, LLD (Dundee and St. Andrews), OSStJ. Member, Court, University of St. Andrews, since 1994; Chairman, Parole Board for Scotland, 1980-92; b. 28.1.29, Kilmarnock; m., Rev. William J. Morris (qv); 1 s. Educ. Kilmarnock Academy; St. Andrews University. Clinical Psychologist: Royal Hospital for Sick Children, Edinburgh, St. David's Hospital, Cardiff, and Church Village, Pontypridd; Member, Bailie and Convener of Housing, Peterhead Town Council; Member, Aberdeen County Council; Columnist, Aberdeen Press and Journal; Chairman, Christian Action Housing Association; Member, Scottish Federation of Housing Associations; Chairman: Government Committee on Links Between Housing and Social Work (Morris Committee), Local Review Committee, Barlinnie Prison, Glasgow Abbeyfield Society; Vice Chairman, TSB Foundation; Director, Scottish Advisory Board, Abbey National; Chairman, Scotia House Development Company. Badminton Blue, St. Andrews University. Recreations: swimming; holidays in France. Address: (h.) 1 Whitehill Grove, Newton Mearns, Glasgow G77 5DH; T.-0141-639 6327.

Morris, Philip T., BSc, FCA. Finance Director, Adam & Company Group PLC, since 1993; b. 23.10.52, Malaysia. Educ. Morrisons Academy, Crieff; St. Andrews University. Arthur Young, Chartered Accountants, London, Stavanger, Norway and Dundee Offices, 1974-87; Royal Bank of Scotland Group (Corporate Finance), 1987-93. Recreations: travel; circuit training; crosswords. Address: (b.) 22 Charlotte Square, Edinburgh EH2 4DF; T.-0131-225 8484.

Morris, Professor Richard Graham Michael, MA, DPhil, FRSE, FRS. Chairman, Department of Neuroscience, Edinburgh University, (Professor, since 1993, Reader, 1989-93); b. 27.6.48, Worthing; m., Hilary Ann; 2 d. Educ. St. Albans, Washington DC; Marlborough College; Cambridge University; Sussex University. Addison Wheeler Fellow, Durham University, 1973-75; SSO, British Museum (Natural History), 1975-77; Researcher, BBC Television, 1977; Lecturer, St. Andrews University, 1977-86; MRC University Research Fellow, 1983-86. Member, MRC Neurosciences Grants Committee, 1981-85, MRC Neurosciences Board, 1993-98; Hon. Secretary, Experimental Psychological Society, 1985-89; Chairman: Brain Research Association, 1990-94, Sectional Committee for Medicine and Biomedical Sciences, Royal Society of

Edinburgh, 1995-97; Member, Council, European Neuroscience Association. Publications: academic papers and books; Learning and Memory (Co-Editor). Recreation: sailing. Address: (b.) Centre for Neuroscience, Edinburgh University, Crichton Street, Edinburgh EH8 9LE; T.-0131-650 3518/4562.

Morris, Professor Robert John, BA, DPhil. Professor of Economic and Social History, Edinburgh University, since 1993; b. 12.10.43, Sheffield; m., Barbara; 1 s.; 1 d. Educ. Acklam Hall, Middlesbrough; Keble and Nuffield Colleges, Oxford. Lecturer and Senior Lecturer in Economic and Social History, Edinburgh University, since 1968. Founding Editor, History and Computing. Recreation: watching vegetables grow. Address: (b.) 55 George Square, Edinburgh EH8 9JU.

Morris, Professor Robert Lyle, BSc, PhD. Professor of Parapsychology, Edinburgh University, since 1985; b. 9.7.42, Canonsburg, Pennsylvania; m., Joanna Du Barry; 2 d. Educ. Crafton High School; University of Pittsburgh; Duke University. Research Fellow, Duke University, 1969-71; Research Co-ordinator, then Research Associate, Psychical Research Foundation, 1971-74; Lecturer in Parapsychology, University of California, Santa Barbara, 1974-78; Lecturer, School of Social Sciences, University of California, Irvine, 1978-80; Research Coordinator, Communication Studies Laboratory, and Senior Research Scientist, School of Computer and Information Sciences, Syracuse University, 1980-85. Member: Council, Parapsychological Association, Council, British Society for Psychical Research; President, Psychology Section, British Association for the Advancement of Science, 1995-96. Publication: Foundations of Parapsychology: Exploring the Boundaries of Human Capability (Co-Author), 1986; Guidelines for Testing Psychic Claimants (Co-Author), 1996. Address: (b.) Psychology Department, University of Edinburgh, 7 George Square, Edinburgh EH8 9JZ; T.-0131 650 3343.

Morris, William, BA (Hons), FIOP, FScotvec, FSQA; b. 15.5.24, Aberdare, Wales; m., Pauline; 1 s.; 2 d. Educ. Aberdare Boys' Secondary School; Cardiff School of Art; Garnet College, London; London School of Printing and Graphic Arts; Open University. Compositor/Typographer; Royal Artillery, 1942-47; Lecturer in Typography, LSP&GA, 1951-58; Head, Department of Typography and Related Subjects; Depute Principal, Glasgow College of Building and Printing, 1959-81; Principal, Anniesland College, 1981-89; Assistant General Secretary, Association of Principals of Colleges, 1991-96. Board Member, Printing and Publishing Industry Training Board, 1968-82; Member, City and Guilds of London Institute; Board Member and Director, Scottish Vocational Education Council, 1987-91; Past Chairman, Association of Principals of Colleges (Scottish Branch); Past Chairman, Association of College Management (Scottish Branch); Secretary, Employers' Association for Scottish Further Education Colleges, 1992-93; Secretary to the Vestry, St. Cyprian's Church, Lenzie, 1981-94; Vice-President, Glasgow Welsh Society, since 1992; President: Probus Club of Kirkintilloch, 1996, Rotary Club of Kelvin, 1997-98. Recreations: golf; gardening; painting. Address: (h.) 26 Laurel Avenue, Lenzie, Kirkintilloch, Glasgow G66 4RU; T.-0141-776 2716.

Morris, Rev. William James, KCVO, ChStJ, JP, BA, BD, PhD, LLD, DD, Hon. FRCP&SGlas. Minister, Glasgow Cathedral, since 1967; Chaplain in Ordinary to The Queen in Scotland, 1969-96, Extra Chaplain, since 1996; Chairman, Iona Cathedral Trust, since 1979; Dean, Chapel Royal in Scotland, 1991-96; Chaplain to The Queen's Body Guard in Scotland (Royal Company of Archers), since 1994; b. 22.8.25, Cardiff; m., Jean Daveena Ogilvy Howie (see Jean Daveena Ogilvy Morris); 1 s. Educ. Cardiff High School; University of Wales (Cardiff and Aberystwyth); Edinburgh University. Ordained, 1951; Assistant, Canongate Kirk, Edinburgh, 1949-51; Minister: Barry Island and Cadoxton Presbyterian Church of Wales, 1951-53, St. David's, Buckhaven, 1953-57, Peterhead Old Parish Church, 1957-67; Chaplain, Peterhead Prison, 1963-67; Chaplain to Lord High Commissioner, 1975-76; Moderator, Deer Presbytery, 1965-66; Chaplain: Strathclyde Police, Glasgow Academy, High School of Glasgow, Glasgow District Council, Trades House of Glasgow, West of Scotland Engineers Association, Royal Scottish Automobile Club; Member, Independent Broadcasting Authority, 1979-84 (Chairman, Scottish Advisory Committee); Member, Convocation, Strathclyde University; Honorary President, Glasgow Society of Social Service; Lord Provost's Award, 1996. Publication: A Walk Through Glasgow Cathedral, 1986. Recreation: being good, careful, and happy (not always simultaneously). Address: (h.) 1 Whitehill Grove, Newton Mearns, Glasgow G77 5DA; T.-0141 639 6327.

Morrison, Alan Stewart, MA (Hons). Editor, The List, since 1998; b. 29.4.66, Falkirk. Educ. Denny High School; University of Edinburgh. Edinburgh International Film Festival: Head of Publications, 1992-95, Programmer, since 1992; Film Editor, The List, since 1992; Deputy Editor, The List, 1995-98. Recreations: cinema; crime novels; following Falkirk F. C. Address: (b.) 14 High Street, Edinburgh EH1 1TE; T.-0131-558 1191.

Morrison, Sir Alexander Fraser, CBE, FRSA, BSc, CEng, FICE, MIHT, FScotvec, FCIOB. Executive Chairman, Morrison Construction plc, since 1996; Director, Clydesdale Bank PLC; Member, Scottish Business Forum; Vice President, Royal Highland and Agricultural Society of Scotland, 1995-96; b. 20.3.48, Dingwall; m., Patricia Janice Murphy; 1 s.; 2 d. Educ. Tain Royal Academy; Edinburgh University. Morrison Construction Group, since 1970; Managing Director, 1976-84. National Federation of Civil Engineering Contractors: Chairman, 1993-94, Vice President, 1994-96; Chairman, Highlands and Islands Enterprise, 1992-98; Director, Aberforth Split Level Trust plc; winner, 1991 Scottish Business Achievement Award; Hon. Doctor of Technology: Napier University, 1995, Glasgow Caledonian University, 1997. Recreations: rugby; golf; skiing; opera; the countryside; theatre; art. Address: (b.) Morrison House, 12 Atholl Crescent, Edinburgh EH3 8HA; T.-0131-228 4188.

Morrison, Rev. Alistair Hogarth, BTh, DipYCS. Minister, St. Mark's-Oldhall, Paisley, since 1989; b. 12.9.43, Glasgow; 1 s.; 1 d. Educ. Jordanhill College School; Aberdeen University; Jordanhill College of Education. City of Glasgow/Strathclyde Police, 1962-81 (resigned with rank of Inspector to train for Ministry); Minister, Elgin High Church, 1985-89. Strathclyde Medal for Bravery, 1976. Recreations: hill-walking; general fitness. Address: 36 Newtyle Road, Paisley PA1 3JX; T.-0141-889 4279.

Morrison, Andrew Neil, CBE. Chief Inspector of Fire Services for Scotland, since 1993; b. 8.9.37, Arbroath; m., Kathleen; 1 s. Educ. Arbroath High School; Dundee College of Technology. Angus Fire Brigade, 1962-75; Tayside Fire Brigade, 1976-80; Deputy Firemaster, then Firemaster, Grampian Fire Brigade, 1980-93. Queen's Fire Service Medal; Hon. Doctor of Technology; Fellow, Institution of Fire Engineers. Recreations: curling; golf. Address: (b.) Scottish Office, Saughton House, Edinburgh EH11 3XD; T.-0131-244 2342.

Morrison, Rev. Angus, MA, BD. Minister, Associated Presbyterian Churches, Viewforth Congregation, Edinburgh, since 1989; b. 30.8.53, Oban; m., Marion Jane Matheson; 3 s.; 1 d. Educ. Oban High School; Glasgow University; London University; Edinburgh University. Minister, Free Presbyterian Church of Scotland Oban Congregation, 1979-86, Edinburgh Congregation, 1986-89; Moderator, Southern Presbytery, Free Presbyterian Church, 1987-88; Moderator, APC General Assembly, 1998-99;

Moderator, APC Scottish Presbytery, 1993-94. Member, Council, Rutherford House, Edinburgh; Contributor, Dictionary of Scottish Church History and Theology, 1993; Member, Gaelic Panel, National Bible Society of Scotland. Recreations: reading; swimming. Address: (h.) 6 Frogston Grove, Edinburgh EH10 7AG; T.-0131-445 3673.

Morrison, Rev. Angus Wilson, MA, BD. Minister, Kildalton and Oa Parish, Islay, since 1989 (Minister, Braid Parish Church, Edinburgh, 1977-89); b. 14.2.34, Glasgow; m., Isobel M.S. Taylor; 1 s.; 2 d. Educ. Epsom College, Surrey; Trinity College, Oxford; New College, Edinburgh. Minister: Whithorn, 1961-67, Cults West, Aberdeen, 1967-77; various periods of service on General Assembly Committees, including Overseas Council, Inter-Church Relations, Board of Education and Selection Schools; Observer for World Alliance of Reformed Churches, Vatican Council II, 1963. Recreations: travel; family. Address: The Manse, Port Ellen, Isle of Islay PA42 7DB; T.-01496 302447.

Morrison, Charles, CA, Director, IBM, since 1997; b. 27.8.53, Glasgow; m., Phyllis Ann Morrison. Educ. St. Columba's High School, Greenock. Reid and Man, 1970-75; Ernst and Whinney, 1975-76; joined IBM, 1976. Recreations: golf; running. Address: Inverkip Road, Spango Valley, Greenock, PA16 0AH.

Morrison, Colin Andrew, BA, MEd, DipM, MCIM, CertEd, FCIBS. Director of Education, Chartered Institute of Bankers in Scotland, since 1991; b. 14.10.61, Ellon; m., Stella Ross Ingram. Educ. Peterhead Academy; Robert Gordon's Institute of Technology; Aberdeen College of Education; Edinburgh University. Former Outdoor Pursuits Instructor and F.E. Lecturer/Senior Lecturer; Head of Business Studies, Stevenson College, 1990-91. Recreations: dinghy sailing; skiing. Address: (b.) 19 Rutland Square, Edinburgh EH1 2DE; T.-0131-229 9869.

Morrison, David Ralston. Writer; b. 4.8.41, Glasgow; m., Edna May Wade; 1 s.; 1 d. Educ. Glasgow High School for Boys; Hamilton Academy; Strathclyde University. Librarian: Lanark County, Edinburgh College of Art, Caithness. Founded and ran Scotia Review, Wick Folk Club, Wick Festival of Poetry, Folk and Jazz; author of numerous books of poetry; edited Essays on Neil M. Gunn, Essays on Fionn MacColla. Recreations: walking; drystanedyking; reading; music. Address: (h.) 18 MacArthur Street, Wick KW1 5AX; T.-01955 603703.

Morrison, Hamish Robertson, OBE. Chief Executive, Scottish Fishermen's Federation, since 1998; b. 24.5.44, Irvine; m., Denise Mary; 1 s.; 2 d. Educ. Kilmarnock Academy; Britannia Royal Naval College, Dartmouth. Royal Navy, 1961-70; Scottish Council Development and Industry, 1970-97 (Chief Executive, 1982-97); Chairman, PJMP Group Ltd., Architects, 1997-98. Recreations: writing and public speaking; hill-walking; gardening. Address: (b.) 14 Regent Quay, Aberdeen AB11 5AE; T.-01224 582583.

Morrison, James, RSA, RSW, DA, DUniv (Stirling). Painter in oil and watercolour; b. 11.4.32, Glasgow; m., Dorothy McCormack; 1 s.; 1 d. Educ. Hillhead High School; Glasgow School of Art. Taught part-time, 1955-58; won Torrance Memorial Prize, RGI, 1958; Visiting Artist, Hospitalfield, 1962-63; Council Member, SSA, 1964-67; staff, Duncan of Jordanstone College of Art, 1965-87; won Arts Council Travelling Scholarship to Greece, 1968; painting in various regions of France, 1976-82; numerous one-man exhibitions since 1956, in Scotland, London, Italy, West Germany, Canada; four works in private collection of Duke of Edinburgh and numerous other works in public and private collections; several group exhibitions since 1980 in UK and Europe; regular series of expeditions to paint in Canadian and Greenland High Arctic, since 1990. Publication: Aff the Squerr. Recreation: playing in a chamber music group. Address: (h.) Craigview House, Usan, Montrose, Angus; T.-Montrose 672639.

Morrison, Neil, MA (Hons), DipEd. Rector, Eyemouth High School, since 1990; b. 5.10.47, Aberdeen; m., Lorna; 2 d. Educ. Robert Gordon's College, Aberdeen; Aberdeen University. Teacher, Principal Teacher, 1971-81; Assistant Rector, Mintlaw Academy, 1981-87; Depute Rector, Culloden Academy, 1987-90. Recreation: gardening. Address: (b.) Eyemouth High School, Eyemouth TD14 5BY.

Morrison, Sheriff Nigel Murray Paton, QC. Sheriff of Lothian and Borders at Edinburgh, since 1996; b. 18.3.48, Paisley. Educ. Rannoch School. Called to the Bar of England and Wales, Inner Temple, 1972; admitted to Scottish Bar, 1975; Assistant Editor, Session Cases, 1976-82; Assistant Clerk, Rules Council, 1978-84; Clerk of Faculty, Faculty of Advocates, 1979-86; Standing Junior Counsel to Scottish Development Department (Planning), 1982-86; Temporary Sheriff, 1982-96; Chairman, Social Security Appeal Tribunals, 1982-91; Second (formerly Junior) Counsel to the Lord President of the Court of Session, 1984-89; First Counsel to the Lord President, 1989-96; Counsel to Secretary of State under Private Legislation Procedure (Scotland) Act 1936, 1986-96; QC, 1988; Chairman, Medical Appeal Tribunals, 1991-96; Trustee, National Library of Scotland, since 1989. Publications: Green's Annotated Rules of the Court of Session; Green's Civil Practice Bulletin; Stair Memorial Encyclopaedia of the Laws of Scotland (Contributor). Recreations: music; riding; Scottish country dancing; being taken by his black labrador for walks. Address: 9 India Street, Edinburgh EH3 6HA; T.-0131-225 2807.

Morrison, Peter, MA, LLB. Singer and Solicitor; b. 14.8.40, Greenock; m., Irene; 1 s.; 1 d. Educ. Greenock Academy; Glasgow University. Private legal practice, since 1968; own legal practice, 1977-96; currently Consultant, Paton Farrell Solicitors, Glasgow; began professional singing engagements at University; first television series, Castles in the Air, 1971; Songs of Scotland, 1973-79; television, theatre and concert appearances throughout UK, USA, Europe, Australia and Far East. Recreations: golf; non-participating cricket and rugby supporter. Address: (b.) 180 Hope Street, Glasgow; T.-0141-331 1798.

Morrison, Rev. Roderick, MA, BD. Minister, Partick Gardner Street Church, Glasgow, since 1994; b. 3.7.43, Lochmaddy; m., Christina Ann MacDonald; 1 s.; 1 d. Educ. Lochportan Public School; Glasgow University and Trinity College. Assistant Minister, Drumchapel Old Parish Church, Glasgow, 1973-74; Minister: Carinish Parish Church, North Uist, 1974-81, High Church, Stornoway, Lewis, 1981-94. Recreations: sailing; fishing; shooting. Address: 148 Beechwood Drive, Broomhill, Glasgow G11 7DX; T.-0141-563 2638.

Morrison, William Garth, CBE, BA, CEng, MIEE, DL. Farmer; Chief Scout, 1988-96; Member, World Scout Committee, since 1992; Chief Commissioner of Scotland, The Scout Association, 1981-88; b. 8.4.43, Edinburgh; m., Gillian Cheetham; 2 s.; 1 d. Educ. Pangbourne College; Pembroke College, Cambridge. Service, Royal Navy, 1961-73, retiring with rank of Lt.; farming, since 1973; Member, Lothian Region Children's Panel, 1976-83 (Chairman, Midlothian/East Lothian Area Panel, 1978-81); Lamp of Lothian Trustee, 1978; Member: Lothian, Borders and Fife Committee, Prince's Trust, 1979, Lothian and Borders Committee, Prince's and Royal Jubilee Trusts, 1983-88, Society of High Constables of Holyroodhouse, 1979; Deputy Lieutenant, East Lothian, 1984; Member, Scottish Community Education Council, 1988-95; Chairman, East and Midlothian NHS Trust, 1993-97; Chairman, Royal Infirmary of Edinburgh NHS Trust, 1997-99; Chairman (Designate) Lothian Primary Care NHS Trust, since 1998;

MacRobert Trustee, 1998; SCEC Honorary Fellowship, 1995; Member, National Lottery Charities Board, since 1995; S.E. Regional Chairman, Scottish Landowners Federation, since 1996; Vice President, Commonwealth Youth Exchange Council, since 1997. Recreations: golf; sailing; Scouting. Address: West Fenton, North Berwick, East Lothian; T.-01620 842154.

Morrow, John, MB, ChB, FRCP(Glas), FRCP(Lond). Chairman, Ayrshire and Arran Health Board, since 1997; b. 19.3.32, Glasgow; m., Clare Patricia; 2 s.; 1 d. Educ. St. Mungo's Academy, Glasgow; University of Glasgow. National Service (RAMC), 1957-59; training posts, Stobhill Hospital and Western Infirmary, Glasgow; Consultant Physician: Ballochmyle Hospital, 1969, Kilmarnock Infirmary, 1981, Crosshouse Hospital, 1983; Clinical Director (Medicine), Crosshouse Hospital, 1992-97; retired 1997. Member, Ayrshire and Arran Health Board, 1981-89; President, Scottish Society of Physicians, 1993. Recreations: reading (biographies and poetry); walking; angling. Address: (h.) 12 Glenpark Place, Ayr KA7 4SQ; T.-01292 441995; (b.) Boswell House, Arthur Street, Ayr; T.-01292 885885.

Morrow, Martin Thomas, LLB (Hons), DipLP, NP. Solicitor; b. 2.7.64, Glasgow; m., Amanda Catherine; 1 s.; 1 d. Educ. St. Aloysius College, Glasgow; University of Strathclyde. Ian McCarry Solicitors, Glasgow, 1986-88; Levy, McRae, Solicitors, Glasgow, 1988-89; Blackadder, McMonagle, Solicitors, Falkirk, 1990-92; Principal, Milligan Telford and Morrow, Solicitors, since 1992. Member, Council, Law Society of Scotland, since 1997. Recreations:, golf; tennis. Address: 1 Cockburn Street, Falkirk FK1 1DJ; T.-01324 633221.

Morton, Rev. Alasdair J., MA, BD, DipEd, DipRE, FEIS. Minister, Bowden linked with Newtown St. Boswells, since 1991; b. 8.6.34, Inverness; m., Gillian M. Richards; 2 s.; 2 d. Educ. Bell-Baxter School, Cupar; St. Andrews University; Hartford Theological Seminary. District Missionary/Minister, Zambia (Northern Rhodesia), 1960-65; Chaplain and Religious Education Lecturer, Malcolm Moffat Teachers' College, Serenje, Zambia, 1966-67; Principal, David Livingstone Teachers' College, Livingstone, Zambia, 1968-72; Minister, Greyfriars Parish Church, Dumfries, 1973-77; General Secretary, Department of Education, Church of Scotland, 1977-91. Recreations: choral singing; gardening. Address: The Manse, Newtown St. Boswells TD6 0SG; T.-01835 822106.

Morton, Rev. Andrew Reyburn, MA, BD, DD. Associate Director, Centre for Theology and Public Issues, University of Edinburgh, since 1994; b. 24.5.28, Kilmarnock; m., Marion Armstrong Chadwin; 2 s.; 2 d. Educ. Kilmarnock Academy; Glasgow University; Edinburgh University; Bonn University. Scottish Secretary, Student Christian Movement, 1953-56; Minister, Moncreiff Parish, East Kilbride, 1956-64; Chaplain, Edinburgh University, 1964-70; Warden, Wolfson Hall and Co-ordinating Warden, Halls of Residence, Glasgow University, 1970-74; Social Responsibility Secretary and, latterly, Secretary, Division of Community Affairs and Assistant General Secretary, British Council of Churches, 1974-81; Secretary, Inter-Church Relations Committee and Assistant Secretary, Overseas Council, subsequently Assistant Secretary, Board of World Mission and Unity, Church of Scotland, 1982-88; Deputy General Secretary, Board of World Mission and Unity, Church of Scotland, 1988-93. Recreation: walking. Address: (h.) 11 Oxford Terrace, Edinburgh, EH4 1PX; T.-0131-332 6592.

Morton, Archibald Campbell, MA, BA (Hons). Director of Education, Argyll and Bute Council, since 1995; b. 15.2.42, Kilmarnock; m., Shirley; 2 s.; 1 d. Educ. Dumfries Academy; Edinburgh University; Moray House College of Education. Teaching, 1964-83, latterly Depute Head Teacher, Cowdenknowes High School, Greenock; Education Officer, Renfrew Division, 1983-89; Senior Education Officer, Glasgow Division, 1990-93; Assistant Director of Education, Strathclyde Regional Council, 1993-95. Recreations: curling; sailing. Address: (b.) Argyll House, Alexandra Parade, Dunoon PA23 8AJ; T.-01369 704000.

Morton, Elizabeth Stewart, NP, LicIPD, FIMgt. Director of Law and Administration, Falkirk Council, since 1995; Solicitor; b. 21.8.56, Glasgow. Educ. Dalmellington High School; Ayr Academy; Glasgow University. Entered local government, 1974, as a legal apprentice; worked for Ayr County, Cunninghame District, Cumnock and Doon Valley District, Kyle and Carrick District; moved to Hamilton District as Chief Administrative Officer, 1990; returned to Ayrshire as Director of Administration and Legal Services, 1993. Address: (b.) Municipal Buildings, Falkirk FK1 5RS; T.-01324 506075.

Morton, 22nd Earl of (John Charles Sholto Douglas), DL; b. 19.3.27; m.; 2 s.; 1 d. Succeeded to title, 1976. Lord-Lieutenant, West Lothian, since 1985.

Morton, William John Keirs, DipTP, MRTPI. Chief Executive, Forth Valley Enterprise, since 1990, and Director, Senior Staff Development, Scottish Enterprise, since 1997; b. 14.6.49, Glasgow; m., Jan; 2 s.; 1 d. Educ. Bearsden Academy; Glasgow College of Art. Planning Assistant, Royal Burgh of Inverness, 1973-75; Project Officer, East Kilbride Development Corporation, 1975-76; SDA, 1976-87, latterly as Project Manager (Coatbridge Project); Chief Executive, Aberdeen Beyond 2000, 1987-89; Head of Urban Regeneration, SDA, 1989-90. Recreations: family; travel; cycling; reading. Address: (b.) Laurel House, Laurelhill Business Park, Stirling FK7 9JQ; T.-01786 451919.

Moule, Rev. Gerald Christopher, BA, BD. Parish Minister, Moffat linked with Wamphray, since 1975; b. 31.8.45, Guildford; m., Patricia Rosemary Parker; 1 s.; 2 d. Educ. Edinburgh Academy; Kelvinside Academy, Glasgow; St. Andrews University; Newcastle upon Tyne University; Edinburgh University (New College). Chartered accountancy articles; Assistant Minister, West Church of St. Nicholas, Aberdeen, 1973-75; Moderator, Presbytery of Annandale and Eskdale, 1980-81 and 1988-89; Convener, Economic Interests Committee, Church and Nation Committee, 1991-95; Secretary and Treasurer, Scottish Journal of Theology; World Council of Churches Consultant for Disaster Preparedness, Central and Eastern Europe, since 1995; Representative, UK Faith Communities in Civil Emergency Planning, Home Office, since 1990. Recreations: cricket; travel; swimming; gardening. Address: St. Andrew's Manse, Moffat DG10 9EJ; T.-01683 220128.

Mounfield, J. Hilary, MA (Hons), MICFM. Chief Executive, Epilepsy Association of Scotland, since 1995; Chair, Joint Epilepsy Council; Convener, ACOSVO; b. 19.7.41, Edinburgh; 2 s.; 1 d. Educ. Boroughmuir School; Edinburgh University. Research, Scottish Development Department and Ministry of Housing, 1963-66; teaching, London, 1973-84; fund-raising for charities, 1984-91; Appeals Director, Penumbra, 1991-95. Chair: ICFM, Scotland, 1993-95, Bighearted Scotland, 1993-96. Recreations: gardening; reading; walking. Address: (b.) 48 Govan Road, Glasgow G51 1JL; T.-0141-427 4911.

Mowat, Ian Robert, MA, BPhil, FLA, FRSA FRSE. Librarian, Edinburgh University, since 1997; b. 20.4.46, Dingwall; m., Margaret Louise; 1 s.; 1 d. Educ. Robert Gordon's College, Aberdeen; Aberdeen University; Sheffield University; St. Andrews University. Assistant Librarian, St. Andrews University, 1970-72, Heriot-Watt University, 1972-75; Assistant Keeper, National Library of Scotland, 1975-78; Sub-Librarian/Associate Librarian,

Glasgow University, 1978-86; Librarian, Hull University, 1986-92, Newcastle University, 1992-97. Recreations: music; architectural history; walking. Address: (b.) Edinburgh University Library, George Square, Edinburgh EH8 9LJ; T.-0131-650 3378.

Mowat, Sheriff Principal John Stuart, MA, LLB, QC. Sheriff Principal of South Strathclyde, Dumfries and Galloway, 1988-93; b. 30.1.23, Manchester; m., Anne Cameron Renfrew; 2 s.; 2 d. Educ. High School of Glasgow; Merchiston Castle School; Glasgow University. Served RAF Transport Command, 1942-46 (Flt.-Lt.); Journalist, 1947-52; Advocate, 1952-60; Sheriff of Fife and Kinross, at Dunfermline, 1960-72, at Cupar and Kinross, 1972-74, of Glasgow and Strathkelvin, 1974-88; Chairman, Sheriff Court Rules Council, 1989-92; Office-Bearer, Scottish Liberal Party, 1954-58; Parliamentary candidate, Caithness and Sutherland, 1955; Secretary, Sheriffs Association, 1968-75 (President, 1988); Trustee: Carnegie Dunfermline Trust, 1967-74, Carnegie United Kingdom Trust, 1970-74. Recreations: golf; curling; watching football. Address: (h.) Old Mill of Camserney, Aberfeldy, Perthshire PH15 2JF.

Mowat, Norman Ashley George, MB, ChB, MRCP (UK), FRCP, FRCP (Edin). Consultant Physician and Gastroenterologist, Aberdeen Teaching Hospitals, since 1975; Clinical Senior Lecturer in Medicine, Aberdeen University, since 1975; b. 11.4.43, Cullen; m., Kathleen Mary Cowie; 1 s.; 2 d. Educ. Fordyce Academy; Aberdeen University. House Officer, then Senior House Officer, then Registrar, Aberdeen Teaching Hospitals, 1966-72; Lecturer in Medicine, Aberdeen University, 1972-73; Lecturer in Gastroenterology and Research Associate, Medical College of St. Bartholomew's, London, 1973-75. Formerly Visiting Physician to Shetland Islands; publications include Integrated Clinical Sciences: Gastroenterology (Co-Editor), 1985. Recreations: sailing; golf; soccer; reading; photography. Address: (h.) Bucholie, 13 Kings Cross Road, Aberdeen AB2 4BF; T.-01224 319223.

Muckart, Rev. Graeme Watson MacKinnon, MSc, MTheol, FSA Scot. Minister, North Church of St. Andrew, Aberdeen, since 1997; b. 11.12.43, Dunfermline; m., 1, Mary Elspeth Small; 1 s.; 1 d.; 2, Elizabeth M. Miller, PhD; 1 d. Educ. Royal Naval Schools, Malta; Willesden County Grammar School; Portsmouth Southern Grammar School; Highbury Technical College, Portsmouth; Leeds College of Art; Open University; St. Andrews University; Stirling University. Barclays Bank, 1962-64; Trainee Architect, 1964-69; architectural appointments, 1969-76; resident staff, Iona Abbey, 1976-78; divinity studies, 1978-82; Assistant Minister, Carrick Knowe, Edinburgh, 1982-83; Minister, Erskine Parish Church, Falkirk, 1983-90; Locum Minister, Carriden Parish Church, Bo'ness, 1990-92; Minister, St. Andrew's Church, Colombo, 1992-96. Chair, Falkirk Council of Churches, 1987-89; Member, Iona Community, since 1978. Recreations: painting; calligraphy; heraldry; reading; walking. Address: The Manse, 51 Osborne Place, Aberdeen AB25 2BX; T.-01224 646429.

Muggoch, Adam, ARTCS. Group Managing Director, J. W. Galloway Ltd., since 1976; b. 17.1.34, London; m., Bernice Mary; 2 s. Educ. Eastbank Academy, Glasgow; Leigh Technical College; Royal Technical College, Salford. Marks and Spencer plc: joined as Trainee, 1955, Senior Executive, 1970-76 (resigned to return to Scotland). Council Member, British Meat Manufacturers Association; Member, Research Steering Committee, Meat and Livestock Commission. Recreations: gardening; sailing. Address: (b.) 27 Glenburn Road, College Milton North, East Kilbride G74 5BA; T.-01355 225381.

Muir, Ian Holstein, OBE, FSQA, MIPD. Chairman, Jewel and Esk Valley College, since 1995; Board Member, Scottish Qualifications Authority, since 1997; Director, Association of Scottish Colleges, since 1996; Technology Management Consultant, since 1995; b. 14.3.37, Edinburgh; m., Pearl; 1 s. Educ. Knox Academy. Development Engineer, 1962-67; Chief Production Engineer, 1967-77; Manufacturing Manager, 1977-87; Company Systems Manager, 1987-89; Training and Education Manager, 1989-95. Chairman, Edinburgh Compact; Member, NTO Recognition Panel. Address: Mavisbank, 46 Edinburgh Road, Tranent, East Lothian EH33 1AW; T.-01875 610444.

Muir, Robert Douglas, MA (Hons), ACIB. Chief Executive, Skye and Lochalsh Enterprise, since 1998; b. 28.8.54, Irvine; m., Nanette Thomson Buchanan; 2 s. Educ. Ardrossan Academy; Glasgow University. Midland Bank plc, from Graduate Trainee to Manager, 1977-92; Head of Development, Skye and Lochalsh Enterprise, 1992-98. Director, An Tuireann Arts Centre; Chairman, Portree Scout Group; Chairman, Skeabost Memorial Hall. Recreations: history; travel; languages; music; following the fortunes of Kilmarnock F. C. Address: (b.) King's House, The Green, Portree, Isle of Skye IV51 9BS; T.-01478 612841.

Muir, Trevor. Chief Executive, Midlothian Council, since 1995; b. 10.7.49, Glasgow; m., Christine Ann; 1 s.; 1 d. Educ. High School of Glasgow; Langside College; Strathclyde University. Scottish Special Housing Association, 1973-77; City of Glasgow District Council, 1977-81; Director of Housing, City of Aberdeen District Council, 1981-87; Chief Executive, Midlothian District Council, 1987-96. Recreations: squash; family life. Address: (b.) Midlothian House, Buccleuch Street, Dalkeith, Midlothian EH22 1DJ.

Mulholland, Francis, LLB (Hons), MBA, DipLP, SSC, NP. Solicitor Advocate; Advocate Depute, since 1997; b. 18.4.59, Coatbridge; m., Marie Elizabeth. Educ. Columba High School, Coatbridge; Aberdeen University; Edinburgh University. Trainee, Bird Semple & Crawford Herron, Solicitors, Glasgow, 1982-84; Procurator Fiscal Depute: Greenock, 1984-87, Glasgow, 1987-91; Solicitor, Crown Office, Edinburgh, 1991-96; Procurator Fiscal Depute, Edinburgh, 1996. First Solicitor Advocate and Member of Procurator Fiscal Service to be appointed to office of Advocate Depute; Member, Council, SSC Society; Member, Council, Society of Solicitor Advocates. Recreations: football; squash; military history. Address: (b.) Crown Office, 25 Chambers Street, Edinburgh; T.-0131-226 2626.

Mullen, Frank, BSc, MPhil, MCP. Director, Scottish Convention Bureau, since 1994; b. 12.5.58, Kilmarnock. Educ. James Hamilton Academy, Kilmarnock; Glasgow University; University of Pennsylvania. Policy Researcher, Strathclyde Regional Council, 1980-85; Area Manager, Scottish Tourist Board, 1985-87; Marketing Director, Greater Glasgow Tourist Board and Convention Bureau, 1987-94. Recreations: keep-fit; theatre. Address: (b.) 23 Ravelston Terrace, Edinburgh EH4 3EU; T.-0131-332 2433.

Mullen, Ian M., BSc, MRPharmS. Freelance consultant on healthcare and pharmaceutical issues; b. 11.5.46, Stirling; m., Veronica Drummond; 2 s.; 1 d. Educ. St. Modan's High School, Stirling; Heriot-Watt University. Registered MPS, 1970; self-employed community pharmacist, 1971-97; elected to Pharmaceutical General Council, 1974; Vice-Chairman, 1983; Chairman, Pharmaceutical General Council (Scotland), 1986-88; Vice-Chairman, National Pharmaceutical Consultative Committee, 1987-89; Member, UK Advisory Committee on Borderline Substances, 1986-89; Vice-Chairman, Forth Valley Health Board, 1989-91; Director, Common Services Agency of the NHS in Scotland, 1991-94, Vice-Chairman, 1993; Director, Central Scotland Chamber of Commerce, 1990-93; Chairman: St. Andrew's School Board, 1990-93, Falkirk and District

Royal Infirmary NHS Trust, 1993-99; Member: Scottish Dental Practice Review Board, 1991-92, Shields Committee for the NHS in Scotland, 1995-96; Chair, Scottish NHS Trust Chairmen's Group, 1998-99; Chairman, Forth Valley Acute NHS Trust. Recreations: walking; golf; swimming. Address: (h.) Ardenlea, 11 Arnothill, Falkirk FK1 5RZ; T.-01324 621806.

Mullen, Veronica C., BA, DipEd, FRSA. Chairman, Scottish Marriage Care, since 1995; Chairman, Scottish Marriage Care, Falkirk and Stirling Centres, since 1991; b. 20.6.46, Stirling; m., Ian M. Mullen; 2 s.; 1 d. Educ. St. Modan's High School, Stirling; Craiglockhart College of Education; Heriot-Watt University. Primary school teaching, 1966-71; partner in retail pharmacy business, 1984-96; partner in healthcare consultancy, since 1990. Recreations: tennis; travel; golf. Address: Ardenlea, 11 Arnothill, Falkirk, FK1 5RZ; T.-01324 621806.

Mullen, William Henry, PhD. Chief Executive, Rowett Research Services, since 1996; b. 3.4.59, Winchester; m., Catherine; 2 d. Educ. Bath University; Sussex University. Postdoctoral Researcher, Newcastle University, 1983-86; Cambridge Life Sciences, Cambridge, 1986-93 (latterly as Head of Collaborative Research and Development); Abbott Laboratories, Chicago, USA, 1993-96. Address: (b.) Greenburn Road, Bucksburn, Aberdeen AB21 9SB; T.-01224 716226.

Mumford, Colin John, BMedSci, DM, FRCP(E), DIMCRCS(Ed). Consultant Neurologist, Western General Hospital, Edinburgh and Royal Infirmary of Edinburgh, since 1996; b. 24.11.59, Liverpool. Educ. St. Margaret's High School, Liverpool; Nottingham University Medical School. Senior House Officer in Medicine, Newcastle upon Tyne teaching hospitals; Registrar in Neurology, Queen's Medical Centre, Nottingham and National Hospital for Neurology, London; Research Fellow, University of Cambridge; Senior Registrar in Neurology, Edinburgh teaching hospitals. Recreations: hillwalking; motorcycling. Address: (b.) Department of Clinical Neurosciences, Western General Hospital, Edinburgh EH4 2XU; T.-0131-537 1169.

Mundell, John Weir. Director of Connect Services, East Dunbartonshire Council; b. Edinburgh; m., Karen; 3 s. Educ. Currie High School; Heriot-Watt University. Entered local government, 1974; Head of Central Contracts, Central Regional Council, 1994-95. Recreations: swimming; karate; gymnastics (coach); farming. Address: (b.) East Dunbartonshire Council, Broomhill Industrial Estate, Kilsyth Road, Kirkintilloch; T.-0141-574 5501.

Munn, Charles William, BA, PhD, FCIBS, FRSA. Chief Executive, Chartered Institute of Bankers in Scotland; b. 26.5.48, Glasgow; m., Andrea Cuthbertson; 1 s.; 1 d. Educ. Queen's Park Secondary School, Glasgow; Langside College; Strathclyde University; Glasgow University; Jordanhill College. British Linen Bank, 1964-67; Glasgow College of Technology, Department of Finance and Accounting, 1975-78; Lecturer in Economic History, Glasgow University, 1978-86, Senior Lecturer, 1986-88. Editor, The Scottish Banker; Member: Church of Scotland Church and Nation Committee, 1990-94, Board, Scottish Qualifications Authority, since 1997. Publications: Clydesdale Bank: the First 150 Years, 1988; The Scottish Provincial Banking Companies 1747-1864, 1981. Recreation: golf. Address: (b.) Drumsheugh House, 38b Drumsheugh Gardens, Edinburgh EH3 7SW.

Munn, Sir James, OBE, MA, DEd, LLD, DUniv; b. 27.7.20, Bridge of Allan; m., Muriel Jean Millar Moles; 1 d. (deceased). Educ. Stirling High School; Glasgow University. Indian Civil Service, 1941-48; various teaching appointments, Glasgow, 1949-57; Principal Teacher of Modern Languages, Falkirk High School, 1957-66 (Depute Rector, 1962-66); Principal Examiner in Modern Languages, Scottish Examination Board, 1965-66; Rector: Rutherglen Academy, 1966-70, Cathkin High School, 1970-83; Member, University Grants Committee, 1973-82; Member, Consultative Committee on the Curriculum, 1968-80, Chairman, 1980-87; Chairman, Committee to review the Structure of the Curriculum at S3 and S4, 1975-77; Member of Court, Strathclyde University, 1983-91; Manpower Services Commission/Training Commission Chairman for Scotland, 1984-88, Chairman, GB, 1987-88; University Commissioner, 1988-95. (h.) 4 Kincath Avenue, Rutherglen, Glasgow G73 4RP; T.-0141-634 4654.

Munn, Professor Pamela, MA, MLitt, CertEd. Professor of Curriculum Research, Moray House Institute of Education, since 1994; b. 31.3.49, Glasgow; m., Graham Hamilton Munn. Educ. Hermitage School, Helensburgh; Aberdeen University. Teacher of History, 1972-78; Research Fellow, Stirling University, 1979-84; Lecturer in Applied Research in Education, York University, 1984-86; Senior Research Officer, then Depute Director, Scottish Council for Research in Education, 1986-94. Member, Scottish Consultative Council on the Curriculum; Fellowship, CIDREE, 1996; SCRE Silver Medal, 1984. Publications: The Changing Face of Education 14-16; Education in Scotland: policy and practice from pre-school to secondary, 1997; Parents and Schools: customers, managers or partners?, 1993. Recreations: hill-walking; gardening; reading, especially crime fiction. Address: (b.) Moray House Institute of Education, Holyrood Road, Edinburgh EH8 8AQ; T.-0131-558 6175.

Munro, Alexander, MB, ChB, ChM, FRCS. Consultant General Surgeon, Raigmore Hospital, Inverness, since 1978; Clinical Senior Lecturer in Surgery, Aberdeen University, since 1978; b. 5.6.43, Ross and Cromarty; m., Maureen E. McCreath; 2 s.; 1 d. Educ. Fortrose Academy; Aberdeen University. Training in General Surgery at Registrar and Senior Registrar level, Aberdeen Hospitals, 1971-78; specialist training, St. Mark's Hospital, 1977. Recreation: gardening. Address: (h.) 23 Eriskay Road, Inverness; T.-Inverness 223804.

Munro, Angus Cunningham, BSc, PhD. Director, Scottish Antibody Production Unit, since 1984; b. 12.1.44, Dundee; m., Christine Renwick; 2 s.; 1 d. Educ. Harris Academy, Dundee; Edinburgh University. Senior Scientist and Project Manager, Beecham Pharmaceuticals, 1969-74; Principal Scientist, Glasgow and West of Scotland Blood Transfusion Service, 1974-84. Recreations: music; astronomy; collecting. Address: (b.) Scottish Antibody Production Unit, Law Hospital, Carluke, Lanarkshire ML8 5QZ; T.-01698 351161.

Munro, Professor Colin Roy, BA, LLB. Professor of Constitutional Law, Edinburgh University, since 1990, Dean, Faculty of Law, 1992-94; Chief Examiner, London University LLB (External) Degree, since 1991; b. 17.5.49, Aberdeen; m., Ruth Elizabeth Pratt; 1 s.; 1 d. Educ. Aberdeen Grammar School; Aberdeen University. Lecturer in Law, Birmingham University, 1971-72, Durham University, 1972-80; Senior Lecturer in Law, then Reader in Law, Essex University, 1980-85; Professor of Law, Manchester University, 1985-90. Publications: Television, Censorship and the Law; Studies in Constitutional Law; Devolution and the Scotland Bill (Co-author). Recreations: sport; cinema and theatre; real ale. Address: (b.) Faculty of Law, Old College, South Bridge, Edinburgh EH8 9YL; T.-0131-650 2056.

Munro, David Mackenzie, BSc, PhD, FRGS, FRSA, FSAScot. Director and Secretary, Royal Scottish Geographical Society, since 1996; Member, Council, National Trust for Scotland; Member, Advisory Board, Graduate School of Environmental Studies, Strathclyde University; Member, Permanent Committee on

Geographical Names for British Official Use; b. 28.5.50, Glasgow. Educ. Daniel Stewart's College; Edinburgh Academy; Edinburgh University. Research Associate, then Research Fellow, Edinburgh University, 1979-96; Leader/Co Leader, Edinburgh University expeditions to Central America, 1981, 1986, 1988, 1991. Chairman, Kinross-shire Civic Trust; Chairman, Michael Bruce Trust. Publications: Chambers World Gazetteer (Editor); Oxford Dictionary of the World (Editor); Gazetteer of the Baltic States; A World Record of Major Conflict Areas; Loch Leven and the River Leven – a Landscape Transformed; numerous articles and reports on land use in Central America. Recreations: walking; travel; exploring landscapes. Address: (b.) 40 George Street, Glasgow G1 1QE; T.-0141-552 3330.

Munro, Rev. David Peacock, MA, BD, STM. Minister, Bearsden North Church, 1967-96; Clerk, Presbytery of Dumbarton, since 1986; b. 7.9.29, Paisley; m., Jessie Scott McPherson; 3 d. Educ. Paisley Grammar School; Glasgow University; Union Theological Seminary, New York. Minister, Aberluthnott Parish Church, 1953-56, Castlehill Church, Ayr, 1956-67. Vice-Convener, General Assembly Council, 1988-90, Convener, 1990-95; Moderator, Dumbarton Presbytery, 1978-79; Chairman, General Assembly Board of Education, 1974-79; Convener, General Assembly Education Committee, 1981-85. Recreations: golf; gardening. Address: (h.) 14 Birch Road, Killearn, Glasgow G63 9SQ; T.-01360 550098.

Munro, Donnie, DA. Former Guitarist and Lead Singer, Runrig; b. Skye; m.; 3 children. Former Art Teacher, Inverness and Edinburgh; Rector, Edinburgh University, 1991-94; contested (Labour) Ross, Skye and Inverness West, 1997. Dr. HC, Edinburgh, 1994.

Munro, Graeme Neil, MA. Director and Chief Executive, Historic Scotland, since 1991; b. 28.8.44, Edinburgh; m., Nicola Susan Wells (qv); 1 s.; 1 d. Educ. Daniel Stewart's College, Edinburgh; St. Andrews University. Assistant Principal, Scottish Development Department, 1968-72; Principal, Scottish Development Department and Scottish Home and Health Department, 1972-79; Assistant Secretary, Department of Agriculture and Fisheries for Scotland, SHHD, and Central Services, 1979-90; Director, Historic Buildings and Monuments, Scottish Office Environment Department, 1990-91. Recreations: walking; reading; local history; gardening; swimming. Address: (b.) Longmore House, Salisbury Place, Edinburgh EH9 1SH; T.-0131-668 8696.

Munro of Foulis, Hector William, ARICS. 31st Chief of Clan Munro; b. 20.2.50; m., Sarah Duckworth; 1 s.; 2 d. Educ. Oratory School; Agricultural College, Cirencester. Farmer and Landowner. Address: (h.) Foulis Castle, Evanton, Ross-shire.

Munro, Hugh Murray, BA, MEng, CA. Office Managing Partner, Ernst & Young, Aberdeen, since 1989; b. 30.12.46, Kirkcaldy; m., Valerie Ingram; 1 s.; 1 d. Educ. Aberdeen Grammar School; Strathclyde University; Glasgow University. Arthur Andersen & Co., Glasgow, 1968-87 (Partner, 1981-87); Arthur Young, Aberdeen, 1987-89 (Office Managing Partner). Recreations: skiing; curling; gardening. Address: (b.) Ernst & Young, 50 Huntly Street, Aberdeen AB10 1ZN; T.-01224 653262.

Munro, Jack, DPE. Chief Executive, Edinburgh and Lothians Tourist Board, since 1997; b. 18.9.49, Cromarty; m., Lynn Prentice Roberts. Educ. Fortrose Academy; Jordanhill College of Education. Assistant Director of Tourism and Recreation, North East Fife District Council, 1975-82; Conference Manager, Inverness District Council, 1984-86; Director, Greater Glasgow Convention Bureau, 1986-90; Director, Edinburgh Convention Bureau, 1990-93. Chief Executive, Greater Glasgow Tourist Board, 1993-96; Chief Executive, Greater Glasgow and Clyde Valley Tourist Board, 1996-97. Chairman, British Association of Conference Towns, 1992-93; Co-Chair, International Task Force, IACVB; Member, Ministerial Advisory Group, Business Tourism. Recreations: rugby; golf; Scottish history; gardening. Address: (b.) 4 Rothesay Terrace, Edinburgh EH3 7RY; T.-0131-473 3600.

Munro, Jean Mary, BA (Hons), PhD. Chairman, Council, Scottish History Society, 1989-93; b. 2.12.23; m., Robert William Munro. Educ. London University; Edinburgh University. WRNS, 1944-47; freelance historical researcher; Member, Council, National Trust for Scotland, 1964-69 and 1987-92 (Executive, 1968-80); Chairman, Council, Scottish Genealogy Society, 1983-86 (Vice-President, since 1987); Chairman, Council, Scottish Local History Forum, 1984-88. Publications (as Jean Dunlop): the British Fisheries Society; the Clan Chisholm; the Clan Mackenzie; the Clan Gordon; the Scotts; the Clan Mackintosh; (with R.W. Munro): Tain through the Centuries; The Scrimgeours; The Acts of the Lords of the Isles. Recreations: reading; walking. Address: (h.) 15a Mansionhouse Road, Edinburgh EH9 1TZ; T.-0131-667 4601.

Munro, Professor J. Forbes, MA, PhD. Associate Director, Centre for Business History, Glasgow University; b. 15.3.40, Grantown-on-Spey. Educ. Dingwall Academy; Edinburgh University; Wisconsin University. Lecturer in Economic History, Senior Lecturer, Reader, Professor, Glasgow University, 1965-96. Editor, Journal of African History, 1982-87; Dean of Social Sciences, 1987-89, Clerk of Senate, 1991-96, Glasgow University. Publications: Colonial Rule and the Kamba, 1975; Africa and the International Economy, 1976; Britain in Tropical Africa, 1984. Recreation: curling. Address: (b.) 4 University Gardens, Glasgow University, Glasgow G12 8QQ.

Munro, John Forbes, OBE, FRCPEdin, FRCPGlas, FRCPLond. Honorary Fellow, Edinburgh University, since 1992; b. 25.6.33, Edinburgh; m., Elizabeth Jean Durell Caird; 3 d. Educ. Edinburgh Academy; Chigwell School, Essex; Edinburgh University. Former Consultant Physician, Eastern General and Edenhall Hospitals and part-time Senior Lecturer, Edinburgh University; Registrar, Royal College of Physicians, Edinburgh, 1993-97. Recreations: art; gardening. Address: (h.) Backhill, Carberry, near Musselburgh, East Lothian; T.-0131-663 4935.

Munro, Rev. John P.L., MA, BD, PhD. Minister, Kinross Parish Church, since 1998; b. 11.5.47, Edinburgh; m., Pat Lawson; 1 s.; 1 d. Educ. Edinburgh Academy; Christ's College, Cambridge; Edinburgh University. Church of Scotland Chaplain, Stirling University, 1977-82; Lecturer, St. Paul's Theological College, Kenya, 1982-85; Minister, St. Vigeans and Knox's Church, Arbroath, 1986-90; Assistant Secretary, Church of Scotland Department of World Mission, 1990-98. Recreations: music; hill-walking; motor-cycle touring. Address: (b.) 15 Station Road, Kinross KY13 8TG; T.-01577 862952.

Munro, Kenneth Alexander, MA, FRSA. Head of Representation in Scotland, European Commission, 1988-98; b. 17.12.36, Glasgow; m., Elizabeth Coats Forrest McCreanor; 2 d. Educ. Hutchesons' Boys' Grammar School; Glasgow University. Economic research, Scottish American Investment Company, 1963-66; Senior Research Officer, ETU, 1966-67; Secretary, Economic Development Committee, NEDO, 1967-69; Industrial Relations Manager, Ford Motor Co., 1969-74; joined European Commission, 1974; Chairman, Centre for Scottish Public Policy; Vice-Chairman, John Smith Memorial Trust. Recreations: walking; swimming; cinema; theatre. Address: (b.) 9 Alva Street, Edinburgh EH2 4PH; T.-0131-225 2058.

Munro, Nicola Susan, BA (Hons). Under Secretary, Scottish Office Public Health Policy, since 1995; b. 11.1.48, Hitchin; m., Graeme Neil Munro (qv); 1 s.; 1 d. Educ. Harrogate Grammar School; Warwick University. Joined Scottish Office, 1970. Recreations: travel; reading; gardening. Address: (b.) St. Andrews House, Edinburgh EH1 3DG; T.-0131-244 2133.

Munro, Robert William. Author and Journalist; b. 3.2.14, Kiltearn, Ross-shire; m., Jean Mary Dunlop. Educ. Edinburgh Academy. War Service, Seaforth Highlanders and Inter-Services Public Relations Directorate (India), 1940-46; Editorial Staff, The Scotsman, 1933-59 and 1963-69; Editor-in-Chief, Highland News Group, 1959-63; Chairman, Edinburgh Press Club, 1955-57 (President, 1969-71); Honorary Editor, Clan Munro Association, 1939-71 (Vice-President, since 1963); former Council Member: Society of Antiquaries of Scotland, Scottish History Society, Scottish Genealogy Society; Trustee, National Museum of Antiquities of Scotland, 1982-85. Publications: Lachlan MacQuarrie of Ulva, 1944; Donald Monro's Western Isles of Scotland and Genealogies of the Clans 1549 (Editor), 1961; Tain Through the Centuries (Co-Author, with wife), 1966; The Glorious Privilege: The History of The Scotsman (Co-Author), 1967; Kinsmen and Clansmen, 1971; The Northern Lighthouses, 1976; Highland Clans and Tartans, 1977; Edinburgh and the Borders, 1977; The Munro Tree 1734, 1978; Scottish Lighthouses, 1979; Taming the Rough Bounds, Knoydart 1745-1784, 1984; Acts of the Lords of the Isles 1336-1493 (Co-Author, with wife), 1986; Clan MacQuarrie: A History, 1996. Recreations: historical research and writing; walking; visiting islands. Address: (h.) 15A Mansionhouse Road, Edinburgh EH9 1TZ; T.-0131-667 4601.

Murby, David Frigast, LLB (Hons). Partner, Shepherd & Wedderburn, WS, since 1974; Procurator Fiscal to Lyon Court; b. 7.3.47, Nigeria; m., Morag; 2 s. Educ. Edinburgh Academy; Edinburgh University. Shepherd & Wedderburn: Trainee Solicitor, 1969-71, Solicitor, 1971-74. Recreations: sport; reading; music. Address: (b.) Saltire Court, 20 Castle Terrace, Edinburgh; T.-0131-228 9900.

Murchison, Lilian Elizabeth, MB, ChB, PhD, FRCPE, FRCP(Lond). Consultant Physician and Honorary Clinical Senior Lecturer in Medicine, Aberdeen University, since 1976; b. 29.4.36, Aultbea. Educ. Invergordon Academy; Edinburgh University; Glasgow University. Member, Scientific Staff, Atheroma Research Unit, Western Infirmary, Glasgow, 1963-68; Senior Tutor/Senior Registrar, Department of Medicine, Queen's University, Belfast, 1969-71; Lecturer, Department of Therapeutics and Clinical Pharmacology, Aberdeen University, 1971-76. Recreations: overseas travel; hill-walking. Address: (h.) 9 Highgate Gardens, Aberdeen, AB11 7TZ; T.-01224 588532.

Murchison, Maurine, OBE, MA (Hons); b. 25.11.35, London; m., Dr. Murdoch Murchison (qv); 3 s.; 2 d. Educ. James Allen's Girls School, Dulwich; Edinburgh University. Secondary school teaching, 1958-59; homemaker and mother, since 1960; Member, Inverness County Children's Panel, 1971-75 (Chairman, 1972-75); Chairman, Highland Region Children's Panel, 1975-80; Member, Inverness Prison Visiting Committee, 1984-85; Member, Panel for Appeals Tribunal, set up under Social Work Scotland Act 1968, since 1983; Assessor under Race Relations Act, since 1982; Church Representative, Grampian Education Committee, 1990-94; Chairman, Children's Panel Advisory Committee, Highland Region, 1980-85; Member: Consultative Committee on the Curriculum, 1980-87, Highlands and Islands Development Consultative Council, 1978-86, Police Advisory Board for Scotland, 1985-93; Lay Member, Schools Inspectorate, 1994; Mediator and Counsellor, A.C.C; Member, Rape/Abuse Line. Publication: Not Without Cost, 1996. Recreations: embroidery; group Bible study; reading (ethics and theology). Address: (h.) Ord House, Strathpeffer, Ross-shire IV14 9AX; T.-01997 421117.

Murdoch, Professor Brian Oliver, BA, PhD, LittD, FRHistS, AMusTCL. Professor of German, Stirling University, since 1991; b. 26.6.44, London; m., Ursula Irene Riffer; 1 s.; 1 d. Educ. Sir George Monoux Grammar School, London; Exeter University; Jesus College, Cambridge. Lecturer in German, Glasgow University; Assistant/Associate Professor of German, University of Illinois; Lecturer/Senior Lecturer in German, Stirling University; Visiting Fellow, Trinity Hall, Cambridge, 1989; Visiting Fellow and Waynflete Lecturer, Magdalen College, Oxford, 1994; Hulsean Lecturer in Divinity, University of Cambridge, 1997-98; author of a number of books and articles on medieval German and Celtic literature, also on literature of the World Wars. Recreations: jazz; numismatics; books. Address: (b.) German Department, Stirling University, Stirling FK9 4LA; T.-01786 467546.

Murdoch, Professor George, MBChB, FRCS (Edin), DSc. Professor Emeritus of Orthopaedic Surgery, since 1966; Visiting Professor, Strathclyde University; b. 30.11.20, Denny; m., Elizabeth Ann Rennie; 2 s.; 3 d. Educ. Falkirk High School; St. Andrews University. Squadron Leader, RAF; Consultant Orthopaedic Surgeon; Professor of Orthopaedic Surgery, Dundee University. Travelling Fellow, World Health Association; Honorary Fellow and Past President, International Society for Prosthetics and Orthotics. Publications: papers on surgery, prosthetics, orthotics; Editor of five books on prosthetics, orthotics. Recreations: reading; writing. Address: (h.) Middle Church, Flat C, 6 Tay Street, Perth PH1 5LQ; T.-01738 445772.

Mure, Kenneth Nisbet, QC. Advocate, Scotland, since 1975; Barrister, Grays Inn, since 1990; Fellow, Institute of Taxation, since 1981; b. 11.4.47, Glasgow. Educ. Glasgow High School; Glasgow University. Address: (b.) Advocates' Library, Edinburgh.

Murning, Lt. Col. Ian Henry, TD, LLB (Hons), DPA, FRICS, MIMgt. Partner, Ian H. Murning Associates, Chartered Surveyors, since 1994; Lecturer, Napier University; b. 24.12.43, Chapelhall; m., Seona Jean Meiklejon; 1 s.; 2 d. Educ. Dalziel High School; Glasgow University; London University; College of Estate Management. Valuer, Stirling Valuation Office, Highlands and Islands; Office of Chief Valuer (Scotland); District Valuer, Dumfries and Galloway, 1988-94. Chairman, Royal Institution of Chartered Surveyors in Scotland, 1995-96; Member, General Council, Royal Institution of Chartered Surveyors, 1994-96; Commander, Royal Engineers (Home Defence), Army HQ Scotland, 1991-95; Commander, District Specialist Training Team, Army HQ Scotland, 1996-97; served with 52(L) Div/Dist Engrs (TA), 1963-67, Royal Monmouthshire Royal Engineers (Militia), 1967-68, 71 (Scottish) Engineer Regt (V), 1968-74; Member: Society of High Constables of Edinburgh, 1993, Merchant Company of Edinburgh, 1995, Territorial Auxiliary and Volunteer Reserve Association for the Lowlands, 1997. Address: (b.) 86 Craiglockhart Drive South, Otterburn Park, Edinburgh EH14 1JY; T.-0131-443 8839.

Murphy, Sheriff Andrew John, MA, LLB. Sheriff of Tayside, Central and Fife at Falkirk, since 1991; b. 16.1.46. Called to Scottish Bar, 1970; called to Bar, Middle Temple, 1990. Address: (b.) Sheriff Court House, Camelon, Falkirk FK1 4AR.

Murphy, Daniel, MA (Hons), MEd. Rector, McLaren High School, Callander, since 1996; Honorary Lecturer, Institute of Education, University of Stirling, since 1996; b. 2.5.51, Edinburgh; m., Joan Telfer; 2 s.; 2 d. Educ. Holy Cross Academy, Edinburgh; Edinburgh University. Teacher, Malaysia, 1974-77 (VSO); Teacher, Social Education Unit,

Stirling, 1977-79; Teacher, History/Learning Support Unit, Wallace High School, 1978-83; Head of History/Modern Studies, McLaren High School, 1983-87; Adviser in Social Subjects, Central Region, 1987-90; Depute Rector, Dunblane High School, 1990-92; Rector, Crieff High School, 1992-96. Past President, Scottish Teachers of History Association; Member, National Curriculum Panels, Environmental Studies, History and Modern Studies. Recreations: running; family; writing; politics. Address: (b.) McLaren High School, Callander FK17 8JH.

Murphy, Hugh Joseph, MA, LLB. Chairman of Industrial Tribunals, since 1992; b. 24.4.42, Kilmarnock; m., Ashley C.; 1 s.; 3 d. Educ. St. Joseph's, Kilmarnock; Glasgow University. Assistant Solicitor, private practice, 1968-75; Partner, R. Maguire Cook & Co., 1975-92. Recreations: music; books; watching football; keep-fit. Address: (b.) 215 Bothwell Street, Glasgow G2 7TS; T.-0141-204 0730.

Murphy, Sheriff James Patrick, BL. Sheriff of Glasgow and Strathkelvin, since 1989; (Sheriff of North Strathclyde, 1976-89); b. 24.1.32.

Murphy, Jim. MP (Labour), Eastwood, since 1997; b. 23.8.67, Glasgow; m., Claire Cook; 1 d. Educ. Milnerton High School, Cape Town; Strathclyde University. President, NUS (Scotland), 1992-94; President, NUS (UK), 1994-96; Director, Endsleigh Insurance, 1994-96. Recreations: football; jazz; popular cinema. Address: (b.) 28 Field Road, Busby, East Renfrewshire G76 8SE; T.-0141-644 3330.

Murphy, Professor John Anthony, BA, PhD, FRSC. Merck-Pauson Professor, Department of Pure and Applied Chemistry, University of Strathclyde, since 1995; b. 30.7.55, Dublin. Educ. University of Dublin; University of Cambridge. University of Nottingham: Lecturer, 1983, Reader, 1993. Address: (b.) 295 Cathedral Street, Glasgow G1 1XZ; T.-0141-548 2389.

Murphy, Vernon Leslie, MA (Cantab), FCIT, FRSA. Chairman and Managing Director, Scottish Airports Ltd., since 1988; Deputy Chairman, Renfrewshire Enterprise, since 1993; b. 28.7.44, Shrewsbury; m., Joan Bridget Mary; 2 d. Educ. Westminster; Gonville and Caius College, Cambridge. Joined B.A.A., 1966; former General Manager, Aberdeen Airport, and Deputy Managing Director, Gatwick Airport Ltd. Recreations: steam engines; photography; music; cricket. Address: (b.) St. Andrews Drive, Glasgow Airport, Paisley PA3 2SW; T.-0141-848 4583.

Murray, Professor Alan Fraser, BSc, PhD, CEng, FIEE, SMIEEE. Professor of Neural Electronics, Edinburgh University, since 1994; b. 26.2.53, Edinburgh; m., Glynis Ruth; 1 s.; 1 d. Educ. Currie High School; Edinburgh University. NATO Fellow, Atomic Energy of Canada, 1978-80; Research Fellow, Edinburgh University, 1980-81; Wolfson Microelectronics Institute, 1981-84; Lecturer, then Reader, Department of Electrical Engineering, Edinburgh University, 1984-94. Publications: 164. Recreations: singer, guitarist, songwriter, and follower of Rupert Bear. Address: (b.) Department of Electrical Engineering, Edinburgh University, Mayfield Road, Edinburgh EH9 3JL; T.-0131-650 5589.

Murray, Alexander George, KStG, KLJ, BSc, FBSC(Lond), FSA Scot. Former National Director, Crossroads (Scotland) Care Attendant Schemes; m., Margaret Elizabeth; 1 d. Educ. Whitehill School, Glasgow; Glasgow University. Former Scottish Manager, British subsidiary of Chase Manhatten Bank of America; formed several companies in investment/credit field. Led first Scottish delegation to UNESCO, 1955-56; established Scottish Worldfriends Society and became its first National Director; active in Highland societies; Scot of the Year, 1986; Founder and Convener, Caledonian Country Dancing Clubs; former Secretary, West of Scotland Refugee Committee; Past President, East Kilbride Sea Cadet Corps; Member, Organising Committee, East Kilbride National Mod, 1974-75; former Provincial Grand Master Mason. Publications: A History of Scottish Contra Dancing; 40 Popular Scottish Dances. Recreations: bowling; swimming; walking. Address: (h.) Failte, 51 Eaglesham Road, Clarkston, Glasgow G76 7TR.

Murray, Athol Laverick, PhD, MA, LLB, FRHistS, FSA Scot. Chairman, Scottish Records Association, since 1997; Vice-President, Society of Antiquaries of Scotland, 1989-92; Keeper of the Records of Scotland, 1985-90; b. 8.11.30, Tynemouth; m., Irene Joyce Cairns; 1 s.; 1 d. Educ. Lancaster Royal Grammar School; Jesus College, Cambridge; Edinburgh University. Research Assistant, Foreign Office, 1953; Scottish Record Office: Assistant Keeper, 1953-83, Deputy Keeper, 1983-84. Recreations: historical research; bowling. Address: (h.) 33 Inverleith Gardens, Edinburgh EH3 5PR; T.-0131-552 4465.

Murray, David Edward. Chairman, Murray International Holdings; Chairman, The Rangers Football Club plc; Founder, David Murray Foundation, 1997; b. 14.10.51, Ayr; m., Louise (deceased); 2 s. Educ. Fettes College; Broughton High School. Young Scottish Business Man of the Year, 1984; Hon. Doctorate, Heriot-Watt University, 1986; Chairman, UK 2000 (Scotland), 1987; Governor, Clifton Hall School, 1987. Recreations: sports sponsorship; collecting wine. Address: (b.) South Gyle, Edinburgh; T.-0131-317 7000.

Murray, Donald, MA. Head Teacher, Sir Edward Scott School, Tarbert, Isle of Harris, since 1981; b. Port of Ness, Isle of Lewis; 2 d. Educ. Nicolson Institute, Stornoway; Glasgow University. Teacher, Calder Street Secondary School, Glasgow; Teacher, Achnamara Residential School, Argyll; Principal Teacher of Guidance, Victoria Drive Secondary School, Glasgow; Assistant Head Teacher (Curriculum), Kingsridge Secondary School, Glasgow. Recreations: angling; gardening; reading. Address: (h.) Balranald, West Tarbert, Isle of Harris; T.-01859 502339.

Murray, Rev. Douglas Millar, MA, BD, PhD. Principal of Trinity College, since 1997, and Lecturer in Ecclesiastical History, Glasgow University, since 1989; b. 1946, Edinburgh; m., Dr. Freya M. Smith. Educ. George Watson's College, Edinburgh; Edinburgh University; New College, Edinburgh; Fitzwilliam and Westminster Colleges, Cambridge. Minister: St. Bride's Church, Callander, 1976-80, John Ker Memorial Church in deferred union with Candlish Church, Edinburgh, 1980-81, and Polwarth Church, 1981-89. Editor, Liturgical Review, 1979-81; Associate Editor, Scottish Journal of Theology, 1981-87; Convener, Panel on Doctrine, General Assembly, Church of Scotland, 1986-90; Chalmers Lecturer, 1991. Publication: Studies in the History of Worship in Scotland (Co-Editor); Freedom to Reform, 1993. Recreations: golf; Scottish country dancing; hill-walking. Address: 28 Sherbrooke Drive, Glasgow G41 5AA; T.-0141-427 9524.

Murray, Frank McDonald, EurEng, BSc (Hons), CEng, FIMinE. Secretary-General, Federation of European Explosives Manufacturers; Director, Ayrshire Chamber of Commerce; Chairman, Comitee Europeen de Normalisation, TC 321 Harmonisation of Explosives Standards, Europe; Secretary General, Safex International; b. 7.9.36, Dunfermline; m., Nancy McDermott; 1 s.; 1 d. Educ. Kirkcaldy High School; Edinburgh University. Coal mining/gold mining, 1957-62; joined ICI as explosives engineer, 1962; Managing Director, ICI Nobel's Explosives Co., 1988-93. Recreation: golf; gardening. Address: (b.) McGowan House, Lundholm Road, Stevenston KA20 3LJ; T.-01294 487287.

Murray, Gordon Lindsay Kevan. Partner, Burness, Solicitors, since 1982; Secretary, Scottish National Orchestra Society Ltd., 1985-90; Director, 1990-93, Secretary and Treasurer, since 1985, Royal Scottish National Orchestra Endowment Trust; b. 23.5.53, Glasgow; m., Susan Patricia; 1 s.; 3 d. Educ. Lenzie Academy; Edinburgh University. President, Scottish Young Lawyers Association, 1977-78. Address: (b.) 50 Lothian Road, Edinburgh EH3 9WJ; T.-0131-473 6000.

Murray, Gregor Cumming, MA, MBA. Executive Director, Midlothian Enterprise Trust, since 1992; Chief Executive, Midlothian Chamber of Commerce; b. 16.4.57, Edinburgh; m., Barbara; 2 d. Educ. George Watson's College, Edinburgh; Trinity College, Oxford; Edinburgh University Management School. Bank of Scotland; Investors in Industry; Leith Enterprise Trust. Board Member, Lothian Investment Fund for Enterprise. Recreations: fly fishing; golf; music; tennis; hill-walking. Address: (b.) 29A Eskbank Road, Dalkeith EH22 1HJ; T.-0131-654 1234.

Murray, Iain McInnes, BSc (Hons), MEd (Hons). Head Teacher, Lanark Grammar School, since 1997; b. 1.3.46, Glasgow; m., Marilyn; 1 s. Educ. Allan Glen's High School; Glasgow University. Teacher of Physics, Paisley Grammar School, 1969-72; Assistant Principal Teacher, Science, Castlehead High School, Paisley, 1972-73; Principal Teacher of Physics, Caldervale High School, Airdrie, 1973-81; Assistant Head Teacher, Vale of Leven Academy, Alexandria, 1981-86; Depute Head Teacher, Braidfield High School, Clydebank, 1986-89; Head Teacher, Wishaw High School, 1989-92; seconded to work with school boards, 1992-94; Head Teacher, Arran High School, 1994-97. Recreations: bridge; golf. Address: (b.) Albany Drive, Lanark ML11 9AQ; T.-01555 662471.

Murray, Isobel (Mary), MA, PhD. Writer and Critic; Reader in English, Aberdeen University; b. 14.2.39, Alloa; m., Bob Tait. Educ. Dollar Academy; Edinburgh University. Assistant Lecturer, Lecturer, Senior Lecturer, Department of English, Aberdeen University; books include several editions of Oscar Wilde, introductions to new editions of J. MacDougall Hay's Gillespie, Ian MacPherson's Shepherds' Calendar and Robin Jenkins' Guests of War; edited, Beyond This Limit: Selected Shorter Fiction of Naomi Mitchison; A Girl Must Live: stories and poems by Naomi Mitchison; Ten Modern Scottish Novels (with Bob Tait), 1984; Scottish Writers Talking, 1996. Address: (b.) Department of English, King's College, Old Aberdeen, Aberdeen AB24 2UB; T.-Aberdeen 272644.

Murray, Professor James, BSc, ARTC, CEng, FIMechE, FIEE, FIM. Vice Principal, Napier University, 1992-95, now Emeritus Professor; b. 25.7.30, Glasgow; m., Emily Lamb Beveridge; 1 s.; 1 d. Educ. Allan Glen's School, Glasgow; Glasgow University. Development Engineer, Ferranti Ltd., Edinburgh, 1952-62; Lecturer, Department of Mechanical Engineering, Heriot-Watt University, 1962-67; Head, Department of Production Engineering, Napier College, 1967-72; Head, Department of Industrial Studies, 1972-74; Assistant Principal and Dean, Faculty of Professional Studies, 1974-82; Assistant Principal/Dean, Faculty of Technology, 1982-92. Former Member, Council: SCOTEC, EITB, IProdE; Past Chairman, IProdE, Edinburgh Section and Scotland Region; Past Chairman: CEI Scotland, CNAA Engineering Board and Research Committee; former Member, Transport Tribunal, Scotland; former Governor, Moray House College of Education; former Member of Convocation, Heriot-Watt University; Trustee, National Museums of Scotland, since 1997; Elder, Church of Scotland, since 1957; former Chairman, Edinburgh Branch, Glasgow Graduates Association; President, Allan Glen's Social Club, since 1998. Recreations: watching rugby; visiting museums; golf; gardening; studying light rail transport systems; opera. Address: (h.) 40 Elliot Road, Edinburgh EH14 1DZ.

Murray, John, BA (Hons), DipED, MEd. Headteacher, Harlaw Academy, since 1993; b. 2.2.52, Irvine; m., Margaret McLaughlin; 2 s.; 1 d. Educ. St. Michael's Academy, Kilwinning; Strathclyde University; Glasgow University; Stirling University. Teacher, Ardrossan Academy, 1975-78; Principal Teacher, St. Mungo's, Alloa, 1978-81; Principal Teacher, Lasswade High School, 1981-86; Assistant Rector, Woodmill High School, 1986-89; Depute Rector, Kirkcaldy High School, 1989-93. Director, Instant Neighbour, Aberdeen. Recreations: family; football; golf. Address: (b.) 18 Albyn Place, Aberdeen AB10 1RG; T.-01224 589251.

Murray, John. Editor, Scottish Express, since 1998; General Manager, Express Newspapers, Scotland, since 1998; b. 10.7.64, Dublin. Educ. Sandymount High School, Dublin. Production Editor, Independent on Sunday, 1990; The Independent: City Reporter, 1992, Assistant Business News Editor, 1993, Business News Editor, 1994; Sunday Express: City Editor, 1995, Business Editor, 1996; The Express: Head of City, 1997, Executive Editor, 1998. Recreations: eating; drinking; singing; the arts; sport. Address: (b.) Park House, Park Circus Place, Glasgow G3 6AN; T.-0141-352 2525.

Murray, Rev. John James, DipTH. Minister, St. Columba's Free Church, Edinburgh, since 1989; b. 11.9.34, Dornoch; m., Cynthia MacPhee; 1 s.; 1 d. Educ. Dornoch Academy; Edinburgh University; Free Church College. Caledonian Insurance Company, 1955-59; Assistant Editor, Banner of Truth Trust, 1960-73; Minister, Free High Church, Oban, 1978-89. Publication: Behind a Frowning Providence. Address: (h.) 10 Esslemont Road, Edinburgh EH16 5PX; T.-0131-667 4730.

Murray, Judy, BA, PCA. National Tennis Coach, since 1997; b. 8.9.59, Bridge of Allan; 2 s. Educ. Morrison's Academy; Edinburgh University. Winner: 65 Scottish titles, 37 Scottish caps (most capped female player); British Hard Court Doubles title, 1981; represented Great Britain, World Student Games, 1981; first female to hold Lawn Tennis Association Performance Coach Award, 1995; former Captain, British Under 14s Girls Team. Recreation: badminton. Address: 23a Kenilworth Road, Bridge of Allan FK9 4DU; T.-01786 834566.

Murray, Leonard G., JP, KHS, BL, SSC. Solicitor; former Senior Partner, now Consultant to, Levy & McRae, Solicitors; b. 16.8.33, Glasgow; m., Elizabeth Wilson; 3 s. Educ. St. Mungo's Academy, Glasgow; Glasgow University. Chairman, Murray Inns Ltd. After-dinner speaker; partner, Murray Enterprises; part-time Chairman, Employment Tribunals. Recreations: golf; gardening. Address: (h.) 23 Courthill, Bearsden, Glasgow G61 3SN.

Murray, Professor Maxwell, BVMS, DVM, FRCPath, FRSE, PhD. Professor of Veterinary Medicine, Glasgow University, since 1985; Head, Department of Veterinary Clinical Studies; b. 3.5.39, Glasgow; m., Christine Madelaine; 1 s.; 2 d. Educ. Shawlands Senior Secondary School; Glasgow University. Animal Health Trust Research Scholarship, 1962-63; Lecturer in Veterinary Pathology, University of Nairobi, 1963-65; Lecturer in Veterinary Pathology, then Senior Lecturer, Glasgow University, 1965-75; Senior Scientist, International Laboratory for Research on Animal Diseases, Nairobi, 1975-85. Address: (b.) Glasgow University Veterinary School, Bearsden Road, Bearsden, Glasgow G61 1QH.

Murray, Professor Noreen Elizabeth, FRS, PhD, FRSE. Professor, Institute of Cell and Molecular Biology, Edinburgh University; b. 26.2.35, Burnley; m., Kenneth Murray (qv). Educ. Lancaster Girls' Grammar School;

King's College, London; Birmingham University. Research Associate, Department of Biological Sciences, Stanford University, 1960-64; Research Fellow, Botany School, Cambridge, 1964-67; Edinburgh University: Member, MRC Molecular Genetics Unit, Department of Molecular Biology, 1968-74, Lecturer, then Senior Lecturer, Department of Molecular Biology, 1974-80; Group Leader, European Molecular Biology Laboratory, Heidelberg, 1980-82; rejoined Edinburgh University as Reader, 1982. Recreation: gardening. Address: (b.) Institute of Cell and Molecular Biology, Edinburgh University, Mayfield Road, Edinburgh EH9 3JR; T.-0131-650 5374.

Murray, Norman Loch, BA, CA, FRSA. Chairman, Morgan Grenfell Development Capital Limited, since 1998 (Deputy Chief Executive, 1989-96, Chief Executive, 1996-98); Executive Director, Deutsche Morgan Grenfell; Non-Executive Director: Morgan Grenfell Development Capital France SA, Deutsche Morgan Grenfell Development Capital Italy SA, Deutsche Morgan Grenfell Private Equity Asia Fund Limited; b. 17.3.48, Kilmarnock; m., Pamela Anne Low; 2 s. Educ. George Watson's College; Heriot-Watt University; Harvard University Graduate School of Business Administration. Scottish & Newcastle Breweries PLC, 1971-73; Arthur Young, 1973-76; Peat Marwick Mitchell & Co. (Hong Kong), 1977-80; Royal Bank of Scotland PLC, 1980-85; Director, Charterhouse Development Capital Ltd., 1985-89. Former directorships (non-executive): Bristow Helicopter Group Limited, Eurodollar (Holdings) Ltd., Taunton Cider plc, Burn Stewart Group Ltd.; Institute of Chartered Accountants of Scotland: Member of Council, Convener, Finance and General Purposes Committee; Member, Research Committee, 1986-91; Chairman, Lothian Borders and Central Area Committee, 1992-95; Chairman, British Venture Capital Association, 1997-98, of its Legal and Technical Committee, 1992-96; Member, Governing Council and Finance Committee, George Watson's College. Publication: Making Corporate Reports Valuable (Co-Author), 1988. Recreations: squash; golf; climbing; travel. Address: (b.) 35 St. Andrew Square, Edinburgh EH2 2AD; T.-0131-557 8600.

Murray, Robert John, MSc, MCIBS, JP. Deputy Leader, Angus Council, and Convenor, Personnel and Property Committee, since 1995; Convenor, Tayside Contracts Joint Committee, since 1998; Vice Convenor: Tayside Valuation Joint Board, since 1995, Tayside Contracts Joint Committee, since 1995; b. 3.2.51, Montrose; 1 s.; 1 d. Educ. Montrose Academy; University of Abertay, Dundee. Recreations: cycling; golf. Address: (h.) 44 Dalhousie Street, Monifieth DD5 4AL; T.-01382 534908.

Murray, Roderick Macpherson, BA (Hons). Director, An Lanntair, since 1985; b. 31.3.56, Coll, Isle of Lewis. Educ. Back Junior Secondary School; Nicolson Institute, Stornoway; Glasgow School of Art. Recreations: cycling; diving (until recently); chess; arts. Address: (b.) An Lanntair, Town Hall, South Beach, Stornoway, Isle of Lewis; T.-01851 703307.

Murray, Rt. Hon. Lord (Ronald King Murray), PC (1974), MA, LLB, Dr.h.c.(Edin). Senator of the College of Justice in Scotland, 1979-95; b. 15.6.22; m., Sheila Winifred Gamlin. Educ. George Watson's College; Edinburgh University; Jesus College, Oxford. Advocate, 1953; QC, 1967; MP (Leith), 1970-79; Lord Advocate, 1974-79. Assessor, Edinburgh University Court, 1981-93 (Vice-Chairman, 1990-93). Recreations: sailing; astronomy. Address: (h.) 1 Inverleith Grove, Edinburgh EH3 5PB; T.-0131-551 5330.

Murray, Professor T. Stuart, MD, PhD, FRCGP, FRCPEdin, FRCPGlas. West of Scotland Director of Postgraduate General Practice Education, since 1985; Professor of General Practice, University of Glasgow, since 1992; b. 22.7.43, Muirkirk, Ayrshire; m., Anne Smith; 1 s.; 2 d. Educ. Muirkirk Junior Secondary School; Cumnock Academy; University of Glasgow. Early training in cardiology; entered general practice, 1971; Senior Lecturer in General Practice, 1979. Publication: Modified Essay Questions for the MRCGP Examination; Guide to Postgraduate Medical Education (Co-author). Recreations: travel; reading; sport. Address: (b.) 1 Horselethill Road, Glasgow G12 9LX; T.-0141-330 5276.

Murray, William James Greig, MBBS, MS, FRCS(Ed), FRCS(Eng). Consultant Surgeon, Perth Royal Infirmary, since 1990; b. 19.10.51, Aberdeen; m., Pamela Jane; 2 s. 2 d. Educ. Robert Gordon's College, Aberdeen; Dulwich College Preparatory School; Westminster School; Middlesex Hospital Medical School, London University. House Surgeon, Middlesex Hospital, 1975; Registrar, Surgery/Urology, King's College Hospital, 1982-87; Senior Registrar, University College Hospital, 1987-90. College Tutor, Royal College of Surgeons of Edinburgh; Chairman, Medical Staff Committee, Perth Royal Infirmary. Recreations: golf; gardening. Address: (b.) Perth Royal Infirmary, Perth PH1 1NX; T.-01738 623311.

Murray-Smith, Professor David James, MSc, PhD, CEng, FIEE, MInstMC. Dean, Faculty of Engineering and Professor of Engineering Systems and Control, Glasgow University; b. 20.10.41, Aberdeen; m., Effie Smith; 2 s. Educ. Aberdeen Grammar School; Aberdeen University; Glasgow University. Engineer, Inertial Systems Department, Ferranti Ltd., Edinburgh, 1964-65; Glasgow University: Assistant, Department of Electrical Engineering, 1965-67, Lecturer, 1967-77, Senior Lecturer, 1977-83, Reader, 1983-85. Past Chairman, United Kingdom Simulation Council. Recreations: hill-walking; photography; strong interest in railways. Address: (b.) Department of Electronics and Electrical Engineering, Glasgow University, Glasgow G12 8QQ; T.-0141-330 5222.

Muscatelli, Professor Vito Antonio, MA (Hons), PhD, FRSA. Daniel Jack Professor of Political Economy, Department of Economics, Glasgow University, since 1994; b. 1.1.62, Bari, Italy; m., Elaine Flood; 1 d. Educ. High School of Glasgow; Glasgow University. Lecturer, Senior Lecturer, Glasgow University, 1984-94; Visiting Professor: University of Parma (Italy), 1989, Catholic University, Milan, 1991, 1997, University of Bari (Italy), since 1995; Editor, Scottish Journal of Political Economy, since 1989; Member, Council, Scottish Economic Society, since 1989; Member, Editorial Advisory Board, International Review of Economics and Business, since 1995. Hon. Fellow, Societa Italiana Degli Economisti, 1996. Publications: Macroeconomic Theory and Stabilisation Policy (Co-author), 1988; Economic and Political Institutions in Economic Policy (Editor of volume), 1996; articles in journals. Recreations: music; literature; football; strategic games. Address: (b.) Department of Economics, Adam Smith Building, Glasgow University, Glasgow G12 8RT; T.-0141-330 5062.

Musson, John Nicholas Whitaker, MA (Oxon). Country Director, Bosnia/Herzogovina, for Mercy Corps/Scottish European Aid, since 1998; Director and Trustee, Scottish European Aid and Mercy Corps Europe, 1996-98; Governor, Clifton College, Bristol, since 1989; b. 2.10.27; m., Ann Priest; 1 s.; 3 d. Educ. Clifton College; Brasenose College, Oxford. Served as Guardsman and Lt., Lancashire Fusiliers, 1945-48; HM Colonial Administrative Service, 1951-59 (District Officer, N. Nigeria and Lecturer, Institute of Administration, Nigeria); British Petroleum Co., London, 1959-61; Assistant Master and Housemaster, Canford School, Dorset, 1961-72; Warden, Glenalmond College, 1972-87; Scottish Division Chairman, Headmasters' Conference, 1981-83; Scottish Director, Independent Schools Careers Organisation, 1987-93; Governor, George

Watson's College, Edinburgh, 1989-98. Recreations: hill-walking; fishing; Egyptology. Address: (h.) 47 Spylaw Road, Edinburgh EH10 5BP; T.-0131-337 0089.

Mutch, Alexander Fyvie, CBE, JP. Member, Grampian Regional Council, 1974-90 (first Convener, 1974-82); b. 23.3.24, Aberdeen; m., Freda Mutch; 1 d. Educ. Aberdeen Central School. Convener, Aberdeen Corporation Cleansing Committee, 1963; Vice-Chairman, North-East Water Board, 1968-70; Magistrate, Aberdeen, 1967; Senior Magistrate, 1968; Chairman, Aberdeen Licensing Court, 1968; Member, Aberdeen University Court, 1974-82; Chairman, South Aberdeen Conservative Association, 1964-68 (President, 1968-72); Senior Vice-President, Conservative Party in Scotland, 1972-73 (President, 1973-74); Leader, Conservative Group, Aberdeen Town Council, 1974-75; Governor, Robert Gordon's College, Aberdeen, 1968-70 and since 1974; Honorary President, Grampian-Houston Association; Honorary Citizen, Houston, Texas. Address: (h.) 28 Salisbury Terrace, Aberdeen; T.-Aberdeen 591520.

Mutch, William Edward Scott, OBE, BSc, PhD, FRSE, FICFor. Forestry and Land Use Consultant; b. 14.8.25, Salford; m., Margaret Isobel McKay; 1 d. Educ. Royal High School, Edinburgh; Edinburgh University. HM Colonial Service (Forest Department, Nigeria, as Assistant Conservator of Forests and Silviculturist), 1946; Research Assistant, Oxford University, 1952; Lecturer in Forestry, Edinburgh University, 1953. Head, Department of Forestry and Natural Resources, Edinburgh University, 1981-87; President, Institute of Chartered Foresters, 1982-84 (Institute Medal, 1986); Member: Countryside Commission for Scotland, 1988-92; National Forestry Research Advisory Committee; Nature Conservancy Council, 1988-91; NCC for Scotland, 1991-92; Scottish Natural Heritage, Chairman S.E. Scotland, 1992-94; Director, Central Scotland Woodlands Ltd., 1989-93, and Central Scotland Countryside Trust, 1992-97. Publications: Farm Woodland Management; Tall Trees and Small Woods. Recreations: cabinet making; travel; painting. Address: (h.) 19 Barnton Grove, Edinburgh EH4 6EQ; T.-0131-339 1400.

Myles, David Fairlie, CBE. Hill Farmer; Member, Angus District Council, 1984-96; Chairman, Dairy Produce Quota Tribunal for Scotland, since 1984; Member, Potato Marketing Board, 1988-97; b. 30.5.25, Cortachy, Kirriemuir; m., Janet I. Gall; 2 s.; 2 d. Educ. Brechin High School. Auctioneer's clerk, 1941-43; Royal Marines, 1943-46; Tenant Hill Farmer, since 1946; Director of auction company, 1963-81; Member, Transport Users Consultative Committee for Scotland, 1973-79; Council Member, NFU of Scotland, 1970-79 (Convener, Organisation and Publicity Committee, 1976-79); Member, Meat Promotion Executive, MLC, 1975-79; Chairman, North Angus and Mearns Constituency Conservative Party, 1971-74; MP (Conservative), Banff, 1979-83; Joint Secretary, Backbench Conservative Agriculture Committee, 1979-83; Secretary, Backbench Conservative European Committee, 1980-83; Member: Select Committee on Agriculture and Select Committee on European Legislation, 1979-83, North of Scotland Hydro-Electric Board, 1985-89, Angus Tourist Board, 1984-92; Dean, Guildry of Brechin, 1993-94; Lord President, Court of Deans of Scotland, 1995-96; Session Clerk, Edzell-Lethnot Parish Church, since 1996; Elder, Edzell-Lethnot Parish Church. Recreations: curling; traditional Scottish fiddle music; works of Robert Burns. Address: (h.) The Gorse, Dunlappie Road, Edzell, Brechin DD9 7UB; T.-0135 64 207.

Myles, William Mackay Stanley, TD (with bar). Senior Partner, Myles Brothers, Wholesale Ironmongers, Edinburgh, since 1954; Member, Executive Committee, National Trust for Scotland, 1988-97; b. 6.3.27, Edinburgh; m., Margaret Shiela Grace Bruce; 3 s. Educ. Sciennes and James Clark's, Edinburgh; Bell-Baxter, Cupar. Royal Scots, 1945-66; India & Pakistan 1st Bn., 1946-47, 7/9 and 8/9 TA Bns., 1948-66, as Rifle Company Commander, 1951-66; Member, Regimental Council, since 1977; Mountaineering Council of Scotland: Training Officer, 1974-90, Hon. Secretary, 1977-83, Vice-President, 1984-88; Chairman: The Royal Scots Club, Edinburgh, since 1977, Edinburgh West End Community Council, 1989-95; Director, Lord Roberts Workshops for Disabled Ex-Servicemen; Council Member, Earl Haig Fund; Elder, Church of Scotland, since 1950; Director, Drumsheugh Baths Club Ltd., Edinburgh, since 1972; President, Rotary Club of Edinburgh, 1983-84. Recreations: hill-walking; swimming; painting in oils; gardening. Address: (h.) 1 Chartwell, 4b Church Hill, Edinburgh EH10 4BQ; T.-0131-452 8331.

N

Naftalin, Norman M. BL, NP, DL. Self-employed Solicitor, since 1961; Managing Director, property companies, since 1978; b. 25.9.39, Glasgow; m., Louise; 2 s.; 1 d. Educ. Glasgow High School; Glasgow University. Established Naftalin Duncan and Company, Solicitors, 1961: Senior Partner, then Consultant, until 1984. Part-time Senior Tutor, Finance and Investment, Strathclyde University; part-time Tutor, Glasgow University; occasional teaching posts in Business Law, Glasgow Caledonian University; International Governor, Hebrew University, Jerusalem, since 1979 (Chairman, Nominations Committee); Member, Greater Glasgow Health Board, since 1989; Member, Business Committee, General Council, University of Glasgow, since 1994; Member Board, Children's Music Foundation in Scotland, since 1995; Accredited Mediator, since 1995; Deputy Lieutenant, Renfrewshire, since 1995. Recreations: squash; tennis. Address: (b.) 537 Sauchiehall Street, Glasgow G3 7PQ; T.-0141-221 3119.

Nagl, Hazel Anna, DA, RSW. Artist/Painter; part-time Tutor, Ayr College; b. 2.11.53, Glasgow; m., James Geoffrey Keanie; 1 d. Educ. North Kelvinside Senior Secondary School; Glasgow School of Art. Exhibits on a regular basis throughout Scotland; RSW, 1988; PAI, 1995; SAAC 1994; RGI Stone Prize, 1987 and 1990; RGI Mackinlay Award, 1994; RGI Eastwood Publications Award, 1994; SAAC Prize, 1994; PAI Prize 1996 and 1998. Address: (h.) Lawmarnock House, Troon Drive, Bridge of Weir PA11 3HF.

Nairn, Nicholas Cameron Abell. Chef/Director, Nairns Restaurant, Glasgow, since 1997; Chef/Director, Braeval Restaurant, Aberfoyle, since 1986; Hon. President, Drambuie Scottish Chefs National Cookery Centre, since 1997; b. 12.1.59, Stirling. Educ. McLaren High School, Callander. Merchant Navy, 1976-83. Presenter: Wild Harvest, BBC2, 1996, Ready Steady Cook, BBC2, since 1996, Celebrity Ready Steady Cook, Who'll Do the Pudding, BBC1, 1996-97, Wild Harvest Two, BBC2, 1997, Island Harvest, BBC2, 1998; Chef/Consultant, Tesco; Winner, Scottish Field/Charles Heidsieck Scottish Restaurant of the Year, 1990; Good Food Guide County Restaurant of the Year, 1991; Macallan/Decanter Scottish Restaurant of the Year, 1992; Scottish Field/Bowmore Restaurant of the Year, 1992; Member, Advisory Board, Scottish Chefs Association; Lifetime Achievement Award, SCA; Hon. President, Chefs' School; Member, Masterchefs of GB. Recreations: cycling; wind-surfing; wine; eating out; travel; Scottish art; theatre; fly fishing; diving. Address: (b.) 13 Woodside Crescent, Glasgow G3 7UP; T.-0141-353 0707.

Nairn, Tom. Sociologist; b. 1932, Freuchie, Fife. Educ. Edinburgh University; Oxford University. Taught social philosophy, Birmingham University, and sociology, Hornsey College of Art; Editor, Bulletin of Scottish Politics, 1981-82; Columnist, The Scotsman. Publications: The Left Against Europe; The Break-Up of Britain?; The Enchanted Glass: Britain and its Monarchy.

Nairne, Andrew, MA (Hons). Director, Dundee Contemporary Arts, since 1997; b. 10.2.60, Guildford; m., Nicola Dandridge; 1 s. Educ. Radley College; St. Andrews University. Assistant Curator, Kettle's Yard, Cambridge University, 1984-85; Deputy Director, Ikon Gallery, Birmingham, 1985-86; Exhibitions Director, Centre for Contemporary Arts, Glasgow, 1986-93; Visual Arts Director, Scottish Arts Council, 1993-97. Recreations: modern history; jazz. Address: (h.) The Schoolhouse, Station Road, Errol PH2 7QB; T.-01821 642434.

Nanjiani, Shereen, MA (Hons). Journalist, Scottish Television, since 1983; b. 4.10.61, Elderslie. Educ. John Neilson High School, Paisley; Glasgow University. Joined STV as a trainee journalist, 1983; moved to reporting two years later; became presenter of Scotland Today, 1985; presented General Election programme, 1997; presented, Secret Scotland documentary series. Address: (b.) Scottish Television, Cowcaddens, Glasgow, G2 3PR.

Napier, 14th Lord, and Etrrick, 5th Baron (Francis Nigel Napier), KCVO, DL. Private Secretary, Comptroller and Equerry to Princess Margaret, Countess of Snowdon, since 1973; b. 5.12.30; m.; 2 s.; 2 d. Succeeded to title, 1987. Address: Thirlestane, Ettrick, Selkirkshire.

Nash, Professor Andrew Samuel, BVMS, PhD, CBiol, FIBiol, DipECVIM, MRCVS. Professor of Small Animal Medicine, Division of Small Animal Clinical Studies, Department of Veterinary Clinical Studies, Glasgow University Veterinary School, since 1992, and Director of the Veterinary Hospital, 1993-96; Royal College of Veterinary Surgeons Recognised Specialist in Small Animal Medicine, since 1993; Vice-Dean for Student Affairs, since 1995; b. 1.8.44, Birmingham; m., Rosemary Truscott Hamilton; 1 s.; 1 d. Educ. Judd School, Tonbridge; Glasgow University. General veterinary practice, Ilfracombe, 1967-72; House Physician, Glasgow University Veterinary School, 1973-75, then Lecturer/Senior Lecturer, 1975-92. Silver Medal in Veterinary Clinical Medicine, 1967; RSPCA Humane Award, 1970; Member, Board of Directors, Glasgow Dog and Cat Home, 1981-95; Hon. President, Scottish Cat Club, since 1990; Member, Glasgow Presbytery, 1991-94; President, European Society of Veterinary Nephrology and Urology, 1992-94; Member, Board of Directors, Scottish Society for the Prevention of Cruelty to Animals, since 1995; author of more than 100 papers, articles, book chapters. Recreations: music; gardening; DIY; church work (church organist). Address: (b.) University of Glasgow Veterinary School, Bearsden Road, Glasgow G61 1QH; T.-0141-330 5700.

Nash, Victoria Jane, BSc, PhD. Director, Scottish Water and Sewerage Customers Council, since 1996; b. 17.6.57, Northampton; m., Robin Campbell; 2 step d. Educ. Cheadle Hulme School; Oxford Polytechnic; Stirling University. Senior Research Officer, Scottish Office Education Department, 1982-83; Project Co-ordinator, Scottish Council for Educational Technology, 1983-85; Policy Analyst, then Assistant Chief Executive, then Chief Executive, Fife Regional Council, 1985-96. Recreations: singing; swimming; cats. Address: (b.) Ochil House, Springkerse Business Park, Stirling FK7 7XE; T.-01786 430200.

Naumann, Laurie M. Director, Scottish Council for Single Homeless; b. 1943, Saffron Walden; m., Barbara; 2 s.; 3 d. Educ. Edinburgh, Gloucester and Nuremberg Rudolf Steiner; Leicester University. Furniture maker, Gloucestershire; Probation and After Care Officer, Leeds; Social Worker, Edinburgh; Council of Europe Social Fellowship to Finland to study services for the drunken offender, 1976; jointly won Rosemary Delbridge Memorial Trophy for influencing Parliament to legislate, 1983; on secondment to Scottish Office Social Work Services Inspectorate, 1992-95; Secretary, Hamish Allan Trust; Board Member, Kingdom and Old Town Housing Associations and Garvald Centre, Edinburgh; Panel Member, Scottish Health Advisory Service. Recreations: travel; reading; walking; woodwork. Address: (h.) St. Ann's, Alexander III Street, Kinghorn, Fife KY3 9SD; T.-01592 890346.

Naylor, Brian, BSc, MPhil. Director (Properties in Care), Historic Scotland, since 1995; b. 10.2.49, Altrincham; m., 1, Mary Halley (deceased); 2 s.; 2, Moira Hillen; 2 step s. Educ. Lymm Grammar School; Leicester University; Edinburgh University. Scottish Office: graduate trainee, 1976-82; Principal, 1982-89; Assistant Secretary, 1989-95. Partner, Naylor's Delicatessen, Gullane. Recreations: fishing; theatre; swimming; walking. Address: (b.) Longmore House, Salisbury Place, Edinburgh EH9 1SH; T.-0131-668 8735.

Naylor, (Charles) John, OBE, MA, CIMgt, FRSA. Secretary and Treasurer, Carnegie United Kingdom Trust, since 1993; b. 17.8.43, Newcastle upon Tyne; m., Margery Thomson; 2 s. Educ. Royal Grammar School, Newcastle upon Tyne; Clare College, Cambridge University. Director, YMCA National Centre, Lakeside, Cumbria, 1975-80; National Council of YMCAs: Deputy Secretary, 1980-82, National Secretary, 1982-93. Member and Chairman, YMCA European and World Committees, 1976-92; Chair, Association of Heads of Outdoor Education Centres, 1979-80; Chair, MSC and DES Working Party on Residential Experience and Unemployment, 1980-81; Member, National Advisory Council for Youth Service, 1985-88; Vice-Chairman, National Council for Voluntary Youth Services, 1985-88; Founding Convener, Scottish Grant-making Trusts' Group, 1994-97; Chairman, Brathay Exploration Group, since 1995; Group Scout Leader, 82nd Inverleith (Cramond) Scouts, since 1996. Publications: Guide to Scottish Grant-making Trusts; Writing Better Fund Raising Applications (Contributor); contributions to other books and periodicals. Address: (b.) Comley Park House, Dunfermline KY12 7EJ; T.-01383 721445.

Neil, Alex., MA (Hons). Policy Vice-Convener, Scottish National Party, since 1994; Economic Consultant; b. 22.8.51, Irvine; m., Isabella Kerr; 1 s. Educ. Dalmellington High School; Ayr Academy; Dundee University. Scottish Research Officer, Labour Party, 1975; General Secretary, Scottish Labour Party (SLP), 1976; Marketing Manager, 1979-83; Director: Cumnock and Doon Enterprise Trust, 1983-87, Prince's Scottish Youth Business Trust, 1987-89; Chairman, Network Scotland Ltd., 1987-93. Recreations: family; golf; gardening; travel. Address: (h.) 26 Overmills Road, Ayr KA7 3LQ; T.-01292 286675.

Neil, Andrew, MA (Hons). Editor-in-Chief, The Scotsman, Scotland on Sunday, Edinburgh Evening News, Sunday Business, since 1996; Presenter, Midnight Hour, BBC2; Thursday Night Live, ITV; Sunday Breakfast, BBC Radio 5; b. 21.5.49. Educ. Paisley Grammar School; Glasgow University. Conservative Research Department, 1971-72; Correspondent in Belfast, London, Washington, New York, for The Economist, 1973-82,UK Editor, London, 1982-83; Editor, Sunday Times, 1983-94; Chairman, Sky TV, 1988-90; author of Full Disclosure (autobiography). Address: (b.) The Scotsman, North Bridge, Edinburgh EH1 1YT.

Neil, Rev. James Duncan, BD. Former Moderator, United Free Church of Scotland; Minister, Cathcart United Free Church, since 1979; b. 25.8.45, Glasgow; m., Janette Wilson Keery; 3 s. Educ. Whitehill Secondary School; Glasgow University and Trinity College. Apprentice, Electricity Board, 1963-68; ordained to charge of Moncrieff U.F. Church, Alloa, 1974-79. Former local Branch Chairman, National Bible Society of Scotland. Recreations: golf; swimming; hill-walking. Address: (h.) 72 Berridale Avenue, Glasgow G44 3AE; T.-0141-637 3944.

Neill, Gordon Webster McCash, DSO, SSC, NP, FInstD. Solicitor and Notary Public; Honorary Sheriff; b. Arbroath; m., Margaret Mary Lamb; 1 s.; 1 d. Educ. Edinburgh Academy. Legal apprenticeship, 1937-39; Pilot, RAF, 1939-46 (DSO, French Croix de Guerres with silver gilt star and silver star); Partner, Neill & Gibb, SSC, 1947; Chairman, Dundee Area Board, British Law Insurance Co. Ltd., 1954; Principal, Neill & Mackintosh, SSC, 1967; Consultant, Thorntons WS, 1989-96; Past Chairman, Scottish Gliding Association and Angus Gliding Club Ltd.; Past President, Chamber of Commerce, Arbroath Rotary Club and Society of Solicitors and Procurators in Angus. Recreations: golf; shooting; fishing. Address: (h.) 29 Duncan Avenue, Arbroath, Angus DD11 2DA; T.-01241 872221.

Neill, William Wilson, MA (Hons). Poet, b. 22.2.22, Prestwick; m., Doris Marie; 2 d. (by pr. m.). Educ. Ayr Academy; Edinburgh University. Served, RAF; won Sloane Verse Prize and Grierson Verse Prize while at Edinburgh University; Teacher; crowned Bard, Aviemore Mod, 1969; former Editor, Catalyst; former Editor, Lallans (Scots Language magazine); SAC Book Award, 1985; broadcasts, essays in Scotland's three tongues. Publications: Scotland's Castle, 1969; Poems, 1970; Four Points of a Saltire (Co-author), 1970; Despatches Home, 1972; Buile Shuibhne, 1974; Galloway Landscape: Poems, 1981; Cnu a Mogaill: Poems, 1983; Wild Places: Poems, 1985; Blossom, Berry, Fall: Poems 1986; Making Tracks: Poems, 1988; Straight Lines, 1992; Tales frae the Odyssey, 1992; Selected Poems, 1994. Address: (h.) Burnside, Crossmichael, Castle Douglas DG7 3AP; T.-055-667 265.

Neilson, Sheriff Hugh S. Floating Sheriff of South Strathclyde Dumfries and Galloway based at Hamilton. Address: (b.) Sheriff Court House, Beckford Street, Hamilton ML3 6AA.

Neilson, Margaret Marion, MA (Hons), LLB, DipLP, SSC, NP. Litigation Partner, Balfour & Manson, since 1987; b. Falkirk; m., Raymond A. McMenamin. Educ. Mary Erskine School, Edinburgh; Edinburgh University. Balfour & Manson: Trainee, 1983, Assistant, 1985. Secretary, Employment Law Group; Fiscal, Society of Solicitors in Supreme Courts of Scotland; Member, Joint Committee of Legal Societies of Edinburgh and Midlothian. Recreations: sport; hill-walking; scuba diving; travel. Address: (b.) 54-64 Frederick Street, Edinburgh EH2 1LS; T.-0131-200 1200.

Nelson, (Peter) Frederick, BSc, CEng, MIEE. Chairman, Scottish Sports Association, 1990-96; Member, Scottish Sports Council, 1990-98; b. 2.9.52, Glasgow; m., (Caroline) Ann; 3 s. Educ. John Neilson; Strathclyde University. President, Scottish Canoe Association, 1980-90; Member, Commonwealth Games Council for Scotland, since 1982; Elder, Davidson's Mains Parish Church. Recreations: canoeing; cycling; DIY. Address: (h.) 11 Barnton Park Place, Edinburgh EH4 6ET; T.-0131-336 4779.

Ness, James Iain, LLB, NP. Solicitor; Member, Council, Law Society of Scotland, since 1990; Senior Partner, Austins, since 1995; b. 5.7.57, Johannesburg; m., Elaine; 1 s.; 1 d. Educ. Robert Gordon's, Aberdeen; Edinburgh University. Apprenticed, Connel & Connel, Edinburgh; Assistant, then Partner, then Senior Partner, Austins. Chairman, Competence Committee, Law Society of Scotland; Past President, Rotary Club of Dalbeattie; Secretary, Cancer Relief Macmillan Fund, Dalbeattie and District; Dean, Faculty of Procurators for the Stewartry of Kirkcudbright. Recreation: skiing. Address: (b.) 52 High Street, Dalbeattie, DG5 4AB; T.-01556 610259.

Neumann, Jan, CBE, BSc, FEng, FIMechE, FIMarE, FIES; b. 26.6.24, Prague; m., 1, Barbara Joyce Gove (deceased); 2 s.; 2, Irene McCusker. Educ. Friends' School, Great Ayton; London University. Flight Engineer, RAF; Design Engineer, English Electric Co., Rugby; various engineering design and management positions in Yarrow Admiralty Research Department; Director: YARD Ltd., 1969-88 (Managing Director, 1978-87), Yarrow PLC, 1978-86; Board Member: SSEB, 1986-88, Scottish Nuclear, 1989-93; President, Institution of Engineers and

Shipbuilders in Scotland, 1993-95; received Denny Gold Medal, IMarE, and Thomas Lowe Gray Prize, IMechE. Recreations: swimming; bowls. Address: (h.) 38 Norwood Park, Bearsden, Glasgow G61 2RZ.

Newall, John, LLB, WS, NP. Solicitor, since 1966; Member, Council, Law Society of Scotland, since 1993; b. 6.8.42, Dumfries; m., Gaye Tuddenham; 1 s.; 2 d. Educ. Dumfries Academy; Edinburgh University. Solicitor, 1966; WS, 1970; Partner, Skene, Edwards and Garson, 1970-78; Partner, McGrigor, Donald, since 1978. Recreations: flying; golf; music. Address: (b.) McGrigor Donald, Erskine House, 68-73 Queen Street, Edinburgh; T.-0131-226 7777.

Newall, Stephen Park, DL, Hon. LLD (Strathclyde). Deputy Chairman, Court, University of Strathclyde, since 1993 (Chairman, Court, 1988-93); Deputy Lieutenant, Dunbartonshire, since 1985; b. 12.4.31, Bearsden, Dunbartonshire; m., Gay Sommerville Craig; 4 s.; 1 d. Educ. Loretto. Commissioned and served with Parachute Regiment, National Service, 1949-51; Sales Manager, A.P. Newall & Co., 1951-57; Managing Director, Bulten-Kanthal Stephen Newall Co. Ltd., 1957-80. Chairman: Epilepsy Association of Scotland, 1982-86, Finance Committee, University of Strathclyde, 1985-88; Council Member: Quarrier's Homes, 1983-88, Scottish Business School, 1983-85; Secretary of State for Scotland's Nominee on Court of Cranfield, 1985-92; Deacon Convener, Trades of Glasgow, 1983-84. Recreations: farming; hill-walking; sailing; music. Address: (h.) Rowaleyn, Rhu, Dunbartonshire; T.-01436 820 521.

Newburgh, 12th Earl of (Don Filippo Giambattista Francesco Aldo Maria Rospigliosi); b. 4.7.42; m.; 1 d. Succeeded to title, 1986; lives in Italy.

Newell, Professor Alan F., BSc, PhD, FIEE, CEng, FBCS, FRSE, HonFCSLT. NCR Professor of Electronics and Microcomputer Systems, Dundee University, since 1980; Director, Dundee University Microcomputer Centre, since 1980; Head, Department of Applied Computing, since 1997 (Head, Applied Computer Studies Division, 1994-97; Deputy Principal, 1993-95); b. 1.3.41, Birmingham; m., Margaret; 1 s.; 2 d. Educ. St. Philip's Grammar School; Birmingham University. Research Engineer, Standard Telecommunication Laboratories; Lecturer, Department of Electronics, Southampton University. Recreations: family life; skiing; sailing. Address: (b.) Department of Applied Computing, Dundee University, Dundee, DD1 4HN; T.-01382 344144 .

Newis, Kenneth, CB, CVO, MA, FRSAMD. President, Queen's Hall (Edinburgh) Ltd.; Trustee, RSAMD Trust; b. 9.11.16, Crewe; m., Kathleen Barrow; 2 d. Educ. Manchester Grammar School; St. John's College, Cambridge. HM Office of Works, London, 1938-70; Under Secretary, Scottish Development Department, 1970-73; Secretary, 1973-76. Recreation: music. Address: (h.) 10/9 St. Margaret's Place, Edinburgh EH9 1AY; T.-0131-447 4138.

Newlands, Rev. Professor George McLeod, MA, BD, PhD. Professor of Divinity, Glasgow University, since 1986 (Dean, Faculty of Divinity, 1988-90); Convener, Panel on Doctrine, Church of Scotland, since 1995; Principal, Trinity College, 1991-97; 12.7.41, Perth; m., Mary Elizabeth Wallace; 3 s. Educ. Perth Academy; Edinburgh University; Heidelberg University; Churchill College, Cambridge. Assistant Minister, Muirhouse, Edinburgh, 1969; Lecturer in Divinity, Glasgow University, 1969; University Lecturer in Divinity, Cambridge, 1973; Dean, Trinity Hall, Cambridge, 1982. Publications: Hilary of Poitiers; Theology of the Love of God; The Church of God; Making Christian Decisions; God in Christian Perspective; Generosity and the Christian Future. Recreations: walking; music. Address: (b.) Faculty of Divinity, 4 The Square, Glasgow University, Glasgow G12 8QQ.

Newlands, William Jeffrey, MB, ChB, FRCSEdin. Consultant Ear, Nose and Throat Surgeon, Grampian Health Board and Orkney and Shetland Health Boards, since 1981; Clinical Senior Lecturer in Otolaryngology, Aberdeen University, since 1981; b. 9.9.29, Edinburgh; m., Patricia Kathleen St. Quintin Gee; 2 s.; 2 d. Educ. Daniel Stewart's College, Edinburgh; Edinburgh University. House Physician and House Surgeon, Western General Hospital, Edinburgh, 1952-53; Captain, RAMC, 1953-55; specialist training, 1958-65, Royal Infirmary, Edinburgh, Western Infirmary, Glasgow, Royal National Throat, Nose and Ear Hospital, London; Otolaryngologist, Brown Clinic, Calgary, 1966; Consultant ENT Surgeon: Grampian Health Board, 1967-77, County Hospital, Uddevalla, Sweden, 1977-78, Lothian Health Board, 1978-79; Professor of Otolaryngology, King Faisal University College of Medicine, Saudi Arabia, 1979-81. Examiner in Otolaryngology, Part 2 Examination, FRCSEdin, 1975-90; Visiting Surgeon, Mount Elizabeth Hospital, Singapore; Visiting Professor, Faculty of Medicine, National University of Malaysis, Kuala Lumpur. Recreations: travel; music. Address: (h.) 43 Westholme Avenue, Aberdeen AB15 6AB; T.-01224 312987.

Newsome, Eric Leslie, LLB, Solicitor of the Supreme Court of England and Wales. Full-time Chairman of Social Security, Disability, Medical and Child Support Appeal Tribunals, since 1993; full-time Chairman of Vaccine Damage Tribunals, since 1996; Deputy Social Security Commissioner, since 1997; b. 2.4.44, Bradford; m., Vivienne Susan; 1 s. Educ. Carlton Grammar School, Bradford; Sheffield University. Local Government Legal Officer, 1966-69; Lecturer in Local Government Law, Norwich College, 1970-72; Lecturer, Senior Lecturer, Principal Lecturer in Law, Manchester Polytechnic/ Manchester Metropolitan University, 1973-93; Consultant in trading standards law, specialising in motor vehicle law, 1975-93; part-time Chairman, Social Security Appeal Tribunals, 1985-93; Consultant in statute law revision, Law Commission of England and Wales, 1988-92; part-time Immigration Adjudicator, 1990-94; Training Consultant, Safeway PLC, 1991-93; Visiting Lecturer in Law, University of Hong Kong, 1991-93; part-time Chairman, Disability Appeal Tribunals, 1991-93. Publications: The Trades Descriptions Acts and the Motor Vehicle, 1977; articles and papers. Recreations: boxing; history of the theatre; snooker; old movies; wining and dining. Address: (b.) Independent Tribunal Service, Wellington House, 134-136 Wellington Street, Glasgow G2 2BR.

Nicholls, Brian, BSc (Econ). Senior Business Consultant, Scottish Enterprise, 1991-98; Vice President, Scottish Council Development and Industry, 1991-98; Director, Scottish Opera, since 1993; b. 21.9.28, London; m., Mary Elizabeth Harley; 1 s.; 2 d. Educ. Haberdashers' Aske's School; London University; Harvard Business School. George Wimpey Ltd., 1951-55; Constructors John Brown Ltd., 1955-75; Director, CJB Projects Ltd., 1972-75; Director, CJB Pipelines Ltd., 1974-75; Deputy Chairman, CJB Mohandessi Iran Ltd., 1974-75; Industrial Adviser to Secretary of State for Trade, 1975-78; Director: John Brown Engineering Ltd., 1978-91, John Brown Engineering Gas Turbines Ltd., 1978-91, Rugby Power Company Ltd., 1990-91; Vice President, John Brown Power Ltd., 1987-90; Member: Council, British Railway Export Group, 1976-78, British Overseas Trade Board, 1978; Fellow, Scottish Council Development and Industry, 1998. Recreations: music; reading; walking. Address: (h.) Blairlogie Park, Blairlogie, by Stirling FK9 5PY; T.-01259 761497.

Nicholson, Sheriff Principal (Charles) Gordon (Brown), QC, MA, LLB. Sheriff Principal of Lothian and Borders, since 1990; Commissioner, Scottish Law Commission,

1982-89; b. 11.9.35, Edinburgh; m., Hazel Mary Nixon; 2 s. Educ. George Watson's College, Edinburgh; Edinburgh University. Admitted to Faculty of Advocates, 1961; Advocate Depute, 1968-70; Sheriff of Dumfries and Galloway, at Dumfries, 1970-76; Sheriff of Lothian and Borders, at Edinburgh, 1976-82; Honorary President: Scottish Association for the Study of Delinquency, Victim Support Scotland; Commissioner, Northern Lighthouse Board, since 1990 (Chairman, 1994-95). Publication: The Law and Practice of Sentencing in Scotland, 1981 (2nd edition, 1992). Recreation: music. Address: (h.) Back O'Redfern, 24C Colinton Road, Edinburgh EH10 5EQ; T.-0131-447 4300.

Nicholson, Liz, MA. Director, Shelter Scotland, since 1995; b. 27.9.46, Birmingham; m., Colin Nicholson; 2 s.; 1 d. Educ. Our Lady of Mercy Grammar School, Wolverhampton; Edinburgh University. Research Associate, Edinburgh University, 1988-89; Housing Campaign Worker, Shelter, 1989-92; Depute Chief Executive, Citizens Advice Scotland, 1989-92. Address: (b.) Shelter, Scotiabank House, 6 South Charlotte Street, Edinburgh EH2 4AW.

Nicholson, Peter Alexander, LLB (Hons). Managing Editor, W. Green, The Scottish Law Publisher, since 1989; General Editor, Scots Law Times, since 1985; Scottish Editor, Current Law, 1985-96; General Editor, Greens Weekly Digest, since 1986; b. 22.5.58, Stirling; m., Morag Ann Fraser; 1 s.; 2 d. Educ. St. David's RC High School, Dalkeith; Edinburgh University. Admitted as Solicitor, 1981. Lay Minister of the Eucharist. Recreations: choral singing; gardening; keeping fit. Address: (h.) 91 Greenbank Road, Edinburgh EH10 5RT; T.-0131-447 1842.

Nickson of Renagour, Lord (David Wigley Nickson), KBE (1987), CBE (1981), DL, CBIM, FRSE. Life Peer; Chairman, Clydesdale Bank, since 1991 (Director, since 1981); Director, General Accident plc, 1971-98 (Deputy Chairman, 1973-98); Director, National Australian Group (UK) Ltd., since 1993; Chancellor, Glasgow Caledonian University, since 1993; Vice Lieutenant, Stirling and Falkirk, since 1997 (Deputy Lieutenant, 1982-97);b. 27.11.29, Eton; m., Helen Louise Cockcraft; 3 d. Educ. Eton College; Royal Military Academy, Sandhurst. Commissioned, Coldstream Guards, 1949-54; William Collins: joined, 1954, Director, 1961-85, Joint Managing Director, 1967, Vice-Chairman, 1976-83, Group Managing Director, 1979-82; Director: Scottish United Investors plc, 1970-83, Scottish & Newcastle Breweries plc, 1981-95 (Chairman, 1983-89), Radio Clyde Ltd., 1982-85, National Australia Bank Ltd., 1991-96, Hambros PLC, 1989-98; Chairman, Pan Books, 1982-83; Chairman, Scottish Enterprise, 1990-93 (SDA, 1988-90); President, CBI, 1986-88; Chairman, CBI in Scotland, 1979-81; Chairman, Countryside Commission for Scotland, 1983-86; Member: Scottish Industrial Development Advisory Board, 1975-80, Scottish Committee, Design Council, 1978-81, Scottish Economic Council, 1980-95, National Economic Development Council, 1985-88; Chairman, Atlantic Salmon Trust, 1988-95; Chairman, Senior Salaries Review Body, 1989-95; President, Association of District Salmon Fisheries Board, since 1996; Chairman, Secretary of State for Scotland's Scottish Salmon Strategy Task Force, 1995-97; Chairman, Scottish Advisory Committee, Imperial Cancer Research Fund, since 1994; Trustee: Princes Youth Business Trust, 1987-90, Princess Royal's Trust for Carers, 1990-94; Director, Countryside Alliance, since 1998; Brigadier, Queen's Bodyguard for Scotland (Royal Company of Archers); D.Univ, Stirling, 1986; Hon. DBA Napier Polytechnic, 1990; Honorary Fellow, Paisley College, 1992. Recreations: fishing; bird-watching; the countryside. Address: (h.) Renagour House, Aberfoyle, Stirling FK8 3TF; T.-01877 382275.

Nicol, Rev. Douglas Alexander Oag, MA, BD (Hons). General Secretary, Church of Scotland Department of National Mission; b. 5.4.48, Dunfermline; m., Anne Wilson Gillespie; 2 s.; 1 d. Educ. Kirkcaldy High School; Edinburgh University; Glasgow University. Assistant Warden, St. Ninian's Centre, Crieff, 1972-76; Minister, Lochside, Dumfries, 1976-82; Minister, St. Columba, Kilmacolm, 1982-91. Chairman, Board of Directors, National Bible Society of Scotland, 1984-87; Convener, Board of National Mission, Church of Scotland, 1990-91. Recreations: family life and family history; travel; athletics. Address: (h.) 24 Corbiehill Avenue, Blackhall, Edinburgh EH4 5DR; T.-0131-336 1965.

Nicol, Rev. James Gerard, PhB, STB, JCL. President, Roman Catholic Scottish National Tribunal, since 1992; Priest, Motherwell Diocese, since 1978; Judicial Vicar of all Scottish R.C. Dioceses, since 1992; b. 8.10.54, Coatbridge. Educ. St. Patrick's High School, Coatbridge; Blairs College, Aberdeen; Pontifical Gregorian University, Rome; Scots College, Rome. Parochial appointments, since 1979; Tribunal: Judge Instructor, 1979-81, Co-ordinator, Motherwell Diocese, 1981-84; Defender of the Bond, 1984-86; Instructor/Defender, 1986-89; Vice-President, 1989-92; Assistant Youth Co-ordinator, Motherwell Diocese, 1979-85. Recreations: cooking; travel; reading; collecting ducks; listening to music. Address: R.C. Scottish National Tribunal, 22 Woodrow Road, Glasgow G41 5PN; T.-0141-427 3036.

Nicol, Rev. John Chalmers, MA, BD, MHSM, DipHSM. Minister, Holy Trinity Church, Bridge of Allan, since 1985; b. 6.4.39, Greenock; m., Anne Morrison MacDonald; 1 s.; 1 d. Educ. Greenock Academy; Glasgow University; Princeton Theological Seminary. Assistant Minister, Westwood Parish Church, East Kilbride, 1964-65; Minister: St. Andrew's Church, Buenos Aires, 1965-69, Bonnyrigg Parish Church, 1970-75; Secretary, Edinburgh Local Health Council, 1975-78; Principal Administrative Assistant, Argyll and Clyde Health Board, 1978-85. Recreations: fishing; Charles Rennie Mackintosh. Address: (h.) 29 Keir Street, Bridge of Allan FK9 4QJ; T.-01786 832093.

Nicol, Rev. Thomas James Trail, LVO, MBE, MC, MA, DD. Minister, Church of Scotland; Extra Chaplain to The Queen, since 1979; b. 24.1.17, Skelmorlie, Ayrshire; m., Mary Barnfather Taylor; 2 d. Educ. Edinburgh Academy; Dundee High School; Glasgow Academy; Aberdeen Grammar School; Aberdeen University. OCTU and Commission, Black Watch, 1939-42; ordained as Chaplain to the Forces, 1942; RAChD, 1942-46, attached 51 (H) Division; Minister, St. Luke's, Broughty Ferry, 1946-49; regular commission, RAChD, 1949-72; Assistant Chaplain-General, HQ Scotland, 1967-72; Minister, Crathie, 1972-77; Domestic Chaplain in Scotland to the Queen, 1972-79. Recreations: hill-walking; gardening; golf. Address: (h.) Beech Cottage, Dalginross, Comrie, Perthshire PH6 2HB; T.-01764 670430.

Nicolaisen, Professor Wilhelm F. H., DrPhil, MLitt. Honorary Professor, University of Aberdeen, since 1998; b. 13.6.27, Halle, Germany; m., Mary; 4 d. Educ. schools in Germany; University of Kiel; University of Tübingen; University of Newcastle upon Tyne; University of Glasgow. Assistant Lecturer, German: University of Glasgow, 1951-52, University College, Dublin, 1952-53; Head, Scottish Place-name Survey, School of Scottish Studies, University of Edinburgh, 1956-69; Visiting Professor, Ohio State University, 1966-67; Professor of English and Folklore, State University of New York at Binghamton, 1969-92 (Distinguished Professor Emeritus, since 1992); Visiting Professor of English, University of Aarhus, Denmark, 1990, 1993, University of Edinburgh, 1996. Publication: Scottish Place-names: Their Study and Significance, 1976; The Picts and their Place-names, 1996; more than 300 scholarly articles. Recreations: swimming; watching Aberdeen F. C.

Address: (b.) Department of English, University of Aberdeen, Aberdeen, AB24 2UB; T.-01224 272957.

Nicoll, Eric Hamilton, CBE, FSA Scot, BSc (Hons), FICE, FCIWEM (Dip). Deputy Chief Engineer, Scottish Development Department, 1976-85; b. 15.5.25, Edinburgh; m., Helen Elizabeth Barnes; 1 s.; 1 d. Educ. George Heriot's School, Edinburgh; Edinburgh University. Engineering Assistant: Midlothian County Council Roads Department, 1945-46, Edinburgh Corporation Water Department, 1946-51; Chief Assistant County Engineer, Midlothian County Council, 1951-62; Scottish Development Department: Engineering Inspector, 1962-68, Senior Engineering Inspector, 1968-72, Assistant Chief Engineer, 1972-75. US Water Pollution Control Federation Arthur Sidney Bedell Award, 1985; Chairman, Edinburgh Recorded Music Society, 1992-95; Chairman (and Archivist), Pictish Arts Society, 1992-95; elected Professional Member of Society, Scottish Artists and Artist Craftsmen, 1995. Publications: Small Water Pollution Control Works: Design and Practice, 1988; A Pictish Panorama (Editor), 1995; Art Without Epoch, 1996; numerous technical and scientific papers. Recreations: wood sculpture; music; antiquities; crosswords. Address: (h.) 35 Wardie Road, Edinburgh EH5 3LJ.

Nicolson, David M., CA. Partner, KPMG Edinburgh, since 1988; b. 22.4.42, Edinburgh; m., Elizabeth Finlay Smith; 1 s.; 1 d. Educ. Royal High School, Edinburgh. Qualified as CA with Robertson & Maxtone Graham, Edinburgh, 1964; Peat Marwick Mitchell & Co., London, 1964-67; returned to Robertson & Maxtone Graham, 1967 (now KPMG). President: Edinburgh Junior Chamber of Commerce, 1975-76, Edinburgh Chamber of Commerce and Enterprise, 1994-96; former Member of Council, Institute of Chartered Accountants of Scotland. Recreations: golf; tennis; skiing; gardening. Address: (b.) Saltire Court, 20 Castle Terrace, Edinburgh EH1 2EG; T.-0131-222 2000.

Nicolson, John Alick (Jan); b. 26.9.45, Inverness; m., Effie; 1 s. Educ. Portree High School. Chairman, Skye and Lochalsh Enterprise, 1991-96; Board Member, Highlands and Islands Enterprise, 1996-98; Chairman, Hi-Screen Ltd., 1997-98; Trustee, Clann Mhicneacail Lands Trust; Scottish Commissioner, Clan Nicolson of Scorrybreac; Director, Jansvans Ltd.; Principal Partner, Jansport; Founder Member and Past Chairman, Isle of Skye Round Table. Recreations: collecting vintage vehicles; community affairs. Address: (h.) Almondbank, Viewfield Road, Portree, Isle of Skye IV51 9E4; T.-01478 612696.

Nicolson, Roy Macdonald, FFA, FPMI. Chief Executive, Scottish Amicable, since 1990; b. 12.6.44, Glasgow; m., Jennifer; 1 s.; 1 d. Educ. Paisley Grammar School. Joined Scottish Amicable, 1960. Recreations: golf; bridge. Address: (b.) Scottish Amicable, Craigforth, Stirling FK9 4UE; T.-01786 448844.

Nimmo, Mae Morrison, DL. President, South Lanarkshire Girl Guides, since 1977; Member, Lanarkshire Health Board, since 1990; Company Director; b. 6.11.34, near Lanrk; m., W. Nimmo, CBE; 3 s.; 1 d. Educ. Lanark Grammar School; Glasgow and West of Scotland College of Domestic Science. Recreations: painting; hill-walking; enjoying the company of grand-children; gardening. Address: (h.) Auchenglen House, Auchenglen Road, Braidwood, Carluke ML8 5PH; T.-01555 772021.

Nimmo, Professor Myra A., BSc, PhD. Professor of Exercise Physiology, Faculty of Education, Strathclyde University; b. 5.1.54, Edinburgh; m., Dr. J.A. Macaskill; 2 s. Educ. Westbourne School for Girls; Glasgow University. Temporary Lecturer, Glasgow University, 1978-80; Wellcome Research Fellow, 1980-82; Lecturer in Physiology, Queen's College, Glasgow, 1982-84, Senior Lecturer in Physiotherapy and research, 1984-87, Acting Head, Department of Physiotherapy, 1987-88; Assistant Director, Scottish Vocational Education Department, 1988-91; Assistant Principal, Jordanhill College, 1991-93; Director, Scottish Institute of Sports Medicine and Sports Science, 1993-96; Member, Scottish Sport Council, Scottish Sport World Class Advisory Group (Member, Scottish Sports Council, 1990-94); Olympic athlete. Recreation: general fitness. Address: (b.) Strathclyde University, Jordanhill Campus, Southbrae Drive, Glasgow G13 1PP; T.-0141-950 3722.

Nimmo, William, CBE, BArch, RIBA, FRIAS, FRSA. Senior Partner, William Nimmo & Partners, since 1956; b. 1.4.29; m., Mae Morrison; 3 s.; 1 d. Educ. Wishaw High School; Mackintosh School of Architecture. Commissioned, Corps of Royal Engineers, 1954-55. Recreations: farming; hill-walking; touring in UK and Europe. Address: (h.) Auchenglen House, Braidwood, Carluke ML8 5PH; T.-01555 772021.

Nimmo Smith, Hon. Lord (William Austin Nimmo Smith), BA, LLB. Senator of the College of Justice, since 1996; b. 6.11.42, Edinburgh; m., Dr. Jennifer Nimmo Smith; 1 s.; 1 d. Educ. Eton; Balliol College, Oxford; Edinburgh University. Advocate, 1969; Standing Junior Counsel, Department of Employment, 1977-82; QC, 1982; Advocate Depute, 1983-86; Chairman, Medical Appeal Tribunals and Vaccine Damage Tribunals, 1986-91; part-time Member, Scottish Law Commission, 1988-96; Temporary Judge, Court of Session, 1995-96; Chairman of Council, Cockburn Association (Edinburgh Civic Trust), since 1996. Recreations: mountaineering; music. Address: (b.) Parliament House, Edinburgh EH1 1RQ.

Nisbet, James Barry Consitt, LLB, NP, JP. Stipendiary Magistrate, Glasgow, since 1984; b. 26.7.42, Forfar; m., Elizabeth McKenzie; 2 d. Educ. Forfar Academy; Edinburgh University. Legal Assistant, Warden Bruce & Co., WS, Edinburgh, 1967-68; Legal Assistant, then Junior Depute Town Clerk, then Depute Town Clerk, Perth City Council, 1968-75; Senior Depute Director of Administration, Perth and Kinross District Council, 1975-84. Lay Elector, Alternate Lay Representative and Head Server, St. Ninian's Episcopal Cathedral, Perth; Secretary-General, Scottish Guild of Servers. Recreations: transport, especially railways and tramways; archaeology; music; foreign travel; genealogy. Address: (b.) District Court Chambers, 21 St. Andrews Street, Glasgow G1 5PW; T.-0141-227 5424.

Niven, Catharine, BSc, AMA, FSA(Scot). Curator, Inverness Museum and Art Gallery, since 1984; b. 23.9.52, Denbigh; m., Roger Niven. Educ. Loughton High School; Leicester University. Freelance archaeologist, working in Britain and Scandinavia; Keeper of Antiquities, Rotherham Museum, 1979-81; Assistant Curator (Archaeology), Inverness Museum and Art Gallery, 1981-84. Recreation: music. Address: (b.) Castle Wynd, Inverness IV2 3ED; T.-01463 237114.

Niven, Stuart Matthew, BSc, DipEd, FIMgt. President Emeritus, International Vocational Education and Training Association; Chairman, Board of Management, Clydebank College; b. 1.3.36, Clydebank; m., Jean K. McPhee; 1 s.; 1 d. Educ. Clydebank High School; Glasgow University. Teacher of Mathematics and Physics: Clydebank High School, 1959, Stow College of Engineering, 1961; Head, Department of Mathematics and Physics, Kilmarnock College, 1964; Jordanhill College of Education: Lecturer in Mathematics, 1967, Senior Lecturer in Further Education, 1968, Principal Lecturer, 1970; Director, Scottish School of Further Education, Strathclyde University, 1983-97. Member, CNAA Further Education Board, 1978-84; Chairman, Editorial Board, Journal for Further and Higher Education in Scotland, 1976-83; Chairman, National Liaison Committee on Training of Teachers of Nursing,

Midwifery and Health Visiting, 1983-88; Member, National Board for Scotland for Nursing, Midwifery and Health Visiting, 1989-93; Member, UK Central Council for Nursing, Midwifery and Health Visiting, since 1989; President, International Vocational Education and Training Association, 1994-96 (Vice President, Europe, 1990-92, President (Elect), 1992-94); President, International Section, American Vocational Association; Member, Royal Philosophical Society of Glasgow. Publications: Vocational Further Education in Scotland, 1982; Professional Development of Further Education Lecturers in Scotland: Towards Comprehensive Provision, 1987. Publication: The First Twenty-Five Years. Recreation: golf. Address: 5 Netherblane, Blanefield, Glasgow G63 9SW; T.-01360 770060.

Nixon, Christopher William, NDA, CertEd, FRAgs. Principal, Oatridge Agricultural College, since 1985; b. 7.11.45, Grappenhall; m., Susan Doreen Presley; 1 s.; 2 d. Educ. Normain College, Chester; Harper Adams Agricultural College. Lecturer in Agriculture/Extra Mural Lecturer, Newton Rigg, Penrith; Lecturer in Sheep Production/Senior Lecturer, Extra Mural, Bishop Burton; Depute Principal, Oatridge Agricultural College. Address: (h.) Woodbank Farm, Bathgate, West Lothian EH48 3BE; T.-01501 733217.

Nixon, Professor Jon, MA (Oxon), MA, PhD. Professor of Education, University of Stirling, since 1997; b. 14.9.50, Pocklington, Yorkshire; m., Elizabeth Margaret O'Brien; 2 s.; 1 d. Educ. Appleby Grammar School; Kirkby Lonsdale Grammar School, 1964-68; University of Oxford; University of London, University of East Anglia. Has worked as teacher, writer and researcher in schools and institutions of higher education. Publications: has written widely on educational equality and social justice, institutional and cultural conditions of learning, alternative models of teacher professionalism. Recreations: good food; good talk; good books. Address: (b.) Institute of Education, University of Stirling, Stirling FK9 4LA; T.-01786 467603.

Nixon, Mary MacKenzie, OBE, MA (Hons), DipEd. Archivist, Scottish Girl Guides Association, 1979-90; b. Port Arthur, Canada. Educ. High School of Stirling; St. Andrews University. Assistant English Teacher, Riverside School, Stirling; Responsible Assistant, History, High School of Stirling, Falkirk High School; Responsible Assistant, English, Falkirk High School; Head, English Department, Grangemouth High School. Girl Guides Association: County Camp Adviser and Chairman, Training Committee, Stirlingshire; Scotland: Ranger Adviser, Training Adviser, Deputy Scottish Chief Commissioner; Co-ordinator, Silver Jubilee Scheme for Unemployed; Chairman, Netherurd Committee, Scottish Girl Guides Association Training Centre, 1981-85. Recreations: genealogy; archaeology; poetry. Address: (h.) Gartlea, 19 Station Road, Bannockburn FK7 8LE.

Noad, Elaine, BA, MSc, DPA, DASS, CQSW. Director of Community Services, South Ayrshire Council, since 1995; b. 7.7.56, London; m., Peter Noad; 2 s.; 1 d. Educ. Chorley College; Newcastle Polytechnic; Aberdeen University. Social Worker: Lothian, 1980-85, Grampian, 1985-87; Development Worker, Scottish Council on Disability, 1987-89; Principal Officer (Corporate Services), City of Edinburgh District Council, 1989-90; Social Work Manager, Tayside Regional Council, 1990-94; Assistant Director of Social Work, Grampian Regional Council, 1994-95. Recreations: swimming; hill-walking; travel; sports. Address: (b.) South Ayrshire Council, County Buildings, Wellington Square, Ayr KA7 1DR; T.-01292 612419.

Noble, Rev. Alexander Buchan, MA, BD (Hons), ThM. Minister, Dunbar Parish Church, since 1993; b. 23.5.55, Fraserburgh; m., Patricia Anne. Educ. Fraserburgh Academy; Dalziel High School, Motherwell; Glasgow University; Aberdeen University; Princeton Theological Seminary. Minister, St. Mark's Parish Church, Stirling, 1982-93. Recreations: football; swimming; reading; writing; travel. Address: Bayswell Road, Dunbar EH42 1AB; T.-01368 863749.

Noble, Sheriff Alistair William, LLB. Sheriff of North Strathclyde at Dunoon, since 1992; b. 10.1.54. Advocate, 1978. Address: (b.) Sheriff Court House, George Street, Dunoon, PA23 8BQ.

Noble, David Hillhouse, LLB, DipMan. Chief Executive, Highlands of Scotland Tourist Board, since 1997; b. 27.4.48, Paisley; m., Hilary; 1 s.; 2 d. Educ. Greenock Academy; Glasgow University. Solicitor in private practice, Glasgow, 1970-72; Legal and Administrative Officer, Argyll County Council, 1972-73; Senior Legal and Administrative Officer, Inverness County Council, 1973-75; Chief Executive, Skye and Lochalsh District Council, 1975-96; Director, Skye and Lochalsh Enterprise, 1992-95; Area Manager, Skye and Lochalsh, The Highland Council, 1996-97. Recreations: music; running. Address: (b.) Peffery House, Strathpeffer, Ross-shire IV14 9HA; T.-01997 421160.

Noble (or Nobail), Sir Iain, Bt. of Ardkinglas and Eilean Iarmain, OBE, MA. Chairman, Noble Group Ltd.; entrepreneur and businessman; b. 8.9.35, Berlin. Educ. in China, Argentina and England; University College, Oxford. Scottish Council (Development and Industry), 1964-69; Co-founder and Joint Managing Director, Noble Grossart Ltd., Edinburgh, 1969-72. Founder and Chairman, Seaforth Maritime PLC, Aberdeen, 1972-77; Co-founder and Director: Adam and Company plc, 1983-94, Independent Insurance Group PLC, since 1986, Premium Trust PLC, since 1993; and other companies; Chairman: Skye Bridge Ltd., 1994-96, Pràban na Linne Ltd ("The Gaelic Whiskies"); Proprietor, Fearann Eilean Iarmain (rural estate in Isle of Skye), since 1972; Member, Edinburgh University Court, 1970-73; Founder, first Chairman and Trustee, Gaelic College of Sabhal Mor Ostaig, Skye, 1975-85; Trustee: National Museums of Scotland, 1986-90, NMS Charitable Trust, since 1990; Scotsman of the Year Award, 1982 (Knights Templar); President, Saltire Society, 1993-96; Chairman, Scots Australian Council, since 1990; Editor, Sources of Finance, 1967-69; other interests: conservation; land management; heritage architecture; community development. Recreations: deasbad, comhradh, orain is ceol le deagh chompanaich. Address: An Oifig, Eilean Iarmain, An t-Eilean Sgitheanach, IV43 8QR; T.-01471 833 266; 76 George Street; T.-0131-225 9677.

Noble, Lillias Mary, BEd, MUniv (Open). Education Advsier, Scottish Prison Service, since 1997; Council Member, Scottish Community Education Council, since 1997; b. 11.9.54, Vancouver. Educ. Larkhall Academy; Hamilton College of Education; Strathclyde University. Formerly English and Guidance Teacher,Thurso High School, 1975-80; Wester Hailes Education Centre, 1980-84; Save the Children Fund, 1985-88; Director, LEAD Scotland, 1988-97; part-time Commissioner, 1992-98, and Vice Chairman, 1995-98, Mental Welfare Commission for Scotland; Chair, Scottish Adult Education Voluntary Organisations Forum, 1995-97. Recreation: climbing mountains. Address: (b.) Scottish Prison Service, Calton House, 5 Redheughs Rigg, Edinburgh EH12 9HW; T.-0131-244 8649.

Noble, Simon John. Owner, Ardkinglas Estate, Argyll, since 1972; Chairman, Loch Fyne Oysters Ltd., since 1977; Director, Noble Group Ltd., since 1977; b. 31.10.36, London. Educ. Eton; Magdalen College, Oxford. S.G. Warburg & Co., 1959-64; wine trade – French and Foreign Wines Ltd. (Founder), 1964-81; Director (non-Executive), Edinburgh Tapestry Co. Ltd., since 1972; Chairman (non-

Executive), Wine Importers Edinburgh Ltd., since 1975. Recreation: country life. Address: (b.) Loch Fyne Oysters Ltd., Cairndow, Argyll PA26 8BH; T.-014996 264.

Noble, Sir (Thomas Alexander) Fraser, Kt (1971), MBE (1947), MA, LLD, FRSE; b. 29.4.18, Cromdale; m., Barbara A.M. Sinclair; 1 s.; 1 d. Educ. Nairn Academy; Aberdeen University. Indian Civil Service, 1940-47; Lecturer in Political Economy, Aberdeen University, 1948-57; Secretary, Carnegie Trust for Scottish Universities, 1957-62; Vice-Chancellor, Leicester University, 1962-76; Principal, Aberdeen University, 1976-81; Past Chairman of numerous public service committees, including Scottish Standing Conference of Youth Service Organisations, Home Office Advisory Committee for Probation and After Care, Television Research Committee; Chairman, UK Committee of Vice Chancellors, 1970-72; former Member of Council, Association of Commonwealth Universities. Publications: Something in India (memoir); articles, mainly on economics, education and India. Recreations: golf; listening to music. Address: (h.) Hedgerley, Victoria Street, Nairn; T.-Nairn 453151.

Noble, Timothy Peter, MA, MBA. Chief Executive, Noble Group Ltd.; Director: Waverley Mining Finance plc; Chairman, British Ski Academy; Chairman, RSNO Endowment Trust; b. 21.12.43; m., Elizabeth Mary Aitken; 2 s.; 1 d. Educ. University College, Oxford; Gray's Inn, London; INSEAD, Fontainebleau. Recreations: skiing; tennis; bridge; wine; astronomy; poetry. Address: (h.) Ardnahane, Barnton Avenue, Edinburgh; T.-0131-336 3565.

Noel-Paton, (Frederick) Ranald, BA, DBA (Hon). Deputy Chairman, John Menzies plc, since 1997 (Group Managing Director, 1986-97); b. 7.11.38, Bombay; m., Patricia Anne Stirling; 4 d. Educ. Rugby School; McGill University. Investment Analyst, Greenshields Inc., 1962-63; Management Trainee, United Biscuits, 1964; various posts, British United Airways Ltd., 1965-70; various senior executive posts, British Caledonian Airways, 1970-86 (General Manager, West Africa, 1975-79, General Manager, Far East, 1980-86, Director, Caledonian Far East Airways, 1984-86); Director: Pacific Assets Trust plc, since 1986 (Chairman, since 1998), General Accident plc, 1987-98. Recreations: fishing; walking; bird-watching; the arts. Address: (b.) 108 Princes Street, Edinburgh EH2 3AA; T.-0131-225 8555.

Norman, Richard, DA, RSW. Teacher of Art, Cleveden Secondary School, Glasgow, since 1983; Painter; b. 15.6.56, Glasgow. Educ. Hillhead Secondary School; Glasgow School of Art. Travelling scholarship, Venice, 1996; one man exhibitions: RGI Kelly Gallery, Glasgow 1990, 1992, Artbank, Glasgow, 1996; various group exhibitions, UK, Hong Kong, Netherlands, France. Cargill Award, RGI, 1991; elected, RSW, 1994. Recreations: good company; Glasgow Art Club; music – particularly the works of Benjamin Britten. Address: (h.) 70 Hotspur Street, Glasgow G20 8LP; T.-0141-945 0755.

Normand, Andrew Christie, MA, LLB, LLM. Crown Agent for Scotland, since 1996; b. 7.2.48, Edinburgh; m., Barbara Jean Smith; 2 d. Educ. George Watson's College, Edinburgh; Edinburgh University; Queen's University, Kingston, Ontario. Address: (b.) Crown Office, 25 Chambers Street, Edinburgh EH1 1LA; T.-0131-226 2626.

Norrie, Rev. Graham, MA, BD. Minister, Forfar: East and Old Parish Church, since 1978; b. 14.5.41, Dundee; m., Irene Seward Pearce; 2 s.; 2 d. Educ. Morgan Academy, Dundee; St. Andrews University; Edinburgh University. Assistant Minister, St. Ninian's Church, Corstorphine, 1965-67; Minister, Alloa: West Church, 1967-78. Recreations: hill-walking; football spectating. Address: (h.) The Manse, Lour Road, Forfar DD8 2BB; T.-01307 464303.

Norrie, Professor Kenneth McKenzie, LLB, DLP, PhD. Professor of Law, University of Strathclyde, since 1995; b. 23.6.59, Dundee. Educ. Kirkton High School, Dundee; University of Dundee; University of Aberdeen. Lecturer in Law: University of Dundee, 1982-83, University of Aberdeen, 1983-90; Gastprofessor, Universität Regensburg, Germany, 1990; Senior Lecturer in Law, University of Strathclyde, 1990-95; Visiting Professor, University of Sydney, Australia, 1997. Member, Children's Panel, City of Glasgow. Publications: Parent and Child; Defamation; Trusts; Children's Hearings. Recreations: philately; travel. Address: (b.) School of Law, University of Strathclyde, Stenhouse Building, 173 Cathedral Street, Glasgow G4 0RQ; T.-0141-548 3393.

North, Michael James, MA, PhD. Reader in Biochemistry, Stirling University, 1989-97; b. 20.1.48, London; m., Barbara Lockwood (deceased); 1 d., Sophie (deceased, victim at Dunblane Primary School). Educ. East Barnet Grammar School; Hertford College, Oxford; Newcastle upon Tyne University. SRC Postdoctoral Fellow, Leicester University and Essex University, 1973-75; Lecturer in Biochemistry, Stirling University, 1975-85; Senior Lecturer, 1985-89. Convener, Scottish Branch, Society for General Microbiology, 1988-93; Editor, Microbiology (formerly Journal of General Microbiology), 1988-94. Founder Member, Gun Control Network. Publication: Biochemical Protozoology (Joint Editor). Recreations: gardening; music; supporting Tottenham Hotspur FC. Address: (h.) Lawers, Aberfeldy, Perthshire PH15 2PA.

Northesk, 14th Earl of (David John MacRae Carnegie); b. 3.11.54; m.; 1 s.; 3 d. Educ. Eton; UCL. Succeeded to title, 1994.

Norwell, Peter Smith, OBE, TD, JP. Honorary Sheriff, Perth; b. 14.4.12, Perth; m., Elisabeth May Edwards; 3 d. Educ. Dollar Academy. Lt.-Col., RASC, 1944; Secretary, Perthshire Territorial Army Association, 1960-62; Assistant Secretary, Angus, Perthshire and Fife Territorial Army Association, 1962-67; Managing Director, Norwells Perth Footwear Ltd., 1935-60; Town Councillor, Perth, 1946-52; Chairman, Perth Theatre Company, 1968-72. Address: (h.) Dura Den, Pitcullen Terrace, Perth PH2 7EQ; T.-Perth 626789.

O

Oatts, Alasdair Henry James, FRICS. Regional Director, National Trust for Scotland, Argyll, Lochaber and Western Isles, since 1995; b. 22.9.53, Nairn; m., Melissa; 1 s.; 1 d. Educ. Wellington College; Royal Agricultural College, Cirencester. Employed by National Trust for Scotland, since 1979. Recreations: golf; squash; shooting. Address: (h.) Glenmore, Kilmelford, by Oban PA34 4XA; T.-01852 200314.

Ó Baoill, Professor Colm, MA, PhD. Professor of Celtic, Aberdeen University, since 1996; b. 22.9.38, Armagh, Ireland; m., Frances G. R.; 3 d. Educ. St. Patrick's College, Armagh; Queen's University of Belfast. Assistant Lecturer, Queen's University of Belfast, 1962; Aberdeen University: Lecturer, 1966, Senior Lecturer, 1980. Chief, Gaelic Society, Inverness, 1993. Address: (h.) 19 King's Crescent, Old Aberdeen AB24 3HJ; T.-01224 637064.

O'Brien, Colin Michael, BA. Rector, Clydebank High School, since 1984; b. 2.1.46, Glasgow; m., Elspeth; 1 s.; 1 d. Educ. Albert Secondary School, Glasgow; Strathclyde University; Jordanhill College of Education. Headteacher, Tiree High School, 1979-84. Recreations: gardening; walking; reading; cinema. Address: (h.) 20 Clairinch Way, Drymen, Stirlingshire G63 0DL; T.-01360 660616.

O'Brien, Sir Frederick William Fitzgerald, QC, MA, LLB. Sheriff Principal, Lothian and Borders, 1978-89; Convener of Sheriffs Principal, 1972-89; b. 19.7.17, Edinburgh; m., Audrey Muriel Owen; 2 s.; 1 d. Educ. Royal High School, Edinburgh; Edinburgh University. Called to Scottish Bar, 1947; QC, 1960; Commissioner, Mental Welfare Commission, 1962-65; Senior Advocate Depute, Crown Office, 1964-65; Sheriff Principal, Caithness, Sutherland, Orkney and Shetland, 1965-75; Interim Sheriff Principal, Aberdeen, Kincardine and Banff, 1969-71; Sheriff Principal, North Strathclyde, 1975-78; Interim Sheriff Principal, South Strathclyde, 1981; Member: Scottish Medical Practices Committee, 1973-76, Scottish Records Advisory Council, 1974-83; Chairman, Sheriff Court Rules Council, 1975-81; Convener, General Council Business Committee, Edinburgh University, 1980-84; Past President, Royal High School FP Club (Honorary President, 1982-91); Chairman, Edinburgh Sir Walter Scott Club, 1989-92; Commissioner, Northern Lighthouse Board, 1965-89 (Chairman, 1983-84 and 1986-87). Recreations: music; golf. Address: (h.) 22 Arboretum Road, Edinburgh EH3 5PN; T.-0131-552 1923.

O'Brien, James Paul, MA (Hons), MEd, PhD, DipEdTech. Vice-Dean, Moray House Institute of Education, Edinburgh University; b. 23.4.50, Stirling; m., Elaine Margaret Kathleen Smith; 1 d. Educ. St. Mirin's Academy, Paisley; Glasgow University. Teacher, 1973-85; Lecturer, St. Andrew's College of Education, 1985-88, Director, 1988-93, Assistant Principal, 1992-93. Recreations: golf; music; reading. Address: (b.) Holyrood Campus, Holyrood Road, Edinburgh EH8 8AQ; T.-0131-558 6164.

O'Brien, Most Rev. Keith Michael Patrick, BSc, DipEd. Archbishop of St. Andrews and Edinburgh, since 1985; b. 17.3.38, Ballycastle, Northern Ireland. Educ. Saint Patrick's, Dumbarton; Holy Cross Academy, Edinburgh; Edinburgh University; St. Andrew's College, Drygrange; Moray House College of Education. Teacher, St. Columba's High School, Fife; Assistant Priest, Kilsyth, then Bathgate; Spiritual Director, St. Andrew's College, Drygrange; Rector, Blairs College, Aberdeen; ordained Archbishop by Cardinal Gray, 1985. Recreations: music; walking. Address: Saint Bennet's, 42 Greenhill Gardens, Edinburgh EH10 4BJ.

O'Callaghan, Frank, MA, CA. Non-Executive Chairman: Macdonald Hotels plc, since 1990, Deep Sealeisure PLC, Outreach plc, Rehab Remanufacturing Services Ltd.; Non-Executive Director: Eagle Taverns Holdings Ltd., Scottish Legal Life Assurance, Rehab Scotland; b. 31.10.39, Glasgow; m., Elizabeth Ann; 1 s.; 1 d. Educ. St. Aloysius College, Glasgow; Glasgow University. Thomson McLintock CA; McLintock Moores and Murray Management Consultants; Stakis PLC. Recreation: golf. Address: 21 Hamilton Avenue, Glasgow G41 4JG, T.-0141-427 0119.

Odoni, Professor Robert Winston Keith, BSc, PhD, FRSE. Professor of Mathematics, University of Glasgow, since 1989; b. 14.7.47, London; m., Josephine Ann; 2 s.; 1 d. Educ. Queen Elizabeth's Grammar School, Barnet; University of Exeter; Downing College, University of Cambridge. Temporary Lecturer, University of Liverpool, 1971-72; Research Fellow, University of Glasgow, 1972-73; University of Exeter: Lecturer, 1973-79, Reader, 1979-85, Personal Chair (Number Theory), 1985-89. Publications: nearly 60 research articles in journals. Member, Editorial Board: London Mathematical Society, 1986-96, Edinburgh Mathematical Society, since 1998, Glasgow Mathematical Journal, since 1991. Recreations: hill-walking; music; literature. Address: (b.) Department of Mathematics, University of Glasgow, University Gardens, Glasgow G12 8QW; T.-0141-330 5179.

O'Donnell, Marjory Ann, MA (Hons). Director, National Asthma Campaign Scotland, since 1996; b. 8.6.49, Glasgow. Educ. Glasgow University. Teacher of Languages, 1972-76; Development Officer, Council for Voluntary Service, 1988-89; Senior Development Officer, Volunteer Development Scotland, 1989-96. Address: (b.) 21 Coates Crescent, Edinburgh EH3 7AF; T.-0131-226 2544.

O'Dwyer, Professor Patrick Joseph, MCh, FRCSI, FRCSGlas. Professor of Surgery, Glasgow University, since 1998; Consultant Surgeon, Western Infirmary, Glasgow, since 1990; b. 24.7.52, Newport, Ireland; m., Marian; 3 s.; 1 d. Educ. Newport Vocational School; University College Cork. Trainee in Surgery, University Hospital, Cork, 1979-83; Research Fellow, Harvard Medical School, 1983-84; Clinical Fellow, Ohio State University, 1984-86; Lecturer in Surgery, University College Dublin, 1986-90; Senior Lecturer and Reader in Surgery, Glasgow University, 1990-98. Publications: 100 papers in journals. Recreations: music; hill-walking. Address: University Department of Surgery, Western Infirmary, Glasgow G11 6NT; T.-0141-211 2163.

O'Farrell, Professor Patrick Neil, BA, PhD, MIPI. Professor of Economics, Heriot-Watt University, since 1986 (Assistant Principal, since 1995, Dean, Faculty of Economic and Social Studies, 1992-95); b. 18.4.41; m.; 3 d. Educ. Trinity College, Dublin. Assistant in Geography, Trinity College, Dublin, 1963-65; Assistant Lecturer and Lecturer in Geography, Queen's University, Belfast, 1965-70; Lecturer in Geography, New University of Ulster, 1971-73; Lecturer, Senior Lecturer and Reader in Planning, UWIST, 1973-86. Recreations: walking; talking; music. Address: (b.) Heriot-Watt University, Riccarton, Edinburgh EH14 4AS.

Ogilvie, Margaret Elizabeth. Owner/Gardener, Pitmuies Gardens, since 1966; b. 21.12.29, Co. Down; m., Douglas Farquhar Ogilvie (deceased); 1 s.; 2 d. Educ. Central School of Art and Crafts, London. Prior to marriage, advertising manager and book designer/typographer; National Trust for Scotland: Member, Council (three times), Member, Executive Committee (twice); Historic Houses Association: Member, Executive Council, Scottish Representative, Gardens Committee; Association for Protection of Rural Scotland: Member, Representative Committee, Member, judging panel for Annual Award; Member, Scottish Council for National Parks; Member, Committee, Scottish Museums of Year Award; Fellow RSA; President, Garden Society of Scotland. Recreations: riding; skiing; music; travelling. Address: (h.) House of Pitmuies, by Forfar, Angus; T.-01241 828245.

Ogilvie-Laing of Kinkell, Gerald, NDD, FRBS. Sculptor; b. 11.2.36; 4 s.; 1 d. Educ. Berkhamsted School; RMA, Sandhurst. Commissioned Fifth Fusiliers, 1955-60; resigned commission and attended St. Martin's School of Art, 1960-64; lived in New York, 1964-69; Artist in Residence, Aspen Institute for Humanistic Studies, Colorado, 1966; moved to north of Scotland, 1969, and restored ruins of Kinkell Castle; Civic Trust Award, 1971; established a tapestry workshop in north of Scotland; Visiting Professor, University of New Mexico, 1976-77; set up bronze foundry, Kinkell Castle, to produce own work; Member, Art Committee, Scottish Arts Council, 1978-80; Professor of Sculpture, Columbia University, New York, 1986-87; Commissioner, Royal Fine Art Commission for Scotland, 1987-95; public sculpture includes Callanish, 1971; Frieze of the Wise and Foolish Virgins, 1980; Fountain of Sabrina, 1982; Conan Doyle Memorial, 1991; Axis Mundi, 1991; Bank Underground Station Dragons, London, 1995; St. George and Dragon Series, Harrow, 1996; Four Rugby Players, Twickenham, 1996; portrait bust, Sir Paul Getty, National Gallery, London, 1997. Address: (h.) Kinkell Castle, Dingwall IV7 8AT; T.-01349 861485.

Ogilvy, Sir Francis (Gilbert Arthur), 14th Bt, ARICS. Chartered Surveyor; b. 22.4.69; m., Dorothy Margaret Stein. Educ. Edinburgh Academy; Glenalmond College; Royal Agricultural College, Cirencester; BSc (Hons) (Reading). Address: (h.) Winton House, Pencaitland, East Lothian EH34 5AT.

Ogston, Rev. David Dinnes, MA, BD. Minister, St. John's Kirk of Perth, since 1980; b. 25.3.45, Ellon, Aberdeenshire; m., Margaret Macleod; 2 d. Educ. Inverurie Academy; King's College and Christ's College, Aberdeen. Assistant Minister: St. Giles' Cathedral, Edinburgh, 1969-73, Balerno, 1973-80. Publication: White Stone Country; Dry Stone Days. Recreations: late-night films on TV; Greek and Russian Ikons. Address: 15 Comely Bank Perth; T.-Perth 621755.

Ogston, Professor Derek, CBE, MA, MD, PhD, DSc, FRCPEdin, FRCP, FIBiol, FRSE, FRSA. Professor of Medicine, Aberdeen University, 1983-97 (Dean, Faculty of Medicine, 1984-87; Vice-Principal, 1987-97); Member, Court, Aberdeen University, since 1998; b. 31.5.32, Aberdeen; m., Cecilia Marie; 1 s.; 2 d. Educ. King's College School, Wimbledon; Aberdeen University. Aberdeen University: Lecturer in Medicine, 1962-69, Senior Lecturer in Medicine, 1969-75, MRC Travelling Fellow, 1967-68, Reader in Medicine, 1975-76, Regius Professor of Physiology, 1977-83. Member, Grampian Health Board, 1991-97 (Vice-Chairman, 1993-97); Member, General Medical Council, 1985-94. Publications: Haemostasis: Biochemistry, Physiology and Pathology (Joint Editor), 1977; The Physiology of Hemostasis, 1983; Antifibrinolytic Drugs: Chemistry, Pharmacology and Clinical Usage, 1984; Venous Thrombosis: Causation and Prediction, 1987. Recreation: gardening. Address: (h.) 64 Rubislaw Den South, Aberdeen AB15 4AY; T.-Aberdeen 316587.

Ohara, Noriko, OBE (1997). Principal Ballerina, Scottish Ballet; b. Japan. New London Ballet, 1974; London Festival Ballet (as principal dancer), 1975; joined Scottish Ballet, 1976; has danced all the major roles in the company's repertoire; regular jury member, Prix de Lausanne; Associate Director, Asami Maki Ballet Company, Tokyo. Address: (b.) 261 West Princes Street, Glasgow, G4 9EE.

Oldham, Professor John David, BSc, PhD. Head, Animal Biology Division, SAC, since 1997; Professor of Animal Biology, SAC, since 1997; Honorary Secretary, The Nutrition Society, since 1996; b. 20.7.49, Stockport; m., Catherine; 3 s. Educ. Cheadle Hulme School; Nottingham University. Post-doctoral Research Fellow, University of Alberta, 1973-74; Research Scientist, National Institute for Research in Dairying, 1974-84; Head, Animal Production Advisory and Development Department, Edinburgh School of Agriculture, 1984-90; Head, Genetics and Behavioural Sciences Department, SAC, 1990-97. Former Vice-President, EAAP Nutrition Commission; Member, Editorial Board, Animal Science; former Member, Editorial Board, British Journal of Nutrition. Sir John Hammond Memorial Prize, 1990; Saltire Society/Royal Bank of Scotland Scottish Science Award, 1995. Recreations: family, home and garden; walking; theatre; reading; music; sketching. Address: Animal Biology Division, SAC, Bush Estate, Penicuik, Midlothian EH26 0QE; T.-0131-535 3201.

Oliver, James Kenneth Murray, OBE. Farmer; b. 1.2.14, Hawick; m., Rhona Mary Purdom Wilkinson; 1 s.; 1 d. Educ. Merchiston Castle, Edinburgh. Army, 1939-46; as racehorse trainer, trained 1,000 winners under National Hunt Rules; rode winner, Scottish Grand National, 1950; trained five winners, Scottish Grand National; four times runner-up, Grand National; trained winners for the Queen Mother; Director and Vice President, Doncaster Bloodstock Sales Ltd. Address: (h.) Hassendean Bank, Hawick.

Olver, Professor Richard Edmund, BSc, MB, FRCP, FRCPE. James Mackenzie Professor of Child Health, Dundee; b. 26.10.41, Ayr; m.; 2 s.; 2 d. Educ. London University. House Officer and Senior House Officer posts, St. Thomas's, Addenbrookes and Brompton Hospitals, 1966-69; Lecturer, Senior Lecturer, Reader, Department of Paediatrics, University College, London, 1969-85; MRC Travelling Fellow, Cardiovascular Research Institute, San Francisco, 1973-74; Consultant Paediatrician, University College Hospital, London, 1975-85. Address: (b.) Dundee University, Dundee.

O'Neil, Brian. Director of Personnel, Historic Scotland, since 1997; b. 14.5.50, Edinburgh; m., Irene; 2 d. Educ. Gracemount Secondary School, Edinburgh. Joined Scottish Office, 1966; Head of Branch, Local Government Division, 1990-95. Recreations: golf; reading; gardening. Address: (b.) Historic Scotland, Longmore House, Salisbury Place, Edinburgh EH9 1SH; T.-0131-668 8667.

O'Neill, Rev. Professor John Cochrane, BA, BD, PhD. Professor of New Testament Language, Literature and Theology, Edinburgh University, 1985-96; b. 8.12.30, Melbourne; m., Judith Beatrice Lyall (see Judith Beatrice O'Neill); 3 d. Educ. Melbourne Church of England Grammar School; Melbourne University; Ormond College Theological Hall; University of Göttingen; Clare College, Cambridge. Senior Tutor in History, Melbourne University, 1953-55; Lecturer in New Testament Studies, Ormond College Theological Hall, Melbourne, 1960-64; Dunn Professor of New Testament Language, Literature and Theology, Westminster College, Cambridge, 1964-85. Publications: Paul's Letter to the Romans, 1975; The Bible's Authority: a portrait gallery of thinkers from Lessing to Bultmann, 1991; Who Did Jesus Think He Was?, 1995. Recreations: swimming; camping. Address: (h.) 9 Lonsdale Terrace, Edinburgh EH3 9HN; T.-0131-229 6070.

O'Neill, Judith Beatrice, MA, PGCE. Author of fiction for older children; b. 30.6.30, Melbourne; m., John Cochrane O'Neill (qv); 3 d. Educ. University of Melbourne; University of London. University Tutor, 1954-56, Melbourne, 1970-72, UK; School Teacher, Cambridge, 1974-82, and part-time author; full-time author, since 1982. Publications: Jess and the River Kids; Stringybark Summer;

Deepwater; The Message; So Far from Skye; Hearing Voices, 1996; Spindle River, 1998. Recreations: reading; walking; music; camping; theatre. Address: (h.) 9 Lonsdale Terrace, Edinburgh EH3 9HN; T.-0131-229 6070.

O'Neill, Martin (John), BA (Econ). MP (Labour), Ochil, since 1997 (Clackmannan, 1983-97, East Stirlingshire and Clackmannan, 1979-83); b. 6.1.45; m., Elaine Samuel; 2 s. Educ. Trinity Academy, Edinburgh; trades union and evening classes; Heriot-Watt University; Moray House College of Education. President, Scottish Union of Students, 1970-71; school teacher, 1974-79; Tutor, Open University, 1976-79. Member, Select Committee, Scottish Affairs, 1979-80; Opposition Spokesman, Scottish Affairs, 1980-84; Opposition Spokesman on Defence, 1984-88; Shadow Defence Secretary, 1988-92; Shadow Spokesman on Energy, 1992-95; Chair, Trade and Industry Select Committee, since 1996. Recreations: watching football; reading; listening to jazz; cinema. Address: (b.) 19 Mar Street, Alloa FK10 1HR; T.-01259 721536.

O'Neill, Maureen Patricia, BA (Hons), DMS. Director, Age Concern Scotland, since 1993; b. 11.5.48, Uganda; m., Jonathan Clogstoun-Willmott; 1 s.; 1 d. Educ. St. Margaret's School, Hastings; Charlton Park School, Cheltenham; Birkbeck College, London University. General Secretary, Edinburgh YWCA, 1982-87; Principal Officer, Policy, Research and Development, Scottish Association for Mental Health, 1987-93; Chairperson, Edinburgh Voluntary Organisations Council; Chairperson, Rowan Alba Association. Recreations: reading; theatre; sport. Address: (b.) 113 Rose Street, Edinburgh EH2 3DT; T.-0131-220 3345.

O'Reilly, Denis St. John, MSc, MD, FRCPath. Consultant Clinical Biochemist, Royal Infirmary, Glasgow, since 1984; b. 30.3.51, Cork; m., Margaret M.P. Lucey; 2 s.; 1 d. Educ. Presentation Brothers College, Cork; University College, Cork; Birmingham University. Registrar, Queen Elizabeth Medical Centre, Birmingham, 1976-78; Senior Registrar, Bristol Royal Infirmary, 1978-84; Ainsworth Scholar-Research Fellow, Norsk Hydro Institute for Cancer Research, Oslo, 1982. Recreation: hill-walking. Address: (h.) 47 Strathblane Road, Milngavie G62 8HA.

O'Reilly, Professor John, BSc (Hons), PhD, DSc. Professor of Control Engineering, University of Glasgow, since 1996; b. 15.2.51, Portadown, Northern Ireland; m., Carol Jane Rogers; 1 s. Educ. St . Patrick's College, Armagh; Queen's University of Belfast. Lecturer, University of Liverpool, 1977-83; Lecturer then Senior Lecturer, University of Strathclyde, 1983-90; Reader, University of Glasgow, 1990-96. Publications: three books on control engineering. Recreations: mountaineering; skiing. Address: Department of Electronics and Electrical Engineering, University of Glasgow, Glasgow G12 8LJ; T.-0141-330 5228.

O'Reilly, Seán, BA (Hons), PhD. Director, Architectural Heritage Society of Scotland, since 1996; b. 27.8.61, Dublin; m., Dr. Deborah Mays. Educ. Christian Brothers School, Kilcock; University College, Dublin. Lecturer, History of Art, Sligo and Dublin; Researcher, Irish Architectural Archive, Dublin; Historic Buildings Consultant, private practice, Dublin. Editor, Journal of the Irish Georgian Society. Publications: New Lease of Life (Co-Author); Irish Houses and Gardens – from the archives of Country Life. Address: (b.) The Glasite Meeting House, 33 Barony Street, Edinburgh EH3 6NX; T.-0131-557 0019.

Ormiston, Linda, MA, DRSAMD. Singer — Mezzo Soprano; b. 15.1.48, Motherwell. Educ. Dalziel High School, Motherwell; Glasgow University; Royal Scottish Academy of Music and Drama; London Opera Centre. Has sung all over Britain, France, Belgium, Italy, Germany, Austria, Holland and Yugoslavia; has sung regularly at Scottish Opera, Opera North, and Glyndebourne; also well-known in lighter vein and as a member of The Music Box; recordings include Noyes Fludde, HMS Pinafore and Ruddigore with New Sadlers Wells Opera and Tell Me Pretty Maiden; has appeared at New York, Vancouver, Monte Carlo, Brussels and Tokyo; debut, Frankfurt Opera, 1993; debut, Salzburg Festival, 1994; debut, English National Opera, 1995; Presenter, BBC Radio 3 and Radio Scotland. Recreations: playing the piano; skating; golf.

O'Rourke, Daniel (Donny), MA. Poet, journalist, film-maker, broadcaster, and teacher; Director, Scottish Cultural Studies, Glasgow School of Art, since 1998; Head of English and Modern Studies, Department of Adult and Continuing Education, Glasgow University, 1996-98; Television Critic, The Scotsman; Member, Editorial Board, Edinburgh University Press, since 1997; Chair, Scottish Book Marketing Group, since 1996; Director, Scottish Book Trust, since 1998; b. 5.7.59, Port Glasgow. Educ. St. Mirin's Academy, Paisley; Glasgow University. Chairman, Scottish Youth Council, 1982-84; Producer, BBC TV and Radio Scotland, 1984-86; Reporter, Scottish Television, 1986-87, Producer, 1987-92, Head of Arts, 1992-93, Head of Arts and Documentaries, 1993-94; Executive Producer, BBC Scotland, 1994-95. Member, Manpower Services Commission Youth Training Board, 1982-84; Member, Scottish Community Education Council, 1981-84; Chairman of Judges, Scottish Writer of the Year Award, 1996, 1997; Director, Tron Theatre Company, 1993-95. Publications: Second City, 1991; Rooming Houses of America, 1993; Dream State, the new Scottish poets, 1994; chapter in Burns Now, 1994; Eftirs/Afters, 1996; The Waist Band and Other Poems, 1997; poems in various anthologies and textbooks. Recreations: playing guitar; Irish literature; Americana. Address: (h.) 63 Barrington Drive, Glasgow, G4 9ES.

Orr, David Campbell, MA. Director, Scottish Federation of Housing Associations, since 1990; b. 27.3.55, Kirkconnel; m., Carol; 1 s.; 2 d. Educ. Dundee University. Deputy Warden, Iona Community, Community House, 1976-77; Team Leader, then Co-ordinator, Centrepoint, Soho, 1977-86; Director, Newlon Housing Trust, 1986-90. Former Chair, Young Homelessness Group, Homeless Network, Threshold H.A. Recreations: watching sport — playing badly; cinema. Address: (b.) 38 York Place, Edinburgh EH1 3HU; T.-0131-556 5777.

Orr, John, OBE, OStJ, QPM, LLD (Glasgow Caledonian), BA, CIMgt. Chief Constable, Strathclyde, since 1996; Hon. President, Association of Chief Police Officers in Scotland, 1997-98; Member, Secretary of State's Crime Prevention Council; b. 3.9.45, Kilmarnock; m., Joan; 2 s.; 1 d. Educ. James Hamilton Academy, Kilmarnock; Open University; Glasgow University. Entered police as cadet, Renfrew and Bute, 1961; progressed through ranks to rank of Detective Chief Superintendent and Joint Head of Strathclyde CID; Deputy Chief Constable, Dumfries and Galloway, 1990-96; seconded 1994 to HM Inspectorate of Constabulary as Assistant Inspector of Constabulary for Scotland. Hon. President, Glasgow Bn., Boys' Brigade. Recreations: Rotary; reading; gardening; angling. Address: (b.) Police Headquarters, 173 Pitt Street, Glasgow G2 4JS.

Orr, John Douglas, MBChB, MBA, FRCSEd. Consultant Paediatric Surgeon, since 1984; Medical Director, Royal Hospital for Sick Children, Edinburgh, since 1995; b. 11.7.45, Edinburgh; m., Elizabeth Erica Yvonne Miklinski; 2 s.; 1 d. Educ. George Heriot's School, Edinburgh; The High School, Dundee; St. Andrews University; Stirling University. Previously: Senior Surgical Registrar, Aberdeen, Senior Paediatric Registrar, Edinburgh and Great Ormond Street, London. Member, Council, Royal College of Surgeons of Edinburgh (Convenor, Examinations Committee). Recreations: golf (Member, Royal and Ancient Golf Club of St. Andrews, Bruntsfield, Luffness Golf

Clubs). Address: (b.) Department of Surgery, Royal Hospital for Sick Children, Sciennes Road, Edinburgh EH9 1LF; T.-0131-536 0667.

Orr, Nigel Wilson, MA, LLB, DipEd. Solicitor, since 1982; Solicitor Advocate, since 1994; b. 11.9.54, Edinburgh. Educ. Jordanhill College School, Glasgow; Glasgow University; Edinburgh University; Besancon University; Freiburg University. Procurator Fiscal Depute: Lanark, 1984, Airdrie, 1988; Senior Legal Assistant, Crown Office, 1990; Principal Procurator Fiscal Depute, Dundee, 1997; currently Manager of Regional Precognition/Fraud Unit, Tayside, Central and Fife. Recreations: sailing; hill-walking. Address: (b.) Caledonian House, Greenmarket, Dundee; T.-01382 227535.

Orr Ewing, Major Edward Stuart, DL, JP. Lord Lieutenant, Wigtown District, since 1989; b. 28.9.31, London; m., 1, F.A.B. Farquhar (m. dissolved); 2, Diana Mary Waters; 1 s.; 2 d. Educ. Sherborne; RMCS, Shrivenham. Black Watch RHR, 1950-69 (Major); Farmer and Landowner, since 1964. Recreations: country sports; skiing; sailing; painting. Address: (h.) Dunskey, Portpatrick, Stranraer; T.-01776 810211.

Orskov, Professor Egil Robert, OBE, BSc, PhD, DSc, FRSE. Director, International Feed Resource Unit, Rowett Research Institute, since 1990; International Consultant, United Nations Organization, since 1980; b. 24.5.34, Denmark; m., Joan P.; 2 s.; 1 d. Post-doctoral work, USDA, Washington, 1966-67; Rowett Research Institute: Head, Sheep Section, 1967-75, Dairy Cattle Section, 1975-85, Head, Ruminant Nutrition, 1985-90. Publications: four books; 510 papers. Recreations: music; travel; antique collector. Address: (b.) Rowett Research Institute, Bucksburn, Aberdeen; T.-01224 716614.

Örücü, Professor Esin, BA, LLB, PhD, Docent. Professor of Comparative Law, Glasgow University, since 1992; Honorary Professor of Turkish Law, Leiden; b. 28.3.40, Istanbul, Turkey. Educ. English High School for Girls, Istanbul; Arnavutkoy American College, Istanbul; Istanbul University; London School of Economics. Law Faculty, Istanbul University: Assistant Professor, 1966-75, Associate Professor, 1975-76; Glasgow University: Lecturer in Commercial Law and Jurisprudence, 1976-83, Senior Lecturer in Commercial Law and Jurisprudence, 1983-92; Professor of Comparative Law, Erasmus University, Rotterdam, 1981. Publications: Studies in Legal Systems: Mixed and Mixing (Joint Editor). Recreations: walking; sailing; reading; classical music; swimming. Address: (b.) School of Law, University of Glasgow, Glasgow G12 8QQ; T.-0141-339 8855.

Osborne, Avril, MA, MSc, PhD. Director, Community Social Services, Orkney, since 1993; b. 9.4.47, Johnstone. Educ. Gourock High School; St. Andrews University; Nottingham University; Lancaster University; Aberdeen University. Child Care Officer, 1969-72; Senior Social Worker, 1972-76; Senior Lecturer, 1976-79; Consultant, 1979-82; Leverhulme Fellow, 1982-84; Assistant Director, Social Work, Highland, 1984-93; seconded to Scottish Office, 1991-93. Recreation: walking. Address: (b.) Orkney Islands Council, School Place, Kirkwall, Orkney; T.-01856 873535.

Osborne, Hon. Lord (Kenneth Hilton Osborne), QC (Scot). Senator of the College of Justice, since 1990; b. 9.7.37. Advocate, 1962; QC, 1976; Chairman, Local Government Boundary Commission, since 1990.

Osborne, Professor Michael John, BSc, PhD, CertEd. Professor of Lifelong Education, University of Stirling, since 1998 (Head, Centre for Lifelong Learning, since 1999); b. 5.7.54, Redruth. Educ. St. Austell Grammar School; University of Reading; University College London. Lecturer: City and East London College, 1980-84, South London College, 1984-89; Research Fellow and Visiting Lecturer, South Bank University, 1986-89; University of Stirling, 1989-98: Lecturer, Senior Lecturer, Acting Head of Educational Policy and Development. Member, Board of Management, Cumbernauld College; Secretary, Universities Association for Continuing Education (Scotland), 1992-96; Member, Editorial Board, Scottish Journal of Adult and Continuing Education, Learning Assistance. Recreations: sports; walking; mycology. Address: Institute of Education, University of Stirling, Stirling FK9 4LA; T.-01786 467618.

Osborne, Sandra. MP (Labour), Ayr, since 1997; b. 23.2.56; m.; 2 d. Educ. Camphill Senior Secondary School, Paisley; Anniesland College; Jordanhill College; Strathclyde University. Former community worker. Address: (b.) House of Commons, London SW1A 0AA.

Osler, Douglas Alexander, MA (Hons). HM Senior Chief Inspector of Schools, Scottish Office Education and Industry Department; b. 11.10.42, Edinburgh; m., Wendy I. Cochrane; 1 s.; 1 d. Educ. Royal High School, Edinburgh; Edinburgh University; Moray House College of Education. Assistant Teacher of History/Careers Master, Liberton Secondary School, Edinburgh, 1965-68; Principal Teacher of History, Dunfermline High School, 1968-74. English Speaking Union Fellowship to USA, 1966; International Visitor Program to USA, 1989. Publications: Queen Margaret of Scotland; Sources for Modern Studies, Volumes 1 and 2. Address: (b.) 3-B01 Victoria Quay, Edinburgh EH6 6QQ.

O'Sullivan, Very Rev. Canon Basil, JCL. Parish Priest, Holy Family Church, Dunblane, since 1988; b. 1932, Fishguard. Educ. St. Finbarr's College, Cork; All Hallow's College, Dublin; Pontifical University of St. Gregory, Rome. Assistant Priest: St. Joseph's, Dundee, 1959-63, St. Andrew's Cathedral, Dundee, 1963-70; R.C. Chaplain, Dundee University, 1964-70; Parish Priest: St. John Vianney's, Alva, 1970-74, St. Columba's, Dundee, 1974-88. Canon of Dunkeld Chapter, since 1992. Recreations: reading; gardening; walking. Address: (h.) St. Clare's, Claredon Place, Dunblane FK15 9HB; T.-01786 822146.

Oswald, Rev. John, BSc, BD, PhD. Minister, Lorne and Lowland Parish Church, since 1997; b. 10.10.47, Glasgow; m., Barbara R.; 1 s. Educ. Kelvinside Academy; Edinburgh University. Management posts, Nickerson Seed Specialists; Managing Director, David Bell Ltd., Penicuik; candidate for ministry; Assistant Minister, Eddleston linked with Peebles Old. Recreations: tennis; gardening; reading. Address: Lorne and Lowland Manse, Castlehill, Campbeltown PA28 6AN; T.-01586 552468.

Ovens, Iain Stanley, BA, MA, DMS, MIPD. Principal, Dundee College, since 1996; b. 9.10.47, Glasgow; m., June Sangster. Educ. Duncanrig Senior Secondary School, East Kilbride; Strathclyde University. Lecturer, Barmulloch College of F.E.; Senior Lecturer, Head of Department, Head of Centre for Industrial Studies, Assistant Principal, Depute Principal, Glenrothes College of F.E.; Principal, Angus College. Address: (b.) Dundee College, Old Glamis Road, Dundee DD3 8LE; T.-01382 834834.

Overing, Professor Joanna Adrienne, BA (Hons), MA, PhD. Professor and Chair, Social Anthropology, St. Andrews University, since 1995; Director, Centre for Indigenous American Studies, St. Andrews University, since 1997; b. 12.8.38, Washington, DC; m., Napier Russell. Educ. University of Connecticut; Brandeis University. Instructor, then Assistant Professor, Anthropology, Vanderbilt University, 1971-74; Lecturer, then Senior Lecturer, Social Anthropology of Latin America, London School of Economics and Institute of Latin American Studies, 1974-92; Senior Lecturer, LSE, 1992-95. Visiting Professor: University of Sao Paulo, 1992,

Eotvos University, Budapest, 1993, University of Goteborg, 1994, UNICAMP, Brazil, 1994. Publications: The Piaroa, a People of the Orinoco Basin, 1975; Social Time and Social Space in Lowland South American Societies, 1977; Reason and Morality, 1985. Address: (b.) Department of Social Anthropology, St. Andrews University, St. Andrews KY16 9AL; T.-01334 462979.

Owen, Professor David Gareth, MA, BD (Hons), PhD, FICE, CEng, FRSA. Professor of Offshore Engineering, Heriot-Watt University, since 1986,Dean of Engineering, since 1996, Assistant Principal, since 1997; b. 6.11.40, Brecon, Wales; m., Ann Valerie Wright; 2 d. Educ. Christ College, Brecon; Downing College, Cambridge. Graduate Engineer, John Laing & Son, London; Aerospace Engineer, Marconi Space and Defence Systems, Portsmouth; Lecturer in Civil Engineering, Heriot-Watt University; Visiting Professor, University of New Hampshire; Senior Lecturer, Department of Offshore Engineering, Heriot-Watt University. Recreations: music; travelling. Address: (h.) 7 Oak Lane, Edinburgh EH12 6XH; T.-0131-339 1740.

Owen, Professor Douglas David Roy, MA, PhD. Professor of French, St. Andrews, 1972-88; b. 17.11.22, Norton, Suffolk; m., Berit Mariann; 2 s. Educ. Cambridge and County High School; Nottingham High Pavement School; Nottingham University; St. Catharine's College, Cambridge. St. Andrews University: Lecturer, 1951-64, Senior Lecturer, 1964-71, Reader, 1971-72; General Editor, Forum for Modern Language Studies. Publications: Fabliaux (Joint Editor), 1957; The Evolution of the Grail Legend, 1968; The Vision of Hell, 1970; Arthurian Romance: Seven Essays (Editor), 1970; Two Old French Gauvain Romances (Joint Editor), 1972; The Song of Roland (Translator), 1972 (new edition, 1990); The Legend of Roland, 1973; Noble Lovers, 1975; Chrétien de Troyes, Arthurian Romances (Translator), 1987; A Chat Round the Old Course, 1990; Guillaume le Clerc, Fergus of Galloway (Translator), 1991; Eleanor of Aquitaine: Queen and Legend, 1993; The Romance of Reynard the Fox (Translator), 1994; William the Lion 1143-1214: Kingship and Culture, 1997. Recreation: golf. Address: (h.) 7 West Acres, St. Andrews, KY16 9UD; T.-01334 473329.

Owens, Agnes. Author; b. 24.5.26, Milngavie; m., Patrick Owens; 2 s.; 4 d. Educ. Bearsden Academy. Worked in shops, factories and offices; came to writing by accident; author of Gentlemen of the West (Autumn Book Award, 1984), Like Birds in the Wilderness, A Working Mother, People Like That, For the Love of Willie; short stories in Lean Tales, The Seven Deadly Sins and The Seven Cardinal Virtues; wrote a play with Liz Lochhead which toured Scotland for three months. Recreations: walking; reading. Address: (h.) 21 Roy Young Avenue, Balloch, Dunbartonshire; T.-Alexandria 50921.

Oxfuird, 13th Viscount of (George Hubbard Makgill), CBE; b. 7.1.34; m.; 1 s.; 3 s. by pr. m. Succceeded to title, 1986.

P

Pacione, Professor Michael, MA, PhD. Professor of Geography, Strathclyde University, since 1990; b. 14.10.47, Dundee; m., Christine Hopper; 1 s.; 1 d. Educ. Lawside Academy, Dundee; Dundee University. Lecturer in Geography, Queens University, Belfast, 1973-75; Lecturer, Senior Lecturer, Reader, Strathclyde University, Glasgow, 1975-89; Visiting Professor, University of Guelph, 1984, and University of Vienna, 1995. Publications: author of three books; editor of 17 books; 90 research papers. Recreations: sport; travel; photography. Address: (b.) Department of Geography, Strathclyde University, 50 Richmond Street, Glasgow G1 1XH; T.-0141-548 3793.

Pack, Professor Donald Cecil, CBE, MA, DSc, FIMA, FEIS, FRSE. Emeritus Professor, Strathclyde University, since 1986; b. 14.4.20, Higham Ferrers; m., Constance Mary Gillam; 2 s.; 1 d. Educ. Wellingborough School; New College, Oxford. Ordnance Board, Cambridge, 1941-43; Armament Research Department, Ministry of Supply, Fort Halstead, 1943-46; Lecturer in Mathematics, St. Andrews University, 1947-52; Visiting Research Associate, Maryland University, 1951-52; Lecturer in Mathematics, Manchester University, 1952-53; Professor of Mathematics, Strathclyde University, 1953-82 (Vice-Principal, 1968-72); Honorary Professor, 1982-86; Member, various Government scientific boards and committees, 1952-84; Member, Defence Scientific Advisory Council, 1975-80; First Hon. Member, European Consortium for Mathematics in Industry, 1988; Chairman, Scottish Certificate of Education Examination Board, 1969-77; Chairman, Committee of Inquiry into Truancy and Indiscipline in Scottish Schools, 1974-77 ("Pack Report" published by HMSO, 1977); Hon. President, National Youth Orchestra of Scotland (Chairman from foundation, 1978-88); Member, Scottish Arts Council, 1980-85; Member, UK Committee for European Music Year 1985 and Chairman, Scotland Advisory Committee, 1983-86; Member: General Teaching Council for Scotland, 1966-73, Dunbartonshire Education Committee, 1960-66; Governor, Hamilton College of Education, 1976-81; Council Member, Royal Society of Edinburgh, 1960-63; Honorary Treasurer and Council Member, Institute of Mathematics and its Applications, 1964-72; Member: International Advisory Committee on Rarefied Gas Dynamics Symposia, 1976-88, British National Committee for Theoretical Mechanics, 1973-78, Council, Gesellschaft fuer angewandte Mathematik und Mechanik, 1977-83; Guest Professor: Technische Universitaet, Berlin, 1967, Bologna University and Politechnico Milan, 1980, Technische Hochschule, Darmstadt, 1981; other visiting appointments, Warsaw University, 1977, Kaiserslautern University, 1980 and 1984. Past President: Edinburgh Mathematical Society, Glasgow Mathematical Association; Honorary President, Milngavie Music Club (President, 1983-93). Recreations: music; gardening; golf. Address: (h.) 18 Buchanan Drive, Bearsden, Glasgow G61 2EW; T.-0141-942 5764.

Pagan, Graeme Henry, MBE, BL, WS. Solicitor, Hosack & Sutherland, Oban, since 1960; Chairman, Oban Housing Association, 1971-98, now Committee Member; Honorary Sheriff of North Strathclyde at Oban, since 1988; b. 20.3.36, Cupar; m., Heather; 1 s.; 2 d. Educ. New Park, St. Andrews; Bedford School; Edinburgh University. Part-time Procurator Fiscal, Oban, 1970-79; Regional Organiser, Shelter Campaign for the Homeless, 1968-75; Founder Member, Oban Abbeyfield Society; Organiser, Scottish Solicitors Will Aid; Chairman, Argyll and Bute Liberal Democrats. Recreations: family; jazz; malt whisky; politics; wandering in the Highlands on foot and bike. Address: (h.) Neaveton, Oban, Argyll; T.-01631 563737.

Page, Professor Alan Chisholm, LLB, PhD. Professor of Public Law, Dundee University, since 1985; b. 7.4.52, Broughty Ferry; m., Sheila Duffus; 1 s.; 1 d. Educ. Grove Academy; Edinburgh University. Lecturer in Law, University College, Cardiff, 1975-80; Senior Lecturer in Law, Dundee University, 1980-85; Head, Department of Law, 1980-95; Dean, Faculty of Law, 1986-89; SHEFC Lead Assessor in Law, 1995-96; Member, Tax Law Review Committee, since 1994. Publications: Legislation; Investor Protection. Recreation: mountaineering. Address: (h.) Westlands, Westfield Road, Cupar, Fife KY15 5DR.

Paine, Nigel, Chief Executive, Scottish Council for Educational Technology, since 1990; b. 25.4.52. Educ. Haberdasher's Aske's Hatcham Boys' School; Reading University; East Anglia University. Visiting Professor, Napier University; English Speaking Union Thyne Scholar, 1984; Trustee, National Extension College, since 1987; Vice-Chair, Anniesland College, since 1993. Board Member, Network Scotland; Chairman, LEAD, LEAD Telematics; Fellow, Institute of Training and Development; Fellow, Royal Society of Arts. Recreations: running; reading. Address: 74 Victoria Crescent Road, Glasgow G12 9JN; T.-0141-337 5000.

Paisley of Westerlea (Duncan Wilson), FRSA, FSA (Scot). Landowner; Company Director; 16th Head of the Name; 5th Laird of the Barony of Westerlea; Captain, Balgonie Castle; Ambassador (Overseas), Capability Scotland; Patron, Westerlea School, Edinburgh; b. 30.8.48, Woodcote; m., Valerie R. Alcantra; 3 d. Educ. Cannock House School; Westwood. Regular Army, 1966-90 (Gordon Highlanders, RAOC) General List; King's Own Scottish Borderers, 1990-95; Regional Liaison Officer, Scottish Landowners' Federation, 1992-93; since 1993: Chief Assessor (Scotland), Guild of Master Craftsmen; Chairman, Westerlea Trust; President, Scottish Tartan Society; Director, Register of all Publicly Known Tartans; Freeman of Glasgow. Recreations: hill-walking; Scottish domestic architecture; family history. Address: (h.) Glen Annan House, Moffat, Dumfriesshire DG10 9RS; T.-01683 220014.

Paisley, Janet, DipCE. Poet; Playwright; Writer; b. 12.1.48, Ilford; 6 s. Educ. Falkirk High School; Callendar Park College of Education. Writing fellowships: Glasgow South Division Libraries, 1990-92, Darnley and Carnwadric, 1992-94, Glasgow South Area, 1994-96; Glasgow University Writing Tutor, since 1993; Margaret Ramsay Memorial Board for best new British play, 1996; plays: Sooans Nicht; For Want of a Nail; Refuge: Winding String. Publications: Pegasus in Flight; Biting Through Skins; Wildfire; Alien Crop; Reading the Bones. Recreations: gardening; sculpting. Address: 12 Hallglen Road, Glenvillage, Falkirk FK1 2AW; T.-01324 638636.

Paling, Edwin. Leader, Royal National Orchestra, since 1973; Member, The Paragon Ensemble, since 1994; Violin Teacher, Royal Scottish Academy of Music and Drama, since 1985; b. 29.12.48, Nottingham; 1 s. 2 d. Educ. Royal Academy of Music. Bournemouth Symphony Orchestra, 1970-71; City of Birmingham Symphony Orchestra, 1971-72; BBC Midland Light Orchestra, 1972. Recreation: walking. Address: 345 Kilmarnock Road, Glasgow G43 2DS; T.-0141-632 0567.

Palmer, Sheriff Charles William, LLB. Sheriff of Tayside, Central and Fife at Dunfermline, since 1992; b. 17.12.45. Sheriff of North Strathclyde at Dunoon and Dumbarton, 1986-92. Address: (b.) Dunfermline Sheriff Court, 1/6 Carnegie Drive, Dunfermline, KY12 7HJ.

Panton, John, MBE. Professional Golfer; b. 9.10.16, Pitlochry. Won PGA Match-Play Championship, 1956 (Runner-up, 1968); PGA British Seniors', 1967-69; World Seniors', 1967 (defeated Sam Snead for title); Silver King,

1950; Daks, 1951; North British-Harrogate, 1952; Goodwin Foursomes, 1952; Yorkshire Evening News, 1954; Gleneagles-Saxone Am.-Pro. Foursomes, 1956; Woodlawn Invitation Open (West Germany), 1958-59-60; leading British player, Open Championship, 1956; Leader, PGA Order of Merit (Vardon Trophy), 1951; won Scottish Professional Championship, seven times (and joint Champion, once); Ryder Cup player, 1951-53-61; awarded Golf Writers' Trophy, 1967; Hon. Professional, Royal and Ancient Golf Club, St. Andrews.

Park, Ian Michael Scott, CBE, MA, LLB. Partner, Paull & Williamsons, Advocates, Aberdeen, 1961-91, Consultant, since 1991; Member: Criminal Injuries Compensation Board, since 1983, Criminal Injuries Compensation Appeals Panel, since 1996; b. 7.4.38, Aberdeen; m., Elizabeth M.L. Struthers; 2 s. Educ. Aberdeen Grammar School; Aberdeen University. Assistant to, subsequently Partner in, Paull & Williamsons; Member, Society of Advocates in Aberdeen, since 1962, Treasurer, 1991-92, President, 1992-93; sometime part-time Assistant, Department of Public Law, Aberdeen University; President, Law Society of Scotland, 1980-81 (Council Member, 1974-85); Chairman, Aberdeen Citizens Advice Bureau, until 1988; Secretary, Aberdeen Granite Association, 1962-84; Temporary Sheriff, 1976-84; Honorary Sheriff at Aberdeen, since 1996; part-time Chairman, Medical Appeals Tribunals, until 1996; frequent broadcaster on legal topics. Recreations: golf; gardening. Address: (h.) 46 Rubislaw Den South, Aberdeen.

Park, Neil Ferguson, BSc, MBA. General Manager, Scottish Athletics Federation; b. 26.9.62, Gosport; m., Judith Frances; 1 s.; 1 d. Educ. Daniel Stewart's and Melville College, Edinburgh; Aberdeen University; Edinburgh University. Former Assistant Secretary, Royal Highland and Agricultural Society; Executive Member: British Institute of Sports Administrators, Scottish Sports Association. Recreations: rugby; golf; road-running. Address: (b.) Caledonia House, South Gyle, Edinburgh EH12 9DQ.

Parker, Cameron Holdsworth, OBE, DL, BSc. Lord Lieutenant of Renfrewshire, since 1998; Managing Director, Lithgows Limited, 1984-92, Vice-Chairman, 1992-97; b. 14.4.32, Dundee; m., Marlyne Honeyman; 3 s. Educ. Morrison's Academy, Crieff; Glasgow University. Managing Director, latterly also Chairman, John G. Kincaid & Co. Ltd., Greenock, 1967-80; Chairman and Chief Executive, Scott Lithgow Ltd., Port Glasgow, 1980-83; Board Member, British Shipbuilders, 1977-80, 1981-83; Chief Executive, Prosper Enginering Ltd., Irvine, 1983-84. Liveryman, Worshipful Company of Shipwrights; Member, Council, CBI Scotland, 1986-92; Member, Argyll and Clyde Health Board, 1991-95; Board Member, Scottish Homes, 1992-96; Director, Clyde Shaw Ltd., 1992-94. Recreation: golf. Address: (h.) Heath House, Kilmacolm, Renfrewshire PA13 4PE; T.-01505 873197.

Parker, Professor Denis Michael, BA, PhD, CPsychol, FBPsS. Professor of Psychology, Glasgow Caledonian University, since 1996; Head, Department of Psychology, since 1996; b. 26. 6.43, Cork; m., Mannell Ruth; 3 s. Educ. St. Ignatius College, London; Durham University. Addison Wheeler Research Fellow, Durham University, 1969-71; Lecturer/Senior Lecturer/Reader in Psychology, Aberdeen University, 1972-95; Visiting Professor, University of Konstanz, 1995. Recreations: hill-walking; reading; cogitating. Address: (b.) Department of Psychology, Glasgow Caledonian University, Cowcaddens Road, Glasgow G4 0BA; T.-0141-331 3120.

Parker, Timothy Robert Walter, LLB. Depute Secretary to Church of Scotland General Trustees, since 1982; b. 7.10.44, Aberdeen; m., Janet Helen Nicol; 3 d. Educ. Trinity College, Glenalmond; Aberdeen University. Private practice as Solicitor, 1969-82. Chairman, Lothian Primary Schools Chess League; Past Chairman, Trinity Academy P.T.A.; Secretary, Lothian Federation of P.T.A.s; Committee Member, Viewpoint Housing Association. Recreations: bowling; walking; watching other sports; listening to music. Address: (h.) 35 Dudley Avenue, Edinburgh EH6 4PL; T.-0131-554 2076.

Parkins, Professor James J., BSc (Hons), PhD, CBiol, FIBiol. Professor of Animal Health, Glasgow Veterinary School (Director, Cochno Farm and Research Centre); b. 27.7.45, Tynemouth; m., Elma; 1 s.; 1 d. Educ. Wolverhampton Grammar School; Glasgow University. Lecturer in Veterinary Animal Husbandry, 1970; Senior Lecturer, 1983, Reader, 1990, Glasgow University Veterinary School. Publications: over 100 papers. Recreations: the country; golf; music. Address: (b.) Glasgow University Veterinary School, Bearsden Road, Glasgow G61 1QH; T.-0141-330 5700.

Parnell, Brian K., BSc, ACGI, DipTP, FRTPI. Planning Consultant; Vice-Chairman and Hon. Secretary, Scottish Council for National Parks, since 1991; Visiting Professor, Centre for Planning, Strathclyde University, since 1991; b. 18.12.22, Brighton; 2 s.; 1 d. Educ. Varndean School, Brighton; London University; Edinburgh College of Art. Captain, EME, 1943-47; Department of Planning, Midlothian County Council, 1949-57; Depute Planning Officer, Stirling County Council, 1957-64; joined Glasgow School of Art, 1964, Head, Department of Planning, 1976-87; Commissioner, Countryside Commission for Scotland, 1968-80; part-time Planning Inquiry Reporter, Scottish Office, 1982-93. Chairman, Scottish Branch, Royal Town Planning Institute, 1972-73; Executive Committee Member, National Trust for Scotland, 1973-83; Trustee, Scottish Civic Trust, since 1985; Convener, Stirling Civic Trust, since 1994. Recreations: sailing; swimming; hill-walking; travel. Address: (h.) 15 Park Terrace, Stirling FK8 2JT; T. 01786 465714.

Parr, Professor John Brian, BSc (Econ), MA, PhD. Professor of Regional and Urban Economics, Glasgow University, since 1989; Chairman, British-Irish Section, Regional Science Association, 1981-85; b. 18.3.41, Epsom; m., Pamela Jean Harkins; 2 d. Educ. Henry Thornton School; London University; University of Washington. Instructor, University of Washington, 1966; Assistant Professor/Associate Professor, University of Pennsylvania, 1967-75; joined Glasgow University as Lecturer, 1975. Editor, Papers of the Regional Science Association, 1968-75; Associate Editor, Journal of Regional Science, since 1979; Co-Editor, European Research in Regional Science, since 1990; Member, Board of Management, Urban Studies, since 1981; Associate Editor, Annals of Regional Science, 1993-96; Member, Editorial Board, International Regional Science Review, since 1995; Member, Editorial Board, Review of Urban and Regional Development Studies, since 1995. Publications: numerous journal articles on urban and regional analysis; Christaller Central Place Structures (Co-Author); Regional Policy: Past Experience and New Directions (Co-Editor); Analysis of Regional Structure: Essays in Honour of August Lösch (Co-Editor); Market Centers and Retail Location (Co-Author). Address: (b.) Department of Urban Studies, Glasgow University, Glasgow G12 8RS; T.-0141-339 8855, Ext. 4724/5048.

Parratt, Professor James Roy, MSc, PhD, DSc, MD (h.c.), DSc (Med), FRCPath, DipRelStudies (Cantab), FRPharmS, FESC, FIBiol, FRPharmS, FRSE. Professor of Cardiovascular Pharmacology, Strathclyde University, since 1983 (Head, Department of Physiology and Pharmacology, 1986-90); b. 19.8.33, London; m., Pamela Joan Lyndon Marels; 2 s.; 1 d. Educ. St. Clement Danes Holborn Estate Grammar School; London University. Spent nine years in Nigeria as Head of Pharmacology, Nigerian School of Pharmacy, then in Physiology, University Medical School, Ibadan; joined Strathclyde University, 1967; appointed

Reader, 1970; Personal Professor, Department of Physiology and Pharmacology, 1975-83. Chairman, Cardiac Muscle Research Group, 1980-83; Vice President, European Shock Society, since 1995; Gold Medal, Szeged University, 1975; Honorary Member, Hungarian Pharmacological Society, 1983; Honorary Doctorate, Albert Szent-Gyorgi Medical University, Hungary, 1989; Gold J.E. Purkyne Honorary Medal, Academy of Sciences of Czech Republic, 1995; Sodalem honoris causa, Slovak Medical and Cardiological Societies, 1997; Chairman, Universities and Colleges Christian Fellowship, 1984-90; former Vice-Chairman, Scripture Union; Past Chairman, SUM Fellowship; Lay Preacher, Baptist Unions of Scotland and Great Britain; Honorary President, Baptist Lay Preachers Association of Scotland, 1985-90. Recreation: music. Address: (h.) 16 Russell Drive, Bearsden, Glasgow G61 3BD; T.-0141-942 7164.

Parsons, Professor Ian, BSc, PhD, FRSE. Professor of Mineralogy, Edinburgh University, since 1988, Head, Department of Geology and Geophysics, 1993-96; b. 5.9.39, Manchester; m., Brenda Mary Reah; 3 s. Educ. Beckenham and Penge Grammar School; Durham University. DSIR Research Fellow, Manchester University, 1963-64; Aberdeen University: Assistant Lecturer, 1964-65, Lecturer, 1965-77, Senior Lecturer, 1977-83, Professor, 1983-88. Member, NERC Earth Sciences Research Grants and Training Awards Committee; President, Mineralogical Society, 1994-95; Member, NCC Committee for Scotland, 1985-90. Recreations: skiing; hill-walking; music. Address: (b.) Department of Geology and Geophysics, Edinburgh University, West Mains Road, Edinburgh, EH9 3JW; T.-0131-650 8512.

Partridge, Professor Stephen. Chair of Media Art, Duncan of Jordanstone College of Art, University of Dundee (Head, School of Television and Imaging, since 1994); Media Artist and Producer; b. 19.3.53, Leicester; separated. Educ. Blackpool Grammar School; Maidstone College of Art; Royal College of Art. Exhibited in: Video Show, Serpentine, 1975, Installation Show, Tate Gallery, 1976, Paris Biennalle, 1977, The Kitchen, New York, 1979; produced Dialogue for Two Players (Channel 4), 1984; Co-founder, Fields and Frames; Co-producer, Not Necessarily (BBC2), 1991; Curator: Video Art 78, Coventry, UK TV New York, National Review of Live Art 1988-90, 19:4:90 Television Interventions, Made in Scotland I, II, Semblances, Passages; has lectured in art colleges for 20 years. Address: University of Dundee DD1 4HT; T.-01382 345249.

Parvin, Gilmour W., MA, AIIMR. Investment Consultant; Chair, Scottish Tory Reform Group. Educ. Glasgow University. Address: (h.) 26 Cramond Avenue, Edinburgh EH4 6NE; T.-0131-312 7803.

Pasley, Anthony de Gard, FLI, FSGD, FSA(Scot); Landscape Architect in private practice, since 1973; b. 10.8.29, Edinburgh. Educ. King's College School. Senior Associate, Sylvia Crowe and Associates, 1967-72; work has included major public projects but specialises in country gardens and estates in UK and Europe; has taught on courses at Kew Gardens, Wisley, Edinburgh and New York Botanic Gardens, Reading University, London University; Senior Lecturer/Consultant, English Gardening School; President, Paisley Family Society. Publications: Summer Flowers, 1977; The English Gardening School (Co-author), 1987. Recreations: gardening; garden and architectural history; collecting books and paintings; opera. Address: Roseburn, Haywood Road, Moffat DG10 9BU; T.-01683 220146.

Pate, James Guy Lindsay, JP, FRIAS, ARIBA, DipTP (Glas), MRTPI (retd). Retired Chartered Architect and Town Planner; Honorary Sheriff, North Strathclyde at Dunoon, since 1992; General Commissioner for Income Tax; Member, Local Valuation Appeal Committee for Argyll and Bute; b. 17.3.27, Ayr; 1st m. diss.; 2 s.; 1 d; m. 2, Christina Margaret MacKay. Educ. Ayr Academy; Glasgow School of Architecture. Royal Marines, 1946-48; Architectural Assistant, Ayr County Council and East Kilbride Development Corporation; Planning Assistant, Renfrew County Council; Founder Partner, Thomas Smith, Gibb and Pate, architects and planning consultants, 1962; Principal, J. G. Lindsay Pate and Associates, 1982-90; Arbiter, Expert Witness, Mediator and Adviser. Former Member, RIAS Practice Committee; past Member, Justices Committee, Argyll and Bute; Chairman, Argyll Conservative and Unionist Association, 1970-72; Member, Argyll County Council, 1971-75; former Member, Argyll and Bute Joint Planning Committee; served on Cowal Licensing Court; Member, Local Board, Armed Services YMCA of the United States of America, 1968-85 (Chairman 1983-84); Steward and Member, Cowal Highland Gathering (Honorary Secretary, Director and Manager, 1982-95); Director, Portavadie Leisure Limited. Recreations: country pursuits; reading; sailing. Address: An Stabull, Woodbine Cottage, Ardhallow, nr Dunoon, Argyll PA23 7QL; T.-01369 704477.

Paternoster, Rev. Canon Michael Cosgrove, MA. Rector, St. James' Episcopal Church, Aberdeen, since 1990; Honorary Canon, St. Paul's Cathedral, Dundee, since 1981; b. 13.5.35, East Molesey, Surrey; m., Careth Osborne. Educ. Kingston Grammar School; Pembroke College, Cambridge; Cuddesdon Theological College. Deacon, 1961; Priest, 1962; Curate, St. Andrew's, Surbiton, 1961-63; Chaplain to Anglican students in Dundee, 1964-68; Secretary, Fellowship of St. Alban and St. Sergius, 1968-71; Rector, St. James', Dollar, 1971-75; Rector, St. James's, Stonehaven, 1975-90; Secretary, Inter-Church Relations Committee, Scottish Episcopal Church, 1975-82; Member, Doctrine Committee, Scottish Episcopal Church, 1980-91; Aberdeen and N.E. Wing Chaplain, Air Training Corps, 1985-92; Director of Ordinands, Diocese of Aberdeen and Orkney, since 1995. Publications: Thou art There Also, 1967; Stronger Than Death, 1972. Recreations: reading; sketching; bird-watching; listening to music. Address: 31 Gladstone Place, Aberdeen AB10 6UX; T.-01224 322631.

Paterson, Professor Alan Alexander, LLB (Hons), DPhil (Oxon), FRSA, FRSE. Solicitor. Professor of Law, Strathclyde University, since 1984; b. 5.6.47, Edinburgh; m., Alison Jane Ross Lowdon; 2 s.; 1 d. Educ. Edinburgh Academy; Edinburgh University; Pembroke College, Oxford. Research Associate, Oxford Centre for Socio-Legal Studies, 1972-73; Lecturer, Law Faculty, Edinburgh University, 1973-84; Visiting Professor, University of New Mexico Law School, 1982, 1986. Former Chairman, Scottish Legal Action Group and British and Irish Legal Education and Technology Association; Chairman, Legal Services Group, Citizens Advice Scotland; Chairman, Committee of Heads of University Law Schools of the UK; Vice-Chair, Joint Standing Conference on Legal Education in Scotland. Publications: The Law Lords, 1982; The Legal System of Scotland (Co-author), 1993. Address: (b.) Strathclyde University Law School, 173 Cathedral Street, Glasgow G4 ORQ; T.-0141-548 3341.

Paterson, Brenda, MA (Hons). News and Current Affairs Presenter, BBC Scotland, since 1991; b. 1.6.59, Aberdeen. Educ. Inverness Royal Academy; Edinburgh University. Reporter, Radio Clyde, 1984-86; BBC Network Radio, 1986-89 (Producer, Today, Radio 4, Newsbeat, Radio 1, and From Our Own Correspondent, Radio 4); Reporter/Presenter, Scottish Television, 1989-91. Recreations: yoga (qualified teacher); theatre; massive amount of reading. Address: (b.) BBC Scotland, Queen Margaret Drive, Glasgow G12 8DG.

Paterson, Calum, BA, MBA, CA. Director, Scottish Development Finance, Scottish Enterprise, since 1996; b.

13.4.63, Edinburgh; m., Amanda McLean. Educ. Linlithgow Academy; University of Strathclyde. Ernst and Young, 1985-88; Scottish Development Agency, 1988-91; Scottish Enterprise, since 1991. Recreations: judo; hillwalking; cinema; keeping fit. Address: (b.) 120 Bothwell Street, Glasgow G2 7JP; T.-0141-248 2700.

Paterson, Douglas McCallum, MA, MEd, DMS, DipM, MIM. Chief Executive, Aberdeen City Council, since 1995; b. 20.11.49, Macduff; m., Isobel Beaton; 2 d. Educ. Banff Academy; Aberdeen University; Robert Gordon University. John Wood Group, 1971-75; Grampian Regional Council: Teacher, 1976-81, Head Teacher, 1981-86, Advisor, 1986-90, Depute Director of Education, 1990-92, Senior Depute Director, 1992-94, Director of Education, 1994-95. Recreations: local history; fishing industry; music; walking; theatre. Address: (b.) Town House, Aberdeen; T.-01224 522500.

Paterson, Lt. Col. Howard Cecil, TD, FSA Scot. International Tourism Consultant and Artist; b. 16.3.20, Edinburgh; m., Isabelle Mary; 1 s. Educ. Daniel Stewart's College, Edinburgh; Edinburgh College of Art. Army, 1939-49; combat duties during War; personnel selection afterwards; Territorial Army, 1949-70; serves on East Scotland TAVR Committee; Founder Member, Gunner Heritage Appeal; Member, City of Edinburgh Artillery Officers' Association; Member, 52nd Lowland Division Officers' Club; Assistant Personnel Manager, Jute Industries Ltd., Dundee, 1949-51; Organising Secretary, Scottish Country Industries Development Trust, 1951-66; Senior Director, Scottish Tourist Board, 1966-81. Chairman, Taste of Scotland Ltd., 1984-86; Vice-Chairman, John Buchan Society, 1990-95; Member, Scottish Committee, British Horse Society; Chairman, Trekking and Riding Society of Scotland. Publications: Tourism in Scotland; Flavour of Edinburgh (with Catherine Brown). Recreations: fishing; shooting; riding; writing; drawing and painting; natural history; history. Address: (h.) Dovewood, West Linton, Peeblesshire, EH46 7DS; T.-01968 60346.

Paterson, Sheriff James Veitch, MA (Oxon), LLB (Edin). Sheriff of Lothian and Borders at Jedburgh, Selkirk and Duns, since 1963; b. 16.4.28; m., Ailie Campbell Clark Hutchison; 1 s.; 1 d. Educ. Edinburgh Academy; Lincoln College, Oxford; Edinburgh University. Admitted Faculty of Advocates, 1953.

Paterson, Rev. John Love, MA, BD, STM, FSA Scot. Minister, St. Michael's Parish Church, Linlithgow, since 1977; Chaplain to The Queen, since 1996; b. 6.5.38, Ayr; m., Lorna Begg (see Lorna Marion Paterson). Educ. Ayr Academy; Glasgow University; Edinburgh University; Union Theological Seminary, New York. Minister: Presbyterian Church of East Africa, 1964-72, St. Andrew's, Nairobi, 1968-72; Chaplain, Stirling University, 1973-77. Moderator, West Lothian Presbytery, 1985. Recreation: gardening. Address: St. Michael's Manse, Linlithgow, West Lothian; T.-01506 842195.

Paterson, Very Rev. John Munn Kirk, ACII, MA, BD, DD. Minister Emeritus, St. Paul's Church, Milngavie; b. 8.10.22, Leeds; m., Geraldine Lilian Parker; 2 s.; 1 d. Educ. Hillhead High School; Edinburgh University. Pilot, RAF, 1940-46; Insurance official, 1946-58; ordained Minister, Church of Scotland, 1964; Minister, St. John's Church, Bathgate, 1964-70; Minister, St. Paul's Church, Milngavie, 1970-87. Moderator, General Assembly, Church of Scotland, 1984-85; Life Member, Chartered Insurance Institute; Hon. Doctorate, Aberdeen University, 1986. Recreations: fishing; gardening. Address: (h.) 58 Orchard Drive, Edinburgh EH4 2DZ; T.-0131-332 5876.

Paterson, Lorna Marion, MA, Dip.Rel.Ed. General Secretary, Church of Scotland Guild, 1985-98; b. 26.1.38, Unst; m., Rev. John L. Paterson (qv). Educ. Inverurie Academy; Aberden University; Aberdeen College of Education. Teacher of English, History, Geography and Religious Education, 1960-62; Teacher of English, 1962-66; Administrative Assistant, Strathclyde University, 1966-68; Deputy Academic Registrar, then Education Administrator, Stirling University, 1968-79. Guider (Division Commissioner, West Lothian, 1982-85); Vice Chairman, Linlithgow Arts Guild, since 1996; Elder, St. Michael's Parish Church, Linlithgow, since 1995. Recreations: singing; homemaking; church activities; the arts; people. Address: (h.) St. Michael's Manse, Kirkgate, Linlithgow EH49 7AL; T.-01506 842195.

Paterson, Stuart Andrew. Dumfries and Galloway Arts Association/Scottish Arts Council Writing Fellow, 1996-98; poet in English and Scots; b. 31.1.66, Truro. Educ. James Hamilton Academy, Kilmarnock; Stirling University. Writing Fellow, Morven Day Care Centre, Kilmarnock, 1995-96; Founder/Editor, Spectrum (poetry/prose review), 1991-97; Writers' Workshop Leader, Harbour Arts Centre, Irvine, 1996; poems anthologised in UK, USA and RSA; Eric Gregory Award, 1992; SAC Writer's Bursary, 1993. Publications: Mulaney of Larne and Other Poems, 1991; Saving Graces, 1997. Recreations: travel; music; football; malts. Address: (h.) 2A Leslie Road, Kilmarnock KA3 7RR; T.-01563 526360.

Paterson, (Thomas) Michael, DA. Artist; Educationist; b. 14.4.38, Kirkcaldy; m., Joan; 1 s.; 2 d. Educ. George Watson's Boys' College; Edinburgh College of Art; Moray House College of Education. Teacher of Art, Waid Academy, Anstruther, 1960-64; Special Assistant, George Heriot's, Edinburgh, 1964-67; Head of Art, Marr College, Troon, 1967-69; Lecturer and Programme Director, College Television Service, Craigie College of Education, 1969-80, Governor, 1979-80; Assistant Head of Educational Programmes, Scottish Television, 1981-89, Head of Education, 1989-91; Educational Television Producer, 1991-98; ETMA: Chairman (Scotland), 1979-80, 1993-95, National Executive, 1978-98, National Chairman, 1994-96; RTS Awards Convener, Scottish Centre, 1981-86, Chairman, RTS Scottish Centre, and Member of Council, 1986-88; Member, Publicity Committee, General Assembly, Church of Scotland, 1983-86, Board of Communication, 1986-90, 1994-95, Convener, A/V Production Committee, 1986-88; Chairman, Editorial Board, Journal of Educational Media, 1994-96; C.O.S. Member, Educational Services Committee, South Ayrshire Council, since 1996. Publication: A Primary Art Course (Co-author). Recreations: golf at Turnberry; travel; gardening; reading. Address: (h.) 1 Laurelbank Road, Maybole KA19 8BE.

Paterson, William, BSc (Eng), CEng, FIEE, MRAeS. Director of Engineering, Northern Lighthouse Board, since 1987; b. 24.7.40, Neilston; m., Margaret Quirie Forrest Gerrard; 2 s.; 2 d. Educ. Paisley Grammar School; Strathclyde University. Radio Officer, Merchant Navy; Technician, then Engineer, Civil Aviation Authority; Head, Radio Department, Northern Lighthouse Board. Recreation: gardening; golf. Address: (b.) 84 George Street, Edinburgh EH2 3DA; T.-0131-226 7051.

Paterson, (William) Guthrie (Wilson), BSc, MSc, CertEd. Vice-Principal, Scottish Agricultural College, since 1990; b. 5.6.40, Blantyre; m., Mary Isabel; 1 s.; 1 d. Educ. Hamilton Academy; Glasgow University; Jordanhill College of Education; Aberdeen University. Lecturer in Crop Husbandry, North of Scotland College of Agriculture, 1965-73; Senior Agronomy Specialist, West of Scotland Agricultural College, 1973-83; Head, Crop Production Department, North of Scotland College of Agriculture, 1983-90. Recreations: golf; gardening; music; reading. Address: (b.) The Scottish Agricultural College, Ferguson Building, Craibstone Estate, Bucksburn, Aberdeen AB21 9YA; T.-01224 711000.

Paterson, Wilma, DRSAM. Freelance Composer/ Writer/Journalist; b. 23.4.44, Dundee; 1 s.; 1 d. Educ. Harris Academy; Royal Scottish Academy of Music. Composition study with Luigi Dallapiccola in Florence; writes all types of music (chamber, orchestral, incidental); music reviews for Glasgow Herald and The Independent; broadcasts and writes on food, plants, travel. Publications: A Country Cup; Was Byron Anorexic?; Shoestring Gourmet; Flowers and Herbs of the Bible; Lord Byron's Relish; Salmon & Women, The Feminine Angle; Songs of Scotland (with Alasdair Gray). Address: Greystones, 30 Kelvinside Gardens, Glasgow G20 6BB; T.-0141-579 0403.

Paterson-Brown, June, CBE, MBChB. Commonwealth Chief Commissioner, Girl Guides Association, 1985-90; Vice-Chairman, Princes Trust, 1982-92; Non-Executive Director, Border Television plc, since 1980; b. 8.2.32, Edinburgh; m., Peter Neville Paterson-Brown (qv); 3 s.; 1 d. Educ. Esdaile School; Edinburgh University. Medical Officer, Family Planning and Well Woman's Clinics, 1959-85; Past Chairman: County of Roxburghshire Youth Committee, Roxburgh Duke of Edinburgh Award Committee; Scottish Chief Commissioner, Girl Guides Association, 1977-82; Chairman, Borders Region Children's Panel Advisory Committee, 1982-85; Chairman, Scottish Standing Conference of Voluntary Youth Organisations, 1983-85; Trustee, MacRobert Trusts, since 1987; Trustee, Prince's Trust, 1982-94; Paul Harris Fellow, 1990; Deputy Lieutenant, Roxburgh, Ettrick and Lauderdale, since 1990. Recreations: golf; skiing; music; fishing; reading; grand-children. Address: (h.) Norwood, Hawick, Roxburghshire TD9 7HP; T.-01450 372352.

Paterson-Brown, Peter Neville, MBChB, DObst RCOG. Medical Practitioner, retired; b. 23.3.31, Hawick; m., June Garden (see June Paterson-Brown); 3 s.; 1 d. Educ. Merchiston Castle School; Edinburgh University. Medical Adviser, Red Cross Scotland, 1981-94; Member, Scottish Committee, Medical Commission on Accident Prevention, 1978-91; Director, Children's Hospice Association Scotland, since 1993; Vice President, React, since 1991. Red Cross Badge of Honour, 1995. Publication: A Matter of Life or Death. Recreations: skiing; shooting; golf; fishing. Address: (h.) Norwood, Hawick, Roxburghshire; T.-01450 372352.

Paterson-Brown, Simon, MB BS, MPhil, MS, FRCS(Ed), FRCS Eng, FCS (UK). Consultant General Surgeon, Royal Infirmary, Edinburgh, since 1994; b. 6.2.58, Edinburgh; m., Dr Sheila Finnerty; 3 d. Educ. Trinity College, Glenalmond; St. Mary's Hospital Medical School, London. Junior doctor posts, London and South East England, 1982-89; Visiting Lecturer in Surgery, Chinese University of Hong Kong, 1989-90; Lecturer in Surgery, Royal Infirmary, Edinburgh, 1990-91; Senior Surgical Registrar, St. Mary's Hospital and Hammersmith Hospital, 1992-94; Senior Lecturer in Surgery, St. Mary's Hospital, London, 1993-94. Chairman, Basic Surgical Training Programme, South East Scotland; Postgraduate Surgical Tutor, Royal Infirmary, Edinburgh; Member, Specialty Advisory Board (General Survery), Royal College of Surgeons of Edinburgh. Publications: Aids to Anatomy; Guide to Practical Procedures in Medicine and Surgery; Principles and Practice of Surgical Laparoscopy (Editor); Emergency Surgery and Critical Care (Editor). Recreations: music; skiing; golf; running. Address: University Department of Surgery, Royal Infirmary, Edinburgh EH3 9YW; T.-0131-536 3819.

Paterson-Nisbet, Mary Sylvia. Secretary, Edinburgh Consumer Group, since 1977; Chairman, Morningside Community Council, since 1995; b. 28.7.37, Hampstead Heath, London; m., 1, Richard Cruickshanks Paterson (deceased); 2 s.; 2, James Bruce Hay Nisbet. Educ. Hornsey High School, London. Westminster Bank Ltd., 1954-55; GPO Continental Telephone Exchange, 1955-56; Scottish Widows Fund, 1957-61; freelance market research. Member, Edinburgh CAB Executive Committee, several years; Member, Post Officers Users' Council for Scotland, 1976-82; Member, Scottish Committee, Meat and Livestock Commission, 1990-95; Member, Executive, National Federation of Consumer Groups, 1992-97.Recreations: music; walking; crosswords. Address: (h.) 4/6 Belhaven Place, Edinburgh EH10 5JN; T.-0131-447 4148.

Paton, Alasdair Chalmers, BSc, CEng, FICE, FCIWEM. Chief Executive, Scottish Environment Protection Agency, since 1995; Director and Chief Engineer, Engineering, Water and Waste Directorate, Scottish Office Environment Department, 1991-95; b. 28.11.44, Paisley; m., Zona G. Gill; 1 s.; 1 d. Educ. John Neilson Institution, Paisley; Glasgow University. Assistant Engineer, Clyde Port Authority, 1967-71; Assistant Engineer, DAFS, 1971-72; Senior Engineer, SDD, 1972-77; Engineer, Public Works Department, Hong Kong Government, 1977-80; Senior Engineer, then Principal Engineer, SDD, 1980-87; Deputy Chief Engineer, 1987-91. Recreations: Rotary; sailing; golf. Address: (b.) Erskine Court, Castle Business Park, Stirling FK9 4TR; T.-01786 457701.

Paton, Alastair George Peter, DL, MBChB, DObstRCOG. Non-Executive Director, Borders Health Board, since 1993; Honorary Sheriff of Lothian and Borders at Peebles, since 1991; General Commissioner of Income Tax, Peebles Division, since 1991; b. 23.5.30, Paisley; m., Ethel Jean Harris; 4 d. Educ. George Watson's College, Edinburgh; Edinburgh University Medical School. House Surgeon and House Physician, Royal Infirmary of Edinburgh, 1954-55; Surgeon Lieutenant, Royal Navy, United Kingdom and South Atlantic Station, 1955-57; House Officer, Sorrento Maternity Hospital, Birmingham, 1958; House Physician, Children's Hospital, Birmingham, 1958; General Medical Practitioner, Peebles, 1959-90. Director, Tweeddale Branch, British Red Cross, 1991-98; Deputy Lieutenant, Lieutenancy of Tweeddale, since 1992; Welfare and Pensions Officer, Peebles Branch, Royal British Legion Scotland, since 1990. Recreations: gardening; music; walking. Address: (h.) Ben Ard, The Mount, Peebles EH45 9EX; T.-01721 720098.

Paton, David Romer, OBE, FRICS, OStJ, IRRV, FSA Scot. Chartered Surveyor; b. 5.3.35, Aberdeen; m., Juliette Burney; 2 s. Educ. Gordonstoun School; Keble College, Oxford. Chartered Surveyor in own practice; Past President, Aberdeen Chamber of Commerce; Past Chairman: Gordon Conservative and Unionist Association, Royal Northern & University Club, Scottish Chambers of Commerce, Aberdeen Beyond 2000, Grampian-Houston Association; former Member: North East River Purification Board, Salmon Advisory Committee; Secretary of State Appointee, Scottish Office Scottish Salmon Strategy Task Force; Chairman: Aberdeen Harbour Board, North East Scotland Preservation Trust, Don District Salmon Fishery Board, Scottish Council (Development and Industry), Aberdeen Committee, Order of St. John, and of Aberdeen Committee, St. John Association; President: Aberdeen Macmillan Cancer Relief, Aberdeen Civic Society, Friends of Grampian Stones; Member: North of Scotland Water Authority, Architectural Heritage Society of Scotland, Association of Scottish District Salmon Fishery Boards; Trustee, Scottish Civic Trust, Aberdeen Foyer; Patron: Bridge of Don Community Trust, Touch of Tartan Ball; Grampian Initiative Ambassador. Address: Grandhome, Aberdeen AB22 8AR; T.-01224 722202.

Paton, George, MA, MEd, FEIS, FITD. Director, Scottish Council for Educational Technology, 1986-90; b. 5.12.31, Rutherglen; m., 1, Barbara Thomson (deceased); 2 s.; 2, J. Honor Smith. Educ. Rutherglen Academy; Glasgow University. National Service, RAEC, 1953-55; Schoolteacher, 1955-61; Lecturer in English, Jordanhill College of Education, 1961-63; Principal Lecturer in English, then Assistant Principal, Dundee College of

Education, 1963-69; Principal, Hamilton College of Education, 1970-81; Depute Director, Scottish Council for Educational Technology, 1982-86. President, International Council for Educational Media, 1989-91; Member, Library Information Service Committee (Scotland), 1984-91; Executive Committee Member, Commonwealth Institute Scotland, 1985-96; Governor, David Livingstone Memorial Trust, since 1971 (Chairman, since 1994); former Convener, Education Committee, General Teaching Council for Scotland; Chairman, Strathclyde Committee, Tenovus–Scotland (for medical research in Scotland), since 1991; Elder, Church of Scotland. Recreations: singing; drama; gardening. Address: (h.) 16 Old Bothwell Road, Bothwell, Glasgow G71 8AW.

Paton, William, BSc (Hons). Chief Executive, TUV Product Service Ltd.; Director, National Engineering Laboratory; b. 29.11.41, Kilwinning; m., Elizabeth Anne; 2 s. Educ. Douglas Ewart School, Newton Stewart; Glasgow University. Consulting Geophysicist, Seismograph Services Ltd., 1963; Management Trainee, Colvilles Ltd., Ravenscraig, 1964; Research Scientist in Materials, NEL, 1965-76; Offshore Supplies Office, 1976-77; Divisional Manager, Materials Engineering Division, then Controller, Design, Materials and Systems Department, NEL, 1977-87. Recreation: golf. Address: (b.) National Engineering Laboratory, East Kilbride, Glasgow; T.-East Kilbride 20222.

Patrick, Bruce Robertson, BA, LLB, WS. Partner, Maclay Murray & Spens, since 1976 (Managing Partner, 1991-94); Vice-Convenor, Law Society Company Law Committee, since 1990; b. 26.11.45, London; m., Hilary Jane Sutton; 1 s.; 2 d. Educ. Glasgow Academy; Edinburgh Academy; Exeter College, Oxford University; Edinburgh University. Apprentice, Mitchells Johnston, Solicitors, Glasgow, 1971-73; Assistant, Maclay Murray and Spens, Solicitors, 1973-75; Assistant, Coward Chance, Solicitors, London, 1975-76. Management Committee Member, Castle Rock Housing Association. Recreations: sailing; golf; hillwalking. Address: (b.) 3 Glenfinlas Street, Edinburgh EH3 6AQ; T.-0131-226 5196.

Patrick, Sheriff (Lilian) Gail, MA, LLB. Sheriff of Tayside, Central and Fife at Kirkcaldy, since 1991; b. 24.12.41. Enrolled as Solicitor, 1966; former Lecturer and Tutor, Glasgow University and Edinburgh University; admitted to Faculty of Advocates, 1981; called to the Bar, Lincoln's Inn, 1990.

Patterson, Professor Henry Desmond, BSc, MSc, DSc, CMath, FIMA, FRSE. Honorary Professor, Mathematics and Statistics Department, Edinburgh University, since 1985; b. 17.7.24, Whitby; m., Janet Mary Roffe; 1 s. Educ. Northallerton Grammar School; Pickering Grammar School; Ripon Grammar School; Leeds University. Department of Scientific and Industrial Research, 1946-47; Rothamsted Experimental Station, 1947-67; Agricultural Research Council Unit of Statistics, Edinburgh University, 1967-85. Recreations: music; mathematical and statistical programming. Address: (h.) 15 Kings Grove, Longniddry EH32 0QW; T.-01875 853012.

Patterson, Rev. John Wallace, BA, BD. Clerk, Presbytery of St. Andrews, since 1974; b. 7.1.23, Coleraine; m., Catherine Mackay Cape; 4 d. Educ. Coleraine Academical Institution; Trinity College, Dublin; St. Andrews University. Minister: Church of the Holy Rude, Stirling, 1948-50; Prestwick North Church, 1950-58; St. Andrews Martyrs Church, 1958-89. Address: 34 Claybraes, St. Andrews KY16 8RS; T.-01334 473606.

Patterson, Lindy Ann, LLB (Hons), ACIArb. Lawyer; Partner, MacRoberts; b. 12.9.58, Berwick-upon-Tweed. Educ. Eyemouth High School; Edinburgh University. UK National Vice-President, Association Internationale de Jeunes Avocats, 1991-94; Member, Commercial Court Consultative Committee; Member, Law Commission Contract Law Advisory Group; Scotland's first female Solicitor Advocate (May, 1993); former Member of number of Law Society Comittees; Member, Napier University Industrial Professional and Advisory Committee. Recreations: skiing; hill-walking. Address: (b.) 27 Melville Street, Edinburgh.

Patterson, Walter Moffat, MSc, BSc. HM Inspector, Post-School Education Quality and Standards; b. 14.6.45, Airdrie; m., Colleen McCrone (Toronto); 1 s.; 1 d. Educ. Coatbridge High School; Strathclyde University. Lecturer in Statistics, Paisley College; Development Officer, Glacier Metal Co., Kilmarnock, 1973-74; Lecturer in Statistics, Paisley College, 1974-83; Senior Lecturer in Information Technology, MEDC, Paisley College, 1983-86; HM Inspector (Computing and IT), 1986-98. Recreations: gardening; cookery. Address: (b.) EID:PS, Floor 1 West, Victoria Quay, Edinburgh, EH6 6QQ; T.-0131-244 0898.

Pattison, David Arnold, BSc, PhD. Director, David A. Pattison Associates; Director of Leisure and Tourism Consulting, Scott Wilson Resource Consultants, 1986-98; Hon. President, Scottish Youth Hostels Association; Hon. Professor, Queen Margaret College, Edinburgh; b. 9.2.41, Kilmarnock; m., Anne Ross Wilson; 2 s.; 1 d. Educ. Kilmarnock Academy; Glasgow University. Planning Assistant, Ayr County Council, 1963-64; PhD studies, Glasgow University, 1964-66; Planning Assistant, Dunbarton County Council, 1966-67; Lecturer, Strathclyde University, 1967-70; Head of Tourism, Highlands and Islands Development Board, 1970-81; Chief Executive, Scottish Tourist Board, 1981-85; Director Leisure & Tourism Consulting, Ernst & Young, 1985-89; Director Leisure and Tourism Consulting, Cobham Resource Consultants, 1989-96; External Examiner for postgraduate tourism courses, Strathclyde University, 1981-84. Recreations: reading; watching soccer and rugby; golf; gardening. Address: (h.) 7 Cramond Glebe Gardens, Cramond, Edinburgh EH4 6NZ.

Pattison, Rev. Kenneth John, MA, BD, STM. Minister, Kilmuir and Logie Easter, Ross-shire, since 1996; b. 22.4.41, Glasgow; m., Susan Jennifer Brierley Jenkins; 1 s.; 2 d. Educ. Lenzie Academy; Glasgow University; Union Theological Seminary, New York. Minister, Church of Central Africa Presbyterian, Malawi, 1967-77; Minister, Park Parish Church, Ardrossan, 1977-84; Chaplain, Glasgow Royal Infirmary, 1984-90; Associate Minister, St. Andrew's and St. George's, Edinburgh, 1990-96. Convener, Chaplaincies Committee, Church of Scotland, 1993-96. Recreations: hill-walking; swimming; gardening; family history. Address: (h.) The Manse, Delny, Invergordon, IV18 0NW; T.-01862 842 280.

Pattullo, Sir (David) Bruce, Kt, CBE, BA, LLD (Hon), DUniv, FRSE, FCIB (Scot). Governor, Bank of Scotland, 1991-98; Director (Non-Executive): British Linen Bank, 1977-98, Bank of Wales PLC, 1986-98, NWS Bank, 1986-98; b. 2.1.38, Edinburgh; m., Fiona Jane Nicholson; 3 s.; 1 d. Educ. Belhaven Hill School; Rugby; Hertford College, Oxford. National Service commission, Royal Scots (seconded to West Africa); joined Bank of Scotland, 1961; winner, first prize, Institute of Bankers in Scotland, 1964; Manager, Investment Services Department, 1967-71; Deputy Manager, Bank of Scotland Finance Co. Ltd., 1971-73; Chief Executive, Group Merchant Banking Activities, 1973-78; Deputy Treasurer, 1978; Treasurer and General Manager, 1979-88; Group Chief Executive and a Deputy Governor, Bank of Scotland, 1988-91. Chairman, Committee of Scottish Clearing Bankers, 1987-89. Recreations: tennis; hill-walking. Address: (h.) 6 Cammo Road, Edinburgh EH4 8EB.

Pawley, Professor G. Stuart, MA, PhD, FRSE, FRS. Professor of Computational Physics, Edinburgh University, since 1985; b. 22.6.37, Ilford; m., Anthea Jean Miller; 2 s.; 1 d. Educ. Bolton School; Corpus Christi College, Cambridge. Lecturer, Edinburgh University, 1964; Reader, 1970; Personal Chair, 1985; Guest Professor, Aarhus University, Denmark, 1969-70. Recreations: choral singing; mountain walking. Address: (b.) Physics Department, Kings Buildings, Edinburgh University EH9 3JZ; T.-0131-650 5300.

Paxton, Professor Roland Arthur, MBE, MSc, CEng, FICE, FRSE, AMCST. Chairman, Institution of Civil Engineers Panel for Historical Engineering Works, since 1990; Commissioner, Royal Commission on the Ancient and Historic Monuments of Scotland, since 1993; Hon. Professor, Civil and Offshore Engineering, Heriot Watt University, since 1994; b. 29.6.32, Altrincham; m., Ann; 2 d. Educ. Altrincham Grammar School; Manchester College of Science and Technology; Heriot Watt University. Cartographical surveyor, Ordnance Survey, 1953-55; Civil Engineer, Corporations of Sale, Manchester, Leicester, Edinburgh, and Lothian Regional Council, retiring as Senior Principal Engineer, 1959-90; Hon. Senior Research Fellow, Heriot Watt University, 1990-94. Chairman, Forth Bridges Visitor Centre Trust; Secretary and Director, Laigh Milton Viaduct Conservation Project; President, Edinburgh Bibliographical Society, 1992-95; author of books and papers on technical innovation and historical engineering. Address: (b.) Civil and Offshore Engineering, Heriot-Watt University, Edinburgh EH14 4AS; T.-0131-449 5111.

Payne, Professor Anthony Philip, BSc, PhD. Professor of Anatomy, Glasgow University, since 1994; Vice-President, Anatomical Society of Great Britain, since 1999; b. 9.7.47, Enfield; m., Ruth Mary; 2 s. Educ. Eastbourne Grammar School; Reading University; Birmingham University; Glasgow University. MRC Junior Fellow, 1971-73; Glasgow University: Lecturer in Anatomy, 1973-84, Senior Lecturer in Anatomy, 1984-94; Head of Anatomy Department, 1990-94. Recreations: birdwatching; reading. Address: Laboratory of Human Anatomy, Glasgow University, Glasgow G12 8QQ; T.-0141-330 5871.

Payne, Professor Peter Lester, BA, PhD, FRHistS, FRSE. Emeritus Professor, Aberdeen University; Professor of Economic History, Aberdeen University, 1969-95; b. 31.12.29, London; m., Enid Christine Rowntree; 1 s.; 1 d. Educ. Brockley County School, London; Nottingham University. Visiting Lecturer in American Economic History, Johns Hopkins University, 1957-58; Lecturer in Economic and Social History, Nottingham University, 1958-59; Colquhoun Lecturer in Business History, Glasgow University, 1959-69; Senior Lecturer in Economic History, Glasgow University, 1964-69; Sherman Fairchild Distinguished Scholar, California Institute of Technology, Pasadena, 1977-78. Vice-President, Business Archives Council; President, Business Archives Council of Scotland; President, Aberdeen and North of Scotland Philatelic Society, 1995-97. Publications include: Rubber and Railways in the Nineteenth Century; British Entrepreneurship in the Nineteenth Century; Colvilles and the Scottish Steel Industry; The Early Scottish Limited Companies; The Hydro; Growth and Contraction: Scottish Industry c. 1860-1990; Northern Scotland (Editor). Recreations: philately; woodwork. Address: (h.) 7 Kirkton Road, Westhill, Skene, Aberdeenshire, AB32 6LF; T.-01224 744703.

Peacock, Professor Sir Alan Turner, Kt (1987), DSC (1945), MA, HonDUniv (Stirling), Hon. DEcon (Zurich), Hon. DScEcon (Buckingham), HonDUniv (Brunel), HonDUniv (York), HonLLD (St. Andrews), HonLLD (Dundee), HonDSc (Edinburgh), Hon. Fellow (LSE), Lib Doc (Catania), FBA, FRSE. Research Professor in Public Finance, Edinburgh Business School, Heriot-Watt University, since 1985; b. 26.6.22, Ryton-on-Tyne; m., Margaret Martha Astell-Burt; 2 s.; 1 d. Educ. Grove Academy; Dundee High School; St. Andrews University. Royal Navy, 1942-45; Lecturer in Economics, St. Andrews, 1947-48; Lecturer, then Reader in Economics, London School of Economics, 1948-56; Professor of Economic Science, Edinburgh University, 1956-62; Professor of Economics, York University, 1962-78 (Deputy Vice Chancellor, 1963-69); Professor of Economics, University College, Buckingham, 1978-80; Principal, then Vice Chancellor, Buckingham University, 1980-84; Chief Economic Adviser, Department of Trade and Industry (on secondment), 1973-76. Member, Royal Commission on the Constitution, 1970-73; Member, Inquiry into Retirement Provision, 1983-85; SSRC Council, 1972-73; President, International Institute of Public Finance, 1966-69; Chairman, Committee on Financing the BBC, 1985-86; Chairman, Rowntree Inquiry on Takeovers, 1989-91; Executive Director, David Hume Institute, Edinburgh, 1985-91; Chairman, Scottish Arts Council, 1986-92; Chairman, Academic Advisory Council, Institute of Economic Affairs, 1991-93; Head, UN Advisory Mission to Russia on Social Protection, 1992; Non-Executive Director, Macdonald Orr Ltd., since 1991; Chairman, Hebrides Ensemble, since 1994; Scottish Free Enterprise Award, 1987; Keynes Lecturer, British Academy, 1994; Fellow, Accademie Nazionale dei Lincei, Rome. Publications: 25 books, over 200 articles on economic questions. Recreations: attempting to write music; hill-walking. Address: (h.) Clinton Grange, 146/4 Whitehouse Loan, Edinburgh EH9 2AN; T.-0131-447 5917.

Peacock, Andrew John, BSc, MPhil, MD, FRCP. Consultant Physician (Respiratory), West Glasgow Hospitals, since 1990; b. 13.11.49, Montreal; m., Jila Pezeshgi; 1 s.; 2 d. Educ. Westminster School; St. Bartholomew's Hospital Medical College, London University; Caius College, Cambridge University. Senior House Officer, St. Bartholomew's, Addenbrookes and Queen Square Hospitals; Registrar, Brompton Hospital; Senior Registrar, Southampton Hospitals; Research Fellow, University of Colorado; Visiting Scientist, National Heart and Lung Institute, London. Physiologist, 1993 British Expedition to Everest. Publication: Pulmonary Circulation: a handbook for clinicians. Recreations: anything to do with mountains; wine; tennis; golf. Address: (b.) Pulmonary Vascular Unit, Level 8, Western Infirmary, Glasgow, G11 6NT; T.-0141-211 3242.

Peacock, Professor Noël A., BA, MA, Marshall Professor of French Language and Literature, University of Glasgow, since 1998; b. 28.9.45, King's Lynn; m., Sandra May Keenan; 1 s. Educ. King Edward VII Grammar School, King's Lynn; University College Cardiff. University of Glasgow: Lecturer, 1970-89, Senior Lecturer, 1989-95, Personal Professor, 1995-98; Head, Department of French, since 1990. Member, Scottish Examination Board: Modern Languages Panel, 1989-94, Universities Assessor of SCE/SYS French; Member, Higher Still Modern Languages Panel, 1995-97; Co-director and Co-founder, Le Nouveau Molieriste, since 1994. Chevalier dans l'Ordre des Palmes Académiques, 1993. Publications: La Jalousie du Barbouille et George Dandin, 1984; L'Ecole des Femmes, 1988; Dépit Amoureux, 1989; Les Femmes Savantes, 1990; Moliere in Scotland, 1993. Recreations: sport (cricket, tennis, football, golf); theatre; gardening. Address: (b.) Department of French, University of Glasgow G12 8QL; T.-0141-330 4589.

Peacock, Peter James, CBE. Convener, Highland Council; Member, Highland Regional Council, 1982-96 (held positions of Vice-Convener, Finance Chairman, Chairman, Policy and Resources Committee); Member, Highlands and Islands Convention; Honorary President, Scottish Library Association; Board Member, Centre for Highlands and Islands Policy Studies; Board Member, Scottish Natural

Heritage; Non-Executive Director, Scottish Post Office Board; Training, Organisation and Policy Consultant; b. 27.2.52, Edinburgh; 2 s. Educ. Hawick High School; Jordanhill College of Education, Glasgow. Community Worker, Orkney Islands, 1973-75; former Area Officer, Highlands, Islands, Grampian, Scottish Association of Citizens Advice Bureaux. Co-author, Vice-Chairman, subsequently Chairman of successful applicant group for Independent Local Radio franchise, Moray Firth; former Member, Highland Area Committee, SCDI; former Chairman, Scottish Library and Information Council; former Vice-President, COSLA; appointed Member, European Committee of the Regions, 1993. Recreations: ornithology; golf; watching rugby union. Address: (h.) 68 Braeside Park, Balloch, Inverness; T.-01463 790371.

Peake, Scott George Angus, BA (Hons), PhD. Head of Classics, Dollar Academy, since 1994; Actor, since 1992; Archaeologist, since 1992; b. 7.2.68, Isle of Raasay. Educ. Bedford College, London University; University of St., Andrews. Millar-Lyell Research Scholar in Classics, St. Andrews University, 1988-91; Law Researcher, Dargan Bullivant Associates, London, 1992-93. Fellow Commoner, Corpus Christi College, Cambridge, 1998; Member, Ancient Monuments Board for Scotland, since 1998. Publications: Archaeology: Theory and Practice, 1998. St. Andrews University Sportsperson of the Year, 1989. Recreations: shinty (first ever shinty blue at St. Andrews University, has played for Scottish Universities and Scotland); politics (SNP); cricket; football (Dundee F. C., shareholder in Charlton Athletic). Address: (b.) Dollar Academy, Dollar FK14 7DU; T.-01259 742511.

Peaker, Professor Malcolm, FRS, DSc, PhD, FZS, FLS, FIBiol, FRSE. Director, Hannah Research Institute, Ayr, since 1981; Hannah Professor, Glasgow University, since 1981; b. 21.8.43, Stapleford, Nottingham; m., Stephanie Jane Large; 3 s. Educ. Henry Mellish Grammar School, Nottingham; Sheffield University, BSc Zoology; DSc; University of Hong Kong, SRC NATO Scholar; PhD. ARC Institute of Animal Physiology, 1968-78; Head, Department of Physiology, Hannah Research Institute, 1978-81. Chairman, London Zoo Board, 1992-93; Vice-President, Zoological Society of London, 1992-94; Member, Editorial Board: Journal of Dairy Science, 1975-78, International Zoo Yearbook, 1978-82, Journal of Endocrinology, 1981-91; Editor, British Journal of Herpetology, 1977-81; Munro Kerr Lecture, 1997; Raine Distinguished Visitor, University of Western Australia, 1998; Scientific Governor, British Nutrition Foundation, since 1997. Publications: Salt Glands in Birds and Reptiles, 1975; Avian Physiology (Editor), 1975; Comparative Aspects of Lactation (Editor), 1977; Physiological Strategies in Lactation (Co-Editor), 1984; Intercellular Signalling in the Mammary Gland (Editor), 1995; Biological Signalling and the Mammary Gland (Editor), 1997; papers. Recreations: vertebrate zoology; natural history; golf; grumbling about bureaucrats. Address: (h.) Hannah Research Institute, Ayr KA6 5HL.

Peakin, Charles William Kelvin. Scotland Editor, The Sunday Times, since 1995; b. 22.8.60, Woking; m., Anna; 1 s. Educ. Durham School. Reporter, Alnwick Advertiser, 1979-80; District Reporter, Darlington and Stockton Times, 1980-83; freelance journalism: Northumberland, 1983-86, Glasgow, 1986-90; Assistant Editor (News), Scotland on Sunday, 1990-95. Address: (b.) 124 Portman Street, Glasgow G41 1EJ; T.-0141-420 5261.

Pears, John Charles, BSc (Hons). Rector, Paisley Grammar School, since 1995; b. 13.10.50, Castle Douglas; m., Margaret Blackwood; 2 s. Educ. Kirkcudbright Academy; Strathclyde University; Jordanhill College. Teacher, Kirkcudbright Academy; Principal Teacher: Braidhurst High School, Lenzie Academy; Assistant Rector, Kilmarnock Academy; Depute Rector, Johnstone High School. Elder, Church of Scotland. Recreations: sport; music; gardening. Address: (b.) Paisley Grammar School, Glasgow Road, Paisley; T.-0141-889 3484.

Pearson, Francis Salmond Gillespie, MA (Oxon). Painter in oils, since 1984; b. 31.7.35, Edinburgh. Educ. Fettes College, Edinburgh; University College, Oxford; Edinburgh University. National Service, Cameron Highlanders; Assistant Master, Harrow School, 1960-61 and 1967-73; Member, Faculty of Advocates, since 1964; Headmaster, Truro Cathedral School, 1974-79; Head of Arts and Languages, Welbeck College, 1979-83. Trustee, Hopetoun House Preservation Trust. Address: (h.) 28 Douglas Crescent, Edinburgh EH12 5BA; T.-0131-225 4736.

Pearson of Rannoch, Lord (Malcolm Everard MacLaren Pearson). Life Peer; b. 20.7.42; m.; 2 d.; 1 d. by pr. m. Chairman, PWS Holdings plc; founded Rannoch Trust, 1984.

Peart, Geoff, BA, MA, MIED, MRTPI. Director of Strategic Services, Falkirk Council; Director: Stirling University Innovation Park, Falkirk Enterprise Action Trust; b. 25.10.46, Jarrow; m., Kathryn; 1 s.; 1 d. Educ. Dame Allan's Boys Grammar School, Newcastle upon Tyne; Southampton University; Nottingham University. Member, Executive Commitee, SSDP, since 1998; Member, Scottish Office/COSLA Scottish Statistical Liaison Committee, 1975-91; Technical Adviser to Scottish Office/COSLA Local Government Finance Distribution Committee, 1985-91; Member, COSLA European Policy Advisory Group, 1989-91; Member, Royal Town Planning Institute Retail Working Party, 1986-87. Recreations: hill-walking; squash; tennis; films; reading. Address: (b.) Abbotsford House, David's Loan, Bainsford, Falkirk; T.-Falkirk 504948.

Peat, George Waddell, CA. Hon. Treasurer, Scottish Football Association, since 1997; Chairman, Airdrieonians Football Club, 1990-97; b. 29.10.40, Coatbridge; m., Evelyn; 1 s.; 1 d. Educ. Coatbridge High School; Glasgow University. CA: General Motors, Transport Development Group, Plessey PLC, J.W. Galloway Ltd.; private practice as CA, first on own account, then in partnership as Peat & McConnachie; Secretary, Airdrieonians FC, since 1978, Director, since 1985. Recreations: sport; music. Address: (b.) Scottish Football Association, 6 Park Gardens, Glasgow G3 7YF.

Peat, Jeremy Alastair, BA, MSc, FRSA. Chief Economist, Royal Bank of Scotland, since 1993; Honorary Professor, Heriot-Watt University; Member, European Commission "GroupEuro"; Fellow, Industry and Parliament Trust; Member, Advisory Board, Scottish Council Foundation; Council Member, Scottish Economic Society; b. 20.3.45, Haywards Heath; m., Philippa Ann; 2 d. Educ. St. Paul's School, London; Bristol University; University College London. Economic Assistant/Economic Adviser, Ministry of Overseas Development, 1969-77; Economic Adviser, Manpower Services Commission, 1978-80; Head, Employment Policy Unit, Ministry of Finance and Development Planning, Government of Botswana, 1980-84; Economic Adviser, HM Treasury, 1984-85; Senior Economic Adviser, Scottish Office, 1985-93. Recreations: walking; reading; tennis; listening to music; conservation of Rosslyn Chapel. Address: (b.) 42 St. Andrew Square, Edinburgh EH2 2YE; T.-0131-523 2277.

Peat, William Wood Watson, CBE, OStJ, JP, FRAgS. Farmer; National Governor for Scotland, BBC, and Chairman, Broadcasting Council for Scotland, 1984-89; b. 14.12.22, Denny; m., Jean McHarrie; 2 s.; 1 d. Educ. Denny Public School. Lt., Royal Signals, NW Europe and India, 1940-46; Broadcaster; National Chairman, subsequently President, Scottish Association of Young Farmers Clubs; Member, Stirling County Council, 1959-75 (Vice Convener, 1967-70); Council Member, NFU of Scotland,

1959-78 (President, 1966-67); Member, Scotish River Purification Advisory Committee, 1960-79; Board of Management, RSNH, 1960-72; General Commissioner of Income Tax, since 1962; Chairman, Scottish Advisory Committee, Association of Agriculture, 1974-79 (Vice-President, since 1979); Council, Hannah Research Institute, 1963-82; Council Member, Scottish Agricultural Organisation Society Ltd., since 1963 (President, 1974-77); Member, British Agricultural Council, 1974-84; Member, Board of Management, Oatridge Agricultural College, 1967-75; Governor, West of Scotland Agricultural College (Chairman, 1983-88); Chairman, Scottish Agricultural Colleges Ltd., 1987-90; Director, FMC plc, 1974-83; Member, Central Council for Agricultural and Horticultural Co-operation, 1967-83; Member, Co-operative Development Board, 1983-89; Member, Board of Management, British Farm Produce Council, 1964-83, BFP Committee, Food from Britain, 1984-87; Chairman, BBC Scottish Agricultural Advisory Committee, 1971-76. Recreations: amateur radio; flying. Address: (h.) 61 Stirling Road, Larbert FK5 4SG.

Peckham, Professor Gordon E., MA, PhD. Professor, Department of Physics, Heriot-Watt University, since 1992; b. 29.10.36, Bristol; 1 s.; 1 d. Educ. Bristol Grammar School; Trinity College, Cambridge. Lecturer: Reading University, 1966, Heriot Watt University, 1971; Reader, Heriot-Watt, 1972. Address: (b.) Physics Department, Heriot-Watt University, Riccarton, Edinburgh EH14 4AS; T.-0131-451 3028.

Peddie, Richard L., MA, MEd, AFBPsS. Retired; Hon. Lecturer, Strathclyde University; formerly Vice Principal, Craigie College of Education; b. 11.6.28, Grangemouth; m., Nan K. Bell; 1 s.; 2 d. Educ. Grangemouth High School; Glasgow University. Royal Signals Officer, Allied Supreme HQ (SHAPE), 1951-53; Teacher, Stirlingshire, 1953-56; Educational Psychologist, Ayrshire, 1956-59; Lecturer, Jordanhill College, 1959-64; Head, Psychology Department, Assistant Principal, Vice-Principal, Craigie College of Education, 1964-88; Member, General Teaching Council for Scotland, 1970-78; External Examiner in Education, London University Institute, 1971-76; External Examiner, Hamilton College of Education, 1977-80; Member, Scottish Examination Board, 1980-84; Member, Education Committee, British Psychological Society, 1964-68; Chairman, Glasgow University Educational Colloquium, 1966-67; Chairman, Association of Lecturers in Colleges of Education in Scotland (ALCES), 1967-69; Member, Scottish Council for Research in Education, 1962-78; Member, Executive Committee, Scottish Division of Educational and Child Psychology, 1979-84; Chairman, Association of Higher Academic Staff in Colleges of Education, 1984-87; Captain, 51 (H) Infantry Division Signals Regiment (TA), 1953-60; Vice-Chairman, Ayr Children's Panel, 1970-74; Paul Harris Fellow, Rotary Award, 1986; Church of Scotland Elder; Dean of Guild, Burgh of Ayr, 1992-93. Recreations: reading; Rotary; driving; golf. Address: (h.) 14 Glenpark Place, Alloway, Ayr KA7 4SQ; T.-01292 441996.

Peden, Professor George Cameron, MA, DPhil. Professor of History, Stirling University, since 1990; b. 16.2.43, Dundee; m., Alison Mary White; 3 s. Educ. Grove Academy, Broughty Ferry; Dundee University; Brasenose College, Oxford. Sub-Editor, Dundee Evening Telegraph, 1960-68; mature student, 1968-75; Tutorial Assistant, Department of Modern History, Dundee University, 1975-76; Temporary Lecturer, School of History, Leeds University, 1976-77; Lecturer in Economic and Social History, then Reader in Economic History, Bristol University, 1977-90; Visiting Fellow, All Souls College, Oxford, 1988-89. Publications: British Rearmament and the Treasury 1932-39, 1979; British Economic and Social Policy: Lloyd George to Margaret Thatcher, 1985; Keynes, The Treasury and British Economic Policy, 1988. Recreation: hill-walking. Address: (h.) Ardvurich, Leny Feus, Callander FK17 8AS; T.-01877 30488.

Peebles, David, FCIBS, MCT, DipM, MCIM. Head of European Regional Bank Treasuries, National Australia Bank Ltd., since 1998; b. 14.2.62, Bridge of Allan; m., Diane; 1 s. Educ. Prince Edward Boys School, Salisbury, Rhodesia. Hong Kong and Shanghai Banking Corporation, 1982-89; Midland Montagu Ltd., 1989-91; Head of Corporate Treasury – Scotland, Royal Bank of Scotland PLC, 1991-95; UK Treasurer, Clydesdale Bank PLC, 1995-98. Address: Clydesdale Bank Treasury Division, 150 Buchanan Street, Glasgow G1 2HL; T.-0141-223 4945.

Peebles, Sheriff I. A. S., QC, LLB. Sheriff of Glasgow and Strathkelvin at Glasgow. Admitted, Faculty of Advocates, 1979. Address: (b.) Sheriff Court House, 1 Carlton Place, Glasgow, G5 9DA.

Peggie, Robert Galloway Emslie, CBE, DUniv, FCCA. Chairman, Board, Edinburgh College of Art, since 1998; Chairman, Local Government Staff Commission for Scotland, 1994-97; b. 5.1.29, Bo'ness; 1 s.; 1 d. Educ. Lasswade High School. Trainee Accountant, 1946-52; Accountant in industry, 1952-57; Edinburgh Corporation, 1957-72: O. and M. Officer, Assistant City Chamberlain, Deputy City Chamberlain, Reorganisation Steering Committee; Chief Executive, Lothian Regional Council, 1974-86; Commissioner (Ombudsman) for Local Administration in Scotland, 1986-94. Former Member, Court, Heriot-Watt University (Convener, Finance Committee); Governor, Edinburgh College of Art; Trustee, Lloyds TSB Foundation. Recreation: golf. Address: 9A Napier Road, Edinburgh EH10 5AZ; T.-0131-229 6775.

Pelham Burn, Angus Maitland, LLD, JP, DL. Director, Bank of Scotland, since 1977, Chairman, Aberdeen Local Board; Chairman, Scottish Provident, 1995-98; Chairman, Aberdeen Asset Management PLC (formerly, Aberdeen Trust PLC); Chairman, Aberdeen Airport Consultative Committee, since 1986; Director, Abtrust Scotland Investment Company, 1989-96; b. 13.12.31, London; m., Anne; 4 d. Educ. Harrow; North of Scotland College of Agriculture. Hudson's Bay Company, 1951-58; Company Director, since 1958; Member, Kincardine County Council, 1967-75 (Vice Convener, 1973-75); Member, Grampian Regional Council, 1974-94; Member, Accounts Commission for Scotland, 1980-94 (Deputy Chairman, 1987-94); Chairman, Aberdeen Airport Consultative Committee, since 1986; Director, Aberdeen Association for Prevention of Cruelty to Animals, 1975-95; Chairman, Order of St. John (Aberdeen) Ltd.; Council Member, Winston Churchill Memorial Trust, 1984-94; Member, Queen's Bodyguard for Scotland (Royal Company of Archers), since 1968; Vice Lord Lieutenant, Kincardineshire, since 1978; Honorary Degree of Doctor of Law, (Robert Gordon University), 1996. Recreations: gardening; wildlife photography. Address: (b.) 68 Station Road, Banchory AB31 5YJ; T.-01330 823343.

Pelly, Frances, RSA. Sculptor; b. 21.7.47, Edinburgh. Educ. Morrison's Academy, Crieff; Duncan of Jordanstone College of Art, Dundee. Part-time lecturing, Dundee, 1974-78; full-time lecturing, Grays School of Art, Aberdeen, 1979-83. Recreations: riding; wildlife; gardening. Address: Costa Schoolhouse, Evie, Orkney; T.-0185 675 1326.

Peltenburg, Professor Edgar, BA, PhD, FSA (Scot). Professor of Archaeology, Edinburgh University, since 1993; b. 28.5.42, Montreal; m., Marie Wright; 3 s.; 1 d. Educ. Montreal; Birmingham University. Assistant Lecturer, Classics, McGill University, Montreal, 1963-66; Research Fellow in Archaeology, Birmingham University, 1966-69; Lecturer in Archaeology, Glasgow University, 1969-78; Lecturer in Near Eastern Archaeology, then Reader, Edinburgh University, 1978-93; director of excavations, Syria and Cyprus. Publications: six books; many scientific papers. Recreations: jazz; skiing. Address: (b.) Department of Archaeology, Old High School, Infirmary Street, Edinburgh; T.-0131-650 2379.

Pender, Sheriff David James, LLB (Hons). Sheriff of North Strathclyde, since 1995; b. 7.9.49, Glasgow; m., Elizabeth; 2 s.; 2 d. Educ. Queen's Park Senior Secondary School, Glasgow; Edinburgh University. Partner, MacArthur Stewart, Solicitors, Oban, 1977. Recreations: reading; travel; bridge. Address: (b.) Sheriff Courthouse, St. James Street, Paisley; T.-0141-887 5291.

Penman, David Roland, DA (Edin), DipTP (Edin), FRTPI, ARIAS, FSAScot. Reporter, Scottish Office Inquiry Reporters' Unit, since 1994; b. 6.6.36, Manchester; m., Tamara Scott; 2 s.; 1 d. Educ. George Watson's Boys' College, Edinburgh; Edinburgh College of Art. Assistant Architect, private practices, 1960-67; Partner, Bamber Hall & Partners, Edinburgh, 1967-71; Depute County Planning Officer, Argyll County Council, 1971-73; County Planning Officer, Perth & Kinross Joint County Council, 1973-75; Director of Planning, Perth and Kinross District Council, 1975-94. Chairman, RTPI Scotland, 1984, Member of Council, 1978-85; President, Dundee Institute of Architects, 1988, Member of Council, 1980-90; Chairman, Scottish Urban Archaeological Trust, since 1990; former Chairman, Duncan of Jordanstone College of Art; former Vice-Chairman, Scottish Conservation Projects Trust; Director, Action Environment Ltd.; former Council Member, National Trust for Scotland. Recreations: hill-walking; art galleries; theatre; DIY; Scots history; travel. Address: (h.) 17 Gannochy Road, Perth, PH2 7EF; T.-01738 627775.

Pennington, Christopher Royston, BSc (Hons), MB, ChB, MRCP, MD, FRCP, FRCPEdin. Consultant Physician (General Medicine and Gastroenterology), since 1979; Clinical Director, General Medicine, since 1995; Honorary Senior Lecturer in Medicine, Dundee University, since 1979; Examiner, MRCP (UK), since 1986; b. 22.2.46, Chard; m., Marcia Jane Barclay; 1 d. Educ. Shebbear College; Manchester University. House Officer, Manchester Royal Infirmary, 1970-71; Registrar in Medicine, Aberdeen Royal Infirmary, 1971-74; Lecturer in Medicine, Dundee University, 1974-79. External Examiner in Medicine, Aberdeen University, 1983-86; Examiner, Edinburgh College of Physicians; Specialty Adviser in Gastroenterology, Medical Defence Union of Scotland. Publications: Therapeutic Nutrition: A Practical Guide, 1988; book chapters and papers. Address: (h.) Balnagowan, Braehead, Invergowrie, Dundee.

Pennington, Professor (Thomas) Hugh, MB BS, PhD, FRCPath, FRCPEdin, FRSA, FMedSci, FRSE. Professor of Bacteriology, University of Aberdeen, since 1979; b. 19.4.38, Edgware, Middlesex; m., Carolyn Ingram Beattie; 2 d. Educ. Lancaster Royal Grammar School; St. Thomas's Hospital Medical School, London University. House appointments, St. Thomas's Hospital, 1962-63; Assistant Lecturer in Medical Microbiology, St. Thomas's Hospital Medical School, 1963-67; Postdoctoral Fellow, University of Wisconsin (Madison), 1967-68; Lecturer then Senior Lecturer in Virology, University of Glasgow, 1969-79; Dean of Medicine University of Aberdeen, 1987-92. Governor, Rowett Research Institute, 1980-88; Chairman, Expert Group on 1996 E.coli Outbreak in Central Scotland; Caroline Walker Trust Consumer Advocate Award, 1997; Royal Institute of Public Health John Kershaw Memorial Prize, 1998. Recreations: collecting books; dipterology. Address: (b.) Department of Medical Microbiology, University of Aberdeen, Aberdeen AB25 2ZD; T.-01224 681818, Ext. 52786.

Penrose, Hon. Lord (George William Penrose), QC (Scot). Senator of the College of Justice, since 1990; b. 2.6.38. Advocate, 1964; QC, 1978; Procurator to General Assembly of Church of Scotland, 1984-90.

Pentland, Brian, BSc, MB, ChB, FRCPE, FRCSLT. Consultant Neurologist in Rehabilitation Medicine, since 1982; Senior Lecturer in Rehabilitation Studies, Edinburgh University, since 1983; b. 24.6.49, Glasgow; m., Gillian Mary Duggua; 4 s. Educ. Liberton High School, Edinburgh; Edinburgh University. Junior hospital appointments in Edinburgh, Cumbria and Dundee; formerly Lecturer in Neurology in Edinburgh. Recreation: hill-walking. Address: (b.) Astley Ainslie Hospital, Grange Loan, Edinburgh EH9 2HL; T.-0131-537 9039.

Peppé, William Lawrence Tosco, OBE, JP, DL, FIMgt; b. 25.11.37, India; m., Deirdre Eva Preston Wakefield; 3 s. Educ. Wellington College; King's College, Cambridge. Naval Officer, 1955-91 – Commander. Recreation: country. Address: (h.) Glendrynoch Lodge, Carbost, Isle of Skye IV47 8SX; T.-01478 640218.

Pepper, Simon Richard, BSc, MSc. Head, WWF Scotland (World Wide Fund for Nature), since 1985; b. 27.9.47, Worthing; m., Morag; 2 s.; 3 d. Educ. Aberdeen University; University College London. Quelea Project, Chad, Central Africa, 1972-73; Country Parks Officer, Essex County Council, 1973-79; Director, Cultullich Holiday Courses, Aberfeldy, 1979-85. Vice Convenor, Millennium Forest for Scotland, since 1995; Member, Secretary of State's Advisory Group on Sustainable Development, since 1994; Member, Environment Advisory Sub-Committee, Forestry Commission, 1993-96. Recreations: enjoying the wild; managing sheep and native woodland of 42 hectare holding. Address: (h.) Upper Brae of Cultullich, Aberfeldy PH15 2EN.

Percy, Professor John Pitkeathly (Ian), CBE, CA, FRSA. Former Senior Partner, Grant Thornton, Scotland; Chairman: The Accounts Commission, MacDonald Orr Ltd.; Deputy Chairman, Scottish Provident Institution; Non-Executive Director: Morgan Grenfell (Scotland) Ltd., Beale Dobie (Scot) Ltd., William Wilson (Holdings) Ltd., The Weir Group PLC, Kiln PLC, The Edinburgh Academy (Chairman, Court of Directors); Vice Chairman, UK Auditing Practices Board; Member, International Auditing Practices Committee; Chairman, International Task Force on Corporate Governance; b. 16.1.42, Southport; m., Sheila; 2 d. Educ. Edinburgh Academy; Edinburgh University. Managing Partner, Grant Thornton, London, 1981-88; Honorary Professor of Accounting, Aberdeen University, 1988. Freeman, City of London; Member, British Academy of Experts; Elder, St. Cuthbert's Church of Scotland; President, Institute of Chartered Accountants of Scotland, 1990-91. Recreations: golf; fishing. Address: (b.) 1 St. Colme Street, Edinburgh EH3 6AA; T.-0131-220 8214; (h.) 30 Midmar Drive, Edinburgh; T.-0131-447 3645.

Perfect, Hugh Epton, BSc. Associate Dean (General), Faculty of Education, Edinburgh University; b. 9.4.41, London; m., Susan; 2 d. Educ. Haberdasher's Askes' School, Hampstead; Imperial College, London. Teacher, Windsor Grammar School; Lecturer, Bulmershe College of Education, Reading; Lecturer/Senior Lecturer, Biology Department, Moray House, and Senior Assistant Principal, until 1998. Recreations: badminton; gardening; micro-computers. Address: (b.) Faculty of Education, Edinburgh University, Holyrood Road, Edinburgh EH8 8AQ; T.-0131-558 6168.

Perman, Ray, BA, MBA. Chief Executive, Scottish Financial Enterprise, since 1999; b. 22.8.47, London; m., Fay Young; 3 s. Educ. Hemel Hempstead Grammar School; University of St. Andrews; Open University; University of Edinburgh. Journalist, 1970-83: The Times, Financial Times, Sunday Standard; Managing Director, Insider Publications, 1983-94; Development Director, Caledonian Publishing, 1994-96. Member: Scottish Council, WWF; Member, Board, Centre for Entrepreneurial Finance. Recreations: painting; forestry; playing the blues guitar.

Address: (b.) 91 George Street, Edinburgh EH2 3ES; T.-0131-225 6990.

Perry, Professor Clive Graham, OBE, MA (Cantab), Hon. MA (Leicester). Festival Director, Pitlochry Festival Theatre, since 1987; Professor of Theatre, Queen Margaret College, Edinburgh, since 1997; (Professor and Head, Department of Drama, Queen Margaret College, Edinburgh, 1990-96); b. 17.3.36, Harrow. Educ. Wolverhampton Grammar School; Harrow County Grammar School; Cambridge University. Awarded Thames TV Scholarship to regional theatre, 1960-61; Assistant Director, Derby Playhouse; Associate Director, Castle Theatre, Farnham; Director of Productions, Phoenix Theatre, Leicester; Director, Royal Lyceum Theatre, Edinburgh, 1966-76 (Director of Theatres in Edinburgh, 1971-76); Director, Birmingham Repertory Theatre, 1976-87. Recreation: theatre. Address: (b.) Pitlochry Festival Theatre, Port-Na-Craig, Pitlochry PH16 5DR; T.-01796 473054.

Perry, John Scott (Jack), BSc, CA, CPA. Office Managing Partner, Ernst and Young, Glasgow, since 1995; b. 23.11.54, Glasgow; m., Lydia Margaret Cox; 1 s.; 2 d. Educ. Glasgow Academy; Glasgow University; Strathclyde University. Joined Ernst and Young, 1976; transferred to Ernst and Young, Dallas, Texas, 1981-83; seconded to Scottish Development Finance, 1987-88; appointed Partner, Ernst and Young, Glasgow, 1988; Head of Audit, 1994-95. Member, CBI Scotland Council, since 1995; Director, Pollok School Company. Recreations: golf; skiing. Address: (b.) George House, 50 George Square, Glasgow G2 1RR; T.-0141-552 3456.

Perry of Walton, Rt. Hon. Lord (Walter Laing Macdonald Perry), Kt, OBE, MB, ChB, MD, DSc, FRCP, FRCPE, FRSE, FRS. President, Videotel Marine International; Life Peer, since 1979; b. 16.6.21, Dundee; m., 1, Anne Grant (m. dissolved); 3 s.; 2, Catherine Crawley; 2 s.; 1 d. Educ. Morgan Academy; Ayr Academy; Dundee High School; University College Dundee, St. Andrews University. Medical Officer, Colonial Service, 1944-46; RAF, 1946-47; Medical Research Council: member of staff, 1947-52, Director, Department of Biological Standards, 1952-58; Professor of Pharmacology, Edinburgh University, 1958-68; Vice-Chancellor, The Open University, 1968-81. Member, Editorial Board, Encyclopaedia Britannica, since 1971; Member of Kuratorium, Fernuniversitat, Hagen, W. Germany, since 1976; Hon. Director, International Centre for Distance Learning, since 1983; Member, Academic Advisory Committee, University of E. Asia, Macau, since 1984; Member, Board, University of the World, since 1987; Member, Select Committee of Science and Technology, House of Lords, since 1997. Recreations: golf; music; reading. Address: (h.) 2 Cramond Road South, Edinburgh EH4 6AD.

Perth, 17th Earl of (John David Drummond), PC (1957); b. 13.5.07; m., Nancy Seymour Fincke; 2 s. Educ. Downside; Cambridge University. Lt., Intelligence Corps, 1940; War Cabinet Offices, 1942-43; Ministry of Production, 1944-45; Minister of State for Colonial Affairs, 1957-62; First Crown Estate Commissioner, 1962-77; Member, Court, St. Andrews University, 1967-86; Trustee, National Library of Scotland, 1968-95. Hon. LLD; Hon. FRIBA; Hon. FRIAS. Address: (h.) Stobhall, by Perth PH2 6DR; T.-01821 640 332.

Petch, Professor Alison Jean, BA, MA, PhD, DipSW. Nuffield Professor of Community Care Studies, Glasgow University, since 1993; b. 5.4.50, Leeds; m., David Jarman; 2 s. Educ. Central Newcastle High School; Cambridge University. Research Planner, Livingston Development Corporation, 1973-75; Research Fellow, Edinburgh University, 1983-86; Research Fellow, then Senior Research Fellow, Social Work Research Centre, Stirling University, 1986-93. Council Member, Alzheimer Scotland. Address: (b.) Nuffield Centre for Community Care Studies, Gregory Building, Glasgow University, Glasgow G12 8RZ; T.-0141-330 5600.

Peterken, Laurence Edwin, CBE, MA. Consultant; Member, Criminal Injuries Compensation Appeal Panel, since 1997; Director, Special Projects, NHS in Scotland, 1993-96; Visiting Professor Elect, Glasgow Caledonian University; b. 2.10.31, London; m., 1, Hanne Birgithe Von Der Recke (deceased); 1 s.; 1 d.; 2, Margaret Raynal Blair; 1 s.; 1 d. Educ. Harrow School (Scholar); Peterhouse, Cambridge (Scholar). Pilot Officer, RAF Regt., Adjt. No. 20 LAA Sqdn., 1950-52; Service Divisional Manager, Hotpoint Ltd., 1961-63; Commercial Director, then Managing Director, British Domestic Appliances Ltd., 1963-68; Director, British Printing Corporation Ltd., 1969-73; Managing Director, Fashion Multiple Division, Debenhams Ltd., 1974-76; Management Auditor, 1976-77; Controller, Operational Services, GLC, 1977-85; President, GLC Chief Officers' Guild, 1983-85; Acting Director, Royal Festival Hall, 1983-85; General Manager, Greater Glasgow Health Board, 1986-93; Chairman, Glasgow and West of Scotland Institute of Public Administration, since 1993; Member, Scottish Committee, Council for Music in Hospitals, since 1996; Trustee, The Rodolfs Choir, since 1998. Recreations: music; cycling. Address: (h.) Langdales, Houston House, Houston, Renfrewshire PA6 7AR.

Peters, Kenneth Jamieson, CBE, JP, DL, FRSA, FSA Scot, Assoc. MCIT. Deputy Lieutenant, City of Aberdeen, since 1978; Vice-Chairman, Peterhead Bay Authority, 1989-96; b. 17.1.23, London; m., Arunda Merle Jane Jones. Educ. Aberdeen Grammar School; Aberdeen University. Served Second World War; commissioned Queen's Own Cameron Highlanders; also King's Own Scottish Borderers; editorial staff, Scottish Daily Record and Evening News Ltd., 1947-51; Assistant Editor, Aberdeen Evening Express, 1951-52; Assistant Editor, Manchester Evening Chronicle, 1952-53; Editor, Aberdeen Evening Express, 1953-56; Editor, Press and Journal, Aberdeen, 1956-60; Managing Director, Aberdeen Journals Ltd., 1960-80, Chairman, 1980-81; Director: Thomson North Sea, 1981-88, Thomson Scottish Petroleum, 1981-86, Thomson Forestry Holdings, 1982-88, Highland Printers Ltd., 1968-83; President, Scottish Daily Newspaper Society, 1964-66 and 1974-76; Member, Press Council, 1974-77; Director, Thomson Regional Newspapers, 1974-81; Director, Aberdeen Association of Social Service, 1973-78; Member, British Railways (Scottish) Board, 1982-92; Member, Girobank, Scotland Board, 1984-90; Member, Executive, Scottish Council (Development and Industry), 1982-88 (Chairman, Aberdeen and North-East Committee, 1982-88); Fellow, SCDI, 1989; Member, Scottish Advisory Committee, British Council, 1967-84; National Committee Member, Films of Scotland, 1970-82; Burgess of Guild, City of Aberdeen, 1963. Publications: The Northern Lights, 1978; Burgess of Guild, 1982; Great North Memories, Vol. 1 and Vol. 2 (Editor). Recreations: walking; cricket; rugby football. Address: 47 Abergeldie Road, Aberdeen AB10 6ED; T.-01224 587647.

Peterson, George Sholto, NP. Solicitor and Notary Public, since 1956; Honorary Sheriff, since 1982; b. 18.9.27, Lerwick; m., Dorothy Hilda Spence; 2 s.; 4 d. Educ. Lerwick Central Public School; Edinburgh University. Secretary, The Shetland Trust; Factor for the Marquess of Zetland; Senior Partner, Tait & Peterson, Solicitors and Estate Agents, Lerwick; Honorary Pastor, Ebenezer Church, Lerwick. Recreations: studying theology; reading; fishing. Address: (b.) Bank of Scotland Buildings, Lerwick, Shetland; T.-01595 693010.

Pethrick, Professor Richard Arthur, BSc, PhD, DSc, FRSC, FRSE. Professor in Chemistry, Strathclyde University, since 1983 (Head of Department, since 1992);

b. 26.10.42; m., Joan Knowles Hume; 1 s. Educ. North Gloucestershire College, Cheltenham; London University; Salford University. Editor: British Polymer Journal, Polymer Yearbook, Polymer International, International Journal of Polymer Materials; Member, Polymer Committee, European Science Foundation; Member, Committee, MACRO Group, 1979-84; Member, SERC Polymer Materials Committee, since 1994; Elder, Merrylea Church of Scotland. Address: (b.) Department of Pure and Applied Chemistry, University of Strathclyde, Thomas Graham Building, Cathedral Street, Glasgow G1 1XL.

Petrie, Professor James Colquhoun, CBE, FRCPEdin, FRCP, FFPM, FRCP Ireland, FAMS (Hon), FCMSA (Hon), FRCGP (Hon). President, Royal College of Physicians of Edinburgh, since 1998; Professor of Clinical Pharmacology, since 1985, Head, Department of Medicine and Therapeutics, Aberdeen University, since 1994; Honorary Consultant Physician, Aberdeen Teaching Hospitals, since 1971; b. 18.9.41, Aberdeen; m., Dr. M. Xanthe P.; 2 s.; 2 d. Educ. Anieres, Geneva; Robert Gordon's College, Aberdeen; Aberdeen University. Senior Lecturer, 1971-81, Reader, 1981-85, Aberdeen University. Chairman, Lecht Ski Company, since 1976. Recreations: ski; golf; fishing. Address: (b.) Department of Medicine and Therapeutics, Aberdeen Royal Infirmary, Foresterhill, Aberdeen AB9 2ZB; T.-01224 681818.

Phelps, Professor Alan David Reginald, MA, DPhil, CPhys, FInstP, FRSE. Professor, Physics and Applied Physics, Strathclyde University, since 1993, Head of Department, since 1998; Chairman, Plasma Physics Group, Institute of Physics, 1995-97; b. 2.6.44, Basingstoke; m., Susan Helen Marshall; 1 d. Educ. Haverfordwest Grammar School; King's College, Cambridge; University College, Oxford. Research Associate, National Academy of Sciences (USA), 1972-73; Research Officer, Oxford University, 1973-78; Lecturer, then Senior Lecturer, then Reader in Physics, Strathclyde University, 1978-93, Deputy Head of Department, 1993-98. Publications: 200 research papers and reports. Recreations: hill-walking; country pursuits. Address: (b.) Department of Physics and Applied Physics, John Anderson Building, Strathclyde University, Glasgow G4 0NG; T.-0141-548 3166.

Philip, Hon. Lord (Alexander Morrison). Senator of the College of Justice, since 1996; b. 3.8.42, Aberdeen; m., Shona Mary Macrae; 3 s. Educ. Glasgow High School; St. Andrews University; Glasgow University. Solicitor, 1967-72; Advocate, 1973; Advocate Depute, 1982-85; QC, 1984; Chairman, Medical Appeal Tribunals, 1988-92; Chairman, Scottish Land Court, 1993-96; President, Lands Tribunal for Scotland, 1993-96. Recreations: piping; golf. Address: (b.) Parliament House, Edinburgh EH1 1RQ; T.-0131-225 2595.

Philips, Douglas John, MHSM, DipHSM. Director of Priority Services and Joint Planning, Argyll and Clyde Health Board, since 1997 (Director of Community Care Development, 1992-97); b. 30.4.53, Edinburgh; m., Morag S. Hall. Educ. Dalkeith High School. Formerly General Manager, Northern Unit, Highland Health Board. Winston Churchill Memorial Trust Fellow, 1996. Recreations: walking the Dalmatians; hill-walking; rambling; cycling; gardening; reading fiction; music; Coronation Street. Address: (h.) Windsong, Blairuskinmore, Kinlochard, Stirling FK8 3TP; T.-01877 387236.

Phillips, Professor John Clifford, BSc, CMath, FIMA, FRSA, MIMgt. Vice-Principal, Glasgow Caledonian University, since 1993; Chief Executive, Glasgow Caledonian University Company, since 1995; Chairman, Glasgow Caledonian University Nominee Company Ltd., since 1996; b. 29.1.43, Dyfed; m., Anne Margaret; 1 s.; 1 d. Educ. Llandeilo Grammar School; University of Wales, Aberystwyth. Lecturer, Lancashire Polytechnic, 1967-69, Leeds Polytechnic, 1969-71; Leeds Polytechnic: Senior Lecturer, 1971-77, Principal Lecturer, 1977-86, Head, School of Mathematics and Computing, 1986-87, Dean, Faculty of Engineering and Computing, 1987-88, Senior Executive, External Development, 1988-90; Principal, The Queen's College, Glasgow, 1991-93. Former Member, North Yorkshire County Council. Recreations: reading; walking; architectural conservation. Address: (b.) Glasgow Caledonian University, Cowcaddens Road, Glasgow G4 0BA.

Phillips, Professor John H., MA, PhD. Professor of Biology Teaching and Vice-Provost of Medicine and Veterinary Medicine, Edinburgh University, since 1996; b. 19.2.41, York; m., Kerstin B. Halling; 2 d. Educ. Leighton Park School, Reading; Christ's College, Cambridge. Lecturer in Biochemistry, Makerere University, Uganda, 1967-69; scientific staff, MRC Laboratory of Molecular Biology, Cambridge, 1969-74; Department of Biochemistry, Edinburgh University, 1974-88, Director of Biology Teaching, 1988-93, Head, Department of Biochemistry, 1993-96. Recreations: natural history; Scottish mountains; visits to Sweden. Address: (h.) 46 Granby Road, Edinburgh EH16 5NW; T.-0131-667 5322.

Pia, Paul Dominic, LLB (Hons), WS. Senior Partner, Burness (formerly W. & J. Burness WS), since 1974; Chairman, Japan Society of Scotland, since 1996; b. 29.3.47, Edinburgh; m., Anne Christine Argent; 3 d. Educ. Holy Cross Academy, Edinburgh; Edinburgh University; University of Perugia. Law apprentice, Lindsays WS, 1968-70; admitted as Solicitor and member of Society of Writers to HM Signet, 1971; Solicitor, W. & J. Burness WS, 1971-74; Associate Member, American Bar Association; Fellow, Institute of Directors. Publication: Care Diligence and Skill (handbook for directors). Recreations: hill walking; travel; foreign languages. Address: (b.) 50 Lothian Road, Edinburgh; T.-0131-473 6000.

Pickard, Willis Ritchie, MA (Hons), Hon. LLD (Aberdeen), FSQA. Editor, Times Educational Supplement Scotland, since 1977; Rector, Aberdeen University, 1988-90; b. 21.5.41, Dunfermline; m., Ann; 2 d. Educ. Daniel Stewart's College; St. Andrews University. The Scotsman: Leader Writer, 1967-72, Features Editor, 1972-77. Former Member, Scottish Arts Council; Chairman, Book Trust Scotland, 1991-95; Liberal candidate, East Fife, 1970 and February, 1974. Address: (b.) Scott House, 10 South St Andrew Street, Edinburgh EH2 2AZ; T.-0131-220 1100.

Pickett, James, BSc (Econ), MLit. Professor Emeritus, Strathclyde University, since 1995; b. 7.6.29, Greenock; m., Janet Clelland; 1 s.; 3 d. Educ. Greenock Academy; School of Economics, Dundee; Edinburgh University; Glasgow University; University of Paris. Statistician, Dominion Bureau of Statistics, Canada; Lecturer, Senior Lecturer, Professor and Director, Livingstone Institute of Overseas Development, Strathclyde University, 1961-95; Special Economic Adviser, UN Economic Commision for Africa; Visiting Professor, University of Saskatchewan; Economic Adviser, African Development Bank; UN Chief Economic Adviser to Ethiopian Government, 1992-95; Consultant to British, Canadian and Ghanian Governments, UN, OECD; author and editor, seven books and numerous papers; FRSA; sometime President, Scottish Union of Students. Recreations: hill-walking; listening to music; photography; computing; long-suffering support of Greenock Morton F.C. Address: (h.) 1 Divert Road, Gourock PA19 1DR; T.-01475 631046.

Pidgeon, Professor Carl R., BSc, PhD, FRSE. Professor of Semiconductor Physics and Head, Physics Department, Heriot Watt University; b. 27.11.37, London; 1 s.; 1 d. Educ. Reading University. Staff Member, National Magnet Laboratory, MIT, 1964-71; Reader in Physics, Heriot Watt

University, 1971-83. Recreations: golf; skiing. Address: (b.) Physics Department, Heriot Watt University, Edinburgh.

Pignatelli, Frank, MA, MEd, DUniv, FIMgt, FSQA, FICPD, FScotVec, FRSA. Chief Executive, Scottish Business in the Community, since 1998; Corporate Consultant, Motorola (Europe, Middle East and Africa), since 1997; Chairman and Managing Director, ESD, since 1997; b. 22.12.46, Glasgow; m., Rosetta Anne; 1 s.; 1 d. Educ. St. Mungo's Academy, Glasgow; University of Glasgow. Executive Director of Education, Strathclyde Regional Council, 1988-96; Group Director, Human Resources, Associated Newspapers, London, 1996-97. Chairman, Association for Management Education and Training in Scotland; President, Scottish Association for Language Teaching; Director, Quality Scotland Foundation; Visiting Professor, Glasgow University. Recreations: genealogy; DIY; stained glass design and construction. Address: (h.) 10 Whittingehame Drive, Glasgow G12 0XX; T.-0141-334 3458.

Pike, (Kathryn) Lorna, MA (Hons). Editor, Dictionary of the Older Scottish Tongue, since 1986; b. 8.8.56, Fort William. Educ. Lochaber High School, Fort William; Edinburgh University. Editor, Concise Scots Dictionary, 1979-83; Assistant Editor, Dictionary of the Older Scottish Tongue, 1984-86. Secretary, Scottish Text Society. Recreations: riding; photography; handicrafts. Address: (b.) 27 George Square, Edinburgh, EH8 9LD; T.-0131-650 4147.

Pilcher, Rosamunde. Author; b. 22.9.24, Lelant, Cornwall. Began publishing short stories in Woman and Home, 1945; since then has published hundreds of short stories. Novels include Sleeping Tiger, Under Gemini, Wild Mountain Thyme, The Carousel, Voices in Summer, The Shell Seekers, September, The Blue Bedroom, Flowers in the Rain, Coming Home; play: The Dashing White Sergeant. Address: (h.) Penrowan, Longforgan, Perthshire; T.-Dundee 360393.

Piper, Professor Ronald Allen, BA, BD, PhD. Principal, St. Mary's College, St. Andrews University, since 1992, Head, School of Divinity, since 1992, Professor of Christian Origins, since 1997; b. 27.3.48, U.S.A.; m., Faith Elizabeth Woodhouse; 1 d. Educ. Pomona College, Claremont, California; London University. Lecturer in New Testament Studies, Aberdeen University, 1979-80; Lecturer in New Testament Language and Literature, St. Andrews University, 1980-92, Reader in New Testament, 1992-97. Secretary, British New Testament Society, 1990-93. Publications: Wisdom in the Q-Tradition, 1989; The Gospel Behind the Gospels, 1995; numerous journal articles. Address: (b.) St. Mary's College, St. Andrews KY16 9JU; T.-01334 462850.

Pippard, Professor Martin John, BSc, MB, ChB, FRCPath, FRCP. Professor of Haematology, Dundee University, since 1989; Honorary Consultant Haematologist, Dundee Teaching Hospitals Trust, since 1989; b. 16.1.48, London; m., Grace Elizabeth; 2 s.; 1 d. Educ. Buckhurst Hill County High School; Birmingham University. House Physician and House Surgeon, 1972-73; Senior Medical House Officer, 1973-75; Research Fellow, Nuffield Department of Clinical Medicine, Oxford, 1975-78; MRC Travelling Research Fellow, University of Washington, Seattle, 1978-80; Wellcome Trust Research Fellow and Clinical Lecturer, Nuffield Department of Clinical Medicine, 1980-83; Consultant Haematologist, MRC Clinical Research Centre and Northwick Park Hospital, 1983-88. Recreations: gardening; fell-walking. Address: (b.) Department of Molecular and Cellular Pathology, Ninewells Hospital and Medical School, Dundee DD1 9SY; T.-01382 660111.

Pirie, Professor Hugh Munro, BVMS, PhD, MRCVS, FRCPath, DipECVP. Professor of Systemic Veterinary Pathology, Department of Veterinary Pathology, Glasgow University; b. 10.4.36, Glasgow; m., Myrtle Elizabeth Stewart Levack; 1 d. Educ. Coatbridge High School; Glasgow University. Scientific Editor, Research in Veterinary Science, 1981-88; British Council Specialist, Argentina, 1982, Ethiopia, 1986-88. President, Association of Veterinary Teachers and Research Workers, 1984; Secretary, European Association of Establishments for Veterinary Education, 1988-92; Chairman, Veterinary Panel, Royal College of Pathologists, 1988-93; Member, Council, Royal College of Veterinary Surgeons, 1993-98; Diplomate, European College of Veterinary Pathologists, 1995; Member, Board, European Society of Veterinary Pathology, 1994-98. Recreations: travel; gardening; hill-walking; swimming; gastronomy. Address: (h.) North East Corner, Buchanan Castle Estate, Drymen G63 0HX; T.-01361 660781.

Pirie, Sheriff Iain Gordon, MA, LLB. Sheriff of Glasgow and Strathkelvin, since 1982; b. 15.1.33, Dundee; m., Dr. Sheila B. Pirie; 2 s.; 1 d. Educ. Harris Academy, Dundee; St. Andrews University. Procurator Fiscal, Dumfries, 1971-76, Ayr, 1976-79; Sheriff of South Strathclyde, Dumfries and Galloway, 1979-82. Address: (b.) Sheriff Court, 1 Carlton Place, Glasgow G5 9DA; T.-0141-429 8888.

Pitcaithly, Mary, LLB. Chief Executive, Falkirk Council, since 1998; b. 17.7.56; m., Euan; 1 d. Educ. Falkirk High School; Edinburgh University. Falkirk District Council: Solicitor, 1980-82, Senior Solicitor, 1982-85, Principal Solicitor, 1985-89, Depute Director of Law and Administration, 1989-95; Assistant Chief Executive, Falkirk Council, 1995-98. Address: 15 Greenhorn's Well Drive, Falkirk FK1 5HJ.

Pitches, Sally Jane, LLB, NP. Executive Director, The Guide Association, since 1997; b. 5.6.57, Edinburgh. Educ. Currie High School; Strathclyde University. Solicitor, private practice, Edinburgh. Founding President, Edinburgh Breakfast Rotary Club; Senator, Junior Chamber International. Recreations: cookery; bridge; travel. Address: (b.) 16 Coates Crescent, Edinburgh; T.-0131-226 4545.

Pitt, Professor Douglas Charles, BA, MA, PhD, FBIM. Professor of Organisational Analysis, Strathclyde University, since 1989; Dean, Strathclyde Business School; b. 13.7.43, Greenock; m., Jean Hamilton Spowart. Educ. Varndean Grammar School, Brighton; Exeter University; Manchester University. Executive Officer, Civil Service, 1961-64; Lecturer, then Senior Lecturer and Reader, Strathclyde University, 1973-89. Current research interest: telecommunications deregulation in Britain and the USA. Publications: The Post Office Telecommunications Function, 1980; Public Administration: An Introduction, 1980; Government Departments: An Organisational Analysis, 1981; The Computer Revolution in Public Administration, 1984. Recreations: German; riding; swimming; fishing; skiing; sailing; traditional jazz; bluegrass; opera. Address: (h.) 19 Waterfoot Road, Newton Mearns, Glasgow G77 5RU; T.-0141-639 5359.

Pittock, Professor Murray G.H., MA, DPhil, FRHistS, FSAScot. Professor in Literature, Strathclyde University, since 1996; Editor, Scottish Literary Journal, since 1995; b. 5.1.62; m., Anne Grace Thornton Martin; 2 d. Educ. Aberdeen Grammar School; Glasgow University; Balliol College, Oxford (Snell Exhibitioner). Lecturer, Pembroke College, Oxford, 1987; British Academy Postdoctoral Fellow, Aberdeen University, 1988; Lecturer, Edinburgh University, 1989, Reader, 1994 (from 1995 Co-ordinator, University in Scotland Initiative). Royal Society of Edinburgh BP Humanities Research Prize, 1992-94. Publications: The Invention of Scotland, 1991; Spectrum of Decadence, 1993; Poetry and Jacobite Politics in Eighteenth-Century Britain and Ireland, 1994; The Myth of the Jacobite Clans, 1995; Inventing and Resisting Britain,

1997; Jacobitism, 1998. Address: (b.) English Studies, Strathclyde University, Richmond Street, Glasgow, G1 1XH; T.-0141-548 4490.

Pitts, Professor Nigel Berry, BDS (Hons), PhD, FDS, RCSEng, FDS, RCSEdin. Director, Dental Health Services Research Unit, since 1985; Head, Department of Dental Health, Dundee University, 1990-97, and Professor of Dental Health, since 1991; Dean of Dentistry, since 1997; b. 1954, London; m., Elizabeth Ann; 3 s. Educ. Royal Liberty School; London Hospital Medical College Dental School, London University. House Officer/Senior House Officer, The London Hospital; Lecturer, Department of Conservative Dentistry, London Hospital Medical College Dental School; Lecturer, then Senior Lecturer, Department of Conservative Dentistry, University of Hong Kong; Director, Chief Scientist's Office Dental Health Services Research Unit; International Director, Behavioral Sciences and Health Services Research Group, International Association for Dental Research; Past President, British Association for the Study of Community Dentistry; President, Diagnostic Systems Group, International Association for Dental Research. Recreations: family; photography. Address: (b.) Dental School, Park Place, Dundee DD1 4HR; T.-01382 635959.

Platt, Joseph, LLB. Founding Partner, Philpott Platt and Niblett and Wight, Solicitors, Dumbarton; part-time Lecturer, Glasgow University; Member, Council, Law Society of Scotland; b. 22.5.51, Dumbarton; m., Christina Susan; 2 s. Educ. Dumbarton Academy; Glasgow University. Qualified as Solicitor, 1974; Partner, J.W. Dunn & Co., 1976. Recreations: hill-walking; photography; reading. Address: 105 Glasgow Road, Dumbarton; T.-01389 733777.

Plotkin, Professor Gordon David, BSc, PhD, FRS, FRSE. Professor in Computer Science, Edinburgh University; b. 9.9.46, Glasgow; m.; 1 s. Educ. Glasgow High School for Boys; Glasgow University; Edinburgh University. Lecturer, then Reader, Edinburgh University; Director, Laboratory for the Foundation of Computer Science; Member, Academia Europaea; Editor: Information and Computation, Mathematical Structures in Computer Science, Theoretical Computer Science. Recreations: chess; hill-walking. Address: (b.) Division of Informatics, King's Buildings, Edinburgh University, Edinburgh; T.-0131-650 5158.

Pollacchi, Derek Albert Paterson. Chief Executive, Central Scotland Healthcare NHS Trust, since 1994; b. 23.7.51, Dumbarton; m., Jean Lindsay Mullan; 2 d. Educ. St. Mungo's Academy, Glasgow. Various junior/middle management positions, 1972-79; Senior Administrator, Mearnskirk General Hospital, Glasgow, 1979-83, Leverndale Hospital, Glasgow, 1983-84; Director of Administrative Services, Lennox Castle Hospital/Stobill General Hospital and associated community health services, 1984-87; General Manager, Mental Handicap Services, Forth Valley Health Board, 1987-92; Chief Executive, Royal Scottish National Hospital and Community NHS Trust, 1993-94. Recreations: swimming; badminton; hill-walking; reading. Address: (b.) Old Denny Road, Larbert FK5 4SD; T.-01324 570700.

Pollock, Sheriff Alexander, MA (Oxon), LLB. Sheriff of Grampian, Highland and Islands, at Aberdeen and Stonehaven, since 1993; b. 21.7.44, Glasgow; m., Verena Francesca Gertraud Alice Ursula Critchley; 1 s.; 1 d. Educ. Rutherglen Academy; Glasgow Academy; Brasenose College, Oxford; Edinburgh University; Perugia University. Partner, Bonar Mackenzie & Kermack, WS, 1971-73; called to Scottish Bar, 1973; Conservative candidate: West Lothian, General Election, February 1974, Moray and Nairn, General Election, October 1974; MP, Moray and Nairn, 1979-83, Moray, 1983-87; Parliamentary Private Secretary to Secretary of State for Scotland, 1982-86; PPS to Secretary of State for Defence, 1986-87; Advocate Depute, 1990-91; Sheriff (Floating) of Tayside, Central and Fife, at Stirling, 1991-93. Member, Queen's Bodyguard for Scotland (Royal Company of Archers), since 1984. Recreations: walking; music. Address: (h.) Drumdarrach, Forres, Moray.

Ponsonby, Bernard Joseph. Reporter/Presenter, Scottish Television, since 1990; b. Glasgow. Educ. Trinity High School, Rutherglen; Strathclyde University. Researcher to Rt. Hon. Dr. Dickson Mabon, 1987; Press Officer, Scottish Liberal Democrats, 1988-89; party's first Parliamentary candidate, Glasgow Govan, 1988; PR and Media Consultant, freelance Reporter for BBC Radio Scotland, 1989-90; Principal Presenter of political, election, and by-election programmes, Scottish Television; presented Platform, since 1996, Scottish Voices, Scottish Questions, Trial by Night. Recreations: golf; Celtic Football Club. Address: (b.) Scottish Television, Cowcaddens, Glasgow G2 3PR; T.-0141 300 3000.

Ponton, Professor John Wylie, BSc, PhD, FIChemE, FEng. Professor of Chemical Engineering, Edinburgh University, since 1989; b. 2.5.43, Edinburgh; m., Katherine Jane Victoria Eachus. Educ. Melville College, Edinburgh; Edinburgh University. Recreations: engineering; amateur radio; music. Address: (b.) Department of Chemical Engineering, Edinburgh University, EH9 3JL; T.-0131-650 4860.

Poole, Sheriff Isobel Anne, LLB. Sheriff of Lothian and Borders; b. 9.12.41, Oxford. Educ. Oxford High School for Girls (GPDST); Edinburgh University. Advocate. Recreations: country; arts; gardens; friends. Address: (b.) Sheriffs' Chambers, Sheriff Court, Edinburgh.

Pope, Professor Malcolm, MS, PRD, DrMedSc, Eur Ing, CEng. Professor and Chair of Health and Safety, University of Aberdeen, since 1998; Director, Liberty Worksafe Centre, Aberdeen, since 1998; b. 11.2.41, London; m., Catherine; 2 s.; 1 d. BAC, UK, 1962-66; United Technologies (NASA), 1966-70; Funded Professor and Director, University of Vermont, 1966-94; Endowed Professor, Director and Chair of Biomedical Engineering, Professor of Mechanical Engineering, Preventive Medicine, Orthopaedic Surgery, University of Iowa, 1994-98. Publications: six books. Awards: Volvo, O'Donogue, Muller, Muybridge, Vienna (two), Kappa Delta (two), Trillat, Donald Julius Gruen, Sir Frederick Bartlett, Borelli, Lissner. Recreations: skiing; travel; gardening. Address: Department of Bio-Medical Physics, University of Aberdeen, Foresterhill, Aberdeen AB25 2ZD; T.-01224 663123, Ext. 51155.

Porteous, Brian William, BSc (Hons), MILAM, DipRM. Depute Director, Cultural and Leisure Services, Glasgow City Council, since 1998, Depute Director of Parks and Recreation, 1994-98; b. 6.2.51, Falkirk; m., Shena; 3 s. Educ. Falkirk High School; St. Andrews University; Moray House College of Education; Loughborough University of Technology. Joined Scottish Sports Council as Development Officer, 1979, appointed Director of Operations, 1989. Honorary Secretary, British Orienteering Federation, 1974-76; former Member, Board, National Coaching Foundation; President, Scottish Orienteering Association, since 1996. Publication: Orienteering, 1979. Recreations: golf; orienteering; amateur opera/musicals; caravanning. Address: (h.) Croft House, 2 Spoker's Loan, Balfron, Glasgow G63 0PA; T.(b.)-0141-287 5520.

Porter, Adrian, MA, BD. Head Master, St. Aloysius' College, Glasgow, since 1995; b. 17.11.59, Bristol. Educ. St. Brendan's, Bristol; Campion Hall, Oxford; Heythrop, London. Member, Society of Jesus (Jesuits), since 1978. Recreation: theatre. Address: (b.) St. Aloysius' College, 45 Hill Street, Glasgow G3 6RJ; T.-0141-332 3190.

Porter, Professor James Whyte, MA, BMus. Director, Elphinstone Institute, University of Aberdeen, since 1996; Professor of Scottish Ethnology, University of Aberdeen; b. 9.6.37, Paisley; m., Christina; 1 s. Educ. Hutcheson's Grammar School; Stirling High School; University of St. Andrews; University of Edinburgh. Assistant Lecturer, University of Edinburgh, 1965-68; University of California, Los Angeles: Assistant Professor, 1968-75, Associate Professor, 1975-81, Professor, 1981-95, Department Chair, 1992-95. Publications: The Ballad Image, 1983; The Traditional Music of Britain and Ireland, 1989; Jeannie Robertson: Emergent Singer, Transformative Voice, 1995. Recreations: golf; croquet; feeding goldfish. Address: Taylor Building, Regent Walk, Aberdeen AB24 3FX; T.-01224 272996.

Potter, Brian Thomas, BSc, MB, ChB,FRCGP. Scottish Secretary, British Medical Association, since 1995; b. 25.8.52, Edinburgh; 1 s.; 2 d. Educ. Scotus Academy, Edinburgh; Edinburgh University Medical School. Registrar posts, Accident and Emergency Medicine, Renal Medicine, Royal Infirmary, Edinburgh, and Geriatric Medicine, City Hospital, Edinburgh; Principal in General Practice, Edinburgh; Medical Officer, Marks and Spencer, Edinburgh; Medical Practitioner, Glencorse Army Depot; Occupational Physician, City Hospital; Senior Medical Officer, Scottish Office Home and Health Department, 1992-95. Former Secretary, Lothian Division, BMA; Secretary, Lothian Area Medical Committee; former Member, Scottish Council, BMA. Recreations: swimming; keep-fit; singing. Address: (b.) BMA, Scottish Office, 3 Hill Place, Edinburgh EH8 9EQ; T.-0131-662 4820.

Pottinger, Graham, LLB, CA, ACMA. Chief Executive, Scottish Mutual Assurance plc, since 1997; Managing Director, Abbey National Financial and Investment Services plc, since 1997; Director, Abbey National Life plc, since 1992; b. 14.6.49, Glasgow; m., Dorothy; 1 s.; 1 d. Educ. Jordanhill College School, Glasgow; Glasgow University. Peat Marwick Mitchell & Co., 1966-72; Partner, Deloitte Haskins & Sells, 1972-79; Controller, UK and Africa, Cargill Plc, 1980-92; Finance Director, Scottish Mutual Assurance plc, 1992-96. Member, Council, Institute of Chartered Accountants of Scotland. Recreations: swimming; gardening. Address: (b.) Abbey National House, 301 St. Vincent Street, Glasgow G2 5HN; T.-0141-275 8654.

Pounder, Professor Derrick John, MB, ChB, FRCPA, FFPathRCPI, FCAP, MRCPath, FHKCPath. Professor of Forensic Medicine, Dundee University, since 1987; b. 25.2.49, Pontypridd; m., Georgina Kelly; 1 s.; 2 d. Educ. Pontypridd Boys' Grammar; Birmingham University. Senior Lecturer (Forensic Pathology), University of Adelaide; Deputy Chief Medical Examiner, Edmonton, Alberta, and Associate Professor, Universities of Alberta and Calgary, 1985-87. Freeman of Llantrisant. Recreations: photography; medieval architecture; almost lost causes. Address: (b.) Department of Forensic Medicine, Dundee University, Dundee DD1 4HN; T.-01382 348020.

Powell, Robert George, MA (Hons). Business Editor, The Herald, since 1998; b. 9.4.54, Cornwall; m., Mary; 1 s.; 1 d. Educ. Frome Grammar School; Edinburgh University; University College Cardiff. Teacher, Muslim Secondary School, Sagamu, Nigeria, 1977-78; Foreign Correspondent, Reuters, 1979-95 (Portugal, 1980-81 and 1991-95, Argentina, 1982-84, Venezuela, 1984-85, Cuba, 1986, Kenya, 1986-90, UK, 1990-91). Recreations: travel; hillwalking; wildlife observation; swimming; reading. Address: (b.) 195 Albion Street, Glasgow G1 1QP; T.-0141-552 6255.

Powell, Shona S. DipRSA. Director, Lemon Tree, Aberdeen, since 1992; b. 10.4.56, Dundee. Educ. Kirkton High School, Dundee; Dundee College of Education; Richmond College, Sheffield. Teacher, Hayshead, Arbroath, 1977-80; Assistant to Director, Sheffield Youth Arts Festival, 1981-82; Acting Arts Co-ordinator, Sheffield Education Department, 1982-83; Administrator, Chesterfield Arts Centre, 1983-86; Co-ordinator, Town Hall Studios, Swindon, 1986-87; Director, West Wiltshire Arts Centre, 1987-90; Director, Newfest '91, Newcastle upon Tyne, 1990-91. Member: Scottish Arts Council Combined Arts Committee, New Directions (Lottery); Board Member, Dance Productions Ltd.; former Member, SAC Capital Lottery Committee. Address: The Lemon Tree, 5 West North Street, Aberdeen AB24 5AT; T.-01224 647999.

Power, Professor David Martin, BCom, MSc(Econ), PhD. Professor of Business Finance, Dundee University, since 1996; b. 20.7.64, Waterford, Ireland. Educ. De La Salle College, Waterford; University College, Cork; London School of Economics. Lecturer/Senior Lecturer, Dundee University, 1987-96. Fellow, Royal Society of Arts. Recreations: golf; tennis. Address: (b.) Department of Accountancy and Business Finance, Dundee University, Dundee DD1 4HN; T.-01382 344854.

Power, Graham, QPM, MA (Oxon). Deputy Chief Constable, Lothian and Borders Police, since 1994; b. 2.6.47, Middlesbrough; m.; 2 s.; 1 d. Educ. Stainsby Boys School, Middlesbrough; Queen's College, Oxford. Constable to Superintendent, Cleveland, 1966-88; Chief Superintendent, North Yorks, Harrogate, 1988-91; Assistant Chief Constable, Lothian and Borders, 1991-94. Recreation: trout fishing. Address: (b.) Police HQ, Fettes Avenue, Edinburgh EH4 1RB; T.-0131-311 3100.

Power, Professor Kevin George, MA, MAppSci, PhD. Consultant Clinical Psychologist, since 1992; Personal Chair in Clinical Psychology, University of Stirling, since 1997; Director, Anxiety and Stress Research Centre, since 1995; b. 19.1.55, Edinburgh; co-habitee: Catherine Kilfedder. Educ. Holy Cross Academy, Edinburgh; St. Augustine's High School, Edinburgh; Edinburgh University; Glasgow University; Stirling University. Clinical Psychologist, Forth Valley Health Board and Scottish Prison Service, 1982-89; Clinical Psychologist, Tayside Health Board/Dundee Healthcare NHS Trust, since 1989; academic posts, University of Stirling, throughout career. Patron (Past Chair), Perth Association for Mental Health. Publications: over 100 in journals and Scottish Office reports. Recreations: squash; hillwalking; fitness training; cigars and malt whisky. Address: Department of Psychology, University of Stirling, Stirling FK9 4LA; T.-01786 467685.

Prag, Thomas Gregory Andrew, MA, FIMgt. Managing Director, Moray Firth Radio; b. 2.1.47, London; m., Angela; 3 s. Educ. Westminster School; Brasenose College, Oxford. Joined BBC, 1968, as Studio Manager; Producer, BBC Radio Oxford; Programme Organiser, BBC Radio Highland; first Chief Executive, Moray Firth Radio, 1981. Trustee, Highland Community Foundation; Past President, Inverness and District Chamber of Commerce; Board Member, Highland Festival. Recreations: good intentions towards restoration of 1950 Daimler; keeping clock collection wound; family; growing vegetables; chasing deer off vegetables. Address: (b.) Moray Firth Radio, PO Box 271, Inverness IV3 8UJ.

Press, Professor Jeffrey Ian, BA (Hons) (Spanish), BA (Hons) (Russian), PhD. Established Professor in Russian (Comparative Linguistics), St. Andrews University, since 1995; b. 23.3.47, Oldham; m., Marie-Christine; 1 s.; 1 d. Educ. Hulme Grammar School, Oldham; London University. Lecturer in Russian, Queen Mary College, London University, 1970-79, SSEES and Queen Mary College, 1979-87, Senior Lecturer, 1987-89; Professor of Slavonic and Comparative Linguistics, London University, 1990-95. Publications: books on Breton, Slavonic languages, Ukrainian and Lithuanian linguistics. Recreations: astronomy; photography; walking; learning languages. Address: (b.) St. Andrews University, St. Andrews KY16 9AL; T.-01334 463631.

Presslie, Sheriff George. Sheriff of Lothian and Borders at Haddington. Address: (b.) Sheriff Court, Court Street, Haddington, EH41 3HN.

Preston, David Michael, LLB, NP. Solicitor, since 1976; b. 26.8.52, Glasgow; m., Sheila Elizabeth; 2 s. Educ. Hillhead High School; Dundee University. Part-time Depute Procurator Fiscal, 1976-79; Clerk to General Commissioners of Income Tax, since 1976; Registrar, Episcopal Diocese of Argyll and the Isles, since 1977; Partner, Hosack and Sutherland, since 1978; Member, Council, Law Society of Scotland, since 1990 (Convenor: Update Committee, 1992-96, Remuneration Committee, since 1996). Past Chairman and first Hon. President, Oban Round Table; Chairman, Oban Youth and Community Association, since 1980; Commodore, Oban Sailing Club, 1992-93; Secretary, Atlantis Leisure, since 1991. Recreations: sailing; skiing; rugby spectating; logistical supporter (travel and finance) of two sons. Address: (h.) Westbank, Duncraggan Road, Oban; T.-01631 563228.

Preston, George Dawson Chrystal, MA. Director and Treasurer, Queen's Nursing Institute Scotland, since 1992; b. 20.4.31, Hampton; m., Elizabeth Anne Rennie; 1 d. Educ. Fettes College; Gonville and Caius College, Cambridge. Science Staff, Fettes College, 1955-91, Housemaster, 1959-64, and 1969-81, Senior Master, 1981-91. Keeper of Records, Fettes College. Recreations: gardening; computing; social court games. Address: (b.) 31 Castle Terrace, Edinburgh, EH1 2EL; T.-0131-229 2333.

Preston, Ian Mathieson Hamilton, CBE, BSc, PhD, FEng, MInstP, FIEE. Chartered Engineer; President, Scottish Council Development and Industry, since 1997; Chairman, Motherwell Bridge Holdings; Chief Executive, Scottish Power, 1990-95; Non-Executive Director: Clydeport plc, Deutsche (Scotland), Hub Power Co. (Pakistan); b. 18.7.32, Bournemouth; m., Sheila Hope Pringle; 2 s. Educ. Kilmarnock Academy; Glasgow University. University Assistant Lecturer, 1957-59; joined SSEB as Assistant Reactor Physicist, 1959; various appointments until Chief Engineer, Generation Design and Construction Division, 1972; Director General, Central Electricity Generating Board, Generation Development and Construction Division, 1977-83; Deputy Chairman, South of Scotland Electricity Board, 1983-90. Address: Motherwell Bridge Holdings, PO Box 4, Logans Road, Motherwell ML1 3NP.

Price, Professor Allan, PhD, MB, BCh, FRCP(Edin), FRCR. Professor of Radiation Oncology, Edinburgh University, since 1996; b. 3.6.58, Cardiff; m., Lesley; 2 s. Educ. Yeovil School; Welsh National School of Medicine. General medical training, Swansea, Middlesborough; oncology training, Edinburgh, Hammersmith and Royal Marsden Hospitals; ICRF Clinical Research Fellow, 1988-92; Consultant Clinical Oncologist, Addenbrooke's and Papworth Hospitals, Cambridge, 1995-96. Scientific Adviser, Melville Trust; Consultant, Lilly Oncology. Recreations: squash; skiing. Address: (b.) Department of Clinical Oncology, Western General Hospital, Edinburgh EH4 2XU; T.-0131-537 2205.

Price, Barclay. Depute Director (Planning and Development), Scottish Arts Council, since 1997; b. 26.7.45, Glasgow; m., Fiona Dick. Educ. Hillhead High School. Head of Development, Crafts Council; Administrator, Hoxton Hall Community Theatre; Visual Arts Subsidy Officer, Arts Council of GB; Officer, Clydesdale Bank. Address: (b.) Scottish Arts Council, 12 Manor Place, Edinburgh EH3 7DD; T.-0131-225 9833.

Price, Janet Elisabeth, BA, PGCE, DipAppLing. Principal, Inverness College, since 1995; Member, North Areas Regional Board, Scottish Natural Heritage, since 1996; b. 24.2.40, Rugby. Educ. London University; Edinburgh University. Lecturer in Languages, London, 1967-70, Oxford, 1970-75 (both in FE sector); Lecturer, Newcastle University, 1975-82; Head of Voluntary Sector Adult Education Institute, Brighton, 1982-86; Assistant Principal, Stevenson College, Edinburgh, 1986-91; Vice-Principal, York College of Further and Higher Education, 1991-95. Recreations: creative writing; hill-walking; languages. Address: (h.) 3 Broadstone Park, Inverness, IV2 3JZ.

Price, Professor Nicholas Charles, MA, DPhil. Professsor of Biochemistry, Stirling University, since 1994; b. 12.8.46, Stafford; m., Margaret Hazel Millen; 1 s.; 2 d. Educ. King Edward VI School, Stafford; Merton College, Oxford. Fereday Fellow, St. John's College, Oxford, 1969-74; Harkness Fellow, University of Pennsylvania, 1971-72; Demonstrator, Department of Biochemistry, Oxford University, 1973-74; Lecturer/Senior Lecturer/Reader in Biochemistry, Stirling University, 1974-94. Publications: three books; over 100 journal articles. Recreations: church activities; fund-raising. Address: (b.) Department of Biological Sciences, Stirling University, Stirling FK9 4LA; T.-01786 467765.

Price, Rev. Peter Owen, CBE, QHC, BA, FPhS. Minister, Blantyre Old Parish Church, Glasgow, 1985-96; b. 18.4.30, Swansea; m., 1, Margaret Winifred Trevan (deceased); 2, Mary Hamill Robertson; 3 d. Educ. Wyggeston School, Leicester; Didsbury Theological College, Bristol; Open University. Chaplain, Royal Navy, 1960-84, latterly Principal Chaplain, Church of Scotland and Free Churches (Naval), Ministry of Defence, 1981-84; appointed Honorary Chaplain to the Queen, 1981. Recreations: clay pigeon shooting; rugby; warm water sailing; golf. Address: Duncraigan, 22 Old Bothwell Road, Bothwell, Glasgow G71 8AW; T.-01698 854032.

Prickett, Professor (Alexander Thomas) Stephen, MA, PhD, DipEd, FAHA. Regius Professor of English Language and Literature, Glasgow University, since 1990; b. 4.6.39, Freetown, Sierra Leone; m., Maria Angelica; 2 d. Educ. Kent College, Canterbury; Trinity Hall, Cambridge; University College, Oxford. English Teacher, Methodist College, Uzuakoli, E. Nigeria, 1962-64; Lecturer/Reader, Sussex University, 1967-82; Professor of English, Australian National University, Canberra, 1983-89. Publications: Do It Yourself Doom, 1962; Coleridge and Wordsworth: the Poetry of Growth, 1970; Romanticism and Religion, 1976; Victorian Fantasy, 1979; Words and the Word: language poetics and Biblical interpretation, 1986; England and the French Revolution, 1988; Reading the Text: Biblical criticism and literary theory, 1991; Origins of Narrative: The Romantic Appropriation of the Bible, 1996; World's Classics Bible (Editor), 1997. Recreations: walking; skiing; tennis; drama. Address: (b.) Department of English Literature, Glasgow University, Glasgow; T.-0141-339 8855.

Pride, Professor Stephen James, BSc, PhD, FRSE. Professor of Mathematics, Glasgow University, since 1992 (Reader in Mathematics, 1987-92); b. 8.1.49, Melbourne. Educ. Hampton High School, Melbourne; Monash University, Melbourne; Australian National University, Canberra. Research Fellow, Open University, 1974-78; Temporary Lecturer in Mathematics, King's College, London University, 1978-79; Lecturer in Mathematics, Glasgow University, 1979-87. Member, Editorial Board, London Mathematical Society; Member, Mathematics College, Engineering and Physical Sciences Research Council. Publications: more than 60 articles on algebra (mainly group theory). Recreations: cycling; travelling; cinema; gardening. Address: (h.) 54 Airlie Street, Glasgow G12 9SN; T.-0141-339 7395.

Priest, Professor Eric Ronald, BSc, MSc, PhD, FRSE. Professor of Theoretical Solar Physics, St. Andrews University, since 1983; b. 7.11.43, Birmingham; m., Clare Wilson; 3 s.; 1 d. Educ. King Edward VI School, Birmingham; Nottingham University; Leeds University. St. Andrews University: Lecturer in Applied Mathematics, 1968, Reader, 1977; SERC Senior Fellow, 1992-97. Elected Member, Norwegian Academy of Sciences and Letters, 1994; Chairman, RSE Mathematics Committee; Member, HEFC Research Assessment Exercise Committee. Recreations: bridge; walking; swimming; swingnastics; children. Address: (b.) Mathematical and Computational Sciences Department, St. Andrews University, St. Andrews KY16 9SS; T.-01334 463709.

Pringle, Ashley Naitby, BEd, MA, DMS, MILAM. Director of Community Services, North Ayrshire Council, since 1997; b. 30.5.48, West Cornforth, Co. Durham; m., Valerie. Educ. Spennymoor Grammar Technical School; Bede College, Durham University; Birmingham University. Teacher of English, Ferryhill, Co. Durham, 1971-73; Activities Officer, Leisure Centre, Teesside CBC, 1973-74; Social Research Officer, Cleveland County Council, 1974; Sports Centres Manager, Darlington, Durham County Council, 1974-85; Assistant Recreation Officer, Tynedale District Council, 1985-88; Assistant Director of Leisure and Recreation, Stirling District Council, 1988-90; Depute Director of Recreation, Edinburgh District Council, 1990-97. Vice-Chair, Scottish Association of Directors of Leisure. Recreations: walking; reading; lecturing. Address: (b.) Nobel House (K31), Ardeer, Stevenston KA20 3LN; T.-01294 485311.

Pringle, Kevin James, MA (Hons). Director of Communications, Scottish National Party, since 1995; b. 30.12.67, Dundee. Educ. Perth High School; Aberdeen University. Research Officer, SNP, 1989-95. Recreations: cinema; reading. Address: (b.) 6 North Charlotte Street, Edinburgh EH2 4JH.

Pritchard, Kenneth William, OBE, BL, WS. Secretary, Law Society of Scotland, 1976-97; Temporary Sheriff, since 1995; b. 14.11.33, London; Honorary Sheriff, Dundee; m., Gretta Murray; 2 s.; 1 d. Educ. Dundee High School; Fettes College; St. Andrews University. National Service, Argyll and Sutherland Highlanders, 1955-57; 2nd Lt., 1956; TA, 1957-62 (Captain); joined J. & J. Scrimgeour, Solicitors, Dundee, 1957; Senior Partner, 1970-76; Member: Sheriff Court Rules Council, 1973-76, Lord Dunpark's Committee considering Reparation upon Criminal Conviction, 1973-77; Hon. Visiting Professor, Law School, Strathclyde University; Hon. Member, Law Institute of Victoria, 1985; Hon. Member, Law Society of New Zealand, 1987; Hon. Member, Faculty of Procurators and Solicitors in Dundee; Member, University Court of Dundee, 1989-93; President, Dundee High School Old Boys Club, 1975-76. Recreation: golf. Address: (h.) 22/4 Kinellan Road, Edinburgh EH12 6ES; T.-0131-337 4294.

Procter, Rev. Robert Hendy, MA. Secretary, Scottish Council, The Scout Association, 1982-96; b. 22.1.31, Alloa; m., Elizabeth Rosemary; 1 s.; 2 d. Educ. Fettes College; Trinity Hall, Cambridge. Commissioned, Royal Corps of Signals, 1950; Patons & Baldwins Ltd., 1954-79 (General Manager, from 1969); Director, John Gladstone & Co. Ltd., Galashiels, 1980-82. General Commissioner of Income Tax, Clackmannan Division, 1976-80; Honorary Sheriff, Tayside Central and Fife, at Alloa, 1975-98; Edinburgh Diocese training for ministry, 1988-91; Team Priest, Christ Church Morningside, 1994; Member, Lothian Valuation Appeal Panel, 1994; Chairman, Garleton Singers, 1996; Chairman, Eric Liddell Centre (Trading) Ltd., since 1997. Recreations: hill-walking; choral singing. Address: (h.) 2 Braid Avenue, Morningside, Edinburgh EH10 6DR; T.-0131-447 1140.

Proctor, Alan. Editor, Evening Telegraph and Sporting Post, Dundee, since 1995; b. 4.9.40, Forfar; m., Sheila Morrison Kerr; 2 d. Educ. Brechin High School. D.C. Thomson, since 1959. Recreations: walking; reading. Address: (b.) D.C. Thomson & Co. Ltd., 80 Kingsway East, Dundee DD4 8SL; T.-01382 223131.

Proctor, Professor John, MA, DPhil, DSc. Professor, Department of Biological and Molecular Science, University of Stirling, since 1996; b. 1.2.44, Accrington; divorced; 1 d. Educ. St. Mary's College, Blackburn; St. Edmund Hall, Oxford. Lecturer, University of Lancaster, 1968-69; Post Doctoral Fellow: Stanford, California, 1969-70, University of Liverpool, 1970-71; University of Stirling, since 1971: subsequently Lecturer, Senior Lecturer, Reader. President, Botanical Society of Scotland, 1996-98. RGS Busk Medal, 1991. Recreations: Vincent motorcycles, E-type Jaguars. Address: (h.) 3 Allanwater Appartments, Bridge of Allan, Stirling FK9 4LA; T.-01786 834042.

Prosser, Professor James Anthony William (Tony), LLB. John Millar Professor of Law, Glasgow University, since 1992; b. 3.5.54, Ludlow. Educ. Ludlow Grammar School; Liverpool University. Research Assistant in Law, Southampton University, 1974-76; Lecturer in Law, Hull University, 1976-79; Lecturer, Senior Lecturer, Sheffield University, 1980-92; Jean Monnet Fellow, European University Institute, Florence, 1987-88. Publications: Test Cases for the Poor; Nationalised Industries and Public Control; Law and the Regulators; Privatizing Public Enterprises (Co-author); Waiving the Rules (Co-editor); Regulating the Changing Media (Co-editor). Recreations: walking; cinema; jazz. Address: (b.) School of Law, Glasgow University, Glasgow G12 8QQ; T.-0141-330 4180.

Prosser, (Leslie) Charles, DFA, DAEd. Secretary, Royal Fine Art Commission for Scotland, since 1976; b. 27.10.39, Harrogate; m., Coral; 1 s.; 2 d. Educ. Bath Academy of Art at Corsham Court; Slade School of Fine Art, London University. Assistant Lecturer in Fine Art, Blackpool School of Art, 1962-64; Fine Art research, Royal Academy, Stockholm, 1964-65; Lecturer in Fine Art, Leeds/Jacob Kramer College of Art, 1965-76; research in Art Education, Leeds University, 1974-75. Leverhulme European Arts Research Award, 1964; FRSA, 1997; Hon. FRIAS, 1997. Recreations: Scottish dancing and hill-walking. Address: (h.) 28 Mayfield Terrace, Edinburgh EH9 1RZ; T.-0131-668 1141.

Prosser, Hon. Lord QC, MA (Oxon), LLB, HonFRIAS. Senator of the College of Justice in Scotland and Lord of Session, since 1986; b. 23.11.34, Edinburgh; m., Vanessa Lindsay; 2 s.; 2 d. Educ. Edinburgh Academy; Corpus Christi College, Oxford; Edinburgh University. Advocate, 1962; Queen's Counsel, 1974; Vice-Dean, Faculty of Advocates, 1979-83, Dean of Faculty, 1983-86. Chairman, Royal Lyceum Theatre Company, 1987-92; Chairman, Scottish Historic Buildings Trust, 1988-98; Chairman, Royal Fine Art Commission for Scotland, 1990-95; Chairman, Scottish Architectural Education Trust; Chairman, Chamber Group of Scotland; Member, Franco-British Council. Address: 7 Randolph Crescent, Edinburgh EH3 7TH; T.-0131-225 2709.

Proud, Professor Christopher Gregory, BSc, PhD. Chair of Biochemical Physiology, University of Dundee, since 1998; b. 29.4.53, Colchester; m., Xuemin Wang; 1 s.; 1 d. Educ. Colchester Royal Grammar School. Junior Lecturer, University of Göttingen, Germany, 1979-80; Research Fellow, University of Sussex, 1980-81; Lecturer in Biochemistry, University of Kent, Canterbury, 1982-85; Lecturer, then Reader in Biochemistry, University of Bristol, 1985-95; Chair, University of Kent, Canterbury, 1995-97. Member, Projects Grants Committee, British Heart Foundation; Editor, European Journal of

Biochemistry. Address: Department of Anatomy and Physiology, University of Dundee, Dundee DD1 5EH; T.-01382 344919.

Proudfoot, Edwina Valmai Windram, MA, DipEd, FSA, FSA Scot, MIFA. Archaeologist; Director, St. Andrews Heritage Services, since 1988; Honorary Research Fellow, St. Andrews University, since 1985; b. 9.3.35, Dover; m., Professor V. Bruce Proudfoot (qv); 2 s. Educ. Invergordon Academy; Inverness Royal Academy; Edinburgh University. Lecturer (including Adult Education) in Archaeology, since 1959; director of excavations, numerous projects; Editor, Discovery and Excavation in Scotland, 1977-90; President, Council for Scottish Archaeology, 1983-89; Founder, first Chairman, Tayside and Fife Archaeological Committee, 1975-82; Member, Ancient Monuments Board for Scotland, 1986-97; Chairman, St. Andrews Preservation Trust, 1988-93; Council Member, National Trust for Scotland, 1984-89 and 1993-97; Chairman, NTS Central, Fife and Tayside Regional Commitee, since 1998; Member, Executive Committee, NTS, since 1994. Recreations: gardening; music; walking. Address: 12 Wardlaw Gardens, St. Andrews, KY16 9DW; T.-01334 473293.

Proudfoot, Professor V. Bruce, OBE, BA, PhD, FSA, FRSE, FRSGS, FSA Scot. Chair of Council, Royal Scottish Geographical Society; Emeritus Professor of Geography, St. Andrews University; b. 24.9.30, Belfast; m., Edwina Valmai Windram Field; 2 s. Educ. Royal Belfast Academical Institution; Queen's University, Belfast. Research Officer, Nuffield Quaternary Research Unit, Queen's University, Belfast, 1954-58; Lecturer in Geography: Queen's University, Belfast, 1958-59, Durham University, 1959-67; Hatfield College, Durham: Tutor, 1960-63, Librarian, 1963-65; Visiting Fellow, University of Auckland and Commonwealth Visiting Fellow, Australia, 1966; Alberta University, Edmonton: Associate Professor, 1967-70, Professor, 1970-74; Co-ordinator, Socio-Economic Opportunity Studies and Staff Consultant, Alberta Human Resources Research Council, 1971-72; Professor of Geography, St. Andrews University, 1974-93. Royal Society of Edinburgh: Convener, Earth Sciences Committee, 1983-85, Vice-President, 1985-88, Convener, Grants Committee, 1988-91, General Secretary, 1991-96, Bicentenary Medal, 1998; Chairman, Society for Landscape Studies, 1979-83; Vice-President, Society of Antiquaries of Scotland, 1982-85; President, Section H, BAAS, 1985; Chairman, Rural Geography Study Group, Institute of British Geographers, 1980-84; Vice-President and Chairman of Council, since 1993, Chairman of Dundee Centre, since 1993, Royal Scottish Geographical Society; Hon. President, Scottish Association of Geography Teachers, 1982-84; Trustee, National Museum of Antiquities of Scotland, 1982-85. Recreation: gardening. Address: (h.) Westgate, Wardlaw Gardens, St. Andrews KY16 9DW; T.-01334 473293.

Provan, James Lyal Clark. Member, European Parliament, South Downs West, since 1994 (Chief Whip EPP Group), Member: Fisheries Committee, Agricultural Committee, Transport and Tourism Committee; Chairman, EP Tourism Group; Chairman, Rowett Research Institute, Aberdeen (Board Member, since 1990); Non-Executive Director, New Holland N.V. and New Holland (Holdings), N.V. Farmer; b. 19.12.36, Glenfarg, Perthshire; m., Roweena Adele Lewis; 2 s.; 1 d. Educ. Ardvreck School, Crieff; Oundle School, Northants; Royal Agricultural College, Cirencester. National Farmers Union of Scotland: Area President, Kinross, 1965, Fife and Kinross, 1971; Tayside Regional Councillor, 1978-81; Member, Tay River Purification Board, 1978-81; Member (Conservative), European Parliament, NE Scotland, 1979-89; European Democratic (Conservative) Spokesman on Agriculture and Fisheries, 1981-87; Questor of European Parliament, 1987-89; former Executive Director, Scottish Financial Enterprise; Chairman, McIntosh of Dyce Ltd., McIntosh Donald Ltd., 1989-94; Member, Agriculture and Food Research Council, 1990-94. Recreations: country pursuits; sailing; flying; politics; agriculture. Address: Summerfield, Glenfarg, Perthshire PH2 9QD; Middle Lodge, Barns Green, Horsham, West Sussex RH13 7NL.

Pugh, Professor John Richard, BSc, PhD, CPhys, CEng, FInstMC, MInstP. Head, Department of Physical Sciences and Professor of Physics, Glasgow Caledonian University, since 1992; Member, Board of Directors, Centre for Industrial Bulk Solids Handling, since 1993; b. 16.4.52, Shrewsbury; m., Christine Haldane; 3 s. Educ. Cumbernauld High School; Whitley Bay Grammar School; Glasgow University. Research Fellow, Glasgow University, 1976-80; Physicist, Barr and Stroud Ltd., Glasgow, 1980-91; Lecturer, then Senior Lecturer, Glasgow College, 1981-90; Professor of Physics and Depute Head, Glasgow Polytechnic, 1990-92. Tuba player, Bellshill Brass Band. Recreations: music; house restoration; gardening. Address: (b.) Department of Physical Sciences, Glasgow Caledonian University, Cowcaddens Road, Glasgow G4 0BA; T.-0141-331 3670.

Pugh, Kenneth Bryan, BSc (Hons), MAgrSc, PhD, CChem, FRSC, FCIWEM. Regional Scientist, Scottish Environment Protection Agency (North), since 1996; b. 13.9.43, Birmingham; m., Susan; 2 s. Educ. Waverley Grammar School, Birmingham; University of Leeds; University of Reading. Scientific Officer, University College of North Wales, 1970-76; North East River Purification Board, Aberdeen: Chief Chemist, 1976-92, Assistant General Manager, 1992-96. Publications: more than 40 scientific papers. Address: (b.) Graesser House, Fodderty Way, Dingwall IV15 9XB; T.-01349 862021.

Punter, Professor David Godfrey, BA, MA, PhD, FRSA. Professor of English Studies, Stirling University, since 1988; b. 19.11.49, London; m., Caroline Mary Case-Punter; 1 s.; 2 d. Educ. John Lyon School, Harrow; Fitzwilliam College, Cambridge. Lecturer, University of East Anglia, 1973-84; Professor, Fudan University, Shanghai, 1983; Senior Lecturer, University of East Anglia, 1984-86; Director, Development of University English Teaching Project, 1985-86; Professor, Chinese University of Hong Kong, 1986-88. Publications: many books of literary criticism, including The Literature of Terror, The Hidden Script, and Gothic Pathologies; articles and essays on romantic and contemporary literature; three books of poetry, China and Glass, Love in the Supermarket, Asleep at the Wheel. Recreations: child-minding; dog-minding; walking; squash. Address: (b.) Stirling University, Stirling, FK9 4LA; T.-01786 467495.

Purser, John Whitley, MA, PhD. Composer and Lecturer; Poet, Playwright, Musicologist, and Broadcaster; b. 10.2.42, Glasgow; 1 s.; 1 d. Educ. Fettes College; Glasgow University; Royal Scottish Academy of Music and Drama. Manager, Scottish Music Information Centre, 1985-87; compositions include two operas, numerous orchestral and chamber works; three books of poetry, The Counting Stick, A Share of the Wind and Amoretti; six radio plays and two radio series, A Change of Tune and Scotland's Music; music history: Is the Red Light On?, Scotland's Music; literary criticism: The Literary Works of Jack B. Yeats; awards: McVitie Scottish Writer of the Year, 1992; Glenfiddich Living Scotland Award, 1991; Giles Cooper Award, 1992; New York International Radio Festival Gold Medal, 1992; Sony Gold Medal, 1993; Oliver Brown Award, 1993; Scottish Heritage Award, 1993; Hon. Life Member, Saltire Society, 1993. Recreations: numerous. Address: (b.) 3 Drinan, Elgol, Isle of Skye IV49 9BG; T.-01471 866262.

Purves, David, BSc, PhD. Editor, Lallans Magazine, 1987-95; Playwright; b. 9.4.24, Selkirk; m., Lilian Rosemary; 3 s. Educ. Galashiels Academy; Edinburgh University. Head, Trace Element Department, Edinburgh School of Agriculture, 1956-82; Supervisor, Central Analytical Department, 1982-87; author of Trace Element Contamination of the Environment, 1985; poetry collections: Thrawart Threipins, 1976, Herts Bluid, 1995; many poems in Scots published; Fringe First play, The Puddok an the Princess and rendering in Scots of Macbeth published, 1992; Joint Editor, Mak It New, anthology of 21 years of writing in Lallans, 1995; author of A Scots Grammar, 1997; Past Preses, Scots Language Society. Address: (h.) 8 Strathalmond Road, Edinburgh EH4 8AD; T.-0131-339 7929.

Purves, Rev. John Peter Sandison, BSc, BD. Parish Minister, Dollar, Glendevon, Muckhart, since 1990; Chaplain, Dollar Academy, since 1990; b. 6.8.48, Edinburgh; m., Patricia Kennedy; 1 s.; 1 d. Educ. Bathgate Academy; Edinburgh University; Aberdeen University. VSO Teacher, Malawi, 1970-72; Adventure Playground Leader, Gorbals, Glasgow, 1972-74; Assistant Minister, Stonelaw Church, Rutherglen, 1977-78; Assistant Chaplain, Aberdeen University, 1978-82; Missionary, Mount Olivet, Jamaica, 1983-89. Kentucky Colonel, 1997. Recreation: gardening. Address: (h.) 2 Manse Road, Dollar FK14 7AJ; T.-01259 743432.

Purves-Hume, Ian Campbell. Director, Royal Scottish Agricultural Benevolent Institution, since 1990; b. 22.7.38, London; m., Jill Cairns Fairbairn; 2 d. Educ. Ottershaw; Royal Military Academy, Sandhurst. Army Officer, Argyll and Sutherland Highlanders, 1958-90, to rank of Brigadier. Recreations: walking; bird-watching. Address: (b.) RSABI, Ingliston, Edinburgh EH28 8NB; T.-0131-333 1023/1027.

Purvis, John Robert, CBE, MA (Hons). International Business Consultant (Managing Partner, Purvis & Co.), since 1973; Director: James River UK Holdings Ltd., 1984-95, Johnson Fry European Utilities Trust PLC, since 1994, Jamont NV, 1994-95, Curtis Fine Papers Ltd., since 1995, Crown Vantage Ltd., since 1995; Chairman, Kingdom FM Radio Ltd., since 1997; b. 6.7.38, St. Andrews; m., Louise Spears Durham; 1 s.; 2 d. Educ. Glenalmond; St. Andrews University. 2nd Lt., Scots Guards, 1956-58; First National City Bank (Citibank NA), London, New York City, Milan, 1962-69; Treasurer, Noble Grossart Ltd., Edinburgh, 1969-73; Director and Secretary, Brigton Farms Ltd., 1969-86; Managing Director, Founder, Owner, Gilmerton Management Services Ltd., 1973-92; Member, European Parliament, Mid Scotland and Fife, 1979-84 (Deputy Chief Whip, Group Spokesman on Monetary Affairs, Energy, Research and Technology) Vice Chairman, European Parliament Delegation to the Gulf States; Chairman, IBA Scottish Advisory Committee, 1985-89; Member for Scotland, IBA, 1985-89; Member of Council, St. Leonards School, St. Andrews, 1981-89; Chairman, Economic Affairs Committee, Scottish Conservative and Unionist Association, 1986-97, Vice-President of Association, 1987-89; Member, Scottish Advisory Committee on Telecommunications, 1990-97. Recreations: Italy and Scotland. Address: Gilmerton House, Dunino, St. Andrews KY16 8NB; T.-01334 75830.

Pyper, Mark Christopher Spring-Rice, BA. Headmaster, Gordonstoun School, since 1990; b. 13.8.47, Seaford; m., Jennifer L.; 1 s.; 2 d. Educ. Winchester College; Oxford University; London University. Assistant Master, Stoke Brunswick School, East Grinstead, 1966-68; Assistant Master, then Joint Headmaster, St. Wilfrid's School, Seaford, 1969-79; Registrar, Housemaster, then Deputy Headmaster, Sevenoaks School, 1979-90; Director, Sevenoaks Summer Festival, 1979-90. Address: (h.) Headmaster's House, Gordonstoun School, Elgin IV30 2RF; T.-01343 837807.

Q

Queensberry, 12th Marquess of (David Harrington Angus Douglas); b. 19.12.29. Educ. Eton. Professor of Ceramics, Royal College of Art, 1959-83; succeeded to title, 1954.

Quigley, Ian Spiers, LLB (Hons). Partner, Maclay Murray and Spens, since 1977; b. 29.11.46, Hamilton; m., Elizabeth Ann Lindsay; 2 d. Educ. Aberdeen Grammar School; Glasgow University. Committee Member, Scottish Outward Bound Association. Recreations: cycling; Nordic skiing; hillwalking; gardening. Address: (b.) 3 Glenfinlas Street, Edinburgh EH3 6AQ; T.-0131-226 5196.

Quinault, Francis Charles, BSc, PhD. Hebdomadar, St. Andrews University, since 1994; former Assistant Principal for External Affairs and Senior Lecturer in Psychology, St. Andrews University; b. 8.5.43, London; m., Wendy Ann Horton; 1 s.; 2 d. Educ. Dulwich College; St. Catharine's College, Cambridge; Bristol University. Ford Foundation Scholar, Oslo University, 1969-70. Member, National Committee for the Training of University Teachers, 1981-87. Recreations: acting; singing; hill-walking. Address: (b.) University of St. Andrews, 71 North Street, St. Andrews KY16 9AJ; T.-01334 462240.

Qureshi, Robina Zia. Director, Positive Action on Housing Ltd., since 1995; b. Glasgow; 1 s. Educ. Bellahouston Academy; Bearsden Academy. Advice Worker, Glasgow West Advisory Service, 1986-87; Welfare Adviser, Woodlands Advice Centre, 1987-90; Project Leader, Race and Housing Project, 1990-92; Race and Housing Officer, Housing Equality Action Unit, 1992-95; Editor, Race and Housing News, 1993-96. Ujima Pookar Award for outstanding contribution to black community, 1996. Recreations: music; horse-riding; photography; going cycling with Ibrahim; a glass of "Irn Bru" in good company. Address: (b.) 98 West George Street, Glasgow G2 1PJ; T.-0141-353 2220.

R

Racey, Professor Paul Adrian, MA, PhD, DSc, FIBiol, FRSE. Regius Professor of Natural History, Aberdeen University, since 1993 (Professor of Zoology, 1985-93); b. 7.5.44, Wisbech, Cambridgeshire; m., Anna Priscilla Notcutt; 3 s. Educ. Ratcliffe College, Leicester; Downing College, Cambridge. Rothamsted Experimental Station, Harpenden, 1965-66; Zoological Society of London, 1966-70; Unit of Reproductive Biology, Liverpool University, 1970-73; joined Department of Zoology, Aberdeen University, 1973. Recreations: riding; sailing; skiing. Address: (b.) Department of Zoology, Aberdeen University, Aberdeen AB24 2TZ; T.-01224 272858.

Radford, Andrew. Chef/Managing Director, Atrium Restaurant, Edinburgh, since 1993; Managing Director, blue bar cafe, since 1997; Founder Member, Scottish Chefs Association, since 1994; b. 9.2.58, Cheltenham; m., Lisa; 2 s.; 1 d. Educ. Maidstone Grammar School; Stafford College of Further Education. Assistant Manager, Cromlix House Hotel, Dunblane, 1984-85; Head Chef, Royal Scotsman Touring Train, 1985-86; Head Chef, Hansel's Restaurant, Edinburgh, 1986-88; Assistant to Sir Bernard Ashley, Ashley Inns, America, 1989; Head Chef, Queen of Scots Touring Train, 1990; Head Chef, Waterloo Place Restaurant, Edinburgh, 1991-92. Winner, Scottish Field Newcomer, 1993; Good Food Guide Newcomer, 1994; Caterer Newcomer, 1994; three AA Rosettes, 1995-98; Michelin Red M, 1996-97; Egon Ronay Star, 1997; Taste of Scotland Personality of Year, 1995; Chef of the Year. Recreations: design; travel; family. Address: (b.) Atrium, 10 Cambridge Street, Edinburgh EH1 2ED; T.-0131-228 8882.

Rae, David, DipTP, MRTPI. Head of Planning, Fife Council, since 1996; b. 10.9.45; m., Ella; 2 s.; 1 d. Educ. Buckhaven High School; Edinburgh College of Art. Various planning posts, Fife, Perth, Dunbarton, 1962-75; Depute Director of Planning/Director of Planning, Kirkcaldy District Council, 1975-90; Divisional Manager, Property and Development Services, Kirkcaldy District Council, 1990-96. Past Chair, Scottish Society of Directors of Planning. Recreations: music; dogs; following East Fife F.C. Address: (b.) Fife Council, Fife House, North Street, Glenrothes KY7 5LT; T.-01592 416200.

Rae, Hugh Crauford. Novelist; b. 22.11.35, Glasgow; m., Elizabeth Dunn; 1 d. Educ. Knightswood School. Prolific popular novelist; author of more than 50 tiles, under a variety of pseudonyms, including Stuart Stern, James Albany and Jessica Stirling; books include (as Hugh C. Rae) Skinner, The Marksman, The Shooting Gallery, Harkfast and Privileged Strangers and (as Jessica Stirling) The Spoiled Earth, The Hiring Fair, The Dark Pasture, Treasures on Earth, Creature Comforts, Hearts of Gold, The Good Provider, The Asking Price, The Wise Child, The Welcome Light, Lantern for the Dark, The Penny Wedding, The Workhouse Girl. Recreation: golf. Address: (h.) Drumore Farm Cottage, Balfron Station, Glasgow G63 0NJ.

Rae, Sheriff Rita Emilia Anna, QC, LLB (Hons). Sheriff of Glasgow and Strathkelvin, since 1997. Educ. St. Patrick's High School, Coatbridge; Edinburgh University. Apprentice, Biggart, Lumsden & Co., Glasgow, 1972-74; Assistant Solicitor: Balfour & Manson, Edinburgh, 1974, Biggart, Baillie & Gifford, Glasgow, 1974-76; Solicitor and Partner, Ross Harper & Murphy, Glasgow, 1976-81; Former Tutor, Advocacy and Pleading, Strathclyde University; Advocate, 1982; Queen's Counsel, 1992. Member, Scottish Council on Human Bioethics; Member, Sacro; Life Member, Scottish Association for the Study of Delinquency. Recreations: theatre; driving; walking; opera; music; Italy; cycling.

Rae, Scott Alexander, LLB (Hons), WS, NP, TEP. Partner, Morton Fraser Milligan WS, Edinburgh, since 1970; b. 17.12.44, Edinburgh; m., Annabel Riach; 3 s. Educ. Daniel Stewarts College, Edinburgh; Edinburgh University. Sometime Tutor and Course Leader, Edinburgh University; Law Society of Scotland Examiner in Taxation and Chairman, Board of Examiners. Member, VAT Tribunal (Scotland); Clerk, Incorporated Trades of Edinburgh; Secretary, International Academy of Estate and Trust Law; Collector, Society of Writers to the Signet; Convener, Law Society of Scotland Tax Law Committee. Recreations: farming; travel. Address: (b.) 15-19 York Place, Edinburgh; T.-0131-556 8444.

Rae, Shelagh, BSc. Director of Education and Leisure, Renfrewshire Council, since 1995; b. Hamilton; m., Ian A. Rae. Educ. St. Joseph's Convent, Hartlepool; St. Andrew's High School, Kirkcaldy; Edinburgh University. Teacher of Mathematics, 1972-74; Assistant Principal Teacher, then Principal Teacher, 1974-85; Curriculum Officer, Lothian Regional Council, 1985-87; Adviser in Mathematics, then Assistant Director of Education, then Head of School Development Services, Central Regional Council, 1987-95. Recreations: reading; walking; swimming; golf. Address: (b.) Renfrewshire Council, Cotton Street, Paisley PA1 1LE; T.-0141-842 5601.

Rae, William, QPM. Chief Constable, Dumfries and Galloway Constabulary. Address: Cornwall Mount, Dumfries DG1 1PZ.

Raeburn, James B., FCIS. Director, Scottish Print Employers' Federation and Scottish Newspaper Publishers' Association, since 1984; Director, Scottish Daily Newspaper Society, since 1996; b. 18.3.47, Jedburgh; m., Rosemary Bisset; 2 d. Educ. Hawick High School. Edinburgh Corporation, 1964-69; Roxburgh County Council, 1969-71; Electrical Contractors' Association of Scotland, 1972-83 (Secretary, 1975-83). Consultative Member, The Press Council, 1984-90; Director, Press Standards Board of Finance Ltd., since 1990; Director, Advertising Standards Board of Finance Ltd., since 1988; Director, National Council for the Training of Journalists, since 1993. Recreation: golf. Address: (b.) 48 Palmerston Place, Edinburgh EH12 5DE; T.-0131-220 4353.

Raeburn, Emeritus Professor John Ross, CBE, FRSE, FIBiol, BSc, MA, PhD. Consultant; b. 20.11.12, Kirkcaldy; m., Mary Roberts; 1 s.; 3 d. Educ. Manchester Grammar School; Edinburgh University; Cornell University. Professor, Agricultural Economics, Nanking University, 1936-37; Research Officer, Oxford University, 1938-39; Statistician, then Head of Agricultural Plans Branch, Ministry of Food, 1939-46; Senior Research Officer, Oxford University, 1946-49; Reader in Agricultural Economics, London University, 1949-59; Professor and Head, Department of Agriculture, Aberdeen University, 1959-78; Principal, North of Scotland College of Agriculture, 1963-78; Consultant to World Bank, 1979-88; Vice-President, International Association of Agricultural Economists, 1964-70; President, Agricultural Economics Society, 1964-65. Publications: Agriculture: Foundations, Principles and Development; The History of the International Association of Agricultural Economists (Co-author). Recreations: travel; gardening; photography. Address: (h.) 30 Morningfield Road, Aberdeen, AB15 4AQ; T.-01224 314010.

Raeburn, Sheriff Susan Adiel Ogilvie, LLB, QC. Sheriff of Glasgow and Strathkelvin, since 1993; b. 23.4.54, Ellon. Educ. St. Margaret's School for Girls, Aberdeen; Edinburgh University. Admitted, Faculty of Advocates, 1977; took silk, 1991; part-time Chairman, Social Security Appeal Tribunals, 1986-91; Temporary Sheriff, 1988-92; part-time Chairman, Medical Appeal Tribunals, 1992-93; Reporter to Scottish Legal Aid Board, 1990-93. Recreations: salmon fishing; the arts; travel. Address: (b.) Sheriff Court, P.O. Box 23, 1 Carlton Place, Glasgow G5 9DA; T.-0141-429 8888.

Raffe, Professor David James, BA, BPhil. Professor of Sociology of Education, University of Edinburgh, since 1992 (Director, Centre for Educational Sociology, since 1987); b., 5.5.51, Felixstowe; m., Shirley; 1 s.; 1 d. Educ. The Leys School, Cambridge; New College and Nuffield College, Oxford University. Centre for Educational Sociology, University of Edinburgh: Research Fellow, 1975-79, Deputy Director, 1979-86, Lecturer in Education, 1979-85, Reader in Education, 1985-92. Publications: Reconstructions of Secondary Education, 1983; Fourteen to Eighteen, 1984; Education and the Youth Labour Market, 1988; British Baccalaureat, 1990; Part-time Higher Education. Address: (b.) 7 Buccleuch Place, Edinburgh EH8 9LW.

Rainey, John Bruce, BSc, MB, ChB, ChM, FRCSEdin. Consultant Surgeon, St. John's Hospital, Howden, Livingston, since 1988; Honorary Senior Lecturer in Surgery, Edinburgh University, since 1988; b. 18.5.52, Belfast; m., Dr. Linda Margaret King; 2 s.; 1 d. Educ. Royal Belfast Academical Institution; Edinburgh University. Trained in general surgery; Examiner in surgery and accident and emergency medicine for Royal College of Surgeons of Edinburgh. Aris and Gale Lecturer, Royal College of Surgeons of England, 1985. Recreations: family; sport; history and military history. Address: (h.) 23 Hatton Place, Edinburgh EH9 1UB, T.-0131-667 6216.

Raistrick, Evlyn, MA. Chairman, Scottish Hockey Union, 1992-96; Tournament Director, Atlanta Olympics, from 1996; Member, Rules Board, Competitions Committee, International Federation, since 1990; Member, Scottish Sports Council, since 1993; Vice-Chairman, Executive, Scottish Sports Association, since 1993; b. 13.8.42, Edinburgh; m., David William; 3 s. Educ. Boroughmuir School; Edinburgh University. Maths Teacher, Liberton High, 1964-72. Recreations: hockey; squash; golf. Address; (h.) Seton Mains House, Longniddry, East Lothian EH32 0PG.

Ralston, Professor Ian Beith McLaren, MA, PhD, FSA, FSA Scot, MIFA. Professor of Archaeology, University of Edinburgh, since 1998 (Director, Centre for Field Archaeology, since 1991); President, Council for Scottish Archaeology, since 1996; b. 11.11.50, Edinburgh; m., Sandra Webb; 1 s.; 1 d. Educ. Edinburgh Academy; Edinburgh University. Aberdeen University: Research Fellow in Archaeology, 1974-77, Lecturer in Geography/Archaeology, 1977-85; University of Edinburgh: Lecturer in Archaeology, 1985-90, Senior Lecturer in Archaeology, 1990-98. Honorary Chair, Institute of Field Archaeologists, 1991-92. Publications: Archaeological Resource Management in the United Kingdom – an introduction (Co-editor), 1993; Scotland – Environment and Archaeology 8000 BC-AD 1000 (Co-editor), 1997; The Archaeology of Britain – an Introduction from the Upper Palaeolithic to the Industrial Revolution, (Co-editor), 1999; exhibition catalogues; papers. Recreations: walking; watching St. Johnstone. Address: (b.) 12 Infirmary Street, Edinburgh EH1 1LT; T.-0131-650 2370.

Ramage, Alan W. Keeper of the Registers of Scotland, since 1994; b. 4.12.43, Edinburgh; m., Fiona Lesslie. Educ. Boroughmuir School, Edinburgh. Recreations: running; reading; working. Address: (b.) Meadowbank House, 153 London Road, Edinburgh EH8 7AU; T.-0131-659 6111.

Ramage, Professor Robert, BSc, PhD, DSc, FRS, CChem, FRSC, FRSA, FRSE. Forbes Professor of Chemistry, University of Edinburgh, since 1984 (Head, Department of Chemistry,since 1997); b. 4.10.35, Glasgow; m., Joan Fraser Paterson; 3 d. Educ. Whitehill Senior Secondary School; University of Glasgow. Lecturer, then Senior Lecturer, University of Liverpool, 1964-77; Professor of Organic Chemistry, then Head of Department, UMIST, 1977-84. Chairman, SERC Organic Chemistry; Member, Panel, SERC Science Board; President, Perkin Division, Royal Society of Chemistry, 1991-93; Member, RAE Chemistry Committee, since 1996; Member, Committees: Royal Society of Edinburgh, Royal Society of London; Director, Edinburgh Centre for Protein Technology, 1996-99; Director, Albachem Ltd. Tilden Lectureship, Royal Society of Chemistry, 1986-87; Society of Chemistry Award for Synthetic Organic Chemistry, 1987. Publication: Peptides (Co-editor), 1996. Recreations: sport; gardening; current affairs. Address: (b.) Department of Chemistry, University of Edinburgh, West Mains Road, Edinburgh EH9 3JJ; T.-0131-650 4721.

Ramsay, Angus Richard James. Principal 2nd Violin, Orchestra of Scottish Opera, since 1985; Artistic Director, Mendelssohn on Mull Festival, since 1994; Teacher of Violin, Royal Scottish Academy of Music and Drama, since 1989; b. 9.3.51, Edinburgh; m., Marianne Tgetgel; 1 s.; 2 d. Educ. George Heriot's School, Edinburgh; Royal Scottish Academy of Music and Drama; Conservatory of Music, Berne, Switzerland. Studied with Leonard Friedman, 1966-70; studied with Professor Max Rostal, 1970-75; Principal 2nd Violin, Würtemberg Chamber Orchestra, 1975-76; Associate Leader, South-West German Chamber Orchestra, 1976-85; Teacher, Fettes College, Edinburgh, since 1994; Founder, Scottish Fiddle Concept, since 1988; Founder, Glasgow Viennese Strings, since 1990; founded Duo Paganini, 1994. Address: (h.) 2 Staikhill, Lanark, ML11 7PW; T.-01555 662645.

Ramsay, Major General Charles Alexander, CB, OBE. Landowner and Company Director; b. 12.10.36, North Berwick; m., Hon. Mary Margaret Hastings MacAndrew; 2 s.; 2 d. Educ. Eton; Sandhurst. Commissioned Royal Scots Greys, 1956; Staff College, Canada, 1967-68; Commanded Royal Scots Dragoon Guards, 1977-79; Commander 12th Armoured Brigade, 1980-82; Dep DMO MOD, 1983-84; GOC Eastern District, 1984-87; Director, General Army Organisation and Territorial Army, 1987-89; Chairman, The Wine Company (Scotland) Ltd., 1992-93, Cockburns of Leith PLC, 1993; Director, John Menzies Plc, Grey Horse Properties Ltd., Edinburgh Military Tattoo Ltd., Potomac Holdings Inc (USA), Morningside Developments Ltd. (USA), Caledonian Eagle. Colonel, The Royal Scots Dragoon Guards, 1992; Member, Royal Company of Archers (Queen's Bodyguard for Scotland). Recreations: field sports; equitation; travel; motor-yachting; motoring. Address: (h.) Bughtrig, Coldstream, Berwickshire TD12 4JP; T.-01890 840678.

Ramsay, Lord (James Hubert Ramsay), DL. Company Director; Brigadier, Queen's Bodyguard for Scotland (Royal Company of Archers); Deputy Lieutenant, Angus; b. 17.1.48; m.; 1 s.; 2 d. Educ. Ampleforth.

Ramsay, Norman James Gemmill, MA, LLB. Sheriff (retired); b. 26.8.16, Kilmarnock; m., Rachael Mary Berkeley Cox. Educ. Merchiston Castle School, Edinburgh; Edinburgh University. WS, 1947; Advocate, 1956; Administrator General, Northern Rhodesia, 1947; Resident, Magistrate, Northern Rhodesia, 1956; Senior Resident Magistrate, Northern Rhodesia, 1958; Puisne Judge, High Court of Northern Rhodesia, later Zambia, 1958; Sheriff, Kirkcudbright, Stranraer and Dumfries, 1971. Recreation: gardening. Address: (h.) Mill of Borgue, Kirkcudbright; T.-01557 870211.

Randall, Rev. David James, MA, BD, ThM. Minister, Church of Scotland, Macduff, since 1971; Vice-Convener, Church of Scotland Board of National Mission; b. 5.6.45, Edinburgh; m., Nan Wardlaw; 3 s.; 1 d. Educ. George

Heriot's School; Edinburgh University; Princeton Theological Seminary. Recreations: jogging; reading; photography. Address: The Manse, Macduff AB45 3QL; T.-01261 832316.

Randall, John Norman, BA, MPhil. Assistant Secretary, Countryside and Natural Heritage Unit, Scottish Office Agriculture, Environment and Fisheries Department, since 1995; b. 1.8.45, Bromley, Kent; 1 s.; 1 d. Educ. Bromley Grammar School; Bristol University; Glasgow University. Department of Economic Affairs; Scottish Office. Recreation: hill-walking. Address: (b.) Pentland House, Edinburgh; T.-0131-244 6416.

Ranicki, Professor Andrew Alexander, MA (Cantab), PhD, FRSE. Professor of Algebraic Surgery, Edinburgh University, since 1995; b. 30.12.48, London; m., Dr. I. Thompson; 1 d. Educ. King's School, Canterbury; Trinity College, Cambridge. Research Fellow, Trinity College, Cambridge, 1972-77; Princeton University, 1977-82. Junior Whitehead Prize, 1983, Senior Berwick Prize, 1994, London Mathematical Society; author of books on algebraic surgery. Address: (b.) Department of Mathematics and Statistics, Edinburgh University, Edinburgh; T.-0131-650 5073.

Rankeillour, Rt. Hon. The Lord. Peer (Conservative); Member, House of Lords, since 1968; descendant of King Robert the Bruce; Rear Commodore, House of Lords Yacht Club; Architectural Adviser, Highland Board; former Lord Commissioner of Scotland; Farmer and Landowner; b. 29.5.35. Educ. Ampleforth. Recreations: agricultural and horticultural equipment/machinery inventor; hunting; grandscale landscaping. Address: (h.) The Achaderry Estate, Roy Bridge, Western Inverness-shire; T.-Spean Bridge 206.

Rankin, Sir Alick Michael. Former Chairman, Scottish & Newcastle plc; b. 23.1.35, London; m., Suzetta Nelson; 1 s.; 3 d. Educ. Eton College; Oxford University. Scots Guards, 1953-55; investment banking, Toronto, 1956-59; Scottish & Newcastle Breweries plc, from 1960.

Rankin, Professor David W.H., MA, PhD, FRSC, CChem, FRSE. Professor of Structural Chemistry, Edinburgh University, since 1989; b. 8.6.45, Birkenhead; m., Stella M. Thomas; 3 s.; 1 d. Educ. Birkenhead School; King's College, Cambridge. Edinburgh University: ICI Research Fellow, 1969, Demonstrator, 1971, Lecturer, 1973, Reader, 1980, Professor, 1989. Publication: Structural Methods in Inorganic Chemistry. Address: (b.) Department of Chemistry, Edinburgh University, West Mains Road, Edinburgh EH9 3JJ; T.-0131-650 4728.

Rankin, Ian. Novelist; b. 1960, Fife; m.; 2 s. Educ. Edinburgh University. Has been employed as grape-picker, swine-herd, taxman, alcohol researcher, hi-fi journalist and punk musician; creator of the Inspector Rebus novels; first Rebus novel, Knots and Crosses, 1987; this series now translated into several languages; elected Hawthornden Fellow; former winner, Chandler-Fulbright Award; two CWA "Daggers"; 1997 CWA Macallan Gold Dagger for fiction for Black and Blue.

Rankin, Rear Admiral Neil Erskine, CB, CBE. Chairman, Caledonian MacBrayne Ltd., since 1996; Chairman, Scottish Seabird Centre, since 1997; Director, Portsmouth Naval Base Property Trust, since 1996; b. 24.12.40, Masjid-I-Suleiman, Persia; m., Jillian Mary; 1 s.; 1 d. Educ. Melville College; Clifton Hall; North Berwick High School; Britannia Royal Naval College. Joined Royal Navy, 1958; pilot's wings, 1963; Commanding Officer: HMS Achilles, 1977, HMS Bacchante, 1978; Commander (Air): RNAS Yeovilton, 1979, HMS Invincible, 1981; Naval Air Warfare, Ministry of Defence, 1983; Chief of Staff, Flag Officer, Third Flotilla, 1984; Commanding Officer, Captain F8, HMS Andromeda, 1985; Senior Naval Officer, Middle East, 1985; Deputy Director, Naval Warfare, Ministry of Defence, 1987; Commanding Officer, HMS Ark Royal, 1991; Commander, British Forces Falkland Isles, 1992; Flag Officer, Portsmouth and Naval Base Commander, 1994; retired RN, 1996; Manchester Business School. Member, Grand Council, KGFS; Younger Brother, Trinity House; Liveryman, Shipwrights' Company; Hammerman of Glasgow. Recreations: sailing (Royal Yacht Squadron, RNSA, East Lothian Yacht Club): golf (North Berwick Golf Club); rugby (Past-President, Combined Services and Royal Navy and United Services, Portsmouth). Address: (h.) 1 May Terrace, North Berwick East Lothian EH39 4BSA; T.-01620 895342.

Rankin, Emeritus Professor Robert Alexander, MA, PhD, ScD, FRSAMD, FRSE. Emeritus Professor of Mathematics, Glasgow University, since 1982; b. 27.10.15, Garlieston, Wigtownshire; m., Mary Ferrier Llewellyn (deceased); 1 s.; 3 d. Educ. Whithorn School; Fettes College; Clare College, Cambridge. Fellow, Clare College, 1939-51; War work on rockets, 1940-45; Lecturer, Cambridge University, 1945-51; Assistant Tutor, Clare College, 1947-51; Mason Professor of Pure Mathematics, Birmingham University, 1951-54; Professor of Mathematics, Glasgow University, 1954-82 (Clerk of Senate, 1971-78, Dean of Faculties, 1985-88). Vice-President, Royal Society of Edinburgh, 1960-63; Keith Prize, RSE, 1961-63; Member, Secretary of State's Advisory Council on Education, 1959-61; Honorary President, Gaelic Society of Glasgow, since 1969; Vice-President, London Mathematical Society, 1966-68; LMS Senior Whitehead Prize, 1987; LMS De Morgan Medal, 1998; President, Edinburgh Mathematical Society, 1957-58 and 1978-79, Honorary member, since 1990. Recreations: music; hill-walking; Gaelic studies. Address: (h.) 98 Kelvin Court, Glasgow G12 0AH; T.-0141-339 2641.

Rankin, Thomas John, MA, MA(Ed), AdvDipEd, FCollP. Head Teacher, Sgoil Dhalabroig, South Uist, since 1981; b. 29.3.47, Glasgow; m., Jean Helen; 2 d. Educ. Strathbungo Secondary School, Glasgow; Glasgow University; Open University. Teacher, Bernard Street Secondary School, Glasgow; taught in Zambia; i/c Cambridge School Certificate and Overseas Examinations, Ministry of Education, Lusaka, Zambia; Head Teacher, Libala Secondary School, Lusaka; Teacher, West Derby Comprehensive School, Liverpool, Chryston High School, Lanarkshire. Recreation: gardening. Address: (b.) Daliburgh School, Isle of South Uist H58 5SS; T.-01878 700276.

Ransford, Tessa, MA, RSA. Poet; Director, Scottish Poetry Library; b. 8.7.38, Bombay; 1 s.; 3 d. Educ. St. Leonard's School, St. Andrews; Edinburgh University; Craiglockhart College of Education. Publicity Department, Oxford University Press, 1958; in Pakistan as wife of missionary, 1960-68; Assistant to the Director, Scottish Institute of Adult Education, 1982-83; Editor, Lines Review, 1988-98; books of poetry: Poetry of Persons, 1975, While It Is Yet Day, 1976, Light of the Mind, 1980, Fools and Angels, 1984; Shadows from the Greater Hill, 1987; A Dancing Innocence, 1988; Seven Valleys, 1991; Medusa Dozen and other poems, 1994; Scottish Selection, 1998; When It Works It Feels Like Play, 1998; first prize, Jubilee poetry competition, Scottish Association for the Speaking of Verse, 1974; Scottish Arts Council Book Award, 1980; Howard Sergeant Award for services to poetry, 1989; Honorary Member, The Saltire Society, 1993; Heritage Society of Scotland Annual Award, 1996; Member, Scottish International PEN; Founder and Organiser, School of Poets (open learning workshop for practising poets). Recreation: grandchildren. Address: (h.) 31 Royal Park Terrace, Edinburgh EH8 8JA; T.-0131-661 1277.

Rapport, Professor Nigel Julian, BA, MA, PhD. Professor of Anthropological and Philosophical Studies, St. Andrews

University, since 1996; b. 8.11.56, Cardiff; m., Elizabeth J.A. Munro; 1 s. Educ. Clifton College, Bristol; Cambridge University; Manchester University. Research Fellow and Associate, Institute of Social and Economic Research, Memorial University of Newfoundland, 1983-87; Lecturer, Blaustein Institute for Desert Research, Ben-Gurion University of the Negev, Israel, 1988; Lecturer, Department of Social Anthropology, Manchester University, 1989; joined St. Andrews University as Lecturer, 1993. Hon. Secretary, Association of Social Anthropologists of the UK and Commonwealth, since 1994; 1996 Royal Society of Edinburgh prize lectureship in the humanities, 1996; Royal Anthropological Institute, Curl Essay Prize, 1996. Publications: Talking Violence: an anthropological interpretation of conversation in the city, 1987; Diverse World-Views in an English Village, 1993; The Prose and the Passion: anthropology, literature and the writing of E.M. Forster, 1994; Transcendent Individual, towards a literary and liberal anthropology, 1997; Questions of Consciousness (Co-editor), 1995; Migrants of Identity: Perceptions of Home in a World of Movement (Co-editor), 1998. Recreations: travel; sport; literature. Address: (b.) Department of Social Anthropology, St. Andrews University, St. Andrews KY16 9AL; T.-01334 462977.

Ratter, James Alexander, BSc, PhD, FRSE, FRGS. Senior Principal Scientific Officer, Head of Tropical Biology, Royal Botanic Garden, Edinburgh, since 1987; b. 15.2.34, Cambridge; m., Pamela Joan Allsop. Educ. Liverpool College; University of Liverpool. University Demonstrator, University of Liverpool, 1958-60; Botanist, Royal Botanic Garden, Edinburgh: Scientific Officer, 1960-64, Senior Scientific Officer, 1964-69, Principal Scientific Officer, 1969-87; Visiting Professor (Co-Founder, Ecology Department), University of Brasilia, 1976-77; Co-Leader of Biodiversity Survey, Anglo-Brazilian Maracá Rainforest Project (INPA/Royal Geographical Society/SEMA), 1987-88. Specialist Adviser, HOC Environment Committee, Climatological and Environmental Effects of Rainforest Destruction, Session 1989-90 and 1990-91; Honorary Citizen, Municipality of Nova Xavantina, Mato Grosso, Brazil, 1997. Recreations; field botany; Portuguese language; ornithology. Publications: Maracá: Rainforest Island (Co- Author), 1993; Maracá: The Biodiversity and Environment of an Amazonian Rainforest (Editor), 1998. Address: (b.) 20A Inverleith Row, Edinburgh EH3 5LR.

Rawson, Simon Christopher, DipRAM. Sub-Principal Viola, Scottish Chamber Orchestra, since 1988; Teacher, since 1989; b. 22.5.58, Halifax; m., Catherine Marwood; 1 s.; 1 d. Educ. Heath School, Halifax; Royal Academy of Music. Member, English Chamber Orchestra, 1981-82; freelance Violist, mainly with Academy of St. Martin in the Fields, London, and City of London Sinfonia; occasional appearances with Hanson and Fairfield Quartets. Recreations: bird-watching; badminton. Address: (h.) 1 The Paddock, North Berwick EH39 4QW; T.-01620 895683.

Read, Professor Andrew Fraser. BSc (Hons), DPhil. Chair of Natural History, University of Edinburgh, since 1998; b. 12.9.62, Hawera, New Zealand; m., Victoria Braithwaite; 2 s. Educ. Otago University, Dunedin, New Zealand; Oxford University. University of Oxford: Commonwealth Scholarship to Merton College, 1985-88, Junior Research Fellowship, Christ Church, 1988-92, Lecturer in Zoology, St. Catherine's College, 1989-90, Lloyd's of London Tercentenary Fellowship, 1991-92; Adjunct Professor in Evolutionary Ecology, University of Tromsø, Norway, 1992-97; BBSRC Advanced Research Fellowship, University of Edinburgh, 1993-97; BBSRC Second Advanced Research Fellowship, 1998. Recreation: hankering after the mountains. Address: (b.) Institute of Cell, Animal and Population Biology, University of Edinburgh, Edinburgh EH9 3JT; T.-0131-650 5506.

Read, Edward Reginald, MIMgt. Consultant, Ayrshire Marketing, since 1989; General Secretary, Tenovus Scotland, since 1986; b. 6.12.29, Sydenham; 1 s.; 3 d. Educ. Ilkley Grammar School; Marr College, Troon. National Service, 1948-50; J. & P. Coats Ltd., 1950-85. Town Councillor, Troon, 1964-71; Past Chairman, Royal Scottish Automobile Club. Recreations: travel; cars; golf. Address: (h.) 3 Windyhaugh, 119 South Beach, Troon KA10 6EH; T.-01292 311276.

Read, Professor Paul, BSc, MSc, PhD, CBiol, FIBiol, CIWEM. Associate Head, Department of Biological Sciences, Napier University, since 1990; b. 1.1.48, Saffron Walden; m., Jane. Educ. Palmers Grammar School, Grays; Hull University; Aston University. Research Technician, Essex Water Authority, 1969-70; Research Assistant, University of Aston, 1971-72; Research Fellow, then Lecturer, Napier College, 1972-82; Senior Lecturer, Napier Polytechnic, 1982-90. Fifty publications. Recreations: offshore sailing/cruising; gardening; hill-walking. Address: (b.) Department of Biological Sciences, Napier University, Colinton Road, Edinburgh EH10 5DT; T.-0131-455 2625.

Reay, 14th Lord (Hugh William Mackay); b. 19.7.37; m.; 2 d.; 2 s., 1 d. by pr. m. Educ. Eton; Christ Church. Succeeded to title, 1963; Member, European Parliament, 1973-79; Parliamentary Under Secretary of State, Department of Trade and Industry, 1991-92.

Reed, Gavin Barras, BA. Chairman, John Menzies plc; b. 13.11.34, Newcastle upon Tyne; m. Muriel Joyce; 1 s.; 3 d. Educ. Eton; Trinity College, Cambridge. National Service, Fleet Air Arm; joined The Newcastle Breweries, 1958; Vice-Chairman, Scottish & Newcastle plc, 1991-94. Director, Hamilton and Inches Ltd. (Chairman), Burtonwood Brewery plc, CNC Properties plc. Recreations: shooting; tennis. Address (h.) Whitehill, Aberdour, Burntisland, Fife KY3 0RW; Broadgate, West Woodburn, Northumberland NE48 2RN.

Reed, Malcolm Christopher, MA, DPhil, FCIT. Director General, Strathclyde Passenger Transport Executive, since 1997; b. 24.11.44, Cardigan, Wales; 2 d. Educ. Royal Grammar School, Newcastle upon Tyne; St. Catherine's College and Nuffield College, Oxford. Assistant, Bodleian Library, Oxford; Lecturer, Glasgow University; Researcher/Associate Director, Planning Exchange, Glasgow; Planner/Chief Public Transport Co-ordinator, Greater Glasgow P.T.E.; Chief Policy Planner/Senior Executive Officer, Strathclyde Regional Council, latterly Assistant Chief Executive. Member, Scottish Section Committee, Chartered Institute of Transport; Deputy Chairman, Railway Heritage Committee. Recreations: hill-walking; listening to music; travel. Address: (b.) Consort House, 12 West George Street, Glasgow G2 1HN; T.-0141-333 3100.

Reed, Professor Peter, BA, RIBA, FRIAS, FRSA. Professor of Architecture, Strathclyde University; b. 31.1.33, Hayes, Middlesex; m., Keow Chim Lim; 2 d. Educ. Southall Grammar School; Manchester University (State Scholar); Open University. Commissioned Officer, RAF, 1960-61; Assistant Lecturer, University of Hong Kong, 1961-64; Architect in practice, Malaysia, 1964-70; joined Strathclyde University as Lecturer, 1970; Professor, 1986; Dean, Faculty of Engineering, 1988-90; Vice-Principal Elect, 1990-92; Vice-Principal, 1992-94. Secretary, Kilsyth Civic Trust, 1975-80; Chairman, Kilsyth Community Council, 1975-78; GIA Council, 1982-84; ARCUK Board of Education, 1985-95; Governor, Glasgow School of Art, 1982-94; Director, Glasgow West Conservation Trust, since 1990, Convener, since 1996; Chairman, Council, Charles Rennie Mackintosh Society, 1991-94. Publications include Glasgow: The Forming of the City (Editor). Recreations: opera; wine; cricket. Address: (b.) Department of

Architecture and Building Science, Strathclyde University, 131 Rottenrow, Glasgow G4 0NG; T.-0141-552 4400.

Reed, Hon. Lord (Rlobert John Reed), LLB, DPhil. Senator of the College of Justice, since 1998; b. 7.9.56, Edinburgh; m., Jane Elizabeth Mylne; 2 d. Educ. George Watson's College, Edinburgh; Edinburgh University; Balliol College, Oxford. Standing Junior Counsel: Scottish Education Department, 1988-89, Scottish Office Home and Health Department, 1989-95; called to English Bar, 1991; QC, 1995; Advocate Depute, 1996-98. Recreations: music; visual arts. Address: (b.) Court of Session, Parliament House, Edinburgh EH1 1RQ.

Reekie, Iain Robert, BA. Artistic Director, 7:84 Theatre Company Scotland; b. 14.2.67, Edinburgh; 1 s. Educ. Firhill High School, Edinburgh; RSAMD. Freelance director, 1989-90; Publicity Officer, Mayfest, 1990; Assistant Director, 7:84 Theatre Company Scotland, 1990-91; Assistant Director, Nottingham Playhouse, 1991. Address: (b.) 2 Port Dundas Place, Glasgow G2 3LB.

Reeks, David Robin, TD, DL, BSc(Eng). Consulting Engineer, Axiom Consulting Engineers Ltd., since 1996; Principal Associate, Avondale Associates, since 1996; b. 15.6.35, Parkstone; m., Kathleen Veronica Stephens; 1 s.; 1 d. Educ. Canford School; London University. Rig Engineer, UKAEA Dounreay, 1962-67; Senior Engineer, SSEB, 1967-90; Reactor Thermal Performance Engineer, Scottish Nuclear Ltd., 1990-94. Committee Member and Volunteer Convoy Leader, Edinburgh Direct Aid to Bosnia; Deputy Lieutenant of Lanarkshire; TA Royal Engineers/Royal Corps of Transport, 1962-90. Recreations: hill-walking; Scottish country dancing. Address: 3 Cedar Place, Strathaven, Lanarkshire ML10 6DW; T.-01357 521695.

Rees, Alan Tait, MBE, MA (Cantab), CQSW; b. 4.8.31, Shanghai, China; m., Alison Margaret; 2 s.; 2 d. Educ. Kingswood School, Bath; Gonville and Caius College, Cambridge; London School of Economics; University College, Swansea. Community Development Officer, Tanzania; Lecturer in Youth and Community Studies, Moray House College; Organising Secretary, Board for Information in Youth and Community Service, Scotland; Senior Community Development Officer, Council of Social Service for Wales; Assistant Director, Edinburgh Voluntary Organisations' Council, retired 1993; Chair, Scotland Yard Adventure Centre, Edinburgh; Member, Scotland Committee, British Association of Social Workers and Editor, Rostrum; Trustee, Seagull Trust; Chair, Handicabs; Scottish National Representative, International Association for the Child's Right to Play; Board Member, Lothian Centre for Integrated Living; Policy Committee, Scottish Council for Voluntary Organisations. Recreations: gardening; painting. Address: (h.) 20 Seaforth Drive, Edinburgh EH4 2BZ; T.-0131-332 7317.

Rees, Professor Elmer Gethin, BA (Cantab), PhD (Warwick), MA (Oxon), FRSE. Professor, Department of Mathematics and Statistics, Edinburgh University, since 1979; Member, Executive Committee, International Centre for Mathematical Sciences, since 1993; Trustee, RSE Scotland Foundation, since 1966; b. 19.11.41, Llandybie, Wales; m., Mary Elene; 2 s. Educ. Llandeilo Grammar School; St. Catharine's College, Cambridge; Warwick University. Lecturer, Department of Pure Mathematics, Hull University, 1967-69; Member, Institute for Advanced Study, Princeton, 1969-70; Lecturer, Department of Pure Mathematics, University College of Swansea, 1970-71; Tutorial Fellow, St. Catherine's College, Oxford and Lecturer in Mathematics, Oxford University, 1971-79. Vice President, London Mathematical Society, 1994-96. Publications: Notes on Geometry; Homotopy Theory. Address: (h.) 23 Blacket Place, Edinburgh EH9 1RJ; T.-0131-667 2747.

Rees, Jennifer Linda, PhD, BSc, FRSS, MIMgt. Assistant Principal (Academic), Bell College of Technology, since 1995; b. 2.7.51, Edinburgh; m., Richard; 1 s.; 1 d. Educ. George Watson's Ladies College, Edinburgh; Edinburgh University. Operational Research Analyst, then Statistical Quality Control Manager, Scottish & Newcastle Breweries Ltd.; Lecturer, Department of Business Studies, Edinburgh University; Head, Department of Management Studies, Scottish College of Textiles. Recreations: swimming; skiing; playing piano badly. Address: (b.) Bell College of Technology, Almada Street, Hamilton ML3 0JB.

Reeves, Philip Thomas Langford, RSA, RSW, RE, RGI, ARCA. Artist; b. 7.7.31, Cheltenham; m., Christine MacLaren (deceased); 1 d. Educ. Naunton Park School, Cheltenham; Cheltenham School of Art; Royal College of Art, London. Lecturer in Graphic Design, Glasgow School of Art, 1954-70, Head of Printmaking, 1970-91. Address: (h.) 13 Hamilton Drive, Glasgow G12 8DN; T.-0141-339 0720.

Reid, Alexander N., WS, NP, LLB. Chairman, Steedman Ramage WS, since 1993; b. 15.9.54, Aberdeen; m., Maria; 2 s. Educ. Robert Gordon's College, Aberdeen; Aberdeen University. Steedman Ramage WS: apprentice lawyer, 1975-77, Assistant, 1977-80, Partner, 1980-93. Recreations: family; sport; music. Address: (b.) 6 Alva Street, Edinburgh; T.-0131-260 6600.

Reid, Alison Hamilton, MA, DMS, MCIM, FRSA. Chief Executive, Scottish Further Education Unit, since 1995; Depute Principal, Perth College. Educ. Montrose Academy; Edinburgh University; Strathclyde University. Marketing and business development in commercial sector, 1973-81; Lecturer and Manager in Further Education, 1981-95. Address: (b.) Argyll Court, Castle Business Park, Stirling; T.-01786 892000.

Reid, Allan William, MBChB, FRCR. Consultant Radiologist: Glasgow Royal Infirmary, since 1989, Ross Hall Hospital, since 1991; Clinical Director of Imaging, Glasgow Royal Infirmary, since 1996; b. 20.6.58, Glasgow. Educ. Glasgow Academy; University of Glasgow. Recreations: photography; swimming; golf. Address: (b.) Department of Radiology, Glasgow Royal Infirmary, Glasgow G31 2ER; T.-0141-211 4783.

Reid, Professor Colin Turriff, MA, LLB. Professor of Environmental Law, Dundee University, since 1995; b. 10.6.58, Aberdeen; m., M. Anne Palin; 2 d. Educ. Robert Gordon's College, Aberdeen; University College, Oxford; Gonville and Caius College, Cambridge. Lecturer in Public Law, Aberdeen University, 1980-90; Senior Lecturer in Law, Dundee University, 1991-95. Publications: Nature Conservation Law; Environmental Law in Scotland (Editor). Recreations: cricket; hockey. Address: (b.) Department of Law, Dundee University, Dundee DD1 4HN; T.-01382 344461.

Reid, David C., MA, MEd. Rector, Kinross High School, since 1985; b. 4.9.43, Motherwell; m., Alison W. Ewing; 1 s.; 1 d. Educ. Wishaw High School; Glasgow University; Jordanhill College; Edinburgh University. Teacher of English, Kirkcaldy High School, 1966-71; Principal Teacher of English, Currie High School, 1971-80; Assistant Rector, Inverkeithing High School, 1980-85. Member/Chairman, English Panel, Scottish Examination Board, 1976-82; Member, IBA Educational Advisory Council (Schools Panels), 1975-86; Chairman, Channel 4 Scottish Schools Committee. Recreations: hill-walking; angling; conversation; reading; Scottish traditional architecture. Address: (b.) Kinross High School, Kinross, Kinross-shire KY13 8AW; T.-01577 862430.

Reid, David Ronald, MA(Hons), LLB. Partner, Burness, since 1965; b. 23.6.37, Larbert; m., Ruth Edith; 1 d. Educ. Daniel Stewart's College, Edinburgh; Edinburgh University. Apprenticeship with W. & J. Burness, 1959-62, Assistant, 1962-65. Former Council Member, WS Society. Recreations: golf; hill-walking; music; reading. Address: (b.) 50 Lothian Road, Festival Square, Edinburgh EH3 9WJ; T.-0131-473 6000.

Reid, Derek Donald, MA. Deputy Chairman, Sea Fish Industry Authority, since 1996; Deputy Chairman, Scotland The Brand, since 1997; various directorships of small companies; b. 30.11.44, Aberdeen; m., Janice Anne Reid; 1 s.; 1 d. Educ. Inverurie Academy; Aberdeen University; Robert Gordon University. Cadbury-Schweppes, 1968-85 (latterly Divisional Director); founding Director/Owner, Premier Brands, 1985-90; Chief Executive, Scottish Tourist Board, 1994-96. Honorary Doctorate, Business Administration, Robert Gordon University; Fellow, George Thomas Society. Recreations: golf; fishing; modern art; fine food/wine. Address: Bonhard House, Scone, Perth PH2 7PQ; T.-01738 553911.

Reid, Rev. Donald, LLB, MPhil, BD. Anglican Chaplain, Universities in Glasgow, since 1995; Team Priest, St. Mary's Cathedral, Glasgow, since 1995; Chair, Jubilee 2000 Scottish Coalition, since 1997; b. 25.2.58, Bellshill. Educ. High School of Glasgow. Curate, St. John's, Greenock, 1985-88; Rector, St. John's, Ballieston, St. Serf's, Shettleston, 1988-95; Convener, Overseas Committee, Scottish Episcopal Church, since 1994; Trustee, Scottish Churches' World Exchange, since 1994; Convener, Scottish Churches' World Action. Recreations: cinema; photography. Address: (h.) 1/2 212 Wilton Street, Glasgow G20 6BL; T.-0141-946 1145.

Reid, Professor Gavin Clydesdale, MA, MSc, PhD. Professor in Economics, St. Andrews University, since 1991; Director, Centre for Research into Industry, Enterprise, Finance and the Firm (CRIEFF), since 1991; b. 25.8.46, Glasgow; m., 1, Margaret Morrice or McGregor (m. diss.); 1 s.; 1 step-s.; 2, Maureen Johnson or Bagnall; 1 s.; 2 d.; 1 step.-s. Educ. Lyndhurst School; Frimley and Camberley Grammar School; Aberdeen University; Southampton University; Edinburgh University. Lecturer, Senior Lecturer, Reader in Economics, Edinburgh University, 1971-91; Visiting Associate Professor: Queen's University, Ontario, 1981-82, Denver University, Colorado, 1984; Visiting Scholar, Darwin College, Cambridge, 1987-88; Visiting Professor, University of Nice, 1998; Leverhulme Trust Research Fellowship, 1989-90; Nuffield Foundation Social Science Research Fellowship, 1997-98. Editorial Board: Scottish Journal of Political Economy, since 1986, Small Business Economics, since 1997, Venture Capital, since 1998; Member, Council, Scottish Economic Society, since 1990. Publications: The Kinked Demand Curve Analysis of Oligopoly, 1981; Theories of Industrial Organization, 1987; The Small Entrepreneurial Firm (Co-author), 1988; Classical Economic Growth, 1989; Small Business Enterprise, 1993; Profiles in Small Business (Co-author), 1993; Venture Capital Investment, 1998. Recreations:music; reading; running; badminton. Address: (h.) 23 South Street, St. Andrews KY16 9QS; T.-01334 472932.

Reid, Harry William, BA (Hons), FRSA. Editor, The Herald, since 1997; b. 23.9.47, Glasgow; m., Julie Davidson (qv); 1 d. Educ. Aberdeen Grammar School; Fettes College; Oxford University. The Scotsman: Education Correspondent, 1973-77, Features Editor, 1977-81; Sports Editor, Sunday Standard, 1981-82; Executive Editor, Glasgow Herald, 1982-83, Deputy Editor, 1983-97. Publication: Dear Country: a quest for England, 1992. Recreations: reading; walking; supporting Aberdeen Football Club. Address: (h.) 15 Albion Buildings, Ingram Street, Glasgow; T.-0141-552 8403.

Reid, Heather M.M., BSc(Hons), MSc, CPhys, MInstP, FRMS. Weather Forecaster, Met Office, since 1993; BBC Scotland Weather Forecaster, since 1994; b. 6.7.69, Paisley. Educ. Camphill High School, Paisley; Edinburgh University. Joined Met Office to work in satellite image research; became forecaster at Glasgow Weather Centre; now known as "Heather the Weather" to viewers. Vice-Chair, Institute of Physics (Scottish Branch), since 1997; active involvement in Edinburgh Science Festival, Techfest, and promoting the public understanding of science. Recreations: apart from lecturing and giving talks in spare time – watch cricket; hill-walking. Address: (b.) Glasgow Weather Centre, 220 St. Vincent Street, Glasgow G2 5QD; T.-0141-248 3451.

Reid, Hugh Watt, BVM&S, DipTVM, PhD, MRCVS. Head, Virology Division, Moredun Research Institute, since 1990; b. 23.6.42, Edinburgh; m., Irene Elisabeth; 1 s.; 2 d. Educ. George Watson's College, Edinburgh; Glasgow Academy; Aberdeen Grammar School; University of Edinburgh. Moredun Research Institute: Veterinary Research Officer, 1968-74, Principal Veterinary Research Officer, 1974-90. Previously officer bearer: Association of Veterinary Teachers and Research Workers, Veterinary Deer Society, Edinburgh South Liberal Party. Publications: 150 papers/book chapters. Recreations: gardening; cycling; walking. Address: Pentlands Science Park, Bush Loan, Penicuik EH26 0PZ; T.-0131-445 5111.

Reid, Professor Ian Cameron, MB, ChB, BMedBiol, PhD, MRCPsych. Professor of Psychiatry, Dundee University, since 1995; b. 13.10.60, Dunfermline; m., Isla; 1 d. Educ. Dollar Academy; Aberdeen University; Edinburgh University. Lecturer in Mental Health, Aberdeen University; Research Fellow, Department of Pharmacology, then Lecturer in Psychiatry, Edinburgh University; Senior Lecturer in Mental Health, Aberdeen University. Recreation: curry. Address: (b.) Department of Psychiatry, Ninewells Hospital and Medical School, Dundee DD1 9SY; T.-01382 632853.

Reid, James Gordon, LLB (Hons), FCIArb. Queen's Counsel (Scotland), since 1993; Barrister, Gray's Inn, London, since 1995; b. 24.7.52, Edinburgh; m., Hannah Hogg Hopkins; 3 s.; 1 d. Educ. Melville College, Edinburgh; Edinburgh University. Solicitor, 1976-80; Advocate, 1980-93; Standing Junior Counsel, Scottish Office Environment Department, 1986-93; admitted as Barrister, Inner Temple, 1991. Recreations: general fitness; computers and music. Address: (h.) Blebo House, by St. Andrews, Fife KY15 5TZ; T.-01334 653274.

Reid, Jimmy. Journalist and Broadcaster; b. 1932. Former Engineer; prominent in campaign to save Upper Clyde Shipbuilders; former Convener of Shop Stewards, AUEW; former (Communist) Member, Clydebank Town Council; joined Labour Party and contested Dundee East, General Election, 1979; Rector, Glasgow University, 1971-74; Founder, Seven Days magazine; Columnist, The Herald, Glasgow.

Reid, Rt. Hon. John, PhD. MP (Labour), Hamilton North and Bellshill, since 1997, Motherwell North, 1987-97; b. 8.5.47, Bellshill; m., Catherine McGowan (deceased); 2 s. Educ. St. Patrick's Senior Secondary School, Coatbridge; Stirling University. Scottish Research Officer, Labour Party, 1979-83; Political Adviser to Rt. Hon. Neil Kinnock, 1983-85; Scottish Organiser, Trade Unionists for Labour, 1986-87. Recreations: crosswords; football; reading. Address: (b.) House of Commons, Westminster, London; Parliamentary Office, Montrose House, 154 Montrose Crescent, Hamilton ML3 6LL; T.-01698 454672.

Reid, Rev. John Kelman Sutherland, CBE, TD, MA, DD. Member, Editorial Board, Scottish Journal of Theology, since 1948; b. 31.3.10, Leith; m., Margaret Winifrid

Brookes (deceased). Educ. George Watson's College, Edinburgh; Edinburgh University; Heidelberg University; Basel University; Marburg University; Strasburg University. Professor of Philosophy, Calcutta University, 1935-37; Minister, Craigmillar Park Parish Church, Edinburgh, 1939-52; Chaplain to the Forces with Parachute Regiment, 1942-46; Professor of Theology, Leeds University, 1952-61; Chaplain, Territorial Army, 1948-62; Professor of Systematic Theology, Aberdeen University, 1961-76. Publications: Calvin's Theological Treatises (Editor and Translator), 1954; The Biblical Doctrine of the Ministry, 1955; The Authority of Scripture, 1957; Calvin's Concerning the Eternal Predestination of God (Editor and Translator), 1961; Our Life in Christ, 1963; Presbyterians and Unity, 1966; Christian Apologetics, 1969. Recreation: golf. Address: (h.) 8 Abbotsford Court, 18 Colinton Road, Edinburgh EH10 5EH; T.-0131-447 6855.

Reid, Professor John Low, MA, DM, FRCP, FRSE. Regius Professor of Medicine, University of Glasgow, since 1989; Consultant Physician, Western Infirmary, Glasgow, since 1989; b. 1.10.43, Glasgow; m., Randa; 1 s.; 1 d. Educ. Kelvinside Academy; Fettes College; Magdalen College, Oxford University. Clinical and research posts, Royal Postgraduate Medical School, London and National Institutes of Health, Bethesda, USA; Regius Chair of Materia Medica, University of Glasgow, 1978-89. Publication: Lecture Notes in Clinical Pharmacology. Editor, Handbook of Hypertension. Recreations: outdoors; gardening; opera. Address: (h.) 5 Princes Terrace, Glasgow G12 9JW; T.-0141-211 2886.

Reid, Professor J.S. Grant, BSc, PhD. Professor of Plant Biochemistry, Stirling University, since 1994; b. 27.3.42, Huntly; m., Mary E. Edwards; 1 s.; 2 d. Educ. Gordon Schools, Huntly; Aberdeen University. Lecturer, University of Fribourg, Switzerland, 1970-73, Lecturer in Biochemistry, Stirling University, 1974-78; Visiting Associate Professor, University of Calgary, 1977-78; Senior Lecturer, then Reader, Stirling University, 1978-94; Visiting Professor, Unilever Research Laboratories, Netherlands, 1988. Address: (b.) Department of Biological Sciences, Stirling University, Stirling FK9 4LA; T.-01786 467755.

Reid, Professor Kenneth Gilbert Cameron, MA, LLB. Professor of Property Law, Edinburgh University, since 1994; Law Commissioner for Scotland, since 1995; b. 25.3.54, Glasgow; m., Elspeth Christie; 2 s.; 1 d. Educ. Loretto; St. John's College, Cambridge; Edinburgh University. Admitted as a Solicitor, 1980; Lecturer in Law, Edinburgh University, 1980. Author of numerous books and papers on the law of property. Recreation: classical music. Address: (b.) Department of Private Law, Old College, South Bridge, Edinburgh EH8 9YL; T.-0131-650 2015.

Reid, Robert Russell, JP. Chairman, Argyll and Bute NHS Trust, formerly Chairman, Argyll and Clyde Health Board; Director, Argyll Training; Member, Bute Housing Association; Honorary Sheriff; Farmer; b. 26.12.32, Campbeltown; m., Rebecca Simpson Hunter; 3 s.; 1 d. Educ. Campbeltown Grammar School; Thorpe House; Rothesay Academy. Address: (h.) Eriskay, 13 Ardmory Road, Rothesay, Bute PA20 0PG; T.-01700 50 3238.

Reid, Seona Elizabeth, BA,DArt, FRSA. Director, Glasgow School of Art, since 1999; Director, Scottish Arts Council, 1990-99; b. 21.1.50, Paisley. Educ. Park School, Glasgow; Strathclyde University; Liverpool University. Business Manager, Theatre Royal, Lincoln, 1972-73; Press Officer, Northern Dance Theatre, Manchester, 1973-76; PRO, Ballet Rambert, London, 1976-79; freelance arts consultant, 1979-81; Director, Shape, London, 1981-87; Assistant Director, Greater London Arts, 1987-90. Recreations: walking; travel; the arts. Address: (b.) 167 Renfrew Street, Glasgow G3 6RQ; T.-0141-353 4500.

Reid, William James, ACII, FBIBA. Chairman, Reid Enterprise Ltd.; Hon. Vice-President, Children 1st; b. 18.9.32, Edinburgh; m., Patricia; 2 s. Educ. George Heriot's School. Director, Collins Halden & Co. Ltd., 1960-68, Joint Managing Director, 1968-72, Chairman and Chief Executive, 1972-78; Director, Halden McQuaker & Co. Ltd., Glasgow, 1964-73; Director, Collins Halden & Burnett Ltd., Aberdeen, 1962-74; Director, Hogg Robinson Ltd., London, 1978-84; Chief Executive, Hogg Robinson (Scotland) Ltd., 1978-84; Chairman and Chief Executive: Collins Halden (Scotland) Ltd., 1984-90, Heath Collins Halden (Scotland) Ltd., 1990-92, C.E. Heath (Scotland) Ltd., 1990-92; Chairman, City Business Venue (Scotland) Ltd., 1992-98; Chairman, Nick Ledya Co. (Scotland) Ltd., 1995-98; President, Insurance Society of Edinburgh, 1978-79; Chairman, Corporation of Insurance Brokers Scotland, 1969-70; Member, National Council, Corporation of Insurance Brokers, 1968-71; Freeman of the City of London. Address: (h.) 33/10 Murrayfield Road, Edinburgh EH12 6EP; T.-0131-337 1220.

Reid, Sir William Kennedy, KCB, MA, LLD (Aberdeen and Reading), FRCPEd. Chairman, Mental Welfare Commission for Scotland; Chairman, Advisory Committee on Distinction Awards; Chairman of Council, St. George's School for Girls; b. 15.2.31, Aberdeen; m., Ann Campbell; 2 s.; 1 d. Educ. Robert Gordon's College; George Watson's College; Edinburgh University; Trinity College, Cambridge. Civil Servant, 1956-89, Department of Education and Science, Cabinet Office, Scottish Office; Member, Council on Tribunals and Its Scottish Committee, 1990-96; Member, Commission for Local Administration in England, 1990-96; Member, Commission for Local Administration in Wales, 1990-96. A Director, International Ombudsman Institute, 1992-96; Parliamentary Commissioner for Administration, 1990-97; Health Service Commissioner for England, Scotland, Wales, 1990-97; Queen Elizabeth the Queen Mother Fellow, Nuffield Trust, 1998; Hon. D. Litt (Napier), 1998. Recreations: verse; hill-walking. Address: (h.) 11 Inverleith Terrace, Edinburgh.

Reid, Sheriff William Macpherson, MA, LLB. Sheriff of Tayside, Central and Fife, since 1983; b. 6.4.38. Advocate, 1963; Sheriff of Lothian and Borders, 1978, Glasgow and Strathkelvin, 1978-83. Address: (b.) Sheriff Court House, County Buildings, Mar Street, Alloa, FK10 1HR.

Reid, (William) Russell. Editor, The Sunday Post, since 1989; b. 27.1.36, Dundee; m., Patricia Rutherford (deceased); 2 d. Educ. Harris Academy, Dundee; Arbroath High School. Joined D.C. Thomson & Co. Ltd. as Reporter on Courier and Evening Telegraph, 1953; joined Sunday Post as Reporter and Feature Writer, 1957; Deputy Editor, 1983; Chairman, Editors' Committee, Scottish Daily Newspaper Society, since 1997; Member, Code Committee, Press Complaints Commission, since 1994. Recreations: music; walking; reading; talking. Address: (b.) Albert Square, Dundee DD1 9QJ; T.-01382 223131.

Reith, David Stewart, LLB, NP, WS. Partner, Lindsays WS, Solicitors, Edinburgh, since 1976; b. 15.4.51, Edinburgh; m., Elizabeth Julia Hawkins; 1 s.; 1 d. Educ. Edinburgh Academy; Fettes College; Aberdeen University. Director: Scottish Historic Buildings Trust, Cockburn Conservation Trust, Scottish Sculpture Trust, Boilerhouse Theatre Company Ltd. (Chair); Secretary: Ponton House Trust, Cockburn Conservation Trust; Clerk, Incorporation of Cordiners; Honorary Solicitor, Architectural Heritage Society of Scotland and Fet-Lor Youth Centre. Recreations: gardening; curling; wine. Address: (h.) Pilmuir House, Haddington, East Lothian EH41 4HS; T.-01875 340008.

Remp, Stephen Edward, BA, MA HonDTech. Chairman and Chief Executive, Ramco Energy plc, since 1977; b. 5.5.47, California, USA; m., Janine Beverley; 2 s.; 1 d. Educ. American International School; Claremont Men's

College; John Hopkins University. Saltire Award, 1977, and Civic Trust Award, 1977 (Harthill Castle); Scottish Business Achievement Award, 1984; Grampian Industrialist of the Year Award, 1996; Burgess of Guild of City of Aberdeen. Recreations: skiing; tennis; shooting; swimming; music. Address: (b.) 4 Rubislaw Place, Aberdeen AB10 1XN; T.-01224 626224.

Rennie, Rev. Adrian James Tait, BA, BD. Minister, Drylaw Parish Church, Edinburgh, since 1996; b. 8.4.63, Aberdeen; m., Jean Gibson; 1 s. Educ. Paisley Grammar School; Strathclyde University; Trinity College, Glasgow University. Minister, Calton, Glasgow, 1988-94; Warden, MacLeod Centre, Isle of Iona, and Warden, Adventure Centre, Isle of Mull, for Iona Community, 1994-95. Chairperson, Scottish CND, 1993-94, Camas (Adventure Centre); Convener, Stewardship and Finance Committee, Edinburgh Presbytery, since 1998. Recreations: fly fishing; swimming; parenting. Address: (h.) 15 House O'Hill Gardens, Blackhall, Edinburgh EH4 2AR; T.-0131-332 3785.

Rennie, Alan Craig. Editor, Stirling Observer, since 1983; b. 28.3.51, Stirling; m., Mary. Educ. High School of Stirling. Joined George Outram & Co. as trainee journalist, 1969; junior reporter, Stirling Journal, 1970; reporter, Perthshire Advertiser, 1971-79; Chief Reporter, Stirling Observer, 1979-83. Scottish Chairman, Guild of Editors, 1992-94; UK Delegate to International Society of Weekly Newspaper Editors, USA, 1992. Publication: edited book on history of Stirling, 1986. Recreations: Member, Stirling County R.F.C., Stirling Golf Club, Carse of Stirling Rotary Club. Address: (b.) 40 Craigs, Stirling FK8 2DW; T.-01786 451110.

Rennie, Alistair Gillies, LLB. Hon. Assoc. RICS. Deputy Keeper, Registers of Scotland, Executive Agency; b. 1.2.44, Edinburgh; m., Eleanor Sutherland; 2 d. Educ. Trinity Academy, Edinburgh; Edinburgh University. Joined Department of Registers of Scotland, 1962; Principal Establishment Officer, 1988; Director, Land Register, 1990; Senior Director, Production, 1992; Deputy Keeper, 1994. Director, East of Scotland Society for Welfare and Teaching of the Blind; Member, Deacon's Court, Royal and Ancient Burgh of Linlithgow. Recreations: reading; walking; swimming. Address: (b.) Meadowbank House, 153 London Road, Edinburgh; T.-0131-659 6111.

Rennie, Archibald Louden, CB, LLD, FDS, RCS(Eng); b. 4.6.24, Guardbridge, Fife; m., Kathleen Harkess; 4 s. Educ. Madras College, St. Andrews; St. Andrews University. Experimental Officer, Minesweeping Research Division, 1944-47; joined Department of Health for Scotland, 1947; Private Secretary to Secretary of State for Scotland, 1962-63; Assistant Secretary, Scottish Home and Health Department, 1963-69; Registrar General for Scotland, 1969-73; Under Secretary, Scottish Economic Planning Department, 1973-77; Secretary, Scottish Home and Health Department, 1977-84. Vice-Chairman, Advisory Committee on Distinction Awards, 1985-94; Chancellor's Assessor, St. Andrews University, 1985-89; Member, Scottish Records Advisory Council, 1985-93; Member, Council on Tribunals, and its Scottish Committee, 1987-88; Trustee, Lockerbie Air Disaster Appeal, 1988-91; Chairman, Disciplined Services Pay Review Committee, Hong Kong, 1988; Chairman, Blacket Association, 1971-73; Commodore, Elie and Earlsferry S.C., 1992-94; Chairman, Elie Harbour Trust, 1993-99. Recreations: sailing; sea-fishing; walking; reading. Address: (h.) Well Wynd House, South Street, Elie, Fife KY9 1DN; T.-01333 330741.

Rennie, Professor Michael John, BSc, MSc, PhD, FRSE. Symers Professor of Physiology, Dundee University, since 1983; b. 28.7.46, Wallsend on Tyne; m., Anne Macgregor Gill; 1 s.; 2 d. Educ. Newcastle Royal Grammar School; Hull University; Manchester University; Glasgow University. MRC Travelling Fellow, Washington University Medical School, St. Louis, 1974-76; Lecturer and Wellcome Senior Lecturer, Department of Medicine, University College London, 1976-83. Editor, British Journal of Intensive Care; Consultant to pharmaceutical industry; medical and scientific writer. Publications: 200 scientific papers. Recreations: walking; cycling; reading; eating. Address: (b.) Department of Anatomy and Physiology, Dundee University, Dundee DD1 4HN; T.-01382 344572.

Rennie, Professor Robert, LLB, PhD, FRSA. Partner, Ballantyne & Copland, Solicitors, Motherwell, since 1972; Professor of Conveyancing, Glasgow University, since 1993; b. 30.6.47, Glasgow; m., Catherine Mary McGregor; 1 s.; 3 d. Educ. Lenzie Academy; Glasgow University. Apprentice then Legal Assistant, Bishop Milne Boyd & Co., Solicitors, Glasgow; joined Ballantyne & Copland as Legal Assistant, 1971; Past Convener, Law Society of Scotland Conveyancing Committee; Board Member, Capability Scotland; Member, Local Interview Committee, Prince's Scottish Youth Business Trust; Director, Taggarts (Motor Holdings) Limited. Recreation: classical music. Address: (b.) Old Bank Chambers, 44 Civic Square, Motherwell M11 1TP.

Rennie, Willie Cowan, BSc. Chief Executive, Scottish Liberal Democrats, since 1997; b. 27.9.67, Perth; m., Janet; 1 s. Educ. Bell Baxter High School, Cupar; Paisley College of Technology. Agent: to Paul Tyler, MP, 1992, Christchurch By-election, 1993, to Robin Teverson, MEP, 1994; Devon and Cornwall Campaigns Officer, Liberal Democrats, 1997. Recreations: running; family. Address: (b.) 4 Clifton Terrace, Edinburgh EH12 5DR; T.-0131-337 2314.

Rennilson, John Douglas, MA, MSc, MRTPI, ARICS, MIMgt. Director of Planning and Development, The Highland Council, since 1998 (formerly Director of Planning); b. 12.2.47, Edinburgh; m., Susan M.; 1 s.; 1. Educ. George Watson's College, Edinburgh; Edinburgh University; University of Wales. Lanarkshire County Council, 1970-74, latterly as Senior Planning Officer; Suffolk County Council, 1974-84, latterly as Assistant County Planning Officer (Environment); County Planning Officer, North Yorkshire County Council, 1984-96. Member, Executive, County Planning Officers Society (Chairman, Committee 3, 1989-91, and from 1995). Recreations: walking; golf; Scottish country dancing; branch line railways. Address: (b.) Glenurquhart Road, Inverness IV3 5NX.

Renshaw, Professor Eric, BSc, ARCS, DipStats, MPhil, PhD, CStat, FRSE. Professor of Statistics, Strathclyde University, since 1991; b. 25.7.45, Preston; m., Anne Renshaw. Educ. Arnold School, Blackpool; Imperial College, London; Manchester University; Sussex University; Edinburgh University. Lecturer, then Senior Lecturer in Statistics, Edinburgh University, 1969-91. Publication: Modelling Biological Populations in Space and Time. Recreations: skiing; golf; hill-walking; photography. Address: (b.) Department of Statistics and Modelling Science, Livingstone Tower, Strathclyde University, 26 Richmond Street, Glasgow G1 1XH; T.-0141-548 3591.

Renton, Rev. Ian Paterson, OStJ, FSA Scot, JP. Minister, St. Colm's Parish Kirk, Dalry, Edinburgh, 1966-91; b. 22.3.26, Kirkcaldy; m., Ann Gordon Mutter Macpherson; 2 s.; 1 d. Educ. Sinclairtown and Viewforth Schools, Kirkcaldy; Newbattle Abbey College; Glasgow University; St. Mary's College, St. Andrews. Shipping Clerk, Robert Wemyss & Co., Kirkcaldy, 1941-44; Sergeant, 3rd Bn., Scots Guards, 1944-47; Ministry of Labour, Kirkcaldy, 1947-48; Newbattle Abbey College, 1948-50; Youth Clubs Organiser, Roxburghshire, 1950-53; divinity studies, 1953-58; Assistant Minister, North Kirk, Aberdeen, 1958-60;

Minister, St. Mark's Church, Greenwich, London, 1960-66. Member, Edinburgh City Education Committee, 1970-76; Governor: Moray House College, 1971-79, Donaldson's School, Edinburgh, 1972-75, Newbattle Abbey College, 1973-76; Member, General Assembly Committee on Education, 1973-79; Joint Chairman, Scottish Joint Committee on Religious Education, 1974-79; Member, Lothian Region Education Committee, 1977-78; Member, Edinburgh Children's Panel, 1971-74; Executive Member, Broadcasting Council, Radio Forth, 1976-79; Member, DHSS Social Security Tribunal, 1978-84; Member, Church of Scotland Board of Education, 1983-85; Member, Lothian Health Board Committee on Medical Ethics, 1984-96; Moderator, Edinburgh Presbytery, 1989-90; Chaplain to Astley Ainslie Hospital, Edinburgh, 1971-98. Recreations: gardening; drystane diking; tai chi. Address: Roseneath, Newbattle Terrace, Edinburgh EH10 4SF.

Renton, Janice Helen, LLB. Deputy Commissioner for Local Administration in Scotland, since 1991; Deputy Local Government Adjudicator for Scotland, since 1990; b. 20.4.47, Falkirk. Educ. Bo'ness Academy; Edinburgh University. Legal Assistant, Clackmannan County Council, 1969; Depute Reporter, Children's Panel, Glasgow Corporation, 1971; Senior Legal Assistant, Aberdeen County Council, 1972; Depute Director of Law and Administration, Grampian Regional Council, 1974; Senior Depute Director of Administration, City of Edinburgh, 1976-84; joined Commissioner's Office, 1989. Secretary, Edinburgh International Festival Society, 1982-84. Recreations: eating; talking. Address: 23 Walker Street, Edinburgh EH3 7HX.

Renton, Joan Forrest, DA, RSW. Painter; b. 11.8.35, Sunderland; m., Ronald Renton; 2 s.; 1 d. Educ. Dumfries Academy; Hawick High School; Edinburgh College of Art. Teacher of Art, primary and secondary schools, Edinburgh, 1960-81. Member, Council: Royal Scottish Society of Painters in Watercolours, Society of Scottish Artists; President: Scottish Society of Women Artists and Artist Craftsmen, 1987-89, Society of Scottish Artists and Artist Craftsmen, 1989-93. Recreation: gardening. Address: Holmcroft, 4 Tweeddale Avenue, Gifford, East Lothian EH41 4QN; T.-01620 810247.

Renton, Stuart, MBE, RSA, DA. Architect; Senior Partner, Reiach and Hall, 1982-97; Royal Scottish Academician, since 1997 (Associate, 1983); Chairman, Board of Governors, Edinburgh College of Art, 1992-98; Visiting Professor, Department of Architecture, Strathclyde University, 1992-98; b. 15.9.29, Edinburgh; m., Ethnie Sloan; 1 s.; 1 d. Educ. Royal High School, Edinburgh; Edinburgh College of Art (Andrew Grant Scholar, 1949-52; Civic Medalist, 1952). Military Service, RAF and RAFVR; Partner, Alan Reiach and Partners, Architects, Edinburgh, 1959; Partner, Reiach and Hall, 1965; three RIBA awards, three Civic Trust awards and commendations among successes in other national award schemes. External Examiner, several universities; Assessor for architectural awards schemes; Member, Visiting Board Panel, RIBA Education Board, 1984-95; Governor, Edinburgh College of Art, since 1985. Recreations: skiing; game fishing; Italian hill villages. Address: Grianan, Killichonan, Rannoch, Perthshire PH17 2QW; T.-01882 633247.

Renwick, Professor John Peter, MA, PhD, DLitt, FRHistS, Officier des Palmes Academiques. John Orr Professor of French, Edinburgh University, since 1980; Director, Centre de Recherches Francophones Belges, since 1995; b. 25.5.39, Gillingham; m., Claudette Gorse; 1 s.; 1 d. Educ. Gillingham Grammar School; St. Bartholomew's Grammar School, Newbury; St. Catherine's College, Oxford; Sorbonne; British Institute in Paris (Leverhulme Research Scholar). Assistant Lecturer, then Lecturer, Glasgow University, 1964-66; Fellow, Churchill College, Cambridge, 1966-72; Maitre de Conferences Associe, Departement de Francais, Universite de Clermont-Ferrand, 1970-71, 1972-74; Professor of French, New University of Ulster, 1974-80 (Pro-Vice-Chancellor, 1978-80); Member, Executive Committee, The Complete Works of Voltaire; Member, Executive Committee, Voltaire Foundation. Publications: La destinee posthume de Jean-Francois Marmontel, 1972; Marmontel, Memoires, 1972; Marmontel, Voltaire and the Belisaire affair, 1974; Marmontel, Correspondence, 1974; Catalogue de la bibliotheque de Jean-Baptiste Massillon, 1977, Voltaire et Morangies, ou les Lumieres l'ont echappe belle, 1982; Chamfort devant La Posterite, 1986; Catalogue de la Bibliotheque du Comte D'Espinchal, 1988; Language and Rhetoric of the French Revolution, 1990; Voltaire, La Guerre Civile de Genève, 1990; Catalogue de la Bibliotheque du College de L'Oratoire de Riom 1619-1792, 1997; Voltaire, Brutus, 1998; Voltaire, Lés Guèbres, 1998. Address: (b.) 60 George Square, Edinburgh EH8 9JU.

Rettie, James Philip, CBE, TD. Farmer; Partner, Rettie Farming Co.; Director, Rettie & Co.; Director, Edinburgh and Glasgow Investment Co.; Trustee, Scottish Civic Trust, since 1982; b. 7.12.26, Dundee; m., 1, Helen Grant; 2, Diana Harvey; 2 s.; 1 d. Educ. Trinity College, Glenalmond. Royal Engineers, 1945-48. Chairman, Sea Fish Industry Authority, 1981-87; Chairman, William Low & Co. PLC, 1980-85. Hon. Colonel, 117 and 277 FDSQNS RE (V), 1983-89. Recreations: shooting; gardening; walking. Address: (h.) Hill House, Ballindean, Inchture, Perthshire PH14 9QS; T.-01828 686337.

Reynolds, Professor Siân, BA, MA, PhD. Professor of French, Stirling University, since 1990; Translator; b. 28.7.40, Cardiff; m., Peter France; 3 d. Educ. Howell's School, Llandaff; St. Anne's College, Oxford. Lecturer and Senior Lecturer, Sussex University, 1974-89; Lecturer, Edinburgh University, 1989-90; President, UK Association for the Study of Modern and Contemporary France, 1993-99. Publications: Women, State and Revolution (Editor); Britannica's Typesetters; France Between the Wars, gender and politics; translations include F. Braudel, The Mediterranean.. Address: (b.) Stirling University, Stirling FK9 4LA; T.-01786 467530.

Rice, Professor C. Duncan, MA, PhD, FRSE, FRHistS, FRSA. Principal and Vice-Chancellor, Aberdeen University, since 1996; b. 20.10.42, Aberdeen; m., Susan Ilene; 2 s.; 1 d. Educ. Aberdeen University; Edinburgh University. Lecturer, Aberdeen University, 1966-69; Assistant Professor of History, then Associate Professor of History, Yale University, New Haven, 1970-79; Professor of History, Hamilton College, Clinton, New York, 1979-85; Professor of History, Dean of Faculty of Arts and Sciences, New York University, 1985-94 (Vice-Chancellor, 1991-96). Board Member: US-UK Fulbright Commission, National Trust for Scotland, UCEA, Socrates-UK Erasmus Council, BT Scotland, Grampian Enterprise Ltd., Rowett Research Institute. Publications: The Rise and Fall of Black Slavery; The Scots Abolitionists 1831-1961; various articles and reviews. Recreations: hill-waking; cycling. Address: (b.) Aberdeen University, Regent Walk, Aberdeen; T.-01224 272134.

Richards, Professor Bryan Edward, BSc (Eng), DIC, PhD, CEng, FRAeSoc, AFAIAA. Mechan Professor of Aerospace Engineering, Glasgow University, since 1980; b. 30.6.38, Hornchurch; m., Margaret Owen; 2 s.; 2 d. Educ. Palmer's School, Grays; Queen Mary College, London University. Aerodynamicist, Bristol Aeroplane Company, Filton, 1960-62; Research Assistant, Imperial College, London University, 1962-66; Assistant Professor, Associate Professor, Professor, Von Karman Institute, Belgium, 1967-79; Head, Department of Aerospace Engineering, Glasgow University, 1980-90; Dean of Engineering, 1984-87. Publications: 110 articles. Recreations: sailing; hill-walking. Address: (h.) Ravenswood, 32 Suffolk Street, Helensburgh G84 9PA; T.-01436 672112.

Richards, John Deacon, CBE, AADip, DUniv, RSA, RIBA, PPRIAS. Architect; Principal, John Richards Associates, Architects, since 1986; b. 7.5.31, Shanghai; m., Margaret Brown; 1 s.; 3 d. Educ. Cranleigh School, Surrey; Architectural Association School of Architecture, London. Partner, Robert Matthew, Johnson-Marshall & Partners, 1964-86 (Chairman, 1983-86); Member, Royal Fine Art Commission for Scotland, 1975-89; Agrement Board, 1980-83; Member, Williams Committee on National Museums and Galleries, 1981; Gold Medallist, RSA, 1972; Past President, Royal Incorporation of Architects in Scotland, 1983-85; Trustee, National Galleries of Scotland, 1986-90; Chairman, Scottish Committee, Housing Corporation, 1983-89; Board Member, Scottish Homes, 1988-93, Deputy Chairman, 1989-93; Housing Association Ombudsman for Scotland, since 1993. Recreations: gardening; fishing. Address: (h.) Lady's Field, Whitekirk, East Lothian; T.-01620 870206.

Richards, Professor Randolph Harvey, MA, VetMB, PhD, MRCVS. Director, Institute of Aquaculture, University of Stirling, since 1996; Roberts Morris Bray Professor of Aquatic Veterinary Studies, since 1991; Veterinary Adviser, Scottish Salmon Growers' Association, since 1986; b. 4.3.48, London; m., Jennifer Halley; 1 d. Educ. Grove Park Grammar School, Wrexham; Jesus College, Cambridge University; University of Stirling. University of Stirling: Deputy Director, Unit of Aquatic Pathobiology, 1976-79, Deputy Director, Institute of Aquaculture, 1979-96. Member, Veterinary Products Committee, Medicines Commission, since 1992. Publications: numerous papers on fish pathology in learned journals. Recreations: fine wine and food; shooting. Address: University of Stirling, Stirling FK9 4LA; T.-01786 467870.

Richards, Professor Robert Michael Edward, OBE, BPharm, PhD, DSc, DPharmSc, FRPharmS, PhC (Thai & Zimb). Professor and Head, School of Pharmacy, Robert Gordon University, Aberdeen, 1986-97, Professor Emeritus, since 1998; b. 5.12.32, Morton, England; m., Joan Mallett Maybrey; 2 s.; 3 d. Educ. Clay Cross Tupton Hall Grammar School; School of Pharmacy, London University. University College Hospital, London, 1954-55; 23rd Parachute Field Ambulance, 1955-57; Medical Missionary and University Lecturer in Thailand with Overseas Missionary Fellowship, 1958-70; Lecturer, Heriot-Watt University, 1970-73; Inaugural Professor of Pharmacy, University of Rhodesia, 1973-78; Senior Lecturer, Strathclyde University, 1978-83; OMF Home Staff and British Council Consultant, Khon Kaen, Thailand and Nanjing, China, 1983-86. Director of project to establish Faculty of Pharmacy, Mahasarakham University, Thailand, since 1998; Director, WHO Collaborating Centre, School of Pharmacy, Robert Gordon University, 1995-97; Chairman, Scottish Council, University and Colleges Christian Fellowship, 1989-95; UK Academic Representative on EC Committee for Training of Pharmacists in Europe, since 1994; Chairman, Scottish Examiners, Pharmacist's Registration Examination, 1993-97. Publications: Clinical Pharmacy and Hospital Drug Management, 1983; Pharmaceutical Practice, 1998; 100 scientific papers. Recreations: travel; languages; classical music; photography; spectator sports. Address: (b.) School of Pharmacy, Robert Gordon University, Schoolhill, Aberdeen AB10 1FR; T.-01224 262500.

Richardson, Professor John Stuart, MA, DPhil, FRSE. Professor of Classics, Edinburgh University, since 1987, Dean, Faculty of Arts, and Provost, Faculty Group of Arts, Divinity and Music, 1992-97; b. 4.2.46, Ilkley; m., Patricia Helen Robotham; 2 s. Educ. Berkhamsted School; Trinity College, Oxford. Lecturer in Ancient History, Exeter College, Oxford, 1969-72, St. Andrews University, 1972-87; Priest, Scottish Episcopal Church, since 1980; Anglican Chaplain, St. Andrews University, 1980-87; Team Priest, St. Columba's, Edinburgh, since 1987. Publications: Roman Provincial Administration, 1976; Hispaniae, 1986; The Romans in Spain, 1996; papers on ancient history. Recreation: choral singing. Address: (h.) 29 Merchiston Avenue, Edinburgh EH10 4PH; T.-0131-228 3094.

Riches, Christopher Gabriel, BSc. Editorial Director, Reference, Harper Collins Publishers, since 1994; b. 25.3.52, Oxford; m., Catherine Mary Gaunt; 3 s. Educ. Marlborough College; Manchester University. Copy Editor, Penguin Books, 1973-74; Oxford University Press: Science Education Editor, 1974-76, Publishing Manager, Hong Kong, 1976-81, Reference Editor, 1981-88; Publishing Manager, Collins Reference, Glasgow, 1989-94. Council Member, Scottish Publishers' Association, since 1995; Hon. Secretary, St. Mary's Episcopal Church, Aberfoyle, 1994-98; Chair, School Board, Killearn Primary School, since 1997. Recreations: book collecting; gardening; walking. Address: (h.) Achadhu House, Main Street, Killearn G63 9RJ; T.-01360 550544.

Riches, Professor John Kenneth, MA. Professor of Divinity and Biblical Criticism, Glasgow University; b. 30.4.39, London; m., Renate Emmy Thermann; 2 s.; 1 d. Educ. Cranleigh School; Corpus Christi College, Cambridge. Assistant Curate, St. Edmund's, Norfolk, 1965-68; Chaplain, Fellow and Director of Studies in Theology, Sidney Sussex College, Cambridge, 1968-72; Lecturer, Department of New Testament Language and Literature, Glasgow University, 1973-86; Senior Lecturer, Department of Biblical Studies, Glasgow University, 1986-91; Chairman, Balmore Trust, since 1980; Convener, Doctrine Committee, Scottish Episcopal Church, 1991-96. Publications: Jesus and the Transformation of Judaism; The World of Jesus; A Century of New Testament Study. Recreations: hill-walking; third world trading. Address: (h.) Viewfield, Balmore, Torrance, Glasgow G64 4AE; T.-01360 620254.

Richmond, Professor John, CBE, MD, FRCPE, FRCP, FRSE. President, Royal College of Physicians of Edinburgh, 1988-91; Emeritus Professor of Medicine, Sheffield University, since 1989; b. 30.5.26, Doncaster; m., Jenny Nicol; 2 s.; 1 d. Educ. Edinburgh University. RAMC, Ethiopia, Kenya, 1st Bn., KAR, N. Rhodesia, 1949-50; rural general practice, Galloway, 1950-52; Lecturer, Senior Lecturer, Reader in Medicine, Edinburgh University, 1954-73; Research Fellow, Memorial Sloan Kettering Cancer Center, New York, 1958-59; Professor of Medicine, Sheffield University, 1973-89 (Dean of Medicine, 1985-88). Senior Censor and Senior Vice-President, Royal College of Physicians of London, 1984-85; Chairman, MRCP (UK) Examining Board, 1984-89; Board of Advisors in Medicine, London University, 1984-93; External Advisor, Chinese University of Hong Kong, since 1982; Department of Health Clinical Standards Advisory Group, 1991-94; Scottish Advisory Board, British Council, 1991-97; Member, Scottish Committee, Marie Curie Cancer Care, since 1992; FRCPSG, FRCPI, FACP(Hon), FFPM(Hon), FRCSE, FFPHM(Hon), FCP(SA)(Hon), FRACP(Hon). Address: (h.) 15 Church Hill, Edinburgh, EH10 4BG.

Richmond, John Kennedy, JP, DL. Chairman, Glasgow Airport Consultative Committee, since 1979; b. 23.4.37, Glasgow; m., Elizabeth Margaret; 1 s.; 1 d. Educ. King's Park Secondary School. Conservative Member, Glasgow Corporation, 1963-75; Member, Glasgow District Council, 1975-84; Deputy Lord Provost, 1977-80; Conservative Group Leader, 1975-77. Recreations: tennis; music; travel. Address: (h.) 84 Merrylee Road, Newlands, Glasgow G43 2QZ; T.-0141-637 7705.

Rickman, David Edwin, BCom (Hons). Rules Secretary, Royal and Ancient Golf Club of St. Andrews, since 1996; b. 9.10.64, St. Andrews; m., Jennifer Mary Cameron; 1 d. Educ. Madras College, St. Andrews; Edinburgh University. Joined R. & A. staff, 1987; appointed Assistant Secretary (Rules), 1990. Recreations: sport, especially golf. Address: (b.) c/o Royal and Ancient Golf Club, St. Andrews, Fife KY16 9JD; T.-01334 472112.

Rickman, Professor Geoffrey Edwin, MA, DPhil (Oxon), FBA, FSA. Professor of Roman History, St. Andrews University, 1981-97; Master of the United College of St. Salvator and St. Leonard, 1992-96; Pro Vice Chancellor, 1996-97; b. 9.10.32, Cherat, India; m., Ann Rosemary Wilson; 1 s.; 1 d. Educ. Peter Symonds' School, Winchester; Brasenose College, Oxford. Junior Research Fellow, Queen's College, Oxford; St. Andrews University: Lecturer in Ancient History, Senior Lecturer, Professor; Visiting Fellow, Brasenose College, Oxford; Member, Institute for Advanced Study, Princeton, 1998; Council Member, Society for Promotion of Roman Studies; British School at Rome: Member, Faculty of Archaeology, History and Letters, (Chairman, 1984-87), Chairman, Council, since 1997. Publications: Roman Granaries and Storebuildings, 1971; The Corn Supply of Ancient Rome, 1980. Recreations: opera; swimming. Address: (h.) 56 Hepburn Gardens, St. Andrews, Fife; T.-St. Andrews 472063.

Riddle, Gordon Stewart, MA. Principal and Chief Ranger, Culzean Country Park, since 1976 (Deputy Administrator, Culzean Castle and Country Park, since 1982); b. 2.10.47, Kelso; m., Rosemary Robb; 1 s.; 1 d. Educ. Kelso High School; Edinburgh University; Moray House College of Education. Biology and History Teacher, Lasswade High School, 1970-71; National Ranger Training Course, 1971-72; Ranger and Depute Principal, Culzean Country Park, 1972-75; National Park Service (USA) Training Course, 1978; Winston Churchill Travelling Fellowship, USA, 1981. Member, Royal Society for the Protection of Birds, Scottish Committee, since 1995; Chairman, South Strathclyde Raptor Study Group, since 1994. Publications: The Kestrel; Seasons with the Kestrel. Recreations: sport; gardening; birds of prey; photography; hill-walking; music; writing. Address: (h.) Swinston, Culzean Country Park, by Maybole, Ayrshire; T.-01655 760 662.

Riddoch, Lesley, BA (Hons). Associate Editor, The Scotsman, 1996-97, Assistant Editor, 1994-96; Presenter, Midnight Hour, BBC2, 1996-98; Presenter, You and Yours, BBC Radio 4, 1996-98; Speaker, The People's Parliament, Channel 4, 1994-98; Presenter, Channel 4's Powerhouse, 1997-98; b. 21.2.60, Wolverhampton; m., George Gunn (separated). Educ. High School of Glasgow; Wadham College, Oxford; University College, Cardiff. Sabbatical President, Oxford University Students Union, 1980; Reporter, BBC Radio Scotland, 1985-88; Co-Presenter, Head On, 1988-90; Presenter, Speaking Out, 1990-94; Founder and Director, Harpies and Quines (feminist magazine). Member, Isle of Eigg Trust, since 1993. Norman McEwen Award, 1992; Cosmopolitan Woman of the Year (Communications), 1992; Plain English Award, 1993. Recreations: drinking; playing pool; walking. Address: (h.) Crannach Ha', Fowlis Wester, Crieff PH7 3NL.

Ridley, Professor Tom, BSc (Eng), BArch, DIC, FRSE, Hon.FRIAS, RIBA, FICE, FIStructE, MConsE. Chartered Architect and Engineer, in private practice; Visiting Professor, Strathclyde University; Member, Royal Fine Art Commission for Scotland, 1992-98; Consultant to Royal Scottish Academy; b. 15.8.27, Gateshead-on-Tyne; m., Carolyn Anne; 3 d. Educ. Imperial College, London University; Strathclyde University. Yorkshire Hennibique Contracting Co., 1948-54; Ove Arup & Partners, 1954-91; opened Scottish Office for Arups, 1960, and responsible for all work in Scotland; won Leverhulme Scholarship. Recreations: fishing; golf. Address: (h.) Marlyn, West Linton EH46 7HW; T.-01968 660604.

Riemersma, Rudolph Arend, BSc, MSc, PhD, FRCPE. Assistant Director, Cardiovascular Research Unit, Edinburgh University, since 1975 (British Heart Foundation Senior Lecturer in Cardiac Biochemistry, since 1979); Professor in Medical Physiology, University of Tromso, Norway, since 1994; b. 9.5.43, Hengelo, Netherlands; m., Eva J. Nieuwenhuis; 1 s.; 1 d. Educ. Charlois Lyceum, Rotterdam; Leyden University; Edinburgh University. Biochemist, Department of Cardiology, Academic Hospital, Utrecht; postgraduate research, Royal Postgraduate Medical School, Hammersmith Hospital, London; Research Fellow, Edinburgh University, 1973. Former Vice-President, European Society of Clinical Investigation. Recreations: orienteering; skiing; hill-walking; botany. Address: (b.) Cardiovascular Research Unit, Hugh Robson Building, George Square, Edinburgh; T.-0131-650 3699.

Rifkind, Rt. Hon Sir Malcolm Leslie, KCMG, QC, LLB, MSc. Secretary of State for Foreign and Commonwealth Affairs, 1995-97; Secretary of State for Defence, 1992-95; Secretary of State for Transport, 1990-92; Secretary of State for Scotland, 1986-90; MP (Conservative), Edinburgh Pentlands, 1974-97; b. 21.6.46, Edinburgh; m., Edith Amalia Steinberg; 1 s.; 1 d. Educ. George Watson's College, Edinburgh; Edinburgh University. Assistant Lecturer, University of Rhodesia, 1967-68; called to Scottish Bar, 1970; Opposition Front-Bench Spokesman on Scottish Affairs, 1975-76; Member, Select Committee on European Secondary Legislation, 1975-76; Chairman, Scottish Conservatives' Devolution Committee, 1976; Joint Secretary, Conservative Parliamentary Foreign and Commonwealth Affairs Committee, 1977-79; Member, Select Committee on Overseas Development, 1978-79; Parliamentary Under-Secretary of State, Scottish Office, 1979-82; Parliamentary Under-Secretary of State, Foreign and Commonwealth Office, 1982-83; Minister of State, Foreign and Commonwealth Office, 1983-86; Member, Queen's Bodyguard for Scotland (Royal Company of Archers); Hon. Col., 162 Movement Control Regiment, Royal Logistic Corps. Address: (h.) Inveresk, East Lothian.

Rigg, David, MA (Hons). University Registrar and Depute Secretary, Paisley University, since 1987; b. 15.3.48, Insch; m., Margaret Taylor Mechie; 1 s.; 1 d. Educ. Daniel Stewart's College, Edinburgh; West Calder High School; Dundee University. British Gas, 1971-73; Administrative Assistant, Strathclyde University, 1973-79; Assistant Secretary, Paisley College, 1979-87. Recreations: cutting grass; reading; theatre; supporting Hibernian Football Club. Address: (b.) Paisley University, High Street, Paisley PA1 2BE; T.-0141-848 3677.

Rigg, John Alexander, BA, MA, PhD. Senior Economic Adviser, Scottish Office Education and Industry Department, since 1995; b. 16.11.54, Leeds; m., Angela Mary English; 1 s.; 1 d. Educ. Roundhay School, Leeds; Trinity College, Cambridge. Research Assistant, Queen Mary College, London University, 1981-82; Senior Economic Analyst, Henley Centre for Forecasting, London, 1982-85; Director, Henley Centre, 1986-92; Economic Adviser, Scottish Office, 1992-95. Recreations: cinema; cricket; family history; rugby league. Address: (b.) Scottish Office Education and Industry Department, Meridian Court, 5 Cadogan Street, Glasgow G2 6AT; T.-0141-242 5565.

Riley, Douglas John, BA. Director, BT Scotland, since 1997; Director, Heritage BT, since 1998; b. 16.6.47, Leeds; m., Louise Isobel. Educ. Templemoor Grammar School; Manchester University; Harvard Business School. Various posts, including positions with Post Office Telephones, 1968-84; Personnel Controller, and Deputy General Manager, West Midlands, 1984-88; Chief Executive, BT Northern Ireland, 1988-95; Chief Executive, BT Ireland,

1995-96; Director, Group Quality and Business Management, 1996-97. Formerly: Chairman, CBI Northern Ireland, Chairman, CBI/IBEC Joint Council, Deputy Chairman, Northern Ireland Growth Challenge, Director, Northern Ireland Quality Care Centre, Director, Northern Ireland Centre in Europe, Director, President's Committee, BITC, Patron, Prince's Youth Business Trust; currently: Director, Scottish Quality Foundation, Member, New Deal Task Force, Member, SCDI Executive Committee, Member, CBI Scotland Council. Recreations: skiing; shooting; cricket; spectating sports; France. Address: (b.) Telephone House, 357 Gorgie Road, Edinburgh EH11 2RP; T.-0131-345 1111.

Rimer, Jennifer, BMusHon, LRAM, DipEd. Headteacher, St. Mary's Music School, Edinburgh, since 1996; SQA Examiner, Setter and Marker, since 1978; b. 16.10.47, Kirkcaldy; m., David Rimer; 3 d. Educ. Buckhaven High School; Edinburgh University. Music Teacher, Newcastle, 1970-72; Principal Music Teacher, Lothian Region, 1972-77; St. Mary's Music School: Piano Teacher/Academic Music Teacher, 1982-93; Head of Guidance, Careers and Academic Music, 1993-95. Governor, George Heriot's School; Director, Edinburgh Youth Orchestra. Recreations: family; reading; yoga; walking; accompanying. Address: (b.) St. Mary's Music School, Coates Hall, 25 Grosvenor Crescent, Edinburgh; T.-0131-538 7766.

Rinning, Andy. Director, Deer Commission for Scotland, since 1990; Chairman, Deer Management Qualifications Ltd., since 1998; b. 15.9.49, Balerno; m., Jeanette Legg; 1 s.; 1 d. Educ. Currie Senior Secondary School. Scottish Office Departments, 1969-85; Assistant Private Secretary to Secretaries of State for Scotland, 1985-88; Scottish Office Finance Division, 1988-90; Scottish Office, 1988-90. Recreations: curling; gardening; golf. Address: (b.) Knowsley, 82 Fairfield Road, Inverness IV3 5LH; T.-01463 231751.

Risk, Sheriff Douglas James, QC, MA, LLB. Sheriff Principal of Grampian, Highland and Islands, since 1993; Honorary Professor, Faculty of Law, Aberdeen University, since 1993; b. 23.1.41; m., Jennifer Hood Davidson; 3 s.; 1 d. Educ. Glasgow Academy; Gonville and Caius College, Cambridge; Glasgow University. Admitted Advocate, 1966; Standing Junior Counsel to Scottish Education Department, 1975; Sheriff of Lothian and Borders at Edinburgh, 1977-79; Sheriff of Grampian, Highland and Islands, at Aberdeen and Stonehaven, 1979-93; Temporary Judge, Court of Session and High Court, 1992-93; QC, 1992; Honorary Lecturer, Faculty of Law, Aberdeen University, 1981-93. Address: (b.) Sheriff Court House, Castle Street, Aberdeen AB10 1WP; T.-01224 648316.

Risk, Sir Thomas Neilson, BL, LLD (Glasgow), Dr. h.c. (Edin), FRSE; b. 13.9.22, Glasgow; m., Suzanne Eiloart; 4 s. (1 dec.) Educ. Kelvinside Academy, Glasgow; Glasgow University. Flt. Lt., RAF, 1941-46; RAFVR, 1946-53; Partner, Maclay, Murray & Spens, Solicitors, 1950-81; Bank of Scotland: Director, 1971-77, Deputy Governor, 1977-81, Governor, 1981-91; Chairman, Standard Life Assurance Company, 1969-77; Director, Shell UK Ltd., 1983-92; Director, The Merchants Trust plc, 1973-94; Director, British Linen Bank Limited, 1977-91 (Governor, 1977-86); Director, Bank of Wales, 1986-91; Director, Howden Group, 1971-87; Chairman, Scottish Financial Enterprise, 1986-89; Director, Barclays Bank, 1983-85; Member, Scottish Economic Planning Council, 1983-91; Member, National Economic Development Council, 1987-91; Member, Scottish Industrial Development Board, 1972-75; Chairman: Edinburgh International Festival Endowment Fund, 1989-97, University of Glasgow Trust; Trustee, Hamilton Bequest. Address: (h.) 10 Belford Place, Edinburgh EH4 3DH.

Ritchie, Alan Sim, Scottish Secretary, Union of Construction, Allied Trades and Technicians, since 1992; b. 12.10.57, Paisley; m., Alison, 1 s.; 1 d. Educ. Anniesland College. President, Anniesland College Students Union; Chairman, STUC Youth Advisory Committee, 1975; Shop Steward and Convenor, 1978; full-time official, since 1983. Recreations: football; reading. Address: (b.) 6 Fitzroy Place, Glasgow G3 7RL.

Ritchie, Alastair Newton Bethune; b. 30.4.21, London; m., Isobel Sinclair; 1 s.; 1 d. Educ. Harrow School; Corpus Christi College, Cambridge; Stirling University. Scots Guards, 1940-58; campaign North-West Europe, 1944-45; wounded; mentioned in Despatches; active service, Malaya and Far East, 1947-49; Canadian Army Staff College, 1951; Assistant Military Attache, Canada, 1952-53; active service, Canal Zone, Egypt, 1954; retired as Major, 1958; Argyll and Sutherland Highlanders TA, 1966-68; Partner, Drunkie Farms, Callander, 1967-81; Partner, Sheppards and Chase, Stock and Money Brokers and Member, Stock Exchange, 1960-85; Member, Stirling District Council, 1977-90; Member, Queen's Bodyguard for Scotland (Royal Company of Archers), 1966; Deputy Lieutenant, Stirling and Falkirk, 1979. Recreations: gardening; fishing; music. Address: (h.) The Steading, Castle Grove, Callander, Perthshire FK17 8AZ; T.-01877 330078.

Ritchie, Alexander John, BSc, DipEd. General Manager, Scottish Cricket Union, since 1991; b. 2.4.35, Alloa; m., Margaret; 1 s.; 1 d. Educ. Dollar Academy; St. Andrews University. Teacher, Larbert High School, 1958-63; Principal Teacher, Grangemouth High School, 1963-69; Assistant Director of Education, Dumfries-shire, 1969-75, Dumfries and Galloway, 1975-82; Senior Education Officer, Strathclyde (Argyll and Bute Division), 1982-91. Address: (h.) 22 South Street, Cambuskenneth, Stirling FK9 5NL; T.-01786 448743.

Ritchie, Andrew, BD, DipMin. Minister, Craiglockhart Parish Church, Edinburgh, since 1991; Assistant Chaplain, Royal Hospital for Sick Children, since 1996; b. 17.4.52, Dunfermline; m., Sheila; 3 s.; 1 d. Educ. Queen Anne School, Dunfermline; Edinburgh University and New College. Assistant Minister, Dundee Parish Church, 1983-84; Minister, Clarkston Parish Church, Airdrie, 1984-91; Convener, Parish Assistance Committee, 1988-90; Vice-Convener, Parish Reappraisal Committee, 1990-93; Convener, Field-Staff Committee, 1993-96; Vice-Convener, New Charge Development Committee, since 1998. Recreations: music; reading; walking. Address: (h.) 202 Colinton Road, Edinburgh EH14 1BP; T.-0131-443 2020.

Ritchie, Anna, OBE, BA, PhD, FSA, FSA Scot. Freelance archaeologist; Member, Ancient Monuments Board for Scotland, since 1990; Trustee, National Museums of Scotland, since 1993; b. 28.9.43, London; m., Graham Ritchie; 1 s.; 1 d. Educ. Woking Grammar School for Girls; University of Wales; Edinburgh University. Excavations on Neolithic, Pictish and Viking sites in Orkney; public and university lectures; archaeological research and writing; Editor, Proceedings of the Society of Antiquaries of Scotland, 1972-79; Secretary, Society of Antiquaries of Scotland, 1986-88; Vice-President, Society of Antiquaries of London, 1988-92; President, Society of Antiquaries of Scotland, 1990-93. Publications: The Kingdom of the Picts, 1977; Orkney and Shetland, 1985; Scotland BC, 1988; Picts, 1989; Viking Scotland, 1993; Prehistoric Orkney, 1995; Iona, 1997; co-author with Graham Ritchie of several works including Scotland: Archaeology and Early History, 1981. Recreations: walking; early music. Address: (h.) 50/1 Spylaw Road, Edinburgh EH10 5BL; T.-0131-228 5962.

Ritchie, Anne Clarke, MA (Hons), DipEd, DCG. Headmistress, St Margaret's School for Girls, Aberdeen, since 1998; b. 5.12.44, Glasgow. Educ. Hutchesons' Girls' Grammar School, Glasgow; Glasgow University. Assistant

Teacher of Modern Languages, Allan Glen's School; Head of Modern Languages, St. Columba's School, Kilmacolm; Principal Teacher of Modern Languages, Jordanhill College School; Senior Mistress, Giggleswick School; Headmistress: Sutherland House School, Norfolk, Runton and Sutherland School, Norfolk; Scottish Director, Independent Schools' Careers Organisation.Director, Craigholme School, Glasgow; Governor, Kilgraston School; Member, Governing Board, Scottish Council of Independent Schools. Recreations: music; painting; theatre; reading; travel; hill-walking. Address: (b.) St Margaret's School for Girls, 17 Albyn Place, Aberdeen AB10 1RU; T.-01224 584466.

Ritchie, Cameron, LLB. Procurator Fiscal, Stirling, since 1996; Solicitor Advocate; b. 25.9.52, Paisley; m., Hazel; 2 s. Educ. John Neilson Institution, Paisley; Glasgow University. Apprentice Solicitor, Wright and Crawford, Paisley, 1972-74; Procurator Fiscal Depute, Ayr, 1974-75, Glasgow, 1975-88; Senior Procurator Fiscal Depute, Hamilton, 1988-93; Assistant Procurator Fiscal, Dundee, 1993-96. Recreations: golf; rugby; watching cricket; military history. Address: (b.) Sheriff Court, Stirling; T.-01786 462021.

Ritchie, Professor David Scarth, MA (Cantab), FRSE. Governor, Paisley University, 1984-95; Trustee and Director, James Clerk Maxwell Foundation; m., 1 Heather McLennan (deceased); 2 s.; 2 d.; 2, Astrid Ilfra Chalmers Watson. Educ. Edinburgh Academy; Cambridge University; Royal Naval College, Greenwich. Lt., Royal Navy, 1944-47; Technical Director, Barr & Stroud Ltd., 1969-85; Chairman, Scottish Education Department survey on industrial liasion in Central Institutions, 1985-88. Visiting Professor in Management of Technological Innovation, Strathclyde University, 1986-94. Address: (h.) Southwood, Newbyth, East Linton EH40 3DU; T.-01620-860-211.

Ritchie, James S., BA. Secretary, Scottish Casec, since 1995 (Secretary, Confederation of Associations of Specialist Engineering Contractors, Scottish Branch, 1991-94); Secretary, Scottish Joint Consultative Committee for Building, 1991-94; b. 20.12.36, Dunfermline; m., Patricia; 2 s.; 1 d. Joined Electrical Contractors' Association of Scotland (ECAS), 1990, following an eclectic career in contracting. Member, Scottish Building Contracts Committee; Member, Committee, Scottish Construction Industry Group. Recreations: reading; contemplating exercise; drafting letters to the editor. Address: (b.) Bush House, Bush Estate, Midlothian EH26 0SB; T.-0131-445 5577.

Ritchie, John Douglas, CA, AMIMC. Partner, Whitelaw Wells, since 1998; Partner, Pannell Kerr Forster, 1985-98 (Chairman, Edinburgh office, 1993-97); Barstow & Millar, CA, 1971-85 (Partner, 1978-85); b. 9.10.52, Edinburgh; m., Joan Moira. Educ. George Watson's College. Member, National Board for Nursing, Midwifery and Health Visiting for Scotland, 1988-93, Hon. Consultant, 1993-97; Member, Management Committee, Viewpoint Housing Association, since 1991; Trustee, Viewpoint Trust, since 1991; President, Rotary Club of Braids, 1991-92; Member, Morningside Christian Council, 1985-92; Member, Church of Scotland Board of Parish Education, since 1994; Treasurer, Scottish Churches Open College, since 1995; Member, Merchant Company of the City of Edinburgh, since 1985, Assistant, Master's Court, since 1998; Trustee, Merchant Company Widows' Fund, since 1997; Member, Board of Management, Edinburgh's Telford College, since 1998; Trustee, Bequest Fund for Ministers in Outlying Districts of the Church of Scotland, since 1994. Address: (b.) 9 Ainslie Place, Edinburgh EH3 6AT; T.-0131-226 5822.

Ritchie, Professor Lewis Duthie, BSc, MSc, MBChB, MD, FRCPEdin, FRCGP, FFPHM, DRCOG, CEng, MBCS, MREHIS. James Mackenzie Professor of General Practice, University of Aberdeen, since 1993; Principal General Practitioner, Peterhead Health Centre, since 1984; Honorary Consultant in Public Health Medicine, Grampian Health Board, since 1993; b. 26.6.52, Fraserburgh; m., Heather. Educ. Fraserburgh Academy; University of Aberdeen; University of Edinburgh. General practitioner vocational training, 1979-82, public health medicine vocational training, 1982-87; Lecturer in General Practice, University of Aberdeen, 1984-92; Consultant in Public Health Medicine, Grampian Health Board, 1987-92. Publications: Computers in Primary Care, 1984; papers on computers, cardiovascular disease, community hospitals and immunisation. John Perry Prize, British Computer Society, 1991; Ian Stokoe Award, Royal College of General Practitioners, 1992; Blackwell Prize, University of Aberdeen, 1995. Recreations: church; art; classical music; naval history; walking. Address: (h.) Cramond, 79 Strichen Road, Fraserburgh AB43 5QJ; T.-01346 510191.

Ritchie, Murray. Scottish Political Editor, The Herald, since 1997; b. 5.9.41, Dumfries; m.; 1 s.; 2 d. Educ. High School of Glasgow. Scottish Farmer, 1958-60; Dumfries and Galloway Standard, 1960-65; Scottish Daily Record, 1965-67; East African Standard, 1967-71; joined Glasgow Herald, 1971. Journalist of the Year, Fraser Press Awards, 1980. Address: (b.) The Herald, 195 Albion Street, Glasgow G1 1QP.

Ritchie, Peter, FCCA. Head of Finance, Fife Council, since 1995; b. 16.3.51; divorced; 1 s.; 1 d. Educ. Kirkland High School; Buckhaven High School; Dundee College of Commerce. Fife County Council, 1969-75; Fife Regional Council: various positions, 1975-80, Chief Accountant, 1980-84, Senior Assistant Director of Finance, 1984-88, Depute Director of Finance, 1988-95. Recreations: hillwalking; travel; photography; theatre/cinema. Address: (h.) 40 Demarco Drive, Glenrothes, Fife KY7 6FD; T.-(h.) 01592 741412, (b.) 01592 413336.

Ritson, Bruce, MD, FRCPsych, FRCP(Ed), DipPsych. Clinical Director and Consultant Psychiatrist, Royal Edinburgh Hospital, since 1972; Senior Lecturer in Psychiatry, Edinburgh University, since 1972; Consultant, Royal Edinburgh Hospital, since 1972; b. 20.3.37, Elgin; m., Eileen Carey; 1 s.; 1 d. Educ. Edinburgh Academy; Edinburgh University; Harvard University. Trained in medicine, Edinburgh; postgraduate training in psychiatry, Edinburgh, Harvard and California; Director, Sheffield Region Addiction Unit, 1968-71; at present Consultant with special responsibility for alcohol-related problems; World Health Organisation consultant; Chairman, Howard League in Scotland; Chairman, Medical Council on Alcoholism; Chairman, Substance Misuse Faculty, Royal College of Psychiatrists; Member, Advisory Group on Substance Misuse, WHO; Chairman, Advisory Panel on Alcohol, DVLA. Recreations: friends; squash; theatre. Address: (b.) Royal Edinburgh Hospital, Morningside Park, Edinburgh; T.-0131-537 6297.

Roach, Professor Gary Francis, OStJ, BSc, MSc, PhD, DSc, ScD. Professor of Mathematics, Strathclyde University, since 1979 (Dean, Faculty of Science, since 1982); b. 8.10.33, Penpedairheol, South Wales; m., Isabella Grace Willins Nicol. Educ. University College, South Wales and Monmouthshire; London University; Manchester University. RAF (Education Branch), Flying Officer, 1955-58; Research Mathematician, British Petroleum Co. Ltd., 1958-61; Lecturer, Manchester University Institute of Science and Technology, 1961-66; Visiting Professor, University of British Columbia, 1966-67; Strathclyde University: Lecturer, 1967-70, Senior Lecturer, 1970-71, Reader, 1971-79. Fellow, Royal Astronomical Society; Fellow, Institute of Mathematics and its Applications; Fellow, Royal Society of Arts; Fellow, Royal Society of Edinburgh; Past President, Edinburgh Mathematical

Society; Deacon, Incorporation of Bonnetmakers and Dyers of Glasgow. Recreations: mountaineering; photography; philately; gardening; music. Address: (b.) Department of Mathematics, Strathclyde University, Livingstone Tower, 26 Richmond Street, Glasgow G1 1XH; T.-0141-552 4400, Ext. 3800.

Roads, Elizabeth Ann, MVO, FSA (Scot). Lyon Clerk and Keeper of the Records, since 1986; Carrick Pursuivant of Arms, since 1992; b. 5.7.51; m., Christopher George William Roads; 2 s.; 1 d. Educ. Lansdowne House School, Edinburgh; Cambridge College of Technology; Study Centre for Fine Art, London. Christie's, Art Auctioneers, 1971-74; Court of the Lord Lyon, since 1975; temporarily Linlithgow Pursuivant Extraordinary, 1987. Recreations: history; reading; countryside activities. Address: (b.) Court of the Lord Lyon, HM New Register House, Edinburgh.

Robb, Professor Alan, DA, MA, RCA. Head, School of Fine Art, Duncan of Jordanstone College of Art, Dundee, since 1983; b. 24.2.46, Glasgow; m., Cynthia J. Neilson; 1 s.; 1 d. Educ. Robert Gordon's College, Aberdeen; Grays School of Art; Royal College of Art. Assistant Art Master, Oundle School, 1972-75; Crawford School of Art, Cork: Lecturer in Painting, 1975-78, Head of Painting, 1978-80, Head of Fine Art, 1980-83. Member, Fine Art Panel, CNAA, 1985-87; Director, Wasps, 1984-94; Specialist Advisor, CNAA, since 1987; Director, Art in Partnership, 1987-92; Director, British Health Care Arts Centre, 1988-93; Member, SHEFC Research Advisory Group, 1993-98; Steering Group, International Cultural Desk, Joint Committee Scottish Arts Council and British Council, since 1998; Lead Assessor for Fine Art, SHEFC Quality Assessment; first one-man exhibition, New 57 Gallery, 1973; Arts Council touring two-man exhibition, 1978-79; regularly exhibits in Scotland; solo exhibitions: In the Mind's Eye, 1996, True Knowledge, East West Gallery, London, 1997. Publications: Irish Contemporary Art, 1980; In the Mind's Eye. Address: (b.) Duncan of Jordanstone College, University of Dundee, Perth Road, Dundee DD1 4HT.

Robb, John Weddell. Chairman, British Energy plc, since 1995; Chairman, Logitron Holdings plc; Non-Executive Director, Unigate plc; Deputy Chairman, Horse Race Betting Levy Board; Non-Executive Director (Chairman Designate), Hewden Stuart PLC; Trustee, Royal Botanic Garden; b. 27.4.36, Edinburgh; m., Janet Teanby; 2 s.; 1 d. Educ. Stewart's College, Edinburgh. Group Managing Director, Beecham Group plc, 1985-88; Wellcome plc, 1989-95 (Chief Executive, 1990-93; Chairman and Chief Executive, 1993-95). Recreations: golf; horse-racing; gardening. Address: (b.) 10 Lochside Place, Edinburgh EH12 9DF; T.-0131-527 2000.

Robb, Kenneth Richard, LLB (Hons), NP. Solicitor; Partner, Marshall, Wilson, Falkirk; b. 3.9.54, Larbert; m., Susan Margaret Ringrose; 1 d. Educ. Falkirk High School; Edinburgh University. Private legal practice, since 1976; Member, Council, Law Society of Scotland, 1987-97; Member, Board, Scottish Child Law Centre; part-time Chairman, Child Support Appeal Tribunals. Recreations: history; hill-walking; gardening. Address: (h.) 9 Bryanston Drive, Dollar, Clackmannanshire; T.-01259 743430.

Robbins, Oliver Charles Gordon, BA (Hons), MIMgt. Principal, Cambuslang College of Further Education, since 1992; b. 28.4.36, Edinburgh; m., Andrewena Henderson Briggs; 4 s.; 1 d. Educ. Bellevue Secondary School; Open University; Napier College. Apprentice engineer, 1952-57; draughtsman, 1957-60; design draughtsman, Rolls Royce/Ferranti Ltd., 1960-69; Lecturer, Senior Lecturer, Head of Department, Moray College of FE. Recreations: caravanning; martial arts. Address: (h.) 11 Strathaven Road, Lesmahagow, Lanarkshire; T.-Lesmahagow 894617.

Roberton, Esther A., BA. Member, Government's Consultative Steering Group on Scottish Parliament; Founder and Director, Scotland Forward, 1996-97; Co-ordinator, Scottish Constitutional Convention, 1995-97; Member, Executive, Scottish Council Development and Industry, since 1991; b. 24.6.56, Kirkcaldy; m., William J. Roberton; 2 s. Educ. Buckhaven High School; Edinburgh University. Recreations: juggling; piano-playing; devouring books. Address: (h.) 15 Pinewood Drive, Dalgety Bay KY11 5SP; T.-01383 820750.

Roberts, Professor Bernard, BSc, PhD, FRAS, FRSE. Professor of Solar Magnetohydrodynamics, since 1994; Chairman, UK Solar Physics Community, since 1992; b. 19.2.46, Cork; m., Margaret Patricia Cartlidge; 4 s. Educ. Bletchley Secondary Modern and Bletchley Grammar Schools; Hull University; Sheffield University. Lecturer in Applied Mathematics, St. Andrews University, 1971-87, Reader, 1987-94. Recreations: hill-walking; squash. Address: (b.) Mathematical Sciences, St. Andrews University, St. Andrews KY16 9SS; T.-01334 463716.

Roberts, Jacqueline Claire, BA (Hons), MSc, MA (Hons), CQSW. Director of Social Work, Dundee City Council, since 1997; b. 8.1.49, Market Harborough; m.; 2 children. Educ. Loughborough High School for Girls; St. Hilda's College, Oxford University; Oxford University Department of Applied Social Studies. Social Worker: Oxford Area Health Authority, 1971-72, Oxfordshire Social Services, Oxford City Area Team, 1974-75; Research Social Worker, Oxfordshire Social Services, 1975-77; Research Co-ordinator and Social Worker, Park Hospital, Oxford Area Health Authority, 1978-83; Social Worker, Lambeth Social Services, 1983-86; Lecturer in Social Work, University of Dundee, 1986-87; Project Head, Polepark Family Counselling Centre, Tayside Regional Council Social Work Department, and Course Director, Child Protection Training, Northern College, 1987-93; Group Manager, Children and Families, Tayside Regional Council Social Work Department, 1993-96; Manager, Older People's Services, Dundee City Council Social Work Department, 1996-97. Member: National Consultation Group on Child Care and Child Care Legislation, 1992-93, Scottish Office Working Party on Practice Guidance in Child Protection, 1992-94; currently Member: Executive Committee, Association of Directors of Social Work, ADSW Standing Committee on Community Care, Tayside Drug Action Team; Associate Editor, Child Abuse and Neglect. 1989 Fidelio Prize. Publications: Consequences of Child Abuse (Co-Author), 1982; many papers, reports and book chapters, especially on child abuse. Address: 67 Camphill Road, Broughty Ferry, Dundee DD5 2LY.

Roberts, James Graeme, MA, PhD, FRSA. Vice Principal and Dean, Faculty of Arts and Divinity, Aberdeen University, since 1996; b. 7.11.42, Glasgow; m., Elizabeth Watson Milo Tucker; 2 s.; 2 d. Educ. Hutchesons' Boys' Grammar School, Glasgow; St. Andrews University; Aberdeen University. Aberdeen University: Assistant Lecturer in English, 1964, Lecturer in English, 1968, Senior Lecturer, 1985, Head, Department of English, 1993; elected Member, University Court, 1981-89, since 1995. Trustee, Aberdeen International Football Festival; Elder, Ferryhill Parish Church, Aberdeen. Recreations: walking; swimming; music. Address: (b.) Aberdeen University, Regent Walk, Aberdeen AB24 3FX; T.-01224 272084.

Roberts, Rev. Maurice Jonathon, BA, BD. Minister, Greyfriars Free Church of Scotland, since 1994; Editor, The Banner of Truth, since 1988; b. 8.3.38, Timperley; m., Alexandra Macleod; 1 d., Educ. Lymm Grammar School; Durham University; London University; Free Church College, Edinburgh. Schoolteacher. Publication: The Thought of God. Recreations: reading; walking. Address: 3 Abertarff Road, Inverness IV2 3NW; T.-01463 220701.

Roberts, Professor Peter Ward, BA, MA, CertEd, MRTPI, FRSA. Professor of European Strategic Planning, Dundee University, since 1995; Member, Scientific Committee on the Regions of Europe, since 1992; Chairman, British Urban Regeneration Association – Best Practice Committee, since 1994; b. 17.7.47, Birkenhead; m., Josephine Blythe; 1 s. Educ. Rock Ferry High School, Birkenhead; Leicester University; Manchester University; Newcastle upon Tyne University. Demonstrator, Newcastle upon Tyne University, 1969-70; Lecturer, Flintshire College of Technology, 1970-71; Senior Lecturer, Department of Town and Country Planning, Liverpool John Moores University, 1971-77; Principal Lecturer/Deputy Head of Department, Department of Urban and Regional Planning, Coventry University, 1978-86; Senior Research Manager, ECOTEC Research and Consulting, Birmingham, 1987; Professor of Urban Planning, Leeds Metropolitan University, and Joint Director, Regional Research Observatory, 1988-94. Trustee and Vice Chairman, Town and Country Planning Association; Board Member, The Planning Exchange; Director, Urban Mines Ltd. Publications include: Environmentally Sustainable Business; Europe: A Handbook for Local Authorities (Co-author); Energy Efficiency in Housing (Co-author); Mineral Resources in Regional and Strategic Planning (Co-author); Metropolitan Planning in Britain (Co-author); Environment, Planning and Land Use (Co-author). Recreations: hill-walking; collecting and reading books; restoring classic cars; listening to opera and classical music; watching cricket. Address: (b.) Centre for Planning Research, School of Town and Regional Planning, 13 Perth Road, Dundee DD1 4HT; T.-01382 345236.

Roberts, Professor Ronald John, BVMS, FRCVS, PhD, FRCPath, FIBiol, FRSE. Professor of Aquatic Pathobiology and Director, Institute of Aquaculture, Stirling University, 1971-96, Emeritus Professor since 1996; Scientific Adviser, Lithgow Group; Non-Executive Director, Landcatch Ltd., since 1996; Hagerman Distinguished Visiting Professor, University of Idaho, since 1997; b. 28.3.41; m., Helen Macgregor; 2 s. Educ. Campbeltown Grammar School; Glasgow University. Lecturer, Glasgow University, 1964-71; Consultant: Department of Agriculture and Fisheries for Scotland, 1967-70, Overseas Development Administration, since 1974, United Nations, since 1976; World Bank, since 1989; Council Member, Royal Society of Edinburgh, 1980-83; Member, Cabinet Office, Scientific Advisory Panel, 1994; Buckland Professor of Fisheries, Buckland Foundation, 1985; BVA Dalrymple-Champneys Medallist, 1990; Scientific Director, Machrihanish Marine Environmental Research Laboratory, 1991-96; Chairman, Kintyre Enterprise Trust; Chairman, Argyll and Bute Countryside Trust; Editor, Journal of Fish Diseases, Aquaculture Research. Commander of Most Noble Order of the Crown (Thailand). Publications: Fish Pathology; Handbook of Salmon and Trout Diseases; Bacterial Diseases of Fishes; Recent Advances in Aquaculture; Diseases of Asian Catfishes (Co-author). Recreations: golf at Machrihanish Golf Club; geriatric squash; forestry; rhododendron culture. Address: (h.) Carrick Point Farm, Ardnacross, Peninver, by Campbeltown, Argyll; T.-01586 554417.

Robertson, Alistair John, BMedBiol (Hons), MB, ChB, FRCPath, MIAC, FRSA. Clinical Director in Pathology, Dundee Teaching Hospitals NHS Trust, since 1993; Consultant Histopathologist, Tayside Health Board, since 1982; Honorary Senior Lecturer in Pathology, Dundee University, since 1982; b. 29.6.50, Aberdeen; m., Frances Elizabeth Smith. Educ. Aberdeen Grammar School; Aberdeen University. House Physician, Ninewells Hospital, Dundee, 1975; House Surgeon, Aberdeen Royal Infirmary, 1976; Senior House Officer in Pathology, Ninewells Hospital, 1976; Lecturer in Pathology, Ninewells Hospital, 1977; Consultant in Administrative Charge, Perth and Kinross Unit Laboratories, 1982. Recreations: golf; curling; caravanning; philately; photography; theatre. Address: (b.) Pathology Department, Ninewells Hospital and Medical School, Dundee; T.-Dundee 660111.

Robertson, Andrew Ogilvie, OBE, LLB. Partner, T.C. Young & Son, Solicitors and Notaries, since 1968; Secretary, Erskine Hospital, since 1976; Chairman, Post Office Users Council for Scotland, since 1988; Secretary, Princess Royal Trust for Carers, since 1990; Chairman, Greater Glasgow Community and Mental Health Services NHS Trust, 1994-97; Chairman, Glasgow Royal Infirmary Univresity NHS Trust, since 1997; Chairman, Scottish Housing Association Charitable Trust, since 1991; Director, Scottish Building Society, since 1994; b. 30.6.43, Glasgow; m., Sheila Sturton; 2 s. Educ Glasgow Academy; Sedbergh School; Edinburgh University. Director, Merchants House of Glasgow, since 1978; Secretary, Clydeside Federation of Community Based Housing Associations, 1978-93; Secretary, The Briggait Company Ltd., 1982-88; Director, Glasgow Chamber of Commerce, 1982-93. Recreations: climbing; swimming; sailing; running; fishing. Address: (b.) 30 George Square, Glasgow, G2 1LH; T.-0141-221 5562.

Robertson, Brenda Margaret, JP. Member, Orkney Islands Council, 1974-94; b. 8.9.24, Scarborough; m., John MacDonald Robertson, BL, NP; 1 s.; 1 d. Educ. Scarborough Girls' High School; University College, St. Andrews. Wartime service, WRNS; decoding, at Bletchley Park; formerly: District Commissioner for Guides, Stromness and West Mainland; Member, Stromness Town Council, 1961-74; Orkney County Councillor; Member, Executive Council, NHS; Governor, Aberdeen College of Education. Recreations: reading; arts generally. Address: (h.) Berridale, Stromness, Orkney.

Robertson, Rev. Charles, JP, MA. Minister, Canongate Kirk, since 1978; Chaplain to The Queen, since 1991; b. 22.10.40, Glasgow; m., Alison Margaret Malloch; 1 s.; 2 d. Educ. Camphill School, Paisley; Edinburgh University. Assistant Minister, North Morningside Church, Edinburgh, 1964-65; Minister, Kiltearn, Ross and Cromarty, 1965-78. Secretary, Panel on Worship, General Assembly, 1982-95, Convener, since 1995; Church of Scotland Representative on Joint Liturgical Group, since 1984, and Chairman, since 1994; Secretary, Committee to Revise the Church Hymnary, since 1995; Chaplain to Lord High Commissioner, 1990, 1991 and to Her Grace The Princess Royal, 1996; Chaplain to: High Constables and Guard of Honour, since 1993, Clan Donnachaidh Society, 1981-96, Elsie Inglis Memorial Maternity Hospital, 1982-89, New Club, since 1986, Moray House, 1986-98, University of Edinburgh at Moray House, since 1998, No. 2 (City of Edinburgh) Maritime HQ Unit RAAF, since 1987, Royal Scots Club, since 1998; President, Church Service Society, 1988-91 (Hon. President, since 1991); Chairman, Board, Queensberry House Hospital, 1989-96; Chairman, Queensberry House Trust, since 1996; Governor, St. Columba's Hospice, Edinburgh, since 1986; Member, Executive Committee, Scottish Veteran's Residences, since 1978; Lecturer in Church Praise, St. Colm's College, 1980-93; Member, Broadcasting Standards Council, 1988-91 and 1992-93; Member, Historic Buildings Council for Scotland, since 1990; Trustee, Church Hymnary Trust, since 1987; Trustee, Edinburgh Old Town Trust, 1987-91; Trustee, Edinburgh Old Town Charitable Trust, since 1991; edited Singing the Faith, 1990, and St Margaret Queen of Scotland and Her Chapel, 1994; Secretary of Committees which compiled Hymns for a Day, 1983, Songs of God's People, 1988, Worshipping Together, 1991, Clann ag Urnaigh, 1997, Common Ground, 1998. Recreations: books; music; history; Canongate. Address: Manse of Canongate, Edinburgh EH8 8BR; T.-0131-556 3515.

Robertson, Sheriff Daphne Jean Black, MA, LLB, WS. Sheriff of Lothian and Borders at Edinburgh (formerly

Sheriff of Glasgow and Strathkelvin); b. 31.3.37. Address: Sheriff Court House, 27 Chambers Street, Edinburgh, EH1 1LB.

Robertson, David Alexander, CA, IRRV. Director of Finance, Orkney Islands Council, since 1994; Finance Director, Orkney Ferries Ltd., since 1992; b. 31.12.59, Glasgow; m., Ruth Elizabeth; 1 s; 1 d. Educ. Inverness Royal Academy; Dundee College of Technology. Address: (b.) Council Offices, Kirkwall, Orkney; T.-01856 873535.

Robertson, David Andrew, MA (Hons). Minister, St. Peter's Free Church of Scotland, Dundee, since 1992; b. 2.5.62, Berwick-upon-Tweed; m., Annabel; 1 s.; 2 d. Educ. Tain Royal Academy, Ross-shire; University of Edinburgh; Free Church College. Minister, Clyne Free Church, Brora, 1986-92; Minister, St. Peter's Free Church, Dundee, 1992-98. Associate Chaplain: University of Dundee, University of Abertay; Member, UCCF Scottish Council. Recreations: football; music; chess; politics. Address: (h.) 14 Shamrock Street, Dundee; T.-01382 861401.

Robertson, Donald Buchanan, QC, BL, FSA(Scot). Advocate; Member, Criminal Injuries Compensation Board, since 1986; Temporary Judge, Court of Session, since 1991; b. 29.3.32, Ardnadam, Argyll; m., 1, Louise Charlotte Limthorst Homan, 2, Daphne Jean Black Kincaid; 1 s.; 1 d. Educ. Dunoon Grammar School; Glasgow University. Solicitor, 1954; National Service, 1954-56; Advocate, 1960; Standing Junior to Registrar of Restrictive Practices, 1970-73; Member, Sheriff Court Rules Council, 1972-75; Member, Royal Commission on Legal Services in Scotland, 1976-80; Member, Legal Aid Central Committee, 1982-85; Chairman, VAT Tribunal, 1978-85; Honorary Sheriff, Lothian and Peebles, since 1982. Recreations: shooting; Scottish history; genealogy; numismatics. Address: (h.) 11 Grosvenor Crescent, Edinburgh EH12 5EL; T.-0131-337 5544; and Cranshaws Castle, by Duns, Berwickshire TD11 3SJ; T.-01361 890268.

Robertson, Professor Edmund Frederick, BSc, MSc, PhD, FRSE. Professor of Mathematics, St. Andrews University, since 1995; b. 1.6.43, St. Andrews; m., Helena Francesca; 2 s. Educ. Madras College, St. Andrews; St. Andrews University; Warwick University. Lecturer in Pure Mathematics, then Senior Lecturer, St. Andrews University, 1968-95. Partnership Award, 1992; European Academic Software Award, 1994; American Computational Engineering and Science Award, 1995. Publications: 26 books; 100 papers. Recreations: history of mathematics; computers. Address: (b.) Mathematical Institute, North Haugh, St. Andrews KY16 9SS; T.-01334 463738.

Robertson, George F., CBE, FRICS. Chartered Surveyor, Arbiter; Sole Principal, G.F. Robertson, Chartered Surveyors; b. 14.7.32, Edinburgh; m., Anne McGonigle; 3 d. Educ. George Heriot's School, Edinburgh; Heriot-Watt College, Edinburgh. Partner, Robertson and Dawson, Chartered Surveyors, Edinburgh, 1970-93; Lecturer (part-time), School of Architecture, Edinburgh College of Art/Heriot-Watt University, 1964-84; Chairman, Joint Standing Committee of Architects, Surveyors and Building Contractors in Scotland, 1976-78; Chairman, Board of Governors, Leith Nautical College, 1976-78; Chairman, Scottish Branch, Royal Institution of Chartered Surveyors, 1984-85; Director, Queensberry House Hospital, Edinburgh, 1983-86; Chairman, Scottish Building Contract Committee, 1983-88; Board Member, Scottish Development Agency, 1987-91; Hon. Secretary, Royal Institution of Chartered Surveyors in Scotland, 1988-90; Lay Member, Scottish Solicitors Discipline Tribunal, 1976-94; President, Rent Assessment Panel for Scotland, 1987-97. Recreations: working; gardening; travel; researching Scottish market crosses. Address: (h.) Gladsheil, Campbell Court, Longniddry, East Lothian EH32 0NR.

Robertson, Rt. Hon. George Islay MacNeill, MA. MP (Labour), Hamilton South; Secretary of State for Defence, since 1997; Member, Shadow Cabinet, 1993-97; Shadow Scottish Secretary, 1993-97; b. 12.4.46, Port Ellen, Islay; m., Sandra Wallace; 2 s.; 1 d. Educ. Dunoon Grammar School; Dundee University; St. Andrews University. Tayside Study Economics Group, 1968-69; Scottish Organiser, General, Municipal, Boilermakers Union, 1969-78; Chairman, Scottish Labour Party, 1977-78; Member, Scottish Executive, Labour Party, 1973-79, 1993-97; MP, Hamilton, 1978-97, Hamilton South, since 1997; PPS to Secretary of State for Social Services, 1979; Opposition Spokesman on Scottish Affairs, 1979-80, on Defence, 1980-81, on Foreign and Commonwealth Affairs, 1981-93, on Scottish Affairs, 1993-97; Principal Spokesman on Europe, 1984-93; Member of Board, Scottish Development Agency, 1976-78, Scottish Tourist Board, 1974-76; Board of Governors, Scottish Police College, 1975-78; Vice Chairman, British Council, 1985-93; Vice-Chairman, Westminster Foundation for Democracy, 1992-93. Recreations: family; photography. Address: (b.) House of Commons, London SW1A 0AA.

Robertson, Harry, CPFA. Chief Executive, Perth and Kinross Council, since 1995; b. 7.9.49, Dunfermline; m., Rosemary Elizabeth; 2 s. Educ. Dunfermline High School; Glasgow College of Commerce. Trainee Accountant, Burgh of Burntisland; Accountancy Assistant, Assistant Town Chamberlain, Depute Town Chamberlain, Burgh of Barrhead; Depute Director of Finance, Director of Finance, Depute Chief Executive, Chief Executive, Perth and Kinross District Council. Secretary/Treasurer, Perth Repertory Theatre Ltd.; Chairman, Scottish Branch, CIPFA, 1987-88; former Council Member, CIPFA; Clerk to Lord Lieutenancy, Perth and Kinross; Chief Executive and Secretary, Perth and Kinross Recreational Facilities Ltd.; Hon. Secretary, Bowerswell Memorial Homes (Perth) Ltd.; Member, Society of High Constables of the City of Perth. Recreations: golf; theatre; badminton; tropical fish. Address: (b.) 2 High Street, Perth PH1 5PH; T.-01738 475001.

Robertson, Iain Alasdair, CBE, LLB. Chief Executive, Highlands and Islands Enterprise, since 1990; Board Member, Locate in Scotland Supervisory Board, since 1992; Board Member, Cairngorm Partnership, since 1998; Board Member, Scottish Tourist Board, 1993-95; b. 30.10.49, Perth; m., Judith Helen Stevenson; 2 s.; 1 d. Educ. Perth Academy; Aberdeen University. Qualified as a Solicitor, 1973; service at home and abroad with British Petroleum, 1975-90, latterly as BP America's Director of Acquisitions. Recreations: skiing; sailing; music. Address: (b.) Bridge House, Bridge Street, Inverness; T.-01463 244204.

Robertson, Iain Samuel, LLB, CA. Chief Executive, UK Bank, Royal Bank of Scotland plc, since 1998; b. 27.12.45, Glasgow; m., Morag; 2 s.; 2 d. Educ. Jordanhill College School; Glasgow University. Civil Servant, Department of Trade and Industry and Department of Energy, 1973-78; Assistant Secretary, Scottish Office, 1978-83; Director, Locate in Scotland, Scottish Office, 1984-87; Chief Executive, Scottish Development Agency, 1987-90; Group Finance Director, County Natwest Ltd., 1990-92; Managing Director, Corporate and Institutional Banking, Royal Bank of Scotland plc, 1992-98. Recreations: golf; football; music and arts.

Robertson, Maj.-Gen. Ian Argyll, CB (1968), MBE (1947), MA. Deputy Lieutenant, Highland Region (Nairn), 1973-88; b. 17.7.13, Richmond, Surrey; m., Marjorie Violet Isobel Duncan; 2 d. Educ. Winchester College; Trinity College, Oxford. Commissioned Seaforth Highlanders, 1934; commanded 1st Bn., 1954-57; commanded School of Infantry, 1963-64; commanded 51 Highland Division,

1964-66; retired, 1968. Vice-Chairman and Chairman, Royal British Legion Scotland, 1971-74. Recreations: golf; gardening. Address: (h.) Gardeners Cottage, Brackla, Cawdor, Nairn.

Robertson, Ian Barr, MA, LLB. Solicitor (retired); Advocate in Aberdeen; Honorary Sheriff, Grampian, Highland and Islands, at Stonehaven; b. Aberdeen; m., Vi L. Johnston; 2 s.; 1 d. Educ. Mackie Academy; Fettes College; Aberdeen University. King's Regiment and KAR, 1939-46 (Captain); Partner, Cunningham & Robertson, Solicitors, Stonehaven, 1951-89; Joint Town Clerk, then Town Clerk, Stonehaven, 1957-75; President, Society of Town Clerks in Scotland, 1973-75; Member, Grampian Regional Council, 1974-86 (Chairman, Transportation and Roads, 1978-86); Member, Aberdeen Harbour Board, 1975-86; Member, Peterhead Bay Authority, 1978-88; Elder, Stonehaven South. Address: (h.) 15 Bath Street, Stonehaven; T.-Stonehaven 762879.

Robertson, Hon. Lord (Ian Macdonald Robertson), TD (1946), BA, LLB, QC. Senator of the College of Justice in Scotland, 1966-87; Chairman of Governors, Merchiston Castle School, 1971-96; b. 30.10.12, Edinburgh; m., Anna Love Glen; 1 s.; 2 d. Educ. Merchiston Castle School, Edinburgh; Balliol College, Oxford; Edinburgh University. Admitted Faculty of Advocates, 1939; served War of 1939-45, 8th Bn., The Royal Scots (The Royal Regiment) - commissioned 1939; Captain/Staff Officer, 44th Lowland Infantry Brigade (15th Scottish Division); Normandy and North West Europe, 1944-45; mentioned in Despatches; Advocate Depute, 1949-51; QC, 1954; Sheriff Principal of Ayr and Bute, 1961-66; Sheriff Principal of Perth and Angus, 1966; Chairman, Medical Appeals Tribunal, 1957-63; Chairman, Scottish Joint Council for Teachers Salaries, 1965-81; Chairman, Scottish Valuation Advisory Council, 1977-86; UK Representative on Central Council, International Association of Judges, 1974-87; General Council Assessor, Edinburgh University Court, 1967-81; Chairman, Edinburgh Centre of Rural Economy and Edinburgh Centre for Tropical Veterinary Medicine, 1967-86; Governor, Merchiston Castle School, 1954-96; Captain, Honourable Company of Edinburgh Golfers at Muirfield, 1970-72. Recreation: golf. Address: (h.) 13 Moray Place, Edinburgh EH3 6DT; T.-0131-225 6637.

Robertson, James. Writer. Educ. Edinburgh University. Former bookseller (Assistant Manager, Waterstone's); Neil Gunn Fellow; author of Close and Other Stories; winner, Sloan Prize, 1991.

Robertson, James Downie, DA, RSA, RSW, RGI. Painter; Resident Painter, Glasgow School of Art, since 1996; b. 2.11.31, Cowdenbeath; m., Ursula Orr Crawford (2nd marriage); 2 step-s.; 1 step-d. Educ. Hillhead High School; Glasgow School of Art. Teacher, Keith Grammar School, Banffshire, 1957-58; Lecturer (part-time), Glasgow School of Art, 1959; elected RSW, 1962; Lecturer in Drawing and Painting, Glasgow School of Art, 1967; elected Associate, Royal Scottish Academy, 1974; Senior Lecturer, Drawing and Painting, Glasgow School of Art, 1975-96; elected, RGI, 1980; elected, RSA, 1989; Visiting Lecturer: Michaelis School of Fine Art, Cape Town University, South Africa, 1970, Grays School of Art, Aberdeen, 1986, Duncan of Jordanstone College of Art, Dundee, 1986, Newcastle-upon-Tyne Polytechnic, 1986, Millersville University, Pennsylvania, USA, 1987. Cargill Award, RGI, 1971; May Marshall Brown Award, RSW, 1976; Sir William Gillies Award, RSW, 1981; Cargill Award, RGI, 1982; Shell Expro Award, 1985; Graham Munro Award, RSW, 1987; Scottish Amicable Award, RGI, 1989; Scottish Post Office Award, RSA, 1993. Many solo and group exhibitions, UK and abroad; work in many public, corporate and private collections. Recreations: drawing; painting; reading. Address: (h.) Carruthmuir, by Kilbarchan, Renfrewshire PA10 2QA; T.-01505 613592.

Robertson, John Davie Manson, CBE, BL, FRSA. Chairman, Robertson Group of Companies, since 1979; Director, Stanley Services Ltd., Falkland Islands, since 1987; Chairman, Lloyds TSB Foundation for Scotland, since 1997; b. 6.11.29, Golspie; m., Elizabeth Amelia Macpherson; 2 s.; 2 d. Educ. Kirkwall Grammar School; Edinburgh University. Anglo-Iranian Oil Co. and BP, UK and Middle East, 1953-58. Honorary Sheriff, Grampian, Highland and Islands, since 1977; Honorary Vice Consul for Denmark, since 1972; Honorary Consul, Federal Republic of Germany, since 1976; Chairman, North of Scotland Water Authority, 1995-98; Trustee, Lloyds TSB Foundation for Scotland, 1989-97; Member, National Health Service Tribunal, 1990-97; Chairman, Highland Health Board, 1991-97; Chairman, Scottish Health Management Efficiency Group (SCOTMEG), 1985-95; Chairman and Vice-Chairman, Scottish Health Boards Chairmen's Group, 1995-97; Chairman, Orkney Health Board, 1983-91 (Vice Chairman, 1979-83, Member, 1974-79); Member, Board of Management, Orkney Hospitals, 1970-74; Board Member, Highlands and Islands Enterprise, 1990-95; Member, Highlands and Islands Development Consultative Council, 1989-91; Chairman, Highlands and Islands Savings Committee, 1975-78; Chairman, Children's Panel for Orkney, 1971-76; Chairman, Children's Panel, Orkney Advisory Committee, 1977-82. OBE, 1978; Royal Order of Knight of Dannebrog, 1982; Cavalier's Cross of the Order of Merit, 1986. Publications: Uppies and Doonies, 1967; An Orkney Anthology, 1991. Recreations: fly fishing; shooting. Address: (h.) Spinningdale House, Spinningdale, Sutherland IV24 3AD; T.-01862 881 240.

Robertson, John Graeme, CBiol, MIBiol, MIMgt, FLS, FRSA. Director, Habitat Scotland, since 1980; Editor, Islander Magazine, since 1995; b. 15.8.54, Edinburgh; m., Anne Christie; 1 s.; 1 d. Educ. Scotus Academy, Edinburgh. Co-ordinator, Environmental Resource Centre; Co-ordinator, Friends of the Earth Scotland. Churchill Fellow, 1996; President, Island Web Consortium. Recreations: exercising his dogs; travel to islands worldwide. Address: Hazelmount, Heron Place, Portree, Isle of Skye IV51 9EU; T.-01478 612898.

Robertson, John Shaw, MA. Rector, Dollar Academy, since 1994; b. 7.4.50, Glasgow; m., Mary; 1 s.; 1 d. Educ. Jordanhill College School; Glasgow University. English Master, Housemaster, Assistant Headmaster, Stewart's Melville, Edinburgh, 1973-87; Deputy Rector, Dollar Academy, 1987-94; HMC Academic Policy Sub-Committee, since 1997; Council Member, SCCC; Governor, Ardvreck School. Publication: Stewart's Melville: the first Ten Years (Co-author). Recreations: cricket (Scottish); music (English); literature (international). Address: 2 Academy Place, Dollar FK14 7DZ; T.-01259 742511.

Robertson, John William, WS, MA. Secretary, British Linen Bank Ltd., since 1986; Solicitor, since 1971; b. 12.11.43, Dunfermline; m., Alice Rudland; 1 s.; 3 d. Educ. Dunfermline High School; Edinburgh University. Assistant Law Secretary, Bank of Scotland, 1975; Manager, Law Department, Bank of Scotland, London, 1978; Assistant Secretary, British Linen Bank Ltd., 1983. Address: (b.) 4 Melville Street, Edinburgh EH3 7NZ.

Robertson, Sir Lewis, CBE, FRSE, FRSA. Chairman, Carnegie Trust for the Universities of Scotland, since 1990; b. 28.11.22, Dundee; m., Elspeth Badenoch; 2 s.; 1 s. (dec.); 1 d. Educ. Trinity College, Glenalmond. Apprentice Chartered Accountant, 1939-42; RAF Intelligence, 1942-46; entered family textile business, 1946; appointed Managing Director, Robertson Industrial Textiles, 1954; first Managing Director, Scott & Robertson, 1965 (Chairman, 1968); resigned, 1970; Chief Executive, Grampian Holdings, Glasgow, 1971-76 (also Deputy Chairman, 1972-76); Non-Executive Director, Scottish &

Newcastle Breweries, 1975-87; Chairman: Triplex Lloyd plc, 1982-90, Girobank Scotland, 1984-90, Borthwicks plc, 1985-89, Lilley plc, 1986-93, Havelock Europe plc, 1989-92, Stakis plc, 1991-95, Posteru Executive Group, 1991-96; Director, Whitman International, Geneva, 1987-90; Chairman, Scottish Board (and UK Council Member), British Institute of Management, 1981-83; Chairman, Eastern Regional Hospitals Board, 1960-70; Member, Committee of Enquiry into the Relationship of the Pharmaceutical Industry with the NHS, 1965-67; Member, Monopolies (later Monopolies and Mergers) Commission, 1969-76; Deputy Chairman and first Chief Executive, Scottish Development Agency, 1976-81; Member, Scottish Economic Council, 1977-83; Member, Restrictive Practices Court, 1983-97; Member, Scottish Post Office Board, 1984-90; Member, Court, Dundee University, 1967-70 (first Finance Chairman); Council Member, Scottish Business School, 1978-83; Chairman, Scottish Arts Council, and Member, Arts Council of GB, 1970-71; Chairman, Scottish Advisory Committee, British Council, 1978-87; Council Member, Scottish History Society, 1984-89; first Chairman, Policy Committee, Scottish Episcopal Church, 1974-76; Trustee, Foundation for the Study of Christianity and Society, 1983-89; Member, Advisory Board, Edinburgh Edition of the Waverley Novels, since 1986; Director, Friends of Royal Scottish Academy, 1986-95; Member, Board, British Executive Service Overseas (Chairman, Scotland), 1995-98; Royal Society of Edinburgh: Fellow, since 1978, Member, Council, since 1992, Treasurer, since 1994; Chairman, Scottish Division, Imperial Society of Knights Bachelor, since 1995; Director and Trustee, Advanced Management Programme Scotland, since 1996; Trustee and Vice-Patron, Scottish Council for Research in Education, since 1997; Hon. Doctorate of Laws, Dundee University, 1971; Hon. Doctorate of Business Administration, Napier University, 1992; Hon. DUniv, Stirling, 1993. Recreations: work; foreign travel; computer use; music; list-making. Address: 32 Saxe Coburg Place, Edinburgh EH3 5BP; T.-0131-332 5221.

Robertson, Professor Noel Farnie, CBE, MA, BSc, PhD, FRSE, FIBiol; b. 24.12.23, Dundalk; m., Doreen Colina Gardner; 2 s.; 2 d. Educ. Trinity Academy; Edinburgh University; Trinity College, Cambridge. Plant Pathologist, West African Cacao Research Institute, Ghana, 1946-48; Lecturer, Plant Pathology, Cambridge University, 1948-59; Professor of Botany, Hull University, 1959-69; Professor of Agriculture, Edinburgh University, and Principal, East of Scotland College of Agriculture, 1969-83. Publications: Britain's First Chair in Agriculture (Co-author), 1990; From Dearth to Plenty (Co-author), 1995. Recreations: gardening; natural history. Address: (h.) Woodend, Juniper Bank, Walkerburn, Peebles-shire EH43 6DE; T.-01896 870523.

Robertson, Raymond Scott, MA. Chairman, Scottish Conservative and Unionist Party, since 1997; b. 11.12.59, Hamilton. Educ. Garrion Academy, Wishaw; University of Glasgow; Jordanhill College of Education. Teacher of History and Modern Studies; MP, Aberdeen South, 1992-97; PPS, Northern Ireland Office, 1993-95; Minister for Education, Housing, Fisheries and Sport, Scottish Office, 1995-97. Recreations: watching football; playing squash; reading. Address: Suite 1/1, 14 Links Place, Edinburgh EH6 7EZ; T.-0131-555 2900.

Robertson, Richard Ross, RSA, FRBS, DA. Sculptor; b. 10.9.14, Aberdeen; m., Kathleen May Matts; 2 d. Educ. Paisley Grammar School; Glasgow School of Art; Aberdeen Art School. Work exhibited in Aberdeen public parks and several public buildings in city and county of Aberdeen; also exhibited in several private collections in Britain, America and Holland; retired Lecturer in Sculpture, Gray's School of Art, Aberdeen. Recreations: carving; gardening; walking. Address: (h.) Creaguir, Woodlands Road, Rosemount, Blairgowrie, Perthshire; T.-01250 4970.

Robertson, Roderick. Managing Director, Robertsons of Tain Ltd.; Honorary Sheriff, Tain and Dingwall, 1976; b. 24.8.35, Tain; m., Elizabeth Martin Steele; 1 s. Educ. Tain Royal Academy. Agricultural engineering, 1951-56; Army, 1956-59; commenced business (agricultural engineering), 1959; elected, Tain Town Council, 1965 (Chairman of Development, Dean of Guild and Senior Bailie); JP, 1975; appointed Member, Valuation Appeal Committee, Ross and Cromarty, Skye and Lochalsh, 1980; Director, Royal Highland and Agricultural Society of Scotland; Director, Ross and Cromarty Enterprise, 1991; Chairman, Justice of the Peace Committee, Ross and Cromarty, 1980; Chairman, Local Royal British Legion Housing Association, 1984; Chairman, Tain Community Council. Recreations: flying; shooting; fishing; judo. Address: (h.) Viewfield Farm, Tain, Ross-shire IV19 1PX; T.-01862 892151.

Robertson, Brigadier Sidney Park, MBE, TD, JP, DL, BCom. Director, S. & J.D. Robertson Group Ltd. (Chairman, 1965-79); Honorary Sheriff, Grampian, Highlands and Islands, since 1969; Vice Lord Lieutenant of Orkney, 1987-90; b. 12.3.14, Kirkwall; m., Elsa Miller Croy (deceased); 1 s.; 1 d. Educ. Kirkwall Grammar School; MIBS; Edinburgh University. Commissioned, Royal Artillery, 1940 (Despatches, NW Europe, 1945); managerial posts, Anglo-Iranian Oil Co., Middle East, 1946-51; Manager Operations/Sales, Southern Division, Shell-Mex and BP, 1951-54; founder, Robertson firm, 1954; Major Commanding 861 (Independent) Light Anti-Aircraft Battery RA (Orkney and Zetland), TA, 1956-61; Lt. Col. Commanding Lovat Scouts, 1962-65; Brigadier, CRA 51st Highland Division, 1966-67; Chairman, Orkney Hospitals Board of Management/Orkney Health Board, 1965-79; DL, 1968; Honorary Vice-President, Royal British Legion Scotland, Highlands and Islands Area, since 1975; President, Royal British Legion Scotland, Kirkwall Branch, 1957-97; Chairman, RNLI, Kirkwall Station Committee, 1972-97 (President, since 1997); Honorary Colonel, 102 (Ulster and Scottish) Light Air Defence Regiment, Royal Artillery, 1975-80; Hon. Colonel Commandant, Royal Regiment of Artillery, 1977-80; Vice President, National Artillery Association, since 1977; Chairman, Royal Artillery Council of Scotland, 1980-84; Honorary President, Orkney Bn., Boys' Brigade; Vice-President, RNLI, since 1985; President, Villars Curling Club, 1978-80, 1986-88; Honorary President: Friends of St. Magnus Cathedral, since 1994, Orkney Family History Society, since 1996; Freedom of Orkney, 1990; Honorary Fellowship, Edinburgh University, since 1996. Recreations: travel; hill-walking; angling. Address: (h.) Daisybank, Kirkwall, Orkney; T.-01856 87 2085.

Robertson, Stephen Andrew Cormack, MBE, MUniv, MA, LLB, NP. Humorist and Actor; founder Member and co-author, Scotland The What?; b. 21.4.33, Aberdeen; m., Eva Mary Stephen; 1 s.; 1 d. Educ. Aberdeen Grammar School; Aberdeen University. National service (2nd Lt. in Royal Signals), 1957-59; supply teaching and legal and administrative assistant in various offices, 1960-63; Solicitor in Aberdeen, 1963-83, mostly as Partner, latterly Consultant, Wilsone & Duffus, Advocates; full-time participation in Scotland The What?, 1983-95; semi-retired, 1996. Recreations: watching sport; country pottering and hill-walking; golf; theatre; reading; drystane dyking. Address: (h.) Flat 1, Sillerton House, 15 Albyn Terrace, Aberdeen AB10 1YP; T.-01224 626728.

Robertson, Sue, BA, MSocSci. Director, One Parent Families Scotland, since 1988; b. 12.7.50, Carlisle; m., Paul Hare; 1 s.; 2 d. Educ. Penrith Queen Elizabeth Grammar School; Oxford University; Birmingham University. Senior Economic Assistant, Scottish Economic Planning Department, 1973-78; Co-ordinator, Scottish Women's Aid, 1978-83; Training Officer, Scottish Council for Single Parents, 1983-88. Committee Member, Cairn Housing Association and PACE. Recreations: hill-walking; cycling;

reading. Address: (b.) 13 Gayfield Square, Edinburgh EH1 3NX; T.-0131-556 3899.

Robertson, William Archibald, QPM, LLB, MPhil. Chief Constable, Northern Constabulary, since 1996; b. 16.10.43, Motherwell; m., Isabel Cook; 3 s. Educ. Hamilton Academy; Glasgow University; University of Strathclyde. Joined Lanarkshire Constabulary, 1962; Head, Fraud Squad, Strathclyde Police, 1980-81; Head of Personnel, 1981-82; appointed Assistant Chief Constable, Strathclyde Police, 1982; Director of Training, Scottish Police College, 1986-88; Deputy Chief Constable, Cleveland Constabulary, 1992. Publication: Scottish Crime Prevention "Strategy for the 90s" (Co-author). Recreations: golf; Rotary. Address: (b.) Police Headquarters, Inverness, IV2 3SY; T.-01463 715555.

Robertson, William Nelson, CBE, MA, FCII. Director: Morrison Construction, since 1995; Director, since 1996: Alliance Investment Trust, Second Alliance Investment Trust, Edinburgh New Tiger Investment Trust, Caledonian Foundation; Member, Advisory Board, Scottish Amicable, since 1997; Member, Court, University of Abertay, Dundee, since 1996; Group Chief Executive, General Accident, 1990-95, Director, 1984-95; Board Member, Association of British Insurers, 1991-95; b. 14.12.33, Berwick upon Tweed; m., Sheila Catherine; 2 d. Educ. Berwick Grammar School; Edinburgh University. Joined General Accident, 1958; Deputy Chief General Manager, 1989-90. Recreations: hill-walking; gardening.

Robertson-Rae, Avril Margaret, FHCIMA. Director, Strathclyde Region Catering Services, 1988-96; b. 17.7.35, Edinburgh; 2 s. Educ. Eastwood Secondary School; Queen's College, Glasgow. Began career as assistant housekeeper, 1956; former domestic science teacher and catering manager; Principal Officer (Catering), Strathclyde Regional Council, 1982-88. Vice-Chairman, Board of Management, Glasgow College of Food Technology; Member, Court, Glasgow Caledonian University; Director, Glasgow Chamber of Commerce, 1994-96. Industrial Caterer of the Year, 1992. Recreations: walking; reading; studying Portuguese; gardening; travel. Address: (h.) 4 Trigoni Court, Largs, Ayrshire; T.-01475 675360.

Robins, Professor David John, BSc, PhD, DSc, CChem, FRSC, FRSE. Professor of Bio-organic Chemistry, since 1990; b. 12.8.45, Purley; m., Helen Dorothy; 1 s.; 1 d. Educ. Purley Grammar School; Exeter University. NIH Postdoctoral Fellow, University of Pittsburgh, USA, 1969-71; SRC Fellowship, University of Surrey, 1971-72; Tutorial Fellow, University of Reading, 1972-73; University of Glasgow: Lecturer, 1974-87, Senior Lecturer, 1987-88, Reader, 1988-90. Flintoff Medal and Prize, Royal Society of Chemistry, 1999. Recreations: cycling; hillwalking; gardening. Address: Department of Chemistry, University of Glasgow, Glasgow G12 8QQ; T.-0141-330 4378.

Robins, John F. Campaigns Consultant, Animal Concern, since 1998 (formerly Secretary); Co-ordinator, Scottish Animal Rights Network, since 1983; Managing Director, Ethical Promotions Ltd., since 1988; Co-ordinator, Save Scotland's Seals Funds, 1988-96; Secretary, Save Our Seals Fund, since 1996; b. 2.1.57, Glasgow; m., Mary E.; 1 s.; 1 d. Educ. St. Ninian's High School. Co-ordinator, Glasgow Energy Group, 1978-80; Company Secretary, Scottisdh Anti-Vivisection Society, 1981-88; Green Party activist and candidate, 1978-81; Delegate, Anti-Nuclear Campaign, 1978-81; Vice-Chair, Friends of the Earth (Scotland) Ltd., 1981-82. Recreation: catching up on lost sleep. Address: (b.) P.O. Box 3982, Glasgow G51 4WD; T.-0141-445 3570.

Robinson, Christopher Peter, FHCIMA. Chief Executive, Heart of Midlothian Football Club, since 1994; Chairman, Wheatsheaf Catering Ltd., since 1978; b. 23.3.51, Edinburgh; m., Elizabeth; 3 d. Educ. Bo'ness Academy; Napier University. Trainee Manager, Open Arms Hotel Group, 1972-78. Guest Lecturer, International Hotel Schools, Paris and Cornell; President, Hotel and Catering Institutional Management Association, 1992-93. Recreations: football; golf. Address: (b.) Tynecastle Stadium, Gorgie Road, Edinburgh EH11 2NL; T.-0131-200 7200.

Robinson, Ernest Thomson, OBE, TD, KLJ, CMLJ, MB, ChB, FRCGP, DRCOG. Chairman, Council, St. Andrew's Ambulance Association, since 1994; retired General Medical Practitioner; b. 18.3.34, Gartcosh; m., Margaret; 4 s.; 3 d. Educ. Coatbridge Secondary School; Glasgow University. Principal General Medical Practitioner, Woodside Health Centre, Glasgow (retired); former Regimental Medical Officer (rank Major), 154 Lowland Regiment RCT (TA). Publication: First Aid Book for Young People. Recreations: salmon and trout fishing. Address: (h.) 132 Prestonfield, Milngavie, Glasgow G62 7QA; T.-0141-563 7409.

Robinson, Helen Mairi Johnstone, MA. Freelance Book Editor, Community Education Worker, Researcher and Lecturer; Managing Editor, Larousse plc, formerly W. & R. Chambers, 1990-96; Research Associate, Edinburgh Edition of the Waverley Novels, 1987-91; Kerr-Fry Award holder, Edinburgh University, 1985-90; b. 21.1.45, Glasgow; 1 s.; 1 d. Educ. George Watson's Ladies' College, Edinburgh; Edinburgh University. Scottish National Dictionary: Junior Assistant Editor, 1966, Assistant Editor, 1967, Senior Assistant Editor, 1972; Editor-in-Chief, Concise Scots Dictionary, 1973-85; Member, Advisory Committee, Private Papers of James Boswell, Yale University, since 1987. Publications: Concise Scots Dictionary, 1985; Chambers 21st Century Dictionary, 1996. Recreations: music; theatre; reading; travel. Address: (b.) 23 Dundas Street, Edinburgh, EH3 6QQ.

Robinson, Ian, BSc, FEng. Chief Executive, Scottish Power plc, since 1995; b. 3.5.42, Boldon, Co. Durham; m., Kay Robinson; 1 s.; 1 d. Educ. Middlesbrough High School; Leeds University. Managing Director, Parsons Corporation, 1985-86; Managing Director, John Brown Engineering and Construction, 1986-92; Chief Executive, John Brown plc, 1992-95; Director, Trafalgar House plc, 1992-95. Non-Executive Director: ASDA plc. Recreations: golf; gardening. Address: (b.) 1 Atlantic Quay, Glasgow G2 8SP; T.-0141-636 4503.

Robson, Agnes, MA. Director, Directorate of Primary Care, NHS Management Executive, Scottish Office Home and Health Department, since 1992; b. 6.10.46, Edinburgh; 1 s. Educ. Holy Cross Academy; Edinburgh University. Civil Servant, since 1968; Head, Energy Division, 1988-89; Head, Nuclear Energy Division, 1989-90; Head, Urban Policy Division, 1990-92. Recreations: music; theatre. Address: (b.) St. Andrews House, Edinburgh.

Robson, Euan Macfarlane, BA, MSc, MICA. Scottish Manager, Gas Consumers' Council, since 1986; b. 17.2.54, Northumberland; m., Valerie; 2 d. Educ. Trinity College, Glenalmond; Newcastle-upon-Tyne University; Strathclyde University. Teacher, 1976-79; Deputy Secretary, Gas Consumers' Northern Council, 1981-86. Member, Northumberland County Council, 1981-89; Honorary Alderman, Northumberland CC, since 1989; Liberal/SDP Alliance candidate, Hexham, 1983, 1987; Liberal Democrat Scottish Parliamentary spokesman on Rural Affairs; River Tweed Commissioner; author. Address: (b.) 86 George Street, Edinburgh, EH2 3BU.

Rochester, Professor Colin Herbert, BSc, PhD, DSc, CChem, FRSC, FRSE. Baxter Professor of Chemistry, Dundee University, since 1980; b. 20.3.37, Coventry; m., Jennifer Mary Orrell; 2 s.; 2 d. Educ. Hymers College, Hull;

Royal Liberty School, Romford; King's College, London University. Nottingham University: Assistant Lecturer in Physical Chemistry, 1962-64, Lecturer, 1964-72, Reader, 1972-80. Publication: Acidity Functions, 1970. Recreations: fossil collecting; swimming. Address: (b.) Chemistry Department, The University, Dundee DD1 4HN; T.-01382 344327.

Rochford, Professor Gerard, BA, BSc. Psychotherapist; b. 17.12.32, Dorking; m., Anne Prime (dec.); 3 s.; 7 d. Educ. Worcester Royal Grammar School; Hull University; Oxford University. Medical Research Council, 1960-63; Lecturer in Psychology: Aberdeen University, 1963-67, Hong Kong University, 1967-70; Lecturer/Senior Lecturer, 1970-78, Professor of Social Work Studies, 1978-88, Aberdeen University. Member, Scottish Association of Psychoanalytical Psychotherapists. Recreations: family; friends; poetry; pottery. Address: (h.) 47 Waverley Place, Aberdeen; T.-Aberdeen 644873.

Rodger of Earlsferry, Rt. Hon. Lord (Alan Ferguson Rodger), QC, MA, LLB, DCL. Lord Justice General; b. 18.9.44. Educ. Kelvinside Academy, Glasgow; Glasgow University; New College, Oxford. Fellow, New College, Oxford, 1970-72; Member, Faculty of Advocates, 1974; Clerk of Faculty, 1976-79; Advocate Depute, 1985-88; Home Advocate Depute, 1986-88; Member, Mental Welfare Commission for Scotland, 1981-84; UK Delegation to CCBE, 1984-89; Maccabaean Lecturer, British Academy, 1991; Solicitor General for Scotland, 1989-92; Lord Advocate, 1992-96. Address: (b.) Supreme Court, 2 Parliament House, Parliament Square, Edinburgh, EH1 1RQ.

Rodger, Professor Albert Alexander, BSc (Eng), PhD, CEng, MICE, FGS. Professor of Civil Engineering, Aberdeen University, since 1997; b. 12.5.51, Greenock; m., Jane Helen; 2 d. Educ. Aberdeen University. Project Engineer, Cementation Research Ltd., London, 1977-79; Aberdeen University: Lecturer in Engineering, 1979-89, Senior Lecturer, 1989-95, Personal Professor, 1995-97. Convenor, Business and Finance Committee, Aberdeen Presbytery. Winner, 1997 National John Logie Baird Award for Innovation; Award for Excellence, Aberdeen University, 1994. Recreations: history of church architecture; photography; swimming. Address: Department of Engineering, King's College, University of Aberdeen, Aberdeen AB24 3UE; T.-01224 272984.

Rodger, Willie, ARSA, RGI, DA (Glas). Artist in lino and woodcuts; b. 3.3.30, Kirkintilloch; m., Anne Charmian Henry; 2 s.; 2 d. Educ. Lenzie Academy; Glasgow School of Art. Visualiser, London advertising agency, 1953-54; Art Teacher, Lenzie Acacady, 1955-68; Head, Art Department, Clydebank High School, 1968-87. Artist in Residence, Sussex University, 1971; Scottish Historical Playing Cards, 1975; Saltire Awards for Art in Architecture, 1984-89; work in permanent collections in Scotland and England; commissions: Enamel Mural Exhibition Station, Glasgow; illustrations and mural, Dallas Dhu Distillery, Forres; design, Stained Glass Windows, St Mary's Parish Church, Kirkintilloch; Street Banners, 200 anniversary, Union Street, Aberdeen. Publications: Scottish Historical Playing Cards; The Field of Thistles (Illustrator); Willie Rodger, Open Eye Gallery. Recreations: gardening; jazz. Address: Stenton, Bellevue Road, Kirkintilloch, Glasgow G66 1AP; T.-0141-776 2116.

Rodgers, Professor Eamonn Joseph, BA, MA, PhD. Professor of Spanish and Latin American Studies, University of Strathclyde, since 1990; b. 4.6.41, Belfast; m., Valerie Ann Goodman; 2 s. Educ. St. Mary's, Belfast; Queen's University, Belfast. Trinity College Dublin: Junior Lecturer in Spanish, 1964-66, Lecturer in Spanish, 1966-78, Senior Lecturer in Spanish, 1978-89. Publications: From Enlightenment to Realism: The Novels of Galdos, 1870-86, 1987; Encyclopedia of Contemporary Spanish Culture, 1999. Recreations: music; walking. Address: University of Strathclyde, 26 Richmond Street, Glasgow G1 1XH; T.-0141-548 3506.

Roe, Professor Nicholas Hugh, MA (Oxon), DPhil (Oxon). Professor of English Literature, St. Andrews University, since 1996; b. 14.12.55, Fareham; m., Dr. Susan Jane Stabler. Educ. Royal Grammar School, High Wycombe; Trinity College, Oxford. Lecturer in English, Queen's University of Belfast, 1982-85; St. Andrews University: Lecturer in English, 1985-94, Reader in English, 1994-96; Visiting Professor, University of Sao Paulo, 1989; Leverhulme Research Fellow, 1994-95; Director, Coleridge Conference, since 1994; Trustee, Keats-Shelley Memorial Association. Publications: Coleridge's Imagination, 1985; Wordsworth and Coleridge, 1988; Wordsworth and Coleridge, The Radical Years, 1988; The Politics of Nature, 1992; Selected Poetry of William Wordsworth, 1992; Keats and History, 1995; Selected Poems of John Keats, 1995; John Keats and the Culture of Dissent, 1997. Recreations: walking; gardening; cookery; France. Address: (b.) School of English, St. Andrews University, St. Andrews KY16 9AL; T.-01334 476161.

Roebuck, Michael Stuart, BSc, MEd, CertEd. Principal, Kilmarnock College, since 1996; b. 5.12.49, Huddersfield; m., Margaret Jane; 1 s.; 1 d. Educ. Marlborough Grammar School; University of Ulster; Edinburgh University. Trainee Town Planner; Lecturer/Senior Lecturer/Depute Head of Department, Stevenson College of F.E.; Assistant to the Director of Education, Lothian Region; TVEI Coordinator, Senior Adviser, Lothian Region; Principal, Lews Castle College; Director, Association of Scottish Colleges; Senior Adviser for Further Education, British Council. Recreation: cricket (retired). Address: (b.) Kilmarnock College, Holehouse Road, Kilmarnock KA3 7AT; T.-01563 523501.

Roger, Peter Charles Marshall, CA. Director, Speirs & Jeffrey Ltd., since 1974; b. 11.4.42, Glasgow; m., Fiona Ann Murray; 2 s.; 1 d. Educ. Glasgow High School. Qualified CA, 1964; Thomson McLintock & Co., 1964-71; joined Speirs & Jeffrey Ltd., 1971. Recreation: golf. Address: (b.) 36 Renfield Street, Glasgow G2 1NA; T.-0141-248 4311.

Rogerson, Robert William Kelly Cupples, OBE, BArch, FRIBA, FRIAS, FSA Scot, MRSH. Vice Chairman, Scottish Council on Disability, 1987-89; Chairman, Committee on Access for Scotland, 1980-89; Council Member, National Trust for Scotland, 1980-86; b. 14.5.17, Glasgow; m., Mary Clark MacNeill; 1 s.; 1 d. Educ. High School of Glasgow; Strathclyde University. Architect in private practice, 1955-56 and 1958-82 (Partner, Watson Salmond & Gray, 1956-58); Lecturer, School of Architecture, Glasgow School of Art; Past Chairman, Glasgow Building Guardian Committee; Past Chairman, RIAS Trustees of The Hill House, Helensburgh; Founder and Chairman, Glasgow Summer School; former Member, Committee on Artistic Matters, Church of Scotland. Publications: A Place at Work (Co-author); Jack Coia, His Life & Work. Recreations: gardening; travelling abroad. Address: (h.) Beinn Bhuidhe House, Glen Shira, Inverary, Argyll PA32 8XH; T.-01499 302472.

Rolfe, Lord Provost Mervyn James, OStJ, MEd, FRSA, FSAScot, JP. Lord Provost of Dundee; b. 31.7.47, Wisbech; m., Christine; 1 s. Educ. Buckhaven High School; Dundee University. Civil servant, until 1983; Co-ordinator, Dundee Resources Centre for the Unemployed, 1983-87; Vice-Chair, Dundee Trades Council, 1981-82; Leader, Labour Group, Tayside Regional Council, 1994-96; Convener, Tayside Education Committee, 1986-94; Member, Executive Committee, COSLA, 1990-96; Governor, Dundee (now Northern) College of Education, 1986-94; Member, Dundee University Court, since 1986; Member,

Scottish Community Education Council, 1986-88; Member, General Teaching Council, 1986-95; Member, Scottish Committee for Staff Development in Education, 1987-91; Board Member, Scottish Enterprise, Tayside, 1991-96; Member, Scottish Cooperative Development Committee, since 1984; Member, Dundee Heritage Trust, since 1986; Executive Member, Campaign for a Scottish Assembly, 1989-91. Recreations: reading; politics. Address: (h.) 17 Mains Terrace, Dundee; T.-01382 450073.

Rolfe, William David Ian, PhD, FRSE, FGS, FMA. Keeper of Geology, National Museums of Scotland, 1986-96; b. 24.1.36; m., Julia Mary Margaret Rayer; 2 d. Educ. Royal Liberty Grammar School, Romford; Birmingham University. Geology Curator, University Lecturer, then Senior Lecturer in Geology, Hunterian Museum, Glasgow University, 1962-81; Deputy Director, 1981-86. President, Geological Society of Glasgow, 1973-76; Editor, Scottish Journal of Geology, 1967-72; President, Edinburgh Geological Society, 1989-91; President, Palaeontological Association, 1992-94; President, Society for the History of Natural History, 1996-99. Recreations: visual arts; walking; swimming; music. Address: 4A Randolph Crescent, Edinburgh, EH3 7TH; T.-0131-226 2094.

Rolland, Lawrence Anderson Lyon, DA, PPRIBA, PPRIAS, FRSE, FRSA. Senior Partner, Hurd Rolland Partnership, 1980-97, Chairman and Consultant, since 1997; General Trustee, Church of Scotland, since 1979; Chairman of Court, Dundee University, and Past Chairman of Audit Committee; b. 6.11.37, Leven; m., Mairi nee Melville; 2 s.; 2 d. Educ. George Watson's Boys College; Duncan of Jordanstone College of Art. Entered father's practice, 1959; joined partnership with Ian Begg bringing L.A. Rolland and Partners and Robert Hurd and Partners together as one partnership; developed the firm into a national practice; President, Royal Incorporation of Architects in Scotland, 1979-81; President, Royal Institute of British Architects, 1985-87. Recreations: music; fishing. Address: (b.) Rossend Castle, Burntisland, Fife KY3 0DF; T.-01592 873535.

Rollo, 14th Lord (David Eric Howard Rollo); b. 1943. Succeeded to title, 1997. Address: Pitcairns, Dunning, Perthshire, PH2 9BX.

Rooke, Matthew Andre Paul, MA (Hons), FRSA. Director, Scottish Cultural Enterprise Ltd., since 1998; Music Director, Scottish Arts Council, 1991-97; b. 14.2.63, Oxford; m., Georgina Vents Dawson. Educ. St. Andrews University; Berklee College of Music. Music Officer, Arts Council of G.B., 1989-91; parallel career as professional composer and performer, recordings including James Taylor, Nitin Sawhney and John Tavener; Member, Royal Society of Musicians of Great Britain. Recreation: cookery; country pursuits. Address: (b.) 90 Constitution Street, Edinburgh EH6 6RP; T.-0131-553 1020.

Rorke, Professor John, CBE, PhD, BSc, DEng, CEng, FIMechE, FRSE. Professor Emeritus, formerly Professor of Mechanical Engineering, Heriot-Watt University, 1980-88, and Vice-Principal, 1984-88; b. 2.9.23, Dumbarton; m., Jane Craig Buchanan; 2 d. Educ. Dumbarton Academy; Royal Technical College, Glasgow. Lecturer, Strathclyde University, 1946-51; Assistant to Engineering Director, Alexander Stephen & Sons Ltd., 1951-56; Technical Manager, then General Manager and Engineering Director, William Denny & Bros. Ltd., 1956-63; Technical Director, then Sales Director, Managing Director and Chairman, Brown Bros. & Co. Ltd. and Chairman, John Hastie of Greenock Ltd., 1963-78; Managing Director, Vickers Offshore Group, 1978 (Director of Planning, Vickers PLC, 1979-80). President, Institution of Engineers and Shipbuilders in Scotland, 1985-87; Chairman, Institute of Offshore Engineering Group, 1990-94. Recreations: bridge; golf. Address: (h.) 3 Barnton Park Grove, Edinburgh; T.-0131-336 3044.

Rose, Barry Michael, BSc, FIA. Chief Executive, Scottish Provident UK, since 1993; b. 10.3.45, Southend; m., Sandra Jane; 2 d. Educ. Manchester University. Assistant Investment Manager, Cooperative Insurance Society, 1971-76; Investment Secretary, then Investment Manager, Scottish Life Assurance, 1976-88; General Manager (Investment), Scottish Provident Institution, 1988-93. Address: (b.) 6 St. Andrew Square, Edinburgh EH2 2YA; T.-0131-556 9181.

Rose, David, BA, NDA, CertEd, FRAgS. Principal, The Barony College, Dumfries, since 1980; b. 6.7.40, Denton, Manchester; m., Pauline Anne Rose; 1 s.; 1 d. Educ. Seale-Hayne College of Agriculture; Open University. Assistant Farm Manager, Wiltshire, 1962-66; Lecturer in Agriculture, Cumbria College of Agriculture and Forestry, 1967-70; Senior Lecturer in Agriculture, Bishop Burton College of Agriculture, 1970-74; Vice-Principal, Oatridge College of Agriculture, 1974-80. Recreation: hill-walking. Address: (b.) Parkgate, Dumfries; T.-01387 860251.

Rose, Dilys Lindsay, BA. Writer of fiction, poetry, drama, since 1980; b. 7.2.54, Glasgow; 2 d. Educ. Edinburgh University. Publications include: fiction: Our Lady of the Pickpockets, Red Tides, War Dolls; poetry: Beauty is a Dangerous Thing, Madame Doubtfire's Dilemma. Winner, first Macallan/Scotland on Sunday short story competition, 1991; Hawthornden Fellow; RLS Memorial Award recipient, 1997. Address: (h.) 12 Panmure Place, Edinburgh; T.-0131-229 0800.

Rose, Professor Richard, BA, DPhil, FBA. Director and Professor of Public Policy, Centre for the Study of Public Policy, Strathclyde University, since 1976; b. 9.4.33; m., Rosemary J.; 2 s.; 1 d. Educ. Clayton High School, Missouri, USA; Johns Hopkins University; London School of Economics; Lincoln and Nuffield Colleges, Oxford University. Political public relations, Mississippi Valley, 1954-55; Reporter, St. Louis Post-Dispatch, 1955-57; Lecturer in Government, Manchester University, 1961-66; Professor of Politics, Strathclyde University, 1966-82; Consultant Psephologist, The Times, Independent Television, Daily Telegraph, STV, UTV, etc., since 1964; Scientific Adviser, Paul Lazarsfeld Society, Vienna, since 1991; American SSRC Fellow, Stanford University, 1967; Visiting Lecturer in Political Sociology, Cambridge University, 1967; Director, ISSC European Summer School, 1973; Secretary, Committee on Political Sociology, International Sociological Association, 1970-85; Founding Member, European Consortium for Political Research, 1970; Member: US/UK Fulbright Commission, 1971-75, Eisenhower Fellowship Programme, 1971; Guggenheim Foundation Fellow, 1974; Visiting Scholar: Woodrow Wilson International Centre, Washington DC, 1974, Brookings Institute, Washington DC, 1976, American Enterprise Institute, Washington, 1980, Fiscal Affairs Department, IMF, Washington, 1984; Visiting Professor, European University Institute, Florence, 1977, 1978; Visitor, Japan Foundation, 1984; Hinkley Professor, Johns Hopkins University, 1987; Guest Professor, Wissenschaftzentrum, Berlin, 1988, 1990, Central European University, Prague, 1992-95, Max Planck Institute, Berlin, 1996; Ransone Lecturer, University of Alabama, 1990; Consultant Chairman, NI Constitutional Convention, 1976; Home Office Working Party on Electoral Register, 1975-77; Co-Founder, British Politics Group, 1974; Convenor, Work Group on UK Politics, Political Studies Association, 1976-88; Member, Council, International Political Science Association, 1976-82; Keynote Speaker, Australian Institute of Political Science, Canberra, 1978; Technical Consultant, OECD, World Bank; Director, ESRC (formerly SSRC) Research Programme, Growth of Government, 1982-86; Honorary Vice President, Political Studies Association, UK, 1986; Editor, Journal of Public Policy, since 1985 (Chairman, 1981-85); Foreign Member, Finnish Academy of Science and Letters, 1985; Member, American Academy of Arts and Sciences, 1994; Robert Marjolin AMEX Prize in International Economics, 1992. Publications: The British General Election of 1959 (Co-author), 1960; Must Labour Lose? (Co-author), 1960; Politics in England, 1964; Studies in British Politics (Editor), 1966; Influencing Voters, 1967; Policy Making in Britain (Editor), 1969; People in Politics, 1970; European Politics (Joint Editor), 1971; Governing Without Consensus — An Irish Perspective, 1971; International Almanack of Electoral History (Co-author), 1974; Electoral Behaviour — A Comparative Handbook (Editor), 1974; Lessons From America (Editor), 1974; The Problem of Party Government, 1974; The Management of Urban Change in Britain and Germany (Editor), 1974; Northern Ireland — A Time of Choice, 1976; Managing Presidential Objectives, 1976; The Dynamics of Public Policy (Editor), 1976; New Trends in British Politics (Joint Editor), 1977; Comparing Public Policies (Joint Editor), 1977; What is Governing? — Purpose and Policy in Washington, 1978; Elections Without Choice (Joint Editor), 1978; Can Government Go Bankrupt? (Co-author), 1978; Britain — Progress and Decline (Joint Editor), 1980; Do Parties Make a Difference?, 1980; Challenge to Governance (Editor), 1980; Electoral Participation (Editor), 1980; Presidents and Prime Ministers (Joint Editor), 1980; Understanding the United Kingdom, 1982; United Kingdom Facts (Co-author), 1982; The Territorial Dimension in United Kingdom Politics (Joint Editor), 1982; Fiscal Stress in Cities (Joint Editor), 1982; Understanding Big Government, 1984; The Nationwide Competition for Votes (Co-author), 1984; Public Employment in Western Nations, 1985; Voters Begin to Choose (Co-author), 1986; Patterns of Parliamentary Legislation (Co-author), 1986; The Welfare State East and West (Joint Editor), 1986; Ministers and Ministries, 1987; Taxation By Political Inertia (Co-author), 1987; The Post-Modern President — The White House Meets the World, 1988; Ordinary People in Public Policy, 1989; Training Without Trainers? (Co-author), 1990; The Loyalty of Voters (Co-author), 1990; Lesson-Drawing in Public Policy, 1993; Inheritance before Choice, 1994; What Is Europe?, 1996; How Russia Votes (Co-author), 1997; Democracy and its Alternatives (Co-author), 1998. Recreations: architecture (historical, Britain; modern, America); music; writing. Address: (b.) CSPP, Strathclyde University, Livingstone Tower, Glasgow G1 1XH; T.-0141-548 3217.

Rosebery, 7th Earl of (Neil Archibald Primrose), DL; b. 11.2.29; m., Alison Mary Deirdre Reid; 1 s.; 4 d. Educ. Stowe; New College, Oxford. Succeeded to title, 1974. Address: (h.) Dalmeny House, South Queensferry, West Lothian.

Rosie, George. Freelance Writer and Broadcaster; b. 27.2.41, Edinburgh; m., Elizabeth Ann Burness; 2 s.; 1 d. Educ. Trinity Academy, Edinburgh; Edinburgh School of Architecture. Editor, Interior Design magazine, 1966-68; freelance magazine writer, 1968-76; Scottish Affairs Correspondent, Sunday Times, 1976-86; Reporter, Channel 4 TV series Down the Line, 1986-87, Scottish Eye, 1988; Reporter/Writer, The Englishing of Scotland, 1988, Selling Scotland, 1989; Scotching the Myth, 1990; Losing the Heid, 1991; Independence Day, 1996; Secret Scotland, 1997-98, Our Friends in the South, 1998; Editor, Observer Scotland, 1988-89; award winner, RSPB birds and countryside awards, 1988. Publications: British in Vietnam, 1970; Cromarty, 1975; The Ludwig Initiative, 1978; Hugh Miller, 1982; The Directory of International Terrorism, 1986; as contributor: Headlines, the Media in Scotland, 1978; Scottish Government Yearbook, 1982; Scotland, Multinationals and the Third World, 1982; World Offshore Oil and Gas Industry Report, 1987; stage plays: The Blasphemer, 1990; Carlucco and the Queen of Hearts, 1991 (winner, Fringe First, The Independent Theatre Award); It Had To Be You, 1994. Recreation: hill-walking. Address: (h.) 70 Comiston Drive, Edinburgh EH10 5QS; T.-0131-447 9660.

Ross, Alastair Robertson, CStJ, DA, ARSA, FRBS, FSA Scot, FRSA, MBIM, Hon. FRIAS. Artist; Lecturer in Fine Art, Duncan of Jordanstone College University of Dundee, since 1994; Lecturer in Fine Art, Duncan of Jordanstone College of Art, Dundee, 1966-94; Honorary Lecturer, Dundee University, 1969-94; Vice President, Royal Society of British Sculptors, 1988-90; Council Member, British School at Rome, 1990-96; b. 8.8.41, Perth; m., Kathryn Margaret Greig Wilson; 1 d. Educ. St. Mary's Episcopal School, Dunblane; McLaren High School, Callander; Duncan of Jordanstone College of Art, Dundee. SED Postgraduate Scholarship, 1965-66; Dickson Prize for Sculpture, 1962; Holokrome (Dundee) Sculpture Prize and Commission, 1962; SED Travelling Scholarship, 1963; Royal Scottish Academy Chalmers Bursary, 1964; Royal Scottish Academy Carnegie Travelling Scholarship, 1965; Duncan of Drumfork Scholarship, 1965; award winner, Paris Salon, 1967; Medaille de Bronze, Societe des Artistes Francais, 1968; Professional Member, Society of Scottish Artists, 1969; Medaille D'Argent, 1970; Membre Associe, Societe des Artistes Francais, 1970; Scottish Representative and Member, Council, Royal Society of British Sculptors, 1972-92; Sir Otto Beit Medal, Royal Society of British Sculptors, 1988; Freeman, City of London, 1989; Sir William Gillies Bequest Award, Royal Scottish Academy, 1989; Council Member, Society of Scottish Artists, 1972-75; Hon. Fellow, Royal Incorporation of Architects in Scotland, 1992; Visiting Lecturer, University of Texas, Arlington, USA, 1996; Member, Board of Directors, Studio and Artists' Workshop Provision Scotland Ltd., since 1997; exhibited work widely in UK and abroad; work in: Scottish Arts Council Collection, Perth Art Gallery and Museum, Dundee Education Authority Collection, Dundee Art Gallery and Museum, private collections in Austria, Switzerland, Egypt, USA, Norway, Bahamas, Canada, Portugal, India, UK. Recreations: genealogy; heraldry; travel. Address: (h.) Ravenscourt, 28 Albany Terrace, Dundee, DD3 6HS; T.-01382 224235.

Ross, Alexander (Sandy), LLB, CYCW. Controller Regional Production, Scottish Media Group, since 1997; Deputy Chief Executive, Scottish Television Enterprises, 1995-97; b. 17.4.48, Grangemouth; m., Alison Fraser; 2 s.; 1 d. Educ. Grangemouth High School; Edinburgh University; Moray House College. Apprentice lawyer, 1971-73; Lecturer, Paisley College, 1974-75; Producer, Granada TV, 1978-86; Controller, Arts and Entertainment, Scottish Television, 1986-95. Member, Edinburgh Town Council, 1971-74; Member, Edinburgh District Council, 1974-78; President, Moray House Students Union, 1976. Recreations: golf; music; reading; watching football. Address: (h.) 7 Murrayfield Avenue, Edinburgh EH12 6AU; T.-0131-539 1192; (b.) 0141-300 3000.

Ross, Rev. Andrew Christian, MA, BD, STM, PhD, FRHistS. Senior Lecturer in Ecclesiastical History, Edinburgh University, since 1966 (Principal of New College and Dean, Faculty of Divinity, 1978-84); b. 10.5.31, Millerhill, Lothian; m., I. Joyce Elder; 4 s.; 1 d. (deceased). Educ. Dalkeith High School; Edinburgh University; Union Theological Seminary, New York. RAF, 1952-54; Minister, Church of Central Africa Presbyterian (Malawi), 1958-65; Chairman, Lands Tribunal of Nyasaland, then Malawi Government, 1963-65; Vice Chairman, National Tenders Board, Nyasaland, then Malawi Government, 1963-65. Member, University Court, 1971-73; Convener, Student Affairs Committee, 1977-83; Kerr Lecturer, Glasgow University, 1984; Lecturer, Assembly's College, Belfast, 1985; Visiting Professor, Yale University and Dartmouth College, 1992. Publications: John Philip: Missions, Race and Politics in South Africa; Vision Betrayed: the Jesuits in China and Japan; Blantyre Mission and the Development of Malawi. Recreation: coaching and watching football. Address: (h.) 27 Colinton Road, Edinburgh; T.-0131-447 5987.

Ross, Professor David Alexander, BSc (Hons), PhD, DipEdTech, CChem, FRSC. Professor of Applied Chemistry, since 1994, and Director, Centre for the Enhancement of Learning and Teaching, University of Abertay, since 1995; b. 6.7.52, Stirling; m., Lyn; 3 d. Educ. Kilsyth Academy; Strathclyde University. Procter and Gamble Ltd., Newcastle, 1977-85; Senior Lecturer, University of Abertay, Dundee, 1985-91; Head, School of Molecular and Life Sciences, 1991-98. Recreations: golf; fishing; gardening. T.-01382 8448.

Ross, David Craib Hinshaw, LLB (Hons), NP. Partner, Biggart Baillie, Solicitors, since 1977 (Head of Corporate, since 1997); Director, Glasgow Chamber of Commerce, since 1996; b. 14.1.48, Glasgow; m., Elizabeth Clark; 2 s.; 1 d. Educ. Kelvinside Academy, Glasgow; Trinity College, Glenalmond; University of Glasgow. Maclay Murray and Spens: Apprenticeship, 1970-72, Assistant, 1972-75; Assistant, Biggart Baillie and Gifford, 1975-77. Member, Executive, Scottish Council Development and Industry; Chairman, Euro-American Lawyers Group, since 1997. Recreation: windsurfing. Address: (h.) Eastfield, 10 Ledcameroch Road, Bearsden, Glasgow G61 4AB; T.-0141-942 2569.

Ross, Donald Forrester, MA, CA. General Treasurer, Church of Scotland, since 1995; b. 14.6.42, Aberdeen; m., Dorothy Reid Nelson; 2 s. Educ. Aberdeen Grammar School; Aberdeen University. CA Apprentice, G. & J. McBain, CA, Aberdeen, 1963-67; Audit Assistant, Thomson McLintock, CA, Glasgow, 1967-69; Assistant Treasurer, Church of Scotland, 1969-75; Deputy General Treasurer, Church of Scotland, 1975-95. Address: (b.) 121 George Street, Edinburgh EH2 4YN; T.-0131-225 5722.

Ross, Rt. Hon. Lord (Donald MacArthur Ross), PC, MA, LLB. Lord Justice Clerk and President of the Second Division of the Court of Session, 1985-97; a Senator of the College of Justice, 1977-97; Chairman, Judicial Studies Committee, Scotland, since 1997; Lord High Commissioner to the General Assembly of the Church of Scotland, 1990 and 1991; b. 29.3.27, Dundee; m., Dorothy Margaret Annand; 2 d. Educ. High School of Dundee; Edinburgh University. Advocate, 1952; QC, 1964; Vice-Dean, Faculty of Advocates, 1967-73; Dean of Faculty, 1973-76; Sheriff Principal of Ayr and Bute, 1972-73; Member, Scottish Committee, Council of Tribunals, 1970-76; Member, Committee on Privacy, 1970; Deputy Chairman, Boundary Commission for Scotland, 1977-85; Member, Court, Heriot-Watt University, 1978-90, Chairman, 1984-90; Member, Parole Board for Scotland, since 1997. Hon. LLD, Edinburgh, Dundee, Abertay Dundee, Aberdeen; Hon. DUniv, Heriot-Watt; FRSE. Recreation: gardening; walking; travel. Address: (h.) 33 Lauder Road, Edinburgh EH9 2JG; T.-0131-667 5731.

Ross, Ernest. MP (Labour), Dundee West, since 1979; Chair, PLP Foreign Affairs Committee; Member, Foreign Affairs Select Committee; Chair, Board of Governors, Westminster Foundation for Democracy; Chair, All Party Group on Poverty; b. 27.7.42, Dundee; m., June; 2 s.; 1 d. Educ. St. John's Junior Secondary School. Apprentice Marine Fitter, Caledon Shipyard; Quality Control Inspector/Engineer, Timex. Recreations: football; cricket. Address: (b.) Constituency Office, 13 Cowgate, Dundee; T.-01382 200329.

Ross, Fiona, MA. Principal, Edinburgh Tutorial College, since 1997; Principal, Regent Edinburgh, since 1997; Singer, Scottish traditional song (Lead Singer, Handsel); b. 16.4.65, Glasgow. Educ. Hyndland Secondary School; University of Glasgow. Taught English overseas; Marketing Manager, Basil Paterson College, 1989-92; Director of Administration and Marketing, Scripps College, California and International House, New York, 1992-95; Educational Marketing Consultant, 1995-97. Recreations: traditional music and song; walking; good food; travel; animals. Address: (h.) 2 The Causeway, Duddingston Village, Edinburgh EH15 3PZ; T.-0131-661 8068.

Ross, George Syme, BSc (Hons). General Secretary, Headteachers' Association of Scotland, since 1998; b. 21.9.42, Glasgow; m., Nanette; 2 s. Educ. Rutherglen Academy; Strathclyde University; Jordanhill College of Education. Rutherglen Academy: Teacher, 1964-67, Special Assistant, 1967-70; Housemaster, Cathkin High School, 1970-72; Principal Teacher of Chemistry, Clydebank High School, 1972-75; Assistant Headteacher, Bannerman High School, 1975-78; Depute Headteacher, Stanley Green High School, 1978-80; Headteacher, Cowdenknowes High School, 1980-85; Headteacher, Gryffe High School, 1985-97. President, Headteachers' Association of Scotland, 1993-94; Depute Session Clerk, St. John's Church of Scotland, Largs. Recreations: hillwalking; classic cars; model railways. Address: (b.) University of Strathclyde, Jordanhill Campus, Southbrae Drive, Glasgow G13 1PP; T.-0141-950 3298/0147 674046.

Ross, Helen Elizabeth, BA, MA (Oxon), PhD (Cantab), FBPsS, CPsychol, FRSE. Honorary Reader, Stirling University, since 1994; b. 2.12.35, London. Educ. South Hampstead High School; Somerville College, Oxford; Newnham College, Cambridge. Assistant Mistress, schools in London and Oxfordshire, 1959-61; Research Assistant and student, Psychological Laboratory, Cambridge University, 1961-65; Lecturer in Psychology: Hull University, 1965-68, Stirling University, 1969-72; Senior Lecturer in Psychology, Stirling University, 1972-83; Research Fellow, DFVLR Institute for Aerospace Medicine, Bonn, 1980-81; Leverhulme Fellowship, 1983-84; Reader in Psychology, Stirling University, 1983-94. Member, S.E. Regional Board, Nature Conservancy Council for Scotland, 1991-92; Fellowship Secretary, Royal Society of Edinburgh, 1994-97. Publications: Behaviour and Perception in Strange Environments, 1974; E.H. Weber: The Sense of Touch (Co-translator), 1978; E.H. Weber on the Tactile Senses (Co-translator), 1996. Recreations: skiing; curling; hill-walking; compleat Munroist, 1998; traditional music; Member, Skelpit Lug Ceilidh Band. Address: (b.) Department of Psychology, Stirling University, Stirling FK9 4LA; T.-01786 467647.

Ross, John Alexander, CBE, FRAgS. President, National Farmers' Union of Scotland, 1990-96; Chairman, Dumfries and Galloway Health Board, since 1997; b. 19.2.45, Stranraer; m., Alison Jean Darling; 2 s.; 1 d. Educ. George Watson's College, Edinburgh. NFU of Scotland: Convener, Hill Farming Sub-Committee, 1984-90, Convener, Livestock Committee, 1987-90, Vice-President, 1986-90, Wigtown Area President, 1985-86. Chairman, Stranraer School Council, 1980-89; Session Clerk, Portpatrick Parish Church, 1975-80; Elder, Church of Scotland; Director, Animal Diseases Research Association; Commissioner, Meat and Livestock Commission, since 1996; Director, NFU Mutual Insurance Society, since 1996. Recreations: golf; curling. Address: Low Auchenree Farm, Portpatrick, Stranraer, Wigtownshire DG9 8TN.

Ross, Sheriff Kenneth A. , LLB (Hons). Sheriff of Lothian and Borders at Linlithgow; b. 21.4.49. Educ. Hutchesons Grammar School, Glasgow; Edinburgh University. Former Partner, Gillespie Gifford and Brown, Solicitors, Dumfries. Address: (b.) Sheriff Court House, High Street, Linlithgow EH49 7EQ.

Ross, Michael David, FFA, CIMgt. Group Chief Executive, Scottish Widows, since 1991; b. 9.7.46, Edinburgh; m., Pamela Marquis Speakman. Joined Scottish Widows, 1964, as Trainee Actuary; Assistant General Manager, 1986-88; appointed Actuary, 1988; General Manager (Finance), 1988-90; Deputy Managing Director, 1990-91. Vice President, Faculty of Actuaries. Fellow,

Royal Society of Arts Manufacture & Commerce. Publication: Transactions of Faculty of Actuaries. Recreations: golf; curling; skiing; gardening. Address: (b.) 69 Morrison Street, Edinburgh EH3 8BW.

Ross, Neil Kilgour, MA, LLB. Partner, Grigor & Young, Solicitors, since 1989; b. 17.5.54, Sutton Coldfield; m., Kathleen Rae; 1 d. Educ. Inverurie Academy; Aberdeen University. Legal apprentice, Western Isles Islands Council, 1977-79; Legal Assistant, Angus District Council, 1979-82; Depute Director of Legal Services, Clerk of the Peace and Clerk to the Licensing Board, Western Isles Islands Council, 1982-85. Director, Moray Council on Addictions; contributor, Stair Memorial Encyclopedia; Member, Council, Law Society of Scotland, since 1994. Recreations: wine; gardening; cricket. Address: (b.) 1 North Street, Elgin IV30 1UA; T.-01343 544077.

Ross, Nicholas Julian, ARCM. Section Principal Clarinet, Orchestra of Scottish Opera, since 1992; b. 29.1.55, Orsett; m., Lorna; 1 s.; 1 d. Educ. Oakham School; Royal Academy of Music, London. Freelance, two years; joined Scottish Opera as 2nd Clarinet, 1980. Recreation: cycling. Address: (h.) 59 Neilston Road, Uplawmoor, Glasgow G78 4AF; T.-01505 850318.

Ross, Philip Wesley, TD, MD, FRCPE, FRCPath, CBiol, FIBiol, FLS. Consultant, Edinburgh Royal Infirmary, and Reader in Medical Microbiology, Edinburgh University; b. 6.6.36, Aberdeen; m., Stella Joyce Shand; 2 s.; 1 d. Educ. Turriff Academy; Robert Gordon's College, Aberdeen; Aberdeen University (President, SRC, 1958-59). Senior Warden, Edinburgh University, 1972-83. Lt.-Col., RAMC (TA); Officer Commanding Medical Division and Edinburgh Detachment 205 Scottish General Hospital, 1975-80; Chairman: Lothian Area Division of Laboratory Medicine, 1986-89, Scottish Branch Institute of Biology, 1991-93; Examiner: Royal College of Surgeons of Edinburgh, Royal College of Pathologists; President, Scottish Microbiology Association; Inspector, Clinical Pathology Accreditation (UK) Ltd.; Liberal Democrat Parliamentary Candidate, Monklands East, 1992; Chairman, Edinburgh East Liberal Democrats; Elder, Duddingston Kirk, Edinburgh. Publications on streptococci, diseases of the mouth, throat and genital tract, infection of the newborn, antibiotics and hospital infection. Recreations: music; playing church organs (organist and choirmaster, Woodside Congregational Church, Bucksburn Parish Church, Holburn Central Church, Aberdeen, 1954-64); travel; walking; old churches; art galleries; politics. Address: (h.) 18 Old Church Lane, Duddingston Village, Edinburgh EH15 3PX; T.-0131-661 5415.

Ross, Raymond, MA, PhD, DipEd. Writer, Editor, Lecturer; b. 17.10.53, Bangour; m., Jennifer; 1 d. Educ. Scotus Academy, Edinburgh; Edinburgh University; Stirling University. Editor, Cencrastus, which he co-founded in 1979; co-editor of books on the poets Sorley MacLean and Norman MacCaig; playwright with more than 12 professional productions in Scotland and Europe; contributor to most Scottish literary publications and newspapers; teaches creative writing, Department of Continuing Education, Edinburgh University; tutor, summer schools in Scottish literature. Address: 42 Spottiswoode Street, Edinburgh; T.-0131-229 4730.

Ross, Robert Fowler. Farming Editor, The Herald, since 1994; b. 9.3.40, Crossgates; m., Jeanette Miller; 1 s.; 1 d. Educ. Dunfermline High School. Trainee Reporter, Dunfermline Press; Reporter, Glasgow Herald, Scottish Daily Mail, Scotsman; Scottish Office Correspondent, The Herald, 1972-87; Edinburgh News Editor, The Herald, 1987-94. Recreations: gardening; walking. Address: (h.) 57 Oatlands Park, Linlithgow EH49 6AS; T.-01506 842892.

Ross, Susan, MA (Hons), MSc, CQSW, PhD. Director of Social Work, East Renfrewshire Council, since 1995; b. 4.7.52, Nottingham; partner, Andy Bilson; 2 d. Educ. Nottingham Bluecoat School; St. Andrews University; Oxford University; Keele University. Social Worker, Newcastle upon Tyne, 1974; Groupworker, Nottinghamshire Social Services Department, 1978; Lecturer, Social Work, Trent Polytechnic, 1983; Principal Officer, Leicestershire Social Services Department, 1985; Children's Society in Wales Director of Wales Centre for Juvenile Justice, 1986; Area Manager, Social Work Department, Fife, 1989; Assistant Director of Social Work, Borders Regional Council, 1995. Recreations: "mummy" things with children, Emma and Anna; ice-skating; listening to 70s music and pretending it's not 20 years old. Address: (h.) 22 Millbrae Crescent, Langside, Glasgow; T.-0141-649 8734.

Ross Stewart, David Andrew, OBE, BA (Cantab). Chairman, Edinburgh Income Trust; b. 30.11.30, Edinburgh; m., Susan Olive Routh; 2 s. Educ. Rugby School; Cambridge University. Assistant General Manager, Alex. Cowan & Sons (NZ) Ltd., 1959-62; General Manager, Alex. Cowan & Sons (Stationery) Ltd., 1962-66; General Manager, Spicers (Stationery) Ltd., 1966-68; Managing Director, John Bartholomew & Son Ltd., 1968-89. Director, Quayle Munro plc; Director, Lothian Investment Fund for Enterprise Ltd.; Hon. Fellow, University of Edinburgh; Fellow, Scottish Council (Development and Industry); Convener, Finance Committee, National Trust for Scotland. Recreations: fishing; gardening; golf. Address: (b.) 13 Blacket Place, Edinburgh EH9 1RN; T.-0131-667 3221.

Rothes, 21st Earl of (Ian Lionel Malcolm Leslie); b. 10.5.32; m.; 2 s. Educ. Eton. Succeeded to title, 1975.

Rotter, Professor John Michael, BA, MA, PhD, FIEAust. Professor of Civil Engineering, Edinburgh University, since 1989; inaugural Director, Division of Engineering, since 1998; Head, Planning Unit for Chemical, Civil and Environmental and Mechanical Engineering, since 1992; b. 31.10.48, Chesterfield; 1 s.; 1 d. Educ. Monkton Combe School, Bath; Cambridge University. Temporary Lecturer in Civil Engineering, then Lecturer, then Senior Lecturer, University of Sydney, 1975-89. Visiting Professor, University of Washington, St. Louis, 1983-84; Visiting Research Fellow, Liverpool University, 1984; Visiting Professor: INSA, Lyon, France, 1996, T.U. Graz, Austria, 1997, University of Nancy, France, 1997; Convener, European Standards Committee on design of silos, tanks and pipelines. Publications: 206 technical papers. Recreations: classical music; eating; foreign places and cultures; hill-walking. Address: (b.) Edinburgh University, King's Buildings, Edinburgh EH9 3JN; T.-0131-650 5719.

Rousseau, Professor George Sebastian, PhD. Regius Professor of English Literature, Aberdeen University, since 1994, and Director, Thomas Reid Institute; b. 23.2.41. Educ. Amherst College; Princeton University. Instructor, then Assistant Professor, Harvard University, 1966-68; University of California, Los Angeles: Assistant Professor of English, 1968-69, Associate Professor, 1969-76, Professor, 1976-94; Fulbright Research Professor, West Germany, 1970; Cambridge University: Hon. Fellow, Wolfson College, 1974-75, Overseas Fellow, 1979; Visiting Fellow Commoner, Trinity College, 1982; Senior Fulbright Research Scholar, Sir Thomas Browne Institute, Netherlands, 1983; Visiting Exchange Professor, King's College, Cambridge, 1984; Clarke Lib Professor, University of California, 1985-86; Senior Fellow, NEH, 1986-87; Visiting Fellow and Waynflete Lecturer, Magdalen College, Oxford, 1993-94; book reviewer, New York Times (Sunday), since 1967; FRSocMed, 1967; FRSA, 1973. Recent publications include: The Languages of Psyche: mind and body in enlightenment thought, 1990; Perilous

Enlightenment: pre- and post-modern discourses – sexual, historical, 1991; Enlightenment Crossings: pre- and post-modern discourses – anthropological, 1991; Enlightenment Borders: pre- and post-modern discourses – medical, scientific, 1991; Hysteria Before Freud (jointly), 1993; Gout: the patrician malady (jointly), 1998. Recreations: chamber music; opera; skiing; walking; hiking. Address: (b.) Department of English, Taylor Building, King's College, Aberdeen University, Aberdeen AB24 3UB; T.-01224 273683.

Rowallan, Lord (John Polson Cameron), ARICS. Director, Rowallan Holdings Ltd., Rowallan Activity Centre Ltd., Rowallan Ltd.; Chairman, British Show Jumping Association; Chairman, Lochgoin Covenanters Trust; Trustee, Charities Shopping Day Trust; b. 8.3.47, Glasgow; m., Claire Rowallan; 2 s.; 2 d; 1 steps.; 1 stepd. Educ. Eton College; Royal Agricultural College. Estate Agent, 1969-74; Farmer, since 1974; Company Director, since 1989; Commentator, since 1986. Recreations: skiing; commentating. Address: (h.) Meiklemosside, Fenwick, Ayrshire KA3 6AY.

Rowan, Professor Alistair John, DipArch, PhD, FRSE. Principal, Edinburgh College of Art, since 1990; Professor, Heriot-Watt University, since 1991; b. 3.6.38, Belfast; m., Ann Martha Wrinch; 1 d. Educ. Campbell College, Belfast; Edinburgh College of Art; Magdalene College, Cambridge; University of Padua. Country Life magazine: Architectural Editor, 1966-67, Scottish Correspondent, 1967-77; Lecturer in Fine Art, Edinburgh University, 1967-77; Professor of History of Art, University College, Dublin, 1977-90; Slade Professor of Fine Art, Oxford University, 1988. Member, Historic Buildings Council for Scotland, 1986-94; President: Society of Architectural Historians of Great Britain, 1992-96, Architectural Heritage Society of Scotland; Chairman, The Paxton Trust; Cavaliere Del Ordine Al Merito, 1983. Publications: The Buildings of Ireland: North West Ulster, 1979, North Leinster, 1994; Designs for Castles and Country Villas by Robert and James Adam, 1985; Catalogue of Robert Adam Drawings (Victoria and Albert Museum), 1988. Recreation: gardening. Address: (b.) Edinburgh College of Art, Lauriston Place, Edinburgh EH3 9DF; T.-0131-221 6060.

Rowan, John O'Donnell, PhD, CPhys, FInstP, CEng, FIEE, FIPEM. Deputy Director, West of Scotland Health Boards Department of Clinical Physics and Bio-Engineering, since 1983; Head, Department of Clinical Physics and Bio-engineering, Glasgow Royal Infirmary NHS Trust, since 1994; Honorary Clinical Senior Lecturer in Clinical Physics, Glasgow University, since 1991; Member, National Panel of Assessors for NHS Scientists in Scotland, 1982-97; b. 5.4.36, Glasgow; m., Anne Kerr Wotherspoon; 2 d. by pr. m. Educ. Victoria Drive Senior Secondary School, Glasgow; Glasgow University. Research Physicist, Barr and Stroud, Glasgow, 1961-63; Electronics Engineer, Scottish Research Reactor Centre, East Kilbride, 1963-66; West of Scotland Health Boards Department of Clinical Physics and Bio-Engineering: Senior Physicist, 1966-71, Principal Physicist, 1971-81, Top Grade Physicist, 1981-83; Chief Physicist, Institute of Neurological Sciences, Glasgow, 1966-83. Honorary Treasurer, Scottish Branch, Institute of Physics, 1972-77; Honorary Secretary, Hospital Physicists Association, 1976-78, and President, 1982-84; Deputy Editor, Physics in Medicine and Biology, 1980-82; President, Institute of Physical Sciences in Medicine, 1982-84; Member, Scottish Health Service National Scientific Services Advisory Committee, 1989-98. Address: (b.) Glasgow Royal Infirmary, Glasgow G4; T.-0141-211 4934.

Rowan-Robinson, Professor Jeremy, MA, LLM. Professor of Planning and Environmental Law, Department of Law, Aberdeen University, since 1989; Director, Centre for Environmental Law and Policy, Aberdeen University, since 1994; Consultant in Planning and Environmental Law, Paull and Williamson, Solicitors, Aberdeen, since 1992; b. 29.3.44, Lasswade; m., Yvonne; 2 s. Educ. University of Kent at Canterbury; Aberdeen University. Assistant Solicitor, London Borough of Redbridge, 1966; Senior Associate Solicitor, London Borough of Hillingdon, 1969; Solicitor then Deputy Clerk, Westmorland County Council, 1972; Solicitor, Lake District Special Planning Board, 1975; Lecturer, Senior Lecturer, Professor of Land Economy, Aberdeen University, 1978-89; Solicitor of the Supreme Court of England and Wales; Legal Associate, Royal Town Planning Institute. Board Member, Scottish Natural Heritage. Publications: author or co-author of seven books on planning law and related topics. Recreations: mountaineering; sailing. Address: (h.) 6 Cairnlee Crescent North, Cults, Aberdeen AB15 9TY; T.-01224 861357.

Rowley, Alexander A.P., MA (Hons), MSc. General Secretary, Scottish Labour Party; b. 30.11.63, Dunfermline; 2 d. Educ. St Columba's High School, Dunfermline; Newbattle Abbey College, Dalkeith; Edinburgh University. Address: 4th Floor, Delta House, 50 West Nile Street, Glasgow G1 2NA.

Rowley, Professor David Ian, MB, ChB, BMedBiol, MD, FRCS. Professor of Orthopaedic and Trauma Surgery, Dundee University, since 1988; b. 4.7.51, Dewsbury; m., Ingrid Ginette; 1 s.; 1 d. Educ. Wheelwright Grammar School, Dewsbury; Aberdeen University; Sheffield University. Lecturer in Orthopaedic Surgery, Sheffield University, 1981; Senior Lecturer in Orthopaedic Surgery, Manchester University, and Senior Lecturer in Orthopaedic Mechanics, Salford University, 1985-88. Orthopaedic Editor, Journal of Royal College of Surgeons of Edinburgh; Regional Advisor in Surgery, NE Region, Royal College of Surgeons of Edinburgh; Examiner, Royal College of Surgeons, Edinburgh. Recreations: gardening; reading history. Address: (h.) Marclann Cottage, Kellie Castle, Arbroath; T.-01241 876466.

Rowlings, Professor Cherry, BA. Professor of Social Work, Stirling University, since 1991; Member, CCETSW Council and Scottish Committee, since 1992; Non-Executive Director, Central Scotland Healthcare NHS Trust, since 1998; b. 10.11.44, Bristol. Educ. Duncan House School, Bristol; York University; Oxford University. Social Worker, London Borough of Croydon; Team Leader, London Borough of Lewisham; Research Officer, Oxford University; Senior Research Fellow, Keele University; Lecturer/Senior Lecturer, Bristol University. Publications: on social work and services for older people and on social work education in Europe. Address: (b.) Department of Applied Social Science, Stirling University, Stirling FK9 4LA; T.-01786 467710.

Rowlinson, Professor Peter, MA, DPhil. Professor of Mathematics, University of Stirling, since 1996; b. 23.10.44, Cambridge; m., Carolyn. Educ. Cambridgeshire High School; New College, Oxford. University of Stirling: Lecturer in Mathematics, 1969-92, Senior Lecturer in Mathematics, 1992-94, Reader in Mathematics, 1994-96. Visiting Associate Professor of Mathematics, California Institute of Technology, 1975-76. Publication: Eigenspaces of Graphs (Co-author), 1997. Recreation: croquet. Address: Department of Computing Science and Mathematics, University of Stirling, Stirling FK9 4LA; T.-01786 467464.

Roxburghe, 10th Duke of (Guy David Innes-Ker), b. 18.11.54; m., 1, Lady Jane Meriel Grosvenor (m. diss.); 2 s.; 1 d.; 2, Virginia Mary Wynn-Williams; 1 s.; 1 d. Educ. Eton; Sandhurst; Magdalene College, Cambridge. Address: (h.) Floors Castle, Kelso.

Roy, Archibald Donald, OBE. Area Director, West of Scotland Benefits Agency, since 1997; b. 9.1.45; m., Morag; 2 s. Educ. Woodside Secondary School, Glasgow.

Management Trainee, Long John Distillers, 1963-66; Department of Social Security: various positions, Glasgow, 1966-83, Principal Inspector, London, 1983-88, Manager, Glasgow, 1988-92, Area Director, Glasgow and Paisley, 1992-97. Member, Strathclyde Steering Committee, Prince's Trust Volunteers; Member, Lomond Mountain Rescue Team. Recreations: reading; music; mountaineering. Address: Corunna House, Cadogan Street, Glasgow G2 7SS; T.-0141-249 3792.

Roy, Frank. MP (Labour), Motherwell and Wishaw, since 1997; b. 29.8.58; m.; 1 s.; 1 d. Educ. Our Lady's High School, Motherwell; Motherwell College; Glasgow Caledonian University. Former steelworker.

Roy, Kenneth. Publisher, Who's Who in Scotland, since 1985; Editor, The Scottish Review, since 1994; Managing Director, European Editions Ltd., since 1999; b. 26.3.45, Falkirk; m., Margaret H. Campbell; 2 s. Educ. Denny High School. Local newspapers, 1962-1965; Glasgow Herald, 1965-67; public relations, 1967-69; Founder Editor, Scottish Theatre magazine, 1969-72; news and current affairs anchorman, BBC Scotland, 1972-80; founder Managing Director, West Sound, 1980-82; founder Editor, The Journalist's Handbook, 1985-93; former weekly Columnist: Scotland on Sunday, The Herald, The Observer; former daily Columnist, The Scotsman. Critic of the Year, Scottish Press Awards, 1990, 1993; Columnist of the Year, UK Press Gazette Awards, 1994; Hon. President, Auchinleck Boswell Society. Publications: Travels in a Small Country, 1987; Conversations in a Small Country, 1989; The Closing Headlines, 1993; Scenes from a Small Country, 1994; Both Sides of the Border, 1998; Dictionary of Scottish Biography, Volume I (Editor), 1999. Address: (b.) Carrick Media, 2/1 Galt House, 31 Bank Street, Irvine KA12 0LL; T.-01294 311322.

Roy, Lindsay Allan, BSc. Rector, Inverkeithing High School, since 1989; Chairman, Higher Still Group Awards Steering Committee, since 1996; Member, Board of Management, Lauder College, and Chairman of its Curriculum and Student Affairs Committee; b. 19.1.49, Perth; m., Irene Elizabeth Patterson; 2 s.; 1 d. Educ. Perth Academy; Edinburgh University. Assistant Rector, Kirkcaldy High School, 1983-86; Depute Rector, Glenwood High School, Glenrothes, 1986-89; Chairman, Modern Studies Association, 1976-79; Chairman, Modern Studies Panel, Scottish Examination Board, 1980-83; Member, Consultative Committee on the Curriculum Central Committee for Social Subjects, 1978-85. Recreation: angling. Address: (b.) Inverkeithing High School, Hillend Road, Inverkeithing, Fife; T.-01383 313400.

Royan, Professor Bruce, BA (Hons), MBA, MBCS, MIInfSc, FLA, FIMgt, FSA(Scot). Chief Executive, Scottish Cultural Resources Access Network, since 1996; Principal Consultant, Infologistix Ltd., since 1988; Visiting Professor of Publishing and Communications, Napier University, since 1997; b. 22.1.47, Luton; m., Ann Elizabeth Wilkins; 1 s.; 1 d. Educ. Dunstable Grammar School; North West Polytechnic; Glasgow University. Systems Development Manager, British Library, 1975-77; Head of Systems, National Library of Scotland, 1977-85; Director, Singapore Integrated Library Automation Service, 1985-88; Director of Information Services and University Librarian, Stirling University, 1989-96. Secretary, Working Party on Access to the National Database, 1980-83; Member, Council, Library Association of Singapore, 1987-88; Convenor, Higher Education IT Directors in Scotland, 1991-93; Executive Chairman, Bath Information and Data Services, 1991-96; Councillor, The Library Association, since 1994; Chair, National Datasets Steering Group, 1994-96; Board Member, Croydon Libraries Internet Project, 1995-96; Chair, Scottish Collaborative On Demand Publishing Enterprise,1996-98; Councillor, Institute of Information Scientists, since 1997; Member, Content Creation Task Group, New Opportunities Fund, 1998. Recreations: choral singing; antique maps; travel. Address: (b.) SCRAN, Abden House, 1 Marchhall Crescent, Edinburgh EH16 5HW.

Royle, Trevor Bridge, MA, FRSE. Author and Journalist; Fellow, Institute for Advanced Studies in the Humanities, Edinburgh University; b. 26.1.45, Mysore, India; m., Dr. Hannah Mary Rathbone; 3 s. Educ. Madras College, St. Andrews; Aberdeen University. Editor, William Blackwood & Sons Ltd.; Literature Director, Scottish Arts Council, 1971-79; Council Member, Scottish National Dictionary Association; Scottish Arts Council Book Award, 1983. Publications: We'll Support You Evermore: The Impertinent Saga of Scottish Fitba' (Co-Editor), 1976; Jock Tamson's Bairns (Editor), 1977; Precipitous City: The Story of Literary Edinburgh, 1980; A Diary of Edinburgh, 1981; Edinburgh, 1982; Death Before Dishonour: The True Story of Fighting Mac, 1982; The Macmillan Companion to Scottish Literature, 1983; James and Jim: The Biography of James Kennaway, 1983; The Kitchener Enigma, 1985; The Best Years of their Lives: The Post-War National Service Experience, 1986; War Report: The War Correspondents' View of Battle from the Crimea to the Falklands, 1987; The Last Days of the Raj, 1989; A Dictionary of Military Quotations, 1989; Anatomy of a Regiment, 1990; In Flanders Fields: Scottish poetry and prose of the First World War, 1990; Glubb Pasha, 1992; Mainstream Companion to Scottish Literature, 1993; Orde Wingate: Irregular Soldier, 1995; Winds of Change, 1996; Scottish War Stories (Editor), 1999; radio plays: Magnificat, 1984; Old Alliances, 1985; Foreigners, 1987; Huntingtower, 1988; A Man Flourishing, 1988; The Pavilion on the Links, 1991; The Suicide Club, 1992; Tunes of Glory, 1995; stage play: Buchan of Tweedsmuir, 1991. Recreations: rugby football; hill-walking; restoring Craigiemeg. Address: (h.) 6 James Street, Edinburgh EH15 2DS; T.-0131-669 2116.

Ruckley, Professor Charles Vaughan, CBE, MB, ChM, FRCSEdin, FRCPEdin. Consultant Surgeon, Royal Infirmary, Edinburgh, since 1971; Professor of Vascular Surgery, Edinburgh University, since 1992; President, Vascular Surgical Society, Great Britain and Ireland, 1993-94; b. 14.5.34, Wallasey; m., Valerie Anne Brooks; 1 s.; 1 d. Educ. Wallasey Grammar School; Edinburgh University. Research Fellow, University of Colorado, 1967-68. Secretary/Treasurer, Vascular Surgical Society of Great Britain and Ireland; Member, Council, Association of Surgeons of Great Britain and Ireland. Recreations: angling; music; skiing. Address: (b.) Vascular Surgery Unit, Royal Infirmary, Edinburgh; T.-0131-229 2477.

Runciman, William Chisholm, LLB. Secretary, Carnegie Dunfermline and Hero Fund Trusts; b. 15.11.41, Greenock; m., Eileen; 2 s. Educ. Greenock Academy; Edinburgh University. Police Officer in Edinburgh and Lothian & Borders, retiring in 1987 as Chief Superintendent; former Director, National Playing Fields Association — Scotland. Recreations: mountaineering; fishing; photography. Address: (h.) 11 East Harbour Road, Charlestown, Fife KY11 3EA.

Rundell, David Richard, BSc, MSc, CStat. Director of Computing Services, Heriot-Watt University, since 1990; b. 5.9.48, Plymouth; 3 d. Educ. Harwich County High, Harwich, Essex; St. Andrews University; Heriot-Watt University. Statistician, Medical School, Edinburgh University, 1970-76; Applications Team, Regional Computing Centre, University of Bath, 1976-79; User Services Manager, Computer Centre, Heriot-Watt University, 1979-90. Address: (b.) Computer Centre, Heriot-Watt University, Riccarton, Edinburgh EH14 4AS; T.-0131-449 5111.

Runnalls, Professor Graham Arthur, BA, MA, DipGenLing, DLitt. Professor of French, Edinburgh

University; b. 21.11.37, Exmouth; m., Anne K.; 2 d. Educ. Exmouth Grammar School; Exeter University. Assistant Lecturer in French, Exeter University, 1962-63; Lecturer in French, North London Polytechnic, 1963-66; joined Edinburgh University as Lecturer, 1966. Honorary President, International Society for the Study of Medieval Theatre. Recreations: opera; walking. Address: (h.) 85A Colinton Road, Edinburgh EH10 5DF; T.-0131-337 1737.

Rush, Christopher, MA (Hons). Writer; Teacher, George Watson's College, Edinburgh, since 1972; b. 23.11.44, St. Monans; m., Patricia Irene Boyd (deceased); 1 s.; 1 d. Educ. Waid Academy; Aberdeen University. Has won three Scottish Arts Council bursaries, two SAC book awards, twice been short-listed for Scottish Book of the Year Award; shortlisted for McVitie Scottish Writer of the Year, 1988; Screenwriter, Venus Peter (based on own book). Publications include: Peace Comes Dropping Slow; A Resurrection of a Kind; A Twelvemonth and A Day; Two Christmas Stories; Into the Ebb; With Sharp Compassion; Venus Peter Saves the Whale; Last Lesson of the Afternoon. Recreations: music; reading; cross-country running; sea-watching. Address: (h.) 2 Peel Terrace, Edinburgh EH9 2AY; T.-0131-667 1248.

Russell, Adrian Paul Grenville, PhD, BEng. Director, UK Astronomy Technology Centre, since 1998; UK Gemini Project Manager, since 1995; b. 11.9.61, Sheffield; m., Lilie Anne. Educ. Newfield School, Sheffield; University of Sheffield; University of Cambridge. Joined Royal Observatory Edinburgh, 1987; posted to Hawaii as Support Scientist, James Clerk Maxwell Telescope (JCMT), 1990; Max Planck Institute, Munich, Germany, 1990; JCMT Instrumentation Programme Manager, Royal Observatory Edinburgh, 1992. Address: Royal Observatory, Blackford Hill, Edinburgh EH9 3HJ; T.-0131-668 8313.

Russell, (Alastair) Muir. Permanent Under-Secretary of State, Scottish Office, since 1998; b. 9.1.49; m., Eileen Alison Mackay. Educ. High School of Glasgow; Glasgow University. Joined Scottish Office, 1970; seconded as Secretary to Scottish Development Agency, 1975-76; Assistant Secretary, 1981; Principal Private Secretary to Secretary of State for Scotland, 1981-83; Under Secretary, 1990; seconded to Cabinet Office, 1990-92; Under Secretary (Housing), Scottish Office Environment Department, 1992-95; Deputy Secretary, Secretary, Scottish Office Agriculture and Fisheries Department, February-October, 1995; Secretary and Head of Department, Scottish Office Agriculture and Fisheries Department, 1995-98; Non-Executive Director, Stagecoach Holdings, 1992-95. Recreations: music; food; wine. Address: (b.) Scottish Office, St Andrew's House, Regent Road, Edinburgh EH1 3DG.

Russell, Sheriff Albert Muir Galloway, CBE, QC, BA (Oxon), LLB. Sheriff, Grampian, Highland and Islands, at Aberdeen, 1971-91; b. 26.10.25, Edinburgh; m., Margaret Winifred Millar; 2 s.; 2 d. Educ. Edinburgh Academy; Wellington College; Brasenose College, Oxford; Edinburgh University. Lt., Scots Guards, 1944-47; Member, Faculty of Advocates, 1951; Standing Junior Counsel to Board of Trade, Department of Agriculture and Forestry Commission; QC (Scot), 1965; Vice Chairman, Board of Management, Southern Group of Hospitals, Edinburgh, 1966-70; Governor, Moray House College of Education, 1965-70. Recreations: golf; music. Address: (h.) Tulloch House, 1 Aultbea, Ross-shire IV22 2JB.

Russell, Sheriff Dan Chapman, MA, LLB. Sheriff of South Strathclyde, Dumfries and Galloway at Hamilton, since 1992; b. 25.12.39. Qualified as Solicitor, 1963; in private practice, 1963-92.

Russell, Professor Elizabeth Mary, MD, DipSocMed, DObstRCOG, FFCM, FRCPGlas, FRCPEdin, FRSE. Professor of Social Medicine, Aberdeen University; Hon. Consultant in Public Health Medicine, since 1972; b. 27.1.36, Preston. Educ. Marr College, Troon; Glasgow University. General practice until 1964; medical management and social medicine, 1964-72; academic public health and health services research, since 1972. Recreations: skiing; gardening; music. Address: (b.) Department of Public Health, Medical School, Foresterhill, Aberdeen AB25 2ZD; T.-01224 681818, Ext. 53861.

Russell, Frank. Councillor, City of Edinburgh Council, since 1996; Convener of Personnel, since 1992; b. 23.2.48, Edinburgh; m., Janice Russell; 1 s.; 1 d. Educ. Forrester High School, Edinburgh. Elected, Edinburgh District Council, 1988; Chair of Personnel, 1992-96; Chair, Labour Group, 1992; Depute Leader of Council, 1993-96. Member, Board, Edinburgh International Jazz Festival. Recreations: reading; watching Hearts F.C. Address: (b.) City Chambers, High Street, Edinburgh; T.-0131-529 3289.

Russell, George Stuart, OBE, BL, CA, WS. Former Senior Partner, Strathern and Blair WS, now Anderson Strathern, WS; b. 21.1.14, Edinburgh; m., Nicholas Mary Gillespie; 1 s.; 3 d. Educ. Edinburgh Academy; Belhaven Hill; Harrow; Edinburgh University. CA, 1937; served Second World War, 1939-45 (Lt. Col.); OBE (Mil); Belgian Ordre de la Couronne; Polish Golden Cross of Merit with Swords; pursued a legal career; Fiscal, WS Society, 1973-79; Solicitor to the National Trust for Scotland, 1951-82, now Councillor Emeritus; Treasurer, Iona Community, 1947-65; President, Edinburgh Abbeyfield Society, 1978-92, now Vice-President; Vice President, UK, Abbeyfield Society, 1975-83; Trustee, New Club; Trustee, Scottish Churches Architectural Heritage Trust, 1982-95; Member, Queen's Bodyguard for Scotland (Royal Company of Archers). Recreations: fishing; walking; erecting plaques and view indicators. Address: 59 Braid Road, Edinburgh EH10 6AR; T.-0131-447 6009.

Russell, Ian Simon Macgregor, BComHons. Finance Director, Scottish Power PLC, since 1994; b. 16.1.53, Edinburgh; m., Fiona; 1 s.; 1 d. Educ. George Heriot's School; Edinburgh University. Recreations: golf; rugby. Address: (b.) 1 Atlantic Quay, Glasgow G2 8SP; T.-0141-636 4511.

Russell, Rev. John, MA. Minister, Tillicoultry Parish Church, since 1978; b. 29.5.33, Glasgow; m., Sheila Spence; 2 s. Educ. Cathedral School, Bombay; High School of Glasgow; Glasgow University. Licensed by Glasgow Presbytery, 1957; ordained by United Church of Canada, 1959; Assistant Minister: Trinity United Church, Kitchener, Ontario, 1958-60, South Dalziel Church, Motherwell, 1960-62; Minister: Scots Church, Rotterdam, 1963-72, Southend Parish Church, Kintyre, 1972-78; Member of various General Assembly Committees, since 1972; Convener, General Assembly's Committee on Unions and Readjustments, 1987-90; Convener, Parish Reappraisal Committee, 1990-94; Vice Convener, Board of National Mission, 1994-95; Convener, Board of National Mission, 1995-96; Moderator, Presbytery of Stirling, 1993-94. Recreations: travel; reading. Address: The Manse, Dollar Road, Tillicoultry, Clackmannanshire FK13 6PD; T.-01259 750340.

Russell, John Graham, FCIT. Chairman and Managing Director, John G. Russell (Transport) Ltd., since 1969; Chairman, Fife Warehousing Ltd., since 1988; Director: Combined Transport Ltd., since 1991, Freight Transport Association, since 1994, Alloa Warehousing, since 1988; Chairman: SCOTIA ATT Limited, since 1995, The Scottish Business Crime Centre, since 1996; b. Edinburgh; m., Isobel Margaret Hogg; 2 s.; 2 d. Educ. Merchiston Castle School, Edinburgh. Address: (b.) Gartcosh, Glasgow G69 8ES; T.-01236 873511.

Russell, John S., BSc. Senior Education Officer, BBC, since 1989; Secretary, Educational Broadcasting Council for Scotland, since 1989; b. 14.11.46, Glasgow; m., Anne Hendry; 2 s. Educ. St. Mungo's Academy, Glasgow; University of Glasgow. Field Marketing Manager, Proctor and Gamble (UK), 1970-74; Principal Teacher, Guidance, Teacher of Geography, St. Mungo's Academy, 1974-82; Assistant Headteacher, St. Patrick's, Coatbridge, 1982-85; Education Officer, BBC, West of Scotland, 1985-89. Prison Visitor; Member, Helping Offenders Prisoners and Families. Recreation: work. Address: BBC, 5 Queen Street, Edinburgh EH2 1JF; T.-0131-248 4243.

Russell, Professor Michael John, EurIng, PhD, FIMM. Dixon Professor of Applied Geology, Glasgow University, since 1989; b. 12.3.39, Sutton, Surrey. Educ. London University; Durham University. Professor and Head, Department of Applied Geology, Strathclyde University, 1984-89; research interests: origin of life, fossilized micro-organisms on Mars. Recreation: science. Address: (h.) 27 Hamilton Drive, Glasgow G12 8DN; T.-0141-339 2711.

Russell, Michael William, MA. Chief Executive, Scottish National Party; b. 9.8.53; m., Cathleen Macaskill; 1 s. Educ. Marr College, Troon; Edinburgh University. Creative Producer, Church of Scotland, 1974-77; Director, Cinema Sgire, Western Isles, 1977-81; Founder and first Director, Celtic Film and Television Festival, 1980; Secretary General, Association for Film and Television in the Celtic Countries, 1981-83; Chief Executive, Network Scotland Ltd., 1983-91; Director, Eala Bhan Ltd., since 1991. Parliamentary candidate (SNP), Clydesdale, 1987, Cunninghame South, Scottish Parliamentary elections, 1999; Executive Vice Convenor in charge of Publicity, SNP, 1987-91; Chairman, Save a Life in Scotland Campaign, 1986-88; Trustee, Celtic Film and TV Association, 1990-95; Board Director, Glasgow Film Theatre, 1992-96. Publications: A Poem of Remote Lives, 1997; In Waiting: travels in the shadow of Edwin Muir, 1998. Recreations: gardening; cookery. Address: (h.) Feorlean, Glendaruel, Argyll PA22 3AH; T.-01369 820139.

Russell, Peter MacLeod, MA. Director, North and East, Scottish Prison Service; b. 22.1.51, Edinburgh; m., Patricia Anne Kelly; 4 s.; 1 d. Educ. Royal High School, Edinburgh; Edinburgh University. Entered Scottish Office, 1973; Private Secretary to Parliamentary Under Secretary of State, 1976-78; Principal, 1978-86: Royal Commission on Legal Services in Scotland, 1978-80, SDD, 1980-84, Industry Department for Scotland, 1985-86; appointed Assistant Secretary, Scottish Office Home and Health Department, 1986. Address: (b.) Calton House, 5 Redheughs Rigg, Edinburgh EH12 9HW; T.-0131-244 8741.

Russell, Sir Robert Mark, MA (Oxon), KCMG. Chairman, Centre for Commonwealth, United Nations and International Affairs, since 1995; Chairman, Margaret Blackwood Housing Association, since 1990; Chairman, C-Mist Ltd. (Centre for Maritime and Industrial Safety Technology), since 1993; b. 3.9.29, India; m., Virginia Mary Rogers; 2 s.; 2 d. Educ. Trinity College, Glenalmond; Exeter College, Oxford University. Royal Artillery, 1952-54; H.M. Diplomatic Service, 1954-89; Assistant Under Secretary of State, F.C.O., 1978-82; H.M. Ambassador to Turkey, 1983-86; Deputy Under Secretary of State, F.C.O., 1986-89. Recreations: music; travel. Address: (h.) 20 Meadow Place, Edinburgh EH9 1JR.

Russell, Robin Irvine, MD, PhD, FRCPEdin, FRCPGlas, FACN, FACP. Consultant in Charge, Department of Gastroenterology, Royal Infirmary, Glasgow, since 1970; Consultant Physician and Gastroenterologist, Royal Infirmary, Glasgow, and Glasgow University, since 1970; b. 21.12.36, Wishaw; m., Ann Tindal Wallace; 1 s.; 1 d. Educ. Glasgow University. Member, medical and scientific staff: Medical Research Council Gastroenterology Unit, London, National Institutes of Health, USA. Chairman, British Digestive Diseases Foundation (Scotland); Member: Association of Physicians, British Society of Gastroenterology, American Gastroenterological Association. Publications: Elemental Diets; Investigative Tests and Techniques in Gastroenterology; Nutrition in Gastro-Intestinal Disease; papers on mechanisms of cellular damage and protection in the gastro-intestinal tract, physiology of intestinal absorption, NSAID and Helicobacter damage in gastrointestinal tract, coeliac disease, Crohn's disease, clinical and experimental nutrition. Recreations: golf; travel; literature; music. Address: (h.) 28 Ralston Road, Bearsden, Glasgow G61 3BA; T.-0141-942 6613.

Russell, Shendl, DCE. Chairman, Scottish Official Board of Highland Dancing, since 1996; Head Teacher; b. 29.3.56, Ayr; m., Robert D. Harvey. Educ. Ayr Academy; Craigie College. Scottish Official Board of Highland Dancing: Delegate, South Africa, Australia; former Scottish champion. Recreations: dancing; football; rugby. Address: (h.) 3 Greenside Avenue, Prestwick KA9 2HB; T.-01292 478577.

Russell, Sheriff Terence Francis, BL. Sheriff, North Strathclyde, at Kilmarnock, since 1983; b. 12.4.31, Glasgow; m., Mary Ann Kennedy; 2 d. Educ. St. Mungo's Academy, Glasgow; Glasgow University. Solicitor: Glasgow, 1955-58, Bombay High Court, 1958-63, Glasgow, 1963-81; Sheriff, North Strathclyde, at Oban and Campbeltown and Grampian, Highland and Islands, at Fort William, 1981-83. Recreations: gardening; painting.

Russell, Thomas, BSc (Hons), MBChB, PhD, FRCS Edin, FRCS Glas. Consultant Neurosurgeon, since 1987; Senior Lecturer in Neurosurgery, Edinburgh University, since 1989; b. 8.3.50, Lanark; m., Donna; 1 d. Educ. Wishaw High School; Glasgow University. MRC Fellow in Neurosurgery, Institute of Neurological Sciences, Glasgow; Senior Registrar, Neurosurgery, Bristol; Exchange Neurosurgical Resident, Memphis; Consultant Neurosurgeon, Western General Hospital, Edinburgh. Recreation: medical ethics/philosophy. Address: (h.) 15 White Dales, Edinburgh EH10 7JQ; T.-0131-445 5920.

Russell-Johnston, Lord (David Russell Russell-Johnston), MA (Hons). MP (Liberal Democrat), Inverness, Nairn and Lochaber (formerly Inverness), 1964-97; b. 28.7.32, Edinburgh; m., Joan Graham Menzies; 3 s. Educ. Carbost Public School; Portree High School; Edinburgh University; Moray House College of Education. National Service: commissioned into Intelligence Corps and 2nd i/c British Intelligence Unit, Berlin, 1958-59; History Teacher, Liberton Secondary School, Edinburgh, 1961-63; Research Assistant, Scottish Liberal Party, 1963-64; Joint Parliamentary Adviser, Educational Institute of Scotland, 1964-70; Member, Royal Commission on Local Government in Scotland, 1966-69; Parliamentary Spokesman for Scottish National Federation for the Welfare of the Blind, since 1967; Parliamentary Representative, Royal National Institute for the Blind, 1977-97; Member, Select Committee on Scottish Affairs, 1969; Parliamentary Adviser, Scottish Police Federation, 1971-75; Scottish Liberal Party: elected to Executive, 1961, and Organisation Committee, 1962, Vice Chairman, 1965, Chairman, 1970-74, Leader, 1974-88, President, 1988-94; Liberal Party Spokesman on Education, 1964-66, on Foreign Affairs, 1970-75 and 1979-85, on Scotland, 1970-73, 1975-83, 1985-88, on Devolution, 1975, on Defence, 1983-88; Member, House of Commons Committee on Privileges, 1988-92; Liberal Democrat Parliamentary Spokesman, Foreign and Commonwealth Affairs, 1988-89, European Affairs, 1988-94, East/West Relations, 1989-94, Central and Eastern Europe, 1994-97; Leader, Council of Europe Liberal Democrat and Reform Group, since 1994; President, Council of Europe Sub Committee on Youth and

Sport, 1992-94; Vice President, WEU Committee on Parliamentary and Public Relations, since 1995; Chairman, Council of Europe Committee on Culture and Education; Vice President, Liberal International, since 1994; Member, European Parliament, 1973-75 and 1976-79; Vice President, European Liberal Group and Group Spokesman on Regional Policy, 1973-75; Vice President of the Parliament's Political Committee, 1976-79; Member, Assemblies of Western European Union and Council of Europe, 1984-85, and since 1987; President, Scottish Liberal Democrats, 1988-94; Deputy Leader, Parliamentary Party, 1988-92; Vice President, ELDR, 1990-92. Created Knight Bachelor, 1985. Recreations: reading; photography; shinty (Vice Chief, Camanachd Association, 1987-90). Address: House of Lords, London, SW1A OPW; T.-0171-219 5353.

Rutherford, Alan Gray, OBE, BSc, PhD, CChem, CEng, FRSC, CEng, FInstE, FRSA. Director, United Distillers and Vintners, UK Operations, since 1988; Hon. Professor, Heriot-Watt University, since 1998; b. 9.10.42, Cramlington; m., Roslyn Anne Moore; 1 s.; 1 d. Educ. Gosforth Grammar School, Newcastle upon Tyne; Sheffield University; Newcastle upon Tyne University. Cookson Group of companies, three years; Scottish & Newcastle Breweries, 14 years, latterly as Group Personnel Director; joined Distillers Company Ltd. as Head of Research and Development, 1984. Executive Member, Scottish Council Development & Industry; Council Member, Scotch Whisky Association, 1990-98; President, Malt Distillers' Association of Scotland, 1991-94; Hon. Col., 4 Para (V); Member, Parachute Regimental Council; President, Ayrshire Branch, Parachute Regimental Association; Co-founder and Chairman, The Airborne Initiative (Scotland) Ltd.; Director, The Medwyn Partnership, since 1997; Director, Chemitech International AB, since 1998; Member, Board of Management, International Centre for Brewing and Distilling. Recreations: TA; hill-walking; rugby football. Address: (b.) United Distillers and Vintners, 33 Ellersly Road, Edinburgh EH12 6JW; T.-0131-337 7373.

Rutherford, Rev. Brian Craig, BSc, BD. Minister, Mastrick Parish, Aberdeen, since 1990; b. 8.6.47, Glasgow; m., Jean Walker; 2 s. Educ. King's Park Secondary School, Glasgow; Glasgow University; Edinburgh University. Assistant Minister, Carrick Knowe Parish, Edinburgh, 1976-77; Minister, Strathbrock Parish, West Lothian, 1977-83; Minister, Greyfriars/St. Ann's Church, Trinidad, 1983-87; General Treasurer, Blantyre Synod, Church of Central Africa Presbyterian, Blantyre, Malawi, 1988-89. Former Member: Edinburgh Corporation, Edinburgh District Council (JP, 1977-80), West Lothian District Council, Aberdeen District Council, 1992-96. Address: (h.) 13 Beechgrove Avenue, Aberdeen AB15 5EZ; T.-01224 638011.

Rutherford, Colin, BA, CA. Chief Executive, RMD Group plc, since 1997; Managing Partner, RMD CAs, since 1986; b. 17.2.59, Edinburgh; m., Karen Elizabeth; 1 s.; 1 d. Educ. Royal High School; Heriot-Watt University. Touche Ross & Co., CAs, Edinburgh and London (Audit and Corporate Finance), 1981-85; Waverley Asset Management, Edinburgh (Unit and Investment Trust), 1985-86; founded Rutherford Manson Dowds (RMD), 1986. Recreations: fishing; shooting; travel; wines; food. Address: (b.) 25 Melville Street, Edinburgh EH3 7PE; T.-0131-225 4727.

Rutherford, William Hay, MA, LLB. Advocate in Aberdeen, since 1949; Consultant, Raeburn Christie & Co. (Partner, 1978-87); Honorary Sheriff, Grampian, Highland and Islands, since 1974; b. 9.11.16, Forres; m., Dr. Jean Aitken Steel Wilson; 1 s.; 2 d. Educ. Forres Academy; Aberdeen University. Law Apprentice, James & George Collie, Advocates, Aberdeen, 1936-39; 51st Highland Division, Royal Signals, 1939-46 (taken prisoner, St. Valery, France, 1940; held prisoner, Stalag VIIIB, Upper Silesia, 1940-45); Legal Assistant, John Angus, Advocate, Aberdeen, 1946-61; Partner, Christie, Buthlay & Rutherford, Advocates, Aberdeen, 1962-78; President, Society of Advocates, Aberdeen, 1985-86; Session Clerk, Kirk of St. Nicholas (City Kirk of Aberdeen), 1954-97; President, Royal Northern Agricultural Society, 1980; Chairman (part-time), Industrial Tribunals (Scotland), 1981-88; holder of British Horse Society 1994 Horse Trials Award for outstanding service to the sport. Recreations: country walking and wildlife study. Address: 38 Gladstone Place, Queen's Cross, Aberdeen AB10 6XA.

Ruthven, Ian Scott, MB, ChB, FRCP, CH, FRCPEdin, FRCPGlas, DObstRCOG. Consultant Paediatrician, Ayrshire and Arran Health Board, since 1969; b. 9.3.37, Glasgow; m., Louisa Mary Jolly; 1 s.; 2 d. Educ. High School of Glasgow; Glasgow University. Junior hospital appointments, various Glasgow hospitals and in New Jersey, USA; Clinical Director, Hospital Paediatric Services in Ayrshire; Chairman, Ayrshire and Arran Division, BMA, 1987-88, currently Ayrshire Representative, Scottish Council, BMA; National Panellist for paediatric appointments in Scotland. Recreations: golf; angling; hill-walking. Address: (h.) Westholme, 10 Victoria Drive, Troon KA10 6EN; T.-01292 313006.

Ryall, Michael Leslie (Mike), BSc, CEng, FIMechE, MInstPet, FRSA. Engineering Consultant (independent and retained by Weir Group), since 1991; Chairman, Scottish Design, since 1994; b. 25.3.31, Carshalton; m., Patricia; 2 s. Educ. George Watson's College; Watford Grammar School; Glasgow University. Research Director, Weir Pumps, 1971-75; Technical Director, Weir Pumps, 1975-91. National runner-up, Prince of Wales Award for Innovation and Production, 1984. Recreations: skiing; windsurfing; hill-walking; music; singing; gardening. Address: 18 Drumbeg Loan, Killearn, Glasgow G63 9LG; T.-01360 550713.

Ryan, Jack, DipComEd. Chief Executive, Crossroads (Scotland), since 1997; b. 9.6.61, Hamilton; m., Janine Barbour; 2 s. Educ. Hamilton Grammar School; Moray House, Edinburgh. Draughtsman, 1978-81; professional musician, 1981-83; Community Musician, Strathclyde Regional Council, 1983-88; Senior Development Officer, Govan Initiative Ltd., 1990-91; Project Manager, CAVOC Motherwell, 1991-92; Director, Govan Community Organisations Council, 1992-96; Lottery Officer, South Lanarkshire Council, 1997. Recreations: musician; computer programming; running/swimming. Address: (b.) 24 George Square, Glasgow; T.-0141-226 3793.

Rycroft, Philip John, MA, DPhil. Assistant Secretary, Scottish Office, Management Group Support Staff Unit, since 1998; b. 22.5.61, Skipton; m., Kate Richards; 2 s. Educ. Leys School, Cambridge; Wadham College, Oxford. Scottish Office Agriculture Department, Research Division, 1989-90; Private Secretary to Scottish Office Agriculture and Fisheries Minister, 1990-91; Principal, Scottish Office Industry Department, European Central Support Unit, 1992-94; Principal, Scottish Office Fisheries Group, Fisheries Policy Branch, 1994; Cabinet of Sir Leon Brittan, European Commission, 1995-97; Head, Agricultural Policy Co-ordination and Rural Development Division and IT Support Division, Agriculture, Environment and Fisheries Department, 1997-98. Recreations: hill-walking; woodwork. Address: (b.) St Andrew's House, Regent Road, Edinburgh EH1 3DG; T.-0131-244 2078.

S

Sadler, Professor Peter John, MA, DPhil, CChem, FRSC. Crum Brown Professor of Chemistry, Edinburgh University, since 1996; UK Representative, EC Technical Committee for COST Chemistry, since 1995; Chairman, EC COST Action on Chemistry of Metals in Medicine, since 1996; Member, Editorial Boards, several international research journals; b. 6.4.46, Norwich; m., Tessa Elizabeth Halstead; 2 s.; 1 d. Educ. City of Norwich School; Magdalen College, Oxford. Medical Research Council Research Fellow, Cambridge University, 1971-72, National Institute for Medical Research, Mill Hill, 1972-73; Lecturer, Reader in Biological Chemistry and Professor of Chemistry, Birkbeck College, London University, 1973-96. Royal Society of Chemistry Award, 1993. Publications: 230 research publications. Recreations: gardening; music; sport. Address: (b.) Department of Chemistry, Edinburgh University, West Mains Road, Edinburgh EH9 3JJ; T.-0131-650 4729.

Salmon, Professor Trevor C., MA (Hons), MLH, PhD, FRSA. Chair of International Relations and Jean Monnet Chair of European Integration, Aberdeen University, since 1996; Professor, College of Europe, since 1995; b. 7.9.48, Cambridge; m., June Veronica Miller; 1 d. Educ. Soham Grammar School; Aberdeen University; St. Andrews University. Lecturer, National Institute for Higher Education, Limerick, 1973-78; Lecturer in International Relations, then Senior Lecturer, St. Andrews University, 1978-90; Jean Monnet Professor of European Integration, St. Andrews University, 1990-95. Elder, Church of Scotland. Publications: Building European Union (Co-author); Understanding the New European Community (Co-author). Address: (b.) Department of Politics and International Relations, Edward Wright Building, Aberdeen University, Aberdeen AB24 3QY; T.-01224 272707.

Salmond, Alexander Elliot Anderson, MA (Hons). Economist; MP (SNP), Banff and Buchan, since 1987; National Convener, Scottish National Party, since 1990; b. 31.12.54, Linlithgow; m., Moira McGlashan. Educ. Linlithgow Academy; St. Andrews University. Vice-President: Federation of Student Nationalists, 1974-77, St. Andrews University SRC, 1977-78; Founder Member, SNP 79 Group, 1979; Assistant Agricultural and Fisheries Economist, DAFS, 1978-80; Economist, Royal Bank of Scotland, 1980-87. Hon. Vice-President, Scottish Centre for Economic and Social Research; former Member, Select Committee on Energy; Parliamentary Spokesman on constitution, fishing. Recreations: golf; reading; football. Address: (b.) 17 Maiden Street, Peterhead, AB42 1EE; T.-01779 470444.

Salmond, Rev. James Sommerville, BA, BD, MTh, ThD. Minister, Holytown Parish Church, since 1979; b. 13.1.51, Broxburn; m., Catherine F. Wildy; 1 s.; 4 d. Educ. West Calder High School; Whitburn Academy; Leeds University; Edinburgh University; Central School of Religion. Serves on the Committees of Scottish Reformation Society, National Church Association, etc. Publications: Evangelicals within the Kirk 1690-1843; Moody Blues; Any Dream Will Do. Recreations: field sports; riding. Address: The Manse, Holytown, Motherwell; T.-Holytown 832622.

Salter, Professor Stephen Hugh, MA (Cantab), FRSE. Personal Chair in Engineering Design, Edinburgh University, since 1986; b. 7.12.38, Johannesburg; m., Professor Margaret Donaldson. Educ. Framlingham College; Sidney Sussex College, Cambridge. Apprentice aircraft fitter and tool-maker; Research Assistant, Department of Psychology, Cambridge University; Research Fellow, then Lecturer, Department of Artificial Intelligence, then Reader in Mechanical Engineering, Edinburgh University. Recreations: photography; inventing and designing instruments and tools. Address: (b.) Department of Mechanical Engineering, Mayfield Road, Edinburgh University, Edinburgh EH9 3JL; T.-0131-650 5703.

Saltoun, Lady (Flora Marjory). Peer of the Realm, since 1979; Chief of the Name of Fraser, since 1979; b. 18.10.30, Edinburgh; 3 d. Educ. St. Mary's School, Wantage. Address: House of Lords, London, SW1A 0PW.

Salvesen, Robin Somervell, DL, FBIM, Chevalier de Dannebrog 1st Class. Director, Christian Salvesen plc; Chairman, Association for the Protection of Rural Scotland; Chairman, Scottish Council, King George's Fund for Sailors; Chairman, Bells Nautical Trust; Chairman, Theodore Salvesen Trust; Trustee, Thistle Trust; Trustee, Noram Trust; b. 4.5.35, Edinburgh; m., Sari; 3 s.; 4 d. Educ. Fettes College; Oxford University. National Service commission, The Royal Scots, Queen's Own Nigeria Regiment; TA, 7/9 Bn., The Royal Scots, 8/9 Bn., The Royal Scots 52 Lowland Volunteers; retired Major; Director, shipping companies, A.F. Henry & Macgregor, Christian Salvesen plc; Lloyds Register of Shipping, 1974-87; Chamber of Shipping, 1974-88; British Shipowners Association, 1969-87; Chairman, Lights Advisory Committee, since 1987; Royal Danish Consul, 1972-87; Elder, Church of Scotland; Chairman, Congregational Board, St Mary's, Haddington. Recreations: archery, shooting. Address: Eaglescairnie House, Haddington, EH41.

Samson, Brian George, DPE, DMS. Director of Sports Development, Scottish Sports Council, since 1994; b. 9.9.47, Cupar; m., Penny; 2 s.; 1 d. Educ. Bell Baxter High School, Cupar; Jordanhill College of Education; Napier University. Principal Teacher of P.E., 1974-84; Development Officer, then Senior Development Officer, Scottish Sports Council, 1984-94. Recreations: rugby; jogging/keep fit; skiing; walking; cycling; music; theatre; ornithology. Address: (b.) South Gyle, Edinburgh EH12 9DQ; T.-0131-317 7200.

Samson, George Carmichael. Director of Administration, Law Society of Scotland, since 1986; b. 17.12.46, Dundee; m., Irene Josephine Ball; 1 d. Sidlaw Industries (Organisation and Methods), 1967-77; Divisional Systems Co-ordinator, Watson & Philip PLC, 1977-86. Law Society of Scotland: Secretary, Practice Management/Client Care Committee, Secretary, Working Party on Electronic Services, Secretary, Services Supra Committee; Member, Scottish Group Committee, Society for Computers and Law; Member, Centre for Law, Computers and Technology Advisory Council, University of Strathclyde Law School. Recreations: guitar; photography; golf; Mah Jong. Address: (b.) 26 Drumsheugh Gardens, Edinburgh EH3 7YR; T.-0131-226 7411.

Sandeman, Robert John, LLB, NP, WS, DL. Solicitor; Deputy Lieutenant, Stirling and Falkirk, since 1986; Member, Southern Area Committee, Highland TA&VRA, since 1978; b. 8.1.29, India; m., Enid; 1 s.; 1 d. Educ. Trinity College, Glenalmond; RMA, Sandhurst; Glasgow University. Infantry Officer, 1948-76; Second-in-Command, 1st Bn., The Royal Scots (The Royal Regiment), 1965-67; staff appointments, 1967-76; retired from Regular Army as Major, 1976; law student, 1976-79; commanded Number One Company, Home Service Force (Black Watch), Territorial Army, 1982-85. Member, Queen's Bodyguard for Scotland (Royal Company of Archers), since 1967; Past Preses, Glasgow, Stirlingshire and Sons of the Rock Society; former Chairman, Stirling Members' Centre, National Trust for Scotland. Recreations: archery; walking; shooting. Address: (h.) Khyber House, Upper Glen Road, Bridge of Allan, FK9 4PX; T.-01786 832180.

Sanderson, Eric Fenton, LLB, CA, FCIBS. Chief Executive, Bank of Scotland Treasury Services PLC, since 1997; Member, Management Board, Bank of Scotland, since 1997; Non-executive Director: Airtours PLC, since 1987, English and Overseas Properties PLC, since 1988, Oriel Leisure Limited, since 1997, Docklands Light Railway Limited, since 1999; b. 14.10.51, Dundee; m., Patricia Ann; 3 d. Educ. Morgan Academy, Dundee; University of Dundee; Harvard Business School. Touche Ross, Edinburgh, 1973-76; British Linen Bank, 1976-97 (Director, 1984-97, Chief Executive, 1989-97). Recreations: tennis player; photography; gardening. Address: (h.) Bowmore, 10 Harelaw Road, Colinton, Edinburgh EH13 0DR; T.-0131-477 0477.

Sanderson, Professor Jeffrey John, BSc, PhD. Professor of Theoretical Plasma Physics, St. Andrews University, since 1985 (Reader in Applied Mathematics, 1975-85); Proctor, since 1997; b. 25.4.37, Birmingham; m., Mirjana Adamovic; 1 s.; 1 d. Educ. George Dixon Grammar School, Birmingham; Birmingham University; Manchester University. Research Associate, Maryland University, 1961-64; Theoretical Physicist, English Electric Co., Whetstone, 1964-66; Lecturer, then Senior Lecturer in Applied Mathematics, St. Andrews University, 1966-75; Visiting Professor, Department of Physics, College of William and Mary, USA, 1976-77. Publications: Plasma Dynamics (Co-author), 1969; Laser Plasma Interactions (Joint Editor), 1979. Recreations: chess; Scottish country dancing; five-a-side football; golf; hill-walking; choral singing. Address: (b.) College Gate, North Street, St. Andrews KY16 9AJ; T.: 01334 472547.

Sanderson, William. Farmer; Director, Royal Highland and Agricultural Society of Scotland; b. 9.3.38, Lanark; m., Netta; 4 d. Educ. Dalkeith High School. Past Chairman, South Midlothian and Lothians and Peeblesshire Young Farmers Clubs; Past Chairman, Dalkeith Agricultural Society; President, Royal Caledonian Curling Club, 1984-85; Past President, Oxenfoord and Edinburgh Curling Clubs; Scottish Curling Champion, 1971 and 1978 (2nd, World Championship, 1971). Recreations: curling; exhibiting livestock. Address: (h.) Blackshiels Farm, Blackshiels, Pathhead, Midlothian; T.-01875 833288.

Sanderson, Very Rev. William Roy, MA, DD. Minister, Church of Scotland; Extra Chaplain to The Queen in Scotland, since 1977 (Chaplain-in-Ordinary, 1965-77); b. 23.9.07, Leith; m., Muriel Easton; 3 s.; 2 d. Educ. Fettes College; Oriel College, Oxford; New College, Edinburgh. Ordained, 1933; Assistant Minister, St. Giles' Cathedral, 1932-34; Minister: St. Andrew's, Lochgelly, 1935-39, The Barony of Glasgow, 1939-63, Stenton with Whittingehame, 1963-73; Moderator, Glasgow Presbytery, 1958 and Haddington and Dunbar Presbytery, 1972-74; Moderator, General Assembly, 1967; Hon. DD (Glasgow), 1959; Chairman, Scottish Religious Advisory Committee, BBC, 1961-71; Member, Central Religious Advisory Committee, BBC and ITA, 1961-71; Governor, Fettes College, 1967-77; Honorary President, Church Service Society; President, New College Union, 1975. Recreations: reading; walking. Address: (h.) 1A York Road, North Berwick, EH39 4LS; T.-01620 892780.

Sanderson of Bowden, Lord (Charles Russell Sanderson), KB. Life Peer; Chairman, Scottish Mortgage and Trust, since 1993; Chairman, Hawick Cashmere Co., since 1990; Deputy Chairman, Clydesdale Bank, since 1996; Director: United Auctions Ltd., Watson and Philip PLC, Morrison Construction PLC; Vice Chairman, Scottish Peers Association, since 1996; Chairman, Scottish Conservative Party, 1990-93; Chairman, Scottish Peers Association, since 1998; b. 30.4.33, Melrose; m., Frances Elizabeth Macaulay; 1 s.; 1 s. deceased; 2 d. Educ. St. Mary's School, Melrose; Glenalmond College; Bradford University; Scottish College of Textiles. Commissioned, Royal Signals; Partner, Charles P. Sanderson, 1958-87; former Director, Johnston of Elgin, Illingworth Morris, Edinburgh Woollen Mills; former Chairman, Shires Investment PLC, Edinburgh Financial Trust, Scottish Pride Holdings; President, Scottish Conservative and Unionist Association, 1977-79; Chairman, National Union of Conservative and Unionist Associations Executive Committee, 1981-86; Minister of State, Scottish Office, 1987-90; Chairman, Eildon Housing Association, 1976-83; Member, Court, Napier University; Chairman, Glenalmond Council, since 1994; Chairman, St Mary's School, Melrose, since 1998; DL. Recreations: golf; amateur dramatics; photography; fishing. Address: (h.) Becketts Field, Bowden, Melrose, Roxburgh, TD6 0ST.

Sandison, Bruce Macgregor. Writer and Journalist; b. 26.9.38, Edinburgh; m., Dorothy Ann Rhodes; 2 s.; 2 d. Educ. Royal High School, Edinburgh. Commissioned into Royal Army Service Corps, 1956-60; sometime poultry farmer and agricultural contractor; full-time writing, since 1981; Angling Correspondent, The Scotsman; Columnist, The Herald; writer on hill-walking and environmental matters; regular contributor to UK game fishing magazines and other journals; Tales of the Loch (series), Radio Scotland and Radio 4. Publications: The Trout Lochs of Scotland; The Sporting Gentleman's Gentleman; Game Fishing in Scotland; The Hillwalker's Guide to Scotland; The Heather Isles; Tales of the Loch; Long Walks with Little People; Trout and Salmon Rivers and Lochs of Scotland. Recreations: hill-walking; game fishing; photography; swimming; music; reading; chess; bridge. Address: Hysbackie, Tongue, by Lairg, IV27 4XJ; T.-01847 55 274.

Sanford, Professor Anthony John, BSc, PhD, FBPsS, CPsychol. Professor of Psychology, Glasgow University, since 1982 (Head, Department of Psychology, 1983-86); b. 5.7.44, Birmingham; m., Linda Mae Moxey; 1 s.; 2 d. Educ. Waverley Grammar School; Leeds University; Cambridge University. MRC Research Scholar, Applied Psychology Unit, Cambridge; Postdoctoral Research Fellow, then Lecturer in Psychology, Dundee University; Senior Lecturer, then Reader in Psychology, Glasgow University. Gifford Lecturer in Natural Theology, Glasgow, 1983. Publications: Understanding Written Language (Co-author); Models, Mind and Man; Cognition and Cognitive Psychology; The Mind of Man; Communicating Quantities (Co-author). Recreations: hill-walking; industrial archaeology; music; cooking. Address: (b.) Department of Psychology, Glasgow University, Glasgow; T.-0141-330 4085.

Sang, Christopher T.M., MB, ChB, FRCSEdin, FRCPEdin. Consultant Cardiothoracic Surgeon, Lothian Health Board, since 1982; b. 14.6.43, Georgetown, Guyana; m., Jean Cowan (divorced); 1 s.; 2 d. Educ. George Watson's College, Edinburgh; Edinburgh University. General surgery training, Edinburgh, and general medicine and cardiology training, Edinburgh and Canada, 1966-73; cardiovascular and thoracic surgery training, Toronto, Edinburgh, London (Guy's) and Baltimore (Johns Hopkins), 1973-82. Address: (h.) 29 Blackford Hill Grove, Edinburgh, EH2 3HA; T.-0131-667 6046.

Sangster, Professor Alan John, BSc (Eng), MSc, PhD, CEng, FIEE. Professor, Electromagnetic Engineering, Heriot Watt University, since 1990; b. 21.11.40, Aberdeen; m., Barbara Macleod Wilkie; 1 s.; 1 d. Educ. Aberdeen Grammar School; Aberdeen University. Research Engineer, Ferranti Ltd., Edinburgh, 1964-69; Plessey Radar Ltd., 1969-72; Lecturer, Heriot Watt University, 1972-79, Senior Lecturer, 1979-86, Reader, 1986-90. Publications: 105 papers. Recreation: golf. Address: (b.) Computing and Electrical Engineering Department, Heriot Watt University, Edinburgh; T.-0131-451 3358.

Sarwar, Mohammed. MP, Glasgow Govan, since 1997; b. 18.8.52; m.; 3 s.; 1 d. Educ. University of Faisalabad. Director, United Wholesalers Ltd., 1983-97; former Glasgow City Councillor. Address: House of Commons, London SW1A 1AA.

Saunders, Professor Alison Marilyn, BA, PhD. Professor of French, Aberdeen University, since 1990; b. 23.12.44, Darlington. Educ. Wimbledon High School GPDST; Durham University. Lectrice, the Sorbonne, 1968-69; Lecturer in French, Aberdeen University, 1970-85; Senior Lecturer in French, 1985-90. Recreations: swimming; gardening; DIY; cooking; antiquarian book-collecting. Address: (h.) 75 Dunbar Street, Old Aberdeen, Aberdeen; T.-01224 494806.

Saunders, Ann Walker, BA, ALA, MIMgt. Director of Community and Leisure, East Renfrewshire Council, since 1995; b. 12.8.52, Glasgow; m., Christopher Saunders; 1 s.; 2 d. Educ. Hutchesons' Grammar School, Glasgow; Strathclyde University, Glasgow. Director of Arts and Libraries, then Director of Leisure Services, Renfrew District Council, 1991-95. Recreations: reading; travelling. Address: (b.) Council Offices, Eastwood Park, Giffnock, G46 6UG; T.-0141-577 3096.

Saunders, Professor David Stanley, BSc, PhD, FIBiol, FRES, FRSE. Professor of Insect Physiology, Edinburgh University, since 1990; b. 12.3.35, Pinner; m., Jean Margaret Comrie Doughty; 3 s. Educ. Pinner County Grammar School; King's College, London; London School of Hygiene and Tropical Medicine. Joined academic staff, Zoology Department, Edinburgh, 1958; Visiting Professor: Stanford University, California, 1971-72, North Carolina University, 1983. Publications: Insect Clocks; Introduction to Biological Rhythms. Recreations: cycling; gardening; photography. Address: (b.) Institute of Cell, Animal and Population Biology, West Mains Road, Edinburgh, EH9 3JT.

Saunders, Professor William Philip, BDS, PhD, FDSRCS(Edin), FDSRCPS(Glas), MRD. Professor in Clinical Dental Practice, Glasgow University, 1993-95, Professor of Endodontology, since 1995; b. 12.10.48, Carlisle; m., Elizabeth; 1 s.; 2 step s.; 1 d.; 1 step d. Educ. Maidstone Grammar School; Royal Dental Hospital of London. Dental Officer, RAF, 1970-75; general dental practice, 1975-81; Lecturer, Department of Conservative Dentistry, Dundee University, 1981-88; Senior Lecturer in Clinical Practice, Glasgow Dental Hospital and School, 1988-93. Postgraduate Dental Hospital Tutor, Glasgow Dental Hospital, 1992-95; Editor, International Endodontic Journal, 1992-98; President, British Endodontic Society, 1997-98. Publications: numerous papers. Recreations: ornithology; natural history; Scottish art; golf; endodontics. Address: (h.) The Old Smiddy, Knapp, Inchture, PH14 9SW; T.-01828 86478.

Savage, Rev. Gordon Matthew Alexander, MA, BD. Minister, Maxwelltown West Church, Dumfries, since 1984; Clerk, Presbytery of Dumfries and Kirkcudbright, since 1987; b. 25.8.51, Old Kilpatrick; m., Mairi Janet MacKenzie; 2 s. Educ. Glasgow Academy; Edinburgh University. Assistant Minister: Dyce Parish Church, 1975-76, Dunblane Cathedral, 1976-77; Minister, Almondbank-Tibbermore with Logiealmond, 1977-84; Junior Clerk, Presbytery of Perth, 1981-84. Recreations: railways; model railways; Clyde steamers; music. Address: Maxwelltown West Manse, 11 Laurieknowe, Dumfries DG2 7AH; T.-01387 252929.

Savidge, Malcolm Kemp, MP, MA (Hons), FRGU. MP (Labour), Aberdeen North, since 1997; b. 9.5.46, Redhill. Educ. Wallington County Grammar School, Surrey; University of Aberdeen; Aberdeen College of Education. Production/ Stock Control and Computer Assistant, Bryans' Electronics Ltd., 1970-71; Mathematics Teacher, Greenwood Dale Secondary School, Nottingham, 1971; Mathematics and Religious and Social Education Teacher, Peterhead Academy, 1972-73; Mathematics Teacher, Kincorth Academy, Aberdeen, 1973-97. Member, Aberdeen City Council, 1980-96: Vice-Chair, Labour Group, 1980-88, Finance Convener, Policy Vice-Convener, Deputy Leader, 1994-96; Governor, Robert Gordon's Institute of Technology, 1980-88; Governor, Aberdeen College of Education, 1980-87; JP, 1984-96; Fellow, Robert Gordon University, 1997. Recreations: exploring life; puzzles; reading; real ale; spectator sport. Address: (b.) House of Commons, London SW1A 0AA; T.-0171-219 3570.

Saville, Alan, BA, FSA, MIFA, FSA Scot. Archaeologist; Senior Curator, National Museums of Scotland, since 1989; b. 31.12.46, London; m., Annette Carruthers. Educ. Colfe's Grammar School, London; Birmingham University. Archaeological Research Assistant, Department of the Environment, London, 1972-74; Archaeologist, Cheltenham Art Gallery and Museum, 1974-76; Field Officer, Western Archaeological Trust, Bristol, 1976-85; Archaeological Consultant, Cheltenham, 1985-89. Treasurer, Society of Antiquaries of Scoland, since 1992; Chairman, The Lithic Studies Society, 1983-90; Conservation Co-ordinator, The Prehistoric Society, 1989-93; Joint Editor, Transactions of the Bristol and Gloucestershire Archaeological Society, 1983-89. Recreations: book collecting; cinema. Address: (b.) Archaeology Department, National Museums of Scotland, Chambers Street, Edinburgh EH1 1JF; T.-0131-247 4054.

Savin, John Andrew, MA, MD (Cantab), FRCP, FRCPEdin, DIH. Consultant Dermatologist, Edinburgh Royal Infirmary, since 1971; Senior Lecturer, Dermatology Department, Edinburgh University, since 1971; b. 10.1.35, London; m., Patricia Margaret Steel; 2 s.; 2 d. Educ. Epsom College; Trinity Hall, Cambridge; St. Thomas's Hospital, London. Royal Naval Medical Service, 1960-64; Registrar to Skin Department, St. George's Hospital, London; Senior Registrar, St. John's Hospital for Diseases of the Skin, and St. Thomas's Hospital, London; Co-Editor, Recent Advances in Dermatology; Associate Editor, British Journal of Dermatology; former Secretary, Scottish Dermatological Society; President, British Association of Dermatologists, 1993-94; President, Section of Dermatology, Royal Society of Medicine, 1987-88. Recreations: golf; literature. Address: (h.) 86 Murrayfield Gardens, Edinburgh; T.-0131-337 7768.

Saxon, Professor David Harold, MA, DPhil, DSc, CPhys, FInstP, FRSE. Kelvin Professor of Physics, Glasgow University, since 1990; Head, Department of Physics and Astronomy, since 1996; b. 27.10.45, Stockport; m., Margaret Flitcroft; 1 s.; 1 d. Educ. Manchester Grammar School; Balliol College, Oxford; Jesus College, Oxford. Research Officer, Nuclear Physics Department, Oxford University, 1969-70; Research Associate, Columbia University, New York, 1970-73; Rutherford Appleton Laboratory, Oxon: Research Associate, 1974-75, Senior Scientific Officer, 1975-76, Principal Scientific Officer, 1976-89; Chairman, PPARC Particle Physics Committee, 1992-95; Member: Scientific Policy Committee, CERN, Geneva, since 1993, Physics Research Committee, DESY, Hamburg, since 1993, Research Assessment Panel (Physics), 1996; PPARC Council Member and Chairman of panel on public understanding of science, since 1997; Chairman, governing committee, Scottish Universities Summer Schools in Physics, since 1997. Address: (b.) Department of Physics and Astronomy, Glasgow University, Glasgow, G12 8QQ; T.-0141-330 4673.

Scaife, Geoffrey Richard. Chief Executive, NHS in Scotland, since 1993; b. 12.1.49, Workington; m. Janet Elizabeth Woodward; 2 s.; 2 d. Educ. Workington Grammar School. Department of Health, London, 1968-71 and 1975-

83; secondment to Prime Minister's Private Office, 1971-74; NHS Manager, Mersey Region, 1983-93 (including 1989-93 as Chief Executive, Mersey Regional Health Authority). Recreations: sport; countryside. Address: (b.) St. Andrew's House, Regent Road, Edinburgh, EH1 3DS; T.-0131-244 2410.

Scanlan, Margaret, LLB. Solicitor, since 1972; b. 10.6.48, Glasgow; m., Michael; 1 s. Educ. Our Lady and St. Francis School; Glasgow University. In private practice except for three years in local government, since 1972. Member, Scottish Legal Aid Board; Member, Sheriff Court Rules Council. Recreation: reading; gardening; golf. Address: (b.) 13 Bath Street, Glasgow G2 1HY; T.-0141-332 4176.

Scanlan, Michael. Solicitor; Vice President, Law Society of Scotland; Senior Partner, Russells Gibson McCaffrey (formerly Russells) Solicitors, Glasgow, since 1982; b. 6.6.46, Glasgow; m., Margaret; 1 s. Educ. St. Aloysius College, Glasgow; Glasgow University. T. F. Russell & Co.: Apprentice, 1965-70, Assistant, 1971-73, Partner, since 1973; Temporary Sheriff, 1986-96; former Member, Glasgow and North Argyll Legal Aid Committee; former Lecturer, Evidence and Procedure, Strathclyde University; former External Examiner, Glasgow University. Recreations: golf; reading. Address: (h.) Willowfield, Kirkintilloch Road, Lenzie; T.-0141-777 7677.

Scanlan, Patrick D., MA. Headteacher, St. Margaret Mary's Secondary School, Glasgow, since 1996; b. 1.3.50, Johnstone; m., Patricia; 2 s. Educ. St. Mirin's Academy, Paisley; Glasgow University; Notre Dame College of Education. Assistant Teacher, St. Cuthbert's High, Johnstone, 1971-73; Principal Teacher of English, then Assistant Head Teacher, St. Brendan's High, Linwood, 1973-90; Depute Head Teacher, St. Mirin's High, Paisley, 1990-96. Recreations: sport; reading; music; travel; theatre and cinema. Address: (b.) 65 Dougrie Road, Glasgow G45 9NJ; T.-0141 634 1169.

Schaw-Miller, Jean-Clare. Deputy Lieutenant, West Lothian, since 1980; Council Member (representing Scotland), Guide Dogs for the Blind Association, since 1992; Executive Committee Member, The Trefoil Holiday Centre for the Disabled, since 1993; Chairman, Association Awards Committee, The Guide Association, since 1998; b. 22.2.37, Gloucestershire; m., Robert Grant Schaw-Miller; 1 s.; 1 d. Educ. Clifton High School for Girls; Edinburgh College of Domestic Science. Scottish Chief Commissioner, Girl Guides Association, 1987-92. Address: (h.) Newgardens House, Dalmeny, South Queensferry, West Lothian, EH30 9TF; T.-0131-331 4612.

Scheunemann, Professor Dietrich F.G., MA, Dr.Phil. Walter H. Bruford Professor of German, University of Edinburgh, since 1990 (Head, Graduate School in Asian and Modern European Languages, since 1995); b. 16.9.39, Schlawe, Germany; m., Sieglinde; 2 s. Educ. Free University of Berlin; Yale University; University of Heidelberg. Taught: University of Heidelberg, Free University of Berlin; Sussex University: Reader in German and Comparative Literature, 1985, Chairman of German, 1987. Publications: Romankrise, 1978; Regelkram und Grenzgänge, 1988; Orality, Literacy and Modern Media, 1996; Text und Ton im Film, 1997; Europäische Kindkunst im Zeitalter des Fernsehens, 1998. Recreations: travel; theatre. Address: (b.) University of Edinburgh, David Hume Tower, George Square, Edinburgh EH8 9JX; T.-0131-650 3639.

Schlesinger, Professor Philip Ronald, BA, PhD, FRSA. Professor of Film and Media Studies, Stirling University, since 1989; b. 31.8.48, Manchester; m., Sharon Joy Rose; 2 d. Educ. North Manchester Grammar School; Queen's College, Oxford; London School of Economics. University of Greenwich: Lecturer, 1974, Senior Lecturer, 1977, Principal Lecturer, 1981; Head, Division of Sociology, 1981-88, Professor of Sociology, 1987-89; Social Science Research Fellow, Nuffield Foundation, 1982-83; Jean Monnet Fellow, European University Institute, Florence, 1985-86; Chair, Research Assessment Panel for Comunication, Cultural and Media Studies, 1995-96; Visiting Professor of Media and Communication, University of Oslo, since 1993; Co-Editor, Media, Culture and Society, since 1982; Media Adviser, Know How Fund, since 1994; Board Member, Scottish Screen, since 1997; Board Member, The Research Centre, Channel 4 Television, Glasgow, since 1998; Member, Film Education Working Group reporting to Department of Culture, Media and Sport, 1998. Publications: Putting "Reality" Together, 1978, 1987; Televising "Terrorism", 1983; Communicating Politics, 1986; Media, Culture and Society, 1986; Los Intelectuales en la Sociedad de la Informacion, 1987; Media, State and Nation, 1991; Women Viewing Violence, 1992; Culture and Power, 1992; Reporting Crime, 1994; European Transformations, 1994; International Media Research, 1997; European Communication Council Report, 1997; Men Viewing Violence, 1998. Recreations: the arts; walking; travel. Address: Department of Film and Media Studies, Stirling University, Stirling FK9 4LA; T.-01786 467520.

Schofield, Rev. Melville Frederick, MA. Chaplain to Western General and Associated Hospitals, Edinburgh, since 1988; b. 3.10.35, Glasgow; m., Christina Skirving Crookston. Educ. Irvine Royal Academy; Dalkeith High School; Edinburgh University and New College. Ordained Assistant, Bathgate High, 1960-61; Minister, Canal Street, Paisley, 1961-67; Minister, Laigh Kirk, Kilmarnock, 1967-88. Former Moderator, Presbytery of Irvine and Kilmarnock; former Moderator, Synod of Ayr; radio and TV broadcaster; Past President, No. 0 Kilmarnock Burns Club. Recreations: international Burns engagements; golf; after-dinner speaking. Address: (h.) 25 Rowantree Grove, Currie, Midlothian, EH14 5AT; T.-0131-449 4745.

Scholes, Thomas Alexander, MSc, IPFA, IRRV, MIMgt. Chief Executive, Renfrewshire Council, since 1995; b. 30.4.49, Glasgow; m., Irene Elizabeth; 2 d. Educ. Hamilton Academy; Central College of Commerce; Strathclyde University. Strathclyde Regional Council: Principal Officer, 1975-80, Assistant Director of Finance, 1981-85, Senior Depute Director of Finance, 1986-95. Recreations: football supporting; watercolour painting; DIY. Address: (H.) 18 Glenfield Crescent, Paisley, PA2; T.-0141-884 5596.

Scobie, Rev. Andrew John, MA, BD. Minister, Cardross Parish Church, since 1965; b. 9.7.35, Windygates; m., Elizabeth Jeannette; 1 s.; 1 d. Educ. Whitehill Senior Secondary School, Glasgow; Glasgow University (Medal in Systematic Theology); Gottingen University; Tubingen University; Marburg University. Assistantship, New Kilpatrick Church, Bearsden; Moderator, Dumbarton Presbytery, 1973-74; Convener, General Assembly's Parish Education Commitee, 1978-80; Convener, General Assembly's Panel on Worship, 1986-90; Member, Joint Liturgical Group, 1987-91; Vice-Convener, General Assembly's Artistic Matters Committee, 1995-98; Chairman or Vice-Chairman, Cardross Community Council, since inception. Publications: Studies in the Historical Jesus (Translator); contributions to New Ways to Worship, 1980, Prayers for Sunday Services, 1980, Three Orders for Holy Communion, 1986, Songs of God's People, 1988; Worshipping Together, 1991; Common Order, 1994. Recreations: golf; photography; wine making; visual arts. Address: The Manse, Cardross, Dumbarton G82 5LB; T.-01389 841289.

Scobie, William Galbraith, MB, ChB, FRCSEdin, FRCSGlas. Consultant Paediatric Surgeon, Lothian Health Board, since 1971; part-time Senior Lecturer, Department of Clinical Surgery, Edinburgh University, 1971-92;

Assistant Director, Edinburgh Postgraduate Board for Medicine, 1986-92; b. 13.10.36, Maybole; m., Elizabeth Caldwell Steel; 1 s.; 1 d. Educ. Carrick Academy, Maybole; Glasgow University. Registrar, General Surgery, Kilmarnock Infirmary; Senior Registrar, Royal Hospital for Sick Children, Glasgow; Senior Registrar, Hospital for Sick Children, London; Senior Paediatric Surgeon, Abu Dhabi, 1980-81. Recreations: fishing; golf; gardening; music. Address: (h.) 133 Caiyside, Fairmilehead, Edinburgh EH10 7HR; T.-0131-445 7404.

Scothorne, Professor Raymond John, BSc, MD, FRSE, FRCSG. Regius Professor of Anatomy, Glasgow University, 1973-90; b. 13.6.20, Nottingham; m., Audrey Gillott; 1 s.; 2 d. Educ. Royal Grammar School, Newcastle-upon-Tyne; Leeds University; Chicago University. Lecturer in Anatomy, Leeds University, 1944-50; Senior Lecturer, Glasgow University, 1950-60; Professor of Anatomy, Newcastle-upon-Tyne University, 1960-73. Anatomical Society of Gt. Britain and Ireland: Honorary Secretary, 1967-71, President, 1971-73; President, British Association of Clinical Anatomists, 1986-89; Hon. Member, American Association of Clinical Anatomists, 1995; Foundation Editor, Clinical Anatomy, since 1988. Recreations: the countryside; labrador dogs. Address: (b.) Southern Knowe, Friars Brae, Linlithgow, West Lothian, EH49 6BQ.

Scothorne, Richard Mark, MA, MPhil. Managing Director, Partners in Economic Development Ltd., since 1992; b. 17.7.53, Glasgow; m., Dr. Sarah Gledhill; 1 s. Educ. Royal Grammar School, Newcastle upon Tyne; St. Catharine's College, Cambridge; Edinburgh University. Various posts in local government, 1977-86; Scottish Director, British Shipbuilders Enterprise Ltd., 1986-87; Economic Development Manager (Depute Director of Planning), Lothian Regional Council, 1987-92; Specialist Adviser to Select Committee on Education and Employment, since 1997. Publication: The Vital Economy: integrating training and enterprise, 1990. Recreations: hill-walking; mountain biking; Scottish art; windsurfing. Address: (h.) 71 Murrayfield Gardens, Edinburgh, EH12 6DL; T.-0131-337 5476.

Scott, Alastair, BA. Travel writer, freelance photographer, and broadcaster; b. 19.3.54, Edinburgh; m., Sheena. Educ. Blairmore; Sedbergh; Stirling University. Travelled around the world, 1978-83; wrote three travel books, 1984-87 – Scot Free, A Scot Goes South, A Scot Returns; cycled 5,000 miles in E. Europe, 1987-88; wrote Tracks Across Alaska (800-mile sled dog journey), 1988-90; travelled Scotland, 1993-94, wrote Native Stranger; presented BBC film version of Native Stranger, 1995. Recreations: reading; running; camping; carpentry; playing concertina. Address: Arroch, Kylerhea, Isle of Skye, IV40 8NH; T.-01599 522329.

Scott, Professor Alexander, MA, MSc, PhD. Professorial Fellow, Heriot-Watt University, since 1989; b. 7.3.45, Lerwick; m., Anne Elliot; 3 d. Educ. Anderson Educational Institute; Boroughmuir Secondary; Edinburgh University. Research Assistant, Edinburgh University, 1967-70; Research Fellow, Heriot-Watt University, 1970-89; Director, The Polecon Co., 1972-89; External Examiner, CNAA, 1981-85; Member, Joint Working Party on Economics, Scottish Examination Board, 1989-90; Chairman, Southfield Housing Society, 1977-80; Executive Director, Edinburgh Business School, since 1997. Publications: four books and numerous papers. Recreations: hill-walking; swimming; music; woodworking. Address: (b.) Edinburgh Business School, Heriot-Watt University, Edinburgh; T.-0131-451 3090.

Scott, Alexander Kemp, MA, LLB. Part Time Chairman, Industrial Tribunals, since 1972; Honorary Sheriff, Dumfries and Galloway, since 1980; Non Executive Director, Dumfries and Galloway Community Health Trust, since 1995; b. 22.9.30, Edinburgh; m., Margo; 1 s.; 1 d. Educ. George Watson's College, Edinburgh; Edinburgh University. Austins Solicitors, Dalbeattie, Castle Douglas and Dumfries, 1957-95 (Senior Partner, 1990-95); Consultant, since 1995. Recreations; family history; bowls; golf. Address: (h.) Rosebank, 312 High Street, Dalbeattie DG5 4DS; T.-01556 610489.

Scott, Professor Bill, RSA. Sculptor; Professor of Sculpture, Edinburgh College of Art (Lecturer, since 1962); b. 16.8.35, Moniaive; m., Phyllis Owen Scott; 1 s.; 2 d. Educ. Dumfries Academy; Edinburgh College of Art; Ecole des Beaux Arts, Paris. One-man exhibitions: Compass Gallery, 1972, Stirling Gallery, 1974, New 57 Gallery, 1979, Lamp of Lothian, 1980, Artspace Gallery, 1980, Kirkcaldy Museum and Gallery, 1985, Talbot Rice Gallery, Edinburgh, 1995; numerous group exhibitions; latest commission: memorial to Sir Alec Douglas-Home at the Hirsel. Address: (h.) 45 St. Clair Crescent, Roslin, Midlothian, EH25 9NG.

Scott, Esme (Lady Scott), CBE, WS, MA, LLB, NP. Chair, The Volunteer Centre UK, 1993-95; b. 7.1.32, Edinburgh; m., 1, Ian Macfarlane Walker (deceased); 1 s.; 2, Kenneth Bertram Adam Scott, KCVO, CMG; 1 step-s.; 1 step-d. Educ. St. George's School for Girls, Edinburgh; Edinburgh University. Lawyer; Vice Chairman, National Consumer Council, 1984-87; Chairman, Scottish Consumer Council, 1980-85; Member, Equal Opportunities Commission, 1985-90; Past Chair, Scottish Association of Citizens Advice Bureaux; Chair, Volunteer Development Scotland, 1989-92; Member, Securities and Investments Board, 1991-93; Member, Court, Edinburgh University, 1989-92; Member, Scottish Committee, Council on Tribunals, 1986-92; Member, Social Security Advisory Committee, 1990-96; Member, National Council for Voluntary Organisations Board, 1993-95. Address: (h.) 13 Clinton Road, Edinburgh.

Scott, Gavin William Thomson, BCom, CA. Secretary and Director of Finance, Scottish Agricultural College, since 1991; b. 19.7.55, Edinburgh; m., Elizabeth Moira Davidson; 2 s. Educ. George Watson's College; Edinburgh University. Deloitte Haskins & Sells, CAs, 1979-82; Keir International Ltd., 1982-87; United Nations Adviser, West Africa, 1987-91. Captain, Gambian Rugby Team, 1987; Scottish International Swimming and Water Polo, 1970s. Recreation: almost any sport. Address: (b.) S.A.C., West Mains Road, Edinburgh, EH9 3JG; T.-0131-535 4000.

Scott, Hugh Johnstone, DA, CertEd. Writer; b. Paisley; m., Mary (Margo) Smith Craig Hamilton; 1 s.; 1 d. Educ. Paisley Grammar School; Glasgow School of Art. Various jobs, then art school; art teacher, until 1984; full-time writing since 1984, including Writing Fellow, City of Aberdeen, 1991; Lecturer in Creative Writing, Glasgow University Adult and Continuing Education Department, since 1988; Tutor in Creative Writing; winner, Woman's Realm children's short story competition, 1982; winner, children's category, Whitbread Book of the Year, 1989, for Why Weeps the Brogan?; short-listed, Mcvitie's Prize, 1990; Tutor, Arvon Foundation Ltd., 1994. Recreations: weight training; exploring England; day-dreaming; reading, of course; painting and exhibiting landscapes.

Scott, Iain William St. Clair, CA, FCIBS. General Manager, Group Office, Bank of Scotland, since 1997; Chairman, Stevenson College, Edinburgh, since 1991; b. 14.5.46, Edinburgh; m., Noelle Margaret Gilmour; 1 s.; 1 d. Educ. George Watson's College. J.W. & R.N. Oswalds, CAs, 1963-70; joined Bank of Scotland, 1970. Recreation: golf. Address: (b.) The Mound, Edinburgh EH1 1YZ; T.-0131-243 5541.

Scott, Ian Edward. Deputy Chief Executive, Scottish Court Service. and Area Director West, for the Sheriffdoms of Glasgow and Strathkelvin, North Strathclyde and South Strathclyde Dumfries and Galloway; m., Maureen Ferrie; 1 s.; 1 d. Educ. Bellahouston Academy. Regional Sheriff Clerk, Lothian and Borders, 1992-95; Sheriff Clerk, Edinburgh, 1992-95; Sheriff Clerk of Chancery, 1992-95; Regional Sheriff Clerk, Glasgow and Strathkelvin, 1996-98; Regional Sheriff Clerk, North Strathclyde, 1997-98. Hon. Member, Royal Faculty of Procurators, Glasgow. Recreations: amateur astronomy; rugby; making changes. Address: (h.) Meadowbank, Annandale Avenue, Lockerbie; T.-01576 203132.

Scott, Rev. Ian Gray, BSc, BD, STM. Minister, Greenbank Parish Church, Edinburgh, since 1983; b. 31.5.41, Kirkcaldy; m., Alexandrina Angus; 1 d. Educ. Kirkcaldy High School; St. Andrews University; Union Theological Seminary, New York. Assistant Minister, St. Mungo's, Alloa, 1965-66; Minister: Holy Trinity Church, Bridge of Allan, 1966-76, Holburn Central, Aberdeen, 1976-83; Convener, Panel on Doctrine, General Assembly, 1978-82; part-time Lecturer, Faculty of Divinity, Aberdeen University, 1977-79; founder Member, Ministry and Psychotherapy Group; Convener, Board of Parish Education, Church of Scotland, 1993-97; Member, Joint Commission on Doctrine, Church of Scotland/Roman Catholic Church. Recreations: reading; photography; caravanning; golf (so called). Address: 112 Greenbank Crescent, Edinburgh, EH10 5SZ; T.-0131-447 4032.

Scott, Irene Mary, DA, BA (Hons), MA, RSW. Painter and Printmaker; b. 31.12.42, Penicuik; m., Brian Snowden Duffield; 4 s.; 1 d. Educ. Lasswade Senior Secondary School; Edinburgh College of Art; Moray House College of Education; Open University; Leeds Metropolitan University. Travelling scholarship to Holland, 1965; Art Teacher, Lothian Region, 1969-74; graphics/cartography, Tourism and Recreation Unit, University of Edinburgh, 1974-76; Assistant Principal Art Teacher, Lothian Region, 1976-89; elected Professional Member: Scottish Society of Artists, 1987, Royal Scottish Society of Painters in Watercolours, 1989; solo exhibitions, Scotland; group exhibitions, Britain and abroad; work in public and private collections, Britain and abroad; commission, Iona Abbey Inc., 1997. Member, Council: SSA, 1986-87, RSW, 1990-93; Member, Board of Directors, AXIS, 1997; Member, Visual Arts Panel, Scottish Arts Council, 1998. Betty Davies Campus Award, RSW, 1990; Whyte and Mackay Purchase Prize, SSA, 1992; Art Media Prize, Highland Open, 1998. Recreations: reading; walking; gardening. Address: 55 Fairfield Road, Inverness IV3 5QP; T.-01463 236 488.

Scott, James Archibald, CB, LVO, FRSE, FScotVec, MA. Director, Dumyat Investment Trust PLC, since 1995; Member of Court, Heriot-Watt University, since 1995; b. 5.3.32, Palestine; m., Dr. Elizabeth Agnes Joyce Scott; 3 s.; 1 d. Educ. Dollar Academy; St. Andrews University; Queen's University of Ontario. RAF Pilot, 1954-56; Commonwealth Relations Office, 1956-65, serving in New Delhi and New York; Scottish Office, 1965; Private Secretary to Secretary of State for Scotland, 1969-71; Secretary, Scottish Education Department, 1984-88; Secretary, Industry Department for Scotland, 1988-91; Chief Executive, Scottish Development Agency, 1991-92; Executive Director, Scottish Financial Enterprise, 1992-95; Director, Scottish Power plc, 1993-96. Recreations: flying; golf. Address: (h.) 38 Queen's Crescent, Edinburgh EH9 2BA; T.-0131-667 8417.

Scott, James Niall, LLB. Partner, McGrigor Donald, since 1979; b. 5.4.52, Glasgow; m., Judith; 2 s.; 2 d. Educ. Jordanhill College School; Aberdeen University. External Examiner, Glasgow University Law School, 1990-92; Managing Partner, McGrigor Donald, 1994-97; currently heads McGrigor Donald's Media Law Group and Scottish Parliament Group. Governor, Glasgow School of Art; Chairman, Mark Scott Foundation; Trustee, Real Young Scots Trust; Member, various working parties, Law Society of Scotland. Recreations: swimming; golf; hill-walking. Address: (b.) Pacific House, 70 Wellington Street, Glasgow G2 2SB; T.-0141-248 6677.

Scott, James Orrock, FCCA. Senior Partner, Henderson Loggie, Chartered Accountants, since 1967; Board Member, Angus, East of Scotland Housing Association, since 1988; Treasurer, SHARP (Scottish Heart and Arterial Disease Risk Prevention), since 1992; b. 13.12.40, Dundee; m., Alva; 1 s. Educ. Grove Academy. President, Scottish Branch Executive, Society of Certified Accountants; first President, Scottish Athletics Federation; Council Member, British Athletic Federation. Recreations: athletics; bowling. Address: (h.) 3 Menzieshill Road, Dundee, DD2 1PS; T.-01382 665813.

Scott, Jayne Patricia, BA, CA. Director of Finance, Fife Health Board, since 1994; b. 25.9.63, Edinburgh. Educ. Glenwood High School, Glenrothes; Napier College. Audit Manager, Coopers and Lybrand, 1988; Contracts and Finance Manager, Lothian Health Board, 1992; Assistant Director of Finance, Fife Health Board, 1993. Address: (b.) Springfield House, Cupar, Fife, KY15 5UP; T.-01334 656200.

Scott, John. Editor, Evening Times, since 1994. Address: (b.) 195 Albion Street, Glasgow G1 1QP.

Scott, John Andrew Ross, JP. Member, Scottish Borders Council, since 1995 (Chairman, Technical Services Committee); Chief Reporter, Southern Reporter, since 1986; b. 6.5.51, Hawick; 2 s. Educ. Hawick High School. Worked on father's farm, 1966-74; Journalist, Hawick News, 1977-78, Tweeddale Press Group, since 1978; first SDP Member, Roxburgh District Council (1980-85) and Borders Regional Council; Chairman, Roxburgh District Licensing Board, 1984-85; first Chairman, Borders Area Party, SDP, 1981-84; Secretary, Roxburgh and Berwickshire Liberal Democrats, 1988-89, Vice Chairman, 1993-94; Chairman, Scottish Association of Direct Labour Organisations Highways Division, 1994-96; Vice-Chairman, South East Scotland Transport Partnership, since 1998; Chairman, COSLA Road Safety Action Group, since 1998. Recreations: writing; music; travel; tennis. Address: (h.) 8 Union Street, Hawick, Roxburghshire; T.-01450 76324.

Scott, John Dominic, LLB, DipLP. Partner, Gilfedder and McInnes, since 1991; Chair, Scottish Human Rights Centre, since 1997; Member, Council, Edinburgh Bar Association; b. 20.7.64, Glasgow. Educ. Holyrood Secondary School, Glasgow; Glasgow University. Trainee and Assistant, Hughes, Dowdall & Company, Glasgow, 1985-88 (qualified Solicitor, since 1987); joined Gilfedder & McInnes, Edinburgh, 1988; Member, Executive Committee, Glasgow Bar Association, since 1997. Recreations: football; tennis. Address: (b.) 34 Leith Walk, Edinburgh EH6 5AA; T.-0131-553 4333.

Scott, John Hamilton. Farmer; Lord-Lieutenant, Shetland; Chairman: Woolgrowers of Shetland Ltd., Sail Shetland Ltd., Shetland Trust, Belmont Trust; b. 30.11.36; m., Wendy Ronald; 1 s.; 1 d. Nature Conservancy Council Committee for Scotland, 1984-91; N.E. Scotland Board, Scottish Natural Heritage, 1992-97; Chairman, Shetland Crofting, Farming and Wildlife Advisory Group, 1984-94; Chairman, Shetland Arts Trust, 1994-98. Recreations: hills; music; pruning. Address: (h.) Gardie House, Bressay, Shetland, ZE2 9EL; T.-01595 820281.

Scott, Rev. John Miller, MA, BD, DD, FSA (Scot). Minister, St. Andrew's Scots Memorial Church, Jerusalem, 1985-88; b. 14.8.22, Glasgow; m., Dorothy Helen Loraine Bushnell; 2 s.; 1 d. Educ. Hillhead High School; Glasgow

University and Trinity College. War Service, Egypt, Italy, India, 1942-46; Assistant Minister, Barony of Glasgow, 1948-49; Minister: Baxter Park Parish, Dundee, 1949-54; High Kirk of Stevenston, 1954-63; Kirk of the Crown of Scotland (Crown Court Church, Westminster), 1963-85; Moderator, Presbytery of England, 1971, 1979; Moderator, Presbytery of Jerusalem, 1986-88; Chairman, Israel Council, 1986-88; various periods of service on General Assembly Committees; Representative, World Alliance of Reformed Churches, Ecumenical Patriarchate, Istanbul, 1988. President, Caledonian Society of London, 1983-84; instituted Kirking Service for Scottish MPs and peers, 1966; Member, UNA Religious Advisory Committee, 1983-85; Convener, St Andrews Council of Churches, 1997. Recreations: travel; historical research; reading; gardening. Address: (h.) St. Martins, 6 Trinity Place, St. Andrews KY16 8SG; T.-01334 479518.

Scott, Sir Kenneth Bertram Adam, KCVO, CMG. Extra Equerry to The Queen, since 1996; b. 23.1.31, Belfast; m., Esme Scott (qv); 1 s.; 1 d.; 1 step. s. Educ. George Watson's College; Edinburgh University. HM Diplomatic Service, 1954-85; HM Ambassador to Yugoslavia, 1982-85; Assistant Private Secretary/Deputy Private Secretary to The Queen, 1985-96; Acting Chairman, Provisional Election Commission for Bosnia, 1996. Deputy Chairman, Hopetoun House Preservation Trust; Governor, George Watson's College; Member, Central Council, Royal Overseas League. Recreations: travel; music; golf; gardening. Address: (h.) 13 Clinton Road, Edinburgh EH9 2AW; T.-0131-447 5191.

Scott, Malcolm Charles Norman, QC, BA, LLB; b. 8.9.51. Advocate, 1978. Address: (b.) Advocates' Library, Parliament House, Edinburgh, EH1 1RF.

Scott, Paul Henderson, CMG, MA, MLitt. Vice-President, Scottish National Party, 1991-97; President, Scottish Centre, International PEN, 1992-97; President, Saltire Society, since 1996; Convener, Advisory Council for the Arts in Scotland, 1981-97; Honorary Fellow, Glasgow University, since 1996; b. 7.11.20, Edinburgh; m., B.C. Sharpe; 1 s.; 1 d. Educ. Royal High School, Edinburgh; Edinburgh University. HM Forces, 1941-47 (Major, RA); HM Diplomatic Service in Foreign Office, Warsaw, La Paz, Havana, Montreal, Vienna, Milan, 1947-80. Rector, Dundee University, 1989-92; Convener, Scottish Centre for Economic and Social Research, 1990-95; President, Edinburgh Sir Walter Scott Club, 1996. Publications: 1707, The Union of Scotland and England, 1979; Walter Scott and Scotland, 1981; John Galt, 1985; The Age of MacDiarmid (Co-Editor), 1980; In Bed with an Elephant: The Scottish Experience, 1985; A Scottish Postbag (Co-Editor), 1986; The Thinking Nation, 1989; Towards Independence — essays on Scotland, 1991; Andrew Fletcher and the Treaty of Union, 1992; Scotland in Europe: a dialogue with a sceptical friend, 1992; Scotland: a Concise Cultural History (Editor), 1993; Defoe in Edinburgh and Other Papers, 1995; Scotland's Ruine (Co-Editor), 1995; Scotland: An Unwon Cause, 1997; Still in Bed with an Elephant, 1998. Recreation: skiing. Address: (h.) 33 Drumsheugh Gardens, Edinburgh, EH3 7RN; T.-0131-225 1038.

Scott, Sheriff Richard John Dinwoodie, MA, LLB. Sheriff of Lothian and Borders at Edinburgh, since 1986 (of Grampian, Highland and Islands, at Aberdeen and Stonehaven, 1977-86); Chairman, Scottish Association for the Study of Delinquency, since 1997; b. 28.5.39, Manchester; m., Josephine Moretta Blake; 2 d. Educ. Edinburgh Academy; Edinburgh University. Lektor, Folkuniversitet of Sweden, 1960-61; admitted to Faculty of Advocates, 1965; Standing Junior Counsel, Ministry of Defence (Air), 1969; Parliamentary candidate, 1974; Honorary Reader, Aberdeen University, 1980-86. Address: (b.) Sheriffs' Chambers, Sheriff Court House, Edinburgh, EH1 1LB; T.-031-226 7181.

Scott, Professor Roger Davidson, BSc, PhD, CPhys, FInstP, FRSE. Personal Professorship, University of Glasgow, 1994; b. 17.12.41, Lerwick; m., Marion McCluckie; 2 s.; 1 d. Educ. Anderson Institute, Lerwick; Edinburgh University. Demonstrator, Edinburgh University, 1965-68; Lecturer, then Depute Director, then Director, SURRC, 1968-98; Recreations: watching football; walking dogs; home maintenance. Address: (h.) 4 Inch Keith, East Kilbride, Glasgow G74 2JZ; T.-01355 229536.

Scott, Sheriff Thomas. Sheriff of North Strathclyde. Address: (b.) Dumbarton Sheriff Court, Sheriff Court House, Church Street, Dumbarton, G82 1QR.

Scott, William, BSc, MSc, MRPharmS. Chief Pharmaceutical Officer, Scottish Office, since 1992; b. 26.10.49, Bellshill; m., Catherine Muir Gilmour; 1 s.; 1 d. Educ. Wishaw High School; Heriot Watt University; Strathclyde University. Resident Pharmacist, Nottingham City Hospital, 1975-76; Staff Pharmacist, Eastern General Hospital, Edinburgh, 1976-79; Principal Pharmacist, Western General Hospital, Edinburgh, 1979-86; Chief Administrative Pharmaceutical Officer, Tayside Health Board, 1986-90; Deputy Chief Pharmacist, Scottish Office, 1990-92. Recreations: walking; reading; golf. Address: (b.) St. Andrews House, Edinburgh; T.-0131-244 2518.

Scott, Professor William Talbot, MA, PhD, DipEd, CertEd. Professor and Head, Department of Language and Media, Glasgow Caledonian University, since 1984; b. 28.2.42, Glasgow; m., Wendy Elizabeth Murray; 1 s.; 1 d. Educ. Woodside Secondary, Glasgow; Glasgow University; Sheffield University. Features Writer, D.C. Thomson & Co.; Lecturer/Senior Lecturer/Principal Lecturer in Communication Studies, Sheffield City Polytechnic. Publication: The Possibility of Communication, 1990. Recreations: running; gardening. Address: (b.) Department of Language and Media, Glasgow Caledonian University, Cowcaddens Road, Glasgow, G4 0BA; T.-0141-331 3260.

Scott Brown, Ronald, MA, LLB, LLD. Director, Aberdeen Asset Management PLC, since 1983, Chairman, 1989-91; b. 14.2.37, Madras; m., Jean Leslie Booth; 3 s. Educ. Aberdeen Grammar School; Aberdeen University. Qualified Solicitor, 1961; Assistant, then Partner, Brander & Cruickshank, Advocates, 1961-83. Member, Board of Governors, Northern College of Education, 1983-95; Member, Court, Aberdeen University, since 1990. Address: (b.) 10 Queen's Terrace, Aberdeen, AB10 1QJ; T.-01224 631999.

Scott Moncrieff, John Kenneth, LLB, WS. Partner, Murray Beith Murray, WS, since 1978; b. 9.2.51, Edinburgh; m., Pilla; 1 s.; 2 d. Educ. Marlborough College; Edinburgh University. Honorary Consul to Monaco; Lecturer and Tutor, Edinburgh University; Chairman, Traverse Theatre, Edinburgh; Board Member, Cheek by Jowl Theatre Co.; Board Member, Scottish Actors Studio; Clerk to the Abbey Court, Holyrood; Trustee, various charitable trusts and companies. Recreations: football; theatre; hillwalking. Address: (b.) 39 Castle Street, Edinburgh EH2 3BH; T.-0131-225 1200.

Scouller, Glen, DA, RGI, RSW. Artist; b. 24.4.50, Glasgow; m., Carol Alison Marsh; 2 d. Educ. Eastbank Academy; Garthamlock Secondary; Glasgow School of Art; Hospitalfield College of Art, Arbroath. RSA Painting Award, 1972; W. O. Hutcheson Prize for Drawing, 1973; travelling scholarship, Greece, 1973; started teaching, Glasgow schools, 1974; started part-time tutoring, Glasgow School of Art, 1986; Lauder Award, Glasgow Art Club, 1987; Scottish Amicable Award, 1987; Royal Glasgow Institute of Fine Arts Award, 1987; elected, RGI, 1989; painting full-time since 1989; elected, Royal Scottish Society of Painters in Watercolours, 1997; solo exhibitions: John D. Kelly Gallery, Glasgow, 1977, The Scottish

Gallery, Edinburgh, 1980, Fine Art Society, Glasgow, 1985, 1988, Harbour Arts Centre, Irvine, 1986, Fine Art Society, Edinburgh, 1989, Portland Gallery, London, 1989, 1992, 1994, 1998, Macauley Gallery, Stenton, 1990, 1993, 1996, French Institute, Edinburgh, 1990, Open Eye Gallery, Edinburgh, 1992, 1994, 1997, Roger Billcliffe Fine Art, Glasgow, 1992, 1995, Everard Read Gallery, Johannesburg, 1997; work in public, corporate and private collections, UK and abroad. Recreations: travel; music. Address: East Loudounhill Farm, Darvel KA17 0LU.

Scrimgeour, John Beocher, MB, ChB, DObst, RCOG, FRCOG, FRCS(Edin), FRCP (Edin). Consultant Obstetrician and Gynaecologist, 1972-97; Honorary Senior Lecturer in Obstetrics and Gynaecology, Edinburgh University, 1972-97; Medical Director, Western General Hospitals Unit, Edinburgh, 1993-97; President, Edinburgh Obstetrical Society, 1996-97; Vice Chairman, Scottish Association of Trust Medical Directors, 1996-97; b. 22.1.39, Elgin; m., Joyce Morrin; 1 s.; 1 d. Educ. Hawick High School; Edinburgh University. General Practitioner, Edinburgh, 1963-65; Senior House Officer: Stirling Royal Infirmary, 1965, and Registrar, Eastern General Hospital, Edinburgh, 1966-69; Senior Registrar, Edinburgh Royal Infirmary, 1970-72; Senior Secretary, Edinburgh Obstetrical Society, 1980-85; Chairman, Area Division of Obstetrics and Gynaecology, 1984-88; Member, Council, Royal College of Obstetricians and Gynaecologists, 1976-81. Publication: Towards the Prevention of Fetal Malformation, 1978. Recreations: gardening; golf. Address: (h.) 16 Belgrave Crescent, Edinburgh EH4 3AJ; T.-0131-332 6480.

Seafield, 13th Earl of (Ian Derek Francis Ogilvie-Grant), b. 20.3.39; m., 1, Mary Dawn Mackenzie Illingworth (m. diss.); 2 s.; 2, Leila Refaat. Succeeded to title, 1969. Educ. Eton. Address: (h.) Old Cullen, Cullen, Banffshire.

Seagrave, David Robert, LLB (Hons), SSC, NP. Solicitor and Notary Public; Council Member, Law Society of Scotland, 1981-87; Partner, Seagrave & Co., Solicitors, Dumfries; b. 29.4.43, Berwick-on-Tweed; m., Fiona Lesley Thomson; 1 s.; 1 d. Educ. Newcastle-upon-Tyne; Glasgow University. Banking, insurance, police; Secretary, Enterprise Trust for Nithsdale, Annandale/Eskdale and the Stewartry, 1984-92. Recreations: choral singing; shooting; fishing; golf. Address: (h.) Amulree, Islesteps, Dumfries; T.-Dumfries 264523.

Sealey, Barry Edward, CBE, BA (Hons) (Cantab), CBIM. Director: Wilson Byard PLC (Chairman), Stagecoach Holdings PLC, The Caledonian Brewing Company Ltd., Scottish Equitable plc, Scottish American Investment Trust plc, Morago Ltd., and other companies; Chairman, Edinburgh Healthcare NHS Trust; b. 3.2.36, Bristol; m., Helen Martyn; 1 s.; 1 d. Educ. Dursley Grammar School; St. John's College, Cambridge. RAF, 1953-55. Joined Christian Salvesen as trainee, 1958; joined Board, Christian Salvesen PLC (responsible for Food Services Division), 1969; appointed Managing Director, 1981, Deputy Chairman and Managing Director, 1987; retired from Christian Salvesen, 1990. Council Member, The Industrial Society. Address: (h.) 4 Castlelaw Road, Edinburgh, EH13 0DN.

Searle, Rev. David Charles, MA, DipTh. Minister of the Church of Scotland, since 1965; Warden, Rutherford House, Edinburgh, since 1993; b. 14.11.37, Swansea; m., Lorna Christine Wilson; 2 s.; 1 d. Educ. Arbroath High School; St. Andrews University; London University; Aberdeen University. Teacher, 1961-64; Assistant Minister, St. Nicholas Church, Aberdeen, 1964-65; Minister: Newhills Parish Church, 1965-75, Larbert Old, 1975-85, Hamilton Road Presbyterian Church, Bangor, Co. Down, 1985-93; Contributor, Presbyterian Herald; Editor, Rutherford Journal of Church and Ministry. Publications: Be Strong in the Lord; Truth and Love in a Sexually Disordered World. Recreations: sail-boarding; gardening; hill-walking. Address: (b.) Rutherford House, 17 Claremont Park, Edinburgh, EH6 7PJ; T.-0131-554 1206.

Seaton, Professor Anthony, CBE, BA, MD (Cantab), FRCPLond, FRCPEdin, FFOM. Professor of Environmental and Occupational Medicine, Aberdeen University, since 1988; b. 20.8.38, London; m., Jillian Margaret Duke; 2 s. Educ. Rossall School, Fleetwood; King's College, Cambridge; Liverpool University. Assistant Professor of Medicine, West Virginia University, 1969-71; Consultant Chest Physician, Cardiff, 1971-77; Director, Institute of Occupational Medicine, Edinburgh, 1978-90. Editor, Thorax, 1977-82; Chairman, Department of Environment Expert Panel on Air Quality Standards, since 1992; Member, Department of Health Committee on Medical Aspects of Air Pollution, MRC Committee on Toxic Hazards in the Environment. Publications: books and papers on occupational and respiratory medicine. Recreations: keeping fit; opera; painting. Address: (h.) 8 Avon Grove, Cramond, Edinburgh, EH4 6RF; T.-031-336 5113; 71 Urquhart Terrace, Aberdeen AB24 1NJ.

Seaton, Robert, MA, LLB. Secretary of the University, Dundee University, since 1973; b. 2.8.37, Clarkston, Renfrewshire; m., Jennifer Graham Jack; 2 s.; 2 d. Educ. Eastwood Secondary School; Glasgow University; Balliol College, Oxford; Edinburgh University. Administrative Assistant, then Senior Administrative Officer, then Assistant Secretary, Edinburgh University, 1962-73. Director, Dundee University Utility Supply Company Ltd., Dundee University Project Management Ltd. Address: (b.) Dundee University, Dundee DD1 4HN.

Seckl, Professor Jonathan Robert, BSc, MB, BS, MRCP(UK), PhD, FRCPE. Moncrieff-Arnott Professor of Molecular Medicine, Edinburgh University, since 1997; Professor of Endocrinology, since 1996; Chairman, Molecular Medicine Centre, since 1996; b. 15.8.56, London; m., Molly; 1 s.; 1 d. Educ. William Ellis School, London; University College Hospital Medical School, London. Sir Jules Thorn Research Fellow in Neuroendocrinology, Charing Cross and Westminster Medical School, 1984-87; Honorary Clinical Assistant, National Hospital for Nervous Diseases, London, 1984-87; Lecturer in Medicine, Edinburgh University, 1987-89; Wellcome Trust/Royal Society of Edinburgh Senior Clinical Research Fellow, 1989-96. Address: (b.) Molecular Medicine Centre, Edinburgh University, Western General Hospital, Crewe Road, Edinburgh EH4 2XU; T.-0131-651 1035.

Sefton, Rev. Henry Reay, MA, BD, STM, PhD. Co-ordinator in Christian Studies, Aberdeen University, 1995-97; Chaplain, College of St Nicholas, Aberdeen, since 1989; b. 15.1.31, Rosehearty. Educ. Brechin High School; St. Andrews University; Glasgow University; Union Theological Seminary, New York. Assistant Minister, Glasgow Cathedral, 1957-58, St. Margaret's, Knightswood, Glasgow, 1958-61; Acting Chaplain, Hope Waddell Training Institution, Nigeria, 1959; Associate Minister, St. Mark's, Wishaw, 1962; Minister, Newbattle, 1962-66; Assistant Secretary, Church of Scotland Department of Education, 1966-72; Lecturer in Church History, Aberdeen University, 1972-90, Senior Lecturer, 1991-92; Master of Christ's College, Aberdeen, 1982-92; Alexander Robertson Lecturer, Glasgow University, 1995; Moderator, Aberdeen Presbytery, 1982-83, Synod of Grampian, 1991-92; Convener, Church of Scotland Board of Education, 1987-91; Clerk, Aberdeen Presbytery, 1993-95; Chairman, Association of University Teachers (Scotland), 1982-84. Recreations: hill-walking; church architecture; stamp and coin collecting. Address: (h.) 25 Albury Place, Aberdeen, AB11 6TQ; T.-01224 572305.

Selkirk of Douglas, Rt. Hon. Lord (James Alexander Douglas-Hamilton), QC. MP (Conservative), Edinburgh West, 1974-97; b. 31.7.42, Strathaven; m., (Priscilla) Susan (Susie) Buchan; 4 s. Educ. Eton; Balliol College, Oxford; Edinburgh University. Officer, TA 6/7 Bn. Cameronians Scottish Rifles, 1961-66, TAVR, 1971-73, Captain 2 Bn. Lowland Volunteers; Advocate, 1968-74; Scottish Conservative Whip, 1977; a Lord Cmnr., HM Treasury, 1979-81, PPS to Malcolm Rifkind MP, at Foreign Office, later as Secretary of State for Scotland, 1983-87; Parliamentary Under Secretary of State: at the Scottish Office for Home Affairs and Environment, 1987-89; for Home Affairs and Environment, 1989-92 (with additional responsibility for local government finance 1989-90, and with additional responsibility for the arts in Scotland, 1990-92); for Education and Housing, Scottish Office, 1992-95; Minister of State for Home Affairs and Health, Scottish Office, 1995-97. Member, Scottish Select Committee Scottish Affairs 1981-83; Honorary Secretary: Conservative Parliamentary Constitutional Committee, Conservative Parliamentary Aviation Committee, since 1983; Chairman, Scottish Parliamentary All-Party Penal Affairs Committee, 1983; Honorary President, Scottish Amateur Boxing Association, 1975-98; President: Royal Commonwealth Society (Scotland), 1979-87, Scottish National Council of UN Association, 1981-87; Member, Council, National Trust for Scotland, 1977-82; Honorary Air Commodore No. 2 (City of Edinburgh) Maritime Headquarters Unit and President International Rescue Corps, 1995. Oxford Boxing Blue, 1961; President, Oxford Union, 1964. Publications: Motive For A Mission: The Story Behind Hess's Flight to Britain, 1971; The Air Battle for Malta: The Diaries of a Fighter Pilot, 1981; Roof of the World: Man's First Flight over Everest, 1983; The Truth about Rudolf Hess, 1993. Recreations: golf; forestry; debating; history; boxing. Address: House of Lords, London.

Sempill, 21st Baron (James William Stuart Whitemore Sempill); b. 25.2.49; m.; 1 s.; 1 d. Educ. St Clare's Hall, Oxford. Succeeded to title, 1995; Company Director.

Semple, Colin Gordon, MA, MBChB, FRCP (Glas), FRCP(Ed), MD. Consultant Physician, Southern General Hospital, Glasgow, since 1988; Honorary Clinical Senior Lecturer, Glasgow University, since 1988; Honorary Secretary, Royal College of Physicians and Surgeons of Glasgow, since 1998; b. 19.3.53, Glasgow; m., Elaine; 1 s.; 1 d. Educ. Loretto School; Brasenose College, Oxford; Glasgow University. General Physician with interest in diabetes and endocrinology and special interest in postgraduate medical education; Secretary, General Medicine Specialist Advisory Committee; Royal College of Physicians and Surgeons of Glasgow: Member, Council, 1986-90, and since 1995, Deputy Honorary Secretary, 1995-98. Recreations: golf; gardening; walking; curling.

Semple, David, WS, LLB, NP. Chairman, Semple Fraser WS, since 1990; b. 29.12.43, Glasgow; m., Jet; 2 s.; 1 d. Educ. Loretto School; Glasgow University. Partner, Bird Son & Semple, 1968-73; Bird Semple and Crawford Herron, 1973-88; Bird Semple Fyfe Ireland, 1988-90. President, Glasgow Chamber of Commerce, 1996-97; Member, Board, Interactive Media Alliance Scotland; accredited ADR Mediator, Centre for Dispute Resolution, Scotland. Recreations: golf; hill-walking; bagpipes. Address: (b.) 130 St. Vincent Street, Glasgow G2 5HF; T.-0141-221 3771.

Semple, Peter d'Almaine, MD, FRCPGlas, FRCPEdin, FRCPLond. Consultant Physician and Chest Specialist, Inverclyde District, since 1979; b. 30.10.45, Glasgow; m., Judith Mairi Abercromby; 2 d. Educ. Belmont House; Loretto School; Glasgow University. Consultant Physician, Inverclyde Royal Hospital, 1979; former Postgraduate Medical Tutor, Inverclyde District; Honorary Clinical Senior Lecturer, Glasgow University. Past Chairman, Medical Audit Sub-Committee, Scottish Office; Past President, Greenock and District Faculty of Medicine; Past Chairman, West of Scotland Branch, British Deer Society; Director, Medical Audit, Royal College of Physicians and Surgeons of Glasgow. Recreations: field sports; gardening; golf. Address: (h.) High Lunderston, Inverkip, PA16 0DU; T.-01475 522342.

Semple, Walter George, BL, NP, ACI Arb. Solicitor; b. 7.5.42, Glasgow; m., Dr. Lena Ohrstrom; 3 d. Educ. Belmont House, Glasgow; Loretto School; Glasgow University. President, Glasgow Juridical Society, 1968; Tutor and Lecturer (part-time), Glasgow University, 1970-79; Council Member, Law Society of Scotland, 1976-80; Chairman, Scottish Lawyers European Group, 1978-81; Member, Commission Consultative des Barreaux Europeens, 1978-80, 1984-87; President, Association Internationale des Jeunes Avocats, 1983-84; Chairman, Scottish Branch, Institute of Arbitrators, 1989-91; Member, Business Committee, Glasgow University General Council; Board Member, Union Internationale des Avocats, since 1997; Dean, Royal Faculty of Procurators in Glasgow, 1998. Recreations: golf; fishing; skiing; music. Address: (h.) 79 Lancefield Quay, Glasgow G3 8HA.

Serafini-Fracassini, Camillo, BSc (Econ). Consumer Affairs Correspondent, The Scotsman, since 1998; b. 25.5.70, Dundee. Educ. Madras College, St Andrews; London School of Economics. Reporter, South East London and Kentish Mercury; Reporter, Hendon Times Group; Court Reporter, national news agency; Reporter, Edinburgh Evening News; Feature Writer, The Scotsman. Recreations: travel; music; photography. Address: (b.) 20 North Bridge, Edinburgh EH1 1YT; T.-0131-243 3531.

Sewel, Lord (John Buttifant Sewel), CBE. Parliamentary Under-Secretary of State, Scottish Office, with responsibility for Agriculture, Environment and Fisheries, since 1997; House of Lords Spokesman on all Scottish Affairs; created Peer, 1996; b. 1946. Educ. Hanson Boys' Grammar School, Bradford; Durham University; University College Swansea; Aberdeen University. Councillor, Aberdeen City Council, 1974-84 (Leader of the Council, 1977-80); President, COSLA, 1982-84; Member, Accounts Commission for Scotland, 1987-96; Member, Scottish Constitutional Convention, 1994-95; successively Research Fellow, Lecturer, Senior Lecturer, Professor, Aberdeen University, from 1969; Dean, Faculty of Economic and Social Sciences, 1989-94; Vice Principal and Dean, Faculty of Social Sciences and Law, 1995-96. Recreations: hill-walking; skiing; watching cricket. Address: (b.) Scottish Office, St Andrew's House, Regent Road, Edinburgh EH1 3DG.

Sewell, Professor John Isaac, PhD, DSc, CEng, FIEEE. Professor of Electronic Systems, Glasgow University, since 1985 (Dean, Faculty of Engineering, 1990-93); b. 13.5.42, Kirkby Stephen; m., Ruth Alexandra Baxter; 1 d. Educ. Kirkby Stephen Grammar School; Durham University; Newcastle-upon-Tyne University. Lecturer, Senior Lecturer, Reader, Department of Electronic Engineering, Hull University, 1968-85. Publications: 133 papers. Recreations: swimming; climbing. Address: (h.) 16 Paterson Place, Bearsden, Glasgow, G61 4RU; T.-0141-943 0729.

Seymour, Professor Philip Herschel Kean, BA, MEd, PhD. Professor of Cognitive Psychology, Dundee University, since 1988; b. 9.3.38, London; m., Margaret Jean Dyson Morris; 2 s.; 2 d. Educ. Kelly College, Tavistock; Exeter College, Oxford; St. Andrews University. Dundee University: Lecturer, 1966-75, Senior Lecturer, 1975-82, Reader, 1982-88. Chairman, Scottish Dyslexia Association, 1982-85. Publications: Human Visual Cognition, 1979; Cognitive Analysis of Dyslexia, 1986.

Address: (b.) Department of Psychology, Dundee University, Dundee; T.-Dundee 223181.

Shand, Sir Jimmy, MBE. Musician and Scottish Country Dance Band Leader; b. 28.1.08, East Wemyss; m., Anne Anderson; 2 s. Educ. East Wemyss School. Has played the accordion and led Scottish danceband at thousands of concert and theatre performances at home and overseas; numerous recordings; several thousand broadcasts. Recreations: motor bikes; sailing.

Shanks, Duncan Faichney, RSA, RGI, RSW. Artist; b. 30.8.37, Airdrie; m., Una Brown Gordon. Educ. Uddingston Grammar School; Glasgow School of Art. Part-time Lecturer, Glasgow School of Art, until 1979; now full-time painter; one-man shows: Stirling University, Scottish Gallery, Fine Art Society, Talbot Rice Art Gallery, Edinburgh University, Crawford Centre, Maclaurin Art Gallery, Glasgow Art Gallery, Fine Art Society, touring exhibition (Wales); taken part in shows of Scottish painting, London, 1986, Toulouse, Rio de Janeiro, 1985, Wales, 1988; Scottish Arts Council Award; Latimer and MacAulay Prizes, RSA; Torrance Award, Cargill Award, MacFarlane Charitable Trust Award, RGI; May Marshall Brown Award, RSW; The Lord Provost's Prize for painting (GOMA), 1996; tapestry commissioned by Coats Viyella, woven by Edinburgh Tapestry Company, presented to Glasgow Royal Concert Hall, 1991. Recreations: music; gardening.

Shanks, Rev. Norman James, MA, BD. Leader, Iona Community, since 1995; b. 15.7.42, Edinburgh; m., Ruth Osborne Douglas; 2 s.; 1 d. Educ. Stirling High School; St. Andrews University; Edinburgh University. Scottish Office, 1964-79; Chaplain, Edinburgh University, 1985-88; Lecturer in Practical Theology, Glasgow University, 1988-95; Convener, Acts Commission on Justice, Peace, Social and Moral Issues, 1991-95; Chairman, Edinburgh Council of Social Service, 1985-88; Chairman, Secretary of State's Advisory Committee on Travelling People, 1985-88; Convener, Church and Nation Committee, Church of Scotland, 1988-92; Member, Broadcasting Council for Scotland, 1988-93. Recreations: armchair cricket; occasional golf. Address: (h.) 1 Marchmont Terrace, Glasgow, G12 9LT; T.-0141-339 4421.

Shanks, Thomas Henry, MA, LLB. Solicitor and Notary Public, since 1956; Honorary Sheriff, Lanark, since 1982; b. 22.10.30, Lanark; m., Marjorie A. Rendall; 1 s.; 1 d. (by pr. m.); 3 step s.; 1 step d. Educ. Lanark Grammar School; Glasgow University. Intelligence Corps (National Service), 1954-56. Depute Clerk of Peace, County of Lanark, 1961-74; Chairman, Royal Burgh of Lanark Community Council, 1977-80 and 1983-86; Captain, Lanark Golf Club, 1962; Lanark Lord Cornet, 1968. Recreation: golf. Address: (h.) Clydesholm Braes, Lanark.

Shanks, Una Brown, DA, RSW. Artist and Illustrator; b. 9.6.40, Hartwood, Lanarkshire; m., Duncan Shanks. Educ. Wishaw High School; Glasgow School of Art. Art Teacher, Coltness High School; Lecturer in Art, Hamilton College of Education. Recreation: gardening. Address: Davingill House, Crossford, by Carluke; T.-01555 860310.

Sharp, Sir George, Kt (1976), OBE, JP, DL. Chairman, Glenrothes Development Corporation, 1978-86; Member, Economic and Social Committee, EEC, 1982-86; b. 8.4.19; m., Elsie May Rodger; 1 s. Educ. Buckhaven High School. Fife County Council: Member, 1945-75, Chairman, Water and Drainage Committee, 1955-61, Chairman, Finance Committee, 1961-72, Convener, 1972-75; Convener, Fife Regional Council, 1974-78; President: Association of County Councils, 1972-74, COSLA, 1975-78; Chairman: Kirkcaldy District Council, 1958-75, Fife and Kinross Water Board, 1967-75, Forth River Purification Board, 1955-67 and 1975-78, Scottish River Purification Advisory Committee, 1967-75, Scottish Tourist Consultative Council, 1979-82; Member, Tay Road Bridge Committee, 1961-72, Vice-Chairman, 1972-78; Vice-Chairman, Forth Road Bridge Committee, 1972-78; Member, Scottish Water Advisory Committee, 1962-69, Potato Marketing Board, 1965-71, Committee of Enquiry into Salmon and Trout Fishing, 1963, Scottish Valuation Advisory Committee, 1972, Committee of Enquiry into Local Government Finance, 1974-76, Scottish Development Agency, 1975-80, Royal Commission on Legal Services in Scotland, 1978-80; Director, Grampian Television, 1975-89; Member, Scottish Board, National Girobank, 1982-90; Managing Trustee, Municipal Mutual Insurance Ltd., 1979-91. Recreations: golf; reading; gardening; football spectating. Address: (h.) Strathlea, 56 Station Road, Thornton, Fife; T.-Glenrothes 774347.

Sharp, Professor Peter Frederick, BSc, PhD, Phys, FInstP, FIPEM, FRSE. Professor of Medical Physics, University of Aberdeen; b. 13.8.47, Spalding; m., Elisabeth Margaret; 2 s. Educ. Spalding Grammar School; Durham University; Aberdeen University. University of Aberdeen: Lecturer in Medical Physics, 1974-83, Senior Lecturer in Medical Physics, 1983-90. Honorary Sheriff, Stonehaven. Publication: Practical Nuclear Medicine (Editor). Address: (b.) Department of Biomedical Physics and Bioengineering, Foresterhill, Aberdeen AB25 2ZD; T.-01224 840733.

Sharratt, John, DPA, DCA, MITSA. Chief Trading Standards Officer, Scottish Borders Council (formerly Borders Regional Council), since 1988; b. 16.8.47, Manchester; m., Yvonne; 4 s. Educ. Horwich Secondary School; Bell College of Technology. Trainee, Lancashire CC, 1964-69; Senior Trading Standards Officer, Glasgow Corporation/Strathclyde RC, 1969-79; Assistant Divisional Trading Standards Officer, 1979-84, Principal TSO (Research, Development and Training), 1984-88, Strathclyde RC. Education Secretary, Institute of Trading Standards Administration (Scottish Branch), 1985-91, Chairman, 1991-92. Recreations: squash; golf; fishing; watching rugby. Address: (b.) St. Dunstan's, High Street, Melrose, TD6 9RU; T.-0189 682 3922.

Shaw, Rev. Alistair Neil, MA (Hons), BD (Hons). Minister, Laigh Kirk, Kilmarnock, since 1988; b. 6.7.53, Kilbarchan; m., Brenda Bruce; 2 d. Educ. Paisley Grammar School; Glasgow University. Minister, Relief Parish Church, Bourtreehill, Irvine, 1982-88; Moderator, Presbytery of Irvine and Kilmarnock, 1995-96. Recreations: wine-making; visiting archaeological sites; foreign travel; swimming. Address: (h.) 1 Holmes Farm Road, Kilmarnock KA1 1TP; T.-01563 525416.

Shaw, Charles M., BA (Economics), DipMktg, MInstM. Director/General Manager, Invergordon Distillers, since 1994; b. 27.3.51, Greenock; m., Elizabeth Shaw; 2 s. Educ. St. Columba's School; Strathclyde University. Product Manager, Golden Wonder Ltd.; Marketing Manager, Canada Dry Corp; Marketing Manager/Marketing Director/Group Marketing and Corporate Development Director, Whyte and Mackay Group. Committee Member, Scotch Whisky Association. Address: (b.) Invergordon Distillers, Salamander Place, Leith, Edinburgh; T.-0131-554 4404.

Shaw, Rev. Professor Douglas William David, MA, LLB, BD, DD, WS. Professor of Divinity, St. Andrews University, 1979-91 (Dean, Faculty of Divinity, 1983-86, Principal, St. Mary's College, 1986-92; Minister, Church of Scotland, since 1960; b. 25.6.28, Edinburgh; m., Edinburgh Academy; Loretto; Ashbury College, Ottawa; St. John's College, Cambridge; Edinburgh University. Practised law as WS (Partner, Davidson and Syme, WS, Edinburgh), 1952-57; Assistant Minister, St. George's West Church, Edinburgh, 1960-63; Official Observer, Second Vatican Council, Rome, 1962; Lecturer in Divinity, Edinburgh University, 1963-79; Principal, New College, and Dean,

Faculty of Divinity, Edinburgh, 1973-78; Visiting Fellow, Fitzwilliam College, Cambridge, 1978; Visiting Lecturer, Virginia University, 1979. Publications: Who is God?, 1968; The Dissuaders, 1978, In Divers Manners (Editor), 1990; Dimensions, 1992; Theology in Scotland. Recreation: golf. Address: (h.) 4 Alexandra Court, St. Andrews, Fife, KY16 9XH; T.-01334 477254.

Shaw, Rev. Duncan, BD (Hons), MTh. Minister, St. John's, Bathgate, since 1978; b. 10.4.47, Blantyre; m., Margaret S. Moore; 2 s.; 1 d. Educ. St. John's Grammar School, Hamilton; Hamilton Academy; Trinity College, Glasgow University. Assistant Minister, Netherlee Parish Church, Glasgow, 1974-77. Clerk, West Lothian Presbytery, since 1982 (Moderator, 1989-90). Recreations: gardening; travel (in Scotland). Address: St. John's Parish Church Manse, Mid Street, Bathgate, EH48 1QD; T.-Bathgate 653146.

Shaw, Professor Duncan James. Professor in Genetics, University of Aberdeen, since 1994; b. 16.10.54, Guildford. Educ. Royal Grammar School, Guildford; University of Bristol; University of Wales. Research Assistant, University of Wales; research posts at Sheffield University, Pittsburgh University, University of Wales College of Medicine. Publications: over 80 scientific and other publications. Recreations: music; food and drink; reading; travel; maths and computing. Address: Department of Molecular and Cell Biology, University of Aberdeen, Aberdeen AB25 2ZD; T.-01224 273191.

Shaw, Professor Sir John Calman, CBE, KStJ, Dr HC, LLD, BL, FRSE, CA, FCMA. Chairman, Scottish Financial Enterprise; Deputy Governor, Bank of Scotland, since 1991; b. 10.7.32, Perth; m., Shirley Botterill; 3 d. Educ. Strathallan; Edinburgh University. Qualified as Chartered Accountant, 1954; Partner, Graham, Smart & Annan, CA, Edinburgh, latterly Deloitte Haskins & Sells, 1960-1987; President, Institute of Chartered Accountants of Scotland, 1983-84; Johnstone Smith Professor of Accountancy, Glasgow University, 1977-83. Director: Scottish Mortgage and Trust PLC, Scottish American Investment Company PLC (Chairman), Scottish Metropolitan Property PLC, Templeton Emerging Markets Investment Trust PLC, Templeton Latin America Investment Trust PLC, TR European Growth Trust PLC, US Smaller Companies Trust PLC (Chairman); Lay Director, Scottish Chamber Orchestra; Deputy Chairman, Edinburgh Festival Society; Chairman, David Hume Institute; former Chairman, Scottish Higher Education Funding Council, 1992-98; Board Member, Scottish Enterprise, 1990-98; Member, Scottish Economic Council, 1996-98; author of various texts and publications on accountancy. Recreations: music; walking; travel. Address: (b.) The Mound, Edinburgh, EH1 1YZ.

Shaw, Mark Robert, BA, MA, DPhil. Keeper of Geology and Zoology, National Museums of Scotland, since 1996; b. 11.5.45, Sutton Coldfield; m., Francesca Dennis Wilkinson; 2 d. Educ. Dartington Hall School; Oriel College, Oxford. Research Assistant (Entomology), Zoology Department, Manchester University, 1973-76; University Research Fellow, Reading University, 1977-80; Assistant Keeper, Department of Natural History, Royal Scottish Museum, 1980-83; Keeper of Natural History, National Museums of Scotland, 1983-96. Recreations: field entomology; family life. Address: (h.) 48 St. Albans Road, Edinburgh, EH9 2LU; T.-0131-667 0577.

Shaw, Neil, BSc, BA (Hons). Head Teacher, Broxburn Academy, since 1998; b. 30.12.53, Airdrie; m., Nan; 1 s.; 1 d. Educ. Airdrie Academy; University of Glasgow; Jordanhill College of Education; Open University. Mathematics Teacher, Caldervale High School, Airdrie, 1977-87; Principal Teacher of Mathematics: Crookston Castle Secondary School, Glasgow, 1987-90, Carluke High School, 1990-93; Assistant Head Teacher, Boclair Academy, Bearsden, 1993-98. Recreations: golf (eight handicap, Airdrie Golf Club); supporter of Airdrieonians F. C. Address: (b.) Cardross Road, Broxburn EH52 6AG; T.-01506 852521.

Shaw, Richard Wright, CBE, MA. Principal, University of Paisley; b. 22.9.41, Preston; m., Susan Angela; 2 s. Educ. Lancaster Royal Grammar School; Sidney Sussex College, Cambridge. Assistant Lecturer in Management, then Lecturer in Economics, Leeds University, 1964-69; Lecturer in Economics, then Senior Lecturer, Stirling University, 1969-84; part-time Lecturer, Glasgow University, 1978-79; Visiting Lecturer, Newcastle University, NSW, 1982; Head, Department of Economics, Stirling University, 1982-84; Professor and Head, Department of Economics and Management, Paisley College, 1984-86; Vice Principal, 1986. Director, Renfrewshire Enterprise; Member, Board of Management, Reid Kerr College; Member, Scottish Business Forum; Convener, Committee of Scottish Higher Education Principals, 1996-98; Fellow, Scottish Vocational Education Council, since 1995. Recreations:walking; listening to music. Address: (b.) University of Paisley, High Street, Paisley, PA1 2BE; T.-0141-848 3670.

Shaw, Professor Susan Angela, MA (Cantab), FCIM. Deputy Principal, Strathclyde University, since 1995; Professor of Marketing, since 1991; b. 1.6.43, Bristol; m., Richard Shaw; 2 s. Educ. Kingswood Grammar School, Bristol; Girton College, Cambridge. Marketing Executive, ICI Fibres; Lecturer, Senior Lecturer, Professor, Stirling University. Council Member, Food from Britain; Member, Food Advisory Committee; Director, Scottish Agricultural Colleges. Recreations: hill-walking; tennis; opera. Address: (b.) Department of Marketing, Strathclyde University, Stenhouse Building, 173 Cathedral Street, Glasgow, G4 0RQ; T.-0141-552 4400.

Shaw-Stewart, Sir Houston (Mark), 11th Bt, MC (1950), TD. Deputy Lieutenant (formerly Vice Lord Lieutenant), Strathclyde Region (Eastwood, Renfrew and Inverclyde Districts); b. 24.4.31; m., Lucinda Victoria Fletcher; 1 s. Educ. Eton. Coldstream Guards, 1949; 2nd Lt., Royal Ulster Rifles, Korea, 1950; Ayrshire Yeomanry, 1952; Member, Queen's Bodyguard for Scotland (Royal Company of Archers). Address: (h.) Ardgowan, Inverkip, Renfrewshire, PA16 0DW.

Shaw-Stewart, Lady (Lucinda Victoria), FRSA. National Trust for Scotland: Vice President, since 1994, Member, Executive Committee, since 1985, Convener, Curatorial Committee, since 1993; Trustee, Wallace Collection, since 1987; Trustee, Sir William Burrell's Trust, since 1992; b. 29.9.49, Harrogate; m., Sir Houston Shaw-Stewart Bt; 1 s. Educ. Cranborne Chase School; diploma from Study Centre for the History of the Fine and Decorative Arts. Freelance Lecturer in Fine and Decorative Arts, 1969-82; National Trust for Scotland: London Representative, 1978-82, Member, Council, 1983-88. Honorary Vice President, Ardgowan Hospice, Greenock. Address: (h.) Ardgowan, Inverkip, Renfrewshire PA16 0DW; T.-01475 521226.

Shea, Michael Sinclair MacAuslan, CVO, MA, PhD. Scottish Member, Independent Television Commission, since 1996; Chairman, Royal Lyceum Theatre, since 1998; Political Consultant, Hanson PLC, since 1993; b. 10.5.38, Carluke; m., Mona Grec Stensen; 2 d. Educ. Lenzie Academy; Gordonstoun; Edinburgh University. Entered Foreign Office, 1963; seconded to Cabinet Office; Deputy Director General, British Information Services, New York; Press Secretary to the Queen; Head of Political and Government Affairs, Hanson PLC; remains Vice-Chairman of Melody Radio Ltd. (wholly-owned Hanson subsidiary). Visiting Professor, Graduate School, Strathclyde University; Trustee, National Galleries of Scotland;

Governor, Gordonstoun; Board Member, Murray Johnstone companies; Non-Excecutive Director, P&A Group; Vice-Chairman, Foundation for Skin Research; Member, Board of Directors, Edinburgh Military Tattoo; has published 21 books of fiction and non-fiction. Address: (b.) 1A Ramsay Garden, Edinburgh EH1 2NA; T.-0131-220 1456.

Shearer, Magnus MacDonald, JP. Lord Lieutenant of Shetland, 1982-94; Honorary Consul for Sweden in Shetland and Orkney, 1958-94; Honorary Consul for Federal Republic of Germany in Shetland, 1972-87; b. 27.2.24; m., Martha Nicolson Henderson; 1 s. Educ. Anderson Educational Institute, Shetland; George Watson's College, Edinburgh. Royal Navy, Atlantic, Mediterranean and Far East, 1942-46; Royal Artillery TA, commissioned 2nd Lt., 1949; TARO, rank Captain, 1959; Honorary Secretary, Lerwick Station, RNLI, 1968-92; Chairman, Lerwick Harbour Trust, 1966-72; Member, Lerwick Town Council, 1963-69; Deputy Lieutenant of Shetland, 1973-82. Recreations: reading; bird watching; ships. Address: (h.) 4 Queens Place, Lerwick, Shetland ZE1 0BZ; T.-01595 696612.

Shedden, Alfred Charles, MA, LLB. Senior Partner, McGrigor Donald, since 1993; b. 30.6.44, Edinburgh; m., Irene; 1 s.; 1 d. Educ. Arbroath High School; Aberdeen University. McGrigor Donald: Apprentice, 1967-69, Assistant, 1969-70, Partner, 1971, Managing Partner, 1985-92. Director, Scottish Financial Enterprise, since 1989; Director, Martin Currie Japan Investment Trust plc, since 1995; Director, Standard Life Assurance Society, since 1992; Non-Executive Director, Scottish Metropolitan Property PLC, since 1998. Address: (b.) Pacific House, 70 Wellington Street, Glasgow; T.-0141-248 6677.

Sheed, Ronald McLean, BSc, CEng, MICE. Director of Commercial Operations, South Ayrshire Council, since 1995; b. 8.5.47, Glasgow; m., Beth; 1 s.; 2 d. Educ. Duncanrig Senior Secondary School, East Kilbride; Strathclyde University. Lanark County Council, 1969-75; Strathclyde Regional Council, 1975-95, latterly as Contracts Manager, Roads Direct. Recreation: sport. Address: (b.) County Buildings, Wellington Square, Ayr, KA7 1DS; T.-01292 012421.

Sheehan, Sheriff Albert Vincent, MA, LLB. Sheriff of Tayside, Central and Fife, at Falkirk, since 1983; b. 23.8.36, Edinburgh; m., Edna Georgina Scott Hastings; 2 d. Educ. Bo'ness Academy; Edinburgh University. 2nd Lt., 1st Bn., Royal Scots (The Royal Regiment), 1960; Captain, Directorate of Army Legal Services, 1961; Depute Procurator Fiscal, Hamilton, 1961-71; Senior Depute Procurator Fiscal, Glasgow, 1971-74; Deputy Crown Agent for Scotland, 1974-79; Scottish Law Commission, 1979-81; Sheriff of Lothian and Borders, at Edinburgh, 1981-83. Leverhulme Fellow, 1971. Publications: Criminal Procedure in Scotland and France, 1975; Criminal Procedure, 1990. Recreations: naval history; travel. Address: (b.) Sheriff Court House, Falkirk; T.-Falkirk 20822.

Shelton, Richard Graham John, BSc, PhD. Officer-in-Charge, Scottish Office Freshwater Fisheries Laboratory, Pitlochry, since 1982; b. 3.7.42, Aylesbury; m., Freda Carstairs; 2 s. Educ. Royal Grammar School, High Wycombe; St. Andrews University. Research work, Burnham-on-Crouch Laboratory, MAFF, 1968-72; Assistant to Controller of Fisheries Research and Development, MAFF Fisheries Laboratory, Lowestoft, 1972-74 and (from 1974) Scottish Office Marine Laboratory, Aberdeen; worked on the population ecology of Crustacea, 1976-82. Address: (b.) Scottish Office Freshwater Fisheries Laboratory, Faskally, Pitlochry, PH16 5LB; T.-01796 2060.

Shepherd, Lt.-Col. Ian. Regional Organiser (Scotland), Army Benevolent Fund; b. 6.4.39; m., Belinda Buchanan-Dunlop; 2 s.; 1 d. Educ. Queen's College of British Guiana; Dollar Academy; RMA Sandhurst. Commissioned into Royal Highland Fusiliers, 1960; Assistant Military Attache (Tech), Moscow, 1981-82; CO Scot Infantry Depot (Bridge of Don), 1984-86; CO, University of Aberdeen OTC, 1986-88, retired 1992. Chairman, Management Committee, Lady Haig's Poppy Factory; Member, North, South, East Committee, Director of The Officers' Association Scotland. Recreation: being an old soldier. Address: c/o Bank of Scotland, The Mound, Edinburgh, EH1 1YZ.

Shepherd, Professor James, BSc, MB, ChB, PhD, FRCPath, FRCP (Glas). Professor in Pathological Biochemistry, Glasgow University, since 1987 (Reader, 1984-87); b. 8.4.44, Motherwell; m., Janet Bulloch Kelly; 1 s.; 1 d. Educ. Hamilton Academy; Glasgow University. Lecturer, Glasgow University: Biochemistry, 1968-72, Pathological Biochemistry, 1972-77; Assistant Professor of Medicine, Baylor College of Medicine, Houston, Texas, 1976-77; Senior Lecturer in Pathological Biochemistry, Glasgow University, 1977-84; Visiting Professor of Medicine, Geneva University, 1984; Director, West of Scotland Coronary Prevention Study; Director, Prospective Study of Pravastation in the Elderly at Risk, since 1997; Chairman, European Atherosclerosis Society, 1993-96; author of textbooks and papers on lipoprotein metabolism and heart disease prevention. Address: (b.) Department of Biochemistry, Royal Infirmary, Glasgow, G4 OSF; T.-0141-304 4628.

Shepherd, Janet, CertEd. Secretary for Scotland, Duke of Edinburgh's Award, since 1994; b. 6.8.52, Chipping Sodbury. Educ. Rodway School; Bognor Regis College of Education. Began career with Royal Forest of Dean Grammar School; Plas Pencelli Outdoor Education Centre; Faskally Outdoor Centre; Dolcorsllwyn Hall Outdoor Education Centre, Knowsley; Howtown Outdoor Education Centre, Co. Durham; Bewerley Park Outdoor Education Centre, North Yorkshire. Recreations: travelling; ornithology; mountaineering; skiing; canoeing; embroidery; Scottish folk music. Address: (b.) 69 Dublin Street, Edinburgh EH3 6NS; T.-0131-556 9097.

Shepherd, Peter Charles, LLB, NP. Solicitor; b. 7.2.58, Aberdeen; m., Sheila Catherine; 2 s.; 1 d. Educ. Robert Gordon's College; Aberdeen University. Apprentice, 1978-80; Assistant, 1980-83; Partner, Aberdein Considine & Co., since 1984. President, Aberdeen Bar Association, since 1997; Member, Society of Advocates in Aberdeen. Recreations: golf; fishing; gardening. Address: (b.) 8 Bon Accord Crescent, Aberdeen; T.-01224 589700.

Shepherd, Robert Horne (Robbie), AScA. Freelance Broadcaster, since 1976; b. 30.4.36, Dunecht, Aberdeen; m., Agnes Margaret (Esma); 1 s. Educ. Robert Gordon's College, Aberdeen. Left school at 15 to work in accountant's office; National Service, two years; joined fish firm as Assistant Accountant, then with fish group for 13 years as Management Accountant; left to become self-employed in that capacity; now full-time on radio and television. Recreations: golf; gardening; traditional music.

Sheridan, Rt. Rev. Mgr. John. Prelate of Honour; Parish Priest, St. Paul's, Whiteinch, Glasgow, since 1986; b. 22.8.29, Clydebank. Educ. Holyrood Senior Secondary School, Glasgow; Campion House, Osterley; Royal Scots College, Valladolid, Spain. Ordained Priest, 1956; Curate in Glasgow, 1956-63; Spiritual Director, Royal Scots College, Valladolid, Spain, 1963-69; Curate in Glasgow, 1969-84; Parish Priest, Our Lady and St. Margaret's, Kinning Park, 1984-86; Chancellor, Archdiocese of Glasgow, 1983-92. Scout Area Chaplain, Glasgow, 1960-63; Scout District Commissioner, N.E. and N.W.II Districts, Glasgow, 1970-78; National Scout Chaplain, 1978-94; Hon. Vice

Chairman, Scottish Catholic Scout Advisory Council, 1995; awarded Scout Silver Acorn, 1987. Recreations: golf; painting; caravanning. Address: St. Paul's, 1213 Dumbarton Road, Glasgow G14 9UP; T.-0141-950 2488.

Sherrard, Mary Stephen, MBE, BA. National President, Woman's Guild, Church of Scotland, 1993-96; Representative on Women's National Commission, 1993-98; b. 22.4.23, Renfrew; m., Rev. John A. Sherrard; 2 s.; 1 d. Educ. Girls' High School, Glasgow; Open University. Journalist; service in W.R.N.S.; playgroup work; Citizens Advice Bureau Manager; Chairman, Angus Citizens Advice Bureau; Vice-Chair, Scottish CAB. Elder, Buckhaven Parish Church. Recreations: crosswords; writing; walking on holiday. Address: (h.) Fair Havens, West Wynd, Buckhaven, KY8 1AS; T.-01592 716457.

Sherriff, Robert Mark, CBE, MSI, BA, DL. Stockbroker, since 1960; Vice Chairman, Executive Committee, Erskine Hospital, since 1988; Chairman, The MacRoberts Trusts Tarland, since 1994; b. 29.3.36, Kilmacolm; m., Margaret Fraser; 2 s.; 2 d. Educ. Cargilfield; Sedbergh; Trinity College, Cambridge. Joined R.C. Greig & Co., Stockbroker, Glasgow, 1959; became a Partner (now Director); Vice Chairman, Greig Middleton & Co. Ltd., Glasgow; Director, Gerrard Group PLC, London; Vice Chairman, Scottish Building Society; retired as Chairman, Highland TAVR, 1996. Member, Erskine Hospital Committee. Recreations: tennis; golf; shooting; skiing. Address: (b.) 155 St. Vincent Street, Glasgow, G2 5NN; T.-0141-240 4000.

Sherwood, Professor John Neil, DSc, PhD, CChem, FRSC, FRSE. Burmah Professor of Physical Chemistry, Strathclyde University, since 1983; b. 8.11.33, Redruth, Cornwall; m., Margaret Enid Shaw; 2 d. Educ. Aireborough Grammar School; Bede College, Durham University. Research Fellow, Hull University, 1958-60; Lecturer, Reader and Personal Professor, Strathclyde University, 1960-83; Vice Principal, 1995-98. Recreations: hill-walking; photography; gardening. Address: (b.) Department of Pure and Applied Chemistry, Strathclyde University, Glasgow, G1 1XL; T.-041-552 4400.

Shiach, Allan G., BA. Chairman, Macallan-Glenlivet PLC, 1979-96; Chairman, Scottish Film Council, 1991-97; Chairman, Scottish Film Production Fund, 1991-96; Chairman, Scottish Screen, 1996-98; b. Elgin; m., Kathleen Breck; 2 s.; 1 d. Educ. Gordonstoun School; McGill University, Montreal. Writer/Producer, since 1970; Writer/Co-Writer: Don't Look Now, The Girl from Petrovia, Daryl, Joseph Andrews, Castaway, The Witches, Cold Heaven, Regeneration, In Love and War, and other films; Member: Broadcasting Council for Scotland, 1988-91; Member, Council, Scotch Whisky Association, 1984-96; Chairman, Writers' Guild of G.B., 1989-91; Director, Rafford Films, since 1982; Director, Scottish Media Group plc, since 1993; Governor, British Film Institute, 1992-98; Freeman, City of London, 1988.

Shiach, Sheriff Gordon Iain Wilson, MA, LLB, BA (Hons). Sheriff of Lothian and Borders, at Edinburgh, 1984-97, and at Peebles, 1996-97; b. 15.10.35, Elgin; m., Margaret Grant Smith; 2 d. (1 deceased). Educ. Lathallan; Gordonstoun; Edinburgh University; Open University. Admitted Advocate, 1960; practised as Advocate, 1960-72; Sheriff of Fife and Kinross, later Tayside, Central and Fife, at Dunfermline, 1972-79; Sheriff of Lothian and Borders, at Linlithgow, 1979-84; Hon. Sheriff, Elgin, since 1986; Member: Council of Sheriffs' Association, 1989-95 (President, 1993-95); Standing Committee on Criminal Procedure, 1989-93; Board, Lothian Family Conciliation Service, 1989-93; Parole Board for Scotland, since 1990 (Vice Chairman, since 1995); Council, Faculty of Advocates, 1993-95; Shrieval Training Group, 1994-95; Review Group on Social Work National Standards for Throughcare, 1994-95; Chairman, The Scottish Society, 1992-93, The Edinburgh Sir Walter Scott Club, 1995-98. Recreations: walking; swimming; music; art; film; theatre.

Shields, Sir Robert, MD, DL, FRCSEd, FRCSEng, FRCPS, DSc, HonFACS, HonFRCSI, HonFRCSHK, HonFRCPEdin, FAcadMedSingap, Hon. FRACS. Professor of Surgery Emeritus, Liverpool University; Consultant Surgeon, Royal Liverpool Hospital; b. 8.11.30, Paisley; m., Marianne; 1 s.; 2 d. Educ. John Neilson Institution, Paisley; Glasgow University. House Officer, Western Infirmary, Glasgow; Research Associate, Mayo Clinic, Rochester, USA; Lecturer in Surgery, Western Infirmary, Glasgow; Senior Lecturer and Reader, Welsh National School of Medicine; Honorary Consultant Surgeon, Royal Infirmary, Cardiff. Past President, James IV Association; Past President, Association of Surgeons of Great Britain and Ireland; Past President, British Society of Gastroenterology; Past President, Surgical Research Society; Past President, Royal College of Surgeons of Edinburgh, 1994-97. Recreations: walking; reading. Address: (b.) Royal College of Surgeons of Edinburgh, Nicolson Street, Edinburgh, EH8 9DW; T.-0131-527 1668; Ardlarig, Tayvallich, Argyll PA31 8PJ; T.-01546 870 308.

Shields, Tom, BA. Diary Writer, The Herald, since 1979; b. 9.2.48, Glasgow; 1 s.; 1 d. Educ. Lourdes Secondary School (no miracle); Strathclyde University. Journalist: Sunday Post, 1969-73, The Herald, since 1973. Publications: Tom Shields' Diary; Tom Shields Too; Tom Shields Free at Last; Just the Three Weeks in Provence (Co-author). Recreation: Celtic studies. Address: (b.) 195 Albion Street, Glasgow G1 1QP; T.-0141-553 3297.

Shinwell, Sir (Maurice) Adrian, Kt, LLB, NP, ACIArb. Solicitor; Senior Partner, Kerr, Barrie & Duncan, Glasgow, since 1991; b. 27.2.51; m., Lesley McLean; 2 s.; 1 d. Educ. Hutchesons' Boys' Grammar School; Glasgow University. Admitted Solicitor, 1975; joined Kerr, Barrie & Duncan, 1976; Notary Public, since 1976; Tutor (part-time), Law Faculty, Glasgow University, 1980-84; ACI Arbitrators, since 1990; Solicitor-Mediator, since 1994; Director, Kerr Barrie Nominees Ltd. Scottish Conservative and Unionist Association: Member, Scottish Council, 1982-98; Chairman, Eastwood Association, 1982-85; Chairman, Cumbernauld and Kilsyth Association, 1989-91; Vice-President, 1989-92; President, 1992-94; Scottish Conservative and Unionist Party: Chairman, Candidates' Board, Member, Scottish Executive and Scottish Council, since 1998; Member, Central Advisory Committee on Justices of the Peace, since 1996. Recreations: family; politics. Address: (h.) Sarona, South Road, Busby, Glasgow, G76 8JB; T.-0141-221 6844.

Shirran, Jane Lindsay, LLB (Hons), DipLP. General Counsel and Secretary, Clydesdale Bank PLC, since 1998; General Counsel, Yorkshire Bank PLC, since 1999; b. 27.6.63, Taiping, Malaysia; m., Angus D. MacRae. Educ. Albyn School; University of Aberdeen. McGrigor Donald, Solicitors, 1988-96; Bank of Scotland, 1996-97; joined Clydesdale Bank, 1997. Recreations: African culture; travel; wildlife photography. Address: (b.) 150 Buchanan Street, Glasgow G1 2NL; T.-0141-223 2883.

Shirreffs, Murdoch John, MB, ChB, DObstRCOG, FRCGP, MFHom. General Medical Practitioner, Aberdeen, since 1974; Medical Hypnotherapist and Homoeopathic Physician; b. 25.5.47, Aberdeen; m., Jennifer McLeod. Educ. Aberdeen Grammar School; Aberdeen University. General Practice Trainer, since 1977; Secretary, Grampian Division, British Medical Association, since 1978; former Member, BMA Scottish Council. Past President, North of Scotland Veterans' Hockey Club. Recreations: hockey; opera and classical music; big band jazz; DIY; gardening; food and wine; travel. Address: (h.) 72 Gray Street, Aberdeen, AB10 6JE; T.-01224 321998.

Short, Agnes Jean, BA (Hons), MLitt. Writer; b. Bradford, Yorkshire; m., Anthony Short (qv); 3 s.; 2 d. Educ. Bradford Girls' Grammar School; Exeter University; Aberdeen University. Various secretarial, research and teaching jobs, both in UK and abroad; took up writing, 1966; 19 novels, most of which have a Scottish setting; also short stories and radio; Constable Award, 1976. Recreations: dog-walking; whisky-tasting; good food; small hills. Address: (h.) Khantore, Crathie, by Ballater, Aberdeenshire, AB35 5TJ.

Shorter, Bob, BA, MHSM, MMS. Director of Primary Care, Lanarkshire Health Board, since 1995; b. 20.8.50, Epsom; m., Hilary; 2 s. Educ. Glyn Grammar School; Heriot-Watt University. Address: (b.) 14 Beckford Street, Hamilton ML3 0TA; T.-01698 281313.

Shucksmith, Professor Mark, MA, MSc, PhD. Professor of Land Economy, University of Aberdeen, since 1993; Co-director, Arkleton Centre for Rural Development Research, University of Aberdeen, since 1995; Programme Adviser, Joseph Rowntree Foundation's Action in Rural Areas Programme, since 1997; b. 25.8.53, London; m., Janet; 2 d. Educ. Sidney Sussex College, University of Cambridge. Department of Agricultural Economics, University of Newcastle upon Tyne, 1977-81; Lecturer then Senior Lecturer then Reader in Land Economy, University of Aberdeen, 1981-93. Former Vice-Chair, Rural Forum. Publications: several books, notably on social exclusion in rural areas, rural housing, agricultural restructuring; over 50 papers in learned journals. Recreations: music; hillwalking; reading. Address: (b.) St. Mary's, University of Aberdeen, Old Aberdeen AB24 3UF; T.-01224 273901.

Siann, Professor Gerda, BSc, MSc, PhD, FBPsS. NCR Professor of Gender Relations, Dundee University, since 1996; b. 2.12.37, Cape Town; m., Julian Siann; 1 s.; 2 d. Educ. Wynberg Girls High School, Cape Town; University of Cape Town; University of Zambia; Edinburgh University. Lecturer in Psychology, Moray House Institute of Education, 1972-84; Senior Lecturer, Reader, Professor of Psychology, Glasgow Caledonian University, 1984-95. Member, British Council Gender and Development Task Force. Publications: Educational Psychology in a Changing World, 1980, 1988; Accounting for Aggression, 1985; Gender, Sex and Sexuality, 1994. Recreations: films; theatre; travel; reading contemporary fiction. Address: (h.) 9 Bay Road, Wormit, Fife DD6 8LU; T.-01382 543041.

Sibbald, Michael Robert, BA, MBA, MInstM. Group Personnel Director, Argos PLC, since 1996; b. 30.8.48, Edinburgh; m., Margaret; 2 s.; 1 d. Educ. George Heriot's School; Heriot-Watt University; Glasgow University. Scottish and Newcastle Breweries, 1972-75; Butler Manufacturing Co., 1975-79; Scottish Brick Corporation Ltd., 1979-81; ICL Plastics Ltd., 1981-82; Grand Metropolitan PLC, 1982-90; Director: Stakis PLC, 1990-91, United Eng Steels Ltd., 1991-94, NHS in Scotland, 1994-96. Member, Advisory Board, Glasgow University Business School, since 1996. Recreations: reading; sports cars; athletics; football. Address: (h.) 18 Craigmount Bank West, Edinburgh, EH4 8HG; T.-0131-538 4513.

Sibbett, Professor Wilson, BSc, PhD. Wardlaw Professor of Natural Philosophy, St. Andrews University (Director of Research, since 1994, Chairman, Department of Physics and Astronomy, 1985-94); b. 15.3.48, Portglenone, N. Ireland; m., Barbara Anne Brown; 3 d. Educ. Ballymena Technical College; Queen's University, Belfast. Postdoctoral Research Fellow, Blackett Laboratory, Imperial College, London, 1973-76; Lecturer in Physics, then Reader, Imperial College, 1976-85. Fellow: Institute of Physics, Royal Society of Edinburgh, Royal Society (of London). Recreation: golf (to low standard). Address: (b.) Department of Physics and Astronomy, St. Andrews University, North Haugh, St. Andrews, KY16 9SS; T.-01334 463100.

Siddiqui, Mona, MA, MIL, PhD. Lecturer in Arabic Studies, Glasgow University, since 1995; Director, Centre for the Study of Islam, Glasgow University, since 1998; b. 3.5.63, Karachi, Pakistan; m., Farhaj; 2 s. Educ. Salendine-Nook High School, Huddersfield; Leeds University; Manchester University. Lecturer in Arabic and Islamic Studies: Manchester Metropolitan University, 1989-90, Glasgow Caledonian University, 1993. Contributor, Thought for the Day, BBC Scotland and Radio 4. Recreations: interior decorating; cooking; reading. Address: (h.) 19 Moorburn Avenue, Giffnock, Glasgow; T.-0141-638 9406.

Sidgwick, Richard Twining, JP, DL, MSc, FRICS. Partner, West Highland Estates Office, since 1974; b. 17.7.44; m., Alison Janet Baggallay; 1 s.; 2 d. Educ. Fort Augustus Abbey School; Reading University. JP, Highland area, 1990; Deputy Lieutenant, Lochaber, Inverness, Badenoch and Strathspey, 1991; Director, Lochaber Limited, 1991, Vice-Chairman, 1992-97; Member, Red Deer Commission, 1993; Honorary Sheriff Fort William, 1994. Recreations: country sports; gardening; amenity woodlands. Address: (h.) Inverlair Lodge, Roy Bridge, Inverness-shire, PH31 4AR; T.-01397 732 246.

Sillars, James. Member, Board, Scottish Enterprise; b. 4.10.37, Ayr; m., Margo MacDonald (qv); 1 s.; 3 d. Educ. Ayr Academy. Member, Ayr Town Council and Ayr County Council Education Committee, 1960s; Member, Western Regional Hospital Board, 1965-70; Head, Organisation Department, Scottish TUC, 1968-70; MP, South Ayrshire, 1970-79; Co-Founder, Scottish Labour Party, 1976; MP, Glasgow Govan, 1988-92.

Silver, Alan William, CEng, DipTE, FICE, FIHT, MRTPI. Assistant Director of Property and Technical Services – Roads, Aberdeen City Council, since 1996; b. 22.6.41, Aberdeen; m., Margaret Eileen; 2 s. Educ. Aberdeen Grammar School; Aberdeen University; Robert Gordon's Institute of Technology. Worked for Sir Robert McAlpine & Sons on M1 Motorway; former Design Engineer, Sir William Halcrow, and Site Agent, C. Bryant & Sons; joined City Engineer's Department, Aberdeen, 1971; Chief Assistant, Traffic/Transporation/Road Safety, Roads Department, Grampian Regional Council, 1975, Director of Roads, 1993. Recreations: amateur opera; bowls; curling; steam vehicles. Address: (b.) Property and Technical Services Department, Roads Section, St. Nicholas House, Broad Street, Aberdeen AB10 1WL.

Silver, Frederick Philip, MA. Editor, Stornoway Gazette, since 1991; b. 15.7.54, Manchester; m., Stephanie Blyth Sargent; 2 d. Educ. Bolton School; Jesus College, Oxford; Victoria University, Wellington. Journalist: Reading Evening Post, Western Mail (Cardiff), Western Daily Press (Bristol), China Daily (Beijing), Dominion/Dominion Sunday Times, Wellington, New Zealand. Address: (b.) 10 Francis Street, Stornoway HS1 2XE.

Silver, Gillian M., LLB, NP. Partner, MacNeill and Critchley, Solicitors, Inverness, since 1983; Member, Local Government Boundary Commission for Scotland, since 1995; b. 13.5.56, Aberdeen; m., Chris. Educ. Inverness Royal Academy; Edinburgh University. Past Chairman, Highland Solicitors Property Centre Ltd.; Past Chairman, Solicitors Property Centres Scotland; Senator, Junior Chamber International. Recreations: golf; curling; choral singing; running; theatre. Address: (h.) Chanonry Green, Kincurdie, Rosemarkie IV10 8SJ; T.-01381 621211.

Sim, Ian Allan, BSc, CA. Secretary General, Scottish Kennel Club, since 1977; Partner, Johnston Smillie, Chartered Accountants, since 1977; b. 2.8.48, Edinburgh; 2 s. Educ. Lochaber High School; Edinburgh University. Manager, Deloittes, Chartered Accountants, 1973-76. Treasurer, St. George's West Church; Chairman,

Association of Independent Accountants in Scotland; Chairman/Vice Chairman, Kennel Club committees. Recreations: swimming; music. Address: (h.) 22 Craigmount Avenue, Edinburgh EH12 8HQ; T.-0131-317 7377.

Sime, Martin, MA. Director, Scottish Council for Voluntary Organisations, since 1991; b. 23.9.53, Edinburgh. Educ. George Heriot's; St. Andrews University; Edinburgh University. Social and Economic History Researcher, 1976-78; Sheep Farmer, 1978-81; Freelance Researcher, 1982; Project Manager, Sprout Market Garden, 1983-85; Development/Principal Officer (Day Services), Scottish Association for Mental Health, then Director, 1985-91; Secretary, Scottish Civic Assembly; Member, Scottish Advisory Task Force for the New Deal; Expert Panel on Procedures for the Scottish Parliament; Board Member, Centre for Scottish Public Policy. Recreations: cinema; food; bridge. Address: (b.) 18/19 Claremont Crescent, Edinburgh, EH7 4QD; T.-0131-556 3882.

Simmers, Graeme Maxwell, CBE, CA. Chairman, Scottish Sports Council, since 1992; Non-Excutive Director, Stirling Royal Infirmary NHS Trust, since 1993; b. 2.5.35, Glasgow; m., Jennifer M.H. Roxburgh; 2 s.; 2 d. Educ. Glasgow Academy; Loretto School. Qualified CA, 1959; commissioned Royal Marines, 1959-61. Former Partner, Kidsons Simmers CA; Chairman, Scottish Highland Hotels Group Ltd., 1972-92; Member, Scottish Tourist Board, 1979-86; Chairman, HCBA (Scotland), 1984-86; Past Chairman, Board of Management, Member of National Executive, BHA; Elder and Treasurer, Killearn Kirk; Governor, Queen's College, Glasgow, 1989-93; Chairman of Governors, Loretto School; Past Chairman, Championship Committee, Royal and Ancient Golf Club of St. Andrews. Recreations: rugby; golf; skiing. Address: (h.) Kincaple, Boquhan, Balfron, near Glasgow, G63 ORW; T.-01360 440375.

Simmons, Professor John Edmund Leonard, BSc, PhD, CEng, FIMechE, FIEE. Professor of Mechanical Engineering, Heriot Watt University, since 1992, and Head, Department of Mechanical and Chemical Engineering, since 1994; Vice-Chairman, Engineering Manufacturing Industries Division, IMechE, since 1995; b. 24.9.47, Faversham; m., Anne; 2 s.; 2 d. Educ. Birmingham University; Cambridge University. Production Manager, Baker Perkins Chemical Machinery, Stoke on Trent, 1977-80; Design Manager, Vickers plc–Michell Bearings, Newcastle upon Tyne, 1981-84; Lecturer in Engineering, Durham University, 1984-91. Recreations: gardening; walking; travelling; cinema. Address: (b.) Heriot Watt University, Edinburgh, EH14 4AS; T.-0131-451 3132.

Simpson, Andrew Rutherford, MB, ChB, D(Obst)RCOG. Principal, general practice, 1965-94; Chairman, Borders Research Ethics Committee; b. 13.7.32, Hawick; m., Helen Margaret Douglas; 3 d. Educ. Merchiston Castle School, Edinburgh; Edinburgh University. BMA: former Member, Scottish Council; Past Chairman, Scottish Borders Division, 1980, former Representative for Borders on Scottish Council; Past President and Life Member, Hawick Rugby Club (club doctor, over 30 years); Past President, Hawick Callants Club; Chairman, Douglas Haig Court. Recreations: rugby involvement; golf; philately; Rotary. Address: (h.) Netherfield, Buccleuch Road, Hawick, TD9 0EL; T.-01450 372459.

Simpson, Brian Middleton, MIBiol, FRAgS. Chief Executive, Scotch Quality Beef and Lamb Association, since 1991; Chairman, Marketing Society in Scotland; b. 24.9.52, Perth; m., Helena; 1 s.; 2 d. Educ. Perth High School; West of Scotland Agricultural College. Agricultural Adviser, Scottish Agricultural College; Marketing Adviser, Kemira Fertilisers; Senior Project Executive, Scottish Enterprise. Recreation: hill-walking. Address: (b.) Rural Centre, West Mains, Ingliston, Newbridge, EH28 8NZ; T.-0131-472 4040.

Simpson, David, CBE, DSc, CEng, FIEE, FRSE, FRSA. Chairman: Simpson Research Ltd., Isocom Components Ltd., Albacom Ltd., Bookham Technology Ltd., PFE Ltd., SDS Ltd., Vibtech Ltd., Sigtronics Ltd., Scotish Opto Electronic Association, Genesis Consultancy Ltd.; Co-Founder, Elvingston Science Centre; b. 23.11.26, Ceres; m., Janice Ann; 1 s.; 2 d. Educ. Bell Baxter School, Cupar; Dundee Technical College; Stanford University. R. & D. Engineer, Marconi, 1952-56; Managing Director, Microcell Electronics, 1956-60; General Manager, Hughes Microelectronics, 1960-62; Managing Director, Hewlett Packard Ltd., 1962-70; President, Gould Corp., Chicago, 1976-88; Chairman, various UK companies, 1988-92. Recreations: hill-walking; wood-carving. Address: (h.) Elvingston House, Tranent, EH33 1EH; T.-01875 852878.

Simpson of Dunkeld, Baron (George Simpson), FCCA, FIMI, FCIT. Managing Director, General Electric Co. plc, since 1996; Life Peer, since 1997; b. 2.7.42; m.; 1 s.; 1 d. Educ. Morgan Academy, Dundee; Dundee Institute of Technology.

Simpson, Professor Graeme Stirling, BSc, PhD, MBA, FGS. Schlumberger Professor of Energy Industry Management, University of Aberdeen, since 1997 (Head, Department of Management Studies, since 1998); b. 27.11.49, Glasgow; m., Nicola; 1 s.; 1 d. Educ. William Hulme's Grammar School, Manchester; Sheffield University; Cranfield University. Geophysicist: Esso Exploration and Production UK, 1975-77, Exxon Co. USA, Houston, Texas, 1977-79, Esso Norge, Stavanger, Norway, 1979-84; Business Analyst, Esso Europe, London, 1984-86; Manager, Business Analysis, Esso Exploration and Production UK, 1986-97. Lacrosse Internationalist: England (1973-74 World Championships, Australia), Scotland (1994 World Championships, Manchester). Recreations: golf (Royal Aberdeen Golf Club); travel; reading; music. Address: (b.) Edward Wright Building, Dunbar Street Aberdeen AB24 3QY; T.-01224 272711.

Simpson, Professor Hugh Walter, MB, ChB, MD, PhD, FRCPath, FRCP(Glas). Head of Pathology, Glasgow Royal Infirmary, 1984-93, now Senior Research Fellow, University Department of Surgery, Glasgow University and Royal Infirmary; b. 4.4.31, Ceres Fife; m., Myrtle Emslie (see Myrtle Simpson); 3 s.; 1 d. Educ. Bryanston; Edinburgh University. Leader of numerous expeditions to polar and tropical regions; awarded Polar Medal, Mungo Park and Pery Medals. Publications: 160 scientific publications, especially on breast cancer. Recreation: skiing. Address: (h.) 7 Cleveden Crescent, Glasgow, G12 0PD; T.-0141-357 1091.

Simpson, Ian Christopher, LLB. Sheriff of South Strathclyde, Dumfries and Galloway, since 1988, at Airdrie, since 1991; b. 5.7.49, Edinburgh; m., Christine Margaret Anne Strang; 2 s. Educ. Glenalmond; Edinburgh University. Admitted to Faculty of Advocates, 1974. Captain, Scottish Universities Golfing Society, 1989-90; President, All Sphere Club, 1989-90. Recreation: golf. Address: (b.) Airdrie Sheriff Court, Graham Street, Airdrie, ML6 6EE; T.-01236 751121.

Simpson, Rev. James Alexander, BSc (Hons), BD, STM, DD. Minister, Dornoch Cathedral, 1976-97; Chaplain to the Queen in Scotland; Moderator, General Assembly of the Church of Scotland, 1994; b. 9.3.34, Glasgow; m., Helen Gray McCorquodale; 3 s.; 2 d. Educ. Eastwood Secondary School; Glasgow University; Union Seminary, New York. Minister: Grahamston Church, Falkirk, 1960-66, St. John's Renfield, Glasgow, 1966-76. Publications: There is a time to ....; Marriage Questions Today; Doubts are not Enough; Holy Wit; Laughter Lines; The Master Mind; Dornoch

Cathedral; More Holy Wit; Keywords of Faith; All About Christmas; The Laugh Shall Be First. Recreations: golf; photography; writing. Address: Cathedral Manse, Chanonry Wynd, Brechin DD9 6JS; T.-01356 622 783.

Simpson, James Walter Thorburn, BArch, RIBA, FRIAS. Partner, Simpson & Brown, Architects, since 1977; Director, Scottish Lime Centre Trust, since 1994; Director, Edinburgh Green Belt Trust, since 1997; Member, Royal Commission on the Ancient and Historical Monuments of Scotland, since 1997; b. 27.7.44, Edinburgh; m., Ann Mary Bunney; 2 d. Educ. Trinity College, Glenalmond; Edinburgh College of Art. Lecturer, Heriot Watt University, 1975-80; co-founded Simpson & Brown, 1977, and Acanthus Associated Architectural Practices, 1985; Architect to St. Giles' Cathedral, 1983-90; Member, Ancient Monuments Board for Scotland, 1983-95; Architectural Adviser, Scottish Historic Buildings Trust, since 1985; Surveyor of the Fabric of York Minster, 1994-95; Chairman, RIAS Conservation Committee, 1992-94; UK Committee Member, International Council for Monuments and Sites, since 1992. Recreations: architectural history and geography; walking; piping; Scotland. Address: (b.) 179 Canongate, Edinburgh, EH8 8BN; T.-0131-557 3880.

Simpson, J.W., BSc, MCIT, MRIN, MNI. Chief Harbour Master, Firth of Forth, and Manager, Marine Services, since 1996; Divisional Manager, Marine Services, Forth Ports PLC, 1986-96; Director, Forth Estuary Towage Ltd., since 1986; b. 30.8.44, St. Andrews; m., Barbara Hutton; 1 s.; 1 d. Educ. Grangemouth High School; Buckhaven High School; Leith Nautical College; Plymouth Polytechnic. Cadet, Furness Prince Lines, 1961-64; Navigating Officer: Shaw Savill Line, 1965-68, Overseas Containers Ltd., 1969-70; Assistant Harbour Master, then Assistant to Port Superintendent, Grangemouth, 1973-77; Port Superintendent, Leith and Granton, 1978-82; Port Manager, Grangemouth, 1982-86. Recreation: sailing. Address: (b.) Forth Ports PLC, Tower Place, Leith, EH6 7DB; T.-0131-554 6473.

Simpson, John Douglas, BSc(Hons). Headteacher, Fortrose Academy, since 1989; b. 2.3.51, Kilbirnie; m., Linda; 2 s.; 2 d. Educ. Spier's School, Beith; Glasgow University. Teacher of Biology, 1975; Principal Teacher, 1979; Assistant Headteacher, Merksworth High School, Paisley, 1983; Depute Headteacher, Cowdenknowes High School, Greenock, 1985. Recreations: golf; snooker. Address: (b.) Fortrose Academy, Fortrose, Ross-shire; T.-01381 620310.

Simpson, Martha, BSc(SocSc). Chief Executive, Scottish Pre-School Play Association, since 1998; b. 30.6.57, New Cumnock; m., Jim; 1.s.; 1.d. Educ. Lanark Grammar School; Bell College of Technology; Open University. Secretary to Director, insurance brokers, 1975; returned to work as Co-ordinator, Home-Start North East Fife, 1987-92; Consultant for Scotland, Home-Start UK, 1992, later Assistant Director (Scotland). Recreations: walking; cycling; music; reading. Address: (b.) 14 Elliot Place, Glasgow G3 8EP; T.-0141-221 4148.

Simpson, Professor Mary, MA, PhD. Professor of Educational Research, Northern College, since 1991 (Director of Educational Research, since 1997); Member, Scottish Consultative Council on the Curriculum, since 1991; b. 4.12.42, Inverurie; 1 s.; 1 d. Educ. Aberdeen Academy; Aberdeen University. Assistant Experimental Officer, Torry Research Station, Aberdeen, 1959-65; Research Officer, Dundee University, 1979-80; Researcher in Education, Northern College, 1976-99. Member: Joint Working Party, Standard Grade Health Studies, 1983-85, Joint Working Party, Standard Grade Science, 1985-87, Committee on Assessment, 5–14, 1989-92, Scottish Council for Research in Education, 1992-98, SOED Task Group on Curriculum and Assessment Higher Still Development Programme, 1994-97, Steering Committee for SOED 5–14 Evaluation Project, 1991-97, Practitioner Award Sub-committee, Scottish Council for Research in Education, 1995-98; External Examiner, St. Andrew's College, Glasgow, 1993-97; Director and Chairman, Cornerstone Community Care Ltd., since 1979; Member, Sitters Service for the Handicapped, since 1975; Director, Partnership Housing, 1988-95; Member, Langstane Housing Association, since 1984. Recreations: gardening; travelling; reading; learning how to be a grandmother. Address: (h.) 223 Clifton Road, Aberdeen, AB24 4ET; T.-01224 492734.

Simpson, Michael John Russell, BA, LLB. Head of Litigation Department, Tods Murray WS, Edinburgh (Partner, since 1970); b. 30.10.41; m., Syä; 2 s.; 1 d. Educ. Rugby School; Oxford University; Edinburgh University. Articled, Messrs Lindsays WS, Edinburgh, 1967. Member, Joint Committee of Legal Societies of Edinburgh and the Lothians; Treasurer, Society of Writers to Her Majesty's Signet. Recreations: reading; shooting; golf (The Honourable Company of Edinburgh Golfers). Address: (b.) 66 Queen Street, Edinburgh EH2 4NE; T.-0131-226 4771.

Simpson, Myrtle Lillias, DL. Author and Lecturer; former Member, Scottish Sports Council; Past Chairman, Scottish National Ski Council; b. 5.7.31, Aldershot; m., Professor Hugh Simpson (qv); 3 s.; 1 d. Educ. 19 schools (father in Army). Writer/Explorer; author of 12 books, including travel, biography, historical and children's; first woman to ski across Greenland; attempted to ski to North Pole (most northerly point reached by a woman unsupported); numerous journeys in polar regions on ski or canoe; exploration in China and Peru; Mungo Park and Pery Medal; former Editor, Avenue (University of Glasgow magazine). Recreations: climbing; skiing; canoeing. Address: (h.) 7 Cleveden Crescent, Glasgow, G12 0PD; T.-0141-357 1091.

Sinclair, Alan, MA, MBA, FRSA. Chief Executive, The Wise Group, since 1987; b. 18.9.54, Bellshill; m., Michele Veldman. Educ. Our Lady's High School, Motherwell; St. Andrews University; Edinburgh University. Member, UK Advisory Group on the New Deal; Member, Scottish Task Force on the New Deal; Director, Glasgow Development Agency; Trustee, Employment Policy Institute; Director, The Main Tool Company; Member, Joseph Rowntree Foundation Steering Groups. Recreation: the great outdoor world. Address: (b.) 72 Charlotte Street, Glasgow G1 5DW; T.-0141-303 3131.

Sinclair, Alexander, OBE, DL, FCII. President, The Golf Foundation, 1991-96; b. 6.7.20, West Kilbride; m., Elizabeth Tennant; 2 s.; 1 d. Educ. Ardrossan Academy. Clerk, Norwich Union, 1938-40; Royal Artillery, 1940-46; joined Alexander Stenhouse Insurance Brokers, 1957 (Director, 1962); Chairman, British Insurance Brokers Association in Scotland, 1985; retired, 1985. Deputy Lieutenant, Lanarkshire, 1988; Captain, Royal & Ancient Golf Club, 1988-89; Chairman, R. & A. Selection Committee, 1969-75; President, European Golf Association, 1981-83; President, Scottish Golf Union, 1976-77; former Scottish golf internationalist and Scottish golf captain; awarded Frank Moran Award, 1979, for contribution to golf; West of Scotland Champion, 1950; semi-finalist, Scottish Amateur Championship, 1947-56; Lanarkshire Champion, three times; Scottish Senior Champion, 1979-84. Recreations: golf; curling; painting. Address: (h.) 17 Blairston Avenue, Bothwell, G71 8RZ; T.-01698 853359.

Sinclair, Lady (Anne Lettice). Vice President, The National Turst for Scotland, since 1996; Chairman, Lothian, Borders, Dumfries and Galloway Region, National Trust for Scotland, since 1995; Director, National Trust for Scotland Trading Company, since 1998; b. 16.10.33, London; m., Lord Sinclair, CVO (qv); 1 s.; 2 d. Recreations: gardening;

gundogs; botany; ornithology. Address: (h.) Knocknalling, St. John's Town of Dalry, by Castle Douglas DG7 3ST; T.-01644 430221.

Sinclair, 17th Lord (Charles Murray Kennedy St. Clair), CVO. Lord Lieutenant, Dumfries and Galloway Region (District of Stewartry), 1982- 89; Extra Equerry to the Queen Mother, since 1953; Member, Queen's Bodyguard for Scotland (Royal Company of Archers); b. 21.6.14; m., Anne Lettice Cotterell; 1 s.; 2 d. Educ. Eton; Magdalene College, Cambridge. Served Second World War (mentioned in Despatches); retired Major, Coldstream Guards. Address: (h.) Knocknalling, St. John's Town of Dalry, Castle Douglas, Kirkcudbrightshire.

Sinclair, Rev. Colin Andrew Macalister, BA (Hons), BD (Hons). Minister, Palmerston Place Church of Scotland, since 1996; b. 16.9.53, Glasgow; m., Ruth Mary Murray; 1 s.; 3 d. Educ. Glasgow Academy; Stirling University; Edinburgh University. Training Officer, Scripture Union, Zambia, 1974-77; Assistant Minister, Palmerston Place Church of Scotland, Edinburgh, 1980-82; Church of Scotland Minister, Newton on Ayr, 1982-88; General Director, Scripture Union Scotland, 1988-96. Vice Chair, Mission Scotland; Chairman, Council of Management, Spring Harvest. Recreations: family; reading; sport. Address: (b.) Annan House, 10 Palmerston Place, Edinburgh EH12 5AA.

Sinclair, Derek Urquhart, MA (Hons), MB, ChB, MRCGP, DPM. Consultant in Learning Disability, Central Scotland Healthcare NHS Trust, since 1992; b. 10.10.40, Falkirk; m., Dorothy Aalbregt; 1 s.; 2 d. Educ. Grangemouth High School; Falkirk High School; Glasgow University. Norwegian State Stipendiary, 1965-66; Principal in general practice, Falkirk, 1972-86; Regional Medical Officer, 1986-87, Medical Officer, 1987-88, Senior Medical Officer, 1988-92, Scottish Office Home and Health Department; Royal Scottish National Hospital and Community NHS Trust, Larbert: Unit Medical Manager, 1992-93, Medical Director, 1993-94; Medical Director, Central Scotland Healthcare NHS Trust, 1994-97. Recreations: gardening; walking; fishing. Address: (b.) Central Scotland Healthcare NHS Trust, Larbert FK5 4SD; T.-01324 570700.

Sinclair, Douglas, MA (Hons). Chief Executive, Convention of Scottish Local Authorities (COSLA), since 1995; b. 28.1.46, Ellon; m., Mairi; 2 d. Educ. Inverness Royal Academy; Edinburgh University. Administrative Assistant, Midlothian CC, 1969-72; Administrative Officer, Barnardo's Scotland, 1972-75; Depute Director of Administration, then Director of Administration, Western Isles Islands Council, 1975-85; Chief Executive, Ross and Cromarty DC, 1985-90; Chief Executive, Central Regional Council, 1990-95. Recreations: gardening; Scottish literature; walking. Address: (h.) 1 Queens Road, Stirling, FK8 2QY.

Sinclair, Eric T.A., MA, DipEd. Rector, Kirkwall Grammar School, since 1991; b. 20.9.48, Edinburgh; m., Johanna Beckley; 3 c. Educ. Bell Baxter High School, Cupar; St. Andrews University; Edinburgh University; Moray House College. Taught, Teacher Training Colleges, Cameroon, Nigeria; Head of English, English High School, Istanbul; Head of English, St Joseph's College, Dumfries; Assistant Rector, Forres Academy; Depute Rector, Bridge of Don Academy. Recreations: orienteering; squash; chess; gardening; reading. Address: (h.) Inganess Cottage, St. Ola, Kirkwall, Orkney; T.-01856 874289.

Sinclair, Isabel Lillias, MA, BL, QC. Honorary Sheriff of Lothian and Borders, since 1979; b. Glasgow; m., J. Gordon MacDonald, BL. Educ. Shawlands Academy; Glasgow University. Newspaperwoman, 1933-46; Scottish Editor, BBC Woman's Hour, 1948; called to Scottish Bar, 1949; appointed Queen's Counsel, 1964; Sheriff Substitute, Lanarkshire at Airdrie, 1966-68; Sheriff of Lothian and Borders at Selkirk and Peebles, then Peebles and Edinburgh, 1968-79. Address: 30 Ravelston Garden, Edinburgh, EH4 3LE; T.-0131-337 9797.

Sinclair, Professor John Henderson, BA, LLB. Professor of Conveyancing, Strathclyde University, since 1991; b. 5.11.35, Glasgow; m., Sandra Gunn Fraser; 1 s.; 1 d. Educ. Strathallan; Queen's University of Belfast; Glasgow University. Admitted Solicitor in Scotland, 1962; Lecturer in Conveyancing, Strathclyde University, 1970; Clerk, Royal Faculty of Procurators in Glasgow, 1983-93. Publications: Handbook of Conveyancing in Scotland; Contributor to Stair Memorial Encyclopaedia. Recreation: walking. Address: (b.) 173 Cathedral Street, Glasgow G4; T.-0141-552 4400.

Sinclair, Martin Fraser, MA, CA. Partner, Chiene & Tait, CA, since 1973; Director, Albyn Trust Ltd., since 1973; Director, NESSCO Ltd., since 1982; b. 18.7.45, Greenock; m., Patricia Anne Ogilvy Smith; 1 s.; 2 d. Educ. Edinburgh Academy; Edinburgh University. Apprentice, Chiene & Tait, CA; qualified, 1970; Peat Marwick Mitchell & Co., Vancouver, 1970-73. President, Institute of Chartered Accountants Benevolent Association, 1983-84. Athletics Blue, Edinburgh University; Captain, Scottish Universities Athletics Team, 1969. Recreations: skiing; squash; orienteering. Address: (b.) 61 Dublin Street, Edinburgh EH3 6NL; T.-0131-558 5800.

Sinclair, Professor Roy Stuart, BSc, MSc, PhD, FSDC, FRSC, CCol, CChem. Personal Professor, Chemistry and Chemical Engineering, 1991-97, Hon. Fellow, Paisley University, since 1998; Assistant Chief Commissioner (Scotland West), Scout Association, 1990-97; b. 21.4.33, Glasgow; m., Ellen Catherine Murray; 2 s. Educ. Allan Glen's School, Glasgow; London University (External); Paisley University; Strathclyde University. Research Assistant, J. & P. Coats, Paisley, 1950-56; Lecturer in Chemistry, Paisley College, 1956-80, Senior Lecturer, 1980-91. President, Paisley Philosophical Institution. Recreations: Scouting; hill-walking; occasional golf. Address: (h.) 1 Hunterhill Avenue, Paisley PA2 6SP; T.-0141-887 5488.

Sischy, Judith, BA, MA. Director, Scottish Council of Independent Schools, since 1990; b. 20.12.47, Halifax; m., Mark Sischy. Educ. Newcastle upon Tyne Church High School; Bristol University; University of Toronto. Previously: Teacher of Modern Languages, Assistant and Deputy Secretary, Edinburgh Merchant Company. Director, Edinburgh Chamber of Commerce and Edinburgh Common Purpose; FRSA. Recreations: walking; swimming; cinema; music. Address: (b.) 21 Melville Street, Edinburgh EH3 7PE; T.-0131-220 2106.

Sizer, Professor John, CBE, DLitt, BA, FCMA, FIM, FRSA. Chief Executive, Scottish Higher Education Funding Council, since 1992; b. 14.9.38, Grimsby; m., Valerie Claire; 3 s. Educ. Grimsby Technical Secondary School; Nottingham and Loughborough Universities. Financial Advisor, GKN PLC; Lecturer, Edinburgh University; Senior Lecturer, London Business School; Professor and Director, Business School, Loughborough University; Member, University Grants Committee. Leverhulme Prize, Chartered Institute of Management Accountants. Publications: An Insight Into Management Accounting; other books and papers. Recreations: walking; enjoying Scotland. Address: (b.) Donaldson House, 97 Haymarket Terrace, Edinburgh, EH12 5HD; T.-0131-313 6502.

Skene, Charles Pirie, OBE, FBIPP, ARPS, FRSA. Chairman, Skene Group of companies, developers and owners of first continuing care retirement community in Scotland; Visiting Professor of Entrepreneurship, Robert

Gordon University; Member, Task Force to investigate under-achievement in schools, 1996-97; Chairman, CBI (Scotland) Enterprise Group, since 1994; b. 30.4.35, Aberdeen; m., Alison; 1 s.; 2 d. Educ. Loretto. Past President of numerous organisations, including Aberdeen Chamber of Commerce and Association of Scottish Chambers of Commerce; Past Chairman, CBI Education and Training Committee; initiated Skene Young Entrepreneur's Award, Grampian, 1986; Member, Board, Young Enterprise; Trustee: Photographic Arts and Science Foundation, Oklahoma City, Haddo Arts Trust, Gordon Cook Foundation. Address: (b.) 23 Rubislaw Den North, Aberdeen, AB15 4AL; T.-01224 326221.

Skinner, Professor Andrew, MA, BLitt, FRSE, FBA. Adam Smith Professor of Political Economy, 1994-97, Emeritus, since 1997, Glasgow University; b. 11.1.35, Glasgow; m., Margaret Mary Robertson. Educ. Keil School, Dumbarton; Glasgow University; Cornell University, New York. Address: (h.) Glen House, Cardross, G82 5ES; T.-0138 9841 603.

Skinner, Angus, MBA, BSc, CQSW. Chief Inspector of Social Work Services, Scotland, since 1991; b. 9.1.50, Pakistan; 1 s.; 2 d. Educ. Daniel Stewart's, Edinburgh; Edinburgh University; London University; Strathclyde University. Cheshire County Council, 1971-72; Kent County Council, 1973-75; Lothian Region Social Work Department, 1976-88; Borders Region Social Work Department, 1988-91. Address: (b.) Scottish Office Home Department, Social Work Services Inspectorate, James Craig Walk, Edinburgh EH1 3BA.

Skinner, Robert Gordon, LLB (Hons). Advocate, since 1987; part-time Chairman, Social Security Appeals Tribunal, since 1988; part-time Chairman, Disability Appeals Tribunal, since 1991; b. 14.6.57, Glasgow; m., Eileen Mary Judith Paterson; 2 s. Educ. Bishopbriggs High School; Glasgow University. Law Apprentice, Hughes, Dowdall & Co., Solicitors, Glasgow; Solicitor, Dorman Jeffrey & Co., Solicitors, Glasgow, 1980-86; called to the Bar, 1987. Recreations: football; swimming; golf; opera. Address: (h.) Whitehall, Springkell Avenue, Pollokshields, Glasgow.

Skorupski, Professor John Maria, MA, PhD. Professor of Moral Philosophy, St. Andrews University, since 1990; b. 19.9.46, Italy; m., Barbara Mary; 2 d. Educ. St. Benedict's, Ealing; Christ's College, Cambridge. Visiting Lectureships, Nigeria and Belgium, 1971-74; University of Wales Research Fellow, University College of Swansea, 1974-76; Lecturer in Philosophy, Glasgow University, 1976-84; Professor of Philosophy, Sheffield University, 1984-90. Fellow, Royal Society of Edinburgh. Publications: Symbol and Theory, 1976; John Stuart Mill, 1989; English Language Philosophy 1750-1945, 1993. Recreations: music; walking; skiing. Address: (h.) Cedar Lodge, Hepburn Gardens, St. Andrews, KY16 9LP; T.-01334 477590.

Slack, Rev. William G., DipTh. General Secretary, Baptist Union of Scotland, since 1995; b. 29.4.49, Edinburgh; m., Vivienne; 1 d. Educ. Trinity Academy, Edinburgh; Hamilton Academy; Baptist Theological College of Scotland. Minister, Ladywell, Livingston, 1974-82; Minister, International Baptist Church, Aberdeen, 1982-95. Recreations: philately; swimming; music. Address: (b.) 14 Aytoun Road, Glasgow, G41 5RT.

Slater, Professor Peter James Bramwell, BSc, PhD, DSc, FIBiol, FRSE. Kennedy Professor of Natural History, St. Andrews University, since 1984, Head, School of Biological and Medical Sciences, 1992-97; Dean, Faculty of Science, since 1998; b. 26.12.42, Edinburgh; m., Elisabeth Vernon Smith; 2 s. Educ. Edinburgh Academy; Glenalmond; Edinburgh University. Demonstrator in Zoology, Edinburgh University, 1966-68; Lecturer in Biology, Sussex University, 1968-84. Secretary, Association for the Study of Animal Behaviour, 1973-78, President, 1986-89; European Editor, Animal Behaviour, 1979-82; Editor, Advances in the Study of Behavior. Recreations: walking; ornithology; music. Address: (b.) School of Environmental and Evolutionary Biology, St. Andrews, Fife; T.-01334 463500.

Slater, Stephen Oakley, BA (Hons). Senior Producer, Tramway, Glasgow City Council, since 1995; b. 13.2.62, Wirksworth, Derbyshire; m., Charlotte Mary Oakley; 1 d. Educ. Anthony Gell Secondary School, Wirksworth; Howard Gardens College of Art, Cardiff. Performance Artist, Stanslat Performance Company, 1985-89; Co-Founder, Situation Cinema, multi media group, Brighton, 1985-88; Art Reach Co-ordinator, Third Eye Centre, Glasgow, 1988-91; Administrator, Paisley Arts Centre, 1992-95. Recreations: painting; hill-walking; cycling; astronomy; science fiction. Address: (h.) 12 Kensington Gate, Dowanhill, Glasgow G12 9LG; T.-0141-357 4363.

Slavin, Rev. William J., MA, STL, CPsychol. Chaplain, Royal Hospital for Sick Children, Glasgow; b. 17.1.40, Bristol. Educ. Blairs College, Aberdeen; Scots College, Rome; Glasgow University. Assistant Priest, Broomhill, Glasgow, 1965-70; Educational Psychologist, Glasgow Child Guidance Service, 1970-75; Deputy Director, Jessore Training Centre, Bangladesh, 1975-80; Secretary, RC Justice and Peace Commission, 1980-85; Co-ordinator, Scottish Drugs Forum, 1986-92; Parish Priest, St. Alphonsus, The Barras, Glasgow, 1992-97. Recreation: An rud Gaidhealach. Address: (h.) 1 Kelvinside Gardens, Glasgow G20 6BG; T.-0141-946 7622.

Sleeman, Professor Derek Henry, BSc, PhD, FBCS, FRSE. Professor of Computing Science, Aberdeen University, since 1986; b. 11.1.41, Penzance; m., Margaret G. Rankine; 1 d. Educ. Penzance Grammar School; King's College, London. Leeds University: Computing Assistant, 1965-67, Lecturer in Computational Science, 1967-82, Associate Director, Computer Based Learning Project, 1969-82; Visiting Scientist: Rutgers University, 1979, Carnegie-Mellon University, 1980-81; Senior Consultant, Teknowledge, Palo Alto, CA, 1983-86; Senior Research Associate/Associate Professor, Stanford University, 1982-86. Secretary, SS AISB, 1979-82; Academic Co-ordinator, European Network of Excellence in Machine Learning, 1992-95. Publications: 100 technical papers. Recreations: hill and coastal path walking; medieval architecture; photography. Address: (b.) Computing Science Department, King's College, Aberdeen University, Aberdeen, AB9 2FX; T.-01224 272288/96.

Sleigh, Daphne Mary Walker. Leader, Conservative Group, City of Edinburgh Council, since 1995; Board Member, Scottish Homes, since 1990; Conservative Party Scottish Spokesman for Local Government, since 1997; b. 26.12.37, Lahore; m., J. Lindsay Walls; 2 s.; 1 d. Educ. Craigmount School for Girls, Hawick. Elected to Edinburgh District Council, 1982; elected to City of Edinburgh Council, 1995. Member, Board, Salvation Army, since 1996. Recreations: travel; walking. Address: (b.) City Chambers, High Street, Edinburgh EH1 1YJ; T.-0131-529 4282.

Sloan, Professor David McPheator, BSc, MSc, PhD, DSc, FRSE. Professor of Mathematics, Strathclyde University; b. 24.12.38, Cronberry; m., Margaret Templeton Kirk; 3 s.; 1 d. Educ. Cumnock Academy; Glasgow University; Keele University; Strathclyde University. Mathematician, English Electric Co., Stafford, 1962-64; Lecturer, Stafford Polytechnic, 1964-65; Lecturer, Senior Lecturer, Reader, Professor, Strathclyde University, from 1965. Recreations: hill-walking; folk music; reading. Address: (b.) Department of Mathematics, Strathclyde University, Glasgow; T.-0141-548 3819.

Sloan, Rev. Robert P., MA, BD. Minister, Braemar linked with Crathie, since 1996; Domestic Chaplain, Balmoral. Ordained, 1968. Address: Crathie, Ballater AB35 5UL.

Sloane, Professor Peter James, BA (Econ), PhD, FRSA, FRSE. Professor of Political Economy, Aberdeen University, since 1984; Vice Principal and Dean, Faculty of Social Sciences and Law, since 1996; b. 6.8.42, Cheadle Hulme; m., Avril Mary Urquhart; 1 s. Educ. Cheadle Hulme School; Sheffield University; Strathclyde University. Assistant Lecturer and Lecturer, Department of Political Economy, Aberdeen University, 1966-69; Lecturer in Industrial Economics, Nottingham University, 1969-75; Economic Adviser, Department of Employment Unit for Manpower Studies (on secondment), 1973-74; Professor of Economics and Management, Paisley College, 1975-84. Member, Economic and Social Research Council, 1979-85; Council Member, Scottish Economic Society, since 1983. Publications: Sex Discrimination in the Labour Market, 1976; Women and Low Pay, 1980; Sport in the Market?, 1980; Equal Employment Issues, 1981; Tackling Discrimination in the Workplace, 1982; Labour Economics, 1985; Low Pay and Earnings Mobility in Europe, 1998. Recreation: sport. Address: (b.) Department of Economics, Aberdeen University, Edward Wright Building, Dunbar Street, Old Aberdeen, Aberdeen, AB24 3QY.

Slowey, Professor Maria, BComm, DipSocSci, M.Litt. Professor and Director, Department of Adult and Continuing Education, University of Glasgow, since 1992; b. 14.10.52, Dublin. Educ. Dominican Convent, Cabra; University College, Dublin; Trinity College, Dublin. Research Fellow, National Association of Adult Education of Ireland, 1976-79; Research Officer, DES National Survey of Adult Learners, 1980-82; Head, Adult Education Centre, LB of Waltham Forest, 1982-83; Lecturer in Adult Education, St Patrick's College, Maynooth, 1983-84; Senior Lecturer in Recurrent Education, subsequently Head, Centre for Continuing Education and External Relations, University of Northumbria, 1985-92. Consultant to international bodies, including OECD, Council of Europe, EC; Visiting Fellow, Centre for Policy Studies in H.E., University of California, Berkeley, also Centre for Policy Studies, University of British Columbia, Vancouver; Honorary Specialist Adviser on Continuing Education to the Committee of Scottish Higher Education Principals. Current and recent committee memberships include: Executive, Universities Association of Continuing Education; Women Returner's Network; Board of Management, Scottish Centre for Community Development; Committee on Community Education Validation and Endorsement, Scottish Community Education Council; Higher Education Policy Group, National Institute of Adult and Continuing Education; Quality Assurance Consultative Group, Higher Education Quality Council; Advisory Group on the Funding of Continuing Education, Scottish Higher Education Funding Council; Chair, Society for Research into Higher Education Continuing Education Research Group. Publications: three co-authored books and numerous official reports, papers and articles on widening access and participation in continuing and higher education. Address: (b.) Department of Adult and Continuing Education, University of Glasgow, 59 Oakfield Avenue, Glasgow, G12 8LW; T.– 0141-330 4392.

Smail, Peter James, MA, BM, BCh, FRCP, DCH. Consultant Paediatrician and Clinical Director of Child Health, Aberdeen Royal Hospitals Trust, since 1992; Honorary Senior Lecturer in Child Health, Aberdeen University, since 1980; b. 10.10.43, Harrow; m., Janice Lockhart; 3 s.; 1 d. Educ. Merchant Taylors', Northwood; St. John's College, Oxford; Oxford Clinical Medical School. Paediatric House Officer, Inverness Hospitals, 1970; Medical Registrar, Royal Cornwall Hospital (Treliske), 1972; Lecturer in Child Health, Dundee University, 1975; Fellow in Paediatric Endocrinology, University of Manitoba, Winnipeg, 1979. Member, Health Services Human Growth Hormone Committee, 1982-87; Secretary, Scottish Study Group for the Care of Young Diabetics, 1984-89. Recreations: Member, Aberdeen Bach Choir; Lay Clerk, St. Andrew's Cathedral, Aberdeen. Address: (b.) Royal Aberdeen Children's Hospital, Aberdeen, AB25 2ZG; T.-0224 681818, Ext. 53037.

Small, Christopher. Writer; b. 15.11.19, London; 3 d. Educ. Dartington Hall; Pembroke College, Oxford. Journalist and miscellaneous writer; Literary Editor and Dramatic Critic, Glasgow Herald, 1955-80. Publications:Ariel Like A Harpy: Shelley, Mary & Frankenstein; The Road to Miniluv: George Orwell, the State & God; The Printed Word. Recreation: gardening. Address: (h.) 26 Bell Place, Edinburgh, EH3 5HT; T.-0131-332 6591.

Small, Professor John Rankin, CBE, DLitt, BSc (Econ), FCCA, FCMA. Professor, Department of Accountancy and Finance, Heriot-Watt University, since 1967; Chairman, Commission for Local Authority Accounts in Scotland, 1983-92; b. 28.2.33, Dundee; m., Catherine Wood; 1 s.; 2 d. Educ. Harris Academy; Dundee School of Economics. Industry and commerce; Lecturer, Edinburgh University; Senior Lecturer, Glasgow University. Director of and Consultant to various organisations; President, Association of Chartered Certified Accountants, 1982-83; Vice-Principal, Heriot-Watt University, 1974-78, 1987-90, Deputy Principal, 1990-94; Chairman, National Appeal Panel for Entry to Pharmaceutical Lists (Scotland), 1987-95; Board Member, Scottish Homes, since 1993. Recreation: golf. Address: (b.) Heriot-Watt University, Riccarton, Edinburgh; T.-0131-451 3362.

Small, Stephen J., CQSW. Director, St Andrew's Children's Society Ltd., since 1996; b. 3.11.61, Edinburgh; m., Kay L. Anderson; 1 s.; 1 d. Educ. Holyrood RC High School, Edinburgh; Moray House College of Education. Social Worker, Humberside County Council, 1986-88; Social Worker, Lothian Regional Council (Midlothian District), 1988-95; Senior Social Worker, St Andrew's Children's Society Ltd., 1995-96. Recreations: most leisure time taken up parenting two small children, but occasionally have a game of tennis. Address: (b.) Gillis Centre, 113 Whitehouse Loan, Edinburgh EH9 1BB; T.-0131-452 8248.

Smart, John Dalziel Beveridge, DL. Chairman, British Polyolefin Textiles Association, 1986-97; b. 12.8.32, Edinburgh; m., Valerie Blaber; 2 s. Educ. Harrow; Administrative Staff College. 2nd Lt., Black Watch (RHR), Korea, 1952; J. & J. Smart (Brechin) Ltd., 1953 (Director, 1954); Director, Don Brothers, Buist & Co. Ltd., 1964 (Managing Director, 1985; retired, 1987). DL, Kincardineshire; Member, Queen's Bodyguard for Scotland, Royal Company of Archers; Dean, Guildry of Brechin, 1991-93; Chairman, Scottish American Community Relations Council, 1990-93. Recreations: shooting; skiing. Address: (h.) Woodmyre, Edzell, Angus, DD9 7UX; T.-01356 648416.

Smethurst, Professor Colin, BA, BLitt, MA, Officier Palmes Academiques. Marshall Professor of French, Glasgow University, since 1980; b. 3.8.37, Bedford; m., Claudine Rozenberg; 2 d. Educ. Slough Grammar School; Keble College, Oxford. Assistant Lecturer, Lecturer, Senior Lecturer in French, Liverpool University, 1962-80. President, Institut Francais D'Ecosse, 1989-96; Secretary, Association of University Professors of French, 1983-87. Publications: Zola: Germinal; Chateaubriand: Atala, René; editions of Balzac novels. Address: (b.) Department of French, Glasgow University, Glasgow G12 8QL; T.-0141-339 8855.

Smillie, Anne. Chief Executive, Scottish Badminton Union, since 1989; b. 17.8.56, Glasgow. Educ. Victoria Drive Secondary School; Anniesland College. Joined Scottish Badminton Union, 1980; Director of major badminton events, including 1992 European Championships, 1994 World Team Championships, 1997 World Team and Individual Championships. Recreations: music; reading. Address: (h.) 55 Westerton Avenue, Westerton, Glasgow; T.-0141-942 9804.

Smillie, Carol. Television Presenter. Credits include: Wheel of Fortune; The Travel Show; Good Morning with Anne and Nick; Holiday; The National Lottery Live; The Big Breakfast; Hearts of Gold; Get It On; Smillie's People; Changing Rooms; Midweek National Lottery Live; Holiday Memories; Holiday Heaven.

Smith of Gilmorehill, Baroness, MA. Peeress, House of Lords, since 1995; Deputy Lieutenant, City of Edinburgh; Non-Executive Director, Morgan Grenfell (Scotland) Ltd.; Chairman, Edinburgh Festival Fringe Society, since 1995; Council Member, Edinburgh International Festival; Member, Press Complaints Commission; Member, BP Scottish Advisory Board; Council Member, British Heart Foundation; Council Member, Russo-British Chamber of Commerce; Trustee, Centre for European Reform; Trustee, Scottish Television Pension Fund; Governor, English Speaking Union; b. 4.6.40, Ayr; m., Rt. Hon. John Smith, MP (deceased); 3 d. Educ. Hutchesons Girls Grammar School; Glasgow University. Recreations: family; garden; the arts. Address: (b.) House of Lords, London, SW1A 0PN.

Smith, Professor Adam Neil, MD, DSc, FRCSE, FRCPE, FIBiol, FRSE. Formerly Wade Professor of Surgical Studies, RCSEd; formerly Consultant Surgeon, Gastro-Intestinal Unit, Edinburgh (retired); b. 27.6.26, Hamilton; m., Sibyl Mary Veitch Johnstone; 1 s.; 3 d. Educ. Lanark Grammar School; Glasgow University. Academic and Health Service appointments, since 1948; Lecturer in Surgery, Glasgow University; Medical Research Council Fellow; Reader, Edinburgh University and Western General Hospital. Vice-President and Council Member, Royal College of Surgeons of Edinburgh; awarded Medal of RCSEd, 1997; Council Member, Association of Coloproctology; Past President, British Group for Research into Pelvic Function and Disease; President, Scottish Society of Coloproctology; former Surgical Traveller, James IV Surgical Association; Commonwealth Fund Travelling Fellow in Medical Education; Trustee, Melville Trust for Care and Cure of Cancer; Trustee, Soutra Achaeo-Medicine. Recreation: golf. Address: (h.) 2 Ravelston House Park, Edinburgh, EH4 3LU; T.-0131-332 4077.

Smith, Agnes Houston, BL. Honorary Sheriff, Dundee, since 1990; Non-Executive Director, Dundee Healthcare NHS Trust, since 1993; b. 27.9.33, Prestwick; m., David Robert Smith; 3 d. Educ. Hutchesons' Girls Grammar School, Glasgow; Glasgow University. Solicitor in Paisley, Edinburgh and Dundee, 1955-92. President, Dundee Society of Glasgow University Graduates. Recreations: golf; gardening; grannying. Address: (h.) Windyridge, Kellas, by Broughty Ferry DD5 3PD; T.-01382 350475.

Smith, Sir Alan, Kt (1982), CBE (1976), DFC (1941) and Bar (1942), DL, JP. President, Dawson International plc, Kinross, since 1982; Chairman, Quayle Munro PLC, Edinburgh, 1982-93; b. 14.3.17, South Shields; m., 1, Margaret Stewart Todd (deceased); 2, Alice Elizabeth Moncur; 3 s.; 2 d. Educ. Bede College, Sunderland. Self-employed, 1931-36; Unilever, 1936-39; RAF, 1939-45; Managing Director, Todd & Duncan Ltd., Kinross, 1946-60; Chairman and Chief Executive, Dawson International, Kinross, 1960-82. Board Member, Scottish Development Agency, 1982-87; Kinross Burgh Councillor, 1952-65; Provost of Kinross, 1959-65; Tayside Regional Councillor, 1979-90; Financial Convenor, Tayside Region, 1980-86. Recreations: work; sailing. Address: (h.) Ardgairney House, Cleish, by Kinross; T.-01577 850265.

Smith, Professor Alan Gordon Rae, MA, PhD, FRAS, FRHistS, FRSE. Professor of Early Modern History, Glasgow University, since 1995; b. 22.12.36, Glasgow; m., Isabel Robertson; 1 s.; 1 d. Educ. Glasgow High School; Glasgow University; University College, London. Research Fellow, Institute of Historical Research, London University, 1961 62; Assistant in History, 1962-64, then Lecturer, Glasgow University, 1964-75; Senior Lecturer in Modern History, 1975-85; Reader, 1985-92, Professor in Modern History, 1992-95; Review Editor, History (Journal of the Historical Association), 1984-87; Member, Council, Royal Historical Society, 1990-94; Member, Governing Board, Institute of Historical Research, London University, since 1994. Publications: The Government of Elizabethan England, 1967; The New Europe, 1969; Science and Society in the Sixteenth and Seventeenth Centuries, 1972; Servant of the Cecils: The Life of Sir Michael Hickes, 1977; The Emergence of a Nation State: The Commonwealth of England 1529-1660, 1984; The Anonymous Life of William Cecil, Lord Burghley, 1990; The Last Years of Mary Queen of Scots, 1990; Tudor Government, 1990; William Cecil, Lord Burghley, Minister of Queen Elizabeth I, 1991. Recreation: watching sport. Address: (h.) 5 Cargil Avenue, Kilmacolm, Renfrewshire; T.-Kilmacolm 3517.

Smith, Alex. Member, European Parliament for South of Scotland, since 1989; b. 2.12.43, Kilwinning; 1 s.; 1 d. Educ. (b.) Damside, Ayr, KA8 8ER; T.-01292 280096.

Smith, Allan Keppie. CBE, DUniv, BSc, FEng, FIMechE, FWeldI. Chairman, Railcare Ltd., since 1995; Managing Director, Facilities Management Division, Babcock International Group PLC, Rosyth Royal Dockyard, until 1997; b. 18.5.32. Joined Army for National Service, 1953; commissioned, REME, 1954; Babcock & Wilcox: joined as Graduate Trainee, 1955; appointed: Industrial Engineering Manager, Renfrew Works, 1965, Production Director, Renfrew Works, 1974, Managing Director, Renfrew and Dumbarton Works, 1976; Managing Director, Babcock Thorn Limited and Chairman, Rosyth Royal Dockyard plc, 1986; Director, Babcock International Group PLC, 1989. Past President, Scottish Engineering; Past Chairman, Council of the Welding Institute; Honorary Doctor, University of Paisley; awarded Institute of Marketing Scottish Marketer of the Year, 1992. Address: (h.) The Forts, Hawes Brae, South Queensferry EH30 9TE; T.-0131-319 1668.

Smith, Bruce Livingstone, BSc, CEng, FIMarE, MRINA, FCMS, ACIArb. Hon. Secretary, Scottish Branch, Chartered Institute of Arbiters, since 1997; Chairman, Yacht Brokers, Designers, Surveyors Association, since 1977; b. 29.8.45, Glasgow; m., Jacqueline McLean; 1 s.; 1 d. Educ. Bearsden Academy; Glasgow University. After honours degree, served apprenticeship as fitter in various Clyde yards and abroad; joined John Brown Engineering as Test Engineer on gas turbines; employed in, and bought, E.K. Wallace and Son Ltd., Marine Consultants (Chairman/Managing Director); Principal Partner, Bruce L. Smith & Associates, since 1992; Past Chairman, Scottish Branch, Chartered Institute of Arbiters. Recreations: sailing; shooting; fishing. Address: (b.) Whittinghame House, 1099 Great Western Road, Glasgow G12 0AA; T.-0141-334 7222.

Smith, Caroline Anne Scott, MB, ChB, LLB, DipLP. Partner, Loudons WS, since 1994; b. 23.6.55, Edinburgh; m., James B. Smith; 1 s.; 1 d. Educ. St Denis School, Edinburgh; Edinburgh University. Hospital doctor, 1979-82; Assistant, Warner & Co., Edinburgh, 1986-88, Morton, Fraser, Milligan, Edinburgh, 1988-93; Associate, Loudons,

Edinburgh, 1993-94. Recreations: horse-riding; reading. Address: 29 St Patrick Square, Edinburgh; T.-0131-662 4193.

Smith, C. Christopher, MB, FRCP, FRCPE. Consultant Physician, Aberdeen Royal Infirmary NHS Trust, since 1973; Honorary Senior Lecturer in Medicine, University of Aberdeen (Elected Member, Senatus Academicus, 1988-92); President, Aberdeen Medical-Chirurgical Society, 1998-99; b. 16.5.39, West Indies; m., Sheila Anne Calder, MRCPsych; 2 s., 1 d. by pr. m. Educ. Lodge School, Barbados; Edinburgh University. Registrar, Department of Medicine, Edinburgh Royal Infirmary; Registrar, Thoracic Medicine, then Senior Registrar, Infectious Diseases, City Hospital, Edinburgh; Senior Registrar, Department of Therapeutics and Clinical Pharmacology, Edinburgh Royal Infirmary. Elected Member, Council, Royal College of Physicians of Edinburgh, 1991-94; Member, Fellowship Committee, 1991-94 and Committees on Examinations and Education/Training, 1992-98; External Examiner, Final MB, University of Dundee, 1992-95; former Member, Part I MRCP Examination Board; Examiner, MRCP, since 1977; External, MRCP, in Hong Kong, Malaysia and Ireland; External Examiner, M.Med., Malaysia, 1996; Member, United Examination Board (UEB) and Member, Examination Committee; Chairman, Written Paper Panel, UEB, 1992-97; Chairman, Specialty Advisory Committee (JCHMT) on Infection and Tropical Medicine, 1991-95 and Member, JCHMT; Chairman, Scottish National Advisory Committee on Hospital Infection, 1996-98; Visitor for JCHMT Accreditation in Internal Medicine, Infection/Tropical Medicine; Regional Adviser, RCPs and Member, Aberdeen and NE Scotland Postgraduate Medical Education Committee; author of papers, chapters and leading articles on topics in medicine, infection, post-infective phenomena, and antimicrobial chemotherapy; Invited Lecturer, Hong Kong, Singapore, Malaysia, Kenya, Zimbabwe, Saudi Arabia, Iceland, South Africa, Holland and Ireland, as well as British universities and societies, since 1980. Recreations: watching cricket; golf; live theatre; jazz music. Address: (b.) Infection Unit, Aberdeen Royal Infirmary, Foresterhill, Aberdeen, AB25 2ZN; T.-Aberdeen 681818.

Smith, David Bruce Boyter, OBE, MA, LLB, FRSA, FInstD, NP. Director and Chief Executive, Dunfermline Building Society, since 1987; b. 11.3.42, St. Andrews; m., Christine Anne; 1 s.; 1 d. Educ. High School, Dunfermline; Edinburgh University. Legal training, Balfour & Manson, Edinburgh; admitted Solicitor, 1968; Solicitor, Standard Life Assurance Co., 1969-73; Dunfermline Building Society: Secretary, 1974-81, General Manager (Admin.), 1981-86, Deputy Chief Executive, 1986. Deputy Chairman, Building Societies Association; Chairman, Northern Association of Building Societies; Member, Council, NHBC (Scotland); Member, Scottish Conveyancing and Executry Services Board; Chairman, Institute of Directors, Scottish Division, 1994-97; Director, Fife Enterprise Ltd.; Director, Scottish Fisheries Museum; Member, Building Societies Investor Protection Board; Vice Chairman of Court and Finance Convener, Edinburgh University; Director, Scottish Opera; Life Trustee, Carnegie Trust. Recreations: golf; sailing; the arts. Address: (b.) Caledonia House, Carnegie Avenue, Dunfermline, Fife; T.-01383 627727.

Smith, Sheriff David Buchanan, MA, LLB, FSAScot. Sheriff of North Strathclyde at Kilmarnock, since 1975; b. 31.10.36, Paisley; m., Hazel Mary Sinclair; 1 s.; 1 d. Educ. Paisley Grammar School; Glasgow University; Edinburgh University. Advocate, 1961; Standing Junior Counsel to Scottish Education Department, 1968-75; Tutor, Faculty of Law, Edinburgh University, 1964-72; Trustee, Scottish Curling Museum Trust, since 1980. President, Kilmarnock and District History Group; Trustee Scottish National Dictionary Association, since 1994; President, Ayr Curling Club, 1995-96. Publications: Curling: An Illustrated History, 1981; The Roaring Game: Memories of Scottish Curling, 1985; contributions to The Laws of Scotland: Stair Memorial Encyclopedia, Vol. 6; George Washington Wilson in Ayrshire, 1991. Recreations: Scotland — history and culture; curling; collecting curliana; music; architecture. Address: (b.) Sheriff Court House, Kilmarnock, KA1 1ED; T.-01563 520211.

Smith, Sir David Cecil, Kt, MA, DPhil, FRS, FRSE. Principal and Vice-Chancellor, Edinburgh University, 1987-94; President, Wolfson College, Oxford, since 1994; m., Lesley Margaret Mollison Mutch; 2 s.; 1 d. Educ. St. Paul's School, London; Queen's College, Oxford. Browne Research Fellow, Queen's College, Oxford, 1956-59; Harkness Fellow, University of California, Berkeley, 1959-60; University Lecturer, Department of Agriculture, Oxford University, 1960-74; Fellow and Tutor, Wadham College, Oxford, 1964-74; Melville Wills Professor of Botany, Bristol University, 1974-80; Sibthorpian Professor of Rural Economy, Oxford University, 1980-87. President, British Lichen Society, 1972-74; President, British Mycological Society, 1980; President, Society for Experimental Biology, 1983-85; President, Scottish Association for Marine Science, since 1993. Publication: The Biology of Symbiosis (Co-author), 1987. Address: Wolfson College, Oxford OX2 6UD; T.-01865 274101; The Steading, Balquhidder, Perthshire FK19 8NY; T.-01877 384316.

Smith, Professor David John, MA. Professor of Criminology, Edinburgh University, since 1994; b. 10.7.41, Egypt; m., Colette Marie Obadia; 1 s. Educ. Bootham School, York; Christ Church, Oxford. Trainee Research Executive, 1963-64; Research Officer, 1964-66; Senior Research Officer, then Board Director, Interscan Ltd., 1966-71; Senior Research Associate, Political and Economic Planning, 1972-78; Senior Fellow, Policy Studies Institute, and Head, Social Justice and Social Order Group, 1979-94. Additional Commissioner, Commission for Racial Equality, 1978-84; Specialist Adviser to Home Affairs and Employment Committees, House of Commons, 1981-82, 1986; Visiting Fellow, Lincoln College, Oxford, 1988-89. Recreations: large format photography; piano; squash. Address: (b.) Faculty of Law, Edinburgh University, Old College, South Bridge, Edinburgh, EH8 9YL; T.-0131-650 2027.

Smith, Donald Alexander, MA, PhD. Director, Netherbow Arts Centre, since 1983; Curator, John Knox House, since 1989; Director, Scottish International Storytelling Festival, since 1987; b. 15.2.56, Glasgow; m., Alison; 3 s.; 2 d. Educ. Stirling High School; Edinburgh University. Researcher, School of Scottish Studies, 1979-82; Administrator, Netherbow, 1982-83. Programme Organiser, St. Margaret 900; Chairperson, Scotland 97 (anniversaries of St. Ninian and St. Columba). Publications: The Scottish Stage, 1994; Edinburgh Old Town Pilgrims' Way, 1995; John Knox House: Gateway to Edinburgh's Old Town,1996; Celtic Travellers: Scotland in the Age of the Saints, 1997; History of Scottish Theatre, 1998. Address: (b.) The Netherbow, 43-45 High Street, Edinburgh EH1 1SR; T.-0131-556 2647.

Smith, (Edward) Alistair, CBE, MA, PhD. Director, Aberdeen University International Office, since 1990 (Director, Aberdeen University University Development Trust, 1982-90); Deputy Chairman, Scottish Conservative Party, 1981-86; b. 16.1.39, Aberdeen. Educ. Aberdeen Grammar School; Aberdeen University. Lecturer in Geography, Aberdeen University, 1963-88; President, Scottish Conservative and Unionist Association, 1979-81; Member, Grampian Health Board, 1983-91; Board Member, SCOTVEC, 1989-93; Member, Committee for Scotland, Nature Conservancy Council, 1989-91; Member, N.E. Regional Committee, Nature Conservancy Council, 1991-92. Publications: Europe: A Geographical Survey of the Continent (Co-author), 1979; Scotland's Future

Development (Contributor), 1983. Recreations: travel; photography; music. Address: (h.) 68A Beaconsfield Place, Aberdeen, AB2 4AJ; T.-01224 642932.

Smith, Elaine Constance. Actress; b. 2.8.58, Baillieston; m., Robert Morton; 2 d. Educ. Braidhurst High School, Motherwell; Royal Scottish Academy of Music and Drama; Moray House College of Education. Teacher of Speech and Drama, Firrhill High School, Edinburgh, 1979-82; joined 7:84 Theatre Company, 1982; moved to Wildcat Stage Productions, 1982; since 1986, worked with Borderline Theatre Co., Royal Lyceum, Dundee Rep., Tron Theatre; TV work includes City Lights and Naked Video; plays Mary Nesbitt in Rab C. Nesbitt (BBC2); original cast member, The Steamie. Board Member, Scottish Youth Theatre; Patron, Family Mediation Scotland. Recreations: swimming; aerobics; reading.

Smith, Rev. Graham Walton, BA, BD, FSA Scot. Minister, Livingston Old Parish Church, since 1995; b. 17.9.46, Edinburgh; m., Rosemary Sheila James. Educ. Lenzie Academy; London University; Glasgow University. Bookseller; sales manager; publisher; company director. Recreations: reading; music; railways. Address: The Manse of Livingston, Livingston EH54 7AJ; T.-01506 420227.

Smith, Professor Grahame Francis, MA, PhD. Professor, Department of English Studies, Stirling University, since 1993; b. 30.5.33, London; m., Angela Mary; 2 s.; 1 d. Educ. Woodside Senior Secondary School, Glasgow; Aberdeen University; Cambridge University. Taught at California University, Los Angeles, 1963-65, University College, Swansea, 1965-70; secondment to Malawi University, 1982-83. Publications: Dickens, Money and Society, 1968; The Novel and Society: From Defoe to George Elliot, 1984; The Achievement of Graham Greene, 1985; A Literary Life of Charles Dickens, 1996. Recreations: cinema; opera; jazz; walking. Address: (b.) Department of English Studies, Stirling University, Stirling, FK9 4LA; T.-01786 467499.

Smith, Gregor, RSW, DA(Edin). Artist and Art Teacher; b. 15.7.44, Renton; m., Elizabeth Stevenson. Educ. Wishaw High School; Edinburgh College of Art. Andrew Grant post-graduate scholarship, 1966-67; teachers included Robin Philipson and James Cumming; exhibits at Royal Scottish Academy, RSW, Compass Gallery, etc.; Chairman, Glasgow Group; works in private and public collections. Address: Auchendarroch House, Shore Road, Kilcreggan G84 0HQ; T.-01436 842727.

Smith, Professor Hamilton, BSc, PhD, CChem, FRSC, FRCPath, FRSE. Professor of Forensic Medicine (Toxicology), Glasgow University, since 1987; b. 27.4.34, Stirling; m., Jacqueline Ann Spittal. Educ. Kilsyth Academy; Glasgow University. Glasgow University: MRC Fellow, 1960, Special Research Fellow, 1963, Lecturer in Forensic Medicine Department, 1964, Senior Lecturer, 1973, Reader, 1984. Publication: Glaister's Medical Jurisprudence and Toxicology, 13th edition. Recreations: golf (New Club, St. Andrews); gardening. Address: (b.) Department of Forensic Medicine and Science, Glasgow University, Glasgow, G12 8QQ; T.-0141-339 8855.

Smith, Ian, BSc, PhD, CBiol, MIBiol. Rector, Kinlochbervie High School, since 1995; b. 2.7.52, Edinburgh; m., Dianne; 2 d. Educ. Galashiels Academy; Heriot Watt University; Glasgow University. Research Biochemist, Knightswood Hospital, Glasgow, 1974-80; Teacher of Biology, Kelso High School, 1981-84; Assistant Principal Teacher of Biology, Nicolson Institute, 1984; Principal Teacher of Biology, Selkirk High School, 1984-88, Hawick High School, 1988-95. Publications: research papers on muscular dystrophy. Recreations: football; rugby; cycling; walking. Address: (b.) Kinlochbervie High School, Kinlochbervie, Sutherland IV27 4RG; T.-01971 521767.

Smith, James Aikman, TD, BA, LLB. Advocate; Honorary Sheriff, since 1976; b. 13.6.14, Kilmarnock; m., Katharine Ann Millar; 3 d. Educ. Glasgow Academy; Oxford University; Edinburgh University. Admitted Faculty of Advocates, 1939; served Royal Artillery, 1939-46 (Lt. Col., 1944), North Africa, Italy and Austria; Despatches, Bronze Star US; Sheriff Substitute, Renfrew and Argyll, 1948-52, Roxburgh, Berwick and Selkirk, 1952-57, Aberdeen, Kincardine and Banff, 1957-68; Sheriff of Lothians and Borders, 1968 76; President, Sheriffs' Association, 1969-72; Member, UK Departmental Committee on Probation Service, 1959-62; Member, After Care Council (Scotland), 1962-65; UK Delegate to UN Congress on Crime, Japan, 1970; Chairman, Edinburgh and East of Scotland Branch, English Speaking Union, 1970-74; Vice-President, Cairngorm Club, 1962-65; Chairman, Allelon Society, 1970-76; Elder, Church of Scotland, 1948-90. Recreations: hill-walking; gardening; travel. Address: (h.) 16 Murrayfield Avenue, Edinburgh, EH12 6AX; T.-0131-337 8205.

Smith, James David, OBE, MA, LLB. Retired Solicitor; b. 27.10.19, Dumbarton; m., Margaret McGregor Grant; 2 s. Educ. Dumbarton Academy; Glasgow University. Commissioned Highland Light Infantry, 1940; Town Clerk, Dumbarton, 1951-67; Chief Executive, Corporation of Greenock, 1967-75; Visiting Lecturer in Law, Paisley College of Technology, 1976-87. Address: (h.) Craigellachie, Balmaha Road, Drymen G63 0BY; T.-01360 660484.

Smith, Sheriff James R., LLB. Sheriff of South Strathclyde, Dumfries and Galloway at Stranraer. Address: (b.) Sheriff Court House, Lewis Street, Stranraer, DG9 7AA.

Smith, Lewis Shand, MA, BD. Rector, St. Magnus Episcopal Church, St. Colman's Church, since 1980; Canon, St. Andrews Cathedral, Aberdeen, since 1993; Convener, Shetland Islands Council, since 1994; Member, Convention of the Highlands and Islands; Member, Executive, Scottish Constitutional Convention; Vice-President, COSLA, since 1998; b. 16.3.52, Lerwick; m., Annette; 1 s. Educ. Anderson Educational Institute, Lerwick; Aberdeen University; Edinburgh University; Edinburgh Theological College. Curate, St. Andrews, Wishaw and Holy Trinity, Motherwell, 1977-80. Convener, Orkney and Shetland Joint Valuation Board, since 1996; Hon. President, Shetland-Vagsoy Twinning Association; Chairman, Hunter-Morrison Trust. Recreations: amateur theatre; music; swimming; gardening. Address: (b.) Papilgarth, 1 Greenrig, Lerwick, Shetland, ZE1 0AW; T.-01595 693862.

Smith, Professor Lorraine Nancy, BScN, MEd, PhD. Professor of Nursing, Glasgow University, since 1990 (Head of Department, since 1990); b. 29.6.49, Ottawa; m., Christopher Murray Smith; 1 s.; 1 d. Educ. Hillcrest High School, Ottawa; University of Ottawa; Manchester University. Co-opted to English National Board, 1988-90; Member, Scottish Alcohol Advisory Group, 1991-95; Member, Clinical and Biomedical Research Committee (Scotland), 1992-94; co-opted to National Board of Scotland for Nursing, Midwifery and Health Visiting; Member, Clinical Standards Advisory Group (UK), since 1994. Recreations: reading; bridge; sailing. Address: (b.) 68 Oakfield Avenue, Glasgow University, Glasgow, G12 8LS; T.-0141-330 4051.

Smith, Matt, JP. Scottish Secretary, UNISON, since 1993; Vice-President, Scottish TUC, since 1997; b. 4.2.52, Irvine; m., Eileen; 1 s.; 1 d. Educ. Stevenston High School; Ardrossan Academy. NALGO employee from 1973; Senior Scottish Officer/Scottish Organiser, 1981-93; Member, STUC General Council, Treasurer, 1995-97; Member, Executive, Scottish Council Development and Industry, Committee on Church and Nation (Church of Scotland),

Scottish Local Government Information Unit, Centre of Scottish Public Policy, Broadcasting Council for Scotland; appointed to Independent Commission on Local Government and a Scottish Parliament, 1997; former Member, Scotland FORward, Scottish Constitutional Convention, Labour for a Scottish Parliament; Member, North Ayrshire Justices Committee; former Stevenston Burgh councillor; Parliamentary candidate, Labour, 1979. Recreations: family; travel; gardening; music; politics. Address: (b.) UNISON House, 14 West Campbell Street, Glasgow, G2 6RX; T.-0141-332 0006.

Smith, Nigel R. Managing Director, David Auld Valves Ltd., since 1976; b. 9.6.41, Girvan; m., Jody; 2 s.; 2 d. Educ. Dollar Academy. Lt., 4/5 Bn., Royal Scots Fusiliers (TA), 1960-67; staff and management appointments, Bowater Paper, Richard Costain, Rank Hovis McDougall. Member, Executive, Scottish Engineering Employers Association, 1985-90; Member, Broadcasting Council for Scotland, 1986-90; Member, BBC General Advisory Council, 1991-93; Member, Glasgow Development Agency, Strategy Review Panel, 1993-94; Member, Scottish Constitutional Commission, 1993-94; Chairman, Broadcasting for Scotland Campaign, 1993-97; Chairman, Scotland Forward Devolution Yes Campaign, 1997. Recreations: hill-walking; offshore sailing; opera and choral; reading, particularly biography. Address: (b.) David Auld Valves, Cowlairs Industrial Estate, Finlas Street, Glasgow, G22 5DQ; T.-0141-557 0515.

Smith, Sir Robert, Bt. MP (Liberal Democrat), Aberdeenshire West and Kincardine; b. 15.4.58; m.; 1 d. Educ. Merchant Taylors' School; Aberdeen University. Runs family estate at Crowmallie. Address: (b.) House of Commons, London SW1A 0AA.

Smith, Robert Graham, MA, DLC. Principal, Scottish National Sports Centre (Cumbrae), since 1995; b. 28.4.44, Rugby; m., Rosemary Ann; 1 s.; 1 d. Educ. Purley Grammar School; Loughborough Colleges; Birmingham University. Address: (b.) Scottish National Sports Centre, Cumbrae, Ayrshire KA28 0HQ; T.-01475 530757.

Smith, Robert Lupton, OBE, FRICS. Vice-President, Association for the Protection of Rural Scotland, since 1993 (Director, 1981-93); Chartered Surveyor in private practice, 1954-96; b. 26.4.24, Cheadle Hulme; m.; 3 d. Educ. George Watson's College; College of Estate Management; Heriot-Watt College. Chairman, Scottish Junior Branch, RICS, 1952; Member, Scottish Executive Committee, RICS, 1952-60; elected, Edinburgh Town Council, 1962-74 and Edinburgh District Council, 1974-77; Governor, Edinburgh College of Art, 1963-89; fought European Election, 1979, as Liberal; Deputy Traffic Commissioner, 1974-78; Chairman, Good Neighbours Housing Association, 1984-87; Scottish Liberal Party: Chairman, Executive Committee, 1971-74, Chairman, 1974, President, 1976-82; Council Member, Royal Scottish Geographical Society, 1957-92; Chairman, A9 Highland Hosts Group, since 1995; Director, Cockburn Conservation Trust Ltd., 1976-90; Chairman, Logierait Bridge Co. Ltd. Recreations: visiting Orkney; reading; looking at fine art. Address: (h.) Charleston, Dalguise, near Dunkeld, PH8 0JX; T.-01350 728968.

Smith, Roger W. Writer and Editor; b. 28.11.38, London; 2 d. Educ. Latymer Upper School, London. Editor, The Great Outdoors, 1977-86; Editor, Environment Now, 1987-89; Editor, Scottish World, 1989-90; Past Chairman, Scottish Wild Land Group; Member, Executive Committee, National Trust for Scotland, and Convenor, NTS Countryside and Nature Conservation Comitteee. Publications include: The Winding Trail, 1981; The Great Outdoors Book of the Walking Year, 1988; Classic Walks in Scotland (Co-author), 1988; Chambers Guide to the Highlands and Islands, 1992; Catastrophes and Disasters, 1992; The Great Flood of Perth, 1993; 25 Walks: Highland Perthshire 1994; 25 Walks: Edinburgh and Lothian, 1995; Mapreading for Beginners, 1996; Insight Guide to the Scottish Highlands, 1997. Recreations: hill-walking; Scottish history. Address: (h.) 43 Kilnknowe Place, Galashiels TD1 1RH; T.-01896 751003.

Smith, Roger Galbraith, MB, ChB, FRCPEdin, FRCPLond, FRCPGlas. Consultant Physician in Geriatric Medicine, Royal Victoria Hospital, Edinburgh, and Honorary Senior Lecturer in Geriatric Medicine, Edinburgh University, since 1989; b. 7.7.42, Edinburgh; m., Margaret Lawson; 1 s.; 1 d. Educ. George Watson's College, Edinburgh; Edinburgh University. Surgeon Lieutenant, Royal Navy, 1967-72; Senior Registrar in Geriatric Medicine, 1973-76; Senior Lecturer, Department of Geriatric Medicine, Edinburgh University, 1976-89. Member, Board of Directors, Queensberry House Hospital, Edinburgh. Recreations: golf; curling. Address: (h.) 56 Alnwickhill Road, Edinburgh; T.-0131-664 1745.

Smith, Ronald A., MA. General Secretary, Educational Institute of Scotland, since 1995; Member, General Council, STUC, since 1995, Chair, STUC Education Committee; Member, Executive Board, European Trade Union Committee for Education, since 1995; Member, European Regional Committee, Education International; b. 9.6.51, Lerwick; m., Mae; 1 s.; 1 d. Educ. Anderson Educational Institute; Aberdeen University; Aberdeen College of Education. Teacher of Latin, then A.P.T. of Latin, then Principal Teacher of Modern Studies, Broxburn Academy, 1973-88; Assistant Secretary, EIS, 1988-95. Address: (b.) 46 Moray Place, Edinburgh, EH3 6BH.

Smith, Sheriff Ronald Good, BL. Sheriff of North Strathclyde, since 1984; b. 24.7.33. Address: (b.) Sheriff Court House, 106 Renfrew Road, Paisley, PA3 4DD.

Smith, Emeritus Professor Stanley Desmond, OBE, BSc, PhD, DSc, FRS, FRSE. Professor of Physics, Heriot-Watt University, 1970-96; Chairman, Edinburgh Instruments Ltd., since 1971; Chairman, Edinburgh Sensors Ltd., since 1988; b. 3.3.31, Bristol; m., Gillian Anne Parish; 1 s.; 1 d. Educ. Cotham Grammar School; Bristol University; Reading University. SSO, RAE, Farnborough, 1956-58; Research Assistant, Department of Meteorology, Imperial College, London, 1958-59; Lecturer, then Reader, Reading University, 1960-70; Head, Department of Physics, Heriot-Watt University, 1970-96. Member: Advisory Council for Applied Research and Development, 1985-87, Advisory Council on Science and Technology, 1987-88, Defence Scientific Advisory Council, 1985-91, SERC Astronomy and Planetary Science and Engineering Boards, 1985-88, Council, Institute of Physics, 1984-87; Chairman, Scottish Optoelectronics Association, 1996-98. Recreations: tennis; skiing; mountaineering; golf; raising the temperature. Address: (b.) Edinburgh Sensors Ltd., 2 Bain Square, Livingston, EH54 7DQ; T.-01506 425300.

Smith, Professor Stanley William, MA, PhD (Cantab). Chair of English, Dundee University, since 1989 (Reader in English, 1988-89, Head of Department, 1989-94); b. 12.1.43, Warrington; 2 s.; 1 d. Educ. Boteler Grammar School, Warrington; Jesus College, Cambridge. Assistant Lecturer in English, Aberdeen University, 1967-68; Lecturer in English, Dundee University, 1968-85; Senior Lecturer, 1985-88; Visiting Professor, University of Florence, 1987; Visiting Professor, University of Zaragoza, 1996; Chair, Council for University English, 1991-93; British Representative, Board, European Society for the Study of English, 1992-93; Member, Board, Standing Committee for Arts and Social Sciences, since 1989; Member, Board, Scotscass, since 1992; Vice-Chair, Scottish Committee of Professors of English, 1992-94; Member, Steering Committee, Council of University Deans of Arts and Humanities, since 1997. Publications: A Sadly Contracted Hero: The Comic Self in Post-War American

Fiction, 1981; Inviolable Voice: History and Twentieth Century Poetry, 1982; 20th Century Poetry, 1983; W.H. Auden, 1985; Edward Thomas, 1986; W.B. Yeats, 1990; The Origins of Modernism, 1994; W.H. Auden, 1997; General Editor, Longman Critical Reader series and Longman Studies in 20th-century Literature series. Recreations: the arts; classical music; history and archaeology; travel. Address: (b.) English Department, Dundee University, Dundee, DD1 4HN; T.-01382 344412.

Smith, William Angus, BEM, FEIS, JP. Chairman, Education Committee, Shetland Islands Council, 1975-97 (Vice Chairman, Housing Committee, 1982-85); Vice-Chairman, Lerwick Harbour Trust; b. 20.8.19, Burra Isle, Shetland; m., Daisy Manson; 3 s. Educ. Anderson Educational Institute. Engineer, British Telecomms, 1937-83; Royal Signals, UK, Middle East, Burma, India, Germany, 1940-46; Member, Lerwick Town Council and Zetland County Council, 1967-75; Member, Lerwick Harbour Trust, since 1967 (except for short break); Provost of Lerwick, 1971-74; Member, Shetland Islands Council, since 1975; Member, Shetland Area Health Board, 1974-89; Member, Electricity Consultative Council for North of Scotland District, 1974-90; Member, Shetland Recreational Trust, 1982-97. Recreations: crosswords; reading. Address: (h.) 14 Bruce Crescent, Lerwick, Shetland, ZE1 OPB; T.-01595 696428.

Smith, Professor William Ewen, BSc, DIC, PhD, DSc, FRSC, FRSE. Professor of Inorganic Chemistry, since 1987, and Head of Department, Strathclyde University, since 1995; b. 21.2.41, Glasgow; m., Frances Helen Williamson; 1 s.; 1 d. Educ. Hutchesons' Boys Grammar School; Strathclyde University. Visiting Scientist, Oak Ridge National Laboratory, 1965-67; SERC and ICI Fellow, University College, London, 1967-69; Lecturer, Reader, Professor, Strathclyde University, since 1969. Publications: 170 papers and reviews. Recreations: golf; sailing. Address: (b.) Department of Pure and Applied Chemistry, Strathclyde University, Glasgow, G1 1XL; T.-0141-552 4400.

Smith, William Leggat, CBE, MC, TD, JP, DL, BA (Oxon), LLB, LLD; b. 30.1.18, Kilmarnock; m., Yvonne Menna Williams; 1 s.; 2 d. Educ. Glasgow Academy; Queen's College, Oxford; Glasgow University. Commissioned (TA), Cameronians (Scottish Rifles), 1939; served Second World War in UK, Europe, USA; Solicitor, 1947-86; Chairman, Governors, Glasgow Academy, 1972-80; Deacon Convener, Trades of Glasgow, 1964-65; Dean, Royal Faculty of Procurators in Glasgow, 1976-79; Member, Reviewing Committee on Export of Works of Art, 1980-82; Convener, Retirement Scheme of Church of Scotland, 1976-80; Chairman, Charles Rennie Mackintosh Society, 1985-88; Chairman, Indigent Gentlewomen of Scotland Fund, 1985-93; Chairman, Glasgow School of Art, 1975-88. Recreations: gardening; salmon fishing. Address: (h.) The Cottage, Clachan of Campsie, Glasgow; T.-01360 311434.

Smith, William Wilson Campbell, MA (Cantab), LLB (Glas). Managing Partner, Biggart Baillie, Solicitors, Glasgow and Edinburgh; b. 17.5.46, Glasgow; m., Elizabeth Margaret Richards; 2 d. Educ. Glasgow Academy; St. Catharine's College, Cambridge; Glasgow University. Qualified as a Solicitor, 1972; Assistant Solicitor, Herbert Smith & Co., London, 1972-73; Partner, Biggart Baillie, since 1974. Member, various committees, Law Society of Scotland; Trustee, Glassford Sheltered Housing Trust; Member of Convocation, Strathclyde University; Member, Joint Insolvency Examination Board, 1986-95; Deacon, Incorporation of Barbers, Glasgow, 1989-90. Recreations: croquet; golf; barbershop singing. Address: (b.) Dalmore House, 310 St. Vincent Street, Glasgow, G2 5QR; T.-0141-228 8000.

Smout, Professor Thomas Christopher, CBE, MA, PhD, FRSE, FSA (Scot), FBA. HM Historiographer in Scotland; Director, Institute for Environmental History; b. 19.12.33. Member, Royal Commission on the Ancient and Historic Monuments of Scotland. Address: (b.) St John's House, South Street, St. Andrews, Fife.

Smuga, George Muirhead Russell, MA (Hons), DipEd. Headteacher, Royal High School, Edinburgh, since 1998; b. 6.11.47, Broughty Ferry; m., Isabel Ann; 1 s.; 1 d. Educ. Kirkcaldy High School; Edinburgh University. Principal Teacher, Modern Studies, then Assistant Headteacher, Portobello High School; Depute Headteacher, Beeslack High School; Headteacher, North Berwick High School and Manager Quality Assurance, East Lothian. Member, Higher Still National Implementation School Sector Group; co-author of four modern studies textbooks. Recreations: golf; supporting Hibernian F.C. Address: (h.) 35 Thornyhall, Dalkeith EH22 2ND.

Smyth, Professor John Crocket, OBE, BSc, PhD, HonDUniv (Paisley), DipEd, CBiol, FIBiol, FLS, FRSA. Emeritus Professor of Biology, Paisley University, since 1988; Honorary Professor (Division of Academic Innovation and Continuing Education), Stirling University; Chairman, Scottish Environmental Education Council, 1983-91, President, since 1991; Chairman, Secretary of State for Scotland's Working Group on Environmental Education, 1990-93; b. 21.3.24, Edinburgh; m., Elizabeth Wallace Learmond; 1 s.; 1 d. Educ. George Watson's College; Edinburgh University. Assistant Lecturer in Zoology, Edinburgh University; Lecturer to Head, Department of Biology, Paisley College; Commissioner, Countryside Commission for Scotland, 1990-92; Vice-President, Royal Zoological Society of Scotland; Institute of Biology Charter Award for 1989; former Secretary and Chairman, Scottish Branch, Institute of Biology; Member, IUCN Commission on Education and Communication; IUCN Tree of Learning Award, 1990; Chairman, N.W. Europe Committee, 1980-85; Consultant for UNESCO-UNEP and UNCED on environmental education; Founder-Leader, Scottish Boys' Club. Address: (h.) Glenpark, Johnstone, Renfrewshire, PA5 0SP; T.-01505 320219.

Smyth, Professor John Fletcher, MA, MB, BChir, MD (Cantab), MSc (Lond), FRCPE, FRCP, FRCSE, FRSE. Professor of Medical Oncology, Edinburgh University, since 1979 (Head, Department of Clinical Oncology, since 1980); Honorary Director, Imperial Cancer Research Fund Medical Oncology Unit, Edinburgh University, since 1980; President, European Society for Medical Oncology, 1992-94; b. 26.10.45, Dursley; m., Catherine Ellis; 2 d. Educ. Bryanston School; Trinity College, Cambridge. Trained, St. Bartholomews Hospital, Royal Postgraduate Medical School and Institute of Cancer Research, London; National Cancer Institute, Bethesda; University of Chicago; Honorary Consultant Physician, Royal Marsden Hospital and Senior Lecturer, Institute of Cancer Research, London, 1976-79. Address: (b.) Department of Clinical Oncology, Western General Hospital, Crew Road, Edinburgh, EH4 2XU.

Snaith, Professor David William, MSc, PhD, CEng, MIM, CChem, FRSC, FInstM, FRSA. Principal, Stow College, Glasgow, since 1983; b. 30.6.40; m., Susan Willoughby Tucker; 1 s.; 2 d. Educ. Kings Norton Grammar School, Birmingham; Aston University. Research Chemist, Birmingham Small Arms Co. Ltd., 1961; Lecturer in Chemistry: Matthew Boulton College, Birmingham, 1965; Suffolk College, 1969; Deputy Head, Department of Science and Metallurgy, North Lindsey College, Scunthorpe, 1974; Head, Department of Science, North East Liverpool Technical College, 1980. Royal Society of Chemistry: Assistant Secretary, East Anglia, and Chairman (Southumbria) Sections, 1972-78; Chair, West of Scotland Access Consortium, 1996. Recreations: hill-walking;

music-making; photography. Address: (b.) Stow College, 43 Shamrock Street, Glasgow, G4 9LD; T.-0141-332 1786.

Sneddon, Hutchison Burt, CBE, JP. Lord Lieutenant of Lanarkshire; b. 17.4.29, Wishaw; m., Elizabeth Jardine; 1 s.; 2 d. Educ. Wishaw High School. Former Scottish Divisional Director, Nationwide Anglia Building Society; Chairman, Cumbernauld Development Corporation, 1979-83; Vice-Chairman, Scottish National Housing and Town Planning Council, 1965-71; Chairman, Burns Heritage Trail, 1971-83; President, World Federation of Burns Clubs, 1989-90; Deputy President, COSLA, 1974-76; Chairman, Motherwell District Council, 1974-77; Provost, Burgh of Motherwell and Wishaw, 1971-75. Recreations: football (watching); philately. Addrerss: (h.) 36 Shand Street, Wishaw, ML2 8HN; T.-01698 373685.

Sneddon, Ian Naismith, OBE (1969), BSc, DSc, BA, MA, FRS, FRSE, FIMA. Honorary Senior Research Fellow and Emeritus Professor of Mathematics, Glasgow University; Board of Directors, Capella Nova; b. 8.12.19, Glasgow; m., Mary Campbell Macgregor; 2 s.; 1 d. Educ. Hyndland School, Glasgow; Glasgow University; Trinity College, Cambridge. Junior Scientific Officer, Ministry of Supply, 1942-45; William Bryce Fellow, Glasgow University, 1945-46; Lecturer in Natural Philosophy, Glasgow University, 1946-50; Professor of Mathematics, University College of North Staffordshire, 1950-56; Simson Professor of Mathematics, Glasgow University, 1956-85. Hon DSc: Warsaw University, Heriot-Watt University, Hull University, Strathclyde University; Kelvin Medal, Glasgow University; Makdougall-Brisbane Prize, Royal Society of Edinburgh, 1959; Eringen Medal, Society of Engineering Science, 1979; Copernicus Medal, Polish Academy of Sciences, 1973; Gold Medal for Culture (Poland), 1983; Member, Order of the Long Leaf Pine (North Carolina), 1964; Commander, Order of Polonia Restituta, 1969; Commander, Order of Merit of Poland, 1979. Recreations: music; painting in oils; photography. Address: (h.) 19 Crown Terrace, Glasgow, G12 9ES; T.-0141-339 4114.

Solomon, Professor Sally Elizabeth, BSc (Hons), PhD. Professor of Poultry Science, Glasgow University, since 1993; President, World Poultry Science Association (UK), since 1998; Chairman, Working Group No. 4, EU Branch, World Poultry Science Association, since 1992; Secretary/Treasurer, British Poultry Science Ltd., since 1994; b. 19.4.44, Glasgow; m., Dr. Roger Tippett. Educ. Rothesay Academy; Woodside Secondary School, Glasgow; University of Glasgow. Glasgow University: Assistant Lecturer in Veterinary Histology, 1968-70, Lecturer in Veterinary Histology, 1970-86, Senior Lecturer in Veterinary Anatomy, 1986-91, Reader in Veterinary Anatomy, 1991-93. Gordon Memorial Medal, 1998; World Poultry Science Education Award, 1996. Publication: Egg and Eggshell Quality. Recreations: gardening; travel; cooking; reading. Address: Department of Veterinary Preclinical Studies, University of Glasgow, Bearsden Road, Bearsden, Glasgow G61 1QH; T.-0141-330 5717.

Somerville, David Wilkie, DipPE. Head of Community Services, Fife Council, since 1995; b. Edinburgh; m., Fiona; 1 s.; 1 d. Educ. Lasswade High School. Football: Hearts, Berwick Rangers; P.E. Teacher, Penicuik High School; Depute Director, National Sports Training Centre; Sport Development, Scottish Sports Council; Senior Assistant Director of Education, Fife Regional Council. Recreations: golf; swimming. Address: (b.) Fife Council, Fife House, North Street, Glenrothes; T.-01592 414141.

Sommerville, John Kenneth, CA. Partner, French Duncan, CA, Glasgow, since 1970; Council Member, Institute of Chartered Accountants of Scotland, 1984-90; Council Member, Association of Accounting Technicians, 1989-98 (President, 1995-96); b. 1.3.42, Glasgow; m., Iris Alexa Hutchison; 3 d. Educ. Kelvinside Academy. Member, Board of Governors, Kelvinside Academy, 1976-94 (Chairman of Board, 1985-94). Recreations: golf; running. Address: (b.) 375 West George Street, Glasgow, G2 4LH; T.-0141-221 2984.

Somerville, Lynda Margaret, RGN, SCM. Director, Mental Health Foundation Scotland, since 1991; b. Paisley. Educ. Paisley Grammar School. Registered general nurse; midwife; medical sales; Marketing Director, Ross Hall Hospital; Director, Mackay Somerville Marketing; Marketing Manager, Britannia Life Ltd. Recreations: studying; music; dance. Address: (b.) 24 George Square, Glasgow, G2 1EG; T.-0141-572 0125.

Souter, William Alexander, MBChB(Hons), FRCSEd. Consultant Orthopaedic Surgeon, Princess Margaret Rose Orthopaedic Hospital, Edinburgh, 1968-1997; Honorary Senior Lecturer in Orthopaedics, Edinburgh University, since 1968; Visiting Professor, Bioengineering Department, Strathclyde University, since 1985; b. 11.5.33, Cupar; m., Kathleen Bruce Georgeson Taylor; 1 s.; 2 d. Educ. Falkirk High School; George Watson's Boys' College, Edinburgh; Medical School, Edinburgh University. Registrar in Hand Surgery, Derbyshire Royal Infirmary, 1964; Senior Registrar, Orthopaedic Department, Edinburgh, 1965-68; Instructor in Orthopaedic Surgery, University of Washington, Seattle, 1967. Member, Council, British Orthopaedic Association, 1986-88 and 1993-95; Member, Council, Royal College of Surgeons of Edinburgh, 1988-98; Inaugural President, British Elbow and Shoulder Society, 1989-90; President, British Society for Surgery of the Hand, 1993; Chairman, Accreditation Committee, Federation of European Societies for Surgery of the Hand, 1992-96; President, European Rheumatoid Arthritis Surgical Society, 1995-99; President, Rheumatoid Arthritis Surgical Society, 1982 and since 1998. Recreations: gardening; music; hill-walking; photography; golf. Address: (h.) Old Mauricewood Mains, Penicuik, Midlothian EH26 0NJ; T.-01968 672609.

Sparks, Professor Leigh, MA, PhD, FRSA. Professor of Retail Studies, Stirling University, since 1992; Dean, Faculty of Management, since 1995; b. 15.2.57, Bridgend, Wales; m., Janice Lewis. Educ. Brynteg C.S.; Christ's College, Cambridge; Lampeter College, Wales. Researcher, Lecturer, Senior Lecturer, Professor, Institute for Retail Studies, Department of Marketing, Stirling University. Recreation: watching sport, especially rugby. Address: (b.) Faculty of Management, Stirling University, Stirling FK9 4LA; T.-01786 467278.

Speirs, Robert, FCIS, FRSA. Non-Executive Director: Macfarlane (Clansman) Group plc, Stagecoach Holdings plc; Chairman, Direct Line Insurance; Finance Director, Royal Bank of Scotland plc, 1993-98, retired; b. 23.10.36, Liverpool; m., Patricia; 2 s. Educ. Alleynes Grammar School. Inland Revenue, 1953-64; Coopers & Lybrand, 1964-68; Texaco Ltd., 1968-77; Treasurer, British National Oil Corporation, 1977-83; Treasurer/Finance Director, Britoil plc, 1983-88; Finance Director, Olympia and York Canary Wharf Ltd., 1988-93. Recreations: DIY; walking; music. Address: (b.) 42 St. Andrew's Square, Edinburgh; T.-0131-523 2033.

Speirs, William MacLeod, BA (Hons), FRSA. General Secretary, Scottish TUC; Member: Scottish Arts Council, Scottish Business Forum, Glasgow Development Agency; Director: Workbase Scotland, Scottish Low Pay Unit; Chairperson, 7:84 Theatre Company (Scotland), since 1988; b. 8.3.52, Dumbarton; 1 s.; 1 d. Educ. John Neilson High School, Paisley; Strathclyde University. Assistant Secretary, Scottish TUC, 1979-88. Chairperson, Labour Party in Scotland, 1987-88; Chairperson, Scottish Friends of Palestine, since 1982; Director, Scottish Trade Union Review. Recreations: reading; losing money on horses; watching St. Mirren F.C. Address: (b.) STUC, 333 Woodlands Road, Glasgow G3 6NG; T.-0141-337 8100.

Spence, Alan, MA. Writer (poet, playwright, novelist, short-story writer); b. 5.12.47, Glasgow; m., Janani (Margaret). Educ. Allan Glen's School, Glasgow; Glasgow University. Writer in Residence, Glasgow University, 1975-77, Deans Community School, 1978, Traverse Theatre, Edinburgh, 1983, City of Edinburgh, 1986-87, Edinburgh University, 1989-82, Aberdeen University, since 1996; winner, People's Prize, 1991; Macallan/Scotland on Sunday Short Story competition, 1993; McVitie's Prize, 1996; TMA Drama Award, 1996. Publications: poetry: ah!; Glasgow Zen; short stories: Its Colours They Are Fine, Stone Garden; novels: The Magic Flute, Way to Go; plays: Sailmaker; Space Invaders; Changed Days. Recreations: meditation; running; playing flute. Address: 21 Waverley Park, Edinburgh, EH8 8ER; T.-0131-661 8403.

Spence, Professor Alastair Andrew, CBE, MD, FRCA, FRCP (Glas & Edin), FRCS (Ed & Eng), Hon FDS, RCS Eng. Professor of Anaesthetics, Edinburgh University, since 1984; Honorary Consultant Anaesthetist, Royal Infirmary, Edinburgh; President, Royal College of Anaesthetists, 1991-94; b. 18.9.36, Glasgow; m., Maureen Isobel Aitchison; 2 s. Educ. Ayr Academy; Glasgow University. Professor and Head, University Department of Anaesthesia, Western Infirmary, Glasgow, 1969-84; Editor, British Journal of Anaesthesia, 1973-83; Hunterian Professor, Royal College of Surgeons of England, 1974; Joseph Clover Lecturer, 1990; Member, Advisory Committee on Distinction Awards, since 1992; Medical Director, since 1996. Recreations: golf; gardening. Address: (h.) Harewood, Kilmacolm, PA13 4HX; T.-Kilmacolm 872962.

Spence, David Lane, CA. London Senior Partner, Grant Thornton, since 1998; President, Institute of Chartered Accountants of Scotland, since 1998; b. 5.10.43, South Africa (raised in Forres); m., Beverley Esther Cardale; 1 s.; 1 d. Educ. Fettes College, Edinburgh; Forres Academy. C.F. Middleton & Co., 1962-67; Grant Thornton (formerly Thornton Baker), since 1967; appointed Partner, 1970; European Practice Partner, 1974-80; Executive Partner, 1983-89; DTI Inspector, 1989 and 1992; Chairman, Chartered Accountants Joint Ethics Committee, 1995-97; Vice-President, Institute of Chartered Accountants of Scotland, 1996-98. Recreations: golf; occasional cycling; tinkering with old MGs. Address: Grant Thornton House, Melton Street, London NW1 2EP; T.-0171-728 2468.

Spence, James Allan Stewart, DA, RGI, RSW. Painter; b. 1.6.29, Glasgow; m., Anda Paterson; 1 s.; 1 d. Educ. Alford Secondary School, Aberdeenshire; Glasgow School of Art. Co-Founder, Glasgow Group of Artists (President, 1958-90); Principal Teacher of Art, Dumbarton Acadedmy, 1973-90; work collected by The Queen, Glasgow and Dundee Art Galleries, Scottish Arts Council; BBC Award, 1989; National Bockingford first prize, 1993; Glasgow Royal Physicians and Surgeons Award, 1994; William Bowie Award, 1994; Scottish Amicable Award (RGI), 1996. Recreations: opera; chess; caravanning; wine-making; Spanish-Portuguese history and culture. Address: (h.) 55 Bainfield Road, Cardross, Argyll and Bute G82 5JQ; T.-0138 9841 768.

Spence, James William, KFO (Norway), RON (Netherlands), DL (Orkney), BSc, MNI, MICS. Master Mariner, since 1971; Shipbroker, since 1975; Company Director, since 1977; b. 19.1.45, St. Ola, Orkney; m., Margaret Paplay Stevenson; 3 s. Educ. Leith Nautical College, Edinburgh; Robert Gordon's Institute of Technology, Aberdeen; University of Wales, Cardiff. Merchant Navy, 1961-74 (Member, Nautical Institute, 1972, Member, Royal Institute of Navigation, 1971); Micoperi SpA, 1974-75 (Temporary Assistant Site Co-ordinator on Scapa Flow Project); John Jolly (Shipbrokers, Stevedores, Shipping and Forwarding Agents) since 1975 (Manager, 1975, Junior Partner, 1976-77, Proprietor and Managing Director, since 1977). Vice-Consul for Norway, 1976, Consul, 1978; Vice-Consul for the Netherlands, 1978-94; Member, Kirkwall Community Council, 1978-82; Member, Orkney Pilotage Committee, 1979-88; Chairman, Kirkwall Port Employers' Association, 1979-87 (Member, since 1975); Chairman, RNLI, Kirkwall Lifeboat Station Branch Committee, 1997 (Station Hon. Secretary, 1987-96, Deputy Launching Authority, 1976-87); Chairman, Pier Arts Centre Trust, 1989-91 (Trustee, 1980-91); Chairman, Association of Honorary Norwegian Consuls in the UK and Ireland, 1993-95. Recreations: oenology; equestrian matters; Orcadian history. Address: (h.) Alton House, Kirkwall, Orkney KW15 1NA; T.-01856 872268.

Spence, Professor John, ARCST, BSc, MEng, PhD, DSc, FEng, FRSE, FIMechE. Vice-Principal, Strathclyde University (Trades House of Glasgow Professor of Mechanics of Materials, since 1982); b. 5.11.37, Chapelhall; m., Margaret Gray Hudson; 2 s. Educ. Airdrie Academy; Royal College of Science and Technology; Sheffield University. Engineering apprenticeship, Stewarts & Lloyds (now British Steel Corporation); Senior Engineer, then Head of Stress Analysis, Babcock & Wilcox Research Division; Strathclyde University: Lecturer, 1966, Senior Lecturer, Reader, Professor since 1979. Serves on several national committees: President, Institution of Mechanical Engineers; EPSRC College; British Standards Institution; Engineering Professors Council (Vice Chairman). Address: (b.) Department of Mechanical Engineering, Strathclyde University, 75 Montrose Street, Glasgow, G1 1XJ; T.-0141-548 4497/2324.

Spence, John Andrew, MBE, ACIB, FRSA. Chief Executive, TSB Bank Scotland plc, since 1998; President, Enable; b. 30.1.51, Edinburgh; m., Yvonne; 1 s.; 2 d. Educ. George Watson's College; Trinity College, Dublin; Harvard Business School. Lloyds Bank PLC: Senior Manager, Employee Communications, 1986-88, Area Director, West London, 1988-90, Regional Manager, Retail Banking, London and South East, 1990-94, Head of Business Banking, 1994-96; Managing Director, Business Banking, Lloyds TSB Group plc, 1996-98. Warden and Chairman, Finance Committee, Chelmsford Cathedral; Chairman, Board of Governors, Rainsford High School; Trustee, Blind in Business. Recreations: cooking; swimming; the arts. Address: (b.) Henry Duncan House, 120 George Street, Edinburgh EH2 4LH; T.-0131-225 4555.

Spence, William Arthur, QPM, LLB, BA. Chief Constable of Tayside; b. 20.11.43, Ellon. Educ. Ellon Academy; Strathclyde University. Served in Renfrew and Bute Constabulary and Strathclyde Police prior to appointment to Tayside Police, 1988; Member, Scottish Victim Support Funding Panel, 1988-96; Chairman, ACPOS Traffic Standing Committee, 1995; Member, Transport Forum for Scotland; President, Association of Chief Police Officers in Scotland, 1996-97; Chairman, Tayside Drugs Action Team; Member, Scottish Advisory Committee on Drugs Misuse; Fellow, RSA; Member of Court, University of Abertay, Dundee. Recreations: reading; genealogy; theatre; gardening. Address: (b.) Tayside Police, PO Box 59, West Bell Street, Dundee, DD1 9JU.

(Spence) Paterson, Anda Carolyn Paterson, DA, RSW, RGI. Painter (full-time), since 1989; b., 2.2.35, Glasgow; m., James Spence; 1 s.; 1 d. Educ. Glasgow High School for Girls; Hillhead High School; Glasgow School of Art. Co-founder with husband of Glasgow Group of Artists, first showing in 1958; Assistant Teacher, Dumbarton Academy, 1975-85; Principal Teacher, Art and Design, Jordanhill College School, 1985-89; special interest in painting people; RSA Award, 1959; Latimer Award, 1961; Glasgow Civic Prize, 1964; Anne Redpath Award, 1971; RSA Maude Gemmell Hutchison Prize, 1995; Compass Gallery Award, 1998. Recreations: music; books; caravanning; bird-watching; geology; fossils; collecting jewelry and ethnic objects. Address: (h.) 55 Bainfield Road, Cardross, Argyll and Bute G82 5JQ; T.-0138 984 768.

Spencely, John Despenser, MA, BArch, DipTP, RIBA, PPRIAS, MRTPI, FCIArb. Chairman, Reiach and Hall; Chairman, Buildings Investigation Centre; b. 5.10.39, Westerham, England; m., Marilyn Anne Read; 1 d. (by pr. m.). Educ. Bryanston School; Cambridge University; Edinburgh University. Architect, Town Planner; former Member, Scottish Building Contract Committee; President: Edinburgh Architectural Association, 1984-86, Royal Incorporation of Architects in Scotland, 1989-91; Lay Member, Scottish Solicitors Discipline Tribunal; Member, Advisory Committee on Arbitration to Scottish Law Commission; Board Member, Scottish Homes; Visiting Professor, Napier University; Freeman of the City of London; Liveryman, Worshipful Company of Arbitrators. Recreations: sailing; reading; collecting some unfashionable 20th century authors; making jam. Address: (b.) 6 Darnaway Street, Edinburgh EH3 6BG; T.-0131-225 8444.

Spencer, Alec P., BA (Hons), MA.Governor, Edinburgh Prison, since 1996; b. 12.3.46, London; m., Joan; 2 s.; 1 d. Educ. Dame Alice Owen School; Keele University. Joined Scottish Prison Service, 1972, as Assistant Governor: Polmont Borstal, Perth Prison, Glenochil; Deputy Governor, Aberdeen Prison, 1978; Prison Department HQ, 1981; Warden, Glenochil D.C., 1983; Deputy Governor, Glenochil Complex, 1987; Governor, Dungavel Prison, 1989; Governor, Peterhead Prison, 1992; Operational Adviser, PFI prison project 8PS HQ, 1996. Chairman, Scottish Forum on Prisons and Families; Butler Trust Award, 1987; Editor, ASPG Journal, 1982-90; Chairman, Governors' Committee, NUCPS, 1991-92; Hon. Senior Research Fellow, Dundee University. Recreations: music; walking; writing; collecting Penguin books. Address: (b.) Edinburgh Prison, 33 Stenhouse Road, Edinburgh EH11 3LN; T.-0131-444 3003.

Spencer, Very Rev. Paul Francis, CP. Rector, Saint Mungo's, Glasgow, since 1996; Provincial Consultor, Congregation of the Passion, since 1992; b. 2.3.54. Educ. Saint Mungo's Academy, Glasgow; University College, Dublin; Milltown Institute, Dublin; Pontifical Gregorian University, Rome. Professed as Member of Passionist Congregation, 1977; Ordained Priest, 1980; Vicar, Saint Mungo's, Glasgow, 1981-86; Master of Novices, Cochin, India, 1986-87; post-graduate studies, Rome, 1987-89; Rector, Mission Anglophone de France, Paris, 1989-96. Advisor to the Passionist Nuns, since 1988; Postulator of the Cause of Canonisation of Elizabeth Prout CP, since 1994; Member, Historical Commission for the Cause of Ignatius Spencer CP, since 1993; awarded Cross Pro piis meritis, Sovereign Military Order of Malta, 1995. Publications: To Heal the Broken-Hearted: The Life of Blessed Charles of Mount Argus, 1988; As a Seal upon your Heart: The Life of Saint Paul of the Cross, Founder of the Passionists, 1994. Recreation: music. Address: (h.) Saint Mungo's Retreat, 52 Parson Street, Glasgow G4 0RX; T.-0141-552 1823.

Spiers, Rev. John McLaren, LTh, MTh. Minister, Orchardhill Church, Giffnock, since 1977; b. 12.12.43, Edinburgh; m., Janet Diane Watson; 2 d. Educ. George Watson's College, Edinburgh; Glasgow University. Probationer Assistant, Drumchapel Old Parish Church, Glasgow, 1971-72; Minister, South Church, Barrhead, 1972-77; Convener, Board of World Mission, since 1996. Recreations: music; art; family life. Address: 23 Huntly Avenue, Giffnock, Glasgow, G46 6LW.

Spilg, Walter Gerson Spence, MB, ChB (Hons), FRCPath, FRCPG. Consultant Pathologist, Victoria Infirmary, Glasgow, since 1972, in Administrative Charge, since 1986; Honorary Clinical Senior Lecturer, Glasgow University, since 1973; b. 27.10.37, Glasgow; m., Vivien Anne Burns; 1 s.; 2 d. Educ. Hutchesons' Boys' Grammar School, Glasgow; Glasgow University. Registrar in Pathology, Glasgow Royal Infirmary, 1965-68; Senior Registrar in Pathology, Victoria Infirmary, Glasgow, 1968-69; Lecturer in Pathology, Glasgow University (Western Infirmary), 1969-72. President, Caledonian Branch, Association of Clinical Pathologists; Examiner, Royal College of Physicians and Surgeons of Glasgow; Member, Forensic Pathology Liaison Committee. Recreation: bridge. Address: (h.) 4B Newton Court, Newton Mearns, Glasgow, G77 5QL.

Spiller, Professor Eric, MA, FRSA. Assistant Principal/Dean, Faculty of Design, Robert Gordon University, since 1992; b. 19.8.46, Staffordshire; m., Carolyn; 2 s.; 1 d. Educ. Central School of Art and Design, London; Royal College of Art. Jewellery designer and lecturer; Head, School of Design, Portsmouth College of Art Design and Further Education, 1985-87, Grays School of Art, Robert Gordon's Institute of Technology, Aberdeen, 1987-92; public collections include: Goldsmiths Hall, Crafts Council, W. Midlands Arts, NW Arts, Aberdeen Art Gallery, Scottish Crafts Collection; private collections worldwide; numerous exhibitions; Council Member and Chair, Craft Committee, Scottish Arts Council. Recreation: hill-walking. Address: (b.) Faculty of Design, Garthdee Road, Aberdeen; T.-01224 263750.

Spratt, Col. Douglas Norman, CBE, TD. Director, Cameo of Edinburgh, since 1984; b. 18.9.20, Ramsgate; m., Margaret; 1 d (deceased). Educ. Sir Roger Manwood's Grammar School, Sandwich, Kent. President, Edinburgh Branch, Chartered Institute of Marketing; Chairman, Friends of the Reserve Forces Association, Scotland; Regional Chairman, Action Research in Scotland; Member, High Constables of Edinburgh; Deputy Lieutenant, City of Edinburgh; Member of the Military Attaches London. Recreations: fishing; sailing. Address: (h.) 6 Fernielaw Avenue, Edinburgh, EH13 OEE; T.-0131-441 1962.

Sprent, Professor Janet I., OBE, BSc, ARCS, PhD, DSc, FRSE. Emeritus Professor of Plant Biology, Dundee University; Leverhulme Emeritus Fellow; Chairman, Board of Governors, Macaulay Land Use Research Institute; b. 10.1.34, Slough; m., Emeritus Professor Peter Sprent. Educ. Slough High School; Imperial College, London; Tasmania University. Has spent 28 years at Dundee University; research focussed on nitrogen fixing legumes, both tree and crop species; currently involved in international collaboration, mainly in Africa and Brazil; Dean of Science and Engineering, 1987-89; Deputy Principal of the University, 1995-98. Council Member, NERC, 1991-95; Member, Scottish Higher Education Funding Council, 1992-96; Member, Joint Nature Conservation Committee, since 1994. Publications:three books and over 200 chapters/papers. Recreations: reseach; hill-walking. Address: Department of Biological Sciences, Dundee University, Dundee DD1 4HN; T.-01382 344279.

Sprot of Haystoun, Lt.-Col. Aidan Mark, MC, JP. Landowner (Haystoun Estate) and Farmer, since 1965; b. 17.6.19, Lilliesleaf. Educ. Belhaven Hill; Stowe. Commissioned, Royal Scots Greys, 1940; served Palestine, 1941-42, Western Desert, 1942-43, Italy, 1943-44, NW Europe, 1944-45; continued serving with Regiment in Germany until 1952, Libya, Egypt and Jordan, 1952-55, UK, 1955-58, Germany, 1958-62; Adjutant, 1944-45; Commanding Officer, 1959-62; retired, 1962. County Councillor, Peeblesshire, 1963-75; DL (Peeblesshire), 1966-80; Lord Lieutenant, Tweeddale, 1980-94; Member, Queen's Bodyguard for Scotland (Royal Company of Archers), since 1950; County Director, Peeblesshire Branch, Red Cross, 1966-74, Patron, since 1983; County Commissioner, Peeblesshire Scout Association, 1968-73, Chairman, 1975-80, President, 1980-94; President, Borders Area Scout Association, since 1994; Scout Medal of Merit,

1994; Honorary Secretary, Royal Caledonian Hunt, 1964-74; President, Lowlands of Scotland TA&VRA, 1986-89; President, Lothian Federation of Boys' Clubs, 1989-96, now Hon. Vice-President; Honorary Freeman, Tweeddale District, 1994. Publication: Swifter than Eagles (war memoirs). Recreations: country sports; motor cycle touring. Address: (h.) Crookston, by Peebles, EH45 9JQ; T.-Kirkton Manor 740209.

Sprott, Gavin, MA, FSAScot. Keeper, Department of Social and Technological History, National Museums of Scotland; b. 23.7.43, Dundee; m., Maureen Turnbull; 2 s.; 1 d. Educ. Edinburgh University. Research Assistant, Scottish Country Life Section, National Museum of Antiquities of Scotland, 1972-79; Curator, Scottish Agricultural Museum, 1979-86. Recreations: cycling; walking. Address: (b.) National Museums of Scotland, Chambers Street, Edinburgh, EH1 1JF; T.-0131-247 4256.

Sproul-Cran, Robert Scott, MA (Cantab), PhD. Director, Northlight Productions Ltd., since 1991; b. 14.8.50; m., Elizabeth Ann; 3 s.; 1 d. Educ. Daniel Stewart's College; Pembroke College, Cambridge; Edinburgh University. Trainee, Phillips & Drew, Stockbrokers, London, 1971-72; Announcer, then Head of Presentation, BBC Radio Scotland, 1979-85; Radio Manager, BBC Aberdeen, 1986-90; Scottish Correspondent, BBC Daytime Television, 1990-91; freelance Graphic Designer and Underwater Photographer, since 1976; Winner, Scottish Corporate Communications Award, RTS Award for video graphics; illustrated Maurice Lindsay's Glasgow; exhibited, Aberdeen Artists' annual exhibition. Recreations: oil painting; printmaking; windsurfing; sub aqua; playing bad rock guitar. Address: (b.) The Media Village, Grampian TV, Queens Cross, Aberdeen AB15 4XJ; T.-01224 646460.

Spry, Christopher John, BA, AHSM. Chief Executive, Greater Glasgow Health Board, since 1996; b. 29.8.46, London; m., Judy; 2 s. Educ. Sir Roger Manwood's School; Exeter University. NHS Management Trainee, 1967-69; Admin Assistant, Doncaster Royal Infirmary, 1969-70; Deputy Hospital Secretary, Lewisham Hospital, 1970-73; Hospital Secretary, Nottingham General Hospital, 1973-75; Assistant District Administrator, then District Administrator, South Nottingham, 1975-81; District Administrator/General Manager, Newcastle Health Authority, 1981-89; Regional General Manager, South West Thames Regional Health Authority, 1989-94; Regional Director, South Thames Regional Office, NHS Executive, 1994-96. Recreations: swimming; arts; enjoying townscapes. Address: (b.) Greater Glasgow Health Board, Dalian House, PO Box 15329, 350 St Vincent Street, Glasgow G3 8YZ; T.-0141-201 4641.

Spurway, Professor Neil Connell, MA, PhD. Professor of Exercise Physiology, University of Glasgow, since 1996; b. 22.8.36, Bradford; m., Alison Katherine Middleton; 3 s. Educ. The Grammar School, Falmouth, Cornwall; Jesus College, Cambridge University. Assistant, then Lecturer, then Senior Lecturer in Physiology, University of Glasgow, 1963-96. Chair, Physiology Section, British Association of Sports Scientists, 1991-93; Chair, Glasgow Gifford Lectureships Committee, 1994-98; Member, Exercise Physiology Steering Group, BOA, since 1991; Fellow, European College of Sports Science. Publications: Humanity, Environment and God; many textbook chapters. Recreations: dinghy racing; distance running; philosophy; theatre. Address: (b.) West Medical Building, University of Glasgow, Glasgow G12 8QQ; T.-0141-330 4499.

Spy, Sheriff James, LLB (Hons). Sheriff of North Strathclyde at Paisley, since 1988; b. 1.12.52. Admitted Solicitor, 1976; Advocate, 1979. Address: (b.) Sheriff Court House, 106 Renfrew Road, Paisley, PA3 4DD.

Squire, Rachel Anne, BA, CQSW. MP (Labour), Dunfermline West, since 1992; b. 13.7.54, Carshalton, Surrey; m., Allan Mason. Educ. Godolphin and Latymer Girls' School; Durham University. Social Worker, Birmingham Social Services, 1975-81; National Union of Public Employees, 1981-92. Address: (b.) House of Commons, London, SW1A 0AA.

Stachura, Peter Desmond, MA, PhD, DLitt, FRHistS. Reader in Modern History, Stirling University, since 1983; b. 2.8.44, Galashiels; m., Kay Higgins; 1 s.; 1 d. Educ. St. Mirin's RC Academy, Paisley; Glasgow University; East Anglia University. Research Fellow, Institut für Europäische Geschichte, Mainz, Germany, 1970-71; Lecturer in History, Stirling University, 1971-83. Chairman (and Founder), The Polish Society, since 1996. Publications: Nazi Youth in the Weimar Republic; The Weimar Era and Hitler: a critical bibliography; The Shaping of the Nazi State (Editor); The German Youth Movement, 1900-1945; Gregor Strasser and the Rise of Nazism; The Nazi Machtergreifung (Editor); Unemployment and the Great Depression in Weimar Germany (Editor); The Weimar Republic and the Younger Proletariat: an economic and social analysis; Political Leaders in Weimar Germany: a biographical study; Themes of Modern Polish History (Editor); Poland Between the Wars, 1918-1939 (Editor); Poland in the Twentieth Century. Recreations: supporting Celtic FC; discovering Poland; gardening. Address: (h.) Ashcroft House, Chalton Road, Bridge of Allan, FK9 4EF; T.-01786 832793.

Stafford, William, MIWM, MREHIS. Director of Community Services, East Ayrshire Council, since 1995; b. 25.3.54, Galston; m., Margaret Ann; 1 s. Educ. Galston High School; Loudoun Academy; College of Food Technology, Glasgow. Ayr County Council, 1971-75; various posts in Environmental Health, Cumnock and Doon Valley District Council, 1975-95. Chairman, Strathclyde Food and Drugs Liaison Group. Recreations: motor sport; gardening. Address: (b.) Council Headquarters, London Road, Kilmarnock; T.-01563 576023.

Stair, 14th Earl of (John David James Dalrymple); b. 4.9.61. Suceeded to title, 1996.

Stakis, Sir Reo. Founder, Stakis plc; b. 13.3.13; m.; 2 s.; 4 d. Educ. American Academy, Larnaca.

Stanners, Ian Cram, FRICS. Chartered Quantity Surveyor; b. 30.11.38, Glasgow; m., Louise Robertson; 2 d. Educ. Hutchesons' Boys' Grammar School. Chairman, Quantity Surveyors Divisional Committee, Scottish Branch, RICS, 1980-81; Chairman, RICS in Scotland, 1986-87; Chairman, Scottish Building Contract Committee. Honorary Vice-President, Clyde Amateur Rowing Club. Recreations: rowing; curling. Address: (b.) 21 Woodlands Terrace, Glasgow, G3 6DF; T.-0141-332 6032.

Stansfeld, John Raoul Wilmot, JP, DL, MA (Oxon), FIFM. Director, Joseph Johnston & Sons Ltd., since 1962; b. 15.1.35, London; m., Rosalinde Rachel Buxton; 3 s. Educ. Eton; Christ Church, Oxford. Lt., Gordon Highlanders, 1954-58; Chairman, North Esk District Salmon Fishery Board, 1967-80; Esk Fishery Board Committee, 1980-85; Vice Chairman, Association of Scottish District Salmon Fishery Boards, 1970-85; Director and Chairman, Montrose Chamber of Commerce, 1984-97; Editor, Salmon Net Magazine, 1978-85; Chairman, Scottish Fish Farmers Association, 1970-73; Secretary, Diocese of Brechin, 1968-76. Member, Royal Company of Archers (Queen's Bodyguard for Scotland). Recreations: reading; jigsaw puzzles; trees. Address: (h.) Dunninald, Montrose, Angus, DD10 9TD; T.-01674 672666.

Stark, Edi, MA (Hons), ALA. Presenter, Fair Deal, Stark Talk, Home Truths, BBC Radio Scotland; Presenter, The

Stark Truth About Everything, Scottish Television; Presenter, Managing Life, Radio 4; b. Edinburgh; m., Gavin Stark; 1 s.; 1 d. Educ. Aberdeen University; RGIT. Community Librarian, Glasgow and Livingston; Northsound Radio: Community Co-ordinator, 1981, Senior Producer, 1982, Head of Speech Programming, 1983-89; freelance journalist, since 1990. Recreations: conversation, food and drink, travel, reading, contemporary art. Address: (b.) c/o BBC Scotland, Beechgrove Terrace, Aberdeen, AB9 2ZT; T.- 01224 625233.

Stark, Robert, CStJ. Honorary Sheriff, Fife; b. 28.8.15, Kirkcaldy; m., Mary Elizabeth M.C. Gray; 1 s.; 1 d. Educ. Kirkcaldy High School; Edinburgh University (not degree course). Joined A. & J. Innes, Solicitors, Kirkcaldy, as a junior clerk, 1930, eventually qualifying as a Solicitor and becoming a Partner; retired, 1985. Secretary, various organisations, including Conservative constituency association. Recreations: cricket; rugby; golf (all long since discontinued). Address: (h.) 2 Mearns Park, Laurencekirk, AB32 1PE; T.-01561 377618.

Starszakowna, Professor Norma, DA, FCSD, FRSA. Textile Designer/Artist; Chair in Design, Duncan of Jordanstone College of Art; b. 9.5.45, Crosshill; m., Andrew Taylor; 2 s. Educ. Kirkcaldy High School; Duncan of Jordanstone College of Art. Design and production of printed and dyed textiles for fashion and interior; commissioned work includes Crest Hotel, Antwerp, General Accident HQ, Perth, Issey Miyake, Winchester, and Scottish Arts Council; exhibited widely, UK and abroad. SAC Award, 1977; Saltire Art in Architecture Award, 1983; Jerwood Prize short-list, 1997; Member: Crafts Council Index, Board of Texprint, Board of ETN (Brussels), Point, Axis, Textile Institute H.E. Committee, ELIA Advisory Group (Brussels), SHEFC Teaching Quality Assessment, HEFCE Research Assessment Panel for Art and Design, Arts and Humanities Research Board, and various other national bodies. Recreation: travel. Address: (h.) 9 Fort Street, Magdalen Green, Dundee, DD2 1BS; T.-01382 644654.

Steedman, Robert Russell, OBE, RSA, RIBA, FRSA, FRIAS, ALI, DA, MLA. Partner, Morris and Steedman, Architects and Landscape Architects; b. 3.1.29, Batu Gajah, Malaysia; m., 1, Susan Scott (m. diss.); 1 s.; 2 d.; 2, Martha Hamilton. Educ. Loretto School; School of Architecture, Edinburgh College of Art; Pennsylvania University. Governor, Edinburgh College of Art, since 1974; Commissioner, Countryside Commission for Scotland, 1980-88; Chairman, Central Scotland Woodlands Project, 1984-88; Association for the Protection of Rural Scotland Award Panel, since 1995; ARSA, 1973, Academician, 1979; Council Member, RSA, 1981 (Deputy President, 1982-83, Secretary, 1983-91); Commissioner, Royal Fine Art Commission for Scotland, 1983-96; former Member, Council, RIAS; nine Civic Trust Awards, 1963-78; British Steel Award, 1971; RIBA Award for Scotland, 1974; European Heritage Medal, 1975; Association for the Protection of Rural Scotland, 1977; Borders Region Award, 1984. Address: (h.) 11B Belford Mews, Edinburgh; T.-0131-225 1697.

Steel, Professor Christopher Michael, BSc, MB, ChB, PhD, DSc, FRCPEdin, FRCPath, FRCSEdin, FRSE. Professor in Medical Science, St. Andrews University, since 1994; b. 25.1.40, Buckhaven; m., Dr. Judith Margaret Spratt; 2 s.; 1 d. Educ. Prince of Wales School, Nairobi; George Watson's College, Edinburgh; Edinburgh University. House Physician/House Surgeon/Resident/Senior House Officer, Edinburgh Teaching Hospitals; Graduate Research Fellow in Medicine, 1968; joined MRC staff, 1971; MRC Travelling Research Fellow, University of Nairobi, 1972-73; Assistant Director, MRC Human Genetics Unit, Edinburgh, 1979. Editor, Disease Markers; published over 200 scientific papers and book chapters; Member, Government Gene Therapy Advisory Committee. Recreations: golf; skiing; music; theatre. Address: (b.) Bute Medical Building, St. Andrews, KY16 9TS; T.-01334 476161.

Steel, Very Rev. David, MA, BD, DD, LLD. Minister Emeritus, St. Michael's, Linlithgow, since 1977; b. 5.10.10, Hamilton; m., Sheila E.N. Martin (deceased); 3 s. (eldest son: Rt. Hon. Lord Steel of Aikwood, KBE, PC, DL (qv)); 2 d. Educ. St. John's Grammar School, Hamilton; Peterhead Academy; Robert Gordon's College, Aberdeen; Aberdeen University. Minister: Denbeath, Fife, 1936-41, Bridgend, Dumbarton, 1941-46; Associate Secretary, Foreign Mission Committee, Edinburgh, 1946-49; Minister, St. Andrew's, Nairobi and East Africa, 1949-57; Locum, St. Cuthbert's, Edinburgh, 1957-58; Minister, St. Michael's, Linlithgow, 1959-76; Moderator, General Assembly of the Church of Scotland, 1974-75; Visiting Preacher and Lecturer: in America, 1953-87, St. Columba's, Pont Street, 1977, Lausanne, 1978, Tanzania, 1980; Chairman, Callendar Park College of Education, 1972-78; Vice-President: Boys' Brigade, National Bible Society of Scotland, West Lothian Historical and Amenity Society. Publications: History of St. Michael's; The Belief; Preaching through the Year. Recreations: trout fishing; travel. Address: (h.) 39 Newbattle Terrace, Edinburgh, EH10 4SF; T.-0131-447 2180.

Steel of Aikwood, Rt. Hon. Lord (David Steel), KBE, PC, DL. MP, Tweeddale, Ettrick and Lauderdale, 1983-97 (Roxburgh, Selkirk and Peebles, 1965-83); Leader, Liberal Party, 1976-88; b. 31.3.38, Kirkcaldy; m., Judith MacGregor; 2 s.; 1 d. Educ. Prince of Wales School, Nairobi; George Watson's College, Edinburgh; Edinburgh University (MA, LLB). Assistant Secretary, Scottish Liberal Party, 1962-64; Interviewer, BBC TV Scotland, 1964-65; Presenter, weekly religious programme, STV, 1966-67, for Granada, 1969, for BBC, 1971-76; Liberal Chief Whip, 1970-75; Sponsor, Private Member's Bill to reform law on abortion, 1966-67; President, Anti-Apartheid Movement of Great Britain, 1966-69; Chairman, Shelter, Scotland, 1969-73; Member, British Council of Churches, 1971-75; Past President, Liberal International (President, 1994-96); Rector, Edinburgh University, 1982-85; Chubb Fellow, Yale, 1987; Hon. DUniv (Stirling), 1991; DLitt, University of Buckingham, 1994; Hon. Doctorate, Heriot Watt University, Edinburgh, 1996; HonLLD, Edinburgh, 1997; awarded Freedom of Tweeddale, 1988, and Ettrick and Lauderdale, 1990; The Commander's Cross of the Order of Merit (Germany), 1992; DL, 1989; contested Central Italy seat, European elections, 1989; President, Liberal International, 1994-96; Vice President, Countryside Alliance, since 1998. Publications: Boost for the Borders, 1964; Out of Control, 1968; No Entry, 1969; The Liberal Way Forward, 1975; Militant for the Reasonable Man, 1977; High Ground of Politics, 1979; A House Divided, 1980; Border Country (with Judy Steel), 1985; The Time Has Come (with David Owen), 1987; Mary Stuart's Scotland (with Judy Steel), 1987; Against Goliath, 1989. Recreations: angling; vintage motoring. Address: (b.) House of Lords, London, SW1A 0PW; T.-0171-219 4433.

Steel, David Robert, MA, DPhil. Head of Health Gain, NHS in Scotland, since 1995; b. 29.5.48, Oxford; m., Susan Elizabeth Easton; 1 s.; 1 d. Educ. Birkenhead School; Jesus and Nuffield Colleges, Oxford. Lecturer in Public Administration, Exeter University, 1972-84; Assistant Director, National Association of Health Authorities, 1984-86; Secretary, Health Board Chairmen's and General Managers' Groups and SCOTMEG, 1986-90; Director of Corporate Affairs, NHS in Scotland, 1990-95. Address: (b.) St. Andrew's House, Edinburgh, EH1 3DG; T.-0131-244 2455.

Steele, Alexander Allison, OBE (1986). Honorary Sheriff, Perth, since 1985; b. 5.10.25, Oakley, Fife; m., Patricia

Joyce Hipkins; 1 s.; 2 d. Educ. Boroughmuir Secondary School. Entered Scottish Home Department, 1942; Royal Navy, 1943-46; Scottish Court Service (Sheriff Clerk's Branch), 1950; Sheriff Clerk: Dingwall, 1969-71, Perth, 1971-81, Dundee, 1981-85; Member, Lord Stewart's Committee on Alternatives to Prosecution, 1977-83; Honorary Life Member, Society of Sheriff Court Auditors. Recreations: gardening; swimming; wine-making. Address: (h.) Lyndhurst, Hillend Road, Perth; T.-01738 626611.

Steele, Professor Robert James Campbell, BSc, MB,ChB, MD, FRCSEd, FRCSEng, FCSHK. Professor of Surgical Oncology, Dundee University, since 1996; b. 5.3.52, Edinburgh; m., Susan Margaret Cachia; 1 s.; 2 d. Educ. Daniel Stewart's College, Edinburgh; Edinburgh University. Surgical training, Edinburgh, 1977-85; Lecturer in Surgery, Chinese University of Hong Kong, 1985-86; Lecturer in Surgery, Aberdeen University, 1986-90; Senior Lecturer and Reader in Surgery, Nottingham University, 1990-96. Publications in: breast cancer, gastrointestinal surgery and colorectal cancer. Recreations: music; Scottish country dancing; country sports. Address:(b.) Department of Surgery, Ninewells Hospital, Dundee DD1 9SY; T.-01382 660111.

Steele, Thomas Graham. Managing Director: Radio Forth, Scottish Radio Network Sales, Cliar Sheanachain; b. 11.5.45, Lanark; m., Fiona MacAuslane; 1 s.; 1 d. Educ. Larkhall Academy, Larkhall; Skerry's College, Glasgow. Lobby Correspondent, Scottish Daily Mail; TV and Radio Presenter, BBC Glasgow; Producer, BBC Local Radio; Broadcaster, Radio Clyde; Head of News and Current Affairs, Radio Forth; Director of Programmes (Group); Creator, Festival City Radio; Member, Radio Academy Council. Recreations: sailing; walking; reading; conversation. Address: (b.) Forth House, Forth Street, Edinburgh; T.-0131-556 9255.

Steer, Christopher Richard, BSc (Hons), MB, ChB, DCH, FRCPE, FRCPCH. Consultant Paediatrician; Clinical Tutor, Department of Child Life and Health, Edinburgh University; Hon. Senior Lecturer, Department of Biomedical Science, St. Andrews University; Clinical Director of Obstetrics, Gynaecology and Paediatrics; b. 30.5.47, Clearbrook, near Plymouth; m., Patricia Mary Lennox. Educ. St. Olaves and St. Saviours Grammar School, London; Edinburgh University. Publications: Textbook of Paediatrics (Contributor); Treatment of Neurological Disorders (Contributor). Recreation: our garden. Address: (b.) Paediatric Unit, Kirkcaldy Acute Hospitals NHS Trust, Victoria Hospital, Kirkcaldy, Fife; T.-01592 643355.

Stein, Sheriff Colin Norman Ralph, BA, LLB. Sheriff of Tayside, Central and Fife, at Arbroath, since 1991; b. 14.6.48, Glasgow; m., Dr Linda McNaught; 1 s. Educ. Glenalmond College; Durham University; Edinburgh University. Admitted Member, Faculty of Advocates, 1975; appointed Sheriff, 1991. Trustee, CAFE Project, Arbroath. Recreations: gardening; fishing. Address: Sheriff's Chambers, Sheriff Court, High Street, Arbroath DD11 1HL; T.-01241 876600.

Stein, Rev. Jock, MA, BD. Joint Warden, Carberry, since 1986 (Minister, Steeple Church, Dundee, 1976-86); b. 8.11.41, Edinburgh; m., Margaret E. Munro; 3 d. Educ. Sedbergh School; Cambridge University; Edinburgh University. Work Study Officer, United Steel Companies, Sheffield; Assistant Warden, St. Ninian's Lay Training Centre, Crieff; publishing and lay training, Presbyterian Church of East Africa. Publications: Ministers for the '80s (Editor); Our One Baptism; In Christ All Things Hold Together (Co-author); Ministry and Mission in the City; Mission and the Crisis of Western Culture (Editor); Scottish Self-Government: Some Christian Viewpoints (Editor). Recreations: music; skiing. Address: Carberry Tower, Musselburgh, EH21 8PY.

Steiner, Eleanor Margaret, MB, ChB, DPH, MFCM, MRCGP, MICGP, FRSH. Formerly General Practitioner at Appin and Easdale, formerly Principal in general practice in Perthshire; Executive Member, Scottish Child Law Centre; Medical Member, Disability Appeals Tribunal; Medical Assessor, Social Security Appeal Tribunals; Aeromedical Doctor, St. John International Air Ambulance; Member, SACOT (Scottish Advisory Committee on Telecommunications); Member, DIEL (OFTEL Committee for Advice on Disabled and Elderly); Founder, National Society of Associate GPs; b. 21.5.37, Glasgow; m., Mark Rudie Steiner (qv); 1 s. Educ. Albyn School, Aberdeen; Aberdeen University. Surgical Assistant, Freiburg; worked in hospitals, Switzerland, Canada, USA; Departmental Medical Officer/Senior Medical Officer, Aberdeen City; Organiser, Family Planning Services, Aberdeen; Member, Rubella Working Party; Adviser, Aberdeen Telephone Samaritans; Assistant, Psychiatry, Murray Royal Hospital, Perth; Contributor, Scientific Congress, Institute of Advanced Medical Sciences, Moscow. Recreations: sailing; hill-walking; international contacts. Address: (h.) Atlantic House, Ellenabeich, Isle of Seil, by Oban, Argyll, PA34 4RF; T.-Balvicar 300 593.

Steiner, Mark Rudie, LLB, NP. Legal Consultant and Defence Lawyer; Chairman, Scotland Patients Association; former part-time Chairman, Social Security Appeal Tribunal and Disability Appeal Tribunal; former Scottish Representative, Consumers in the European Community Group; Member, Potato Marketing Board Consumer Liaison Committee; Member, National Pharmaceutical Consultative Committee Working Group on Quality Assurance; m., Dr. Eleanor Steiner, DPH, MFCM, MRCGP, MICGP; 1 s. Educ. Aberdeen University. Editor, Canadian Broadcasting Corporation, Toronto and Montreal; Editor, Swiss Broadcasting Corporation, Berne; Procurator Fiscal in Scotland; Partner and Director of various firms and companies, Past Chairman, Perth Community Relations Council; Delegate, Scottish Council for Racial Equality; neutral observer at various overseas political trials; contributor to various international journals; retired Principal, Goodman Steiner & Co., Defence Lawyers and Notaries in Central Scotland; former Member, Scottish Consumer Council. Recreations: sailing; developing international exchanges. Address: (h.) Atlantic House, Ellenabeich, Isle of Seil, by Oban, Argyll, PA34 4RF; T.-Balvicar 300 593.

Stell, Geoffrey Percival, BA, FSA, FSA Scot. Head of Architecture, Royal Commission on the Ancient and Historical Monuments of Scotland, since 1991; b. 21.11.44, Keighley; m., Evelyn Florence Burns; 1 s.; 1 d. Educ. Keighley Boys' Grammar School; Leeds University; Glasgow University. Historic Buildings Investigator, RCAHMS, since 1969; sometime Chairman, Scottish Vernacular Buildings Working Group; sometime Chairman, Scottish Urban Archaeological Trust; sometime Vice-President, Council for Scottish Archaeology. Publications include: Dumfries and Galloway, 1986; Monuments of Industry (Co-author); Buildings of St. Kilda (Co-author); Loads and Roads in Scotland (Co-editor); The Scottish Medieval Town (Co-editor); Galloway, Land and Lordship (Co-Editor); Materials and Traditions in Scottish Building (Co-Editor). Recreations: gardening; music; travel, particularly in Scotland and France. Address: (h.) Beechmount, Borrowstoun, Bo'ness, West Lothian, EH51 9RS; T.-01506 510366.

Stenhouse, Charlotte, JP. Chairman, Fife Health Board, since 1997 (Board Member, since 1970); Member, JP Advisory Committee, since 1979; Member, Health Service National Training Organisation, since 1999; b. 23.4.35, Buckhaven; m., George, 1 step-s.; 1 d. Educ. Buckhaven High School. Industrial radiographer and local government officer; full-time GMB trade union officer, 1977-92. Town Councillor, Burntisland, 1969-75; Member, Labour Party

Scottish Executive, 1972-82; Chairman, Labour Party in Scotland, 1976-77; Member: Social Security Appeals Tribunal, 1982-86, Scottish Advisory Committee, IBA, 1986-89, Local Government Staff Commission (Scotland), 1994-97. Labour Party Candidate, Edinburgh South, October 1974. Recreations: golf; gardening. Address: (h.) 29 Cromwell Road, Burntisland, Fife; T.-(b.) 01334 656200/(h.) 01592 873402.

Stenning, Professor Keith, MA, PhD. Founding Director, Human Communication Research Centre, Edinburgh and Glasgow Universities, 1989-98; Personal Chair, Edinburgh University, 1989-97; b. 15.6.48, London; m., Dr. Lynn Michell; 2 s. Educ. High Wycombe Grammar School; Oxford University; Rockefeller University, NY. Lecturer in Psychology, Liverpool University; Lecturer in Psychology and Cognitive Science, Edinburgh University, 1983-88. Publications: papers on human information processing. Recreation: being blown hither and thither. Address: (b.) H.C.R.C., 2 Buccleuch Place, Edinburgh, EH8 9LW; T.-0131-650 4444.

Stephen, Alex, FCCA. Chief Executive, Dundee City Council, since 1995; (Chief Executive, City of Dundee District Council, 1991-95); b. 17.9.48, Dundee; m., Joyce; 1 s.; 1 d. Local government since 1970. Recreation: voluntary work. Address: (b.) 21 City Square, Dundee; T.-01382 434201.

Stephen, Rev. Donald Murray, TD, MA, BD, ThM. Minister, Marchmont St. Giles' Parish Church, Edinburgh, since 1974; b. 1.6.36, Dundee; m., Hilda Swan Henriksen; 2 s.; 1 d. Educ. Brechin High School; Richmond Grammar School, Yorkshire; Edinburgh University; Princeton Theological Seminary. Assistant Minister, Westover Hills Presbyterian Church, Arkansas, 1962-64; Minister, Kirkoswald, 1964-74; Chaplain, TA, 1965-85 (attached to 4/5 Bn., RSF, 205 Scottish General Hospital, 2nd Bn., 52nd Lowland Volunteers); Convener, Committee on Chaplains to Her Majesty's Forces, General Assembly, 1985-89. Recreations: golf; curling. Address: 19 Hope Terrace, Edinburgh, EH9 2AP; T.-0131-447 2834.

Stephen, Eric John. Farmer; Director, McIntosh Donald Ltd., since 1995; b. 2.1.38, Turriff; m., Norah Winifred Anderson; 1 s.; 3 d. Educ. Inverurie Academy. Former Member, Scottish Agricultural Wages Board; former Convener, Employment and Technology Committee, National Farmers Union of Scotland; Elder, Auchterless Parish Church, 35 years; Past President, Aberdeen and Kincardine Executive, NFU of Scotland; Past President, Royal Northern Agricultural Society; Past President, Aberdeen Fatstock Club; former Director: Aberdeen and Northern Marts, Aberdeen and Northern Estates; President, Turriff Show, 1992; elected Grampian Regional Councillor, 1993; Regional Member, British Wool Marketing Board, since 1993. Recreation: bowling. Address: Lower Thorneybank, Rothienorman, Inverurie, AB51 8XT; T.-018885 11233.

Stephen, Professor Kenneth William, BDS, DDSc, HDDRCPS, FDSRCS. Professor of Dental Public Health, Glasgow University; b. 1.10.37, Glasgow; m., Anne Seymour Gardiner; 1 s.; 1 d. Educ. Hillhead High School, Glasgow; Glasgow University. General Dental Practitioner, 1960-64; House Officer, Department of Oral Surgery, Glasgow Dental Hospital, 1964-65; Lecturer, Department of Conservative Dentistry, 1965-68, Lecturer, Department of Oral Medicine and Pathology, Glasgow University, 1968-71; Visiting Lecturer, Department of Oral Physiology, Newcastle-upon-Tyne University, 1969-70; Senior Lecturer, Department of Oral Medicine and Pathology, Glasgow University, 1971-80; Reader, 1980-84. Co-President, European Organisation for Caries Research, 1978-79. Recreations: swimming; hill-walking; skiing; gardening. Address: (b.) Dental School, 378 Sauchiehall Street, Glasgow, G2 3JZ; T.-0141-211 9854.

Stephen, Mark, DSD. Presenter, The Scottish Connection, Radio Scotland, since 1997; b. 11.9.60, Aberdeen; m., Jean; 3 d. Educ. Inverurie Academy; Royal Scottish Academy of Music and Drama. Commercial Producer, Northsound ILR; Assistant Floor Manager, Researcher, Trails Producer, Senior Announcer (TV), Radio Producer, BBC Scotland. Recreations: reading; water colour painting; DIY.

Stephen, Sheriff Mhairi Margaret, BA, LLB. Sheriff at Edinburgh, since 1997; b. 22.1.54, Falkirk. Educ. George Watson's Ladies College; Edinburgh University. Allan McDougall and Co., SSC, 1976-97 (Partner, 1981-97). Recreations: curling; golf; hill-walking; music. Address: Sheriff's Chambers, Sheriff Court, 27 Chambers Street, Edinburgh EH1 1LB; T.-0131-225 2525.

Stephens, Professor William Peter, MA, BD, DesSR. Professor of Church History, Aberdeen University, since 1986 (Dean, Faculty of Divinity, 1987-89, Provost, Faculty of Divinity, 1989-90); Methodist Minister, since 1958; President, Conference of the British Methodist Church; b. 16.5.34, Penzance. Educ. Truro School; Clare College, Cambridge, and Wesley House, Cambridge; Universities of Lund, Strasbourg, Muenster. Assistant Tutor, Hartley Victoria College, Manchester, 1958-61; Minister and University Chaplain, Nottingham University, 1961-65; Minister, Shirley Methodist Church, Croydon, 1967-71; Chair of Church History, Hartley Victoria College, Manchester, 1971-73; Chair of Historical and Systematic Theology, Wesley College, Bristol, 1973-80; Research Fellow, then Lecturer in Church History, The Queen's College, Birmingham, 1980-86. Secretary, Society for the Study of Theology, 1963-77; President, Society for Reformation Studies,1995-98; Max Geilinger Prize, 1997. Publications: The Holy Spirit in the Theology of Martin Bucer; Faith and Love; Methodism in Europe; The Theology of Huldrych Zwingli; Zwingli: an Introduction to His Thought; The Bible, the Reformation and the Church (Editor); Huldrych Zwingli: Einfuetirung in sein Denken. Recreations: squash; tennis; hill-walking; skiing; swimming; theatre. Address: (b.) Faculty of Divinity, King's College, Aberdeen University, Aberdeen; T.-01224 272383.

Stevely, Professor William Stewart, BSc, DPhil, DipEd, FIBiol. Principal and Vice Chancellor, The Robert Gordon University, since 1997; b. 6.4.43, West Kilbride; m., Sheila Anne Stalker; 3 s.; 2 d. Educ. Ardrossan Academy; Glasgow University; Oxford University. Lecturer and Senior Lecturer in Biochemistry, Glasgow University, 1968-88; Professor and Head, Department of Biology, Paisley College, 1988-92; Vice Principal, Paisley University, 1992-97. Member, Scottish Higher Education Funding Council, 1994-97; Member, National Board for Nursing, Midwifery and Health Visiting for Scotland, since 1993. Address: (b.) The Robert Gordon University, Schoolhill, Aberdeen, AB10 1FR; T.-01224 262001.

Steven, George, MBE. Convener, North Ayrshire Council, since 1995; b. 19.11.29, Glengarnock; m., Janet Ferguson Wilson; 2 s.; 1 d. Educ. Kilbirnie Central School; Glasgow University. Probation Officer, 1963-68; Residential Social Work (Officer in Charge), 1968-88; Assistant Director of Social Work, Salvation Army, 1988-94; Cunninghame District Council: Vice-Chairman, Leisure Committee, 1980-84, Chairman, Planning Committee, 1984-88, Vice-Convener of Council, 1992-96. Recreations: hill-walking; bowling; swimming; football (spectator); music. Address: (h.) 13 Western Crescent, Kilbirnie, KA25 6JE; T.-01505 682698.

Steven, Ian Rollo, BL. Dean, Faculty of Solicitors and Procurators, Dundee, since 1997; b. 5.2.35, Dundee; m.,

Hilary Joy; 2 d. Educ. Glenalmond; St. Andrews University. Qualified, 1957; Senior Partner, Rollo, Steven & Bond, since 1975. Recreations: skiing; sailing; hill-walking. Address: (b.) 21 Dock Street, Dundee.

Steven, John Douglas, MB, ChB, FRCOG. Consultant Obstetrician and Gynaecologist, Stirling Royal Infirmary, since 1981; Member, Scottish Council, British Medical Association; b. 20.4.46, Perth. Educ. Douglas Ewart High School, Newton Stewart; Edinburgh University. Registrar in Obstetrics and Gynaecology, Western General Hospital, Edinburgh; Senior Registrar, Obstetrics and Gynaecology, Ninewells Hospital, Dundee. Address: (b.) Stirling Royal Infirmary, Stirling, FK8 2AU; T.-01786 434000.

Stevens, Claire, BA (Hons). Director–Scotland, Community Service Volunteers, since 1998; b. 26.7.58, Sudbury, Suffolk. Educ. Sudbury Girls High; Sudbury Upper School; University of Warwick. Strathclyde Regional Council, 1981-84; Basildon District Council, 1984-85; Shelter Scotland, 1985-89; Age Concern Scotland, 1989-92; Scottish Council for Single Homeless, 1992-96; The Prince's Trust, 1996-98. Member, Management Committee, Muirhouse Housing Association, since 1990. Recreations: on-going study with Open University Business School. Address: (b.) Wellgate House, 200 Cowgate, Edinburgh EH1 1NQ; T.-0131-622 7766.

Stevens, Professor Paul John, BA (Cantab), MA, PhD. Professor of Petroleum Policy and Economics, Dundee University, since 1993; b. 30.4.47, Liverpool; m., Cassie Stevens; 1 s.; 1 d. Educ. Alsop High School, Liverpool; Clare College, Cambridge; London University. Assistant Professor, American University of Beirut, 1973-75; oil consultant, Beirut, 1975-77; Assistant Professor, American University of Beirut, 1977-79; Lecturer in Economics, then Senior Lecturer, University of Surrey, 1979-93. Publications: numerous books and papers on oil and gas. Recreations: travel; food and drink; golf; carpentry. Address: (b.) CPMLP, Dundee University, Dundee, DD1 4HN; T.-01382 344300.

Stevenson, Celia Margaret Stirton. Director of Locations, Scottish Screen, since 1997, Head of Press and Public Relations, since 1998; Director, Scottish Screen Locations Ltd., 1995-97; b. Ballantrae; m., Charles William Forbes Judge; 2 s.; 1 d. Educ. Wellington School, Ayr; Edinburgh College of Art. Interior design business, 1970-80; Reporter/Presenter, West Sound, Ayr, 1981-84; Scottish Television: Reporter/Presenter, 1984-86, Promotions trailer-maker, 1987-89, Head of Programme Planning and Film Acquisition, 1990-95. Board Member, British Film Commission, since 1997; Member, Steering Group, UK Film Commission Network. Recreations: cooking; reading; study of 20th-century art; interior design. Address: (b.) 249 West George Street, Glasgow G2.

Stevenson, Professor David, BA, PhD, DLitt. Emeritus Professor, Scottish History, St. Andrews University, since 1994; b. 30.4.42, Largs; m., Wendy B. McLeod; 2 s. Educ. Gordonstoun; Dublin University; Glasgow University. Aberdeen University: Lecturer in History, 1970-80, Senior Lecturer in History, 1980-84; Reader in Scottish History, 1984-90; St. Andrews University: Reader in Scottish History, 1990-91; Professor of Scottish History, 1991-94. Honorary Secretary, Scottish History Society, 1976-84; Fellow, Royal Historical Society. Publications: The Scottish Revolution 1637-44, 1973; Revolution and Counter-Revolution in Scotland 1644-51, 1977; Alasdair MacColla and the Highland Problem in the 17th Century, 1980; Scottish Covenanters and Irish Confederates, 1981; The Government of Scotland under the Covenanters 1637-51, 1982; Scottish Texts and Calendars (with Wendy B. Stevenson), 1987; The Origins of Freemasonry, 1988; The First Freemasons: The Early Scottish Lodges and their members, 1988; The Covenanters: the National Covenant and Scotland, 1988; King's College, Aberdeen, 1560-1641, 1990; Scotland's Lost Royal Wedding, 1997; King or Covenant, 1998; Union, Revolution and Religion in 17th Century Scotland, 1998. Address: (h.) 5 Forgan Way, Newport on Tay, Fife DD6 8JQ.

Stevenson, David Deas, CBE, DSc, BCom, CA. Chairman Edinburgh Woollen Mill; b. 28.11.41, Hawick; m., Alix Jamieson; 2 d. Educ. Langholm Academy; Dumfries Academy; Edinburgh University. British Steel Corporation, 1966-67; Langholm Dyeing Co., 1967-70. Recreations: golf; horses; running. Address: (b.) Waverley Mills, Langholm, Dumfriesshire, DG13 OEB; T. 013873 80611.

Stevenson, Gerda. Actress, Singer, Writer, Book Illustrator, Director; b. 10.4.56, West Linton; m., Aonghas MacNeacail; 1 s. Educ. Peebles High School; Royal Academy of Dramatic Art, London (DDA, Vanbrugh Award). Has performed with 7:84 Theatre Co., Scottish Theatre Company, Royal Lyceum Theatre (Edinburgh), Traverse Theatre, Communicado, Monstrous Regiment, Victoria Theatre (Stoke on Trent), Contact Theatre (Manchester) and with Freefall at Lilian Baylis Theatre, London, and Birmingham Rep; directed Uncle Jesus for Edinburgh Festival Fringe; Assistant Director, Royal Lyceum, on Merchant of Venice and A Doll's House; Founder Member and Director, Stellar Quines Theatre Co.; TV work includes Clay, Smeddum and Greenden, Square Mile of Murder, Grey Granite, Horizon: Battered Baby, The Old Master, Taggart, Dr. Finlay, The Bill; films: The Stamp of Greatness, Tickets to the Zoo, Blue Black Permanent (BAFTA Scotland Best Film Actress Award, 1993), Braveheart; directed short film, An Iobairt, in Gaelic for BBC; extensive radio work includes title roles in Bride of Lammermoor and Catriona; freelance producer for Radio Scotland; wrote and illustrated children's book, The Candlemaker. Recreation: walking in the country.

Stevenson, John Meikle, DL, FRAgS, BSc (Agric), FInstD. Farmer; b. 20.1.31, Aberlady; m., Eileen A.; 2 s.; 1 d. Educ. Trinity College, Glenalmond; Aberdeen University. Councillor, East Lothian County Council, 1961-66; President, East Lothian, National Farmers' Union, 1968-69; Council Member, NFU, 1966-70; Member, Governing Body, British Society for Research in Agricultural Engineering, 1968-96; Chairman, Committee, Scottish Centre of Agricultural Engineering, 1987-95; Governor, East of Scotland College of Agriculture; Chairman, Royal Scottish Agricultural Benevolent Institution, 1991-97; Deputy Lieutenant, East Lothian, since 1993. Recreations: shooting; fishing; gardening; golf. Address: (h.) Luffness Mains, Aberlady, East Lothian EH32 OPZ; T.-01875 870212.

Stevenson, Peter David, MA (Cantab); b. 6.3.47, Edinburgh; m., The Hon. Susan Blades; 1 s.; 1 d. Educ. Edinburgh Academy; Trinity College, Cambridge. Chairman: Mackays Stores (Holdings) PLC; Director, British Energy plc; Director, Scottish Nuclear Ltd. Address: (b.) 22 Rutland Street, Edinburgh EH1 2AN; T.-0131-229 0550.

Stevenson, Ronald, DUniv (Stirling), **DMus (Aberdeen), LLD (Dundee),** FRMCM, HonFRIAS. Composer and Pianist; Broadcaster; Author; b. 6.3.28, Blackburn; m., Marjorie Spedding; 1 s.; 2 d. Educ. Royal Manchester College of Music; Conservatorio Di Santa Cecilia, Rome. Senior Lecturer, Cape Town University, 1963-65; BBC Prom debut in own 2nd Piano Concerto, 1972; Aldeburgh Festival recital with Sir Peter Pears, 1973; Busoni documentary, BBC TV, 1974; BBC Radio Scotland extended series on the bagpipe, clarsach and fiddle music of Scotland, 1980-84; Artist in Residence: Melbourne University, 1980, University of W. Australia, 1982, Conservatory of Shanghai, 1985; York University, 1987; published and recorded compositions: Passacaglia for

Piano, two Piano Concertos, Violin Concerto (commissioned by Menuhin), Prelude, Fugue and Fantasy for Piano, Prelude and Fugue for Organ, In Memoriam Robert Carver, St. Mary's May Songs, A Child's Garden of Verse (BBC commission), Voces Vagabundae, Salute to Nelson Mandela (march for brass band), Cello Concerto (RSNO commission), A Carlyle Suite (piano), Le Festin d'Alkan (piano). Publications: Western Music; Alan Bush - a symposium; The Paderewski Paradox. Recreations: hill-walking; reading poetry, biographies and politics. Address: (h.) Townfoot House, West Linton, Peeblesshire; T.-01968 660511.

Stevenson, William Trevor, CBE, DL, FCIT; b. 21.3.21, Peebles; m., Alison Wilson Roy. Educ. Edinburgh Academy. Apprentice Engineer, 1937-41; Engineer, 1941-45; entered family food manufacturing business, Cottage Rusks, 1945; Managing Director, 1948-54; Chairman, 1954-59; Chief Executive, Cottage Rusks Associates, 1965-69; Regional Director, Ranks Hovis McDougall, 1969-74; Director, various companies in food, engineering, hotel and aviation industries, since 1974; Chairman, Alex. Wilkie Ltd., 1977-90; founder Chairman, Gleneagles Hotels, 1981-83; Chairman, Scottish Transport Group, 1981-86; Master, Company of Merchants of City of Edinburgh, 1978-80; Vice President, Edinburgh Chamber of Commerce, 1983-87; Chairman, Scottish Export Association, since 1993. Recreations: flying; sailing; curling. Address: (h.) 42 Spylaw Road, Edinburgh EH10 5BL.

Stewart, A.J. (Ada F. Kay). Playwright and Author; b. 5.3.29, Tottington, Lancashire. Educ. Grammar School, Fleetwood. ATS Scottish Command; first produced play, 1951; repertory actress, 1952-54; BBC TV Staff Writer/Editor/Adaptor, Central Script Section, 1956-59; returned to Scotland, 1959, as stage and TV writer; winner, BBC New Radio Play competition, 1956; The Man from Thermopylae, presented in Festival of Contemporary Drama, Rheydt, West Germany, 1959, as part of Edinburgh International Festival, 1965, and at Masquers' Theatre, Hollywood, 1972; first recipient, Wendy Wood Memorial Grant, 1982; Polish Gold Cross for achievements in literary field. Publications: Falcon - The Autobiography of His Grace, James the 4, King of Scots, 1970; Died 1513-Born 1929 - The Autobiography of A.J. Stewart, 1978; The Man from Thermopylae, 1981. Recreation: work. Address: (h.) 33 Howe Street, Edinburgh EH3 6TF.

Stewart, Sheriff Alastair Lindsay, QC, BA (Oxon), LLB(Edin). Sheriff of Tayside, Central and Fife at Dundee, since 1990; Temporary Judge, Court of Session and High Court of Justiciary, since 1996; b. 28.11.38, Aberdeen; m., 1, Annabel Claire Stewart (m. diss.); 2 s.; 2, Sheila Anne Mackinnon. Educ. Edinburgh Academy; St. Edmund Hall, Oxford; Edinburgh University. Admitted to Faculty of Advocates, 1963; Tutor, Faculty of Law, Edinburgh University, 1963-73; Standing Junior Counsel to the Registrar of Restrictive Trading Agreements, 1968-70; Advocate Depute, 1970-73; Sheriff of Lanarkshire (later South Strathclyde, Dumfries and Galloway) at Airdrie, 1973-79; Sheriff of Grampian, Highland and Islands at Aberdeen and Stonehaven, 1979-90. Chairman, Scottish Association of Family Conciliation Services, 1986-89; Editor, Scottish Civil Law Reports, 1992-95. Publications: Sheriff Court Practice (Contributor), 1988; The Scottish Criminal Courts in Action, 1990, 1997; Sheriff Court Practice (Joint General Editor and Contributor), 1998. Recreations: music; reading; walking. Address: (b.) Sheriffs' Chambers, Sheriff Court House, 6 West Bell Street, Dundee DD1 9AD; T.-01382 229961.

Stewart, Alexander Donald, BA, LLB, WS, DL. Director, Prudential Corporation PLC; Chairman, Murray Extra Return Investment Trust PLC; b. 18.6.33, Edinburgh; m., Virginia Mary Washington; 1 s.; 5 d. Educ. Wellington College, Berkshire; Oxford University; Edinburgh University. Hon. Consul for Thailand in Scotland; DL, Perthshire. Recreations: music; field sports; winter sports. Address: (h.) Ardvorlich, Lochearnhead, Perthshire.

Stewart, Alexander Reavell Macdonald, FRICS. Chartered Surveyor; Chairman, Scottish Branch, Royal Institution of Chartered Surveyors, 1985-86; b. 14.2.29, Bearsden; m., Keris Duguid Keir; 2 s.; 2 d. Educ. Merchiston Castle School. President: Property Owners and Factors Association Glasgow, 1968-69, National Federation of Property Owners Scotland, 1978-80. Recreations: trout fishing; piping. Address: (b.) 21 Winton Lane, Glasgow; T.-0141-357 1272.

Stewart, Archibald Ian Balfour, CBE, BL (Dist), FSA (Scot). Retired Solicitor; Honorary Sheriff; b. 19.5.15, Campbeltown; m., Ailsa Rosamund Mary Massey; 3 s. Educ. Cheltenham College; Glasgow University. Solicitor, 1938; Town Clerk, Lochgilphead, 1939-46, Campbeltown, 1947-54; Procurator Fiscal of Argyll at Campbeltown, 1941-74; Temporary Sheriff, 1975-88; Secretary, Clyde Fishermen's Association, 1941-70; Churchill Fellow, 1966; President, Scottish Fishermen's Federation, 1970-75; Hon. President, Clyde Fishermen's Association and Scottish Fishermen's Federation; former Director, Scottish Fishermen's Organisation and Scottish Board, Phoenix Insurance Co. Ltd.; Past President, Kintyre Antiquarian Society; Past Chairman, Argyll and Bute National Insurance Committee, Kintyre Employment Committee; Adviser, North East Atlantic Fisheries Conference, UN Law of Sea Conference; Editor, List of Inhabitants upon the Duke of Argyle's Kintyre Estates 1792. Recreations: local history; genealogy; wine; gardening; idling. Address: (h.) Askomel End, Campbeltown, Argyll PA28 6EP; T.-01586 52353.

Stewart (nee Muir), Professor Averil M., BA, FCOT, TDip, SROT. Head, Department of Occupational Therapy and Art Therapy, Queen Margaret College, Edinburgh, since 1986; b. 7.4.43, Edinburgh; m., J. Gavin Stewart. Educ. Dunfermline High School; Occupational Therapy Training Centre, Edinburgh. Lecturer, Glasgow School of Occupational Therapy, 1972-74; Senior Occupational Therapist, Head and District Occupational Therapist, Worthing District, 1975-83; Educational Development Officer, Council for Professions Supplementary to Medicine (secondment), 1978-80; Senior Lecturer, Department of Occupational Therapy, Queen Margaret College, 1983-86. Member, Vice-Chairman and Chairman, Occupational Therapists Board, CPSM, 1980-92; Trustee, Dementia Services Development Centre, since 1996; Chairman, CAB Leith, since 1997. Publications: Occupational Therapy Teaching Resources in UK; Contributor: Occupational Therapy in Short-Term Psychiatry; Occupational Therapy in Mental Health. Recreations: wilderness travel; gardening. Address: (b.) Queen Margaret College, Edinburgh EH6 8HF.

Stewart, Brian John, CBE, MSc, CA. Group Chief Executive and Deputy Chairman, Scottish & Newcastle plc, since 1991; Director (Non-Executive), Standard Life and Booker PLC, since 1993; b. 9.4.45, Stirling; m., Shona (Seonaid); 2 s.; 1 d. Educ. Perth Academy; Edinburgh University. J. & R. Morrison, CA, Perth, 1962-67; Chief Management Accountant, Ethicon Ltd., 1969-76; joined Scottish & Newcastle plc, 1976; Corporate Development Director, 1985; Group Finance Director, 1988. Recreations: skiing; golf. Address: (b.) 111 Holyrood Road, Edinburgh EH8 8YS; T.-0131-556 2591.

Stewart, Brian West, BSc, MRTPI. Chief Executive, Western Isles Islands Council, now Western Isles Council, now Comhairle nan Eilean Siar, since 1993; b. 27.6.58, Edinburgh; m., Alicia Dolores Giles-Stewart; 1 s.; 1 d. Educ. George Heriot's, Edinburgh; Heriot-Watt University, Edinburgh. Graduate Trainee, UK Atomic Energy Authority, Risley; entered local government with posts in

Newbury, Farnborough, Dingwall and Stornoway. Recreations: reading; current affairs; planning foreign holidays. Address: (b.) Council Offices, Sandwick Road, Stornoway, Isle of Lewis; T.-01851 703773.

Stewart, David John, MP, BA (Hons). MP (Labour), Inverness East, Nairn and Lochaber, since 1997; b. 5.5.56; m., Linda; 1 s.; 1 d. Educ. Inverness High School; Paisley College; Stirling University; Open University Business School. Lecturer in Community Care, Esk Valley College, 1981; Social Worker, Dumfries and Dingwall, 1981-87; Social Work Team Manager, Highland Council, 1987-97. Patron, Shopmobility Highland. Recreations: sport; keep-fit; travel; reading. Address: (b.) Queensgate Business Centre, Fraser Street, Inverness; T.-01463 237441.

Stewart, David Roger, TD, MA, BA (Hons), FEIS. Honorary Sheriff, Selkirk, since 1983; b. 3.2.20, Glasgow; m., Gwyneth Ruth Morris; 2 s.; 1 d. Educ. Hyndland Secondary School; Glasgow High School; Glasgow University; London University. Army, 1939-46; Schoolmaster, 1947-65 (Kelvinside Academy, Galashiels Academy); Rector, Selkirk High School, 1965-81; Member: Selkirk Town Council, 1967-75, Borders Education Committee, 1975-81, Borders Regional Council, 1982-86; TA, 1939-64; Chairman, Selkirk Committee, Cancer Research Campaign. Recreations: golf; gardening; reading. Address: (h.) Cairncoed, Hillside Terrace, Selkirk TD7 4ND; T.-01750 21755.

Stewart, Ena Lamont. Playwright; b. 10.2.12, Glasgow; m., Jack Stewart (deceased); 1 s. Educ. Woodside School, Glasgow; Esdaile School, Edinburgh. Assistant, Public Library, Aberdeen, 1930-34; Medical Secretary, Radcliffe, Lancashire, 1934-37; Secretary/Receptionist, Royal Hospital for Sick Children, Glasgow, 1937-41; Baillie's Reference Library, Glasgow: Assistant Librarian, 1953-57, Librarian-in-charge, 1957-66; author of plays: Starched Aprons, Men Should Weep, The Heir to Ardmally, Business in Edinburgh, After Tomorrow (unperformed), Walkies Time, Knocking on the Wall, Towards Evening, High Places. Recreations: reading; listening to music. Address: (h.) 5a Monkton Road, Prestwick KA9 1AP.

Stewart, Francis John, MA (Oxon), LLB, TD. Writer to the Signet (retired); Member, Queen's Bodyguard for Scotland (Royal Company of Archers); b. 11.5.17, Edinburgh; m., Olga Margaret Mounsey (deceased); 3 s.; 1 d. Educ. Cargilfield School, Edinburgh; Loretto School; Trinity College, Oxford; Edinburgh University. 1st Bn., Lothians and Borders Yeomanry; Senior Partner, Murray Beith & Murray, WS, Edinburgh (retired); Past Chairman of Governors, Loretto School; Honorary Consul for Principality of Monaco, 1964-85; Chevalier of the Order of St. Charles. Recreation: gardening. Address: (b.) 39 Castle Street, Edinburgh; T.-0131-225 1200.

Stewart, Sir Frederick Henry, KB, BSc, PhD, FRSA, DSc Hon. (Aberdeen, Leicester, Heriot-Watt, Durham, Glasgow), FRS, FRSE, FGS. Professor Emeritus, Edinburgh University, since 1982; Trustee, British Museum (Natural History), 1983-88; Council Member, Scottish Marine Biological Association, 1983-89; b. 16.1.16, Aberdeen; m., Mary Florence Elinor Rainbow. Educ. Fettes College, Edinburgh; Robert Gordon's College, Aberdeen; Aberdeen University; Emmanuel College, Cambridge. Mineralogist, Research Department, Imperial Chemical Industries, 1941-43; Lecturer in Geology, Durham University, 1943-56; Regius Professor of Geology and Mineralogy, Edinburgh University, 1956-82; Member, Council for Scientific Policy, 1967-71 (Assessor, 1971-73); Chairman, Natural Environment Research Council, 1971-73; Chairman, Advisory Board for the Research Councils, 1973-79; Member, Advisory Council for Research and Development, 1976-79; University Grants Committee Earth Sciences Review, 1986-87. Lyell Fund Award, 1951 and Lyell Medal, 1970, Geological Society of London; Mineralogical Society of America Award, 1952; Clough Medal, Edinburgh Geological Society; Sorby Medal, Yorkshire Geological Society. Publications: The British Caledonides, 1963; Marine Evaporites, 1963. Recreations: fishing; collecting fossil fish. Address: (h.) House of Letterawe, Lochawe, Argyll, PA33 1AH; T.-01838 200 329.

Stewart, George Girdwood, CB, MC, TD, BSc, FICFor, Hon. FLI. Cairngorm Estate Adviser to Highlands and Islands Enterprise, since 1988-98; b. 12.12.19, Glasgow; m., Shelagh Jean Morven Murray; 1 s.; 1 d. Educ. Kelvinside Academy, Glasgow; Glasgow University; Edinburgh University. Royal Artillery, 1940-46 (mentioned in Despatches); Forestry Commission: District Officer, 1949-60, Assistant Conservator, 1960-67, Conservator (West Scotland), 1967-69, Commissioner, Forest and Estate Management, 1969-79. Commanding Officer, 278 (Lowland) Field Regiment RA (TA), 1956-59; President, Scottish Ski Club, 1971-75; Vice President, National Ski Federation of Great Britain and Chairman, Alpine Racing Committee, 1975-78; National Trust for Scotland: Member of Council, 1975-79, Representative, Branklyn Garden, 1980-84, Regional Representative, Central and Tayside, 1984-88; Forestry Consultant, 1989-93; Chairman, Scottish Wildlife Trust, 1981-87; Member, Countryside Commission for Scotland, 1981-88; Member, Environment Panel, British Railways Board, 1980-90; Associate Director, Oakwood Environmental, since 1990; Member, Cairngorm Recreation Trust, since 1986; President, Scottish National Ski Council, 1988-94, Hon. Vice-President, since 1997; Specialist Adviser to House of Lords Select Committee on EEC Forestry Policy, 1986; National Service to Sport Award, 1995. Fellow, Royal Society of Arts. Recreations: skiing; veterans' tennis; studying Scottish painting. Address: (h.) Stormont House, 11 Mansfield Road, Scone, Perth PH2 6SA; T. 01738 551815.

Stewart, Gillian Mary, BA (Hons). Head of Group, Scottish Office Home Department, since 1992; b. 2.6.45, Gosforth; 2 s. Educ. Blyth Grammar School; Durham University. Joined Scottish Office, 1970, as Assistant Principal; posts held in Education, Social Work Services Group, Environment. Recreations: swimming; walking; theatre; music. Address: (b.) James Craig Walk, Edinburgh EH1 3BA; T.-0131-244 3670.

Stewart, Professor Graham George, BSc, PhD, DSc, FIBrew, FIBiol. Director, International Centre for Brewing and Distilling, since 1994; b. 22.3.42, Cardiff; m., Olga Leonara. Educ. Cathays High School, Cardiff; University College Cardiff; Bath University. Lecturer in Biochemistry, Portsmouth College of Technology, 1967-69; various technical positions, J. Labatt Ltd., Canada, 1969-94. Recreations: rugby; music; travel. Address: (b.) Heriot-Watt University, Riccarton, Edinburgh, EH14 4AS; T.-0131-451 3184.

Stewart, Rev. James Charles, MA, BD, STM. Minister, Kirk of St. Nicholas, Aberdeen (The City Kirk), since 1980; b. 29.3.33, Glasgow. Educ. Glasgow Academy; St. Andrews University; Union Theological Seminary, New York. Assistant Minister, St. John's Kirk of Perth, 1959-64; Minister: St. Andrew's Church, Drumchapel, 1964-74, East Parish Church of St. Nicholas, Aberdeen, 1974-80. Trustee, Aberdeen Endowments Trust and other trusts; President, Church Service Society; Past Chairman, Aberdeen Civic Society; Past Chairman, Third World Centre, Aberdeen. Address: (b.) The New Vestry, Kirk of St. Nicholas, Back Wynd, Aberdeen AB10 1JZ; T.-01224 314056.

Stewart, John Barry Bingham, LVO, OBE, BA, CA. Past Chairman, Martin Currie Ltd.; b. 21.2.31, Edinburgh; m., Ailsa Margaret Crawford. Educ. The Leys School, Cambridge; Magdalene College, Cambridge. Accountancy training, Edinburgh; worked in London, United States and Canada; joined Martin Currie, 1960. Recreations: fishing; shooting; golf; skiing. Address: 18 Hope Terrace, Edinburgh EH9 2AR; T.-0131-447 1626.

Stewart, Sheriff John Hall, LLB. Sheriff of Strathclyde, Dumfries and Galloway, at Hamilton, since 1985; b. 15.3.44, Bellshill; m., Marion MacCalman; 1 s.; 2 d. Educ. Airdrie Academy; St. Andrews University. Admitted Solicitor, 1971; Advocate, 1978; Past President, Uddingston RFC; Past President, Uddingston Cricket and Sports Club. Address: (b.) Sheriff Court House, Beckford Street, Hamilton, ML3 6AA.

Stewart, Rev. Kenneth, MA, DipTh. Minister, Stornoway Free Church of Scotland, since 1996; b. 10.10.64, North Uist; m., Anna; 2 s.; 2 d. Educ. Paible Secondary School; Nicolson Institute; Glasgow University. Free Church minister: Scalpay, Isle of Harris, 1991-93, Toronto, Canada, 1993-96. Recreations: music; reading; current affairs. Address: Free Church Manse, 46 Francis Street, Stornoway, Western Isles; T.-01851 702279.

Stewart, Rev. Norma Drummond, MA, MEd, DipTh, BD. Minister, Strathbungo Queen's Park Church, Glasgow, since 1979; b. 20.5.36, Glasgow. Educ. Hyndland Secondary School, Glasgow; Glasgow University; Bible Training Institute, Glasgow; University of London (External); Trinity College, Glasgow. Teacher, Garrioch Secondary School, Glasgow, 1958-62; Missionary, Overseas Missionary Fellowship, West Malaysia, 1965-74; ordained to ministry, Church of Scotland, 1977. Selection School Assessor; Convener, Education for the Ministry Committee, Glasgow Presbytery; Member, Church of Scotland Panel on Doctrine; occasional Lecturer and Tutor in Old Testament, Glasgow University; Participant in Congress on World Evangelisation, Manila, 1989; Member, Council, Evangelical Alliance Scotland; Pastoral Adviser, Glasgow Presbytery; Member, Council of Christians and Jews; Member, Judicial Commission, Church of Scotland. Recreation: research in Old Testament studies. Address: 5 Newark Drive, Glasgow G41 4QJ; T.-0141-423 4818.

Stewart, Norman MacLeod, BL, SSC. Consultant, Allan, Black & McCaskie, Solicitors, Elgin (Senior Partner, 1984-97); Chairman, Elgin and Lossiemouth Harbour Board, since 1993; President, Law Society of Scotland, 1985-86; b. 2.12.34, Lossiemouth; m., Mary Slater Campbell; 4 d. Educ. Elgin Academy; Edinburgh University. Training and Legal Assistant, Alex. Morison & Co., WS, Edinburgh, 1954-58; Legal Assistant: McLeod, Solicitor, Portsoy, 1958-59, Allan, Black & McCaskie, Solicitors, Elgin, 1959-61 (Partner, 1961-97); Council Member, Law Society of Scotland, 1976-87 (Convener, Public Relations Committee, 1979-81, and Professional Practice Committee, 1981-84). Past President, Elgin Rotary Club; Past Chairman, Moray Crime Prevention Panel; President, Edinburgh University Club of Moray, 1987-89. Recreations: walking; golf; music; Spanish culture. Address: (h.) Argyll Lodge, Lossiemouth, Moray; T.-0134381 3150.

Stewart, Patrick Loudon McIain, LLB, WS, DL. Senior Partner, Stewart Balfour & Sutherland, Solicitors, since 1982; Secretary, Clyde Fishermen's Association, since 1970; Honorary Sheriff at Campbeltown; b. 25.7.45, Campbeltown; m., Mary Anne McLellan; 1 s.; 1 d. Educ. Edinburgh Academy; Edinburgh University. Partner, Stewart Balfour & Sutherland, Campbeltown, 1970; former Executive Member, Scottish Fishermen's Federation; former Director, Scottish Fishermen's Organisation Ltd.; member of many Scottish fishing industry committees; Chairman, Argyll & Bute Trust; Secretary, Campbeltown and Kintyre Enterprise Trust Ltd.; Clerk, General Commissioners of Income Tax — Islay; HQ Staff Officer Legal Affairs, Sea Cadet Corps; Honorary Legal Adviser, Sea Cadet Association; Cadet Forces Medal. Recreations: sailing; shooting; youth work. Address: Craigadam, Campbeltown, Argyll PA28 6EP; T.-01586 552161.

Stewart, Robert Armstrong, BA, DipTP, FRTPI, MIMgt. Director of Economic Development and Planning, The Moray Council; formerly Director of Planning and Development, Moray District Council; b. Stirling. Planning Assistant, Lanark County Council, 1968-69; Planner, Glasgow, 1969-70; Senior Assistant, then Group Leader: Development Control, West Lothian County, 1970-75; Depute Director: Planning, East Lothian District, 1975-79; joined Moray District Council, 1979. Address: (b.) Council Office, High Street, Elgin, IV30 1BX.

Stewart, Lt. Col. Robert Christie, CBE, TD; Lord Lieutenant, Clackmannanshire, since 1994; b. 3.8.26, Dollar; m., Ann Grizel Cochrane; 3 s.; 2 d. Educ. Eton; University College, Oxford. Lt., Scots Guards, 1944-49; 7th Bn., Argyll and Sutherland Highlanders TA, 1951-66; Lt.-Col., 1963-66; Hon. Col., 1/51 Highland Volunteers, 1972-75; Landowner; Lord Lieutenant, Kinross-shire, 1966-74; Member, Perth and Kinross County Council, 1953-75; Chairman, Kinross County Council, 1963-73; Chairman and President, Board of Governors, East of Scotland College of Agriculture, 1970-83. Recreations: shooting; golf; the countryside. Address: (h.) Arndean, by Dollar, FK14 7NH; T.-01259 742527.

Stewart-Clark, Sir Jack, Bt, MEP. Member of European Parliament for East Sussex and Kent South, since 1979; Vice President, European Parliament, 1992-97; b. 17.9.29, West Lothian; m., Lydia Loudon; 1 s.; 4 d. Educ. Eton; Balliol College, Oxford; Harvard Business School. Coldstream Guards, 1948-49; J. & P. Coats, 1952-70; Philips Industries, 1970-79 (Managing Director, Philips Electrical Ltd., 1970-74, Pye of Cambridge Ltd., 1974-79). Member, Queen's Bodyguard for Scotland, Royal Company of Archers. Publications: European Competition Law; Drugs Education, It's My Problem as Well. Recreations: golf; tennis; photography; classic cars. Address: (h.) Dundas Castle, South Queensferry, near Edinburgh, EH30 9SP; T.-0131-331 1114.

Steyn, John H., CStJ, PhD, MB, ChB, FRCSEd, FRCSEng. Hon. Treasurer, Royal College of Surgeons, Edinburgh, 1993-97; Chairman, Albyn Hospital, Aberdeen, since 1985; b. 3.10.29, Johannesburg; m., Daphne Mary Nelson; 5 s.; 2 d. Educ. St. John's College, Johannesburg; Cape Town University. Consultant in Administrative Charge, Department of Urology, Aberdeen Royal Infirmary, 1969-93. Address: (b.) Albyn Hospital, 21 Albyn Place, Aberdeen AB10 1RW; T.-01224 595993.

Stimson, Professor William Howard, BSc, PhD, CBiol, FIBiol, FRSE. Professor of Immunology and Head, Department of Immunology, Strathclyde University, since 1981; Director, Immunogene Biomedical Ltd.; b. 2.11.43, Liverpool; m., Jean Scott Baird; 1 s.; 1 d. Educ. Prince of Wales School, Nairobi; St. Andrews University. Research Fellow, Department of Obstetrics and Gynaecology, Dundee University, 1970-72; Lecturer, then Senior Lecturer, Biochemistry Department, Strathclyde University, 1973-80. Patron, Scottish Motor Neurone Disease Association; holder, Glasgow Loving Cup, 1982-83; Member, Editorial Boards,five scientific journals. Recreations: mechanical engineering; walking; golf. Address: (b.) Department of Immunology, Strathclyde University, 31 Taylor Street, Glasgow G4 ONR; T.-0141-552 4400, Ext. 3729.

Stirling, Sheriff Hamish, MA, LLB. Sheriff of South Strathclyde Dumfries and Galloway, at Hamilton, since 1992; b. 9.7.38, Liverpool; m., Margaret Davidson Bottomley; 2 s.; 1 d. Educ. Liverpool College; Robert Gordon's College, Aberdeen; Aberdeen University. Solicitor, 1961-62; Procurator Fiscal Depute: Dundee,

1963-70, Borders, 1970-74, Glasgow, 1974-75; Advocate, 1975-92; Temporary Sheriff, 1987-92. Recreations: foreign travel; golf. Address: (b.) Sheriff Court House, Beckford Street, Hamilton ML3 6AA; T.-01698 282957.

Stirling of Garden, Col. James, CBE, TD, KStJ, BA, FRICS. Lord Lieutenant of Stirling and Falkirk, since 1983; Chartered Surveyor; b. 8.9.30; m., Fiona; 2 s.; 2 d. Educ. Rugby; Trinity College, Cambridge. Partner, Ryden and Partners, 1962-89; Director, Scottish Widows Life Assurance Society, 1974-96. President, Highland TAVRA, 1990-96; Director, Woolwich Building Society, 1975-95. Address: (h.) Garden, Buchlyvie, Stirlingshire.

Stirling, Robin Colin Baillie, OBE, JP; b. 6.4.25, Bo'ness; m., Jean R. Hendrie, MA. Educ. Dalziel High School, Motherwell. Editor: Motherwell Times, 1957-85, Motherwell Times Series, 1959-85. Former Secretary, Lanarkshire Branch, NUJ; elected Life Member, NUJ, 1985; Guild of British Newspaper Editors: former Scottish Secretary, Chairman, 1967-70; NCTJ: Member, Scottish Training Committee, 1961-85, Chairman, Scottish Committee, 1978-81. Convener, Motherwell Guild of Help, since 1953; Chairman, Strathclyde Police P Division Crime Prevention Panel, 1976-84; Member: Management Committee, Motherwell and Wishaw CAB, 1971-95 (Chairman, 1978-80), Motherwell and District Christian Aid Committee 1970-82; Honorary Vice President: Motherwell ASC, since 1986, Motherwell CC, since 1985, Lanarkshire Little Theatre; President, Motherwell Probus Club, 1987-88; Founder Chairman, Motherwell and District Music Society (Chairman, 1984-93). Recreations: gardening; music (including jazz); steam locomotives; Motherwell FC; Scottish Opera; cinema organs. Address: (h.) 37 The Loaning, Motherwell ML1 3HE; T.-63762.

Stirling of Fairburn, Roderick William Kenneth, TD, JP. Lord Lieutenant, Ross and Cromarty and Skye and Lochalsh, since 1988; Landowner and Estate Manager; Member, Red Deer Commission, 1964-89; Chairman, Highland Region Valuation Appeal Committee, 1983-91; Chairman, Scottish Salmon and White Fish Co. Ltd., 1980-91; b. 17.6.32; m., Penelope Jane Wright; 4 d. Educ. Wellesley House; Harrow; Aberdeen University. National Service, Scots Guards, 1950-52 (commissioned, 1951); TA service, Seaforth and Queen's Own Highlanders, 1953-69 (retired with rank of Captain); Member, Regional Advisory Committee to Forestry Commission, 1964-85; Local Director, Eagle Star Insurance Co., 1966-85; Director, Moray Firth Salmon Fishing Co. Ltd., 1973-91; Member, Highland River Purification Board, 1975-90; Ross and Cromarty County Councillor, 1970-74 (Chairman of Highways, 1973-74); Member, Ross and Cromarty District Council, and its Representative on Scottish Accident Prevention Council, 1984-96. Recreations: wild life management; gardening; curling. Address: (h.) Arcan, Muir of Ord, Ross-shire IV6 7UL; T.-01997 433207.

Stirrups, Professor David Robert, MSc, BA, BDS, FDS, DOrth(RCSEng), FDS, MOrth(RCPS) Glasgow. Professor of Orthodontics, Dundee University, since 1993; b. 23.6.48, Gillingham; m., Anne; 1 s.; 1 d. Educ. Gillingham Grammar School; Sheffield University. Senior Registrar, Northern Health Authority, 1977-80; Consultant Orthodontist, Greater Glasgow Health Board, 1980-93. Recreations: orienteering; mountain marathons; philately. Address: (b.) Dundee University, Dundee DD1 4HN; T.-01382 635961.

Stobie, David Henry, BSc, MSc, DMS, FIMgt. Head, Postgraduate Programmes, Napier University, since 1997; Chairman, Edinburgh Branch, British Institute of Management, 1988-91, President, 1991-94; b. 21.10.41, Edinburgh; m., June Moffat; 1 s.; 1 d. Educ. Tynecastle Senior Secondary School, Edinburgh; Heriot-Watt University, Edinburgh. Production Planning Engineer, Ferranti Ltd., 1965; various line management positions, Hewlett-Packard Ltd., 1966-73; Works Manager, Hall and Hall Ltd., 1973-74; Senior Systems Analyst, Hewlett-Packard Ltd., 1974-75; joined Napier as Lecturer, 1975; Head, Department of Management Studies, 1984-97. Recreations: hill-walking; classical music; wine-tasting. Address: (b.) Napier University Business School, Bevan Villa, Craighouse Road, Edinburgh, EH10 5LG.

Stobie, David Johnston, FRSA, MCIBS. Non-Executive Director, Shaw Marketing & Design Ltd., since 1994; Non-Executive Chairman, Macnaughton Holdings Ltd., since 1997; Chairman, Queen Margaret NHS Trust, since 1997; Chairman, Children 1st (RSSPCC), since 1996; Trustee: Carnegie Dunfermline and Hero Fund Trust, since 1990, Carnegie United Kingdom Trust, since 1995; b. 29.6.37, Galashiels; m., Nancy R. McIntosh; 1 s.; 1 d. Educ. George Heriot's School, Edinburgh. British Linen Bank, 1954-71; Noble Grossart Ltd., 1971-81 (Treasurer, 1976-81); British Linen Bank Ltd., 1981-96 (Business Development Director, 1986-96). Recreations: family; walking; gardening. Address: (h.) Strathmore, 17 Venturefair Avenue, Dunfermline KY12 OPF; T.-01383 721396.

Stobo, James, CBE, DL, FRAgS. Farmer; Chairman, Moredun Foundation for Animal Health and Welfare, since 1994; Chairman of Governors, Longridge Towers School, since 1982; Chairman, Scottish Seed Potato Development Council, 1988-95; Director, Pentland Science Park Ltd.; Director, New Park Management Ltd., since 1995; b. 9.12.34, Lanark; m., Pamela Elizabeth Mary Herriot; 1 s.; 2 d. Educ. Edinburgh Academy. Farming, since 1951; Past Chairman and President, Scottish Association of Young Farmers Clubs; Member, Home-Grown Cereals Authority, 1971-76; President, National Farmers' Union of Scotland, 1973-74; President, Animal Diseases Research Foundation, 1980-95; Director, John Hogarth Ltd., Kelso Mills; Member, Secretary of State for Scotland's Panel of Agricultural Arbiters. Vice-President: Scottish National Fat Stock Club, Royal Smithfield Club; Deputy Lieutenant, County of Berwick, 1987. Recreation: photography. Address: Nabdean, Berwick-upon-Tweed TD15 1SZ; T.-01289 386224.

Stockdale, Elizabeth Joan Noel, MB, ChB, DMRD, FRCR, FRCPCH, MBA. Consultant Radiologist, Royal Aberdeen Children's Hospital and Aberdeen Royal Infirmary, since 1980; Clinical Senior Lecturer, Aberdeen University, since 1980; b. Chippenham; m., Christopher Leo Stockdale; 2 s.; 1 d. Educ. Aberdeen University. House Surgeon, Aberdeen Royal Infirmary; Senior House Surgeon, Professorial Surgical Unit, Hospital for Sick Children, Great Ormond Street; Registrar, St. George's Hospital; Senior Registrar, Royal National Orthopaedic Hospital, Royal Marsden Hospital, Atkinson Morley's Hospital; Chairman, Grampian Division, BMA, 1995-97; Member, BMA Scottish Council and SCHMS, since 1997; Member, RCR Standing Scottish Committee, since 1997. Recreations: theatre; classical music; travel. Address: (h.) 1 Grant Road, Banchory, Kincardineshire AB31 5UW; T.-013302 823096.

Stodart of Leaston, Rt. Hon. Lord (James Anthony Stodart), PC (1974); b. 6.6.16, Exeter; m., Hazel Usher (deceased). Educ. Wellington. MP (Conservative), Edinburgh West, 1959-74; Joint Under Secretary of State, Scottish Office, 1963-64; Parliamentary Secretary, later Minister of State, Ministry of Agriculture, Fisheries and Food, 1970-74; Chairman: Agricultural Credit Corporation Ltd., 1975-87, Committee of Enquiry into Local Government in Scotland, 1980, Manpower Review of Veterinary Profession in UK, 1984-85. Publication: Land of Abundance: a study of Scottish agriculture in the 20th century. Recreations: music; preserving a sense of humour. Addresses: Lorimers, North Berwick; Leaston, Humbie, East Lothian.

Stoddart, Sheriff Charles Norman, LLB, LLM, PhD. Sheriff of Lothian and Borders at Edinburgh, since 1995; b. 4.4.48, Dunfermline; m., Anne Lees; 1 d. Educ. Dunfermline High School; Edinburgh University; McGill University, Montreal. Private practice as Solicitor, 1972-73; Lecturer in Scots Law, Edinburgh University, 1973-80; private practice, 1980-88; Sheriff of North Strathclyde at Paisley, 1988-95; Director of Judicial Studies in Scotland, since 1997. Publications: (as Co-author) The Law and Practice of Legal Aid in Scotland; Cases and Materials on Criminal Law; Cases and Materials on Criminal Procedure; (as author) Criminal Warrants; Bible John. Recreations: music; sport. Address: (b.) Sheriff's Chambers, Sheriff Court, 27 Chambers Street, Edinburgh, EH1 1LB; T.-0131-225 2525.

Stoddart, Sheila Grahame, LLB, WS, NP. Solicitor, since 1980; b. 20.11.43, Duns. Educ. Esdaile School for Girls, Edinburgh; Edinburgh University. Travel representative; beautician; BBC make-up artist; solicitor. Member, Council, Law Society of Scotland. Recreations: breeder/exhibitor/judge of Australian terriers; travel; reading. Address: (b.) Ayton, Berwickshire TD14 5QH; T.-018907 81209.

Stone, David, MD, FRCP, FFPHM, FRCPCH. Founding Director, Paediatric Epidemiology and Community Health Unit, Department of Child Health, Glasgow University, since 1995; b. 13.5.49, Glasgow; m., Dr Susan V. Carr; 2 s.; 2 d. Educ. High School of Glasgow; Edinburgh University. Trained in general medicine and public health, Glasgow and London; Senior Lecturer in Epidemiology, Ben Gurion University of the Negev, Israel, 1981-85; Senior Lecturer, Glasgow University, since 1985. Recreations: music; dining; current affairs. Address: PEACH Unit, Yorkhill Hospital, Glasgow G3 8SJ; T.-0141-201 0178.

Stone, Professor Frederick Hope, OBE, MB, ChB, FRCP, FRCPsych, FRCPCH. Professor of Child and Adolescent Psychiatry, Glasgow University, 1977-86; Consultant Psychiatrist, Royal Hospital for Sick Children, Glasgow, since 1954; b. 11.9.21, Glasgow; m., Zelda Elston, MA; 2 s.; 1 d. Educ. Hillhead High School, Glasgow; Glasgow University. Acting Director, Lasker Mental Hygiene Clinic, Hadassah, Jerusalem, 1952-54; World Health Organisation Visiting Consultant, 1960, 1964; Member, Kilbrandon Committee, 1963-65; Secretary-General, International Association of Child Psychiatry, 1962-66; Member, Houghton Committee on Adoption, 1968-72; Chairman, Scottish Division, Royal College of Psychiatrists, 1981-84; President, Young Minds; Chairman, Strathclyde Children's Panel Advisory Committee, 1988-94. Publications: Child Psychiatry for Students (Co-author); Juvenile Justice in Scotland (Co-author). Address: (h.) 14A Hamilton Avenue, Pollokshields, Glasgow, G41 4JF; T.-0141-427 0115.

Stone, Gordon Victor, MBChB, FFCM, MFCMI, DCM. General Manager, Highland Health Board, since 1994; b. 4.10.45, London; m., Aileen S. Wilson; 1 s.; 1 d. Educ. Aberdeen Grammar School; Aberdeen University; Edinburgh University. Medical Officer, RAF, 1970-75; Scottish Health Service Fellow in Community Medicine, 1975-78; Specialist in Community Medicine, Grampian Health Board, 1978-89; Chief Administrative Medical Officer/Director of Public Health Medicine, Highland Health Board, 1989-94. Recreations: golf; skiing. Address: (b.) Beechwood Park, Inverness, IV2 3NG; T.-01463 717123.

Stone, Sheriff Marcus, MA, LLB. Accredited Mediator, since 1993; Director, The Mediation Bureau; Hon. President, Association of Mediators; b. 22.3.21, Glasgow; m., Jacqueline Barnoin; 3 s.; 2 d. Educ. High School of Glasgow; Glasgow University. Served Second World War; admitted Solicitor, 1949; admitted Faculty of Advocates, 1965; Sheriff of North Strathclyde, at Dumbarton, 1971-76; Sheriff of Glasgow and Strathkelvin, at Glasgow, 1976-84; Sheriff of Lothian and Borders, at Linlithgow, 1984-93. Publications: Proof of Fact in Criminal Trials, 1984; Cross-examination in Criminal Trials, 1988; Fact-Finding for Magistrates, 1990; Representing Clients in Mediation, 1998. Publication: Mediation Advocacy. Recreations: swimming; music. Address: (b.) Advocates Library, Parliament House, Edinburgh.

Stone, Professor Trevor W., BPharm, PhD, DSc. Professor and Head of Pharmacology, Glasgow University, since 1989; b. 7.10.47, Mexborough; m., Anne Corina. Educ. Mexborough Grammar School; London University; Aberdeen University. Lecturer in Physiology, Aberdeen University, 1970-77; Senior Lecturer/Reader in Neuroscience, then Professor of Neuroscience, London University, 1977-88. Editor, British Journal of Pharmacology, 1980-86. Publications: Microiontophoresis and Pressure Ejection, 1985; Purines: Basic and Clinical Aspects, 1991. Recreations: photography; snooker; working. Address: (b.) Department of Pharmacology, Glasgow University, Glasgow G12; T.-0141-330 4481.

Stormonth Darling, Sir Jamie Carlisle, Kt, CBE, MC, TD, WS, LLB, MA, Hon. FRIAS, DUniv (Stirling), Hon. LLD (Aberdeen); b. 18.7.18, Battle, Sussex; m., Mary Finella Gammell, BEM, DL; 1 s.; 2 d. Educ. Winchester College; Christ Church, Oxford; Edinburgh University. 2nd Lt., KOSB (Territorial), 1937: Adjutant, 1941, to Lt.-Col. Commanding 52nd (L) Division; Reconnaissance Regiment, RAC, 1945-46; studied law, Edinburgh University, 1946-49; appointed Chief Executive as Secretary, then Director, National Trust for Scotland, 1949-83, then Vice-President (Emeritus); Scottish Conservation Projects Trust: first President, 1984-89, Vice-President, 1989-97; oncerned with various Scottish charities such as Scotland's Churches Scheme (Vice Chairman, 1994, Trustee, since 1994), Scottish Churches Architectural Heritage Trust, Scotland's Gardens Scheme, Pollok Trust (Glasgow), Edinburgh Old Town Charitable Trust; Patron, The Woodland Trust, Edinburgh Green Belt Trust. Recreations: gardening; countryside; golf. Address: (h.) Chapelhill House, Dirleton, North Berwick EH39 5HG; T.-01620 850 296.

Stormonth Darling, Lady (Mary Finella), BEM, DL (East Lothian); b. 15.4.24, Farnborough; m., Sir Jamie Carlisle Stormonth Darling, qv; 1 s.; 2 d. Educ. Southover Manor School, Lewes; Architectural Association, London. Special Operations Executive (SOE), 1942-45. Designed own house, 1974; Elder, Dirleton Kirk and Convener, Fabric Committee, since 1976; Member, Church and Nation Committee, Church of Scotland, 1978-86; Convener, Sub-Committee on International Interests, 1982-84; Member, British Council of Churches, 1980-83; voluntary and charitable work. Recreations: painting, sculpting and gardening. Address: Chapelhill House, Dirleton, North Berwick EH39 5HG; T.-01620 850 296.

Stott, Professor David James, MB, ChB, MD(Glas), FRCP(Glas), FRCP(Edin). Professor of Geriatric Medicine, Glasgow University, since 1994; b. 4.6.59, Rugby; m., Shiona; 1 s.; 1 d. Educ. Eastwood High School; Glasgow University. Trained in research methodology, MRC Blood Pressure Unit, 1982-84; Senior Lecturer (Honorary Consultant) in Geriatric Medicine, 1991-94. Recreations: golf; hill-walking; acoustic guitar. Address: (b.) Academic Section of Geriatric Medicine, Glasgow Royal Infirmary G4 0SF; T.-0141-211 4976.

Stott, Rt. Hon. Lord (George Gordon Stott), PC (1964), QC (Scot), MA, LLB, DipEd; b. 22.12.09; m., Nancy Braggins; 1 s.; 1 d. Educ. Edinburgh Academy; Edinburgh University. Advocate, 1936; QC (Scot), 1950; Advocate Depute, 1947-51; Sheriff of Roxburgh, Berwick and Selkirk, 1961-64; Lord Advocate, 1964-67; Senator of the

College of Justice, 1967-85. Publications: Lord Advocate's Diary, 1992; Judge's Diary, 1995; QC's Diary, 1997; Editor, Edinburgh Clarion. Address: (h.) 12 Midmar Gardens, Edinburgh; T.-0131-447 4251.

Stott, Rev. Kenneth David, MA (Hons), BD (Hons). Parish Minister, Chalmers Ardler, Dundee, since 1997; b. 14.12.62, Montrose; m., Anne Herron; 3 d. Educ. Tynecastle High School, Edinburgh; Edinburgh University. Probationery period, Brightons, Falkirk, 1985-89; ordained and inducted into Partick South, Glasgow, 1989. Recreations: modern history; politics; football; reading. Address: The Manse, Turnberry Avenue, Dundee DD2 3TP; T.-01382 827439.

Strachan, Professor Hew Francis Anthony, MA, PhD, FRHistS. Professor of Modern History, Glasgow University, since 1992; Director, Scottish Centre for War Studies, since 1996; Life Fellow, Corpus Christi College, Cambridge, since 1992; b. 1.9.49, Edinburgh; m., Pamela Dorothy Tennant (née Symes); 1 s.; 1 step s.; 2 d.; 1 step d. Educ. Rugby School; Corpus Christi College, Cambridge. Senior Lecturer, Department of War Studies and International Affairs, Royal Military Academy, Sandhurst, 1978-79; Research Fellow, Corpus Christi College, Cambridge, 1975-78; Fellow, Corpus Christi College, since 1979: Tutor for Admissions, 1981-88, Director of Studies in History, 1986-92, Senior Tutor, 1987 and 1989-92. Governor, Rugby School, since 1985, and Stowe School, since 1990; Member, Council, Society for Army Historical Research, 1980-95, Army Records Society, 1990-94, Council, National Army Museum, since 1994; Joint Editor, War in History; Member, Queen's Bodyguard for Scotland (Royal Company of Archers). Publications: British Military Uniforms; History of the Cambridge University Officers Training Corps; European Armies and the Conduct of War; Wellington's Legacy: the Reform of the British Army 1830-54; From Waterloo to Balaclava: Tactics, Technology, and the British Army 1815-1854 (Templer Medal, 1986); The Politics of the British Army (Westminster Medal, 1998); numerous articles and reviews. Recreations: shooting; rugby football. Address: (b.) Department of History, Glasgow University, Glasgow G12 8QQ; T.-0141-339 8855.

Strachan, Michael Francis, CBE (Civil), MBE (Military), MA, FRSE. Writer; b. 23.10.19, Watford; m., Iris Winifred Hemingway; 2 s.; 2 d. Educ. Rugby School; Corpus Christi College, Cambridge. Served in Army, 1939-46; demobilised (Lt.-Col.), 1946; joined Wm. Thomson & Co., Edinburgh, managers of Ben Line, 1946; Partner, 1950-64; Joint Managing Director, Ben Line Steamers Ltd., 1964; Chairman, Ben Line Steamers Ltd. and Ben Line Containers Ltd., 1970-82; Director, Bank of Scotland, 1972-90; Chairman, Associated Container Transportation Ltd., 1971-75; Trustee: National Galleries of Scotland, 1972-74, National Library of Scotland, since 1974 (Chairman, 1974-90), Carnegie Trust for Universities of Scotland, since 1976; Member, Queen's Bodyguard for Scotland (Royal Company of Archers. Publications: The Life and Adventures of Thomas Coryate, 1962; The East India Company Journals of Captain William Keeling and Master Thomas Bonner 1615-17, (Joint Editor), 1971; Sir Thomas Roe (1581-1644), A Life, 1989; contributor to Oxford Book of Military Anecdotes, 1987; The Ben Line, 1825-1982, 1992; Esmond S. de Beer (1895-1990), Scholar and Benefactor, 1995; contributor to various journals. Recreations: country pursuits; silviculture. Address: (h.) Glenhighton, Broughton, by Biggar ML12 6JF; T.-01899 830 273.

Strang, Gavin Steel, BSc (Hons), DipAgriSci, PhD. MP (Labour), East Edinburgh, since 1970; Minister for Transport, 1997-98; b. 10.7.43, Dundee; m., Bettina Smith; 1 s. Educ. Morrison's Academy, Crieff; Edinburgh University. Parliamentary Under Secretary of State, Department of Energy, February to October, 1974; Parliamentary Secretary, Ministry of Agriculture, 1974-79; Principal Labour Agriculture Spokesman, 1992-97. Recreations: golf; swimming; the countryside. Address: (b.) House of Commons, Westminster, London; T.-0171-219 3000.

Strang, William Frank Gourlay, BA (Oxon). Secretary to Forestry Commission, since 1997; b. 30.6.61, Glasgow; m., Eleanor Ann Munro-Faure. Educ. Loretto; St. Edmund Hall, Oxford. Administration Trainee, Ministry of Agriculture Fisheries and Food, 1984; Private Secretary to Permanent Secretary, 1987-88; Private Secretary to Parliamentary Secretary, 1988-89; Agricultural Attache, British Embassy, Paris, 1990-94; Principal Private Secretary to Minister of Agriculture, 1994-97. Recreations: hill-walking; bagpipes. Address: (b.) Forestry Commission, 231 Corstorphine Road, Edinburgh; T.-0131-314 6432.

Strange, Lady (Jean Cherry), MA, FIMarE, FSAScot. Peer of the Realm, since 1986; President, War Widows Association of Great Britain, since 1990; b. 17.12.28, London; m., Humphrey Drummond of Megginch; 3 s.; 3 d. Educ. Oxenfoord Castle School; St. Andrews University; Cambridge University. Member, All Party Parliamentary Defence Group; Member, Executive Committee, Association of Conservative Peers, 1990-93; Member, All Party Committee for Children. Publications: Love from Belinda; Lalage in Love; Creatures Great and Small; Love is Forever (poems); The Remarkable Life of Victoria Drummond, Marine Engineer. Address: (b.) Megginch Castle, Errol, Perthshire.

Strang Steel, Sir (Fiennes) Michael, 3rd Bt; b. 22.2.43; m., Sally Russell; 2 s.; 1 d. Educ. Eton. Retired Major, 17th/21st Lancers, 1962-80. Forestry Commissioner, since 1988; DL. Address: (h.) Philiphaugh, Selkirk, TD7 5LX.

Strang Steel, Malcolm Graham, BA (Cantab), LLB, WS. Partner, W. & J. Burness, WS, 1973-97; Partner, Turcan Connell, WS, since 1997; b. 24.11.46, Selkirk; m., Margaret Philippa Scott; 1 s.; 1 d. Educ. Eton; Trinity College, Cambridge; Edinburgh University. Sometime Chairman, Albyn Housing Society Ltd., Scottish Dyslexia Trust; Member, Council, Law Society of Scotland, 1984-90; Secretary, Scottish Agricultural Arbiters Association. Recreations: shooting; fishing; skiing; tennis; reading. Address: (b.) Saltire Court, 20 Castle Terrace, Edinburgh EH1 2EF; T.-0131-228 8111.

Strathclyde, 2nd Baron of (Thomas Galloway Dunlop du Roy de Blicquy Galbraith), PC. Leader of Conservative Group, House of Lords, since 1999; b. 22.2.60; m.; 2 d. Educ. Wellington College; University of East Anglia; Univresité d'Aix-en-Provence. Insurance Broker; Scottish Office Minister for Agriculture and Fisheries, 1990-92; DTI, 1993-94.

Strathmore and Kinghorne, 18th Earl of (Michael Fergus Bowes Lyon); b. 7.6.57; m.; 3 s. President, Boys' Brigade, since 1994; DL, Angus, since 1993. Address: Glamis Castle, Forfar, DD8 1QJ.

Straton, Timothy Duncan, TD, CA, ATII. Partner, Scott-Moncrieff Downie Wilson, Chartered Accountants; Treasurer, Scottish Society for the Prevention of Cruelty to Animals; b. 1.10.42, Edinburgh; m., Gladys Margaret George; 1 s.; 1 d. Educ. Edinburgh Academy. Honorary Treasurer: Bruntsfield Links Golfing Society, Royal British Legion Scotland, SSAFA Forces Help (Edinburgh and Midlothian Branch). Recreations: driving; photography; golf. Address: (b.) 17 Melville Street, Edinburgh EH3 7PH; T.-0131-473 3500.

Street, Margaret Dobson; b. 18.10.20, Hawick; m., Richard Andrew Rutherford Street (deceased); 2 s. Educ.

Hawick High School; Alva Academy. Civil Servant, 1938-48; Ministry of Labour and National Service, 1938-47; Ministry of National Insurance (Inspectorate), 1947-48; voluntary work since 1948, apart from freelance writing on household and conservation topics; Honorary Secretary Leith Civic Trust, until 1997, Patron, since 1998; Convener, Friends of North Carr Lightship; Member, North East Fife District Council, North Carr Management Committee; Saltire Society Representative, Council, National Trust for Scotland, 1986-95; Secretary, Mungo Park Commemoration Committee; Trustee, Robert Hurd Memorial Fund; Appeal Convener, Wallace Statue, Lanark; Member, Steering Committee, Brownsbank; Appeal Convener, Wallace Statue, Dryburgh; Vice-Chairman, Saltire Society, 1983-94, Chairman, 1995-97; Saltire Society's Andrew Fletcher of Saltoun Award for services to Scotland, 1992; Honorary Member, Saltire Society, 1997. Recreations: promotion of Scottish cultural activity; conservation; good cooking. Address: (h.) 115 Trinity Road, Edinburgh; T.-0131-552 2409.

Stretton, James, BA, FFA. Chief Executive (UK Operations), Standard Life Assurance Company, since 1994; b. 16.12.43, Peterborough; m., Isobel Robertson; 2 d. Educ. Laxton Grammar School, Oundle; Worcester College, Oxford. Joined Standard Life, 1965. Recreations: music; gardening; reading; golf. Address: (b.) Standard Life House, 30 Lothian Road, Edinburgh, EH1 2DH; T.-0131-245 6012.

Stringer, Joan Kathleen, BA, CertEd, PhD, MIMgt, FRSA. Principal, Queen Margaret College, Edinburgh, since 1996; Commissioner (with responsibility for Scotland), Equal Opportunities Commission, since 1995; Member, Human Fertilisation and Embryology Authority, since 1996; Member, CVCP Commission on University Career Opportunities; Deputy Convener, Committee of Scottish Higher Education Principals, since 1998; Member, Executive Committee, Scottish Council Development and Industry, since 1998; b. 12.5.48, Stoke on Trent; m., Roel Mali. Educ. Portland House High School, Stoke on Trent; Stoke on Trent College of Art; Keele University. Assistant Principal, Robert Gordon University, 1991-96, having joined as Lecturer, 1980; Visiting Lecturer, Aberdeen University, 1984-86; Member, Management Board, North of Scotland Consortium on Wider Access, 1988-92; Auditor, Higher Education Quality Council, 1992-95; Member, Royal Institute of Public Administration, 1984-91; Member, Joint University Council for Social and Public Administration, 1982-91; Member, Scottish Committee, National Committee of Inquiry into Higher Education (The Dearing Committee), 1996-97; Member, Grampian Health Board, 1994-96; Member, Board of Management, Aberdeen College, 1993-96. Address: (b.) Queen Margaret College, Clerwood Terrace, Edinburgh, EH12 8TS; T.-01651 842430.

Strong, Hilary. Director, Edinburgh Festival Fringe, since 1994; b. 3.6.57, Chichester. Educ. Chichester High School for Girls; Lombard School of Dancing, Chichester; Avery Hill College of Education, London. Stage manager and actress, 1979-83; administration and PR, 1984-85; Administrator: Merlin Theatre, Frome, 1986-88, Natural Theatre Company, Bath, 1989-94; freelance lecturer and director, 1987-94. Member, Board of Directors, National Campaign for the Arts, 1991-93; Member, Arts Council of England, since 1998. Recreations: travel; cooking; dancing. Address: (b.) Festival Fringe Society Ltd., 180 High Street, Edinburgh, EH1 1QS; T.-0131-226 5257.

Strudwick, Major General Mark Jeremy, CBE. General Officer Commanding, Army in Scotland, and Governor, Edinburgh Castle, since 1997; b. 19.4.45; m., Janet Elizabeth Coleridge Vivers; 1 s.; 1 d. Educ. St. Edmund's School, Canterbury; Royal Military Academy, Sandhurst. Commissioned, The Royal Scots (The Royal Regiment), 1966 (Colonel, 1995); served UK, BAOR, Cyprus, Canada, India, Northern Ireland (Despatches twice); Commanded, 1st Bn. The Royal Scots, 1984-87; Instructor, Staff College Camberley, 1987-88; Assistant Chief of Staff, G1/G4 HQ Northern Ireland 1988-90; Higher Command and Staff Course, 1989; Commanded, 3 Infantry Bde., 1990-91; NDC New Delhi, 1992; Deputy Military Secretary, Ministry of Defence, 1993-95; Director of Infantry, 1996-97. ADC to HM The Queen, 1996-97; Colonel Commandant, The Scottish Division, since 1997; Member, Royal Company of Archers, Queen's Bodyguard for Scotland; Commodore Infantry Sailing Association, since 1997; Her Majesty's Commissioner, Queen Victoria School, Dunblane, since 1997; Governor, Royal School, Bath, since 1993. Recreations: golf; shooting; sailing. Address: (b.) Army HQ Scotland, Craigiehall, South Queensferry, West Lothian EH30 9TN; T.-0131-310 2063.

Stuart, Charles Murray. Chairman, Scottish Power PLC, since 1992; Chairman, Intermediate Capital Group, since 1993; Chairman, Hammersmith Hospitals NHS Trust, since 1996; Non-Executive Director: Willis Corroon Group PLC, 1996-97, Royal Bank of Scotland plc, since 1996, CMG plc, since 1998, Royal Scottish National Orchestra Society Ltd., since 1998, Glasgow Academicals War Memorial Trust Ltd., since 1996; b. 28.7.33, Gourock; m., Netta Caroline; 1 s.; 1 d. Educ. Glasgow Academy; Glasgow University. MB Group PLC (formerly Metal Box), 1981-90, latterly as Executive Chairman; Chief Executive, Berisford International plc, 1990-91. Recreations: sailing; ballet; theatre. Address: (b.) 1 Atlantic Quay, Glasgow G2 8SP; T.-0141-248 8200.

Stuart of Findhorn, 2nd Viscount (David Randolph Moray Stuart); b. 20.6.24; m.; 2 s.; 3 d. Succeeded to title, 1971. Address: Findhorn, Forres, IV36 0YE.

Stuart, Jamie. Author of A Glasgow Bible; b. 10.9.20, Glasgow; widower; 2 d. Educ. Whitehill School, Glasgow. Flying Officer/Wireless Operator/Air Gunner, RAF, 1941-46; Actor/Social Worker/Evangelist; athlete: Scottish two-miles steeplechase champion, 1948. Address: (h.) 436 Edinburgh Road, Glasgow G33 2PW; T.-0141-778 2437.

Stuart, John Forester, MA (Cantab). Secretary General, General Synod, Scottish Episcopal Church, since 1996; b. 26.5.59, Broughty Ferry; m., Sally Ann Bell; 1 s. Educ. Dundee High School; Daniel Stewart's and Melville College; Queens' College Cambridge, College of Law, Guildford.Articled Clerk and subsequently Solicitor, MacFarlanes, London, 1982-86; Solicitor and subsequently Partner, J. & F. Anderson, Solicitors, Edinburgh (merged, 1992, to become Anderson Strathern), 1986-96. Recreations: music; walking; astronomy. Address: (b.) 21 Grosvenor Crescent, Edinbrugh EH12 5EE; T.-0131-225 6357.

Stuart, Michael John, BSc (Hons). Headteacher, Kincorth Academy, since 1990; b. 24.11.46, Fraserburgh; m., Daniele Madeleine; 2 s.; 1 d. Educ. Fraserburgh Academy; Aberdeen University. Assistant Teacher, Fraserburgh Academy, 1970-71, Kelvinside Academy, Glasgow, 1971-72; Principal Teacher, Greenwood Academy, Irvine, 1972-81; Assistant Head Teacher, Loudoun Academy, Galston, 1981-89; Depute Head Teacher, Carrick Academy, Maybole, 1989-90. Recreations: golf; angling; hill-walking. Address: (b.) Kincorth Academy, Kincorth Circle, Aberdeen, AB1 5NL; T.-01224 872881.

Stubbs, Ian Michael, LLB, CA, FTII. Partner, Maclay Murray & Spens, Solicitors, since 1973; b. 14.11.43, Birmingham; m., Joan Baird Crowther; 2 s.; 1 d. Educ. Marr College, Troon; Glasgow University. Thomson McLintock, Glasgow, 1965-68; Apprentice/Assistant, Maclay Murray & Spens, 1968-73. Council Member, Law Society of Scotland, since 1995; Council Member, Institute of Chartered Accountants of Scotland, 1986-92; Past Chairman, Board of Examiners, Law Society of Scotland; Senior Tutor, Wills Trusts and Executries, Glasgow University, 1980-86. Address: (h.) Suffolk Lodge, Methven Road, Whitecraigs, Glasgow, G46; T.-0141-639 6580.

Sturgeon, David, BL, MLitt. Registrar and Deputy Secretary, Heriot-Watt University, 1967-95; b. 10.12.35, Kilwinning; m., Nancy McDougall; 1 d.; 2 s. Educ. Dalry High School, Ayrshire (Blair Medallist, 1950); Glasgow University. National Service (RASC - War Office), 1957-59; Trainee Actuary, Scottish Widows Fund, 1959-61; Administrative Assistant, Royal College of Science and Technology (later, Strathclyde University), 1961-67. Secretary and Treasurer, Edinburgh Society of Glasgow University Graduates, since 1971; Hon. degree, Heriot-Watt University, 1996. Recreations: golf; music (particularly Scottish country dance music). Address: (h.) 10 Dalhousie Road, Eskbank, Midlothian EH22 3AS; T.-0131-663 1059.

Sturgeon, Nicola, LLB (Hons), DipLP. Vice Convener, Publicity, Scottish National Party, since 1997, Education Spokesperson, since 1997; b. 19.7.70, Irvine. Educ. Greenwood Academy, Irvine; University of Glasgow. Trainee Solicitor, Glasgow, 1993-95; Solicitor, Stirling, 1995-97; Solicitor, Drumchapel Law Centre, Glasgow, 1997-99. Recreations: reading; theatre; badminton. Address: (h.) 2467 Dumbarton Road, Glasgow; T.-0141-952 0845.

Sturrock, Professor Robert Ralph, MB, ChB, DSc. Professor of Anatomy, Dundee University, since 1992; b. 1.7.43, Dundee; m., Norma Duncan; 1 d. Educ. Dundee High School; St. Andrews University. House Surgeon, Perth Royal Infirmary, 1967-68; House Physician, Stirling Royal Infirmary, 1968; Demonstrator, then Lecturer, Anatomy Department, Dundee University, 1968-77; Visiting Associate Professor of Neuroanatomy, Iowa University, 1976; Senior Lecturer, Dundee, 1977-81, Reader in Anatomy, 1981-92. Symington Memorial Prize in Anatomy, 1978; Convener, Tayforth Universities Military Education Committee, since 1997. Address: (b.) Dundee University, Dundee, DD1 4HN.

Sturrock, Professor Roger Davidson, MB, BS, MRCS, MD, FRCPLond, FRCPGlas. McLeod/ARC Professor of Rheumatology, Glasgow University, since 1990; b. 20.10.46, Dundee; m., Helen; 3 d. Educ. Llanelli Boys' Grammar School; Queen Mary's School, Basingstoke; London University. Senior Lecturer and Hon. Consultant, Westminster Medical School, 1977-79; Senior Lecturer in Medicine and Hon. Consultant, Centre for Rheumatic Diseases, Glasgow Royal Infirmary, 1979-90; President, British Society for Rheumatology, 1996-98. Recreations: hill-walking; music; choral singing. Address: (b.) University Department of Medicine, Royal Infirmary, Glasgow G31 2ER; T.-0141-211 4687.

Subak-Sharpe, Professor John Herbert, CBE, FInstBiol, BSc, PhD, FRSE. Professor Emeritus, Glasgow University and Honorary Senior Research Fellow in Virology, since 1994; Professor of Virology, Glasgow University, 1968-94; Honorary Director, MRC Virology Unit, Institute of Virology, Glasgow, 1968-94; b. 14.2.24, Vienna; m., Barbara Naomi Morris; 2 s.; 1 d. Educ. Humanistisches Gymnasium, Vienna; Birmingham University. Assistant Lecturer, Glasgow University, 1954-56; Member, ARC scientific staff, AVRI Pirbright, 1956-61; Visiting Fellow, California Institute of Technology, 1961; Member, MRC Experimental Virus Unit scientific staff, Glasgow, 1961-68; Visiting Professor, NIH, Bethesda, 1967-68. Visiting Fellow, Clare Hall, Cambridge, 1986; elected Member (Past Chairman, Course and Workshops Committee), EMBO, since 1969; Trustee (former Secretary and Vice-President), Genetical Society, since 1971; Member, Genetic Manipulation Advisory Group, 1976-80; Chairman, MRC Training Awards Panel, 1986-89; Member, Governing Body, West of Scotland Oncological Organisation, since 1974, and Governing Body, Animal Virus Research Institute, Pirbright, 1986-88; Member, Scientific Advisory Group, Equine Virology Research Foundation, 1987-98; Member, Medical Research Council Cell Biology and Disorders Board, 1988-92; Biochemical Society CIBA Medal and Prize, 1994. Recreations: travel; bridge. Address: (h.) 63 Kelvin Court, Glasgow G12 0AG; T.-0141-339 1863.

Suckling, Professor Colin James, BSc, PhD, DSc, CChem, FRSC, FRSA, FRSE. Professor of Chemistry, Strathclyde University, since 1984 (Pro-Vice Principal, 1998); b. 24.3.47, Birkenhead; m., Catherine Mary Faulkner; 2 s.; 1 d. Educ. Quarry Bank High School, Liverpool; Liverpool University. Lecturer, Department of Pure and Applied Chemistry, Strathclyde University, 1972; Royal Society Smith and Nephew Senior Research Fellow, 1980; Dean, Faculty of Science, 1992-96; Deputy Principal, 1996-98; Convener, RSE Chemistry Committee, 1989-91; Member of Council, RSE, 1989-92; Member, General Teaching Council, 1993-95; Member of Board, Systems Level Integration Ltd., Lanarkshire Technology and Innovation Centre; Chairman, West of Scotland Schools Symphony Orchestra Board.Publications: Chemistry Through Models (Co-author), 1978; Biological Chemistry (Co-author), 1980; Enzyme Chemistry, Impact and Applications (Co-author), 1984, 1989, 1998. Recreations: music; horn playing. Address: (b.) Department of Pure and Applied Chemistry, Strathclyde Universtiy, 295 Cathedral Street Glasgow, G1 1XL; T.-0141-548 2271.

Suckling, David E., CBiol, MIBiol. Member, Scottish Borders Council, since 1995 (Chairman of Education, since 1996); Chairman, Scottish Borders Careers; Convener, Tweeddale District Council, 1992-96; b. 6.4.43, New Quay, Dyfed; m., Anne E. Robertson; 1 s.; 1 d. Educ. Dulwich College. District Council 1988; Board Member: Garvald Home Farm, since 1989 (Chairman, since 1997), Scottish Museums Council, 1991-97 (Vice Chair, 1992-97), Borders 1996 Ltd., since 1996, Borders Careers Ltd., since 1996; COSLA appointment to Board of Governors, Moray House College, 1997-98, Board of Scottish Maritime Museum, since 1998; Chairman, West Linton Community Council, 1986-91; West Linton Whipman, 1987; President, Whipman Play, since 1992. Recreations: gardening; walking; MGBs, reading. Address: (h.) The Dean, West Linton, Peeblesshire EH46 7AU.

Sugden, Chris, BA. Rector, Buckie High School; b. 25.5.46, Paignton; m., Lynne; 1 s.; 1 d. Educ. Newcastle upon Tyne University. Gordonstoun School, Moray; Castlebrae High School, Edinburgh; Knox Academy, Haddington; Harlaw Academy, Aberdeen. Recreations: exploration and outdoor activities. Address: (b.) Buckie High School, West Cathcart Street, Buckie, AB56 1QB; T.-Buckie 832605.

Suggett, Gavin Robert, MA, MSc, FCA. Director (Managing), The Alliance Trust PLC, since 1995, The Second Alliance Trust PLC, since 1995; Director, Alliance Trust Savings Ltd., since 1986; b. 11.5.44, Sunderland; m., Louise Thomson; 1 s.; 2 d. Educ. Felsted; Christ's College Cambridge; London Business School. Deloitte Haskins & Sells; Weir Group PLC; Alliance Trust PLC: Assistant Company Secretary, Company Secretary, Director, Deputy Managing Director. Recreations: skiing; golf; gardening; keep-fit. Address: (b.) Meadow House, 64 Reform Street, Dundee DD1 1TJ; T.-01382 201700.

Suleiman, Professor Yasir, BA, PhD, BA, DipTFLA. Professor of Arabic and Islamic Studies, University of Edinburgh, since 1990 (Director, Edinburgh Institute for Advanced Study of Islam and the Middle East, since 1997); b. Jerusalem (East), Palestine; m., Shahla Awad; 2 s. Educ.

Amman University, Jordan; St. Andrews University; Durham University. Banker, 1973-74; Teacher of English as a Foreign Language, Kuwait, 1974-75; University of St. Andrews: Teaching Fellow in Lingusitics, 1977-80, Lecturer in Linguistics, 1980-83, Lecturer in Linguistics and Arabic, 1984-90. Publications: Language and Identity in the Middle East and North Africa, 1996; Arabic Grammatical Tradition, 1999; Language and Society in Middle East and North Africa, 1999. Recreations: squash; walking. Address: (b.) David Hume Tower, George Square, Edinburgh EH8 9JX; T.-0131-650 4181/2.

Summers, John P., FREHIS, MIWM. Director, Technical and Leisure Services, Moray Council, since 1996; b. 22.12.46, Rhynie; m., Alison; 1 s.; 1 d. Educ. Aberdeen Academy; Napier College, Edinburgh. Assistant Environmental Health Officer, Aberdeen County Council, 1972-74; Divisional Environmental Health Officer, Kincardine and Deeside District, 1974-79; Depute Director of Environmental Health, Banff and Buchan District Council, 1979-90; Director of Environmental Health, Moray District Council, 1990-94; Chief Executive, Moray District Council, 1994-96. President, Royal Environmental Health Institute of Scotland, 1995-96 (Fellow, 1997). Recreations: rambling; enjoying traditional Scottish folk music and bagpipe playing; family; travelling. Address: (h.) 14 Fleurs Road, Elgin, Moray; T.-541955 (b.) Council HQ, High Street, Elgin, Moray; T.-563340.

Summerton, Edward, ARSA. Lecturer in Fine Art, Duncan of Jordanstone College, since 1994; Member, Council, Society of Scottish Artists; b. 9.2.62, Dundee; m., Rosalie Dow; 1 s.; 1 d. Educ. Kirkton High School, Dundee; Dundee University. Lecturer, Edinburgh College of Art, 1991-93; exhibited in group and solo exhibitions nationally and internationally, since 1986; elected ARSA, 1977; travelled extensively, funded by travelling scholarships and artistic exchanges, since 1987. Publications: North of Normal (catalogue of paintings); Line Controller (artists' book). Address: (h.) Mains of Airlie, Airlie, Kirriemuir, Angus; T.-01575 530219.

Sunter, Thomas Lacey Murray, FIMgt, FRSA, MNI. Director, Institute of Directors (Scotland), since 1997; Chief Executive, Business Enterprise Scotland, 1996-97; Deputy Lieutenant, Fife; b. 14.8.41, Liverpool; m., Margaret; 3 d. Educ. Merchant Taylors School, Crosby; Royal Naval College, Dartmouth. Royal Navy, 1960-96, including command of HMS Scylla, 1984-86 and HMS Endurance, 1987-89; UN Treaty Inspector, Antarctica, 1987-89; Ministry of Defence, 1989-91; Commander, RN Forces Hong Kong, 1991-94; Naval Base Commander, Rosyth, 1994-96. Trustee, Scottish Fisheries Museum. Recreations: golf; tennis; reading. Address: (h.) Kirklands Cottage, Saline, Fife; T.-01383 723444.

Surber, Elizabeth, MA (Hons). Headmistress, Laurel Park School, Glasgow, since 1995; b. 10.5.54, Kingston upon Thames. Educ. Tiffin Girls' School, Kingston upon Thames; Exeter University; Oxford University. Teacher of French, Hadleigh High School, 1976-77; Lectrice, Universite de Haute-Bretagne, 1977-78; Teacher of French, Tiffin Girls' School, Kingston upon Thames, 1979-82, Cheltenham Ladies' College, 1982-88; Second Deputy Headmistress, Bedford High School, 1988-94. Recreations: ballet; walking; travel. Address: (b.) Laurel Park School, 4 Lilybank Terrace, Glasgow, G12 8RX.

Sutherland, David I.M., MA, MEd, DLitt, FCCEAM, FIMgt, FRSA. Registrar, The General Teaching Council for Scotland, since 1985; b. 22.1.38, Wick; m., Janet H. Webster; 2 s. Educ. Aberdeen Grammar School; Aberdeen University; University of Zurich. Teacher of Modern Languages, Aberdeen Grammar School, 1962-66; Lecturer in Education, Stranmillis College of Education, Belfast, 1966-69; Lecturer in Educational Psychology, Craigie College of Education, Ayr, 1969-72; Assistant Director of Education, Sutherland County Council, 1972-75; Divisional Education Officer (Inverness), then Depute Director of Education, Highland Regional Council, 1975-85. Assessor, Scottish Teacher Education Committe; Member: Scottish Education Department Planning Group on Teacher Supply, Scottish Association for Educational Management and Administration, Council, British Educational Management and Administration Society, Board, Commonwealth Council for Educational Administration and Management, Standing Conference on Studies in Education, Scottish Educational Research Association, Professional Advisory Committee to Department of Education, Stirling University; Associate Member: Association of Directors of Education in Scotland; Consultant, National Board for Nursing, Midwifery and Health Visiting for Scotland. Recreations: golf; walking; theatre; reading. Address: (b.) 5 Royal Terrace, Edinburgh EH7 5AF; T.-0131-556 0072.

Sutherland, Donald Gilmour, CA. Regional Managing Partner — South, Ernst & Young, 1990-95; b. 15.4.40, Edinburgh; m., Linda Malone; 2 s.; 1 d. Educ. George Watson's College. Joined Brown Fleming & Murray, London, 1963; Partner, Whinney Murray & Co., Glasgow, 1968, Edinburgh, 1974; Managing Partner, Ernst & Whinney, Edinburgh, 1985; Regional Managing Partner, 1987; Director, Murray Johnstone Ltd., Murray International Trust plc, Murray Income plc, Murray Smaller Markets Trust plc, 1987-89; Regional Managing Partner — North, Ernst & Young, 1989-90; Chairman, E. & Y. Trustees Ltd., since 1997; Director: Standard Life Assurance Company, since 1990, CALA plc, since 1995, Murray Smaller Markets Trust plc, since 1995, Alexander Russell plc, since 1995, Quayle Munro Holdings plc, since 1995 (Chairman, since 1996). Recreations: conservation: golf; antiques. Address: (h.) Woodside House, Gladsmuir, East Lothian, EH33 2AL; T.-01875 852327.

Sutherland, Elizabeth (Elizabeth Margaret Marshall), FSA Scot. Writer; b. 24.8.26, Kemback, Cupar; m., Rev. John D. Marshall; 2 s.; 1 d. Educ. St. Leonard's Girls' School, St. Andrews; Edinburgh University. Social Worker for Scottish Episcopal Church, 1974-80; Curator, Groam House Museum, Rosemarkie, 1982-93; author of: Lent Term (Constable Trophy), 1973, The Seer of Kintail, 1974, Hannah Hereafter (Scottish Arts Council Book Award), 1976, The Eye of God, 1977, The Weeping Tree, 1980, Ravens and Black Rain: The Story of Highland Second Sight, 1985, The Gold Key and The Green Life, 1986; In Search of the Picts, 1994; Guide to the Pictish Stones, 1997; Five Euphemias: Women in Scotland in Medieval Scotland, 1999. Recreations: Highland history; Gaelic language; the Picts; walking. Address: (h.) 17 Mackenzie Terrace, Rosemarkie, Ross-shire IV10 8UH; T.-Fortrose 620924.

Sutherland, Countess of (Elizabeth Millicent Sutherland). Chief of Clan Sutherland; b. 30.3.21; m., Charles Noel Janson; 2 s.; 1 s. (deceased); 1 d. Educ. Queen's College, London; abroad. Land Army, 1939-41; Laboratory Technician, Raigmore Hospital, Inverness, and St. Thomas's Hospital, London, 1941-45. Address: (h.) Dunrobin Castle, Sutherland; House of Tongue, Lairg, Sutherland.

Sutherland, George O., CA, MCT, FIMgt, FRSA. Director of Finance, Edinburgh University, since 1994; b. 5.11.44, Dundee; m., Jane; 1 s.; 3 d. Educ. Morgan Academy; St.Andrews University. TA, 1962-72. Shell International Petroleum Co. Ltd., 1969-92, serving in Libya, Hong Kong, United Arab Emirates, Norway, Brunei and Syria; set up a major World Bank power project in Pakistan, 1992-93; Member of Lowland Territorial Auxiliary and Volunteer Reserves Association; Joint Universities of Edinburgh Military Education Committee; Member, Advisory Board, Centre for Second World War Studies; Member, ICAS committees. Recreations: military and aviation history;

organised and led expeditions in Sahara desert and Borneo jungle, the latter identifying historically significant aircraft wrecks; battlefields; flying; hill-walking; water sports; a young family; an old Morgan sports car. Address: (b.) Old College, South Bridge, Edinburgh, EH8 9YL; T.-0131-650 2182.

Sutherland, George William Douglas, FCMA. Managing Director – Finance – North of Scotland Water, since 1995; b. 7.3.53, Dunoon; m., Mary; 1 s.; 2 d. Educ. Inverness High School. Dunlops; Rediffusion; Black and Decker (senior finance posts, latterly Group Financial Controller); Director of Financial Control, Grand Met; Finance Director, Express Foods Group; Finance Director, latterly Managing Director, Dairy Crest Dairies. Recreations: music; family; art. Address: (b.) North of Scotland Water, Cairngorm House, Beechwood Park, Inverness IV2 3ED; T.-01463 245400.

Sutherland, Ian, DL, DipYCS; b. 22.11.38, Edinburgh. Educ. Boroughmuir Secondary School; Moray House College of Education. Clerical, book-keeping, administrative posts, 1956-65; youth and community course, 1965-67; Youth Leader, Greenock and Kirkcaldy, 1967-71; Area Youth and Community Officer, Clackmannan County Council, 1971-73; Area Community Education Officer, Central Regional Council, 1973-93. Trustee and Hon. Secretary, Scottish Silver Jubilee and Children's Bursary Fund; Elder, St. Serf's Church of Scotland, Tullibody; Deputy Lieutenant, Clackmannanshire. Recreations: singing; gardening; hand-crafts. Address: (h.) 1 Woodside Road, Tullibody, Alloa, FK10 2QQ; T.-01259 723935.

Sutherland, Ian Douglas, FRICS. Managing Partner, D.M. Hall & Son, Chartered Surveyors, Partner since 1975 (joined as Trainee Surveyor, 1965); b. 23.10.45, Colombo, Ceylon; m., Kathryn Wallace; 1 s.; 1 d. Educ. St. Bees School, Cumberland. Member, Company of Merchants of the City of Edinburgh. Address: (b.) 36 Melville Street, Edinburgh EH3 7HA; T.-0131-477 6000.

Sutherland, Professor Ian Wishart, BSc, PhD, DSc. Professor of Microbial Physiology, Edinburgh University, since 1991; b. 6.12.35, Perth; m., Ann Mary Barker; 1 d. Educ. Pitlochry High School; Dollar Academy; Edinburgh University. Lecturer in Bacteriology, Edinburgh University Medical School, 1961-75, Senior Lecturer, then Reader, in Microbiology, 1975-91. Member, Council, Society of General Microbiology, 1984-93; Chair, British Co-ordinating Committee for Biotechnology, 1993-96. Recreations: mountain walking; photography. Address: (b.) Institute of Cell and Molecular Biology, Edinburgh University, Edinburgh EH9 3JH; T.-0131-650 5331.

Sutherland, James, CBE (1974), MA, LLB, LLD. McClure Naismith, Solicitors, Glasgow, Edinburgh and London (Partner, 1951-87, Consultant, 1987-90); b. 15.2.20; m., 1, Elizabeth Kelly Barr; 2 s.; 2, Grace Williamson Dawson. Educ. Queens Park Secondary School, Glasgow; Glasgow University. Royal Signals, 1940-46; Examiner in Scots Law, 1951-55, and Mercantile Law and Industrial Law, 1968-69, Glasgow University; Chairman, Glasgow South National Insurance Tribunal, 1964-66; Member, Board of Management, Glasgow Maternity and Women's Hospitals, 1964-74 (Chairman, 1966-74); Council Member, Law Society of Scotland, 1959-77 (Vice-President, 1969-70, President, 1972-74); Council Member, International Bar Association, since 1972 (Chairman, General Practice Section, 1978-80, Secretary General, 1980-84, President, 1984-86); Vice-Chairman, Glasgow Eastern Health Council, 1975-77; Council Member, General Dental Council, 1975-89; Deacon, Incorporation of Barbers, Glasgow, 1962-63; Dean, Royal Faculty of Procurators in Glasgow, 1977-80; Member, Court, Strathclyde University, 1977-92. Recreation: golf. Address: (h.) Greenacres, 20/1 Easter Belmont Road, Edinburgh EH12 6EX; T.-0131-337 1888.

Sutherland, Hon. Lord (Ranald Iain Sutherland), QC (Scot). Senator of the College of Justice, since 1985; b. 23.1.32. Advocate Depute, 1962-64, 1971-77; QC (Scot), 1969.

Sutherland, Professor Sir Stewart Ross, FBA, FRSE, MA. Principal and Vice-Chancellor, Edinburgh University, since 1994; b. 25.2.41, Aberdeen; m., Sheena Robertson; 1 s.; 2 d. Educ. Robert Gordon's College; Aberdeen University; Cambridge University. Assistant Lecturer, Philosophy, UCNW, 1965-68; Lecturer, Senior Lecturer, Reader, Stirling University, 1968-77; Professor, Philosophy of Religion, King's College, London, 1977-90 (Vice-Principal, 1981-85, Principal, 1985-90); Vice-Chancellor, London University, 1990-94, and HM Chief Inspector of Schools (England), 1992-94; Visiting Fellow, Australian National University, 1974; Chairman, Brit. Acad. Postgraduate Studentships, 1987-94; Member, Council for Science and Technology, since 1993, Hong Kong Univrsity Grants Com., since 1995, Higher Education Funding Council, England, since 1996; Editor, Religious Studies, 1984-90; Chairman, Royal Commission on the Funding of Long-Term Care of the Elderly, since 1997; Chairman, Secretary of State's Committee on Appeal Procedures, 1994-96; Chairman, Royal Institute of Philosophy, since 1988; President, Society for Study of Theology, 1985, 1986. Publications: several books and papers. Recreations: jazz; theatre; rough gardening. Address: (b.) Edinburgh University, Old College, South Bridge, EH8 9YL; T.-0131-650 2150.

Sutherland, Sir William George MacKenzie, Kt. (1988), QPM. HM Chief Inspector of Constabulary for Scotland, 1996-98; Chief Constable, Lothian and Borders Police, 1983-96; b. 12.11.33, Inverness; m., Jennie Abbott; 2 d. Educ. Inverness Technical High School. Cheshire Police, 1954-73; Surrey Police, 1973-75; Hertfordshire Police, 1975-79; Chief Constable, Bedfordshire Police, 1979-83. Recreations: squash; hill-walking.

Sutter, Art. Broadcaster; b. 27.8.41, Airdrie; m., Janette; 2 d. Educ. Airdrie Academy. Studied piano/organ/voice; most of career spent in Scotch whisky industry (sales); Presenter, BBC Radio Scotland, 1985-93; chatshow, Grampian TV, since 1989. Recreations: golf; badminton; gardening.

Suttie, James Michael Peter, MRTPI. Director of Planning and Economic Development, Aberdeenshire Council, since 1995; b. 24.3.48, Arbroath; m., Sylvia; 1 s.; 2 d. Educ. Dundee High School; Duncan of Jordanstone College of Art, Dundee. Principal Planning Officer, Dundee Corporation, 1973-75; Principal Planning Assistant, Tayside Regional Council, 1975; Chief Assistant Planning Officer, Fife Regional Council, 1975-80; Director of Planning and Development, Banff and Buchan District Council, 1980-95. Recreations: golf; hill-walking; orienteering; driving. Address: (b.) Woodhill House, Westburn Road, Aberdeen; T.-01224 665540.

Swaffield, Professor John Arthur, BSc, MPhil, PhD, CEng, MRAeS, FIWEM, MCIBSE. Professor of Building Services Engineering, Heriot-Watt University, Edinburgh, since 1985; b. 4.3.43, Aberystwyth; m., Jean Winnan; 2 d. Educ. Ardwyn Grammar School, Aberystwyth; Bristol University. Research Fellow, Mechanical Engineering Department, City University, London, 1966-70; Deputy Head, Systems Laboratory, British Aircraft Corporation, Filton, Bristol, 1970-72; Senior Lecturer, South Bank Polytechnic, 1972-74; Lecturer and Senior Lecturer, Department of Building Technology, Brunel University, 1974-83; Reader in Mechanical Engineering, Brunel University, 1983-85; Dean of Engineering, Heriot-Watt University, 1990-93; Head, Department of Building

Engineering and Surveying, Heriot-Watt University, 1995; Chairman, Water Regulations Advisory Committee, DETR, 1996-99. Recreations: skiing; hill-walking; cinema; political/military history. Address: (b.) Department of Building Engineering and Surveying, Heriot-Watt University, Riccarton, Edinburgh EH14 4AS; T.-0131-449 5111.

Swainson, Charles P., MBChB, FRCPE. Consultant Renal Physician, since 1981; b. 18.5.48, Gloucester; m., Marie Irwin; 1 s. Educ. St. Edward's School, Cheltenham; Edinburgh University. Senior Lecturer, Christchurch, NZ, 1981-86; Consultant Physician, Royal Infirmary of Edinburgh, since 1986. Member, Lothian Children's Panel, 1987-95. Recreations: wine; golf; skiing. Address: (b.) Royal Infirmary of Edinburgh, Lauriston Place, Edinburgh EH3 9YW; T.-0131-536 3008.

Swan, Iain Ruairidh Cameron, MD, FRCS(Edin). Senior Lecturer in Otolaryngology, Glasgow University, since 1986; Consultant Otologist, MRC Institute of Hearing Research, since 1986; Honorary Consultant Otolaryngologist, Glasgow Royal Infirmary, since 1986; b. 19.5.52, Motherwell; m., Helen Buchanan; 1 s.; 1 d. Educ. Glasgow Academy; Glasgow University. SHO/Registrar, Glasgow, 1978-81; Clinical Research Fellow, MRC Institute of Hearing Research, 1981; Senior Registrar in Otolaryngology, Glasgow, 1981-86; clinical attachment, University of Tubingen, 1984-85. Examiner, Final Fellowship, Royal College of Surgeons of Edinburgh and Royal College of Physicians and Surgeons, Glasgow. Recreations: bridge; opera; mountain biking. Address: (b.) Department of Otolaryngology, Royal Infirmary, Glasgow G31 2ER; T.-0141-211 4695.

Swanson, Alexander James Grenville, MB, ChB, FRCS Edin. Consultant Orthopaedic Surgeon, since 1980; b. 18.10.41, Ecclefechan; 2 s. Educ. Dingwall Academy; St. Andrews University. Postgraduate training: St. Andrews, 1967-68, Edinburgh, 1968-69, Glasgow, 1969-70, Edinburgh, 1970-74, Dunfermline, 1974-75; Lecturer, then Senior Lecturer and Honorary Consultant, Dundee University, 1975-83. Recreations: downhill skiing; cross-country skiing; travel. Address: (b.) Department of Orthopaedic and Trauma Surgery, Royal Infirmary, Dundee DD1 9ND; T.-01382 660111.

Swanson, Carol Barbara, MA, MSc, PhD, MRTPI, MIFA, FSAScot. Member, Ancient Monuments Board, since 1997; Manager, West of Scotland Archaeology Service, since 1996; b. 2.12.51, Thurso; m., Ian Johnson. Educ. Thurso High School; Edinburgh University; Strathclyde University. Planner: Lanark County Council, 1974-75, Strathclyde Regional Council, 1975-85; Regional Archaeologist, Strathclyde Regional Council, 1985-96. Address: (b.) West of Scotland Archaeology Service, 20 India Street, Glasgow G2 4PF; T.-0141-287 8334.

Swanson, Kenneth M., BSc, PhD, JP, DL. Farmer; Assistant Director, Technology, Dounreay Nuclear Power Development Establishment, 1986-91; Vice Lord Lieutenant, Caithness, since 1996; b. 14.2.30, Canisbay, Caithness; m., Elspeth J.W. Paton; 2 s.; 1 d. Educ. Wick High School; St. Andrews University. Flying Officer, Pilot, RAF, 1952; Lecturer in Physics, University of Wales, 1955; joined UKAEA, Dounreay, on Fast Reactors, 1958; appointed JP, 1970; DL, Caithness, 1977; Chairman, Caithness Jobs Commission, 1988; Director, Caithness and Sutherland Local Enterprise Company, 1990 (Vice-Chairman, 1994); Member, N.W. Board, Scottish Natural Heritage, 1992; author of papers and patents on the development of plutonium fuels for electricity production. Address: Knockglass, Westfield, Thurso; T.-0184 787 1201.

Swanson, Professor Philip, BA, PhD. Professor of Hispanic Studies, University of Aberdeen, since 1997; b. 26.5.59, Liverpool. Educ. St. Edward's College; University of Liverpool; University of Edinburgh. Previous posts at: University College Galway; University of Edinburgh; Queen Mary and Westfield College, University of London; State University of New York (Albany); University of Leeds. Publications: The New Novel in Latin America; Landmarks in Modern Latin American Fiction; José Donoso: The Boom and Beyond; Cómo Ceer and Gabriel Garcia Márquez. Recreations: cinema; walking; socialising. Address: (b.) Department of Hispanic Studies, University of Aberdeen, Aberdeen AB24 3UB; T.-01224 272549.

Swanston, Professor Michael Timothy, MA (Cantab), PhD. Professor, University of Abertay Dundee, since 1995; Head, School of Social and Health Sciences, since 1995; b. 6.6.47, Bristol; m., Georgina Mary; 1 s.; 2 d. Educ. Rugby School; Cambridge University (Pembroke College). Psychologist, Army Personnel Research Establishment, 1969-72; Lecturer in Psychology, Dundee Institute of Technology, 1972-84; Reader in Psychology, 1984-95; Honorary Research Fellow, Dundee university, since 1989. Publications: one book; 40 papers. Recreations: golf; gardening. Address: (b.) School of Social and Health Sciences, University of Abertay Dundee, Marketgait House, 158 Marketgait, Dundee DD1 1NJ.

Swapp, George David, OBE, DL, MA (Hons), DipEd. Deputy Lieutenant, Kincardineshire, since 1990; Member Aberdeenshire Council, since 1995; b. 25.5.31, Labuan; m., Eva Jane MacNab; 2 s.; 2 d. Educ. Mackie Academy, Stonehaven; Aberdeen University. RAF Staff College, graduate and directing staff, 1965-68; Ministry of Defence (Training Policy), 1971-74 and 1978-80; promoted Wing Commander, 1971; Board Chairman, RAF Officer and Aircrew Selection Centre, 1974-78; Head, RAF Officer Training Establishment, Bracknell, 1980-83; retired from RAF, 1983. Former Member, Grampian Regional Council, 1986-96; President, Stonehaven Branch, Royal British Legion; founder Member, Stonehaven Heritage Society and Dunnottar Woodland Park Association; Church Elder. Recreations: hill-walking; local history; travel; geography; protection and enhancement of amenities and woodlands. Address: (h.) 9 Urie Crescent, Stonehaven AB39 2DY; T.-Stonehaven 764124.

Sweeney, Sister Dorothea, MA (Hons), BA(Soc) (Hons), PhD. Consultant and former Vice Principal, St. Andrew's College, 1985-96; b. Glasgow. Educ. Notre Dame High School, Glasgow; Glasgow University; Notre Dame College of Education; Bedford College and LSE, London University; Strathclyde University. Assistant Teacher of English, Our Lady & St. Francis Secondary School, Glasgow, 1960-63; entered Congregation of Sisters of Notre Dame, Sussex, 1963; Assistant Teacher of English, Notre Dame High School, London, 1966-67; Notre Dame College of Education: Lecturer, Department of Psychology, 1970-76, Senior Lecturer, Department of Educational Science, 1976-80, Assistant Principal, 1980-85. Member, Board of Governors, St. Andrew's College, 1980-96; Member, CNAA Inservice Education Board, 1982-87, Committee for Teacher Education, 1987-89, and Committee for Scotland, 1990-92; Member, National Inter-College Committee for Educational Research, 1982-89; Convener, School Boards, Headteacher Training, Steering Committee, 1988-89; School Boards Members Training, 1989-90; Training Consultant, National Staff Development & Appraisal Training, 1991-92; Myers-Briggs Qualified Trainer, since 1990; part-time Counsellor, since 1968; Sabbatical Semester, Weston Jesuit School of Theology, Cambridge, Massachusetts, 1998. Recreations: creative writing; dance; music; art; sport; drama; technology.

Sweeney, Patrick, MA (Hons). Head Teacher, Holy Rood High School, Edinburgh, since 1994; b. 13.4.49, Wanlockhead; m., May Grant. Educ. Blairs College, Aberdeen; Glasgow University. Taught French and Latin in various schools, 1973-85; Assistant Head Teacher, St. Augustine's High School, Edinburgh, 1985-88; on staff of Quality Assurance Division, Lothian Regional Council, 1988-94, as Co-ordinator of Lothian TVEI Project and then Regional Adviser. Recreations: travel; squash; poor golf; regular contributor of articles to educational press; books of all descriptions. Address: (b.) Holy Rood High School, Duddingston Road, Edinburgh, EH15 1ST.

Swinborn, Albert Victor, MA, MEd. Headteacher, Portlethen Academy, since 1997; b. 24.9.52, Aberdeen; m., Patricia. Educ. Aberdeen Grammar School; Aberdeen University. Teacher of English: Lossiemouth High School, Inverurie Academy; Principal Teacher of English, Hilton Academy; Assistant Headteacher/Depute Headteacher, Westhill Academy. Recreations: travel; Aberdeen FC; Burmese cats. Address: (b.) Portlethen Academy, Bruntland Road, Portlethen, Aberdeen AB12 4QL; T.-01224 782174.

Swinfen, Professor David Berridge, MA, DPhil, FRHistS. Professor of Commonwealth History, Dundee University, since 1990 (Head, Department of Modern History, 1988-92, Deputy Principal, 1992-94, Vice Principal, since 1994); Chairman, Scottish Advisory Committee on Credit and Access, since 1997; b. 8.11.36, Kirkcaldy; m., Ann Pettit; 2 s.; 3 d. Educ. Fettes College, Edinburgh; Hertford College, Oxford. 2/Lt., KOSB, 1956-57; Assistant Lecturer in Modern History, then Lecturer, Queen's College, Dundee, 1963-75; Director, School of American Studies, Dundee University, 1970-85; Senior Lecturer, Modern History, Dundee University, 1975-90. Publications: five books. Recreation: music. Address: (h.) 14 Cedar Road, Broughty Ferry, Dundee, DD5 3BB; T.-01382 776496.

Swinney, John Ramsay, MP, MA (Hons). MP (SNP), North Tayside, since 1997; SNP Treasury Spokesman, since 1995; b. 13.4.64, Edinburgh; 1 s.; 1 d. Educ. Forrester High School, Edinburgh; Edinburgh University. Research Officer, Scottish Coal Project, 1987-88; Senior Managing Consultant, Development Options Ltd., 1998-92; Strategic Planning Principal, Scottish Amicable, 1992-97. Recreation: hill-walking. Address: (b.) 35 Perth Street, Blairgowrie PH10 6DL; T.-01250 876576.

Swinton, Major General Sir John, KCVO, OBE, JP. Lord Lieutenant, Berwickshire, since 1989; President, Royal Highland and Agricultural Society of Scotland, 1993-94; Member, Queen's Bodyguard for Scotland (Royal Company of Archers), since 1977 (Ensign, since 1996); President, Borders Branch, SSAFA, since 1993; Council Member, Commonwealth Ex-Services League, 1984-98; Trustee, Scottish National War Memorial, since 1988 (Chairman, since 1995); President, Berwickshire Civic Society (Chairman, 1982-96); President, Lowland TA & VRA, 1992-96; Chairman, Berwickshire Recreation Sports Trust, since 1997; Chairman, St. Abbs Head National Nature Reserve Joint Management Committee, since 1991; Trustee, The Scots at War Trust, since 1996; Trustee, Berwick Military Tattoo, since 1996; President, Berwickshire Naturalists Club, 1996-97; Patron, POWER, since 1995; b. 21.4.25, London; m., Judith Balfour Killen; 3 s.; 1 d. Educ. Harrow School. Enlisted Scots Guards, 1943; commissioned, 1944; served NW Europe (twice wounded); Malaya, 1948-51 (Despatches); ADC to Field Marshal Sir William Slim, Governor General of Australia, 1953-54; Regimental Adjutant, Scots Guards, 1960-62; Adjutant, RMA, Sandhurst, 1962-64; comd. 2nd Bn., Scots Guards, 1966-68; Lt.-Col. commanding Scots Guards, 1970-71; Commander, 4th Guards Armoured Brigade, BAOR, 1972-73; Brigadier, Lowlands and Commander, Edinburgh and Glasgow Garrisons, 1975-76; GOC London District and Major General comd. Household Division, 1976-79. Honorary Colonel, 2nd Bn., 52nd Lowland Volunteers, 1983-90; National Chairman, Royal British Legion Scotland, 1986-89; Coordinator for Scotland, Duke of Edinburgh's Award 25th Anniversary Appeal, 1980 (Honorary Liaison Officer for the Borders, 1983-85); Chairman, Roxburgh and Berwickshire Conservative Association, 1983-85; Chairman, Thirlestane Castle Trust, 1984-90; Trustee, Army Museums Ogilby Trust, 1978-91; Member, Central Advisory Committee on War Pensions, 1986-89. Address: (h.) Kimmerghame, Duns, Berwickshire; T.-01361 883277.

Sword, Ian Pollock, BSc, PhD, CChem, FRSC, FRSE, FRCP (Edin). Chairman, Inveresk Research International, since 1979; Director, Inveresk Clinical Research, since 1988; Director, SGS UK Holding Ltd., since 1989; Senior Executive Vice President, SGS Geneva, since 1994; Member, Medical Research Council, 1994-98, Scottish Higher Educational Funding Council, 1996-98; b. 6.3.42, Kilmarnock; m., Flora Collins; 2 s.; 1 d. Educ. Coatbridge High School; Glasgow University. Princeton University, New Jersey, 1967-69; Oxford University, 1969-70; Huntingdon Research Centre, 1970-73; Inveresk Research International, since 1973. Publications: editor of two books; scientific papers. Recreations: music; golf. Address: (b.) Inveresk Research International Ltd., Tranent EH33 2NE; T.-01875 614545.

Sykes, Diana Antoinette, MA (Hons). Director, Crawford Arts Centre, since 1988; b. 12.9.59, Stirling. Educ. Stirling High School; St Andrews University; Sweet Briar College, Virginia; Manchester University. Curator/Driver, Scottish Arts Council Travelling Gallery, 1983-88. Chair, Mobile Projects Association Scotland, 1986-88; Member/Chair, Scottish Arts Council Exhibitions Panel, since 1995. Recreation: travel. Address: (b.) 93 North Street, St Andrews KY16 9AL; T.-01334 474610.

Syme, Peter William, MA, DipAfrSts. Scottish Director, The Open University, and Vice-Chancellor's Delegate in Scotland, since 1997; b. 27.1.50, Brechin. Educ. Brechin High School; Trinity College, Glenalmond; Trinity College, Cambridge; Edinburgh University. VSO, Nigeria, 1972-74; Department of Education and Science, London, 1975-89, including Private Secretary to Sir James Hamilton, Permanent Secretary, 1979-80; seconded to Edinburgh University, 1983-85; Secretary to Review of University Grants Committee, 1985-87; Regional Director, Open University, London, 1990-97. Recreations: travel; photography; Africa. Address: (b.) The Open University in Scotland, 10 Drumsheugh Gardens, Edinburgh EH3 7QJ; T.-0131-226 3851.

Symington, Rev. Alastair Henderson, MA, BD. Minister, Old Parish Church of Troon, since 1998, of New Kilpatrick Parish Church, Bearsden, 1985-98; Chaplain to The Queen in Scotland, since 1996; b. 15.4.47, Edinburgh; m., Eileen Margaret Jenkins; 2 d. Educ. Daniel Stewart's College, Edinburgh; Edinburgh University; Tubingen University, West Germany. Assistant Minister, Wellington Church, Glasgow, 1971-72; Chaplain, RAF, 1972-76; Minister, Craiglockhart Parish Church, Edinburgh, 1976-85. Contributor, Scottish Liturgical Review. Publications: Westminster Church Sermons, 1984; Reader's Digest Family Guide to the Bible (Co-author), 1985; For God's Sake, Ask!, 1993. Recreations: golf; rugby; music; computing. Address: 85 Bentinck Drive, Troon KA10 6HZ; T.-01292 313644.

T

Tait, A. Margaret, BSc. Convenor, General Council, University of Edinburgh Business Committee; Member, Women in Scotland Forum and its Research Advisory Group; Member, St. Margaret's Chapel Guild, Edinburgh Castle; Vice Chairman, Lothian Healthy Volunteers Medical Ethics Committee; Member, Lothian Health Council; Public Affairs Consultant, Scotland, British Federation of Women Graduates; b. 8.10.44, Edinburgh; m., J. Haldane Tait; 1 s.; 1 d. Educ. George Watson's Ladies' College, Edinburgh; Edinburgh University; Jordanhill College of Education. Teacher of Mathematics, Bellahouston Academy, Glasgow; former Member, Lothian Children's Panel; former Honorary Secretary, Scottish Association of Children's Panels; former Chairman, Dean House Children's Home, Edinburgh; Volunteer, Edinburgh Citizens' Advice Bureau; former Member, Edinburgh Youth Orchestra Committee; formerly Secretary of State's Nominee to General Teaching Council; former Member, Scottish Legal Aid Board. Recreations: golf; speaking in Spanish and Japanese. Address: (h.) 6 Ravelston House Park, Edinburgh EH4 3LU; T.-0131-332 6795.

Tait, Rev. Thomas William, BD, RAFVR (Rtd). Parish Minister, Rattray, Blairgowrie, 1972-97; Chairman, Tayside Health Council, since 1992; Convener, Scottish Association of Health Councils; Principal Chaplain, Scotland and Northern Ireland, Air Training Corps, since 1996; b. 11.11.31, Dunfermline; m., Irene Pope; 1 s.; 2 d. Educ. Dunfermline High School; St. Colm's College, Edinburgh; Edinburgh University; Christ's College, Aberdeen; Aberdeen University. HQ Staff, Boys' Brigade, 1954-61; Missionary, Church of Scotland, South Arabia, 1962-67; ordained and inducted, 1972; Member, Assembly Council, 1984-88; Chaplain, 2519 (Strathmore) Squadron, Air Training Corps, since 1974; Chairman, Blairgowrie Schools Council, 1975-89; Member, Perth and Kinross Health Council, 1980-91 (Chairman, 1984-91); Chairman, Blairgowrie and District Branch, Royal British Legion Scotland, and Chaplain, Angus and Perthshire Area; commissioned RAFVR, 1977 (retired Flt. Lt., 1988); Moderator, Dunkeld and Meigle Presbytery, 1978; Member, Secretary of State's Consultative Panel on Registration of Nursing Homes and Private Hospitals, since 1993; Member, Tayside Health Board Quality Monitoring Team, 1993-98; Member, CRAG (Clinical Research and Audit Group); Member, Multi Research Ethics Committee for Scotland, since 1997. Recreations: encouraging others to work in voluntary organisations; swimming; reading; overseas travel. Address: 20 Cedar Avenue, Blairgowrie, Perthshire; T.-01250 4833.

Tallach, Rev James Ross, MB, ChB. Free Presbyterian Minister, Raasay, since 1983; occasional locum, general practitioner, Raasay; b. Tighnabruaich, Argyll; m., Mairi McCuish Martin; 2 d. Educ. Nicolson Institute, Stornoway; Aberdeen University. House jobs in surgery, medicine and obstetrics, Inverness, Aberdeen, and Bellshill, 1967-69; Medical Missionary, Mbuma, Zimbabwe, 1969-76; training for ministry, 1976-80; ordained medical missionery, Mbuma, 1980-83. Moderator of Synod, 1996; Clerk to Foreign Mission Committee of F.P. Church, since 1989. Recreations: gardening; walking. Address: Free Presbyterian Manse, Raasay, Kyle, Ross-shire IV40 8PB; T.-01478 660216.

Tankel, Henry I., OBE, MD, FRCSEdin, FRCSGlas. Chairman, Glasgow Jewish Housing Association, since 1996; Surgeon, Southern General Hospital, Glasgow, 1962-91; b. 14.1.26, Glasgow; m., Judith Woolfson; 2 s.; 2 d. Educ. High School of Glasgow; Glasgow University. Fulbright Scholar, 1954-55; President, Glasgow Jewish Representative Council, 1974-77; Chairman, Glasgow Hospital Medical Services Committee, 1974-79; Board of Science and Education, 1978-81; President, United Synagogues of Scotland, 1978-85; Treasurer, Scottish Committee for Hospital Medical Services, 1978-91; Member, National Panel of Specialists, 1978-82 and 1987-91; invited to address General Assembly of Church of Scotland, 1984; Chairman, Scottish Joint Consultants Committee, 1989-92; Member, Scottish Health Service Advisory Council, 1989-93; Non-Executive Director, Southern General Hospital NHS Trust, 1993-97; Chairman, Glasgow Board of Jewish Education, 1985-90. Recreations: walking; making model boats. Address: (h.) 26 Dalziel Drive, Glasgow G41 4PU; T.-0141-423 5830.

Tannahill, Professor Andrew James, MB, ChB, MSc, FFPHM, FRCPE, MHSM. Chief Executive, Health Education Board for Scotland, since 1991; Visiting Professor, Glasgow University, since 1997; Honorary Senior Lecturer, Department of Epidemiology and Public Health, University of Dundee, since 1993; Honorary Fellow, Department of Public Health Sciences, University of Edinburgh, since 1994; Honorary Clinical Senior Lecturer, Department of Public Health, Glasgow University, since 1996; b. 28.4.54, Inchinnan; m., Carol Elizabeth Fyfe. Educ. John Neilson Institution, Paisley; Glasgow University; Edinburgh University. Lecturer in Pathology, Glasgow University; Senior Registrar in Community Medicine, Lothian Health Board/Honorary Clinical Tutor, Edinburgh University; Regional Specialist in Community Medicine, East Anglian Regional Health Authority/Associate Lecturer, Cambridge University; Senior Lecturer in Public Health Medicine, Glasgow University/Honorary Consultant in Public Health Medicine, Greater Glasgow Health Board. Publications: Health Promotion: Models and Values (Co-author); contributor to Health Promotion: Disciplines and Diversity; papers on health education, prevention and health promotion. Recreations: countryside and bird-watching; music; theatre; photography; drawing and painting; reading (especially humour). Address: (b.) Health Education Board for Scotland, Woodburn House, Canaan Lane, Edinburgh EH10 4SG; T.-0131-536 5500.

Tarbert, Andrew, BSc. Head Teacher, St Gerard's Secondary School, Glasgow, since 1989; b. 12.6.37, Glasgow; m., Margaret A. Martin; 1 s.; 2 d. Educ. St Gerard's Secondary School; Glasgow University. Teacher, St Gregory's Secondary School, 1959-65; Teacher, St Mary's, Toronto, 1965-66; Special Assistant, Holyrood Secondary, Glasgow, 1966-70; Principal Teacher, Physics, St Roch's Secondary, Glasgow, 1970-77; Assistant Head, St Gregory's Secondary, Glasgow, 1977-81; Depute Head, St Gerard's Secondary, Glasgow, 1981-89. Recreations: hill-walking; golf; bowls; bridge; Celtic. Address: (h.) 59 Courthill Avenue, Glasgow G44 5AA; T.-0141-637 1909.

Tate, Professor Austin, BA (Hons), PhD, CEng, MBCS, FBIS. Technical Director, AIAI (Artificial Intelligence Applications Institute), since 1985; Chair in Knowledge-Based Systems, Edinburgh University, since 1995; b. 12.5.51, Knottingley, West Yorkshire; m., Margaret. Educ. King's School, Pontefract; Lancaster University; Edinburgh University. Elected Fellow, American Association of Artificial Intelligence, since 1993. Address: (b.) AIAI, University of Edinburgh, 80 South Bridge, Edinburgh EH1 1HN; T.-0131-650 2732.

Tavener, Alan, MA, ARCO, ARCM. Director of Music, Strathclyde University, since 1980; Artistic Director, Cappella Nova, since 1982; b. 22.4.57, Weston-Super-Mare; m., Rebecca Jane Gibson. Educ. City of Bath Boys' School; Brasenose College, Oxford. Conducted several world premieres of choral works and several CDs of early and contemporary music. Recreations: architecture; exhibitions; Scottish country dancing; food and drink.

Address: (b.) Strathclyde University, Livingstone Tower, Richmond Street, Glasgow G1 1XH; T.-0141-548 3444.

Tavener, Rebecca Jane. Soprano; Co-Artistic Director and Manager, Cappella Nova; b. 3.5.58, Trowbridge; m., Alan Tavener. Co-founded Cappella Nova, 1982; Concert Manager, Glasgow University, 1983-89; Founder and Director, Chorus International, 1990-94; founded Canty (medieval vocal ensemble), 1998; launched new early music consortium for Scotland, 1998. Recreations: Italophilia; retail therapy; gourmandising; reading history books. Address: (h.) 172 Hyndland Road, Glasgow G12 9HZ; T.-(b.) 0141-552 0634.

Taylor, Brian, MA (Hons). Political Editor, BBC Scotland; b. 9.1.55, Dundee; m., Pamela Moira Niven; 2 s. Educ. High School of Dundee; St. Andrews University. Reporter, Press and Journal, Aberdeen, 1977-80; Lobby Correspondent, Thomson Regional Newspapers, Westminster, 1980-85; Reporter, BBC Scotland, Glasgow, 1985-86; Co-Presenter, Left, Right and Centre, BBC Scotland, 1986-88; Political Correspondent, BBC Scotland, 1988-90. Recreations: golf; theatre. Address: (b.) BBC Scotland, Queen Margaret Drive, Glasgow G12 8DG.

Taylor, Charles Edwin, CBE, BSc, PhD, FRSE, CBiol, FIBiol. Director, Scottish Crop Research Institute, 1972-86; President, Association of Applied Biologists, 1989; NATO Senior Research Fellow, Istituto di Nematologia Agraria CNR, Bari, Italy; b. 11.9.23, Oystermouth; 1 d. Educ. Cardiff High School; University College, Cardiff. Pilot, RAF, 1943-46; Lecturer in Applied Zoology, Nottingham University School of Agriculture, 1949-56; Senior Entomologist, Federation of Rhodesia and Nyasaland, 1956-59; Head, Zoology Section, Scottish Horticultural Research Institute, 1959-72. President, European Society of Nematologists, 1980-84; Editor, Nematologica, 1990-96. Address: (b.) Westcroft, Longforgan, Dundee DD2 5EX; T.-01382 360 243.

Taylor, David Alexander, LLB (Hons), MSc, MBA. Director, Scottish Trade International, since 1994; Chairman, Scottish Development Overseas Ltd.; Director, Trade Development Centre Ltd.; b. 14.3.54, Forfar; m., Catherine Taylor; 2 s. Educ. Dundee High School; Edinburgh University; Strathclyde University. Senior Solicitor, City of Glasgow Council, 1979-84; SDA, 1985-91; Head of Consumer Products, Scottish Enterprise, 1991-94 (also part-time Tutor, Open University). Recreations: Partick Thistle; golf; the pursuit of knowledge. Address: (b.) 123 Bothwell Street, Glasgow, G2 7JP; T.-0141-228 2747.

Taylor, Elizabeth (Liz) Dewar, MA (Hons). Journalist and Author; b. 25.4.31, Newport, Fife; m., Adam McNeill Taylor (deceased); 1 s.; 3 d. Educ. Morgan Academy, Dundee; Galashiels Academy; King's College, Aberdeen. Reporter, Edinburgh Evening Dispatch, 1954-56; freelance stringer, Bombay, 1960-65; freelance journalist and broadcaster, since 1971. Publications include: Living with Loss; Bringing Up Children On Your Own; Living Alone; The Writing Business; 20th Century Antiques; also several books as Elisabeth McNeill. Recreations: gardening; crossword puzzles; bridge; Scrabble; cinema; horse-racing. Address: (h.) Cairnhill, Newstead, Melrose TD6 9DX; T.-0189682 2972.

Taylor, Rev. Howard, BSc (Hons), BD (Hons), MTh. Chaplain, Heriot-Watt University, since 1998; Minister, St. David's Church, Knightswood, Glasgow, 1986-98; Part-time Lecturer in Apologetics, International Christian College, since 1989; b. 6.6.44, Stockport; m., Eleanor Clark; 3 s. Educ. Gravesend Technical School, Kent; Nottingham University; Edinburgh University. Maths and Physics Teacher, Malawi University; Missionary in Malawi (minister of town and rural African churches, theological teacher, teacher of African languages to missionaries); Minister, Toward and Innellan Churches, Argyll. Publications: Faith Seeks Understanding, 1980; Pray Today 1982/83, 1982; In Christ All Things Hold Together; World Hope in the Middle East; The Delusion of Unbelief in a Scientific Age; Faith and Understanding; Israel — People of God; The Uniqueness of Christ in a Pluralist World, 1994; Is the New Testament the Source of Anti-Semitism?,1994. Recreations: hill walking; reading; classical music. Address: (b.) Chaplaincy Centre, Heriot-Watt University, Edinburgh EH14 4AF; T.-0131-449 5111.

Taylor, Rev. Ian, BSc, MA, LTh, DipEd. Lecturer on music and the arts, broadcaster, opera producer; b. 12.10.32, Dundee; m., Joy Coupar, LRAM; 2 s.; 1 d. Educ. Dundee High School; St. Andrews University; Durham University; Sheffield University; Edinburgh University. Teacher, Mathematics Department, Dundee High School; Lecturer in Mathematics, Bretton Hall College of Education; Senior Lecturer in Education, College of Ripon and York St. John; Assistant Minister, St. Giles' Cathedral, Edinburgh; Minister, Abdie & Dunbog and Newburgh, 1983-97; Moderator, Presbytery of St. Andrews, 1995-96; Secretary, History of Education Society, 1968-73; extensive work in adult education (appreciation of music and the arts); Director, Summer Schools in Music, St. Andrews University; numerous courses for St. Andrews, Edinburgh and Hull Universities and WEA; has played principal roles in opera and operetta; Producer, Gilbert and Sullivan Society of Edinburgh, 1979-87; compiled Theatre Music Quiz series, Radio Tay; presented own operetta, My Dear Gilbert...My Dear Sullivan, BBC; Writer of revues and documentary plays with music, including Tragic Queen (Mary Queen of Scots), St. Giles' Cathedral, Edinburgh Festival Fringe, 1982, and John Knox (Church of Scotland Video). Publications: How to Produce Concert Versions of Gilbert Sullivan; The Gilbert and Sullivan Quiz Book; The Opera Lover's Quiz Book. Address: Lundie Cottage, Arncroach, Fife KY10 2RN; T.-01333 720 222.

Taylor, Sheriff James Alastair, BSc, LLB. Sheriff of Lothian and Borders at Edinburgh, since 1998; Convener, Rights of Audience Civil Training Course, 1995-98; b. 21.2.51, Inverness; m., Lesley Macleod; 2 s. Educ. Nairn Academy; Aberdeen University. Apprenticed to Brander & Cruickshank, Advocates in Aberdeen, 1975-77; apprenticed to, Assistant with, Lefevre & Co., Advocates in Aberdeen, 1977-78; Assistant, later Partner, A.C. Morrison & Richards, Advocates in Aberdeen, 1978-87; Partner and latterly Head of Litigation Department, McGrigor Donald, 1988-98; attained rights of audience in Supreme Courts in Scotland, 1993. Recreations: golf; music; good food and wine. Address: (b.) Sheriff's Chambers, Sheriff Court House, 27 Chambers Street, Edinburgh EH1 1LB.

Taylor, James Bradley. Chief Executive, Northern Lighthouse Board, since 1993; Nautical Assessor to the Court of Session, since 1996; Trustee, Scotland's Lighthouse Museum, since 1995; Trustee, Bell's Nautical Trust, since 1996; b. 12.8.45, Paisley; m., Elizabeth Sherwood. Educ. George Watson's College, Edinburgh; Britannia Royal Naval College; Defence School of Languages; Royal College of Defence Studies. Royal Navy, 1963-93; commanded HM submarines: Grampus, 1974-75, Orpheus, 1975-77, Spartan, 1980-82, HM ship London, 1989-90; Chief of Staff, Submarine Flotilla, 1990-91; Royal College of Defence Studies, 1992. Recreations: shooting; stalking; history; classic cars. Address: (b.) 84 George Street, Edinburgh, EH2 3DA; T.-0131-473 3100.

Taylor, Rev. John Henry Bindon, MA, BD, DipEd, DipScotLit, FEIS. Vice-President, Christian Education Movement (Scotland), since 1990; b. 4.11.26, Swansea; m., Jean Taylor, MBE; 3 s.; 1 d. Educ. Swansea Grammar School; Worcester College, Oxford; Glasgow University. Minister, Lincluden, Cumfries, 1952-56; St. Mary's,

Woolston, Southampton, 1956-60; St. Andrew's, Irvine, 1960-69; Teacher, Ravenspark Academy, Irvine, 1969 (Assistant Rector, 1974); Depute Rector, Garnock Academy, 1978; Rector, Auchenharvie Academy, Stevenston, 1980, till retirement, 1989; Associate Minister, Galston Parish Church, since 1991; Convener, Scottish Examination Board Panel on Religious Studies, 1982-88; Convener, Church of Scotland Education Committee, 1989-95; Chairman, Forum on Scottish Education, 1989-96. Recreations: walking; railway history. Address: (h.) 62 Woodlands Grove, Kilmarnock; T.-01563 526698.

Taylor, Rt. Rev. John Mitchell, MA. Bishop of Glasgow and Galloway, retired 1998; b. 23.5.32, Aberdeen; m., Edna Elizabeth Maitland; 1 s.; 1 d. Educ. Banff Academy; Aberdeen University; Theological College, Edinburgh. Curate, St. Margaret's, Aberdeen; Rector: Holy Cross, Knightswood, Glasgow, St. Ninian's, Pollokshields, Glasgow, St. John the Evangelist, Dumfries; Canon, St. Mary's Cathedral, Glasgow. Recreations: angling; hill-walking; sketching; music. Address: (h.) 10 St Georges, Castle Douglas DG7 1LN.

Taylor, John Murray, MA, DipEd, MIM, FRSA. Principal, Clackmannan College, since 1987; b. 18.7.42; m., Katie Forsyth; 2 d. Educ. Banchory Academy; Aberdeen University. Teacher, Dunfermline High School, 1965-70; Principal Teacher of Classics, Kirkcudbright, Liberton, Callander, 1970-78; Assistant Director of Education, Central Region, 1978-87. Recreations: music; cycling; travel; railways; DX radio. Address: (b.) Clackmannan College of Further Education, Branshill Road, Alloa FK10 3BT; T.-01259 215121.

Taylor, Malcolm John, TD, MA (Hons), ARICS. Chartered Surveyor/Land Agent, Youngs Chartered Surveyors, since 1987; Member, Ancient Monuments Board for Scotland, since 1998; b. 21.11.61, Glasgow; m., Helen McKay; 2 s.; 1 d. Educ. Dumfries Academy; Aberdeen University. Trainee, C.G. Grieve & Co., Dumfries, 1985-87; joined Youngs, 1987; appointed Associate, 1991, Partner, 1998. Vice-Chairman, RICS Rural Practice Division. Recreations: field sports; music; natural history. Address: (b.) Youngs Chartered Surveyors, Manor Street, Forfar; T.-01307 462516.

Taylor, Margie, MSc, MBA, FDSRCSEQ. Consultant in Dental Public Health, Lanarkshire Health Board, since 1994; Honorary Senior Lecturer, Glasgow University; b. Edinburgh. Educ. James Gillespie's High School for Girls; Edinburgh University; Heriot-Watt University. Formerly Chief Administrative Dental Officer, Fife Health Board, and Honorary Senior Lecturer, St. Andrews University. President, Royal Odonto-Chirurgical Society of Scotland; Board Member, Health Education Board for Scotland. Recreations: calligraphy; golfing (badly); cooking. Address: (b.) Lanarkshire Health Board, 14 Beckford Street, Hamilton ML3 0TA; T.-01698 281313.

Taylor, Rt. Rev. Maurice, STD. Bishop of Galloway, since 1981; b. 5.5.26, Hamilton. Educ. St. Aloysius College, Glasgow; Our Lady's High School, Motherwell; Pontifical Gregorian University, Rome. Royal Army Medical Corps, UK, India, Egypt, 1944-47; Assistant Priest: St. Bartholomew's, Coatbridge, 1951-52, St. Bernadette's, Motherwell, 1954-55; Lecturer, St. Peter's College, Cardross, 1955-65; Rector, Royal Scots College, Spain, 1965-74; Parish Priest, Our Lady of Lourdes, East Kilbride, 1974-81. Episcopal Secretary, Bishops' Conference of Scotland; Vice President, Catholic Institute for International Relations; Chairman, Episcopal Board, International Commission on English in the Liturgy. Publications: The Scots College in Spain, 1971; Guatemala, A Bishop's Journey, 1991; El Salvador: Portrait of a Parish, 1992; Opening Our Lives to the Saviour (Co-author), 1995; Listening at the Foot of the Cross (Co-author), 1996. Address: 8 Corsehill Road, Ayr KA7 2ST; T.-01292 266750.

Taylor, Michael Thomas, MA, MEd. Rector, Dyce Academy, Aberdeen, since 1980; b. 17.2.47, Newcastle upon Tyne; m., Sheena Robertson; 1 s.; 2 d. Educ. Rutherford Grammar School, Newcastle upon Tyne; Trinity College, Cambridge; Aberdeen University. Teacher of Chemistry, Cannock Grammar School, 1969-75; Ellon Academy: Principal Teacher of Guidance, 1975-76, Assistant Head Teacher, 1977-78, Depute Rector, 1978-80. Secretary, Newmachar Community Council. Recreations: hill-walking; music; sailing. Address: (h.) Loch-An-Eilein, Newmachar, Aberdeenshire AB21 OUQ; T.-01651 862234.

Taylor, Paul Doyle, MA, MEd. Head Teacher, Menzieshill High School, Dundee, since 1996; b. 27.9.43, Bognor Regis; m., Jean; 1 s.; 1 d. Educ. Chichester High School for Boys; Edinburgh University; University of Manitoba; Stirling University. Teacher, Gillam School, Manitoba, 1968-69; Teacher of History, Forrester High School, Edinburgh, 1969-74; Principal Teacher of History: Gracemount High School, Edinburgh, 1974-79, Inveralmond Community High School, Livingston, 1979-83; Assistant Head Teacher: Ainslie Park High School, Edinburgh, 1983-87, Inveralmond Community High School, Livingston, 1987-89; Deputy Head, Gracemount High School, Edinburgh, 1989-94; Head Teacher, Linlathen High School, Dundee, 1994-96. Recreations: walking; gardening; ornithology; photography. Address: (h.) 8 Woodburne, Ceres, Cupar KY15 5PY; T.-01334 828925.

Taylor, Professor Rex, BA, PhD. Director of Crichton College, University of Glasgow, since 1997; Chairman, Dumfries and Galloway NHS Trust (Primary Care), since 1998; b. 30.12.39, Orkney Isles; m., Judith; 1 s.; 1 d. Educ. King James's Grammar School, Knaresborough; University College, Durham University. Lecturer in Social Anthropology, University of Durham; Lecturer in Sociology, University of Kent at Canterbury; Senior Lecturer in Sociology, University of Aberdeen; Research Scientist, Medical Research Council; Professor of Social Policy, University of Glasgow. Visiting Professor: University of Virginia, University of Texas; Member, Dumfries and Galloway Enterprise Board. Publications: 50 scientific papers; four books. Recreations: music; chess; building; woodwork. Address: Dalswinton Mill, Dalswinton, Dumfries DG2 0XY; T.-01387 740421.

Taylor, Professor Samuel Sorby Brittain, BA, PhD, Officier dans l'Ordre des Palmes Academiques. Professor of French, St. Andrews University, 1977-95; b. 20.9.30, Dore and Totley, Derbyshire; m., Agnes McCreadie Ewan; 2 d. Educ. High Storrs Grammar School, Sheffield; Birmingham University; Paris University. Royal Navy, 1956-58 (Sub Lt., RNVR); Personnel Research Officer, Dunlop Rubber Co., 1958-60; Institut et Musee Voltaire, Geneva, 1960-63; St. Andrews University: Lecturer, 1963, Reader, 1972, Professor, 1977, retired 1995; Chairman, National Council for Modern Languages, 1981-85; Member, Executive Committee, Complete Works of Voltaire, 1970-85; Project Leader, Inter-University French Language Teaching Research and Development Project, 1980-88; Director, Nuffield Foundation project ("Nuffield French for science students"), 1991-97; Chairman, Scottish Joint Working Party for Standard Grade in Modern Languages, 1982-84; Secretary, Scottish Applied French Language Association, since 1965. Publication: definite iconography of Voltaire, 1998. Recreations: athletics timekeeping; photography. Address: (h.) 11 Irvine Crescent, St. Andrews KY16 8LG; T.-01334 472588.

Taylor, Sheena Barbara, MA, BA, MEd. Headteacher, Albyn School for Girls, Aberdeen, since 1997; b. Stromness, Orkney; m., Michael Taylor; 1 s.; 2 d. Educ. Inverurie Academy; Kirkwall Grammar School; Edinburgh

University; Open University; Aberdeen University. Cannock Grammar School, 1968-73; Ellon Academy, 1980-83; Principal Teacher of Guidance, Banchory Academy, 1983-90; Assistant Headteacher, Torry Academy, Aberdeen, 1990-97. Member, SCCC Deliberative Committee/COSAC, 1990-93. Recreations: sailing; hill-walking. Address: (b.) 17-23 Queen's Road, Aberdeen AB15 4PB; T.-01224 322408.

Taylor of Gryfe, Lord (Thomas Johnston Taylor), Hon. LLD (Strathclyde); b. 27.4.12, Glasgow; m., Isobel. Educ. Bellahouston Academy. Member, Board, Scottish Television, 1968-83; Director: Whiteaway Laidlaw (Bankers), since 1971, Friends Provident, 1972-83, Scottish Metropolitan Property, 1972-88; Member, International Advisory Board, Morgan Grenfell, 1972-88; Chairman, Forestry Commission, 1967-72; Chairman, Economic Forestry, 1972-82; Chairman, Scottish Railways Board, 1969-80; Chairman, Wolfson Trust (Scotland), since 1975; Trustee, Dulverton Trust, since 1979; Chairman, Scottish Peers Association, 1988; Chairman, All-Party Parliamentary Group on Forestry; Commander Order of merit — Federal Republic of Germany.

Taylor, William James, QC, QC (England and Wales), MA (Hons), LLB. Advocate, since 1971; Barrister, since 1990; b. 13.9.44, Nairn. Educ. Robert Gordon's College; Aberdeen University. Called to Scots Bar, 1971; called to Bar of England and Wales, 1990. Councillor, Edinburgh Corporation, 1973-75, Lothian Regional Council, 1974-82. Recreations: music; theatre; hill-walking. Address: (b.) Parliament House, Parliament Square, Edinburgh, EH1 1RF.

Teasdale, Professor Graham Michael, MB, BS, MRCP, FRCSEdin, FRCSGlas. Professor and Head, Department of Neurosurgery, Glasgow University, since 1981; Consultant Neurosurgeon, Institute of Neurological Sciences, Glasgow, since 1975; b. 23.9.40, Spennymoor; m.; 3 s. Educ. Johnston Grammar School, Durham; Durham University. Postgraduate clinical training, Newcastle-upon-Tyne, London and Birmingham, 1963-69; Assistant Lecturer in Anatomy, Glasgow University, 1969-71; specialist training in surgery and neurosurgery, Southern General Hospital, Glasgow, 1971-75; Senior Lecturer, then Reader in Neurosurgery, Glasgow University, 1975-81. President, International Neurotrauma Society, 1993; Chairman, European Brain Injury Consortium, 1995. Publication: The Management of Head Injuries. Recreations: hill-walking; inshore fishing. Address: (b.) University Department of Neurosurgery, Institute of Neurological Sciences, Southern General Hospital, Glasgow; T.-0141-445 2466.

Tedford, Professor David John, OBE, BSc, PhD, ScD, ARCST, CEng, FIEE, SMIEEE, CPhys, FInstP, FRSE, FRSA, Order of Merit of Poland, DTech (Hon. Abertay, Dundee), DSc (Hon. Robert Gordon University); DUniv (Strathclyde University). Chairman of Court, University of Abertay Dundee, since 1997, Scottish Science Trust, since 1997, Dundee Science Trust, since 1998; Director, Scottish Academic Consultants, since 1996; Non-Executive Director, Startech Partners Ltd., since 1997; Chairman, Technology Education Advisory Group (Scottish Consultative Council on the Curriculum), since 1996; Member, Steering Group, Skills Strategy for Electronics Industry, since 1996; Emeritus Professor; formerly Professor of Electrical Engineering (Foundation Chair), Strathclyde University; Chief Scientific Adviser to Secretary of State for Scotland, 1994-96; Secretary of State Scientific Adviser to Scottish Office Industry Department, 1992-94; b. 12.7.31, Coatbridge; m., Mary White Gardner; 3 s.; 1 d. Educ. Coatbridge High School; Royal Technical College; Glasgow University. Research Engineer, Ferranti Ltd., Edinburgh, 1955-57; joined Strathclyde University as Lecturer, 1957; Deputy Principal, 1982-84, Vice-Principal, 1986-88, Deputy Principal (International Affairs), 1988-91; Special Adviser to Principal, 1991-92; Member: Standing Conference on University Entrance, 1989-93, Scottish Examination Board, 1986-93, Council, IEE, 1992-95; British National Committee and Executive Committee, CIGRE, 1985-96; Council and Vice President, Royal Society of Edinburgh, 1992-95; Education and International Relations Committees, Royal Society, 1992-95; Management Board, Bell College of Technology, Hamilton, since 1990 (Chairman of Council, 1990-93); Management Board, SCOTVEC, 1993-97. Recreations: hill-walking; music; amateur astronomy. Address: (h.) 76 Woodlands Drive, Coatbridge, ML5 1LB; T.-01236 422016.

Templeton, Professor Allan, MBChB, MD (Hons), FRCOG. Regius Professor of Obstetrics and Gynaecology, University of Aberdeen, since 1985; Honorary Secretary, Royal College of Obstetricians and Gynaecologists, since 1998; b. 28.6.46, Glasgow.; m., Gillian Penney; 3 s.; 1 d. Educ. Aberdeen Grammar School; University of Aberdeen. Junior hospital posts, Aberdeen Royal Infirmary; Lecturer then Senior Lecturer, University of Edinburgh. Member, Human Fertilisation and Embryology Authority. Publications: books and scientific papers on human infertility. Recreation: mountaineering. Address: (b.) Department of Obstetrics and Gynaecology, University of Aberdeen, Aberdeen Maternity Hospital, Foresterhill, Aberdeen AB25 9ZD; T.-01224 840590.

Templeton, Ian Godfrey, MA, BA. Warden, Glenalmond College, Perth, since 1992; b. 1.2.44, Edinburgh; m., Elisabeth Aline Robin; 1 s.; 1 d. Educ. Gordonstoun; Edinburgh University; Bedford College, London University. Assistant Master, then Housemaster, Melville College, Edinburgh, 1969-73; Housemaster, Daniel Stewart's and Melville College, Edinburgh, 1973-78; Assistant Headmaster, Robert Gordon's College, Aberdeen, 1978-85; Headmaster, Oswestry School, 1985-92. Governor, Belhaven Preparatory School; Director, Lathallan Preparatory School. Recreations: golf; skiing; choral singing. Address: Glenalmond College, Glenalmond, Perth PH1 3RY; T.-01738 880227.

Tennant, Sir Iain Mark, KT (1986). Chairman, Grampian Television PLC, 1968-89 (Vice-Chairman, 1960-68); Director, Caledonian Associated Cinemas PLC, 1950-90; Director, Clydesdale Bank PLC, 1969-89; Director, Abbey National Building Society (Chairman, Scottish Advisory Board, 1969-89); Director, Moray and Nairn Newspaper Company Ltd.; Member, Royal Company of Archers (Queen's Bodyguard in Scotland), since 1950; Crown Estate Commissioner, 1969-89; Honorary Director, Seagram Company Ltd., Montreal; Lord Lieutenant of Morayshire, 1963-94; Lord High Commissioner to the General Assembly of the Church of Scotland, 1988, 1989; b. 11.3.19, North Berwick; m., Lady Margaret Ogilvy; 2 s.; 1 d. Educ. Eton College; Magdalene College, Cambridge. Learned about film production, Welwyn Garden City Film Studios; served in Egypt with 2nd Bn., Scots Guards, 1940-42; became Intelligence Officer, 201 Guard's Brigade; captured at the surrender of Tobruk; prisoner of war, Italy and Germany, until 1945; Founder Member, Moray Sea School, 1949; Council Member, Outward Bound Trust, 15 years; joined Board, Gordonstoun School, 1951 (Chairman, 1957-72); Member, Moray and Nairn County Council, 1956-64 (latterly Vice-Chairman, Education Committee); Member, The Times Publishing Co. Ltd., 1962-66; Member, Board, Cairngorm Sports Development Ltd., 1964-76; appointed Chairman, local Disablement Advisory Committee, 1964; Chairman, Glenlivet and Glen Grant Distilleries Ltd., 1964-70; Chairman, Glenlivet Distillers Ltd., 1970-77; Trustee, King George's Jubilee Trust, London, 1967-71; FRSA, 1971; Trustee, Churchill Trust, 1973-76; Member, Board, Courage Ltd., 1974-77; Chairman, Seagram Distillers Ltd. (in London), 1977-82; CBIM, 1983; Freeman of Moray District, 1994.

Recreations: shooting; fishing. Address: (b.) Lochnabo, Lhanbryde, Moray; T.-01343 842228.

Terrasse, Dr. Jean-Marc-André. Director, French Institut of Scotland, since 1997; b. 23.6.48, Paris; 1 s.; 2 d. Educ. Ecole Alsacienne, Paris; Lycée Louis-le-Grand, Paris; Paris VII. Teacher of Mathematics; Ethnologist; Radio Broadcaster; Journalist, since 1974 and Writer since 1972 (nouvelles litteraires, periodicals, newspapers); Film and Television Writer; Theatre Writer; previously Director, French Institut, Innsbruck, Austria. Publications: five novels. Recreations: rugby; swimming; sailing. Address: (h.) 54 Bruntsfield Gardens, Edinburgh EH10 4DY; T.-0131-466 0797.

Terrell, Harry, MA, JP. Chief Executive, Dundee and Tayside Chamber of Commerce and Industry, since 1978; Non-Executive Member, Tayside Health Board, since 1998; Member, Industrial Tribunals, since 1986; b. 2.8.38, Dundee; m., Patricia Mary Milgate; 1 s. Educ. Royal High School, Edinburgh; Dundee University. H.M. Diplomatic Service, 1955-66; Confederation of British Industry, 1970-76; Export Group for the Constructional Industries, 1976-77. Member, Advisory Board, Salvation Army, Dundee; Vice Chairman, Dundee Citizens' Advice Bureau Ltd. Recreations: curling; reading. Address: (b.) Panmure Street, Dundee, DD1 1ED; T.-01382 201122.

Terry, Peter Brian, MB, ChB, MD, FRCS Edin, FRCOG. Consultant Obstetrician and Gynaecologist, since 1986; b. 3.6.52, Hillingdon; m., Gillian Margaret; 3 s. Educ. Merchant Taylors'; Edinburgh University Medical School. SHO, Simpson Memorial Maternity Pavilion, Edinburgh, 1977, Cumberland Infirmary, Carlisle, 1978; Registrar, Obstetrics and Gynaecology, Dudley Road Hospital, Birmingham, 1979; Research Registrar, 1982; Senior Registrar, Obstetrics and Gynaecology, Aberdeen, 1983; Consultant, 1986. Recreations: gardening; golf; walking. Address: (h.) 60 Forest Road, Aberdeen, AB15 4BP; T.-01224 317560.

Tervet, David John, BSc, MSc, PhD, CChem, MRSC, FCIWEM, MIMgt. Divisional Manager, Scottish Environment Protection Agency, since 1996 (Director, Solway River Purification Board, 1994-96); b. 29.6.47, Woodford Green; m., Janie; 3 s. Educ. Chigwell; Edinburgh University; Strathclyde University; Dundee University. Assistant Chemist, Fife and Kinross Water Board, 1973-74; Chemist, Chief Chemist, Chief Scientist/Depute Director, Solway River Purification Board, 1974-94. Publications: papers on water quality. Recreations: cricket; music; gardening; railways (Life Member, Festiniog Railway Society). Address: (b.) Rivers House, Irongray Road, Dumfries, DG2 0JE; T.-01387 720502.

Thin, David Ainslie, BSc. Chairman, James Thin Ltd.; Chairman, Book Tokens Ltd., 1987-95; Director, Edinburgh Book Festival; Member, Executive Committee and Finance Committee, National Trust for Scotland; b. 9.7.33, Edinburgh; m., Elspeth J.M. Scott; 1 s.; 2 d. Educ. Edinburgh Academy; Loretto School; Edinburgh University. President, Booksellers Association of GB and Ireland, 1976-78. Recreations: golf; travelling; reading. Address: (h.) 60 Fountainhall Road, Edinburgh EH9 2LP; T.-0131-667 2725.

Thomaneck, Professor Jurgen Karl Albert, JP, MEd, Drphil, FRSA. Professor in German, Aberdeen University, since 1992; Aberdeen City Councillor, since 1996; President, Aberdeen Trades Council, since 1982; Convenor, Grampian Joint Police Board, 1995-98; b. 12.6.41, Germany; m., Guinevere Ronald; 2 d. Educ. Universities of Kiel, Tubingen, Aberdeen. Lecturer in German, Aberdeen University, since 1968. Grampian Regional Councillor, 1984-96; Board Member, Grampian Enterprise Ltd., until 1995; President, KIMO UK, since 1996; author/editor of eight books, 13 contributions to books, 30 articles in learned journals, all in German studies. Recreation: football. Address: (b.) Aberdeen University, Aberdeen AB25 3UB.

Thomas, Jeremy St. John, MA (Oxon), FRCPE, FRCPath. Consultant Pathologist, Western General Hospital, Edinburgh, since 1988; Secretary, Royal College of Physicians of Edinburgh, since 1993; b. 29.8.53, Cardiff; m., Dr. Valerie Doherty; 1 s.; 1 d. Educ. Lincoln College, Oxford; St. Thomas's Hospital, London. Trained in general medicine and pathology, Western Infirmary, Glasgow, 1979-88. Recreations: rugby football; photography. Address: (b.) Department of Pathology, Western General Hospital, Edinburgh; T.-0131-537 1961.

Thomas, Joseph Healy. Provost, West Lothian Council, since 1995; b. 13.10.36, Fauldhouse; m., Mary Anna Welsh; 2 s.; 3 d. Educ. St. Mary's Senior Secondary School, Bathgate; Falkirk Technical College. JP, 1977-97; mine deputy, 1984-85; Depute Leader, West Lothian District Council, 1992-95. Recreations: walking; hill-climbing; reading; football as a spectator. Address: (b.) West Lothian House, Almondvale Boulevard, Livingston EH54 6QG; T.-01506 777022.

Thomas, Professor Lyn Carey, MA, DPhil (Oxon), FIMA, FRSE. Professor of Management Science, Edinburgh University, since 1985 (Head, Department of Business Studies, 1987-90); b. 10.8.46, Dowlais; m., Margery Wynn Bright; 2 s.; 1 d. Educ. Lewis School, Pengam; Jesus College, Oxford. Research Fellow, University College, Swansea, 1971-74; Lecturer in Decision Theory, then Senior Lecturer, Manchester University, 1974-85; Senior NRC Fellow, Naval Postgraduate School, Monterey, California, 1982-83; President, Operational Research Society, 1994-95; Associate Editor, Naval Research Logistics; Editor, IMA Journal of Mathematics applied in Business and Industry, 1986-96. Publications: Games, Theory and Applications, 1984; Operational Research Techniques, 1986; Credit Scoring and Credit Control, 1992. Recreations: reading; rugby; walking. Address: (b.) Department of Business Studies, William Robertson Building, 50 George Square, Edinburgh; T.-0131-650 3798.

Thomas, Professor Michael Frederic, MA, PhD, FGS, FRSE. Professor of Environmental Science, Stirling University, since 1980; b. 15.9.33, London; m., Elizabeth Anne Dadley (deceased); 1 s.; 1 d. Educ. Royal Grammar School, Guildford; Reading University. Assistant Lecturer in Geography, Magee University College, Londonderry, 1957-60; Lecturer, Ibadan University, Nigeria, 1960-64; Lecturer, then Senior Lecturer, St. Andrews University, 1964-79; visiting appointments, Universities of Canterbury (New Zealand), New South Wales, Natal, and Sierra Leone. Council Member, Royal Scottish Geographical Society; Past Chairman, British Geomorphological Research Group; Vice Chairman, Scottish Environmental Education Council. Publications: Tropical Geomorphology, 1974; Geomorphology in the Tropics, 1994; Progress in Environmental Science (Joint Managing Editor). Recreations: listening to music; hill-walking; travel. Address: (b.) Department of Environmental Science, Stirling University, Stirling FK9 4LA; T.-01786 67840.

Thomas, Professor Michael James, OM (Poland), BSc, MBA, FRSA, FCIM. Professor of Marketing, Strathclyde University, since 1987; b. 15.7.33; m.; 1 s.; 1 d. Educ. University College London; Indiana University. Metal Box Co. Ltd., London, 1957-60; Syracuse University Management School, 1960-71; Lancaster University, 1972-86; former National Chairman, Chartered Institute of Marketing. Recreation: ornithology. Address: (b.) Strathclyde University, Glasgow G4 ORQ.

Thomas, Professor Phillip Charles, BSc, PhD, FIBiol, CBiol, FRAgS, FRSE. Principal and Chief Executive, The

Scottish Agricultural College, since 1990; Professor of Agriculture, Glasgow University, since 1987; Honorary Professor, Edinburgh University, since 1991; b. 17.6.42, Pontypool; m., Pamela Mary Hirst; 1 s.; 1 d. Educ. Abersychan Grammar School; University College of North Wales, Bangor. Lecturer, Department of Animal Nutrition and Physiology, Leeds University, 1966-71; Research Scientist, Hannah Research Institute, Ayr, 1971-87; Principal, West of Scotland College, Ayr, 1987-90. Publications: Nutritional Physiology of Farm Animals, 1983; Silage for Milk Production, 1983. Address: (b.) The Scottish Agricultural College, Central Office, West Mains Road, Edinburgh EH9 3JG.

Thompson, Professor Alan Eric, MA (Hons), PhD, FRSA, FSA(Scot). Emeritus Professor of the Economics of Government, Heriot-Watt University; b. 16.9.24; m., Mary Heather Long; 3 s.; 1 d. Educ. Edinburgh University. Edinburgh University: Assistant in Political Economy, 1952-53, Lecturer in Economics, 1953-59 and 1964-71; Professor of the Economics of Government, Heriot-Watt University, 1972-87; Parliamentary Labour candidate, Galloway, 1950, 1951; MP (Labour), Dunfermline, 1959-64; Member, Royal Fine Art Commission for Scotland, 1975-80; Chairman, Northern Offshore Maritime Resources Study, 1974-83; Governor, Newbattle Abbey College, 1975-85 (Chairman, 1980-83); Member, Local Government Boundaries Commission for Scotland, 1975-80; Member, Scottish Council for Adult Education in HM Forces, since 1973; BBC National Governor for Scotland, 1975-79; Governor, Leith Nautical College, 1981-85; Trustee, Bell's Nautical Trust, 1981-85; Parliamentary Adviser, Scottish Pharmaceutical General Council, since 1984. Publications: Development of Economic Doctrine (Co-author), 1980; articles in academic journals. Recreation: writing children's stories and plays. Address: (h.) 11 Upper Gray Street, Edinburgh EH9 1SN; T.-0131-667 2140.

Thompson, Colin, CBE, DUniv, FRSE, MA, FMA. Writer, Lecturer and Broadcaster on art and museums; b. 2.11.19, Berkhamstead; m., Jean A.J. O'Connell; 1 s.; 1 d. Educ. Sedbergh; King's College, Cambridge; Chelsea Polytechnic. Lecturer, Bath Academy of Art, Corsham, 1948-54; joined National Gallery of Scotland as Assistant Keeper, 1954; Director, National Galleries of Scotland, 1977-84. Member: Scottish Arts Council, 1976-83, Edinburgh Festival Society, since 1979, Expert Advisory Panel on Museums to Heritage Lottery Fund, 1995-98; Chairman, Scottish Museums Council, 1984-87; Chairman, Board of Governors, Edinburgh College of Art, 1989-91; Trustee, Buccleuch Heritage Trust, since 1988; Member, Scottish Mining Museum Trust, since 1987 (Chairman, 1992-96). Publications: Pictures for Scotland, 1972; Hugo Van Der Goes and the Trinity Panels in Edinburgh (Co-author), 1974; Exploring Museums: Scotland, 1990. Address: (h.) Edenkerry, Lasswade, Midlothian EH18 1LW; T.-0131-663 7927.

Thompson, David George, MITSA, MAPEA, DCA, FIMgt. Director of Protective Services, Highland Council, since 1996 (Director of Trading Standards, Highland Regional Council, 1986-96); b. 20.9.49, Lossiemouth; m., Veronica; 1 s.; 3 d. Educ. Lossiemouth High School. Trainee, then Trading Standards Officer, Banff, Moray and Nairn Joint CC, 1967-73; Assistant Chief Trading Standards Officer, Ross & Cromarty County Council, 1973-75; Chief Trading Standards Officer, Western Isles Islands Council, 1975-83; Depute Director of Trading Standards, Highland Regional Council, 1983-86. Secretary/Treasurer, Scottish Branch, Institute of Trading Standards Administration, 1985-87, Chairman, 1988-89; Secretary/Treasurer, Society of Directors of Trading Standards in Scotland, 1987-89, Chairman, 1991-93. Recreations: golf; DIY; reading; Speakers' Club. Address: (h.) Balnafettack Farmhouse, Leachkin Road, Inverness; T.-01463 221555.

Thompson, Francis George, IEng, FIElecIE, MIExE, FSA (Scot). Author of books on Highland subjects; retired Senior Lecturer, Lews Castle College, Stornoway; Director, Western Isles Development Fund; b. 29.3.31, Stornoway; m., Margaret Elaine Pullar; 1 s.; 3 d. Educ. Nicolson Institute, Stornoway. From 1946: supply maintenance electrician, technical writer, assistant publicity manager, lecturer; has held various offices within An Comann Gaidhealach, including editorship of Sruth, bilingual newspaper, 1967-71; books include: Harris and Lewis, 1999; Harris Tweed, 1969; Highlands and Islands, 1974; Crofting Years, 1998; Shell Guide to Northern Scotland, 1987; The Western Isles, 1988; The First Hundred, 1992. Recreation: writing! Address: Am Fasgadh, 5 Rathad na Muilne, Stornoway, Lewis; T.-01851 703812.

Thompson, Professor Paul Ian, BA (Hons), PhD. Head, Department of Business Studies, Edinburgh University, since 1994; b. 1.1.51, Wallasey; 1 d. Educ. Maghull Grammar School; Liverpool University. Lecturer in Sociology, St. Helen's College of Technology, 1974-84; appointed Senior Lecturer in Organisation Studies, Lancashire Polytechnic, 1984, going on to become Principal Lecturer and Professor in new University of Central Lancashire; Visiting Professor, Institute for Advanced Studies, Vienna, 1987, Institute of Business, Beijing, 1989; Visiting Principal Fellow, University of Wollongong, Australia, 1997; Editor, Renewal (A Journal of New Labour Politics), since 1993. Recreations: music; cinema; playing and watching football, especially Everton F.C. Address: (b.) Department of Business Studies, Edinburgh University, 50 George Square, Edinburgh EH8 9JY; T.-0131-650 3811.

Thoms, Lisbeth Margaret, BSc, DipArch, FSAScot. Freelance archaeologist and heritage advisor; b. Kirkcaldy. Educ. Barnsley High School for Girls; Alloa Academy; Edinburgh University; St Mary's College, Durham University. Field Archaeological Officer, Dundee Art Galleries and Museums, 1972-83; Depute Curator, Dundee Art Galleries and Museums, 1983-96. Vice-Chairman, Scottish Urban Archaeological Trust; Member, Ancient Monuments Board for Scotland; Member, Advisory Panel on Treasure Trove. Recreations: golf; opera; gardening; travel. Address: 4 Portpatrick Terrace, Monifieth, Angus DD5 4TU; T.-01382 535212.

Thomson, Adam Riddell, LDS, RCS. Chairman, Scottish Society for Prevention of Cruelty to Animals, since 1998; Trustee, Cattanach Charitable Trust, since 1996; b. 4.3.30, Linton; m., Judy Jacob, BDS; 1 s.; 2 d. Educ. Berwickshire High School; Edinburgh University. Private dental practitioner, London and Edinburgh, 1955-83; part-time clinical tutor in Dentistry, 1980-84; inventor and developer of Ewesplint; Chief of Dentistry, Tabuk Military Hospital, Saudi Arabia, 1985-89; part-time clinical tutor and practitioner, Edinburgh, 1989-95; retired, 1995. Recreations: country pursuits; travel. Address:(h.) Tyne Steading, Ormiston EH35 5NQ; T.-01875 611267.

Thomson, Brian M. Managing Director, D. C. Thomson & Co. Ltd. Address: (b.) Courier Buildings, 2 Albert Square, Dundee, DD1 9QJ.

Thomson, Professor Derick S., MA (Aberdeen), BA (Cantab), DLitt (Univ. of Wales), DLitt (Univ. of Aberdeen), FRSE, FBA. Professor of Celtic, Glasgow University, 1963-91; b. 5.8.21, Stornoway; m., Carol Galbraith; 5 s.; 1 d. Educ. Nicolson Institute, Stornoway; Aberdeen University; Cambridge University; University College of North Wales, Bangor. Taught at Edinburgh, Glasgow and Aberdeen Universities before returning to Glasgow as Professor, 1963; Chairman, Gaelic Books Council, 1968-91; Hon. President, Scottish Gaelic Texts Society; former Member, Scottish Arts Council; first recipient, Ossian Prize, 1974; author of numerous books and articles, including An Introduction to Gaelic Poetry,

The Companion to Gaelic Scotland, European Poetry in Gaelic and collections of Gaelic poetry, including collected poems Creachadh na Clarsaich and Meall Garbh/Rugged Mountain; Editor, Gairm, since 1952. Address: (h.) 15 Struan Road, Cathcart, Glasgow G44 3AT; T.-0141-637 3704.

Thomson, Sir (Frederick Douglas) David, Bt, BA. Chairman, Britannia Steam Ship Insurance Association Limited, since 1986 (Director, since 1965); Director, Cairn Energy PLC, since 1971; Chairman, Through Transport Marine Mutual Assurance Association (Bermuda) Ltd., since 1983 (Director, since 1973); Director, Danae Investment Trust Ltd., since 1979; Chairman, Jove Investment Trust PLC, since 1983; Director, Martin Currie Pacific Trust PLC, since 1985; Chairman, Aberdeen European Index Investment Trust PLC, since 1990; Chairman, Ptarmigan International Capital Trust PLC, since 1990; Director, Kynoch Group PLC, since 1991; Chairman, Wright & Jobson (Galashiels) Ltd., since 1996; Chairman, S.A. Meacock & Co. Ltd., since 1996; Director, Ionian Group Ltd., since 1994, Bolero Operations Ltd., since 1999; Chairman, Laurence J. Smith Ltd., since 1993; Director, Asset Management Investment Company PLC, since 1994; Member, Royal Company of Archers (Queen's Bodyguard for Scotland); b. 14.2.40, Edinburgh; 2 s.; 1 d. Educ. Eton; University College, Oxford. Recreations: shooting; skiing; tennis; bonfires. Address: (h.) Holylee, Walkerburn, Peeblesshire; T.-01896 870673.

Thomson, Geddes, MA (Hons). Writer, former teacher; b. 20.9.39, Dalry; m., Lucy Faulkner; 2 s. Educ. Dalry High School; Glasgow University. Principal Teacher of English, Allan Glen's School, Glasgow, 1972-89, Shawlands Academy, Glasgow, 1989-93; Extra-Mural Lecturer, Department of Adult and Continuing Education, Glasgow University, 1985-93. Publications include: A Spurious Grace, 1981; Identities (Editor), 1981; The Poetry of Edwin Morgan, 1986. Recreations: supporting Partick Thistle; fishing; browsing in bookshops. Address: (h.) 48 Windyedge Crescent, Glasgow G13 1YF; T.-0141-959 5277.

Thomson, George Buchanan, FCIBS; b. 10.1.24, Glasgow; m., Margaret Irene Williams. Educ. Eastwood Secondary School. Joined Union Bank of Scotland, 1940; War Service, 1942-46 with RAF (Navigator, Bomber Command); held various banking appointments, 1947-86; retired as Assistant General Manager (Branch Administration, West), Bank of Scotland; Past President, Institute of Bankers in Scotland; Director and Chairman, Association for the Relief of Incurables; Hon. Treasurer, Scottish Civic Trust; former Convener, Board of Stewardship and Finance, Church of Scotland; Director, Ian Skelly Holdings Ltd., 1986-89; Director, Clydesdale Development Company, 1988-95. Recreations: curling; bowling. Address: (h.) Kingswood, 26 Waverley Avenue, Helensburgh G84 7JU; T.-01436 672915.

Thomson, George Preston. Commercial Director, Scotland, United Distillers and Vintners UK; b. 31.5.54, Lenzie; m., Gillian Kidd; 1 s.; 1 d. Educ. Lenzie Academy; Glasgow College of Technology. Export Correspondent, White Horse Distillers, 1973-78; Sales Administration Manager, Export Sales Manager, Bass Export Ltd., 1978-84; External Accounts Manager, Charles Wells Ltd., 1984-87; joined United Distillers, 1987. Director, Benevolent Society of the Licensed Trade of Scotland; Chairman, Cherrybank Gardens Trust. Recreations: reading; music (eclectic); running; rugby; football. Address: (b.) United Distillers and Vintners UK, Royal British House, Leonard Street, Perth PH2 8HA.

Thomson, Rev. Iain Urquhart. Minister, Parish of Skene, since 1972; Clerk, Presbytery of Gordon, since 1988; b. 13.12.45, Dundee; m., Christine Freeland; 1 s.; 2 d. Educ. Harris Academy, Dundee; Inverness Royal Academy; Aberdeen University; Christ's College, Aberdeen. Assistant Minister, Castlehill Church, Ayr, 1970-72. Clerk and Treasurer, Synod of Grampian Trusts Committee, since 1993; Member, Skene School Board. Recreations: golf; theatre. Address: The Manse, Kirkton of Skene, Westhill, Aberdeenshire AB32 6LX; T.-01224 743277.

Thomson, James Ewing, MBChB, FRCP(Glas), FRCP(Edin). Consultant Physician, Inverclyde Royal Hospital, since 1978; b. 7.12.45, Glasgow; m., Ann. Educ. Lenzie Academy; Glasgow University. Registrar in Medicine, Law Hospital; Registrar in Endocrinology and Diabetes, Royal Infirmary, Glasgow; Senior Registrar, Stobhill Hospital, Glasgow. Recreations: church work; gardening; music; theatre. Address: (b.) Inverclyde Royal Hospital, Greenock; T.-01475 633777.

Thomson, Sir John Adam, GCMG. Chairman, Minority Rights Group, since 1991; b. 27.4.27, Bieldside, Aberdeen; m., 1, Elizabeth Anne McClure (deceased); 3 s.; 1 d.; 2, Judith Ogden Bullitt. Educ. Aberdeen University; Trinity College, Cambridge. Joined Foreign Office, 1950; seconded to Cabinet Office as Chief of Assessment Staff, 1968-71; Minister and Deputy Permanent Representative, NATO, 1972; Head of UK Delegation, MBFR Exploratory Talks, Vienna, 1973; Assistant Under Secretary for Defence and Disarmament, 1973-76; British High Commissioner in India, 1977-82; British Permanent Representative and Ambassador to UN, 1982-87; Principal Director, 21st Century Trust, 1987-90; Director, ANZ Grindlays, 1987-96; International Adviser, ANZ Grindleys Bank, 1996-98; Chairman, Felmings Emerging Markets Investment Trust, 1990-97; Director's Visitor, Institute for Advanced Studies, Princeton, 1995-96. Trustee, National Museums of Scotland; Member, Council, International Institute of Strategic Studies; Trustee, Aberdeen University Development Trust; Trustee, Indian National Trust for Art and Cultural Heritage; Member, Governing Body, IDS and ODI. Recreations: hill-walking; tennis. Address: (h.) Kirkpatrick Durham, Castle Douglas, Dumfries and Galloway.

Thomson, Professor John Aidan Francis, MA, DPhil, FRHistS. Professor of Mediaeval History, Glasgow University, since 1995; b. 26.7.34, Edinburgh; m., Katherine J.V. Bell; 1 s.; 1 d. Educ. George Watson's Boys' College, Edinburgh; Edinburgh University; Balliol College, Oxford. Glasgow University: Assistant in Mediaeval History, 1960, Lecturer, 1961, Senior Lecturer, 1974, Reader, 1983, Titular Professor, 1994. President, Glasgow Archaeological Society, 1978-81. Publications: The Later Lollards 1414-1520, 1965; Popes and Princes 1417-1517, 1980; The Transformation of Mediaeval England 1370-1529, 1983; Towns and Townspeople in the Fifteenth Century (Editor), 1988; The Early Tudor Church and Society, 1485-1529, 1993; The Western Church in the Middle Ages, 1998. Recreations: travel and sightseeing; walking; gardening. Address: (b.) Department of Medieval History, Glasgow University, Glasgow G12 8QQ; T.-0141-339 8855.

Thomson, Rev. John Morria Arnott, TD, BD, ThM. Minister, Lanark St. Nicholas, since 1988; b. 27.2.49, Buckhaven; m., Marlene Jeffrey Logan; 1 s.; 1 d. Educ. Irvine Royal Academy; Glasgow University; Columbia Theological Seminary, Atlanta, Georgia. Journalist, Irvine Herald; Executive Officer, Environment Research Council; Finance/Administration Officer, Irvine New Town Corporation; Assistant Project Co-ordinator, Wiltshire County Council; Minister, Houston and Killellan Kirk, 1978-88. Chaplain, Clyde Division RNR, 1986-92; Chaplain, 105 Regt. RA (V), since 1992; Chaplain, Lanark Lord Cornets Club; Depute Clerk, Lanark Presbytery. Recreations: sailing; writing; music; Romanian and Eastern

Europe aid. Address: St. Nicholas Manse, 32 Braxfield Road, Lanark ML11 9BS; T.-01555 662600.

Thomson, Professor Joseph McGeachy, LLB, FRSE, FRSA. Regius Professor of Law, Glasgow University, since 1991; Deputy General Editor, Stair Memorial Encyclopaedia of the Laws of Scotland, since 1985; b. 6.5.48, Campbeltown. Educ. Keil School, Dumbarton; Edinburgh University. Lecturer in Law, Birmingham University, 1970-74; Lecturer in Laws, King's College, London, 1974-84; Professor of Law, Strathclyde University, 1984-90. Recreations: opera; ballet; food and wine. Address: (h.) 2 Kew Terrace, Glasgow; T.-0141-334 6682.

Thomson, Kirsteen Isabel Scott, MSc, AADip, ARIAS, MRTPI. Executive Director, Edinburgh Old Town Renewal Trust, since 1996; b. 31.8.49, Cardiff; 1 s.; 1 d. Educ. Malvern Girls College; Architectural Association, London; Edinburgh University. Principal, Scott Thomson, 1980-85; Programme Manager, The Planning Exchange, Glasgow, 1985-87; Principal, Scott Thomson, 1987-90; Economic Development Officer, Stirling District Council, 1990-92; Project Executive, Edinburgh Old Town Renewal Trust, 1992-96. Recreations: family; gardening; old buildings; walking; rock climbing. Address: (b.) 343 High Street, Edinburgh, EH1 1PW; T.-0131-225 8818.

Thomson, Lesley Ann. Partner, Liddell Thomson Management Consultants, since 1996; b. 11.2.59, Glasgow. Educ. Greenock Academy. Journalist: D. C. Thomson and Co. Ltd., 1978-82, Scottish Licensed Trade News, 1982-85; public relations, Scottish Development Agency, 1985-87; Communications Manager, Guinness PLC/United Distillers, 1987-92; Director, PR Consultants Scotland, 1992-93; Corporate Communications Manager, Scottish Power, 1993-96. Member: Scottish Arts Council, 1992-97, Board, Scottish Ballet, since 1997, Board, Arches Theatre, since 1997, Council, CBI (Scotland). Recreations: the arts; music; reading; walking; cooking. Address: (b.) 225 West George Street, Glasgow G2 2ND; T.-0141-221 5775.

Thomson, Malcolm George, QC, LLB. Practice at Scottish Bar, since 1974; b. 6.4.50, Edinburgh; m., Susan Gordon; 2 d. Educ. Edinburgh Academy; Edinburgh University. Standing Junior Counsel, Department of Agriculture and Fisheries and Forestry Commission, 1982-87; QC (Scotland), 1987; called to the Bar, Lincoln's Inn, 1991; Chairman, National Health Service Tribunal, Scotland, since 1995; Member, Scottish Legal Aid Board, since 1998; Editor, Scots Law Times Reports, since 1989; Scottish Case Editor, Current Law, since 1977. Recreations: sailing; skiing. Address: (h.)12 Succoth Avenue, Edinburgh EH12 6BT; T.-0131-337 4911.

Thomson, Michael Stuart MacGregor, MA, CA. Director of Finance and Administration, Royal Scottish Society for Prevention of Cruelty to Children, since 1991; b. 4.5.38, Perth; m., Rosemary; 2 s.; 1 d. Educ. Gordonstoun; St. Andrews University. CA apprenticeship, 1960-63; Director, then Managing Director, Peter Thomson (Perth) Ltd., 1963-85; Michael Thomson & Co., 1985-91; Balbirnie House Hotel Ltd., 1987-91. Lord Dean of the Guildry Incorporation of Perth, 1973-76, Publication: Background to Collecting Doulton Art Pottery. Recreations: grandparenting; footering; adventures; travel; sport. Address: (b.) 41 Polwarth Terrace, Edinburgh EH11 1NU; T.-0131-337 8539.

Thomson, Sheriff Nigel Ernest Drummond, CBE, MA, LLB. Sheriff of Lothian and Borders, at Edinburgh, 1976-96; b. 19.6.26, Aberdeen; m., Snjolaug Magnusson; 1 s.; 1 d. Educ. George Watson's Boys' College; St. Andrews University; Edinburgh University. Called to Scottish Bar, 1953; appointed Sheriff at Hamilton, 1966; Member, Scottish Arts Council, 1978 (Chairman, Music Committee, 1979-84). Hon. President, Strathaven Arts Guild; Hon. Vice-President, Tenovus-Scotland; Hon. President, Scottish Association for Counselling, 1986-89; Vice President, British Association for Counselling, since 1992; Chairman, Edinburgh Youth Orchestra Society, 1986-92; Convenor, Council for Music in Hospitals in Scotland, since 1992; Honorary Texas Ranger, 1994. Recreations: music; woodwork; golf. Address: (h.) 50 Grange Road, Edinburgh; T.-0131-667 2166.

Thomson, Paul William, BSc, PhD, DipEd. Rector, Jordanhill School, Glasgow, since 1997; Board Member, Scottish Qualifications Authority, since 1997 (Convenor, National Qualifications Committee, since 1998); b. 25.7.57, Glasgow; m., Mary; 2 s. Educ. Dollar Academy; University of Glasgow. Teacher of Physics, Boclair Academy, 1983-87; Principal Teacher of Physics, Chryston High School, 1987-90; Assistant Head Teacher, Vale of Leven Academy, 1990-94; Depute Head Teacher, Hermitage Academy, 1994-97; Board Member, Scottish Examination Board, 1990-97. Recreations: golf; bridge. Address: (b.) Jordanhill School, Chamberlain Road, Glasgow G13 1SP; T.-0141-576 2500.

Thomson, Rev. Peter David, MA, BD. Minister, Comrie and Strowan with Dundurn, since 1978; b. 4.11.41, St. Andrews; m., Margaret Celia Murray; 1 s.; 1 d. Educ. Dundee High School; Edinburgh University; Glasgow University; Tubingen University. Minister, Balmaclellan with Kells, 1968-78; Moderator, Kirkcudbright Presbytery, 1974-75; Convener, Nomination Committee, General Assembly, 1982-85. Chairman, New Galloway and Kells Community Council, 1976-78; Moderator, Perth Presbytery, 1988-89. Recreations: haphazardly pursued interests in photography, wildlife, music, theology, current affairs. Address: The Manse, Comrie, Perthshire, PH6 2HE; T.-01764 670269.

Thomson, Professor Richard Ian, MA, DipHistArt (Oxon), MA, PhD, FRSE. Watson Gordon Professor of Fine Art, Edinburgh University, since 1996; b. 1.3.53, Tenterden; m., Belina Jane Greaves; 2 s. Educ. Dragon School, Oxford; Shrewsbury School; St. Catherine's College, Oxford; Courtauld Institute of Art, London University. Lecturer/Senior Lecturer/Reader, Manchester University, 1977-96; Curator or Co-Curator of several exhibitions: The Private Degas, 1987, Camille Pissarro: Impressionist Landscape and Rural Labour, 1990, Monet to Matisse, 1994. Publications: Toulouse-Lautrec, 1977; Seurat, 1985; Degas: The Nudes, 1988; Edgar Degas: Waiting, 1995; Framing France (Editor), 1998. Recreations: jazz; gardening. Address: (b.) Department of Fine Art, Edinburgh University, 19 George Square, Edinburgh EH8 9LD; T.-0131-650 4124.

Thomson, Roy Hendry, CStJ, MA (Hons). President, Scottish Liberal Democrats; President, Mental Health Aberdeen; Chairman, Friends of Aberdeen University Library; Chairman, Kaleidoscope, Aberdeen International Children's Festival; Marketing Director, Aberdeen International Youth Festival; b. 27.8.32, Aberdeen; m., Nancy; 3 d. Educ. Aberdeen Grammar School; Aberdeen University. National Service, Gordon Highlanders, 1955-57; personnel and market research, Rowntree & Co. Ltd., 1957-60; Chairman/Director, family motor business, until 1986; former Director, The Scottish Ballet (Chairman, 1983-87); former Member, City of Aberdeen District Council; Past President: Rotary Club of Aberdeen, Mountain Rescue Association, Aberdeen; former Chairman, Scottish Liberal Democrats. Recreations: skiing; hill-walking. Address: (h.) 5 Baillieswells Grove, Bieldside, Aberdeen AB15 9BH; T.-Aberdeen 861628.

Thomson, Professor Samuel J., BSc, PhD, DSc, CChem, FRSC, FRSE. Professor Emeritus, Glasgow University, since 1987; Honorary Senior Research Fellow, since 1987; Adviser to BR Transrail, then to EWS Railway, since 1996;

b. 27.9.22, Hamilton; m., Christina M. Mactaggart, BSc, PhD; 1 s.; 1 d. Educ. Hamilton Academy; Glasgow University. Lt., Royal Signals, 1944; Lecturer in Radiochemistry, Durham University, 1951; Lecturer, Senior Lecturer, Reader, Titular Professor, Glasgow University, 1957-87. Member, British Railways Board, Scottish Committee, 1989-94; Adviser to BR Railfreight Distribution, 1994-96, and to EWS Railway, 1997-98. Publications: books and papers on surface chemistry and catalysis, etc. Recreations: visual perception; reading. Address: (h.) 10 Balfleurs Street, Milngavie, Glasgow G62 8HW; T.-0141-956 2622.

Thomson, S. Kenneth, MHSM, DipHSM. Chief Executive, Yorkhill NHS Trust, since 1997; Conductor, Glasgow Gaelic Musical Association, since 1983; b. 20.8.49, Campbeltown; m., Valerie Ferguson; 1 s.; 1 d. Educ. Keil School, Dumbarton. Administrative trainee, Scottish Health Service; various administrative and management posts, Glasgow and West of Scotland; Chief Executive, Law Hospital NHS Trust. National Mod Gold Medallist, 1979; Governor, Keil School, since 1995. Recreations: opera; Gaelic language and culture; theatre; The Archers; swimming. Address: (b.) Yorkshire NHS Trust, Royal Hospital for Sick Children, Yorkhill, Glasgow G3 8SJ; T.-0141-201 0473.

Thomson, Stuart James, HND (Agric). Chief Executive, Ayrshire Cattle Society of GB and Ireland, since 1984; Managing Director, Cattle Services (Ayr) Ltd.; Managing Director, Ayrshire's Milk Marketing Ltd.; Executive Director, World Federation Ayrshire Breed Societies; b. 29.8.54, Kirkwall; m., Carolynne Henderson; 1 s. Educ. Kirkwall Grammar School; School of Agriculture, Aberdeen. Regional Officer, North of Scotland Milk Marketing Board, 1976-84. served, Executive Committee, National Cattle Association. Recreations: gardening; golf; fishing. Address: (b.) 1 Racecourse Road, Ayr KA7 2DE; T.-01292 267123.

Thomson, Sir Thomas James, Kt (1991), CBE (1983), OBE (1978), MB, ChB, FRCPGlas, FRCPLond, FRCPEdin, FRCPIre. Chairman, Greater Glasgow Health Board, 1987-93; Member, Court, University of Strathclyde, 1992-97; b. 8.4.23, Airdrie; m., Jessie Smith Shotbolt; 2 s.; 1 d. Educ. Airdrie Academy; Glasgow University. Lecturer, Department of Materia Medica, Glasgow University, 1953-61; Postgraduate Adviser to Glasgow Northern Hospitals, 1961-80; Honorary Secretary, RCPSGlas, 1965-73; Secretary, Specialist Advisory Committee for General Internal Medicine for UK, 1970-74; Chairman: Medico-Pharmaceutical Forum, 1978-80 (Chairman, Education Advisory Board, 1979-83); Conference of Royal Colleges and Faculties in Scotland, 1982-85; National Medical Consultative Committee for Scotland, 1982-87; President, RCPSGlas, 1982-84; Hon.FACP, 1983; Hon. LLD, Glasgow University, 1988; DUniv, Strathclyde University, 1997. Publications: Dilling's Pharmacology (Co-Editor); Gastroenterology - an integrated course. Recreations: swimming; golfing. Address: (h.) 1 Varna Road, Glasgow G14 9NE; T.-0141-959 5930.

Thomson, Walter Nigel Jamieson, LLB, NP, WS. Partner and Head of Private Client Services, Robson McLean W.S., since 1998 (Quality Controller, since 1997); b. 5.3.44, Galashiels; m., Elizabeth (separated); 2 s. Educ. George Watson's College, Edinburgh; Edinburgh University. Apprentice, McNeill and Sime W. S., 1969-71; Partner, McNeill and Sime W. S. and Kilgour McNeill and Sime, 1971-89. Musical Director, JUBILO, an Edinburgh choir. Recreations: music; walking. Address: (b.) 28 Abercromby Place, Edinburgh; T.-0131-556 0556.

Thomson,. William P. L., OBE, MA, MUniv, DipEd; b. 9.5.33, Newmilns; m., Elizabeth Watson; 1 s.; 3 d. Educ. Dundee High School; St. Andrews University. Teacher of History and Geography/Deputy Head Teacher, Anderson High School, Shetland, 1958-71; Rector, Kirkwall Grammar School, Orkney, 1971-91; Historian. Honorary Sheriff. Publications: The Little General and the Rousay Crofters, 1981; Kelp-Making in Orkney, 1983; History of Orkney, 1987; Lord Henry Sinclair's 1492 Rental of Orkney, 1996. Address: (h.) South Manse, Burray, Orkney KW17 2SS; T.-01856 731330.

Thorley, George William Faulds, BA (Hons), DipTP, MSc, FRSA, MRTPI. Chief Executive, South Ayrshire Council, since 1995; Assistant Chief Executive, Strathclyde Regional Council, 1990-95; b. 19.1.48, Dundee; m., Anne; 2 d. Educ. St. Michael's Secondary School, Dundee; Lawside Academy, Dundee; Strathclyde University. Joined Strathclyde Regional Council, 1975, as Senior Planner/Economist; joined Chief Executive's Department, 1980, as Senior Executive (Economic Strategy). Recreations: gardening; badminton; music; visual arts. Address: (b.) County Buildings, Wellington Square, Ayr, KA7 1DR; T.-01292 612170.

Thorne, Professor Michael Philip, BSc (Hons), PhD, FIMA, FBCS, FRSA. Vice Principal, Napier University, since 1998; b. 19.10.51, Colchester; m., Val; 3 s. Educ. Hinchingbrooke School; University of London; University of Birmingham. South East Derbyshire College; University College, London; University of Wales, Cardiff; University of Sunderland. Recreations: music; theatre; hillwalking. Address: (b.) Craiglockhart Campus, 219 Colinton Road, Edinburgh EH12 1DJ; T.-0131-455 4247.

Thorpe, John Elton, BA, PhD. Leverhulme Emeritus Fellow, 1995-97, and Visiting Professor, Glasgow University Institute of Biomedical and Life Sciences; Professor, University of Bergen Institute of Biology; Emeritus Fellow, American Institute of Fishery Biologists; formerly Senior Principal Scientific Officer, Freshwater Fisheries Laboratory, Pitlochry; b. 24.1.35, Wolverhampton; m., Judith Anne Johnson; 2 s. Educ. Kingswood School, Bath; Jesus College, Cambridge. Cambridge Expedition to British Honduras, 1959-60 (Leader); Shell International Chemical Co. Ltd., London, 1960-62; joined DAFS Freshwater Fisheries Laboratory, Pitlochry, 1963. Vice-President, Fisheries Society of British Isles, 1988-93; Editor, Journal of Fish Biology, since 1991; Member, Editorial Board: Fisheries Management, 1978-84, Journal of Animal Ecology, 1988-97, Reviews in Fish and Fisheries, since 1989, Folia Zoologica, since 1991, Sarsia, since 1996, and Aquaculture and Fisheries Management, since 1985; Chairman, Killiecrankie and Fincastle Community Council, 1976-78. Special Medal, University of Lodz, Poland, 1992. Publications: nine books; 220 scientific papers. Recreations: travelling; Baroque music. Address: (h.) Piper's Croft, Killiecrankie, Perthshire PH16 5LW; T.-01796 47 3886.

Thrower, Rev. Charles George, BSc. Minister, Carnbee linked with Pittenweem, since 1970; Moderator, St. Andrews Presbytery, 1991-92; b. 22.11.37, Barton Turf, Norfolk; m., Dr. Stephanie A.M. Thrower; 1 s.; 3 d. Educ. King Edward VI School, Norwich; Britannia Royal Naval College, Dartmouth. Electrical branch training H.M.S. Girdle-Ness (Malta), 1960-61; divinity student, St. Mary's, 1961-64; probationer, St. Andrews Church, Dundee, 1964-65; missionary appointment, Hampden with Falmouth, Trelawny, Jamaica, 1966-70. Synod of Fife Youth Adviser, 1971-74; Chairman, East Neuk of Fife Committee, Children 1st, since 1974, and Member of Council. Recreations: art; photography; sailing; gardening; local church history. Address: The Manse, 2 Milton Place, Pittenweem, Fife, KY10 2LR; T.-01333 311255.

Thrower, Professor James Arthur, BLitt, MA, PhD, FRAS. Professor of the History of Religions and Director, Centre for the Study of Religions, Aberdeen University, since 1994; b. 5.10.36, Guisborough; m., Judith Elizabeth Gauss; 3 d. Educ. Guisborough Grammar School; St. Chad's College, Durham; St. Edmund Hall, Oxford. Staff-Tutor, Eastern District, WEA, 1962-64; Lecturer in Philosophy of Religion, Ghana University, 1964-68; Lecturer in Religious Studies, Bede College, Durham, 1968-70; Lecturer in Religious Studies, Aberdeen University, 1970 (Senior Lecturer, 1981, Reader, 1993, Head of Department, 1984-87); Riddoch Lecturer, since 1984; Visiting Professor: Helsinki University, 1974, Polish Academy of Sciences, 1976, Aligarh Muslim University, India, 1988; British Council Exchange Scholar, Leningrad University, 1976 and 1978; Visiting Scholar, Gdansk University, 1981 and 1982; British Academy exchange scholar Chinese Academy of Social Sciences, 1989; GLCA-Scotland, Visiting Fellow, De Pauw University, Indiana, 1998; Warden, Balgownie Lodge, Aberdeen University, 1971-82. Author of a number of books and articles about the history of religions. Recreations: travel and exploration; classical music; opera; ballet. (h.) 2 Riverside Mill Cottages, Bridge of Don AB23 8LZ; T.-Aberdeen 822127.

Thurso, 3rd Viscount of (John Archibald Sinclair); b. 10.9.53; m.; 2 s.; 1 d. Educ. Eton. Managing Director, Fitness and Leisure Holdings, since 1995.

Tiefenbrun, Ivor Sigmund, MBE. Managing Director, Linn Products Ltd., Glasgow; Member, Design Council; b. 18.3.46, Glasgow; m., Evelyn Stella Balarksy; 2 s.; 1 d. Educ. Strathbungo Senior Secondary School; Strathclyde University (Sixties dropout). Worked overseas, 1971-73; founded Linn Products, 1973. Chairman, Federation of British Audio, 1983-87; Council Member, Design Council, since 1995. Recreations: thinking; music; reading; sailing. Address: (b.) Linn Products Ltd., Floors Road, Waterfoot, Eaglesham, Glasgow G76 0EP; T.-0141-307 7777.

Tierney, David A., BA (Hons). Rector, Speyside High School, Aberlour, since 1987; b. 15.1.50, Glasgow; m., Valerie Lauder; 2 s. Educ. Queen's Park School, Glasgow; Strathclyde University; Jordanhill College of Education; Glasgow University. Teacher, Govan High School, Glasgow, 1973-76; Principal Teacher of Modern Studies, Mackie Academy, 1976-83; Depute Rector, Speyside High School, 1983-87. Recreations: hill-walking; cycling; reading; gardening. Address: (b.) Speyside High School, Mary Avenue, Aberlour, Banff; T.-01340 871522.

Tildesley, James Michael. Director, Scottish Maritime Museum, since 1989; b. 10.3.47, Southminster; m., Janet Birks; 2 s.; 1 d. Educ. Chelmsford Technical High School; Goldsmiths' College, London University. Assistant Master, Mayfield School, Redbridge; Assistant Curator, then Deputy Curator, Passmore Edwards Museum; Assistant Director of Leisure, L.B. of Newham. Address: (b.) Scottish Maritime Museum, Laird Forge, Gottries Road, Irvine, KA12 8QE; T.-01294 278283.

Timms, Professor Peter Kenneth, CBE. Chairman, Board of Management, Glasgow University Business School, since 1991; Chairman and Managing Director, Flexible Technology Ltd., Bute, since 1981; Chairman, Murray VCT3 plc, since 1998; Director, Argyll and the Islands Enterprise, since 1998; Director, Smartpower Ltd., since 1998; Member, Scottish Industrial Development Advisory Board, since 1989; b. 2.12.43, Witney, Oxon; m., Patricia; 3 s. Educ. St. Edmund's School, Canterbury, Kent. Production Engineer, Texas Instruments Ltd., 1964; Manufacturing Engineer, then Process Engineering Manager, IBM UK Ltd., 1967; Director and General Manager, AFA Minerva, 1978. Non-Executive Director: Ferranti Technologies Ltd (Chairman, since 1995), Murray Enterprise plc, Scottish Electronics Technology Group Ltd. Recreations: boating; travel. Address: Millbrae, Ascog, Rothesay, Bute PA20 9ET; T.-01700 504515.

Titterington, Professor (Donald) Michael, BSc, PhD, DipMathStat, FRSE. Professor of Statistics, Glasgow University, since 1988; b. 20.11.45, Marple, Cheshire; m., Mary Hourie Philp; 1 s. Educ. High School of Stirling; Edinburgh University; Cambridge University. Lecturer, then Senior Lecturer, then Titular Professor, Department of Statistics, Glasgow University, 1972-88; visiting appointments: Princeton University, 1978, State University of New York, 1980, Wisconsin University, 1982, Australian National University, 1982, 1994, 1995; Associate Editor, Biometrika, 1979-85, Annals of Statistics, 1983-85 and 1995-96, Journal, American Statistical Association, 1986-88 and 1991-96, and IEEE Transactions on Pattern Analysis and Machine Intelligence, 1994-96; Joint Editor, Journal of the Royal Statistical Society, Series B, 1986-89, and Statistical Science, 1992-94; Editor, Biometrika, since 1996; Council Member, Royal Statistical Society, 1987-92; elected Fellow, Institute of Mathematical Statistics, 1986; elected Member, International Statistical Institute, 1991. Publications: Statistical Analysis of Finite Mixture Distributions (Co-author); many journal articles. Recreation: being a father. Address: (b.) Department of Statistics, Glasgow University, Glasgow, G12 8QQ; T.-0141-330 5022.

Tobin, Patrick Francis John, MA, PGCE, FRSA. Principal, Mary Erskine School and Daniel Stewart's & Melville College, since 1989; b. 4.10.41, London; m., Margery Ann Sluce; 1 s.; 3 d. Educ. St. Benedict's, Ealing; Christ Church, Oxford; London University. Head of Economics, St. Benedict's, Ealing, 1963-71; Head of History, Christ College, Brecon, 1971-75; Head of History, Tonbridge School, 1975-81; The King's School, Parramatta, NSW, 1980; Headmaster, Prior Park College, Bath, 1981-89. Chairman, HMC. Recreations: reading; writing; canal boating; hill-walking; travel. Address: (h.) 11 Queensferry Terrace, Edinburgh EH4 3EQ

Tod, Stewart, DA (Edin), RIBA, FRIAS, FSA Scot. Consultant to Stewart Tod & Partners, Architects, Edinburgh, formerly David Carr Architects; b. 30.4.27, West Wemyss; m., A. Vivienne J. Nixon; 2 s.; 2 d. Educ. Buckhaven High School; Edinburgh College of Art. RAF, 1945-48; Stratton Davis & Yates, 1952-55; Falkirk District Council, 1955-57; Carr and Matthew, 1957-60; David Carr Architects, 1960-77. Executive Committee Member, Association for the Protection of Rural Scotland, Chairman, Historic Roads and Bridges Committee; General Trustee, Church of Scotland. Recreations: bee-keeping; gardening; sketching. Address: (b.) 43 Manor Place, Edinburgh; T.-0131-225 7988.

Todd, Professor Adrian Christopher, BTech, PhD, CEng, FIChemE, FInstPet. Professor of Petroleum Engineering, Heriot Watt University, since 1990 (Head of Department, 1991-96); b. 1944, Leicester; m., Valerie H. Todd; 1 d. Educ. Lutterworth Grammar School; Loughborough University of Technology. Research Scientist, Shell, 1969-72; joined Heriot Watt University as Lecturer in Chemical Engineering, 1972. Recreation: Christian activities. Address: (b.) Department of Petroleum Engineering, Heriot Watt University, Riccarton, Edinburgh; T.-0131-451 3124.

Todd, Rev. Andrew Stewart, MA, BD, DD. Minister, St. Machar's Cathedral, Old Aberdeen, 1967-93; Extra Chaplain to The Queen in Scotland, since 1996 (Chaplain-in-Ordinary, 1991-96); b. 26.5.26, Alloa; m., Janet Agnes Brown Smith; 2 s.; 2 d. Educ. High School of Stirling; Edinburgh University; Basel University. Assistant Minister, St. Cuthbert's, Edinburgh, 1951-52; Minister: Symington, Lanarkshire, 1952; North Leith, 1960; Member, Church Hymnary Revision Comittee, 1963-73; Convener, General Assembly's Committee on Public Worship and Aids to Devotion, 1974-78; Moderator, Aberdeen Presbytery, 1980-81; Convener, Panel on Doctrine, 1990-95; Member, Church Hymnary Trust; awarded Honorary Doctorate,

Aberdeen University, 1982; translator of three theological books from German into English; Honorary President, Church Service Society; Honorary President, Scottish Church Society. Recreations: music; gardening. Address: (h.) Culearn, Balquhidder, Lochearnhead, Perthshire FK19 8PB; T.-01877 384662.

Toft, Anthony Douglas, CBE, BSc, MD, FRCPE, FRCPGlas, FRCPLond, FRCPI, FACP(Hon), FRACP(Hon), FRCSE, FRCPC(Hon), FRCGP(Hon), FFPM (Hon), FFAEM (Hon), FCPS Pakistan (Hon), FCPS Bangladesh (Hon), FAM Singapore (Hon), MAM Malaysia (Hon). Consultant Physician, Royal Infirmary, Edinburgh, since 1978; Physician to the Queen in Scotland, since 1996; Chief Medical Officer, Scottish Equitable Life Assurance, since 1987; President, British Thyroid Association, since 1996; President, Royal College of Physicians of Edinburgh, 1991-94; b. 29.10.44, Perth; m., Maureen Darling; 1 s.; 1 d. Educ. Perth Academy; Edinburgh University. Chairman, Collegiate Members' Committee, Royal College of Physicians of Edinburgh, 1978; Vice-President, Royal College of Physicians, 1989-91; Chairman, Scottish Royal Colleges, 1992-94; Chairman, Joint Committee of Higher Medical Training, 1993-96; Member, Health Appointments Advisory Committee, since 1994. Recreations: golf; gardening. Address: (h.) 41 Hermitage Gardens, Edinburgh EH10 6AZ; T.-0131-447 2221.

Tolley, David Anthony, MB, BS (Lond), FRCS, FRCSEdin. Consultant Urological Surgeon, Western General Hospital, Edinburgh, since 1980; Honorary Senior Lecturer, Department of Surgery/Urology, Edinburgh University, since 1980; Director, Scottish Lithotriptor Centre; b. 29.11.47, Warrington; m., Judith Anne Finn; 3 s.; 1 d. Educ. Manchester Grammar School; Kings College Hospital Medical School, London University. House Surgeon and Physician, Kings College Hospital; Lecturer in Human Morphology, Southampton University; Lecturer in Anatomy and Fulbright Fellow, University of Texas at Houston; Surgical Registrar, Hammersmith and Ealing Hospitals, London; Senior Surgical Registrar (Urology), Kings College Hospital, London; Senior Urological Registrar, Yorkshire Regional Training Scheme. Member: MRC Working Party on Urological Cancer; MRC Working Party on Superficial Bladder Cancer; Editorial Board, British Journal of Urology; Member, Council, British Association of Urological Surgeons; Standing Commitee on Postgraduate Education, British Association of Urological Surgeons; President, British Society for Endourology; Board, Minimal Access Therapy Training Unit Scotland; Education Committee, Royal College of Surgeons of Edinburgh; Past Chairman, Scottish Urological Oncology Group. Recreations: golf; motor racing; sailing. Address: (b.) Murrayfield Hospital, Corstorphine Road, Edinburgh; T.-0131-334 0363.

Tombs, Sebastian Martineau, BArch, DipArch (Cantab), FRIAS, ACIArb. Secretary, Royal Incorporation of Architects in Scotland, since 1995; b. 11.10.49, Sussex; m., Eva Hierman; 4 s.; 2 d. Educ. Bryanston; Cambridge University. RMJM, Edinburgh, 1975-76; Roland Wedgwood, Edinburgh, 1976-77; Fountainbridge Housing Association, Edinburgh, 1977-78; Housing Corporation, 1978-81; Edinburgh District Council Housing Department, 1982-86; Depute Secretary, RIAS, 1986-94; Founder and first Secretary, Scottish Ecological Design Association, 1991-94, Chairman, 1994-97. Founder and first Chairman, Association of Planning Supervisors, 1995-97. Recreation: choral music. Address: (b.) 15 Rutland Square, Edinburgh, EH1 2BE; T.-0131-229 7545.

Toner, Mary Catherine, BEd (Hons), DPSE. Chief Executive, Scottish Marriage Care, since 1999; b. 14.5.46, Shotts; m., Thomas; 2 s. Educ. St. Andrew's College; Jordanhill College. Training in industry, leading to middle management and production, posts, 1967-79; Primary School Teacher, Glasgow and Lanarkshire, 1984-91; Head Teacher, St. Anthony's Primary School, West Lothian, 1991-94; Education Officer, Lothian Region and West Lothian, 1994-98. Former Counsellor, Supervisor, Tutor, Scottish Marriage Care. Recreations: travelling; good restaurants; fine wines. Address: (b.) 50 Greenock Road, Paisley PA3 2LE; T.-0141-849 6183.

Topping, Professor Barry H.V., BSc, PhD, CEng, CMath, MBCS, MICE, MIStructE, MIMechE, FIMA. Professor of Computational Mechanics, Department of Mechanical and Chemical Engineering, Heriot-Watt University, Edinburgh, since 1995; b. 14.2.52, Manchester. Educ. Bedford Modern School; City University, London. Lecturer in Civil Engineering, Edinburgh University, 1978-88; Von-Humboldt Research Fellow, Stuttgart University, 1986-87; Senior Lecturer, Heriot-Watt University, 1988-89, Reader, 1989-90, Professor of Structural Engineering, 1990-95. Co-Editor, Computers and Structures; Co-Editor, Advances in Engineering Software. Address: (b.) Department of Mechanical and Chemical Engineering, Heriot-Watt University, Riccarton, Edinburgh EH14 4AS; T.-0131-449 5111.

Torphichen, 15th Lord (James Andrew Douglas Sandilands); b. 27.8.46; m.; 4 d. Address: Calder House, Mid Calder, West Lothian.

Torrance, Rev. Dr. Iain Richard, TD, MA, BD, DPhil. Senior Lecturer in Divinity, Aberdeen University, since 1997 (Lecturer, 1993-97); Co-Editor, Scottish Journal of Theology, since 1982; b. 13.1.49, Aberdeen; m., Morag Ann MacHugh; 1 s.; 1 d. Educ. Edinburgh Academy; Monkton Combe School, Bath; Edinburgh University; St. Andrews University; Oriel College, Oxford University. Minister, Northmavine, Shetland, 1982-85; Lecturer in New Testament and Ethics, Queen's College, Birmingham, 1985-89; Lecturer in New Testament and Patristics, Birmingham University, 1989-93; Chaplain to the Moderator of the General Assembly, 1976; Member, International Dialogue between the Orthodox and the Reformed Churches, since 1992; Member, General Assembly's Panel on Doctrine, since 1993; Member, Ethics Committee, Grampian Health Board, since 1996; Hon. Secretary, Aberdeen A.U.T., 1995-98, Hon. President, 1998-99; Secretary, Society for the Study of Christian Ethics, 1995-98; Judge, Templeton (UK) Awards, since 1994; TA Chaplain, 1982-97; ACF Chaplain, since 1996; Member, Academie Internationale des Sciences Religieuses, since 1997; Convener, General Assembly's Committee on Chaplains to HM Forces, since 1998. Publications: Christology after Chalcedon, 1988; Human Genetics: a Christian perspective (Co-author), 1995; Ethics and the Military Community, 1998. Recreations: historical Scottish culture (tartan, castles, battles, literature, art). Address: (h.) Concraig Smiddy, Clinterty, Kingswells, AB15 8RN; T.-01224 790902.

Torrance, Rev. Professor James Bruce, MA (Hons), BD. Professor of Systematic Theology, Aberdeen University, 1977-89 (Dean, Faculty of Divinity, 1978-81); Minister, Church of Scotland, since 1950; b. 3.2.23, Chengtu, Szechwan, West China; m., Mary Heather Aitken; 1 s.; 2 d. Educ. Royal High School, Edinburgh; Edinburgh University and New College; Marburg University; Basle University; Oxford University. RAF, 1943-45; ordained, Invergowrie, Dundee, 1954; Lecturer in Divinity and Dogmatics in History of Christian Thought, 1961, and Senior Lecturer in Christian Dogmatics, 1972, New College, Edinburgh; Visiting Professor of New Testament, Union Theological Seminary, Richmond, Virginia, 1960, of Theology, Columbia Theological Seminary, 1965, and Vancouver School of Theology, 1974-75; Visiting Professor in South Africa, USA, New Zealand, Australia, Fiji, W. Samoa, Canada. Convenor, Panel on Doctrine, General Assembly, 1982-86; Joint Convener, British Council of Churches Commission on Doctrine of the Trinity, 1983-89; Joint

Convenor, World Alliance of Reformed Churches, Lutheran World Federation Conversations, 1985-88. Publications: John Duns Scotus in a Nutshell (Co-author), 1992; Worship, Community and the Triune God of Grace, 1994; Nature of Atonement (Editor), 1995; Scottish Theology, 1996. Recreations: bee-keeping; fishing; swimming; gardening. Address: (h.) 3 Greenbank Crescent, Edinburgh EH10 5TE; T.-0131-447 3230.

Torrance, Very Rev. Professor Thomas Forsyth, MBE, MA, BD, DrTheol, DLitt, DD, DrTeol, DTheol, DSc, FBA, FRSE. Emeritus Professor, Edinburgh University, since 1979; b. 30.8.13, Chengdu, Sichuan, China; m., Margaret Edith Spear; 2 s.; 1 d. Educ. Canadian School, Chengdu, China; Bellshill Academy, Lanarkshire; Edinburgh University; Basel University; Oriel College, Oxford. Minister: Alyth Barony Parish Church, 1940-47; served as Church of Scotland Chaplain, 1943-45; Minister, Beechgrove Parish Church, Aberdeen, 1947-50; Edinburgh University: Professor of Church History, 1950-52, Professor of Christian Dogmatics, 1952-79; Templeton Prize, 1978; Moderator, General Assembly of the Church of Scotland, 1976-77. Cross of St. Mark, First Class, 1970; Protoprebyter of Greek Orthodox Church (Hon.), 1973; President, Academie Internationale des Sciences Religieuses, 1972-81. Publications: The Doctrine of Grace in the Apostolic Fathers, 1949; Calvin's Doctrine of Man, 1949; Royal Priesthood, 1955; Kingdom and Church, 1956; The School of Faith, 1959; Conflict and Agreement in the Church, 1959; Karl Barth: An Introduction to his Early Theology, 1962; Theology in Reconstruction, 1965; Theological Science, 1969 (Collins Prize); Space, Time and Incarnation, 1969; God and Rationality, 1971; Theology in Reconciliation, 1975; Space, Time and Resurrection, 1976; The Ground and Grammar of Theology, 1980; Christian Theology and Scientific Culture, 1980; Divine and Contingent Order, 1981; Reality and Evangelical Theology, 1982; Juridical and Physical Law, 1982, The Mediation of Christ, 1983; Transformation and Convergence in the Frame of Knowledge, 1984; Reality and Scientific Theology, 1985; The Trinitarian Faith, 1988; The Hermeneutics of John Calvin, 1988; Karl Barth: Biblical and Evangelical Theologian, 1990; Trinitarian Perspectives, 1993; Preaching Christ Today, 1993; Divine Meaning, 1995; The Christian Doctrine of God, 1995. Founding Editor of Scottish Journal of Theology. Recreations: formerly golf, squash, fishing; now walking. Address: (h.) 37 Braid Farm Road, Edinburgh EH10 6LE; T.-0131-447 3224.

Toth, Professor Akos George, Dr. Jur., PhD. Professor of Law, Strathclyde University, since 1984; Jean Monnet Chair of European Law, since 1991; b. 9.2.36, Mezotur, Hungary; m., Sarah Kurucz. Educ. Budapest University; Szeged University; Exeter University. Strathclyde University: Lecturer in Law, 1971-76, Senior Lecturer, 1976-82, Reader, 1982-84; British Academy Research Readership, 1993-95. Publications: Legal Protection of Individuals in the European Communities, 1978; The Oxford Encyclopaedia of European Community Law, 1990. Recreations: travel; music; opera; theatre; swimming; walking. Address: (b.) Strathclyde University, Law School, 173 Cathedral Street, Glasgow, G4 ORQ; T.-0141-552 4400, Ext. 3338.

Townell, Nicholas Howard, MB, BS (Lond), FRCS (Eng), FRCS (Edin). Consultant Urologist, Dundee and Angus Hospitals, since 1985; Honorary Senior Lecturer in Surgery, Dundee University Medical School, since 1985; b. 19.4.49, Redhill; m., Hoang Anh Vuong; 1 s.; 2 d. Educ. Davenant Foundation Grammar School; London University; Royal Free Hospital School of Medicine. Various House Surgeon, House Physician and Registrar posts; Senior Registrar in General Surgery and Urology, Royal Free Hospital. Fellow, Royal Society of Medicine. Specialist interest: minimally invasive urology. Recreations: classical music; golf; squash; hill-walking. Address: (h.) Rosebank, Hillside, Angus, DD10 9HZ; T.-0167 4830296.

Trainer, Professor James, MA, PhD. Professor of German, Stirling University, 1969-97 (Emeritus) (Deputy Principal, 1973-78, 1981-87, 1989-92); b. 2.3.32; m., Barbara Herta Reinhard (deceased); 2 s.; 1 d. Educ. St. Andrews University; Free University of Berlin. Lecturer in German, St. Andrews University, 1958-67; Visiting Professor, Yale University, 1964-65; Visiting Scholar, University of California at Santa Barbara, 1989; Vice-Convener, SUCE, 1987-94; Convener, SUCE Modern Languages Panel, 1979-86; Member, Inter University and Polytechnic Council, since 1983; Member, Scottish Examination Board, 1975-82; Chairman, SED Postgraduate Awards Committee, since 1989; Member, UK Fulbright Committee, 1985-93; Trustee, National Library of Scotland, 1986-91; Chairman, Scottish Conference of University Teachers of German, 1978-80; Member, National Academic Audit Unit; Member, SHEFCO Quality Assessment Committee; Member Overseas Research Students Awards Committee, CVCP; Governor, Morrison's Academy, Crieff, 1994-98. Recreations: music; cricket; translating. Address: (b.) Stirling University, Stirling; T.-01786 473171.

Trainor, Professor Richard Hughes, BA, MA., DPhil, FRHistS, FRSA. Vice-Principal, Glasgow University, since 1996; Professor of Social History, Glasgow University, since 1995; b. 31.12.48, New Jersey; m., Dr. Marguerite Wright Dupree; 1 s.; 1 d. Educ. Calvert Hall High School, Maryland; Brown University; Princeton University; Merton and Nuffield Colleges, Oxford University. Junior Research Fellow, Wolfson College, Oxford, 1977-79; Lecturer, Balliol College, Oxford, 1978-79; Glasgow University: Lecturer in Economic History, 1979-89, Senior Lecturer in Economic and Social History, 1989-95, Director, Design and Implementation of Software in History Project, 1985-89, Co-Director, Computers in Teaching Initiative Centre for History, since 1989, Dean of Social Sciences, 1992-96. Rhodes Scholar; Honorary Secretary, Economic History Society, since 1998; Council Member, Royal Historical Society, since 1997; Joint Editor, Scottish Economic and Social History, 1989-94. Publication: Black Country Elites: the exercise of authority in an industrialised area 1830-1900, 1993. Recreations: parenting; observing politics; tennis. Address: (h.) 45 Mitre Road, Glasgow G14 9LE; T.-0141-959 0006.

Tranter, Nigel, OBE, KCLJ, DLitt, MA (Hon.). Author and Novelist, since 1935; b. 23.11.09, Glasgow; m., May Jean Campbell Grieve (deceased); 1 s. (deceased); 1 d. Educ. St. James' Episcopal School; George Heriot's, Edinburgh. Professional Writer, since 1946; published more than 120 books, including over 80 novels; Vice-Convener, Scottish Covenant Association, 1951-55; President, East Lothian Liberal Association, 1960-70; Chairman, National Forth Road Bridge Committee, 1953-57; Chairman, St. Andrew Society of East Lothian, since 1966; President, Scottish PEN, 1962-66 (now Honorary President); Chairman, Society of Authors, Scotland, 1966-70; Chairman, National Book League, Scotland, 1971-73. Vice-Chancellor, Order of St. Lazarus of Jerusalem, 1982-88; Hon. Vice-President, Scottish Association of Teachers of History; Honorary Freeman of Blackstone, Virginia, USA, 1980; BBC Radio Scot of the Year, 1989; Hon. President, Saltire Society; Trustee, Scottish Flag Fund; Hon. Member, Scottish Library Association; President, Scottish Castles Association. Recreations: walking; castle architecture. Address: (h.) Quarry House, Aberlady, East Lothian; T.-Aberlady 258.

Travers, Andrew Keith Buchanan, BSc. Chief Executive, Scottish Design Ltd., since 1996; b. 3.1.62, Lanark. Educ. Earnock High School, Hamilton; Strathclyde University. Consultant Engineer, IBM Greenock, 1989-94; Director, Centre for Integrated Product Development, 1994-96.

Recreations: rugby; tennis; sailing; skiing. Address: (b.) Scottish Design, Stock Exchange House, 7 Nelson Mandela Place, Glasgow, G2 7JN; T.-0141-221 6121.

Travers, John, BA, MA. Director of Education, North Ayrshire Council, since 1995; b. 22.1.48, Catterick; m., Joy; 1 s.; 2 d. Educ. St. Patrick's High School, Dumbarton; Glasgow University. Teaching, Glasgow and Barrhead, 1977-82; Assistant Head Teacher, St. Patrick's High School, Coatbridge, 1982-84; TVEI Coordinator, James Watt College, Greenock, 1984-86; Strathclyde Regional Council: Education Officer, Renfrew Division, 1986-89, Assistant Director of Education, 1989-90, Senior Education Officer, 1990-92; Senior Depute Director of Education, Fife Regional Council, 1992-95. Address: (b.) Cunninghame House, Irvine, KA12 8EE; T.-01294 324412.

Travis, Christopher Douglas, BSc (Soc Sci), MBA. Chief Executive, Kincardine and Deeside Enterprise Trust Ltd.; b. 12.5.59, Kaduna, Nigeria. Educ. Dollar Academy; Edinburgh University. Previously: Lecturer in Economics/ research student, Dundee College of Technology, Business Counsellor, SDA, Economic Development Manager, Gordon District Council, Executive Director, Clydesdale Development Co. Ltd., Chairman, Lanarkshire Enterprise Training Ltd. Recreations: cooking; reading; hill-walking; golf. Address: (b.) Unit 1, Aboyne Business Centre, Huntly Road, Aboyne AB34 5HE; T.-013398 87222.

Trayhurn, Professor Paul, BSc, DPhil, DSc, FRSE. Assistant Director (Academic Affairs) and Head, Division of Biomedical Science, Rowett Research Institute, since 1988; Department of Biomedical Sciences and Department of Molecular and Cell Biology, Aberdeen University, since 1992 (Honorary); b. 6.5.48, Exeter; m., Deborah Hartland Gigg; 3 s.; 1 d. Educ. Colyton Grammar School, Devon; Reading University; Oxford University. Graduate student, Linacre College, Oxford, 1969-72; NATO European Research Fellow, Strasbourg, 1972-73; Postdoctoral Fellow, Oxford, 1973-75; MRC Scientific/Senior Scientific Staff, Dunn Nutrition Laboratory, Cambridge, 1975-86; Professor and Heritage Scholar, University of Alberta, 1986-88; Evelyn Williams Visiting Professor, University of Sydney, 1992. Member, Council, Nutrition Society, 1982-84, 1991-93; Chairman, Scottish Section, Nutrition Society, 1993-95; Executive Council, Korean Collaboration Centre; Member, BBSRC Agri-Food Directorate. Publications: over 300 scientific publications. Address: (b.) Division of Biomedical Science, Rowett Research Institute, Bucksburn, Aberdeen, AB21 9SB; T.-01224 716610.

Trewavas, Professor Anthony James, BSc, PhD, FRSE., FRSA. Professor, Institute of Cell and Molecular Biology, Edinburgh University, since 1990; b. 17.6.39, London; m., Valerie; 1 s.; 2 d. Educ. Roan Grammar School; University College, London. Lecturer/Reader, Edinburgh University; Visiting Professor, Universities of Michigan State, Calgary, California (Davis), Bonn, Illinois, North Carolina, National University of Mexico; University of Milan. Publications: 170 scientific papers; two books. Recreations: music (particularly choral); reading. Address: (h.) 1 Rullion Road, Penicuik, Midlothian; T.-01968 673372.

Trotter, Alexander Richard, DL, FRSA; President, Scottish Landowners' Federation, since 1996; b. 20.2.39, London; m., Julia Henrietta Greenwell; 3 s. Educ. Eton College; City of London Technical College. Royal Scots Greys, 1958-68; Member, Berwickshire County Council, 1969-75 (Chairman, Roads Committee, 1974-75); Manager, Charterhall Estate and Farm, since 1969; Chairman, Meadowhead Ltd. (formerly Mortonhall Park Ltd.), since 1974; Director, Timber Growers' GB Ltd., 1977-82; Vice Chairman, Border Grain Ltd., since 1984; Council Member, Scottish Landowners' Federation, since 1975 (Chairman, Land Use Committee, 1975-78, Convener, 1982-85); Member, Department of Agriculture Working Party on the Agricultural Holding (Scotland) Legislation, 1981-82; Chairman, Scottish Committee, Nature Conservancy Council, 1985-90; Member, UK Committee for Euro Year of the Environment, 1986-88; Member, Scottish Tourist Board Graded Holiday Parks Overseeing Committee, since 1993; Member, Queen's Bodyguard for Scotland (Royal Company of Archers). Recreations: skiing; golf; hunting; shooting. Address: Charterhall, Duns, Berwickshire, TD11 3RE; T.-01890 840210.

Trudgill, David L., BSc, PhD, CBiol, FBIBiol. Head, Nematology Department, Scottish Crop Research Institute, since 1972; b. 2.5.42, Leeds; m., Margaret Jean Luckraft; 3 s. Educ. Leeds Grammar School; Ulverston Grammar School; Leeds University; London University. Nematologist, Rothamsted Experimental Station, 1966-72. Chairman, European Plant Protection Organisation ad hoc committee on potato cyst nematodes; President, European Society of Nematologists. Recreations:hill-walking; fishing. Address: (b.) Nematology Department, Scottish Crop Research Institute, Invergowrie, Dundee DD2 5DA; T.-01382 562731.

Trueland, Jennifer, MA. Health Correspondent, The Scotsman, since 1997; b. 13.2.66, Dundee. Educ. Menzieshill High School, Dundee; Edinburgh University. Reporter and Feature Writer, Leicester Mercury, 1990-94; Health Editor, Newcastle Journal, 1994-95; UK News, 1995-96; News Editor, Pulse, 1996-97. Recreations: American comedies; red wine. Address: (b.) 20 North Bridge, Edinburgh EH1 1YT; T.-0131-243 3365.

Truman, Donald Ernest Samuel, BA, PhD, FIBiol, CBiol, FRSA. Assistant Principal, University of Edinburgh, since 1998; b. 23.10.36, Leicester; m., Kathleen Ramsay; 1 s.; 1 d. Educ. Wyggeston School, Leicester; Clare College, Cambridge. NATO Research Fellow, Wenner-Grenn Institute, Stockholm, 1962-63; MRC Epigenetics Research Group, Edinburgh, 1963-72; Lecturer, Department of Genetics, Edinburgh University, 1972-78; Senior Lecturer, 1978-89, Head of Department, 1984-89, Director of Biology Teaching Unit, 1985-89; Vice-Dean and Vice-Provost, Faculty of Science and Engineering, 1989-98; Aneurin Bevan Memorial Fellow, Government of India, 1978; Chairman, Edinburgh Centre for Rural Research, since 1993; Member, Council, Scottish Agricultural College, since 1995; Chairman, Purchasing Consortium of Universities of Scotland and Northern Ireland, since 1996; Director, Edinburgh Technopole Company Ltd., since 1996. Publications: The Biochemistry of Cytodifferentiation, 1974; Differentiation in Vitro (Joint Editor), 1982; Stability and Switching in Cellular Differentiation, 1982; Coordinated Regulation of Gene Expression, 1986. Recreation: gardening; books. Address: (b.) Institute of Cell and Molecular Biology, Mayfield Road, Edinburgh EH9 3JR; T.-0131-650 7066.

Tuck, Ronald Moore Sinclair, MA, DMS, TQFE. Chief Executive, Scottish Qualifications Authority, since 1997; b. 20.3.49, Edinburgh; m., Anne; 1 s.; 1 d. Educ. George Heriot's; Edinburgh University; Dundee Institute of Technology. Lecturer/Senior Lecturer, Angus College, 1974-85; H.M. Inspector of Schools, 1985-92; HM Chief Inspector of Schools, 1992-96. Recreations: watching football; travelling; reading; cooking. Address: (b.) Hanover House, 24 Douglas Street, Glasgow G2 7NQ.

Tucker, Derek Alan. Editor, Press and Journal, Aberdeen, since 1992; b. 31.10.53, Liverpool; 1 s.; 1 d. Educ. Quarry Bank High School, Liverpool; Municipal Grammar School, Wolverhampton. Reporter/Chief Reporter/News Editor/Deputy Editor, Express and Star, Wolverhampton, 1972-92. Member, Press Complaints Commission, 1995-97. Recreations: golf; travel; watching any sport not involving horses. Address: (b.) Lang Stracht, Mastrick, Aberdeen; T.-01224 690222.

Tucker, Professor John Barry, BA, MA, PhD, FRSE. Professor of Cell Biology, St. Andrews University, since 1990; b. 17.3.41, Arundel; m., Janet Stephen Murray; 1 s. Educ. Queen Elizabeth Grammar School, Atherstone; Peterhouse, Cambridge. Fulbright Travel Scholar and Research Associate, Department of Zoology, Indiana University, 1966-68; SERC Research Fellow, Department of Zoology, Cambridge, 1968-69; Lecturer in Zoology, St. Andrews University, 1969-79 (Chairman, Zoology Department, 1982-84); Reader in Zoology, 1979-90. Member: SERC Advisory Group II, 1977-80, SERC Molecular Biology and Genetics Sub-committee, 1986-89, Editorial Board of Development, 1979-88. Recreations: cycling; hill-walking; tennis; reluctant gardener. Address: (b.) School of Biomedical Sciences, Bute Building, St. Andrews University, St. Andrews, Fife KY16 9TS; T.-01334 463560.

Tudhope, James Mackenzie, CB, BL; b. 11.2.27, Glasgow; m., Margaret W.; 2 s. Educ. Dunoon Grammar School; Glasgow University. Solicitor, 1951; private legal practice, 1951-55; Procurator Fiscal Depute, 1955; Senior Procurator Fiscal Depute, 1962; Assistant Procurator Fiscal, Glasgow, 1968-70; Procurator Fiscal: Kilmarnock 1970-73, Dumbarton, 1973-76; Regional Procurator Fiscal: South Strathclyde, Dumfries and Galloway at Hamilton, 1976-80, Glasgow and Strathkelvin, 1980-87. Member, Council, Law Society of Scotland, 1983-86; Honorary Sheriff, Kilmarnock, since 1989. Recreations (include): serendipity; worrying. Address: (h.) Point House, Dundonald Road, Kilmarnock;T.-01563 523727.

Turley, Mark John, BSc (Hons), MBA, MCIOH. Director of Housing, City of Edinburgh Council, since 1996; Executive Director of Housing, City of Edinburgh District Council, since 1993; b. 25.6.60, Dudley. Educ. High Arcal Grammar School, Sedgley; Leicester University. Sheffield City Council, 1981-91; Head of Tenant Services, York City Council, 1991-93. Recreations: playing violin; reading. Address: (b.) Housing Department, 23 Waterloo Place, Edinburgh, EH1 3BH; T.-0131-529 7325.

Turmeau, Professor William Arthur, CBE, FRSE, Dr. h.c. (Edinburgh University), Doctor of Education (Napier University), BSc, PhD, CEng, FIMechE. Chairman, Scottish Environment Protection Agency, since 1995; Principal and Vice-Chancellor, Napier University, 1982-94; b. 19.9.29, London; m., Margaret Moar Burnett; 1 d. Educ. Stromness Academy, Orkney; Edinburgh University; Moray House College of Education; Heriot-Watt University. Royal Signals, 1947-49; Research Engineer, Northern Electric Co. Ltd., Montreal, 1952-54; Mechanical Engineer, USAF, Goose Bay, Labrador, 1954-56; Contracts Manager, Godfrey Engineering Co. Ltd., Montreal, 1956-61; Lecturer, Bristo Technical Institute, Edinburgh, 1962-64; Napier College: Lecturer and Senior Lecturer, 1964-68, Head, Department of Mechanical Engineering, 1968-75, Assistant Principal and Dean, Faculty of Technology, 1975-82. Member, Steering Committee, University of the Highlands and Islands Project; Member, IMechE Academic Standards Committee; Trustee, Dynamic Earth Charitable Trust; Vice Chairman, ASH (Scotland). Recreations: modern jazz; Leonardo da Vinci. Address: (h.) 71 Morningside Park, Edinburgh, EH10 5EZ; T.-0131-447 4639.

Turnbull, Wilson Mark, DipArch, MLA (Penn), MBCS, RIBA, FRIAS, FLI. Turnbull Jeffrey Partnership, Landscape Architects, since 1982; b. 1.4.43, Edinburgh. Educ. George Watson's; Edinburgh College of Art; University of Pennsylvania. Assistant Professor of Architecture, University of Southern California, 1970-74; Partner, W.J. Cairns and Partners, Environmental Consultants, 1974-82; Partner, Design Innovations Research, 1976-81; Council Member, Cockburn Association (Edinburgh Civic Trust), 1986-95; Commissioner, Countryside Commission for Scotland, 1988-92; Commissioner, Royal Fine Art Commission for Scotland, 1996; Chairman, Edinburgh Greenbelt Initiative, 1988-91; Director, Edinburgh Greenbelt Trust, since 1991, Vice-Chairman, since 1993. Recreation: sailing. Address: (b.) Sandeman House, 55 High Street, Edinburgh EH1 1SR; T.-0131-557 5050.

Turner, Professor (Andrew) Neil, MA, BMBCh, PhD, FRCP (Lond.), FRCPEdin. Professor of Nephrology, University of Edinburgh, since 1998; Honorary Consultant, Royal Infirmary of Edinburgh, since 1998; b. 28.4.56, Alnwick; m., Helen Cameron; 3 s. Educ. Cambridge University; Oxford University. SHO in Medicine, Norfolk and Norwich Hospital, 1982; SHO in Renal Medicine and Transplantation, Churchill Hospital, Oxford, 1983; Registrar in Medicine, York District Hospital, 1984; Hammersmith Hospital/Royal Postgraduate Medical School, London: Registrar, Research Fellow, Senior Registrar, 1989-93; Senior Lecturer, Honorary Consultant, 1993-94; Senior Lecturer, University of Aberdeen, and Honorary Consultant, Aberdeen Royal Infirmary, 1994-98. Address: (b.) Renal Medicine, Royal Infirmary, Lauriston Place, Edinburgh EH3 9YW; T.-0131-536 2313.

Turner, Donald Ian, CA. Regional Managing Partner Scotland and Northern Ireland, Ernst and Young, since 1986; b. 20.9.44, Kilmarnock; m., Trish; 1 s.; 1 d. Educ. Strathallan School. McClelland Moores & Co., 1962-67; Peat Marwick Mitchell & Co., Paris, 1967-69; Turner Hutton & Lawson, 1969-81; Arthur Young, 1981-89. Non-Executive Director, Scottish Knowledge plc; Board Member, Scottish Council Development and Industry; Chairman, Scottish Fundraising Committee, Princess Royal Trust for Carers. Recreations: golf; fishing; shooting. Address: (b.) Ernst and Young, George House, 50 George Square, Glasgow G2 1RR; T.-0141-553 4363.

Turner, John R., MA, HonMA, MusB, FRCO. Organist and Director of Music, Glasgow Cathedral, since 1965; Lecturer, Royal Scottish Academy of Music, since 1965; Organist, Strathclyde University, since 1965; b. Halifax. Educ. Rugby; Jesus College, Cambridge. Recreations: gardening; travel. Address: (h.) Binchester, 1 Cathkin Road, Rutherglen, Glasgow G73 4SE; T.-0141-634 7775.

Turner, Professor Kenneth John, BSc, PhD. Professor of Computing Science, Stirling University, since 1987; b. 21.2.49, Glasgow; m., Elizabeth Mary Christina; 2 s. Educ. Hutchesons' Boys Grammar School; Glasgow University; Edinburgh University. Data Communications Designer, International Computers Ltd., 1974-76; Senior Systems Analyst, Central Regional Council, 1976-77; Data Communications Consultant, International Computers Ltd., 1977-87. Recreations: choral singing; craft work; sailing. Address: (b.) Department of Computing Science and Mathematics, Stirling University, Stirling, FK9 4LA; T.-01786 467420.

Turner, Malcolm, OBE, JP, DL. Deputy Lieutenant, Dunbartonshire, since 1989; Vice Chairman, Scottish National Housing and Town Planning Council; Vice-President, Clydebank Rugby Club; b. 13.12.21, Clydebank; m., Margaret Balfour; 1 s. Educ. Clydebank High School. Member: Clydebank Town Council, 1957-75 (Provost, 1966-69), Dunbarton County Council, 1957-75; Strathclyde Regional Council, 1974-95; Member, Cumbernauld Development Corporation, 1975-83; former Chairman, Central Water Development Board; Vice-Chairman, Convention of Royal Burghs, 1967-73; Hon. Freeman, Clydebank District; former Chairman, Forth and Clyde Advisory Committee. Recreations: angling; caravanning; bowling; golf. Address: (h.) 14 Mossgiel Drive, Clydebank, Dunbartonshire G81 2BY; T.-0141-952 3992.

Turner, Norman William, LLB, MILAM, ALA, FIMgt, FSA(Scot). Director of Leisure Services, North Lanarkshire Council, since 1995; Past Chairman, Association of Directors of Leisure, Recreation and Tourism; b. 12.4.48, Portsmouth; m. Ann Malloy. Educ. Portsmouth Technical High School; Brighton Polytechnic; Strathclyde University. District Librarian, Motherwell District Council; Depute Director of Libraries and Museums, Falkirk District Council; Deputy District Librarian, City of Southampton District; Deputy Borough Librarian, Andover Borough Council; Director of Leisure, Motherwell District Council, 1985-95. Former Vice-Chairman, Public Libraries Group; former Hon. Treasurer, Scottish Library Association. Recreations: season ticket holder, Motherwell FC; sport; theatre; cinema; music; natural history. Address: (b.) Buchanan Tower, Buchanan Business Park, Stepps, G33 6HR.

Turner, Susan Morag, MA, DipEd, DIDCE, CTD, FISW, FCollP, FRSA. Consultant in deafness issues, since 1997; Director, Scottish Association for the Deaf, 1991-97; b. 5.4.35, Glasgow. Educ. Rutherglen Academy; Glasgow University; Manchester University. Teacher of hearing-impaired children, Glasgow School for the Deaf; Head Teacher: Paisley School for the Deaf, Dundee School for the Deaf; Lecturer, Professional Curriculum Support Services Department, Moray House College; Director, Scottish Centre for the Education of the Deaf, 1971-91. Vice President, Scottish Association for the Deaf, 1971-91; Scottish President, National Association of Special Educational Needs; Council Member, International Centre for Special Education; Member, Board of Trustees, Royal National Institute for Deaf People; Member, Church Advisorate on Special Educational Needs; Chairman, J.S. Lochrie Memorial Trust. Address: (h.) 15 Bonaly Brae, Colinton, Edinburgh EH13 0QF; T.-0131-441 7520.

Turner Thomson, Ann Denise. Interior Designer; b. 23.5.29, Molesey; m., Gordon Turner Thomson; 1 s.; 3 d. Educ. Sherborne School for Girls, Dorset; St. James's Secretarial College, London. Council Member, Scottish Arts Council, 1983-88; Council Member, National Trust for Scotland, 1990-95; Council Member, Edinburgh International Festival, 1991-97; Member, Board of Directors, Art in Partnership; Member, Saltire Society Housing Awards Panel, Art in Architecture Award Panel; Convenor, Saltire Society/Royal Scottish Academy Permanent Collection Award; Convenor, Scottish Committee, Iwate Art Festival UK, 1998. Recreations: theatre; opera; visual arts. Address: 8 Middleby Street, Edinburgh EH9 1TD; T.-0131-667 3997.

Turok, Professor Ivan Nicholas, BSc, MSc, PhD, MRTPI. Professor of Urban Economic Development, Glasgow University, since 1996; b. 7.8.56, Cape Town; m., Elizabeth; 1 s.; 2 d. Educ. William Ellis School, London; Bristol University. Lecturer, Glasgow University, 1984-87; Senior Lecturer and Professor, Strathclyde University, 1987-96. Publications; over 40 articles and books. Recreations: hill-walking; cycling; current affairs. Address: (b.) 25 Bute Gardens, Glasgow G12 8RS; T.-0141-330 6274.

Tweeddale, 13th Marquis of (Edward Douglas John Hay); b. 6.8.47. Insurance broker; succeeded to title, 1979.

Tweedie, Douglas Kay, DL. Land Owner; farming, since 1963; estate management, since 1991; b. 30.3.42, Gordon; m., Senga Anne; 1 s.; 1 d. Educ. Tabley House, Cheshire. M.F.H., Berwickshire Hunt, 1982-92; Church Elder and Treasurer. Recreation: hunting. Address: Middlethird, Gordon, Berwickshire, TD3 6JX; T.-01573 410297.

Tyre, Alistair McKenzie, FHCIMA, DipSHS, MIMgt. Principal and Chief Executive, Langside College, Glasgow, since 1991; b. 6.12.40, Glasgow; m., Jenice Elizabeth Cleat; 1 d. Educ. Dunoon Grammar School; Strathclyde University. Hotel management, 1960-67; Lecturer and Head of Department, Ayr College, 1967-87; Depute Principal, James Watt College, Greenock, 1987-91. Director, Association of Scottish Colleges; Director and Company Secretary, West of Scotland Colleges Partnership; Hampden Training Enterprises Ltd.; Member, General Convocation, Strathclyde University. Recreations: golf; squash; hill-walking; gardening; theatre. Address: (b.) 50 Prospecthill Road, Glasgow, G42 9LB; T.-0141-649 4991.

Tyre, Colin Jack, QC, LLB, DESU. Advocate, since 1987; b. 17.4.56, Dunoon; m., Elaine Patricia Carlin; 1 s.; 2 d. Educ. Dunoon Grammar School; Edinburgh University; Universite d'Aix Marseille. Lecturer in Scots Law, Edinburgh University, 1980-83; Tax Editor, CCH Editions Ltd., Bicester, 1983-86. Publications: CCH Inheritance Tax Reporter; contributor to Stair Memorial Encyclopaedia; Standing Junior Counsel to Scottish Office Environment Department in planning matters, 1995-98. Recreations: orienteering; golf; mountain walking; popular music. Address: (b.) Advocates' Library, 1 Parliament Square, Edinburgh; T.-0131-226 5071.

U

Ullrich, Kay Morrison. Vice President, Scottish National Party; SNP Cabinet Spokesperson, Health Housing and Social Policy; b. 5.5.43, Prestwick; m., Grady; 1 s.; 1 d. Educ. Ayr Academy; Queen's College, Glasgow. Butlins Redcoat, 1961-64; Swimming Instructor, schools in North Ayrshire, 1973-81; Social Worker: Easterhouse (schools), 1984-86, Crosshouse Hospital (paediatric), 1986-88, Stevenston, Saltcoats, Ardrossan (child care), 1988-92; Senior Social Worker, Kilmarnock (Sheriff Court), 1992-97. Recreations: swimming; reading (politics and Scottish history); travel. Address: (h.) Tulsa, Montgomeryfield, Dreghorn, Irvine KA11 4HB; T.-01294 213331.

Underhill, Professor John Richard, BSc, PhD, FGS. Chair of Stratigraphy, University of Edinburgh, since 1998; b. 5.1.61, Portsmouth; m., Rosemary Anne Gigg; 1 s.; 1 d. Educ. Portsmouth Grammar School; University of Bristol; University of Wales. Exploration Geologist/Geophysicist, Shell International, Den Haag, Netherlands, 1985-89; University of Edinburgh: Lecturer, 1989-92, Senior Lecturer, 1992-98. Geological Society President's Award, 1990; European Association of Petroleum Geologists' Distinguished Lecturer Award, 1989, 1992, 1995; American Association of Petroleum Geologists' Matson Award for Excellence in Presentation, 1992; American Association of Petroleum Geologists Distinguished Lecturer, 1999. Grade one football referee, SFA, since 1993 (officiating in Scottish Premier League and European football). Address: (b.) Department of Geology and Geophysics, Grant Institute, King's Buildings, West Mains Road, Edinburgh EH9 3JW; T.-0131-650 8518.

U'ren, William Graham, BSc (Hons), DipTP, FRTPI. Director and Scottish Policy Officer, Royal Town Planning Institute in Scotland; b. 28.12.46, Glasgow; m., Wendy; 2 d. Educ. Aberdeen Grammar School; Aberdeen University; Strathclyde University. Planning Assistant: Clackmannan County Council, 1970-72, Lanark County Council, 1972-75; Principal and Chief Planning Officer, Clydesdale District Council, 1975-82; Director of Planning and Technical Services, Clydesdale District Council, 1982-96; Environment Services Manager, Planning and Economic Development, South Lanarkshire Council, 1996-97. Past Chairman, Scottish Society of Directors of Planning; Vice Convener, Historic Burghs Association of Scotland; Member, Heritage Lottery Fund Committee for Scotland. Recreations: town-twinning; cricket; bird watching; philately. Address: (b.) 125 Hyndford Road, Lanark ML11 9AU.

Urquhart, Celia Margaret Lloyd. Chief Executive, Urquhart Ltd. and C U Group of Companies; Vice President, Glasgow Chamber of Commerce; Member, Merchants House, Glasgow; Member, Advisory Committee, Imperial Cancer Research. b. 7.4.47, Glasgow; 1 s.; 2 d. Founded C U Data, 1986; Winner, Scottish Free Enterprise Award, 1990; Fellow, Institute of Management; Patron, Arran Cancer Support. Recreations: hill-walking; sailing; working late. Address: (b.) 6 Woodside Place, Glasgow G3 7QF.

Urwin, Professor Derek William, BA, MA (Econ), PhD. Professor of Politics and International Relations, Aberdeen University, since 1990; b. 27.10.39, Consett; m., Patricia Anne Ross; 2 s. Educ. Consett Grammar School; Wolsingham Grammar School; Keele University; Manchester University. Lecturer, Strathclyde University, 1963-72; Associate Professor, University of Bergen, 1972-80; Professor, Warwick University, 1981-90. Publications: Western Europe since 1945; The Community of Europe; From Ploughshare to Ballot Box; Politics in Western Europe Today; Centre-Periphery Structures in Europe; Dictionary of European History and Politics, since 1945; Scottish Political Behaviour. Recreations: walking; reading; marquetry. Address: (b.) Department of Politics and International Relations, Aberdeen University, Old Aberdeen, AB9 2TY; T.-01224 272716/272713.

Usher, Professor Michael Barham, BSc, PhD, DUniv, CBiol, FIBiol, MIEEM, FRES. Chief Scientist, Scottish Natural Heritage, since 1991; b. 19.11.41, Old Colwyn; m., Kathleen Fionna Munro; 1 s.; 1 d. Educ. Portsmouth Grammar School; Edinburgh University. Lecturer, Senior Lecturer, Reader, Department of Biology, University of York, 1967-91; Adviser on termite research, British Technical Assistance to the Government of Ghana, 1971-73; research in Antarctica and Sub-Antarctica, 1980-81; joined Nature Conservancy Council for Scotland as Chief Scientific Adviser, 1991. Member/Chairman, several Natural Environment Research Council and Economic and Social Research Council Committees. Publications: 205 scientific papers; 10 books. Recreations: walking; gardening; natural history photography; philately. Address: (b.) Scottish Natural Heritage, 2 Anderson Place, Edinburgh, EH6 5NP; T.-0131-446 2401.

Uttamchandani, Professor Deepak, BEng, MSc, PhD, CEng, FIEE. Professor of Optoelectronic Systems, University of Strathclyde, since 1998; b. 27.8.58, Bombay; m., Barbara. Educ. primary, secondary and tertiary levels in Nigeria; University College London. University of Strathclyde, Department of Electronic and Electrical Engineering: Lecturer, 1985, Senior Lecturer, 1991, Reader, 1995. Publications: author or co-author of nearly 200 scientific and technical publications in optoelectronic systems. Recreations: travel; sport. Address: Department of Electronic and Electrical Engineering, University of Strathclyde, 204 George Street, Glasgow G1 1XW; T.-0141-548 2211.

V

Valentine, Ian Balfour, CA, FRSA. Scottish Senior Partner, BDO Stoy Hayward, Chartered Accountants; Non-Executive Board Member, Ayrshire and Arran Health Board, 1981-93; b. 17.10.40, Glasgow; m., Elaine; 1 s.; 1 d. Educ. Hutchesons' Boys' Grammar School. Partner, J. Wyllie Guild & Ballantine, 1965 (subsequently BDO Stoy Hayward). Member, Council, Institute of Chartered Accountants of Scotland, 1989-97; Chairman, Ayrshire Association of Chartered Accountants of Scotland, 1976-78; President, Junior Chamber Ayr, 1972-73; Member, Ayr Schools Council, 1976-78; Director, Federation of Scottish Junior Chambers of Commerce, 1973-74; Honorary Secretary and Treasurer, Ayr Rugby Football Club, 1979-84; Captain, Royal Troon Golf Club, 1994-97. Recreations: golf; rugby (as spectator); bridge. Address: (b.) 64 Dalblair Road, Ayr; T.-01292 263277.

Vanezis Professor Peter, MD, PhD, FRCPath, FRCP (Glas), DMJ. Regius Professor of Forensic Medicine and Science, Glasgow University, since 1993; Director, Human Identification Centre, since 1996; Senior Civilian Consultant in Forensic Medicine to the British Army, since 1992; b. 11.12.47, Nicosia; m., Maria; 1 s.; 1 d. Educ. Wanstead High School, London; Bristol University. Lecturer/Senior Lecturer in Forensic Medicine, London Hospital Medical College, 1974-90; Reader in Forensic Medicine, Charing Cross and Westminster Medical School, 1990-93; Hon. Consultant to Cyprus Government, since 1985, Kenyons International Emergency Services, since 1993; Honorary Consultant, Medico-Legal Institute, Santiago, Chile, since 1994. Publications: Pathology of Neck Injury, 1989; Suspicious Death – Scene Investigation, 1996; various publications in forensic medicine. Recreations: golf; painting. Address: (b.) Department of Forensic Medicine and Science, Glasgow University, Glasgow G12 8QQ; T.-0141-330 4573.

van Heyningen, Veronica, MA, MS, DPhil, FRSE. Staff Scientist, MRC Human Genetics Unit, Edinburgh, since 1977; Hon. Treasurer, The Genetical Society, since 1994; Trustee, National Museums of Scotland, since 1994; b. 12.11.46, Hungary; m., Dr. Simon van Heyningen; 1 s.; 1 d. Educ. Humphrey Perkins School, Leicestershire; Girton College, Cambridge; Northwestern University, Illinois; Lady Margaret Hall, Oxford. Beit Memorial Fellow, 1973-76; Howard Hughes International Research Scholar, 1993-98; Honorary Professor, Edinburgh University, 1995. Recreations: visiting museums; travel; talking to people. Address: (b.) MRC Human Genetics Unit, Edinburgh, EH4 2XU; T.-0131-467 8405.

Vannet, Alfred Douglas, LLB, FRSA. Regional Procurator Fiscal, Glasgow and Strathkelvin, since 1997; b. 31.7.49, Dundee; m., Pauline Margaret Renfrew; 1 s.; 1 d. Educ. High School of Dundee; Dundee University. Procurator Fiscal Depute, Dundee, 1976-77; Procurator Fiscal Depute, then Senior Procurator Fiscal Depute, Glasgow, 1977-84; Assistant Solicitor, Crown Office, 1984-90; Deputy Crown Agent, 1990-94; Regional Procurator Fiscal, Grampian, Highland and Islands at Aberdeen, 1994-97. Recreations: music; walking. Address: (b.) 10 Ballater Street, Glasgow G5 9PS.

Vardy, Professor Alan Edward, BSc, PhD, DEng, EurIng, CEng, FICE, FASCE, MIAHR, FRSA. Research Professor in Civil Engineering, Dundee University, since 1995; Professor of Civil Engineering, 1979-95 (Deputy Principal, 1985-89, Vice-Principal, 1988-89); Director, Wolfson Bridge Research Unit, 1980-90; b. 6.11.45, Sheffield; m., Susan Janet; 2 s.; 1 d. Educ. High Storrs Grammar School, Sheffield; Leeds University. Lecturer in Civil Engineering, Leeds University, 1972-75; Royal Society Warren Research Fellow, Cambridge University, 1975-79; Royal Society/SERC Industrial Fellow, 1990-94. Dunholm, 512 Perth Road, Dundee, DD2 1LW; T.-Dundee 566123.

Varwell, Rev. Dr. Adrian P.J., BA, BD. Director, St. Ninian's Centre, Crieff, since 1997. Educ. Aberdeen University; Durham University; Edinburgh University. Research Fellow, Aberdeen University, 1969-73; Social Development Officer, Ross and Cromarty County Council/Highland Regional Council, 1973-78; Research Fellow, Edinburgh University, 1978-79; Assistant Minister, Dunblane Cathedral, 1982-83; Minister, Benbecula, 1983-97; Clerk, Presbytery of Uist, 1985-97. Address: (b.) St. Ninian's Centre, Comrie Road, Crieff; T.-01764 653766.

Vas, Peter, MSc, PhD, CSc, DSc, MIEEE, FIEE. Professor in Engineering, Department of Engineering, Aberdeen University, since 1990; b. 1.6.48, Budapest; m., S. Vasne; 2 s. Educ. Technical University of Budapest. United Electrical Machine Works, 1973-77; Newcastle University, 1977-87; Chalmers University of Technology, Lund University of Technology, 1987-90. Laureate of George Montefiore International Award, Belgium, 1990. Publications: over 140 papers; five books; several patents. Address: (b.) Department of Engineering, University of Aberdeen, Aberdeen; T.-01224 272818.

Vaughan, Barbara, BSc, MA. Former Chairman, Scottish Community Education Council; b. 12.2.40, Thornton Heath; m., Dr. Robin A. Vaughan; 2 s.; 2 d. Educ. St. Anne's College, Sanderstead; Nottingham University; Dundee University. Teacher, Derbyshire, 1962-64; Lecturer in Economics, Dundee Institute of Technology, 1979-83; Councillor, Tayside Region, 1980; Chairman, Further Education Sub-Committee, 1981-82; Chairman, Education Committee, 1982-86; Member, MSC Committee for Scotland, 1983-86; Commissioner, MSC, 1986.

Veal, Sheriff Kevin Anthony, KSG, KCHS, LLB. Sheriff of Tayside Central and Fife at Forfar, since 1993; b. 16.9.46, Chesterfield; m., Monica Flynn; 2 s.; 2 d. Educ. Lawside Academy, Dundee; St. Andrews University. Partner, Burns Veal and Gillan, Dundee, 1971-93; Legal Aid Reporter, 1978-93; Temporary Sheriff, 1984-93; Tutor, Department of Law, Dundee University, 1978-85; Dean, Faculty of Procurators and Solicitors in Dundee, 1991-93. Musical Director, Cecilian Choir, Dundee, since 1975; Member, University Court, Abertay Dundee, since 1998. Recreations: organ and classical music; hill-walking. Address: (h.) Viewfield, 70 Blackness Avenue, Dundee, DD2 1JL; T.-01382 668633.

Veitch, William Hood, Honorary Sheriff, Jedburgh Sheriff Court; b. 18.5.18, Jedburgh; m., Evelyn; 2 s. Educ. Jedburgh Grammar School; Hawick High School. Trained as Inspector of Weights and Measures, 1936-39; King's Own Scottish Borderers, 1939-47; Borders Region: Inspector of Weights and Measures, 1947-69, Chief Inspector, 1969-83. Recreations: gardening; illustrated talks to voluntary organisations; Jedforest Historical Society. Address: Inchbonny, Jedburgh; T.-01835 863539.

Vernon, Kenneth Robert, CBE, BSc, FEng, FIEE, FIMechE. Deputy Chairman and Chief Executive, North of Scotland Hydro-Electric Board, 1973-88; b. 15.3.23, Dumfries; m., Pamela Hands; 1 s.; 3 d.; 1 d. deceased. Educ. Dumfries Academy; Glasgow University. BTH Co., Edinburgh Corporation, British Electricity Authority, 1948-55; South of Scotland Electricity Board, 1955-56; North of Scotland Hydro Electric Board: Chief Electrical and Mechanical Engineer, 1964, General Manager, 1966, Board Member, 1970; Director, British Electricity International Ltd., 1976-88; Board Member, Northern Ireland Electricity Service, 1979-85. Recreation: fishing. Address: (h.) 10 Keith Crescent, Edinburgh EH4 3NH; T.-0131-332 4610.

Vernon, Richard Geoffrey, BSc, PhD, FIBiol. Head, Science Planning and Development and Head, Molecular Homeorhesis Group, Hannah Research Intitute; Honorary Lecturer, Glasgow University; b. 19.2.43, Maidstone; m., Mary Christine Cunliffe; 1 s.; 1 d. Educ. Newcastle High School; Birmingham University. Research Fellow, University of Toronto, 1969-72; Senior Scientist then Head of Department, Hannah Research Institute, 1972-95; Consultant Editor, Journal of Dairy Research; Member, Editorial Board, British Journal of Nutrition, 1981-87, Domestic Animal Endocrinology (USA), 1992-95; Chairman, Scottish Section, Nutrition Society, 1989-91; Member, AFRC Animals Research Grants Board, 1991-94; Past President, Birmingham University Mountaineering Club; Chairman, Belmont Academy School Board, 1989-93. Publications: Physiological Strategies in Lactation (Co-editor); 200 scientific papers. Recreations: hill-walking; ornithology; bridge; photography. Address: (h.) 29 Knoll Park, Ayr, KA7 4RH; T.-01292 42195.

Vettese, Raymond John, DipEd, BA (Hons). Teacher and Writer; b. 1.11.50, Arbroath; m., Maureen Elizabeth. Educ. Montrose Academy; Dundee College of Education; Open Univesity. Journalist, Montrose Review, 1968-72; student, 1972-75; barman, 1975-77; factory worker/farmer, 1977-78; clerical officer, 1978-85; teacher, since 1985; Preses, Scots Language Society, 1991-94; William Soutar Fellowship, 1989-90. Publications: Four Scottish Poets, 1985; The Richt Noise, 1988 (Saltire Society Best First Book); A Keen New Air, 1995. Recreations: reading; music; cooking; chess. Address: (h.) 9 Tayock Avenue, Montrose, DD10 9AP; T.-01674 678943.

Vickerman, Professor Keith, BSc, PhD, DSc, FLS, FRSE, FRS. Regius Professor of Zoology, Glasgow University, 1984-98; Consultant Expert on Parasitic Diseases, World Health Organisation, 1973-98; b. 21.3.33, Huddersfield; m., Moira Dutton; 1 d. Educ. King James Grammar School, Almondbury; University College, London (Fellow, 1985). Wellcome Lecturer in Protozoology, University College, London, 1958-63; Tropical Research Fellow, Royal Society, 1963-68; Glasgow University: Reader in Zoology, 1968-74; Professor of Zoology, 1974-84, Head, Department of Zoology, 1979-85. Leeuwenhoek Lecturer, Royal Society, 1994; Linnean Society Gold Medal for contributions to science, 1996. Publications: The Protozoa (Co-author), 1967; many papers in scientific and medical journals. Recreations: drawing and painting; gardening. Address: (h.) 16 Mirrlees Drive, Glasgow G12 OSH; T.-0141-334 2794.

Vincent, Catherine Lindsey, BA (Hons). Director of Corporate Strategy, Scottish Sports Council, since 1989; b. 30.7.56, Oxford; m., Jonathan Nicholas Crook; 2 d. Educ. Rosebery Grammar School, Epsom; Newnham College, Cambridge. Research Assistant, Sheffield University, 1978; Assistant Editor, Athlone Press, 1979; Freelance Writer, 1980; Development Officer, Scottish Community Education Council, 1981; Senior Policy Analyst, Fife Regional Council, 1986. Former Chairman, Spiritual Assembly of the Baha'is of Edinburgh; former Director, Baha'i Information Scotland. Publication: Discovering Edinburgh, 1981. Recreations: reading; walking; tennis; badminton; enjoying family. Address: (b.) Scottish Sports Council, Caledonia House, South Gyle, Edinburgh EH12 9DQ; T.-0131-317 7200.

Vowles, Kenneth Leslie, FIME, FIEE, MBIM, CEng. Executive Director, Scottish Power, since 1996; b. 22.3.42, Newport, Gwent; m., Christine; 2 d. Educ. University of Wales. Generation Manager, National Power (Northern Group); Station Manager, Rugeley and Ironbridge Power Station.Vice-President, Scottish Engineering. Recreation: golf. Address: (b.) 1 Atlantic Quay, Glasgow; T.-0141-636 4509.

W

Waddell, John MacLaren Ogilvie, LLB, WS. Director, Special Duties, International Division, Bank of Scotland; b. 12.4.56, Inverness; m., Alice Emily Bain; 1 s.; 1 d. Educ. Inverness Royal Academy; George Watson's College; Edinburgh University. Qualified as a Solicitor, 1980; Assistant, 1980, Partner, 1983, Steedman Ramage WS; Director of Legal Services, 1989, Member of Management Board, Christian Salvesen PLC. Recreations: shooting; reading. Address: (b.) Orchard Brae House, 30 Queensferry Road, Edinburgh EH4 2UG; T.-0131-343 7000.

Waddell, William A.H., BA (Hons). Head Teacher, Bishopbriggs High School, since 1994; b. 22.6.51, Paisley; m., Alison; 2 d. Educ. John Neilson, Paisley; Strathclyde University. Teacher of Mathematics, then Assistant Principal Teacher of Mathematics, Park Mains High School, 1974-80; Principal Teacher of Mathematics, Dumbarton Academy, 1980-85; Assistant Head Teacher, Boclair Academy, 1985-90; Depute Head Teacher, Hermitage Academy, 1990-94. Recreations: sport; gardening; family pursuits. Address: (h.) 66 Stuart Road, Bishopton, Renfrewshire.

Wade, Professor Nicholas James, BSc, PhD, FRSE. Professor of Visual Psychology, Dundee University, since 1991; b. 27.3.42, Retford, Nottinghamshire; m., Christine Whetton; 2 d. Educ. Queen Elizabeth's Grammar School, Mansfield; Edinburgh University; Monash University. Postdoctoral Research Fellow, Max-Planck Institute for Behavioural Physiology, Germany, 1969-70; Lecturer in Psychology, Dundee University, 1970-78, Reader, 1978-91. Publications: The Art and Science of Visual Illusions, 1982; Brewster and Wheatstone on Vision, 1983; Visual Allusions: Pictures of Perception, 1990; Visual Perception: an introduction, 1991; Psychologists in Word and Image, 1995; A Natural History of Vision, 1998. Recreations: golf; cycling. Address: (h.) 36 Norwood, Newport-on-Tay, Fife DD6 8DW; T.-01382 543136.

Wade, Paul Francis Joseph, LLB. Solicitor, since 1976; Solicitor Advocate, since 1993; b. 19.3.53, Derby; m., Gilllian Ann; 1 s.; 1 d. Educ. Queen Margaret Academy, Ayr; Glasgow University. Biggart, Baillie and Gifford, 1974-79; Partner, Cochran Sayers & Cook, Glasgow, 1981-93; Partner, Simpson & Marwick WS, Glasgow, since 1993. Recreations: sailing; rural pursuits; travel; eating shellfish; cooking wine. Address: (b.) 93 West George Street, Glasgow G2 1PB; T.-0141-248 2666.

Wade, Professor Terence Leslie Brian, BA, PhD, FIL. Emeritus Professor in Russian Studies, Strathclyde University; b. 19.5.30, Southend-on-Sea; m., Mary Isobel McEwan; 2 d. Educ. Southend-on-Sea High School for Boys; Durham University; Cologne University; London University. National Service, Intelligence Corps, 1953-55; War Office Language Instructor, 1955-63; Lecturer, Scottish College of Commerce, Glasgow, 1963-64; Lecturer, Senior Lecturer, Reader, Professor, Strathclyde University, from 1964; Chairman, Department of Modern Languages, 1986-94; Professor, Research Fellow, since 1995. Convener, West of Scotland Association of Teachers of Russian; Editor, Journal of Russian Studies, 1980-86: Chairman, Association of Teachers of Russian, 1986-89; President, Association of Teachers of Russian, 1989-90; Member, Presidium, International Association of Teachers of Russian Language and Literature, since 1991. Publications: Russian Exercises for Language Laboratories (Co-author); The Russian Preposition "do" and the Concept of Extent; Prepositions in Modern Russian; Russia Today (Co-Editor); The Gender of Soft-Sign Nouns in Russian; A Comprehensive Russian Grammar; A Russian Grammar Workbook; Russian Etymological Dictionary. Address: 1 Cleveden Crescent, Glasgow, G12 OPD; T.-0141-339 3947.

Waigh, Professor Roger David, BPharm, PhD, FRPharmS, CChem, FRSC. Professor of Medicinal Chemistry, Strathclyde University, since 1991; b. 8.8.44, Loughborough; m., Sally Joy Bembridge; 1 s.; 1 d. Educ. Sir George Monoux Grammar School, Walthamstow; Bath University. Lecturer, Strathclyde University, 1970-76; Lecturer, then Senior Lecturer, Manchester University, 1976-91. Recreations: bird-watching; golf; photography. Address: (b.) Strathclyde Institute for Biomedical Sciences, 27 Taylor Street, Glasgow G4 ONR; T.-0141-548 4355.

Waite, James A., MA. Rector, Perth Academy, since 1986; b. 9.10.42, Edinburgh; m., Sandra R. MacKenzie; 1 s.; 2 d. Educ. Royal High School, Edinburgh; Edinburgh University. Teacher of English, George Heriot's School, 1965-70; Principal Teacher of English, Campbeltown Grammar School, 1970-71; Principal Teacher of English, then Assistant Head Teacher, Boroughmuir High School, 1971-83; Depute Head Teacher, James Gillespie's High School, 1983-86. Recreations: theatre; literature; music; hill-walking. Address: (b.) Perth Academy, Murray Place, Perth, PH1 1NJ; T.-01738 623491.

Wake, Joseph Robert, MA, CPA. Secretary, Scotland, Central Bureau for Educational Visits and Exchanges, since 1972; b. 16.5.42, Corbridge; 1 s.; 2 d. Educ. Royal Grammar School, Newcastle upon Tyne; Edinburgh University; Moray House College of Education. Teacher, Kirkcaldy High School, 1966-69, St. Modan's High School, Stirling, 1969-71; Principal Teacher of Modern Languages, Grangemouth High School, 1971-72. Recreations: cricket; philately; Scottish dancing. Address: (b.) 3 Bruntsfield Crescent, Edinburgh EH10 4HD; T.-0131-447 8024.

Wakeford, Air Marshal Sir Richard (Gordon), KCB (1976), LVO (1961), OBE (1958), AFC (1952). Chairman, MacRobert Trustees, 1982-94; b. 20.4.22, Torquay; m., Anne Butler; 2 s.; 1 d.; 1 d. (deceased). Educ. Montpelier School, Paignton; Kelly College, Tavistock. Entered RAF, 1941; Coastal Command, 1941-45; Transport Command, 1945-47; King's Commendation, 1946; Training Command, 1947-52; staff duties, including Director of Ops Staff, Malaya, 1952-58; CO, The Queens' Flight, 1958-61; IDC, 1969; Director, Service Intelligence, 1970-73; Commander, Anzuk Force Singapore, 1974-75; Deputy Chief of Defence Staff (Intelligence), 1975-78; retired Air Marshal, 1978. Director, RAF Benevolent Fund, Scotland, 1978-89; Commissioner, Queen Victoria School, Dunblane, 1980-90; Director, Thistle Foundation; Director, Cromar Nominess; Commander, Order of St. John, 1986. Recreation: fishing. Address: (h.) Sweethome Cottage, Inchberry Road, Fochabers, IV32 7QA; T.-01343 820 436.

Walde, Professor Thomas W., LLM, Driur. Professor of International Economic, Natural Resources and Energy Law, University of Dundee, since 1991; Executive Director, Centre for Energy, Petroleum and Mineral Law and Policy; b. 1949, Germany; 1 s. Educ. Universities of Heildelberg, Frankfurt and Harvard. Institute for International Economic Law, Frankfurt, 1975-80; U.N. Natural Resources and Energy Division, 1980-85; Adviser to Governments on mineral development policies, legislation, and contract negotiations; Interregional Advisor on Petroleum and Mineral Legislation, U.N. (D.T.C.D.); EC Jean Monnet Professor of European Economic and Energy Law; Editor, Journal of Energy and Natural Resources Law; Visiting Professor, Universite de Paris II - Pantheon; Corresponding Editor, International Legal Materials; Editor, CEPMCP On-line Journal. Address: (b.) Park Place, Dundee DD1 4HN; T.-01382 344300.

Wale, Andrew Charles, BA, ALA. Director of Library Services and Keeper of the Hunterian Books and

Manuscripts, University of Glasgow, since 1998; b. 25.11.40, Leicester; m., Margaret Smart Pitkeathly; 2 s. Educ. Haberdashers Aske's Hampstead School; Keble College, Oxford University; University College London. Assistant Librarian: University of Kent at Canterbury, 1966-69, University of the South Pacific, 1969-72, University of York, 1972-78; Joint Deputy Librarian, Manchester Polytechnic, 1978-80; Deputy Librarian, University of Glasgow, 1980-88. Recreations: theology; hillwalking; needlepoint. Address: (h.) 35 North Birbiston Road, Lennoxtown, Glasgow G66 7LZ; T.-01360 310310.

Walker, Professor Andrew Charles, BA, MSc, PhD, FInstP, FRSE, CPhys. Professor of Modern Optics, Heriot-Watt University, since 1988; b. 24.6.48, Wembley; m., Margaret Elizabeth; 1 s.; 1 d. Educ. Kingsbury County Grammar School; Essex University. Postdoctoral Fellowship, National Research Council of Canada, 1972-74; SRC Research Fellowship, Essex University, 1974-75; Higher/Senior Scientific Officer, UKAEA Culham Laboratory, 1975-83; Lecturer/Reader, Heriot-Watt University, 1983-88. Honorary Secretary, Quantum Electronics Group, Institute of Physics, 1982-85; Chairman, Scottish Branch, Institute of Physics, 1993-95. Recreations: music; skiing; sailing. Address: (b.) Department of Physics, Heriot-Watt University, Riccarton, Edinburgh EH14 4AS; T.-0131-451 3036.

Walker, Audrey R., BA, ALA. Librarian, Signet Library, since 1994; b. 18.10.57, Glasgow. Educ. Clydebank High School; Robert Gordon University, Aberdeen. Library Assistant, 1975-80; Senior Library Assistant, Telford College, Edinburgh, 1980-84; Assistant Librarian: Scottish Office Library, 1987, Post-Graduate Medical Library, 1988-90, Advocates Library, 1990-94. Scottish Library Association: Chair, East Branch, and Chair, Membership Services Committee; Committee Member, Meadowbank National Track League. Recreations: cycling; reading; cross-stitch; cinema. Address: (b.) Signet Library, Parliament Square, Edinburgh EH1 1RF; T.-0131-225 4923.

Walker, Professor David Maxwell, CBE, QC, MA, PhD, LLD, Hon. LLD, FBA, FRSE, FRSA, FSA Scot. Regius Professor of Law, Glasgow University, 1958-90; Honorary Senior Research Fellow, since 1990; b. 9.4.20, Glasgow; m., Margaret Knox, OBE. Educ. High School of Glasgow; Glasgow University; Edinburgh University; London University. HLI and Indian Army, 1939-46; Advocate, 1948; in practice, Scottish Bar, 1948-54; Professor of Jurisprudence, Glasgow University, 1954-58; Barrister (Middle Temple), 1957; QC (Scot), 1958; Dean, Faculty of Law, Glasgow University, 1956-59; Convener, School of Law, 1984-88. Chairman, High School of Glasgow Trust. Publications: Law of Damages in Scotland; The Scottish Legal System; Law of Delict in Scotland; Law of Civil Remedies in Scotland; Law of Prescription in Scotland; Law of Contracts in Scotland; Oxford Companion to Law; Principles of Scottish Private Law (four volumes); The Scottish Jurists; Stair's Institutions (Editor); Stair Tercentenary Studies (Editor); A Legal History of Scotland, (5 Vols). Recreations: book collecting; Scottish history; motoring. Address: (b.) School of Law, Glasgow University, Glasgow G12 8QQ; T.-0141-339 8855, Ext. 4556.

Walker, Professor David Morrison, OBE, DA, FSA, FSA Scot, FRSE, HFRIAS, Hon. LLD (Dundee). Honorary Professor of Art History, University of St. Andrews, since 1994; Chief Inspector of Historic Buildings, Scottish Office Environment Department, 1988-93; b. 31.1.33, Dundee; m., Averil Mary Stewart McIlwraith (deceased); 1 s. Educ. Morgan Academy, Dundee; Dundee College of Art. Voluntary work for National Buildings Record, Edinburgh, 1952-56; National Service, Royal Engineers, 1956-58; Glasgow Education Authority, 1958-59; Dundee Education Authority, 1959-61; Historic Buildings Branch, Scottish Office: Senior Investigator of Historic Buildings, 1961-76, Principal Investigator of Historic Buildings, 1976-78; Principal Inspector of Historic Buildings, 1978-88. Alice Davis Hitchcock Medallion, 1970. Publications: Dundee Nineteenth Century Mansions, 1958; Architecture of Glasgow (Co-author), 1968 (revised and enlarged edition, 1987); Buildings of Scotland: Edinburgh (Co-author), 1984; Dundee: An Illustrated Introduction (Co-author), 1984; St. Andrew's House: an Edinburgh Controversy 1912-1939, 1989; Central Glasgow: an illustrated architectural guide (Co-author), 1989. Address: (h.) 22 Inverleith Row, Edinburgh EH3 5QH.

Walker, Douglas William, TD, BSc, CEng, MICE, MIBC. Director of Technical Services, East Dunbartonshire Council, since 1995; b. 18.6.50, Edinburgh; 2 d. Educ. George Heriot's School, Edinburgh; Edinburgh University. Perth and Kinross County Surveyor's Department, 1972-75; T. Harley Haddow and Partners, Consulting Engineers, 1975-80; Strathclyde Regional Council Roads Department, 1980-83; Glasgow City Council Building Control Department, 1984-95 (Depute Director, 1991-95). Service with TA Royal Engineers, 1968-86, retired 1986 with rank of Major. Recreations: golf; cycling; travel; reading. Address: (b.) East Dunbartonshire Council, Technical Services, Cleddens House, Wester Cleddens Road, Bishopbriggs, Glasgow G64 2LW.

Walker, (Edward) Michael, FRICS. Chairman, Walker Group (Scotland) Ltd., Westerwood Ltd., and associated companies, since 1986 (Founder, 1969); Chairman, Lothian and Edinburgh Ltd. (LEEL), since 1996 (Director, since 1991); b. 12.4.41, Aberdeen; m., Flora Margaret; 2 s.; 1 d. Educ. Aberdeen Grammar School. President, Edinburgh and District Master Builders Association, 1987 and 1996; Past President, Scottish House Builders Association; former Committee Member, NHBC (Scotland) Ltd., 1990-96; former Lord Dean of Guild, City of Edinburgh, 1992-96; Captain of Industry Award, Livingston Industrial and Commercial Association, 1987; Chairman, Livingston Youth Trust, since 1993. Recreations: skiing; scuba diving; walking; reading. Address: (b.) Walker Group (Scotland) Ltd., Westerwood House, Royston Road, Deans Industrial Estate, Livingston, W. Lothian; T.-01506 413101.

Walker, Ernest John Munro, CBE. Chairman, UEFA Stadia Committee; b. 20.7.28, Glasgow; m., Anne; 1 s.; 2 d. Educ. Queen's Park Secondary School. Army (Royal Horse Artillery), 1946-48; Assistant Secretary, industrial textile company, 1948-58; Assistant Secretary, Scottish Football Association, 1958-77, Secretary, 1977-90. Director, Euro-Sporting; Director, Scotball Travel and Leisure Ltd.; Director, The National Stadium (Hampden); Trustee, English National Stadium (Wembley); Director, Eastern European Assistance Bureau; Member: FIFA Board of Appeal; Chairman, Scottish Stadia Committee; Chairman, Scottish Football's Independent Rview Commission; Vice-President, Newspaper Press Fund; Independent Adviser to Secretary of State for Scotland on Appointments to Public Bodies. Recreations: golf (past Captain, Haggs Castle GC); fishing; music; travel.

Walker, Hugh A.D. Principal, Clydebank College, since 1997; b. 26.10.43. Educ. Bournemouth School; St. David's College, Lampeter; Institute of Education, London. Taught in comprehensive school and adult education, London, 1968-71; taught in school and continuing education centre, Mid West State, Nigeria; Diploma, Applied Linguistics, Edinburgh University, 1974; Appleton Scholar, Edinburgh, 1975; Teacher, Stevenson College, 1975-85; Assistant to Director of Education, Lothian Region, 1985-88; Head of Department, West Lothian College, 1988-89; Depute Principal, Anniesland College, 1989, Principal, 1992-97; Chair, Higher Still Further Education Implementation Studies Group; Director, Leven Valley Initiative.

Recreations: hill-running; tennis; squash. Address: (b.) Kilbowie Road, Clydebank G81 2AA; T.-0141-952 7771.

Walker, Irene, MBA, BSc (Hons). Chief Executive, Dumfries and Galloway Enterprise Ltd., since 1994; b. 28.1.52, Larbert; m., Neil Walker. Educ. Larbert High School; Edinburgh University; St. Andrews University. Local government, 1975-86; Glasgow Garden Festival, 1986-88; Scottish Development Agency, 1989-91; Grampian Enterprise Ltd., 1991-93. Recreations: windsurfing; skiing. Address: (b.) Solway House, Dumfries Enterprise Park, Tinwald Downs Road, Heathhall, Dumfries DG1 3SJ. Tel.: 01387 245000.

Walker, Rev. James Bernard, MA, BD, DPhil. Chaplain, St. Andrews University, since 1993; b. 7.5.46, Malawi; m., Sheila Mary Easton; 3 s. Educ. Hamilton Academy; Edinburgh University; Merton College, Oxford. Church of Scotland Minister: Mid Craigie linked with Wallacetown, Dundee, 1975-78, Old and St. Paul's, Galashiels, 1978-87; Principal, The Queen's College, Birmingham, 1987-93. Publication: Israel — Covenant and Land, 1988. Recreations: hill-walking; tennis; golf. Address: 3A St. Mary's Place, St. Andrews KY16 9UY; T.-01334 462865.

Walker, Leslie Gresson, MA, PhD, DipClinPsychol, CPsychol, CBiol, MIBiol, AFBPsS. Reader, Department of Mental Health, Aberdeen University, since 1998; Director, Behavioural Oncology Unit, Departments of Mental Health and Surgery, Aberdeen University; Honorary Consultant Clinical Psychologist, Aberdeen Royal Hospitals NHS Trust; b. 17.5.49, Glasgow; m., Mary Birnie Durno; 2 s. Educ. Banff Academy; Aberdeen University. Clinical Psychologist, Grampian Health Board, 1974-76; Lecturer, Aberdeen University, 1976-89; Senior Lecturer, 1989-98; elected Member, National Committee of Scientists in Professions Allied to Medicine (Clinical Psychology Sub-Committee), Scottish Home and Health Department, 1979-85; External Assessor, Children's Panel Advisory Committee, Grampian Regional Council, 1982-90; Council Member, British Society of Experimental and Clinical Hypnosis, since 1991; Consultant Editor, Contemporary Hypnosis, since 1991; Editorial Advisory Board Member, Psycho-Oncology, since 1996; Chairman, British Psychosocial Oncology Society, since 1996; Co-Chair, Nominations Committee, International Psychosocial Oncology Society, since 1998; Elder, Church of Scotland. Publications: numerous scientific papers and three books, including Police Stress at Work (Co-author), 1993. Address: (b.) Behavioural Oncology Unit, Departments of Mental Health and Surgery, Medical School, Foresterhill, Aberdeen AB25 2ZD; T.-01224 681818, Ext. 53881.

Walker, Michael John, LLB. Managing Partner, Maclay Murray and Spens, since 1994 (Partner, since 1981); b. 23.10.52, Glasgow; m., Elspeth Raeburn Lyle Reid; 1 s.; 1 d. Educ. Glenalmond; Dundee University. Apprenticeship, Dundas and Wilson, 1974-76; joined Maclay Murray and Spens, 1976 (secondment to Lovell White and King, 1980). Various non-executive directorships including John Menzies plc. Recreations: golf; travel. Address: 151 St. Vincent Street, Glasgow; T.-0141-248 5011.

Walker, Professor Stephen Paul, BA, PhD, CA. Professor of Accounting History, University of Edinburgh, since 1998 (Head, Department of Accounting and Business Method, since 1998); b. 20.6.60, King's Lynn; m., Liz; 1 s. Educ. Gaywood Park School, King's Lynn; University of Kent; University of Edinburgh. Postdoctoral Research Fellow, University of Edinburgh, 1987-88; CA student, Ernst and Young, Chartered Accountants, Edinburgh, 1988-91; University of Edinburgh: Lecturer in Accounting, 1991-96, Senior Lecturer in Accounting, 1996-98. Academic Fellow, Institute of Chartered Accountants in England and Wales, 1994-98. Publications: The Society of Accountants in Edinburgh 1854–1914, 1988; Accountancy at the University of Edinburgh – The Emergence of a Viable Academic Department, 1994; Professional Reconstruction (Co-Author), 1998. Recreations: music; photography; walking. Address: William Robertson Building, 50 George Square, Edinburgh EH8 9JY; T.-0131-650 8342.

Walker, Stewart. Director, Edinburgh Convention Bureau, since 1994; b. 13.10.53, Glasgow; m., Linda McPherson; 2 d. Educ. Queen's Park Secondary School, Glasgow; Glasgow College of Food Technology. Resident Manager, Caledonian Hotel, 1985-88; General Manager, North British Hotel, 1988-89; General Manager, St. James Club, Los Angeles, 1989-90; Managing Director, HCI Ltd., 1991-94. Recreations: golf; skiing. Address: (b.) 4 Rothesay Terrace, Edinburgh EH3 7RY; T.-0131-473 3666.

Walker, Susan McFarlane, BEd. Headteacher, Castlehead High School, since 1997; b. 14.9.51, Glasgow; m., Dr. Allan Paterson Walker; 1 d. Educ. Hillhead High School, Glasgow; Glasgow University. Waverley Secondary School, Glasgow 1973-85 (Teacher of Chemistry and Biology, Assistant Principal Teacher, Guidance); Castlehead High School, since 1985 (successively as Principal Teacher, Guidance, Staff Tutor in Guidance, Assistant Headteacher, Adviser in Guidance (Argyll and Bute and Renfrew), Depute Headteacher. Recreations: family; garden; golf. Address: (h.) Camphill, Paisley PA1 2HL; T.-0141-887 4261.

Walker, Timothy Frederick. Principal, Glenmore Lodge, Aviemore (Scottish Sports Council), since 1995; b. 11.12.48, Stannington; m., Helen; 2 d. Royal Marines (Mountain and Arctic Warfare Cadre); Outward Bound, Eskdale; Joint Services Mountain Training Centre, Scotland; Tutor, Seneca College, Ontario, Canada; Instructional Officer, Scottish Sports Council. Publications: Cross Country Skiing; Chairman, BASI Nordic; Vice Chairman, Boat of Garten Community Council; Representative, Action of Churches Together in Scotland. Recreations: all aspects of mountaineering; skiing. Address: (h.) Drumullie Steading, Boat of Garten, Inverness-shire PH24 3BX; T.-(b.) 01479 861 256; (h.) 01479 831 316.

Walker, Professor William Barclay, BSc, MSc. Professor of International Relations, St. Andrews University, since 1996; b. 7.12.46, Longforgan; m., Carolyn Scott; 1 s. Educ. Shrewsbury School; Edinburgh University. Design Engineer, Ferranti Ltd., 1970-72; Research Fellow, Science Policy Research Unit, Sussex University, 1974-78; Research Fellow, Royal Institute of International Affairs, and Secretary, International Consultative Group on Nuclear Energy, 1978-80; Science Policy Research Unit, Sussex University: Senior Fellow, 1981-92, Professorial Fellow and Director of Research, 1993-96. Publications: Plutonium and Highly Enriched Uranium: World Inventories, Capabilities and Policies (Co-author), 1997. Recreations: piano-playing; tennis; ornithology. Address: (b.) Department of International Relations, University of St. Andrews, St. Andrews KY16 9AL; T.-01334 462934.

Walkinshaw, Professor Malcolm Douglas, BSc, PhD. Professor of Structural Biochemistry, Edinburgh University, since 1995; b. 3.11.50, Edinburgh; m., Pamela; 1 s.; 1 d. Educ. George Heriot's School, Edinburgh; Edinburgh University. Alexander von Homboldt Fellow, Göttingen, Germany, 1977-79; Research Fellow, Edinburgh University, 1979-85; Head of Structure-based Design, Sandoz A G, Switzerland, 1985-95. Recreation: walking. Address: (h.) 68 Spylaw Bank Road, Edinburgh EH13 0JB; T.-0131-441 3780.

Wallace, Archibald Duncan, MB, ChB. Medical Practitioner, Campbeltown, since 1950; Hon. Sheriff of North Strathclyde at Campbeltown, since 1980; b. 4.1.26, Glasgow; m., Rona B. MacLennan; 1 s.; 2 d. Educ. High School of Glasgow; Glasgow University. Sector Medical

Officer, Argyll and Clyde Health Board, until 1988; Civilian MO to RAF Machrihanish, until 1988. Chairman, Campbeltown Branch, RNLI; Past President, Campbeltown Rotary Club; Past Captain, Machrihanish Golf Club. Recreations: golf; gardening. Address: (h.) Lilybank House, Low Askomil, Campbeltown; T.-01586 52658.

Wallace, James Fleming, QC, MA, LLB. Counsel (Draftsman), Scottish Law Commission, 1979-93; Part-time Chairman, Industrial Tribunals, since 1993; b. 19.3.31, Edinburgh; m., Valerie Mary Lawrence (deceased); 2 d.; 2, Linda Ann Lilleker. Educ. Edinburgh Academy; Edinburgh University. National Service, 1954-56 (2nd Lt., Royal Artillery); TA (Lt., Royal Artillery), 1956-60; practised at Scottish Bar, 1957-60; Parliamentary Draftsman and Legal Secretary to Lord Advocate, 1960-79. Publications: The Businessman's Lawyer (Scottish Supplement); Stair Memorial Encyclopaedia (Contributor). Recreations: hill-walking; choral singing; golf; badminton. Address: (h.) 24 Corrennie Gardens, Edinburgh EH10 6DB; T.-0131-447 1224.

Wallace, James Robert, QC, MA (Cantab), LLB (Edinburgh). MP (Liberal Democrat, formerly Liberal), Orkney and Shetland, since 1983; Leader, Scottish Liberal Democrats, since 1992; Advocate, 1979; QC (Scot.), 1997; b. 25.8.54, Annan; m., Rosemary Janet Fraser; 2 d. Educ. Annan Academy; Downing College, Cambridge; Edinburgh University. Called to Scottish Bar, 1979; contested Dumfries, 1979, and South of Scotland Euro Constituency, 1979; Member, Scottish Liberal Party Executive, 1976-85 (Vice-Chairman, Policy, 1982-85); Honorary President, Scottish Young Liberals, 1984-85; Liberal Democrat Spokesman on Fisheries, 1988-97, and on Scotland, since 1992; jointly awarded Andrew Fletcher Award for services to Scotland, 1998. Publication: New Deal for Rural Scotland (Co-Editor), 1983. Recreations: golf; reading; travelling (especially between London and the Northern Isles). Address: (h.) Northwood House, Tankerness, Orkney KW17 2QS; T.-01856 861383.

Wallace, Rev. William Fitch, BDS, BD. Minister, Pulteneytown and Thrumster Church, since 1990; Convener, Church of Scotland Board of Social Responsibility, 1993-97; b. 6.10.39, Falkirk; m., Jean Wyness Hill; 1 s.; 3 d. Educ. Allan Glen's School; Glasgow University; Edinburgh University. Minister, Wick St. Andrew's and Thrumster Church, 1974-90; former missionary dentist. Vice-Convener, Board of Social Responsibility, 1989-92. Recreations: family; golf; gardening. Address: The Manse, Coronation Street, Wick KW1 5LS; T.-01955 603166.

Wallace, Professor William Villiers, MA, FRHistS. Director, Institute of Russian and East European Studies, Glasgow University, 1979-92, now Senior Research Fellow; Visiting Professor, Sunderland University, since 1995; Vice-President, Council for Education in World Citizenship, since 1996; Features Editor, eurobüro, since 1997; b. 15.12.26, Glasgow; m., Gulli Fyfe; 2 s.; 1 d. Educ. Hutchesons' Boys' Grammar School; Glasgow University; London University. RNVR, 1944-47; appointments in History, Pittsburgh University, London University, Aberdeen University, Durham University, 1953-67; Professor of History, New University of Ulster, 1967-79. Foreign Member, Russian Academy of Technological Sciences. Address: (b.) Institute of Russian and East European Studies, Glasgow University, 29 Bute Gardens, Glasgow G12 8RS; T.-0141-330 5585.

Walls, Professor Andrew Finlay, OBE, MA, BLitt, DD, FSA Scot. Curator of Collections, Centre for the Study of Christianity in the Non-Western World, since 1996; b. 21.4.28; m., Doreen Mary Harden; 1 s.; 1 d. Librarian, Tyndale House, Cambridge, 1952-57; Lecturer in Theology, Fourah Bay College, Sierra Leone, 1957-62; Head, Department of Religion, Nigeria University, 1962-65; Aberdeen University: Lecturer in Church History, 1966-69, Senior Lecturer, 1969, first Head, Department of Religious Studies, and Riddoch Lecturer in Comparative Religion, 1970, Reader, 1975, Professor of Religious Studies, 1979-85, Emeritus Professor, 1985; Director, Centre for the Study of Christianity in the Non-Western World, 1982-96; Honorary Professor, Edinburgh University, 1987-96; Visiting Professor of World Christianity, Yale University, 1988; Visiting Professor of Ecumenics and Mission, Princeton Theological Seminary, since 1997; Co opted Member, Aberdeen Education Committee, 1971-74; Aberdeen City Councillor, 1974-80; Convener, Arts and Recreation, COSLA, 1978-80; Chairman, Council for Museums and Galleries in Scotland, 1978-81; Vice-Chairman, Committee of Area Museums Councils, 1980-81; Member, Williams Committee on the future of the national museums, 1979-82; Trustee, National Museum of Antiquities of Scotland, 1982-85; Member, Museums Advisory Board for Scotland, 1984-85; Trustee, National Museums of Scotland, 1985-87; Methodist Preacher; Past Chairman, Disablement Income Group, Scotland; President, British Association for the History of Religions, 1977-80; Secretary, Scottish Institute of Missionary Studies; Editor, Journal of Religion in Africa, 1967-86; Henry Martyn Lectures, Cambridge University, 1988; Margaret Harris Lectures, Dundee University, 1989; Annual Missiology Lecturer, Fuller Theological Seminary, 1996; Co-chair, Yale-Edinburgh Group on the History of the Missionary Movement. Address: (b.) Centre for the Study of Christianity in the Non-Western World, Edinburgh University, New College, Mound Place, Edinburgh EH1 2LX; T.-0131-650 8952.

Walters, Professor David Gareth, BA, PhD. Stevenson Professor of Hispanic Studies, Glasgow University, since 1995; b. 1.1.48, Neath; m., Christine Ellen Knott; 1 s.; 1 d. Educ. Rhondda County Grammar School for Boys; University College, Cardiff. Temporary Lecturer in Spanish, Leeds University, 1972-73; Glasgow University, 1973-95: Lecturer in Hispanic Studies, Senior Lecturer, Titular Professor. Publications: books on Francisco de Quevedo and Francisco de Aldana; editor, Poems to Lisi and collection of essays on Antonio Machado; numerous articles on Spanish, Portuguese and Catalan literature. Recreations:music; playing the piano; poetry; travel; tennis and most sports. Address: (h.) 32 Golf View, Bearsden, Glasgow G61 4HJ; T.-0141-942 4948.

Walton, Professor Henry John, MD, PhD, FRCPE, FRCPsych, DPM, Hon.MD. Physician; Emeritus Professor of International Medical Education, Edinburgh University; b. 15.2.24, South Africa; m., Sula Wolff. Educ. University of Cape Town; London University; Columbia University, NY; Edinburgh University. Registrar in Neurology and Psychiatry, University of Cape Town, 1946-54; Head, Department of Psychiatry, 1957-60; Senior Registrar, Maudsley Hospital, London, 1955-57; Senior Lecturer in Psychiatry, then Professor of Psychiatry, Edinburgh University, 1962-85; appointed Professor of International Medical Education, 1986; Editor, Medical Education, since 1976; President, Association for Medical Education in Europe, 1972-86, Hon. Life President, since 1986; Immediate Past-President, World Federation for Medical Education (Member, Executive Council); frequent Consultant to WHO; Member, Academies of Medicine of Argentina, Belgium and Poland. Publications: as Editor: Small Group Psychotherapy, 1974; Dictionary of Psychiatry, 1985; as Co-Editor: Newer Developments in Assessing Clinical Competence, 1986; as Co-Author: Alcoholism, 1988; Report of the World Conference on Medical Education, 1988; Report on World Summit of Medical Education, 1993; International Medical Education in Graduate Prospects in a Changing World, 1998. Recreations: literature; visual arts, particularly Western painting and Chinese and Japanese art. Address: 38 Blacket Place, Edinburgh, EH9 1RL; T.-0131-667 7811.

Walton, Professor John Christopher, BSc, PhD, DSc, FRSE. Professor of Reactive Chemistry, St. Andrews University, since 1997; b. 4.12.41, St. Albans; m., Jane Lehman; 1 s.; 1 d. Educ. Watford Grammar School for Boys; Sheffield University. Assistant Lecturer: Queen's College, St. Andrews, 1966-67, Dundee University, 1967-69; Lecturer in Chemistry, United College, St. Andrews, 1969-80; Senior Lecturer, 1980-86, Reader, 1986-96. Elder, Seventh-day Adventist Church. Recreations: music; philosophy. Address: (b.) School of Chemistry, St. Andrews University, St. Andrews, Fife, KY16 9ST; T.-01334 463864.

Wannop, Professor Urlan Alistair, MA, MCD, MRTPI. Emeritus Professor of Urban and Regional Planning, Strathclyde University; b. 16.4.31, Newtown St. Boswells; 1 s.; 1 d. Educ. Aberdeen Grammar School; Edinburgh University; Liverpool University. Appointments in public and private practice, 1956-68; Team Leader, Coventry-Solihull-Warwickshire Sub-Regional Planning Study, 1968-71; Director, West Central Scotland Plan, 1972-74; Senior Deputy Director of Planning, Strathclyde Regional Council, 1975-81; appointed Professor of Urban and Regional Planning, Strathclyde University, 1981. Member, Parliamentary Boundary Commission for Scotland, since 1983. Address: (h.) 43 Lomond Street, Helensburgh G84 7ES; T.-01436 74622.

Ward, Colin, BA, CA. Chief Executive, Student Loans Company, Glasgow, since 1996; b. 23.6.47, Edinburgh; m., Marjory. Educ. Daniel Stewart's College, Edinburgh; Heriot-Watt University. Ernst and Young, 1970-74; Price Waterhouse, Glasgow, 1974-75; British Steel Corporation, 1975-77; Scottish Development Agency, 1977-90, latterly as Chief Accountant; Student Loans Company, since 1990. Recreations: sailing; gardening; classical music. Address: (b.) 100 Bothwell Street, Glasgow, G2 7JD; T.-0141-306 2010.

Ward, David Romen, MA, CertEd. Rector, Hutchesons' Grammar School, since 1987; b. 21.12.35, Newcastle upon Tyne; m., Stella Barbara Anderson; 1 s.; 2 d. Educ. St. Mary's, Melrose; Sedbergh School; Emmanuel College, Cambridge. Assistant Master: Winchester College, Wellington College; Senior History Master, City of London School; Deputy Headmaster, Portsmouth Grammar School; Head Master, Hulme Grammar School. Member, Admiralty Interview Board; Deputy Chairman (Staff), Court, Strathclyde University; Member, Quality Assessment Committee, Scottish Higher Education Funding Council, 1994-97; Freeman, City of London. Publications: Fall of Metternich and the Revolution of 1848; British Foreign Policy 1815-1865; Explorations. Address: (h.) 192 Nithsdale Road, Glasgow, G41 5EU; (b.) Hutchesons' Grammar School, Beaton Road, Glasgow G41 4NW; T.-0141-423 2933.

Ward, Professor Geoffrey Christopher, BA, MA. Professor of English and Head of Department, Dundee University, since 1995; b. 18.2.54, Oldham; m., Marion Wynne-Davies; 2 s. Educ. Manchester Grammar School; Clare College, Cambridge. Lecturer, then Senior Lecturer, English Department, Liverpool University, 1978-95. Member, Editorial Board, The Cambridge Quarterly; has lectured widely. Publications: Statutes of Liberty: the New York School of Poets, 1992; Language Poetry and the American Avant-Garde, 1993; Bloomsbury Guide to Romantic Literature (Editor). Recreations: poetry; music; food; beach-combing. Address: (b.) English Department, Dundee University, Dundee DD1 4HN; T.-01382 344412.

Ward, Professor John Macqueen, CBE, CA, Companion, IEE. Chairman, Scottish Post Office Board; Chairman, Scottish Homes; Chairman, European Assets Trust NV; Director: Macfarlane Group (Clansman) PLC, Dunfermline Building Society; former Resident Director, Scotland and North of England, IBM United Kingdom Ltd; Professor, Heriot Watt University; b. 1.8.40, Edinburgh; m., Barbara Macintosh; 1 s.; 3 d. Educ. Edinburgh Academy; Fettes College. Joined IBM UK Ltd. at Greenock plant, 1966; worked in France and UK; appointed European Director of Information Systems, 1975, and Havant Site Director, 1981. Past Chairman, Scottish CBI; Chairman, Quality Scotland Foundation, Advisory Scottish Council for Education and Training Targets, Scottish Electronics Forum; Chairman, Institute of Technology Management; Director, Scottish Business in the Community; Director, Greater Easterhouse Development Company, 1991-93. Honorary Doctorate, Napier University, Strathclyde University. Address: (b.) 102 West Port, Edinburgh EH3 9HS; T.-0131-228 7300.

Ward, Leslie Graeme. Director, Advocates for Animals, since 1989; Secretary, St.Andrew Animal Fund, since 1994; b. 12.1.51, Dunbar; m., Erika Gillian; 1 d. Educ. Dunbar Grammar School. RAF, 1969-79. Member, Home Secretary's Animal Procedures Committee; Fellow, Winston Churchill Travelling Fellowship Trust. Recreations: sports; walking the dogs. Address: (b.) 10 Queensferry Street, Edinburgh. EH2 4PG; T.-0131-225 6039.

Ward, Professor Mark Gordon, BA. Dean, Faculty of Arts, since 1995, Professor of German Language and Literature, since 1997, Glasgow University; Principal Examiner, CSYS German, since 1987; b. 4.2.51, Hemel Hempstead; m., Janet Helen; 2 s. Educ. Leeds Grammar School; King's College, London University. Tutorial Research Scholar, Bedford College, London University, 1974-75; Lecturer, then Senior Lecturer, Department of German, Glasgow University, 1975-97. Publications include: Theodor Storm: Der Schimmelreiter, 1988; Laughter, Comedy and Aesthetics: Kleist's Der Zerbrochne Krug, 1995; Perspectives on German Realism. Recreations: music; gardening; sport. Address: (b.) Faculty of Arts, Glasgow University, Glasgow G12 8QQ; T.-0141-330 5253.

Ward, Maxwell Colin Bernard, MA. Partner, Baillie Gifford & Co., since 1975; Director, Scottish Equitable Policyholders' Trust, since 1994; Director, Scottish Equitable plc, since 1995; Director, Scottish Equitable Life Assurance Society, 1988-94; b. 22.8.49, Sherborne; m., Sarah Marsham; 2 s.; 2 d. Educ. Harrow; St. Catharine's, Cambridge. Trainee, Baillie Gifford & Co., 1971-75. Board Member, Capability Scotland. Recreations: tennis; squash; bridge; country pursuits. Address: (h.) Stobshiel House, Humbie, East Lothian EH36 5PD; T.-01875 833646.

Wardrop, James Arneil, DL, FCIBS, FSA (Scot). Retired Banker; Deputy Lieutenant, Renfrewshire; Chairman, Peter Brough Bequest Fund; Vice Chairman, Accord, The Renfrewshire Hospice, since 1993; Vice Chairman, Japan Society of Scotland, since 1990; Secretary, Society of Friends of Paisley Abbey, since 1969; b. 19.4.40, Paisley. Educ. John Neilson Institution, Paisley. Joined National Bank of Scotland, by a process of mergers absorbed into Royal Bank of Scotland; Deputy Agent, San Francisco, 1978-81; Manager, Business Development International Division, 1981-94. Elder, Paisley Abbey; Trustee, Miss Kibble's Trust; Director, Past Chairman, Incorporated Glasgow Renfrewshire Society; Director, Kibble Education and Care Centre; Council Member, Society of Friends of Glasgow Cathedral; Member, Committee, Scotland's Gardens Scheme, Renfrewshire and Inverclyde; Member, Master Court, Paisley Hammermen Society (Deacon, 1996-97); Lay Member of Council, Paisley Art Institute. Recreations: country pursuits; gardening; music. Address: (h.) Saint Kevins, Meikleriggs, Paisley, PA2 9PT; T.-0141-887 3627.

Ward Thompson, Catharine J., BSc, DipLA, MLI. Head, School of Landscape Architecture, Edinburgh College of Art/Heriot Watt University, since 1989; b. 5.12.52; m., Henry Swift Thompson; 3 c. Educ. Holy Cross Convent, Chalfont St. Peter; Southampton University; Edinburgh University. Landscape Assistant/Landscape Architect/ Senior Landscape Architect, 1973-81; Lecturer and Studio Instructor, School of Landscape Architecture, Edinburgh College of Art, 1981-88. Consultant, Landscape Design and Research Unit, Heriot-Watt University, since 1989. Recreations: dance; choreography. Address: (h.) 11 Douglas Crescent, Edinburgh EH12 5BB; T.-0131-337 6818.

Wark, Kirsty, BA. Partner, Wark, Clements and Company, since 1990; b. 1955, Dumfries; m., Alan Clements; 1 s.; 1 d. Former Researcher and Producer, BBC; presented Seven Days, Reporting Scotland, Left Right and Centre, Up Front, Breakfast Time, etc.; formed production company with husband, presenting Words with Wark, One Foot in the Past; General Election night and Referendum coverage; Presenter, The Late Show, 1990-93, Newsnight, since 1993. BAFTA Scotland Journalist of the Year, 1993; BAFTA Scotland Best Television Presenter, 1997. Publication: Restless Nation (Co-author). Recreations: family; tennis; swimming; cooking; beach-combing; reading. Address: (b.) Wark, Clements and Co. Ltd., The Production Centre, The Tollgate, 19 Marine Crescent, Glasgow G51 1HD.

Warlow, Professor Charles Picton, BA, MB, BChir, MD, FRCP (Lond), FRCP (Edin), FRCP (Glas). Professor of Medical Neurology, Edinburgh, since 1987; Honorary Consultant Neurologist, Western General Hospital; b. 29.9.43; m.; 2 s.; 1 d. Educ. Cambridge University. Lecturer in Medicine, Aberdeen University, 1971-74; Registrar and Senior Registrar in Neurology, National Hospitals for Nervous Diseases, London, and University College Hospital, London, 1974-76; Clinical Lecturer in Neurology, then Clinical Reader, Oxford University, 1976-86. Recreations: sailing; photography; mountains. Address: 3 Mortonhall Hall Road, Edinburgh EH9 2HS.

Warner, Gerald, OStJ, MA, FSAScot. Author; Columnist, Scotland on Sunday, since 1997; b. 22.3.45, Falkirk. Educ. St. Aloysius' College, Glasgow; Glasgow University. Vice-Chairman, Una Voce (International Latin Mass Federation), Scotland, 1965-66; Administrative Assistant, Glasgow University, 1971-74; author and broadcaster, 1974-89; Diarist (under pseudonym Henry Cockburn), Sunday Times Scotland, 1989-95; columnist, 1992-95; Special Adviser to Secretary of State for Scotland, 1995-97. Council Member, 1745 Association, 1967-70; Member, Scottish Council of Monarchist League, 1969-71; Chairman, The Monday Club – Scotland, 1973-74; Secretary, Conservative Party's Scottish Policy Committee on Education, 1976-77; Parliamentary candidate, Hamilton, October 1974. Knight of Grace and Devotion, Sovereign Military Order of Malta, 1979; Knight, Jure Sanguinis, Sacred Military Constantinian Order of St. George, 1994. Publications: Homelands of the Clans, 1980; Being of Sound Mind, 1980; Tales of the Scottish Highlands, 1982; Conquering by Degrees, 1985; The Scottish Tory Party: A History, 1988. Recreations: literature; genealogy; Brummelliana. Address: 17 Huntly Gardens, Glasgow G12 9AT.

Watchman, Karen, BA. Director, Scottish Down's Syndrome Association, since 1998; b. 9.1.65, Stockton-on-Tees; m., Mark Smith; 2 s. Educ. Ian Ramsey Comprehensive School, Stockton-on-Tees; Stockton Sixth Form College; University of Stirling; Jordanhill College of Education. NCH Action for Children: Depute Manager, Stirling Stopover, 1988-94, Depute Manager, Raploch Family Centre, 1994-96; Manager, Quality Action Group, Stirling, 1996-98; Manager, Scottish Down's Syndrome Association Central Branch Befriending Scheme. Recreations: family; vegetarian cooking; sport (Middlesbrough Football Club). Address: (b.) 158/160 Balgreen Road, Edinburgh EH11 3AU; T.-0131-313 4225.

Waterman, Professor Peter George, BPharm (Hons), PhD, FLS, DSc, FRSE. Professor in Phytochemistry, Department of Pharmaceutical Sciences, Strathclyde University, since 1987; b. 28.4.46, Langley, Kent; m., Margaret Humble. Educ. Judd School, Tonbridge; London University. Postgraduate Research Assistant, London University, 1968-69; Lecturer, Senior Lecturer, Reader, Department of Pharmacy, Strathclyde University, 1969-87. Pharmaceutical Society Young Scientist of the Year Award, 1979; Phytochemical Society of Europe Tate & Lyle Award for contribution to Phytochemistry, 1984; Executive Editor, Journal of Biochemical Systematics and Ecology; Dhc, Universite de Franche-Compte, 1995. Recreations: travel; ornithology; walking. Address: (b.) Phytochemistry Research Laboratories, Department of Pharmaceutical Sciences, Strathclyde University, Glasgow G1 1XW; T.-0141-548 2028.

Waters, Donald Henry, OBE, CA. Director, Scottish Media Group, since 1997; Deputy Chairman and Chief Executive, Grampian Television PLC, 1993-97 (Chief Executive and Director, 1987-93); b. 17.12.37, Edinburgh; m., June Leslie Hutchison; 1 s.; 2 d. Educ. George Watson's, Edinburgh; Inverness Royal Academy. Director, John M. Henderson and Co. Ltd., 1972-75; Grampian Television PLC: Company Secretary, 1975, Director of Finance, 1979; Director: Scottish Television and Grampian Sales Ltd., 1980-97, Moray Firth Radio Ltd., 1982-97, Independent Television Publications Ltd., 1987-90, Cablevision Scotland PLC, 1987-91; Chairman, Celtic Film and Television Association, 1994-96; Vice-Chairman, BAFTA Scotland; Visiting Professor of Film and Media Studies, Stirling University; Chairman, Police Dependant Trust for Grampian, 1992-96; Past Chairman, Royal Northern and University Club, Aberdeen; Chairman, Glenburnie Properties Ltd., 1993-97; Director: Central Scotland Radio Ltd., 1994-96 (Chairman, 1995-96), GRT Bus Group PLC, 1994-96, British Linen Bank Ltd., since 1995, Scottish Post Office Board, since 1996; Member, ITV Council and ITV Broadcast Board; Fellow, Royal Society of Arts; Council Member, CBI Scotland, since 1994; Director, Aberdeen Royal Hospital NHS Trust, since 1996; Member of Council, Aberdeen Chamber of Commerce, since 1996; Governor, Aberdeen University, since 1998; Governor, Robert Gordon's, Aberdeen, since 1998; Member, Grampian and Islands Family Trust, since 1988; Member of Council, SATRO; Burgess of Guild Assessor, since 1997. Address: (h.) Balquhidder, 141 North Deeside Road, Milltimber, Aberdeen AB13 0JS; T.-Aberdeen 867131.

Waters, Fergus Cameron. Director, Scottish Mining Museum, since 1996; b. 15.2.57, Tanzania; m., Alison Crawford. Educ. Rannoch School; Moray College of Further Education. Marketing Manager, Castlewynd Studios, 1984-88; Commercial and Marketing Manager, Ford and Etal Estates, 1988-94; General Manager, Hartlepool Historic Quay, 1994-96. Recreations: motor-biking; skiing; sailing. Address: (b.) Scottish Mining Museum, Lady Victoria Colliery, Newtongrange EH22 4QN; T.-0131-663 7519.

Watson, Adam, BSc, PhD, DSc, DUniv (Stirling), FRSE. Senior Principal Scientific Officer and Leader of grouse research team, Institute of Terrestrial Ecology, 1971-90; Environmental Consultant; Member, Cairngorms Partnership Board, 1995-97; b. 14.4.30, Turriff; m., Jenny; 1 s.; 1 d. Educ. Aberdeen University. Demonstrator in Zoology, McGill University, Montreal, 1952-53; Zoologist on Baird expedition to Baffin Island, 1953; Assistant Lecturer in Zoology, Aberdeen University, 1953-55; Teacher of Science, Aberdeen Academy, 1957; Senior Research Fellow, Aberdeen University, 1957-60; Senior

Scientific Officer, then Principal Scientific Officer, Nature Conservancy, 1961-66; Officer in charge, Nature Conservancy Council Mountain and Moorland Ecology Station, Banchory, 1968-71; Neill Prize, Royal Society of Edinburgh, for "outstanding contribution to natural history". Recreations: mountaineering; skiing. Address: (h.) Clachnaben, Crathes, Banchory AB31 5JE.

Watson, Professor Alan Albert, JP, MA, BD, MB, BS, FRCP, FRCPath, DMJ, DTM&H. Emeritus Regius Professor of Forensic Medicine, Glasgow University; Honorary Consultant in Forensic Medicine, Greater Glasgow Health Board, since 1978; Committee Member, Forensic Medicine (Scotland) Committee, since 1982; b. 20.2.29, Reading; m., Jeannette Anne Pitts; 3 s. Educ. Reading School; St. Mary's Hospital, London; Queens' College, Cambridge. Lecturer in Pathology, Glasgow University, 1964-69; University Senior Assistant Pathologist, Cambridge University, 1969-71; elected Fellow of Queen's College and Assistant Director of Studies, 1970; Consultant in Forensic Medicine, SE Asia Region, Delhi, WHO, 1977. Hon. President, Scottish Band of Hope Union. Recreations: Church activities (Baptist lay preacher). Address: (h.) 76 Arrol Drive, Ayr KA7 4AW; T.-01292 266365.

Watson, Alexander Bell, MA, MEd, FIMgt, FSA Scot, FRSA. Chief Executive, Angus Council, since 1995 (Chief Executive, Tayside Regional Council, 1995); b. 20.5.45, Airdrie; m., Jean; 3 s. Educ. Airdrie Academy; Glasgow University; Jordanhill College of Education. Teacher of Classics, Morrison's Academy, Crieff, 1968; Principal Teacher of Classics: Portree High School, 1971, McLaren High School, Callander, 1973; Assistant Director of Education: Central, 1975, Strathclyde, 1983; Senior Depute Director of Education, Central Regional Council, 1986; Director of Education, Tayside Regional Council, 1990-94. General Secretary, Association of Directors of Education in Scotland, 1993-95; Chair, National Co-ordinating Committee on Staff Development of Teachers, 1994-95; Member, Board of Management and Chair, Personnel Committee, Angus College, since 1997; Hon. Secretary, Society of Local Authority Chief Executives and Senior Managers (Scotland), since 1997. Recreations: music; reading; fishing; Scottish heritage; DIY. Address: (b.) Angus Council, The Cross, Forfar DD8 1BX; T.-01307 473020.

Watson, Garry Sanderson, CA. Scottish Legal Services Ombudsman, since 1994; b. 31.7.40, Glasgow; m., Elizabeth Ann; 4 d. Educ. Glasgow Academy. Hill Samuel Bank, 1969-91: Chairman, All Seasons Wholefoods, 1993-94. Director, Macaulay Land Use Research Institute, since 1997; Director, Business in the Community, 1985-88; Hon. Treasurer, National Association of Citizens' Advice Bureaux, 1986-91; Hon. Treasurer, Scottish Association of CAB, 1992-95; Director, Edinvar Housing Association, 1992 (Chair, 1997). Recreations: tennis; hill-walking; shooting. Address: (h.) Newlandburn House, Newlandrig, by Gorebridge, Midlothian, EH23 4NS; T.-01875 820939.

Watson, Professor George Alistair, BSc, MSc, PhD, FIMA, FRSE. Professor, Department of Mathematics, Dundee University, since 1988; b. 30.9.42, Aberfeldy; m., Hilary Mackay; 1 d. Educ. Breadalbane Academy; Edinburgh University; Australian National University. Demonstrator, Computer Unit, Edinburgh University, 1964-66; Dundee University: Research Fellow, then Lecturer, Mathematics Department, 1969-82; Senior Lecturer, Mathematical Sciences Department, 1982-84; Reader, Department of Mathematics and Computer Science, 1984-88. Recreation: gardening. Address: (h.) 7 Albany Road, West Ferry, Dundee DD5 1NS; T.-Dundee 779473.

Watson, Harry Duff, MA, BA, DipEd, FSAScot. Senior Editor, Dictionary of the Older Scottish Tongue, Edinburgh University, since 1985; b. 17.6.46, Crail; m., Susan Margaret Saul; 2 s. Educ. Waid Academy, Anstruther; Edinburgh University; University College, London. Teacher of English/English as a Foreign Language, Scotland, England, Sweden, West Germany, 1970-79; appointed Editor, Dictionary of the Older Scottish Tongue, 1979. Past Senior Vice-President, Scottish Swedish Society; Member, Council, Scottish Text Society; Member, Board, Scottish Studies, Edinburgh University. Publication: Kilrenny and Cellardyke. Recreations: reading; writing; music; genealogy; literary translation. Address: (h.) 14 Braehead Grove, Edinburgh EH4 6BG; T.-0131-339 6911.

Watson, Professor John, BSc, ARCST, PhD, DSc. Professor in Biochemistry, Strathclyde University, since 1988 (Reader, 1985-88); Head, Department of Bioscience and Biotechnology; b. 17.6.42, Glasgow; m., Anne Brown; 2 d. Educ. Whitehill Secondary, Glasgow; Glasgow University; Strathclyde University. MRC Research Fellow, Glasgow University; Lecturer, Senior Lecturer, Reader, Professor, Strathclyde University. Recreations: golf; swimming; skiing; reading. Address: (b.) Royal College, Glasgow G1 1XW; T.-0141-548 3822.

Watson of Invergowrie, Lord (Michael Goodall Watson), BA (Hons). MP (Labour), Glasgow Central, 1989-97; b. 1.5.49, Cambuslang; m., Lorraine Therese McManus. Educ. Dundee High School; Heriot-Watt University. Development Officer, WEA East Midlands District, 1974-77; Industrial Officer, ASTMS, 1977-79; Regional Officer, ASTMS (latterly MSF), 1979-89. Member, Scottish Executive Committee, Labour Party, 1987-90; Hon. Doctorate, University of Abertay Dundee, 1998. Publication: Rags to Riches: the official history of Dundee United FC. Recreations: watching Dundee United FC; jogging; reading, especially political biographies. Address: (b.) House of Lords, London SW1A 0PW.

Watson, Peter, BA, LLB, SSC. Solicitor (Levy & McRae); b. 22.1.54, Greenock; m., Claire Watson; 2 d. Educ. Eastwood High School, Glasgow; Strathclyde University; Edinburgh University; Scandinavian Maritime Law Institute, Norway; Dundee Petroleum Law Institute. Qualified, 1981; Solicitor to the Supreme Courts; Notary Public; Temporary Sheriff; President, Society of Solicitor Advocates, 1997; Hon. Vice-President and former Chairman, Association of Mediators; Visiting Professor, Nova University, Fort Lauderdale, Florida; Member, Steering Committee, and Negotiator, Piper Alpha Disaster Group; Secretary, Braer Disaster Group; Secretary, Lockerbie Air Disaster Group; former Official Collaborator, International Labour Organisation, Geneva; Member, Criminal Rules Council; Member, Board, Sports Law Centre, Anglia University; Honorary Citizen of Nashville, Tennessee; large media practice based in Glasgow. Publications: Civil Justice System in Britain; Crimes of War – The Antony Gecas Story; The Truth Written in Blood; Dunblane – A Predictable Tragedy; DNA and the Criminal Trial; In Pursuit of Pan Am. Recreations: working out; drinking fine wine. Address: (b.) Levy & McRae, 266 St. Vincent Street, Glasgow G2 5RL; T.-0141-307 2311.

Watson, Professor Roderick, MA, PhD, FRSE. Poet; Literary Critic and Writer; Professor in English, Stirling University; Director, Stirling Institute for International Scottish Studies; b. 12.5.43, Aberdeen; m., Celia Hall Mackie; 1 s.; 1 d. Educ. Aberdeen Grammar School; Aberdeen University; Peterhouse, Cambridge. Lecturer in English, Victoria University, British Columbia, 1965-66; collections of poetry include Trio and True History on the Walls; other books include The Penguin Book of the Bicycle, The Literature of Scotland, MacDiarmid, The Poetry of Norman MacCaig and The Poetry of Scotland (Editor). Recreation: cycling; motor cycling. Address: (h.) 19 Millar Place, Stirling; T.-Stirling 475971.

Watson, Tom. Actor, Playwright, Poet; b. 21.3.32, Auchinleck; m., Joyce; 2 d. Educ. Hamilton Academy. Byre Theatre/Perth Theatre, 1955-57; BBC Radio Repertory Company; television work includes: The Physicist, Dr Finlay's Casebook, Treasure Island, Churchill's People, Village Hall, Benny Lynch, The Mourning Brooch, The Standard, Govan Ghost Story, Prime Suspect, Cardiac Arrest, Hamish MacBeth, Your Cheating Heart; stage work includes: Fool for Love, National Theatre and West End; The Treatment, Some Voices, A Wholly Healthy Glasgow, Royal Court; Translations, Lyceum; The Government Inspector, Almeida; film: Lord Fauntleroy, The Big Man, The Slab Boys, Winter Guest. Gold Medal, New York International Radio Awards. Publication: The Dark Whistle (poetry). Recreations: natural history; observing; old-time music hall. Address: (b.) Kerry Gardner Management, 15 Kensington High Street, London.

Watt, Archibald, MBE, JP, MA, MEd, FEIS, FSA Scot. Honorary Sheriff, Grampian, Highlands and Islands, since 1979; b. 20.5.14, Aberdeen; m., 1, Anne D.M. Ashton (deceased); 2, Elizabeth P. White. Educ. Robert Gordon's College, Aberdeen; Aberdeen University; Aberdeen College of Education. Teacher of English, Elgin Academy, 1938; Flt.-Lt., RAF Administrative and Special Duties Branch and RAF Regiment, 1941-46; Mackie Academy: Principal Teacher of English, 1949, Deputy Rector, 1962, retired, 1977; Organist, HM Prison, Aberdeen, 1930-38; WEA Organiser for Adult Education, Elgin, 1946-49; WEA Tutor in Psychology, 1946-51; Founder and Organising Secretary, Stonehaven Music Club, since 1949; Member, National Council, and Chairman, Regional and District Committees, Scottish Community Drama Association, 1949-67; Member, National Executive and District Chairman, School Library Association in Scotland, 1952-73; Elder, Church of Scotland, since 1954; Chairman and/or Member, Kincardine District Committee, EIS, 1956-77; Member, Joint Consultative Committee, Kincardine County Council, 1965-77; Queen's Jubilee Medal, 1977; Organist, South Church, Stonehaven, 1976-94; Director, Kinneff Old Church Preservation Trust Ltd., since 1979; Founder Member and President, Stonehaven Probus Club, 1981-82; Committee Member, National Trust for Scotland (Kincardine and Deeside Centre), 1984-88; Member, Aberdeen Choral Society, 1978-91, Aberdeen Proms Chorus, since 1985, BB Centenary Band, since 1991; Chairman, Stonehaven Heritage Society, since 1988; author of Reading Lists for the Secondary School, 1966; Highways and Byways Round Stonehaven, 1976; Highways and Byways Round Kincardine, 1985; A Goodly Heritage, 1991; The Roman Camp of Raedykes, 1992; Early Stonehaven Settlers, 1994. Recreations: concert and theatre-going; travel; antiquities and archaeology; brass bands; research; golf; choral singing. Address: (h.) Rutlands, Arduthie Road, Stonehaven; T.-Stonehaven 762712.

Watt, Archie Sutter, RSW, DA. Painter/Printmaker; b. 31.3.15, Edinburgh; m., Morag McLeod Miller (deceased). Educ. Dunfermline High School; Glasgow School of Art; Edinburgh College of Art; Moray House College. Served in arms, 1939-46; Teacher, Stewartry of Kirkcudbright; set up teaching studio at Kirkgunzeon, 1976, running classes and summer schools, also occasionally at St. Andrews University; elected to RSW, 1966; Professional Member, SSA, SAAC; work in public and private collections, UK and abroad. Founder Member, Stewartry Art Society; Founder Member and Honorary Vice President, Dumfries and Galloway Arts Festival. Recreations: books; listening to music. Address: Bankhead, Kirkgunzeon, Dumfries DG2 8LA; T.- 01387 760283.

Watt, Brian, MD, FRCPath, FRCP Edin, CBiol, FIBiol. Consultant Bacteriologist, City Hospital, Edinburgh, since 1982; Honorary Senior Lecturer, Department of Bacteriology, Edinburgh University, since 1974; Director, Scottish Mycobacteria Reference Laboratory; Clinical Director, Medical Microbiology Services, RIE Unit; b. 6.12.41, Edinburgh; m., Hilary Watt; 2 d. Educ. Rudolf Steiner School; Edinburgh University. Lecturer, Department of Bacteriology, Edinburgh University, 1968-73; Consultant Microbiologist, Western General Hospital, 1973-82. Recreations: fishing; gardening; golf; tennis; singing. Address: (h.) Silverburn House, by Penicuik, Midlothian; T.-01968 672085.

Watt, Professor Graham Charles Murray, MD, FRCP, MRCGP, FFPHM. Professor of General Practice, University of Glasgow, since 1994; b. 3.1.52, Aberdeen; m., Elizabeth Munro; 2 d. Educ. Aberdeen Grammar School; Aberdeen University. Address: 15 Banavie Road, Glasgow G11 5AW; T.-0141-334 2476.

Watt, Iain Alasdair, BSc (Econ). Chief Executive, Edinburgh Fund Managers; b. 30.3.45, Edinburgh; m., Lynne Neilson; 3 s.; 1 d. Educ. Edinburgh Academy; Hull University. Recreations: golf; tennis. Address: (b.) Donaldson House, 97 Haymarket Terrace, Edinburgh; T.-0131-313 1000.

Watt, Jim, MBE (1980). Boxer; b. 18.7.48, Glasgow. Turned professional, 1968; British Lightweight Champion, 1972-73, 1975-77; European Lightweight Champion, 1977-79; World Lightweight Champion, 1979-81; four successful defences of World title; Freedom of Glasgow, 1981.

Watters, Michael. Chief Executive, West Dunbartonshire Council. Address: (b.) Council Offices, Garshake Road, Dumbarton, G82 3PU.

Waugh, Alan, BSc (Hons), DipEd, FRSA. Head Teacher, Penicuik High School, since 1992; b. 9.2.49, Loanhead; m., Margo Watt; 1 s.; 1 d. Educ. Lasswade Senior Secondary School; Edinburgh University. Head of Chemistry, then Assistant Head Teacher, Lasswade High School Centre, 1976-86; Depute Head Teacher, James Gillespie's High School, 1986-92. Address: (b.) Penicuik High School, Carlops Road, Penicuik EH26 9EP; T.-Penicuik 674165.

Waugh, David Reginald, BSc, PhD. Director, Royal Zoological Society of Scotland, since 1998; b. 13.6.51, Colchester; m., Marian Diaz de Waugh; 1 s. Educ. Earl's Colne Grammar School; University College of Swansea; University of Stirling. Director of Training, Jersey Wildlife Preservation Trust, Jersey, 1981-92; Director, Tangara Asesores Ecólogos, C. A., Venezuela, 1992-95; Scientific Director, Loro Parque Fundación, Tenerife, 1995-98. Honorary Research Fellow, Durrell Institute of Conservation and Ecology, University of Kent; Member, IUCN Conservation Breeding Specialist Group and Reintroduction Specialist Group; Honorary Life Member, Jersey Wildlife Preservation Trust; Member, Edinburgh Centre for Rural Research. Recreations: bird-watching; exploration of wild places; photography; travel. Address: (b.) Royal Zoological Society of Scotland, Edinburgh EH12 6TS; T.-0131-314 0302.

Way of Plean, George Alexander, LLB (Hons), FSAScot, FRSA, NP, SSC. Senior Litigation Partner, Beveridge and Kellas, SSC, since 1985; Secretary, Standing Council of Scottish Chiefs, since 1984; b. 22.5.56, Edinburgh; m., Rosemary Calder; 1 s. Educ. Boroughmuir School; University of Edinburgh. Apprenticed to W. F. M. Whitelaw, W. S., 1978-80; Solicitor, Beveridge and Kellas, 1980-85. Member, Convention of the Baronage of Scotland. Publications: Collins Clans and Family Encyclopaedia (Editor-in-Chief); Homelands of the Clans. Recreations: heraldry and orders of chivalry. Address: (b.) Hope Chambers, 52 Leith Walk, Leith, Edinburgh EH6 5HW; T.-0131-554 6321.

Weatherhead, Alexander Stewart, OBE, TD, MA, LLB. Solicitor; formerly Senior Partner, Brechin Tindal Oatts (formerly Tindal Oatts), Solicitors, Glasgow, since 1997 (Partner, 1960-97, Consultant, 1997-98); b. 3.8.31, Edinburgh; m., Harriett Foye; 2 d. Educ. Glasgow Academy; Glasgow University. Royal Artillery, 1950-52; TA, 1952; Lt. Col. Commanding 277 (A&SH) Field Regiment, RA (TA), 1965-67, The Lowland Regiment, RA (T), 1967 and Glasgow and Strathclyde Universities OTC, 1970-73; Colonel, 1974; TAVR Colonel, Lowlands (West), 1974-76; ADC (TAVR) to The Queen, 1977-81; Honorary Colonel, Glasgow and Strathclyde Universities OTC, 1982-98; Chairman, Lowlands TAVRA, 1990-93; Council Member, Law Society of Scotland, 1971-84 (Honorary Vice-President, 1983-84); Member, Royal Commission on Legal Services in Scotland, 1976-80; Council Member, Society for Computers and Law, 1973-86 (Chairman, 1981-84); Temporary Sheriff, 1985-92; Dean, Royal Faculty of Procurators in Glasgow, 1991-95; Commodore, Royal Western Yacht Club, 1995-98. Recreations: tennis; sailing; reading; music. Address: (h.) 52 Partickhill Road, Glasgow, G11 5AB; T.-0141-334 6277.

Weatherhead, Very Rev. Dr. James Leslie, CBE, MA, LLB. Former Principal Clerk, General Assembly of the Church of Scotland; Moderator, General Assembly, 1993; b. 29.3.31, Dundee; m., Dr. Anne Elizabeth Shepherd (see Anne E. Weatherhead); 2 s. Educ. High School of Dundee; Edinburgh University and New College, Edinburgh. Temporary Sub-Lt., RNVR (National Service), 1955-56. Licensed by Presbytery of Dundee, 1960, Presbytery of Ayr, 1960; Assistant Minister, Auld Kirk of Ayr, 1960-62; Minister: Trinity Church, Rothesay, 1962-69, Old Church, Montrose, 1969-85. Member, Broadcasting Council for Scotland, 1978-82.

Weaver, C. Giles H., FCA, MBA. Murray Johnstone Ltd., since 1990, Managing Director, 1993; Proprietor, Greywalls Hotel, Gullane, since 1976; b. 4.4.46; m., Rosamund B. Mayhew; 2 s.; 2 d. Educ. Eton College; London Business School. Ernst & Young, 1966-70; London Business School, 1971-73; Jessel Securities/Berry Wiggins, 1973-76; Director, Ivory & Sime plc, 1976-86; Managing Director Pensions, Prudential Portfolio Managers, 1986-90. Trustee, Lutyens Trust; Trustee, National Galleries of Scotland; Director: James Finlay PLC, Charter European Trust PLC, Helical Bar PLC. Recreations: golf; bridge; skiing; stalking. Address: (b.) Murray Johnstone Ltd., 7 West Nile Street, Glasgow G1 2PX; T.-0141-226 3131.

Weaver, Professor Lawrence Trevelyan, MA, MB BChir, DObstRCOG, DCH, MD, FRCP, FRCPGlas. Honorary Consultant Paediatrician, Royal Hospital for Sick Children, Yorkhill, Glasgow, since 1994; Samson Gemmell Professor of Child Health, University of Glasgow, since 1996; b. 13.10.48; m., Camilla Simmons; 1 s.; 1 d. Educ. Clifton College, Bristol; Corpus Christi College, Cambridge University. Newcastle University Hospitals: House Physician, House Surgeon, SHO, Registrar in Medicine, Surgery, Obstetrics and Gynaecology, General Practice and Paediatrics, 1973-81, Research Registrar in Child Health, 1982-83, Senior Registrar in Child Health, 1983-84; MRC Training Fellow, Dunn Nutritional Laboratory and Honorary Senior Registrar, Department of Paediatrics, Addenbrooke's Hospital, Cambridge, 1984-86; Clinical Research Fellow, Harvard Medical School Departments of Pediatric Gastroenterology and Nutrition, Children's Hospital and Massachusetts General Hospital, Boston, 1987-88; Member, MRC Scientific Staff, Dunn Nutrition Laboratory and Honorary Consultant Paediatrician, Addenbrooke's Hospital and University of Cambridge, 1988-94; Reader in Human Nutrition, University of Glasgow, 1994-96. Member, Academic Panel, RCPCH; Member, Nutrition Committees, RCPCH and ESPGHAN. Recreations: walking; shooting; fishing. Address: (b.) Department of Child Health, Royal Hospital for Sick Children, Yorkhill, Glasgow G3 8SJ; T.-0141-201 0236.

Webb, Professor David John, MD, FRCP, FRCPE, FFPM. Christison Professor of Therapeutics and Clinical Pharmacology, Clinical Pharmacology Unit and Research Centre, Edinburgh University, since 1995; Head, University Department of Medical Sciences, Western General Hospital, Edinburgh, since 1998; Head, Centre for Research in Cardiovascular Biology, Edinburgh University, since 1997; Director, Clinical Research Centre and Honorary Consultant Physician, Western General Hospital, Edinburgh, since 1990; b. 1.9.53, Greenwich; m., Dr. Margaret Jane Cullen. Educ. Dulwich College, London; London University: Royal London Hospital. Junior hospital appointments, 1977-79; Medical Registrar, Royal London rotation, 1979-82; MRC Research Fellow, MRC Blood Pressure Unit, Glasgow, and Honorary Lecturer, Glasgow University, 1982-85; Lecturer in Pharmacology and Clinical Pharmacology, St. George's Hospital Medical School, London, and Honorary Medical Senior Registrar, St. George's Hospital, London, 1985-89; Senior Lecturer in Medicine, Edinburgh University. Executive Member, British Hypertension Society, since 1991; Member, MRC Scientific Advisory Board, since 1996; Member, Wellcome Trust Physiology and Pharmacology Panel, since 1997; Member, Multi-Centre Research Ethics Committee for Scotland, since 1997; Honorary Trustee and Joint Research Director, High Blood Pressure Foundation and Endocrine Research Trust, since 1991; Member, Association of Clinical Professors of Medicine and of Association of Physicians of Great Britain and Ireland. Recreations: opera; bridge; summer and winter mountaineering. Address: (h.) 26 Inverleith Gardens, Edinburgh EH3 5PS; T.-0131-332 1205.

Webb, Professor Jeffrey R.L., BSc, DPhil, FRSE. Professor of Mathematics, Glasgow University, since 1987 (Reader, 1982-87); b. 19.12.45, Stourport-on-Severn; m., Angela Millard; 1 s.; 1 d. Educ. King Charles I School, Kidderminster; Sussex University. Royal Society European Programme Fellowship, 1970-71; Science Research Council Fellowship, Sussex University, 1971-73; Lecturer in Mathematics, Glasgow University, 1973-78 and 1979-82; Visiting Associate Professor, Indiana University, 1978-79; Visiting Professor, Tulane University, New Orleans, 1982. Member, Editorial Board, Glasgow Mathematical Journal. Recreations:chess; books; listening to music. Address: (b.) Mathematics Department, Glasgow University, Glasgow G12 8QW; T.-0141-339 8855, Ext. 5181.

Webster, Ann, BSc (Hons). National Secretary, Girls' Brigade in Scotland, since 1996; b. 16.11.43, Oxford; m., Robert Webster; 1 s.; 2 d. Educ. Stobswell Girls' Junior Secondary School, Dundee; Scottish College of Textiles, Galashiels. Analyst, WRAC, 1963-68; Assistant Domestic Services Manager, Ninewells Hospital, 1973-78. Girls' Brigade Officer, 19 years. Recreations: reading; cross-stitch; knitting; bird-watching. Address: (b.) Girls' Brigade Scotland, Boys' Brigade House, 168 Bath Street, Glasgow G2 4TQ; T.-0141-332 1765.

Webster, David Pirie, OBE, DPE. Author; Chairman, Commonwealth Games Council for Scotland, 1990-95; b. 18.9.28, Aberdeen; 4 s.; 2 d. Educ. Crowlees Boys School; Aberdeen Training College; Woolmanhill College. Senior Technical Representative, Scottish Council of Physical Recreation, 1954-72; Head of Facilities Planning Division, Scottish Sports Council, 1972-74; Director/Administrator, Magnum Leisure Centre, 1974-75; Director of Leisure, Recreation and Tourism, Cunninghame District Council, 1975-87. Director of Weightlifting, Commonwealth Games; Secretary General, International Federation of Strength Athletes. Recreations: writing (more than 30 books); Highland Games; fitness and weight training. Address: (h.) 43 West Road, Irvine KA12 8RE; T.-01294 272257.

Webster, Jack (John Barron). Author and Journalist; Columnist, The Herald; b. 8.7.31, Maud, Aberdeenshire;

m., Eden Keith; 3 s. Educ. Maud School; Peterhead Academy; Robert Gordon's College, Aberdeen. Reporter, Turriff Advertiser; Reporter/Sub Editor, Aberdeen Press & Journal/Evening Express; Chief Sub-Editor, Scottish Sunday Express; Feature Writer, Scottish Daily Express; Feature Writer, Sunday Standard. Columnist of the Year, 1996; Speaker of the Year, 1996. Publications: The Dons, 1978; A Grain of Truth, 1981; Gordon Strachan, 1984; Another Grain of Truth, 1988; 'Tis Better to Travel, 1989; Alistair MacLean (biography), 1991; Famous Ships of the Clyde, 1993; The Flying Scots, 1994; The Express Years, 1994; In the Driving Seat, 1996; The Herald Years, 1996; From Dali to Burrell, 1997; television films: The Roup, 1985; As Time Goes By, 1987; Northern Lights, 1989; Webster Goes West, 1991; John Brown: The Man Who Drew a Legend, 1994; Walking Back to Happiness, 1996; video film: The Glory of Gothenburg, 1993. Address: (b.) The Herald, 195 Albion Street, Glasgow G1; T.-0141-552 6255.

Webster, Michael Alan, BA, DMS, MIMgt, FRSA. Principal, Perth College, since 1991; b. 7.12.45, Manchester. Educ. Chetham's School, Manchester; Moseley Hall Grammar School; Exeter University. FE Lecturer and Head of Department, 1972-84; Education Adviser, Shropshire County Council, 1984-88, Principal Adviser, 1988-91. Recreations: hill-walking; skiing; theatre; fishing. Address: (b.) Perth College, Crieff Road, Perth, PH1 2NX; T.-01738 621171.

Webster, Professor Nigel Robert, BSc, MB, ChB, PhD, FRCA, FRCPEdin. Professor of Anaesthesia and Intensive Care, Aberdeen University, since 1994; b. 14.6.53, Walsall; m., Diana C.S. Webster; 1 s.; 2 d. Educ. Edward Shelley High School, Walsall; Leeds University. Member, scientific staff/Consultant, Clinical Research Centre, Northwick Park Hospital, Harrow; Consultant in Anaesthesia and Intensive Care, St. James's University Hospital, Leeds. Address: (b.) Institute of Medical Sciences, Foresterhill, Aberdeen AB25 2ZD; T.-01224 681818.

Webster, Professor Robin Gordon Maclennan, MA (Cantab), MA (Arch), RIBA, FRIAS, ARSA. Professor of Architecture and Head of School, Scott Sutherland School of Architecture, The Robert Gordon University, Aberdeen, since 1984; Senior Partner, Robin Webster & Associates, Aberdeen, since 1984; Member, The Designers' Collaborative, since 1994; Commissioner, Royal Fine Art Commission for Scotland, 1992-98; b. 24.12.39, Glasgow; m., Katherine S. Crichton; 1 s.; 2 d. Educ. Glasgow Academy; Rugby School; St. John's College, Cambridge; University College London. Assistant, Gillespie Kidd & Coia, Architects, Glasgow, 1963-64; National Building Agency, London, 1965-67; Senior Partner, Spence and Webster, Architects, 1972-84; Lecturer, Bartlett School of Architecture, 1969-74; Visiting Lecturer, Washington University, St. Louis, 1975, Cambridge University, 1976-77, and Mackintosh School, Glasgow School of Art, 1978-84. Winner, New Parliamentary Building Competition, Westminster, 1972; 1st prize, New York Waterfront Competition, 1988; Winner, 1997 Sellic library competition for University of Edinburgh; Chairman, Association of Scottish Schools of Architecture, 1986-90; President, Aberdeen Society of Architects, 1989-91. Recreations: looking and drawing. Address: (h.) 6 Park Road, Cults, Aberdeen; T.-01224 867140.

Webster, Robin Maclean, MBE, RD, BA (Cantab), FCIArb. Employment Tribunal Chairman, Edinburgh, since 1994; b. 22.4.40; m., Janice Helen Reid; 2 d. Educ. Fettes College, Edinburgh; Christ's College, Cambridge University. Solicitor (Scotland), 1966; NP, 1970; Partner, Haddow & McLay, Solicitors, Glasgow, 1968-70; Deputy Secretary, Law Society of Scotland, 1970-76; Secretary, Scottish Lawyers' European Group, 1971-77; Office of Solicitor to Secretary of State for Scotland, 1976-88; seconded as Legal Draftsman, Seychelles Government, 1980-82; Assistant Parliamentary Draftsman, Lord Advocate's Department, 1982-83; Senior Parliamentary Counsel, Kenya Government, 1985-86; Attorney-General, Tuvalu, S. Pacific, 1986-88; Judge of the Supreme Court of Tonga, S. Pacific, 1988-91; Temporary Sheriff, 1991-96; part-time Industrial Tribunal Chairman, 1991-94; Legal Consultant, Overseas Development Administration, 1992-95. Royal Naval Reserve, 1962-90; Lt. Commander (Rtd); Chairman, Queensferry and District Unit, Sea Cadet Corps, since 1994; Hon. Secretary, Royal Scottish Pipers' Society, 1973-76; Elder, Palmerston Place Church of Scotland. Recreations: piping and piobaireachd; Scottish dancing; reading; dog walking. Address: (b.) Employment Tribunals, 54-56 Melville Street, Edinburgh EH3 7HF; T.-0131-226 5584.

Webster, Roderick Brenton. Managing Director, Northsound Radio, since 1997; b. 22.12.44, Inverness; m., Elizabeth Anne; 2 s.; 1 d. Educ. Portobello Secondary School. Moray Firth Radio, Inverness, 1980-89 (Head of Sales); on award of licence, established Radio Borders, 1989-97 (Managing Director); Sony "Station of the Year", 1991. Address: (b.) 45 Kingsgate, Aberdeen AB15 4EL; T.-01224 337000.

Weeple, Edward John, MA. Under Secretary, Lifelong Learning Group, The Scottish Office Education and Industry Department, since 1995; b. 15.5.45, Glasgow; 3 s.; 1 d. Educ. St. Aloysius' College, Glasgow; Glasgow University. Entered DHSS, London, 1968; Assistant Principal, 1968-73 (Private Secretary to Minister of Health, 1971-73); Principal, 1973-78; transferred to Scottish Office, 1978; Principal (Industrial Development Division, SEPD), 1978-80; Assistant Secretary, Scottish Home and Health Department, 1980-85; Assistant Secretary, Department of Agriculture and Fisheries for Scotland, 1985-90; Head, Local Economic Development Group, Industry Department, 1990-95. Address: (b.) Victoria Quay, Edinburgh, EH6 6QQ; T.-0131-244 0623.

Weir, Professor Alexander Douglas, MA, MEd, FRSA. Professor of Education, Strathclyde University, since 1993; Dean, Faculty of Education, since 1997; b. 2.9.42, Falkirk; m., Alison Marion Cook; 1 s.; 1 d. Educ. Falkirk High School; Edinburgh University. Lecturer, Falkirk College of Technology, 1965-67; Senior Research Officer, Scottish Council for Research in Education, 1967-74; Lecturer, Glasgow University, 1974-79; Director, Scottish Vocational Preparation Unit, 1979-85; Director, Vocational Initiatives Unit, Glasgow University, 1985-88; Director of Research, Jordanhill College of Education, 1988-91, Assistant Principal, 1991-93; Vice Dean (Research), Faculty of Education, Strathclyde University, 1993-97. Member, National Executive, Boys' Brigade, 1976-84; Chair, Strathclyde Regional Conference of Voluntary Youth Organisations, 1991-94; author of five books and 75 articles. Recreation: youth work. Address: (b.) Faculty of Education, Strathclyde University, Southbrae Drive, Glasgow G13 1PP; T.-0141-950 3200.

Weir, Sharman Elizabeth, BMus (Hons), FRSA. General Manager, Citizens' Theatre, Glasgow, since 1994; b. 31.3.59, Barrhead. Educ. John Neilson High School, Paisley; Glasgow University. Professional musician, 1981-85; Project Manager and Consultant, BP Exploration, 1985-92; Business Manager, Citizens' Theatre, Glasgow, 1992-94. Recreations: music (flute, singing, piano); travel. Address: (b.) Citizens' Theatre, 119 Gorbals Street, Glasgow, G5; T.-0141-429 5561.

Weir, Tom, MBE, FRSGS. Journalist and Photographer. Former Ordnance Surveyor; climbed in the Himalayas and began professional photography; author of several books on climbing and Scotland; Presenter, Weir's Way, Scottish Television.

Weir, Viscount (William Kenneth James Weir), BA, Hon. DEng (Glasgow), Hon. FEng. Director, The Weir Group PLC, since 1966; Director and former Vice-Chairman, St. James' Place Capital plc; Chairman, BICC plc, since 1996 (Deputy Chairman, 1992-96, Director, since 1977); Director, Canadian Pacific Limited; b. 9.11.33, Glasgow; m., 1, Diana MacDougall (m. diss.); 2, Jacqueline Mary Marr (m. diss.); 3, Marina Sevastopoulo; 2 s.; 1 d. Educ. Eton; Trinity College, Cambridge. Member, London Advisory Committee, Hongkong and Shanghai Banking Corporation, 1980-92; Deputy Chairman, Charterhouse J. Rothschild PLC, 1983-85; Member, Court, Bank of England, 1972-84; Co-Chairman, RIT and Northern PLC, 1982-83; Director, 1970, Chairman, 1975-82, Great Northern Investment Trust Ltd.; Member, Scottish Economic Council, 1972-85; Director, British Steel Corporation, 1972-76; Chairman, Patrons of National Galleries of Scotland, 1984-95; Member, Queen's Bodyguard for Scotland (Royal Company of Archers). Recreations: shooting; golf; fishing. Address: (h.) Rodinghead, Mauchline, Ayrshire.

Wells, Margaret J., MA, CQSW. Director of Housing and Social Work, Aberdeenshire, since 1995; b. 22.7.55, Berwick upon Tweed; m., Tony Wells. Educ. Berwickshire High School, Duns; Edinburgh University; Glasgow University. Social worker, Perth, 1977-87; Area Fieldwork Manager (Hospitals), Tayside, 1987-89; District Manager, Dundee, 1989-92; Assistant Director of Social Work, then Depute Director, Grampian, 1992-95. Recreation: singing. Address: (h.) 257 Union Grove, Aberdeen; T.-01224 665490.

Welsh, Andrew Paton, MA (Hons), DipEd. MP (SNP), Angus East, since 1987; National Vice-President, SNP, since 1987; b. 19.4.44, Glasgow; m., Sheena Margaret Cannon (see Sheena Margaret Welsh); 1 d. Educ. Govan High School; Glasgow University. Member, Stirling District Council, 1974; MP (SNP), South Angus, 1974-79; SNP Parliamentary Spokesman on Housing, 1974-78 and since 1987, Self-Employed and Small Businesses, 1975-79 and 1987-97, Agriculture, 1975-79 and 1987-97, Education, since 1997; Parliamentary Chief Whip, 1977-79 and since 1987; Member, Select Committee on Members' Interests, 1989-92; Member, House of Commons Chairmen's Panel, since 1997; Member, Scottish Affairs Committee, since 1992; SNP Executive Vice Chairman for Administration, 1979-83, for Local Government, 1984-87; Parliamentary candidate, East Angus, 1983; Member, Church and Nation Committee, Church of Scotland, 1984-85; Member, Dundee University Court, 1984-87; Provost, Angus District Council, 1984-87; Member, Angus District Health Council; Member, SCOTVEC Public Administration and Moderating Committees. Recreations: music; horse riding. Address: (h.) Montquhir, Carmyllie, Arbroath; T.-01241 860317.

Welsh, Frederick Wright, JP. Member, Dundee City Council, since 1995; Spokesperson, Joint Boards (Police, Fire, Valuation); Director/Chairman, Taywide Services, Dundee, since 1991; Member, Central Advisory Committee on Justices of the Peace, since 1991; Member, Justices Committee, Dundee District; Member, Scottish Housing Forum; Vice-Chair, Post Office and Telecommunications Advisory Committee for Tayside; b. Dundee; m., Margaret; 3 s. Educ. Rockwell Secondary School, Dundee. Member, Dundee Corporation, 1973-75 (Convener, Public Libraries, Museums and Art Galleries, 1973-75); Member, Tayside Regional Council, 1974-77 (Labour Group Chief Whip and Further Education Opposition Spokesman, 1974-77); Member, Dundee District Council, 1977-95 (Chairman, Community Services Committee, 1990-95, Convener of Housing, 1992-95); Director, Local Government Information Unit, 1991-92; National Chair, Association of Direct Labour Organisations, 1991-92; Chair, Dundee East Constituency Labour Party; Member, Central Committee, Gas Consumers Council for Scotland; Member, Perth Prison Visiting Committee; Member, Management Committee, Dundee Resources Centre for Unemployed; Chairman, ADLO Scottish Region and Member, National Council, ADLO; Vice Convener, COSLA Miscellaneous Services Committee; Depute Chair, Heat Development (Dundee) Ltd., since 1986; Member, Fire Services Scotland Examination Board, 1973-75; Member, British Standards Institute OC/4 Committee. Recreations: gardening; DIY; watching all sports; walking. Address: (h.) 2 McKinnon Street, Dundee DD3 6JN; T.-01382 27669.

Welsh, Ian, MA (Hons), MA, DPSE, FRSA. Leader, South Ayrshire Council; Chief Executive, Kilmarnock Football Club; Director, Enterprise Ayrshire; Director, Ayr College; b. 23.11.53, Ayr; m., Elizabeth; 2 s. Educ. Prestwick Academy; Ayr Academy; Glasgow University; Jordanhill College; Open University. Councillor, Kyle and Carrick, 1984-95, Leader, 1990-92. Former Governor, Craigie College of Education; former professional footballer; former Director of Human Resources and Public Affairs, Glasgow Prestwick International Airport; Director, Prestwick International Airport, since 1992; Director, Borderline Theatre Company, since 1990; Member, Council, National Trust for Scotland; Member, COSLA Strategy Forum; Chair, Ayrshire Economic Forum; Chair, North Ayr Partnership. Recreations: reading non-fiction, crime fiction. Address: (h.) 35 Ayr Road, Prestwick, Ayrshire; T.-01292 476502.

Wemyss and March, Earl of (Francis David Charteris), KT (1966), Hon. LLD (St. Andrews), Hon. DUniv (Edinburgh), JP, BA. Lord Lieutenant, East Lothian, 1967-87; b. 19.1.12, London; m., Mavis Lynette Gordon Murray (deceased); 1 s.; 1 d.; 1 s. (deceased); 1 d. (deceased); 2, Shelagh Kennedy. Educ. Eton; Balliol College, Oxford. Commissioned, Lovat Scouts (TA), 1932-44; Basutoland Administrative Service, 1937-44; War Service, African Auxiliary Pioneer Corps, Middle East, 1941-44; Chairman, Council, National Trust for Scotland, 1947-67 (President, 1967-91, President Emeritus, 1991); Chairman, Scottish Churches Council, 1964-71; Chairman, Royal Commission on Ancient and Historical Monuments of Scotland, 1949-84; Vice-President, Marie Curie Memorial Foundation; President, Royal Scottish Geographical Society, 1958-62; President, National Bible Society of Scotland, 1960-83; Lieutenant, Queen's Bodyguard for Scotland (Royal Company of Archers). Recreations: countryside and conservation. Address: (h.) Gosford House, Longniddry, East Lothian EH32 0PX; T.-01875 870200.

West, Professor Anthony Roy, BSc, PhD, DSc, CChem, FRSC, FIM, FRSE. Professor of Chemistry, Aberdeen University, since 1989; b. 21.1.47, Sandwich; m., Sheena Cruickshank; 1 s.; 1 d. Educ. Harvey Grammar School, Folkestone; University College Swansea; Aberdeen University. Lecturer, 1971, Senior Lecturer, 1984, Reader, 1986, Professor, 1989, Aberdeen University; Visiting Professor: National University of Mexico, 1976-77, University of Stockholm, 1986, Moscow State University, 1991, Tokyo Institute of Technology, 1993, University of Barcelona, 1996, University of Bahia Blanca, 1997; Founding Editor, Journal of Materials Chemistry, 1991-94; Founding Chairman, Materials Chemistry Forum, since 1993; Member, various Engineering and Physical Sciences Research Council committees, since 1989; Member, SEB Chemistry Panel, 1990-96. Recreations: athletics; gardening. Address: (b.) Department of Chemistry, Meston Walk, Aberdeen AB24 3UE; T.-01224 272918.

West, Peter William Alan, MA, DUniv. Secretary to the University, Strathclyde University, since 1990; b. 16.3.49, Edinburgh; m., Margaret Clark; 1 s.; 1 d. Educ. Edinburgh Academy; St. Andrews University. Administrator, Edinburgh University, 1972-77; Assistant Secretary, Leeds University, 1977-83; Deputy Registrar, Strathclyde

University, 1983-89. Doctor of the University of Rostov. Recreations: supporting Scotland's leading football team (Hibernian) through thick and thin. Address: (b.) Strathclyde University, McCance Building, 16 Richmond Street, Glasgow G1 1XQ; T.-0141-548 2001.

West, Professor Thomas Summers, CBE, BSc, PhD, DSc, FRSC, FRSE, FRS. Emeritus Professor of Chemistry, Aberdeen University; former Director, Macaulay Institute for Soil Research, Aberdeen; b. 18.11.27, Peterhead; m., Margaret O. Lawson; 1 s.; 2 d. Educ. Tarbat School, Portmahomack; Tain Royal Academy; Aberdeen University; Birmingham University. Lecturer in Chemistry, Birmingham University, 1955-63; Imperial College of Science and Technology, London: Reader in Chemistry, 1963-65, Professor of Chemistry, 1965-75. Meldola Medal, Royal Institute of Chemistry; Gold Medal, Society of Analytical Chemistry; President, Society for Analytical Chemistry, 1969-71; Honorary Secretary, Royal Society of Chemistry, 1972-75; President, Analytical Division, International Union of Pure and Applied Chemistry, 1979-81; Secretary General, IUPAC, 1983-91; Honorary Research Professor, Aberdeen University, 1983-87; Chairman, Royal Society, Intrenational Exchanges, Panel III. Recreations: gardening; motoring; reading; music; family history research. Address:(h.) 31 Baillieswells Drive, Bieldside, Aberdeen AB15 9AT; T.-01224 868294.

Westcott, Michael John Herbert, BSc (Hons) (Glasgow), Hon. MA (Edinburgh). Chairman, Management Committee, The Ark (providing food for those caught in the poverty trap); retired Assistant Secretary, Edinburgh University; b. 16.4.19, Plymouth. Educ. Hillhead High School; Glasgow University. Ministry of Home Grown Timber Production, 1940-43; Army (Royal Signals), 1943-48 (retired as Major); Colonial Service, Sierra Leone (Administrative Officer), 1948-61; Administrative Officer, Edinburgh University, 1962-86. Honorary Vice-President, National Youth Music Theatre; Honorary President, Edinburgh and SE Scotland VSO Group. Recreations: walking; theatre; music. Address: (h.) 2 Kilgraston Court, Kilgraston Road, Edinburgh EH9 2ES; T.-0131-447 8282.

Whalley, David William McRae, BEM. Chairman, Scottish Mountain Rescue Committee, since 1998 (Member, Executive Committee, since 1990); b. 17.12.52, Ayr. Educ. Belmont Academy; Mainholm High School. Member, Scottish Mountain Rescue and RAF Mountain Rescue, since 1973; Mountain Rescue Team Leader, RAF Leuchars, 1986-89; Team Leader, RAF Kinloss, 1989-92; has attended over 600 mountain rescues and over 50 aircraft crashes over 26 years (Senior Team Leader, Lockerbie aircraft disaster); awarded two Commendations for Services to Mountain Rescue. Recreations: mountaineering; football; golf; tennis; photography; squash. Address: (h.) 92 Forbeshill, Forres, Moray IV36 1YL; T.-01309 674181.

Whatley, Professor Christopher Allan, BA, PhD, FRHistS. Professor in Scottish History and Head, Department of Modern History, Dundee University, since 1995; b. 29.5.48, Birmingham; 1 s.; 1 d. Educ. Bearsden Academy; Strathclyde University. Lecturer, Ayr College, 1975-79, Dundee University, 1979-88, St. Andrews University, 1988-92, Dundee University, 1992-94; Senior Lecturer, 1994. Editor, Scottish Economic and Social History; Chairman, SCCC Review Group, Scottish History in the Curriculum. Publications: The Industrial Revolution in Scotland; The Scottish Salt Industry, 1570-1850; Onwards from Osnaburgs: the rise and progress of a Scottish textile company; Bought and Sold for English Gold?: explaining the union of 1707; The Manufacture of Scottish History (Co-editor); The Life and Times of Dundee (Co-author); The Remaking of Juteopolis: Dundee 1891-1991 (Editor); John Galt. Recreations: walking; watching Dundee United FC; theatre. Address: (h.) Tayfield Cottage, Main Street, Longforgan, by Dundee DD2 5EW; T.-01382 360794.

Wheater, Professor Roger John, OBE, CBiol, FIBiol, FRSA, FRSGS (Hon), FRSE. Director, Royal Zoological Society of Scotland, 1972-98; Honorary Professor, Edinburgh University, since 1993; b. 24.11.33, Brighton; m., Jean Ord Troup; 1 s.; 1 d. Educ. Brighton, Hove and Sussex Grammar School; Brighton Technical College. Commissioned, Royal Sussex Regiment, 1953; served Gold Coast Regiment, 1953-54; 4/5th Bn., Royal Sussex Regiment (TA), 1954-56; Colonial Police, Uganda, 1956-61; Chief Warden, Murchison Falls National Park, 1961-70; Director, Uganda National Parks, 1970-72; Member, Co-ordinating Committee, Nuffield Unit of Tropical Animal Ecology; Member, Board of Governors, Mweka College of Wildlife Management, Tanzania; Director, National Park Lodges Ltd.; Member, Uganda National Research Council; Vice Chairman, Uganda Tourist Association; Council Member, 1980, and President, 1988-91, International Union of Directors of Zoological Gardens; Chairman, Federation of Zoological Gardens of Great Britain and Ireland, 1993-96; Chairman, Anthropoid Ape Advisory Panel, 1977-91; Member, International Zoo Year Book Editorial Board, since 1987; President, Association of British Wild Animal Keepers, since 1984; Chairman, Membership and Licensing Committee, 1984-91; Chairman, Working Party on Zoo Licensing Act, 1981-84; Council Member, Zoological Society of London, 1991-92, since 1995, Vice President, since 1999; Member, Board, Whipsnade Wild Animal Park; Vice-President, World Pheasant Association, since 1994; Trustee Dian Fossey Gorilla Fund, since 1995; Chairman, European Association of Zoos and Aquaria, 1994-97; Member of Council, National Trust for Scotland, 1973-78, Executive Committee, 1982-87; Chairman, Cammo Estate Advisory Committee, 1980-95; ESU William Thyne Scholar, 1975 (Trustee, Thyne Scholarship, since 1997); Assessor, Council, Scottish Wildlife Trust, 1973-92; Consultant, World Tourist Organisation (United Nations), since 1980; Member, Secretary of State for Scotland's Working Group on Environmental Education, 1990-94; Board Member, Scottish Natural Heritage, since 1995 (Deputy Chairman, since 1997); Chairman, Access Forum, since 1996; Founder Patron, Dynamic Earth, since 1994; Vice-Chairman, Edinburgh Branch, English Speaking Union, 1977-81; President, Edinburgh Special Mobile Angling Club, 1982-86; President, Cockburn Trout Angling Club, since 1997. Recreations: country pursuits; painting; gardening. Address: (h.) 26 Dovecot Road, Edinburgh EH12 6LE; T.-0131-334 9171.

Wheatley, Sheriff John Francis, QC, BL. Sheriff, Perthshire and Kinross-shire, at Perth, since 1980; b. 9.5.41, Edinburgh; m., Bronwen Catherine Fraser; 2 s. Educ. Mount St. Mary's College, Derbyshire; Edinburgh University. Called to Scottish Bar, 1966; Standing Counsel to Scottish Development Department, 1968-74; Advocate Depute, 1974-78. Recreations: music; gardening. Address: Braefoot Farmhouse, Fossoway, Kinross-shire; T.-Fossoway 212.

Wheeler, Sir (Harry) Anthony, Kt (1988), OBE, PPRSA, Hon. RA, Hon. RHA, Hon. RGI, Hon. DDes, Hon. RBS, PPRIAS, FRIBA, FRSA, BArch, MRTPI, DipTP. Consultant, Wheeler & Sproson, Architects and Town Planners, Edinburgh and Kirkcaldy, since 1986; Hon. President, Saltire Society, since 1995; b. 7.11.19, Stranraer; m., Dorothy Jean Campbell; 1 d. Educ. Stranraer High School; Glasgow School of Architecture; Strathclyde University. War Service, Royal Artillery, 1939-46; John Keppie Scholar and Sir Rowand Anderson Studentship, RIBA Grissell Medallist, Neale Bursar; Assistant to City Architect, Oxford, to Sir Herbert Baker & Scott, London; Senior Architect, Glenrothes Development Corporation; began private practice in Fife; Senior Lecturer, Dundee School of Architecture, 1952-58; Saltire Awards and

Commendations (22), Civic Trust Awards and Commendations (12); Trustee, Scottish Civic Trust, 1970-83; Member, Royal Fine Art Commission for Scotland, 1967-85; President, Royal Scottish Academy, 1983-90. Recreations: sketching and water colours; fishing; music; drama; gardens. Address: (h.) Hawthornbank House, Dean Village, Edinburgh EH4 3BH.

Wheeler, Professor Simon Jonathan, MA, DPhil, CEng, MICE. Cormack Professor of Civil Engineering, Glasgow University, since 1996; b. 30.4.58, Warlingham, Surrey; m., Noelle Patricia O'Rourke; 2 d. Educ. Whitehaven Grammar School; St. John's College, Cambridge; Balliol College, Oxford. University Lecturer in Soil Mechanics, Queen's University of Belfast, 1984-88; Lecturer in Soil Mechanics, Sheffield University, 1988-92; Lecturer in Civil Engineering, Oxford University, and Fellow of Keble College, Oxford, 1992-95. Committee Member, British Geotechnical Society, Scottish Geotechnical Group. Recreation: mountaineering. Address: (b.) Department of Civil Engineering, Rankine Building, Glasgow G12 8LT; T.-0141-330 5202.

Wherrett, Professor Brian Spencer, BSc, PhD, FInstP, FRSE. Chair of Theoretical Physics, Heriot-Watt University, since 1986; b. 8.5.46, Bromley; m., Shirley Ruth; 1 s.; 1 d. Educ. Westcliff High School; Reading University. Lecturer, Department of Physics, Heriot-Watt University, 1971; promoted to Senior Lecturer and Reader; Visiting Professor, North Texas State University, 1981-82; Past Chairman, SERC Committee on Atomic, Molecular and Plasma Physics and Optical Sciences. Recreation: golf. Address: (b.) Department of Physics, Heriot-Watt University, Riccarton, Edinburgh EH14 4AS; T.-0131-451 3039.

White, Iain, BSc (Hons), MEd, MIBiol, CBiol. Head Teacher, Govan High School, Glasgow, since 1994; b. 2.2.54, Greenock; m., Gail. Educ. Greenock High School; Glasgow University. Biology Teacher, then Principal Biology Teacher, Cowdenknowes High School, Greenock, 1977-87; Assistant Rector, Rothesay Academy, 1987-92; Depute Head Teacher, Port Glasgow High School, 1992-94. Captain, Greenock Golf Club. Recreations: golf; skiing; travel; watching football; Robert Burns; after-dinner speaking. Address: (b.) Govan High School, 12 Ardnish Street, Glasgow G51 4NB; T.-0141-445 4464.

White, Michael, MA (Hons), CertEd, MIPD. Director of Education and Recreation, Aberdeenshire Council, since 1995; b. 3.7.47, Llwynpia; 3 s. Educ. Grangemouth High School; Falkirk High School; Edinburgh University. Teacher, 1969-77; Headteacher, 1977-84; Divisional Education Officer, Grampian, 1984-90; Assistant Director, Dumfries and Galloway Regional Council, 1990-95. Recreations: sport; pop music; hospital radio; football history. Address: (b.) Woodhill House, Westburn Road, Aberdeen, AB16 5GB; T.-01224 665420.

White, Norman Hugh, CA. Honorary Sheriff, since 1983; b. 19.7.31, Liverpool; m., Fiona Shearer; 2 d. Educ. Hillhead High School. National Service (2nd Lt., Highland Light Infantry), 1957-58; employed in a professional capacity, 1959-66; Partner, Victor T. Fraser and Co., CA, 1966-94. Former Member, Supplementary Benefits Appeals Tribunal. Recreations: golf; travel. Address: (h.) 7 West Park, Wick, Caithness KW1 5QE; T.-01955 603162.

White, Paul Charles, BA, IPFA, MBA. Director of Finance/Deputy General Manager, Lothian Health Board, since 1993; b. 9.8.49, Londonderry; m., Alison Perry (deceased); 4 d. Educ. St. Columb's College, Londonderry; Queen's University, Belfast; Henley Business School. Director of Finance and Information, Western Health Board, N.I., 1985-90; General Manager, Altnagelvin Group of Hospitals, Londonderry, 1990-93. Recreations: family; cooking. Address: (h.) 13 Macnair Avenue, North Berwick, East Lothian.

White, Professor Stephen Leonard, MA, PhD, DPhil. Professor of Politics, Glasgow University, since 1991; b. 1.7.45, Dublin; m., Ishbel MacPhie; 1 s. Educ. St. Andrew's College, Dublin; Trinity College, Dublin; Glasgow University; Wolfson College, Oxford. Lecturer in Politics, Glasgow University, 1971-85, Reader, 1985-91; Head of Department, 1992-98. President, British Association for Slavonic and East European Studies, 1994-97; General Editor, Cambridge Russian, Soviet and Post-Soviet Series; Chief Editor, Journal of Communist Studies and Transition Politics. Publications include: Political Culture and Soviet Politics, 1979; Britain and the Bolshevik Revolution, 1980; Origins of Detente, 1986; The Bolshevik Poster, 1988; After Gorbachev, 1993; Russia Goes Dry, 1996; How Russia Votes (with others), 1996; Values and Political Change in Postcommunist Europe (with others), 1998. Address: (h.) 11 Hamilton Drive, Glasgow G12 8DN; T.-0141-334 9541.

Whitehead, Professor Rex Raymond, MSc, PhD, DSc, FRSE. Clerk of Senate, University of Glasgow, since 1996; Professor of Theoretical Physics, University of Glasgow, since 1986; b. 30.5.41, Melbourne, Australia; m., Hilary Joan; 1 s.; 1 d. Educ. Essendon High School; University of Melbourne. University of Glasgow: Research Fellow, 1967-70, Lecturer in Theoretical Physics, 1970-78, Reader, 1978-86; Dean, Faculty of Science, 1994-96. Address: (b.) Senate Office, University of Glasgow, Glasgow G12 8QQ; T.-0141-330 4242.

Whitelaw, Brian Murray, LLB, DipLP, MIMgt, NP. Caithness Area Manager, The Highland Council, since 1995; Clerk to Lord Lieutenant of Caithness; Depute Chief Executive, Caithness District Council, 1990-95; Solicitor and Notary Public; b. 25.12.53, Glasgow; m., Joan Harte; 1 s.; 2 d. Educ. St. Columba's, Clydebank; Strathclyde University. Trainee Solicitor, Joseph Mellick, Solicitors, Glasgow, 1981-83; Assistant Solicitor, Borders Regional Council, 1983-85; Senior Solicitor, Dumbarton District Council, 1985-86; Principal Solicitor, Dumbarton District Council, 1986-90. Recreations: photography; cycling. Address: (b.) The Highland Council – Caithness, Market Square, Wick, KW1 4AB; T.-01955 607701.

Whitelaw, Robert George, MA, MD, FRCOG, DL. Deputy Lieutenant, Fife, since 1969; Honorary Sheriff, since 1978; b. 29.4.13, Motherwell; m., Cicely Mary Ballard; 1 s. Educ. Wishaw High School; Glasgow University. Consultant Obstetrician and Gynaecologist, West Fife Group of Hospitals, 1956-78; External Examiner, Edinburgh University, 1967-71; Examiner: Central Midwives Board for Scotland, General Nursing Council for Scotland, Royal College of Surgeons of Edinburgh, PLAB. Past President, Fife Branch, BMA; Past President, Dunfermline Rotary Club. Publications: various papers, mainly on obstetrical and gynaecological subjects. Recreations: golf; photography; travel. Address: (h.) 64 Garvock Hill, Dunfermline, Fife KY12 7UU; T.-01383 721209.

Whiteman, Professor Arthur John, BSc, PhD. Professor Emeritus, Aberdeen University, since 1993; Professor of Petroleum Geology, 1974-93; b. 1.1.28, Ormskirk; m., Sally Janet Pettet; 2 s.; 2 d. Educ. University College, London; Stanford University; Columbia University. Geologist, Humble Oil and Refining Co. Research Fellowship, Columbia University, 1949-51; Geologist, HM Geologist Survey, Great Britain, 1951-56; Exploration Geologist, Compagnie Des Petroles D'Algerie, Royal Dutch Shell, 1956-60; Consultant Petroleum Geologist, since 1960; Professor of Geology, Khartoum, 1960-68; Professor of Petroleum Geology, Ibadan University, 1968-72; Professor of Petroleum Geology, Bergen University, 1972-74.

Publications: Geology of Sudan Republic, 1971; Nigeria: Its Petroleum Geology, Resources and Potential, 1982; Rift Systems — Hydrocarbon Habitat and Potential, 1989. Recreation: gardening; water colour. Address: (h.) Garden Cottage, Inchmarlo, Banchory AB31 4BT; T.-01330 825214.

Whiten, Professor David Andrew, BSc, PhD, FBPS. Professor of Evolutionary and Developmental Psychology, St. Andrews University, since 1997; b. 20.4.48, Grimsby; m., Dr. Susie Challoner; 2 d. Educ. Wintringham School, Grimsby; Sheffield University; Bristol University; Oxford University. Research Fellow, Oxford University, 1972-75; Lecturer, then Reader, St. Andrews University, 1975-97; Visiting Professor, Zurich University, 1992, Emory University, 1996. Publications: Machiavellian Intelligence (Co-author), 1988; Natural Theories of Mind, 1991; Foraging Strategies of Monkeys, Apes and Humans (Co-author), 1992; Machiavellian Intelligence II, 1997. Recreations: painting; walking; wildlife; good-lifing. Address: (b.) School of Psychology, St. Andrews University, St. Andrews KY16 9JU.

Whitley, Rev. Laurence Arthur Brown, MA, BD, PhD. Minister, Montrose Old Parish, since 1985 (Busby East and West, 1975-85); b. 19.9.49, Port Glasgow; m., Catherine MacLean MacFadyen; 1 s.; 1 d. Educ. Edinburgh Academy; Edinburgh University; St. Andrews University. Assistant Minister, St. Andrews, Dundee, 1974-75. Parliamentary candidate (SNP), Dumfriesshire, February and October, 1974. Recreation: Sesquipedalianism. Address: (h.) 2 Rosehill Road, Montrose, Angus DD10 8ST; T.-Montrose 672447.

Whittemore, Professor Colin Trengove, BSc, PhD, DSc, NDA, CBiol, FIBiol, FRSE. Head, Institute of Ecology and Resource Management, Edinburgh University, since 1990, and Professor of Agriculture and Rural Economy, since 1990; b. 16.7.42, Chester; m., Chris; 1 s.; 3 d. Educ. Rydal School; Newcastle-upon-Tyne University. Lecturer in Agriculture, Edinburgh University and Head, Animal Production, Advisory and Development, Edinburgh School of Agriculture; Professor of Animal Production, Head, Animal Division, Edinburgh School of Agriculture; Head, Department of Agriculture, Edinburgh University. Sir John Hammond Memorial Prize for scientific contribution to an understanding of nutrition and growth; President, British Society of Animal Science, 1998; Royal Agricultural Society of England Gold Medal for research; Mignini Oscar; David Black Award. Publications: author of five text books of animal sciences. Recreations: skiing; riding. Address: (b.) Edinburgh University, School of Agriculture, West Mains Road, Edinburgh EH9 3JG; T.-0131-667 1041.

Whoriskey, Margaret, BA (Hons), MPhil, PhD. Advisor, Disability Services, Scottish Health Advisory Services, since 1998; Mental Welfare Commissioner, since 1996; Clinical Psychologist, since 1980; b. 11.6.58, Galway, Ireland; m., Colin Harkins; 1 s.; 2 d. Educ. Dominican Convent, Galway; University College Galway; Edinburgh University; St. Andrews University. Clinical Psychologist: Galway, Ireland, 1980-82, Fife, 1982-93; Director of Clinical Psychology, Fife, 1993-98. Recreations: shopping; activities with children; Irish holidays; walking; keep fit; golf widow.

Whyte, Christopher, MA (Hons), PhD. Writer and Critic; Lecturer in Scottish Literature, Glasgow University, since 1990; b. 29.10.52, Glasgow. Educ. St. Aloysius College, Glasgow; Pembroke College, Cambridge. Lector, Rome University, 1977-85; Lecturer in English Literature, Edinburgh University, 1986-89. Publications: In The Face of Eternity: Eight Gaelic Poets, 1991; Uirsgeul/Myth, 1991; Euphemia MacFarrigle and the Laughing Virgin, 1995; Gendering the Nation, 1995; The Warlock of Strathearn, 1997; The Gay Decameron, 1998. Recreations: classical music; walking; cooking. Address: (h.) 15 Hart Street, Edinburgh EH1 3RN; T.-0131-558 3907.

Whyte, David James, MA. Rector, Golspie High School, since 1983; b. 21.2.40, Cupar; m., Judith; 4 s. Educ. Bell Baxter High School; St. Andrews University. Assistant Teacher of English, Strathallan School, 1964-67; Special Assistant, Kirkcaldy High School, 1967-69; Principal Teacher of English, Brechin High School, 1969-73; Assistant Headteacher, Arbroath Academy, 1973-79; Depute Rector, Peterhead Academy, 1979-83. British Athletics International, 1958-61; Scottish Rugby International, 1964-67; President, Rotary Club of East Sutherland, 1996. Recreations: bridge; tennis. Address: (b.) Golspie High School, Main Street, Golspie KW10 6RF; T.-01408 633451.

Whyte, Donald, JP, FHG, FSG. Consultant Genealogist, Author and Lecturer; b. 13.3.26, Newtongrange; m., Mary Burton; 3 d. Educ. Crookston School, Musselburgh; Institute of Heraldic and Genealogical Studies, Canterbury. Agricultural and horticultural work, 1940-68; professional genealogist, 1968-76; Member, Kirkliston and Winchburgh District Council, 1964-75 (Chairman, 1970-73); Member, West Lothian County Council, 1970-75; founder Member and Vice-President, Scottish Genealogy Society; President, Association of Scottish Genealogists and Record Agents, since 1981. Publications: Kirkliston: A Short Parish History; Dictionary of Scottish Emigrants to USA; Introducing Scottish Genealogical Research; Dictionary of Scottish Emigrants to Canada before Confederation, 2 vols; Walter MacFarlane: Clan Chief and Antiquary; Scottish Clock and Watchmakers, 1453-1900; Scottish Surnames and Families. Address: (h.) 4 Carmel Road, Kirkliston EH29 9DD; T.-0131-333 3245.

Whyte, Rev. Iain Alexander, BA, BD, STM. Chaplain, University of Edinburgh, since 1994; b. 3.9.40, Stirling; m., Isabel Helen Martin; 2 s.; 1 d. Educ. Sherborne School, Dorset; St. Peter's College, Oxford; Glasgow University; Union Theological Seminary, NY. Assistant Minister, Kildrum, Cumbernauld, 1967-69; Minister and Youth Worker in Ghana, 1969-71; Chaplain to Overseas Students in Glasgow, 1971-74; Lecturer, Falkirk Technical College, 1974-75; Minister, Merksworth Parish Church, Paisley, 1976-81; Chaplain, St. Andrews University, 1981-87; Minister, Blairhill Dundyvan Parish Church, Coatbridge, 1987-90; National Secretary for Scotland, Christian Aid, 1990-94. Scottish Churches Representative, Board, Christian Aid, 1980-86 (Chairman, Christian Aid Middle East Committee, 1982-86); Chairman, Scottish Churches Council Race and Community Relations Group, 1981-83; Scottish Representative, Britain/Zimbabwe Society; former Chair, Glasgow Anti-Apartheid Group. Recreations: travel; squash; watching St. Mirren; numismatics; candle-making. Address: (h.) 34 Shandon Crescent, Edinburgh EH11 1QF; T.-0131-337 0886.

Whyte, Iain Wilson, BA, DCE, DMS. Director and General Secretary, Church of Scotland Board of Parish Education, since 1993; b. 2.12.56, Johnstone; m., Elaine; 2 d. Educ. Paisley Grammar School; Jordanhill College; Open University. Adult Education Tutor, Glasgow, 1978-82; Development Officer, Priesthill, Glasgow, 1982-84; Adult Education Officer, European Social Fund Project, Strathclyde, 1984-86; Lecturer, Cardonald College, Glasgow, 1986-90, Senior Lecturer, 1990-93. Elder, Colinton Parish Church, Edinburgh. Recreations: playing guitar, piano, organ; singing; songwriting; golf. Address: (b.) 18 Inverleith Terrace, Edinburgh, EH3 5NS; T.-0131-332 0343.

Whyte, Rev. James, BD, DipCE. Parish Minister, Broom, Newton Mearns, since 1987; b. 26.4.46, Glasgow; m., Norma Isabella West; 1 s.; 2 d. Educ. Glasgow; Jordanhill College; Glasgow University. Trained as planning engineer;

studied community education (Glasgow and Boston, Mass., USA); Community Organiser with Lamp of Lothian Collegiate Trust, Haddington; Organiser of Community Education, Dumbarton, 1971-73; Assistant Principal Community Education Officer, Renfrew Division, Strathclyde Region, 1973-77; entered ministry, Church of Scotland, 1977; Assistant Minister: Barrhead Arthurlie, 1977-78, St. Marks, Oldhall, Paisley, 1978-80; Minister, Coupar Angus Abbey, 1981-87. Recreations: gardening; reading. Address: Manse of Broom, 3 Laigh Road, Newton Mearns, Glasgow G77; T.-0141-639 2916.

Whyte, Very Rev. Professor James Aitken, MA, LLD, DD, DUniv. Moderator, General Assembly of the Church of Scotland, 1988-89; Professor of Practical Theology and Christian Ethics, St. Andrews University, 1958-87; b. 28.1.20, Leith; m., 1, Elisabeth Wilson Mill (deceased); 2 s.; 1 d.; 2, Ishbel Christina Macaulay or Rathie. Educ. Daniel Stewart's College, Edinburgh; Edinburgh University. Ordained and commissioned as Chaplain to the Forces, 1945; Minister: Dunollie Road Church, Oban, 1948-54, Mayfield North Church, Edinburgh, 1954-58; Dean of Divinity, St. Andrews University, 1968-72; Principal, St. Mary's College, 1978-82; Kerr Lecturer, Glasgow University, 1969-72; Croall Lecturer, Edinburgh University, 1972-73; Hon. LLD, Dundee University, 1981; Hon.DD, St. Andrews University, 1989; Hon. DUniv., Stirling University, 1994; President, Society for the Study of Theology, 1983-84; Margaret Harris Lecturer, Dundee University, 1990. Publication: Laughter and Tears, 1993. Address: (h.) 13 Hope Street, St. Andrews, Fife; T.-St. Andrews 472323.

Whyte, Richard Brodie, LLB, DFM, SSC, NP. Solicitor Advocate, since 1995; Solicitor, since 1981; b. 1.8.47, Edinburgh; m., Gail; 2 s.; 1 d. Educ. Broxburn High School; Edinburgh University; Glasgow University. Principal in private practice, since 1983. Recreations: reading; golf; football; cinema; art galleries. Address: (b.) Lammermuir House, Livingston EH54 6NB; T.-01506 415281.

Whyte, Robert, MB, ChB, FRCPsych, DPM. Consultant Psychotherapist, Carswell House, Glasgow, since 1979; b. 1.6.41, Edinburgh; m., Susan Frances Milburn; 1 s.; 1 d. Educ. George Heriot's, Edinburgh; St. Andrews University. House Officer in Surgery, Arbroath Infirmary, 1966; House Officer in Medicine, Falkirk and District Royal Infirmary, 1967; Trainee in Psychiatry, Dundee Psychiatric Services, 1967-73; Consultant Psychiatrist, Duke Street Hospital, Glasgow, 1973. Past Chairman, Scottish Association of Psychoanalytical Psychotherapists; Member, Scottish Institute of Human Relations. Address: (h.) Waverley, 70 East Kilbride Road, Busby, Glasgow G76 8HU; T.-0141-644 1659.

Wickham-Jones, Caroline R., MA, MIFA, FSA, FSA Scot. Archaeologist; b. 25.4.55, Middlesborough; m.; 1 s. Educ. Teesside High School; Edinburgh University. Freelance archaeologist and author with research interests in early (postglacial) settlement of Scotland, stone tools, and the preservation of the cultural heritage; former Council Member, National Trust for Scotland; Council Member, Institute of Field Archaeologists, 1986-90; former Secretary, Society of Antiquaries of Scotland; former Trustee, John Muir Trust; Livery Woman of the City of London (Skinners Company). Publications: Scotland's First Settlers; Arthurs Seat and Holyrood Park, a Visitor's Guide. Recreations: travel; wilderness walking; socialising. Address: (h.) 21 Dudley Gardens, Edinburgh EH6 4PU.

Wight, Robin A.F., MA, FCA. Chairman, Arville Holdings, since 1995; b. 5.6.38, Edinburgh; m., Sheila; 3 s.; 1 d. Educ. Dollar Academy; Magdalene College, Cambridge. Partner, Coopers & Lybrand, 1971-96; Regional Partner, Scotland, 1977-95; Member, Executive Committee, 1978-87; Member, Governing Board, 1987-89; Member, Council, 1989-93. Recreations: skiing; golf; reading; theatre. Address: (h.) 22 Regent Terrace, Edinburgh; T.-0131-556 2100.

Wightman, John Watt, CVO, CBE, RD, MA, LLB, WS, NP. Chairman, Morton Fraser Partnership, since 1988; Solicitor to H. M. The Queen in Scotland, since 1984; Chairman, Craig & Rose PLC, since 1993; b. 20.11.33, Leith; m., Isla Macleod; 1 s.; 2 d. Educ. Daniel Stewart's College; St. Andrews University; Edinburgh University. Morton Fraser Partnership, since 1960 (Partner, then Finance Director). Commodore, Royal Naval Reserve, 1982-85; Chairman, Lowland TAVRA, 1992-95; Elder, St. George's West Church; Trustee: Sea Cadet Association, Douglas Haig Memorial Homes. Recreations: sailing; ornithology. Address: 19 York Place, Edinburgh EH1 3EL; T.-0131-550 1014.

Wightman, Very Rev. William David, BA (Hons). Provost, St. Andrews Cathedral, Aberdeen, since 1991, also Priest-in-Charge, St. Ninian's, Aberdeen; Hon. Canon, Christchurch Cathedral, Hartford, Conn., since 1991; b. 29.1.39, Leicester; m., Karen Elizabeth Harker; 2 s.; 2 d. Educ. Alderman Newton's Grammar School, Leicester; George Dixon Grammar School, Birmingham; Birmingham University; Wells Theological College. Ordained Deacon, 1963; ordained Priest, 1964. Director, Training for Ministry (Diocese of Aberdeen and Orkney), 1989-91. Recreations: fishing; swimming; choral music. Address: (h.) 15 Morningfield Road, Aberdeen AB15 4AP; T.-01224 314765.

Wilcox, Christine Alison, BA (Hons), ALA. Librarian, S.S.C. Library, Edinburgh, since 1991; b. 18.7.63, New Zealand; m., Michael Wilcox; 2 s.; 1 d. Educ. South Wilts Grammar School, Salisbury; Manchester Polytechnic Library School. Assistant Librarian, Barlow Lyde and Barlow Gilbert, Solicitors, London, 1984-86; Librarian, Beaumont and Son, Solicitors, London, 1986-89; posting to Bahrain accompanying husband, 1989-91. Secretary, Scottish Law Librarians Group, 1993-95. Publications: Directory of Legal Libraries in Scotland; Union List of Periodical and Law Report Holdings in Scotland. Recreations: needlework; hill-walking. Address: (b.) S.S.C. Library, 11 Parliament Square, Edinburgh EH1 1RF; T.-0131-225 6268.

Wild, John Robin, JP, BDS, DPD, FDSRCS(Edin), DGDP. Chief Dental Officer, Department of Health, since 1997; Chief Dental Officer, Scottish Office Department of Health, and Director of Dental Services for the NHS in Scotland, 1993-97 (Deputy Chief Dental Officer, 1987-93); b. 12.9.41, Scarborough; m., Eleanor Daphne Kerr; 1 s.; 2 d. Educ. Sedbergh School; Edinburgh University; Dundee University. General Dental Practitioner, Scarborough, 1965-71; Dental Officer, East Lothian, 1971-74;Chief Administrative Dental Officer, Borders Health Board, 1974-87; Regional Dental Postgraduate Adviser, S.E. Regional Committee for Postgraduate Medical Education, 1982-87; Hon. Senior Lecturer, Dundee Dental School, since 1993; JP for District of Ettrick and Lauderdale, since 1982; Past Chairman, Scottish Council, British Dental Association. Recreations: vintage cars (restoration and driving); music; gardening. Address: (h.) Braehead House, St. Boswells, Roxburghshire; T.-01835 823203.

Wildgoose, James Richmond, BSc, DPhil. Head of Food Safety and Standards Division, Scottish Office Agriculture, Environment and Fisheries Department; formerly Chief Agricultural Economist; b. 17.4.49, Edinburgh; m., Charlotte Dorothy; 1 s.; 1 d. Educ. Melville College; Edinburgh University; Oxford University. Economic Assistant/Economic Adviser, Ministry of Agriculture, Fisheries and Food, 1976-86; Administrative Principal, MAFF Tropical Foods Division, 1986-90; Admnistrative Principal, Scottish Office (SDD), 1990. Address: (b.) Room

352, Pentland House, Robb's Loan, Edinburgh; T.-0131-244 6128.

Wildsmith, Professor John Anthony Winston, MD, FRCA, FRCPEd. Foundation Professor of Anaesthesia, Dundee University, since 1995; Honorary Consultant Anaesthetist, Dundee Teaching Hospitals, since 1995; b. 22.2.46, Newent, Glos; m., Angela Fay Smith; 3 d. Educ. King's School, Gloucester; Edinburgh University Medical School. Spent greater part of early professional career in Edinburgh, either at University or Royal Infirmary, apart from a year at Brigham and Women's Hospital, Boston, USA; final post in Edinburgh, Consultant/Senior Lecturer; Clinical Director for Anaesthetics, Intensive Care and Operating Theatres, Royal Infirmary, Edinburgh, 1992-95. Member, Council, Royal College of Anaesthetists; Member, Editorial Board, British Journal of Anaesthesia. Recreations: golf; wine; travel. Address: (b.) University Department of Anaesthesia, Ninewells Hospital and Medical School, Dundee DD1 9SY; T.-01382 632427.

Wilkie, Alex Joseph. Managing Director, Radio Tay Ltd., since 1991; Treasurer, Association of Fife Youth Football Clubs, since 1996; b. 8.7.48, Stirling; m., Jill; 2 s. Educ. Royal High School of Stirling; Falkirk Technical College; Telford College. Sterlini Radio Ltd., 1963-69; Graham and Morton, 1969-70; Callander Park College (CCTV), 1970-74; Radio Forth Ltd., 1974-86. Recreations: boating; fishing; clay pigeon shooting; youth football; reading. Address: (h.) 21 Glamis Gardens, Dalgety Bay, Fife KY11 5TD; T.-01383 823600.

Wilkie, Rev. James Lindsay, MA, BD. Secretary for relations with churches in Africa, Board of World Mission, Church of Scotland, 1984-98; b. 30.1.34, Dunfermline; m., Dr. Irene A. Wilkie; 1 s.; 3 d. Educ. Aberdeen Grammar School; Aberdeen University and Christ's College. Assistant Minister, St. Machar's Cathedral, Aberdeen, 1959-60; District Missionary and Minister, United Church of Zambia, 1961-70; Chaplain, University of Zambia, 1970-76; Africa Secretary, then Divisional Secretary and Deputy General Secretary, British Council of Churches, 1976-84; member of team which translated Bible into Chinamwanga language of Zambia. Recreation: DIY. Address: (h.) 7 Comely Bank Avenue, Edinburgh EH4 1EW; T.-0131-343 1552.

Wilkie, Neil Keith, OBE, MA (Hons), FRSA. Headmaster, Gairloch High School, since 1978; b. 5.4.39, Perth; m., Margaret Rawlinson; 1 s. Educ. Perth Academy; Dundee University; Dundee College of Education; East of Scotland College of Agriculture. Sugar planter, Trinidad, six years; resumed academic studies, 1966; Teacher of History and Modern Studies, then Principal Teacher of History, Golspie High School, 1972-78. Elder, Gairloch and Dundonnell Parish Church; Member, Gairloch Community Council. Recreations: sport; travel; gardening. Address: (h.) Rohallion, Achtercairn, Gairloch, Ross-shire; T.-01445 712221.

Wilkie, Professor (William) Roy, MA. Emeritus Professor, Department of Human Resource Management, Strathclyde University, since 1974; b. 10.6.30, Rutherglen; m., Jill Henzell; 1 s.; 3 d. Educ. Rutherglen Academy; Aberdeen University. Lecturer and Senior Lecturer, Department of Administration, Strathclyde University, 1963-66; Director, J. & J. Denholm (Management) Ltd., 1966-70; Reader and Head, Department of Administration, Strathclyde University, 1966-73. Publications: The Concept of Organization, 1974; Managing the Police, 1986. Recreations: swimming; movies; jazz; reading. Address: (b.) Graham Hill Building, 50 Richmond Street, Glasgow; T.-0141-552 4400.

Wilkin, Andrew, BA, MA, MIL. Senior Lecturer in Italian Studies, University of Strathclyde, since 1986; b. 30.5.44, Farnborough; m., Gaynor Carole Gray; 1 s.; 1 d. Educ. Royal Naval School, Malta; University of Manchester; Open University. Assistant Lecturer, then Lecturer in Italian Studies, University of Strathclyde, 1967-86; Associate Dean, Faculty of Arts and Social Sciences, 1986-93; Course Director, BA European Studies, 1989-97. Governor, Craigie College of Education, 1985-91; Editor, Tuttitalia, 1992-97; Member, Modern Languages Panel, UCAS Scotland, since 1993. Publications: Harrap's Italian Verbs (Compiler), 1990; G. Verga, Little Novels of Sicily (Editor), 1973; 25 Years Emancipation? – Women in Switzerland 1971-96 (Co-Editor), 1997. Invested Cavaliere dell'Ordine al Merito della Repubblica Italiana, 1975. Recreations: travel; reading; Scottish History; supporting Partick Thistle F. C. Address: (b.) Department of Modern Languages, University of Strathclyde, Glasgow G1 1XH; T.-0141-548 3914.

Wilkins, Professor Malcolm Barrett, BSc, PhD, DSc, AKC, FRSE. Regius Professor of Botany, Glasgow University, since 1970 (Dean, Faculty of Science, 1985-87; Member, University Court, since 1993); b.27.2.33, Cardiff; m., Mary Patricia Maltby; 1 s.; 1 d. (deceased). Educ. Monkton House School, Cardiff; King's College, London University. Lecturer in Botany, King's College, London, 1958-64; Lecturer in Biology, then Professor of Biology, East Anglia University, 1964-67; Professor of Plant Physiology, Nottingham University, 1967-70. Rockefeller Foundation Fellow, Yale University, 1961-62; Corporation Research Fellow, Harvard University, 1962-63; Darwin Lecturer, British Association for the Advancement of Science, 1967; elected Corresponding (Honorary) Member, American Society of Plant Physiologists, 1984; Chairman, Life Science Working Group, European Space Agency, 1987-89; Trustee, Royal Botanic Garden, Edinburgh, since 1990, Chairman, since 1994; Vice President, Royal Society of Edinburgh, since 1994; Member, Advisory Council, Scottish Agricultural College, since 1992. Recreations: sailing; fishing; model engineering. Address: (b.) Botany Department, Glasgow University, Glasgow G12 8QQ; T.-0141-330 4450.

Wilkinson, Sheriff Alexander Birrell, QC, MA, LLB. Sheriff of Lothian and Borders at Edinburgh (formerly of Glasgow and Strathkelvin at Glasgow); Temporary Judge, Court of Session, since 1993; b. 2.2.32, Perth; m., Wendy Imogen Barrett; 1 s.; 1 d. Educ. Perth Academy; St. Andrews University; Edinburgh University. Advocate, 1959; practised at Scottish Bar, 1959-69; Lecturer in Scots Law, Edinburgh University, 1965-69; Sheriff of Stirling, Dunbarton and Clackmannan, at Stirling and Alloa, 1969-72; Professor of Private Law, Dundee University, 1972-86 (Dean, Faculty of Law, 1974-76 and 1986); Sheriff of Tayside, Central and Fife at Falkirk, 1986-91; a Chairman, Industrial Tribunals (Scotland), 1972-86; Chancellor, Dioceses of Brechin, 1990-98, and of Argyll and the Isles, 1985-98, Scottish Episcopal Church; Chairman, Scottish Marriage Guidance Council, 1974-77; Chairman, Legal Services Group, Scottish Association of CAB, 1979-83; President, The Sheriffs' Association, since 1997. Publications: Gloag and Henderson's Introduction to the Law of Scotland, 8th and 9th editions (Co-editor); The Scottish Law of Evidence; The Law of Parent and Child in Scotland (Co-author). Recreations: collecting books and pictures; reading; travel.

Wilkinson, Professor Paul, MA. Professor of International Relations, St. Andrews University; Writer on conflict and terrorism; b. 9.5.37, Harrow, Middlesex; m., Susan; 2 s.; 1 d. Educ. John Lyon School; University College, Swansea; University of Wales. RAF, 1959-65; Assistant Lecturer in Politics, University College, Cardiff, 1966-68; University of Wales: Lecturer, 1968-75, Senior Lecturer, 1975-77, Reader in Politics, 1978-79; Professor of International Relations, Aberdeen University, 1979-89; Editor, Terrorism and Political Violence; Member, Editorial Board, Security Handbook, Social Intelligence, and Violence and

Aggression; Editor, Key Concepts in International Relations; Scottish Free Enterprise Award, 1982; Honorary Fellow, University College, Swansea, 1986; Special Consultant, CBS America, 1989-90, BBC, since 1989; Aviation Security Adviser to IFAPA, 1988; Safety Adviser, World Tourism and Travel Council; FRSA, 1995; Visiting Fellow, Trinity Hall, Cambridge, 1997-98. Publications: Social Movement, 1971; Political Terrorism, 1974; Terrorism and the Liberal State, 1986 (revised edition); The New Fascists, 1983; Terrorism: Theory and Practice (Co-author), 1979; British Perspectives on Terrorism (Editor), 1981; Contemporary Research on Terrorism (Joint Editor), 1987; Technology and Terrorism (Editor), 1994; Terrorism: British Perspectives (Editor), 1993; Research Report for Inquiry into Legislation Against Terrorism, Vol. II, 1996; Aviation Terrorism and Security (Joint Editor). Recreations: modern art; poetry; walking. Address: (b.) Department of International Relations, St. Andrews University, St. Andrews KY16 9AL; T.-01334 462900.

Wilkinson, (William) Roderick, DAA, FIPM. Novelist and Scriptwriter; b. 31.3.17, Glasgow; 1 s.; 2 d. Educ. North Kelvinside Secondary, Glasgow. Director of advertising agency, 1946-59; Director of Personnel, 1959-80. Publications: 10 books, fiction and non-fiction; plays, articles and stories. Recreation: fishing. Address: (h.) 61 Norwood Park, Bearsden, Glasgow G61 2RZ; T.-0141-570 1689.

Wilks, Antony Hugh Francis, MBE, FNI. Chairman, Scottish Coastal Forum; Chairman, Forth Estuary Forum; Member, Board, Scottish Environment Protection Agency (East); Member, Board, Scottish Natural Heritage (East); Direct, CoastNet; b. 29.12.36, Watford; m., Susan Chaloner Reed; 1 s.; 1 d. Educ. Oundle. Royal Navy, 1958-90, latterly Naval Base Commander, Rosyth, 1985-90. Contributor, The Naval Review; knighthood, State of Brunei. Recreations: lawn tennis and rackets. Address: (b.) Easter Fossoway, Kinross-shire KY13 0PA; T.-01577 840255.

Will, David Houston, BL, NP. Vice-President, FIFA, since 1990; Chairman, FIFA Referees Committee, and Legal Matters Committee; Member, FIFA Executive Committee, World Cup Organising Committee and Security Committee; b. 20.11.36, Glasgow; m., Margaret; 2 d. Educ. Brechin High School; Edinburgh University. Chairman, Brechin City FC, 1966-91; appointed to SFA Council, 1970; President, SFA, 1984-89; Vice-President, UEFA, 1986-90. Recreations: golf; curling. Address: (h.) Norandale, 32 Airlie Street, Brechin, Angus; T.-01356 622273.

Will, Professor Robert George, MA, MD, MB BChir, FRCPE, FRCP, FRSA. Consultant Neurologist, Western General Hospital NHS Trust, Edinburgh, since 1987; Director, National Creutzfeldt-Jakob Disease Surveillance Unit, since 1990; Professor of Clinical Neurology, University of Edinburgh, since 1998; b. 30.7.50, Glasgow; m., Jayne; 1 s.; 1 d. Educ. Trinity College Glenalmond; Cambridge University. National Hospital for Nervous Diseases: Registrar in Neurosurgery, 1978-79, Senior House Officer, 1979; Honorary Registrar in Neurology, Department of Clinical Neurology, University of Oxford, 1979-82; Registrar in Neurology/Psychiatry, St. Thomas's Hospital, 1982-83; Registrar in Neurology, National Hospital for Nervous Diseases, 1983-85; Senior Registrar in Neurology, National Hospital for Nervous Diseases/Guy's Hospital, 1985-87. Publications: scientific papers on Creutzfeldt-Jakob disease; Member, Spongiform Encephalopathy Advisory Committee, 1990-98 (Deputy Chairman, 1994-98). Recreations: travel; cinema. Address: (h.) 4 Saint Catherine's Place, Edinburgh EH9 1NU; T.-0131-667 3667.

Willett, Emeritus Professor Frank, CBE, MA, FRSE. Hon. Senior Research Fellow, since 1990, Director, Hunterian Museum & Art Gallery, Glasgow, 1976-90; b. 18.8.25, Bolton; m., Mary Constance Hewitt; 1 s.; 3 d. Educ. Bolton Municipal Secondary School; University College, Oxford. Keeper of Ethnology and General Archaeology, Manchester Museum, 1950-58; Government Archaeologist, Nigeria, 1958-63; Leverhulme Research Fellow, 1964; Research Fellow, Nuffield College, Oxford, 1964-66; Professor of Art History, African Studies and Interdisciplinary Studies, Northwestern University, Evanston, Illinois, 1966-76; Visiting Fellow, Clare Hall, Cambridge, 1970-71; Hon. Corresponding Member, Manchester Literary and Philosophical Society, since 1958; Vice Chairman, Scottish Museums Council, 1986-89; Fellow, Royal Anthropological Institute; Fellow, Royal Society of Edinburgh, 1979, Curator, RSE, 1992-97; Leadership Award, Arts Council of the African Studies Association, 1995. Publications: Ife in the History of West African Sculpture, 1967; African Art: An Introduction, 1971; Treasures of Ancient Nigeria, Co-author, 1980. Recreation: walking. Address: (b.) Hunterian Museum, University of Glasgow, Glasgow G12 8QQ; T.-0141-330 4221.

Willetts, Professor Brian Benjamin, MA, PhD, CEng, FICE, FRSE. Professor of Civil Engineering, Aberdeen University, since 1985 (Head, Engineering Department, 1991-94); b. 12.6.36, Old Hill; m., Patricia Margaret Jones; 1 s.; 1 d. Educ. King Edward VI School, Stourbridge; Emmanuel College, Cambridge. Assistant Engineer, City of Birmingham, 1959-61; Executive Engineer, Government of Northern Nigeria, 1961-63; Lecturer/Senior Lecturer, Lanchester Polytechnic, 1963-66; Lecturer/Senior Lecturer, Aberdeen University, 1967-85. Address: (h.) Mosscroft, Upper Lochton, Banchory, Kincardineshire; T.-0133 082 2674.

Williams, Sir Alwyn, Kt, PhD, FRS, FRSE, MRIA, FGS, Hon. FRCPS, Hon. DSc, Hon. LLD. Honorary Research Fellow, Department of Geology, Glasgow University (Principal and Vice-Chancellor, Glasgow University, 1976-88); Non-Executive Director, Scottish Daily Record and Sunday Mail Ltd., 1984-90; b. 8.6.21, Aberdare, Wales; m., Edythe Joan Bevan; 1 s.; 1 d. Educ. Aberdare Boys' Grammar School; University College of Wales, Aberystwyth. Commonwealth Fund Fellow, US National Museum, 1948-50; Lecturer in Geology, Glasgow University, 1950-54; Professor of Geology, Queen's University, Belfast, 1954-74; Lapworth Professor of Geology, Birmingham University, 1974-76; Chairman, Scottish Hospital Endowments Research Trust, 1989-96; Member, Scottish Tertiary Education Advisory Council, 1984-86; President, Palaeontological Association, 1968-70; President, Royal Society of Edinburgh, 1985-88; Trustee and Chairman, Board of British Museum (Natural History), 1971-79; Chairman, Committee on National Museums and Galleries of Scotland, 1979-81; Honorary Fellow, Geological Society of America, since 1970; Foreign Member, Polish Academies of Science, since 1981; Hon. DSc, Universities of Wales, Queen's (Belfast) and Edinburgh; Hon. DCL, Oxford; Hon. LLD, Glasgow, Strathclyde; Hon. DUniv, Paisley; Hon. FRSAMD; Hon. FDS RCPSG; Hon. FRCPSG; Fellow, University College of Wales. Address: (h.) 25 Sutherland Avenue, Pollokshields, Glasgow G41 4HG; T.-0141-427 0589.

Williams, Anthony E. BSc, PhD, MICFM. Director of Fundraising and Publicity, Quarriers, since 1995; b. 6.5.37, Rhyl; m., Jean Grant; 1 s.; 1 d. Educ. Rhyl Grammar School; University College London. Scientific Officer, MRE, Portondown, Wilts., 1958-65; Lecturer in Mircobiology, University of Birmingham 1965-73; Senior Lecturer, University of Edinburgh, 1973-83; Appeals Officer/Fundraising Manager, Scottish Conservation Projects, 1985-95. Vice-Chair, ICFM (Scotland), 1996-98. Recreations: birdwatching; gardening; computers; real ale.

Address: (b.) Quarriers, Quarriers Village, Bridge of Weir, Renfrewshire PA11 3SX; T.-01505 612224.

Williams, Professor Howard Peter, MSc. Professor, Management Science Department, Strathclyde University, since 1990; Director, Network and Resource Management Centre; b. 27.2.54, St. Albans. Educ. Exeter University; Newcastle upon Tyne University. Economist, ICI Plant Protection Division, International Wool Secretariat, British Ship Research Association; Senior Research Fellow, Newcastle-upon-Tyne University. Member, Scottish Advisory Committee on Telecommunications, Glasgow Advisory Committee on Posts and Telecommunications. Recreations: windsurfing; opera; breadmaking. Address: (b.) Department of Management Science, Sir Graham Hills Building, Strathclyde University, Glasgow G1 1XH; T.-0141-548 3141.

Williams, John, BSc, MIFireE, MCGI. Firemaster, Grampian Fire Brigade, since 1998; b. 28.2.54, Carmarthen, Wales; m., Yvette; 3 d. Educ. Gwendraeth Grammar School. Joined Dyfed Fire Brigade, 1974: Leading Firefighter, 1978, Sub Officer, 1979, Station Officer, 1983, Assistant Divisional Officer – Emergency Planning, 1987, Divisional Officer – Deputy Senior Fire Safety Officer, 1988, Divisional Officer – Senior Fire Safety Officer, 1993; Senior Divisional Officer – Area Commander, Midland West Wales Fire Brigade, 1996; Deputy Firemaster, Grampian Fire Brigade, 1997. Member, Board of Trustees, Prince's Trust, Aberdeen; Member, Board of Trustees, Common Purpose, Aberdeen. Recreations: rugby football; DIY; golf; walking. Address: (h.) 15 Crombie Place, Westhill, Aberdeen AB32 6PX, T.-01224 749114; (b.) 19 North Anderson Drive, Aberdeen AB15 6DW, T.-01224 696666.

Williams, Professor Morgan Howard, BSc Hons, PhD, DSc, CEng, FBCS, FRSA. Professor of Computer Science, Heriot-Watt University, since 1980 (Head of Department, 1980-88); b. 15.12.44, Durban; 2 s. Educ. Grey High School, Port Elizabeth; Rhodes University, Grahamstown. Physicist in Antarctic Expedition, 1968-69; Rhodes University: Lecturer in Computer Science, 1970-72, Senior Lecturer, 1972-77, Professor and Head of Department, 1977-80. Address: Department of Computing and Electrical Engineering, Heriot-Watt University, Riccarton, Edinburgh EH14 4AS; T.-0131-451 3430.

Williams, Roger Bevan, PhD, BMus, FRCO, FTCL, ARCM, PGCE, FGMS. Conductor, Composer, Musician; Director of Music and Organist, University of Aberdeen, since 1991; Head, Music Department, University of Aberdeen, since 1988; b. 30.8.43, Swansea; m., Katherine Ellen; 2 s.; 1 d. Educ. Mirfield Grammar School, Yorkshire; Huddersfield School of Music; University College, Cardiff; Goldsmiths' College, University of London; King's College, Cambridge. Assistant Organist, Holy Trinity Church, Brompton, 1971; Lecturer, 1971, Director, 1973-75, Chiswick Music Centre; Organist, St. Patrick's Church, Soho, 1973; Musical Director, Sacred Heart Church, Wimbledon, 1975; Lecturer, West London Institute, 1975-78; Organist, Our Lady of Victories, Kensington, 1978-97; Lecturer, University of Aberdeen, 1978-88; Chorus Master, SNO Chorus, 1984-88; Harpsichordist, Aberdeen Sinfonietta, since 1988; first recording of Arne's Six Organ Concertos, 1988; Music at Castle Fraser: catalogue, 1995, CDs, 1997; numerous compositions, editions, catalogues of music holdings in North East Scotland. Recreations: board games; cooking; gardening. Address: (h.) The Old Hall, Barthol Chapel, Old Meldrum, Inverurie AB51 8TD; T.-01651 806634.

Williamson, Professor Edwin Henry, MA, PhD. Professor of Hispanic Studies, Edinburgh University, since 1990; b. 2.10.49; m., Susan Jane Fitchie; 2 d. Educ. Edinburgh University. Lecturer in Spanish, Trinity College, Dublin, 1974-77; Lecturer in Spanish, Birkbeck College, London, 1977-90. Publications: The Half-Way House of Fiction: Don Quixote and Arthurian Romance, 1984; El Quijote Y Los Libros de Caballerias, 1991; The Penguin History of Latin America, 1992; Cervantes and the Modernists, 1994. Recreations: theatre; art; film; hill-walking. Address: (b.) School of European Languages and Cultures (Hispanic Studies), Edinburgh University, David Hume Tower, George Square, Edinburgh EH8 9JX; T.-0131-650 3673.

Williamson, Professor James, CBE, MB, ChB, FRCPEdin, DSc (Hon.). Past Chairman, Chest, Heart and Stroke, Scotland; Past President, British Geriatrics Society; Past Chairman, Age Concern Scotland; Professor Emeritus, Geriatric Medicine, Edinburgh University; b. 22.11.20, Wishaw; m., Sheila Mary Blair; 3 s.; 2 d. Educ. Wishaw High School; Glasgow University. General medical training in Glasgow hospitals; general practice; training in respiratory medicine, becoming Consultant in Edinburgh, 1954; converted to geriatric medicine, 1959; Consultant, Edinburgh, until 1973; first occupant, Chair of Geriatric Medicine, Liverpool University; first occupant, Chair of Geriatric Medicine, Edinburgh University, 1976-86; Visiting Professor to several North American medical schools. Recreations: reading; walking. Address: (h.) 8 Chester Street, Edinburgh EH3 7RA; T.-0131-477 0282.

Williamson, Raymond MacLeod, MA, LLB, FRSA. Solicitor, since 1968 (Partner, MacRoberts, Solicitors, Glasgow and Edinburgh, since 1972); Secretary, High School of Glasgow Educational Trust; Governor, Royal Scottish Academy of Music and Drama; Chairman, John Currie Singers Ltd.; b. 24.12.42, Glasgow; m., Brenda; 1 s.; 1 d. Educ. High School of Glasgow; Glasgow University. Chairman, Royal Scottish National Orchestra, 1985-91; Chairman, Children's Music Foundation in Scotland; Chairman, National Youth Choir of Scotland; Deputy Chairman, Scottish International Piano Competition. Recreation: music. Address: (h.) 11 Islay Drive, Newton Mearns, Glasgow G77 6UD; T.-0141-639 4133.

Williamson, Professor Timothy, MA, DPhil, FBA, FRSE. Professor of Logic and Metaphysics, Edinburgh University, since 1995; b. 6.8.55, Uppsala, Sweden; m., Elisabetta Perosino; 1 s.; 1 d. Educ. Henley Grammar School; Balliol College and Christ Church, Oxford. Lecturer in Philosophy, Trinity College Dublin, 1980-88; Fellow in Philosophy, University College Oxford, 1988-94; Visiting Professor, MIT, 1994, Princeton, 1998-99; Visiting Fellow, Australian National University, 1990 and 1995; Erskine Visiting Fellow, University of Canterbury (NZ), 1995. Publications: Identity and Discrimination, 1990; Vagueness, 1994; articles in learned journals. Recreation: conventional behaviour. Address: (b.) Department of Philosophy, Edinburgh University, David Hume Tower, George Square, Edinburgh EH8 9JX; T.-0131-650 3665.

Wilson, Alan Oliver Arneil, MB, ChB, DPM, FRCPsych. Consultant in private practice, Murrayfield Hospital, Edinburgh; Consultant Psychiatrist, Bangour Hospitals, 1977-89; former Member, Clinical Teaching Staff, Faculty of Medicine, Edinburgh University; Member, Executive Group of Board of Directors, and Past President, World Association for Psychosocial Rehabilitation; Consultant (in Scotland), Ex-Services Mental Welfare Society; b. 4.1.30, Douglas; m., Dr. Fiona Margaret Davidson; 3 s. Educ. Biggar High School; Edinburgh University. RAMC, 1953-55; psychiatric post, Stobhill General Hospital, Glasgow, and Garlands Hospital, Carlisle, 1955-63; Consultant Psychiatrist and Deputy Physician Superintendent, St. George's Hospital, Morpeth, 1963-77. Joint Honorary Secretary, Northern Counties Psychiatric Association; Chairman, Group for Study of Rehabilitation and Community Care, Scottish Division, RCPsych; Member, Ethics Committee, World Association for Social Psychiatry; Chairman, Psychosocial Rehabilitation Scotland. V.M.

Bekhterev Medal awarded by Bekhterev Psychoneurological Research Institute, St. Petersburg; Co-Founder, Morpeth Northumbrian Gathering. Recreations: classical music; opera; folk song. Address: (h.) 14 Cammo Hill, Edinburgh EH4 8EY; T.-0131-339 2244.

Wilson, Brian, MA (Hons), FSA (Scot). MP (Labour), Cunninghame North, since 1987; Minister for Trade, Department of Trade and Industry, since 1998; Minister of State, Scottish Office (Minister for Education and Industry), 1997-98; b. 13.12.48, Dunoon; m., Joni Buchanan; 2 s.; 1 d. Educ. Dunoon Grammar School; Dundee University; University College, Cardiff. Journalist; Publisher and Founding Editor, West Highland Free Press; Contributor to The Guardian, Glasgow Herald, etc.; first winner, Nicholas Tomalin Memorial Award for Journalism; contested Ross and Cromarty, Oct., 1974, Inverness, 1979, Western Isles, 1983; front-bench spokesman on Scottish Home Affairs etc., 1988-92, Transport, 1992-94 and 1995-96, Trade and Industry, 1994-95. Address: House of Commons, London SW1A 0AA.

Wilson, Christina Kerr. Joint Managing Director and Co-Editor, Books in Scotland, since 1987; b. 7.1.24, Edinburgh; m., Norman Wilson (deceased); 2 d. Educ. Leith Academy. Compiled monthly magazine, New Books, for John Menzies & Co. Ltd., 1943; continued working for Menzies until 1960 (left to raise family); contributor, Books in Scotland, 1976. Recreations: cinema; swimming; reading. Address: (h.) 15 Gloucester Place, Edinburgh; T.-0131-225 5646.

Wilson of Tillyorn, Baron (David Clive Wilson), GCMG, MA (Oxon), PhD. Life Peer (1992); Chairman, Scottish Hydro Electric PLC, since 1993; Chairman, Scottish Committee, British Council, since 1993; Chancellor, Aberdeen University, since 1997; Member, Council, Glenalmond College, since 1994; President, Bhutan Society of the UK, since 1993; President, Hong Kong Society and Hong Kong Association, since 1994; Member, Council, CBI Scotland, since 1993; Vice-President, Royal Scottish Geographical Society, since 1998; Member, Board, Martin Currie Pacific Trust; Member, Governing Body, School of Oriental and African Studies, 1992-97; b. 14.2.34, Alloa; m., Natasha Helen Mary Alexander; 2 s. Educ. Trinity College, Glenalmond; Keble College, Oxford. Entered Foreign Service, 1958; Third Secretary, Vientiane, 1959-60; language student, Hong Kong, 1960-62; Second, later First Secretary, Peking, 1963-65; FCO, 1965-68; resigned, 1968; Editor, China Quarterly, 1968-74; Visiting Scholar, Columbia University, New York, 1972; rejoined Diplomatic Service, 1974; Cabinet Office, 1974-77; Political Adviser, Hong Kong, 1977-81; Head, S. European Department, FCO, 1981-84; Assistant Under Secretary of State, FCO, 1984-87. Hon.LLD (Aberdeen); Hon.DLitt (Sydney); Hon.DLitt (Abertay, Dundee); Hon. LLD, Chinese University, Hong Kong. KStJ. Recreations: mountaineering; skiing; reading. Address: (b.) Scottish Hydro Electric plc, Dunkeld Road, Perth PH1 5WA; T.-01738 455200.

Wilson, David John Rowland, MA (Hons), MA (Econ). Deputy Director General for Scotland, Office of Electricity Regulation, since 1998; b. 8.5.63, Hamilton; m., Lynn Reid Torrance; 2 s.; 1 d. Educ. Strathaven Academy; Larkhall Academy; Edinburgh University; Manchester University. Scottish Office: Economist, 1986-97, Principal, 1997-98. Recreations: films; music; changing electricity supplier. Address: (b.) OFFER, Regent Coiurt, 70 West Regent Street, Glasgow G2 2QZ.

Wilson, David Steel, DipM. Chef/Proprietor, The Peat Inn, since 1972; Director, Taste of Scotland Ltd., since 1996; Director, Scottish Chefs Association, since 1997; b. 21.1.36, Bishopbriggs; m., Patricia Ann; 1 s.; 1 d. Educ. Bishopbriggs High School; Glasgow College of Commerce. Sales/Marketing Manager in industry, 1967-71; trainee chef, 1971-72. Master Chef of G.B.; Chef Laureate; Fellow, RSA, 1992; Hon. Doctor of Laws, Dundee University, 1997. Recreations: travel; art; sport; music; theatre. Address: (b.) The Peat Inn, by Cupar, Fife KY15 5LH; T.-0133840 206.

Wilson, Gerald R., CB, MA. Secretary, The Scottish Office Education and Industry Department, since 1988; b. 7.9.39, Edinburgh; m., Margaret; 1 s.; 1 d. Educ. Holy Cross Academy; Edinburgh University. Assistant Principal, Scottish Home and Health Department, 1961-65; Private Secretary, Minister of State for Scotland, 1965-66; Principal, Scottish Home and Health Department, 1966-72; Private Secretary to Lord Privy Seal, 1972-74, to Minister of State, Civil Service Department, 1974; Assistant Secretary, Scottish Economic Planning Department, 1974-77; Counsellor, Office of the UK Permanent Representative to the Economic Communities, Brussels, 1977-82; Assistant Secretary, Scottish Office, 1982-84; Under Secretary, Industry Department for Scotland, 1984-88. Recreation: music. Address: (b.) Victoria Quay, Edinburgh EH6 6QQ; T.-0131-244 7114.

Wilson, Professor Gordon McAndrew, MA, PhD, FRSA. Assistant Principal and Director of Craigie Campus in Ayr, Paisley University, since 1993; b. 4.12.39, Glasgow; m., Alison Rosemary Cook; 2 s.; 1 d. Educ. Eastwood Secondary School; Glasgow University; Jordanhill College of Education. Teacher of History and Modern Studies: Eastwood Secondary School, 1963-65, Eastwood High School, 1965-67; Lecturer in Social Studies, Hamilton College of Education, 1967-73 (Head of Department, 1973-81); Principal Lecturer in Inservice Education, then Assistant Principal, Jordanhill College of Education, 1981-88; Principal, Craigie College of Education, 1988-93; Member, Committee on Curriculum and Examinations S5-S6 (Howie Committee), 1990-92; Chairman, South Ayrshire Hospitals NHS Trust, since 1997; Member: Board of Directors, Ayrshire Chamber of Commerce and Industry, Board of Directors, Enterprise Ayrshire, since 1994. Publications: Teaching Local History in Lanarkshire, 1972; Alexander McDonald, Leader of the Miners, 1982; Dictionary of Scottish Business Biography (Contributor), 1986. Recreations: reading; gardening; walking; music. Address: (b.) Paisley University, Craigie Campus in Ayr, Beech Grove, Ayr KA8 0SR; T.-01292 886200.

Wilson, Hamish Robert McHattie, MA (Aberdeen), MA, PhD (Cantab), FHSM. Director of Primary Care, Grampian Health Board, since 1991 (Unit General Manager, 1987-90); b. 19.1.46, Aberdeen. Educ. Robert Gordon's College, Aberdeen; Aberdeen University; Emmanuel College, Cambridge. Entered Health Service administration, 1972; held posts with Grampian Health Board in planning, primary care and as Secretary. Recreations: music; reading; theatre; cinema; good food and wine. Address: (b.) Summerfield House, 2 Eday Road, Aberdeen AB15 6RE; T.-01224 663456.

Wilson, Helen Frances, DA, RSW, RGI. Artist; b. 25.7.54, Pailsey; 1 d. Educ. John Neilson High School, Paisley; Glasgow School of Art. Drawings and paintings in public and private collections; awards and prizes include: Cargill Travelling Scholarship (Colonsay and Italy), 1976; First Prize, Scottish Drawing Competition, 1997; elected: RGI, 1984, RSW, 1997. Recreations: working with pre-school children; watching theatre, ballet, pantomime and people. Address: (h.) 1 Partickhill Road, Glasgow; T.-0141-339 5827.

Wilson, Ian Matthew, CB, MA. Secretary of Commissions for Scotland, 1987-92 (Under Secretary, Scottish Education Department, 1977-86); Member, RSAMD Governing Body, since 1992; President, University of Edinburgh Graduates' Association, 1995-97; b. 12.12.26, Edinburgh; m., 1, Anne Chalmers (deceased); 3 s.; 2, Joyce Town. Educ. George

Watson's College; Edinburgh University. Assistant Principal, Scottish Home Department, 1950; Private Secretary to Permanent Under Secretary of State, Scottish Office, 1953-55; Principal, Scottish Home Department, 1955; Assistant Secretary: Scottish Education Department, 1963, Scottish Home and Health Department, 1971; Assistant Under Secretary of State, Scottish Office, 1974-77. Address: (h.) 1 Bonaly Drive, Edinburgh EH13 OEJ; T.-0131-441 2541.

Wilson, James Wiseman, OBE, OStJ. Director, Barcapel Foundation, since 1970; Director, Wilson Management Ltd., since 1970; b. 31.5.33, Glasgow; m., Valerie Grant; 1 s.; 3 d. Educ. Trinity College, Glenalmond; Harvard Business School. Marketing Director, Scottish Animal Products, 1959-63; Sales Director, then Managing Director, then Chairman, Robert Wilson & Sons (1849) Ltd., 1964-85. National Trust for Scotland: Member of Council, 1977-82 and 1984-89, President, Ayrshire Members' Centre; Chairman, Management Committee, Scottish Civic Trust; Honorary President, Skelmorlie Golf Club and Irvine Pipe Band; won Aims of Industry Free Enterprise Award (Scotland), 1980. Recreations: golf; backgammon; skiing; bridge; travelling. Address: (h.) Skelmorlie Castle, Skelmorlie, Ayrshire PA17 5EY; T.-01475 521127.

Wilson, Janette Sylvia, LLB, NP. Solicitor of the Church of Scotland and Law Agent to the General Assembly, since 1995; b. 15.1.51, Inverness; m., Stuart Ronald Wilson. Educ. Inverness Royal Academy; Edinburgh University. Law Apprentice, then Assistant, Dundas & Wilson, CS, Edinburgh, 1973-77; Assistant, then Partner, Ross Harper & Murphy, Edinburgh, 1977-81; Depute Solicitor, Church of Scotland, 1981-95. Member, Law Society Conveyancing Committee and Public Service and Commerce Group. Recreations: keeping fit; reading; gardening. Address: (b.) 121 George Street, Edinburgh; T.-0131-225 5722.

Wilson, Les. Documentary Producer/Director, since 1980; Director, Caledonia, Sterne and Wyld Ltd., since 1992; b. 17.7.49, Glasgow; m., Adrienne Cochrane; 2 d. Educ. Grove Academy, Broughty Ferry. Trainee Journalist, 1969-70; hippy trail, 1970-71; Reporter, Greenock Telegraph, 1972-73; Reporter, STV, 1973-78; Editor, STV political programme, Ways and Means, 1979-80; Producer/Director, STV, 1981-92. Winner, Celtic Film Festival Award, 1991; BAFTA Scotland and British Telecom Factual/Current Affairs awards, 1997; British Telecom Factual/Current Affairs award, 1998. Publication: Scotland's War (Co-author), 1995. Recreation: Islay – the island, its people, its malts. Address: (b.) 5 Queens Crescent, Glasgow G4 9BW; T.-0141-353 3153.

Wilson, Leslie, BSc, FCCA, MIMIS, DipStat, DipMS. Director of Finance, Historic Scotland, since 1997; b. 10.5.47, Glasgow; m., Maureen S. Borrowman; 1 s.; 2 d. Educ. Allan Glen's School; Glasgow University. British Gas (Edinburgh and London), 1969-91; Head of Finance, Scottish Homes, 1991-92; Head of Finance and Information Systems, Historic Scotland, 1992-97. Recreations: golf; music; languages. Address: (b.) Longmore House, Salisbury Place, Edinburgh EH9 1SH; T.-0131-668 8874.

Wilson, Professor Lindsay, BA, DipEd, PhD, CPyschol. Professor of Psychology, University of Stirling, since 1998 (Head, Department of Psychology, since 1995); b. 24.6.51, Aberdeen; m., Jean; 2 s. Educ. Biggar High School; University of Stirling; University of Edinburgh. Research Fellow, Max Planck Institute for Psychiatry, Munich, 1979-80; University of Stirling: Medical Research Council Training Fellow, 1980-83, Lecturer then Senior Lecturer, 1983-98. Recreations: sailing; hillwalking. Address: (b.) Department of Psychology, University of Stirling, Stirling FK9 4LA; T.-01786 467640.

Wilson, Paul, MBA, DMS, DN, RGN, RMN. Director of NHS Trusts, NHS in Scotland, since 1994; b. 2.8.47, Newcastle upon Tyne; 1 s. Educ. Brunel University; Henley Management College. Registered mental nurse training and registered general nurse training; nursing appointments; Divisional Nursing Officer, Roehampton Health District, 1977-82; Chief Nursing Officer, then Director Policy and Planning, Maidstone Health Authority, 1982-87; General Manager, Mental Health Services, Greater Glasgow Health Board, 1987-91; Director of Operations, then Director, Health Care Contracting, Lothian Health Board, 1991-95. Recreations: cats; children; food; travel; music. Address: (b.) Scottish Office, St. Andrews House, Edinburgh, EH1 3OG; T.-0131-244 2179.

Wilson, Peter Liddell, BSc, MA, FIMgt, FIPD. Secretary, Heriot-Watt University, since 1991; b. 8.12.42, Douglas; m., Joy Janet Gibson; 2 d. Educ. Lanark Grammar School; Glasgow University; Birkbeck College, London University. Mathematics Teacher, Lanark Grammar School, 1964-67; Royal Navy (Instructor Lieutenant), 1967-70; Army (Royal Army Educational Corps), 1970-90: Commander Education, 1st Armoured Division (Lt. Col.), 1983-85, SOI Education HQ BAOR (Lt. Col.), 1986-88, MOD (Resettlement) (Colonel), 1988-90. Chairman, Edinburgh Conference Centre, since 1991. Recreations: golf; jogging; hill-walking; theatre. Address: (b.) Heriot-Watt University, Riccarton, Edinburgh EH14 4AS; T.-0131-449 5111.

Wilson, Professor Peter Northcote, CBE, BSc, MSc, Dip. Animal Genetics, PhD, CBiol, FBiol, FRSE. Emeritus Professor of Agriculture and Rural Economy, Edinburgh University; General Secretary, Royal Society of Edinburgh, since 1996; b. 4.4.28, Beckenham, Kent; m., Maud Ethel Bunn; 2 s.; 1 d. Educ. Whitgift School, Croydon; Wye College, London University; Edinburgh University. Lecturer in Agriculture, Makerere College, East Africa; Senior Lecturer in Agriculture, Imperial College of Tropical Agriculture, Trinidad; Professor of Tropical Agriculture, University of West Indies, Trinidad; Head of Biometrics, Unilever Research Laboratory, Bedford; Agricultural Development Director, SLF Ltd., Liverpool; Chief Agricultural Adviser, BOCM Silcock Ltd., Basingstoke. Life Fellow, Wye College, University of London; Past President, British Society of Animal Production; Past Vice President, Institute of Biology; Chairman, Frank Parkinson Agricultural Trust, since 1978; Hon. Secretary, Institute of Biology, 1992-96; Scientific Director, Edinburgh Centre for Rural Research, 1990-95; Past President, Edinburgh Agricultural Society; Member, Council, SAC, since 1995; Vice-Convener, Business Committee, University of Edinburgh Council, since 1996; Member, Scottish Committee, RSPB, since 1996. Publications: Agriculture in the Tropics (Co-author); Improved Feeding of Cattle and Sheep (Co-author). Recreations: walking; photography; natural history. Address: 8 St. Thomas Road, Edinburgh EH9 2LQ.

Wilson, Robert Gordon, BL, LLD. Vice-President, Scottish National Party, 1992-97; Solicitor; b. 16.4.38, Glasgow; m., Edith M. Hassall; 2 d. Educ. Douglas High School for Boys; Edinburgh University. National Secretary, SNP, 1963-71; MP, Dundee East, 1974-87; Chairman and National Convener, SNP, 1979-90; Rector, Dundee University, 1983-86; Member, Court, University of Abertay Dundee 1992-96. Recreation: reading; sailing; walking. Address: (h.) 48 Monifieth Road, Dundee DD5 2RX.

Wilson, Roy. General Manager, Pitlochry Festival Theatre, 1961-95, Art Exhibitions Director, since 1995; b. St. Andrews. Educ. Burgh School and Madras College, St. Andrews. Proprietor, grocer's business, St. Andrews, 1953-58; Assistant Manager, Pitlochry Festival Theatre, 1958-61. Winner David K. Thomson Award, 1995, in recognition of his contribution to Pitlochry Festival Theatre. Recreations: plays and theatre in general; most forms of classical music, with particular interest in choral singing; listening to records; reading; art and antiques. Address: (h.) Kilrymont, Bruach Lane, Pitlochry, Perthshire PH16 5DG; T.-Pitlochry 472897.

Wilson, R. Ross, BSc, PhD, MInstP, CPhys. Chief Executive, Howden Process Compressors, since 1998; Managing Director, James Howden & Co. Ltd., since 1992; Director, Renfrewshire Enterprise, since 1996; b. 13.3.47, Glasgow; m., Margaret; 2 s. Educ. Hamilton Academy; Glasgow University. Research Officer, then Vibration Group Leader, Central Electricity Research Laboratories, CEGB; Section Head, Design Analysis, Corporate Engineering Laboratory, British Steel; Design Manager, then Technical Director, James Howden Ltd. Recreations: golf; collecting Penguin books; gardening. Address: (b.) Old Govan Road, Renfrew PA4 8XJ; T.-0141-886 6711.

Wilson, Thomas Black, BSc (Hons), CEng, MBCS. Principal, Glasgow College of Building and Printing, since 1989; b. 23.12.43, Airdrie; m., Barbara Smith; 1 s.; 1 d. Educ. Cumnock Academy; Glasgow University; Jordanhill College. Principal Teacher, Prestwick Academy, 1969-74; Head, Computing Department, Ayr College, 1974-84; Depute Principal: Barmulloch College, Glasgow, 1984-86, Cardonald College, Glasgow, 1986-89. Member, Scottish Central Committee (Mathematics), 1975-82; Governor, Scottish Council for Educational Technology, since 1995; Hon. Professor, Glasgow Caledonian University, since 1995. Recreations: reading; writing; music. Address: (b.) 60 North Hanover Street, Glasgow G1 2BP; T.-0141-332 9969.

Wilson, Emeritus Professor Thomas Brendan, CBE, MA, BMus, ARCM, FRSE. Composer; b. 10.10.27, Trinidad, Colorado; m., Margaret Rayner; 3 s. Educ. St. Mary's College, Aberdeen; Glasgow University; Royal College of Music. RAF, 1945-48; Glasgow University: Lecturer in Music, Extra-Mural Studies, 1957, Reader in Music, Extra-Mural Studies, 1972, Professor, 1977; Member, Scottish Arts Council, 1966-72; Past Chairman, Composers Guild; President, Scottish Society of Composers; elected Member, Royal Society of Musicians; compositions include orchestral, choral-orchestral, chamber-orchestral, opera (including The Confessions of a Justified Sinner), ballet, brass band, vocal music of different kinds, and works for a wide variety of chamber ensembles and solo instruments; numerous commissions; Hon. Doctorate of Music, Glasgow University, 1991; Fellow, Royal Scottish Academy of Music and Drama, since 1991. Recreations: golf; talking shop. Address: (h.) 120 Dowanhill Street, Glasgow G12 9DN; T.-0141-339 1699.

Wilson, Professor Thomas Michael Aubrey, BSc (Hons), PhD, CBiol, MIBiol. Deputy Director, Scottish Crop Research Institute, since 1995; b. 10.10.51, Hawick; m., Judith Lindsey Dring; 2 s.; 1 d. Educ. Hawick High School; Edinburgh University; Cambridge University. Lecturer in Biochemistry, Liverpool University; Senior Scientific Officer, then Principal Scientific Officer, John Innes Institute, Norwich; Professor, AgBiotech Center, Rutgers University, NJ; Head, Virology Department, SCRI, Dundee, 1992-95; Senior Editor, Journal of General Virology; published 85 papers, reviews, and book chapters; edited or co-authored two books; first recipient, SGM Herpes Vaccine Research Trust Prize, 1985. Recreations: light movies; books; DIY; dog-walking. Address: (b.) Invergowrie, Dundee, DD2 5DA; T.-01382 562731.

Wilson, William John McKinley, QPM. Chief Constable, Central Scotland Police, since 1990; b. 27.6.43, Kinghorn; m., Catherine; 3 s. Educ. Kirkcaldy High School. Joined Fife Constabulary, 1962: Chief Superintendent, 1981, Deputy Chief Constable, 1984. Recreations: football; golf. Address: (b.) Central Scotland Police, Randolphfield, Stirling; T.-01786 456000.

Wilson, William Murray, MB, ChB, MRCGP. General Medical Practitioner, Dalry, Ayrshire, 1949-89; Medical Advisor, Roche Products, Dalry, Ayrshire, since 1965; Medical Referee, Cunninghame District Council, since 1972; Member, Ayrshire and Arran Health Board; b. 19.1.25, Glasgow; m., Elizabeth Carbine; 3 s. Educ. Eastwood Secondary School; Glasgow University. Past Chairman, Local Medical Committee/GP Committee, Area Medical Committee, BMA Ayrshire Division; former Member, General Medical Services Committee, London and Edinburgh; Elder, St. Margaret's Church, Dalry; former Member, Education for the Ministry Committee, Church of Scotland; Honorary Lecturer, British Red Cross Society, St. Andrew's Ambulance Association. Recreations: travel; photography. Address: (h.) 22 Courthill Street, Dalry, Ayrshire KA24 5AN; T.-Dalry 832165.

Windsor, Malcolm L., PhD, FRSC. Secretary, North Atlantic Salmon Conservation Organization, since 1984; b. 12.4.38, Bristol; m., Sally; 2 d. Educ. Cotham Grammar School, Bristol; Bristol University. Researcher, University of California, 1965-67; fisheries research, Humber Laboratory, Hull, 1967-75; Fisheries Adviser to Chief Scientist, Ministry of Agriculture and Fisheries, London, 1975-84. Secretary, Duddingston Village Conservation Society. Publication: book on fishery products. Recreations: local conservation work; jazz; walking. Address: (b.) 11 Rutland Square, Edinburgh EH1 2AS; T.-0131-228 2551.

Windsor, Col. Rodney Francis Maurice, CBE, DL. Farmer; b. 22.2.25, Redhill; m., Deirdre Chichester (deceased); m. Angela Stainton; 2 s.; 1 d. Educ. Tonbridge School. Enlisted Royal Armoured Corps, 1943; commissioned The Queen's Bays, 1944-52; Captain, 1949; ADC to CINC and High Commissioner Austria, 1949-50; served in North Irish Horse (TA), 1959-67; Lt. Col. Commanding, 1964-67; Colonel TA N. Ireland, 1967-71; ADC (TA) to HM The Queen, 1970-75; Member, Highland TA Association, 1971-77; Member, Banff and Buchan District Valuation Appeal Committee, 1982-96 (Chairman, 1989-96); Deputy Lieutenant:, Co. Antrim, 1967-97, Aberdeenshire, since 1989; Hon. President, Turiff Branch, Royal British Legion Scotland, since 1997. Recreations: field sports; golf. Address: (h.) Byth House, New Byth, Turiff, Aberdeenshire AB53 7XN; T.-01888 544230.

Winney, Robin John, MB, ChB, FRCPEdin. Consultant Renal Physician, Edinburgh Royal Infirmary, since 1978; b. 8.5.44, Dunfermline. Educ. Dunfermline High School; Edinburgh University. Recreations: badminton; curling. Address: (h.) 74 Lanark Road West, Currie, Midlothian EH14 5JZ.

Winning, His Eminence Thomas Joseph Cardinal, STL, DCL, DD, DUniv, GCHS, FEIS. Archbishop of Glasgow and Metropolitan, since 1974; President, Bishops' Conference of Scotland, since 1985; b. 3.6.25, Wishaw. Educ. Our Lady's High School, Motherwell; St. Mary's College, Blairs; St. Peter's College; Scots College; Gregorian University, Rome. Ordained Priest, Rome, 1948; Assistant Priest, Chapelhall, 1949-50; Rome (DCL, "Cum Laude"), 1953; Assistant Priest, St. Mary's Hamilton, 1953-57; Cathedral, Motherwell, 1957-58; Chaplain, Franciscans of the Immaculate Conception, Bothwell, 1958-61; Diocesan Secretary, Motherwell, 1956-61; Spiritual Director, Scots College, Rome, 1961-66; Advocate of the Sacred Roman Rota, 1965; Parish Priest, St. Luke's Motherwell, 1966-70; Officialis and Vicar Episcopal, Motherwell Diocese, 1966-70; first President, Scottish Catholic Marriage Tribunal, 1970; nominated Titular Bishop of Louth and Bishop Auxiliary, 1971, and ordained by James Donald Scanlan, Archbishop of Glasgow, November, 1971; Parish Priest, Our Holy Redeemer's Clydebank, 1972-74; translated to Glasgow as Archbishop, 1974; created Cardinal Priest of the title of S. Andrea delle Frate, 1994; Honorary DD (Glasgow), 1983; awarded

Glasgow Loving Cup, 1983; Grand Prior of Scotland, Equestrian Order of the Holy Sepulchre of Jerusalem, 1989; Hon. D.Univ. (Strathclyde), 1992; Hon. LLD, Aberdeen University, 1996; Hon. Professor, Glasgow University, 1996. Recreations: watching football; listening to music. Address: (h.) 40 Newlands Road, Glasgow G43 2JD; T.-0141-226 5898.

Winter, Michael, BA, AKC. Artistic Director, Perth Theatre, since 1996; b. Winchelsea, Sussex. Educ. Rye Grammar School; King's College, London. Director, York Theatre Royal, 1978-84; Artistic Director, Mercury Theatre, Colchester, Essex, 1984-94. Address: (b.) 185 High Street, Perth PH1 5UW; T.-01738 472701.

Wiseman, Alan William. Director and Chairman, Robert Wiseman Dairies, since 1979; President, Scottish Dairy Trade Federation, 1988-95; b. 20.8.50, Giffnock; m., Margaret. Educ. Duncanrig Senior Secondary School, East Kilbride. Left school to be one of his father's milkmen, 1967; has been a milkman ever since. Scottish Businessman of the Year, 1992; former Chairman, Scottish Dairy Council; Scottish Business Achievement Award, 1994. Recreations: golf; shooting. Address: (b.) Cadzow House, High Parks Farm, Hamilton; T.-01698 425481.

Wishart, David, BSc, PhD, CEng, CStat. Director, Clustan Ltd.; b. 5.7.43, London; m., Doreen Pamela Craig Wishart; 3 s. Educ. Kilburn Grammar School; Truro School; St. Andrews University. Statistician, Civil Service Department, London, 1970-75; Principal, Scottish Office, 1975-77; Chief Statistician, Scottish Office, 1977-81; Director of Statistics, Scottish Office, 1981-84; Assistant Secretary, Scottish Office, 1984-95; Honorary Research Fellow, Department of Management, St Andrews University; Fellow: British Computer Society, Royal Statistical Society (Vice President, 1986-88), Royal Society of Arts; Member, Institute of Directors; Director, Wishart Society. Recreations: golf; skiing; opera. Address: (h.) 16 Kingsburgh Road, Edinburgh EH12; T.-0131-337 1448.

Wishart, Professor Jennifer Grant, MA, PhD, CPsychol. Professor of Special Education, University of Edinburgh, since 1998; b. 9.5.48, Dundee; m., Thomas Arrol. Educ. Harris Academy, Dundee; University of Edinburgh. Research Psychologist, University of Edinburgh, 1970-96 (Research Associate, 1970-79, Research Fellow, 1979-90, Senior Research Fellow, 1990-95, Reader, 1995-96); first Scottish Chair in Special Education, Moray House Institute of Education, Heriot-Watt University, 1996-98. Advisor to Scottish UK and European Down's Syndrome associations, International Society on Early Intervention, Partners in Advocacy, and other charities. Publications: numerous papers and chapters in psychology in education and medical journals and textbooks. Recreations: wine; food; English pointers. Address: Faculty of Education, Moray House Institute of Education, Holyrood Road, Edinburgh EH8 8AQ; T.-0131-651 6099.

Wishart, Ruth. Columnist, The Herald; Broadcaster, BBC Radio, since 1989; b. Glasgow; m., Rod McLeod. Educ. Eastwood Senior Secondary School. TV Editor, Daily Record, 1970-73; Woman's Editor, Daily Record, 1973-78; Assistant Editor, Sunday Mail, 1978-82; Assistant Editor, Sunday Standard, 1982-83; Freelance Writer, 1983-86; Senior Assistant Editor, The Scotsman, 1986-88.

Wiszniewski, Adrian, BA (Hons). Artist/Designer; b. 31.3.58, Glasgow; m., Diane Foley; 2 s.; 1 d. Educ. Mackintosh School of Architecture, Glasgow School of Art. Around 40 solo exhibitions throughout the world, since 1983; commissions include: two large paintings for Liverpool Anglican Cathedral 1996, Gallery of Modern Art, Glasgow, 1996, Millennium Tower, Hamilton, 1997-98; work purchased by museums worldwide including Tate Gallery, London and MOMA, New York. New York Design Award for designs of six rugs in collaboration with Edinburgh Tapestry Workshop; has created limited edition books. Recreations: looking at pictures; cinema; family. Address: (h.) 2 Shields, Castle Semple, Lochwinnoch PA12 4HL.

Withers, Professor Charles William John, BSc, PhD, FRGS. Professor of Geography, Edinburgh University, since 1992; b. 6.12.54, Edinburgh; m., Anne; 2 s.; 1 d. Educ. Daniel Stewart's College, Edinburgh; St. Andrews University; Cambridge University. Lecturer, Senior Lecturer, Principal Lecturer, Professor of Geography, College of St. Paul and St. Mary/Cheltenham and Gloucester College of Higher Education Author of five books, 80 academic articles. Recreations: reading; hill-walking. Address: (b.) Department of Geography, Edinburgh University, Drummond Street, Edinburgh; T.-0131-650 2559.

Withers, John Alexander (Jack), FCIL. Writer; b. Glasgow; m., Beate (Bea) Haertel. Educ. North Kelvinside School; Jordanhill College of Education (Youth and Community Diploma). Left school at 14; worked in garage, electrical industry, labouring, National Service, unemployment, razor-blade salesman; long periods abroad, wandering, wondering, working: France, FRG, Italy, Scandinavia, Spain, North Africa; youth worker; freelance writer; ski instructor; librarian; performance poet; Scottish republican and radical; plays for radio, TV, theatre; James Kennoway Screenplay Award (shared); Scottish Arts Council Awards; short stories published in numerous journals in UK, Denmark and West Germany; Editor, Two Tongues — Two Cities; books: Glasgow Limbo, A Real Glasgow Archipelago, Balancing on a Barbed Wire Fence. Address: (h.) 16 Belmont Crescent, Glasgow; T.-0141-339 9492.

Witney, Eur. Ing. Professor Brian David, BSc, MSc, PhD, CEng, FIMechE, Hon.FIAgrE, MemASAE. Director, Land Technology Ltd., since 1995; Hon. Professor of Agricultural Engineering, Edinburgh University, since 1989; Professor of Terramechanics, Scottish Agricultural College, Edinburgh, since 1994; b. 8.6.38, Edinburgh; m., Maureen M.I. Donnelly; 1 s.; 2 d. Educ. Daniel Stewart's College, Edinburgh; Edinburgh University; Durham University; Newcastle University. Senior Research Associate, Newcastle upon Tyne University, 1962-66; Research Fellow, US Army Research Office, Duke Univ., 1966-67; Senior Scientific Officer, Military Engineering Experimental Establishment, Christchurch, 1967-70; Head, Agricultural Engineering Department, East of Scotland College of Agriculture, Edinburgh, 1970-86; Director, Scottish Centre of Agricultural Engineering, 1987-95, and Vice-Dean, Scottish Agricultural College, 1990-95. President, Institution of Agricultural Engineers, 1988-90; President, European Society of Agricultural Engineers, 1993-94; Managing Editor, Landwards, since 1996; Managing Editor, Land Technology, 1994-96; Editor and Chairman, Editorial Board, Journal of Agricultural Engineering Research, since 1998; Chairman, Douglas Bomford Trust, since 1998. Publication: Choosing and Using Farm Machines. Address: (b.) Land Technology Ltd., 33 South Barnton Avenue, Edinburgh EH4 6AN; T.-0131-336 3129.

Wolfe, William Cuthbertson, CA, JP. Member, National Council, since 1991; Member, National Executive Committee, since 1998, Scottish National Party; b. 22.2.24; 2 s.; 2 d. Educ. Bathgate Academy; George Watson's College, Edinburgh. Army Service, 1942-47, NW Europe and Far East; Air OP Pilot. Hon. Publications Treasurer, Saltire Society, 1953-60; Scout County Commissioner, West Lothian, 1960-64; Hon. President (Rector), Students' Association, Heriot-Watt University, 1966-69; contested (SNP) West Lothian, 1962, 1964, 1966, 1970, Feb. and Oct. 1974, 1979, North Edinburgh, Nov. 1973; Chairman, SNP,

1969-79, President, 1980-82; Treasurer, Scottish CND, 1982-85; Secretary, Scottish Poetry Library, 1985-91; Member, Forestry Commission's National Committee for Scotland, 1974-87. Publication: Scotland Lives.

Wolfram, Professor Julian, BSc, CEng, PhD, FRINA, MSaRS. Total Oil Marine Chair of Offshore Research and Development, Heriot-Watt University, since 1990; b. 2.8.46, London; m., Margaret Mary Lockhart; 1 s., 1 d., by pr. m. Educ. Gordonstoun; Reading University; Newcastle University. Research and Development Officer, Vickers Shipbuilders Ltd.; Lecturer (latterly Senior Lecturer) in Naval Architecture, Sunderland Polytechnic; Lecturer (latterly Senior Lecturer) in Marine Technology, Strathclyde University; Tutor, Open University; Chief Examiner, Ship Structures and Dynamics, Engineering Council; Consultant to several companies in the marine field. Publications: over 50 technical papers and reports. Recreations: sailing; squash; hill walking. Address: (b.) Heriot-Watt University, Edinburgh EH14 4AS; T.-0131-449 5111.

Wong, Professor Henry H.Y., BSc, PhD, DIC, CEng, FRAeS. Emeritus Professor, Department of Aeronautics and Fluid Mechanics, Glasgow University; Senior Research Fellow, since 1987; Adviser to the Guangdong Higher Education Bureau, China, since 1985; Adviser to Glasgow University on Chinese Affairs, since 1986; Chair Professor, Nanjing University of Aeronautics and Astronautics, since 1987; "Concurrent" Professor, National University of Defense Technology, Changsha, since 1989; b. 23.5.22, Hong Kong; m., Joan Anstey; 2 s.; 1 d. Educ. St. Stephen College, Hong Kong; Jiao-Tong University, Shanghai; Imperial College, London; Glasgow University. Assistant Lecturer, Jiao-Tong University, 1947-48; Engineer, Armstrong Siddeley, 1949; Structural Engineer, Hunting Percival Aircraft, 1949-51; Senior Structural Engineer, de Havilland Aircraft, 1952-57; Senior Lecturer, Hatfield Polytechnic, 1957-59; Lecturer, Senior Lecturer, then Reader in Aeronautics and Fluid Mechanics, Glasgow University, from 1960; Economic and Technological Consultant to Shantou Special Economic Zone, China, since 1988. Former Treasurer and Vice-Chairman, Kilmardinny Music Circle; Chairman, Glasgow Summer School, 1979-95; City of Glasgow Lord Provost's Award, 1988. Recreations: reading; music; painting; swimming. Address: (h.) 77 Antonine Road, Bearsden, Glasgow; T.-0141-942 8346.

Wood, Brian Charles Thallon, BL (Dist.), NP. Solicitor, since 1955; Consultant, Charles Wood & Son, Solicitors, Kirkcaldy; Honorary Sheriff; b. 8.8.34, Kirkcaldy; m., Tessa; 1 s.; 1 d. Educ. Fettes; Edinburgh University. Part-time Chairman, Industrial Tribunals, 1972-77; part-time Chairman, Rent Assessment Committee, 1987-96; Member, Council, Law Society of Scotland, 1992-94; Accredited ADR Mediator. Recreations: gardens; skiing; curling; country dancing; mending anything. Address: (h.) 4 Kilcruik Road, Kinghorn, Fife; T.-01592 891218.

Wood, Brian James, JP, BSc (Hons), FRSA. Rector, Hazlehead Academy, Aberdeen, since 1993 (Rector, Mearns Academy, 1989-93); Chairman, Justices of the Peace, Aberdeenshire; Hon. Sheriff, Stonehaven; b. 6.12.49, Banff; m., Doreen A. Petrie; 1 s.; 1 d. Educ. Banff Academy; Aberdeen Academy; Aberdeen University; Aberdeen College of Education. Teacher of Physics, George Heriot's School, Edinburgh, 1972-75; Mackie Academy, 1975-89, latterly as Depute Rector. Chairman, Justices of the Peace for Kincardine and Deeside; Member, Chairmen of Justices Committee for Scotland; Elder, Church of Scotland. Recreations: sport; reading; music; travel; theatre; DIY. Address: (h.) 13 Edinview Gardens, Stonehaven; T.-01569 763888.

Wood, David Crawford, BCom. Development and Communications Director, Royal Botanic Garden Edinburgh, since 1996; Managing Director, Botanics Trading Company Ltd., since 1996; b. 14.8.61, Odense, Denmark; m., Patricia; 2 s.; 1 d. Educ. Kirkcudbright Academy; Edinburgh University. General Manager, Local Investment Networking Company, 1986; Business Development Manager, Peter Dominic Ltd., 1989; Regional Manager, Thorntons PLC, 1992. Recreations: current affairs; sport; playing with my children. Address: (b.) Royal Botanic Garden Edinburgh, 20a Inverleith Row, Edinburgh EH3 5LR; T.-0131-248 2944.

Wood, Graham Allan, MBChB, BDS, FDSRCPS, FRSC(Ed). Consultant Oral and Maxillofacial Surgeon, Canniesburn Hospital, Glasgow, since 1995; Honorary Clincial Senior Lecturer, University of Glasgow, since 1995; Clinical Professor, University of Texas, USA, since 1990; b. 15.8.46, Glasgow; m., Lindsay Balfour; 1 s.; 1 d. Educ. Hillhead High School, Glasgow; University of Glasgow; University of Dundee. General dental practice, Glasgow, 1968-70; House Officer, Senior House Officer, Registrar, dental specialties, Glasgow Dental Hospital, Glasgow Victoria Infirmary and Canniesburn Hospital, 1970-72; Dental Surgeon, Grenfell Mission, Labrador, Canada, 1972-73; House Officer (plastic surgery), Dundee Royal Infirmary, 1978; Senior Registrar (oral and maxillofacial surgery), North Wales, 1979-83; Consultant, Oral and Maxillofacial Surgeon, North Wales, 1983-95. Fellow, International Association of Oral and Maxillofacial Surgeons; Fellow, British Association of Oral and Maxillofacial Surgeons. Recreations: hillwalking; golf; sailing; skiing. Address: (h.) Abbotsford, Broomknowe Road, Kilmacolm PA13 4HX; T.-01505 873954.

Wood, Emeritus Professor Hamish Christopher Swan, CBE, BSc, PhD, CChem, FRSC, FRSE, DUniv, LLD, FScotvec, FSQA; b. 8.5.26, Hawick; m., Jean Dumbreck Mitchell; 1 s.; 1 d. Educ. Hawick High School; St. Andrews University. Lecturer in Chemistry, St. Andrews University, 1950-51; Research Fellow, Australian National University, 1951-53; Lecturer, Senior Lecturer and Reader, Strathclyde University, 1953-69, Professor of Organic Chemistry, 1969-91, Deputy Principal, 1982-84, Vice-Principal, 1984-86; Member, Universities Funding Council, 1989-92; Chairman, Court, Glasgow Caledonian University, 1993-94; Member, Council, Royal Society of Edinburgh, 1992-95. Address: (b.) Thomas Graham Building, Strathclyde University, 295 Cathedral Street, Glasgow G1 1XL; T.-0141-552 4400.

Wood, Sir Ian Clark, CBE (1982), LLD, BSc, DBA, CBIM. Chairman and Managing Director, John Wood Group PLC, since 1967; Chairman, J.W. Holdings, since 1982; Chairman, Scottish Enterprise Board, since 1997; b. 21.7.42, Aberdeen; m., Helen Macrae; 3 s. Educ. Robert Gordon's College, Aberdeen; Aberdeen University. Joined family business, John Wood & Sons, 1964; Member, Scottish Business Forum; Chairman, Oil, Gas and Petrochemicals Supplies Office Board; Fellow, Royal Society of Arts; Board Director, Royal Bank of Scotland; Grampian Industrialist of the Year, 1978; Young Scottish Businessman of the Year, 1979; Scottish Free Enterprise Award, 1985; Scottish Business Achievement Award Trust — joint winner, 1992, corporate elite leadership award services category; Hon. LLD, 1984; Hon. DBA, 1998; Corporate Elite "World Player" Award, 1996; Fellow: Scottish Vocational Educational Council, Scottish Qualifications Authority. Recreations: tennis; family; art. Address: (b.) John Wood Group PLC, John Wood House, Greenwell Road, East Tullos, Aberdeen; T.-01224 851000.

Wood, Professor Robert Anderson, BSc, MB, ChB, FRCPEdin and Glas, FRCSEdin. Postgraduate Medical Dean and Professor of Clinical Medicine, Aberdeen University, since 1992; b. 26.5.39, Edinburgh; m., Dr.

Sheila Pirie; 1 s.; 3 d. Educ. Edinburgh Academy; Edinburgh University. Consultant Physician, Perth Royal Infirmary, 1972-92; Deputy Director of Postgraduate Medical Education, Dundee University, 1985-91; Dean, RCPE, 1992-95, and Councillor, 1990-92; Member, Harveian Society (President, 1998-99). Address: (h.) Ballomill House, Abernethy, Perthshire; T.-Abernethy 0201.

Wood, Professor Roy Christopher, BA, MPhil, PhD, PGDipHCA, MHCIMA. Professor of Hospitality Management, Scottish Hotel School, University of Strathclyde, since 1996; b. 29.7.59, Lancaster. Educ. Higham Lane School, Nuneaton; University of York; University of Bath; University of Strathclyde; Manchester Polytechnic. Lecturer in Applied Social Science, Oxford Polytechnic, 1983; Lecturer, Scottish Hotel School, University of Strathclyde, 1984-91; Senior Lecturer, Duncan of Jordanstone College of Art, 1992; Scottish Hotel School, University of Strathclyde: Senior Lecturer, 1992, Reader, 1995. Publications: author or co-author of seven books, numerous academic papers. Recreations: music; literature; travel; art. Address: (b.) 94 Cathedral Street, Glasgow G4 0LG; T.-0141-548 3945.

Wood, Stephen Charles, BA, MA, FSA, FRSA, FSA Scot, Chevalier de l'Ordre des Palmes Académiques, France. Keeper, Scottish United Services Museum, Edinburgh Castle, since 1983; b. 29.1.52, Wells, Somerset; 1 s. Educ. The Blue School, Wells; Bishop Wordsworth's School, Salisbury; Birkbeck College, London University. Curator, Department of Uniform, National Army Museum, London, 1971-83. Publications: The Scottish Soldier, 1987; In the Finest Tradition, 1988; The Auld Alliance, 1989; The Legendary 51st, 1990. Recreations: travel; gastronomy; historical research. Address: (b.) Edinburgh Castle, Edinburgh.

Woodcock, Brian, BEd (Hons). Director of Arts and Recreation, Aberdeen City Council, since 1996; Hon. Chairman, Scottish Association of Directors of Leisure Services, 1995-98; b. 22.4.59, St. Andrews; m., Susan; 1 s.; 1 d. Educ. Waid Academy, Anstruther; Jordanhill College. Sports Development Assistant, Central Regional Council, 1983-87; Sports Officer, Stirling District Council, 1987-89; Sport and Leisure Manager, Strathkelvin District Council, 1989-90; Chief Leisure Officer, Derwentside District Council, 1990-92; Director of Leisure Services, Kilmarnock and Loudoun District Council, 1992-96. Recreations: sport; music; theatre. Address: (b.) Aberdeen City Council, St. Nicholas House, Broad Street, Aberdeen AB10 1XJ; T.-01224 522472.

Woodruff, Professor Sir Michael (Francis Addison), Kt (1969), DSc, MD, MS, FRCS, FRCSE, FRACS, Hon. FACS, FRSE, FRS. Professor Emeritus, Surgery, Edinburgh University; b. 3.4.11, London; m., Hazel Gwenyth Ashby; 2 s.; 1 d. Educ. Wesley College, Melbourne; Queens College, Melbourne University. House Physician and House Surgeon, Royal Melbourne Hospital; Captain, Australian Army Medical Corps (PoW, Singapore); Tutor in Surgery, Sheffield University, 1946; Lecturer in Surgery, Aberdeen University, 1948; Professor of Surgery, Otago University, 1953; Edinburgh University, 1957-76; research worker, MRC Clinical and Population Cytogenetics Unit, Edinburgh, 1976-86. President, The Transplantation Society, 1972-74. Publications: Deficiency Diseases in Japanese Prison Camps; Surgery for Dental Students; The Transplantation of Tissues and Organs; On Science and Surgery; The Interaction of Cancer and Host; Cellular Variation and Adaptation in Cancer, 1990. Recreations: sailing; music; tennis. Address: (h.) The Bield, 506 Lanark Road, Juniper Green, Edinburgh EH14 5DH; T.-0131-453 3653.

Woods, (Adrien) Charles, MA. Director, Strategy and Planning, Scottish Enterprise, since 1997; b. 22.9.55, London. Educ. St. Andrews University. Various posts, Scottish Development Agency, 1981-91; Scottish Enterprise: Director, Policy and Planning, 1991-92, Director, Operations, 1992-94; Chief Executive, Scotland Europa, 1994-97. Recreations: golf; cycling. Address: (b.) 120 Bothwell Street, Glasgow G2 7JP; T.-0141-248 2700.

Woods, Kevin James, BSc, PhD, MHSM. Director of Strategy and Performance Management, NHS Management Executive, Scottish Office, since 1995; Hon. Fellow, Health Services Management Unit, Manchester University, since 1990; b. 9.2.53, Sale; m., Helen Denise; 3 d. Educ. Sale County Grammar School; Queen Mary College, London University. Lecturer in Health Care, Queen Mary College and London Hospital Medical College, 1979-85; Consumer and Operational Research Officer/Deputy District General Manager, North Derbyshire Health Authority, 1985-89; District General Manager, Chester Health Authority, 1990; Regional Director of Corporate Planning/Regional General Manager, Trent Regional Health Authority, 1991-94. Recreations: gardening; golf; soccer. Address: (b.) NHS Management Executive, Scottish Office, St. Andrews House, Edinburgh, EH1 3DG; T.-0131-244 1727.

Woodward, Michael Trevor, PhD, MA (Hons), MBA. Director, Ivory and Sime Investment Management plc; Investment Director, Ivory and Sime plc, 1990-94; b. 25.11.57, Birmingham; m., Anne McWalter Russell; 2 d. Educ. Dartmouth Comprehensive School; Aberdeen University; Edinburgh University. Ivory and Sime plc, since 1983. Recreations: family; golf; squash; racketball. Address: (b.) 1 Charlotte Square, Edinburgh EH2 4DZ; T.-0131-225 1357.

Woolhouse, Professor Mark Edward John, MA, MSc, PhD. Chair of Veterinary Public Health and Quantitative Epidemiology, University of Edinburgh, since 1997; b. 25.4.59, Shrewsbury. Educ. Tiffin School, Kingston, Surrey; New College, University of Oxford; University of York; Queen's University, Canada. Research Fellow: University of Zimbabwe, 1985-86, Imperial College, London, 1986-89, University of Oxford, 1989-97. Recreations: walking; fly-fishing; tennis. Address: (b.) Centre for Tropical Veterinary Medicine, University of Edinburgh, Easter Bush, Roslin, Midlothian; T.-0131-650 6264.

Wooton, Professor Ian, MA, MA, MPhil, PhD. Bonar-Macfie Professor of Economics, Glasgow University, since 1995; Research Fellow, Centre for Economic Policy Research, London, since 1994; b. 4.4.57, Kirkcaldy; 1 s.; 1 d. Educ. Kirkcaldy High School; St. Andrews University; Columbia University, New York. Associate Professor of Economics, University of Western Ontario, London, Canada, 1982-95. Recreations: reading; architecture; calligraphy. Address: (b.) Department of Economics, Adam Smith Building, Glasgow University, Glasgow G12 8RT; T.-0141-330 4672.

Worthington, Tony, BA, MEd. MP (Labour), Clydebank and Milngavie, since 1987; Parliamentary Under Secretary of State, Northern Ireland Office, 1997-98; b. 11.10.41, Hertfordshire; m., Angela; 1 s.; 1 d. Educ. City School, Lincoln; London School of Economics; York University; Glasgow University. Recreations: running; fishing; gardening. Address: (h.) 24 Cleddans Crescent, Hardgate, Clydebank; T.-01389 73195.

Wotherspoon (John Munro) Iain, TD, DL. Senior Partner, MacAndrew & Jenkins, WS, since 1954; Deputy Lieutenant, Districts of Lochaber, Inverness, Badenoch and Strathspey, now Inverness, since 1982, and Clerk, since 1985; b. 19.7.24, Inverness; m., Victoria Avril Jean Edwards; 2 s.; 2 d. Educ. Inverness Royal Academy;

Loretto School; Trinity College, Oxford; Edinburgh University. Lt., Royal Signals, Europe and Burma, 1944-46; TA, 1948-78; Lt.-Col. commanding 51 (Highland) Division Signals, 1963-70; Col. Dep. Cdr. 13 Signals Gp., 1970-72; Hon. Col. 32 (Scottish) Signal Regiment, 1972-78; ADC to The Queen, 1972-76; WS, 1950; Solicitor and Land Owner. Recreations: shooting; fishing; stalking. Address: (h.) Maryfield, 62 Midmills Road, Inverness IV2 3QL; T.-01463 233642.

Wray, Professor David, MD (Hons), BDS, MB, ChB, FDSRCPS, FDSRCS (Edin). Professor of Oral Medicine, Glasgow University, since 1993; Hon. Consultant, Greater Glasgow Health Board, since 1993; b. 3.1.51, Carshalton; m., Alyson P.M. Wray; 3 s. Educ. Uddingston Grammar School; Glasgow University. Fogarty Fellow, N.I.H. Bethesda, USA, 1979-81; Wellcome Research Fellow, Royal Dental, London, 1982; Senior Lecturer, Edinburgh University, 1983-92. Recreations: golf; curling; skiing. Address: (h.) 3 Kirklee Gardens, Glasgow G12 0SG.

Wray, James. MP (Labour), Glasgow Baillieston (formerly Glasgow Provan); b. 28.4.38; m.; 1 s.; 2 d. Former heavy goods vehicle driver; former Strathclyde Regional Councillor. Address: (b.) House of Commons, London SW1A 0AA.

Wright, Andrew Paul Kilding, BArch, RIBA, PPRIAS, FRSA. Partner, Law & Dunbar-Nasmith, since 1981; President, Royal Incorporation of Architects in Scotland, 1995-97; b. 11.2.47, Walsall; m., Jean Patricia; 1 s.; 2 d. Educ. Queen Mary's Grammar School, Walsall; Liverpool University School of Architecture. Practising architect, since 1972; President, Inverness Architectural Association, 1986-88; Council, RIAS, 1985-94 and since 1995; External Examiner, Robert Gordon University, since 1990; Council, Royal Institute of British Architects, 1988-94 and 1995-97; Diocesan Architect, Diocese of Moray, Ross and Caithness, 1989-98; UK Delegate, Architects Council of Europe, 1995-96; Consultant Architect to National Trust for Scotland for Mar Lodge Estate, since 1995; Board Director, Glasgow 1999 Festival Company; Member, Ancient Monuments Board for Scotland, since 1996; Commissioner, Royal Fine Art Commission for Scotland, since 1997; Hon. Adviser, Scottish Redundant Churches Trust, since 1996; Member, Civic Trust National Awards Panel, since 1997. Recreations: music; railway history; fishing. Address: (b.) 29 St. Leonards Road, Forres, IV36 1EN; T.-01309 673221.

Wright, Bill, RSW, RGI, PAI, DA. Painter; b. 1.9.31, Glasgow; m., Anne Elizabeth; 3 d. Educ. Hyndland Secondary School; Glasgow School of Art. Work in several public and private collections in Norway, USA, Germany, Switzerland, Sarajavo, Saudi Arabia, Belgium; included in exhibitions in Wales, Poland, Germany, Norway, Yugoslavia, Netherlands; elected: RSW, 1977, RGI, 1990, PAI, 1995; formerly Adviser in Art, Strathclyde Regional Council; formerly Lecturer, Scottish Arts Council; Vice President, Scottish Artists Benevolent Society. Recreations: opera; gardening; lobster fishing. Address: (h.) Old Lagalgarve Cottage, Bellochantuy, Argyll PA28 6QE; T.-01586 820372.

Wright, Professor Crispin James Garth, MA, PhD, FBA, BPhil, DLitt, FRSE. Professor of Logic and Metaphysics, St. Andrews University, since 1978; Leverhulme Personal Research Professor, since 1998; Bishop Wardlaw Professor, since 1997; b. 21.12.42, Bagshot, Surrey; m., Catherine; 2 s. Educ. Birkenhead School; Trinity College, Cambridge. Junior Research Fellow, Trinity College, Oxford, 1967-69; Fellow/Research Fellow, All Souls College, Oxford, 1969-78. Publications: Wittgenstein on the Foundations of Mathematics, 1980; Frege's Conception of Numbers as Objects, 1983; Realism, Meaning and Truth, 1986; Truth and Objectivity, 1992. Recreations: mountaineering; gardening; travel. Address: (b.) Department of Logic and Metaphysics, St. Andrews University, St. Andrews KY16 9AL.

Wright, David, BEd, MEd. Headteacher, Dunbar Grammar School, since 1997; b. 21.7.55, Kirkcaldy; m., Katrina; 1 s.; 1 d. Educ. Kirkcaldy High School; Edinburgh University; Moray House. Biology Teacher, Ainslie Park High School, 1979; Principal Teacher of Biology, Balerno Community High School, 1983; Assistant Head, Musselburgh Grammar School, 1988; Depute Head, Firrhill High School, 1993. Publication: The Biosphere, 1989. Recreations: golf; football. Address: (b.) Dunbar Grammar School, Summerfield Road, Dunbar EH42 1NJ; T.-01368 863339.

Wright, David Frederick, MA (Cantab), DD (Edin). Senior Lecturer in Ecclesiastical History, Edinburgh University, since 1973; b. 2.10.37, Hayes, Kent; m., Anne-Marie; 1 s.; 1 d. Educ. Christ's College, Cambridge; Lincoln College, Oxford. Edinburgh University: Lecturer, 1964-73, Associate Dean, Faculty of Divinity, 1972-76, Dean, 1988-92, Member, University Court, 1984-87; External Examiner, Universities of Sussex, Liverpool, Durham, Cambridge, etc.; Member, Council of Management, Keston College; Chairman, Tyndale Fellowship for Biblical and Theological Research; Associate Editor, Tyndale Bulletin; Editor, Scottish Bulletin of Evangelical Theology; Member of Praesidium, International Congress on Calvin Research; recipient of Festschrift, 1997. Publications: Common Places of Martin Bucer, 1972; Essays in Evangelical Social Ethics (Editor), 1979; Lion Handbook History of Christianity (Consultant Editor), 1977; New Dictionary of Theology (Joint Editor), 1988; The Bible in Scottish Life and Literature (Contributor and Editor), 1988; Chosen by God: Mary in Evangelical Perspective (Contributor and Editor), 1989; Dictionary of Scottish Church History and Theology (Chief General Editor), 1993; Calvin's Old Testament Commentaries (General Editor), 1993; Martin Bucer: Reforming Church and Community (Contributor and Editor), 1994; Disruption to Diversity: Edinburgh Divinity 1846-1996 (Co-Editor and Contributor), 1996. Recreations: walking; gardening; DIY. Address: (h.) 3 Camus Road East, Edinburgh EH10 6RE; T.-0131-445 1960.

Wright, David John, MB, BS, FRCA. Consultant Anaesthetist, Western General Hospital, Edinburgh, since 1979; b. 13.4.44, Oswestry; m., Bronwen; 2 s.; 1 d. Educ. Bristol Grammar School; St. Bartholomew's Hospital Medical College, London. Honorary Editor, Scottish Society of the History of Medicine. Address: (h.) 20 Lennox Row, Edinburgh EH5 3JW; T.-0131-552 3439.

Wright, Rev. David Livingston, MA, BD. Minister of Religion, Church of Scotland, since 1957; b. 18.5.30, Aberdeen; m., Margaret Brown; 2 s.; 1 d. Educ. Robert Gordon's College, Aberdeen; King's College, Aberdeen University. Assistant, Garthdee, Aberdeen, 1955-56, West St. Andrew's, 1956-57; licensed by Aberdeen Presbytery, 1957; Assistant, St. Andrew's, Dundee, till December 1957; Minister: Cockenzie Chalmers Memorial, 1957-64, Forfar Lowson Memorial, 1964-71, Hawick Old, 1971-72, linked with Teviothead, 1972-86, Stornoway St. Columba's Old Parish, 1986-98. Former Moderator, Jedburgh Presbytery and Synod of Borders; twice Moderator, Lewis Presbytery; Chairman, Scottish Reformation Society; former Chairman, National Church Association. Publications: Reformed and Evangelical (Editor), 1992; The Difference Christ Makes, 1997. Recreations: golf; walking dog; reading; occasional TV; playing piano and organ. Address: (h.) 84 Wyvis Drive, Nairn IV12 4TP; T.-01667 451613.

Wright, Professor George, BSc, MPhil, PhD. Deputy Director and Professor of Business Administration, Strathclyde Graduate Business School, since 1991; b. 24.11.52, Louth; m., Josephine Elizabeth; 2 s. Educ. Queen Elizabeth I Grammar School; NE London Polytechnic;

Brunel University. Research Assistant, Brunel University, 1974-79; Research Fellow, Huddersfield Polytechnic, 1979-81; Senior Lecturer, City of London Polytechnic, 1981-86; Reader, then Professor, Bristol Business School, 1986-91. Publications: seven books; 100 journal articles. Recreation: renovating historic houses. Address: (b.) Strathclyde Graduate Business School, 199 Cathedral Street, Glasgow G4 0QU; T.-0141-553 6000.

Wright, George Gordon. Publisher; b. 25.6.42, Edinburgh; m., Carmen Ilie; 1 s. Educ. Darroch Secondary School; Heriot Watt College. Started publishing as a hobby, 1969; left printing trade, 1973, to develop own publishing company; founder Member, Scottish General Publishers Association; Past Chairman, Scottish Young Publishers Society; Oliver Brown Award, 1994; Secretary/Treasurer, 200 Burns Club, since 1991. Publications: MacDiarmid: An Illustrated Biography, 1977; A Guide to the Royal Mile, 1979; Orkney From Old Photographs, 1981; A Guide to Holyrood Park and Arthur's Seat, 1987. Recreations: history of Edinburgh; photography; jazz. Address: (h.) 25 Mayfield Road, Edinburgh EH9 2NQ; T.-0131-667 1300.

Wright, Grahame Alan, BA (Econ), MPhil (Cantab). Assistant Principal External Relations, University of Abertay Dundee, since 1993; Chairman, Product Development Tayside Ltd., since 1994; Director, Dundee Incubator Ltd., since 1997; Trustee, Dundee Heritage Trust, since 1997; b. 5.8.47, Sunderland; m., Joan Margaret; 2 s.; 1 d. Educ. Mortimer County Secondary, South Shields; Open University; Newcastle Polytechnic; Clare College, Cambridge. Musical instrument retailer, 1963-77; Research Assistant, Lecturer, Senior Lecturer, Principal Lecturer, Newcastle Polytechnic, 1980-91; Head, Department of Accountancy, Economics and Law, Dundee Institute of Technology, 1991-93. Recreations: music; preacher, Methodist Church. Address: (h.) 12 Woodlands Park, Blairgowrie, PH10 6UW; T.-01250 875243.

Wright, Professor Howard David, BEng, PhD, CEng, FIStructE, FICE, FRSA. Professor of Structures (in association with Thorburn Colquhoun), Strathclyde University, since 1991; b. 5.10.52, Holmes Chapel; m., Elizabeth Mary Warren Baynham; 2 s.; 1 d. Educ. Sandbach School; Sheffield University. Assistant Engineer, CEGB, 1974-78; Structural Engineer, Boots the Chemists, 1978-82; Lecturer in Structural Design, University of Wales, Cardiff, 1982-91. Council Member, Institution of Structural Engineers, 1988-91; Committee Member, Building Standards Advisory Board, 1991-97. Publications: papers on composite construction and engineering education. Recreations: hill-walking; music; mechanics. Address: (b.) Department of Civil Engineering, 107 Rottenrow, Glasgow G4 0NG; T.-0141-598 3251.

Wright, John Robertson, Chief Executive and Director, Clydesdale Bank PLC and Yorkshire Bank PLC, since 1998; b. 10.9.41, London; m., Christine; 1 s.; 1 d. Educ. Daniel Stewart's College, Edinburgh. Vice President, First Interstate Bank of California, 1974-79; Assistant General Manager, Bank of Scotland, 1979-86; Director and Chief Executive Officer, Oman International Bank, 1986-93; Chief Executive and Director: Northern Bank Ltd., 1993-97, Northern Bank and National Irish Banks, 1996-97; Chief Executive and Chief General Manager, Gulf Bank KSC, Kuwait, 1997-98; President, Institute of Bankers in Ireland, 1996-97. Recreations: rugby spectating. Address: (b.) 30 St. Vincent Place, Glasgow G1 2HL; T.-0141-248 7070.

Wright, Rev. Kenyon Edward, MA, BA, BSc, MTh. Director, Kairos (Centre for a Sustainable Society), since 1990; Convener, Vision 21; Consultant on Justice and Peace to ACTS (Action of Churches Together in Scotland); Chair, Executive, Scottish Constitutional Convention; Co-ordinating Secretary, The Christian Peace Conference (International); Patron, Scottish Refugee Council; Canon Emeritus and Companion of the Order of the Cross of Nails, Coventry Cathedral; b. 31.8.32, Paisley; m., Betty Robinson; 3 d. Educ. Paisley Grammar School; Glasgow University; Cambridge University. Missionary in India, 1955-70; Director, Ecumenical Social and Industrial Institute, Durgapur, India, 1963-70; Director, Urban Ministry, Coventry Cathedral, 1970-74; Canon Residentiary and Director of International Ministry, Coventry Cathedral, 1974-81; General Secretary, Scottish Churches Council and Director, Scottish Churches House, 1981-90. Recreations: reading; walking; travel; living life to the full. Address: (b.) Kairos Centre, c/o The Rectory, Glencarse, Perth, PH2 7LX; T.-01738 860386.

Wright, Malcolm Robert, MHSM, DipHSM. Chief Executive, Edinburgh and Sick Children's NHS Trust, since 1994; b. 1.9.57, Blyth; m., Hilary; 1 s.; 1 d. Educ. Kings School, Tynemouth; Penicuik High School. Hospital Manager, Great Ormond Street, London, 1989-92; Unit General Manager, Lothian Health Board, 1992-94. Chairman, National Association for Child Health Services, 1995-98. Recreations: cycling; reading; architecture. Address: (h.) Royal Hospital for Sick Children, Sciennes Road, Edinburgh; T.-0131-536 0002.

Wright, Philip, BSc, CEng, MICE. Head, European Environment and Engineering Unit, and Chief Water Engineer, Scottish Office Agriculture Environment and Fisheries Department, since 1997; b. 15.4.49, Edinburgh; m., Anne Margaret; 3 d. Educ. St. Anthony's Secondary School; Tynecastle Secondary School; Heriot Watt University. Civil Engineer, Edinburgh Corporation, 1971-75, Lothian Regional Council, 1975-82; joined Scottish Office as Senior Civil Engineer, 1982; Assistant Chief Engineer, 1991. Director, Scotland and Northern Ireland Forum for Environmental Research; Director, Foundation for Water Research. Recreations: football; squash; golf; walking. Address: (b.) Victoria Quay, Edinburgh EH6 6QQ; T.-0131-244 0193.

Wright, Professor Robert Edward, BA, MA, PhD, FRSA. Professor of Economics, University of Stirling, since 1995; b. 28.4.58, Trenton, Ontario, Canada. Educ. Trenton High School; University of Western Ontario; University of Stockholm; INED, Paris; University of Michigan. Research Fellow, Birkbeck College, London University, 1987; Lecturer/Senior Lecturer in Economics, University of Glasgow, 1991-95. Recreation: mountaineering. Address: Department of Economics, University of Stirling, Stirling FK9 4LA.

Wright, Tom, BA (Hons). Writer; b. 8.3.23, Glasgow. Educ. Coatbridge High School; Strathclyde University. Served apprenticeship in embossing and stained glass; Army, 1943-47; served in Europe and Far East, including Japan; began to publish poems and short stories after demobilisation; had first play performed, Edinburgh Festival, 1960; author of There Was A Man; began to write radio and television drama, 1963; former Creative Writing Fellow; former Script Editor, BBC Scotland Drama Department; has also been Script Editor and Story Line Editor, Take The High Road, STV; won Festival Fringe Award, 1984, for Talk of the Devil; recent work includes The Hunter and the Hill, 1994, and Forgotten Army, 1995; Past Chairman, Scottish Committee, Writers' Guild, and Scottish Society of Playwrights. Recreation: listening to music. Address: 318 Churchill Drive, Glasgow G11.

Wright, W. J. (Bill), ACII, MSFA. Practice Leader, Ernst and Young Financial Management Ltd., Glasgow, since 1995; Director/Trustee, Sustrans, since 1996; b. 8.8.50, Falkirk; 2 d. Educ. Falkirk High School; Glasgow University. CA training followed by 25 years in financial services industry including: Eagle Star, Scottish Amicable, Parsons Penney, Stockbrokers, 1986-89; Ernst and Young

Financial Management, since 1989. Recreations: cycling; golf; reading. Address: (b.) George House, 50 George Square, Glasgow G2 1RR; T.-0141-553 4345.

Wunsch, Nigel John, BA. Business Development Manager, Railtrack, since 1998; b. 21.5.58, Bellshill; m., Linda. Educ. St. Aloysius College; Dundee College of Technology. Various local management jobs, ScotRail, 1981-91; resource planning, ScotRail, 1991-94; timetable planning, Railtrack, 1994-98. Recreations: amateur theatre. Address: (b.) Buchanan House, 58 Port Dundas Road, Glasgow; T.-0141-335 2790.

Wyke, John Anthony, MA, PhD, VetMB, MRCVS, FRSE. Director, Beatson Institute for Cancer Research, since 1987; Visiting Professor, Glasgow University; b. 5.4.42, Cleethorpes. Educ. Dulwich College; Cambridge University; Glasgow University; London University. Leukemia Society of America Fellow, Universities of Washington and Southern California, 1970-72; Staff Scientist, Imperial Cancer Research Fund, 1972-85; Assistant Director of Research, 1985-87. Address: (b.) Beatson Institute for Cancer Research, CRC Beatson Laboratories, Garscube Estate, Switchback Road, Bearsden, Glasgow G61 1BD; T.-0141-330 3950.

Wylie, Alexander Featherstonhaugh, QC, LLB, FCIArb. Lawyer; Member of the Scottish Bar, since 1978; b. 2.6.51, Perth; m., Gail Elizabeth Watson Duncan; 2 d. Educ. Edinburgh University. Qualified Solicitor in Scotland, 1976; called to Scottish Bar, 1978; Standing Junior Counsel to Accountant of Court, 1986-89; Advocate Depute, 1989-92; called to English Bar, 1990; QC (Scot), 1991. Part-time Joint Chairman, Discipline Committee, Institute of Chartered Accountants of Scotland, since 1994; Member, Scottish Legal Aid Board, since 1994. Address: (b.) Advocates Library, Parliament House, Edinburgh, EH1 1RF; T.-0131-226 2881.

Wylie, Rt. Hon. Lord (Norman Russell Wylie), PC (1970), VRD (1961), BA (Oxon), LLB (Glas). Senator of the College of Justice in Scotland, 1974- 90; b. 26.10.23, Elderslie; m., Gillian Mary Verney; 3 s. Educ. Paisley Grammar School; St. Edmund Hall, Oxford (Hon. Fellow, since 1975); Glasgow University; Edinburgh University. Fleet Air Arm, 1942-46 (subsequently RNR, Lt.-Cdr, 1954). Admitted Faculty of Advocates, 1952; Standing Junior Counsel to Air Ministry, 1956; Advocate Depute, 1958; QC, 1964; Solicitor General for Scotland, April to October, 1964; MP (Conservative), Edinburgh Pentlands, 1964-74; Lord Advocate, 1970-74. Chairman, Scottish National Committee, English Speaking Union of Commonwealth, 1978-84; Trustee, Carnegie Trust for Universities of Scotland, 1975-95; Justice of Appeal, Republic of Botswana, 1994-96. Recreations: shooting; sailing. Address: (h.) 30 Lauder Road, Edinburgh; T.-0131-667 8377.

Wylie, Rev. William Andrew, MA. Crisis Management Consultant; b. 17.5.27, London; m., Jennifer Barclay Mack; 4 d. by pr. m. Educ. Glasgow Academy; Glasgow University and Trinity College. Royal Navy, 1944-47; Chaplain, Clyde Division, RNVR, 1954-59; Minister: Stepps, 1953-59, Scots Kirk, Lausanne, 1959-67; General Secretary, Scottish Churches Council, 1967-71; Minister, St. Andrew's and St. George's, Edinburgh, 1972-85; Chaplain, Inverclyde Industrial Mission, 1985-86; Chaplain to the offshore oil industry, 1986-91; founded Prioritas Consultants, 1991; elected Hon. Fellow, Institute of Petroleum, 1990; elected Burgess of Aberdeen, 1990; Co-Founder and Chairman, Lausanne International School, 1962-67; Chairman of Governors, Aiglon College, Switzerland, 1984-91 (Hon. Chaplain, 1991); Governor, Fettes College, 1978-85; Hon. Citizen, Indianapolis, 1970. Recreations: gardening; writing; music; labradors; not playing golf. Address: (h.) Wellrose Cottage, Peat Inn, Fife KY15 5LH; T.-01334 840600.

Wyllie, George. Artist; b. 1921, Glasgow. Installations; performances; events; best known for "paper boat" installation and exhibition, Glasgow, Liverpool, London and New York, 1989-90; Visiting Lecturer, Glasgow School of Art; Associate, Royal Scottish Academy; Hon. DLitt, Strathclyde University, Glasgow.

Wyllie, Gordon Hope, DA, RSW. Painter; b. 12.2.30, Greenock; m., Helen; 2 s. Educ. Highlanders' Academy, Greenock; Greenock High School; Glasgow School of Art; Hospitalfield College of Art, Arbroath; Jordanhill College of Education. Teacher of Art and Design, Paisley Grammar School; Principal Teacher of Art and Design: St. Columba's School, Kilmacolm, Greenock Academy; former Examiner, Scottish Examination Board (Principal Examiner, Art and Design, 1980-92). Newbery Medallist, GSA, 1953, Post-diploma Award, GSA, 1953, Royal Scottish Academy Award, GSA, 1953; paintings in collections worldwide; widely exhibited. Recreations: music (Member, Bach Choir, RSAM and RSNO Choir for many years). Address: 17 Fox Street, Greenock PA16 8BS; T.-01475 723033.

Wyllie, Gordon Malcolm, LLB, FSA Scot, NP, TEP, WS. Partner, Biggart Baillie, Solicitors; Clerk to the Trades House of Glasgow and to Grand Antiquity Society of Glasgow; Clerk to General Commissioners of Inland Revenue, Glasgow North and South Divisions; b. Newton Mearns. Educ. Dunoon Grammar School; Glasgow University. Honorary Treasurer, Edinburgh Summer School in Ancient Greek; Director, Bailford Trustees Ltd.; Chairman, Edinburgh Subscription Ball Committee; Freeman of Glasgow; Deacon, Incorporation of Hammermen of Edinburgh; Member, Edinburgh West End Community Council; wrote Scottish contribution to International Bar Association's International Dictionary of Succession Terms; Trustee, Britannia Panopticon Music Hall Trust. Recreations: music; history and the arts generally; country walks; foreign travel. Address: (b.) 310 St. Vincent Street, Glasgow; T.-0141-228 8000.

Wyllie, Very Rev. Hugh Rutherford, MA, Hon.DD (Aberdeen), FCIBS. Minister, Old Parish Church of Hamilton, since 1981; Moderator, General Assembly of the Church of Scotland, 1992-93; admitted as Hon. Freeman, District of Hamilton, 1992; b. 11.10.34, Glasgow; m., Eileen E. Cameron, MA; 2 d. Educ. Shawlands Academy; Hutchesons' Grammar School, Glasgow. Union Bank of Scotland, 1951-53; RAF, 1953-55; Glasgow University, 1956-62; Assistant Minister, Glasgow Cathedral, 1962-65; Minister, Dunbeth Church, Coatbridge, 1965-72; Minister, Cathcart South Church, Glasgow, 1972-81; Moderator, Presbytery of Hamilton, 1989-90, Convener, Business Committee, 1991-95; President, Hamilton Burns Club, 1990; founder Member, Hamilton Centre for Information for the Unemployed, 1983; introduced Dial-a-Fact on drugs and alcohol, 1986; established Hamilton Church History Project, 1984-87; Convener, General Assembly's Stewardship and Budget Committee, 1978-83; Convener, Stewardship and Finance Board, 1983-86; Convener, Assembly Council, 1987-91; Member, Board of Nomination to Church Chairs, 1985-91 and since 1993; Member, General Assembly's Board of Practice and Procedure, 1991-95; Non-Executive Director, Lanarkshire Health Care NHS Trust, since 1995, Vice-Chairman, since 1996; Dr William Barclay Memorial Lecturer, 1994; elected Member, Council, Scout Association, 1993; Master, Hamilton Hospital, since 1982; Chaplain, Royal British Legion, Hamilton, since 1981, Lanarkshire Burma Star Association, since 1983. Recreations: gardening; DIY; yellow labrador. Address: Mansewood, Union Street, Hamilton ML3 6NA; T.-01698 420002.

Wyllie, James Hogarth, BA, MA. Senior Lecturer in International Relations and Director, Postgraduate Strategic Studies Programme, Aberdeen University, since 1979; International Affairs Analyst, Grampian Television, 1989-94; Specialist Correspondent, Jane's Intelligence Review, since 1992; Member, JDM Marketing Associates, Aberdeen, since 1992; b. 7.3.51, Dumfries; m., Claire Helen Beaton; 2 s. Educ. Sanquhar Academy; Dumfries Academy; Stirling University; Lancaster University. Research Officer, Ministry of Defence, 1974-75; Tutor in Politics, Durham University, 1975-77; Lecturer in Politics, University of East Anglia, 1977-79; freelance journalism; frequent current affairs comment and analysis, BBC Radio; Commonwealth Fellow, University of Calgary, 1988. Publications: Influence of British Arms; European Security in the Nuclear Age; Economist Pocket Guide to Defence (Co-author); International Politics since 1945 (Contributor); European Security in the New Political Environment. Recreations: travelling; cinema; badminton; walking. Address: (b.) Department of Politics and International Relations, Aberdeen University, Aberdeen AB24 3QY; T.-01224 272725.

Wyllie, Willilam, JP, DL. Dean of Guild, City of Aberdeen, 1981-98; Governor, Robert Gordon University, Aberdeen, since 1991; b. 5.2.32, Aberdeen; m., Mary Anne; 3 d. Educ. Robert Gordon's College, Aberdeen; Gordonstoun School, Elgin; North of Scotland College of Agriculture. W. Smith & Son, seedsmen; Hazlehead Nurseries, Aberdeen, 1952-85, retiring as Managing Director. Secretary, NE Scotland Horticultural Training Board; former Chairman, Aberdeen Airport Consultative Committee; Chairman, British Chambers of Commerce Aviation Committee. Recreations: gardening; swimming; reading. Address: (h.) 156 Kings Gate, Aberdeen, AB15 6BR; T.-01224 317811.

Wynd, Andrew H.D., DipSW (CQSW). Chief Executive, Scottish Spina Bifida Association, since 1989; b. 7.10.53, Hamilton. Educ. Bellshill Academy; Stirling University. Local government officer; Senior Officer, National Voluntary Childcare Organisation. Past Chair, Scottish Association of Voluntary Service Co-ordinators; former Chair, Strathclyde Regional Council Pre-five Voluntary Sector Forum. Address: (b.) Scottish Spina Bifida Association, 190 Queensferry Road, Edinburgh EH4 2BW; T.-0131-332 0743.

Y

Yadav, Professor Pradeep Kumar, BSc (Hons), MSc (Physics), MSc (Financial Studies), PhD. Professor of Finance, since 1993, Head, Department of Accounting and Finance, 1995-98, Strathclyde University; Director, Scottish Institute for Research in Investment and Finance, since 1998; b. 31.8.53, India; m., Mamta; 1 s.; 1 d. Educ. St. Xaviers School, Delhi; St. Stephen's College, University of Delhi; Strathclyde University. Member, Indian Administrative Service (formerly Indian Civil Service), 1976-86; Lecturer in Finance/Senior Lecturer in Finance, Department of Accounting and Finance, Strathclyde University, 1987-93. Publications: 25 articles in journals and books. Address: (b.) Department of Accounting and Finance, Strathclyde University, 100 Cathedral Street, Glasgow G4 0LN; T.-0141-548 3939.

Yarrow, Sir Eric Grant, MBE, DL, CEng, MRINA, FRSE. Chairman, Clydesdale Bank PLC, 1985-91 (Director, since 1962); Director, National Australia Bank Ltd., 1987-91; b. 23.4.20, Glasgow; m., 1, Rosemary Ann Young (deceased); 1 s. (deceased); 2, Annette Elizabeth Francoise Steven (m. diss.); 3 s.; 3, Joan Botting; 3 step d. Educ. Marlborough College; Glasgow University. Served engineering apprenticeship, G. & J. Weir, 1938-39; Royal Engineers, 1939-45; served Burma, 1942-45 (Major, RE, 1945); Yarrow & Co. Ltd. (later Yarrow PLC): Assistant Manager, 1946, Director, 1948, Managing Director, 1958-67, Chairman, 1962-85, President, 1985-87; Director, Standard Life Assurance Company, 1958-91; Chairman, Princess Louise Scottish Hospital, Erskine, 1980-86, Hon. President, since 1986; President, Scottish Convalescent Home for Children, 1957-70; Council Member, Royal Institution of Naval Architects, since 1957 (Vice President, 1965, Honorary Vice President, 1972); Member, General Committee, Lloyd's Register of Shipping, 1960-89; Deacon, Incorporation of Hammermen in Glasgow, 1961-62; Chairman, Yarrow (Shipbuilders) Ltd., 1962-79; Officer (Brother), Order of St. John, since 1965; Deputy Lieutenant, County of Renfrewshire, 1970-96; Prime Warden, Worshipful Company of Shipwrights, 1970-71; Council Member, Institute of Directors, 1983-90; President, Smeatonican Society of Civil Engineers, 1983-84; President, The Marlburian Club, 1984; President, Scottish Area, Burma Star Association, since 1990; Vice President, Royal Highland and Agricultural Society for Scotland, 1990. Recreation: golf. Address: (h.) Cloak, Kilmacolm, Renfrewshire PA13 4SD; T.-Kilmacolm 2067.

Yates, Keith, BSc (Hons). Chief Executive, Stirling Council, since 1995; b. 13.3.48, Preston; m., Aileen; 1 s.; 2 d. Educ. Preston Grammar School; Sheffield University; Liverpool University. Consultant, Peat Marwick Kates, 1971; Planning Officer, Oxfordshire County Council, 1971; Consultant, Colin Buchanan and Partners, 1972; Planning Officer, Scottish Office, 1974; Group Leader, Regional Report, Strathclyde Regional Council, 1975; senior executive posts, Strathclyde Regional Council, 1980-91; Assistant Chief Executive, Central Regional Council, 1991-95. Recreations: reading; current affairs; runing; hillwalking (Munroist). Address: (b.) Viewforth, Stirling FK8 2ET; T.-01786 443320.

Yewe-Dyer, Mervyn Richard, BDS, BSc, FDS, MSc, MGDS. Deputy Chief Dental Officer, Scottish Office, since 1994; Chief Dental Adviser, since 1996; b. 4.8.43, London; m., Melanie Dorcas Gould; 1 s.; 2 d. Educ. Christ's Hospital; London University. Nuffield Research Fellow, 1966-68; Lecturer, Manchester University, 1969-73; general dental practice, 1974-93; Lecturer (part-time), Guy's Hospital Dental School, 1979-87; Board Member, Dental Practice Board England, 1985-91. Publication: Notes on Prosthetic Dentistry. Recreations: photography; golf; bee-keeping. Address: (b.) Room 54 H, St. Andrew's House, Edinburgh, EH1 3DG; T.-0131-244 2305.

Young, Alastair Duncan, BSc (Hons), CEng, MICE. Director of Land Services, Glasgow City Council, since 1995; Director, RTI Focus, since 1996; Director, Susiephone Ltd., since 1997; b. 7.6.48, Glasgow; m., Janet U.H. Young; 1 s. Educ. Uddingston Grammar School; Strathclyde University. Technician, Leitch and Sharp; Strathclyde Regional Council, joining as Technician/Engineer, latterly as Regional Network Manager. Recreations: golf; cooking. Address: (b.) Richmond Exchange, 20 Cadogan Street, Glasgow, G2 7AD; T.-0141-287 9100.

Young, Alexander Grant, MA (Hons). Head Teacher, Kyle Academy, Ayr, since 1996; b. 9.6.51, Stornoway; m., Patricia; 1 s.; 1 d. Educ. Ayr Academy; Edinburgh University; Moray House College of Education. Began teaching, Penicuik High School; moved to Cumnock Academy, 1975; exchange teacher, Orange County, S. California, 1979-80; Principal Teacher of Geography, James Hamilton Academy, Kilmarnock, 1982-86; Assistant Head Teacher, Kilwinning Academy, 1986-91; Area Development Officer, TVE1 Extension Team, Ayrshire, 1991-94; Depute Head Teacher, Grange Academy, Kilmarnock, 1994-96. Member, Higher Still Specialist Group on Guidance; former Vice President, Ayr Seaforth Athletic Club; President, Mauchline Burns Club. Recreations: sport; family; reading; music; travel; gardening. Address: (b.) Kyle Academy, Overmills Road, Ayr KA7 3LR; T.-01292 262234.

Young, Professor Archie, BSc, MBChB, MD, FRCP (Glas), FRCP (Lond). Professor of Geriatric Medicine, University of Edinburgh, since 1998; b. 19.9.46, Glasgow; 1 s.; 1 d. Educ. High School of Glasgow. Training posts, Glasgow, London, Oxford; Consultant/Honorary Consultant posts: Oxford Rehabilitation Research Unit, University of Oxford, Royal Free Hospital and Medical School, London; Professor of Geriatric Medicine, Royal Free Hospital Medical School. Recreations: physical. Address: (b.) Geriatric Medicine Unit, 21 Chalmers Street, Edinburgh EH3 9EW.

Young, Chick. Football Correspondent, BBC Television and Radio, since 1988; b. 4.5.51, Glasgow. Educ. Glasgow High School; Bellahouston Academy, Glasgow. Daily Record, 1969-72; Carrick Herald, Girvan, 1972; Irvine Herald, 1972-73; Charles Buchan's Football Monthly, London, 1973-74; Editor, Scottish Football magazine, 1974-75; Scottish Daily News, 1975; Scottish Daily Express, 1976; Evening Times, Glasgow, 1977-88; Radio Clyde, 1977-95; BBC, since 1988; Sunday People, 1988-89; Scotland on Sunday, 1989-91; Columnist, Daily Star, since 1996. Fraser Award, Young Journalist of the Year, 1973; British Provincial Sports Journalist of the Year, 1987; Sony Award, British Sports Broadcaster of the Year (Bronze), 1997; Scottish Sports Journalist of the Year (Runner-up), 1997. Publications: Rebirth of the Blues; Mo. Address: (b.) BBC TV Sport, Queen Margaret Drive, Glasgow G12 8DG; T.-0141-338 2622.

Young, Professor Daniel Greer, MB, ChB, FRCSEdin, FRCSGlas, DTM&H. Professor of Paediatric Surgery, Glasgow University; Honorary Consultant Paediatric Surgeon; former President, British Association of Paediatric Surgeons; b. Skipness, Argyll; m., Agnes Gilchrist Donald; 1 s.; 1 d. Educ. Wishaw High School; Glasgow University. Resident Assistant Surgeon, Hospital for Sick Children, London; Senior Lecturer, Institute of Child Health, London University; Honorary Consultant Surgeon, Hospital for Sick Children, London, and Queen Elizabeth Hospital, Hackney, London; Senior Lecturer and Head, Department of Paediatric Surgery, Glasgow University, Honorary

Consultant Surgeon, Royal Hospital for Sick Children and Stobhill General Hospital, Glasgow. Honorary Secretary, Lanarkshire Division, British Medical Association; Past President, Royal Medico-Chirurgical Society of Glasgow; Honorary President, Scottish Spina Bifida Association; Member of Council, Royal College of Physicians and Surgeons; Past Chairman, Intercollegiate Board in Paediatric Surgery; Past Chairman, National Paramedic Training Board, Scottish Ambulance Service; former Member, Professional Advisory Group, Scottish Ambulance Service; Past Chairman, West of Scotland Surgical Association; Honorary Member: Hungarian Paediatric Surgical Association, South African Paediatric Surgical Association, American Surgical Paediatric Association. Recreations: curling; fishing; gardening. Address: (b.) Department of Paediatric Surgery, Royal Hospital for Sick Children, Yorkhill, Glasgow G3 8SJ; T.-0141-201 0170.

Young, Lt.-Gen. Sir David (Tod), KBE (1980), CB (1977), DFC (1952). Chairman, Cairntech Ltd., Edinburgh, 1983-93, Director, 1993-96; b. 17.5.26, Edinburgh; m., 1, Joyce Marian Melville (deceased); 2 s.; 2, Joanna Myrtle Oyler (nee Torin). Educ. George Watson's College, Edinburgh. Commissioned The Royal Scots, 1945; Brevet Lt.-Col., 1964; Mil. Assistant, MoD, 1964-67; commanded 1st Bn., The Royal Scots, 1967-69; Col. GS, Staff College, 1969-70; Commander, 12 Mechanized Brigade, 1970-72; Deputy Military Secretary, MoD, 1972-74; Commander Land Forces, Northern Ireland, 1975-77; Director of Infantry, MoD, 1977-80; GOC Scotland and Governor, Edinburgh Castle, 1980-82; Colonel, The Royal Scots, 1975-80; Colonel Commandant: Scottish Division, 1980-82, Ulster Defence Regiment, 1986-91; Honorary Colonel, Northern Ireland Regiment Army Air Corps, 1988-93; Vice President, Scottish Partnership Agency for Palliative and Cancer Care, 1993-98; Member, Scottish Committee, Marie Curie Foundation, since 1983 (Chairman, 1986 98); Trustee, Marie Curie, since 1986; President, Army Cadet Force Association Scotland, 1984-97; HM Commissioner, Queen Victoria School, 1984-93; Chairman, St. Mary's Cathedral Workshop, 1986-92; Member, Board of Governors, St. Columba's Hospice, since 1986; Honorary President, St. Mary's Cathedral Workshop, since 1993. Recreations: golf; sports; music. Address: c/o Adam & Company plc, 22 Charlotte Square, Edinburgh EH2 4DF.

Young, Dennis James, MA, LLB, TEP. Senior Partner, Blackadder Reid Johnston, Solicitors, Dundee; b. 23.1.42, Forfar; m., Enid; 2 s. Educ. Brechin High School; St. Andrews University. Lectured part-time, Dundee University, for several years; trained, Gray Robertson & Wilkie, Dundee; joined present firm, 1967, becoming Partner, 1969; Founder Secretary, Committee, Dundee Solicitors' Property Centre, Chairman, 1978-86; Member, Society of Trust and Estates Practitioners (Leader, Tayside and Aberdeen Regional Discussion Group); Dean, Faculty of Procurators and Solicitors in Dundee, 1993-95; Member, Council, Law Society of Scotland, 1996-97. Member, Executive Committee, Scottish Heart and Arterial Disease Risk Prevention (charity). Recreations: golf; football/rugby spectating; listening to music. Address: (b.) 30-34 Reform Street, Dundee DD1 1RJ; T.-01382 229222.

Young, Hugh Kenneth, TD, CA, FCIBS. Vice-Chairman, Lowland Employers Liaison Committee; Chairman, Trustees, Royal Scots Benevolent Society; Trustee, Royal Scots (War Memorial) Club; General Manager and Secretary and Member, Management Board, Bank of Scotland, 1984-96; b. 6.5.36, Galashiels; m., Marjory Bruce Wilson; 2 s.; 1 d. Educ. Edinburgh Academy. National Service, 1959-61; commissioned as 2nd Lt., Royal Scots; TA service, 1957-59, 1961-69 and 1986-92, latterly as Major; with ICFC Ltd., 1962-67; with Schroders Ltd. group, 1967-73, latterly as Manager, J. Henry Schroder Wagg & Co. Ltd.; Local Director in Edinburgh, Edward Bates & Sons Ltd., 1973-75; joined Bank of Scotland, 1975; Head of Corporate Finance, Bank of Scotland Finance Company Ltd., 1976; Director, The British Linen Bank Ltd., 1978-84 (Deputy Chief Executive, 1982-84). Recreations: squash; tennis; hill-walking. Address: (h.) 30 Braid Hills Road, Edinburgh EH10 6HY; T.-0131-447 3101.

Young, James Drummond, LLB, NP. Solicitor (Partner, McGrigor Donald, since 1985); b. 26.2.50, Broughty Ferry; m., Gillian Anne Boyd; 1 s.; 1 d. Educ. Hutchesons' Grammar School; Glasgow University. Apprentice, then Legal Assistant, McGrigor Donald & Co., 1971-75; Legal Officer, West Lothian District Council, 1975-77; Legal Assistant, then Partner, Moncrieff Warren Paterson & Co., 1977-85. Elder, Greenbank Church; Scottish Editor, Employment Precedents and Company Policy Documents. Recreations: golf; contemporary art; cricket. Address: (b.) Erskine House, 68/73 Queen Street, Edinburgh; T.-0131-226 7777.

Young, John Graeme Bennett, MA (Hons), PhD, DipEd. Director of Education Services, Falkirk Council, since 1995; b. 31.10.50, Bridge of Allan; m., Shena; 2 s. Educ. Striling High School; University of Glasgow; University of Edinburgh. Teacher of History and Modern Studies, Dalziel High School, Motherwell, 1976-81; Principal Teacher of History and Modern Studies, Tain Royal Academy, Ross-shire, 1981-85; Assistant Divisional Education Officer, Inverness, Highland Region, 1985-88; Assistant Director of Education/Head of Resources, Central Region, 1988-95. Recreations: reading; gardening; walking; sport (as a spectator). Address: (h.) Morven, Doune Road, Dunblane FK15 9AT; T.-01786 822305.

Young, John Henderson, OBE, JP, DL, KSJ, MIMgt. Deputy Lieutenant of Glasgow, since 1981; Chairman, Association of Scottish Conservative Councillors, 1991-94, Hon. President, since 1994; Member, SPTA, since 1996; Local Government Commissioner, Rifkind Policy Commission, 1998; Scottish Conservative Transport Spokesman, since 1998; Member, Strathclyde Passenger Transport Authority; b. 21.12.30, Glasgow; m., Doris Paterson; 1 s. Educ. Hillhead High School, Glasgow; Scottish College of Commerce. RAF, 1949-51. Councillor, Glasgow Corporation, 1964-73, Glasgow District Council, 1974-96, City of Glasgow Council, from 1996; Police Judge, 1971-72; Bailie/Magistrate of Glasgow on four occasions; Leader, Glasgow City Council, 1977-79, Leader of the Opposition, 1979-80, 1988-92, from 1996 (new City of Glasgow Council); former Chairman/Vice-Chairman, Council committees; Parliamentary candidate (Conservative), Rutherglen, 1966, Cathcart, 1992; Chairman, Cathcart Conservatives, 1964-65, 1968-71, 1987-88; Chairman, Glasgow Euro Constituency, 1987-91; Vice-Chairman, Scottish Tory Reform Group, since 1993; Vice Chairman, Glasgow Conservatives, 1969-72; Export Manager, Teacher's Whisky; Public Relations Consultant; former Vice-Chairman, Scottish Pakistani Association; Secretary, Scottish/South African Society, 1986-88; Governor, Hutcheson's Educational Trust, 1991-97; Member, Glasgow Sports Promotion Council; Life Member, Merchants House of Glasgow; Kentucky Colonel, 1984; Hon. Don Cossack (Russia), 1989; Lord Provost's Award, 1989. Publication: A History of Cathcart Conservative Association, 1918-93. Recreations: meeting people; history; reading; animal welfare. Address: (h.) 4 Deanwood Avenue, Netherlee, Glasgow G44 3RJ; T.-0141-637 9535.

Young, Provost John Maclennan, OBE, JP. Farmer, since 1949; Caithness Area Provost, The Highland Council (Member of Housing Committee, Environmental Health Committee, Special Programmes Committee, Leisure and General Purposes Committee, Caithness District Licensing Board); Honorary Sheriff, Grampian, Highland and Islands;

b. 6.6.33, Thurso. Educ. Thurso Miller Academy. Member, Caithness County Council, 1961-75 (Chairman, Housing Committee, 1968-73, Chairman, Planning Committee, 1973-75); Member, Caithness Western District Council, 1961-75 (Chairman, 1968-75); Convener, Caithness District Council, 1975-96; Member, Highland Regional Council, 1974-90 (Chairman, Manpower Committee, 1974-78, Chairman, Roads and Transport Committee, 1978-90, Member of Roads and Transport Committee, 1974-90, Policy and Resources Committee, 1974-90, Finance Committee, 1974-90, Water and Sewerage Committee, 1986-90, Planning Committee, 1974-90, Development Committee, 1974-90, Northern Joint Police Committee, 1975-90); Member, Council, National Farmers Union of Scotland, 1961-69 (President, Thurso Branch, 1961 and 1962, President, Caithness Area Executive Committee, 1963 and 1964); Conservative Candidate, Caithness and Sutherland, 1970. Address: (h.) Sordale, Halkirk, Caithness KW12 6XB; T.-01847 831228.

Young, Rev. John Nicol, MA, PhD, BD. Minister, Liberton Kirk, Edinburgh, since 1996; b. 5.12.55, W. Pakistan; m., C.S. Lindsay Wormald; 1 s.; 1 d. Educ. George Heriot's School, Edinburgh; Edinburgh University. Co-ordinator, Multi-Cultural Education Centre, Leith, 1982-88; Research Worker, Diocese of Hyderabad, Church of Pakistan, 1988-92. Address: (b.) The Manse, 7 Kirk Park, Edinburgh EH16 6HZ; T.-0131-664 3067.

Young, Laurence Mitchell, MBE (1998). Director, Discovery Award Association, since 1995; b. 2.7.27, Dundee; m., Margaret Thomson Fawns; 1 s.; 1 d. Educ. Stobswell Junior Secondary School; Dundee Training College. Early career in building industry; military service, King's Own Scottish Borderers, 1945-48; joined Stobswell Boys' School, 1956; Technical Teacher, 1956-67, Special Assistant, 1967-73; Principal Teacher of Guidance, Craigie High School, Dundee, 1973-87; retired, 1987; involved with Duke of Edinburgh Award, since 1964: Group Scheme Leader to Stobswell Boys' School, 1964-73, Group Leader, Craigie High School, 1973-87, Duke of Edinburgh Counsellor and Advisor for Dundee, 1969-92, Secretary/Treasurer, Dundee District Award Co-ordination Committee, since 1974; Co-Founder, Tay Award, 1985-96; Founder Member, Discovery Award, since 1987: Group Leader, Pilot Group, 1987-89, Chairman, Dundee Group, 1989-93; Chairman, Association Steering Group, 1993-95; Elder, Church of Scotland, since 1968. Recreations: family; people. Address: (h.) 124 Tweed Crescent, Menzieshill, Dundee DD2 4DS; T.-01382 641800.

Young, Margaret Rose, JP, DMH, DHyp, PNLP, DipCouns. Hypnotherapist and Counsellor; Honorary Sheriff; BAC Accredited Counsellor; b. 5.1.51, Canada; m., Simon George Young; 3 d. Educ. St. Mary's School, Calne; St. Andrews University. Member, Justice of the Peace Committee, Ross and Cromarty, since 1985. Recreations: reading; music; theatre; walking. Address: (h.) Tarrel, by Tain, Ross-shire, IV20 1SL; T.-01862 871248.

Young, Mark Richard, BSc, PhD, FRES, FIBiol, CBiol. Senior Lecturer, Aberdeen University, since 1989; Director, Culterty Field Station, since 1996; Member, North Board, Scottish Environment Protection Agency, since 1996; b. 27.10.48, Worcester; m., Jennifer Elizabeth Tully; 1 s.; 1 d. Educ. Kings School, Worcester; Birmingham University. Lecturer, Aberdeen University, 1973-89. Recreations: natural history; walking; ball sports; visiting Hebridean islands. Address: (b.) Culterty Field Station, Department of Zoology, University of Aberdeen, Newburgh, Ellon, Aberdeenshire AB41 6AA; T.-01358 789631.

Young, Roger, BSc, MBA. Chief Executive, Scottish Hydro-Electric plc, since 1988; Non-Executive Director: Friends Ivory and Sime PLC, since 1993, Bank of Scotland, since 1994; b. 14.1.44, Edinburgh; m., Sue; 1 s.; 2 d. Educ. Gordonstoun School; Edinburgh University; Cranfield Business School. Rolls-Royce Ltd.; Alidair Ltd.; Wavin Plastics Ltd.; Aurora Holdings Ltd.; Low and Bonar plc. Recreations: hill-walking; aviation; family. Address: (b.) 10 Dunkeld Road, Perth PH1 5WA; Tel.: 01738 455040.

Young, Professor Stephen, BCom, MSc. Professor of International Business, Strathclyde University, since 1987, Head, Department of Marketing, 1992-96; b. 20.8.44, Berwick upon Tweed; 1 s.; 1 d. Educ. Berwick Grammar School; Liverpool University; Newcastle University. Economist, Government of Tanzania; Head, International Economics Department, Milk Marketing Board, 1969-73; Lecturer/Senior Lecturer, Paisley College of Technology, 1973-79; Senior Lecturer, Department of Marketing, Strathclyde Business School, 1980-87 (Director, Strathclyde International Business Unit, from 1983); Director, Licensing Centre Ltd. Recreations: mountaineering; cycling; running. Address: (h.) 42 Brierie Gardens, Crosslee, Johnstone PA6 7BZ; T.-01505 615554.

Young, Sheriff Sir Stephen Stewart Templeton, 3rd Bt. Sheriff of North Strathclyde at Greenock, since 1984; b. 24.5.47; m.; 2 s. Educ. Rugby; Trinity College, Oxford; Edinburgh University. Sheriff, Glasgow and Strathkelvin, 1984. Address: (b.) Sheriff Court House, Nelson Street, Greenock, PA15 1TR.

Young, William Smith Geates, LLB (Hons), NP. Managing Partner, Brechin Tindal Oatts, since 1997; b. 21.12.55, Girvan; m., Margot Glanville Jones. Educ. Girvan Academy; Glasgow University. Joined Tindal Oatts & Rodger, 1978; admitted as Solicitor, 1980; Managing Partner, Tindal Oatts, 1993. SFA Class 1 Referee List, 1990; FIFA List of International Linesmen, 1992; FIFA List of International Referees, 1994. Recreations: football; golf; after-dinner speaking. Address: (b.) 48 St. Vincent Street, Glasgow G2 5HS; T.-0141-221 8012.

Younger of Leckie, Rt. Hon. Viscount (George Kenneth Hotson Younger), KT, KCVO, TD, DL. Chairman, The Royal Bank of Scotland Group plc, since 1991; b. 22.9.31; m., Diana Rhona Tuck; 3 s.; 1 d. Educ. Cargilfield School, Edinburgh; Winchester College; New College, Oxford. Argyll and Sutherland Highlanders, 1950-51; 7th Bn., Argyll and Sutherland Highlanders (TA), 1951-65; Honorary Colonel, 154 (Lowland) Transport Regiment, RCT T&AVR, 1977-85; Director: George Younger & Son Ltd., 1958-68; J.G. Thomson & Co. Ltd., Leith, 1962-66; Maclachlans Ltd., 1968-70; Tennant Caledonian Breweries, 1977-79; Non Executive Director: The Royal Bank of Scotland Group plc, 1989; Murray International Trust PLC, 1989 (Chairman); Murray Smaller Markets Trust PLC, 1989 (Chairman); Murray Income Trust PLC, 1989 (Chairman); Murray Ventures PLC, 1989 (Chairman); Banco Santander S.A., 1991; Royal Armouries Board of Trustees, 1994 (Chairman); The Fleming Mercantile Investment Trust PLC, 1994; contested North Lanarkshire, 1959; Unionist Candidate, Kinross and West Perthshire, 1963 (stood down in favour of Sir Alec Douglas-Home); MP (Conservative), Ayr, 1964-92; Scottish Conservative Whip, 1965-67; Parliamentary Under-Secretary of State for Development, Scottish Office, 1970-74; Minister of State for Defence, 1974; Secretary of State for Scotland, 1979-86; Chairman, Conservative Party in Scotland, 1974-75 (Deputy Chairman, 1967-70); Secretary of State for Defence, 1986-89; President, National Union of Conservative and Unionist Associations, 1987-88. Brigadier, Queen's Bodyguard for Scotland (Royal Company of Archers); DL, Stirlingshire, 1968. Recreations: music; tennis; sailing; golf. Address: (b.) 42 St. Andrew Square, Edinburgh EH2 2YE; T.-0131-556 8555.

Younger, John David Bingham. Lord Lieutenant of Tweeddale, since 1994; Managing Director, Broughton Brewery Ltd., 1979-95; Director, Broughton Ales, 1995-96;

b. 20.5.39, Doune; m., Anne Rosaleen Logan; 1 s.; 2 d. Educ. Eton College; Royal Military Academy, Sandhurst. Argyll and Sutherland Highlanders, 1957-69; Scottish and Newcastle Breweries, 1969-79; Broughton Brewery Ltd., 1979-95; Deputy Lieutenant, Tweeddale, 1987. Chairman, Board of Governors, Belhaven Hill School Trust, 1988; Chairman, Scottish Borders Tourist Board, 1989; Member, A&SH Regimental Trust and Committee, 1985; Director, Queen's Hall (Edinburgh) Ltd; Member, Queen's Bodyguard for Scotland (Royal Company of Archers) since 1969, Secretary, since 1993; Vice President, RHASS, 1994. Recreation: the countryside. Address: (h.) Kirkurd House, Blyth Bridge, Peeblesshire EH46 7AH; T.-01721 752223.

Younger, Sheriff Robert Edward Gilmour, MA, LLB. Sheriff of Tayside, Central and Fife, at Stirling, since 1992 (Stirling and Alloa, 1987-92); b. 25.9.40, Stirling; m., Helen Jane Hayes; 1 s.; 1 d. Educ. Winchester; New College, Oxford; Edinburgh University; Glasgow University. Advocate, 1968-79; Sheriff of Glasgow and Strathkelvin, at Glasgow, 1979-82, and of Tayside, Central and Fife, at Stirling and Falkirk, 1982-87. Recreations: out of doors. Address: (h.) Old Leckie, Gargunnock, Stirling; T.-01786 860213.

Youngson, George Gray, MB, ChB, PhD, FRCSEdin. Consultant Surgeon, Royal Aberdeen Children's Hospital and Aberdeen Royal Infirmary, since 1985; Honorary Senior Lecturer in Clinical Surgery, Aberdeen University, since 1985; b. 13.5.49, Glasgow; m., Sandra Jean Lister; 1 s.; 2 d. Educ. Buckhaven High School; Aberdeen University. House Officer to Professor George Smith, 1973; Research Fellow, 1975; Registrar in General Surgery, 1975-77; Senior Resident in Cardiac and Thoracic Surgery, University Hospital, London, Ontario, 1979; Lecturer in Clinical Surgery, Aberdeen University, 1981; Clinical Fellow, Paediatric Surgery, Hospital for Sick Children, Toronto, 1983; Lecturer in Surgical Paediatrics and Transplantation, Aberdeen University, 1984; Regional Advisor and Examiner, Royal College of Surgeons of Edinburgh. Recreations: sport (tennis and squash); music (piobaireachd, guitar). Address: (h.) 10 Kennerty Park, Peterculter, Aberdeen.

Z

Zealley, Andrew King, MB, ChB, FRCP, FRCPsych, DPM. Consultant Psychiatrist, Lothian Health Board, since 1971, and Honorary Senior Lecturer, Edinburgh University; b. 28.10.35, Stockton-on-Tees; m., Dr. Helen Elizabeth Zealley (qv); 1 s.; 1 d. Educ. Sherborne School; Edinburgh University. Chairman, Lothian Area Medical Committee, 1978-88; Chairman, Lothian Research Ethics Committee, since 1988; Physician Superintendent, Royal Edinburgh Hospital, 1984-94; Medical Director, Edinburgh Healthcare NHS Trust, 1994-96. Publications include: Companion to Psychiatric Studies, 6th edition (Co-editor). Recreations: running; sailing; skiing. Address: (h.) Viewfield House, Tipperlinn Road, Edinburgh EH10 5ET; T.-0131-447 5545.

Zealley, Helen Elizabeth, OBE, QHP, MD, FRCPE, FFPHM. Chief Administrative Medical Officer and Director of Public Health, Lothian Health Board, since 1988; Honorary Senior Lecturer, Edinburgh University, since 1988; b. 10.6.40; m., Dr. Andrew Zealley (qv); 1 s.; 1 d. Educ. St. Albans High School; Edinburgh University. Former Member, Council, Royal College of Physicians, Edinburgh; former Member, Board, Faculty of Public Health Medicine; Hon. President, Lothian Branch, British Association of Early Childhood; former Member, Court, Edinburgh University. Recreations: family and home; sailing; skiing; travel. Address: (b.) Lothian Health Board, 148 Pleasance, Edinburgh EH8 9RS; T.-0131-536 9163.

von Zugbach de Sugg, Professor Reginald (Reggie) Gordon Leslie, KLJ, MA, PhD, MBIM, FMS, ACP. Professor in Management, Paisley University, since 1990; b. 20.2.44, Derbyshire; m., Theda Claudia Susanna Stapelfeldt. Educ. City of London College; Brighton Polytechnic; London University Institute of Education; UMIST. Regular Army Officer (Major), 1968-86; Director of Undergraduate Studies, Glasgow Business School, Glasgow University, 1986-90; author of numerous papers; books: Power and Prestige in the British Army, 1988; The Winning Manager, 1995; Nur Einzelkampfer siesen, 1996; Mr Downsizing, 1998; Knight Commander, Military and Hospitaler Order of St. Lazarus of Jerusalem. Recreations: horses; dogs; real tennis; literature. Address: (h.) 7 Dowanside Road, Dowanhill, Glasgow; T.-0141-337 2228.